The
Oxford Dictionary of
Quotations

THIRD EDITION

Oxford   New York   Toronto   Melbourne

OXFORD UNIVERSITY PRESS

PREFACE TO THE THIRD EDITION

Many a home and library in the English-speaking world has a copy of the *Oxford Dictionary of Quotations* in the first or, more frequently, second edition. Those should not be dispensed with nor superseded; but need will be found to make room for this new, third edition. For over a quarter of a century has passed since the publication of the last revision, and much that is quoted or quotable has been said or written or simply come into wider cognizance during this period. Add that the second edition, published in 1953, was about 95% the same in content as the first edition of 1941 — the differences consisting then chiefly of the addition of Second World War quotations (essentially of course those of Winston Churchill),[1] correction of errors, rearrangement of certain sections, and much more full and precise indexing — and it will be seen that this volume presents the first substantial revision of the *Dictionary* since its original compilation.

To have simply incorporated modern and freshly recognized quotations into the preceding edition in like measure to its ingredients would have resulted in a volume which, on account of the present costs of producing so bulky a work, must have been priced beyond the book-purchasing powers of all but the wealthier owners of libraries, private or even public. To have published a separate supplement to the second edition would have been unfair to those (mostly younger) readers and writers who did not already possess a copy of a previous edition, and might reasonably seek a single-volume coverage of what they heard or saw quoted from all periods and places that impinged on their own conversation or culture. It was resolved therefore that space must be made for new inclusions by considerable cutting of the contents of the second edition.

Besides, there were positive reasons for omitting parts of the earlier selection of quotations in fairly extensive quantity. The first edition was compiled within the Oxford University Press in the decade of the 1930s by men and women imbued with the history and politics, the culture whether educated or popular, of the first quarter of the twentieth century in Britain, and especially the literature of the ancient and the English-speaking worlds that was then read and studied at home, school, and university. They had mostly been to Oxford or Cambridge and before that to schools where learning poetry (and even prose) by heart for repetition was regular. Some had served in the First World War and the songs they knew were those of marching soldiers or of the music-hall; drawing-room ballads too were not forgotten. Hymns, though, when church-going was still the rule, were probably the most widely known forms of song for the compilers of the first edition; and constant acquaintance with

[1] The first edition contained only the one 'terminological inexactitude' part-sentence; the second edition added another 25 quotations from the then Prime Minister; in this new edition appear 41 Churchill items, including enough context for the original one to explain its sense and correct those who often misuse 'terminological inexactitude'.

the Bible and the Book of Common Prayer enabled them to assume that 'five smooth stones out of the brook' or ' sat in the seat of the scornful' needed no context for their recognition and the understanding of their significance. The Greek and Latin classics were still then drawn on for quotations by Members of Parliament, or elsewhere in debating or after-dinner speeches. Dr. Johnson's observation in the first sentence of the prefatory pages of 'The Compilers to the Reader' of this *Dictionary* in 1941 — see p. x — was still, if not strictly, true.

Much of that lettered world of reference has disappeared. The *Dictionary* was claimed to be one of *familiar* quotations. But take now any page that has two or more authors represented on it, in the second edition, and ask someone of great general knowledge and wide reading, someone even of an older generation, and they will find several quotations quite unknown to them. Every generation, every decade perhaps, needs its new *Dictionary of Quotations.*

In order to select and accommodate the desired new quotations, a team of revisers consisting of a few members of the Press, together with a greater number of alert, enthusiastic, and variously interested members of the public, was asked during 1975—7 to suggest cuts to be made from the contents of the second edition and additions to be inserted in the third. Apart from the publishing editors, they included a former literary editor and other active or retired journalists, writers, and representatives of Parliament and the professions, the universities, the Church, Whitehall and the City, the British Museum, and even another publishing house. No definition of what constitutes a quotation was imposed; we suggest that a quotation is what is recognized for one (even without quotation marks) by some at least of its hearers or readers, or else what is welcomed as quotable, and then probably quoted. The claim that this is a dictionary of *familiar* quotations is, moreover, hereby dropped. (It would have been unkind to set a ban on the 'innocent vanity' Bernard Darwin refers to in the first paragraph of his Introduction, of those who know a quotation that may be unfamiliar to others.)[1] But neither is it simply an anthology displaying the choice and taste of one man, or even of a small committee of the Press such as compiled the first edition of the *Dictionary. Popularity,* rather, is the word (not eschewed even by the original compilers — see p. x): every quotation or passage excluded had been marked for omission by a majority of those who read right through the second edition, and all quotations added have likewise had a majority vote in favour of them.

The method of revision was, first, to issue some ten copies of the second edition, interleaved with blank pages, to the core of the revision team, each of whom read through every single quotation and marked their recommended deletions, corrections, or additions; these were then collated and the balance of opinion calculated by the editors in the Press. Secondly, suggestions for quotations to be added were sought on specially prepared forms, with a voting box for each item; the suggestions lists were then photocopied and distributed to the full team of revisers,

---

[1] Bernard Darwin in his second paragraph used a quotation from Charles Lamb that has never been included in this *Dictionary;* his quotation from *The Wrecker* (p.xvii) was inserted in the second edition, but not in the first; nor in this.

about twenty in all, whose votes in favour or against each provided the editors, when the forms were returned to them, with at least a sample poll for that popularity which had seemed the only valid criterion. A twenty-five years' accumulation of correspondence from readers of the second edition had also brought to the Press a small harvest of quotations offered by members of the public in general; these were likewise given the suggestions-list treatment and voted on.

Public opinion and discussion within the Press had helped to evolve too some new principles for whole classes of 'quotations' to be excluded. The original compilers of the *Dictionary* had claimed — see p. xi — that 'proverbs and phrases are not included, since these have been dealt with fully in the *Oxford Dictionary of English Proverbs'*; this was not altogether true, and several so-called quotations have been removed because they are found in proverbial form much earlier than the authors to whom they were attributed.

Nursery rhymes, as a section, have been ousted. In the second edition reference was made to the *Oxford Dictionary of Nursery Rhymes,* edited by Iona and Peter Opie, as having provided the sources for many rhymes. Since these rarely have a named author, and the sources given were those of earliest written or published appearance, the information the *Dictionary of Quotations* supplied was not only largely drawn from but duplicated the Opies' *Dictionary of Nursery Rhymes,* to which masterly work the reader is commended.

Songs, with some regret, have also been excluded. The writers of the words of music-hall or popular songs identified in the preceding editions were often so obscure that the reader was informed of no more than their names, not even their dates. To have extended the citing of snatches of song on the scale of the earlier editions would have been a boundless venture: if 'my dear old Dutch' had been kept to the credit of Albert Chevalier, why not 'We'll gather lilacs...' added to Ivor Novello's or 'It's been a hard day's night' to the Beatles'? And how could justice be done then to the galaxy of shining, singing phrases, from the Gershwins to Cole Porter to Bob Dylan, in America's greatest contribution to Western civilization? The reader will look in vain to know who 'had plenty of privilege' — or was it 'twenty years' privilege'? — 'taken away from him' or when and where; and if authors and sources of popular songs had been given, why should the reader not also have expected to be told who wrote, 'How beautiful they are, the lordly ones', or even *'Che gelida manina'* ? No: the rule of thumb, given to the revision team and followed by the editors, has been that if the words cannot be said without the tune (*a* tune, in the case of many hymns) coming to mind, they are *not* quotations in the same sense as the others. Try 'Night and Day'.... This rule has not prevented the inclusion of poems that have subsequently been set to music; nor verses which, though written for musical setting, such as John Gay's, W. S. Gilbert's, or Noël Coward's, may now be quoted without a tune in the mental background.

Broadcasting and other mass-media have, in the past forty years, vastly multiplied the use and recognition and even therefore the 'quoting' of advertisements, slogans, and other catch-phrases. It would have been an equally vast and pointless task to try to record even the most familiar of them, apart from the near impossibility of ascribing each to the actual copywriter, speechwriter, or scriptwriter. This applies as much to the cinema and popular theatre as to radio and television. 'After you, Claude!' 'A funny thing happened on the way...'; yes, but not in the *O.D.Q.,* for lack of space and time.

Titles of books, films, and plays have been excised for similar reasons. Two or three exceptions may be found, where a title has come to be used in quotation often by people with no inkling that it was a title. (But no one would ever say, for example, *'Mourning Becomes Electra'* without that awareness.)

There will indeed probably be found places where all these guide-lines for the revisers have been departed from. One principle, however, of exclusion was not formulated or imposed but does seem to have emerged from the collective spirit of all the revisers: much that was sententious moralizing, homely wisdom, or merely uplifting reflection has been omitted.

But what of what remains? About 60% of the contents of the second edition is retained, not surprisingly. Well-known passages of the drama and literature of the past, from the Authorized Version of the Bible and from Shakespeare, together naturally with many famous historical *mots,* dicta, quips, and other utterances, still form the solid core of the universe of discourse in quotations, and the major part of this *Dictionary*.

Readers acquainted with the earlier editions may be interested (as the original compilers expected they would be) in the most quoted writers: they are still largely the same as those listed for the first edition on p. xi in alphabetical order before the Bible and the Book of Common Prayer. Less is quoted in this edition than in its predecessors in the case of every author in that list. But there are very nearly the same number of quotations from the two leading prose-writers, Dr. Johnson and Dickens. Wordsworth has suffered most; one of the revisers wrote of the 'huge snowdrifts of Wordsworth' that needed to be cleared, and indeed there were: beautiful, but not useful, and in the way! Cowper is the other poet who has (to change the metaphor) taken the biggest tumble. Both these illustrate certainly the decline in learning of English verse by heart. Cowper actually had no more space given to him in the second edition than Keats or Pope, though they are not listed by the first edition compilers; those two are well ahead of him in this new edition. The order of most quoted writers (the Bible and Prayer Book apart) is: Shakespeare, Tennyson, Milton, Johnson, Browning, Kipling, Dickens, Byron, Wordsworth, Pope, Keats, and Shelley. There are recent poets with more space given to them here than Cowper. The four novelists mentioned by the compilers of the first edition — Trollope, Henry James, Jane Austen and P. G. Wodehouse — all have more quotations in this third one (in each case continuing the trend of the second).

If proportionately more space has been given here to passages from the Bible of 1611 and the Prayer Book of 1662 (in which quotations from the Psalms appear) that is because English speaking and English writing are both shot through with phrases that derive from those books, still used, often unwittingly, even though the amount of church-going or Bible-reading has certainly diminished; indeed, for that very reason, as has been implied, more of the context of a biblical phrase, or one, say, from the Collects, has now been provided. It is no longer true, as the compilers were able to claim in 1941, that, in great part, both books are familiar to most people.

Not many concessions have been made, however, to the fact that the Greek and Latin classics are less studied in the original than they were; it is likely that rather more people are acquainted now, through translation, with Homer and Plato, Catullus and Martial, for example, and for the sake of those who do know the original languages they are for the most part quoted in Greek or Latin (with a translation supplied). Horace still has the 'array of columns' Bernard Darwin refers to, though half are English-made. Many more quotations from other modern European languages have been included. In all cases where a translator has not been named, the translation has in this edition been newly supplied by the publishing editors, in it is hoped a livelier rendering than earlier versions (but a close one).

In general it has been thought helpful in many instances to give more context to a quotation retained from the previous edition consisting only of a phrase or fragment of words; and the same principle has been applied to the few thousand newly added quotations. The length of the average quotation will thus probably be greater than in the earlier editions.

Beneath each quotation its source is given or is deducible from those immediately above it, and it has proved possible often to supply a better source reference than before. But in many cases (many more than for earlier editions) this annotation also includes some explanation of circumstances, a cross-reference to a related quotation, or some added point of quirky interest.

Throughout, the editors have endeavoured to correct errors perpetrated in the preceding editions. Many have been pointed out by members of the public since the last corrected impression of the second edition, and many discovered by the revisers in preparing this one. Others have doubtless lurked, or even slipped in; and for these the editors only are to blame, not the contributory revisers from outside the Press. The attempt was made to check the texts and verify the references of all new quotations elected for inclusion. The *Dictionary,* however, cannot aspire to be a work of scholarship in the strictest sense; no claim is made that the best or most authoritative text has been sought out and used in each case. It is a general work of reference, and normally a standard twentieth-century text, such as a World's Classics or an Oxford Classical Texts edition, has been followed. The editors will of course welcome corrections of their errors.

In the interests of book-production economy the index is neither as intensive nor as extensive as in the second edition, but it still occupies over a third of the volume and contains nearly 70,000 entries. The selection of words to be indexed has been made more after careful consideration of the salient word likely to be recalled in any quotation, and less at the mechanical rate of about two words per line. The actual process of printing and numbering the index has, moreover, been ingeniously achieved by computer; and a new attempt to assist the user of the index has also thus been contrived by the printing, before each page and quotation number reference, of the first few letters of the author's name. Thus a search under 'hill' to discover what manner of man Stevenson described as being 'home from the hill' will be promptly ended by the letters 'STEV' and sight of the 'hunter'.

But it will inevitably be upon the quotations newly chosen for inclusion that attention will be principally focused. Whether they are drawn from authors and works that have appeared in the last forty years or so, from the political and social memorabilia of the last quarter-century, or from areas neglected in preceding editions (writers now more widely known, foreign literature and drama, passages earlier evidently considered indelicate), it is hoped that for their familiarity or relevance or sheer appeal they resonate a bell in the memory, or carry a ring of aptness and truth, or just simply entertain and amuse.

It remains to record and renew the thanks of the Press to the team of scrutineers and contributors who agreed to take part in the process of revision described above, naming first the one who first took up the challenge and undertaking, and who by his example and zest influenced the whole new edition; the other names follow, in reverse alphabetical order:

the late Mr. T. C. Worsley; Mr. John Sparrow; Mr. Alan Ryan; the Hon. Sir Steven Runciman; Mrs. M. C. Rintoul; Mr. John Rayner; Mr. Charles Monteith; Mr. Colin Leach; Miss Marghanita Laski; Mr. Antony Jay; the Revd. Gerard Irvine; Miss Phyllis Hartnoll; Mr. John Gere; Miss Bertha Gaster; the late Lord Bradwell (Tom Driberg); Mr. Richard Boston; and Lord Annan.

As has been mentioned, many members of the public have contributed some few or more quotations or corrections, and the editors have not been without recourse to other published collections of quotations; it would be invidious to name some and not all, but the Press is grateful to all who have helped, and (it is expected and hoped) will continue to help the *Dictionary* in this way. But special thanks are due to the following who, at the editors' request, sought sources or supplied quotations in particular sections or otherwise made this a more accurate reference book:

Dr. Raymond Tyner; the late Mr. Oliver Stallybrass; Professor Richard Ellmann; Lady Donaldson; Mr Nevill Coghill; Mr. George Chowdharay-Best; and Professor Mortimer Chambers.

There has proved no need to reprint the 'Note to the Second Edition' (1953), but thanks were there recorded to two distinguished officers of the Press, Dr. R. W. Chapman and Sir Humphrey Milford, for their help in preparing that edition; also to Mr. S. H. Moore for French, German, and Spanish quotations. Much of their work probably survives in this third edition. The members of the past or present staff of the Press who have been principally concerned in the preparation of this edition are Andrew Thomson, Ena Sheen, Richard Sabido (and the Computer Department), Betty Palmer, Christina Lacey, Bob Knowles, Derek Hudson, Judy Gough, Roy Girling (and the Computer Typesetting Unit), and Richard Brain.

March 1979   R.T.B.

CONTENTS

THE COMPILERS TO THE READER
(1941)

'Classical quotation', said Johnson, 'is the *parole* of literary men all over the world.' Although this is no longer strictly true the habit of quoting, both in speech and writing, has steadily increased since his day, and Johnson would undoubtedly be surprised to find here eight and a half pages of his own work that have become part of the *parole* of the reading public. Small dictionaries of quotations have been published for many years — in 1799 D. E. Macdonnel brought out a *Dictionary of Quotations chiefly from Latin and French translated into English* — and during comparatively recent years several large works of American editorship have been produced. In this book the Oxford Press publishes what it is hoped will be a valuable addition to the Oxford Books of Reference already in existence.

The work remained in contemplation for some time before it first began to take shape under the general editorship of Miss Alice Mary Smyth, who worked, for purposes of selection, with a small committee formed of members of the Press itself. The existing dictionaries were taken as a foundation and the entries, pasted on separate cards, considered individually for rejection or inclusion. With these as a basis the most important authors were again dealt with either by the expert, or in committee, or by both. The Press is indebted for a great deal of work to the late Charles Fletcher, who among others made the original selections from Shakespeare, Milton, Pope, Tennyson, and Dryden: among those who dealt with single authors were Lady Charnwood and Mr. Bernard Darwin, who did the Dickens entries, Professor Dewar the Burns, Professor Ernest de Selincourt the Wordsworth: Mr. Colin Ellis did the Surtees, Sterne, and Whyte-Melville, Mr. E. Latham contributed the French quotations, and Mr. Harold Child made many valuable suggestions. A great many people, whom it is impossible to name individually, sent in one or more quotations.

During the whole work of selection a great effort was made to restrict the entries to actual current quotations and not to include phrases which the various editors or contributors believed to be quotable or wanted to be quoted: the work is primarily intended to be a dictionary of *familiar* quotations and not an anthology of every author good and bad; popularity and not merit being the password to inclusion. The selections from the Bible and Shakespeare were the most difficult because a great part of both are familiar to most people; but as concordances of both the Bible and Shakespeare are in print the quotations here included are meant to be the most well known where all is well known.

It has been found very difficult to put into precise words the standard of familiarity that has been aimed at or to imagine one man who might be asked whether or not the particular words were known to him. But it is believed that any of the quotations here printed might be found at some time in one or other of the leading articles of the daily and weekly papers with their wide range of matter — political, literary, descriptive, humorous, &c. So much for the very elastic standard to which the quotations conform. No one person having been imagined to whom everything included in this book would be familiar, the committee have tried to keep in mind that a number of different kinds of readers would be likely to use the book: these are the 'professionals', such as journalists, writers, public speakers, &c.; the cross-word devotee, since this form of intellectual amusement appears to have come to stay; the man who has in his mind either a few or many half-completed or unidentified quotations which he would like to complete or verify; and (since, as Emerson wrote — 'By necessity, by proclivity — and by delight, we all quote') everyone who has found joy and beauty in the words of the writers and wishes to renew that pleasure by using the words again — he whom perhaps Johnson meant by 'the literary man'. The book is not intended as a substitute for the complete works nor as an excuse to anyone not to drink deep of the Pierian spring. But it *is* hoped that the lover of Dickens, for instance, may find pleasure in reading through his entries and that even his detractors will have to admit how good he is in quotation: that the man who has always regarded Milton as a heavy and dull poet may here come across some lovely line and be inclined to read *Paradise Lost*. If the book serves to start people reading the poets it will have accomplished a great deal besides being a work of reference.

It is interesting to observe that the following are the most quoted writers (arranged in the order in which they appear here): Browning, Byron, Cowper, Dickens, Johnson, Kipling, Milton, Shakespeare, Shelley, Tennyson, Wordsworth, the Bible, and the Book of Common Prayer. On the other hand, certain authors of accepted merit or favour such as Trollope, Henry James, Jane Austen, and P. G. Wodehouse have none of them as much as one page to their credit: it would seem that their charm depends on character and atmosphere and that quotability is no real criterion of either popularity or merit in a writer.[1]

The arrangement of authors is alphabetical and not chronological. Under each author the arrangement of the extracts is alphabetical according to the title of the poem or work from which the quotation is taken. The text is, wherever possible, the acknowledged authoritative text and the source of the quotation is always given as fully as possible. Some quotations have had to be omitted because every effort to trace their source has failed — e.g. 'Home, James, and don't spare the horses'. Proverbs and phrases are not included, since these have been dealt with fully in the *Oxford Dictionary of English Proverbs*.

It is to be expected that almost every reader will be shocked by what he considers obvious omissions. Should the reader's indignation be strong enough to prompt him to write pointing these out it is to be hoped that he will give the source of all his suggestions. It is not possible to give all the quotations familiar to every reader;

[1] But see p. vi for a change now (3rd edn.).

almost all households have favourite books and authors from whom they frequently quote: to one family Stevenson is known and quoted by heart, to another the whole of the *Beggar's Opera* is as familiar as the extracts given here. Nor must the user expect to find here every quotation given in cross-word puzzles: compilers of these often seek to be obscure rather than familiar.

Latin is no longer a normal part of the language of educated people as it was in the eighteenth century; but from that age certain classical phrases have survived to become part of contemporary speech and writing. It is these 'survivals' that have been included here together with a few of the sayings or writings of the Schoolmen and early theologians. In many places more of the context of the actual familiar phrase has been given than is strictly necessary; but this has been a practice throughout the book, and one which it was thought would add to its value and charm. The translations are usually taken from the works of the better-known translators. Some one or two of the Greek quotations may be known to the general reader in their English version — e.g. 'The half is better than the whole' or 'Call no man happy till he dies'; but no apology is needed for the inclusion of two pages of matter most of which cannot pretend to be familiar to any but classical scholars.

The foreign quotations are not intended to satisfy the foreigner: they include such things as have become part of the speech and writings of English-speaking people either in their own language, such as 'les enfants terribles', or in an English translation, such as 'We will not go to Canossa'. As hardly any Spanish and no Russian or Swedish quotations are familiar to English readers most of these have been given only in translation.[1]

The index occupies approximately one-third of the total bulk of the book. A separate note will be found at the beginning of the index explaining the arrangement that has been adopted. Of the Latin quotations only those phrases that are familiar to the reader have been indexed; the unfamiliar context has not. In the English translations much the same principle has been followed: where the quotation is known to the reader in its English equivalent it has been indexed; where only the Latin is familiar and a translation is merely supplied to assist the reader it is left unindexed. A great deal of care has been spent on the index and the compilers look at it with some pride, believing that unless the searcher has to say 'Iddy tiddity' for every important word in the quotation he is looking for he will be able to find it; if, like Pig-wig (in Beatrix Potter's *Pigling Bland*), he has only forgotten some of the words, the index is full enough for him to trace it.

[1]At least for Spanish, there are more English readers now, and they have been honoured accordingly (3rd edn.).

INTRODUCTION
By Bernard Darwin

Quotation brings to many people one of the intensest joys of living. If they need any encouragement they have lately received it from the most distinguished quarters. Mr. Roosevelt quoted Longfellow to Mr. Churchill; Mr. Churchill passed on the quotation to us and subsequently quoted Clough on his own account. Thousands of listeners to that broadcast speech must have experienced the same series of emotions. When the Prime Minister said that there were some lines that he deemed appropriate we sat up rigid, waiting in mingled pleasure and apprehension. How agreeable it would be if we were acquainted with them and approved the choice! How flat and disappointing should they be unknown to us! A moment later we heard 'For while the tired waves, vainly breaking' and sank back in a pleasant agony of relief. We whispered the lines affectionately to ourselves, following the speaker, or even kept a word or two ahead of him in order to show our familiarity with the text. We were if possible more sure than ever that Mr. Churchill was the man for our money. He had given his ultimate proofs by flattering our vanity. He had chosen what we knew and what, if we had thought of it, we could have quoted ourselves. This innocent vanity often helps us over the hard places in life; it gives us a warm little glow against the coldness of the world and keeps us snug and happy. It certainly does its full share in the matter of quotations. We are puffed up with pride over those that we know and, a little illogically, we think that everyone else must know them too. As to those which lie outside our line of country we say, with Jowett as pictured by some anonymous genius[1] at Balliol, 'What I don't know isn't knowledge.' Yet here again we are illogical and unreasonable, for we allow ourselves to be annoyed by those who quote from outside our own small preserves. We accuse them in our hearts, as we do other people's children at a party, of 'showing off'. There are some departments of life in which we are ready to strike a bargain of mutual accommodation. The golfer is prepared to listen to his friend's story of missed putts, in which he takes no faintest interest, on the understanding that he may in turn impart his own heart-rending tale, and the bargain is honourably kept by both parties. The same rule does not apply to other people's quotations, which are not merely tedious but wound us in our tenderest spot. And the part played by vanity is perhaps worth pointing out because everybody, when he first plunges adventurously into this great work, ought in justice to the compilers to bear it in mind.

It is safe to say that there is no single reader who will not have a mild grievance or two, both as to what has been put in and what has been left out. In particular he will 'murmur a little sadly' over some favourite that is not there. I, for instance, have a

[1] Since identified as H. C. Beeching.

small grievance. William Hepworth Thompson, sometime Master of Trinity, the author of many famous and mordant sayings on which I have been brought up, is represented by but a single one.[1] Can it be, I ask myself, that this is due to the fact that an Oxford Scholar put several of the Master's sayings into his Greek exercise book but attributed them to one Talirantes? Down, base thought! I only mention this momentary and most unworthy suspicion to show other readers the sort of thing they should avoid as they would the very devil. It is not that of which any one of us is fondest that is entitled as of right to a place. As often as he feels ever so slightly aggrieved, the reader should say to himself, if need be over and over again, that this is not a private anthology, but a collection of the quotations which the public knows best. In this fact, moreover, if properly appreciated, there ought to be much comfort. 'My head', said Charles Lamb, 'has not many mansions nor spacious',[2] and is that not true of most of us? If in this book there are a great many quotations that we do not know, there are also a great many that we do. There is that example of Clough with which I began. We may have to admit under cross-examination that we have only a rather vague acquaintance with Clough's poems, but we do know 'Say not the struggle'; and there on page so-and-so it is. Both we and the dictionary's compilers are thereupon seen to be persons of taste and discrimination.

If I may be allowed to harp a little longer on this string of vanity, it is rather amusing to fancy the varied reception given to the book by those who are quoted in it. They will consist largely of more or less illustrious shades, and we may picture them looking over one another's pale shoulders at the first copy of the dictionary to reach the asphodel. What jealousies there will be as they compare the number of pages respectively allotted to them! What indignation at finding themselves in such mixed company! Alphabetical order makes strange bedfellows. Dickens and Dibdin must get on capitally and convivially together, but what an ill-assorted couple are Mrs. Humphry Ward and the beloved Artemus of the same name![3] George Borrow may ask, 'Pray, who is this John Collins Bossidy?'[4] Many readers may incidentally echo his question, and yet no man better merits his niche, for Mr. Bossidy wrote the lines ending 'And the Cabots talk only to God', which have told the whole world of the blue blood of Boston. John Hookham Frere, singing of the mailed lobster clapping his broad wings, must feel his frivolity uncomfortably hushed for a moment by his next-door neighbour, Charles Frohman, on the point of going down with the *Lusitania*.[5] And apropos of Frere, there rises before me the portentous figure of my great-great-grandfather, Erasmus Darwin. He was thought a vastly fine poet in his day and there is a family legend that he was paid a guinea a line for his too fluent verses. And yet he is deservedly forgotten, while those who parodied him in the

---

[1] Two in the 2nd edn., three in this 3rd.
[2] *The Essays of Elia* (1820-23), 'The Old and the New Schoolmaster'.
[3] 'Propinquity does it, indeed.
[4] These two were already separated in the 2nd edn. by the admission of foreign quotations among the English and thus by Maréchal Bosquet's magnificent put-down of the Light Brigade.
[5] For this pathetic juxtaposition readers must refer to the 1st or 2nd edn.

Anti-Jacobin attain an equally well-deserved immortality. He was a formidable old gentleman, with something of the Johnson touch, but not without a sense of humour, and I do not think he will be greatly hurt.

The most famous poets must be presumed to be above these petty vanities, though it would be agreeable to think of Horace contemplating his array of columns and saying, 'I told you so — Exegi monumentum'. In any case the number of columns or pages does not constitute the only test. Another is the number of words in each line by which any particular quotation can be identified, and this gives me a chance of making my compliments to the ingenuity and fullness of the index. The searcher need never despair and should he draw blank under 'swings' he is pretty sure to find what he wants under 'roundabouts'. There is a little game to be played (one of the many fascinating games which the reader can devise for himself) by counting the number of 'key words' in each line and working out the average of fame to which any passage is entitled. Even a short time so spent shows unexpected results, likely to spread envy and malice among the shades. It might be imagined that Shakespeare would be an easy winner. It has been said that every drop of the Thames is liquid history and almost every line of certain passages in Shakespeare is solid quotation. Let us fancy that his pre-eminence is challenged, that a sweepstake is suggested, and that he agrees to be judged by 'To be or not to be'. It seems a sufficiently sound choice and is found to produce fifty-five key words[1] in thirty-three lines. All the other poets are ready to give in at once; they cannot stand against such scoring as that and Shakespeare is about to pocket the money when up sidles Mr. Alexander Pope. What, he asks, about that bitter little thing of his which he sent to Mr. Addison? And he proves to be right, for in those two and twenty lines to Atticus there are fifty-two key words.[2] I have not played this game nearly long enough to pronounce Pope the winner. Very likely Shakespeare or someone else can produce a passage with a still higher average, but here at any rate is enough to show that it is a good game and as full of uncertainties as cricket itself.

Though the great poets may wrangle a little amongst themselves, they do not stand in need of anything that the dictionary can do for them. Very different is the case of the small ones, whose whole fame depends upon a single happy line or even a single absurd one. To them exclusion from these pages may virtually mean annihilation, while inclusion makes them only a little lower than the angels. Their anxiety therefore must be pitiful and their joy when they find themselves safe in the haven proportionately great. Sometimes that joy may be short-lived. Think of Mr. Robert Montgomery, who was highly esteemed till the ruthless Macaulay fell upon him. With trembling hand he turns the pages and finds no less than four extracts from 'The Omnipresence of the Deity'.[3] Alas! under his own letter M the traducer is waiting for him, and by a peculiar refinement of cruelty there are quoted no less than five[4] of Lord Macaulay's criticisms on that very poem. This is a sad case; let us take a

---

[1] Now only forty-one since many fewer phrases have had words indexed (3rd edn.).

[2] In this 3rd edn. thirty-one in only twenty of those lines.

[3] *The...Deity* now (3rd edn.) virtually annihilated.   [4] Reduced to three (3rd edn.).

more cheerful one and still among the M's. Thomas Osbert Mordaunt has full recognition as the author of 'Sound, sound the clarion, fill the fife', after having for years had to endure the attribution of his lines to Sir Walter Scott, who in pure innocency put them at the head of a chapter. This to be sure was known already, but whoever heard before the name of the author of 'We don't want to fight', the man who gave the word 'Jingo' to the world? We know that the Great McDermott sang it, but even he may not have known who wrote it, just as Miss Fotheringay did not know who wrote 'The Stranger'. Now G. W. Hunt comes into his kingdom and with him another who helped many thousands of soldiers on their way during the last war. Mr. George H. Powell[1] is fortunately still alive to enjoy the celebrity of 'Pack up your troubles in your old kit bag'. How many thousands, too, have sung 'Wrap me up in my tarpaulin jacket' without realizing that it was by Whyte-Melville?[2] To him, however, recognition is of less account. His place was already secure.

Among the utterers of famous sayings some seem to have been more fortunate than others. Lord Westbury, for instance, has always had the rather brutal credit of telling some wretched little attorney to turn the matter over 'in what you are pleased to call your mind'; but how many of us knew who first spoke of a 'blazing indiscretion' or called the parks 'the lungs of London'? We may rejoice with all these who, having for years been wronged, have come into their rights at last, but there are others with whom we can only sympathize. They must be contented with the fact that their sayings or their verses have been deemed worth recording, even though their names 'shall be lost for evermore'. The Rugby boy who called his headmaster 'a beast but a just beast' sleeps unknown, while through him Temple lives. He can only enjoy what the dynamiter Zero called 'an anonymous infernal glory'. So do the authors of many admirable limericks, though some of the best are attributed to a living divine of great distinction, who has not disclaimed such juvenile frolics.[3] So again do those who have given us many household words from the advertisement hoardings, the beloved old jingle of 'the Pickwick, the Owl, and the Waverley pen', the alluring alliteration of 'Pink Pills for Pale People'.[4] Let us hope that it is enough for them that they did their duty and sent the sales leaping upward.

So much for the authors without whom this book could never have been. Now for the readers and some of the happy uses to which they will put it. 'Hand me over the Burton's *Anatomy*', said Captain Shandon, 'and leave me to my abominable devices.' It was Greek and Latin quotations that he sought for his article, but fashion has changed and today it would rather be English ones. Here is one of the most obvious purposes for which the dictionary will be used. It cannot accomplish impossibilities. It will not prevent many an honest journalist from referring to 'fresh fields and pastures new' nor from describing a cup-tie as an example of 'Greek meeting Greek'. There is a fine old crusted tradition of misquoting not lightly to be

[1] Georg Asaf.
[2] Both these verses are omitted from this 3rd edn. as songs: see p. v.
[3] The late Mgr. Ronald Knox (1888-1957).
[4] The latter, like most advertising (see p. v), has been excluded from the 3rd edn.

broken and it might almost seem pedantry to deck these ancient friends in their true but unfamiliar colours. Misquoting may even be deemed an amiable weakness, since Dickens in one of his letters misquoted Sam Weller; but here at least is a good chance of avoiding it. There is likewise a chance of replenishing a stock grown somewhat threadbare. 'Well, you're a boss word', exclaimed Jim Pinkerton,[1] when he lighted on 'Hebdomadary' in a dictionary. 'Before you're very much older I'll have you in type as long as yourself.' So the hard-pressed writer in turning over these pages may find and note many excellent phrases against future contingencies, whether to give a pleasing touch of erudition or to save the trouble of thinking for himself. These, however, are sordid considerations, and the mind loves rather to dwell on fireside quoting-matches between two friends, each of whom thinks his own visual memory the more accurate. There are certain writers well adapted to this form of contest and among the moderns Conan Doyle must, with all respect to Mr. Wodehouse, be assigned the first place. Sherlock Holmes scholars are both numerous and formidable; they set themselves and demand of others a high standard. It is one very difficult to attain since there often seems no reason why any particular remark should have been made on any particular occasion. This is especially true of Dr. Watson. He was constantly saying that his practice was not very absorbing or that he had an accommodating neighbour, but when did he say which? Even the most learned might by a momentary blunder confuse 'A Case of Identity' with 'The Final Problem'. It would be dry work to plough through all the stories, even though the supreme satisfaction of being right should reward the search. Now a glance at the dictionary will dispose of an argument which would otherwise 'end only with the visit'.

It is incidentally curious and interesting to observe that two authors may each have the same power of inspiring devotion and the competitive spirit, and yet one may be, from the dictionary point of view, infinitely more quotable than the other. Hardly any prose writer, for instance, produces a more fanatical adoration than Miss Austen, and there are doubtless those who can recite pages of her with scarce a slip; but it is perhaps pages rather than sentences that they quote. Mr. Bennet provides an exception, but generally speaking she is not very amenable to the treatment by scissors and paste. George Eliot, if we leave out Mrs. Poyser, a professed wit and coiner of aphorisms, is in much poorer case. Another and a very different writer, Borrow, can rouse us to a frantic pitch of romantic excitement, but it is the whole scene and atmosphere that possess this magic and we cannot take atmosphere to pieces. These are but three examples of writers who do not seem to lend themselves to brief and familiar quotations.[2] They have jewels in plenty, but these form part of a piece of elaborate ornament from which they cannot be detached without irreparable damage. The works of some other writers may by contrast be said to consist of separate stones, each of which needs no setting and can sparkle on its own acount.

[1] Robert Louis Stevenson (with Lloyd Osbourne), *The Wrecker* (1892), ch. 7.
[2] A good many more quotations from both Jane Austen and George Eliot are included in this 3rd than in the preceding editions.

Dickens is an obvious and unique instance. Stevenson, too, has the gift of producing characters such as Prince Florizel and Alan Breck, John Silver and Michael Finsbury, whose words can stand memorable by themselves, apart from context or atmosphere. Those who share my love for Florizel will rejoice to observe that he has had some faithful friend among the compilers. As for Michael I cannot help feeling that he has been rather scurvily used, for *The Wrong Box* is admirably suited to competition and even learned Judges of the Court of Appeal have been known, all unsuspected by their ignorant auditors, to bandy quotations from it on the Bench. Here, however, I take leave to give any indignant reader a hint. Let him not cry too loudly before he is hurt! It is true that 'nothing like a little judicious levity' is not in the main body of the dictionary, but someone awoke just in time and it is among the addenda.[1]

To return to those friends by the fireside whom I pictured indulging in a heated quoting-match, it may be that they will presently become allies and unite to use the dictionary over a cross-word puzzle. It is hardly too much to say that the setters of these problems should not use a quotation unless it is to be found in the dictionary. A cross-word quotation should not be too simple, but it should be such that that hypothetical personage, the reasonable man, might have heard of it. The solver demands fair play, and the setter who takes a volume of verse at haphazard, finds a word that fits, and substitutes a blank for it, is not playing the game. There are solvers whose standard of sportsmanship is so high that they would as soon allow themselves to cheat at patience as have recourse to a book. We may admire though we cannot emulate this fine austere arrogance. It is the best fun to win unaided, but there is good fun too in ferreting out a quotation. It well repays the ardours of the chase. Moreover a setter of puzzles who oversteps honourable limits should be fought with his own weapons. He has palpably used books and this is an epoch of reprisals. Then let us use books too and hoist him with his own petard.

It is difficult today not to deal in warlike metaphors, but perhaps the truest and most perfect use of the dictionary is essentially peaceful. Reviewers are apt to say of a detective story that it is 'impossible to lay it down till the last page is reached'. It is rather for books of reference that such praise should be reserved. No others are comparable with them for the purposes of eternal browsing. They suggest all manner of lovely, lazy things, in particular the watching of a cricket match on a sunshiny day. We have only dropped in for half an hour, but the temptation to see just one more over before we go is irresistible. Evening draws on, the shadows of the fielders lengthen on the grass, nothing much is happening, a draw becomes every minute more inevitable, and still we cannot tear ourselves away. So it is with works of reference, even with the most arid, even with Bradshaw, whose vocabulary, as Sherlock Holmes remarked, is 'nervous and terse but limited'. Over the very next page of Bradshaw there may be hidden a Framlingham Admiral; adventure may always be in wait a little farther down the line. So, but a thousand times more so, is

---

[1] In the main body all right in the 2nd edn., and further amends have been made to *The Wrong Box* in this new edn.

some exciting treasure-trove awaiting us over the next page of this dictionary. What it is we cannot guess, but it is for ever calling in our ears to turn over just one more. We have only taken down the book to look up one special passage, but it is likely enough that we shall never get so far. Long before we have reached the appropriate letter we shall have been waylaid by an earlier one, and shall have clean forgotton our original quest. Nor is this all, for, if our mood changes as we browse, it is so fatally, beautifully easy to change our pasture. We can play a game akin to that 'dabbing' cricket, so popular in private-school days, in which the batsman's destiny depended or was supposed to depend — for we were not always honest — on a pencil delivered with eyes tightly shut. We can close the book and open it again at random, sure of something that shall set us off again on a fresh and enchanting voyage of not too strenuous discovery.

Under this enchantment I have fallen deep. I have pored over the proofs so that only by a supreme effort of will could I lay them down and embark on the impertinent task of trying to write about them. I now send them back to their home with a sense of privation and loneliness. Here seems to me a great book. Then

> Deem it not all a too presumptuous folly,

this humble tribute to Oxford from another establishment over the way.

B.D.

May 1941

HOW TO USE THE DICTIONARY

The arrangement is alphabetical by the names of authors; their surnames mostly, but sometimes their titles, monarchs by their imperial or royal titles, writers sometimes by their pseudonyms. In general the best-known names are given, and usually in the form most used: T. S. (rather than Thomas Stearns) Eliot and no Fingal O'Flahertie Wills for Oscar. Sections such as the Anonymous one, Ballads, the Bible, the Mass in Latin, etc., are included in the alphabetical order.

Under each author, quotations are arranged by the alphabetical order of the titles of the works from which they come: books, plays, poems. These are printed in bold italic type. Titles of pieces (e.g., articles, essays, short stories) that constitute part of a published volume are in bold roman (the volume title having been given in bold italic). Quotations from diaries, letters, speeches, etc., however, are given in chronological order, and normally follow the literary works quoted. Poetry quotations precede prose ones for poets; and vice versa for writers most of whose work was in prose. Quotations cited from biographies or other writers' works are kept to the end under each author; sources are then given conventionally with titles of books or plays in italic (not bold) type.

Numerical source references are given for the first line of each quotation, by, e.g., act, scene, and, if appropriate, line number; by chapter or by page or section or verse number. But references are not repeated for every single quotation. The use of 'Ib.' — ubiquitous in the earlier editions — has been avoided. Each quotation without a full source given depends from its immediate predecessor. If no source reference is given at all, that is an invisible 'Ib.': the quotation is from the same poem or chapter or whatever as the last preceding named or numbered one.

A date in brackets is of the first performance or publication of the work cited.

Italic has been used for all quotations in foreign languages and Latin. Throughout, spelling and capitalization have been modernized, except in English writers of the Middle Ages.

Running headlines give the names of the first and last authors *starting* a section on each page (not usually of the author of the first quotation on a page).

Sub-headings have been used under Dickens with the titles of novels, under the Bible with the books named — kept in canonical order, not alphabetically — followed by the Vulgate, and under Shakespeare with the titles of plays and poems.

QUOTATIONS

PETER ABELARD 1079–1142

1 *O quanta qualia sunt illa sabbata,*
Quae semper celebrat superna curia.
O how great and glorious are those sabbaths which the
heavenly court for ever celebrates!
Hymnus Paraclitensis

2 *Quis rex, quae curia, quale palatium,*
Quae pax, quae requies, quod illud gaudium.
What a king, what a court, how fine a palace, what
peace, what rest, what rejoicing is there!

ACCIUS 170–c.90 B.C.

3 *Oderint, dum metuant.*
Let them hate, so long as they fear.
Atreus. Seneca, *De Ira*, I, 20, 4

DEAN ACHESON 1893–1971

4 Great Britain has lost an Empire and has not yet found
a role.
Speech at the Military Academy, West Point, 5 Dec. 1962

LORD ACTON 1834–1902

5 Power tends to corrupt and absolute power corrupts
absolutely.
Letter to Bishop Mandell Creighton, 3 Apr. 1887. See *Life and
Letters of Mandell Creighton* (1904), i.372. See 373:23

CHARLES FRANCIS ADAMS 1807–1886

6 It would be superfluous in me to point out to your
lordship that this is war.
Dispatch to Earl Russell, 5 Sept. 1863. C.F. Adams, *Charles
Francis Adams*, p.342

HENRY ADAMS 1838–1918

7 A friend in power is a friend lost.
The Education of Henry Adams, ch.7

PRESIDENT JOHN QUINCY ADAMS 1767–1848

8 Think of your forefathers! Think of your posterity!
Speech, 22 Dec. 1802

SAMUEL ADAMS 1722–1803

9 A nation of shop-keepers are very seldom so
disinterested.
Oration said to have been delivered at Philadelphia, 1 Aug. 1776.
See 359:15, 509:12

SARAH F. ADAMS 1805–1848

10 Nearer, my God, to thee,
Nearer to thee!
Nearer My God to Thee

JOSEPH ADDISON 1672–1719

11 Pray consider what a figure a man would make in the
republic of letters.
Ancient Medals, 1

12 There is nothing more requisite in business than
dispatch.
5

13 'Twas then great Marlbro's mighty soul was prov'd.
The Campaign, 1.279

14 And, pleas'd th' Almighty's orders to perform,
Rides in the whirl-wind, and directs the storm.
1.291

15 And those who paint 'em truest praise 'em most.
1.476

16 'Tis not in mortals to command success,
But we'll do more, Sempronius; we'll deserve it.
Cato, I.ii.43

17 Blesses his stars, and thinks it luxury.
iv.70

18 'Tis pride, rank pride, and haughtiness of soul;
I think the Romans call it stoicism.
82

19 Were you with these, my prince, you'd soon forget
The pale, unripened beauties of the north.
134

20 The woman that deliberates is lost.
IV.i.31

21 Curse on his virtues! they've undone his country.
Such popular humanity is treason.
iv.35

22   What pity is it
That we can die but once to serve our country!
81

23 Content thyself to be obscurely good.
When vice prevails, and impious men bear sway,
The post of honour is a private station.
139

24 It must be so—Plato, thou reason'st well!—
Else whence this pleasing hope, this fond desire,
This longing after immortality?
Or whence this secret dread, and inward horror,
Of falling into naught? Why shrinks the soul
Back on herself, and startles at destruction?
'Tis the divinity that stirs within us;
'Tis heaven itself, that points out an hereafter,
And intimates eternity to man.
Eternity! thou pleasing, dreadful thought!
V.i.1

25 From hence, let fierce contending nations know
What dire effects from civil discord flow.
iv.111

1 Round-heads and Wooden-shoes are standing jokes.
The Drummer, Prologue

2 I should think my self a very bad woman, if I had done what I do, for a farthing less.
I

3 He more had pleas'd us, had he pleas'd us less.
English Poets. Of Cowley

4 For wheresoe'er I turn my ravished eyes,
Gay gilded scenes and shining prospects rise,
Poetic fields encompass me around,
And still I seem to tread on classic ground.
Letter from Italy

5 A painted meadow, or a purling stream.

6 Music, the greatest good that mortals know,
And all of heaven we have below.
A Song for St. Cecilia's Day, st. 3

7 A reader seldom peruses a book with pleasure until he knows whether the writer of it be a black man or a fair man, of a mild or choleric disposition, married or a bachelor.
The Spectator, 1

8 Thus I live in the world rather as a spectator of mankind than as one of the species.

9 As a perfect tragedy is the noblest production of human nature, so it is capable of giving the mind one of the most delightful and most improving entertainments.
39

10 In all thy humours, whether grave or mellow,
Thou'rt such a touchy, testy, pleasant fellow;
Hast so much wit, and mirth, and spleen about thee,
There is no living with thee, nor without thee.
68. See 331:13

11 The infusion of a China plant sweetened with the pith of an Indian cane.
69

12 As Sir Roger is landlord to the whole congregation, he keeps them in very good order, and will suffer nobody to sleep in it [the church] besides himself; for if by chance he has been surprised into a short nap at sermon, upon recovering out of it, he stands up, and looks about him; and if he sees anybody else nodding, either wakes them himself, or sends his servant to them.
112

13 Sir Roger told them, with the air of a man who would not give his judgment rashly, that much might be said on both sides.
122

14 My friends Sir Roger de Coverley and Sir Andrew Freeport are of different principles, the first of them inclined to the *landed* and the other to the *monied* interest.
126

15 It was a saying of an ancient philosopher, which I find some of our writers have ascribed to Queen Elizabeth, who perhaps might have taken occasion to repeat it, that a good face is a letter of recommendation.
221. See 402:4

16 I have often thought, says Sir Roger, it happens very well that Christmas should fall out in the Middle of Winter.
269

17 Dr Busby, a great man! he whipped my grandfather; a very great man! I should have gone to him myself, if I had not been a blockhead; a very great man!
329

18 These widows, Sir, are the most perverse creatures in the world.
335

19 The Knight in the triumph of his heart made several reflections on the greatness of the *British* Nation; as, that one *Englishman* could beat three *Frenchmen;* that we cou'd never be in danger of Popery so long as we took care of our fleet; that the *Thames* was the noblest river in *Europe;* that *London Bridge* was a greater piece of work than any of the Seven Wonders of the World; with many other honest prejudices which naturally cleave to the heart of a true *Englishman.*
383

20 Through all Eternity to Thee
A joyful Song I'll raise,
For oh! Eternity's too short
To utter all thy Praise.
453

21 We have in England a particular bashfulness in every thing that regards religion.
458

22 The spacious firmament on high,
With all the blue ethereal sky.
465

23 A woman seldom asks advice before she has bought her wedding clothes.
475

24 Our disputants put me in mind of the skuttle fish, that when he is unable to extricate himself, blackens all the water about him, till he becomes invisible.
476

25 I value my garden more for being full of blackbirds than of cherries, and very frankly give them fruit for their songs.
477

26 If we may believe our logicians, man is distinguished from all other creatures by the faculty of laughter.
494

27 'We are always doing', says he, 'something for Posterity, but I would fain see Posterity do something for us.'
583

28 I remember when our whole island was shaken with an earthquake some years ago, there was an impudent mountebank who sold pills which (as he told the country people) were very good against an earthquake.
The Tatler, 240

29 See in what peace a Christian can die.
Dying words to his stepson Lord Warwick. Young, *Conjectures on Original Composition,* 1759

30 Should the whole frame of nature round him break,
In ruin and confusion hurled,
He, unconcerned, would hear the mighty crack,
And stand secure amidst a falling world.
Translation of Horace, Odes, III.iii. See 260:18, 376:21

AESCHYLUS 525/4–456 B.C.

1 ἐλέναυς ἔλανδρος ἐλέπτολις.
Hell to ships, hell to men, hell to cities.
Agamemnon, 689. Of Helen; literally 'Ship-destroyer, (etc.)'.

2 ὤμοι, πέπληγμαι καιρίαν πληγὴν ἔσω.
Oh me, I have been struck a mortal blow right inside.
1343

3 ποντίων τε κυμάτων ἀνήριθμον γέλασμα.
Innumerable twinkling of the waves of the sea.
Prometheus Bound, 89

AGATHON 446?–c.401 B.C.

4 Even God cannot change the past.
Aristotle, *Nicomachean Ethics*, VI.2.1139b

MARIA, MARCHIONESS OF AILESBURY
d.1902

5 My dear, my dear, you never know when any
beautiful young lady may not blossom into a Duchess!
Duke of Portland, *Men, Women, and Things*, ch.3

CANON AINGER 1837–1904

6 No flowers, by request.
Speech, 8 July 1897. *D.N.B.* Summary of principle of
conciseness for its contributors.

ALBERT, PRINCE CONSORT 1819–1861

7 The works of art, by being publicly exhibited and
offered for sale, are becoming articles of trade,
following as such the unreasoning laws of markets and
fashion; and public and even private patronage is
swayed by their tyrannical influence.
Speech at the Royal Academy Dinner, 3 May 1851

SCIPIONE ALBERTI fl. 1550–1590

8 *I pensieri stretti ed il viso sciolto* will go safely over
the whole world.
Secret thoughts and open countenance...
On being asked how to behave in Rome. Sir Henry Wotton, letter
to Milton, 13 Apr. 1638, prefixed to *Comus*.

ALCUIN c.735–804

9 *Nec audiendi qui solent dicere, Vox populi, vox Dei,
quum tumultuositas vulgi semper insaniae proxima sit.*
And those people should not be listened to who keep
saying the voice of the people is the voice of God,
since the riotousness of the crowd is always very close
to madness.
Letter to Charlemagne, A.D.800. *Works*, Epist.127

DEAN ALDRICH 1647–1710

10 If all be true that I do think,
There are five reasons we should drink;
Good wine—a friend—or being dry—
Or lest we should be by and by—
Or any other reason why.
Reasons for Drinking

THOMAS BAILEY ALDRICH 1836–1907

11   The fair, frail palaces,
The fading alps and archipelagoes,
And great cloud-continents of sunset-seas.
Sonnet: Miracles

ALEXANDER THE GREAT 356–323 B.C.

12 εἰ μὴ 'Αλέξανδρος ἤμην, Διογένης ἂν ἤμην.
If I were not Alexander, I would be Diogenes.
Plutarch, *Life of Alexander*, xiv.3

MRS. ALEXANDER 1818–1895

13 All things bright and beautiful,
    All creatures great and small,
All things wise and wonderful,
    The Lord God made them all.
All Things Bright and Beautiful (1848)

14 The rich man in his castle,
    The poor man at his gate,
God made them, high or lowly,
    And order'd their estate.

SIR WILLIAM ALEXANDER, EARL OF STIRLING 1567?–1640

15 The weaker sex, to piety more prone.
Doomsday, Hour v, lv

ALFONSO THE WISE, KING OF CASTILE
1221–1284

16 Had I been present at the Creation, I would have given
some useful hints for the better ordering of the
universe.
Said after studying the Ptolemaic system. Attr.

KING ALFRED 849–901

17 Then began I...to turn into English the book that is
named in Latin *Pastoralis*...one-while word for word,
another-while meaning for meaning.
Whole Works (Jubilee Edition, 1852), vol.III, p.64. Preface to
the Anglo-Saxon version of Gregory's *Pastoral Care*.

RICHARD ALISON fl. c.1606

18 There cherries grow, that none can buy
Till cherry ripe themselves do cry.
An Hour's Recreation in Music. See 129:22, 248:21

ABBÉ D'ALLAINVAL 1700–1753

19 *L'embarras des richesses.*
The more alternatives, the more difficult the choice.
Title of comedy, 1726

WILLIAM ALLINGHAM 1828–1889

20 Up the airy mountain,
Down the rushy glen,
We daren't go a-hunting,
For fear of little men.
The Fairies

21 Four ducks on a pond,
A grass-bank beyond,

A blue sky of spring,
White clouds on the wing:
What a little thing
To remember for years—
To remember with tears!
A Memory

ST. AMBROSE c.339–397

1 *Ubi Petrus, ibi ergo ecclesia.*
Where Peter is, there must be the Church.
Explanatio psalmi 40, 30. *Corpus Scriptorum Ecclesiasticorum Latinorum* 64, 250

2 *Si fueris Romae, Romano vivito more;*
Si fueris alibi, vivito sicut ibi.
If you are at Rome live in the Roman style; if you are elsewhere live as they live elsewhere.
Jeremy Taylor, *Ductor Dubitantium*, I.i.5. Usually quoted as 'When in Rome, do as the Romans do.'

FISHER AMES 1758–1808

3 A monarchy is a merchantman which sails well, but will sometimes strike on a rock, and go to the bottom; a republic is a raft which will never sink, but then your feet are always in the water.
House of Representatives, 1795

KINGSLEY AMIS 1922–

4 More will mean worse.
Encounter, July 1960

HANS CHRISTIAN ANDERSEN 1805–1875

5 'But the Emperor has nothing on at all!' cried a little child.
The Emperor's New Clothes

BISHOP LANCELOT ANDREWES 1555–1626

6 But we are not so much to regard the *Ecce*, how great it is, as *Gaudium*, what joy is in it; that is the point we are to speak to.
Sermon 5, Of the Nativity (1610)

7 It was no summer progress. A cold coming they had of it, at this time of the year; just, the worst time of the year, to take a journey, and specially a long journey, in. The ways deep, the weather sharp, the days short, the sun farthest off *in solstitio brumali*, the very dead of Winter.
Sermon 15, Of the Nativity (1622)

8 The nearer the Church the further from God.

ANONYMOUS

ENGLISH

9 A beast, but a just beast.
Of Dr. Temple, Headmaster of Rugby, 1857-69

10 Absence makes the heart grow fonder.
Davison, *Poetical Rhapsody*, 1602

11 A Company for carrying on an undertaking of Great Advantage, but no one to know what it is.
The South Sea Company Prospectus, 1711. Cowles, *The Great Swindle* (1963), ch.5

12 Adam

Had 'em.
On the antiquity of Microbes. (Claimed as the shortest poem.)

13 A gentleman haranguing on the perfection of our law, and that it was equally open to the poor and the rich, was answered by another, 'So is the London Tavern'.
Tom Paine's Jests... (1794), 23. Also attr. to John Horne Tooke (1736–1812) in W. Hazlitt, *The Spirit of the Age* (1825), 'Mr. Horne Tooke'.

14 All human beings are born free and equal in dignity and rights.
Universal Declaration of Human Rights (1948), Article 1

15 All present and correct.
King's Regulations (Army). Report of the Orderly Sergeant to the Officer of the Day

16 All this buttoning and unbuttoning.
18th Century suicide note

17 Along the electric wire the message came:
He is not better—he is much the same.
Said to be from a poem on the illness of the Prince of Wales, afterwards Edward VII, often attr. to Alfred Austin (1835–1913), Poet Laureate. Gribble, *Romance of the Cambridge Colleges* (1913), p.226

18 An abomination unto the Lord, but a very present help in time of trouble. [A lie.]
(Cf. Proverbs 12:22; Psalms 46:1)

19 An old song made by an aged old pate,
Of an old worshipful gentleman who had a great estate.
The Old Courtier

20 Any officer who shall behave in a scandalous manner, unbecoming the character of an officer and a gentleman shall...be CASHIERED.
Articles of War (1872), *Disgraceful Conduct*, 79. The Naval Discipline Act (10 Aug. 1860), Article 24, contained the words 'conduct unbecoming the character of an Officer'.

21 A place within the meaning of the Act.
Betting Act

22 Appeal from Philip drunk to Philip sober.
Valerius Maximus, *Facta ac Dicta Memorabilia* (c. A.D. 32), VI, ii

23 Are we downhearted? No!
Expression much used by British soldiers in 1914-18, probably based on 139:7

24 A sympathetic Scot summed it all up very neatly in the remark, 'You should make a point of trying every experience once, excepting incest and folk-dancing'.
Sir Arnold Bax (1883–1953), *Farewell My Youth* (1943), 'Cecil Sharp'

25 A was an apple-pie;
B bit it;
C cut it.
John Eachard, *Some Observations* (1671)

26 A willing foe and sea room.
Naval toast in the time of Nelson. Beckett, *A Few Naval Customs, Expressions, Traditions, and Superstitions* (1931)

27 Be happy while y'er leevin,
For y'er a lang time deid.
Scottish motto for a house. N. & Q. 7 Dec. 1901, 469

28 Conduct...to the prejudice of good order and military discipline.
Army Act, 40

29 Dear Sir, Your astonishment's odd:
I am always about in the Quad.
And that's why the tree
Will continue to be,

Since observed by Yours faithfully, God.
Reply to limerick on idealism. See 305:22

1 Defence, not defiance.
Motto of the Volunteers Movement, 1859

2 Dollar Diplomacy.
Term applied to Secretary Knox's activities in securing opportunities for the investment of American capital abroad, particularly in Latin America and China. *Harper's Weekly*, 23 Apr. 1910, 8

3 Early one morning, just as the sun was rising,
I heard a maid sing in the valley below:
'Oh, don't deceive me; Oh, never leave me!
How could you use a poor maiden so?'
Early One Morning

4 Earned a precarious living by taking in one another's washing.
Attr. Mark Twain by William Morris in *The Commonweal*, 6 Aug. 1887

5 An intelligent Russian once remarked to us, 'Every country has its own constitution; ours is absolutism moderated by assassination.'
Georg Herbert, Count Münster, *Political Sketches of the State of Europe, 1814–1867* (1868), 19

6 *Knowledge:* Everyman, I will go with thee, and be thy guide.
In thy most need to go by thy side.
Everyman (c.500), l.522

7 Father of his Country. [George Washington.]
Francis Bailey, *Nord Americanische Kalender*, 1779

8 From ghoulies and ghosties and long-leggety beasties
And things that go bump in the night,
     Good Lord, deliver us!
Cornish

9 God be in my head,
And in my understanding;

God be in my eyes,
And in my looking;

God be in my mouth,
And in my speaking;

God be in my heart,
And in my thinking;

God be at my end,
And at my departing.
Sarum Missal

10 Great Chatham with his sabre drawn
Stood waiting for Sir Richard Strachan;
Sir Richard, longing to be at 'em,
Stood waiting for the Earl of Chatham.
At Walcheren, 1809

11 Greensleeves was all my joy,
     Greensleeves was my delight,
Greensleeves was my heart of gold,
     And who but Lady Greensleeves?
A new Courtly Sonnet of the Lady Greensleeves, to the new tune of 'Greensleeves'. From *A Handful of Pleasant Delites* (1584)

12 Happy is that city which in time of peace thinks of war. (Inscription in the armoury of Venice.)
Burton, *Anatomy of Melancholy*, pt.ii, 3, memb.6. See 556:3

13 Here lies a poor woman who always was tired,
For she lived in a place where help wasn't hired.
Her last words on earth were, Dear friends I am going
Where washing ain't done nor sweeping nor sewing,
And everything there is exact to my wishes,

For there they don't eat and there's no washing of dishes...
Don't mourn for me now, don't mourn for me never,
For I'm going to do nothing for ever and ever.
Epitaph in Bushey churchyard, before 1860, destroyed by 1916. Quoted in a letter to the *Spectator*, 2 Sept. 1922

14 Here lies a valiant warrior
Who never drew a sword;
Here lies a noble courtier
Who never kept his word;
Here lies the Earl of Leicester
Who governed the estates
Whom the earth could never living love,
And the just heaven now hates.
Attr. Ben Jonson in Tissington, *Collection of Epitaphs* (1857), p.377

15 Here lies Fred,
Who was alive and is dead:
Had it been his father,
I had much rather;
Had it been his brother,
Still better than another;
Had it been his sister,
No one would have missed her;
Had it been the whole generation,
Still better for the nation:
But since 'tis only Fred,
Who was alive and is dead,—
There's no more to be said.
Horace Walpole, *Memoirs of George II* (1847), I, 436

16 Here's tae us; wha's like us?
Gey few, and they're a' deid.
Scottish Toast, probably of nineteenth-century origin. The first line appears in Crosland, *The Unspeakable Scot* (1902), p.24n. Various versions of the second line are current.

17 He talked shop like a tenth muse.
Of Gladstone's Budget speeches. G.W.E. Russell, *Collections and Recollections*, ch.12

18   He tickles this age that can
Call Tullia's ape a marmasyte
     And Leda's goose a swan.
Fara diddle dyno, from Thomas Weelkes, *Airs or Fantastic Spirits* (1608). See N. Ault, *Elizabethan Lyrics*

19 Hierusalem, my happy home
     When shall I come to thee?
When shall my sorrows have an end,
     Thy joys when shall I see?
Hierusalem. See *Songs of Praise Discussed*

20 'How different, how very different from the home life of our own dear Queen!'
Irvin S. Cobb, *A Laugh a Day*. Comment by a middle-aged British matron at a performance of Cleopatra by Sarah Bernhardt. The story is probably apocryphal.

21 I can not eat but little meat,
     My stomach is not good:
But sure I think, that I can drink
     With him that wears a hood.
Though I go bare, take ye no care,
     I am nothing acold:
I stuff my skin, so full within,
     Of jolly good ale and old,
Back and side go bare, go bare,
     Both foot and hand go cold:
But belly God send thee good ale enough,

5

Whether it be new or old.
Song from *Gammer Gurton's Needle* (acted 1566, printed 1575),
Act II. The play has been attr. to William Stevenson
(1530?–1575) and to John Still (1543–1608); the song may be
earlier in origin.

1 I feel no pain dear mother now
But oh, I am so dry!
O take me to a brewery
And leave me there to die.
Parody of 209:21

2 If God were to take one or other of us, I should go and
live in Paris.
Reported in S. Butler, *Notebooks*, ed. G. Keynes and B. Hill,
1951, p.193

3 If he only knew a little of law, he would know a little
of everything.
Of Lord Brougham. Emerson, *Quotation and Originality* (1877)

4 I'm arm'd with more than complete steel—The justice
of my quarrel.
Lust's Dominion (1657), IV.iii

5 I'll sing you twelve O.
Green grow the rushes O.
What is your twelve O?
Twelve for the twelve apostles,
Eleven for the eleven who went to heaven,
Ten for the ten commandments,
Nine for the nine bright shiners,
Eight for the eight bold rangers,
Seven for the seven stars in the sky,
Six for the six proud walkers,
Five for the symbol at your door,
Four for the Gospel makers,
Three for the rivals,
Two, two, the lily-white boys,
Clothed all in green O,
One is one and all alone
And ever more shall be so.
The Dilly Song. See G. Grigson, *The Faber Book of Popular
Verse;* see also Revd. S. Baring-Gould and Revd. H. Fleetwood
Sheppard, *Songs and Ballads of the West* (1891), no.78, for a
variant version.

6 I met wid Napper Tandy, and he took me by the hand,
And he said, 'How's poor ould Ireland, and how does
she stand?'
She's the most disthressful country that iver yet was
seen,
For they're hangin' men an' women there for the
wearin' o' the Green.
The Wearin' o' the Green. (Famous street ballad, later added to
by Boucicault.)

7   I saw my lady weep,
And Sorrow proud to be exalted so
In those fair eyes where all perfections keep.
        Her face was full of woe;
But such a woe, believe me, as wins more hearts,
Than Mirth can do with her enticing parts.
Songs set by John Dowland, *Oxford Book of 16th Cent. Verse*

8 It is positively dangerous to sit to Sargent. It's taking
your face in your hands.
W. Graham Robertson, *Time Was* (1931), ch.21

9 The children of Lord Lytton organized a charade. The
scene displayed a Crusader knight returning from the
wars. At his gate he was welcomed by his wife to
whom he recounted his triumphs and the number of
heathen he had slain. His wife, pointing to a row of

dolls of various sizes, replied with pride, 'And I too,
my lord, have not been idle'.
G.W.E. Russell, *Collections and Recollections*, ch.31

10 Like a fine old English gentleman,
All of the olden time.
The Fine Old English Gentleman. Oxford Song Book

11 The newly-elected mayor who…said that during his
year of office he should lay aside all his political
prepossessions and be 'like Caesar's wife, all things to
all men'.
G.W.E. Russell, *Collections and Recollections*, ch.30

12 Lizzie Borden took an axe
And gave her mother forty whacks;
When she saw what she had done
She gave her father forty-one!
Lizzie Borden was acquitted of murdering her father and
stepmother on 4 Aug. 1892 in Fall River, Massachusetts

13 Love me little, love me long,
Is the burden of my song.
Love me Little, Love me Long (1569–70)

14 *Child:* Mamma, are Tories born wicked, or do they
grow wicked afterwards?
Mother: They are born wicked, and grow worse.
G.W.E. Russell, *Collections and Recollections*, ch.10

15 Matthew, Mark, Luke, and John,
The Bed be blest that I lie on.
Four angels to my bed,
Four angels round my head,
One to watch, and one to pray,
And two to bear my soul away.
Thomas Ady, *A Candle in the Dark* (1656)

16 Miss Buss and Miss Beale
Cupid's darts do not feel.
How different from us,
Miss Beale and Miss Buss.
Of the Headmistress of the North London Collegiate School and
the Principal of the Ladies' College, Cheltenham, c. 1884

17 Most Gracious Queen, we thee implore
To go away and sin no more,
But if that effort be too great,
To go away at any rate.
Epigram on Queen Caroline, quoted in Lord Colchester's Diary,
15 Nov. 1820

18 Multiplication is vexation,
Division is as bad;
The Rule of three doth puzzle me,
And Practice drives me mad.
Elizabethan MS. dated 1570

19 My sledge and anvil lie declined
My bellows too have lost their wind
My fire's extinct, my forge decayed,
And in the Dust my Vice is laid
My coals are spent, my iron's gone
My Nails are Drove, My Work is done.
Epitaph in Nettlebed churchyard on William Strange, d. 6 June
1746, and used similarly for other blacksmiths.

20 My Love in her attire doth show her wit,
    It doth so well become her:
For every season she hath dressings fit,
    For winter, spring, and summer.
No beauty she doth miss,
    When all her robes are on;
But beauty's self she is,
    When all her robes are gone.
Madrigal

1 My name is George Nathaniel Curzon,
I am a most superior person.
The Masque of Balliol, composed by and current among members
of Balliol College in the late 1870's. See 37:8, 517:11–12

2 My face is pink, my hair is sleek,
I dine at Blenheim once a week.
(A later addition.)

3 Now I lay me down to sleep;
I pray the Lord my soul to keep.
If I should die before I wake,
I pray the Lord my soul to take.
First printed in a late edition of the *New England Primer*, 1781

4 O Death, where is thy sting-a-ling-a-ling,
O Grave, thy victoree?
The bells of Hell go ting-a-ling-a-ling
For you but not for me.
Song popular in the British Army, 1914-18

5 O God, if there be a God, save my soul, if I have a
soul!
Prayer of a common soldier before the battle of Blenheim (see N.
& Q., clxxiii.264). Quoted in Newman's *Apologia*

6 Oh my dear fellow, the noise...and the people!
Of the Battle of Bastogne. Attr. to a Captain Strahan. See Griffin,
'Dialogue with W.H. Auden', *Hudson Review* III, iv, Winter 51,
p.583

7 One Cartwright brought a Slave from Russia, and
would scourge him, for which he was questioned: and
it was resolved, That England was too pure an Air for
Slaves to breathe in.
'In the 11th of Elizabeth' (17 Nov. 1568–16 Nov. 1569).
Rushworth, *Historical Collections* (1680–1722), II, p.468

8 On Waterloo's ensanguined plain
Full many a gallant man was slain,
But none, by sabre or by shot,
Fell half so flat as Walter Scott.
On Scott's *Field of Waterloo*. 1815

9 Please do not shoot the pianist. He is doing his best.
Oscar Wilde, *Impressions of America*. 'Leadville'

10 Please to remember the Fifth of November,
Gunpowder Treason and Plot.
We know no reason why gunpowder treason
Should ever be forgot.
Traditional since 17th cent.

11 Raise the stone, and there thou shalt find me, cleave
the wood and there am I.
Oxyrhynchus Papyri, B.P. Grenfell and A.S. Hunt (eds.) *Sayings
of Our Lord* (1897) Logion 5, l.23

12 Says Tweed to Till—
'What gars ye rin sae still?'
Says Till to Tweed—
'Though ye rin with speed
And I rin slaw,
For ae man that ye droon
I droon twa'.
Two Rivers, Oxford Book of English Verse

13 See the happy moron,
He doesn't give a damn.
I wish I were a moron.
My God! Perhaps I am!
Eugenics Review, July 1929, 86/2

14 Seven wealthy Towns contend for HOMER Dead

Through which the Living HOMER begged his Bread.
Epilogue to *Aesop at Tunbridge; or, a Few Selected Fables in
Verse*. By No Person of Quality, 1698. See 250:22

15 Since first I saw your face, I resolved to honour and
renown ye;
If now I be disdained, I wish my heart had never
known ye.
What? I that loved and you that liked, shall we begin
to wrangle?
No, no, no, my heart is fast, and cannot disentangle.
Music of Sundry Kinds (1607)

16 Since wars begin in the minds of men, it is in the
minds of men that the defences of peace must be
constructed.
Constitution of the United Nations Educational, Scientific and
Cultural Organisation (1946)

17 Spheres of influence.
Hertslet, *Map of Africa by Treaty*, 3rd edn., 868. See 234:10

18 Sumer is icumen in,
Lhude sing cuccu!
Groweth sed, and bloweth med,
And springth the wude nu.
Cuckoo Song, c. 1250, sung annually at Reading Abbey
gateway. First recorded by John Fornset, a monk of Reading
Abbey

19 That this house will in no circumstances fight for its
King and country.
Motion passed at the Oxford Union, 9 Feb. 1933

20 That we spent, we had:
That we gave, we have:
That we left, we lost.
Epitaph of the Earl of Devonshire, as quoted by Spenser in *The
Shepherd's Calendar*, May, l.70. See 8:17

21 The almighty dollar is the only object of worship.
Philadelphia Public Ledger, 2 Dec. 1836

22 The children in Holland take pleasure in making
What the children in England take pleasure in
breaking.
Nursery Rhyme

23 The eternal triangle.
Book review in the *Daily Chronicle*, 5 Dec. 1907

24 The fault is great in man or woman
Who steals a goose from off a common;
But what can plead that man's excuse
Who steals a common from a goose?
The Tickler Magazine, 1 Feb. 1821

25 The King over the Water.
Jacobite Toast, 18th cent.

26 The ministry of all the talents.
A name given ironically to Grenville's coalition of 1806; also
applied to later coalitions

27 The nature of God is a circle of which the centre is
everywhere and the circumference is nowhere.
Said to have been traced to a lost treatise of Empedocles. Quoted
in the *Roman de la Rose*, and by S. Bonaventura in *Itinerarius
Mentis in Deum*, cap.v, *ad fin.*

28 Therefore let us sing and dance a galliard,
To the remembrance of the mallard:
And as the mallard dives in pool,
Let us dabble, dive, and duck in Bowl.
Oh! by the blood of King Edward,
Oh! by the blood of King Edward,
It was a swapping, swapping mallard.
All Souls College, Oxford, song (perhaps of Tudor date). See *The
Oxford Sausage* (1764), pp.83-84. Manuscript sources suggest

that the song was first printed in 1752. Hearne's Diaries, 17, p.46, May 1708 (see *Collections*, ed. C.E. Doble, ii, O.H.S. vii, 1886, p.111), have the order 'duck and dive' in the last line of the verse.

1 There is a lady sweet and kind,
   Was never face so pleased my mind;
   I did but see her passing by,
   And yet I love her till I die.
   Found on back of leaf 53 of 'Popish Kingdome or reigne of Antichrist', in Latin verse by Thomas Naogeorgus, and Englished by Barnabe Googe. Printed 1570. See N. & Q., 9th series, x.427

2 There is so much good in the worst of us,
   And so much bad in the best of us,
   That it hardly becomes any of us
   To talk about the rest of us.
   Good and Bad. Attr. to Edward Wallis Hoch (1849–1925) but disclaimed by him; and to many others.

3 There's nae luck about the house,
      There's nae luck at a',
   There's nae luck about the house
      When our gudeman's awa'.
   The Mariner's Wife

4 The Sun himself cannot forget
   His fellow traveller.
   On Sir Francis Drake. *Wit's Recreations* (1640), Epigrams, No.146

5 They come as a boon and a blessing to men,
   The Pickwick, the Owl, and the Waverley pen.
   Advertisement by MacNiven and Cameron Ltd, Edinburgh and Birmingham

6 Thirty days hath September,
   April, June, and November;
   All the rest have thirty-one,
   Excepting February alone,
   And that has twenty-eight days clear
   And twenty-nine in each leap year.
   Stevins MS. (c.1555)

7 The singer not the song.
   From a West Indian calypso and used as the title of a novel (1959) by Audrey Erskine Lindop

8 This is a rotten argument, but it should be good enough for their lordships on a hot summer afternoon.
   Annotation to ministerial brief, said to have been read inadvertently in the House of Lords. Lord Home, *The Way the Wind Blows* (1976), p.204

9 Thought shall be the harder, heart the keener, courage the greater, as our might lessens.
   The Battle of Maldon. Tr. R.K. Gordon (1926) from Anglo-Saxon.

10 To many people Victorian wit and humour is summed up by *Punch*, when every joke is supposed to end with 'Collapse of Stout Party', though this phrase tends to be as elusive as 'Elementary, my dear Watson' in the Sherlock Holmes sagas.
   R. Pearsall, *Collapse of Stout Party* (1975), Introduction

11 Too small to live in and too large to hang on a watch-chain. [Of Chiswick House.]
   Cecil Roberts, *And so to Bath* (1940), ch.4. 'By Way of Chiswick', attr. to 'one guest'

12 Two men wrote a lexicon, Liddell and Scott;
   Some parts were clever, but some parts were not.
   Hear, all ye learned, and read me this riddle,
   How the wrong part wrote Scott, and the right part
      wrote Liddell.
   On Henry Liddell (1811–98) and Robert Scott (1811–87), co-authors of the Greek Lexicon, 1843

13 Weep you no more, sad fountains;
      What need you flow so fast?
   Songs set by John Dowland, *Oxford Book of 16th Cent. Verse*

14 We hold these truths to be self-evident, that all men are created equal, that they are endowed by their Creator with certain unalienable rights, that among these are life, liberty and the pursuit of happiness.
   The American Declaration of Independence, 4 July 1776. See 272:6

15 'Well, what sort of sport has Lord — had?'
   'Oh, the young Sahib shot divinely, but God was very merciful to the birds.'
   G.W.E. Russell, *Collections and Recollections*, ch.30

16 Western wind, when wilt thou blow,
      The small rain down can rain?
   Christ, if my love were in my arms
      And I in my bed again!
   Oxford Book of 16th Cent. Verse

17 What wee gave, wee have;
   What wee spent, wee had;
   What wee kept, wee lost.
   Epitaph on Edward Courtenay, Earl of Devonshire (d. 1419), and his wife, at Tiverton. See 7:20

18 When Israel was in Egypt land,
   Let my people go,
   Oppressed so hard they could not stand,
   Let my people go.
      Go down, Moses,
      Way-down in Egypt land,
      Tell old Pharaoh
      To let my people go.
   Negro Spiritual. See 47:13

19 When I was a little boy, I had but a little wit,
   'Tis a long time ago, and I have no more yet;
   Nor ever ever shall, until that I die,
   For the longer I live the more fool am I.
   Wit and Mirth, an Antidote against Melancholy (1684)

20 Where is the man who has the power and skill
   To stem the torrent of a woman's will?
   For if she will, she will, you may depend on't;
   And if she won't, she won't; so there's an end on't.
   From the Pillar Erected on the Mount in the Dane John Field, Canterbury *Examiner*, 31 May 1829

21 Whilst Adam slept, Eve from his side arose:
   Strange his first sleep should be his last repose.
   The Consequence

22 Whose Finger do you want on the Trigger When the World Situation Is So Delicate?
   Headline in the *Daily Mirror*, see H. Cudlipp, *Publish and Be Damned* (1953), p.263

23 Would you like to sin
   With Elinor Glyn
   On a tiger-skin?
   Or would you prefer
   to err
   with her
   on some other fur?
   c. 1907. A. Glyn, *Elinor Glyn* (1955), pt.II.30

24 Yet, if his majesty our sovereign lord
   Should of his own accord
   Friendly himself invite,
   And say 'I'll be your guest tomorrow night',
   How should we stir ourselves, call and command

All hands to work!
From Christ Church MS.

1 But at the coming of the King of Heaven
All's set at six and seven:
We wallow in our sin.
Christ cannot find a chamber in the inn.
We entertain Him always like a stranger,
And as at first still lodge Him in the manger.

2 You pays your money and you takes your choice.
From a peepshow rhyme. See V.S. Lean, *Collectanea* (1902-4)

FRENCH

3 An army marches on its stomach.
Attr. Napoleon in, e.g., *Windsor Magazine*, 1904, p.268.
Probably condensed from a long passage in Las Cases, *Mémorial de Ste-Hélène* (Nov. 1816)

4 *Cet animal est très méchant,*
Quand on l'attaque il se défend.
This animal is very bad; when attacked it defends itself.
La Ménagerie, by Théodore P.K., 1828

5 *Chevalier sans peur et sans reproche.*
Knight without fear and without blemish.
Description in contemporary chronicles of Pierre Bayard, 1476–1524

6 *Honi soit qui mal y pense.*
Evil be to him who evil thinks [of it].
Motto of the Order of the Garter, originated by Edward III probably on 23 Apr. of 1348 or 1349.

7 *Il y avait un jeune homme de Dijon,*
Qui n'avait que peu de religion.
Il dit: 'Quant à moi,
Je déteste tous les trois,
Le Père, et le Fils, et le Pigeon.'
The Norman Douglas limerick book (1969, first privately printed in 1928 under the title *Some Limericks*), introduction.

8 *Je suis le capitaine de vingt-quatre soldats, et sans moi Paris serait pris?* [Answer:] *A.*
Hugh Rowley, *Puniana: or thoughts wise and otherwise a new collection of the best* (1867), p.42. The saying 'With twenty-six lead soldiers [the characters of the alphabet set up for printing] I can conquer the world' may be derived from this riddle, but probably arose independently.

9 *La grande phrase reçue, c'est* qu'il ne faut pas être plus royaliste que le roi. *Cette phrase n'est pas du moment; elle fut inventée sous Louis XVI: elle enchaîna les mains des fidèles, pour ne laisser libre que le bras du bourreau.*
The big catch-phrase is *that you mustn't be more of a royalist than His Royal Highness*. This expression is not new; it was coined under the reign of Louis XVI: it chained up the hands of the loyal, leaving free only the arm of the hangman.
Chateaubriand, *De La Monarchie selon la Charte*, II, xli

10 *Laisser-nous-faire.*
M. Colbert assembla plusieurs Deputés de commerce chez lui pour leur demander ce qu'il pourroit faire pour le commerce; le plus raisonnable et le moins flatteur d'entre eux, lui dit ce seul mot: '*Laissez-nous-faire.*' *Journal Oeconomique*, Paris, Apr. 1751

11 *L'amour est aveugle; l'amitié ferme les yeux.*
Love is blind; friendship closes its eyes.
See 11:25, 402:22

12 *Le monde est plein de fous, et qui n'en veut pas voir*
Doit se tenir tout seul, et casser son miroir.
The world is full of fools, and he who would not see it should live alone and smash his mirror.
An adaptation from an original form attr. to Claude Le Petit (1640–1665) in *Discours Satiriques*, 1686

13 *Liberté! Égalité! Fraternité!*
Freedom! Equality! Brotherhood!
Motto of the French Revolution, but of earlier origin. The Club des Cordeliers passed a motion, 30 June 1793, '*que les propriétaires seront invités,…de faire peindre sur la façade de leurs maisons, en gros caractères, ces mots: Unité, indivisibilité de la République, Liberté, Égalité, Fraternité ou la mort*':*Journal de Paris*, 182. From 1795 the words '*ou la mort*' were dropped from this prescription. See 139:18

14 *L'ordre règne à Varsovie.*
Order reigns in Warsaw.
After the brutal suppression of an uprising, the newspaper *Moniteur* reported (16 Sept. 1831) '*L'ordre et la tranquillité sont entièrement rétablis dans la capitale.*' On the same day Count Sebastiani, minister of foreign affairs said '*La tranquillité règne à Varsovie.*'

15 *Nous n'irons plus aux bois, les lauriers sont coupés.*
We'll to the woods no more,
The laurels all are cut.
Old nursery rhyme quoted by Banville in *Les Cariatides, les stalactites*. Tr. Housman, *Last Poems*, introductory

16 *Revenons à ces moutons.*
Let us return to our sheep. (Let us get back to the subject.)
Maistre Pierre Pathelin (line 1191). Often quoted as '*Retournons à nos moutons*'

17 *Si le Roi m'avait donné,*
Paris, sa grand'ville,
Et qu'il me fallût quitter
L'amour de ma mie,
Je dirais au roi Henri:
'Reprenez votre Paris:
J'aime mieux ma mie, au gué,
J'aime mieux ma mie.'
If the king had given me Paris, his great city, and if I were required to give up my darling's love, I would say to King Henry: 'Take your Paris back; I prefer my darling, by the ford, I prefer my darling'.
Popular song, attr. Antoine de Bourbon (1518–1562), father of Henri IV; see Ampère, *Instructions relatives aux poésies populaires de la France*. Quoted in this form in Molière, *Le Misanthrope*, I.ii

18 *Taisez-vous! Méfiez-vous! Les oreilles ennemies vous écoutent.*
Keep your mouth shut! Be on your guard! Enemy ears are listening to you.
Official Notice in France in 1915

19 *Toujours perdrix!*
Always partridge!
Said to originate in a story of Henri IV's having ordered that nothing but partridge should be served to his confessor, who had rebuked the king for his liaisons.

20 *Tout passe, tout casse, tout lasse.*
Everything passes, everthing perishes, everthing palls.
Cahier, *Quelques six mille proverbes*

GREEK

21 γνῶθι σεαυτόν.
Know thyself.
Inscribed on the temple of Apollo at Delphi. Plato, *Protagoras*, 343 b, ascribes the saying to the Seven Wise Men.

22 μηδὲν ἄγαν.
Nothing in excess.

1 ὅταν δ᾽ ὁ δαίμων ἀνδρὶ πορσύνῃ κακά,
τὸν νοῦν ἔβλαψε πρῶτον, ᾧ βουλεύεται.

Whenever God prepares evil for a man, He first
damages his mind.
Scholiast on Sophocles, *Antigone*, 622 ff. See R.C. Jebb's edn.
(1906), Appendix, pp.255-6. Perhaps best known in Latin
translation. See 199:15

2 ἀγεωμέτρητος μηδεὶς εἰσίτω.

Let no one enter who does not know geometry
[mathematics].
Inscription on Plato's door, probably at the Academy at Athens.
Elias Philosophus, *In Aristotelis Categorias Commentaria*, 118.18
(A. Busse ed., *Comm. in Arist. Graeca*, Berlin, 1900, XVIII, i.)

ITALIAN

3 *Se non è vero, è molto ben trovato.*
If it is not true, it is a happy invention.
Apparently a common saying in the sixteenth century. Found in
Giordano Bruno (1585) in the above form, and in Antonio Doni
(1552) as '*Se non è vero, egli è stato un bel trovato.*'

LATIN

4 *Adeste, fideles,*
　　Laeti triumphantes;
Venite, venite in Bethlehem.
　　O come, all ye faithful,
　　Joyful and triumphant,
O come, ye, O come ye to Bethlehem.
French or German hymn of 18th Cent. Trans. F. Oakeley in
Murray's Hymnal, 1852. See *Songs of Praise Discussed*

5 *Venite adoremus, venite adoremus,*
Venite adoremus Dominum.
O come, let us adore him! O come, let us adore him!
O come, let us adore him, Christ the Lord!

6 *Ad majorem Dei gloriam.*
To the greater glory of God.
Motto of the Society of Jesus

7 *Ave Caesar, morituri te salutant.*
Hail Caesar; those who are about to die salute you.
Gladiators saluting the Roman Emperor. See Suetonius, *Claudius*,
21

8 *Ave Maria, gratia plena, Dominus tecum: Benedicta*
tu in mulieribus, et benedictus fructus ventris tui,
Jesus.
Hail Mary, full of grace, the Lord is with thee: Blessed
art thou among women, and blessed is the fruit of thy
womb, Jesus.
Ave Maria, also known as *The Angelic Salutation*, dating from
the 11th cent.

9 *Ave verum corpus,*
Natum Ex Maria Virgine.
Hail the true body, born of the Virgin Mary.
Eucharistic hymn, dating probably from the 14th cent.

10 *Caveant consules ne quid res publica detrimenti*
caperet.
Let the consuls see to it that no harm come to the
state.
Senatorial 'ultimate decree' in the Roman Republic. See, e.g.,
Cicero, *Pro Milone*, 26, 70

11 *Cras amet qui nunquam amavit, quique amavit cras*
amet!
Let those love now, who never lov'd before:
Let those who always lov'd, now love the more.
Pervigilium Veneris, 1. Tr. Parnell

12 *Et in Arcadia ego.*
And I too in Arcadia.
Tomb inscription often depicted in classical paintings. The
meaning is disputed.

13 *Gaudeamus igitur,*
Juvenes dum sumus
Post jucundam juventutem,
Post molestam senectutem,
Nos habebit humus.
Let us then rejoice,
While we are young.
After the pleasures of youth
And the tiresomeness of old age
Earth will hold us.
Medieval students' song, traced to 1267, but revised in the 18th
cent.

14 *Meum est propositum*
　　In taberna mori,
Ut sint vina proxima
　　Morientis ori.
Tunc cantabunt laetius
　　Angelorum chori:
'Sit Deus propitius
　　Huic potatori!'
I desire to end my days in a tavern drinking,
May some Christian hold for me the glass when I am
　　shrinking;
That the Cherubim may cry, when they see me
　　sinking,
'God be merciful to a soul of this gentleman's way of
　　thinking.'
'The Archpoet' (fl. 1159-67), *Estuans intrinsecus ira vehementi.*
Tr. Leigh Hunt.

15 *Nemo me impune lacessit.*
No one provokes me with impunity.
Motto of the Crown of Scotland and of all Scottish regiments

16 *Per ardua ad astra.*
Hard and high to the stars!
Motto of the Mulvany family, quoted in Rider Haggard, *The*
People of the Mist (1894), ch.1, proposed by J.S. Yule in 1912,
adopted as official motto of the Royal Flying Corps and approved
by King George V in 1913, still in use as motto of the R.A.F. See
P.G. Hering, *Customs and Traditions of the Royal Air Force*
(1961). Rider Haggard's rendering was 'Through Struggle to the
Stars'.

17 *Post coitum omne animal triste.*
After coition every animal is sad.
Post-classical

18 *Quidquid agas, prudenter agas, et respice finem.*
Whatever you do, do cautiously, and look to the end.
Gesta Romanorum, 103

19 *Salve, regina, mater misericordiae,*
Vita, dulcedo et spes nostra, salve!
Ad te clamamus exsules filii Evae,
Ad te suspiramus gementes et flentes
In hac lacrimarum valle.
Eia ergo, advocata nostra,
Illos tuos misericordes oculos ad nos converte.
Et Iesum, benedictum fructum ventris tui,
Nobis post hoc exsilium ostende,
O clemens, o pia,
O dulcis virgo Maria.
Hail holy queen, mother of mercy, hail our life, our
　　sweetness, and our hope! To thee do we cry, poor
banished children of Eve; to thee do we send up our
sighs, mourning and weeping in this vale of tears.

Turn then, most gracious advocate, thine eyes of mercy towards us; and after this our exile show unto us the blessed fruit of thy womb, Jesus, O clement, O loving, O sweet virgin Mary.
Attr. to various eleventh-century authors. See *Analecta Hymnica...* vol.50 (1907), p.318.

1 *Sic transit gloria mundi.*
Thus passes the glory of the world.
Spoken during the coronation of a new Pope, while flax is burned to represent the transitoriness of earthly glory. Used at the coronation of Alexander V, Pisa, 7 July 1409, but earlier in origin. See 546:7

2 *Si monumentum requiris, circumspice.*
If you seek for a monument, gaze around.
Inscription in St. Paul's Cathedral, London, attr. to the son of the architect, Sir Christopher Wren.

3 *Te Deum laudamus: Te Dominum confitemur.*
We praise thee, God: we own thee Lord.
Te Deum. Hymn traditionally ascribed to St. Ambrose and St. Augustine in 387, but some modern scholars attribute it to St. Niceta (d.c.414). See 384:16

4 *In te Domine, speravi: non confundar in aeternum.*
Lord, I have set my hopes in thee, I shall not be destroyed for ever.
See 384:18

5 *Tempora mutantur, et nos mutamur in illis.*
Times change, and we change with them.
Harrison, *Description of Britain* (1577), III, iii, 99. Attributed to the Emperor Lothar I (795-855) in the form *Omnia mutantur, nos et mutamur in illis*

6 *Vox et praeterea nihil.*
A voice and nothing more.
Of a nightingale. See also Plutarch, *Moralia*, 'Sayings of Spartans', 233a

CHRISTOPHER ANSTEY 1724–1805

7 If ever I ate a good supper at night,
I dream'd of the devil, and wak'd in a fright.
The New Bath Guide. Letter 4. A Consultation of the Physicians

8 You may go to Carlisle's, and to Almack's too;
And I'll give you my head if you find such a host,
For coffee, tea, chocolate, butter, and toast:
How he welcomes at once all the world and his wife,
And how civil to folk he ne'er saw in his life.
Letter 13. A Public Breakfast

F. ANSTEY 1856–1934

9 Drastic measures is Latin for a whopping.
Vice Versa, ch.7

GUILLAUME APOLLINAIRE 1880–1918

10 *Les souvenirs sont cors de chasse*
Dont meurt le bruit parmi le vent.
Memories are hunting horns whose sound dies on the wind.
Cors de Chasse

11 *Sous le pont Mirabeau coule la Seine*
Et nos amours
Faut-il qu'il m'en souvienne
La joie venait toujours après la peine

Vienne nuit sonne l'heure
Les jours s'en vont je demeure.
Under Mirabeau Bridge flows the Seine.

Why must I be reminded again
Of our love?
Doesn't happiness issue from pain?

Bring on the night, ring out the hour.
The days wear on but I endure.
Le Pont Mirabeau, tr. William Meredith

THOMAS GOLD APPLETON 1812–1884

12 A Boston man is the east wind made flesh.
Attr.

13 Good Americans, when they die, go to Paris.
O.W. Holmes, *Autocrat of the Breakfast Table*, 6

ARABIAN NIGHTS

14 Who will change old lamps for new ones?...new lamps for old ones?
The History of Aladdin

15 Open Sesame!
The History of Ali Baba

WILLIAM ARABIN 1773–1841

16 If ever there was a case of clearer evidence than this of persons acting in concert together, this case is that case.
Sir R. Megarry, *Arabinesque at Law* (1969)

17 They will steal the very teeth out of your mouth as you walk through the streets. I know it from experience.
[The citizens of Uxbridge.]

18 Prisoner, God has given you good abilities, instead of which you go about the country stealing ducks.
See N. & Q., clxx.310

DR. ARBUTHNOT 1667–1735

19 He warns the heads of parties against believing their own lies.
The Art of Political Lying (1712)

20 Law is a bottomless pit.
The History of John Bull (1712), ch.24

21 Here continueth to rot the body of Francis Chartres.
See A. Pope, note to 1.20 of *Epistles to Several Persons*, iii. 'To Lord Bathhurst' (1733)

ARCHILOCHUS fl. c.650 B.C.

22 πολλ᾽ οἶδ᾽ ἀλώπηξ, ἀλλ᾽ ἐχῖνος ἓν μέγα.
The fox knows many things—the hedgehog one *big* one.
E. Diehl (ed.), *Anth. Lyr. Gr.*, I, p.241, no.103

ARCHIMEDES 287–212 B.C.

23 εὕρηκα.
Eureka! (I've got it!)
Vitruvius Pollio, *De Architectura*, ix.215

24 δός μοι ποῦ στῶ καὶ κινῶ τὴν γῆν.
Give me somewhere to stand, and I will move the earth.
Pappus, *Synagoge*, ed. F. Hultsch, Berlin, 1876-8, VIII, 10, xi

COMTE D'ARGENSON 1652–1721

25 *Laisser-faire.*

No interference.
Mémoires, vol.5, p.364. See 9:10, 403:22

1 Abbé Guyot Desfontaines: *Il faut que je vive.*
D'Argenson: *Je n'en vois pas la nécessité.*
Desfontaines: I must live.
D'Argenson: I do not see the necessity.
Voltaire, *Alzire, Discours Préliminaire*

LUDOVICO ARIOSTO 1474–1533

2 *Natura il fece, e poi roppe la stampa.*
Nature made him, and then broke the mould.
Orlando Furioso, x.84

ARISTOPHANES c.444–c.380 B.C.

3 βούλει Νεφελοκοκκυγίαν;
How about 'Cloudcuckooland'?
Birds, 819. Naming the capital city of the Birds.

4 ὁ δ' εὔκολος μὲν ἐνθάδ', εὔκολος δ' ἐκεῖ.
But he was contented there, is contented here.
(Sophocles)
Frogs, 82

5 βρεκεκεκὲξ κοὰξ κοάξ.
Brekekekex koax koax.
209 and elsewhere. Cry of the Frogs.

ARISTOTLE 384–322 B.C.

6 διὸ καλῶς ἀπεφήναντο τἀγαθόν, οὗ πάντ' ἐφίεται.
So the good has been well explained as that at which all things aim.
Nicomachean Ethics, I.1.1094a

7 ἄνθρωπος φύσει πολιτικὸν ζῷον.
Man is by nature a political animal.
Politics, i.2.1253a

8 Where some people are very wealthy and others have nothing, the result will be either extreme democracy or absolute oligarchy, or despotism will come from either of those excesses.
4.1296a

9 ἔστιν οὖν τραγῳδία μίμησις πράξεως σπουδαίας καὶ τελείας μέγεθος ἐχούσης ... δι' ἐλέου καὶ φόβου περαίνουσα τὴν τῶν τοιούτων παθημάτων κάθαρσιν.
Tragedy is thus a representation of an action that is worth serious attention, complete in itself and of some amplitude...by means of pity and fear bringing about the purgation of such emotions.
Poetics, 6.1449b

10 διὸ καὶ φιλοσοφώτερον καὶ σπουδαιότερον ποίησις ἱστορίας ἐστίν.
For this reason poetry is something more philosophical and more worthy of serious attention than history.
9.1451b

11 προαιρεῖσθαί τε δεῖ ἀδύνατα εἰκότα μᾶλλον ἢ δυνατὰ ἀπίθανα.
Probable impossibilities are to be preferred to improbable possibilites.
24.1460a

12 *Amicus Plato, sed magis amica veritas.*
Plato is dear to me, but dearer still is truth.
Greek original ascribed to Aristotle

LEWIS ADDISON ARMISTEAD 1817–1863

13 Give them the cold steel, boys!
Attr. during Amer. Civil War, 1863

DR. JOHN ARMSTRONG 1709–1779

14 Virtuous and wise he was, but not severe;
He still remember'd that he once was young.
Art of Preserving Health (1744), bk.iv, 1.226

15   Much had he read,
Much more had seen; he studied from the life,
And in th'original perus'd mankind.
1.231

16 Of right and wrong he taught
Truths as refin'd as ever Athens heard;
And (strange to tell!) he practis'd what he preach'd.
1.303

17 'Tis not too late to-morrow to be brave.
1.460

NEIL A. ARMSTRONG 1930–

18 That's one small step for a man, one giant leap for mankind.
On landing on the moon, 21 July 1969. First reported without the word 'a'.

SIR EDWIN ARNOLD 1832–1904

19   Nor ever once ashamed
    So we be named
Press-men; Slaves of the Lamp; Servants of Light.
The Tenth Muse (1895), st.18

GEORGE ARNOLD 1834–1865

20 The living need charity more than the dead.
The Jolly Old Pedagogue

MATTHEW ARNOLD 1822–1888

21 And we forget because we must
And not because we will.
Absence

22 A bolt is shot back somewhere in our breast,
And a lost pulse of feeling stirs again.
The eye sinks inward, and the heart lies plain,
And what we mean, we say, and what we would, we
    know.
A man becomes aware of his life's flow,
And hears its winding murmur; and he sees
The meadows where it glides, the sun, the breeze.

And there arrives a lull in the hot race
Wherein he doth forever chase
That flying and elusive shadow, rest.
An air of coolness plays upon his face,
And an unwonted calm pervades his breast.
And then he thinks he knows
The hills where his life rose,
And the sea where it goes.
The Buried Life, 1.84

23 The Sea of Faith
Was once, too, at the full, and round earth's shore
Lay like the folds of a bright girdle furl'd.
But now I only hear
Its melancholy, long, withdrawing roar,
Retreating, to the breath
Of the night-wind, down the vast edges drear
And naked shingles of the world.

Ah, love, let us be true
To one another! for the world, which seems
To lie before us like a land of dreams,
So various, so beautiful, so new,
Hath really neither joy, nor love, nor light,
Nor certitude, nor peace, nor help for pain;
And we are here as on a darkling plain
Swept with confused alarms of struggle and flight,
Where ignorant armies clash by night.
Dover Beach, l.21

1 Be neither saint nor sophist-led, but be a man.
Empedocles on Etna (1852), I.ii.136

2 Not here, O Apollo!
Are haunts meet for thee.
But, where Helicon breaks down
In cliff to the sea.
II.421

3 'Tis Apollo comes leading
His choir, the Nine.
—The leader is fairest,
But all are divine.
445

4 Let beam upon my inward view
Those eyes of deep, soft, lucent hue—
Eyes too expressive to be blue,
Too lovely to be grey.
Faded Leaves, 4. **On the Rhine**

5 Now the great winds shoreward blow;
Now the salt tides seaward flow;
Now the wild white horses play,
Champ and chafe and toss in the spray.
The Forsaken Merman, l.4

6 Sand-strewn caverns, cool and deep,
Where the winds are all asleep;
Where the spent lights quiver and gleam;
Where the salt weed sways in the stream;
Where the sea-beasts rang'd all round
Feed in the ooze of their pasture-ground...
Where great whales come sailing by,
Sail and sail, with unshut eye,
Round the world for ever and aye.
l.35

7 She will start from her slumber
When gusts shake the door;
She will hear the winds howling,
Will hear the waves roar.
We shall see, while above us
The waves roar and whirl,
A ceiling of amber,
A pavement of pearl.
Singing, 'Here came a mortal,
But faithless was she!
And alone dwell for ever
The kings of the sea.'
l.112

8 Not as their friend or child I speak!
But as on some far northern strand,
Thinking of his own Gods, a Greek
In pity and mournful awe might stand
Before some fallen Runic stone—
For both were faiths, and both are gone.

Wandering between two worlds, one dead,
The other powerless to be born,
With nowhere yet to rest my head,

Like these, on earth I wait forlorn.
The Grande Chartreuse, l.79

9 What helps it now, that Byron bore,
With haughty scorn which mock'd the smart,
Through Europe to the Aetolian shore
The pageant of his bleeding heart?
That thousands counted every groan,
And Europe made his woe her own?
l.133

10 What shelter to grow ripe is ours?
What leisure to grow wise?
In Memory of the Author of Obermann, l.71

11 This truth—to prove, and make thine own:
'Thou hast been, shalt be, art, alone.'
Isolation. To Marguerite, l.29

12 Yes! in the sea of life enisled,
With echoing straits between us thrown,
Dotting the shoreless watery wild,
We mortal millions live *alone*.
To Marguerite—Continued, l.1

13 A God, a God their severance ruled!
And bade betwixt their shores to be
The unplumb'd, salt, estranging sea.
l.22

14 Creep into thy narrow bed,
Creep, and let no more be said!
Vain thy onset! all stands fast.
Thou thyself must break at last.

Let the long contention cease!
Geese are swans, and swans are geese.
Let them have it how they will!
Thou art tired; best be still.
The Last Word

15 Let the victors, when they come,
When the forts of folly fall,
Find thy body by the wall.

16 When Byron's eyes were shut in death,
We bow'd our head and held our breath.
He taught us little: but our soul
Had *felt* him like the thunder's roll.
Memorial Verses, l.6

17 He spoke, and loos'd our heart in tears.
He laid us as we lay at birth
On the cool flowery lap of earth. [Wordsworth.]
l.47

18 Time may restore us in his course
Goethe's sage mind and Byron's force:
But where will Europe's latter hour
Again find Wordsworth's healing power?
l.60

19 Ere the parting hour go by,
Quick, thy tablets, Memory!
A Memory Picture

20 With women the heart argues, not the mind.
Merope (1858), l.341

21 He bears the seed of ruin in himself.
l.856

22 For this is the true strength of guilty kings,
When they corrupt the souls of those they rule.
l.1436

23 With aching hands and bleeding feet
We dig and heap, lay stone on stone;

We bear the burden and the heat
 Of the long day, and wish 'twere done.
Not till the hours of light return,
All we have built do we discern.
Morality, st.2. See 67:15

1 Say, has some wet bird-haunted English lawn
 Lent it the music of its trees at dawn?
 Parting, l.19

2 Hark! ah, the Nightingale!
 The tawny-throated!
 Hark! from that moonlit cedar what a burst!
 What triumph! hark—what pain!
 Philomela, l.1

3 Listen, Eugenia—
 How thick the bursts come crowding through the
  leaves!
 Again—thou hearest!
 Eternal Passion!
 Eternal Pain!
 l.28

4 Cruel, but composed and bland,
 Dumb, inscrutable and grand,
 So Tiberius might have sat,
 Had Tiberius been a cat.
 Poor Matthias, l.40

5 Strew on her roses, roses,
  And never a spray of yew.
 In quiet she reposes:
  Ah! would that I did too.
 Requiescat

6 Her cabin'd ample Spirit,
  It flutter'd and fail'd for breath.
 To-night it doth inherit
  The vasty hall of death.

7 Not deep the Poet sees, but wide.
 Resignation, l.214

8 Coldly, sadly descends
 The autumn evening. The Field
 Strewn with its dank yellow drifts
 Of wither'd leaves, and the elms,
 Fade into dimness apace,
 Silent.
 Rugby Chapel, l.1

9 Friends who set forth at our side,
 Falter, are lost in the storm.
 We, we only, are left!
 l.102

10 Go, for they call you, Shepherd, from the hill.
 The Scholar-Gipsy (1853), l.1

11 All the live murmur of a summer's day.
 l.20

12 Tired of knocking at Preferment's door.
 l.35

13 In hat of antique shape, and cloak of grey,
  The same the Gipsies wore.
 l.55

14 Crossing the stripling Thames at Bab-lock-hithe,
  Trailing in the cool stream thy fingers wet,
   As the slow punt swings round.
 l.74

15 Rapt, twirling in thy hand a wither'd spray,
  And waiting for the spark from heaven to fall.
 l.119

16 The line of festal light in Christ-Church hall.
 l.129

17 Thou waitest for the spark from heaven! and we,
 Light half-believers in our casual creeds...
 Who hesitate and falter life away,
 And lose to-morrow the ground won to-day—
  Ah, do not we, Wanderer, await it too?
 l.171

18 With close-lipp'd Patience for our only friend,
  Sad Patience, too near neighbour to Despair.
 l.194

19 This strange disease of modern life.
 l.203

20 Still nursing the unconquerable hope,
  Still clutching the inviolable shade.
 l.211

21 As some grave Tyrian trader, from the sea,
  Descried at sunrise an emerging prow
 Lifting the cool-hair'd creepers stealthily,
  The fringes of a southward-facing brow
   Among the Aegean isles;
 And saw the merry Grecian coaster come,
 Freighted with amber grapes, and Chian wine,
 Green bursting figs, and tunnies steep'd in brine;
  And knew the intruders on his ancient home,

 The young light-hearted Masters of the waves;
  And snatch'd his rudder, and shook out more sail,
  And day and night held on indignantly
   O'er the blue Midland waters with the gale,
    Betwixt the Syrtes and soft Sicily,
     To where the Atlantic raves
   Outside the Western Straits, and unbent sails
   There, where down cloudy cliffs, through sheets
    of foam,
    Shy traffickers, the dark Iberians come;
    And on the beach undid his corded bales.
 l.232

22 Resolve to be thyself: and know, that he
 Who finds himself, loses his misery.
 Self-Dependence, l.31

23 Others abide our question. Thou art free.
 We ask and ask: Thou smilest and art still,
 Out-topping knowledge.
 Shakespeare

24 And thou, who didst the stars and sunbeams know,
 Self-school'd, self-scann'd, self-honour'd, self-secure,
 Didst tread on Earth unguess'd at.—Better so!
 All pains the immortal spirit must endure,
 All weakness which impairs, all griefs which bow,
 Find their sole speech in that victorious brow.

25 Curl'd minion, dancer, coiner of sweet words!
 Sohrab and Rustum (1853), l.458

26   And Ruksh, the horse,
 Who stood at hand, utter'd a dreadful cry:
 No horse's cry was that, most like the roar
 Of some pain'd desert lion, who all day
 Hath trail'd the hunter's javelin in his side,
 And comes at night to die upon the sand.
 l.501

27 Truth sits upon the lips of dying men.
 l.656

28 But the majestic River floated on,
 Out of the mist and hum of that low land,

Into the frosty starlight.
1.875

1 Oxus, forgetting the bright speed he had
In his high mountain cradle in Pamere,
A foil'd circuitous wanderer—till at last
The long'd-for dash of waves is heard, and wide
His luminous home of waters opens, bright
And tranquil, from whose floor the new-bathed stars
Emerge, and shine upon the Aral Sea.
1.886

2 Still bent to make some port he knows not where,
Still standing for some false impossible shore.
A Summer Night, 1.68

3 The signal-elm, that looks on Ilsley downs,
The Vale, the three lone weirs, the youthful
Thames.
Thyrsis, 1.14

4 And that sweet City with her dreaming spires,
She needs not June for beauty's heightening.
1.19

5 So have I heard the cuckoo's parting cry,
From the wet field, through the vext garden-trees,
Come with the volleying rain and tossing breeze:
'The bloom is gone, and with the bloom go I.'
1.57

6 Too quick despairer, wherefore wilt thou go?
Soon will the high Midsummer pomps come on,
Soon will the musk carnations break and swell,
Soon shall we have gold-dusted snapdragon,
Sweet-William with his homely cottage-smell,
And stocks in fragrant blow.
1.61

7 For Time, not Corydon, hath conquer'd thee.
1.80

8 I know what white, what purple fritillaries
The grassy harvest of the river-fields,
Above by Ensham, down by Sandford, yields,
And what sedg'd brooks are Thames's tributaries.
1.107

9 The foot less prompt to meet the morning dew,
The heart less bounding at emotion new,
And hope, once crushed, less quick to spring again.
1.138

10 Who saw life steadily, and saw it whole:
The mellow glory of the Attic stage;
Singer of sweet Colonus, and its child. [Sophocles.]
To a Friend

11 France, fam'd in all great arts, in none supreme.
To a Republican Friend. Continued.

12 Nor bring, to see me cease to live,
Some doctor full of phrase and fame,
To shake his sapient head and give
The ill he cannot cure a name.
A Wish

13 And sigh that one thing only has been lent
To youth and age in common—discontent.
Youth's Agitations

14 Our society distributes itself into Barbarians,
Philistines, and Populace; and America is just
ourselves, with the Barbarians quite left out, and the
Populace nearly.
Culture and Anarchy (1869), preface

15 The pursuit of perfection, then, is the pursuit of

sweetness and light…He who works for sweetness and
light united, works to make reason and the will of God
prevail.
i. See 525:33

16 The men of culture are the true apostles of equality.

17 One has often wondered whether upon the whole earth
there is anything so unintelligent, so unapt to perceive
how the world is really going, as an ordinary young
Englishman of our upper class.
ii

18 For this [Middle] class we have a designation which
now has become pretty well known, and which we
may as well still keep for them, the designation of
Philistines.
iii

19 I often, therefore, when I want to distinguish clearly
the aristocratic class from the Philistines proper, or
middle class, name the former, in my own mind *the
Barbarians.*

20 But that vast portion, lastly, of the working-class
which, raw and half-developed, has long lain
half-hidden amidst its poverty and squalor, and is now
issuing from its hiding-place to assert an Englishman's
heaven-born privilege of doing as he likes, and is
beginning to perplex us by marching where it likes,
meeting where it likes, bawling what it likes, breaking
what it likes—to this vast residuum we may with great
propriety give the name of Populace.

21 Hebraism and Hellenism—between these two points
of influence moves our World…they are, each of
them, contributions to human development.
iv

22 'He knows' says Hebraism, 'his Bible!'—whenever
we hear this said, we may, without any elaborate
defence of culture, content ourselves with answering
simply: 'No man, who knows nothing else, knows
even his Bible.'

23 The magnificent roaring of the young lions of the
Daily Telegraph.
Essays in Criticism, First Series (1865), preface

24 Passionate, absorbing, almost blood-thirsty clinging to
life.

25 Beautiful city! so venerable, so lovely, so unravaged
by the fierce intellectual life of our century, so
serene!…whispering from her towers the last
enchantments of the Middle Age…Home of lost
causes, and forsaken beliefs, and unpopular names,
and impossible loyalties! [Oxford.]

26 What a touch of grossness in our race, what an
original shortcoming in the more delicate spiritual
perceptions, is shown by the natural growth amongst
us of such hideous names as Higginbottom, Stiggins,
Bugg!
The Function of Criticism at the Present Time

27 'Our unrivalled happiness';—what an element of
grimness, bareness, and hideousness mixes with it and
blurs it; the workhouse, the dismal Mapperly
Hills,—how dismal those who have seen them will
remember;—the gloom, the smoke, the cold, the
strangled illegitimate child!…And the final
touch,—short, bleak and inhuman: *Wragg is in
custody.* The sex lost in the confusion of our unrivalled

happiness; or (shall I say?) the superfluous Christian name lopped off by the straightforward vigour of our old Anglo-Saxon breed!
Prompted by a newspaper report of the murder of her illegitimate child by a girl named Wragg.

1 I am bound by my own definition of criticism: a disinterested endeavour to learn and propagate the best that is known and thought in the world.

2 It always seems to me that the right sphere for Shelley's genius was the sphere of music, not of poetry.
Maurice de Guérin, footnote

3 Philistine must have originally meant, in the mind of those who invented the nickname, a strong, dogged, unenlightened opponent of the chosen people, of the children of the light.
Heinrich Heine

4 Philistinism!—We have not the expression in English. Perhaps we have not the word because we have so much of the thing.

5 The absence, in this country, of any force of educated literary and scientific opinion.
Literary Influence of Academies

6 The great apostle of the Philistines, Lord Macaulay.
Joubert

7 His expression may often be called bald...but it is bald as the bare mountain tops are bald, with a baldness full of grandeur.
Second Series (1888), preface to **Poems of Wordsworth**

8 Nature herself seems, I say, to take the pen out of his hand, and to write for him with her own bare, sheer, penetrating power.

9 The difference between genuine poetry and the poetry of Dryden, Pope, and all their school, is briefly this: their poetry is conceived and composed in their wits, genuine poetry is conceived and composed in the soul.
Thomas Gray

10 In poetry, no less than in life, he is 'a beautiful and ineffectual angel, beating in the void his luminous wings in vain'.
Shelley. (Quoting his own sentence in his essay on Byron, **Essays on Criticism,** Second Series)

11 The translator of Homer should above all be penetrated by a sense of four qualities of his author:—that he is eminently rapid; that he is eminently plain and direct both in the evolution of his thought and in the expression of it, that is, both in his syntax and in his words; that he is eminently plain and direct in the substance of his thought, that is, in his matter and ideas; and, finally, that he is eminently noble.
On Translating Homer (1861), i

12 Wordsworth says somewhere that wherever Virgil seems to have composed 'with his eye on the object', Dryden fails to render him. Homer invariably composes 'with his eye on the object', whether the object be a moral or a material one: Pope composes with his eye on his style, into which he translates his object, whatever it is.

13 He [the translator] will find one English book and one only, where, as in the *Iliad* itself, perfect plainness of speech is allied with perfect nobleness; and that book is the Bible.
iii

14 Nothing has raised more questioning among my critics than these words—noble, the grand style....I think it will be found that the grand style arises in poetry, when a noble nature, poetically gifted, treats with simplicity or with severity a serious subject.
Final words

15 The theatre is irresistible; organise the theatre!
Irish Essays. **The French Play in London**

16 Miracles do not happen.
Literature and Dogma, preface to 1883 edition, last words

17 Culture, the acquainting ourselves with the best that has been known and said in the world, and thus with the history of the human spirit.
Preface to 1873 edition

18 Terms like grace, new birth, justification...terms, in short, which with St Paul are literary terms, theologians have employed as if they were scientific terms.
i, 1

19 When we are asked further, what is conduct?—let us answer: Three-fourths of life.

20 The true meaning of religion is thus not simply morality, but morality touched by emotion.
2

21 Conduct is three-fourths of our life and its largest concern.
3

22 But there remains the question: what righteousness really is. The method and secret and sweet reasonableness of Jesus.
xii, 2

23 So we have the Philistine of genius in religion—Luther; the Philistine of genius in politics—Cromwell; the Philistine of genius in literature—Bunyan.
Mixed Essays, **Lord Falkland**

24 I am past thirty, and three parts iced over.
Letter to A.H. Clough, 12 Feb. 1853

25 People think that I can teach them style. What stuff it all is! Have something to say, and say it as clearly as you can. That is the only secret of style.
G.W.E. Russell, *Collections and Recollections,* ch.13

DR. THOMAS ARNOLD 1795–1842

26 What we must look for here is, 1st, religious and moral principles: 2ndly, gentlemanly conduct: 3rdly, intellectual ability.
Arnold of Rugby (ed. J.J. Findlay), p.65

27 My object will be, if possible, to form Christian men, for Christian boys I can scarcely hope to make.
Letter, in 1828, on appointment to Headmastership of Rugby

28 As for rioting, the old Roman way of dealing with that is always the right one; flog the rank and file, and fling the ringleaders from the Tarpeian rock.
From an unpublished letter written before 1828, quoted by M. Arnold, *Cornhill Magazine,* Aug. 1868

ANTONIN ARTAUD 1896–1948

29 *Il faut nous laver de la littérature. Nous voulons être hommes avant tout, être humains.*
We must wash literature off ourselves. We want to be

men first of all; to be human.
Les Oeuvres et les Hommes, unpublished ms., 17 May 1922

ROGER ASCHAM 1515–1568

1 I said...how, and why, young children, were sooner allured by love, than driven by beating, to attain good learning.
The Schoolmaster (1570), preface

2 There is no such whetstone, to sharpen a good wit and encourage a will to learning, as is praise.
1

3 *Inglese Italianato, è un diavolo incarnato,* that is to say, you remain men in shape and fashion, but become devils in life and condition.
Of Englishmen travelling in Italy

4 He that will write well in any tongue, must follow this counsel of Aristotle, to speak as the common people do, to think as wise men do; and so should every man understand him, and the judgment of wise men allow him.
Toxophilus (1545), **To all gentlemen and yeomen of England**

DAISY ASHFORD 1881-1972

5 Mr Salteena was an elderly man of 42 and was fond of asking peaple to stay with him.
The Young Visiters (1919), ch.1

6 I do hope I shall enjoy myself with you...I am parshial to ladies if they are nice I suppose it is my nature. I am not quite a gentleman but you would hardly notice it.

7 You look rather rash my dear your colors dont quite match your face.
ch.2

8 My own room is next the bath room said Bernard it is decerated dark red as I have somber tastes. The bath room has got a tip up bason and a hose thing for washing your head.

9 Bernard always had a few prayers in the hall and some whiskey afterwards as he was rarther pious but Mr Salteena was not very addicted to prayers so he marched up to bed.
ch.3

10 It was a sumpshous spot all done up in gold with plenty of looking glasses.
ch.5

11 Oh I see said the Earl but my own idear is that these things are as piffle before the wind.

12 My dear Clincham, The bearer of this letter is an old friend of mine not quite the right side of the blanket as they say in fact he is the son of a first rate butcher but his mother was a decent family called Hyssopps of the Glen so you see he is not so bad and is desireus of being the correct article.

13 Ethel patted her hair and looked very sneery.
ch.8

14 My life will be sour grapes and ashes without you.

15 Take me back to the Gaierty hotel.
ch.9

H.H. ASQUITH 1852–1928

16 We had better wait and see.

Phrase used repeatedly in speeches in 1910, referring to the rumour that the House of Lords was to be flooded with new Liberal peers to ensure the passage of the Finance Bill. R.Jenkins, *Asquith*, ch.14

17 We shall never sheathe the sword which we have not lightly drawn until Belgium receives in full measure all and more than all that she has sacrificed, until France is adequately secured against the menace of aggression, until the rights of the smaller nationalities of Europe are placed upon an unassailable foundation, and until the military domination of Prussia is wholly and finally destroyed.
Guildhall, 9 Nov. 1914

MARGOT ASQUITH 1865–1945

18 Ettie has told enough white lies to ice a cake.
Nicholas Mosley, *Julian Grenfell* (1976), ch.3. Of Lady Desborough (1867–1952)

19 Mrs Asquith remarked indiscreetly that if Kitchener was not a great man, he was, at least, a great poster.
Said in 1914. Sir Philip Magnus, *Kitchener: Portrait of an Imperialist* (1958), ch.14

SIR JACOB ASTLEY 1579–1652

20 O Lord! thou knowest how busy I must be this day: if I forget thee, do not thou forget me.
Prayer before the Battle of Edgehill. Sir Philip Warwick, *Memoires*, 1701, p.229

SURGEON-CAPTAIN E.L. ATKINSON 1882–1929
and APSLEY CHERRY-GARRARD 1882–1959

21 Hereabouts died a very gallant gentleman, Captain L.E.G. Oates of the Inniskilling Dragoons. In March 1912, returning from the Pole, he walked willingly to his death in a blizzard, to try and save his comrades, beset by hardships.
Epitaph on a cairn and cross erected in the Antarctic, November 1912

JOHN AUBREY 1626–1697

22 How these curiosities would be quite forgot, did not such idle fellows as I am put them down.
Brief Lives. **Venetia Digby**

23 The parliament intended to have hanged him; and he expected no less, but resolved to be hanged with the Bible under one arm and Magna Carta under the other.
David Jenkins

24 He was so fair that they called him *the lady of* Christ's College.
John Milton

25 Sciatica: he cured it, by boiling his buttock.
Sir Jonas Moore

26 Sir Walter, being strangely surprised and put out of his countenance at so great a table, gives his son a damned blow over the face. His son, as rude as he was, would not strike his father, but strikes over the face the gentleman that sat next to him and said 'Box about: 'twill come to my father anon'.
Sir Walter Raleigh

27 When he killed a calf he would do it in a high style, and make a speech.
William Shakespeare

1 He was a handsome, well-shaped man: very good
company, and of a very ready and pleasant smooth
wit.

2 Anno 1670, not far from Cirencester, was an
apparition; being demanded whether a good spirit or a
bad? returned no answer, but disappeared with a
curious perfume and most melodious twang. Mr W.
Lilly believes it was a fairy.
Miscellanies. Apparitions (1696)

W.H. AUDEN 1907–1973

3 In a garden shady this holy lady
With reverent cadence and subtle psalm,
Like a black swan as death came on
Poured forth her song in perfect calm:
And by ocean's margin this innocent virgin
Constructed an organ to enlarge her prayer,
And notes tremendous from her great engine
Thundered out on the Roman air.

Blonde Aphrodite rose up excited,
Moved to delight by the melody,
White as an orchid she rode quite naked
In an oyster shell on top of the sea.
Anthem for St. Cecilia's Day, I. Dedicated to Benjamin Britten,
and set to music by Britten as *Hymn to St. Cecilia*, op.27 (1942)

4 *Blessed Cecilia, appear in visions*
To all musicians, appear and inspire:
Translated Daughter, come down and startle
Composing mortals with immortal fire.

5 *O dear white children casual as birds,*
Playing among the ruined languages,
So small beside their large confusing words,
So gay against the greater silences
Of dreadful things you did.
III

6 *Weep for the lives your wishes never led.*

7 Reindeer are coming to drive you away
Over the snow on an ebony sleigh,
Over the mountains and over the sea
You shall go happy and handsome and free.
The Ascent of F.6 (with Christopher Isherwood) (1936), II.v

8 *Mother:* Over the green pastures there
You shall go hunting the beautiful deer,
You shall pick flowers, the white and the blue,
Shepherds shall flute their sweetest for you.
Chorus: True, Love finally is great,
Greater than all; but large the hate,
Far larger than Man can ever estimate.

9 I'll love you, dear, I'll love you
      Till China and Africa meet,
And the river jumps over the mountain
      And the salmon sing in the street.

I'll love you till the ocean
      Is folded and hung up to dry
And the seven stars go squawking
      Like geese about the sky.
As I Walked Out One Evening

10 O let not Time deceive you,
      You cannot conquer Time.

In the burrows of the Nightmare
      Where Justice naked is,
Time watches from the shadow

And coughs when you would kiss.

In headaches and in worry
      Vaguely life leaks away,
And Time will have his fancy
      To-morrow or today.

Into many a green valley
      Drifts the appalling snow;
Time breaks the threaded dances
      And the diver's brilliant bow.

O plunge your hands in water,
      Plunge them in up to the wrist;
Stare, stare in the basin
      And wonder what you've missed.

The glacier knocks in the cupboard,
      The desert sighs in the bed,
And the crack in the tea-cup opens
      A lane to the land of the dead.

11 O stand, stand at the window
      As the tears scald and start;
You shall love your crooked neighbour
      With your crooked heart.

12 August for the people and their favourite islands.
Birthday Poem

13 The desires of the heart are as crooked as corkscrews,
      Not to be born is the best for man;
The second-best is a formal order,
      The dance's pattern; dance while you can.
Dance, dance, for the figure is easy,
      The tune is catching and will not stop;
Dance till the stars come down from the rafters;
      Dance, dance, dance till you drop.
Death's Echo

14 Happy the hare at morning, for she cannot read
The Hunter's waking thoughts.
The Dog Beneath the Skin (with Christopher Isherwood) (1935),
Chorus following II.ii

15 Perfection, of a kind, was what he was after,
And the poetry he invented was easy to understand;
He knew human folly like the back of his hand,
And was greatly interested in armies and fleets;
When he laughed, respectable senators burst with
      laughter,
And when he cried the little children died in the
      streets.
Epitaph on a Tyrant. See 358:20

16 Altogether elsewhere, vast
Herds of reindeer move across
Miles and miles of golden moss,
Silently and very fast.
The Fall of Rome

17 'O where are you going?' said reader to rider,
'That valley is fatal where furnaces burn,
Yonder's the midden whose odours will madden,
That gap is the grave where the tall return.'
Five Songs, V

18 Behind you swiftly the figure comes softly,
The spot on your skin is a shocking disease.

19   Clutching a little case,
He walks out briskly to infect a city
Whose terrible future may have just arrived.
Gare du Midi

20 Lawrence was brought down by smut-hounds, Blake

went dotty as he sang,
Homer Lane was killed in action by the Twickenham
Baptist gang.
Get there if you can and see the land

1 As it is, plenty.
His Excellency

2 He disappeared in the dead of winter:
The brooks were frozen, the airports almost deserted,
And snow disfigured the public statues;
The mercury sank in the mouth of the dying day.
What instruments we have agree
The day of his death was a dark cold day.
In Memory of W.B. Yeats, I

3 The provinces of his body revolted,
The squares of his mind were empty,
Silence invaded the suburbs,
The current of his feeling failed; he became his
admirers.

4 The words of a dead man
Are modified in the guts of the living.

5 You were silly like us; your gift survived it all:
The parish of rich women, physical decay,
Yourself.
II

6   Now Ireland has her madness and her weather still,
For poetry makes nothing happen.

7 Earth, receive an honoured guest:
William Yeats is laid to rest.
Let the Irish vessel lie
Emptied of its poetry.

Time that is intolerant
Of the brave and innocent,
And indifferent in a week
To a beautiful physique,

Worships language and forgives
Everyone by whom it lives.
III

8 Time that with this strange excuse
Pardoned Kipling and his views,
And will pardon Paul Claudel,
Pardons him for writing well.

9 In the deserts of the heart
Let the healing fountain start,
In the prison of his days
Teach the free man how to praise.

10 Certainly the growth of the fore-brain has been a
success:
He has not got lost in a backwater like the lampshell
Or the limpet; he has not died out like the
super-lizards.

His boneless worm-like ancestors would be amazed
At the upright position, the breasts, the
four-chambered heart,
The clandestine evolution in the mother's shadow.
In Time of War, Commentary, from *Journey to a War* (1939)

11 By wire and wireless, in a score of bad translations,
They give their simple message to the world of man:
'*Man can have Unity if Man will give up Freedom.*

The State is real, the Individual is wicked;
Violence shall synchronize your movements like a
tune,

And Terror like a frost shall halt the flood of thinking.

Barrack and bivouac shall be your friendly refuge,
And racial pride shall tower like a public column
And confiscate for safety every private sorrow.'

12 '*Leave Truth to the police and us; we know the Good;*
We build the Perfect City time shall never alter;
Our Law shall guard you always like a cirque of
mountains,

Your Ignorance keep off evil like a dangerous sea;
You shall be consummated in the General Will,
Your children innocent and charming as the beasts.'

13 And, if we care to listen, we can always hear them:
'*Men are not innocent as beasts and never can be,*
Man can improve himself but never will himself be
perfect,

Only the free have disposition to be truthful,
Only the truthful have the interest to be just,
Only the just possess the will-power to be free.'

14 It's no use raising a shout.
No, Honey, you can cut that right out.
I don't want any more hugs;
Make me some fresh tea, fetch me some rugs.
Here am I, here are you:
But what does it mean? What are we going to do?
It's no use raising a Shout

15 It wasn't always like this?
Perhaps it wasn't, but it is.
Put the car away; when life fails,
What's the good of going to Wales?

16   To me Art's subject is the human clay,
And landscape but a background to a torso;
All Cézanne's apples I would give away
For one small Goya or a Daumier.
Letter to Lord Byron, III

17 Lay your sleeping head, my love,
Human on my faithless arm;
Time and fevers burn away
Individual beauty from
Thoughtful children, and the grave
Proves the child ephemeral:
But in my arms till break of day
Let the living creature lie,
Mortal, guilty, but to me
The entirely beautiful.
Lullaby

18 About suffering they were never wrong,
The Old Masters: how well they understood
Its human position; how it takes place
While someone else is eating or opening a window or
just walking dully along.
Musée des Beaux Arts

19 They never forgot
That even the dreadful martyrdom must run its course
Anyhow in a corner, some untidy spot
Where the dogs go on with their doggy life and the
torturer's horse
Scratches its innocent behind on a tree.

20 Only God can tell the saintly from the suburban,
Counterfeit values always resemble the true;
Neither in Life nor Art is honesty bohemian,
The free behave much as the respectable do.
New Year Letter (1941), note to line 1277

1 This is the Night Mail crossing the Border
Bringing the cheque and the postal order.

Letters for the rich, letters for the poor,
The shop at the corner, the girl next door.

Pulling up Beattock, a steady climb:
The gradient's against her, but she's on time.

Past cotton-grass and moorland border,
Shovelling white steam over her shoulder.
Night Mail, I

2 Letters of thanks, letters from banks,
Letters of joy from girl and boy,
Receipted bills and invitations
To inspect new stock or to visit relations,
And applications for situations,
And timid lovers' declarations,
And gossip, gossip from all the nations.
III

3 Look, stranger, on this island now
The leaping light for you discovers,
Stand stable here
And silent be,
That through the channels of the ear
May wander like a river
The swaying sound of the sea.
On This Island

4 O what is that sound which so thrills the ear
Down in the valley drumming, drumming?
Only the scarlet soldiers, dear,
The soldiers coming.
O What is That Sound

5 O it's broken the lock and splintered the door,
O it's the gate where they're turning, turning;
Their boots are heavy on the floor
And their eyes are burning.

6 O Love, the interest itself in thoughtless Heaven,
Make simpler daily the beating of man's heart; within,
There in the ring where name and image meet,

Inspire them with such a longing as will make his
thought
Alive like patterns a murmuration of starlings,
Rising in joy over wolds, unwittingly weave.
Perhaps (**Prologue** from **On This Island**)

7 Send to us power and light...
Harrow the house of the dead; look shining at
New styles of architecture, a change of heart.
Petition

8 It's not only this we praise, it's the general love:
Let cat's mew rise to a scream on the tool-shed roof.
Prothalamion

9 Hunger allows no choice
To the citizen or the police;
We must love one another or die.
September 1, 1939

10 Out of the air a voice without a face
Proved by statistics that some cause was just
In tones as dry and level as the place.
The Shield of Achilles

11 Let us honour if we can
The vertical man,
Though we value none
But the horizontal one.
Collected Poems, II *1927–1932, Shorts*

12 Private faces in public places
Are wiser and nicer
Than public faces in private places.

13 To the man-in-the-street, who, I'm sorry to say,
Is a keen observer of life,
The word 'Intellectual' suggests straight away
A man who's untrue to his wife.
IV *1939-47, Shorts*

14 A poet's hope: to be,
like some valley cheese,
local, but prized elsewhere.
XII *1958–1971, Shorts II*

15 And the poor in their fireless lodgings, dropping the
sheets
Of the evening paper: 'Our day is our loss, O show us
History the operator, the
Organizer, Time the refreshing river.'

And the nations combine each cry, invoking the life
That shapes the individual belly and orders
The private nocturnal terror:
'Did you not found once the city state of the sponge,

'Raise the vast military empires of the shark
And the tiger, establish the robin's plucky canton?
Intervene. O descend as a dove or
A furious papa or a mild engineer, but descend.'
Spain 1937

16 Tomorrow for the young the poets exploding like
bombs,
The walks by the lake, the weeks of perfect
communion;
Tomorrow the bicycle races
Through the suburbs on summer evenings. But to-day
the struggle.

17 The stars are dead. The animals will not look.
We are left alone with our day, and the time is short,
and
History to the defeated
May say Alas but cannot help nor pardon.

18 Out on the lawn I lie in bed,
Vega conspicuous overhead.
A Summer Night

19 That later we, though parted then,
May still recall those evenings when
Fear gave his watch no look;
The lion griefs loped from the shade
And on our knees their muzzles laid,
And Death put down his book.

20 He still loves life
But O O O O how he wishes
The good Lord would take him.
Thank You, Fog (1974), in introductory Note

21 Let a florid music praise,
The flute and the trumpet,
Beauty's conquest of your face:
In that land of flesh and bone,
Where from citadels on high
Her imperial standards fly
Let the hot sun
Shine on, shine on.
Twelve Songs, III

22 At last the secret is out, as it always must come in the
end,

The delicious story is ripe to tell to the intimate friend;
Over the tea-cups and in the square the tongue has its desire;
Still waters run deep, my dear, there's never smoke without fire.
VIII

1 For the clear voice suddenly singing, high up in the convent wall,
The scent of elder bushes, the sporting prints in the hall,
The croquet matches in summer, the handshake, the cough, the kiss,
There is always a wicked secret, a private reason for this.

2 When it comes, will it come without warning
Just as I'm picking my nose?
Will it knock on my door in the morning,
Or tread in the bus on my toes?
Will it come like a change in the weather?
Will its greeting be courteous or rough?
Will it alter my life altogether?
O tell me the truth about love.
XII

3 Nerves that steeled themselves for slaughter
Are shot to pieces by the shorter
Poems of Donne.
Under Which Lyre

4 Thou shalt not do as the dean pleases,
Thou shalt not write thy doctor's thesis
On education.

5   Thou shalt not sit
With statisticians nor commit
A social science.

6 Thou shalt not live within thy means
Nor on plain water and raw greens.
If thou must choose
Between the chances, choose the odd:
Read *The New Yorker*, trust in God;
And take short views.
See 510:31

7 He stood there above the body,
He stood there holding the knife;
And the blood ran down the stairs and sang:
'I'm the Resurrection and the Life'.

They tapped Victor on the shoulder,
They took him away in a van;
He sat as quiet as a lump of moss
Saying, 'I am the Son of Man'.

Victor sat in a corner
Making a woman of clay;
Saying: 'I am Alpha and Omega, I shall come
To judge the earth one day.'
Victor

8 A shilling life will give you all the facts.
Who's Who

9 Some of the last researchers even write
Love made him weep his pints like you and me.

With all his honours on, he sighed for one
Who, say astonished critics, lived at home;
Did little jobs about the house with skill
And nothing else; could whistle; would sit still
Or potter round the garden; answered some

Of his long marvellous letters but kept none.

10 The sky is darkening like a stain;
Something is going to fall like rain,
And it won't be flowers.
The Witnesses (1932 poem)

ÉMILE AUGIER 1820–1889

11 Marquis: *Mettez un canard sur un lac au milieu des cygnes, vous verrez qu'il regrettera sa mare et finira par y retourner.*
Montrichard: *La nostalgie de la boue!*
Marquis: Put a duck on a lake in the midst of some swans, and you'll see he'll miss his pond and eventually return to it.
Montrichard: Longing to be back in the mud!
Le Mariage d'Olympe, I.i

ST. AUGUSTINE 354–430

12 *Nondum amabam, et amare amabam...quaerebam quid amarem, amans amare.*
I loved not yet, yet I loved to love...I sought what I might love, in love with loving.
Confessions, bk.iii, ch.1

13 *Et illa erant fercula, in quibus mihi esurienti te inferebatur sol et luna.*
And these were the dishes wherein to me, hunger-starven for thee, they served up the sun and moon.
ch.6

14 *Da mihi castitatem et continentiam, sed noli modo.*
Give me chastity and continency—but not yet!
bk.viii, ch.7

15 *Tolle lege, tolle lege.*
Take up and read, take up and read.
ch.12

16 *Sero te amavi, pulchritudo tam antiqua et tam nova, sero te amavi! et ecce intus eras et ego foris, et ibi te quaerebam.*
Too late came I to love thee, O thou Beauty both so ancient and so fresh, yea too late came I to love thee. And behold, thou wert within me, and I out of myself, where I made search for thee.
bk.x, ch.27

17 *Da quod iubes et iube quod vis. Imperas nobis continentiam.*
Give what you command, and command what you will. You impose continency upon us.
ch.29

18 *Securus iudicat orbis terrarum.*
The verdict of the world is conclusive.
Contra Epist. Parmen., iii.24

19 *Salus extra ecclesiam non est.*
There is no salvation outside the church.
De Bapt. IV, c.xvii.24. See 170:19

20 *Audi partem alteram.*
Hear the other side.
De Duabus Animabus, XIV.ii

21 *Dilige et quod vis fac.*
Love and do what you will.
(Often quoted as *Ama et fac quod vis*.)
In Epist. Joann. Tractatus, vii, 8

22 *Multi quidem facilius se abstinent ut non utantur, quam*

temperent ut bene utantur.
To many, total abstinence is easier than perfect
moderation.
On the Good of Marriage, xxi

1 *Cum dilectione hominum et odio vitiorum.*
With love for mankind and hatred of sins.
Often quoted in the form: Love the sinner but hate the sin. **Opera
Omnia,** vol.II. col.962, letter 211. Migne's *Patrologiae* (1845),
vol.XXXIII

2 *Roma locuta est; causa finita est.*
Rome has spoken; the case is concluded.
Sermons, bk.i

3 We make ourselves a ladder out of our vices if we
trample the vices themselves underfoot.
iii. **De Ascensione**

EMPEROR AUGUSTUS 63 B.C.–A.D. 14

4 Quintilius Varus, give me back my legions.
Suetonius, *Divus Augustus, 23*

5 I inherited it brick and left it marble.
(Of the city of Rome.) 28

6 It will be paid at the Greek Kalends.
(Meaning, Never.) 87

JANE AUSTEN 1775–1817

7 An egg boiled very soft is not unwholesome. [Mr.
Woodhouse.]
Emma, ch.3

8 One half of the world cannot understand the pleasures
of the other. [Emma.]
ch.9

9 With men he can be rational and unaffected, but when
he has ladies to please, every feature works. [Mr. John
Knightley of Mr. Elton.]
ch.13

10 A man...must have a very good opinion of himself
when he asks people to leave their own fireside, and
encounter such a day as this, for the sake of coming to
see him. He must think himself a most agreeable
fellow. [Mr. John Knightley.]

11 She believed he had been drinking too much of Mr
Weston's good wine.
ch.15

12 My mother's deafness is very trifling, you see, just
nothing at all. By only raising my voice, and saying
anything two or three times over, she is sure to hear.
[Miss Bates.]
ch.19

13 The sooner every party breaks up the better. [Mr.
Woodhouse.]
ch.25

14 That young man...is very thoughtless. Do not tell his
father, but that young man is not quite the thing. He
has been opening the doors very often this evening and
keeping them open very inconsiderately. He does not
think of the draught. I do not mean to set you against
him, but indeed he is not quite the thing. [Mr.
Woodhouse.]
ch.29

15 Open the windows! But, surely Mr Churchill, nobody
would think of opening the windows at Randalls.
Nobody could be so imprudent. [Mr. Woodhouse.]

16 They will have their barouche-landau, of course.
[Mrs. Elton.]
ch.32

17 Young ladies should take care of themselves. Young
ladies are delicate plants. They should take care of
their health and their complexion. My dear, did you
change your stockings? [Mr. Woodhouse.]
ch.34

18 One has no great hopes from Birmingham. I always
say there is something direful in the sound. [Mrs.
Elton.]
ch.36

19 N.B. There will be very few Dates in this History.
The History of England (1791)

20 Henry the 4th ascended the throne of England much to
his own satisfaction in the year 1399.

21 One of Edward's Mistresses was Jane Shore, who has
had a play written about her, but it is a tragedy and
therefore not worth reading.

22 Nothing can be said in his vindication, but that his
abolishing Religious Houses and leaving them to the
ruinous depredations of time has been of infinite use to
the landscape of England in general.

23 Lady Jane Grey, who has been already mentioned as
reading Greek.

24 It was too pathetic for the feelings of Sophia and
myself—we fainted Alternately on a Sofa.
Love and Freindship. Letter the 8th

25 She was nothing more than a mere good-tempered,
civil and obliging young woman; as such we could
scarcely dislike her—she was only an Object of
Contempt.
Letter the 13th

26 There certainly are not so many men of large fortune
in the world, as there are pretty women to deserve
them.
Mansfield Park, ch.1

27 You must give my compliments to him. Yes—I think
it must be compliments. Is there not a something
wanted, Miss Price, in our language—a something
between compliments and—and love—to suit the sort
of friendly acquaintance we have had together? [Mary
Crawford.]
ch.11

28 A large income is the best recipe for happiness I ever
heard of. It certainly may secure all the myrtle and
turkey part of it.
ch.22

29 Let other pens dwell on guilt and misery.
ch.48

30 She was of course only too good for him; but as
nobody minds having what is too good for them, he
was very steadily earnest in the pursuit of the blessing.

31 'And what are you reading, Miss —?' 'Oh! it is only a
novel!' replies the young lady: while she lays down
her book with affected indifference, or momentary
shame.—'It is only Cecilia, or Camilla, or Belinda:'
or, in short, only some work in which the most
thorough knowledge of human nature, the happiest
delineation of its varieties, the liveliest effusions of
wit and humour are conveyed to the world in the best

chosen language.
***Northanger Abbey*, ch.5**

1 But are they all horrid, are you sure they are all horrid? [Catherine.]
ch.6

2 Oh, Lord! not I; I never read much; I have something else to do. [John Thorpe.]
ch.7

3 Oh! who can ever be tired of Bath?
ch.10

4 Real solemn history, I cannot be interested in...The quarrels of popes and kings, with wars or pestilences, in every page; the men all so good for nothing, and hardly any women at all.
ch.14

5 Where people wish to attach, they should always be ignorant. To come with a well-informed mind, is to come with an inability of administering to the vanity of others, which a sensible person would always wish to avoid. A woman especially, if she have the misfortune of knowing any thing, should conceal it as well as she can.

6 From politics, it was an easy step to silence.

7 Sir Walter Elliot, of Kellynch-hall, in Somersetshire, was a man who, for his own amusement, never took up any book but the Baronetage; there he found occupation for an idle hour, and consolation in a distressed one;...this was the page at which the favourite volume always opened: ELLIOT OF KELLYNCH-HALL.
***Persuasion*, ch.1**

8 'My idea of good company, Mr Elliot, is the company of clever, well-informed people, who have a great deal of conversation; that is what I call good company.'
'You are mistaken,' said he gently, 'that is not good company, that is the best.'
ch.16

9 My sore throats are always worse than anyone's. [Mary Musgrove.]
ch.18

10 All the privilege I claim for my own sex...is that of loving longest, when existence or when hope is gone. [Anne.]
ch.23

11 It is a truth universally acknowledged, that a single man in possession of a good fortune, must be in want of a wife.
***Pride and Prejudice*, ch.1**

12 'Kitty has no discretion in her coughs,' said her father: 'she times them ill.'
'I do not cough for my own amusement,' replied Kitty fretfully.
ch.2

13 May I ask whether these pleasing attentions proceed from the impulse of the moment, or are the result of previous study? [Mr. Bennet.]
ch.14

14 You have delighted us long enough. [Mr. Bennet.]
ch.18

15 An unhappy alternative is before you, Elizabeth. From this day you must be a stranger to one of your parents.—Your mother will never see you again if you do *not* marry Mr Collins, and I will never see you

again if you *do*. [Mr. Bennet.]
ch.20

16 Nobody is on my side, nobody takes part with me: I am cruelly used, nobody feels for my poor nerves. [Mrs. Bennet.]
ch.20

17 'It is very hard to think that Charlotte Lucas should ever be mistress of this house, that *I* should be forced to make way for *her*, and live to see her take my place in it.'
'My dear, do not give way to such gloomy thoughts. Let us hope for better things. Let us flatter ourselves that *I* may be the survivor.'
ch.23

18 No arguments shall be wanting on my part, that can alleviate so severe a misfortune: or that may comfort you, under a circumstance that must be of all others most afflicting to a parent's mind. The death of your daughter would have been a blessing in comparison of this. [Mr. Collins.]
ch.48

19 You ought certainly to forgive them as a christian, but never to admit them in your sight, or allow their names to be mentioned in your hearing. [Mr. Collins.]
ch.57

20 For what do we live, but to make sport for our neighbours, and laugh at them in our turn? [Mr. Bennet.]

21 I have been a selfish being all my life, in practice, though not in principle. [Mr. Darcy.]
ch.58

22 If any young men come for Mary or Kitty, send them in, for I am quite at leisure. [Mr. Bennet.]
ch.59

23 Dear, dear Lizzy. A house in town! Every thing that is charming! Three daughters married! Ten thousand a year! Oh, Lord! What will become of me? I shall go distracted. [Mrs. Bennet.]

24 An annuity is a very serious business. [Mrs. Dashwood.]
***Sense and Sensibility*, ch.2**

25 'I am afraid,' replied Elinor, 'that the pleasantness of an employment does not always evince its propriety.'
ch.13

26 Lady Middleton...exerted herself to ask Mr Palmer if there was any news in the paper.
'No, none at all,' he replied, and read on.
ch.19

27 Where so many hours have been spent in convincing myself that I am right, is there not some reason to fear I may be wrong?
ch.31

28 A person and face, of strong, natural, sterling insignificance, though adorned in the first style of fashion.
ch.33

29 We met...Dr Hall in such very deep mourning that either his mother, his wife, or himself must be dead.
Letter to Cassandra Austen, 17 May 1799

30 I am proud to say that I have a very good eye at an Adultress, for tho' repeatedly assured that another in the same party was the *She,* I fixed upon the right one

from the first.
12 May 1801

1 How horrible it is to have so many people
killed!—And what a blessing that one cares for none
of them!
31 May 1811, after the battle of Albuera, 16 May 1811

2 I think I may boast myself to be, with all possible
vanity, the most unlearned and uninformed female who
ever dared to be an authoress.
Letter to James Stanier Clarke. 11 Dec. 1815

3 The little bit (two inches wide) of ivory on which I
work with so fine a brush as produces little effect after
much labour.
Letter, 16 Dec. 1816

SIR ROBERT AYTOUN 1570–1638

4 I loved thee once. I'll love no more,
 Thine be the grief, as is the blame;
Thou art not what thou wast before,
 What reason I should be the same?
To an Inconstant Mistress

W.E. AYTOUN 1813–1865

5 They bore within their breasts the grief
 That fame can never heal—
The deep, unutterable woe
 Which none save exiles feel.
The Island of the Scots, xii

6 Fhairshon swore a feud
 Against the clan M'Tavish;
Marched into their land
 To murder and to rafish;
For he did resolve
 To extirpate the vipers,
With four-and-twenty men
 And five-and-thirty pipers.
The Massacre of the Macpherson, i

7 Fhairshon had a son,
 Who married Noah's daughter,
And nearly spoiled ta Flood,
 By trinking up ta water:

Which he would have done,
 I at least pelieve it,
Had the mixture peen
 Only half Glenlivet.
vii

8 And some that came to scoff at him
 Now turned aside and wept.
The Execution of Montrose, vi

9 'He is coming! he is coming!'
 Like a bridegroom from his room,
Came the hero from his prison
 To the scaffold and the doom.
xiv

10 The grim Geneva ministers
 With anxious scowl drew near,
As you have seen the ravens flock
 Around the dying deer.
xvii

11 Like a brave old Scottish Cavalier,
 All of the olden time!
The Old Scottish Cavalier. See 6:10

12 The earth is all the home I have,
The heavens my wide roof-tree.
The Wandering Jew, l.49

CHARLES BABBAGE 1792–1871

13 Every moment dies a man,
Every moment $1\frac{1}{16}$ is born.
See *New Scientist*, 4 Dec. 1958, p.1428. Unpublished letter to
Tennyson, whose *Vision of Sin* this parodies. See 544:8

FRANCIS BACON 1561–1626

14 For all knowledge and wonder (which is the seed of
knowledge) is an impression of pleasure in itself.
Advancement of Learning, I.i.3

15 So let great authors have their due, as time, which is
the author of authors, be not deprived of his due,
which is further and further to discover truth.
iv.12

16 If a man will begin with certainties, he shall end in
doubts; but if he will be content to begin with doubts,
he shall end in certainties.
v.8

17 [Knowledge is] a rich storehouse for the glory of the
Creator and the relief of man's estate.
11

18 Antiquities are history defaced, or some remnants of
history which have casually escaped the shipwreck of
time.
II.ii.1

19 Poesy was ever thought to have some participation of
divineness, because it doth raise and erect the mind, by
submitting the shows of things to the desires of the
mind; whereas reason doth buckle and bow the mind
unto the nature of things.
iv.2

20 The knowledge of man is as the waters, some
descending from above, and some springing from
beneath; the one informed by the light of nature, the
other inspired by divine revelation.
v.1

21 They are ill discoverers that think there is no land,
when they can see nothing but sea.
vii.5

22 Words are the tokens current and accepted for
conceits, as moneys are for values.
xvi.3

23 A dance is a measured pace, as a verse is a measured
speech.
5

24 But men must know, that in this theatre of man's life
it is reserved only for God and angels to be lookers on.
xx.8

25 We are much beholden to Machiavel and others, that
write what men do, and not what they ought to do.
xxi.9

26 Men must pursue things which are just in present, and
leave the future to the divine Providence.
11

27 Did not one of the fathers in great indignation call
poesy *vinum daemonum*?
xxii.13

28 All good moral philosophy is but an handmaid to

religion.
14

1 Man seeketh in society comfort, use, and protection.
xxiii.2

2 A man must make his opportunity, as oft as find it.
3

3 Fortunes...come tumbling into some men's laps.
43

4 It is in life as it is in ways, the shortest way is commonly the foulest, and surely the fairer way is not much about.
45

5 The inseparable propriety of time, which is ever more and more to disclose truth.
xxiv

6 Books must follow sciences, and not sciences books.
Proposition touching Amendment of Laws

7 Wise nature did never put her precious jewels into a garret four stories high: and therefore...exceeding tall men had ever very empty heads.
Apophthegms, 17

8 Hope is a good breakfast, but it is a bad supper.
36

9 Riches are a good handmaid, but the worst mistress.
De Dignitate et Augmentis Scientiarum, I, vi, 3. Antitheta, 6 (ed. 1640, tr. Gilbert Watts)

10 *Antiquitas saeculi juventus mundi.*
Ancient times were the youth of the world.
vii, 81

11 The voice of the people hath some divineness in it, else how should so many men agree to be of one mind?
9

12 No terms of moderation takes place with the vulgar.
30

13 Silence is the virtue of fools.
31

14 The worst solitude is to be destitute of sincere friendship.
37

15 It is sufficiently agreed that all things change, and that nothing really disappears, but that the sum of matter remains exactly the same.
Cogitationes de Natura Rerum, 5; translated from the Latin.

16 I hold every man a debtor to his profession.
The Elements of the Common Law, preface

17 My essays, which of all my other works have been most current; for that, as it seems, they come home, to men's business, and bosoms.
Essays. Dedication of 1625 edition

18 Prosperity is the blessing of the Old Testament, adversity is the blessing of the New.
5. **Of Adversity**

19 The pencil of the Holy Ghost hath laboured more in describing the afflictions of Job than the felicities of Solomon.

20 Prosperity is not without many fears and distastes; and adversity is not without comforts and hopes.

21 Prosperity doth best discover vice, but adversity doth best discover virtue.

22 I had rather believe all the fables in the legend, and the

Talmud, and the Alcoran, than that this universal frame is without a mind.
16. **Atheism**

23 God never wrought miracle to convince atheism, because his ordinary works convince it.

24 A little philosophy inclineth man's mind to atheism, but depth in philosophy bringeth men's minds about to religion.

25 They that deny a God destroy man's nobility; for certainly man is of kin to the beasts by his body; and, if he be not of kin to God by his spirit, he is a base and ignoble creature.

26 Virtue is like a rich stone, best plain set.
43. **Of Beauty**

27 That is the best part of beauty, which a picture cannot express.

28 There is no excellent beauty that hath not some strangeness in the proportion.

29 There is in human nature generally more of the fool than of the wise.
12. **Boldness**

30 He said it that knew it best. (Demosthenes)

31 In civil business; what first? boldness; what second and third? boldness: and yet boldness is a child of ignorance and baseness.

32 Boldness is an ill keeper of promise.

33 Mahomet made the people believe that he would call a hill to him, and from the top of it offer up his prayers for the observers of his law. The people assembled: Mahomet called the hill to come to him again and again; and when the hill stood still, he was never a whit abashed, but said, 'If the hill will not come to Mahomet, Mahomet will go to the hill.' (Proverbially, 'If the mountain will not...')

34 Houses are built to live in and not to look on; therefore let use be preferred before uniformity, except where both may be had.
45. **Of Building**

35 Light gains make heavy purses.
52. **Of Ceremonies and Respects**

36 Small matters win great commendation.

37 He that is too much in anything, so that he giveth another occasion of satiety, maketh himself cheap.

38 A wise man will make more opportunities than he finds.

39 Books will speak plain when counsellors blanch.
20. **Of Counsel**

40 There be that can pack the cards and yet cannot play well; so there are some that are good in canvasses and factions, that are otherwise weak men.
22. **Of Cunning**

41 In things that are tender and unpleasing, it is good to break the ice by some whose words are of less weight, and to reserve the more weighty voice to come in as by chance.

42 I knew one that when he wrote a letter he would put that which was most material in the postscript, as if it had been a bymatter.

43 Nothing doth more hurt in a state than that cunning

men pass for wise.

1 Men fear death as children fear to go in the dark; and as that natural fear in children is increased with tales, so is the other.
2. **Of Death**

2 There is no passion in the mind of man so weak, but it mates and masters the fear of death. And therefore death is no such terrible enemy, when a man hath so many attendants about him that can win the combat of him. Revenge triumphs over death; love slights it; honour aspireth to it; grief flieth to it.

3 It is as natural to die as to be born; and to a little infant, perhaps, the one is as painful as the other.

4 Above all, believe it, the sweetest canticle is *Nunc dimittis*, when a man hath obtained worthy ends and expectations. Death hath this also, that it openeth the gate to good fame, and extinguisheth envy.

5 If you dissemble sometimes your knowledge of that you are thought to know, you shall be thought, another time, to know that you know not.
32. **Of Discourse**

6 I knew a wise man that had it for a by-word, when he saw men hasten to a conclusion. 'Stay a little, that we may make an end the sooner.'
25. **Of Dispatch**

7 To choose time is to save time.

8 It is a miserable state of mind to have few things to desire and many things to fear.
19. **Of Empire**

9 Riches are for spending.
28. **Of Expense**

10 A man ought warily to begin charges which once begun will continue.

11 There is little friendship in the world, and least of all between equals.
48. **Of Followers and Friends**

12 Chiefly the mould of a man's fortune is in his own hands.
40. **Of Fortune**

13 If a man look sharply, and attentively, he shall see Fortune: for though she be blind, yet she is not invisible.

14 It had been hard for him that spake it to have put more truth and untruth together, in a few words, than in that speech: 'Whosoever is delighted in solitude is either a wild beast, or a god.'
27. **Of Friendship.** See Aristotle, *Politics*, i, 14, 1253a

15 A crowd is not company, and faces are but a gallery of pictures, and talk but a tinkling cymbal, where there is no love.

16 It [friendship] redoubleth joys, and cutteth griefs in halves.

17 As if you would call a physician, that is thought good for the cure of the disease you complain of but is unacquainted with your body, and therefore may put you in the way for a present cure but overthroweth your health in some other kind; and so cure the disease and kill the patient.

18 God Almighty first planted a garden; and, indeed, it is the purest of human pleasures.
46. **Of Gardens**

19 The inclination to goodness is imprinted deeply in the nature of man: insomuch, that if it issue not towards men, it will take unto other living creatures.
13. **Goodness, and Goodness of Nature**

20 If a man be gracious and courteous to strangers, it shows he is a citizen of the world.

21 Men in great place are thrice servants: servants of the sovereign or state, servants of fame, and servants of business.
11. **Of Great Place**

22 It is a strange desire to seek power and to lose liberty.

23 The rising unto place is laborious, and by pains men come to greater pains; and it is sometimes base, and by indignities men come to dignities. The standing is slippery, and the regress is either a downfall, or at least an eclipse.

24 Set it down to thyself, as well to create good precedents as to follow them.

25 Severity breedeth fear, but roughness breedeth hate. Even reproofs from authority ought to be grave, and not taunting.

26 All rising to great place is by a winding stair.

27 As the births of living creatures at first are ill-shapen, so are all innovations, which are the births of time.
24. **Of Innovations**

28 He that will not apply new remedies must expect new evils; for time is the greatest innovator.

29 The speaking in a perpetual hyperbole is comely in nothing but in love.
10. **Of Love**

30 It has been well said that 'the arch-flatterer with whom all the petty flatterers have intelligence is a man's self.'

31 He that hath wife and children hath given hostages to fortune; for they are impediments to great enterprises, either of virtue or mischief.
8. **Of Marriage and Single Life.** See 319:25

32 There are some other that account wife and children but as bills of charges.

33 A single life doth well with churchmen, for charity will hardly water the ground where it must first fill a pool.

34 Wives are young men's mistresses, companions for middle age, and old men's nurses.

35 He was reputed one of the wise men that made answer to the question when a man should marry? 'A young man not yet, an elder man not at all.'

36 Nature is often hidden, sometimes overcome, seldom extinguished.
38. **Of Nature in Men**

37 It is generally better to deal by speech than by letter.
47. **Of Negotiating**

38 It is a reverend thing to see an ancient castle or building not in decay.
14. **Of Nobility**

39 New nobility is but the act of power, but ancient nobility is the act of time.

1 Nobility of birth commonly abateth industry.

2 The joys of parents are secret, and so are their griefs and fears.
   7. **Of Parents and Children**

3 Children sweeten labours, but they make misfortunes more bitter.

4 The noblest works and foundations have proceeded from childless men, which have sought to express the images of their minds where those of their bodies have failed.

5 Fame is like a river, that beareth up things light and swollen, and drowns things weighty and solid.
   53. **Of Praise**

6 Age will not be defied.
   30. **Of Regimen of Health**

7 Revenge is a kind of wild justice, which the more man's nature runs to, the more ought law to weed it out.
   4. **Of Revenge**

8 Why should I be angry with a man for loving himself better than me?

9 A man that studieth revenge keeps his own wounds green.

10 The four pillars of government...(which are religion, justice, counsel, and treasure).
   15. **Of Seditions and Troubles**

11 The surest way to prevent seditions (if the times do bear it) is to take away the matter of them.

12 Money is like muck, not good except it be spread.

13 The remedy is worse than the disease.

14 The French are wiser than they seem, and the Spaniards seem wiser than they are.
   26. **Of Seeming Wise**

15 Studies serve for delight, for ornament, and for ability.
   50. **Of Studies**

16 To spend too much time in studies is sloth.

17 They perfect nature and are perfected by experience.

18 Read not to contradict and confute, nor to believe and take for granted, nor to find talk and discourse, but to weigh and consider.

19 Some books are to be tasted, others to be swallowed, and some few to be chewed and digested; that is, some books are to be read only in parts; others to be read but not curiously; and some few to be read wholly, and with diligence and attention. Some books also may be read by deputy, and extracts made of them by others.

20 Reading maketh a full man; conference a ready man; and writing an exact man.

21 Histories make men wise; poets, witty; the mathematics, subtile; natural philosophy, deep; moral, grave; logic and rhetoric, able to contend.

22 There is a superstition in avoiding superstition.
   17. **Of Superstition**

23 Suspicions amongst thoughts are like bats amongst birds, they ever fly by twilight.
   31. **Of Suspicion**

24 There is nothing makes a man suspect much, more than to know little.

25 Neither is money the sinews of war (as it is trivially said).
   29. **Of the True Greatness of Kingdoms.** See 151:30

26 Neither will it be, that a people overlaid with taxes should ever become valiant and martial.

27 Travel, in the younger sort, is a part of education; in the elder, a part of experience. He that travelleth into a country before he hath some entrance into the language, goeth to school, and not to travel.
   18. **Of Travel**

28 What is truth? said jesting Pilate; and would not stay for an answer.
   1. **Of Truth.** See 72:44

29 A mixture of a lie doth ever add pleasure.

30 It is not the lie that passeth through the mind, but the lie that sinketh in, and settleth in it, that doth the hurt.

31 The inquiry of truth, which is the love-making, or wooing of it, the knowledge of truth, which is the presence of it, and the belief of truth, which is the enjoying of it, is the sovereign good of human nature.

32 All colours will agree in the dark.
   3. **Of Unity in Religion**

33 It was prettily devised of Aesop, 'The fly sat upon the axletree of the chariot-wheel and said, what a dust do I raise.'
   54. **Of Vain-Glory**

34 In the youth of a state arms do flourish; in the middle age of a state, learning; and then both of them together for a time; in the declining age of a state, mechanical arts and merchandise.
   58. **Of Vicissitude of Things**

35 Be so true to thyself as thou be not false to others.
   23. **Of Wisdom for a Man's Self**

36 It is a poor centre of a man's actions, himself.

37 It is the nature of extreme self-lovers, as they will set a house on fire, and it were but to roast their eggs.

38 It is the wisdom of the crocodiles, that shed tears when they would devour.

39 Young men are fitter to invent than to judge, fitter for execution than for counsel, and fitter for new projects than for settled business.
   42. **Of Youth and Age**

40 I have often thought upon death, and I find it the least of all evils.
   An Essay on Death, 1

41 I do not believe that any man fears to be dead, but only the stroke of death.
   3

42 Why should a man be in love with his fetters, though of gold?
   4

43 He is the fountain of honour.
   Essay of a King

44 For they thought generally that he was a Prince as ordained, and sent down from heaven to unite and put to an end the long dissensions of the two houses; which although they had had, in the times of Henry the Fourth, Henry the Fifth, and a part of Henry the Sixth on the one side, and the times of Edward the Fourth on the other, lucid intervals and happy pauses; yet they did ever hang over the kingdom, ready to break forth

in new perturbations and calamities.
History of King Henry VII, par.3

1 I have taken all knowledge to be my province.
Letter to Lord Burleigh, 1592

2 Opportunity makes a thief.
Letter to the Earl of Essex, 1598

3 I am too old, and the seas are too long, for me to double the Cape of Good Hope.
Memorial of Access

4 I would live to study, and not study to live.

5 God's first Creature, which was Light.
New Atlantis (1627)

6 The end of our foundation is the knowledge of causes, and secret motions of things; and the enlarging of the bounds of human Empire, to the effecting of all things possible.

7 *Quod enim mavult homo verum esse, id potius credit.*
For what a man would like to be true, that he more readily believes.
Novum Oganum, bk.I, Aphor.49. See 126:27

8 *Magna ista scientiarum mater.*
That great mother of sciences.
80. [Of natural philosophy]

9 *Vim et virtutem et consequentias rerum inventarum notare juvat; quae non in aliis manifestius occurrunt, quae in illis tribus quae antiquis incognitae, et quarum primordia, licet recentia, obscura et ingloria sunt: Artis nimirum Imprimendi, Pulveris Tormentarii, et Acus Nauticae.*
It is well to observe the force and virtue and consequence of discoveries, and these are to be seen nowhere more conspicuously than in those three which were unknown to the ancients, and of which the origin, though recent, is obscure and inglorious; namely, printing, gunpowder and the magnet [i.e. Mariner's Needle]. For these three have changed the whole face and state of things throughout the world.
129, tr. Spedding. See 131:3

10 *Naturae enim non imperatur, nisi parendo.*
Nature cannot be ordered about, except by obeying her.

11 *Nam et ipsa scientia potestas est.*
Knowledge itself is power.
Religious Meditations. **Of Heresies**

12 Universities incline wits to sophistry and affectation.
Valerius Terminus of the Interpretation of Nature, ch.26

13 I have rather studied books than men.
Works, ed. 1765, II, 258

14 For my name and memory, I leave it to men's charitable speeches, and to foreign nations, and the next ages.
III, 677. Last Will (19 Dec. 1625)

15 The world's a bubble; and the life of man
    Less than a span.
The World

16 Who then to frail mortality shall trust,
But limns the water, or but writes in dust.

17 What is it then to have or have no wife,
But single thraldom, or a double strife?

18 What then remains, but that we still should cry,
Not to be born, or being born, to die?

KARL BAEDEKER 1801–1859

19 Oxford is on the whole more attractive than Cambridge to the ordinary visitor; and the traveller is therefore recommended to visit Cambridge first, or to omit it altogether if he cannot visit both.
Baedeker's Great Britain (1887), 30. **From London to Oxford**

WALTER BAGEHOT 1826–1877

20 There is a glare in some men's eyes which seems to say, 'Beware, I am dangerous; *Noli me tangere.*' Lord Brougham's face has this. A mischievous excitability is the most obvious expression of it. If he were a horse, nobody would buy him; with that eye no one could answer for his temper.
Biographical Studies. Essay II, **Lord Brougham**

21 The mystic reverence, the religious allegiance, which are essential to a true monarchy, are imaginative sentiments that no legislature can manufacture in any people.
The English Constitution (1867), 1. **The Cabinet**

22 The Crown is according to the saying, the 'fountain of honour'; but the Treasury is the spring of business.
See 27:43

23 It has been said that England invented the phrase, 'Her Majesty's Opposition'; that it was the first government which made a criticism of administration as much a part of the polity as administration itself. This critical opposition is the consequence of cabinet government.

24 The *Times* has made many ministries.

25 The great qualities, the imperious will, the rapid energy, the eager nature fit for a great crisis are not required—are impediments—in common times. A Lord Liverpool is better in everyday politics than a Chatham—a Louis Philippe far better than a Napoleon.

26 We turned out the Quaker (Lord Aberdeen), and put in the pugilist (Lord Palmerston). (Change of Ministry, 1855).

27 The best reason why Monarchy is a strong government is, that it is an intelligible government. The mass of mankind understand it, and they hardly anywhere in the world understand any other.
2. **The Monarchy**

28 The characteristic of the English Monarchy is that it retains the feelings by which the heroic kings governed their rude age, and has added the feeling by which the constitutions of later Greece ruled in more refined ages.

29 Women—one half the human race at least—care fifty times more for a marriage than a ministry.

30 Royalty is a government in which the attention of the nation is concentrated on one person doing interesting actions. A Republic is a government in which that attention is divided between many, who are all doing uninteresting actions. Accordingly, so long as the human heart is strong and the human reason weak, Royalty will be strong because it appeals to diffused feeling, and Republics weak because they appeal to the understanding.

31 An Englishman whose heart is in a matter is not easily baffled.

1 Throughout the greater part of his life George III was a kind of 'consecrated obstruction'.

2 But of all nations in the world the English are perhaps the least a nation of pure philosophers.

3 The Sovereign has, under a constitutional monarchy such as ours, three rights—the right to be consulted, the right to encourage, the right to warn.
3. **The Monarchy** (continued)

4 The order of nobility is of great use, too, not only in what it creates, but in what it prevents. It prevents the rule of wealth—the religion of gold. This is the obvious and natural idol of the Anglo-Saxon.
4. **The House of Lords**

5 The House of Peers has never been a House where the most important peers were most important.

6 A severe though not unfriendly critic of our institutions said that 'the cure for admiring the House of Lords was to go and look at it.'

7 Nations touch at their summits.

8 Years ago Mr Disraeli called Sir Robert Peel's Ministry—the last Conservative Ministry that had real power—'an organized hypocrisy', so much did the ideas of its 'head' differ from the sensations of its 'tail'.
See 184:16

9 It has been said, not truly, but with a possible approximation to truth, 'that in 1802 every hereditary monarch was insane.'

10 Queen Anne was one of the smallest people ever set in a great place.
7. **Checks and Balances**

11 The soldier—that is, the great soldier—of to-day is not a romantic animal, dashing at forlorn hopes, animated by frantic sentiment, full of fancies as to a love-lady or a sovereign; but a quiet, grave man, busied in charts, exact in sums, master of the art of tactics, occupied in trivial detail; thinking, as the Duke of Wellington was said to do, *most* of the shoes of his soldiers; despising all manner of *éclat* and eloquence; perhaps, like Count Moltke, 'silent in seven languages'.

12 No real English gentleman, in his secret soul, was ever sorry for the death of a political economist.
Estimates of some Englishmen and Scotchmen (1858), **The First Edinburgh Reviewers**

13 Writers, like teeth, are divided into incisors and grinders.

14 To a great experience one thing is essential, an experiencing nature.
Shakespeare—The Individual

15 A constitutional statesman is in general a man of common opinion and uncommon abilities.
Historical Essays. **The Character of Sir Robert Peel**

16 No man [Sir R. Peel] has come so near our definition of a constitutional statesman—the powers of a first-rate man and the creed of a second-rate man.

17 He believes, with all his heart and soul and strength, that there *is* such a thing as truth; he has the soul of a martyr with the intellect of an advocate.
Mr. Gladstone

18 The most melancholy of human reflections, perhaps, is that, on the whole, it is a question whether the benevolence of mankind does most good or harm.
Physics and Politics, No.v

19 One of the greatest pains to human nature is the pain of a new idea.

20 Wordsworth, Tennyson and Browning; or, Pure, Ornate, and Grotesque Art in English Poetry.
Essay, *National Review,* Nov. 1864

PHILIP JAMES BAILEY 1816–1902

21 We should count time by heart-throbs.
Festus (1839), v

22 America, thou half-brother of the world;
With something good and bad of every land.
x

BRUCE BAIRNSFATHER 1888–1959

23 Well, if you knows of a better 'ole, go to it.
Fragments from France, No.1 (1915)

MICHAEL BAKUNIN 1814–1876

24 *Die Lust der Zerstörung ist zugleich eine schaffende Lust!*
The urge for destruction is also a creative urge!
'Die Reaktion in Deutschland' in *Jahrbuch für Wissenschaft und Kunst* (1842), under the pseudonym 'Jules Elysard'

25 We wish, in a word, equality—equality in fact as corollary, or rather, as primordial condition of liberty. From each according to his faculties, to each according to his needs; that is what we wish sincerely and energetically.
Declaration signed by forty-seven anarchists on trial after the failure of their uprising at Lyons in 1870. See J. Morrison Davidson, *The Old Order and the New,* 1890. See 333:5

STANLEY BALDWIN 1867–1947

26 A lot of hard-faced men who look as if they had done very well out of the war.
Of the House of Commons returned after the election of 1918.
J.M. Keynes, *Economic Consequences of the Peace,* ch.5; and see Middlemass and Barnes, *Baldwin* p.72n.

27 I think it is well also for the man in the street to realise that there is no power on earth that can protect him from being bombed. Whatever people may tell him, the bomber will always get through, and it is very easy to understand that, if you realise the area of space.
House of Commons, 10 Nov. 1932. A reference to the effectiveness of air power in modern warfare

28 When you think about the defence of England you no longer think of the chalk cliffs of Dover. You think of the Rhine. That is where our frontier lies to-day.
30 July 1934

29 I shall be but a short time to-night. I have seldom spoken with greater regret, for my lips are not yet unsealed. Were these troubles over I would make a case, and I guarantee that not a man would go into the Lobby against us.
10 Dec. 1935, speech on the Abyssinian crisis. Usually quoted as 'My lips are sealed.'

A.J. BALFOUR 1848–1930

1 Do not hesitate to shoot.
Attr. to Balfour, actually part of a telegram sent by the Divisional Magistrate for Cork district in 1888: 'Deal very summarily with any organized resistance to lawful authority. If necessary do not hesitate to shoot. Plunkett.'

2 I thought he was a young man of promise; but it appears he was a young man of promises. (Said of Winston Churchill in 1899.)
R.S. Churchill, *Winston Churchill* (1966), I, 449

3 The energies of our system will decay, the glory of the sun will be dimmed, and the earth, tideless and inert, will no longer tolerate the race which has for a moment disturbed its solitude. Man will go down into the pit, and all his thoughts will perish.
The Foundations of Belief, I, 1

4 It is unfortunate, considering that enthusiasm moves the world, that so few enthusiasts can be trusted to speak the truth.
Letter to Mrs. Drew, 1918

5 Frank Harris…said…: 'The fact is, Mr Balfour, all the faults of the age come from Christianity and journalism.' 'Christianity, of course but why journalism?'
Margot Asquith, *Autobiography*, I, 10

6 This is a singularly ill-contrived world, but not so ill-contrived as all that.
W.S. Churchill, *Into Battle* (1941), p. 123

BALLADS

7 There was a youth, and a well-beloved youth,
   And he was an esquire's son,
He loved the bailiff's daughter dear,
   That lived in Islington.
The Bailiff's Daughter of Islington

8 But when his friends did understand
   His fond and foolish mind,
They sent him up to fair London,
   An apprentice for to bind.

9 She stept to him, as red as any rose,
   And took him by the bridle-ring:
'I pray you, kind sir, give me one penny,
   To ease my weary limb.'

'I prithee, sweetheart, canst thou tell me,
   Where thou wast born?'
'At Islington, kind sir,' said she,
   'Where I have had many a scorn.'

'I prithee, sweetheart, canst thou tell me
   Whether thou dost know
The bailiff's daughter of Islington?'
   'She's dead, sir, long ago.'

'Then will I sell my goodly steed,
   My saddle and my bow;
I will into some far countrey,
   Where no man doth me know.'

'O stay, O stay, thou goodly youth!
   She's alive, she is not dead;
Here she standeth by thy side,
   And is ready to be thy bride.'

10 In Scarlet town, where I was born,
   There was a fair maid dwellin',
Made every youth cry *Well-a-way!*

Her name was Barbara Allen.

All in the merry month of May,
When green buds they were swellin',
Young Jemmy Grove on his death-bed lay,
For love of Barbara Allen.
Barbara Allen's Cruelty

11 So slowly, slowly rase she up,
   And slowly she came nigh him,
And when she drew the curtain by—
   'Young man, I think you're dyin'!'.

12 'O mother, mother, make my bed,
   O make it soft and narrow:
My love has died for me to-day,
   I'll die for him to-morrow.'

13 'Farewell,' she said, 'ye virgins all,
   And shun the fault I fell in:
Henceforth take warning by the fall
   Of cruel Barbara Allen.'

14 There were twa sisters sat in a bour;
   Binnorie, O Binnorie!
There came a knight to be their wooer,
   By the bonnie milldams o' Binnorie.
Binnorie

15 Ye Highlands and ye Lawlands,
   O where hae ye been?
They hae slain the Earl of Murray,
   And hae laid him on the green.
The Bonny Earl of Murray

16 He was a braw gallant,
   And he rid at the ring;
And the bonny Earl of Murray,
   O he might hae been a king!

17 He was a braw gallant,
   And he play'd at the gluve;
And the bonny Earl of Murray,
   O he was the Queen's luve!

O lang will his Lady
   Look owre the Castle Downe,
Ere she see the Earl of Murray
   Come sounding through the town!

18 She hadna sail'd a league, a league,
   A league but barely three,
Till grim, grim grew his countenance
   And gurly grew the sea.

'What hills are yon, yon pleasant hills,
   The sun shines sweetly on?'—
'O yon are the hills o' Heaven,' he said,
   'Where you will never won.'
The Daemon Lover

19 He strack the top-mast wi' his hand,
   The fore-mast wi' his knee;
And he brake that gallant ship in twain,
   And sank her in the sea.

20 O well's me o' my gay goss-hawk,
   That he can speak and flee!
He'll carry a letter to my love,
   Bring another back to me.
The Gay Gosshawk

21 But ne'er a word wad ane o' them speak,
   For barring of the door.
Get Up and Bar the Door

1 Goodman, you've spoken the foremost word!
    Get up and bar the door.

2 A ship I have got in the North Country
    And she goes by the name of the *Golden Vanity*,
O I fear she will be taken by a Spanish Ga-la-lee,
    As she sails by the Low-lands low.
The Golden Vanity

3 He bored with his augur, he bored once and twice,
    And some were playing cards, and some were playing
      dice,
When the water flowed in it dazzled their eyes,
    And she sank by the Low-lands low.

So the Cabin-boy did swim all to the larboard side,
    Saying 'Captain! take me in, I am drifting with the
      tide!'
'I will shoot you! I will kill you!' the cruel Captain
    cried,
    'You may sink by the Low-lands low.'

4 I wish I were where Helen lies,
    Night and day on me she cries;
O that I were where Helen lies,
    On fair Kirkconnell lea!

Curst be the heart that thought the thought,
And curst the hand that fired the shot,
When in my arms burd Helen dropt,
    And died to succour me!
Helen of Kirkconnell

5 'What gat ye to your dinner, Lord Randal, my Son?
    What gat ye to your dinner, my handsome young
      man?'
'I gat eels boil'd in broo'; mother, make my bed soon,
    For I'm weary wi' hunting, and fain wald lie down.'
Lord Randal

6 This ae nighte, this ae nighte,
    —*Every nighte and alle,*
Fire and fleet and candle-lighte,
    And Christe receive thy saule.
Lyke-Wake Dirge

        fleet;floor. Other readings are 'sleet' and 'salt'

7 From Brig o' Dread when thou may'st pass,
    —*Every nighte and alle,*
To Purgatory fire thou com'st at last;
    And Christe receive thy saule.

If ever thou gavest meat or drink,
    —*Every nighte and alle,*
The fire sall never make thee shrink
    And Christe receive thy saule.

8 When captains couragious whom death could not
    daunte,
Did march to the seige of the city of Gaunt,
They mustered their soldiers by two and by three,
And the foremost in battle was Mary Ambree.
Mary Ambree

9 For in my mind, of all mankind
    I love but you alone.
The Nut Brown Maid

10 For I must to the greenwood go
    Alone, a banished man.

11 Marie Hamilton's to the kirk gane
    Wi' ribbons on her breast;
The King thought mair o' Marie Hamilton

Than he listen'd to the priest.
The Queen's Maries

12 Yestreen the Queen had four Maries,
    The night she'll hae but three;
There was Marie Seaton, and Marie Beaton,
    And Marie Carmichael, and me.

13 There are twelve months in all the year,
    As I hear many men say,
But the merriest month in all the year
    Is the merry month of May.
Robin Hood and the Widow's Three Sons

14 'Let me have length and breadth enough,
    And under my head a sod;
That they may say when I am dead,
    —*Here lies bold Robin Hood!*'
The Death of Robin Hood

15 Fight on, my men, sayes Sir Andrew Bartton,
I am hurt but I am not slain;
Ile lay mee downe and bleed a while
And then Ile rise and fight againe.
Sir Andrew Bartton

16 The king sits in Dunfermline town
    Drinking the blude-red wine.
Sir Patrick Spens

17 Our king has written a braid letter,
    And seal'd it with his hand,
And sent it to Sir Patrick Spens,
    Was walking on the strand.

'To Noroway, to Noroway,
    To Noroway o'er the faem;
The king's daughter o' Noroway,
    'Tis thou must bring her hame.'

The first word that Sir Patrick read
    So loud, loud laughed he;
The neist word that Sir Patrick read
    The tear blinded his e'e.

18 'I saw the new moon late yestreen
    Wi' the auld moon in her arm;
And if we gang to sea master,
    I fear we'll come to harm.'

Go fetch a web o' the silken claith,
    Another o' the twine,
And wap them into our ship's side,
    And let nae the sea come in.

    wap;wrap.

19 O laith, laith were our gude Scots lords
    To wat their cork-heel'd shoon;
But lang or a' the play was play'd
    They wat their hats aboon.

20 O lang, lang may the ladies sit,
    Wi' their fans into their hand,
Before they see Sir Patrick Spens
    Come sailing to the strand!

And lang, lang may the maidens sit
    Wi' their gowd kames in their hair,
A-waiting for their ain dear loves!
    For them they'll see nae mair.

Half-owre, half-owre to Aberdour,
    'Tis fifty fathoms deep;
And there lies good Sir Patrick Spens,
    Wi' the Scots lords at his feet!

1 And she has kilted her green kirtle
    A little abune her knee;
And she has braided her yellow hair
    A little abune her bree.
Tam Lin, v

2 About the dead hour of the night
    She heard the bridles ring;
And Janet was as glad at that
    As any earthly thing.
xli

3 'But what I ken this night, Tam Lin,
    Gin I had kent yestreen,
I wad ta'en out thy heart o' flesh,
    And put in a heart o' stane.'
l

4 She's mounted on her milk-white steed,
    She's ta'en true Thomas up behind.
Thomas the Rhymer, viii

5 'And see ye not yon braid, braid road,
    That lies across the lily leven?
That is the Path of Wickedness,
    Though some call it the Road to Heaven.'
xii

6 It was mirk, mirk night, there was nae starlight,
    They waded thro' red blude to the knee;
For a' the blude that's shed on the earth
    Rins through the springs o' that countrie.
xvi

7 There were three ravens sat on a tree,
They were as black as they might be.
The one of them said to his make,
'Where shall we our breakfast take?'
The Three Ravens

8 As I was walking all alane,
I heard twa corbies making a mane:
The tane unto the tither did say,
'Where sall we gang and dine the day?'

'—In behint yon auld fail dyke
I wot there lies a new-slain knight;
And naebody kens that he lies there
But his hawk, his hound, and his lady fair.

'His hound is to the hunting gane,
His hawk to fetch the wild-fowl hame,
His lady's ta'en anither mate,
So we may make our dinner sweet.

'Ye'll sit on his white hause-bane,
And I'll pike out his bonny blue e'en:
Wi' ae lock o' his gowden hair
We'll theek our nest when it grows bare.'
The Twa Corbies

corbies;ravens. fail;turf. hause;neck. theek;thatch.

9 'The wind doth blow to-day, my love,
    And a few small drops of rain;
I never had but one true love;
    In cold grave she was lain.

'I'll do as much for my true-love
    As any young man may;
I'll sit and mourn all at her grave
    For a twelvemonth and a day.'
The Unquiet Grave

10 O waly, waly, up the bank,
    And waly, waly, doun the brae,
And waly, waly, yon burn-side,
    Where I and my Love wont to gae!

I lean'd my back unto an aik,
    I thocht it was a trustie tree;
But first it bow'd and syne it brake—
    Sae my true love did lichtlie me.

O waly, waly, gin love be bonnie
    A little time while it is new!
But when 'tis auld it waxeth cauld,
    And fades awa' like morning dew.

O wherefore should I busk my heid,
    Or wherefore should I kame my hair?
For my true Love has me forsook,
    And says he'll never lo'e me mair.
Waly, Waly

11 But had I wist, before I kist,
    That love had been sae ill to win,
I had lock'd my heart in a case o' gowd,
    And pinn'd it wi' a siller pin.

And O! if my young babe were born,
    And set upon the nurse's knee;
And I mysel' were dead and gane,
    And the green grass growing over me!

12 'Tom Pearse, Tom Pearse, lend me your grey mare,
All along, down along, out along, lee.
For I want for to go to Widdicombe Fair,
Wi' Bill Brewer, Jan Stewer, Peter Gurney, Peter
    Davey, Dan'l Whiddon, Harry Hawk,
    Old Uncle Tom Cobbleigh and all.
    Old Uncle Tom Cobbleigh and all.'
Widdicombe Fair

GEORGE BANCROFT 1800–1891

13 It [Calvinism in Switzerland] established a religion
without a prelate, a government without a king.
History of the United States (1834–40), vol.iii, ch.6

RICHARD BANCROFT 1544–1610

14 Where Christ erecteth his Church, the devil in the
same churchyard will have his chapel.
Sermon at Paul's Cross, 9 Feb. 1588

EDWARD BANGS fl. 1775

15 Yankee Doodle keep it up,
    Yankee Doodle dandy;
Mind the music and the step,
    And with the girls be handy.
Yankee Doodle; or Father's Return to Camp. See Nicholas
Smith, *Stories of Great National Songs*

16 Yankee Doodle came to town
    Riding on a pony;
Stuck a feather in his cap
    And called it Macaroni.

THÉODORE FAULLAIN DE BANVILLE
1823–1891

1 *Jeune homme sans mélancolie,*
Blond comme un soleil d'Italie,
Garde bien ta belle folie.
Young man untroubled by melancholy, fair as an
Italian sun, take good care of your fine carelessness.
A Adolphe Gaïffe

2 Licences poétiques. *Il n'y en a pas.*
Poetic licence. There's no such thing.
Petit traité de poésie française (1872)

JOHN BARBOUR 1316?–1395

3 Storys to rede ar delitabill,
Suppos that thai be nocht bot fabill.
The Bruce (1375), I, l.1

4 A! fredome is a noble thing!
Fredome mayse man to haiff liking.
l.225

REVD. R.H. BARHAM 1788–1845

5 Like a blue-bottle fly on a rather large scale,
With a rather large corking-pin stuck through his tail.
The Ingoldsby Legends. The Auto-da-Fé

6 She help'd him to lean, and she help'd him to fat,
And it look'd like hare—but it might have been cat.
The Bagman's Dog

7 Though I've always considered Sir Christopher Wren,
As an architect, one of the greatest of men;
And, talking of Epitaphs,—much I admire his,
'Circumspice, si Monumentum requiris';
Which an erudite Verger translated to me,
'If you ask for his Monument, Sir-come-spy-see!'
The Cynotaph. See 11:2

8 What Horace says is,
Eheu fugaces
Anni labuntur, Postume, Postume!
Years glide away, and are lost to me, lost to me!
Epigram: Eheu fugaces. See 260:10

9 What *was* to be done?—'twas perfectly plain
That they could not well hang the man over again;
What *was* to be done?—The man was dead!
Nought *could* be done—nought could be said;
So—my Lord Tomnoddy went home to bed!
Hon. Mr. Sucklethumbkin's Story

10 A servant's too often a negligent elf;
—If it's business of consequence, do it yourself!
The Ingoldsby Penance. Moral

11 The Jackdaw sat on the Cardinal's chair!
Bishop, and abbot, and prior were there;
　Many a monk, and many a friar,
　Many a knight, and many a squire,
With a great many more of lesser degree,—
In sooth a goodly company;
And they served the Lord Primate on bended knee.
　　Never, I ween,
　　Was a prouder seen,
Read of in books, or dreamt of in dreams,
Than the Cardinal Lord Archbishop of Rheims!
The Jackdaw of Rheims

12 And six little Singing-boys,—dear little souls!
In nice clean faces, and nice white stoles.

13 He cursed him in sleeping, that every night
He should dream of the devil, and wake in a fright.

14 Never was heard such a terrible curse!
　But what gave rise to no little surprise,
Nobody seem'd one penny the worse!

15 Heedless of grammar, they all cried, 'That's him!'

16 Here's a corpse in the case with a sad swell'd face,
And a Medical Crowner's a queer sort of thing!
A Lay of St. Gengulphus

17 　　A German,
Who smoked like a chimney.
Lay of St. Odille

18 So put that in your pipe, my Lord Otto, and smoke it!

19 'Twas in Margate last July, I walk'd upon the pier,
I saw a little vulgar Boy—I said, 'What make you
　here?'
Misadventures at Margate

20 And now I'm here, from this here pier it is my fixed
　intent
To jump, as Mr Levi did from off the Monu-ment!

21 I could not see my little friend—because he was not
　there!

22 But when the Crier cried, 'O Yes!' the people cried, 'O
　No!'

23 It's very odd that Sailor-men should talk so very
　queer—
And then he hitch'd his trousers up, as is, I'm told,
　their use,
It's very odd that Sailor-men should wear those things
　so loose.

24 He smiled and said, 'Sir, does your mother know that
　you are out?'

25 They were a little less than 'kin', and rather more than
　'kind'.
Nell Cook. See 429:21

26 She drank Prussic acid without any water,
And died like a Duke-and-a-Duchess's daughter!
The Tragedy

BARNABE BARNES 1569?–1609

27 Ah, sweet Content! where doth thine harbour hold?
Parthenophil and Parthenophe (1593), Sonnet lxvi

WILLIAM BARNES 1801–1886

28 An' there vor me the apple tree
Do leän down low in Linden Lea.
My Orcha'd in Linden Lea

29 But still the neäme do bide the seäme—
'Tis Pentridge—Pentridge by the river.
Pentridge by the River

30 My love is the maïd ov all maïdens,
Though all mid be comely.
In the Spring

31 Since I noo mwore do zee your feäce.
The Wife A-Lost

RICHARD BARNFIELD 1574–1627

32 As it fell upon a day
In the merry month of May,

Sitting in a pleasant shade,
Which a grove of myrtles made.
Beasts did leap and birds did sing,
Trees did grow and plants did spring,
Everything did banish moan,
Save the nightingale alone.
She, poor bird, as all forlorn,
Lean'd her breast up-till a thorn,
And there sung the dolefull'st ditty
That to hear it was great pity.
Fie, fie, fie, now would she cry;
Tereu, Tereu, by and by.
An Ode. Also attr. Shakespeare

1 King Pandion, he is dead,
All thy friends are lapp'd in lead.

2 If Music and sweet Poetry agree,
As they must needs (the Sister and the Brother)
Then must the love be great, 'twixt thee and me,
Because thou lov'st the one, and I the other.
Sonnet

3 Nothing more certain than incertainties;
Fortune is full of fresh variety:
Constant in nothing but inconstancy.
The Shepherd's Content, xi

4 My flocks feed not,
My ewes breed not,
My rams speed not,
　　　All is amiss.
Love is dying,
Faith's defying,
Heart's denying,
　　　Causer of this.
A Shepherd's Complaint

5 The waters were his winding sheet, the sea was made
his tomb;
Yet for his fame the ocean sea, was not sufficient
room.
(On the death of Hawkins.) **Encomion of Lady Pecunia. To the
Gentlemen Readers**

PHINEAS T. BARNUM 1810–1891

6 There's a sucker born every minute.
Attr.

J.M. BARRIE 1860–1937

7 His Lordship may compel us to be equal upstairs, but
there will never be equality in the servants' hall.
The Admirable Crichton, I

8 I'm a second eleven sort of chap.
III

9 Never ascribe to an opponent motives meaner than
your own.
'**Courage**', Rectorial Address, St. Andrews, 3 May 1922

10 Courage is the thing. All goes if courage goes.

11 Facts were never pleasing to him. He acquired them
with reluctance and got rid of them with relief. He was
never on terms with them until he had stood them on
their heads.
Love Me Never or For Ever

12 I do loathe explanations.
My Lady Nicotine, 16

13 When the first baby laughed for the first time, the
laugh broke into a thousand pieces and they all went
skipping about, and that was the beginning of fairies.
Peter Pan, I

14 Every time a child says 'I don't believe in fairies'
there is a little fairy somewhere that falls down dead.

15 To die will be an awfully big adventure.
III

16 Do you believe in fairies?...If you believe, clap your
hands!
IV

17 Oh the gladness of her gladness when she's glad,
And the sadness of her sadness when she's sad,
But the gladness of her gladness
And the sadness of her sadness
Are as nothing, Charles,
To the badness of her badness when she's bad.
Rosalind

18 It's a sort of bloom on a woman. If you have it
[charm], you don't need to have anything else; and if
you don't have it, it doesn't much matter what else you
have.
What Every Woman Knows, I

19 A young Scotsman of your ability let loose upon the
world with £300, what could he not do? It's almost
appalling to think of; especially if he went among the
English.

20 You've forgotten the grandest moral attribute of a
Scotsman, Maggie, that he'll do nothing which might
damage his career.
II

21 There are few more impressive sights in the world than
a Scotsman on the make.

22 Every man who is high up loves to think that he has
done it all himself; and the wife smiles, and lets it go
at that. It's our only joke. Every woman knows that.
IV

GEORGE BARRINGTON b. 1755

23 From distant climes, o'er widespread seas we come,
Though not with much *éclat* or beat of drum;
True patriots we; for be it understood,
We left our country for our country's good.
No private views disgraced our generous zeal,
What urged our travels was our country's weal;
And none will doubt but that our emigration
Has proved most useful to the British nation.
D.N.B. Prologue for the opening of the Playhouse, Sydney, New
South Wales, 16 Jan. 1796, when the actors were principally
convicts. Also attr. Henry Carter (d. 1806): see *Annual Register,*
1801. See 212:4

CHARLES BARTLETT 1921–

24 The hawks favoured an air strike to eliminate the
Cuban missile bases.... The doves opposed the air
strike and favoured a blockade.
Saturday Evening Post, 8 Dec. 1962

BERNARD M. BARUCH 1870–1965

25 Let us not be deceived—we are today in the midst of a
cold war.
Speech before South Carolina Legislature, 16 Apr. 1947. Mr.
Baruch said the expression 'cold war' was suggested to him by
H.B. Swope, former editor of the New York *World.*

WILLIAM BASSE d. 1653?

1 Renowned Spenser, lie a thought more nigh
To learned Chaucer, and rare Beaumont lie,
A little nearer Spenser, to make more room
For Shakespeare, in your threefold, fourfold tomb.
On Shakespeare

THOMAS BASTARD 1566–1618

2 Age is deformed, youth unkind,
We scorn their bodies, they our mind.
Chrestoleros (1598), Bk.7, Epigram 9

EDGAR BATEMAN nineteenth century

3 Wiv a ladder and some glasses,
You could see to 'Ackney Marshes,
If it wasn't for the 'ouses in between.
If it wasn't for the 'Ouses in between

KATHERINE LEE BATES 1859–1929

4 America! America!
   God shed His grace on thee
And crown thy good with brotherhood
   From sea to shining sea!
America the Beautiful

CHARLES BAUDELAIRE 1821–1867

5 *Hypocrite lecteur,—mon semblable,—mon frère.*
Hypocrite reader—my likeness—my brother.
Les Fleurs du Mal, Préface

6 *Le poète est semblable au prince des nuées
Qui haute la tempète et se rit de l'archer;
Exilé sur le sol, au milieu des huées,
Ses ailes de géant l'empêchent de marcher.*
The poet is like the prince of the clouds, who rides out
   the tempest and laughs at the archer. But when he is
   exiled on the ground, amidst the clamour, his
   giant's wings prevent him from walking.
ii, *L'Albatros*

7 *Là, tout n'est qu'ordre et beauté,
Luxe, calme et volupté.*
Everything there is simply order and beauty, luxury,
   peace and sensual indulgence.
liii, *L'Invitation au Voyage*

8 *Quelle est cette île triste et noire? C'est Cythère,
Nous dit-on, un pays fameux dans les chansons,
Eldorado banal de tous les vieux garçons.
Regardez, après tout, c'est un pauvre terre.*
What sad, black isle is that? It's Cythera, so they say,
   a land celebrated in song, the banal Eldorado of all
   the old fools. Look, after all, it's a land of poverty.
cxvi, *Un Voyage à Cythère*

LILIAN BAYLIS 1874–1937

9 I do like to see the Jews coming, don't you dear? Even
if they aren't Christians, it must do them good, but I
wish we didn't have to give them *The Merchant of
Venice*, the Christians all behave so badly.
Richard Findlater, *Lilian Baylis: The Lady of the Old Vic* (1975)

THOMAS HAYNES BAYLY 1797–1839

10 Oh! no! we never mention her,

Her name is never heard;
My lips are now forbid to speak
That once familiar word.
Oh! No! We Never Mention Her

AUBREY BEARDSLEY 1872–1898

11 Really I believe I'm so affected, even my lungs are
affected.
O. Sitwell, *Noble Essences* (1950, vol.5 of *Left Hand, Right
Hand!*), 6

EARL BEATTY 1871–1936

12 There's something wrong with our bloody ships
to-day, Chatfield.
Remark during the Battle of Jutland, 1916: Winston Churchill,
The World Crisis (1927), I, 129. The additional words commonly
attributed: 'Steer two points nearer the enemy' are denied by Lord
Chatfield

TOPHAM BEAUCLERK 1739–1780

13 [On Boswell saying that a certain man had good
principles.] Then he does not wear them out in
practice.
Boswell, *Life of Johnson*, 14 Apr. 1778

PIERRE-AUGUSTIN CARON DE
BEAUMARCHAIS 1732–1799

14 *Aujourd'hui ce qui ne vaut pas la peine d'être dit, on
le chante.*
Today if something is not worth saying, people sing it.
Le Barbier de Séville, I.ii

15 *Je me presse de rire de tout, de peur d'être obligé d'en
pleurer.*
I make myself laugh at everything, for fear of having
to weep.

16 *Est-ce qu'un homme comme vous ignore quelque
chose?*
Can anything be beyond the knowledge of a man like
you?
(Figaro to Count Almaviva.)
vi

17 *Boire sans soif et faire l'amour en tout temps,
madame, il n'y a que ça qui nous distingue des autres
bêtes.*
Drinking when we are not thirsty and making love all
year round, madam; that is all there is to distinguish us
from other animals.
Le Mariage de Figaro, II.xxi

18 *Parce que vous êtes un grand seigneur, vous vous
croyez un grand génie!...Vous vous êtes donné la
peine de naître, et rien de plus.*
Because you are a great lord, you believe yourself to
be a great genius!...You took the trouble to be born,
but no more.

FRANCIS BEAUMONT 1584–1616

19   What things have we seen,
Done at the Mermaid! heard words that have been
So nimble, and so full of subtil flame,
As if that every one from whence they came,
Had meant to put his whole wit in a jest,
And had resolv'd to live a fool, the rest

Of his dull life.
Letter to Ben Jonson

1 Here are sands, ignoble things,
Dropt from the ruin'd sides of Kings;
Here's a world of pomp and state,
Buried in dust, once dead by fate.
On the Tombs in Westminster Abbey

FRANCIS BEAUMONT 1584–1616
and
JOHN FLETCHER 1579–1625
(see also under FLETCHER)

2 You are no better than you should be.
The Coxcomb, IV.iii

3 I care not two-pence.

4 It is always good
When a man has two irons in the fire.
The Faithful Friends, I.ii (attr.)

5 Nose, nose, jolly red nose,
Who gave thee this jolly red nose?...
Nutmegs and ginger, cinnamon and cloves,
And they gave me this jolly red nose.
The Knight of the Burning Pestle, I, 1.334

6 This is a pretty flim-flam.
II.iii

7 The sturdy steed now goes to grass and up they hang
his saddle.
IV, interlude

8 Upon my buried body lay
Lightly gently earth.
The Maid's Tragedy, II.i

9 Those have most power to hurt us, that we love.
V.iv

10 *Philaster:* Oh, but thou dost not know
What 'tis to die.
Bellario: Yes, I do know, my Lord:
'Tis less than to be born; a lasting sleep;
A quiet resting from all jealousy,
A thing we all pursue; I know besides,
It is but giving over of a game,
That must be lost.
Philaster, III.i

11 Kiss till the cow comes home.
The Scornful Lady, II.ii

12 There is no other purgatory but a woman.
III.i

13 It would talk:
Lord how it talk't!
IV.i

LORD BEAVERBROOK 1879–1964

14 Our cock won't fight.
Said to W.S. Churchill during the abdication crisis, 1936. Frances
Donaldson, *Edward VIII,* ch.22

SAMUEL BECKETT 1906–

15 *Estragon:* Let's go.
Vladimir: We can't.
Estragon: Why not?
Vladimir: We're waiting for Godot.
Waiting for Godot (1954), I

16 We always find something, eh, Didi, to give us the

impression that we exist?
II

17 If I had the use of my body I would throw it out of the
window.
Malone Dies, English version (1956), p.44

PETER BECKFORD 1740–1811

18 The colour I think of little moment; and am of opinion
with our friend Foote, respecting his negro friend, that
a good dog, like a good candidate, cannot be of a bad
colour.
Thoughts upon Hare and Fox Hunting (1781), letter 3

WILLIAM BECKFORD 1759–1844

19 When he was angry, one of his eyes became so
terrible, that no person could bear to behold it; and the
wretch upon whom it was fixed, instantly fell
backward, and sometimes expired. For fear, however,
of depopulating his dominions and making his palace
desolate, he but rarely gave way to his anger.
Vathek (1782, 3rd edn. 1816), 1st para.

20 He did not think, with the Caliph Omar Ben Adalaziz,
that it was necessary to make a hell of this world to
enjoy paradise in the next.
2nd para.

21 Your presence I condescend to accept; but beg you
will let me be quiet; for, I am not over-fond of
resisting temptation.
215th para.

THOMAS BECON 1512–1567

22 For when the wine is in, the wit is out.
Catechism, 375

THOMAS LOVELL BEDDOES 1803–1849

23 If thou wilt ease thine heart
Of love and all its smart,
Then sleep, dear, sleep.
Death's Jest Book, II.ii

24 But wilt thou cure thine heart
Of love and all its smart,
Then die, dear, die.

25 I have a bit of FIAT in my soul,
And can myself create my little world.
V.i

26 Old Adam, the carrion crow.
iv

27 King Death hath asses' ears.

28 If there were dreams to sell,
What would you buy?
Some cost a passing bell;
Some a light sigh,
That shakes from Life's fresh crown
Only a roseleaf down.
If there were dreams to sell,
Merry and sad to tell,
And the crier rung the bell,
What would you buy?
Dream-Pedlary

THE VENERABLE BEDE c.673–735

1 The present life of men on earth, O king, as compared
with the whole length of time which is unknowable to
us, seems to me to be like this: as if, when you are
sitting at dinner with your chiefs and ministers in
wintertime,…one of the sparrows from outside flew
very quickly through the hall; as if it came in one door
and soon went out through another. In that actual time
it is indoors it is not touched by the winter's storm;
but yet the tiny period of calm is over in a moment,
and having come out of the winter it soon returns to
the winter and slips out of your sight. Man's life
appears to be more or less like this; and of what may
follow it, or what preceded it, we are absolutely
ignorant.
Ecclesiastical History (completed 731), 2, 13

2 *'Magister dilecte, restat adhuc una sententia non
descripta.' At ille inquit 'Scribe.' Et post modicum
dixit puer: 'Modo descripta est.' At ille 'Bene' inquit,
'consummatum est; veritatem dixisti.'*
'There is still one sentence, dear master, that we
haven't written down.' And he said, 'Write it.' After a
little while the boy said, 'There, now it is written.'
'Good' he replied, 'It is finished, you have spoken the
truth.'
Cuthbert's letter to Cuthwin on the death of Bede, A.D.735. See
Ecclesiastical History, Colgrave and Mynors (eds) (1969), p.579
ff.

BARNARD ELLIOTT BEE 1823–1861

3 Let us determine to die here, and we will conquer.
There is Jackson standing like a stone wall. Rally
behind the Virginians.
First Battle of Bull Run, 1861. Poore, *Reminiscences of
Metropolis*, II.85

SIR THOMAS BEECHAM 1879–1961

4 Too much counterpoint; what is worse, Protestant
counterpoint. [Of Bach.]
Neville Cardus, *Guardian*, 8 Mar. 1971

5 When the history of the first half of this century comes
to be written—properly written—it will be
acknowledged the most stupid and brutal in the history
of civilisation.
H. Proctor-Gregg, *Beecham Remembered* (1976), p.153

6 A musicologist is a man who can read music but can't
hear it.
p.154

7 In the first movement alone, I took note of six
pregnancies and at least four miscarriages. [Of
Bruckner's 7th Symphony.]
Oral trad.

REVD. H.C. BEECHING 1859–1919

8 First come I; my name is Jowett.
There's no knowledge but I know it.
I am Master of this college:
What I don't know isn't knowledge.
The Masque of Balliol, composed by and current among members
of Balliol College in the late 1870's. See 7:1, 517:11–12

9 Not when the sense is dim,
  But now from the heart of joy,
I would remember Him:

Take the thanks of a boy.
Prayers

MAX BEERBOHM 1872–1956

10 Most women are not so young as they are painted.
A Defence of Cosmetics

11 I belong to the Beardsley period.
Diminuendo

12 There is always something rather absurd about the
past.
1880

13 To give an accurate and exhaustive account of that
period would need a far less brilliant pen than mine.

14 She swam to the bell-rope and grasped it for a tinkle.
(Parody of Meredith.) *Euphemia Clashthought*

15 A swear-word in a rustic slum
A simple swear-word is to some,
To Masefield something more.
(Caption to a cartoon) *Fifty Caricatures*, 1913. See 579:19

16 None, it is said, of all who revelled with the Regent,
was half so wicked as Lord George Hell.
The Happy Hypocrite, ch.1

17 Mankind is divisible into two great classes: hosts and
guests.
Hosts and Guests

18 I maintain that though you would often in the fifteenth
century have heard the snobbish Roman say, in a
would-be off-hand tone, 'I am dining with the Borgias
to-night,' no Roman ever was able to say, 'I dined last
night with the Borgias.'

19 The Nonconformist Conscience makes cowards of us
all.
King George the Fourth. See 573:12

20 Fate wrote her [Queen Caroline] a most tremendous
tragedy, and she played it in tights.

21 Not that I had any special reason for hating school.
Strange as it may seem to my readers, I was not
unpopular there. I was a modest, good-humoured boy.
It is Oxford that has made me insufferable.
More. Going back to School

22 Undergraduates owe their happiness chiefly to the fact
that they are no longer at school…The nonsense which
was knocked out of them at school is all put gently
back at Oxford or Cambridge.

23 They so very indubitably *are,* you know!
(Parody of Henry James.) *Mote in the Middle Distance*

24 'After all', as a pretty girl once said to me, 'women
are a sex by themselves, so to speak'.
The Pervasion of Rouge

25 Enter Michael Angelo. Andrea del Sarto apears for a
moment at a window. Pippa passes.
Savonarola Brown, III

26 The fading signals and grey eternal walls of that
antique station, which, familiar to them and
insignificant, does yet whisper to the tourist the last
enchantment of the Middle Age.
Zuleika Dobson, ch.1

27 Zuleika, on a desert island, would have spent most of
her time in looking for a man's foot-print.
ch.2

28 The dullard's envy of brilliant men is always assuaged

by the suspicion that they will come to a bad end.
ch.4

1 Your mentality, too, is bully, as we all predicate.
ch.8

2 Deeply regret inform your grace last night two black owls came and perched on battlements remained there through night hooting at dawn flew away none knows whither awaiting instructions Jellings.
ch.14

3 Prepare vault for funeral Monday Dorset.

4 The Socratic manner is not a game at which two can play.
ch.15

5 'Ah, say that again,' she murmured. 'Your voice is music.'
He repeated his question.
'Music!' she said dreamily; and such is the force of habit that 'I don't', she added, 'know anything about music, really. But I know what I like.'
ch.16

6 Of course he was a wonderful all-round man, but the act of walking round him has always tired me.
Of William Morris. S.N. Behrman, *Conversations with Max*, ch.2

7 Only the insane take themselves quite seriously.
Lord David Cecil, *Max* (1964), ch.2

ETHEL LYNN BEERS 1827–1879

8 All quiet along the Potomac to-night,
    No sound save the rush of the river,
While soft falls the dew on the face of the dead—
    The picket's off duty forever.
The Picket Guard. See 324:29

LUDWIG VAN BEETHOVEN 1770–1827

9 *Muss es sein? Es muss sein.*
Must it be? It must be.
Epigraph to String Quartet in F Major, Opus 135

MRS. APHRA BEHN 1640–1689

10 Oh, what a dear ravishing thing is the beginning of an Amour!
The Emperor of the Moon, I.i

11 Of all that writ, he was the wisest bard, who spoke this mighty truth—
He that knew all that ever learning writ,
Knew only this—that he knew nothing yet.
iii

12 Love ceases to be a pleasure, when it ceases to be a secret.
The Lover's Watch, Four o'clock

13 Faith, Sir, we are here to-day, and gone to-morrow.
The Lucky Chance, IV

14 I owe a duty, where I cannot love.
The Moor's Revenge, III.iii

15 A brave world, Sir, full of religion, knavery, and change: we shall shortly see better days.
The Roundheads, I.i

16 Variety is the soul of pleasure.
The Rover, Part II, Act I

17 Come away; poverty's catching.

18 Money speaks sense in a language all nations understand.
III.i

19 Beauty unadorn'd.
IV.ii

20 'Sure, I rose the wrong way to-day, I have had such damn'd ill luck every way'.
The Town Fop, V.i

21 The soft, unhappy sex.
The Wandering Beauty

W.H. BELLAMY nineteenth century

22 Old Simon the Cellarer keeps a rare store
Of Malmsey and Malvoisie.
Song: *Simon the Cellarer*

HILAIRE BELLOC 1870–1953

23 Child! do not throw this book about;
Refrain from the unholy pleasure
Of cutting all the pictures out!
Preserve it as your chiefest treasure.
Bad Child's Book of Beasts, dedication

24 Your little hands were made to take
The better things and leave the worse ones:
They also may be used to shake
The massive paws of elder persons.

25 A manner rude and wild
Is common at your age.
introduction

26 Who take their manners from the Ape,
Their habits from the Bear,
Indulge the loud unseemly jape,
And never brush their hair.

27 The Dromedary is a cheerful bird:
I cannot say the same about the Kurd.
The Dromedary

28 When people call this beast to mind,
They marvel more and more
At such a little tail behind,
So large a trunk before.
The Elephant

29 The Frog is justly sensitive
    To epithets like these.
The Frog

30 I shoot the Hippopotamus
With bullets made of platinum,
Because if I use leaden ones
His hide is sure to flatten 'em.
The Hippopotamus

31 Mothers of large families (who claim to common sense)
Will find a Tiger well repay the trouble and expense.
The Tiger

32 The nicest child I ever knew
Was Charles Augustus Fortescue.
Cautionary Tales. Charles Augustus Fortescue

33 Godolphin Horne was nobly born;
He held the human race in scorn.
Godolphin Horne

34 The chief defect of Henry King
Was chewing little bits of string.
Henry King

1 Physicians of the utmost fame
Were called at once, but when they came
They answered, as they took their fees,
'There is no cure for this disease.'

2 'Oh, my friends, be warned by me,
That breakfast, dinner, lunch, and tea
Are all the human frame requires...'
With that the wretched child expires.

3 And always keep a hold of Nurse
For fear of finding something worse.
Jim

4 In my opinion Butlers ought
To know their place, and not to play
The Old Retainer night and day.
Lord Lundy

5 Towards the age of twenty-six,
They shoved him into politics.

6 We had intended you to be
The next Prime Minister but three:
The stocks were sold; the Press was squared;
The Middle Class was quite prepared.
But as it is!...My language fails!
Go out and govern New South Wales!

7 Matilda told such Dreadful Lies,
It made one Gasp and Stretch one's Eyes;
Her Aunt, who, from her Earliest Youth,
Had kept a Strict Regard for Truth,
Attempted to Believe Matilda:
The effort very nearly killed her.
Matilda

8 Summoned the Immediate Aid
Of London's Noble Fire Brigade.

9 Until Matilda's Aunt succeeded
In showing them they were not needed;
And even then she had to pay
To get the Men to go away!

10 It happened that a few Weeks later
Her Aunt was off to the Theatre
To see that Interesting Play
The Second Mrs Tanqueray.

11 For every time she shouted 'Fire!'
They only answered 'Little Liar!'

12 She was not really bad at heart,
But only rather rude and wild;
She was an aggravating child.
Rebecca

13 Her funeral sermon (which was long
And followed by a sacred song)
Mentioned her virtues, it is true,
But dwelt upon her vices too.

14 Of Courtesy—it is much less
Than courage of heart or holiness;
Yet in my walks it seems to me
That the Grace of God is in Courtesy.
Courtesy

15 From quiet homes and first beginning,
Out to the undiscovered ends,
There's nothing worth the wear of winning,
But laughter and the love of friends.
Dedicatory Ode

16 The moon on the one hand, the dawn on the other:
The moon is my sister, the dawn is my brother.
The moon on my left and the dawn on my right.
My brother, good morning: my sister, good night.
The Early Morning

17 I said to Heart, 'How goes it?' Heart replied:
'Right as a Ribstone Pippin!' But it lied.
Epigrams. The False Heart

18 I'm tired of Love: I'm still more tired of Rhyme.
But Money gives me pleasure all the time.
Fatigue

19 When I am dead, I hope it may be said:
'His sins were scarlet, but his books were read.'
On his Books

20 Of this bad world the loveliest and the best
Has smiled and said 'Good Night,' and gone to rest.
On a Dead Hostess

21 The accursed power which stands on Privilege
(And goes with Women, and Champagne, and Bridge)
Broke—and Democracy resumed her reign:
(Which goes with Bridge, and Women and
   Champagne).
On a Great Election

22 Sleep your fill—but when you wake
Dawn shall over Lethe break.
On a Sleeping Friend

23 I am a sundial, and I make a botch
Of what is done far better by a watch.
On a Sundial

24 The Devil, having nothing else to do,
Went off to tempt my Lady Poltagrue.
My Lady, tempted by a private whim,
To his extreme annoyance, tempted him.
On Lady Poltagrue, a Public Peril

25 Pale Ebenezer thought it wrong to fight,
But Roaring Bill (who killed him) thought it right.
The Pacifist

26 Sally is gone that was so kindly,
Sally is gone from Ha'nacker Hill.
Ha'nacker Mill

27 Remote and ineffectual Don
That dared attack my Chesterton.
Lines to a Don

28 Don different from those regal Dons!
With hearts of gold and lungs of bronze,
Who shout and bang and roar and bawl
The Absolute across the hall,
Or sail in amply billowing gown,
Enormous through the Sacred Town.

29 Lord Finchley tried to mend the Electric Light
Himself. It struck him dead: and serve him right!
It is the business of the wealthy man
To give employment to the artisan.
Lord Finchley

30 Lord Heygate had a troubled face,
His furniture was commonplace—
The sort of Peer who well might pass
For someone of the middle class.
I do not think you want to hear
About this unimportant Peer.
Lord Heygate

31 The nuisance of the tropics is
The sheer necessity of fizz.
The Modern Traveller (1898), iv

1 Whatever happens, we have got
The Maxim Gun, and they have not.
vi

2 The Llama is a woolly sort of fleecy hairy goat,
With an indolent expression and an undulating throat
Like an unsuccessful literary man.
More Beasts for Worse Children. The Llama

3 Oh! let us never, never doubt
What nobody is sure about!
The Microbe

4 I had an aunt in Yucatan
Who bought a Python from a man
And kept it for a pet.
She died, because she never knew
These simple little rules and few;—
The Snake is living yet.
The Python

5 Like many of the upper class
He liked the sound of broken glass.
New Cautionary Tales. About John

6 Birds in their little nests agree
With Chinamen, but not with me.
On Food. See 565:20

7 A smell of burning fills the startled air—
The Electrician is no longer there!
Newdigate Poem

8 Strong Brother in God, and last Companion: Wine.
**Short Talks with the Dead, The Good Poet and the Bad Poet.
Heroic Poem on Wine.** (An adaptation from the Heroic Poem in Praise of Wine.)

9 When I am living in the Midlands
That are sodden and unkind...
The great hills of the South Country
Come back into my mind.
The South Country

10 A lost thing could I never find,
Nor a broken thing mend.

11 If I ever become a rich man,
Or if ever I grow to be old,
I will build a house with deep thatch
To shelter me from the cold,
And there shall the Sussex songs be sung
And the story of Sussex told.
I will hold my house in the high wood
Within a walk of the sea,
And the men that were boys when I was a boy
Shall sit and drink with me.

12 Do you remember an Inn,
Miranda?
Tarantella

13 The fleas that tease in the high Pyrenees.

14 Balliol made me, Balliol fed me,
Whatever I had she gave me again;
And the best of Balliol loved and led me,
God be with you, Balliol men.
To the Balliol men still in Africa

15 It is the best of all trades, to make songs, and the second best to sing them.
On Everything. On Song

16 From the towns all Inns have been driven: from the villages most...Change your hearts or you will lose your Inns and you will deserve to have lost them. But when you have lost your Inns drown your empty

selves, for you will have lost the last of England.
This and That. On Inns

P.-L. B. DU BELLOY 1725–1775

17 *Plus je vis d'étrangers, plus j'aimai ma patrie.*
The more foreigners I saw, the more I loved my homeland.
Le Siège de Calais (1765), II.iii

JULIEN BENDA 1868–1956

18 *La trahison des clercs.*
The intellectuals' betrayal.
Title of book (1927)

STEPHEN VINCENT BENÉT 1898–1943

19 I have fallen in love with American names,
The sharp names that never get fat,
The snakeskin-titles of mining-claims,
The plumed war-bonnet of Medicine Hat,
Tucson and Deadwood and Lost Mule Flat.
American Names

20 I shall not rest quiet in Montparnasse.
I shall not lie easy at Winchelsea.
You may bury my body in Sussex grass,
You may bury my tongue at Champmédy.
I shall not be there, I shall rise and pass.
Bury my heart at Wounded Knee.

ARNOLD BENNETT 1867-1931

21 'Ye can call it influenza if ye like,' said Mrs Machin. 'There was no influenza in my young days. We called a cold a cold.'
The Card, ch.8

22 Being a husband is a whole-time job.
The Title, Act I

23 Journalists say a thing that they know isn't true, in that hope that if they keep on saying it long enough it will be true.
Act II

A.C. BENSON 1862–1925

24 Land of Hope and Glory, Mother of the Free,
How shall we extol thee, who are born of thee?
Wider still and wider shall thy bounds be set;
God who made thee mighty, make thee mightier yet.
Words written to be sung as the Finale of Elgar's *Coronation Ode* (1902) to music derived from the *Pomp and Circumstance March,* op.39, No.1 in D major

JEREMY BENTHAM 1748–1832

25 The greatest happiness of the greatest number is the foundation of morals and legislation.
The Commonplace Book (*Works*, x.142). See 268:20

26 The Fool had stuck himself up one day, with great gravity, in the King's throne; with a stick, by way of a sceptre, in one hand, and a ball in the other: being asked what he was doing? he answered *'reigning'.* Much of the same sort of reign, I take it would be that of our Author's [Blackstone's] Democracy.
Fragment on Government (1776), ch.2, note to sect. 34

27 All punishment is mischief: all punishment in itself is

evil.
Principles of Morals and Legislation, ch.13, 2

1 He rather hated the ruling few than loved the suffering many.
Of James Mill. *Journals of Caroline Fox*, 17 Aug. 1840

2 Prose is when all the lines except the last go on to the end. Poetry is when some of them fall short of it.
M. St.J. Packe, *Life of John Stuart Mill*, bk.I, ch.ii

EDMUND CLERIHEW BENTLEY 1875–1956

3 The art of Biography
Is different from Geography.
Geography is about maps,
But Biography is about chaps.
Biography for Beginners

4 Chapman and Hall
Swore not at all.
Mr Chapman's yea was yea,
And Mr Hall's nay was nay.

5 What I like about Clive
Is that he is no longer alive.
There is a great deal to be said
For being dead.

6 Sir Humphrey Davy
Abominated gravy.
He lived in the odium
Of having discovered Sodium.

7 Edward the Confessor
Slept under the dresser.
When that began to pall
He slept in the hall.

8 John Stuart Mill
By a mighty effort of will
Overcame his natural bonhomie
And wrote 'Principles of Political Economy'

9 Sir Christopher Wren
Said, 'I am going to dine with some men.
If anybody calls
Say I am designing St Paul's.'

10 George the Third
Ought never to have occurred.
One can only wonder
At so grotesque a blunder.
More Biographies

RICHARD BENTLEY 1662–1742

11 He is believed to have liked port, but to have said of claret that 'it would be port if it could'.
R.C. Jebb, *Bentley*, p.200

12 It is a pretty poem, Mr Pope, but you must not call it Homer.
Johnson, *Life of Pope*

13 I hold it as certain, that no man was ever written out of reputation but by himself.
William Warburton, *The Works of Alexander Pope*, iv.159

PIERRE-JEAN DE BÉRANGER 1780–1857

14 *Il était un roi d'Yvetot*
Peu connu dans l'histoire.
There was a king of Yvetot

Little known to history.
Le Roi d'Yvetot (1815)

15 *Nos amis, les ennemis.*
Our friends, the enemy.
L'Opinion de ces demoiselles

LORD CHARLES BERESFORD 1846–1919

16 The idea of a Commercial Alliance with England based on the integrity of China and the open door for all nations' trade.
The Break-Up of China (1899)

17 Very sorry can't come. Lie follows by post.
Telegram to the Prince of Wales after an eleventh-hour summons to dine. R. Nevill, *The World of Fashion 1837–1922* (1923), ch 5. See 401:24

BISHOP BERKELEY 1685–1753

18 We have first raised a dust and then complain we cannot see.
Principles of Human Knowledge, introduction, 3

19 All the choir of heaven and furniture of earth—in a word, all those bodies which compose the mighty frame of the world—have not any subsistence without a mind.
Principles of Human Knowledge

20 Westward the course of empire takes its way;
The first four acts already past,
A fifth shall close the drama with the day:
Time's noblest offspring is the last.
On the Prospect of Planting Arts and Learning in America

21 [Tar water] is of a nature so mild and benign and proportioned to the human constitution, as to warm without heating, to cheer but not inebriate.
Siris, par.217

22 Truth is the cry of all, but the game of the few.
par.368

SIR ISAIAH BERLIN 1909–

23 Injustice, poverty, slavery, ignorance—these may be cured by reform or revolution. But men do not live only by fighting evils. They live by positive goals, individual and collective, a vast variety of them, seldom predictable, at times incompatible.
Four Essays on Liberty, **Political Ideas in the Twentieth Century**

ST. BERNARD 1091–1153

24 *Liberavi animam meam.*
I have freed my soul.
Epistle 371

BERNARD OF CHARTRES d. c.1130

25 Bernard of Chartres used to say that we are like dwarfs on the shoulders of giants, so that we can see more than they, and things at a greater distance, not by virtue of any sharpness of sight on our part, or any physical distinction, but because we are carried high and raised up by their giant size.
John of Salisbury, *Metalogicon* (1159), bk.III.ch.iv. See also R.K. Merton, *On the Shoulders of Giants* (1965)

LORD BERNERS 1883–1950

1 He's always backing into the limelight.
Oral tradition, of T.E. Lawrence

CHARLES BEST fl. 1602

2 Look how the pale Queen of the silent night
Doth cause the Ocean to attend upon her,
And he, as long as she is in his sight,
With his full tide is ready her to honour.
A Sonnet of the Moon

THEOBALD VON BETHMANN HOLLWEG 1856–1921

3 Just for a word—'neutrality', a word which in wartime
has so often been disregarded, just for a scrap of
paper—Great Britain is going to make war.
To Sir Edward Goschen, 4 Aug. 1914

SIR JOHN BETJEMAN 1906–

4 He sipped at a weak hock and seltzer,
     As he gazed at the London skies
Through the Nottingham lace of the curtains
     Or was it his bees-winged eyes?
The Arrest of Oscar Wilde at the Cadogan Hotel

5 Green Shutters, shut your shutters! Windyridge,
Let winds unnoticed whistle round your hill!
Beside the Seaside

6 From the geyser ventilators
     Autumn winds are blowing down
On a thousand business women
     Having baths in Camden Town.
Business Girls

7 Rest you there, poor unbelov'd ones,
     Lap your loneliness in heat.
All too soon the tiny breakfast,
     Trolley-bus and windy street!

8 And girls in slacks remember Dad,
     And oafish louts remember Mum,
And sleepless children's hearts are glad,
     And Christmas morning bells say 'Come!'
Even to shining ones who dwell
Safe in the Dorchester Hotel.

And is it true? And is it true,
     This most tremendous tale of all,
Seen in a stained-glass window's hue,
     A Baby in an ox's stall?
Christmas

9 And Nurse came in with the tea-things
     Breast high 'mid the stands and chairs—
But Nurse was alone with her own little soul,
     And the things were alone with theirs.
Death in Leamington

10 Oh! chintzy, chintzy cheeriness,
     Half dead and half alive!

11 Spirits of well-shot woodcock, partridge, snipe
     Flutter and bear him up the Norfolk sky.
Death of King George V

12 Old men in country houses hear clocks ticking
     Over thick carpets with a deadened force;

Old men who never cheated, never doubted,
Communicated monthly, sit and stare

At the new suburb stretched beyond the run-way
Where a young man lands hatless from the air.

13 Rime Intrinsica, Fontmell Magna, Sturminster Newton
     and Melbury Bubb,
Whist upon whist upon whist upon whist drive, in
     Institute, Legion and Social Club.
Horny hands that hold the aces which this morning
     held the plough—
While Tranter Reuben, T.S. Eliot, H.G. Wells and
     Edith Sitwell lie in Mellstock churchyard now.
Dorset. See 239:17

14 You ask me what it is I do. Well actually, you know,
I'm partly a liaison man and partly P.R.O.
Essentially I integrate the current export drive
And basically I'm viable from ten o'clock till five.
Executive

15 Glow, white lily in London,
     You are high in our hearts today!
14 November, 1973. On Princess Anne's wedding

16 When melancholy Autumn comes to Wembley
     And electric trains are lighted after tea
The poplars near the Stadium are trembly
     With their tap and tap and whispering to me,
          Like the sound of little breakers
          Spreading out along the surf-line
When the estuary's filling
          With the sea.

Then Harrow-on-the-Hill's a rocky island
     And Harrow churchyard full of sailors' graves
And the constant click and kissing of the trolley buses
     hissing
Is the level to the Wealdstone turned to waves.
Harrow-on-the-Hill

17 There's a storm cloud to the westward over Kenton,
     There's a line of harbour lights at Perivale,
Is it rounding rough Pentire in a flood of sunset fire
     The little fleet of trawlers under sail?

18 When shall I see the Thames again?
The prow-promoted gems again,
     As beefy ATS
     Without their hats
Come shooting through the bridge?
     And 'cheerioh' and 'cheeri-bye'
     Across the waste of waters lie
And lightly skims the midge.
Henley-on-Thames

19 Phone for the fish-knives, Norman,
     As Cook is a little unnerved;
You kiddies have crumpled the serviettes
     And I must have things daintily served.
How to Get On in Society

20 Milk and then just as it comes dear?
     I'm afraid the preserve's full of stones;
Beg pardon, I'm soiling the doileys
     With afternoon tea-cakes and scones.

21 It's awf'lly bad luck on Diana,
     Her ponies have swallowed their bits;
She fished down their throats with a spanner
     And frightened them all into fits.
Hunter Trials

22 Oh wasn't it naughty of Smudges?
     Oh, Mummy, I'm sick with disgust.
She threw me in front of the judges

And my silly old collarbone's bust.

1 In the Garden City Café with its murals on the wall
Before a talk on 'Sex and Civics' I meditated on the
Fall.
Huxley Hall

2 The Church's Restoration
In eighteen-eighty-three
Has left for contemplation
Not what there used to be.
Hymn

3 Sing on, with hymns uproarious,
Ye humble and aloof,
Look up! and oh how glorious
He has restored the roof!

4 'Let us not speak, for the love we bear one another—
Let us hold hands and look.'
She, such a very ordinary little woman;
He, such a thumping crook;
But both, for a moment, little lower than the angels
In the teashop's ingle-nook.
In a Bath Teashop. See 244:10

5 Gracious Lord, oh bomb the Germans.
Spare their women for Thy Sake,
And if that is not too easy
We will pardon Thy Mistake.
But, gracious Lord, whate'er shall be,
Don't let anyone bomb me.
In Westminster Abbey

6 Think of what our Nation stands for,
Books from Boots' and country lanes,
Free speech, free passes, class distinction,
Democracy and proper drains.
Lord, put beneath Thy special care
One-eighty-nine Cadogan Square.

7 Bells are booming down the bohreens,
White the mist along the grass.
Now the Julias, Maeves and Maureens
Move between the fields to Mass.
Twisted trees of small green apple
Guard the decent whitewashed chapel.
Ireland with Emily

8 Where a Stone Age people breeds
The last of Europe's stone age race.

9 There in pinnacled protection,
One extinguished family waits
A Church of Ireland resurrection
By the broken, rusty gates
Sheepswool, straw and droppings cover,
Graves of spinster, rake and lover,
Whose fantastic mausoleum
Sings its own seablown Te Deum,
In and out the slipping slates.

10 I made hay while the sun shone.
My work sold.
Now, if the harvest is over
And the world cold,
Give me the bonus of laughter
As I lose hold.
The Last Laugh

11 Take me, Lieutenant, to that Surrey homestead!
Love in a Valley

12 Belbroughton Road is bonny, and pinkly bursts the
spray

Of prunus and forsythia across the public way,
For a full spring-tide of blossom seethed and departed
hence,
Leaving land-locked pools of jonquils by sunny garden
fence.

And a constant sound of flushing runneth from
windows where
The toothbrush too is airing in this new North Oxford
air.
May-Day Song for North Oxford

13 Gaily into Ruislip Gardens
Runs the red electric train,
With a thousand Ta's and Pardon's
Daintily alights Elaine.
Middlesex

14 Well-cut Windsmoor flapping lightly,
Jacqmar scarf of mauve and green
Hiding hair which, Friday nightly,
Delicately drowns in Drene.

15 Dear Mary,
Yes, it will be bliss
To go with you by train to Diss,
Your walking shoes upon your feet;
We'll meet, my sweet, at Liverpool Street.
A Mind's Journey to Diss. Addressed to Mrs. Harold Wilson
(Lady Wilson)

16 Pink may, double may, dead laburnum
Shedding an Anglo-Jackson shade,
Shall we ever, my staunch Myfanwy,
Bicycle down to North Parade?
Kant on the handle-bars, Marx in the saddlebag,
Light my touch on your shoulder-blade.
Myfanwy at Oxford

17 Rumbling under blackened girders, Midland, bound
for Cricklewood,
Puffed its sulphur to the sunset where the Land of
Laundries stood.
Rumble under, thunder over, train and tram alternate
go.
Parliament Hill Fields

18 Outside Charrington's we waited, by the 'STOP HERE
IF REQUIRED',
Launched aboard the shopping basket, sat precipitately
down,
Rocked past Zwanziger the baker's, and the terrace
blackish-brown,
And the curious Anglo-Norman parish church of
Kentish Town.

19 Oh the after-tram-ride quiet, when we heard a mile
beyond,
Silver music from the bandstand, barking dogs by
Highgate Pond;
Up the hill where stucco houses in Virginia creeper
drown—
And my childish wave of pity, seeing children carrying
down
Sheaves of drooping dandelions to the courts of
Kentish Town.

20 Pam, I adore you, Pam, you great big mountainous
sports girl,
Whizzing them over the net, full of the strength of
five.
Pot Pourri from a Surrey Garden

1 Oh would I could subdue the flesh
   Which sadly troubles me!
And then perhaps could view the flesh
As though I never knew the flesh
And merry misery.
Senex

2 The gas was on in the Institute,
   The flare was up in the gym,
A man was running a mineral line,
   A lass was singing a hymn,
When Captain Webb the Dawley man,
   Captain Webb from Dawley,
Came swimming along the old canal
   That carried the bricks to Lawley.
A Shropshire Lad

3 We saw the ghost of Captain Webb,
   Webb in a water sheeting,
Come dripping along in a bathing dress
   To the Saturday evening meeting.
      Dripping along—
      Dripping along—
      To the Congregational Hall;
Dripping and still he rose over the sill and faded away
   in a wall.

4 Come, friendly bombs, and fall on Slough
It isn't fit for humans now,
There isn't grass to graze a cow
   Swarm over, Death!
Slough

5 Come, friendly bombs, and fall on Slough
To get it ready for the plough.
The cabbages are coming now:
   The earth exhales.

6 Miss J. Hunter Dunn, Miss J. Hunter Dunn,
Furnish'd and burnish'd by Aldershot sun,
What strenuous singles we played after tea
We in the tournament—you against me!

Love-thirty, love-forty, oh! weakness of joy,
The speed of a swallow, the grace of a boy,
With carefullest carelessness, gaily you won,
I am weak from your loveliness, Joan Hunter Dunn.

Miss Joan Hunter Dunn, Miss Joan Hunter Dunn,
How mad I am, sad I am, glad that you won.
The warm-handled racket is back in its press,
But my shock-headed victor, she loves me no less.
A Subaltern's Love Song

7 Her father's euonymus shines as we walk.

8 By roads 'not adopted', by woodlanded ways,
She drove to the club in the late summer haze,
Into nine-o'clock Camberley, heavy with bells
And mushroomy, pine-woody, evergreen smells.

Miss Joan Hunter Dunn, Miss Joan Hunter Dunn,
I can hear from the car-park the dance has begun.
Oh! full Surrey twilight! importunate band!
Oh! strongly adorable tennis-girl's hand!

9 I heard the church bells hollowing out the sky,
Deep beyond deep, like never-ending stars,
And turned to Archibald, my safe old bear,
Whose woollen eyes looked sad or glad at me.
Summoned by Bells, ch.I, l.37

10 Balkan Sobranies in a wooden box,
The college arms upon the lid; Tokay

And sherry in the cupboard; on the shelves
The University Statutes bound in blue,
Crome Yellow, Prancing Nigger, Blunden, Keats.
ch.IX, l.1

11 While Sandy Lindsay from his lodge looks down
   Dreaming of Adult Education where
      The pottery chimneys flare
On lost potential firsts in some less favoured town.
Oxford Ode, l.41. Of A.D. Lindsay

12 Lunching with poets, dining late with peers,
   I felt that I had come into my own.
l.96

13 There was sun enough for lazing upon beaches,
   There was fun enough for far into the night.
But I'm dying now and done for,
What on earth was all the fun for?
   For I'm old and ill and terrified and tight.
Sun and Fun

14 Broad of Church and broad of mind,
Broad before and broad behind,
A keen ecclesiologist,
A rather dirty Wykehamist.
The Wykehamist

15 *Ghastly Good Taste,* or *A Depressing Story of the
Rise and Fall of English Architecture.*
Book title (1933)

ANEURIN BEVAN 1897–1960

16 No amount of cajolery, and no attempts at ethical and
social seduction, can eradicate from my heart a deep
burning hatred for the Tory Party…So far as I am
concerned they are lower than vermin.
Speech at Manchester, 4 July 1948

17 If you carry this resolution and follow out all its
implications and do not run away from it you will send
a Foreign Minister, whoever he may be, naked into the
conference chamber.
M. Foot, *Aneurin Bevan*, vol. ii (1973), ch 15. Speech at Labour
Party Conference, 3 Oct. 1957, against motion proposing
unilateral nuclear disarmament by the U.K.

ERNEST BEVIN 1881–1951

18 My [foreign] policy is to be able to take a ticket at
Victoria Station and go anywhere I damn well please.
Spectator, 20 Apr. 1951

19 If you open that Pandora's Box you never know what
Trojan 'orses will jump out.
On the Council of Europe. Sir Roderick Barclay, *Ernest Bevin and
the Foreign Office* (1975), p.67

THE BIBLE

20 Upon the setting of that bright *Occidental Star,* Queen
Elizabeth of most happy memory.
Authorized Version, Epistle Dedicatory

21 The appearance of Your Majesty, as of the Sun in his
strength.

OLD TESTAMENT. GENESIS

22 In the beginning God created the heaven and the earth.
And the earth was without form, and void; and
darkness was upon the face of the deep. And the Spirit
of God moved upon the face of the waters.

And God said, Let there be light: and there was light.
1:1

1 And the evening and the morning were the first day.
5

2 And God saw that it was good.
10

3 And God made two great lights; the greater light to rule the day, and the lesser light to rule the night: he made the stars also.
16

4 And God said, Let us make man in our image, after our likeness: and let them have dominion over the fish of the sea, and over the fowl of the air, and over the cattle, and over all the earth and over every creeping thing that creepeth upon the earth.
26

5 Male and female created he them.
27

6 Be fruitful, and multiply, and replenish the earth, and subdue it.
28

7 And the Lord God formed man of the dust of the ground, and breathed into his nostrils the breath of life; and man became a living soul.
And the Lord God planted a garden eastward in Eden.
2:7

8 And out of the ground made the Lord God to grow every tree that is pleasant to the sight, and good for food; the tree of life also in the midst of the garden, and the tree of knowledge of good and evil.
9

9 But of the tree of the knowledge of good and evil, thou shalt not eat of it: for in the day that thou eatest thereof thou shalt surely die.
17

10 It is not good that the man should be alone; I will make him an help meet for him.
18

11 And the Lord God caused a deep sleep to fall upon Adam, and he slept: and he took one of his ribs, and closed up the flesh instead thereof;
And the rib, which the Lord God had taken from man, made he a woman.
21

12 This is now bone of my bones, and flesh of my flesh: she shall be called Woman, because she was taken out of Man.
23

13 Therefore shall a man leave his father and his mother, and shall cleave unto his wife: and they shall be one flesh.
24

14 Now the serpent was more subtil than any beast of the field.
3:1

15 Ye shall be as gods, knowing good and evil.
5

16 And they sewed fig leaves together, and made themselves aprons [breeches in Genevan Bible, 1560].
And they heard the voice of the Lord God walking in the garden in the cool of the day.
7

17 The woman whom thou gavest to be with me, she

gave me of the tree, and I did eat.
12

18 What is this that thou hast done?
13

19 The serpent beguiled me, and I did eat.

20 It shall bruise thy head, and thou shalt bruise his heel.
15

21 In sorrow thou shalt bring forth children.
16

22 In the sweat of thy face shalt thou eat bread.
19

23 For dust thou art, and unto dust shalt thou return.

24 The mother of all living.
20

25 Am I my brother's keeper?
4:9

26 The voice of thy brother's blood crieth unto me from the ground.
10

27 My punishment is greater than I can bear.
13

28 And the Lord set a mark upon Cain.
15

29 And Cain went out from the presence of the Lord, and dwelt in the land of Nod, on the east of Eden.
16

30 And Enoch walked with God: and he was not; for God took him.
5:24

31 And all the days of Methuselah were nine hundred sixty and nine years: and he died.
27

32 And Noah begat Shem, Ham, and Japheth.
32

33 There were giants in the earth in those days; and also after that, when the sons of God came in unto the daughters of men, and they bare children to them, the same became mighty men which were of old, men of renown.
6:4

34 There went in two and two unto Noah into the Ark, the male and the female.
7:9

35 But the dove found no rest for the sole of her foot.
8:9

36 For the imagination of man's heart is evil from his youth.
21

37 While the earth remaineth, seedtime and harvest, and cold and heat, and summer and winter, and day and night shall not cease.
22

38 At the hand of every man's brother will I require the life of man.
9:5

39 Whoso sheddeth man's blood, by man shall his blood be shed.
6

40 I do set my bow in the cloud, and it shall be for a token of a covenant between me and the earth. And it shall come to pass, when I bring a cloud over the

earth, that the bow shall be seen in the cloud.
13

1 Even as Nimrod the mighty hunter before the Lord.
10:9

2 Let there be no strife, I pray thee, between thee and me...for we be brethren.
13:8

3 An horror of great darkness fell upon him.
15:12

4 Thou shalt be buried in a good old age.
15

5 His [Ishmael's] hand will be against every man, and every man's hand against him.
16:12

6 Now Abraham and Sarah were old and well stricken in age; and it ceased to be with Sarah after the manner of women.
18:11

7 Shall not the Judge of all the earth do right.
25

8 But his wife looked back from behind him, and she became a pillar of salt.
19:26

9 Take now thy son, thine only son Isaac, whom thou lovest.
22:2

10 My son, God will provide himself a lamb.
8

11 Behold behind him a ram caught in a thicket by his horns.
13

12 Esau selleth his birthright for a mess of potage.
Heading to chapter 25 in Genevan Bible

13 Esau was a cunning hunter, a man of the field; and Jacob was a plain man, dwelling in tents.
25:27

14 And he sold his birthright unto Jacob.
33

15 Behold, Esau my brother is a hairy man, and I am a smooth man.
27:11

16 The voice is Jacob's voice, but the hands are the hands of Esau.
22

17 Thy brother came with subtilty, and hath taken away thy blessing.
35

18 And he dreamed, and behold a ladder set up on the earth, and the top of it reached to heaven: and behold the angels of God ascending and descending on it.
28:12

19 Surely the Lord is in this place; and I knew it not.
16

20 This is none other but the house of God, and this is the gate of heaven.
17

21 And Jacob served seven years for Rachel; and they seemed unto him but a few days, for the love he had to her.
29:20

22 Mizpah; for he said, The Lord watch between me and

thee, when we are absent one from another.
31:49

23 There wrestled a man with him until the breaking of the day.
And when he saw that he prevailed not against him, he touched the hollow of his thigh; and the hollow of Jacob's thigh was out of joint, as he wrestled with him.
32:24

24 I will not let thee go, except thou bless me.
26

25 For I have seen God face to face, and my life is preserved.
30

26 Now Israel loved Joseph more than all his children, because he was the son of his old age; and he made him a coat of many colours.
37:3

27 Behold, your sheaves stood round about, and made obeisance to my sheaf.
7

28 Behold, this dreamer cometh.
19

29 Some evil beast hath devoured him.
20

30 And she caught him by his garment, saying, Lie with me; and he left his garment in her hand, and fled.
39:12

31 And the lean and the ill favoured kine did eat up the first seven fat kine.
41:20

32 And the thin ears devoured the seven good ears.
24

33 Jacob saw that there was corn in Egypt.
42:1

34 Ye are spies; to see the nakedness of the land ye are come.
9

35 My son shall not go down with you; for his brother is dead, and he is left alone: if mischief befell him by the way in which ye go, then shall ye bring down my gray hairs with sorrow to the grave. [Jacob, of Benjamin.]
38

36 Ye shall eat the fat of the land.
45:18

37 See that ye fall not out by the way.
24

38 Few and evil have the days of the years of my life been.
47:9

39 Unstable as water, thou shalt not excel.
49:4

EXODUS

40 Now there arose up a new king over Egypt, which knew not Joseph.
1:8

41 She took for him an ark of bulrushes, and daubed it with slime.
2:3

1 Who made thee a prince and a judge over us?
14

2 I have been a stranger in a strange land.
22. See Exodus 18:3

3 Behold, the bush burned with fire, and the bush was not consumed.
3:2

4 Put off thy shoes from off thy feet, for the place whereon thou standest is holy ground.
5

5 And Moses hid his face; for he was afraid to look upon God.
6

6 A land flowing with milk and honey; unto the place of the Canaanites, and the Hittites, and the Amorites, and the Perizzites, and the Hivites, and the Jebusites.
8

7 I AM THAT I AM.
14

8 The Lord God of your fathers, the God of Abraham, the God of Isaac, and the God of Jacob.
15

9 But I am slow of speech, and of a slow tongue.
4:10

10 I know not the Lord, neither will I let Israel go.
5:2

11 And I will harden Pharaoh's heart, and multiply my signs and my wonders in the land of Egypt.
7:3

12 Aaron's rod swallowed up their rods.
And he hardened Pharaoh's heart, that he hearkened not.
12

13 Let my people go.
7:16

14 A boil breaking forth with blains.
9:10

15 Stretch out thine hand toward heaven, that there may be darkness over the land of Egypt, even darkness which may be felt.
10:21

16 Your lamb shall be without blemish.
12:5

17 And they shall eat the flesh in that night, roast with fire, and unleavened bread; and with bitter herbs they shall eat it.
Eat not of it raw, nor sodden at all with water, but roast with fire; his head with his legs, and with the purtenance thereof.
8

18 With your loins girded, your shoes on your feet, and your staff in your hand; and ye shall eat it in haste; it is the Lord's passover.
For I will pass through the land of Egypt this night, and will smite all the firstborn in the land of Egypt, both man and beast.
11

19 And Pharaoh rose up in the night, he, and all his servants, and all the Egyptians; and there was a great cry in Egypt; for there was not a house where there was not one dead.
30

20 And they spoiled the Egyptians.
36

21 And the Lord went before them by day in a pillar of a cloud, to lead them the way; and by night in a pillar of fire, to give them light.
13:21

22 The Lord is a man of war.
15:3

23 Would to God we had died by the hand of the Lord in the land of Egypt, when we sat by the flesh pots, and when we did eat bread to the full.
16:3

24 And God spake all these words, saying,
I am the Lord thy God, which have brought thee out of the land of Egypt, out of the house of bondage.
Thou shalt have no other gods before me.
Thou shalt not make unto thee any graven image, or any likeness of any thing that is in heaven above, or that is in the earth beneath, or that is in the water under the earth:
Thou shalt not bow down thyself to them, nor serve them: for I the Lord thy God am a jealous God, visiting the iniquity of the fathers upon the children unto the third and fourth generation of them that hate me;
And showing mercy unto thousands of them that love me, and keep my commandments.
Thou shalt not take the name of the Lord thy God in vain; for the Lord will not hold him guiltless that taketh his name in vain.
Remember the sabbath day, to keep it holy.
Six days shalt thou labour, and do all thy work:
But the seventh day is the sabbath of the Lord thy God: in it thou shalt not do any work, thou, nor thy son, nor thy daughter, thy manservant, nor thy maidservant, nor thy cattle, nor thy stranger that is within thy gates:
For in six days the Lord made heaven and earth, the sea, and all that in them is, and rested the seventh day: wherefore the Lord blest the sabbath day, and hallowed it.
Honour thy father and thy mother: that thy days may be long upon the land which the Lord thy God giveth thee.
Thou shalt not kill.
Thou shalt not commit adultery.
Thou shalt not steal.
Thou shalt not bear false witness against thy neighbour.
Thou shalt not covet thy neighbour's house, thou shalt not covet thy neighbour's wife, nor his manservant, nor his maidservant, nor his ox, nor his ass, nor any thing that is thy neighbour's.
20:1

25 Life for life,
Eye for eye, tooth for tooth, hand for hand, foot for foot,
Burning for burning, wound for wound, stripe for stripe.
21:23

26 Thou shalt not suffer a witch to live.
22:18

27 Thou shalt not seethe a kid in his mother's milk.
23:19

1 And thou shalt put in the breastplate of judgment the Urim and the Thummin. [Sacred symbols worn on the breastplate of the high priest.]
28:30

2 These be thy gods, O Israel.
32:4

3 And the people sat down to eat and to drink, and rose up to play.
6

4 I will not go up in the midst of thee; for thou art a stiffnecked people: lest I consume thee in the way.
33:3

5 There shall no man see me and live.
20

LEVITICUS

6 And the swine, though he divide the hoof, and be cloven-footed, yet he cheweth not the cud; he is unclean to you.
11:7

7 Let him go for a scapegoat into the wilderness.
16:10

8 Thou shalt love thy neighbour as thyself.
19:18. See Matt. 19:19

NUMBERS

9 The Lord bless thee, and keep thee:
The Lord make his face shine upon thee, and be gracious unto thee:
The Lord lift up his countenance upon thee, and give thee peace.
6:24

10 These are the names of the men which Moses sent to spy out the land.
13:16

11 And there we saw the giants, the sons of Anak, which come of the giants: and we were in our own sight as grasshoppers, and so we were in their sight.
33

12 And Israel smote him with the edge of the sword, and possessed his land.
21:24

13 He whom thou blessest is blessed, and he whom thou cursest is cursed.
22:6

14 God is not a man, that he should lie.
23:19

15 What hath God wrought!
23. Quoted by Samuel Morse in the first electric telegraph message, Washington, 24 May 1844

16 I called thee to curse mine enemies, and, behold, thou hast altogether blessed them these three times.
24:10

17 Be sure your sin will find you out.
32:23

DEUTERONOMY

18 I call heaven and earth to witness against you this day.
4:26

19 Remember that thou wast a servant in the land of Egypt, and that the Lord thy God brought thee out

thence through a mighty hand and by a stretched out arm.
5:15

20 Hear, O Israel: The Lord our God is one Lord.
6:4

21 For the Lord thy God is a jealous God.
15

22 Man doth not live by bread only, but by every word that proceedeth out of the mouth of the Lord doth man live.
8:3. See 64:1

23 If there arise among you a prophet, or a dreamer of dreams...Thou shalt not hearken.
13:1

24 If thy brother, the son of thy mother, or thy son, or thy daughter, or the wife of thy bosom, or thy friend, which is as thine own soul, entice thee secretly...Thou shalt not consent.
6

25 Thou shalt not muzzle the ox when he treadeth out the corn.
25:4

26 Cursed be he that removeth his neighbour's landmark.
27:17

27 In the morning thou shalt say, Would God it were even! and at even thou shalt say, Would God it were morning!
28:67

28 The secret things belong unto the Lord our God.
29:29

29 I have set before you life and death, blessing and cursing: therefore choose life that both thou and thy seed may live.
30:19

30 He found him in a desert land, and in the waste howling wilderness; he led him about, he kept him as the apple of his eye.
32:10

31 For they are a very froward generation, children in whom is no faith.
20

32 I will heap mischiefs upon them; I will spend mine arrows upon them.
23

33 The eternal God is thy refuge, and underneath are the everlasting arms.
33:27

34 No man knoweth of his [Moses'] sepulchre unto this day.
34:6

JOSHUA

35 As I was with Moses, so I will be with thee: I will not fail thee, nor forsake thee.
1:5

36 Be strong and of a good courage; be not afraid, neither be thou dismayed: for the Lord thy God is with thee, whithersoever thou goest.
9

37 This line of scarlet thread.
2:18

1 All the Israelites passed over on dry ground.
3:17

2 When the people heard the sound of the trumpet, and the people shouted with a great shout, that the wall fell down flat, so that the people went up into the city.
6:20

3 Let them live; but let them be hewers of wood and drawers of water unto all the congregation.
9:21

4 Sun, stand thou still upon Gibeon; and thou, Moon, in the valley of Ajalon.
10:12

5 I am going the way of all the earth.
13:14

JUDGES

6 He delivered them into the hands of spoilers.
2:14

7 Then Jael Heber's wife took a nail of the tent, and took an hammer in her hand, and went softly unto him, and smote the nail into his temples, and fastened it into the ground: for he was fast asleep and weary.
4:21

8 I arose a mother in Israel.
5:7

9 The stars in their courses fought against Sisera.
20

10 He asked water, and she gave him milk; she brought forth butter in a lordly dish. [Jael.]
25

11 At her feet he bowed, he fell, he lay down.
27

12 The mother of Sisera looked out at a window, and cried through the lattice, Why is his chariot so long in coming? why tarry the wheels of his chariots?
28

13 Have they not divided the prey; to every man a damsel or two?
30

14 The Lord is with thee, thou mighty man of valour.
6:12

15 The Spirit of the Lord came upon Gideon, and he blew a trumpet.
34

16 The host of Midian was beneath him in the valley.
7:8

17 Is not the gleaning of the grapes of Ephraim better than the vintage of Abi-ezer?
8:2

18 Faint, yet pursuing.
4

19 Let fire come out of the bramble and devour the cedars of Lebanon.
9:15

20 Then said they unto him, Say now Shibboleth: and he said Sibboleth: for he could not frame to pronounce it right. Then they took him, and slew him.
12:6

21 Out of the eater came forth meat, and out of the strong came forth sweetness.
14:14

22 If ye had not plowed with my heifer, ye had not found out my riddle.
18

23 He smote them hip and thigh.
15:8

24 With the jawbone of an ass, heaps upon heaps, with the jaw of an ass have I slain a thousand men.
16

25 The Philistines be upon thee, Samson.
16:9

26 He wist not that the Lord was departed from him.
20

27 He did grind in the prison house.
21

28 The dead which he slew at his death were more than they which he slew in his life.
30

29 In those days there was no king in Israel, but every man did that which was right in his own eyes.
17:6

30 From Dan even to Beer-sheba.
20:1

31 The people arose as one man.
8

RUTH

32 Intreat me not to leave thee, or to return from following after thee: for whither thou goest, I will go; and where thou lodgest, I will lodge: thy people shall be my people, and thy God my God:
Where thou diest, will I die, and there will I be buried: the Lord do so to me, and more also, if ought but death part thee and me.
1:16

1 SAMUEL

33 All the increase of thy house shall die in the flower of their age.
2:33

34 The Lord called Samuel: and he answered, Here am I.
3:4

35 Here am I; for thou calledst me. And he said, I called not; lie down again.
5

36 Speak, Lord; for thy servant heareth.
9

37 The ears of every one that heareth it shall tingle.
11

38 Quit yourselves like men, and fight.
4:9

39 He fell from off the seat backward by the side of the gate, and his neck brake.
18

40 And she named the child I-chabod, saying, The glory is departed from Israel.
21

41 Is Saul also among the prophets?
10:11

42 God save the king.
24

1 A man after his own heart.
13:14

2 Come up to us and we will shew you a thing.
14:12

3 I did but taste a little honey with the end of the rod that was in mine hand, and, lo, I must die.
43

4 To obey is better than sacrifice, and to hearken than the fat of rams.
For rebellion is as the sin of witchcraft.
15:22

5 Agag came unto him delicately. And Agag said, Surely the bitterness of death is past.
32

6 For the Lord seeth not as man seeth: for man looketh on the outward appearance, but the Lord looketh on the heart.
16:7

7 Now he was ruddy, and withal of a beautiful countenance, and goodly to look to.
12

8 I know thy pride, and the naughtiness of thine heart.
17:28

9 Let no man's heart fail because of him [Goliath].
32

10 Go, and the Lord be with thee.
37

11 And he took his staff in his hand and chose him five smooth stones out of the brook. [David.]
40

12 Am I a dog, that thou comest to me with staves?
43

13 Saul hath slain his thousands, and David his ten thousands.
18:7

14 And Saul said, God hath delivered him into mine hand.
23:7

15 Behold, I have played the fool, and have erred exceedingly. [Saul.]
26:21

2 SAMUEL

16 The beauty of Israel is slain upon thy high places: how are the mighty fallen!
Tell it not in Gath, publish it not in the streets of Askelon; lest the daughters of the Philistines rejoice, lest the daughters of the uncircumcised triumph.
Ye mountains of Gilboa, let there be no dew, neither let there be rain, upon you, nor fields of offerings: for there the shield of the mighty is vilely cast away.
1:19

17 Saul and Jonathan were lovely and pleasant in their lives, and in their death they were not divided: they were swifter than eagles, they were stronger than lions.
Ye daughters of Israel, weep over Saul, who clothed you in scarlet, with other delights, who put on ornaments of gold upon your apparel.
How are the mighty fallen in the midst of the battle! O Jonathan, thou wast slain in thine high places.
I am distressed for thee, my brother Jonathan: very

pleasant hast thou been unto me: thy love to me was wonderful, passing the love of women.
How are the mighty fallen, and the weapons of war perished!
23

18 And David danced before the Lord with all his might.
6:14

19 Set ye Uriah in the forefront of the hottest battle, and retire ye from him, that he may be smitten, and die.
11:15

20 The poor man had nothing, save one little ewe lamb.
12:3

21 Thou art the man.
7

22 While the child was yet alive, I fasted and wept... But now he is dead, wherefore should I fast? can I bring him back again? I shall go to him but he shall not return to me.
22

23 For we needs must die, and are as water spilt on the ground, which cannot be gathered up again; neither doth God respect any person.
14:14

24 Come out, come out, thou bloody man, thou son of Belial.
16:7

25 And when Ahithophel saw that his counsel was not followed, he saddled his ass, and arose, and gat him home to his house, to his city, and put his household in order, and hanged himself.
17:23

26 And the king was much moved, and went up to the chamber above the gate, and wept: and as he went, thus he said, O my son Absalom, my son, my son Absalom! would God I had died for thee, O Absalom, my son, my son!
18:33

27 By my God have I leaped over a wall.
22:30

28 David...the sweet psalmist of Israel.
23:1

29 Went in jeopardy of their lives.
17

1 KINGS

30 And Zadok the priest took an horn of oil out of the tabernacle, and anointed Solomon. And they blew the trumpet; and all the people said, God save king Solomon.
1:39

31 Then will I cut off Israel out of the land which I have given them; and this house, which I have hallowed for my name, will I cast out of my sight; and Israel shall be a proverb and a byword among all people.
9:7

32 And when the queen of Sheba had seen all Solomon's wisdom...there was no more spirit in her.
10:4

33 Behold, the half was not told me.
7

34 Once in three years came the navy of Tharshish, bringing gold, and silver, ivory, and apes, and

peacocks.
22

1 But king Solomon loved many strange women.
11:1

2 My little finger shall be thicker than my father's loins.
12:10

3 My father hath chastised you with whips, but I will chastise you with scorpions.
11

4 To your tents, O Israel: now see to thine own house, David.
16

5 He slept with his fathers.
14:20

6 He went and dwelt by the brook Cherith, that is before Jordan.
And the ravens brought him bread and flesh in the morning, and bread and flesh in the evening; and he drank of the brook.
17:5

7 An handful of meal in a barrel, and a little oil in a cruse.
12

8 How long halt ye between two opinions?
18:21

9 He is talking, or he is pursuing, or he is in a journey, or peradventure he sleepeth, and must be awaked.
27

10 There is a sound of abundance of rain.
41

11 There ariseth a little cloud out of the sea, like a man's hand.
44

12 He girded up his loins, and ran before Ahab.
46

13 He himself went a day's journey into the wilderness, and came and sat down under a juniper tree.
19:4

14 But the Lord was not in the wind: and after the wind an earthquake; but the Lord was not in the earthquake: And after the earthquake a fire: but the Lord was not in the fire: and after the fire a still small voice.
11

15 Elijah passed by him, and cast his mantle upon him.
19

16 Let not him that girdeth on his harness boast himself as he that putteth it off.
20:11

17 Naboth the Jezreelite had a vineyard, which was in Jezreel, hard by the palace of Ahab King of Samaria. And Ahab spake unto Naboth, saying, Give me thy vineyard, that I may have it for a garden of herbs, because it is near unto my house.
21:1

18 Hast thou found me, O mine enemy?
20

19 I saw all Israel scattered upon the hills, as sheep that have not a shepherd.
22:17

20 Feed him with bread of affliction and with water of affliction, until I come in peace.
And Micaiah said, If thou return at all in peace, the

Lord hath not spoken by me.
27

21 And a certain man drew a bow at a venture, and smote the king of Israel between the joints of the harness.
34

2 KINGS

22 Elijah went up by a whirlwind into heaven.
And Elisha saw it, and he cried, My father, my father, the chariot of Israel, and the horsemen thereof.
2:11

23 The spirit of Elijah doth rest on Elisha.
15

24 Go up, thou bald head.
23

25 Is it well with the child? And she answered, It is well.
4:26

26 There is death in the pot.
40

27 He shall know that there is a prophet in Israel.
5:8

28 Are not Abana and Pharpar, rivers of Damascus, better than all the waters of Israel?
12

29 I bow myself in the house of Rimmon.
18

30 Whence comest thou, Gehazi?
25

31 Is thy servant a dog, that he should do this great thing?
8:13

32 Is it peace? And Jehu said, What hast thou to do with peace? turn thee behind me.
9:18

33 The driving is like the driving of Jehu, the son of Nimshi; for he driveth furiously.
20

34 She painted her face, and tired her head, and looked out at a window.
30

35 Had Zimri peace, who slew his master?
31

36 Who is on my side? who?
32

37 They found no more of her than the skull, and the feet, and the palms of her hands.
35

38 Thou trustest upon the staff of this bruised reed, even upon Egypt, on which if a man lean, it will go into his hand, and pierce it.
18:21

1 CHRONICLES

39 For we are strangers before thee, and sojourners, as were all our fathers: our days on the earth are as a shadow, and there is none abiding.
29:15

40 He died in a good old age, full of days, riches, and honour.
28

NEHEMIAH

1 Every one with one of his hands wrought in the work, and with the other hand held a weapon.
4:17

ESTHER

2 And if I perish, I perish.
4:16

3 Thus shall it be done to the man whom the king delighteth to honour.
6:6

4 Behold also, the gallows fifty cubits high.
7:9

JOB

5 The sons of God came to present themselves before the Lord, and Satan came also among them.
And the Lord said unto Satan, Whence comest thou? Then Satan answered the Lord, and said, From going to and fro in the earth, and from walking up and down in it.
1:6

6 Doth Job fear God for naught?
9

7 The Lord gave, and the Lord hath taken away; blessed be the name of the Lord.
21

8 All that a man hath will he give for his life.
2:4

9 And he took him a potsherd to scrape himself withal.
8

10 Curse God, and die.
9

11 Let the day perish wherein I was born, and the night in which it was said, There is a man child conceived.
3:3

12 For now should I have lain still and been quiet, I should have slept: then had I been at rest,
With kings and counsellors of the earth, which built desolate places for themselves.
13

13 There the wicked cease from troubling, and there the weary be at rest.
17

14 Wherefore is light given to him that is in misery, and life unto the bitter in soul?
20

15 Then a spirit passed before my face; the hair of my flesh stood up.
4:15

16 Shall mortal man be more just than God? shall a man be more pure than his maker?
17

17 Man is born unto trouble, as the sparks fly upward.
5:7

18 My days are swifter than a weaver's shuttle.
7:6

19 He shall return no more to his house, neither shall his place know him any more.
10

20 Let me alone, that I may take comfort a little,

Before I go whence I shall not return, even to the land of darkness and the shadow of death.
10:20

21 A land...where the light is as darkness.
22

22 Canst thou by searching find out God?
11:7

23 No doubt but ye are the people, and wisdom shall die with you.
12:2

24 With the ancient is wisdom; and in length of days understanding.
12

25 Though he slay me, yet will I trust in him: but I will maintain mine own ways before him.
13:15

26 Man that is born of a woman is of few days, and full of trouble.
He cometh forth like a flower, and is cut down: he fleeth also as a shadow, and continueth not.
14:1. See 389:11

27 Miserable comforters are ye all.
16:2

28 I also could speak as ye do: if your soul were in my soul's stead.
4

29 I am escaped with the skin of my teeth.
19:20

30 Oh that my words were now written! oh that they were printed in a book!
23

31 I know that my redeemer liveth, and that he shall stand at the latter day upon the earth:
And though after my skin worms destroy this body, yet in my flesh shall I see God.
25

32 Ye should say, Why persecute we him, seeing the root of the matter is found in me?
28

33 But where shall wisdom be found? and where is the place of understanding?
28:12

34 The price of wisdom is above rubies.
18

35 I was eyes to the blind, and feet was I to the lame.
29:15

36 For I know that thou wilt bring me to death, and to the house appointed for all living.
30:23

37 I am a brother to dragons, and a companion to owls.
29

38 My desire is...that mine adversary had written a book.
31:35

39 Great men are not always wise.
32:9

40 He multiplieth words without knowledge.
35:16

41 Who is this that darkeneth counsel by words without knowledge?
38:2

1 Gird up now thy loins like a man.
3

2 Where wast thou when I laid the foundations of the earth? declare, if thou hast understanding.
4

3 When the morning stars sang together, and all the sons of God shouted for joy.
7

4 Hath the rain a father? or who hath begotten the drops of dew?
28

5 Canst thou bind the sweet influences of Pleiades, or loose the bands of Orion?
31

6 He paweth in the valley, and rejoiceth in his strength: he goeth on to meet the armed men.
39:21

7 He swalloweth the ground with fierceness and rage: neither believeth he that it is the sound of the trumpet. He saith among the trumpets, Ha, ha; and he smelleth the battle afar off, the thunder of the captains, and the shouting.
24

8 Behold now behemoth. which I made with thee; he eateth grass as an ox.
40:15

9 He is the chief of the ways of God: he that made him can make his sword to approach unto him.
19

10 He lieth under the shady trees, in the covert of the reed, and fens.
The shady trees cover him with their shadow; the willows of the brook compass him about.
Behold, he drinketh up a river, and hasteth not.
21

11 Canst thou draw out leviathan with an hook?
41:1

12 I have heard of thee by the hearing of the ear: but now mine eye seeth thee.
42:5

13 So the Lord blessed the latter end of Job more than his beginning.
12

For psalms in the Book of Common Prayer see PRAYER BOOK.

PROVERBS

14 Surely in vain the net is spread in the sight of any bird.
1:17

15 For whom the Lord loveth he correcteth.
3:12

16 Length of days is in her right hand; and in her left hand riches and honour.
16

17 Her ways are ways of pleasantness, and all her paths are peace.
17

18 Wisdom is the principal thing; therefore get wisdom: and with all thy getting get understanding.
4:7

19 The path of the just is as the shining light, that shineth

more and more unto the perfect day.
18

20 For the lips of a strange woman drop as an honeycomb, and her mouth is smoother than oil:
But her end is bitter as wormwood, sharp as a twoedged sword.
Her feet go down to death; her steps take hold on hell.
5:3

21 Go to the ant thou sluggard; consider her ways, and be wise.
6:6

22 How long wilt thou sleep, O sluggard? When wilt thou arise out of thy sleep?
Yet a little sleep, a little slumber, a little folding of the hands to sleep:
So shall thy poverty come as one that travelleth, and thy want as an armed man.
9. See Prov. 24:33

23 Can a man take fire in his bosom, and his clothes not be burned?
27

24 Come, let us take our fill of love until the morning: let us solace ourselves with loves.
For the goodman is not at home, he is gone a long journey.
7:18

25 He goeth after her straightway, as an ox goeth to the slaughter.
22

26 Wisdom is better than rubies.
8:11

27 Wisdom hath builded her house, she hath hewn out her seven pillars.
9:1

28 Stolen waters are sweet, and bread eaten in secret is pleasant.
17

29 A wise son maketh a glad father: but a foolish son is the heaviness of his mother.
10:1

30 The destruction of the poor is their poverty.
15

31 He that is surety for a stranger shall smart for it.
11:15

32 As a jewel of gold in a swine's snout, so is a fair woman which is without discretion.
22

33 A virtuous woman is a crown to her husband.
12:4

34 A righteous man regardeth the life of his beast: but the tender mercies of the wicked are cruel.
10

35 Hope deferred maketh the heart sick: but when the desire cometh, it is a tree of life.
13:12

36 The way of transgressors is hard.
15

37 The desire accomplished is sweet to the soul.
19

38 He that spareth his rod hateth his son.
24

1 Even in laughter the heart is sorrowful.
14:13

2 In all labour there is profit.
23

3 Righteousness exalteth a nation.
34

4 A soft answer turneth away wrath.
15:1

5 A merry heart maketh a cheerful countenance.
13

6 Better is a dinner of herbs where love is, than a stalled ox and hatred therewith.
17. Better is a mess of pottage with love, than a fat ox with evil will. (Matthew's Bible, 1535)

7 A word spoken in due season, how good is it!
23

8 Pride goeth before destruction, and an haughty spirit before a fall.
16:18

9 He that is slow to anger is better than the mighty; and he that ruleth his spirit than he that taketh a city.
32

10 He that repeateth a matter separateth very friends.
17:9

11 A friend loveth at all times, and a brother is born for adversity.
17

12 A merry heart doeth good like a medicine.
22

13 A wounded spirit who can bear?
18:14

14 There is a friend that sticketh closer than a brother.
24

15 Wine is a mocker, strong drink is raging.
20:1

16 Every fool will be meddling.
3

17 Even a child is known by his doings.
11

18 The hearing ear, and the seeing eye, the Lord hath made even both of them.
12

19 It is naught, it is naught, saith the buyer: but when he is gone his way, then he boasteth.
14

20 It is better to dwell in a corner of the housetop, than with a brawling woman in a wide house.
21:9

21 A good name is rather to be chosen than great riches.
22:1

22 Train up a child in the way he should go: and when he is old, he will not depart from it.
6

23 Remove not the ancient landmark, which thy fathers have set.
28

24 Look not thou upon the wine when it is red, when it giveth his colour in the cup,...
At the last it biteth like a serpent, and stingeth like an adder.
23:31

25 The heart of kings is unsearchable.
25:3

26 A word fitly spoken is like apples of gold in pictures of silver.
11

27 Whoso boasteth himself of a false gift is like clouds and wind without rain.
14

28 Withdraw thy foot from thy neighbour's house; lest he be weary of thee, and so hate thee.
17

29 If thine enemy be hungry, give him bread to eat; and if he be thirsty, give him water to drink.
For thou shalt heap coals of fire upon his head, and the Lord shall reward thee.
21

30 As cold waters to a thirsty soul, so is good news from a far country.
25

31 Answer not a fool according to his folly, lest thou also be like unto him.
Answer a fool according to his folly, lest he be wise in his own conceit.
26:4

32 As a dog returneth to his vomit, so a fool returneth to his folly.
11

33 Seest thou a man wise in his own conceit? There is more hope of a fool than of him.
12

34 The slothful man saith, There is a lion in the way: a lion is in the streets.
13

35 The sluggard is wiser in his own conceit than seven men that can render a reason.
16

36 Boast not thyself of to morrow; for thou knowest not what a day may bring forth.
27:1

37 Open rebuke is better than secret love.
5

38 Faithful are the wounds of a friend.
6

39 A continual dropping in a very rainy day and a contentious woman are alike.
15

40 Iron sharpeneth iron; so a man sharpeneth the countenance of his friend.
17

41 The wicked flee when no man pursueth: but the righteous are bold as a lion.
28:1

42 He that maketh haste to be rich shall not be innocent.
20

43 A fool uttereth all his mind.
29:11

44 Where there is no vision, the people perish.
18

45 Give me neither poverty nor riches; feed me with food convenient for me.
30:8

46 There are three things that are never satisfied, yea,

four things say not, It is enough:
The grave; and the barren womb; the earth that is not filled with water; and the fire that saith not, It is enough.
15

1 There be three things which are too wonderful for me, yea, four which I know not:
The way of an eagle in the air; the way of a serpent upon a rock; the way of a ship in the midst of the sea; and the way of a man with a maid.
18

2 It is not for kings, O Lemuel, it is not for kings to drink wine; nor for princes strong drink:
Lest they drink and forget the law, and pervert the judgment of any of the afflicted.
Give strong drink unto him that is ready to perish, and wine unto those that be of heavy hearts.
Let him drink, and forget his poverty, and remember his misery no more.
31:4

3 Who can find a virtuous woman? for her price is far above rubies.
10

4 Her children arise up, and call her blessed.
28

ECCLESIASTES

5 Vanity of vanities, saith the Preacher, vanity of vanities; all is vanity.
What profit hath a man of all his labour which he taketh under the sun?
One generation passeth away, and another generation cometh.
1:2. See 83:14

6 All the rivers run into the sea; yet the sea is not full.
7

7 All things are full of labour; man cannot utter it: the eye is not satisfied with seeing, nor the ear filled with hearing.
The thing that hath been, it is that which shall be; and that which is done is that which shall be done: and there is no new thing under the sun.
8

8 All is vanity and vexation of spirit.
14

9 He that increaseth knowledge increaseth sorrow.
18

10 Wisdom excelleth folly, as far as light excelleth darkness.
2:13

11 One event happeneth to them all.
14

12 To every thing there is a season, and a time to every purpose under the heaven:
A time to be born, and a time to die; a time to plant, and a time to pluck up that which is planted;
A time to kill, and a time to heal; a time to break down, and a time to build up;
A time to weep, and a time to laugh; a time to mourn, and a time to dance;
A time to cast away stones, and a time to gather stones together; a time to embrace, and a time to refrain from embracing;

A time to get, and a time to lose; a time to keep, and a time to cast away;
A time to rend, and a time to sew; a time to keep silence, and a time to speak;
A time to love, and a time to hate; a time of war, and a time of peace.
3:1

13 For that which befalleth the sons of men befalleth beasts; even one thing befalleth them: as the one dieth, so dieth the other; yea, they have all one breath; so that a man hath no preeminence above a beast: for all is vanity.
19

14 Wherefore I praised the dead which are already dead more than the living which are yet alive.
4:2

15 A threefold cord is not quickly broken.
12

16 God is in heaven, and thou upon earth: therefore let thy words be few.
5:2

17 The sleep of a labouring man is sweet.
12

18 As the crackling of thorns under a pot, so is the laughter of a fool.
7:6

19 Better is the end of a thing than the beginning thereof.
8

20 Say not thou, What is the cause that the former days were better than these? for thou dost not enquire wisely concerning this.
10

21 In the day of prosperity be joyful, but in the day of adversity consider.
14

22 Be not righteous over much.
16

23 One man among a thousand have I found; but a woman among all those have I not found.
28

24 God hath made man upright; but they have sought out many inventions.
29

25 There is no man that hath power over the spirit to retain the spirit; neither hath he power in the day of death; there is no discharge in that war.
8:8

26 A man hath no better thing under the sun, than to eat, and to drink, and to be merry.
15. See 58:15, 70:4, 76:24

27 A living dog is better than a dead lion.
9:4

28 Go thy way, eat thy bread with joy, and drink thy wine with a merry heart; for God now accepteth thy works.
7

29 Whatsoever thy hand findeth to do, do it with thy might; for there is no work, nor device, nor knowledge, nor wisdom, in the grave, whither thou goest.
10

30 The race is not to the swift, nor the battle to the strong.
11

1 Dead flies cause the ointment of the apothecary to send forth a stinking savour.
10:1

2 He that diggeth a pit shall fall into it.
8

3 Woe to thee, O land, when thy king is a child, and thy princes eat in the morning!
16

4 Wine maketh merry: but money answereth all things.
19

5 Cast thy bread upon the waters: for thou shalt find it after many days.
11:1

6 In the place where the tree falleth, there it shall be.
3

7 He that observeth the wind shall not sow; and he that regardeth the clouds shall not reap.
4

8 In the morning sow thy seed, and in the evening withhold not thine hand.
6

9 Truly the light is sweet, and a pleasant thing it is for the eyes to behold the sun.
7

10 Rejoice, O young man, in thy youth; and let thy heart cheer thee in the days of thy youth.
9

11 Remember now thy Creator in the days of thy youth, while the evil days come not, nor the years draw nigh, when thou shalt say, I have no pleasure in them;
While the sun, or the light, or the moon, or the stars, be not darkened, nor the clouds return after the rain:
In the day when the keepers of the house shall tremble, and the strong men shall bow themselves, and the grinders cease because they are few, and those that look out of the windows be darkened,
And the doors shall be shut in the streets, when the sound of the grinding is low, and he shall rise up at the voice of the bird, and all the daughters of musick shall be brought low;
Also when they shall be afraid of that which is high, and fears shall be in the way, and the almond tree shall flourish, and the grasshopper shall be a burden, and desire shall fail: because man goeth to his long home, and the mourners go about the streets:
Or ever the silver cord be loosed, or the golden bowl be broken, or the pitcher be broken at the fountain, or the wheel broken at the cistern.
Then shall the dust return to the earth as it was: and the spirit shall return unto God who gave it.
12:1

12 The words of the wise are as goads.
11

13 Of making many books there is no end; and much study is a weariness of the flesh.
12

14 Fear God, and keep his commandments: for this is the whole duty of man.
For God shall bring every work into judgment, with every secret thing, whether it be good, or whether it be evil.
13

SONG OF SOLOMON

15 The song of songs, which is Solomon's.
Let him kiss me with the kisses of his mouth: for thy love is better than wine.
1:1

16 I am black, but comely, O ye daughters of Jerusalem, as the tents of Kedar, as the curtains of Solomon.
5

17 O thou fairest among women.
8

18 A bundle of myrrh is my wellbeloved unto me; he shall lie all night betwixt my breasts.
13

19 I am the rose of Sharon, and the lily of the valleys.
2:1

20 His banner over me was love.
4

21 Stay me with flagons, comfort me with apples: for I am sick of love.
His left hand is under my head, and his right hand doth embrace me.
5

22 Rise up, my love, my fair one, and come away.
For, lo, the winter is past, the rain is over and gone;
The flowers appear on the earth; the time of the singing of birds is come, and the voice of the turtle is heard in our land.
2:10

23 Take us the foxes, the little foxes, that spoil the vines.
15

24 My beloved is mine, and I am his: he feedeth among the lilies.
Until the day break, and the shadows flee away.
16

25 By night on my bed I sought him whom my soul loveth.
3:1

26 Behold, thou art fair, my love; behold, thou art fair; thou hast doves' eyes within thy locks: thy hair is as a flock of goats, that appear from mount Gilead.
Thy teeth are like a flock of sheep that are even shorn, which came up from the washing; whereof every one bear twins, and none is barren among them.
Thy lips are like a thread of scarlet, and thy speech is comely: thy temples are like a piece of a pomegranate within thy locks.
Thy neck is like the tower of David builded for an armoury, whereon there hang a thousand bucklers, all shields of mighty men.
Thy breasts are like two young roes that are twins, which feed among the lilies.
4:1

27 Thou art all fair, my love; there is no spot in thee.
7

28 A garden inclosed is my sister, my spouse; a spring shut up, a fountain sealed.
12

29 Awake, O north wind; and come, thou south; blow upon my garden, that the spices thereof may flow out.

Let my beloved come into his garden, and eat his pleasant fruits.
16

1 I sleep, but my heart waketh: it is the voice of my beloved that knocketh, saying, Open to me, my sister, my love, my dove, my undefiled.
5:2

2 The watchmen that went about the city found me, they smote me, they wounded me; the keepers of the walls took away my veil from me.
I charge you, O daughters of Jerusalem, if ye find my beloved, that ye tell him, that I am sick of love.
What is thy beloved more than another beloved, O thou fairest among women?
7

3 My beloved is white and ruddy, the chiefest among ten thousand.
10

4 His hands are as gold rings set with the beryl: his belly is as bright ivory overlaid with sapphires.
His legs are as pillars of marble, set upon sockets of fine gold: his countenance is as Lebanon, excellent as the cedars.
His mouth is most sweet: yea, he is altogether lovely. This is my beloved, and this is my friend, O daughters of Jerusalem.
14

5 Who is she that looketh forth as the morning, fair as the moon, clear as the sun, and terrible as an army with banners?
6:10

6 Return, return, O Shulamite; return, return, that we may look upon thee.
13

7 How beautiful are thy feet with shoes, O prince's daughter!
7:1

8 Thy navel is like a round goblet, which wanteth not liquor: thy belly is like an heap of wheat set about with lilies.
2

9 Thy neck is as a tower of ivory; thine eyes like the fishpools in Heshbon, by the gate of Bath-rabbim: thy nose is as the tower of Lebanon which looketh toward Damascus.
4

10 Like the best wine, for my beloved, that goeth down sweetly, causing the lips of those that are asleep to speak.
9

11 Set me as a seal upon thine heart, as a seal upon thine arm: for love is strong as death; jealousy is cruel as the grave.
8:6

12 Many waters cannot quench love, neither can the floods drown it: if a man would give all the substance of his house for love, it would utterly be contemned.
7

13 We have a little sister, and she hath no breasts.
8

14 Make haste, my beloved, and be thou like to a roe or to a young hart upon the mountain of spices.
14

ISAIAH

15 The ox knoweth his owner, and the ass his master's crib.
1:3

16 The daughter of Zion is left as a cottage in a vineyard, as a lodge in a garden of cucumbers, as a besieged city.
8

17 Bring no more vain oblations; incense is an abomination unto me; the new moons and sabbaths, the calling of assemblies, I cannot away with.
13

18 Though your sins be as scarlet, they shall be as white as snow.
18

19 They shall beat their swords into plowshares, and their spears into pruninghooks: nation shall not lift up sword against nation, neither shall they learn war any more.
2:4

20 What mean ye that ye beat my people to pieces, and grind the faces of the poor?
3:15

21 My wellbeloved hath a vineyard in a very fruitful hill.
5:1

22 And he looked that it should bring forth grapes, and it brought forth wild grapes.
2

23 And he looked for judgment, but behold oppression; for righteousness, but behold a cry.
7

24 Woe unto them that join house to house, that lay field to field, till there be no place.
8

25 Woe unto them that rise up early in the morning, that they may follow strong drink.
11

26 Woe unto them that call evil good, and good evil.
20

27 For all this his anger is not turned away, but his hand is stretched out still.
25

28 In the year that king Uzziah died I saw also the Lord sitting upon a throne, high and lifted up, and his train filled the temple.
Above it stood the seraphims: each one had six wings; with twain he covered his face, and with twain he covered his feet, and with twain he did fly.
And one cried unto another, and said, Holy, holy, holy, is the Lord of hosts: the whole earth is full of his glory.
6:1

29 Then said I, Woe is me! for I am undone; because I am a man of unclean lips, and I dwell in the midst of a people of unclean lips.
5

30 Then flew one of the seraphims unto me, having a live coal in his hand...And he laid it upon my mouth, and said, Lo, this hath touched thy lips.
6

1 Whom shall I send, and who will go for us? Then said I, Here am I; send me.
8

2 Then said I, Lord, how long?
11

3 Behold, a virgin shall conceive, and bear a son, and shall call his name Immanuel.
Butter and honey shall he eat, that he may know to refuse the evil, and choose the good.
7:14

4 Sanctify the Lord of hosts himself; and let him be your fear, and let him be your dread.
And he shall be for a sanctuary; but for a stone of stumbling and for a rock of offence to both the houses of Israel.
8:13

5 Wizards that peep and that mutter.
19

6 The people that walked in darkness have seen a great light: they that dwell in the land of the shadow of death, upon them hath the light shined.
Thou hast multiplied the nation, and not increased the joy: they joy before thee according to the joy in harvest, and as men rejoice when they divide the spoil.
9:2

7 For unto us a child is born, unto us a son is given: and the government shall be upon his shoulder: and his name shall be called Wonderful, Counsellor, The mighty God, The everlasting Father, The Prince of Peace.
Of the increase of his government and peace there shall be no end.
6

8 The zeal of the Lord of hosts will perform this.
7

9 And there shall come forth a rod out of the stem of Jesse, and a Branch shall grow out of his roots:
And the spirit of the Lord shall rest upon him, the spirit of wisdom and understanding, the spirit of counsel and might, the spirit of knowledge and of the fear of the Lord.
11:1

10 The wolf also shall dwell with the lamb, and the leopard shall lie down with the kid; and the calf and the young lion and the fatling together; and a little child shall lead them.
6

11 And the lion shall eat straw like the ox.
And the sucking child shall play on the hole of the asp, and the weaned child shall put his hand on the cockatrice' den.
They shall not hurt nor destroy in all my holy mountain: for the earth shall be full of the knowledge of the Lord, as the waters cover the sea.
7

12 Dragons in their pleasant palaces.
13:22

13 How art thou fallen from heaven, O Lucifer, son of the morning!
14:12

14 Watchman, what of the night? Watchman, what of the night?
The watchman said, The morning cometh, and also the night.
21:11

15 Let us eat and drink; for to morrow we shall die.
22:13. See 55:26, 70:4, 76:24

16 Tyre, the crowning city, whose merchants are princes.
23:8

17 Howl, ye ships of Tarshish.
14

18 In this mountain shall the Lord of hosts make unto all people a feast of fat things, a feast of wine on the lees, of fat things full of marrow, of wine on the lees well refined.
25:6

19 He will swallow up death in victory; and the Lord God will wipe away tears from off all faces.
8

20 We have as it were brought forth wind.
26:18

21 For precept must be upon precept, precept upon precept; line upon line, line upon line; here a little, and there a little.
28:10

22 We have made a covenant with death, and with hell are we at agreement.
15

23 They are drunken, but not with wine.
29:9

24 Their strength is to sit still.
30:7

25 Now go, write it before them in a table, and note it in a book.
8

26 Speak unto us smooth things, prophesy deceits.
10

27 In quietness and in confidence shall be your strength.
15

28 The bread of adversity, and the waters of affliction.
20

29 This is the way, walk ye in it.
21

30 And a man shall be as an hiding place from the wind, and a covert from the tempest; as rivers of water in a dry place, as the shadow of a great rock in a weary land.
32:2

31 And thorns shall come up in her palaces, nettles and brambles in the fortresses thereof: and it shall be an habitation of dragons, and a court for owls.
34:13

32 The wilderness and the solitary place shall be glad for them; and the desert shall rejoice, and blossom as the rose.
35:1

33 Strengthen ye the weak hands, and confirm the feeble knees.
3

34 Then shall the lame man leap as an hart, and the tongue of the dumb sing: for in the wilderness shall waters break out, and streams in the desert.
6

35 The wayfaring men, though fools, shall not err

therein.
8

1 They shall obtain joy and gladness, and sorrow and sighing shall flee away.
10

2 Set thine house in order: for thou shalt die, and not live.
38:1

3 I shall go softly all my years in the bitterness of my soul.
15

4 Comfort ye, comfort ye my people, saith your God. Speak ye comfortably to Jerusalem, and cry unto her, that her warfare is accomplished.
40:1

5 The voice of him that crieth in the wilderness, Prepare ye the way of the Lord, make straight in the desert a highway for our God.
Every valley shall be exalted, and every mountain and hill shall be made low: and the crooked shall be made straight, and the rough places plain:
And the glory of the Lord shall be revealed, and all flesh shall see it together: for the mouth of the Lord hath spoken it.
3. See 63:36 ·

6 The voice said, Cry. And he said, What shall I cry? All flesh is grass, and all the goodliness thereof is as the flower of the field:
The grass withereth, the flower fadeth: because the spirit of the Lord bloweth upon it: surely the people is grass.
6. See 80:21

7 He shall feed his flock like a shepherd: he shall gather the lambs with his arm, and carry them in his bosom, and shall gently lead those that are with young.
11

8 The nations are as a drop of a bucket, and are counted as the small dust of the balance: behold, he taketh up the isles as a very little thing.
15

9 Have ye not known? have ye not heard? hath it not been told you from the beginning?
21

10 But they that wait upon the Lord shall renew their strength: they shall mount up with wings as eagles; they shall run, and not be weary; and they shall walk, and not faint.
31

11 A bruised reed shall he not break, and the smoking flax shall he not quench.
42:3

12 He warmeth himself, and saith, Aha, I am warm, I have seen the fire.
44:16

13 Woe unto him that striveth with his maker! Let the potsherd strive with the potsherds of the earth. Shall the clay say to him that fashioneth it, What makest thou?
45:9

14 I have chosen thee in the furnace of affliction.
48:10

15 O that thou hadst hearkened to my commandments! then had thy peace been as a river, and thy

righteousness as the waves of the sea.
18

16 There is no peace, saith the Lord, unto the wicked.
22

17 Can a woman forget her sucking child, that she should not have compassion on the son of her womb? yea, they may forget, yet will I not forget thee.
49:15

18 How beautiful upon the mountains are the feet of him that bringeth good tidings, that publisheth peace; that bringeth good tidings of good, that publisheth salvation; that saith unto Zion, Thy God reigneth!
52:7

19 For they shall see eye to eye, when the Lord shall bring again Zion.
Break forth into joy, sing together, ye waste places of Jerusalem: for the Lord hath comforted his people, he hath redeemed Jerusalem.
8

20 Who hath believed our report? and to whom is the arm of the Lord revealed?
53:1

21 He hath no form nor comeliness; and when we shall see him there is no beauty that we should desire him.
He is despised and rejected of men; a man of sorrows, and acquainted with grief: and we hid as it were our faces from him; he was despised, and we esteemed him not.
Surely he hath borne our griefs, and carried our sorrows.
2

22 But he was wounded for our transgressions, he was bruised for our iniquities: the chastisement of our peace was upon him; and with his stripes we are healed.
All we like sheep have gone astray; we have turned every one to his own way; and the Lord hath laid on him the iniquity of us all.
He was oppressed, and he was afflicted, yet he opened not his mouth: he is brought as a lamb to the slaughter, and as a sheep before her shearers is dumb, so he openeth not his mouth.
5

23 He was cut off out of the land of the living.
8

24 He was numbered with the transgressors; and he bare the sin of many, and made intercession for the transgressors.
12

25 Ho, every one that thirsteth, come ye to the waters, and he that hath no money; come ye, buy, and eat; yea, come, buy wine and milk without money and without price.
Wherefore do ye spend money for that which is not bread? and your labour for that which satisfieth not?
55:1

26 Seek ye the Lord while he may be found, call ye upon him while he is near.
6

27 For my thoughts are not your thoughts, neither are your ways my ways, saith the Lord.
8

28 Instead of the thorn shall come up the fir tree, and

instead of the brier shall come up the myrtle tree.
13

1 I will give them an everlasting name, that shall not be cut off.
56:5

2 The righteous perisheth, and no man layeth it to heart.
57:1

3 Peace to him that is far off, and to him that is near.
19

4 Is not this the fast that I have chosen? to loose the bands of wickedness, to undo the heavy burdens, and to let the oppressed go free, and that ye break every yoke?
58:6

5 Then shall thy light break forth as the morning, and thine health shall spring forth speedily.
8

6 They make haste to shed innocent blood.
59:7

7 Arise, shine; for thy light is come, and the glory of the Lord is risen upon thee.
60:1

8 The Spirit of the Lord God is upon me...
To bind up the brokenhearted, to proclaim liberty to the captives, and the opening of the prison to them that are bound;
To proclaim the acceptable year of the Lord, and the day of vengeance of our God; to comfort all that mourn.
61:1

9 To give unto them beauty for ashes, the oil of joy for mourning, the garment of praise for the spirit of heaviness.
3

10 Who is this that cometh from Edom, with dyed garments from Bozrah?
63:1

11 I have trodden the winepress alone.
3

12 All our righteousnesses are as filthy rags; and we all do fade as a leaf.
64:6

13 [A people] Which say, Stand by thyself, come not near to me; for I am holier than thou.
65:5

14 For, behold, I create new heavens and a new earth.
17

JEREMIAH

15 Can a maid forget her ornaments, or a bride her attire?
2:32

16 They were as fed horses in the morning: every one neighed after his neighbour's wife.
5:8

17 This people hath a revolting and a rebellious heart.
23

18 The prophets prophesy falsely, and the priests bear rule by their means; and my people love to have it so: and what will ye do in the end thereof?
31

19 They have healed also the hurt of the daughter of my people slightly, saying, Peace, peace; when there is no

peace.
6:14

20 The harvest is past, the summer is ended, and we are not saved.
8:20

21 Is there no balm in Gilead?
22

22 Can the Ethiopian change his skin, or the leopard his spots?
13:23

23 Woe is me, my mother, that thou hast borne me a man of strife and a man of contention to the whole earth!
15:10

24 The heart is deceitful above all things, and desperately wicked.
17:9

25 As the partridge sitteth on eggs, and hatcheth them not: so he that getteth riches, and not by right, shall leave them in the midst of his days.
11

26 Behold, I will make thee a terror to thyself, and to all thy friends.
20:4

LAMENTATIONS

27 How doth the city sit solitary, that was full of people!
1:1

28 Is it nothing to you, all ye that pass by? behold, and see if there be any sorrow like unto my sorrow.
12

29 And I said, My strength and my hope is perished from the Lord:
Remembering mine affliction and my misery, the wormwood and the gall.
3:18

30 It is good for a man that he bear the yoke in his youth.
27

31 He giveth his cheek to him that smiteth him.
30

32 O Lord, thou hast seen my wrong: judge thou my cause.
4:59

EZEKIEL

33 As is the mother, so is her daughter.
16:44

34 The fathers have eaten sour grapes, and the children's teeth are set on edge.
18:2

35 When the wicked man turneth away from his wickedness that he hath committed, and doeth that which is lawful and right, he shall save his soul alive.
27

36 The king of Babylon stood at the parting of the ways.
21:21

37 She doted upon the Assyrians her neighbours, captains and rulers clothed most gorgeously, horsemen riding upon horses, all of them desirable young men.
23:12

38 The hand of the Lord was upon me, and carried me out in the spirit of the Lord, and set me down in the

midst of the valley which was full of bones.
37:1

1 Can these bones live?
3

2 Again he said unto me, Prophesy upon these bones,
and say unto them, O ye dry bones, hear the word of
the Lord.
4

DANIEL

3 To you it is commanded, O peoples, nations, and
languages,
That at what time ye hear the sound of the cornet,
flute, harp, sackbut, psaltery, dulcimer, and all kinds
of musick, ye fall down and worship the golden image
that Nebuchadnezzar the king hath set up:
And whoso falleth not down and worshippeth shall the
same hour be cast into the middle of a burning fiery
furnace.
3:4

4 Shadrach, Meshach, and Abed-nego, ye servants of
the most high God, come forth and come hither.
26

5 In the same hour came forth fingers of a man's hand,
and wrote over against the candlestick upon the
plaister of the wall of the king's palace.
5:5

6 And this is the writing that was written, MENE,
MENE, TEKEL, UPHARSIN.
This is the interpretation of the thing: MENE; God
hath numbered thy kingdom, and finished it.
TEKEL; Thou art weighed in the balances and art
found wanting.
PERES; Thy kingdom is divided, and given to the
Medes and Persians.
25

7 Now, O king, establish the decree, and sign the
writing, that it be not changed, according to the law of
the Medes and Persians, which altereth not.
6:8

8 The Ancient of days did sit, whose garment was white
as snow, and the hair of his head like the pure wool:
his throne was like the fiery flame, and his wheels as
burning fire.
A fiery steam issued and came forth from behind him:
thousand thousands ministered unto him, and ten
thousand times ten thousand stood before him: the
judgment was set, and the books were opened.
7:9

9 O Daniel, a man greatly beloved.
10:11

10 Many shall run to and fro, and knowledge shall be
increased.
12:4

HOSEA

11 They have sown the wind, and they shall reap the
whirlwind.
8:7

12 I drew them...with bands of love.
11:4

JOEL

13 That which the palmerworm hath left hath the locust
eaten.
1:4

14 I will restore to you the years that the locust hath
eaten, the cankerworm, and the caterpillar, and the
palmerworm, my great army which I sent among you.
2:25

15 And it shall come to pass afterward, that I will pour
out my spirit upon all flesh; and your sons and your
daughters shall prophesy, your old men shall dream
dreams, your young men shall see visions.
28

16 Beat your plowshares into swords, and your
pruninghooks into spears.
3:10

17 Multitudes, multitudes in the valley of decision: for
the day of the Lord is near in the valley of decision.
14

AMOS

18 Can two walk together, except they be agreed?
3:3

19 Shall there be evil in a city, and the Lord hath not
done it?
6

20 I have overthrown some of you, as God overthrew
Sodom and Gomorrah, and ye were as a firebrand
plucked out of the burning.
4:11

JONAH

21 Come, and let us cast lots, that we may know for
whose cause this evil is upon us. So they cast lots, and
the lot fell upon Jonah.
1:7

22 Jonah was in the belly of the fish three days and three
nights.
17

MICAH

23 They shall sit every man under his vine, and under his
fig tree.
4:4

24 But thou, Beth-lehem Ephratah, though thou be little
among the thousands of Judah, yet out of thee shall he
come forth unto me that is to be ruler in Israel.
5:2

25 What doth the Lord require of thee, but to do justly,
and to love mercy, and to walk humbly with thy God?
6:8

NAHUM

26 Woe to the bloody city! it is all full of lies and
robbery; the prey departeth not.
3:1

ZEPHANIAH

27 Woe to her that is filthy and polluted, to the

oppressing city!
3:1

HABAKKUK

1 Write the vision, and make it plain upon tables, that he may run that readeth it.
2:2

HAGGAI

2 Ye have sown much, and bring in little; ye eat but ye have not enough...and he that earneth wages earneth wages to put it into a bag with holes.
1:6

MALACHI

3 But unto you that fear my name shall the Sun of righteousness arise with healing in his wings.
4:2

APOCRYPHA. 1 ESDRAS

4 The first wrote, Wine is the strongest.
The second wrote, The king is strongest.
The third wrote, Women are strongest: but above all things Truth beareth away the victory.
3:10

5 Great is Truth, and mighty above all things.
4:41

2 ESDRAS

6 Nourish thy children, O thou good nurse; stablish their feet.
2:25

7 For the world has lost his youth, and the times begin to wax old.
14:10

8 I shall light a candle of understanding in thine heart, which shall not be put out.
25

TOBIT

9 So they went forth both, and the young man's dog with them.
5:16

WISDOM OF SOLOMON

10 The ear of jealousy heareth all things.
1:10

11 Let us crown ourselves with rosebuds, before they be withered.
2:8

12 Through envy of the devil came death into the world.
24

13 But the souls of the righteous are in the hand of God, and there shall no torment touch them.
In the sight of the unwise they seemed to die: and their departure is taken for misery,
And their going from us to be utter destruction: but they are in peace.
For though they be punished in the sight of men, yet is their hope full of immortality.

And having been a little chastised, they shall be greatly rewarded: for God proved them, and found them worthy for himself.
3:1

14 And in the time of their visitation they shall shine, and run to and fro like sparks among the stubble.
7

15 He, being made perfect in a short time, fulfilled a long time.
4:13

16 We fools accounted his life madness, and his end to be without honour:
How is he numbered among the children of God, and his lot is among the saints!
5:4

17 Even so we in like manner, as soon as we were born, began to draw to our end.
13

18 For the hope of the ungodly...passeth away as the remembrance of a guest that tarrieth but a day.
14

19 And love is the keeping of her laws; and the giving heed unto her laws is the assurance of incorruption.
6:18

ECCLESIASTICUS

20 For the same things uttered in Hebrew, and translated into another tongue, have not the same force in them: and not only these things, but the law itself, and the prophets, and the rest of the books, have no small difference, when they are spoken in their own language.
The Prologue

21 For the Lord is full of compassion and mercy, long-suffering, and very pitiful, and forgiveth sins, and saveth in time of affliction.
2:11

22 We will fall into the hands of the Lord, and not into the hands of men: for as his majesty is, so is his mercy.
18

23 Be not curious in unnecessary matters: for more things are shewed unto thee than men understand.
3:23

24 Be not ignorant of any thing in a great matter or a small.
5:15

25 A faithful friend is the medicine of life.
6:16

26 Laugh no man to scorn in the bitterness of his soul.
7:11

27 Miss not the discourse of the elders.
8:9

28 Open not thine heart to every man.
19

29 Give not thy soul unto a woman.
9:2

30 Forsake not an old friend; for the new is not comparable to him; a new friend is as new wine; when it is old, thou shalt drink it with pleasure.
10

31 Many kings have sat down upon the ground; and one

that was never thought of hath worn the crown.
11:5

1 Judge none blessed before his death.
28

2 He that toucheth pitch shall be defiled therewith.
13:1

3 For how agree the kettle and the earthen pot together?
2

4 When a rich man is fallen, he hath many helpers: he speaketh things not to be spoken, and yet men justify him: the poor man slipped, and yet they rebuked him too; he spake wisely, and could have no place.
14:22

5 When thou hast enough, remember the time of hunger.
18:25

6 Be not made a beggar by banqueting upon borrowing.
33

7 He that contemneth small things shall fall by little and little.
19:1

8 All wickedness is but little to the wickedness of a woman.
25:19

9 Neither [give] a wicked woman liberty to gad abroad.
25

10 A merchant shall hardly keep himself from doing wrong.
26:29

11 Many have fallen by the edge of the sword: but not so many as have fallen by the tongue.
28:18

12 And weigh thy words in a balance, and make a door and bar for thy mouth.
25

13 Envy and wrath shorten the life.
30:24

14 Leave off first for manners' sake.
31:17

15 Wine is as good as life to a man, if it be drunk moderately: what life is then to a man that is without wine? for it was made to make men glad.
27

16 Leave not a stain in thine honour.
33:22

17 Honour a physician with the honour due unto him for the uses which ye may have of him: for the Lord hath created him.
38:1

18 He that sinneth before his Maker, Let him fall into the hand of the physician.
15

19 The wisdom of a learned man cometh by opportunity of leisure: and he that hath little business shall become wise.
24

20 How can he get wisdom...whose talk is of bullocks?
25

21 Let us now praise famous men, and our fathers that begat us.
44:1

22 Such as did bear rule in their kingdoms.
3

23 Such as found out musical tunes, and recited verses in writing:
Rich men furnished with ability, living peaceably in their habitations.
5

24 There be of them, that have left a name behind them.
8

25 And some there be, which have no memorial.
9

26 Their bodies are buried in peace; but their name liveth for evermore.
14

27 As the flower of roses in the spring of the year, as lilies by the rivers of waters, and as the branches of the frankincense tree in the time of summer.
50:8

28 Get learning with a great sum of money, and get much gold by her.
51:28

2 MACCABEES

29 It is a foolish thing to make a long prologue, and to be short in the story itself.
2:32

30 When he was at the last gasp.
7:9

NEW TESTAMENT. ST. MATTHEW

31 There came wise men from the east to Jerusalem, Saying, Where is he that is born King of the Jews? for we have seen his star in the east, and are come to worship him.
2:1

32 They presented unto him gifts; gold, and frankincense, and myrrh.
11

33 They departed into their own country another way.
12

34 In Rama was there a voice heard, lamentation, and weeping, and great mourning, Rachel weeping for her children, and would not be comforted, because they are not.
18 and Jer. 31:15

35 Repent ye: for the kingdom of heaven is at hand.
3:2

36 The voice of one crying in the wilderness, Prepare ye the way of the Lord, make his paths straight.
3. See 59:5

37 John had his raiment of camel's hair, and a leathern girdle about his loins; and his meat was locusts and wild honey.
4

38 O generation of vipers, who hath warned you to flee from the wrath to come?
7

39 And now also the axe is laid unto the root of the trees.
10

40 This is my beloved Son, in whom I am well pleased.
17

1 Man shall not live by bread alone, but by every word that proceedeth out of the mouth of God.
4:4. See 48:22

2 Thou shalt not tempt the Lord thy God.
7 and Deut. 6:16

3 The devil taketh him up into an exceeding high mountain, and sheweth him all the kingdoms of the world, and the glory of them.
8

4 Angels came and ministered unto him.
11

5 [Jesus] saith unto them, Follow me, and I will make you fishers of men.
19

6 Blessed are the poor in spirit: for theirs is the kingdom of heaven.
Blessed are they that mourn: for they shall be comforted.
Blessed are the meek: for they shall inherit the earth.
Blessed are they which do hunger and thirst after righteousness: for they shall be filled.
Blessed are the merciful: for they shall obtain mercy.
Blessed are the pure in heart: for they shall see God.
Blessed are the peacemakers: for they shall be called the children of God.
5:3

7 Ye are the salt of the earth: but if the salt have lost his savour, wherewith shall it be salted?
13

8 Ye are the light of the world. A city that is set on an hill cannot be hid.
14

9 Let your light so shine before men, that they may see your good works.
16

10 Think not that I am come to destroy the law, or the prophets: I am come not to destroy, but to fulfil.
17

11 Except your righteousness shall exceed the righteousness of the scribes and Pharisees, ye shall in no case enter into the kingdom of heaven.
20

12 Whosoever shall say, Thou fool, shall be in danger of hell fire.
22

13 Agree with thine adversary quickly, whiles thou art in the way with him.
25

14 Till thou hast paid the uttermost farthing.
26

15 Swear not at all; neither by heaven; for it is God's throne:
Nor by the earth; for it is his footstool.
34

16 Let your communication be Yea, yea; Nay, nay.
37

17 Resist not evil: but whosoever shall smite thee on thy right cheek, turn to him the other also.
39

18 Whosoever shall compel thee to go a mile, go with him twain.
41

19 He maketh his sun to rise on the evil and on the good, and sendeth rain on the just and on the unjust.
45

20 For if ye love them which love you, what reward have ye? do not even the publicans the same?
46

21 Be ye therefore perfect, even as your Father which is in heaven is perfect.
48

22 When thou doest alms, let not thy left hand know what thy right hand doeth.
That thine alms may be in secret: and thy Father which seeth in secret himself shall reward you openly.
6:3

23 Use not vain repetitions, as the heathen do: for they think that they shall be heard for their much speaking.
7

24 After this manner therefore pray ye: Our Father which art in heaven, Hallowed be thy name.
Thy kingdom come. Thy will be done in earth, as it is in heaven.
Give us this day our daily bread.
And forgive us our debts, as we forgive our debtors.
And lead us not into temptation, but deliver us from evil: For thine is the kingdom, and the power, and the glory, for ever. Amen.
9 and Luke 11:2

25 Lay not up for yourselves treasures upon earth, where moth and rust doth corrupt, and where thieves break through and steal:
But lay up for yourselves treasures in heaven.
19

26 Where your treasure is, there will your heart be also.
21

27 No man can serve two masters...Ye cannot serve God and mammon.
24

28 Is not the life more than meat, and the body than raiment?
Behold the fowls of the air: for they sow not, neither do they reap, nor gather into barns.
25

29 Which of you by taking thought can add one cubit unto his stature?
27

30 Consider the lilies of the field, how they grow; they toil not, neither do they spin:
And yet I say unto you, That even Solomon in all his glory was not arrayed like one of these.
28

31 Seek ye first the kingdom of God, and his righteousness; and all these things shall be added unto you.
33

32 Take therefore no thought for the morrow: for the morrow shall take thought for the things of itself. Sufficient unto the day is the evil thereof.
34

33 Judge not, that ye be not judged.
7:1. See 69:22

34 Why beholdest thou the mote that is in thy brother's eye, but considerest not the beam that is in thine own

eye?
3

1 Neither cast ye your pearls before swine.
6

2 Ask, and it shall be given you; seek, and ye shall find; knock, and it shall be opened unto you.
7

3 Every one that asketh receiveth; and he that seeketh findeth.
8

4 Or what man is there of you, whom if his son ask bread, will he give him a stone?
9

5 Therefore all things whatsoever ye would that men should do to you, do ye even so to them: for this is the law and the prophets.
12

6 Wide is the gate, and broad is the way, that leadeth to destruction, and many there be that go in thereat.
13

7 Strait is the gate, and narrow is the way, which leadeth unto life, and few there be that find it.
14

8 Beware of false prophets, which come to you in sheep's clothing, but inwardly they are ravening wolves.
15

9 Do men gather grapes of thorns, or figs of thistles?
16

10 By their fruits ye shall know them.
20

11 The winds blew, and beat upon that house; and it fell not: for it was founded upon a rock.
25

12 Every one that heareth these sayings of mine, and doeth them not, shall be likened unto a foolish man, which built his house upon the sand:
And the rain descended, and the floods came, and the winds blew, and beat upon that house; and it fell: and great was the fall of it.
27

13 For he taught them as one having authority, and not as the scribes.
29

14 Lord I am not worthy that thou shouldest come under my roof.
8:8

15 I am a man under authority, having soldiers under me: and I say to this man, Go, and he goeth; and to another, Come, and he cometh; and to my servant, Do this, and he doeth it.
9

16 I have not found so great faith, no, not in Israel.
10

17 But the children of the kingdom shall be cast out into outer darkness: there shall be weeping and gnashing of teeth.
12

18 The foxes have holes, and the birds of the air have nests; but the Son of man hath not where to lay his head.
20

19 Let the dead bury their dead.
22

20 The whole herd of swine ran violently down a steep place into the sea, and perished in the waters.
32

21 He saw a man, named Matthew, sitting at the receipt of custom: and he saith unto him, Follow me. And he arose and followed him.
9:9

22 Why eateth your Master with publicans and sinners?
11

23 They that be whole need not a physician, but they that are sick.
12

24 I am not come to call the righteous, but sinners to repentance.
13

25 Neither do men put new wine into old bottles.
17

26 Thy faith hath made thee whole.
22

27 The maid is not dead, but sleepeth.
24

28 He casteth out devils through the prince of the devils.
34

29 The harvest truly is plenteous, but the labourers are few.
37

30 Go rather to the lost sheep of the house of Israel.
10:6

31 Freely ye have received, freely give.
8

32 When ye depart out of that house or city, shake off the dust of your feet.
14

33 Be ye therefore wise as serpents, and harmless as doves.
16

34 The disciple is not above his master, nor the servant above his lord.
24

35 Are not two sparrows sold for a farthing? and one of them shall not fall on the ground without your Father.
29. See 70:3

36 The very hairs of your head are all numbered.
30

37 Fear ye not therefore, ye are of more value than many sparrows.
31

38 I came not to send peace, but a sword.
34

39 A man's foes shall be they of his own household.
36

40 He that findeth his life shall lose it: and he that loseth his life for my sake shall find it.
39

41 Whosoever shall give to drink unto one of these little ones a cup of cold water only in the name of a disciple, verily I say unto you, he shall in no wise lose his reward.
42

1 Art thou he that should come, or do we look for another?
11:3

2 What went ye out into the wilderness to see? A reed shaken with the wind?
But what went ye out for to see? A man clothed in soft raiment?...
But what went ye out for to see? A prophet? yea, I say unto you, and more than a prophet.
7

3 We have piped unto you, and ye have not danced; we have mourned unto you, and ye have not lamented.
17

4 Wisdom is justified of her children.
19

5 Come unto me, all ye that labour and are heavy laden, and I will give you rest.
Take my yoke upon you, and learn of me; for I am meek and lowly in heart: and ye shall find rest unto your souls.
For my yoke is easy, and my burden is light.
28

6 He that is not with me is against me.
12:30 and Luke 11:23

7 The blasphemy against the Holy Ghost shall not be forgiven unto men.
31

8 The tree is known by his fruit.
33

9 Out of the abundance of the heart the mouth speaketh.
34

10 Every idle word that men shall speak, they shall give account thereof in the day of judgment.
36

11 An evil and adulterous generation seeketh after a sign.
39

12 Behold, a greater than Solomon is here.
42

13 When the unclean spirit is gone out of a man, he walketh through dry places, seeking rest, and findeth none.
Then he saith, I will return into my house from whence I came out; and when he is come, he findeth it empty, swept, and garnished.
43

14 Then goeth he, and taketh with himself seven other spirits more wicked than himself, and they enter in and dwell there: and the last state of that man is worse than the first.
45

15 Behold my mother and my brethren!
49

16 Behold, a sower went forth to sow;
And when he sowed, some seeds fell by the wayside, and the fowls came and devoured them up:
Some fell upon stony places, where they had not much earth: and forthwith they sprung up, because they had no deepness of earth:
And when the sun was up, they were scorched; and because they had no root, they withered away.
And some fell among thorns; and the thorns sprang up and choked them:
But other fell into good ground, and brought forth fruit, some an hundredfold, some sixtyfold, some thirtyfold.
13:3

17 He also that received the seed among the thorns is he that heareth the word; and the care of this world, and the deceitfulness of riches, choke the word, and he becometh unfruitful.
22

18 His enemy came and sowed tares.
25

19 An enemy hath done this.
28

20 The kingdom of heaven is like to a grain of mustard seed, which a man took, and sowed in his field:
Which indeed is the least of all seeds: but when it is grown, it is the greatest among herbs, and becometh a tree, so that the birds of the air come and lodge in the branches thereof.
31

21 The kingdom of heaven is like unto a merchant man, seeking goodly pearls:
Who, when he had found one pearl of great price, went and sold all that he had, and bought it.
45

22 Is not this the carpenter's son?
55

23 A prophet is not without honour, save in his own country, and in his own house.
57

24 They took up of the fragments that remained twelve baskets full.
14:20

25 In the fourth watch of the night Jesus went unto them, walking on the sea.
25

26 Be of good cheer; it is I; be not afraid.
27

27 O thou of little faith, wherefore didst thou doubt?
31

28 Not that which goeth into the mouth defileth a man; but that which cometh out of the mouth, this defileth a man.
15:11

29 They be blind leaders of the blind. And if the blind lead the blind, both shall fall into the ditch.
14

30 Truth, Lord: yet the dogs eat of the crumbs which fall from their masters' table.
27

31 When it is evening, ye say, It will be fair weather: for the sky is red.
16:2

32 Ye can discern the face of the sky; but can ye not discern the signs of the times?
3

33 Thou art Peter, and upon this rock I will build my church; and the gates of hell shall not prevail against it.
18

34 Get thee behind me, Satan.
23

35 What is a man profited, if he shall gain the whole

world, and lose his own soul?
26. See 68:34

1 If ye have faith as a grain of mustard seed, ye shall say unto this mountain, Remove hence to yonder place; and it shall remove.
17:20

2 Except ye be converted, and become as little children, ye shall not enter into the kingdom of heaven.
18:3

3 Whoso shall receive one such little child in my name receiveth me.
But whoso shall offend one of these little ones which believe in me, it were better for him that a millstone were hanged abut his neck, and that he were drowned in the depth of the sea.
5

4 It must needs be that offences come; but woe to that man by whom the offence cometh!
7

5 If thine eye offend thee, pluck it out, and cast it from thee: it is better for thee to enter into life with one eye, rather than having two eyes to be cast into hell fire.
9

6 For where two or three are gathered together in my name, there am I in the midst of them.
20

7 Lord, how oft shall my brother sin against me, and I forgive him? till seven times?
Jesus saith unto him I say not unto thee, Until seven times: but Until seventy times seven. [To Peter.]
21

8 What therefore God hath joined together, let not man put asunder.
19:6

9 If thou wilt be perfect, go and sell that thou hast, and give to the poor, and thou shalt have treasure in heaven.
21

10 He went away sorrowful: for he had great possessions.
22

11 It is easier for a camel to go through the eye of a needle, than for a rich man to enter into the kingdom of God.
24

12 With men this is impossible; but with God all things are possible.
26

13 But many that are first shall be last; and the last shall be first.
30

14 Why stand ye here all the day idle?
20:6

15 These last have wrought but one hour, and thou hast made them equal unto us, which have borne the burden and heat of the day.
12

16 I will give unto this last, even as unto thee.
Is it not lawful for me to do what I will with mine own?
14

17 It is written, My house shall be called the house of

prayer; but ye have made it a den of thieves.
21:13 and Is. 56:7

18 For many are called, but few are chosen.
22:14

19 Whose is this image and superscription?
20

20 Render therefore unto Caesar the things which are Caesar's; and unto God the things that are God's.
21

21 For in the resurrection they neither marry, nor are given in marriage.
30

22 They make broad their phylacteries, and enlarge the borders of their garments,
And love the uppermost rooms at feasts, and the chief seats in the synagogues.
23:5

23 Whosoever shall exalt himself shall be abased; and he that shall humble himself shall be exalted.
12. See 70:9

24 Woe unto you, scribes, and Pharisees, hypocrites! for ye pay tithe of mint and anise and cummin, and have omitted the weightier matters of the law, judgment, mercy, and faith: these ought ye to have done, and not to leave the other undone.
Ye blind guides, which strain at a gnat, and swallow a camel.
23

25 Ye are like unto whited sepulchres, which indeed appear beautiful outward, but are within full of dead men's bones, and of all uncleanness.
27

26 O Jerusalem, Jerusalem, thou that killest the prophets, and stonest them which are sent unto thee, how often would I have gathered thy children together, even as a hen gathereth her chickens under her wings, and ye would not!
37

27 Ye shall hear of wars and rumours of wars: see that ye be not troubled: for all these things must come to pass but the end is not yet.
24:6

28 For nation shall rise against nation, and kingdom against kingdom.
7

29 When ye therefore shall see the abomination of desolation, spoken of by Daniel the prophet, stand in the holy place, (whoso readeth, let him understand:).
15 and Dan. 12:11

30 Wheresoever the carcase is, there will the eagles be gathered together.
28

31 Heaven and earth shall pass away, but my words shall not pass away.
35

32 For as in the days that were before the flood they were eating and drinking, marrying and giving in marriage, until the day that Noe entered into the ark,
And knew not until the flood came, and took them all away; so shall also the coming of the Son of Man be.
38

33 One shall be taken, and the other left.
40

1 Watch therefore: for ye know not what hour your Lord doth come.
42

2 Well done, thou good and faithful servant: thou hast been faithful over a few things, I will make thee a ruler over many things: enter thou into the joy of thy lord.
25:21

3 Lord, I knew thee that thou art an hard man, reaping where thou hast not sown, and gathering where thou hast not strawed.
24

4 Unto every one that hath shall be given, and he shall have abundance: but from him that hath not shall be taken away even that which he hath.
29

5 And he shall set the sheep on his right hand, but the goats on the left.
33

6 For I was an hungred, and ye gave me meat: I was thirsty and ye gave me drink: I was a stranger, and ye took me in:
Naked, and ye clothed me: I was sick, and ye visited me: I was in prison, and ye came unto me.
35

7 Inasmuch as ye have done it unto one of the least of these my brethren, ye have done it unto me.
40

8 There came unto him a woman having an alabaster box of very precious ointment, and poured it on his head, as he sat at meat.
But when his disciples saw it, they had indignation saying, To what purpose is this waste?
For this ointment might have been sold for much, and given to the poor.
26:7

9 What will ye give me, and I will deliver him unto you? And they covenanted with him for thirty pieces of silver.
15

10 It had been good for that man if he had not been born.
24

11 Jesus took bread, and blessed it, and brake it, and gave it to the disciples, and said, Take, eat; this is my body.
26

12 This night, before the cock crow, thou shalt deny me thrice.
34

13 Though I should die with thee, yet will I not deny thee.
35

14 If it be possible, let this cup pass from me.
39

15 What, could ye not watch with me one hour?
40

16 Watch and pray, that ye enter not into temptation: the spirit indeed is willing but the flesh is weak.
41

17 Friend, wherefore art thou come?
50

18 All they that take the sword shall perish with the

19 Thy speech bewrayeth thee.
Then began he to curse and to swear, saying, I know not the man. And immediately the cock crew.
73

20 Have thou nothing to do with that just man.
27:19

21 He took water, and washed his hands before the multitude, saying, I am innocent of the blood of this just person: see ye to it.
24

22 His blood be on us, and on our children.
25

23 He saved others; himself he cannot save.
42

24 Eli, Eli, lama sabachthani?...My God, my God, why hast thou forsaken me?
46. See 390:16

25 And, lo, I am with you alway, even unto the end of the world.
28:20

ST. MARK

26 The sabbath was made for man, and not man for the sabbath.
2:27

27 If a house be divided against itself, that house cannot stand.
3:25

28 He that hath ears to hear, let him hear.
4:9

29 With what measure ye mete, it shall be measured to you.
24

30 My name is Legion: for we are many.
5:9

31 Clothed, and in his right mind.
15

32 Jesus, immediately knowing in himself that virtue had gone out of him, turned him about in the press, and said, Who touched my clothes?
30

33 I see men as trees, walking.
8:24

34 For what shall it profit a man, if he shall gain the whole world, and lose his own soul?
36. See 66:35

35 Lord, I believe; help thou mine unbelief.
9:24

36 Suffer the little children to come unto me, and forbid them not: for of such is the kingdom of God.
10:14

37 Beware of the scribes, which love to go in long clothing, and love salutations in the marketplaces,
And the chief seats in the synagogues, and the uppermost rooms at feasts:
Which devour widows' houses, and for a pretence make long prayers.
12:38

38 And there came a certain poor widow, and she threw

in two mites.
42

1 Watch ye therefore: for ye know not when the master
of the house cometh...
Lest coming suddenly he find you sleeping.
13:35

2 Go ye into all the world, and preach the gospel to
every creature.
16:15

ST. LUKE

3 It seemed good to me also...to write unto thee...most
excellent Theophilus.
1:3

4 Hail, thou art highly favoured, the Lord is with thee:
blessed art thou among women.
28

5 My soul doth magnify the Lord,
And my spirit hath rejoiced in God my Saviour.
For he hath regarded the low estate of his handmaiden:
for, behold, from henceforth all generations shall call
me blessed.
46

6 He hath shewed strength with his arm; he hath
scattered the proud in the imagination of their hearts.
He hath put down the mighty from their seats, and
exalted them of low degree.
He hath filled the hungry with good things; and the
rich he hath sent empty away.
51

7 To give light to them that sit in darkness and in the
shadow of death, to guide our feet into the way of
peace.
79

8 And it came to pass in those days, that there went out
a decree from Caesar Augustus, that all the world
should be taxed.
2:1

9 She brought forth her firstborn son, and wrapped him
in swaddling clothes, and laid him in a manger;
because there was no room for them in the inn.
And there were in the same country shepherds abiding
in the field, keeping watch over their flock by night.
And, lo, the angel of the Lord came upon them, and
the glory of the Lord shone round about them: and they
were sore afraid.
7

10 Behold, I bring you good tidings of great joy.
10

11 Glory to God in the highest, and on earth peace, good
will toward men.
14

12 Lord, now lettest thou thy servant depart in peace,
according to thy word.
29

13 Wist ye not that I must be about my Father's business?
49

14 Jesus increased in wisdom and stature, and in favour
with God and man.
52

15 Be content with your wages.
3:14

16 And the devil, taking him up into a high mountain,
shewed unto him all the kingdoms of the world in a
moment of time.
4:5

17 Physician, heal thyself.
23

18 Master, we have toiled all the night, and have taken
nothing: nevertheless at thy word I will let down the
net.
5:5

19 No man...having drunk old wine straightway desireth
new: for he saith, The old is better.
39

20 Woe unto you, when all men shall speak well of you!
6:26

21 Love your enemies, do good to them which hate you.
27

22 Judge not, and ye shall not be judged.
37. See 64:33

23 Give, and it shall be given unto you; good measure,
pressed down, and shaken together, and running over,
shall men give into your bosom.
38

24 Her sins, which are many, are forgiven; for she loved
much.
7:47

25 No man, having put his hand to the plough, and
looking back, is fit for the kingdom of God.
9:62

26 Peace be to this house.
10:5

27 For the labourer is worthy of his hire.
7

28 I beheld Satan as lightning fall from heaven.
18

29 Blessed are the eyes which see the things which ye
see:
For I tell you, that many prophets and kings have
desired to see those things which ye see, and have not
seen them; and to hear those things which ye hear, and
have not heard them.
23

30 A certain man went down from Jerusalem to Jericho,
and fell among thieves.
30

31 He passed by on the other side.
31

32 He took out two pence, and gave them to the
host...whatsoever thou spendeth more, when I come
again, I will repay thee.
35

33 Go, and do thou likewise.
37

34 But Martha was cumbered about much serving, and
came to him, and said, Lord, dost thou not care that
my sister hath left me to serve alone? bid her therefore
that she help me.
40

35 But one thing is needful: and Mary hath chosen that
good part, which shall not be taken away from her.
42

36 When a strong man armed keepeth his palace, his

goods are in peace,
But when a stronger than he shall come upon him,
and overcome him, he taketh from him all his armour
wherein he trusted, and divideth his spoils.
11:21

1 No man, when he hath lighted a candle, putteth it in a
secret place, neither under a bushel, but on a
candlestick, that they which come in may see the light.
33

2 Woe unto you, lawyers! for ye have taken away the
key of knowledge.
52

3 Are not five sparrows sold for two farthings, and not
one of them is forgotten before God?
12:6. See 65:35

4 Soul, thou hast much goods laid up for many years;
take thine ease, eat, drink, and be merry.
19. See 55:26, 58:15, 76:24

5 Thou fool, this night thy soul shall be required of
thee.
20

6 Let your loins be girded about, and your lights
burning.
35

7 When thou art bidden of any man to a wedding, sit
not down in the highest room; lest a more honourable
man than thou be bidden of him;
And he that bade thee and him come and say to thee,
Give this man place; and thou begin with shame to
take the lowest room.
14:8

8 Friend, go up higher.
10

9 For whosoever exalteth himself shall be abased; and
he that humbleth himself shall be exalted.
11. See 67:23

10 They all with one consent began to make excuse…I
pray thee have me excused.
18

11 I have married a wife, and therefore I cannot come.
20

12 Go out quickly into the streets and lanes of the city,
and bring in hither the poor, and the maimed, and the
halt, and the blind.
21

13 Go out into the highways and hedges, and compel them
to come in.
23

14 For which of you, intending to build a tower, sitteth
not down first, and counteth the cost, whether he have
sufficient to finish it?
28

15 Leave the ninety and nine in the wilderness.
15:4

16 Rejoice with me; for I have found my sheep which
was lost.
6

17 Joy shall be in heaven over one sinner that repenteth,
more than over ninety and nine just persons, which
need no repentance.
7

18 The younger son gathered all together, and took his

journey into a far country, and there wasted his
substance with riotous living.
13

19 He would fain have filled his belly with the husks that
the swine did eat: and no man gave unto him.
And when he came to himself, he said, How many
hired servants of my father's have bread enough and to
spare, and I perish with hunger!
I will arise and go to my father, and will say unto him,
Father, I have sinned against heaven, and before thee,
And am no more worthy to be called thy son: make me
as one of thy hired servants.
16

20 Bring hither the fatted calf, and kill it.
23

21 This my son was dead, and is alive again; he was lost,
and is found.
24

22 Which hath devoured thy living with harlots.
30

23 I cannot dig; to beg I am ashamed.
16:3

24 Take thy bill, and sit down quickly, and write fifty.
6

25 And the Lord commended the unjust steward, because
he had done wisely: for the children of this world are
in their generation wiser than the children of light.
8

26 Make to yourselves friends of the mammon of
unrighteousness; that, when ye fail, they may receive
you into everlasting habitations.
9

27 He that is faithful in that which is least is faithful also
in much.
10

28 There was a certain rich man, which was clothed in
purple and fine linen, and fared sumptuously every
day:
And there was a certain beggar named Lazarus, which
was laid at his gate, full of sores,
And desiring to be fed with the crumbs which fell from
the rich man's table: moreover the dogs licked his
sores.
And it came to pass that the beggar died, and was
carried by the angels into Abraham's bosom.
19

29 Between us and you there is a great gulf fixed.
26

30 It were better for him that a millstone were hanged
about his neck, and he cast into the sea.
17:2

31 The kingdom of God is within you.
21

32 Remember Lot's wife.
32

33 Men ought always to pray, and not to faint.
18:1

34 God, I thank thee, that I am not as other men are.
11

35 God be merciful to me a sinner.
13

36 How hardly shall they that have riches enter into the

kingdom of God!
24

1 Out of thine own mouth will I judge thee...Thou
knewest that I was an austere man.
19:22

2 If these should hold their peace, the stones would
immediately cry out.
40

3 If thou hadst known, even thou, at least in this thy
day, the things which belong unto thy peace! but now
they are hid from thy eyes.
42

4 And when they heard it, they said, God forbid.
20:16

5 In your patience possess ye your souls.
21:19

6 He shall shew you a large upper room furnished.
22:12

7 I am among you as he that serveth.
27

8 Nevertheless, not my will, but thine, be done.
42

9 And the Lord turned, and looked upon Peter.
61

10 For if they do these things in a green tree, what shall
be done in the dry.
23:31

11 Father, forgive them: for they know not what they do.
34

12 Lord, remember me when thou comest into thy
kingdom.
42

13 To day shalt thou be with me in paradise.
43

14 Father, into thy hands I commend my spirit.
46. See 391:15

15 He was a good man, and a just.
50

16 Why seek ye the living among the dead?
24:5

17 Their words seemed to them as idle tales.
11

18 Did not our heart burn within us, while he talked with
us by the way?
32

19 He was known of them in breaking of bread.
35

20 A piece of a broiled fish, and of an honeycomb.
42

ST. JOHN

21 In the beginning was the Word, and the Word was
with God, and the Word was God.
1:1

22 All things were made by him; and without him was
not any thing made that was made.
3

23 And the light shineth in darkness; and the darkness
comprehended it not.
5

24 There was a man sent from God, whose name was
John.
6

25 He was not that Light, but was sent to bear witness of
that Light.
That was the true Light, which lighteth every man that
cometh into the world.
8

26 He was in the world, and the world was made by him,
and the world knew him not.
He came unto his own, and his own received him not.
10

27 And the Word was made flesh, and dwelt among us,
(and we beheld his glory, the glory as of the only
begotten of the Father,) full of grace and truth.
14

28 No man hath seen God at any time.
18. See 1 John 4:12

29 I baptize with water: but there standeth one among
you, whom ye know not;
He it is, who coming after me is preferred before me,
whose shoe's latchet I am not worthy to unloose.
26

30 Behold the Lamb of God, which taketh away the sin
of the world.
29

31 Can there any good thing come out of Nazareth?
46

32 Behold an Israelite indeed, in whom is no guile!
47

33 Woman, what have I to do with thee? mine hour is
not yet come.
2:4

34 Every man at the beginning doth set forth good wine;
and when men have well drunk, then that which is
worse: but thou hast kept the good wine until now.
10

35 When he had made a scourge of small cords, he drove
them all out of the temple.
15

36 The wind bloweth where it listeth, and thou hearest the
sound thereof, but canst not tell whence it cometh, and
whither it goeth.
3:8

37 How can these things be?
9

38 God so loved the world, that he gave his only begotten
Son, that whosoever believeth in him should not
perish, but have everlasting life.
16

39 Men loved darkness rather than light, because their
deeds were evil.
19

40 God is a Spirit: and they that worship him must
worship him in spirit and in truth.
4:24

41 They are white already to harvest.
35

42 Other men laboured, and ye are entered into their
labours.
38

43 Except ye see signs and wonders, ye will not believe.
48

1 Rise, take up thy bed, and walk.
5:8

2 He was a burning and a shining light.
35

3 Search the scriptures; for in them ye think ye have eternal life: and they are which testify of me.
39

4 What are they among so many?
6:9

5 Gather up the fragments that remain, that nothing be lost.
12

6 Him that cometh to me I will in no wise cast out.
37

7 Verily, verily, I say unto you, He that believeth on me hath everlasting life.
47

8 It is the spirit that quickeneth.
63

9 And the scribes and the Pharisees brought unto him a woman taken in adultery.
8:3

10 He that is without sin among you, let him first cast a stone at her.
7

11 Neither do I condemn thee: go, and sin no more.
11

12 And ye shall know the truth, and the truth shall make you free.
32

13 Ye are of your father the devil, and the lusts of your father ye will do. He was a murderer from the beginning, and abode not in the truth, because there is no truth in him. When he speaketh a lie, he speaketh of his own: for he is a liar, and the father of it.
44

14 The night cometh, when no man can work.
9:4

15 He is of age; ask him: he shall speak for himself.
21

16 One thing I know, that, whereas I was blind, now I see.
25

17 I am the door.
10:9

18 I am the good shepherd: the good shepherd giveth his life for the sheep.
11

19 The hireling fleeth, because he is an hireling, and careth not for the sheep.
13

20 Other sheep I have, which are not of this fold.
16

21 Though ye believe not me, believe the works.
38

22 I am the resurrection, and the life.
11:25

23 Jesus wept.
35

24 Ye know nothing at all,
Nor consider that it is expedient for us, that one man should die for the people, and that the whole nation perish not.
49

25 Why was not this ointment sold for three hundred pence, and given to the poor?
12:5

26 The poor always ye have with you.
8

27 Lord, dost thou wash my feet?
13:6

28 Now there was leaning on Jesus' bosom one of his disciples, whom Jesus loved.
23

29 That thou doest, do quickly.
27

30 Let not your heart be troubled: ye believe in God, believe also in me.
14:1

31 In my Father's house are many mansions...I go to prepare a place for you.
2

32 I am the way, the truth, and the life: no man cometh unto the Father, but by me.
6

33 Have I been so long time with you, and yet hast thou not known me, Philip?
9

34 Judas saith unto him, not Iscariot.
22

35 Peace I leave with you, my peace I give unto you: not as the world giveth, give I unto you.
27

36 Greater love hath no man than this, that a man lay down his life for his friends.
15:13

37 Ye have not chosen me, but I have chosen you.
16

38 It is expedient for you that I go away: for if I go not away, the Comforter will not come unto you.
16:7

39 I have yet many things to say unto you, but ye cannot bear them now.
12

40 A little while, and ye shall not see me: and again, a little while, and ye shall see me, because I go to the Father.
16

41 In the world ye shall have tribulation: but be of good cheer; I have overcome the world.
33

42 While I was with them in the world, I kept them in thy name: those that thou gavest me I have kept, and none of them is lost but the son of perdition.
17:12

43 Put up thy sword into the sheath.
18:11

44 Pilate saith unto him, What is truth?
38

45 Now Barabbas was a robber.
40

1   What I have written I have written.
19:22

2   Woman, behold thy son!...
Behold thy mother!
26

3   I thirst.
28

4   It is finished.
30

5   The first day of the week cometh Mary Magdalene
early, when it was yet dark, unto the sepulchre, and
seeth the stone taken away from the sepulchre.
20:1

6   So they ran both together: and the other disciple did
outrun Peter, and came first to the sepulchre.
4

7   They have taken away my Lord, and I know not where
they have laid him.
13

8   Jesus saith unto her, Woman, why weepest thou?
whom seekest thou? She supposing him to be the
gardener saith unto him, Sir, if thou have borne him
hence, tell me where thou hast laid him, and I will take
him away. [Mary Magdalene.]
15

9   Touch me not.
17. See 83:24

10   Except I shall see in his hands the print of the nails,
and put my finger into the print of the nails, and thrust
my hand into his side, I will not believe.
25

11   Be not faithless, but believing.
27

12   Thomas, because thou hast seen me, thou hast
believed: blessed are they that have not seen, and yet
have believed.
29

13   Simon Peter saith unto them, I go a fishing.
21:3

14   Simon, son of Jonas, lovest thou me more that
these?...Feed my lambs.
15

15   Feed my sheep.
16

16   Lord, thou knowest all things; thou knowest that I love
thee.
17

17   When thou wast young, thou girdedst thyself, and
walkedst whither thou wouldest: but when thou shalt
be old, thou shalt stretch forth thy hands, and another
shall gird thee, and carry thee whither thou wouldest
not.
18

18   Peter, turning about, seeth the disciple whom Jesus
loved following; which also leaned on his breast at
supper, and said Lord, which is he that betrayeth thee?
20

19   What shall this man do?
Jesus saith unto him, If I will that he tarry till I come,
what is that to thee?
21

ACTS OF THE APOSTLES

20   The former treatise have I made, O Theophilus, of all
that Jesus began both to do and teach,
Until the day in which he was taken up.
1:1

21   Ye men of Galilee, why stand ye gazing up into
heaven?
11

22   And suddenly there came a sound from heaven as of a
rushing mighty wind, and it filled all the house where
they were sitting.
And there appeared unto them cloven tongues like as
of fire.
2:2

23   Parthians, and Medes, and Elamites, and the dwellers
in Mesopotamia, and in Judaea, and Cappadocia, in
Pontus, and Asia.
Phrygia, and Pamphylia, in Egypt, and in the parts of
Libya about Cyrene, and strangers of Rome, Jews and
proselytes,
Cretes and Arabians, we do hear them speak in our
tongues the wonderful works of God.
9

24   And all that believed were together, and had all things
common.
44

25   Silver and gold have I none; but such as I have give I
thee.
3:6

26   Walking, and leaping, and praising God
8

27   It is not reason that we should leave the word of God,
and serve tables.
6:2

28   The witnesses laid down their clothes at a young
man's feet, whose name was Saul.
7:58

29   Saul was consenting unto his death.
8:1

30   Thy money perish with thee, because thou hast
thought that the gift of God may be purchased with
money.
20

31   Thou hast neither part nor lot in this matter.
21

32   Breathing out threatenings and slaughter.
9:1

33   Saul, Saul, why persecutest thou me?
4

34   It is hard for thee to kick against the pricks.
5

35   The street which is called Straight.
11

36   Dorcas: this woman was full of good works.
36

37   He fell into a trance,
And saw heaven opened, and a certain vessel
descending unto him, as it had been a great sheet knit
at the four corners, and let down to the earth:
Wherein were all manner of four-footed beasts of the
earth, and wild beasts, and creeping things, and fowls

of the air.
10:10

1 What God hath cleansed, that call not thou common.
15

2 God is no respecter of persons.
34. See 74:34

3 He was eaten of worms, and gave up the ghost. [Herod Agrippa I.]
23

4 The gods are come down to us in the likeness of men.
14:11

5 We also are men of like passions with you.
15

6 Come over into Macedonia, and help us.
16:9

7 What must I do to be saved?
30

8 The Jews which believed not, moved with envy, took unto them certain lewd fellows of the baser sort, and gathered a company, and set all the city on an uproar.
17:5

9 Those that have turned the world upside down are come hither also;
Whom Jason hath received: and these all do contrary to the decrees of Caesar, saying that there is another king, one Jesus.
6

10 What will this babbler say?
18

11 For all the Athenians and strangers which were there spent their time in nothing else, but either to tell, or to hear some new thing.
21

12 Ye men of Athens, I perceive that in all things ye are too superstitious.
For as I passed by, and beheld your devotions, I found an altar with this inscription, TO THE UNKNOWN GOD. Whom therefore ye ignorantly worship, him declare I unto you.
22

13 God that made the world and all things therein, seeing that he is Lord of Heaven and earth, dwelleth not in temples made with hands.
24

14 For in him we live, and move, and have our being.
28

15 Gallio cared for none of those things.
18:17

16 We have not so much as heard whether there be any Holy Ghost.
19:2

17 All with one voice about the space of two hours cried out, Great is Diana of the Ephesians.
34

18 I go bound in the spirit unto Jerusalem.
20:22

19 It is more blessed to give than to receive.
35

20 But Paul said, I am a man which am a Jew of Tarsus, a city in Cilicia, a citizen of no mean city.
21:39

21 And the chief captain answered, With a great sum

obtained I this freedom. And Paul said, But I was free born.
22:28

22 A conscience void of offence toward God, and toward men.
24:16

23 I appeal unto Caesar.
25:11

24 Hast thou appealed unto Caesar? unto Caesar shalt thou go.
12

25 Paul, thou art beside thyself; much learning doth make thee mad.
26:24

26 For this thing was not done in a corner.
26

27 Almost thou persuadest me to be a Christian.
28

28 I would to God, that not only thou, but also all that hear me this day, were both almost, and altogether such as I am, except these bonds.
29

ROMANS

29 Without ceasing I make mention of you always in my prayers.
1:9

30 I am debtor both to the Greeks, and to the Barbarians; both to the wise, and to the unwise.
14

31 The just shall live by faith.
17

32 Worshipped and served the creature more than the Creator.
25

33 Patient continuance in well doing.
2:7

34 For there is no respect of persons with God.
11. See 74:2

35 These...are a law unto themselves.
14

36 Let God be true, but every man a liar.
3:4

37 Let us do evil, that good may come.
8

38 For all have sinned, and come short of the glory of God.
23

39 For where no law is, there is no transgression.
4:15

40 Who against hope believed in hope, that he might become the father of many nations. [Abraham.]
18

41 Hope maketh not ashamed; because the love of God is shed abroad in our hearts by the Holy Ghost which is given unto us.
5:5

42 Where sin abounded, grace did much more abound.
20

43 Shall we continue in sin, that grace may abound? God forbid. How shall we, that are dead to sin, live

any longer in sin?
6:1

1 We also should walk in newness of life.
4

2 Christ being raised from the dead dieth no more; death
   hath no more dominion over him.
   For in that he died, he died unto sin once: but in that
   he liveth, he liveth unto God.
   9

3 The wages of sin is death.
   23

4 Is the law sin? God forbid. Nay, I had not known sin,
   but by the law.
   7:7

5 For the good that I would I do not: but the evil which
   I would not, that I do.
   19. See 366:17

6 O wretched man that I am! who shall deliver me from
   the body of this death?
   24

7 They that are after the flesh do mind the things of the
   flesh; but they that are after the Spirit the things of the
   Spirit.
   For to be carnally minded is death.
   8:5

8 For ye have not received the spirit of bondage again to
   fear; but ye have received the Spirit of adoption,
   whereby we cry, Abba, Father.
   15

9 We are the children of God:
   And if the children, then heirs; heirs of God, and
   joint-heirs with Christ.
   16

10 For we know that the whole creation groaneth and
   travaileth in pain together until now.
   22

11 All things work for good to them that love God.
   28

12 If God be for us, who can be against us?
   31

13 For I am persuaded, that neither death, nor life, nor
   angels, nor principalities, nor powers, nor things
   present, nor things to come,
   Nor height, nor depth, nor any other creature, shall be
   able to separate us from the love of God, which is in
   Christ Jesus our Lord.
   38

14 Shall the thing formed say to him that formed it, Why
   hast thou made me thus?
   Hath not the potter power over the clay, of the same
   lump to make one vessel unto honour, and another
   unto dishonour?
   9:20

15 I beseech you therefore, brethren, by the mercies of
   God, that ye present your bodies a living sacrifice,
   holy, acceptable unto God.
   12:1

16 Rejoice with them that do rejoice, and weep with them
   that weep.
   15

17 Mind not high things, but condescend to men of low

estate. Be not wise in you own conceits.
16

18 Vengeance is mine; I will repay, saith the Lord.
   19

19 Be not overcome of evil, but overcome evil with
   good.
   21

20 Let every soul be subject unto the higher powers...the
   powers that be are ordained of God.
   13:1

21 For rulers are not a terror to good works, but to the
   evil.
   3

22 Render therefore to all their dues: tribute to whom
   tribute is due; custom to whom custom; fear to whom
   fear; honour to whom honour.
   Owe no man anything, but to love one another: for he
   that loveth another hath fulfilled the law.
   7

23 Love is the fulfilling of the law.
   10

24 Now it is high time to awake out of sleep: for now is
   our salvation nearer than when we believed.
   The night is far spent, the day is at hand: let us
   therefore cast off the works of darkness, and let us put
   on the armour of light.
   11

25 Make not provision for the flesh, to fulfil the lusts
   thereof.
   14

26 Doubtful disputations.
   14:1

27 Let every man be fully persuaded in his own mind.
   5

28 Salute one another with an holy kiss.
   16:16

1 CORINTHIANS

29 The foolishness of preaching to save them that
   believe.
   1:21

30 God hath chosen the foolish things of the world to
   confound the wise; and God hath chosen the weak
   things of the world to confound the things which are
   mighty.
   27

31 I have planted, Apollos watered; but God gave the
   increase.
   3:6

32 Stewards of the mysteries of God.
   4:1

33 A spectacle unto the world, and to angels.
   9

34 Absent in body, but present in spirit.
   5:3

35 Know ye not that a little leaven leaveneth the whole
   lump?
   6

36 Christ our passover is sacrificed for us:
   Therefore let us keep the feast, not with the old
   leaven, neither with the leaven of malice and
   wickedness; but with the unleavened bread of sincerity

and truth.
7

1 Your body is the temple of the Holy Ghost.
6:19

2 It is better to marry than to burn.
7:9

3 The unbelieving husband is sanctified by the wife.
14

4 The fashion of this world passeth away.
31

5 Knowledge puffeth up, but charity edifieth.
8:1

6 Who goeth a warfare any time at his own charges? who planteth a vineyard, and eateth not of the fruit thereof?
9:7

7 I am made all things to all men.
22

8 Know ye not that they which run in a race run all, but one receiveth the prize?
24

9 Now they do it to obtain a corruptible crown; but we an incorruptible.
I therefore so run, not as uncertainly; so fight I, not as one that beateth the air:
But I keep under my body, and bring it into subjection: lest that by any means, when I have preached to others, I myself should be a castaway.
25

10 All things are lawful for me, but all things are not expedient.
10:23

11 For the earth is the Lord's, and the fulness thereof.
26. See Ps. 24:1

12 Doth not even nature itself teach you, that, if, a man have long hair, it is a shame unto him?
But if a woman have long hair, it is a glory to her.
11:14

13 Now there are diversities of gifts, but the same Spirit.
12:4

14 Though I speak with the tongues of men and of angels, and have not charity, I am become as sounding brass, or a tinkling cymbal.
And though I have the gift of prophecy, and understand all mysteries, and all knowledge; and though I have all faith, so that I could remove mountains, and have not charity, I am nothing.
And though I bestow all my goods to feed the poor, and though I give my body to be burned, and have not charity, it profiteth me nothing.
Charity suffereth long, and is kind; charity envieth not; charity vaunteth not itself, is not puffed up,
Doth not behave itself unseemly, seeketh not her own, is not easily provoked, thinketh no evil;
Rejoiceth not in iniquity, but rejoiceth in the truth;
Beareth all things, believeth all things, hopeth all things, endureth all things.
Charity never faileth: but whether there be prophecies, they shall fail; whether there be tongues, they shall cease; whether there be knowledge, it shall vanish away.
For we know in part, and we prophesy in part.
But when that which is perfect is come, then that

which is in part shall be done away.
When I was a child, I spake as a child, I understood as a child, I thought as a child: but when I became a man, I put away childish things.
For now we see through a glass, darkly; but then face to face: now I know in part; but then shall I know even as also I am known.
And now abideth faith, hope, charity, these three; but the greatest of these is charity.
13:1

15 If the trumpet give an uncertain sound, who shall prepare himself to the battle?
14:8

16 Let your women keep silence in the churches: for it is not permitted unto them to speak.
34

17 If they will learn any thing, let them ask their husbands at home: for it is a shame for women to speak in the church.
35

18 Let all things be done decently and in order.
40

19 Last of all he was seen of me also, as of one born out of due time.
For I am the least of the apostles, that am not meet to be called an apostle, because I persecuted the church of God.
But by the grace of God I am what I am.
15:8

20 I laboured more abundantly than they all: yet not I, but the grace of God which was with me
10

21 If in this life only we have hope in Christ, we are of all men most miserable.
19

22 But now is Christ risen from the dead, and become the firstfruits of them that slept.
For since by man came death, by man came also the resurrection of the dead.
For as in Adam all die, even so in Christ shall all be made alive.
20

23 The last enemy that shall be destroyed is death.
26

24 If after the manner of men I have fought with beasts at Ephesus, what advantageth it me, if the dead rise not? let us eat and drink; for to morrow we die.
32. See 55:26, 58:15, 70:4

25 Evil communications corrupt good manners.
33

26 One star differeth from another star in glory.
41

27 So also is the resurrection of the dead. It is sown in corruption; it is raised in incorruption.
42

28 The first man is of the earth, earthy.
47

29 Behold, I shew you a mystery; We shall not all sleep, but we shall all be changed,
In a moment, in the twinkling of an eye, at the last trump: for the trumpet shall sound, and the dead shall be raised incorruptible, and we shall be changed.
For this corruptible must put on incorruption, and this

mortal must put on immortality.
51

1 O death, where is thy sting? O grave, where is thy victory?
55

2 Quit you like men, be strong.
16:13

3 Let him be Anathema Maran-atha.
22

2 CORINTHIANS

4 Our sufficiency is of God;
Who also hath made us able ministers of the new testament; not of the letter, but of the spirit: for the letter killeth, but the spirit giveth life.
3:5

5 We have this treasure in earthen vessels.
4:7

6 We know that if our earthly tabernacle of this house were dissolved, we have a building of God, an house not made with hands, eternal in the heavens.
5:1

7 Now is the accepted time.
6:2

8 As having nothing, and yet possessing all things.
10

9 God loveth a cheerful giver.
9:7

10 For ye suffer fools gladly, seeing ye yourselves are wise.
19

11 Are they Hebrews? so am I. Are they Israelites? so am I. Are they the seed of Abraham? so am I.
Are they ministers of Christ? (I speak as a fool) I am more.
11:22

12 Of the Jews five times received I forty stripes save one.
Thrice was I beaten with rods, once was I stoned, thrice I suffered shipwreck, a night and a day have I been in the deep;
In journeyings often, in perils of waters, in perils of robbers, in perils by mine own countrymen, in perils by the heathen, in perils of the city, in perils in the wilderness, in perils in the sea, in perils among false brethren;
In weariness and painfulness, in watchings often, in hunger and thirst, in fastings often, in cold and nakedness.
Beside those things that are without, that which cometh upon me daily, the care of all the churches.
24

13 There was given to me a thorn in the flesh, the messenger of Satan to buffet me.
12:7

14 My strength is made perfect in weakness.
9

GALATIANS

15 The right hands of fellowship.
2:9

16 It is written, that Abraham had two sons, the one by a

bondmaid, the other by a freewoman.
But he who was of the bondwoman was born after the flesh; but he of the freewoman was by promise.
Which things are an allegory.
4:22

17 Ye are fallen from grace.
5:4

18 But the fruit of the Spirit is love, joy, peace, longsuffering, gentleness, goodness, faith,
Meekness, temperance.
22

19 Be not deceived; God is not mocked: for whatsoever a man soweth, that shall he also reap.
6:7

20 Let us not be weary in well doing: for in due season we shall reap, if we faint not.
9. See 2 Thess. 3:13

21 Ye see how large a letter I have written unto you with mine own hand.
11

EPHESIANS

22 Christ came and preached peace to you which were afar off, and to them that were nigh.
2:17

23 Unto me, who am less than the least of all saints, is this grace given, that I should preach among the Gentiles the unsearchable riches of Christ.
3:8

24 I bow my knees unto the Father of our Lord Jesus Christ,
Of whom the whole family in heaven and earth is named,
That he would grant you, according to the riches of his glory, to be strengthened with might by his Spirit in the inner man.
14

25 The love of Christ, which passeth knowledge.
19

26 Now unto him that is able to do exceeding abundantly above all that we ask or think, according to the power that worketh in us,
Unto him be glory in the church by Christ Jesus throughout all ages, world without end. Amen.
20

27 I therefore, the prisoner of the Lord, beseech you that ye walk worthy of the vocation wherewith ye are called.
4:1

28 He gave some, apostles; and some, prophets; and some, evangelists; and some, pastors and teachers;
For the perfecting of the saints, for the work of the ministry, for the edifying of the body of Christ:
Till we all come in the unity of the faith, and of the knowledge of the Son of God, unto a perfect man, unto the measure of the stature of the fulness of Christ:
That we henceforth be no more carried about with every wind of doctrine, by the sleight of men, and cunning craftiness, whereby they lie in wait to deceive.
11

29 We are members one of another.
25

1 Be ye angry and sin not: let not the sun go down upon your wrath.
26

2 Fornication, and all uncleanness, or covetousness, let it not once be named among you, as becometh saints; Neither filthiness, nor foolish talking, nor jesting, which are not convenient.
5:3

3 Let no man deceive you with vain words: for because of these things cometh the wrath of God upon the children of disobedience.
6

4 See then that ye walk circumspectly, not as fools, but as wise,
Redeeming the time, because the days are evil.
15

5 Be not drunk with wine, wherein is excess; but be filled with the Spirit;
Speaking to yourselves in psalms and hymns and spiritual songs, singing and making melody in your heart to the Lord.
18

6 Wives, submit yourselves to your own husbands, as unto the Lord.
22

7 Ye fathers, provoke not your children to wrath.
6:4

8 Not with eyeservice, as menpleasers.
6

9 Put on the whole armour of God.
11

10 For we wrestle not against flesh and blood, but against principalities, against powers, against the rulers of the darkness of this world, against spiritual wickedness in high places.
Wherefore take unto you the whole armour of God, that ye may be able to withstand in the evil day, and having done all, to stand.
Stand therefore, having your loins girt about with truth, and having on the breastplate of righteousness;
And your feet shod with the preparation of the gospel of peace;
Above all, taking the shield of faith, wherewith ye shall be able to quench all the fiery darts of the wicked.
12

PHILIPPIANS

11 For me to live is Christ, and to die is gain.
1:21

12 Having a desire to depart, and to be with Christ; which is far better.
23

13 Let this mind be in you, which was also in Christ Jesus:
Who, being in the form of God, thought it not robbery to be equal with God:
But made himself of no reputation, and took upon him the form of a servant and was made in the likeness of men.
2:5

14 God hath also highly exalted him, and given him a name which is above every name:

That at the name of Jesus every knee should bow, of things in heaven, and things in earth, and things under the earth.
9

15 Work out your own salvation with fear and trembling.
12

16 If any other man thinketh that he hath whereof he might trust in the flesh, I more:
Circumcised the eighth day, of the stock of Israel, of the tribe of Benjamin, an Hebrew of the Hebrews; as touching the law, a Pharisee.
3:4

17 But what things were gain to me, those I counted loss for Christ.
7

18 Forgetting those things which are behind, and reaching forth unto those things which are before,
I press toward the mark.
13

19 Whose God is their belly, and whose glory is their shame.
19

20 Rejoice in the Lord alway: and again I say, Rejoice.
4:4

21 The peace of God, which passeth all understanding, shall keep your hearts and minds through Christ Jesus.
7

22 Whatsoever things are true, whatsoever things are honest, whatsoever things are just, whatsoever things are pure, whatsoever things are lovely, whatsoever things are of good report; if there be any virtue and if there be any praise, think on these things.
8

23 I can do all things through Christ which strengtheneth me.
13

COLOSSIANS

24 Touch not; taste not; handle not.
2:21

25 Set your affection on things above, not on things on the earth.
3:2

26 Ye have put off the old man with his deeds:
And have put on the new man, which is renewed in knowledge after the image of him that created him:
Where there is neither Greek nor Jew, circumcision nor uncircumcision, Barbarian, Scythian, bond nor free: but Christ is all, and in all.
9

27 Husbands, love your wives, and be not bitter against them.
19

28 Let your speech be alway with grace, seasoned with salt.
4:6

29 Luke, the beloved physician, and Demas, greet you.
14

1 THESSALONIANS

30 We give thanks to God always for you all, making mention of you in our prayers;

Remembering without ceasing your work of faith and labour of love, and patience of hope in our Lord Jesus Christ.
1:2

1 Study to be quiet, and to do your own business.
4:11

2 But let us, who are of the day, be sober, putting on the breastplate of faith and love; and for an helmet, the hope of salvation.
5:8

3 Pray without ceasing.
17

4 Prove all things; hold fast that which is good.
21

2 THESSALONIANS

5 If any would not work, neither should he eat.
3:10

1 TIMOTHY

6 Fables and endless genealogies.
1:4

7 I did it ignorantly in unbelief.
13

8 Sinners; of whom I am chief.
15

9 Let the woman learn in silence with all subjection. But I suffer not a woman to teach, nor to usurp authority over the man, but to be in silence.
2:11

10 And Adam was not deceived, but the woman being deceived was in the transgression.
14

11 If a man desire the office of a bishop, he desireth a good work.
3:1

12 A bishop then must be blameless, the husband of one wife, vigilant, sober, of good behaviour, given to hospitality, apt to teach;
Not given to wine, no striker, not greedy of filthy lucre; but patient, not a brawler, not covetous.
2

13 Giving heed to seducing spirits, and doctrines of devils.
4:1

14 Refuse profane and old wives' fables, and exercise thyself rather unto godliness.
7

15 But the younger widows refuse: for when they have begun to wax wanton against Christ, they will marry;
Having damnation, because they have cast off their first faith.
5:11

16 Drink no longer water, but use a little wine for thy stomach's sake and thine often infirmities.
23

17 For we brought nothing into this world, and it is certain we can carry nothing out.
6:7

18 The love of money is the root of all evil.
10

19 Fight the good fight of faith, lay hold on eternal life.
12

20 Rich in good works.
18

21 Science falsely so called.
20

2 TIMOTHY

22 For God hath not given us the spirit of fear; but of power, and of love, and of a sound mind.
1:7

23 Hold fast the form of sound words.
13

24 Silly women laden with sins, led away with divers lusts.
3:6

25 Be instant in season, out of season.
4:2

26 I have fought a good fight, I have finished my course, I have kept the faith.
7

TITUS

27 Unto the pure all things are pure.
1:15

HEBREWS

28 God, who at sundry times and in divers manners spake in time past unto the fathers by the prophets,
Hath in these last days spoken unto us by his Son, whom he hath appointed heir of all things, by whom he also made the worlds:
Who being the brightness of his glory, and the express image of his person, and upholding all things by the word of his power, when he had by himself purged our sins, sat down on the right hand of the Majesty on high.
1:1

29 Without shedding of blood is no remission.
9:22

30 It is a fearful thing to fall into the hands of the living God.
10:31

31 Faith is the substance of things hoped for, the evidence of things not seen.
11:1

32 For he looked for a city which hath foundations, whose maker and builder is God.
10

33 These all died in faith, not having received the promises, but having seen them afar off, and were persuaded of them, and embraced them, and confessed that they were strangers and pilgrims on the earth.
13

34 Of whom the world was not worthy.
38

35 Wherefore seeing we also are compassed about with so great a cloud of witnesses, let us lay aside every weight, and the sin which doth so easily beset us, and let us run with patience the race that is set before us,
Looking unto Jesus the author and finisher of our

faith; who for the joy that was set before him endured the cross, despising the shame, and is set down at the right hand of God.
12:1

1 Whom the Lord loveth he chasteneth.
6

2 The spirits of just men made perfect.
23

3 Let brotherly love continue.
Be not forgetful to entertain strangers: for thereby some have entertained angels unawares.
13:1

4 Jesus Christ the same yesterday, and to day, and for ever.
8

5 For here have we no continuing city, but we seek one to come.
14

6 To do good and to communicate forget not.
16

JAMES

7 Let patience have her perfect work.
1:4

8 Blessed is the man that endureth temptation: for when he is tried, he shall receive the crown of life.
12

9 Every good gift and every perfect gift is from above, and cometh down from the Father of lights, with whom is no variableness, neither shadow of turning.
.17

10 Be swift to hear, slow to speak, slow to wrath:
For the wrath of man worketh not the righteousness of God.
Wherefore lay apart all filthiness and superfluity of naughtiness, and receive with meekness the engrafted word, which is able to save your souls,
But be ye doers of the word, and not hearers only, deceiving your own selves.
For if any be a hearer of the word, and not a doer, he is like unto a man beholding his natural face in a glass:
For he beholdeth himself, and goeth his way, and straightway forgetteth what manner of man he was.
19

11 If any man among you seem to be religious, and bridleth not his tongue, but deceiveth his own heart, this man's religion is vain.
Pure religion and undefiled before God and the Father is this, To visit the fatherless and widows in their affliction, and to keep himself unspotted from the world.
26

12 Faith without works is dead.
2:20

13 How great a matter a little fire kindleth.
3:5

14 The tongue can no man tame; it is an unruly evil.
8

15 Doth a fountain send forth at the same place sweet water and bitter?
11

16 For what is your life? It is even a vapour, that

appeareth for a little time, and then vanisheth away.
4:14

17 Ye have heard of the patience of Job.
5:11

18 Let your yea be yea; and your nay, nay.
12

19 The effectual fervent prayer of a righteous man availeth much.
16

1 PETER

20 Jesus Christ:
Whom having not seen, ye love; in whom, though now ye see him not, yet believing, ye rejoice with joy unspeakable and full of glory.
1:7

21 All flesh is as grass, and all the glory of man as the flower of grass. The grass withereth, and the flower thereof falleth away.
24. See 59:6

22 As newborn babes, desire the sincere milk of the word, that ye may grow thereby:
If so be ye have tasted that the Lord is gracious.
2:2

23 But ye are a chosen generation, a royal priesthood, an holy nation, a peculiar people.
9

24 Abstain from fleshly lusts, which war against the soul.
11

25 Honour all men. Love the brotherhood. Fear God. Honour the king.
17

26 For what glory is it, if, when ye be buffeted for your faults, ye shall take it patiently? but if, when ye do well, and suffer for it, ye take it patiently, this is acceptable with God.
20

27 Ye were as sheep going astray; but are now returned unto the Shepherd and Bishop of your souls.
25

28 Ornament of a meek and quiet spirit.
3:4

29 Giving honour unto the wife, as unto the weaker vessel.
7

30 Not rendering evil for evil, or railing for railing: but contrariwise blessing.
9

31 The end of all things is at hand.
4:7

32 Charity shall cover the multitude of sins.
8

33 Be sober, be vigilant; because your adversary the devil, as a roaring lion, walketh about, seeking whom he may devour.
5:8

2 PETER

34 And the day star arise in your hearts.
1:19

1 Not afraid to speak evil of dignities.
2:10

2 The dog is turned to his own vomit again.
22

1 JOHN

3 If we say that we have no sin, we deceive ourselves, and the truth is not in us.
1:8

4 But whoso hath this world's good, and seeth his brother have need, and shutteth up his bowels of compassion from him, how dwelleth the love of God in him?
3:17

5 He that loveth not knoweth not God; for God is love.
4:8

6 There is no fear in love; but perfect love casteth out fear.
18

7 If a man say, I love God, and hateth his brother, he is a liar: for he that loveth not his brother whom he hath seen, how can he love God whom he hath not seen?
20

3 JOHN

8 He that doeth good is of God: but he that doeth evil hath not seen God.
11

REVELATION

9 John to the seven churches which are in Asia: Grace be unto you, and peace, from him which is, and which was, and which is to come.
1:4

10 Behold, he cometh with clouds; and every eye shall see him, and they also which pierced him: and all kindreds of the earth shall wail because of him. Even so, Amen.
I am Alpha and Omega, the beginning and the ending, saith the Lord.
7

11 I was in the Spirit on the Lord's day, and heard behind me a great voice as of a trumpet.
10

12 What thou seest, write in a book, and send it unto the seven churches which are in Asia.
11

13 Being turned, I saw seven golden candlesticks.
12

14 His head and his hairs were white like wool, as white as snow; and his eyes were as a flame of fire;
And his feet like unto fine brass, as if they burned in a furnace; and his voice as the sound of many waters.
And he had in his right hand seven stars: and out of his mouth went a sharp twoedged sword: and his countenance was as the sun shineth in his strength.
And when I saw him, I fell at his feet as dead.
14

15 I am he that liveth, and was dead; and, behold, I am alive for evermore, Amen; and have the keys of hell and of death.
18

16 I have somewhat against thee, because thou hast left thy first love.
2:4

17 Be thou faithful unto death, and I will give thee a crown of life.
10

18 I will not blot out his name out of the book of life.
3:5

19 I will write upon him my new name.
12

20 I know thy works, that thou art neither cold nor hot: I would thou wert cold or hot.
So then because thou art lukewarm, and neither cold nor hot, I will spue thee out of my mouth.
15

21 Behold, I stand at the door, and knock.
20

22 And he that sat was to look upon like a jasper and a sardine stone: and there was a rainbow round about the throne, in sight like unto an emerald.
4:3

23 And before the throne there was a sea of glass like unto crystal: and in the midst of the throne, and round about the throne, were four beasts full of eyes before and behind.
6

24 They were full of eyes within: and they rest not day and night, saying, Holy, holy, holy, Lord God Almighty, which was, and is, and is to come.
8

25 Thou hast created all things, and for thy pleasure they are and were created.
11

26 Who is worthy to open the book, and to loose the seals thereof?
5:2

27 The four beasts and four and twenty elders fell down before the Lamb, having every one of them harps, and golden vials full of odours, which are the prayers of saints.
8

28 He went forth conquering, and to conquer.
6:2

29 And I looked, and behold a pale horse: and his name that sat on him was Death.
8

30 The kings of the earth, and the great men, and the rich men, and the chief captains, and the mighty men, and every bondman, and every free man, hid themselves in the dens and in the rocks of the mountains;
And said to the mountains and rocks, Fall on us, and hide us from the face of him that sitteth upon the throne, and from the wrath of the Lamb:
For the great day of his wrath is come; and who shall be able to stand?
15

31 A great multitude, which no man could number, of all nations, and kindreds, and people, and tongues, stood before the throne, and before the Lamb.
7:9

32 And all the angels stood round about the throne, and about the elders and the four beasts, and fell before the

throne on their faces, and worshipped God.
11

1 And one of the elders answered, saying unto me, What are these which are arrayed in white robes? and whence came they?
13

2 These are they which came out of great tribulation, and have washed their robes, and made them white in the blood of the Lamb.
14

3 They shall hunger no more, neither thirst any more; neither shall the sun light on them, nor any heat.
16

4 God shall wipe away all tears from their eyes.
17

5 And when he had opened the seventh seal, there was silence in heaven about the space of half an hour.
8:1

6 And the name of the star is called Wormwood.
11

7 And in those days shall men seek death, and shall not find it; and shall desire to die, and death shall flee from them.
9:6

8 And there were stings in their tails.
10

9 It was in my mouth sweet as honey: and as soon as I had eaten it, my belly was bitter.
10:10

10 And there appeared a great wonder in heaven; a woman clothed with the sun, and the moon under her feet, and upon her head a crown of twelve stars.
12:1

11 And there was war in heaven: Michael and his angels fought against the dragon; and the dragon fought and his angels.
7

12 Who is like unto the beast? who is able to make war with him?
13:4

13 And that no man might buy or sell, save he that had the mark, or the name of the beast, or the number of his name.
17

14 Let him that hath understanding count the number of the beast: for it is the number of a man; and his number is Six hundred threescore and six.
18

15 And I heard a voice from heaven, as the voice of many waters, and as the voice of a great thunder: and I heard the voice of harpers harping with their harps:
And they sung as it were a new song...and no man could learn that song but the hundred and forty and four thousand, which were redeemed from the earth.
14:2

16 Babylon is fallen, is fallen, that great city.
8

17 And the smoke of their torment ascendeth up for ever and ever: and they have no rest day or night, who worship the beast and his image.
11

18 Blessed are the dead which die in the Lord from

henceforth: Yea, saith the Spirit, that they may rest from their labours; and their works do follow them.
13

19 And I saw as it were a sea of glass mingled with fire.
15:2

20 Behold, I come as a thief.
16:15

21 And he gathered them together into a place called in the Hebrew tongue Armageddon.
16

22 I will shew unto thee the judgment of the great whore that sitteth upon many waters.
17:1

23 MYSTERY, BABYLON THE GREAT, THE MOTHER OF HARLOTS AND ABOMINATIONS OF THE EARTH.
5

24 And a mighty angel took up a stone like a great millstone, and cast it into the sea, saying, Thus with violence shall that great city Babylon be thrown down, and shall be found no more at all.
18:21

25 And I saw heaven opened, and behold a white horse; and he that sat upon him was called Faithful and True.
19:11

26 And he hath on his vesture and on his thigh a name written, KING OF KINGS, AND LORD OF LORDS.
16

27 And he laid hold on the dragon, that old serpent, which is the Devil, and Satan, and bound him a thousand years.
20:2

28 And I saw a great white throne.
11

29 And the sea gave up the dead which were in it; and death and hell delivered up the dead which were in them: and they were judged every man according to their works.
13

30 And I saw a new heaven and a new earth: for the first heaven and the first earth were passed away; and there was no more sea.
And I John saw the holy city, new Jerusalem, coming down from God out of heaven, prepared as a bride adorned for her husband.
21:1

31 And God shall wipe away all tears from their eyes; and there shall be no more death, neither sorrow, nor crying, neither shall there be any more pain: for the former things are passed away.
And he that sat upon the throne said, Behold, I make all things new. And he said unto me, Write: for these words are true and faithful.
4

32 I will give unto him that is athirst of the fountain of the water of life freely.
6

33 The street of the city was pure gold.
21

34 And the gates of it shall not be shut at all by day: for there shall be no night there.
25

35 And he shewed me a pure river of water of life, clear

as crystal, proceeding out of the throne of God and of the Lamb.
22:1

1 And the leaves of the tree were for the healing of the nations.
2

2 And, behold, I come quickly.
12

3 For without are dogs, and sorcerers, and whoremongers, and murderers, and idolaters, and whosoever loveth and maketh a lie.
15

4 Amen. Even so, come, Lord Jesus.
20

VULGATE

5 *Dominus illuminatio mea, et salus mea, quem timebo?*
The Lord is the source of my light and my safety, so whom shall I fear?
Psalm 26:1. See 391:7

6 *Asperges me hyssopo, et mundabor; lavabis me, et super nivem dealbabor.*
You will sprinkle me with hyssop, and I shall be made clean; you will wash me and I shall be made whiter than snow.
50:9 (A.V. Psalm 51:7)

7 *Cantate Domino canticum novum, quia mirabilia fecit.*
Sing to the Lord a new song, because he has done marvellous things.
97:1. See 396:7

8 *Jubilate Deo, omnis terra; servite Domino in laetitia.*
Sing joyfully to God, all the earth; serve the Lord with gladness.
99:2. See 396:11

9 *Beatus vir qui timet Dominum, in mandatis ejus volet nimis!*
Happy is the man who fears the Lord, who is only too willing to follow his orders.
111:1 (A.V. Psalm 112:1)

10 *Non nobis, Domine, non nobis; sed nomini tuo da gloriam.*
Not unto us, Lord, not unto us; but to thy name give glory.
113:(9). See 397:17

11 *Laudate Dominum, omnes gentes; laudate eum, omnes populi.*
Praise the Lord, all nations; praise him, all people.
116:1 (A.V. Psalm 117:1)

12 *Nisi Dominus aedificaverit domum, in vanum laboraverunt qui aedificant eam.*
Nisi Dominus custodierit civitatem, frustra vigilat qui custodit eam.
Unless the Lord has built the house, its builders have laboured in vain. Unless the Lord guards the city, it's no use its guard staying awake.
126:1. See 398:18 [Shortened to *Nisi Dominus frustra* as the motto of the city of Edinburgh.]

13 *De profundis clamavi ad te, Domine;*
Domine, exaudi vocem meam.
Up from the depths I have cried to thee, Lord; Lord, hear my voice.
129:1. See 398:23

14 *Vanitas vanitatum, dixit Ecclesiastes; vanitas vanitatum, et omnia vanitas.*
Vanity of vanities, said the preacher; vanity of vanities, and everything is vanity.
Ecclesiastes 1:2. See 55:5

15 *Rorate, coeli, desuper, et nubes pluant Justum; aperiatur terra, et germinet Salvatorem.*
Drop down dew, heavens, from above, and let the clouds rain down righteousness; let the earth be opened, and a saviour spring to life.
Is. 45:8

16 *Benedicite, omnia opera Domini, Domino; laudate et superexaltate eum in secula.*
Bless the Lord, all the works of the Lord; praise him and exalt him above all things for ever.
Dan. 3:57. See 384:19

17 *Magnificat anima mea Dominum;*
Et exsultavit spiritus meus in Deo salutari meo.
My soul doth magnify the Lord: and my spirit hath rejoiced in God my Saviour. [Tr. Book of Common Prayer]
Ev. S. Luc. 1:46

18 *Esurientes implevit bonis, et divites dimisit inanes.*
He hath filled the hungry with good things: and the rich he hath sent empty away. [Tr. Book of Common Prayer]
53

19 *Nunc dimittis servum tuum, Domine, secundum verbum tuum in pace.*
Lord, now lettest thou thy servant depart in peace: according to thy word. [Tr. Book of Common Prayer]
2:29

20 *Pax Vobis.*
Peace be unto you.
24:36

21 *Quo vadis?*
Where are you going?
Ev. S. Joann. 16:5

22 *Ecce homo.*
Behold the man.
19:5

23 *Consummatum est.*
It is achieved.
30

24 *Noli me tangere.*
Do not touch me.
20:17. See 73:9

25 *Sicut modo geniti infantes, rationabile, sine dolo lac concupiscite.*
After the fashion of newborn babes, desire the sincere milk of the word.
1 Pet. 2:2

26 *Magna est veritas, et praevalet.*
Great is truth, and it prevails.
3 Esdr. 4:41

ISAAC BICKERSTAFFE 1735?–1812?

27 Perhaps it was right to dissemble your love,
But—why did you kick me downstairs?
An Expostulation

28 There was a jolly miller once,
　　Lived on the river Dee;
He worked and sang from morn till night;

No lark more blithe than he.
Love in a Village (1762), I.v

1 And this the burthen of his song,
   For ever us'd to be,
I care for nobody, not I,
   If no one cares for me.

2 We all love a pretty girl—under the rose.
II.ii

3 In every port he finds a wife.
Thomas and Sally (1761), ii

REVD. E.H. BICKERSTETH 1825–1906

4 Peace, perfect peace, in this dark world of sin?
The Blood of Jesus whispers peace within.
Songs in the House of Pilgrimage (1875)

ROGER BIGOD, EARL OF NORFOLK 1245-1306

5 By God, O King, I will neither go nor hang!
Reply to King Edward I's expostulation, 'By God, earl, you shall either go or hang', 24 Feb. 1297, when Edward required the barons to invade France through Gascony while he took command in Flanders. *Hemingburgh's Chronicle*, ii.121

JOSH BILLINGS (HENRY WHEELER SHAW) 1818–1885

6 Thrice is he armed that hath his quarrel just,
But four times he who gets his blow in fust.
Josh Billings, his Sayings (1865). See 446:6

7 The trouble with people is not that they don't know but that they know so much that ain't so.
Josh Billings' Encyclopedia of Wit and Wisdom (1874)

LAURENCE BINYON 1869–1943

8 Now is the time for the burning of the leaves.
The Burning of the Leaves

9 With proud thanksgiving, a mother for her children,
England mourns for her dead across the sea.
Poems For the Fallen

10 They shall grow not old, as we that are left grow old:
Age shall not weary them, nor the years condemn.
At the going down of the sun and in the morning
We will remember them.

NIGEL BIRCH 1906–

11 For the second time the Prime Minister has got rid of a Chancellor of the Exchequer who tried to get expenditure under control.
Once is more than enough.
Letter, *The Times*, 14 July 1962

EARL OF BIRKENHEAD (F.E. SMITH) 1872–1930

12 We have the highest authority for believing that the meek shall inherit the Earth; though I have never found any particular corroboration of this aphorism in the records of Somerset House.
Contemporary Personalities (1924). **Marquess Curzon**

13 Nature has no cure for this sort of madness [Bolshevism], though I have known a legacy from a rich relative work wonders.
Law, Life and Letters (1927), ii. ch.19

14 The world continues to offer glittering prizes to those who have stout hearts and sharp swords.
Rectorial Address, Glasgow University, 7 Nov. 1923

15 *Judge Willis:* You are extremely offensive, young man.
F.E. Smith: As a matter of fact, we both are, and the only difference between us is that I am trying to be, and you can't help it.
Birkenhead, *Frederick Elwin, Earl of Birkenhead* (1933), vol.I, ch.9

16 *Judge Willis:* What do you suppose I am on the Bench for, Mr Smith?
Smith: It is not for me to attempt to fathom the inscrutable workings of Providence.

AUGUSTINE BIRRELL 1850–1933

17 That great dust-heap called 'history'
Obiter Dicta. **Carlyle**

18 In the name of the Bodleian.
Dr. Johnson

PRINCE BISMARCK 1815–1898

19 *Die Politik ist keine exakte Wissenschaft.*
Politics is not an exact science.
Prussian Chamber, 18 Dec. 1863

20 *Die Politik ist die Lehre von Möglichen.*
Politics is the art of the possible.
In conversation with Meyer von Waldeck, 11 Aug. 1867

21 *Nach Canossa gehen wir nicht.*
We will not go to Canossa.
Reichstag, 14 May 1872

22 *Die gesunden Knochen eines einzigen pommerschen Musketiers.*
The healthy bones of a single Pomeranian grenadier.
5 Dec. 1876

23 *Ehrlicher Makler.*
An honest broker.
19 Feb. 1878

24 *Die Politik ist keine Wissenschaft…sondern eine Kunst.*
Politics is not a science…but an art.
15 Mar. 1884

25 *Legt eine möglichst starke militärische Kraft…in die Hand des Königs von Preussen, dann wird er die Politik machen können, die Ihr wünscht; mit Reden und Schützenfesten und Liedern macht sie sich nicht, sie macht sich nur durch Blut und Eisen.*
Place in the hands of the King of Prussia the strongest possible military power, then he will be able to carry out the policy you wish; this policy cannot succeed through speeches, and shooting-matches, and songs; it can only be carried out through blood and iron.
Prussian House of Deputies, 28 Jan. 1886. Used by Bismarck in the form *Eisen und Blut*, 30 Sept. 1862

26 If there is ever another war in Europe, it will come out of some damned silly thing in the Balkans.
Said to Herr Ballen 'towards the end of [Bismarck's] life', and related by Ballen to Winston S. Churchill a fortnight before World War I. See *Hansard*, Vol.413, col.84

27 I may avail myself of the opportunity of denying once more the truth of the story that Prince Bismarck had ever likened Lord Salisbury to a lath of wood painted

to look like iron.
Sidney Whitman, *Personal Reminiscences of Prince Bismarck* (1902), p.252

SIR WILLIAM BLACKSTONE 1723–1780

1 Man was formed for society.
Commentaries on the Laws of England, introd. 2

2 Mankind will not be reasoned out of the feelings of humanity.
bk.i.5

3 The king never dies.
7

4 The royal navy of England hath ever been its greatest defence and ornament; it is its ancient and natural strength; the floating bulwark of the island.
13

5 That the king can do no wrong, is a necessary and fundamental principle of the English constitution.
iii.17

6 It is better that ten guilty persons escape than one innocent suffer.
iv.27

WILLIAM BLAKE 1757–1827

7 When Sir Joshua Reynolds died
All Nature was degraded:
The King dropped a tear into the Queen's ear,
And all his pictures faded.
Annotations to Reynolds, *Discourses*, p.109

8 To see a World in a Grain of Sand,
  And a Heaven in a Wild Flower,
Hold Infinity in the palm of your hand,
  And Eternity in an hour.
Auguries of Innocence, 1

9 A Robin Redbreast in a Cage
Puts all Heaven in a Rage.
5

10 A dog starv'd at his master's gate
Predicts the ruin of the State,
A horse misus'd upon the road
Calls to Heaven for human blood.
Each outcry of the hunted hare
A fibre from the brain does tear,
A skylark wounded in the wing,
A cherubim does cease to sing.
9

11 The bat that flits at close of eve
Has left the brain that won't believe.
25

12 He who shall hurt the little wren
Shall never be belov'd by men.
He who the ox to wrath has mov'd
Shall never be by woman lov'd.
29

13 The caterpillar on the leaf
Repeats to thee thy mother's grief.
Kill not the moth nor butterfly,
For the Last Judgement draweth nigh.
37

14 A truth that's told with bad intent
Beats all the lies you can invent.
It is right it should be so;

15 Man was made for Joy and Woe;
And when this we rightly know,
Thro' the World we safely go,
Joy and woe are woven fine,
A clothing for the soul divine.
53

15 The bleat, the bark, bellow, and roar
Are waves that beat on Heaven's shore.
71

16 The strongest poison ever known
Came from Caesar's laurel crown.
97

17 He who doubts from what he sees
Will ne'er believe, do what you please.
If the Sun and Moon should doubt,
They'd immediately go out.
To be in a passion you good may do,
But no good if a passion is in you.
The whore and gambler, by the state
Licensed, build that nation's fate.
The harlot's cry from street to street
Shall weave old England's winding sheet.
107

18 God appears, and God is Light,
To those poor souls who dwell in Night;
But does a Human Form display
To those who dwell in realms of Day.
129

19 Does the Eagle know what is in the pit
Or wilt thou go ask the Mole?
Can Wisdom be put in a silver rod,
Or Love in a golden bowl?
The Book of Thel, Thel's motto

20   Everything that lives,
Lives not alone, nor for itself.
xi.26

21 The Vision of Christ that thou dost see
Is my vision's greatest enemy.
Thine has a great hook nose like thine,
Mine has a snub nose like to mine.
The Everlasting Gospel, a, l.1

22 Both read the Bible day and night,
But thou read'st black where I read white.
l.13

23 This life's five windows of the soul
Distorts the Heavens from pole to pole,
And leads you to believe a lie
When you see with, not thro', the eye.
d, l.103

24 Jesus was sitting in Moses' chair.
They brought the trembling woman there.
Moses commands she be ston'd to death.
What was the sound of Jesus' breath?
He laid His hand on Moses' law;
The ancient Heavens, in silent awe,
Writ with curses from pole to pole,
All away began to roll.
e, l.7

25 I am sure this Jesus will not do,
Either for Englishman or Jew.
f

26 Mutual Forgiveness of each vice,

Such are the Gates of Paradise.
The Gates of Paradise, prologue

1 Truly, my Satan, thou art but a dunce,
And dost not know the garment from the man;
Every harlot was a virgin once,
Nor canst thou ever change Kate into Nan.

Tho' thou art worshipp'd by the names divine
Of Jesus and Jehovah, thou art still
The Son of Morn in weary Night's decline,
The lost traveller's dream under the hill.
epilogue

2 I must Create a System, or be enslav'd by another
Man's;
I will not Reason and Compare: my business is to
Create.
Jerusalem, pl.10, l.20

3   Near mournful
Ever-weeping Paddington.
pl.12, l.27

4 The fields from Islington to Marybone,
To Primrose Hill and Saint John's Wood,
Were builded over with pillars of gold;
And there Jerusalem's pillars stood.
pl.27, l.1

5 Pancras and Kentish Town repose
Among her golden pillars high,
Among her golden arches which
Shine upon the starry sky.
l.9

6 For a tear is an intellectual thing,
And a sigh is the sword of an Angel King,
And the bitter groan of the martyr's woe
Is an arrow from the Almighty's bow.
pl.52, l.25

7 He who would do good to another must do it in
Minute Particulars.
General Good is the plea of the scoundrel, hypocrite,
and flatterer;
For Art and Science cannot exist but in minutely
organized Particulars.
pl.55, l.60

8 I give you the end of a golden string;
Only wind it into a ball,
It will lead you in at Heaven's gate,
Built in Jerusalem's wall.
pl.77

9 O ye Religious, discountenance every one among you
who shall pretend to despise Art and Science!

10 Let every Christian, as much as in him lies, engage
himself openly and publicly, before all the World, in
some mental pursuit for the Building up of Jerusalem.

11 England! awake! awake! awake!
Jerusalem thy sister calls!
Why wilt thou sleep the sleep of death,
And close her from thy ancient walls?

12 And now the time returns again:
Our souls exult, and London's towers
Receive the Lamb of God to dwell
In England's green and pleasant bowers.

13 I care not whether a man is Good or Evil; all that I
care
Is whether he is a Wise man or a Fool. Go! put off

Holiness,
And put on Intellect.
pl.91, l.55

14 For double the vision my eyes do see,
And a double vision is always with me.
With my inward eye 'tis an old Man grey,
With my outward, a Thistle across my way.
Letter to Thomas Butts, 22 Nov. 1802, l.27

15 O why was I born with a different face?
Why was I not born like the rest of my race?
Letter to Thomas Butts, 16 Aug. 1803

16 And did those feet in ancient time
Walk upon England's mountains green?
And was the holy Lamb of God
On England's pleasant pastures seen?

And did the Countenance Divine
Shine forth upon our clouded hills?
And was Jerusalem builded here
Amoung these dark Satanic mills?

Bring me my bow of burning gold!
Bring me my arrows of desire!
Bring me my spear! O clouds, unfold!
Bring me my chariot of fire!

I will not cease from Mental Fight,
Nor shall my Sword sleep in my hand,
Till we have built Jerusalem,
In England's green & pleasant Land.
Milton, preface

17 What is it men in women do require?
The lineaments of gratified desire.
What is it women do in men require?
The lineaments of gratified desire.
MS. Notebooks, 1793, p.99

18 He who binds to himself a Joy
Doth the winged life destroy;
But he who kisses the Joy as it flies
Lives in Eternity's sunrise.

19 The sword sung on the barren heath,
The sickle in the fruitful field:
The sword he sung a song of death,
But could not make the sickle yield.
p.105

20 Abstinence sows sand all over
The ruddy limbs and flaming hair,
But Desire gratified
Plants fruits of life and beauty there.

21 Never pain to tell thy love,
Love that never told can be;
For the gentle wind does move
Silently, invisibly.
p.115

22 Soon as she was gone from me,
A traveller came by,
Silently, invisibly:
He took her with a sigh.

23 Mock on, mock on, Voltaire, Rousseau;
Mock on, mock on, 'tis all in vain!
You throw the sand against the wind,
And the wind blows it back again.
1800-03, p.7

24 The Atoms of Democritus
And Newtons Particles of Light

Are sands upon the Red sea shore
Where Israel's tents do shine so bright.

1 [On William Haines]
   The Sussex men are noted fools,
   And weak is their brain-pan;
   I wonder if H— the painter
   Is not a Sussex man?
   1808-11, p.24

2 [Of Hayley's birth]
   Of H—'s birth this was the happy lot:
   His mother on his father him begot.
   p.27

3 [On Cromek]
   A petty sneaking knave I knew—
   O! Mr Cr—, how do ye do?
   p.29

4 He has observ'd the golden rule,
   Till he's become the golden fool.
   p.30

5 [On Hayley]
   To forgive enemies H— does pretend,
   Who never in his life forgave a friend.
   p.34

6 On H[ayle]y's Friendship.
   When H—y finds out what you cannot do,
   This is the very thing he'll set you to.
   p.35

7 To H[ayley]
   Thy friendship oft has made my heart to ache:
   Do be my enemy—for friendship's sake.
   p.37

8 I understood Christ was a carpenter
   And not a brewer's servant, my good Sir.
   p.38

9 The errors of a wise man make your rule,
   Rather than the perfections of a fool.
   p.42

10 Great things are done when men and mountains meet;
   This is not done by jostling in the street.
   p.43

11 When I tell any Truth it is not for the sake of
   convincing those who do not know it, but for the sake
   of defending those who do.
   Public Address

12 O Rose, thou art sick!
   The invisible worm
   That flies in the night,
   In the howling storm,

   Has found out thy bed
   Of crimson joy:
   And his dark secret love
   Does thy life destroy.
   The Sick Rose

13 Hear the voice of the Bard!
   Who present, past, and future sees.
   Songs of Experience, introduction

14 Tyger! Tyger! burning bright
   In the forests of the night,
   What immortal hand or eye
   Could frame thy fearful symmetry?
   The Tyger

15 What the hand dare seize the fire?

And what shoulder, and what art,
Could twist the sinews of thy heart?
And when thy heart began to beat,
What dread hand? and what dread feet?

16 When the stars threw down their spears,
   And water'd heaven with their tears,
   Did he smile his work to see?
   Did he who made the Lamb make thee?

17 Children of the future age,
   Reading this indignant page,
   Know that in a former time,
   Love, sweet love, was thought a crime.
   A Little Girl Lost

18 Love seeketh not itself to please,
   Nor for itself hath any care,
   But for another gives its ease,
   And builds a Heaven in Hell's despair.
   The Clod and the Pebble

19 Love seeketh only Self to please,
   To bind another to its delight,
   Joys in another's loss of ease,
   And builds a Hell in Heaven's despite.

20 Then the Parson might preach, and drink, and sing,
   And we'd be as happy as birds in the spring;
   And modest Dame Lurch, who is always at church,
   Would not have bandy children, nor fasting, nor birch.
   The Little Vagabond

21 I was angry with my friend
   I told my wrath, my wrath did end.
   I was angry with my foe:
   I told it not, my wrath did grow.
   A Poison Tree

22 Ah, Sun-flower! weary of time,
   Who countest the steps of the Sun;
   Seeking after that sweet golden clime,
   Where the traveller's journey is done;

   Where the Youth pined away with desire,
   And the pale Virgin shrouded in snow,
   Arise from their graves and aspire
   Where my Sun-flower wishes to go.
   Ah, Sun-Flower!

23 My mother groan'd, my father wept,
   Into the dangerous world I leapt;
   Helpless, naked, piping loud,
   Like a fiend hid in a cloud.
   Infant Sorrow

24 Piping down the valleys wild,
   Piping songs of pleasant glee,
   On a cloud I saw a child,
   And he laughing said to me:

   'Pipe a song about a Lamb!'
   So I piped with merry cheer.
   'Piper, pipe that song again;'
   So I piped: he wept to hear.

   'Drop thy pipe, thy happy pipe;
   Sing thy songs of happy cheer:'
   So I sang the same again,
   While he wept with joy to hear.
   Songs of Innocence, introduction

25 And I wrote my happy songs
   Every child may joy to hear.

26 Little Lamb, who made thee?

Dost thou know who made thee?
Gave thee life, and bid thee feed,
By the stream and o'er the mead;
Gave thee clothing of delight,
Softest clothing, woolly, bright;
Gave thee such a tender voice,
Making all the vales rejoice?
The Lamb

1 'I have no name;
I am but two days old.'
What shall I call thee?
'I happy am,
Joy is my name.'
Sweet joy befall thee!
Infant Joy

2 My mother bore me in the southern wild,
And I am black, but O! my soul is white;
White as an angel is the English child,
But I am black, as if bereav'd of light.
The Little Black Boy

3 When the voices of children are heard on the green,
And laughing is heard on the hill.
Nurse's Song

4 Then cherish pity, lest you drive an angel from your door.
Holy Thursday

5 When my mother died I was very young,
And my father sold me while yet my tongue
Could scarcely cry, ''weep! 'weep! 'weep! 'weep!'
So your chimneys I sweep, and in soot I sleep.
The Chimney Sweeper

6 To Mercy, Pity, Peace, and Love
All pray in their distress.
The Divine Image

7 For Mercy has a human heart,
Pity a human face,
And Love, the human form divine,
And Peace, the human dress.

8 Can I see another's woe,
And not be in sorrow too?
Can I see another's grief,
And not seek for kind relief?
On Another's Sorrow

9 Cruelty has a human heart,
And Jealousy a human face;
Terror the human form divine,
And Secrecy the human dress.
Appendix to *Songs of Innocence and of Experience.* **A Divine Image**

10 Whether on Ida's shady brow,
Or in the chambers of the East,
The chambers of the sun, that now
From ancient melody have ceas'd...
How have you left the ancient love
That bards of old enjoy'd in you!
The languid strings do scarcely move!
The sound is forc'd, the notes are few!
To the Muses

11 Energy is Eternal Delight.
The Marriage of Heaven and Hell: **The Voice of the Devil**

12 The reason Milton wrote in fetters when he wrote of Angels and God, and at liberty when of Devils and Hell, is because he was a true Poet, and of the Devil's party without knowing it.
(note)

13 The road of excess leads to the palace of wisdom.
Proverbs of Hell

14 Prudence is a rich, ugly, old maid courted by Incapacity.

15 He who desires but acts not, breeds pestilence.

16 A fool sees not the same tree that a wise man sees.

17 Eternity is in love with the productions of time.

18 Bring out number, weight, and measure in a year of dearth.

19 If the fool would persist in his folly he would become wise.

20 Prisons are built with stones of Law, brothels with bricks of Religion.

21 The pride of the peacock is the glory of God.
The lust of the goat is the bounty of God.
The wrath of the lion is the wisdom of God.
The nakedness of woman is the work of God.

22 The tigers of wrath are wiser than the horses of instruction.

23 Damn braces. Bless relaxes.

24 Sooner murder an infant in its cradle than nurse unacted desires.

25 Truth can never be told so as to be understood, and not be believ'd.

26 Then I asked: 'Does a firm persuasion that a thing is so, make it so?'
He replied: 'All Poets believe that it does, and in ages of imagination this firm persuasion removed mountains; but many are not capable of a firm persuasion of anything.'
A Memorable Fancy, pl.12-13

27 I was in a printing house in Hell, and saw the method in which knowledge is transmitted from generation to generation.

28 If the doors of perception were cleansed everthing would appear as it is, infinite.
pl.14

29 'What,' it will be questioned, 'when the sun rises, do you not see a round disc of fire somewhat like a guinea?' 'O no, no, I see an innumerable host company of the heavenly host crying, ''Holy, Holy, Holy is the Lord God Almighty.'''
A Vision of the Last Judgement, **Descriptive Catalogue** (1810)

LESLEY BLANCH 1907–

30 She was an Amazon. Her whole life was spent riding at breakneck speed along the wilder shores of love.
The Wilder Shores of Love, 2. **Jane Digby El Mezrab**

PHILIP PAUL BLISS 1838–1876

31 Hold the fort, for I am coming.
The Charm. **Ho, My Comrades, See the Signal!**

PRINCE BLÜCHER 1742–1819

32 *Was für plunder!*

What rubbish!
Of London seen from the Monument, June 1814. Often misquoted
as *'Was für plündern!'* (What a place to plunder!) Prince Gebhard
Lebrecht Blücher, *Memoirs* (1932), p. 33

1 Blücher and I met near La Belle Alliance; we were
both on horseback; but he embraced and kissed me
exclaiming *Mein lieber Kamerad,* and then *quelle
affaire!* which was pretty much all he knew of French.
Stanhope, *Conversations with the Duke of Wellington,* 4 Nov.
1840. (In 1816 Wellington said the meeting took place at
Genappe.)

EDMUND BLUNDEN 1896–1974

2 All things they have in common being so poor,
And their one fear, Death's shadow at the door.
Each sundown makes them mournful, each sunrise
Brings back the brightness in their failing eyes.
Almswomen

3 I have been young, and now am not too old;
And I have seen the righteous forsaken,
His health, his honour and his quality taken.
    This is not what we formerly were told.
Report on Experience. See 391:28

WILFRID SCAWEN BLUNT 1840–1922

4 I like the hunting of the hare
Better than that of the fox.
The Old Squire

5 I like to be as my fathers were,
In the days ere I was born.

BOETHIUS c.480–c.524

6 *Nam in omni adversitate fortunae infelicissimum
genus est infortunii, fuisse felicem.*
For in every ill-turn of fortune the most unhappy sort
of misfortune is to have been happy.
Consolation of Philosophy, bk.ii, prose 4

HUMPHREY BOGART 1899–1957

7 If she can stand it I can. Play it!
Casablanca (1942), script by Julius J. Epstein, Philip G. Epstein,
Howard Koch. Often quoted as 'Play it again, Sam.'

8 Here's looking at you, kid.

JOHN B. BOGART 1845–1921

9 When a dog bites a man that is not news, but when a
man bites a dog that is news.
Oral tradition: also attr. Charles Dana and Amos Cummings

NICOLAS BOILEAU 1636–1711

10 *Enfin Malherbe vint, et, le premier en France,
Fit sentir dans les vers une juste cadence.*
At last came Malherbe, and, first ever in France, made
    a proper flow felt in verse.
L'Art Poétique, i.131

11 *Qu'en un lieu, qu'en un jour, un seul fait accompli
Tienne jusqu'à la fin le théâtre rempli.*
Let a single completed action, all in one place, all in
    one day, keep the theatre packed to the end of your
    play.
iii.45

12 *Si j'écris quatre mots, j'en effacerai trois.*
Of every four words I write, I strike out three.
Satires, ii

HENRY ST. JOHN, VISCOUNT BOLINGBROKE
1678–1751

13 What a world is this, and how does fortune banter us!
Letter, 3 Aug. 1714

14 Pests of society; because their endeavours are directed
to loosen the bands of it, and to take at least one curb
out of the mouth of that wild beast man.
12 Sept. 1724

15 Truth lies within a little and certain compass, but error
is immense.
Reflections upon Exile

16 They make truth serve as a stalking-horse to error.
On the Study of History, letter 1

17 Nations, like men, have their infancy.
letter 4

18 They [Thucydides and Xenophon] maintained the
dignity of history.
letter 5

SIR DAVID BONE 1874–1959

19 It's 'Damn you, Jack—I'm all right!' with you chaps.
The Brassbounder (1910), ch.3

DANIEL J. BOORSTIN 1914–

20 The celebrity is a person who is known for his
well-knownness.
The Image (1961), ch.2, **From Hero to Celebrity: The Human
Pseudo-event,** pt.iii

21 A best-seller was a book which somehow sold well
simply because it was selling well.
ch.4, **From Shapes to Shadows: Dissolving Forms,** pt.viii

GENERAL WILLIAM BOOTH 1829–1912

22 This Submerged Tenth—is it, then, beyond the reach
of the nine-tenths in the midst of whom they live.
In Darkest England (1890), I.ii.23

JORGE LUIS BORGES 1899–

23 *Que el cielo exista, aunque nuestro lugar sea el
infierno.*
Let heaven exist, even though our estate be hell.
La Biblioteca de Babel

24 *El original es infiel a la traducción.*
The original is unfaithful to the translation (Henley's
translation of Beckford's *Vathek*).
Sobre el 'Vathek' de William Beckford

CESARE BORGIA 1476–1507

25 *Aut Caesar, aut nihil.*
Caesar or nothing.
Motto

GEORGE BORROW 1803–1881

26 The author of 'Amelia', the most singular genius
which their island ever produced, whose works it has
long been the fashion to abuse in public and to read in
secret.
The Bible in Spain, ch.1

1 My favourite, I might say, my only study, is man.
ch.5

2 The poor Ferrolese, with the genuine spirit of localism so prevalent in Spain, boast that their town contains a better public walk than Madrid.
ch.31

3 There are no countries in the world less known by the British than these selfsame British Islands.
Lavengro, preface

4 There's night and day, brother, both sweet things; sun, moon, and stars, brother, all sweet things; there's likewise a wind on the heath. Life is very sweet, brother; who would wish to die?
ch.25

5 There's the wind on the heath, brother; if I could only feel that, I would gladly live for ever.

6 Let no one sneer at the bruisers of England. What were the gladiators of Rome, or the bull-fighters of Spain, in its palmiest days, compared to England's bruisers?
ch.26

7 A losing trade, I assure you, sir: literature is a drug.
ch.30

8 Good ale, the true and proper drink of Englishmen. He is not deserving of the name of Englishman who speaketh against ale, that is good ale.
ch.48

9 Youth will be served, every dog has his day, and mine has been a fine one.
ch.92

10 Fear God, and take your own part.
The Romany Rye, ch.16

11 So when folks are disposed to ill-treat you, young man, say, 'Lord have mercy upon me!' and then tip them to Long Melford, which, as the saying goes, there is nothing comparable for shortness all the world over.

MARÉCHAL BOSQUET 1810–1861

12 *C'est magnifique, mais ce n'est pas la guerre.*
It is magnificent, but it is not war.
Remark on the charge of the Light Brigade, 1854

JOHN COLLINS BOSSIDY 1860–1928

13 And this is good old Boston,
   The home of the bean and the cod,
Where the Lowells talk only to Cabots,
   And the Cabots talk only to God.
Toast at Holy Cross Alumni dinner, 1910

JACQUES-BÉNIGNE BOSSUET 1627–1704

14 *L'Angleterre, ah, la perfide Angleterre, que le rempart de ses mers rendoit inaccessible aux Romains, la foi du Sauveur y est abordée.*
England, ah, faithless England, which the protection afforded by its seas rendered inaccessible to the Romans, the faith of the Saviour spread even there.
Premier Sermon pour La Fête de la Circoncision de Notre Seigneur

JAMES BOSWELL 1740–1795

15 *Johnson:* Well, we had a good talk.
Boswell: Yes, Sir; you tossed and gored several persons.
Life of Johnson, vol.ii, p.66. 1769

16 A man, indeed, is not genteel when he gets drunk; but most vices may be committed very genteelly: a man may debauch his friend's wife genteelly: he may cheat at cards genteelly.
p.340. 6 Apr. 1775

GORDON BOTTOMLEY 1874–1948

17 When you destroy a blade of grass
You poison England at her roots:
Remember no man's foot can pass
Where evermore no green life shoots.
To Ironfounders and Others

DION BOUCICAULT 1820?–1890

18 Men talk of killing time, while time quietly kills them.
London Assurance (1841), II.i

ANTOINE BOULAY DE LA MEURTHE 1761–1840

19 *C'est pire qu'un crime, c'est une faute.*
It is worse than a crime, it is a blunder.
On hearing of the execution of the Duc d'Enghien, 1804

MATTHEW BOULTON 1728–1809

20 I sell here, Sir, what all the world desires to have—POWER.
[To Boswell, of his engineering works.]
Boswell, *Life of Johnson,* vol.ii, p.459. 22 Mar. 1776

F.W. BOURDILLON 1852–1921

21 The night has a thousand eyes,
   And the day but one;
Yet the light of the bright world dies,
   With the dying sun.

The mind has a thousand eyes,
   And the heart but one;
Yet the light of a whole life dies,
   When love is done.
Light. See 321:15

LORD BOWEN 1835–1894

22 The rain it raineth on the just
   And also on the unjust fella:
But chiefly on the just, because
   The unjust steals the just's umbrella.
Walter Sichel, *Sands of Time*

23 On a metaphysician: A blind man in a dark room—looking for a black hat—which isn't there.
Attr. See N. & Q., clxxxii.153

E.E. BOWEN 1836–1901

24 Forty years on, when afar and asunder
Parted are those who are singing to-day.
Forty Years On. Harrow School Song

25 Follow up! Follow up! Follow up! Follow up! Follow up!

Till the field ring again and again,
With the tramp of the twenty-two men,
Follow up!

ELIZABETH BOWEN 1899–1973

1 One can live in the shadow of an idea without grasping it.
The Heat of the Day (1949), ch.10

2 Art is the only thing that can go on mattering once it has stopped hurting.
ch.16

3 There is no end to the violations committed by children on children, quietly talking alone.
The House in Paris (1935), pt.I, ch.2

4 Nobody speaks the truth when there's something they must have.
ch.5

5 Fate is not an eagle, it creeps like a rat.
pt.II, ch.2

6 No, it is not only our fate but our business to lose innocence, and once we have lost that, it is futile to attempt a picnic in Eden.
'Out of a Book', *Orion III* (1946), eds. R. Lehmann and others

REVD. WILLIAM LISLE BOWLES 1762–1850

7 The cause of Freedom is the cause of God!
Edmund Burke, 1.78

REVD. E.E. BRADFORD 1860–1944

8 I walked with Will through bracken turning brown,
  Pale yellow, orange, dun and golden-red.
'God made the country and man made the town—
  And woman made Society,' he said.
Society. See 166:31

JOHN BRADFORD 1510?–1555

9 But for the grace of God there goes John Bradford.
D.N.B. Exclamation on seeing some criminals taken to execution.

F.H. BRADLEY 1846–1924

10 Unearthly ballet of bloodless categories.
The Principles of Logic, vol.III, ch.2, iv

11 The secret of happiness is to admire without desiring. And that is not happiness.
Aphorisms (1930), 33

JOHN BRADSHAW 1602–1659

12 Rebellion to tyrants is obedience to God.
Supposititious epitaph. Randall, *Life of Jefferson,* vol.III, appendix IV, p.585

ANNE BRADSTREET 1612–1672

13 I am obnoxious to each carping tongue,
Who sayes my hand a needle better fits,
A Poet's Pen, all scorne, I should thus wrong;
For such despight they cast on female wits:
If what I doe prove well, it won't advance,
They'l say it's stolne, or else, it was by chance.
The Prologue

14 Let *Greeks* be *Greeks,* and Women what they are,
Men have precedency, and still excell.

15 This meane and unrefined stuffe of mine,
Will make your glistering gold but more to shine.

JOHN BRAHAM 1774?–1856

16 England, home and beauty.
The Americans (1811). Song, **The Death of Nelson**

HARRY BRAISTED nineteenth century

17   If you want to win her hand,
   Let the maiden understand
That she's not the only pebble on the beach.
You're Not the Only Pebble on the Beach

ERNEST BRAMAH 1868–1942

18 It is a mark of insincerity of purpose to spend one's time in looking for the sacred Emperor in the low-class tea-shops.
The Wallet of Kai Lung. **Transmutation of Ling**

19 An expression of no-encouragement.
Confession of Kai Lung

20 The whole narrative is permeated with the odour of joss-sticks and honourable high-mindedness.
Kin Yen

21 It has been said…that there are few situations in life that cannot be honourably settled, and without loss of time, either by suicide, a bag of gold, or by thrusting a despised antagonist over the edge of a precipice upon a dark night.
Kai Lung's Golden Hours. **The Incredible Obtuseness…**

22 However entrancing it is to wander unchecked through a garden of bright images, are we not enticing your mind from another subject of almost equal importance?
Story of Hien

REVD. JAMES BRAMSTON 1694?–1744

23 What's not destroy'd by Time's devouring hand?
Where's Troy, and where's the Maypole in the Strand?
The Art of Politicks (1729), 1.71

RICHARD BRATHWAITE 1588?–1673

24 To Banbury came I, O profane one!
Where I saw a Puritane-one
Hanging of his cat on Monday
For killing of a mouse on Sunday.
Barnabee's Journal (1638), pt.i

BERTOLT BRECHT 1898–1956

25 *Erst kommt das Fressen, dann kommt die Moral.*
First comes fodder, then comes morality.
Die Dreigroschenoper, II, finale

26 *Ich will mit ihm gehen, den ich liebe.*
Ich will nicht ausrechnen, was es kostet.
Ich will nicht nachdenken, ob es gut ist.
Ich will nicht wissen, ob er mich liebt.
Ich will mit ihm gehen, den ich liebe.
It is my will to go with the man I love. I do not wish to count the cost. I do not wish to consider whether it is good. I do not wish to know whether he loves

me. It is my will to go with him whom I love.
Der gute Mensch von Sezuan, V

1 Andrea: *Unglücklich das Land, das keine Helden hat!*...
Galileo: *Nein, unglücklich das Land, das Helden nötig hat.*
Andrea: Unhappy the land that has no heroes.
Galileo: No, unhappy the land that needs heroes.
Leben des Galilei, sc.13

NICHOLAS BRETON 1545?–1626?

2 We rise with the lark and go to bed with the lamb.
The Court and Country, par.8

3 I wish my deadly foe, no worse
Than want of friends, and empty purse.
A Farewell to Town

4 He is as deaf as a door.
Miseries of Mavillia, v

5 In the merry month of May,
In a morn by break of day,
Forth I walked by the wood side,
Whenas May was in his pride:
There I spied all alone,
Phillida and Coridon.
Phillida and Coridon

6 Come little babe, come silly soul,
Thy father's shame, thy mother's grief,
Born as I doubt to all our dole,
And to thy self unhappy chief:
    Sing lullaby and lap it warm,
    Poor soul that thinks no creature harm.
A Sweet Lullaby

ROBERT BRIDGES 1844–1930

7 Awake, my heart, to be loved, awake, awake!
Awake, My Heart, To be Loved

8 Awake, the land is scattered with light, and see,
Uncanopied sleep is flying from field and tree:
And blossoming boughs of April in laughter shake.

9 Thus may I think the adopting Muses chose
Their sons by name, knowing none would be heard
Or writ so oft in all the world as those,—
Dan Chaucer, mighty Shakespeare, then for third
The classic Milton, and to us arose
Shelley with liquid music in the word.
Growth of Love, 4

10 I love all beauteous things,
I seek and adore them;
God hath no better praise,
And man in his hasty days
    Is honoured for them.

I too will something make
And joy in the making;
Altho' to-morrow it seem
Like the empty words of a dream
    Remembered on waking.
I Love All Beauteous Things

11 I will not let thee go.
Ends all our month-long love in this?
Can it be summed up so,
Quit in a single kiss?

12 I will not let thee go.
I Will Not Let Thee Go

12 When men were all asleep the snow came flying,
In large white flakes falling on the city brown,
Stealthily and perpetually settling and loosely lying,
    Hushing the latest traffic of the drowsy town.
London Snow

13 All night it fell, and when full inches seven
It lay in the depth of its uncompacted lightness,
The clouds blew off from a high and frosty heaven;
    And all woke earlier for the unaccustomed
        brightness
Of the winter dawning, the strange unheavenly glare.

14 Or peering up from under the white-mossed wonder,
'O look at the trees!' they cried, 'O look at the trees!'

15   The daily word is unspoken,
The daily thoughts of labour and sorrow slumber
At the sight of the beauty that greets them, for the
    charm they have broken.

16 My delight and thy delight
Walking, like two angels white,
In the gardens of the night.
My Delight and Thy Delight

17 Beautiful must be the mountains whence ye come,
And bright in the fruitful valleys the streams,
    wherefrom
        Ye learn your song:
Where are those starry woods? O might I wander
    there,
Among the flowers, which in that heavenly air
        Bloom the year long!
Nightingales

18 Rejoice ye dead, where'er your spirits dwell,
Rejoice that yet on earth your fame is bright,
And that your names, remembered day and night,
Live on the lips of those who love you well.
Ode to Music

19 Whither, O splendid ship, thy white sails crowding,
Leaning across the bosom of the urgent West,
That fearest nor sea rising, nor sky clouding,
Whither away, fair rover, and what thy quest?
A Passer-By

20 So sweet love seemed that April morn,
When first we kissed beside the thorn,
So strangely sweet, it was not strange
We thought that love could never change.

But I can tell—let truth be told—
That love will change in growing old;
Though day by day is nought to see,
So delicate his motions be.
So Sweet Love Seemed

21 When Death to either shall come,—
    I pray it be first to me,—
Be happy as ever at home,
    If so, as I wish, it be.
Possess thy heart, my own;
    And sing to the child on thy knee
Or read to thyself alone
    The songs that I made for thee.
When Death to Either Shall Come

22 When first we met we did not guess
That Love would prove so hard a master;
Of more than common friendliness

When first we met we did not guess.
Who could foretell this sore distress,
This irretrievable disaster
When first we met?—We did not guess
That Love would prove so hard a master.
Triolet

JOHN BRIGHT 1811–1889

1 The angel of death has been abroad throughout the land; you may almost hear the beating of his wings.
House of Commons, 23 Feb. 1855

2 I am for 'Peace, retrenchment, and reform', the watchword of the great Liberal party 30 years ago.
Birmingham, 28 Apr. 1859

3 My opinion is that the Northern States will manage somehow to muddle through.
During the American Civil War. Justin McCarthy, *Reminiscences* (1899)

4 England is the mother of Parliaments.
Birmingham, 18 Jan. 1865

5 The right hon Gentleman…has retired into what may be called his political Cave of Adullam—and he has called about him every one that was in distress and every one that was discontented.
House of Commons, 13 Mar. 1866

6 This party of two is like the Scotch terrier that was so covered with hair that you could not tell which was the head and which was the tail.

7 Force is not a remedy.
Birmingham, 16 Nov. 1880

8 The knowledge of the ancient languages is mainly a luxury.
Letter in *Pall Mall Gazette*, 30 Nov. 1886

ANTHELME BRILLAT-SAVARIN 1755–1826

9 *Dis-moi ce que tu manges, je te dirai ce que tu es.*
Tell me what you eat and I will tell you what you are.
Physiologie du Goût (1825), **Aphorismes…pour servir de prolégomènes**… iv. See 210:35

ALEXANDER BROME 1620–1666

10 I have been in love, and in debt, and in drink,
This many and many a year.
The Mad Lover, l.1

RICHARD BROME d. 1652?

11 You rose o' the wrong side to-day.
The Court Beggar (1632), Act II

12 I am a gentleman, though spoiled i' the breeding. The Buzzards are all gentlemen. We came in with the Conqueror.
English Moor, III.ii

ANNE BRONTË 1820–1849

13 Because the road is rough and long,
Shall we despise the skylark's song?
Views of Life

CHARLOTTE BRONTË 1816–1855

14 Conventionality is not morality. Self-righteousness is not religion. To attack the first is not to assail the last.

To pluck the mask from the face of the Pharisee, is not to lift an impious hand to the Crown of Thorns.
Jane Eyre. Preface to 2nd edition, 1847

15 Reader, I married him.
ch.38

16 Of late years an abundant shower of curates has fallen upon the North of England.
Shirley, ch.1, opening words

17 One day, in the autumn of 1845, I accidentally lighted on a MS volume of verse in my sister Emily's handwriting…I looked it over, and something more than surprise seized me,—a deep conviction that these were not common effusions, nor at all like the poetry women generally write. I thought them condensed and terse, vigorous and genuine. To my ear, they had also a peculiar music—wild, melancholy, and elevating.
Biographical Notice of Ellis and Acton Bell by Currer Bell. Published in the 1850 reprint of *Wuthering Heights* and *Agnes Grey.*

EMILY BRONTË 1818–1848

18 No coward soul is mine,
No trembler in the world's storm-troubled sphere:
    I see Heaven's glories shine,
And faith shines equal, arming me from fear.
Last Lines

19 O God within my breast,
Almighty! ever-present Deity!
    Life—that in me has rest,
As I—undying Life—have power in Thee!

20 Vain are the thousand creeds
That move men's hearts: unutterably vain;
    Worthless as withered weeds,
Or idlest froth amid the boundless main.

21 Oh! dreadful is the check—intense the agony—
When the ear begins to hear, and the eye begins to see;
When the pulse begins to throb, the brain to think again;
The soul to feel the flesh, and the flesh to feel the chain.
The Prisoner

22 Cold in the earth—and fifteen wild Decembers,
From those brown hills, have melted into spring.
Remembrance

23 Sweet Love of youth, forgive, if I forget thee,
While the world's tide is bearing me along;
Other desires and other hopes beset me,
Hopes which obscure, but cannot do thee wrong!

24 But when the days of golden dreams had perished,
And even Despair was powerless to destroy,
Then did I learn how existence could be cherished,
Strengthened, and fed without the aid of joy.

25 If all else perished, and he remained, I should still continue to be; and if all else remained, and he were annihilated, the universe would turn to a mighty stranger: I should not seem a part of it. My love for Linton is like the foliage in the woods; time will change it, I'm well aware, as winter changes the trees—My love for Heathcliff resembles the eternal rocks beneath:—a source of little visible delight, but necessary.
Wuthering Heights, ch.9

1 I lingered round them, under that benign sky: watched
the moths fluttering among the heath and hare-bells;
listened to the soft wind breathing through the grass;
and wondered how any one could ever imagine
unquiet slumbers for the sleepers in that quiet earth.
last words

REVD. PATRICK BRONTË 1777–1861

2 Girls, do you know Charlotte has been writing a book,
and it is much better than likely?
Elizabeth Gaskell, *Life of Charlotte Brontë*, ch.16

3 No quailing, Mrs Gaskell! no drawing back!
About her undertaking to write the life of Charlotte Brontë.
Elizabeth Gaskell, letter to Ellen Nussey, 24 July 1855

HENRY BROOKE 1703?–1783

4 For righteous monarchs,
Justly to judge, with their own eyes should see;
To rule o'er freemen, should themselves be free.
Earl of Essex (1749), I

RUPERT BROOKE 1887–1915

5 The hawthorn hedge puts forth its buds,
And my heart puts forth its pain.
All Suddenly the Spring Comes Soft

6 Now that we've done our best and worst, and parted.
The Busy Heart

7 Blow out, you bugles, over the rich Dead!
  There's none of these so lonely and poor of old,
    But, dying, has made us rarer gifts than gold.
These laid the world away; poured out the red
Sweet wine of youth; gave up the years to be
  Of work and joy, and that unhoped serene,
    That men call age; and those who would have been,
Their sons, they gave, their immortality.
The Dead

8 The cool kindliness of sheets, that soon
Smooth away trouble; and the rough male kiss of
  blankets.
The Great Lover

9 The benison of hot water.

10 Fish say, they have their stream and pond;
But is there anything beyond?
Heaven

11 One may not doubt that, somehow, good
Shall come of water and of mud;
And, sure, the reverent eye must see
A purpose in liquidity.

12 But somewhere, beyond space and time,
Is wetter water, slimier slime!

13 Immense, of fishy form and mind,
Squamous, omnipotent, and kind;
And under that Almighty Fin,
The littlest fish may enter in.
Oh! never fly conceals a hook,
Fish say, in the Eternal Brook,
But more than mundane weeds are there,
And mud, celestially fair.

14 Unfading moths, immortal flies,
And the worm that never dies.
And in that Heaven of all their wish,

There shall be no more land, say fish.

15 Breathless, we flung us on the windy hill,
Laughed in the sun, and kissed the lovely grass.
The Hill

16 With snuffle and sniff and handkerchief,
  And dim and decorous mirth,
With ham and sherry, they'll meet to bury
  The lordliest lass of earth.
Lines Written in the Belief that the Ancient Roman Festival of the Dead was called Ambarvalia

17 Oh! there the chestnuts, summer through,
Beside the river make for you
A tunnel of green gloom, and sleep
Deeply above.
The Old Vicarage, Grantchester

18 Here tulips bloom as they are told;
Unkempt about those hedges blows
An English unofficial rose.

19 And there the unregulated sun
Slopes down to rest when day is done,
And wakes a vague unpunctual star,
A slippered Hesper.

20 εἴθε γενοίμην …would I were
In Grantchester, in Grantchester!

21 Curates, long dust, will come and go
On lissom, clerical, printless toe;
And oft between the boughs is seen
The sly shade of a Rural Dean.

22 God! I will pack, and take a train,
And get me to England once again!

23 For Cambridge people rarely smile,
Being urban, squat, and packed with guile.

24 They love the Good; they worship Truth;
They laugh uproariously in youth;
(And when they get to feeling old,
They up and shoot themselves, I'm told.)

25 Stands the Church clock at ten to three?
And is there honey still for tea?

26 Now, God be thanked Who has matched us with His
  hour,
And caught our youth, and wakened us from sleeping.
Peace

27 Leave the sick hearts that honour could not move,
And half-men, and their dirty songs and dreary,
And all the little emptiness of love.

28 Naught broken save this body, lost but breath;
Nothing to shake the laughing heart's long peace there
But only agony, and that has ending;
And the worst friend and enemy is but Death.

29 Some white tremendous daybreak.
Second Best

30 If I should die, think only this of me:
That there's some corner of a foreign field
That is for ever England. There shall be
In that rich earth a richer dust concealed;
A dust whom England bore, shaped, made aware,
Gave, once, her flowers to love, her ways to roam,
A body of England's, breathing English air,
Washed by the rivers, blest by suns of home.
And think, this heart, all evil shed away,
A pulse in the eternal mind, no less

Gives somewhere back the thoughts by England given.
Her sights and sounds; dreams happy as her day;
And laughter, learnt of friends; and gentleness,
In hearts at peace, under an English heaven.
The Soldier

1 And there's an end, I think, of kissing,
When our mouths are one with Mouth.
Tiare Tahiti

THOMAS BROOKS 1608–1680

2 For (magna est veritas et praevalebit) great is truth,
and shall prevail.
The Crown and Glory of Christianity (1662), p.407. See 83:26

ROBERT BARNABAS BROUGH 1828–1860

3 My Lord Tomnoddy is thirty-four;
The Earl can last but a few years more.
My Lord in the Peers will take his place:
Her Majesty's councils his words will grace.
Office he'll hold and patronage sway;
Fortunes and lives he will vote away;
And what are his qualifications?—ONE!
He's the Earl of Fitzdotterel's eldest son.
My Lord Tomnoddy

LORD BROUGHAM 1778–1868

4 In my mind, he was guilty of no error,—he was
chargeable with no exaggeration,—he was betrayed by
his fancy into no metaphor, who once said, that all we
see about us, Kings, Lords, and Commons, the whole
machinery of the State, all the apparatus of the system,
and its varied workings, end in simply bringing twelve
good men into a box.
Speech on the Present State of the Law, 7 Feb. 1828

5 Look out, gentlemen, the schoolmaster is abroad!
Speech, London Mechanics' Institute, 1825

6 Education makes a people easy to lead, but difficult to
drive; easy to govern, but impossible to enslave.
Attr.

JOHN BROWN 1715–1766

7 Altogether upon the high horse.
Letter to Garrick, 27 Oct. 1765

THOMAS BROWN 1663–1704

8 In the reign of King Charles the Second, a certain
worthy Divine at Whitehall, thus address'd himself to
the auditory at the conclusion of his sermon: 'In short,
if you don't live up to the precepts of the Gospel, but
abandon your selves to your irregular appetites, you
must expect to receive your reward in a certain place,
which 'tis not good manners to mention here.'
Laconics

9 A little before you made a leap into the dark.
Letters from the Dead. See 251:24

10 I do not love you, Dr Fell,
But why I cannot tell;
But this I know full well,
I do not love you, Dr Fell.
Works (1719), vol.IV, p.113. See 331:9

T.E. BROWN 1830–1897

11 O blackbird, what a boy you are!
How you do go it.
The Blackbird

12 A garden is a lovesome thing, God wot!
My Garden

CECIL BROWNE

13 But not so odd
As those who choose
A Jewish God,
But spurn the Jews.
Reply to 209:13

SIR THOMAS BROWNE 1605–1682

14 Oblivion is a kind of Annihilation.
Christian Morals, pt.i, xxi

15 He who discommendeth others obliquely commendeth
himself.
xxxiv

16 As for that famous network of Vulcan, which enclosed
Mars and Venus, and caused that unextinguishable
laugh in heaven, since the gods themselves could not
discern it, we shall not pry into it.
The Garden of Cyrus (1658), ch.2

17 Life itself is but the shadow of death, and souls
departed but the shadows of the living. All things fall
under this name. The sun itself is but the dark
simulacrum, and light but the shadow of God.
ch.4

18 Flat and flexible truths are beat out by every hammer;
but Vulcan and his whole forge sweat to work out
Achilles his armour.
ch.5

19 But the quincunx of heaven runs low, and 'tis time to
close the five ports of knowledge.

20 All things began in order, so shall they end, and so
shall they begin again; according to the ordainer of
order and mystical mathematics of the city of heaven.

21 Nor will the sweetest delight of gardens afford much
comfort in sleep; wherein the dullness of that sense
shakes hands with delectable odours; and though in the
bed of Cleopatra, can hardly with any delight raise up
the ghost of a rose.

22 Though Somnus in Homer be sent to rouse up
Agamemnon, I find no such effects in these drowsy
approaches of sleep. To keep our eyes open longer
were but to act our Antipodes. The huntsmen are up in
America, and they are already past their first sleep in
Persia. But who can be drowsy at that hour which
freed us from everlasting sleep? or have slumbering
thoughts at that time, when sleep itself must end, and,
as some conjecture, all shall awake again?

23 That children dream not in the first half year, that men
dream not in some countries, are to me sick men's
dreams, dreams out of the ivory gate, and visions
before midnight.
On Dreams

24 Half our days we pass in the shadow of the earth; and
the brother of death exacteth a third part of our lives.

25 That the Jews stink naturally…is a received opinion

we know not how to admit.
Pseudodoxia Epidemica, Bk.4, 10

1 Half our days we pass in the shadow of the earth; and the brother of death exacteth a third part of our lives.

2 I dare, without usurpation, assume the honourable style of a Christian.
Religio Medici (1643), pt.i, 1

3 At my devotion I love to use the civility of my knee, my hat, and hand.
3

4 I could never divide my self from any man upon the difference of an opinion, or be angry with his judgment for not agreeing with me in that, from which perhaps within a few days I should dissent my self.
6

5 Many...have too rashly charged the troops of error, and remain as trophies unto the enemies of truth.

6 A man may be in as just possession of truth as of a city, and yet be forced to surrender.

7 There is another man within me, that's angry with me, rebukes, commands, and dastards me.
7

8 As for those wingy mysteries in divinity, and airy subtleties in religion, which have unhinged the brains of better heads, they never stretched the *pia mater* of mine. Methinks there be not impossibilities enough in Religion for an active faith.
9

9 I love to lose myself in a mystery; to pursue my reason to an *O altitudo!*
10

10 Who can speak of eternity without a solecism, or think thereof without an ecstasy? Time we may comprehend, 'tis but five days elder than ourselves.
11

11 I have often admired the mystical way of Pythagoras, and the secret magic of numbers.
12

12 We carry within us the wonders we seek without us: There is all Africa and her prodigies in us.
15

13 All things are artificial, for nature is the art of God.
16

14 'Twill be hard to find one that deserves to carry the buckler unto Samson.
21

15 Obstinacy in a bad cause, is but constancy in a good.
25

16 Persecution is a bad and indirect way to plant religion.

17 There are many (questionless) canonized on earth, that shall never be Saints in Heaven.
26

18 Not wrung from speculations and subtleties, but from common sense and observation—not pickt from the leaves of any author, but bred amongst the weeds and tares of mine own brain.
36

19 When I take a full view and circle of myself, without this reasonable moderator and equal piece of justice, Death, I do conceive myself the miserablest person

extant.
38

20 I am not so much afraid of death, as ashamed thereof; 'tis the very disgrace and ignominy of our natures, that in a moment can so disfigure us that our nearest friends, wife, and children, stand afraid and start at us.
40

21 Certainly there is no happiness within this circle of flesh, nor is it in the optics of these eyes to behold felicity; the first day of our Jubilee is death.
44

22 He forgets that he can die who complains of misery—we are in the power of no calamity while death is in our own.

23 I have tried if I could reach that great resolution...to be honest without a thought of Heaven or Hell.
47

24 To believe only possibilities, is not faith, but mere Philosophy.
48

25 There is no road or ready way to virtue.
55

26 My desires only are, and I shall be happy therein, to be but the last man, and bring up the rear in heaven.
57

27 I am of a constitution so general, that it consorts and sympathiseth with all things. I have no antipathy, or rather idiosyncrasy, in diet, humour, air, any thing.
pt.ii, 1

28 I feel not in myself those common antipathies that I can discover in others; those national repugnances do not touch me, nor do I behold with prejudice the French, Italian, Spaniard, or Dutch; but where I find their actions in balance with my countrymen's, I honour, love and embrace them in the same degree.

29 All places, all airs make unto me one country; I am in England, everywhere, and under any meridian.

30 If there be any among those common objects of hatred I do contemn and laugh at, it is that great enemy of reason, virtue, and religion, the multitude; that numerous piece of monstrosity, which, taken asunder, seem men, and the reasonable creatures of God, but, confused together, make but one great beast, and a monstrosity more prodigious than Hydra.

31 It is the common wonder of all men, how among so many millions of faces, there should be none alike.
2

32 No man can justly censure or condemn another, because indeed no man truly knows another.
4

33 I could be content that we might procreate like trees, without conjunction, or that there were any way to perpetuate the World without this trivial and vulgar way of coition: it is the foolishest act a wise man commits in all his life; nor is there any thing that will more deject his cool'd imagination, when he shall consider what an odd and unworthy piece of folly he hath committed.
9

34 Sure there is music even in the beauty, and the silent note which Cupid strikes, far sweeter than the sound of an instrument. For there is a music wherever there is a harmony, order or proportion; and thus far we may maintain the music of the spheres; for those well ordered motions, and regular paces, though they give no sound unto the ear, yet to the understanding they strike a note most full of harmony.

1 For even that vulgar and tavern music, which makes one man merry, another mad, strikes in me a deep fit of devotion, and a profound contemplation of the first Composer, there is something in it of divinity more than the ear discovers.

2 We all labour against our own cure, for death is the cure of all diseases.

3 For the world, I count it not an inn, but an hospital, and a place, not to live, but to die in.
11

4 There is surely a piece of divinity in us, something that was before the elements, and owes no homage unto the sun.

5 [Sleep is] in fine, so like death, I dare not trust it without my prayers.
12

6 Sleep is a death, O make me try,
By sleeping what it is to die.
And as gently lay my head
On my grave, as now my bed.

7 Old mortality, the ruins of forgotten times.
Urn Burial (1658), Epistle Dedicatory

8 With rich flames, and hired tears, they solemnized their obsequies.
ch.3

9 Men have lost their reason in nothing so much as their religion, wherein stones and clouts make martyrs.
ch.4

10 They carried them out of the world with their feet forward.

11 Were the happiness of the next world as closely apprehended as the felicities of this, it were a martyrdom to live.

12 Time, which antiquates antiquities, and hath an art to make dust of all things, hath yet spared these minor monuments.
ch.5

13 The long habit of living indisposeth us for dying.

14 What song the Syrens sang, or what name Achilles assumed when he hid himself among women, though puzzling questions, are not beyond all conjecture.

15 But to subsist in bones, and be but pyramidally extant, is a fallacy in duration.

16 Generations pass while some tree stands, and old families last not three oaks.

17 To be nameless in worthy deeds exceeds an infamous history.

18 But the iniquity of oblivion blindly scattereth her poppy, and deals with the memory of men without distinction to merit of perpetuity.

19 Herostatus lives that burnt the Temple of Diana—he is almost lost that built it.

20 The night of time far surpasseth the day, and who knows when was the equinox?

21 Diuturnity is a dream and a folly of expectation.

22 Mummy is become merchandise, Mizraim cures wounds, and Pharaoh is sold for balsams.

23 Man is a noble animal, splendid in ashes, and pompous in the grave.

24 Ready to be any thing, in the ecstasy of being ever, and as content with six foot as the *moles* of Adrianus.

WILLIAM BROWNE 1591–1643

25 Underneath this sable hearse
Lies the subject of all verse,
Sidney's sister, Pembroke's mother;
Death! ere thou hast slain another,
Fair and learn'd, and good as she,
Time shall throw a dart at thee.
Epitaph. On the Countess of Pembroke

SIR WILLIAM BROWNE 1692–1774

26 The King to Oxford sent a troop of horse,
For Tories own no argument but force:
With equal skill to Cambridge books he sent,
For Whigs admit no force but argument.
Reply to Trapp's epigram See 552:5. Nichols' *Literary Anecdotes*, vol.III, p.330

ELIZABETH BARRETT BROWNING 1806–1861

27   Near all the birds
Will sing at dawn,—and yet we do not take
The chaffering swallow for the holy lark.
Aurora Leigh (1857), bk.i

28 God answers sharp and sudden on some prayers,
And thrusts the thing we have prayed for in our face,
A gauntlet with a gift in't.
bk.ii

29 The music soars within the little lark,
And the lark soars.
bk.iii

30 I think it frets the saints in heaven to see
How many desolate creatures on the earth
Have learnt the simple dues of fellowship
And social comfort, in a hospital.

31 Since when was genius found respectable?
bk.vi

32 The devil's most devilish when respectable.
bk.vii

33   Earth's crammed with heaven,
And every common bush afire with God;
But only he who sees, takes off his shoes,
The rest sit round it and pluck blackberries,
And daub their natural faces unaware
More and more from the first similitude.

34 'Jasper first,' I said,
'And second sapphire; third chalcedony;
The rest in order,—last an amethyst.'
bk.ix

35 And kings crept out again to feel the sun.
Crowned and Buried

36 But the young, young children, O my brothers,
They are weeping bitterly!
They are weeping in the playtime of the others,

In the country of the free.
The Cry of the Children (1843)

1 And lips say, 'God be pitiful,'
Who ne'er said, 'God be praised.'
Cry of the Human

2 And that dismal cry rose slowly
And sank slowly through the air,
Full of spirit's melancholy
And eternity's despair!
And they heard the words it said—
Pan is dead! great Pan is dead!
Pan, Pan is dead!
The Dead Pan

3 Or from Browning some 'Pomegranate', which, if cut
deep down the middle,
Shows a heart within blood-tinctured, of a veined
humanity.
Lady Geraldine's Courtship, xli

4 By thunders of white silence, overthrown.
Hiram Power's Greek Slave

5 'Yes,' I answered you last night;
'No,' this morning, sir, I say.
Colours seen by candle-light
Will not look the same by day.
The Lady's Yes

6 What was he doing, the great god Pan,
Down in the reeds by the river?
Spreading ruin and scattering ban,
Splashing and paddling with hoofs of a goat,
And breaking the golden lilies afloat
With the dragon-fly on the river.
A Musical Instrument

7 I tell you, hopeless grief is passionless.
Sonnets. Grief

8　　　　Deep-hearted man, express
Grief for thy dead in silence like to death;
Most like a monumental statue set
In everlasting watch and moveless woe,
Till itself crumble to the dust beneath.
Touch it: the marble eyelids are not wet—
If it could weep, it could arise and go.

9　　　　Straightway I was 'ware,
So weeping, how a mystic shape did move
Behind me, and drew me backward by the hair
And a voice said in mastery while I strove…
'Guess now who holds thee?'—'Death', I said, but
there
The silver answer rang…'Not Death, but Love.'
Sonnets from the Portuguese, 1

10　　　　For frequent tears have run
The colours from my life.
8

11 If thou must love me, let it be for naught
Except for love's sake only.
14

12 First time he kissed me, he but only kissed
The fingers of this hand wherewith I write;
And, ever since, it grew more clean and white.
38

13 How do I love thee? Let me count the ways.
43

14　　　　If God choose,
I shall but love thee better after death.

15 Thou large-brained woman and large-hearted man.
To George Sand. A Desire

16 And the rolling anapaestic
Curled like vapour over shrines!
Wine of Cyprus, x

ROBERT BROWNING 1812–1889

17 Burrow awhile and build, broad on the roots of things.
Abt Vogler, ii

18 On the earth the broken arcs; in the heaven, a perfect
round.
ix

19 All we have willed or hoped or dreamed of good shall
exist.
x

20 The high that proved too high, the heroic for earth too
hard,
The passion that left the ground to lose itself in the
sky,
Are music sent up to God by the lover and the bard;
Enough that he heard it once: we shall hear it by and
by.

21 But God has a few of us whom he whispers in the ear;
The rest may reason and welcome; 'tis we musicians
know.
xi

22　　　　I feel for the common chord again…
The C Major of this life.
xii

23 So free we seem, so fettered fast we are!
Andrea del Sarto, l.51

24 Ah, but a man's reach should exceed his grasp,
Or what's a heaven for?
l.97

25 It all comes to the same thing at the end.
Any Wife to Any Husband, xvi

26 Why need the other women know so much?
xvii

27 A minute's success pays the failure of years.
Apollo and the Fates, prologue

28 But, thanks to wine-lees and democracy,
We've still our stage where truth calls spade a spade!
Aristophanes' Apology, l.392

29 But flame? The Bush is bare.
Asolando, Prologue

30 All the breath and the bloom of the year in the bag of
one bee.
Summum Bonum

31 At the midnight in the silence of the sleep-time,
When you set your fancies free.
Epilogue

32 One who never turned his back but marched breast
forward,
Never doubted clouds would break,
Never dreamed, though right were worsted, wrong
would triumph,
Held we fall to rise, are baffled to fight better,
Sleep to wake.

33 Greet the unseen with a cheer.

34　　　　I find earth not grey but rosy,
Heaven not grim but fair of hue.

Do I stoop? I pluck a posy.
Do I stand and stare? All's blue.
At the 'Mermaid'

1 There up spoke a brisk little somebody,
Critic and whippersnapper, in a rage
To set things right.
Balaustion's Adventure, pt.i, l.308

2   Don't you know,
I promised, if you'd watch a dinner out,
We'd see truth dawn together?—truth that peeps
Over the glass's edge when dinner's done,
And body gets its sop and holds its noise
And leaves soul free a little.
Bishop Blougram's Apology, l.15

3 A piano-forte is a fine resource,
All Balzac's novels occupy one shelf,
The new edition fifty volumes long.
l.107

4 Just when we're safest, there's a sunset-touch,
A fancy from a flower-bell, some one's death,
A chorus-ending from Euripides,—
And that's enough for fifty hopes and fears
As old and new at once as nature's self,
To rap and knock and enter in our soul,
Take hands and dance there, a fantastic ring,
Round the ancient idol, on his base again,—
The grand Perhaps.
l.182

5 All we have gained then by our unbelief
Is a life of doubt diversified by faith,
For one of faith diversified by doubt:
We called the chess-board white—we call it black.
l.209

6   Demirep
That loves and saves her soul in new French books.
l.397

7   You, for example, clever to a fault,
The rough and ready man who write apace,
Read somewhat seldomer, think perhaps even less.
l.420

8 And that's what all the blessed Evil's for.
l.655

9 How you'd exult if I could put you back
Six hundred years, blot out cosmogeny,
Geology, ethnology, what not…
And set you square with Genesis again.
l.678

10 No, when the fight begins within himself,
A man's worth something.
l.693

11 He said true things, but called them by wrong names.
l.996

12 Saint Praxed's ever was the church for peace.
The Bishop Orders His Tomb at Saint Praxed's Church, l.14

13 And have I not Saint Praxed's ear to pray
Horses for ye, and brown Greek manuscripts,
And mistresses with great smooth marbly limbs?
—That's if ye carve my epitaph aright.
l.73

14 And then how I shall lie through centuries,
And hear the blessed mutter of the mass,
And see God made and eaten all day long,
And feel the steady candle-flame, and taste

Good strong thick stupefying incense-smoke!
l.80

15 Aha, ELUCESCEBAT quoth our friend?
No Tully, said I, Ulpian at the best.
l.99

16 I was so young, I loved him so, I had
No mother, God forgot me, and I fell.
A Blot in the 'Scutcheon (1843), I.iii.l.508

17 How well I know what I mean to do
When the long dark autumn-evenings come.
By the Fireside, i

18 I shall be found by the fire, suppose,
O'er a great wise book as beseemeth age,
While the shutters flap as the cross-wind blows
And I turn the page, and I turn the page,
Not verse now, only prose!
ii

19   That great brow
And the spirit-small hand propping it.
xxiii

20 When earth breaks up and heaven expands,
How will the change strike me and you
In the house not made with hands?
xxvii. See 77:6

21 We two stood there with never a third.
xxxviii

22 Oh, the little more, and how much it is!
And the little less, and what worlds away!
xxxix

23 If two lives join, there is oft a scar.
They are one and one, with a shadowy third;
One near one is too far.
xlvi

24 Letting the rank tongue blossom into speech.
Setebos, Setebos, and Setebos!
'Thinketh, He dwelleth i' the cold o' the moon.
'Thinketh He made it, with the sun to match,
But not the stars; the stars came otherwise.
Caliban upon Setebos, l.24

25 'Let twenty pass, and stone the twenty-first.
Loving not, hating not, just choosing so.
l.103

26 Kentish Sir Byng stood for his King,
Bidding the crop-headed Parliament swing:
And, pressing a troop unable to stoop
And see the rogues flourish and honest folk droop,
Marched them along, fifty-score strong,
Great-hearted gentlemen, singing this song.

God for King Charles! Pym and such carles
To the Devil that prompts 'em their treasonous parles!
Cavalier Tunes, 1. **Marching Along**

27 Boot, saddle, to horse, and away!
3. **Boot and Saddle**

28 One stiff blind horse, his every bone a-stare.
Childe Roland to the Dark Tower Came, xiii

29 I never saw a brute I hated so;
He must be wicked to deserve such pain.
xiv

30 Dauntless the slug-horn to my lips I set,
And blew. '*Childe Roland to the Dark Tower came.*'
xxxiv. See 454:27

1 In the natural fog of the good man's mind.
Christmas Eve, l.226

2 Some thrilling view of the surplice-question.
l.839

3 The raree-show of Peter's successor.
l.1242

4 For the preacher's merit or demerit,
It were to be wished the flaws were fewer
  In the earthen vessel, holding treasure,
Which lies as safe in a golden ewer;
  But the main thing is, does it hold good measure?
Heaven soon sets right all other matters!
l.1311

5 I have written three books on the soul,
Proving absurd all written hitherto,
And putting us to ignorance again.
Cleon, l.57

6 What is he buzzing in my ears?
  'Now that I come to die,
Do I view the world as a vale of tears?'
  Ah, reverend sir, not I!
Confessions

7 To mine, it serves for the old June weather
  Blue above lane and wall;
And that farthest bottle labelled 'Ether'
  Is the house o'ertopping all.

8 We loved, sir—used to meet:
How sad and bad and mad it was—
  But then, how it was sweet!

9 Stung by the splendour of a sudden thought.
A Death in the Desert, l.59

10 For I say, this is death and the sole death,
When a man's loss comes to him from his gain,
Darkness from light, from knowledge ignorance,
And lack of love from love made manifest.
l.482

11 Progress, man's distinctive mark alone,
Not God's, and not the beasts': God is, they are,
Man partly is and wholly hopes to be.
l.586

12 Your ghost will walk, you lover of trees,
  (If our loves remain)
  In an English lane.
De Gustibus

13 The bean-flowers' boon,
And the blackbird's tune,
And May, and June!

14 Italy, my Italy!
Queen Mary's saying serves for me—
  (When fortune's malice
  Lost her—Calais)—
Open my heart and you will see
Graved inside of it, 'Italy'.

15 Reads verse and thinks she understands.
Dis aliter visum, iv

16 Schumann's our music-maker now.
viii

17 Ingres's the modern man who paints.

18 Heine for songs; for kisses, how?

19 Sure of the Fortieth spare Arm-chair

20 When gout and glory seat me there.
xii

20 Here comes my husband from his whist.
xxx

21   'Tis well averred,
A scientific faith's absurd.
Easter Day, vi

22 At last awake
From life, that insane dream we take
For waking now.
xiv

23 A fierce vindictive scribble of red.
xv

24 Karshish, the picker-up of learning's crumbs,
The not-incurious in God's handiwork.
An Epistle

25 Beautiful Evelyn Hope is dead!
Evelyn Hope

26 You will wake, and remember, and understand.

27 Truth never hurts the teller.
Fifine at the Fair, xxxii

28 I must learn Spanish, one of these days,
  Only for that slow sweet name's sake.
The Flower's Name

29 If you get simple beauty and nought else,
You get about the best thing God invents.
Fra Lippo Lippi, l.217

30 You should not take a fellow eight years old
And make him swear to never kiss the girls.
l.224

31   This world's no blot for us,
Nor blank; it means intensely, and means good:
To find its meaning is my meat and drink.
l.313

32 Let us begin and carry up this corpse,
  Singing together.
A Grammarian's Funeral, l.1

33 Our low life was the level's and the night's;
  He's for the morning.
l.23

34 This is our master, famous, calm, and dead,
  Born on our shoulders.
l.27

35 Yea, but we found him bald too, eyes like lead,
  Accents uncertain:
'Time to taste life,' another would have said,
  'Up with the curtain!'
l.53

36 Yea, this in him was the peculiar grace...
Still before living he'd learn how to live.
l.75

37 He said, 'What's time? Leave Now for dogs and apes!
  Man has Forever.'
l.83

38 That low man seeks a little thing to do,
  Sees it and does it:
This high man, with a great thing to pursue,
  Dies ere he knows it:
That low man goes on adding one to one,
  His hundred's soon hit;
This high man, aiming at a million,
  Misses an unit.

That, has the world here—should he need the next,
  Let the world mind him!
This, throws himself on God, and unperplext
  Seeking shall find Him.
  l.113

1 He settled *Hoti's* business—let it be!--
   Properly based *Oun*—
   Gave us the doctrine of the enclitic *De*,
   Dead from the waist down.
   l.129

2 Lofty designs must close in like effects:
     Loftily lying,
   Leave him—still loftier than the world suspects,
     Living and dying.
   l.145

3 The Lord will have mercy on Jacob yet,
   And again in his border see Israel set.
   Holy-Cross Day, xiii

4 We withstood Christ then? Be mindful how
   At least we withstand Barabbas now!
   xviii

5 Oh, to be in England
   Now that April's there,
   And whoever wakes in England
   Sees, some morning, unaware,
   That the lowest boughs and the brushwood sheaf
   Round the elm-tree bole are in tiny leaf,
   While the chaffinch sings on the orchard bough
   In England—now!
   Home-Thoughts, from Abroad

6 That's the wise thrush; he sings each song twice over,
   Lest you should think he never could recapture
   The first fine careless rapture!

7 All will be gay when noontide wakes anew
   The buttercups, the little children's dower
   —Far brighter than this gaudy melon-flower!

8 Nobly, nobly Cape St Vincent to the North-west died
     away;
   Sunset ran, one glorious blood-red, reeking into Cadiz
     Bay.
   Home-Thoughts, from the Sea

9 'Here and here did England help me: how can I help
     England?'—say,
   Whoso turns as I, this evening, turn to God to praise
     and pray,
   While Jove's planet rises yonder, silent over Africa.

10   'With this same key
   Shakespeare unlocked his heart' once more!
   Did Shakespeare? If so, the less Shakespeare he!
   House, x. See 582:14

11 He took such cognizance of men and things.
   How it Strikes a Contemporary, l.30

12 I sprang to the stirrup, and Joris, and he;
   I galloped, Dirck galloped, we galloped all three.
   How they brought the Good News from Ghent to Aix

13 A man can have but one life and one death,
   One heaven, one hell.
   In a Balcony, l.13

14   I count life just a stuff
   To try the soul's strength on.
   l.651

15 The moth's kiss, first!

Kiss me as if you made believe
You were not sure, this eve,
How my face, your flower, had pursed
Its petals up...
The bee's kiss, now!
Kiss me as if you entered gay
My heart at some noonday.
In a Gondola

16 'You're wounded!' 'Nay,' the soldier's pride
     Touched to the quick, he said:
   'I'm killed, Sire!' And his chief beside
     Smiling the boy fell dead.
   Incident of the French Camp

17 Ignorance is not innocence but sin.
   The Inn Album, v

18 Just my vengeance complete,
   The man sprang to his feet,
   Stood erect, caught at God's skirts, and prayed!
   —So, *I* was afraid!
   Instans Tyrannus

19 The swallow has set her six young on the rail,
     And looks seaward.
   James Lee's Wife, III.i

20 Oh, good gigantic smile o' the brown old earth,
     This autumn morning!
   VII.i

21 I should be dead of joy, James Lee.
   IX.viii

22 I said—Then, dearest, since 'tis so,
   Since now at length my fate I know,
   Since nothing all my love avails,
   Since all, my life seemed meant for, fails,
     Since this was written and needs must be—
   My whole heart rises up to bless
   Your name in pride and thankfulness!
   Take back the hope you gave,—I claim
   Only a memory of the same.
   The Last Ride Together, i

23 Who knows but the world may end to-night?
   ii

24   My soul
   Smoothed itself out, a long-cramped scroll
   Freshening and fluttering in the wind...
   Had I said that, had I done this,
   So might I gain, so might I miss.
   Might she have loved me? just as well
   She might have hated, who can tell!
   iv

25 Look at the end of work, contrast
   The petty done, the undone vast,
   This present of theirs with the hopeful past!
   v

26 What hand and brain went ever paired?
   vi

27 They scratch his name on the Abbey-stones.
   My riding is better, by their leave.

28 Sing, riding's a joy! For me, I ride.
   vii

29 Ride, ride together, for ever ride?
   x

30 Escape me?
   Never—

Beloved!
Life in a Love

1 But what if I fail of my purpose here?
It is but to keep the nerves at strain,
   To dry one's eyes and laugh at a fall,
And, baffled, get up and begin again.

2 So, I gave her eyes my own eyes to take,
   My hand sought hers as in earnest need,
And round she turned for my noble sake,
   And gave me herself indeed.
A Light Woman

3 'Tis an awkward thing to play with souls,
And matter enough to save one's own.

4 Just for a handful of silver he left us,
   Just for a riband to stick in his coat.
The Lost Leader

5 We that had loved him so, followed him, honoured
      him,
   Lived in his mild and magnificent eye,
Learned his great language, caught his clear accents,
   Made him our pattern to live and to die!
Shakespeare was of us, Milton was for us,
   Burns, Shelley, were with us—they watch from their
      graves!

6 We shall march prospering,—not thro' his presence;
   Songs may inspirit us,—not from his lyre;
Deeds will be done,—while he boasts his quiescence,
   Still bidding crouch whom the rest bade aspire.

7 One more devils'-triumph and sorrow for angels,
One wrong more to man, one more insult to God!

8 Never glad confident morning again!

9 All's over, then; does truth sound bitter
   As one at first believes?
The Lost Mistress

10 Oppression makes the wise man mad.
Luria, iv

11 Argument's hot to the close.
Master Hugues of Saxe-Gotha, xiii

12 One dissertates, he is candid;
   Two must discept,—has distinguished.
xiv

13 And find a poor devil has ended his cares
At the foot of your rotten-runged rat-riddled stairs?
   Do I carry the moon in my pocket?
xxix

14 As I gain the cove with pushing prow,
   And quench its speed i' the slushy sand.

Then a mile of warm sea-scented beach;
Three fields to cross till a farm appears;
A tap at the pane, the quick sharp scratch
And blue spurt of a lighted match,
And a voice less loud, thro' its joys and fears,
Than the two hearts beating each to each!
Meeting at Night

15 Ah, did you once see Shelley plain,
   And did he stop and speak to you
And did you speak to him again?
   How strange it seems, and new!
Memorabilia

16 A moulted feather, an eagle-feather!
Well, I forget the rest.

17 If such as came for wool, sir, went home shorn,
Where is the wrong I did them?
Mr. Sludge, 'The Medium', l.630

18   Solomon of saloons
And philosophic diner-out.
l.773

19 This trade of mine—I don't know, can't be sure
But there was something in it, tricks and all!
Really, I want to light up my own mind.
l.809

20 Boston's a hole, the herring-pond is wide,
V-notes are something, liberty still more.
Beside, is he the only fool in the world?
l.1523

21 That's my last Duchess painted on the wall,
Looking as if she were alive.
My Last Duchess, l.1

22   She had
A heart—how shall I say?—too soon made glad,
Too easily impressed; she liked whate'er
She looked on, and her looks went everywhere.
l.21

23 All I can say is—I saw it!
Natural Magic

24 Never the time and the place
   And the loved one all together!
Never the Time and the Place

25   A lion who dies of an ass's kick,
The wronged great soul of an ancient Master.
Old Pictures in Florence, vi

26   What's come to perfection perishes.
Things learned on earth, we shall practise in heaven.
   Works done least rapidly, Art most cherishes.
xvii

27   Lose who may—I still can say,
Those who win heaven, blest are they!
One Way of Love

28 Rafael made a century of sonnets,
Made and wrote them in a certain volume
Dinted with the silver-pointed pencil
Else he only used to draw Madonnas.
One Word More, ii

29 Suddenly, as rare things will, it vanished.
iv

30 Dante once prepared to paint an angel:
Whom to please? You whisper 'Beatrice'.
v

31 Dante, who loved well because he hated,
Hated wickedness that hinders loving.

32 Does he paint? he fain would write a poem,—
Does he write? he fain would paint a picture.
viii

33 Never dares the man put off the prophet.
x

34 Where my heart lies, let my brain lie also.
xiv

35 Blank to Zoroaster on his terrace,
Blind to Galileo on his turret,
Dumb to Homer, dumb to Keats—him, even!
xvi

36 God be thanked, the meanest of his creatures
Boasts two soul-sides, one to face the world with,

One to show a woman when he loves her!
xvii

1 Oh, their Rafael of the dear Madonnas,
Oh, their Dante of the dread Inferno,
Wrote one song—and in my brain I sing it,
Drew one angel—borne, see, on my bosom!
xix

2 Truth is within ourselves.
Paracelsus, pt.I, l.726

3 *Paracelsus:*
I am he that aspired to KNOW: and thou?
Aprile:
I would LOVE infinitely, and be loved!
pt.II, l.384

4 God is the perfect poet,
Who in his person acts his own creations.
l.648

5 Measure your mind's height by the shade it casts!
pt.III, l.821

6 I give the fight up: let there be an end,
A privacy, an obscure nook for me.
I want to be forgotten even by God.
pt.V, l.363

7 Like plants in mines which never saw the sun,
But dream of him, and guess where he may be,
And do their best to climb and get to him.
l.882

8 If I stoop
Into a dark tremendous sea of cloud,
It is but for a time; I press God's lamp
Close to my breast; its splendour, soon or late,
Will pierce the gloom: I shall emerge one day.
l.899

9 Round the cape of a sudden came the sea,
And the sun looked over the mountain's rim;
And straight was a path of gold for him,
And the need of a world of men for me.
Parting at Morning

10 It was roses, roses, all the way.
The Patriot

11 The air broke into a mist with bells.

12 Sun-treader, life and light be thine for ever!
(Shelley) *Pauline,* l.151

13 Ah, thought which saddens while it soothes!
Pictor Ignotus

14 Hamelin Town's in Brunswick,
By famous Hanover city;
The river Weser, deep and wide,
Washes its walls on the southern side.
The Pied Piper of Hamelin, st.i

15 Rats!
They fought the dogs and killed the cats,
And bit the babies in the cradles,
And ate the cheeses out of the vats,
And licked the soup from the cooks' own ladles,
Split open the kegs of salted sprats,
Made nests inside men's Sunday hats,
And even spoiled the women's chats
By drowning their speaking
With shrieking and squeaking
In fifty different sharps and flats.
ii

16 A plate of turtle green and glutinous.
iv

17 Anything like the sound of a rat
Makes my heart go pit-a-pat!

18 'Come in!'—the Mayor cried, looking bigger:
And in did come the strangest figure!
v

19 So munch on, crunch on, take your nuncheon,
Breakfast, supper, dinner, luncheon.
vii

20 So, Willy, let me and you be wipers
Of scores out with all men, especially pipers!
xv

21 The year's at the spring
And day's at the morn;
Morning's at seven;
The hill-side's dew-pearled;
The lark's on the wing;
The snail's on the thorn:
God's in his heaven,
All's right with the world!
Pippa Passes, pt.I, l.222

22 God must be glad one loves His world so much!
pt.III, l.73

23 No need that sort of king should ever die!
l.178

24 You'll look at least on love's remains,
A grave's one violet:
Your look?—that pays a thousand pains.
What's death? You'll love me yet!
l.314

25 All service ranks the same with God—
With God, whose puppets, best and worst,
Are we; there is no last nor first.
pt.IV, l.113

26 Stand still, true poet that you are!
I know you; let me try and draw you.
Some night you'll fail us: when afar
You rise, remember one man saw you,
Knew you, and named a star!
Popularity

27 Hobbs hints blue,—straight he turtle eats:
Nobbs prints blue,—claret crowns his cup:
Nokes outdares Stokes in azure feats,—
Both gorge. Who fished the murex up?
What porridge had John Keats?

28 The rain set early in to-night.
Porphyria's Lover

29 All her hair
In one long yellow string I wound
Three times her little throat around,
And strangled her. No pain felt she;
I am quite sure she felt no pain.

30 And all night long we have not stirred,
And yet God has not said a word!

31 Fear death?—to feel the fog in my throat,
The mist in my face.
Prospice

32 I was ever a fighter, so—one fight more,
The best and the last!
I would hate that death bandaged my eyes, and
forbore,

And bade me creep past.

1 No! let me taste the whole of it, fare like my peers
   The heroes of old,
Bear the brunt, in a minute pay glad life's arrears
   Of pain, darkness and cold.

2   Grow old along with me!
   The best is yet to be,
The last of life, for which the first was made:
   Our times are in His hand
   Who saith, 'A whole I planned,
Youth shows but half; trust God: see all, nor be
   afraid!'
   Rabbi ben Ezra, i

3 Irks care the crop-full bird? Frets doubt the
   maw-crammed beast?
   iv

4 For thence,—a paradox
   Which comforts while it mocks,—
Shall life succeed in that it seems to fail:
   What I aspired to be,
   And was not, comforts me:
A brute I might have been, but would not sink i' the
   scale.
   vii

5 Once more on my adventure brave and new.
   xiv

6   When evening shuts,
   A certain moment cuts
The deed off, calls the glory from the grey.
   xvi

7   Now, who shall arbitrate?
   Ten men love what I hate.
Shun what I follow, slight what I receive;
   Ten, who in ears and eyes
   Match me: we all surmise,
They this thing, and I that: whom shall my soul
   believe?
   xxii

8 Fancies that broke through language and escaped.
   xxv

9   All that is, at all,
   Lasts ever, past recall;
Earth changes, but thy soul and God stand sure.
   xxvii

10 Time's wheel runs back or stops: Potter and clay
   endure.

11 He fixed thee mid this dance
   Of plastic circumstance.
   xxviii

12 Look not thou down but up!
   To uses of a cup.
   xxx

13 My times be in Thy hand!
   Perfect the cup as planned!
Let age approve of youth, and death complete the
   same!
   xxxii

14 Do you see this square old yellow Book, I toss
   I' the air, and catch again.
   The Ring and the Book, bk.i, l.33

15 The Life, Death, Miracles of Saint Somebody,

Saint Somebody Else, his Miracles, Death and Life.
l.80

16 Well, British Public, ye who like me not,
   (God love you!).
l.410

17 'Go get you manned by Manning and new-manned
By Newman and, mayhap, wise-manned to boot
By Wiseman.'
l.444

18   Youth means love,
Vows can't change nature, priests are only men.
l.1056

19 O lyric Love, half-angel and half-bird
   And all a wonder and a wild desire.
l.1391

20 The story always old and always new.
bk.ii, l.214

21 But facts are facts and flinch not.
l.1049

22   Go practise if you please
With men and women: leave a child alone
For Christ's particular love's sake!—so I say.
bk.iii, l.88

23 In the great right of an excessive wrong.
l.1055

24 Everyone soon or late comes round by Rome.
bk.v, l.296

25 'T was a thief said the last kind word to Christ:
Christ took the kindness and forgave the theft.
bk.vi, l.869

26 The uncomfortableness of it all.
bk.vii, l.400

27   Through such souls alone
God stooping shows sufficient of His light
For us i' the dark to rise by. And I rise.
l.1843

28 Faultless to a fault.
bk.ix, l.1175

29   Of what I call God,
And fools call Nature.
bk.x, l.1072

30 Why comes temptation but for man to meet
And master and make crouch beneath his foot,
And so be pedestalled in triumph?
l.1184

31 White shall not neutralize the black, nor good
Compensate bad in man, absolve him so:
Life's business being just the terrible choice.
l.1235

32   There's a new tribunal now
Higher than God's—the educated man's!
l.1975

33   That sad obscure sequestered state
Where God unmakes but to remake the soul
He else made first in vain; which must not be.
l.2129

34   It is the glory and good of Art,
That Art remains the one way possible
Of speaking truth, to mouths like mine at least.
bk.xii, l.838

35 Good, to forgive;
   Best, to forget!

Living, we fret;
Dying, we live.
La Saisiaz, dedication

1 How good is man's life, the mere living! how fit to
  employ
  All the heart and the soul and the senses, for ever in
  joy!
  Saul, ix

2 'Tis not what man Does which exalts him, but what
  man Would do!
  xviii

3   Because a man has shop to mind
  In time and place, since flesh must live,
     Needs spirit lack all life behind,
  All stray thoughts, fancies fugitive,
  All loves except what trade can give?
  Shop, xx

4 I want to know a butcher paints,
  A baker rhymes for his pursuit,
  Candlestick-maker much acquaints
  His soul with song, or, haply mute,
  Blows out his brains upon the flute.
  xxi

5 Gr-r-r- there go, my heart's abhorrence!
  Water your damned flower-pots, do!
  Soliloquy of the Spanish Cloister

6 I the Trinity illustrate,
     Drinking watered orange-pulp—
  In three sips the Arian frustrate;
     While he drains his at one gulp.

7 There's a great text in Galatians,
     Once you trip on it, entails
  Twenty-nine distinct damnations,
     One sure, if another fails.

8 My scrofulous French novel
     On grey paper with blunt type!

9 'St, there's Vespers! *Plena gratiâ*
     Ave, Virgo! Gr-r-r—you swine!

10 Nay but you, who do not love her,
   Is she not pure gold, my mistress?
   Song

11 Who will, may hear Sordello's story told.
   Sordello, bk.i, l.1

12 Sidney's self, the starry paladin.
   l.69

13 Still more labyrinthine buds the rose.
   l.476

14   A touch divine—
   And the scaled eyeball owns the mystic rod;
   Visibly through his garden walketh God.
   l.502

15   Any nose
   May ravage with impunity a rose.
   bk.vi, l.881

16 Who would has heard Sordello's story told.
   l.886

17 You are not going to marry your old friend's love,
   after all?
   A Soul's Tragedy, Act II

18 The world and its ways have a certain worth.
   The Statue and the Bust, l.138

19 The glory dropped from their youth and love,
   And both perceived they had dreamed a dream.
   l.152

20 The soldier-saints, who row on row,
   Burn upward each to his point of bliss.
   l.222

21 The sin I impute to each frustrate ghost
   Is—the unlit lamp and the ungirt loin,
   Though the end in sight was a vice, I say.
   l.246

22 As I ride, as I ride.
   Through the Metidja to Abd-el-kadr

23 There may be heaven; there must be hell;
   Meantime, there is our earth here—well!
   Time's Revenges

24 Hark, the dominant's persistence till it must be
   answered to!
   A Toccata of Galuppi's, viii

25 What of soul was left, I wonder, when the kissing had
   to stop?
   xiv

26 Dear dead women, with such hair, too—what's
   become of all the gold
   Used to hang and brush their bosoms? I feel chilly and
   grown old.
   xv

27 Grand rough old Martin Luther
      Bloomed fables—flowers on furze,
   The better the uncouther:
      Do roses stick like burrs?
   The Twins

28 I would that you were all to me,
   You that are just so much, no more.
   Two in the Campagna, 8

29   I pluck the rose
   And love it more than tongue can speak—
   Then the good minute goes.
   10

30   Only I discern—
   Infinite passion, and the pain
   Of finite hearts that yearn.
   12

31 *Bang-whang-whang* goes the drum, *tootle-te-tootle* the
   fife.
   Oh, a day in the city-square, there is no such pleasure
   in life!
   Up at a Villa—Down in the City

32 What's become of Waring
   Since he gave us all the slip?
   Waring, I.i

33 In Vishnu-land what Avatar?
   vi

34 'When I last saw Waring...'
   (How all turned to him who spoke!
   You saw Waring? Truth or joke?
   In land-travel or sea-faring?)
   II.i

35 Let's contend no more, Love,
      Strive nor weep:
   All be as before, Love,
      —Only sleep!
   A Woman's Last Word

36 I knew you once: but in Paradise,

If we meet, I will pass nor turn my face.
The Worst of It, xix

1 I chanced upon a new book yesterday:
I opened it, and where my finger lay
'Twixt page and uncut page those words I read,
Some six or seven at most, and learned thereby
That you, FitzGerald, whom by ear and eye
She never knew, 'thanked God my wife was dead.'
Ay, dead! and were yourself alive, good Fitz,
How to return your thanks would pass my wits.
Kicking you seems the common lot of curs—
While more appropriate greeting lends you grace:
Surely to spit there glorifies your face—
Spitting from lips once sanctified by Hers.
Rejoinder to 213:19. *Athenaeum,* 13 July 1889

ROBERT BRUCE 1274–1329

2 Now, God be with you, my dear children: I have
breakfasted with you and shall sup with my Lord Jesus
Christ.
Oral tradition

BEAU BRUMMELL 1778–1840

3 Who's your fat friend? (Of the Prince of Wales.)
Gronow, *Reminiscences* (1862), p.63

4 I always like to have the morning well-aired before I
get up.
Charles Macfarlane, *Reminiscences of a Literary Life,* 27

5 No perfumes, but very fine linen, plenty of it, and
country washing.
Harriette Wilson, *Memoirs,* ch.2

6 Shut the door, Wales.
(To the Prince.) Attr.

WILLIAM JENNINGS BRYAN 1860–1925

7 The humblest citizen of all the land, when clad in the
armor of a righteous cause, is stronger than all the
hosts of error.
National Democratic Convention, Chicago, 1896

8 You shall not press down upon the brow of labour this
crown of thorns, you shall not crucify mankind upon a
cross of gold.

WILLIAM CULLEN BRYANT 1794–1878

9   They seemed
Like old companions in adversity.
A Winter Piece, l.26

ROBERT BUCHANAN 1841–1901

10   She just wore
Enough for modesty—no more.
White Rose and Red, I, v, l.60

11 The sweet post-prandial cigar.
De Berny

GEORGE VILLIERS, SECOND DUKE OF BUCKINGHAM 1628–1687

12 The world is made up for the most part of fools and
knaves.
To Mr. Clifford, on his Humane Reason

13 What the devil does the plot signify, except to bring in

fine things?
The Rehearsal (1671), III.i

14 Ay, now the plot thickens very much upon us.
ii

JOHN SHEFFIELD, FIRST DUKE OF BUCKINGHAM AND NORMANBY 1648–1721

15 Learn to write well, or not to write at all.
Essay on Satire, l.281

H. J. BUCKOLL 1803–1871

16 Lord, behold us with Thy blessing
Once again assembled here.
**Psalms and Hymns for the Use of Rugby School Chapel. Lord,
Behold us with Thy Blessing**

17 Lord, dismiss us with Thy blessing,
Thanks for mercies past receive.
Lord, Dismiss us with Thy Blessing

J. B. BUCKSTONE 1802–1879

18 On such an occasion as this,
All time and nonsense scorning,
Nothing shall come amiss,
And we won't go home till morning.
Billy Taylor, I.ii

EUSTACE BUDGELL 1686–1737

19 What Cato did, and Addison approved
Cannot be wrong.
Lines found on his desk after his suicide, 4 May 1737

COMTE DE BUFFON 1707–1788

20 *Ces choses sont hors de l'homme, le style est l'homme
même.*
These things [subject matter] are external to the man;
style is the man.
Discours sur le Style, address given to the Académie française, 25
Aug. 1753

21 *Le génie n'est qu'une plus grande aptitude à la
patience.*
Genius is only a greater aptitude for patience.
Hérault de Séchelles, *Voyage à Montbar* (1803), p.15

PROF. ARTHUR BULLER 1874–1944

22 There was a young lady named Bright,
Whose speed was far faster than light;
   She set out one day
   In a relative way,
And returned home the previous night.
Punch, 19 Dec. 1923

COUNT VON BÜLOW 1849–1929

23 *Mit einem Worte: wir wollen niemand in den Schatten
stellen aber wir verlangen auch unseren Platz an der
Sonne.*
In a word, we desire to throw no one into the shade [in
East Asia], but we also demand our own place in the
sun.
Reichstag, 6 Dec. 1897

EDWARD GEORGE BULWER-LYTTON, BARON LYTTON 1803–1873

1 Ah, never can fall from the days that have been
A gleam on the years that shall be!
A Lament

2 Here Stanley meets,—how Stanley scorns, the glance!
The brilliant chief, irregularly great,
Frank, haughty, rash,—the Rupert of Debate.
Of Edward Stanley, 14th Earl of Derby. *The New Timon*
(1845-7), pt.I.vi. See 184:13

3 Out-babying Wordsworth and out-glittering Keats.
(Tennyson.)

4 Beneath the rule of men entirely great
The pen is mightier than the sword.
Richelieu (1838), II.ii

5 In the lexicon of youth, which Fate reserves
For a bright manhood, there is no such word
As—*fail*!

6 Poverty has strange bedfellows.
The Caxtons (1850), pt.iv, ch.4

7 There is no man so friendless but what he can find a
friend sincere enough to tell him disagreeable truths.
What Will He Do With It? (1858), bk.iii, ch.15 (heading)

EDWARD ROBERT BULWER, EARL OF LYTTON
see OWEN MEREDITH

ALFRED BUNN 1796?–1860

8 Alice, where art thou?
Song

9 I dreamt that I dwelt in marble halls,
With vassals and serfs at my side.
The Bohemian Girl, Act II

JOHN BUNYAN 1628–1688

10 As I walk'd through the wilderness of this world.
The Pilgrim's Progress (1678), pt.i

11 The name of the slough was Despond.

12 *Christian:* Gentlemen, Whence came you, and whither
do you go?
Formalist and *Hypocrisy:* We were born in the land of
Vainglory, and we are going for praise to Mount Sion.

13 The valley of Humiliation.

14 A foul Fiend coming over the field to meet him; his
name is Apollyon.

15 Then Apollyon straddled quite over the whole breadth
of the way.

16 It beareth the name of Vanity-Fair, because the town
where 'tis kept, is lighter than vanity.
See 393:20

17 Hanging is too good for him, said Mr Cruelty.

18 Yet my great-grandfather was but a water-man,
looking one way, and rowing another: and I got most
of my estate by the same occupation. [Mr. By-Ends.]
See 116:15

19 They are for religion when in rags and contempt; but I
am for him when he walks in his golden slippers, in
the sunshine and with applause.

20 A castle, called Doubting-Castle, the owner whereof
was Giant Despair.

21 Now Giant Despair had a wife, and her name was
Diffidence.

22 A grievous crab-tree cudgel.

23 They came to the Delectable Mountains.

24 Sleep is sweet to the labouring man.
See 55:17

25 A great horror and darkness fell upon Christian.

26 Then I saw that there was a way to Hell, even from the
gates of heaven.

27 So I awoke, and behold it was a dream.

28 A man that could look no way but downwards, with a
muckrake in his hand.
pt.ii

29 One leak will sink a ship, and one sin will destroy a
sinner.

30 A young Woman her name was Dull.

31 One Great-heart.

32 He that is down needs fear no fall,
He that is low no pride.
He that is humble ever shall
Have God to be his guide.
Shepherd Boy's Song

33 A very zealous man...Difficulties, Lions, or
Vanity-Fair he feared not at all; 'Twas only Sin,
Death, and Hell that was to him a terror. [Mr.
Fearing.]

34 A man there was, tho' some did count him mad,
The more he cast away, the more he had.

35 An ornament to her profession.

36 Who would true valour see,
Let him come hither;
One here will constant be,
Come wind, come weather.
There's no discouragement
Shall make him once relent
His first avow'd intent
To be a pilgrim.

Who so beset him round
With dismal stories,
Do but themselves confound—
His strength the more is.

37 The last words of Mr Despondency were, Farewell
night, welcome day. His daughter went through the
river singing, but none could understand what she
said.

38 Though with great difficulty I am got hither, yet now I
do not repent me of all the trouble I have been at to
arrive where I am. My sword, I give to him that shall
succeed me in my pilgrimage, and my courage and
skill to him that can get it. My marks and scars I carry
with me, to be a witness for me, that I have fought his
battles, who will now be my rewarder...So he passed
over, and the trumpets sounded for him on the other
side. [Mr. Valiant-for-Truth.]

39 I have formerly lived by hearsay, and faith, but now I
go where I shall live by sight, and shall be with Him in
whose company I delight myself. [Mr. Standfast.]

REVD. SAMUEL DICKINSON BURCHARD
1812–1891

1 We are Republicans and don't propose to leave our party and identify ourselves with the party whose antecedents are rum, Romanism, and rebellion.
Speech, New York City, 29 Oct. 1884

GELETT BURGESS 1866–1951

2 I never saw a Purple Cow,
  I never hope to see one;
But I can tell you, anyhow,
  I'd rather see than be one!
Burgess Nonsense Book. **The Purple Cow**

3 Ah, yes! I wrote the 'Purple Cow'—
  I'm sorry, now, I wrote it!
But I can tell you anyhow,
  I'll kill you if you quote it!

DEAN BURGON 1813–1888

4 Match me such marvel save in Eastern clime,
A rose-red city 'half as old as Time'!
Petra (1845). See 407:9

GENERAL BURGOYNE 1722–1792

5 You have only, when before your glass, to keep pronouncing to yourself nimini-pimini—the lips cannot fail of taking their plie.
The Heiress (1786), III.ii

EDMUND BURKE 1729–1797

6 I would rather sleep in the southern corner of a little country church-yard, than in the tomb of the Capulets. I should like, however, that my dust should mingle with kindred dust.
Letter to Matthew Smith, 1750

7 There are others so continually in the agitation of gross and merely sensual pleasures, or so occupied in the low drudgery of avarice, or so heated in the chase of honours and distinction, that their minds, which had been used continually to the storms of these violent and tempestuous passions, can hardly be put in motion by the delicate and refined play of the imagination.
On the Sublime and Beautiful (1756), introduction

8 I am convinced that we have a degree of delight, and that no small one, in the real misfortunes and pains of others.
pt.i, xiv

9 No passion so effectually robs the mind of all its powers of acting and reasoning as fear.
pt.ii, ii

10 Custom reconciles us to everything.
pt.iv, xviii

11 The fabric of superstition has in our age and nation received much ruder shocks than it had ever felt before; and through the chinks and breaches of our prison we see such glimmerings of light, and feel such refreshing airs of liberty, as daily raise our ardour for more.
A Vindication of Natural Society (1756)

12 A good parson once said, that where mystery begins, religion ends. Cannot I say, as truly at least, of human laws, that where mystery begins, justice ends? It is hard to say whether the doctors of law or divinity have made the greater advance in the lucrative business of mystery.

13 There is, however, a limit at which forbearance ceases to be a virtue.
Observations on a Publication, 'The present state of the nation' (1769)

14 It is piteously doleful, nodding every now and then towards dulness; well stored with pious frauds, and, like most discourses of the sort, much better calculated for the private advantage of the preacher than the edification of the hearers.

15 It is a general popular error to imagine the loudest complainers for the public to be the most anxious for its welfare.

16 People not very well grounded in the principles of public morality find a set of maxims in office ready made for them, which they assume as naturally and inevitably as any of the insignia or instruments of the situation. A certain tone of the solid and practical is immediately acquired. Every former profession of public spirit is to be considered as a debauch of youth, or, at best, as a visionary scheme of unattainable perfection. The very idea of consistency is exploded. The convenience of the business of the day is to furnish the principle for doing it.

17 To complain of the age we live in, to murmur at the present possessors of power, to lament the past, to conceive extravagant hopes of the future, are the common dispositions of the greatest part of mankind.
Thoughts on the Cause of the Present Discontents (1770)

18 I am not one of those who think that the people are never in the wrong. They have been so, frequently and outrageously, both in other countries and in this. But I do say, that in all disputes between them and their rulers, the presumption is at least upon a par in favour of the people.

19 The power of the crown, almost dead and rotten as Prerogative, has grown up anew, with much more strength, and far less odium, under the name of Influence.

20 We must soften into a credulity below the milkiness of infancy to think all men virtuous. We must be tainted with a malignity truly diabolical, to believe all the world to be equally wicked and corrupt.

21 The circumstances are in a great measure new. We have hardly any landmarks from the wisdom of our ancestors to guide us.

22 When bad men combine, the good must associate; else they will fall, one by one, an unpitied sacrifice in a contemptible struggle.

23 Of this stamp is the cant of *Not men, but measures;* a sort of charm by which many people get loose from every honourable engagement.

24 It is therefore our business carefully to cultivate in our minds, to rear to the most perfect vigour and maturity, every sort of generous and honest feeling that belongs to our nature. To bring the dispositions that are lovely in private life into the service and conduct of the commonwealth; so to be patriots, as not to forget we are gentlemen.

1 The greater the power, the more dangerous the abuse.
Speech on the Middlesex Election, 7 Feb. 1771

2 Would twenty shillings have ruined Mr Hampden's fortune? No! but the payment of half twenty shillings, on the principle it was demanded, would have made him a slave.
Speech on American Taxation (1774)

3 It is the nature of all greatness not to be exact, and great trade will always be attended with considerable abuses.

4 Falsehood has a perennial spring.

5 Sir, the venerable age of this great man, his merited rank, his superior eloquence, his splendid qualities, his eminent services, the vast space he fills in the eye of mankind, and, more than all the rest, his fall from power, which like death canonizes and sanctifies a great character, will not suffer me to censure any part of his conduct. I am afraid to flatter him; I am sure I am not disposed to blame him. Let those who have betrayed him by their adulation insult him with their malevolence. But what I do not presume to censure I may have leave to lament. For a wise man, he seemed to me at that time to be governed too much by general maxims. I speak with the freedom of history, and I hope without offence.
(Of Lord Chatham.)

6 For even then, sir, even before this splendid orb was entirely set, and while the western horizon was in a blaze with his descending glory, on the opposite quarter of the heavens arose another luminary, and, for his hour, became lord of the ascendant.
(Of Lord Chatham and Charles Townshend.)

7 Great men are the guide-posts and landmarks in the state.

8 He had no failings which were not owing to a noble cause; to an ardent, generous, perhaps an immoderate passion for fame; a passion which is the instinct of all great souls.
(Of Charles Townshend.)

9 To tax and to please, no more than to love and to be wise, is not given to men.

10 The only liberty I mean, is a liberty connected with order; that not only exists along with order and virtue, but which cannot exist at all without them.
Speech at his arrival at Bristol, 13 Oct. 1774

11 Your representative owes you, not his industry only, but his judgement; and he betrays, instead of serving you, if he sacrifices it to your opinion.
Speech to the Electors of Bristol, 3 Nov. 1774

12 Parliament is not a *congress* of ambassadors from different and hostile interests; which interests each must maintain, as an agent and advocate, against other agents and advocates; but parliament is a *deliberative* assembly of *one* nation, with *one* interest, that of the whole; where, not local purposes, not local prejudices ought to guide, but the general good, resulting from the general reason of the whole. You choose a member indeed; but when you have chosen him, he is not member of Bristol, but he is a member of *parliament*.

13 I have in general no very exalted opinion of the virtue of paper government.
Speech on Conciliation with America, (22 Mar. 1775)

14 The concessions of the weak are the concessions of fear.

15 Young man, there is America—which at this day serves for little more than to amuse you with stories of savage men, and uncouth manners; yet shall, before you taste of death, show itself equal to the whole of that commerce which now attracts the envy of the world.

16 When we speak of the commerce with our colonies, fiction lags after truth; invention is unfruitful, and imagination cold and barren.

17 Neither the perseverance of Holland, nor the activity of France, nor the dexterous and firm sagacity of English enterprise, ever carried this most perilous mode of hard industry to the extent to which it has been pushed by this recent people; a people who are still, as it were, but in the gristle and not yet hardened into the bone of manhood.
(Of Americans and their fishing industry.)

18 Through a wise and salutary neglect [of the colonies], a generous nature has been suffered to take her own way to perfection; when I reflect upon these effects, when I see how profitable they have been to us, I feel all the pride of power sink and all presumption in the wisdom of human contrivances melt and die away within me. My rigour relents, I pardon something to the spirit of liberty.

19 The use of force alone is but *temporary.*It may subdue for a moment; but it does not remove the necessity of subduing again; and a nation is not governed, which is perpetually to be conquered.

20 Nothing less will content me, than *whole America.*

21 Abstract liberty, like other mere abstractions, is not to be found.

22 All protestantism, even the most cold and passive, is a sort of dissent. But the religion most prevalent in our northern colonies is a refinement on the principle of resistance; it is the dissidence of dissent, and the protestantism of the Protestant religion.

23 In no country perhaps in the world is the law so general a study...This study renders men acute, inquisitive, dexterous, prompt in attack, ready in defence, full of resources...They augur misgovernment at a distance, and snuff the approach of tyranny in every tainted breeze.

24 The mysterious virtue of wax and parchment.

25 I do not know the method of drawing up an indictment against an whole people.

26 It is not, what a lawyer tells me I *may* do; but what humanity, reason, and justice, tell me I ought to do.

27 Govern two millions of men, impatient of servitude, on the principles of freedom.

28 I am not determining a point of law; I am restoring tranquillity.

29 The march of the human mind is slow.

30 Freedom and not servitude is the cure of anarchy; as religion, and not atheism, is the true remedy for superstition.

31 Instead of a standing revenue, you will have therefore a perpetual quarrel.

1 Parties must ever exist in a free country.

2 My hold of the colonies is in the close affection which grows from common names, from kindred blood, from similar privileges, and equal protection. These are ties which, though light as air, are as strong as links of iron.

3 Slavery they can have anywhere. It is a weed that grows in every soil.

4 Deny them this participation of freedom, and you break that sole bond, which originally made, and must still preserve the unity of the empire.

5 It is the love of the people; it is their attachment to their government, from the sense of the deep stake they have in such a glorious institution, which gives you your army and your navy, and infuses into both that liberal obedience, without which your army would be a base rabble, and your navy nothing but rotten timber.

6 Magnanimity in politics is not seldom the truest wisdom; and a great empire and little minds go ill together.

7 By adverting to the dignity of this high calling, our ancestors have turned a savage wilderness into a glorious empire: and have made the most extensive, and the only honourable conquests, not by destroying, but by promoting the wealth, the number, the happiness of the human race.

8 People crushed by law have no hopes but from power. If laws are their enemies, they will be enemies to laws; and those, who have much to hope and nothing to lose, will always be dangerous, more or less.
Letter to the Hon. C.J. Fox, 8 Oct. 1777

9 I know many have been taught to think that moderation, in a case like this, is a sort of treason.
Letter to the Sheriffs of Bristol (1777)

10 Between craft and credulity, the voice of reason is stifled.

11 If any ask me what a free government is, I answer, that for any practical purpose, it is what the people think so.

12 Liberty, too, must be limited in order to be possessed.

13 Nothing in progression can rest on its original plan. We may as well think of rocking a grown man in the cradle of an infant.

14 Among a people generally corrupt, liberty cannot long exist.

15 The coquetry of public opinion, which has her caprices, and must have her way.
Letter to Thos. Burgh, New Year's Day, 1780

16 Corrupt influence, which is itself the perennial spring of all prodigality, and of all disorder; which loads us, more than millions of debt; which takes away vigour from our arms, wisdom from our councils, and every shadow of authority and credit from the most venerable parts of our constitution.
Speech on the Economical Reform, 11 Feb. 1780

17 Individuals pass like shadows; but the commonwealth is fixed and stable.

18 The people are the masters.

19 Applaud us when we run; console us when we fall; cheer us when we recover; but let us pass on—for God's sake, let us pass on!
Speech at Bristol previous to the Election, 1780

20 Bad laws are the worst sort of tyranny.

21 The worthy gentleman [Mr. Coombe], who has been snatched from us at the moment of the election, and in the middle of the contest, whilst his desires were as warm, and his hopes as eager as ours, has feelingly told us, what shadows we are, and what shadows we pursue.
Speech at Bristol on Declining the Poll, 1780

22 Not merely a chip of the old 'block', but the old block itself.
On Pitt's First Speech, 1781

23 The arrogance of age must submit to be taught by youth.
Letter to Fanny Burney, 29 July, 1782

24 Every other conqueror of every other description has left some monument, either of state or beneficence, behind him. Were we to be driven out of India this day, nothing would remain to tell that it had been possessed, during the inglorious period of our dominion, by anything better than the orang-outang or the tiger.
Speech on Fox's East India Bill, 1 Dec. 1783

25 Your governor stimulates a rapacious and licentious soldiery to the personal search of women, lest these unhappy creatures should avail themselves of the protection of their sex to secure any supply for their necessities.
(Of Warren Hastings in India).

26 He has put to hazard his ease, his security, his interest, his power, even his darling popularity, for the benefit of a people whom he has never seen.

27 The people never give up their liberties but under some delusion.
Speech at County Meeting of Buckinghamshire, 1784

28 What the greatest inquest of the nation has begun, its highest Tribunal [the British House of Commons] will accomplish.
Impeachment of Warren Hastings, 15 Feb. 1788

29 Religious persecution may shield itself under the guise of a mistaken and over-zealous piety.
17 Feb. 1788

30 An event has happened, upon which it is difficult to speak, and impossible to be silent.
5 May 1789

31 Resolved to die in the last dyke of prevarication.
7 May 1789

32 There is but one law for all, namely, that law which governs all law, the law of our Creator, the law of humanity, justice, equity—the law of nature, and of nations.
28 May 1794

33 I impeach him in the name of the people of India, whose rights he has trodden under foot, and whose country he has turned into a desert. Lastly, in the name of human nature itself, in the name of both sexes, in the name of every age, in the name of every rank, I impeach the common enemy and oppressor of all!
Impeachment of Warren Hastings, as recorded by Macaulay in his essay on Warren Hastings

34 I flatter myself that I love a manly, moral, regulated

liberty as well as any gentleman.
Reflections on the Revolution in France (1790)

1 Whenever our neighbour's house is on fire, it cannot be amiss for the engines to play a little on our own.

2 Politics and the pulpit are terms that have little agreement. No sound ought to be heard in the church but the healing voice of Christian charity.

3 Surely the church is a place where one day's truce ought to be allowed to the dissensions and animosities of mankind.

4 A state without the means of some change is without the means of its conservation.

5 Make the Revolution a parent of settlement, and not a nursery of future revolutions.

6 We, on our parts, have learned to speak only the primitive language of the law, and not the confused jargon of their Babylonian pulpits.

7 People will not look forward to posterity, who never look backward to their ancestors.

8 Government is a contrivance of human wisdom to provide for human *wants*. Men have a right that these wants should be provided for by this wisdom.

9 It is now sixteen or seventeen years since I saw the Queen of France, then the Dauphiness, at Versailles; and surely never lighted on this orb, which she hardly seemed to touch, a more delightful vision. I saw her just above the horizon, decorating and cheering the elevated sphere she just began to move in,—glittering like the morning star, full of life, and splendour, and joy. Oh! what a revolution! and what a heart I must have, to comtemplate without emotion that elevation and that fall! Little did I dream when she added titles of veneration to those of enthusiastic, distant, respectful love, that she should ever be obliged to carry the sharp antidote against disgrace concealed in that bosom; little did I dream that I should have lived to see disasters fallen upon her in a nation of gallant men, in a nation of men of honour, and of cavaliers. I thought ten thousand swords must have leaped from their scabbards to avenge even a look that threatened her with insult. But the age of chivalry is gone. That of sophisters, economists, and calculators, has succeeded; and the glory of Europe is extinguished for ever.

10 The unbought grace of life, the cheap defence of nations, the nurse of manly sentiment and heroic enterprise is gone! It is gone, that sensibility of principle, that chastity of honour, which felt a stain like a wound, which inspired courage whilst it mitigated ferocity, which ennobled whatever it touched, and under which vice itself lost half its evil, by losing all its grossness.

11 This barbarous philosophy, which is the offspring of cold hearts and muddy understandings.

12 In the groves of *their* academy, at the end of every vista, you see nothing but the gallows.

13 Kings will be tyrants from policy, when subjects are rebels from principle.

14 Learning will be cast into the mire, and trodden down under the hoofs of a swinish multitude.

15 France has always more or less influenced manners in England; and when your fountain is choked up and polluted, the stream will not run long, or will not run clear with us, or perhaps with any nation.

16 Because half a dozen grasshoppers under a fern make the field ring with their importunate chink, whilst thousands of great cattle, reposed beneath the shadow of the British oak, chew the cud and are silent, pray do not imagine that those who make the noise are the only inhabitants of the field; that, of course, they are many in number; or that, after all, they are other than the little, shrivelled, meagre, hopping, though loud and troublesome *insects* of the hour.

17 Who now reads Bolingbroke? Who ever read him through? Ask the booksellers of London what is become of all these lights of the world.

18 Man is by his constitution a religious animal.

19 A perfect democracy is therefore the most shameless thing in the world.

20 The men of England, the men, I mean, of light and leading in England, whose wisdom (if they have any) is open and direct, would be ashamed, as of a silly, deceitful trick, to profess any religion in name, which, by their proceedings, they appear to contemn.
See 352:7

21 Nobility is a graceful ornament to the civil order. It is the Corinthian capital of polished society.

22 Superstition is the religion of feeble minds.

23 He that wrestles with us strengthens our nerves, and sharpens our skill. Our antagonist is our helper.

24 Our patience will achieve more than our force.

25 Good order is the foundation of all good things.

26 Every politician ought to sacrifice to the graces; and to join compliance with reason.

27 The conduct of a losing party never appears right: at least it never can possess the only infallible criterion of wisdom to vulgar judgments—success.
Letter to a Member of the National Assembly (1791)

28 Those who have been once intoxicated with power, and have derived any kind of emolument from it, even though but for one year, can never willingly abandon it.

29 Cromwell was a man in whom ambition had not wholly suppressed, but only suspended the sentiments of religion.

30 Tyrants seldom want pretexts.

31 You can never plan the future by the past.

32 Old religious factions are volcanoes burnt out.
Speech on the Petition of the Unitarians, 11 May 1792

33 Dangers by being despised grow great.

34 The cold neutrality of an impartial judge.
Preface to the Address of M. Brissot, 1794

35 Nothing is so fatal to religion as indifference, which is, at least, half infidelity.
Letter to Wm. Smith, 29 Jan. 1795

36 The silent touches of time.

37 Somebody had said, that a king may make a nobleman, but he cannot make a gentleman.

1 The grand Instructor, Time.
Letter to Sir H. Langrishe, 26 May 1795

2 To innovate is not to reform.
A Letter to a Noble Lord (1796)

3 These gentle historians, on the contrary, dip their pens in nothing but the milk of human kindness.

4 The storm has gone over me; and I lie like one of those old oaks which the late hurricane has scattered about me. I am stripped of all my honours; I am torn up by the roots, and lie prostrate on the earth!

5 The king, and his faithful subjects, the lords and commons of this realm,—the triple cord, which no man can break.
See 55:15

6 All men that are ruined are ruined on the side of their natural propensities.
Letters on a Regicide Peace, letter 1 (1796)

7 Example is the school of mankind, and they will learn at no other.

8 Never, no never, did Nature say one thing and Wisdom say another.
No.3 (1797)

9 Well is it known that ambition can creep as well as soar.

10 And having looked to government for bread, on the very first scarcity they will turn and bite the hand that fed them.
Thoughts and Details on Scarcity (1797)

11 Laws, like houses, lean on one another.
Tracts on the Popery Laws, ch.3, pt.i

12 In all forms of Government the people is the true legislator.

13 His virtues were his arts.
Inscription on the statue of the Marquis of Rockingham in Wentworth Park

14 'No,no', said he, 'it is not a good imitation of Johnson; it has all his pomp, without his force; it has all the nodosities of the oak without its strength; it has all the contortions of the Sibyl without the inspiration.'
Remark to Boswell who had spoken of Croft's *Life of Dr. Young* as a good imitation of Johnson's style. Boswell, *Life of Johnson,* vol.iv, p.59

WILLIAM CECIL, LORD BURLEIGH 1520–1598

15 What! all this for a song?
To Queen Elizabeth, when ordered to give a pension of £100 to Spenser. Birch, *Life of Spenser*, p.xiii

FANNY BURNEY 1752–1840

16 In the bosom of her respectable family resided Camilla.
Camilla (1796), bk.i, ch.1

17 Travelling is the ruin of all happiness! There's no looking at a building here after seeing Italy. [Mr. Meadows.]
Cecilia (1782), bk.iv, ch.2

18 'True, very true, ma'am,' said he [Mr. Meadows], yawning, 'one really lives no where; one does but vegetate, and wish it all at an end.'
bk.vii, ch.5

19 'The whole of this unfortunate business,' said Dr Lyster, 'has been the result of PRIDE AND PREJUDICE.'
bk.x, ch.10

20 Indeed, the freedom with which Dr Johnson condemns whatever he disapproves is astonishing.
Diary, 23 Aug. 1778

21 All the delusive seduction of martial music.
5-6 May, 1802

22 'Do you come to the play without knowing what it is?' 'O yes, Sir, yes, very frequently: I have no time to read play-bills; one merely comes to meet one's friends, and show that one's alive.'
Evelina, letter 20

JOHN BURNS 1858–1943

23 I have seen the Mississippi. That is muddy water. I have seen the St Lawrence. That is crystal water. But the Thames is liquid history.
Oral trad.

ROBERT BURNS 1759–1796

24 O thou! whatever title suit thee,
Auld Hornie, Satan, Nick, or Clootie.
Address to the Devil

25 Then gently scan your brother man,
    Still gentler sister woman;
Tho' they may gang a kennin wrang,
    To step aside is human.
Address to the Unco Guid

26 Then at the balance let's be mute,
    We never can adjust it;
What's done we partly may compute,
    But know not what's resisted.

27 Ae fond kiss, and then we sever;
Ae fareweel, and then for ever!
Ae Fond Kiss

28 But to see her was to love her,
Love but her, and love for ever.

29 Had we never lov'd sae kindly,
Had we never lov'd sae blindly,
Never met—or never parted,
We had ne'er been broken-hearted.

30 Should auld acquaintance be forgot,
    And never brought to mind?
Auld Lang Syne

31 We'll tak' a right gude-willie waught
    For auld lang syne.

32 We'll tak a cup o' kindness yet,
    For auld lang syne.

33 And there's a hand, my trusty fiere,
    And gie's a hand o'thine.

34 But tell me whisky's name in Greek,
        I'll tell the reason.
The Author's Earnest Cry and Prayer, xxx

35 Freedom and Whisky gang thegither!
xxxi

36 Sleep I can get nane
    For thinking on my dearie.
Ay Waukin O

37 O saw ye bonnie Lesley

As she gaed o'er the border?
She's gane, like Alexander,
  To spread her conquests farther.
To see her is to love her,
  And love but her for ever,
For Nature made her what she is,
  And ne'er made anither!
Bonnie Lesley

1 Bonnie wee thing, cannie wee thing,
    Lovely wee thing, wert thou mine,
  I wad wear thee in my bosom,
    Lest my jewel I should tine.
  The Bonnie Wee Thing

2 She draiglet a' her petticoatie,
    Coming through the rye.
  Coming Through the Rye (taken from an old song, *The Bob-tailed Lass*).

3 Gin a body meet a body
    Coming through the rye;
  Gin a body kiss a body,
    Need a body cry?

4 Contented wi' little and cantie wi' mair,
  Whene'er I forgather wi' Sorrow and Care,
  I gie them a skelp, as they're creeping alang,
  Wi' a cog o' gude swats and an auld Scotish sang.
  Contented wi' Little

5 Th' expectant wee-things, toddlin', stacher through
    To meet their Dad, wi' flichterin' noise an' glee.
  His wee bit ingle, blinkin bonnilie,
    His clean hearth-stane, his thrifty wifie's smile,
  The lisping infant prattling on his knee,
    Does a' his weary kiaugh and care beguile,
  An' makes him quite forget his labour an' his toil.
  The Cotter's Saturday Night, iii

6 They never sought in vain that sought the Lord aright!
  vi

7 Is there, in human-form, that bears a heart—
    A wretch! a villain! lost to love and truth!
  That can, with studied, sly, ensnaring art,
    Betray sweet Jenny's unsuspecting youth?
  x

8 The halesome parritch, chief of Scotia's food.
  xi

9 The sire turns o'er, wi' patriarchal grace,
    The big ha'-Bible, ance his father's pride.
  xii

10 From scenes like these old Scotia's grandeur springs,
    That makes her loved at home, revered abroad:
  Princes and Lords are but the breath of kings,
    'An honest man's the noblest work of God.'
  xix. See 379:24

11 I wasna fou, but just had plenty.
  Death and Dr. Hornbook, iii

12 On ev'ry hand it will allow'd be,
  He's just—nae better than he should be.
  A Dedication to Gavin Hamilton, l.25

13 There's threesome reels, there's foursome reels,
    There's hornpipes and strathspeys, man,
  But the ae best dance e'er cam to the Land
    Was, the de'il's awa wi' th'Exciseman.
  The De'il's awa wi' th'Exciseman

14 But Facts are chiels that winna ding,

An' downa be disputed.
  A Dream

15 A Gentleman who held the patent for his honours
  immediately from Almighty God.
  Elegy on Capt. Matthew Henderson: from the title

16 Perhaps it may turn out a sang,
    Perhaps turn out a sermon.
  Epistle to a Young Friend, 1786

17 I wave the quantum o' the sin,
    The hazard of concealing;
  But och; it hardens a' within,
    And petrifies the feeling!

18 An atheist-laugh's a poor exchange
    For Deity offended.

19 What's a' your jargon o' your schools,
  Your Latin names for horns and stools;
  If honest Nature made you fools,
      What sairs your grammars?
  First Epistle to John Lapraik

20 Gie me ae spark o' Nature's fire,
  That's a' the learning I desire.

21 For thus the royal mandate ran,
  When first the human race began,
  'The social friendly, honest man,
      Whate'er he be,
  'Tis he fulfils great Nature's plan,
      And none but he!'
  Second Epistle to Lapraik

22 A Workhouse! ah, that sound awakes my woes,
  And pillows on the thorn my racked repose!
  In durance vile here must I wake and weep,
  And all my frowzy couch in sorrow steep.
  Epistle from Esopus to Maria, l.57

23 Just now I've taen the fit o' rhyme,
  My barmie noddle's working prime.
  Epistle to James Smith

24 Some rhyme a neebor's name to lash;
  Some rhyme (vain thought!) for needfu' cash;
  Some rhyme to court the country clash,
      An' raise a din;
  For me, an aim I never fash;
      I rhyme for fun.

25 Farewell dear, deluding Woman,
  The joy of joys!

26 If there's another world, he lives in bliss;
  If there is none, he made the best of this.
  Epitaph on Wm. Muir

27 Flow gently, sweet Afton, among thy green braes,
  Flow gently, I'll sing thee a song in thy praise.
  My Mary's asleep by thy murmuring stream,
  Flow gently, sweet Afton, disturb not her dream.
  Flow gently, sweet Afton

28 The rank is but the guinea's stamp,
    The man's the gowd for a' that!
  For a' that and a' that

29 A man's a man for a' that.

30 There's Death in the cup—so beware!
  On a Goblet

31 Go fetch to me a pint o' wine,
  An' fill it in a silver tassie.
  Go Fetch to Me a Pint

1 Green grow the rashes O,
    Green grow the rashes O;
The sweetest hours that e'er I spend,
Are spent among the lasses O!
Green Grow the Rashes

2 But gie me a canny hour at e'en,
    My arms about my dearie O;
An' warly cares, an' warly men,
    May a' gae tapsalteerie O!

3 The wisest man the warl' saw,
    He dearly lov'd the lasses O.

4 Auld nature swears, the lovely dears
    Her noblest work she classes O;
Her prentice han' she tried on man,
    An' then she made the lasses O.

5 It's guid to be merry and wise,
    It's guid to be honest and true,
It's guid to support Caledonia's cause,
    And bide by the buff and the blue.
Here's a Health to Them that's Awa'

6 O, gie me the lass that has acres o' charms,
O, gie me the lass wi' the weel-stockit farms.
Hey for a Lass wi' a Tocher

7 Here some are thinkin' on their sins,
    An' some upo' their claes.
The Holy Fair, x

8 Leeze me on drink! it gi'es us mair
    Than either school or college.
    xix

9 There's some are fou o' love divine,
    There's some are fou o' brandy.
    xxvii

10 It was a' for our rightfu' King
    We left fair Scotland's strand.
It was a' for our Rightfu' King

11 The soger frae the wars returns,
    The sailor frae the main,
But I hae parted frae my Love,
    Never to meet again, my dear,
    Never to meet again.

12 John Anderson my jo, John,
    When we were first acquent,
Your locks were like the raven,
    Your bonny brow was brent.
John Anderson My Jo

13 There were three kings into the east,
Three kings both great and high;
And they hae sworn a solemn oath
John Barleycorn should die.
John Barleycorn

14 Some have meat and cannot eat,
    Some cannot eat that want it:
But we have meat and we can eat,
    Sae let the Lord be thankit.
The Kirkudbright Grace. (Also known as the Selkirk Grace.)

15 I've seen sae mony changefu' years,
    On earth I am a stranger grown;
I wander in the ways of men,
    Alike unknowing and unknown.
Lament for James, Earl of Glencairn

16 Cease, ye prudes, your envious railing,
    Lovely Burns has charms—*confess*;

True it is, she had one failing,
    Had ae woman ever less?
Lines written under the Picture of Miss Burns

17 I once was a maid, tho' I cannot tell when,
And still my delight is in proper young men.
Love and Liberty—A Cantata, l.57

18 Partly wi' love o'ercome sae sair,
    And partly she was drunk.
l.183

19 A fig for those by law protected!
    Liberty's a glorious feast!
Courts for cowards were erected,
    Churches built to please the priest.
l.254

20 Life is all a variorum,
    We regard not how it goes;
Let them cant about decorum
    Who have characters to lose.
l.270

21 May coward shame distain his name,
    The wretch that dares not die!
Macpherson's Farewell

22   Nature's law,
That man was made to mourn!
Man was made to Mourn

23 Man's inhumanity to man
    Makes countless thousands mourn!

24 O Death, the poor man's dearest friend,
    The kindest and the best!

25 My heart's in the Highlands, my heart is not here;
My heart's in the Highlands a-chasing the deer;
Chasing the wild deer, and following the roe,
My heart's in the Highlands, wherever I go.
My Heart's in the Highlands

26 Farewell to the Highlands, farewell to the North,
The birth-place of valour, the country of worth.

27 O, my Luve's like a red red rose
    That's newly sprung in June:
O my Luve's like the melodie
    That's sweetly play'd in tune.
My Love is like a Red Red Rose

28 The minister kiss'd the fiddler's wife,
    An' could na preach for thinkin' o't.
My Love she's but a Lassie yet

29 An idiot race to honour lost,
Who know them best, despise them most.
On Seeing Stirling Palace in Ruins

30 The wan moon sets behind the white wave,
And time is setting with me, Oh.
Open the door to me, Oh

31 Or were I in the wildest waste,
    Sae black and bare, sae black and bare,
The desert were a paradise,
    If thou wert there, if thou wert there.
O, Wert Thou in the Could Blast

32 The mair they talk I'm kent the better.
The Poet's Welcome (to his bastard child)

33 O Luve will venture in, where it daur na weel be seen.
The Posie

34 Scots, wha hae wi' Wallace bled,
Scots, wham Bruce has aften led,
Welcome to your gory bed,

Or to victorie.
Now's the day, and now's the hour;
See the front o' battle lour!
See approach proud Edward's power—
Chains and slaverie!
Scots, Wha Hae (Robert Bruce's March to Bannockburn)

1 Liberty's in every blow!
Let us do or die!

2 Good Lord, what is man! for as simple he looks,
Do but try to develop his hooks and his crooks,
With his depths and his shallows, his good and his
evil,
All in all, he's a problem must puzzle the devil.
Sketch: inscribed to C.J. Fox

3 While we sit bousing at the nappy,
And getting fou and unco happy,
We think na on the lang Scots miles,
The mosses, waters, staps, and styles,
That lie between us and our hame,
Whare sits our sulky sullen dame,
Gathering her brows like gathering storm,
Nursing her wrath to keep it warm.
Tam o' Shanter, l.10

4 Auld Ayr, wham ne'er a town surpasses
For honest men and bonnie lasses.
l.15

5 His ancient, trusty, drouthy crony;
Tam lo'ed him like a vera brither;
They had been fou for weeks thegither.
l.43

6 Kings may be blest, but Tam was glorious,
O'er a' the ills o' life victorious!
l.57

7 But pleasures are like poppies spread—
You seize the flow'r, its bloom is shed;
Or like the snow falls in the river—
A moment white—then melts for ever.
l.59

8 Nae man can tether time or tide.
l.67

9 Inspiring bold John Barleycorn!
What dangers thou canst make us scorn!
Wi' tippenny, we fear nae evil;
Wi' usquebae, we'll face the devil!
l.105

10 As Tammie glowr'd, amaz'd, and curious,
The mirth and fun grew fast and furious.
l.143

11 Ev'n Satan glowr'd, and fidg'd fu' fain,
An' hotched an' blew wi' might an' main:
Till first ae caper, syne anither,
Tam tint his reason a' thegither,
And roars out, 'Weel done, Cutty-sark!'
l.185

12 Ah, Tam! ah, Tam! thou'll get thy fairin'!
In hell they'll roast thee like a herrin'!
l.201

13 A man may drink and no be drunk;
A man may fight and no be slain;
A man may kiss a bonnie lass,
And aye be welcome back again.
There was a Lass, they ca'd her Meg

14 Come, Firm Resolve, take thou the van,

Thou stalk o' carl-hemp in man!
And let us mind, faint heart ne'er wan
A lady fair;
Wha does the utmost that he can,
Will whyles do mair.
To Dr. Blacklock

15 To make a happy fire-side clime
To weans and wife,
That's the true pathos and sublime
Of human life.

16 Fair fa' your honest sonsie face,
Great chieftain o' the puddin'-race!
Aboon them a' ye tak your place,
Painch, tripe, or thairm:
Weel are ye wordy o' a grace
As lang's my arm.
To a Haggis

17 His spindle shank a guid whip-lash,
His nieve a nit.

18 O wad some Pow'r the giftie gie us
To see oursels as others see us!
It wad frae mony a blunder free us,
And foolish notion.
To a Louse

19 Ev'n thou who mourn'st the Daisy's fate,
That fate is thine—no distant date;
Stern Ruin's ploughshare drives elate
Full on thy bloom,
Till crush'd beneath the furrow's weight
Shall be thy doom!
To a Mountain Daisy

20 Wee, sleekit, cow'rin', tim'rous beastie,
O what a panic's in thy breastie!
Thou need na start awa sae hasty,
Wi' bickering brattle!
I wad be laith to rin an' chase thee,
Wi' murd'ring pattle!
To a Mouse

21 I'm truly sorry Man's dominion
Has broken Nature's social union,
An' justifies th' ill opinion
Which makes thee startle
At me, thy poor, earth-born companion
An' fellow-mortal!

22 The best laid schemes o' mice an' men
Gang aft a-gley.

23 Their sighin', cantin', grace-proud faces,
Their three-mile prayers, and half-mile graces.
To the Rev. John M'Math

24 We labour soon, we labour late,
To feed the titled knave, man,
And a' the comfort we're to get,
Is that ayont the grave, man.
The Tree of Liberty

25 His lockèd, lettered, braw brass collar,
Shew'd him the gentleman and scholar.
The Twa Dogs, l.13

26 And there began a lang digression
About the lords of the creation.
l.45

27 But human bodies are sic fools,
For a' their colleges and schools,
That when nae real ills perplex them,

They mak enow themsels to vex them.
l.195

1 Rejoiced they were na men but dogs.
l.236

2 Up in the morning's no' for me,
Up in the morning early.
Up in the Morning

3 What can a young lassie, what shall a young lassie,
What can a young lassie do wi' an auld man?
What can a Young Lassie

4 O whistle, and I'll come to you, my lad:
O whistle, and I'll come to you, my lad:
Tho' father and mither and a' should gae mad,
O whistle, and I'll come to you, my lad.
Whistle, and I'll come to you, my Lad

5 It is the moon, I ken her horn,
  That's blinkin' in the lift sae hie;
She shines sae bright to wyle us hame,
  But, by my sooth! she'll wait a wee.
Willie Brewed a Peck o' Maut

6 Ye banks and braes o' bonny Doon,
  How can ye bloom sae fresh and fair?
How can ye chant, ye little birds,
  And I sae weary fu' o' care?
Ye Banks and Braes o' Bonny Doon

7 Thou minds me o' departed joys,
Departed never to return.

8 And my fause lover stole my rose,
But ah! he left the thorn wi' me.

9 Don't let the awkward squad fire over me.
A. Cunningham, *Works of Burns; with his Life*, 1834, vol.i,
p.344

SIR FRED BURROWS 1887–1973

10 Unlike my predecessors, I have devoted more of my
life to shunting and hooting than to hunting and
shooting.
Speech as last Governor of undivided Bengal (1946-7), having
been President of the National Union of Railwaymen. Obituary,
Daily Telegraph, 24 Apr. 1973

SIR RICHARD BURTON 1821–1890

11 Don't be frightened; I am recalled. Pay, pack, and
follow at convenience.
Note to Isabel Burton, 19 August 1871 on being replaced as
Consul to Damascus. Isabel Burton, *Life of Sir Richard Burton*,
ch.21

ROBERT BURTON 1577–1640

12 All my joys to this are folly,
Naught so sweet as Melancholy.
Anatomy of Melancholy. **Author's Abstract of Melancholy**

13 They lard their lean books with the fat of others'
works.
Democritus to the Reader

14 I had no time to lick it into form, as she [a bear] doth
her young ones.

15 Like watermen, that row one way and look another.

16 Him that makes shoes go barefoot himself.

17 All poets are mad.

18 A loose, plain, rude writer.

19 Cookery is become an art, a noble science: cooks are
gentlemen.
pt.i, 2, memb.2, subsect.2

20 Die to save charges.
memb.3, subsect.12

21 I may not here omit those two main plagues, and
common dotages of human kind, wine and women,
which have infatuated and besotted myriads of people.
They go commonly together.
subsect.13

22 *Hinc quam sit calamus saevior ense patet.*
From this it is clear how much the pen is worse than
the sword.
memb.4, subsect.4

23 One was never married, and that's his hell; another is,
and that's his plague.
subsect.7

24 Seneca thinks he takes delight in seeing thee. The
gods are well pleased when they see great men
contending with adversity.
pt.ii, 3, memb.1, subsect.1

25 Every thing, saith Epictetus, hath two handles, the one
to be held by, the other not.
memb.3

26 Who cannot give good counsel? 'tis cheap, it costs
them nothing.

27 What is a ship but a prison?
memb.4

28 All places are distant from Heaven alike.

29 Tobacco, divine, rare, superexcellent tobacco, which
goes far beyond all their panaceas, potable gold, and
philosopher's stones, a sovereign remedy to all
diseases…But, as it is commonly abused by most
men, which take it as tinkers do ale, 'tis a plague, a
mischief, a violent purger of goods, lands, health,
hellish, devilish, and damned tobacco, the ruin and
overthrow of body and soul.
4, memb.2, subsect.1

30 Let me not live, saith Aretine's Antonia, if I had not
rather hear thy discourse than see a play!
pt.iii, 1, memb.1, subsect.1

31 And this is that Homer's golden chain, which reacheth
down from Heaven to earth, by which every creature is
annexed, and depends on his Creator.
subsect.2

32 To enlarge or illustrate this—is to set a candle in the
sun.
2, memb.1, subsect.2

33 No chord, nor cable can so forcibly draw, or hold so
fast, as love can do with a twined thread.

34 Cornelia kept her in talk till her children came from
school, and these, said she, are my jewels.
memb.2, subsect.3

35 To these crocodile's tears, they will add sobs, fiery
sighs, and sorrowful countenance.
subsect.4

36 Diogenes struck the father when the son swore.

37 England is a paradise for women, and hell for horses:
Italy a paradise for horses, hell for women, as the
diverb goes.
3, memb.1, subsect.2

1 The fear of some divine and supreme powers, keeps
men in obedience.
4, memb.1, subsect.2

2 One religion is as true as another.
memb.2, subsect.1

3 Be not solitary, be not idle.
final words

HERMANN BUSENBAUM 1600–1668

4 *Cum finis est licitus, etiam media sunt licita.*
The end justifies the means.
Medulla Theologiae Moralis (1650)

COMTE DE BUSSY-RABUTIN 1618–1693

5 *L'amour vient de l'aveuglement,*
L'amitié de la connaissance.
Love comes from blindness, friendship from
knowledge.
Histoire Amoureuse des Gaules. Maximes d'Amour, pt.I

6 *L'absence est à l'amour ce qu'est au feu le vent;*
Il éteint le petit, il allume le grand.
Absence is to love what wind is to fire; it extinguishes
the small, it enkindles the great.
pt.II. See 218:2, 310:15

7 *Comme vous savez, Dieu est d'ordinaire pour les gros*
escadrons contre les petits.
As you know, God is usually on the side of the big
squadrons against the small.
Letter to the Comte de Limoges, 18 Oct. 1677

BISHOP BUTLER 1692–1752

8 It has come, I know not how, to be taken for granted,
by many persons, that Christianity is not so much as a
subject of inquiry; but that it is, now at length,
discovered to be fictitious.
The Analogy of Religion (1756), Advertisement

9 But to *us,* probability is the very guide of life.
Introduction

10 Things and actions are what they are, and the
consequences of them will be what they will be: why
then should we desire to be deceived?
Fifteen Sermons. No.7, 16

11 Sir, the pretending to extraordinary revelations and
gifts of the Holy Ghost is a horrid thing, a very horrid
thing. [To John Wesley.]
Wesley, *Works,* xiii.449

NICHOLAS MURRAY BUTLER 1862–1947

12 ...a society like ours [U.S.A.] of which it is truly said
to be often but three generations 'from shirt-sleeves to
shirt-sleeves'.
True and False Democracy

13 An expert is one who knows more and more about less
and less.
attr. to a Commencement Address. Columbia University

SAMUEL BUTLER 1612–1680

14 He'd run in debt by disputation,
And pay with ratiocination.
Hudibras, pt.I, c.1, l.77

15 For rhetoric he could not ope

His mouth, but out there flew a trope.
1.81

16 For all a rhetorician's rules·
Teach nothing but to name his tools.
1.89

17 A Babylonish dialect
Which learned pedants much affect.
1.93

18 Beside, he was a shrewd philosopher,
And had read ev'ry text and gloss over.
1.127

19 What ever sceptic could inquire for;
For every why he had a wherefore.
1.131

20 He knew what's what, and that's as high
As metaphysic wit can fly.
1.149

21 Such as take lodgings in a head
That's to be let unfurnished.
1.160

22 And still be doing, never done:
As if Religion were intended
For nothing else but to be mended.
1.202

23 Compound for sins, they are inclin'd to
By damning those they have no mind to.
1.213

24 The trenchant blade, Toledo trusty,
For want of fighting was grown rusty,
And eat into it self, for lack
Of some body to hew and hack.
1.357

25 For rhyme the rudder is of verses,
With which like ships they steer their courses.
1.457

26 For what is Worth in anything,
But so much Money as 'twill bring.
1.465

27 He ne'er consider'd it, as loth
To look a gift-horse in the mouth.
1.483

28 Great actions are not always true sons
Of great and mighty resolutions.
1.885

29 Ay me! what perils do environ
The man that meddles with cold iron!
c.3, l.1

30   I'll make the fur
Fly 'bout the ears of the old cur.
1.277

31 Cheer'd up himself with ends of verse,
And sayings of philosophers.
1.1011

32 Cleric before, and Lay behind;
A lawless linsy-woolsy brother,
Half of one order, half another.
1.1226

33 Learning, that cobweb of the brain,
Profane, erroneous, and vain.
1.1339

34 For nothing goes for sense, or light,
That will not with old rules jump right;

As if rules were not in the schools
Derived from truth, but truth from rules.
1.1353

1 She that with poetry is won
Is but a desk to write upon.
pt.II, c.1, 1.591

2 Love is a boy, by poets styl'd,
Then spare the rod, and spoil the child.
1.844

3 The sun had long since in the lap
Of Thetis, taken out his nap,
And like a lobster boil'd, the morn
From black to red began to turn.
c.2, 1.29

4 Oaths are but words, and words but wind.
1.107

5 For saints may do the same things by
The Spirit, in sincerity,
Which other men are tempted to.
1.235

6 Doubtless the pleasure is as great
Of being cheated, as to cheat.
As lookers-on feel most delight,
That least perceive a juggler's sleight,
And still the less they understand,
The more th' admire his sleight of hand.
c.3, 1.1

7 Still amorous, and fond, and billing,
Like Philip and Mary on a shilling.
pt.III, c.1, 1.687

8 For in what stupid age or nation
Was marriage ever out of fashion?
1.817

9 Discords make the sweetest airs.
1.919

10 What makes all doctrines plain and clear?
About two hundred pounds a year.
And that which was prov'd true before,
Prove false again? Two hundred more.
1.1277

11 For if it be but half denied,
'Tis half as good as justified.
c.2, 1.803

12 For, those that fly, may fight again,
Which he can never do that's slain.
c.3, 1.243

13 He that complies against his will,
Is of his own opinion still.
1.547

14 For Justice, though she's painted blind,
Is to the weaker side inclin'd.
1.709

15 For money has a power above
The stars and fate, to manage love.
1.1279

16 The best of all our actions tend
To the preposterousest end.
Genuine Remains: Satire upon the Weakness and Misery of Man, 1.41

17 All love at first, like generous wine,
Ferments and frets until 'tis fine;
But when 'tis settled on the lee,
And from th' impurer matter free,

Becomes the richer still the older,
And proves the pleasanter the colder.
Miscellaneous Thoughts

18 The souls of women are so small,
That some believe they've none at all.

19 The law can take a purse in open court,
While it condemns a less delinquent for't.

20 For trouts are tickled best in muddy water.
On a Hypocritical Nonconformist, iv

SAMUEL BUTLER 1835–1902

21 It has been said that though God cannot alter the past,
historians can; it is perhaps because they can be useful
to Him in this respect that He tolerates their existence.
Erewhon Revisited, ch.14

22 I keep my books at the British Museum and at
Mudie's.
The Humour of Homer. Ramblings in Cheapside

23 The most perfect humour and irony is generally quite
unconscious.
Life and Habit, ch.2

24 It has, I believe, been often remarked, that a hen is
only an egg's way of making another egg.
ch.8

25 Life is one long process of getting tired.
Note Books, selected and edited by H. Festing Jones (1912), ch.I

26 Life is the art of drawing sufficient conclusions from
insufficient premises.

27 All progress is based upon a universal innate desire on
the part of every organism to live beyond its income.

28 When the righteous man turneth away from his
righteousness that he hath committed and doeth that
which is neither lawful nor quite right, he will
generally be found to have gained in amiability what
he has lost in holiness.
ch.II

29 I believe that more unhappiness comes from this
source than from any other—I mean from the attempt
to prolong family connection unduly and to make
people hang together artificially who would never
naturally do so. The mischief among the lower classes
is not so great, but among the middle and upper
classes it is killing a large number daily. And the old
people do not really like it much better than the young.

30 It costs a lot of money to die comfortably.

31 The healthy stomach is nothing if not conservative.
Few radicals have good digestions.
ch.VI

32 How thankful we ought to feel that Wordsworth was
only a poet and not a musician. Fancy a symphony by
Wordsworth! Fancy having to sit it out! And fancy
what it would have been if he had written fugues!
ch.VIII

33 The history of art is the history of revivals.

34 Genius...has been defined as a supreme capacity for
taking trouble...It might be more fitly described as a
supreme capacity for getting its possessors into pains
of all kinds, and keeping them therein so long as the
genius remains.
ch.XI

35 Talking it over, we agreed that Blake was no good

because he learnt Italian at over 60 to study Dante, and we knew Dante was no good because he was so fond of Virgil, and Virgil was no good because Tennyson ran him, and as for Tennyson—well, Tennyson goes without saying.
ch. XII

1 An Apology for the Devil: It must be remembered that we have only heard one side of the case. God has written all the books.
ch.XIV

2 God is Love, I dare say. But what a mischievous devil Love is.

3 To live is like to love—all reason is against it, and all healthy instinct for it.

4 The public buys its opinions as it buys its meat, or takes in its milk, on the principle that it is cheaper to do this than to keep a cow. So it is, but the milk is more likely to be watered.
ch.XVII

5 I do not mind lying but I hate inaccuracy.
ch.XIX

6 The world will, in the end, follow only those who have despised as well as served it.
ch.XXIV

7 An honest God's the noblest work of man.
Further extracts from the Note Books, selected and edited by A. Bartholomew (1934), p.26. See 270:17, 379:24

8 'Man wants but little here below' but likes that little good—and not too long in coming.
p.61. See 231:7, 588:8

9 Dulce et decorum est desipere in loco.
p.92. See 260:17, 261:20

10 Jesus! with all thy faults I love thee still.
p.117

11 My Lord, I do not believe. Help thou mine unbelief.
Note Books, selected and edited by G. Keynes and B. Hill (1951), p.284

12 Taking numbers into account, I should think more mental suffering had been undergone in the streets leading from St George's, Hanover Square, than in the condemned cells of Newgate.
The Way of All Flesh, ch.13

13 They would have been equally horrified at hearing the Christian religion doubted, and at seeing it practised.
ch.15

14 The advantage of doing one's praising for oneself is that one can lay it on so thick and exactly in the right places.
ch.34

15 There's many a good tune played on an old fiddle.
ch.61

16 'Tis better to have loved and lost, than never to have lost at all.
ch.77. See 536:16

17 Yet meet we shall, and part, and meet again, Where dead men meet on lips of living men.
Life after Death

18 I would not be—not quite—so pure as you.
A Prayer

19 O God! Oh Montreal!
Psalm of Montreal

20 Preferrest thou the gospel of Montreal to the gospel of Hellas,
The gospel of thy connexion with Mr Spurgeon's haberdasher to the gospel of the Discobolus?
Yet none the less blasphemed he beauty saying, 'The Discobolus hath no gospel,
But my brother-in-law is haberdasher to Mr Spurgeon.'

21 Not on sad Stygian shore, nor in clear sheen Of far Elysian plain, shall we meet those Among the dead whose pupils we have been, Nor those great shades whom we have held as foes.
Seven Sonnets (1904), I

22 It was very good of God to let Carlyle and Mrs Carlyle marry one another and so make only two people miserable instead of four, besides being very amusing.
Letter to Miss Savage, 21 Nov. 1884

WILLIAM BUTLER 1535–1618

23 Doubtless God could have made a better berry [strawberry], but doubtless God never did.
Walton, *Compleat Angler,* pt.i, ch.5

JOHN BYROM 1692–1763

24 Some say, that Signor Bononcini,
Compar'd to Handel's a mere ninny;
Others aver, to him, that Handel
Is scarcely fit to hold a candle.
Strange! that such high dispute shou'd be
'Twixt Tweedledum and Tweedledee.
Epigram on the Feuds between Handel and Bononcini

25 God bless the King, I mean the Faith's Defender;
God bless—no harm in blessing—the Pretender;
But who Pretender is, or who is King,
God bless us all—that's quite another thing.
To an Officer in the Army

LORD BYRON 1788–1824

26 For what were all these country patriots born?
To hunt, and vote, and raise the price of corn?
The Age of Bronze, xiv

27 Year after year they voted cent per cent,
Blood, sweat, and tear-wrung millions—why? for rent!

28 And wilt thou weep when I am low?
And Wilt Thou Weep?

29 Just like a coffin clapt in a canoe. [A gondola.]
Beppo, st.19

30 In short, he was a perfect cavaliero,
And to his very valet seem'd a hero.
st.33. See 162:24

31 His heart was one of those which most enamour us,
Wax to receive, and marble to retain.
st.34

32 'Tis true, your budding Miss is very charming,
But shy and awkward at first coming out,
So much alarm'd, that she is quite alarming,
All Giggle, Blush; half Pertness and half Pout;
And glancing at Mamma, for fear there's harm in
What you, she, it, or they, may be about,
The nursery still leaps out in all they utter—
Besides, they always smell of bread and butter.
st.39

1 Know ye the land where the cypress and myrtle
  Are emblems of deeds that are done in their clime?
Where the rage of the vulture, the love of the turtle,
  Now melt into sorrow, now madden to crime!
The Bride of Abydos, c.I.st.1

2 Where the virgins are soft as the roses they twine,
And all, save the spirit of man, is divine?

3 The blind old man of Scio's rocky isle.
c.II.st.2

4 Mark! where his carnage and his conquests cease!
He makes a solitude, and calls it—peace!
st.20. See 531:7

5 Adieu, adieu! my native shore
  Fades o'er the waters blue.
Childe Harold's Pilgrimage, c.I.st.13

6 My native land—Good Night!

7 Here all were noble, save Nobility.
st.85

8 War, war is still the cry, 'War even to the knife!'
st.86. See 368:8

9 A schoolboy's tale, the wonder of an hour!
c.II.st.2

10 Well didst thou speak, Athena's wisest son!
'All that we know is, nothing can be known.'
st.7

11 Ah! happy years! once more who would not be a boy?
st.23

12 None are so desolate but something dear,
  Dearer than self, possesses or possess'd
A thought, and claims the homage of a tear.
st.24

13 Fair Greece! sad relic of departed worth!
Immortal, though no more; though fallen, great!
st.73

14 Hereditary bondsmen! know ye not
Who would be free themselves must strike the blow?
st.76

15 Where'er we tread 'tis haunted, holy ground.
st.88

16 What is the worst of woes that wait on age?
  What stamps the wrinkle deeper on the brow?
To view each loved one blotted from life's page,
  And be alone on earth, as I am now.
st.98

17 Ada! sole daughter of my house and heart.
c.III.st.1

18 Once more upon the waters! yet once more!
And the waves bound beneath me as a steed
That knows his rider.
st.2

19   Years steal
Fire from the mind as vigour from the limb;
And life's enchanted cup but sparkles near the brim.
st.8

20 There was a sound of revelry by night,
  And Belgium's capital had gather'd then
Her beauty and her chivalry, and bright
  The lamps shone o'er fair women and brave men;
A thousand hearts beat happily; and when
Music arose with its voluptuous swell,
Soft eyes look'd love to eyes which spake again,
  And all went merry as a marriage bell;

But hush! hark! a deep sound strikes like a rising
  knell!
st.11

21 Did ye not hear it?—No; 'twas but the wind,
  Or the car rattling o'er the stony street;
On with the dance! let joy be unconfined;
  No sleep till morn, when Youth and Pleasure meet
To chase the glowing Hours with flying feet.
st.12

22 Arm! Arm! it is—it is—the cannon's opening roar!

23 Within a window'd niche of that high hall
Sate Brunswick's fated chieftain.
st.23

24 He rush'd into the field, and, foremost fighting, fell.

25 Or whispering, with white lips—'The foe! they come!
  they come!'
st.25

26 Grieving, if aught inanimate e'er grieves,
Over the unreturning brave,—alas!
st.27

27   The earth is cover'd thick with other clay,
  Which her own clay shall cover, heap'd and pent,
Rider and horse,—friend, foe,—in one red burial
  blent!
st.28

28   Life will suit
Itself to Sorrow's most detested fruit,
Like to the apples on the Dead Sea's shore,
All ashes to the taste.
st. 34

29 There sunk the greatest, nor the worst of men,
Whose spirit, antithetically mixt,
One moment of the mightiest, and again
On little objects with like firmness fixt. [Napoleon.]
st.36

30 Quiet to quick bosoms is a hell.
st.42

31 The castled crag of Drachenfels
Frowns o'er the wide and winding Rhine.
st.55

32 But these are deeds which should not pass away,
And names that must not wither.
st.67

33 Lake Leman woos me with its crystal face.
st.68

34 To fly from, need not be to hate, mankind.
st.69

35 I live not in myself, but I become
Portion of that around me; and to me
High mountains are a feeling, but the hum
Of human cities torture.
st.72

36 The self-torturing sophist, wild Rousseau.
st.77

37 Sapping a solemn creed with solemn sneer. [Gibbon.]
st.107

38 I have not loved the world, nor the world me;
  I have not flatter'd its rank breath, nor bow'd
To its idolatries a patient knee.
st.113

39   I stood
Among them, but not of them; in a shroud

Of thoughts which were not their thoughts.

1 I stood in Venice, on the Bridge of Sighs:
A palace and a prison on each hand.
c.IV.st.1

2 Where Venice sate in state, throned on her hundred
isles!

3 The spouseless Adriatic mourns her lord.
st.11

4 The moon is up, and yet it is not night;
Sunset divides the sky with her; a sea
Of glory streams along the Alpine height
Of blue Friuli's mountains; Heaven is free
From clouds, but of all colours seems to be,—
Melted to one vast Iris of the West,—
Where the day joins the past Eternity.
st.27

5 The Ariosto of the North. [Scott.]
st.40

6 Italia! oh Italia! thou who hast
The fatal gift of beauty.
st.42

7 Love watching Madness with unalterable mien.
st.72

8 Then farewell, Horace; whom I hated so,
Not for thy faults, but mine.
st.77

9 Oh Rome! my country! city of the soul!
st.78

10 The Niobe of nations! there she stands,
Childless and crownless, in her voiceless woe.
st.79

11 Yet, Freedom! yet thy banner, torn, but flying,
Streams like the thunder-storm *against* the wind.
st.98

12 Alas! our young affections run to waste,
Or water but the desert.
st.120

13 Of its own beauty is the mind diseased.
st.122

14 Time, the avenger!
st.130

15 The arena swims around him— he is gone,
Ere ceased the inhuman shout which hail'd the wretch
who won.
st.140

16 He heard it, but he heeded not—his eyes
Were with his heart, and that was far away;
He reck'd not of the life he lost nor prize,
But where his rude hut by the Danube lay,
There were his young barbarians all at play,
There was their Dacian mother— he, their sire,
Butcher'd to make a Roman holiday.
st.141

17 A ruin—yet what ruin! from its mass
Walls, palaces, half-cities, have been rear'd.
st.143

18 While stands the Coliseum, Rome shall stand;
When falls the Coliseum, Rome shall fall;
And when Rome falls—the World.
st.145

19 The Lord of the unerring bow,

The God of life, and poesy, and light.
st.161

20 So young, so fair,
Good without effort, great without a foe.
st.172

21 Oh! that the desert were my dwelling-place,
With one fair spirit for my minister,
That I might all forget the human race,
And, hating no one, love but only her!
st.177

22 There is a pleasure in the pathless woods,
There is a rapture on the lonely shore,
There is society, where none intrudes,
By the deep sea and music in its roar:
I love not man the less, but Nature more,
From these our interviews, in which I steal
From all I may be, or have been before,
To mingle with the Universe, and feel
What I can ne'er express, yet cannot all conceal.
st.178

23 Roll on, thou deep and dark blue Ocean—roll!
Ten thousand fleets sweep over thee in vain;
Man marks the earth with ruin—his control
Stops with the shore.
st.179

24 He sinks into thy depths with bubbling groan,
Without a grave, unknell'd, uncoffin'd, and unknown.

25 Time writes no wrinkle on thine azure brow:
Such as creation's dawn beheld, thou rollest now.
st.182

26 Dark-heaving—boundless, endless, and sublime,
The image of eternity.
st.183

27 And I have loved thee, Ocean! and my joy
Of youthful sports was on thy breast to be
Borne, like thy bubbles, onward: from a boy
I wanton'd with thy breakers.
st.184

28 The glory and the nothing of a name.
Churchill's Grave

29 The fatal facility of the octo-syllabic verse.
The Corsair, preface

30 Such hath it been—shall be—beneath the sun
The many still must labour for the one.
c.I.st.8

31 There was a laughing devil in his sneer.
st.9

32 Much hath been done, but more remains to do—
Their galleys blaze—why not their city too?
c.II.st.4

33 The weak alone repent.
st.10

34 Oh! too convincing—dangerously dear—
In woman's eye the unanswerable tear!
st.15

35 She for him had given
Her all on earth, and more than all in heaven!
c.III.st.17

36 He left a Corsair's name to other times,
Link'd with one virtue, and a thousand crimes.
st.24

37 Slow sinks, more lovely ere his race be run,

Along Morea's hills the setting sun;
Not, as in northern climes, obscurely bright,
But one unclouded blaze of living light.
Curse of Minerva, I.1, and **The Corsair**, III.1

1 The Assyrian came down like the wolf on the fold,
And his cohorts were gleaming in purple and gold;
And the sheen of their spears was like stars on the sea,
When the blue wave rolls nightly on deep Galilee.
Destruction of Sennacherib

2 For the Angel of Death spread his wings on the blast,
And breathed in the face of the foe as he pass'd.

3 I wish he would explain his explanation.
Don Juan, c.I, dedication st.2

4 The intellectual eunuch Castlereagh.
st.11

5 My way is to begin with the beginning.
st.7

6 In virtues nothing earthly could surpass her,
Save thine 'incomparable oil', Macassar!
st.17

7 But—Oh! ye lords of ladies intellectual,
Inform us truly, have they not hen-peck'd you all?
st.22

8   She,
Was married, charming, chaste, and twenty-three.
st.59

9 What men call gallantry, and gods adultery,
Is much more common where the climate's sultry.
st.63

10 Christians have burnt each other, quite persuaded
That all the Apostles would have done as they did.
st.83

11 A little still she strove, and much repented,
And whispering 'I will ne'er consent'—consented.
st.117

12 Sweet is revenge—especially to women.
st.124

13 Pleasure's a sin, and sometimes sin's a pleasure.
st.133

14 Man's love is of man's life a thing apart,
'Tis woman's whole existence.
st.194

15 So for a good old-gentlemanly vice,
I think I must take up with avarice.
st.216

16 There's nought, no doubt, so much the spirit calms
As rum and true religion.
c.II.st.34

17 'Twas twilight, and the sunless day went down
Over the waste of waters.
st.49

18 A solitary shriek, the bubbling cry
Of some strong swimmer in his agony.
st.53

19   If this be true, indeed,
Some Christians have a comfortable creed.
st.86

20 He could, perhaps, have pass'd the Hellespont,
As once (a feat on which ourselves we prided)
Leander, Mr Ekenhead, and I did.
st.105

21 Let us have wine and women, mirth and laughter,

Sermons and soda-water the day after.
st.178

22 Man, being reasonable, must get drunk;
The best of life is but intoxication.
st.179

23   A group that's quite antique,
Half naked, loving, natural, and Greek.
st.194

24 Alas! the love of women! it is known
To be a lovely and a fearful thing!
st.199

25 In her first passion woman loves her lover,
In all the others all she loves is love.
c.III.st.3

26 'Tis melancholy, and a fearful sign
Of human frailty, folly, also crime,
That love and marriage rarely can combine,
Although they both are born in the same clime;
Marriage from love, like vinegar from wine—
A sad, sour, sober beverage—by time
Is sharpen'd from its high celestial flavour,
Down to a very homely household savour.
st.5

27 Romances paint at full length people's wooings,
But only give a bust of marriages:
For no one cares for matrimonial cooings,
There's nothing wrong in a connubial kiss:
Think you, if Laura had been Petrarch's wife,
He would have written sonnets all his life?
st.8

28 All tragedies are finish'd by a death,
All comedies are ended by a marriage.
st.9

29 Dreading that climax of all human ills,
The inflammation of his weekly bills.
st.35

30 He was the mildest manner'd man
That ever scuttled ship or cut a throat,
With such true breeding of a gentleman,
You never could divine his real thought.
st.41

31 But Shakspeare also says, 'tis very silly
'To gild refined gold, or paint the lily.'
st.76. See 452:25

32 The isles of Greece, the isles of Greece!
Where burning Sappho loved and sung,
Where grew the arts of war and peace,
Where Delos rose, and Phoebus sprung!
Eternal summer gilds them yet,
But all, except their sun, is set.
st.86, 1

33 The mountains look on Marathon—
And Marathon looks on the sea;
And musing there an hour alone,
I dream'd that Greece might still be free.
3

34 A king sate on the rocky brow
Which looks o'er sea-born Salamis;
And ships, by thousands, lay below,
And men in nations;—all were his!
He counted them at break of day—
And when the sun set where were they?
4

1 For what is left the poet here?
   For Greeks a blush—for Greece a tear.
   6

2 Earth! render back from out thy breast
   A remnant of our Spartan dead!
   Of the three hundred grant but three,
   To make a new Thermopylae!
   7

3 Fill high the cup with Samian wine!
   9

4 Place me on Sunium's marbled steep,
     Where nothing, save the waves and I,
   May hear our mutual murmurs sweep;
     There, swan-like, let me sing and die:
   A land of slaves shall ne'er be mine—
   Dash down yon cup of Samian wine!
   16

5 Milton's the prince of poets—so we say;
     A little heavy, but no less divine.
   st.91

6 A drowsy frowzy poem, call'd the 'Excursion',
   Writ in a manner which is my aversion.
   st.94

7 We learn from Horace, 'Homer sometimes sleeps';
   We feel without him, Wordsworth sometimes wakes.
   st.98

8 Ave Maria! 'tis the hour of prayer!
   Ave Maria! 'tis the hour of love!
   st.103

9 Imagination droops her pinion.
   c.IV.st.3

10 And if I laugh at any mortal thing,
   'Tis that I may not weep.
   st.4

11 'Whom the gods love die young' was said of yore.
   st.12. See 336:25

12 'Arcades ambo', *id est*—blackguards both.
   st.93. See 560:3

13 I've stood upon Achilles' tomb,
   And heard Troy doubted; time will doubt of Rome.
   st.101

14 When amatory poets sing their loves
     In liquid lines mellifluously bland,
   And pair their rhymes as Venus yokes her doves.
   c.V.st.1

15 I have a passion for the name of 'Mary',
     For once it was a magic sound to me:
   And still it half calls up the realms of fairy
     Where I beheld what never was to be.
   st.4

16 And put himself upon his good behaviour.
   st.47

17 That all-softening, overpowering knell,
   The tocsin of the soul—the dinner-bell.
   st.49

18 Not to admire is all the art I know.
   st.101. See 258:17, 380:10

19 Why don't they knead two virtuous souls for life
   Into that moral centaur, man and wife?
   st.158

20 There is a tide in the affairs of women,
     Which, taken at the flood, leads—God knows

where.
c.VI.st.2. See 451:27

21 A lady of a 'certain age', which means
   Certainly aged.
   st.69

22 A 'strange coincidence', to use a phrase
   By which such things are settled now-a-days.
   st.78

23 'Let there be light' said God, 'and there was light!'
   'Let there be blood!' says man, and there's a sea!
   c.VII.st.41

24 Oh, Wellington! (or 'Villainton')—for Fame
   Sounds the heroic syllables both ways.
   c.IX.st.1

25 Call'd 'Saviour of the Nations'—not yet saved,
   And 'Europe's Liberator'—still enslaved.
   [Wellington.]
   st.5

26 Never had mortal man such opportunity,
   Except Napoleon, or abused it more.
   st.9

27 That water-land of Dutchmen and of ditches.
   c.X.st.63

28 When Bishop Berkeley said 'there was no matter',
     And proved it—'twas no matter what he said.
   c.XI.st.1

29 But Tom's no more—and so no more of Tom.
   st.22

30 And, after all, what is a lie? 'Tis but
     The truth in masquerade.
   st.37

31   I—albeit I'm sure I did not know it,
   Nor sought of foolscap subjects to be king.—
   Was reckon'd, a considerable time,
   The grand Napoleon of the realms of rhyme.
   st.55

32 John Keats, who was kill'd off by one critique,
   Just as he really promised something great,
   If not intelligible, without Greek
   Contrived to talk about the Gods of late,
   Much as they might have been supposed to speak.
   Poor fellow! His was an untoward fate;
   'Tis strange the mind, that very fiery particle,
   Should let itself be snuff'd out by an article.
   st.60

33 Nought's permanent among the human race,
   Except the Whigs *not* getting into place.
   st.82

34 For talk six times with the same single lady,
   And you may get the wedding dresses ready.
   c.XII.st.59

35   Merely innocent flirtation,
   Not quite adultery, but adulteration.
   st.63

36 A Prince...
   With fascination in his very bow.
   st.84

37 A finish'd gentleman from top to toe.

38 Now hatred is by far the longest pleasure;
   Men love in haste, but they detest at leisure.
   c.XIII.st.4

1 Cervantes smiled Spain's chivalry away.
st.11

2 I hate to hunt down a tired metaphor.
st.36

3 The English winter—ending in July,
To recommence in August.
st.42

4 Society is now one polish'd horde,
Form'd of two mighty tribes, the *Bores* and *Bored*.
st.95

5 I for one venerate a petticoat.
c.XIV.st.26

6 Of all the horrid, hideous notes of woe,
Sadder than owl-songs or the midnight blast,
Is that portentous phrase, 'I told you so.'
st.50

7 'Tis strange—but true; for truth is always strange;
Stranger than fiction.
st.101

8 A lovely being, scarcely form'd or moulded,
A rose with all its sweetest leaves yet folded.
c.XV.st.43

9 Between two worlds life hovers like a star,
'Twixt night and morn, upon the horizon's verge.
How little do we know that which we are!
How less what we may be!
st.99

10 The antique Persians taught three useful things,
To draw the bow, to ride, and speak the truth.
c.XVI.st.1

11 The loudest wit I e'er was deafen'd with.
st.81

12 And both were young, and one was beautiful.
The Dream, st.2

13 A change came o'er the spirit of my dream.
st.5

14 Still must I hear?—shall hoarse Fitzgerald bawl
His creaking couplets in a tavern hall.
English Bards and Scotch Reviewers, l.1

15　　　　　I'll publish, right or wrong:
Fools are my theme, let satire be my song.
l.5

16 'Tis pleasant, sure, to see one's name in print;
A book's a book, although there's nothing in 't.
l.51

17 A man must serve his time to every trade
Save censure—critics all are ready made.
Take hackney'd jokes from Miller, got by rote,
With just enough of learning to misquote.
l.63

18　　　　　As soon
Seek roses in December—ice in June;
Hope constancy in wind, or corn in chaff;
Believe a woman or an epitaph,
Or any other thing that's false, before
You trust in critics, who themselves are sore.
l.75

19 Better to err with Pope, than shine with Pye.
l.102

20 Sense and wit with poesy allied.
l.105

21 Who both by precept and example, shows
That prose is verse, and verse is merely prose.
[Wordsworth.]
l.241

22 Be warm, but pure: be amorous, but be chaste.
l.306

23 Perverts the Prophets, and purloins the Psalms.
l.326

24 Oh, Amos Cottle!—Phoebus! what a name
To fill the speaking trump of future fame!
l.399

25 The petrifactions of a plodding brain.
l.416

26 To sanction Vice, and hunt Decorum down.
l.621

27 Lords too are bards, such things at times befall,
And 'tis some praise in peers to write at all.
l.719

28 Forsook the labours of a servile state.
Stemm'd the rude storm, and triumph'd over fate.
l.779

29 Let simple Wordsworth chime his childish verse,
And brother Coleridge lull the babe at nurse.
l.917

30 Glory, like the phoenix 'midst her fires,
Exhales her odours, blazes, and expires.
l.959

31 I too can hunt a poetaster down.
l.1064

32 The world is a bundle of hay,
Mankind are the asses who pull;
Each tugs it a different way,
And the greatest of all is John Bull.
Epigram

33 Fare thee well! and if for ever,
Still for ever, fare thee well.
Fare Thee Well!

34 I only know we loved in vain—
I only feel—Farewell!—Farewell!
Farewell! if ever Fondest Prayer

35 Dark tree, still sad when others' grief is fled,
The only constant mourner o'er the dead! [A cypress.]
The Giaour, l.286

36 Or lend fresh interest to a twice-told tale.
Hints from Horace, l.184

37 Friendship is Love without his wings!
Hours of Idleness. L'Amitié

38 I have tasted the sweets and the bitters of love.
To Rev. J.T. Becher

39 Though women are angels, yet wedlock's the devil.
To Eliza

40 But the poor dog, in life the firmest friend,
The first to welcome, foremost to defend.
Inscription on a Newfoundland Dog

41 Then receive him as best such an advent becomes,
With a legion of cooks, and an army of slaves!
The Irish Avatar

42 More happy, if less wise.
The Island, c.II.st.11

43 Jack was embarrassed—never hero more,
And as he knew not what to say, he swore.
c.IV.st.5

1 Who killed John Keats?
  'I,' says the Quarterly,
    So savage and Tartarly;
'Twas one of my feats.'
John Keats

2 His madness was not of the head, but heart.
Lara, c.I.st.18

3 Maid of Athens, ere we part,
  Give, oh give me back my heart!
Or, since that has left my breast,
  Keep it now, and take the rest!
Maid of Athens

4 By thy cold breast and serpent smile,
By thy unfathom'd gulfs of guile,
By that most seeming virtuous eye,
By thy shut soul's hypocrisy;
By the perfection of thine art
Which pass'd for human thine own heart;
By thy delight in others' pain,
And by thy brotherhood of Cain,
I call upon thee! and compel
Thyself to be thy proper Hell!
Manfred, I.i.242

5 Old man! 'tis not so difficult to die.
III.iv.151

6   You have deeply ventured;
But all must do so who would greatly win.
Marino Faliero, I.ii

7 'Tis done—but yesterday a King!
And arm'd with Kings to strive—
And now thou art a nameless thing:
So abject—yet alive!
Ode to Napoleon Bonaparte

8 The Arbiter of others' fate
A Suppliant for his own!

9 The Cincinnatus of the West. [Washington.]

10 It is not in the storm nor in the strife
  We feel benumb'd, and wish to be no more,
  But in the after-silence on the shore,
When all is lost, except a little life.
On Hearing Lady Byron was Ill

11 My days are in the yellow leaf;
  The flowers and fruits of love are gone;
The worm, the canker, and the grief
  Are mine alone!
On This Day I Complete my Thirty-Sixth Year

12 Seek out—less often sought than found—
  A soldier's grave, for thee the best;
Then look around, and choose thy ground,
  And take thy rest.

13 Yet in my lineaments they trace
Some features of my father's face.
Parisina

14 Eternal spirit of the chainless mind!
Brightest in dungeons, Liberty! thou art.
Sonnet on Chillon

15 Chillon! thy prison is a holy place,
  And thy sad floor an altar—for 'twas trod,
Until his very steps have left a trace
  Worn, as if thy cold pavement were a sod,
By Bonnivard! May none those marks efface!
  For they appeal from tyranny to God.

16 My hair is grey, but not with years,
  Nor grew it white
    In a single night,
As men's have grown from sudden fears.
The Prisoner of Chillon, st.1

17 Regain'd my freedom with a sigh.
st.14

18 Thy Godlike crime was to be kind,
  To render with thy precepts less
  The sum of human wretchedness.
Prometheus

19 Man in portions can foresee
His own funereal destiny.

20 I am the very slave of circumstance
And impulse—borne away with every breath!
Sardanapalus, IV.i

21 She walks in beauty, like the night
  Of cloudless climes and starry skies;
And all that's best of dark and bright
  Meet in her aspect and her eyes:
Thus mellow'd to that tender light
  Which heaven to gaudy day denies.
She Walks in Beauty

22 And on that cheek, and o'er that brow,
  So soft, so calm, yet eloquent,
The smiles that win, the tints that glow
  But tell of days in goodness spent,
A mind at peace with all below,
  A heart whose love is innocent!

23 We were a gallant company,
Riding o'er land, and sailing o'er sea.
Oh! but we went merrily!
Siege of Corinth, prologue

24 Born in the garret, in the kitchen bred,
Promoted thence to deck her mistress' head.
A Sketch

25 So, we'll go no more a roving
  So late into the night,
Though the heart be still as loving,
  And the moon be still as bright.
So, We'll Go No More a Roving

26 Though the night was made for loving,
  And the day returns too soon,
Yet we'll go no more a-roving
  By the light of the moon.

27 There be none of Beauty's daughters
  With a magic like thee.
Stanzas for Music. There be none of Beauty's daughters

28 There's not a joy the world can give like that it takes
  away.
There's not a joy the world can give

29 Oh, talk not to me of a name great in story;
The days of our youth are the days of our glory;
And the myrtle and ivy of sweet two-and-twenty
Are worth all your laurels, though ever so plenty.
Stanzas Written on the Road between Florence and Pisa

30 I knew it was love, and I felt it was glory.

31 I am ashes where once I was fire.
To the Countess of Blessington

32 My boat is on the shore,
  And my bark is on the sea;
But, before I go, Tom Moore,

Here's a double health to thee!
To Thomas Moore

1 Here's a sigh to those who love me,
    And a smile to those who hate;
And, whatever sky's above me,
    Here's a heart for every fate.

2 My Murray.
To Mr. Murray

3 The fault was Nature's fault not thine,
    Which made thee fickle as thou art.
To a Youthful Friend

4 And when we think we lead, we are most led.
The Two Foscari, II.i.361

5 The angels all were singing out of tune,
And hoarse with having little else to do,
Excepting to wind up the sun and moon,
Or curb a runaway young star or two.
The Vision of Judgement, st.2

6 In whom his qualities are reigning still,
Except that household virtue, most uncommon,
Of constancy to a bad, ugly woman.
st.12

7 As he drew near, he gazed upon the gate
Ne'er to be entered more by him or Sin,
With such a glance of supernatural hate
As made Saint Peter wish himself within;
He patter'd with his keys at a great rate,
And sweated through his apostolic skin:
Of course his perspiration was but ichor,
Or some such other spiritual liquor.
st.25

8 Yet still between his Darkness and his Brightness
There pass'd a mutual glance of great politeness.
st.35

9   Satan met his ancient friend
With more hauteur, as might an old Castilian
Poor noble meet a mushroom rich civilian.
st.36

10 And when the tumult dwindled to a calm,
I left him practising the hundredth psalm.
st.106

11 Seductive Waltz!
The Waltz

12 Voluptuous Waltz!

13 When we two parted
    In silence and tears,
Half broken-hearted
    To sever for years,
Pale grew thy cheek and cold,
    Colder thy kiss.
When We Two Parted

14 If I should meet thee
    After long years,
How should I greet thee?—
    With silence and tears.

15 Through life's road, so dim and dirty,
I have dragg'd to three-and-thirty.
What have these years left to me?
Nothing—except thirty-three.
Diary, 21 Jan. 1821. In Moore, *Life of Byron*

16 You should have a softer pillow than my heart.
To his wife. E.C. Mayne, ed., *The Life and Letters of Anne Isabella, Lady Noel Byron,* ch.11

17 Wordsworth—stupendous genius! damned fool.
Letter to James Hogg, 1816

18 Love in this part of the world is no sinecure.
Letter to John Murray from Venice, 27 Dec. 1816

19 No *Manual,* no letters, no tooth-powder, no *extract* from Moore's *Italy* concerning Marino Falieri, no *nothing*—as a man hallooed out at one of Burdett's elections, after a long ululatus of No Bastille! No Governor Aris! No '—God knows what';—but his *ne plus ultra* was, 'no nothing!'
Letter to Murray, 4 June 1817

20 I am sure my bones would not rest in an English grave, or my clay mix with the earth of that country. I believe the thought would drive me mad on my deathbed, could I suppose that any of my friends would be base enough to convey my carcass back to your soil.
7 June 1819

21 The Princess of Parallelograms.
(Of Annabella Milbanke, to Lady Melbourne)

22 I awoke one morning and found myself famous.
(Referring to the instantaneous success of *Childe Harold*). Moore, *Life of Byron,* I, 347

H.J. BYRON 1834–1884

23 Life's too short for chess.
Our Boys, Act I

JAMES BRANCH CABELL 1879–1958

24 A man possesses nothing certainly save a brief loan of his own body: and yet the body of man is capable of much curious pleasure.
Jurgen, ch.20

25 The optimist proclaims that we live in the best of all possible worlds; and the pessimist fears this is true.
The Silver Stallion, bk.iv, ch.26

AUGUSTUS CAESAR
see AUGUSTUS

JULIUS CAESAR 102?–44 B.C.

26 *Gallia est omnis divisa in partes tres.*
Gaul as a whole is divided into three parts.
De Bello Gallico, I.i

27 *Fere libenter homines id quod volunt credunt.*
Men willingly believe what they wish.
iii.18

28 *Et tu, Brute?*
You too Brutus?
Oral trad. See 450:1 and Philemon Holland, trans., Suetonius, *Historie of Twelve Caesars* (1606), 'Some have written that as M. Brutus came running upon him, he said "καὶ σύ, τέκνον", "And you, my son."'

29 *Veni, vidi, vici.*
I came, I saw, I conquered.
Suetonius, *Divus Julius,* xxxvii.2. (Inscription displayed in Caesar's Pontic triumph, or, according to Plutarch, 1.2, written in a letter by Caesar, announcing the victory of Zela which concluded the Pontic campaign)

30 The die is cast.
xxxii. At the crossing of the Rubicon. Often quoted in Latin, '*Iacta alea est,*' but originally spoken in Greek: Plutarch, *Pompey,* 60.2

1 Caesar's wife must be above suspicion.
Oral trad. See Plutarch, *Lives*, Julius Caesar, x.6

2 Thou hast Caesar and his fortune with thee.
xxxviii.3. Tr. North

3 Caesar, when he first went into Gaul, made no scruple to profess 'That he had rather be first in a village than second at Rome'.
Bacon, *Advancement of Learning*, II, xxiii, 36

PEDRO CALDERÓN DE LA BARCA 1600–1681

4   *Aún en sueños*
no se pierde el hacer bien.
Even in dreams good works are not wasted.
La Vida es Sueño (1636), II

5 *Qué es la vida? Un frenesí.*
Qué es la vida? Una ilusión,
una sombra, una ficción,
y el mayor bien es pequeño;
que toda la vida es sueño,
y los sueños, sueños son.
What is life? a frenzy. What is life? An illusion, a shadow, a fiction. And the greatest good is of slight worth, as all life is a dream, and dreams are dreams.
See 355:5

CALIGULA A.D. 12–41

6 *Utinam populus Romanus unam cervicem haberet!*
Would that the Roman people had but one neck!
Suetonius, *Life of Caligula*, 30

CALLIMACHUS c.305–c.240 B.C.

7

I abhor, too, the roaming lover, nor do I drink from every well; I loathe all things held in common.
Epigrams, ed. R. Pfeiffer (1949-53), 28. *Anth. Pal.*, 12.43

8 μέγα βιβλίον ἴσον τῷ μεγάλῳ κακῷ.
A great book is like great evil.
Fragments, ed. R. Pfeiffer, 465. Proverbially reduced to μέγα βιβλίον μέγα κακόν. 'Great book, great evil'

CHARLES ALEXANDRE DE CALONNE 1734–1802

9 *Madame, si c'est possible, c'est fait; impossible? cela se fera.*
Madam, if a thing is possible, consider it done; the impossible? that will be done.
J. Michelet, *Histoire de la Révolution Française* (1847), vol.I, pt.ii, sect 8. Better known as the U.S. Armed Forces slogan, 'The difficult we do immediately; the impossible takes a little longer.'

C.S. CALVERLEY 1831–1884

10 The farmer's daughter hath soft brown hair;
    (Butter and eggs and a pound of cheese)
And I met with a ballad, I can't say where,
    Which wholly consisted of lines like these.
Ballad

11 And this song is consider'd a perfect gem,
    And as to the meaning, it's what you please.

12 O Beer! O Hodgson, Guinness, Allsopp, Bass!
Names that should be on every infant's tongue!
Beer

13 I cannot sing the old songs now!
    It is not that I deem them low;
'Tis that I can't remember how
        They go.
Changed. See 152:23

14 Aspect anything but bland.
Charades, vi

15 You see this pebble-stone? It's a thing I bought
Of a bit of a chit of a boy i' the mid o' the day—
I like to dock the smaller parts-o'-speech,
As we curtail the already curtail'd cur
(You catch the paronomasia, play 'po' words?).
The Cock and the Bull

16 Donn'd galligaskins, antigropeloes,
And so forth; and, complete with hat and gloves,
One on and one a'dangle in my hand,
And ombrifuge (Lord love you!), case o' rain.

17 A bare-legg'd beggarly son of a gun.

18 Fiddlepin's end! Get out, you blazing ass!
Gabble o' the goose. Don't bugaboo-baby *me*!

19 Life is with such all beer and skittles;
They are not difficult to please
About their victuals.
Contentment

20 For king-like rolls the Rhine,
And the scenery's divine,
And the victuals and the wine
                Rather good.
Dover to Munich

21 Forever! 'Tis a single word!
    Our rude forefathers deemed it two:
Can you imagine so absurd
                A view?
Forever

22 For I've read in many a novel that, unless they've souls that grovel,
Folks *prefer* in fact a hovel to your dreary marble halls.
In the Gloaming

23 Grinder, who serenely grindest
    At my door the Hundredth Psalm.
Lines on Hearing the Organ

24 Meaning, however, is no great matter.
Lovers, and a Reflection

25 Thro' the rare red heather we dance together,
    (O love my Willie!) and smelt for flowers:
I must mention again it was gorgeous weather,
    Rhymes are so scarce in this world of ours.

26 Study first propriety.
Of Propriety

27 How Eugene Aram, though a thief, a liar, and a murderer,
Yet, being intellectual, was amongst the noblest of mankind.
Of Reading

28 Thou, who when fears attack,
Bidst them avaunt, and Black
Care, at the horseman's back
        Perching, unseatest;
Sweet, when the morn is grey;
Sweet, when they've cleared away
Lunch; and at close of day

Possibly sweetest.
Ode to Tobacco

1 I have a liking old
For thee, though manifold
Stories, I know, are told
Not to thy credit.

GENERAL CAMBRONNE 1770–1842

2 *La Garde meurt, mais ne se rend pas.*
The Guards die but do not surrender.
Attr. to Cambronne when called upon to surrender at Waterloo.
Cambronne denied the saying at a banquet at Nantes, 19 Sept. 1830

3 *Merde!*
Said to be Cambronne's actual reply to the call to surrender:
euphemistically known as '*Le mot de Cambronne*'.

CHARLES PRATT, LORD CAMDEN 1714–1794

4 [The British parliament has no right to tax the
Americans.] Taxation and representation are
inseparable...whatever is a man's own, is absolutely
his own; no man hath a right to take it from him
without his consent either expressed by himself or
representative; whoever attempts to do it, attempts an
injury; whoever does it, commits a robbery; he throws
down and destroys the distinction between liberty and
slavery.
House of Lords, 7 Mar. 1766. See 365:25

WILLIAM CAMDEN 1551–1623

5 My friend, judge not me,
Thou seest I judge not thee.
Betwixt the stirrup and the ground
Mercy I asked, mercy I found.
Remains. Epitaph for a Man Killed by Falling from His Horse

BARON CAMPBELL 1779–1861

6 So essential did I consider an Index to be to every
book, that I proposed to bring a Bill into parliament to
deprive an author who publishes a book without an
Index of the privilege of copyright; and, moreover, to
subject him, for his offence, to a pecuniary penalty.
Lives of the Chief Justices, preface to vol.iii, which included an
index to the previously published vols.

MRS. PATRICK CAMPBELL 1865–1940

7 Some day you'll eat a pork chop, Joey, and then God
help all women.
To George Bernard Shaw, a vegetarian. Alexander Woollcott,
While Rome Burns, Some Neighbours, 3

8 I don't mind where people make love, so long as they
don't do it in the street and frighten the horses.
Oral tradition

9 Marriage is the result of the longing for the deep, deep
peace of the double bed after the hurly-burly of the
chaise-longue.
Oral tradition

ROY CAMPBELL 1901–1957

10   Giraffes! —a People
Who live between the earth and skies,
Each in his lone religious steeple,

Keeping a light-house with his eyes.
Dreaming Spires

11 Write with your spade, and garden with your pen,
Shovel your couplets to their long repose.
And type your turnips down the field in rows.
The Georgiad (1931), pt.ii

12 You praise the firm restraint with which they write—
I'm with you there, of course:
They use the snaffle and the curb all right,
But where's the bloody horse?
On Some South African Novelists

13 South Africa, renowned both far and wide
For politics and little else beside.
The Wayzgoose (1928)

THOMAS CAMPBELL 1777–1844

14 Of Nelson and the North
Sing the glorious day's renown,
When to battle fierce came forth
All the might of Denmark's crown,
And her arms along the deep proudly shone,—
By each gun the lighted brand
In a bold determined hand;
And the Prince of all the land
Led them on.
Battle of the Baltic

15 There was silence deep as death,
And the boldest held his breath
For a time.

16 Let us think of them that sleep,
Full many a fathom deep,
By thy wild and stormy steep,
Elsinore!

17 O leave this barren spot to me!
Spare, woodman, spare the beechen tree.
The Beech-Tree's Petition

18 To-morrow let us do or die!
Gertrude of Wyoming, pt.iii, 37

19 To live in hearts we leave behind
Is not to die.
Hallowed Ground

20 On the green banks of Shannon, when Sheelah was
nigh,
No blithe Irish lad was so happy as I;
No harp like my own could so cheerily play,
And wherever I went was my poor dog Tray.
The Harper

21 On Linden, when the sun was low,
All bloodless lay the untrodden snow,
And dark as winter was the flow
Of Iser, rolling rapidly.
Hohenlinden

22 The combat deepens. On, ye brave,
Who rush to glory, or the grave!
Wave, Munich! all thy banners wave,
And charge with all thy chivalry!

23 Better be courted and jilted
Than never be courted at all.
The Jilted Nymph

24 'Tis the sunset of life gives me mystical lore,
And coming events cast their shadows before.
Lochiel's Warning

1 A chieftain to the Highlands bound
   Cries, 'Boatman, do not tarry!
And I'll give thee a silver pound
   To row us o'er the ferry.'
Lord Ullin's Daughter

2 O, I'm the chief of Ulva's isle,
And this Lord Ullin's daughter.

3 I'll meet the raging of the skies,
   But not an angry father.

4 One lovely hand she stretched for aid,
   And one was round her lover.

5 The waters wild went o'er his child,
   And he was left lamenting.

6 'Tis distance lends enchantment to the view,
And robes the mountain in its azure hue.
Pleasures of Hope, pt.i, l.7

7 Hope, for a season, bade the world farewell,
And Freedom shrieked—as Kosciusko fell!
l.381

8 What millions died—that Caesar might be great!
pt.ii, l.174

9 Truth, ever lovely,—since the world began
The foe of tyrants, and the friend of man.
l.347

10 What though my winged hours of bliss have been,
Like angel-visits, few and far between?
l.375

11 It was not strange; for in the human breast
Two master-passions cannot co-exist.
Theodric, l.488

12 Ye Mariners of England
That guard our native seas,
Whose flag has braved, a thousand years,
The battle and the breeze—
Your glorious standard launch again
To match another foe!
And sweep through the deep,
While the stormy winds do blow,—
While the battle rages loud and long,
And the stormy winds do blow.
Ye Mariners of England

13 With thunders from her native oak
She quells the floods below.

14 An original something, fair maid, you would win me
To write—but how shall I begin?
For I fear I have nothing original in me—
Excepting Original Sin.
To a Young Lady, Who Asked Me to Write Something Original for Her Album

15 Now Barabbas was a publisher.
Often attributed to Byron

THOMAS CAMPION d. 1620

16 Rose-cheeked Laura, come;
Sing thou smoothly with thy beauty's
Silent music, either other
   Sweetly gracing.
Observations in the Art of English Poesie. **Laura**

17 When to her lute Corinna sings,
Her voice revives the leaden strings,
And both in highest notes appear,
As any challeng'd echo clear.

But when she doth of mourning speak,
Ev'n with her sighs the strings do break.
A Book of Airs, vi

18 Follow your Saint, follow with accents sweet;
Haste you, sad notes, fall at her flying feet.
x

19 Good thoughts his only friends,
   His wealth a well-spent age,
The earth his sober inn
   And quiet pilgrimage.
xviii

20 Never weather-beaten sail more willing bent to shore,
Never tired pilgrim's limbs affected slumber more.
Two Books of Airs. **Divine and Moral Songs,** xi

21   Kind are her answers,
But her performance keeps no day;
   Breaks time, as dancers
From their own Music when they stray.
Third Book of Airs, vii

22 There is a garden in her face,
Where roses and white lilies grow;
A heav'nly paradise is that place,
Wherein all pleasant fruits do flow.
There cherries grow, which none may buy
Till 'Cherry ripe' themselves do cry.
Fourth Book of Airs, vii. See 3:18, 248:21

23 Those cherries fairly do enclose
Of orient pearl a double row;
Which when her lovely laughter shows,
They look like rosebuds fill'd with snow.

ALBERT CAMUS 1913–1960

24 *La lutte elle-même vers les sommets suffit à remplir un coeur d'homme. Il faut imaginer Sisyphe heureux.*
The struggle to the top alone will make a human heart swell. Sisyphus must be regarded as happy.
Le Mythe de Sisyphe (1942), last words

GEORGE CANNING 1770–1827

25 In matters of commerce the fault of the Dutch
Is offering too little and asking too much.
The French are with equal advantage content,
So we clap on Dutch bottoms just twenty per cent.
Dispatch, in Cipher, To Sir Charles Bagot, English Ambassador at the Hague, 31 Jan. 1826

26 Needy Knife-grinder! whither are you going?
Rough is the road, your wheel is out of order—
Bleak blows the blast;—your hat has got a hole in't.
   So have your breeches.
The Friend of Humanity and the Knife-Grinder

27 *I* give thee sixpence! I will see thee damn'd first—
Wretch! whom no sense of wrongs can rouse to
   vengeance;
Sordid, unfeeling, reprobate, degraded,
       Spiritless outcast!

28 A steady patriot of the world alone,
The friend of every country but his own. [The Jacobin.]
New Morality, l.113. See 185:14, 366:6

29 And finds, with keen discriminating sight,
Black's not so black;—nor white so very white.
l.199

1 Give me the avowed, erect and manly foe;
Firm I can meet, perhaps return the blow;
But of all plagues, good Heaven, thy wrath can send,
Save me, oh, save me, from the candid friend.
l.207

2 Pitt is to Addington
As London is to Paddington.
The Oracle, c.1803-4

3 Man, only—rash, refined, presumptuous man,
Starts from his rank, and mars creation's plan.
Progress of Man, l.55

4 A sudden thought strikes me, let us swear an eternal
friendship.
The Rovers, I.i

5 Whene'er with haggard eyes I view
This Dungeon, that I'm rotting in,
I think of those Companions true
Who studied with me at the U-
     -NIVERSITY OF GOTTINGEN,-
     -NIVERSITY OF GOTTINGEN.
Song

6 Sun, moon, and thou vain world, adieu.

7 Away with the cant of 'Measures not men'!—the idle
supposition that it is the harness and not the horses
that draw the chariot along. If the comparison must be
made, if the distinction must be taken, men are
everything, measures comparatively nothing.
House of Commons, 1801

8 I called the New World into existence, to redress the
balance of the Old.
Speech, 12 Dec. 1826

KING CANUTE 994?–1035

9 Merrily sang the monks in Ely
When Cnut, King, rowed thereby;
Row, my knights, near the land,
And hear we these monks' song.
Attr. **Song of the Monks of Ely**, *Historia Eliensis* (1066). Green,
Conquest of England, ix

MARQUIS DOMENICO CARACCIOLO
1715–1789

10 *Il y a en Angleterre soixante sectes religieuses
différentes, et une seule sauce.*
In England there are sixty different religions, and only
one sauce.
Attr. N. & Q., Dec. 1968

RICHARD CAREW 1555–1620

11 Take the miracle of our age, Sir Philip Sidney.
An Epistle on the Excellency of the English Tongue

THOMAS CAREW 1595?–1639?

12 He that loves a rosy cheek,
    Or a coral lip admires,
Or, from star-like eyes, doth seek
    Fuel to maintain his fires;
As old Time makes these decay,
So his flames must waste away.
Disdain Returned

13 Know, Celia (since thou art so proud,)
'Twas I that gave thee thy renown.

Thou had'st in the forgotten crowd
Of common beauties liv'd unknown,
Had not my verse extoll'd thy name,
And with it imped the wings of fame.
Ingrateful Beauty Threatened

14 Good to the poor, to kindred dear,
To servants kind, to friendship clear,
To nothing but herself severe.
Inscription on Tomb of Lady Mary Wentworth

15 So though a virgin, yet a bride
To every Grace, she justified
A chaste polygamy, and died.

16 Give me more love or more disdain;
The torrid or the frozen zone:
Bring equal ease unto my pain;
The temperate affords me none.
Mediocrity in Love Rejected

17 The purest soul that e'er was sent
Into a clayey tenement.
On the Lady Mary Villiers

18 Ask me no more where Jove bestows,
When June is past, the fading rose;
For in your beauty's orient deep
These flowers, as in their causes, sleep.
A Song

19 Ask me no more whither doth haste
The nightingale when May is past;
For in your sweet dividing throat
She winters and keeps warm her note.

20 Ask me no more if east or west
The Phoenix builds her spicy nest;
For unto you at last she flies,
And in your fragrant bosom dies.

HENRY CAREY 1693?–1743

21 Aldiborontiphoscophornio!
Where left you Chrononhotonthologos?
Chrononhotonthologos, I.i

22 His cogitative faculties immers'd
In cogibundity of cogitation.

23 To thee, and gentle Rigdum-Funnidos,
Our gratulations flow in streams unbounded.
iii

24 God save our gracious king!
Long live our noble king!
    God save the king!
God Save the King. (But see 252:24)

25 Confound their politics,
Frustrate their knavish tricks.

26 Of all the girls that are so smart
    There's none like pretty Sally,
She is the darling of my heart,
    And she lives in our alley.
Sally in our Alley

27 Of all the days that's in the week
    I dearly love but one day—
And that's the day that comes betwixt
    A Saturday and Monday.

WILLIAM CARLETON 1794–1869

28 Things at home are crossways, and Betsey and I are

out.
***Farm Ballads.* Betsey and I Are Out**

JANE WELSH CARLYLE 1801–1866

1 I am not at all the sort of person you and I took me for.
Letter to Thomas Carlyle, 7 May 1822

THOMAS CARLYLE 1795–1881

2 A well-written Life is almost as rare as a well-spent one.
Critical and Miscellaneous Essays, vol.i. **Richter**

3 The three great elements of modern civilization, Gunpowder, Printing, and the Protestant Religion.
State of German Literature. See 28:9

4 The 'golden-calf of Self-love.'
Burns

5 It is the Age of Machinery, in every outward and inward sense of that word.
vol.ii. **Signs of the Times**

6 The Bible-Society...is found, on inquiry, to be...a machine for converting the Heathen.

7 Thought, he [Dr. Cabanis] is inclined to hold, is still secreted by the brain; but then Poetry and Religion (and it is really worth knowing) are 'a product of the smaller intestines'!

8 What is all knowledge too but recorded experience, and a product of history; of which, therefore, reasoning and belief, no less than action and passion, are essential materials?
On History

9 History is the essence of innumerable biographies.
See 131:31

10 The foul sluggard's comfort: 'It will last my time.'
vol.iii. **Count Cagliostro. Flight Last**

11 This Mirabeau's work, then, is done. He sleeps with the primeval giants. He has gone over to the majority: *Abiit ad plures.*
Mirabeau. See 373:1

12 There is no life of a man, faithfully recorded, but is a heroic poem of its sort, rhymed or unrhymed.
vol.iv. **Sir Walter Scott**

13 Under all speech that is good for anything there lies a silence that is better. Silence is deep as Eternity; speech is shallow as Time.

14 It can be said of him [Scott], When he departed, he took a man's life along with him. No sounder piece of British manhood was put together in that eighteenth century of Time.

15 A witty statesman said, you might prove anything by figures.
Chartism, ch.2

16 Surely of all 'rights of man', this right of the ignorant man to be guided by the wiser, to be, gently or forcibly, held in the true course by him, is the indisputablest.
ch.6

17 In epochs when cash payment has become the sole nexus of man to man.

18 'Genius' (which means transcendent capacity of taking trouble, first of all).
Frederick the Great, bk.iv, ch.3. See 106:21

19 If they could forget, for a moment, the correggiosity of Correggio, and the learned babble of the saleroom and varnishing auctioneer.
ch.6. See 519:29

20 Happy the people whose annals are blank in history-books!
bk.xvi, ch.1

21 France was long a despotism tempered by epigrams.
History of the French Revolution, pt.I, bk.i, ch.1

22 A whiff of grapeshot.
bk.v, ch.3

23 History a distillation of rumour.
bk.vii, ch.5

24 The gospel according to Jean Jacques.
pt.II, bk.i, ch.6

25 The difference between Orthodoxy or My-doxy and Heterodoxy or Thy-doxy.
bk.iv, ch.2

26 The seagreen Incorruptible. [Robespierre.]
ch.4

27 Aristocracy of the Moneybag.
bk.vii, ch.7

28 It is well said, in every sense, that a man's religion is the chief fact with regard to him.
Heroes and Hero-Worship, i. **The Hero as Divinity**

29 Worship is transcendent wonder.

30 No sadder proof can be given by a man of his own littleness than disbelief in great men.

31 No great man lives in vain. The history of the world is but the biography of great men.
See 131:9

32 The greatest of faults, I should say, is to be conscious of none.
ii. **The Hero as Prophet**

33 The Hero can be Poet, Prophet, King, Priest or what you will, according to the kind of world he finds himself born into.
iii. **The Hero as Poet**

34 In books lies the *soul* of the whole Past Time; the articulate audible voice of the Past, when the body and material substance of it has altogether vanished like a dream.
v. **The Hero as Man of Letters**

35 The true University of these days is a collection of books.

36 Adversity is sometimes hard upon a man; but for one man who can stand prosperity, there are a hundred that will stand adversity.

37 I hope we English will long maintain our *grand talent pour le silence.*
vi. **The Hero as King**

38 Maid-servants, I hear people complaining, are getting instructed in the 'ologies'.
Inaugural Address at Edinburgh, 1866

39 Speech is human, silence is divine, yet also brutish and dead: therefore we must learn both arts.
Journal

40 Respectable Professors of the Dismal Science.

[Political Economy.]
Latter-Day Pamphlets, No.1. **The Present Time**

1 Little other than a redtape Talking-machine, and unhappy Bag of Parliamentary Eloquence.

2 A healthy hatred of scoundrels.
No.2. **Model Prisons**

3 Nature admits no lie.
No.5. **Stump Orator**

4 A Parliament speaking through reporters to Buncombe and the twenty-seven millions mostly fools.
No.6. **Parliaments**

5 'May the Devil fly away with the fine arts!' exclaimed…in my hearing, one of our most distinguished public men.
No.8

6 The unspeakable Turk should be immediately struck out of the question.
Letter to G. Howard, 24 Nov. 1876

7 Transcendental moonshine.
Life of John Sterling, pt.i, ch.15

8 The progress of human society consists…in…the better and better apportioning of wages to work.
Past and Present, bk.i, ch.3

9 Brothers, I am sorry I have got no Morrison's Pill for curing the maladies of Society.
ch.4

10 Blessed is he who has found his work; let him ask no other blessedness.
bk.iii, ch.11

11 Captains of industry.
bk.iv, ch.4

12 He who first shortened the labour of copyists by device of *Movable Types* was disbanding hired armies, and cashiering most Kings and Senates, and creating a whole new democratic world: he had invented the art of printing.
Sartor Resartus, bk.i, ch.5

13 Man is a tool-using animal…Without tools he is nothing, with tools he is all.

14 Whoso has sixpence is sovereign (to the length of sixpence) over all men; commands cooks to feed him, philosophers to teach him, kings to mount guard over him,—to the length of sixpence.

15 Language is called the garment of thought: however, it should rather be, language is the flesh-garment, the body, of thought.
ch.11

16 The end of man is an action and not a thought, though it were the noblest.
bk.ii, ch.6

17 The everlasting No.
ch.7, title

18 The folly of that impossible precept, 'Know thyself'; till it be translated into this partially possible one, 'Know what thou canst work at'.
See 9:21

19 Man's unhappiness, as I construe, comes of his greatness; it is because there is an Infinite in him, which with all his cunning he cannot quite bury under the Finite.
ch.9

20 Close thy Byron; open thy Goethe.

21 'Do the duty which lies nearest thee', which thou knowest to be a duty! Thy second duty will already have become clearer.

22 Be no longer a chaos, but a world, or even worldkin. Produce! Produce! Were it but the pitifullest infinitesimal fraction of a product, produce it in God's name! 'Tis the utmost thou hast in thee: out with it, then.

23 As the Swiss Inscription says: *Sprechen ist silbern, Schweigen ist golden* (Speech is silvern, Silence is golden); or as I might rather express it: Speech is of Time, Silence is of Eternity.
bk.iii, ch.3

24 A *big,* fierce, weeping, hungry man, not a strong one.
(Of Thackeray.) Letter to R.W. Emerson, 9 Sept. 1853

25 I don't pretend to understand the Universe—it's a great deal bigger than I am…People ought to be modester.
To Wm. Allingham. D.A. Wilson and D. Wilson MacArthur, *Carlyle in Old Age*

26 If Jesus Christ were to come to-day, people would not even crucify him. They would ask him to dinner, and hear what he had to say, and make fun of it.
D.A. Wilson, *Carlyle at his Zenith*

27 It were better to perish than to continue schoolmastering.
D.A. Wilson, *Carlyle Till Marriage*

28 Macaulay is well for a while, but one wouldn't *live* under Niagara.
R.M. Milnes, *Notebook,* 1838

29 A good book is the purest essence of a human soul.
Speech in support of the London Library, 1840. F. Harrison, *Carlyle and the London Library*

30 *Margaret Fuller:* I accept the universe.
Carlyle: Gad! she'd better!
Attr.

ANDREW CARNEGIE 1835–1919

31 Of every thousand dollars spent in so-called charity today, it is probable that nine hundred and fifty dollars is unwisely spent.
North American Review, June 1889, **'The Gospel of Wealth'**, pt.I

32 The man who dies…rich dies disgraced.

JULIA A. CARNEY 1823–1908

33 Little drops of water,
    Little grains of sand,
Make the mighty ocean
    And the beauteous land.

And the little moments,
    Humble though they be,
Make the mighty ages
    Of eternity.
Little Things (1845). Reprinted in *Juvenile Missionary Magazine,* 10, Apr. 1853

JOSEPH EDWARDS CARPENTER 1813–1885

34 What are the wild waves saying
    Sister, the whole day long,

That ever amid our playing,
I hear but their low lone song?
What are the Wild Waves Saying?

LEWIS CARROLL 1832–1898

1 What I tell you three times is true.
The Hunting of the Snark, Fit 1. **The Landing**

2 He had forty-two boxes, all carefully packed,
With his name painted clearly on each:
But, since he omitted to mention the fact,
They were all left behind on the beach.

3 He would answer to 'Hi!' or to any loud cry,
Such as 'Fry me!' or 'Fritter-my-wig!'

4 His intimate friends called him 'Candle-ends',
And his enemies, 'Toasted-cheese'.

5 Then the bowsprit got mixed with the rudder
sometimes.

6 But the principal failing occurred in the sailing,
And the Bellman, perplexed and distressed,
Said he *had* hoped, at least, when the wind blew due
East,
That the ship would *not* travel due West!
Fit 2. **The Bellman's Speech**

7 But oh, beamish nephew, beware of the day,
If your Snark be a Boojum! For then
You will softly and suddenly vanish away,
And never be met with again!
Fit 3. **The Baker's Tale**

8 They sought it with thimbles, they sought it with care;
They pursued it with forks and hope;
They threatened its life with a railway-share;
They charmed it with smiles and soap.
Fit 5. **The Beaver's Lesson**

9 For the Snark *was* a Boojum, you see.
Fit 8. **The Vanishing**

10 He thought he saw an Elephant,
That practised on a fife:
He looked again, and found it was
A letter from his wife.
'At length I realize,' he said,
'The bitterness of life!'
Sylvie and Bruno, ch.5

11 He thought he saw a Buffalo
Upon the chimney-piece:
He looked again, and found it was
His sister's husband's niece.
'Unless you leave this house,' he said,
'I'll send for the Police!'
ch.6

12 He thought he saw a Rattlesnake
That questioned him in Greek,
He looked again and found it was
The Middle of Next Week.
'The one thing I regret,' he said,
'Is that it cannot speak!'

13 He thought he saw a Banker's Clerk
Descending from the bus:
He looked again, and found it was
A Hippopotamus:
'If this should stay to dine,' he said,
'There won't be much for us.'
ch.7

14 'What is the use of a book', thought Alice, 'without
pictures or conversations?'
Alice's Adventures in Wonderland, ch.1

15 Do cats eat bats?…Do bats eat cats?

16 'Curiouser and curiouser!' cried Alice.
ch.2

17 How doth the little crocodile
Improve his shining tail,
And pour the waters of the Nile
On every golden scale!
See 565:21

18 How cheerfully he seems to grin,
How neatly spreads his claws,
And welcomes little fishes in
With gently smiling jaws!

19 'I'll be judge, I'll be jury,' said cunning old Fury;
'I'll try the whole cause, and condemn you to death.'
ch.3

20 The Duchess! The Duchess! Oh my dear paws! Oh my
fur and whiskers!
ch.4

21 'I can't explain *myself,* I'm afraid, sir,' said Alice,
'because I'm not myself, you see.' 'I don't see,' said
the Caterpillar.
ch.5

22 'You are old, Father William,' the young man said,
'And your hair has become very white;
And yet you incessantly stand on your head—
Do you think, at your age, it is right?'

'In my youth,' Father William replied to his son,
'I feared it might injure the brain;
But now that I'm perfectly sure I have none,
Why, I do it again and again.'
See 514:7

23 'I have answered three questions, and that is enough,'
Said his father; 'don't give yourself airs!
Do you think I can listen all day to such stuff?
Be off, or I'll kick you downstairs!'
See 83:27

24 'I shall sit here,' he said, 'on and off, for days and
days.'
ch.6

25 'If everybody minded their own business,' said the
Duchess in a hoarse growl, 'the world would go round
a deal faster than it does.'

26 Speak roughly to your little boy,
And beat him when he sneezes;
He only does it to annoy,
Because he knows it teases.

27 This time it vanished quite slowly, beginning with the
end of the tail, and ending with the grin, which
remained some time after the rest of it had gone. [The
Cheshire Cat.]

28 'Have some wine,' the March Hare said in an
encouraging tone. Alice looked all round the table, but
there was nothing on it but tea. 'I don't see any wine,'
she remarked. 'There isn't any,' said the March Hare.
ch.7

29 'Then you should say what you mean,' the March
Hare went on. 'I do,' Alice hastily replied; 'at
least—at least I mean what I say—that's the same
thing, you know.'

'Not the same thing a bit!' said the Hatter. 'Why, you might just as well say that "I see what I eat" is the same thing as "I eat what I see!"'

1 'It was the *best* butter,' the March Hare meekly replied.

2 Twinkle, twinkle, little bat!
How I wonder what you're at!
Up above the world you fly!
Like a teatray in the sky.
See 532:1

3 'Take some more tea,' the March Hare said to Alice, very earnestly.
'I've had nothing yet,' Alice replied in an offended tone, 'so I can't take more.'
'You mean you can't take *less*,' said the Hatter: 'it's very easy to take *more* than nothing.'

4 Let's all move one place on.

5 The Queen was in a furious passion, and went stamping about, and shouting, 'Off with his head!' or 'Off with her head!' about once in a minute.
ch.8

6 Everything's got a moral, if you can only find it.
ch.9

7 Take care of the sense, and the sounds will take care of themselves.

8 'That's nothing to what I could say if I chose,' the Duchess replied.

9 'Just about as much right,' said the Duchess, 'as pigs have to fly.'

10 I only took the regular course...the different branches of Arithmetic—Ambition, Distraction, Uglification and Derision.

11 The Drawling-master was an old conger-eel, that used to come once a week: *he* taught us Drawling, Stretching, and Fainting in Coils.

12 'That's the reason they're called lessons,' the Gryphon remarked: 'because they lessen from day to day.'

13 'Will you walk a little faster?' said a whiting to a snail,
'There's a porpoise close behind us, and he's treading on my tail.'
ch.10

14 Will you, won't you, will you, won't you, will you join the dance?

15 The further off from England the nearer is to France—
Then turn not pale, beloved snail, but come and join the dance.

16 'Tis the voice of the lobster; I heard him declare,
'You have baked me too brown, I must sugar my hair.'
See 565:25

17 Soup of the evening, beautiful Soup!

18 'Write that down,' the King said to the jury, and the jury eagerly wrote down all three dates on their slates, and then added them up, and reduced the answer to shillings and pence.
ch.11

19 'Where shall I begin, please your Majesty?' he asked.
'Begin at the beginning,' the King said, gravely, 'and go on till you come to the end: then stop.'

20 '*Un*important, of course, I meant,' the King hastily said, and went on to himself in an undertone, 'important—unimportant—unimportant—important—' as if he were trying which word sounded best.
ch.12

21 'That's not a regular rule: you invented it just now.'
'It's the oldest rule in the book,' said the King.
'Then it ought to be Number One,' said Alice.

22 They told me you had been to her,
And mentioned me to him:
She gave me a good character,
But said I could not swim.

23 No! No! Sentence first—verdict afterwards.

24 I never loved a dear Gazelle—
Nor anything that cost me much:
High prices profit those who sell,
But why should I *be fond of such?*
Phantasmagoria (1911 ed.), **Tema con Variazioni**. See 356:25

25 Yet what are all such gaieties to me
Whose thoughts are full of indices and surds?
$$x^2 + 7x + 53 = \tfrac{11}{3}$$
from **Four Riddles**, I

26 'The horror of that moment,' the King went on, 'I shall never, *never* forget!' 'You will, though,' the Queen said, 'if you don't make a memorandum of it.'
Through the Looking-Glass, ch.1

27 'My precious Lily! My imperial kitten!'—
'Imperial fiddlestick!'

28 'Twas brillig, and the slithy toves
Did gyre and gimble in the wabe;
All mimsy were the borogoves,
And the mome raths outgrabe.

'Beware the Jabberwock, my son!
The jaws that bite, the claws that catch!'

29 And as in uffish thought he stood,
The Jabberwock, with eyes of flame,
Came whiffling through the tulgey wood,
And burbled as it came!

One, two! One, two! And through and through
The vorpal blade went snicker-snack!
He left it dead, and with its head
He went galumphing back.

'And hast thou slain the Jabberwock?
Come to my arms, my beamish boy!
O frabjous day! Callooh! Callay!'
He chortled in his joy.

30 Curtsey while you're thinking what to say. It saves time.
ch.2

31 Speak in French when you can't think of the English for a thing.

32 Now, *here*, you see, it takes all the running *you* can do, to keep in the same place. If you want to get somewhere else, you must run at least twice as fast as that!

33 Tweedledum and Tweedledee
Agreed to have a battle;
For Tweedledum said Tweedledee
Had spoilt his nice new rattle.

Just then flew down a monstrous crow,
　　As black as a tar-barrel;
Which frightened both the heroes so,
　　They quite forgot their quarrel.
ch.4

1 If you think we're wax-works, you ought to pay, you
know. Wax-works weren't made to be looked at for
nothing. Nohow!

2 'Contrariwise,' continued Tweedledee, 'if it was so, it
might be; and if it were so, it would be: but as it isn't,
it ain't. That's logic.'

3 The sun was shining on the sea,
　　Shining with all his might:
He did his very best to make
　　The billows smooth and bright—
And this was odd, because it was
　　The middle of the night.

4 'It's very rude of him,' she said
　　'To come and spoil the fun!'

5 The Walrus and the Carpenter
　　Were walking close at hand;
They wept like anything to see
　　Such quantities of sand:
'If this were only cleared away,'
　　They said, 'it would be grand!'

'If seven maids with seven mops
　　Swept it for half a year,
Do you suppose,' the Walrus said,
　　'That they could get it clear?'
'I doubt it,' said the Carpenter,
　　And shed a bitter tear.

6 But four young Oysters hurried up,
　　All eager for the treat:
Their coats were brushed, their faces washed,
　　Their shoes were clean and neat—
And this was odd, because, you know,
　　They hadn't any feet.

7 'The time has come,' the Walrus said,
　　'To talk of many things:
Of shoes—and ships—and sealing wax—
　　Of cabbages—and kings—
And why the sea is boiling hot—
　　And whether pigs have wings.'

8 'A loaf of bread,' the Walrus said,
　　'Is what we chiefly need:
Pepper and vinegar besides
　　Are very good indeed—
Now if you're ready, Oysters dear,
　　We can begin to feed.'

9 The Carpenter said nothing but
　　'The butter's spread too thick!'

10 'I weep for you,' the Walrus said:
　　'I deeply sympathize.'
With sobs and tears he sorted out
　　Those of the largest size,
Holding his pocket-handkerchief
　　Before his streaming eyes.

11 　　But answer came there none—
And this was scarcely odd because
　　They'd eaten every one.
See 415:21

12 'Let's fight till six, and then have dinner,' said
Tweedledum.

13 'You know,' he said very gravely, 'it's one of the
most serious things that can possibly happen to one in
a battle—to get one's head cut off.'

14 'I'm very brave generally,' he went on in a low voice:
'only to-day I happen to have a headache.'

15 The rule is, jam to-morrow and jam yesterday—but
never jam to-day.
ch.5

16 'It's a poor sort of memory that only works
backwards,' the Queen remarked.

17 Consider anything, only don't cry!

18 Why, sometimes I've believed as many as six
impossible things before breakfast.

19 With a name like yours, you might be any shape,
almost.
ch.6

20 They gave it me,—for an un-birthday present.

21 'There's glory for you!' 'I don't know what you mean
by "glory",' Alice said. 'I meant, "there's a nice
knock-down argument for you!"' 'But "glory"
doesn't mean "a nice knock-down argument",' Alice
objected. 'When *I* use a word,' Humpty Dumpty said
in a rather scornful tone, 'it means just what I choose
it to mean—neither more nor less.'

22 'The question is,' said Humpty Dumpty, 'which is to
be master—that's all.'

23 I can explain all the poems that ever were
invented—and a good many that haven't been invented
just yet.

24 '*I* can repeat poetry as well as other folk if it comes to
that—' 'Oh, it needn't come to that!' Alice hastily
said.

25 The little fishes of the sea,
　　They sent an answer back to me.

The little fishes' answer was
'We cannot do it, Sir, because—'

26 I took a kettle large and new,
　　Fit for the deed I had to do.

27 I said it very loud and clear;
　　I went and shouted in his ear.

But he was very stiff and proud;
　　He said 'You needn't shout so loud!'

And he was very proud and stiff;
　　He said 'I'd go and wake them, if—'

28 You see it's like a portmanteau—there are two
meanings packed up into one word.

29 He's an Anglo-Saxon Messenger—and those are
Anglo-Saxon attitudes.
ch.7

30 The other Messenger's called Hatta. I must have *two*
you know—to come and go. One to come, and one to
go.

31 'There's nothing like eating hay when you're
faint.'…'I didn't say there was nothing *better*,' the
King replied, 'I said there was nothing *like* it.'

32 'I'm sure nobody walks much faster than I do!'

'He can't do that,' said the King, 'or else he'd have been here first.'

1 It's as large as life, and twice as natural!

2 If you'll believe in me, I'll believe in you.

3 The [White] Knight said…'It's my own invention.'
ch.8

4 But you've no idea what a difference it makes, mixing it with other things—such as gunpowder and sealing-wax.

5 I'll tell thee everything I can:
    There's little to relate.
I saw an aged, aged man,
    A-sitting on a gate.

6 He said, 'I look for butterflies
    That sleep among the wheat:
I make them into mutton-pies,
    And sell them in the street.'

7 Or madly squeeze a right-hand foot
    Into a left-hand shoe.

8 'Speak when you're spoken to!' the Red Queen sharply interrupted her.
ch.9

9 No admittance till the week after next!

10 It isn't etiquette to cut any one you've been introduced to. Remove the joint.

11 Un-dish-cover the fish, or dishcover the riddle.

12 I am fond of children (except boys).
Letter to Kathleen Eschwege. S.D. Collingwood, *The Life and Letters of Lewis Carroll* (1898), p.416

JOHN CARTWRIGHT 1740–1824

13 One man shall have one vote.
People's Barrier Against Undue Influence (1780), p.5

PHOEBE CARY 1824–1871

14 And though hard be the task,
    'Keep a stiff upper lip'.
Keep a Stiff Upper Lip

REVD. EDWARD CASWALL 1814–1878

15 Jesu, the very thought of Thee
With sweetness fills the breast.
Jesu, The Very Thought of Thee (tr. from Latin)

16 My God, I love Thee; not because
I hope for heaven thereby.
My God, I Love Thee (tr. from Latin)

EMPRESS CATHERINE THE GREAT 1729–1796

17 *Moi, je serai autocrate: c'est mon métier. Et le bon Dieu me pardonnera: c'est son métier.*
I shall be an autocrat: that's my trade. And the good Lord will forgive me: that's his.
Attr. See also 244:13

THE ELDER CATO, THE CENSOR 234–149 B.C

18 *Delenda est Carthago.*

Carthage must be destroyed.
Pliny the Elder, *Naturalis Historia*, xv.18.74

CATULLUS 87–54? B.C.

19 *Cui dono lepidum novum libellum
Arido modo pumice expolitum?*
Here's my small book out, nice and new,
Fresh-bound—whom shall I give it to?
Carmina, i, tr. Sir William Marris

20   *Namque tu solebas
Meas esse aliquid putare nugas.*
For you used to think my trifles were worth something.

21 *Plus uno maneat perenne saeclo.*
May it live and last for more than a century.

22 *Lugete, O Veneres Cupidinesque,
Et quantum est hominum venustiorum.
Passer mortuus est meae puellae,
Passer, deliciae meae puellae.*
Mourn, you powers of Charm and Desire, and all you who are endowed with charm. My lady's sparrow is dead, the sparrow which was my lady's darling.
iii

23 *Qui nunc it per iter tenebricosum
Illuc, unde negant redire quemquam.*
Now he goes along the darksome road, thither whence they say no one returns.

24 *Sed haec prius fuere.*
All this is over now.
iv

25 *Vivamus, mea Lesbia, atque amemus,
Rumoresque senum severiorum
Omnes unius aestimemus assis.
Soles occidere et redire possunt:
Nobis cum semel occidit brevis lux
Nox est perpetua una dormienda.*
My sweetest Lesbia let us live and love,
And though the sager sort our deeds reprove,
Let us not weigh them: Heav'n's great lamps do dive
Into their west, and straight again revive,
But soon as once set is our little light,
Then must we sleep one ever-during night.
v. Tr. Campion, *A Book of Airs*, i

26 *Da mi basia mille, deinde centum,
Dein mille altera, dein secunda centum,
Deinde usque altera mille, deinde centum.*
Give me a thousand kisses, then a hundred, then another thousand, then a second hundred, then yet another thousand, then a hundred.

27 *Miser Catulle, desinas ineptire,
Et quod vides perisse perditum ducas.*
Poor Catullus, drop your silly fancies, and what you see is lost let it be lost.
viii

28 *Paene insularum, Sirmio, insularumque
Ocelle…
O quid solutis est beatius curis?
Cum mens onus reponit, ac peregrino
Labore fessi venimus larem ad nostrum,
Desideratoque acquiescimus lecto.
Hoc est quod unum est pro laboribus tantis.
Salve O venusta Sirmio atque hero gaude;
Gaudete vosque O Lydiae lacus undae;*

Ridete quidquid est domi cachinnorum.
Sirmio, bright eye of peninsulas and islands…Ah, what is more blessed than to put cares away, when the mind lays by its burden, and tired with labour of far travel we have come to our own home and rest on the couch we have longed for? This it is which alone is worth all these toils. Hail, sweet Sirmio, and make cheer for your master. Rejoice ye too, waters of the Lydian lake, and laugh out aloud all the laughter you have at your command.
xxxi

1 *Nam risu inepto res ineptior nulla est.*
For there is nothing sillier than a silly laugh.
xxxix

2 *Iam ver egelidos refert tepores.*
Now Spring restores balmy warmth.
xlvi

3 *Gratias tibi maximas Catullus*
Agit pessimus omnium poeta,
Tanto pessimus omnium poeta,
Quanto tu optimus omnium's patronum.
Catullus gives you warmest thanks,
And he the worst of poets ranks;
As much the worst of bards confessed,
As you of advocates the best.
xlix, tr. Sir William Marris

4 *Ille mi par esse deo videtur,*
Ille, si fas est, superare divos,
Qui sedens adversus identidem te
         Spectat et audit
Dulce ridentem, misero quod omnis
Eripit sensus mihi.
Like to a god he seems to me,
Above the gods, if so may be,
Who sitting often close to thee
      May see and hear
Thy lovely laugh: ah, luckless man!
li, tr. Sir William Marris. Itself a translation of 414:6

5 *Caeli, Lesbia nostra, Lesbia illa,*
Illa Lesbia, quam Catullus unam
Plus quam se atque suos amavit omnes,
Nunc in quadriviis et angiportis
Glubit magnanimos Remi nepotes.
O Caelius, our Lesbia, that Lesbia whom Catullus once loved uniquely, more than himself and more than all his own, now at the crossroads and in the alleyways has it off with the high-minded descendants of Remus.
lviii

6 *Ut flos in saeptis secretus nascitur hortis,*
Ignotus pecori, nullo contusus aratro,
Quem mulcent aurae, firmat sol, educat imber;
Multi illum pueri, multae optavere puellae.
As a flower grows concealed in an enclosed garden, unknown to the cattle, bruised by no plough, which the breezes caress, the sun makes strong, and the rain brings out; many boys and many girls long for it.
lxii.39

7   *Sed mulier cupido quod dicit amanti,*
In vento et rapida scribere oportet aqua.
But what a woman says to her lusting lover it is best to write in wind and swift-flowing water.
lxx

8 *Desine de quoquam quicquam bene velle mereri,*
   Aut aliquem fieri posse putare pium.
Give up wanting to deserve any thanks from anyone, or thinking that anybody can be grateful.
lxxiii

9 *Siqua recordanti benefacta priora voluptas*
Est homini.
If a man can take any pleasure in recalling the thought of kindnesses done.
lxxvi

10 *Difficile est longum subito deponere amorem.*
It is difficult suddenly to lay aside a long-cherished love.

11 *Si vitam puriter egi.*
If I have led a pure life.

12 *O di, reddite mi hoc pro pietate mea.*
O gods, grant me this in return for my piety.

13 *Chommoda dicebat, si quando commoda vellet*
Dicere.
'Hamenities' he used to say, meaning 'amenities'. (Of Arrius.)
lxxxiv

14 *Odi et amo: quare id faciam, fortasse requiris.*
Nescio, sed fieri sentio et excrucior.
I hate and I love: why I do so you may well ask. I do not know, but I feel it happen and am in agony.
lxxxv

15 *Multas per gentes et multa per aequora vectus*
   Advenio has miseras, frater, ad inferias,
Ut te postremo donarem munere mortis
   Et mutam nequiquam alloquerer cinerem.
Quandoquidem fortuna mihi tete abstulit ipsum,
   Heu miser indigne frater adempte mihi,
Nunc tamen interea haec prisco quae more parentum
   Tradita sunt tristi munere ad inferias,
Accipe fraterno multum manantia fletu,
   Atque in perpetuum, frater, ave atque vale.
By many lands and over many a wave
I come, my brother, to your piteous grave,
To bring you the last offering in death
And o'er dumb dust expend an idle breath;
For fate has torn your living self from me,
And snatched you, brother, O, how cruelly!
Yet take these gifts, brought as our fathers bade
For sorrow's tribute to the passing shade;
A brother's tears have wet them o'er and o'er;
And so, my brother, hail, and farewell evermore!
ci, tr. Sir William Marris

16 *At non effugies meos iambos.*
You shan't evade
These rhymes I've made.
Fragments, tr. Sir William Marris

CONSTANTINE CAVAFY 1863–1933

17 What shall become of us without any barbarians?
Those people were a kind of solution.
Expecting the Barbarians

EDITH CAVELL 1865–1915

18 Standing, as I do, in the view of God and eternity I realize that patriotism is not enough. I must have no

hatred or bitterness towards anyone.
Spoken to the chaplain who attended her before her execution by firing squad, 12 Oct. 1915. *The Times*, 23 Oct. 1915

COUNT CAVOUR 1810–1861

1 *Noi siamo pronti a proclamare nell' Italia questo gran principio: Libera Chiesa in libero Stato.*
We are ready to proclaim throughout Italy this great principle: a free church in a free state.
Speech, 27 Mar. 1861. William de la Rive, *Remin. of Life and Character of Count Cavour* (1862), ch.13, p.276

WILLIAM CAXTON c.1421–1491

2 The worshipful father and first founder and embellisher of ornate eloquence in our English, I mean Master Geoffrey Chaucer.
Epilogue to Caxton's edition (?1478) of Chaucer's translation of Boethius, *The Consolacion of Philosophie*, 93 verso

3 It is notoriously known through the universal world that there be nine worthy and the best that ever were. That is to wit three paynims, three Jews, and three Christian men. As for the paynims they were...the first Hector of Troy,...the second Alexander the Great; and the third Julius Caesar....As for the three Jews...the first was Duke Joshua...; the second David, King of Jerusalem; and the third Judas Maccabaeus.... And sith the said Incarnation...was first the noble Arthur.... The second was Charlemagne or Charles the Great...; and the third and last was Godfrey of Bouillon.
Malory, *Le Morte D'Arthur*, Original Preface

4 I, according to my copy, have done set it in imprint, to the intent that noble men may see and learn the noble acts of chivalry, the gentle and virtuous deeds that some knights used in those days.

ROBERT CECIL
see SALISBURY

THOMAS OF CELANO c.1190–1260

5 *Dies irae, dies illa,*
Solvet saeclum in favilla,
Teste David cum Sibylla.
That day, the day of wrath, will turn the universe to ashes, as David foretells (and the Sibyl too).
Dies irae, 1. Attr. Printed in Missal, Mass for the Dead

6 *Tuba mirum sparget sonum*
Per sepulchra regionum,
Coget omnes ante thronum.

Mors stupebit et natura,
Cum resurget creatura
Iudicanti responsura.

Liber scriptus proferetur,
In quo totum continetur
Unde mundus iudicetur.
The trumpet will fling out a wonderful sound through the tombs of all regions, it will drive everyone before the throne. Death will be aghast and so will nature, when creation rises again to make answer to the judge. The written book will be brought forth, in which everything is included whereby the world

will be judged.
7

7 *Rex tremendae maiestatis,*
Qui salvandos salvas gratis,
Salva me, fons pietatis!
O King of tremendous majesty, who freely saves those who should be saved, save me, O source of pity!
22

8 *Inter oves locum praesta*
Et ab haedis me sequestra
Statuens in parte dextra.
Among the sheep set me a place and separate me from the goats, standing me on the right-hand side.
43

MRS. CENTLIVRE 1667?–1723

9 The real Simon Pure.
A Bold Stroke for a Wife, V.i

10 And lash the vice and follies of the age.
The Man's Bewitched, prologue. See 159:20

11 He is as melancholy as an unbrac'd drum.
Wonder, II.i

MIGUEL DE CERVANTES 1547–1616

12 *El Caballero de la Triste Figura.*
The Knight of the Doleful Countenance.
Don Quixote, pt.i, ch.19

13 *La mejor salsa del mundo es el hambre.*
Hunger is the best sauce in the world.
pt.ii, ch.5

14 *El pan comido y la compañía deshecha.*
With the bread eaten up, up breaks the company.
ch.7

15 [Sancho asks whether, to get to heaven, we ought not all to become monks.]
No todos podemos ser frailes y muchos son los caminos por donde lleva Dios a los suyos al cielo. Religión es la caballería.
We cannot all be friars, and many are the ways by which God leads his own to eternal life. Religion *is* knight-errantry.
ch.8

16 *Es un entreverado loco, lleno de lúcidos intervalos.*
He's a muddle-headed fool, with frequent lucid intervals.
(Sancho Panza, of Don Quixote). ch.18

17 *Dos linages sólos hay en el mundo, como decía una abuela mía, que son el tener y el no tener.*
There are only two families in the world, as a grandmother of mine used to say: the haves and the have-nots.
ch.20

18 *Digo, paciencia y barajar.*
What I say is, patience, and shuffle the cards.
ch.23

19 *La diligencia es madre de la buena ventura y la pereza, su contrario, jamás llegó al término que pide un buen deseo.*
Diligence is the mother of good fortune, and idleness, its opposite, never led to good intention's goal.

20 *Bien haya el que inventó el sueño, capa que cubre todos los humanos pensamientos, manjar que quita la*

hambre, agua que ahuyenta la sed, fuego que calienta el frío, frío que templa el ardor, y, finalmente, moneda general con que todas las cosas se compran, balanza y peso que iguala al pastor con el rey y al simple con el discreto.

Blessings on him who invented sleep, the mantle that covers all human thoughts, the food that satisfies hunger, the drink that slakes thirst, the fire that warms cold, the cold that moderates heat, and, lastly, the common currency that buys all things, the balance and weight that equalises the shepherd and the king, the simpleton and the sage.
ch.68

1 *Los buenos pintores imitan la naturaleza, pero los malos la vomitan.*
Good painters imitate nature, bad ones spew it up.
El Licenciado Vidriera

2 *Puesto ya el pie en el estribo.*
With one foot already in the stirrup.
Preface to **Persiles y Sigismunda** (four days before his death)

PATRICK REGINALD CHALMERS 1872–1942

3 What's lost upon the roundabouts we pulls up on the swings!
Green Days and Blue Days: Roundabouts and Swings

JOSEPH CHAMBERLAIN 1836–1914

4 Provided that the City of London remains as it is at present, the clearing-house of the world.
Guildhall, London, 19 Jan. 1904

5 Learn to think Imperially.

6 The day of small nations has long passed away. The day of Empires has come.
Birmingham, 12 May 1904

7 We are not downhearted. The only trouble is, we cannot understand what is happening to our neighbours.
Smethwick, 18 Jan. 1906

NEVILLE CHAMBERLAIN 1869–1940

8 In war, whichever side may call itself the victor, there are no winners, but all are losers.
Kettering, 3 July 1938

9 How horrible, fantastic, incredible, it is that we should be digging trenches and trying on gas-masks here because of a quarrel in a far-away country between people of whom we know nothing.
(Of Germany's annexation of the Sudetenland.) Radio broadcast, 27 Sept. 1938. K.Feiling, *Life of Neville Chamberlain*, bk.iv, ch.28

10 I believe it is peace for our time…peace with honour.
After Munich Agreement. 30 Sept. 1938. See 185:15

11 Hitler has missed the bus.
Central Hall, Westminster, 4 April 1940

HADDON CHAMBERS 1860–1921

12 The long arm of coincidence.
Captain Swift (1888), Act II

NICOLAS-SÉBASTIEN CHAMFORT 1741–1794

13 *Vivre est une maladie dont le sommeil nous soulage toutes les 16 heures. C'est un palliatif. La mort est le remède.*
Living is an illness to which sleep provides relief every sixteen hours. It's a palliative. The remedy is death.
Maximes et Pensées (1796), ch.2

14 *Des qualités trop supérieures rendent souvent un homme moins propre à la société. On ne va pas au marché avec des lingots; on y va avec de l'argent ou de la petite monnaie.*
Qualities too elevated often unfit a man for society. We don't take ingots with us to market; we take silver or small change.
ch.3

15 *L'amour, tel qu'il existe dans la société, n'est que l'échange de deux fantaisies et le contact de deux épidermes.*
Love, in the form in which it exists in society, is nothing but the exchange of two fantasies and the superficial contact of two bodies.
ch.6

16 *Je dirais volontiers des métaphysiciens ce que Scalinger disait des Basques, on dit qu'ils s'entendent, mais je n'en crois rien.*
I am tempted to say of metaphysicians what Scalinger used to say of the Basques: they are said to understand one another, but I don't believe a word of it.
ch.7

17 *Les pauvres sont les nègres de l'Europe.*
The poor are Europe's blacks.
ch.8

18 *Sois mon frère, ou je te tue.*
Be my brother, or I kill you.
Oeuvres, I, *'Notice sur la vie de Chamfort'*. Interpretation of *'Fraternité ou la mort'*. See 9:13

JOHN CHANDLER 1806–1876

19 Conquering kings their titles take
From the foes they captive make:
Jesu, by a nobler deed,
From the thousands He hath freed.
Hymns Ancient and Modern. (Tr. from Latin)

RAYMOND CHANDLER 1888–1959

20 It was about eleven o'clock in the morning, mid-October, with the sun not shining and a look of hard wet rain in the clearness of the foothills. I was wearing my powder-blue suit, with dark blue shirt, tie and display handkerchief, black brogues, black wool socks with dark blue clocks on them. I was neat, clean, shaved and sober, and I didn't care who knew it.
The Big Sleep, ch.1

21 The demand was for constant action; if you stopped to think you were lost. When in doubt have a man come through a door with a gun in his hand. This could get to be pretty silly but somehow it didn't seem to matter.
The Simple Art of Murder (1950), preface, referring to the policy of light crime fiction magazines

22 Down these mean streets a man must go who is not himself mean; who is neither tarnished nor afraid.
The Simple Art of Murder

CHARLES CHAPLIN 1889–1977

1 *Priest:* May the Lord have mercy on your soul.
Verdoux: Why not? After all, it belongs to Him.
Monsieur Verdoux (1947)

ARTHUR CHAPMAN 1873–1935

2 Out where the handclasp's a little stronger,
Out where the smile dwells a little longer,
   That's where the West begins.
Out where the West Begins

GEORGE CHAPMAN 1559?–1634?

3   I know an Englishman,
Being flatter'd, is a lamb; threaten'd, a lion.
Alphonsus, Emperor of Germany, I.ii

4 Berenice's ever-burning hair.
Blind Beggar of Alexandria

5 Speed his plough.
Bussy D'Ambois, I.i

6 Who to himself is law, no law doth need,
Offends no law, and is a king indeed.
II.i

7 Terror of darkness! O, thou king of flames!
V.i

8 There is no danger to a man, that knows
What life and death is; there's not any law,
Exceeds his knowledge; neither is it lawful
That he should stoop to any other law.
He goes before them, and commands them all,
That to himself is a law rational.
Byron's Conspiracy, III.i

9 O incredulity! the wit of fools,
That slovenly will spit on all things fair,
The coward's castle, and the sluggard's cradle.
De Guiana, l.82

10 We have watered our horses in Helicon.
May-Day, III.iii

11 For one heat, all know, doth drive out another,
One passion doth expel another still.
Monsieur D'Olive, V.i

12 I am ashamed the law is such an ass.
Revenge for Honour, III.ii

13 They're only truly great who are truly good.
V.ii

14 A poem, whose subject is not truth, but things like
truth.
Revenge of Bussy D'Ambois, dedication

15 Danger, the spur of all great minds.
V.i

16 And let a scholar all Earth's volumes carry,
He will be but a walking dictionary.
Tears of Peace, l.266

KING CHARLES I 1600–1649

17 Never make a defence or apology before you be
accused.
Letter to Lord Wentworth, 3 Sept. 1636

18 I see all the birds are flown.
Said in the House of Commons, 4 Jan. 1642, after attempting to
arrest the Five Members. *Parliamentary History*, vol.II (1807),
col.1010

19 As to the King, the Laws of the Land will clearly
instruct you for that…For the People; and truly I desire
their Liberty and Freedom, as much as any Body: but
I must tell you, that their Liberty and Freedom consists
in having the Government of those Laws, by which
their Life and their Goods may be most their own; 'tis
not for having share in Government [Sirs] that is
nothing pertaining to 'em. A Subject and a Sovereign
are clean different things…If I would have given way
to an arbitrary way, for to have all Laws chang'd
according to the Power of the Sword, I needed not to
have come here; and therefore I tell you (and I pray
God it be not laid to your Charge) that I am the Martyr
of the People.
Speech on the scaffold, 30 Jan. 1649. Rushworth, *Historical
Collections* (1703-8), vol.vi

20 I die a Christian, according to the Profession of the
Church of England, as I found it left me by my Father.

KING CHARLES II 1630–1685

21 It is upon the navy under the Providence of God that
the safety, honour, and welfare of this realm do chiefly
attend.
Articles of War (1652), Preamble

22 Better than a play.
(On the Debates in the House of Lords on Lord Ross's Divorce
Bill, 1670.) A. Bryant, *King Charles II*

23 This is very true: for my words are my own, and my
actions are my ministers'.
Reply to Lord Rochester's Epitaph on him. See 406:18

24 He [Charles II] said once to myself, he was no atheist,
but he could not think God would make a man
miserable only for taking a little pleasure out of the
way.
Burnet, *History of My Own Time*, vol.I, bk.ii, ch.1

25 He [Lauderdale] told me, the king spoke to him to let
that [Presbytery] go, for it was not a religion for
gentlemen.
ch.2

26 His nonsense suits their nonsense.
ch.11. Of Woolly, afterward Bishop of Clonfert, ('a very honest
man, but a very great blockhead') who had gone from house to
house trying to persuade Nonconformists to go to church.

27 King Charles gave him [Godolphin] a short character
when he was page, which he maintained to his life's
end, of being never *in* the way, nor *out* of the way.
vol.II, bk.iii, ch.11, n. (The Earl of Dartmouth)

28 Let not poor Nelly starve.
ch.17

29 I am sure no man in England will take away my life to
make you King. [To his brother James.]
W. King, *Political & Lit. Anecdotes*

30 He had been, he said, an unconscionable time dying;
but he hoped that they would excuse it.
Macaulay, *Hist. England*, 1849, vol.i, ch.4, p.437

EMPEROR CHARLES V 1500–1558

31 *Je parle espagnol à Dieu, italien aux femmes, français
aux hommes et allemand à mon cheval.*
To God I speak Spanish, to women Italian, to men
French, and to my horse—German.
Attr.

PIERRE CHARRON 1541–1603

1 *La vraye science et le vray étude de l'homme, c'est l'homme.*
The true science and study of man is man.
De la Sagesse (1601), bk.I, ch.i

SALMON PORTLAND CHASE 1808–1873

2 No more slave States: no slave Territories.
Platform of the Free Soil National Convention, 1848

3 The Constitution, in all its provisions, looks to an indestructible Union composed of indestructible States.
Decision in Texas v. White, 7 Wallace, 725

4 The way to resumption is to resume.
Letter to Horace Greeley, 17 May 1866

EARL OF CHATHAM
see WILLIAM PITT

FRANÇOIS-RENÉ DE CHATEAUBRIAND 1768–1848

5 *L'écrivain original n'est pas celui qui n'imite personne, mais celui que personne ne peut imiter.*
The original writer is not he who refrains from imitating others, but he who can be imitated by none.
Génie du Christianisme

GEOFFREY CHAUCER 1340?–1400
All line references are to the various fragments as collected in *The Works of Geoffrey Chaucer*, ed. F.N. Robinson, 2nd edition (1957)

6 Ful craftier to pley she was
Than Athalus, that made the game
First of the ches, so was his name.
The Book of the Duchess, l.662

7 Whan that Aprill with his shoures soote
The droghte of March hath perced to the roote.
The Canterbury Tales, **General Prologue,** l.1

8 And smale foweles maken melodye,
That slepen al the nyght with open ye
(So priketh hem nature in hir corages);
Thanne longen folk to goon on pilgrimages.
l.9

9   He loved chivalrie,
Trouthe and honour, freedom and curteisie.
l.45

10 He was a verray, parfit gentil knyght.
l.72

11 He was as fressh as is the month of May.
l.92

12 He koude songes make and wel endite.
l.95

13 Curteis he was, lowely, and servysable,
And carf biforn his fader at the table.
l.99

14 Hire gretteste ooth was but by Seinte Loy.
l.120

15 Ful weel she soong the service dyvyne,
Entuned in hir nose ful semely,
And Frenssh she spak ful faire and fetisly,
After the scole of Stratford atte Bowe,

For Frenssh of Parys was to hire unknowe.
l.122

16 She wolde wepe, if that she saugh a mous
Kaught in a trappe, if it were deed or bledde.
Of smale houndes hadde she that she fedde
With rosted flessh, or milk and wastel-breed.
But soore wepte she if oon of hem were deed.
l.144

17 Of smal coral aboute hire arm she bar
A peire of bedes, gauded al with grene,
And theron heng a brooch of gold ful sheene,
On which ther was first write a crowned A,
And after *Amor vincit omnia.*
l.158

18 He yaf nat of that text a pulled hen,
That seith that hunters ben nat hooly men.
l.177

19 A Frere there was, a wantowne and a merye.
l.208

20 He knew the tavernes well in every toun.
l.240

21 He was the beste beggere in his hous.
l.252

22 Somwhat he lipsed, for his wantownesse,
To make his Englissh sweete upon his tonge.
l.264

23 A Clerk ther was of Oxenford also,
That unto logyk hadde longe ygo.
As leene was his hors as is a rake,
And he nas nat right fat, I undertake,
But looked holwe, and therto sobrely.
l.285

24 For hym was levere have at his beddes heed
Twenty bookes, clad in blak or reed
Of Aristotle and his philosophie,
Than robes riche, or fithele, or gay sautrie.
But al be that he was a philosophre,
Yet hadde he but litel gold in cofre.
l.293

25 And gladly wolde he lerne and gladly teche.
l.308

26 Nowher so bisy a man as he ther nas,
And yet he semed bisier than he was.
l.321

27 For he was Epicurus owene sone.
l.336

28 It snewed in his hous of mete and drynke.
l.345

29 A Shipman was ther, wonynge fer by weste;
For aught I woot, he was of Dertemouthe.
l.388

30 His studie was but litel on the Bible.
l.438

31 She was a worthy womman al hir lyve:
Housbondes at chirche dore she hadde fyve,
Withouten oother compaignye in youthe,—
But thereof nedeth nat to speke as nowthe.
And thries hadde she been at Jerusalem;
She hadde passed many a straunge strem;
At Rome she hadde been, and at Boloigne,
In Galice at Seint-Jame, and at Coloigne.
l.459

32 A good man was ther of religioun,

And was a povre Persoun of a Toun.
l.477

1 This noble ensample to his sheep he yaf,
That first he wroghte, and afterward he taughte.
l.496

2 If gold ruste, what shall iren do?
l.500

3 But Cristes loore and his apostles twelve
He taughte, but first he folwed it hymselve.
l.527

4 A Somonour was ther with us in that place,
That hadde a fyr-reed cherubynnes face,
For saucefleem he was, with eyen narwe.
As hoot he was and lecherous as a sparwe.
l.623

5 Wel loved he garleek, oynons, and eek lekes,
And for to drynken strong wyn, reed as blood.
l.634

6 His walet lay biforn hym in his lappe,
Bretful of pardoun, comen from Rome al hoot.
l.686

7 He hadde a croys of latoun ful of stones,
And in a glas he hadde pigges bones.
But with thise relikes, whan that he fond
A povre person dwellynge upon lond,
Upon a day he gat hym moore moneye
Than that the person gat in monthes tweye;
And thus, with feyned flaterye and japes,
He made the person and the peple his apes.
l.699

8 'O stormy peple! unsad and evere untrewe!'
The Clerk's Tale, l.995

9 Grisilde is deed, and eek hire pacience,
And bothe atones buryed in Ytaille;
For which I crie in open audience,
No wedded man so hardy be t'assaille
His wyves pacience in trust to fynde
Grisildis, for in certein he shal faille.
The Clerk's Tale: Lenvoy de Chaucer, l.1177

10 Ye archewyves, stondeth at defense,
Syn ye be strong as is a greet camaille;
Ne suffreth nat that men yow doon offense.
And sklendre wyves, fieble as in bataille,
Beth egre is a tygre yond in Ynde;
Ay clappeth as a mille, I yow consaille.
l.1195

11 Be ay of chiere as light as leef on lynde,
And lat hym care, and wepe, and wrynge, and waille!
l.1211

12 For o thyng, sires, saufly dar I seye,
That freendes everych oother moot obeye,
If they wol longe holden compaignye.
Love wol nat been constreyned by maistrye.
Whan maistrie comth, the God of Love anon
Beteth his wynges, and farewel, he is gon!
Love is a thyng as any spirit free.
Wommen, of kynde, desiren libertee,
And nat to been constreyned as a thral;
And so doon men, if I sooth seyen shal.
The Franklin's Tale, l.761

13 Til that the brighte sonne loste his hewe;
For th'orisonte hath reft the sonne his lyght;

This is as muche to seye as it was nyght!
l.1016

14 Trouthe is the hyest thing that man may kepe.
l.1479

15 The carl spak oo thing, but he thoghte another.
The Friar's Tale, l.1568

16 And therefore, at the kynges court, my brother,
Ech man for hymself, ther is noon oother.
The Knight's Tale, l.1181

17 And whan a beest is deed he hath no peyne;
But man after his deeth moot wepe and pleyne.
l.1319

18 The bisy larke, messager of day.
l.1491

19 For pitee renneth soone in gentil herte.
l.1761

20 The smylere with the knyf under the cloke.
l.1999

21 Up roos the sonne, and up roos Emelye.
l.2273

22 What is this world? what asketh men to have?
Now with his love, now in his colde grave.
l.2777

23 She is mirour of alle curteisye.
The Man of Law's Tale, l.166

24 Have ye nat seyn somtyme a pale face,
Among a prees, of hym that hath be lad
Toward his deeth, wher as hym gat no grace,
And swich a colour in his face hath had,
Men myghte knowe his face that was bistad,
Amonges alle the faces in that route?
l.645

25 Lat take a cat, and forstre hym wel with milk
And tendre flessh, and make his couche of silk,
And lay hym seen a mous go by the wal,
Anon he weyveth milk and flessh and al,
And every deyntee that is in that hous,
Swich appetit hath he to ete a mous.
The Manciple's Tale, l.175

26 Kepe wel they tonge, and thenk upon the crowe.
l.362

27 And what is bettre than wisedoom? Womman. And
what is bettre than a good womman? Nothyng.
The Tale of Melibee, l.1107

28 'Tehee!' quod she, and clapte the wyndow to.
The Miller's Tale, l.3740

29 For certein, whan that Fortune list to flee,
Ther may no man the cours of hire withholde.
The Monk's Tale, l.1995

30 Ful wys is he that kan hymselven knowe!
l.2139

31 Redeth the grete poete of Ytaille
That highte Dant, for he kan al devyse
Fro point to point, nat o word wol he faille.
l.2460

32 His coomb was redder than the fyn coral,
And batailled as it were a castle wal;
His byle was blak, and as the jeet it shoon;
Lyk asure were his legges and his toon;
His nayles whitter than the lylye flour,
And lyk the burned gold was his colour.
This gentil cok hadde in his governaunce

Sevene hennes for to doon al his plesaunce,
Whiche were his sustres and his paramours,
And wonder lyk to hym, as of colours;
Of whiche the faireste hewed on hir throte
Was cleped fair damoysele Pertelote.
The Nun's Priest's Tale, 1.2859

1 Whan that the month in which the world bigan,
That highte March, whan God first maked man.
1.3187

2 And daun Russell the fox stirte up atones.
1.3334

3 And on a Friday fil al this meschaunce.
1.3341

4 Mordre wol out, that se we day by day.
1.4241

5 Thanne peyne I me to strecche forth the nekke,
And est and west upon the peple I bekke.
The Pardoner's Prologue, 1.395

6 O wombe! O bely! O stynkyng cod
Fulfilled of dong and of corrupcioun!
The Pardoner's Tale, 1.534

7 'What, carl, with sory grace!'
1.717

8 And lightly as it comth, so wol we spende.
1.781

9 He kan nat stynte of syngyng by the weye.
The Prioress's Tale, 1.557

10 Yet in oure asshen olde is fyr yreke.
The Reeve's Prologue, 1.3882

11 'The gretteste clerkes been noght wisest men.'
The Reeve's Tale, 1.4054

12 So was hir joly whistle wel ywet.
1.4155

13 Thou lookest as thou woldest fynde an hare,
For evere upon the ground I se thee stare.
Prologue to Sir Thopas, 1.696

14 He hadde a semely nose.
Sir Thopas, 1.729

15 'By God,' quod he, 'for pleynly, at a word,
Thy drasty rymyng is nat worth a toord!'
1.929

16 Experience though noon auctoritee
Were in this world, is right ynogh for me
To speke of wo that is in mariage.
The Wife of Bath's Prologue, 1.1

17 Yblessed be god that I have wedded fyve!
Welcome the sixte, whan that evere he shal.
For sothe, I wol nat kepe me chaast in al.
Whan myn housbonde is fro the world ygon,
Som Cristen man shall wedde me anon.
1.44

18 The bacon was nat fet for hem, I trowe,
That som men han in Essex at Dunmowe.
1.217

19 But, Lord Crist! whan that it remembreth me
Upon my yowthe, and on my jolitee,
It tikleth me aboute myn herte roote
Unto this day it dooth myn herte boote
That I have had my world as in my tyme.
1.469

20 And for to se, and eek for to be seye

Of lusty folk.
1.552

21 But yet I hadde alwey a coltes tooth.
Gat-tothed I was, and that bicam me weel.
1.602

22 This is a long preamble of a tale!
1.831

23 Of which mayde anon, maugree hir heed,
By verray force, he rafte hire maydenhed.
The Wife of Bath's Tale, 1.887

24 'My lige lady, generally,' quod he,
'Wommen desiren to have sovereynetee
As wel over hir housbond as hir love.'
1.1037

25 That he is gentil that dooth gentil dedis.
1.1170

26   Venus clerk, Ovide,
That hath ysowen wonder wide
The grete god of Loves name.
The House of Fame, 1.1487

27 And she was fayr as is the rose in May.
The Legend of Cleopatra, 1.613

28 A thousand tymes have I herd men telle
That ther ys joy in hevene and peyne in helle,
And I acorde wel that it ys so;
But, natheless, yet wot I wel also
That ther nis noon dwellyng in this contree,
That eyther hath in hevene or helle ybe,
Ne may of hit noon other weyes witen,
But as he hath herd seyd, or founde it writen;
For by assay ther may no man it preve.
But God forbede but men shulde leve
Wel more thing then men han seen with ye!
Men shal not wenen every thing a lye
But yf himself yt seeth, or elles dooth;
For, God wot, thing is never the lasse sooth,
Thogh every wight ne may it nat ysee.
Bernard the monk ne saugh nat all, pardee!
The Legend of Good Women, The Prologue, 1.1

29 And as for me, though that I konne but lyte,
On bokes for to rede I me delyte,
And to hem yive I feyth and ful credence,
And in myn herte have hem in reverence
So hertely, that ther is game noon
That fro by bokes maketh me to goon,
But yt be seldom on the holyday,
Save, certeynly, whan that the month of May
Is comen, and that I here the foules synge,
And that the floures gynnen for to sprynge,
Farewel my bok, and my devocioun!
1.29

30   Of al the floures in the mede,
Thanne love I most thise floures white and rede,
Swiche as men callen daysyes in our toun.
1.41

31 That wel by reson men it calle may
The 'dayesye,' or elles the 'ye of day,'
The emperice and flour of floures alle.
I pray to God that faire mote she falle,
And alle that lovel floures, for hire sake!
1.183

32 That lyf so short, the craft so long to lerne,

Th' assay so hard, so sharp the conquerynge.
The Parliament of Fowls, l.1. See 251:8

1 Thou shalt make castels thanne in Spayne,
And dreme of joye, all but in vayne.
The Romaunt of the Rose, l.2573

2 For it is seyd, 'man maketh ofte a yerde
With which the maker is hymself ybeten.'
Troilus and Criseyde, i, l.740

3 But love a womman that she woot it nought,
And she wol quyte it that thow shalt nat fele;
Unknowe, unkist, and lost, that is unsought.
l.807

4 O wynd, o wynd, the weder gynneth clere.
ii, l.2

5 So longe mote ye lyve, and alle proude,
Til crowes feet be growen under youre yë.
l.402

6 And we shall speek of the somwhat, I trow,
Whan thow art gon, to don thyn eris glow!
l.1021

7 It is nought good a slepyng hound to wake.
iii, l.764

8 For I have seyn, of a ful misty morwe
Folowen ful ofte a myrie someris day.
l.1060

9 Right as an aspes leef she gan to quake.
l.1200

10 And as the newe abaysed nyghtyngale,
That stynteth first whan she bygynneth to synge.
l.1233

11 For of fortunes sharpe adversitee
The worst kynde of infortune is this,
A man to han ben in prosperitee,
And it remembren, whan it passed is.
l.1625. See 89:6, 171:8

12 Oon ere it herde, at tothir out it wente.
iv, l.434

13 But manly sette the world on six and sevene;
And if thow deye a martyr, go to hevene!
l.622

14 For tyme ylost may nought recovered be.
l.1283

15 Ye, fare wel al the snow of ferne yere!
v, l.1176

16 Ek gret effect men write in place lite;
Th' entente is al, and nat the letrres space.
l.1629

17 Go, litel bok, go, litel myn tragedye,
Ther God thi makere yet, er that he dye,
So sende myght to make in som comedye!
But litel bok, no makyng thow n'envie,
But subgit be to alle poesye;
And kis the steppes, where as thow seest pace
Virgile, Ovide, Omer, Lucan, and Stace.

And for ther is so gret diversite
In Englissh and in writyng of oure tonge,
So prey I God that non myswrite the,
Ne the mysmetre for defaute of tonge.
And red wherso thow be, or elles songe,
That thow be understonde, God I biseche!
l.1786

18 And whan that he was slayn in this manere,

His lighte goost ful blisfully is went
Up to the holughnesse of the eighthe spere,
In convers letyng everich element;
And ther he saugh, with ful avysement,
The erratik sterres, herkenyng armonye
With sownes ful of hevenyssh melodie.

And down from thennes faste he gan avyse
This litel spot of erthe, that with the se
Embraced is, and fully gan despise
This wrecched world, and held al vanite
To respect of the pleyn felicite
That is in hevene above.
l.1807

19 O yonge, fresshe folkes, he or she,
In which that love up groweth with youre age,
Repeyreth hom fro worldly vanyte,
And of youre herte up casteth the visage
To thilke God that after his ymage
Yow made, and thynketh al nys but a faire
This world, that passeth soone as floures faire.

And loveth hym, the which that right for love
Upon a crois, our soules for to beye,
First start, and roos, and sit in hevene above;
For he nyl falsen no wight, dar I seye,
That wol his herte al holly on hym leye.
And syn he best to love is, and most meke,
What nedeth feynede loves for to seke?

Lo here, of payens corsed olde rites,
Lo here, what alle hire goddes may availle;
Lo here, thise wrecched worldes appetites;
Lo here, the fyn and guerdoun for travaille
Of Jove, Appollo, of Mars, of swich rascaille!
l.1835

20 O moral Gower, this book I directe
To the.
l.1856

21 Flee fro the prees, and dwelle with sothfastnesse.
Truth: Balade de Bon Conseyle, l.1

22 Forth, pilgrim, forth! Forth, beste, out of they stal!
Know thy contree, look up, thank God of al;
Hold the heye wey, and lat thy gost thee lede;
And trowth thee shal delivere, it is no drede.
l.18

ANTON CHEKHOV 1860–1904

23 When a lot of remedies are suggested for a disease,
that means it can't be cured.
The Cherry Orchard (1903-4), II.i

24 Great God in Heaven, the Cherry Orchard is now
mine...I've bought the estate where my father and
grandfather were slaves, where they weren't even
allowed inside the kitchen. I must be dreaming, I must
be imagining it all.
III

25 *Medvedenko:* Why do you wear black all the time?
Masha: I'm in mourning for my life, I'm unhappy.
The Seagull (1896), I

26 *Nina:* Your play's hard to act, there are no living
people in it.
Treplev: Living people! We should show life neither
as it is nor as it ought to be, but as we see it in our
dreams.

1 Women can't forgive failure.
II

2 *Nina:* I'm a seagull. No, that's wrong. Remember you shot a seagull? A man happened to come along, saw it and killed it, just to pass the time. A plot for a short story.
IV

3 People don't notice whether it's winter or summer when they're happy. If I lived in Moscow I don't think I'd care what the weather was like.
Three Sisters (1900-1), II

4 Man has been endowed with reason, with the power to create, so that he can add to what he's been given. But up to now he hasn't been a creator, only a destroyer. Forests keep disappearing, rivers dry up, wild life's become extinct, the climate's ruined and the land grows poorer and uglier every day.
Uncle Vanya, I

5 A woman can become a man's friend only in the following stages—first an acquaintance, next a mistress, and only then a friend.
II

6 *Sonya:* I'm not beautiful.
Helen: You have lovely hair.
Sonya: No, when a woman isn't beautiful, people always say, 'You have lovely eyes, you have lovely hair.'
III

EARL OF CHESTERFIELD 1694–1773

7 Unlike my subject will I frame my song,
It shall be witty and it sha'n't be long.
Epigram on 'Long' Sir Thomas Robinson. D.N.B.

8 The picture plac'd the busts between,
   Adds to the thought much strength;
Wisdom and Wit are little seen,
   But Folly's at full length.
Wit and Wisdom of Lord Chesterfield. Epigrams. On the Picture of Richard Nash...between the Busts of...Newton and...Pope...at Bath. (Attr. also to Mrs. Jane Brereton)

9 In scandal, as in robbery, the receiver is always thought as bad as the thief.
Advice to his Son. Rules for Conversation, Scandal

10 In my mind, there is nothing so illiberal and so ill-bred, as audible laughter.
Graces, Laughter. See 137:1, 159:22

11 In my opinion, parsons are very like other men, and neither the better nor the worse for wearing a black gown.
Letter to his son, 5 Apr. 1746

12 The knowledge of the world is only to be acquired in the world, and not in a closet.
4 Oct. 1746

13 An injury is much sooner forgotten than an insult.
9 Oct. 1746

14 Courts and camps are the only places to learn the world in.
2 Oct. 1747

15 There is a Spanish proverb, which says very justly, Tell me whom you live with, and I will tell you who you are.
9 Oct. 1747

16 Take the tone of the company that you are in.

17 Do as you would be done by is the surest method that I know of pleasing.
16 Oct. 1747

18 I recommend you to take care of the minutes: for hours will take care of themselves.
6 Nov. 1747

19 Advice is seldom welcome; and those who want it the most always like it the least.
29 Jan. 1748

20 Speak of the moderns without contempt, and of the ancients without idolatry.
22 Feb. 1748

21 Wear your learning, like your watch in a private pocket: and do not merely pull it out and strike it; merely to show that you have one.

22 If you happen to have an Elzevir classic in your pocket, neither show it nor mention it.

23 I am neither of a melancholy nor a cynical disposition, and am as willing and as apt to be pleased as anybody; but I am sure that, since I have had the full use of my reason, nobody has ever heard me laugh.
9 Mar. 1748

24 If Shakespeare's genius had been cultivated, those beauties, which we so justly admire in him, would have ben undisgraced by those extravagancies, and that nonsense, with which they are so frequently accompanied.
1 Apr. 1748

25 Women, then, are only children of a larger growth: they have an entertaining tattle, and sometimes wit; but for solid, reasoning good-sense, I never knew in my life one that had it, or who reasoned or acted consequentially for four and twenty hours together.
5 Sept. 1748. See 195:15

26 A man of sense only trifles with them [women], plays with them, humours and flatters them, as he does with a sprightly and forward child; but he neither consults them about, nor trusts them with, serious matters.

27 It must be owned, that the Graces do not seem to be natives of Great Britain; and I doubt, the best of us here have more of rough than polished diamond.
18 Nov. 1748

28 Idleness is only the refuge of weak minds.
20 July 1749

29 Women are much more like each other than men: they have, in truth, but two passions, vanity and love; these are their universal characteristics.
19 Dec. 1749

30 Putting moral virtues at the highest, and religion at the lowest, religion must still be allowed to be a collateral security, at least, to virtue; and every prudent man will sooner trust to two securities than to one.
8 Jan. 1750

31 Knowledge may give weight, but accomplishments give lustre, and many more people see than weigh.
8 May 1750

32 Is it possible to love such a man? No. The utmost I can do for him is to consider him as a respectable Hottentot. [Lord Lyttelton.]
28 Feb. 1751

33 It is commonly said, and more particularly by Lord

Shaftesbury, that ridicule is the best test of truth.
6 Feb. 1752

1 Every woman is infallibly to be gained by every sort
of flattery, and every man by one sort or other.
16 Mar. 1752

2 A chapter of accidents.
16 Feb. 1753

3 In matters of religion and matrimony I never give any
advice; because I will not have anybody's torments in
this world or the next laid to my charge.
Letter to A.C. Stanhope, 12 Oct. 1765

4 Religion is by no means a proper subject of
conversation in a mixed company.
Undated Letter to his Godson, No.112

5 Cunning is the dark sanctuary of incapacity.
Letters from a Celebrated Nobleman to his Heir (1783), **Letter
to his godson and heir, to be delivered after his own death**

6 I...could not help reflecting in my way upon the
singular ill-luck of this my dear country, which, as
long as ever I remember it, and as far back as I have
read, has always been governed by the only two or
three people, out of two or three millions, totally
incapable of governing, and unfit to be trusted.
Works, ed. M. Maty (1777-9), vol.II. **Miscellaneous Pieces,** xlv.
First published in *The World,* 7 Oct. 1756.

7 Tyrawley and I have been dead these two years; but
we don't choose to have it known.
Boswell's *Johnson,* 3 Apr. 1773

8 He once exclaimed to Anstis, Garter King at Arms,
'You foolish man, you do not even know your own
foolish business.'
Jesse, *Memoirs of the Court of England from 1688 to Geo. II,*
vol.ii

9 Give Dayrolles a chair.
Last words. W.H. Craig, *Life of Chesterfield*

G.K. CHESTERTON 1874–1936

10 Are they clinging to their crosses,
F.E. Smith?
Antichrist, or the Reunion of Christendom

11 Talk about the pews and steeples
And the cash that goes therewith!
But the souls of Christian peoples...
Chuck it, Smith!

12 They spoke of progress spiring round,
Of Light and Mrs Humphry Ward—
It is not true to say I frowned,
Or ran about the room and roared;
I might have simply sat and snored—
I rose politely in the club
And said, 'I feel a little bored;
Will some one take me to a pub?'
A Ballade of an Anti-Puritan

13 Prince, Prince-Elective on the modern plan,
Fulfilling such a lot of people's Wills,
You take the Chiltern Hundreds while you can—
A storm is coming on the Chiltern Hills.
A Ballade of the First Rain

14 The strangest whim has seized me...After all
I think I will not hang myself to-day.
A Ballade of Suicide

15 Before the gods that made the gods
Had seen their sunrise pass,

The White Horse of the White Horse Vale
Was cut out of the grass.
Ballad of the White Horse, bk.i

16 I tell you naught for your comfort,
Yea, naught for your desire,
Save that the sky grows darker yet
And the sea rises higher.

17 For the great Gaels of Ireland
Are the men that God made mad,
For all their wars are merry,
And all their songs are sad.
bk.ii

18 The thing on the blind side of the heart,
On the wrong side of the door,
The green plant groweth, menacing
Almighty lovers in the spring;
There is always a forgotten thing,
And love is not secure.
bk.iii

19 Because it is only Christian men
Guard even heathen things.

20 'The high tide!' King Alfred cried.
'The high tide and the turn!'
bk.vii

21 Nelson turned his blindest eye
On Naples and on liberty.
Blessed are the Peacemakers

22 When fishes flew and forests walked
And figs grew upon thorn,
Some moment when the moon was blood
Then surely I was born.

With monstrous head and sickening cry
And ears like errant wings,
The devil's walking parody
On all four-footed things.
The Donkey

23 Fools! For I also had my hour;
One far fierce hour and sweet:
There was a shout about my ears,
And palms before my feet.

24 The men that worked for England
They have their graves at home...
And they that rule in England,
In stately conclave met,
Alas, alas for England
They have no graves as yet.
Elegy in a Country Churchyard

25 They died to save their country and they only saved
the world.
The English Graves

26 But since he stood for England
And knew what England means,
Unless you give him bacon
You must not give him beans.
The Englishman

27 When Man is the Turk, and the Atheist,
Essene, Erastian Whig,
And the Thug and the Druse and the Catholic
And the crew of the Captain's gig.
The Higher Unity. See 225:16

28 White founts falling in the courts of the sun,

And the Soldan of Byzantium is smiling as they run.
Lepanto

1 The cold queen of England is looking in the glass;
The shadow of the Valois is yawning at the Mass.

2 Strong gongs groaning as the guns boom far,
Don John of Austria is going to the war.

3 Then the tuckets, then the trumpets, then the cannon, and he comes.
Don John laughing in the brave beard curled,
Spurning of his stirrups like the thrones of all the world,
Holding his head up for a flag of all the free.
Love-light of Spain—hurrah!
Death-light of Africa!
Don John of Austria
Is riding to the sea.

4 It is he that saith not 'Kismet'; it is he that knows not Fate;
It is Richard, it is Raymond, it is Godfrey in the gate!

5 The walls are hung with velvet that is black and soft as sin,
And little dwarfs creep out of it and little dwarfs creep in.

6 Cervantes on his galley sets the sword back in the sheath
(*Don John of Austria rides homeward with a wreath.*)

7 And they think we're burning witches when we're only burning weeds.
Me Heart

8 The legend of an epic hour
A child I dreamed, and dream it still,
Under the great grey water-tower
That strikes the stars on Campden Hill.
The Napoleon of Notting Hill, dedication

9 John Grubby, who was short and stout
And troubled with religious doubt,
Refused about the age of three
To sit upon the curate's knee.
The New Freethinker

10 Before the Roman came to Rye or out to Severn strode,
The rolling English drunkard made the rolling English road.
The Rolling English Road

11 The night we went to Birmingham by way of Beachy Head.

12 My friends, we will not go again or ape an ancient rage,
Or stretch the folly of our youth to be the shame of age,
But walk with clearer eyes and ears this path that wandereth,
And see undrugged in evening light the decent hall of death;
For there is good news yet to hear and fine things to be seen,
Before we go to Paradise by way of Kensal Green.

13 And a few men talked of freedom, while England talked of ale.
The Secret People

14 We only know the last sad squires ride slowly towards the sea,

And a new people takes the land: and still it is not we.

15 Smile at us, pay us, pass us; but do not quite forget.
For we are the people of England, that never have spoken yet.

16 Lord Lilac thought it rather rotten
That Shakespeare should be quite forgotten,
And therefore got on a Committee
With several chaps out of the City.
The Shakespeare Memorial

17 The souls most fed with Shakespeare's flame
Still sat unconquered in a ring,
Remembering him like anything.

18 God made the wicked Grocer
For a mystery and a sign.
That men might shun the awful shops
And go to inns to dine.
Song Against Grocers

19 He keeps a lady in a cage
Most cruelly all day,
And makes her count and calls her 'Miss'
Until she fades away.

20 He crams with cans of poisoned meat
The subjects of the King
And when they die by thousands
Why, he laughs like anything.

21 The righteous minds of innkeepers
Induce them now and then
To crack a bottle with a friend
Or treat unmoneyed men.

22 And I dream of the days when work was scrappy,
And rare in our pockets the mark of the mint,
And we were angry and poor and happy,
And proud of seeing our names in print.
A Song of Defeat

23 They haven't got no noses,
The fallen sons of Eve.
The Song of Quoodle

24 And goodness only knowses
The Noselessness of Man.

25 But I, I cannot read it
(Although I run and run)
Of them that do not have the faith,
And will not have the fun.
The Song of the Strange Ascetic

26 Where his aunts, who are not married,
Demand to be divorced.

27 Tea, although an Oriental,
Is a gentleman at least;
Cocoa is a cad and coward,
Cocoa is a vulgar beast.
The Song of Right and Wrong

28 And Noah he often said to his wife when he sat down to dine,
'I don't care where the water goes if it doesn't get into the wine.'
Wine and Water

29 All slang is metaphor, and all metaphor is poetry.
The Defendant. A Defence of Slang

30 One sees great things from the valley; only small things from the peak.
The Hammer of God

1 The artistic temperament is a disease that afflicts amateurs.
Heretics (1905), ch.17

2 The human race, to which so many of my readers belong.
The Napoleon of Notting Hill, ch.1

3 Mr Blatchford is not only an early Christian, he is the only early Christian who ought really to have been eaten by lions.
Orthodoxy (1909), 3. **Suicide of Thought**

4 Mr Shaw is (I suspect) the only man on earth who has never written any poetry.

5 Tradition means giving votes to the most obscure of all classes, our ancestors. It is the democracy of the dead. Tradition refuses to submit to the small and arrogant oligarchy of those who merely happen to be walking about. All democrats object to men being disqualified by the accident of birth; tradition objects to their being disqualified by the accident of death.
4. **The Ethics of Elfland**

6 There is nothing the matter with Americans except their ideals. The real American is all right; it is the ideal American who is all wrong.
New York Times, 1 Feb. 1931. Reprinted in *Sidelights*

7 Hardy went down to botanize in the swamp, while Meredith climbed towards the sun. Meredith became, at his best, a sort of daintily dressed Walt Whitman: Hardy became a sort of village atheist brooding and blaspheming over the village idiot.
The Victorian Age in Literature, ch.2

8 He [Tennyson] could not think up to the height of his own towering style.
ch.3

9 The Christian ideal has not been tried and found wanting. It has been found difficult; and left untried.
What's Wrong with the World (1910), i.5. **The Unfinished Temple**

10 If a thing is worth doing, it is worth doing badly.
iv.14. **Folly and Female Education**

11 Chesterton taught me this: the only way to be sure of catching a train is to miss the one before it.
P. Daninos, *Vacances à tous prix* (1958), 'Le supplice de l'heure'

WILLIAM CHILLINGWORTH 1602–1644

12 The Bible and the Bible only is the religion of Protestants.
The Religion of Protestants (1637)

13 I once knew a man out of courtesy help a lame dog over a stile, and he for requital bit his fingers.

RUFUS CHOATE 1799–1859

14 Its constitution the glittering and sounding generalities of natural right which make up the Declaration of Independence.
Letter to the Maine Whig State Central Committee, 9 Aug. 1856. See 208:14

PROFESSOR NOAM CHOMSKY 1928–

15 Colourless green ideas sleep furiously.
An example of a sentence which, though grammatically acceptable, is without meaning. *Syntactic Structures* (1957), 2.3

16 As soon as questions of will or decision or reason or choice of action arise, human science is at a loss.
Television interview, 30 Mar. 1978. See *The Listener,* 6 Apr. 1978

CHUANG TSE 4th–3rd cent. B.C.

17 I do not know whether I was then a man dreaming I was a butterfly, or whether I am now a butterfly dreaming I am a man.
H.A. Giles, *Chuang Tse,* ch.2

CHARLES CHURCHILL 1731–1764

18 Greatly his foes he dreads, but more his friends;
He hurts me most who lavishly commends.
The Apology, l.19

19 Though by whim, envy, or resentment led,
They damn those authors whom they never read.
The Candidate, l.57

20 The only difference, after all their rout,
Is, that the one is in, the other out.
The Conference, l.165

21 The danger chiefly lies in acting well;
No crime's so great as daring to excel.
An Epistle to William Hogarth, l.51

22 Candour, who, with the charity of Paul,
Still thinks the best, whene'er she thinks at all,
With the sweet milk of human kindness bless'd,
The furious ardour of my zeal repress'd.
l.55

23 By different methods different men excel;
But where is he who can do all things well?
l.573

24   Be England what she will,
With all her faults, she is my country still.
The Farewell, l.27. See 166:33

25 It can't be Nature, for it is not sense.
l.200

26 England—a happy land we know,
Where follies naturally grow.
The Ghost, bk.i, l.111

27 And adepts in the speaking trade
Keep a cough by them ready made.
bk.ii, l.545

28 Who wit with jealous eye surveys,
And sickens at another's praise.
l.663

29 Just to the windward of the law.
bk.iii, l.56

30 [Johnson:] He for subscribers baits his hook,
And takes your cash; but where's the book?
No matter where; wise fear, you know,
Forbids the robbing of a foe;
But what, to serve our private ends,
Forbids the cheating of our friends?
l.801

31 A joke's a very serious thing.
bk.iv, l.1386

32 Old-age, a second child, by Nature curs'd
With more and greater evils than the first,
Weak, sickly, full of pains; in ev'ry breath
Railing at life, and yet afraid of death.
Gotham, i, l.212

33 Keep up appearances; there lies the test;

The world will give thee credit for the rest.
Outward be fair, however foul within;
Sin if thou wilt, but then in secret sin.
Night, 1.311

1 As one with watching and with study faint,
Reel in a drunkard, and reel out a saint.
1.323

2 Who often, but without success, have pray'd
For apt Alliteration's artful aid.
The Prophecy of Famine, 1.85

3 And Nature gave thee, open to distress,
A heart to pity, and a hand to bless.
1.177

4 He sicken'd at all triumphs but his own.
The Rosciad, 1.64

5 To mischief trained, e'en from his mother's womb,
Grown old in fraud, tho' yet in manhood's bloom.
Adopting arts, by which gay villains rise,
And reach the heights, which honest men despise;
Mute at the bar, and in the senate loud,
Dull 'mongst the dullest, proudest of the proud;
A pert, prim Prater of the *northern* race,
Guilt in his heart, and famine in his face.
1.69. [Alexander Wedderburn, later Lord Loughborough.]

6 Ne'er blush'd unless, in spreading Vice's snares,
She blunder'd on some virtue unawares.
1.137

7 Genius is of no country.
1.207

8 He mouths a sentence, as curs mouth a bone.
1.322

9 Fashion—a word which knaves and fools may use,
Their knavery and folly to excuse.
1.455

10 So much they talk'd, so very little said.
1.550

11 Learn'd without sense, and venerably dull.
1.592

12 Not without Art, but yet to Nature true,
She charms the town with humour just, yet new.
1.699

13 But, spite of all the criticizing elves,
Those who would make us feel, must feel themselves.
1.961

14 The two extremes appear like man and wife,
Coupled together for the sake of strife.
1.1005

15 Where he falls short, 'tis Nature's fault alone;
Where he succeeds, the merit's all his own.
1.1025

16 The best things carried to excess are wrong.
1.1039

17 With the persuasive language of a tear.
The Times, 1.308

LORD RANDOLPH CHURCHILL 1849–1894

18 Ulster will fight; Ulster will be right.
Letter, 7 May 1886

19 The old gang. [Members of the Conservative
Government.]
House of Commons, 7 Mar. 1878

20 For the purposes of recreation he [Mr. Gladstone] has
selected the felling of trees, and we may usefully
remark that his amusements, like his politics, are
essentially destructive...The forest laments in order
that Mr Gladstone may perspire.
Speech on Financial Reform, Blackpool, 24 Jan. 1884.

21 He [Gladstone] told them that he would give them and
all other subjects of the Queen much legislation, great
prosperity, and universal peace, and he has given them
nothing but chips. Chips to the faithful allies in
Afghanistan, chips to the trusting native races of South
Africa, chips to the Egyptian fellah, chips to the
British farmer, chips to the manufacturer and the
artisan, chips to the agricultural labourer, chips to the
House of Commons itself.

22 An old man in a hurry. [Gladstone.]
To the Electors of South Paddington, June 1886

23 All great men make mistakes. Napoleon forgot
Blücher, I forgot Goschen.
Leaves from the Notebooks of Lady Dorothy Nevill, p.21

24 I never could make out what those damned dots
meant. (Decimal points.)
W.S.Churchill, *Lord Randolph Churchill,* vol.ii, p.184

WINSTON CHURCHILL 1874–1965

25 A labour contract into which men enter voluntarily for
a limited and for a brief period, under which they are
paid wages which they consider adequate, under which
they are not bought or sold and from which they can
obtain relief...on payment of £17.10s., the cost of
their passage, may not be a desirable contract, may
not be a healthy or proper contract, but it cannot in the
opinion of His Majesty's Government be classified as
slavery in the extreme acceptance of the word without
some risk of terminological inexactitude.
House of Commons, 22 Feb. 1906. See R.S. Churchill, *Winston
S. Churchill* (1967), II.167: 'This celebrated example of
polysyllabic humour was always to be misunderstood and to be
regarded as a nice substitute for "lie" which it plainly was not
intended to be.'

26 The maxim of the British people is 'Business as
usual'.
Guildhall, 9 Nov. 1914

27 I remember, when I was a child, being taken to the
celebrated Barnum's circus, which contained an
exhibition of freaks and monstrosities, but the
exhibit...which I most desired to see was the one
described as 'The Boneless Wonder'. My parents
judged that that spectacle would be too revolting and
demoralising for my youthful eyes, and I have waited
50 years to see the boneless wonder sitting on the
Treasury Bench.
House of Commons, 28 Jan. 1931

28 I cannot forecast to you the action of Russia. It is a
riddle wrapped in a mystery inside an enigma.
Broadcast talk, 1 Oct. 1939

29 I would say to the House, as I said to those who have
joined this Government, 'I have nothing to offer but
blood, toil, tears and sweat'.
House of Commons, 13 May 1940

30 Victory at all costs, victory in spite of all terror,
victory however long and hard the road may be; for
without victory there is no survival.

31 We shall go on to the end, we shall fight in France, we
shall fight on the seas and oceans, we shall fight with

growing confidence and growing strength in the air, we shall defend our island, whatever the cost may be, we shall fight on the beaches, we shall fight on the landing grounds, we shall fight in the fields and in the streets, we shall fight in the hills; we shall never surrender.
4 June 1940

1 Let us therefore brace ourselves to our duties and so bear ourselves that if the British Empire and its Commonwealth last for a thousand years men will still say, 'This was their finest hour'.
18 June 1940

2 Never in the field of human conflict was so much owed by so many to so few.
20 Aug. 1940

3 The British Empire and the United States will have to be somewhat mixed up together in some of their affairs for mutual and general advantage. For my own part, looking out for the future, I do not view the process with any misgivings. I could not stop it if I wished; no one can stop it. Like the Mississippi, it just keeps rolling along. Let it roll. Let it roll on full flood, inexorable, irresistible, benignant, to broader lands and better days.

4 We are waiting for the long-promised invasion. So are the fishes.
Radio Broadcast to the French people, 21 Oct. 1940

5 I do not resent criticism, even when, for the sake of emphasis, it parts for the time with reality.
House of Commons, 22 Jan. 1941

6 Give us the tools, and we will finish the job.
Radio Broadcast, 9 Feb. 1941. (Addressing President Roosevelt.)

7 This whipped jackal [Mussolini], who, to save his own skin, has made of Italy a vassal state of Hitler's Empire, is frisking up by the side of the German tiger with yelps not only of appetite—that could be understood—but even of triumph.
House of Commons, Apr. 1941

8 Do not let us speak of darker days; let us rather speak of sterner days. These are not dark days: these are great days—the greatest days our country has ever lived; and we must all thank God that we have been allowed, each of us according to our stations, to play a part in making these days memorable in the history of our race.
Harrow School, 29 Oct. 1941

9 What kind of people do they [the Japanese] think we are?
To U.S. Congress, 24 Dec. 1941

10 When I warned them [the French Government] that Britain would fight on alone whatever they did, their Generals told their Prime Minister and his divided Cabinet: 'In three weeks England will have her neck wrung like a chicken.'
Some chicken! Some neck!
To the Canadian Parliament, 30 Dec. 1941

11 This is not the end. It is not even the beginning of the end. But it is, perhaps, the end of the beginning.
Mansion House, 10 Nov. 1942. (Of the Battle of Egypt.)

12 I have not become the King's First Minister in order to preside over the liquidation of the British Empire.

13 The soft under-belly of the Axis.
Report on the War Situation, House of Commons, 11 Nov. 1942

14 Not a seat but a springboard. (North Africa.)
Radio Broadcast, 29 Nov. 1942

15 There is no finer investment for any community than putting milk into babies.
21 Mar. 1943

16 You may take the most gallant sailor, the most intrepid airman, or the most audacious soldier, put them at a table together—what do you get? *The sum of their fears.*
On the Chiefs of Staffs system, 16 Nov. 1943. H. Macmillan, *The Blast of War*, ch.16

17 There are few virtues that the Poles do not possess—and there are few mistakes they have ever avoided.
House of Commons, 16 Aug. 1945

18 An iron curtain has descended across the Continent.
Address at Westminster College, Fulton, U.S.A., 5 Mar. 1946. The expression 'iron curtain' had been previously applied by others to the Soviet Union or its sphere of influence, e.g., Ethel Snowden, *Through Bolshevik Russia* (1920); Dr. Goebbels, *Das Reich* (25 Feb. 1945); and by Churchill himself in a cable to President Truman (4 June 1945).

19 Many forms of government have been tried, and will be tried in this world of sin and woe. No one pretends that democracy is perfect or all-wise. Indeed, it has been said that democracy is the worst form of Government except all those other forms that have been tried from time to time.
House of Commons, 11 Nov. 1947

20 To jaw-jaw is better than to war-war.
Washington, 26 June 1954

21 It was the nation and the race dwelling all round the globe that had the lion's heart. I had the luck to be called upon to give the roar.
Speech at Palace of Westminster on his 80th birthday, 30 Nov. 1954

22 Headmasters have powers at their disposal with which Prime Ministers have never yet been invested.
My Early Life (1930), ch.2

23 By being so long in the lowest form [at Harrow] I gained an immense advantage over the cleverer boys...I got into my bones the essential structure of the normal British sentence—which is a noble thing. Naturally I am biased in favour of boys learning English; and then I would let the clever ones learn Latin as an honour, and Greek as a treat.

24 It is a good thing for an uneducated man to read books of quotations.
ch.9

25 In war, resolution; in defeat, defiance; in victory, magnanimity; in peace, goodwill.
Epigram after the Great War, 1914–18. Sir Edward Marsh, *A Number of People* (1939), p.152. Later used as the 'Moral of the Work' in each volume of *The Second World War*.

26 On the night of the tenth of May [1940], at the outset of this mighty battle, I acquired the chief power in the State, which henceforth I wielded in ever-growing measure for five years and three months of world war, at the end of which time, all our enemies having surrendered unconditionally or being about to do so, I was immediately dismissed by the British electorate from all further conduct of their affairs.
vol.i, *The Gathering Storm* (1948), p.526

27 The loyalties which centre upon number one are enormous. If he trips he must be sustained. If he

makes mistakes they must be covered. If he sleeps he must not be wantonly disturbed. If he is no good he must be pole-axed.
vol.ii, *Their Finest Hour* (1949), p.15

1 No one can guarantee success in war, but only deserve it.
p.484

2 When you have to kill a man it costs nothing to be polite.
(On the ceremonial form of the declaration of war against Japan, 8 Dec. 1941.) vol.iii, *The Grand Alliance* (1950), p.543

3 Dictators ride to and fro upon tigers which they dare not dismount. And the tigers are getting hungry.
While England Slept (1936)

4 I have watched this famous island descending incontinently, fecklessly, the stairway which leads to a dark gulf. It is a fine broad stairway at the beginning, but after a bit the carpet ends. A little farther on there are only flagstones, and a little farther on still these break beneath your feet.

5 In defeat, unbeatable; in victory, unbearable.
(Of Viscount Montgomery.) Edward Marsh, *Ambrosia and Small Beer*, ch.5

6 This is the sort of English up with which I will not put.
Attr. comment against clumsy avoidance of a preposition at the end of a sentence. E. Gowers, *Plain Words*, ch.9, 'Troubles with Prepositions', i

7 Don't talk to me about naval tradition. It's nothing but rum, sodomy and the lash.
Sir Peter Gretton, *Former Naval Person*, ch.1. Sometimes quoted as 'Rum, buggery and the lash'; compare 'Rum, bum, and bacca' and 'Ashore it's wine women and song, aboard it's rum, bum and concertina', naval catch-phrases dating from the nineteenth century.

COLLEY CIBBER 1671–1757

8 Whilst thus I sing, I am a King,
Altho' a poor blind boy.
The Blind Boy

9 Oh! how many torments lie in the small circle of a wedding-ring!
The Double Gallant, I.ii

10 One had as good be out of the world, as out of the fashion.
Love's Last Shift, Act II

11 What! now your fire's gone, you would knock me down with the butt-end, would you?
The Refusal, Act I

12 Off with his head—so much for Buckingham.
Richard III, (adapted from Shakespeare) IV.iii

13 Conscience avaunt, *Richard's* himself again:
Hark! the shrill trumpet sounds, to horse, away,
My soul's in arms, and eager for the fray.
V.iii

14 Perish the thought!
v

15 Stolen sweets are best.
The Rival Fools, Act I

CICERO 106–43 B.C.

16 *Dicit enim tamquam in Platonis πολιτείᾳ, non tamquam in Romuli faece sententiam.*

For he delivers his opinions as though he were living in Plato's Republic rather than among the dregs of Romulus. (Of M. Porcius Cato, the Younger.)
Ad Atticum, II.i.8

17 There is nothing so absurd but some philosopher has said it.
De Divinatione, ii.58

18 *Vulgo enim dicitur: Iucundi acti labores.*
For it is commonly said: completed labours are pleasant.
De Finibus, ii.105

19 *Salus populi suprema est lex.*
The good of the people is the chief law.
De Legibus, III.iii.8

20 *'Ipse dixit.' 'Ipse' autem erat Pythagoras.*
'He himself said it', and this 'himself' was Pythagoras.
De Natura Deorum, I.v.10

21 *Summum bonum.*
The highest good.
De Officiis, I.ii.5

22 *Cedant arma togae, concedant laurea laudi.*
Let war yield to peace, laurels to paeans.
xxii.82

23 *Numquam se minus otiosum esse quam cum otiosus, nec minus solum quam cum solus esset.*
Never less idle than when wholly idle, nor less alone than when wholly alone.
III.i.1

24 *Mens cuiusque is est quisque.*
The spirit is the true self.
De Republica, vi.26

25 *Quousque tandem abutere, Catilina, patientia nostra?*
How long will you abuse our patience, Catiline?
In Catilinam, I.i.1

26 *O tempora, O mores!*
Oh, the times! Oh, the manners!

27 *Abiit, excessit, evasit, erupit.*
He departed, he withdrew, he strode off, he broke forth.
II.i.1

28 *Civis Romanus sum.*
I am a Roman citizen.
In Verrem, V.lvii.147

29 *Quod di omen avertant.*
May the gods avert this omen.
Philippic, III.xiv.35

30 *Nervos belli, pecuniam infinitam.*
The sinews of war, unlimited money.
V.ii.5

31 *Silent enim leges inter arma.*
Laws are inoperative in war.
Pro Milone, IV.xi

32 *Cui bono?*
To whose profit?
XII.xxxii (Quoting L. Cassius Longinus)

33 *Id quod est praestantissimum maximeque optabile omnibus sanis et bonis et beatis, cum dignitate otium.*
The thing which is the most outstanding and chiefly to be desired by all healthy and good and well-off persons, is leisure with honour.
Pro Sestio, xlv.98

1 I would rather be wrong, by God, with Plato than be correct with those men. (The Pythagoreans.)
Tusculanae disputationes, I.xvii.39

2 *O fortunatam natam me consule Romam!*
O happy Rome, born when I was consul!
Juvenal, x.122

JOHN CLARE 1793–1864

3 When badgers fight then everyone's a foe.
Badger

4 He could not die when the trees were green,
    For he loved the time too well.
The Dying Child

5 My life hath been one chain of contradictions,
Madhouses, prisons, whore-shops.
The Exile

6 They took me from my wife, and to save trouble
I wed again, and made the error double.

7 Here let the Muse oblivion's curtain draw,
    And let man think—for God hath often saw
Things here too dirty for the light of day;
    For in a madhouse there exists no law.
Now stagnant grows my too refinèd clay;
I envy birds their wings to fly away.

8 Pale death, the grand physician, cures all pain;
The dead rest well who lived for joys in vain.

9 Hopeless hope hopes on and meets no end,
Wastes without springs and homes without a friend.

10 When words refuse before the crowd
    My Mary's name to give,
The muse in silence sings aloud:
    And there my love will live.
First Love

11 A quiet, pilfering, unprotected race.
Gypsies

12 I am—yet what I am, none cares or knows;
    My friends forsake me like a memory lost:
I am the self-consumer of my woes.
I Am

13 Untroubling and untroubled where I lie
The grass below, above, the vaulted sky.

14 When fishes leap in silver stream...
And forest bees are humming near,
And cowslips in boys' hats appear...
We then may say that May is come.
May. See N. Ault, *A Treasury of Unfamiliar Lyrics* (1938),
p.473

15 The present is the funeral of the past,
And man the living sepulchre of life.
The Past

16 Summers pleasures they are gone like to visions every
    one
And the cloudy days of autumn and of winter cometh
    on
I tried to call them back but unbidden they are gone
Far away from heart and eye and for ever far away.
Remembrances

17 Dear Sir,—I am in a Madhouse and quite forget your
name or who you are.
Letter, 1860

EARL OF CLARENDON 1609–1674

18 Without question, when he [Hampden] first drew the
sword, he threw away the scabbard.
History of the Rebellion, ed. Macray (1888), III.vii.84

19 He [Hampden] had a head to contrive, a tongue to
persuade, and a hand to execute any mischief.

20 He [Falkland]...would, with a shrill and sad accent,
ingeminate the word *Peace, Peace.*
233

21 So enamoured on peace that he would have been glad
the King should have bought it at any price.

22 He [Cromwell] will be looked upon by posterity as a
brave bad man.
xv, last line

CLARIBEL (MRS. C.A. BARNARD) 1840–1869

23 I cannot sing the old songs
I sang long years ago,
For heart and voice would fail me,
And foolish tears would flow.
Fireside Thoughts

JOHN CLARKE fl. 1639

24 He that would thrive
Must rise at five;
He that hath thriven
May lie till seven.
Paraemiologia Anglo-Latina (1639)

25 Home is home, though it be never so homely.

APPIUS CLAUDIUS CAECUS fl. 312–279 B.C.

26 *Faber est suae quisque fortunae.*
Each man is the smith of his own fortune.
'Sallust', *Epistulae ad Caesarem senem*, I.i.2

KARL VON CLAUSEWITZ 1780–1831

27 *Der Krieg ist nichts als eine Fortsetzung der
politschen Verkehrs mit Einmischung anderer Mittel.*
War is nothing but the continuation of politics with the
admixture of other means.
Vom Kriege, (memorial ed. 1952) p.888, commonly rendered in
the form 'War is the continuation of politics by other means'.

HENRY CLAY 1777–1852

28 I had rather be right than be President.
To Senator Preston of South Carolina, 1839

29 The gentleman [Josiah Quincy] can not have forgotten
his own sentiments, uttered even on the floor of this
House, 'peaceably if we can, forcibly if we must'.
Speech, 8 Jan. 1813. See 403:24

GEORGES CLEMENCEAU 1841–1929

30 *Quatorze? Le bon Dieu n'a que dix.*
Fourteen? The good Lord has only ten.
Attr. comment on hearing of Woodrow Wilson's Fourteen Points
(1918)

31 War is much too serious a thing to be left to the
military.
Attr. Also attr. Talleyrand and Briand. See, e.g., John Bailey,
Letters and Diaries (1935), p.176

POPE CLEMENT XIII 1693–1769

1 *Sint ut sunt aut non sint.*
Let them be as they are or not be at all.
Reply to request for changes in the constitutions of the Society of Jesus, 27 Jan. 1762. See J.A.M. Crétineau-Joly, *Clément XIV et les Jésuites* (1847), p.370n.

GROVER CLEVELAND 1837–1908

2 I have considered the pension list of the republic a roll of honour.
Veto of Dependent Pension Bill, 5 July 1888

JOHN CLEVELAND 1613–1658

3 Here lies wise and valiant dust,
Huddled up, 'twixt fit and just:
Strafford, who was hurried hence
'Twixt treason and convenience.
He spent his time here in a mist,
A *Papist*, yet a *Calvinist*.
His Prince's nearest joy and grief;
He had, yet wanted, all relief:
The Prop and Ruin of the State,
The people's violent love and hate:
One in extremes lov'd and abhor'd.
Riddles lie here, or in a word,
Here lies blood; and let it lie
Speechless still, and never cry.
Epitaph on the Earl of Strafford

4 Had Cain been Scot, God would have changed his doom,
Nor forced him wander, but confined him home.
The Rebel Scot

LORD CLIVE 1725–1774

5 By God, Mr Chairman, at this moment I stand astonished at my own moderation!
Reply during Parliamentary cross-examination, 1773

6 I feel that I am reserved for some end or other.
Words when his pistol failed to go off twice, in his attempt to commit suicide. G.R. Gleig, *Life*, ch.1

ARTHUR HUGH CLOUGH 1819–1861

7 Rome, believe me, my friend, is like its own Monte Testaceo,
Merely a marvellous mass of broken and castaway wine-pots.
Amours de Voyage, c.I.ii

8 The horrible pleasure of pleasing inferior people.
xi

9 Am I prepared to lay down my life for the British female?
Really, who knows?...
Ah, for a child in the street I could strike; for the full-blown lady—
Somehow, Eustace, alas! I have not felt the vocation.
c.II.iv

10 But for his funeral train which the bridegroom sees in the distance,
Would he so joyfully, think you, fall in with the marriage-procession?
c.III.vi

11 Allah is great, no doubt, and Juxtaposition his prophet.

12 Mild monastic faces in quiet collegiate cloisters.
ix

13 Whither depart the souls of the brave that die in the battle,
Die in the lost, lost fight, for the cause that perishes with them?
c.V.vi

14 The grave man, nicknamed Adam.
The Bothie of Tober-na-Vuolich, i

15 Petticoats up to the knees, or even, it might be, above them,
Matching their lily-white legs with the clothes that they trod in the wash-tub!
ii

16 Good, too, Logic, of course; in itself, but not in fine weather.

17 Sesquipedalian blackguard.

18 Grace is given of God, but knowledge is bought in the market.
iv

19 They are married, and gone to New Zealand.
ix

20   Delicious. Ah!
What else is like the gondola?
Dipsychus, sc.v

21 They may talk as they please about what they call pelf,
And how one ought never to think of one's self,
And how pleasures of thought surpass eating and drinking—
My pleasure of thought is the pleasure of thinking
How pleasant it is to have money, heigh ho!
How pleasant it is to have money.

22 'There is no God,' the wicked saith,
'And truly it's a blessing,
For what he might have done with us
It's better only guessing.'
vi

23 But country folks who live beneath
The shadow of the steeple;
The parson and the parson's wife,
And mostly married people;

Youths green and happy in first love,
So thankful for illusion;
And men caught out in what the world
Calls guilt, in first confusion;

And almost every one when age,
Disease, or sorrows strike him,
Inclines to think there is a God,
Or something very like Him.

24 Home, Rose, and home, Provence and La Palie.
Les Vaches

25 Thou shalt have one God only; who
Would be at the expense of two?
The Latest Decalogue

26 Thou shalt not kill; but need'st not strive
Officiously to keep alive.

27 Do not adultery commit;
Advantage rarely comes of it.

28 Thou shalt not steal; an empty feat,

When it's so lucrative to cheat.

1 Thou shalt not covet; but tradition
Approves all forms of competition.

2 What voice did on my spirit fall,
Peschiera, when thy bridge I crost?
''Tis better to have fought and lost,
Than never to have fought at all.'
Peschiera. See 536:16

3 As ships, becalmed at eve, that lay
With canvas drooping, side by side,
Two towers of sail at dawn of day
Are scarce long leagues apart descried.
Qua Cursum Ventus

4 Say not the struggle naught availeth,
The labour and the wounds are vain,
The enemy faints not, nor faileth,
And as things have been, things remain.

If hopes were dupes, fears may be liars;
It may be, in yon smoke concealed,
Your comrades chase e'en now the fliers,
And, but for you, possess the field.

For while the tired waves, vainly breaking,
Seem here no painful inch to gain,
Far back through creeks and inlets making
Comes silent, flooding in, the main.

And not by eastern windows only,
When daylight comes, comes in the light,
In front the sun climbs slow, how slowly,
But westward, look, the land is bright.
Say Not the Struggle Naught Availeth

5 That out of sight is out of mind
Is true of most we leave behind.
Songs in Absence, That Out of Sight

6 What shall we do without you? Think where we are.
Carlyle has led us all out into the desert, and he has
left us there.
Parting words to Emerson, 15 July 1848. See E.E. Hale, *James
Russell Lowell and his Friends* (1889), ch.19

WILLIAM COBBETT 1762–1835

7 The slavery of the tea and coffee and other slop-kettle.
Advice to Young Men, letter i, 31

8 Nouns of number, or multitude, such as *Mob*,
Parliament, Rabble, House of Commons, Regiment,
Court of King's Bench, Den of Thieves, and the like.
English Grammar, letter xvii, **Syntax as Relating to Pronouns**

9 From a very early age, I had imbibed the opinion, that
it was every man's duty to do all that lay in his power
to leave his country as good as he had found it.
Political Register, 22 Dec. 1832

10 But what is to be the fate of the great wen [London] of
all? The monster, called…'the metropolis of the
empire'?
Rural Rides

RICHARD COBDEN 1804–1865

11 I believe it has been said that one copy of *The Times*
contains more useful information than the whole of the
historical works of Thucydides.
Speech, Manchester, 27 Dec. 1850

JEAN COCTEAU 1889–1963

12 *Vivre est une chute horizontale.*
Life is falling sideways.
Opium, 1930 ed., p.37

13 *Victor Hugo…un fou qui se croyait Victor Hugo.*
Victor Hugo…A madman who thought he was Victor
Hugo.
See **Opium,** 1930 ed., p.77

SIR ASTON COKAYNE 1608–1684

14 Sydney, whom we yet admire
Lighting our little torches at his fire.
Funeral Elegy on Mr. Michael Drayton

DESMOND COKE 1879–1931

15 His blade struck the water a full second before any
other…until…as the boats began to near the
winning-post, his own was dipping into the water *twice*
as often as any other.
Sandford of Merton (1903), ch.xii. Often quoted as 'All rowed
fast but none so fast as stroke', and attr. to Ouida.

SIR EDWARD COKE 1552–1634

16 Magna Charta is such a fellow, that he will have no
sovereign.
On the Lords' Amendment to the Petition of Right, 17 May 1628.
Rushworth, *Hist. Coll.,* 1659, i

17 How long soever it hath continued, if it be against
reason, it is of no force in law.
Institutes: Commentary upon Littleton. First Institute, 62a

18 Reason is the life of the law, nay the common law
itself is nothing else but reason…The law, which is the
perfection of reason.
97b

19 The gladsome light of Jurisprudence.
epilogus

20 Syllables govern the world.

21 For a man's house is his castle, *et domus sua cuique
est tutissimum refugium.*
Third Institute, cap.73

22 Six hours in sleep, in law's grave study six,
Four spend in prayer, the rest on Nature fix.
Pandects, lib.II, tit.iv, **De in Jus vocando.** See 283:13

23 The house of every one is to him as his castle and
fortress.
Semayne's Case, 5 Rep.91b

24 They [corporations] cannot commit treason, nor be
outlawed, nor excommunicate, for they have no souls.
Sutton's Hospital Case, 10 Rep.32b

HARTLEY COLERIDGE 1796–1849

25 But what is Freedom? Rightly understood,
A universal licence to be good.
Liberty

26 She is not fair to outward view
As many maidens be;
Her loveliness I never knew
Until she smiled on me.
Oh! then I saw her eye was bright,
A well of love, a spring of light.
Song. She is not Fair

1 Her very frowns are fairer far,
Than smiles of other maidens are.

LORD COLERIDGE 1820–1894

2 I speak not of this college or of that, but of the
University as a whole; and, gentlemen, what a *whole*
Oxford is!
G.W.E. Russell, *Collections and Recollections*, ch.29

MARY COLERIDGE 1861–1907

3 Egypt's might is tumbled down
    Down a-down the deeps of thought;
Greece is fallen and Troy town,
Glorious Rome hath lost her crown,
    Venice' pride is nought.

But the dreams their children dreamed
    Fleeting, unsubstantial, vain.
Shadowy as the shadows seemed
Airy nothing, as they deemed,
    These remain.
Poems (1908), cxxi

4 Some hang above the tombs,
Some weep in empty rooms,
I, when the iris blooms,
    Remember.
cxlvi

SAMUEL TAYLOR COLERIDGE 1772–1834

5 It is an ancient Mariner,
And he stoppeth one of three.
'By thy long grey beard and glittering eye,
Now wherefore stopp'st thou me?'
The Ancient Mariner, pt.i

6 He holds him with his skinny hand,
'There was a ship,' quoth he.
'Hold off! unhand me, grey-beard loon!'
Eftsoons his hand dropt he.

He holds him with his glittering eye…
He cannot choose but hear;
And thus spake on that ancient man,
The bright-eyed Mariner.

7 The Sun came up upon the left.
Out of the sea came he!
And he shone bright, and on the right
Went down into the sea.

8 The Wedding-Guest here beat his breast,
For he heard the loud bassoon.

9 And ice, mast-high, came floating by,
As green as emerald.

10 'God save thee, ancient Mariner!
From the fiends that plague thee thus!—
Why look'st thou so?'—With my cross-bow
I shot the Albatross.

11 Nor dim nor red, like God's own head,
The glorious Sun uprist.
pt.ii

12 We were the first that ever burst
Into that silent sea.

13 As idle as a painted ship
Upon a painted ocean.

14 Water, water, every where,
And all the boards did shrink;
Water, water, every where.
Nor any drop to drink.

The very deep did rot: O Christ!
That ever this should be!
Yea, slimy things did crawl with legs
Upon the slimy sea.

15 *Her* lips were red, *her* looks were free,
Her locks were yellow as gold:
Her skin was white as leprosy,
The Night-mare LIFE-IN-DEATH was she,
Who thicks man's blood with cold.

16 The Sun's rim dips; the stars rush out:
At one stride comes the dark.

17 We listened and looked sideways up!

18 The hornèd Moon, with one bright star
Within the nether tip.

19 'I fear thee, ancient Mariner!
I fear thy skinny hand!
And thou art long, and lank, and brown,
As is the ribbed sea-sand.'
pt.iv

20 Alone, alone, all, all alone,
Alone on a wide wide sea!
And never a saint took pity on
My soul in agony.

21 And a thousand thousand slimy things
Lived on; and so did I.

22 A spring of love gushed from my heart,
And I blessed them unaware.

23 Oh Sleep! it is a gentle thing,
Beloved from pole to pole,
To Mary Queen the praise be given!
She sent the gentle sleep from Heaven,
That slid into my soul.
pt.v

24 Sure I had drunken in my dreams,
And still my body drank.

25 We were a ghastly crew.

26 It ceased; yet still the sails made on
A pleasant noise till noon,
A noise like of a hidden brook
In the leafy month of June,
That to the sleeping woods all night
Singeth a quiet tune.

27 Like one, that on a lonesome road
Doth walk in fear and dread,
And having once turned round walks on,
And turns no more his head;
Because he knows, a frightful fiend
Doth close behind him tread.
pt.vi

28 No voice; but oh! the silence sank
Like music on my heart.

29 I pass, like night, from land to land;
I have strange power of speech.
pt.vii

30 He prayeth well, who loveth well
Both man and bird and beast.

He prayeth best, who loveth best
All things both great and small;
For the dear God who loveth us,
He made and loveth all.

1 He went like one that hath been stunned,
And is of sense forlorn:
A sadder and a wiser man,
He rose the morrow morn.

2 And the Spring comes slowly up this way.
Christabel, pt.i

3 A sight to dream of, not to tell!

4 Alas! they had been friends in youth;
But whispering tongues can poison truth;
And constancy lives in realms above;
And life is thorny; and youth is vain;
And to be wroth with one we love
Doth work like madness in the brain.
pt.ii

5 In Köhln, a town of monks and bones,
And pavements fang'd with murderous stones
And rags, and hags, and hideous wenches;
I counted two and seventy stenches,
All well defined, and several stinks!
Ye Nymphs that reign o'er sewers and sinks,
The river Rhine, it is well known,
Doth wash your city of Cologne;
But tell me, Nymphs, what power divine
Shall henceforth wash the river Rhine?
Cologne

6 Well! If the Bard was weatherwise, who made
The grand old ballad of Sir Patrick Spence.
Dejection: an Ode

7 I see them all so excellently fair,
I see, not feel, how beautiful they are!

8 I may not hope from outward forms to win
The passion and the life, whose fountains are within.

9 O Lady! we receive but what we give,
And in our life alone does Nature live.

10 From his brimstone bed at break of day
A walking the Devil is gone,
To visit his snug little farm the earth,
And see how his stock goes on.
The Devil's Thoughts. (Written jointly with Southey.)

11 His jacket was red and his breeches were blue,
And there was a hole where the tail came through.

12 He saw a Lawyer killing a viper
On a dunghill hard by his own stable;
And the Devil smiled, for it put him in mind
Of Cain and his brother, Abel.

13 He saw a cottage with a double coach-house,
A cottage of gentility;
And the Devil did grin, for his darling sin
Is pride that apes humility.

14 As he went through Cold-Bath Fields he saw
A solitary cell;
And the Devil was pleased, for it gave him a hint
For improving his prisons in Hell.

15 What is an Epigram? a dwarfish whole,
Its body brevity, and wit its soul.
Epigram

16 Swans sing before they die—'twere no bad thing,

Did certain persons die before they sing.
Epigram on a Volunteer Singer

17 That he who many a year with toil of breath
Found death in life, may here find life in death.
Epitaph for Himself

18 Ere sin could blight or sorrow fade,
Death came with friendly care:
The opening bud to Heaven convey'd
And bade it blossom *there*.
Epitaph on an Infant

19 Forth from his dark and lonely hiding-place
(Portentous sight!) the owlet Atheism,
Sailing on obscene wings athwart the noon,
Drops his blue-fringèd lids, and holds them close,
And hooting at the glorious sun in Heaven,
Cries out, 'Where is it?'
Fears in Solitude

20 With what deep worship I have still adored
The spirit of divinest Liberty.
France

21 The frost performs its secret ministry,
Unhelped by any wind.
Frost at Midnight

22 Only that film, which fluttered on the grate,
Still flutters there, the sole unquiet thing.

23 Therefore all seasons shall be sweet to thee,
Whether the summer clothe the general earth
With greenness, or the redbreast sit and sing
Betwixt the tufts of snow on the bare branch
Of mossy apple-tree, while the nigh thatch
Smokes in the sun-thaw; whether the eave-drops fall
Heard only in the trances of the blast,
Or if the secret ministry of frost
Shall hang them up in silent icicles,
Quietly shining to the quiet moon.

24 And visited all night by troops of stars.
Hymn before Sun rise, in the Vale of Chamouni

25 On awaking he...instantly and eagerly wrote down the
lines that are here preserved. At this moment he was
unfortunately called out by a person on business from
Porlock.
Kubla Khan, Preliminary note

26 In Xanadu did Kubla Khan
A stately pleasure-dome decree:
Where Alph, the sacred river, ran
Through caverns measureless to man
Down to a sunless sea.
So twice five miles of fertile ground
With walls and towers were girdled round.

27 But oh! that deep romantic chasm which slanted
Down the green hill athwart a cedarn cover!
A savage place! as holy and enchanted
As e'er beneath a waning moon was haunted
By woman wailing for her demon-lover!
And from this chasm, with ceaseless turmoil seething,
As if this earth in fast thick pants were breathing,
A mighty fountain momently was forced.

28 Five miles meandering with a mazy motion
Through wood and dale the sacred river ran.

29 And 'mid this tumult Kubla heard from far
Ancestral voices prophesying war!

30 A damsel with a dulcimer

In a vision once I saw:
It was an Abyssinian maid,
And on her dulcimer she played,
Singing of Mount Abora.

1 Weave a circle round him thrice,
And close your eyes with holy dread,
For he on honey-dew hath fed,
And drunk the milk of Paradise.

2 All thoughts, all passions, all delights,
    Whatever stirs this mortal frame,
All are but ministers of Love,
    And feed his sacred flame.
Love

3 Trochee trips from long to short.
Metrical Feet

4 Iambics march from short to long;—
With a leap and a bound the swift Anapaests throng.

5 Choose thou whatever suits the line;
Call me Sappho, call me Chloris,
Call me Lalage or Doris,
    Only, only call me thine.
Names (from Lessing's *Die Namen*.)

6 With Donne, whose muse on dromedary trots,
Wreathe iron pokers into true-love knots.
On Donne's Poetry

7 In the hexameter rises the fountain's silvery column;
    In the pentameter aye falling in melody back.
Ovidian Elegiac Metre

8 But still the heart doth need a language, still
Doth the old instinct bring back the old names.
Piccolomini, II.iv (from Schiller.)

9 So for the mother's sake the child was dear,
And dearer was the mother for the child.
**Sonnet to a Friend Who Asked How I Felt When the Nurse
First Presented My Infant to Me**

10 Well, they are gone, and here must I remain,
This lime-tree bower my prison!
This Lime-Tree Bower my Prison, l.1

11   When the last rook
Beat its straight path along the dusky air.
1.68

12   A charm
For thee, my gentle-hearted Charles, to whom
No sound is dissonant which tells of Life.
1.74

13 We ne'er can be
Made happy by compulsion.
The Three Graves, pt.IV.xii

14 All Nature seems at work. Slugs leave their lair—
    The bees are stirring—birds are on the wing—
And Winter slumbering in the open air,
    Wears on his smiling face a dream of Spring!
And I the while, the sole unbusy thing,
Nor honey make, nor pair, nor build, nor sing.
Work Without Hope

15 Work without hope draws nectar in a sieve,
And hope without an object cannot live.

16 Poor little Foal of an oppressed race!
I love the languid patience of thy face.
To a Young Ass

17 Like some poor nigh-related guest,
That may not rudely be dismist;

Yet hath outstay'd his welcome while,
And tells the jest without the smile.
Youth and Age

18 He who begins by loving Christianity better than Truth
will proceed by loving his own sect or church better
than Christianity, and end by loving himself better than
all.
Aids to Reflection: Moral and Religious Aphorisms, XXV

19 The most happy marriage I can picture or imagine to
myself would be the union of a deaf man to a blind
woman.
Allsop, *Recollections* (1836)

20 If men could learn from history, what lessons it might
teach us! But passion and party blind our eyes, and the
light which experience gives is a lantern on the stern,
which shines only on the waves behind us!
(18 Dec. 1831)

21 Until you understand a writer's ignorance, presume
yourself ignorant of his understanding.
Biographia Literaria, ch.12

22 That willing suspension of disbelief for the moment,
which constitutes poetic faith.
ch.14

23 Our *myriad-minded* Shakespeare. *Note*
'Ανὴρ μυριόνους, a phrase which I have borrowed
from a Greek monk, who applies it to a Patriarch of
Constantinople.
ch.15

24 No man was ever yet a great poet, without being at the
same time a profound philosopher.

25 The dwarf sees farther than the giant, when he has the
giant's shoulder to mount on.
The Friend, i, Essay 8. See 41:25

26 Reviewers are usually people who would have been
poets, historians, biographers, &c., if they could; they
have tried their talents at one or at the other, and have
failed; therefore they turn critics.
Lectures on Shakespeare and Milton, i

27 Summer has set in with its usual severity.
Quoted in Lamb's letter to V. Novello, 9 May 1826

28 The last speech, [Iago's soliloquoy] the
motive-hunting of motiveless malignity—how awful!
Notes on the Tragedies of Shakespeare, Othello

29 From whatever place I write you will expect that part
of my 'Travels' will consist of excursions in my own
mind.
Satyrane's Letters, ii. [*The Friend,* 7 Dec. 1809 No. 16.
Biographia Literaria]

30 You abuse snuff! Perhaps it is the final cause of the
human nose.
Table Talk, 4 Jan. 1823

31 To see him [Kean] act, is like reading Shakespeare by
flashes of lightning.
27 Apr. 1823

32 I wish our clever young poets would remember my
homely definitions of prose and poetry; that is prose ;
words in their best order;—poetry ; the *best* words in
the best order.
12 July 1827

33 The man's desire is for the woman; but the woman's
desire is rarely other than for the desire of the man.
23 July 1827

34 My mind is in a state of philosophical doubt as to

animal magnetism.
30 Apr. 1830

1 Poetry is certainly something more than good sense,
but it must be good sense at all events; just as a palace
is more than a house, but it must be a house, at least.
9 May 1830

2 Swift was *anima Rabelaisii habitans in sicco*—the
soul of Rabelais dwelling in a dry place.
15 June 1830

3 In politics, what begins in fear usually ends in folly.
5 Oct. 1830

4 The misfortune is, that he [Tennyson] has begun to
write verses without very well understanding what
metre is.
24 Apr. 1833

5 I am glad you came in to punctuate my discourse,
which I fear has gone on for an hour without any stop
at all.
29 June 1833

6 When I was a boy, I was fondest of Aeschylus; in
youth and middle-age I preferred Euripides; now in my
declining years I prefer Sophocles. I can now at length
see that Sophocles is the most perfect. Yet he never
rises to the sublime simplicity of Aeschylus—a
simplicity of design, I mean—nor diffuses himself in
the passionate outpourings of Euripides.
1 July 1833

7 That passage is what I call the sublime dashed to
pieces by cutting too close with the fiery four-in-hand
round the corner of nonsense.
20 Jan. 1834

8 I believe Shakespeare was not a whit more intelligible
in his own day than he is now to an educated man,
except for a few local allusions of no consequence. He
is of no age—nor of any religion, or party or
profession. The body and substance of his works came
out of the unfathomable depths of his own oceanic
mind: his observation and reading, which was
considerable, supplied him with the drapery of his
figures.
15 Mar. 1834

9 Poor Lamb, if he wants any *knowledge,* he may apply
to me.
Ascribed by Lamb in a letter to Southey, 28 July 1798

WILLIAM COLLINGBOURNE d 1484

10 The Cat, the Rat, and Lovell our dog
Rule all England under a hog.
R. Holinshed, *Chronicles* (1586), iii.746. Of Sir William Catesby
(d.1485), Sir Richard Ratcliffe (d.1485), Lord Lovell
(1454–?1487) (whose crest was a dog), and King Richard III
(whose emblem was a wild boar). Collingbourne was executed on
Tower Hill.

JESSE COLLINGS 1831–1920

11 Three acres and a cow.
Phrase used in his land-reform propaganda of 1885. See 339:16

ADMIRAL COLLINGWOOD 1750–1810

12 Now, gentlemen, let us do something today which the
world may talk of hereafter.
Said before the Battle of Trafalgar, 21 Oct. 1805. G.L. Newnham
Collingwood, ed., *Correspondence and Memoir of Lord
Collingwood*

R.G. COLLINGWOOD 1889–1943

13 Perfect freedom is reserved for the man who lives by
his own work, and in that work does what he wants to
do.
Speculum Mentis, Prologue

CHURTON COLLINS 1848–1908

14 To ask advice is in nine cases out of ten to tout for
flattery.
Maxims and Reflections, No.59

MORTIMER COLLINS 1827–1876

15 A man is as old as he's feeling,
A woman as old as she looks.
The Unknown Quantity

WILLIAM COLLINS 1721–1759

16 To fair Fidele's grassy tomb
Soft maids and village hinds shall bring
Each opening sweet of earliest bloom,
And rifle all the breathing spring.
Dirge in Cymbeline

17 If aught of oaten stop, or pastoral song,
May hope, O pensive Eve, to soothe thine ear.
Ode to Evening

18 Now air is hush'd, save where the weak-ey'd bat,
With short shrill shriek flits by on leathern wing,
Or where the beetle winds
His small but sullen horn,
As oft he rises 'midst the twilight path,
Against the pilgrim borne in heedless hum.

19 How sleep the brave, who sink to rest,
By all their country's wishes blest!
Ode Written in the Year 1746

20 By fairy hands their knell is rung,
By forms unseen their dirge is sung.

21 With eyes up-rais'd, as one inspir'd,
Pale Melancholy sate retir'd,
And from her wild sequester'd seat,
In notes by distance made more sweet,
Pour'd thro' the mellow horn her pensive soul.
The Passions, an Ode for Music

22 In hollow murmurs died away.

23 Too nicely Jonson knew the critic's part,
Nature in him was almost lost in Art.
Verses to Sir Thomas Hanmer

GEORGE COLMAN 1732–1794

24 Love and a cottage! Eh, Fanny! Ah, give me
indifference and a coach and six!
The Clandestine Marriage, I.ii

GEORGE COLMAN THE YOUNGER 1762–1836

25 Oh, London is a fine town,
A very famous city,
Where all the streets are paved with gold,
And all the maidens pretty.
The Heir at Law (1797), I.ii

1 Not to be sneezed at.
II.i

2 Says he, 'I am a handsome man, but I'm a gay deceiver.'
Love Laughs at Locksmiths (1808), Act II

3 Johnson's style was grand and Gibbon's elegant; the stateliness of the former was sometimes pedantic, and the polish of the latter was occasionally finical. Johnson marched to kettle-drums and trumpets; Gibbon moved to flutes and hautboys: Johnson hewed passages through the Alps, while Gibbon levelled walks through parks and gardens.
Random Records (1830), i.121

4 My father was an eminent button maker—but I had a soul above buttons—I panted for a liberal profession.
Sylvester Daggerwood (1795), I.x

5 His heart runs away with his head.
Who Wants a Guinea? (1805), I.i

6 Impaling worms to torture fish.
Lady of the Wreck, c.II.1.18

7 When taken, To be well shaken.
My Nightgown and Slippers (1797), **Newcastle Apothecary**

CHARLES CALEB COLTON 1780?-1832

8 When you have nothing to say, say nothing.
Lacon (1820), vol.i, No.183

9 Examinations are formidable even to the best prepared, for the greatest fool may ask more than the wisest man can answer.
No.322

10 If you would be known, and not know, vegetate in a village; if you would know, and not be known, live in a city.
No.334

11 Man is an embodied paradox, a bundle of contradictions.
No.408

IVY COMPTON-BURNETT 1892–1969

12 'Time has too much credit,' said Bridget. 'I never agree with the compliments paid to it. It is not a great healer. It is an indifferent and perfunctory one. Sometimes it does not heal at all. And sometimes when it seems to, no healing has been necessary.'
Darkness and Day (1951), ch.7

13 'We may as well imagine the scene.'
'No, my mind baulks at it.'
'Mine does worse. It constructs it.'
A Family and a Fortune (1939), ch.9

14 'She still seems to me in her own way a person born to command,' said Luce...
'I wonder if anyone is born to obey,' said Isabel.
'That may be why people command rather badly, that they have no suitable material to work on.'
Parents and Children (1941), ch.3

AUGUSTE COMTE 1798–1857

15 M. Comte used to reproach his early English admirers with maintaining the 'conspiracy of silence' concerning his later performances.
J.S. Mill, *Auguste Comte and Positivism* (1865), p.199

PRINCE DE CONDÉ 1621–1686

16 *Silence! Voilà l'ennemi!*
Hush! Here comes the enemy!
As Bourdaloue mounted the pulpit at St. Sulpice

WILLIAM CONGREVE 1670–1729

17 Is there in the world a climate more uncertain than our own? And, which is a natural consequence, is there any where a people more unsteady, more apt to discontent, more *saturnine, dark,* and *melancholic* than our selves? Are we not of all people the most unfit to be alone, and most unsafe to be trusted with our selves?
Amendments of Mr. Collier's False and Imperfect Citations

18 Careless she is with artful care,
Affecting to seem unaffected.
Amoret

19 She likes her self, yet others hates
For that which in herself she prizes;
And while she laughs at them, forgets
She is the thing that she despises.

20 It is the business of a comic poet to paint the vices and follies of human kind.
The Double Dealer (1694), Epistle Dedicatory. See 138:10

21 Retired to their tea and scandal, according to their ancient custom.
I.i

22 There is nothing more unbecoming a man of quality than to laugh; Jesu, 'tis such a vulgar expression of the passion!
iv. See 137:1

23 Tho' marriage makes man and wife one flesh, it leaves 'em still two fools.
II.iii

24 She lays it on with a trowel.
III.x

25 When people walk hand in hand there's neither overtaking nor meeting.
IV.ii

26 See how love and murder will out.
vi

27 No mask like open truth to cover lies,
As to go naked is the best disguise.
V.vi

28 I cannot help it, if I am naturally more delighted with any thing that is amiable, than with any thing that is wonderful.
Preface to Dryden

29 What he [Dryden] has done in any one species, or distinct kind, would have been sufficient to have acquired him a great name. If he had written nothing but his Prefaces, or nothing but his Songs, or his Prologues, each of them would have intituled him to the preference and distinction of excelling in his kind.

30 The good receiv'd, the giver is forgot.
Epistle to Lord Halifax, l.40

31 Music alone with sudden charms can bind
The wand'ring sense, and calm the troubled mind.
Hymn to Harmony

32 Ah! Madam,...you know every thing in the world but your perfections, and you only know not those,

because 'tis the top of perfection not to know them.
Incognita (1692)

1 I am always of the opinion with the learned, if they speak first.

2 But soon as e'er the beauteous idiot spoke,
Forth from her coral lips such folly broke,
Like balm the trickling nonsense heal'd my wound,
And what her eyes enthral'd, her tongue unbound.
Lesbia

3 I confess freely to you, I could never look long upon a monkey, without very mortifying reflections.
Letter to Dennis, concerning Humour in Comedy, 1695

4 Has he not a rogue's face?...a hanging-look to me...has a damn'd Tyburn-face, without the benefit o' the Clergy...
Love for Love (1695), II.vii

5 I came upstairs into the world; for I was born in a cellar.

6 What, wouldst thou have me turn pelican, and feed thee out of my own vitals?

7 I know that's a secret, for it's whispered every where.
III.iii

8 He that first cries out stop thief, is often he that has stoln the treasure.
xiv

9 Women are like tricks by slight of hand,
Which, to admire, we should not understand.
IV.xxi

10 A branch of one of your antediluvian families, fellows that the flood could not wash away.
V.ii

11 To find a young fellow that is neither a wit in his own eye, nor a fool in the eye of the world, is a very hard task.

12 Aye, 'tis well enough for a servant to be bred at an University. But the education is a little too pedantic for a gentleman.
iii

13 Nay, for my part I always despised Mr *Tattle* of all things; nothing but his being my husband could have made me like him less.
xi

14 Music has charms to sooth a savage breast.
The Mourning Bride (1697), I.i

15 Heav'n has no rage, like love to hatred turn'd,
Nor Hell a fury, like a woman scorn'd.
III.viii

16 Is he then dead?
What, dead at last, quite, quite for ever dead!
V.xi

17 In my conscience I believe the baggage loves me, for she never speaks well of me her self, nor suffers any body else to rail at me.
The Old Bachelor (1693), I.i

18 One of love's April-fools.

19 The Devil watches all opportunities.
vi

20 Man was by Nature Woman's cully made:
We never are, but by ourselves, betrayed.
III.i

21 Bilbo's the word, and slaughter will ensue.
vii

22 Ask all the tyrants of thy sex, if their fools are not known by this party-coloured livery—I am melancholy when thou art absent; look like an ass when thou art present; wake for thee, when I should sleep, and even dream of thee, when I am awake; sigh much, drink little, eat less, court solitude, am grown very entertaining to my self, and (as I am informed) very troublesome to everybody else. If this be not love, it is madness, and then it is pardonable—Nay yet a more certain sign than all this; I give thee my money.
x

23 Eternity was in that moment.
IV.vii

24 You were about to tell me something, child—but you left off before you began.
viii

25 Now am I slap-dash down in the mouth.
ix

26 Well, Sir Joseph, you have such a winning way with you.
V.vii

27 *Sharper:* Thus grief still treads upon the heels of pleasure:
Marry'd in haste, we may repent at leisure.
Setter: Some by experience find those words mis-plac'd:
At leisure marry'd, they repent in haste.
viii and ix

28 I could find it in my heart to marry thee, purely to be rid of thee.
x

29 Courtship to marriage, as a very witty prologue to a very dull Play.

30 Wou'd I were free from this restraint,
Or else had hopes to win her;
Wou'd she cou'd make of me a saint,
Or I of her a sinner.
Song: Pious Selinda Goes to Prayers

31 For 'tis some virtue, virtue to commend.
To Sir Godfrey Kneller

32 They come together like the Coroner's Inquest, to sit upon the murdered reputations of the week.
The Way of the World (1700), I.i

33 Ay, ay, I have experience: I have a wife, and so forth.
iii

34 I always take blushing either for a sign of guilt, or of ill breeding.
ix

35 Say what you will, 'tis better to be left than never to have been loved.
II.i

36 Here she comes i' faith full sail, with her fan spread and streamers out, and a shoal of fools for tenders.
iv

37 *Millamant:* O ay, letters—I had letters—I am persecuted with letters—I hate letters—no body knows how to write letters; and yet one has 'em, one does not know why—They serve one to pin up one's hair.
Witwoud: ...Pray, Madam, do you pin up your hair with all your letters: I find I must keep copies.
Millamant: Only with those in verse, Mr Witwoud. I

never pin up my hair with prose.

1 Beauty is the lover's gift.

2 A little disdain is not amiss; a little scorn is alluring.
III.v

3 Love's but a frailty of the mind
When 'tis not with ambition join'd.
xii

4 O, nothing is more alluring than a levee from a couch
in some confusion.
IV.i

5 I nauseate walking; 'tis a country diversion, I loathe
the country.
iv

6 My dear liberty, shall I leave thee? My faithful
solitude, my darling contemplation, must I bid you
then adieu? Ay-h adieu—My morning thoughts,
agreeable wakings, indolent slumbers, all ye *douceurs,*
ye *sommeils du matin,* adieu—I can't do't, 'tis more
than impossible.
v

7 Don't let us be familiar or fond, nor kiss before folks,
like my Lady Fadler and Sir Francis: Nor go to
Hyde-Park together the first Sunday in a new chariot,
to provoke eyes and whispers, and then never be seen
there together again; as if we were proud of one
another the first week, and asham'd of one another
ever after...Let us be very strange and well-bred: Let
us be as strange as if we had been married a great
while, and as well-bred as if we were not married at
all.

8 These articles subscrib'd, if I continue to endure you a
little longer, I may by degrees dwindle into a wife.

9 I hope you do not think me prone to any iteration of
nuptials.
xii

JAMES M. CONNELL 1852–1929

10 The people's flag is deepest red;
It shrouded oft our martyred dead,
And ere their limbs grew stiff and cold,
Their heart's blood dyed its every fold.
Then raise the scarlet standard high!
Within its shade we'll live or die.
Tho' cowards flinch and traitors sneer,
We'll keep the red flag flying here.
The Red Flag (1889), in H.E. Piggot, *Songs that made History,*
ch.6

CYRIL CONNOLLY 1903–1974

11 The Mandarin style...is beloved by literary pundits, by
those who would make the written word as unlike as
possible to the spoken one. It is the title of those
writers whose tendency is to make their language
convey more than they mean or more than they feel.
Enemies of Promise (1938), pt.I. **Predicament,** ch.ii

12 She [the artist's wife] will know that there is no more
sombre enemy of good art than the pram in the hall.
pt.II. **The Charlock's Shade,** ch.xiv

13 There is no fury like an ex-wife searching for a new
lover.
The Unquiet Grave (1944), Part I. **Ecce Gubernator**

14 Arrival-Angst is closely connected with guilt, with the
dread of something terrible having happened during
our absence. Death of parents. Entry of bailiffs. Flight
of loved one. Sensations worse at arriving in the
evening than in the morning, and much worse at
Victoria and Waterloo, than at Paddington.

15 Imprisoned in every fat man a thin one is wildly
signalling to be let out.
Part II. **Te Palinure Petens.** See 365:11

16 It is closing time in the gardens of the West and from
now on an artist will be judged only by the resonance
of his solitude or the quality of his despair.
'Comment', *Horizon,* Nos. 120-121, Dec. 1949–Jan. 1950. (Final
Issue)

JOSEPH CONRAD 1857–1924

17 The conquest of the earth, which mostly means the
taking it away from those who have a different
complexion or slightly flatter noses than ourselves, is
not a pretty thing when you look into it too much.
The Heart of Darkness (1902), ch.1

18 Mistah Kurtz—he dead.
ch.3

19 In the destructive element immerse...that was the
way.
Lord Jim (1900), ch.20

20 The terrorist and the policeman both come from the
same basket.
The Secret Agent (1907), ch.4

21 He walked frail, insignificant, shabby, miserable—and
terrible in the simplicity of his idea calling madness
and despair to the regeneration of the world. Nobody
looked at him. He passed on unsuspected and deadly,
like a pest in the street full of men.
closing words

22 The scrupulous and the just, the noble, humane, and
devoted natures; the unselfish and the intelligent may
begin a movement—but it passes away from them.
They are not the leaders of a revolution. They are its
victims.
Under Western Eyes (1911), Part II, ch.3

23 There was a completeness in it, something solid like a
principle, and masterful like an instinct—a disclosure
of something secret—of that hidden something, that
gift of good and evil that makes racial difference, that
shapes the fate of nations.
Youth (1898)

24 I remember my youth and the feeling that will never
come back any more—the feeling that I could last for
ever, outlast the sea, the earth, and all men; the
deceitful feeling that lures us on to perils, to love, to
vain effort—to death; the triumphant conviction of
strength, the heat of life in the handful of dust, that
glow in the heart that with every year grows dim,
grows cold, grows small, and expires—and expires,
too soon, too soon—before life itself.

HENRY CONSTABLE 1562–1613

25 Diaphenia, like the daffadowndilly,
White as the sun, fair as the lily,
Heigh ho, how I do love thee!
I do love thee as my lambs
Are beloved of their dams;

How blest were I if thou wouldst prove me!
Diaphenia

JOHN CONSTABLE 1776–1837

1 The sound of water escaping from mill-dams, etc,
willows, old rotten planks, slimy posts, and
brickwork, I love such things....those scenes made me
a painter and I am grateful.
Leslie, *Life of John Constable* (1843), ch.5. Letter to John Fisher,
23 Oct. 1821

2 There is nothing ugly; *I never saw an ugly thing in my
life:* for let the form of an object be what it
may,—light, shade, and perspective will always make
it beautiful.
ch.17

3 The amiable but eccentric Blake...said of a beautiful
drawing of an avenue of fir trees...'Why, this is not
drawing, but *inspiration.*'...[Constable] replied, 'I
never knew it before; I meant it for drawing'.

4 In Claude's landscape all is lovely—all amiable—all is
amenity and repose;—the calm sunshine of the heart.
ch.18. A Course of Lectures to the Royal Institution. Lecture II, 2
June 1836.

BENJAMIN CONSTANT 1767–1834

5 *Dîner avec Robinson, écolier de Schelling. Son
travail sur l'esthétique du Kant. Idées très
ingénieuses. L'art pour l'art et sans but; tout but
dénature l'art. Mais l'art atteint au but qu'il n'a pas.*
Dinner with [Crabb] Robinson, a pupil of Schelling.
His work on Kant's aesthetics. Very clever notions.
Art for art's sake and with no purpose; any purpose
perverts art. But art achieves a purpose which is not its
own.
Journal intime, 11 février 1804

EMPEROR CONSTANTINE 288?–337

6 *In hoc signo vinces.*
In this sign shalt thou conquer.
Traditional form of words of Constantine's vision (312). Reported
in Greek, τούτῳ νίκα, 'By this, conquer', Eusebius, *Life of
Constantine*, i.28

ELIZA COOK 1818–1889

7 I love it, I love it; and who shall dare
To chide me for loving that old arm-chair?
The Old Arm-chair

8 Better build schoolrooms for 'the boy',
Than cells and gibbets for 'the man'.
A Song for the Ragged Schools

CALVIN COOLIDGE 1872–1933

9 I do not choose to run for President in 1928.
Announcement in 1927

10 He said he was against it.
On being asked what had been said by a clergyman who preached
on sin.

11 The business of America is business.
Speech before Society of American Newspaper Editors, 17 Jan.
1925

12 They hired the money, didn't they?
With reference to the war debts incurred by England and others
(1925)

BISHOP RICHARD CORBET 1582–1635

13 Farewell, rewards and Fairies,
   Good housewives now may say,
For now foul sluts in dairies
   Do fare as well as they.
The Fairies' Farewell

14   Who of late for cleanliness,
Finds sixpence in her shoe?

15 By which we note the Fairies
   Were of the old profession;
Their songs were Ave Marys,
   Their dances were procession.

PIERRE CORNEILLE 1606–1684

16 *A vaincre sans péril, on triomphe sans gloire.*
When there is no peril in the fight, there is no glory in
the triumph.
Le Cid (1637), II.ii

17 *Faites votre devoir et laissez faire aux dieux.*
Do your duty, and leave the issue to the Gods.
Horace (1640), II.viii

18 *Un premier mouvement ne fut jamais un crime.*
A first impulse was never a crime.
V.iii. See 355:11

FRANCES CORNFORD 1886–1960

19 Whoso maintains that I am humbled now
   (Who wait the Awful Day) is still a liar;
I hope to meet my Maker brow to brow
   And find my own the higher.
Epitaph for a Reviewer

20 How long ago Hector took off his plume,
Not wanting that his little son should cry,
Then kissed his sad Andromache goodbye—
And now we three in Euston waiting-room.
Parting in Wartime

21 A young Apollo, golden-haired,
Stands dreaming on the verge of strife,
Magnificently unprepared
For the long littleness of life.
Rupert Brooke

22 O fat white woman whom nobody loves,
Why do you walk through the fields in gloves...
Missing so much and so much?
To a Fat Lady Seen from a Train

F.M. CORNFORD 1874–1943

23 Every public action which is not customary, either is
wrong or, if it is right, is a dangerous precedent. It
follows that nothing should ever be done for the first
time.
Microcosmographia Academica, vii

MME CORNUEL 1605–1694

24 *Il n'y a point de héros pour son valet de chambre.*
No man is a hero to his valet.
Lettres de Mlle Aïssé, xii, 13 août, 1728

CORONATION SERVICE

25 We present you with this Book, the most valuable
thing that this world affords. Here is wisdom; this is

the royal Law; these are the lively Oracles of God.
The Presenting of the Holy Bible. See L.G. Wickham Legge, *English Coronation Records* (1901), p.334

CORREGGIO c.1489–1534

1 *Anch' io sono pittore!*
I, too, am a painter.
On seeing Raphael's 'St. Cecilia' at Bologna, c.1525

WILLIAM CORY 1823–1892

2 Jolly boating weather,
And a hay harvest breeze,
Blade on the feather,
Shade off the trees
Swing, swing together
With your body between your knees.
Eton Boating Song, see E. Parker, *Floreat* (1923), p.109. First published in *Eton Scrap Book,* 1865

3   Nothing in life shall sever
The chain that is round us now.

4 They told me, Heraclitus, they told me you were
     dead,
They brought me bitter news to hear and bitter tears to
     shed.
I wept as I remembered how often you and I
Had tired the sun with talking and sent him down the
     sky.
Heraclitus. Translation of Callimachus, *Epigrams,* 2

5 You promise heavens free from strife,
     Pure truth, and perfect change of will;
But sweet, sweet is this human life,
     So sweet, I fain would breathe it still;
Your chilly stars I can forgo,
This warm kind world is all I know.
Mimnermus in Church

6 All beauteous things for which we live
     By laws of space and time decay.
But Oh, the very reason why
I clasp them, is because they die.

CHARLES COTTON 1630–1687

7 The shadows now so long do grow,
That brambles like tall cedars show,
Molehills seem mountains, and the ant
Appears a monstrous elephant.
Evening Quatrains, iii

ÉMILE COUÉ 1857–1926

8 *Tous les jours, à tous points de vue, je vais de mieux
en mieux.*
Every day, in every way, I am getting better and
better.
Formula in his clinic at Nancy

VICTOR COUSIN 1792–1867

9 *Il faut de la religion pour la religion, de la morale
pour la morale, comme de l'art pour l'art...le beau ne
peut être la voie ni de l'utile, ni du bien, ni du saint; il
ne conduit qu'à lui-même.*
We must have religion for religion's sake, morality for
morality's sake, as with art for art's sake...the
beautiful cannot be the way to what is useful, or to

what is good, or to what is holy; it leads only to itself.
Du vrai, du beau, et du bien (Sorbonne lecture, 1818). See 162:5

THOMAS COVENTRY, BARON COVENTRY 1578–1640

10 The dominion of the sea, as it is an ancient and
undoubted right of the crown of England, so it is the
best security of the land. The wooden walls are the
best walls of this kingdom.
Speech to the Judges, 17 June 1635. See Rushworth, *Hist. Coll.*
(1680), vol.ii, p.297

NOËL COWARD 1899–1973

11 Very flat, Norfolk.
Private Lives, I

12 Extraordinary how potent cheap music is.

13 It didn't look like a biscuit box did it? I've always felt
that it might. [Of the Taj Mahal.]

14 Certain women should be struck regularly, like gongs.
III

15 Don't let's be beastly to the Germans
When our Victory is ultimately won.
Don't Let's Be Beastly to the Germans (1943)

16 They had him thrown out of a club in Bombay
For, apart from his Mess-bills exceeding his pay,
He took to pig-sticking in *quite* the wrong way.
I wonder what happened to him!
I Wonder what Happened to Him from *Sigh No More* (1945)

17 I believe that since my life began
The most I've had is just a talent to amuse.
Heigh-o,
If love were all.
If Love were all from *Bitter Sweet* (1929)

18 Mad about the boy,
It's pretty funny but I'm mad about the boy.
He has a gay appeal
That makes me feel
There may be something sad about the boy.
Mad about the Boy from *Words and Music* (1932)

19 Mad dogs and Englishmen go out in the mid-day sun;
The Japanese don't care to, the Chinese wouldn't dare
     to;
Hindus and Argentines sleep firmly from twelve to
     one,
But Englishmen detest a
Siesta.
Mad Dogs and Englishmen

20 In the mangrove swamps where the python romps
There is peace from twelve till two.
Even caribous lie around and snooze,
For there's nothing else to do.
In Bengal, to move at all
Is seldom, if ever done.

21 Don't put your daughter on the stage, Missis
     Worthington
Don't put your daughter on the stage.
Mrs. Worthington

22 She refused to begin the 'Beguine'
Tho' they besought her to
And with language profane and obscene
She curs'd the man who taught her to

She curs'd Cole Porter too!
Nina from *Sigh No More* (1945)

1 Poor little rich girl
You're a bewitched girl,
Better beware!
Poor Little Rich Girl from *Charlot's Revue* of 1926

2 We have been able to dispose of
Rows and rows and rows of
Gainsboroughs and Lawrences
Some sporting prints of Aunt Florence's
Some of which were rather rude.
The Stately Homes of England from *Operette* (1938)

3 The Stately Homes of England
How beautiful they stand,
To prove the upper classes
Have still the upper hand.
See 244:21

4 Tho' the pipes that supply the bathroom burst
And the lavat'ry makes you fear the worst
It was used by Charles the First
Quite informally
And later by George the Fourth
On a journey North.

5 The Stately Homes of England,
Tho' rather in the lurch,
Provide a lot of chances
For Psychical Research—
There's the ghost of a crazy younger son
Who murder'd in Thirteen Fifty-One,
An extremely rowdy Nun
Who resented it,
And people who come to call
Meet her in the hall.

ABRAHAM COWLEY 1618–1667

6 Love in her sunny eyes does basking play;
Love walks the pleasant mazes of her hair;
Love does on both her lips for ever stray;
And sows and reaps a thousand kisses there.
In all her outward parts Love's always seen;
    But, oh, he never went within.
The Change

7 The thirsty earth soaks up the rain,
And drinks, and gapes for drink again.
The plants suck in the earth, and are
With constant drinking fresh and fair.
Drinking

8 Fill all the glasses there, for why
Should every creature drink but I,
Why, man of morals, tell me why?

9 God the first garden made, and the first city Cain.
The Garden

10 The world's a scene of changes, and to be
Constant, in Nature were inconstancy.
Inconstancy

11 Well then; I now do plainly see
This busy world and I shall ne'er agree;
The very honey of all earthly joy
Does of all meats the soonest cloy,
    And they (methinks) deserve my pity,
Who for it can endure the stings,
The crowd, and buz, and murmurings

Of this great hive, the city.
The Mistress, or Love Verses

12 Nothing so soon the drooping spirits can raise
As praises from the men, whom all men praise.
Ode upon a Copy of Verses of My Lord Broghill's

13 This only grant me, that my means may lie
Too low for envy, for contempt too high.
Of Myself

14 Acquaintance I would have, but when't depends
Not on the number, but the choice of friends.

15 Poet and Saint! to thee alone are given
The two most sacred names of earth and Heaven.
On the Death of Mr. Crashaw

16 Hail, Bard triumphant! and some care bestow
On us, the Poets Militant below!

17 Ye fields of Cambridge, our dear Cambridge, say,
Have ye not seen us walking every day?
Was there a tree about which did not know
    The love betwixt us two?
On William Harvey

18 Lukewarmness I account a sin
As great in love as in religion.
The Request

19 Life is an incurable disease.
To Dr. Scarborough, vi

20 Hence, ye profane; I hate ye all;
Both the great vulgar, and the small.
Trans. of Horace, bk.iii, ode 1. See 260:13

MRS. HANNAH COWLEY 1743–1809

21 Five minutes! Zounds! I have been five minutes too
late all my life-time!
The Belle's Stratagem (1780), I.i

22 Vanity, like murder, will out.
iv

23 But what is woman?—only one of Nature's agreeable
blunders.
Who's the Dupe?, II

WILLIAM COWPER 1731–1800

24 Regions Caesar never knew
    Thy posterity shall sway,
Where his eagles never flew,
    None invincible as they.
Boadicea

25 Grief is itself a med'cine.
Charity, l.159

26 He found it inconvenient to be poor.
l.189

27 India's spicy shores.
l.442

28 No learned disputants would take the field,
Sure not to conquer, and sure not to yield;
Both sides deceiv'd, if rightly understood,
Pelting each other for the public good.
l.620

29 Spare the poet for his subject's sake.
l.636

30 Though syllogisms hang not on my tongue,
I am not surely always in the wrong!
'Tis hard if all is false that I advance—

A fool must now and then be right, by chance.
Conversation, l.93

1 A noisy man is always in the right.
l.114

2 A tale should be judicious, clear, succinct;
The language plain, and incidents well link'd;
Tell not as new what ev'ry body knows;
And, new or old, still hasten to a close.
l.235

3 The pipe, with solemn interposing puff,
Makes half a sentence at a time enough;
The dozing sages drop the drowsy strain,
Then pause, and puff—and speak, and pause again.
l.245

4 Pernicious weed! whose scent the fair annoys,
Unfriendly to society's chief joys,
Thy worst effect is banishing for hours
The sex whose presence civilizes ours.
l.251

5 His wit invites you by his looks to come,
But when you knock it never is at home.
l.303

6 Whose only fit companion is his horse.
l.412

7 War lays a burden on the reeling state,
And peace does nothing to relieve the weight.
Expostulation, l.306

8 And hast thou sworn, on ev'ry slight pretence,
Till perjuries are common as bad pence,
While thousands, careless of the damning sin,
Kiss the book's outside who ne'er look within.
l.386

9 The man that hails you Tom or Jack,
And proves by thumps upon your back
    How he esteems your merit,
Is such a friend, that one had need
Be very much his friend indeed
    To pardon or to bear it.
Friendship

10 Pleasure is labour too, and tires as much.
Hope, l.20

11 Men deal with life as children with their play,
Who first misuse, then cast their toys away.
l.127

12   The multitudes beguil'd
In vain opinion's waste and dang'rous wild.
Ten thousand rove the brakes and thorns among,
Some eastward, and some westward, and all wrong.
l.278

13 Could he with reason murmur at his case,
Himself sole author of his own disgrace?
l.316

14 And diff'ring judgements serve but to declare
That truth lies somewhere, if we knew but where.
l.423

15 John Gilpin was a citizen
    Of credit and renown,
A train-band captain eke was he
    Of famous London town.
John Gilpin

16 My sister and my sister's child,
    Myself and children three,
Will fill the chaise; so you must ride

On horseback after we.

17   O'erjoy'd was he to find
That, though on pleasure she was bent,
    She had a frugal mind.

18 So down he came; for loss of time,
    Although it griev'd him sore,
Yet loss of pence, full well he knew,
    Would trouble him much more.

19 Nor stopp'd till where he had got up
    He did again get down.

20 Beware of desp'rate steps. The darkest day
(Live till tomorrow) will have pass'd away.
The Needless Alarm, l.132

21 Hence jarring sectaries may learn
    Their real int'rest to discern;
That brother should not war with brother,
And worry and devour each other.
The Nightingale and Glow-Worm

22 No dancing bear was so genteel,
    Or half so dégagé.
Of Himself

23 Oh! for a closer walk with God,
    A calm and heav'nly frame;
A light to shine upon the road
    That leads me to the Lamb!
Olney Hymns, 1

24 There is a fountain fill'd with blood
    Drawn from Emmanuel's veins,
And sinners, plunged beneath that flood,
    Lose all their guilty stains.
15

25 Hark, my soul! it is the Lord;
'Tis thy Saviour, hear his word;
Jesus speaks, and speaks to thee;
'Say, poor sinner, lov'st thou me?'
18

26 God moves in a mysterious way
    His wonders to perform;
He plants his footsteps in the sea,
    And rides upon the storm.
35

27 Ye fearful saints fresh courage take,
    The clouds ye so much dread
Are big with mercy, and shall break
    In blessings on your head.

28 Behind a frowning providence
    He hides a smiling face.

29 Blind unbelief is sure to err,
    And scan his work in vain;
God is his own interpreter,
    And he will make it plain.

30 Toll for the brave—
    The brave! that are no more:
All sunk beneath the wave,
    Fast by their native shore.
On the Loss of the Royal George

31 His sword was in the sheath,
    His fingers held the pen,
When Kempenfelt went down
    With twice four hundred men.

32 Oh, fond attempt to give a deathless lot

To names ignoble, born to be forgot!
On Observing Some Names of Little Note Recorded in the Biographia Britannica

1 There goes the parson, oh! illustrious spark,
And there, scarce less illustrious, goes the clerk!

2 Oh that those lips had language! Life has pass'd
With me but roughly since I heard thee last.
Those lips are thine—thy own sweet smiles I see,
The same that oft in childhood solac'd me.
On the Receipt of My Mother's Picture, l.1

3 Thy morning bounties ere I left my home,
The biscuit, or confectionary plum.
l.60

4 Perhaps a frail memorial, but sincere,
Not scorn'd in heav'n, though little notic'd here.
l.72

5 I shall not ask Jean Jacques Rousseau,
If birds confabulate or no.
Pairing Time Anticipated

6 Unmiss'd but by his dogs and by his groom.
The Progress of Error, l.95

7 Oh, laugh or mourn with me the rueful jest,
A cassock'd huntsman and a fiddling priest!
l.110

8 Himself a wand'rer from the narrow way,
His silly sheep, what wonder if they stray?
l.118

9 Remorse, the fatal egg by pleasure laid.
l.239

10 As creeping ivy clings to wood or stone,
And hides the ruin that it feeds upon.
l.285

11 How much a dunce that has been sent to roam
Excels a dunce that has been kept at home.
l.415

12 Judgment drunk, and brib'd to lose his way,
Winks hard, and talks of darkness at noon-day.
l.450

13 Thou god of our idolatry, the press...
Thou fountain, at which drink the good and wise;
Thou ever-bubbling spring of endless lies;
Like Eden's dread probationary tree,
Knowledge of good and evil is from thee.
l.461

14 Laugh at all you trembled at before.
l.592

15 Then, shifting his side, (as a lawyer knows how).
Report of a Adjudged Case

16 The disencumber'd Atlas of the state.
Retirement, l.394

17 He likes the country, but in truth must own,
Most likes it, when he studies it in town.
l.573

18 Philologists who chase
A panting syllable through time and space,
Start it at home, and hunt it in the dark,
To Gaul, to Greece, and into Noah's ark.
l.619

19 Absence of occupation is not rest,
A mind quite vacant is a mind distress'd.
l.623

20 Beggars invention and makes fancy lame.
l.709

21 I praise the Frenchman, his remark was shrewd—
How sweet, how passing sweet, is solitude!
But grant me still a friend in my retreat,
Whom I may whisper—solitude is sweet.
l.739

22 The lie that flatters I abhor the most.
Table Talk, l.88

23 Admirals, extoll'd for standing still,
Or doing nothing with a deal of skill.
l.192

24 The Frenchman, easy, debonair, and brisk,
Give him his lass, his fiddle, and his frisk,
Is always happy, reign whoever may,
And laughs the sense of mis'ry far away.
l.236

25 Freedom has a thousand charms to show,
That slaves, howe'er contented, never know.
l.260

26 Stamps God's own name upon a lie just made,
To turn a penny in the way of trade.
l.420

27 But he (his musical finesse was such,
So nice his ear, so delicate his touch)
Made poetry a mere mechanic art;
And ev'ry warbler has his tune by heart. [Pope.]
l.654

28 Thus first necessity invented stools,
Convenience next suggested elbow-chairs,
And luxury the accomplish'd Sofa last.
The Task, bk.i, **The Sofa**, l.86

29 The nurse sleeps sweetly, hir'd to watch the sick,
Whom, snoring, she disturbs.
l.89

30 He, not unlike the great ones of mankind,
Disfigures earth; and, plotting in the dark,
Toils much to earn a monumental pile,
That may record the mischiefs he has done. [The mole.]
l.274

31 God made the country, and man made the town.
l.749

32 Slaves cannot breathe in England, if their lungs
Receive our air, that moment they are free;
They touch our country, and their shackles fall.
bk.ii, **The Timepiece**, l.40. See 7:7

33 England, with all thy faults, I love thee still—
My country!
l.206. See 148:24

34 I would not yet exchange thy sullen skies,
And fields without a flow'r, for warmer France
With all her vines.
l.212

35 There is a pleasure in poetic pains
Which only poets know.
l.285

36 Variety's the very spice of life,
That gives it all its flavour.
l.606

37 Let her pass, and, chariotted along

In guilty splendour, shake the public ways.
bk.iii, **The Garden**, l.69

1 I was a stricken deer, that left the herd
Long since.
l.108. See 434:16

2   Charge
His mind with meanings that he never had.
l.148

3 Great contest follows, and much learned dust
Involves the combatants.
l.161

4 From reveries so airy, from the toil
Of dropping buckets into empty wells,
And growing old in drawing nothing up!
l.188

5   Newton, childlike sage!
Sagacious reader of the works of God.
l.252

6   Detested sport,
That owes its pleasures to another's pain.
l.326

7 How various his employments, whom the world
Calls idle.
l.352

8 Studious of laborious ease.
l.361

9 Who loves a garden loves a greenhouse too.
l.566

10 To combat may be glorious, and success
Perhaps may crown us; but to fly is safe.
l.686

11 Now stir the fire, and close the shutters fast,
Let fall the curtains, wheel the sofa round,
And, while the bubbling and loud-hissing urn
Throws up a steamy column, and the cups,
That cheer but not inebriate, wait on each,
So let us welcome peaceful ev'ning in.
bk.iv, **The Winter Evening**, l.34. See 41:21

12 'Tis pleasant through the loopholes of retreat
To peep at such a world; to see the stir
Of the great Babel, and not feel the crowd.
l.88

13 I crown thee king of intimate delights,
Fire-side enjoyments, home-born happiness.
l.139

14   A Roman meal;...
               a radish and an egg.
ll.168-73

15 The slope of faces, from the floor to th' roof,
(As if one master-spring controll'd them all),
Relax'd into a universal grin.
l.202

16 With spots quadrangular of di'mond form,
Ensanguin'd hearts, clubs typical of strife,
And spades, the emblem of untimely graves.
l.217

17 I never fram'd a wish, or form'd a plan,
That flatter'd me with hopes of earthly bliss,
But there I laid the scene.
l.695

18 Shaggy, and lean, and shrewd, with pointed ears

And tail cropp'd short, half lurcher and half cur.
bk.v, **The Winter Morning Walk**, l.45

19 Great princes have great playthings.
l.175

20 But war's a game, which, were their subjects wise,
Kings would not play at.
l.187

21 And the first smith was the first murd'rer's son.
l.219

22 He is the freeman whom the truth makes free.
l.733

23   Knowledge dwells
In heads replete with thoughts of other men;
Wisdom in minds attentive to their own.
bk.vi, **The Winter Walk at Noon**, l.89

24 Knowledge is proud that he has learn'd so much;
Wisdom is humble that he knows no more.
l.96

25 Books are not seldom talismans and spells.
l.98

26 Nature is but a name for an effect,
Whose cause is God.
l.223

27 A cheap but wholesome salad from the brook.
l.304

28 I would not enter on my list of friends
(Tho' grac'd with polish'd manners and fine sense,
Yet wanting sensibility) the man
Who needlessly sets foot upon a worm.
l.560

29   Stillest streams
Oft water fairest meadows, and the bird
That flutters least is longest on the wing.
l.929

30 Public schools 'tis public folly feeds.
Tirocinium, l.250

31 The parson knows enough who knows a duke.
l.403

32   As a priest,
A piece of mere church furniture at best.
l.425

33   Tenants of life's middle state,
Securely plac'd between the small and great.
l.807

34 Greece, sound thy Homer's, Rome thy Virgil's name,
But England's Milton equals both in fame.
To John Milton

35 Humility may clothe an English dean.
Truth, l.118

36 He has no hope who never had a fear.
l.298

37 His mind his kingdom, and his will his law.
l.406

38 I am monarch of all I survey,
My right there is none to dispute;
From the centre all round to the sea
I am lord of the fowl and the brute.
Oh, solitude! where are the charms
That sages have seen in thy face?
Better dwell in the midst of alarms,
Than reign in this horrible place.
Verses Supposed to be Written by Alexander Selkirk

1 [On Johnson's inadequate treatment of *Paradise Lost*]
Oh! I could thresh his old jacket till I made his pension
jingle in his pockets.
Letters. To the Revd. W. Unwin, 31 Oct. 1779

2 Our severest winter, commonly called the spring.
8 June 1783

3 He kissed likewise the maid in the kitchen, and
seemed upon the whole a most loving, kissing,
kind-hearted gentleman.
To the Revd. J. Newton, 29 Mar. 1784

GEORGE CRABBE 1754–1832

4 What is a church?—Our honest sexton tells,
'Tis a tall building, with a tower and bells.
The Borough, letter ii, **The Church,** l.11

5 Virtues neglected then, adored become,
And graces slighted, blossom on the tomb.
l.133

6 Intrigues half-gather'd, conversation-scraps,
Kitchen-cabals, and nursery-mishaps.
letter iii, **The Vicar,** l.71

7 Habit with him was all the test of truth,
'It must be right: I've done it from my youth.'
l.138

8 Lo! the poor toper whose untutor'd sense,
Sees bliss in ale, and can with wine dispense;
Whose head proud fancy never taught to steer,
Beyond the muddy ecstasies of beer.
Inebriety, l.120. Imitation of Pope: see 379:5

9 This, books can do—nor this alone: they give
New views to life, and teach us how to live;
They soothe the grieved, the stubborn they chastise;
Fools they admonish, and confirm the wise.
Their aid they yield to all: they never shun
The man of sorrow, nor the wretch undone;
Unlike the hard, the selfish, and the proud,
They fly not sullen from the suppliant crowd;
Nor tell to various people various things,
But show to subjects, what they show to kings.
The Library, l.41

10 With awe around these silent walks I tread:
These are the lasting mansions of the dead.
l.105

11 And mighty folios first, a lordly band,
Then quartos, their well-order'd ranks maintain,
And light octavos fill a spacious plain;
See yonder, ranged in more frequented rows,
A humbler band of duodecimos.
l.128

12 Fashion, though Folly's child, and guide of fools,
Rules e'en the wisest, and in learning rules.
l.167

13 Coldly profane, and impiously gay.
l.265

14 The murmuring poor, who will not fast in peace.
The Newspaper, l.158

15 A master-passion is the love of news.
l.279

16 Our farmers round, well pleased with constant gain,
Like other farmers, flourish and complain.
The Parish Register, pt.i, **Baptisms,** l.273

17 Who often reads, will sometimes wish to write.
Tales, xi, **Edward Shore,** l.109

18 The wife was pretty, trifling, childish, weak;
She could not think, but would not cease to speak.
xiv, **Struggles of Conscience,** l.343

19 But 'twas a maxim he had often tried,
That right was right, and there he would abide.
xv, **The Squire and the Priest,** l.365

20 That all was wrong because not all was right.
xix, **The Convert,** l.313

21 He tried the luxury of doing good.
Tales of the Hall, iii, **Boys at School,** l.139

22 Secrets with girls, like loaded guns with boys,
Are never valued till they make a noise.
xi, **The Maid's Story,** l.84

23 'The game', he said, 'is never lost till won.'
xv, **Gretna Green,** l.334

24 The face the index of a feeling mind.
xvi, **Lady Barbara,** l.124

25 Love warps the mind a little from the right.
xxi, **Smugglers and Poachers,** l.216

26 Lo! where the heath, with withering brake grown o'er,
Lends the light turf that warms the neighbouring poor;
From thence a length of burning sand appears,
Where the thin harvest waves its wither'd ears;
Rank weeds, that every art and care defy,
Reign o'er the land, and rob the blighted rye:
There thistles stretch their prickly arms afar,
And to the ragged infant threaten war;
There poppies, nodding, mock the hope of toil;
There the blue bugloss paints the sterile soil;
Hardy and high, above the slender sheaf,
The slimy mallow waves her silky leaf;
O'er the young shoot the charlock throws a shade,
And clasping tares cling round the sickly blade.
The Village, bk.i, l.63

27 And the cold charities of man to man.
l.245

28 A potent quack, long versed in human ills,
Who first insults the victim whom he kills;
Whose murd'rous hand a drowsy Bench protect,
And whose most tender mercy is neglect.
l.282

HART CRANE 1899–1932

29 O Sleepless as the river under thee,
Vaulting the sea, the prairies' dreaming sod,
Unto us lowliest sometime sweep, descend
And of the curveship lend a myth to God.
The Bridge

30 You who desired so much—in vain to ask—
Yet fed your hunger like an endless task,
Dared dignify the labor, bless the quest—
Achieved that stillness ultimately best,

Being, of all, least sought for: Emily, Hear!
To Emily Dickinson

31 And yet this great wink of eternity,
Of rimless floods, unfettered leewardings,
Samite sheeted and processioned where
Her undinal vast belly moonward bends,
Laughing the wrapt inflections of our love;

Take this Sea, whose diapason knells
On scrolls of silver snowy sentences,
The sceptered terror of whose session rends
As her demeanors motion well or ill,

All but the pieties of lovers' hands.
Voyages, II

ARCHBISHOP CRANMER 1489–1556

1 This was the hand that wrote it, therefore it shall
suffer first punishment.
At the stake, 21 March 1556. Green, *Short History of the English
People,* p.367

RICHARD CRASHAW 1612?–1649

2 *Nympha pudica Deum vidit, et erubuit.*
The conscious water saw its God, and blushed.
Epigrammata Sacra. **Aquae in Vinum Versae** (His own
translation.)

3 Love's passives are his activ'st part.
The wounded is the wounding heart.
The Flaming Heart upon the Book of Saint Teresa, l.73

4 By all the eagle in thee, all the dove.
l.95

5 Love, thou art absolute sole Lord
Of life and death.
Hymn to the Name & Honour of the Admirable Saint Teresa,
l.1

6 Gloomy night embrac'd the place
Where the noble Infant lay.
The Babe look't up and shew'd his face;
In spite of darkness, it was day.
It was Thy day, sweet! and did rise
Not from the East, but from thine eyes.
Hymn of the Nativity, l.17

7 Poor World (said I) what wilt thou do
To entertain this starry stranger?
Is this the best thou canst bestow?
A cold, and not too cleanly, manger?
Contend, ye powers of heav'n and earth
To fit a bed for this huge birth.
l.37

8 Welcome, all wonders in one sight!
Eternity shut in a span.
l.79

9 I would be married, but I'd have no wife,
I would be married to a single life.
On Marriage

10 Lo here a little volume, but large book.
Prayer...prefixed to a little Prayer-book

11 It is love's great artillery
Which here contracts itself and comes to lie
Close couch'd in your white bosom.

12 Two walking baths; two weeping motions;
Portable, and compendious oceans.
Saint Mary Magdalene, or The Weeper, xix

13 All is Caesar's; and what odds
So long as Caesar's self is God's?
Steps to the Temple, Mark 12

14 And when life's sweet fable ends,
Soul and body part like friends;
No quarrels, murmurs, no delay;
A kiss, a sigh, and so away.
Temperance

15 Whoe'er she be,
That not impossible she
That shall command my heart and me;

Where'er she lie,
Lock'd up from mortal eye,
In shady leaves of destiny.
Wishes to His Supposed Mistress

JULIA CRAWFORD fl. 1835

16 Kathleen Mavourneen! the grey dawn is breaking,
The horn of the hunter is heard on the hill;
The lark from her light wing the bright dew is shaking;
Kathleen Mavourneen! what, slumbering still?
Oh! hast thou forgotten how soon we must sever?
Oh! hast thou forgotten this day we must part?
It may be for years, and it may be for ever,
Oh! why art thou silent, thou voice of my heart?
Kathleen Mavourneen. Metropolitan Magazine, London, 1835

BISHOP MANDELL CREIGHTON 1843–1901

17 No people do so much harm as those who go about
doing good.
Life (1904), vol.ii, p.503

SIR RANULPHE CREWE 1558–1646

18 And yet time hath his revolution; there must be a
period and an end to all temporal things, *finis rerum,*
an end of names and dignities and whatsoever is
terrene; and why not of De Vere? Where is Bohun,
where's Mowbray, where's Mortimer? Nay, which is
more and most of all, where is Plantagenet? They are
entombed in the urns and sepulchres of mortality. And
yet let the name and dignity of De Vere stand so long
as it pleaseth God.
Oxford Peerage Case, 1625. See D.N.B.

OLIVER CROMWELL 1599–1658

19 A few honest men are better than numbers.
Letter to Sir W. Spring, Sept. 1643

20 Such men as had the fear of God before them and as
made some conscience of what they did...the plain
russet-coated captain that knows what he fights for and
loves what he knows.
Letter of Sept. 1643. Carlyle, *Letters and Speeches of Oliver
Cromwell*

21 I beseech you, in the bowels of Christ, think it
possible you may be mistaken.
Letter to the General Assembly of the Church of Scotland, 3 Aug.
1650

22 The dimensions of this mercy are above my thoughts.
It is, for aught I know, a crowning mercy.
Letter for the Honourable William Lenthall, 4 Sept. 1651

23 Not what they want but what is good for them.
Attr.

24 Mr Lely, I desire you would use all your skill to paint
my picture truly like me, and not flatter me at all; but
remark all these roughnesses, pimples, warts, and
everything as you see me, otherwise I will never pay a
farthing for it.
Walpole, *Anecdotes of Painting,* ch.12

25 Take away that fool's bauble, the mace.
At the dismissal of the Rump Parliament, 20 Apr. 1653. Bulstrode
Whitelock, *Memorials* (1682), p.554. Often quoted as 'Take away
these baubles'.

26 You have sat too long here for any good you have
been doing. Depart, I say, and let us have done with

you. In the name of God, go!
Addressing the Rump Parliament, 20 Apr. 1653. See Bulstrode
Whitelock, *Memorials* (1682), p.554. Quoted by L.S. Amery from
the back benches of Neville Chamberlain's Government, House of
Commons, 7 May 1940.

1 It's a maxim not to be despised, 'Though peace be
made, yet it's interest that keeps peace.'
Speech to Parliament, 4 Sept. 1654

2 Necessity hath no law. Feigned necessities, imaginary
necessities,…are the greatest cozenage that men can
put upon the Providence of God, and make pretences
to break known rules by.
12 Sept. 1654

3 Your poor army, those poor contemptible men, came
up hither.
21 Apr. 1657

4 You have accounted yourselves happy on being
environed with a great ditch from all the world
besides.
25 Jan. 1658

5 My design is to make what haste I can to be gone.
Last words. Morley, *Life*, v, ch.10

RICHARD ASSHETON, VISCOUNT CROSS
1823–1914

6 [When the House of Lords laughed at his speech in
favour of Spiritual Peers]
I hear a smile.
G.W.E. Russell, *Collections and Recollections*, ch.29

BISHOP RICHARD CUMBERLAND 1631–1718

7 It is better to wear out than to rust out.
G. Horne, *The Duty of Contending for the Faith*

E.E. CUMMINGS 1894–1962

8 who knows if the moon's
a balloon, coming out of a keen city
in the sky—filled with pretty people?
& [AND] (1925), N&:VII

9 the Cambridge ladies who live in furnished souls.
the Cambridge ladies

10 'next to of course god america i
love you land of the pilgrims' and so forth oh
say can you see by the dawn's early my
country 'tis of centuries come and go
and are no more what of it we should worry
in every language even deafanddumb
thy sons acclaim your glorious name by gorry
by jingo by gee by gosh by gum
why talk of beauty what could be more beautiful than these heroic happy dead
who rushed like lions to the roaring slaughter
they did not stop to think they died instead
then shall the voice of liberty be mute?'

He spoke. And drank rapidly a glass of water.
next to of course god

11 pity this busy monster, manunkind,

not. Progress is a comfortable disease.
pity this busy monster, manunkind

12 listen: there's a hell
of a good universe next door; let's go.

ALLAN CUNNINGHAM 1784–1842

13 A wet sheet and a flowing sea,
A wind that follows fast
And fills the white and rustling sail
And bends the gallant mast.
A Wet Sheet and a Flowing Sea

14 It's hame and it's hame, hame fain wad I be,
O, hame, hame, hame to my ain countree!
It's hame and It's hame. Hogg includes this poem among his
Jacobite Relics, i.135. In his notes, i.294, he says he took it from
Cromek's *Galloway and Nithsdale Relics*, and supposes that it
owed much to Allan Cunningham

WILL CUPPY 1884–1949

15 The Dodo never had a chance. He seems to have been
invented for the sole purpose of becoming extinct and
that was all he was good for.
How to Become Extinct

JOHN PHILPOT CURRAN 1750–1817

16 The condition upon which God hath given liberty to
man is eternal vigilance; which condition if he break,
servitude is at once the consequence of his crime, and
the punishment of his guilt.
Speech on the Right of Election of Lord Mayor of Dublin, 10 July
1790

LORD CURZON OF KEDLESTON 1859–1925

17 I hesitate to say what the functions of the modern
journalist may be; but I imagine that they do not
exclude the intelligent anticipation of facts even before
they occur.
House of Commons, 29 Mar. 1898

18 No gentleman has soup at luncheon.
Attr. by Evelyn Waugh in *Noblesse oblige* by A.S.C. Ross and
others (1956), p.73

ST. CYPRIAN d. 258

19 *Habere non potest Deum patrem qui ecclesiam non
habet matrem.*
He cannot have God for his father who has not the
church for his mother.
De Cath. Eccl. Unitate, vi. See 21:19

SAMUEL DANIEL 1562–1619

20 Princes in this case
Do hate the traitor, though they love the treason.
Tragedy of Cleopatra, IV.i

21 Unless above himself he can
Erect himself, how poor a thing is man!
To the Lady Margaret, Countess of Cumberland, xii

22 Custom that is before all law, Nature that is above all
art.
A Defence of Rhyme

23 And who, in time, knows whither we may vent
The treasure of our tongue, to what strange shores
This gain of our best glory shall be sent,
T'enrich unknowing nations with our stores?
What worlds in th'yet unformed Occident
May come refin'd with th'accents that are ours?
Musophilus, l.957

24 But years hath done this wrong,

To make me write too much, and live too long.
Philotas, [Ded.] **To the Prince,** l.108

1 Care-charmer Sleep, son of the sable Night,
Brother to Death, in silent darkness born:
Relieve my languish, and restore the light,
With dark forgetting of my care return,
And let the day be time enough to mourn
The shipwreck of my ill adventured youth:
Let waking eyes suffice to wail their scorn,
Without the torment of the night's untruth.
Sonnets to Delia, liv

DANTE 1265–1321

2 *Nel mezzo del cammin di nostra vita.*
In the middle of the road of our life.
Divina Commedia (ed. Sinclair, 1971). **Inferno,** i.1

3 *PER ME SI VA NELLA CITTÀ DOLENTE,*
PER ME SI VA NELL' ETERNO DOLORE,
PER ME SI VA TRA LA PERDUTA GENTE...
LASCIATE OGNI SPERANZA VOI CH'ENTRATE!
This way for the sorrowful city. This way for eternal
suffering. This way to join the lost
people...Abandon all hope, you who enter!
iii.1. Inscription at the entrance to Hell

4 *Non ragioniam di lor, ma guarda, e passa.*
Let us not speak of them, but look, and pass on.
51

5 *Il gran rifiuto.*
The great refusal.
60

6 *Onorate l'altissimo poeta.*
Honour to the greatest poet.
iv.80

7 *Il maestro di color che sanno.*
The master of them that know. [Aristotle.]
131

8 *Nessun maggior dolore,*
Che ricordarsi del tempo felice
Nella miseria.
There is no greater sorrow than to recall a time of
happiness in misery.
v.121. See 89:6

9 *Noi leggiavamo un giorno per diletto*
Di Lancialotto, come amor lo strinse:
Soli eravamo, e sanza alcun sospetto.
We were reading one day for recreation of Lancelot,
how love constrained him: we were alone and
completely unsuspecting.
127

10 *Galeotto fu il libro e chi lo scrisse:*
Quel giorno più non vi leggemmo avante.
A Galeotto [a pander] was the book and writer too:
that day therein we read no more.
137

11 *Siete voi qui, ser Brunetto?*
Are *you* here, Advocate Brunetto?
xv.30. Brunetto Latini, old and respected friend of Dante,
encountered in hell with other 'Sodomites'.

12 *La cara e buona imagine paterna.*
The dear and kindly paternal image.
83

13 *Considerate la vostra semenza:*
Fatti non foste a viver come bruti,

Ma per seguir virtute e canoscenza.
Consider your origins: you were not made that you
might live as brutes, but so as to follow virtue and
knowledge.
xxvi.118

14 *E quindi uscimmo a riveder le stelle.*
Thence we came forth to see the stars again.
xxxiv.139

15 *Puro e disposto a salire alle stelle.*
Pure and ready to mount to the stars.
Purgatorio, xxxiii.145

16 *E'n la sua volontade è nostra pace.*
In His will is our peace.
Paradiso, iii.85

17 *Tu proverai sì come sa di sale*
Lo pane altrui, e come'è duro calle
Lo scendere e'l salir per l'altrui scale.
You shall find out how salt is the taste of another
man's bread, and how hard is the way up and down
another man's stairs.
xvii.58

18 *L'amor che muove il sole e l'altre stelle.*
The love that moves the sun and the other stars.
xxxiii.145

DANTON 1759–1794

19 *De l'audace, et encore de l'audace, et toujours de*
l'audace!
Boldness, and again boldness, and always boldness!
Speech to the Legislative Committee of General Defence, 2 Sept.
1792. *Le Moniteur,* 4 Sept. 1792

20 Thou wilt show my head to the people: it is worth
showing.
5 Apr. 1794. Carlyle, *French Revolution,* bk.VI, ch.2

GEORGE DARLEY 1795–1846

21   O blest unfabled Incense Tree,
That burns in glorious Araby.
Nepenthe, l.147

CHARLES DARWIN 1809–1882

22 I have tried lately to read Shakespeare, and found it so
intolerably dull that it nauseated me.
Autobiography (ed. G. de Beer, 1974), p.83

23 A hairy quadruped, furnished with a tail and pointed
ears, probably arboreal in its habits.
Descent of Man (1871), ch.21

24 We must, however, acknowledge, as it seems to me,
that man with all his noble qualities,...still bears in his
bodily frame the indelible stamp of his lowly origin.
final words

25 I have called this principle, by which each slight
variation, if useful, is preserved, by the term of
Natural Selection.
The Origin of Species (1859), ch.3

26 We will now discuss in a little more detail the struggle
for existence.

27 The expression often used by Mr Herbert Spencer of
the Survival of the Fittest is more accurate, and is
sometimes equally convenient.
See 514:30

28 It is interesting to contemplate an entangled bank,

clothed with many plants of many kinds, with birds singing on the bushes, with various insects flitting about, and with worms crawling through the damp earth, and to reflect that these elaborately constructed forms, so different from each other, and dependent upon each other in so complex a manner, have all been produced by laws acting around us...Growth with Reproduction; Inheritance...Variability...a Ratio of Increase so high as to lead to a Struggle for Life, and as a consequence to Natural Selection, entailing Divergence of Character and the Extinction of less-improved forms.
ch.15

1 What a book a devil's chaplain might write on the clumsy, wasteful, blundering, low, and horribly cruel works of nature!
Letter to J.D. Hooker, 13 July 1856

ERASMUS DARWIN 1731–1802

2 A fool...is a man who never tried an experiment in his life.
Letter from Maria Edgeworth to Sophy Ruxton, 9 Mar. 1792

3 No, Sir, because I have time to think before I speak, and don't ask impertinent questions. [When asked if he found his stammering very inconvenient.]
Sir Francis Darwin, *Reminiscences of My Father's Everyday Life,* appendix to his edition of Charles Darwin, *Autobiography* (1877)

CHARLES DAVENANT 1656–1714

4 Custom, that unwritten law,
By which the people keep even kings in awe.
Circe, II.iii

SIR WILLIAM DAVENANT 1606–1668

5 Had laws not been, we never had been blam'd;
For not to know we sinn'd is innocence.
Dryden Miscellany, vi.1.226

6 In ev'ry grave make room, make room!
The world's at an end, and we come, we come.
The Law against Lovers, III.i

7 For I must go where lazy Peace
Will hide her drowsy head;
And, for the sport of kings, increase
The number of the dead.
The Soldier Going to the Field

JOHN DAVIDSON 1857–1909

8 A runnable stag, a kingly crop.
A Runnable Stag

SIR JOHN DAVIES 1569–1626

9 Wedlock, indeed, hath oft compared been
To public feasts where meet a public rout,
Where they that are without would fain go in
And they that are within would fain go out.
A Contention Betwixt a Wife, a Widow, and a Maid for Precedence, l.193

10 Skill comes so slow, and life so fast doth fly,
    We learn so little and forget so much.
Nosce Teipsum, xix

11 I know my life's a pain and but a span,
I know my sense is mock'd in every thing;

And to conclude, I know myself a man,
Which is a proud and yet a wretched thing.
xlv

12 Wit to persuade, and beauty to delight.
Orchestra, v

SCROPE DAVIES c.1783–1852

13 Babylon in all its desolation is a sight not so awful as that of the human mind in ruins.
Letter to Thomas Raikes, May 1835. See T. Raikes, *Journal, 1831 to 1847* (1856), vol.ii

W.H. DAVIES 1870–1940

14 The simple bird that thinks two notes a song.
April's Charms

15 A rainbow and a cuckoo's song
May never come together again;
        May never come
        This side the tomb.
A Great Time

16 It was the Rainbow gave thee birth,
And left thee all her lovely hues.
The Kingfisher

17 What is this life if, full of care,
We have no time to stand and stare?
Leisure

BETTE DAVIS 1908–

18 Fasten your seatbelts. It's going to be a bumpy night.
All About Eve (1950), script by Joseph Mankiewicz

JEFFERSON DAVIS 1808–1889

19 All we ask is to be let alone.
Attr., Inaugural Address as President of the Confederate States of America, 18 Feb. 1861

THOMAS DAVIS 1814–1845

20 Come in the evening, or come in the morning,
Come when you're looked for, or come without
    warning.
The Welcome

CECIL DAY-LEWIS 1904–1972

21   Hurry! We burn
For Rome so near us, for the phoenix moment
When we have thrown off this traveller's trance
And mother-naked and ageless-ancient
Wake in her warm nest of renaissance.
Flight to Italy

22 Tempt me no more; for I
Have known the lightning's hour,
The poet's inward pride,
The certainty of power.
The Magnetic Mountain (1933), pt.III

23 It is the logic of our times,
No subject for immortal verse—
That we who lived by honest dreams
Defend the bad against the worse.
Where are the War Poets?

STEPHEN DECATUR 1779–1820

1 Our country! In her intercourse with foreign nations,
 may she always be in the right; but our country, right
 or wrong.
 Decatur's Toast (1816), see A.S. Mackenzie, *Life of Decatur*,
 ch.xiv

DANIEL DEFOE 1661?–1731

2 The best of men cannot suspend their fate:
 The good die early, and the bad die late.
 Character of the late Dr. S. Annesley

3 We lov'd the doctrine for the teacher's sake.

4 Nature has left this tincture in the blood,
 That all men would be tyrants if they could.
 The Kentish Petition, addenda, 1.11

5 I was born in the year 1632, in the city of York, of a
 good family, though not of that county, my father
 being a foreigner of Bremen, who settled first at Hull.
 The Life and Adventures of Robinson Crusoe, pt.i

6 Robin, Robin, Robin Crusoe, poor Robin Crusoe!
 Where are you, Robin Crusoe? Where are you? Where
 have you been? [The parrot.]

7 It happened one day, about noon, going towards my
 boat, I was exceedingly surprised with the print of a
 man's naked foot on the shore, which was very plain to
 be seen in the sand. I stood like one thunderstruck, or
 as if I had seen an apparition.

8 I takes my man Friday with me.

9 In trouble to be troubl'd
 Is to have your trouble doubl'd.
 Robinson Crusoe, The Farther Adventures

10 Necessity makes an honest man a knave.
 Serious Reflections of Robinson Crusoe, ch.2

11 Wherever God erects a house of prayer,
 The Devil always builds a chapel there;
 And 'twill be found, upon examination,
 The latter has the largest congregation.
 The True-Born Englishman, pt.i, 1.1. See 32:14

12 From this amphibious ill-born mob began
 That vain, ill-natur'd thing, an Englishman.
 1.132

13 Your Roman-Saxon-Danish-Norman English.
 1.139

14 Great families of yesterday we show,
 And lords whose parents were the Lord knows who.
 1.374

15 And of all plagues with which mankind are curst,
 Ecclesiastic tyranny's the worst.
 pt.ii, 1.299

16 When kings the sword of justice first lay down,
 They are no kings, though they possess the crown.
 Titles are shadows, crowns are empty things,
 The good of subjects is the end of kings.
 1.313

CHARLES DE GAULLE 1890–1970

17 *On ne peut rassembler les français que sous le coup de
 la peur. On ne peut pas rassembler à froid un pays qui
 compte 265 spécialités de fromages.*
 The French will only be united under the threat of
 danger. Nobody can simply bring together a country
 that has 265 kinds of cheese.
 Speech after the *recul* of the R.P.P. at the elections of 1951

THOMAS DEKKER 1570?–1641?

18 That great fishpond (the sea).
 The Honest Whore, pt.i.I.ii

19   The best of men
 That e'er wore earth about him, was a sufferer,
 A soft, meek, patient, humble, tranquil spirit,
 The first true gentleman that ever breath'd.

20 Art thou poor, yet hast thou golden slumbers?
         Oh sweet content!
 Art thou rich, yet is thy mind perplexed?
         Oh, punishment!
 Dost thou laugh to see how fools are vexed
 To add to golden numbers, golden numbers?
 O, sweet content, O, sweet, O, sweet content!
         Work apace, apace, apace, apace;
         Honest labour bears a lovely face;
 Then hey nonny, nonny; hey nonny, nonny.
 Patient Grissil, Act I

21 Canst drink the waters of the crisped spring?
         O sweet content!
 Swim'st thou in wealth, yet sink'st in thine own tears?
         O punishment!

22 Golden slumbers kiss your eyes,
 Smiles awake you when you rise:
 Sleep, pretty wantons, do not cry,
 And I will sing a lullaby:
 Rock them, rock them, lullaby.
 IV.ii

WALTER DE LA MARE 1873–1956

23 Ann, Ann!
     Come! quick as you can!
 There's a fish that *talks*
     In the frying-pan.
 Alas, Alack

24 Oh, no man knows
 Through what wild centuries
 Roves back the rose.
 All That's Past

25 Very old are we men;
 Our dreams are tales
 Told in dim Eden
 By Eve's nightingales;
 We wake and whisper awhile,
 But, the day gone by,
 Silence and sleep like fields
 Of amaranth lie.

26 He is crazed with the spell of far Arabia,
 They have stolen his wits away.
 Arabia

27 Here lies a most beautiful lady,
     Light of step and heart was she;
 I think she was the most beautiful lady
     That ever was in the West Country.
 But beauty vanishes; beauty passes;
     However rare—rare it be;
 And when I crumble, who will remember
     This lady of the West Country?
 Epitaph

1 When I lie where shades of darkness
Shall no more assail mine eyes.
Fare Well, i

2 Memory fades, must the remembered
Perishing be?

3 Look thy last on all things lovely,
Every hour—let no night
Seal thy sense in deathly slumber
Till to delight
Thou have paid thy utmost blessing;
Since that all things thou wouldst praise
Beauty took from those who loved them
In other days.
iii

4 In Hans' old Mill his three black cats
Watch the bins for the thieving rats.
Whisker and claw, they crouch in the night,
Their five eyes smouldering green and bright:...
Jekkel, and Jessup, and one-eyed Jill.
Five Eyes

5 Nought but vast sorrow was there—
The sweet cheat gone.
The Ghost

6 Three jolly gentlemen,
In coats of red,
Rode their horses
Up to bed.
The Huntsmen

7 'Is there anybody there?' said the traveller,
Knocking on the moonlit door.
The Listeners

8 'Tell them I came, and no one answered,
That I kept my word,' he said.

9 Never the least stir made the listeners.

10 Ay, they heard his foot upon the stirrup,
And the sound of iron on stone,
And how the silence surged softly backward,
When the plunging hoofs were gone.

11 It's a very odd thing—
As odd as can be—
That whatever Miss T eats
Turns into Miss T.
Miss T

12 What is the world, O soldiers?
It is I:
I, this incessant snow,
This northern sky;
Soldiers, this solitude
Through which we go
Is I.
Napoleon

13 And there, in the moonlight, dark with dew,
Asking not wherefore nor why,
Would brood like a ghost, and as still as a post,
Old Nicholas Nye.
Nicholas Nye

14 Three jolly Farmers
Once bet a pound
Each dance the others would
Off the ground.
Off the Ground

15 And still would remain

My wit to try—
My worn reeds broken,
The dark tarn dry,
All words forgotten—
Thou, Lord, and I.
The Scribe

16 Slowly, silently, now the moon
Walks the night in her silver shoon.
Silver

17 Of all the trees in England,
Oak, Elder, Elm, and Thorn,
The Yew alone burns lamps of peace
For them that lie forlorn.
Trees

18 Of all the trees in England,
Her sweet three corners in,
Only the Ash, the bonnie Ash
Burns fierce while it is green.

DEMETRIUS THE CYNIC 1st cent. A.D.

19 *...si sociale animal et in commune genitus mundum ut
unam omnium domum spectat...*
...if [man], being a social animal and created for a
communal existence, regards the world as the one and
only home for everyone...
One of the prerequisites for a balanced stoical philosophy. Seneca,
De Beneficiis, VII.i.7

SIR JOHN DENHAM 1615–1669

20 Youth, what man's age is like to be doth show;
We may our ends by our beginnings know.
Of Prudence, l.225

21 Such is our pride, our folly, or our fate,
That few, but such as cannot write, translate.
To Richard Fanshaw (c. 1643, first printed 1648)

LORD DENMAN 1779–1854

22 Trial by jury itself, instead of being a security to
persons who are accused, will be a delusion, a
mockery, and a snare.
Judgement in O'Connell v. the Queen, 4 Sept. 1844

C.J. DENNIS 1876–1938

23 Me name is Mud.
The Sentimental Bloke: A Spring Song, st.2 (1916)

JOHN DENNIS 1657–1734

24 A man who could make so vile a pun would not
scruple to pick a pocket.
The Gentleman's Magazine (1781), p.324 (Edit. note)

25 Damn them! They will not let my play run, but they
steal my thunder!
W.S. Walsh, *Handy-book of Literary Curiosities*

THOMAS DE QUINCEY 1785–1859

26 The burden of the incommunicable.
Confessions of an English Opium Eater, pt.i

27 So, then, Oxford Street, stony-hearted stepmother,
thou that listenest to the sighs of orphans, and drinkest
the tears of children, at length I was dismissed from
thee.

1 It was a Sunday afternoon, wet and cheerless: and a duller spectacle this earth of ours has not to show than a rainy Sunday in London.
pt.ii, **The Pleasures of Opium**

2 Thou hast the keys of Paradise, oh just, subtle, and mighty opium!

3 Everlasting farewells! and again, and yet again reverberated—everlasting farewells!
pt.iii, **The Pains of Opium**

4 Murder Considered as One of the Fine Arts.
Essay

5 If once a man indulges himself in murder, very soon he comes to think little of robbing; and from robbing he comes next to drinking and sabbath-breaking, and from that to incivility and procrastination.
Supplementary Papers

6 There is first the literature of *knowledge*, and secondly, the literature of *power*.
Essays on the Poets; Pope

7 Books, we are told, propose to *instruct* or to *amuse*. Indeed!...The true antithesis to knowledge, in this case, is not *pleasure*, but *power*. All that is literature seeks to communicate power; all that is not literature, to communicate knowledge.
Letters to a Young Man, letter iii. De Quincey adds that he is indebted for this distinction to 'many years' conversation with Mr. Wordsworth'.

EDWARD STANLEY, EARL OF DERBY 1799–1869

8 When I first came into Parliament, Mr Tierney, a great Whig authority, used always to say that the duty of an Opposition was very simple—it was, to oppose everything, and propose nothing.
House of Commons, 4 June 1841

9 The foreign policy of the noble Earl [Russell]...may be summed up in two short homely but expressive words:—'meddle and muddle'.
Speech on the Address, House of Lords, 4 Feb. 1864

DESCARTES 1596–1650

10 *Cogito, ergo sum.*
I think, therefore I am.
Le Discours de la Méthode

11 *Le bon sens est la chose du monde la mieux partagée, car chacun pense en être bien pourvu.*
Common sense is the best distributed commodity in the world, for every man is convinced that he is well supplied with it.

12 *Repugnare ut detur vacuum sive in quo nulla plane sit res.*
[That] it is contrary to reason to say that there is a vacuum or space in which there is absolutely nothing.
Principia Philosophica, pt.II, xvi, tr. E.S. Haldane and G.R.T. Ross

CAMILLE DESMOULINS 1760–1794

13 My age is that of the *bon Sansculotte Jésus*; an age fatal to Revolutionists.
Answer at his trial. Carlyle, *French Revolution*, bk.vi, ch.2

PHILIPPE NÉRICAULT called DESTOUCHES 1680–1754

14 *Les absents ont toujours tort.*
The absent are always in the wrong.
L'Obstacle imprévu, I.vi

EDWARD DE VERE, EARL OF OXFORD
see OXFORD

ROBERT DEVEREUX, EARL OF ESSEX
see ESSEX

SERGE DIAGHILEV 1872–1929

15 *Étonne-moi.*
Said to Jean Cocteau who was questioning his lack of praise and encouragement in 1912. Cocteau continues, 'In 1917, the evening of the première of *Parade*, I surprised him'.
The Journals of Jean Cocteau, 1

CHARLES DIBDIN 1745–1814

16 Did you ever hear of Captain Wattle?
He was all for love and a little for the bottle.
Captain Wattle and Miss Roe

17 For a soldier I listed, to grow great in fame,
And be shot at for sixpence a-day.
Charity

18 In every mess I finds a friend,
In every port a wife.
Jack in his Element

19 What argufies sniv'ling and piping your eye?
Poor Jack

20 But the standing toast that pleased the most
Was—The wind that blows, the ship that goes,
And the lass that loves a sailor!
The Round Robin

21 Here, a sheer hulk, lies poor Tom Bowling,
The darling of our crew.
Tom Bowling

22 Faithful, below, he did his duty;
But now he's gone aloft.

THOMAS DIBDIN 1771–1841

23 Oh! what a snug little Island,
A right little, tight little Island!
The Snug Little Island

CHARLES DICKENS 1812–1870

BARNABY RUDGE

24 Rather a tough customer in argeyment, Joe, if anybody was to try and tackle him. [Parkes.]
ch.1

25 Something will come of this. I hope it mayn't be human gore. [Simon Tappertit.]
ch.4

26 Polly put the kettle on, we'll all have tea. [Grip.]
ch.17

27 'There are strings,' said Mr Tappertit, '...in the human

heart that had better not be wibrated.'
ch.22

1 Oh gracious, why wasn't I born old and ugly? [Miss Miggs.]
ch.70

BLEAK HOUSE

2 Jarndyce and Jarndyce still drags its dreary length before the Court, perennially hopeless.
ch.1

3 This is a London particular...A fog, miss.
ch.3

4 Educating the natives of Borrioboola-Gha, on the left bank of the Niger. [Mrs. Jellyby.]
ch.4

5 The wind's in the east...I am always conscious of an uncomfortable sensation now and then when the wind is blowing in the east. [Mr. Jarndyce.]
ch.6

6 I only ask to be free. The butterflies are free. Mankind will surely not deny to Harold Skimpole what it concedes to the butterflies!

7 'Not to put too fine a point upon it'—a favourite apology for plain-speaking with Mr Snagsby.
ch.11

8 He wos wery good to me, he wos! [Jo.]

9 He [Mr. Turveydrop] is celebrated, almost everywhere, for his Deportment. [Caddy.]
ch.14

10 'It was a maxim of Captain Swosser's', said Mrs Badger, 'speaking in his figurative naval manner, that when you make pitch hot, you cannot make it too hot; and that if you only have to swab a plank, you should swab it as if Davy Jones were after you.'
ch.17

11 The Professor made the same remark, Miss Summerson, in his last illness; when (his mind wandering) he insisted on keeping his little hammer under the pillow, and chipping at the countenances of the attendants. The ruling passion! [Mrs. Badger.]
See 377:13

12 What is peace? Is it war? No. Is it strife? No. [Mr. Chadband.]
ch.19

13 The Chadband style of oratory is widely received and much admired.

14 You are a human boy, my young friend. A human boy. O glorious to be a human boy!...
   O running stream of sparkling joy
   To be a soaring human boy! [Mr. Chadband.]

15 Jobling, there *are* chords in the human mind. [Guppy.]
ch.20

16 'It is,' says Chadband, 'the ray of rays, the sun of suns, the moon of moons, the star of stars. It is the light of Terewth.'
ch.25

17 Lo, the city is barren, I have seen but an eel.

18 It's my old girl that advises. She has the head. But I never own to it before her. Discipline must be

maintained. [Mr. Bagnet.]
ch.27

19 It is a melancholy truth that even great men have their poor relations.
ch.28

20 Never have a mission, my dear child. [Mr. Jellyby.]
ch.30

21 England has been in a dreadful state for some weeks. Lord Coodle would go out, and Sir Thomas Doodle wouldn't come in, and there being nobody in Great Britain (to speak of) except Coodle and Doodle, there has been no Government.
ch.40

22 She's Colour-Sergeant of the Nonpareil battalion. [Mr. Bagnet.]
ch.52

THE CHIMES

23 O let us love our occupations,
Bless the squire and his relations,
Live upon our daily rations,
And always know our proper stations.
2nd Quarter

A CHRISTMAS CAROL

24 'God bless us every one!' said Tiny Tim, the last of all.
stave 3

25 It *was* a turkey! He could never have stood upon his legs, that bird. He would have snapped 'em off short in a minute, like sticks of sealing-wax.
stave 5

DAVID COPPERFIELD

26 'Somebody's sharp.' 'Who is?' asked the gentleman, laughing. I looked up quickly; being curious to know. 'Only Brooks of Sheffield,' said Mr Murdstone. I was relieved to find that it was only Brooks of Sheffield; for, at first, I really thought it was I.
ch.2

27 'I am a lone lorn creetur',' were Mrs Gummidge's words,...'and everythink goes contrairy with me.'
ch.3

28 'I feel it more than other people,' said Mrs Gummidge.

29 I'd better go into the house, and die and be a riddance! [Mrs. Gummidge.]

30 She's been thinking of the old 'un! [Mr. Peggotty, of Mrs. Gummidge.]

31 Barkis is willin'.
ch.5

32 'There was a gentleman here yesterday,' he said—'a stout gentleman, by the name of Topsawyer...he came in here,...ordered a glass of this ale—*would* order it—I told him not—drank it, and fell dead. It was too old for him. It oughtn't to be drawn; that's the fact.' [The Waiter.]

33 I live on broken wittles—and I sleep on the coals. [The Waiter.]

34 'When a man says he's willin',' said Mr Barkis,...'it's

as much as to say, that a man's waitin' for a answer.'
ch.8

1 Experientia does it—as papa used to say. [Mrs. Micawber.]
ch.11

2 I have known him [Micawber] come home to supper with a flood of tears, and a declaration that nothing was now left but a jail; and go to bed making a calculation of the expense of putting bow-windows to the house, 'in case anything turned up,' which was his favourite expression.

3 I never will desert Mr Micawber. [Mrs. Micawber.]
ch.12

4 Annual income twenty pounds, annual expenditure nineteen nineteen six, result happiness. Annual income twenty pounds, annual expenditure twenty pounds ought and six, result misery. [Mr. Micawber]

5 Mr Dick had been for upwards of ten years endeavouring to keep King Charles the First out of the Memorial; but he had been constantly getting into it, and was there now.
ch.14

6 I am well aware that I am the 'umblest person going....My mother is likewise a very 'umble person. We live in a numble abode. [Uriah Heep.]
ch.16

7 The mistake was made of putting some of the trouble out of King Charles's head into my head.
ch.17

8 We are so very 'umble. [Uriah Heep].

9 'Orses and dorgs is some men's fancy. They're wittles and drink to me—lodging, wife, and children—reading, writing and 'rithmetic—snuff, tobacker, and sleep.
ch.19

10 I only ask for information. [Miss Rosa Dartle.]
ch.20

11 'It was as true', said Mr Barkis, '...as taxes is. And nothing's truer than them.'
ch.21. See 218:18

12 What a world of gammon and spinnage it is, though, ain't it! [Miss Mowcher.]
ch.22

13 Other things are all very well in their way, but give me Blood! [Mr. Waterbrook.]
ch.25

14 I assure you she's the dearest girl. [Traddles.]
ch.27

15 Accidents will occur in the best-regulated families; and in families not regulated by that pervading influence which sanctifies while it enhances the—a—I would say, in short, by the influence of Woman, in the lofty character of Wife, they may be expected with confidence, and must be borne with philosophy. [Mr. Micawber.]
ch.28

16 He told me, only the other day, that it was provided for. That was Mr Micawber's expression, 'Provided for.' [Traddles.]

17 'People can't die, along the coast,' said Mr Peggotty, 'except when the tide's pretty nigh out. They can't be born, unless it's pretty nigh in—not properly born, till

flood. He's a going out with the tide.'
ch.30

18 Mrs Crupp had indignantly assured him that there wasn't room to swing a cat there; but, as Mr Dick justly observed to me, sitting down on the foot of the bed, nursing his leg, 'You know, Trotwood, I don't want to swing a cat. I never do swing a cat. Therefore, what does that signify to *me*!'
ch.35

19 It's only my child-wife. [Dora.]
ch.44

20 Circumstances beyond my individual control. [Mr. Micawber.]
ch.49

21 I'm Gormed—and I can't say no fairer than that! [Mr. Peggotty.]
ch.63

DOMBEY AND SON

22 He's tough, ma'am, tough is J.B. Tough, and devilish sly! [Major Bagstock.]
ch.7

23 There was no light nonsense about Miss Blimber...She was dry and sandy with working in the graves of deceased languages. None of your live languages for Miss Blimber. They must be dead—stone dead—and then Miss Blimber dug them up like a Ghoul.
ch.11

24 As to Mr Feeder, B.A., Doctor Blimber's assistant, he was a kind of human barrel-organ, with a little list of tunes at which he was continually working, over and over again, without any variation.

25 If I could have known Cicero, and been his friend, and talked with him in his retirement at Tusculum (beautiful Tusculum), I could have died contented. [Mrs. Blimber.]

26 'Wal'r, my boy,' replied the Captain, 'in the Proverbs of Solomon you will find the following words, "May we never want a friend in need, nor a bottle to give him!" When found, make a note of.' [Captain Cuttle.]
ch.15

27 Train up a fig-tree in the way it should go, and when you are old sit under the shade of it. [Captain Cuttle.]
ch.19

28 Cows are my passion. [Mrs. Skewton.]
ch.21

29 Mr Toots devoted himself to the cultivation of those gentle arts which refine and humanize existence, his chief instructor in which was an interesting character called the Game Chicken, who was always to be heard of at the bar of the Black Badger, wore a shaggy white great-coat in the warmest weather, and knocked Mr Toots about the head three times a week.
ch.22

30 It's of no consequence. [Mr. Toots.]

31 The bearings of this observation lays in the application of it. [Bunsby.]
ch.23

32 Say, like those wicked Turks, there is no What's-his-name but Thingummy, and

What-you-may-call-it is his prophet! [Mrs. Skewton.]
ch.27

1 I positively adore Miss Dombey;—I—I am perfectly sore with loving her. [Mr. Toots.]
ch.30

2 If you could see my legs when I take my boots off, you'd form some idea of what unrequited affection is. [Mr. Toots.]
ch.48

EDWIN DROOD

3 Stranger, pause and ask thyself the question, Canst thou do likewise? If not, with a blush retire.
ch.4

4 'Dear me,' said Mr Grewgious, peeping in, 'it's like looking down the throat of Old Time.'
ch.9

5 'Umps', said Mr Grewgious.
ch.11

GREAT EXPECTATIONS

6 Much of my unassisted self...I struggled through the alphabet as if it had been a bramble-bush; getting considerably worried and scratched by every letter. After that, I fell among those thieves, the nine figures, who seemed every evening to do something new to disguise themselves and baffle recognition.
ch.7

7 Your sister is given to government. [Joe Gargery.]

8 'He calls the knaves, Jacks, this boy,' said Estella with disdain, before our first game was out.
ch.8

9 I had cherished a profound conviction that her bringing me up by hand, gave her no right to bring me up by jerks.

10 On the Rampage, Pip, and off the Rampage, Pip; such is Life! [Joe Gargery.]
ch.15

11 Get hold of portable property. [Wemmick.]
ch.24

12 You don't object to an aged parent, I hope? [Wemmick.]
ch.25

13 'Have you seen anything of London, yet?' [Herbert.] 'Why, yes: Sir—but we didn't find that it come up to its likeness in the red bills—it is there drawd too architectooralooral.' [Joe Gargery.]
ch.27

14 'Halloa! Here's a church!...Let's go in!...Here's Miss Skiffins! Let's have a wedding.' [Wemmick.]
ch.55

HARD TIMES

15 Now, what I want is, Facts...Facts alone are wanted in life. [Mr. Gradgrind.]
bk.i, ch.1

LITTLE DORRIT

16 Whatever was required to be done, the Circumlocution Office was beforehand with all the public departments

in the art of perceiving—HOW NOT TO DO IT.
bk.i, ch.10

17 Look here. Upon my soul you mustn't come into the place saying you want to know, you know. [Barnacle Junior.]

18 One remark...I wish to make, one explanation I wish to offer, when your Mama came and made a scene of it with my Papa and when I was called down into the little breakfast-room where they were looking at one another with your Mama's parasol between them seated on two chairs like mad bulls what was I to do? [Flora Finching.]
ch.13

19 The Great Fire of London was not the fire in which your Uncle George's workshops was burned down. [Mr. F.'s Aunt]

20 I hate a fool! [Mr. F.'s Aunt.]

21 Take a little time—count five-and-twenty, Tattycoram. [Mr. Meagles.]
ch.16

22 There's milestones on the Dover Road! [Mr. F.'s Aunt.]
ch.23

23 You can't make a head and brains out of a brass knob with nothing in it. You couldn't when your Uncle George was living; much less when he's dead. [Mr. F.'s Aunt.]

24 He [Mr. Finching] proposed seven times once in a hackney-coach once in a boat once in an pew once on a donkey at Tunbridge Wells and the rest on his knees. [Flora Finching.]
ch.24

25 I revere the memory of Mr F. as an estimable man and most indulgent husband, only necessary to mention Asparagus and it appeared or to hint at any little delicate thing to drink and it came like magic in a pint bottle it was not ecstasy but it was comfort. [Flora Finching.]

26 Father is rather vulgar, my dear. The word Papa, besides, gives a pretty form to the lips. Papa, potatoes, poultry, prunes, and prism, are all very good words for the lips: especially prunes and prism. [Mrs. General.]
bk.ii, ch.5

27 Dante—known to that gentleman [Mr. Sparkler] as an eccentric man in the nature of an Old File, who used to put leaves round his head, and sit upon a stool for some unaccountable purpose, outside the cathedral at Florence.
ch.6

28 Once a gentleman, and always a gentleman. [Rigaud.]
ch.28

MARTIN CHUZZLEWIT

29 The Lord No Zoo. [Toby Chuzzlewit.]
ch.1

30 'The name of those fabulous animals (pagan, I regret to say) who used to sing in the water, has quite escaped me.' Mr George Chuzzlewit suggested 'Swans.' 'No,' said Mr Pecksniff. 'Not swans. Very like swans, too. Thank you.' The nephew...propounded 'Oysters.' 'No,' said Mr

Pecksniff,...'nor oysters. But by no means unlike oysters; a very excellent idea; thank you, my dear sir, very much. Wait. Sirens! Dear me! sirens, of course.'
ch.4

1 Any man may be in good spirits and good temper when he's well dressed. There an't much credit in that. [Mark Tapley.]
ch.5

2 Some credit in being jolly. [Mark Tapley.]

3 A highly geological home-made cake.

4 'Let us be merry.' Here he took a captain's biscuit. [Mr. Pecksniff.]

5 With affection beaming in one eye, and calculation shining out of the other. [Mrs. Todgers.]
ch.8

6 Charity and Mercy. Not unholy names, I hope? [Mr. Pecksniff.]
ch.9

7 'Do not repine, my friends,' said Mr Pecksniff, tenderly. 'Do not weep for me. It is chronic.'

8 Let us be moral. Let us contemplate existence. [Mr. Pecksniff.]

9 Here's the rule for bargains: 'Do other men, for they would do you.' That's the true business precept. [Jonas Chuzzlewit.]
ch.11

10 'Mrs Harris,' I says, 'leave the bottle on the chimley-piece, and don't ask me to take none, but let me put my lips to it when I am so dispoged.' [Mrs. Gamp.]
ch.19

11 Some people...may be Rooshans, and others may be Prooshans; they are born so, and will please themselves. Them which is of other naturs thinks different. [Mrs. Gamp.]

12 Therefore I *do* require it, which I makes confession, to be brought reg'lar and draw'd mild. [Mrs. Gamp.]
ch.25

13 'She's the sort of woman now,' said Mould,...'one would almost feel disposed to bury for nothing: and do it neatly, too!'

14 He'd make a lovely corpse. [Mrs. Gamp.]

15 All the wickedness of the world is print to him. [Mrs. Gamp.]
ch.26

16 'Sairey,' says Mrs Harris, 'sech is life. Vich likeways is the hend of all things!' [Mrs. Gamp.]
ch.29

17 We never knows wot's hidden in each other's hearts; and if we had glass winders there, we'd need keep the shutters up, some on us, I do assure you! [Mrs Gamp.]

18 Our backs is easy ris. We must be cracked-up, or they rises, and we snarls...You'd better crack up, you had! [Chollop.]
ch.33

19 Our fellow-countryman is a model of a man, quite fresh from Natur's mould!...Rough he may be. So air our Barrs. Wild he may be. So air our Buffalers. [Pogram.]
ch.34

20 A lane was made; and Mrs Hominy, with the aristocratic stalk, the pocket handkerchief, the clasped hands, and the classical cap, came slowly up it, in a procession of one.

21 'To be presented to a Pogram,' said Miss Codger, 'by a Hominy, indeed, a thrilling moment is it in its impressiveness on what we call our feelings.'

22 'Mind and matter,' said the lady in the wig, 'glide swift into the vortex of immensity. Howls the sublime, and softly sleeps the calm Ideal, in the whispering chambers of Imagination.'

23 'The Ankworks package,'...'I wish it was in Jonadge's belly, I do,' cried Mrs Gamp; appearing to confound the prophet with the whale in this miraculous aspiration.
ch.40

24 Oh Sairey, Sairey, little do we know wot lays afore us! [Mrs. Gamp.]

25 I know'd she wouldn't have a cowcumber! [Betsey Prig.]
ch.49

26 'Who deniges of it?' Mrs Gamp enquired.

27 Ever since afore her First, which Mr Harris who was dreadful timid went and stopped his ears in a empty dog-kennel, and never took his hands away or come out once till he was showed the baby, wen bein' took with fits, the doctor collared him and laid him on his back upon the airy stones, and she was told to ease her mind, his owls was organs. [Mrs. Gamp.]

28 No, Betsey! Drink fair, wotever you do! [Mrs. Gamp.]

29 'Bother Mrs Harris!' said Betsey Prig....'I don't believe there's no sich a person!'

30 The words she spoke of Mrs Harris, lambs could not forgive...nor worms forget. [Mrs. Gamp.]

31 Which fiddle-strings is weakness to expredge my nerves this night! [Mrs. Gamp.]
ch.51

32 Farewell! Be the proud bride of a ducal coronet, and forget me!... Unalterably, never yours, Augustus. [Augustus Moddle.]
ch.54

NICHOLAS NICKLEBY

33 United Metropolitan Improved Hot Muffin and Crumpet Baking and Punctual Delivery Company.
ch.2

34 EDUCATION.—At Mr Wackford Squeers's Academy, Dotheboys Hall, at the delightful village of Dotheboys, near Greta Bridge in Yorkshire, Youth are boarded, clothed, booked, furnished with pocket-money, provided with all necessaries, instructed in all languages living and dead, mathematics, orthography, geometry, astronomy, trigonometry, the use of the globes, algebra, single stick (if required), writing, arithmetic, fortification, and every other branch of classical literature. Terms, twenty guineas per annum. No extras, no vacations, and diet unparalleled.
ch.3

35 He had but one eye, and the popular prejudice runs in

favour of two. [Mr. Squeers.]
ch.4

1 Serve it right for being so dear. [Mr. Squeers.]
ch.5

2 Subdue your appetites my dears, and you've conquered human natur. [Mr. Squeers.]

3 Here's richness! [Mr. Squeers.]

4 C-l-e-a-n, clean, verb active, to make bright, to scour. W-i-n, win, d-e-r, der, winder, a casement. When the boy knows this out of the book, he goes and does it. [Mr. Squeers.]
ch.8

5 As she frequently remarked when she made any such mistake, it would be all the same a hundred years hence. [Mrs. Squeers.]
ch.9

6 There are only two styles of portrait painting; the serious and the smirk. [Miss La Creevy.]
ch.10

7 Oh! they're too beautiful to live, much too beautiful! [Mrs. Kenwigs.]
ch.14

8 Sir, My pa requests me to write to you, the doctors considering it doubtful whether he will ever recuvver the use of his legs which prevents his holding a pen. [Fanny Squeers.]
ch.15

9 I am screaming out loud all the time I write and so is my brother which takes off my attention rather and I hope will excuse mistakes. [Fanny Squeers.]

10 I pity his ignorance and despise him. [Fanny Squeers.]

11 This is all very well, Mr Nickleby, and very proper, so far as it goes—so far as it goes, but it doesn't go far enough. [Mr. Gregsbury.]
ch.16

12 We've got a private master comes to teach us at home, but we ain't proud, because ma says it's sinful. [Mrs. Kenwigs.]

13 'What's the water in French, sir?' 'L'eau,' replied Nicholas. 'Ah!' said Mr Lillywick, shaking his head mournfully. 'I thought as much. Lo, eh? I don't think anything of that language—nothing at all.'

14 'It's very easy to talk,' said Mrs Mantalini. 'Not so easy when one is eating a demnition egg,' replied Mr Mantalini; 'for the yolk runs down the waistcoat, and yolk of egg does not match any waistcoat but a yellow waistcoat, demmit.'
ch.17

15 What's the demd total? [Mr Mantalini.]
ch.21

16 Language was not powerful enough to describe the infant phenomenon.
ch.23

17 'The unities, sir,...are a completeness—a kind of a universal dovetailedness with regard to place and time.' [Mr. Curdle.]
ch.24

18 She's the only sylph I ever saw, who could stand upon one leg, and play the tambourine on her other knee, like a sylph. [Mr. Crummles.]
ch.25

19 I am a demd villain! I will fill my pockets with change for a sovereign in half-pence and drown myself in the Thames...I will become a demd, damp, moist, unpleasant body! [Mr. Mantalini.]
ch.34

20 Bring in the bottled lightning, a clean tumbler, and a corkscrew. [The Gentleman in the Small-clothes.]
ch.49

21 All is gas and gaiters. [The Gentleman in the Small-clothes.]

22 My life is one demd horrid grind! [Mr. Mantalini.]
ch.64

23 He has gone to the demnition bow-wows. [Mr. Mantalini.]

THE OLD CURIOSITY SHOP

24 Is the old min agreeable? [Dick Swiveller.]
ch.2

25 What is the odds so long as the fire of soul is kindled at the taper of conwiviality, and the wing of friendship never moults a feather! [Dick Swiveller.]

26 Fan the sinking flame of hilarity with the wing of friendship; and pass the rosy wine. [Dick Swiveller.]
ch.7

27 Codlin's the friend, not Short. [Codlin.]
ch.19

28 If I know'd a donkey wot wouldn't go
To see Mrs Jarley's waxwork show,
Do you think I'd acknowledge him,
                              Oh no no!
ch.27

29 I never nursed a dear Gazelle, to glad me with its soft black eye, but when it came to know me well, and love me, it was sure to marry a market-gardener. [Dick Swiveller.]
ch.56. See 356:25

30 'Did you ever taste beer?' 'I had a sip of it once,' said the small servant. 'Here's a state of things!' cried Mr Swiveller....'She never tasted it—it can't be tasted in a sip!'
ch.57

31 It was a maxim with Foxey—our revered father, gentlemen—'Always suspect everybody.' [Sampson Brass.]
ch.66

OLIVER TWIST

32 Oliver Twist has asked for more! [Bumble.]
ch.2

33 Known by the sobriquet of 'The artful Dodger.'
ch.8

34 'Hard,' replied the Dodger. 'As nails,' added Charley Bates.
ch.9

35 There is a passion for hunting something deeply implanted in the human breast.
ch.10

36 I'll eat my head. [Mr. Grimwig.]
ch.14

37 I only know two sorts of boys. Mealy boys, and beef-faced boys. [Mr. Grimwig.]

1 Oh, Mrs Corney, what a prospect this opens! What a opportunity for a jining of hearts and house-keepings! [Bumble.]
ch.27

2 'If the law supposes that,' said Mr Bumble…'the law is a ass—a idiot.'
ch.51. See 140:12

OUR MUTUAL FRIEND

3 A literary man—*with* a wooden leg. [Mr. Boffin on Silas Wegg.]
bk.1, ch.5

4 Professionally he declines and falls, and as a friend he drops into poetry. [Mr. Boffin on Silas Wegg.]

5 Why then we should drop into poetry. [Boffin.]

6 Decline-and-Fall-Off-The-Rooshan-Empire. [Mr. Boffin.]

7 'Mrs Boffin, Wegg,' said Boffin, 'is a highflyer at Fashion.'

8 Meaty jelly, too, especially when a little salt, which is the case when there's ham, is mellering to the organ. [Silas Wegg.]

9 'It is Rooshan; ain't it, Wegg?'
'No, sir. Roman. Roman.'
'What's the difference, Wegg?'
'The difference, sir?—There you place me in a difficulty, Mr Boffin. Suffice it to observe, that the difference is best postponed to some other occasion when Mrs Boffin does not honour us with her company.'

10 Mr Podsnap settled that whatever he put behind him he put out of existence.…Mr Podsnap had even acquired a peculiar flourish of his right arm in often clearing the world of its most difficult problems, by sweeping them behind him.
ch.11

11 The question [with Mr. Podsnap] about everything was, would it bring a blush into the cheek of the young person?

12 'This Island was Blest, Sir, to the Direct Exclusion of such Other Countries as—as there may happen to be. And if we were all Englishmen present, I would say,' added Mr Podsnap…'that there is in the Englishman a combination of qualities, a modesty, an independence, a responsibility, a repose, combined with an absence of everything calculated to call a blush into the cheek of a young person, which one would seek in vain among the Nations of the Earth.'

13 I think…that it is the best club in London. [Mr. Twemlow, on the House of Commons.]
bk.ii, ch.3

14 I don't care whether I am a Minx, or a Sphinx. [Lavvy.]
ch.8

15 A slap-up gal in a bang-up chariot.

16 O Mrs Higden, Mrs Higden, you was a woman and a mother, and a mangler in a million million. [Sloppy.]
bk.iii, ch.9

17 He'd be sharper than a serpent's tooth, if he wasn't as dull as ditch water. [Fanny Cleaver.]
ch.10

18 T'other governor. [Mr Riderhood.]
bk.iv, ch.1

19 I want to be something so much worthier than the doll in the doll's house. [Bella.]
ch.5

20 The dodgerest of the dodgers. [Mr. Fledgeby.]
ch.8

21 The Golden Dustman.
ch.11

PICKWICK PAPERS

22 He had used the word in its Pickwickian sense…He had merely considered him a humbug in a Pickwickian point of view. [Mr Blotton.]
ch.1

23 Heads, heads…!…five children—mother—tall lady, eating sandwiches—forgot the arch—crash—knock—children look round—mother's head off—sandwich in her hand—no mouth to put it in—head of a family off—shocking, shocking! [Jingle.]
ch.2

24 'I am ruminating,' said Mr Pickwick, 'on the strange mutability of human affairs.'
'Ah, I see—in at the palace door one day, out at the window the next. Philosopher, sir?'
'An observer of human nature, sir,' said Mr Pickwick.

25 Half-a-crown in the bill, if you look at the waiter.—Charge you more if you dine at a friend's than they would if you dined in the coffee-room. [Jingle.]

26 Not presume to dictate, but broiled fowl and mushrooms—capital thing! [Jingle.]

27 Kent, sir—everybody knows Kent—apples, cherries, hops, and women. [Jingle.]

28 'It wasn't the wine,' murmured Mr Snodgrass, in a broken voice, 'It was the salmon.'
ch.8

29 I wants to make your flesh creep. [The Fat Boy.]

30 'It's always best on these occasions to do what the mob do.' 'But suppose there are two mobs?' suggested Mr Snodgrass. 'Shout with the largest,' replied Mr Pickwick.
ch.13

31 'Can I unmoved see thee dying
      On a log,
      Expiring frog!' [Mrs. Leo Hunter.]
ch.15

32 'Sir,' said Mr Tupman, 'you're a fellow.' 'Sir,' said Mr Pickwick, 'you're another!'

33 Tongue; well that's a wery good thing when it an't a woman's. [Mr Weller.]
ch.19

34 Battledore and shuttlecock's a wery good game, when you an't the shuttlecock and two lawyers the battledores, in which case it gets too excitin' to be pleasant.
ch.20

35 Mr Weller's knowledge of London was extensive and peculiar.

36 Be wery careful o' vidders all your life. [Mr. Weller.]

1 The wictim o' connubiality, as Blue Beard's domestic chaplain said, with a tear of pity, ven he buried him. [Mr. Weller.]

2 'It's a wery remarkable circumstance, sir,' said Sam, 'that poverty and oysters always seem to go together.' ch.22

3 It's over, and can't be helped, and that's one consolation, as they always says in Turkey, ven they cuts the wrong man's head off. [Sam Weller.] ch.23

4 Dumb as a drum vith a hole in it, sir. [Sam Weller.] ch.25

5 Wery glad to see you, indeed, and hope our acquaintance may be a long 'un, as the gen'l'm'n said to the fi'pun' note. [Sam Weller.]

6 Our noble society for providing the infant negroes in the West Indies with flannel waistcoats and moral pocket handkerchiefs. ch.27

7 Wen you're a married man, Samivel, you'll understand a good many things as you don't understand now; but vether it's worth while goin' through so much to learn so little, as the charity-boy said ven he got to the end of the alphabet, is a matter o' taste. [Mr. Weller.]

8 'Eccentricities of genius, Sam,' said Mr Pickwick. ch.30

9 Keep yourself *to* yourself. [Mr. Raddle.] ch.32

10 Pursuit of knowledge under difficulties, Sammy? [Mr. Weller.] ch.33

11 A double glass o' the inwariable, [Mr. Weller.]

12 Poetry's unnat'ral; no man ever talked poetry 'cept a beadle on boxin' day, or Warren's blackin' or Rowland's oil, or some o' them low fellows. [Mr. Weller.]

13 Wot's the good o' callin' a young 'ooman a Wenus or a angel, Sammy? [Mr. Weller.]

14 'That's rather a sudden pull up, ain't it, Sammy?' inquired Mr Weller.
'Not a bit on it,' said Sam; 'she'll vish there wos more, and that's the great art o' letter writin'.'

15 If your governor don't prove a alleybi, he'll be what the Italians call reg'larly flummoxed. [Mr. Weller.]

16 She's a swellin' wisibly before my wery eyes. [Mr. Weller.]

17 It's my opinion, sir, that this meeting is drunk, sir! [Mr. Stiggins.]

18 A Being, erect upon two legs, and bearing all the outward semblance of a man, and not of a monster. [Buzfuz.] ch.34

19 Chops and Tomata sauce. Yours, Pickwick.

20 'Do you spell it with a "V" or a "W"?' inquired the judge.
'That depends upon the taste and fancy of the speller, my Lord,' replied Sam.

21 Put it down a we, my Lord, put it down a we. [Mr. Weller.]

22 'Little to do, and plenty to get, I suppose?' said Sergeant Buzfuz, with jocularity.
'Oh, quite enough to get, sir, as the soldier said ven they ordered him three hundred and fifty lashes,' replied Sam.
'You must not tell us what the soldier, or any other man, said, sir,' interposed the judge; 'it's not evidence.'

23 'Yes, I have a pair of eyes,' replied Sam, 'and that's just it. If they wos a pair o' patent double million magnifyin' gas microscopes of hextra power, p'raps I might be able to see through a flight o' stairs and a deal door; but bein' only eyes, you see my wision's limited.'

24 Oh Sammy, Sammy, vy worn't there a alleybi! [Mr. Weller.]

25 Miss Bolo rose from the table considerably agitated, and went straight home, in a flood of tears and a Sedan chair. ch.35

26 A friendly swarry, consisting of a boiled leg of mutton with the usual trimmings. ch.37

27 'That 'ere young lady,' replied Sam. 'She knows wot's wot, she does.'

28 *We* know, Mr Weller—we, who are men of the world—that a good uniform must work its way with the women, sooner or later. [The Gentleman in Blue.]

29 You're a amiably-disposed young man, sir, I don't think. [Sam Weller.] ch.38

30 'And a bird-cage, sir,' says Sam. 'Veels vithin veels, a prison in a prison.' ch.40

31 'It would make anyone go to sleep, that bedstead would, whether they wanted to or not.' [Mr. Roker.]
'I should think,' said Sam,…'poppies was nothing to it.' ch.41

32 *They* don't mind it; it's a regular holiday to them—all porter and skittles. [Sam Weller.]

33 The have-his-carcase, next to the perpetual motion, is vun of the blessedest things as was ever made. [Sam Weller.] ch.43

34 Anythin' for a quiet life, as the man said wen he took the sitivation at the lighthouse. [Sam Weller.]

35 Wich puts me in mind o' the man as killed hisself on principle, wich o' course you've heerd on, sir. [Sam Weller.] ch.44

36 Which is your partickler wanity? Vich wanity do you like the flavour on best, sir? [Sam Weller.] ch.45

37 You've got the key of the street, my friend. [Lowten.] ch.47

38 'Never…see…a dead postboy, did you?' inquired Sam…'No,' rejoined Bob, 'I never did.' 'No!' rejoined Sam triumphantly. 'Nor never vill; and there's another thing that no man never see, and that's

a dead donkey.'
ch.51

1 'Vell, gov'ner, ve must all come to it, one day or another.'
'So we must, Sammy,' said Mr Weller the elder.
'There's a Providence in it all,' said Sam.
'O' course there is,' replied his father with a nod of grave approval. 'Wot 'ud become of the undertakers vithout it, Sammy?'
ch.52

2 ''Cos a coachman's a privileged indiwidual,' replied Mr Weller, looking fixedly at his son. ''Cos a coachman may do vithout suspicion wot other men may not; 'cos a coachman may be on the wery amicablest terms with eighty mile o' females, and yet nobody think that he ever means to marry any vun among them.'

SKETCHES BY BOZ

3 A smattering of everything, and a knowledge of nothing. [Minerva House.]
Tales, ch.3. **Sentiment**

4 Grief never mended no broken bones, and as good people's wery scarce, what I says is, make the most on 'em.
Scenes, ch.22. **Gin-Shops**

A TALE OF TWO CITIES

5 It was the best of times, it was the worst of times, it was the age of wisdom, it was the age of foolishness, it was the epoch of belief, it was the epoch of incredulity, it was the season of Light, it was the season of Darkness, it was the spring of hope, it was the winter of despair, we had everything before us, we had nothing before us, we were all going direct to Heaven, we were all going direct the other way.
bk.i, ch.1

6 I pass my whole life, miss, in turning an immense pecuniary Mangle. [Mr. Lorry.]
ch.4

7 A likely thing...If it was ever intended that I should go across salt water, do you suppose Providence would have cast my lot in an island? [Miss Pross.]

8 If you must go flopping yourself down, flop in favour of your husband and child, and not in opposition to 'em. [Jerry Cruncher.]
bk.ii, ch.1

9 'I tell thee,' said madame—'that although it is a long time on the road, it is on the road and coming. I tell thee it never retreats, and never stops.' [Mme Defarge.]
ch.16

10 'It is possible—that it may not come, during our lives...We shall not see the triumph.' [Defarge.]
'We shall have helped it,' returned madame.

11 There might be medical doctors...a cocking their medical eyes. [Jerry Cruncher.]
bk.iii, ch.9

12 It is a far, far better thing that I do, than I have ever done; it is a far, far better rest that I go to, than I have ever known. [Sydney Carton's thoughts on the scaffold.]
ch.15

EMILY DICKINSON 1830–1886

13 After great pain, a formal feeling comes—
The Nerves sit ceremonious, like Tombs—
The stiff Heart questions was it He, that bore,
And Yesterday, or Centuries before?
After great pain, a formal feeling comes

14 This is the Hour of Lead—
Remembered, if outlived,
As Freezing persons, recollect the Snow—
First—Chill—then Stupor—then the letting go.

15 Because I could not stop for Death—
He kindly stopped for me—
The Carriage held but just Ourselves—
And Immortality.
Because I could not stop for Death

16 Since then—'tis Centuries—and yet
Feels shorter than the Day
I first surmised the Horses Heads
Were toward Eternity.

17 The Bustle in a House
The Morning after Death
Is solemnest of industries
Enacted upon Earth—

The Sweeping up the Heart
And putting love away
We shall not want to use again
Until Eternity.
The Bustle in a House

18 What fortitude the Soul contains,
That it can so endure
The accent of a coming Foot—
The opening of a Door.
Elysium is as far as to

19 I heard a Fly buzz—when I died...
With Blue—uncertain stumbling Buzz—
Between the light—and me—
And then the Windows failed—and then
I could not see to see.
I heard a Fly buzz—when I died

20 My life closed twice before its close;
It yet remains to see
If Immortality unveil
A third event to me,

So huge, so hopeless to conceive
As these that twice befel.
Parting is all we know of heaven
And all we need of hell.
My life closed twice before its close

21 The Soul selects her own Society—
Then—shuts the Door—
To her divine Majority—
Present no more.
The Soul selects her own Society

22 I've known her—from an ample nation—
Choose One—
Then—close the Valves of her attention—
Like Stone.

23 Success is counted sweetest
By those who ne'er succeed.
To comprehend a nectar
Requires sorest need.
Success is counted sweetest

1 There's a certain Slant of light,
Winter Afternoons—
That oppresses like the Heft
Of Cathedral Tunes—

Heavenly Hurt, it gives us—
We can find no scar,
But internal difference,
Where the Meanings, are.
There's a certain Slant of light

2 This quiet Dust was Gentlemen and Ladies
           And Lads and Girls—
Was laughter and ability and Sighing,
           And Frocks and Curls.
This quiet Dust was Gentlemen and Ladies

3 What Soft—Cherubic Creatures—
These Gentlewomen are—
One would as soon assault a Plush—
Or violate a Star—

Such Dimity Convictions—
A Horror so refined
Of freckled Human Nature—
Of Deity—ashamed.
What Soft—Cherubic Creatures

JOHN DICKINSON 1732–1808

4 Our cause is just. Our union is perfect.
Declaration on Taking Up Arms in 1775

5 Then join hand in hand, brave Americans all,—
By uniting we stand, by dividing we fall.
The Liberty Song (1768). *Memoirs of the Historical Soc. of Pennsylvania*, vol.xiv

DENIS DIDEROT 1713–1784

6 *L'esprit de l'escalier.*
Staircase wit.
An untranslatable phrase, the meaning of which is that one only thinks on one's way downstairs of the smart retort one might have made in the drawing-room. ***Paradoxe sur le Comédien***

7 *Voyez-vous cet oeuf. C'est avec cela qu'on renverse toutes les écoles de théologie, et tous les temples de la terre.*
See this egg. It is with this that all the schools of theology and all the temples of the earth are to be overturned.
Le Rêve de d'Alembert, pt.i

WENTWORTH DILLON, EARL OF ROSCOMMON
see ROSCOMMON

DIOGENES c.400–c.325 B.C.

8 "μικρόν", εἶπεν, "ἀπὸ τοῦ ἡλίου μετάστηθι."
Alexander...asked him if he lacked anything. 'Yea,' said he, 'that I do: that you stand out of my sun a little.'
Plutarch, *Life of Alexander*, 14 (North's translation)

DIONYSIUS OF HALICARNASSUS fl. 30–7 B.C.

9 History is philosophy from examples.
Ars Rhetorica, xi.2

BENJAMIN DISRAELI 1804–1881

10 Though I sit down now, the time will come when you will hear me.
Maiden speech, 7 Dec. 1837. Meynell, *Disraeli*, i.43

11 The Continent will not suffer England to be the workshop of the world.
House of Commons, 15 Mar. 1838

12 Thus you have a starving population, an absentee aristocracy, and an alien Church, and in addition the weakest executive in the world. That is the Irish Question.
16 Feb. 1844

13 The noble Lord [Lord Stanley] is the Rupert of Parliamentary discussion.
24 Apr. 1844. See 107:2

14 The right hon Gentleman [Sir Robert Peel] caught the Whigs bathing, and walked away with their clothes.
28 Feb. 1845

15 Protection is not a principle, but an expedient.
17 Mar. 1845

16 A Conservative Government is an organized hypocrisy.

17 He traces the steam-engine always back to the tea-kettle.
11 Apr. 1845

18 Justice is truth in action.
11 Feb. 1851

19 I read this morning an awful, though monotonous, manifesto in the great organ of public opinion, which always makes me tremble: Olympian bolts; and yet I could not help fancying amid their rumbling terrors I heard the plaintive treble of the Treasury Bench.
13 Feb. 1851

20 He [Sir C. Wood] has to learn that petulance is not sarcasm, and that insolence is not invective.
16 Dec. 1852

21 England does not love coalitions.

22 Finality is not the language of politics.
28 Feb. 1859

23 This shows how much easier it is to be critical than to be correct.
24 Jan. 1860

24 To put an end to these bloated armaments.
8 May 1862

25 He seems to think that posterity is a pack-horse, always ready to be loaded.
3 June 1862

26 Colonies do not cease to be colonies because they are independent.
5 Feb. 1863

27 You are not going, I hope, to leave the destinies of the British Empire to prigs and pedants.

28 Never take anything for granted.
Salthill, 5 Oct. 1864

29 I hold that the characteristic of the present age is craving credulity.
Meeting of Society for Increasing Endowments of Small Livings in the Diocese of Oxford, 25 Nov. 1864

30 Man, my Lord [Bishop Wilberforce], is a being born to believe.

1 Party is organized opinion.

2 Is man an ape or an angel? Now I am on the side of the angels.

3 Assassination has never changed the history of the world.
House of Commons, 1 May 1865

4 Change is inevitable. In a progressive country change is constant.
Edinburgh, 29 Oct. 1867

5 I had to prepare the mind of the country, and...to educate our party.

6 We have legalized confiscation, consecrated sacrilege, and condoned high treason.
House of Commons, 27 Feb. 1871

7 I believe that without party Parliamentary government is impossible.
Manchester, 3 Apr. 1872

8 You behold a range of exhausted volcanoes. (Of the Treasury Bench.)

9 Increased means and increased leisure are the two civilizers of man.

10 A University should be a place of light, of liberty, and of learning.
House of Commons, 11 Mar. 1873

11 An author who speaks about his own books is almost as bad as a mother who talks about her own children.
At Banquet given by Glasgow to Lord Rector, 19 Nov. 1873

12 Upon the education of the people of this country the fate of this country depends.
House of Commons, 15 June 1874

13 He is a great master of gibes and flouts and jeers. (The Marquis of Salisbury.)
5 Aug. 1874

14 Cosmopolitan critics, men who are the friends of every country save their own.
Guildhall, 9 Nov. 1877. See 129:28, 366:6

15 Lord Salisbury and myself have brought you back peace—but a peace I hope with honour.
House of Commons, 16 July 1878. See 412:19

16 A series of congratulatory regrets. (Lord Harrington's Resolution on the Berlin Treaty.)
At Banquet in Riding School, Knightsbridge, 27 July 1878

17 A sophistical rhetorician, inebriated with the exuberance of his own verbosity. (Gladstone.)

18 The hare-brained chatter of irresponsible frivolity.
Guildhall, London, 9 Nov. 1878

19 One of the greatest of Romans, when asked what were his politics, replied, *Imperium et Libertas*. That would not make a bad programme for a British Ministry.
Mansion House, London, 10 Nov. 1879

20 The key of India is London.
House of Lords, 5 Mar. 1881

21 Damn your principles! Stick to your party.
Attr. (To Bulwer Lytton.) Latham, *Famous Sayings*

22 Protection is not only dead, but damned. (c. 1850)
Monypenny and Buckle, *Life of Disraeli*, iii.241

23 Pray remember, Mr Dean, no dogma, no Dean.
iv.368

24 We authors, Ma'am. (To Queen Victoria.)
v.49

25 I am dead: dead, but in the Elysian fields. (Said to a peer on his elevation to the House of Lords.)
522

26 When I want to read a novel I write one.
vi.636

27 She is an excellent creature, but she never can remember which came first, the Greeks or the Romans. [Of his wife.]
G.W.E. Russell, *Collections and Recollections*, ch.1

28 Everyone likes flattery; and when you come to Royalty you should lay it on with a trowel.
(To Matthew Arnold.) ch.23

29 Your Majesty is the head of the literary profession. (To Queen Victoria.)

30 Never complain and never explain.
J. Morley, *Life of Gladstone*, i.122

31 Between ourselves, I could floor them all. This *entre nous*: I was never more confident of anything than that I could carry everything before me in that House. The time will come.
Letters, 7 Feb. 1833

32 In the 'Town' yesterday, I am told 'some one asked Disraeli, in offering himself for Marylebone, on what he intended *to stand*. "On my head," was the reply.'
8 Apr. 1833

33 There can be no economy where there is no efficiency.
To Constituents, 3 Oct. 1868

34 Tadpole and Taper were great friends. Neither of them ever despaired of the Commonwealth.
Coningsby (1844), bk.i, ch.1

35 No Government can be long secure without a formidable Opposition.
bk.ii, ch.1

36 The Arch-Mediocrity who presided, rather than ruled, over this Cabinet of Mediocrities.

37 Conservatism discards Prescription, shrinks from Principle, disavows Progress; having rejected all respect for antiquity, it offers no redress for the present, and makes no preparation for the future.
ch.5

38 'A sound Conservative government,' said Taper, musingly. 'I understand: Tory men and Whig measures.'
ch.6

39 Almost everything that is great has been done by youth.
bk.iii, ch.1

40 Youth is a blunder; Manhood a struggle; Old Age a regret.

41 It seems to me a barren thing this Conservatism—an unhappy cross-breed, the mule of politics that engenders nothing.
ch.5

42 I have been ever of opinion that revolutions are not to be evaded.
bk.iv, ch.11

43 The depositary of power is always unpopular.

1 Where can we find faith in a nation of sectaries?
ch.13

2 Man is only truly great when he acts from the passions.

3 I grew intoxicated with my own eloquence.
Contarini Fleming (1832), pt.i, ch.7

4 Read no history: nothing but biography, for that is life without theory.
ch.23

5 The practice of politics in the East may be defined by one word—dissimulation.
pt.v, ch.10

6 His Christianity was muscular.
Endymion (1880), ch.14

7 The Athanasian Creed is the most splendid ecclesiastical lyric ever poured forth by the genius of man.
ch.54

8 The sweet simplicity of the three per cents.
ch.91. See 524:2

9 I believe they went out, like all good things, with the Stuarts.
ch.99

10 What we anticipate seldom occurs; what we least expected generally happens.
Henrietta Temple (1837), bk.ii, ch.4

11 Time is the great physician.
bk.vi, ch.9

12 They [the Furies] mean well; their feelings are strong, but their hearts are in the right place.
The Infernal Marriage (1834), pt.i, 1

13 The blue ribbon of the turf. [The Derby.]
Life of Lord George Bentinck (1854), ch.26

14 Every day when he looked into the glass, and gave the last touch to his consummate toilette, he offered his grateful thanks to Providence that his family was not unworthy of him.
Lothair (1870), ch.1

15 'I could have brought you some primroses, but I do not like to mix violets with anything.'
'They say primroses make a capital salad,' said Lord St Jerome.
ch.13

16 A Protestant, if he wants aid or advice on any matter, can only go to his solicitor.
ch.27

17 London; a nation, not a city.

18 The gondola of London. [A hansom.]

19 When a man fell into his anecdotage it was a sign for him to retire from the world.
ch.28

20 He was not an intellectual Croesus, but his pockets were full of sixpences.

21 The greatest misfortune that ever befell man was the invention of printing. Printing has destroyed education...The essence of education is the education of the body...What I admire in the order to which you belong is that they do live in the air; that they excel in athletic sports; that they can only speak one language; and that they never read. This is not a complete education, but it is the highest education since the

Greek.
ch.29

22 Every woman should marry—and no man.
ch.30

23 You know who the critics are? The men who have failed in literature and art.
ch.35. See 157:26

24 'My idea of an agreeable person,' said Hugo Bohun, 'is a person who agrees with me.'
ch.41

25 St Aldegonde had a taste for marriages and public executions.
ch.88

26 'I rather like bad wine,' said Mr Mountchesney; 'one gets so bored with good wine.'
Sybil (1845), bk.i, ch.1

27 The Egremonts had never said anything that was remembered, or done anything that could be recalled.
ch.3

28 To do nothing and get something, formed a boy's ideal of a manly career.
ch.5

29 'Two nations; between whom there is no intercourse and no sympathy; who are as ignorant of each other's habits, thoughts, and feelings, as if they were dwellers in different zones, or inhabitants of different planets; who are formed by a different breeding, are fed by a different food, are ordered by different manners, and are not governed by the same laws.'
'You speak of—' said Egremont, hesitatingly.
'THE RICH AND THE POOR.'
bk.ii, ch.5

30 Little things affect little minds.
bk.iii, ch.2

31 Mr Kremlin himself was distinguished for ignorance, for he had only one idea,—and that was wrong.
bk.iv, ch.5. See 275:34

32 I was told that the Privileged and the People formed Two Nations.
ch.8

33 The Youth of a Nation are the trustees of Posterity.
bk.vi, ch.13

34 That fatal drollery called a representative government.
Tancred (1847), bk.ii, ch.13

35 A majority is always the best repartee.
ch.14

36 All is race; there is no other truth.

37 The East is a career.

38 London is a modern Babylon.
bk.v, ch.5

39 The microcosm of a public school.
Vivian Grey (1826), bk.i, ch.2

40 I hate definitions.
bk.ii, ch.6

41 Experience is the child of Thought, and Thought is the child of Action. We cannot learn men from books.
bk.v, ch.1

42 There is moderation even in excess.
bk.vi, ch.1

43 I repeat...that all power is a trust—that we are accountable for its exercise—that, from the people,

and for the people, all springs, and all must exist.
ch.7

1 All Paradise opens! Let me die eating ortolans to the
sound of soft music!
The Young Duke (1831), bk.i, ch.10

2 A *dark* horse, which had never been thought of, and
which the careless St James had never even observed
in the list, rushed past the grand stand in sweeping
triumph.
bk.ii, ch.5

3 'The age of chivalry is past,' said May Dacre. 'Bores
have succeeded to dragons.'

4 A man may speak very well in the House of
Commons, and fail very completely in the House of
Lords. There are two distinct styles requisite: I intend,
in the course of my career, if I have time, to give a
specimen of both.
bk.v, ch.6

5 I never deny; I never contradict; I sometimes forget.
Said to Lord Esher of his relations with Queen Victoria. Elizabeth
Longford, *Victoria R.I*, ch.27

6 I will not go down to posterity talking bad grammar.
Said while correcting proofs of his last Parliamentary speech, 31
March 1881. Blake, *Disraeli, ch.32*

7 There are three kinds of lies: lies, damned lies and
statistics.
Attr. Mark Twain, *Autobiography*, I.246

ISAAC D'ISRAELI 1766–1848

8 He wreathed the rod of criticism with roses. [Bayle.]
Curiosities of Literature, 1834, vol.i, p.20

9 There is an art of reading, as well as an art of
thinking, and an art of writing.
Literary Character, ch.11

AUSTIN DOBSON 1840–1921

10 And where are the galleons of Spain?
Ballad to Queen Elizabeth

11 Fame is a food that dead men eat,—
I have no stomach for such meat.
Fame is a Food that Dead Men Eat

12 The ladies of St James's!
They're painted to the eyes,
Their white it stays for ever,
Their red it never dies:
But Phyllida, my Phyllida!
Her colour comes and goes;
It trembles to a lily,—
It wavers to a rose.
The Ladies of St. James's

13 Time goes, you say? Ah no!
Alas, Time stays, *we* go.
The Paradox of Time

14 I intended an Ode,
And it turned to a Sonnet.
It began *à la mode*,
I intended an Ode;
But Rose crossed the road
In her latest new bonnet;
I intended an Ode;

And it turned to a Sonnet.
Rose-Leaves

PHILIP DODDRIDGE 1702–1751

15 O God of Bethel, by whose hand
Thy people still are fed,
Who through this weary pilgrimage
Hast all our fathers led.
Hymns (1755). **O God of Bethel**

MARY ABIGAIL DODGE
see GAIL HAMILTON

BUBB DODINGTON 1691–1762

16 Love thy country, wish it well,
Not with too intense a care,
'Tis enough, that when it fell,
Thou its ruin didst not share.
Spence, *Anecdotes*

AELIUS DONATUS fl. 4th cent. A.D.

17 *Pereant, inquit, qui ante nos nostra dixerunt.*
Confound those who have said our remarks before us.
St. Jerome, *Commentary on Ecclesiastes*, 1. Migne, *Patrologiae
Lat. Cursus*, 23.390. See 544:16

JOHN DONNE 1571?–1631

18 Twice or thrice had I loved thee,
Before I knew thy face or name.
So in a voice, so in a shapeless flame,
Angels affect us oft, and worshipped be.
Air and Angels

19 And new philosophy calls all in doubt,
The element of fire is quite put out;
The sun is lost, and th'earth, and no man's wit
Can well direct him where to look for it.
And freely men confess that this world's spent,
When in the planets and the firmament
They seek so many new; they see that this
Is crumbled out again to his atomies.
'Tis all in pieces, all coherence gone;
All just supply and all relation.
An Anatomy of the World, First Anniversary, 1.205

20 She, she is dead; she's dead; when thou know'st this,
Thou know'st how dry a cinder this world is.
1.427

21 Cloth'd in her virgin white integrity.
Funeral Elegy, 1.75

22   Just such disparity
As is 'twixt air and Angels' purity,
'Twixt women's love, and men's will ever be.

23 All other things, to their destruction draw,
Only our love hath no decay;
This, no to-morrow hath, nor yesterday,
Running it never runs from us away,
But truly keeps his first, last, everlasting day.
The Anniversary

24 Come live with me, and be my love,
And we will some new pleasures prove
Of golden sands, and crystal brooks,
With silken lines, and silver hooks.
The Bait. See 329:23, 404:9, 495:16

1 A naked thinking heart, that makes no show,
   Is to a woman, but a kind of ghost.
   The Blossom, l.27

2   Meet me at London, then,
   Twenty days hence, and thou shalt see
   Me fresher, and more fat, by being with men,
   Than if I had stayed still with her and thee.
   l.33

3 The day breaks not, it is my heart.
   Break of Day (Attr. also to John Dowland)

4 For God's sake hold your tongue, and let me love.
   The Canonization

5 Dear love, for nothing less than thee
   Would I have broke this happy dream,
        It was a theme
   For reason, much too strong for fantasy,
   Therefore thou wak'd'st me wisely; yet
   My dream thou brok'st not, but continued'st it.
   The Dream

6 Love built on beauty, soon as beauty, dies.
   Elegies, No.2. **The Anagram**

7 No Spring, nor Summer beauty hath such grace,
   As I have seen in one Autumnal face.
   No.9. **The Autumnal**

8 So, if I dream I have you, I have you.
   For, all our joys are but fantastical.
   No.10. **The Dream**

9 I will not look upon the quick'ning sun,
   But straight her beauty to my sense shall run;
   The air shall note her soft, the fire most pure;
   Water suggest her clear, and the earth sure;
   Time shall not lose our passages; the spring
   How fresh our love was in the beginning;
   The summer how it ripened in the ear;
   And autumn, what our golden harvests were.
   The winter I'll not think on to spite thee,
   But count it a lost season, so shall she.
   No. 12. **His Parting from Her**

10 By our first strange and fatal interview
   By all desires which thereof did ensue.
   No.16. **On His Mistress**

11   All will spy in thy face
   A blushing womanly discovering grace.

12 Nurse, O! my love is slain; I saw him go
   O'er the white Alps alone.

13 Whoever loves, if he do not propose
   The right true end of love, he's one that goes
   To sea for nothing but to make him sick.
   No.18. **Love's Progress**

14   The straight Hellespont between
   The Sestos and Abydos of her breasts.

15   We easily know
   By this these angels from an evil sprite,
   Those set our hairs, but these our flesh upright.
   No.19. **Going to Bed**

16 Licence my roving hands, and let them go,
   Before, behind, between, above, below.
   O my America! my new-found-land,
   My kingdom, safliest when with one man mann'd.

17 O strong and long-liv'd death, how cam'st thou in?
   Epicedes and Obsequies. Elegy on Mrs. Boulstred, l.21

18 Hail, Bishop Valentine, whose day this is,

   All the air is thy Diocese.
   Epithalamions. 1, **On the Lady Elizabeth and Count Palatine being Married on St. Valentine's Day**

19 The household bird, with the red stomacher.

20 So, so, break off this last lamenting kiss,
   Which sucks two souls, and vapours both away,
   Turn thou ghost that way, and let me turn this,
   And let our selves benight our happiest day.
   The Expiration

21 Where, like a pillow on a bed,
   A pregnant bank swelled up, to rest
   The violet's reclining head,
   Sat we two, one another's best.
   The Extasy

22 So to'entergraft our hands, as yet
   Was all the means to make us one,
   And pictures in our eyes to get
   Was all our propagation.

23 And whilst our souls negotiate there,
   We like sepulchral statues lay;
   All day, the same our postures were,
   And we said nothing, all the day.

24 But O alas, so long, so far
   Our bodies why do we forbear?
   They're ours, though they're not we, we are
   The intelligencies, they the sphere.

25 So must pure lovers' souls descend
   T'affections, and to faculties,
   Which sense may reach and apprehend,
   Else a great Prince in prison lies.

26 O wrangling schools, that search what fire
   Shall burn this world, had none the wit
   Unto this knowledge to aspire,
   That this her fever might be it?
   A Fever

27 Who ever comes to shroud me, do not harm
   Nor question much
   That subtle wreath of hair, which crowns my arm;
   The mystery, the sign you must not touch,
        For 'tis my outward soul,
   Viceroy to that, which then to heaven being gone,
        Will leave this to control,
   And keep these limbs, her Province, from dissolution.
   The Funeral

28 What ere she meant by it, bury it with me,
        For since I am
   Love's martyr, it might breed idolatry,
   If into other's hands these relics came;
        As 'twas humility
   To afford to it all that a soul can do,
        So, 'tis some bravery,
   That since you would save none of me, I bury some of
        you.

29 I wonder by my troth, what thou, and I
   Did, till we lov'd? were we not wean'd till then?
   But suck'd on country pleasures, childishly?
   Or snorted we in the Seven Sleepers den?
   The Good-Morrow

30 And now good morrow to our waking souls,
   Which watch not one another out of fear.

31 Without sharp North, without declining West.

32 That All, which always is All everywhere,

Which cannot sin, and yet all sins must bear,
Which cannot die, yet cannot choose but die.
Holy Sonnets (1). **Annunciation**

1 Immensity cloistered in thy dear womb,
Now leaves his well belov'd imprisonment.
Nativity

2 I am a little world made cunningly
Of elements, and an angelic sprite.
Holy Sonnets (2), v

3 At the round earth's imagined corners, blow
Your trumpets, Angels, and arise, arise
From death, you numberless infinities
Of souls, and to your scattered bodies go.
vii

4 All whom war, dearth, age, agues, tyrannies,
Despair, law, chance, hath slain.

5 Death be not proud, though some have called thee
Mighty and dreadful, for thou art not so,
For those whom thou think'st thou dost overthrow,
Die not, poor death, nor yet canst thou kill me.
From rest and sleep, which but thy pictures be,
Much pleasure, then from thee much more must flow,
And soonest our best men with thee do go,
Rest of their bones and soul's delivery.
x

6 One short sleep past, we wake eternally,
And death shall be no more; death, thou shalt die.

7 What if this present were the world's last night?
xiii

8 Batter my heart, three person'd God; for, you
As yet but knock, breathe, shine, and seek to mend.
xiv

9 Take me to you, imprison me, for I
Except you enthrall me, never shall be free,
Nor ever chaste, except you ravish me.

10   As thou
Art jealous, Lord, so I am jealous now,
Thou lov'st not, till from loving more, thou free
My soul: whoever gives, takes liberty:
    O, if thou car'st not whom I love
Alas, thou lov'st not me.
Hymn to Christ, at the author's last going into Germany

11 Seal then this bill of my Divorce to all.

12 To see God only, I go out of sight:
    And to scape stormy days, I choose
    An everlasting night.

13 Wilt thou forgive that sin, where I begun,
Which is my sin, though it were done before?
Wilt thou forgive those sins through which I run
And do them still, though still I do deplore?
When thou hast done, thou hast not done,
    For I have more.

Wilt thou forgive that sin, by which I'have won
Others to sin, and made my sin their door?
Wilt thou forgive that sin which I did shun
A year or two, but wallowed in a score?
When thou hast done, thou hast not done,
    For I have more.
Hymn to God the Father

14 Since I am coming to that holy room,
Where, with thy quire of Saints for evermore,
I shall be made thy Music; as I come

I tune the instrument here at the door,
And what I must do then, think here before.
Hymn to God my God in My Sickness

15 Will no other vice content you?
The Indifferent

16 Rob me, but bind me not, and let me go.

17 And by Love's sweetest part, Variety, she swore.

18 And said, alas, some two or three
Poor heretics in love there be,
Which think to stablish dangerous constancy.

19 Stand still, and I will read to thee
A lecture, Love, in love's philosophy.
A Lecture in the Shadow

20 Love is a growing or full constant light;
And his first minute, after noon, is night.

21 When I died last, and, Dear, I die
As often as from thee I go,
Though it be but an hour ago,
And lovers' hours be full eternity.
The Legacy

22 Sir, more than kisses, letters mingle souls.
Letters to Severall Personages, **To Sir Henry Wotton**

23 And seeing the snail, which everywhere doth roam,
Carrying his own house still, still is at home,
Follow (for he is easy paced) this snail,
Be thine own palace, or the world's thy gaol.

24 If yet I have not all thy love,
Dear, I shall never have it all.
Lovers' Infiniteness

25 I long to talk with some old lover's ghost,
Who died before the god of love was born.
Love's Deity

26 Rebel and Atheist too, why murmur I,
As though I felt the worst that love could do?

27 'Tis the year's midnight, and it is the day's.
Nocturnal upon St. Lucy's Day

28   The world's whole sap is sunk:
The general balm th'hydroptic earth hath drunk.

29 As till God's great *Venite* change the song.
Of the Progress of the Soul, **Second Anniversary**, 1.44

30 Think then, my soul, that death is but a groom,
Which brings a taper to the outward room.
1.85

31   Her pure and eloquent blood
Spoke in her cheeks, and so distinctly wrought,
That one might almost say, her body thought.
1.244

32 Whose twilights were more clear, than our mid-day.
1.463

33 Thou art the proclamation; and I am
The trumpet, at whose voice the people came.
1.527

34 I sing the progress of a deathless soul.
Progress of the Soul, i

35 Great Destiny the Commissary of God.
iv

36 To my six lustres almost now outwore.
v

37 This soul to whom Luther, and Mahomet were

Prisons of flesh.
vii

1   So, of a lone unhaunted place possesst,
    Did this soul's second inn, built by the guest,
    This living buried man, this quiet mandrake, rest.
    xvi

2   Is any kind subject to rape like fish?
    xxix

3   Nature's great masterpiece, an Elephant,
    The only harmless great thing...
    Still sleeping stood; vexed not his fantasy
    Black dreams; like an unbent bow, carelessly,
    His sinewy proboscis did remissly lie.
    xxxix

4   She knew treachery,
    Rapine, deceit, and lust, and ills enow
    To be a woman.
    li

5   When my grave is broke up again
    Some second guest to entertain,
    (For graves have learnt that woman-head
    To be to more than one a bed)
                And he that digs it spies
    A bracelet of bright hair about the bone,
                Will he not let us alone?
    The Relic

6   On a huge hill,
    Cragged, and steep, Truth stands, and he that will
    Reach her, about must, and about must go.
    Satyre III, l.79

7   Sweetest love, I do not go,
    For weariness of thee,
    Nor in hope the world can show
    A fitter Love for me;
        But since that I
    Must die at last, 'tis best,
    To use my self in jest
    Thus by feigned deaths to die.
    Song

8   Go, and catch a falling star,
    Get with child a mandrake root,
    Tell me, where all past years are,
    Or who cleft the Devil's foot.
    Song, Go and Catch a Falling Star

9   And swear
                No where
    Lives a woman true and fair.

10 Though she were true, when you met her,
    And last, till you write your letter,
                Yet she
                Will be
    False, ere I come, to two, or three.

11   Busy old fool, unruly Sun,
                Why dost thou thus,
    Through windows, and through curtains call on us?
    Must to thy motions lovers' seasons run?
    The Sun Rising

12 Love, all alike, no season knows, nor clime,
    Nor hours, days, months, which are the rags of time.

13 This bed thy centre is, these walls thy sphere.

14 Send me not this, nor that, t'increase my store,

But swear thou think'st I love thee, and no more.
The Token

15 I am two fools, I know,
    For loving, and for saying so
    In whining Poetry.
    The Triple Fool

16 I have done one braver thing
    Than all the Worthies did,
    And yet a braver thence doth spring,
    Which is, to keep that hid.
    The Undertaking

17 So let us melt, and make no noise,
    No tear-floods, nor sigh-tempests move,
    'Twere profanation of our joys
    To tell the laity our love.
    A Valediction Forbidding Mourning

18 Thy firmness makes my circle just,
    And makes me end, where I begun.

19 But I do nothing upon my self, and yet I am mine own
    Executioner.
    Devotions upon Emergent Occasions. Meditation XII

20 No man is an *Island*, entire of it self; every man is a
    piece of the *Continent*, a part of the *main*; if a *clod* be
    washed away by the *sea*, *Europe* is the less, as well as
    if a *promontory* were, as well as if a *manor* of thy
    friends or of *thine own* were; any man's *death*
    diminishes *me*, because I am involved in *Mankind*;
    And therefore never send to know for whom the *bell*
    tolls; It tolls for *thee*.
    Meditation XVII

21 John Donne, Anne Donne, Un-done.
    Letter to his Wife

22 Man is but earth; 'Tis true; but earth is the centre.
    That man who dwells upon himself, who is always
    conversant in himself, rests in his true centre.
    LXXX Sermons (1640), v, Christmas Day, 1627

23 It [Death] comes equally to us all, and makes us all
    equal when it comes. The ashes of an Oak in the
    Chimney, are no epitaph of that Oak, to tell me how
    high or how large that was; It tells me not what flocks
    it sheltered while it stood, nor what men it hurt when
    it fell. The dust of great persons' graves is speechless
    too, it says nothing, it distinguishes nothing: As soon
    the dust of a wretch whom thou wouldest not, as of a
    Prince whom thou couldest not look upon, will trouble
    thine eyes, if the wind blow it thither; and when a
    whirlwind hath blown the dust of the Churchyard into
    the Church, and the man sweeps out the dust of the
    Church into the Churchyard, who will undertake to sift
    those dusts again, and to pronounce, This is the
    Patrician, this is the noble flower, and this the
    yeomanly, this the Plebeian bran.
    xv, 8 March 1621/2

24 There is nothing that God hath established in a
    constant course of nature, and which therefore is done
    every day, but would seem a Miracle, and exercise our
    admiration, if it were done but once.
    xxii, Easter Day, 25 March 1627

25 Poor intricated soul! Riddling, perplexed,
    labyrinthical soul!
    xlviii, 25 Jan. 1628/9

26 A day that hath no *pridie*, nor *postridie*, yesterday
    doth not usher it in, nor tomorrow shall not drive it

out. *Methusalem*, with all his hundreds of years, was but a mushroom of a night's growth, to this day, And all the four Monarchies, with all their thousands of years, and all the powerful Kings and all the beautiful Queens of this world, were but as a bed of flowers, some gathered at six, some at seven, some at eight, All in one Morning, in respect of this Day.
lxxiii, 30 Apr. 1626. **Eternity**

1 I throw myself down in my Chamber, and I call in, and invite God, and his Angels thither, and when they are there, I neglect God and his Angels, for the noise of a fly, for the rattling of a coach, for the whining of a door.
lxxx, 12 Dec. 1626. **At the Funeral of Sir William Cokayne**

2 A memory of yesterday's pleasures, a fear of tomorrow's dangers, a straw under my knee, a noise in mine ear, a light in mine eye, an anything, a nothing, a fancy, a Chimera in my brain, troubles me in my prayer. So certainly is there nothing, nothing in spiritual things, perfect in this world.

3 They shall awake as *Jacob* did, and say as *Jacob* said, *Surely the Lord is in this place,* and *this is no other but the house of God, and the gate of heaven,* And into that gate they shall enter, and in that house they shall dwell, where there shall be no Cloud nor Sun, no darkness nor dazzling, but one equal light, no noise nor silence, but one equal music, no fears nor hopes, but one equal possession, no foes nor friends, but one equal communion and Identity, no ends nor beginnings, but one equal eternity.
XXVI Sermons (1660), x, 29 Feb 1627/8

LORD ALFRED DOUGLAS 1870–1945

4 I am the Love that dare not speak its name.
Two Loves

BISHOP GAVIN DOUGLAS 1474?–1522

5 And all small fowlys singis on the spray:
Welcum the lord of lycht and lamp of day.
Eneados, bk.xii, prol.l.251

JAMES DOUGLAS, EARL OF MORTON d. 1581

6 Here lies he who neither feared nor flattered any flesh.
Of John Knox, said as he was buried, 26 Nov. 1572. G.R. Preedy, *Life of John Knox,* VII

KEITH DOUGLAS 1920–1944

7 If at times my eyes are lenses
through which the brain explores
constellations of feeling
my ears yielding like swinging doors
admit princes to the corridors
into the mind, do not envy me.
I have a beast on my back.
Fragment from *Bête Noire,* England, 1944

8 And all my endeavours are unlucky explorers
come back, abandoning the expedition;
the specimens, the lilies of ambition
still spring in their climate, still unpicked:
but time, time is all I lacked
to find them, as the great collectors before me.
On a Return from Egypt, England, 1944

9 Remember me when I am dead
and simplify me when I'm dead.
Simplify me when I'm dead, ?May 1941

10 But she would weep to see today
how on his skin the swart flies move;
the dust upon the paper eye
and the burst stomach like a cave.

For here the lover and killer are mingled
who had one body and one heart.
And death who had the soldier singled
has done the lover mortal hurt.
Vergissmeinnicht, Tunisia, 1943

LORENZO DOW 1777–1834

11 Observing the doctrine of Particular Election...and those who preached it up to make the Bible clash and contradict itself, by preaching somewhat like this:
You can and you can't—You shall and you shan't—You will and you won't—And you will be damned if you do—
And you will be damned if you don't.
Reflections on the Love of God, vi (1836), 30

ERNEST DOWSON 1867–1900

12 I have forgot much, Cynara! gone with the wind,
Flung roses, roses, riotously, with the throng,
Dancing, to put thy pale, lost lilies out of mind;
But I was desolate and sick of an old passion,
  Yea, all the time, because the dance was long:
I have been faithful to thee, Cynara! in my fashion.
Non Sum Qualis Eram

13 They are not long, the weeping and the laughter,
  Love and desire and hate:
I think they have no portion in us after
  We pass the gate.

They are not long, the days of wine and roses:
  Out of a misty dream
Our path emerges for a while, then closes
  Within a dream.
Vitae Summa Brevis

SIR ARTHUR CONAN DOYLE 1859–1930

14 What of the bow?
The bow was made in England:
Of true wood, of yew-wood,
The wood of English bows.
Song of the Bow

15 Singularity is almost invariably a clue. The more featureless and commonplace a crime is, the more difficult is it to bring it home.
The Adventures of Sherlock Holmes. **The Boscombe Valley Mystery**

16 A little monograph on the ashes of one hundred and forty different varieties of pipe, cigar, and cigarette tobacco.

17 The husband was a teetotaller, there was no other woman, and the conduct complained of was that he had drifted into the habit of winding up every meal by taking out his false teeth and hurling them at his wife.
A Case of Identity

18 It has long been an axiom of mine that the little things are infinitely the most important.

1 It is my belief, Watson, founded upon my experience, that the lowest and vilest alleys of London do not present a more dreadful record of sin than does the smiling and beautiful countryside.
Copper Beeches

2 A man should keep his little brain attic stocked with all the furniture that he is likely to use, and the rest he can put away in the lumber room of his library, where he can get it if he wants it.
Five Orange Pips

3 It is quite a three-pipe problem.
The Red-Headed League

4 I have nothing to do to-day. My practice is never very absorbing.

5 To Sherlock Holmes she [Irene Adler] is always *the* woman.
Scandal in Bohemia

6 You see, but you do not observe.

7 It is a capital mistake to theorize before one has data.

8 You know my methods, Watson.
The Memoirs of Sherlock Holmes. The Crooked Man

9 'Excellent!' I [Dr. Watson] cried. 'Elementary,' said he [Holmes].

10 'It is my duty to warn you that it will be used against you,' cried the Inspector, with the magnificent fair play of the British criminal law.
Dancing Men

11 He [Professor Moriarty] is the Napoleon of crime.
The Final Problem

12 'The practice is quiet,' said I [Dr. Watson], 'and I have an accommodating neighbour.'

13 My practice could get along very well for a day or two.
The Naval Treaty

14 You mentioned your name as if I should recognize it, but beyond the obvious facts that you are a bachelor, a solicitor, a Freemason, and an asthmatic, I know nothing whatever about you.
The Norwood Builder

15 A long shot, Watson; a very long shot!
Silver Blaze

16 'Is there any other point to which you would wish to draw my attention?'
'To the curious incident of the dog in the night-time.'
'The dog did nothing in the night-time.'
'That was the curious incident,' remarked Sherlock Holmes.

17 We have not yet met our Waterloo, Watson, but this is our Marengo.
The Return of Sherlock Holmes. Abbey Grange

18 You will ruin no more lives as you ruined mine. You will wring no more hearts as you wrung mine. I will free the world of a poisonous thing. Take that, you hound, and that!—and that!—and that!—and that!
Charles Augustus Milverton

19 Now, Watson, the fair sex is your department.
The Second Stain

20 There is a spirituality about the face, however...which the typewriter does not generate. The lady is a musician.
The Solitary Cyclist

21 All other men are specialists, but his specialism is omniscience.
His Last Bow. Bruce-Partington Plans

22 'I [Sherlock Holmes] followed you—' 'I saw no one.' 'That is what you may expect to see when I follow you.'
The Devil's Foot

23 Good old Watson! You are the one fixed point in a changing age.
His Last Bow

24 But here, unless I am mistaken, is our client.
Wisteria Lodge

25 There is but one step from the grotesque to the horrible.

26 The giant rat of Sumatra, a story for which the world is not yet prepared.
The Case Book. Sussex Vampire

27 They were the footprints of a gigantic hound!
The Hound of the Baskervilles, ch.2

28 Detection is, or ought to be, an exact science, and should be treated in the same cold and unemotional manner. You have attempted to tinge it with romanticism, which produces much the same effect as if you worked a love-story or an elopement into the fifth proposition of Euclid.
The Sign of Four

29 An experience of women which extends over many nations and three separate continents.

30 How often have I said to you that when you have eliminated the impossible, whatever remains, *however improbable*, must be the truth?

31 You know my methods. Apply them.

32 The Baker Street irregulars.

33 London, that great cesspool into which all the loungers of the Empire are irresistibly drained.
A Study in Scarlet

34 'Wonderful!' I [Dr. Watson] ejaculated. 'Commonplace,' said Holmes.

35 'I should have more faith,' he said; 'I ought to know by this time that when a fact appears opposed to a long train of deductions it invariably proves to be capable of bearing some other interpretation.'

36 'I am inclined to think—' said I [Dr Watson]. 'I should do so,' Sherlock Holmes remarked, impatiently.
The Valley of Fear

37 The vocabulary of 'Bradshaw' is nervous and terse, but limited.

38 Mediocrity knows nothing higher than itself, but talent instantly recognizes genius.

SIR FRANCIS DOYLE 1810–1888

39 Last night, among his fellow roughs,
He jested, quaff'd, and swore.
The Private of the Buffs

40 His creed no parson ever knew,
For this was still his 'simple plan,'
To have with clergymen to do

As little as a Christian can.
The Unobtrusive Christian

SIR FRANCIS DRAKE 1540?–1596

1 There must be a beginning of any great matter, but the continuing unto the end until it be thoroughly finished yields the true glory.
Dispatch to Sir Francis Walsingham, 17 May 1587. Navy Records Society, vol. XI (1898), p.134

2 There is plenty of time to win this game, and to thrash the Spaniards too.
Attr. D.N.B.

3 I remember Drake, in the vaunting style of a soldier, would call the Enterprise the singeing of the King of Spain's Beard. (Of the expedition to Cadiz, 1587.)
Bacon, *Considerations touching a War with Spain* (*Harleian Misc.* 1745, vol.v, p.85, col.1)

4 I must have the gentleman to haul and draw with the mariner, and the mariner with the gentleman…I would know him, that would refuse to set his hand to a rope, but I know there is not any such here.
Corbett, *Drake and the Tudor Navy*, i.249

JOSEPH RODMAN DRAKE 1795–1820

5 Forever float that standard sheet!
Where breathes the foe but falls before us,
With Freedom's soil beneath our feet,
And Freedom's banner streaming o'er us?
The American Flag, New York Evening Post, 29 May 1819.
Attr. also to Fitz-Greene Halleck

MICHAEL DRAYTON 1562–1631

6 Ill news hath wings, and with the wind doth go,
Comfort's a cripple and comes ever slow.
The Barrons' Wars, bk.II, xxviii

7 He of a temper was so absolute,
As that it seem'd when Nature him began,
She meant to shew all, that might be in man.
bk.III, xl

8 The mind is free, whate'er afflict the man,
A King's a King, do Fortune what she can.
bk.V, xxxvi

9 Thus when we fondly flatter our desires,
Our best conceits do prove the greatest liars.
bk.VI, xciv

10 Fair stood the wind for France
When we our sails advance,
Nor now to prove our chance
    Longer will tarry.
To the Cambro-Britons. Agincourt

11 O when shall English men
With such acts fill a pen?
Or England breed again
    Such a King Harry?

12 When Time shall turn those amber locks to grey,
My verse again shall gild and make them gay.
England's Heroic Epistles. Henry Howard, Earl of Surrey, to the Lady Geraldine, 1.123

13 Had in him those brave translunary things,
That the first poets had. [Marlowe.]
To Henry Reynolds, of Poets and Poesy, 1.106

14 For that fine madness still he did retain

Which rightly should possess a poet's brain.
1.109

15 Next these, learn'd Jonson, in this list I bring,
Who had drunk deep of the Pierian spring.
1.129

16 I pray thee leave, love me no more,
    Call home the heart you gave me,
I but in vain the saint adore,
    That can, but will not, save me.
To His Coy Love

17 These poor half-kisses kill me quite.

18 That shire which we the heart of England well may call. [Warwickshire.]
Poly-olbion, song xiii, 1.2

19 Crave the tuneful nightingale to help you with her lay,
The ousel and the throstlecock, chief music of our May.
Shepherd's Garland, eclogue iii, 17-18

20 Queens hereafter shall be glad to live
Upon the alms of thy superfluous praise.
Sonnets. **Idea,** vi

21 Since there's no help, come let us kiss and part,
Nay, I have done: you get no more of me,
And I am glad, yea glad with all my heart,
That thus so cleanly, I myself can free,
Shake hands for ever, cancel all our vows,
And when we meet at any time again,
Be it not seen in either of our brows,
That we one jot of former love retain;
Now at the last gasp of Love's latest breath,
When his pulse failing, Passion speechless lies,
When Faith is kneeling by his bed of death,
And Innocence is closing up his eyes,
Now if thou wouldst, when all have given him over,
From death to life, thou might'st him yet recover.
lxi

WILLIAM DRENNAN 1754–1820

22 The men of the Emerald Isle.
Erin

JOHN DRINKWATER 1882–1937

23 Moon-washed apples of wonder.
Moonlit Apples

THOMAS DRUMMOND 1797–1840

24 Property has its duties as well as its rights.
Letter to the Earl of Donoughmore, 22 May 1838

WILLIAM DRUMMOND 1585–1649

25 Only the echoes which he made relent,
Ring from their marble caves repent, repent.
For the Baptist

26 Phoebus, arise,
And paint the sable skies,
With azure, white, and red.
Song (ii)

27 I long to kiss the image of my death.
Sonnet ix, **Sleep, Silence Child**

28   A morn
Of bright carnations did o'erspread her face.
xlvi

JOHN DRYDEN 1631–1700

1 In pious times, ere priestcraft did begin,
Before polygamy was made a sin.
Absalom and Achitophel, pt.i, l.1

2 Then Israel's monarch, after Heaven's own heart,
His vigorous warmth did, variously, impart
To wives and slaves: and, wide as his command,
Scatter'd his Maker's image through the land.
l.7

3 Whate'er he did was done with so much ease,
In him alone, 'twas natural to please.
l.27

4 The Jews, a headstrong, moody, murmuring race
As ever tried the extent and stretch of grace,
God's pampered people, whom, debauched with ease,
No king could govern nor no God could please.
l.45

5 Plots, true or false, are necessary things,
To raise up commonwealths and ruin kings.
l.83

6 Of these the false Achitophel was first,
A name to all succeeding ages curst.
For close designs and crooked counsels fit,
Sagacious, bold, and turbulent of wit,
Restless, unfixed in principles and place,
In power unpleas'd, impatient of disgrace;
A fiery soul, which working out its way,
Fretted the pigmy body to decay:
And o'er informed the tenement of clay.
A daring pilot in extremity;
Pleased with the danger, when the waves went high
He sought the storms; but for a calm unfit,
Would steer too nigh the sands to boast his wit.
Great wits are sure to madness near alli'd,
And thin partitions do their bounds divide.
l.150

7 Why should he, with wealth and honour blest,
Refuse his age the needful hours of rest?
Punish a body which he could not please;
Bankrupt of life, yet prodigal of ease?
And all to leave what with his toil he won
To that unfeather'd two-legged thing, a son.
l.165

8 In friendship false, implacable in hate:
Resolv'd to ruin or to rule the state.
l.173

9 The people's prayer, the glad diviner's theme,
The young men's vision and the old men's dream!
l.238

10 All empire is no more than power in trust.
l.411

11 Better one suffer, than a nation grieve.
l.416

12 But far more numerous was the herd of such
Who think too little and who talk too much.
l.533

13 A man so various that he seem'd to be
Not one, but all mankind's epitome.
Stiff in opinions, always in the wrong;
Was everything by starts, and nothing long:
But, in the course of one revolving moon,
Was chemist, fiddler, statesman, and buffoon.
l.545

14 Railing and praising were his usual themes;
And both (to show his judgement) in extremes:
So over violent, or over civil,
That every man, with him, was God or Devil.
l.555

15 In squandering wealth was his peculiar art:
Nothing went unrewarded, but desert.
Beggar'd by fools, whom still he found too late:
He had his jest, and they had his estate.
l.559

16 During his office treason was no crime,
The sons of Belial had a glorious time.
l.597

17 Youth, beauty, graceful action seldom fail:
But common interest always will prevail:
And pity never ceases to be shown
To him, who makes the people's wrongs his own.
l.723

18 For who can be secure of private right,
If sovereign sway may be dissolv'd by might?
Nor is the people's judgement always true:
The most may err as grossly as the few.
l.779

19 Never was patriot yet, but was a fool.
l.968

20 Beware the fury of a patient man.
l.1005

21 Doeg, though without knowing how or why,
Made still a blund'ring kind of melody;
Spurr'd boldly on, and dash'd through thick and thin,
Through sense and nonsense, never out nor in;
Free from all meaning, whether good or bad,
And in one word, heroically mad.
pt.ii, l.412

22 Rhyme is the rock on which thou art to wreck.
l.486

23   The god-like hero sate
    On his imperial throne;
    His valiant peers were plac'd around;
Their brows with roses and with myrtles bound.
   (So should desert in arms be crowned:)
The lovely Thais by his side,
Sate like a blooming Eastern bride
In flow'r of youth and beauty's pride.
   Happy, happy, happy, pair!
    None but the brave,
    None but the brave,
   None but the brave deserves the fair.
Alexander's Feast, l.4

24   With ravish'd ears
    The monarch hears,
    Assumes the god,
    Affects to nod,
And seems to shake the spheres.
l.42

25 Bacchus ever fair, and ever young.
l.48

26 Sound the trumpets; beat the drums;
   Flush'd with a purple grace;
   He shows his honest face:
Now give the hautboys breath; he comes, he comes.
l.50

1 Drinking is the soldier's pleasure;
   Rich the treasure;
   Sweet the pleasure;
Sweet is pleasure after pain.
1.57

2 And thrice he routed all his foes, and thrice he slew
   the slain.
1.68

3 Fallen from his high estate,
   And welt'ring in his blood:
Deserted at his utmost need
By those his former bounty fed;
On the bare earth expos'd he lies,
With not a friend to close his eyes.
1.78

4 Revolving in his alter'd soul
   The various turns of chance below.
1.85

5 Softly sweet, in Lydian measures,
Soon he sooth'd his soul to pleasures.
War, he sung, is toil and trouble;
Honour but an empty bubble.
   Never ending, still beginning,
Fighting still, and still destroying,
   If the world be worth thy winning,
Think, oh think, it worth enjoying.
   Lovely Thais sits beside thee,
   Take the good the gods provide thee.
1.97

6 Sigh'd and look'd, and sigh'd again.
1.120

7 And, like another Helen, fir'd another Troy.
1.154

8 Could swell the soul to rage, or kindle soft desire.
1.160

9 Let old Timotheus yield the prize,
   Or both divide the crown:
He rais'd a mortal to the skies;
   She drew an angel down.
1.177

10 Errors, like straws, upon the surface flow;
He who would search for pearls must dive below.
All for Love, Prologue

11 My love's a noble madness.
II.i

12 Fool that I was, upon my eagle's wings
I bore this wren, till I was tired with soaring,
And now he mounts above me.

13   Give, you gods,
Give to your boy, your Caesar,
The rattle of a globe to play withal,
This gewgaw world, and put him cheaply off:
I'll not be pleased with less than Cleopatra.

14 The wretched have no friends.
III.i

15 Men are but children of a larger growth;
Our appetites as apt to change as theirs,
And full as craving too, and full as vain.
IV.i

16 Your Cleopatra; Dolabella's Cleopatra; every man's
Cleopatra.

17 Welcome, thou kind deceiver!
Thou best of thieves; who, with an easy key,
Dost open life, and, unperceived by us,
Even steal us from ourselves.
V.i

18 I am devilishly afraid, that's certain; but...I'll sing,
that I may seem valiant.
Amphitryon, II.i

19 Whistling to keep myself from being afraid.
III.i

20 I never saw any good that came of telling truth.

21 As one that neither seeks, nor shuns his foe.
Annus Mirabilis, xli

22 By viewing nature, nature's handmaid art,
   Makes mighty things from small beginnings grow:
Thus fishes first to shipping did impart,
   Their tail the rudder, and their head the prow.
clv

23 And on the lunar world securely pry.
clxiv

24 An horrid stillness first invades the ear,
And in that silence we the tempest fear.
Astraea Redux, l.7

25 He made all countries where he came his own.
1.76

26 Death, in itself, is nothing; but we fear,
To be we know not what, we know not where.
Aureng-Zebe, IV.i

27   None would live past years again,
Yet all hope pleasure in what yet remain;
And, from the dregs of life, think to receive,
What the first sprightly running could not give.

28 And made almost a sin of abstinence.
Character of a Good Parson, l.11

29 I am as free as nature first made man,
Ere the base laws of servitude began,
When wild in woods the noble savage ran.
The Conquest of Granada, pt.i, I.i

30 Forgiveness to the injured does belong;
But they ne'er pardon, who have done the wrong.
pt.ii, I.ii

31 Thou strong seducer, opportunity!
IV.iii

32 Old as I am, for ladies' love unfit,
The power of beauty I remember yet.
Cymon and Iphigenia, l.1

33 When beauty fires the blood, how love exalts the
   mind.
1.41

34 He trudg'd along unknowing what he sought,
And whistled as he went, for want of thought.
1.84

35 She hugg'd th' offender, and forgave th' offence.
1.367. See 22:1

36 Ill fortune seldom comes alone.
1.392

37 Of seeming arms to make a short essay,
Then hasten to be drunk, the business of the day.
1.407

38 Bold knaves thrive without one grain of sense,

But good men starve for want of impudence.
Epilogue to Constantine the Great

1 Theirs was the giant race before the flood.
Epistles, To Mr. Congreve, l.5

2 Heav'n, that but once was prodigal before,
To Shakespeare gave as much; she could not give him
    more.
l.62

3 How blessed Is he, who leads a country life,
Unvex'd with anxious cares, and void of strife!
Who studying peace, and shunning civil rage,
Enjoy'd his youth, and now enjoys his age:
All who deserve his love, he makes his own;
And, to be lov'd himself, needs only to be known.
To John Driden of Chesterton, l.1

4 Lord of yourself, uncumber'd with a wife.
l.18

5 Better to hunt in fields, for health unbought,
Than fee the doctor for a nauseous draught.
The wise, for cure, on exercise depend;
God never made his work, for man to mend.
l.92

6 Ev'n victors are by victories undone.
l.164

7 His colours laid so thick on every place,
As only showed the paint, but hid the face.
To Sir R. Howard, l.75

8 Here lies my wife: here let her lie!
Now she's at rest, and so am I.
Epitaph Intended for Dryden's Wife

9 For he was great, ere fortune made him so.
Heroic Stanzas (On the Death of Oliver Cromwell), vi

10 She fear'd no danger, for she knew no sin.
The Hind and the Panther, pt.i, l.4

11 And doom'd to death, though fated not to die.
l.8

12 For truth has such a face and such a mien
As to be lov'd needs only to be seen.
l.33

13 My thoughtless youth was winged with vain desires,
My manhood, long misled by wandering fires,
Followed false lights; and when their glimpse was
    gone
My pride struck out new sparkles of her own.
Such was I, such by nature still I am;
Be Thine the glory, and be mine the shame!
Good life be now my task: my doubts are done;
(What more could fright my faith than Three in One?)
l.72

14 Reason to rule, but mercy to forgive:
The first is law, the last prerogative.
l.261

15 For all have not the gift of martyrdom.
pt.ii, l.59

16 Either be wholly slaves or wholly free.
l.285

17 Much malice mingled with a little wit
Perhaps may censure this mysterious writ.
pt.iii, l.1

18 For present joys are more to flesh and blood
Than a dull prospect of a distant good.
l.364

19 By education most have been misled;
So they believe, because they so were bred.
The priest continues what the nurse began,
And thus the child imposes on the man.
l.389

20 The wind was fair, but blew a mack'rel gale.
l.456

21 T'abhor the makers, and their laws approve,
Is to hate traitors and the treason love.
l.706

22 For those whom God to ruin has design'd,
He fits for fate, and first destroys their mind.
l.1093. See 10:1, 199:15

23 And love's the noblest frailty of the mind.
The Indian Emperor, II.ii. See 420:20

24 Repentance is the virtue of weak minds.
III.i

25 For all the happiness mankind can gain
Is not in pleasure, but in rest from pain.
IV.i

26 That fairy kind of writing which depends only upon
the force of imagination.
King Arthur, Dedication

27 All heiresses are beautiful.
I.i

28 War is the trade of kings.
II.ii

29 Fairest Isle, all isles excelling,
Seat of pleasures, and of loves;
Venus here will choose her dwelling,
And forsake her Cyprian groves.
V. Song of Venus

30 Three poets, in three distant ages born,
Greece, Italy and England did adorn.
The first in loftiness of thought surpass'd;
The next in majesty, in both the last:
The force of nature could no farther go;
To make a third she join'd the former two.
Lines on Milton

31 Ovid, the soft philosopher of love.
Love Triumphant, II.i

32 Thou tyrant, tyrant Jealousy,
Thou tyrant of the mind!
Song of Jealousy

33 All human things are subject to decay,
And, when fate summons, monarchs must obey.
Mac Flecknoe, l.1

34 The rest to some faint meaning make pretence,
But Shadwell never deviates into sense.
Some beams of wit on other souls may fall,
Strike through and make a lucid interval;
But Shadwell's genuine night admits no ray,
His rising fogs prevail upon the day.
l.19

35 Thy genius calls thee not to purchase fame
In keen iambics, but mild anagram:
Leave writing plays, and choose for thy command
Some peaceful province in Acrostic Land.
There thou mayest wings display and altars raise,
And torture one poor word ten thousand ways.
l.203

36 I am resolved to grow fat and look young till forty,
and then slip out of the world with the first wrinkle and

the reputation of five-and-twenty.
The Maiden Queen, III.i

1 I am to be married within these three days; married
past redemption.
Marriage à la Mode, I.i

2 We loathe our manna, and we long for quails.
The Medal, l.131

3 But treason is not own'd when 'tis descried;
Successful crimes alone are justified.
l.207

4 Whatever is, is in its causes just.
Oedipus (1679), III.i

5 We know not what you can desire or hope,
To please you more, but burning of a *Pope.*
Epilogue

6 But love's a malady without a cure.
Palamon and Arcite, bk.ii, l.110

7 Fool, not to know that love endures no tie,
And Jove but laughs at lovers' perjury.
l.148. See 366:11

8 And Antony, who lost the world for love.
l.607

9 Repentance is but want of power to sin.
bk.iii, l.813

10 Since ev'ry man who lives is born to die,
And none can boast sincere felicity,
With equal mind, what happens, let us bear,
Nor joy nor grieve too much for things beyond our
care.
Like pilgrims to th' appointed place we tend;
The world's an inn, and death the journey's end.
l.883

11 A virgin-widow and a *Mourning Bride.*
l.927

12 But 'tis the talent of our English nation,
Still to be plotting some new reformation.
Prologue at Oxford, 1680

13 So poetry, which is in Oxford made
An art, in London only is a trade.
Prologue to the University of Oxon, 1684

14 Oxford to him a dearer name shall be,
Than his own mother University.
Thebes did his green unknowing youth engage,
He chooses Athens in his riper age.
Prologue to the University of Oxford

15 And this unpolished rugged verse I chose
As fittest for discourse and nearest prose.
Religio Laici, ad fin.

16 I strongly wish for what I faintly hope:
Like the day-dreams of melancholy men,
I think and think on things impossible,
Yet love to wander in that golden maze.
Rival Ladies, III.i

17 A very merry, dancing, drinking,
Laughing, quaffing, and unthinking time.
Secular Masque, l.39

18 Joy rul'd the day, and Love the night.
l.81

19 *Momus:* All, all of a piece throughout;
Thy chase had a beast in view; [pointing to Diana]
Thy wars brought nothing about; [to Mars]
Thy lovers were all untrue. [to Venus]

Janus: 'Tis well an old age is out,
Chronos: And time to begin a new.
l.86

20 For secrets are edged tools,
And must be kept from children and from fools.
Sir Martin Mar-All, II.ii

21 From harmony, from heavenly harmony
This universal frame began:
From harmony to harmony
Through all the compass of the notes it ran,
The diapason closing full in Man.
A Song for St. Cecilia's Day, i

22 What passion cannot Music raise and quell?
ii

23 The trumpet's loud clangour
Excites us to arms.
iii

24 The soft complaining flute.
iv

25 The trumpet shall be heard on high,
The dead shall live, the living die,
And Music shall untune the sky.
Grand Chorus

26 There is a pleasure sure,
In being mad, which none but madmen know!
The Spanish Friar, I.i

27 And, dying, bless the hand that gave the blow.
II.ii

28 They say everything in the world is good for
something.
III.ii

29 Mute and magnificent, without a tear.
Threnodia Augustalis, ii

30 Men met each other with erected look,
The steps were higher that they took;
Friends to congratulate their friends made haste;
And long inveterate foes saluted as they passed.
iv

31 Freedom which in no other land will thrive,
Freedom an English subject's sole prerogative.
x

32 Thou youngest virgin-daughter of the skies,
Made in the last promotion of the blest.
To the Memory of Mrs. Killigrew, l.1

33 Wit will shine
Through the harsh cadence of a rugged line.
To the Memory of Mr. Oldham

34 And he, who servilely creeps after sense,
Is safe, but ne'er will reach an excellence.
Tyrannic Love, Prologue

35 All delays are dangerous in war.
I.i

36 Pains of love be sweeter far
Than all other pleasures are.
IV.i

37 We must beat the iron while it is hot, but we may
polish it at leisure.
Aeneis, Dedication

38 I trade both the living and the dead, for the
enrichment of our native language.

39 Every age has a kind of universal genius, which

inclines those that live in it to some particular studies.
Essay of Dramatic Poesy (1688)

1 A thing well said will be wit in all languages.

2 He was the man who of all modern, and perhaps
ancient poets, had the largest and most comprehensive
soul...He was naturally learn'd; he needed not the
spectacles of books to read Nature: he looked inwards,
and found her there...He is many times flat, insipid;
his comic wit degenerating into clenches, his serious
swelling into bombast. But he is always great.
[Shakespeare.]

3 He invades authors like a monarch; and what would be
theft in other poets, is only victory in him. [Ben
Jonson.]

4 If by the people you understand the multitude, the *hoi
polloi*, 'tis no matter what they think; they are
sometimes in the right, sometimes in the wrong: their
judgement is a mere lottery.

5 He [Shakespeare] is the very Janus of poets; he wears
almost everywhere two faces; and you have scarce
begun to admire the one, ere you despise the other.
Essay on the Dramatic Poetry of the Last Age

6 One of the greatest, most noble, and most sublime
poems which either this age or nation has produced.
[Paradise Lost.]
Essays, Apology for Heroic Poetry

7 What judgment I had increases rather than diminishes;
and thoughts, such as they are, come crowding in so
fast upon me, that my only difficulty is to choose or
reject; to run them into verse or to give them the other
harmony of prose.
Fables, Preface

8 'Tis sufficient to say [of Chaucer], according to the
proverb, that here is God's plenty.

9 He [Chaucer] is a perpetual fountain of good sense.

10 One of our late great poets is sunk in his reputation,
because he could never forgive any conceit which
came in his way; but swept like a drag-net, great and
small. There was plenty enough, but the dishes were
ill-sorted; whole pyramids of sweetmeats, for boys and
women; but little of solid meat for men.

11 How easy it is to call rogue and villain, and that
wittily! But how hard to make a man appear a fool, a
blockhead, or a knave, without using any of those
opprobrious terms! To spare the grossness of the
names, and to do the thing yet more severely, is to
draw a full face, and to make the nose and cheeks
stand out, and yet not to employ any depth of
shadowing.
Of Satire

12 Sure the poet...spewed up a good lump of clotted
nonsense at once.
On Settle

13 A man may be capable, as Jack Ketch's wife said of
his servant, of a plain piece of work, a bare hanging;
but to make a malefactor die sweetly was only
belonging to her husband.

14 There are many who understand Greek and Latin, and
yet are ignorant of their Mother Tongue.
Sylvae (Poetical Miscellanies, pt.II. 1685), preface

15 Happy the man, and happy he alone,

He, who can call to-day his own:
He who, secure within, can say,
To-morrow do thy worst, for I have lived to-day.
Trans. of Horace, III, xxix

16 Not Heav'n itself upon the past has pow'r;
But what has been, has been, and I have had my hour.

17 I can enjoy her while she's kind;
But when she dances in the wind,
And shakes the wings, and will not stay,
I puff the prostitute away. [Fortune.]

18 Look round the habitable world! how few
Know their own good; or knowing it, pursue.
Trans. of Juvenal, X

19 To see and be seen, in heaps they run;
Some to undo, and some to be undone.
Trans. of Ovid, Art of Love, I.109

20 Who, for false quantities, was whipt at school.
Trans. of Persius, Satires, I.135

21 She knows her man, and when you rant and swear,
Can draw you to her *with a single hair*.
V.246

22 Arms, and the man I sing, who, forced by fate,
And haughty Juno's unrelenting hate...
Trans. of Virgil, Aeneid, I.i

23 Cousin Swift, you will never be a poet.
Johnson, Lives of the Poets: Swift

ALEXANDER DUBCEK 1921–

24 Communism with a human face.
Attr. A resolution by the party group in the Ministry of Foreign
Affairs, in 1968, referred to Czechoslovak foreign policy acquiring
'its own defined face'. *Rudé právo*, 14 Mar. 1968

JOACHIM DU BELLAY 1522–1560

25 *France, mère des arts, des armes et des lois.*
France, mother of arts, of warfare, and of laws.
Sonnets

26 *Heureux qui comme Ulysse a fait un beau voyage
Ou comme cestuy là qui conquit la toison,
Et puis est retourné, plein d'usage et raison,
Vivre entre ses parents le reste de son aage!*
Happy he who like Ulysses has made a great journey,
or like that man who won the Fleece and then came
home, full of experience and good sense, to live the
rest of his time among his family!

27 *Plus que le marbre dur me plaist l'ardoise fine,*
*Plus mon Loyre Gaulois, que le Tybre Latin,
Plus mon petit Lyré, que le mont Palatin,
Et plus que l'air marin la doulceur Angevin.*
I love thin slate more than hard marble, my Gallic
Loire more than the Latin Tiber, my little Liré more
than the Palatine Hill, and more than the sea air the
sweetness of Anjou.

MME DU DEFFAND 1697–1780

28 *La distance n'y fait rien; il n'y a que le premier pas
qui coûte.*
The distance is nothing; it is only the first step that is
difficult.
Commenting on the legend that St. Denis, carrying his head in his
hands, walked two leagues. Letter to d'Alembert, 7 July 1763

GEORGE DUFFIELD 1818–1888

1 Stand up!—stand up for Jesus!
The Psalmist, **Stand Up, Stand Up for Jesus**

ALEXANDRE DUMAS 1802–1870

2 *Cherchons la femme.*
Let us look for the woman.
Les Mohicans de Paris, passim (*Cherchez la femme.* Attributed to Joseph Fouche.)

3 *Tous pour un, un pour tous.*
All for one, one for all.
Les Trois Mousquetiers, passim

GEORGE DU MAURIER 1834–1894

4 Life ain't all beer and skittles, and more's the pity;
but what's the odds, so long as you're happy?
Trilby, pt.1

5 The salad, for which, like everybody else I ever met,
he had a special receipt of his own.

6 A little work, a little play
To keep us going—and so, good-day!

A little warmth, a little light
Of love's bestowing—and so, good-night!

A little fun, to match the sorrow
Of each day's growing—and so, good-morrow!

A little trust that when we die
We reap our sowing! and so—good-bye!

GENERAL DUMOURIEZ 1739–1823

7 *Les courtisans qui l'entourent n'ont rien oublié et n'ont rien appris.*
The courtiers who surround him have forgotten nothing and learnt nothing.
Of Louis XVIII, at the time of the Declaration of Verona, Sept. 1795. *Examen.* Later used by Napoleon in his Declaration to the French on his return from Elba. See 531:17

WILLIAM DUNBAR 1465?–1530?

8 I that in heill wes and gladnes
Am trublit now with gret seiknes
And feblit with infirmitie:
Timor mortis conturbat me.
Lament for the Makaris

9 London, thou art of townes *A per se.*
London, l.1

10 London, thou art the flower of cities all!
Gemme of all joy, jasper of jocunditie.
l.16

11 Fair be their wives, right lovesom, white and small.
l.46

12 Thy famous Maire, by pryncely governaunce,
With sword of justice thee ruleth prudently.
No Lord of Parys, Venyce, or Floraunce
In dignitye or honour goeth to hym nigh.
l.49

13 All love is lost but upon God alone.
The Merle and the Nightingale, ii

JOHN DUNNING, BARON ASHBURTON 1731–1783

14 The influence of the Crown has increased, is increasing, and ought to be diminished.
Motion passed in the House of Commons, 1780

JAMES DUPORT 1606–1679

15 *Quem Jupiter vult perdere, dementat prius.*
Whom God would destroy He first sends mad.
Homeri Gnomologia (1660), p.282. See 10:1

RICHARD DUPPA 1770–1831

16 In language, the ignorant have prescribed laws to the learned.
Maxims (1830), 252

SIR EDWARD DYER c.1540–1607

17 My mind to me a kingdom is,
Such present joys therein I find,
That it excels all other bliss
That earth affords or grows by kind.
Though much I want which most would have,
Yet still my mind forbids to crave.
My Mind to Me a Kingdom Is

JOHN DYER 1700?–1758

18 A little rule, a little sway,
A sunbeam in a winter's day,
Is all the proud and mighty have
Between the cradle and the grave.
Grongar Hill, l.89

JOHN DYER fl. 1714

19 And he that will this health deny,
Down among the dead men let him lie.
Toast: Here's a Health to the King

MARIA EDGEWORTH 1767–1849

20 Well! some people talk of morality, and some of religion, but give me a little snug property.
The Absentee, ch.2

21 And all the young ladies...said...that to be sure a love match was the only thing for happiness, where the parties could any way afford it.
Castle Rackrent (Continuation of Memoirs)

22 I've a great fancy to see my own funeral afore I die.

23 Come when you're called;
And do as you're bid;
Shut the door after you;
And you'll never be chid.
The Contrast, ch.1

24 Business was his aversion; pleasure was his business.
ch.2

THOMAS ALVA EDISON 1847–1931

25 Genius is one per cent inspiration and ninety-nine per cent perspiration.
Life (1932), ch.24

JAMES EDMESTON 1791–1867

26 Lead us, Heavenly Father, lead us
O'er the world's tempestuous sea;

Guard us, guide us, keep us, feed us,
For we have no help but Thee.
Sacred Lyrics, Set 2. **Lead Us, Heavenly Father**

KING EDWARD III 1312–1377

1 Also say to them, that they suffre hym this day to
wynne his spurres, for if god be pleased, I woll this
journey be his, and the honoure therof.
(Of the Black Prince at Crécy, 1345. Commonly quoted as 'Let
the boy win his spurs.') Berners, *Froissart's Chronicle*, 1812, I,
cxxx, 158

KING EDWARD VII 1841–1910

2 I thought everyone must know that a *short* jacket is
always worn with a silk hat at a private view in the
morning.
Sir P. Magnus, *Edward VII*, ch.19

KING EDWARD VIII 1894–1972

3 These works [derelict steel-works] brought all these
people here. Something must be done to find them
work.
Speaking in S. Wales during the Depression. F. Donaldson,
Edward VIII (1974), ch.19

4 I have found it impossible to carry the heavy burden
of responsibility and to discharge my duties as King as
I would wish to do without the help and support of the
woman I love.
Broadcast, 11 Dec. 1936

RICHARD EDWARDES 1523?–1566

5 In going to my naked bed, as one that would have
   slept,
I heard a wife sing to her child, that long before had
   wept.
She sighed sore, and sang full sweet, to bring the babe
   to rest,
That would not cease, but cried still in sucking at her
   breast.
She was full weary of her watch and grieved with her
   child,
She rocked it, and rated it, till that on her it smiled.
Then did she say, 'Now have I found this proverb true
   to prove:
The falling out of faithful friends, renewing is of
   love.'
Amantium Irae, ed. 1580

JONATHAN EDWARDS 1629–1712

6 The bodies of those that made such a noise and tumult
when alive, when dead, lie as quietly among the
graves of their neighbours as any others.
Procrastination

JONATHAN EDWARDS 1703–1758

7 Of all Insects no one is more wonderfull than the
spider especially with Respect to their sagacity and
admirable way of working...I...once saw a very large
spider to my surprise swimming in the air...and Others
have assured me that they Often have seen spiders fly,
the appearance is truly very Pretty and Pleasing.
Of Insects, written in his early youth, see *Andover Review* XIII,
pp.5–13 (1890)

OLIVER EDWARDS 1711–1791

8 I have tried too in my time to be a philosopher; but, I
don't know how, cheerfulness was always breaking in.
Boswell's *Johnson*, 17 Apr. 1778

9 For my part now, I consider supper as a turnpike
through which one must pass, in order to get to bed.
[Boswell's note: I am not absolutely sure but this was
my own suggestion, though it is truly in the character
of Edwards.]

ALBERT EINSTEIN 1879–1955

10 *Gott würfelt nicht.*
God does not play dice. [Einstein's habitually
expressed reaction to the quantum theory.]
B. Hoffman, *Albert Einstein, Creator and Rebel*, ch.10

GEORGE ELIOT 1819–1880

11 It was a pity he couldna be hatched o'er again, an'
hatched different.
Adam Bede (1859), ch.18

12 Our deeds determine us, as much as we determine our
deeds.
ch.29

13 Mrs Poyser 'has her say out'.
ch.32

14 It's them as take advantage that get advantage i' this
world.

15 A maggot must be born i' the rotten cheese to like it.

16 He was like a cock who thought the sun had risen to
hear him crow.
ch.33

17 We hand folks over to God's mercy, and show none
ourselves.
ch.42

18 I'm not one o' those as can see the cat i' the dairy, an'
wonder what she's come after.
ch.52

19 I'm not denyin' the women are foolish: God Almighty
made 'em to match the men.
ch.53

20 Gossip is a sort of smoke that comes from the dirty
tobacco-pipes of those who diffuse it: it proves nothing
but the bad taste of the smoker.
Daniel Deronda (1874–6), bk.ii, ch.13

21 A difference of taste in jokes is a great strain on the
affections.
ch.15

22 There is a great deal of unmapped country within us
which would have to be taken into account in an
explanation of our gusts and storms.
bk.iii, ch.24

23 Friendships begin with liking or gratitude—roots that
can be pulled up.
bk.iv, ch.32

24 Half the sorrows of women would be averted if they
could repress the speech they know to be useless; nay,
the speech they have resolved not to make.
Felix Holt (1866), ch.2

25 An election is coming. Universal peace is declared,
and the foxes have a sincere interest in prolonging the

lives of the poultry.
ch.5

1 A little daily embroidery had been a constant element in Mrs Transome's life; that soothing occupation of taking stitches to produce what neither she nor any one else wanted, was then the resource of many a well-born and unhappy woman.
ch.7

2 Speech is often barren; but silence also does not necessarily brood over a full nest. Your still fowl, blinking at you without remark, may all the while be sitting on one addled egg; and when it takes to cackling will have nothing to announce but that addled delusion.
ch.15

3 A woman can hardly ever choose...she is dependent on what happens to her. She must take meaner things, because only meaner things are within her reach.
ch.27

4 There's many a one who would be idle if hunger didn't pinch him; but the stomach sets us to work.
ch.30

5 'Abroad', that large home of ruined reputations.
epilogue

6 A woman dictates before marriage in order that she may have an appetite for submission afterwards.
Middlemarch (1871–2), ch.9

7 He said he should prefer not to know the sources of the Nile, and that there should be some unknown regions preserved as hunting-grounds for the poetic imagination.
ch.7

8 Among all forms of mistake, prophecy is the most gratuitous.
ch.10

9 A woman, let her be as good as she may, has got to put up with the life her husband makes for her.
ch.25

10 A man is seldom ashamed of feeling that he cannot love a woman so well when he sees a certain greatness in her: nature having intended greatness for men.
ch.39

11 Though, as we know, she was not fond of pets that must be held in the hands or trodden on, she was always attentive to the feelings of dogs, and very polite if she had to decline their advances.

12 Poor Dagley read a few verses [of the Bible] sometimes on a Sunday evening, and the world was at least not darker to him than it had been before.

13 It was a room where you had no reason for sitting in one place rather than in another.
ch.54

14 Our deeds still travel with us from afar,
And what we have been makes us what we are.
heading to ch.70

15 This is a puzzling world, and Old Harry's got a finger in it.
The Mill on the Floss (1860), bk.iii, ch.9

16 It was written down by a hand that waited for the heart's prompting: it is the chronicle of a solitary hidden anguish, struggle, trust and triumph. [*The Imitation of Christ*.]
bk.iv, ch.3

17 I've never any pity for conceited people, because I think they carry their comfort about with them.
bk.v, ch.4

18 The happiest women, like the happiest nations, have no history.
bk.vi, ch.3

19 If you please to take the privilege o' sitting down.
ch.4

20 I should like to know what is the proper function of women, if it is not to make reasons for husbands to stay at home, and still stronger reasons for bachelors to go out.
ch.6

21 'Character', says Novalis, in one of his questionable aphorisms—'character is destiny.'
See 364:9

22 In every parting there is an image of death.
Scenes of Clerical Life (1857), Amos Barton, ch.10

23 Errors look so very ugly in persons of small means—one feels they are taking quite a liberty in going astray; whereas people of fortune may naturally indulge in a few delinquencies.
Janet's Repentance, ch.25

24 Animals are such agreeable friends—they ask no questions, they pass no criticisms.
Mr. Gilfil's Love-Story, ch.7

25 Nothing is so good as it seems beforehand.
Silas Marner (1861), ch.18

26 Debasing the moral currency.
Essay in *Theophrastus Such* (1879)

27 Oh may I join the choir invisible
Of those immortal dead who live again
In minds made better by their presence.
Poems: Oh May I Join the Choir Invisible

28 'Tis God gives skill,
But not without men's hands: He could not make
Antonio Stradivari's violins
Without Antonio.
Stradivarius, l.140

29 By the time you receive this letter I shall...have been married to Mr J.W. Cross...who now that I am alone sees his happiness in the dedication of his life to me.
Letter to Barbara Bodichon, 5 May 1880

30 She, stirred somewhat beyond her wont, and taking as her text the three words which have been used so often as the inspiring trumpet-calls of men—the words *God, Immortality, Duty*—pronounced, with terrible earnestness, how inconceivable was the *first*, how unbelievable the *second*, and yet how peremptory and absolute the third. Never, perhaps, have sterner accents affirmed the sovereignty of impersonal and unrecompensing Law.
F.W.H. Myers, 'George Eliot', *Century Magazine*, Nov. 1881

31 I am not an optimist but a meliorist.
Laurence Housman, *A.E.H.* (1937), p.72

T.S. ELIOT 1888–1965

32 Because I do not hope to turn again
Because I do not hope
Because I do not hope to turn.
Ash Wednesday, 1

33 Because I do not hope to know again

The infirm glory of the positive hour.

1 Because these wings are no longer wings to fly
But merely vans to beat the air
The air which is now thoroughly small and dry
Smaller and dryer than the will
Teach us to care and not to care
Teach us to sit still.

2   Turning
Wearily, as one would turn to nod good-bye to
   Rochefoucauld,
If the street were time and he at the end of the street.
The Boston Evening Transcript

3 Where is the Life we have lost in living?
Where is the wisdom we have lost in knowledge?
Where is the knowledge we have lost in information?
Choruses from 'The Rock', I

4 I shall not want Capital in Heaven,
   For I shall meet Sir Alfred Mond.
We two shall lie together, lapt
   In a five per cent Exchequer Bond.
A Cooking Egg

5 Where are the eagles and the trumpets?

   Buried beneath some snow-deep Alps.
Over buttered scones and crumpets
   Weeping, weeping multitudes
Droop in a hundred A.B.C.'s.

6 Stone, bronze, stone, steel, stone, oakleaves, horses'
   heels
Over the paving.
Coriolan, I. **Triumphal March**

7 (And Easter Day, we didn't get to the country,
So we took young Cyril to church. And they rang a
   bell
And he said right out loud, *crumpets*.)

8   Don't throw away that sausage,
It'll come in handy. He's artful. Please, will you
Give us a light?
Light
Light
Et les soldats faisaient la haie? ILS LA FAISAIENT.

9 The clock has stopped in the dark.
The Family Reunion, II.iii

10 Round and round the circle
Completing the charm
So the knot be unknotted
The crossed be uncrossed
The crooked be made straight
And the curse be ended.

11 Sometimes these cogitations still amaze
The troubled midnight and the noon's repose.
La Figlia Che Piange

12 Time present and time past
Are both perhaps present in time future,
And time future contained in time past.
Four Quartets. Burnt Norton, 1

13 Footfalls echo in the memory
Down the passage which we did not take
Towards the door we never opened
Into the rose-garden. My words echo
Thus, in your mind.

14   Human kind

Cannot bear very much reality.

15 At the still point of the turning world. Neither flesh
   nor fleshless;
Neither from nor towards; at the still point, there the
   dance is,
But neither arrest nor movement.
2

16   Time past and time future
Allow but a little consciousness.
To be conscious is not to be in time
But only in time can the moment in the rose-garden,
The moment in the arbour where the rain beat,
The moment in the draughty church at smokefall
Be remembered; involved with past and future.
Only through time time is conquered.

17   Words strain,
Crack and sometimes break, under the burden,
Under the tension, slip, slide, perish,
Decay with imprecision, will not stay in place,
Will not stay still.
5

18 In my beginning is my end.
East Coker, 1

19   A way of putting it—not very satisfactory:
A periphrastic study in a worn-out poetical fashion,
Leaving one still with the intolerable wrestle
With words and meanings.
2

20   We are only undeceived
Of that which, deceiving, could no longer harm.

21 The wounded surgeon plies the steel
That questions the distempered part;
Beneath the bleeding hands we feel
The sharp compassion of the healer's art
Resolving the enigma of the fever chart.
4

22 The whole earth is our hospital
Endowed by the ruined millionaire,
Wherein, if we do well, we shall
Die of the absolute paternal care
That will not leave us, but prevents us everwhere.

23   Each venture
Is a new beginning, a raid on the inarticulate
With shabby equipment always deteriorating
In the general mess of imprecision of feeling.
5

24 There is only the fight to recover what has been lost
And found and lost again and again: and now, under
   conditions
That seem unpropitious. But perhaps neither gain nor
   loss.
For us, there is only the trying. The rest is not our
   business.

25   Our concern was speech, and speech impelled us
To purify the dialect of the tribe
And urge the mind to aftersight and foresight.
Little Gidding, 2

26 From wrong to wrong the exasperated spirit
   Proceeds, unless restored by the refining fire
Where you must move in measure, like a dancer.

27 We cannot revive old factions
We cannot restore old policies

Or follow an antique drum.

1 What we call the beginning is often the end
And to make an end is to make a beginning.
The end is where we start from.
5

2 We shall not cease from exploration
And the end of all our exploring
Will be to arrive where we started
And know the place for the first time.

3 An old man in a dry month.
Gerontion

4 Signs are taken for wonders. 'We would see a sign!'
The word within a word, unable to speak a word,
Swaddled with darkness. In the juvescence of the
     year
Came Christ the tiger.

In depraved May, dogwood and chestnut, flowering
     judas,
To be eaten, to be divided, to be drunk
Among whispers.

5 After such knowledge, what forgiveness?

6   Unnatural vices
Are fathered by our heroism.

7 And he'll say, as he scratches himself with his claws,
'Well, the Theatre's certainly not what it was.
These modern productions are all very well,
But there's nothing to equal, from what I hear tell,
     That moment of mystery
     When I made history
As Firefrorefiddle, the Fiend of the Fell.'
Gus: The Theatre Cat

8 We are the hollow men
We are the stuffed men
Leaning together
Headpiece filled with straw. Alas!
The Hollow Men, 1

9 *Here we go round the prickly pear
Prickly pear prickly pear.*
5

10 Between the idea
And the reality
Between the motion
And the act
Falls the Shadow.

11 This is the way the world ends
Not with a bang but a whimper.

12 A cold coming we had of it,
Just the worst time of the year
For a journey, and such a long journey:
The ways deep and the weather sharp,
The very dead of winter.
Journey of the Magi. See 4:7

13 And the cities hostile and the towns unfriendly
And the villages dirty and charging high prices.

14 And an old white horse galloped away in the meadow.

15   But set down
This set down
This: were we led all that way for
Birth or Death? There was a Birth, certainly,
We had evidence and no doubt. I had seen birth and
death,
But had thought they were different; this Birth was
Hard and bitter agony for us, like Death, our death.
We returned to our places, these Kingdoms,
But no longer at ease here, in the old dispensation,
With an alien people clutching their gods.
I should be glad of another death.

16 Cling, swing,
Spring, sing,
Swing up into the apple-tree.
Landscapes. I. **New Hampshire**

17   Let us go then, you and I,
When the evening is spread out against the sky
Like a patient etherized upon a table.
The Love Song of J. Alfred Prufrock

18 In the room the women come and go
Talking of Michelangelo.

     The yellow fog that rubs its back upon the
        window-panes,
The yellow smoke that rubs its muzzle on the
      window-panes,
Licked its tongue into the corners of the evening.

19 There will be time, there will be time
To prepare a face to meet the faces that you meet;
There will be a time to murder and create,
And time for all the works and days of hands
That lift and drop a question on your plate.

20 I have measured out my life with coffee spoons.

21 I should have been a pair of ragged claws
Scuttling across the floors of silent seas.

22 Should I, after tea and cakes and ices,
Have the strength to force the moment to its crisis?

23 I have seen the moment of my greatness flicker,
And I have seen the eternal Footman hold my coat, and
     snicker,
And in short, I was afraid.

24 No! I am not Prince Hamlet, nor was meant to be;
Am an attendant lord, one that will do
To swell a progress, start a scene or two.

25   I grow old...I grow old...
I shall wear the bottoms of my trousers rolled.

     Shall I part my hair behind? Do I dare to eat a
       peach?
I shall wear white flannel trousers, and walk upon the
     beach.
I have heard the mermaids singing, each to each;

I do not think that they will sing to me.

26 Macavity, Macavity, there's no one like Macavity,
There never was a Cat of such deceitfulness and
     suavity.
He always has an alibi, and one or two to spare:
At whatever time the deed took place—MACAVITY
     WASN'T THERE!
Macavity: The Mystery Cat

27 I am aware of the damp souls of housemaids
Sprouting despondently at area gates.
Morning at the Window

28 When Mr Apollinax visited the United States
His laughter tinkled among the teacups.
I thought of Fragilion, that shy figure among the
     birch-trees,

And of Priapus in the shrubbery
Gaping at the lady in the swing.
Mr. Apollinax

1 Polyphiloprogenitive
The sapient sutlers of the Lord
Drift across the window-panes
In the beginning was the Word.
Mr. Eliot's Sunday Morning Service

2 Yet we have gone on living,
Living and partly living.
Murder in the Cathedral, pt.I

3 Friendship should be more than biting Time can sever.

4 The last temptation is the greatest treason:
To do the right deed for the wrong reason.

5 The Naming of Cats is a difficult matter,
    It isn't just one of your holiday games;
At first you may think I'm as mad as a hatter
When I tell you a cat must have THREE DIFFERENT
    NAMES.
The Naming of Cats

6 When you notice a cat in profound meditation,
    The reason, I tell you, is always the same:
His mind is engaged in a rapt contemplation
    Of the thought, of the thought, of the thought of his
    name:
        His ineffable effable
        Effanineffable
Deep and inscrutable singular Name.

7 The winter evening settles down
With smell of steaks in passageways.
Six o'clock.
The burnt-out ends of smoky days.
Preludes, I

8 The worlds revolve like ancient women
Gathering fuel in vacant lots.

9 Every street lamp that I pass
Beats like a fatalistic drum,
And through the spaces of the dark
Midnight shakes the memory
As a madman shakes a dead geranium.

Half-past one,
The street-lamp sputtered,
The street-lamp muttered,
The street-lamp said, 'Regard that woman
Who hesitates toward you in the light of the door
Which opens on her like a grin.'
Rhapsody on a Windy Night

10 Regard the moon,
La lune ne garde aucune rancune.

11 Paint me the bold anfractuous rocks
    Faced by the snarled and yelping seas.
Sweeney Erect

12   You'd be bored.
Birth, and copulation, and death.
That's all the facts when you come to brass tacks:
Birth, and copulation and death.
I've been born, and once is enough.
Sweeney Agonistes, Fragment of an Agon

13 *Where the breadfruit fall*
And the penguin call
And the sound is the sound of the sea
Under the bam

Under the boo
Under the bamboo tree.

14 Apeneck Sweeney spreads his knees
Letting his arms hang down to laugh,
The zebra stripes along his jaw
Swelling to maculate giraffe.
Sweeney Among the Nightingales

15 Gloomy Orion and the Dog
Are veiled; and hushed the shrunken seas;
The person in the Spanish cape
Tries to sit on Sweeney's knees.

16 The host with someone indistinct
Converses at the door apart,
The nightingales are singing near
The convent of the Sacred Heart,

And sang within the bloody wood
When Agamemnon cried aloud
And let their liquid siftings fall
To stain the stiff dishonoured shroud.

17 April is the cruellest month, breeding
Lilacs out of the dead land, mixing
Memory and desire, stirring
Dull roots with spring rain.
Winter kept us warm, covering
Earth in forgetful snow, feeding
A little life with dried tubers.
The Waste Land. 1. **The Burial of the Dead**

18 I read, much of the night, and go south in the winter.

19 And I will show you something different from either
Your shadow at morning striding behind you,
Or your shadow at evening rising to meet you
I will show you fear in a handful of dust.

20   Unreal City,
Under the brown fog of a winter dawn,
A crowd flowed over London Bridge, so many,
I had not thought death had undone so many.

21 Flowed up the hill and down King William Street,
To where Saint Mary Woolnoth kept the hours
With a dead sound on the final stroke of nine.

22 'O keep the Dog far hence, that's friend to men,
'Or with his nails he'll dig it up again!
'You! hypocrite lecteur!—mon semblable,—mon
    frère!'
See 35:5, 567:9

23   The Chair she sat in, like a burnished throne,
Glowed on the marble.
2. **A Game of Chess.** See 422:2

24 And still she cried, and still the world pursues,
'Jug Jug' to dirty ears.

25 O O O O that Shakespeherian Rag—
It's so elegant
So intelligent.

26 A rat crept softly through the vegetation
Dragging its slimy belly on the bank
While I was fishing in the dull canal
On a winter evening round behind the gashouse
Musing upon the king my brother's wreck
And on the king my father's death before him.
3. **The Fire Sermon**

27 But at my back from time to time I hear
The sound of horns and motors, which shall bring

Sweeney to Mrs Porter in the spring.
O the moon shone bright on Mrs Porter
And on her daughter
They wash their feet in soda water.
See 332:19

1 I Tiresias, old man with wrinkled dugs
Perceived the scene, and foretold the rest—
I too awaited the expected guest.
He, the young man carbuncular, arrives,
A small house agent's clerk, with one bold stare,
One of the low on whom assurance sits
As a silk hat on a Bradford millionaire.

2 And I Tiresias have foresuffered all
Enacted on this same divan or bed.

3 When lovely woman stoops to folly and
Paces about her room again, alone,
She smoothes her hair with automatic hand,
And puts a record on the gramophone.
See 231:31

4 O City city, I can sometimes hear
Beside a public bar in Lower Thames Street,
The pleasant whining of a mandoline
And a clatter and a chatter from within
Where fishermen lounge at noon: where the walls
Of Magnus Martyr hold
Inexplicable splendour of Ionian white and gold.

5 'Trams and dusty trees.
Highbury bore me. Richmond and Kew
Undid me. By Richmond I raised my knees
Supine on the floor of a narrow canoe.'

6 Phlebas the Phoenician, a fortnight dead,
Forgot the cry of gulls, and the deep sea swell
And the profit and loss.
4. Death by Water

7 Consider Phlebas, who was once handsome and tall as
you.

8 Who is the third who walks always beside you?
When I count, there are only you and I together
But when I look ahead up the white road
There is always another one walking beside you.
5. What the Thunder Said

9 A woman drew her long black hair out tight
And fiddled whisper music on those strings.

10 In this decayed hole among the mountains
In the faint moonlight, the grass is singing
Over the tumbled graves, about the chapel
There is the empty chapel, only the wind's home.

11 The awful daring of a moment's surrender.

12 These fragments have I shored against my ruins.

13 Webster was much possessed by death
And saw the skull beneath the skin;
And breastless creatures under ground
Leaned backward with a lipless grin.
Whispers of Immortality

14 Grishkin is nice: her Russian eye
Is underlined for emphasis;
Uncorseted, her friendly bust
Gives promise of pneumatic bliss.

15 The critic, one would suppose, if he is to justify his
existence, should endeavour to discipline his personal
prejudices and cranks—tares to which we are all

subject—and compose his differences with as many of
his fellows as possible, in the common pursuit of true
judgement.
The Function of Criticism (1923), i

16 The only way of expressing emotion in the form of art
is by finding an 'objective correlative'; in other words,
a set of objects, a situation, a chain of events which
shall be the formula of that *particular* emotion; such
that when the external facts, which must terminate in
sensory experience, are given, the emotion is
immediately evoked.
Hamlet (1919)

17 In the seventeenth century a dissociation of sensibility
set in from which we have never recovered.
The Metaphysical Poets

18 Poetry is not a turning loose of emotion, but an escape
from emotion; it is not the expression of personality,
but an escape from personality.
Tradition and the Individual Talent, II

QUEEN ELIZABETH I 1533–1603

19 'Twas God the word that spake it,
He took the Bread and brake it;
And what the word did make it;
That I believe, and take it.
Answer on being asked her opinion of Christ's presence in the
Sacrament. S. Clarke, *Marrow of Ecclesiastical History,* pt.ii,
Life of Queen Elizabeth, ed. 1675

20 The queen of Scots is this day leichter of a fair son,
and I am but a barren stock.
Memoirs of Sir James Melville (1549–93)

21 Anger makes dull men witty, but it keeps them poor.
Bacon, *Apophthegms,* 5

22 Like strawberry wives, that laid two or three great
strawberries at the mouth of their pot, and all the rest
were little ones.
54

23 Good-morning, gentlemen both. [To a delegation of
eighteen tailors.]
Chamberlin, *Sayings of Queen Elizabeth,* p.28

24 To your text, Mr Dean! to your text!
p.137

25 I am your anointed Queen. I will never be by violence
constrained to do anything. I thank God that I am
endued with such qualities that if I were turned out of
the Realm in my petticoat I were able to live in any
place in Christome.
p.142

26 I will make you shorter by the head.
p.224

27 The daughter of debate, that eke discord doth sow.
[Mary Queen of Scots.]
p.301

28 Madam I may not call you; mistress I am ashamed to
call you; and so I know not what to call you; but
howsoever, I thank you. [To the wife of the
Archbishop of Canterbury. The Queen did not approve
of married clergy.]
Harington, *Brief View of the State of the Church,* 1607

29 God may pardon you, but I never can. [To the
Countess of Nottingham.]
See Hume, *History of England under the House of Tudor,* vol.ii,
ch.7

1 If thy heart fails thee, climb not at all.
Lines written on a window after 404:14. Fuller, *Worthies of England*, vol.i, p.419

2 *Semper eadem*. (Ever the same.)
Motto

3 As for me, I see no such great cause why I should either be fond to live or fear to die. I have had good experience of this world, and I know what it is to be a subject and what to be a sovereign. Good neighbours I have had, and I have met with bad: and in trust I have found treason.
Speech to Parliament, 1586. Camden's *Annals*, p.98

4 I know I have the body of a weak and feeble woman, but I have the heart and stomach of a king, and of a king of England too; and think foul scorn that Parma or Spain, or any prince of Europe, should dare to invade the borders of my realm.
Speech to the Troops at Tilbury on the Approach of the Armada, 1588

5 Though God hath raised me high, yet this I count the glory of my crown: that I have reigned with your loves.
The Golden Speech, 1601. D'Ewes's *Journal*, p.659

6 Must! Is *must* a word to be addressed to princes? Little man, little man! thy father, if he had been alive, durst not have used that word.
To Robert Cecil, on her death-bed. J.R. Green, *A Short History of the English People*, ch.vii

JOHN ELLERTON 1826–1893

7 The day Thou gavest, Lord, is ended,
The darkness falls at Thy behest.
A Liturgy for Missionary Meetings

JANE ELLIOT 1727–1805

8 I've heard them lilting, at the ewe milking.
  Lasses a' lilting, before dawn of day;
But now they are moaning, on ilka green loaning;
  The flowers of the forest are a' wede away.
The Flowers of the Forest (1756) (Popular version of the traditional lament for Flodden.)

CHARLOTTE ELLIOTT 1789–1871

9 'Christian! seek not yet repose,'
Hear thy guardian angel say;
Thou art in the midst of foes—
  'Watch and pray.'
Morning and Evening Hymns

10 Just as I am, without one plea
But that Thy blood was shed for me,
And that Thou bidd'st me come to Thee,
  O Lamb of God, I come!
Invalid's Hymn Book (1834)

EBENEZER ELLIOTT 1781–1849

11 What is a communist? One who hath yearnings
For equal division of unequal earnings.
Epigram

12 When wilt thou save the people?
  Oh, God of Mercy! when?
The people, Lord, the people!

Not thrones and crowns, but men!
The People's Anthem

GEORGE ELLIS 1753–1815

13 Snowy, Flowy, Blowy,
Showery, Flowery, Bowery,
Hoppy, Croppy, Droppy,
Breezy, Sneezy, Freezy.
The Twelve Months

HAVELOCK ELLIS 1859–1939

14 Every artist writes his own autobiography.
The New Spirit. Tolstoi II

ELSTOW

15 Elstow ['One Elstow, a friar of the order of Observant Friars'] smiling said...'With thanks to God we know the way to heaven, to be as ready by water as by land, and therefore we care not which way we go.'
When threatened with drowning by Henry VIII. Stow, *Annales*, 1615, p.543

PAUL ELUARD 1895–1952

16 *Adieu tristesse*
Bonjour tristesse
Tu es inscrite dans les lignes du plafond.
Farewell sadness
Good day sadness
You are inscribed in the lines of the ceiling.
A peine défigurée

RALPH WALDO EMERSON 1803–1882

17 If the red slayer think he slays,
  Or if the slain think he is slain,
They know not well the subtle ways
  I keep, and pass, and turn again.
Brahma

18 I am the doubter and the doubt,
  And I the hymn the Brahmin sings.

19 By the rude bridge that arched the flood,
  Their flag to April's breeze unfurl'd,
Here once the embattled farmers stood,
  And fired the shot heard round the world.
Hymn Sung at the Completion of the Concord Monument

20 Good-bye, proud world! I'm going home:
Thou art not my friend, and I'm not thine.
Good-bye

21 Things are in the saddle,
  And ride mankind.
Ode, Inscribed to W.H. Channing

22 I like a church; I like a cowl;
I love a prophet of the soul;
And on my heart monastic aisles
Fall like sweet strains, or pensive smiles;
Yet not for all his faith can see,
Would I that cowlèd churchman be.
The Problem

23 He builded better than he knew;—
The conscious stone to beauty grew.

24 The frolic architecture of the snow.
The Snowstorm

1 Wilt thou seal up the avenues of ill?
Pay every debt, as if God wrote the bill.
Solution

2 So nigh is grandeur to our dust,
    So near is God to man,
When Duty whispers low, *Thou must,*
    The youth replies, *I can.*
Voluntaries, iii

3 Make yourself necessary to someone.
Conduct of Life. **Considerations by the way**

4 All sensible people are selfish, and nature is tugging at every contract to make the terms of it fair.

5 A person seldom falls sick, but the bystanders are animated with a faint hope that he will die.

6 Art is a jealous mistress.
Wealth

7 We say the cows laid out Boston. Well, there are worse surveyors.

8 The louder he talked of his honour, the faster we counted our spoons.
Worship. See 275:1

9 London is the epitome of our times, and the Rome of to-day.
English Traits, xviii. **Result**

10 This aged England…pressed upon by transitions of trade and…competing populations,—I see her not dispirited, not weak, but well remembering that she has seen dark days before;—indeed, with a kind of instinct that she sees a little better in a cloudy day, and that, in storm of battle and calamity, she has a secret vigour and a pulse like a cannon.
xix. **Speech at Manchester** (1847)

11 Nothing astonishes men so much as common-sense and plain dealing.
Essays, xii. **Art**

12 Though we travel the world over to find the beautiful we must carry it with us or we find it not.

13 Beware when the great God lets loose a thinker on this planet.
x. **Circles**

14 Conversation is a game of circles. In conversation we pluck up the *termini* which bound the common of silence on every side.

15 People wish to be settled: only as far as they are unsettled is there any hope for them.

16 Nothing great was ever achieved without enthusiasm.

17 To fill the hour—that is happiness.
xiv. **Experience**

18 The wise through excess of wisdom is made a fool.

19 The years teach much which the days never know.

20 A friend may well be reckoned the masterpiece of Nature.
vi. **Friendship**

21 The only reward of virtue is virtue; the only way to have a friend is to be one.

22 Tart, cathartic virtue.
viii. **Heroism**

23 It was a high counsel that I once heard given to a young person, 'Always do what you are afraid to do.'

24 There is properly no history; only biography.
i. **History**

25 Men are conservatives when they are least vigorous, or when they are most luxurious. They are conservatives after dinner.
New England Reformers

26 The reward of a thing well done, is to have done it.

27 We are wiser than we know.
ix. **The Over-Soul**

28 Words are also actions, and actions are a kind of words.
xiii. **The Poet**

29 It is not metres, but a metre-making argument, that makes a poem.

30 We are symbols, and inhabit symbols.

31 Language is fossil poetry.

32 Good men must not obey the laws too well.
xix. **Politics**

33 In skating over thin ice, our safety is in our speed.
vii. **Prudence**

34 To believe your own thought, to believe that what is true for you in your private heart is true for all men,—that is genius.
ii. **Self-Reliance**

35 To-morrow a stranger will say with masterly good sense precisely what we have thought and felt all the time, and we shall be forced to take with shame our own opinion from another.

36 Society everywhere is in conspiracy against the manhood of every one of its members.

37 Whoso would be a man must be a nonconformist.

38 A foolish consistency is the hobgoblin of little minds, adored by little statesmen and philosophers and divines. With consistency a great soul has simply nothing to do.

39 Is it so bad, then, to be misunderstood? Pythagoras was misunderstood, and Socrates, and Jesus, and Luther, and Copernicus, and Galileo, and Newton, and every pure and wise spirit that ever took flesh. To be great is to be misunderstood.

40 I like the silent church before the service begins, better than any preaching.

41 If you would not be known to do anything, never do it.
iv. **Spiritual Laws**

42 What is a weed? A plant whose virtues have not been discovered.
Fortune of the Republic

43 We are always getting ready to live, but never living.
Journals, 13 Apr. 1834

44 I hate quotations.
May 1849

45 Old age brings along with its uglinesses the comfort that you will soon be out of it,—which ought to be a substantial relief to such discontented pendulums as we are. To be out of the war, out of debt, out of the drouth, out of the blues, out of the dentist's hands, out of the second thoughts, mortifications, and remorses that inflict such twinges and shooting pains,—out of the next winter, and the high prices, and company

below your ambition,—surely these are soothing hints.
1864

1 By necessity, by proclivity,—and by delight, we all
quote.
Letters and Social Aims. **Quotation and Originality**

2 Next to the originator of a good sentence is the first
quoter of it.

3 When Nature has work to be done, she creates a
genius to do it.
Method of Nature

4 Every hero becomes a bore at last.
Representative Men. **Uses of Great Men**

5 Talent alone cannot make a writer. There must be a
man behind the book.
Goethe

6 Is not marriage an open question, when it is alleged,
from the beginning of the world, that such as are in the
institution wish to get out; and such as are out wish to
get in.
Montaigne

7 Never read any book that is not a year old.
Society and Solitude. **Books**

8 Hitch your wagon to a star.
Civilization

9 We boil at different degrees.
Eloquence

10 One of our statesmen said, 'The curse of this country
is eloquent men.'

11 America is a country of young men.
Old Age

12 'Tis the good reader that makes the good book.
Success

13 Invention breeds invention.
Works and Days

14 Glittering generalities! They are blazing ubiquities.
Attr. remark on 148:14

15 If a man write a better book, preach a better sermon,
or make a better mouse-trap than his neighbour, tho'
he build his house in the woods, the world will make a
beaten path to his door.
Mrs. Sarah S.B. Yule (1856–1916) credits the quotation to
Emerson in her *Borrowings* (1889), stating in *The Docket*, Feb.
1912, that she copied this in her handbook from a lecture delivered
by Emerson. The quotation was the occasion of a long
controversy, owing to Elbert Hubbard's claim to its authorship.

WILLIAM EMPSON 1906–

16 Waiting for the end, boys, waiting for the end.
What is there to be or do?
What's become of me or you?
Are we kind or are we true?
Sitting two and two, boys, waiting for the end.
Just a Smack at Auden

17 Slowly the poison the whole blood stream fills.
It is not the effort nor the failure tires.
The waste remains, the waste remains and kills.
Missing Dates

FRIEDRICH ENGELS 1820–1895

18 *Der Staat wird nicht 'abgeschaft', er stirbt ab.*

The State is not 'abolished', *it withers away.*
Anti-Dühring, III.ii

THOMAS DUNN ENGLISH 1819–1902

19 Oh! don't you remember sweet Alice, Ben Bolt,
Sweet Alice, whose hair was so brown,
Who wept with delight when you gave her a smile,
And trembled with fear at your frown?
Ben Bolt

ENNIUS 239–169 B.C.

20 *O Tite tute Tati tibi tanta tyranne tulisti!*
O tyrant Titus Tatius, what a lot you brought upon
yourself!
Annals 1. Priscianus (*Grammatici Latini*, ed. H. Keil *et al.*,
Leipzig, 1857-80, II, 591, 5)

21 *At tuba terribili sonitu taratantara dixit.*
And the trumpet in terrible tones went taratantara.
Annals 2. Priscianus (*Grammatici Latini*, ed. H. Keil *et al.*,
Leipzig, 1857-80, II, 450, 2)

22 *Unus homo nobis cunctando restituit rem.*
One man by delaying put the state to rights for us.
Annals 12. Cicero, *De Off.*, I, 24, 84

23 *Moribus antiquis res stat Romana virisque.*
The Roman state survives by its ancient customs and
its manhood.
Annals. St. Augustine, *De Civ. Dei*, 2, 21

ROBERT DEVEREUX, EARL OF ESSEX
1566–1601

24 Reasons are not like garments, the worse for wearing.
To Lord Willoughby, 4 Jan. 1598-9. See N. & Q., Ser.X, vol.ii,
p.23

HENRI ESTIENNE 1531–1598

25 *Si jeunesse savoit; si vieillesse pouvoit.*
If youth knew; if age could.
Les Prémices, Épigramme cxci

SIR GEORGE ETHEREGE 1635?–1691

26 I must confess I am a fop in my heart; ill customs
influence my very senses, and I have been so used to
affectation that without the help of the air of the court
what is natural cannot touch me.
Letter to Mr. Poley, 2/12 Jan. 1687/8

27 Few of our plays can boast of more wit than I have
heard him speak at a supper. [Sir Charles Sedley.]
Letter to Mr. Will. Richards, undated

28 I walk within the purlieus of the Law.
Love in a Tub, I.iii

29 When love grows diseas'd, the best thing we can do is
put it to a violent death; I cannot endure the torture of
a lingring and consumptive passion.
The Man of Mode, II.ii

30 Writing, Madam, 's a mechanic part of wit! A
gentleman should never go beyond a song or a billet.
IV.i

31 What e'er you say, I know all beyond High-Park's a
desart to you.
V.ii

EUCLID fl. c.300 B.C.

1 *Quod erat demonstrandum.* (trans. from the Greek).
Which was to be proved.

2 A line is length without breadth.

3 There is no 'royal road' to geometry.
Said to Ptolemy I. Proclus, *Comment on Euclid*, Prol. G.20

EURIPIDES 480–406 B.C.

4 ἡ γλῶσσ' ὀμώμοχ', ἡ δὲ φρὴν ἀνώμοτος.
My tongue swore, but my mind's unsworn.
Hippolytus, 612

ABEL EVANS 1679–1737

5 Under this stone, Reader, survey
Dead Sir John Vanbrugh's house of clay.
Lie heavy on him, Earth! for he
Laid many heavy loads on thee!
Epitaph on Sir John Vanbrugh, Architect of Blenheim Palace

JOHN EVELYN 1620–1706

6 This knight was indeed a valiant gentleman; but not a
little given to romance, when he spake of himself.
Diary, 6 Sept. 1651

7 Mulberry Garden, now the only place of refreshment
about the town for persons of the best quality to be
exceedingly cheated at.
10 May 1654

8 That miracle of a youth, Mr Christopher Wren.
11 July 1654

9 I saw Hamlet Prince of Denmark played, but now the
old plays began to disgust this refined age.
26 Nov. 1661

DAVID EVERETT 1769–1813

10 You'd scarce expect one of my age
To speak in public on the stage;
And if I chance to fall below
Demosthenes or Cicero,
Don't view me with a critic's eye,
But pass my imperfections by.
Large streams from little fountains flow,
Tall oaks from little acorns grow.
Lines Written for a School Declamation

VISCOUNT EVERSLEY
see CHARLES SHAW-LEFEVRE

GAVIN EWART 1916–

11 Miss Twye was soaping her breasts in the bath
When she heard behind her a meaning laugh
And to her amazement she discovered
A wicked man in the bathroom cupboard.
Miss Twye

WILLIAM NORMAN EWER 1885–1976

12 I gave my life for freedom—This I know:
For those who bade me fight had told me so.
Five Souls, 1917

13 How odd
Of God

To choose
The Jews.
How Odd. See 95:13

F.W. FABER 1814–1863

14 The music of the Gospel leads us home.
Oratory Hymns. **The Pilgrims of the Night**

ROBERT FABYAN d. 1513

15 Finally he paid the debt of nature.
New Chronicles, pt.i, xli

16 King Henry [I] being in Normandy, after some
writers, fell from or with his horse, whereof he caught
his death; but Ranulphe says he took a surfeit by eating
of a lamprey, and thereof died.
ccxxix. Ranulphus Higden's account, *Polychronicon* VII.xvii,
does not attribute Henry's death to any direct cause. Fabyan may
have derived the notion of 'surfeit' from an anonymous and rather
fanciful translation of Higden's *nocuerat* as 'chargede his
stomake'. See Harleian ms 2261, f.354.b.

17 The Duke of Clarence...then being a prisoner in the
Tower, was secretly put to death and drowned in a
barrel of Malmesey wine within the said Tower.
vol.II, **1477**. Early editions have the spelling 'malvesye'.

CLIFTON FADIMAN

18 I encountered the mama of dada again. [Gertrude
Stein.]
Appreciations, **Gertrude Stein**

LUCIUS CARY, VISCOUNT FALKLAND
1610?–1643

19 When it is not necessary to change, it is necessary not
to change.
A Speech concerning Episcopacy [delivered 1641]. *A Discourse
of Infallibility*, 1660

MICHAEL FARADAY 1791–1867

20 Tyndall, I must remain plain Michael Faraday to the
last; and let me now tell you, that if I accepted the
honour which the Royal Society desires to confer upon
me, I would not answer for the integrity of my
intellect for a single year.
On being offered the Presidency of the Royal Society. J. Tyndall,
Faraday as a Discoverer (1868), 'Illustrations of Character'

EDWARD FARMER 1809?–1876

21 I have no pain, dear mother, now;
But oh! I am so dry:
Just moisten poor Jim's lips once more;
And, mother, do not cry!
The Collier's Dying Child. See 6:1

GEORGE FARQUHAR 1678–1707

22 Sir, you shall taste my *Anno Domini*.
The Beaux' Stratagem, I.i

23 I have fed purely upon ale; I have eat my ale, drank
my ale, and I always sleep upon ale.

24 My Lady Bountiful.

25 Says little, thinks less, and does—nothing at all, faith.

26 'Tis still my maxim, that there is no scandal like rags,

nor any crime so shameful as poverty.

1 There's some diversion in a talking blockhead; and
since a woman must wear chains, I would have the
pleasure of hearing 'em rattle a little.
II.ii

2 No woman can be a beauty without a fortune.

3 I believe they talked of me, for they laughed
consumedly.
III.i

4 'Twas for the good of my country that I should be
abroad.—Anything for the good of one's country—I'm
a Roman for that.
ii

5 Captain is a good travelling name, and so I take it.

6 *Aimwell:* Then you understand Latin, Mr Bonniface?
Bonniface: Not I, Sir, as the saying is, but he talks it
so very fast that I'm sure it must be good.

7 There are secrets in all families.
iii

8 How a little love and good company improves a
woman!
IV.i

9 It is a maxim that man and wife should never have it in
their power to hang one another.
ii

10 Spare all I have, and take my life.
V.ii

11 I hate all that don't love me, and slight all that do.
The Constant Couple, I.ii

12 Grant me some wild expressions, Heavens, or I shall
burst—...Words, words or I shall burst.
V.iii

13 Charming women can true converts make,
We love the precepts for the teacher's sake.
See 173:3

14 Crimes, like virtues, are their own rewards.
The Inconstant, IV.ii

15 'Tis an old saying, Like master, like man; why not as
well, Like mistress, like maid?
Love and a Bottle, I.i

16 Money is the sinews of love, as of war.
II.i. See 151:30

17 Poetry's a mere drug, Sir.
III.ii

18 He answered the description the page gave to a T, Sir.
IV.iii

19 Hanging and marriage, you know, go by Destiny.
The Recruiting Officer, III.ii

20 I cou'd be mighty foolish, and fancy my self mighty
witty; Reason still keeps its throne, but it nods a little,
that's all.

21 A lady, if undrest at Church, looks silly,
One cannot be devout in dishabilly.
The Stage Coach, prologue

22 I'm privileg'd to be very impertinent, being an
Oxonian.
Sir Harry Wildair, II.i

23 The King of Spain is dead.
ii

DAVID GLASGOW FARRAGUT 1801–1870

24 Damn the torpedoes! Full speed ahead.
At the battle of Mobile Bay, 5 Aug. 1864. 'Torpedoes' were
mines. But see Capt. A.T. Mahan, *Admiral Farragut* (1892),
ch.10

DEAN FARRAR 1831–1903

25 Russell...acted invariably from the highest principles.
Eric, or Little by Little, pt.i, ch.3

26 Russell, let me always call you Edwin, and call me
Eric.
ch.4

27 'What a surly devil that is,' said Eric,...
'A surly—? Oh, Eric, that's the first time I ever heard
you swear.
ch.8

28 'By heavens, this is *too* bad!' he exclaimed, stamping
his foot with anger. 'What have I ever done to you
young blackguards, that you should treat me thus?'
pt.ii, ch.1

29 They all drank his health with the usual honours:—
'...For he's a jolly good fe-el-low, which nobody can
deny.'
Julian Home, ch.21

WILLIAM FAULKNER 1897–1962

30 He [the writer] must teach himself that the basest of
all things is to be afraid; and, teaching himself that,
forget it forever leaving no room in his workshop for
anything but the old verities and truths of the heart, the
old universal truths lacking which any story is
ephemeral and doomed—love and honor and pity and
pride and compassion and sacrifice.
Nobel Prize Speech, Stockholm, 10 Dec. 1950

GUY FAWKES 1570–1606

31 A desperate disease requires a dangerous remedy.
6 Nov. 1605. See D.N.B.

GEOFFREY FEARON

32 The 'angry young men' of England (who refuse to
write grammatically and syntactically in order to flaunt
their proletarian artistry).
Times Literary Supplement, 4 Oct. 1957 but see also R. West,
Black Lamb and Grey Falcon (1941), 'Dalmatia'

EMPEROR FERDINAND I 1503–1564

33 *Fiat justitia et pereat mundus.*
Let justice be done, though the world perish.
Motto. Johannes Manlius, *Locorum Communium Collectanea*
(Basle, 1563), II, 290. See 565:8

WILLIAM PITT FESSENDEN 1806–1869

34 Repudiate the repudiators.
Presidential Campaign Slogan, 1868

LUDWIG FEUERBACH 1804–1872

35 *Der Mensch ist, was er isst.*
Man is what he eats.
Advertisement to Moleschott, *Lehre der Nahrungsmittel: Für das
Volk* (1850). See 93:9

EUGENE FIELD 1850–1895

1 But I, when I undress me
    Each night, upon my knees,
Will ask the Lord to bless me,
    With apple pie and cheese.
Apple Pie and Cheese

2 Wynken, Blynken, and Nod one night
    Sailed off in a wooden shoe—
Sailed on a river of crystal light,
    Into a sea of dew.
Wynken, Blynken, and Nod

3 He played the King as though under momentary
apprehension that someone else was about to play the
ace.
Of Creston Clarke as King Lear. Attr. to a review in the *Denver
Tribune*, c.1880

HENRY FIELDING 1707–1754

4 '*Tace*, madam,' answered Murphy, 'is Latin for a
candle.'
Amelia, bk.i, ch.10

5 It hath been often said, that it is not death, but dying,
which is terrible.
bk.iii, ch.4

6 When widows exclaim loudly against second
marriages, I would always lay a wager, that the man,
if not the wedding-day, is absolutely fixed on.
bk.vi, ch.8

7 One fool at least in every married couple.
bk.ix, ch.4

8 There is not in the universe a more ridiculous, nor a
more contemptible animal, than a proud clergyman.
ch.10

9 One of my illustrious predecessors.
Covent-Garden Journal, No.3, 11 Jan. 1752

10 Oh! The roast beef of England,
And old England's roast beef.
The Grub Street Opera, III.iii

11 He in a few minutes ravished this fair creature, or at
least would have ravished her, if she had not, by a
timely compliance, prevented him.
Jonathan Wild, bk.iii, ch.7

12 But pray, Mr Wild, why bitch?
ch.8

13 To whom nothing is given, of him can nothing be
required.
Joseph Andrews, bk.ii, ch.8

14 I describe not men, but manners; not an individual,
but a species.
bk.iii, ch.1

15 They are the affectation of affectation.
ch.3

16 Public schools are the nurseries of all vice and
immorality.
ch.5

17 Some folks rail against other folks, because other folks
have what some folks would be glad of.
bk.iv, ch.6

18 Love and scandal are the best sweeteners of tea.
Love in Several Masques, IV.xi

19 Yes, I had two strings to my bow; both golden ones,

agad! and both cracked.
V.xiii

20 I have lived long enough in the world to see that
necessity is a bad recommendation to favours...which
as seldom fall to those who really want them, as to
those who really deserve them.
The Modern Husband (first performed 1731), II.v

21 Map me no maps, sir, my head is a map, a map of the
whole world.
Rape upon Rape, II.v

22 Every physician almost hath his favourite disease.
Tom Jones, bk.ii, ch.9

23 When I mention religion, I mean the Christian
religion; and not only the Christian religion, but the
Protestant religion; and not only the Protestant religion
but the Church of England.
bk.iii, ch.3

24 Thwackum was for doing justice, and leaving mercy to
heaven.
ch.10

25 What is commonly called love, namely the desire of
satisfying a voracious appetite with a certain quantity
of delicate white human flesh.
bk.vi, ch.1

26 O! more than Gothic ignorance.
bk.vii, ch.3

27 'I did not mean to abuse the cloth; I only said your
conclusion was a *non sequitur*.'—
'You are another,' cries the sergeant, 'an you come to
that, no more a *sequitur* than yourself.'
bk.ix, ch.6

28 An amiable weakness.
bk.x, ch.8

29 His designs were strictly honourable, as the phrase is;
that is, to rob a lady of her fortune by way of
marriage.
bk.xi, ch.4

30 Composed that monstrous animal a husband and wife.
bk.xv, ch.9

31 Nay, you may call me coward if you will; but if that
little man there upon the stage is not frightened, I
never saw any man frightened in my life.
bk.xvi, ch.5

32 'He the best player!' cries Partridge, with a
contemptuous sneer. 'Why, I could act as well as he
myself. I am sure, if I had seen a ghost, I should have
looked in the very same manner, and done just as he
did...The king for my money! He speaks all his words
distinctly, half as loud again as the other. Anybody
may see he is an actor.'

33 All Nature wears one universal grin.
Tom Thumb the Great, I.i

34 To sun my self in Huncamunca's eyes.
iii

35 When I'm not thank'd at all, I'm thank'd enough,
I've done my duty, and I've done no more.

36 The dusky night rides down the sky,
    And ushers in the morn;
The hounds all join in glorious cry,
    The huntsman winds his horn:

And a-hunting we will go.
A-Hunting We Will Go

RONALD FIRBANK 1886–1926

1 There was a pause—just long enough for an angel to pass, flying slowly.
Vainglory, 6

L'ABBÉ EDGEWORTH DE FIRMONT 1745–1807

2 *Fils de Saint Louis, montez au ciel.*
Son of Saint Louis, ascend to heaven.
Attr. words to Louis XVI as he mounted the steps of the guillotine at his execution, 1793. No documentary proof at all.

LORD FISHER 1841–1920

3 Sack the lot!
The Times, 2 Sept. 1919

CHARLES FITZGEFFREY 1575?–1638

4 And bold and hard adventures t' undertake,
Leaving his country for his country's sake.
Sir Francis Drake (1596), st.213

EDWARD FITZGERALD 1809–1883

5 Awake! for Morning in the Bowl of Night
Has flung the Stone that puts the Stars to Flight:
    And Lo! the Hunter of the East has caught
The Sultan's Turret in a Noose of Light.
The Rubáiyát of Omar Khayyám (1859), 1

6 Dreaming when Dawn's Left Hand was in the Sky
I heard a Voice within the Tavern cry,
    'Awake, my Little ones, and fill the Cup
Before Life's Liquor in its Cup be dry.'
2

7   In divine
High piping Pehlevi, with 'Wine! Wine! Wine!
    Red Wine!'—the Nightingale cries to the Rose
That yellow Cheek of hers to incarnadine.
6
That sallow cheek of hers to incarnadine. (ed.4 1879)

8 And look—a thousand Blossoms with the Day
Woke—and a thousand scatter'd into Clay.
8

9 But come with old Khayyám and leave the Lot
Of Kaikobad and Kaikhosru forgot:
    Let Rustum lay about him as he will,
Or Hatim Tai cry Supper—heed them not.
9

10 Each Morn a thousand Roses brings, you say;
Yes, but where leaves the Rose of Yesterday?
    And this first Summer month that brings the Rose,
Shall take Jamshyd and Kaikobad away.
9 (ed.4)

11 Here with a Loaf of Bread beneath the bough,
A Flask of Wine, a Book of Verse—and Thou
    Beside me singing in the Wilderness—
And Wilderness is Paradise enow.
11
A Book of Verses underneath the Bough,
A Jug of Wine, a Loaf of Bread—and Thou
  Beside me singing in the Wilderness—
Oh, Wilderness were Paradise enow! 12 (ed.4)

12 Ah, take the Cash in hand and waive the Rest;
Oh, the brave Music of a *distant* Drum!
12
Ah, take the Cash, and let the Credit go,
Nor heed the rumble of a distant Drum! 13 (ed.4)

13 Think, in this batter'd Caravanserai
Whose Doorways are alternate Night and Day,
    How Sultan after Sultan with his Pomp
Abode his Hour or two, and went his way.
15
Think, in this batter'd Caravanserai
Whose Portals are alternate Night and Day,
  How Sultan after Sultan with his Pomp
Abode his destin'd Hour, and went his way. 17 (ed.4)

14 They say the Lion and the Lizard keep
The Courts where Jamshyd gloried and drank deep:
    And Bahram, that great Hunter—the Wild Ass
Stamps o'er his Head, and he lies fast asleep.
17
...but cannot break his Sleep. 18 (ed.4)

15 I sometimes think that never blows so red
The Rose as where some buried Caesar bled;
    That every Hyacinth the Garden wears
Dropt in her Lap from some once lovely Head.
18

16 Ah, my Belovéd, fill the Cup that clears
TO-DAY of past Regrets and Future Fears:
    To-morrow! —Why, To-morrow I may be
Myself with Yesterday's Sev'n thousand Years.
20

17 Lo! some we loved, the loveliest and best
That Time and Fate of all their Vintage prest,
    Have drunk their Cup a Round or two before,
And one by one crept silently to Rest.
21
For some we loved, the loveliest and the best
That from his Vintage rolling Time hath prest. 22 (ed.4)

18 Ah, make the most of what we yet may spend,
Before we too into the Dust descend;
    Dust into Dust, and under Dust, to lie,
Sans Wine, sans Song, sans Singer, and—sans End!
23

19 Oh, come with old Khayyám, and leave the Wise
To talk; one thing is certain, that Life flies;
    One thing is certain, and the Rest is Lies;
The Flower that once hath blown for ever dies.
26
Oh threats of Hell and Hopes of Paradise!
One thing at least is certain—*This* Life flies;
  One thing is certain and the rest is Lies;
The Flower that once has blown for ever dies. 63 (ed.4)

20 Myself when young did eagerly frequent
Doctor and Saint, and heard great argument
    About it and about: but evermore
Came out by the same Door as I went.
27
Came out by the same Door wherein I went. (ed.4)

21 With them the Seed of Wisdom did I sow,
And with mine own hand wrought to make it grow;
    And this was all the Harvest that I reap'd—
'I came like Water, and like Wind I go'.
28

22 Ah, fill the Cup:—what boots it to repeat
How Time is slipping underneath our Feet:
    Unborn TO-MORROW, and dead YESTERDAY,

Why fret about them if TO-DAY be sweet!
37

1 You know, my Friends, with what a brave Carouse
I made a Second Marriage in my house;
    Divorced old barren Reason from my Bed,
And took the Daughter of the Vine to Spouse.
55 (ed.4)

2 The Grape that can with Logic absolute
The Two-and-Seventy jarring Sects confute.
43

3 For in and out, above, about, below,
'Tis nothing but a Magic Shadow-show,
    Played in a Box whose Candle is the Sun,
Round which we Phantom Figures come and go.
46

4 Strange, is it not? that of the myriads who
Before us pass'd the door of Darkness through,
    Not one returns to tell us of the Road,
Which to discover we must travel too.
64 (ed.4)

5 'Tis all a Chequer-board of Nights and Days
Where Destiny with Men for Pieces plays:
    Hither and thither moves, and mates, and slays,
And one by one back in the Closet lays.
49
But helpless Pieces of the Game He plays
Upon this Chequer-board of Nights and Days;
    Hither and thither moves, and checks, and slays,
And one by one back in the Closet lays. 69 (ed.4)

6 The Ball no question makes of Ayes and Noes,
But Here or There as strikes the Player goes;
    And He that toss'd you down into the Field,
He knows about it all—HE knows—HE knows!
70 (ed.4)

7 The Moving Finger writes; and, having writ,
Moves on: nor all thy Piety nor Wit
    Shall lure it back to cancel half a Line,
Nor all thy Tears wash out a Word of it.
51 ...your Tears... 71 (ed.4)

8 And that inverted Bowl we call The Sky,
Whereunder crawling coop't we live and die,
    Lift not thy hands to *It* for help—for It
Rolls impotently on as Thou or I.
52
...they call the Sky...
As impotently moves as you or I. 72 (ed.4)

9 Drink! for you know not whence you came, nor why:
Drink! for you know not why you go, nor where.
74 (ed.4)

10 After a momentary silence spake
Some Vessel of a more ungainly Make;
    'They sneer at me for leaning all awry;
What! did the Hand then of the Potter shake?'
86 (ed.4)

11 'Who *is* the Potter, pray, and who the Pot?'
60

12 Then said another—'Surely not in vain
My Substance from the common Earth was ta'en,
    That He who subtly wrought me into Shape,
Should stamp me back to common Earth again'.
61

13 Indeed the Idols I have loved so long
Have done my credit in this World much wrong:
Have drown'd my Glory in a Shallow Cup

And sold my Reputation for a Song.
93 (ed.4)

14 And much as Wine has play'd the Infidel,
And robb'd me of my Robe of Honour—Well,
    I often wonder what the Vintners buy
One half so precious as the Goods they sell.
71 ...the stuff they sell. 95 (ed.4)

15 Alas, that Spring should vanish with the Rose!
That Youth's sweet-scented Manuscript should close!
    The Nightingale that in the Branches sang,
Ah, whence, and whither flown again, who knows!
72

16 Ah Love! could thou and I with Fate conspire
To grasp this sorry Scheme of Things entire,
    Would not we shatter it to bits—and then
Re-mould it nearer to the Heart's Desire!
73
Ah Love! could you and I with Him conspire. 94 (ed.4)

17 Ah, Moon of my Delight who know'st no wane,
The Moon of Heav'n is rising once again:
    How oft hereafter rising shall she look
Through this same Garden after me—in vain!
74
Yon rising Moon that looks for us again.
How oft hereafter will she wax and wane;
    How oft hereafter rising look for us
Through this same Garden—and for *one* in vain! 100 (ed.4)

18 And when Thyself with shining Foot shall pass
Among the Guests Star-scattered on the Grass,
    And in thy joyous Errand reach the Spot
Where I made one—turn down an empty Glass!
75
And when like her, O Saki, you shall pass...
And in your joyous errand reach the spot. 101 (ed.4)

19 Mrs Browning's death is rather a relief to me, I must
say: no more Aurora Leighs, thank God! A woman of
real genius, I know; but what is the upshot of it all?
She and her sex had better mind the kitchen and their
children; and perhaps the poor: except in such things
as little novels, they only devote themselves to what
men do much better, leaving that which men do worse
or not at all.
Letter to W.H. Thompson, 15 July 1861. For Browning's
rejoinder see 106:1

20 Taste is the feminine of genius.
To J.R. Lowell, Oct. 1877

21 A Mr Wilkinson, a clergyman.
Hallam Tennyson, *Tennyson*, ii.276. An imitation of
Wordsworth's worst style.

F. SCOTT FITZGERALD 1896–1940

22 In the real dark night of the soul it is always three
o'clock in the morning.
The Crack-Up, ed. E. Wilson (1945), John Peale Bishop, *The
Hours*. The phrase 'dark night of the soul' was used as the Spanish
title of a work by St. John of the Cross known in English as *The
Ascent of Mount Carmel* (1578-80)

23 Her voice is full of money.
The Great Gatsby, ch.7

24 Let me tell you about the very rich. They are different
from you and me.
The Rich Boy. 'Notebooks E' in *The Crack-Up* records Ernest
Hemingway's rejoinder: 'Yes, they have more money.'

ROBERT FITZSIMMONS 1862–1917

1 The bigger they come, the harder they fall.
Said before his fight with Jefferies in San Francisco, 9 June 1899

GUSTAVE FLAUBERT 1821–1880

2 *Nous ferons tout ce qui nous plaira! nous laisserons pousser notre barbe!*
We'll do just as we like! We'll grow beards!
Bouvard et Pécuchet, ch.1

3 *Les livres ne se font pas comme les enfants, mais comme les pyramides…et ça ne sert à rien! et ça reste dans le désert!…Les chacals pissent au bas et les bourgeois montent dessus.*
Books are made not like children but like pyramids…and they're just as useless! and they stay in the desert!…Jackals piss at their foot and the bourgeois climb up on them.
Letter to Ernest Feydeau (1821–73), Nov./Dec. 1857

JAMES ELROY FLECKER 1884–1915

4 For pines are gossip pines the wide world through.
Brumana

5 Half to forget the wandering and the pain,
Half to remember days that have gone by,
And dream and dream that I am home again!

6 Noon strikes on England, noon on Oxford town,
Beauty she was statue cold—there's blood upon her
     gown:
Noon of my dreams, O noon!
Proud and godly kings had built her, long ago,
With her towers and tombs and statues all arow,
With her fair and floral air and the love that lingers
     there,
And the streets where the great men go.
The Dying Patriot

7 West of these out to seas colder than the Hebrides I
     must go
Where the fleet of stars is anchored and the young
     star-captains glow.

8 The dragon-green, the luminous, the dark, the
     serpent-haunted sea.
The Gates of Damascus. West Gate

9 We who with songs beguile your pilgrimage
And swear that Beauty lives though lilies die,
We Poets of the proud old lineage
Who sing to find your hearts, we know not why,—
What shall we tell you? Tales, marvellous tales
Of ships and stars and isles where good men rest.
The Golden Journey to Samarkand (1913), Prologue

10 When the great markets by the sea shut fast
     All that calm Sunday that goes on and on:
When even lovers find their peace at last,
     And Earth is but a star, that once had shone.

11 How splendid in the morning glows the lily; with
     what grace he throws
His supplication to the rose.
Hassan (1922), I.i

12 And some to Meccah turn to pray, and I toward thy
     bed, Yasmin.

13   For one night or the other night
Will come the Gardener in white, and gathered flowers
are dead, Yasmin.

14 For lust of knowing what should not be known,
We take the Golden Road to Samarkand.
V.ii

15 And once I touched a broken girl
     And knew that marble bled.
Oak and Olive

16 I have seen old ships sail like swans asleep
Beyond that village which men still call Tyre,
With leaden age o'ercargoed, dipping deep
For Famagusta and the hidden sun
That rings black Cyprus with a lake of fire.
The Old Ships (1915)

17 But now through friendly seas they softly run,
Painted the mid-sea blue or the shore-sea green,
Still patterned with the vine and grapes in gold.

18 And with great lies about his wooden horse
     Set the crew laughing, and forgot his course.

19 It was so old a ship—who knows, who knows?
     And yet so beautiful, I watched in vain
To see the mast burst open with a rose,
     And the whole deck put on its leaves again.

20 And walk with you, and talk with you, like any other
     boy.
Rioupéroux

21 A ship, an isle, a sickle moon—
     With few but with how splendid stars
The mirrors of the sea are strewn
     Between their silver bars.
A Ship, an Isle, and a Sickle Moon

22 And old Maeonides the blind
Said it three thousand years ago.
To a Poet a Thousand Years Hence

23 O friend unseen, unborn, unknown,
     Student of our sweet English tongue,
Read out my words at night, alone:
     I was a poet, I was young.

RICHARD FLECKNOE d. 1678?

24 Still-born Silence! thou that art
Floodgate of the deeper heart.
Miscellania (1653)

MARJORY FLEMING 1803–1811

25 A direful death indeed they had
That would put any parent mad
But she was more than usual calm
She did not give a singel dam.
Journal, p.29

26 The most devilish thing is 8 times 8 and 7 times 7 it is
what nature itselfe cant endure.
p.47

27 To-day I pronounced a word which should never come
out of a lady's lips it was that I called John a Impudent
Bitch.
p.51

28 I am going to turn over a new life and am going to be
a very good girl and be obedient to Isa Keith, here
there is plenty of gooseberries which makes my teeth
watter.
p.76

29 I hope I will be religious again but as for regaining my

character I despare.
p.80

1 An annibabtist is a thing I am not a member of.
p.99

2 Sentiment is what I am not acquainted with.

3 My dear Isa,
  I now sit down on my botom to answer all your kind
  and beloved letters which you was so good as to
  write to me.
Letters. I, To Isabella

4 O lovely O most charming pug
  Thy graceful air and heavenly mug...
  His noses cast is of the roman
  He is a very pretty weoman
  I could not get a rhyme for roman
  And was obliged to call it weoman.
Poems

PAUL FLEMING 1609–1640

5 *Des grossen Vaters Helm ist viel zu weit dem Sohne.*
  The mighty father's helm is far too big for his son.
Die jetzigen Deutschen

ANDREW FLETCHER OF SALTOUN 1655–1716

6 I knew a very wise man so much of Sir Chr—'s
  sentiment, that he believed if a man were permitted to
  make all the ballads, he need not care who should
  make the laws of a nation.
Political Works. **Letter to the Marquis of Montrose, and
Others** (1703)

JOHN FLETCHER 1579–1625
See also under BEAUMONT

7 Best while you have it use your breath,
  There is no drinking after death.
The Bloody Brother (with Jonson and others), II.ii, song

8 And he that will go to bed sober,
  Falls with the leaf still in October.

9 Three merry boys, and three merry boys,
  And three merry boys are we,
  As ever did sing in a hempen string
  Under the Gallows-Tree.
III.ii

10 Come, we are stark naught all, bad's the best of us.
IV.ii

11 Death hath so many doors to let out life.
The Custom of the Country (with Massinger), II.ii. See
336:1, 420:11, 566:26

12 But what is past my help, is past my care.
The Double Marriage (with Massinger), I.i

13 Our acts our angels are, or good or ill,
  Our fatal shadows that walk by us still.
An Honest Man's Fortune, Epilogue

14 *Leon:* I have heard you are poetical.
  Mallfort: Something given that way.
The Lover's Progress (rev. Massinger), I.i

15 Deeds, not words shall speak me.
III.vi

16 I find the medicine worse than the malady.
III.ii

17 Nothing's so dainty sweet, as lovely melancholy.
The Nice Valour (with Middleton), III.iii, song

18 'Tis virtue, and not birth that makes us noble:
  Great actions speak great minds, and such should
    govern.
The Prophetess (with Massinger), II.iii

19 Are you at ease now? Is your heart at rest?
  Now you have got a shadow, an umbrella
  To keep the scorching world's opinion
  From your fair credit.
Rule a Wife and Have a Wife, III.i

20 I'll have a fling.
v

21 Daisies smell-less, yet most quaint,
                And sweet thyme true,
  Primrose first born child of Ver,
  Merry Springtime's Harbinger.
Two Noble Kinsmen (with Shakespeare), I.i

22 Care-charming Sleep, thou easer of all woes,
  Brother to Death.
Valentinian, V.ii, song

23 Come sing now, sing; for I know ye sing well,
  I see ye have a singing face.
The Wild-Goose Chase, II.ii

24 Whistle and she'll come to you.
Wit Without Money, IV.iv

25 Charity and beating begins at home.
V.ii

26 Have you not maggots in your brains?
Women Pleased, III.iv

PHINEAS FLETCHER 1582–1650

27 Poorly (poor man) he liv'd; poorly (poor man) he
    di'd.
The Purple Island (1633), I.xix

28 His little son into his bosom creeps,
  The lively picture of his father's face.
XII.vi

29 Drop, drop, slow tears,
      And bathe those beauteous feet,
  Which brought from Heav'n
      The news and Prince of Peace.
An Hymn

30 In your deep floods
      Drown all my faults and fears;
  Not let His eye
      See sin, but through my tears.

31 Love is like linen often chang'd, the sweeter.
Sicelides (1614), III.v

32 The coward's weapon, poison.
V.iii

33 Love's tongue is in the eyes.
Piscatory Eclogues (1633), eclog. V, xiii

JEAN-PIERRE CLARIS DE FLORIAN 1755–1794

34 *Plaisir d'amour ne dure qu'un moment,*
  Chagrin d'amour dure toute la vie.
  Love's pleasure lasts but a moment; love's sorrow
    lasts all through life.
Celestine. See 327:19

JOHN FLORIO 1553?–1625

1 England is the paradise of women, the purgatory of men, and the hell of horses.
Second Frutes (1591)

DR F.J. FOAKES JACKSON 1855–1941

2 It's no use trying to be *clever*—we are all clever here; just try to be *kind*—a little kind.
Said to a recently elected young don at Jesus College, Cambridge. Oral tradition. Noted in A.C. Benson's Commonplace Book

MARSHAL FOCH 1851–1929

3 *Mon centre cède, ma droite recule, situation excellente. J'attaque!*
My centre is giving way, my right is in retreat; situation excellent. I shall attack.
Aston, *Biography of Foch* (1929), ch.13

JOSÉ DA FONSECA
and PEDRO CAROLINO fl. 1855

4 The walls have hearsay.
O Novo Guia da Conversação em Portuguez e Inglez (1855), **Idiotisms and Proverbs.** Selections from this book were first published in England by James Millington in 1883 under the title *English as she is spoke: or a Jest in sober earnest.*

5 *Por dinheiro baila o perro.* Nothing some money nothing of Swiss.
A literal translation of the Portuguese proverb would be *The dog dances for money*. It is suspected that the *Novo Guia* was prepared with the help of a French-English dictionary. See 404:5

SAMUEL FOOTE 1720–1777

6 Born in a cellar,...and living in a garret.
The Author (1757), II

7 So she went into the garden to cut a cabbage-leaf, to make an apple-pie; and at the same time a great she-bear, coming up the street, pops its head into the shop. 'What! no soap?' So he died, and she very imprudently married the barber; and there were present the Picninnies, and the Joblillies, and the Garyalies, and the grand Panjandrum himself, with the little round button at top, and they all fell to playing the game of catch as catch can, till the gun powder ran out at the heels of their boots.
Farrago composed by Foote to test the vaunted memory of the actor Charles Macklin. See *Quarterly Review* (1854), 95.516

8 For as the old saying is,
When house and land are gone and spent
Then learning is most excellent.
Taste (1752), I.i

9 He is not only dull in himself, but the cause of dullness in others.
Boswell, *Life of Johnson*, ed. Powell, IV, p.178. Parody of 441:3

MISS C.F. FORBES 1817–1911

10 The sense of being well-dressed gives a feeling of inward tranquillity which religion is powerless to bestow.
Emerson, *Social Aims*

HENRY FORD 1863–1947

11 History is more or less bunk.
Chicago Tribune, 25 May 1916

JOHN FORD c.1586–1639

12 Tempt not the stars, young man, thou canst not play
With the severity of fate.
The Broken Heart (1633), I.iii

13 I am...a mushroom
On whom the dew of heaven drops now and then.

14 The joys of marriage are the heaven on earth,
Life's paradise, great princess, the soul's quiet,
Sinews of concord, earthly immortality,
Eternity of pleasures; no restoratives
Like to a constant woman.
II.ii

15   There's not a hair
Sticks on my head but, like a leaden plummet,
It sinks me to the grave: I must creep thither;
The journey is not long.
IV.ii

16 He hath shook hands with time.
V.ii

17 We can drink till all look blue.
The Lady's Trial (1638), IV.ii

18   Tell us, pray, what devil
This melancholy is, which can transform
Men into monsters.
III.i

19 Parthenophil is lost, and I would see him;
For he is like to something I remember,
A great while since, a long, long time ago.
The Lover's Melancholy (1629)

20   Why, I hold fate
Clasp'd in my fist, and could command the course
Of time's eternal motion, hadst thou been
One thought more steady than an ebbing sea.
'Tis Pity She's a Whore (1633), V.iv

HOWELL FORGY 1908–

21 Praise the Lord, and pass the ammunition.
Attr. when a Naval Lt., at Pearl Harbor, 7 Dec. 1941

E.M. FORSTER 1879–1970

22 They go forth into it [the world] with well-developed bodies, fairly developed minds, and undeveloped hearts. [Public schoolboys.]
Abinger Harvest (1936), pt.I, **Notes on the English Character,** first published 1920

23 Everything must be like something, so what is this like?
Our Diversions, 3 'The Doll Souse', first published 1924

24 Yes—oh dear yes—the novel tells a story.
Aspects of the Novel, ch.2

25 I felt for a moment that the whole Wilcox family was a fraud, just a wall of newspapers and motor-cars and golf-clubs, and that if it fell I should find nothing behind it but panic and emptiness.
Howards End, ch.4

26 All men are equal—all men, that is to say, who

possess umbrellas.
ch.6

1 Personal relations are the important thing for ever and
ever, and not this outer life of telegrams and anger.
ch.19

2 Only connect! That was the whole of her sermon. Only
connect the prose and the passion, and both will be
exalted, and human love will be seen at its highest.
ch.22

3 Death destroys a man; the idea of Death saves him.
ch.27

4 The good societies say, 'I tell you to do this because I
am Cambridge'. The bad ones say, 'I tell you to do
that because I am the great world'—not 'because I am
Peckham', or 'Billingsgate', or 'Park Lane', but
'because I am the great world'. They lie.
The Longest Journey, ch.7

5 The very wood seems to be made of mud, the
inhabitants of mud moving.
A Passage to India, ch.1

6 'I don't think I understand people very well. I only
know whether I like or dislike them.' 'Then you are an
Oriental.'
ch.2

7 The so-called white races are really pinko-gray.
ch.7

8 The echo in a Marabar cave…is entirely devoid of
distinction…Hope, politeness, the blowing of a nose,
the squeak of a bat, all produce 'boum'
ch.14

9 God si Love. Is this the final message of India?
ch.33

10 I do not believe in Belief…Lord I disbelieve—help
thou my unbelief.
Two Cheers for Democracy, pt.2. **What I Believe.** See 119:11

11 My law-givers are Erasmus and Montaigne, not Moses
and St Paul.

12 I hate the idea of causes, and if I had to choose
between betraying my country and betraying my
friend, I hope I should have the guts to betray my
country.

13 So Two cheers for Democracy: one because it admits
variety and two because it permits criticism. Two
cheers are quite enough: there is no occasion to give
three. Only Love the Beloved Republic deserves that.

14 Works of art, in my opinion, are the only objects in
the material universe to possess internal order, and
that is why, though I don't believe that only art
matters, I do believe in Art for Art's sake.
Art for Art's Sake. See 162:5, 163:9

15 Creative writers are always greater than the causes
that they represent.
Gide and George

CHARLES FOSTER 1828–1904

16 Isn't this a billion dollar country?
At the 51st Congress; retorting to a Democratic gibe about a
'million dollar Congress'. Also attr. Thomas B. Reed.

SIR GEORGE FOSTER 1847–1931

17 In these somewhat troublesome days when the great

Mother Empire stands splendidly isolated in Europe.
Canadian House of Commons, 16 Jan. 1896

CHARLES FOURIER 1772–1837

18 *L'extension des privilèges des femmes est le principe
général de tous progrès sociaux.*
The extension of women's rights is the basic principle
of all social progress.
Théorie des Quatre Mouvements (1808), II.iv

CHARLES JAMES FOX 1749–1806

19 How much the greatest event it is that ever happened
in the world! and how much the best!
On the Fall of the Bastille. Letter to Fitzpatrick, 30 July 1789.
Russell, *Life and Times of C.J. Fox*, vol.ii, p.361

20 He was uniformly of an opinion which, though not a
popular one, he was ready to aver, that the right of
governing was not property but a trust.
On Pitt's scheme of Parliamentary Reform. J.L. Hammond, *C.J.
Fox* (1903), p.75

21 No man could be so wise as Thurlow looked.
Campbell, *Lives of the Lord Chancellors* (1846), vol.v, p.661

22 I die happy.
Last Words, Russell, *op.cit.,* vol.iii, ch.69

GEORGE FOX 1624–1691

23 I told them I lived in the virtue of that life and power
that took away the occasion of all wars.
Fox had been offered a captaincy in the army of the
Commonwealth, against the forces of the King, in 1651. *Journal,*
ed. N. Penney (1911), vol.I, p.11

HENRY FOX
see 1ST LORD HOLLAND

HENRY RICHARD VASSALL FOX
see 3RD LORD HOLLAND

HENRY STEPHEN FOX 1791–1846

24 I am so changed that my oldest creditors would hardly
know me.
After an illness. Quoted by Byron in a letter to John Murray, 8
May 1817

ANATOLE FRANCE 1844–1924

25 *Désarmer les forts et armer les faibles ce serait
changer l'ordre social que j'ai mission de conserver.
La justice est la sanction des injustices établies.*
To disarm the strong and arm the weak would be to
change the social order which it's my job to preserve.
Justice is the means by which established injustices are
sanctioned.
Crainquebille, iv

26 *La majestueuse égalité des lois, qui interdit au riche
comme au pauvre de coucher sous les ponts, de
mendier dans les rues et de voler du pain.*
The majestic egalitarianism of the law, which forbids
rich and poor alike to sleep under bridges, to beg in the
streets, and to steal bread.
Le Lys Rouge (1894), ch.7

27 *Il fut des temps barbares et gothiques où les mots
avaient un sens; alors les écrivains exprimaient des*

pensées.
It was in the barbarous, gothic times when words had a meaning; in those days, writers expressed thoughts.
La Vie Littéraire (1888-92), vol.II. **M. Charles Morice**

FRANCIS I 1494–1547

1 *De toutes choses ne m'est demeuré que l'honneur et la vie qui est saulve.*
Of all I had, only honour and life have been spared.
Letter to his mother after his defeat at Pavia, 1525. *Collection des Documents Inédits sur l'Histoire de France* (1847), I, 129.
Usually cited as *'Tout est perdu fors l'honneur'* (All is lost save honour).

ST. FRANCIS DE SALES 1567–1622

2 *Ce sont les grans feux qui s'enflamment au vent, mays les petitz s'esteignent si on ne les y porte a couvert.*
Big fires flare up in a wind, but little ones are blown out unless they are carried in under cover.
Introduction à la vie dévote (1609), pt.III, ch.34

BENJAMIN FRANKLIN 1706–1790

3 Remember, that time is money.
Advice to Young Tradesman (1748)

4 No nation was ever ruined by trade.
Essays. Thoughts on Commercial Subjects

5 The having made a young girl miserable may give you frequent bitter reflection; none of which can attend the making of an old woman happy.
On the Choice of a Mistress (i.e. wife)

6 A little neglect may breed mischief,...for want of a nail, the shoe was lost; for want of a shoe the horse was lost; and for want of a horse the rider was lost.
Maxims...Prefixed to *Poor Richard's Almanack* (1758)

7 Some are weather-wise, some are otherwise.
Poor Richard's Almanack, Feb. 1735

8 Necessity never made a good bargain.
Apr. 1735

9 Three may keep a secret, if two of them are dead.
July 1735

10 At twenty years of age, the will reigns; at thirty, the wit; and at forty, the judgement.
June 1741

11 Dost thou love life? Then do not squander time, for that's the stuff life is made of.
June 1746

12 Many have been ruined by buying good pennyworths.
Sept. 1747

13 He that lives upon hope will die fasting.
1758, preface

14 We must indeed all hang together, or, most assuredly, we shall all hang separately.
Remark to John Hancock, at the Signing of the Declaration of Independence, 4 July 1776

15 Man is a tool-making animal.
Boswell, *Life of Johnson*, 7 Apr. 1778

16 Here Skugg
Lies snug
As a bug
In a rug.
Letter to Georgiana Shipley on the death of her squirrel, 26 Sept. 1772. 'Skug' was a dialect word meaning 'squirrel'.

17 There never was a good war, or a bad peace.
Letter to Quincy, 11 Sept. 1783

18 But in this world nothing can be said to be certain, except death and taxes.
Letter to Jean Baptiste Le Roy, 13 Nov. 1789

19 What is the use of a new-born child?
When asked what was the use of a new invention. J. Parton, *Life and Times of Benjamin Franklin* (1864), pt.IV, ch.17

20   The body of
              Benjamin Franklin, printer,
           (Like the cover of an old book,
                Its contents worn out,
        And stript of its lettering and gilding)
              Lies here, food for worms!
        Yet the work itself shall not be lost,
     For it will, as he believed, appear once more
                      In a new
              And more beautiful edition,
                Corrected and amended
                    By its Author!
Epitaph for himself. See 553:22

21 *Ça ira.*
That will go its way.
Oral trad. Remark made in Paris, 1776-7, on the American War of Independence. Taken up in the French Revolution and used as the refrain of the song to the tune *'Carillon national'* by 1790. Ladré later claimed to have written the words.

FREDERICK THE GREAT 1712–1786

22 My people and I have come to an agreement which satisfies us both. They are to say what they please, and I am to do what I please.
Ascribed

23 *Ihr Racker, wollt ihr ewig leben?*
Rascals, would you live for ever?
When the Guards hesitated, at Kolin, 18 June 1757

E.A. FREEMAN 1823–1892

24 A saying which fell from myself in one of the debates in Congregation on the Modern Language Statute has been quoted in several places...'chatter about Shelley'...I mentioned that I had lately read a review of a book about Shelley in which the critic...praised or blamed the author...for his 'treatment of the Harriet problem'.
Contemporary Review, Oct. 1887: 'Literature and Language'. The two phrases are often telescoped as 'chatter about Harriet'.

JOHN HOOKHAM FRERE 1769–1846

25 The feather'd race with pinions skim the air—
Not so the mackerel, and still less the bear!
Progress of Man, l.34

26 Ah! who has seen the mailed lobster rise,
Clap her broad wings, and soaring claim the skies?
l.44

ROBERT FROST 1874–1963

27 I have been one acquainted with the night.
I have walked out in rain—and back in rain.
I have outwalked the furthest city light.

I have looked down the saddest city lane.
I have passed by the watchman on his beat

And dropped my eyes, unwilling to explain.
Acquainted with the Night

1 I'd like to get away from earth awhile
And then come back to it and begin over.
May no fate willfully misunderstand me
And half grant what I wish and snatch me away
Not to return. Earth's the right place for love:
I don't know where it's likely to get better.
I'd like to go by climbing a birch tree,
And climb black branches up a snow-white trunk
Toward heaven, till the tree could bear no more,
But dipped its top and set me down again.
That would be good both going and coming back.
One could do worse than be a swinger of birches.
Birches

2 'Home is the place where, when you have to go there,
They have to take you in'.

         'I should have called it
Something you somehow haven't to deserve.'
The Death of the Hired Man

3 They cannot scare me with their empty spaces
Between stars—on stars where no human race is.
I have it in me so much nearer home
To scare myself with my own desert places.
Desert Places

4 Spades take up leaves
No better than spoons,
And bags full of leaves
Are light as balloons.
Gathering Leaves

5 The land was ours before we were the land's.
The Gift Outright

6 Such as we were we gave ourselves outright
(The deed of gift was many deeds of war)
To the land vaguely realizing westward,
But still unstoried, artless, unenhanced,
Such as she was, such as she would become.

7 Forgive, O Lord, my little jokes on Thee
And I'll forgive Thy great big one on me.
In the clearing, **Cluster of Faith**

8 Something there is that doesn't love a wall.
North of Boston (1914). **Mending Wall**

9 My apple trees will never get across
And eat the cones under his pines, I tell him.
He only says, 'Good fences make good neighbours.'

10 Two roads diverged in a wood, and I—
I took the one less traveled by,
And that has made all the difference.
The Road Not Taken

11 Whoever it is that leaves him out so late,
When other creatures have gone to stall and bin,
Ought to be told to come and take him in.
The Runaway

12 The woods are lovely, dark, and deep,
But I have promises to keep,
And miles to go before I sleep,
And miles to go before I sleep.
Stopping by Woods on a Snowy Evening

13 To err is human, not to, animal.
The White-tailed Hornet

14 The ruling passion in man is not as Viennese as is
claimed. It is rather a gregarious instinct to keep

together by minding each other's business. Grex rather
than sex.
The Constant Symbol

15 Writing free verse is like playing tennis with the net
down.
Address at Milton Academy, Milton, Mass., 17 May 1935

16 Poetry is what gets lost in translation.
Attr.

J.A. FROUDE 1818–1894

17 Wild animals never kill for sport. Man is the only one
to whom the torture and death of his fellow-creatures
is amusing in itself.
Oceana (1886), ch.5

18 Men are made by nature unequal. It is vain, therefore,
to treat them as if they were equal.
Short Studies on Great Subjects. 3rd Ser (1877). **Party Politics**

19 Experience teaches slowly, and at the cost of
mistakes.

20 Fear is the parent of cruelty.

CHRISTOPHER FRY 1907–

21 This is the morning to take the air.
The Boy with a Cart (1938)

22 You can't be beaten by a piece of timber; it isn't
princely in a man to be beaten by a piece of timber.

23 There's a dreariness in dedicated spirits
That makes the promised land seem older than the
fish.
The Dark is Light Enough (1954), Act I

24   I sometimes think
His critical judgement is so exquisite
It leaves us nothing to admire except his opinion.
Act II

25   In our plain defects
We already know the brotherhood of man.

26 Out there, in the sparkling air, the sun and the rain
Clash together like the cymbals clashing
When David did his dance. I've an April blindness.
You're hidden in a cloud of crimson catherine-wheels.
The Lady's Not For Burning (1948), Act I

27   What, after all,
Is a halo? It's only one more thing to keep clean.

28   You bubble-mouthing, fog-blathering,
Chin-chuntering, chap-flapping, liturgical,
Turgidical, base old man!

29   Am I invisible?
Am I inaudible? Do I merely festoon
The room with my presence?

30   Using words
That are only fit for the Bible.
Act II

31 We should be like stars now that it's dark;
Use ourselves up to the last bright dregs
And vanish in the morning.

32   The moon is nothing
But a circumambulating aphrodisiac
Divinely subsidized to provoke the world
Into a rising birth-rate.
Act III

1   I hear
A gay modulating anguish, rather like music.

2 The Great Bear is looking so geometrical
One would think that something or other could be
    proved.

3 *Margaret:* She must be lost.
Nicholas: Who isn't? The best
Thing we can do is to make wherever we're lost in
Look as much like home as we can.

4 It's all this smell of cooped-up angels
Worries me.
A Sleep of Prisoners (1951)

5 Run on, keep your head down, cross at the double
The bursts of open day between the nights.

6   I hope
I've done nothing so monosyllabic as to cheat.
A spade is never so merely a spade as the word
Spade would imply.
Venus Observed (1950), II.i

7 Over all the world
Men move unhoming, and eternally
Concerned: a swarm of bees who have lost their
    queen.

8   What a minefield
Life is! One minute you're taking a stroll in the sun,
The next your legs and arms are all over the hedge.
There's no dignity in it.
A Yard of Sun (1970), Act II

9 There may always be another reality
To make fiction of the truth we think we've arrived at.

RICHARD BUCKMINSTER FULLER 1895–

10   God, to me, it seems,
is a verb
not a noun,
proper or improper.
No More Secondhand God. See 267:9

THOMAS FULLER 1608–1661

11 A proverb is much matter decocted into few words.
The History of the Worthies of England (1662), ch.2

12 Worldly wealth he cared not for, desiring only to make
both ends meet. [Of Edmund Grindall.]
Worthies of Cumberland

13 Know most of the rooms of thy native country before
thou goest over the threshold thereof.
The Holy State and the Profane State (1642), bk.ii, ch.4. **Of
Travelling**

14 A little skill in antiquity inclines a man to Popery; but
depth in that study brings him about again to our
religion.
ch.6. **The True Church Antiquary**

15 But our captain counts the Image of God nevertheless
his image, cut in ebony as if done in ivory.
ch.20. **The Good Sea-Captain**

16 Light (God's eldest daughter) is a principal beauty in
building.
bk.iii, ch.7. **Of Building**

17 Anger is one of the sinews of the soul.
ch.8. **Of Anger**

18 Learning hath gained most by those books by which

the printers have lost.
ch.18. **Of Books**

19 He was one of a lean body and visage, as if his eager
soul, biting for anger at the clog of his body, desired to
fret a passage through it.
bk.v, ch.19. **Life of the Duke of Alva**

THOMAS FULLER 1654–1734

20 It is a silly game where nobody wins.
Gnomologia (1732), No. 2880

21 We are all Adam's children but silk makes the
difference.
No.5425

HENRY FUSELI 1741–1825

22 Blake is damned good to steal from!
Gilchrist, *Life of Blake* (1863), ch.vii

ROSE FYLEMAN 1877–1957

23 There are fairies at the bottom of our garden.
Fairies and Chimneys

THOMAS GAINSBOROUGH 1727–1788

24 We are all going to Heaven, and Vandyke is of the
company.
Attr. last words. Boulton, *Thomas Gainsborough*, ch.9

REVD. THOMAS GAISFORD 1779–1855

25 Nor can I do better, in conclusion, than impress upon
you the study of Greek literature, which not only
elevates above the vulgar herd, but leads not
infrequently to positions of considerable emolument.
Christmas Day Sermon in the Cathedral, Oxford. Revd. W.
Tuckwell, *Reminiscences of Oxford* (2nd ed., 1907), p.124

HUGH GAITSKELL 1906–1963

26 There are some of us who will fight and fight and
fight again to save the party we love.
Speech, Labour Party Conference, Scarborough, 5 Oct. 1960

GAIUS 2nd cent. A.D.

27 *Damnosa hereditas.*
Ruinous inheritance.
Institutes, ii.163

J.K. GALBRAITH 1908–

28 In the affluent society no useful distinction can be
made between luxuries and necessaries.
The Affluent Society, ch.21.iv

GALILEO GALILEI 1564–1642

29 *Eppur si muove.*
But it does move.
Attr. to Galileo after his recantation in 1632. The earliest
apppearance of the phrase is perhaps in Baretti, *Italian Library*
(1757), p.52

JOHN GALSWORTHY 1867–1933

30 He [Jolyon] was afflicted by the thought that where
Beauty was, nothing ever ran quite straight, which, no

doubt, was why so many people looked on it as immoral.
In Chancery (1920), ch.13

1 Nobody tells me anything. [James Forsyte.]
The Man of Property (1906), pt.I, ch.i

JOHN GALT 1779–1839

2 From the lone shieling of the misty island
Mountains divide us, and the waste of seas—
Yet still the blood is strong, the heart is Highland,
And we in dreams behold the Hebrides!
Fair these broad meads, these hoary woods are grand;
But we are exiles from our fathers' land.
Attr. *Canadian Boat Song ('The Lone Shieling')*. 'Noctes
Ambrosianae', XLVI, Blackwoods Magazine, Sept. 1829

GRETA GARBO 1905–

3 I want to be alone.
Grand Hotel (1932), script by William A. Drake.
The phrase had frequently been attributed to Garbo before being
used in the film; she seems in fact to have said on various
occasions (off screen) 'I want to be left alone' and 'Why don't
they leave me alone.'

FEDERICO GARCÍA LORCA 1899–1936

4 *Verte desnuda es recordar la Tierra.*
To see you naked is to recall the Earth.
Casida de la mujer tendida

5 *A las cinco de la tarde.*
A las cinco en punto de la tarde.
At five in the afternoon. At exactly five in the
afternoon.
Llanto por Ignacio Sánchez Mejías, 1

6 *Que no quiero verla!*
I don't want to see it!
2

7 *Verde que te quiero verde,*
Verde viento. Verde ramas.
Green I love you green. Green wind. Green branches.
Romance sonámbulo

RICHARD GARDINER b. c.1533

8 Sowe Carrets in your Gardens, and humbly praise God
for them, as for a singular and great blessing.
*Profitable Instructions for the Manuring, Sowing and Planting
of Kitchen Gardens* (1599)

JAMES A. GARFIELD 1831–1881

9 Fellow-citizens: God reigns, and the Government at
Washington lives!
Speech on Assassination of Lincoln, 1865

GIUSEPPE GARIBALDI 1807–1882

10 *Soldati, io esco da Roma. Chi vuole continuare la
guerra contro lo straniero venga con me. Non posso
offrirgli nè onori nè stipendi; gli offro fame, sete,
marcie forzate, battaglie e morte. Chi ama la patria
mi segua.*
Men, I'm getting out of Rome. Anyone who wants to
carry on the war against the outsiders, come with me.
I can't offer you either honours or wages; I offer you
hunger, thirst, forced marches, battles and death.

Anyone who loves his country, follow me.
Guerzoni, *Garibaldi* (1882), I. p.331. (The speech was not
recorded verbatim.)

DAVID GARRICK 1717–1779

11 Prologues precede the piece—in mournful verse;
As undertakers—walk before the hearse.
Apprentice, prologue

12 Are these the choice dishes the Doctor has sent us?
Is this the great poet whose works so content us?
This Goldsmith's fine feast, who has written fine
books?
Heaven sends us good meat, but the Devil sends
cooks.
On Doctor Goldsmith's Characteristical Cookery

13 Here lies Nolly Goldsmith, for shortness call'd Noll,
Who wrote like an angel, but talk'd like poor Poll.
Impromptu Epitaph. See 231:16, 278:19

14 I've that within—for which there are no plaisters.
Prologue to Goldsmith's *She Stoops to Conquer*

15 A fellow-feeling makes one wond'rous kind.
An Occasional Prologue on Quitting the Theatre, 10 June 1776

16 Kitty, a fair, but frozen maid,
    Kindled a flame I still deplore;
The hood-wink'd boy I call'd in aid,
Much of his near approach afraid.
    So fatal to my suit before.
A Riddle. *Lady's Magazine*, June 1762

WILLIAM LLOYD GARRISON 1805–1879

17 I am in earnest—I will not equivocate—I will not
excuse—I will not retreat a single inch—and I will be
heard!
Salutatory Address of *The Liberator*, 1 Jan. 1831

18 Our country is the world—our countrymen are all
mankind.
Prospectus of *The Liberator*, 15 Dec. 1837

19 The compact which exists between the North and the
South is 'a covenant with death and an agreement with
hell'.
Resolution adopted by the Massachusetts Anti-Slavery Society, 27
Jan. 1843. See 58:22

SIR SAMUEL GARTH 1661–1719

20 Hard was their lodging, homely was their food;
For all their luxury was doing good.
Claremont (1715), 1.148

21 A barren superfluity of words.
The Dispensary (1699), c.2, 1.95

MRS. GASKELL 1810–1865

22 A man...is *so* in the way in the house!
Cranford (1851-3), ch.1

23 [The Cranford ladies'] dress is very independent of
fashion; as they observe, 'What does it signify how we
dress here at Cranford, where everybody knows us?'
And if they go from home, their reason is equally
cogent: 'What does it signify how we dress here,
where nobody knows us?'

24 Get her a flannel waistcoat and flannel drawers,
ma'am, if you wish to keep her alive. But my advice
is, kill the poor creature at once. [Capt. Brown on

Miss Betsey Barker's cow.]

1 We were none of us musical, though Miss Jenkyns beat time, out of time, by way of appearing to be so.

2 'It is very pleasant dining with a bachelor,' said Miss Matty, softly, as we settled ourselves in the counting-house. 'I only hope it is not improper; so many pleasant things are!'
ch.4

3 Bombazine would have shown a deeper sense of her loss. [Miss Jenkyns.]
ch.7

4 That kind of patriotism which consists in hating all other nations.
Sylvia's Lovers (1863), ch.1

GAVARNI 1804–1866

5 *Les enfants terribles.*
The embarrassing young.
Title of a series of prints

JOHN GAY 1685–1732

6   I rage, I melt, I burn,
The feeble God has stabb'd me to the heart.
Acis and Galatea (c.1720), ii

7 Bring me an hundred reeds of decent growth,
To make a pipe for my capacious mouth.

8 O ruddier than the cherry,
O sweeter than the berry,

9 Wou'd you gain the tender creature?
Softly, gently, kindly treat her,
    Suff'ring is the lover's part.
Beauty by constraint, possessing,
You enjoy but half the blessing,
    Lifeless charms, without the heart.

10 Love sounds the alarm, and Fear is a flying.

11 How, like a moth, the simple maid
    Still plays about the flame!
The Beggar's Opera (1728), Act I, sc.iv, air iv

12 Our Polly is a sad slut! nor heeds what we have taught her.
I wonder any man alive will ever rear a daughter!
sc.viii, air vii

13 Do you think your mother and I should have liv'd comfortably so long together, if ever we had been married?

14 Can Love be controll'd by advice?
air viii

15 Well, Polly; as far as one woman can forgive another, I forgive thee.
air ix

16 *Polly:* Then all my sorrows are at an end.
Mrs Peachum: A mighty likely speech, in troth, for a wench who is just married!

17 Money, wife, is the true fuller's earth for reputations, there is not a spot or a stain but what it can take out.
sc.ix

18 The comfortable estate of widowhood, is the only hope that keeps up a wife's spirits.
sc.x

19 Away, hussy. Hang your husband and be dutiful.

20 Even butchers weep!
sc.xii

21 Pretty Polly, say,
When I was away,
Did your fancy never stray
    To some newer lover?
sc.xiii, air xiv

22 If with me you'd fondly stray.
Over the hills and far away.
air xvi

23 O what pain it is to part!
air xvii

24 We retrench the superfluities of mankind.
Act II, sc.i

25 Fill ev'ry glass, for wine inspires us,
    And fires us
With courage, love and joy.
Women and wine should life employ.
Is there ought else on earth desirous?
air xix

26 If the heart of a man is deprest with cares,
The mist is dispell'd when a woman appears.
sc.iii, air xxi

27 I must have women. There is nothing unbends the mind like them.

28 Youth's the season made for joys,
    Love is then our duty.
sc.iv, air xxii

29 To cheat a man is nothing; but the woman must have fine parts indeed who cheats a woman!

30 Man may escape from rope and gun;
    Nay, some have outliv'd the doctor's pill:
Who takes a woman must be undone,
    That basilisk is sure to kill.
The fly that sips treacle is lost in the sweets,
So he that tastes woman, woman, woman,
    He that tastes woman, ruin meets.
sc.viii, air xxvi

31 *Macheath:* Have you no bowels, no tenderness, my dear Lucy, to see a husband in these circumstances?
Lucy: A husband!
Macheath: In ev'ry respect but the form.
sc.ix

32 I am ready, my dear Lucy, to give you satisfaction—if you think there is any in marriage?

33 In one respect indeed, our employment may be reckoned dishonest, because, like great Statesmen, we encourage those who betray their friends.
sc.x

34 I think you must ev'n do as other widows—buy yourself weeds, and be cheerful.
sc.xi

35 How happy could I be with either,
    Were t'other dear charmer away!
But while ye thus tease me together,
    To neither a word will I say.
sc.xiii, air xxxv

36 One wife is too much for one husband to hear,
But two at a time there's no mortal can bear.
This way, and that way, and which way I will,
What would comfort the one, t'other wife would take

ill.
Act III, sc.xi, air liii

1 The charge is prepar'd; the lawyers are met;
The Judges all rang'd (a terrible show!).
air lvii

2 She who has never lov'd, has never liv'd.
The Captives (1724), II.i

3 If e'er your heart has felt the tender passion
You will forgive this just, this pious fraud.
IV.x

4 She who trifles with all
Is less likely to fall
Than she who but trifles with one.
The Coquet Mother and the Coquet Daughter

5 Then nature rul'd, and love, devoid of art,
Spoke the consenting language of the heart.
Dione, prologue

6 Behold the victim of Parthenia's pride!
He saw, he sigh'd, he lov'd, was scorn'd and died.
I.i

7 He best can pity who has felt the woe.
II.ii

8   Woman's mind
Oft' shifts her passions, like th'inconstant wind;
Sudden she rages, like the troubled main,
Now sinks the storm, and all is calm again.
v

9 A woman's friendship ever ends in love.
IV.vi

10 Whence is thy learning? Hath thy toil
O'er books consum'd the midnight oil?
Fables (1727), introduction, l.15. See 403:10

11 Where yet was ever found a mother,
Who'd give her booby for another?
iii. **The Mother, the Nurse, and the Fairy**, l.33

12 Envy's a sharper spur than pay,
No author ever spar'd a brother,
Wits are gamecocks to one another.
x. **The Elephant and the Bookseller**, l.74

13 An open foe may prove a curse,
But a pretended friend is worse.
xvii. **The Shepherd's Dog and the Wolf**, l.33

14 Those who in quarrels interpose,
Must often wipe a bloody nose.
xxxiv. **The Mastiff**, l.1

15 Fools may our scorn, not envy raise,
For envy is a kind of praise.
xliv. **The Hound and the Huntsman**, l.29

16 And when a lady's in the case,
You know, all other things give place.
l. **The Hare and Many Friends**, l.41

17 Give me, kind heaven, a private station,
A mind serene for contemplation.
(1738), ii. **The Vulture, the Sparrow, and Other Birds**, l.69

18 Studious of elegance and ease,
Myself alone I seek to please.
viii. **The Man, the Cat, the Dog, and the Fly**, l.127

19 Behold the bright original appear.
A Letter to a Lady, l.85

20 Praising all alike, is praising none.
l.114

21 One always zealous for his country's good.
l.118

22 Life is a jest; and all things show it.
I thought so once; but now I know it.
My Own Epitaph

23 Variety's the source of joy below,
From whence still fresh revolving pleasures flow.
In books and love, the mind one end pursues,
And only change th'expiring flame renews.
On a Miscellany of Poems

24 Whether we can afford it or no, we must have
superfluities.
Polly (1729), I.i

25 No, sir, tho' I was born and bred in England, I can
dare to be poor, which is the only thing now-a-days
men are asham'd of.
xi

26 An inconstant woman, tho' she has no chance to be
very happy, can never be very unhappy.
xiv

27   No retreat.
      No retreat.
They must conquer or die who've no retreat.
II.x

28 All in the Downs the fleet was moor'd,
The streamers waving in the wind,
When black-ey'd Susan came aboard.
Sweet William's Farewell to Black-Eyed Susan

29 They'll tell thee, sailors, when away,
In ev'ry port a mistress find.

30 Adieu, she cries! and wav'd her lily hand.

31 A miss for pleasure, and a wife for breed.
The Toilette

SIR ERIC GEDDES 1875–1937

32 The Germans, if this Government is returned, are
going to pay every penny; they are going to be
squeezed, as a lemon is squeezed—until the pips
squeak. My only doubt is not whether we can squeeze
hard enough, but whether there is enough juice.
Speech, Cambridge, 10 Dec. 1918. *Cambridge Daily News*, 3/2

LLOYD GEORGE 1863–1945

33 What is our task? To make Britain a fit country for
heroes to live in.
Speech, Wolverhampton, 24 Nov. 1918

KING GEORGE I 1660–1727

34 I hate all Boets and Bainters.
Campbell, *Lives of the Chief Justices*, ch.30, Lord Mansfield

KING GEORGE II 1683–1760

35 *Non, j'aurai des maîtresses.*
No, I shall have mistresses.
Reply to Queen Caroline when, as she lay dying, she urged him to
marry again. Her reply to this was '*Ah! mon dieu! cela n'empêche
pas*'. Hervey, *Memoirs of George the Second* (1848), vol.ii

36 Mad, is he? Then I hope he will *bite* some of my other
generals.
Reply to the Duke of Newcastle who complained that General
Wolfe was a madman. Willson, *The life and letters of James
Wolfe*, ch.17

KING GEORGE III 1738–1820

1 Born and educated in this country I glory in the name of Briton.
Speech from the Throne, 1760

2 'Was there ever,' cried he, 'such stuff as great part of Shakespeare? Only one must not say so! But what think you?—what?—Is there not sad stuff? what?—what?'
To Fanny Burney (in her *Diary*, 19 Dec. 1785)

KING GEORGE IV 1762–1830

3 Harris, I am not well; pray get me a glass of brandy.
On first seeing Caroline of Brunswick. Earl of Malmesbury, *Diaries*, 5 Apr. 1795

KING GEORGE V 1865–1936

4 I have many times asked myself whether there can be more potent advocates of peace upon earth through the years to come than this massed multitude of silent witnesses to the desolation of war.
On the battlefield cemeteries in Flanders, 1922. Gavin Stamp (ed.), *Silent Cities* (1977), p.19

5 How is the Empire?
Last words. *The Times*, 21 Jan. 1936

EDWARD GIBBON 1737–1794

6 My early and invincible love of reading, which I would not exchange for the treasures of India.
Autobiography (World's Classics ed.), p.27

7 To the University of Oxford I acknowledge no obligation; and she will as cheerfully renounce me for a son, as I am willing to disclaim her for a mother. I spent fourteen months at Magdalen College: they proved the fourteen months the most idle and unprofitable of my whole life.
p.36

8 If I inquire into the manufactures of the monks of Magdalen, if I extend the inquiry to the other colleges of Oxford and Cambridge, a silent blush, or a scornful frown, will be the only reply. The fellows or monks of my time were decent easy men, who supinely enjoyed the gifts of the founder.

9 Their dull and deep potations excused the brisk intemperance of youth.

10 Dr — well remembered that he had a salary to receive, and only forgot that he had a duty to perform.
p.44

11 It was here that I suspended my religious inquiries (aged 17).
p.63

12 I saw and loved.
p.83

13 I sighed as a lover, I obeyed as a son.

14 Crowds without company, and dissipation without pleasure. [Of London.]
p.90

15 The captain of the Hampshire grenadiers…has not been useless to the historian of the Roman empire.
p.106. (Referring to his own army service.)

16 It was at Rome, on the 15th of October, 1764, as I sat musing amidst the ruins of the Capitol, while the barefoot friars were singing vespers in the Temple of Jupiter, that the idea of writing the decline and fall of the city first started to my mind.
p.160

17 The first of earthly blessings, independence.
p.176

18 I will not dissemble the first emotions of joy on the recovery of my freedom, and, perhaps, the establishment of my fame. But my pride was soon humbled, and a sober melancholy was spread over my mind, by the idea that I had taken an everlasting leave of an old and agreeable companion, and that whatsoever might be the future date of my History, the life of the historian must be short and precarious.
p.205

19 My English text is chaste, and all licentious passages are left in the decent obscurity of a learned language.
p.212

20 I must reluctantly observe that two causes, the abbreviation of time, and the failure of hope, will always tinge with a browner shade the evening of life.
p.221

21 The various modes of worship, which prevailed in the Roman world, were all considered by the people as equally true; by the philosopher, as equally false; and by the magistrate, as equally useful. And thus toleration produced not only mutual indulgence, but even religious concord.
The Decline and Fall of the Roman Empire (1776–88), ch.2

22 The principles of a free constitution are irrecoverably lost, when the legislative power is nominated by the executive.
ch.3

23 His reign is marked by the rare advantage of furnishing very few materials for history; which is, indeed, little more than the register of the crimes, follies, and misfortunes of mankind.
(Of Antoninus Pius, Roman Emperor, 137–161 A.D.) See 561:10

24 If a man were called to fix the period in the history of the world during which the condition of the human race was most happy and prosperous, he would, without hesitation, name that which elapsed from the death of Domitian to the accession of Commodus.

25 Twenty-two acknowledged concubines, and a library of sixty-two thousand volumes attested the variety of his inclinations; and from the productions which he left behind him, it appears that both the one and the other were designed for use rather than for ostentation. [Emperor Gordian the Younger.]
ch.7

26 All taxes must, at last, fall upon agriculture.
ch.8

27 Corruption, the most infallible symptom of constitutional liberty.
ch.21

28 In every deed of mischief he [Comenus] had a heart to resolve, a head to contrive, and a hand to execute.
ch.48. See 152:19

29 All that is human must retrograde if it does not advance.
ch.71

ORLANDO GIBBONS 1583–1625

1 The silver swan, who, living had no note,
  When death approached unlocked her silent throat.
  from *The First Set of Madrigals and Motets of Five Parts*
  (1612)

STELLA GIBBONS 1902–

2 Something nasty in the woodshed.
  Cold Comfort Farm (1932), *passim*

3 Every year, in the fulness o'summer, when the
  sukebind hangs heavy from the wains…'tes the same.
  And when the spring comes her hour is upon her
  again. 'Tes the hand of Nature, and we women cannot
  escape it.
  ch.5

4 [Mr. Mybug] said that, by god, D.H. Lawrence was
  right when he had said there must be a dumb, dark,
  dull, bitter belly-tension between a man and a woman,
  and how else could this be achieved save in the long
  monotony of marriage?
  ch.20

WILFRED GIBSON 1878–1962

5 The heart-break in the heart of things.
  Lament (1926). See 557:17

ANDRÉ GIDE 1869–1951

6 *Hugo—hélas!*
  When asked to name the greatest poet of the nineteenth century.
  André Gide–Paul Valéry Correspondance 1890–1942, p.494

SIR HUMPHREY GILBERT 1539?–1583

7 We are as near to heaven by sea as by land!
  Richard Hakluyt, *Voyages* (1600), iii, p.159. See 206:15

W.S. GILBERT 1836–1911

8 Down went the owners—greedy men whom hope of
    gain allured:
  Oh, dry the starting tear, for they were heavily
    insured.
  The 'Bab' Ballads (1866–71), **Etiquette**

9 He had often eaten oysters, but had never had enough.

10 There were captains by the hundred, there were
    baronets by dozens.
  Ferdinando and Elvira

11 Only find out who it is that writes those lovely cracker
  mottoes!

12 The padre said, 'Whatever have you been and gone
    and done?'
  Gentle Alice Brown

13 From a highly impossible tree
  In a highly impossible scene.
  Only a Dancing Girl

14 Which is pretty, but I don't know what it means.
  Story of Prince Agib

15 Then they began to sing
  That extremely lovely thing,
  'Scherzando! ma non troppo ppp.'

16 Oh, I am a cook and a captain bold,
    And the mate of the *Nancy* brig,

And a bo'sun tight, and a midshipmite,
    And the crew of the captain's gig.
  The Yarn of the 'Nancy Bell'

17 He led his regiment from behind—
    He found it less exciting.
  The Gondoliers (1899), I

18 That celebrated,
  Cultivated,
  Underrated
        Nobleman,
  The Duke of Plaza Toro!

19 Of that there is no manner of doubt—
  No probable, possible shadow of doubt—
  No possible doubt whatever.

20 His terrible taste for tippling.

21 A taste for drink, combined with gout,
  Had doubled him up for ever.

22 Oh, 'tis a glorious thing, I ween,
  To be a regular Royal Queen!
  No half-and-half affair, I mean,
  But a right-down regular Royal Queen!

23 All shall equal be.
  The Earl, the Marquis, and the Dook,
  The Groom, the Butler, and the Cook,
  The Aristocrat who banks with Coutts,
  The Aristocrat who cleans the boots.

24   But the privilege and pleasure
        That we treasure beyond measure
  Is to run on little errands for the Ministers of State.
  II

25 With the gratifying feeling that our duty has been
    done!

26 Take a pair of sparkling eyes,
        Hidden, ever and anon,
            In a merciful eclipse.

27 Take my counsel, happy man;
  Act upon it, if you can!

28 He wished all men as rich as he
  (And he was as rich as he could be),
  So to the top of every tree
        Promoted everybody.

29 Ambassadors cropped up like hay,
  Prime Ministers and such as they
  Grew like asparagus in May,
        And dukes were three a penny.

30 When every blessed thing you hold
  Is made of silver, or of gold,
        You long for simple pewter.
  When you have nothing else to wear
  But cloth of gold and satins rare,
  For cloth of gold you cease to care—
        Up goes the price of shoddy.

31 When every one is somebodee,
  Then no one's anybody.

32 I see no objection to stoutness, in moderation.
  Iolanthe (1882), I

33 For I'm to be married to-day—to-day—
  Yes, I'm to be married to-day!

34 Thou the singer; I the song!

35 Bow, bow, ye lower middle classes!

Bow, bow, ye tradesmen, bow, ye masses.

1 The Law is the true embodiment
Of everything that's excellent.
It has no kind of fault or flaw,
And I, my Lords, embody the Law.

2 The constitutional guardian I
Of pretty young wards in Chancery,
All very agreeable girls—and none
Are over the age of twenty-one.
A pleasant occupation for
A rather susceptible Chancellor!

3 For I'm not so old, and not so plain,
And I'm quite prepared to marry again.

4 Spurn not the nobly born
With love affected,
Nor treat with virtuous scorn
The well-connected.

5 Hearts just as pure and fair
May beat in Belgrave Square
As in the lowly air
Of Seven Dials.

6 When I went to the Bar as a very young man,
(Said I to myself—said I),
I'll work on a new and original plan,
(Said I to myself—said I).

7 My son in tears—and on his wedding day!

8 When all night long a chap remains
On sentry-go, to chase monotony
He exercises of his brains,
That is, assuming that he's got any.
Though never nurtured in the lap
Of luxury, yet I admonish you,
I am an intellectual chap,
And think of things that would astonish you.
I often think it's comical
How Nature always does contrive
That every boy and every gal,
That's born into the world alive,
Is either a little Liberal,
Or else a little Conservative!
II

9 When in that House MPs divide,
If they've a brain and cerebellum too,
They have to leave that brain outside,
And vote just as their leaders tell 'em to.

10 The prospect of a lot
Of dull MPs in close proximity,
All thinking for themselves is what
No man can face with equanimity.

11 The House of Peers, throughout the war,
Did nothing in particular,
And did it very well:
Yet Britain set the world ablaze
In good King George's glorious days!

12 When you're lying awake with a dismal headache, and
repose is taboo'd by anxiety,
I conceive you may use any language you choose to
indulge in, without impropriety.

13 For you dream you are crossing the Channel, and
tossing about in a steamer from Harwich—
Which is something between a large bathing machine

and a very small second class carriage.

14 And you're giving a treat (penny ice and cold meat) to
a party of friends and relations—
They're a ravenous horde—and they all came on board
at Sloane Square and South Kensington Stations.
And bound on that journey you find your attorney
(who started that morning from Devon);
He's a bit undersized, and you don't feel surprised
when he tells you he's only eleven.

15 In your shirt and your socks (the black silk with gold
clocks), crossing Salisbury Plain on a bicycle.

16 The shares are a penny, and ever so many are taken by
Rothschild and Baring,
And just as a few are allotted to you, you awake with a
shudder despairing.

17 The darkness is gone
Ditto ditto my song.

18 A wandering minstrel I—
A thing of shreds and patches,
Of ballads, songs and snatches,
And dreamy lullaby!
The Mikado (1885), I

19 And I am right,
And you are right,
And all is right as right can be!

20 I can trace my ancestry back to a protoplasmal
primordial atomic globule. Consequently, my family
pride is something in-conceivable. I can't help it. I
was born sneering.

21 It revolts me, but I do it!

22 I accept refreshment at any hands, however lowly.

23 I am happy to think that there will be no difficulty in
finding plenty of people whose loss will be a distinct
gain to society at large.

24 As some day it may happen that a victim must be
found,
I've got a little list—I've got a little list
Of society offenders who might well be under ground
And who never would be missed—who never would
be missed!

25 The idiot who praises, with enthusiastic tone,
All centuries but this, and every country but his own.
See 129:28, 185:14, 366:6

26 They wouldn't be sufficiently degraded in their own
estimation unless they were insulted by a very
considerable bribe.

27 Three little maids from school are we,
Pert as a schoolgirl well can be,
Filled to the brim with girlish glee.

28 Life is a joke that's just begun.

29 Three little maids who, all unwary,
Come from a ladies' seminary.

30 Modified rapture!

31 Awaiting the sensation of a short, sharp shock,
From a cheap and chippy chopper on a big black
block.

32 Ah, pray make no mistake,
We are not shy;
We're very wide awake,

    The moon and I!
II

1 Sing a merry madrigal.

2 Here's a how-de-doo!

3 Matrimonial devotion
Doesn't seem to suit her notion.

4 Ha! ha! Family Pride, how do you like *that*, my buck?

5   My object all sublime
  I shall achieve in time—
To let the punishment fit the crime—
    The punishment fit the crime;
  And make each prisoner pent
  Unwillingly represent
A source of innocent merriment!
  Of innocent merriment.

6 The music-hall singer attends a series
  Of masses and fugues and 'ops'
    By Bach, interwoven
    With Spohr and Beethoven,
At classical Monday Pops.

7 The billiard sharp whom any one catches,
  His doom's extremely hard—
    He's made to dwell—
    In a dungeon cell
On a spot that's always barred.
And there he plays extravagant matches
  In fitless finger-stalls
    On a cloth untrue
    With a twisted cue
And elliptical billiard balls.

8 I drew my snickersnee!

9   Though trunkless, yet
  It couldn't forget
The deference due to me!

10 I have a left shoulder-blade that is a miracle of
loveliness. People come miles to see it. My right elbow
has a fascination that few can resist.

11 Something lingering, with boiling oil in it, I fancy.

12 Merely corroborative detail, intended to give artistic
verisimilitude to an otherwise bald and unconvincing
narrative.

13 The flowers that bloom in the spring,
    Tra la,
Have nothing to do with the case.

14 I've got to take under my wing,
    Tra la,
A most unattractive old thing,
    Tra la,
With a caricature of a face.
And that's what I mean when I say, or I sing,
'Oh bother the flowers that bloom in the spring.'

15 On a tree by a river a little tom-tit
Sang 'Willow, titwillow, titwillow!'
And I said to him, 'Dicky-bird, why do you sit
Singing Willow, titwillow, titwillow?'

16 'Is it weakness of intellect, birdie?' I cried,
'Or a rather tough worm in your little inside?'
With a shake of his poor little head he replied,
  'Oh, willow, titwillow, titwillow!'

17 He sobbed and he sighed, and a gurgle he gave,

Then he plunged himself into the billowy wave,
And an echo arose from the suicide's grave—
  'Oh willow, titwillow, titwillow!'

18   There's a fascination frantic
  In a ruin that's romantic;
Do you think you are sufficiently decayed?

19 Twenty love-sick maidens we,
Love-sick all against our will.
Patience (1881), I

20 If you're anxious for to shine in the high aesthetic line
  as a man of culture rare.

21 You must lie upon the daisies and discourse in novel
  phrases of your complicated state of mind,
The meaning doesn't matter if it's only idle chatter of
  a transcendental kind.
    And everyone will say,
    As you walk your mystic way,
'If this young man expresses himself in terms too deep
  for *me*,
Why, what a very singularly deep young man this deep
  young man must be!'

22 For Art stopped short in the cultivated court of the
  Empress Josephine.

23 Then a sentimental passion of a vegetable fashion
  must excite your languid spleen,
An attachment à la Plato for a bashful young potato, or
  a not too French French bean!
Though the Philistines may jostle, you will rank as an
  apostle in the high aesthetic band,
If you walk down Piccadilly with a poppy or a lily in
  your medieval hand.
    And everyone will say,
    As you walk your flowery way,
'If he's content with a vegetable love which would
  certainly not suit *me*,
Why, what a most particularly pure young man this
  pure young man must be!'

24 While this magnetic,
  Peripatetic
Lover, he lived to learn,
  By no endeavour
  Can magnet ever
Attract a Silver Churn!
II

25 'High diddle diddle'
Will rank as an idyll,
If I pronounce it chaste!

26 Francesca di Rimini, miminy, piminy,
Je-ne-sais-quoi young man!

27 A greenery-yallery, Grosvenor Galley,
Foot-in-the-grave young man!

28 A Sewell & Cross young man,
A Howell & James young man,
A pushing young particle—'What's the next article?'
Waterloo House young man!

29 I'm called Little Buttercup—dear Little Buttercup,
Though I could never tell why.
H.M.S. *Pinafore* (1878), I

30 I am the Captain of the *Pinafore*;
And a right good captain too!

31 And I'm never, never sick at sea!

What, never?
No, never!
What, *never*?
Hardly ever!
He's hardly ever sick at sea!
Then give three cheers, and one cheer more,
For the hardy Captain of the *Pinafore*!

1 You're exceedingly polite,
And I think it only right
To return the compliment.

2 Though 'Bother it' I may
Occasionally say,
I never use a big, big D—

3 And so do his sisters, and his cousins and his aunts!
His sisters and his cousins,
Whom he reckons up by dozens,
And his aunts!

4 When I was a lad I served a term
As office boy to an Attorney's firm.
I cleaned the windows and I swept the floor,
And I polished up the handle of the big front door.
I polished up that handle so carefullee
That now I am the Ruler of the Queen's Navee!

5 And I copied all the letters in a big round hand.

6 I always voted at my party's call,
And I never thought of thinking for myself at all.

7 Stick close to your desks and never go to sea,
And you all may be Rulers of the Queen's Navee!

8 Things are seldom what they seem,
Skim milk masquerades as cream.
II

9 He is an Englishman!
For he himself has said it,
And it's greatly to his credit,
That he is an Englishman!

10 For he might have been a Roosian,
A French, or Turk, or Proosian,
Or perhaps Ital-ian!
But in spite of all temptations
To belong to other nations,
He remains an Englishman!

11 The other, upper crust,
A regular patrician.

12 It is, it is a glorious thing
To be a Pirate King.
The Pirates of Penzance (1879), I

13 The question is, had he not been
A thing of beauty,
Would she be swayed by quite as keen
A sense of duty?

14 Poor wandering one!
Though thou hast surely strayed,
Take heart of grace,
Thy steps retrace,
Poor wandering one!

15 Take heart, fair days will shine;
Take any heart, take mine!

16 I'm very good at integral and differential calculus,
I know the scientific names of beings animalculous;
In short, in matters vegetable, animal, and mineral,

I am the very model of a modern Major-General.

17 About binomial theorems I'm teeming with a lot of news,
With many cheerful facts about the square on the hypoteneuse.

18 When the foeman bares his steel,
Tarantara, tarantara!
We uncomfortable feel,
Tarantara.
II

19 When constabulary duty's to be done,
A policeman's lot is not a happy one.

20 When the enterprising burglar's not a-burgling.

21 When the coster's finished jumping on his mother—
He loves to lie a-basking in the sun.

22 They are no members of the common throng;
They are all noblemen who have gone wrong!

23 No Englishman unmoved that statement hears,
Because, with all our faults, we love our House of Peers.

24 With all our faults, we love our Queen.

25 Politics we bar,
They are not our bent:
On the whole we are
Not intelligent.
Princess Ida (1884), I

26 Yet everybody says I'm such a disagreeable man!
And I can't think why!

27 To everybody's prejudice I know a thing or two;
I can tell a woman's age in half a minute—and I do!

28 Man is Nature's sole mistake!
II

29 Oh, don't the days seem lank and long
When all goes right and nothing goes wrong,
And isn't your life extremely flat
With nothing whatever to grumble at!
III

30 All baronets are bad.
Ruddigore (1887), I

31 I'll wager in their joy they kissed each other's cheek
(Which is what them furriners do).

32 You must stir it and stump it,
And blow your own trumpet,
Or trust me, you haven't a chance.

33 He combines the manners of a Marquis with the morals of a Methodist.

34 When he's excited he uses language that would make your hair curl.

35 If a man can't forge his own will, whose will can he forge?
II

36 Some word that teems with hidden meaning—like Basingstoke.

37 This particularly rapid, unintelligible patter
Isn't generally heard, and if it is it doesn't matter.

38 Time was when Love and I were well acquainted.
The Sorcerer (1877), I

39 Forsaking even military men.

1 I was a pale young curate then.

2   Oh! My name is John Wellington Wells,
I'm a dealer in magic and spells.

3 So I fell in love with a rich attorney's
Elderly ugly daughter.
Trial by Jury (1875)

4 She may very well pass for forty-three
In the dusk with a light behind her!

5 For now I am a Judge,
And a good Judge too.

6 And a good job too!

7 Is life a boon?
If so, it must befall
That Death, whene'er he call,
Must call too soon.
The Yeoman of the Guard (1888), I

8 I have a song to sing O!
Sing me your song, O!

9 It's a song of a merryman, moping mum,
Whose soul was sad, and whose glance was glum,
Who sipped no sup, and who craved no crumb,
As he sighed for the love of a ladye.

10 'Tis ever thus with simple folk—an accepted wit has
but to say 'Pass the mustard', and they roar their ribs
out!
II

ERIC GILL 1882–1940

11 That state is a state of Slavery in which a man does
what he likes to do in his spare time and in his working
time that which is required of him.
Slavery and Freedom (1918)

W.E. GLADSTONE 1809–1898

12 You cannot fight against the future. Time is on our
side.
Speech on the Reform Bill, 1866

13 [The Turks] one and all, bag and baggage, shall, I
hope, clear out from the province they have desolated
and profaned.
House of Commons, 7 May 1877

14 The resources of civilization are not yet exhausted.
Leeds, Speech at Banquet, 7 Oct. 1881

15 It is perfectly true that these gentlemen [the Irish Land
League] wish to march through rapine to disintegration
and dismemberment of the Empire, and, I am sorry to
say, even to the placing of different parts of the
Empire in direct hostility one with the other.
Knowsley, 27 Oct. 1881

16 I would tell them of my own intention to keep my own
counsel…and I will venture to recommend them, as an
old Parliamentary hand, to do the same.
House of Commons, 21 Jan. 1886

17 All the world over, I will back the masses against the
classes.
Liverpool, 28 June 1886

18 We are part of the community of Europe, and we must
do our duty as such.
Carnarvon, 10 Apr. 1888

19 This is the negation of God erected into a system of
Government.
*First Letter to the Earl of Aberdeen on the State persecutions of
the Neapolitan Government,* 8, 1851, p.9n

20 It is not a Life at all. It is a Reticence, in three
volumes.
On J.W. Cross's *Life of George Eliot.* E.F. Benson, *As We Were*
(1930), ch.6

MRS. HANNAH GLASSE fl. 1747

21 Take your hare when it is cased…
The Art of Cookery Made Plain and Easy (1747), ch.1. Cased ;
skinned. The proverbial 'First catch your hare', recorded since
c. 1300, has frequently been misattributed to Mrs. Glasse.

DUKE OF GLOUCESTER 1743–1805

22 Another damned, thick, square book! Always
scribble, scribble, scribble! Eh! Mr Gibbon?
Best's *Literary Memorials.* (Boswell's *Johnson,* vol.ii, p.2n)

**WILLIAM FREDERICK, 2nd DUKE OF
GLOUCESTER** 1776–1834

23 Who's Silly Billy now?
Lending his own nick-name to William IV, his nephew. G. Smith,
Lectures and Essays (1881), 'A Wirepuller of Kings'

A.D. GODLEY 1856–1925

24 What is this that roareth thus?
Can it be a Motor Bus?
Yes, the smell and hideous hum
Indicat Motorem Bum…
How shall wretches live like us
Cincti Bis Motoribus?
Domine, defende nos
Contra hos Motores Bos!
The Motor Bus. Letter to C.R.L.F., 10 Jan. 1914

HERMANN GOERING 1893–1946

25 Guns will make us powerful; butter will only make us
fat.
Radio Broadcast, summer of 1936, often misquoted as 'Guns
before butter'.

JOHANN WOLFGANG VON GOETHE
1749–1832

26 Lord Byron is only great as a poet; as soon as he
reflects, he is a child.
Conversations with Eckermann, 18 Jan. 1825

27 *Im übrigen ist es zuletzt die grösste Kunst, sich zu
beschränken und zu isolieren.*
For the rest of it, the last and greatest art is to limit and
isolate oneself.
20 Apr. 1825

28 *Ich kenne mich auch nicht und Gott soll mich auch
davor behüten.*
I do not know myself, and God forbid that I should.
10 Apr. 1829. See 9:21

29 *Es irrt der Mensch, so lang er strebt.*
Man is in error throughout his strife.
Faust, pt.i (1808). Prolog im Himmel

30 *Zwei Seelen wohnen, ach! in meiner Brust.*
Two souls dwell, alas! in my breast.
Vor dem Thor

1 *Ich bin der Geist der stets verneint.*
I am the spirit that always denies.
Studierzimmer

2 *Entbehren sollst Du! sollst entbehren!*
Das ist der ewige Gesang.
Deny yourself! You must deny yourself!
That is the song that never ends.

3 *Grau, teurer Freund, ist alle Theorie*
Und grün des Lebens goldner Baum.
All theory, dear friend, is grey, but the golden tree of
actual life springs ever green.

4 *Meine Ruh' ist hin,*
Mein Herz ist schwer.
My peace is gone,
My heart is heavy.
Gretchen am Spinnrad

5 *Die Tat ist alles, nichts der Ruhm.*
The deed is all, and not the glory.
pt. ii (1832). **Hochgebirg**

6 *Das Ewig-Weibliche zieht uns hinan.*
Eternal Woman draws us upward.
last line

7 *Du musst herrschen und gewinnen,*
Oder dienen und verlieren,
Leiden oder triumphieren
Amboss oder Hammer sein.
You must be master and win, or serve and lose, grieve
or triumph, be the anvil or the hammer.
Der Gross-Cophta (1791), Act ii

8 *Wenn es eine Freude ist das Gute zu geniessen, so ist*
es eine grössere das Bessere zu empfinden, und in der
Kunst ist das Beste gut genug.
Since it is a joy to have the benefit of what is good, it
is a greater one to experience what is better, and in art
the best is good enough.
Italienische Reise (1816–17), 3 Mar. 1787

9 *Der Aberglaube ist die Poesie des Lebens.*
Superstition is the poetry of life.
Sprüche in Prosa (1819)

10 *Es bildet ein Talent sich in der Stille,*
Sich ein Charakter in dem Strom der Welt.
Talent develops in quiet places, character in the full
current of human life.
Torquato Tasso (1790), i.2

11 *Über allen Gipfeln*
Ist Ruh'.
Over all the mountain tops is peace.
Wanderers Nachtlied

12 *Wer nie sein Brot mit Tränen ass,*
Wer nie die kummervollen Nächte
Auf seinem Bette weinend sass,
Der kennt euch nicht, ihr himmlischen Mächte.
Who never ate his bread in sorrow,
Who never spent the darksome hours
Weeping and watching for the morrow
He knows ye not, ye heavenly powers.
Wilhelm Meisters Lehrjahre (1795–6), II.13. Tr. Carlyle

13 *Kennst du das Land, wo die Zitronen blühn?*
Im dunkeln Laub die Gold-Orangen glühn,
Ein sanfter Wind vom blauen Himmel weht,
Die Myrte still und hoch der Lorbeer steht—
Kennst du es wohl?
　　　Dahin! Dahin!

Möcht ich mit dir, o mein Geliebter, ziehn!
Know you the land where the lemon-trees bloom? In
the dark foliage the gold oranges glow; a soft wind
hovers from the sky, the myrtle is still and the laurel
stands tall—do you know it well? There, there, I
would go, O my beloved, with thee!
III.i

14 *Mehr Licht!*
More light!
Attr. dying words. (Actually: *'Macht doch den zweiten*
Fensterladen auch auf, damit mehr Licht hereinkomme': 'Open
the second shutter, so that more Licht can come in.')

15 *Ohne Hast, aber ohne Rast.*
Without haste, but without rest.
Motto

OLIVER GOLDSMITH 1730–1774

16 Sweet Auburn, loveliest village of the plain,
Where health and plenty cheered the labouring swain,
Where smiling spring its earliest visit paid,
And parting summer's lingering blooms delayed.
The Deserted Village (1770), l.1

17 The bashful virgin's side-long looks of love,
The matron's glance that would those looks reprove.
l.29

18 Ill fares the land, to hast'ning ills a prey,
Where wealth accumulates, and men decay;
Princes and lords may flourish, or may fade;
A breath can make them, as a breath has made;
But a bold peasantry, their country's pride,
When once destroy'd, can never be supplied.
A time there was, ere England's griefs began,
When every rood of ground maintain'd its man;
For him light labour spread her wholesome store,
Just gave what life requir'd, but gave no more;
His best companions, innocence and health;
And his best riches, ignorance of wealth.
l.51

19 How happy he who crowns in shades like these,
A youth of labour with an age of ease.
l.99

20 Bends to the grave with unperceiv'd decay,
While resignation gently slopes the way;
And, all his prospects bright'ning to the last,
His heaven commences ere the world be pass'd.
l.109

21 The watchdog's voice that bay'd the whisp'ring wind,
And the loud laugh that spoke the vacant mind.
l.121. See 137:1

22 A man he was to all the country dear,
And passing rich with forty pounds a year;
Remote from towns he ran his godly race,
Nor e'er had chang'd nor wished to change his place;
Unpractis'd he to fawn, or seek for power,
By doctrines fashion'd to the varying hour;
Far other aims his heart had learned to prize,
More skill'd to raise the wretched than to rise.
l.141

23 He chid their wand'rings, but reliev'd their pain.
l.150

24 At church, with meek and unaffected grace,
His looks adorn'd the venerable place;
Truth from his lips prevail'd with double sway,

And fools, who came to scoff, remain'd to pray.
l.177

1 Even children follow'd with endearing wile,
And pluck'd his gown, to share the good man's smile.
l.183

2 A man severe he was, and stern to view;
I knew him well, and every truant knew;
Well had the boding tremblers learn'd to trace
The day's disasters in his morning face;
Full well they laugh'd with counterfeited glee,
At all his jokes, for many a joke had he;
Full well the busy whisper, circling round,
Convey'd the dismal tidings when he frown'd;
Yet he was kind; or if severe in aught,
The love he bore to learning was in fault.
l.197

3 In arguing too, the parson own'd his skill,
For e'en though vanquish'd, he could argue still;
While words of learned length, and thund'ring sound
Amazed the gazing rustics rang'd around,
And still they gaz'd, and still the wonder grew,
That one small head could carry all he knew.
l.211

4 The white-wash'd wall, the nicely sanded floor,
The varnish'd clock that click'd behind the door;
The chest contriv'd a double debt to pay,
A bed at night, a chest of drawers by day.
l.227

5 How wide the limits stand
Between a splendid and a happy land.
l.267

6 In all the silent manliness of grief.
l.384

7 Man wants but little here below,
Nor wants that little long.
Edwin and Angelina, or the Hermit (1766). See 588:8

8 The doctor found, when she was dead,—
Her last disorder mortal.
Elegy on Mrs. Mary Blaize

9 Good people all, of every sort,
Give ear unto my song;
And if you find it wond'rous short,
It cannot hold you long.
Elegy on the Death of a Mad Dog

10 That still a godly race he ran,
Whene'er he went to pray.

11 The naked every day he clad,
When he put on his clothes.

12 And in that town a dog was found,
As many dogs there be,
Both mongrel, puppy, whelp, and hound,
And curs of low degree.

13 The dog, to gain some private ends,
Went mad and bit the man.

14 The man recover'd of the bite,
The dog it was that died.

15 Brutes never meet in bloody fray,
Nor cut each other's throats, for pay.
Logicians Refuted, l.39

16 Our Garrick's a salad; for in him we see
Oil, vinegar, sugar, and saltness agree.
Retaliation (1774), l.11. See 221:13

17 Who, too deep for his hearers, still went on refining,
And thought of convincing, while they thought of dining;
Though equal to all things, for all things unfit,
Too nice for a statesman, too proud for a wit. [Edmund Burke].
l.35

18 Here lies David Garrick, describe me, who can,
An abridgement of all that was pleasant in man.
l.93

19 As a wit, if not first, in the very first line. [Garrick.]
l.96

20 On the stage he was natural, simple, affecting;
'Twas only that when he was off he was acting.
[Garrick.]
l.101

21 When they talk'd of their Raphaels, Correggios, and stuff,
He shifted his trumpet, and only took snuff.
[Reynolds.]
l.145

22 Let schoolmasters puzzle their brain,
With grammar, and nonsense, and learning,
Good liquor, I stoutly maintain,
Gives genius a better discerning.
She Stoops to Conquer, I.i, song

23 Remote, unfriended, melancholy, slow,
Or by the lazy Scheldt, or wandering Po.
The Traveller (1764), l.1

24 Where'er I roam, whatever realms to see,
My heart untravell'd fondly turns to thee;
Still to my brother turns with ceaseless pain,
And drags at each remove a lengthening chain.
l.7

25 Such is the patriot's boast, where'er we roam,
His first, best country ever is, at home.
l.73

26 At night returning, every labour sped,
He sits him down the monarch of a shed;
Smiles by his cheerful fire, and round surveys
His children's looks, that brighten at the blaze;
While his lov'd partner, boastful of her hoard,
Displays her cleanly platter on the board.
l.191

27 To men of other minds my fancy flies,
Embosom'd in the deep where Holland lies.
Methinks her patient sons before me stand,
Where the broad ocean leans against the land.
l.282

28 Pride in their port, defiance in their eye,
I see the lords of human kind pass by.
l.327

29 Laws grind the poor, and rich men rule the law.
l.386

30 In every government, though terrors reign,
Though tyrant kings, or tyrant laws restrain,
How small, of all that human hearts endure,
That part which laws or kings can cause or cure!
l.427

31 When lovely woman stoops to folly
And finds too late that men betray,
What charm can soothe her melancholy,
What art can wash her guilt away?

The only art her guilt to cover,
 To hide her shame from every eye,
To give repentance to her lover
 And wring his bosom—is to die.
Song from *The Vicar of Wakefield,* ch.29

1 As writers become more numerous, it is natural for readers to become more indolent.
The Bee (1759), No. 175. **Upon Unfortunate Merit**

2 He writes indexes to perfection.
The Citizen of the World (1762), letter 29

3 To a philosopher no circumstance, however trifling, is too minute.
letter 30

4 'Did I say so?' replied he coolly; 'to be sure, if I said so, it was so.'
letter 54

5 The true use of speech is not so much to express our wants as to conceal them.
Essays, v. **The Use of Language**

6 I hate the French because they are all slaves, and wear wooden shoes.
xxiv. **Distresses of a Common Soldier**

7 This same philosophy is a good horse in the stable, but an arrant jade on a journey.
The Good-Natured Man (1768), I

8 We must touch his weaknesses with a delicate hand. There are some faults so nearly allied to excellence, that we can scarce weed out the fault without eradicating the virtue.

9 All his faults are such that one loves him still the better for them.

10 I'm now no more than a mere lodger in my own house.

11 Friendship is a disinterested commerce between equals; love, an abject intercourse between tyrants and slaves.

12 Don't let us make imaginary evils, when you know we have so many real ones to encounter.

13 *Leontine:* An only son, sir, might expect more indulgence.
Croaker: An only father, Sir, might expect more obedience.

14 I am told he makes a very handsome corpse, and becomes his coffin prodigiously.

15 Silence is become his mother tongue.
II

16 All men have their faults; too much modesty is his.

17 You, that are going to be married, think things can never be done too fast; but we, that are old, and know what we are about, must elope methodically, madam.

18 In my time, the follies of the town crept slowly among us, but now they travel faster than a stagecoach.
She Stoops to Conquer (1773), I

19 I love every thing that's old; old friends, old times, old manners, old books, old wines.

20 As for disappointing them I should not so much mind; but I can't abide to disappoint myself.

21 Is it one of my well-looking days, child? Am I in face to-day?

22 The very pink of perfection.

23 In a concatenation accordingly.

24 I'll be with you in the squeezing of a lemon.

25 It's a damned long, dark, boggy, dirty, dangerous way.

26 This is Liberty-Hall, gentlemen.
II

27 The first blow is half the battle.

28 Was there ever such a cross-grained brute?
III

29 Women and music should never be dated.

30 As for murmurs, mother, we grumble a little now and then, to be sure. But there's no love lost between us.
IV

31 A book may be amusing with numerous errors, or it may be very dull without a single absurdity.
The Vicar of Wakefield (1761–2, published 1766) advertisement

32 I was ever of opinion, that the honest man who married and brought up a large family, did more service than he who continued single and only talked of population.
ch.1

33 I chose my wife, as she did her wedding gown, not for a fine glossy surface, but such qualities as would wear well.

34 All our adventures were by the fire-side, and all our migrations from the blue bed to the brown.

35 The virtue which requires to be ever guarded is scarcely worth the sentinel.
ch.5

36 With other fashionable topics, such as pictures, taste, Shakespeare, and the musical glasses.

37 Mr Burchell...at the conclusion of every sentence would cry out '*Fudge!*'—an expression which displeased us all.
ch.11

38 Conscience is a coward, and those faults it has not strength enough to prevent it seldom has justice enough to accuse.
ch.13

39 It seemed to me pretty plain, that they had more of love than matrimony in them.
ch.16

40 There is no arguing with Johnson; for when his pistol misses fire, he knocks you down with the butt end of it.
Boswell, *Life of Johnson,* 26 Oct. 1769. See 151:11

41 As I take my shoes from the shoemaker, and my coat from the tailor, so I take my religion from the priest.
9 Apr. 1773

SAMUEL GOLDWYN 1882–1974

42 In two words: im possible.
Alva Johnson, *The Great Goldwyn*

43 You can include me out.
See Zierold, *The Hollywood Tycoons* (1969), ch.3

44 For years I have been known for saying 'Include me out'; but today I am giving it up for ever.
Address at Balliol College, Oxford, 1 Mar. 1945

ADAM LINDSAY GORDON 1833–1870

1 Life is mostly froth and bubble,
　　Two things stand like stone,
Kindness in another's trouble,
　　Courage in your own.
Ye Wearie Wayfarer, Fytte 8

1ST LORD GOSCHEN 1831–1907

2 I have the courage of my opinions, but I have not the
temerity to give a political blank cheque to Lord
Salisbury.
House of Commons, 19 Feb. 1884

3 We have stood alone in that which is called
isolation—our splendid isolation, as one of our
colonial friends was good enough to call it.
Lewes, 26 Feb. 1896. See 217:17

EDMUND GOSSE 1849–1928

4 A sheep in sheep's clothing.
Of T. Sturge Moore, c.1906. Ferris Greenslet, *Under the Bridge*,
ch.12. Also attr. Winston Churchill of Clement Attlee.

DEAN GOULBURN 1818–1897

5 Let the scintillations of your wit be like the
coruscations of summer lightning, lambent but
innocuous.
Sermon at Rugby. Revd. W. Tuckwell, *Reminiscences of Oxford*
(2nd ed., 1907), p.272

JOHN GOWER 1330?–1408

6 It hath and schal ben evermor
That love is maister wher he wile.
Confessio Amantis (1386–90), prologue, l.34

SIR ERNEST GOWERS 1880–1966

7 It is not easy nowadays to remember anything so
contrary to all appearances as that officials are the
servants of the public; and the official must try not to
foster the illusion that it is the other way round.
Plain Words, ch. 3, The Elements

CLEMENTINA STIRLING GRAHAM 1782–1877

8 The best way to get the better of temptation is just to
yield to it.
Mystifications (1859), **Soirée at Mrs Russel's**

HARRY GRAHAM 1874–1936

9 Weep not for little Léonie
Abducted by a French *Marquis!*
Though loss of honour was a wrench
Just think how it's improved her French.
More Ruthless Rhymes for Heartless Homes. **Compensation**

10 O'er the rugged mountain's brow
　　Clara threw the twins she nursed,
And remarked, 'I wonder now
　　Which will reach the bottom first?'
Ruthless Rhymes for Heartless Homes. **Calculating Clara**

11 Aunt Jane observed, the second time
　　She tumbled off a bus,
The step is short from the Sublime
To the Ridiculous.
Equanimity

12 'There's been an accident!' they said,
'Your servant's cut in half; he's dead!'
'Indeed!' said Mr Jones, 'and please
Send me the half that's got my keys.'
Mr. Jones

13 Billy, in one of his nice new sashes,
Fell in the fire and was burnt to ashes;
Now, although the room grows chilly,
I haven't the heart to poke poor Billy.
Tender-Heartedness

JAMES GRAHAM, MARQUIS OF MONTROSE 1612–1650

14 He either fears his fate too much,
　　Or his deserts are small,
That puts it not unto the touch
　　To win or lose it all.
My Dear and Only Love

15 But if thou wilt be constant then,
　　And faithful of thy word,
I'll make thee glorious by my pen,
　　And famous by my sword.

16 Let them bestow on every airth a limb;
Then open all my veins, that I may swim
To thee, my Maker! in that crimson lake;
Then place my parboiled head upon a stake—
Scatter my ashes—strew them in the air;—
Lord! since thou know'st where all these atoms are,
I'm hopeful thou'lt recover once my dust,
And confident thou'lt raise me with the just.
Lines written on the Window of his Jail the Night before his Execution

KENNETH GRAHAME 1859–1932

17 Aunt Maria flung herself on him [the curate]. 'O Mr
Hodgitts!' I heard her cry, 'you are brave! for my sake
do not be rash!' He was not rash.
The Golden Age (1895). **The Burglars**

18 Believe me, my young friend, there is
nothing—absolutely nothing—half so much worth
doing as simply messing about in boats.
The Wind in the Willows (1908), ch.1

19 The clever men at Oxford
　　Know all that there is to be knowed.
But they none of them know one half as much
　　As intelligent Mr Toad.
ch.10

JAMES GRAINGER 1721?–1766

20 What is fame? an empty bubble;
Gold? a transient, shining trouble.
Solitude, l.96

ULYSSES S. GRANT 1822–1885

21 I purpose to fight it out on this line, if it takes all
summer.
Dispatch to Washington, from head-quarters in the field, 11 May
1864

22 I know no method to secure the repeal of bad or
obnoxious laws so effective as their stringent

execution.
Inaugural Address, 4 Mar. 1869

1 No terms except unconditional and immediate
surrender can be accepted. I propose to move
immediately upon your works.
*To Simon Bolivar Buckner, whom he was besieging in Fort
Donelson, 16 Feb. 1862*

2 Let us have peace.
Letter of acceptance of nomination, 29 May 1868

3 Let no guilty man escape, if it can be avoided…No
personal considerations should stand in the way of
performing a public duty.
Indorsement of a letter relating to the Whiskey Ring, 29 July 1875

GEORGE GRANVILLE, BARON LANSDOWNE
1666–1735

4 I'll be this abject thing no more;
    Love, give me back my heart again.
Adieu l'Amour

5 Of all the plagues with which the world is curst,
Of every ill, a woman is the worst.
The British Enchanters (1706), II.i

6 Bright as the day, and like the morning, fair,
Such Cloe is…and common as the air.
Cloe

7 O Love! thou bane of the most generous souls!
Thou doubtful pleasure, and thou certain pain.
Heroic Love (1698), II.i

8 'Tis the talk, and not the intrigue, that's the crime.
The She Gallants (1696), III.i

9 Cowards in scarlet pass for men of war.
V

LORD GRANVILLE 1819–1907

10 Spheres of action.
*Letter to Count Münster, 29 April 1885. Sir Edward Hertslet, Map
of Africa by Treaty* (1894), vol.ii, p.596. See 7:17

ROBERT GRAVES 1895–

11 His eyes are quickened so with grief,
He can watch a grass or leaf
Every instant grow.
Lost Love

12 'Complaints is many and various
And my feet are cold,' says Aquarius,
'There's Venus objects to Dolphin-scales,
And Mars to Crab-spawn found in my pails,
    And the pump has frozen to-night,
    And the pump has frozen to-night.'
Star-talk

PATRICK, 6TH LORD GRAY d.1612

13 A dead woman bites not.
*Oral tradition. Gray advocated the execution of Mary, Queen of
Scots, 1587. See J.B. Black, The Reign of Elizabeth
(1558–1603), 2nd edn. (1959), ch.10: The Master of Gray
whispered…'Mortui non mordent'.*

THOMAS GRAY 1716–1771

14 Ruin seize thee, ruthless King!
    Confusion on thy banners wait,
Tho' fann'd by Conquest's crimson wing

They mock the air with idle state.
The Bard (1757), I.i

15 Weave the warp, and weave the woof,
    The winding-sheet of Edward's race.
Give ample room, and verge enough
    The characters of hell to trace.
II.i

16 Fair laughs the morn, and soft the zephyr blows,
    While proudly riding o'er the azure realm
In gallant trim the gilded vessel goes,
    Youth on the prow, and Pleasure at the helm;
Regardless of the sweeping whirlwind's sway,
That, hush'd in grim repose, expects his evening prey.
ii

17 Ye towers of Julius, London's lasting shame,
With many a foul and midnight murther fed.
iii

18 The curfew tolls the knell of parting day,
    The lowing herd wind slowly o'er the lea,
The ploughman homeward plods his weary way,
    And leaves the world to darkness and to me.

Now fades the glimmering landscape on the sight,
    And all the air a solemn stillness holds,
Save where the beetle wheels his droning flight,
    And drowsy tinklings lull the distant folds.
Elegy in a Country Churchyard (1742–50), 1

19 Save that from yonder ivy-mantled tow'r,
    The moping owl does to the moon complain.
3

20 Beneath those rugged elms, that yew-tree's shade,
    Where heaves the turf in many a mouldering heap,
Each in his narrow cell for ever laid,
    The rude forefathers of the hamlet sleep.

The breezy call of incense-breathing Morn,
    The swallow twitt'ring from the straw-built shed,
The cock's shrill clarion, or the echoing horn,
    No more shall rouse them from their lowly bed.
4

21 Let not ambition mock their useful toil,
    Their homely joys, and destiny obscure;
Nor grandeur hear with a disdainful smile,
    The short and simple annals of the poor.

The boast of heraldry, the pomp of pow'r,
    And all that beauty, all that wealth e'er gave,
Awaits alike th' inevitable hour,
    The paths of glory lead but to the grave.
8

22 Can storied urn or animated bust
    Back to its mansion call the fleeting breath?
Can honour's voice provoke the silent dust,
    Or flatt'ry soothe the dull cold ear of death?
11

23 Full many a gem of purest ray serene,
    The dark unfathom'd caves of ocean bear:
Full many a flower is born to blush unseen,
    And waste its sweetness on the desert air.

Some village-Hampden, that with dauntless breast
    The little tyrant of his fields withstood;
Some mute inglorious Milton here may rest,
    Some Cromwell guiltless of his country's blood.
14

24   Nor circumscrib'd alone

Their growing virtues, but their crimes confin'd;
Forbad to wade through slaughter to a throne,
And shut the gates of mercy on mankind.
17

1 Far from the madding crowd's ignoble strife,
   Their sober wishes never learn'd to stray;
Along the cool sequester'd vale of life
   They kept the noiseless tenor of their way.
19

2 For who to dumb Forgetfulness a prey,
   This pleasing anxious being e'er resign'd,
Left the warm precincts of the cheerful day,
   Nor cast one longing ling'ring look behind?
22

3 Mindful of th' unhonour'd dead.
24

4 Here rests his head upon the lap of Earth
   A youth to fortune and to fame unknown.
Fair Science frown'd not on his humble birth,
   And Melancholy mark'd him for her own.
30

5 He gave to Mis'ry all he had, a tear,
   He gain'd from Heav'n ('twas all he wish'd) a
      friend.
31

6 What female heart can gold despise?
   What cat's averse to fish?
Ode on the Death of a Favourite Cat (1747)

7 A fav'rite has no friend!

8 Not all that tempts your wand'ring eyes
And heedless hearts, is lawful prize;
Nor all, that glisters, gold.

9 Ye distant spires, ye antique towers,
   That crown the wat'ry glade.
Ode on a Distant Prospect of Eton College (1742, published
1747), l.1

10 Urge the flying ball.
l.30

11 Still as they run they look behind,
They hear a voice in every wind,
   And snatch a fearful joy.
l.38

12 Alas, regardless of their doom,
   The little victims play!
No sense have they of ills to come,
   Nor care beyond to-day.
l.51

13 To each his suff'rings, all are men,
   Condemn'd alike to groan;
The tender for another's pain,
   Th' unfeeling for his own.

Yet ah! why should they know their fate?
Since sorrow never comes too late,
   And happiness too swiftly flies.
Thought would destroy their paradise.
No more; where ignorance is bliss,
   'Tis folly to be wise.
l.91

14 Servitude that hugs her chain.
Ode for Music, l.6

15 The meanest flowret of the vale,
The simplest note that swells the gale,

The common sun, the air, and skies,
To him are opening paradise.
Ode on the Pleasure Arising from Vicissitude, l.49

16 The Attic warbler pours her throat,
Responsive to the cuckoo's note.
Ode on the Spring, l.5

17 The bloom of young desire and purple light of love.
The Progess of Poesy (1754, published 1757), i.3

18   Far from the sun and summer-gale,
In thy green lap was Nature's darling laid,
What time, where lucid Avon stray'd,
To him the mighty Mother did unveil
Her aweful face: the dauntless child
Stretch'd forth his little arms, and smiled.
iii.1 (Shakespeare.)

19 Nor second he, that rode sublime
   Upon the seraph-wings of ecstasy,
   The secrets of th' abyss to spy.
He pass'd the flaming bounds of place and time:
The living throne, the sapphire-blaze,
Where angels tremble, while they gaze,
He saw; but blasted with excess of light,
Closed his eyes in endless night.
2 (Milton.)

20 Beyond the limits of a vulgar fate,
Beneath the good how far—but far above the great.
3

21 Too poor for a bribe, and too proud to importune,
He had not the method of making a fortune.
Sketch of his own Character

22 The language of the age is never the language of
poetry, except among the French, whose verse, where
the thought or image does not support it, differs in
nothing from prose.
Letters. 103, To West [8] Apr., [1742]

23 It has been usual to catch a mouse or two (for form's
sake) in public once a year.
[On refusing the Laureateship.] 259, To Mason, 19 Dec. 1757

24 Any fool may write a most valuable book by chance,
if he will only tell us what he heard and saw with
veracity.
475, To Walpole, 25 Feb. 1768

25 I shall be but a shrimp of an author.

HORACE GREELY 1811–1872

26 Go West, young man, and grow up with the country.
Hints toward Reform. See 513:11

MATTHEW GREEN 1696–1737

27 They politics like ours profess,
The greater prey upon the less.
The Grotto (1732), l.69

28 To cure the mind's wrong biass, spleen,
Some recommend the bowling green,
Some, hilly walks; all, exercise;
Fling but a stone, the giant dies.
Laugh and be well.
The Spleen (1737), l.89

29 Or to some coffee-house I stray,
For news, the manna of a day,
And from the hipp'd discourses gather

That politics go by the weather.
l.168

1 Who their ill-tasted, home-brewed prayer
To the State's mellow forms prefer.
l.336

2 By happy alchemy of mind
They turn to pleasure all they find.
l.610

GRAHAM GREENE 1904–

3 Against the beautiful and the clever and the
successful, one can wage a pitiless war, but not
against the unattractive.
The Heart of the Matter (1948), bk.1, pt.1, ch.2

4 They had been corrupted by money, and he had been
corrupted by sentiment. Sentiment was the more
dangerous, because you couldn't name its price. A
man open to bribes was to be relied upon below a
certain figure, but sentiment might uncoil in the heart
at a name, a photograph, even a smell remembered.

5 Any victim demands allegiance.
bk.3, pt.1, ch.1

6 His hilarity was like a scream from a crevasse.

7 Perhaps if I wanted to be understood or to understand
I would bamboozle myself into belief, but I am a
reporter; God exists only for leader-writers.
The Quiet American (1955), pt.I, ch.iv.2

ROBERT GREENE 1560?–1592

8 Cupid abroad was lated in the night,
His wings were wet with ranging in the rain.
Sonnet: Cupid Abroad was Lated

9 Hangs in the uncertain balance of proud time.
Friar Bacon and Friar Bungay (1594), 111.i

10 Ah! were she pitiful as she is fair,
Or but as mild as she is seeming so.
Pandosto, or Dorastus and Fawnia (1588)

11 Ah! what is love! It is a pretty thing,
As sweet unto a shepherd as a king,
　　And sweeter too;
For kings have cares that wait upon a crown,
And cares can make the sweetest love to frown.
　　Ah then, ah then,
If country loves such sweet desires do gain,
What lady would not love a shepherd swain?
The Shepherd's Wife's Song

12 For there is an upstart crow, beautified with our
feathers, that with his tiger's heart wrapped in a
player's hide, supposes he is as well able to bumbast
out a blank verse as the best of you; and being an
absolute *Iohannes fac totum,* is in his own conceit the
only Shake-scene in a country.
Groatsworth of Wit Bought with a Million of Repentance
(1592)

POPE GREGORY THE GREAT c.540–604

13 *Non Angli sed Angeli.*
Not Angles but Angels.
Bede, *Historia Ecclesiastica*, II.i, recorded: *Responsum est, quod
Angli vocarentur. At ille: 'Bene,' inquit; 'nam et angelicam
habent faciem, et tales angelorum in caelis decet esse coheredes.'*
They answered that they were called Angles. 'It is well,' he said,
'for they have the faces of angels, and such should be the co-heirs
of the angels of heaven.'

STEPHEN GRELLET 1773–1855

14 I expect to pass through this world but once; any good
thing therefore that I can do, or any kindness that I can
show to any fellow-creature, let me do it now; let me
not defer or neglect it, for I shall not pass this way
again.
Attr. See John o' London's *Treasure Trove* (1925). Many other
claimants to authorship

JULIAN GRENFELL 1888–1915

15 The naked earth is warm with Spring,
　　And with green grass and bursting trees
Leans to the sun's kiss glorying,
　　And quivers in the sunny breeze;

And life is colour and warmth and light
　　And a striving evermore for these;
And he is dead, who will not fight;
　　And who dies fighting has increase.

The fighting man shall from the sun
Take warmth, and life from the glowing earth.
Into Battle, published in *The Times,* 27 May 1915

SIR FULKE GREVILLE 1554–1628

16 Oh wearisome condition of humanity!
Born under one law, to another bound.
Mustapha (1609), V.iv

17 Silence augmenteth grief, writing increaseth rage,
Stal'd are my thoughts, which loved and lost, the
　　wonder of our age,
Yet quick'ned now with fire, though dead with frost
　　ere now,
Enraged I write, I know not what: dead, quick, I know
　　not how.
Elegy on the Death of Sir Philip Sidney

18 Fulke Greville, Servant to Queen Elizabeth,
Councillor to King James, and Friend to Sir Philip
Sidney.
Epitaph written for himself, on his Monument in Warwick

LORD GREY OF FALLODON 1862–1933

19 The lamps are going out all over Europe; we shall not
see them lit again in our lifetime.
3 Aug. 1914. *Twenty-Five Years, 1892–1916* (1925), vol.ii,
ch.18

NICHOLAS GRIMALD 1519–1562

20 Of all the heavenly gifts that mortal men commend,
What trusty treasure in the world can countervail a
　　friend?
Of Friendship

GEORGE GROSSMITH 1847–1912
and WEEDON GROSSMITH 1854–1919

21 What's the good of a home if you are never in it?
The Diary of a Nobody (1894), ch.1

22 I...recognized her as a woman who used to work years
ago for my old aunt at Clapham. It only shows how
small the world is.
ch.2

1 He [Gowing] suggested we should play 'Cutlets', a game we never heard of. He sat on a chair, and asked Carrie to sit on his lap, an invitation which dear Carrie rightly declined.
ch.7

2 I left the room with silent dignity, but caught my foot in the mat.
ch.12

3 I am a poor man, but I would gladly give ten shillings to find out who sent me the insulting Christmas card I received this morning.
ch.13

PHILIP GUEDALLA 1889–1944

4 The little ships, the unforgotten Homeric catalogue of *Mary Jane* and *Peggy IV*, of *Folkestone Belle*, *Boy Billy*, and *Ethel Maud*, of *Lady Haig* and *Skylark*...the little ships of England brought the Army home.
Mr. Churchill (1941). (Evacuation of Dunkirk.)

5 The work of Henry James has always seemed divisible by a simple dynastic arrangement into three reigns: James I, James II, and the Old Pretender.
Collected Essays, vol.iv. **Men of Letters: Mr. Henry James**

TEXAS GUINAN 1884–1933

6 Fifty million Frenchmen can't be wrong.
Attr. *New York World-Telegram*, 21 Mar. 1931

MRS. DOROTHY FRANCES GURNEY 1858–1932

7 The kiss of the sun for pardon,
   The song of the birds for mirth,
One is nearer God's Heart in a garden
   Than anywhere else on earth.
God's Garden

NELL GWYN 1650–1687

8 Pray, good people, be civil. I am the Protestant whore.
In Oxford, during the Popish Terror, 1681. Bevan, *Nell Gwyn*, ch.xiii

EMPEROR HADRIAN A.D. 76–138

9 *Animula vagula blandula,*
Hospes comesque corporis,
Quae nunc abibis in loca
Pallidula rigida nudula,
Nec ut soles dabis iocos!
Ah! gentle, fleeting, wav'ring sprite,
Friend and associate of this clay!
   To what unknown region borne,
Wilt thou now wing thy distant flight?
No more with wonted humour gay,
   But pallid, cheerless, and forlorn.
J.W. Duff (ed.), *Minor Latin Poets* (1934), 445. Trans. Byron, *Adrian's Address to His Soul When Dying*

C.F.S. HAHNEMANN 1755–1843

10 *Similia similibus curantur.*
Like cures like.
Motto of homoeopathic medicine. Hahnemann seems to have used this formula, but with *curentur:* Let similars be treated by similars. Paracelsus (1493–1541), not acknowledged as an influence by Hahnemann, wrote *Simile similis cura: non contrarium (Fragmenta Medica).*

EARL HAIG 1861–1928

11 Every position must be held to the last man: there must be no retirement. With our backs to the wall, and believing in the justice of our cause, each one of us must fight on to the end.
Order to the British Troops, 12 Apr. 1918

EDWARD EVERETT HALE 1822–1909

12 'Do you pray for the senators, Dr Hale?' 'No, I look at the senators and I pray for the country.'
Van Wyck Brooks, *New England Indian Summer* (1940), p.418n.

SIR MATTHEW HALE 1609–1676

13 Christianity is part of the Common Law of England.
Historia Placitorum Coronae, ed. Sollom Emlyn (1736). Also in W. Blackstone *Commentaries on the Laws of England*, iv, 1765

NATHAN HALE 1755–1776

14 I only regret that I have but one life to lose for my country.
Speech before being executed as a spy by the British, 22 Sept. 1776. See 1:22

MRS. SARAH JOSEPHA HALE 1788–1879

15 Mary had a little lamb,
   Its fleece was white as snow,
And everywhere that Mary went
   The lamb was sure to go.
Poems for Our Children (1830). **Mary's Little Lamb**

T.C. HALIBURTON 1796–1865

16 I want you to see Peel, Stanley, Graham, Shiel, Russell, Macaulay, Old Joe, and so on. These men are all upper crust here.
The Attaché, or Sam Slick in England (1843-4), ch.24

GEORGE SAVILE, MARQUIS OF HALIFAX 1633–1695

17 Love is a passion that hath friends in the garrison.
Advice to a Daughter (1688). **Behaviour and Conversation**

18 This innocent word 'Trimmer' signifies no more than this, that if men are together in a boat, and one part of the company would weigh it down on one side, another would make it lean as much to the contrary.
Character of a Trimmer (1685, printed 1688), preface

19 There is...no fundamental, but that *every supreme power must be arbitrary.*
Political, Moral, and Miscellaneous Thoughts and Reflections (1750). **Of Fundamentals**

20 When the People contend for their Liberty, they seldom get anything by their Victory but new masters.
Of Prerogative, Power and Liberty

21 Power is so apt to be insolent and Liberty to be saucy, that they are very seldom upon good Terms.

22 Men are not hanged for stealing horses, but that horses may not be stolen.
Of Punishment

23 Most men make little other use of their speech than to

give evidence against their own understanding.
Of Folly and Fools

1 Anger is never without an argument, but seldom with
a good one.
Of Anger

2 Malice is of a low stature, but it hath very long arms.
Of Malice and Envy

3 The best way to suppose what may come, is to
remember what is past.
Miscellaneous, 'Experience'

4 To the question, What shall we do to be saved in this
World? there is no other answer but this, Look to your
Moat.
A Rough Draft of a New Model at Sea

5 He [Halifax] had said he had known many kicked
down stairs, but he never knew any kicked up stairs
before.
Burnet, *Original Memoirs* (c.1697)

BISHOP JOSEPH HALL 1574–1656

6 I first adventure, follow me who list
And be the second English satirist.
Virgidemiae (1597), Prologue

7 Perfection is the child of Time.
Works (1625), p.670

FITZ-GREENE HALLECK 1790–1867

8 They love their land because it is their own,
    And scorn to give aught other reason why;
Would shake hands with a king upon his throne,
    And think it kindness to his Majesty.
Connecticut

9 Green be the turf above thee,
Friend of my better days!
None knew thee but to love thee,
Nor named thee but to praise.
On the Death of J.R. Drake

FRIEDRICH HALM 1806–1871

10 *Mein Herz ich will dich fragen:*
Was ist denn Liebe? Sag'!—
'Zwei Seelen und ein Gedanke,
Zwei Herzen und ein Schlag!'
What love is, if thou wouldst be taught,
    Thy heart must teach alone—
Two souls with but a single thought,
    Two hearts that beat as one.
Der Sohn der Wildnis (1842), Act II *ad fin.* Trans. by Maria
Lovell in *Ingomar the Barbarian*

ADMIRAL W.F. ('BULL') HALSEY 1882-1959

11 Our ships have been salvaged and are retiring at high
speed toward the Japanese fleet.
Radio Message, Oct. 1944 after Japanese claims that most of the
American Third Fleet had been sunk or were retiring

P.G. HAMERTON 1834–1894

12 The art of reading is to skip judiciously.
The Intellectual Life (1873), pt.iv, letter iv

ALEXANDER HAMILTON 1755?–1804

13 A national debt, if it is not excessive, will be to us a
national blessing.
Letter to Robert Morris, 30 Apr. 1781

GAIL HAMILTON (MARY A. DODGE) 1833–1896

14 The total depravity of inanimate things.
Epigram

SIR WILLIAM HAMILTON 1788–1856

15 Truth, like a torch, the more it's shook it shines.
Discussions on Philosophy (1852), title page

16 On earth there is nothing great but man; in man there
is nothing great but mind.
Lectures on Metaphysics (1859-60)

CHRISTOPHER HAMPTON 1946–

17 If I had to give a definition of capitalism I would say:
the process whereby American girls turn into American
women.
Savages (1973), 16

JOHN HANCOCK 1737–1793

18 There, I guess King George will be able to read that.
Remark on signing the Declaration of Independence, 4 July 1776

MINNY MAUD HANFF 1880–1942

19 Since then they called him Sunny Jim.
Advertisement for Force, a breakfast food, c.1902

EDMOND HARAUCOURT 1856–1941

20 *Partir c'est mourir un peu,*
C'est mourir à ce qu'on aime:
On laisse un peu de soi-même
En toute heure et dans tout lieu.
To go away is to die a little, it is to die to that which
    one loves: everywhere and always, one leaves
    behind a part of oneself.
Seul (1891), **Rondel de l'Adieu**

KEIR HARDIE 1856–1915

21 From his childhood onward this boy [the future
Edward VIII] will be surrounded by sycophants and
flatterers by the score—[*Cries of* 'Oh, oh!']—and will
be taught to believe himself as of a superior creation.
[*Cries of* 'Oh, oh!'] A line will be drawn between him
and the people whom he is to be called upon some day
to reign over. In due course, following the precedent
which has already been set, he will be sent on a tour
round the world, and probably rumours of a
morganatic alliance will follow—[*Loud cries of* 'Oh,
oh!' *and* 'Order!']—and the end of it all will be that
the country will be called upon to pay the bill. [*Cries
of* Divide!]
House of Commons, 28 June 1894

THOMAS HARDY 1840–1928

22   Come again, with the feet
That were light on the green as a thistledown ball,

And those mute ministrations to one and to all
    Beyond a man's saying sweet.
After the Visit

1 When the Present has latched its postern behind my
      tremulous stay,
    And the May month flaps its glad green leaves like
      wings,
  Delicate-filmed as new-spun silk, will the neighbours
    say,
    'He was a man who used to notice such things'?
Afterwards

2 Some nocturnal blackness, mothy and warm,
  When the hedgehog travels furtively over the lawn.

3 'Peace upon earth!' was said. We sing it,
  And pay a million priests to bring it.
  After two thousand years of mass
  We've got as far as poison-gas.
Christmas: 1924

4   In a solitude of the sea
        Deep from human vanity,
  And the Pride of Life that planned her, stilly couches
    she.

        Steel chambers, late the pyres
        Of her salamandrine fires,
  Cold currents thrid, and turn to rhythmic tidal lyres.

        Over the mirrors meant
        To glass the opulent
  The sea-worm crawls—grotesque, slimed, dumb,
    indifferent.
The Convergence of the Twain. Lines on the Loss of the *Titanic*,
I

5   Dim moon-eyed fishes near
        Gaze at the gilded gear
  And query: 'What does this vaingloriousness down
    here?'
V

6   And as the smart ship grew
        In stature, grace, and hue,
  In shadowy silent distance grew the Iceberg too.

        Alien they seemed to be:
        No mortal eye could see
  The intimate welding of their later history,

        Or sign that they were bent
        By paths coincident
  On being twin halves of one august event,

        Till the Spinner of the Years
        Said 'Now!' And each one hears,
  And consummation comes, and jars two hemispheres.
VIII

7 At once a voice arose among
    The bleak twigs overhead
  In a full-hearted evensong
    Of joy illimited;
  An aged thrush, frail, gaunt, and small,
    In blast-beruffled plume,
  Had chosen thus to fling his soul
    Upon the growing gloom.

  So little cause for carollings
    Of such ecstatic sound
  Was written on terrestrial things
    Afar or nigh around,
  That I could think there trembled through

His happy good-night air
Some blessed Hope, whereof he knew
    And I was unaware.
The Darkling Thrush

8 Young Hodge the Drummer never knew—
    Fresh from his Wessex home—
  The meaning of the broad Karoo,
    The Bush, the dusty loam.
Drummer Hodge

9 Yet portion of that unknown plain
    Will Hodge for ever be;
  His homely Northern breast and brain
    Grow to some Southern tree,
  And strange-eyed constellations reign
    His stars eternally.

10   Ah, no; the years, the years;
  Down their carved names the rain-drop ploughs.
During Wind and Rain

11 What of the Immanent Will and its designs?—
  It works unconsciously as heretofore,
  Eternal artistries in Circumstance.
The Dynasts (1903–08), pt.i. Fore-Scene

12   Like a knitter drowsed,
  Whose fingers play in skilled unmindfulness,
  The Will has woven with an absent heed
  Since life first was; and ever so will weave.

13 The nether sky opens, and Europe is disclosed as a
  prone and emaciated figure, the Alps shaping like a
  backbone, and the branching mountain-chains like
  ribs, the peninsular plateau of Spain forming a head.
Stage Direction

14 A local cult called Christianity.
I.vi

15 My argument is that War makes rattling good history;
  but Peace is poor reading.
II.v

16 But O, the intolerable antilogy
  Of making figments feel!
IV.vi

17 William Dewy, Tranter Reuben, Farmer Ledlow late
    at plough,
      Robert's kin, and John's, and Ned's,
  And the Squire, and Lady Susan, lie in Mellstock
    churchyard now!
Friends Beyond

18   Yet at mothy curfew-tide,
  And at midnight when the noon-heat breathes it back
    from walls and leads,
  They've a way of whispering to me—fellow-wight
    who yet abide—
      In the muted, measured note
  Of a ripple under archways, or a lone cave's stillicide.

19 Ye mid burn the old bass-viol that I set such value by.

20 If ye break my best blue china, children, I shan't care
  or ho.

21 Well, World, you have kept faith with me,
    Kept faith with me;
  Upon the whole you have proved to be
    Much as you said you were.
He Never Expected Much [or] *A Consideration.* On his 86th
birthday

22   'I do not promise overmuch,

Child; overmuch;
   Just neutral-tinted haps and such,'
   You said to minds like mine.

1 I am the family face;
   Flesh perishes, I live on.
   Heredity

2 But Time, to make me grieve,
   Part steals, lets part abide;
   And shakes this fragile frame at eve
   With throbbings of noontide.
   I Look Into My Glass

3 Let him in whose ears the low-voiced Best is killed by
      the clash of the First,
   Who holds that if way to the Better there be, it exacts
      a full look at the worst,
   Who feels that delight is a delicate growth cramped by
      crookedness, custom, and fear,
   Get him up and be gone as one shaped awry; he
      disturbs the order here.
   In Tenebris

4 I'm a labouring man, and know but little,
      Or nothing at all;
   But I can't help thinking that stone once echoed
      The voice of Paul.
   In the British Museum

5 Only a man harrowing clods
      In a slow silent walk
   With an old horse that stumbles and nods
      Half asleep as they stalk.

   Only thin smoke without flame
      From the heaps of couch grass;
   Yet this will go onward the same
      Though Dynasties pass.

   Yonder a maid and her wight
      Come whispering by:
   War's annals will cloud into night
      Ere their story die.
   In Time of 'The Breaking of Nations'

6 Let me enjoy the earth no less
   Because the all-enacting Might
   That fashioned forth its loveliness
   Had other aims than my delight.
   Let Me Enjoy the Earth

7 Here's not a modest maiden elf
      But dreads the final Trumpet,
   Lest half of her should rise herself,
      And half some sturdy strumpet!
   The Levelled Churchyard

8 What of the faith and fire within us
      Men who march away
      Ere the barn-cocks say
      Night is growing gray?
   Men Who March Away

9 In the third-class seat sat the journeying boy
   And the roof-lamp's oily flame
   Played on his listless form and face,
   Bewrapt past knowing to what he was going,
   Or whence he came.
   Midnight on the Great Western

10 Your face, and the God-curst sun, and a tree,
      And a pond edged with grayish leaves.
   Neutral Tones

11 A car comes up, with lamps full-glare,

That flash upon a tree:
   It has nothing to do with me,
And whangs along in a world of its own,
   Leaving a blacker air.
Nobody Comes

12 That long drip of human tears.
   On an Invitation to the United States

13 Christmas Eve, and twelve of the clock.
   'Now they are all on their knees,'
An elder said as we sat in a flock
   By the embers in hearthside ease.
   The Oxen

14 So fair a fancy few would weave
   In these years! Yet, I feel,
If someone said on Christmas Eve,
   'Come; see the oxen kneel,

'In the lonely barton by yonder coomb
   Our childhood used to know',
I should go with him in the gloom,
   Hoping it might be so.

15 Queer are the ways of a man I know:
      He comes and stands
      In a careworn craze,
      And looks at the sands
      And the seaward haze
      With moveless hands
      And face and gaze,
      Then turns to go…
And what does he see when he gazes so?
   The Phantom Horsewoman

16 We shall see her no more
         On the balcony
Smiling, while hurt, at the roar
         As of a surging sea
From the stormy sturdy band
         Who have doomed her lord's cause,
Though she waves her little hand
         As it were applause.
The Rejected Member's Wife (Jan. 1906)

17 Read that moderate man Voltaire.
   The Respectable Burgher

18 Love is lame at fifty years.
   The Revisitation

19 —'You left us in tatters, without shoes or socks,
   Tired of digging potatoes, and spudding up docks;
   And now you've gay bracelets and bright feathers
      three!'—
   'Yes: that's how we dress when we're ruined,' said
      she.
   The Ruined Maid

20 A little ball of feather and bone.
   Shelley's Skylark

21   Every branch big with it,
            Bent every twig with it;
         Every fork like a white web-foot;
         Every street and pavement mute:
   Some flakes have lost their way, and grope back
      upward, when
   Meeting those meandering down they turn and descend
      again.
   Snow in the Suburbs

22 A baby watched a ford, whereto
      A wagtail came for drinking;

A blaring bull went wading through,
The wagtail showed no shrinking.
Wagtail and Baby

1 A perfect gentleman then neared;
The wagtail, in a winking,
With terror rose and disappeared;
The baby fell a-thinking.

2 This is the weather the cuckoo likes,
And so do I;
When showers betumble the chestnut spikes,
And nestlings fly:
And the little brown nightingale bills his best,
And they sit outside at 'The Travellers' Rest'.
Weathers

3 This is the weather the shepherd shuns,
And so do I.

4 And drops on gate-bars hang in a row,
And rooks in families homeward go,
And so do I.

5 When I set out for Lyonnesse,
A hundred miles away,
The rime was on the spray,
And starlight lit my lonesomeness
When I set out for Lyonnesse
A hundred miles away.
When I Set Out for Lyonnesse

6 When I came back from Lyonnesse
With magic in my eyes,
All marked with mute surmise
My radiance rare and fathomless,
When I came back from Lyonnesse
With magic in my eyes!

7 Goodbye is not worth while.
Without Ceremony

8 It says that Life would signify
A thwarted purposing:
That we come to live, and are called to die.
Yes, that's the thing
In fall, in spring,
That Yell'ham says:—
'Life offers—to deny!'
Yell'ham-Wood's Story

9 The kingly brilliance of Sirius pierced the eye with a
steely glitter, the star called Capella was yellow,
Aldebaran and Betelgueux shone with a fiery red. To
persons standing alone on a hill during a clear
midnight such as this, the roll of the world eastward is
almost a palpable movement.
Far From the Madding Crowd (1874), ch.2

10 A nice unparticular man.
ch.8

11 We ought to feel deep cheerfulness that a happy
Providence kept it from being any worse.

12 Ah! stirring times we live in—stirring times.
ch.15

13 Five decades hardly modified the cut of a gaiter, the
embroidery of a smock-frock, by the breadth of a hair.
Ten generations failed to alter the turn of a single
phrase. In these Wessex nooks the busy outsider's
ancient times are only old; his old times are still new;
his present is futurity.
ch.22

14 Ethelberta breathed a sort of exclamation, not right
out, but stealthily, like a parson's damn.
The Hand of Ethelberta (1875), ch.26

15 Done because we are too menny.
Jude the Obscure (1895), pt.vi, ch.2

16 'Well, poor soul; she's helpless to hinder that or
anything now,' answered Mother Cuxsom: 'And all
her shining keys will be took from her, and her
cupboards opened, and things a' didn't wish seen,
anybody will see; and her little wishes and ways will
all be as nothing.'
The Mayor of Casterbridge (1894), ch.18

17 Dialect words—those terrible marks of the beast to the
truly genteel.
ch.20

18   Michael Henchard's Will.
That Elizabeth-Jane Farfrae be not told of my death,
or made to grieve on account of me.
& that I be not buried in consecrated ground.
& that no sexton be asked to toll the bell.
& that nobody is wished to see my dead body.
& that no murners walk behind me at my funeral.
& that no flours be planted on my grave.
& that no man remember me.
To this I put my name.
ch.45

19 The heaven being spread with this pallid screen and
the earth with the darkest vegetation, their meeting-line
at the horizon was clearly marked. In such contrast the
heath wore the appearance of an instalment of night
which had taken up its place before its astronomical
hour was come: darkness had to a great extent arrived
hereon, while day stood distinct in the sky.
The Return of the Native (1878), ch.1

20 In fact, precisely at this transitional point of its nightly
roll into darkness the great and particular glory of the
Egdon waste began, and nobody could be said to
understand the heath who had not been there at such a
time.

21 The great inviolate place had an ancient permanence
which the sea cannot claim. Who can say of a
particular sea that it is old? Distilled by the sun,
kneaded by the moon, it is renewed in a year, in a
day, or in an hour. The sea changed, the fields
changed, the rivers, the villages, and the people
changed, yet Egdon remained.

22 A little one-eyed, blinking sort o' place.
Tess of the D'Urbervilles (1891), ch.1

23 Always washing, and never getting finished.
ch.4

24 The New Testament was less a Christiad than a
Pauliad to his intelligence.
ch.25

25 'Justice' was done, and the President of the Immortals
(in Aeschylean phrase) had ended his sport with Tess.
ch.59

26 Good, but not religious-good.
Under the Greenwood Tree (1872), ch.2

27 That man's silence is wonderful to listen to.
ch.14

1 You was a good man, and did good things.
The Woodlanders (1887), ch.48

JULIUS HARE 1795–1855
and AUGUSTUS HARE 1792–1834

2 Truth, when witty, is the wittiest of all things.
Guesses at Truth (1827), Series 1

3 The ancients dreaded death: the Christian can only fear dying.

4 Half the failures in life arise from pulling in one's horse as he is leaping.

5 Purity is the feminine, Truth the masculine, of Honour.

6 Every Irishman, the saying goes, has a potato in his head.

MAURICE EVAN HARE 1886–1967

7 Alfred de Musset
Used to call his cat Pusset.
His accent was affected.
That was only to be expected.
Byway in Biography

8 There once was a man who said, 'Damn!
It is borne in upon me I am
 An engine that moves
 In predestinate grooves,
I'm not even a bus, I'm a tram.'
Written, as above, at St. John's College, Oxford, in 1905

SIR JOHN HARINGTON 1561–1612

9   When I make a feast,
I would my guests should praise it, not the cooks.
Epigrams (1618), bk.i, No.5. **Against Writers that Carp at Other Men's Books**

10 Treason doth never prosper, what's the reason?
For if it prosper, none dare call it treason.
bk.iv, No.5. **Of Treason**

KING HAROLD OF ENGLAND 1022–1066

11 He will give him seven feet of English ground, or as much more as he may be taller than other men.
His offer to Harald Sigurdson, invading England. Snorri Sturluson, *Heimskringla*, X. xci

JOEL CHANDLER HARRIS 1848–1908

12 'Law, Brer Tarrypin!' sez Brer Fox, sezee, 'you ain't see no trouble yit. Ef you wanter see sho' nuff trouble, you des oughter go 'longer me; I'm de man w'at kin show you trouble,' sezee.
Nights with Uncle Remus (1883), ch.17

13 W'en folks git ole en strucken wid de palsy, dey mus speck ter be laff'd at.
ch.23

14 Hit look lak sparrer-grass, hit feel like sparrer-grass, hit tas'e lak sparrer-grass, en I bless ef 'taint sparrer-grass.
ch.27

15 All by my own-alone self.
ch.36

16 We er sorter po'ly, Sis Tempy, I'm 'blige ter you.

You know w'at de jay-bird say ter der squinch-owl!
'I'm sickly but sassy.'
ch.50

17 Oh, whar shill we go w'en de great day comes,
Wid de blowin' er de trumpits en de bangin' er de drums?
How many po' sinners'll be kotched out late
En find no latch ter de golden gate?
Uncle Remus: His Songs and Sayings (1880), i

18 How duz yo' sym'tums seem ter segashuate?
Uncle Remus. Legends of the Old Plantation (1881), ch.2. **Tar-Baby Story**

19 Tar-baby ain't sayin' nuthin', en Brer Fox, he lay low.

20 Bred en bawn in a brier-patch!
ch.4

21 Lounjun 'roun' en suffer'n'.
ch.12

22 Ole man Know-All died las' year.
ch.34, **Plantation Proverbs**

23 Licker talks mighty loud w'en it git loose fum de jug.

24 Hongry rooster don't cackle w'en he fine a wum.

25 Youk'n hide de fier, but w'at you gwine do wid de smoke?

BRET HARTE 1836–1902

26 And on that grave where English oak and holly
 And laurel wreaths entwine
Deem it not all a too presumptuous folly,—
 This spray of Western pine!
Dickens in Camp

27 Thar ain't no sense
In gittin' riled!
Jim

28 If, of all words of tongue and pen,
The saddest are, 'It might have been,'
More sad are these we daily see:
'It is, but hadn't ought to be!'
Mrs. Judge Jenkins. See 571:19

29 Which I wish to remark,
And my language is plain,
That for ways that are dark
And for tricks that are vain,
The heathen Chinee is peculiar,
Which the same I would rise to explain.
Plain Language from Truthful James (1870)

30 We are ruined by Chinese cheap labour.

31 He wore, I think, a chasuble, the day when first we met.
The Ritualist

32 I reside at Table Mountain, and my name is Truthful James;
I am not up to small deceit, or any sinful games.
The Society upon the Stanislaus

33 And he smiled a kind of sickly smile, and curled up on the floor,
And the subsequent proceedings interested him no more.

L.P. HARTLEY 1895–1972

34 The past is a foreign country: they do things

differently there.
The Go-Between, Prologue

M. LOUISE HASKINS 1875–1957

1 And I said to the man who stood at the gate of the
year: 'Give me a light that I may tread safely into the
unknown'. And he replied: 'Go out into the darkness
and put your hand into the hand of God. That shall be
to you better than light and safer than a known way.'
The Desert (c.1908), Introduction. Quoted by King George VI in
a Christmas Broadcast, 25 Dec. 1939

STEPHEN HAWES d. 1523?

2 When the lytle byrdes swetely dyd syng
Laudes to their maker early in the mornyng.
Passetyme of Pleasure (1506, printed 1509), cap.33, xxxiii

3 For though the day be never so longe,
At last the belles ringeth to evensonge.
cap.42

REVD. R.S. HAWKER 1803–1875

4 And have they fixed the where and when?
   And shall Trelawny die?
Here's twenty thousand Cornish men
   Will know the reason why!
Song of the Western Men. The last three lines have existed since
the imprisonment by James II, 1688, of the seven Bishops,
including Trelawny, Bishop of Bristol.

NATHANIEL HAWTHORNE 1804–1864

5 Dr Johnson's morality was as English an article as a
beefsteak.
Our Old Home (1863), **Lichfield and Uttoxeter**

IAN HAY 1876–1952

6 What do you mean, funny? Funny-peculiar or
funny-ha-ha?
The Housemaster (1936), Act III

J. MILTON HAYES fl. 1911

7 There's a one-eyed yellow idol to the north of
   Khatmandu,
There's a little marble cross below the town;
There's a broken-hearted woman tends the grave of
   Mad Carew
And the Yellow God forever gazes down.
The Green Eye of the Yellow God (1911)

WILLIAM HAZLITT 1778–1830

8 His sayings are generally like women's letters; all the
pith is in the postscript. [Charles Lamb.]
Conversations of Northcote. (Boswell Redivivus, 1826-7)

9 The only specimen of Burke is, *all that he wrote.*
English Literature, ch.ix. **Character of Mr. Burke**

10 He writes as fast as they can read, and he does not
write himself down.
ch.xiv. **Sir Walter Scott**

11 His worst is better than any other person's best.

12 His works (taken together) are almost like a new
edition of human nature. This is indeed to be an
author!

13 The round-faced man in black entered, and dissipated
all doubts on the subject, by beginning to talk. He did
not cease while he stayed; nor has he since, that I know
of. [Coleridge.]
ch.xvii. **My First Acquaintance with Poets**

14 'For those two hours,' he [Coleridge] afterwards was
pleased to say, 'he was conversing with W.H.'s
forehead!'

15 So have I loitered my life away, reading books,
looking at pictures, going to plays, hearing, thinking,
writing on what pleased me best. I have wanted only
one thing to make me happy, but wanting that have
wanted everything.

16 You will hear more good things on the outside of a
stagecoach from London to Oxford than if you were to
pass a twelvemonth with the undergraduates, or heads
of colleges, of that famous university.
The Ignorance of the Learned

17 He [Coleridge] talked on for ever; and you wished him
to talk on for ever.
Lectures on the English Poets. Lecture viii, **On the Living Poets**

18 The dupe of friendship, and the fool of love; have I
not reason to hate and to despise myself? Indeed I do;
and chiefly for not having hated and despised the world
enough.
The Plain Speaker (1826). **On the Pleasure of Hating**

19 The love of liberty is the love of others; the love of
power is the love of ourselves.
Political Essays (1819). **'The Times' Newspaper**

20 Those who make their dress a principal part of
themselves, will, in general, become of no more value
than their dress.
On the Clerical Character

21 There is nothing good to be had in the country, or if
there is, they will not let you have it.
1817. **Observations on Mr. Wordsworth's Excursion**

22 The art of pleasing consists in being pleased.
Round Table, vol.i. **On Manner**

23 The greatest offence against virtue is to speak ill of it.
Sketches and Essays (1839). **On Cant and Hypocrisy**

24 The most fluent talkers or most plausible reasoners are
not always the justest thinkers.
On Prejudice

25 We never do anything well till we cease to think about
the manner of doing it.

26 There is an unseemly exposure of the mind, as well as
of the body.
On Disagreeable People

27 A nickname is the heaviest stone that the devil can
throw at a man.
Nicknames

28 Rules and models destroy genius and art.
On Taste

29 But of all footmen the lowest class is *literary footmen.*
Footmen

30 One of the pleasantest things in the world is going on
a journey; but I like to go by myself.
Table Talk, xix. **On Going a Journey**

31 When I am in the country I wish to vegetate like the
country.

32 Give me the clear blue sky over my head, and the

green turf beneath my feet, a winding road before me,
and a three hours' march to dinner—and then to
thinking! It is hard if I cannot start some game on these
lone heaths.

1 The English (it must be owned) are rather a
foul-mouthed nation.
xxii. **On Criticism**

2 We can scarcely hate any one that we know.

3 No young man believes he shall ever die.
Uncollected Essays, xviii. **On the Feeling of Immortality in
Youth**

4 Well, I've had a happy life.
Last words. W.C. Hazlitt, *Memoirs of William Hazlitt,* 1867

EDWARD HEATH 1916–

5 It is the unpleasant and unacceptable face of capitalism
but one should not suggest that the whole of British
industry consists of practices of this kind.
House of Commons, 15 May 1973

BISHOP REGINALD HEBER 1783–1826

6 What though the spicy breezes
Blow soft o'er Ceylon's isle;
Though every prospect pleases,
And only man is vile:

In vain with lavish kindness
The gifts of God are strown;
The heathen in his blindness
Bows down to wood and stone.
From Greenland's Icy Mountains. This is the most familiar
version. Bishop Heber originally wrote 'The savage in his
blindness'. He altered this, and also altered 'Ceylon's' to 'Java's'.

7 They climb'd the steep ascent of Heav'n
Through peril, toil and pain;
O God, to us may grace be given
To follow in their train.
The Son of God Goes Forth

G.W.F. HEGEL 1770–1831

8 What experience and history teach is this—that people
and governments never have learned anything from
history, or acted on principles deduced from it.
Philosophy of History. Introduction

HEINRICH HEINE 1797–1856

9 *Ich weiss nicht, was soll es bedeuten,*
Dass ich so traurig bin;
Ein Märchen aus alten Zeiten,
Das kommt mir nicht aus dem Sinn.
I know not why I am so sad; I cannot get out of my
head a fairy-tale of olden times.
Die Loreley

10 *Sie hatten sich beide so herzlich lieb,*
Spitzbübin war sie, er war ein Dieb.
They loved each other beyond belief—
She was a strumpet, he was a thief.
Neue Gedichte (1844), **Romanzen,** I. 'Ein Weib'. Trans. Louis
Untermeyer (1938)

11 *Hört ihr das Glöckchen klingeln? Kniet nieder—Man*
bringt die Sakramente einem sterbenden Gotte.
Do you hear the little bell tinkle? Kneel down. They

are bringing the sacraments to a dying god.
Zur Geschichte der Religion und Philosophie in Deutschland
(1834), bk.2

12 *Dieses merkt Euch, Ihr stolzen Männer det Tat. Ihr*
seid nichts als unbewusste Handlanger der
Gedankenmänner. . .Maximilan Robespierre war
nichts als die Hand von Jean Jacques Rousseau, die
blutige Hand, die aus dem Schosse der Zeit den Leib
hervorzog, dessen Seele Rousseau geschaffen.
Note this, you proud men of action. You are nothing
but the unconscious hodmen of the men of
ideas. . .Maximilian Robespierre was nothing but the
hand of Jean Jacques Rousseau, the bloody hand that
drew from the womb of time the body whose soul
Rousseau had created.
bk. 3

13 *Dieu me pardonnera. C'est son métier.*
God will pardon me. It is His trade.
On his deathbed. Edmond and Charles Goncourt, *Journal,* 23 Feb. 1863

14   *Dort, wo man Bücher*
Verbrennt, verbrennt man auch am Ende Menschen.
Whenever books are burned men also, in the end, are
burned.
Almansor (1820–1), l. 245

LILLIAN HELLMAN 1905–

15 I cannot and will not cut my conscience to fit this
year's fashions.
Letter to the Honourable John S. Wood, Chairman of the House
Committee on un-American Activities, 19 May 1952

SIR ARTHUR HELPS 1813–1875

16 Reading is sometimes an ingenious device for avoiding
thought.
Friends in Council (1847,1853), bk.ii, ch.1

17 What a blessing this smoking is! perhaps the greatest
that we owe to the discovery of America.
series II, 1859, vol.i, ch.1, **Worry**

18 There is one statesman of the present day, of whom I
always say that he would have escaped making the
blunders that he has made if he had only ridden more
in omnibuses.
vol.ii, ch.9, **On Government**

C.-A. HELVÉTIUS 1715–1771

19 *L'éducation nous faisait ce que nous sommes.*
Education makes us what we are.
Discours XXX, ch.30

MRS. HEMANS 1793–1835

20 The boy stood on the burning deck
Whence all but he had fled;
The flame that lit the battle's wreck
Shone round him o'er the dead.
Casabianca

21 The stately homes of England,
How beautiful they stand!
Amidst their tall ancestral trees,
O'er all the pleasant land.
The Homes of England

JOHN HEMING d.1630
and HENRY CONDELL d.1627

1 Well! it is now public, and you will stand for your privileges we know: to read, and censure. Do so, but buy it first. That doth best commend a book, the stationer says.
Preface to the First Folio Shakespeare, 1623

2 Who, as he was a happy imitator of Nature, was a most gentle expresser of it. His mind and hand went together: And what he thought, he uttered with that easiness, that we have scarce received from him a blot.

ERNEST HEMINGWAY 1898–1961

3 But did thee feel the earth move?
For Whom the Bell Tolls (1940), ch.13

W.E. HENLEY 1849–1903

4 Out of the night that covers me,
Black as the Pit from pole to pole,
I thank whatever gods may be
For my unconquerable soul.

In the fell clutch of circumstance,
I have not winced nor cried aloud:
Under the bludgeonings of chance
My head is bloody, but unbowed.
Echoes (1888), iv. **Invictus. In Mem. R.T.H.B.**

5 It matters not how strait the gate,
How charged with punishments the scroll,
I am the master of my fate:
I am the captain of my soul.

6 Madam Life's a piece in bloom
Death goes dogging everywhere;
She's the tenant of the room,
He's the ruffian on the stair.
ix. **To W.R.**

7 A late lark twitters from the quiet skies.
xxxv. **Margaritae Sororis**

8 Night with her train of stars.
And her great gift of sleep.

9 So be my passing!
My task accomplished and the long day done,
My wages taken, and in my heart
Some late lark singing,
Let me be gathered to the quiet west,
The sundown splendid and serene,
Death.

10 Or ever the Knightly years were gone
With the old world to the grave,
I was a King in Babylon
And you were a Christian Slave.
xxxvii. **To W.A.**

11 What have I done for you,
England, my England?
What is there I would not do,
England, my own?
For England's Sake (1900), iii. **Pro Rege Nostro**

12 Valiant in velvet, light in ragged luck,
Most vain, most generous, sternly critical,
Buffoon and poet, lover and sensualist:
A deal of Ariel, just a streak of Puck,

Much Antony, of Hamlet most of all,
And something of the Shorter-Catechist. [Stevenson.]
In Hospital, xxv. **Apparition**

HENRI IV 1553–1610

13 *Je veux qu'il n'y ait si pauvre paysan en mon royaume qu'il n'ait tous les dimanches sa poule au pot.*
I want there to be no peasant in my kingdom so poor that he is unable to have a chicken in his pot every Sunday.
Hardouin de Péréfixe, *Hist. de Henry le Grand,* 1681

14 *Pends-toi, brave Crillon; nous avons combattu à Arques et tu n'y étais pas.*
Hang yourself, brave Crillon; we fought at Arques and you were not there.
Traditional form given by Voltaire to a letter of Henri to Crillon. *Lettres missives de Henri IV, Collection des documents inédits de l'histoire de France,* vol.iv, 1847, p.848. Henri's actual words, in a letter to Crillon of 20 Sept. 1597, were *Brave Crillon, pendez-vous de n'avoir été ici près de moi lundi dernier à la plus belle occasion qui se soit jamais vue et qui peut-être se verra jamais.*

15 *Paris vaut bien une messe.*
Paris is well worth a mass.
Attr. either to Henri IV or to his minister Sully, in conversation with Henri. *Caquets de l'Accouchée,* 1622

16 The wisest fool in Christendom.
Of James I of England. Remark attr. to Henri IV and Sully. The French is not known

MATTHEW HENRY 1662–1714

17 The better day, the worse deed.
Exposition of the Old and New Testaments (1708-10), Genesis III.vi

18 To their own second and sober thoughts.
Job VI.xxix

19 He rolls it under his tongue as a sweet morsel.
Ps. XXXVI.ii

20 They that die by famine die by inches.
Ps. LIX.xv

21 Men of polite learning and a liberal education.
Acts X.i

22 All this and heaven too.
Attr.

O. HENRY 1862–1910

23 Life is made up of sobs, sniffles, and smiles, with sniffles predominating.
The Gift of the Magi

24 Turn up the lights, I don't want to go home in the dark.
Last words, quoting popular song. C.A. Smith, *O. Henry,* ch.9

PATRICK HENRY 1736–1799

25 Caesar had his Brutus—Charles the First, his Cromwell—and George the Third—('Treason,' cried the Speaker)...*may profit by their example.* If *this* be treason, make the most of it.
Speech in the Virginia Convention, May 1765. Wirt, *Patrick Henry* (1818), p.65

26 I am not a Virginian, but an American.
Speech in the Virginia Convention, Sept. 1774

27 I know not what course others may take; but as for

me, give me liberty, or give me death!
20 Mar. 1775. Wirt, *Patrick Henry* (1818), p.123

KING HENRY II 1133–1189

1 Will no one revenge me of the injuries I have sustained
from one turbulent priest?
Of St. Thomas Becket (Dec. 1170). Oral trad. See G. Lyttelton,
History of the Life of King Henry the Second (1769), IV, p.353;
also Herbert of Bosham, *Vita S. Thomae* in *Materials for the
History of Archbishop Thomas Becket* (Rolls Series), III (1887),
p.487

KING HENRY VIII 1491–1547

2 The King found her so different from her
picture…that…he swore they had brought him a
Flanders mare. [Anne of Cleves.]
Smollett, *Hist. of England* (ed.3, 1759), vi.68

3 This man hath the right sow by the ear. [Of Cranmer.]
Attr.

BISHOP JOSEPH HENSHAW 1603–1679

4 One doth but breakfast here, another dines, he that
liveth longest doth but sup; we must all go to bed in
another world.
Horae Succisivae (1631), pt.I

HERACLITUS fl. 513 B.C.

5 πάντα χωρεῖ, ὀυδὲν μένει.
Everything flows and nothing stays.
Plato, *Cratylus*, 402a

6 δὶς ἐς τὸν ἀυτὸν ποταμὸν οὐκ ἂν ἐμβαίης.
You can't step twice into the same river.

A.P. HERBERT 1890–1971

7 Don't let's go to the dogs to-night,
For mother will be there.
Don't Let's Go to the Dogs

8 Don't tell my mother I'm living in sin,
Don't let the old folks know:
Don't tell my twin that I breakfast on gin,
He'd never survive the blow.
Don't Tell My Mother

9 Let's find out what everyone is doing,
And then stop everyone from doing it.
Let's Stop Somebody

10 As my poor father used to say
In 1863,
Once people start on all this Art
Good-bye, moralitee!
And what my father used to say
Is good enough for me.
Lines for a Worthy Person

11 Well, fancy giving money to the Government!
Might as well have put it down the drain.
Fancy giving money to the Government!
Nobody will see the stuff again.
Well, they've no idea what money's for—
Ten to one they'll start another war.
I've heard a lot of silly things, but, Lor'!
Fancy giving money to the Government!
Too Much!

12 He didn't ought to come to bed in boots.
Riverside Nights

13 The Common Law of England has been laboriously
built about a mythical figure—the figure of 'The
Reasonable Man'.
Uncommon Law (1935), p.1

14 People must not do things for fun. We are not here for
fun. There is no reference to fun in any Act of
Parliament.
p.28

15 If elderly bishops were seen leaving the Athenaeum
with jugs of stout in their hands the casual observer
would form an impression of the character of that
institution which would be largely unjust.
p.33

16 The critical period in matrimony is breakfast-time.
p.98

17 The Englishman never enjoys himself except for a
noble purpose.
p.198

18 For any ceremonial purposes the otherwise excellent
liquid, water, is unsuitable in colour and other
respects.
p.272

19 An Act of God was defined as *something which no
reasonable man could have expected.*
p.316

LORD HERBERT OF CHERBURY 1583–1648

20 Now that the April of your youth adorns
The garden of your face.
Ditty: Now That the April

GEORGE HERBERT 1593–1633

21 He that makes a good war makes a good peace.
Outlandish Proverbs, 420

22 He that lives in hope danceth without musick.
1006

23 I read, and sigh, and wish I were a tree—
For sure then I should grow
To fruit or shade; at least some bird would trust
Her household to me, and I should be just.
The Temple (1633). **Affliction**

24 Ah, my dear God, though I am clean forgot,
Let me not love Thee, if I love Thee not.

25 How well her name an 'Army' doth present.
In whom the 'Lord of Hosts' did pitch His tent!
Anagram, Mary

26 Let all the world in ev'ry corner sing
My God and King.
The heav'ns are not too high,
His praise may thither fly;
The earth is not too low,
His praises there may grow.
Let all the world in ev'ry corner sing
My God and King.
The Church with psalms must shout,
No door can keep them out:
But above all, the heart
Must bear the longest part.
Antiphon

27 Hearken unto a Verser, who may chance

Rhyme thee to good, and make a bait of pleasure:
A verse may find him who a sermon flies,
And turn delight into a sacrifice.
The Church Porch, i

1   Drink not the third glass—which thou
canst not tame
When once it is within thee.
v

2 Dare to be true: nothing can need a lie;
A fault, which needs it most, grows two thereby.
xiii

3 O England, full of sin, but most of sloth;
Spit out thy phlegm, and fill thy breast with glory.
xvi

4 Wit's an unruly engine, wildly striking
Sometimes a friend, sometimes the engineer.
xli

5 But love is lost, the way of friendship's gone,
Though David had his Jonathan, Christ his John.
xlvi

6 Be calm in arguing; for fierceness makes
Error a fault and truth discourtesy.
lii

7 Calmness is great advantage; he that lets
Another chafe, may warm him at his fire.
liii

8   Who aimeth at the sky
Shoots higher much than he that means a tree.
lvi

9 Man is God's image; but a poor man is
Christ's stamp to boot.
lxiv

10 Kneeling ne'er spoil'd silk stocking; quit thy state;
All equal are within the Church's gate.
lxviii

11   O, be drest;
Stay not for th' other pin! Why, thou hast lost
A joy for it worth worlds.
lxix

12 Judge not the preacher, for he is thy Judge;
If thou mislike him, thou conceiv'st him not:
God calleth preaching folly: do not grudge
To pick out treasures from an earthen pot:
The worst speaks something good; if all want sense,
God takes a text, and preacheth patience.
lxxii

13 Look not on pleasures as they come, but go.
lxxvii

14 I struck the board, and cried, 'No more;
     I will abroad.'
What, shall I ever sigh and pine?
My lines and life are free; free as the road,
Loose as the wind, as large as store.
     Shall I be still in suit?
Have I no harvest but a thorn
To let me blood, and not restore
What I have lost with cordial fruit?
     Sure there was wine
Before my sighs did dry it; there was corn
Before my tears did drown it;
Is the year only lost to me?
Have I no bays to crown it?
The Collar

15   Away! take heed;
     I will abroad.
Call in thy death's-head there, tie up thy fears;
     He that forbears
To suit and serve his need
     Deserves his load.
But as I rav'd and grew more fierce and wild
     At every word,
Methought I heard one calling, 'Child';
     And I replied, 'My Lord.'

16 Love is swift of foot;
Love's a man of war,
     And can shoot,
And can hit from far.
Discipline

17 I got me flowers to strew Thy way,
I got me boughs off many a tree;
But Thou wast up by break of day,
And brought'st Thy sweets along with Thee.
Easter Song

18 Teach me, my God and King,
In all things Thee to see,
And what I do in any thing
To do it as for Thee.

A man that looks on glass,
On it may stay his eye;
Or if he pleaseth, through it pass,
And then the heaven espy.
The Elixir

19 A servant with this clause
Makes drudgery divine;
Who sweeps a room as for Thy laws
Makes that and th' action fine.

20 Oh that I were an orange-tree,
          That busy plant!
Then I should ever laden be,
          And never want
Some fruit for Him that dressed me.
Employment

21 Who would have thought my shrivel'd heart
Could have recovered greenness?
The Flower

22 And now in age I bud again,
After so many deaths I live and write;
I once more smell the dew and rain,
And relish versing: O, my only Light,
          It cannot be
          That I am he
On whom Thy tempests fell all night.

23 Death is still working like a mole,
And digs my grave at each remove.
Grace

24 I made a posy while the day ran by;
Here will I smell my remnant out, and tie
     My life within this band;
But Time did beckon to the flow'rs, and they
By noon most cunningly did steal away,
     And wither'd in my hand.
Life

25 Love bade me welcome; yet my soul drew back,
          Guilty of dust and sin.
But quick-ey'd Love, observing me grow slack
          From my first entrance in,

Drew nearer to me, sweetly questioning
       If I lack'd any thing.
Love

1 'You must sit down,' says Love, 'and taste My meat.'
       So I did sit and eat.

2   For us the winds do blow,
The earth resteth, heav'n moveth, fountains flow;
   Nothing we see but means our good,
   As our delight or as our treasure;
The whole is either our cupboard of food
   Or cabinet of pleasure.
Man

3 Oh mighty love! Man is one world, and hath
   Another to attend him.

4   When boyes go first to bed,
They step into their voluntarie graves.
Mortification

5 Prayer the Church's banquet...
Exalted manna, gladness of the best,
Heaven in ordinary, man well drest,
The Milkie Way, the bird of Paradise...
The land of spices; something understood.
Prayer

6 When God at first made man,
Having a glass of blessings standing by;
Let us (said he) pour on him all we can:
Let the world's riches, which dispersed lie,
   Contract into a span.
The Pulley

7 He would adore my gifts instead of Me,
And rest in Nature, not the God of Nature:
   So both should losers be.

8   Yet let him keep the rest,
But keep them with repining restlessness;
Let him be rich and weary, that at least,
If goodness lead him not, yet weariness
   May toss him to My breast.

9 But who does hawk at eagles with a dove?
The Sacrifice, xxiii

10 Lord, with what care Thou hast begirt us round!
Parents first season us; then schoolmasters
Deliver us to laws; they send us, bound
To rules of reason, holy messengers,

Pulpits and Sundays, sorrow dogging sin,
Afflictions sorted, anguish of all sizes,
Fine nets and stratagems to catch us in,
Bibles laid open, millions of surprises.
Sin

11 Yet all these fences and their whole array
One cunning bosom sin blows quite away.

12 Grasp not at much, for fear thou losest all.
The Size

13 The God of love my Shepherd is,
And He that doth me feed,
While He is mine, and I am His,
What can I want or need?
23rd Psalm

14 Lord, make me coy and tender to offend:
In friendship, first I think if that agree
      Which I intend
Unto my friend's intent and end;

I would not use a friend as I use Thee.
Unkindness

15 My friend may spit upon my curious floor;
Would he have gold? I lend it instantly;
      But let the poor,
And Thou within them, starve at door:
I cannot use a friend as I use Thee.

16 Sweet day, so cool, so calm, so bright,
The bridal of the earth and sky,
The dew shall weep thy fall to-night;
      For thou must die.

Sweet rose, whose hue angry and brave
Bids the rash gazer wipe his eye,
Thy root is ever in its grave,
      And thou must die.

Sweet spring, full of sweet days and roses,
A box where sweets compacted lie.
Virtue

17 Only a sweet and virtuous soul,
Like season'd timber, never gives;
But though the whole world turn to coal,
      Then chiefly lives.

ROBERT HERRICK 1591–1674

18 I sing of brooks, of blossoms, birds, and bowers:
Of April, May, of June, and July-flowers.
I sing of May-poles, Hock-carts, wassails, wakes,
Of bride-grooms, brides, and of their bridal-cakes.
***Hesperides* (1648). Argument of his Book**

19 And once more yet (ere I am laid out dead)
Knock at a star with my exalted head.
The Bad Season Makes the Poet Sad

20 Fair pledges of a fruitful tree,
Why do ye fall so fast?
Your date is not so past;
But you may stay yet here a while,
To blush and gently smile;
And go at last.
Blossoms

21 Cherry-ripe, ripe, ripe, I cry,
Full and fair ones; come and buy:
If so be, you ask me where
They do grow? I answer, there,
Where my Julia's lips do smile;
There's the land, or cherry-isle.
Cherry-Ripe. See 3:18, 129:22

22 Get up, get up for shame, the blooming morn
Upon her wings presents the god unshorn.
Corinna's Going a-Maying

23 Get up, sweet Slug-a-bed, and see
The dew bespangling herb and tree.

24   'Tis sin,
Nay, profanation to keep in.

25 Come, let us go, while we are in our prime;
And take the harmless folly of the time.

26 So when or you or I are made
A fable, song, or fleeting shade;
All love, all liking, all delight
Lies drown'd with us in endless night.
Then while time serves, and we are but decaying;
Come, my Corinna, come, let's go a-Maying.

1 With thousand such enchanting dreams, that meet
   To make sleep not so sound, as sweet.
   A Country Life: to his Brother, M. Tho. Herrick

2 A sweet disorder in the dress
   Kindles in clothes a wantonness:
   A lawn about the shoulders thrown
   Into a fine distraction...
   A careless shoe-string, in whose tie
   I see a wild civility:
   Do more bewitch me, than when Art
   Is too precise in every part.
   Delight in Disorder

3 More discontents I never had
   Since I was born, than here;
   Where I have been, and still am sad,
     In this dull Devonshire.
   Discontents in Devon

4 It is the end that crowns us, not the fight.
   The End

5 Only a little more
   I have to write,
   Then I'll give o'er,
   And bid the world Good-night.
   His Poetry his Pillar

6 When I a verse shall make,
   Know I have prayed thee
   For old religion's sake,
   Saint Ben, to aid me.
   His Prayer to Ben Jonson

7 Roses at first were white,
     Till they co'd not agree,
   Whether my Sappho's breast,
     Or they more white sho'd be.
   How Roses Came Red

8 'Twixt kings and tyrants there's this difference
       known;
   Kings seek their subjects' good: tyrants their own.
   Kings and Tyrants

9 Love is a circle that doth restless move
   In the same sweet eternity of love.
   Love What It Is

10 Good morrow to the day so fair;
   Good morning, Sir, to you:
   Good morrow to mine own torn hair
     Bedabbled with the dew.
   The Mad Maid's Song

11 Her eyes the glow-worm lend thee,
   The shooting-stars attend thee;
       And the elves also,
       Whose little eyes glow,
   Like the sparks of fire, befriend thee.
   The Night-Piece, to Julia

12 Night makes no difference 'twixt the Priest and Clerk;
   Joan as my Lady is as good i' th' dark.
   No Difference i' th' Dark

13 Made us nobly wild, not mad.
   Ode for Ben Jonson

14 Out-did the meat, out-did the frolic wine.

15 Fain would I kiss my Julia's dainty leg,
   Which is as white and hairless as an egg.
   On Julia's Legs

16 Men are suspicious; prone to discontent:

Subjects still loathe the present Government.
Present Government Grievous

17 Praise they that will times past, I joy to see
   My self now live: this age best pleaseth me.
   The Present Time Best Pleaseth

18 Some ask'd how pearls did grow, and where?
   Then spoke I to my girl,
   To part her lips, and shew'd them there
   The quarelets of pearl.
   The Rock of Rubies, and the Quarry of Pearls

19 Attempt the end, and never stand to doubt;
   Nothing's so hard, but search will find it out.
   Seek and Find

20 A little saint best fits a little shrine,
   A little prop best fits a little vine,
   As my small cruse best fits my little wine.
   A Ternary of Littles, upon a Pipkin of Jelly sent to a Lady

21 A little stream best fits a little boat;
   A little lead best fits a little float;
   As my small pipe best fits my little note.

   A little meat best fits a little belly,
   As sweetly, Lady, give me leave to tell ye,
   This little pipkin fits this little jelly.

22 Give me a kiss, add to that kiss a score;
   Then to that twenty, add a hundred more:
   A thousand to that hundred: so kiss on,
   To make that thousand up a million,
   Treble that million, and when that is done,
   Let's kiss afresh, as when we first begun.
   To Anthea: Ah, My Anthea! See 136:26

23 Now is the time, when all the lights wax dim;
   And thou (Anthea) must withdraw from him
   Who was thy servant.
   To Anthea: Now is the Time

24 For my Embalming (Sweetest) there will be
   No Spices wanting, when I'm laid by thee.

25 Bid me to live, and I will live
   Thy Protestant to be:
   Or bid me love, and I will give
   A loving heart to thee.
   To Anthea, Who May Command Him Anything

26 Bid me to weep, and I will weep,
   While I have eyes to see.

27 Bid me despair, and I'll despair,
   Under that cypress tree:
   Or bid me die, and I will dare
   E'en Death, to die for thee.

   Thou art my life, my love, my heart,
   The very eyes of me:
   And hast command of every part,
   To live and die for thee.

28 Fair daffodils, we weep to see
   You haste away so soon:
   As yet the early-rising sun
   Has not attain'd his noon.
       Stay, stay,
   Until the hasting day
       Has run
   But to the even-song;
   And, having pray'd together, we
   Will go with you along.

   We have short time to stay, as you,

We have as short a Spring;
As quick a growth to meet decay,
As you or any thing.
To Daffodils

1 Sweet, be not proud of those two eyes,
Which star-like sparkle in their skies.
To Dianeme

2 That ruby which you wear
Sunk from the tip of your soft ear
Will last to be a precious stone
When all your world of beauty's gone.

3 I dare not ask a kiss;
I dare not beg a smile;
Lest having that, or this,
I might grow proud the while.

No, no, the utmost share
Of my desire, shall be
Only to kiss that air,
That lately kissed thee.
To Electra

4 He loves his bonds, who when the first are broke,
Submits his neck unto a second yoke.
To Love

5 Gather ye rosebuds while ye may,
Old Time is still a-flying:
And this same flower that smiles to-day,
To-morrow will be dying.
To the Virgins, to Make Much of Time

6 Then be not coy, but use your time;
And while ye may, go marry:
For having lost but once your prime,
You may for ever tarry.

7 Her pretty feet
Like snails did creep
A little out, and then,
As if they started at bo-peep,
Did soon draw in agen.
Upon her Feet

8 Whenas in silks my Julia goes,
Then, then (methinks) how sweetly flows
That liquefaction of her clothes.

Next, when I cast mine eyes and see
That brave vibration each way free;
O how that glittering taketh me!
Upon Julia's Clothes

9 So smooth, so sweet, so silv'ry is thy voice,
As, could they hear, the damn'd would make no noise,
But listen to thee (walking in thy chamber)
Melting melodious words, to lutes of amber.
Upon Julia's Voice

10 Here a little child I stand,
Heaving up my either hand;
Cold as paddocks though they be,
Here I lift them up to Thee,
For a benison to fall
On our meat, and on us all. Amen.
Noble Numbers. Another Grace for a Child

11 In prayer the lips ne'er act the winning part,
Without the sweet concurrence of the heart.
The Heart

12 When the artless doctor sees
No one hope, but of his fees,

And his skill runs on the lees;
Sweet Spirit, comfort me!

When his potion and his pill,
Has, or none, or little skill,
Meet for nothing, but to kill;
Sweet Spirit, comfort me!
His Litany to the Holy Spirit

13 But, for Man's fault, then was the thorn,
Without the fragrant rose-bud, born;
But ne'er the rose without the thorn.
The Rose

14 Lord, Thou hast given me a cell
Wherein to dwell,
A little house, whose humble roof
Is weather-proof;
Under the spars of which I lie
Both soft, and dry.
A Thanksgiving to God for his House

15 If any thing delight me for to print
My book, 'tis this; that Thou, my God, art in't.
To God

16 To work a wonder, God would have her shown,
At once, a bud, and yet a rose full-blown.
The Virgin Mary

JAMES HERVEY 1714–1758

17 E'en crosses from his sov'reign hand
Are blessings in disguise.
Reflections on a Flower-Garden

LORD HERVEY 1696–1743

18 Whoever would lie usefully should lie seldom.
Memoirs of the Reign of George II, vol.I, ch.19

HESIOD c.700 B.C.

19 πλέον ἥμισυ παντός.
The half is greater than the whole.
Works and Days, 40

LORD HEWART 1870–1943

20 It is not merely of some importance but is of
fundamental importance that justice should not only be
done, but should manifestly and undoubtedly be seen
to be done.
Rex v. Sussex Justices, 9 Nov. 1923 (King's Bench Reports,
1924, vol.i, p.259)

JOHN HEYWOOD 1497?–1580?

21 All a green willow, willow;
All a green willow is my garland.
The Green Willow

THOMAS HEYWOOD 1574?–1641

22 Seven cities warr'd for Homer, being dead,
Who, living, had no roof to shroud his head.
The Hierarchy of the Blessed Angels (1635). See 7:14

SIR SEYMOUR HICKS 1871–1949

23 You will recognize, my boy, the first sign of old age:
it is when you go out into the streets of London and
realize for the first time how young the policemen

look.
Attr. C. Pulling, *They Were Singing*, 7

W.E. HICKSON 1803–1870

1 'Tis a lesson you should heed,
Try, try again.
If at first you don't succeed,
Try, try again.
Try and Try Again

AARON HILL 1685–1750

2 Tender-handed stroke a nettle,
    And it stings you for your pains;
Grasp it like a man of mettle,
    And it soft as silk remains.
Verses Written on Window

JOE HILL 1879–1914

3 You will eat (You will eat)
    Bye and bye (Bye and bye)
In that glorious land above the sky (Way up high)
    Work and pray (Work and pray)
Live on hay (Live on hay)
    You'll get pie in the sky when you die (That's a
    lie.)
The Preacher and the Slave

REVD. ROWLAND HILL 1744–1833

4 He did not see any reason why the devil should have
all the good tunes.
E.W.Broome, *Rev. Rowland Hill*, vii

HILLEL 'THE ELDER' ?70 B.C.–A.D. 10?

5 A name made great is a name destroyed.
Pirque Aboth. See *Sayings of the Jewish Fathers*, ed. C. Taylor
(1877), i.14

6 If I am not for myself who is for me; and being for my
own self what am I? If not now when?
15

HIPPOCLEIDES 6th cent. B.C.

7 οὐ φροντὶς ʽΙπποκλείδῃ.
Hippocleides doesn't care.
Herodotus, *Histories*, vi.129.4

HIPPOCRATES 5th cent. B.C.

8 ὁ βίος βραχύς, ἡ δὲ τέχνη μακρή.
The life so short, the craft so long to learn.
Aphorisms, I.i. Trans. by Chaucer. See 143:32.
Often quoted in Latin as *Ars longa, vita brevis*. See Seneca, *De
Brevitate Vitae*, 1

ADOLF HITLER 1889–1945

9 *Die breite Masse eines Volkes...einer grossen Lüge
leichter zum Opfer fällt als einer kleinen.*
The broad mass of a nation...will more easily fall
victim to a big lie than to a small one.
Mein Kampf, I.x

10 I go the way that Providence dictates with the
assurance of a sleepwalker.
Speech in Munich, 15 Mar. 1936, after the successful
re-occupation of the Rhineland, against the experts' advice. See
Alan Bullock, *Hitler, A Study in Tyranny* (1952), ch.7, pt.i

11 My patience is now at an end.
Speech, 26 Sept. 1938

12 It is the last territorial claim which I have to make in
Europe. [The Sudetenland.]

THOMAS HOBBES 1588–1679

13 True and False are attributes of speech, not of things.
And where speech is not, there is neither Truth nor
Falsehood.
Leviathan (1651), pt.i, ch.4

14 Geometry (which is the only science that it hath
pleased God hitherto to bestow on mankind).

15 Words are wise men's counters, they do but reckon by
them: but they are the money of fools, that value them
by the authority of an Aristotle, a Cicero, or a
Thomas, or any other doctor whatsoever, if but a man.

16 They that approve a private opinion, call it opinion;
but they that mislike it, heresy: and yet heresy
signifies no more than private opinion.
ch.11

17 During the time men live without a common power to
keep them all in awe, they are in that condition which
is called war; and such a war as is of every man
against every man...the nature of war consisteth not in
actual fighting, but in the known disposition thereto
during all the time there is no assurance to the
contrary.
ch.13

18 No arts; no letters; no society; and which is worst of
all, continual fear and danger of violent death; and the
life of man, solitary, poor, nasty, brutish, and short.

19 Force, and fraud, are in war the two cardinal virtues.

20 They that are discontented under *monarchy,* call it
tyranny; and they that are displeased with *aristocracy,*
call it *oligarchy:* so also, they which find themselves
grieved under a *democracy,* call it *anarchy,* which
signifies the want of government; and yet I think no
man believes, that want of government, is any new
kind of government.
pt.ii, ch.19

21 The Papacy is not other than the Ghost of the deceased
Roman Empire, sitting crowned upon the grave
thereof.
pt.iv, ch.47

22 Laughter is nothing else but sudden glory arising from
some sudden conception of some eminency in
ourselves, by comparison with the infirmity of others,
or with our own formerly.
Human Nature (1640, published 1650), ix

23 He was wont to say that if he had read as much as
other men, he should have known no more than other
men.
Aubrey, *Life of Hobbes*

24 I am about to take my last voyage, a great leap in the
dark.
Last words. Watkins, *Anecdotes of Men of Learning*

JOHN CAM HOBHOUSE, BARON BROUGHTON
1786–1869

1 When I invented the phrase 'His Majesty's
Opposition' [Canning] paid me a compliment on the
fortunate hit.
Recollections of a Long Life (1865), ii, ch.12

RALPH HODGSON 1871–1962

2 'Twould ring the bells of Heaven
The wildest peal for years,
If Parson lost his senses
And people came to theirs,
And he and they together
Knelt down with angry prayers
For tamed and shabby tigers
And dancing dogs and bears,
And wretched, blind, pit ponies,
And little hunted hares.
The Bells of Heaven

3 See an old unhappy bull,
Sick in soul and body both.
The Bull

4 Eve, with her basket, was
Deep in the bells and grass,
Wading in bells and grass
Up to her knees,
Plucking a dish of sweet
Berries and plums to eat,
Down in the bells and grass
Under the trees.
Eve

5 Reason has moons, but moons not hers,
    Lie mirror'd on her sea,
Confounding her astronomers,
    But, O! delighting me.
Reason Has Moons

6 I climbed a hill as light fell short,
And rooks came home in scramble sort,
And filled the trees and flapped and fought
And sang themselves to sleep.
The Song of Honour

7 When stately ships are twirled and spun
Like whipping tops and help there's none
And mighty ships ten thousand ton
Go down like lumps of lead.

8 I stood upon that silent hill
And stared into the sky until
My eyes were blind with stars and still
I stared into the sky.

9 Time, you old gypsy man,
    Will you not stay,
Put up your caravan
    Just for one day?
Time, You Old Gypsy Man

10 Last week in Babylon,
    Last night in Rome,
Morning, and in the crush
    Under Paul's dome.

HEINRICH HOFFMANN 1809-1894

11 Augustus was a chubby lad;
Fat ruddy cheeks Augustus had:

And everybody saw with joy
The plump and hearty, healthy boy.
He ate and drank as he was told,
And never let his soup get cold.
But one day, one cold winter's day,
He screamed out, 'Take the soup away!
O take the nasty soup away!
I won't have any soup today.'
Struwwelpeter (1845, translated 1848). **Augustus**

12 Here is cruel Frederick, see!
A horrid wicked boy was he.
Cruel Frederick

13 At this, good Tray grew very red,
And growled, and bit him till he bled.

14 Let me see if Philip can
Be a little gentleman;
Let me see, if he is able
To sit still for once at table.
Fidgety Philip

15 But fidgety Phil,
He won't sit still;
He wriggles
And giggles,
And then, I declare,
Swings backwards and forwards,
And tilts up his chair,
Just like any rocking-horse—
'Philip! I am getting cross!'

16 Look at little Johnny there,
Little Johnny Head-In-Air!
Johnny Head-In-Air

17 Silly little Johnny, look,
You have lost your writing-book!

18 The door flew open, in he ran,
The great, long, red-legged scissor-man.
The Little Suck-a-Thumb

19 'Ah!' said Mamma, 'I knew he'd come
To naughty little Suck-a-Thumb.'

20 He finds it hard, without a pair
Of spectacles, to shoot the hare.
The hare sits snug in leaves and grass,
And laughs to see the green man pass.
The Man Who Went Out Shooting

21 And now she's trying all she can,
To shoot the sleepy, green-coat man.

22 Anything to me is sweeter
Than to see Shock-headed Peter.
Shock-Headed Peter

JAMES HOGG 1770–1835

23 Where the pools are bright and deep
Where the gray trout lies asleep,
Up the river and o'er the lea
That's the way for Billy and me.
A Boy's Song

24 God bless our Lord the King!
God save our lord the king!
    God save the king!
Make him victorious,
Happy, and glorious,
Long to reign over us:

God save the king!
Jacobite Relics of Scotland (1819-20), ii.50. **God Save The King.** See 130:24

1 We'll o'er the water, we'll o'er the sea,
We'll o'er the water to Charlie;
Come weel, come wo, we'll gather and go,
And live or die wi' Charlie.
76. **O'er the Water to Charlie**

2 Cock up your beaver, and cock it fu' sprush;
We'll over the Border and gi'e them a brush;
There's somebody there we'll teach better behaviour.
Hey, Johnnie lad, cock up your beaver!
127. **Cock Up Your Beaver**

1ST LORD HOLLAND 1705–1774

3 If Mr Selwyn calls again, shew him up: if I am alive I shall be delighted to see him; and if I am dead he would like to see me.
During his last illness. J.H. Jesse, *George Selwyn and his Contemporaries*, 1844, vol.iii, p.50

3RD LORD HOLLAND 1733–1840

4 Nephew of Fox, and friend of Grey,—
Enough my meed of fame
If those who deign'd to observe me say
I injur'd neither name.
Lady Holland, *Memoir of Rev. Sydney Smith* (1855), i.334

REVD. JOHN H. HOLMES 1879–1964

5 The universe is not hostile, nor yet is it friendly. It is simply indifferent.
A Sensible Man's View of Religion (1933)

OLIVER WENDELL HOLMES 1809–1894

6 Sweet is the scene where genial friendship plays
The pleasing game of interchanging praise.
An After-Dinner Poem

7 Fate tried to conceal him by naming him Smith.
[Samuel Francis Smith.] *The Boys*

8 Have you heard of the wonderful one-hoss shay,
That was built in such a logical way
It ran a hundred years to a day?
The Deacon's Masterpiece

9 A general flavor of mild decay.

10 Lean, hungry, savage anti-everythings.
A Modest Request

11 Wisdom has taught us to be calm and meek,
To take one blow, and turn the other cheek;
It is not written what a man shall do
If the rude caitiff smite the other too!
Non-Resistance

12 And, when you stick on conversation's burrs,
Don't strew your pathway with those dreadful *urs*.
A Rhymed Lesson

13 Man wants but little drink below,
But wants that little strong.
A Song of other Days. See 231:7, 588:8

14 To be seventy years young is sometimes far more cheerful and hopeful than to be forty years old.
On the Seventieth Birthday of Julia Ward Howe

15 Man has his will,—but woman has her way.
The Autocrat of the Breakfast-Table (1858), ch.1

16 The axis of the earth sticks out visibly through the centre of each and every town or city.
ch.6

17 The world's great men have not commonly been great scholars, nor its great scholars great men.

18 His humid front the cive, anheling, wipes.
And dreams of erring on ventiferous ripes.
ch.11. **Aestivation**

19 Depart,—be off,—excede,—evade,—erump!
See 151:27

20 It is the province of knowledge to speak and it is the privilege of wisdom to listen.
The Poet at the Breakfast Table (1872), ch.10

21 A moment's insight is sometimes worth a life's experience.
The Professor at the Breakfast Table (1860), ch.10

JOHN HOME 1722–1808

22 My name is Norval; on the Grampian hills
My father feeds his flocks; a frugal swain,
Whose constant cares were to increase his store.
Douglas (1756), II.1

23   He seldom errs
Who thinks the worst he can of womankind.
III.iii

24 Like Douglas conquer, or like Douglas die.
v

25 Bold and erect the Caledonian stood,
Old was his mutton and his claret good;
Let him drink port, the English Statesman cried—
He drank the poison and his spirit died.
Lockhart, *Life of Scott*, IV, ch.v

HOMER 8th cent. B.C.

26 μῆνιν ἄειδε, θεά, Πηληϊάδεω Ἀχιλῆος
οὐλομένην, ἣ μυρί᾽ Ἀχαιοῖς ἄλγε᾽ ἔθηκε.
Achilles' cursed anger sing, O goddess, that son of Peleus, which started a myriad sufferings for the Achaeans.
Achilles' wrath, to Greece the direful spring
Of woes unnumbered, heavenly goddess, sing.
(Alexander Pope's translation.)
Iliad, i.1

27 ἔπεα πτερόεντα.
Winged words.
201

28 οὐ νέμεσις Τρῶας καὶ ἐϋκνήμιδας Ἀχαιοὺς
τοιῇδ᾽ ἀμφὶ γυναικὶ πολὺν χρόνον ἄλγεα πάσχειν·
αἰνῶς ἀθανάτῃσι θεῇς εἰς ὦπα ἔοικεν.
It is no cause for anger that the Trojans and the well-greaved Achaeans have suffered for so long over *such* a woman: she is wondrously like the immortal goddesses to look upon.
iii.156. Of Helen

29 οἵη περ φύλλων γενεή, τοίη δὲ καὶ ἀνδρῶν.
Like that of leaves is a generation of men.
vi.146

30 αἰὲν ἀριστεύειν καὶ ὑπείροχον ἔμμεναι ἄλλων.

Always to be best, and to be distinguished above the rest.
208

1 δακρυόεν γελάσασα.
Smiling through her tears.
484

2 εἷς οἰωνὸς ἄριστος, ἀμύνεσθαι περὶ πάτρης.
This is the one best omen, to fight in defence of one's country.
xii.243

3 κεῖτο μέγας μεγαλωστὶ, λελασμένος ἱπποσυνάων.
He lay great and greatly fallen, forgetful of his chivalry.
xvi.776

4 ἄνδρα μοι ἔννεπε, Μοῦσα, πολύτροπον, ὃς μάλα πολλὰ
πλάγχθη, ἐπεὶ Τροίης ἱερὸν πτολίεθρον ἔπερσε,
πολλῶν δ' ἀνθρώπων ἴδεν ἄστεα καὶ νόον ἔγνω.
Tell me, Muse, of the man of many tricks, who wandered far and wide after he had sacked Troy's sacred city, and saw the towns of many men and knew their mind.
Odyssey, i.1. Of Odysseus

5 ῥοδοδάκτυλος Ἠώς.
Rosy-fingered dawn.
ii.1, and elsewhere

6 βουλοίμην κ' ἐπάρουρος ἐὼν θητευέμεν ἄλλω
ἀνδρὶ παρ' ἀκλήρω, ᾧ μὴ βίοτος πολὺς εἴη,
ἢ πᾶσιν νεκύεσσι καταφθιμένοισιν ἀνάσσειν.
I would rather be tied to the soil as another man's serf, even a poor man's, who hadn't much to live on himself, than be King of all these the dead and destroyed.
xi.489

WILLIAM HONE 1780–1842

7 John Jones may be described as 'one of the *has beens.*'
Every-Day Book (1826-7), vol.ii, 820

THOMAS HOOD 1799–1845

8 It was not in the winter
  Our loving lot was cast!
It was the time of roses,
  We plucked them as we passed!
Ballad: It Was Not in the Winter

9 Take her up tenderly,
Lift her with care;
Fashion'd so slenderly,
'Young, and so fair!
The Bridge of Sighs

10 Mad from life's history,
Glad to death's mystery,
Swift to be hurl'd—
Anywhere, anywhere,
Out of the world!

11 Much study had made him very lean,
  And pale, and leaden-ey'd.
The Dream of Eugene Aram

12 Two stern-faced men set out from Lynn,
  Through the cold and heavy mist;
And Eugene Aram walked between,
  With gyves upon his wrist.

13 Ben Battle was a soldier bold,
  And used to war's alarms:
But a cannon-ball took off his legs,
  So he laid down his arms!
Faithless Nelly Gray

14 For here I leave my second leg,
  And the Forty-second Foot!

15 The love that loves a scarlet coat
  Should be more uniform.

16 His death, which happen'd in his berth,
  At forty-odd befell:
They went and told the sexton, and
  The sexton toll'd the bell.
Faithless Sally Brown

17 I remember, I remember,
The house where I was born,
The little window where the sun
Came peeping in at morn;
He never came a wink too soon,
Nor brought too long a day,
But now, I often wish the night
Had borne my breath away!
I Remember

18 I remember, I remember,
The fir trees dark and high;
I used to think their slender tops
Were close against the sky:
It was a childish ignorance,
But now 'tis little joy
To know I'm farther off from heav'n
Than when I was a boy.

19 He never spoils the child and spares the rod,
But spoils the rod and never spares the child.
The Irish Schoolmaster, xii

20 But evil is wrought by want of thought,
  As well as want of heart!
The Lady's Dream

21 For that old enemy the gout
  Had taken him in toe!
Lieutenant Luff

22 Alas! my everlasting peace
  Is broken into pieces.
Mary's Ghost

23 And then, in the fulness of joy and hope,
Seem'd washing his hands with invisible soap,
  In imperceptible water.
Miss Kilmansegg (1841-3). **Her Christening**

24 There's Bardus, a six-foot column of fop,
A lighthouse without any light atop.
Her First Step

25 For one of the pleasures of having a rout,
Is the pleasure of having it over.
Her Dream

26 Home-made dishes that drive one from home.
Her Misery

27 No sun—no moon!
No morn—no noon
No dawn—no dusk—no proper time of day.
No!

28 No warmth, no cheerfulness, no healthful ease,
No comfortable feel in any member—
No shade, no shine, no butterflies, no bees,

No fruits, no flowers, no leaves, no birds,—
November!

1   I saw old Autumn in the misty morn
Stand shadowless like Silence, listening
To silence.
Ode: Autumn

2   The bird forlorn,
That singeth with her breast against a thorn.
The Plea of the Midsummer Fairies (1827), xxx

3   When Eve upon the first of Men
The apple press'd with specious cant,
Oh! what a thousand pities then
That Adam was not Adamant!
A Reflection

4   She stood breast high amid the corn,
Clasp'd by the golden light of morn,
Like the sweetheart of the sun,
Who many a glowing kiss had won.
Ruth

5   Sure, I said, heav'n did not mean,
Where I reap thou shouldst but glean,
Lay thy sheaf adown and come,
Share my harvest and my home.

6   With fingers weary and worn,
With eyelids heavy and red,
A woman sat, in unwomanly rags,
Plying her needle and thread—
Stitch! stitch! stitch!
In poverty, hunger, and dirt.
The Song of the Shirt (1843)

7   O! men with sisters dear,
O! men with mothers and wives!
It is not linen you're wearing out,
But human creatures' lives!

8   Oh! God! that bread should be so dear,
And flesh and blood so cheap!

9   No blessed leisure for love or hope,
But only time for grief!

10 My tears must stop, for every drop
Hinders needle and thread!

11 There is a silence where hath been no sound,
There is a silence where no sound may be,
In the cold grave—under the deep deep sea,
Or in the wide desert where no life is found.
Sonnet. Silence

12 A wife who preaches in her gown,
And lectures in her night-dress!
The Surplice Question

13 Our hands have met, but not our hearts;
Our hands will never meet again.
To a False Friend

14 What is a modern poet's fate?
To write his thoughts upon a slate;
The critic spits on what is done,
Gives it a wipe—and all is gone.
See Hallam Tennyson, *Alfred Lord Tennyson, A Memoir* (1897),
vol.ii, ch.3. Not found in Hood's *Complete Works*.

15 There are three things which the public will always
clamour for, sooner or later: namely, Novelty,
novelty, novelty.
Announcement of *Comic Annual* for 1836

16 The sedate, sober, silent, serious, sad-coloured sect.
[Quakers.]
The Doves and the Crows

17 'Extremes meet', as the whiting said with its tail in its
mouth.

18 Holland...lies so low they're only saved by being
dammed.
Up the Rhine. To Rebecca Page (1839)

RICHARD HOOKER 1554?–1600

19 He that goeth about to persuade a multitude, that they
are not so well governed as they ought to be, shall
never want attentive and favourable hearers.
Of the Laws of Ecclesiastical Polity (1594,1597), bk.I.i

20 Of Law there can be no less acknowledged, than that
her seat is the bosom of God, her voice the harmony
of the world: all things in heaven and earth do her
homage, the very least as feeling her care, and the
greatest as not exempted from her power.
xvi

21 Change is not made without inconvenience, even from
worse to better.
Quoted by Johnson, as from Hooker, in the Preface to the *English
Dictionary*

ELLEN STURGIS HOOPER 1816–1841

22 I slept, and dreamed that life was Beauty;
I woke, and found that life was Duty.
Beauty and Duty (1840)

PRESIDENT HERBERT HOOVER 1874–1964

23 The American system of rugged individualism.
Campaign speech, New York, 22 Oct. 1928

24 Our country has deliberately undertaken a great social
and economic experiment, noble in motive and
far-reaching in purpose. [The Eighteenth Amendment,
enacting Prohibition.]
Letter to Senator W.H. Borah, 28 Feb. 1928

25 Older men declare war. But it is youth that must fight
and die.
Speech to Republican National Convention, Chicago, 27 June
1944

ANTHONY HOPE 1863–1933

26 Economy is going without something you do want in
case you should, some day, want something you
probably won't want.
The Dolly Dialogues (1894), No.12

27 'You oughtn't to yield to temptation.'
'Well, somebody must, or the thing becomes absurd.'
No. 14

28 'Boys will be boys—'
'And even that...wouldn't matter if we could only
prevent girls from being girls.'
No. 16

29 '*Bourgeois,*' I observed, 'is an epithet which the
riff-raff apply to what is respectable, and the
aristocracy to what is decent.'
No. 17

30 I wish you would read a little poetry sometimes. Your
ignorance cramps my conversation.
No. 22

1 Good families are generally worse than any others.
The Prisoner of Zenda (1894), ch.1

2 His foe was folly and his weapon wit.
Inscription on the tablet to W.S. Gilbert, Victoria Embankment, London (1915)

LAURENCE HOPE (MRS. M.H. NICOLSON) 1865–1904

3 Pale hands I loved beside the Shalimar,
Where are you now? Who lies beneath your spell?
The Garden of Kama and other Love Lyrics from India (1901). **Pale Hands I Loved**

4 Pale hands, pink-tipped, like lotus-buds that float
On those cool waters where we used to dwell,
I would have rather felt you round my throat
Crushing out life than waving me farewell.

5 Less than the dust beneath thy chariot wheel,
Less than the weed that grows beside thy door,
Less than the rust that never stained thy sword,
Less than the need thou hast in life of me,
   Even less am I.
Less than the Dust

GERARD MANLEY HOPKINS 1844–1889

6 Wild air, world-mothering air,
Nestling me everywhere.
The Blessed Virgin Compared to the Air We Breathe

7 Not, I'll not, carrion comfort, Despair, not feast on thee;
Not untwist—slack they may be—these last strands of man
In me or, most weary, cry *I can no more*. I can;
Can something, hope, wish day come, not choose not to be.
Carrion Comfort

8   That night, that year
Of now done darkness I wretch lay wrestling with (my God!) my God.

9 Towery city and branchy between towers.
Duns Scotus' Oxford

10 Cuckoo-echoing, bell-swarmèd, lark-charmèd,
rook-racked, river-rounded.

11 Didst fettle for the great grey drayhorse his bright and battering sandal!
Felix Randal

12 The world is charged with the grandeur of God.
   It will flame out like shining from shook foil;...
Generations have trod, have trod, have trod;
   And all is seared with trade; bleared, smeared with toil;
   And wears man's smudge and shares man's smell: the soil
Is bare now, nor can foot feel, being shod.
God's Grandeur

13   Because the Holy Ghost over the bent
World broods with warm breast and with ah! bright wings.

14 Elected Silence, sing to me
And beat upon my whorlèd ear,
Pipe me to pastures still and be
The music that I care to hear.
The Habit of Perfection

15 Palate, the hutch of tasty lust,
Desire not to be rinsed with wine:
The can must be so sweet, the crust
So fresh that come in fasts divine!

16 And you unhouse and house the Lord.

17   I have desired to go
      Where springs not fail,
To fields where flies no sharp and sided hail
   And a few lilies blow.

      And I have asked to be
      Where no storms come,
Where the green swell is in the havens dumb,
   And out of the swing of the sea.
Heaven-Haven

18 What would the world be, once bereft
Of wet and wildness? Let them be left,
O let them be left, wildness and wet;
Long live the weeds and the wilderness yet.
Inversnaid

19 No worst, there is none. Pitched past pitch of grief,
More pangs will, schooled at forepangs, wilder wring.
Comforter, where, where is your comforting?
No Worst, there is None

20 O the mind, mind has mountains; cliffs of fall
Frightful, sheer, no-man-fathomed. Hold them cheap
May who ne'er hung there.

21   Here! creep,
Wretch, under a comfort serves in a whirlwind: all
Life death does end and each day dies with sleep.

22 Glory be to God for dappled things.
Pied Beauty

23 All things counter, original, spare, strange;
   Whatever is fickle, freckled (who knows how?)
   With swift, slow; sweet, sour; adazzle, dim;
He fathers-forth whose beauty is past change:
   Praise him.

24   The glassy peartree leaves and blooms, they brush
      The descending blue; that blue is all in a rush
With richness.
Spring

25 Margaret, are you grieving
Over Goldengrove unleaving?
Spring and Fall. To a young child

26 Ah! as the heart grows older
It will come to such sights colder
By and by, not spare a sigh
Though worlds of wanwood leafmeal lie,
And yet you *will* weep and know why.

27 It is the blight man was born for,
It is Margaret you mourn for.

28 Look at the stars! look, look up at the skies!
O look at all the fire-folk sitting in the air!
The bright boroughs, the circle-citadels there!
The Starlight Night

29 Ah well! it is all a purchase, all is a prize.
Buy then! bid then!—What?— Prayer, patience, alms, vows.
Look, look: a May-mess, like on orchard boughs!
Look! March-bloom, like on mealed-with-yellow sallows!
These are indeed the barn; withindoors house

The shocks. This piece-bright paling shuts the spouse
Christ home, Christ and his mother and all his
   hallows.

1 I am all at once what Christ is, since he was what I
   am, and
This Jack, joke, poor potsherd, patch, matchwood,
   immortal diamond,
      Is immortal diamond.
That Nature is a Heraclitean Fire

2 Thou art indeed just, Lord, if I contend
With thee; but, sir, so what I plead is just.
Why do sinners' ways prosper? and why must
Disappointment all I endeavour end?
Thou Art Indeed Just, Lord

3   Birds build—but not I build; no, but strain,
Time's eunuch, and not breed one work that wakes.
Mine, O thou lord of life, send my roots rain.

4 I caught this morning morning's minion, kingdom of
   daylight's dauphin, dapple-dawn-drawn Falcon.
The Windhover

5   My heart in hiding
Stirred for a bird,—the achieve of, the mastery of the
   thing!

6   I did say yes
O at lightning and lashed rod;
Thou heardst me truer than tongue confess
   Thy terror, O Christ, O God.
The Wreck of the Deutschland, I.2

7   How a lush-kept plush-capped sloe
   Will, mouthed to flesh-burst,
Gush!—flush the man, the being with it, sour or
   sweet,
Brim, in a flash, full!
8

JOSEPH HOPKINSON 1770–1842

8 Hail, Columbia! happy land!
Hail, ye heroes! heaven-born band!
Hail, Columbia! Porcupine's Gazette, 20 Apr. 1798

HORACE 65–8 B.C.

9   *Ut turpiter atrum*
Desinat in piscem mulier formosa superne.
So that what is a beautiful woman on top ends in a
   black and ugly fish.
Ars Poetica, 3

10   *'Pictoribus atque poetis*
Quidlibet audendi semper fuit aequa potestas.'
Scimus, et hanc veniam petimusque damusque
   vicissim.
'Painters and poets alike have always had licence to
   dare anything.' We know that, and we both claim
   and allow to others in their turn this indulgence.
9

11 *Inceptis gravibus plerumque et magna professis*
Purpureus, late qui splendeat, unus et alter
Adsuitur pannus.
Frequently with serious works and ones of great
   import, some purple patch or other is stitched on, to
   show up far and wide.
14

12   *Brevis esse laboro,*

Obscurus fio.
I strive to be brief, and I become obscure.
25

13 *Dixeris egregie notum si callida verbum*
Reddiderit iunctura novum.
You will have written exceptionally well if, by skilful
   arrangement of your words, you have made an
   ordinary one seem original.
47

14 *Multa renascentur quae iam cecidere, cadentque*
Quae nunc sunt in honore vocabula, si volet usus,
Quem penes arbitrium est et ius et norma loquendi.
Many terms which have now dropped out of favour,
   will be revived, and those that are at present
   respectable will drop out, if usage so choose, with
   whom resides the decision and the judgement and
   the code of speech.
70

15 *Grammatici certant et adhuc sub iudice lis est.*
Scholars dispute, and the case is still before the courts.
78

16 *Proicit ampullas et sesquipedalia verba.*
Throws aside his paint-pots and his words a foot and a
   half long.
97

17 *Difficile est proprie communia dicere.*
It is hard to utter common notions in an individual
   way.
128

18 *Parturient montes, nascetur ridiculus mus.*
Mountains will heave in childbirth, and a silly little
   mouse will be born.
139

19 *Non fumum ex fulgore, sed ex fumo dare lucem*
Cogitat.
His thinking does not result in smoke after the flashing
   fire, but in light emerging from the smoke.
143

20 *Semper ad eventum festinat et in medias res*
Non secus ac notas auditorem rapit.
He always hurries to the main event and whisks his
   audience into the middle of things as though they
   knew already.
148

21 *Difficilis, querulus, laudator temporis acti*
Se puero, castigator censorque minorum.
Multa ferunt anni venientes commoda secum,
Multa recedentes adimunt.
Tiresome, complaining, a praiser of the times that
   were when he was a boy, a castigator and censor of
   the young generation. The years as they come bring
   a lot of advantages with them, but as they go by they
   take a lot away too.
173

22   *Vos exemplaria Graeca*
Nocturna versate manu, versate diurna.
For your own good, turn the pages of your Greek
   exemplars by night and by day.
268

23 *Grais ingenium, Grais dedit ore rotundo*
Musa loqui.
To the Greeks the Muse gave native wit, to the Greeks

the gift of graceful eloquence.
323

1 *Omne tulit punctum qui miscuit utile dulci,*
Lectorem delectando pariterque monendo.
He has gained every point who has mixed practicality
with pleasure, by delighting the reader at the same
time as instructing him.
343

2 *Indignor quandoque bonus dormitat Homerus.*
I'm aggrieved when sometimes even excellent Homer
nods.
359

3 *Ut pictura poesis.*
The making of a poem is like that of a painting.
361

4 *Mediocribus esse poetis*
Non homines, non di, non concessere columnae.
Not gods, nor men, nor even booksellers have put up
with poets' being second-rate.
372

5 *Tu nihil invita dices faciesve Minerva.*
You will get nothing written or created unless Minerva
helps.
385

6 *Nonumque prematur in annum,*
Membranis intus positis: delere licebit
Quod non edideris; nescit vox missa reverti.
Let it be kept till the ninth year, the manuscript put
away at home: you may destroy whatever you
haven't published; once out, what you've said can't
be stopped.
388. See 258:22

7 *Nullius addictus iurare in verba magistri,*
Quo me cumque rapit tempestas, deferor hospes.
Not bound to swear allegiance to any master, wherever
the wind takes me I travel as a visitor.
Epistles, I.i.14. *Nullius in verba* is the motto of the Royal
Society.

8 *Condicio dulcis sine pulvere palmae.*
The happy state of getting the victor's palm without
the dust of racing.
51

9 *Hic murus aeneus esto,*
Nil conscire sibi, nulla pallescere culpa.
Let this be your wall of brass, to have nothing on your
conscience, no guilt to make you turn pale.
60

10 *Si possis recte, si non, quocumque modo rem.*
If possible honestly, if not, somehow, make money.
66

11 *Olim quod vulpes aegroto cauta leoni*
Respondit referam: 'quia me vestigia terrent,
Omnia te adversum spectantia, nulla retrorsum.'
Let me remind you what the wary fox said once upon a
time to the sick lion: 'Because those footprints scare
me, all directed your way, none coming back.'
73

12 *Quidquid delirant reges plectuntur Achivi.*
For any madness of their kings, it is the Greeks who
take the beating.
ii.14

13 *Nos numerus sumus et fruges consumere nati.*

We are just statistics, born to consume resources.
27

14 *Dimidium facti qui coepit habet: sapere aude.*
To have begun is half the job: be bold and be sensible.
40

15 *Ira furor brevis est.*
Anger is a short madness.
62

16 *Omnem crede diem tibi diluxisse supremum.*
Grata superveniet quae non sperabitur hora.
Me pinguem et nitidum bene curata cute vises
Cum ridere voles Epicuri de grege porcum.
Believe each day that has dawned is your last. Some
hour to which you have not been looking forward
will prove lovely. As for me, if you want a good
laugh, you will come and find me fat and sleek, in
excellent condition, one of Epicurus' herd of pigs.
iv.13

17 *Nil admirari prope res est una, Numici,*
Solaque quae possit facere et servare beatum.
To marvel at nothing is just about the one and only
thing, Numicius, that can make a man happy and
keep him that way.
vi.1

18 *Naturam expellas furca, tamen usque recurret.*
You may drive out nature with a pitchfork, yet she'll
be constantly running back.
x.24

19 *Caelum non animum mutant qui trans mare currunt.*
Strenua nos exercet inertia: navibus atque
Quadrigis petimus bene vivere. Quod petis hic est,
Est Ulubris, animus si te non deficit aequus.
They change their clime, not their frame of mind, who
rush across the sea. We work hard at doing nothing:
we look for happiness in boats and carriage rides.
What you are looking for is here, is at Ulubrae, if
only peace of mind doesn't desert you.
xi.27

20 *Concordia discors.*
Harmony in discord.
xii.19

21 *Principibus placuisse viris non ultima laus est.*
Non cuivis homini contingit adire Corinthum.
It is not the least praise to have pleased leading men.
Not everyone is lucky enough to get to Corinth.
xvii.35

22 *Et semel emissum volat irrevocabile verbum.*
And once sent out a word takes wing irrevocably.
xviii.71. See 258:6

23 *Nam tua res agitur, paries cum proximus ardet.*
For it is your business, when the wall next door
catches fire.
84

24 *Fallentis semita vitae.*
The pathway of a life unnoticed.
103

25 *Prisco si credis, Maecenas docte, Cratino,*
Nulla placere diu nec vivere carmina possunt
Quae scribuntur aquae potoribus.
If you believe Cratinus from days of old, Maecenas,
(as you must know) no verse can give pleasure for
long, nor last, that is written by drinkers of water.
xix.1

1 *O imitatores, servum pecus.*
O imitators, you slavish herd.
19

2 *Graecia capta ferum victorem cepit et artes*
Intulit agresti Latio.
Greece, once overcome, overcame her wild conqueror,
and brought the arts into rustic Latium.
II.i.156

3 *Si foret in terris, rideret Democritus.*
If he were on earth, Democritus would laugh at the
sight.
194

4 *Atque inter silvas Academi quaerere verum.*
And seek for truth in the groves of Academe.
ii.45

5 *Multa fero, ut placem genus irritabile vatum.*
I have to put up with a lot, to please the sensitive race
of poets.
102

6 *Quid te exempta iuvat spinis de pluribus una?*
Vivere si recte nescis, decede peritis.
Lusisti satis, edisti satis atque bibisti:
Tempus abire tibi est.
What pleasure does it give to be rid of one thorn out of
many? If you don't know how to live right, give
way to those who are expert at it. You have had
enough fun, eaten and drunk enough: time you were
off.
212

7 *Beatus ille, qui procul negotiis,*
    Ut prisca gens mortalium,
Paterna rura bubus exercet suis,
    Solutus omni faenore.
He's happy who, far away from business, like the race
of men of old, tills his ancestral fields with his own
oxen, unbound by any interest to pay.
Epodes, ii.1

8 *Maecenas atavis edite regibus,*
O et praesidium et dulce decus meum.
Maecenas, descended from royal forebears, oh and my
stronghold and my pride and joy!
Odes, I.i.1

9 *Indocilis pauperiem pati.*
Hard to train to accept being poor.
18

10 *Quodsi me lyricis vatibus inseres,*
Sublimi feriam sidera vertice.
And if you include me among the lyric poets, I'll hold
my head so high it'll strike the stars.
35

11 *Animae dimidium meae.*
The half of my own life.
iii.8. Of Virgil.

12   *Illi robur et aes triplex*
Circa pectus erat, qui fragilem truci
    Commisit pelago ratem
Primus.
His breast must have been protected all round with oak
and three-ply bronze, who first launched his frail
boat on the rough sea.
9

13 *Pallida Mors aequo pulsat pede pauperum tabernas*
    Regumque turris.

Pale Death kicks his way equally into the cottages of
the poor and the castles of kings.
iv.13

14 *Vitae summa brevis spem nos vetat incohare longam.*
Life's short span forbids us to enter on far-reaching
hopes.
15

15 *Quis multa gracilis te puer in rosa*
Perfusus liquidis urget odoribus
    Grato, Pyrrha, sub antro?
        Cui flavam religas comam,
Simplex munditiis?
Who's the slim boy now, dripping with scent, who's
pressing you down, Pyrrha, on a pile of rose-petals,
in the pleasant shade of some rock? For whom are
you dressing your golden hair, simply but with such
style?
v.1

16 *Nil desperandum Teucro duce et auspice.*
Teucer shall lead and his star shall preside.
No cause for despair, then.
vii.27. Tr. James Michie

17 *Cras ingens iterabimus aequor.*
Tomorrow we'll be back on the vast ocean.
32

18 *Quid sit futurum cras fuge quaerere et*
Quem Fors dierum cumque dabit lucro
Appone.
Drop the question what tomorrow may bring, and
count as profit every day that Fate allows you.
ix.13

19 *Tu ne quaesieris, scire nefas, quem mihi, quem tibi*
Finem di dederint.
Do not try to find out—we're forbidden to
know—what end the gods have in store for me, or
for you.
xi.1

20   *Dum loquimur, fugerit invida*
Aetas: carpe diem, quam minimum credula postero.
While we're talking, time will have meanly run on:
pick today's fruits, not relying on the future in the
slightest.
7

21   *Felices ter et amplius*
Quos irrupta tenet copula nec malis
            Divulsus querimoniis
Suprema citius solvet amor die.
Thrice blest (and more) are the couple whose ties are
unbroken and whose love, never strained by nasty
quarrels, will not slip until their dying day.
xiii.17

22 *O matre pulchra filia pulchrior.*
What a beautiful mother, and yet more beautiful
daughter!
xvi.1

23 *Integer vitae scelerisque purus.*
Of unblemished life and spotless record.
xxii.1

24 *Dulce ridentem Lalagen amabo,*
    Dulce loquentem.
I will go on loving Lalage, who laughs so sweetly and
talks so sweetly.
23

1 *Multis ille bonis flebilis occidit,*
Nulli flebilior quam tibi.
Many good men should weep for his death, but you
most of all.
xxiv.9

2 *Parcus deorum cultor et infrequens.*
Not a devoted or regular worshipper of the gods.
xxxiv.1

3 *Nunc est bibendum, nunc pede libero*
Pulsanda tellus.
Now for drinks, now for some dancing with a good
beat.
xxxvii.1

4 *Persicos odi, puer, apparatus.*
I hate all that Persian gear, boy.
xxxviii.1

5 *Mitte sectari, rosa quo locorum*
Sera moretur.
Stop looking for the place where a late rose may yet
linger.
3

6 *Aequam memento rebus in arduis*
Servare mentem.
When things are steep, remember to stay level-headed.
II.iii.1

7 *Omnes eodem cogimur, omnium*
Versatur urna serius ocius
Sors exitura et nos in aeternum
Exsilium impositura cumbae.
Sheep driven deathward. Sooner or later Fate's
Urn shakes, the lot comes leaping for each of us
And books a one-way berth in Charon's
Boat on the journey to endless exile.
25. Tr. James Michie

8 *Ille terrarum mihi praeter omnis*
Angulus ridet.
That corner of the world smiles for me more than
anywhere else.
vi.13

9 *Auream quisquis mediocritatem*
Diligit.
Someone who loves the golden mean.
x.5

10 *Eheu fugaces, Postume, Postume,*
Labuntur anni.
Ah me, Postumus, Postumus, the fleeting years are
slipping by.
xiv.1

11 *Nihil est ab omni*
Parte beatum.
Nothing is an unmixed blessing.
xvi.27

12 *Credite posteri.*
Believe me, you who come after me!
xix.2

13 *Odi profanum vulgus et arceo;*
Favete linguis; carmina non prius
Audita Musarum sacerdos
Virginibus puerisque canto.
I hate the unholy masses and I keep away from them.
Hush your tongues; as a priest of the Muses, I sing
songs never heard before to virgin girls and boys.
III.i.1

14 *Omne capax movet urna nomen.*
The enormous tombola shakes up everyone's name.
16

15 *Post equitem sedet atra Cura.*
At the rider's back sits dark Anxiety.
40

16 *Cur valle permutem Sabina*
Divitias operosiores?
Why should I exchange my Sabine valley for riches
which just make more trouble?
47

17 *Dulce et decorum est pro patria mori.*
Lovely and honourable it is to die for one's country.
ii.13

18 *Iustum et tenacem propositi virum*
Non civium ardor prava iubentium,
Non vultus instantis tyranni
Mente quatit solida.
For a just man and one with a firm grasp of his
intentions, neither the heated passions of his
fellow-citizens ordaining something awful, nor the
face of a tyrant before his very eyes, will shake him
in his firm-based mind.
iii.1

19 *Si fractus illabatur orbis,*
Impavidum ferient ruinae.
If the world should break and fall on him, its ruins
would strike him unafraid.
7

20 *Aurum irrepertum et sic melius situm.*
Gold undiscovered (and all the better for being so).
49

21 *Non sine dis animosus infans.*
An adventurous child, thanks to the gods.
iv.20

22 *Fratresque tendentes opaco*
Pelion imposuisse Olympo.
And the brothers attempting to get Pelion perched on
top of shady Olympus.
51. Of two gigantic heroes trying to reach heaven.

23 *Vis consili expers mole ruit sua.*
Force, if unassisted by judgement, collapses through
its own mass.
65

24 *O magna Carthago, probrosis*
Altior Italiae ruinis!
O mighty Carthage, all the loftier for the shocking
collapse of Italy!
v.39

25 *Delicta maiorum immeritus lues.*
Undeservedly you will atone for the sins of your
fathers.
vi.1

26 *Damnosa quid non imminuit dies?*
Aetas parentum peior avis tulit
Nos nequiores, mox daturos
Progeniem vitiosiorem.
What do the ravages of time not injure? Our parents'
age (worse than our grandparents') has produced us,
more worthless still, who will soon give rise to a yet
more vicious generation.
45

27 *Donec gratus eram tibi.*

In the days when I was dear to you.
ix.1

1 *Tecum vivere amem, tecum obeam libens.*
With you I should love to live, with you be ready to
die.
24

2 *Splendide mendax et in omne virgo*
Nobilis aevum.
Gloriously deceitful and a virgin renowned for ever.
xi.35. Of the Danaid Hypermestra.

3 *O fons Bandusiae splendidior vitro.*
O spring of Bandusia, glinting more than glass.
xiii.1

4 *Non ego hoc ferrem calidus iuventa*
Consule Planco.
I shouldn't have put up with this when I was a
hot-blooded youth (and Plancus was consul).
xiv.27

5 *O nata mecum consule Manlio*
...pia testa.
O trusty wine-jar, born the same year as I (when
Manlius was consul).
xxi.1

6 *Vixi puellis nuper idoneus*
Et militavi non sine gloria;
Nunc arma defunctumque bello
Barbiton hic paries habebit.
My life with girls has ended, though till lately I was up
to it and soldiered on not ingloriously; now on this
wall will hang my weapons and my lyre, discharged
from the war.
xxvi.1

7 *Fumum et opes strepitumque Romae.*
The smoke and wealth and din of Rome.
xxix.12

8 *Exegi monumentum aere perennius.*
I have executed a memorial longer lasting than bronze.
xxx.1

9 *Non omnis moriar.*
I shall not altogether die.
6

10 *Non sum qualis eram bonae*
Sub regno Cinarae. Desine, dulcium
Mater saeva Cupidinum.
I am not as I was when dear Cinara was my queen.
Don't force me, cruel mother of the lovely Cupids.
IV.i.3

11 *Quod spiro et placeo, si placeo, tuum est.*
That I make poetry and give pleasure (if I give
pleasure) are because of you.
iii.24

12 *Merses profundo: pulchrior evenit.*
Plunge it in deep water: it comes up more beautiful.
iv.65

13 *Occidit, occidit*
Spes omnis et fortuna nostri
Nominis Hasdrubale interempto.
All our hope is fallen, fallen, and the luck of our name
lost with Hasdrubal.
70

14 *Diffugere nives, redeunt iam gramina campis*
Arboribusque comae.
The snows have dispersed, now grass returns to the
fields and leaves to the trees.
vii.1

15 *Immortalia ne speres, monet annus et almum*
Quae rapit hora diem.
Not to hope for things to last for ever, is what the year
teaches and even the hour which snatches a nice day
away.
7

16 *Damna tamen celeres reparant caelestia lunae:*
Nos ubi decidimus
Quo pater Aeneas, quo Tullus dives et Ancus,
Pulvis et umbra sumus.
Yet moons swiftly wax again after they have waned.
We, when we have gone down to join our father
Aeneas, and Tullus who was so rich, and Ancus, we
are but dust and a shadow.
13

17 *Dignum laude virum Musa vetat mori.*
The man worthy of praise the Muse forbids to die.
viii.28

18 *Vixere fortes ante Agamemnona*
Multi; sed omnes illacrimabiles
Urgentur ignotique longa
Nocte, carent quia vate sacro.
Many brave men lived before Agamemnon's time; but
they are all, unmourned and unknown, covered by
the long night, because they lack their sacred poet.
ix.25

19 *Non possidentem multa vocaveris*
Recte beatum: rectius occupat
Nomen beati, qui deorum
Muneribus sapienter uti
Duramque callet pauperiem pati
Peiusque leto flagitium timet.
Not the owner of many possessions will you be right to
call happy: he more rightly deserves the name of
happy who knows how to use the gods' gifts wisely
and to put up with rough poverty, and who fears
dishonour more than death.
45

20 *Misce stultitiam consiliis brevem:*
Dulce est desipere in loco.
Mix a little foolishness with your serious plans: it's
lovely to be silly at the right moment.
xii.27

21 *Qui fit, Maecenas, ut nemo, quam sibi sortem*
Seu ratio dederit seu fors obiecerit, illa
Contentus vivat, laudet diversa sequentis?
How is it, Maecenas, that no one lives contented with
his lot, whether he has planned it for himself or fate
has flung him into it, but yet he praises those who
follow different paths?
Satires, I.i.1

22 *Mutato nomine de te*
Fabula narratur.
Change the name and it's about you, that story.
69

23 *Est modus in rebus, sunt certi denique fines,*
Quos ultra citraque nequit consistere rectum.
Things have their due measure; there are ultimately
fixed limits, beyond which, or short of which,
something must be wrong.
106

24 *Hoc genus omne.*

All that tribe.
ii.2

1   *Ab ovo*
Usque ad mala.
From the egg right through to the apples.
iii.6. Meaning, from the start to the finish (of a meal).

2 *Etiam disiecti membra poetae.*
Even though broken up, the limbs of a poet.
iv.62. Of Ennius.

3 *Hic niger est, hunc tu, Romane, caveto.*
That man's a blackguard; Roman, watch out for that
   man.
85

4   *Ad unguem*
Factus homo.
An accomplished man to his finger-tips.
v.32

5   *Credat Iudaeus Apella,*
Non ego.
Let Apella the Jew believe it; I shan't.
100

6 *Sic me servavit Apollo.*
Thus did Apollo rescue me.
ix.78

7 *Solventur risu tabulae, tu missus abibis.*
The case will be dismissed with a laugh. You will get
   off scot-free.
II.i.86. Tr. H.R. Fairclough

8 *Par nobile fratrum.*
A noble pair of brothers.
iii.243

9 *Hoc erat in votis: modus agri non ita magnus,*
Hortus ubi et tecto vicinus iugis aquae fons
Et paulum silvae super his foret.
This was one of my prayers: for a parcel of land not so
   very large, which should have a garden and a spring
   of ever-flowing water near the house, and a bit of
   woodland as well as these.
vi.1

10 *Responsare cupidinibus, contemnere honores*
Fortis, et in se ipso totus, teres, atque rotundus.
Strong enough to answer back to desires, to despise
   distinctions, and a whole man in himself, polished
   and well-rounded.
vii.85

BISHOP SAMUEL HORSLEY 1733–1806

11 In *this* country, my Lords,...the individual
subject...'has nothing to do with the laws but to obey
them.'
House of Lords, 13 Nov. 1795. Bishop Horsley was defending a
maxim which he had earlier used in committee.

A.E. HOUSMAN 1859–1936

12 From Clee to heaven the beacon burns,
   The shires have seen it plain,
From north and south the sign returns
   And beacons burn again.
A Shropshire Lad (1896), 1. **1887**

13 The saviours come not home tonight:
   Themselves they could not save.

It dawns in Asia, tombstones show

And Shropshire names are read;
And the Nile spills his overflow
   Beside the Severn's dead.

14 Loveliest of trees, the cherry now
Is hung with bloom along the bough,
And stands about the woodland ride
Wearing white for Eastertide.

Now of my threescore years and ten,
Twenty will not come again,
And take from seventy springs a score,
It only leaves me fifty more.

And since to look at things in bloom
Fifty springs are little room,
About the woodlands I will go
To see the cherry hung with snow.
2

15 Up, lad: thews that lie and cumber
   Sunlit pallets never thrive;
Morns abed and daylight slumber
   Were not meant for man alive.

Clay lies still, but blood's a rover;
   Breath's a ware that will not keep.
Up, lad: when the journey's over
   There'll be time enough to sleep.
4. **Reveillé**

16 They hang us now in Shrewsbury jail:
   The whistles blow forlorn,
And trains all night groan on the rail
   To men that die at morn.
9

17 And naked to the hangman's noose
   The morning clocks will ring
A neck God made for other use
   Than strangling in a string.

18 So here I'll watch the night and wait
   To see the morning shine,
When he will hear the stroke of eight
   And not the stroke of nine.

19 Afield for palms the girls repair,
And sure enough the palms are there,
And each will find by hedge or pond
Her waving silver-tufted wand.
10. **March**

20 When I was one-and-twenty
   I heard a wise man say,
'Give crowns and pounds and guineas
   But not your heart away;
Give pearls away and rubies,
   But keep your fancy free.'
But I was one-and-twenty,
   No use to talk to me.
13

21 Look not in my eyes, for fear
   They mirror true the sight I see,
And there you find your face too clear
   And love it and be lost like me.
One the long night through must lie
   Spent in star-defeated sighs,
But why should you as well as I
   Perish? gaze not in my eyes.
15

22 Twice a week the winter thorough

Here stood I to keep the goal:
Football then was fighting sorrow
For the young man's soul.

Now in Maytime to the wicket
Out I march with bat and pad:
See the son of grief at cricket
Trying to be glad.
17

1 Oh, when I was in love with you,
Then I was clean and brave,
And miles around the wonder grew
How well did I behave.

And now the fancy passes by,
And nothing will remain,
And miles around they'll say that I
Am quite myself again.
18

2 Eyes the shady night has shut
Cannot see the record cut,
And silence sounds no worse than cheers
After earth has stopped the ears.
19. **To an Athlete Dying Young**

3 And round that early-laurelled head
Will flock to gaze the strengthless dead,
And find unwithered on its curls
The garland briefer than a girl's.

4 In summertime on Bredon
The bells they sound so clear;
Round both the shires they ring them
In steeples far and near,
A happy noise to hear.

Here of a Sunday morning
My love and I would lie,
And see the coloured counties,
And hear the larks so high
About us in the sky.
21. **Bredon Hill**

5 'Come all to church, good people,'—
Oh, noisy bells, be dumb;
I hear you, I will come.

6 The lads in their hundreds to Ludlow come in for the
fair,
There's men from the barn and the forge and the
mill and the fold,
The lads for the girls and the lads for the liquor are
there,
And there with the rest are the lads that will never
be old.
23

7 I wish one could know them, I wish there were tokens
to tell
The fortunate fellows that now you can never
discern.

8 They carry back bright to the coiner the mintage of
man,
The lads that will die in their glory and never be
old.

9 'Is my team ploughing,
That I was used to drive
And hear the harness jingle
When I was man alive?'
27

10 The goal stands up, the keeper
Stands up to keep the goal.

11 Yes, lad, I lie easy,
I lie as lads would choose;
I cheer a dead man's sweetheart,
Never ask me whose.

12 High the vanes of Shrewsbury gleam
Islanded in Severn stream.
28. **The Welsh Marches**

13 Others, I am not the first,
Have willed more mischief than they durst.
30

14 On Wenlock Edge the wood's in trouble;
His forest fleece the Wrekin heaves;
The gale, it plies the saplings double,
And thick on Severn snow the leaves.
31

15 There, like the wind through woods in riot,
Through him the gale of life blew high;
The tree of man was never quiet:
Then 'twas the Roman, now 'tis I.

The gale, it plies the saplings double,
It blows so hard, 'twill soon be gone:
Today the Roman and his trouble
Are ashes under Uricon.

16 From far, from eve and morning
And yon twelve-winded sky,
The stuff of life to knit me
Blew hither: here am I.
32

17 Speak now, and I will answer;
How shall I help you, say;
Ere to the wind's twelve quarters
I take my endless way.

18 On the idle hill of summer,
Sleepy with the flow of streams,
Far I hear the steady drummer
Drumming like a noise in dreams.
35

19 East and west on fields forgotten
Bleach the bones of comrades slain,
Lovely lads and dead and rotten;
None that go return again.

20 White in the moon the long road lies,
The moon stands blank above;
White in the moon the long road lies
That leads me from my love.
36

21 You and I must keep from shame
In London streets the Shropshire name;
On banks of Thames they must not say
Severn breeds worse men than they.
37

22 Into my heart an air that kills
From yon far country blows:
What are those blue remembered hills,
What spires, what farms are those?

That is the land of lost content,
I see it shining plain,
The happy highways where I went
And cannot come again.
40

1   And bound for the same bourn as I,
    On every road I wandered by,
    Trod beside me, close and dear,
    The beautiful and death-struck year.
    41

2   Shot? so quick, so clean an ending?
        Oh that was right, lad, that was brave.
    44

3   Be still, my soul, be still; the arms you bear are
            brittle,
    Earth and high heaven are fixt of old and founded
            strong.
    48

4   Men loved unkindness then, but lightless in the quarry
    I slept and saw not; tears fell down, I did not
            mourn;
    Sweat ran and blood sprang out and I was never sorry:
    Then it was well with me, in days ere I was born.

5   Be still, be still, my soul; it is but for a season:
    Let us endure an hour and see injustice done.

6   Think no more; 'tis only thinking
        Lays lads underground.
    49

7   *Clunton and Clunbury,*
        Clungunford and Clun,
    Are the quietest places
        Under the sun.
    50. Version of a traditional rhyme.

8   'Tis a long way further than Knighton,
        A quieter place than Clun,
    Where doomsday may thunder and lighten
        And little 'twill matter to one.

9   For when the knife has slit
    The throat across from ear to ear
        'Twill bleed because of it.
    53

10 With rue my heart is laden
        For golden friends I had,
    For many a rose-lipt maiden
        And many a lightfoot lad.

    By brooks too broad for leaping
        The lightfoot lads are laid;
    The rose-lipt girls are sleeping
        In fields where roses fade.
    54

11 'Terence, this is stupid stuff:
    You eat your victuals fast enough;
    There can't be much amiss, 'tis clear,
    To see the rate you drink your beer.
    But oh, good Lord, the verse you make,
    It gives a chap the belly-ache.'
    62

12 Say, for what were hop-yards meant,
    Or why was Burton built on Trent?
    Oh many a peer of England brews
    Livelier liquor than the Muse,
    And malt does more than Milton can
    To justify God's ways to man.

13 Oh I have been to Ludlow fair
    And left my necktie God knows where,
    And carried half way home, or near,
    Pints and quarts of Ludlow beer:

Then the world seemed none so bad,
And I myself a sterling lad;
And down in lovely muck I've lain,
Happy till I woke again.

14 Therefore, since the world has still
    Much good, but much less good than ill,
    And while the sun and moon endure
    Luck's a chance, but trouble's sure,
    I'd face it as a wise man would,
    And train for ill and not for good.

15 They put arsenic in his meat
    And stared aghast to watch him eat;
    They poured strychnine in his cup
    And shook to see him drink it up.

16 —I tell the tale that I heard told.
    Mithridates, he died old.

17 I hoed and trenched and weeded,
        And took the flowers to fair:
    I brought them home unheeded;
        The hue was not the wear.

18 Comrade, look not on the west:
    'Twill have the heart out of your breast.
    Last Poems (1922), 1. **The West**

19 I 'listed at home for a lancer,
        Oh who would not sleep with the brave?
    6. **Lancer**

20 The chestnut casts his flambeaux, and the flowers
        Stream from the hawthorn on the wind away,
    The doors clap to, the pane is blind with showers.
        Pass me the can, lad; there's an end of May.
    9

21 We for a certainty are not the first
        Have sat in taverns while the tempest hurled
    Their hopeful plans to emptiness, and cursed
        Whatever brute and blackguard made the world.

22 The troubles of our proud and angry dust
        Are from eternity, and shall not fail.
    Bear them we can, and if we can we must.
        Shoulder the sky, my lad, and drink your ale.

23 But men at whiles are sober
        And think by fits and starts,
    And if they think, they fasten
        Their hands upon their hearts.
    10

24 The laws of God, the laws of man,
    He may keep that will and can.
    12

25 I, a stranger and afraid
    In a world I never made.

26 And since, my soul, we cannot fly
    To Saturn nor to Mercury,
    Keep we must, if keep we can,
    These foreign laws of God and man.

27 Oh let not man remember
        The soul that God forgot,
    But fetch the county kerchief
        And noose me in the knot
    And I will rot.
    14

28 He stood, and heard the steeple
    Sprinkle the quarters on the morning town.

One, two, three, four, to market-place and people
   It tossed them down.

Strapped, noosed, nighing his hour,
   He stood and counted them and cursed his luck;
And then the clock collected in the tower
   Its strength, and struck.
15. **Eight O'Clock**

1 The night is freezing fast,
   Tomorrow comes December;
      And winterfalls of old
Are with me from the past;
   And chiefly I remember
      How Dick would hate the cold.

Fall, winter, fall; for he,
   Prompt hand and headpiece clever,
      Has woven a winter robe,
And made of earth and sea
   His overcoat for ever,
      And wears the turning globe.
20

2 The candles burn their sockets,
   The blinds let through the day,
The young man feels his pockets
   And wonders what's to pay.
21

3 *The King with half the East at heel is marched from*
   lands of morning;
   Their fighters drink the rivers up, their shafts
      benight the air.
And he that stands will die for nought, and home
   there's no returning.
   The Spartans on the sea-wet rock sat down and
      combed their hair.
25. **The Oracles**

4 Many things I thought of then,
Battle, and the loves of men,
Cities entered, oceans crossed,
Knowledge gained and virtue lost,
Careless folly done and said,
And the lovely way that led
To the slimepit and the mire
And the everlasting fire.
31. **Hell Gate**

5 And the portress foul to see
Lifted up her eyes on me
Smiling, and I made reply:
'Met again, my lass,' said I.
Then the sentry turned his head,
Looked, and knew me, and was Ned.

6 I sought them far and found them,
   The sure, the straight, the brave,
The hearts I lost my own to,
   The souls I could not save.
They braced their belts about them,
   They crossed in ships the sea,
They sought and found six feet of ground,
   And there they died for me.
32

7 These, in the day when heaven was falling,
   The hour when earth's foundations fled,
Followed their mercenary calling
   And took their wages and are dead.

Their shoulders held the sky suspended;

They stood, and earth's foundations stay;
What God abandoned, these defended,
   And saved the sum of things for pay.
37. **Epitaph on an Army of Mercenaries**

8 Tell me not here, it needs not saying,
   What tune the enchantress plays
In aftermaths of soft September
   Or under blanching mays,
For she and I were long acquainted
   And I knew all her ways.
40

9 The cuckoo shouts all day at nothing
   In leafy dells alone;
And traveller's joy beguiles in autumn
   Hearts that have lost their own.

10 For nature, heartless, witless nature,
   Will neither care nor know
What stranger's feet may find the meadow
   And trespass there and go,
Nor ask amid the dews of morning
   If they are mine or no.

11 Wenlock Edge was umbered
   And bright was Abdon Burf,
And warm between them slumbered
   The smooth green miles of turf.
41. **Fancy's Knell**

12 Tomorrow, more's the pity,
   Away we both must hie,
To air the ditty,
   And to earth I.

13 They say my verse is sad: no wonder;
   Its narrow measure spans
Tears of eternity, and sorrow,
   Not mine, but man's.

This is for all ill-treated fellows
   Unborn and unbegot,
For them to read when they're in trouble
   And I am not.
More Poems (1936), epigraph

14 I to my perils
   Of cheat and charmer
   Came clad in armour
      By stars benign.
6

15 When green buds hang in the elm like dust
   And sprinkle the lime like rain,
Forth I wander, forth I must,
   And drink of life again.
9

16 The weeping Pleiads wester,
   And the moon is under seas.
10

17 The rainy Pleiads wester,
   Orion plunges prone,
The stroke of midnight ceases,
   And I lie down alone.
11

18 Crossing alone the nighted ferry
   With the one coin for fee,
Whom, on the wharf of Lethe waiting,
   Count you to find? Not me.

The brisk fond lackey to fetch and carry,

The true, sick-hearted slave,
Expect him not in the just city
And free land of the grave.
23

1 Because I liked you better
    Than suits a man to say,
It irked you, and I promised
    To throw the thought away.
31

2 Halt by the headstone naming
    The heart no longer stirred,
And say the lad that loved you
    Was one that kept his word.

3 Here dead lie we because we did not choose
    To live and shame the land from which we sprung.
Life, to be sure, is nothing much to lose;
    But young men think it is, and we were young.
36

4 I did not lose my heart in summer's even,
    When roses to the moonrise burst apart:
When plumes were under heel and lead was flying,
    In blood and smoke and flame I lost my heart.

I lost it to a soldier and a foeman,
    A chap that did not kill me, but he tried;
That took the sabre straight and took it striking
    And laughed and kissed his hand to me and died.
37

5 Good-night; ensured release,
Imperishable peace,
    Have these for yours.
48. **Parta Quies**

6 When the bells justle in the tower
    The hollow night amid,
Then on my tongue the taste is sour
    Of all I ever did.
Collected Poems (1939), **Additional Poems**, 9

7 The stars have not dealt me the worst they could do:
My pleasures are plenty, my troubles are two.
But oh, my two troubles they reave me of rest,
The brains in my head and the heart in my breast.
17

8 Oh who is that young sinner with the handcuffs on his
    wrists?
And what has he been after that they groan and shake
    their fists?
And wherefore is he wearing such a
    conscience-stricken air?
Oh they're taking him to prison for the colour of his
    hair.

'Tis a shame to human nature, such a head of hair as
    his;
In the good old time 'twas hanging for the colour that
    it is;
Though hanging isn't bad enough and flaying would be
    fair
For the nameless and abominable colour of his hair.
18

9 O suitably attired in leather boots
Head of a traveller, wherefore seeking whom
Whence by what way how purposed art thou come
To this well-nightingaled vicinity?
My object in enquiring is to know.
But if you happen to be deaf and dumb

And do not understand a word I say,
Nod with your hand to signify as much.
Fragment of a Greek Tragedy, *Trinity Magazine*, Feb. 1921;
first published in *The Bromsgrovian*, 1883

10 Mud's sister, not himself, adorns my shoes.

11 Reader, behold! this monster wild
Has gobbled up the infant child.
The infant child is not aware
It has been eaten by the bear.
Infant Innocence. Laurence Housman, *A.E.H.* (1937), p.256

12 Three minutes' thought would suffice to find this out,
but thought is irksome and three minutes is a long
time.
Juvenalis Saturae (ed.) (1905), Preface

13 The arsenals of divine vengeance, if I may so describe
the Bodleian library.

14 Gentlemen who use MSS as drunkards use
lamp-posts—not to light them on their way but to
dissimulate their instability.
M. Manilii Astronomicon Liber Primus (ed.) (1903),
introduction, I

15 If a man will comprehend the richness and variety of
the universe, and inspire his mind with a due measure
of wonder and of awe, he must contemplate the human
intellect not only on its heights of genius but in its
abysses of ineptitude; and it might be fruitlessly
debated to the end of time whether Richard Bentley or
Elias Stoeber was the more marvellous work of the
Creator: Elias Stoeber, whose reprint of Bentley's
text, with a commentary intended to confute it, saw the
light in 1767 at Strasbourg, a city still famous for its
geese.
II. Of earlier editors of Manilius

16 *Ueberlieferungsgeschichte*...is a longer and nobler
name than fudge.
Preface to his (1927) edition of Lucan, *De Bello Civili*

17 Experience has taught me, when I am shaving of a
morning, to keep watch over my thoughts, because, if
a line of poetry strays into my memory, my skin
bristles so that the razor ceases to act.
The Name and Nature of Poetry (1933)

18 The University which once saw Wordsworth drunk and
once saw Porson sober will see a better scholar than
Wordsworth, and a better poet than Porson, betwixt
and between.
Speech at farewell dinner, University College, London, before
going to Cambridge as Kennedy Professor of Latin, 1911.
Laurence Housman, *A.E.H.* (1937), p.101

JULIA WARD HOWE 1819–1910

19 Mine eyes have seen the glory of the coming of the
    Lord:
He is trampling out the vintage where the grapes of
    wrath are stored.
Battle Hymn of the American Republic (Dec. 1861)

JAMES HOWELL 1594?–1666

20 Some hold translations not unlike to be
The wrong side of a Turkey tapestry.
Familiar Letters (1645–55), bk.i, let.6

21 One hair of a woman can draw more than a hundred
pair of oxen.
bk.ii, let.4

1 This life at best is but an inn,
And we the passengers.
let.73

MARY HOWITT 1799–1888

2 Buttercups and daisies,
Oh, the pretty flowers;
Coming ere the Springtime,
To tell of sunny hours.
Buttercups and Daisies

3 'Will you walk into my parlour?' said a spider to a
fly:
''Tis the prettiest little parlour that ever you did spy.'
The Spider and the Fly

EDMOND HOYLE 1672–1769

4 When in doubt, win the trick.
Hoyle's Games (c. 1756). **Whist, Twenty-four Short Rules for
Learners**

FRIEDRICH VON HÜGEL 1852–1926

5 The golden rule is, to help those we love to escape
from us; and never try to begin to help people, or
influence them till they ask, but wait for them. (To his
niece, in conversation.)
Letters...to a Niece (1928), introduction

THOMAS HUGHES 1822–1896

6 Tom and his younger brothers as they grew up, went
on playing with the village boys without the idea of
equality or inequality (except in wrestling, running,
and climbing) ever entering their heads, as it doesn't
till it's put there by Jack Nastys or fine ladies' maids.
Tom Brown's Schooldays, pt.i, ch.3

7 He never wants anything but what's right and fair;
only when you come to settle what's right and fair, it's
everything that he wants and nothing that you want.
And that's his idea of a compromise. Give me the
Brown compromise when I'm on his side.
pt.ii, ch.2

8 It's more than a game. It's an institution. [Cricket.]
ch.7

VICTOR HUGO 1802–1885

9 *Le mot, c'est le Verbe, et le Verbe, c'est Dieu.*
The word is the Verb, and the Verb is God.
Contemplations (1856), I.viii

10 *Souffrons, mais souffrons sur les cimes.*
If suffer we must, let's suffer on the heights.
Les Malheureux

11 *On résiste à l'invasion des armées; on ne résiste pas à
l'invasion des idées.*
A stand can be made against invasion by an army; no
stand can be made against invasion by an idèa.
Histoire d'un Crime, La Chute, X

12 *La symétrie, c'est l'ennui, et l'ennui est le fond même
du deuil. Le désespoir baîlle.*
Symmetry is tedious, and tedium is the very basis of
mourning. Despair yawns.
Les Misérables, vol.II, bk.iv, ch.1

13 *Jésus a pleuré, Voltaire a souri; c'est de cette larme
divine et de ce sourire humain qu'est faite la douceur
de la civilisation actuelle.* (Applaudissements
prolongés.)
Jesus wept; Voltaire smiled. Of that divine tear and of
that human smile the sweetness of present civilisation
is composed. (*Hearty applause.*)
Transcript of centenary oration on Voltaire, 30 May 1878

DAVID HUME 1711–1776

14 Custom, then, is the great guide of human life.
An Enquiry Concerning Human Understanding (1748), sec.5,
pt.1

15 If we take in our hand any volume; of divinity or
school metaphysics, for instance; let us ask, *Does it
contain any abstract reasoning concerning quantity or
number?* No. *Does it contain any experimental
reasoning, concerning matter of fact and existence?*
No. Commit it then to the flames: for it can contain
nothing but sophistry and illusion.
sec.12, pt.III

16 Avarice, the spur of industry, is so obstinate a
passion, and works its way through so many real
dangers and difficulties, that it is not likely to be
scared by an imaginary danger, which is so small that
it scarcely admits of calculation.
Essays (1741–2). **Of Civil Liberty**

17 Beauty in things exists in the mind which
contemplates them.
Of Tragedy

18 There is not to be found, in all history, any miracle
attested by a sufficient number of men, of such
unquestioned good sense, education, and learning, as
to secure us against all delusion in themselves; of such
undoubted integrity, as to place them beyond all
suspicion of any design to deceive others; of such
credit and reputation in the eyes of mankind, as to
have a great deal to lose in case of their being detected
in any falsehood; and at the same time attesting facts,
performed in such a public manner, and in so
celebrated a part of the world, as to render the
detection unavoidable.
Of Miracles, Pt.2

19 Their credulity increases his impudence: and his
impudence overpowers their credulity.

20 We soon learn that there is nothing mysterious or
supernatural in the case, but that all proceeds from the
usual propensity of mankind towards the marvellous,
and that, though this inclination may at intervals
receive a check from sense and learning, it can never
be thoroughly extirpated from human nature.

21 The Christian religion not only was at first attended
with miracles, but even at this day cannot be believed
by any reasonable person without one. Mere reason is
insufficient to convince us of its veracity: and whoever
is moved by faith to assent to it, is conscious of a
continued miracle in his own person, which subverts
all the principles of his understanding, and gives him a
determination to believe what is most contrary to
custom and experience.

22 It cannot reasonably be doubted, but a little miss,
dressed in a new gown for a dancing-school ball,
receives as complete enjoyment as the greatest orator,
who triumphs in the splendour of his eloquence, while
he governs the passions and resolutions of a numerous

assembly.
The Sceptic

1 Never literary attempt was more unfortunate than my Treatise of Human Nature. It fell *dead-born from the Press*.
My Own Life (1777), ch.1

2 Opposing one species of superstition to another, set them a quarrelling; while we ourselves, during their fury and contention, happily make our escape into the calm, though obscure, regions of philosophy.
The Natural History of Religion (1757), xv

G.W. HUNT 1829?–1904

3 We don't want to fight, but, by jingo if we do,
We've got the ships, we've got the men, we've got the money too.
We've fought the Bear before, and while Britons shall be true,
The Russians shall not have Constantinople.
We Don't Want to Fight. Music hall song, 1878

LEIGH HUNT 1784–1859

4 Abou Ben Adhem (may his tribe increase!)
Awoke one night from a deep dream of peace,
And saw, within the moonlight in his room,
Making it rich, and like a lily in bloom,
An angel writing in a book of gold:—
Exceeding peace had made Ben Adhem bold,
And to the presence in the room he said,
'What writest thou?'—The vision raised its head,
And with a look made of all sweet accord,
Answered, 'The names of those who love the Lord.'
Abou Ben Adhem and the Angel

5   'I pray thee then,
Write me as one that loves his fellow-men.'

6 And lo! Ben Adhem's name led all the rest.

7 You strange, astonished-looking, angle-faced,
Dreary-mouthed, gaping wretches of the sea.
The Fish, the Man, and the Spirit

8 'By God!' said Francis, 'rightly done!' and he rose from where he sat:
'No love,' quoth he, 'but vanity, sets love a task like that.'
The Glove and the Lions

9 The laughing queen that caught the world's great hands.
The Nile

10 Jenny kissed me when we met,
Jumping from the chair she sat in;
Time, you thief, who love to get
Sweets into your list, put that in:
Say I'm weary, say I'm sad,
Say that health and wealth have missed me,
Say I'm growing old, but add,
Jenny kissed me.
Rondeau

11 Stolen sweets are always sweeter,
Stolen kisses much completer,
Stolen looks are nice in chapels,
Stolen, stolen, be your apples.
Song of Fairies Robbing an Orchard

12 Where the light woods go seaward from the town.
The Story of Rimini, i, 1.18

13 The two divinest things this world has got,
A lovely woman in a rural spot!
iii, 1.257

14 A pleasure so exquisite as almost to amount to pain.
Letter to Alexander Ireland, 2 June 1848

ANNE HUNTER 1742–1821

15 My mother bids me bind my hair
With bands of rosy hue,
Tie up my sleeves with ribbons rare,
And lace my bodice blue.
My Mother Bids Me Bind My Hair

WILLIAM HUNTER 1718–1783

16 Some physiologists will have it that the stomach is a mill;—others, that it is a fermenting vat;—others again that it is a stew-pan;—but in my view of the matter, it is neither a mill, a fermenting vat, nor a stew-pan—but a *stomach,* gentlemen, a *stomach.*
MS. note from his lectures. Epigraph to J.A. Paris, *A Treatise on Diet* (1824)

SIR GERALD HURST 1877–1957

17 One of the mysteries of human conduct is why adult men and women all over England are ready to sign documents which they do not read, at the behest of canvassers whom they do not know, binding them to pay for articles which they do not want, with money which they have not got.
Closed Chapters (1942), p.141

JOHN HUSS c.1372–1415

18 *O sancta simplicitas!*
O holy simplicity!
At the stake, seeing an old peasant bringing a faggot to throw on the pile. Zincgreff-Weidner, *Apophthegmata,* (Amsterdam, 1653), pt.iii, p.383. See 272:20

FRANCIS HUTCHESON 1694–1746

19 Wisdom denotes the pursuing of the best ends by the best means.
Inquiry into the Original of our Ideas of Beauty and Virtue (1725). Treatise I, sec.v, 18

20 That action is best, which procures the greatest happiness for the greatest numbers.
Treatise II. **Concerning Moral Good and Evil,** sec.3, 8

ALDOUS HUXLEY 1894–1963

21 A million million spermatozoa,
All of them alive:
Out of their cataclysm but one poor Noah
Dare hope to survive.
Fifth Philosopher's Song

22   But when the wearied Band
Swoons to a waltz, I take her hand,
And there we sit in peaceful calm,
Quietly sweating palm to palm.
Frascati's

23 Your maiden modesty would float face down,

And men would weep upon your hinder parts.
Leda

1 Beauty for some provides escape,
Who gain a happiness in eyeing
The gorgeous buttocks of the ape
Or Autumn sunsets exquisitely dying.
Ninth Philosopher's Song

2 Then brim the bowl with atrabilious liquor!
We'll pledge our Empire vast across the flood:
For Blood, as all men know, than water's thicker,
But water's wider, thank the Lord, than Blood.

T.H. HUXLEY 1825–1895

3 Science is nothing but trained and organized common sense, differing from the latter only as a veteran may differ from a raw recruit: and its methods differ from those of common sense only as far as the guardsman's cut and thrust differ from the manner in which a savage wields his club.
Collected Essays, iv. **The Method of Zadig**

4 Every variety of philosophical and theological opinion was represented there [the Metaphysical Society], and expressed itself with entire openness; most of my colleagues were *-ists* of one sort or another; and, however kind and friendly they might be, I, the man without a rag of a label to cover himself with, could not fail to have some of the uneasy feelings which must have beset the historical fox when, after leaving the trap in which his tail remained, he presented himself to his normally elongated companions. So I took thought, and invented what I conceived to be the appropriate title of 'agnostic'.
v. **Agnosticism**

5 The great tragedy of Science—the slaying of a beautiful hypothesis by an ugly fact.
viii. **Biogenesis and Abiogenesis**

6 The chess-board is the world; the pieces are the phenomena of the universe; the rules of the game are what we call the laws of Nature. The player on the other side is hidden from us. We know that his play is always fair, just, and patient. But also we know, to our cost, that he never overlooks a mistake, or makes the smallest allowance for ignorance.
Lay Sermons, &c., iii. **A Liberal Education**

7 Some experience of popular lecturing had convinced me that the necessity of making things plain to uninstructed people was one of the very best means of clearing up the obscure corners in one's own mind.
Man's Place in Nature, Preface to 1894 edition

8 If some great Power would agree to make me always think what is true and do what is right, on condition of being turned into a sort of clock and wound up every morning before I got out of bed, I should instantly close with the offer.
On Descartes' Discourse on Method. **Method & Results,** iv

9 If a little knowledge is dangerous, where is the man who has so much as to be out of danger?
On Elementary Instruction in Physiology (1877)

10 Logical consequences are the scarecrows of fools and the beacons of wise men.
Science and Culture, ix. **On the Hypothesis that Animals are Automata**

11 Irrationally held truths may be more harmful than reasoned errors.
xii. **The Coming of Age of the Origin of Species**

12 It is the customary fate of new truths to begin as heresies and to end as superstitions.

13 I asserted—and I repeat—that a man has no reason to be ashamed of having an ape for his grandfather. If there were an ancestor whom I should feel shame in recalling it would rather be a *man*—a man of restless and versatile intellect—who, not content with an equivocal success in his own sphere of activity, plunges into scientific questions with which he has no real acquaintance, only to obscure them by an aimless rhetoric, and distract the attention of his hearers from the real point at issue by eloquent digressions and skilled appeals to religious prejudice.
Replying to Bishop Samuel Wilberforce in the debate on Darwin's theory of evolution during the meeting of the British Association at Oxford, 30 June 1860. See *Life and Letters of Thomas Henry Huxley* (1900), vol.i, p.185, letter from J.R. Green to Professor Boyd Dawkins. Huxley, in a letter to Francis Darwin agreed that this account was fair if not wholly accurate: there is no reliable verbatim transcript.

14 I am too much of a sceptic to deny the possibility of anything.
Letter to Herbert Spencer, 22 March 1886

EDWARD HYDE
see EARL OF CLARENDON

DOLORES IBÁRRURI 'LA PASIONARIA'
1895–

15 *No pasarán!*
They shall not pass.
H. Thomas, *The Spanish Civil War* (1961), ch.16. See 363:17

16 It is better to die on your feet than to live on your knees.
Speech in Paris, 3 Sept. 1936

HENRIK IBSEN 1828–1906

17 The worst enemy of truth and freedom in our society is the compact majority. Yes, the damned, compact, liberal majority.
An Enemy of the People (1882), Act 4

18 The majority has the might—more's the pity—but it hasn't right...The minority is always right.

19 You should never have your best trousers on when you turn out to fight for freedom and truth.
Act 5

20 The strongest man in the world is the man who stands alone.

21 It's not just what we inherit from our mothers and fathers that haunts us. It's all kinds of old defunct theories, all sorts of old defunct beliefs, and things like that. It's not that they actually *live* on in us; they are simply lodged there, and we cannot get rid of them. I've only to pick up a newspaper and I seem to see ghosts gliding between the lines.
Ghosts (1881), Act 2

22 Mother, give me the sun.
Act 3

23 Ten o'clock...and back he'll come. I can just see him. With vine leaves in his hair. Flushed and confident.
Hedda Gabler (1890), Act 2

1 People don't do such things!
Act 4

2 Youth will come here and beat on my door, and force its way in.
The Master Builder (1892), Act 1

3 Castles in the air—they're so easy to take refuge in. So easy to build, too.
Act 3

4 Take the life-lie away from the average man and straight away you take away his happiness.
The Wild Duck (1884), Act 5

IVAN ILLICH 1926–

5 In a consumer society there are inevitably two kinds of slaves: the prisoners of addiction and the prisoners of envy.
Tools for Conviviality (1973)

DEAN INGE 1860–1954

6 To become a popular religion, it is only necessary for a superstition to enslave a philosophy.
Outspoken Essays, Second Series (1922), ch.III. **The Idea of Progress.** First published as the Romanes Lecture, 1920

7 Democracy is only an experiment in government, and it has the obvious disadvantage of merely counting votes instead of weighing them.
Possible Recovery?

8 Literature flourishes best when it is half a trade and half an art.
The Victorian Age (1922), p.49

9 A man may build himself a throne of bayonets, but he cannot sit on it.
Marchant (ed.), *Wit and Wisdom of Dean Inge*, No. 108

10 The nations which have put mankind and posterity most in their debt have been small states—Israel, Athens, Florence, Elizabethan England.
No.181

11 *Nisi monumentum requiris, circumspice.* (Of the traffic outside St. Paul's.)
Attr.

JEAN INGELOW 1820–1897

12 Play uppe, play uppe, O Boston bells! Play all your changes, all your swells.
The High Tide on the Coast of Lincolnshire, 1571

13 Play uppe 'The Brides of Enderby'.

14 'Cusha! Cusha! Cusha!' calling
E'er the early dews were falling,
Farre away I heard her song.

15 Come uppe, Whitefoot, come uppe Lightfoot,
Come uppe Jetty, rise and follow,
Jetty, to the milking shed.

16 But each will mourn her own (she saith)
And sweeter woman ne'er drew breath
Than my sonne's wife, Elizabeth.

ROBERT G. INGERSOLL 1833–1899

17 An honest God is the noblest work of man.
Gods, pt.1, p.2. See 119:7, 379:24

18 In nature there are neither rewards nor punishments—there are consequences.
Lectures & Essays, 3rd Series. **Some Reasons Why,** viii

J.A.D. INGRES 1780–1867

19 *Le dessin est la probité de l'art.*
Drawing is the true test of art.
Pensées d'Ingres, 1922, p.70

WASHINGTON IRVING 1783–1859

20 A woman's whole life is a history of the affections.
The Sketch Book (1819–20). **The Broken Heart**

21 A tart temper never mellows with age, and a sharp tongue is the only edged tool that grows keener with constant use.
Rip Van Winkle

22 They who drink beer will think beer.
Stratford-on-Avon

23 Free-livers on a small scale; who are prodigal within the compass of a guinea.
The Stout Gentleman

24 I am always at a loss to know how much to believe of my own stories.
Tales of a Traveller (1824), To the Reader

25 There is a certain relief in change, even though it be from bad to worse; as I have found in travelling in a stage-coach, that it is often a comfort to shift one's position and be bruised in a new place.

26 The almighty dollar, that great object of universal devotion throughout our land, seems to have no genuine devotees in these peculiar villages.
Wolfert's Roost (1855). **The Creole Village**

CHRISTOPHER ISHERWOOD 1904–

27 The common cormorant or shag
Lays eggs inside a paper bag
The reason you will see no doubt
It is to keep the lightning out.
But what these unobservant birds
Have never noticed is that herds
Of wandering bears may come with buns
And steal the bags to hold the crumbs.
The Common Cormorant

28 I am a camera with its shutter open, quite passive, recording, not thinking.
Goodbye to Berlin, A Berlin Diary, Autumn 1930

PRESIDENT ANDREW JACKSON 1767–1845

29 You are uneasy; you never sailed with *me* before, I see.
J. Parton, *Life of Jackson,* vol.iii, ch.35

30 Our Federal Union: it must be preserved.
Toast given on the Jefferson Birthday Celebration, 13 Apr. 1830. Benton, *Thirty Years' View,* vol.1

JACOPONE DA TODI c.1230–1306

31 *Stabat Mater dolorosa,*
Iuxta crucem lacrimosa
  Dum pendebat Filius.
There was standing the sorrowing Mother, beside the cross weeping while her Son hung upon it.
Stabat Mater dolorosa. Hymn also ascribed to Pope Innocent III and St. Bonaventure

REVD. RICHARD JAGO 1715–1781

1 With leaden foot time creeps along
   While Delia is away.
Absence

KING JAMES I OF ENGLAND AND VI OF SCOTLAND 1566–1625

2 A branch of the sin of drunkenness, which is the root
   of all sins.
A Counterblast to Tobacco (1604)

3 A custom loathsome to the eye, hateful to the nose,
   harmful to the brain, dangerous to the lungs, and in the
   black, stinking fume thereof, nearest resembling the
   horrible Stygian smoke of the pit that is bottomless.

4 Herein is not only a great vanity, but a great contempt
   of God's good gifts, that the sweetness of man's
   breath, being a good gift of God, should be wilfully
   corrupted by this stinking smoke.

5 I will govern according to the common weal, but not
   according to the common will.
December, 1621. J.R. Green, *History of the English People*,
Vol.III, bk.vii, ch.4

6 Dr Donne's verses are like the peace of God; they pass
   all understanding.
Saying recorded by Archdeacon Plume (1630–1704)

KING JAMES V OF SCOTLAND 1512–1542

7 It cam' wi' a lass, it will gang wi' a lass.
Said on his deathbed of the crown of Scotland; David Hume,
History of England, vol.iv, ch.33 records 'It came with a
woman...and it will go with one.' It is unlikely that James V
spoke with a strong Scottish accent.

HENRY JAMES 1843–1916

8 It takes a great deal of history to produce a little
   literature.
Life of Nathaniel Hawthorne (1879)

9 [Thoreau] was worse than provincial—he was
   parochial.
ch.4

10 The only obligation to which in advance we may hold
   a novel, without incurring the accusation of being
   arbitrary, is that it be interesting.
Partial Portraits. **The Art of Fiction**

11 Experience is never limited, and it is never complete;
   it is an immense sensibility, a kind of huge spider-web
   of the finest silken threads suspended in the chamber
   of consciousness, and catching every air-borne particle
   in its tissue.

12 What is character but the determination of incident?
   what is incident but the illustration of character?

13 We must grant the artist his subject, his idea, his
   donné: our criticism is applied only to what he makes
   of it.

14 Dramatise, dramatise!
Prefaces (1909). **The Altar of the Dead** (1909), and elsewhere

15 The note I wanted; that of the strange and sinister
   embroidered on the very type of the normal and easy.

16 The terrible *fluidity* of self-revelation.
The Ambassadors (1903)

17 The deep well of unconscious cerebration.
The American (1877)

18 The historian, essentially, wants more documents than
   he can really use; the dramatist only wants more
   liberties than he can really take.
The Aspern Papers, &c (1888)

19 The fatal futility of Fact.
The Spoils of Poynton, &c (1897)

20 Live all you can; it's a mistake not to. It doesn't so
   much matter what you do in particular, so long as you
   have your life. If you haven't had that what *have* you
   had?
The Ambassadors (1903), bk.5, ch.2

21 She was a woman who, between courses, could be
   graceful with her elbows on the table.
bk.7, ch.16

22 Vereker's secret, my dear man—the general intention
   of his books: the string the pearls were strung on, the
   buried treasure, the figure in the carpet.
The Figure in the Carpet (1897), ch.11

23 The black and merciless things that are behind the
   great possessions.
The Ivory Tower (1917), Notes, p.287

24 Cats and monkeys, monkeys and cats—all human life
   is there.
The Madonna of the Future (1879)

25 Tennyson was not Tennysonian.
Terminations (1895). **The Middle Years**

26 Print it as it stands—beautifully.
The Death of the Lion, x

27 To kill a human being is, after all, the least injury you
   can do him.
My Friend Bingham (1867)

28 The superiority of one man's opinion over another's is
   never so great as when the opinion is about a woman.
The Tragic Muse (1890), ch.9

29 The perfect presence of mind, unconfused, unhurried
   by emotion, that any artistic performance requires and
   that all, whatever the instrument, require in exactly the
   same degree.
ch.19

30 Summer afternoon—summer afternoon; to me those
   have always been the two most beautiful words in the
   English language.
Edith Wharton, *A Backward Glance*, ch.10

31 So here it is at last, the distinguished thing. [Of his
   own death.]
ch.14

32 I remember once saying to Henry James, in reference
   to a novel of the type that used euphemistically to be
   called 'unpleasant': 'You know, I was rather
   disappointed; that book wasn't nearly as bad as I
   expected'; to which he replied, with his incomparable
   twinkle: 'Ah, my dear, the abysses are all so shallow.'
Edith Wharton, *The House of Mirth.* Introduction to the World's
Classics edition (1936), ii

33 I can stand a great deal of gold. [On seeing a
   particularly grand drawing room.]
Attr. by D. McCarthy, *The Legend of the Master* (compiled by S.
Nowell-Smith, 1947) 'Social Occasions'.

34 Some beflagged jam pots, I understand, my dear Fred,
   let into the soil at long but varying distances. A
   swoop, a swing, a flourish of steel, a dormy. [On

golf.]
Attr. by E.F. Benson, 'Lamb House'.

1 Poor Gissing...struck me as quite particularly marked out for what is called in his and my profession an unhappy ending.
Letter to Sir Sidney Colvin, 1903

2 It is art that *makes* life, makes interest, makes importance, for our consideration and application of these things, and I know of no substitute whatever for the force and beauty of its process.
Letter to H.G. Wells, 10 July 1915

WILLIAM JAMES 1842–1910

3 The moral flabbiness born of the bitch-goddess SUCCESS. That—with the squalid cash interpretation put on the word success—is our national disease.
Letter to H.G. Wells, 11 Sept. 1906

JEAN PAUL (J.P.F. RICHTER) 1763–1825

4 Providence has given to the French the empire of the land, to the English that of the sea, and to the Germans that of the air.
Quoted by Thomas Carlyle, in the *Edinburgh Review,* 1827

PRESIDENT THOMAS JEFFERSON 1743–1826

5 When in the course of human events, it becomes necessary for one people to dissolve the political bonds which have connected them with another, and to assume among the powers of the earth the separate and equal station to which the laws of nature and of Nature's God entitle them, a decent respect to the opinions of mankind requires that they should declare the causes which impel them to the separation.
Declaration of Independence, 4 July 1776: Preamble

6 We hold these truths to be sacred and undeniable; that all men are created equal and independent, that from that equal creation they derive rights inherent and inalienable, among which are the preservation of life, and liberty, and the pursuit of happiness.
Original draft for the Declaration of Independence. See 8:14

7 In the full tide of successful experiment.
First Inaugural Address, 4 March 1801

8 Peace, commerce, and honest friendship with all nations—entangling alliances with none.

9 A little rebellion now and then is a good thing.
Letter to James Madison, 30 Jan. 1787

10 The tree of liberty must be refreshed from time to time with the blood of patriots and tyrants. It is its natural manure.
To W.S. Smith, 13 Nov. 1787

11 Whenever a man has cast a longing eye on them [offices], a rottenness begins in his conduct.
To Tench Coxe, 1799

12 If the principle were to prevail of a common law [i.e a single government] being in force in the United States...it would become the most corrupt government on the earth.
To Gideon Granger, 13 Aug. 1800

13 To seek out the best through the whole Union we must resort to other information, which, from the best of men, acting disinterestedly and with the purest motives, is sometimes incorrect.
Letter to Elias Shipman and others of New Haven, 12 July 1801

14 To attain all this [universal republicanism], however, rivers of blood must yet flow, and years of desolation pass over; yet the object is worth rivers of blood, and years of desolation.
To John Adams, 4 Sept. 1823

15 If a due participation of office is a matter of right, how are vacancies to be obtained? Those by death are few; by resignation none.
Usually quoted, 'Few die and none resign'.

16 Indeed I tremble for my country when I reflect that God is just.
Notes on Virginia (1784), Query xviii. **Manners**

17 When a man assumes a public trust, he should consider himself as public property.
Remark to Baron von Humboldt, 1807. Rayner, *Life of Jefferson* (1834), p.356

18 No duty the Executive had to perform was so trying as to put the right man in the right place.
J.B. MacMaster, *History of the People of the U.S.*, vol.ii, ch.13, p.586

FRANCIS, LORD JEFFREY 1773–1850

19 This will never do.
On Wordsworth's 'Excursion'. *Edinburgh Review*, Nov. 1814, p.1

ST. JEROME c.342–420

20 *Venerationi mihi semper fuit non verbosa rusticitas, sed sancta simplicitas.*
I have revered always not crude verbosity, but holy simplicity.
Letters, 57, xii (*Patrologia Latina* xxii, 579)

21 Hooly writ is the scripture of puplis, for it is maad, that alle puplis schulden knowe it.
Attr. See J. Forshall and F. Madden (eds.), *The Holy Bible...in the Earliest English Versions...* Oxford (1850), Prologue (probably by John Purvey, c.1353–c.1428), ch.xv

JEROME K. JEROME 1859–1927

22 It is impossible to enjoy idling thoroughly unless one has plenty of work to do.
The Idle Thoughts of an Idle Fellow (1889). **On Being Idle**

23 Love is like the measles; we all have to go through it.
On Being in Love

24 George goes to sleep at a bank from ten to four each day, except Saturdays, when they wake him up and put him outside at two.
Three Men in a Boat (1889), ch.2

25 But there, everything has its drawbacks, as the man said when his mother-in-law died, and they came down on him for the funeral expenses.
ch.3

26 I like work: it fascinates me. I can sit and look at it for hours. I love to keep it by me: the idea of getting rid of it nearly breaks my heart.
ch.15

DOUGLAS JERROLD 1803–1857

27 Honest bread is very well—it's the butter that makes the temptation.
The Catspaw (1850), Act III

1 Religion's in the heart, not in the knees.
The Devil's Ducat (1830), I.ii

2 He is one of those wise philanthropists who, in a time of famine, would vote for nothing but a supply of toothpicks.
Wit and Opinions of Douglas Jerrold (1859), **A Philanthropist**

3 Love's like the measles—all the worse when it comes late in life.

4 The best thing I know between France and England is—the sea.
The Anglo-French Alliance

5 That fellow would vulgarize the day of judgment.
A Comic Author

6 The ugliest of trades have their moments of pleasure. Now, if I were a grave-digger, or even a hangman, there are some people I could work for with a great deal of enjoyment.
Ugly Trades

7 Earth is here [Australia] so kind, that just tickle her with a hoe and she laughs with a harvest.
A Land of Plenty

8 Some people are so fond of ill-luck that they run half-way to meet it.
Meeting Troubles Half-way

9 He was so good he would pour rose-water over a toad.
A Charitable Man

10 Talk to him of Jacob's ladder, and he would ask the number of the steps.
A Matter-of-fact Man

11 We love peace, as we abhor pusillanimity; but not peace at any price. There is a peace more destructive of the manhood of living man than war is destructive of his material body. Chains are worse than bayonets.
Peace

12 If an earthquake were to engulf England to-morrow, the English would manage to meet and dine somewhere among the rubbish, just to celebrate the event.
Blanchard Jerrold, *Life of D. Jerrold*, ch.14

13 The only athletic sport I ever mastered was backgammon.
W. Jerrold, *Douglas Jerrold* (1914), vol.i, ch.1, p.22

BISHOP JOHN JEWEL 1522–1571

14 In old time we had treen [wooden] chalices and golden priests, but now we have treen priests and golden chalices.
Certain Sermons Preached Before the Queen's Majesty (1609), p.176

ST. JOHN OF THE CROSS 1542–1591

15 *Muero porque no muero.*
I die because I do not die.
Coplas del alma que pena por ver a dios

16 *Con un no saber sabiendo.*
With a knowing ignorance.
Coplas hechas sobre un éxtasis de alta contemplación

JOHN OF SALISBURY c.1115–1180

17 *Siquidem uita breuis, sensus hebes, neglegentiae torpor, inutilis occupatio, nos paucula scire*
permittunt, et eadem iugiter excutit et auellit ab animo fraudatrix scientiae, inimica et infida semper memoriae nouerca, obliuio.
The brevity of our life, the dullness of our senses, the torpor of our indifference, the futility of our occupation, suffer us to know but little: and that little is soon shaken and then torn from the mind by that traitor to learning, that hostile and faithless stepmother to memory, oblivion.
Prologue to the Policraticus (C.C.J. Webb's edition, vol.i, p.12, ll.13-16) Tr. Helen Waddell

HIRAM JOHNSON 1866–1945

18 The first casualty when war comes is truth.
Speech, U.S. Senate, 1917

LIONEL JOHNSON 1867–1902

19 There Shelley dream'd his white Platonic dreams.
Oxford

20   In her ears the chime
Of full, sad bells brings back her old springtide.

21 I know you: solitary griefs,
Desolate passions, aching hours.
The Precept of Silence

22 The saddest of all Kings
Crown'd, and again discrown'd.
By the Statue of King Charles I at Charing Cross

23 Alone he rides, alone,
The fair and fatal king.

PHILANDER CHASE JOHNSON 1866–1939

24 Cheer up, the worst is yet to come.
Shooting Stars. See *Everybody's Magazine*, May 1920

SAMUEL JOHNSON 1709–1784

25 The rod produces an effect which terminates in itself. A child is afraid of being whipped, and gets his task, and there's an end on't; whereas, by exciting emulation and comparisons of superiority, you lay the foundation of lasting mischief; you make brothers and sisters hate each other.
Boswell, *Life of Johnson* (L.F. Powell's revision of G.B. Hill's edition), vol.i, p.46

26 In my early years I read very hard. It is a sad reflection, but a true one, that I knew almost as much at eighteen as I do now.
p.56. 20 July 1763

27 *Johnson*: I had no notion that I was wrong or irreverent to my tutor.
Boswell: That, Sir, was great fortitude of mind.
Johnson: No, Sir; stark insensibility.
p.60. 5 Nov. 1728

28 Sir, we are a nest of singing birds.
Of Pembroke College, Oxford. p.75. 1730

29 It is incident to physicians, I am afraid, beyond all other men, to mistake subsequence for consequence.
Review of Dr. Lucas's *Essay on Waters*. p.91n. 25 Nov. 1734

30 He was a vicious man, but very kind to me. If you call a dog *Hervey*, I shall love him.
p.106. 1737

31 My old friend, Mrs Carter, could make a pudding as

well as translate Epictetus.
p.123n. 1738

1 Tom Birch is as brisk as a bee in conversation; but no
sooner does he take a pen in his hand, than it becomes
a torpedo to him, and benumbs all his faculties.
p.159. 1743

2 I'll come no more behind your scenes, David; for the
silk stockings and white bosoms of your actresses
excite my amorous propensities.
p.201. 1750

3 A man may write at any time, if he will set himself
doggedly to it.
p.203. Mar. 1750

4 Thy body is all vice, and thy mind all virtue.
To Beauclerk. p.250. 1752

5 I had done all I could; and no man is well pleased to
have his all neglected, be it ever so little.
p.261. Letter to Lord Chesterfield, 7 Feb. 1755

6 The shepherd in Virgil grew at last acquainted with
Love, and found him a native of the rocks.

7 Is not a Patron, my Lord, one who looks with
unconcern on a man struggling for life in the water,
and, when he has reached ground, encumbers him with
help? The notice which you have been pleased to take
of my labours, had it been early, had been kind; but it
has been delayed till I am indifferent, and cannot enjoy
it; till I am solitary, and cannot impart it; till I am
known, and do not want it.

8 A fly, Sir, may sting a stately horse and make him
wince; but one is but an insect, and the other is a horse
still.
p.263. n.3

9 This man I thought had been a Lord among wits; but,
I find, he is only a wit among Lords.
Of Lord Chesterfield. p.266. 1754

10 They teach the morals of a whore, and the manners of
a dancing master.
Of Lord Chesterfield's *Letters*. p.266. 1754

11 There are two things which I am confident I can do
very well: one is an introduction to any literary work,
stating what it is to contain, and how it should be
executed in the most perfect manner; the other is a
conclusion, shewing from various causes why the
execution has not been equal to what the author
promised to himself and to the public.
p.292. 1755

12 Ignorance, madam, pure ignorance.
When asked by a lady why he defined 'pastern' as the 'knee' of a
horse, in his Dictionary. p.293. 1755

13 Lexicographer: a writer of dictionaries, a harmless
drudge.
p.296. 1755

14 I have protracted my work till most of those whom I
wished to please have sunk into the grave; and success
and miscarriage are empty sounds.
p.297. 1755

15 If a man does not make new acquaintance as he
advances through life, he will soon find himself left
alone. A man, Sir, should keep his friendship in
constant repair.
p.300. 1755

16 The booksellers are generous liberal-minded men.
p.304. 1756

17 The worst of Warburton is, that he has a rage for
saying something, when there's nothing to be said.
p.329. 1758

18 No man will be a sailor who has contrivance enough to
get himself into a jail; for being in a ship is being in a
jail, with the chance of being drowned...A man in a
jail has more room, better food, and commonly better
company.
p.348. 16 Mar. 1759

19 'Are you a botanist, Dr Johnson?'
'No, Sir, I am not a botanist; and (alluding, no doubt,
to his near sightedness) should I wish to become a
botanist, I must first turn myself into a reptile.'
p.377. 20 July 1762

20 *Boswell*: I do indeed come from Scotland, but I
cannot help it...
Johnson: That, Sir, I find, is what a very great many
of your countrymen cannot help.
p.392. 16 May 1763

21 The notion of liberty amuses the people of England,
and helps to keep off the *taedium vitae*. When a
butcher tells you that *his heart bleeds for his country*
he has, in fact, no uneasy feeling.
p.394. 16 May 1763

22 Yes, Sir, many men, many women, and many
children.
On Dr. Blair's asking whether any man of a modern age could
have written *Ossian*. p.396. 24 May 1763

23 It was like leading one to talk of a book when the
author is concealed behind the door.

24 He insisted on people praying with him; and I'd as lief
pray with Kit Smart as any one else.
p.397. 24 May 1763

25 He did not love clean linen; and I have no passion for
it.
Of Kit Smart

26 You *may* abuse a tragedy, though you cannot write
one. You may scold a carpenter who has made you a
bad table, though you cannot make a table. It is not
your trade to make tables.
Of literary criticism. p.409. 25 June 1763

27 I am afraid he has not been in the inside of a church
for many years; but he never passes a church without
pulling off his hat. This shews that he has good
principles.
Of Dr. John Campbell. p.418. 1 July 1763

28 He is the richest author that ever grazed the common
of literature.
Of Dr. John Campbell

29 Great abilities are not requisite for an
Historian...Imagination is not required in any high
degree.
p.424. 6 July 1763

30 Norway, too, has noble wild prospects; and Lapland is
remarkable for prodigious noble wild prospects. But,
Sir, let me tell you, the noblest prospect which a
Scotchman ever sees, is the high road that leads him to
England!
p.425. 6 July 1763

31 A man ought to read just as inclination leads him; for

what he reads as a task will do him little good.
p.428. 14 July 1763

1 But if he does really think that there is no distinction
between virtue and vice, why, Sir, when he leaves our
houses let us count our spoons.
p.432. 14 July 1763

2 You never find people labouring to convince you that
you may live very happily upon a plentiful fortune.
p.441. 20 July 1763

3 Truth, Sir, is a cow, which will yield such people
[sceptics] no more milk, and so they are gone to milk
the bull.
p.444. 21 July 1763

4 Young men have more virtue than old men; they have
more generous sentiments in every respect.
p.445. 22 July 1763

5 Your levellers wish to level *down* as far as
themselves; but they cannot bear levelling *up* to
themselves.
p.448. 21 July 1763

6 It is no matter what you teach them [children] first,
any more than what leg you shall put into your
breeches first.
p.452. 26 July 1763

7 Why, Sir, Sherry [Thomas Sheridan] is dull, naturally
dull; but it must have taken him a great deal of pains to
become what we now see him. Such an excess of
stupidity, Sir, is not in Nature.
p.453. 28 July 1763

8 It is burning a farthing candle at Dover, to shew light
at Calais.
Of Thomas Sheridan's influence on the English language. p.454.
28 July 1763

9 [To a woman of the town, accosting him]
No, no, my girl...it won't do.
p.457. 28 July 1763

10 A woman's preaching is like a dog's walking on his
hinder legs. It is not done well; but you are surprised
to find it done at all.
p.463. 31 July 1763

11 I look upon it, that he who does not mind his belly
will hardly mind anything else.
p.467. 5 Aug. 1763

12 This was a good dinner enough, to be sure; but it was
not a dinner to *ask* a man to.
p.470. 5 Aug. 1763

13 We could not have had a better dinner had there been
a *Synod of Cooks.*

14 Don't, Sir, accustom yourself to use big words for
little matters. It would *not* be *terrible,* though I *were* to
be detained some time here.
p.471. 6 Aug. 1763

15 [Of Bishop Berkeley's theory of the non-existence of
matter, Boswell observed that though they were
satisfied it was not true, they were unable to refute it.
Johnson struck his foot against a large stone, till he
rebounded from it, saying]
I refute it *thus.*

16 A very unclubable man.
Sir John Hawkins. p.480n. 1764

17 That all who are happy, are equally happy, is not true.
A peasant and a philosopher may be equally *satisfied,*

but not equally *happy.* Happiness consists in the
multiplicity of agreeable consciousness.
vol.ii, p.9. Feb. 1766

18 It is our first duty to serve society, and, after we have
done that, we may attend wholly to the salvation of
our own souls. A youthful passion for abstracted
devotion should not be encouraged.
p.10. Feb. 1766

19 Our tastes greatly alter. The lad does not care for the
child's rattle, and the old man does not care for the
young man's whore.
p.14. Spring, 1766

20 It was not for me to bandy civilities with my
Sovereign.
p.35. Feb. 1767

21 I love Robertson, and I won't talk of his book.
p.53. 1768

22 Sir, if a man has a mind to *prance,* he must study at
Christ-Church and All-Souls.
p.68n. Autumn, 1769

23 Let me smile with the wise, and feed with the rich.
p.79. 6 Oct. 1769

24 We *know* our will is free, and *there's* an end on't.
p.82. 16 Oct. 1769

25 Inspissated gloom.
p.90

26 I do not know, Sir, that the fellow is an infidel; but if
he be an infidel, he is an infidel as a dog is an infidel;
that is to say, he has never thought upon the subject.
p.95. 19 Oct. 1769

27 Shakespeare never had six lines together without a
fault. Perhaps you may find seven, but this does not
refute my general assertion.
p.96. 19 Oct. 1769

28 I would not *coddle* the child.
p.101. 26 Oct. 1769

29 Why, Sir, most schemes of political improvement are
very laughable things.
p.102. 26 Oct. 1769

30 There is no idolatry in the Mass. They believe God to
be there, and they adore him.
p.105. 26 Oct. 1769

31 It matters not how a man dies, but how he lives. The
act of dying is not of importance, it lasts so short a
time.
p.106. 26 Oct. 1769

32 Burton's *Anatomy of Melancholy,* he said, was the
only book that ever took him out of bed two hours
sooner than he wished to rise.
p.121. 1770

33 Want of tenderness is want of parts, and is no less a
proof of stupidity than depravity.
p.122. 1770

34 That fellow seems to me to possess but one idea, and
that is a wrong one.
p.126. 1770

35 Johnson observed, that 'he did not care to speak ill of
any man behind his back, but he believed the
gentleman was an *attorney.'*

36 The triumph of hope over experience.
Of a man who remarried immediately after the death of a wife with
whom he had been very unhappy. p.128. 1770

1 Every man has a lurking wish to appear considerable in his native place.
p.141. Letter to Sir Joshua Reynolds, 17 July 1771

2 It is so far from being natural for a man and woman to live in a state of marriage that we find all the motives which they have for remaining in that connection, and the restraints which civilized society imposes to prevent separation, are hardly sufficient to keep them together.
p.165. 31 Mar. 1772

3 Nobody can write the life of a man, but those who have eat and drunk and lived in social intercourse with him.
p.166. 31 Mar. 1772

4 I would not give half a guinea to live under one form of government rather than another. It is of no moment to the happiness of an individual.
p.170. 31 Mar. 1772

5 Sir, I perceive you are a vile Whig.
To Sir Adam Fergusson

6 There is a remedy in human nature against tyranny, that will keep us safe under every form of government.

7 A man who is good enough to go to heaven, is good enough to be a clergyman.
p.171. 5 Apr. 1772

8 There is more knowledge of the heart in one letter of Richardson's, than in all *Tom Jones*.
p.174. 6 Apr. 1772

9 Why, Sir, if you were to read Richardson for the story, your impatience would be so much fretted that you would hang yourself.
p.175. 6 Apr. 1772

10 Much may be made of a Scotchman, if he be *caught* young.
On Lord Mansfield, who was educated in England. p.194. Spring 1772

11 He has, indeed, done it very well; but it is a foolish thing well done.
On Goldsmith's apology in the *London Chronicle* for beating Evans the bookseller. p.210. 3 Apr. 1773

12 All intellectual improvement arises from leisure.
p.219. 13 Apr. 1773

13 *Elphinston:* What, have you not read it through?...
Johnson: No, Sir, do *you* read books *through*?
p.226. 19 Apr. 1773

14 Read over your compositions, and where ever you meet with a passage which you think is particularly fine, strike it out.
Quoting a college tutor. p.237. 30 Apr. 1773

15 The woman's a whore, and there's an end on't.
Of Lady Diana Beauclerk. p.247. 7 May 1773

16 I hope I shall never be deterred from detecting what I think a cheat, by the menaces of a ruffian.
p.298. Letter to James Macpherson, 20 Jan. 1775

17 The Irish are a fair people;—they never speak well of one another.
p.307. 1775

18 There are few ways in which a man can be more innocently employed than in getting money.
p.323. 27 Mar. 1775

19 He [Thomas Gray] was dull in a new way, and that made many people think him *great*.
p.327. 28 Mar. 1775

20 I never think I have hit hard, unless it rebounds.
p.335. 2 Apr. 1775

21 I think the full tide of human existence is at Charing-Cross.
p.337. 2 Apr. 1775

22 George the First knew nothing, and desired to know nothing; did nothing, and desired to do nothing; and the only good thing that is told of him is, that he wished to restore the crown to its hereditary successor.
p.342. 6 Apr. 1775

23 It is wonderful, when a calculation is made, how little the mind is actually employed in the discharge of any profession.
p.344. 6 Apr. 1775

24 A man will turn over half a library to make one book.

25 Patriotism is the last refuge of a scoundrel.
p.348. 7 Apr. 1775

26 That is the happiest conversation where there is no competition, no vanity, but a calm quiet interchange of sentiments.
p.359. 14 Apr. 1775

27 Their learning is like bread in a besieged town: every man gets a little, but no man gets a full meal.
On the Scots. p.363. 18 Apr. 1775

28 Knowledge is of two kinds. We know a subject ourselves, or we know where we can find information upon it.
p.365. 18 Apr. 1775

29 Politics are now nothing more than a means of rising in the world.
p.369. 1775

30 Players, Sir! I look upon them as no better than creatures set upon tables and joint stools to make faces and produce laughter, like dancing dogs.
p.404. 1775

31 In lapidary inscriptions a man is not upon oath.
p.407. 1775

32 There is now less flogging in our great schools than formerly, but then less is learned there; so that what the boys get at one end they lose at the other.

33 When men come to like a sea-life, they are not fit to live on land.
p.438. 18 Mar. 1776

34 Nothing odd will do long. *Tristram Shandy* did not last.
p.449. 20 Mar. 1776

35 There is nothing which has yet been contrived by man, by which so much happiness is produced as by a good tavern or inn.
p.452. 21 Mar. 1776

36 Marriages would in general be as happy, and often more so, if they were all made by the Lord Chancellor.
p.461. 22 Mar. 1776

37 Questioning is not the mode of conversation among gentlemen.
p.472. Mar. 1776

38 Fine clothes are good only as they supply the want of other means of procuring respect.
p.475. 27 Mar. 1776

1 If a madman were to come into this room with a stick in his hand, no doubt we should pity the state of his mind; but our primary consideration would be to take care of ourselves. We should knock him down first, and pity him afterwards.
vol.iii, p.11. 3 Apr. 1776

2 Consider, Sir, how should you like, though conscious of your innocence, to be tried before a jury for a capital crime, once a week.

3 We would all be idle if we could.
p.13. 3 Apr. 1776

4 No man but a blockhead ever wrote, except for money.
p.19. 5 Apr. 1776

5 It is better that some should be unhappy than that none should be happy, which would be the case in a general state of equality.
p.26. 7 Apr. 1776

6 A man who has not been in Italy, is always conscious of an inferiority, from his not having seen what it is expected a man should see. The grand object of travelling is to see the shores of the Mediterranean.
p.36. 11 Apr. 1776

7 'Sir, what is poetry?'
'Why Sir, it is much easier to say what it is not. We all *know* what light is; but it is not easy to *tell* what it is.'
p.38 10 Apr. 1776

8 Nay, Madam, when you are declaiming, declaim; and when you are calculating, calculate.
To Mrs. Thrale, who had interrupted him and Boswell by a lively extravagant sally on the expense of clothing children. p.49. 26 Apr. 1776

9 Every man of any education would rather be called a rascal, than accused of deficiency in *the graces*.
p.54. May 1776

10 Sir, you have but two topics, yourself and me. I am sick of both.
p.57. May 1776

11 Dine with Jack Wilkes, Sir! I'd as soon dine with Jack Ketch.
p.66. 'This has been circulated as if actually said by Johnson; when the truth is, it was only *supposed* by me.' (Boswell's note.)

12 Sir, it is not so much to be lamented that Old England is lost, as that the Scotch have found it.
p.78. 15 May 1776

13 *Olivarii Goldsmith, Poetae, Physici, Historici, Qui nullum fere scribendi genus non tetigit, Nullum quod tetigit non ornavit.*
To Oliver Goldsmith, A Poet, Naturalist, and Historian, who left scarcely any style of writing untouched, and touched none that he did not adorn.
p.82. 22 June 1776. Epitaph on Goldsmith

14 Hermit hoar, in solemn cell,
    Wearing out life's evening gray;
    Smite thy bosom, sage, and tell,
    What is bliss, and which the way?
Thus I spoke; and speaking sigh'd;
    —Scarce repressed the starting tear;—
When the smiling sage reply'd—
    —Come, my lad, and drink some beer.
p.159. 18 Sept. 1777

15 If I had no duties, and no reference to futurity, I would spend my life in driving briskly in a post-chaise with a pretty woman.
p.162. 19 Sept. 1777

16 Depend upon it, Sir, when a man knows he is to be hanged in a fortnight, it concentrates his mind wonderfully.
p.167. 19 Sept. 1777

17 When a man is tired of London, he is tired of life; for there is in London all that life can afford.
p.178. 20 Sept. 1777

18 He who praises everybody praises nobody.
p.225n.

19 Round numbers are always false.
p.226, n.4. 30 Mar. 1778

20 Accustom your children constantly to this; if a thing happened at one window and they, when relating it, say that it happened at another, do not let it pass, but instantly check them; you do not know where deviation from truth will end.
p.228. 31 Mar. 1778

21 All argument is against it; but all belief is for it.
Of the appearance of the spirit of a person after death. p.230. 31 Mar. 1778

22 John Wesley's conversation is good, but he is never at leisure. He is always obliged to go at a certain hour. This is very disagreeable to a man who loves to fold his legs and have out his talk, as I do.

23 Though we cannot out-vote them we will out-argue them.
p.234. 3 Apr. 1778

24 Seeing Scotland, Madam, is only seeing a worse England.
p.248. 7 Apr. 1778

25 Goldsmith, however, was a man, who, whatever he wrote, did it better than any other man could do.
p.253. 9 Apr. 1778

26 Every man thinks meanly of himself for not having been a soldier, or not having been at sea.
p.265. 10 Apr. 1778

27 A mere antiquarian is a rugged being.
p.278. Letter to Boswell, 23 Apr. 1778

28 Johnson had said that he could repeat a complete chapter of 'The Natural History of Iceland', from the Danish of Horrebow, the whole of which was exactly thus:—'CHAP. LXXII. *Concerning snakes.* There are no snakes to be met with throughout the whole island.'
p.279. 13 Apr. 1778

29 A country governed by a despot is an inverted cone.
p.283. 14 Apr. 1778

30 I am willing to love all mankind, *except an American.*
p.290. 15 Apr. 1778

31 As the Spanish proverb says, 'He, who would bring home the wealth of the Indies, must carry the wealth of the Indies with him.' So it is in travelling; a man must carry knowledge with him, if he would bring home knowledge.
p.302. 17 Apr. 1778

32 Sir, the insolence of wealth will creep out.
p.316. 18 Apr. 1778

33 All censure of a man's self is oblique praise. It is in order to shew how much he can spare.
p.323. 25 Apr. 1778

1 Sir, there are rascals in all countries.
On Boswell's expressing surprise at finding a Staffordshire Whig.
p.326. 28 Apr. 1778

2 I have always said, the first Whig was the Devil.

3 It is thus that mutual cowardice keeps us in peace.
Were one half of mankind brave and one half cowards,
the brave would be always beating the cowards. Were
all brave, they would lead a very uneasy life; all would
be continually fighting; but being all cowards, we go
on very well.

4 Were it not for imagination, Sir, a man would be as
happy in the arms of a chambermaid as of a Duchess.
p.341. 9 May 1778

5 There are innumerable questions to which the
inquisitive mind can in this state receive no answer:
Why do you and I exist? Why was this world created?
Since it was to be created, why was it not created
sooner?

6 Dr Mead lived more in the broad sunshine of life than
almost any man.
p.355. 16 May 1778

7 Claret is the liquor for boys; port for men; but he who
aspires to be a hero must drink brandy.
p.381. 7 Apr. 1779

8 A man who exposes himself when he is intoxicated,
has not the art of getting drunk.
p.389. 24 Apr. 1779

9 Remember that all tricks are either knavish or
childish.
p.396. Letter to Boswell, 9 Sept. 1779

10 Worth seeing? yes; but not worth going to see.
Of the Giant's Causeway. p.410. 12 Oct. 1779

11 If you are idle, be not solitary; if you are solitary, be
not idle.
p.415. Letter to Boswell, 27 Oct. 1779. See 117:3

12 When Charles Fox said something to me once about
Catiline's Conspiracy, I withdrew my attention and
thought about Tom Thumb.
p.512. Letter from Mrs. Piozzi to W.A. Conway, 21 Aug. 1819

13 Among the anfractuosities of the human mind, I know
not if it may not be one, that there is a superstitious
reluctance to sit for a picture.
vol.iv, p.4. 1780

14 Clive, sir, is a good thing to sit by; she always
understands what you say.
Of Kitty Clive. p.7. 1780

15 I have got no further than this: Every man has a right
to utter what he thinks truth, and every other man has
a right to knock him down for it. Martyrdom is the
test.
p.12. 1780

16 They are forced plants, raised in a hot-bed; and they
are poor plants; they are but cucumbers after all.
Of Gray's *Odes*. p.13. 1780

17 A Frenchman must be always talking, whether he
knows anything of the matter or not; an Englishman is
content to say nothing, when he has nothing to say.
p.15. 1780

18 Sir, your wife, under pretence of keeping a
bawdy-house, is a receiver of stolen goods.
During an exchange of coarse raillery customary among people
travelling upon the Thames. p 26. 1780

19 No man was more foolish when he had not a pen in
his hand, or more wise when he had.
Of Goldsmith. See 221:13

20 Depend upon it that if a man talks of his misfortunes
there is something in them that is not disagreeable to
him; for where there is nothing but pure misery there
never is any recourse to the mention of it.
p.31. 1780

21 Supposing…a wife to be of a studious or
argumentative turn, it would be very troublesome: for
instance,—if a woman should continually dwell upon
the subject of the Arian heresy.
p.32. 1780

22 No man speaks concerning another, even suppose it be
in his praise, if he thinks he does not hear him, exactly
as he would, if he thought he was within hearing.

23 I believe that is true. The dogs don't know how to
write trifles with dignity.
Reply to Fowke who had observed that in writing biography,
Johnson infinitely exceeded his contemporaries. p.34, n.5

24 Mrs Montagu has dropt me. Now, Sir, there are
people whom one should like very well to drop, but
would not wish to be dropped by.
p.73. Mar. 1781

25 This merriment of parsons is mighty offensive.
p.76. Mar. 1781

26 He fills a chair.
Of Mr. Dudley Long. p.81. 1 Apr. 1781

27 We are not here to sell a parcel of boilers and vats,
but the potentiality of growing rich, beyond the dreams
of avarice.
At the sale of Thrale's brewery. p.87. 6 Apr. 1781. See 355:14

28 'The woman had a bottom of good sense.'
The word '*bottom*' thus introduced, was so
ludicrous,…that most of us could not forbear tittering…
'Where's the merriment?…I say the *woman* was
fundamentally sensible.'
p.99. 20 Apr. 1781

29 Classical quotation is the *parole* of literary men all
over the world.
p.102. 8 May 1781

30 Why, that is, because, dearest, you're a dunce.
To Miss Monckton, afterwards Lady Corke, who said that
Sterne's writings affected her. p.109. May 1781

31 I have two very cogent reasons for not printing any
list of subscribers;—one, that I have lost all the
names,—the other, that I have spent all the money.
p.111. May 1781

32 My friend [Johnson] was of opinion, that when a man
of rank appeared in that character [as an author], he
deserved to have his merit handsomely allowed.
p.114. May 1781

33 Always, Sir, set a high value on spontaneous
kindness. He whose inclination prompts him to
cultivate your friendship of his own accord, will love
you more than one whom you have been at pains to
attach to you.
p.115. May 1781

34 A wise Tory and a wise Whig, I believe, will agree.
Their principles are the same, though their modes of
thinking are different.
p.117. Written statement given to Boswell, May 1781

35 Officious, innocent, sincere,

Of every friendless name the friend.

Yet still he fills affection's eye,
Obscurely wise, and coarsely kind.
p.127. 20 Jan. 1782. On the death of Mr. Levett

1 Then, with no throbs of fiery pain,
No cold gradations of decay,
Death broke at once the vital chain,
And freed his soul the nearest way.

2 Resolve not to be poor: whatever you have, spend
less. Poverty is a great enemy to human happiness; it
certainly destroys liberty, and it makes some virtues
impracticable and others extremely difficult.
p.157. 7 Dec. 1782

3 I hate a fellow whom pride, or cowardice, or laziness
drives into a corner, and who does nothing when he is
there but sit and *growl*; let him come out as I do, and
bark.
p.161, n.3. 14 Nov. 1782

4 I never have sought the world; the world was not to
seek me.
p.172. 23 Mar. 1783

5 How few of his friends' houses would a man choose to
be at when he is sick.
p.181. 1783

6 There is a wicked inclination in most people to
suppose an old man decayed in his intellects. If a
young or middle-aged man, when leaving a company,
does not recollect where he laid his hat, it is nothing;
but if the same inattention is discovered in an old man,
people will shrug up their shoulders, and say, 'His
memory is going.'

7 A man might write such stuff for ever, if he would
abandon his mind to it.
Of Ossian. p.183. 1783

8 Sir, there is no settling the point of precedency
between a louse and a flea.
To Maurice Morgann who asked him whether he reckoned Derrick
or Smart the better poet. p.192. 1783

9 When I observed he was a fine cat, saying, 'why yes,
Sir, but I have had cats whom I liked better than this';
and then as if perceiving Hodge to be out of
countenance, adding, 'but he is a very fine cat, a very
fine cat indeed.'
p.197. 1783

10 Sir, I have never slept an hour less, nor eat an ounce
less meat. I would have knocked the factious dogs [the
Whigs] on the head, to be sure; but I was not *vexed*.
p.220. 15 May 1783

11 My dear friend, clear your *mind* of cant...You may
talk in this manner; it is a mode of talking in Society:
but don't *think* foolishly.
p.221. 15 May 1783

12 As I know more of mankind I expect less of them, and
am ready now to call a man *a good man*, upon easier
terms than I was formerly.
p.239. Sept. 1783

13 Boswell is a very clubable man.
p.254n. 1783

14 I should as soon think of contradicting a Bishop.
Of George Psalmanazar, whom he reverenced for his piety. p.274.
15 May 1784

15 If a man were to go by chance at the same time with
[Edmund] Burke under a shed, to shun a shower, he

would say—'this is an extraordinary man.'
p.275

16 It is as bad as bad can be: it is ill-fed, ill-killed,
ill-kept, and ill-drest.
The roast mutton he had for dinner at an inn. p.284. 3 June 1784

17 *Johnson*: As I cannot be sure that I have fulfilled the
conditions on which salvation is granted, I am afraid I
may be one of those who shall be damned (looking
dismally).
Dr. Adams: What do you mean by damned?
Johnson (passionately and loudly): Sent to Hell, Sir,
and punished everlastingly.
p.299. 1784

18 Milton, Madam, was a genius that could cut a
Colossus from a rock; but could not carve heads upon
cherry-stones.
To Miss Hannah More, who had expressed a wonder that the poet
who had written *Paradise Lost* should write such poor Sonnets.
p.305. 13 June 1784

19 Don't cant in defence of savages.
p.308. 15 June 1784

20 It might as well be 'Who drives fat oxen should
himself be fat.'
p.313. June 1784. Parody of 94:4

21 Sir, I have found you an argument; but I am not
obliged to find you an understanding.

22 No man is a hypocrite in his pleasures.
p.316. June 1784

23 Dublin, though a place much worse than London, is
not so bad as Iceland.
Letter to Mrs. Christopher Smart. p.359n. 1791

24 Who can run the race with Death?
p.360. Letter to Dr. Burney, 2 Aug. 1784

25 Sir, I look upon every day to be lost, in which I do
not make a new acquaintance.
p.374. Nov. 1784

26 I will be conquered; I will not capitulate.
Talking of his illness

27 Are you sick or are you sullen?
p.380. Letter to Boswell, 3 Nov. 1784

28 Long-expected one-and-twenty,
Ling'ring year, at length is flown;
Pride and pleasure, pomp and plenty
Great [Sir John], are now your own.
p.413. Dec. 1784

29 An odd thought strikes me:—we shall receive no
letters in the grave.

30 A lawyer has no business with the justice or injustice
of the cause which he undertakes, unless his client
asks his opinion, and then he is bound to give it
honestly. The justice or injustice of the cause is to be
decided by the judge.
Boswell, *Tour to the Hebrides (Life,* vol.v), 15 Aug. 1773, p.175

31 Let him go abroad to a distant country; let him go to
some place where he is *not* known. Don't let him go to
the devil where he is known!
18 Aug., p.194

32 I have, all my life long, been lying till noon; yet I tell
all young men, and tell them with great sincerity, that
nobody who does not rise early will ever do any good.
14 Sept., p.299

33 I inherited a vile melancholy from my father, which

has made me mad all my life, at least not sober.
16 Sept., p.302

1 I am always sorry when any language is lost, because languages are the pedigree of nations.
18 Sept., p.310

2 No, Sir; there were people who died of dropsies, which they contracted in trying to get drunk.
Johnson, railing against Scotland, had said that the wine the Scots had before the Union would not make them drunk. Boswell assured Johnson there was much drunkenness. 23 Sept., p.326

3 A cucumber should be well sliced, and dressed with pepper and vinegar, and then thrown out, as good for nothing.
5 Oct., p.354

4 Come, let me know what it is that makes a Scotchman happy!
Calling for a gill of whisky. 23 Oct., p.393

5 Sir, are you so grossly ignorant of human nature, as not to know that a man may be very sincere in good principles, without having good practice?
25 Oct., p.403

6 I am sorry I have not learned to play at cards. It is very useful in life: it generates kindness and consolidates society.
21 Nov., p.433

7 This world where much is to be done and little to be known.
Johnsonian Miscellanies ed. G.B. Hill (1897), vol.i. Prayers and Meditations. Against inquisitive and perplexing Thoughts, p.118

8 Corneille is to Shakespeare...as a clipped hedge is to a forest.
Anecdotes of Johnson by Mrs. Piozzi, p.187

9 Wheresoe'er I turn my view,
All is strange, yet nothing new;
Endless labour all along,
Endless labour to be wrong;
Phrase that time hath flung away,
Uncouth words in disarray,
Trick'd in antique ruff and bonnet,
Ode, and elegy, and sonnet.
p.190

10 If the man who turnips cries,
Cry not when his father dies,
'Tis a proof that he had rather
Have a turnip than his father.
Burlesque of Lope de Vega's lines, '*Si a quien los leones vence,*' &c. p.193

11 Dear Bathurst (said he to me one day) was a man to my very heart's content: he hated a fool, and he hated a rogue, and he hated a whig; he was a very good hater.
p.204

12 He will not, whither he is now gone, find much difference, I believe, either in the climate or the company.
Of a Jamaica gentleman, then lately dead. p.211

13 One day at Streatham...a young gentleman called to him suddenly, and I suppose he thought disrespectfully, in these words: 'Mr Johnson, would you advise me to marry?' 'I would advise no man to marry, Sir,' returns for answer in a very angry tone Dr Johnson, 'who is not likely to propagate understanding.'
p.213

14 *Goldsmith*: Here's such a stir about a fellow that has written one book [Beattie's *Essay on Truth*], and I have written many.
Johnson: Ah, Doctor, there go two-and-forty sixpences you know to one guinea.
p.269

15 It is very strange, and very melancholy, that the paucity of human pleasures should persuade us ever to call hunting one of them.
p.288

16 Was there ever yet anything written by mere man that was wished longer by its readers, excepting *Don Quixote, Robinson Crusoe,* and the *Pilgrim's Progress*?
p.332

17 Books that you may carry to the fire, and hold readily in your hand, are the most useful after all.
vol.ii. Apophthegms from Hawkins's edition of Johnson's works, p.2

18 A man is in general better pleased when he has a good dinner upon his table, than when his wife talks Greek.
p.11

19 I would rather see the portrait of a dog that I know, than all the allegorical paintings they can shew me in the world.
p.15

20 I have heard him assert, that a tavern chair was the throne of human felicity.
Extracts from Hawkins's *Life of Johnson*, p.91

21 I dogmatise and am contradicted, and in this conflict of opinions and sentiments I find delight.
p.92

22 Abstinence is as easy to me, as temperance would be difficult.
Anecdotes by Hannah More, p.197

23 Of music Dr Johnson used to say that it was the only sensual pleasure without vice.
Anecdotes by William Seward, p.301

24 Difficult do you call it, Sir? I wish it were impossible.
Of the performance of a celebrated violinist. p.308

25 What is written without effort is in general read without pleasure.
p.309

26 As with my hat upon my head
I walk'd along the Strand,
I there did meet another man
With his hat in his hand.
Anecdotes by George Steevens, p.315

27 Love is the wisdom of the fool and the folly of the wise.
From William Cooke's '*Life of Samuel Foote*', p.393

28 Fly fishing may be a very pleasant amusement; but angling or float fishing I can only compare to a stick and a string, with a worm at one end and a fool at the other.
Attrib. Johnson by Hawker in *Instructions to Young Sportsmen* (1859), p.197. Not found in his works. See N. & Q., 11 Dec. 1915

29 Madam, before you flatter a man so grossly to his face, you should consider whether or not your flattery is worth his having.
Remark to Hannah More. Mme D'Arblay, *Diary and Letters* (1891 edn.), vol.i, ch.ii, p.55 (Aug. 1778)

1 A general anarchy prevails in my kitchen.
ch.iii, p.63 (Sept. 1778)

2 Every man has, some time in his life, an ambition to
be a wag.
vol.iii, ch.xlvi, p.413 (1 June 1792)

3 I know not, madam, that you have a right, upon moral
principles, to make your readers suffer so much.
To Mrs. Sheridan, after publication of her novel *Memoirs of Miss
Sydney Biddulph* (1763)

4 In all pointed sentences, some degree of accuracy
must be sacrificed to conciseness.
On the Bravery of the English Common Soldier. *Works*
(1787), vol.x, p.286

5 It is the fate of those who toil at the lower
employments of life...to be exposed to censure,
without hope of praise; to be disgraced by miscarriage,
or punished for neglect...Among these unhappy
mortals is the writer of dictionaries...Every other
author may aspire to praise; the lexicographer can only
hope to escape reproach.
Dictionary of the English Language (1775), Preface

6 I am not yet so lost in lexicography, as to forget that
words are the daughters of earth, and that things are
the sons of heaven. Language is only the instrument of
science, and words are but the signs of ideas: I wish,
however, that the instrument might be less apt to
decay, and that signs might be permanent, like the
things which they denote.
See 326:19

7 Every quotation contributes something to the stability
or enlargement of the language.
Of citations of usage in a dictionary

8 But these were the dreams of a poet doomed at last to
wake a lexicographer.

9 If the changes that we fear be thus irresistible, what
remains but to acquiesce with silence, as in the other
insurmountable distresses of humanity? It remains that
we retard what we cannot repel, that we palliate what
we cannot cure.

10 The chief glory of every people arises from its
authors.

11 *Dull.* 8. To make dictionaries is dull work.

12 *Excise.* A hateful tax levied upon commodities.

13 *Net.* Anything reticulated or decussated at equal
distances, with interstices between the intersections.

14 *Oats.* A grain, which in England is generally given to
horses, but in Scotland supports the people.

15 *Patron.* Commonly a wretch who supports with
insolence, and is paid with flattery.

16 *Whig.* The name of a faction.

17 Every man is, or hopes to be, an idler.
The Idler (1758-60), No.1

18 When two Englishmen meet, their first talk is of the
weather.
No.11

19 Promise, large promise, is the soul of an
advertisement.
No.41

20 He is no wise man who will quit a certainty for an
uncertainty.
No.57

21 Nothing is more hopeless than a scheme of merriment.
No.58

22 A Scotchman must be a very sturdy moralist who does
not love Scotland better than truth.
Journey to the Western Islands of Scotland (1775). **Col**

23 At seventy-seven it is time to be in earnest.

24 Whatever withdraws us from the power of our senses;
whatever makes the past, the distant, or the future,
predominate over the present, advances us in the
dignity of thinking beings.
Inch Kenneth

25 I do not much wish well to discoveries, for I am
always afraid they will end in conquest and robbery.
Letter to W.S. Johnson, 4 Mar. 1773

26 Grief is a species of idleness.
To Mrs. Thrale, 17 Mar. 1773

27 There is no wisdom in useless and hopeless sorrow.
To Mrs. Thrale, 12 Apr. 1781

28 A hardened and shameless tea-drinker, who has for
twenty years diluted his meals with only the infusion
of this fascinating plant; whose kettle has scarcely time
to cool; who with tea amuses the evening, with tea
solaces the midnight, and with tea welcomes the
morning.
Review in the *Literary Magazine*, vol.ii, No.xiii. 1757

29 The reciprocal civility of authors is one of the most
risible scenes in the farce of life.
Life of Sir Thomas Browne, first published as preface to his 1756
edition of *Christian Morals*·

30 The true genius is a mind of large general powers,
accidentally determined to some particular direction.
Lives of the English Poets (1779-81). **Cowley**

31 Language is the dress of thought.
See 568:25

32 We are perpetually moralists, but we are
geometricians only be chance. Our intercourse with
intellectual nature is necessary; our speculations upon
matter are voluntary, and at leisure.
Milton

33 An acrimonious and surly republican.

34 The great source of pleasure is variety.
Butler

35 The father of English criticism.
Dryden

36 I am disappointed by that stroke of death, which has
eclipsed the gaiety of nations and impoverished the
public stock of harmless pleasure. [Garrick's death.]
Edmund Smith

37 About things on which the public thinks long it
commonly attains to think right.
Addison

38 Whoever wishes to attain an English style, familiar
but not coarse, and elegant but not ostentatious, must
give his days and nights to the volumes of Addison.

39 In the character of his Elegy I rejoice to concur with
the common reader; for by the common sense of
readers uncorrupted with literary prejudices...must be
finally decided all claim to poetical honours.
Gray

40 A man, doubtful of his dinner, or trembling at a
creditor, is not much disposed to abstracted

meditation, or remote enquiries.
Collins

1 This play [*The Beggar's Opera*]...was first offered to
   Cibber and his brethren at Drury-Lane, and rejected; it
   being then carried to Rich, had the effect, as was
   ludicrously said, of making Gay *rich* and Rich *gay*.
   John Gay

2 He washed himself with oriental scrupulosity.
   Swift

3 Friendship is not always the sequel of obligation.
   James Thomson

4 There are minds so impatient of inferiority that their
   gratitude is a species of revenge, and they return
   benefits, not because recompense is a pleasure, but
   because obligation is a pain.
   The Rambler, 15 Jan. 1751

5 I have laboured to refine our language to grammatical
   purity, and to clear it from colloquial barbarisms,
   licentious idioms, and irregular combinations.
   14 Mar. 1752

6 The business of a poet, said Imlac, is to examine, not
   the individual, but the species;...he does not number
   the streaks of the tulip, or describe the different shades
   in the verdure of the forest.
   Rasselas (1759), ch.10

7 He [the poet] must write as the interpreter of nature,
   and the legislator of mankind, and consider himself as
   presiding over the thoughts and manners of future
   generations; as a being superior to time and place.

8 Human life is everwhere a state in which much is to be
   endured, and little to be enjoyed.
   ch.11

9 Marriage has many pains, but celibacy has no
   pleasures.
   ch.26

10 Example is always more efficacious than precept.
   ch.29

11 Integrity without knowledge is weak and useless, and
   knowledge without integrity is dangerous and
   dreadful.
   ch.41

12 The endearing elegance of female friendship.
   ch.45

13 The power of punishment is to silence, not to confute.
   Sermons (1788), No.xxiii

14 Notes are often necessary, but they are necessary
   evils.
   Plays of William Shakespeare, with Notes (1765), preface

15 A quibble is to Shakespeare what luminous vapours
   are to the traveller: he follows it at all adventures; it is
   sure to lead him out of his way and sure to engulf him
   in the mire.

16 It must be at last confessed that, as we owe everything
   to him [Shakespeare], he owes something to us; that,
   if much of our praise is paid by perception and
   judgement, much is likewise given by custom and
   veneration. We fix our eyes upon his graces and turn
   them from his deformities, and endure in him what we
   should in another loathe or despise.

17 I have always suspected that the reading is right which
   requires many words to prove it wrong, and the
   emendation wrong that cannot without so much labour

appear to be right.

18 How is it that we hear the loudest yelps for liberty
   among the drivers of negroes?
   Taxation No Tyranny (1775)

19 A generous and elevated mind is distinguished by
   nothing more certainly than an eminent degree of
   curiosity.
   Dedication of his English trans. of Fr. J. Lobo's *Voyage to
   Abyssinia* (1735), signed 'the editor' but attr. to Johnson in
   Boswell's *Life*, i.89

20 Unmov'd tho' witlings sneer and rivals rail;
   Studious to please, yet not asham'd to fail.
   Irene (1736-7, produced 1749), prologue

21 How small, of all that human hearts endure,
   That part which laws or kings can cause or cure!
   Still to ourselves in every place consigned,
   Our own felicity we make or find:
   With secret course, which no loud storms annoy,
   Glides the smooth current of domestic joy.
   Lines added to Goldsmith's 'Traveller' (1764). See 231:30

22 Here falling houses thunder on your head,
   And here a female atheist talks you dead.
   London (1738), l.17

23 Of all the griefs that harrass the distress'd,
   Sure the most bitter is a scornful jest;
   Fate never wounds more deep the gen'rous heart,
   Than when a blockhead's insult points the dart.
   l.166

24 This mournful truth is ev'rywhere confess'd,
   Slow rises worth by poverty depress'd.
   l.176

25 When learning's triumph o'er her barb'rous foes
   First rear'd the Stage, immortal Shakespeare rose;
   Each change of many-colour'd life he drew,
   Exhausted worlds, and then imagin'd new:
   Existence saw him spurn her bounded reign,
   And panting Time toil'd after him in vain.
   Prologue at the Opening of the Theatre in Drury Lane, 1747

26 Hard is his lot, that here by fortune plac'd,
   Must watch the wild vicissitudes of taste;
   With ev'ry meteor of caprice must play,
   And chase the new-blown bubbles of the day.

27 The stage but echoes back the public voice.
   The drama's laws the drama's patrons give,
   For we that live to please, must please to live.

28 Let observation with extensive view,
   Survey mankind, from China to Peru;
   Remark each anxious toil, each eager strife,
   And watch the busy scenes of crowded life.
   The Vanity of Human Wishes (1749), l.1

29 Deign on the passing world to turn thine eyes,
   And pause awhile from letters to be wise;
   There mark what ills the scholar's life assail,
   Toil, envy, want, the patron, and the jail.
   See nations slowly wise, and meanly just,
   To buried merit raise the tardy bust.
   l.157

30 A frame of adamant, a soul of fire,
   No dangers fright him and no labours tire.
   l.193

31 His fall was destined to a barren strand,
   A petty fortress, and a dubious hand;
   He left the name, at which the world grew pale,

To point a moral, or adorn a tale. [Charles XII of
Sweden.]
l.219

1 'Enlarge my life with multitude of days!'
In health, in sickness, thus the suppliant prays:
Hides from himself its state, and shuns to know,
That life protracted is protracted woe.
Time hovers o'er, impatient to destroy,
And shuts up all the passages of joy.
l.225

2 Superfluous lags the vet'ran on the stage.
l.308

3 In life's last scene what prodigies surprise,
Fears of the brave, and follies of the wise!
From Marlb'rough's eyes the streams of dotage flow,
And Swift expires a driv'ler and a show.
l.315

4 What ills from beauty spring.
l.321

5 Still raise for good the supplicating voice,
But leave to Heaven the measure and the choice.
l.351

6 With these celestial Wisdom calms the mind,
And makes the happiness she does not find.
l.367

JOHN BENN JOHNSTONE 1803–1891

7 I want you to assist me in forcing her on board the
lugger; once there, I'll frighten her into marriage.
Since quoted as: Once aboard the lugger and the maid is mine.
The Gipsy Farmer

HANNS JOHST 1890–

8 *Wenn ich Kultur höre...entsichere ich meinen
Browning!*
Whenever I hear the word 'culture'...I release the
safety-catch on my pistol.
Schlageter (1934), I.i. Often attrib. Goering

AL JOLSON 1886–1950

9 You ain't heard nothin' yet, folks.
In the first talking film, *The Jazz Singer*, July 1927

HENRY ARTHUR JONES 1851–1929
and HENRY HERMAN 1832–1894

10 O God! Put back Thy universe and give me yesterday.
The Silver King

JOHN PAUL JONES 1747–1792

11 I have not yet begun to fight.
On being hailed to know whether he had struck his flag, as his
ship was sinking, 23 Sept. 1779. De Koven, *Life and Letters of
J.P. Jones*, vol.i

SIR WILLIAM JONES 1746–1794

12 My opinion is, that power should always be
distrusted, in whatever hands it is placed.
Lord Teignmouth, *Life of Sir W. Jones* (1835), vol.i. Letter to
Lord Althorpe, 5 Oct. 1782

13 Seven hours to law, to soothing slumber seven,

Ten to the world allot, and *all* to Heaven.
vol.ii. Lines in substitution for Sir E. Coke's lines: Six hours in
sleep, [&c.]. See 154:22

BEN JONSON 1573?–1637

14 Fortune, that favours fools.
The Alchemist (1610), prologue

15 Thou look'st like Antichrist in that lewd hat.
IV.vii

16 I will eat exceedingly, and prophesy.
Bartholomew Fair (1614), I.vi

17 Neither do thou lust after that tawney weed tobacco.
II.vi

18 When I mock poorness, then heaven make me poor.
The Case is Altered (1598-9), III.i

19 *People:* The Voice of Cato is the voice of Rome.
Cato: The voice of Rome is the consent of heaven!
Catiline his Conspiracy (1611), III.i

20   Where it concerns himself,
Who's angry at a slander makes it true.

21 Slow, slow, fresh fount, keep time with my salt tears:
   Yet, slower, yet; O faintly, gentle springs:
List to the heavy part the music bears,
Woe weeps out her division, when she sings.
Cynthia's Revels (1600), I.i

22   So they be ill men,
If they spake worse, 'twere better: for of such
To be dispraised, is the most perfect praise.
III.ii

23   True happiness
Consists not in the multitude of friends,
But in the worth and choice.

24 Queen and huntress, chaste and fair,
Now the sun is laid to sleep,
Seated in thy silver chair,
State in wonted manner keep:
   Hesperus entreats thy light,
   Goddess, excellently bright.
v.iii

25   If he were
To be made honest by an act of parliament,
I should not alter in my faith of him.
The Devil is an Ass (1616), IV.i

26 Alas, all the castles I have, are built with air, thou
know'st.
Eastward Ho (1604), II.ii.226

27 Still to be neat, still to be drest,
As you were going to a feast;
Still to be powder'd, still perfum'd,
Lady, it is to be presumed,
Though art's hid causes are not found,
All is not sweet, all is not sound.

Give me a look, give me a face,
That makes simplicity a grace;
Robes loosely flowing, hair as free:
Such sweet neglect more taketh me,
Than all the adulteries of art;
They strike mine eyes, but not my heart.
Epicoene (1609), I.i

28 Rest in soft peace, and, ask'd say here doth lye
Ben Jonson his best piece of poetrie.
Epigrams (1672), xlv. **On My First Son**

1 But that which most doth take my Muse and me,
Is a pure cup of rich Canary wine,
Which is the Mermaid's now, but shall be mine.
ci. **Inviting a Friend to Supper**

2 Weep with me, all you that read
    This little story:
And know for whom a tear you shed
    Death's self is sorry.
'Twas a child that so did thrive
    In grace and feature,
As Heaven and Nature seem'd to strive
    Which own'd the creature.
Years he number'd scarce thirteen
    When Fates turn'd cruel,
Yet three fill'd Zodiacs had he been
    The stage's jewel;
And did act, what now we moan,
    Old men so duly,
As sooth the Parcae thought him one,
    He play'd so truly.
So, by error, to his fate
    They all consented;
But viewing him since, alas, too late!
    They have repented;
And have sought (to give new birth)
    In baths to steep him;
But being so much too good for earth,
    Heaven vows to keep him.
cxx. **An Epitaph on Salomon Pavy, a Child of Queen Elizabeth's Chapel**

3 Underneath this stone doth lie
As much beauty as could die;
Which in life did harbour give
To more virtue than doth live.
cxxiv. **Epitaph on Elizabeth L.H.**

4 Helter skelter, hang sorrow, care'll kill a cat, up-tails all, and a louse for the hangman.
Every Man in His Humour (1598), I.iii

5 Ods me, I marvel what pleasure or felicity they have in taking their roguish tobacco. It is good for nothing but to choke a man, and fill him full of smoke and embers.
III.v

6 I do honour the very flea of his dog.
IV.ii

7 I have it here in black and white.

8 It must be done like lightning.
v

9 There shall be no love lost.
Every Man out of His Humour (1599), II.i

10   Blind Fortune still
Bestows her gifts on such as cannot use them.
ii

11 Follow a shadow, it still flies you,
    Seem to fly it, it will pursue:
So court a mistress, she denies you;
    Let her alone, she will court you.
Say, are not women truly, then,
Styl'd but the shadows of us men?
The Forest (1616), vii. **Song: That Women are but Men's Shadows**

12 Drink to me only with thine eyes,
    And I will pledge with mine;
Or leave a kiss but in the cup,

And I'll not look for wine.
The thirst that from the soul doth rise
    Doth ask a drink divine;
But might I of Jove's nectar sup,
    I would not change for thine.

I sent thee late a rosy wreath,
    Not so much honouring thee,
As giving it a hope that there
    It could not wither'd be.
ix. **To Celia**

13 Ramp up my genius, be not retrograde;
But boldly nominate a spade a spade.
The Poetaster (1601), v.i

14 Detraction is but baseness' varlet;
And apes are apes, though clothed in scarlet.

15 This is Mab, the Mistress-Fairy
That doth nightly rob the dairy.
The Satyr (1603)

16   Tell proud Jove,
Between his power and thine there is no odds:
'Twas only fear first in the world made gods.
Sejanus (1603), II.ii

17 This figure that thou here seest put,
It was for gentle Shakespeare cut,
Wherein the graver had a strife
With Nature, to out-do the life:
O could he but have drawn his wit
As well in brass, as he has hit
His face; the print would then surpass
All that was ever writ in brass:
But since he cannot, reader, look
Not on his picture, but his book.
On the Portrait of Shakespeare, To the Reader

18 While I confess thy writings to be such,
    As neither man, nor muse, can praise too much.
To the Memory of My Beloved, the Author, Mr. William Shakespeare

19   Soul of the Age!
The applause! delight! the wonder of our stage!
My Shakespeare, rise; I will not lodge thee by
    Chaucer, or Spenser, or bid Beaumont lie
A little further, to make thee a room:
    Thou art a monument, without a tomb,
And art alive still, while thy book doth live,
    And we have wits to read, and praise to give.

20 Marlowe's mighty line.

21 And though thou hadst small Latin, and less Greek.

22   To hear thy buskin tread,
And shake a stage: or, when thy socks were on,
    Leave thee alone, for the comparison
Of all that insolent Greece or haughty Rome
    Sent forth, or since did from their ashes come.

23 He was not of an age, but for all time!

24 For a good poet's made, as well as born.

25 Sweet Swan of Avon! what a sight it were
    To see thee in our waters yet appear,
And make those flights upon the banks of Thames,
    That so did take Eliza, and our James!

26 Well, they talk we shall have no more Parliaments,
    God bless us!
The Staple of News (1625), III.i

1 I remember the players have often mentioned it as an honour to Shakespeare that in his writing (whatsoever he penned) he never blotted out a line. My answer hath been 'Would he had blotted a thousand'. Which they thought a malevolent speech. I had not told posterity this, but for their ignorance, who chose that circumstance to commend their friend by wherein he most faulted; and to justify mine own candour: for I loved the man, and do honour his memory, on this side idolatry, as much as any. He was (indeed) honest, and of an open and free nature; had an excellent phantasy, brave notions, and gentle expressions; wherein he flowed with that facility, that sometimes it was necessary he should be stopped: *sufflaminandus erat,* as Augustus said of Haterius. His wit was in his own power, would the rule of it had been so too...But he redeemed his vices with his virtues. There was ever more in him to be praised than to be pardoned.
Timber, or Discoveries made upon Men and Matter (1641). **De Shakespeare Nostrati. Augustus in Haterium.** See 245:2

2 The fear of every man that heard him was, lest he should make an end. [Bacon.]
Dominus Verulamius

3 Talking and eloquence are not the same: to speak, and to speak well, are two things.
Praecept. Element

4 Have you seen but a bright lily grow,
    Before rude hands have touch'd it?
Have you mark'd but the fall o' the snow
    Before the soil hath smutch'd it?...
O so white! O so soft! O so sweet is she!
The Underwood (1640). **Celebration of Charis,** iv. **Her Triumph**

5 She is Venus when she smiles;
But she's Juno when she walks,
And Minerva when she talks.
v. **His Discourse with Cupid**

6 Greek was free from rhyme's infection,
Happy Greek, by this protection,
    Was not spoiled:
Whilst the Latin, queen of tongues,
Is not yet free from rhyme's wrongs,
    But rests foiled.
29. **A Fit of Rhyme against Rhyme**

7 England's high Chancellor: the destin'd heir,
In his soft cradle, to his father's chair.
51. **On Lord Bacon's [Sixtieth] Birthday**

8 It is not growing like a tree
In bulk, doth make men better be;
Or standing long an oak, three hundred year,
To fall a log at last, dry, bald, and sere:
    A lily of a day,
    Is fairer far in May,
Although it fall and die that night;
It was the plant and flower of light.
In small proportions we just beauties see;
And in short measures, life may perfect be.
70. **To the Immortal Memory...of...Sir Lucius Carey and Sir H. Morison**

9 What gentle ghost, besprent with April dew,
Hails me so solemnly to yonder yew?
83. **Elegy on the Lady Jane Pawlet**

10 The voice so sweet, the words so fair,
As some soft chime had stroked the air;

And though the sound were parted thence,
Still left an echo in the sense.
84. **Eupheme**

11 Calumnies are answered best with silence.
Volpone (1605), II.ii

12 Come, my Celia, let us prove,
While we can, the sports of love.
III.v. See 136:25

13 Suns, that set, may rise again;
But if once we lose this light,
'Tis with us perpetual night.

14 Our drink shall be prepared gold and amber;
Which we will take, until my roof whirl around
With the *vertigo:* and my dwarf shall dance.

15 You have a gift, sir, (thank your education,)
Will never let you want, while there are men,
And malice, to breed causes. [To a lawyer.]
V.i

16   Mischiefs feed
Like beasts, till they be fat, and then they bleed.
viii

17 His censure of the English poets was this...
That Donne...deserved hanging.
That Shakespeare wanted Art.
Conversations with William Drummond of Hawthornden (1619), III

THOMAS JORDAN 1612?–1685

18 They pluck't communion tables down
    And broke our painted glasses;
They threw our altars to the ground
    And tumbled down the crosses.
They set up Cromwell and his heir—
    The Lord and Lady Claypole—
Because they hated Common Prayer,
    The organ and the maypole.
How the War began (1664)

JOHN JORTIN 1698–1770

19 *Palmam qui meruit, ferat.*
Let him who has won it bear the palm.
Lusus Poetici (1722): **Ad Ventos.** Adopted as motto by Lord Nelson.

BENJAMIN JOWETT 1817–1893

20 One man is as good as another until he has written a book.
Abbott and Campbell, *Letters of B. Jowett* (1899), i.248

21 At Oxford, as you know, we follow the Cambridge lead, sometimes with uncertain steps.
Letter to Professor Marshall, 5 Jan. 1886

22 I hope our young men will not grow into such *dodgers* as these old men are. I believe everything a *young* man says to me. (Attr.)
'Notes and Sayings'

23 Nowhere probably is there more true feeling, and nowhere worse taste, than in a churchyard—both as regards the monuments and the inscriptions. Scarcely a word of true poetry anywhere.

24 Young men make great mistakes in life; for one thing, they idealize love too much.

1 My dear child, you must believe in God in spite of what the clergy tell you.
Private conversation with Margot Asquith, shortly after the near-fatal illness a year before his death. Asquith, *Autobiography*, ch.8

JAMES JOYCE 1882–1941

2 Riverrun, past Eve and Adam's, from swerve of shore to bend of bay, brings us by a commodius vicus of recirculation back to Howth Castle and Environs.
Finnegans Wake (1939), standard edition. Opening words.

3 That ideal reader suffering from an ideal insomnia.
p.120

4 When is a man not a man?...when he is a—yours till the rending of the rocks—Sham.
p.170

5 The flushpots of Euston and the hanging garments of Marylebone.
p.192

6   O
          tell me all about
       Anna Livia! I want to hear all
about Anna Livia. Well, you know Anna Livia?
Yes, of course, we all know Anna Livia. Tell me all.
Tell me now.
p.196

7 If you don't like my story get out of the punt.
p.206

8 Can't hear with the waters of. The chittering waters of. Flittering bats, fieldmice bawk talk. Ho! Are you not gone ahome?...Dark hawks hear us. Night! Night! My ho head halls. I feel as heavy as yonder stone...Beside the rivering waters of, hitherandthithering waters of. Night!
p.215

9 Quiet takes back her folded fields.
p.244

10 Loud, heap miseries upon us yet entwine our arts with laughters low!
p.259

11 All moanday, tearsday, wailsday, thumpsday, frightday, shatterday.
p.301

12 Three quarks for Muster Mark!
p.383

13 The Gracehoper was always jigging ajog, hoppy on akkant of his joyicity.
p.414

14 Soft morning, city!
p.619

15 Poor Parnell! he cried loudly. My dead King!
A Portrait of the Artist as a Young Man (1916), ch.1

16 Ireland is the old sow that eats her farrow.
ch.5

17 Pity is the feeling which arrests the mind in the presence of whatsoever is grave and constant in human sufferings and unites it with the human sufferer. Terror is the feeling which arrests the mind in the presence of whatsoever is grave and constant in human sufferings and unites it with the secret cause.

18 The mystery of esthetic like that of material creation is accomplished. The artist, like the God of the creation, remains within or behind or beyond or above his handiwork, invisible, refined out of existence, indifferent, paring his fingernails.

19 April 26...Welcome, O life! I go to encounter for the millionth time the reality of experience and to forge in the smithy of my soul the uncreated conscience of my race.
April 27. Old father, old artificer, stand me now and ever in good stead.
closing words

20 The snotgreen sea. The scrotumtightening sea.
Ulysses (1922). **Telemachus**

21 It is a symbol of Irish art. The cracked lookingglass of a servant.

22 I fear those big words, Stephen said, which make us so unhappy.
Nestor

23 History is a nightmare from which I am trying to awake.

24 Lawn Tennyson, gentleman poet.
Proteus

25 The statue of the onehandled adulterer. [Nelson.]
Aeolus

26 A base barreltone voice.
Lestrygonians

27 A man of genius makes no mistakes. His errors are volitional and are the portals of discovery.
Scylla and Charybdis

28 Greater love than this, he said, no man hath that a man lay down his wife for a friend. Go thou and do likewise. Thus, or words to that effect, saith Zarathustra, sometime regius professor of French letters to the University of Oxtail.
Oxen of the Sun

29 The heaventree of stars hung with humid nightblue fruit.
Ithaca

30 And I thought well as well him as another and then I asked him with my eyes to ask again yes and then he asked me would I yes to say yes my mountain flower and first I put my arms around him yes and drew him down to me so he could feel my breasts all perfume yes and his heart was going like mad and yes I said yes I will Yes.
Penelope, closing words

EMPEROR JULIAN THE APOSTATE c.332–363

31 *Vicisti, Galilaee.*
You have won, Galilean.
Supposed dying words; but a late embellishment of Theodoret, *Hist. Eccles.*, iii.25

DAME JULIAN OF NORWICH 1343–1443

32 Sin is behovely, but all shall be well and all shall be well and all manner of thing shall be well.
Revelations of Divine Love, ch.27

33 Wouldest thou wit thy Lord's meaning in this thing? Wit it well: Love was his meaning. Who shewed it thee? Love. What shewed He thee? Love. Wherefore shewed it He? for Love...Thus was I learned that Love

is our Lord's meaning.
ch.86

'JUNIUS' fl. 1770

1 The liberty of the press is the *Palladium* of all the civil, political, and religious rights of an Englishman.
Letters, Public Advertiser (1769–71), dedication

2 The right of election is the very essence of the constitution.
Letter 11, 24 Apr. 1769

3 Is this the wisdom of a great minister? or is it the ominous vibration of a pendulum?
Letter 12, 30 May 1769

4 There is a holy mistaken zeal in politics as well as in religion. By persuading others, we convince ourselves.
Letter 35, 19 Dec. 1769

5 Whether it be the heart to conceive, the understanding to direct, or the hand to execute.
Letter 37, 19 Mar. 1770. See 152:19

6 The injustice done to an individual is sometimes of service to the public.
Letter 41, 14 Nov. 1770

7 As for Mr Wedderburne, there is something about him, which even treachery cannot trust.
Letter 49, 22 June 1771

EMPEROR JUSTINIAN c.482–565

8 Justice is the constant and perpetual wish to render to every one his due.
Institutes, I.i.1

JUVENAL A.D. c.60–c.130

9 *Difficile est saturam non scribere.*
It's hard not to write satire.
Satires, i.30

10 *Probitas laudatur et alget.*
Honesty is praised and left to shiver.
i.74. Tr. G.G. Ramsay

11 *Si natura negat, facit indignatio versum.*
Even if nature says no, indignation makes me write verse.
79

12 *Quidquid agunt homines, votum timor ira voluptas Gaudia discursus nostri farrago libelli est.*
Everything mankind does, their hope, fear, rage, pleasure, joys, business, are the hotch-potch of my little book.
85

13 *Quis tulerit Gracchos de seditione querentes?*
Who would put up with the Gracchi complaining about subversion?
ii.24

14 *Nemo repente fuit turpissimus.*
No one ever suddenly became depraved.
83

15 *Iam pridem Syrus in Tiberim defluxit Orontes Et linguam et mores.*
The Syrian Orontes has now for long been pouring into the Tiber, with its own language and ways of behaving.

16 *Grammaticus, rhetor, geometres, pictor, aliptes,*

Augur, schoenobates, medicus, magus, omnia novit Graeculus esuriens: in caelum iusseris ibit.
Scholar, public speaker, geometrician, painter, physical training instructor, diviner of the future, rope-dancer, doctor, magician, the hungry little Greek can do everything: send him to—Heaven (and he'll go there).
iii.76

17 *Nil habet infelix paupertas durius in se Quam quod ridiculos homines facit.*
The misfortunes of poverty carry with them nothing harder to bear than that it exposes men to ridicule.
152

18 *Haud facile emergunt quorum virtutibus obstat Res angusta domi.*
It's not easy for people to rise out of obscurity when they have to face straitened circumstances at home.
164

19 *Omnia Romae Cum pretio.*
Everything in Rome is expensive.
183

20 *Rara avis in terris nigroque simillima cycno.*
A rare bird on this earth, like nothing so much as a black swan.
vi.165

21 *Hoc volo, sic iubeo, sit pro ratione voluntas.*
I will have this done, so I order it done; let my will replace reasoned judgement.
223

22 *'Pone seram, cohibe.' Sed quis custodiet ipsos Custodes? Cauta est et ab illis incipit uxor.*
'Bolt her in, keep her indoors.' But who is to guard the guards themselves? Your wife arranges accordingly and begins with them.
347

23 *Tenet insanabile multos Scribendi cacoethes et aegro in corde senescit.*
Many suffer from the incurable disease of writing, and it becomes chronic in their sick minds.
vii.51

24 *Occidit miseros crambe repetita magistros.*
That cabbage hashed up again and again proves the death of the wretched teachers.
154

25 *Summum crede nefas animam praeferre pudori Et propter vitam vivendi perdere causas.*
Count it the greatest sin to prefer mere existence to honour, and for the sake of life to lose the reasons for living.
viii.83

26 *Cantabit vacuus coram latrone viator.*
Travel light and you can sing in the robber's face.
x.22

27 *Verbosa et grandis epistula venit A Capreis.*
A huge wordy letter came from Capri.
71. The Emperor Tiberius's letter to the Senate that caused the downfall of Sejanus, A.D. 31.

28 *Duas tantum res anxius optat, Panem et circenses.*
Only two things does he worry about or long

for—bread and the big match.
80. Of the citizen these days.

1 *Expende Hannibalem: quot libras in duce summo*
Invenies?
Weigh Hannibal: how many pounds will you find in
that great general?
147

2 *I, demens, et saevas curre per Alpes*
Ut pueris placeas et declamatio fias.
Off you go, madman, and hurry across the horrible
Alps, duly to delight schoolboys and become a
subject for practising speech-making.
166

3   *Mors sola fatetur*
Quantula sint hominum corpuscula.
Death alone reveals how small are men's poor bodies.
172

4 *Orandum est ut sit mens sana in corpore sano.*
You should pray to have a sound mind in a sound
body.
356

5   *Prima est haec ultio, quod se*
Iudice nemo nocens absolvitur.
This is the first of punishments, that no guilty man is
acquitted if judged by himself.
xiii.2

6   *Quippe minuti*
Semper et infirmi est animi exiguique voluptas
Ultio. Continuo sic collige, quod vindicta
Nemo magis gaudet quam femina.
Indeed, it's always a paltry, feeble, tiny mind that
takes pleasure in revenge. You can deduce it
without further evidence than this, that no one
delights more in vengeance than a woman.
189

7 *Maxima debetur puero reverentia, siquid*
Turpe paras, nec tu pueri contempseris annos.
A child deserves the maximum respect; if you ever
have something disgraceful in mind, don't ignore
your son's tender years.
xiv.47

IMMANUEL KANT 1724–1804

8 Two things fill the mind with ever new and increasing
wonder and awe, the more often and the more
seriously reflection concentrates upon them: the starry
heaven above me and the moral law within me.
Critique of Practical Reason, conclusion

9 *Ich soll niemals anders verfahren, als so, dass ich*
auch wollen könne, meine Maxime solle ein
allgemeines Gesetz werden.
I am never to act otherwise than so *that I could also*
will that my maxim should become a universal law.
Grundlegung zur Metaphysik der Sitten, trans. T.K. Abbott,
Section I

10 *Endlich gibt es einen Imperativ, der, ohne irgend eine*
andere durch ein gewisses Verhalten zu erreichende
Absicht als Bedingung zum Grunde zu legen, dieses
Verhalten unmittelbar gebietet. Dieser Imperativ ist
kategorisch…Dieser Imperativ mag der der
Sittlichkeit heissen.
Finally, there is an imperative which commands a
certain conduct immediately, without having as its
condition any other purpose to be attained by it. This

imperative is Categorical…This imperative may be
called that of Morality.
Section II

11 *Wer den Zweck will, will (so fern die Vernunft auf*
seine Handlungen entscheidenden Einfluss hat) auch
das dazu unentbehrlich notwendige Mittel, das in
seiner Gewalt ist.
Whoever wills the end, wills also (so far as reason
decides his conduct) the means in his power which are
indispensably necessary thereto.

12 *…weil Glückseligkeit nicht ein Ideal der Vernunft,*
sondern der Einbildung ist.
…because happiness is not an ideal of reason but of
imagination.

13 *Handle so, dass du die Menschheit, sowohl in deiner*
Person, als in der Person eines jeden andern, jederzeit
zugleich als Zweck, niemals bloss als Mittel brauchest.
So act as to treat humanity, whether in thine own
person or in that of any other, in every case as an end
withal, never as means only.

14 *Aus so krummem Holze, als woraus der Mensch*
gemacht ist, kann nichts ganz gerades gezimmert
werden.
Out of the crooked timber of humanity no straight
thing can ever be made.
Idee zu einer allgemeinen Geschichte in weltbürgerlicher
Absicht

ALPHONSE KARR 1808–1890

15 *Plus ça change, plus c'est la même chose.*
The more things change, the more they are the same.
Les Guêpes, Jan. 1849. vi

16 *Si l'on veut abolir la peine de mort en ce cas, que MM*
les assassins commencent.
If we are to abolish the death penalty, I should like to
see the first step taken by our friends the murderers.

CHRISTOPH KAUFMANN 1753–1795

17 *Sturm und Drang.*
Storm and stress.
Phrase suggested to F.M. Klinger (1752–1831) as a better title for
his play originally called *Der Wirrwarr*, the suggestion was
adopted, the play produced in 1777, and a literary period was thus
named.

DENIS KEARNEY 1847–1907

18 Horny-handed sons of toil.
Speech, San Francisco, c.1878. See 319:9

JOHN KEATS 1795–1821

19 The imagination of a boy is healthy, and the mature
imagination of a man is healthy; but there is a space of
life between, in which the soul is in a ferment, the
character undecided, the way of life uncertain, the
ambition thick-sighted: thence proceeds mawkishness.
Endymion (1818), preface

20 A thing of beauty is a joy for ever:
Its loveliness increases; it will never
Pass into nothingness; but still will keep
A bower quiet for us, and a sleep
Full of sweet dreams, and health, and quiet breathing.
bk.i, l.1

1   The grandeur of the dooms
We have imagined for the mighty dead.
1.20

2 They must be always with us, or we die.
1.33

3   Who, of men, can tell
That flowers would bloom, or that green fruit would
     swell
To melting pulp, that fish would have bright mail,
The earth its dower of river, wood, and vale,
The meadows runnels, runnels pebble-stones,
The seed its harvest, or the lute its tones,
Tones ravishment, or ravishment its sweet
If human souls did never kiss and greet?
1.835

4   Here is wine,
Alive with sparkles—never, I aver,
Since Ariadne was a vintager,
So cool a purple.
bk.ii, 1.442

5 To Sorrow,
     I bade good-morrow,
And thought to leave her far away behind;
     But cheerly, cheerly,
     She loves me dearly;
She is so constant to me, and so kind.
bk.iv, 1.173

6   Their smiles,
Wan as primroses gather'd at midnight
By chilly finger'd spring.
1.969

7 Sweet are the pleasures that to verse belong,
And doubly sweet a brotherhood in song.
Epistle to G.F. Mathew

8   It is a flaw
In happiness, to see beyond our bourn,—
It forces us in summer skies to mourn,
It spoils the singing of the nightingale.
Epistle to J.H. Reynolds, 1.82

9 St Agnes' Eve—Ah, bitter chill it was!
The owl, for all his feathers, was a-cold;
The hare limp'd trembling through the frozen grass,
And silent was the flock in woolly fold.
The Eve of Saint Agnes, 1

10 The sculptur'd dead on each side seem to freeze,
Emprison'd in black, purgatorial rails.
2

11 The silver, snarling trumpets 'gan to chide.
4

12 Soft adorings from their loves receive
Upon the honey'd middle of the night.
6

13 The music, yearning like a God in pain.
7

14 A poor, weak, palsy-stricken, churchyard thing.
18

15 Out went the taper as she hurried in;
Its little smoke, in pallid moonshine, died.
23

16 A casement high and triple-arch'd there was,
All garlanded with carven imag'ries
Of fruits, and flowers, and bunches of knot-grass,
And diamonded with panes of quaint device,

Innumerable of stains and splendid dyes,
As are the tiger-moth's deep-damask'd wings.
24

17   By degrees
Her rich attire creeps rustling to her knees.
26

18 Her soft and chilly nest.
27

19 As though a rose should shut, and be a bud again.

20 And still she slept an azure-lidded sleep,
In blanched linen, smooth, and lavender'd,
While he from forth the closet brought a heap
Of candied apple, quince, and plum, and gourd,
With jellies soother than the creamy curd,
And lucent syrops, tinct with cinnamon;
Manna and dates, in argosy transferr'd
From Fez; and spiced dainties, every one,
From silken Samarcand to cedar'd Lebanon.
30

21 He play'd an ancient ditty, long since mute,
In Provence call'd, 'La belle dame sans mercy'.
33

22 And the long carpets rose along the gusty floor.
40

23 And they are gone: aye, ages long ago
These lovers fled away into the storm.
42

24 The Beadsman, after thousand aves told,
For aye unsought-for slept among his ashes cold.

25 Dry your eyes—O dry your eyes,
For I was taught in Paradise
To ease my breast of melodies.
Fairy's Song

26 Fanatics have their dreams, wherewith they weave
A paradise for a sect.
The Fall of Hyperion, 1.1

27 'None can usurp this height', return'd that shade,
'But those to whom the miseries of the world
Are misery, and will not let them rest.'
1.147

28 The poet and the dreamer are distinct,
Diverse, sheer opposite, antipodes.
The one pours out a balm upon the world,
The other vexes it.
1.199

29 Ever let the fancy roam,
Pleasure never is at home.
Fancy, 1.1

30 O sweet Fancy! let her loose;
Summer's joys are spoilt by use.
1.9

31 Where's the cheek that doth not fade,
Too much gaz'd at? Where's the maid
Whose lip mature is ever new?
1.69

32   Where's the face
One would meet in every place?
1.73

33 Deep in the shady sadness of a vale
Far sunken from the healthy breath of morn,
Far from the fiery noon, and eve's one star,

Sat gray-hair'd Saturn, quiet as a stone.
Hyperion, bk.i, l.1

1   No stir of air was there,
Not so much life as on a summer's day
Robs not one light seed from the feather'd grass,
But where the dead leaf fell, there did it rest.
l.7

2   The Naiad 'mid her reeds
Press'd her cold finger closer to her lips.
l.13

3 That large utterance of the early Gods.
l.51

4 O aching time! O moments big as years!
l.64

5 As when, upon a trancèd summer-night,
Those green-rob'd senators of mighty woods,
Tall oaks, branch-charmèd by the earnest stars,
Dream, and so dream all night without a stir.
l.72

6   Sometimes eagle's wings,
Unseen before by Gods or wondering men,
Darken'd the place.
l.182

7 And still they were the same bright, patient stars.
l.353

8 Knowledge enormous makes a God of me.
bk.iii, l.113

9   Why were they proud? again we ask aloud,
Why in the name of Glory were they proud?
Isabella, 16

10 So the two brothers and their murder'd man
        Rode past fair Florence.
27

11 And she forgot the stars, the moon, the sun,
        And she forgot the blue above the trees,
And she forgot the dells where waters run,
        And she forgot the chilly autumn breeze;
She had no knowledge when the day was done,
        And the new morn she saw not: but in peace
Hung over her sweet Basil evermore.
53

12   'For cruel 'tis,' said she,
'To steal my Basil-pot away from me.'
62

13   And then there crept
A little noiseless noise among the leaves,
Born of the very sigh that silence heaves.
I Stood Tip-toe upon a Little Hill

14 Here are sweet peas, on tiptoe for a flight.

15 Oh, what can ail thee, Knight at arms
        Alone and palely loitering;
The sedge is wither'd from the lake,
        And no birds sing.
La Belle Dame Sans Merci

16 I see a lily on thy brow,
        With anguish moist and fever dew;
And on thy cheek a fading rose
        Fast withereth too.

I met a lady in the meads
        Full beautiful, a faery's child;
Her hair was long, her foot was light,
        And her eyes were wild.

17 I set her on my pacing steed,
        And nothing else saw all day long;
For sideways would she lean, and sing
        A faery's song.

18 She look'd at me as she did love,
        And made sweet moan.

19 And sure in language strange she said,
        'I love thee true!'

20 And there I shut her wild, wild eyes
        With kisses four.

21   'La belle Dame sans Merci
        Hath thee in thrall!'

I saw their starv'd lips in the gloam
        With horrid warning gapèd wide,
And I awoke, and found me here
        On the cold hill side.

22 She was a gordian shape of dazzling hue,
Vermilion-spotted, golden, green, and blue;
Striped like a zebra, freckled like a pard,
Eyed like a peacock, and all crimson barr'd.
Lamia, pt.i, l.47

23 Real are the dreams of Gods, and smoothly pass
Their pleasures in a long immortal dream.
l.127

24 Love in a hut, with water and a crust,
Is—Love, forgive us!—cinders, ashes, dust;
Love in a palace is perhaps at last
More grievous torment than a hermit's fast.
pt.ii, l.1

25 That purple-lined palace of sweet sin.
l.31

26 In pale contented sort of discontent.
l.135

27   Do not all charms fly
At the mere touch of cold philosophy?
There was an awful rainbow once in heaven:
We know her woof, her texture; she is given
In the dull catalogue of common things.
Philosophy will clip an Angel's wings.
l.229

28 Souls of poets dead and gone,
What Elysium have ye known,
Happy field or mossy cavern,
Choicer than the Mermaid Tavern?
Have ye tippled drink more fine
Than mine host's Canary wine?
Lines on the Mermaid Tavern

29 Pledging with contented smack
The Mermaid in the Zodiac.

30 This living hand, now warm and capable
Of earnest grasping, would, if it were cold
And in the icy silence of the tomb,
So haunt thy days and chill thy dreaming nights
That thou wouldst wish thine own heart dry of blood
So in my veins red life might stream again,
And thus be conscience-calm'd—see here it is—
I hold it towards you.
Lines Supposed to have been Addressed to Fanny Brawne

31 Bards of Passion and of Mirth,
Ye have left your souls on earth!

Have ye souls in heaven too?
Ode. Written on the blank page before Beaumont and Fletcher's
Fair Maid of the Inn.

1 Where the nightingale doth sing
   Not a senseless, tranced thing,
   But divine melodious truth.

2 Thou still unravish'd bride of quietness,
     Thou foster-child of silence and slow time.
   Ode on a Grecian Urn

3   What men or gods are these? What maidens loth?
   What mad pursuit? What struggle to escape?
     What pipes and timbrels? What wild ecstasy?

4 Heard melodies are sweet, but those unheard
     Are sweeter; therefore, ye soft pipes, play on;
   Not to the sensual ear, but, more endear'd,
     Pipe to the spirit ditties of no tone.

5 For ever wilt thou love, and she be fair!

6 For ever piping songs for ever new.

7   For ever warm and still to be enjoy'd,
        For ever panting and for ever young;
   All breathing human passion far above,
        That leaves a heart high-sorrowful and cloy'd,
          A burning forehead, and a parching tongue.

8 Who are these coming to the sacrifice?
     To what green altar, O mysterious priest,
   Lead'st thou that heifer lowing at the skies,
     And all her silken flanks with garlands drest?
   What little town by river or sea shore,
     Or mountain-built with peaceful citadel,
   Is emptied of this folk, this pious morn?

9 O Attic shape! Fair attitude!

10 Thou, silent form, dost tease us out of thought
     As doth eternity: Cold Pastoral!

11 'Beauty is truth, truth beauty,'—that is all
     Ye know on earth, and all ye need to know.

12 Rich in the simple worship of a day.
   Ode to May

13 No, no, go not to Lethe, neither twist
     Wolf's-bane, tight-rooted, for its poisonous wine.
   Ode on Melancholy

14 Nor let the beetle, nor the death-moth be
     Your mournful Psyche.

15 But when the melancholy fit shall fall
     Sudden from heaven like a weeping cloud,
   That fosters the droop-headed flowers all,
     And hides the green hill in an April shroud;
   Then glut thy sorrow on a morning rose,
     Or on the rainbow of the salt sand-wave,
       Or on the wealth of globèd peonies.
   Or if thy mistress some rich anger shows,
     Emprison her soft hand and let her rave,
       And feed deep, deep upon her peerless eyes.

She dwells with Beauty—Beauty that must die;
  And Joy, whose hand is ever at his lips
Bidding adieu; and aching Pleasure nigh,
  Turning to Poison while the bee-mouth sips:
Ay, in the very temple of delight
  Veil'd Melancholy has her sovran shrine.
    Though seen of none save him whose strenuous
      tongue
Can burst Joy's grape against his palate fine;

His soul shall taste the sadness of her might,
  And be among her cloudy trophies hung.

16 My heart aches, and a drowsy numbness pains
     My sense, as though of hemlock I had drunk.
   Ode to a Nightingale

17 'Tis not through envy of thy happy lot,
     But being too happy in thine happiness,—
       That thou, light-winged Dryad of the trees,
         In some melodious plot
   Of beechen green, and shadows numberless,
     Singest of summer in full-throated ease.

18 O, for a draught of vintage! that hath been
     Cool'd a long age in the deep-delved earth,
   Tasting of Flora and the country green,
     Dance, and Provençal song, and sunburnt mirth!
   O for a beaker full of the warm South,
     Full of the true, the blushful Hippocrene,
       With beaded bubbles winking at the brim,
         And purple-stained mouth;
   That I might drink, and leave the world unseen,
     And with thee fade away into the forest dim.

Fade far away, dissolve, and quite forget
  What thou among the leaves hast never known,
The weariness, the fever, and the fret,
  Here, where men sit and hear each other groan.

19   Where youth grows pale, and spectre-thin, and dies.
        Where but to think is to be full of sorrow
          And leaden-eyed despairs.

20 Away! away! for I will fly to thee,
     Not charioted by Bacchus and his pards,
   But on the viewless wings of Poesy,
     Though the dull brain perplexes and retards:
   Already with thee! tender is the night,
     And haply the Queen-Moon is on her throne,
       Clustered around by all her starry Fays;
         But here there is no light,
   Save what from heaven is with the breezes blown
     Through verdurous glooms and winding mossy
       ways.

I cannot see what flowers are at my feet,
  Nor what soft incense hangs upon the boughs.

21   Fast fading violets cover'd up in leaves;
        And mid-May's eldest child,
   The coming musk-rose, full of dewy wine,
     The murmurous haunt of flies on summer eves.

22 Darkling I listen; and, for many a time
     I have been half in love with easeful Death,
   Call'd him soft names in many a mused rhyme,
     To take into the air my quiet breath;
   Now more than ever seems it rich to die,
     To cease upon the midnight with no pain,
       While thou art pouring forth thy soul abroad
         In such an ecstasy!
   Still wouldst thou sing, and I have ears in vain—
     To thy high requiem become a sod.

23 Thou wast not born for death, immortal Bird!
     No hungry generations tread thee down;
   The voice I hear this passing night was heard
     In ancient days by emperor and clown:
   Perhaps the self-same song that found a path
     Through the sad heart of Ruth, when sick for home,
       She stood in tears amid the alien corn;

The same that oft-times hath
Charm'd magic casements, opening on the foam
Of perilous seas, in faery lands forlorn.

Forlorn! the very word is like a bell
To toll me back from thee to my sole self!
Adieu! the fancy cannot cheat so well
As she is fam'd to do, deceiving elf.
Adieu! adieu! thy plaintive anthem fades
Past the near meadows, over the still stream,
Up the hill-side; and now 'tis buried deep
In the next valley-glades:
Was it a vision, or a waking dream?
Fled is that music:—Do I wake or sleep?

1 'Mid hush'd, cool-rooted flowers, fragrant-eyed,
Blue, silver-white, and budded Tyrian.
Ode to Psyche

2 Nor virgin-choir to make delicious moan
Upon the midnight hour.

3 Yes, I will be thy priest, and build a fane
In some untrodden region of my mind,
Where branched thoughts, new grown with pleasant pain,
Instead of pines shall murmur in the wind.

4 A bright torch, and a casement ope at night,
To let the warm Love in!

5 O fret not after knowledge—I have none,
And yet my song comes native with the warmth.
O fret not after knowledge—I have none,
And yet the Evening listens.
O Thou Whose Face

6 Stop and consider! life is but a day;
A fragile dew-drop on its perilous way
From a tree's summit; a poor Indian's sleep
While his boat hastens to the monstrous steep
Of Montmorenci.
Sleep and Poetry, 1.85

7 O for ten years, that I may overwhelm
Myself in poesy; so I may do the deed
That my own soul has to itself decreed.
1.96

8 They sway'd about upon a rocking horse,
And thought it Pegasus.
1.186

9 They shall be accounted poet kings
Who simply tell the most heart-easing things.
1.267

10 I had a dove and the sweet dove died;
And I have thought it died of grieving:
O, what could it grieve for? Its feet were tied,
With a silken thread of my own hand's weaving.
Song

11 Bright star, would I were steadfast as thou art—
Not in lone splendour hung aloft the night
And watching, with eternal lids apart,
Like nature's patient, sleepless Eremite,
The moving waters at their priestlike task
Of pure ablution round earth's human shores.
Sonnets. Bright Star

12 Still, still to hear her tender-taken breath,
And so live ever—or else swoon to death.

13 The day is gone, and all its sweets are gone!
Sweet voice, sweet lips, soft hand, and softer
breast.
The Day Is Gone

14 Four seasons fill the measure of the year;
There are four seasons in the mind of men.
Four Seasons

15 Happy is England! I could be content
To see no other verdure than its own;
To feel no other breezes than are blown
Through its tall woods with high romances blent.
Happy is England!

16 Happy is England, sweet her artless daughters;
Enough their simple loveliness for me.

17 Much have I travell'd in the realms of gold,
And many goodly states and kingdoms seen.
On First Looking into Chapman's Homer

18 Then felt I like some watcher of the skies
When a new planet swims into his ken;
Or like stout Cortez when with eagle eyes
He star'd at the Pacific—and all his men
Look'd at each other with a wild surmise—
Silent, upon a peak in Darien.

19 Mortality
Weighs heavily on me like unwilling sleep.
On Seeing the Elgin Marbles

20 Yet the sweet converse of an innocent mind,
Whose words are images of thought refin'd,
Is my soul's pleasure; and it sure must be
Almost the highest bliss of human-kind,
When to thy haunts two kindred spirits flee.
O Solitude!

21 The poetry of earth is never dead:
When all the birds are faint with the hot sun,
And hide in cooling trees, a voice will run
From hedge to hedge about the new-mown mead.
On the Grasshopper and Cricket

22 It keeps eternal whisperings around
Desolate shores, and with its mighty swell
Gluts twice ten thousand Caverns.
On the Sea

23 O Chatterton! how very sad thy fate!
To Chatterton

24 Other spirits there are standing apart
Upon the forehead of the age to come.
To Haydon, ii

25 Aye on the shores of darkness there is light,
And precipices show untrodden green,
There is a budding morrow in midnight,
There is a triple sight in blindness keen.
To Homer

26 Glory and loveliness have pass'd away.
To Leigh Hunt. Dedication of *Poems*, 1817

27 To one who has been long in city pent;
'Tis very sweet to look into the fair
And open face of heaven.
To One Who Has Been Long

28 O soft embalmer of the still midnight,
Shutting, with careful fingers and benign,
Our gloom-pleas'd eyes.
To Sleep

29 Turn the key deftly in the oiled wards,
And seal the hushed Casket of my Soul.

30 When I have fears that I may cease to be

Before my pen has glean'd my teeming brain.
When I Have Fears

1 When I behold upon the night's starr'd face,
   Huge cloudy symbols of a high romance.

2   Then on the shore
   Of the wide world I stand alone, and think
   Till love and fame to nothingness do sink.

3 In a drear-nighted December,
      Too happy, happy tree,
   Thy branches ne'er remember
      Their green felicity.
   Stanzas

4 But were there ever any
         Writh'd not at passing joy?
   To know the change and feel it,
   When there is none to heal it,
   Nor numbed sense to steel it,
         Was never said in rhyme.

5 Season of mists and mellow fruitfulness,
      Close bosom-friend of the maturing sun;
   Conspiring with him how to load and bless
      With fruit the vines that round the thatch-eaves run.
   To Autumn

6 Who hath not seen thee oft amid thy store?
      Sometimes whoever seeks abroad may find
   Thee sitting careless on a granary floor,
      Thy hair soft-lifted by the winnowing wind;
   Or on a half-reap'd furrow sound asleep,
      Drows'd with the fume of poppies, while thy hook
      Spares the next swath and all its twined flowers.

7 Where are the songs of Spring? Ay, where are they?
   Think not of them, thou hast thy music too.

8 Then in a wailful choir the small gnats mourn
      Among the river sallows, borne aloft
      Or sinking as the light wind lives or dies.

9 The red-breast whistles from a garden-croft;
   And gathering swallows twitter in the skies.

10 Woman! when I behold thee flippant, vain,
   Inconstant, childish, proud, and full of fancies.
   Woman! When I Behold Thee

11 I remember your saying that you had notions of a good
   Genius presiding over you. I have of late had the same
   thought—for things which [I] do half at random are
   afterwards confirmed by my judgment in a dozen
   features of propriety. Is it too daring to fancy
   Shakespeare this Presider?
   Letters. To B.R. Haydon, 10/11 May 1817

12 I am quite disgusted with literary men.
   To Benjamin Bailey, 8 Oct. 1817

13 A long poem is a test of invention which I take to be
   the Polar star of poetry, as fancy is the sails, and
   imagination the rudder.

14 A man should have the fine point of his soul taken off
   to become fit for this world.
   To J.H. Reynolds, 22 Nov. 1817

15 I am certain of nothing but the holiness of the heart's
   affections and the truth of imagination—what the
   imagination seizes as beauty must be truth—whether it
   existed before or not.
   To Benjamin Bailey, 22 Nov. 1817

16 I have never yet been able to perceive how anything

can be known for truth by consecutive reasoning—and
yet it must be.

17 O for a life of sensations rather than of thoughts!

18 The excellency of every art is its intensity, capable of
   making all disagreeables evaporate, from their being in
   close relationship with beauty and truth.
   To G. and T. Keats, 21 Dec. 1817

19 Negative Capability, that is, when a man is capable of
   being in uncertainties, mysteries, doubts, without any
   irritable reaching after fact and reason—Coleridge, for
   instance, would let go by a fine isolated verisimilitude
   caught from the Penetralium of mystery, from being
   incapable of remaining content with half-knowledge.

20 There is nothing stable in the world; uproar's your
   only music.
   To G. and T. Keats, 13 Jan. 1818

21 So I do believe…that works of genius are the first
   things in this world.

22 For the sake of a few fine imaginative or domestic
   passages, are we to be bullied into a certain philosophy
   engendered in the whims of an egotist.
   To J.H. Reynolds, 3 Feb. 1818

23 We hate poetry that has a palpable design upon
   us—and if we do not agree, seems to put its hand in its
   breeches pocket. Poetry should be great and
   unobtrusive, a thing which enters into one's soul, and
   does not startle or amaze it with itself, but with its
   subject.

24 Poetry should surprise by a fine excess, and not by
   singularity; it should strike the reader as a wording of
   his own highest thoughts, and appear almost a
   remembrance. Its touches of beauty should never be
   half-way, thereby making the reader breathless, instead
   of content. The rise, the progress, the setting of
   imagery should, like the sun, come natural to him.
   To John Taylor, 27 Feb. 1818

25 If poetry comes not as naturally as leaves to a tree it
   had better not come at all.

26 I have good reason to be content, for thank God I can
   read and perhaps understand Shakespeare to his
   depths.

27 Scenery is fine—but human nature is finer.
   To Benjamin Bailey, 13 Mar. 1818

28 It is impossible to live in a country which is
   continually under hatches…Rain! Rain! Rain!
   To J.H. Reynolds, 10 Apr. 1818 (from Devon)

29 I have been hovering for some time between the
   exquisite sense of the luxurious and a love for
   philosophy—were I calculated for the former I should
   be glad—but as I am not I shall turn all my soul to the
   latter.
   To John Taylor, 24 Apr. 1818

30 Axioms in philosophy are not axioms until they are
   proved upon our pulses: we read fine things but never
   feel them to the full until we have gone the same steps
   as the author.
   To J.H. Reynolds, 3 May 1818

31 I am in that temper that if I were under water I would
   scarcely kick to come to the top.
   To Benjamin Bailey, 21 May 1818

32 Were it in my choice I would reject a petrarchal

coronation—on account of my dying day, and because women have cancers.
To Benjamin Bailey, 10 June 1818

1 I do think better of womankind than to suppose they care whether Mister John Keats five feet high likes them or not.
To Benjamin Bailey, 18 July 1818

2 I wish I could say Tom was any better. His identity presses upon me so all day that I am obliged to go out.
Of his youngest brother. To C.W. Dilke, 21 Sept. 1818

3 I never was in love—yet the voice and the shape of a woman has haunted me these two days.
To J.H. Reynolds, 22 Sept. 1818

4 There is an awful warmth about my heart like a load of immortality.

5 In Endymion, I leaped headlong into the sea, and thereby have become better acquainted with the soundings, the quicksands, and the rocks, than if I had stayed upon the green shore, and piped a silly pipe, and took tea and comfortable advice.
To James Hessey, 9 Oct. 1818

6 I would sooner fail than not be among the greatest.

7 As to the poetical character itself (I mean that sort of which, if I am anything, I am a member; that sort distinguished from the Wordsworthian or egotistical sublime; which is a thing *per se* and stands alone) it is not itself—it has no self...It has as much delight in conceiving an Iago as an Imogen.
To Richard Woodhouse, 27 Oct. 1818

8 A poet is the most unpoetical of anything in existence, because he has no identity; he is continually informing [?] and filling some other body.

9 I think I shall be among the English Poets after my death.
To George and Georgiana Keats, 14 Oct. 1818

10 The roaring of the wind is my wife and the stars through the window pane are my children. The mighty abstract idea I have of beauty in all things stifles the more divided and minute domestic happiness...The opinion I have of the generality of women—who appear to me as children to whom I would rather give a sugar plum than my time, forms a barrier against matrimony which I rejoice in.

11 I never can feel certain of any truth but from a clear perception of its beauty.
To George and Georgiana Keats, 16 Dec. 1818–4 Jan. 1819

12 A man's life of any worth is a continual allegory.
To George and Georgiana Keats, 18 Feb. 1819

13 Shakespeare led a life of allegory: his works are the comments on it.

14 I have come to this resolution—never to write for the sake of writing or making a poem, but from running over with any little knowledge or experience which many years of reflection may perhaps give me; otherwise I shall be dumb.
To B.R. Haydon, 8 Mar. 1819

15 It is true that in the height of enthusiasm I have been cheated into some fine passages: but that is not the thing.

16 I should like the window to open onto the Lake of Geneva—and there I'd sit and read all day like the picture of somebody reading.
To Fanny Keats, 13 Mar. 1819

17 I go among the fields and catch a glimpse of a stoat or a fieldmouse peeping out of the withered grass—The creature hath a purpose and its eyes are bright with it—I go amongst the buildings of a city and I see a man hurrying along—to what? The Creature has a purpose and his eyes are bright with it.
To George and Georgiana Keats, 19 Mar. 1819

18 Nothing ever becomes real till it is experienced—even a proverb is no proverb to you till your life has illustrated it.

19 Call the world if you please 'The vale of Soul-making'.

20 I have met with women whom I really think would like to be married to a poem, and to be given away by a novel.
To Fanny Brawne, 8 July 1819

21 I have two luxuries to brood over in my walks, your loveliness and the hour of my death. O that I could have possession of them both in the same minute.
To Fanny Brawne, 25 July 1819

22 My friends should drink a dozen of Claret on my Tomb.
To Benjamin Bailey, 14 Aug. 1819

23 I am convinced more and more day by day that fine writing is next to fine doing, the top thing in the world.
To. J.H. Reynolds, 24 Aug. 1819

24 Give me books, fruit, french wine and fine weather and a little music out of doors, played by somebody I do not know.
To Fanny Keats, 29 Aug. 1819

25 All clean and comfortable I sit down to write.
To George and Georgiana Keats, 17 Sept. 1819

26 The only means of strengthening one's intellect is to make up one's mind about nothing—to let the mind be a thoroughfare for all thoughts. Not a select party.

27 You have ravished me away by a power I cannot resist; and yet I could resist till I saw you; and even since I have seen you I have endeavoured often 'to reason against the reason of my Love'.
To Fanny Brawne, 13 Oct. 1819

28 'If I should die', said I to myself, 'I have left no immortal work behind me—nothing to make my friends proud of my memory—but I have loved the principle of beauty in all things, and if I had had time I would have made myself remembered.'
To Fanny Brawne, Feb. 1820?

29 I long to believe in immortality...If I am destined to be happy with you here—how short is the longest life. I wish to believe in immortality—I wish to live with you for ever.
To Fanny Brawne, July 1820

30 I wish you could invent some means to make me at all happy without you. Every hour I am more and more concentrated in you; every thing else tastes like chaff in my mouth.
To Fanny Brawne, Aug. 1820

31 You, I am sure, will forgive me for sincerely remarking that you might curb your magnanimity, and be more of an artist, and load every rift of your subject

with ore.
To Shelley, Aug. 1820

1 He already seemed to feel the flowers growing over him.
Words reported by Severn. W. Sharp, *Life and Letters of Severn*, ch.4

2 I shall soon be laid in the quiet grave—thank God for the quiet grave—O! I can feel the cold earth upon me—the daisies growing over me—O for this quiet—it will be my first.
Joseph Severn, letter to John Taylor, 6 Mar. 1821

3 Here lies one whose name was writ in water.
Epitaph. Lord Houghton, *Life of Keats*, ii.91

JOHN KEBLE 1792–1866

4 The trivial round, the common task,
Would furnish all we ought to ask;
Room to deny ourselves; a road
To bring us, daily, nearer God.
The Christian Year (1827). **Morning**

5 There is a book, who runs may read,
Which heavenly truth imparts,
And all the lore its scholars need,
Pure eyes and Christian hearts.
Septuagesima

6 The voice that breathed o'er Eden.
Holy Matrimony

GEORGE KEITH, 5th EARL MARISCHAL 1553–1623

7 They haif said: Quhat say they? Lat thame say.
Motto of the Earls Marischal of Scotland, inscribed at Marischal College, founded by the fifth Earl at Aberdeen in 1593. A similarly defiant motto in Greek has been found engraved in remains from classical antiquity.

FRANK B. KELLOGG 1856–1937

8 The high contracting parties solemnly declare in the names of their respective peoples that they condemn recourse to war for the solution of international controversies, and renounce it as an instrument of national policy in their relations with one another. The high contracting parties agree that the settlement or solution of all disputes or conflicts of whatever nature or of whatever origin they may be, which may rise among them, shall never be sought except by pacific means.
Peace Pact, signed at Paris, 27 Aug. 1928

THOMAS À KEMPIS
See THOMAS

BISHOP THOMAS KEN 1637–1711

9 Teach me to live, that I may dread
The grave as little as my bed.
Evening Hymn. Glory to Thee My God This Night

JOHN FITZGERALD KENNEDY 1917–1963

10 And so, my fellow Americans: ask not what your country can do for you—ask what you can do for your country. My fellow citizens of the world: ask not what America will do for you, but what together we can do

for the freedom of man.
Inaugural address, 20 Jan. 1961. Not the first use of this form of words: a similiar exhortation may be found in the funeral oration for John Greenleaf Whittier.

11 All free men, wherever they may live, are citizens of Berlin. And therefore, as a free man, I take pride in the words *Ich bin ein Berliner*.
Speech at City Hall, West Berlin, 26 June 1963

LADY CAROLINE KEPPEL 1735–?

12 What's this dull town to me?
Robin's not near.
He whom I wished to see,
Wished for to hear;
Where's all the joy and mirth
Made life a heaven on earth?
O! they're all fled with thee,
Robin Adair.
Robin Adair

RALPH KETTELL 1563–1643

13 Here is Hey for Garsington! and Hey for Cuddesdon! and Hey Hockley! but here's nobody cries, Hey for God Almighty!
Sermon at Garsington Revel. Aubrey, *Brief Lives*

FRANCIS SCOTT KEY 1779–1843

14 'Tis the star-spangled banner; O long may it wave
O'er the land of the free, and the home of the brave!
The Star-Spangled Banner (1814)

J.M. KEYNES 1883–1946

15 I do not know which makes a man more conservative—to know nothing but the present, or nothing but the past.
The End of Laisser-Faire (1926), I

16 Marxian Socialism must always remain a portent to the historians of Opinion—how a doctrine so illogical and so dull can have exercised so powerful and enduring an influence over the minds of men, and, through them, the events of history.
III

17 The important thing for Government is not to do things which individuals are doing already, and to do them a little better or a little worse; but to do those things which at present are not done at all.
IV. See 365:22, 549:31

18 I think that Capitalism, wisely managed, can probably be made more efficient for attaining economic ends than any alternative system yet in sight, but that in itself it is in many ways extremely objectionable.
V

19 This goat-footed bard, this half-human visitor to our age from the hag-ridden magic and enchanted woods of Celtic antiquity. [Lloyd George.]
Essays and Sketches in Biography (1933)

20 Practical men, who believe themselves to be quite exempt from any intellectual influences, are usually the slaves of some defunct economist. Madmen in authority, who hear voices in the air, are distilling their frenzy from some academic scribbler of a few

years back.
The General Theory of Employment Interest and Money
(1936), ch.24.v

1 There are the *Trade-Unionists*, once the oppressed,
 now the tyrants, whose selfish and sectional
 pretensions need to be bravely opposed.
 Liberalism and Labour (1926)

2 For him [Keynes] the short run was much more
 significant than the long run—that long run in which,
 as he used to say, 'we are all dead'.
 A.C. Pigou, *Proceedings of the British Academy*, v.32, p.13

[ALFRED] JOYCE KILMER 1886–1918

3 I think that I shall never see
 A poem lovely as a tree.
 Trees (1914)

4 Poems are made by fools like me,
 But only God can make a tree.

REVD. FRANCIS KILVERT 1840–1879

5 Of all noxious animals, too, the most noxious is a
 tourist. And of all tourists the most vulgar, ill-bred,
 offensive and loathsome is the British tourist.
 Diary, 5 Apr. 1870

6 The Vicar of St Ives says the smell of fish there is
 sometimes so terrific as to stop the church clock.
 21 July 1870

7 An angel satyr walks these hills.
 20 June 1871

8 It is a fine thing to be out on the hills alone. A man
 can hardly be a beast or a fool alone on a great
 mountain.
 On the Black Mountain in Wales. 29 May 1871

BENJAMIN FRANKLIN KING 1857–1894

9 Nothing to do but work,
 Nothing to eat but food,
 Nothing to wear but clothes
 To keep one from going nude.
 The Pessimist

10 Nothing to breathe but air,
 Quick as a flash 'tis gone;
 Nowhere to fall but off,
 Nowhere to stand but on!

BISHOP HENRY KING 1592–1669

11 Sleep on, my Love, in thy cold bed,
 Never to be disquieted!
 My last good night! Thou wilt not wake
 Till I thy fate shall overtake:
 Till age, or grief, or sickness must
 Marry my body to that dust
 It so much loves; and fill the room
 My heart keeps empty in thy tomb.
 The Exequy

12 But hark! My pulse like a soft drum
 Beats my approach, tells thee I come.

13 We that did nothing study but the way
 To love each other, with which thoughts the day
 Rose with delight to us, and with them set,

Must learn the hateful art, how to forget.
The Surrender

REVD. MARTIN LUTHER KING 1929–1968

14 A riot is at bottom the language of the unheard.
 Chaos or Community (1967), ch.4

15 I have a dream that one day this nation will rise up,
 live out the true meaning of its creed: we hold these
 truths to be self-evident, that all men are created
 equal.
 Washington, 27 Aug. 1963. The phrase 'I have a dream' was used
 by him in other speeches during the summer of that year.

CHARLES KINGSLEY 1819–1875

16 Airly Beacon, Airly Beacon;
 Oh the pleasant sight to see
 Shires and towns from Airly Beacon,
 While my love climb'd up to me!
 Airly Beacon

17 Airly Beacon, Airly Beacon;
 Oh the weary haunt for me,
 All alone on Airly Beacon,
 With his baby on my knee!

18 The merry brown hares came leaping
 Over the crest of the hill,
 Where the clover and corn lay sleeping
 Under the moonlight still.
 The Bad Squire

19 Be good, sweet maid, and let who can be clever;
 Do lovely things, not dream them, all day long;
 And so make Life, and Death, and that For Ever,
 One grand sweet song.
 A Farewell. To C.E.G.

20 Leave to Robert Browning
 Beggars, fleas, and vines;
 Leave to squeamish Ruskin
 Popish Apennines,
 Dirty stones of Venice
 And his gas-lamps seven;
 We've the stones of Snowdon
 And the lamps of heaven.
 Letter to Thomas Hughes

21 What we can we will be,
 Honest Englishmen.
 Do the work that's nearest,
 Though it's dull at whiles,
 Helping, when we meet them,
 Lame dogs over stiles.

22 Welcome, wild North-easter!
 Shame it is to see
 Odes to every zephyr;
 Ne'er a verse to thee.
 Ode to the North-East Wind

23 'Tis the hard grey weather
 Breeds hard English men.

24 Come; and strong within us
 Stir the Vikings' blood;
 Bracing brain and sinew;
 Blow, thou wind of God!

25 'O Mary, go and call the cattle home,
 And call the cattle home,
 And call the cattle home,

Across the sands of Dee.'
The western wind was wild and dank with foam,
And all alone went she.
The Sands of Dee

1 The western tide crept up along the sand,
And o'er and o'er the sand,
And round and round the sand,
As far as eye could see.
The rolling mist came down and hid the land:
And never home came she.

2 Three fishers went sailing away to the west,
Away to the west as the sun went down;
Each thought on the woman who loved him the best,
And the children stood watching them out of the town.
The Three Fishers

3 For men must work, and women must weep,
And there's little to earn, and many to keep,
Though the harbour bar be moaning.

4 I once had a sweet little doll, dears
The prettiest doll in the world;
Her cheeks were so red and so white, dears,
And her hair was so charmingly curled.
Songs from **The Water Babies** (1863). **My Little Doll**

5 When all the world is young, lad,
And all the trees are green;
And every goose a swan, lad,
And every lass a queen;
Then hey for boot and horse, lad,
And round the world away:
Young blood must have its course, lad,
And every dog his day.
Young and Old

6 To be discontented with the divine discontent, and to
be ashamed with the noble shame, is the very germ and
first upgrowth of all virtue.
Health and Education (1874), p.20

7 We have used the Bible as if it was a constable's
handbook—an opium-dose for keeping beasts of
burden patient while they are being overloaded.
Letters to the Chartists, no.2. See 333:6

8 He did not know that a keeper is only a poacher turned
outside in, and a poacher a keeper turned inside out.
The Water Babies (1863), ch.1

9 As thorough an Englishman as ever coveted his
neighbour's goods.
ch.4

10 And still the lobster held on.
ch.5

11 Mrs Bedonebyasyoudid is coming.

12 The loveliest fairy in the world; and her name is Mrs
Doasyouwouldbedoneby.

13 All the butterflies and cockyolybirds would fly past
me.
ch.8

14 Till the coming of the Cocqcigrues.

15 More ways of killing a cat than choking her with
cream.
Westward Ho! (1855), ch.20

16 Eustace is a man no longer; he is become a thing, a
tool, a Jesuit.
ch.23

17 Truth, for its own sake, had never been a virtue with
the Roman clergy.
Review of Froude's *History of England,* in *Macmillan's
Magazine,* Jan. 1864

18 Some say that the age of chivalry is past, that the
spirit of romance is dead. The age of chivalry is never
past, so long as there is a wrong left unredressed on
earth.
Mrs C. Kingsley, *Life* (1879), vol.ii, ch.28

HUGH KINGSMILL 1889–1949

19 What, still alive at twenty-two,
A clean upstanding chap like you?
Sure, if your throat 'tis hard to slit,
Slit your girl's, and swing for it.
Two Poems after A.E. Housman, 1

20 But bacon's not the only thing
That's cured by hanging from a string.

21 'Tis Summer Time on Bredon,
And now the farmers swear;
The cattle rise and listen
In valleys far and near,
And blush at what they hear.

But when the mists in autumn
On Bredon top are thick,
The happy hymns of farmers
Go up from fold and rick,
The cattle then are sick.
2

RUDYARD KIPLING 1865–1936

22 When you've shouted 'Rule Britannia', when you've
sung 'God save the Queen',
When you've finished killing Kruger with your mouth.
The Absent-Minded Beggar

23 He's an absent-minded beggar, and his weaknesses are
great—
But we and Paul must take him as we find him—
He's out on active service, wiping something off a
slate—
And he's left a lot of little things behind him!

24 Duke's son—cook's son—son of a hundred Kings—
(Fifty thousand horse and foot going to Table Bay!)

25 Pass the hat for your credit's sake, and
pay—pay—pay!

26 England's on the anvil—hear the hammers ring—
Clanging from the Severn to the Tyne!
Never was a blacksmith like our Norman King—
England's being hammered, hammered, hammered
into line!
The Anvil

27 Oh, East is East, and West is West, and never the
twain shall meet,
Till Earth and Sky stand presently at God's great
Judgment Seat;
But there is neither East nor West, Border, nor Breed,
nor Birth,
When two strong men stand face to face, though they
come from the ends of earth!
The Ballad of East and West

28 And the talk slid north, and the talk slid south,
With the sliding puffs from the hookah-mouth.
Four things greater than all things are,—

Women and Horses and Power and War.
Ballad of the King's Jest

1 It was not part of their blood,
    It came to them very late
With long arrears to make good,
    When the English began to hate.
The Beginnings

2 Ah! What avails the classic bent
    And what the cultured word,
Against the undoctored incident
    That actually occurred?
The Benefactors. See 308:26

3 And a woman is only a woman, but a good cigar is a
    Smoke.
The Betrothed

4 'Oh, where are you going to, all you Big Steamers,
    With England's own coal, up and down the salt seas?'
'We are going to fetch you your bread and your butter,
    Your beef, pork, and mutton, eggs, apples, and
    cheese.'
Big Steamers

5 'For the bread that you eat and the biscuits you nibble,
    The sweets that you suck and the joints that you carve,
They are brought to you daily by all us Big Steamers—
    And if any one hinders our coming you'll starve!'

6 We're foot—slog—slog—slog—sloggin' over Africa—
    Foot—foot—foot—foot—sloggin' over Africa—
(Boots—boots—boots—boots—movin' up an' down
    again!)
There's no discharge in the war!
Boots. See 55:25

7 I've a head like a concertina, I've a tongue like a
    button-stick,
I've a mouth like an old potato, and I'm more than a
    little sick,
But I've had my fun o' the Corp'ral's Guard; I've
    made the cinders fly,
And I'm here in the Clink for a thundering drink and
    blacking the Corporal's eye.
Cells

8 Take of English earth as much
As either hand may rightly clutch.
In the taking of it breathe
Prayer for all who lie beneath...
Lay that earth upon thy heart,
And thy sickness shall depart!
A Charm

9 These were our children who died for our lands...
    But who shall return us the children?
The Children

10 Land of our birth, we pledge to thee
Our love and toil in the years to be;
When we are grown and take our place,
As men and women with our race.
The Children's Song

11 That we, with Thee, may walk uncowed
By fear or favour of the crowd.

12 Teach us delight in simple things,
And mirth that has no bitter springs;
Forgiveness free of evil done,
And love to all men 'neath the sun!

13 High noon behind the tamarisks—the sun is hot above
    us—

As at Home the Christmas Day is breaking wan.
They will drink our healths at dinner—those who tell
    us how they love us,
And forget us till another year be gone!
Christmas in India

14 We must go back with Policeman Day—
    Back from the City of Sleep!
The City of Sleep

15 Gold is for the mistress—silver for the maid—
Copper for the craftsman cunning at his trade.
'Good!' said the Baron, sitting in his hall,
'But Iron—Cold Iron—is master of them all.'
Cold Iron

16 We know that the tail must wag the dog, for the horse
    is drawn by the cart;
But the Devil whoops, as he whooped of old: 'It's
    clever, but is it Art?'
The Conundrum of the Workshops

17 By the favour of God we might know as much—as
    our father Adam knew!

18 It is always a temptation to a rich and lazy nation,
    To puff and look important and to say:-
'Though we know we should defeat you, we have not
    the time to meet you.
    We will therefore pay you cash to go away.'

And that is called paying the Dane-geld;
But we've proved it again and again,
That if once you have paid him the Dane-geld
You never get rid of the Dane.
Dane-Geld

19 'What are the bugles blowin' for?' said
    Files-on-Parade.
'To turn you out, to turn you out,' the
    Colour-Sergeant said.
Danny Deever

20 'For they're hangin' Danny Deever, you can hear the
    Dead March play,
The Regiment's in 'ollow square—they're hangin' 'im
    to-day;
They've taken of 'is buttons off an' cut 'is stripes
    away,
An' they're hangin' Danny Deever in the mornin'.'

21 The 'eathen in 'is blindness bows down to wood an'
    stone;
'E don't obey no orders unless they is 'is own;
'E keeps 'is side-arms awful: 'e leaves 'em all about,
An' then comes up the Regiment an' pokes the 'eathen
    out.
The 'Eathen. See 244:6

22 The 'eathen in 'is blindness must end where 'e began,
But the backbone of the Army is the
    Non-commissioned man!

23 Who are neither children nor Gods, but men in a world
    of men!
England's Answer

24 Winds of the World, give answer! They are
    whimpering to and fro—
And what should they know of England who only
    England know?
The English Flag

25 I could not look on Death, which being known,

Men led me to him, blindfold and alone.
Epitaphs of the War. The Coward

1 But it never really mattered till the English grew
polite.
Et Dona Ferentes

2 'Something hidden. Go and find it. Go and look
behind the Ranges—
Something lost behind the Ranges. Lost and waiting
for you. Go.'
The Explorer

3 Yes, your 'Never-never country'—yes, your 'edge of
cultivation'
And 'No sense in going further'—till I crossed the
range to see.
God forgive me! No I didn't. It's God's present to our
nation.
Anybody might have found it, but—His whisper
came to Me!

4 When the Himalayan peasant meets the he-bear in his
pride,
He shouts to scare the monster, who will often turn
aside.
But the she-bear thus accosted rends the peasant tooth
and nail
For the female of the species is more deadly than the
male.
The Female of the Species

5 Man propounds negotiations, Man accepts the
compromise.
Very rarely will he squarely push the logic of a fact
To its ultimate conclusion in unmitigated act.

6 For all we have and are,
For all our children's fate,
Stand up and take the war.
The Hun is at the gate!
For All We Have and Are

7 There is but one task for all—
One life for each to give.
What stands if Freedom fall?
Who dies if England live?

8 So 'ere's to you, Fuzzy-Wuzzy, at your 'ome in the
Soudan;
You're a pore benighted 'eathen but a first-class
fightin' man;
An' 'ere's to you, Fuzzy-Wuzzy, with your 'ayrick
'ead of 'air—
You big black boundin' beggar—for you broke a
British square!
Fuzzy-Wuzzy

9 'E's all 'ot sand an' ginger when alive,
An' 'e's generally shammin' when 'e's dead.

10 We're poor little lambs who've lost our way,
Baa! Baa! Baa!
We're little black sheep who've gone astray,
Baa-aa-aa!
Gentleman-rankers out on the spree,
Damned from here to Eternity,
God ha' mercy on such as we,
Baa! Yah! Bah!
Gentleman-Rankers

11 We have done with Hope and Honour, we are lost to
Love and Truth,
We are dropping down the ladder rung by rung;

And the measure of our torment is the measure of our
youth.
God help us, for we knew the worst too young!
See 113:7

12 Our England is a garden that is full of stately views,
Of borders, beds and shrubberies and lawns and
avenues,
With statues on the terraces and peacocks strutting by;
But the Glory of the Garden lies in more than meets
the eye.
The Glory of the Garden

13 The Glory of the Garden it abideth not in words.

14 Our England is a garden, and such gardens are not
made
By singing:—'Oh, how beautiful!' and sitting in the
shade,
While better men than we go out and start their
working lives
At grubbing weeds from gravel paths with broken
dinner-knives.

15 Oh, Adam was a gardener, and God who made him
sees
That half a proper gardener's work is done upon his
knees,
So when your work is finished, you can wash your
hands and pray
For the Glory of the Garden, that it may not pass
away!
And the Glory of the Garden it shall never pass away!

16 In the Carboniferous Epoch we were promised
abundance for all,
By robbing selected Peter to pay for collective Paul;
But though we had plenty of money, there was nothing
our money could buy,
And the Gods of the Copybook Headings said: *'If you
don't work, you die'.*
The Gods of the Copybook Headings

17 The uniform 'e wore
Was nothin' much before,
An' rather less than 'arf o' that be'ind.
Gunga Din

18 An' for all 'is dirty 'ide
'E was white, clear white, inside
When 'e went to tend the wounded under fire!

19 So I'll meet 'im later on
At the place where 'e is gone—
Where it's always double drills and no canteen.
'E'll be squattin' on the coals
Givin' drink to poor damned souls,
An' I'll get a swig in Hell from Gunga Din.

20 Though I've belted you an' flayed you,
By the livin' Gawd that made you,
You're a better man than I am, Gunga Din!

21 What is a woman that you forsake her,
And the hearth-fire and the home-acre,
To go with the old grey Widow-maker?
Harp Song of the Dane Women

22 If you can keep your head when all about you
Are losing theirs and blaming it on you,
If you can trust yourself when all men doubt you,
But make allowance for their doubting too;
If you can wait and not be tired by waiting,
Or being lied about, don't deal in lies,

Or being hated, don't give way to hating,
And yet don't look too good, nor talk too wise:

If you can dream—and not make dreams your master;
If you can think—and not make thoughts your aim;
If you can meet with Triumph and Disaster
And treat those two impostors just the same.
If—

1 If you can make one heap of all your winnings
And risk it on one turn of pitch-and-toss,
And lose, and start again at your beginnings
And never breathe a word about your loss.

2 If you can talk with crowds and keep your virtue,
Or walk with Kings—nor lose the common touch,
If neither foes nor loving friends can hurt you,
If all men count with you, but none too much;
If you can fill the unforgiving minute
With sixty seconds' worth of distance run,
Yours is the Earth and everything that's in it,
And—which is more—you'll be a Man, my son!

3 There are nine and sixty ways of constructing tribal
lays,
And—every—single—one—of—them—is—right!
In the Neolithic Age

4 Then ye returned to your trinkets; then ye contented
your souls
With the flannelled fools at the wicket or the muddied
oafs at the goals.
The Islanders

5 He wrote that monarchs were divine,
And left a son who—proved they weren't!
James I

6 For agony and spoil
Of nations beat to dust,
For poisoned air and tortured soil
And cold, commanded lust,
And every secret woe
The shuddering waters saw—
Willed and fulfilled by high and low—
Let them relearn the Law.
Justice. October, 1918

7 Yes, weekly from Southampton,
Great steamers, white and gold,
Go rolling down to Rio
(Roll down—roll down to Rio!).
And I'd like to roll to Rio
Some day before I'm old!
Just-So Stories (1902). **Beginning of the Armadilloes**

8 I've never seen a Jaguar,
Nor yet an Armadill-
o dilloing in his armour,
And I s'pose I never will.

9 The Camel's hump is an ugly lump
Which well you may see at the Zoo;
But uglier yet is the Hump we get
From having too little to do.
How the Camel Got His Hump

10 We get the Hump—
Cameelious Hump—
The Hump that is black and blue!

11 The cure for this ill is not to sit still,
Or frowst with a book by the fire;
But to take a large hoe and a shovel also,
And dig till you gently perspire.

12 I keep six honest serving-men
(They taught me all I knew);
Their names are What and Why and When
And How and Where and Who.
I keep six honest serving-men

13 Old Man Kangaroo first, Yellow-Dog Dingo behind.
Sing-Song of Old Man Kangaroo

14 For Allah created the English mad—the maddest of all
mankind!
Kitchener's School

15 But the things you will learn from the Yellow an'
Brown,
They'll 'elp you a lot with the White!
The Ladies

16 An' I learned about women from 'er!

17 I've taken my fun where I've found it,
An' now I must pay for my fun,
For the more you 'ave known o' the others
The less will you settle to one;
An' the end of it's sittin' and thinkin',
An' dreamin' Hell-fires to see.
So be warned by my lot (which I know you will not),
An' learn about women from me!

18 For the Colonel's Lady an' Judy O'Grady
Are sisters under their skins!

19 And Ye take mine honour from me if Ye take away
the sea!
The Last Chantey

20 Now this is the Law of the Jungle—as old and as true
as the sky;
And the Wolf that shall keep it may prosper, but the
Wolf that shall break it must die.
The Law of the Jungle

21 It was our fault, and our very great fault—and now we
must turn it to use.
We have forty million reasons for failure, but not a
single excuse.
So the more we work and the less we talk the better
results we shall get.
We have had an Imperial lesson; it may make us an
Empire yet!
The Lesson

22 And that's how it all began, my dears,
And that's how it all began!
The Light that Failed (1890), chapter heading

23 There's a whisper down the field where the year has
shot her yield,
And the ricks stand grey to the sun,
Singing:—'Over then, come over, for the bee has quit
the clover,
And your English summer's done.'

You have heard the beat of the off-shore wind,
And the thresh of the deep-sea rain;
You have heard the song—how long? how long?
Pull out on the trail again!
Ha' done with the Tents of Shem, dear lass,
We've seen the seasons through,
And it's time to turn on the old trail, our own trail, the
out trail,
Pull out, pull out, on the Long Trail—the trail that is
always new!
The Long Trail

24 It's North you may run to the rime-ringed sun,

Or South to the blind Horn's hate;
Or East all the way into Mississippi Bay,
Or West to the Golden Gate.

1   There be triple ways to take, of the eagle or the snake,
    Or the way of a man with a maid;
    But the sweetest way to me is a ship's upon the sea
    In the heel of the North-East Trade.
    See 55:1

2   Lord, Thou hast made this world below the shadow of
        a dream,
    An', taught by time, I tak' it so—exceptin' always
        Steam.
    From coupler-flange to spindle-guide I see Thy Hand,
        O God—
    Predestination in the stride o' yon connectin'-rod.
    McAndrew's Hymn

3   Yon's strain, hard strain, o' head an' hand, for though
        Thy Power brings
    All skill to naught, Ye'll understand a man must think
        o' things.

4   Mister McAndrew, don't you think steam spoils
        romance at sea?

5   By the old Moulmein Pagoda, lookin' eastward to the
        sea,
    There's a Burma girl a-settin', and I know she thinks
        o' me;
    For the wind is in the palm-trees, an' the temple-bells
        they say:
    'Come you back, you British soldier; come you back
        to Mandalay!'
    Come you back to Mandalay,
    Where the old Flotilla lay:
    Can't you 'ear their paddles chunkin' from Rangoon to
        Mandalay?
    On the road to Mandalay,
    Where the flyin'-fishes play,
    An' the dawn comes up like thunder outer China 'crost
        the Bay!
    Mandalay

6   An' I seed her first a-smokin' of a whackin' white
        cheroot,
    An' a-wastin' Christian kisses on an 'eathen idol's
        foot.

7   I am sick o' wastin' leather on these gritty
        pavin'-stones,
    An' the blasted English drizzle wakes the fever in my
        bones;
    Tho' I walks with fifty 'ousemaids outer Chelsea to the
        Strand,
    An' they talks a lot o' lovin', but wot do they
        understand?
        Beefy face an' grubby 'and—
        Law! Wot do they understand?
    I've a neater, sweeter maiden in a cleaner, greener
        land!

8   Ship me somewheres east of Suez, where the best is
        like the worst,
    Where there aren't no Ten Commandments, an' a man
        can raise a thirst:
    For the temple-bells are callin', an' it's there that I
        would be—
    By the old Moulmein Pagoda, looking lazy at the sea.

9   For a man he must go with a woman, which women

don't understand—
    Or the sort that say they can see it, they aren't the
        marrying brand.
    The 'Mary Gloster'

10 I'm sick of the hired women. I'll kiss my girl on her
        lips!

11 Nice while it lasted, an' now it is over—
    Tear out your 'eart an' good-bye to your lover!
    What's the use o' grievin', when the mother that bore
        you
    (Mary, pity women!) knew it all before you?
    Mary, Pity Women

12 Mines reported in the fairway,
    Warn all traffic and detain.
    'Sent up *Unity, Claribel, Assyrian, Stormcock,* and
        Golden Gain.
    Mine Sweepers

13   Good rest to all
    That keep the Jungle Law.
    Morning Song in the Jungle

14 If I were hanged on the highest hill,
    Mother o' mine, O mother o' mine!
    I know whose love would follow me still,
    Mother o' mine, O mother o' mine!
    Mother O' Mine

15 'Have you news of my boy Jack?'
        Not this tide.
    'When d'you think that he'll come back?'
        Not with this wind blowing, and this tide.
    My Boy Jack

16 The depth and dream of my desire,
    The bitter paths wherein I stray—
    Thou knowest Who hast made the Fire,
    Thou knowest Who hast made the Clay.
    My New-cut Ashlar

17 One stone the more swings into place
    In that dread Temple of Thy worth.
    It is enough that, through Thy Grace,
    I saw nought common on Thy Earth.

18 Now it is not good for the Christian's health to hustle
        the Aryan brown,
    For the Christian riles, and the Aryan smiles, and it
        weareth the Christian down;
    And the end of the fight is a tombstone white with the
        name of the late deceased,
    And the epitaph drear: 'A Fool lies here who tried to
        hustle the East.'
    The Naulahka (1892), heading of ch.5

19 The Saxon is not like us Normans. His manners are
        not so polite.
    But he never means anything serious till he talks about
        justice and right,
    When he stands like an ox in the furrow with his sullen
        set eyes on your own,
    And grumbles, 'This isn't fair dealing,' my son, leave
        the Saxon alone.
    Norman and Saxon

20 A Nation spoke to a Nation,
    A Throne sent word to a Throne:
    'Daughter am I in my mother's house,
    But mistress in my own.
    The gates are mine to open,
    As the gates are mine to close,

And I abide by my Mother's House.'
Said our Lady of the Snows.
Our Lady of the Snows

1 The toad beneath the harrow knows
Exactly where each tooth-point goes;
The butterfly upon the road
Preaches contentment to that toad.
Pagett M.P.

2 The Three in One, the One in Three? Not so!
To my own Gods I go.
It may be they shall give me greater ease
Than your cold Christ and tangled Trinities.
Plain Tales from the Hills (1888). Chapter heading to **Lispeth**

3 There is sorrow enough in the natural way
From men and women to fill our day;
But when we are certain of sorrow in store,
Why do we always arrange for more?
Brothers and Sisters, I bid you beware
Of giving your heart to a dog to tear.
The Power of the Dog

4 The Celt in all his variants from Builth to Ballyhoo,
His mental processes are plain—one knows what he will do,
And can logically predicate his finish by his start.
The Puzzler

5 For undemocratic reasons and for motives not of
　State,
They arrive at their conclusions—largely inarticulate.
Being void of self-expression they confide their views
　to none;
But sometimes in a smoking room, one learns why
　things were done.
Of the English

6 Valour and Innocence
Have latterly gone hence
To certain death by certain shame attended.
The Queen's Men

7 God of our fathers, known of old,
Lord of our far-flung battle-line,
Beneath whose awful Hand we hold
Dominion over palm and pine—
Lord God of Hosts, be with us yet,
Lest we forget—lest we forget!

The tumult and the shouting dies;
The Captains and the Kings depart:
Still stands Thine ancient sacrifice,
An humble and a contrite heart.
Lord God of Hosts, be with us yet,
Lest we forget—lest we forget!
Recessional (1897)

8 Lo, all our pomp of yesterday
Is one with Nineveh and Tyre!

9 If, drunk with sight of power, we loose
Wild tongues that have not Thee in awe,
Such boastings as the Gentiles use,
Or lesser breeds without the Law.

10 For heathen heart that puts her trust
In reeking tube and iron shard,
All valiant dust that builds on dust,
And, guarding, calls not Thee to guard,
For frantic boast and foolish word—
Thy mercy on Thy People, Lord!

11 If England was what England seems,

An' not the England of our dreams,
But only putty, brass, an' paint,
'Ow quick we'd drop 'er! But she ain't!
The Return

12 English they be and Japanee that hang on the Brown
　Bear's flank,
And some be Scot, but the worst of the lot, and the
　boldest thieves, be Yank!
The Rhyme of the Three Sealers

13 And I've lost Britain, and I've lost Gaul,
And I've lost Rome and, worst of all,
I've lost Lalage!
Rimini

14 Brother, thy tail hangs down behind!
Road Song of the Bandar-Log

15 No one thinks of winter when the grass is green!
A St. Helena Lullaby

16 You can go where you please, you can skid up the
　trees, but you don't get away from the guns!
Screw-guns

17 But remember, please, the Law by which we live,
We are not built to comprehend a lie,
We can neither love nor pity nor forgive,
If you make a slip in handling us you die!
The Secret of the Machines

18 Cheer for the Sergeant's weddin'—
　Give 'em one cheer more!
Grey gun-'orses in the lando,
　An' a rogue is married to a whore.
The Sergeant's Weddin'

19 Shillin' a day,
Bloomin' good pay—
Lucky to touch it, a shillin' a day!
Shillin' a Day

20 Give 'im a letter—
Can't do no better,
Late Troop-Sergeant-Major an'—runs with a letter!
Think what 'e's been,
Think what 'e's seen.
Think of 'is pension an'—
GAWD SAVE THE QUEEN!

21 There was two-an'-thirty Sergeants,
　There was Corp'rals forty-one,
There was just nine 'undred rank an' file
　To swear to a touch o' sun.
The Shut-Eye Sentry

22 If you wake at midnight, and hear a horse's feet,
Don't go drawing back the blind, or looking in the
　street,
Them that asks no questions isn't told a lie.
Watch the wall, my darling, while the Gentlemen go
　by!
　Five and twenty ponies,
　Trotting through the dark—
　Brandy for the Parson,
　'Baccy for the Clerk;
Laces for a lady, letters for a spy,
Watch the wall, my darling, while the Gentlemen go
　by!
A Smuggler's Song

23 'E's a kind of a giddy harumfrodite—soldier an' sailor
　too!
Soldier an' Sailor too!

1 I'm the Prophet of the Utterly Absurd,
   Of the Patently Impossible and Vain.
   The Song of the Banjo

2 I am all that ever went with evening dress!

3 There's never a wave of all her waves
   But marks our English dead.
   The Song of the Dead, ii

4 If blood be the price of admiralty,
   Lord God, we ha' paid in full!

5 For the Lord our God Most High
   He hath made the deep as dry,
   He hath smote for us a pathway to the ends of all the
      earth!
   A Song of the English

6 Keep ye the law—be swift in all obedience—
   Clear the land of evil, drive the road and bridge the
      ford.
   Make ye sure to each his own
   That he reap where he hath sown;
   By the peace among our peoples let men know we
      serve the Lord!

7 Ere Mor the Peacock flutters, ere the Monkey People
      cry,
   Ere Chil the Kite swoops down a furlong sheer,
   Through the Jungle very softly flits a shadow and a
      sigh—
   He is Fear, O Little Hunter, he is Fear!
   The Song of the Little Hunter

8 But thy throat is shut and dried, and thy heart against
      thy side
   Hammers: 'Fear, O Little Hunter—this is Fear!'

9 Mithras, God of the Morning, our trumpets waken the
      Wall!
   'Rome is above the Nations, but Thou art over all!'
   A Song to Mithras

10 They sit at the Feet—they hear the Word—they see
      how truly the Promise runs.
   They have cast their burden upon the Lord, and—the
      Lord He lays it on Martha's Sons!
   The Sons of Martha

11 An' it all goes into the laundry,
   But it never comes out in the wash,
   'Ow we're sugared about by the old men
   ('Eavy-sterned amateur old men!)
   That 'amper an' 'inder an' scold men
   For fear o' Stellenbosch!
   Stellenbosch

12 The barrow and the camp abide,
   The sunlight and the sward.
   Sussex

13 And here the sea-fogs lap and cling
   And here, each warning each,
   The sheep-bells and the ship-bells ring
   Along the hidden beach.

14 Little, lost, Down churches praise
   The Lord who made the hills.

15 Huge oaks and old, the which we hold
   No more than Sussex weed.

16 God gives all men all earth to love,
   But, since man's heart is small,
   Ordains for each one spot shall prove
   Belovèd over all.

Each to his choice, and I rejoice
   The lot has fallen to me
In a fair ground—in a fair ground—
   Yea, Sussex by the sea!
See 390:6

17 One man in a thousand, Solomon says,
   Will stick more close than a brother.
   The Thousandth Man

18 But the Thousandth Man will stand by you side
   To the gallows-foot—and after!

19 Though we called your friend from his bed this night,
      he could not speak to you,
   For the race is run by one and one and never by two
      and two.
   Tomlinson

20 For the sin ye do by two and two ye must pay for one
      by one!

21 And—the God that you took from a printed book be
      with you, Tomlinson!

22 Oh, it's Tommy this, an' Tommy that, an' 'Tommy,
      go away';
   But it's 'Thank you, Mister Atkins,' when the band
      begins to play.
   Tommy

23 It's Tommy this, an' Tommy that, an' 'Chuck him
      out, the brute!'
   But it's 'Saviour of 'is country' when the guns begin to
      shoot.

24 Then it's Tommy this, an' Tommy that, an' 'Tommy
      'ow's yer soul?'
   But it's 'Thin red line of 'eroes' when the drums begin
      to roll.

25 Of all the trees that grow so fair,
      Old England to adorn,
   Greater are none beneath the Sun,
      Than Oak, and Ash, and Thorn.
   A Tree Song. The association of these trees is traditional

26 Ellum she hateth mankind and waiteth
      Till every gust be laid
   To drop a limb on the head of him
      That anyway trusts her shade.

27 England shall bide till Judgement Tide,
      By Oak, and Ash, and Thorn!

28 I tell this tale, which is strictly true,
   Just by way of convincing you
   How very little, since things were made,
   Things have altered in the building trade.
   A Truthful Song

29 A fool there was and he made his prayer
      (Even as you and I!)
   To a rag and a bone and a hank of hair
   (We called her the woman who did not care)
   But the fool he called her his lady fair—
      (Even as you and I!)
   The Vampire

30 Oh, was there ever sailor free to choose,
      That didn't settle somewhere near the sea?
   The Virginity

31 They shut the road through the woods
   Seventy years ago.
   Weather and rain have undone it again,
   And now you would never know

There was once a road through the woods.
The Way Through the Woods

1 You will hear the beat of a horse's feet,
And the swish of a skirt in the dew,
Steadily cantering through
The misty solitudes,
As though they perfectly knew
The old lost road through the woods—
But there is no road through the woods!

2 Father, Mother, and Me,
Sister and Auntie say
All the people like us are We,
And every one else is They.
We and They

3 And only The Master shall praise us, and only The
Master shall blame;
And no one shall work for money, and no one shall
work for fame,
But each for the joy of the working, and each, in his
separate star,
Shall draw the Thing as he sees It for the God of
Things as They are!
When Earth's Last Picture

4 When 'Omer smote 'is bloomin' lyre,
'E'd 'eard men sing by land an' sea;
An' what 'e thought 'e might require,
'E went an' took—the same as me!
When 'Omer Smote. (Barrack-Room Ballads (1892):
Introduction)

5 They knew 'e stole; 'e knew they knowed.
They didn't tell, nor make a fuss,
But winked at 'Omer down the road,
An' 'e winked back—the same as us!

6 Take up the White Man's burden—
Send forth the best ye breed—
Go, bind your sons to exile
To serve your captives' need;
To wait in heavy harness
On fluttered folk and wild—
Your new-caught, sullen peoples,
Half-devil and half-child.
The White Man's Burden

7 By all ye cry or whisper,
By all ye leave or do,
The silent, sullen peoples
Shall weigh your Gods and you.

8 Take up the White Man's burden—
And reap his old reward:
The blame of those ye better,
The hate of those ye guard.

9 'Ave you 'eard o' the Widow at Windsor
With a hairy gold crown on 'er 'ead?
She 'as ships on the foam—she 'as millions at 'ome,
An' she pays us poor beggars in red.
The Widow at Windsor

10 Take 'old o' the Wings o' the Mornin',
An' flop round the earth till you're dead;
But you won't get away from the tune that they play
To the bloomin' old rag over 'ead.

11 Down to Gehenna or up to the Throne,
He travels the fastest who travels alone.
The Winners

12 Good hunting!
The Jungle Book (1894). **Kaa's Hunting**

13 We be of one blood, thou and I.

14 'Nice,' said the small 'stute Fish. 'Nice but nubbly.'
Just So Stories (1902). **How the Whale Got His Throat**

15 You must *not* forget the Suspenders, Best Beloved.

16 He had his Mummy's leave to paddle, or else he
would never have done it, because he was a man of
infinite-resource-and-sagacity.

17 Most 'scruciating idle.
How the Camel Got His Hump

18 'Humph yourself!'
And the Camel humphed himself.

19 There lived a Parsee from whose hat the rays of the
sun were reflected in more-than-oriental-splendour.
How the Rhinoceros Got His Skin

20 An Elephant's Child—who was full of 'satiable
curtiosity.
The Elephant's Child

21 The great grey-green, greasy Limpopo River, all set
about with fever-trees.

22 Led go! You are hurtig be!

23 He walked by himself, and all places were alike to
him.
The Cat That Walked by Himself

24 He went back through the Wet Wild Woods, waving
his wild tail, and walking by his wild lone. But he
never told anybody.

25 The mad all are in God's keeping.
Kim (1901), ch.2

26 What's the good of argifying?
Life's Handicap (1891). **On Greenhow Hill**

27 Asia is not going to be civilized after the methods of
the West. There is too much Asia and she is too old.
The Man Who Was

28 Let it be clearly understood that the Russian is a
delightful person till he tucks in his shirt.

29 Man that is born of woman is small potatoes and few
in the hill.
The Head of the District

30 Some were married, which was bad, and some did
other things which were worse.
The Mark of the Beast

31 You haf too much Ego in your Cosmos.
Bertran and Bimi

32 She was as immutable as the Hills. But not quite so
green.
Plain Tales from the Hills (1888). **Venus Annodomini**

33 Every one is more or less mad on one point.
On the Strength of a Likeness

34 Open and obvious devotion from any sort of man is
always pleasant to any sort of woman.

35 Take my word for it, the silliest woman can manage a
clever man; but it needs a very clever woman to
manage a fool.
Three and—an Extra

36 Lalun is a member of the most ancient profession in
the world.
Soldiers Three (1888). **On the City Wall**

37 Being kissed by a man who didn't wax his moustache

was—like eating an egg without salt.
The Gadsbys. Poor Dear Mamma

1 Steady the Buffs.

2 Been trotting out the Gorgonzola!

3 Almost inevitable Consequences.
Fatima

4 I gloat! Hear me gloat!
Stalky & Co. (1899). **The Ambush**

5 It's boy; only boy.
An Unsavoury Interlude

6 We ain't goin' to have any beastly Erickin'.
The Moral Reformers

7 'This man,' said M'Turk, with conviction, 'is *the*
Gadarene Swine.'
The Flag of Their Country

8 A Jelly-bellied Flag-flapper.

9 'Tisn't beauty, so to speak, nor good talk necessarily.
It's just IT. Some women'll stay in a man's memory if
they once walked down a street.
Traffics and Discoveries (1904). **Mrs. Bathurst**

10 Once upon a time there was a Man and his Wife and a
Tertium Quid.
Wee Willie Winkie (1888). **At the Pit's Mouth**

11 Gawd knows, an' 'E won't split on a pal.
Drums of the Fore and Aft

12 A Soldier of the Great War Known unto God.
Inscription on gravestones above unidentified bodies, chosen by
Kipling as literary adviser for the Imperial War Graves
Commission, 1919. Gavin Stamp (ed.), *Silent Cities* (1977), p.13

13 Power without responsibility—the prerogative of the
harlot throughout the ages.
In conversation with Max Aitken (Lord Beaverbrook); later used
by Stanley Baldwin. See Lord Baldwin, *Address to the Kipling
Society*, Oct. 1971

LORD KITCHENER 1850–1916

14 You are ordered abroad as a soldier of the King to help
our French comrades against the invasion of a common
enemy. You have to perform a task which will need
your courage, your energy, your patience. Remember
that the honour of the British Army depends on your
individual conduct. It will be your duty not only to set
an example of discipline and perfect steadiness under
fire but also to maintain the most friendly relations
with those whom you are helping in this struggle. In
this new experience you may find temptations both in
wine and women. You must entirely resist both
temptations, and, while treating all women with
perfect courtesy, you should avoid any intimacy. Do
your duty bravely. Fear God. Honour the King.
A message to the soldiers of the British Expeditionary Force,
1914, to be kept by each soldier in his Active Service Pay-Book.
Sir G. Arthur, *Life of Kitchener*, vol.iii, p.27. See 80:25

PAUL KLEE 1879–1940

15 An *active* line on a walk moving freely, without goal.
A walk for a walk's sake.
Pedagogical Sketchbook (1925), 1.1

FRIEDRICH KLOPSTOCK 1724–1803

16 God and I both knew what it meant once; now God

alone knows.
C. Lombroso, *The Man of Genius* (1891), pt.I, ch.2. Also attr. to
Browning in the form 'When [*Sordello*] was written, God and
Robert Browning knew what it meant; now only God knows.'

MARY KNOWLES 1733–1807

17 He [Dr. Johnson] gets at the substance of a book
directly; he tears out the heart of it.
Boswell's *Johnson* (ed. 1934), vol.iii, p.284. 15 Apr. 1778

JOHN KNOX 1505–1572

18 *Un homme avec Dieu est toujours dans la majorité.*
A man with God is always in the majority.
Inscription on the Reformation Monument, Geneva, Switzerland

19 The First Blast of the Trumpet Against the Monstrous
Regiment of Women.
Title of Pamphlet, 1558

MGR. RONALD KNOX 1888–1957

20 When suave politeness, tempering bigot zeal,
Corrected *I believe* to *One does feel.*
Absolute and Abitofhell (1913)

21 O God, for as much as without Thee
We are not enabled to doubt Thee,
  Help us all by Thy grace
  To convince the whole race
It knows nothing whatever about Thee.
Attr. Langford Reed, *The Limerick Book*

22 There once was a man who said 'God
Must think it exceedingly odd
  If he find that this tree
  Continues to be
When there's no one about in the Quad.'
For the answer see 4:29

23 Evangelical vicar, in want of a portable, second-hand
font,would dispose, for the same, of a portrait, in frame,
of the Bishop, elect, of Vermont.
Advertisement placed in a newspaper. See W.S. Baring-Gould,
The Lure of the Limerick, pt. I. ch. 1. n. 5

VICESIMUS KNOX 1752–1821

24 That learning belongs not to the female character, and
that the female mind is not capable of a degree of
improvement equal to that of the other sex, are narrow
and unphilosophical prejudices.
Essays, vol.3, 142. (*The British Essayists* (1823), vol.37)

25 All sensible people agree in thinking that large
seminaries of young ladies, though managed with all
the vigilance and caution which human abilities can
exert, are in danger of great corruption.
Liberal Education, vol.I. sect.27, **On the literary education of
women**

26 Can anything be more absurd than keeping women in
a state of ignorance, and yet so vehemently to insist on
their resisting temptation?
See Mary Wollstonecraft, *A Vindication of the Rights of Woman*
(1792)

ALEXANDER KORDA 1893–1956

27 It's not enough to be Hungarian, you must have talent
too.
c.1935. See K. Kulik, *Alexander Korda* (1975), p.142

PAUL KRUGER 1825–1904

1 A bill of indemnity...for raid by Dr Jameson and the British South Africa Company's troops. The amount falls under two heads—first material damage, total of claim, £577,938 3s.3d.; second, moral or intellectual damage, total of claim, £1,000,000.
Communicated to House of Commons by Joseph Chamberlain, 18 Feb. 1897

THOMAS KYD 1558?–1594?

2 What outcries pluck me from my naked bed?
The Spanish Tragedy (1592), II.v.1

3 Oh eyes, no eyes, but fountains fraught with tears;
Oh life, no life, but lively form of death;
Oh world, no world, but mass of public wrongs.
III.ii.1

4 Thus must we toil in other men's extremes,
That know not how to remedy our own.
vi.1

5 I am never better than when I am mad. Then methinks
I am a brave fellow; then I do wonders. But reason
abuseth me, and there's the torment, there's the hell.
vii a.169 (1602 edn.)

6 My son—and what's a son? A thing begot
Within a pair of minutes, thereabout,
A lump bred up in darkness.
xi. Additions, l.5

7   Duly twice a morning
Would I be sprinkling it with fountain water.
At last it grew, and grew, and bore, and bore,
Till at the length
It grew a gallows and did bear our son,
It bore thy fruit and mine: O wicked, wicked plant.
xii. Additions, l.66

8 Why then I'll fit you.
IV.i.69

9 For what's a play without a woman in it?
96

HENRY LABOUCHERE 1831–1912

10 He [Labouchere] did not object, he once said, to Gladstone's always having the ace of trumps up his sleeve, but only to his pretence that God had put it there.
D.N.B. See also Thorold, *Life of Henry Labouchere*, ch.15:
'[Gladstone] cannot refrain from perpetually bringing an ace down his sleeve, even when he has only to play fair to win the trick.'

JEAN DE LA BRUYÈRE 1645–1696

11 *Tout est dit et l'on vient trop tard depuis plus de sept mille ans qu'il y a des hommes et qui pensent.*
Everything has been said, and we are more than seven thousand years of human thought too late.
Les Caractères (1688). Des Ouvrages de l'Esprit

12 *C'est un métier que de faire un livre, comme de faire une pendule: il faut plus que de l'esprit pour être auteur.*
Making a book is a craft, as is making a clock; it takes more than wit to become an author.

13 *Le commencement et le déclin de l'amour se font sentir par l'embarras où l'on est de se trouver seuls.*
The onset and the waning of love make themselves felt in the uneasiness experienced at being alone together.
Du Coeur

14 *Le peuple n'a guère d'esprit et les grands n'ont point d'âme...faut-il opter, je ne balance pas, je veux être peuple.*
The people have little intelligence, the great no heart...if I had to choose I should have no hesitation: I would be of the people.
Des Grands

15 *Entre le bon sens et le bon goût il y a la différence de la cause et son effet.*
Between good sense and good taste there is the same difference as between cause and effect.
Des Jugements

NIVELLE DE LA CHAUSSÉE 1692–1754

16 *Quand tout le monde a tort, tout le monde a raison.*
When everyone is wrong, everyone is right.
La Gouvernante (1747), I.iii

JEAN DE LA FONTAINE 1621–1695

17 *Aide-toi, le ciel t'aidera.*
Help yourself, and heaven will help you.
Fables (1668), vi.18. **Le Chartier Embourbé**

18 *Je plie et ne romps pas.*
I bend and I break not.
i.22. **Le Chêne et le Roseau**

19 *C'est double plaisir de tromper le trompeur.*
It is doubly pleasing to trick the trickster.
ii.15. **Le Coq et le Renard**

20 *Il connaît l'univers et ne se connaît pas.*
He knows the world and does not know himself.
(1678–9), viii.26. **Démocrite et les Abdéritains**

21 *La raison du plus fort est toujours la meilleure.*
The reason of the strongest is always the best.
i.10. **Le Loup et l'Agneau**

22 *La mort ne surprend point le sage,*
Il est toujours prêt à partir.
Death never takes the wise man by surprise; he is always ready to go.
viii.1. **La Mort et le Mourant**. See 354:13

JULES LAFORGUE 1860–1887

23 *Ah! que la vie est quotidienne.*
Oh, what a day-to-day business life is.
Complainte sur certains ennuis (1885)

ALPHONSE DE LAMARTINE 1790–1869

24 *Un seul être vous manque, et tout est dépeuplé.*
Only one being is wanting, and your whole world is bereft of people.
Premières Méditations poétiques (1820), **L'Isolement**

LADY CAROLINE LAMB 1785–1828

25 Mad, bad, and dangerous to know.
Of Byron, in her journal after their first meeting at a ball in March 1812. See Jenkins, *Lady Caroline Lamb* (1932), ch.6

CHARLES LAMB 1775–1834

1 I have no ear.
Essays of Elia (1820–23). **A Chapter on Ears**

2 I even think that sentimentally I am disposed to harmony. But organically I am incapable of a tune.

3 'Presents', I often say, 'endear Absents.'
A Dissertation upon Roast Pig

4 It argues an insensibility.

5 Why have we none [i.e. no grace] for books, those spiritual repasts—a grace before Milton—a grace before Shakspeare—a devotional exercise proper to be said before reading the Faerie Queene?
Grace Before Meat

6 Coleridge holds that a man cannot have a pure mind who refuses apple-dumplings. I am not certain but he is right.

7 I am, in plainer words, a bundle of prejudices—made up of likings and dislikings.
Imperfect Sympathies

8 I have been trying all my life to like Scotchmen, and am obliged to desist from the experiment in despair.

9 She unbent her mind afterwards—over a book.
Mrs. Battle's Opinions on Whist

10 In everything that relates to science, I am a whole Encyclopaedia behind the rest of the world.
The Old and the New Schoolmaster

11 A votary of the desk—a notched and cropt scrivener—one that sucks his substance, as certain sick people are said to do, through a quill.
Oxford in the Vacation

12 The human species, according to the best theory I can form of it, is composed of two distinct races, *the men who borrow,* and *the men who lend.*
The Two Races of Men

13 What a liberal confounding of those pedantic distinctions of *meum* and *tuum!*

14 I mean your *borrowers of books*—those mutilators of collections, spoilers of the symmetry of shelves, and creators of odd volumes.

15 To lose a volume to C[oleridge] carries some sense and meaning in it. You are sure that he will make one hearty meal on your viands, if he can give no account of the platter after it.

16 I love to lose myself in other men's minds. When I am not walking, I am reading; I cannot sit and think. Books think for me.
Last Essays of Elia (1833). **Detached Thoughts on Books and Reading**

17 I can read any thing which I call a book. There are things in that shape which I cannot allow for such. In this catalogue of books which are no books—biblia a-biblia—I reckon Court Calendars, Directories…the works of Hume, Gibbon, Robertson, Beattie, Soame Jenyns, and, generally, all those volumes which 'no gentleman's library should be without'.

18 Things in books' clothing.

19 Milton almost requires a solemn service of music to be played before you enter upon him.

20 A poor relation—is the most irrelevant thing in nature.
Poor Relations

21 Cultivate simplicity, Coleridge.
Letter to Coleridge, 8 Nov. 1796

22 Separate from the pleasure of your company, I don't much care if I never see another mountain in my life.
Letter to William Wordsworth, 30 Jan. 1801

23 The man must have a rare recipe for melancholy, who can be dull in Fleet Street.
The Londoner, in letter to Thomas Manning, 15 Feb. 1802

24 Nursed amid her noise, her crowds, her beloved smoke—what have I been doing all my life, if I have not lent out my heart with usury to such scenes?

25 I have made a little scale, supposing myself to receive the following various accessions of dignity from the king, who is the fountain of honour—As at first, 1, Mr C. Lamb;…10th, Emperor Lamb; 11th, Pope Innocent, higher than which is nothing but the Lamb of God.
Letter to Thomas Manning, 2 Jan. 1810

26 Nothing puzzles me more than time and space; and yet nothing troubles me less, as I never think about them.

27 I was at Hazlitt's marriage, and had like to have been turned out several times during the ceremony. Anything awful makes me laugh. I misbehaved once at a funeral.
Letter to Southey, 9 Aug. 1815

28 This very night I am going to leave off tobacco! Surely there must be some other world in which this unconquerable purpose shall be realized. The soul hath not her generous aspirings implanted in her in vain.
Letter to Thomas Manning, 26 Dec. 1815

29 His face when he repeats his verses hath its ancient glory, an Archangel a little damaged. [Coleridge.]
Letter to Wordsworth, 26 Apr. 1816

30 The rogue gives you Love Powders, and then a strong horse drench to bring 'em off your stomach that they mayn't hurt you. [Coleridge.]
23 Sept. 1816

31 Fanny Kelly's divine plain face.
Letter to Mrs. Wordsworth, 18 Feb. 1818

32 How I like to be liked, and what I do to be liked!
Letter to D. Wordsworth, 8 Jan. 1821

33 Who first invented Work—and tied the free
And holy-day rejoicing spirit down
To the ever-haunting importunity
Of business, in the green fields, and the town—
To plough—loom—anvil—spade—and, oh, most sad,
To this dry drudgery of the desk's dead wood?
Letter to Barton, Sept. 1822

34 Those fellows hate us. [Booksellers and authors.]
9 Jan. 1823

35 We should be modest for a modest man—as he is for himself.
Letter to Mrs. Montagu, Summer 1827

36 You are knee deep in clover.
Letter to C.C. Clarke, Dec. 1828

37 When my sonnet was rejected, I exclaimed, 'Damn the age; I will write for Antiquity!'
Letter to B.W. Procter, 22 Jan. 1829

38 Books of the true sort, not those things in boards that moderns mistake for books—what they club for at

book clubs.
Letter to J. Gillman, 30 Nov. 1829

1 Half as sober as a judge.
Letter to Mr. and Mrs. Moxon, Aug. 1833

2 The greatest pleasure I know, is to do a good action by
stealth, and to have it found out by accident.
Table Talk by the late Elia. *The Athenaeum,* 4 Jan. 1834

3 What a lass that were to go a-gipseying through the
world with.
The Jovial Crew. *The Examiner,* July 1819

4 The uncommunicating muteness of fishes.
A Quakers' Meeting

5 For thy sake, Tobacco, I
Would do any thing but die.
A Farewell to Tobacco, l.122

6 I have had playmates, I have had companions,
In my days of childhood, in my joyful school-days,—
All, all are gone, the old familiar faces.
The Old Familiar Faces

7 If ever I marry a wife,
I'll marry a landlord's daughter,
For then I may sit in the bar,
And drink cold brandy and water.
Written in a copy of *Coelebs in Search of a Wife*

8 At Godwin's…they [Lamb, Holcroft, and Coleridge]
were disputing fiercely which was the best—Man as he
was, or man as he is to be. 'Give me,' says Lamb,
'man as he is *not* to be.'
Hazlitt, *English Literature,* ch.xvii. My First Acquaintance with
Poets

9 Martin, if dirt were trumps, what hands you would
hold!
Leigh Hunt, *Lord Byron and his Contemporaries* (1828), p.299

10 I do not [know the lady]; but damn her at a venture.
E.V. Lucas, *Charles Lamb* (1905), vol.i, p.320, note

11 I noted one odd saying of Lamb's that 'the last breath
he drew in he wished might be through a pipe and
exhaled in a pun'.
Macready, *Journal,* 9 Jan. 1834

12 Dr Parr…asked him, how he had acquired his power
of smoking at such a rate? Lamb replied, 'I toiled after
it, sir, as some men toil after virtue.'
Talfourd, *Memoirs of Charles Lamb* (1892), p.262

MARY LAMB 1764–1847

13 He [Henry Crabb Robinson] says he never saw a man
so happy in *three wives* as Mr Wordsworth is.
Letter to Sarah Hutchinson, Nov. 1816

14 A child's a plaything for an hour.
Parental Recollections

JOHN GEORGE LAMBTON, FIRST EARL OF DURHAM 1792–1840

15 £40,000 a year a moderate income—such a one as
a man *might jog on with.*
The Creevey Papers (13 Sept. 1821), ii.32

LETITIA ELIZABETH LANDON 1802–1838

16 Few, save the poor, feel for the poor.
The Poor

WALTER SAVAGE LANDOR 1775–1864

17 Around the child bent all the three
Sweet Graces: Faith, Hope, Charity.
Around the man bend other faces:
Pride, Envy, Malice, are his Graces.
Around the Child

18 Hail, ye indomitable heroes, hail!
Despite of all your generals ye prevail.
The Crimean Heroes

19 Death stands above me, whispering low
I know not what into my ear;
Of his strange language all I know
Is, there is not a word of fear.
Epigrams, c. **Death**

20 I strove with none; for none was worth my strife;
Nature I loved, and, next to Nature, Art;
I warmed both hands before the fire of life;
It sinks, and I am ready to depart.
Finis

21 He says, *my reign is peace,* so slays
A thousand in the dead of night.
Are you all happy now? he says,
And those he leaves behind cry *quite.*
He swears he will have no contention,
And sets all nations by the ears;
He shouts aloud, *No intervention*!
Invades, and drowns them all in tears.
A Foreign Ruler (1863)

22 Past ruin'd Ilion Helen lives,
Alcestis rises from the shades;
Verse calls them forth; 'tis verse that gives
Immortal youth to mortal maids.
Ianthe

23 Ireland never was contented…
Say you so? You are demented.
Ireland was contented when
All could use the sword and pen,
And when Tara rose so high
That her turrets split the sky,
And about her courts were seen
Liveried Angels robed in green,
Wearing, by St Patrick's bounty,
Emeralds big as half a county.
The Last Fruit Off an Old Tree (1853), **Epigrams** LXXXIV

24 I loved him not; and yet now he is gone
I feel I am alone.
I check'd him while he spoke; yet, could he speak,
Alas! I would not check.
The Maid's Lament

25 Proud word you never spoke, but you will speak
Four not exempt from pride some future day.
Resting on one white hand a warm wet cheek
Over my open volume you will say,
'This man loved *me*!' then rise and trip away.
Proud Word You Never Spoke

26 Ah, what avails the sceptred race!
Ah, what the form divine!
What every virtue, every grace!
Rose Aylmer, all were thine.

Rose Aylmer, whom these wakeful eyes
May weep, but never see,
A night of memories and of sighs

I consecrate to thee.
Rose Aylmer

1 There is delight in singing, tho' none hear
Beside the singer.
To Robert Browning

2 Thee gentle Spenser fondly led;
But me he mostly sent to bed.
To Wordsworth: Those Who Have Laid the Harp Aside

3 How many verses have I thrown
Into the fire because the one
Peculiar word, the wanted most,
Was irrecoverably lost.
Verses Why Burnt

4 Well I remember how you smiled
    To see me write your name upon
The soft sea-sand—'O! what a child!
    You think you're writing upon stone!'

I have since written what no tide
    Shall ever wash away, what men
Unborn shall read o'er ocean wide
    And find Ianthe's name again.
Well I Remember How You Smiled

5 I know not whether I am proud,
But this I know, I hate the crowd.
With an Album. See 260:13

6 George the First was always reckoned
Vile, but viler George the Second;
And what mortal ever heard
Any good of George the Third?
When from earth the Fourth descended
God be praised the Georges ended!
Epigram in The Atlas, 28 Apr. 1855. See N. & Q., 3 May 1902, pp.318, 354

7 Laodameia died; Helen died; Leda, the beloved of Jupiter, went before.
Imaginary Conversations (1824–29). **Aesop and Rhodope,** i

8 There are no fields of amaranth on this side of the grave: there are no voices, O Rhodope! that are not soon mute, however tuneful: there is no name, with whatever emphasis of passionate love repeated, of which the echo is not faint at last.

9 He who first praises a good book becomingly, is next in merit to the author.
Alfieri and Salomon the Florentine Jew

10 Prose on certain occasions can bear a great deal of poetry: on the other hand, poetry sinks and swoons under a moderate weight of prose.
Archdeacon Hare and Walter Landor

11 I hate false words, and seek with care, difficulty, and moroseness, those that fit the thing.
Bishop Burnet and Humphrey Hardcastle

12 Goodness does not more certainly make men happy than happiness makes them good.
Lord Brooke and Sir Philip Sidney

13 States, like men, have their growth, their manhood, their decrepitude, their decay.
Pollio and Calvus

14 Clear writers, like clear fountains, do not seem so deep as they are; the turbid look the most profound.
Southey and Porson (1823).

15 Fleas know not whether they are upon the body of a giant or upon one of ordinary size.

SIR EDWIN LANDSEER 1802–1873

16 If people only knew as much about painting as I do, they would never buy my pictures.
Said to W.P. Frith. Campbell Lennie, Landseer the Victorian Paragon, ch.12

ANDREW LANG 1844–1912

17 St Andrews by the Northern Sea,
That is a haunted town to me!
Almae Matres

18   And through the music of the languid hours
They hear like Ocean on a western beach
    The surge and thunder of the Odyssey.
As One That for a Weary Space has Lain

19 If the wild bowler thinks he bowls,
    Or if the batsman thinks he's bowled,
They know not, poor misguided souls,
    They too shall perish unconsoled.
I am the batsman and the bat,
    I am the bowler and the ball,
The umpire, the pavilion cat,
    The roller, pitch, and stumps, and all.
Brahma. See 206:17

JULIA S. LANG 1921–

20 Are you sitting comfortably? Then I'll begin.
Preamble to children's story in Listen With Mother, B.B.C. radio programme, from 1950

FREDERICK LANGBRIDGE 1849–1923

21 Two men look out through the same bars:
One sees the mud, and one the stars.
A Cluster of Quiet Thoughts (1896) (Religious Tract Society Publication)

WILLIAM LANGLAND 1330?–1400?

22 In a somer seson whan soft was the sonne.
The Vision of William concerning Piers the Plowman (ed. Skeat), B Text, Prologue, l.1

23 A faire felde ful of folke fonde I there bytwene
Of alle manner of men, the mene and riche,
Worchyng and wandryng as the worlde asketh.
l.17

24 A glotoun of wordes.
l.139

25 Ac on a May morwenyng on Maluerne hulles
Me byfel for to slepe for weyrynesse of wandryng.
C Text, Passus 1, l.6

26 Bakers and brewers, bouchers and cokes—
For thees men doth most harme to the mene puple.
Passus 4, l.80

27 Grammere, that grounde is of alle.
Passus 18, l.107

28 'After sharpest shoures,' quath Pees [Peace] 'most sheene is the sonne;
Ys no weder warmer than after watery cloudes.'
Passus 21, l.456

ARCHBISHOP STEPHEN LANGTON d. 1228

29 *Veni, Sancte Spiritus,*
Et emitte coelitus
Lucis tuae radium.

Come, Holy Spirit, and send out from heaven the beam
of your light.
The 'Golden Sequence' for Whitsunday. Attr.

1 *Lava quod est sordidum,*
Riga quod est aridum,
Sana quod est saucium.
Flecte quod est rigidum,
Fove quod est frigidum,
Rege quod est devium.
Wash what is dirty, water what is dry, heal what is
wounded. Bend what is stiff, warm what is cold,
guide what goes off the road.

LÂO TSE ?6th cent. B.C.

2 Heaven and Earth are not ruthful;
To them the Ten Thousand Things are but as straw
dogs.
Tao-te-ching, 5. Tr. Arthur Waley. (The Ten Thousand Things:
all life forms. Straw dogs: sacrificial tokens.)

PHILIP LARKIN 1922–

3 What are days for?
Days are where we live
They come they wake us
Time and time over.
They are to be happy in;
Where can we live but days?
Days

4 Nothing, like something, happens anywhere.
I Remember, I Remember

5 Perhaps being old is having lighted rooms
Inside your head, and people in them, acting.
People you know, yet can't quite name.
The Old Fools

6 Why should I let the toad *work*
    Squat on my life?
Can't I use my wit as a pitchfork
    And drive the brute off?
Toads

7 Give me your arm, old toad;
Help me down Cemetery Road.
Toads Revisited

DUC DE LA ROCHEFOUCAULD 1613–1680

8 *Dans l'adversité de nos meilleurs amis, nous trouvons*
toujours quelque chose qui ne nous déplaît pas.
In the misfortune of our best friends, we always find
something which is not displeasing to us.
Réflexions ou Maximes Morales (1665), 99

9 *Nous avons tous assez de force pour supporter les*
maux d'autrui.
We are all strong enough to bear the misfortunes of
others.
Réflexions ou Sentences et Maximes Morales (1678), 19

10 *Il est plus honteux de se défier de ses amis que d'en*
être trompé.
It is more shameful to spurn one's friends than to be
duped by them.
84

11 *Il y a de bons mariages, mais il n'y en a point de*
délicieux.

There are good marriages, but no delightful ones.
113

12 *L'hypocrisie est un hommage que le vice rend à la*
vertu.
Hypocrisy is a tribute which vice pays to virtue.
218

13 *C'est une grande habileté que de savoir cacher son*
habileté.
The height of cleverness is to be able to conceal it.
245

14 *Il n'y a guère d'homme assez habile pour connaître*
tout le mal qu'il fait.
There is scarcely a single man sufficiently aware to
know all the evil he does.
269

15 *L'absence diminue les médiocres passions, et*
augmente les grandes, comme le vent éteint les
bougies, et allume le feu.
Absence diminishes commonplace passions and
increases great ones, as the wind extinguishes candles
and kindles fire.
276. See 117:6, 218:2

16 *La reconnaissance de la plupart des hommes n'est*
qu'une secrète envie de recevoir de plus grands
bienfaits.
In most of mankind gratitude is merely a secret hope
for greater favours.
298

17 *L'accent du pays où l'on est né demeure dans l'esprit*
et dans le coeur comme dans le langage.
The accent of one's birthplace lingers in the mind and
in the heart as it does in one's speech.
342

18 *On n'est jamais si malheureux qu'on croit, ni si*
heureux qu'on espère.
One is never as unhappy as one thinks, nor as happy as
one hopes.
Sentences et Maximes de Morale, Dutch edition (1664), 128

DUC DE LA ROCHEFOUCAULD-LIANCOURT
1747–1827

19 Louis XVI: *C'est une grande révolte.*
La Rochefoucauld-Liancourt: *Non, Sire, c'est une*
grande révolution.
('It is a big revolt.' 'No, Sir, a big revolution.')
When the Fall of the Bastille was reported at Versailles, 1789. F.
Dreyfus, *La Rochefoucauld-Liancourt* (1903), ch.II, sect iii

BISHOP HUGH LATIMER c.1485–1555

20 *Gutta cavat lapidem, non vi sed saepe cadendo.*
The drop of rain maketh a hole in the stone, not by
violence, but by oft falling.
7th Sermon preached before Edward VI (1549). See 366:27

21 Be of good comfort Master Ridley, and play the man.
We shall this day light such a candle by God's grace in
England, as (I trust) shall never be put out.
16 Oct. 1555. Foxe, *Actes and Monuments* (1562–3), 1570 edn.,
p.1937

BONAR LAW 1858–1923

22 If, therefore, war should ever come between these two
countries [Great Britain and Germany], which Heaven
forbid! it will not, I think, be due to irresistible natural

laws, it will be due to the want of human wisdom.
House of Commons, 27 Nov. 1911

1 I said [in 1911] that if ever war arose between Great Britain and Germany it would not be due to inevitable causes, for I did not believe in inevitable war. I said it would be due to human folly.
6 Aug. 1914

D.H. LAWRENCE 1885–1930

2 To the Puritan all things are impure, as somebody says.
Etruscan Places (1932). **Cerveteri**

3 She is dear to me in the middle of my being. But the gold and flowing serpent is coiling up again, to sleep at the root of my tree.
The Man Who Died (1931), pt.ii

4 Be a good animal, true to your animal instincts.
The White Peacock (1911), pt.ii, ch.2. See 514:25

5 Along the avenue of cypresses,
All in their scarlet cloaks and surplices
Of linen, go the chanting choristers,
The priests in gold and black, the villagers.
Giorno dei Morti

6 How beastly the bourgeois is
especially the male of the species.
How beastly the bourgeois is

7 So now it is vain for the singer to burst into clamour
With the great black piano appassionato. The glamour
Of childish days is upon me, my manhood is cast
Down in the flood of remembrance, I weep like a child
for the past.
Piano

8 Now it is autumn and the falling fruit
and the long journey towards oblivion…
Have you built your ship of death, O have you?
O build your ship of death, for you will need it.
The Ship of Death

9 Not I, not I, but the wind that blows through me!
Song of a man who has come through

10 Never trust the artist. Trust the tale. The proper function of a critic is to save the tale from the artist who created it.
Studies in Classic American Literature (1924), ch.1

11 It is lurid and melodramatic, but it is true.
ch.6

T.E. LAWRENCE 1888–1935

12 I loved you, so I drew these tides of men into my hands
and wrote my will across the sky in stars
To earn you Freedom, the seven pillared worthy house,
that your eyes might be shining for me
When we came.
Epigraph to *The Seven Pillars of Wisdom*. 'To S.A.'

EMMA LAZARUS 1849–1887

13 　　　　　Give me your tired, your poor,
Your huddled masses yearning to breathe free.
The New Colossus

STEPHEN LEACOCK 1869–1944

14 Lord Ronald…flung himself upon his horse and rode madly off in all directions.
Nonsense Novels (1911). **Gertrude the Governess**

EDWARD LEAR 1812–1888

15 There was an Old Man with a beard,
Who said, 'It is just as I feared!—
　Two Owls and a Hen,
　Four Larks and a Wren,
Have all built their nests in my beard!'
Book of Nonsense (1846)

16 There was an Old Man in a tree,
Who was horribly bored by a bee;
　When they said, 'Does it buzz?'
　He replied, 'Yes, it does!
It's a regular brute of a bee!'

17 There was an old Lady of Chertsey,
Who made a remarkable curtsey;
　She whirled round and round,
　Till she sunk underground,
Which distressed all the people of Chertsey.

18 There was an old man who said, 'Hush!
I perceive a young bird in this bush!'
　When they said, 'Is it small?'
　He replied, 'Not at all!
It is four times as big as the bush!'

19 Nasticreechia Krorluppia.
Nonsense Botany (1870)

20 'How pleasant to know Mr Lear!'
　Who has written such volumes of stuff!
Some think him ill-tempered and queer,
　But a few think him pleasant enough.
Nonsense Songs (1871), preface

21 He has ears, and two eyes, and ten fingers,
　Leastways if you reckon two thumbs;
Long ago he was one of the singers,
　But now he is one of the dumbs.

22 He drinks a good deal of Marsala
　But never gets tipsy at all.

23 He has many friends, laymen and clerical.
　Old Foss is the name of his cat:
His body is perfectly spherical,
　He weareth a runcible hat.

24 He reads but he cannot speak Spanish,
　He cannot abide ginger-beer:
Ere the days of his pilgrimage vanish,
　How pleasant to know Mr Lear!

25 On the coast of Coromandel
Where the early pumpkins blow,
　In the middle of the woods,
　Lived the Yonghy-Bonghy-Bó.
Two old chairs, and half a candle;—
One old jug without a handle,—
　These were all his worldly goods.
The Courtship of the Yonghy-Bonghy-Bó

26 'Gaze upon the rolling deep
　(Fish is plentiful and cheap)
　As the sea my love is deep!'
Said the Yonghy-Bonghy-Bó.
Lady Jíngly answered sadly,

And her tears began to flow—
'Your proposal comes too late.'

1 I can merely be your friend.

2 When awful darkness and silence reign
Over the great Gromboolian plain,
   Through the long, long wintry nights.
When the angry breakers roar
As they beat on the rocky shore;—
When Storm-clouds brood on the towering heights
   Of the Hills of the Chankly Bore.
The Dong with the Luminous Nose

3 And those who watch at that midnight hour
From Hall or Terrace or lofty Tower,
Cry as the wild light passes along,—
   'The Dong!—the Dong!
The wandering Dong through the forest goes!
   The Dong!—the Dong!
The Dong with Luminous Nose!'

4 And who so happy,—O who,
As the Duck and the Kangaroo?
The Duck and the Kangaroo

5 O My agéd Uncle Arly!
Sitting on a heap of Barley
   Thro' the silent hours of night,—
Close beside a leafy thicket:—
On his nose there was a Cricket,—
In his hat a Railway-Ticket;—
   (But his shoes were far too tight.)
Incidents in the Life of my Uncle Arly

6 Far and few, far and few,
Are the lands where the Jumblies live;
   Their heads are green, and their hands are blue,
And they went to sea in a Sieve.
The Jumblies

7   In spite of all their friends could say,
On a winter's morn, on a stormy day,
   In a Sieve they went to sea!

8 They called aloud 'Our Sieve ain't big,
But we don't care a button! We don't care a fig!'

9 And they brought an Owl, and a useful Cart,
And a pound of Rice, and a Cranberry Tart,
   And a hive of silvery Bees.
And they brought a Pig, and some green Jack-daws,
And a lovely Monkey with lollipop paws,
And forty bottles of Ring-Bo-Ree,
   And no end of Stilton Cheese.

10   Till Mrs Discobbolos said
   'Oh! W! X! Y! Z!
It has just come into my head—
Suppose we should happen to fall!!!!
           Darling Mr Discobbolos?'
Mr. and Mrs. Discobbolos

11 The Owl and the Pussy-Cat went to sea
   In a beautiful pea-green boat.
They took some honey, and plenty of money,
   Wrapped up in a five-pound note.
The Owl looked up to the Stars above
   And sang to a small guitar,
'Oh lovely Pussy! O Pussy, my love,
   What a beautiful Pussy you are.'
The Owl and the Pussy-Cat

12 Pussy said to the Owl, 'You elegant fowl!

How charmingly sweet you sing!
O let us be married! too long we have tarried:
   But what shall we do for a ring?'
They sailed away for a year and a day,
   To the land where the Bong-tree grows,
And there in a wood a Piggy-wig stood
   With a ring at the end of his nose.

13 'Dear Pig, are you willing to sell for one shilling
   Your ring?' Said the Piggy, 'I will.'

14 They dined on mince, and slices of quince,
   Which they ate with a runcible spoon;
And hand in hand, on the edge of the sand,
   They danced by the light of the moon.

15 Ploffskin, Pluffskin, Pelican jee!
We think no birds so happy as we!
Plumpskin, Plashkin, Pelican jill!
We think so then, and we thought so still!
The Pelican Chorus

16 We live on the Nile. The Nile we love.
By night we sleep on the cliffs above.
By day we fish, and at eve we stand
On long bare islets of yellow sand.

17 The Pobble who has no toes
Had once as many as we;
When they said, 'Some day you may lose them all';—
He replied,—'Fish fiddle de-dee!'

His Aunt Jobiska made him drink
Lavender water tinged with pink,
For she said, 'The world in general knows
There's nothing so good for a Pobble's toes!'
The Pobble Who Has No Toes

18 For his Aunt Jobiska said, 'No harm
Can come to his toes if his nose is warm,
And it's perfectly known that a Pobble's toes
Are safe, provided he minds his nose.'

19   When boats or ships came near him
He tinkledy-binkledy-winkled a bell.

20 He has gone to fish, for his Aunt Jobiska's
Runcible Cat with crimson whiskers!

21 And she made him a feast at his earnest wish
Of eggs and buttercups fried with fish;—
And she said, 'It's a fact the whole world knows,
That Pobbles are happier without their toes.'

22 'But the longer I live on this Crumpetty Tree
The plainer than ever it seems to me
That very few people come this way
And that life on the whole is far from gay!'
   Said the Quangle-Wangle Quee.
The Quangle-Wangle's Hat

23 Two old Bachelors were living in one house;
One caught a Muffin, the other caught a Mouse.
The Two Old Bachelors

24 And what can we expect if we haven't any dinner,
But to lose our teeth and eyelashes and keep on
   growing thinner?

25 Who, or why, or which, or what,
Is the Akond of Swat?
1888 edn. **The Akond of Swat**

26 There was an old person of Slough,
Who danced at the end of a bough;
   But they said, 'If you sneeze,

You might damage the trees,
You imprudent old person of Slough.'
One Hundred Nonsense Pictures and Rhymes

1 There was an old person of Ware,
Who rode on the back of a bear:
    When they asked,—'Does it trot?'—
He said, 'Certainly not!
He's a Moppsikon Floppsikon bear.'

2 There was an old person of Dean,
Who dined on one pea and one bean;
    For he said, 'More than that,
    Would make me too fat,'
That cautious old person of Dean.

3 There was an old man of Thermopylae,
Who never did anything properly;
    But they said, 'If you choose
    To boil eggs in your shoes,
You shall never remain in Thermopylae.'

MARY ELIZABETH LEASE 1853–1933

4 Kansas had better stop raising corn and begin raising
hell.
Attr.

LE CORBUSIER 1887–1965

5 *La maison est une machine à habiter.*
A house is a living-machine.
Vers une architecture (1923), p.ix

ALEXANDRE AUGUSTE LEDRU-ROLLIN
1807–1874

6 *Eh! je suis leur chef, il fallait bien les suivre.*
Ah well! I am their leader, I really ought to follow
them!
E. de Mirecourt, *Histoire Contemporaine* no.79, 'Ledru-Rollin'
(1857)

HENRY LEE 1756–1818

7 A citizen, first in war, first in peace, and first in the
hearts of his countrymen.
*Resolutions Adopted by the Congress on the Death of
Washington*, 19 Dec. 1799; moved by John Marshall and
misquoted in his *Life of Washington* as '...first in the hearts of his
fellow citizens.'

NATHANIEL LEE 1653?–1692

8 When the sun sets, shadows, that showed at noon
But small, appear most long and terrible.
Oedipus (1679), IV.i

9 He speaks the kindest words, and looks such things,
Vows with so much passion, swears with so much
    grace.
That 'tis a kind of Heaven to be deluded by him.
The Rival Queens (1677), I

10 'Tis beauty calls and glory leads the way.

11 Then he will talk, Good Gods,
    How he will talk.
III

12 When Greeks joined Greeks, then was the tug of war!
IV.ii

13 Philip fought men, but Alexander women.

14 Man, false man, smiling, destructive man.
Theodosius (1680), III.ii

HENRY SAMBROOKE LEIGH 1837–1883

15 The rapturous, wild, and ineffable pleasure
Of drinking at somebody else's expense.
Carols of Cockayne (1869). **Stanzas to an Intoxicated Fly**

CHARLES G. LELAND 1824–1903

16 Hans Breitmann gife a barty—
    Vhere ish dat barty now?
Hans Breitmann's Barty (1857)

17 All goned afay mit de lager-beer—
Afay in de ewigkeit!

18 They saw a Dream of Loveliness descending from the
train.
Brand New Ballads. The Masher

LENIN (VLADIMIR ILYICH ULYANOV)
1870–1924

19 The methods of the liberals were aptly and graphically
hit off by the Trudovik Sedelnikov at a meeting on
May 9 in the Panina Palace. When a liberal is abused,
he says: Thank God they didn't beat me. When he is
beaten, he thanks God they didn't kill him. When he is
killed, he will thank God that his immortal soul has
been delivered from its mortal clay.
**The Government's Falsification of the Duma and the Tasks of
the Social-Democrats.** Proletary, no.10, Dec. 1906. Tr. in
Collected Works, Moscow (1962), ed. C. Dutt, Vol.11

20 We shall now proceed to construct the socialist order.
Opening words of congress after the capture of the Winter Palace,
26 Oct. 1917, Trotsky, *History of the Russian Revolution*, ch.10

21 The substitution of the proletarian for the bourgeois
state is impossible without a violent revolution.
State and Revolution, (1917), ch.1.4

22 Communism is Soviet power plus the electrification of
the whole country.
Report at the eighth All-Russia Congress of Soviets on the work
of the Council of People's Commissars, 22 Dec. 1920

SPEAKER WILLIAM LENTHALL 1591–1662

23 I have neither eye to see, nor tongue to speak here,
but as the House is pleased to direct me.
4 Jan. 1642. Said to Charles I, who had asked if he saw any of the
five M.P.s whom the King had ordered to be arrested. Rushworth,
Historical Collections (1703–08), iv.238

LEONARDO DA VINCI 1452–1519

24 The poet ranks far below the painter in the
representation of visible things, and far below the
musician in that of invisible things.
Selections from the Notebooks, World's Classics edn., p.198

25 Every man at three years old is half his height.
MS. in Library of Institute of France, H. 31 recto

G.E. LESSING 1729–1781

26 *Gestern lieb' ich,
Heute leid' ich,
Morgen sterb' ich:
Dennoch denk' ich
Heut und morgen
Gern an gestern.*

Yesterday I loved, today I suffer, tomorrow I die: but I still think fondly, today and tomorrow, of yesterday.
Lied aus dem Spanischen

1 *Ein einziger dankbarer Gedanke gen Himmel ist das vollkommenste Gebet.*
One single grateful thought raised to heaven is the most perfect prayer.
Minna von Barnhelm (1767), ii.7

2 *Wenn Gott in seiner Rechten alle Wahrheit und in seiner Linken den einzigen, immer regen Trieb nach Wahrheit, obgleich mit dem Zusatz, mich immer und ewig zu irren, verschlossen hielte und spräche zu mir: Wähle! ich fiele ihm mit Demut in seine Linke und sagte: Vater, gieb! Die reine Wahrheit ist ja doch nur für Dich allein.*
If God were to hold out enclosed in His right hand all Truth, and in His left hand just the active search for Truth, though with the condition that I should ever err therein, and should say to me: Choose! I should humbly take His left hand and say: Father! Give me this one; absolute Truth belongs to Thee alone.
Wolfenbüttler Fragmente

ADA LEVERSON 1865–1936

3 The last gentleman in Europe.
Of Oscar Wilde. Wilde, *Letters to the Sphinx*. 'Reminiscences', 2

DUC DE LÉVIS 1764–1830

4 *Noblesse oblige.*
Nobility has its obligations.
Maximes et Réflexions, 1812 ed., **Morale**, 'Maximes et Préceptes', lxxiii

5 *Gouverner, c'est choisir.*
To govern is to make choices.
Politique, 'Maximes de Politique', xix

G.H. LEWES 1817–1878

6 Murder, like talent, seems occasionally to run in families.
The Physiology of Common Life (1859), ch.12

7 We must never assume that which is incapable of proof.
ch.13

C.S. LEWIS 1898–1963

8 A sensible human once said...'She's the sort of woman who lives for others—you can tell the others by their hunted expression.'
The Screwtape Letters (1942), XXVI

9 Term, holidays, term, holidays, till we leave school, and then work, work, work till we die.
Surprised by Joy, ch.4

SIR GEORGE CORNEWALL LEWIS 1806–1863

10 Life would be tolerable but for its amusements.
D.N.B.

WLAZIU VALENTINO ('LEE') LIBERACE 1920–

11 I cried all the way to the bank.
Liberace: An Autobiography, ch.2. After hostile criticism

CHARLES-JOSEPH, PRINCE DE LIGNE 1735–1814

12 *Le congrès ne marche pas, il danse.*
The Congress makes no progress; it dances.
La Garde-Chambonas, *Souvenirs du Congrès de Vienne, 1814–1815,* c.I

ABRAHAM LINCOLN 1809–1865

13 The ballot is stronger than the bullet.
Speech, 19 May 1856

14 'A house divided against itself cannot stand.' I believe this government cannot endure permanently, half slave and half free.
Speech, 16 June 1858. See 68:27

15 You can fool all the people some of the time, and some of the people all the time, but you can not fool all the people all of the time.
Attr. words in a speech at Clinton, 8 Sept. 1858. N.W. Stephenson, *Autobiography of A. Lincoln* (1927). Attr. also to Phineas Barnum

16 What is conservatism? Is it not adherence to the old and tried, against the new and untried?
Speech, 27 Feb. 1860

17 Let us have faith that right makes might; and in that faith let us to the end, dare to do our duty as we understand it.

18 I take the official oath to-day with no mental reservations, and with no purpose to construe the Constitution or laws by any hypercritical rules.
First Inaugural Address, 4 Mar. 1861

19 This country, with its institutions, belongs to the people who inhabit it. Whenever they shall grow weary of the existing government, they can exercise their constitutional right of amending it, or their revolutionary right to dismember or overthrow it.

20 I think the necessity of being *ready* increases.—Look to it.
The whole of a letter to Governor Andrew Curtin of Pennsylvania, 8 Apr. 1861

21 My paramount object in this struggle is to save the Union...If I could save the Union without freeing any slave, I would do it; and if I could save it by freeing all the slaves, I would do it; and if I could save it by freeing some and leaving others alone, I would also do that...I have here stated my purpose according to my views of official duty and I intend no modification of my oft-expressed personal wish that all men everywhere could be free.
Letter to Horace Greeley, 22 Aug. 1862

22 In giving freedom to the slave, we assure freedom to the free,—honourable alike in what we give and what we preserve.
Annual Message to Congress, 1 Dec. 1862

23 Fourscore and seven years ago our fathers brought forth upon this continent a new nation, conceived in liberty, and dedicated to the proposition that all men are created equal...In a larger sense we cannot dedicate, we cannot consecrate, we cannot hallow this ground. The brave men, living and dead, who struggled here, have consecrated it far above our power to add or detract. The world will little note, nor long remember, what we say here, but it can never forget what they did here. It is for us, the living, rather

to be dedicated here to the unfinished work which they who fought here have thus far so nobly advanced. It is rather for us to be here dedicated to the great task remaining before us, that from these honoured dead we take increased devotion to that cause for which they gave the last full measure of devotion; that we here highly resolve that the dead shall not have died in vain, that this nation, under God, shall have a new birth of freedom; and that government of the people, by the people, and for the people, shall not perish from the earth.
Address at Dedication of National Cemetery at Gettysburg, 19 Nov. 1863. See 368:26

1 I claim not to have controlled events, but confess plainly that events have controlled me.
Letter to A.G. Hodges, 4 Apr. 1864

2 It is not best to swap horses while crossing the river.
Reply to National Union League, 9 June 1864. J.G. Nicolay and J. Hay, *Abraham Lincoln*, bk.ix

3 With malice toward none; with charity for all; with firmness in the right, as God gives us to see the right, let us strive on to finish the work we are in: to bind up the nation's wounds; to care for him who shall have borne the battle, and for his widow and his orphan, to do all which may achieve and cherish a just and lasting peace among ourselves, and with all nations.
Second Inaugural Address, 4 Mar. 1865

4 People who like this sort of thing will find this the sort of thing they like.
Judgement on a book. G.W.E. Russell, *Collections and Recollections*, ch.30

5 The Lord prefers common-looking people. That is why he makes so many of them.
James Morgan, *Our President*, ch.6

6 So you're the little woman who wrote the book that made this great war!
On meeting Harriet Beecher Stowe. Carl Sandburg, *Abraham Lincoln: The War Years*, vol.II, ch.39

7 As President, I have no eyes but constitutional eyes; I cannot see you.
Attr. reply to the South Carolina Commissioners

GEORGE LINLEY 1798–1865

8 Among our ancient mountains,
And from our lovely vales,
Oh, let the prayer re-echo:
'God bless the Prince of Wales!'
God Bless the Prince of Wales

WALTER LIPPMANN 1889–

9 I doubt whether the student can do a greater work for his nation in this grave moment of its history than to detach himself from its preoccupations, refusing to let himself be absorbed by distractions about which, as a scholar, he can do almost nothing.
The Scholar in a Troubled World, (1932)

MAXIM LITVINOFF 1876–1951

10 Peace is indivisible.
First used publicly 25 Feb. 1920. A.U. Pope, *Maxim Litvinoff*, p.234. Also used in a speech to the 16th Plenum of the League of Nations on 1 July 1936. See *Against Aggression* (1939), p.45

LIVY 59 B.C.–A.D. 17 or 64 B.C.–A.D. 12

11 *Vae victis.*
Down with the defeated.
Ab Urbe Condita, 5.48.9. Shouted by Brennus, the Gallic King, who had captured Rome (390 B.C.), but a proverbial cry.

12 *Pugna magna victi sumus.*
In a battle, a big one, the defeated were us!
22.7.8. The announcement of the Roman disaster in Hannibal's ambush at Lake Trasimene (217 B.C.)

JOHN LOCKE 1632–1704

13 New opinions are always suspected, and usually opposed, without any other reason but because they are not already common.
An Essay concerning Human Understanding (1690), dedicatory epistle

14 Nature never makes excellent things for mean or no uses.
bk.ii, ch.1, sec.15

15 No man's knowledge here can go beyond his experience.
sec.19

16 It is one thing to show a man that he is in an error, and another to put him in possession of truth.
bk.iv, ch.7, sec.11

17 All men are liable to error; and most men are, in many points, by passion or interest, under temptation to it.
ch.20, sec.17

FREDERICK LOCKER-LAMPSON 1821–1895

18 If you lift a guinea-pig up by the tail
His eyes drop out!
A Garden Lyric

19 The world's as ugly, ay, as sin,
And almost as delightful.
The Jester's Plea

20 And many are afraid of God—
And more of Mrs Grundy.

21 Some men are good for righting wrongs,—
And some for writing verses.

JOHN GIBSON LOCKHART 1794–1854

22 It is a better and a wiser thing to be a starved apothecary than a starved poet; so back to the shop Mr John, back to 'plasters, pills, and ointment boxes.'
Review of Keats's *Endymion* in *Blackwood's Magazine*, 1818; authorship attr. to Lockhart.

23 Here, early to bed, lies kind William Maginn,
Who with genius, wit, learning, life's trophies to win,
Had neither great Lord nor rich cit of his kin,
Nor discretion to set himself up as to tin...
But at last he was beat, and sought help of the bin
(All the same to the Doctor, from claret to gin),
Which led swiftly to gaol, with consumption therein;
It was much, when the bones rattled loose in his skin,
He got leave to die here, out of Babylon's din.
Barring drink and the girls, I ne'er heard of a sin:
Many worse, better few, than bright, broken Maginn.
Epitaph for William Maginn (1794–1842), in William Maginn, *Miscellanies* (1885), vol.I, p.xviii

1 Here lies that peerless peer Lord Peter,
    Who broke the laws of God and man and metre.
Epitaph for Patrick ('Peter'), Lord Robertson. Sir Walter Scott,
Journal, vol.i, p.259, n.2

FRANCIS LOCKIER 1667–1740

2 In all my travels I never met with any one Scotchman
but what was a man of sense. I believe everybody of
that country that has any, leaves it as fast as they can.
Joseph Spence, *Anecdotes* (1858), p.55

THOMAS LODGE 1558?–1625

3 Love, in my bosom, like a bee,
    Doth suck his sweet.
Love, In My Bosom

4 Heigh ho, would she were mine!
Rosalind's Description

FRIEDRICH VON LOGAU 1604–1655

5 *Gottesmühlen mahlen langsam, mahlen aber trefflich
klein;*
*Ob aus Langmut Er sich säumet, bringt mit Schärf' Er
alles ein.*
Though the mills of God grind slowly, yet they grind
exceeding small;
Though with patience He stands waiting, with
exactness grinds He all.
Sinngedichte (1653), III.ii.24 (tr. H.W. Longfellow)

HENRY WADSWORTH LONGFELLOW
1807–1882

6 I shot an arrow into the air,
It fell to earth, I knew not where.
The Arrow and the Song

7 Thou, too, sail on, O Ship of State!
Sail on, O Union, strong and great!
Humanity with all its fears,
With all the hopes of future years,
Is hanging breathless on thy fate!
The Building of the Ship

8 Ye are better than all the ballads
    That ever were sung or said;
For ye are living poems,
    And all the rest are dead.
Children

9 Between the dark and the daylight,
    When the night is beginning to lower,
Comes a pause in the day's occupations,
    That is known as the Children's Hour.
The Children's Hour

10   The cares that infest the day
Shall fold their tents, like the Arabs,
    And as silently steal away.
The Day is Done

11 If you would hit the mark, you must aim a little above
    it;
Every arrow that flies feels the attraction of earth.
Elegiac Verse

12 This is the forest primeval.
Evangeline (1847), introduction, l.1

13 Sorrow and silence are strong, and patient endurance

is godlike.
pt.II, l.60

14 The shades of night were falling fast,
As through an Alpine village passed
A youth, who bore, 'mid snow and ice,
A banner with the strange device,
                    Excelsior!
Excelsior

15 'Try not the Pass!' the old man said;
'Dark lowers the tempest overhead.'

16 A traveller, by the faithful hound,
Half-buried in the snow was found.

17   Giotto's tower,
The lily of Florence blossoming in stone.
Giotto's Tower

18 I like that ancient Saxon phrase, which calls
    The burial-ground God's-Acre!
God's-Acre

19 The heights by great men reached and kept
    Were not attained by sudden flight,
But they, while their companions slept,
    Were toiling upward in the night.
The Ladder of Saint Augustine

20 Standing, with reluctant feet,
Where the brook and river meet,
Womanhood and childhood fleet!
Maidenhood

21   The men that women marry,
And why they marry them, will always be
A marvel and a mystery to the world.
Michael Angelo, pt.I, vi

22 I remember the black wharves and the slips,
    And the sea-tides tossing free;
And Spanish sailors with bearded lips,
And the beauty and mystery of the ships,
    And the magic of the sea.
        And the voice of that wayward song
        Is singing and saying still:
    'A boy's will is the wind's will
And the thoughts of youth are long, long thoughts.'
My Lost Youth

23 A solid man of Boston.
A comfortable man, with dividends,
And the first salmon and the first green peas.
New England Tragedies (1868), **John Endicott**, IV.i

24 *Emigravit* is the inscription on the tombstone where he
    lies;
Dead he is not, but departed,—for the artist never
    dies. [Of Albrecht Dürer.]
Nuremberg, xiii

25 Listen, my children, and you shall hear
Of the midnight ride of Paul Revere,
On the eighteenth of April in Seventy-five.
Paul Revere's Ride (1861)

26 A hurry of hoofs in a village street,
A shape in the moonlight, a bulk in the dark,
And beneath, from the pebbles, in passing, a spark
Struck out from a steed flying fearless and fleet:
That was all! And yet, through the gloom and the
    light,
The fate of a nation was riding that night.

27 Not in the clamour of the crowded street,
Not in the shouts and plaudits of the throng,

But in ourselves, are triumph and defeat.
The Poets

1 Tell me not, in mournful numbers,
  Life is but an empty dream!
For the soul is dead that slumbers,
  And things are not what they seem.

Life is real! Life is earnest!
  And the grave is not its goal;
Dust thou art, to dust returnest,
  Was not spoken of the soul.
A Psalm of Life

2 Art is long, and Time is fleeting,
  And our hearts, though stout and brave,
Still, like muffled drums, are beating
  Funeral marches to the grave.
See 251:8

3 Trust no Future, howe'er pleasant!
  Let the dead Past bury its dead!
Act,—act in the living Present!
  Heart within, and God o'erhead!

4 Lives of great men all remind us
  We can make our lives sublime,
And, departing, leave behind us
  Footprints on the sands of time.

5 Let us, then, be up and doing,
  With a heart for any fate;
Still achieving, still pursuing,
  Learn to labour and to wait.

6 There is no flock, however watched and tended,
  But one dead lamb is there!
There is no fireside, howsoe'er defended,
  But has one vacant chair!
Resignation

7 A Lady with a Lamp shall stand
In the great history of the land,
  A noble type of good,
  Heroic womanhood.
Santa Filomena

8 The forests, with their myriad tongues,
  Shouted of liberty;
And the Blast of the Desert cried aloud,
  With a voice so wild and free,
That he started in his sleep and smiled
  At their tempestuous glee.
The Slave's Dream

9 Gitche Manito, the mighty.
The Song of Hiawatha (1855), i. **The Peace-Pipe**

10 By the shore of Gitche Gumee,
By the shining Big-Sea-Water,
Stood the wigwam of Nokomis,
Daughter of the Moon, Nokomis.
Dark behind it rose the forest,
Rose the black and gloomy pine-trees,
Rose the firs with cones upon them;
Bright before it beat the water,
Beat the clear and sunny water,
Beat the shining Big-Sea-Water.
iii. **Hiawatha's Childhood**

11 From the waterfall he named her,
Minnehaha, Laughing Water.
iv. **Hiawatha and Mudjekeewis**

12 As unto the bow the cord is,
  So unto the man is woman;

Though she bends him, she obeys him,
Though she draws him, yet she follows;
Useless each without the other!
x. **Hiawatha's Wooing**

13 Onaway! Awake, beloved!
xi. **Hiawatha's Wedding-feast**

14 He is dead, the sweet musician!
He the sweetest of all singers!
He has gone from us for ever,
He has moved a little nearer
To the Master of all music,
To the Master of all singing!
O my brother, Chibiabos!
xv. **Hiawatha's Lamentation**

15 The secret anniversaries of the heart.
Sonnets. **Holidays**

16 He seemed the incarnate 'Well, I told you so!'
Tales of a Wayside Inn, pt.I (1863), **The Poet's Tale. The Birds of Killingworth**

17 Ships that pass in the night, and speak each other in
    passing;
Only a signal shown and a distant voice in the
    darkness;
So on the ocean of life we pass and speak one another,
Only a look and a voice; then darkness again and a
    silence.
pt.III (1874), **The Theologian's Tale. Elizabeth,** iv

18 Under the spreading chestnut tree
  The village smithy stands;
The smith, a mighty man is he,
  With large and sinewy hands;
And the muscles of his brawny arms
  Are strong as iron bands.
The Village Blacksmith

19 Each morning sees some task begin,
  Each evening sees it close;
Something attempted, something done,
  Has earned a night's repose.

20 It was the schooner Hesperus,
  That sailed the wintry sea;
And the skipper had taken his little daughter,
  To bear him company.
The Wreck of the Hesperus

21 But the father answered never a word,
  A frozen corpse was he.

22 There was a little girl
Who had a little curl
Right in the middle of her forehead,
When she was good
She was very, very good,
But when she was bad she was horrid.
B.R.T. Machetta, *Home Life of Longfellow*

23 The square root of half a number of bees, and also
eight-ninths of the whole, alighted on the jasmines,
and a female buzzed responsive to the hum of the male
inclosed at night in a water-lily. O, beautiful damsel,
tell me the number of bees.
Kavanagh, ch.4

FREDERICK LONSDALE 1881–1934

24 Don't keep finishing your sentences. I am not a bloody

fool.
Frances Donaldson, *Child of the Twenties* (1959), p.11

ANITA LOOS 1893–

1 A girl like I.
Gentlemen Prefer Blondes (1925), *passim*

2 Fate keeps on happening.
ch.2 (heading)

3 Kissing your hand may make you feel very very good
but a diamond and safire bracelet lasts forever.
ch.4

4 You have got to be a Queen to get away with a hat like
that.

5 Fun is fun but no girl wants to laugh all of the time.

6 So then Dr Froyd said that all I needed was to cultivate
a few inhibitions and get some sleep.
ch.5

FEDERICO GARCÍA LORCA
see GARCÍA LORCA

LOUIS XIV 1638–1715

7 *Il n'y a plus de Pyrénées.*
The Pyrenees have ceased to exist.
At the accession of his grandson to the throne of Spain, 1700.
Attr. Voltaire, *Siècle de Louis XIV*, ch.28

8 *L'État c'est moi.*
I am the State.
Attr. remark before the Parlement de Paris, 13 Apr. 1655.
Dulaure, *Histoire de Paris* (1834), vol.6, p.298. Probably
apocryphal.

9 *Toutes les fois que je donne une place vacante, je fais
cent mécontents et un ingrat.*
Every time I make an appointment, I make one
ungrateful person and a hundred with a grievance.
Voltaire, *Siècle de Louis XIV*, ch.26

10 *J'ai failli attendre.*
I almost had to wait.
Attrib. expression of impatience. Attribution doubted by e.g. E.
Fournier, *L'Esprit dans l'Histoire* (4th edition, 1884), ch.xlviii

LOUIS XVIII 1755–1824

11 *L'exactitude est la politesse des rois.*
Punctuality is the politeness of kings.
Attr. *Souvenirs de J. Lafitte* (1844), bk.1, ch.3

RICHARD LOVELACE 1618–1658

12   Am not I shot
With the self-same artillery?
Amyntor from Beyond the Sea to Alexis

13 Lucasta that bright northern star.

14 Forbear, thou great good husband, little ant.
The Ant

15 When Love with unconfined wings
Hovers within my gates;
And my divine Althea brings
To whisper at the grates:
When I lie tangled in her hair,
And fettered to her eye;
The Gods, that wanton in the air,

Know no such liberty.
To Althea, From Prison

16 When flowing cups run swiftly round
With no allaying Thames.

17 When thirsty grief in wine we steep,
When healths and draughts go free,
Fishes, that tipple in the deep,
Know no such liberty.

18 Stone walls do not a prison make
Nor iron bars a cage;
Minds innocent and quiet take
That for an hermitage;
If I have freedom in my love,
And in my soul am free,
Angels alone, that soar above,
Enjoy such liberty.

19 If to be absent were to be
Away from thee;
Or that when I am gone,
You or I were alone;
Then my Lucasta might I crave
Pity from blust'ring wind, or swallowing wave.
To Lucasta, Going Beyond the Seas

20 Tell me not (Sweet) I am unkind,
That from the nunnery
Of thy chaste breast, and quiet mind,
To war and arms I fly.

True; a new mistress now I chase,
The first foe in the field;
And with a stronger faith embrace
A sword, a horse, a shield.

Yet this inconstancy is such,
As you too shall adore;
I could not love thee (Dear) so much,
Lov'd I not honour more.
To Lucasta, Going to the Wars

SAMUEL LOVER 1797–1868

21 When once the itch of literature comes over a man,
nothing can cure it but the scratching of a pen.
Handy Andy (1842), ch.36

22 'Now women are mostly troublesome cattle to deal
with mostly', said Goggins.

ROBERT LOWE, VISCOUNT SHERBROOKE
1811–1892

23 I believe it will be absolutely necessary that you
should prevail on our future masters to learn their
letters.
House of Commons, 15 July 1867, on the passing of the Reform
Bill. Popularized as 'We must educate our masters.'

24 The Chancellor of the Exchequer is a man whose
duties make him more or less of a taxing machine. He
is intrusted with a certain amount of misery which it is
his duty to distribute as fairly as he can.
House of Commons, 11 Apr. 1870

AMY LOWELL 1856–1943

25 And the softness of my body will be guarded from
embrace
By each button, hook, and lace.

For the man who should loose me is dead,
Fighting with the Duke in Flanders,
In a pattern called a war.
Christ! What are patterns for?
Patterns

JAMES RUSSELL LOWELL 1819–1891

1 An' you've gut to git up airly
    Ef you want to take in God.
  The Biglow Papers, First Series (1848), No.1

2 You've a darned long row to hoe.

3 I du believe in Freedom's cause,
    Ez fur away ez Payris is;
  I love to see her stick her claws
    In them infarnal Phayrisees;
  It's wal enough agin a king
    To dror resolves an' triggers,—
  But libbaty's a kind o' thing
    Thet don't agree with niggers.
  No.6. **The Pious Editor's Creed**

4 I *don't* believe in princerple,
    But O, I *du* in interest.

5 It ain't by princerples nor men
    My preudunt course is steadied,—
  I scent wich pays the best, an' then
    Go into it baldheaded.

6 She thought no v'ice hed sech a swing
    Ez hisn in the choir;
  My! when he made Ole Hundred ring,
    She *knowed* the Lord was nigher.
  Introduction to the Second Series (1867), **The Courtin'**

7 We've a war, an' a debt, an' a flag; an' ef this
  Ain't to be inderpendunt, why, wut on airth is?
  Second Series, No.4

8 There comes Poe with his raven like Barnaby Rudge,
  Three-fifths of him genius, and two-fifths sheer fudge.
  A Fable for Critics (1848), l.1215

9 No man is born into the world, whose work
  Is not born with him; there is always work,
  And tools to work withal, for those who will:
  And blessèd are the horny hands of toil!
  A Glance Behind the Curtain, l.201

10 These pearls of thought in Persian gulfs were bred,
  Each softly lucent as a rounded moon;
  The diver Omar plucked them from their bed,
  Fitzgerald strung them on an English thread.
  In a Copy of Omar Khayyám

11 Before Man made us citizens, great Nature made us
  men.
  On the Capture of Fugitive Slaves

12 Once to every man and nation comes the moment to
    decide,
  In the strife of Truth with Falsehood, for the good or
    evil side.
  The Present Crisis

13 Truth forever on the scaffold, Wrong forever on the
    throne,—
  Yet that scaffold sways the future, and, behind the dim
    unknown,
  Standeth God within the shadow, keeping watch above
    his own.

14 New occasions teach new duties: Time makes ancient
  good uncouth;
  They must upward still, and onward, who would keep
  abreast of Truth.

15 May is a pious fraud of the almanac.
  Under the Willows, l.21

16 A wise scepticism is the first attribute of a good critic.
  Among My Books. Shakespeare Once More

17 Let us be of good cheer, however, remembering that
  the misfortunes hardest to bear are those which never
  come.
  Democracy and Addresses. Democracy

18 There is no good in arguing with the inevitable. The
  only argument available with an east wind is to put on
  your overcoat.

ROBERT LOWELL 1917–1977

19 I saw the spiders marching through the air,
  Swimming from tree to tree that mildewed day
    In latter August when the hay
    Came creaking to the barn…

          Let there pass
  A minute, ten, ten trillion; but the blaze
  Is infinite, eternal, this is death,
  To die and know it. This is the Black Widow, death.
  Mr. Edwards and the Spider. See 200:7

20 These are the tranquillized *Fifties*,
  and I am forty. Ought I to regret my seedtime?
  I was a fire-breathing Catholic C.O.,
  and made my manic statement,
  telling off the state and president, and then
  sat waiting sentence in the bull pen
  beside a negro boy with curlicues
  of marijuana in his hair.
  Memories of West Street and Lepke

WILLIAM LOWNDES 1652–1724

21 Take care of the pence, and the pounds will take care
  of themselves.
  Lord Chesterfield, letter to his son, 5 Feb. 1750. In an earlier
  letter (6 Nov. 1747) the formula is given as '…for the pounds…'

LUCAN A.D. 39–65

22   *Quis iustis induit arma*
  Scire nefas, magno se iudice quisque tuetur:
  Victrix causa deis placuit, sed victa Catoni.
  It is not granted to know which man took up arms with
    more right on his side. Each pleads his cause before
    a great judge: the winning cause pleased the gods,
    but the losing one pleased Cato.
  Bellum Civile, I.126

23 *Stat magni nominis umbra.*
  There stands the ghost of a great name.
  Works, I.135

24 *Nil actum credens, dum quid superesset agendum.*
  Thinking nothing done while anything remained to be
    done.
  II.657

25   *Coniunx*
  Est mihi, sunt nati: dedimus tot pignora fatis.
  I have a wife, I have sons: all of them hostages given
    to fate.
  VII.661

1   *Jupiter est quodcumque vides, quocumque moveris.*
    Jupiter is whatever you see, whichever way you move.
    IX.580

LUCILIUS d.102/1 B.C.

2   *Maior erat natu; non omnia possumus omnes.*
    He was older; there are some things we cannot all do.
    See Macrobius, *Saturnalia,* VI.i.35

LUCRETIUS 94?–55 B.C.

3   *Ergo vivida vis animi pervicit, et extra*
    Processit longe flammantia moenia mundi
    Atque omne immensum peragravit, mente animoque.
    So the vital strength of his spirit won through, and he
    made his way far outside the flaming walls of the
    world and ranged over the measureless whole, both
    in mind and spirit.
    De Rerum Natura, i.72. Of Epicurus.

4   *Tantum religio potuit suadere malorum.*
    So much wrong could religion induce.
    101

5   *Nil posse creari*
    De nilo.
    Nothing can be created out of nothing.
    155

6   *Suave, mari magno turbantibus aequora ventis,*
    E terra magnum alterius spectare laborem;
    Non quia vexari quemquamst iucunda voluptas,
    Sed quibus ipse malis careas quia cernere suave est.
    Suave etiam belli certamina magna tueri
    Per campos instructa tua sine parte pericli.
    Sed nil dulcius est, bene quam munita tenere
    Edita doctrina sapientum templa serena,
    Despicere unde queas alios passimque videre
    Errare atque viam palantis quaerere vitae,
    Certare ingenio, contendere nobilitate,
    Noctes atque dies niti praestante labore
    Ad summas emergere opes rerumque potiri.
    Lovely it is, when the winds are churning up the
    waves on the great sea, to gaze out from the land on
    the great efforts of someone else; not because it's an
    enjoyable pleasure that somebody is in difficulties,
    but because it's lovely to realize what troubles you
    are yourself spared. Lovely also to witness great
    battle-plans of war, carried out across the plains,
    without your having any share in the danger. But
    nothing is sweeter than to occupy the quiet precincts
    that are well protected by the teachings of the wise,
    from where you can look down on others and see
    them wandering all over the place, getting lost and
    seeking the way in life, striving by their wits, pitting
    their noble birth, by night and by day struggling by
    superior efforts to rise to power at the top and make
    all theirs.
    ii.1

7   *Augescunt aliae gentes, aliae minuuntur,*
    Inque brevi spatio mutantur saecla animantum
    Et quasi cursores vitai lampada tradunt.
    Some races increase, others are reduced, and in a short
    while the generations of living creatures are changed
    and like runners relay the torch of life.
    7

8   *Nil igitur mors est ad nos neque pertinet hilum,*

Quandoquidem natura animi mortalis habetur.
Death therefore is nothing to us nor does it concern us
    a scrap, seeing that the nature of the spirit we
    possess is something mortal.
    iii.830

9   *Scire licet nobis nil esse in morte timendum*
    Nec miserum fieri qui non est posse neque hilum
    Differre an nullo fuerit iam tempore natus,
    Mortalem vitam mors cum immortalis ademit.
    We can know there is nothing to be feared in death,
    that one who is not cannot be made unhappy, and
    that it matters not a scrap whether one might ever
    have been born at all, when death that is immortal
    has taken over one's mortal life.
    866

10 *Vitaque mancipio, nulli datur, omnibus usu.*
    And life is given to none freehold, but it is leasehold
    for all.
    971

11   *Medio de fonte leporum*
    Surgit amari aliquid quod in ipsis floribus angat.
    From the midst of the fountain of delights rises
    something bitter that chokes them all amongst the
    flowers.
    iv.1133

FRAY LUIS DE LEÓN c.1527–1591

12 *Que descansada vida*
    la del que huye el mundanal ruido,
    y sigue la escondida
    senda, por donde han ido
    los pocos sabios que en el mundo han sido!
    What a relaxed life is that which flees the worldly
    clamour, and follows the hidden path down which
    have gone the few wise men there have been in the
    world!
    Vida Retirada

13 *Dicebamus hesterno die.*
    We were saying yesterday.
    On resuming a lecture at Salamanca University (1577) after five
    years' imprisonment. Attr. in, e.g., A.F.G. Bell, *Luis de León,*
    ch.8

MARTIN LUTHER 1483–1546

14 *Darum gibt unser Herr Gott gemeiniglich Reichtum*
    den grossen Eseln, denen er sonst nichts gönnt.
    So our Lord God commonly gives riches to those gross
    asses to whom He vouchsafes nothing else.
    Colloquia (collected 1566, J. Aurifaber), ch.XX

15 *Esto peccator et pecca fortiter, sed fortius fide et*
    gaude in Christo.
    Be a sinner and sin strongly, but more strongly have
    faith and rejoice in Christ.
    Letter to Melanchthon. **Epistolae,** Jena (1556), i.345

16 *Hier stehe ich. Ich kann nicht anders. Gott helfe mir.*
    Amen.
    Here stand I. I can do no other. God help me. Amen.
    Speech at the Diet of Worms, 18 Apr. 1521

17 The confidence and faith of the heart alone make both
    God and an idol.
    Large Catechism, pt.I. 'The First Commandment', 1

18 Whatever your heart clings to and confides in that is
    really your God.

1 *Wer nicht liebt Wein, Weib und Gesang,*
Der bleibt ein Narr sein Leben lang.
Who loves not woman, wine, and song
Remains a fool his whole life long.
<small>Attr. Written in the Luther room in the Wartburg, but no proof exists of its authorship</small>

2 *Ein' feste Burg ist unser Gott,*
Ein' gute Wehr und Waffen.
A safe stronghold our God is still,
A trusty shield and weapon.
Klug'sche Gesangbuch (1529). Tr. Carlyle

3 *Wenn ich gewusst hätte, dass so viel Teufel auf mich*
gezielet hätten, als Ziegel auf den Dächern waren zu
Worms, wäre ich dennoch eingeritten.
If I had heard that as many devils would set on me in
Worms as there are tiles on the roofs, I should none
the less have ridden there.
Luthers Sämmtliche Schriften (1745), xvi.14

JOHN LYDGATE 1370?–1451?

4 Woord is but wynd; leff woord and tak the dede.
Secrees of Old Philisoffres, l.1224

5 Sithe off oure language he [Chaucer] was the
lodesterre.
Falls of Princes (1430–38), prol. l.252

6 Sithe he off Inglissh in makyng was the beste,
Preie onto God to yiue his soule good reste.
l.356

7 Comparisouns doon offte gret greuaunce.
bk.iii, l.2188

8 Love is mor than gold or gret richesse.
The Story of Thebes (c.1420), pt.III, l.2716

JOHN LYLY 1554?–1606

9 *Campaspe:* Were women never so fair, men would be
false.
Apelles: Were women never so false, men would be
fond.
Campaspe (1584), III.iii

10 Cupid and my Campaspe play'd
At cards for kisses, Cupid paid.
III.v

11 At last he set her both his eyes;
She won, and Cupid blind did rise.
O Love! has she done this to thee?
What shall, alas! become of me?

12 What bird so sings, yet so does wail?
O 'tis the ravish'd nightingale.
Jug, jug, jug, jug, tereu, she cries,
And still her woes at midnight rise.
V.i

13 How at heaven's gates she claps her wings,
The morn not waking till she sings. [The lark.]

14 Be valiant, but not too venturous. Let thy attire be
comely, but not costly.
Euphues: the Anatomy of Wit (1578, Arber), p.39

15 Night hath a thousand eyes.
Maides Metamorphose (1600), III.i

16 If all the earth were paper white
And all the sea were ink
'Twere not enough for me to write

As my poor heart doth think.
Works, ed. Bond (1902), vol.iii, p.452

BARON LYNDHURST 1772–1863

17 Campbell has added another terror to death.
<small>On being assured that he had not yet been included in Lord Campbell's *Lives of the Lord Chancellors;* attr. by Sir H. Poland. See E. Bowen-Rowlands, *Seventy-Two Years At the Bar,* ch.10. See 569:6</small>

LYSANDER d. 395 B.C.

18 Deceive boys with toys, but men with oaths.
Plutarch, *Lives, Lysander,* 8

H.F. LYTE 1793–1847

19 Abide with me; fast falls the eventide;
The darkness deepens; Lord, with me abide;
When other helpers fail, and comforts flee,
Help of the helpless, O, abide with me.

Swift to its close ebbs out life's little day;
Earth's joys grow dim, its glories pass away;
Change and decay in all around I see;
O Thou, who changest not, abide with me.
Abide with Me

GEORGE, LORD LYTTELTON 1709–1773

20 What is your sex's earliest, latest care,
Your heart's supreme ambition?—To be fair.
Advice to a Lady (1733), l.17

21 Seek to be good, but aim not to be great;
A woman's noblest station is retreat.
l.51

22 Where none admire, 'tis useless to excel;
Where none are beaux, 'tis vain to be a belle.
Soliloquy of a Beauty in the Country

E.R. BULWER, 1ST EARL OF LYTTON
see OWEN MEREDITH

WARD McALLISTER 1827–1895

23 There are only about four hundred people in New York
society.
<small>Interview with Charles H. Crandall in the *New York Tribune,* 1888. D. Amer. B.</small>

GENERAL DOUGLAS MACARTHUR 1880–1964

24 I shall return.
Message on leaving Corregidor for Australia. 11 Mar. 1942

LORD MACAULAY 1800–1859

25 Attend, all ye who list to hear our noble England's
praise;
I tell of the thrice famous deeds she wrought in ancient
days.
The Armada (1842)

26 Night sank upon the dusky beach, and on the purple
sea,
Such night in England ne'er had been, nor e'er again
shall be.

27 The rugged miners poured to war from Mendip's
sunless caves.

1 The sentinel on Whitehall gate looked forth into the
  night.

2 At once on all her stately gates arose the answering
  fires;
  At once the wild alarum clashed from all her reeling
  spires.

3 And broader still became the blaze, and louder still the
  din,
  As fast from every village round the horse came
  spurring in;
  And eastward straight from wild Blackheath the
  warlike errand went,
  And roused in many an ancient hall the gallant squires
  of Kent.

4 Till Belvoir's lordly terraces the sign to Lincoln sent,
  And Lincoln sped the message on o'er the wide vale of
  Trent;
  Till Skiddaw saw the fire that burned on Gaunt's
  embattled pile,
  And the red glare on Skiddaw roused the burghers of
  Carlisle.

5 Obadiah Bind-their-kings-in-chains-and-their-
  nobles-with-links-of-iron.
  The Battle of Naseby. (Name of the supposed author. See
  399:24)

6 Oh, wherefore come ye forth in triumph from the
  north,
  With your hands, and your feet, and your raiment all
  red?
  And wherefore doth your rout send forth a joyous
  shout?
  And whence be the grapes of the wine-press which ye
  tread?

7 And the Man of Blood was there, with his long
  essenced hair,
  And Astley, and Sir Marmaduke, and Rupert of the
  Rhine.

8 To my true king I offer'd free from stain
  Courage and faith; vain faith, and courage vain.
  A Jacobite's Epitaph

9 For him I languished in a foreign clime,
  Grey-haired with sorrow in my manhood's prime;
  Heard on Lavernia Scargill's whispering trees,
  And pined by Arno for my lovelier Tees.

10 By those white cliffs I never more must see,
   By that dear language which I spake like thee,
   Forget all feuds, and shed one English tear
   O'er English dust. A broken heart lies here.

11 Lars Porsena of Clusium
     By the nine gods he swore
   That the great house of Tarquin
     Should suffer wrong no more.
   By the Nine Gods he swore it,
     And named a trysting day,
   And bade his messengers ride forth,
   East and west and south and north,
     To summon his array.
   Lays of Ancient Rome (1842). Horatius, 1

12 The harvests of Arretium,
     This year, old men shall reap.
   This year, young boys in Umbro
     Shall plunge the struggling sheep;

And in the vats of Luna,
  This year, the must shall foam
Round the white feet of laughing girls
  Whose sires have marched to Rome.
8

13 And with a mighty following
     To join the muster came
   The Tusculan Mamilius,
     Prince of the Latian name.
   12

14 But the Consul's brow was sad,
     And the Consul's speech was low,
   And darkly looked he at the wall,
     And darkly at the foe.
   26

15 Then out spake brave Horatius,
     The Captain of the Gate:
   'To every man upon this earth
     Death cometh soon or late.
   And how can man die better
     Than facing fearful odds,
   For the ashes of his fathers,
     And the temples of his Gods?'
   27

16 To save them from false Sextus
     That wrought the deed of shame.
   28

17 'Now who will stand on either hand,
     And keep th﹍ bridge with me?'
   29

18 Then none was for a party;
     Then all were for the state;
   Then the great man helped the poor,
     And the poor man loved the great:
   Then lands were fairly portioned;
     Then spoils were fairly sold:
   The Romans were like brothers
     In the brave days of old.
   31

19 Was none who would be foremost
     To lead such dire attack;
   But those behind cried 'Forward!'
     And those before cried 'Back!'
   50

20 'Come back, come back, Horatius!'
     Loud cried the Fathers all.
   'Back, Lartius! back, Herminius!
     Back, ere the ruin fall!'
   53

21 'Oh, Tiber! father Tiber
     To whom the Romans pray,
   A Roman's life, a Roman's arms,
     Take thou in charge this day!'
   59

22 And even the ranks of Tuscany
     Could scarce forbear to cheer.
   60

23 When the oldest cask is opened,
     And the largest lamp is lit;...
   With weeping and with laughter
     Still is the story told,
   How well Horatius kept the bridge

In the brave days of old.
69-70

1 Those trees in whose dim shadow
 The ghastly priest doth reign,
The priest who slew the slayer,
 And shall himself be slain.
The Battle of Lake Regillus, 10

2 Let no man stop to plunder,
 But slay, and slay, and slay;
The Gods who live for ever
 Are on our side to-day.
35

3 Knowledge advances by steps, and not by leaps.
Essays and Biographies. History (*Edinburgh Review*, May 1828)

4 The English Bible, a book which, if everything else in our language should perish, would alone suffice to show the whole extent of its beauty and power.
John Dryden (Jan. 1828)

5 His imagination resembled the wings of an ostrich. It enabled him to run, though not to soar.

6 The business of everybody is the business of nobody.
Historical Essays Contributed to the 'Edinburgh Review'. **Hallam's 'Constitutional History'** (Sept. 1828)

7 The gallery in which the reporters sit has become a fourth estate of the realm.

8 He knew that the essence of war is violence, and that moderation in war is imbecility. [John Hampden.]
Lord Nugent's 'Memorials of Hampden' (Dec. 1831)

9 The reluctant obedience of distant provinces generally costs more than it [the territory] is worth.
War of the Succession in Spain (Jan. 1833)

10 Biographers, translators, editors, all, in short, who employ themselves in illustrating the lives or writings of others, are peculiarly exposed to the *Lues Boswelliana,* or disease of admiration.
William Pitt, Earl of Chatham (Jan. 1834)

11 The highest intellects, like the tops of mountains, are the first to catch and to reflect the dawn.
Sir James Mackintosh (July 1835)

12 The history of England is emphatically the history of progress.

13 The rising hope of those stern and unbending Tories who follow, reluctantly and mutinously, a leader whose experience and eloquence are indispensable to them, but whose cautious temper and moderate opinions they abhor. [Sir Robert Peel.]
Gladstone on Church and State (Apr. 1839)

14 Every schoolboy knows who imprisoned Montezuma, and who strangled Atahualpa.
Lord Clive (Jan. 1840)

15 They [the Nabobs] raised the price of everything in their neighbourhood, from fresh eggs to rotten boroughs.

16 She [the Roman Catholic Church] may still exist in undiminished vigour when some traveller from New Zealand shall, in the midst of a vast solitude, take his stand on a broken arch of London Bridge to sketch the ruins of St Paul's.
Von Ranke (Oct. 1840). See 563:9

17 She [the Church of Rome] thoroughly understands what no other church has ever understood, how to deal with enthusiasts.

18 The Chief Justice was rich, quiet, and infamous.
Warren Hastings (Oct. 1841)

19 The great Proconsul.

20 That temple of silence and reconciliation where the enmities of twenty generations lie buried.
[Westminster Abbey.]

21 In order that he might rob a neighbour whom he had promised to defend, black men fought on the coast of Coromandel, and red men scalped each other by the Great Lakes of North America.
Frederic the Great (Apr. 1842)

22 As civilization advances, poetry almost necessarily declines.
Literary Essays Contributed to the 'Edinburgh Review'. Milton (Aug. 1825)

23 Perhaps no person can be a poet, or can even enjoy poetry, without a certain unsoundness of mind.

24 There is only one cure for the evils which newly acquired freedom produces; and that is freedom.

25 Many politicians of our time are in the habit of laying it down as a self-evident proposition, that no people ought to be free till they are fit to use their freedom. The maxim is worthy of the fool in the old story, who resolved not to go into the water till he had learnt to swim. If men are to wait for liberty till they become wise and good in slavery, they may indeed wait for ever.

26 On the rich and the eloquent, on nobles and priests, they looked down with contempt: for they esteemed themselves rich in a more precious treasure, and eloquent in a more sublime language, nobles by the right of an earlier creation, and priests by the imposition of a mightier hand. [The Puritans.]

27 Out of his surname they have coined an epithet for a knave, and out of his Christian name a synonym for the Devil.
Machiavelli (Mar. 1827)

28 Nothing is so useless as a general maxim.

29 We have heard it said that five per cent is the natural interest of money.
Southey's 'Colloquies on Society' (Jan. 1830)

30 His writing bears the same relation to poetry which a Turkey carpet bears to a picture. There are colours in the Turkey carpet out of which a picture might be made. There are words in Mr Montgomery's writing which, when disposed in certain orders and combinations, have made, and will make again, good poetry. But, as they now stand, they seem to be put together on principle in such a manner as to give no image of anything 'in the heavens above, or in the earth beneath, or in the waters under the earth.'
Mr. Robert Montgomery's Poems (Apr. 1830). See 47:24

31 The use of a mirror, we submit, is not to be painted upon.

32 His theory is therefore this, that God made the thunder, but that the lightning made itself.

33 He had a head which statuaries loved to copy, and a foot the deformity of which the beggars in the street mimicked.
Moore's 'Life of Lord Byron' (June 1830)

1 We know no spectacle so ridiculous as the British public in one of its periodical fits of morality.

2 We prefer a gipsy by Reynolds to his Majesty's head on a sign-post.

3 From the poetry of Lord Byron they drew a system of ethics, compounded of misanthropy and voluptuousness, a system in which the two great commandments were, to hate your neighbour, and to love your neighbour's wife.

4 It is not easy to make a simile go on all fours.
John Bunyan (Dec. 1830)

5 The Life of Johnson is assuredly a great, a very great work. Homer is not more decidedly the first of heroic poets, Shakespeare is not more decidedly the first of dramatists, Demosthenes is not more decidedly the first of orators, than Boswell is the first of biographers.
Samuel Johnson (Sept. 1831)

6 They knew luxury; they knew beggary; but they never knew comfort.

7 In the foreground is that strange figure which is as familiar to us as the figures of those among whom we have been brought up, the gigantic body, the huge massy face, seamed with the scars of disease, the brown coat, the black worsted stockings, the grey wig with the scorched foretop, the dirty hands, the nails bitten and pared to the quick.

8 The conformation of his mind was such that whatever was little seemed to him great, and whatever was great seemed to him little.
Horace Walpole (Oct. 1833)

9 With the dead there is no rivalry. In the dead there is no change. Plato is never sullen. Cervantes is never petulant. Demosthenes never comes unseasonably. Dante never stays too long. No difference of political opinion can alienate Cicero. No heresy can excite the horror of Bossuet.
Lord Bacon (July 1837)

10 An acre in Middlesex is better than a principality in Utopia.

11 We now turn away from the checkered spectacle of so much glory and so much shame.

12 What schoolboy of fourteen is ignorant of this remarkable circumstance?
Sir William Temple (Oct. 1838)

13 He was a rake among scholars, and a scholar among rakes. [Richard Steele.]
The Life and Writings of Addison (July 1843)

14 The old philosopher is still among us in the brown coat with the metal buttons and the shirt which ought to be at wash, blinking, puffing, rolling his head, drumming with his fingers, tearing his meat like a tiger, and swallowing his tea in oceans.
Life of Johnson, (ad fin.)

15 I shall cheerfully bear the reproach of having descended below the dignity of history.
History of England, vol.i (1849), ch.1

16 Thus our democracy was, from an early period, the most aristocratic, and our aristocracy the most democratic in the world.

17 Persecution produced its natural effect on them. It found them a sect; it made them a faction.

18 It was a crime in a child to read by the bedside of a sick parent one of those beautiful collects which had soothed the griefs of forty generations of Christians.
ch.2

19 The Puritan hated bear-baiting, not because it gave pain to the bear, but because it gave pleasure to the spectators.

20 The object of oratory alone is not truth, but persuasion.
Works (1898), vol.xi. **Essay on Athenian Orators**

21 History, abounding with kings thirty feet high, and reigns thirty thousand years long—and geography made up of seas of treacle and seas of butter.
Minute, as Member of Supreme Council of India, 2 Feb. 1835

22 Dark and terrible beyond any season within my remembrance of political affairs was the day of their flight. Far darker and far more terrible will be the day of their return. [The Tory Government, defeated in Nov. 1830.]
Speech, 20 Sept. 1831

23 A broken head in Cold Bath Fields produces a greater sensation among us than three pitched battles in India.
10 July 1833

24 Thank you, madam, the agony is abated. [Reply, aged four.]
Trevelyan, *Life and Letters of Macaulay,* ch.1

25 I shall not be satisfied unless I produce something which shall for a few days supersede the last fashionable novel on the tables of young ladies.
ch.9

26 We were regaled by a dogfight...How odd that people of sense should find any pleasure in being accompanied by a beast who is always spoiling conversation.
ch.14

ROSE MACAULAY 1889–1958

27 'Take my camel, dear,' said my aunt Dot as she climbed down from this animal on her return from High Mass.
The Towers of Trebizond (1956), p.1

GENERAL McAULIFFE 1898–1975

28 Nuts!
Reply to German demand for surrender of 101st Airborne Division men trapped at Bastogne, Belgium, 23 Dec. 1944

GENERAL GEORGE B. McCLELLAN 1826–1885

29 All quiet along the Potomac.
Attr. in the American Civil War. See 38:8

DR. JOHN McCRAE 1872–1918

30 In Flanders fields the poppies blow
Between the crosses, row on row,
  That mark our place.
In Flanders Fields. Ypres Salient, 3 May 1915

31   If ye break faith with us who die
We shall not sleep, though poppies grow
  In Flanders fields.

C.B. MACDONALD 1855–1939

1 When ye come to play golf ye maun hae a heid!
Scotland's Gift—Golf (1928)
(A caddy at St. Andrews named Lang Willie was teaching one of the professors of the university the noble game. The professor was not a promising pupil.—Willie fairly got out of patience and said to him: 'Ye see, Professor, as long as ye are learning thae lads at the College Latin and Greek it is easy work, but when ye come to play golf ye maun hae a heid!')

GEORGE MACDONALD 1824–1905

2 Where did you come from, baby dear?
Out of the everywhere into here.
At the Back of the North Wind (1871), xxxiii, Song

3 Here lie I, Martin Elginbrodde:
Hae mercy o' my soul, Lord God;
As I wad do, were I Lord God,
And ye were Martin Elginbrodde.
David Elginbrod (1863), bk.i, ch.13

4 They all were looking for a king
To slay their foes, and lift them high;
Thou cam'st, a little baby thing,
That made a woman cry.
That Holy Thing

WILLIAM McGONAGALL 1825–1902

5 Alas! Lord and Lady Dalhousie are dead, and buried at last,
Which causes many people to feel a little downcast.
The Death of Lord and Lady Dalhousie

6 Beautiful Railway Bridge of the Silv'ry Tay!
Alas, I am very sorry to say
That ninety lives have been taken away
On the last Sabbath day of 1879,
Which will be remember'd for a very long time.
The Tay Bridge Disaster

ANTONIO MACHADO 1875–1939

7 *Yo vivo en paz con los hombres
y en guerra con mis entrañas.*
I am living at peace with men and at war with my innards.
Campos de Castilla (1917), **Proverbios y Cantares**, xxii

NICCOLÒ MACHIAVELLI 1469–1527

8 As a prince must be able to act just like a beast, he should learn from the fox and the lion; because the lion does not defend himself against traps, and the fox does not defend himself against wolves. So one has to be a fox in order to recognize traps, and a lion to frighten off wolves.
The Prince, XVIII

CHARLES MACKAY 1814–1889

9 There's a good time coming, boys,
A good time coming.
The Good Time Coming

SIR COMPTON MACKENZIE 1883–1972

10 You are offered a piece of bread and butter that feels like a damp handkerchief and sometimes, when cucumber is added to it, like a wet one. [An English tea party.]
Vestal Fire (1927), ch.3

SIR JAMES MACKINTOSH 1765–1832

11 Men are never so good or so bad as their opinions.
Ethical Philosophy (1830), 6. **Bentham**

12 The Commons, faithful to their system, remained in a wise and masterly inactivity.
Vindiciae Gallicae (1791), 1

ARCHIBALD MACLEISH 1892–

13 A Poem should be palpable and mute
As a globed fruit,

Dumb
As old medallions to the thumb,

Silent as the sleeve-worn stone
Of casement ledges where the moss has grown—

A poem should be wordless
As the flight of birds.
Ars poetica

14 A poem should not mean
But be.

MURDOCH McLENNAN fl. 1715

15 There's some say that we wan, some say that they wan,
Some say that nane wan at a', man;
But one thing I'm sure, that at Sheriffmuir
A battle there was which I saw, man:
And we ran, and they ran, and they ran, and we ran,
And we ran; and they ran awa', man!
Sheriffmuir. Roxburghe Ballads (1889), vol.vi. In Hogg's *Jacobite Relics*, 1821, vol.ii, the last line is: 'But Florence ran fastest of a', man.' (Florence was the Marquis of Huntley's horse)

MARSHALL McLUHAN 1911–

16 In a culture like ours, long accustomed to splitting and dividing all things as a means of control, it is sometimes a bit of a shock to be reminded that, in operational and practical fact, the medium is the message.
Understanding Media (1964), pt.i, ch.1

MARSHAL MACMAHON 1808–1893

17 *J'y suis, j'y reste.*
Here I am, and here I stay.
At the taking of the Malakoff, 8 Sept. 1855. MacMahon later cast doubt on the attribution: *'Je ne crois pas…avoir donné à ma pensée cette forme lapidaire.'* See Hanoteaux, *Histoire de la France Contemporaine*, vol.II, ch.1, sect.i

HAROLD MACMILLAN 1894–

18 Let's be frank about it; most of our people have never had it so good.
Speech at Bedford, 20 July 1957. 'You Never Had It So Good' was the Democratic Party slogan in the U.S. election campaign of 1952.

19 On 7 January [1958]…I made a short and carefully prepared statement…I referred to 'some recent difficulties' in our affairs at home which had 'caused me a little anxiety'. However, 'I thought the best thing

to do was to settle up these little local difficulties and
then to turn to the wider vision of the
Commonwealth.'
Referring to the sterling crisis and to Thorneycroft's resignation.
Riding The Storm, 1956–1959 (1971), ch.11, **Money and Men**

1 The most striking of all the impressions I have formed
since I left London a month ago is of the strength of
this African national consciousness…The wind of
change is blowing through this continent.
Speech to the South African Houses of Parliament, Cape Town, 3
Feb. 1960. The speech was drafted by Sir David Hunt as described
by him in *On the Spot: An Ambassador Remembers* (1975)

LEONARD MACNALLY 1752–1820

2 This lass so neat, with smiles so sweet,
Has won my right good-will,
I'd crowns resign to call thee mine,
Sweet lass of Richmond Hill.
The Lass of Richmond Hill. E. Duncan, *Minstrelsy of England*
(1905), i.254. Attr. also to W. Upton in *Oxford Song Book*, and to
W. Hudson in Baring-Gould, *English Minstrelsie* (1895), iii.54

LOUIS MACNEICE 1907–1963

3 All of London littered with remembered kisses.
Autumn Journal, iv

4 Better authentic mammon than a bogus god.
xii

5 Good-bye now, Plato and Hegel,
    The shop is closing down;
They don't want any philosopher-kings in England,
    There ain't no universals in this man's town.
xiii

6   There will be time to audit
The accounts later, there will be sunlight later
    And the equation will come out at last.
xxiv

7 It's no go the merrygoround, it's no go the rickshaw,
All we want is a limousine and a ticket for the
    peepshow.
Bagpipe Music

8 It's no go the picture palace, it's no go the stadium,
It's no go the country cot with a pot of pink
    geraniums,
It's no go the Government grants, it's no go the
    elections,
Sit on your arse for fifty years and hang your hat on a
    pension.

It's no go my honey love, it's no go my poppet;
Work your hands from day to day, the winds will blow
    the profit.
The glass is falling hour by hour, the glass will fall for
    ever,
But if you break the bloody glass, you won't hold up
    the weather.

9 Why, then, do I loiter round these chartered
    sanctuaries,
Holding the basin to gowned and spectacled Pilates
While they suffer those ghosts [classical authors] to be
    martyred over and over.
A Classical Education

10 A poet like a pale candle guttering
On a worn window-sill in the wind.

11 Time was away and somewhere else,

There were two glasses and two chairs
And two people with the one pulse
(Somebody stopped the moving stairs):
Time was away and somewhere else.
Meeting Point

12 So they were married—to be the more together—
And found they were never again so much together.
Novelettes, II. Les Sylphides

13 I am not yet born; O fill me
With strength against those who would freeze my
humanity, would dragoon me into a lethal automaton,
would make me a cog in a machine, a thing with
one face, a thing, and against all those
who would dissipate my entirety, would
blow me like thistledown hither and
thither or hither and thither
like water held in the
hands would spill me.

let them not make me a stone and let them not spill me
Otherwise kill me.
Prayer before Birth

14 World is crazier and more of it than we think,
Incorrigibly plural.
Snow

15 The sunlight on the garden
Hardens and grows cold,
We cannot cage the minute
Within its nets of gold,
When all is told
We cannot beg for pardon.
The Sunlight on the Garden

16 Our freedom as free lances
Advances towards its end;
The earth compels, upon it
Sonnets and birds descend;
And soon, my friend,
We shall have no time for dances.

GEOFFREY MADAN 1895–1947

17 The devil finds some mischief still for hands that have
not learnt how to be idle.
L.S.N., *Twelve Reflections* (privately printed, 1934)

18 The dust of exploded beliefs may make a fine sunset.

SAMUEL MADDEN 1686–1765

19 Words are men's daughters, but God's sons are
things.
Boulter's Monument (1745), I.377

MAURICE MAETERLINCK 1862–1949

20 *Il n'y a pas de morts.*
There are no dead.
L'Oiseau bleu (1909), IV.ii

ARCHBISHOP MAGEE 1821–1891

21 It would be better that England should be free than
that England should be compulsorily sober.
Speech on the Intoxicating Liquor Bill, House of Lords, 2 May
1872

MAGNA CARTA 1215

1 *Quod Anglicana ecclesia libera sit.*
That the English Church shall be free.
1

2 *Nullus liber homo capiatur, vel imprisonetur, aut dissaisiatur, aut utlagetur, aut exuletur, aut aliquo modo destruator, nec super eum ibimus, nec super eum mittemus, nisi per legale judicium parium suorum vel per legem terrae.*
No free man shall be taken or imprisoned or dispossessed, or outlawed or exiled, or in any way destroyed, nor will we go upon him, nor will we send against him except by the lawful judgement of his peers or by the law of the land.
39

3 *Nulli vendemus, nulli negabimus aut differemus, rectum aut justitiam.*
To no man will we sell, or deny, or delay, right or justice.
40

SIR JOHN PENTLAND MAHAFFY 1839–1919

4 [On distinguishing the Irish bull from similar freaks of language.] The Irish bull is always pregnant.
Oral trad.

ALFRED T. MAHAN 1840–1914

5 Those far distant, storm-beaten ships, upon which the Grand Army never looked, stood between it and the dominion of the world.
The Influence of Sea Power upon the French Revolution and Empire, 1793–1812 (1892), ii.118

GUSTAV MAHLER 1860–1911

6 *Endlich fortissimo!*
At last, *fortissimo!*
On visiting Niagara. K. Blankopf, *Mahler*, ch.8

SIR HENRY MAINE 1822–1888

7 Except the blind forces of Nature, nothing moves in this world which is not Greek in its origin.
Village Communities (1871)

JOSEPH DE MAISTRE 1753–1821

8 *Toute nation a le gouvernement qu'elle mérite.*
Every country has the government it deserves.
Lettres et Opuscules Inédits, i. p.215, 15 Aug. 1811

STÉPHANE MALLARMÉ 1842–1898

9 *La chair est triste, hélas! et j'ai lu tous les livres.*
The flesh, alas, is wearied; and I have read all the books there are.
Brise Marin

10 *Le vierge, le vivace et le bel aujourd'hui.*
That virgin, vital, fine day: today.
Plusieurs Sonnets

11 *Un coup de dés jamais n'abolira le hasard.*
A throw of the dice will never eliminate chance.
Cosmopolis, May 1897

DAVID MALLET 1705?–1765

12 O grant me, Heaven, a middle state,
Neither too humble nor too great;
More than enough, for nature's ends,
With something left to treat my friends.
Imitation of Horace. See 262:9

GEORGE LEIGH MALLORY 1886–1924

13 Because it is there.
Answer to the question repeatedly asked him on his American lecture tour of 1923, 'Why do you want to climb Mt. Everest?' D. Robertson, *George Mallory* (1969), p.215

SIR THOMAS MALORY d. 1471

14 Whoso pulleth out this sword of this stone and anvil is rightwise King born of all England.
Le Morte D'Arthur (finished 1469–70, printed 1485), bk.i, ch.4

15 This beast went to the well and drank, and the noise was in the beast's belly like unto the questing of thirty couple hounds, but all the while the beast drank there was no noise in the beast's belly.
ch.19

16 Me repenteth, said Merlin; because of the death of that lady thou shalt strike a stroke most dolorous that ever man struck, except the stroke of our Lord, for thou shalt hurt the truest knight and the man of most worship that now liveth, and through that stroke three kingdoms shall be in great poverty, misery and wretchedness twelve years, and the knight shall not be whole of that wound for many years.
bk.ii, ch.8

17 Ah, my little son, thou hast murdered thy mother! And therefore I suppose thou that art a murderer so young, thou art full likely to be a manly man in thine age...when he is christened let call him Tristram, that is as much to say as a sorrowful birth.
bk.viii, ch.1

18 Meanwhile came Sir Palomides, the good knight, following the questing beast that had in shape like a serpent's head and a body like a leopard, buttocked like a lion and footed like a hart. And in his body there was such a noise as it had been twenty couple of hounds questing [yelping], and such noise that beast made wheresomever he went.
bk.ix, ch.12

19 God defend me, said Dinadan, for the joy of love is too short, and the sorrow thereof, and what cometh thereof, dureth over long.
bk.x, ch.56

20 Now I thank God, said Sir Launcelot, for His great mercy of that I have seen, for it sufficeth me. For, as I suppose, no man in this world hath lived better than I have done, to achieve that I have done.
bk.xvii, ch.16

21 Fair lord, salute me to my lord, Sir Launcelot, my father, and as soon as ye see him, bid him remember of this unstable world.
ch.22

22 Thus endeth the story of the Sangreal, that was briefly drawn out of French into English, the which is a story chronicled for one of the truest and the holiest that is in this world.
ch.23, end

1 The month of May was come, when every lusty heart beginneth to blossom, and to bring forth fruit; for like as herbs and trees bring forth fruit and flourish in May, in likewise every lusty heart that is in any manner a lover, springeth and flourisheth in lusty deeds.
bk.xviii, ch.25

2 Therefore all ye that be lovers call unto your remembrance the month of May, like as did Queen Guenevere, for whom I make here a little mention, that while she lived she was a true lover, and therefore she had a good end.

3 Through this man and me hath all this war been wrought, and the death of the most noblest knights of the world; for through our love that we have loved together is my most noble lord slain.
bk.xxi, ch.9

4 Wherefore, madam, I pray you kiss me and never no more. Nay, said the queen, that shall I never do, but abstain you from such works: and they departed. But there was never so hard an hearted man but he would have wept to see the dolour that they made.
ch.10

5 And Sir Launcelot awoke, and went and took his horse, and rode all that day and all night in a forest, weeping.

6 Then Sir Launcelot never after ate but little meat, ne drank, till he was dead.
ch.12

7 I saw the angels heave up Sir Launcelot unto heaven, and the gates of heaven opened against him.

8 Said Sir Ector…Sir Launcelot…thou wert never matched of earthly knight's hand; and thou wert the courteoust knight that ever bare shield; and thou wert the truest friend to thy lover that ever bestrad horse; and thou wert the truest lover of a sinful man that ever loved woman; and thou wert the kindest man that ever struck with sword; and thou wert the goodliest person that ever came among press of knights; and thou wert the meekest man and the gentlest that ever ate in hall among ladies; and thou wert the sternest knight to thy mortal foe that ever put spear in the rest.
ch.13

THOMAS ROBERT MALTHUS 1766–1834

9 Population, when unchecked, increases in a geometrical ratio. Subsistence only increases in an arithmetical ratio.
The Principle of Population (1798), 1

W.R. MANDALE nineteenth century

10 Up and down the City Road,
In and out the Eagle,
That's the way the money goes—
Pop goes the weasel!
Pop Goes the Weasel

MANILIUS 1st cent. A.D.

11 *Eripuitque Jovi fulmen viresque tonandi.*
And snatched from Jove the lightning shaft and power

to thunder.
Astronomica, i.104. Of human intelligence

MRS. MANLEY 1663–1724

12 No time like the present.
The Lost Lover (1696), IV.i

HORACE MANN 1796–1859

13 The object of punishment is, prevention from evil; it never can be made impulsive to good.
Lectures and Reports on Education (1845), 1867 edn., lecture vii

14 Lost, yesterday, somewhere between Sunrise and Sunset, two golden hours, each set with sixty diamond minutes. No reward is offered, for they are gone forever.
Lost, Two Golden Hours

LORD JOHN MANNERS, DUKE OF RUTLAND 1818–1906

15 Let wealth and commerce, laws and learning die,
But leave us still our old nobility!
England's Trust (1841), pt.III, 1.227

LORD MANSFIELD 1705–1793

16 The constitution does not allow reasons of state to influence our judgments: God forbid it should! We must not regard political consequences; however formidable soever they might be: if rebellion was the certain consequence, we are bound to say '*fiat justitia, ruat caelum*'.
Rex v. Wilkes, 8 June 1768

17 Consider what you think justice requires, and decide accordingly. But never give your reasons; for your judgement will probably be right, but your reasons will certainly be wrong.
Advice to a newly appointed colonial governor ignorant in the law. Campbell, *Lives of the Chief Justices,* ch.40

MAO TSE-TUNG 1893–1976

18 Letting a hundred flowers blossom and a hundred schools of thought contend is the policy.
Speech, 2 May 1956. Roderick MacFarquhar, *Origins of the Cultural Revolution* (1974), vol. 1, p. 51

19 Every Communist must grasp the truth, 'Political power grows out of the barrel of a gun.'
Selected Works (Peking, 1961), vol.II. **Problems of War and Strategy,** ii, 6 Nov. 1938

20 The atomic bomb is a paper tiger which the US reactionaries use to scare people. It looks terrible, but in fact it isn't. . .All reactionaries are paper tigers.
vol. IV. **Talk with Anna Louise Strong,** Aug. 1946

WILLIAM LEARNED MARCY 1786–1857

21 To the victor belong the spoils of the enemy.
Parton, *Life of Jackson* (1860), vol.iii, p.378

QUEEN MARIE-ANTOINETTE 1755–1793

22 *Qu'ils mangent de la brioche.*
Let them eat cake.
On being told that her people had no bread. Attributed to Marie-Antoinette, but much older. Rousseau refers in his

Confessions, 1740, to a similar remark, as a well known saying. Louis XVIII in his *Relation d'un Voyage à Bruxelles et à Coblentz en 1791* (1823, p.59) attributes to Marie-Thérèse (1638–83), wife of Louis XIV, *'Que ne mangent-ils de la croûte de pâté?'* ('Why don't they eat pastry?')

SARAH, 1ST DUCHESS OF MARLBOROUGH
1660–1744

1 The Duke returned from the wars today and did pleasure me in his top-boots.
Oral trad. Attr. in various forms

2 For painters, poets and builders have very high flights, but they must be kept down.
Letter to the Duchess of Bedford, 21 June 1734. Gladys Scott Thomson, *The Russells in Bloomsbury (1669–1771)* (1940), ch.9

CHRISTOPHER MARLOWE 1564–1593

3 Sweet Analytics, 'tis thou hast ravished me.
Doctor Faustus (1588?, published 1604), I.i.6

4 I'll have them fly to India for gold,
Ransack the ocean for orient pearl.
80

5 I'll have them wall all Germany with brass,
And make swift Rhine circle fair Wertenberg.
I'll have them fill the public schools with silk,
Wherewith the students shall be bravely clad.
86

6 *Faustus:* And what are you that live with Lucifer?
Mephistopheles: Unhappy spirits that fell with Lucifer,
Conspired against our God with Lucifer,
And are for ever damned with Lucifer.
iii.69

7 Why this is hell, nor am I out of it:
Thinkst thou that I who saw the face of God,
And tasted the eternal joys of heaven,
Am not tormented with ten thousand hells
In being deprived of everlasting bliss!
76

8 Hell hath no limits nor is circumscrib'd
In one self place, where we are is Hell,
And where Hell is, there must we ever be.
And to be short, when all the world dissolves,
And every creature shall be purified,
All places shall be hell that are not heaven.
II.i.120

9 Have not I made blind Homer sing to me?
ii.26

10 Was this the face that launch'd a thousand ships,
And burnt the topless towers of Ilium?
Sweet Helen, make me immortal with a kiss!
Her lips suck forth my soul: see, where it flies!
Come Helen, come give me my soul again.
Here will I dwell, for heaven be in these lips,
And all is dross that is not Helena.
V.i.97

11 Now hast thou but one bare hour to live,
And then thou must be damned perpetually;
Stand still you ever-moving spheres of heaven,
That time may cease, and midnight never come.
Fair nature's eye, rise, rise again and make
Perpetual day, or let this hour be but
A year, a month, a week, a natural day,
That Faustus may repent and save his soul.
O lente, lente currite noctis equi:

The stars move still, time runs, the clock will strike,
The devil will come, and Faustus must be damn'd.
O I'll leap up to my God: who pulls me down?
See see where Christ's blood streams in the firmament.
One drop would save my soul, half a drop, ah my Christ.
ii.127

12 Mountains and hills, come, come and fall on me,
And hide me from the heavy wrath of God.
146

13 You stars that reigned at my nativity,
Whose influence hath allotted death and hell,
Now draw up Faustus like a foggy mist,
Into the entrails of yon labouring cloud,
That when you vomit forth into the air,
My limbs may issue from your smoky mouths,
So that my soul may but ascend to heaven.
151

14 Ah, Pythagoras' metempsychosis, were that true,
This soul should fly from me, and I be chang'd
Unto some brutish beast.
168

15 O soul, be changed into little water drops,
And fall into the ocean, ne'er be found:
My God, my God, look not so fierce on me.
179

16 Cut is the branch that might have grown full straight,
And burnèd is Apollo's laurel bough,
That sometime grew within this learned man.
epilogue

17 My men, like satyrs grazing on the lawns,
Shall with their goat feet dance an antic hay.
Edward II (1593), I.i.59

18 It lies not in our power to love, or hate,
For will in us is over-rul'd by fate.
When two are stripped, long ere the course begin,
We wish that one should lose, the other win;
And one especially do we affect
Of two gold ingots, like in each respect.
The reason no man knows; let it suffice,
What we behold is censured by our eyes.
Where both deliberate, the love is slight;/
Who ever loved that loved not at first sight?
Hero and Leander (published 1598). First Sestiad, l.167. See 426:19

19 I count religion but a childish toy,
And hold there is no sin but ignorance.
The Jew of Malta (c. 1592), prologue

20 Thus methinks should men of judgement frame
Their means of traffic from the vulgar trade,
And, as their wealth increaseth, so enclose
Infinite riches in a little room.
I.i.34

21 As for myself, I walk abroad o' nights
And kill sick people groaning under walls:
Sometimes I go about and poison wells.
II.iii.172

22 *Barnadine:* Thou hast committed—
Barabas: Fornication? But that was in another country: and besides, the wench is dead.
IV.i.40

23 Come live with me, and be my love,
And we will all the pleasures prove,

That valleys, groves, hills and fields,
Woods or steepy mountain yields.
The Passionate Shepherd to his Love. See
187:24, 404:9, 495:16

1 By shallow rivers, to whose falls,
Melodious birds sing madrigals.

2 From jigging veins of rhyming mother-wits,
And such conceits as clownage keeps in pay,
We'll lead you to the stately tents of war.
Tamburlaine the Great (1587 or earlier, published 1590),
prologue

3 Zenocrate, lovelier than the Love of Jove,
Brighter than is the silver Rhodope,
Fairer than whitest snow on Scythian hills.
pt.I, l.283

4 Our swords shall play the orators for us.
l.328

5 With Nature's pride, and richest furniture,
His looks do menace heaven and dare the Gods.
l.351

6 Accurst be he that first invented war.
l.664

7 Is it not passing brave to be a King,
And ride in triumph through Persepolis?
l.758

8 Nature that fram'd us of four elements,
Warring within our breasts for regiment,
Doth teach us all to have aspiring minds:
Our souls, whose faculties can comprehend
The wondrous Architecture of the world:
And measure every wand'ring planet's course,
Still climbing after knowledge infinite,
And always moving as the restless Spheres,
Will us to wear ourselves and never rest,
Until we reach the ripest fruit of all,
That perfect bliss and sole felicity,
The sweet fruition of an earthly crown.
l.869

9 Virtue is the fount whence honour springs.
l.1769

10 Ah fair Zenocrate, divine Zenocrate,
Fair is too foul an epithet for thee.
l.1916

11 What is beauty saith my sufferings, then?
If all the pens that ever poets held
Had fed the feeling of their masters' thoughts,
And every sweetness that inspir'd their hearts,
Their minds, and muses on admired themes:
If all the heavenly quintessence they still
From their immortal flowers of Poesy,
Wherein as in a mirror we perceive
The highest reaches of a human wit;
If these had made one poem's period,
And all combin'd in beauty's worthiness,
Yet should there hover in their restless heads
One thought, one grace, one wonder at the least,
Which into words no virtue can digest.
But how unseemly is it for my sex,
My discipline of arms and chivalry,
My nature, and the terror of my name,
To harbour thoughts effeminate and faint!
Save only that in Beauty's just applause,
With whose instinct the soul of man is touched,
And every warrior that is rapt with love

Of fame, of valour, and of victory,
Must needs have beauty beat on his conceits:
I thus conceiving and subduing both,
That which hath stopp'd the tempest of the Gods,
Even from the fiery-spangled veil of heaven,
To feel the lovely warmth of shepherds' flames,
And march in cottages of strowed reeds,
Shall give the world to note, for all my birth,
That Virtue solely is the sum of glory,
And fashions men with true nobility.
l.1941

12 Now walk the angels on the walls of heaven,
As sentinels to warn th' immortal souls,
To entertain divine Zenocrate.
pt.II, l.2983

13 Yet let me kiss my Lord before I die,
And let me die with kissing of my Lord.
l.3037

14 Helen, whose beauty summoned Greece to arms,
And drew a thousand ships to Tenedos.
l.3055

15 More childish valourous than manly wise.
l.3690

16 Holla, ye pampered Jades of Asia:
What, can ye draw but twenty miles a day?
l.3980. See 441:25

17 Tamburlaine, the Scourge of God, must die.
l.4641

SHACKERLEY MARMION 1603–1639

18 Familiarity begets boldness.
The Antiquary (1636 or earlier, published 1641), Act I

19 Great joys, like griefs, are silent.
Holland's Leaguer (1632), V.i

DON MARQUIS 1878–1937

20 girls we was all of us ladies
we was o what the hell
and once a lady always game
by crikey blood will tell.
archy and mehitabel, xxxv. mehitabel dances with boreas

21 but wotthehell archy wotthehell
jamais triste archy jamais triste
that is my motto.
xlvi. mehitabel sees paris

22 toujours gai, archy, toujours gai.
archys life of mehitabel, i. the life of mehitabel the cat

23 the great open spaces
where cats are cats.
xiv. mehitabel has an adventure

24 honesty is a good
thing but
it is not profitable to
its possessor
unless it is
kept under control.
xl. archygrams

25 as I was crawling
through the holes in
a swiss cheese
the other
day it occurred to

me to wonder
what a swiss cheese
would think if
a swiss cheese
could think and after
cogitating for some
time I said to myself
if a swiss cheese
could think
it would think that
a swiss cheese
was the most important
thing in the world
just as everything that
can think at all
does think about itself.

1 did you ever
notice that when
a politician
does get an idea
he usually
gets it all wrong.

2 now and then
there is a person born
who is so unlucky
that he runs into accidents
which started out to happen
to somebody else.
xli. **archy says**

CAPTAIN MARRYAT 1792–1848

3 There's no getting blood out of a turnip.
Japhet in Search of a Father (1836), ch.4

4 As savage as a bear with a sore head.
The King's Own (1830), ch.26

5 If you please, ma'am, it was a very little one. [The nurse excusing her illegitimate baby.]
Mr. Midshipman Easy (1836), ch.3

6 All zeal...all zeal, Mr Easy.
ch.9

7 I never knows the children. It's just six of one and half-a-dozen of the other.
The Pirate (1836), ch.4

MARTIAL b. A.D. 43

8 *Non est, crede mihi, sapientis dicere 'Vivam':*
   Sera nimis vita est crastina: vive hodie.
Believe me, wise men don't say 'I shall live to do that', tomorrow's life's too late; live today.
Epigrammata, I.xv

9 *Non amo te, Sabidi, nec possum dicere quare:*
   Hoc tantum possum dicere, non amo te.
I don't love you, Sabidius, and I can't tell you why; all I can tell you is this, that I don't love you.
xxxii

10 *Laudant illa sed ista legunt.*
They praise those works, but they're not the ones they read.
IV.xlix

11   *Bonosque*
   Soles effugere atque abire sentit,
   Qui nobis pereunt et imputantur.

Each of us feels the good days speed and depart, and they're lost to us and counted against us.
V.xx

12 *Non est vivere, sed valere vita est.*
Life's not just being alive, but being well.
VI.lxx

13 *Difficilis facilis, iucundus acerbus es idem:*
   Nec tecum possum vivere nec sine te.
Difficult or easy, pleasant or bitter, you are the same you: I cannot live with you—nor without you.
XII.xlvi (xlvii)

14 *Rus in urbe.*
Country in the town.
lvii

ANDREW MARVELL 1621–1678

15 Where the remote Bermudas ride
In th' ocean's bosom unespied.
Bermudas

16 He hangs in shades the orange bright,
Like golden lamps in a green night. . .
And makes the hollow seas, that roar,
Proclaim the ambergris on shore.
He cast (of which we rather boast)
The Gospel's pearls upon our coast.

17 O let our voice his praise exalt,
Till it arrive at Heaven's vault:
Which thence (perhaps) rebounding, may
Echo beyond the Mexique Bay.

18 My love is of a birth as rare
As 'tis for object strange and high:
It was begotten by despair
Upon impossibility.

Magnanimous Despair alone
Could show me so divine a thing,
Where feeble Hope could ne'er have flown
But vainly flapt its tinsel wing.
The Definition of Love

19 As lines so loves oblique may well
Themselves in every angle greet
But ours so truly parallel,
Though infinite can never meet.

Therefore the love which us doth bind,
But Fate so enviously debars,
Is the conjunction of the mind,
And opposition of the stars.

20 Choosing each stone, and poising every weight,
Trying the measures of the breadth and height;
Here pulling down, and there erecting new,
Founding a firm state by proportions true.
The First Anniversary of the Government under Oliver Cromwell, l.245

21 How vainly men themselves amaze
To win the palm, the oak, or bays;
And their uncessant labours see
Crown'd from some single herb or tree,
Whose short and narrow vergèd shade
Does prudently their toils upbraid;
While all flowers and all trees do close
To weave the garlands of repose.
The Garden, 1

22 Fair quiet, have I found thee here,

And Innocence thy Sister dear!

2

1 Society is all but rude,
To this delicious solitude.

2 The Gods, that mortal beauty chase,
Still in a tree did end their race.
Apollo hunted Daphne so,
Only that she might laurel grow.
And Pan did after Syrinx speed,
Not as a nymph, but for a reed.

4

3 What wond'rous life is this I lead!
Ripe apples drop about my head;
The luscious clusters of the vine
Upon my mouth do crush their wine;
The nectarine and curious peach,
Into my hands themselves do reach;
Stumbling on melons, as I pass,
Insnar'd with flow'rs, I fall on grass.

5

4 Meanwhile the mind, from pleasure less,
Withdraws into its happiness.

6

5 Annihilating all that's made
To a green thought in a green shade.

6

6 Here at the fountain's sliding foot,
Or at some fruit-tree's mossy root,
Casting the body's vest aside,
My soul into the boughs does glide.

7

7 Such was that happy garden-state,
While man there walk'd without a mate.

8

8 But 'twas beyond a mortal's share
To wander solitary there:
Two Paradises 'twere in one
To live in Paradise alone.

9 He nothing common did or mean
Upon that memorable scene:
    But with his keener eye
    The axe's edge did try. [Charles I.]
An Horatian Ode upon Cromwell's Return from Ireland
(1650), l.57

10 But bowed his comely head,
Down as upon a bed.
l.63

11 And now the Irish are ashamed
To see themselves in one year tamed:
    So much one man can do
    That does both act and know.
l.75

12 Ye living lamps, by whose dear light
The nightingale does sit so late,
And studying all the summer night,
Her matchless songs does meditate.

Ye country comets, that portend
No war, nor prince's funeral,
Shining unto no higher end
Then to presage the grasses' fall.
The Mower to the Glow-worms

13 It is a wond'rous thing, how fleet
'Twas on those little silver feet.
With what a pretty skipping grace,

It oft would challenge me the race:
And when 't had left me far away,
'Twould stay, and run again, and stay.
For it was nimbler much than hinds;
And trod, as on the four winds.
The Nymph Complaining for the Death of her Fawn

14 I have a garden of my own,
But so with roses overgrown,
And lilies, that you would it guess
To be a little wilderness.

15 Had it liv'd long, it would have been
Lilies without, roses within.

16 For though the whole world cannot shew such
    another,
    Yet we'd better by far have him than his brother. [Of
    Charles II.]
The Statue in Stocks-Market

17 He is Translation's thief that addeth more,
As much as he that taketh from the store
Of the first author.
To...Dr. Witty

18 Had we but world enough, and time,
This coyness, Lady, were no crime.
We would sit down, and think which way
To walk, and pass our long love's day.
Thou by the Indian Ganges' side
Shouldst rubies find: I by the tide
Of Humber would complain. I would
Love you ten years before the Flood:
And you should if you please refuse
Till the conversion of the Jews.
My vegetable love should grow
Vaster than empires, and more slow.
To His Coy Mistress

19 But at my back I always hear
Time's wingèd chariot hurrying near.
And yonder all before us lie
Deserts of vast eternity.
Thy beauty shall no more be found;
Nor, in thy marble vault, shall sound
My echoing song: then worms shall try
That long preserved virginity:
And your quaint honour turn to dust;
And into ashes all my lust.
The grave's a fine and private place,
But none I think do there embrace.

20 Let us roll all our strength and all
Our sweetness up into one ball,
And tear our pleasures with rough strife
Thorough the iron gates of life:
Thus, though we cannot make our sun
Stand still, yet we will make him run.

21 What need of all this marble crust
T' impark the wanton mote of dust?
Upon Appleton House, to my Lord Fairfax, iii

22 Thrice happy he who, not mistook,
Hath read in Nature's mystic book.
lxxiii

23 But now the salmon-fishers moist
Their leathern boats begin to hoist;
And, like Antipodes in shoes,
Have shod their heads in their canoes.
How tortoise-like, but not so slow,

These rational amphibii go!
lxxxxvii

GROUCHO MARX 1895–1977

1 Either he's dead or my watch has stopped.
A Day at the Races (1937), script by Robert Pirosh, George
Seaton, George Oppenheim

KARL MARX 1818–1883

2 A spectre is haunting Europe—The spectre of
Communism.
The Communist Manifesto (1848), opening words

3 The history of all hitherto existing society is the
history of class struggle.

4 The workers have nothing to lose in this [revolution]
but their chains. They have a world to gain. Workers
of the world, unite!
closing words

5 From each according to his abilities, to each according
to his needs.
Criticism of the Gotha Programme (1875). See 29:25

6 Religion…is the opium of the people.
Critique of Hegel's Philosophy of Right (1843–4), Introduction.
See 297:7

7 Mankind always sets itself only such problems as it
can solve; since, looking at the matter more closely, it
will always be found that the task itself arises only
when the material conditions for its solution already
exist or are at least in the process of formation.
A Critique of Political Economy (1859), preface, tr. D. McLellan

8 And even when a society has got upon the right track
for the discovery of the natural laws of its
movement—and it is the ultimate aim of this work, to
lay bare the economic law of motion of modern
society—it can neither clear by bold leaps, nor remove
by legal enactments, the obstacles offered by the
successive phases of its normal development. But it
can shorten and lessen the birth-pangs.
Das Kapital, Preface (25 July 1865) to the 1st German edn.
(1867)

9 Hegel says somewhere that all great events and
personalities in world history reappear in one fashion
or another. He forgot to add: the first time as tragedy,
the second as farce.
The Eighteenth Brumaire of Louis Napoleon (1852), 1

10 The philosophers have only interpreted the world in
various ways; the point is to change it.
Theses on Feuerbach (1888), xi

11 What I did that was new was to prove…that the class
struggle necessarily leads to the dictatorship of the
proletariat.
Letter to Weydemeyer 5 Mar. 1852. The phrase 'dictatorship of
the proletariat' had earlier been used in the Constitution of the
World Society of Revolutionary Communists (1850), signed by
Marx, Engels, Adam and J. Vidil, G. Julian Harney, and August
Willich. Marx claimed that the phrase had been coined by Auguste
Blanqui (1805–1881), but it has not been found in this form in
Blanqui's work. See Marx, *Political Writings* (ed. Fernbach,
1973), vol.1, p.24.

12 All I know is that I am not a Marxist.
Attr. in Engels, letter to C. Schmidt, 5 Aug. 1890

MARY TUDOR 1516–1558

13 When I am dead and opened, you shall find 'Calais'

lying in my heart.
Holinshed, *Chronicles,* iii.1160

QUEEN MARY 1867–1953

14 Well, Mr Baldwin! *this* is a pretty kettle of fish!
(The abdication crisis, 1936.) James Pope-Hennessy, *Life of
Queen Mary* (1959), ch.7.i

15 Really! this might be Roumania!
ii

16 So *that's* what hay looks like.
ch.8.i

JOHN MASEFIELD 1878–1967

17 I have seen dawn and sunset on moors and windy hills
Coming in solemn beauty like slow old tunes of Spain.
Beauty

18 Quinquireme of Nineveh from distant Ophir
Rowing home to haven in sunny Palestine,
With a cargo of ivory,
And apes and peacocks,
Sandalwood, cedarwood, and sweet white wine.
Cargoes. See 50:34

19 Dirty British coaster with a salt-caked smoke stack,
Butting through the Channel in the mad March days,
With a cargo of Tyne coal,
Road-rail, pig-lead,
Firewood, iron-ware, and cheap tin trays.

20 Oh some are fond of Spanish wine, and some are fond
of French,
And some'll swallow tay and stuff fit only for a
wench.
Captain Stratton's Fancy

21 Oh some are fond of fiddles, and a song well sung,
And some are all for music for to lilt upon the tongue;
But mouths were made for tankards, and for sucking
at the bung,
Says the old bold mate of Henry Morgan.

22 In the dark womb where I began
My mother's life made me a man.
Through all the months of human birth
Her beauty fed my common earth.
I cannot see, nor breathe, nor stir,
But through the death of some of her.
C.L.M.

23 I have seen flowers come in stony places
And kind things done by men with ugly faces,
And the gold cup won by the worst horse at the races,
So I trust, too.
An Epilogue

24 To get the whole world out of bed
And washed, and dressed, and warmed, and fed,
To work, and back to bed again,
Believe me, Saul, costs worlds of pain.
The Everlasting Mercy (1911)

25 And he who gives a child a treat
Makes joy-bells ring in Heaven's street,
And he who gives a child a home
Builds palaces in Kingdom come,
And she who gives a baby birth
Brings Saviour Christ again to Earth.

26 The corn that makes the holy bread
By which the soul of man is fed,

The holy bread, the food unpriced,
Thy everlasting mercy, Christ.

1 Death opens unknown doors. It is most grand to die.
Pompey the Great (1910). i. **The Chief Centurions. 'Man is a sacred city'**

2 One road leads to London,
  One road runs to Wales,
My road leads me seawards
  To the white dipping sails.
Roadways

3 Most roads lead men homewards,
  My road leads me forth.

4 I must down to the seas again, to the lonely sea and
  the sky,
And all I ask is a tall ship and a star to steer her by,
And the wheel's kick and the wind's song and the
  white sail's shaking,
And a grey mist on the sea's face and a grey dawn
  breaking.
Sea Fever

5 I must down to the seas again, for the call of the
  running tide
Is a wild call and a clear call that may not be denied.

6 I must down to the seas again, to the vagrant gypsy
  life,
To the gull's way and the whale's way where the
  wind's like a whetted knife;
And all I ask is a merry yarn from a laughing
  fellow-rover,
And quiet sleep and a sweet dream when the long
  trick's over.

7 Friends and loves we have none, nor wealth, nor
  blessed abode,
But the hope of the City of God at the other end of the
  road.
The Seekers

8 It is good to be out on the road, and going one knows
  not where,
  Going through meadow and village, one knows not
    whither nor why.
Tewkesbury Road

9 It's a warm wind, the west wind, full of birds' cries;
I never hear the west wind but tears are in my eyes.
For it comes from the west lands, the old brown hills,
And April's in the west wind, and daffodils.
The West Wind

THE MASS IN LATIN

10 *Asperges me, Domine, hyssopo, et mundabor.*
Sprinkle me with hyssop, O Lord, and I shall be
cleansed.
Anthem at Sprinkling the Holy Water. See 393:5

11 *Dominus vobiscum.*
  Et cum spiritu tuo.
The Lord be with you.
  And with thy spirit.

12 *In Nomine Patris, et Filii, et Spiritus Sancti.*
In the Name of the Father, and of the Son, and of the
Holy Ghost.
The Ordinary of the Mass

13 *Introibo ad altare Dei.*

I will go unto the altar of God.
See 392:11

14 *Gloria Patri, et Filio, et Spiritui Sancto.*
  *Sicut erat in principio, et nunc, et semper, et in
  saecula saeculorum.*
Glory be to the Father, and to the Son, and to the Holy
Ghost.
  As it was in the beginning, is now, and ever shall
  be, world without end.
See 384:15

15 *Confiteor Deo omnipotenti, beatae Mariae semper
Virgini, beato Michaeli Archangelo, beato Joanni
Baptistae, sanctis Apostolis Petro et Paulo, omnibus
sanctis, et tibi, Pater, quia peccavi nimis cogitatione,
verbo, et opere, mea culpa, mea culpa, mea maxima
culpa.*
I confess to almighty God, to blessed Mary ever
Virgin, to blessed Michael the Archangel, to blessed
John the Baptist, to the holy Apostles Peter and Paul,
to all the saints, and to you, Father, that I have sinned
exceedingly in thought, word, and deed, through my
fault, through my fault, through my most grievous
fault.

16 *Kyrie eleison, Kyrie eleison, Kyrie eleison.*
  Christe eleison, Christe eleison, Christe eleison.
Lord, have mercy upon us.
  Christ, have mercy upon us.

17 *Requiem aeternam dona eis, Domine: et lux perpetua
luceat eis.*
Grant them eternal rest, O Lord; and let perpetual light
shine on them.
[To be said only at Masses for the dead.]

18 *Gloria in excelsis Deo, et in terra pax hominibus
bonae voluntatis. Laudamus te, benedicimus te,
adoramus te, glorificamus te.*
Glory be to God on high, and on earth peace to men of
good will. We praise thee, we bless thee, we adore
thee, we glorify thee.

19 *Deo gratias.*
Thanks be to God.

20 *Credo in unum Deum, Patrem omnipotentem, factorem
coeli et terrae, visibilium omnium et invisibilium.
Et in unum Dominum Jesum Christum Filium Dei
unigenitum, et ex Patre natum ante omnia saecula:
Deum de Deo, lumen de lumine, Deum verum de Deo
vero; genitum non factum, consubstantialem Patri, per
quem omnia facta sunt. Qui propter nos homines, et
propter nostram salutem, descendit de coelis; et
incarnatus est de Spiritu Sancto, ex Maria Virgine; ET
HOMO FACTUS EST. Crucifixus etiam pro nobis,
sub Pontio Pilato passus, et sepultus est. Et resurrexit
tertia die, secundum Scripturas; et ascendit in coelum;
sedet ad dexteram Patris; et iterum venturus est cum
gloria, judicare vivos et mortuos; cuius regni non erit
finis.
Et in Spiritum Sanctum, Dominum vivificantem, qui ex
Patre Filioque procedit; qui cum Patre et Filio simul
adoratur, et conglorificatur; qui locutus est per
Prophetas. Et unam sanctam Catholicam et
Apostolicam Ecclesiam. Confiteor unum Baptisma in
remissionem peccatorum. Et expecto resurrectionem
mortuorum, et vitam venturi saeculi.*
I believe in one God, the Father almighty, maker of
heaven and earth, and of all things visible and

invisible.
And in one Lord Jesus Christ, the only begotten Son
of God, and born of the Father before all ages; God of
God, light of light; true God of true God; begotten,
not made; consubstantial to the Father, by whom all
things were made. Who for us men, and for our
salvation, came down from heaven; and became
incarnate by the Holy Ghost, of the Virgin Mary; AND
WAS MADE MAN. He was crucified also for us,
suffered under Pontius Pilate, and was buried. And the
third day he rose again according to the Scriptures; and
ascended into heaven, sitteth at the right hand of the
Father; and he is to come again with glory, to judge
both the living and the dead; of whose kingdom there
shall be no end.
And in the Holy Ghost, the Lord and giver of life, who
proceedeth from the Father and the Son; who together
with the Father and the Son, is adored and glorified;
who spoke by the Prophets. And one holy Catholic and
Apostolic Church. I confess one Baptism for the
remission of sins. And I expect the resurrection of the
dead, and the life of the world to come.
See 384:26, 387:10

1 *Oremus.*
Let us pray.

2 *Sursum corda.*
Lift up your hearts.
See 387:21

3 *Dignum et justum est.*
It is right and fitting.
See 387:23

4 *Sanctus, sanctus, sanctus, Dominus Deus Sabaoth.*
Pleni sunt coeli et terra gloria tua. Hosanna in
excelsis. Benedictus qui venit in nomine Domini.
Holy, holy, holy, Lord God of Hosts. Heaven and
earth are full of thy glory. Hosanna in the highest.
Blessed is he that cometh in the name of the Lord.
See 81:24, 387:23

5 *Pater noster, qui es in coelis, sanctificetur nomen*
tuum; adveniat regnum tuum; fiat voluntas tua sicut in
coelo, et in terra; panem nostrum quotidianum da
nobis hodie; et dimitte nobis debita nostra, sicut et nos
dimittimus debitoribus nostris; et ne nos inducas in
tentationem.
    Sed libera nos a malo.
Our Father, who art in heaven, hallowed be thy name;
thy kingdom come; thy will be done on earth, as it is
in heaven; give us this day our daily bread; and forgive
us our trespasses, as we forgive them that trespass
against us; and lead us not into temptation.
    But deliver us from evil.
See 64:24

6 *Pax Domini sit semper vobiscum.*
The peace of the Lord be always with you.

7 *Agnus Dei, qui tollis peccata mundi, miserere nobis.*
Agnus Dei, qui tollis peccata mundi, dona nobis
pacem.
Lamb of God, who takest away the sins of the world,
have mercy on us.
Lamb of God, who takest away the sins of the world,
give us peace.

8 *Domine, non sum dignus ut intres sub tectum meum;*
sed tantum dic verbo, et sanabitur anima mea.
Lord, I am not worthy that thou shouldst enter under

my roof; but say only the word, and my soul shall be
healed.
See 65:14

9 *Ite missa est.*
Go, you are dismissed.

10 *Requiescant in pace.*
May they rest in peace.
[In Masses for the dead.]

11 *In principio erat Verbum, et Verbum erat apud*
Deum, et Deus erat Verbum.
In the beginning was the Word, and the Word was with
God, and the Word was God.
See 71:21

12 VERBUM CARO FACTUM EST.
THE WORD WAS MADE FLESH.
See 71:27

PHILIP MASSINGER 1583–1640

13 Ambition, in a private man a vice,
Is, in a prince, the virtue.
The Bashful Lover (licensed 1636, published 1655), I.ii

14 He that would govern others, first should be
The master of himself.
The Bondman (licensed 1623, printed 1624), I.iii

15 Pray enter
You are learned Europeans and we worse
Than ignorant Americans.
The City Madam (1658), III.iii

16 Soar not too high to fall; but stoop to rise.
The Duke of Milan (1623), I.ii

17   Greatness, with private men
Esteem'd a blessing, is to me a curse;
And we, whom, for our high births, they conclude
The only freemen, are the only slaves.
Happy the golden mean!
The Great Duke of Florence (1627, printed 1635), I.i. See 260:9

18   I am driven
Into a desperate strait and cannot steer
A middle course.
III.i

19   Verity, you brach!
The devil turned precisian?
A New Way to Pay Old Debts (c.1625, printed 1632), I.i

20 Patience, the beggar's virtue.
V.i

21 Some undone widow sits upon my arm,
And takes away the use of 't; and my sword,
Glued to my scabbard with wrong'd orphans' tears,
Will not be drawn.

22   View yourselves
In the deceiving mirror of self-love.
The Parliament of Love (licensed 1624), I.v

23 What pity 'tis, one that can speak so well,
Should in his actions be so ill!
III.iii

24   All words,
And no performance!
IV.ii

25   Serves and fears
The fury of the many-headed monster,

The giddy multitude.
The Unnatural Combat (c.1619, printed 1639), III.ii

1 Death has a thousand doors to let out life:
I shall find one.
A Very Woman, V.iv. See 215:11, 420:11, 566:26

LORD JUSTICE SIR JAMES MATHEW
1830–1908

2 In England, Justice is open to all, like the Ritz hotel.
R.E. Megarry, *Miscellany-at-Law* (1955), p.254. See 4:13

SOMERSET MAUGHAM 1874–1965

3 People ask you for criticism, but they only want praise.
Of Human Bondage (1915), ch.50

4 Dying is a very dull, dreary affair. And my advice to you is to have nothing whatever to do with it.
Robin Maugham, *Escape from the Shadows,* 5

BILL MAULDIN 1921–

5 I feel like a fugitive from th' law of averages.
Up Front (1946), p.39

JONATHAN MAYHEW 1720–1766

6 Rulers have no authority from God to do mischief.
A Discourse Concerning Unlimited Submission and Non-Resistance to the Higher Powers, 30 Jan. 1750

HUGHES MEARNS 1875–1965

7 As I was going up the stair
I met a man who wasn't there.
He wasn't there again to-day.
I wish, I wish he'd stay away.
The Psychoed

COSIMO DE MEDICI 1389–1464

8 We read that we ought to forgive our enemies; but we do not read that we ought to forgive our friends.
Bacon, *Apophthegms,* 206

LORENZO DE' MEDICI 1449–1492

9 *Quant' è bella giovinezza*
Che si fugge tuttavia!
Chi vuol esser lieto, sia:
Di doman non c'è certezza.
How beautiful is youth, that is always slipping away!
Whoever wants to be happy, let him be so: about tomorrow there's no knowing.
Trionfo di Bacco ed Arianna

LORD MELBOURNE 1779–1848

10 I wish I was as cocksure of anything as Tom Macaulay is of everything.
Earl Cowper, *Preface to Lord Melbourne's Papers* (1889), p.xii

11 What all the wise men promised has not happened, and what all the d—d fools said would happen has come to pass.
Of Catholic Emancipation. H. Dunckley, *Lord Melbourne* (1890)

12 I like the Garter; there is no damned merit in it.
On the Order of the Garter

13 Things have come to a pretty pass when religion is allowed to invade the sphere of private life.
Remark on hearing an evangelical sermon. G.W.E. Russell, *Collections and Recollections,* ch.6

14 Now, is it to lower the price of corn, or isn't it? It is not much matter which we say, but mind, we must all say *the same.*
(At a Cabinet meeting.) Attr. See Bagehot, *The English Constitution,* ch.1

15 Nobody ever did anything very foolish except from some strong principle.
Lord David Cecil, *The Young Melbourne,* ch.9

16 God help the Minister that meddles with art!
Lord David Cecil, *Lord M,* ch.3

17 What I want is men who will support me when I am in the wrong.
ch.4. 'Reply to a politician' who said 'I will support you as long as you are in the right.'

18 I have always thought complaints of ill-usage contemptible, whether from a seduced disappointed girl or a turned out Prime Minister.
After his dismissal by William IV. See letter from Emily Eden to Mrs. Lister, 23 Nov. 1834, in *Miss Eden's Letters,* ed. V. Dickinson (1919)

19 Damn it all, another Bishop dead,—I verily believe they die to vex me.
Attr.

20 The worst of the present day [1835] is that men hate one another so damnably. For my part I love them all.
Attr.

21 I don't know, Ma'am, why they make all this fuss about education; none of the Pagets can read or write, and they get on well enough. [To the Queen.]
Attr.

22 While I cannot be regarded as a pillar, I must be regarded as a buttress of the church, because I support it from the outside.
Attr.

HERMAN MELVILLE 1819–1891

23 Call me Ishmael.
Moby Dick, ch.1, opening words

GILLES MÉNAGE 1613–1692

24 *Comme nous nous entretenions de ce qui pouvait rendre heureux, je lui dis; Sanitas sanitatum, et omnia sanitas.*
While we were discussing what could make one happy, I said to him: *Sanitas sanitatum et omnia sanitas.*
Ménagiana (1693), p.166. Part of a conversation with Jean-Louis Guez de Balzac (1594–1654). See 83:14

MENANDER 342/1–293/89 B.C.

25 ὃν οἱ θεοὶ φιλοῦσιν ἀποθνῄσκει νέος.
Whom the gods love dies young.
Dis Exapaton, fr.4

GEORGE MEREDITH 1828–1909

26 Overhead, overhead
Rushes life in a race,
As the clouds the clouds chase;
    And we go,

And we drop like the fruits of the tree,
   Even we,
   Even so.
Dirge in Woods

1 Under yonder beech-tree single on the greensward,
   Couched with her arms behind her golden head,
Knees and tresses folded to slip and ripple idly,
   Lies my young love sleeping in the shade.
Love in the Valley, i

2 She whom I love is hard to catch and conquer,
   Hard, but O the glory of the winning were she won!
ii

3 Lovely are the curves of the white owl sweeping
   Wavy in the dusk lit by one large star.
Lone on the fir-branch, his rattle-note unvaried,
   Brooding o'er tne gloom, spins the brown eve-jar.
Darker grows the valley, more and more forgetting:
   So were it with me if forgetting could be willed.
Tell the grassy hollow that holds the bubbling
   well-spring,
   Tell it to forget the source that keeps it filled.
v

4 Love that so desires would fain keep her changeless;
   Fain would fling the net, and fain have her free.
vi

5 On a starred night Prince Lucifer uprose.
Tired of his dark dominion swung the fiend...
He reached a middle height, and at the stars,
Which are the brain of heaven, he looked, and sank.
Around the ancient track marched, rank on rank,
The army of unalterable law.
Lucifer in Starlight

6 He fainted on his vengefulness, and strove
To ape the magnanimity of love.
Modern Love (1862), ii

7 Not till the fire is dying in the grate,
Look we for any kinship with the stars.
iv

8 And if I drink oblivion of a day,
So shorten I the stature of my soul.
xii

9 'I play for Seasons; not Eternities!'
Says Nature.
xiii

10 A kiss is but a kiss now! and no wave
Of a great flood that whirls me to the sea.
But, as you will! we'll sit contentedly,
And eat our pot of honey on the grave.
xxix

11   That rarest gift
To Beauty, Common Sense.
xxxii

12 O have a care of natures that are mute!
xxxv

13 God, what a dancing spectre seems the moon.
xxxix

14   In tragic life, God wot,
No villain need be! Passions spin the plot:
We are betrayed by what is false within.
xliii

15 Love, that had robbed us of immortal things,
This little moment mercifully gave,
Where I have seen across the twilight wave

The swan sail with her young beneath her wings.
xlvii

16 Their sense is with their senses all mixed in,
Destroyed by subtleties these women are!
xlviii

17 Thus piteously Love closed what he begat:
The union of this ever diverse pair!
These two were rapid falcons in a snare,
Condemned to do the flitting of a bat.
l

18 Ah, what a dusty answer gets the soul
When hot for certainties in this our life!

19 Narrows the world to my neighbour's gate.
Seed Time

20 We spend our lives in learning pilotage,
And grow good steersmen when the vessel's crank!
The Wisdom of Eld

21 Enter these enchanted woods,
   You who dare.
The Woods of Westermain

22 Thoughts of heroes were as good as warming-pans.
Beauchamp's Career (1874-5), ch.4

23 They that make of his creed a strait jacket for
humanity.
ch.29

24 'Tis Ireland gives England her soldiers, her generals
too.
Diana of the Crossways (1885), ch.2

25 She did not seduce, she ravished.
ch.7

26 She was a lady of incisive features bound in stale
parchment.
ch.14

27 Between the ascetic rocks and the sensual whirlpools.
ch.37

28 There is nothing the body suffers the soul may not
profit by.
ch.43

29 A Phoebus Apollo turned fasting friar.
The Egoist (1879), ch.2

30 A dainty rogue in porcelain.
ch.5

31 Cynicism is intellectual dandyism.
ch.7

32 In...the book of Egoism, it is written, Possession
without obligation to the object possessed approaches
felicity.
ch.14

33 None of your dam punctilio.
One of Our Conquerors (1890-91), ch.1

34 I expect that Woman will be the last thing civilized by
Man.
The Ordeal of Richard Feverel (1859), ch.1

35 In action Wisdom goes by majorities.

36 Who rises from prayer a better man, his prayer is
answered.
ch.12

37 Away with Systems! Away with a corrupt world! Let
us breathe the air of the Enchanted island.
Golden lie the meadows; golden run the streams; red
gold is on the pine-stems. The sun is coming down to

earth, and walks the fields and the waters.
The sun is coming down to earth, and the fields and
the waters shout to him golden shouts.
ch.19

1 Kissing don't last: cookery do!
ch.28

2 Speech is the small change of silence.
ch.34

3 Italia, Italia shall be free.
Vittoria (1866), ch.21

4 Much benevolence of the passive order may be traced
to a disinclination to inflict pain upon oneself.
ch.42

OWEN MEREDITH (E.R.B. LYTTON, EARL OF LYTTON) 1831–1891

5 Genius does what it must, and Talent does what it
can.
Last Words of a Sensitive Second-Rate Poet

6 We may live without poetry, music and art;
We may live without conscience, and live without
heart;
We may live without friends; we may live without
books;
But civilized man cannot live without cooks.
Lucile (1860), pt.1, c.2.xix

7 He may live without books,—what is knowledge but
grieving?
He may live without hope,—what is hope but
deceiving?
He may live without love,—what is passion but
pining?
But where is the man that can live without dining?
xxiv

DIXON LANIER MERRITT 1879–1954

8 A wonderful bird is the pelican,
His bill will hold more than his belican.
He can take in his beak
Food enough for a week,
But I'm damned if I see how the helican.
The Pelican

LE CURÉ MESLIER 1664?–1733

9 *Il me souvient à ce sujet d'un souhait que faisait
autrefois un homme, qui n'avait ni science ni
étude...Il souhaitait, disait-il...que tous les grands de
la terre et que tous les nobles fussent pendus et
étranglés avec les boyaux des prêtres. Pour ce qui est
de moi...je souhaitais d'avoir les bras et la force
d'Hercule pour purger le monde de tout vice et de
toute iniquité, et pour avoir le plaisir d'assommer tous
ces monstres d'erreurs et d'iniquité qui font gémir si
pitoyablement tous les peuples de la terre.*
I remember, on this matter, the wish made once by an
ignorant, uneducated man...He said he wished...that
all the great men in the world and all the nobility could
be hanged, and strangled in the guts of priests. For
myself...I wish I could have the strength of Hercules to
purge the world of all vice and sin, and the pleasure of
destroying all those monsters of error and sin [priests]
who make all the peoples of the world groan so

pitiably.
Testament (ed. R. Charles, 1864), I.ch.2. Often quoted as *'Je
voudrais... que le dernier des rois fût étranglé avec les boyaux du
dernier prêtre'* or in Diderot's version:
*Et des boyaux du dernier prêtre
Serrons le cou du dernier roi.*

PRINCE METTERNICH 1773–1859

10 *L'erreur n'a jamais approché de mon esprit.*
Error has never approached my spirit.
(Spoken to Guizot in 1848.) Guizot, *Mémoires* (1858–1867),
vol.IV, p.21

11 *Italien ist ein geographischer Begriff.*
Italy is a geographical expression.
Letter, 19 Nov. 1849

CHARLOTTE MEW 1869–1928

12 She sleeps up in the attic there
Alone, poor maid. 'Tis but a stair
Betwixt us. Oh! my God! the down,
The soft young down of her, the brown,
The brown of her—her eyes, her hair, her hair!
The Farmer's Bride

ALICE MEYNELL 1847–1922

13 I must not think of thee; and, tired yet strong,
I shun the thought that lurks in all delight—
The thought of thee—and in the blue heaven's height,
And in the sweetest passage of a song.
Renouncement

14 With the first dream that comes with the first sleep
I run, I run, I am gathered to thy heart.

15 She walks—the lady of my delight—
A shepherdess of sheep.
The Shepherdess

HUGO MEYNELL 1727–1808

16 The chief advantage of London is, that a man is
always so near his burrow.
Boswell, *Johnson* (ed. 1934), vol.iii, p.379. 1 Apr. 1779

17 For anything I see, foreigners are fools.
vol.iv, p.15. 1780

THOMAS MIDDLETON 1570?–1627

18 I never heard
Of any true affection, but 'twas nipt
With care.
Blurt, Master-Constable (published 1602), III.i.39

19 By many a happy accident.
No Wit, No Help, Like a Woman's (1613?, published 1657),
IV.i.66

20 There's no hate lost between us.
The Witch (before 1627, printed 1778), IV.iii.10

JOHN STUART MILL 1806–1873

21 Ask yourself whether you are happy, and you cease to
be so.
Autobiography (1873), ch.5

22 No great improvements in the lot of mankind are
possible, until a great change takes place in the

fundamental constitution of their modes of thought.
ch.7

1 As often as a study is cultivated by narrow minds, they
will draw from it narrow conclusions.
Auguste Comte and Positivism (1865), p.82

2 The Conservatives...being by the law of their
existence the stupidest party.
Considerations on Representative Government (1861), ch.vii,
footnote

3 When society requires to be rebuilt, there is no use in
attempting to rebuild it on the old plan.
Dissertations and Discussions, vol.i (1859), **Essay on
Coleridge,** p.423

4 Unearned increment.
vol.iv (1876), p.299

5 I will call no being good, who is not what I mean
when I apply that epithet to my fellow-creatures; and
if such a being can sentence me to hell for not so
calling him, to hell I will go.
Examination of Sir William Hamilton's Philosophy (1865), ch.7

6 The sole end for which mankind are warranted,
individually or collectively, in interfering with the
liberty of action of any of their number, is
self-protection.
On Liberty (1859), ch.1

7 The only purpose for which power can be rightfully
exercised over any member of a civilized community,
against his will, is to prevent harm to others. His own
good, either physical or moral, is not a sufficient
warrant.

8 If all mankind minus one, were of one opinion, and
only one person were of the contrary opinion, mankind
would be no more justified in silencing that one
person, than he, if he had the power, would be
justified in silencing mankind.
ch.2

9 We can never be sure that the opinion we are
endeavouring to stifle is a false opinion; and if we
were sure, stifling it would be an evil still.

10 A party of order or stability, and a party of progress or
reform, are both necessary elements of a healthy state
of political life.

11 The liberty of the individual must be thus far limited;
he must not make himself a nuisance to other people.
ch.3

12 All good things which exist are the fruits of
originality.

13 Liberty consists in doing what one desires.
ch.5

14 The worth of a State, in the long run, is the worth of
the individuals composing it.

15 A State which dwarfs its men, in order that they may
be more docile instruments in its hands even for
beneficial purposes—will find that with small men no
great thing can really be accomplished.

16 When the land is cultivated entirely by the spade and
no horses are kept, a cow is kept for every three acres
of land.
Principles of Political Economy (1848). **A Treatise on Flemish
Husbandry**

17 The great majority of those who speak of perfectibility
as a dream, do so because they feel that it is one which

would afford them no pleasure if it were realized.
Speech on Perfectibility (1828)

18 The principle which regulates the existing social
relations between the two sexes—the legal
subordination of one sex to the other—is wrong in
itself, and now one of the chief hindrances to human
improvement; and...it ought to be replaced by a
principle of perfect equality, admitting no power or
privilege on the one side, nor disability on the other.
The Subjection of Women (1869), ch.1

19 The moral regeneration of mankind will only really
commence, when the most fundamental of the social
relations [marriage] is placed under the rule of equal
justice, and when human beings learn to cultivate their
strongest sympathy with an equal in rights and
cultivation.
ch.4

20 If we may be excused the antithesis, we should say
that eloquence is *heard,* poetry is *overheard.*
Thoughts on Poetry and its varieties (1859)

21 The most important thing women have to do is to stir
up the zeal of women themselves.
Letter to Alexander Bain, 14 July 1869

22 Were there but a few hearts and intellects like hers this
earth would already become the hoped-for heaven.
Epitaph (1858-9) for his wife Harriet, cemetery of St. Véran, near
Avignon. See M. St.J. Packe, *Life of John Stuart Mill* (1954),
bk.VII, ch. iii

EDNA ST. VINCENT MILLAY 1892–1950

23 Gently they go, the beautiful, the tender, the kind;
Quietly they go, the intelligent, the witty, the brave.
I know. But I do not approve. And I am not resigned.
The Buck in the Snow, III, **Dirge without Music**

24 Childhood is not from birth to a certain age and at a
    certain age
The child is grown, and puts away childish things,

Childhood is the kingdom where nobody dies.

Nobody that matters, that is.
Childhood is the Kingdom where Nobody dies

25 Man has never been the same since God died.

He has taken it very hard. Why, you'd think it was
    only yesterday,
The way he takes it.
Not that he says much, but he laughs much louder than
    he used to,
And he can't bear to be left alone even for a minute,
    and he can't
Sit still.
Conversation at Midnight, IV

26 My candle burns at both ends;
    It will not last the night;
But ah, my foes, and oh my friends—
    It gives a lovely light!
A Few Figs from Thistles (1920). **First Fig**

27 Was it for this I uttered prayers,
And sobbed and cursed and kicked the stairs,
That now, domestic as a plate,
I should retire at half-past eight?
Grown-up

28 Euclid alone has looked on Beauty bare.
The Harp-Weaver (1923), 4, sonnet 22

29 Death devours all lovely things:

Lesbia with her sparrow
Shares the darkness,—presently
Every bed is narrow.
Passer Mortuus Est. See 136:22

1 After all, my erstwhile dear,
My no longer cherished,
Need we say it was not love,
Just because it perished?

ALICE DUER MILLER 1874–1942

2 I am American bred,
I have seen much to hate here—much to forgive,
But in a world where England is finished and dead,
I do not wish to live.
The White Cliffs (1940)

WILLIAM MILLER 1810–1872

3 Wee Willie Winkie rins through the town,
Up stairs and down stairs in his nicht-gown,
Tirling at the window, crying at the lock,
Are the weans in their bed, for it's now ten o'clock?
Willie Winkie (1841)

A.A. MILNE 1882–1956

4 They're changing guard at Buckingham Palace—
Christopher Robin went down with Alice.
Alice is marrying one of the guard.
'A soldier's life is terrible hard,'
          Says Alice.
When We Were Very Young (1924). **Buckingham Palace**

5 James James
Morrison Morrison
Weatherby George Dupree
Took great
Care of his Mother
Though he was only three.
Disobedience

6 You must never go down to the end of the town if you
don't go down with me.

7 The King asked
The Queen, and
The Queen asked
The Dairymaid:
'Could we have some butter for
The Royal slice of bread?'
The King's Breakfast

8 I do like a little bit of butter to my bread!

9 The King said
'Butter, eh?'
And bounced out of bed.

10 *What* is the matter with Mary Jane?
She's perfectly well and she hasn't a pain,
And it's lovely rice pudding for dinner again,—
What *is* the matter with Mary Jane?
Rice Pudding

11 Little Boy kneels at the foot of the bed,
Droops on the little hands, little gold head;
Hush! Hush! Whisper who dares!
Christopher Robin is saying his prayers.
Vespers

12 Isn't it funny

How a bear likes honey?
Buzz! Buzz! Buzz!
I wonder why he does?
Winnie-the-Pooh (1926), ch.1

13 I am a Bear of Very Little Brain, and long words
Bother me.
ch.4

14 'Pathetic', he said. 'That's what it is. Pathetic'.
ch.6

15 Time for a little something.

16 On Monday, when the sun is hot,
I wonder to myself a lot:
'Now is it true, or is it not,
'That what is which and which is what?'
ch.7

17 When I was young, we *always* had mornings like this.
Toad of Toad Hall (1929), II.3. Milne's dramatization of Kenneth
Grahame's *The Wind in the Willows*.

LORD MILNER 1854–1925

18 If we believe a thing to be bad, and if we have a right
to prevent it, it is our duty to try to prevent it and to
damn the consequences. [The Peers and the Budget.]
Speech at Glasgow, 26 Nov. 1909

JOHN MILTON 1608–1674

19 Such sweet compulsion doth in music lie.
Arcades (?1633), 1.68

20 Blest pair of Sirens, pledges of Heaven's joy,
Sphere-born harmonious sisters, Voice and Verse.
At a Solemn Music

21 Where the bright Seraphim in burning row
Their loud up-lifted Angel trumpets blow.

22 Before the starry threshold of Jove's Court
My mansion is.
Comus (1634), 1.1

23 Above the smoke and stir of this dim spot,
Which men call Earth.
1.5

24 Yet some there be that by due steps aspire
To lay their just hands on that golden key
That opes the palace of Eternity.
1.12

25 Rich and various gems inlay
The unadornèd bosom of the deep.
1.22

26 An old, and haughty nation proud in arms.
1.33

27 And the gilded car of day,
His glowing axle doth allay
In the steep Atlantic stream.
1.95

28 What hath night to do with sleep?
1.122

29 Come, knit hands, and beat the ground,
In a light fantastic round.
1.143

30   When the grey-hooded Even
Like a sad votarist in palmer's weed,
Rose from the hindmost wheels of Phoebus' wain.
1.188

1   O thievish Night,
Why shouldst thou, but for some felonious end,
In thy dark lantern thus close up the stars
That nature hung in heaven, and filled their lamps
With everlasting oil, to give due light
To the misled and lonely traveller?
l.195

2 Was I deceived, or did a sable cloud
Turn forth her silver lining on the night?
l.221

3 Sweet Echo, sweetest nymph, that liv'st unseen
       Within thy airy shell
By slow Meander's margent green,
       And in the violet-embroidered vale.
l.230

4 Can any mortal mixture of earth's mould
Breathe such divine enchanting ravishment?
l.244

5 Such sober certainty of waking bliss
I never heard till now.
l.263

6   Shepherd, I take thy word,
And trust thy honest offer'd courtesy,
Which oft is sooner found in lowly sheds
With smoky rafters, than in tap'stry halls
And courts of princes.
l.321

7 With thy long levell'd rule of streaming light.
l.340

8 Virtue could see to do what virtue would
By her own radiant light, though sun and moon
Were in the flat sea sunk. And Wisdom's self
Oft seeks to sweet retired solitude,
Where with her best nurse Contemplation
She plumes her feathers, and lets grow her wings
That in the various bustle of resort
Were all to-ruffled, and sometimes impair'd.
He that has light within his own clear breast
May sit i' th' centre and enjoy bright day;
But he that hides a dark soul and foul thoughts
Benighted walks under the midday sun.
l.373

9 Where an equal poise of hope and fear
Does arbitrate th' event, my nature is
That I incline to hope rather than fear,
And gladly banish squint suspicion.
l.410

10 'Tis Chastity, my brother, Chastity:
She that has that, is clad in complete steel.
l.420

11 How charming is divine philosophy!
Not harsh, and crabbed as dull fools suppose,
But musical as is Apollo's lute,
And a perpetual feast of nectared sweets,
Where no crude surfeit reigns.
l.476

12 What the sage poets taught by th' heavenly Muse,
Storied of old in high immortal verse
Of dire chimeras and enchanted isles
And rifted rocks whose entrance leads to Hell,—
For such there be, but unbelief is blind.
l.515

13 And fill'd the air with barbarous dissonance.
l.550

14   I was all ear,
And took in strains that might create a soul
Under the ribs of Death.
l.560

15   Against the threats
Of malice or of sorcery, or that power
Which erring man call chance, this I hold firm:
Virtue may be assailed, but never hurt,
Surprised by unjust force, but not enthralled.
l.586

16 O foolishness of men! that lend their ears
To those budge doctors of the Stoic fur,
And fetch their precepts from the Cynic tub,
Praising the lean and sallow Abstinence.
l.706

17 Beauty is Nature's coin, must not be hoarded,
But must be current, and the good thereof
Consists in mutual and partaken bliss.
l.739

18 Beauty is Nature's brag, and must be shown
In courts, at feasts, and high solemnities,
Where most may wonder at the workmanship;
It is for homely features to keep home,
They had their name thence; coarse complexions
And cheeks of sorry grain will serve to ply
The sampler, and to tease the huswife's wool.
What need a vermeil-tinctur'd lip for that,
Love-darting eyes, or tresses like the morn?
l.745

19 Obtruding false rules pranked in reason's garb.
l.759

20 Sabrina fair,
       Listen where thou art sitting
Under the glassy, cool, translucent wave,
       In twisted braids of lilies knitting
The loose train of thy amber-dropping hair.
l.859

21 Thus I set my printless feet
O'er the cowslip's velvet head,
That bends not as I tread.
l.897

22 Love virtue, she alone is free,
She can teach ye how to climb
Higher than the sphery chime;
Or, if virtue feeble were,
Heaven itself would stoop to her.
l.1019

23 Hence, vain deluding joys,
The brood of Folly without father bred.
Il Penseroso (1632), l.1

24 As thick and numberless
       As the gay motes that people the sunbeams.
l.7

25 Hail divinest Melancholy.
l.12

26 Come, pensive Nun, devout and pure,
Sober, steadfast, and demure.
l.31

27 And join with thee calm Peace, and Quiet,
Spare Fast, that oft with gods doth diet.
l.45

1 And add to these retired Leisure,
That in trim gardens takes his pleasure.
l.49

2 Sweet bird, that shunn'st the noise of folly,
Most musical, most melancholy!
l.61

3   I walk unseen
On the dry smooth-shaven green,
To behold the wandering moon,
Riding near her highest noon,
Like one that had been led astray
Through the heav'n's wide pathless way;
And oft, as if her head she bow'd,
Stooping through a fleecy cloud.
l.65

4 Oft, on a plat of rising ground,
I hear the far-off curfew sound
Over some wide-watered shore,
Swinging slow with sullen roar.
l.73

5 Where glowing embers through the room
Teach light to counterfeit a gloom,
Far from all resort of mirth,
Save the cricket on the hearth.
l.79

6 Or bid the soul of Orpheus sing
Such notes as, warbled to the string,
Drew iron tears down Pluto's cheek.
l.105

7 Where more is meant than meets the ear.
l.120

8 While the bee with honied thigh,
That at her flowery work doth sing,
And the waters murmuring
And such consort as they keep,
Entice the dewy-feather'd sleep.
l.142

9 But let my due feet never fail
To walk the studious cloister's pale.
l.155

10 With antique pillars massy proof,
And storied windows richly dight,
Casting a dim religious light.
There let the pealing organ blow,
To the full-voiced quire below,
In service high, and anthems clear
As may, with sweetness, through mine ear,
Dissolve me into ecstasies,
And bring all Heaven before mine eyes.
l.158

11 Till old experience do attain
To something like prophetic strain.
l.173

12 Hence, loathed Melancholy,
   Of Cerberus, and blackest Midnight born,
In Stygian cave forlorn,
   'Mongst horrid shapes, and shrieks, and sights
       unholy.
   L'Allegro (1632), l.1

13 So buxom, blithe, and debonair.
l.24

14 Haste thee Nymph, and bring with thee
Jest and youthful jollity,

Quips and cranks, and wanton wiles,
Nods, and becks, and wreathed smiles.
l.25

15 Sport that wrinkled Care derides,
And Laughter holding both his sides.
Come, and trip it as ye go
On the light fantastic toe,
And in thy right hand lead with thee
The mountain nymph, sweet Liberty.
l.31

16 Mirth, admit me of thy crew,
To live with her, and live with thee,
In unreproved pleasures free.
l.38

17 While the cock with lively din
Scatters the rear of darkness thin,
And to the stack, or the barn door,
Stoutly struts his dames before.
l.49

18 Right against the eastern gate,
Where the great Sun begins his state.
l.59

19   The ploughman near at hand,
Whistles o'er the furrowed land,
And the milkmaid singeth blithe,
And the mower whets his scythe,
And every shepherd tells his tale
Under the hawthorn in the dale.
l.63

20 Meadows trim with daisies pied,
Shallow brooks and rivers wide.
Towers, and battlements it sees
Bosom'd high in tufted trees,
Where perhaps some beauty lies,
The cynosure of neighbouring eyes.
l.75

21 Of herbs, and other country messes,
Which the neat-handed Phyllis dresses.
l.85

22 To many a youth, and many a maid,
Dancing in the chequered shade.
And young and old come forth to play
On a sunshine holiday.
l.95

23 Then to the spicy nut-brown ale.
l.100

24 Towered cities please us then,
And the busy hum of men.
l.117

25 Store of ladies, whose bright eyes
Rain influence, and judge the prize
Of wit or arms.
l.121

26 And pomp, and feast, and revelry,
With mask, and antique pageantry,
Such sights as youthful poets dream,
On summer eves by haunted stream.
Then to the well-trod stage anon,
If Jonson's learnèd sock be on,
Or sweetest Shakespeare, Fancy's child,
Warble his native wood-notes wild,
And ever against eating cares,
Lap me in soft Lydian airs,

Married to immortal verse
Such as the meeting soul may pierce
In notes, with many a winding bout
Of linked sweetness long drawn out.
l.127

1 Such strains as would have won the ear
Of Pluto, to have quite set free
His half regain'd Eurydice.
l.148

2 Yet once more, O ye laurels, and once more
Ye myrtles brown, with ivy never sere,
I come to pluck your berries harsh and crude,
And with forc'd fingers rude,
Shatter your leaves before the mellowing year.
Bitter constraint and sad occasion dear
Compels me to disturb your season due,
For Lycidas is dead, dead ere his prime,
Young Lycidas and hath not left his peer.
Who would not sing for Lycidas? he knew
Himself to sing and build the lofty rhyme.
He must not float upon his watery bier
Unwept, and welter to the parching wind
Without the meed of some melodious tear.
Lycidas (1637), l.1

3 Hence with denial vain, and coy excuse.
l.18

4 For we were nursed upon the self-same hill.
l.23

5 But, O the heavy change, now thou art gone,
Now thou art gone, and never must return!
l.37

6   The woods and desert caves,
With wild thyme and the gadding vine o'ergrown.
l.39

7 Where were ye, Nymphs, when the remorseless deep
Closed o'er the head of your loved Lycidas?
l.50

8 Alas! what boots it with uncessant care
To tend the homely, slighted, shepherd's trade,
And strictly meditate the thankless Muse?
Were it not better done, as others use,
To sport with Amaryllis in the shade,
Or with the tangles of Neaera's hair.
Fame is the spur that the clear spirit doth raise
(That last infirmity of noble mind)
To scorn delights, and live laborious days;
But the fair guerdon when we hope to find,
And think to burst out into sudden blaze,
Comes the blind Fury with th' abhorred shears
And slits the thin-spun life.
l.64

9 Fame is no plant that grows on mortal soil.
l.78

10 It was that fatal and perfidious bark
Built in th' eclipse, and rigged with curses dark,
That sunk so low that sacred head of thine.
l.100

11 Last came, and last did go,
The Pilot of the Galilean lake,
Two massy keys he bore of metals twain,
The golden opes, the iron shuts amain.
l.108

12   Such as for their bellies' sake,

Creep and intrude, and climb into the fold.
Of other care they little reckoning make,
Than how to scramble at the shearers' feast,
And shove away the worthy bidden guest.
Blind mouths! that scarce themselves know how to
  hold
A sheep-hook, or have learn'd aught else the least
That to the faithful herdman's art belongs!
l.114

13   Their lean and flashy songs
Grate on their scrannel pipes of wretched straw,
The hungry sheep look up, and are not fed,
But, swoln with wind and the rank mist they draw,
Rot inwardly and foul contagion spread;
Besides what the grim wolf with privy paw
Daily devours apace, and nothing said.
But that two-handed engine at the door
Stands ready to smite once, and smite no more.
l.123

14   Return, Alpheus, the dread voice is past
That shrunk thy streams; return Sicilian Muse.
l.132

15 Bring the rathe primrose that forsaken dies,
The tufted crow-toe, and pale jessamine,
The white pink, and the pansy freakt with jet,
The glowing violet,
The musk-rose, and the well-attir'd woodbine,
With cowslips wan that hang the pensive head,
And every flower that sad embroidery wears.
Bid amaranthus all his beauty shed,
And daffadillies fill their cups with tears,
To strew the laureate hearse where Lycid lies.
l.142

16 Whether beyond the stormy Hebrides,
Where thou perhaps under the whelming tide
Visit'st the bottom of the monstrous world;
Or whether thou, to our moist vows denied,
Sleepst by the fable of Bellerus old,
Where the great Vision of the guarded mount
Looks toward Namancos and Bayona's hold.
Look homeward, Angel, now, and melt with ruth.
l.156

17 For Lycidas your sorrow is not dead,
Sunk though he be beneath the watery floor;
So sinks the day-star in the ocean bed,
And yet anon repairs his drooping head,
And tricks his beams, and with new spangled ore,
Flames in the forehead of the morning sky:
So Lycidas sunk low, but mounted high,
Through the dear might of Him that walked the waves.
l.166

18 There entertain him all the saints above,
In solemn troops and sweet societies
That sing, and singing in their glory move,
And wipe the tears for ever from his eyes.
l.178

19 Thus sang the uncouth swain to th' oaks and rills,
While the still morn went out with sandals gray;
He touch'd the tender stops of various quills,
With eager thought warbling his Doric lay.
l.186

20 At last he rose, and twitch'd his mantle blue;
To-morrow to fresh woods, and pastures new.
l.192

1 What needs my Shakespeare for his honour'd bones,
The labour of an age in piled stones,
Or that his hallow'd relics should be hid
Under a star-y-pointing pyramid?
On Shakespeare (1630)

2 O fairest flower, no sooner blown but blasted,
Soft silken primrose fading timelessly.
On the Death of a Fair Infant, Dying of a Cough (1628), 1.1

3 This is the month, and this the happy morn,
Wherein the Son of Heaven's eternal King,
Of wedded maid, and virgin mother born,
Our great redemption from above did bring;
For so the holy sages once did sing,
That He our deadly forfeit should release,
And with His Father work us a perpetual peace.
On the Morning of Christ's Nativity (1629), 1.1

4 The star-led wizards haste with odours sweet!
1.23

5 It was the winter wild
While the Heav'n-born child
All meanly wrapt in the rude manger lies,
Nature in awe to him
Had doff't her gawdy trim
With her great Master so to sympathize.
1.29

6 Nor war, nor battle's sound
Was heard the world around,
The idle spear and shield were high uphung.
1.53

7 The stars with deep amaze
Stand fixt in stedfast gaze
Bending one way their precious influence
And will not take their flight
For all the morning light,
Or Lucifer that often warned them thence,
But in their glimmering orbs did glow
Until their Lord himself bespake and bid them go.
1.69

8 Perhaps their loves, or else their sheep,
Was all that did their silly thoughts so busy keep.
1.91

9 The helmed Cherubim
And sworded Seraphim,
Are seen in glittering ranks with wings display'd.
1.112

10 Ring out ye crystal spheres,
Once bless our human ears
(If ye have power to touch our senses so)
And let your silver chime
Move in melodious time;
And let the base of heav'n's deep organ blow,
And with your ninefold harmony
Make up full consort to th' angelic symphony.
1.125

11 For if such holy song
Enwrap our fancy long,
Time will run back, and fetch the age of gold
And speckled Vanity
Will sicken soon and die.
1.133

12 Swinges the scaly horror of his folded tail.
1.172

13 The oracles are dumb,

No voice or hideous hum
Runs through the arched roof in words deceiving.
Apollo from his shrine
Can no more divine,
With hollow shriek the steep of Delphos leaving.
1.173

14 So when the sun in bed,
Curtain'd with cloudy red,
Pillows his chin upon an orient wave.
1.229

15 But see the Virgin blest,
Hath laid her Babe to rest,
Time is our tedious song should here have ending.
1.237

16 Showed him his room where he must lodge that night,
Pulled off his boots, and took away the light.

If any ask for him, it shall be said,
'Hobson has supped, and's newly gone to bed.'
On the University Carrier

17 Fly, envious Time, till thou run out thy race:
Call on the lazy leaden-stepping hours.
On Time, 1.1

18 Rhyme being no necessary adjunct or true ornament of
poem or good verse, in longer works especially, but
the invention of a barbarous age, to set off wretched
matter and lame metre.
The Verse. Preface to *Paradise Lost* (1667), 1668 ed.

19 The troublesome and modern bondage of Rhyming.

20 Of Man's first disobedience, and the fruit
Of that forbidden tree, whose mortal taste
Brought death into the world, and all our woe,
With loss of Eden.
bk.i, 1.1

21 Things unattempted yet in prose or rhyme.
1.16

22   What in me is dark
Illumine, what is low raise and support;
That to the highth of this great argument
I may assert eternal Providence,
And justify the ways of God to Men.
1.22

23 The infernal serpent; he it was, whose guile,
Stirr'd up with envy and revenge, deceived
The mother of mankind.
1.34

24   Him the Almighty Power
Hurled headlong flaming from th' ethereal sky
With hideous ruin and combustion down
To bottomless perdition, there to dwell
In adamantine chains and penal fire
Who durst defy th' Omnipotent to arms.
1.44

25 A dungeon horrible, on all sides round
As one great furnace flam'd; yet from those flames
No light, but rather darkness visible
Serv'd only to discover sights of woe,
Regions of sorrow, doleful shades, where peace
And rest can never dwell, hope never comes
That comes to all.
1.60

26   But O how fall'n! how changed
From him who, in the happy realms of light,
Clothed with transcendent brightness didst outshine

Myriads though bright.
1.84

1 United thoughts and counsels, equal hope,
And hazard in the glorious enterprise.
1.88

2   Yet not for those
Nor what the potent victor in his rage
Can else inflict do I repent or change,
Though changed in outward lustre; that fixed mind
And high disdain, from sense of injured merit.
1.94

3   What though the field be lost?
All is not lost; th' unconquerable will,
And study of revenge, immortal hate,
And courage never to submit or yield:
And what is else not to be overcome?
1.105

4 Vaunting aloud, but racked with deep despair.
1.126

5 Fall'n Cherub, to be weak is miserable
Doing or suffering; but of this be sure,
To do ought good never will be our task,
But ever to do ill our sole delight.
1.157

6 And out of good still to find means of evil.
1.165

7 What reinforcement we may gain from hope,
If not, what resolution from despair.
1.190

8   The will
And high permission of all-ruling Heaven
Left him at large to his own dark designs,
That with reiterated crimes he might
Heap on himself damnation.
1.211

9 Is this the region, this the soil, the clime,
Said then the lost Archangel, this the seat
That we must change for Heav'n, this mournful gloom
For that celestial light?
1.242

10   Farewell happy fields
Where joy for ever dwells: Hail horrors, hail
Infernal world, and thou profoundest Hell
Receive thy new possessor: one who brings
A mind not to be changed by place or time.
The mind is its own place, and in it self
Can make a Heav'n of Hell, a Hell of Heav'n.
1.249

11 Here we may reign secure, and in my choice
To reign is worth ambition though in hell:
Better to reign in hell, than serve in heav'n.
1.261

12 His spear, to equal which the tallest pine
Hewn on Norwegian hills, to be the mast
Of some great ammiral, were but a wand,
He walk'd with to support uneasy steps
Over the burning marle.
1.292

13 Thick as autumnal leaves that strow the brooks
In Vallombrosa, where th' Etrurian shades
High over-arch'd embower.
1.302

14 First Moloch, horrid king, besmear'd with blood

Of human sacrifice, and parents' tears.
1.392

15   For spirits when they please
Can either sex assume, or both; so soft
And uncompounded is their essence pure...
       in what shape they choose,
Dilated or condensed, bright or obscure,
Can execute their aery purposes.
1.423

16 Astarte, Queen of Heav'n, with crescent horns.
1.439

17   Thammuz came next behind,
Whose annual wound in Lebanon allur'd
The Syrian damsels to lament his fate
In amorous ditties all a summer's day,
While smooth Adonis from his native rock
Ran purple to the sea.
1.446

18   And when night
Darkens the streets, then wander forth the sons
Of Belial, flown with insolence and wine.
1.500

19 Th' imperial ensign, which full high advanced
Shone like a meteor streaming to the wind.
1.536

20 Sonorous metal blowing martial sounds:
At which the universal host upsent
A shout that tore hell's concave, and beyond
Frighted the reign of Chaos and old Night.
1.540

21   Anon they move
In perfect phalanx to the Dorian mood
Of flutes and soft recorders.
1.549

22   That small infantry
Warred on by cranes. [Pygmies.]
1.575

23   What resounds
In fable or romance of Uther's son
Begirt with British and Armoric knights;
And all who since, baptized or infidel
Jousted in Aspramont or Montalban,
Damasco, or Marocco, or Trebisond,
Or whom Biserta sent from Afric shore
When Charlemain with all his peerage fell
By Fontarabbia.
1.579

24   The sun...
In dim eclipse disastrous twilight sheds
On half the nations, and with fear of change
Perplexes monarchs.
1.594

25   Who overcomes
By force, hath overcome but half his foe.
1.648

26   Mammon led them on,
Mammon, the least erected Spirit that fell
From heav'n, for ev'n in heav'n his looks and thoughts
Were always downward bent, admiring more
The riches of heaven's pavement, trodden gold,
Than aught divine or holy else enjoy'd
In vision beatific.
1.678

1   Let none admire
That riches grow in hell; that soil may best
Deserve the precious bane.
1.690

2 Anon out of the earth a fabric huge
Rose like an exhalation.
1.710

3   From morn
To noon he fell, from noon to dewy eve,
A summer's day; and with the setting sun
Dropt from the zenith like a falling star.
1.742

4   Nor aught availed him now
To have built in heav'n high tow'rs nor did he scape
By all his engines, but was headlong sent
With his industrious crew to build in hell.
1.748

5 Pandoemonium, the high capitol
Of Satan and his peers.
1.756

6 High on a throne of royal state, which far
Outshone the wealth of Ormus and of Ind,
Or where the gorgeous East with richest hand
Showers on her kings barbaric pearl and gold,
Satan exalted sat, by merit raised
To that bad eminence; and from despair
Thus high uplifted beyond hope.
bk.ii, 1.1

7 The strongest and the fiercest Spirit
That fought in Heav'n; now fiercer by despair.
His trust was with th' Eternal to be deemed
Equal in strength, and rather than be less
Cared not to be at all.
1.44

8 My sentence is for open war: of wiles
More unexpert, I boast not.
1.51

9 Belial, in act more graceful and humane;
A fairer person lost not Heav'n; he seemed
For dignity compos'd and high exploit:
But all was false and hollow; though his tongue
Dropt manna, and could make the worse appear
The better reason.
1.109

10   For who would lose,
Though full of pain, this intellectual being,
Those thoughts that wander through eternity,
To perish rather, swallowed up and lost
In the wide womb of uncreated night,
Devoid of sense and motion?
1.146

11 There to converse, with everlasting groans,
Unrespited, unpitied, unreprieved,
Ages of hopeless end.
1.184

12 Thus Belial with words clothed in reason's garb
Counselled ignoble ease, and peaceful sloth,
Not peace.
1.226

13 Our torments also may in length of time
Become our elements.
1.274

14   With grave

Aspect he rose, and in his rising seem'd
A pillar of state; deep on his front engraven
Deliberation sat and public care;
And princely counsel in his face yet shone,
Majestic though in ruin.
1.300

15   To sit in darkness here
Hatching vain empires.
1.377

16 Who shall tempt with wand'ring feet
The dark unbottom'd infinite abyss
And through the palpable obscure find out
His uncouth way.
1.404

17   Long is the way
And hard, that out of hell leads up to light.
1.432

18 O shame to men! devil with devil damn'd
Firm concord holds, men only disagree
Of creatures rational.
1.496

19   In discourse more sweet
(For eloquence the soul, song charms the sense,)
Others apart sat on a hill retir'd,
In thoughts more elevate, and reason'd high
Of providence, foreknowledge, will, and fate,
Fix'd fate, free will, foreknowledge absolute,
And found no end, in wand'ring mazes lost.
1.555

20 Of good and evil much they argued then,
Of happiness and final misery,
Passion and apathy, and glory and shame,
Vain wisdom all, and false philosophy.
1.562

21   The parching air
Burns frore, and cold performs th' effect of fire.
1.594

22   Feel by turns the bitter change
Of fierce extremes, extremes by change more fierce.
1.598

23 O'er many a frozen, many a fiery Alp,
Rocks, caves, lakes, fens, bogs, dens, and shades of
   death,
A universe of death, which God by curse
Created evil, for evil only good,
Where all life dies, death lives, and Nature breeds,
Perverse, all monstrous, all prodigious things,
Abominable, unutterable, and worse
Than fables yet have feigned, or fear conceived,
Gorgons and Hydras, and Chimaeras dire.
1.620

24   The other shape,
If shape it might be call'd that shape had none
Distinguishable in member, joint, or limb,
Or substance might be call'd that shadow seem'd,
For each seem'd either; black it stood as night,
Fierce as ten furies, terrible as hell,
And shook a dreadful dart; what seem'd his head
The likeness of a kingly crown had on.
1.666

25 Whence and what art thou, execrable shape?
1.681

26 Incens'd with indignation Satan stood

Unterrifi'd, and like a comet burn'd
That fires the length of Ophiucus huge
In th' arctic sky, and from his horrid hair
Shakes pestilence and war.
1.707

1   Their fatal hands
No second stroke intend.
1.712

2   I fled, and cry'd out, *Death*;
Hell trembled at the hideous name, and sigh'd
From all her caves, and back resounded, *Death*.
1.787

3   On a sudden open fly
With impetuous recoil and jarring sound
Th' infernal doors, and on their hinges grate
Harsh thunder.
1.879

4   Chaos umpire sits,
And by decision more embroils the fray
By which he reigns: next him high arbiter
Chance governs all.
1.907

5 Sable-vested Night, eldest of things.
1.962

6 With ruin upon ruin, rout on rout,
Confusion worse confounded.
1.995

7 So he with difficulty and labour hard
Moved on, with difficulty and labour he.
1.1021

8 Then feed on thoughts, that voluntary move
Harmonious numbers; as the wakeful bird
Sings darkling, and in shadiest covert hid,

Tunes her nocturnal note. Thus with the year
Seasons return, but not to me returns
Day, or the sweet approach of ev'n or morn,
Or sight of vernal bloom, or summer's rose,
Or flocks, or herds, or human face divine;
But cloud instead, and ever-during dark

Surrounds me, from the cheerful ways of men
Cut off, and for the book of knowledge fair
Presented with a universal blank
Of Nature's works to me expung'd and raz'd,
And wisdom at one entrance quite shut out.
bk.iii, 1.37

9 Dark with excessive bright.
1.380

10 So on this windy sea of land, the Fiend
Walked up and down alone bent on his prey.
1.440

11 Into a Limbo large and broad, since called
The Paradise of Fools, to few unknown.
1.495

12 For neither man nor angel can discern
Hypocrisy, the only evil that walks
Invisible, except to God alone.
1.682

13   At whose sight all the stars
Hide their diminished heads.
bk.iv, 1.34

14 Warring in Heav'n against Heav'n's matchless King.
1.41

15 Me miserable! which way shall I fly

Infinite wrath, and infinite despair?
Which way I fly is Hell; myself am Hell;
And in the lowest deep a lower deep
Still threatening to devour me opens wide,
To which the Hell I suffer seems a Heaven.
1.73

16 So farewell hope, and with hope farewell fear,
Farewell remorse: all good to me is lost;
Evil be thou my Good.
1.108

17   When to them who sail
Beyond the Cape of Hope, and now are past
Mozambic, off at sea north-east winds blow
Sabean odours from the spicy shore

Of Araby the Blest, with such delay
Well pleased they slack their course, and many a
    league
Cheered with the grateful smell old Ocean smiles.
1.159

18 So clomb this first grand thief into God's fold:
So since into his church lewd hirelings climb.
Thence up he flew, and on the tree of life,
The middle tree and highest there that grew,
Sat like a cormorant.
1.192

19 Groves whose rich trees wept odorous gums and balm,
Others whose fruit burnished with golden rind
Hung amiable, Hesperian fables true,
If true, here only.
1.248

20 Flowers of all hue, and without thorn the rose.
1.256

21   Not that fair field
Of Enna, where Proserpin gathering flowers
Herself a fairer flower by gloomy Dis
Was gathered, which cost Ceres all that pain.
1.268

22 For contemplation he and valour formed;
For softness she and sweet attractive grace,
He for God only, she for God in him:
His fair large front and eye sublime declared
Absolute rule.
1.297

23   Which implied
Subjection, but required with gentle sway
And by her yielded, by him best received;
Yielded with coy submission, modest pride,
And sweet reluctant amorous delay.
1.307

24 Adam, the goodliest man of men since born
His sons; the fairest of her daughters Eve.
1.323

25 The savoury pulp they chew, and in the rind
Still as they thirsted scooped the brimming stream.
1.335

26 Sporting the lion ramped, and in his paw,
Dandled the kid; bears, tigers, ounces, pards
Gamboll'd before them, th' unwieldy elephant
To make them mirth us'd all his might, and wreathed
His lithe proboscis.
1.343

27 So spake the Fiend, and with necessity,

The tyrant's plea, excus'd his devilish deeds.
1.393

1   These two
Imparadised in one another's arms,
The happier Eden, shall enjoy their fill
Of bliss on bliss.
1.505

2 Now came still evening on, and twilight gray
Had in her sober livery all things clad;
Silence accompanied, for beast and bird,
They to their grassy couch, these to their nests,
Were slunk, all but the wakeful nightingale;
She all night long her amorous descant sung;
Silence was pleas'd: now glow'd the firmament
With living sapphires: Hesperus that led
The starry host, rode brightest, till the moon,
Rising in clouded majesty, at length
Apparent queen unveil'd her peerless light,
And o'er the dark her silver mantle threw.
1.598

3 God is thy law, thou mine: to know no more
Is woman's happiest knowledge and her praise.
With thee conversing I forget all time.
1.637

4 Sweet is the breath of morn, her rising sweet,
With charm of earliest birds.
1.641

5   Sweet the coming on
Of grateful evening mild, then silent night
With this her solemn bird and this fair moon,
And these the gems of Heav'n, her starry train.
1.646

6 Millions of spiritual creatures walk the earth
Unseen, both when we wake, and when we sleep.
1.677

7   Into their inmost bower
Handed they went; and eas'd the putting off
These troublesome disguises which we wear,
Strait side by side were laid, nor turned I ween
Adam from his fair spouse, nor Eve the rites
Mysterious of connubial love refus'd:
Whatever hypocrites austerely talk
Of purity and place and innocence,
Defaming as impure what God declares
Pure, and commands to some, leaves free to all.
1.738

8 Hail wedded love, mysterious law, true source
Of human offspring, sole propriety,
In Paradise of all things common else.
1.750

9   Sleep on,
Blest pair; and O yet happiest if ye seek
No happier state, and know to know no more.
1.773

10   Him there they found
Squat like a toad, close at the ear of Eve.
1.799

11 But wherefore thou alone? Wherefore with thee
Came not all hell broke loose?
1.917

12 Then when I am thy captive talk of chains,
Proud limitary Cherub.
1.970

13   His sleep
Was aery light, from pure digestion bred.
bk.v, l.3

14 My fairest, my espoused, my latest found,
Heaven's last best gift, my ever new delight.
1.18

15 Best image of myself and dearer half.
1.95

16 On earth join all ye creatures to extol
Him first, him last, him midst, and without end.
1.164

17 A wilderness of sweets.
1.294

18 So saying, with despatchful looks in haste
She turns, on hospitable thoughts intent.
1.331

19   Nor jealousy
Was understood, the injured lover's hell.
1.449

20   Freely we serve,
Because we freely love, as in our will
To love or not; in this we stand or fall.
1.538

21   What if earth
Be but the shadow of Heaven, and things therein
Each to other like, more than on earth is thought?
1.574

22 Hear all ye Angels, progeny of light,
Thrones, Dominations, Princedoms, Virtues, Powers.
1.600

23 All seemed well pleased, all seemed but were not all.
1.617

24   Yonder starry sphere
Of planets and of fixed in all her wheels
         ...mazes intricate,
Eccentric, intervolved, yet regular
Then most, when most irregular they seem;
And in their motions harmony divine
So smoothes her charming tones that God's own ear
Listens delighted.
1.620

25 Satan, so call him now, his former name
Is heard no more in heaven.
1.655

26 Servant of God, well done, well hast thou fought
The better fight, who singly hast maintained
Against revolted multitudes the cause
Of truth, in word mightier than they in arms.
bk.vi, 1.29

27   Headlong themselves they threw
Down from the verge of Heaven, eternal wrath
Burnt after them to the bottomless pit.
1.864

28 Standing on earth, not rapt above the Pole,
More safe I sing with mortal voice, unchang'd
To hoarse or mute, though fall'n on evil days,
On evil days though fall'n, and evil tongues.
bk.vii, 1.23

29   Drive far off the barb'rous dissonance
Of Bacchus and his revellers.
1.32

30   Necessity and chance

Approach not me, and what I will is fate.
1.172

1   There Leviathan
Hugest of living creatures, on the deep
Stretch'd like a promontory sleeps or swims,
And seems a moving land, and at his gills
Draws in, and at his trunk spouts out a sea.
1.412

2   The Planets in their stations list'ning stood,
While the bright Pomp ascended jubilant.
Open, ye everlasting gates, they sung,
Open, ye heavens, your living doors; let in
The great Creator from his work return'd
Magnificent, his six days' work, a world.
1.563

3   He his fabric of the Heavens
Hath left to their disputes, perhaps to move
His laughter at their quaint opinions wide
Hereafter, when they come to model Heaven
And calculate the stars, how they will wield
The mighty frame, how build, unbuild, contrive
To save appearances, how gird the sphere
With centric and eccentric scribbled o'er,
Cycle and epicycle, orb in orb.
bk.viii, 1.76

4   Heaven is for thee too high
To know what passes there; be lowly wise:
Think only what concerns thee and thy being.
1.172

5   Tell me, how may I know him, how adore,
From whom I have that thus I move and live,
And feel that I am happier than I know?
1.280

6   In solitude
What happiness? Who can enjoy alone,
Or all enjoying, what contentment find?
1.364

7   So absolute she seems
And in herself complete, so well to know
Her own, that what she wills to do or say
Seems wisest, virtuousest, discreetest, best.
1.547

8   Oft-times nothing profits more
Than self-esteem, grounded on just and right
Well manag'd.
1.571

9   My celestial Patroness, who deigns
Her nightly visitation unimplor'd,
And dictates to me slumb'ring, or inspires
Easy my unpremeditated verse:
Since first this subject for heroic song
Pleas'd me long choosing, and beginning late.
bk.ix, 1.21

10   Unless an age too late, or cold
Climate, or years damp my intended wing.
1.44

11 The serpent subtlest beast of all the field.
1.86

12 For solitude sometimes is best society,
And short retirement urges sweet return.
1.249

13 As one who long in populous city pent,
Where houses thick and sewers annoy the air,

Forth issuing on a summer's morn to breathe
Among the pleasant villages and farms
Adjoin'd, from each thing met conceives delight.
1.445

14 She fair, divinely fair, fit love for Gods.
1.489

15 God so commanded, and left that command
Sole daughter of his voice; the rest, we live
Law to ourselves, our reason is our law.
1.652

16   Her rash hand in evil hour
Forth reaching to the fruit, she pluck'd, she eat:
Earth felt the wound, and Nature from her seat
Sighing through all her works gave signs of woe
That all was lost.
1.780

17 O fairest of creation! last and best
Of all God's works! creature in whom excell'd
Whatever can to sight or thought be form'd,
Holy, divine, good, amiable, or sweet!
1.896

18   For with thee
Certain my resolution is to die;
How can I live without thee, how forgo
Thy sweet converse and love so dearly joined,
To live again in these wild woods forlorn?
1.906

19   Flesh of flesh,
Bone of my bone thou art, and from thy state
Mine never shall be parted, weal or woe.
1.915

20   What thou art is mine;
Our state cannot be sever'd, we are one,
One flesh; to lose thee were to lose myself.
1.957

21   Yet I shall temper so
Justice with mercy.
bk.x, 1.77

22   He hears
On all sides, from innumerable tongues,
A dismal universal hiss, the sound
Of public scorn.
1.506

23   Oh! why did God,
Creator wise, that peopled highest Heaven
With Spirits masculine, create at last
This novelty on Earth, this fair defect
Of Nature?
1.888

24 Demoniac frenzy, moping melancholy,
And moon-struck madness.
bk.xi, 1.485

25 Nor love thy life, nor hate; but what thou liv'st
Live well, how long or short permit to Heaven.
1.553

26   The evening star,
Love's harbinger.
1.588

27   For now I see
Peace to corrupt no less than war to waste.
1.779

28 In me is no delay; with thee to go,
Is to stay here; without thee here to stay,

Is to go hence unwilling; thou to me
Art all things under Heaven, all places thou,
Who for my wilful crime art banished hence.
bk.xii, l.615

1 They looking back, all th' eastern side beheld
Of Paradise, so late their happy seat,
Wav'd over by that flaming brand, the Gate
With dreadful faces throng'd and fiery arms.
Some natural tears they dropped, but wiped them
   soon;
The world was all before them, where to choose
Their place of rest, and Providence their guide:
They hand in hand with wandering steps and slow
Through Eden took their solitary way.
l.641

2 Skill'd to retire, and in retiring draw
Hearts after them tangled in amorous nets.
Paradise Regained (1671), bk.ii, l.161

3 Ladies of th' Hesperides, that seemed
Fairer than feign'd of old, or fabled since
Of faery damsels met in forest wide
By knights of Logres, or of Lyones,
Lancelot or Pelleas, or Pellenore.
l.357

4 Of whom to be dispraised were no small praise.
bk.iii, l.56

5 But on Occasion's forelock watchful wait.
l.173

6 As he who, seeking asses, found a kingdom. [Saul.]
l.242

7   The childhood shows the man,
As morning shows the day. Be famous then
By wisdom; as thy empire must extend,
So let extend thy mind o'er all the world.
bk.iv, l.220

8 Athens, the eye of Greece, mother of arts
And eloquence, native to famous wits
Or hospitable, in her sweet recess,
City or suburban, studious walks and shades;
See there the olive grove of Academe,
Plato's retirement, where the Attic bird
Trills her thick-warbled notes the summer long.
l.240

9 The first and wisest of them all professed
To know this only, that he nothing knew.
l.293

10   Who reads
Incessantly, and to his reading brings not
A spirit and judgment equal or superior
(And what he brings, what needs he elsewhere seek?)
Uncertain and unsettled still remains,
Deep versed in books and shallow in himself.
l.322

11 In them is plainest taught, and easiest learnt,
What makes a nation happy, and keeps it so.
l.361

12 But headlong joy is ever on the wing.
The Passion, l.5

13 A little onward lend thy guiding hand
To these dark steps, a little further on.
Samson Agonistes (1671), l.1

14 Ask for this great deliverer now, and find him

Eyeless in Gaza, at the mill with slaves.
l.40

15 O dark, dark, dark, amid the blaze of noon,
Irrecoverably dark, total eclipse
Without all hope of day!
l.80

16 The sun to me is dark
And silent as the moon,
When she deserts the night
Hid in her vacant interlunar cave.
l.86

17 To live a life half dead, a living death.
l.100

18 Ran on embattled armies clad in iron,
And, weaponless himself,
Made arms ridiculous.
l.129

19   Wisest men
Have erred, and by bad women been deceived;
And shall again, pretend they ne'er so wise.
l.210

20 Just are the ways of God,
And justifiable to men;
Unless there be who think not God at all.
l.293

21   Of such doctrine never was there school,
But the heart of the fool,
And no man therein doctor but himself.
l.297

22 But what availed this temperance, not complete
Against another object more enticing?
What boots it at one gate to make defence,
And at another to let in the foe?
l.558

23 My race of glory run, and race of shame,
And I shall shortly be with them that rest.
l.597

24   That grounded maxim
So rife and celebrated in the mouths
Of wisest men; that to the public good
Private respects must yield.
l.865

25 Yet beauty, though injurious, hath strange power,
After offence returning, to regain
Love once possess'd.
l.1003

26 Love-quarrels oft in pleasing concord end.
l.1008

27 Lords are lordliest in their wine.
l.1418

28 For evil news rides post, while good news baits.
l.1538

29 And as an ev'ning dragon came,
Assailant on the perched roosts
And nests in order rang'd
Of tame villatic fowl.
l.1692

30 Like that self-begotten bird
In the Arabian woods embost,
That no second knows nor third,
And lay erewhile a holocaust.
l.1699

31 And though her body die, her fame survives,

A secular bird, ages of lives.
l.1706

1   Samson hath quit himself
Like Samson, and heroically hath finish'd
A life heroic.
l.1709

2 Nothing is here for tears, nothing to wail
Or knock the breast; no weakness, no contempt,
Dispraise or blame; nothing but well and fair,
And what may quiet us in a death so noble.
l.1721

3 All is best, though we oft doubt,
What th' unsearchable dispose
Of highest wisdom brings about,
And ever best found in the close.
l.1745

4 His servants he with new acquist
Of true experience from this great event
With peace and consolation hath dismiss'd,
And calm of mind all passion spent.
l.1752

5 O nightingale, that on yon bloomy spray
Warbl'st at eve, when all the woods are still.
Sonnet i. **To the Nightingale**

6 How soon hath Time, the subtle thief of youth
Stoln on its wing my three and twentieth year.
ii. **On his having arrived at the age of twenty-three**

7 I did but prompt the age to quit their clogs,
By the known rules of ancient liberty,
When straight a barbarous noise environs me
Of owls and cuckoos, asses, apes, and dogs.
xii. **On the Same [Detraction, etc.]**

8 Licence they mean when they cry Liberty;
For who loves that, must first be wise and good.

9 Avenge, O Lord, thy slaughtered saints, whose bones
Lie scattered on the Alpine mountains cold;
Ev'n them who kept thy truth so pure of old,
When all our fathers worshipped stocks and stones,
Forget not.
xv. **On the late Massacre in Piedmont**

10 When I consider how my light is spent,
E're half my days, in this dark world and wide,
And that one Talent which is death to hide,
Lodg'd with me useless, though my Soul more bent
To serve therewith my Maker, and present
My true account, lest He returning chide;
'Doth God exact day-labour, light deny'd?'
I fondly ask; But Patience, to prevent
That murmur, soon replies, 'God doth not need
Either man's work or his own gifts. Who best
Bear his mild yoke, they serve him best, his State
Is Kingly. Thousands at his bidding speed
And post o'er Land and Ocean without rest:
They also serve who only stand and wait.
xvi. **On His Blindness**

11 In mirth, that after no repenting draws.
xviii. **To Cyriac Skinner**

12 Methought I saw my late espousèd Saint
Brought to me like Alcestis from the grave.
xix. **On His Deceased Wife**

13 Love, sweetness, goodness, in her person shined.

14 But O as to embrace me she inclined,
I waked, she fled, and day brought back my night.

15 New Presbyter is but old Priest writ large.
On the New Forcers of Conscience under the Long Parliament

16 For what can war but endless war still breed?
On the Lord General Fairfax

17   Peace hath her victories
No less renowned than war.
To the Lord General Cromwell, May 1652

18 He who would not be frustrate of his hope to write
well hereafter in laudable things ought himself to be a
true poem.
An Apology against a Pamphlet…against Smectymnuus (1642),
introd. to 1

19 His words…like so many nimble and airy servitors trip
about him at command.
12

20 For this is not the liberty which we can hope, that no
grievance ever should arise in the Commonwealth,
that let no man in this world expect; but when
complaints are freely heard, deeply considered, and
speedily reformed, then is the utmost bound of civil
liberty attained that wise men look for.
Areopagitica (1644)

21 Books are not absolutely dead things, but do contain a
potency of life in them to be as active as that soul was
whose progeny they are; nay they do preserve as in a
vial the purest efficacy and extraction of that living
intellect that bred them.

22 As good almost kill a man as kill a good book: who
kills a man kills a reasonable creature, God's image;
but he who destroys a good book, kills reason itself,
kills the image of God, as it were in the eye.

23 A good book is the precious life-blood of a master
spirit, embalmed and treasured up on purpose to a life
beyond life.

24 He that can apprehend and consider vice with all her
baits and seeming pleasures, and yet abstain, and yet
distinguish, and yet prefer that which is truly better, he
is the true wayfaring Christian. I cannot praise a
fugitive and cloistered virtue, unexercised and
unbreathed, that never sallies out and sees her
adversary, but slinks out of the race, where that
immortal garland is to be run for, not without dust and
heat. Assuredly we bring not innocence into the world,
we bring impurity much rather: that which purifies us
is trial, and trial is by what is contrary.

25 If we think to regulate printing thereby to rectify
manners, we must regulate all recreations and
pastimes, all that is delightful to man…It will ask more
than the work of twenty licensers to examine all the
lutes, the violins, and the guitars in every house…and
who shall silence all the airs and madrigals, that
whisper softness in chambers?

26 To be still searching what we know not by what we
know, still closing up truth to truth as we find it (for
all her body is homogeneal and proportional), this is
the golden rule in theology as well as in arithmetic,
and makes up the best harmony in a church.

27 God is decreeing to begin some new and great period
in His Church, even to the reforming of Reformation
itself. What does He then but reveal Himself to His
servants, and as His manner is, first to His
Englishmen?

1 Behold now this vast city [London]; a city of refuge, the mansion-house of liberty, encompassed and surrounded with His protection.

2 Where there is much desire to learn, there of necessity will be much arguing, much writing, many opinions; for opinion in good men is but knowledge in the making.

3 Methinks I see in my mind a noble and puissant nation rousing herself like a strong man after sleep, and shaking her invincible locks. Methinks I see her as an eagle mewing her mighty youth, and kindling her undazzled eyes at the full midday beam.

4 Give me the liberty to know, to utter, and to argue freely according to conscience, above all liberties.

5 Though all the winds of doctrine were let loose to play upon the earth, so Truth be in the field, we do injuriously by licensing and prohibiting to misdoubt her strength. Let her and Falsehood grapple; who ever knew Truth put to the worse, in a free and open encounter?

6 Let not England forget her precedence of teaching nations how to live.
The Doctrine and Discipline of Divorce (1643)

7 I owe no light or leading received from any man in the discovery of this truth.
The Judgement of Martin Bucer Concerning Divorce

8 I call therefore a complete and generous education that which fits a man to perform justly, skilfully and magnanimously all the offices both private and public of peace and war.
Of Education (1644)

9 Ornate rhetorick taught out of the rule of Plato,...To which poetry would be made subsequent, or indeed rather precedent, as being less subtle and fine, but more simple, sensuous and passionate.

10 In those vernal seasons of the year, when the air is calm and pleasant, it were an injury and sullenness against Nature not to go out, and see her riches, and partake in her rejoicing with Heaven and Earth.

11 What I have spoken, is the language of that which is not called amiss *The good old Cause.*
The Ready and Easy Way to Establish a Free Commonwealth (1660)

12 But because about the manner and order of this government, whether it ought to be Presbyterial, or Prelatical, such endless question, or rather uproar is arisen in this land, as may be justly termed, what the fever is to the physicians, the eternal reproach of the divines.
The Reason of Church Government Urged Against Prelaty (1641), preface

13 This manner of writing [i.e. prose] wherein knowing myself inferior to myself...I have the use, as I may account it, but of my left hand.
bk.ii, introd. to ch.1

14 By labour and intent study (which I take to be my portion in this life) joined with the strong propensity of nature, I might perhaps leave something so written to after-times, as they should not willingly let it die.

15 The land had once enfranchised herself from this impertinent yoke of prelaty, under whose inquisitorious and tyrannical duncery no free and splendid wit can flourish.

16 Beholding the bright countenance of truth in the quiet and still air of delightful studies.

17 None can love freedom heartily, but good men; the rest love not freedom, but licence.
The Tenure of Kings and Magistrates (1648-9)

18 No man who knows aught, can be so stupid to deny that all men naturally were born free.

COMTE DE MIRABEAU 1749-1791

19 *La guerre est l'industrie nationale de la Prusse.*
War is the national industry of Prussia.
Attr. to Mirabeau by Albert Sorel, based on his Introduction to his *Monarchie Prussienne*

MISSAL

20 *O felix culpa, quae talem ac tantum meruit habere Redemptorem.*
O happy fault, which has deserved to have such and so mighty a Redeemer.
'Exsultet' on Holy Saturday

MARGARET MITCHELL 1900-1949

21 After all, tomorrow is another day.
Gone with the Wind (1936), closing words.

MARY RUSSELL MITFORD 1787-1855

22 I have discovered that our great favourite, Miss Austen, is my country-woman...with whom mamma before her marriage was acquainted. Mamma says that she was then the prettiest, silliest, most affected, husband-hunting butterfly she ever remembers.
Letter to Sir William Elford, 3 Apr. 1815

NANCY MITFORD 1904-1973

23 'Always be civil to the girls, you never know who they may marry' is an aphorism which has saved many an English spinster from being treated like an Indian widow.
Love in a Cold Climate, pt.1, ch.2. See 3:5

24 'Twenty-three and a quarter minutes past', Uncle Matthew was saying furiously, 'in precisely six and three-quarter minutes the damned fella will be late.'
ch.13

25 When the loo paper gets thicker and the writing paper thinner it's always a bad sign, at home.
pt.2, ch.2

26 Like all the very young we took it for granted that making love is child's play.
The Pursuit of Love, ch.3

27 I loathe abroad, nothing would induce me to live there...and, as for foreigners, they are all the same, and they all make me sick.
ch.10

28 Abroad is unutterably bloody and foreigners are fiends.
ch.15

EMILIO MOLA d. 1937

29 *La quinta columna.*

The fifth column.
A reference to Mola's expectation of help from civilians in
Madrid, reported in *Mundo Obrero* in the first week of Oct. 1936;
but the phrase may not have been coined with direct reference to
the Madrid offensive, since there is doubt over the number of
columns deployed in his march on the city. See, e.g., G. Hills,
The Battle for Madrid (1976), p.85n, and *Madrid: Servicio
Histórico Militar*, La Marcha sobre Madrid (1968), p.88 n.70

MOLIÈRE (J.-B. POQUELIN) 1622–1673

1 *Présentez toujours le devant au monde.*
   Always show your front to the world.
   L'Avare (1668), III.ii

2 *Il faut manger pour vivre et non pas vivre pour
   manger.*
   One should eat to live, and not live to eat.
   v

3 M. Jourdain: *Quoi? quand je dis: 'Nicole,
   apportez-moi mes pantoufles, et me donnez mon
   bonnet de nuit', c'est de la prose?*
   Maître de Philosophie: *Oui, Monsieur.*
   M. Jourdain: *Par ma foi! il y a plus de quarante ans
   que je dis de la prose sans que j'en susse rien.*
   M. Jourdain: What? when I say: 'Nicole, bring me my
   slippers, and give me my night-cap,' is that prose?
   Philosophy Teacher: Yes, Sir.
   M. Jourdain: Good heavens! For more than forty years
   I have been speaking prose without knowing it.
   Le Bourgeois Gentilhomme (1670), II.iv

4 *Tout ce qui n'est point prose est vers; et tout ce qui
   n'est point vers est prose.*
   All that is not prose is verse; and all that is not verse is
   prose.

5 *Ah, la belle chose que de savoir quelque chose.*
   Ah, it's a lovely thing, to know a thing or two.
   vi

6 *Je voudrais bien savoir si la grande règle de toutes les
   règles n'est pas de plaire.*
   I shouldn't be surprised if the greatest rule of all
   weren't to give pleasure.
   Critique de L'École des Femmes (1663), vii

7 *C'est une étrange entreprise que celle de faire rire les
   honnêtes gens.*
   It's an odd job, making decent people laugh.

8 *On ne meurt qu'une fois, et c'est pour si longtemps!*
   One dies only once, and it's for such a long time!
   Le Dépit Amoureux (1656), V.iii

9 *Qui vit sans tabac n'est pas digne de vivre.*
   He who lives without tobacco is not worthy to live.
   Dom Juan (1665), I.i

10 *Je vis de bonne soupe et non de beau langage.*
   It's good food and not fine words that keeps me alive.
   Les Femmes Savantes (1672), II.vii

11 *Guenille, si l'on veut: ma guenille m'est chère.*
   Rags and tatters, if you like: I am fond of my rags and
   tatters.

12 *Un sot savant est sot plus qu'un sot ignorant.*
   A knowledgeable fool is a greater fool than an
   ignorant fool.
   IV.iii

13 *Les livres cadrent mal avec le mariage.*
   Reading goes ill with the married state.
   V.iii

14 *Que diable allait-il faire dans cette galère?*
   What the devil would he be doing in this gang?
   Les Fourberies de Scapin (1671), II.vii

15 *Vous l'avez voulu, Georges Dandin, vous l'avez
   voulu.*
   You asked for it, George Dandin, you asked for it.
   Georges Dandin (1668), I.ix

16 *L'on a le temps d'avoir les dents longues, lorsqu'on
   attend pour vivre le trépas de quelqu'un.*
   You've time to get hungry, while you're waiting for
   someone's death to get a living.
   Le Médecin malgré lui (1666), II.ii

17 Géronte: *Il me semble que vous les placez autrement
   qu'ils ne sont: que le coeur est du côté gauche, et le
   foie du côté droit.*
   Sganarelle: *Oui, cela était autrefois ainsi, mais nous
   avons changé tout cela, et nous faisons maintenant la
   médecine d'une méthode toute nouvelle.*
   Géronte: It seems to me you are locating them
   wrongly: the heart is on the left and the liver is on the
   right.
   Sganarelle: Yes, in the old days that was so, but we
   have changed all that, and we now practise medicine
   by a completely new method.
   iv

18 *Il faut, parmi le monde, une vertu traitable.*
   Virtue, in the great world, should be amenable.
   Le Misanthrope (1666), I.i

19 *C'est une folie à nulle autre seconde,
   De vouloir se mêler à corriger le monde.*
   Of all human follies there's none could be greater
   Than trying to render our fellow-men better.

20 *On doit se regarder soi-même un fort long temps,
   Avant que de songer à condamner les gens.*
   We should look long and carefully at ourselves before
      we pass judgement on others.
   III.vii

21 *C'est un homme expéditif, qui aime à dépêcher ses
   malades; et quand on a à mourir, cela se fait avec lui
   le plus vite du monde.*
   He's an expeditious man, who likes to hurry his
   patients along; and when you have to die, he sees to
   that quickest in all the world.
   Monsieur de Pourceaugnac (1669), I.vii

22 *Ils commencent ici par faire pendre un homme et puis
   ils lui font son procès.*
   Here [in Paris] they hang a man first, and try him
   afterwards.
   III.ii

23 *Les gens de qualité savent tout sans avoir jamais rien
   appris.*
   People of quality know everything without ever having
   been taught anything.
   Les Précieuses Ridicules (1659), X

24 *Assassiner c'est le plus court chemin.*
   Assassination is the quickest way.
   Le Sicilien (1668), XIII

25 *Ah, pour être dévot, je n'en suis pas moins homme.*
   I am not the less human for being devout.
   Le Tartuffe (1664), III.iii

26 *Le ciel défend, de vrai, certains contentements
   Mais on trouve avec lui des accommodements.*
   God, it is true, does some delights condemn,

But 'tis not hard to come to terms with Him.
IV.v

1 *Le scandale du monde est ce qui fait l'offense,*
Et ce n'est pas pécher que pécher en silence.
It is public scandal that constitutes offence, and to sin
in secret is not to sin at all.

2 *L'homme est, je vous l'avoue, un méchant animal.*
Man, I can assure you, is a nasty creature.
V.vi

3 *Il m'est permis de reprendre mon bien où je le trouve.*
It is permitted me to take good fortune where I find it.
Grimarest, *Vie de Molière* (1704), p.14

HELMUTH VON MOLTKE 1800–1891

4 *Der ewige Friede ist ein Traum, und nicht einmal ein*
schöner und der Krieg ein Glied in Gottes
Weltordnung...Ohne den Krieg wurde die Welt in
Materialismus versumpfen.
Everlasting peace is a dream, and not even a pleasant
one; and war is a necessary part of God's arrangement
of the world...Without war, the world would slide
dissolutely into materialism.
Letter to Dr. J.K. Bluntschli, 11 Dec. 1880

DUKE OF MONMOUTH 1649–1685

5 Do not hack me as you did my Lord Russell.
Words to his Executioner. Macaulay, *History of England*, vol.i,
ch.5

LADY MARY WORTLEY MONTAGU 1689–1762

6 This world consists of men, women, and Herveys.
Letters, vol.i, p.67

7 But the fruit that can fall without shaking,
     Indeed is too mellow for me.
Letters and Works. Answered, for Lord William Hamilton

8 And we meet, with champagne and a chicken, at last.
The Lover

9 General notions are generally wrong.
Letter to Mr. Wortley Montagu, 28 Mar. 1710

10 Civility costs nothing and buys everything.
Letter to the Countess of Bute, 30 May 1756

11 People wish their enemies dead—but I do not; I say
give them the gout, give them the stone!
Letter from Horace Walpole to the Earl of Harcourt, 17 Sept. 1778

MONTAIGNE 1533–1592

12 *Pour juger des choses grandes et hautes, il faut une*
âme de même, autrement nous leur attribuons le vice
qui est le nôtre.
To make judgements about great and high things, a
soul of the same stature is needed; otherwise we
ascribe to them that vice which is our own.
Essais, I.xiv. [References are to M. Rat's edition of the **Essais**
(1958) which, in accordance with the Strowski and Gebelin text
(1906–1933), conflates the 1580 edition of books I and II, the
revised and enlarged 1588 edition of all three books, and later
manuscript additions published posthumously.]

13 *Il faut être toujours botté et prêt à partir.*
One should always have one's boots on, and be ready
to leave.
xx

14 *Je veux...que la mort me trouve plantant mes choux,*

mais nonchalant d'elle, et encore plus de mon jardin
imparfait.
I want death to find me planting my cabbages, but
caring little for it, and much more for my imperfect
garden.

15 *'Le continuel ouvrage de votre vie, c'est bâtir la*
mort.'
The ceaseless labour of your life is to build the house
of death.

16 *'L'utilité du vivre n'est pas en l'espace, elle est en*
l'usage; tel a vécu longtemps qui a peu vécu...Il gît en
votre volonté, non au nombre des ans, que vous ayez
assez vécu.'
The value of life lies not in the length of days but in
the use you make of them; he has lived for a long time
who has little lived. Whether you have lived enough
depends not on the number of your years but on your
will.

17 *Il faut noter, que les jeux d'enfants ne sont pas jeux:*
et les faut juger en eux, comme leurs plus sérieuses
actions.
It should be noted that children at play are not playing
about; their games should be seen as their most
serious-minded activity.
xxiii

18 *Si on me presse de dire pourquoi je l'aimais, je sens*
que cela ne se peut s'exprimer, qu'en répondant:
'Parce que c'était lui; parce que c'était moi.'
If I am pressed to say why I loved him, I feel it can
only be explained by replying: 'Because it was he;
because it was me.'
[Of his friend Étienne de la Boétie.] xxviii

19 *Il n'y a guère moins de tourment au gouvernement*
d'une famille que d'un état entier...et, pour être les
occupations domestiques moins importantes, elles n'en
sont pas moins importunes.
There is scarcely any less bother in the running of a
family than in that of an entire state. And domestic
business is no less importunate for being less
important.
xxxix

20 *Il se faut réserver une arrière boutique toute notre,*
toute franche, en laquelle nous établissons notre vraie
liberté et principale retraite et solitude.
A man should keep for himself a little back shop, all
his own, quite unadulterated, in which he establishes
his true freedom and chief place of seclusion and
solitude.

21 *La plus grande chose du monde, c'est de savoir être à*
soi.
The greatest thing in the world is to know how to be
one's own.

22 *La gloire et le repos sont choses qui ne peuvent loger*
en même gîte.
Fame and tranquillity can never be bedfellows.

23 *Mon métier et mon art c'est vivre.*
Living is my job and my art.
II.vi

24 *La vertue refuse la facilité pour compagne...elle*
demande un chemin âpre et épineux.
Virtue shuns ease as a companion. It demands a rough
and thorny path.
xi

1 *Notre religion est faite pour extirper les vices; elle les couvre, les nourrit, les incite.*
Our religion is made so as to wipe out vices; it covers them up, nourishes them, incites them.
xii

2 *Quand je me joue à ma chatte, qui sait si elle passe son temps de moi plus que je ne fais d'elle?*
When I play with my cat, who knows whether she isn't amusing herself with me more than I am with her?

3 *'Que sais-je?'*
What do I know?

4 *L'homme est bien insensé. Il ne saurait forger un ciron, et forge des Dieux à douzaines.*
Man is quite insane. He wouldn't know how to create a maggot, and he creates Gods by the dozen.

5 *Ceux qui ont apparié notre vie à un songe, ont eu de la raison, à l'aventure plus qu'ils ne pensaient...Nous veillons dormants, et veillants dormons.*
Those who have likened our life to a dream were more right, by chance, than they realised. We are awake while sleeping, and waking sleep.

6 *Quelqu'un pourrait dire de moi que j'ai seulement fait ici un amas de fleurs étrangères, m'y ayant fourni du mien que le filet à les lier.*
It could be said of me that in this book I have only made up a bunch of other men's flowers, providing of my own only the string that ties them together.
III.xii

BARON DE MONTESQUIEU 1689–1755

7 *Les grands seigneurs ont des plaisirs, le peuple a de la joie.*
Great lords have their pleasures, but the people have fun.
Pensées Diverses

8 *Les Anglais sont occupés; ils n'ont pas le temps d'être polis.*
The English are busy; they don't have time to be polite.

FIELD-MARSHAL MONTGOMERY 1887–1976

9 The U.S. has broken the second rule of war. That is, don't go fighting with your land army on the mainland of Asia. Rule One is don't march on Moscow. I developed these two rules myself.
Of American policy in Vietnam. Chalfont, *Montgomery of Alamein* (1976), p.318

ROBERT MONTGOMERY 1807–1855

10 The solitary monk who shook the world.
Luther, Man's Need and God's Supply (1842), l.68

CASIMIR, COMTE DE MONTROND 1768–1843

11 *Défiez-vous des premiers mouvements parce qu'ils sont bons.*
Have no truck with first impulses as they are always generous ones.
Attr., Comte J. d'Estournel, *Derniers Souvenirs*. Also attr. Talleyrand. See 162:18

MARQUIS OF MONTROSE
see JAMES GRAHAM

PROFESSOR CLEMENT C. MOORE 1779–1863

12 'Twas the night before Christmas, when all through the house
Not a creature was stirring, not even a mouse;
The stockings were hung by the chimney with care,
In hopes that St Nicholas soon would be there.
A Visit from St. Nicholas. Troy Sentinel, 23 Dec. 1823

EDWARD MOORE 1712–1757

13 This is adding insult to injuries.
The Foundling (1747–8), V.ii

14 I am rich beyond the dreams of avarice.
The Gamester (1753), II.ii

GEORGE MOORE 1852–1933

15 All reformers are bachelors.
The Bending of the Bough (1900), Act I

16 Art must be parochial in the beginning to become cosmopolitan in the end.
Hail and Farewell! (1911–14), 1925 edn., vol.i, p.5

17 Acting is therefore the lowest of the arts, if it is an art at all.
Mummer-Worship

MARIANNE MOORE 1887–1972

18   O to be a dragon
a symbol of the power of Heaven.
O to Be a Dragon

19 I, too, dislike it: there are things that are important beyond all this fiddle.
Reading it, however, with a perfect contempt for it, one discovers in
it after all, a place for the genuine.
Poetry

20   Nor till the poets among us can be
'literalists of
the imagination'—above
insolence and triviality and can present

for inspection, 'imaginary gardens with real toads in them,' shall we have
it. [Poetry.]

21 My father used to say
'Superior people never make long visits.'
Silence

22 Self-reliant like the cat—
that takes its prey to privacy,
the mouse's limp tail hanging like a shoelace from its mouth.

STURGE MOORE 1870–1944

23 Then, cleaving the grass, gazelles appear
(The gentler dolphins of kindlier waves)
With sensitive heads alert of ear;
Frail crowds that a delicate hearing saves.
The Gazelles

THOMAS MOORE 1779–1852

1 For you know, dear—I may, without vanity, hint—
Though an angel should write, still 'tis *devils* must
print.
The Fudges in England (1835), letter iii, l.64

2 Yet, who can help loving the land that has taught us
Six hundred and eighty-five ways to dress eggs?
The Fudge Family in Paris (1818), letter viii, l.64

3 A Persian's Heaven is easily made;
'Tis but black eyes and lemonade.
Intercepted Letters, vi

4 Believe me, if all those endearing young charms,
    Which I gaze on so fondly today,
Were to change by tomorrow, and fleet in my arms,
    Like fairy gifts fading away!
Thou wouldst still be ador'd as this moment thou art,
    Let thy loveliness fade as it will,
And, around the dear ruin, each wish of my heart
    Would entwine itself verdantly still.
Irish Melodies (1807). **Believe Me, if all those Endearing
Young Charms**

5 No, the heart that has truly lov'd never forgets,
    But as truly loves on to the close,
As the sun-flower turns on her god, when he sets,
    The same look which she turn'd when he rose.

6 Eyes of most unholy blue!
By that Lake

7 You may break, you may shatter the vase, if you will,
But the scent of the roses will hang round it still.
Farewell! But Whenever

8 Go where glory waits thee,
But, while fame elates thee,
    Oh! still remember me.
Go Where Glory

9 The harp that once through Tara's halls
    The soul of music shed,
Now hangs as mute on Tara's walls
    As if that soul were fled.—
So sleeps the pride of former days,
    So glory's thrill is o'er;
And hearts, that once beat high for praise,
    Now feel that pulse no more.
The Harp that Once

10 Thus freedom now so seldom wakes,
    The only throb she gives,
Is when some heart indignant breaks,
    To show that still she lives.

11 Lesbia hath a beaming eye,
    But no one knows for whom it beameth.
Lesbia Hath

12 No, there's nothing half so sweet in life
As love's young dream.
Love's Young Dream

13 The Minstrel Boy to the war is gone,
    In the ranks of death you'll find him;
His father's sword he has girded on,
    And his wild harp slung behind him.
The Minstrel Boy

14 Oh! blame not the bard.
Oh! Blame Not

15 Oh! breathe not his name, let it sleep in the shade,

Where cold and unhonour'd his relics are laid.
Oh! Breathe not his Name

16 Rich and rare were the gems she wore,
And a bright gold ring on her wand she bore.
Rich and Rare

17 She is far from the land where her young hero sleeps,
    And lovers are round her, sighing:
But coldly she turns from their gaze, and weeps,
    For her heart in his grave is lying.
She is Far

18   My only books
    Were woman's looks,
And folly's all they've taught me.
The Time I've Lost

19 'Tis sweet to think, that, where'er we rove,
We are sure to find something blissful and dear,
And that, when we're far from the lips we love,
We've but to make love to the lips we are near.
'Tis Sweet to Think

20 'Tis the last rose of summer
    Left blooming alone;
All her lovely companions
    Are faded and gone.
'Tis the Last Rose

21 Then awake! the heavens look bright, my dear;
'Tis never too late for delight, my dear;
    And the best of all ways
    To lengthen our days
Is to steal a few hours from the night, my dear!
The Young May Moon

22 Where I love I must not marry;
Where I marry, cannot love.
Juvenile Poems. Love and Marriage

23 'Twere more than woman to be wise;
'Twere more than man to wish thee so!
The Ring (ed. 1882)

24 To love you was pleasant enough,
And, oh! 'tis delicious to hate you!
To—When I Lov'd You

25 Oh! ever thus, from childhood's hour,
    I've seen my fondest hopes decay;
I never lov'd a tree or flow'r,
    But 'twas the first to fade away.
I never nurs'd a dear gazelle,
    To glad me with its soft black eye,
But when it came to know me well,
    And love me, it was sure to die!
Lalla Rookh (1817). **The Fire-Worshippers**, i. l.279

26 Like Dead Sea fruits, that tempt the eye,
    But turn to ashes on the lips!
l.484

27 One Morn a Peri at the gate
Of Eden stood, disconsolate.
Paradise and the Peri, l.1

28 But Faith, fanatic Faith, once wedded fast
To some dear falsehood, hugs it to the last.
The Veiled Prophet, iii. l.356

29 'Come, come', said Tom's father, 'at your time of
life,
    'There's no longer excuse for thus playing the rake—
'It is time you should think, boy, of taking a wife'—
    'Why, so it is, father—whose wife shall I take?'
Miscellaneous Poems. A Joke Versified

1 Disguise our bondage as we will,
   'Tis woman, woman, rules us still.
   Sovereign Woman

2 Oft, in the stilly night,
        Ere Slumber's chain has bound me,
   Fond Memory brings the light
        Of other days around me.
   National Airs (1815). **Oft in the Stilly Night**

3 There was a little Man, and he had a little Soul,
   And he said, 'Little Soul, let us try, try, try'.
   Satirical and Humorous Poems. **Little Man and Little Soul**

4 Your priests, whate'er their gentle shamming,
   Have always had a taste for damning.
   The Twopenny Post-Bag (1813), letter iv

5 Good at a fight, but better at a play,
   Godlike in giving, but—the devil to pay!
   *On a Cast of Sheridan's Hand. Memoirs of the Life of R.B.
   Sheridan* (1825), p.712

THOMAS OSBERT MORDAUNT 1730–1809

6 Sound, sound the clarion, fill the fife,
        Throughout the sensual world proclaim,
        One crowded hour of glorious life
             Is worth an age without a name.
   Verses Written During the War, 1756–1763. The Bee, 12 Oct.
   1791

HANNAH MORE 1745–1833

7 For you'll ne'er mend your fortunes, nor help the just
        cause,
   By breaking of windows, or breaking of laws.
   Address to the Meeting in Spa Fields (1817). H. Thompson, *Life*
   (1838), p.398

8 Small habits, well pursued betimes,
   May reach the dignity of crimes.
   Florio, l.77

9 He lik'd those literary cooks
   Who skim the cream of others' books;
   And ruin half an author's graces
   By plucking bon-mots from their places.
   l.123

10   Did not God
   Sometimes withhold in mercy what we ask,
   We should be ruined at our own request.
   Moses in the Bulrushes (1782), pt.i, l.34

11 The sober comfort, all the peace which springs
   From the large aggregate of little things;
   On these small cares of daughter, wife, or friend,
   The almost sacred joys of home depend.
   Sensibility, l.315

SIR THOMAS MORE 1478–1535

12 'In good faith, I rejoiced, son,' quoth he, 'that I had
   given the devil a foul fall, and that with those Lords I
   had gone so far, as without great shame I could never
   go back again.'
   Roper, *Life of Sir Thomas More* (1935), p.69

13 'By god body, master More, *Indignatio principis mors
   est*.'
   'Is that all, my Lord?' quoth he. 'Then in good faith is
   there no more difference between your grace and me,
   but that I shall die to-day, and you to-morrow.'
   p.71

14 Son Roper, I thank our Lord the field is won.
   p.73

15 Is not this house [the Tower of London] as nigh
   heaven as my own?
   p.83

16 I pray you, master Lieutenant, see me safe up, and my
   coming down let me shift for my self. [On mounting
   the scaffold.]
   p.103

17 Pluck up thy spirits, man, and be not afraid to do thine
   office; my neck is very short; take heed therefore thou
   strike not awry, for saving of thine honesty. [To the
   Executioner.]

18 This hath not offended the king. [As he drew his beard
   aside on placing his head on the block.]
   Bacon, *Apophthegms*, 22

19 Your sheep, that were wont to be so meek and tame,
   and so small eaters, now, as I hear say, be become so
   great devourers, and so wild, that they eat up and
   swallow down the very men themselves.
   Utopia (1516), bk.I

20 I cumber you goode Margaret muche, but I woulde be
   sorye, if it shoulde be any lenger than to morrowe, for
   it is S. Thomas evin and the vtas of Sainte Peter and
   therefore to morowe longe I to goe to God, it were a
   daye very meete and conveniente for me. I neuer liked
   your maner towarde me better then when you kissed
   me laste for I loue when doughterly loue and deere
   charitie hathe no laisor to looke to worldely curtesye.
   Fare well my deere childe and praye for me, and I
   shall for you and all your freindes that we maie merily
   meete in heaven.
   Last letter to Margaret Roper, his daughter, 5 July 1535 (ed. E.F.
   Rogers, 1947). More was beheaded the following morning.

THOMAS MORELL 1703–1784

21 See, the conquering hero comes!
   Sound the trumpets, beat the drums!
   Joshua (1748), pt.iii (Libretto for Handel's oratorio)

CHRISTIAN MORGENSTERN 1871–1914

22 *Es war einmal ein Lattenzaun,
   mit Zwischenraum, hindurchzuschaun.*

   *Ein Architekt, der dieses sah,
   stand eines Abends plötzlich da—*

   *und nahm den Zwischenraum heraus
   und baute draus ein grosses Haus.*

   One time there was a picket fence
   with space to gaze from hence to thence.

   An architect who saw this sight
   approached it suddenly one night,

   removed the spaces from the fence
   and built of them a residence.
   Galgenlieder (1905), **Der Lattenzaun**; tr. Max Knight, 1963

LORD MORLEY (VISCOUNT MORLEY OF BLACKBURN) 1838–1923

23 That most delightful way of wasting time.
   [Letter-writing.]
   Critical Miscellanies (1886), ii. **Life of Geo. Eliot**, p.96

24 The whole of the golden Gospel of Silence is now

effectively compressed in thirty-five volumes.
Carlyle, p.195

LORD MORLEY (3rd EARL OF MORLEY) 1843–1905

1 I am always very glad when Lord Salisbury makes a great speech,…It is sure to contain at least one blazing indiscretion which it is a delight to remember.
Speech, Hull, 25 Nov. 1887

'COUNTESS MORPHY' (MARCELLE AZRA FORBES) fl. 1930–50

2 The tragedy of English cooking is that 'plain' cooking cannot be entrusted to 'plain' cooks.
English Recipes (1935), p.17

CHARLES MORRIS 1745–1838

3 If one must have a villa in summer to dwell,
Oh, give me the sweet shady side of Pall Mall!
The Contrast

4 A house is much more to my taste than a tree,
And for groves, oh! a good grove of chimneys for me.

DESMOND MORRIS 1928–

5 There are one hundred and ninety-three living species of monkeys and apes. One hundred and ninety-two of them are covered with hair. The exception is a naked ape self-named *Homo sapiens*.
The Naked Ape (1967), Introduction

GENERAL GEORGE POPE MORRIS 1802–1864

6 Woodman, spare that tree!
  Touch not a single bough!
In youth it sheltered me,
  And I'll protect it now.
Woodman, Spare That Tree (1830)

WILLIAM MORRIS 1834–1896

7 What is this, the sound and rumour? What is this that all men hear,
Like the wind in hollow valleys when the storm is drawing near,
Like the rolling on of ocean in the eventide of fear?
  'Tis the people marching on.
Chants for Socialists (1885), **The March of the Workers**

8 Nor for my words shall ye forget your tears,
Or hope again for aught that I can say,
The idle singer of an empty day.
The Earthly Paradise (1868–70). **An Apology**

9 Dreamer of dreams, born out of my due time,
Why should I strive to set the crooked straight?
Let it suffice me that my murmuring rhyme
Beats with light wing against the ivory gate,
Telling a tale not too importunate
To those who in the sleepy region stay,
Lulled by the singer of an empty day.
See 48:23

10 Forget six counties overhung with smoke,
Forget the snorting steam and piston stroke,
Forget the spreading of the hideous town;
Think rather of the pack-horse on the down,

And dream of London, small and white and clean,
The clear Thames bordered by its gardens green.
Prologue. **The Wanderers**, l.1

11 Had she come all the way for this,
To part at last without a kiss?
Yea, had she borne the dirt and rain
That her own eyes might see him slain
Beside the haystack in the floods?
The Haystack in the Floods

12 But lo, the old inn, and the lights, and the fire,
And the fiddler's old tune and the shuffling of feet;
Soon for us shall be quiet and rest and desire,
And to-morrow's uprising to deeds shall be sweet.
The Message of the March Winds

13 And ever she sung from noon to noon,
'Two red roses across the moon.'
Two Red Roses Across the Moon

14 Have nothing in your houses that you do not know to be useful, or believe to be beautiful.
Hopes and Fears for Art (1882), p.108

J.B. MORTON ('BEACHCOMBER') 1893–1979

15 Hush, hush,
Nobody cares!
Christopher Robin
Has
  Fallen
    Down-
      Stairs.
By the Way (1931), 18 Dec. **Now We are Sick.** See 340:11

THOMAS MORTON 1764?–1838

16 Approbation from Sir Hubert Stanley is praise indeed.
A Cure for the Heartache (1797), V.ii

17 I eat well, and I drink well, and I sleep well—but that's all.
A Roland for an Oliver (1819), I.ii

18 Always ding, dinging Dame Grundy into my ears—what will Mrs Grundy zay? What will Mrs Grundy think?
Speed the Plough (1798), I.i

SIR OSWALD MOSLEY 1896–

19 I am not, and never have been, a man of the right. My position was on the left and is now in the centre of politics.
Letter to *The Times*, 26 Apr. 1968

JOHN LOTHROP MOTLEY 1814–1877

20 As long as he lived, he was the guiding-star of a whole brave nation, and when he died the little children cried in the streets. [William of Orange.]
Rise of the Dutch Republic (1856), pt.vi, ch.vii

21 Give us the luxuries of life, and we will dispense with its necessities.
O.W. Holmes, *Autocrat of the Breakfast-Table*, ch.6

PETER ANTHONY MOTTEUX 1660–1718

22 The devil was sick, the devil a monk wou'd be;
The devil was well, and the devil a monk he'd be.
Translation of Rabelais, *Gargantua and Pantagruel* (1693), bk.iv (1708 edn.) ch.24. Version of a medieval Latin proverb.

WILHELM MÜLLER 1794–1827

1 *Vom Abendrot zum Morgenlicht*
Ward mancher Kopf zum Greise.
Wer glaubt's? Und meiner ward es nicht
Auf dieser ganzen Reise.
Between dusk and dawn many a head has turned
white. Who can believe it? And mine has not
changed on all this long journey.
Die Winterreise, 14. **Der greise Kopf**

ALFRED DE MUSSET 1810–1857

2 *Mon verre n'est pas grand mais je bois dans mon*
verre.
The glass I drink from is not large, but at least it is my
own.
La Coupe et les Lèvres

3 *Le seul bien qui me rest au monde*
Est d'avoir quelquefois pleuré.
The only good thing left to me is that I have
sometimes wept.
Poèmes

4 *Malgré moi l'infini me tourmente.*
I can't help it, the idea of the infinite torments me.
Premières Poésies. L'Espoir en Dieu

VLADIMIR NABOKOV 1891–1977

5 Lolita, light of my life, fire of my loins.
Lolita, ch.1

IAN NAIRN 1930–

6 If what is called development is allowed to multiply at
the present rate, then by the end of the century Great
Britain will consist of isolated oases of preserved
monuments in a desert of wire, concrete roads, cosy
plots and bungalows...Upon this new Britain the
REVIEW bestows a name in the hope that it will
stick—SUBTOPIA. [Making an ideal of suburbia.]
Architectural Review, June 1955, p.365

SIR WILLIAM NAPIER 1785–1860

7 Then was seen with what a strength and majesty the
British soldier fights.
History of the War in the Peninsula (1828–40), bk.xii, ch.6,
Albuera

NAPOLEON I 1769–1821

8 *Soldats, songez que, du haut de ces pyramides,*
quarante siècles vous contemplent.
Think of it, soldiers; from the summit of these
pyramids, forty centuries look down upon you.
Speech to the Army of Egypt on 21 July 1798, before the Battle of
the Pyramids. Gourgaud, *Mémoires, Guerre d'Orient,* i, p.160

9 *Tout soldat français porte dans sa giberne le bâton de*
maréchal de France.
Every French soldier carries in his cartridge-pouch the
baton of a marshal of France.
E. Blaze, *La Vie Militaire sous l'Empire,* I.v

10 *A la guerre, les trois quarts sont des affaires morales,*
la balance des forces réelles n'est que pour un autre
quart.
In war, three-quarters turns on personal character and
relations; the balance of manpower and materials

counts only for the remaining quarter.
Correspondance de Napoléon Ier, xvii, no.14276 (Observations
sur les affaires d'Espagne, Saint-Cloud, 27 août 1808)

11 *Du sublime au ridicule il n'y a qu'un pas.*
There is only one step from the sublime to the
ridiculous.
To De Pradt, Polish ambassador, after the retreat from Moscow in
1812. De Pradt, *Histoire de l'Ambassade dans le grand-duché de
Varsovie en 1812,* ed.1815, p.215. See 367:21

12 *Quant au courage moral, il avait trouvé fort rare,*
disait-il, celui de deux heures après minuit;
c'est-à-dire le courage de l'improviste.
As to moral courage, I have very rarely met with two
o'clock in the morning courage: I mean instantaneous
courage.
Las Cases, Mémorial de Ste-Hélène, Dec. 4-5, 1815

13 *Les savants conçurent une autre idée tout-à-fait*
étrangère au bienfait de l'unité de poids et de
mesures; ils y adaptérent la numération décimale, en
prenant le métre pour unité; ils supprimèrent tous les
nombres complexes. Rien n'est plus contraire à
l'organisation de l'esprit, de la mémoire et de
l'imagination...Le nouveau système de poids et
mesures sera un sujet d'embarras et de difficultés pour
plusieurs générations...C'est tourmenter le peuple par
des vétilles!!!
The scientists had another idea which was totally at
odds with the benefits to be derived from the
standardization of weights and measures; they adapted
to them the decimal system, on the basis of the metre
as a unit; they suppressed all complicated numbers.
Nothing is more contrary to the organization of the
mind, of the memory, and of the imagination...The
new system of weights and measures will be a
stumbling block and the source of difficulties for
several generations...It's just tormenting the people
with trivia!!!
Of the introduction of the metric system. **Mémoires...écrits à
Ste-Hélène**...(*Paris 1823–25*), vol.IV. ch.xvi.4

14 *La carrière ouverte aux talents.*
The career open to talents.
O'Meara, *Napoleon in Exile* (1822), vol.i, p.103

15 *L'Angleterre est une nation de boutiquiers.*
England is a nation of shopkeepers.
Attr. by B.E. O'Meara, *Napoleon at St. Helena,* vol. ii. See
1:9, 509:12

16 Has he luck?
Attr. Habitually asked, to assess a man's probable practical value.
See A.J.P. Taylor, *Politics in Wartime* (1964), ch.16

17 An army marches on its stomach.
Attr. See, e.g., *Windsor Magazine,* 1904, p.268. Probably
condensed from a long passage in Las Cases, *Mémorial de
Ste-Hélène* (Nov. 1816). Also attr. to Frederick the Great.

OGDEN NASH 1902–1971

18 One would be in less danger
From the wiles of a stranger
If one's own kin and kith
Were more fun to be with.
Family Court

19 Candy
Is dandy
But liquor
Is quicker.
Reflections on Ice-Breaking

1 When I consider how my life is spent,
  I hardly ever repent.
  Reminiscent Reflection. See 351:10

2 I think that I shall never see
  A billboard lovely as a tree
  Indeed, unless the billboards fall
  I'll never see a tree at all.
  Song of the Open Road. See 296:3

3 Mr Lionel Fortague said he would settle down on
    Innisfree, the home of iridescent chitchat,
  He said he would a small cabin build there, of clay and
    wattles made.
  Everyone said did he mean he would build a small
    cabin there, made of clay and wattles?
  Mr Lionel Fortague said yes, but his way of putting it
    was more poetic.
  Everyone said maybe, but they were all out of wattles…
  He a fierce-looking dog at an annual clearance sale
    bought, and it the people of Innisfree one by one to
    bite he instructed.
  My, he was disappointed.
  He had forgotten that a bargain dog never bites.
  The Strange Case of Mr. Fortague's Disappointment

4 The turtle lives 'twixt plated decks
  Which practically conceal its sex.
  I think it clever of the turtle
  In such a fix to be so fertile.
  The Turtle

5 Sure, deck your lower limbs in pants;
  Yours are the limbs, my sweeting.
  You look divine as you advance—
  Have you seen yourself retreating?
  What's the Use?

THOMAS NASHE 1567–1601

6 O, tis a precious apothegmaticall Pedant, who will
  finde matter inough to dilate a whole day of the first
  invention of *Fy, fa, fum,* I smell the bloud of an
  English-man.
  Have with you to Saffron-walden (1596), fol.iii

7 Brightness falls from the air;
  Queens have died young and fair;
  Dust hath closed Helen's eye.
  I am sick, I must die.
    Lord have mercy on us.
  In Time of Pestilence

8 From winter, plague and pestilence, good lord, deliver
  us!
  Songs from *Summer's Last Will and Testament* (1592?,
  published 1600)

9 Spring, the sweet spring, is the year's pleasant king;
  Then blooms each thing, then maids dance in a ring,
  Cold doth not sting, the pretty birds do sing:
    Cuckoo, jug-jug, pu-we, to-witta-woo

JAMES BALL NAYLOR 1860–1945

10 King David and King Solomon
   Led merry, merry lives,
   With many, many lady friends
     And many, many wives;
   But when old age crept over them,
     With many, many qualms,
   King Solomon wrote the Proverbs

And King David wrote the Psalms.
David and Solomon

HORATIO, LORD NELSON 1758–1805

11 It is my turn now; and if I come back, it is yours.
   Exercising his privilege, as second lieutenant, to board a prize ship
   before the Master. Southey, *Life of Nelson,* ch.1, Nelson's
   Memoir of His Services.

12 You must consider every man your enemy who speaks
   ill of your king: and…you must hate a Frenchman as
   you hate the devil.
   ch.3

13 Westminster Abbey or victory!
   At the battle of Cape St. Vincent, ch.4

14 Before this time to-morrow I shall have gained a
   peerage, or Westminster Abbey.
   Battle of the Nile, ch.5

15 Victory is not a name strong enough for such a scene.
   At the battle of the Nile

16 It is warm work; and this day may be the last to any of
   us at a moment. But mark you! I would not be
   elsewhere for thousands.
   At the battle of Copenhagen, ch.7

17 I have only one eye,—I have a right to be blind
   sometimes:…I really do not see the signal!
   At the battle of Copenhagen

18 In honour I gained them, and in honour I will die with
   them.
   When asked to cover the stars on his uniform, ch.9

19 I believe my arrival was most welcome, not only to
   the Commander of the Fleet but almost to every
   individual in it; and when I came to explain to them
   the *'Nelson touch',* it was like an electric shock. Some
   shed tears, all approved—'It was new—it was
   singular—it was simple!'…Some may be Judas's; but
   the majority are much pleased with my commanding
   them.
   Letter to Lady Hamilton, 1 Oct. 1805

20 England expects that every man will do his duty.
   At the battle of Trafalgar

21 This is too warm work, Hardy, to last long.

22 Thank God, I have done my duty.

23 Kiss me, Hardy.

EMPEROR NERO A.D. 37–68

24 *Qualis artifex pereo!*
   What an artist dies with me!
   Suetonius, *Life of Nero,* xlix.1

GÉRARD DE NERVAL 1808–1855

25 *Dieu est mort! le ciel est vide—*
   Pleurez! enfants, vous n'avez plus de père.
   God is dead! Heaven is empty—Weep, children, you
     no longer have a father.
   Epigraph to **Le Christ aux Oliviers,** Les Chimères (1854).
   Nerval's summary of a passage in Jean Paul, **Blumen- Frucht- und
   Dornstücke** (1796-7), in which God's children are referred to as
   'orphans'

26 *Je suis le ténébreux,—le veuf,—l'inconsolé,*
   Le prince d'Aquitaine à la tour abolie:
   Ma seule étoile *est morte, et mon luth constellé*
   Porte le soleil *noir de la* mélancholie.

I am the darkly shaded, the bereaved, the inconsolate,
  the prince of Aquitaine, with the blasted tower. My
  only *star* is dead, and my star-strewn lute carries on
  it the black *sun* of *melancholy*.
  El Desdichado

1 *En quoi un homard est-il plus ridicule qu'un
  chien...ou [que] toute autre bête dont on se fait suivre?
  J'ai le goût des homards, qui sont tranquilles, sérieux,
  savent les secrets de la mer, n'aboient pas et n'avalent
  pas la monade des gens comme les chiens, si
  antipathiques à Goethe, lequel pourtant n'était pas
  fou.*
  Why should a lobster be any more ridiculous than a
  dog...or any other animal that one chooses to take for
  a walk? I have a liking for lobsters. They are peaceful,
  serious creatures. They know the secrets of the sea,
  they don't bark, and they don't gnaw upon one's
  monadic privacy like dogs do. And Goethe had an
  aversion to dogs, and he wasn't mad.
  In justification of his walking a lobster, on a lead, in the gardens
  of the Palais Royal. T. Gautier, *Portraits et Souvenirs Littéraires*
  (1875). Tr. Richard Holmes, in Gautier, *My Phantoms* (1976),
  p.149

PROFESSOR ALLAN NEVINS 1890–1971

2 The former allies had blundered in the past by offering
  Germany too little, and offering even that too late,
  until finally Nazi Germany had become a menace to
  all mankind.
  Article in *Current History*, May 1935

SIR HENRY NEWBOLT 1862–1938

3 Admirals all, for England's sake,
    Honour be yours, and fame!
  And honour, as long as waves shall break,
    To Nelson's peerless name!
  Admirals All, i

4 He clapped the glass to his sightless eye,
  And 'I'm damned if I see it', he said.
  See 360:17

5 'Qui procul hinc', the legend's writ,—
    The frontier-grave is far away—
  'Qui ante diem periit:
    Sed miles, sed pro patria.'
  The Island Race. **Clifton Chapel**

6 'Take my drum to England, hang et by the shore,
    Strike et when your powder's runnin' low;
  If the Dons sight Devon, I'll quit the port o' Heaven,
    An' drum them up the Channel as we drummed them
      long ago.'
  Drake's Drum (1896)

7 Drake he's in his hammock till the great Armadas
    come.
    (Capten, art tha sleepin' there below?)
  Slung atween the round shot, listenin' for the drum,
    An' dreamin' arl the time o' Plymouth Hoe.
  Call him on the deep sea, call him up the Sound,
    Call him when ye sail to meet the foe;
  Where the old trade's plyin' an' the old flag flyin'
    They shall find him ware an' wakin', as they found
      him long ago!

8 There's a breathless hush in the Close to-night—
    Ten to make and the match to win—
  A bumping pitch and a blinding light,

An hour to play and the last man in.
  And it's not for the sake of a ribboned coat,
    Or the selfish hope of a season's fame,
  But his Captain's hand on his shoulder smote—
    'Play up! play up! and play the game!'
  Vitaï Lampada

9 The voice of the schoolboy rallies the ranks:
    'Play up! play up! and play the game!'

10 Now the sunset breezes shiver,
    And she's fading down the river,
  But in England's song for ever
    She's the Fighting Téméraire.
  The Fighting Téméraire

11 'Ye have robb'd,' said he, 'ye have slaughter'd and
    made an end,
  Take your ill-got plunder, and bury the dead.'
  He Fell Among Thieves

12 But cared greatly to serve God and the King,
    And keep the Nelson touch.
  Minora Sidera. See 360:19

CARDINAL NEWMAN 1801–1890

13 It is very difficult to get up resentment towards
  persons whom one has never seen.
  Apologia pro Vita Sua (1864). **Mr. Kingsley's Method of
  Disputation**

14 There is such a thing as legitimate warfare: war has its
  laws; there are things which may fairly be done, and
  things which may not be done...He has attempted (as I
  may call it) to *poison the wells*.

15 I will vanquish, not my Accuser, but my judges.
  True Mode of meeting Mr. Kingsley

16 I used to wish the Arabian Tales were true.
  History of My Religious Opinions to the Year 1833

17 Two and two only supreme and luminously
  self-evident beings, myself and my Creator.

18 For years I used almost as proverbs what I considered
  to be the scope and issue of his [Thomas Scott's]
  doctrine, 'Holiness rather than peace', and 'Growth the
  only evidence of life'.

19 It would be a gain to the country were it vastly more
  superstitious, more bigoted, more gloomy, more fierce
  in its religion than at present it shows itself to be.
  History of My Religious Opinions from 1833 to 1839

20 From the age of fifteen, dogma has been the
  fundamental principle of my religion: I know no other
  religion; I cannot enter into the idea of any other sort
  of religion; religion, as a mere sentiment, is to me a
  dream and a mockery.

21 This is what the Church is said to want, not party
  men, but sensible, temperate, sober, well-judging
  persons, to guide it through the channel of
  no-meaning, between the Scylla and Charybdis of Aye
  and No.
  History of My Religious Opinions from 1839 to 1841

22 I recollect an acquaintance saying to me that 'the Oriel
  Common Room stank of Logic'.
  History of My Religious Opinions from 1841 to 1845

23 Trinity had never been unkind to me. There used to be
  much snap-dragon growing on the walls opposite my
  freshman's rooms there, and I had for years taken it as
  the emblem of my own perpetual residence even unto

death in my University.
On the morning of the 23rd I left the Observatory. I have never seen Oxford since, excepting its spires, as they are seen from the railway.

1 Ten thousand difficulties do not make one doubt.
Position of my Mind since 1845

2 What must be the face-to-face antagonist, by which to withstand and baffle the fierce energy of passion and the all-corroding, all-dissolving scepticism of the intellect in religious enquiries.

3 It is almost a definition of a gentleman to say that he is one who never inflicts pain.
The Idea of a University (1852). **Knowledge and Religious Duty**

4 She [the Catholic Church] holds that it were better for sun and moon to drop from heaven, for the earth to fail, and for all the many millions who are upon it to die of starvation in extremest agony, as far as temporal affliction goes, than that one soul, I will not say, should be lost, but should commit one single venial sin, should tell one wilful untruth,...or steal one poor farthing without excuse.
Lectures on Anglican Difficulties (1852). Lecture VIII

5 And this is all that is known, and more than all—yet nothing to what the angels know—of the life of a servant of God, who sinned and repented, and did penance and washed out his sins, and became a Saint, and reigns with Christ in heaven.
Lives of the English Saints: Hermit Saints. 'The Legend of Saint Bettelin'. This passage attr. to Newman; the phrase 'and more than all' may have been added by J.A. Froude.

6 *Ex umbris et imaginibus in veritatem.*
From shadows and types to the reality.
Motto

7 *Cor ad cor loquitur.*
Heart speaks to heart.
Motto adopted for his coat-of-arms as cardinal. 1879

8 It is as absurd to argue men, as to torture them, into believing.
Sermon at Oxford, 11 Dec. 1831

9 May He support us all the day long, till the shades lengthen, and the evening comes, and the busy world is hushed, and the fever of life is over, and our work is done! Then in His mercy may He give us a safe lodging, and a holy rest, and peace at the last.
Sermon, 1834. 'Wisdom and Innocence'

10 When men understand what each other mean, they see, for the most part, that controversy is either superfluous or hopeless.
Sermon at Oxford, Epiphany, 1839

11 Firmly I believe and truly
  God is Three, and God is One;
And I next acknowledge duly
  Manhood taken by the Son.
The Dream of Gerontius (1865)

12 Praise to the Holiest in the height,
  And in the depth be praise;
In all his words most wonderful,
  Most sure in all His ways.

13 O wisest love! that flesh and blood
  Which did in Adam fail,
Should strive afresh against their foe,
  Should strive and should prevail.

14 Lead, kindly Light, amid the encircling gloom,

Lead thou me on;
The night is dark, and I am far from home,
  Lead thou me on.
Keep Thou my feet; I do not ask to see
The distant scene; one step enough for me.
The Pillar of Cloud. Lead Kindly Light (1833)

15 And with the morn those Angel faces smile,
Which I have loved long since, and lost awhile.

16 *We can believe what we choose.* We are answerable for what we choose to believe.
Letter to Mrs. William Froude, 27 June 1848

17 Though you can believe what you choose, you must believe what you ought.
3 July 1848

SIR ISAAC NEWTON 1642–1727

18 Nature is very consonant and conformable with herself.
Opticks (1730 ed.), bk.III, pt.i, qu.30

19 If I have seen further it is by standing on the shoulders of giants.
Letter to Robert Hooke, 5 Feb. 1675/6. See 41:25

20 I do not know what I may appear to the world, but to myself I seem to have been only like a boy playing on the sea-shore, and diverting myself in now and then finding a smoother pebble or a prettier shell than ordinary, whilst the great ocean of truth lay all undiscovered before me.
L.T. More, *Isaac Newton* (1934), p.664

21 O Diamond! Diamond! thou little knowest the mischief done!
Remark to a dog who knocked down a candle and so set fire to some papers and 'destroyed the almost finished labours of some years'. Thomas Maude, *Wensley-Dale...a Poem* (1780), p.28, note

EMPEROR NICHOLAS I OF RUSSIA 1796–1855

22 *Nous avons sur les bras un homme malade—un homme gravement malade.*
We have on our hands a sick man—a very sick man. [The sick man of Europe, the Turk.]
Parliamentary Papers. Accounts and Papers, vol.lxxi, pt.5. Eastern Papers, p.2. Sir G.H. Seymour to Lord John Russell, 11 Jan. 1853

23 Russia has two generals in whom she can confide—Generals Janvier and Février.
Attr. See *Punch*, 10 Mar. 1853

ROBERT NICHOLS 1893–1944

24 Was there love once? I have forgotten her.
Was there grief once? grief yet is mine.
Fulfilment

NICIAS c.470–413 B.C.

25 ἄνδρες γὰρ πόλις, καὶ οὐ τείχη οὐδὲ νῆες ἀνδρῶν κεναί.
For a city consists in its men, and not in its walls nor ships empty of men.
Speech to the defeated Athenian army at Syracuse, 413 B.C. Thucydides, vii.77

REINHOLD NIEBUHR 1892–1971

26 Man's capacity for justice makes democracy possible, but man's inclination to injustice makes democracy

necessary.
The Children of Light and the Children of Darkness (1944),
foreword

FRIEDRICH NIETZSCHE 1844–1900

1 *Ich lehre euch den Übermenschen. Der Mensch ist*
Etwas, das überwunden werden soll.
I teach you the superman. Man is something to be
surpassed.
Also Sprach Zarathustra. Prologue (1883)

2 *Auf Andere warte ich. . .auf Höhere, Stärkere,*
Sieghaftere, Wohlgemutere, Solche, die rechtwinklig
gebaut sind an Leib und Seele: lachende Löwen
müssen kommen.
For others do I wait. . .for higher ones, stronger ones,
more triumphant ones, merrier ones, for such as are
built squarely in body and soul: laughing lions must
come
IV, Die Begrüssung

3 *Das Erbarmen Gottes mit der einzigen Not, die alle*
Paradiese an sich haben, kennt keine Grenzen: er
schuf alsbald noch andere Tiere. Erster Fehlgriff
Gottes: der Mensch fand die Tiere nicht
unterhaltend,—er herrschte über sie, er wollte nicht
einmal 'Tier' sein.
[Man found a solitary existence tedious.] There are no
limits to God's compassion with Paradises over their
one universally felt want: he immediately created
other animals besides. God's first blunder: Man didn't
find the animals amusing,—he dominated them, and
didn't even want to be an 'animal'.
Der Antichrist, 48

4 *Das Weib war der zweite Fehlgriff Gottes.*
Woman was God's second blunder.

5 *Wie ich den Philosophen verstehe, als einen*
furchtbaren Explosionsstoff, vor dem Alles in Gefahr
ist.
What I understand by 'philosopher': a terrible
explosive in the presence of which everything is in
danger.
Ecce Homo, Die Unzeitgemässen

6 *Gott ist tot: aber so wie die Art der Menschen ist,*
wird es vielleicht noch jahrtausendlang Höhlen geben,
in denen man seinen Schatten zeigt.
God is dead: but considering the state the species Man
is in, there will perhaps be caves, for ages yet, in
which his shadow will be shown.
Die Fröhliche Wissenschaft, III, 108

7 *Moralität ist Herden-Instinkt im Einzelnen.*
Morality is the herd-instinct in the individual.
116

8 *Der christliche Entschluss, die Welt hässlich und*
schlecht zu finden, hat die Welt hässlich und schlecht
gemacht.
The Christian resolution to find the world ugly and bad
has made the world ugly and bad.
130

9 *Glaubt es mir!—das Geheimniss, um die grösste*
Fruchtbarkeit und den grössten Genuss vom Dasein
einzuernten, heisst: gefährlich leben!
Believe me! The secret of reaping the greatest
fruitfulness and the greatest enjoyment from life is to

live dangerously!
IV, 283

10 *Wer mit Ungeheuern kämpft, mag zusehn, dass er*
nicht dabei zum Ungeheuer wird. Und wenn du lange
in einen Abgrund blickst, blickt der Abgrund auch in
dich hinein.
He who fights with monsters might take care lest he
thereby become a monster. And if you gaze for long
into an abyss, the abyss gazes also into you.
Jenseits von Gut und Böse, IV, 146

11 *Der Gedanke an den Selbstmord ist ein starkes*
Trostmittel: mit ihm kommt man gut über manche böse
Nacht hinweg.
The thought of suicide is a great source of comfort:
with it a calm passage is to be made across many a bad
night.
157

12 *Herren-Moral und Sklaven-Moral.*
Master-morality and slave-morality.
IX.260

13 *Der Witz ist das Epigramm auf den Tod eines*
Gefühls.
Wit is the epitaph of an emotion.
Menschliches, Allzumenschliches, II.i, 202

14 *Auf dem Grunde aller dieser vornehmen Rassen ist*
das Raubtier, die prachtvolle nach Beute und Sieg
lüstern schweifende blonde Bestie nicht zu verkennen.
At the base of all these aristocratic races the predator is
not to be mistaken, the splendorous blond beast, avidly
rampant for plunder and victory.
Zur Genealogie der Moral, I, 11

FLORENCE NIGHTINGALE 1820–1910

15 Sir Douglas Dowson, after a short speech, stepped
forward and handed the insignia of the Order [of
Merit] to Miss Nightingale. Propped up by pillows she
dimly recognized that some kind of compliment was
being paid her. 'Too kind—too kind,' she murmured;
and she was not ironical.
Lytton Strachey, *Eminent Victorians*, 'Florence Nightingale

16 To understand God's thoughts we must study
statistics, for these are the measure of his purpose.
Attr. See K. Pearson, *Life...of Francis Galton*, vol.II, ch.xiii,
sect.i

GENERAL R.-G. NIVELLE 1856–1924

17 *Ils ne passeront pas.*
They shall not pass.
Used as a slogan throughout the defence of Verdun and often
attributed to Marshal Pétain. Nivelle's Order of the Day in late
June 1916 read '*Vous ne les laisserez pas passer.*' Taken up by
the Republicans in the Spanish Civil War as '*No pasarán!*'

ALBERT J. NOCK 1873–1945

18 It is an economic axiom as old as the hills that goods
and services can be paid for only with goods and
services.
Memoirs of a Superfluous Man, III, ch.3

THOMAS NOEL 1799–1861

19 Rattle his bones over the stones;

He's only a pauper, whom nobody owns!
Rhymes and Roundelays (1841), The Pauper's Drive

CHARLES HOWARD, DUKE OF NORFOLK
1746–1815

1 I cannot be a good Catholic; I cannot go to heaven;
and if a man is to go to the devil, he may as well go
thither from the House of Lords as from any other
place on earth.
Henry Best, *Personal and Literary Memorials* (1829), ch.18

CHRISTOPHER NORTH (PROFESSOR JOHN WILSON) 1785–1854

2 Minds like ours, my dear James, must always be
above national prejudices, and in all companies it
gives me true pleasure to declare, that, as a people, the
English are very little indeed inferior to the Scotch.
Noctes Ambrosianae, No.28 (Oct. 1826)

3 Laws were made to be broken.
No.24 (May 1830)

4 Insultin the sun, and quarrellin wi' the equawtor.
[Ettrick Shepherd.]

5 Animosities are mortal, but the Humanities live for
ever.
No.35 (Aug. 1834)

6 I cannot sit still, James, and hear you abuse the
shopocracy.
No.39 (Feb. 1835)

SIR STAFFORD NORTHCOTE, 1ST EARL OF IDDESLEIGH 1818–1887

7 Argue as you please, you are nowhere, that grand old
man, the Prime Minister, insists on the other thing.
Of Gladstone. Speech at Liverpool, 12 Apr. 1882

MRS. CAROLINE NORTON 1808–1877

8 For death and life, in ceaseless strife,
    Beat wild on this world's shore,
And all our calm is in that balm—
    Not lost but gone before.
Not Lost but Gone Before

NOVALIS (FRIEDRICH VON HARDENBERG) 1772–1801

9 *Oft fühl ich jetzt...[und] je tiefer ich einsehe, dass
Schicksal und Gemüt Namen eines Begriffes sind.*
I often feel, and ever more deeply I realize, that fate
and character are the same conception.
Heinrich von Ofterdingen (1802), bk.II. Often quoted as
'Character is destiny' or 'Character is fate'. See, e.g., 201:21

10 *Ein Gott-betrunkener Mensch.*
A God-intoxicated man.
Attr. remark about Spinoza

ALFRED NOYES 1880–1958

11 Go down to Kew in lilac-time, in lilac-time, in
    lilac-time;
    Go down to Kew in lilac-time (it isn't far from
        London!)
Barrel Organ

12 The wind was a torrent of darkness among the gusty

trees,
The moon was a ghostly galleon tossed upon cloudy
    seas,
The road was a ribbon of moonlight over the purple
    moor,
And the highwayman came riding—
        Riding—riding—
The highwayman came riding, up to the old inn-door.
The Highwayman

13   The landlord's black-eyed daughter,
        Bess, the landlord's daughter,
Plaiting a dark red love-knot into her long black hair.

14   Look for me by moonlight;
        Watch for me by moonlight;
I'll come to thee by moonlight, though hell should bar
    the way!

SEAN O'CASEY 1884–1964

15 I ofen looked up at the sky an' assed meself the
question—what is the stars, what is the stars? [Boyle.]
Juno and the Paycock (1924), I

16 The whole counthry's in a state of chassis. [Boyle.]
II. Meaning 'a state of chaos'. In Act I and Act III (last line) used
of the whole world.

17 Sacred Heart of the Crucified Jesus, take away our
hearts o' stone...an' give us hearts o' flesh!...Take
away this murdherin' hate...an' give us Thine own
eternal love! [Mrs. Tancred.]

18 The Polis as Polis, in this city, is Null an' Void! [Mrs
Madigan.]
III. Of the Police

WILLIAM OCCAM c.1280–1349

19 *Entia non sunt multiplicanda praeter necessitatem.*
No more things should be presumed to exist than are
absolutely necessary.
'Occams's Razor'. Ancient philosophical principle, often
attributed to Occam, but used by many earlier thinkers. Not found
in this form in his writings, though he frequently used similar
expressions, e.g. *Pluralitas non est ponenda sine necessitate*
(**Quodlibeta**, c.1324, V, Q.i).

ADOLPH S. OCHS 1858–1935

20 All the news that's fit to print.
Motto of the *New York Times*

JAMES OGILVY, FIRST EARL OF SEAFIELD 1664–1730

21 Now there's ane end of ane old song.
As he signed the engrossed exemplification of the Act of Union,
1706. *Lockhart Papers* (1817), i.223

DANIEL O'CONNELL 1775–1847

22 [Sir Robert] Peel's smile: like the silver plate on a
coffin.
Hansard, 26 Feb. 1835, quoting J.P. Curran (1750—1817), Irish
politician and lawyer

JOHN O'KEEFFE 1747–1833

23 Amo, amas, I love a lass,
As a cedar tall and slender;
Sweet cowslip's grace

Is her nom'native case,
And she's of the feminine gender.
The Agreeable Surprise (1781), II.ii

1 Fat, fair and forty were all the toasts of the young
men.
Irish Mimic (1795), ii

2 You should always except the present company.
London Hermit (1793), I.ii

DENNIS O'KELLY 1720?–1787

3 Eclipse first, the rest nowhere.
Epsom, 3 May 1769. *Annals of Sporting*, vol.ii, p.271. D.N.B.
gives the occasion as the Queen's Plate at Winchester, 1769.

WILLIAM OLDYS 1696–1761

4 Busy, curious, thirsty fly,
Gently drink, and drink as I;
Freely welcome to my cup.
The Fly (1732)

FRANK WARD O'MALLEY 1875–1932

5 Life is just one damned thing after another.
Attr. See *Literary Digest*, 5 Nov. 1932. Also attr. Elbert Hubbard

JOHN OPIE 1761–1807

6 [When asked with what he mixed his colours.]
I mix them with my brains, sir.
Samuel Smiles, *Self-Help*, ch.4

BARONESS ORCZY 1865–1947

7 We seek him here, we seek him there,
Those Frenchies seek him everywhere.
Is he in heaven?—Is he in hell?
That demmed, elusive Pimpernel?
The Scarlet Pimpernel (1905), ch.12

GEORGE ORWELL 1903–1950

8 Four legs good, two legs bad.
Animal Farm (1945), ch.3

9 All animals are equal but some animals are more
equal than others.
ch.10

10 Whatever is funny is subversive, every joke is
ultimately a custard pie... A dirty joke is...a sort of
mental revolution.
The Art of Donald McGill (1945)

11 I'm fat, but I'm thin inside. Has it ever struck you that
there's a thin man inside every fat man, just as they
say there's a statue inside every block of stone?
Coming Up For Air (1939), Part I, ch.3. See 161:15

12 Big Brother is watching you.
1984 (1949), p.1

13 *Doublethink* means the power of holding two
contradictory beliefs in one's mind simultaneously, and
accepting both of them.
pt.II, ch.9

14 If you want a picture of the future, imagine a boot
stamping on a human face—for ever.
pt.III, ch.3

15 Good prose is like a window pane.
Collected Essays (1968), vol.I. **Why I Write**

16 Nine times out of ten a revolutionary is merely a
climber with a bomb in his pocket.
Review of F.C. Green, *Stendhal*

17 To see what is in front of one's nose needs a constant
struggle.
vol.IV. **In Front of Your Nose**

18 At 50, everyone has the face he deserves.
Closing words, MS Notebook, 17 Apr. 1949

DOROTHY OSBORNE (LADY TEMPLE) 1627–1695

19 All letters, methinks, should be as free and easy as
one's discourse, not studied as an oration, nor made up
of hard words like a charm.
Letter to Sir Wm. Temple, Oct. 1653

ARTHUR O'SHAUGHNESSY 1844–1881

20 We are the music makers,
We are the dreamers of dreams,
Wandering by lone sea-breakers,
And sitting by desolate streams;—
World-losers and world-forsakers,
On whom the pale moon gleams:
We are the movers and shakers
Of the world for ever, it seems.
Ode

21 For each age is a dream that is dying,
Or one that is coming to birth.

JOHN L. O'SULLIVAN 1813–1895

22 Understood as a central consolidated power, managing
and directing the various general interests of the
society, all government is evil, and the parent of
evil...The best government is that which governs least.
Introduction to *The United States Magazine and Democratic
Review* (1837)

23 Our manifest destiny to overspread the continent
allotted by Providence for the free development of our
yearly multiplying millions.
vol.xvii, July-Aug. 1845, p.5

24 A torchlight procession marching down your throat.
Description of some whisky. G.W.E. Russell, *Collections and
Recollections*, ch.19

JAMES OTIS 1725–1783

25 Taxation without representation is tyranny.
Watchword (coined 1761?) of the American Revolution. See
Samuel Eliot Morison, 'James Otis', *Dict. Am. Biog.*, xiv.102

THOMAS OTWAY 1652–1685

26 These are rogues that pretend to be of a religion now!
Well, all I say is, honest atheism for my money.
The Atheist, Act III, l.31

27 Ere man's corruptions made him wretched, he
Was born most noble that was born most free;
Each of himself was lord; and unconfin'd
Obey'd the dictates of his godlike mind.
Don Carlos (1676), Act II, l.3

1 Destructive, damnable, deceitful woman!
The Orphan (1680), Act III, l.586

2 And for an apple damn'd mankind.
l.594

3 You wags that judge by rote, and damn by rule.
Titus and Berenice (1677), prologue, l.3

4 Oh woman! lovely woman! Nature made thee
To temper man: we had been brutes without you;
Angels are painted fair, to look like you;
There's in you all that we belive of heav'n,
Amazing brightness, purity, and truth,
Eternal joy, and everlasting love.
Venice Preserv'd (1681/2), Act I, l.337

5 No praying, it spoils business.
Act II, l.87

SIR THOMAS OVERBURY 1581–1613

6 He disdains all things above his reach, and preferreth
all countries before his own.
Miscellaneous Works. An Affectate Traveller

7 You cannot name any example in any heathen author
but I will better it in Scripture.
Crumms Fal'n From King James's Table, 10

OVID 43 B.C–A.D. 17

8 *Procul omen abesto!*
Far be that fate from us!
Amores, I.xiv.41

9 *Procul hinc, procul este, severae!*
Far hence, keep far from me, you grim women!
II.i.3

10 *Spectatum veniunt, veniunt spectentur ut ipsae.*
The women come to see the show, they come to make
a show themselves.
Ars Amatoria, i.99

11 *Iuppiter ex alto periuria ridet amantum.*
Jupiter from on high laughs at lovers' perjuries.
633

12 *Forsitan et nostrum nomen miscebitur istis.*
Perhaps my name too will be linked with theirs.
iii.339

13 *Chaos, rudis indigestaque moles.*
Chaos, a rough and unordered mass.
Metamorphoses, i.7

14 *Medio tutissimus ibis.*
A middle course is the safest for you to take.
ii.137

15 *Inopem me copia fecit.*
Plenty has made me poor.
iii.466

16 *Ipse docet quid agam; fas est et ab hoste doceri.*
He himself teaches what I should do; it is right to be
taught by the enemy.
iv.428

17 *Video meliora, proboque;*
Deteriora sequor.
I see the better way, and approve it; I follow the
worse.
vii.20

18 *Tempus edax rerum.*

Time the devourer of everything.
xv.234

19 *Iamque opus exegi, quod nec Iovis ira, nec ignis,*
Nec poterit ferrum, nec edax abolere vetustas.
And now I have finished the work, which neither the
wrath of Jove, nor fire, nor the sword, nor
devouring age shall be able to destroy.
871

20 *Principiis obsta; sero medicina paratur*
Cum mala per longas convaluere moras.
Stop it at the start, it's late for medicine to be prepared
when disease has grown strong through long delays.
Remedia Amoris, 91

21 *Qui finem quaeris amoris,*
Cedet amor rebus; res age, tutus eris.
You who seek an end of love, love will yield to
business: be busy, and you will be safe.
143

22 *Teque, rebellatrix, tandem, Germania, magni*
Triste caput pedibus supposuisse ducis!
How you, rebellious Germany, laid your wretched
head beneath the feet of the great general.
Tristia, III.xii.47

23 *Sponte sua carmen numeros veniebat ad aptos,*
Et quod temptabam dicere versus erat.
Of its own accord my song would come in the right
rhythms, and what I was trying to say was poetry.
IV.x.25

24 *Vergilium vidi tantum.*
I just saw Virgil.
51

25 *Adde quod ingenuas didicisse fideliter artes*
Emollit mores nec sinit esse feros.
Add the fact that to have conscientiously studied the
liberal arts refines behaviour and does not allow it to
be savage.
Epistulae Ex Ponto, II.ix.47

26 *Ut desint vires, tamen est laudanda voluntas.*
Though the strength is lacking, yet the willingness is to
be praised.
III.iv.79

27 *Gutta cavat lapidem, consumitur anulus usu.*
Dripping water hollows out a stone, a ring is worn
away by use.
IV.x.5

JOHN OWEN 1560?–1622

28 God and the doctor we alike adore
But only when in danger, not before;
The danger o'er, both are alike requited,
God is forgotten, and the Doctor slighted.
Epigrams

ROBERT OWEN 1771–1858

29 All the world is queer save thee and me, and even thou
art a little queer.
To his partner, W. Allen on severing business relations at New
Lanark 1828. Attr.

WILFRED OWEN 1893–1918

30 Above all, this book is not concerned with Poetry.
The subject of it is War, and the Pity of War.
The Poetry is in the pity.
Poems (1920), Preface

1 All the poet can do today is to warn.
That is why the true Poets must be truthful.

2 What passing-bells for these who die as cattle?
    Only the monstrous anger of the guns.
    Only the stuttering rifles' rapid rattle
Can patter out their hasty orisons.
Anthem for Doomed Youth

3   The pallor of girls' brows shall be their pall;
Their flowers the tenderness of patient minds,
And each slow dusk a drawing-down of blinds.

4 Move him into the sun...
If anything might rouse him now
The kind old sun will know.
Futility

5 Was it for this the clay grew tall?
—O what made fatuous sunbeams toil
    To break earth's sleep at all?

6 Red lips are not so red
As the stained stones kissed by the English dead.
Greater Love

7 So secretly, like wrongs hushed-up, they went:
They were not ours.
We never heard to which front these were sent.

Nor, there, if they yet mock what women meant
Who gave them flowers.
The Send-Off

8 Hour after hour they ponder the warm field,—
And the far valley behind, where the buttercup
Had blessed with gold their slow boots coming up.
Spring Offensive

9 It seemed that out of battle I escaped
Down some profound dull tunnel, long since scooped
Through granites which titanic wars had groined.
Strange Meeting

10 'Strange friend,' I said, 'here is no cause to mourn.'
'None,' said the other, 'save the undone years,
The hopelessness. Whatever hope is yours
Was my life also; I went hunting wild
After the wildest beauty in the world.'

11 For by my glee might many men have laughed,
And of my weeping something have been left,
Which must die now. I mean the truth untold,
The pity of war, the pity war distilled.
Now men will go content with what we spoiled,
Or, discontent, boil bloody, and be spilled.
They will be swift with swiftness of the tigress,
None will break ranks, though nations trek from
    progress.

12 I am the enemy you killed, my friend.

COUNT OXENSTIERNA 1583–1654

13 Dost thou not know, my son, with how little wisdom
the world is governed?
Letter to his son, 1648

EDWARD DE VERE, EARL OF OXFORD
1550–1604

14 If women could be fair and yet not fond.
Women's Changeableness

BARRY PAIN 1864–1928

15 The cosy fire is bright and gay,
The merry kettle boils away
    And hums a cheerful song.
I sing the saucer and the cup;
Pray, Mary, fill the teapot up,
    And do not make it strong.
The Poets at Tea. Cowper

16 Pour, varlet, pour the water,
The water steaming hot!
A spoonful for each man of us,
Another for the pot!
Macaulay

17 As the sin that was sweet in the sinning
Is foul in the ending thereof,
As the heat of the summer's beginning
Is past in the winter of love:
O purity, painful and pleading!
O coldness, ineffably gray!
O hear us, our handmaid unheeding,
And take it away!
Swinburne

18 I think that I am drawing to an end:
For on a sudden came a gasp for breath,
And stretching of the hands, and blinded eyes,
And a great darkness falling on my soul.
O Hallelujah!...Kindly pass the milk.
Tennyson

19 'Come, little cottage girl, you seem
To want my cup of tea;
And will you take a little cream?
Now tell the truth to me.'

She had a rustic, woodland grin
Her cheek was soft as silk,
And she replied, 'Sir, please put in
A little drop of milk.'
Wordsworth

TOM PAINE 1737–1809

20 It is necessary to the happiness of man that he be
mentally faithful to himself. Infidelity does not consist
in believing, or in disbelieving, it consists in
professing to believe what one does not believe.
The Age of Reason (1794), pt.i

21 The sublime and the ridiculous are often so nearly
related, that it is difficult to class them separately. One
step above the sublime, makes the ridiculous; and one
step above the ridiculous, makes the sublime again.
pt.ii (1795), p.20

22 Government, even in its best state, is but a necessary
evil; in its worst state, an intolerable one.
Government, like dress, is the badge of lost
innocence; the palaces of kings are built upon the ruins
of the bowers of paradise.
Common Sense (1776), ch.1

23 As to religion, I hold it to be the indispensable duty of
government to protect all conscientious professors
thereof, and I know of no other business which
government hath to do therewith.
ch.4

1 These are the times that try men's souls. The summer
soldier and the sunshine patriot will, in this crisis,
shrink from the service of their country; but he that
stands it *now*, deserves the love and thanks of men and
women.
The Crisis, Intro. (Dec. 1776)

2 The final event to himself [Mr Burke] has been, that
as he rose like a rocket, he fell like the stick.
Letter to the Addressers on the late Proclamation (1792), p.4

3 [Burke] is not affected by the reality of distress
touching his heart, but by the showy resemblance of it
striking his imagination. He pities the plumage, but
forgets the dying bird. [Of Burke's *Reflections on the
Revolution in France.*]
The Rights of Man (1791), p.26

4 Lay then the axe to the root, and teach governments
humanity. It is their sanguinary punishments which
corrupt mankind.
p.33

5 My country is the world, and my religion is to do
good.
pt.ii (1792), ch.5

6 A share in two revolutions is living to some purpose.
See Eric Foner, *Tom Paine and Revolutionary America* (1976),
ch.7

7 The religion of humanity.
Attr. by Edmund Gosse

JOSÉ DE PALAFOX 1780–1847

8 War to the knife.
On 4 Aug. 1808, at the siege of Saragossa, the French general
Verdier sent a one-word suggestion: 'Capitulation'. Palafox
replied '*Guerra y cuchillo*' (War and the knife), later reported as
'*Guerra a cuchillo*' and commonly rendered as above. The
correctness of the former is confirmed by its appearance, at the
behest of Palafox himself, on survivors' medals. Gómez de
Arteche, *Guerra de la Independencia* (1868–1903), II, iv

REVD. WILLIAM PALEY 1743–1805

9 Who can refute a sneer?
Principles of Moral and Political Philosophy (1785), bk.v, ch.9

LORD PALMERSTON 1784–1865

10 I therefore fearlessly challenge the verdict which this
House...is to give...whether, as the Roman, in days of
old, held himself free from indignity, when he could
say *Civis Romanus sum*; so also a British subject, in
whatever land he may be, shall feel confident that the
watchful eye and the strong arm of England will
protect him against injustice and wrong.
House of Commons, 25 June 1850, in the Don Pacifico debate

11 You may call it coalition, you may call it the
accidental and fortuitous concurrence of atoms.
Of a projected Palmerston-Disraeli coalition. House of Commons,
5 Mar. 1857

12 What is merit? The opinion one man entertains of
another.
Carlyle, *Critical and Miscellaneous Essays,* viii, 'Shooting
Niagara'

13 Die, my dear Doctor, that's the last thing I shall do!
Attr. last words

DOROTHY PARKER 1893–1967

14 Oh, life is a glorious cycle of song,
A medley of extemporanea;
And love is a thing that can never go wrong,
And I am Marie of Roumania.
Comment

15 Four be the things I'd been better without:
Love, curiosity, freckles, and doubt.
Inventory

16 Men seldom make passes
At girls who wear glasses.
News Item

17 Why is it no one ever sent me yet
One perfect limousine, do you suppose?
Ah no, it's always just my luck to get
One perfect rose.
One Perfect Rose

18 Razors pain you;
Rivers are damp;
Acids stain you;
And drugs cause cramp.
Guns aren't lawful;
Nooses give;
Gas smells awful;
You might as well live.
Résumé

19 By the time you swear you're his,
Shivering and sighing,
And he vows his passion is
Infinite, undying—
Lady, make a note of this:
One of you is lying.
Unfortunate Coincidence

20 And I'll stay off Verlaine too; he was always chasing
Rimbauds.
The Little Hours (The Penguin Dorothy Parker, 1977)

21 She ran the whole gamut of the emotions from A to B.
Of Katharine Hepburn in a Broadway play

22 Dear Mary, We all knew you had it in you.
Telegram sent after a much-publicised pregnancy

23 How could they tell?
[On being told of the death of President Coolidge.]
John Keats, *You might as well live* (1971), Foreword

24 If all the girls attending it [the Yale Prom] were laid
end to end, I wouldn't be at all surprised.
A. Woollcott, *While Rome Burns*, 'Some Neighbours', IV: Our
Mrs. Parker

MARTIN PARKER d. 1656?

25 You gentlemen of England
Who live at home at ease,
How little do you think
On the dangers of the seas.
The Valiant Sailors. See *Early Naval Ballads* (Percy Society,
1841), p.34

THEODORE PARKER 1810–1860

26 There is what I call the American idea...This idea
demands...a democracy, that is, a government of all
the people, by all the people, for all the people; of
course, a government after the principles of eternal
justice, the unchanging law of God; for shortness'

sake, I will call it the idea of freedom.
Speech at N.E. Anti-Slavery Convention, Boston, 29 May 1850.
Discourses of Slavery (1863), i

C. NORTHCOTE PARKINSON 1909–

1 Work expands so as to fill the time available for its
completion.
Parkinson's Law (1958), I, opening words

CHARLES STEWART PARNELL 1846–1891

2 No man has a right to fix the boundary of the march of
a nation; no man has a right to say to his
country—thus far shalt thou go and no further.
Speech at Cork, 21 Jan. 1885

BLAISE PASCAL 1623–1662

3 *La dernière chose qu'on trouve en faisant un ouvrage,
est de savoir celle qu'il faut mettre la première.*
The last thing one knows in constructing a work is
what to put first.
Pensées, ed. L. Brunschvicg (5th edn. 1909), i.19

4 *Quand on voit le style naturel, on est tout étonné et
ravi, car on s'attendait de voir un auteur, et on trouve
un homme.*
When we see a natural style, we are quite surprised
and delighted, for we expected to see an author and we
find a man.
29

5 *Tout le malheur des hommes vient d'une seule chose,
qui est de ne savoir pas demeurer en repos dans une
chambre.*
All the misfortunes of men derive from one single
thing, which is their inability to be at ease in a room
[at home].
ii.139

6 *Le nez de Cléopâtre: s'il eût été plus court, toute la
face de la terre aurait changé.*
Had Cleopatra's nose been shorter, the whole face of
the world would have changed.
162

7 *Le silence éternel de ces espaces infinis m'effraie.*
The eternal silence of these infinite spaces [the
heavens] terrifies me.
iii.206

8 *Le dernier acte est sanglant, quelque belle que soit la
comédie en tout le reste.*
The last act is bloody, however charming the rest of
the play may be.
210

9 *On mourra seul.*
We shall die alone.
211

10 *Le coeur a ses raisons que la raison ne connaît point.*
The heart has its reasons which reason knows nothing
of.
iv.277

11 *L'homme n'est qu'un roseau, le plus faible de la
nature; mais c'est un roseau pensant.*
Man is only a reed, the weakest thing in nature; but he
is a thinking reed.
vi.347

12 *Le moi est haïssable.*

'I' is hateful.
vii.455

13 *Tu ne me chercherais pas si tu ne me possédais.
Ne t'inquiete donc pas.*
You would not be looking for Me if you did not
possess Me. So do not be uneasy.
555

14 *Je n'ai fait celle-ci plus longue que parce que je n'ai
pas eu le loisir de la faire plus courte.*
I have made this letter longer than usual, only because
I have not had the time to make it shorter.
Lettres Provinciales (1657), xvi

15 *FEU. Dieu d'Abraham, Dieu d'Isaac, Dieu de Jacob,
non des philosophes et savants. Certitude. Certitude.
Sentiment. Joie. Paix.*
FIRE. God of Abraham, God of Isaac, God of Jacob,
not of the philosophers and scholars. Certainty.
Certainty. Feeling. Joy. Peace.
On a paper dated 23 Nov. 1654, stitched into the lining of his coat
and found after his death.

LOUIS PASTEUR 1822–1895

16 *Dans les champs de l'observation le hasard ne
favorise que les esprits préparés.*
Where observation is concerned, chance favours only
the prepared mind.
Address given on the inauguration of the Faculty of Science,
University of Lille, 7 Dec. 1854.
*De nos jours, le hasard ne favorise l'invention que pour des
esprits préparés aux découvertes par de patientes études et de
persévérants efforts. 'Pourquoi la France n'a pas trouvé
d'hommes supérieurs au moment du péril,' La Salut public,*
Lyons, Mar. 1871

17 *Il n'existe pas de sciences appliquées, mais seulement
des applications de la science.*
There are no such things as applied sciences, only
applications of science.
Address, 11 Sept. 1872, *Comptes rendus des travaux du Congrès
viticole et séricicole de Lyon, 9–14 septembre 1872,* p.49

WALTER PATER 1839–1894

18 Hers is the head upon which all 'the ends of the world
are come', and the eyelids are a little weary. [Mona
Lisa.]
Studies in the History of the Renaissance (1873) **Leonardo da
Vinci** (1869)

19 She is older than the rocks among which she sits; like
the vampire, she has been dead many times, and
learned the secrets of the grave; and has been a diver in
deep seas, and keeps their fallen day about her; and
trafficked for strange webs with Eastern merchants:
and, as Leda, was the mother of Helen of Troy, and as
Saint Anne, the mother of Mary; and all this has been
to her but as the sound of lyres and flutes, and lives
only in the delicacy with which it has moulded the
changing lineaments, and tinged the eyelids and the
hands.

20 All art constantly aspires towards the condition of
music.
The School of Giorgione

21 To burn always with this hard, gemlike flame, to
maintain this ecstasy, is success in life.
Conclusion

22 Not to discriminate every moment some passionate

attitude in those about us, and in the brilliance of their gifts some tragic dividing of forces on their ways is, on this short day of frost and sun, to sleep before evening.

COVENTRY PATMORE 1823–1896

1 Kind souls, you wonder why, love you,
    When you, you wonder why, love none.
We love, Fool, for the good we do,
    Not that which unto us is done!
The Angel in the House (1854–62), 1904 edn., bk.I, c.vi, Prelude 4, **A Riddle Solved**

2 I drew my bride, beneath the moon,
    Across my threshold; happy hour!
But, ah, the walk that afternoon
    We saw the water-flags in flower!
c.viii, Prelude 3, **The Spirit's Epochs**, l.9

3 'I saw you take his kiss!' ''Tis true.'
    'O modesty!' ''Twas strictly kept:
He thought me asleep; at least, I knew
    He thought I thought he thought I slept.'
bk.II, c.viii, Prelude 3, **The Kiss**

4 Some dish more sharply spiced than this
Milk-soup men call domestic bliss.
Olympus, l.15

5 So, till to-morrow eve, my Own, adieu!
Parting's well-paid with soon again to meet,
Soon in your arms to feel so small and sweet,
Sweet to myself that am so sweet to you!
The Unknown Eros (1877), bk.I, vii, **The Azalea**, l.22

6 With all my will, but much against my heart,
We two now part.
My Very Dear,
Our solace is, the sad road lies so clear.
It needs no art,
With faint, averted feet
And many a tear,
In our opposed paths to persevere.
xvi, **A Farewell**, l.1

7 He that but once too nearly hears
The music of forfended spheres
Is thenceforth lonely, and for all
His days as one who treads the Wall
Of China, and, on this hand, sees
Cities and their civilities
And, on the other, lions.
The Victories of Love, bk.I.ii. **From Mrs. Graham**, l.15

MARK PATTISON 1813–1884

8 In research the horizon recedes as we advance, and is no nearer at sixty than it was at twenty. As the power of endurance weakens with age, the urgency of the pursuit grows more intense…And research is always incomplete.
Isaac Casaubon (1875), ch.10

JAMES PAYN 1830–1898

9 I had never had a piece of toast
Particularly long and wide,
But fell upon the sanded floor,

And always on the buttered side.
Chambers's Journal, 2 Feb. 1884. See 356:25

J.H. PAYNE 1791–1852

10 Mid pleasures and palaces though we may roam,
Be it ever so humble, there's no place like home;
A charm from the skies seems to hallow us there,
Which, seek through the world, is ne'er met with elsewhere.
Home, home, sweet, sweet home!
There's no place like home! there's no place like home!
Clari, the Maid of Milan (1823), **Home, Sweet Home**

THOMAS LOVE PEACOCK 1785–1866

11 Ancient sculpture is the true school of modesty. But where the Greeks had modesty, we have cant; where they had poetry, we have cant; where they had patriotism, we have cant; where they had anything that exalts, delights, or adorns humanity, we have nothing but cant, cant, cant.
Crotchet Castle (1831) ch.7

12 A book that furnishes no quotations is, *me judice*, no book—it is a plaything.
ch.9

13 The march of mind has marched in through my back parlour shutters, and out again with my silver spoons, in the dead of night. The policeman, who was sent down to examine, says my house has been broken open on the most scientific principles.
ch.17

14 A Sympathizer would seem to imply a certain degree of benevolent feeling. Nothing of the kind. It signifies a ready-made accomplice in any species of political villainy.
Gryll Grange (1861), ch.1

15 Nothing can be more obvious than that all animals were created solely and exclusively for the use of man.
Headlong Hall (1816), ch.2

16 'Indeed, the loaves and fishes are typical of a mixed diet; and the practice of the Church in all ages shows—'
'That it never loses sight of the loaves and the fishes.

17 'I distinguish the picturesque and the beautiful, and I add to them, in the laying out of grounds, a third and distinct character, which I call *unexpectedness*.'
'Pray, sir,' said Mr Milestone, 'by what name do you distinguish this character, when a person walks round the grounds for the second time?'
ch.4

18 Sir, I have quarrelled with my wife; and a man who has quarrelled with his wife is absolved from all duty to his country.
Nightmare Abbey (1818), ch.11

19 He remembered too late on his thorny green bed,
Much that well may be thought cannot wisely be said.
Crotchet Castle (1831): **The Priest and the Mulberry Tree**, st.5

20 Long night succeeds thy little day
    Oh blighted blossom! can it be,
That this gray stone and grassy clay
    Have closed our anxious care of thee?
Epitaph on his Daughter. Works of Peacock, ed. Henry Cole (1875), Biographical Notice by E. Nicolls

1 Frail as thy love, the flowers were dead
　　Ere yet the evening sun was set:
But years shall see the cypress spread,
　　Immutable as my regret.
The Grave of Love

2 The mountain sheep are sweeter,
　　But the valley sheep are fatter;
We therefore deemed it meeter
　　To carry off the latter.
The Misfortunes of Elphin (1823), ch.11. **The War-Song of Dinas Vawr**

3 In a bowl to sea went wise men three,
　　On a brilliant night in June:
They carried a net, and their hearts were set
　　On fishing up the moon.
The Wise Men of Gotham

PEDRO I, EMPEROR OF BRAZIL (PEDRO IV OF PORTUGAL) 1798–1834

4 *Como é para o bem de todos e a felicidade geral da nação, estou pronto. Diga ao povo que fico.*
As it is for the good of all and the general happiness of the nation, I am ready and willing. Tell the people I'm staying.
In response to a popular delegation, and in defiance of a decree from Lisbon requiring his return, 9 Sept. 1822. Commonly rendered *Fico* (I'm staying).

SIR ROBERT PEEL 1788–1850

5 I may be a Tory. I may be an illiberal—but...Tory as I am, I have the further satisfaction of knowing that there is not a single law connected with my name which has not had as its object some mitigation of the criminal law; some prevention of abuse in the exercise of it; or some security for its impartial administration.
House of Commons, 1 May 1827

GEORGE PEELE 1558?–1597?

6 Fair and fair, and twice so fair,
　　As fair as any may be;
The fairest shepherd on our green,
　　A love for any lady.
Works, ed. A.H. Bullen, vol.i. **The Arraignment of Paris** (c.1581), I.ii.55 Song of Oenone and Paris

7 What thing is love for (well I wot) love is a thing.
It is a prick, it is a sting,
It is a pretty, pretty thing;
It is a fire, it is a coal
Whose flame creeps in at every hole.
vol.ii. **Miscellaneous Poems. The Hunting of Cupid,** 1.1

8 His golden locks time hath to silver turn'd;
　　O time too swift, O swiftness never ceasing!
His youth 'gainst time and age hath ever spurn'd
　　But spurn'd in vain; youth waneth by increasing:
Beauty, strength, youth, are flowers but fading seen;
Duty, faith, love, are roots, and ever green.

His helmet now shall make a hive for bees,
　　And, lovers' sonnets turn'd to holy psalms,
A man-at-arms must now serve on his knees,
　　And feed on prayers, which are age his alms:
But though from court to cottage he depart,
His saint is sure of his unspotted heart...

Goddess, allow this aged man his right,

To be your beadsman now that was your knight.
Polyhymnia (1590), **Sonnet ad finem. A Farewell to Arms**

9 When as the rye reach to the chin,
And chopcherry, chopcherry ripe within,
Strawberries swimming in the cream,
And schoolboys playing in the stream,
Then O, then O, then O, my true love said,
Till that time come again,
She could not live a maid.
The Old Wives' Tale, 1.81

1ST EARL OF PEMBROKE 1501?–1570

10 Out ye whores, to work, to work, ye whores, go spin.
Aubrey, *Brief Lives.* Commonly quoted as 'Go spin, you jades, go spin.' See Sir W. Scott, *Journal,* 9 Feb. 1826

2ND EARL OF PEMBROKE c.1534–1601

11 A parliament can do any thing but make a man a woman, and a woman a man.
Quoted in Speech made by his son, the 4th Earl on 11 Apr. 1648, proving himself Chancellor of Oxford. *Harleian Miscellany* (1810), Vol.5, p.113

10th EARL OF PEMBROKE 1734–1794

12 Dr Johnson's sayings would not appear so extraordinary, were it not for his *bow-wow way.*
Boswell, *Life of Johnson,* 27 Mar. 1775, note

VLADIMIR PENIAKOFF 1897–1951

13 A message came on the wireless for me. It said 'SPREAD ALARM and DESPONDENCY'...The date was, I think, May 18th, 1942.
Private Army, II, v.128. See also Army Act 42 & 43 Vict.33 sect.5 (1879): 'Every person subject to military law who...spreads reports calculated to create unnecessary alarm or despondency...shall...be liable to suffer penal servitude.'

WILLIAM PENN 1644–1718

14 It is a reproach to religion and government to suffer so much poverty and excess.
Some Fruits of Solitude, in Reflections and Maxims relating to the conduct of Humane Life (1693), pt.i, No.52

15 Men are generally more careful of the breed of their horses and dogs than of their children.
No.85

16 The taking of a Bribe or Gratuity, should be punished with as severe Penalties as the defrauding of the State.
No.384

SAMUEL PEPYS 1633–1703

17 Strange the difference of men's talk!
Diary, 4 Jan. 1659–60

18 I stayed up till the bell-man came by with his bell just under my window as I was writing of this very line, and cried, 'Past one of the clock, and a cold, frosty, windy morning.'
16 Jan. 1659–60

19 And so to bed.
20 Apr. 1660

20 A silk suit, which cost me much money, and I pray God to make me able to pay for it.
1 July 1660

1 I went out to Charing Cross, to see Major-general Harrison hanged, drawn, and quartered; which was done there, he looking as cheerful as any man could do in that condition.
13 Oct. 1660

2 Very merry, and the best fritters that ever I eat in my life.
26 Feb: 1660–1 (Shrove Tues.)

3 A good honest and painful sermon.
17 Mar. 1661

4 If ever I was foxed it was now.
23 Apr. 1661

5 But methought it lessened my esteem of a king, that he should not be able to command the rain.
19 July 1662

6 I see it is impossible for the King to have things done as cheap as other men.
21 July 1662

7 But Lord! to see the absurd nature of Englishmen, that cannot forbear laughing and jeering at everything that looks strange.
27 Nov. 1662

8 My wife, who, poor wretch, is troubled with her lonely life.
19 Dec. 1662

9 Went to hear Mrs Turner's daughter...play on the harpsichon; but, Lord! it was enough to make any man sick to hear her; yet was I forced to commend her highly.
1 May 1663

10 A woman sober, and no high flyer, as he calls it.
27 May 1663

11 Most of their discourse was about hunting, in a dialect I understand very little.
22 Nov. 1663

12 While we were talking came by several poor creatures carried by, by constables, for being at a conventicle...I would to God they would either conform, or be more wise, and not be catched!
7 Aug. 1664

13 Pretty witty Nell. [Nell Gwynne.]
3 Apr. 1665

14 Strange to see how a good dinner and feasting reconciles everybody.
9 Nov. 1665

15 Strange to say what delight we married people have to see these poor fools decoyed into our condition.
25 Dec. 1665

16 Music and women I cannot but give way to, whatever my business is.
9 Mar. 1665–6

17 And mighty proud I am (and ought to be thankful to God Almighty) that I am able to have a spare bed for my friends.
8 Aug. 1666

18 I bless God I do find that I am worth more than ever I yet was, which is £6,200, for which the Holy Name of God be praised!
31 Oct. 1666

19 But it is pretty to see what money will do.
21 Mar. 1667–8

20 This day my wife made it appear to me that my late

entertainment this week cost me above £12, an expense which I am almost ashamed of, though it is but once in a great while, and is the end for which, in the most part, we live, to have such a merry day once or twice in a man's life.
6 Mar. 1669

21 And so I betake myself to that course, which is almost as much as to see myself go into my grave—for which, and all the discomforts that will accompany my being blind, the good God prepare me!
Closing words, 31 May 1669

PERICLES c.495–429 B.C.

22 φιλοκαλοῦμέν τε γὰρ μετ' εὐτελείας καὶ φιλοσοφοῦμεν ἄνευ μαλακίας.
Our love of what is beautiful does not lead to extravagance; our love of the things of the mind does not make us soft.
Funeral Oration, Athens, 430 B.C., as reported by Thucydides, Histories ii.40, 1. Trans. Rex Warner

23 ἀνδρῶν γὰρ ἐπιφανῶν πᾶσα γῆ τάφος.
For famous men have the whole earth as their memorial.
43, 3. Trans. Rex Warner

24 τῆς τε γὰρ ὑπαρχούσης φύσεως μὴ χείροσι γενέσθαι ὑμῖν μεγάλη ἡ δόξα καὶ ἧς ἂν ἐπ' ἐλάχιστον ἀρετῆς πέρι ἢ ψόγου ἐν τοῖς ἄρσεσι κλέος ᾖ.
Your great glory is not to be inferior to what God has made you, and the greatest glory of a woman is to be least talked about by men, whether they are praising you or criticizing you.
45, 2. Trans. Rex Warner

CHARLES PERRAULT 1628–1703

25 'Anne, ma soeur Anne, ne vois-tu rien venir?' Et la soeur Anne lui répondit, 'Je ne vois rien que le soleil qui poudroye, et l'herbe qui verdoye.'
'Anne, sister Anne, do you see nothing coming?' And her sister Anne replied, 'I see nothing but the sun making a dust, and the grass looking green.'
Histoires et Contes du Temps Passé (1697)

PERSIUS A.D. 34–62

26 Nec te quaesiveris extra.
And don't consult anyone's opinions but your own.
Satires, i.7

27 Virtutem videant intabescantque relicta.
Let them recognize virtue and rot for having lost it.
iii.38

28 Venienti occurrite morbo.
Confront disease at its onset.
64. See 366:20

29 Tecum habita: noris quam sit tibi curta supellex.
Live with yourself: get to know how poorly furnished you are.
iv.52

PETRONIUS A.D. 1st cent.

30 Canis ingens, catena vinctus, in pariete erat pictus superque quadrata littera scriptum 'Cave canem.'
A huge dog, tied by a chain, was painted on the wall and over it was written in capital letters 'Beware of the

dog.'
Satyricon: Cena Trimalchionis, 29.1

1 *Abiit ad plures.*
He's gone to join the majority.
42.5. Meaning the dead.

2 *Nam Sibyllam quidem Cumis ego ipse oculis meis vidi
in ampulla pendere, et cum illi pueri dicerent:
Σίβυλλα, τί θελεις; respondebat illa: ἀποθανεῖν
θέλω*
'I saw the Sibyl at Cumae'
(One said) 'with mine own eye.
She hung in a cage, and read her rune
    To all the passers-by.
Said the boys, "What wouldst thou, Sibyl?"
    She answered, "I would die."'
48.8. Tr. D.G. Rossetti, *Fragments. The Sibyl*

3 *Horatii curiosa felicitas.*
Horace's precisely lucky strikes.
Satyricon, 118

4 *Habes confitentem reum.*
Your prisoner admits the crimes.
130

5 *Foeda est in coitu et brevis voluptas
Et taedet Veneris statim peractae.*
Delight of lust is gross and brief
And weariness treads on desire.
A. Baehrens, *Poetae Latinae Minores*, vol.IV, no.101. Tr. Helen
Waddell.

PHEIDIPPIDES or PHILIPPIDES d. 490 B.C.

6 *χαίρετε, νικῶμεν.*
Greetings, we win.
Lucian, III.64, *Pro Lapsu inter salutandum*, para.iii. Before
dying, having run to Athens with news of the Battle of Marathon.

EDWARD JOHN PHELPS 1822–1900

7 The man who makes no mistakes does not usually
make anything.
Speech at Mansion House, 24 Jan. 1899

REAR ADMIRAL 'JACK' PHILIP 1840–1900

8 Don't cheer, men; those poor devils are dying.
At the Battle of Santiago, 4 July 1898. Allan Westcott, John
Woodward Philip, *Dict. Am. Biog.*

AMBROSE PHILIPS 1675?–1749

9 The flowers anew, returning seasons bring!
But beauty faded has no second spring.
The First Pastoral (1709), Lobbin, 1.55

STEPHEN PHILLIPS 1864–1915

10 A man not old, but mellow, like good wine.
Ulysses (1902), III.ii

WENDELL PHILLIPS 1811–1884

11 Every man meets his Waterloo at last.
Speeches (1880), Lecture at Brooklyn, N.Y., 1 Nov. 1859

12 We live under a government of men and morning
newspapers.
Address: The Press

PINDAR 518–438 B.C.

13 ἄριστον μὲν ὕδωρ.
Water is excellent.
Olympian Odes, I.1

14 φωνᾶντα συνετοῖσιν. ἐς δὲ τὸ πᾶν ἑρμηνέων
χατίζει.
(Weapons) that speak to the wise; but in general they
need interpreters.
II.85

15 μή, φίλα ψυχά, βίον ἀθάνατον
σπεῦδε, τὰν δ' ἔμπρακτον ἄντλει μαχανάν.
My soul, do not seek immortal life, but exhaust the
realm of the possible.
Pythian Odes, III.109

SIR ARTHUR WING PINERO 1855–1934

16 Put me into something loose.
The Gay Lord Quex (1899), III

17 What beautiful fruit! I love fruit when it's expensive.
The Second Mrs. Tanqueray (1893), Act I

HAROLD PINTER 1930–

18 I can't drink Guinness from a thick mug. I only like it
out of a thin glass.
The Caretaker (1959), Act I

19 If only I could get down to Sidcup. I've been waiting
for the weather to break.

WILLIAM PITT, EARL OF CHATHAM
1708–1778

20 The atrocious crime of being a young man...I shall
neither attempt to palliate nor deny.
House of Commons, 27 Jan. 1741

21 I rejoice that America has resisted. Three millions of
people, so dead to all the feelings of liberty, as
voluntarily to submit to be slaves, would have been fit
instruments to make slaves of the rest.
14 Jan. 1766

22 I cannot give them my confidence; pardon me,
gentlemen, confidence is a plant of slow growth in an
aged bosom: youth is the season of credulity.

23 Unlimited power is apt to corrupt the minds of those
who possess it.
House of Lords, 9 Jan. 1770. See 1:5

24 There is something behind the throne greater than the
King himself.
2 Mar. 1770

25 We have a Calvinistic creed, a Popish liturgy, and an
Arminian clergy.
19 May 1772

26 If I were an American, as I am an Englishman, while
a foreign troop was landed in my country, I never
would lay down my arms,—never—never—never!
18 Nov. 1777

27 You cannot conquer America.

28 I invoke the genius of the Constitution!

29 The poorest man may in his cottage bid defiance to all
the forces of the Crown. It may be frail—its roof may
shake—the wind may blow through it—the storm may
enter—the rain may enter—but the King of England

cannot enter!—all his force dares not cross the threshold of the ruined tenement!
Date unknown. Lord Brougham, *Statesmen in the Time of George III* (1839), vol.I

1 Our watchword is security.
Attr.

2 The lungs of London. [The parks.]
William Windham, in a Speech in House of Commons, 30 June 1808

WILLIAM PITT 1759–1806

3 Necessity is the plea for every infringement of human freedom. It is the argument of tyrants; it is the creed of slaves.
House of Commons, 18 Nov. 1783

4 We must recollect…what it is we have at stake, what it is we have to contend for. It is for our property, it is for our liberty, it is for our independence, nay, for our existence as a nation; it is for our character, it is for our very name as Englishmen, it is for everything dear and valuable to man on this side of the grave.
22 July 1803

5 England has saved herself by her exertions, and will, as I trust, save Europe by her example.
Guildhall, 1805

6 Roll up that map; it will not be wanted these ten years.
On a map of Europe, after hearing the news of the Battle of Austerlitz Dec. 1805. Lord Stanhope, *Life of the Rt. Hon. William Pitt* (1862), vol.iv, p.369

7 Oh, my country! how I leave my country!
Last words. Stanhope (1879), iii. p.397; in the 1st edn. (1862), iv, p.369, the words were given as 'How I love my country' and in G. Rose, *Diaries and Correspondence*, 23 Jan. 1806, as simply 'My country! oh, my country!' Oral tradition reports the alternative, 'I think I could eat one of Bellamy's veal pies.'

PLATO c.429–347 B.C.

8 Σωκράτη φησὶν ἀδικεῖν τούς τε νέους διαφθείροντα καὶ θεοὺς οὓς ἡ πόλις νομίζει οὐ νομίζοντα, ἕτερα δὲ δαιμόνια καινά.
It is said that Socrates commits a crime by corrupting the young men and not recognizing the gods that the city recognizes, but some other new religion.
Apologia, 24b

9 Socrates, I shall not accuse you as I accuse others, of getting angry and cursing me when I tell them to drink the poison imposed by the authorities. I know you on the contrary in your time here to be the noblest and gentlest and best man of all who ever came here; and now I am sure you are not angry with me, for you know who are responsible, but with them.
Phaedo, 116c. Spoken by Socrates' jailor

10 This was the end, Echecrates, of our friend; a man of whom we may say that of all whom we met at that time he was the wisest and justest and best.
118. Of Socrates' death

11 οὐ γὰρ περὶ τοῦ ἐπιτυχόντος ὁ λόγος, ἀλλὰ περὶ τοῦ ὄντινα τρόπον χρὴ ζῆν.
For our discussion is on no trifling matter, but on the right way to conduct our lives.
Republic, VIII, 352d

12 οὐ μὲν οὖν τῇ ἀληθείᾳ, φάναι, ὦ φιλούμενε Ἀγάθων, δύνασαι ἀντιλέγειν, ἐπεὶ Σωκράτει γε οὐδὲν χαλεπόν.

But, my dearest Agathon, it is truth which you cannot contradict; you can without any difficulty contradict Socrates.
Symposium, 201

PLAUTUS d. c.184 B.C.

13 *Lupus est homo homini, non homo, quom qualis sit non novit.*
A man is a wolf rather than a man to another man, when he hasn't yet found out what he's like.
Asinaria, 495. Often cited simply as *Homo homini lupus* (A man is a wolf to another man.)

14 *Dictum sapienti sat est.*
What's been said is enough for anyone with sense.
Persa, 729. Proverbially later, *Verbum sapienti sat est*, A word is enough for the wise.

15 Labrax: *Una littera plus sum quam medicus.*
Gripus: *Tum tu Mendicus es?*
Labrax: *Tetigisti acu.*
Labrax: One letter more than a medical man, that's what I am.
Gripus: Then you're a mendicant?
Labrax: You've hit the point.
Rudens, 1305

PLINY A.D. 23/24–79

16 *Brutum fulmen.*
A harmless thunderbolt.
Historia Naturalis, II.xliii

17 *Sal Atticum.*
Attic wit.
xxxi.87

WILLIAM PLOMER 1903–1973

18 A rose-red sissy half as old as time.
The Playboy of the Demi-World (1938). See 108:4

19 Fissures appeared in football fields
And houses in the night collapsed.
The Thames flowed backward to its source,
The last trickle seemed to disappear
Swiftly, like an adder to its hole,
And here and there along the river-bed
The stranded fish gaped among empty tins;
Face downward lay the huddled suicides
Like litter that a riot leaves.
The Silent Sunday

PLUTARCH A.D.c.50–c. 120

20 He who cheats with an oath acknowledges that he is afraid of his enemy, but that he thinks little of God.
Lives: Lysander, 8. See 321:18

EDGAR ALLAN POE 1809–1849

21 This maiden she lived with no other thought
   Than to love and be loved by me.
Annabel Lee (1849)

22 I was a child and she was a child,
   In this kingdom by the sea;
But we loved with a love which was more than love—
   I and my Annabel Lee.

23 And so, all the night-tide, I lie down by the side
Of my darling, my darling, my life and my bride

In her sepulchre there by the sea,
In her tomb by the side of the sea.

1 Keeping time, time, time,
   In a sort of Runic rhyme,
To the tintinnabulation that so musically wells
   From the bells, bells, bells.
   The Bells (1849), l.9

2 All that we see or seem
Is but a dream within a dream.
   A Dream within a Dream, l.10

3 The fever call'd 'Living'
Is conquer'd at last.
   For Annie

4 Once upon a midnight dreary, while I pondered, weak
   and weary,
Over many a quaint and curious volume of forgotten
   lore,
While I nodded, nearly napping, suddenly there came
   a tapping,
As of some one gently rapping, rapping at my
   chamber door.
   The Raven (1845), i

5 Eagerly I wished the morrow,—vainly had I sought to
   borrow
From my books surcease of sorrow—sorrow for the
   lost Lenore—
For the rare and radiant maiden whom the angels name
   Lenore—
       Nameless here for evermore.
   ii

6 Take thy beak from out my heart, and take thy form
   from off my door!
       Quoth the Raven, 'Nevermore'.
   xvii

7 Helen, thy beauty is to me
   Like those Nicean barks of yore,
That gently, o'er a perfumed sea,
   The weary, wayworn wanderer bore
   To his own native shore.

On desperate seas long wont to roam,
   Thy hyacinth hair, thy classic face,
Thy Naiad airs have brought me home,
   To the glory that was Greece
   And the grandeur that was Rome.
   To Helen, l.1

JOHN POMFRET 1667–1702

8 We live and learn, but not the wiser grow.
   Reason (1700), l.112

MADAME DE POMPADOUR 1721–1764

9 *Après nous le déluge.*
After us the deluge.
   Madame de Hausset, *Mémoires,* p.19

JOHN POOLE 1786?–1872

10 I hope I don't intrude?
   Paul Pry (1825), I.ii

ALEXANDER POPE 1688–1744

11 To wake the soul by tender strokes of art,

To raise the genius, and to mend the heart;
To make mankind, in conscious virtue bold,
Live o'er each scene, and be what they behold:
For this the Tragic Muse first trod the stage.
   Prologue to Addison's *Cato* (1713), l.1

12 A brave man struggling in the storms of fate,
And greatly falling with a falling state.
While Cato gives his little senate laws,
What bosom beats not in his country's cause?
   l.21

13 Poetic Justice, with her lifted scale;
Where, in nice balance, truth with gold she weighs,
And solid pudding against empty praise.
   The Dunciad (1728), bk.i, l.52

14 Now night descending, the proud scene was o'er,
But liv'd, in Settle's numbers, one day more.
   l.89

15 While pensive poets painful vigils keep,
Sleepless themselves, to give their readers sleep.
   l.93

16 Or where the pictures for the page atone,
And Quarles is sav'd by beauties not his own.
   l.139

17 And gentle dullness ever loves a joke.
   bk.ii, l.34

18 A brain of feathers, and a heart of lead.
   l.44

19 All crowd, who foremost shall be damn'd to fame.
   bk.iii, l.158

20 Flow Welsted, flow! like thine inspirer, beer,
Tho' stale, not ripe; tho' thin, yet never clear;
So sweetly mawkish, and so smoothly dull;
Heady, not strong; o'erflowing tho' not full.
   l.169

21 Proceed, great days! 'till learning fly the shore,
'Till Birch shall blush with noble blood no more,
'Till Thames see Eaton's sons for ever play,
'Till Westminster's whole year be holiday,
'Till Isis' elders reel, their pupils sport,
And Alma Mater lie dissolv'd in port!
   l.333

22 A wit with dunces, and a dunce with wits.
   bk.iv (1742), l.90

23 May you, may Cam, and Isis, preach it long,
The Right Divine of Kings to govern wrong.
   l.187

24 With the same cement, ever sure to bind,
We bring to one dead level ev'ry mind.
Then take him to develop, if you can,
And hew the block off, and get out the man.
   l.267

25   She mark'd thee there,
Stretch'd on the rack of a too easy chair,
And heard thy everlasting yawn confess
The pains and penalties of idleness.
   l.341

26 See skulking Truth to her old cavern fled,
Mountains of casuistry heap'd o'er her head!
Philosophy, that lean'd on Heav'n before,
Shrinks to her second cause, and is no more.
Physic of Metaphysic begs defence,
And Metaphysic calls for aid on Sense!
   l.641

1 Religion blushing veils her sacred fires,
And unawares Morality expires.
1.649

2 Lo! thy dread empire, Chaos! is restor'd;
Light dies before thy uncreating word;
Thy hand, great Anarch! lets the curtain fall,
And universal darkness buries all.
1.653

3 Vital spark of heav'nly flame!
Quit, oh quit this mortal frame:
Trembling, hoping, ling'ring, flying,
Oh the pain, the bliss of dying!
The Dying Christian to his Soul (1713). See 237:9

4 Tell me, my soul, can this be death?

5 What beck'ning ghost, along the moonlight shade
Invites my step, and points to yonder glade?
Elegy to the Memory of an Unfortunate Lady (1717), l.1

6 Is it, in heav'n, a crime to love too well?
1.6

7 Is there no bright reversion in the sky,
For those who greatly think, or bravely die?
1.9

8 Ambition first sprung from your blest abodes;
The glorious fault of angels and of gods.
1.13

9 On all the line a sudden vengeance waits,
And frequent hearses shall besiege your gates.
1.37

10 By foreign hands thy dying eyes were clos'd,
By foreign hands thy decent limbs compos'd,
By foreign hands thy humble grave adorn'd,
By strangers honour'd, and by strangers mourn'd!
1.51

11 No, make me mistress to the man I love;
If there be yet another name more free,
More fond than mistress, make me that to thee!
Eloisa to Abelard (1717), 1.88

12 Of all affliction taught a lover yet,
'Tis sure the hardest science to forget!
How shall I lose the sin, yet keep the sense,
And love the offender, yet detest th'offence?
How the dear object from the crime remove,
Or how distinguish penitence from love?
1.189. See 22:1

13 How happy is the blameless Vestal's lot?
The world forgetting, by the world forgot.
1.207

14 See my lips tremble, and my eye-balls roll,
Suck my last breath, and catch my flying soul!
1.323

15 You beat your pate, and fancy wit will come;
Knock as you please, there's nobody at home.
Epigram

16 I am his Highness' dog at Kew;
Pray, tell me sir, whose dog are you?
Epigram Engraved on the Collar of a Dog which I gave to his Royal Highness

17 Sir, I admit your gen'ral rule
That every poet is a fool;
But you yourself may serve to show it,
That every fool is not a poet.
Epigram from the French

18 Shut, shut the door, good John! fatigu'd I said,

Tie up the knocker; say I'm sick, I'm dead.
The Dog-star rages!
Epistle to Dr. Arbuthnot (1735), l.1 (Imitation of Horace)

19 Is there a parson, much bemus'd in beer,
A maudlin poetess, a rhyming peer,
A clerk, foredoom'd his father's soul to cross,
Who pens a stanza, when he should engross?
1.15

20 Fir'd that the house reject him, "Sdeath I'll print it,
And shame the fools.'
1.61

21 You think this cruel? take it for a rule,
No creature smarts so little as a fool.
Let peals of laughter, Codrus! round thee break,
Thou unconcern'd canst hear the mighty crack:
Pit, box, and gall'ry in convulsions hurl'd,
Thou stand'st unshook amidst a bursting world.
1.83. See 2:30, 260:18

22 Destroy his fib or sophistry—in vain!
The creature's at his dirty work again.
1.91

23 As yet a child, nor yet a fool to fame,
I lisp'd in numbers, for the numbers came.
I left no calling for this idle trade,
'No duty broke, no father disobey'd.
The Muse but serv'd to ease some friend, not wife,
To help me thro' this long disease, my life.
1.127. See 366:23

24 Pretty! in amber to observe the forms
Of hairs, or straws, or dirt, or grubs, or worms!
The things, we know, are neither rich nor rare,
But wonder how the Devil they got there.
1.169

25 And he, whose fustian's so sublimely bad,
It is not poetry, but prose run mad.
1.187

26   Were there one whose fires
True genius kindles, and fair fame inspires;
Blest with each talent, and each art to please,
And born to write, converse, and live with ease:
Should such a man, too fond to rule alone,
Bear, like the Turk, no brother near the throne,
View him with scornful, yet with jealous eyes,
And hate for arts that caus'd himself to rise;
Damn with faint praise, assent with civil leer,
And, without sneering, teach the rest to sneer;
Willing to wound, and yet afraid to strike,
Just hint a fault, and hesitate dislike. [Addison.]
1.193. See 584:2

27 Alike reserv'd to blame, or to commend,
A tim'rous foe, and a suspicious friend;
Dreading ev'n fools, by flatterers besieged,
And so obliging, that he ne'er oblig'd;
Like Cato, give his little senate laws,
And sit attentive to his own applause. [Addison.]
1.207

28 Who but must laugh, if such a man there be?
Who would not weep, if Atticus were he! [Addison.]
1.215

29 But still the great have kindness in reserve,
He help'd to bury whom he help'd to starve.
1.247

30 Let Sporus tremble—'What? that thing of silk,

Sporus, that mere white curd of ass's milk?
Satire or sense, alas! can Sporus feel?
Who breaks a butterfly upon a wheel?' [Lord Hervey.]
l.305

1 Yet let me flap this bug with gilded wings,
   This painted child of dirt, that stinks and stings. [Lord
      Hervey.]
   l.309

2 Eternal smiles his emptiness betray,
   As shallow streams run dimpling all the way. [Lord
      Hervey.]
   l.315

3 And he himself one vile antithesis.
   l.325

4 A cherub's face, a reptile all the rest. [Lord Hervey.]
   l.331

5 Unlearn'd, he knew no schoolman's subtle art,
   No language, but the language of the heart.
   By nature honest, by experience wise,
   Healthy by temp'rance, and by exercise.
   l.398

6 Such were the notes, thy once-loved Poet sung,
   Till Death untimely stopp'd his tuneful tongue.
   Epistle to the Earl of Oxford and Earl Mortimer (1721), l.1

7 She went, to plain-work, and to purling brooks,
   Old-fashion'd halls, dull aunts, and croaking rooks:
   She went from op'ra, park, assembly, play,
   To morning-walks, and pray'rs three hours a day;
   To part her time 'twixt reading and Bohea,
   To muse, and spill her solitary tea,
   Or o'er cold coffee trifle with the spoon,
   Court the slow clock, and dine exact at noon;
   Divert her eyes with pictures in the fire,
   Hum half a tune, tell stories to the squire.
   *Epistle to Miss Blount, on her leaving the Town after the
   Coronation,* l.11

8 To observations which ourselves we make,
   We grow more partial for th' observer's sake.
   Epistles to Several Persons Ep.i. **To Lord Cobham** (1734), l.11

9 Like following life thro' creatures you dissect,
   You lose it in the moment you detect.
   l.29

10 Alas! in truth the man but chang'd his mind,
   Perhaps was sick, in love, or had not din'd.
   l.127

11 'Tis from high life high characters are drawn;
   A saint in crape is twice a saint in lawn.
   l.135

12 'Tis Education forms the common mind,
   Just as the twig is bent, the tree's inclin'd.
   l.149

13 Search then the Ruling Passion: There, alone,
   The wild are constant and the cunning known;
   The fool consistent, and the false sincere;
   Priests, princes, women, no dissemblers here.
   This clue once found, unravels all the rest.
   l.174

14 Old politicians chew on wisdom past,
   And totter on in bus'ness to the last.
   l.228

15 'Odious! in woollen! 'twould a saint provoke!'
   l.246

16 'One would not, sure, be frightful when one's dead:

And—Betty—give this cheek a little red.'
l.250

17 Most women have no characters at all.
   Ep.ii. **To a Lady** (1735), l.2

18 Choose a firm cloud, before it fall, and in it
   Catch, ere she change, the Cynthia of this minute.
   l.19

19 A very heathen in the carnal part,
   Yet still a sad, good Christian at her heart.
   l.67

20 Chaste to her husband, frank to all beside,
   A teeming mistress, but a barren bride.
   l.71

21 Wise wretch! with pleasures too refin'd to please,
   With too much spirit to be e'er at ease,
   With too much quickness ever to be taught;
   With too much thinking to have common thought:
   You purchase pain with all that joy can give,
   And die of nothing but a rage to live.
   l.95

22 'With ev'ry pleasing, ev'ry prudent part,
   Say, what can Cloe want?'—She wants a heart.
   l.159

23 Virtue she finds too painful an endeavour,
   Content to dwell in decencies for ever.
   l.163

24 In men, we various ruling passions find,
   In women, two almost divide the kind;
   Those, only fix'd, they first or last obey,
   The love of pleasure, and the love of sway.
   l.207

25 Men, some to bus'ness, some to pleasure take;
   But ev'ry woman is at heart a rake:
   Men, some to quiet, some to public strife;
   But ev'ry lady would be Queen for life.
   l.215

26 Still round and round the ghosts of beauty glide,
   And haunt the places where their honour died.
   See how the world its veterans rewards!
   A youth of frolics, an old age of cards.
   l.241

27 She who ne'er answers till a husband cools,
   Or, if she rules him, never shows she rules;
   Charms by accepting, by submitting sways,
   Yet has her humour most, when she obeys.
   l.261

28 And mistress of herself, though China fall.
   l.268

29 Woman's at best a contradiction still.
   l.270

30 Who shall decide, when doctors disagree,
   And soundest casuists doubt, like you and me?
   Ep.iii. **To Lord Bathurst** (1733), l.1

31 But thousands die, without or this or that,
   Die, and endow a college, or a cat.
   l.95

32 The ruling passion, be it what it will,
   The ruling passion conquers reason still.
   l.153

33 In the worst inn's worst room, with mat half-hung,
   The floors of plaister, and the walls of dung,
   On once a flock-bed, but repaired with straw,
   With tape-tied curtains, never meant to draw,

The George and Garter dangling from that bed
Where tawdry yellow strove with dirty red,
Great Villiers lies.
l.299

1 Gallant and gay, in Cliveden's proud alcove,
The bow'r of wanton Shrewsbury and love.
l.307

2 Where London's column, pointing at the skies,
Like a tall bully, lifts the head, and lies.
l.339

3 Consult the genius of the place in all.
Ep.iv. **To Lord Burlington** (1731), l.57

4 To rest, the cushion and soft Dean invite,
Who never mentions Hell to ears polite.
l.149

5 Another age shall see the golden ear
Imbrown the slope, and nod on the parterre,
Deep harvests bury all his pride has plann'd,
And laughing Ceres re-assume the land.
l.173

6 Statesman, yet friend to truth! of soul sincere,
In action faithful, and in honour clear;
Who broke no promise, serv'd no private end,
Who gain'd no title, and who lost no friend.
Ep.v. **To Mr. Addison** (1721), l.67

7 Nature, and Nature's laws lay hid in night:
God said, *Let Newton be!* and all was light.
Epitaphs. Intended for Sir Isaac Newton. See 517:14

8 Of manners gentle, of affections mild;
In wit, a man; simplicity, a child:
With native humour temp'ring virtuous rage,
Form'd to delight at once and lash the age.
On Mr. Gay

9 Here rests a woman, good without pretence,
Blest with plain reason, and with sober sense.
On Mrs. Corbet

10 Let such teach others who themselves excel,
And censure freely who have written well.
An Essay on Criticism (1711), l.15

11 Some are bewilder'd in the maze of schools,
And some made coxcombs nature meant but fools.
l.26

12 Some have at first for wits, then poets pass'd,
Turn'd critics next, and prov'd plain fools at last.
l.36

13 A little learning is a dang'rous thing;
Drink deep, or taste not the Pierian spring:
There shallow draughts intoxicate the brain,
And drinking largely sobers us again.
l.215. See 193:15

14 Hills peep o'er hills, and Alps on Alps arise!
l.232

15 Whoever thinks a faultless piece to see
Thinks what ne'er was, nor is, nor e'er shall be.
l.253

16 Poets, like painters, thus unskill'd to trace
The naked nature and the living grace,
With gold and jewels cover ev'ry part,
And hide with ornaments their want of art.
l.293

17 True wit is nature to advantage dress'd,

What oft was thought, but ne'er so well express'd.
l.297

18 Such labour'd nothings, in so strange a style,
Amaze th' unlearn'd, and make the learned smile.
l.326

19 Be not the first by whom the new are tried,
Nor yet the last to lay the old aside.
l.335

20 As some to church repair,
Not for the doctrine, but the music there,
These equal syllables alone require,
Tho' oft the ear the open vowels tire;
While expletives their feeble aid do join;
And ten low words oft creep in one dull line.
l.342

21 Where'er you find 'the cooling western breeze',
In the next line, it 'whispers through the trees':
If crystal streams 'with pleasing murmurs creep',
The reader's threaten'd, not in vain, with 'sleep':
Then, at the last and only couplet fraught
With some unmeaning thing they call a thought,
A needless Alexandrine ends the song,
That, like a wounded snake, drags its slow length
    along.
l.350

22 True ease in writing comes from art, not chance,
As those move easiest who have learn'd to dance.
'Tis not enough no harshness gives offence,
The sound must seem an echo to the sense.
l.362

23 But when loud surges lash the sounding shore,
The hoarse, rough verse should like the torrent roar:
When Ajax strives, some rock's vast weight to throw,
The line too labours, and the words move slow.
l.368

24 Yet let not each gay turn thy rapture move;
For fools admire, but men of sense approve.
l.390

25 What woeful stuff this madrigal would be,
In some starv'd hackney sonneteer, or me?
But let a lord once own the happy lines,
How the wit brightens! how the style refines!
l.418

26 Some praise at morning what they blame at night;
But always think the last opinion right.
l.430

27 To err is human, to forgive, divine.
l.525

28 All seems infected that th'infected spy,
As all looks yellow to the jaundic'd eye.
l.558

29 Men must be taught as if you taught them not,
And things unknown propos'd as things forgot.
l.574

30 The bookful blockhead, ignorantly read,
With loads of learned lumber in his head.
l.612

31 For fools rush in where angels fear to tread.
l.625

32 But where's the man, who counsel can bestow,
Still pleas'd to teach, and yet not proud to know?
Unbiass'd, or by favour, or by spite:
Not dully prepossess'd, nor blindly right;

Tho' learn'd, well-bred; and tho' well-bred, sincere;
Modestly bold, and humanly severe:
Who to a friend his faults can freely show,
And gladly praise the merit of a foe?
l.631

1 Awake, my St John! leave all meaner things
To low ambition, and the pride of kings.
Let us (since Life can little more supply
Than just to look about us and to die)
Expatiate free o'er all this scene of man;
A mighty maze! but not without a plan.
An Essay on Man. Epistle i (1733), l.1

2 Eye Nature's walks, shoot folly as it flies,
And catch the manners living as they rise.
Laugh where we must, be candid where we can;
But vindicate the ways of God to man.
Say first, of God above or man below,
What can we reason, but from what we know.
l.13

3 Observe how system into system runs,
What other planets circle other suns.
l.25

4 Who sees with equal eye, as God of all,
A hero perish, or a sparrow fall,
Atoms or systems into ruin hurl'd,
And now a bubble burst, and now a world.
l.87

5 Hope springs eternal in the human breast;
Man never Is, but always To be blest.
The soul, uneasy, and confin'd from home,
Rests and expatiates in a life to come.
Lo, the poor Indian! whose untutor'd mind
Sees God in clouds, or hears him in the wind;
His soul proud Science never taught to stray
Far as the solar walk or milky way;
Yet simple Nature to his hope has giv'n,
Behind the cloud-topp'd hill, an humbler heav'n.
l.95

6 But thinks, admitted to that equal sky,
His faithful dog shall bear him company.
l.111

7 Pride still is aiming at the bless'd abodes,
Men would be angels, angels would be gods.
Aspiring to be gods if angels fell,
Aspiring to be angels men rebel.
l.125

8 Why has not man a microscopic eye?
For this plain reason, man is not a fly.
l.193

9 The spider's touch, how exquisitely fine!
Feels at each thread, and lives along the line.
l.217

10 All are but parts of one stupendous whole,
Whose body Nature is, and God the soul.
l.267

11 All nature is but art unknown to thee;
All chance, direction which thou canst not see;
All discord, harmony not understood;
All partial evil, universal good;
And, spite of pride, in erring reason's spite,
One truth is clear, 'Whatever IS, is RIGHT.'
l.289

12 Know then thyself, presume not God to scan,

The proper study of mankind is man.
Plac'd on this isthmus of a middle state,
A being darkly wise, and rudely great:
With too much knowledge for the sceptic side,
With too much weakness for the stoic's pride,
He hangs between; in doubt to act or rest,
In doubt to deem himself a god, or beast;
In doubt his mind or body to prefer;
Born but to die, and reas'ning but to err;
Alike in ignorance, his reason such,
Whether he thinks too little or too much.
Ep.ii (1733), l.1. See 141:1

13 Created half to rise, and half to fall;
Great lord of all things, yet a prey to all;
Sole judge of truth, in endless error hurl'd;
The glory, jest, and riddle of the world!
l.15

14 Go, teach eternal wisdom how to rule—
Then drop into thyself, and be a fool!
l.29

15 Fix'd like a plant on his peculiar spot,
To draw nutrition, propagate, and rot.
l.63

16 Vice is a monster of so frightful mien,
As, to be hated, needs but to be seen;
Yet seen too oft, familiar with her face,
We first endure, then pity, then embrace.
But where th' extreme of vice, was ne'er agreed:
Ask where's the North? at York, 'tis on the Tweed;
In Scotland, at the Orcades; and there,
At Greenland, Zembla, or the Lord knows where.
l.217

17 The learn'd is happy nature to explore,
The fool is happy that he knows no more.
l.263

18 Behold the child, by nature's kindly law
Pleas'd with a rattle, tickled with a straw.
l.275

19 Scarfs, garters, gold, amuse his riper stage,
And beads and pray'r-books are the toys of age:
Pleas'd with this bauble still, as that before;
Till tir'd, he sleeps, and life's poor play is o'er.
l.279

20 For forms of government let fools contest;
Whate'er is best administer'd is best:
For modes of faith, let graceless zealots fight;
His can't be wrong whose life is in the right:
In faith and hope the world will disagree,
But all mankind's concern is charity.
Ep.iii (1733), l.303

21 O Happiness! our being's end and aim!
Good, pleasure, ease, content! whate'er thy name:
That something still which prompts th' eternal sigh,
For which we bear to live, or dare to die.
Ep.iv (1734), l.1

22 Worth makes the man, and want of it, the fellow;
The rest is all but leather or prunella.
l.203

23 What can ennoble sots, or slaves, or cowards?
Alas! not all the blood of all the Howards.
l.215

24 A wit's a feather, and a chief a rod;

An honest man's the noblest work of God.
l.247

1 If parts allure thee, think how Bacon shin'd,
The wisest, brightest, meanest of mankind:
Or ravish'd with the whistling of a name,
See Cromwell, damn'd to everlasting fame!
l.281

2 Slave to no sect, who takes no private road,
But looks through Nature, up to Nature's God.
l.331

3 Form'd by thy converse, happily to steer
From grave to gay, from lively to severe.
l.379

4 Shall then this verse to future age pretend
Thou wert my guide, philosopher, and friend?
That urg'd by thee, I turn'd the tuneful art
From sounds to things, from fancy to the heart;
For wit's false mirror held up nature's light;
Shew'd erring pride, whatever is, is right;
That reason, passion, answer one great aim;
That true self-love and social are the same;
That virtue only makes our bliss below;
And all our knowledge is, ourselves to know.
l.389

5 There St John mingles with my friendly bowl
The feast of reason and the flow of soul.
Imitations of Horace. Hor.II, Sat.1 (1733). **To Mr. Fortescue,**
l.127

6 For I, who hold sage Homer's rule the best,
Welcome the coming, speed the going guest.
Hor.II, Sat.2 (1734). **To Mr. Bethel,** l.159. See 380:25

7 Our Gen'rals now, retir'd to their estates,
Hang their old trophies o'er the garden gates,
In life's cool ev'ning satiate of applause.
Hor.I, Ep.1 (1738). **To Lord Bolingbroke,** l.7

8 Not to go back, is somewhat to advance,
And men must walk at least before they dance.
l.53

9 Get place and wealth, if possible, with grace;
If not, by any means get wealth and place.
l.103

10 Not to admire, is all the art I know,
To make men happy, and to keep them so.
Hor.I, Ep.6 (1738). **To Mr. Murray,** l.1. See 258:17

11 The worst of madmen is a saint run mad.
l.27

12 Shakespeare (whom you and ev'ry play-house bill
Style the divine, the matchless, what you will)
For gain, not glory, wing'd his roving flight,
And grew immortal in his own despite.
Hor.II, Ep.1 (1737). **To Augustus,** l.69

13 Who now reads Cowley? if he pleases yet,
His moral pleases, not his pointed wit.
l.75

14   The people's voice is odd,
It is, and it is not, the voice of God.
l.89. See 3:9

15 Waller was smooth; but Dryden taught to join
The varying verse, the full-resounding line,
The long majestic march, and energy divine.
l.267

16 Ev'n copious Dryden wanted, or forgot,

The last and greatest art, the art to blot.
l.280

17 There still remains, to mortify a wit,
The many-headed monster of the pit.
l.304

18 Let humble Allen, with an awkward shame,
Do good by stealth, and blush to find it fame.
Epilogue (1738), Dial.i, l.135

19 Ask you what provocation I have had?
The strong antipathy of good to bad.
Dial.ii, l.197

20 Yes, I am proud; I must be proud to see
Men not afraid of God, afraid of me.
l.208

21 Vain was the chief's and sage's pride.
They had no poet and they died!
Hor.IV, Ode 9, l.12

22 Ye gods! annihilate but space and time,
And make two lovers happy.
Martinus Scriblerus...or The Art of Sinking in Poetry, ch.11
(Miscellanies, 1727)

23 Happy the man, whose wish and care
        A few paternal acres bound,
Content to breathe his native air,
                In his own ground.
Ode on Solitude (1717)

24 Thus let me live, unseen, unknown,
        Thus unlamented let me die;
Steal from the world, and not a stone
                Tell where I lie.

25 Welcome the coming, speed the parting guest.
Odyssey (1725–6), xv.83

26 'Has she no faults then (Envy says) Sir?'
        Yes, she has one, I must aver:
When all the world conspires to praise her,
        The woman's deaf, and does not hear.
On a Certain Lady at Court (1727–8)

27   Where'er you walk, cool gales shall fan the
        glade,
Trees, where you sit, shall crowd into a shade:
Where'er you tread, the blushing flow'rs shall rise,
And all things flourish where you turn your eyes.
Pastorals (1709), **Summer,** l.73

28 What dire offence from am'rous causes springs,
What mighty contests rise from trivial things.
The Rape of the Lock (1714), c.i, l.1

29 Now lap-dogs give themselves the rousing shake,
And sleepless lovers, just at twelve, awake:
Thrice rung the bell, the slipper knock'd the ground,
And the press'd watch return'd a silver sound.
l.15

30 They shift the moving Toyshop of their heart.
l.100

31 Here files of pins extend their shining rows,
Puffs, powders, patches, bibles, billet-doux.
l.137

32 Bright as the sun, her eyes the gazers strike,
And, like the sun, they shine on all alike.
c.ii, l.13

33 If to her share some female errors fall,
Look on her face, and you'll forget 'em all.
l.17

1 Fair tresses man's imperial race insnare,
And beauty draws us with a single hair.
l.27

2 Here thou, great Anna! whom three realms obey,
Dost sometimes counsel take—and sometimes tea.
c.iii, l.7

3 At ev'ry word a reputation dies.
l.16

4 The hungry judges soon the sentence sign,
And wretches hang that jury-men may dine.
l.21

5 Let Spades be trumps! she said, and trumps they were.
l.46

6 For lo! the board with cups and spoons is crown'd,
The berries crackle, and the mill turns round;
On shining altars of Japan they raise
The silver lamp; the fiery spirits blaze:
From silver spouts the grateful liquors glide,
While China's earth receives the smoking tide:
At once they gratify their scent and taste,
And frequent cups prolong the rich repast.
l.105

7 Coffee, (which makes the politician wise,
And see through all things with his half-shut eyes)
Sent up in vapours to the Baron's brain
New stratagems, the radiant lock to gain.
l.117

8 Not louder shrieks to pitying heav'n are cast,
When husbands, or when lapdogs breathe their last.
l.157

9 Here in a grotto, shelter'd close from air,
And screen'd in shades from day's detested glare,
She sighs for ever on her pensive bed,
Pain at her side, and Megrim at her head.
c.iv, l.21

10 Sir Plume, of amber snuff-box justly vain,
And the nice conduct of a clouded cane.
l.123

11 Beauties in vain their pretty eyes may roll;
Charms strike the sight, but merit wins the soul.
c.v, l.33

12 Thou Great First Cause, least understood!
Who all my sense confin'd
To know but this, that Thou art good,
And that myself am blind.
The Universal Prayer

13 Teach me to feel another's woe,
To hide the fault I see;
That mercy I to others show,
That mercy show to me.

14 See! from the brake the whirring pheasant springs,
And mounts exulting on triumphant wings:
Short is his joy; he feels the fiery wound,
Flutters in blood, and panting beats the ground.
Ah! what avail his glossy, varying dyes,
His purple crest, and scarlet-circled eyes,
The vivid green his shining plumes unfold,
His painted wings and breast that flames with gold?
Windsor Forest, l.111

15 This is the Jew
That Shakespeare drew.
Of Macklin's performance of Shylock, 14 Feb. 1741. Baker, Reed & Jones, Biographia Dramatica (1812), vol.I, pt.ii, p.469

16 Party-spirit, which at best is but the madness of many for the gain of a few.
Letters. To E. Blount, 27 Aug. 1714

17 How often are we to die before we go quite off this stage? In every friend we lose a part of ourselves, and the best part.
To Swift, 5 Dec. 1732

18 To endeavour to work upon the vulgar with fine sense, is like attempting to hew blocks with a razor.
Thoughts on Various Subjects (1706)

19 A man should never be ashamed to own he has been in the wrong, which is but saying, in other words, that he is wiser to-day than he was yesterday.

20 It is with narrow-souled people as with narrow-necked bottles: the less they have in them, the more noise they make in pouring it out.

21 When men grow virtuous in their old age, they only make a sacrifice to God of the devil's leavings.

22 The most positive men are the most credulous.

23 Here am I, dying of a hundred good symptoms.
15 May 1744. Joseph Spence, Anecdotes by and about Alexander Pope, p.637

SIR KARL POPPER 1902–

24 The open society and its enemies.
Book title (1945)

25 Piecemeal social engineering resembles physical engineering in regarding the ends as beyond the province of technology.
The Poverty of Historicism, III, 21

RICHARD PORSON 1759–1808

26 When Dido found Aeneas would not come,
She mourn'd in silence, and was Di-do-dum.
Epigram: On Latin Gerunds. J.S. Watson, Life of Porson (1861), p.418

27 The Germans in Greek
Are sadly to seek:
Not five in five score,
But ninety-five more:
All, save only Herman,
And Herman's a German.
M.L. Clarke, Life of Porson, ch.vii

28 Madoc will be read,—when Homer and Virgil are forgotten. [To Southey.]
Samuel Rogers, Table Talk, p.330

29 I went to Frankfort, and got drunk
With that most learn'd professor, Brunck;
I went to Worts, and got more drunken
With that more learn'd professor, Ruhnken.
Facetiae Cantabrigienses (1825)

30 Life is too short to learn German.
T.L. Peacock, Gryll Grange, ch.3

BEILBY PORTEUS 1731–1808

31 One murder made a villain,
Millions a hero.
Death (1759), l.155

32 War its thousands slays, Peace its ten thousands.
l.179

33 Teach him how to live,

And, oh! still harder lesson! how to die.
1.319

BEATRIX POTTER 1866–1943

1 Don't go into Mr McGregor's garden: your Father had
an accident there; he was put in a pie by Mrs
McGregor.
The Tale of Peter Rabbit (1902)

BISHOP HENRY CODMAN POTTER 1835–1908

2 We have exchanged the Washingtonian dignity for the
Jeffersonian simplicity, which in due time came to be
only another name for the Jacksonian vulgarity.
Address, Washington Centennial, 30 Apr. 1889

EUGÈNE POTTIER 1816–1887

3 *Debout! les damnés de la terre!*
   Debout! les forçats de la faim!
La raison tonne en son cratère,
C'est l'éruption de la fin.
Du passé faisons table rase,
   Foule esclave, debout, debout,
Le monde va changer de base,
   Nous ne sommes rien, soyons tout!
      C'est la lutte finale
      Groupons-nous, et, demain,
      L'Internationale
         Sera le genre humain.
On your feet, you damned souls of the earth! On your
feet, inmates of hunger's prison! Reason is rumbling
in its crater, and its final eruption is on its way. Let
us wipe clean the slate of the past—on your feet,
you enslaved multitude, on your feet—the world is
to undergo a fundamental change: we are nothing,
let us be everything! This is the final conflict: let us
form up and, tomorrow, the International will
encompass the human race.
L'Internationale, in H.E. Piggot, *Songs that made History*
(1937), ch.6

EZRA POUND 1885–1972

4 Winter is icummen in,
Lhude sing Goddamm,
Raineth drop and staineth slop,
And how the wind doth ramm!
   Sing: Goddamm.
Ancient Music. See 7:18

5 Blue, blue is the grass about the river
And the willows have overfilled the close garden.
And within, the mistress, in the midmost of her youth,
White, white of face, hesitates, passing the door.
Slender, she puts forth a slender hand;

And she was a courtezan in the old days,
And she has married a sot,
Who now goes drunkenly out
And leaves her too much alone.
The Beautiful Toilet, By Mei Sheng B.C. 140

6 Hang it all, Robert Browning,
      there can but be the one 'Sordello'.
Cantos, 2

7 Palace in smoky light,

Troy but a heap of smouldering boundary stones.
4

8 *With Usura*

With usura hath no man a house of good stone
each block cut smooth and well fitting
that design might cover their face.
45

9 WITH USURA
wool comes not to market
sheep bringeth no gain with usura
Usura is a murrain, usura
blunteth the needle in the maid's hand
and stoppeth the spinner's cunning.

10 Usura rusteth the chisel
It rusteth the craft and the craftsman.

11 Azure hath a canker by usura; cramoisi is unbroidered
Emerald findeth no Memling
Usura slayeth the child in the womb
It stayeth the young man's courting
It hath brought palsey to bed, lyeth
between the young bride and her bridegroom
                CONTRA NATURA
They have brought whores for Eleusis
Corpses are set to banquet
at behest of usura.

12 What thou lovest well remains,
            the rest is dross
What thou lov'st well shall not be reft from thee
What thou lov'st well is thy true heritage.
81

13 The ant's a centaur in his dragon world.
Pull down thy vanity, it is not man
Made courage, or made order, or made grace.
      Pull down thy vanity, I say pull down.
Learn of the green world what can be thy place
In scaled invention or true artistry,
Pull down thy vanity,
            Paquin pull down!
The green casque has outdone your elegance.

14 But to have done instead of not doing
            this is not vanity
To have, with decency, knocked
That a Blunt should open
            To have gathered from the air a live tradition
or from a fine old eye the unconquered flame
This is not vanity.
      Here error is all in the not done,
all in the diffidence that faltered.

15 Yet you ask on what account I write so many
      love-lyrics
And whence this soft book comes into my mouth.
Neither Calliope nor Apollo sung these things into my
      ear,
      My genius is no more than a girl.

If she with ivory fingers drive a tune through the lyre,
      We look at the process.
How easy the moving fingers; if hair is mussed on her
      forehead,
If she goes in a gleam of Cos, in a slither of dyed
      stuff,
There is a volume in the matter.
Homage to Sextus Propertius (1917), V, 2

1 For three years, out of key with his time,
   He strove to resuscitate the dead art
   Of poetry; to maintain the 'sublime'
   In the old sense.
   Hugh Selwyn Mauberley, I

2 Bent resolutely on wringing lilies from the acorns;
   Capaneus; trout for factitious bait.

3 His true Penelope was Flaubert,
   He fished by obstinate isles;
   Observed the elegance of Circe's hair
   Rather than the mottoes on sun-dials.

4 Better mendacities
   Than the classics in paraphrase!
   II

5 The tea-rose tea-gown, etc.
   Supplants the *mousseline* of Cos,
   The pianola 'replaces'
   Sappho's barbitos.
   III

6 Christ follows Dionysus,
   Phallic and ambrosial
   Made way for macerations;
   Caliban casts out Ariel.

7 All things are a flowing,
   Sage Heracleitus says;
   But a tawdry cheapness
   Shall outlast our days.
   See 246:5

8 Even the Christian beauty
   Defects—after Samothrace;
   We see $\tau\grave{o}$ $\kappa\alpha\lambda\acute{o}\nu$
   Decreed in the market place.

9 O bright Apollo,
   $\tau\acute{\iota}\nu'$ $\check{\alpha}\nu\delta\rho\alpha$, $\tau\acute{\iota}\nu$ $\mathring{\eta}\rho\omega\alpha$, $\tau\iota\nu\alpha$ $\theta\epsilon\acute{o}\nu$,
   What god, man, or hero
   Shall I place a tin wreath upon!

10 There died a myriad,
   And of the best, among them,
   For an old bitch gone in the teeth,
   For a botched civilization.
   V

11 The apparition of these faces in the crowd;
   Petals, on a wet, black bough.
   Lustra (1915), **In a Station of the Metro**

12 I make a pact with you, Walt Whitman—
   I have detested you long enough…
   It was you that broke the new wood,
   Now is a time for carving.
   We have one sap and one root—
   Let there be commerce between us.
   A Pact

13 Even in my dreams you have denied yourself to me
   And sent me only your handmaids.
   $\tau\grave{o}$ $\kappa\alpha\lambda\acute{o}\nu$ [Good]

14 Suddenly discovering in the eyes of the very beautiful
   Normande cocotte
   The eyes of the very learned British Museum assistant.
   Pagani's, November 8

15 O woe, woe,
   People are born and die,
   We also shall be dead pretty soon

Therefore let us act as if we were dead already.
   Mr. Housman's Message

16 At fourteen I married My Lord you.
   I never laughed, being bashful.
   Lowering my head, I looked at the wall.
   Called to, a thousand times, I never looked back.

   At fifteen I stopped scowling,
   I desired my dust to be mingled with yours
   Forever and forever and forever.
   Why should I climb the look out?

   At sixteen you departed,
   You went into far Ku-to-yen, by the river of swirling
        eddies,
   And you have been gone five months.
   The monkeys make sorrowful noise overhead.
   The River Merchant's Wife: A Letter, By Rihaku

17 The leaves fall early this autumn, in wind.
   The paired butterflies are already yellow with August
   Over the grass in the West garden;
   They hurt me. I grow older.
   If you are coming down through the narrows of the
        river Kiang,
   Please let me know beforehand,
   And I will come out to meet you
                    As far as Cho-fu-sa.

18 He hath not heart for harping, nor in ring-having
   Nor winsomeness to wife, nor world's delight
   Nor any whit else save the wave's slash,
   Yet longing comes upon him to fare forth on the
        water.
   Bosque taketh blossom, cometh beauty of berries,
   Fields to fairness, land fares brisker,
   All this admonisheth man eager of mood,
   The heart turns to travel so that he then thinks
   On flood-ways to be far departing.
   Cuckoo calleth with gloomy crying,
   He singeth summerward, bodeth sorrow,
   The bitter heart's blood.
   The Seafarer. From the Anglo-Saxon

19 There come now no Kings nor Caesars
   Nor gold-giving lords like those gone.
   Howe'er in mirth most magnified,
   Whoe'er lived in life most lordliest,
   Drear all this excellence, delights undurable!
   Waneth the watch, but the world holdeth.
   Tomb hideth trouble. The blade is layed low.
   Earthly glory ageth and seareth.

20 I had over-prepared the event,
        that much was ominous.
   With middle-ageing care
        I had laid out just the right books.
   I had almost turned down the pages.
   Villanelle: the psychological hour

21 Music begins to atrophy when it departs too far from
   the dance;…poetry begins to atrophy when it gets too
   far from music.
   ABC of Reading (1934), Warning

22 One of the pleasures of middle age is to *find out* that
   one WAS right, and that one was much righter than
   one knew at say 17 or 23.
   ch.1, 2

23 Literature is news that STAYS news.
   ch.2

1 Great literature is simply language charged with meaning to the utmost possible degree.
How to Read (1931), Pt.II

SIR JOHN POWELL 1645–1713

2 Let us consider the reason of the case. For nothing is law that is not reason.
Coggs v. Bernard, 2 Lord Raymond, 911

JOHN O'CONNOR POWER

3 The mules of politics: without pride of ancestry, or hope of posterity.
Quoted in H.H. Asquith, *Memories and Reflections*, i.123. See 185:41

WINTHROP MACKWORTH PRAED 1802–1839

4 My own Araminta, say 'No!'
A Letter of Advice

5 Of science and logic he chatters
As fine and as fast as he can;
Though I am no judge of such matters,
I'm sure he's a talented man.
The Talented Man

6 For all who understood admired,
And some who did not understand them.
The Vicar

PRAYER BOOK 1662

7 It hath been the wisdom of the Church of England, ever since the first compiling of her Publick Liturgy, to keep the mean between the two extremes, of too much stiffness in refusing, and of too much easiness in admitting any variation from it.
The Preface

8 There was never any thing by the wit of man so well devised, or so sure established, which in continuance of time hath not been corrupted.
Concerning the Service of the Church

9 Dearly beloved brethren, the Scripture moveth us in sundry places to acknowledge and confess our manifold sins and wickedness; and that we should not dissemble nor cloke them before the face of Almighty God our heavenly Father; but confess them with an humble, lowly, penitent, and obedient heart.
Morning Prayer. After the beginning Sentences

10 I pray and beseech you, as many as are here present, to accompany me with a pure heart, and humble voice, unto the throne of the heavenly grace.

11 We have erred, and strayed from thy ways like lost sheep. We have followed too much the devices and desires of our own hearts.
General Confession

12 We have left undone those things which we ought to have done; And we have done those things which we ought not to have done; And there is no health in us.

13 Restore thou them that are penitent; According to thy promises declared unto mankind in Christ Jesu our Lord. And grant, O most merciful Father, for his sake; That we may hereafter live a godly, righteous, and sober life.

14 And forgive us our trespasses, As we forgive them that trespass against us.
The Lord's Prayer. See 64:24

15 Glory be to the Father, and to the Son: and to the Holy Ghost; As it was in the beginning, is now, and ever shall be: world without end. Amen.
Gloria. See 334:14

16 We praise thee, O God: we acknowledge thee to be the Lord.
All the earth doth worship thee: the Father everlasting.
To thee all Angels cry aloud: the Heavens, and all the Powers therein.
To thee Cherubin, and Seraphin: continually do cry, Holy, Holy, Holy: Lord God of Sabaoth;
Heaven and earth are full of the Majesty: of thy Glory.
The glorious company of the Apostles: praise thee.
The goodly fellowship of the Prophets: praise thee.
The noble army of Martyrs: praise thee.
Te Deum. See 11:3

17 When thou hadst overcome the sharpness of death: thou didst open the Kingdom of Heaven to all believers.

18 Day by day: we magnify thee;
And we worship thy Name: ever world without end.
Vouchsafe, O Lord: to keep us this day without sin.
O Lord, have mercy upon us: have mercy upon us.
O Lord, let thy mercy lighten upon us: as our trust is in thee.
O Lord, in thee have I trusted: let me never be confounded.
See 11:4

19 O all ye Works of the Lord, bless ye the Lord.
Benedicite. See 83:16

20 O ye Waters that be above the Firmament, bless ye the Lord.

21 O ye Showers, and Dew, bless ye the Lord: praise him, and magnify him for ever.
O ye Winds of God, bless ye the Lord: praise him, and magnify him for ever.

22 O ye Dews, and Frosts, bless ye the Lord: praise him, and magnify him for ever.
O ye Frost and Cold, bless ye the Lord: praise him and magnify him for ever.
O ye Ice and Snow, bless ye the Lord: praise him and magnify him for ever.
O ye Nights, and Days, bless ye the Lord: praise him, and magnify him for ever.

23 O let the Earth bless the Lord: yea, let it praise him, and magnify him for ever.

24 O all ye Green Things upon the Earth, bless ye the Lord: praise him, and magnify him for ever.

25 O ye Whales, and all that move in the Waters, bless ye the Lord: praise him, and magnify him for ever.

26 I believe in God the Father Almighty, Maker of heaven and earth: And in Jesus Christ his only Son our Lord, Who was conceived by the Holy Ghost, Born of the Virgin Mary, Suffered under Pontius Pilate, Was crucified, dead, and buried, He descended into hell; The third day he rose again from the dead, He ascended into heaven, And sitteth on the right hand of God the Father Almighty; From thence he shall come to judge the quick and the dead.
I believe in the Holy Ghost; The holy Catholick Church; The Communion of Saints; The Forgiveness

of sins; The Resurrection of the body, And the life everlasting. Amen.
The Apostles' Creed. See 334:20, 387:10

1 Give peace in our time, O Lord.
Versicle

2 O God, who art the author of peace and lover of concord, in knowledge of whom standeth our eternal life, whose service is perfect freedom; Defend us thy humble servants in all assaults of our enemies.
Second Collect, for Peace

3 Grant that this day we fall into no sin, neither run into any kind of danger.
Third Collect, for Grace

4 In Quires and Places where they sing, here followeth the Anthem.
Rubric after Third Collect

5 Endue her plenteously with heavenly gifts; grant her in health and wealth long to live.
Prayer for the Queen's Majesty

6 Almighty God, the fountain of all goodness.
Prayer for the Royal Family

7 Almighty and everlasting God, who alone workest great marvels; Send down upon our Bishops, and Curates, and all Congregations committed to their charge, the healthful Spirit of thy grace; and that they may truly please thee, pour upon them the continual dew of thy blessing.
Prayer for the Clergy and People

8 Almighty God, who hast given us grace at this time with one accord to make our common supplications unto thee; and dost promise, that when two or three are gathered together in thy Name thou wilt grant their requests: Fulfil now, O Lord, the desires and petitions of thy servants, as may be most expedient for them.
Prayer of St. Chrysostom

9 O God, from whom all holy desires, all good counsels, and all just works do proceed; Give unto thy servants that peace which the world cannot give.
Evening Prayer. Second Collect

10 Lighten our darkness, we beseech thee, O Lord; and by thy great mercy defend us from all perils and dangers of this night.
Third Collect

11 Whosoever will be saved: before all things it is necessary that he hold the Catholick Faith.
At Morning Prayer. Athanasian Creed. Quicunque vult

12 And the Catholick Faith is this: That we worship one God in Trinity, and Trinity in Unity;
Neither confounding the Persons: nor dividing the Substance.

13 There are not three incomprehensibles, nor three uncreated: but one uncreated, and one incomprehensible.

14 Perfect God, and perfect Man: of a reasonable soul and human flesh subsisting; Equal to the Father, as touching his Godhead: and inferior to the Father, as touching his Manhood.

15 Have mercy upon us miserable sinners.
The Litany

16 From all evil and mischief; from sin, from the crafts and assaults of the devil; from thy wrath, and from everlasting damnation,

Good Lord, deliver us.
From all blindness of heart; from pride, vain-glory, and hypocrisy; from envy, hatred, and malice, and from all uncharitableness,
Good Lord, deliver us.
From fornication, and all other deadly sin; and from all the deceits of the world, the flesh, and the devil,
Good Lord, deliver us.
From lightning and tempest; from plague, pestilence, and famine; from battle and murder, and from sudden death,
Good Lord, deliver us.

17 By thine Agony and bloody Sweat; by thy Cross and Passion; by thy precious Death and Burial; by thy glorious Resurrection and Ascension; and by the coming of the Holy Ghost,
Good Lord, deliver us.
In all time of our tribulation; in all time of our wealth; in the hour of death, and in the day of judgement,
Good Lord, deliver us.

18 That it may please thee to illuminate all Bishops, Priests, and Deacons, with true knowledge and understanding of thy Word; and that both by their preaching and living they may set it forth, and show it accordingly;
We beseech thee to hear us, good Lord.

19 That it may please thee to strengthen such as do stand; and to comfort and help the weak-hearted; and to raise up them that fall; and finally to beat down Satan under our feet;
We beseech thee to hear us, good Lord.

20 That it may please thee to preserve all that travel by land or by water, all women labouring of child, all sick persons, and young children; and to shew thy pity upon all prisoners and captives;
We beseech thee to hear us, good Lord.
That it may please thee to defend, and provide for, the fatherless children, and widows, and all that are desolate and oppressed;
We beseech thee to hear us, good Lord.

21 That it may please thee to give and preserve to our use the kindly fruits of the earth, so as in due time we may enjoy them;
We beseech thee to hear us, good Lord.

22 O God, merciful Father, that despisest not the sighing of a contrite heart, not the desire of such as be sorrowful; Mercifully assist our prayers that we make before thee in all our troubles and adversities, whensoever they oppress us.

23 O God, whose nature and property is ever to have mercy and to forgive, receive our humble petitions; and though we be tied and bound by the chain of our sins, yet let the pitifulness of thy great mercy loose us; for the honour of Jesus Christ, our Mediator and Advocate.
Prayers and Thanksgivings, upon Several Occasions

24 O God, the Creator and Preserver of all mankind, we humbly beseech thee for all sorts and conditions of men.
Collect or Prayer for all Conditions of Men

25 We pray for the good estate of the Catholick Church; that it may be so guided and governed by thy good Spirit, that all who profess and call themselves

Christians may be led into the way of truth.

1 We commend to thy fatherly goodness all those, who are any ways afflicted, or distressed, in mind, body, or estate; that it may please thee to comfort and relieve them, according to their several necessities, giving them patience under their sufferings, and a happy issue out of all their afflictions.

2 We bless thee for our creation, preservation, and all the blessings of this life; but above all, for thine inestimable love in the redemption of the world by our Lord Jesus Christ; for the means of grace, and for the hope of glory.
General Thanksgiving

3 O God our heavenly Father, who by thy gracious providence dost cause the former and the latter rain to descend upon the earth, that it may bring forth fruit for the use of man; We give thee humble thanks that it hath pleased thee, in our great necessity, to send us at the last a joyful rain upon thine inheritance, and to refresh it when it was dry.
Thanksgiving for Rain

4 Almighty God, give us grace that we may cast away the works of darkness, and put upon us the armour of light, now in the time of this mortal life, in which thy Son Jesus Christ came to visit us in great humility.
Collects. 1st Sunday in Advent

5 Blessed Lord, who hast caused all holy Scriptures to be written for our learning; Grant that we may in such wise hear them read, mark, learn, and inwardly digest them, that by patience, and comfort of thy holy Word, we may embrace, and ever hold fast the blessed hope of everlasting life.
2nd Sunday in Advent

6 That whereas, through our sins and wickedness, we are sore let and hindered in running the race that is set before us, thy bountiful grace and mercy may speedily help and deliver us.
4th Sunday in Advent

7 O Lord, we beseech thee mercifully to receive the prayers of thy people which call upon thee; and grant that they may both perceive and know what things they ought to do, and also may have grace and power faithfully to fulfil the same.
1st Sunday after Epiphany

8 O God, who knowest us to be set in the midst of so many and great dangers, that by reason of the frailty of our nature we cannot always stand upright; Grant to us such strength and protection, as may support us in all dangers, and carry us through all temptations.
4th Sunday after Epiphany

9 Almighty God, who seest that we have no power of ourselves to help ourselves; Keep us both outwardly in our bodies, and inwardly in our souls; that we may be defended from all adversities which may happen to the body, and from all evil thoughts which may assault and hurt the soul.
2nd Sunday in Lent

10 We humbly beseech thee, that, as by thy special grace preventing us thou dost put into our minds good desires, so by thy continued help we may bring the same to good effect.
Easter Day

11 Grant us so to put away the leaven of malice and

wickedness, that we may alway serve thee in pureness of living and truth.
1st Sunday after Easter

12 O Almighty God, who alone canst order the unruly wills and affections of sinful men; Grant unto thy people, that they may love the thing which thou commandest, and desire that which thou dost promise; that so, among the sundry and manifold changes of the world, our hearts may surely there be fixed, where true joys are to be found.
4th Sunday after Easter

13 We beseech thee, leave us not comfortless; but send to us thine Holy Ghost to comfort us, and exalt us unto the same place whither our Saviour Christ is gone before.
Sunday after Ascension Day

14 God, who as at this time, didst teach the hearts of thy faithful people, by the sending to them the light of thy Holy Spirit; Grant us by the same Spirit to have a right judgement in all things.
Whit-Sunday

15 Because through the weakness of our mortal nature we can do no good thing without thee, grant us the help of thy grace, that in keeping of thy commandments we may please thee, both in will and deed.
1st Sunday after Trinity

16 O God, the protector of all that trust in thee, without whom nothing is strong, nothing is holy; Increase and multiply upon us thy mercy; that, thou being our ruler and guide, we may so pass through things temporal, that we finally lose not the things eternal.
4th Sunday after Trinity

17 Grant, O Lord, we beseech thee, that the course of this world may be so peaceably ordered by thy governance, that thy Church may joyfully serve thee in all godly quietness.
5th Sunday after Trinity

18 O God, who hast prepared for them that love thee such good things as pass man's understanding; Pour into our hearts such love toward thee, that we, loving thee above all things, may obtain thy promises, which exceed all that we can desire.
6th Sunday after Trinity

19 Lord of all power and might, who art the author and giver of all good things; Graft in our hearts the love of thy Name, increase in us true religion, nourish us with all goodness, and of thy great mercy keep us in the same.
7th Sunday after Trinity

20 Pour down upon us the abundance of thy mercy; forgiving us those things whereof our conscience is afraid.
12th Sunday after Trinity

21 O God, forasmuch as without thee we are not able to please thee; Mercifully grant, that thy Holy Spirit may in all things direct and rule our hearts.
19th Sunday after Trinity

22 Grant, we beseech thee, merciful Lord, to thy faithful people pardon and peace, that they may be cleansed from all their sins, and serve thee with a quiet mind.
21st Sunday after Trinity

23 Lord, we beseech thee to keep thy household the

Church in continual godliness.
22nd Sunday after Trinity

1 Grant that those things which we ask faithfully we may obtain effectually.
23rd Sunday after Trinity

2 Stir up, we beseech thee, O Lord, the wills of thy faithful people; that they, plenteously bringing forth the fruit of good works, may of thee be plenteously rewarded.
25th Sunday after Trinity

3 Give us grace, that, being not like children carried away with every blast of vain doctrine, we may be established in the truth of thy holy Gospel.
St. Mark's Day. 25 April

4 O Almighty God, who hast knit together thine elect in one communion and fellowship, in the mystical body of thy Son Christ our Lord; Grant us grace so to follow thy blessed Saints in all virtuous and godly living, that we may come to those unspeakable joys, which thou hast prepared for them that unfeignedly love thee.
All Saints' Day. 1 November

5 So many as intend to be partakers of the holy Communion shall signify their names to the Curate, at least some time the day before.
And if any of those be an open and notorious evil liver, or have done any wrong to his neighbours by word or deed, so that the Congregation be thereby offended; the Curate, having knowledge thereof, shall call him and advertise him, that in any wise he presume not to come to the Lord's Table, until he have openly declared himself to have truly repented and amended his former naughty life.
Holy Communion. Introductory rubric

6 The Table, at the Communion-time having a fair white linen cloth upon it, shall stand in the Body of the Church, or in the Chancel.

7 Almighty God, unto whom all hearts be open, all desires known, and from whom no secrets are hid; Cleanse the thoughts of our hearts by the inspiration of thy Holy Spirit, that we may perfectly love thee, and worthily magnify thy holy Name.
Collect

8 Incline our hearts to keep this law.
Response to Commandments

9 Thou shalt do no murder.
6th Commandment. See 47:24

10 I believe in one God the Father Almighty, Maker of heaven and earth, And of all things visible and invisible:
And in one Lord Jesus Christ, the only-begotten Son of God, Begotten of his Father before all worlds, God of God, Light of Light, Very God of very God, Begotten, not made, Being of one substance with the Father, By whom all things were made.
Nicene Creed. See 334:20, 384:26

11 And I believe in the Holy Ghost, the Lord and giver of life, Who proceedeth from the Father and the Son, Who with the Father and the Son together is worshipped and glorified, Who spake by the Prophets. And I believe one Catholick and Apostolick Church.

12 Let us pray for the whole state of Christ's Church

militant here in earth.
Prayer for the Church Militant

13 We humbly beseech thee most mercifully to accept our alms and oblations, and to receive these our prayers, which we offer unto thy Divine Majesty; beseeching thee to inspire continually the universal Church with the spirit of truth, unity, and concord: And grant, that all they that do confess thy holy Name may agree in the truth of thy holy Word, and live in unity, and godly love.

14 Grant unto her whole Council, and to all that are put in authority under her, that they may truly and indifferently minister justice.
(Of the Queen's government.)

15 Give grace, O heavenly Father, to all Bishops and Curates, that they may both by their life and doctrine set forth thy true and lively Word.

16 We most humbly beseech thee of thy goodness, O Lord, to comfort and succour all them, who in this transitory life are in trouble, sorrow, need, sickness, or any other adversity. And we also bless thy holy Name for all thy servants departed this life in thy faith and fear.

17 Because it is requisite, that no man should come to the holy Communion, but with a full trust in God's mercy, and with a quiet conscience; therefore if there be any of you, who by this means cannot quiet his own conscience herein, but requireth further comfort or counsel, let him come to me, or to some other discreet and learned Minister of God's Word, and open his grief.
First Exhortation

18 Ye that do truly and earnestly repent you of your sins, and are in love and charity with your neighbours, and intend to lead a new life, following the commandments of God, and walking from henceforth in his holy ways; Draw near with faith, and take this holy Sacrament to your comfort; and make your humble confession to Almighty God, meekly kneeling upon your knees.
The Invitation

19 We do earnestly repent, And are heartily sorry for these our misdoings; The remembrance of them is grievous unto us; The burden of them is intolerable.
General Confession

20 Hear what comfortable words our Saviour Christ saith unto all that truly turn to him.
The Comfortable Words

21 Lift up your hearts.
Versicles and Responses. See 335:2

22 It is meet and right so to do.

23 It is very meet, right, and our bounden duty, that we should at all times, and in all places, give thanks unto thee, O Lord, Holy Father, Almighty, Everlasting God.
Therefore with Angels and Archangels, and with all the company of heaven, we laud and magnify thy glorious Name; evermore praising thee, and saying, Holy, holy, holy, Lord God of hosts, heaven and earth are full of thy glory: Glory be to thee, O Lord most High.
Hymn of Praise. See 81:24, 335:3

24 Almighty God, our heavenly Father, who of thy

tender mercy didst give thine only Son Jesus Christ to suffer death upon the cross for our redemption; who made there (by his one oblation of himself once offered) a full, perfect, and sufficient sacrifice, oblation, and satisfaction, for the sins of the whole world.
Prayer of Consecration

1 Who, in the same night that he was betrayed, took Bread; and, when he had given thanks, he brake it, and gave it to his disciples, saying, Take, eat, this is my Body which is given for you: Do this in remembrance of me. Likewise after supper he took the Cup; and, when he had given thanks, he gave it to them, saying, Drink ye all of this; for this is my Blood of the New Testament, which is shed for you and for many for the remission of sins: Do this, as oft as ye shall drink it, in remembrance of me.

2 Although we be unworthy, through our manifold sins, to offer unto thee any sacrifice, yet we beseech thee to accept this our bounden duty and service; not weighing our merits, but pardoning our offences.
1st Prayer of Oblation

3 We are very members incorporate in the mystical body of thy Son, which is the blessed company of all faithful people; and are also heirs through hope of thy everlasting kingdom.
2nd (alternative) Prayer of Oblation

4 The blessing of God Almighty, the Father, the Son, and the Holy Ghost, be amongst you and remain with you always.
The Blessing

5 Assist us mercifully, O Lord, in these our supplications and prayers, and dispose the way of thy servants towards the attainment of everlasting salvation; that, among all the changes and chances of this mortal life, they may ever be defended by thy most gracious and ready help.
Collects after the Offertory, 1

6 Prevent us, O Lord, in all our doings with thy most gracious favour, and further us with thy continual help; that in all our works, begun, continued, and ended in thee, we may glorify thy holy Name.
4

7 Those things, which for our unworthiness we dare not, and for our blindness we cannot ask, vouchsafe to give us, for the worthiness of thy Son Jesus Christ our Lord.
5

8 It is expedient that Baptism be administered in the vulgar tongue.
Publick Baptism of Infants. Introductory rubric

9 O merciful God, grant that the old Adam in this Child may be so buried, that the new man may be raised up in him.
Invocation of blessing on the child

10 Humbly we beseech thee to grant, that he, being dead unto sin, and living unto righteousness, and being buried with Christ in his death, may crucify the old man, and utterly abolish the whole body of sin.
Thanksgiving

11 And as for you, who have now by Baptism put on Christ, it is your part and duty also, being made the children of God and of the light, by faith in Jesus

Christ, to walk answerably to your Christian calling, and as becometh the children of light.
Publick Baptism of Such as are of Riper Years. Priest's final address

12 Question. What is your Name?
Answer. N or M.
Question. Who gave you this Name?
Answer. My Godfathers and Godmothers in my Baptism; wherein I was made a member of Christ, the child of God, and an inheritor of the kingdom of heaven.
Catechism

13 I should renounce the devil and all his works, the pomps and vanity of this wicked world, and all the sinful lusts of the flesh.

14 Question. What dost thou chiefly learn by these Commandments?
Answer. I learn two things: my duty towards God, and my duty to my Neighbour.

15 My duty towards my Neighbour, is to love him as myself, and to do to all men, as I would they should do unto me.

16 To submit myself to all my governors, teachers, spiritual pastors and masters.

17 To keep my hands from picking and stealing, and my tongue from evil-speaking, lying, and slandering.

18 Not to covet nor desire other men's goods; but to learn and labour truly to get mine own living, and to do my duty in that state of life, unto which it shall please God to call me.

19 Question. How many Sacraments hath Christ ordained in his Church?
Answer. Two only, as generally necessary to salvation, that is to say, Baptism, and the Supper of the Lord.
Question. What meanest thou by this word Sacrament?
Answer. I mean an outward and visible sign of an inward and spiritual grace.

20 Our help is in the name of the Lord;
Who hath made heaven and earth.
Order of Confirmation. See 398:9

21 Lord, hear our prayers.
And let our cry come unto thee.

22 Defend, O Lord, this thy Child [or this thy Servant] with thy heavenly grace, that he may continue thine for ever; and daily increase in thy holy Spirit more and more, until he come unto thy everlasting kingdom.

23 If any of you know cause, or just impediment, why these two persons should not be joined together in holy Matrimony, ye are to declare it. This is the first [second, or third] time of asking.
Solemnization of Matrimony. The Banns

24 Dearly beloved, we are gathered together here in the sight of God, and in the face of this congregation, to join together this Man and this Woman in holy Matrimony.
Exhortation

25 Which holy estate Christ adorned and beautified with his presence, and first miracle that he wrought, in Cana of Galilee; and is commended of Saint Paul to be honourable among all men: and therefore not by any to be enterprised, nor taken in hand, unadvisedly, lightly,

or wantonly, to satisfy men's carnal lusts and appetites, like brute beasts that have no understanding.

1 First, It was ordained for the procreation of children, to be brought up in the fear and nurture of the Lord, and to the praise of his holy Name.

2 If any man can shew any just cause, why they may not lawfully be joined together, let him now speak, or else hereafter for ever hold his peace.

3 Wilt thou have this Woman to thy wedded wife, to live together after God's ordinance in the holy estate of Matrimony? Wilt thou love her, comfort her, honour, and keep her in sickness and in health; and, forsaking all other, keep thee only unto her, so long as ye both shall live?
Betrothal

4 I *N* take thee *N* to my wedded husband, to have and to hold from this day forward, for better for worse, for richer for poorer, in sickness and in health, to love, cherish, and to obey, till death us do part, according to God's holy ordinance; and thereto I give thee my troth.
The Man will have used the words 'I plight thee my troth' and not 'to obey'.

5 With this Ring I thee wed, with my body I thee worship, and with all my worldly goods I thee endow.
Wedding

6 Those whom God hath joined together let no man put asunder.

7 Forasmuch as *N* and *N* have consented together in holy wedlock, and have witnessed the same before God and this company, and thereto have given and pledged their troth either to other, and have declared the same by giving and receiving of a Ring, and by joining of hands; I pronounce that they be Man and Wife together.
Minister's declaration

8 Peace be to this house, and to all that dwell in it.
Visitation of the Sick

9 Unto God's gracious mercy and protection we commit thee.

10 The Office ensuing is not to be used for any that die unbaptized, or excommunicate, or have laid violent hands upon themselves.
Burial of the Dead. Introductory rubric

11 Man that is born of a woman hath but a short time to live, and is full of misery.
First anthem. See 52:26

12 In the midst of life we are in death.

13 Forasmuch as it hath pleased Almighty God of his great mercy to take unto himself the soul of our dear brother here departed, we therefore commit his body to the ground; earth to earth, ashes to ashes, dust to dust; in sure and certain hope of the Resurrection to eternal life, through our Lord Jesus Christ; who shall change our vile body, that it may be like unto his glorious body, according to the mighty working, whereby he is able to subdue all things to himself.
Interment

14 Blessed is the man that hath not walked in the counsel of the ungodly, nor stood in the way of sinners: and hath not sat in the seat of the scornful.
Psalms 1:1

15 Why do the heathen so furiously rage together: and why do the people imagine a vain thing?
2:1

16 Let us break their bonds asunder: and cast away their cords from us.
3

17 The Lord shall have them in derision.
4

18 Thou shalt bruise them with a rod of iron: and break them in pieces like a potter's vessel.
9

19 Kiss the Son, lest he be angry, and so ye perish from the right way: if his wrath be kindled, (yea, but a little,) blessed are all they that put their trust in him.
12

20 Stand in awe, and sin not: commune with your own heart, and in your chamber, and be still.
4:4

21 Lord, lift thou up: the light of thy countenance upon us.
7

22 I will lay me down in peace, and take my rest.
9

23 The Lord will abhor both the bloodthirsty and deceitful man.
5:6

24 Make thy way plain before my face.
8

25 Let them perish through their own imaginations.
11

26 I am weary of my groaning; every night wash I my bed: and water my couch with my tears.
6:6

27 Away from me, all ye that work vanity.
8

28 Out of the mouth of very babes and sucklings hast thou ordained strength, because of thine enemies: that thou mightest still the enemy, and the avenger.
For I will consider thy heavens, even the works of thy fingers: the moon and the stars, which thou hast ordained.
What is man, that thou art mindful of him: and the son of man, that thou visitest him?
Thou madest him lower than the angels: to crown him with glory and worship.
8:2

29 Up, Lord, and let not man have the upper hand.
9:19

30 He that said in his heart, Tush, I shall never be cast down: there shall no harm happen unto me.
10:6

31 Upon the ungodly he shall rain snares, fire and brimstone, storm and tempest: this shall be their portion to drink.
11:7

32 Help me, Lord, for there is not one godly man left: for the faithful are minished from among the children of men.
They talk of vanity every one with his neighbour: they do but flatter with their lips, and dissemble in their double heart.
12:1

1 How long wilt thou forget me, O Lord, for ever: how long wilt thou hide thy face from me?
13:1

2 The fool hath said in his heart: There is no God. They are corrupt, and become abominable in their doings: there is none that doeth good, no not one.
14:1

3 They are all gone out of the way, they are altogether become abominable.
4

4 Lord, who shall dwell in thy tabernacle: or who shall rest upon thy holy hill?
Even he, that leadeth an uncorrupt life: and doeth the thing which is right, and speaketh the truth from his heart.
He that hath used no deceit in his tongue, nor done evil to his neighbour: and hath not slandered his neighbour.
15:1

5 He that sweareth unto his neighbour, and disappointeth him not: though it were to his own hindrance.
He that hath not given his money upon usury: nor taken reward against the innocent.
Whoso doeth these things: shall never fall.
5

6 The lot is fallen unto me in a fair ground: yea, I have a goodly heritage.
16:7. The Authorized Version of the Bible (Psalms 16:6) has 'The lines are fallen unto me in pleasant places'.

7 Thou shalt not leave my soul in hell: neither shalt thou suffer thy Holy One to see corruption.
11

8 He rode upon the cherubims, and did fly: he came flying upon the wings of the wind.
18:10

9 At the brightness of his presence his clouds removed: hailstones, and coals of fire.
12

10 With the help of my God I shall leap over the wall.
29

11 The heavens declare the glory of God: and the firmament sheweth his handy-work.
One day telleth another: and one night certifieth another.
There is neither speech nor language: but their voices are heard among them.
Their sound is gone out into all lands: and their words into the ends of the world.
In them hath he set a tabernacle for the sun: which cometh forth as a bridegroom out of his chamber, and rejoiceth as a giant to run his course.
19:1

12 The law of the Lord is an undefiled law, converting the soul: the testimony of the Lord is sure, and giveth wisdom unto the simple.
The statutes of the Lord are right, and rejoice the heart: the commandment of the Lord is pure, and giveth light unto the eyes.
The fear of the Lord is clean, and endureth for ever: the judgements of the Lord are true, and righteous altogether.
More to be desired are they than gold, yea, than much fine gold: sweeter also than honey, and the

honey-comb.
7

13 Who can tell how oft he offendeth: O cleanse thou me from my secret faults.
Keep thy servant also from presumptuous sins, lest they get the dominion over me: so shall I be undefiled, and innocent from the great offence.
Let the words of my mouth, and the meditation of my heart: be alway acceptable in thy sight,
O Lord: my strength, and my redeemer.
12

14 Some put their trust in chariots, and some in horses: but we will remember the Name of the Lord our God.
20:7

15 They intended mischief against thee: and imagined such a device as they are not able to perform.
21:11

16 My God, my God, look upon me; why hast thou forsaken me: and art so far from my health, and from the words of my complaint?
O my God, I cry in the day-time, but thou hearest not: and in the night-season also I take no rest.
22:1. See 68:24

17 But as for me, I am a worm, and no man: a very scorn of men, and the out-cast of the people.
All they that see me laugh me to scorn: they shoot out their lips, and shake their heads, saying,
He trusted in God, that he would deliver him: let him deliver him, if he will have him.
6

18 Many oxen are come about me: fat bulls of Basan close me in on every side.
12

19 I am poured out like water, and all my bones are out of joint: my heart also in the midst of my body is even like melting wax.
14

20 They pierced my hands and my feet; I may tell all my bones: they stand staring and looking upon me.
They part my garments among them: and cast lots upon my vesture.
17

21 The Lord is my shepherd: therefore can I lack nothing.
He shall feed me in a green pasture: and lead me forth beside the waters of comfort.
23:1

22 Yea, though I walk through the valley of the shadow of death, I will fear no evil: for thou art with me; thy rod and thy staff comfort me.
Thou shalt prepare a table before me against them that trouble me: thou hast anointed my head with oil, and my cup shall be full.
But thy loving-kindness and mercy shall follow me all the days of my life: and I will dwell in the house of the Lord for ever.
4

23 The earth is the Lord's, and all that therein is: the compass of the world, and they that dwell therein.
24:1

24 Lift up your heads, O ye gates, and be ye lift up, ye everlasting doors: and the King of glory shall come in.
Who is the King of glory: it is the Lord strong and

mighty, even the Lord mighty in battle.
7

1 Even the Lord of hosts, he is the King of glory.
10

2 O remember not the sins and offences of my youth.
25:6

3 Deliver Israel, O God: out of all his troubles.
21

4 Examine me, O Lord, and prove me: try out my reins and my heart.
26:2

5 I will wash my hands in innocency, O Lord: and so will I go to thine altar;
That I may shew the voice of thanksgiving: and tell of all thy wondrous works.
6

6 My foot standeth right: I will praise the Lord in the congregation.
12

7 The Lord is my light, and my salvation; whom then shall I fear: the Lord is the strength of my life; of whom then shall I be afraid?
27:1. See 83:5

8 Teach me thy way, O Lord: and lead me in the right way, because of mine enemies.
13

9 I should utterly have fainted: but that I believe verily to see the goodness of the Lord in the land of the living.
15

10 The voice of the Lord breaketh the cedar-trees: yea, the Lord breaketh the cedars of Libanus.
He maketh them also to skip like a calf: Libanus also, and Sirion, like a young unicorn.
29:5

11 The voice of the Lord maketh the hinds to bring forth young, and discovereth the thick bushes.
8

12 The Lord shall give strength unto his people: the Lord shall give his people the blessing of peace.
10

13 Sing praises unto the Lord, O ye saints of his: and give thanks unto him for a remembrance of his holiness.
For his wrath endureth but the twinkling of an eye, and in his pleasure is life: heaviness may endure for a night, but joy cometh in the morning.
30:4

14 Then cried I unto thee, O Lord: and gat me to my Lord right humbly.
8

15 Into thy hands I commend my spirit.
31:6. See 71:14

16 Blessed is the man unto whom the Lord imputeth no sin: and in whose spirit there is no guile.
For while I held my tongue: my bones consumed away through my daily complaining.
32:2

17 For this shall every one that is godly make his prayer unto thee, in a time when thou mayest be found: but in the great water-floods they shall not come nigh him.
7

18 I will inform thee, and teach thee in the way wherein thou shalt go: and I will guide thee with mine eye.
Be ye not like to horse and mule, which have no understanding: whose mouths must be held with bit and bridle, lest they fall upon thee.
Great plagues remain for the ungodly: but whoso putteth his trust in the Lord, mercy embraceth him on every side.
9

19 Sing unto the Lord a new song: sing praises lustily unto him with a good courage.
33:3

20 A horse is counted but a vain thing to save a man: neither shall he deliver any man by his great strength.
16

21 O taste and see, how gracious the Lord is: blessed is the man that trusteth in him.
34:8

22 The lions do lack, and suffer hunger: but they who seek the Lord shall want no manner of thing that is good.
10

23 What man is he that lusteth to live: and would fain see good days?
Keep thy tongue from evil: and thy lips, that they speak no guile.
Eschew evil, and do good: seek peace, and ensue it.
12

24 They rewarded me evil for good: to the great discomfort of my soul.
35:12

25 O deliver my soul from the calamities which they bring on me, and my darling from the lions.
17

26 Fret not thyself because of the ungodly.
37:1

27 The meek-spirited shall possess the earth: and shall be refreshed in the multitude of peace.
11

28 I have been young, and now am old: and yet saw I never the righteous forsaken, nor his seed begging their bread.
25

29 I myself have seen the ungodly in great power: and flourishing like a green bay-tree.
I went by, and lo, he was gone: I sought him, but his place could no where be found.
Keep innocency, and take heed unto the thing that is right: for that shall bring a man peace at the last.
36

30 I held my tongue, and spake nothing: I kept silence, yea, even from good words; but it was pain and grief to me.
My heart was hot within me, and while I was thus musing the fire kindled: and at the last I spake with my tongue;
Lord, let me know mine end, and the number of my days: that I may be certified how long I have to live.
39:3

31 For man walketh in a vain shadow, and disquieteth himself in vain: he heapeth up riches, and cannot tell who shall gather them.
7

1 I waited patiently for the Lord: and he inclined unto me, and heard my calling.
He brought me also out of the horrible pit, out of the mire and clay: and set my feet upon the rock, and ordered my goings.
40:1

2 Sacrifice, and meat-offering, thou wouldest not: but mine ears hast thou opened.
Burnt-offerings, and sacrifice for sin, hast thou not required: then said I, Lo, I come.
In the volume of the book it is written of me, that I should fulfil thy will, O my God.
8

3 Thou art my helper and redeemer: make no long tarrying, O my God.
21

4 Blessed is he that considereth the poor and needy: the Lord shall deliver him in the time of trouble.
41:1

5 Yea, even mine own familiar friend, whom I trusted: who did also eat of my bread, hath laid great wait for me.
9. The Authorized Version of the Bible has '...hath lifted up his heel against me'.

6 Like as the hart desireth the water-brooks: so longeth my soul after thee, O God.
42:1

7 Why art thou so full of heaviness, O my soul: and why art thou so disquieted within me?
6

8 My God, my soul is vexed within me: therefore will I remember thee concerning the land of Jordan, and the little hill of Hermon.
One deep calleth another, because of the noise of the water-pipes: all thy waves and storms are gone over me.
8

9 I will say unto the God of my strength, Why hast thou forgotten me: why go I thus heavily, while the enemy oppresseth me?
My bones are smitten asunder as with a sword: while mine enemies that trouble me cast me in the teeth;
Namely, while they say daily unto me: Where is now thy God?
11. See 234:13

10 Give sentence with me, O God, and defend my cause against the ungodly people: O deliver me from the deceitful and wicked man.
43:1

11 O send out thy light and thy truth, that they may lead me: and bring me unto thy holy hill, and to thy dwelling.
And that I may go unto the altar of God, even unto the God of my joy and gladness: and upon the harp will I give thanks unto thee, O God, my God.
3

12 O put thy trust in God: for I will yet give him thanks, which is the help of my countenance, and my God.
6

13 We have heard with our ears, O God, our fathers have told us: what thou hast done in their time of old.
44:1

14 My heart is inditing of a good matter: I speak of the things which I have made unto the King.
My tongue is the pen: of a ready writer.
45:1

15 Thou hast loved righteousness, and hated iniquity: wherefore God, even thy God, hath anointed thee with the oil of gladness above thy fellows.
8

16 Kings' daughters were among thy honourable women: upon thy right hand did stand the queen in a vesture of gold, wrought about with divers colours.
10

17 The King's daughter is all glorious within: her clothing is of wrought gold.
She shall be brought unto the King in raiment of needlework: the virgins that be her fellows shall bear her company, and shall be brought unto thee.
14

18 Instead of thy fathers thou shalt have children: whom thou mayest make princes in all lands.
17

19 God is our hope and strength: a very present help in trouble.
Therefore will we not fear, though the earth be moved: and though the hills be carried into the midst of the sea.
46:1

20 God is in the midst of her, therefore shall she not be removed: God shall help her, and that right early.
The heathen make much ado, and the kingdoms are moved: but God hath shewed his voice, and the earth shall melt away.
The Lord of hosts is with us: the God of Jacob is our refuge.
5

21 He maketh wars to cease in all the world: he breaketh the bow, and knappeth the spear in sunder, and burneth the chariots in the fire.
Be still then, and know that I am God: I will be exalted among the heathen, and I will be exalted in the earth.
9

22 O clap your hands together, all ye people: O sing unto God with the voice of melody.
47:1

23 He shall subdue the people under us: and the nations under our feet.
3

24 God is gone up with a merry noise: and the Lord with the sound of the trump.
5

25 For lo, the kings of the earth: are gathered, and gone by together.
They marvelled to see such things: they were astonished, and suddenly cast down.
48:3

26 Thou shalt break the ships of the sea: through the east-wind.
6

27 Walk about Sion, and go round about her: and tell the towers thereof.
Mark well her bulwarks, set up her houses: that ye may tell them that come after.
11

28 Wise men also die, and perish together: as well as the

ignorant and foolish, and leave their riches for other.
And yet they think that their houses shall continue for
ever: and that their dwelling-places shall endure from
one generation to another; and call the lands after their
own names.
Nevertheless, man will not abide in honour: seeing he
may be compared unto the beasts that perish; this is the
way of them.
49:10

1 They lie in the hell like sheep, death gnaweth upon
them, and the righteous shall have domination over
them in the morning: their beauty shall consume in the
sepulchre out of their dwelling.
14

2 All the beasts of the forest are mine: and so are the
cattle upon a thousand hills.
50:10

3 Thinkest thou that I will eat bulls' flesh: and drink the
blood of goats?
13

4 Wash me throughly from my wickedness: and cleanse
me from my sin.
For I acknowledge my faults: and my sin is ever before
me.
Against thee only have I sinned, and done this evil in
thy sight.
51:2

5 Behold, I was shapen in wickedness: and in sin hath
my mother conceived me.
But lo, thou requirest truth in the inward parts: and
shalt make me to understand wisdom secretly.
Thou shalt purge me with hyssop, and I shall be clean:
thou shalt wash me, and I shall be whiter than snow.
Thou shalt make me hear of joy and gladness: that the
bones which thou hast broken may rejoice.
5. See 334:10

6 Make me a clean heart, O God: and renew a right
spirit within me.
Cast me not away from thy presence: and take not thy
holy Spirit from me.
O give me the comfort of thy help again: and stablish
me with thy free Spirit.
10

7 Deliver me from blood-guiltiness, O God.
14

8 Thou shalt open my lips, O Lord: and my mouth shall
shew thy praise.
For thou desirest no sacrifice, else would I give it
thee: but thou delightest not in burnt-offerings.
The sacrifice of God is a troubled spirit: a broken and
contrite heart, O God, shalt thou not despise.
O be favourable and gracious unto Sion: build thou the
walls of Jerusalem.
15

9 Then shall they offer young bullocks upon thine altar.
19

10 O that I had wings like a dove: for then would I flee
away, and be at rest.
55:6

11 It was even thou, my companion: my guide, and mine
own familiar friend.
We took sweet counsel together: and walked in the
house of God as friends.
14

12 The words of his mouth were softer than butter, having
war in his heart: his words were smoother than oil, and
yet they be very swords.
22

13 Thou tellest my flittings; put my tears into thy bottle:
are not these things noted in thy book?
56:8

14 Under the shadow of thy wings shall be my refuge,
until this tyranny be over-past.
57:1

15 God shall send forth his mercy and truth: my soul is
among lions.
And I lie even among the children of men, that are set
on fire: whose teeth are spears and arrows, and their
tongue a sharp sword.
Set up thyself, O God, above the heavens: and thy
glory above all the earth.
They have laid a net for my feet, and pressed down my
soul: they have digged a pit before me, and are fallen
into the midst of it themselves.
4

16 Awake up, my glory; awake, lute and harp: I myself
will awake right early.
9

17 They are as venomous as the poison of a serpent: even
like the deaf adder that stoppeth her ears;
Which refuseth to hear the voice of the charmer: charm
he never so wisely.
58:4

18 Gilead is mine, and Manasses is mine: Ephraim also is
the strength of my head; Judah is my law-giver;
Moab is my wash-pot; over Edom will I cast out my
shoe: Philistia, be thou glad of me.
60:7

19 Their delight is in lies; they give good words with
their mouth, but curse with their heart.
62:4

20 As for the children of men, they are but vanity: the
children of men are deceitful upon the weights, they
are altogether lighter than vanity itself.
O trust not in wrong and robbery, give not yourselves
unto vanity: if riches increase, set not your heart upon
them.
God spake once, and twice I have also heard the same:
that power belongeth unto God;
And that thou, Lord, art merciful: for thou rewardest
every man according to his work.
9

21 My soul thirsteth for thee, my flesh also longeth after
thee: in a barren and dry land where no water is.
63:2

22 These also that seek the hurt of my soul: they shall go
under the earth.
Let them fall upon the edge of the sword: that they
may be a portion for foxes.
10

23 Thou, O God, art praised in Sion: and unto thee shall
the vow be performed in Jerusalem.
Thou that hearest the prayer: unto thee shall all flesh
come.
65:1

1 Thou that art the hope of all the ends of the earth, and of them that remain in the broad sea.
Who in his strength setteth fast the mountains: and is girded about with power.
Who stilleth the raging of the sea: and the noise of his waves, and the madness of the people.
5

2 Thou visitest the earth, and blessest it: thou makest it very plenteous.
9

3 Thou waterest her furrows, thou sendest rain into the little valleys thereof: thou makest it soft with the drops of rain, and blessest the increase of it.
Thou crownest the year with thy goodness: and thy clouds drop fatness.
They shall drop upon the dwellings of the wilderness: and the little hills shall rejoice on every side.
The folds shall be full of sheep: the valleys also shall stand so thick with corn, that they shall laugh and sing.
11

4 God be merciful unto us, and bless us: and shew us the light of his countenance, and be merciful unto us;
That thy way may be known upon earth: thy saving health among all nations.
Let the people praise thee, O God: yea, let all the people praise thee.
67:1

5 Then shall the earth bring forth her increase: and God, even our own God, shall give us his blessing.
6

6 Let God arise, and let his enemies be scattered: let them also that hate him flee before him.
68:1

7 O sing unto God, and sing praises unto his name: magnify him that rideth upon the heavens, as it were upon an horse; praise him in his name JAH, and rejoice before him.
He is a Father of the fatherless, and defendeth the cause of the widows: even God in his holy habitation.
He is the God that maketh men to be of one mind in an house, and bringeth the prisoners out of captivity: but letteth the runagates continue in scarceness.
O God, when thou wentest forth before the people: when thou wentest through the wilderness,
the earth shook, and the heavens dropped at the presence of God.
4

8 The Lord gave the word: great was the company of the preachers.
Kings with their armies did flee, and were discomfited: and they of the household divided the spoil.
Though ye have lien among the pots, yet shall ye be as the wings of a dove: that is covered with silver wings, and her feathers like gold.
11

9 Why hop ye so, ye high hills? this is God's hill, in which it pleaseth him to dwell.
16

10 Thou art gone up on high, thou hast led captivity captive, and received gifts for men.
18

11 The zeal of thine house hath even eaten me.
69:9

12 Thy rebuke hath broken my heart; I am full of heaviness: I looked for some to have pity on me, but there was no man, neither found I any to comfort me.
They gave me gall to eat: and when I was thirsty they gave me vinegar to drink.
21

13 Let their habitation be void: and no man to dwell in their tents.
26

14 Let them be wiped out of the book of the living: and not be written among the righteous.
29

15 Let them be ashamed and confounded that seek after my soul: let them be turned backward and put to confusion that wish me evil.
Let them for their reward be soon brought to shame: that cry over me, There, there.
70:2

16 I am become as it were a monster unto many: but my sure trust is in thee.
71:6

17 Cast me not away in the time of age: forsake me not when my strength faileth me.
8

18 Give the King thy judgements, O God: and thy righteousness unto the King's son.
72:1

19 The mountains also shall bring peace: and the little hills righteousness unto the people.
3

20 His dominion shall be also from the one sea to the other: and from the flood unto the world's end.
They that dwell in the wilderness shall kneel before him: his enemies shall lick the dust.
The Kings of Tharsis and of the isles shall give presents: the kings of Arabia and Saba shall bring gifts.
All kings shall fall down before him: all nations shall do him service.
8

21 He shall live, and unto him shall be given of the gold of Arabia.
15

22 Therefore fall the people unto them: and thereout suck they no small advantage.
Tush, say they, how should God perceive it: is there knowledge in the most High?
73:10

23 Then thought I to understand this: but it was too hard for me.
Until I went into the sanctuary of God: then understood I the end of these men.
15

24 O deliver not the soul of thy turtle-dove unto the multitude of the enemies: and forget not the congregation of the poor for ever.
74:20

25 The earth is weak, and all the inhabiters thereof: I bear up the pillars of it.
75:4

26 For promotion cometh neither from the east, nor from

the west: nor yet from the south.
And why? God is the Judge: he putteth down one, and setteth up another.
7

1 In Jewry is God known: his Name is great in Israel.
At Salem is his tabernacle: and his dwelling in Sion.
76:1

2 I have considered the days of old: and the years that are past.
77:5

3 Hear my law, O my people: incline your ears unto the words of my mouth.
I will open my mouth in a parable: I will declare hard sentences of old;
Which we have heard and known: and such as our fathers have told us.
78:1

4 Not to be as their forefathers, a faithless and stubborn generation: a generation that set not their heart aright, and whose spirit cleaveth not stedfastly unto God.
9

5 He divided the sea, and let them go through: he made the waters to stand on an heap.
14

6 He rained down manna also upon them for to eat: and gave them food from heaven.
So man did eat angels' food: for he sent them meat enough.
25

7 So the Lord awaked as one out of sleep: and like a giant refreshed with wine.
66

8 Turn us again, O God: shew the light of thy countenance, and we shall be whole.
80:3

9 Sing we merrily unto God our strength: make a cheerful noise unto the God of Jacob.
Take the psalm, bring hither the tabret: the merry harp with the lute.
Blow up the trumpet in the new-moon: even in the time appointed, and upon our solemn feast-day.
81:1

10 I have said, Ye are gods: and ye are all children of the most Highest.
But ye shall die like men: and fall like one of the princes.
82:6

11 O how amiable are thy dwellings: thou Lord of hosts!
My soul hath a desire and longing to enter into the courts of the Lord: my heart and my flesh rejoice in the living God.
Yea, the sparrow hath found her an house, and the swallow a nest where she may lay her young: even thy altars, O Lord of hosts, my King and my God.
84:1

12 Blessed is the man whose strength is in thee: in whose heart are thy ways.
Who going through the vale of misery use it for a well: and the pools are filled with water.
They will go from strength to strength: and unto the God of gods appeareth every one of them in Sion.
5

13 For one day in thy courts: is better than a thousand.

I had rather be a door-keeper in the house of my God: than to dwell in the tents of ungodliness.
10

14 Wilt thou not turn again, and quicken us: that thy people may rejoice in thee?
85:6

15 Mercy and truth are met together: righteousness and peace have kissed each other.
Truth shall flourish out of the earth: and righteousness hath looked down from heaven.
10

16 Very excellent things are spoken of thee: thou city of God.
87:2

17 Lord, thou hast been our refuge: from one generation to another.
Before the mountains were brought forth, or ever the earth and the world were made: thou art God from everlasting, and world without end.
90:1

18 For a thousand years in thy sight are but as yesterday: seeing that is past as a watch in the night.
As soon as thou scatterest them they are even as a sleep: and fade away suddenly like the grass.
In the morning it is green, and groweth up: but in the evening it is cut down, dried up, and withered.
4

19 The days of our age are threescore years and ten; and though men be so strong that they come to fourscore years: yet is their strength then but labour and sorrow; so soon passeth it away, and we are gone.
10

20 So teach us to number our days: that we may apply our hearts unto wisdom.
12

21 For he shall deliver thee from the snare of the hunter: and from the noisome pestilence.
He shall defend thee under his wings, and thou shalt be safe under his feathers: his faithfulness and truth shall be thy shield and buckler.
Thou shalt not be afraid for any terror by night: nor for the arrow that flieth by day;
For the pestilence that walketh in darkness: nor for the sickness that destroyeth in the noon-day.
A thousand shall fall beside thee, and ten thousand at thy right hand: but it shall not come nigh thee.
91:3

22 For thou, Lord, art my hope: thou hast set thine house of defence very high.
There shall no evil happen unto thee: neither shall any plague come nigh thy dwelling.
For he shall give his angels charge over thee: to keep thee in all thy ways.
They shall bear thee in their hands: that thou hurt not thy foot against a stone.
Thou shalt go upon the lion and adder: the young lion and the dragon shalt thou tread under thy feet.
9

23 With long life will I satisfy him: and shew him my salvation.
16

24 The Lord is King, and hath put on glorious apparel: the Lord hath put on his apparel, and girded himself with strength.

He hath made the round world so sure: that it cannot
be moved.
93:1

1 The floods are risen, O Lord, the floods have lift up
their voice: the floods lift up their waves.
The waves of the sea are mighty, and rage horribly:
but yet the Lord, who dwelleth on high, is mightier.
Thy testimonies, O Lord, are very sure: holiness
becometh thine house for ever.
4

2 He that planted the ear, shall he not hear: or he that
made the eye, shall he not see?
94:9

3 O come, let us sing unto the Lord: let us heartily
rejoice in the strength of our salvation.
Let us come before his presence with thanksgiving:
and shew ourselves glad in him with psalms.
95:1. See 83:7

4 In his hand are all the corners of the earth: and the
strength of the hills is his also.
The sea is his, and he made it: and his hands prepared
the dry land.
O come, let us worship and fall down: and kneel
before the Lord our Maker.
For he is the Lord our God: and we are the people of
his pasture, and the sheep of his hand.
To-day if ye will hear his voice, harden not your
hearts: as in the provocation, and as in the day of
temptation in the wilderness;
When your fathers tempted me: proved me, and saw
my works.
Forty years long was I grieved with this generation,
and said: It is a people that do err in their hearts, for
they have not known my ways;
Unto whom I sware in my wrath: that they should not
enter into my rest.
4

5 Ascribe unto the Lord the honour due unto his Name:
bring presents, and come into his courts.
O worship the Lord in the beauty of holiness: let the
whole earth stand in awe of him.
96:8

6 The Lord is King, the earth may be glad thereof: yea,
the multitude of the isles may be glad thereof.
97:1

7 O sing unto the Lord a new song: for he hath done
marvellous things.
With his own right hand, and with his holy arm: hath
he gotten himself the victory.
98:1

8 Praise the Lord upon the harp: sing to the harp with a
psalm of thanksgiving.
With trumpets also, and shawms: O shew yourselves
joyful before the Lord the King.
6

9 With righteousness shall he judge the world: and the
people with equity.
10

10 The Lord is King, be the people never so impatient: he
sitteth between the cherubims, be the earth never so
unquiet.
99:1

11 O be joyful in the Lord, all ye lands: serve the Lord
with gladness, and come before his presence with a
song.
Be ye sure that the Lord he is God: it is he that hath
made us, and not we ourselves; we are his people, and
the sheep of his pasture.
100:1. See 83:8

12 I am become like a pelican in the wilderness: and like
an owl that is in the desert.
I have watched, and am even as it were a sparrow:
that sitteth alone upon the house-top.
102:6

13 Thou, Lord, in the beginning hast laid the foundation
of the earth: and the heavens are the work of thy
hands.
They shall perish, but thou shalt endure: they all shall
wax old as doth a garment;
And as a vesture shalt thou change them, and they
shall be changed: but thou art the same, and thy years
shall not fail.
25

14 Praise the Lord, O my soul: and forget not all his
benefits.
103:2

15 Who satisfieth thy mouth with good things: making
thee young and lusty as an eagle.
5

16 The Lord is full of compassion and mercy:
long-suffering, and of great goodness.
He will not alway be chiding: neither keepeth he his
anger for ever.
8

17 For look how high the heaven is in comparison of the
earth: so great is his mercy also toward them that fear
him.
Look how wide also the east is from the west: so far
hath he set our sins from us.
Yea, like as a father pitieth his own children: even so
is the Lord merciful unto them that fear him.
For he knoweth whereof we are made: he remembereth
that we are but dust.
The days of man are but as grass: for he flourisheth as
a flower of a field.
For as soon as the wind goeth over it, it is gone: and
the place thereof shall know it no more.
11

18 Who layeth the beams of his chambers in the waters:
and maketh the clouds his chariot, and walketh upon
the wings of the wind.
He maketh his angels spirits: and his ministers a
flaming fire.
He laid the foundations of the earth: that it never
should move at any time.
Thou coveredst it with the deep like as with a garment:
the waters stand in the hills.
104:3

19 Thou hast set them their bounds which they shall not
pass: neither turn again to cover the earth.
He sendeth the springs into the rivers: which run
among the hills.
All beasts of the field drink thereof: and the wild asses
quench their thirst.
Beside them shall the fowls of the air have their
habitation: and sing among the branches.
9

20 He bringeth forth grass for the cattle: and green herb

for the service of men;

That he may bring food out of the earth, and wine that maketh glad the heart of man: and oil to make him a cheerful countenance, and bread to strengthen man's heart.

The trees of the Lord also are full of sap: even the cedars of Libanus which he hath planted.
14

1 The high hills are a refuge for the wild goats: and so are the stony rocks for the conies.

He appointed the moon for certain seasons: and the sun knoweth his going down.

Thou makest darkness that it may be night: wherein all the beasts of the forest do move.

The lions roaring after their prey: do seek their meat from God.

The sun ariseth, and they get them away together: and lay them down in their dens.

Man goeth forth to his work, and to his labour: until the evening.

O Lord, how manifold are thy works, in wisdom hast thou made them all; the earth is full of thy riches.

So is the great and wide sea also: wherein are creeping things innumerable, both small and great beasts.

There go the ships, and there is that Leviathan: whom thou hast made to take his pastime therein.

These wait all upon thee: that thou mayest give them meat in due season.
18

2 The earth shall tremble at the look of him: if he do but touch the hills, they shall smoke.
32

3 He had sent a man before them: even Joseph, who was sold to be a bond-servant;

Whose feet they hurt in the stocks: the iron entered into his soul.
105:17

4 The king sent, and delivered him: the prince of the people let him go free.

He made him lord also of his house: and ruler of all his substance;

That he might inform his princes after his will: and teach his senators wisdom.
20

5 Yea, they thought scorn of that pleasant land: and gave no credence to his word;

But murmured in their tents: and hearkened not unto the voice of the Lord.
106:24

6 Thus were they stained with their own works: and went a whoring with their own inventions.
38

7 O that men would therefore praise the Lord for his goodness: and declare the wonders that he doeth for the children of men!

For he satisfieth the empty soul: and filleth the hungry soul with goodness.

Such as sit in darkness, and in the shadow of death: being fast bound in misery and iron;

Because they rebelled against the words of the Lord: and lightly regarded the counsel of the most Highest.
107:8

8 Their soul abhorred all manner of meat: and they were

even hard at death's door.
18

9 They that go down to the sea in ships: and occupy their business in great waters;

These men see the works of the Lord: and his wonders in the deep.
23

10 They reel to and fro, and stagger like a drunken man: and are at their wit's end.

So when they cry unto the Lord in their trouble: he delivereth them out of their distress.

For he maketh the storm to cease: so that the waves thereof are still.

Then are they glad, because they are at rest: and so he bringeth them unto the heaven where they would be.
27

11 The Lord said unto my Lord: Sit thou on my right hand, until I make thine enemies thy footstool.
110:1

12 Thou art a Priest for ever after the order of Melchisedech.
4

13 The fear of the Lord is the beginning of wisdom: a good understanding have all they that do thereafter; the praise of it endureth for ever.
111:10

14 A good man is merciful, and lendeth: and will guide his words with discretion.

For he shall never be moved: and the righteous shall be had in everlasting remembrance.
112:5

15 He maketh the barren woman to keep house: and to be a joyful mother of children.
113:8

16 When Israel came out of Egypt: and the house of Jacob from among the strange people,

Judah was his sanctuary: and Israel his dominion.

The sea saw that, and fled: Jordan was driven back.

The mountains skipped like rams: and the little hills like young sheep.
114:1

17 Not unto us, O Lord, not unto us, but unto thy Name give the praise.
115:1. See 83:10

18 They have mouths, and speak not: eyes have they, and see not.

They have ears, and hear not: noses have they, and smell not.

They have hands, and handle not: feet have they, and walk not: neither speak they through their throat.
5

19 The snares of death compassed me round about: and the pains of hell gat hold upon me.
116:3

20 And why? thou hast delivered my soul from death: mine eyes from tears, and my feet from falling.
8

21 I said in my haste, All men are liars.
10

22 I will pay my vows now in the presence of all his people: right dear in the sight of the Lord is the death of his saints.
13

1 The right hand of the Lord hath the pre-eminence: the right hand of the Lord bringeth mighty things to pass.
118:16

2 The same stone which the builders refused: is become the head-stone in the corner.
This is the Lord's doing: and it is marvellous in our eyes.
This is the day which the Lord hath made: we will rejoice and be glad in it.
22

3 Blessed be he that cometh in the Name of the Lord: we have wished you good luck, ye that are of the house of the Lord.
26

4 Wherewithal shall a young man cleanse his way: even by ruling himself after thy word.
119:9

5 The law of thy mouth is dearer unto me: than thousands of gold and silver.
72

6 Thy word is a lantern unto my feet: and a light unto my paths.
105

7 Woe is me that I am constrained to dwell with Mesech: and to have my habitation among the tents of Kedar.
120:4

8 I labour for peace, but when I speak unto them therof: they make them ready to battle.
6

9 I will lift up mine eyes unto the hills: from whence cometh my help.
My help cometh even from the Lord: who hath made heaven and earth.
He will not suffer thy foot to be moved: and he that keepeth thee will not sleep.
Behold, he that keepeth Israel: shall neither slumber not sleep.
The Lord himself is thy keeper: the Lord is thy defence upon thy right hand;
So that the sun shall not burn thee by day: neither the moon by night.
121:1

10 The Lord shall preserve thy going out, and thy coming in: from this time forth for evermore.
8

11 I was glad when they said unto me: We will go into the house of the Lord.
Our feet shall stand in thy gates: O Jerusalem.
Jerusalem is built as a city: that is at unity in itself.
For thither the tribes go up, even the tribes of the Lord.
122:1

12 O pray for the peace of Jerusalem: they shall prosper that love thee.
Peace be within thy walls: and plenteousness with thy palaces.
For my brethren and companions' sakes: I will wish thee prosperity.
6

13 If the Lord himself had not been on our side, now may Israel say: if the Lord himself had not been on our side, when men rose up against us;

They had swallowed us up quick: when they were so wrathfully displeased at us.
124:1

14 Our soul is escaped even as a bird out of the snare of the fowler: the snare is broken, and we are delivered.
Our help standeth in the Name of the Lord: who hath made heaven and earth.
6

15 The hills stand about Jerusalem: even so standeth the Lord round about his people, from this time forth for evermore.
125:2

16 When the Lord turned again the captivity of Sion: then were we like unto them that dream.
Then was our mouth filled with laughter: and our tongue with joy.
126:1

17 Turn our captivity, O Lord: as the rivers in the south.
They that sow in tears: shall reap in joy.
He that now goeth on his way weeping, and beareth forth good seed: shall doubtless come again with joy, and bring his sheaves with him.
5

18 Except the Lord build the house: their labour is but lost that build it.
Except the Lord keep the city: the watchman waketh but in vain.
127:1. See 83:12

19 Like as the arrows in the hand of the giant: even so are the young children.
Happy is the man that hath his quiver full of them: they shall not be ashamed when they speak with their enemies in the gate.
5

20 Thy wife shall be as the fruitful vine: upon the walls of thine house.
Thy children like the olive-branches: round about thy table.
128:3

21 Many a time have they fought against me from my youth up: may Israel now say.
129:1

22 But they have not prevailed against me.
The plowers plowed upon my back: and made long furrows.
2

23 Out of the deep have I called unto thee, O Lord: Lord, hear my voice.
O let thine ears consider well: the voice of my complaint.
If thou, Lord, wilt be extreme to mark what is done amiss: O Lord, who may abide it?
130:1. See 83:13

24 My soul fleeth unto the Lord: before the morning watch, I say, before the morning watch.
6

25 Lord, I am not high-minded: I have no proud looks.
I do not exercise myself in great matters: which are too high for me.
131:1

26 Behold, how good and joyful a thing it is: brethren, to dwell together in unity!
133:1

1 He smote divers nations: and slew mighty kings;
Sehon king of the Amorites, and Og the king of
Basan: and all the kingdoms of Canaan;
And gave their land to be an heritage: even an heritage
unto Israel his people.
135:10

2 O give thanks unto the Lord, for he is gracious: and
his mercy endureth for ever.
136:1

3 By the waters of Babylon we sat down and wept: when
we remembered thee, O Sion.
As for our harps, we hanged them up: upon the trees
that are therein.
For they that led us away captive required of us then a
song, and melody, in our heaviness: Sing us one of the
songs of Sion.
How shall we sing the Lord's song: in a strange land?
If I forget thee, O Jerusalem: let my right hand forget
her cunning.
If I do not remember thee, let my tongue cleave to the
roof of my mouth: yea, if I prefer not Jerusalem in my
mirth.
137:1

4 O Lord, thou hast searched me out, and known me:
thou knowest my down-sitting, and mine up-rising;
thou understandest my thoughts long before.
139:1

5 Such knowledge is too wonderful and excellent for
me: I cannot attain unto it.
Whither shall I go then from thy Spirit: or whither
shall I go then from thy presence?
If I climb up into the heaven, thou art there: if I go
down to hell, thou art there also.
If I take the wings of the morning: and remain in the
uttermost parts of the sea;
Even there also shall thy hand lead me: and thy right
hand shall hold me.
If I say, Peradventure the darkness shall cover me:
then shall my night be turned to day.
Yea, the darkness is no darkness with thee, but the
night is as clear as the day: the darkness and light to
thee are both alike.
5

6 I will give thanks unto thee, for I am fearfully and
wonderfully made.
13

7 Thine eyes did see my substance, yet being imperfect:
and in thy book were all my members written;
Which day by day were fashioned: when as yet there
were none of them.
15

8 Try me, O God, and seek the ground of my heart:
prove me, and examine my thoughts.
23

9 Let the lifting up of my hands be an evening sacrifice.
Set a watch, O Lord, before my mouth: and keep the
door of my lips.
141:2

10 Let the ungodly fall into their own nets together: and
let me ever escape them.
11

11 Enter not into judgement with thy servant: for in thy
sight shall no man living be justified.
143:2

12 Save me, and deliver me from the hand of strange
children: whose mouth talketh of vanity, and their
right hand is a right hand of iniquity.
That our sons may grow up as the young plants: and
that our daughters may be as the polished corners of
the temple.
144:11

13 That our sheep may bring forth thousands and ten
thousands in our streets.
That our oxen may be strong to labour, that there be no
decay: no leading into captivity, and no complaining in
our streets.
13

14 The Lord upholdeth all such as fall: and lifteth up all
those that are down.
145:14

15 Thou givest them their meat in due season.
Thou openest thine hand: and fillest all things living
with plenteousness.
15

16 O put not your trust in princes, nor in any child of
man: for there is no help in them.
146:2

17 The Lord looseth men out of prison: the Lord giveth
sight to the blind.
7

18 The Lord careth for the strangers; he defendeth the
fatherless and widow: as for the way of the ungodly,
he turneth it upside down.
9

19 A joyful and pleasant thing it is to be thankful.
The Lord doth build up Jerusalem: and gather together
the out-casts of Israel.
He healeth those that are broken in heart: and giveth .
medicine to heal their sickness.
He telleth the number of the stars: and calleth them all
by their names.
147:1

20 He hath no pleasure in the strength of an horse:
neither delighteth he in any man's legs.
10

21 He giveth snow like wool: and scattereth the
hoar-frost like ashes.
He casteth forth his ice like morsels: who is able to
abide his frost?
16

22 Praise the Lord upon earth: ye dragons, and all deeps;
Fire and hail, snow and vapours: wind and storm,
fulfilling his word.
148:7

23 Young men and maidens, old men and children, praise
the Name of the Lord: for his Name only is excellent,
and his praise above heaven and earth.
12

24 Let the saints be joyful with glory: let them rejoice in
their beds.
Let the praises of God be in their mouth: and a
two-edged sword in their hands;
To be avenged of the heathen: and to rebuke the
people;
To bind their kings in chains: and their nobles with
links of iron.
149:5

1 Praise him upon the well-tuned cymbals: praise him
   upon the loud cymbals.
   Let every thing that hath breath: praise the Lord.
   150:5

2 Be pleased to receive into thy Almighty and most
   gracious protection the persons of us thy servants, and
   the Fleet in which we serve.
   Forms of Prayer to be Used at Sea. 1st prayer

3 That we may be...a security for such as pass on the
   seas upon their lawful occasions.

4 We therefore commit his body to the deep, to be
   turned into corruption, looking for the resurrection of
   the body (when the Sea shall give up her dead).
   At the Burial of their Dead at Sea

5 Come, Holy Ghost, our souls inspire,
   And lighten with celestial fire.
   Thou the anointing Spirit art,
   Who dost thy seven-fold gifts impart.

   Thy blessed Unction from above,
   Is comfort, life, and fire of love.
   Enable with perpetual light
   The dulness of our blinded sight.

   Anoint and cheer our soiled face
   With the abundance of thy grace.
   Keep far our foes, give peace at home:
   Where thou art guide, no ill can come.
   Ordering of Priests. Veni, Creator Spiritus

6 Holy Scripture containeth all things necessary to
   salvation.
   Articles of Religion (1562). 6

7 Man is very far gone from original righteousness.
   9

8 It is a thing plainly repugnant to the Word of God, and
   the custom of the Primitive Church, to have publick
   Prayer in the Church, or to minister the Sacraments in
   a tongue not understood of the people.
   24

9 The sacrifices of Masses, in the which it was
   commonly said, that the Priest did offer Christ for the
   quick and the dead, to have remission of pain or guilt,
   were blasphemous fables, and dangerous deceits.
   31

10 The Bishop of Rome hath no jurisdiction in this Realm
    of England.
    37

11 It is lawful for Christian men, at the commandment of
    the Magistrate, to wear weapons, and serve in the
    wars.

12 The Riches and Goods of Christians are not common,
    as touching the right, title, and possession of the same,
    as certain Anabaptists do falsely boast.
    38

13 A Man may not marry his Mother.
    Table of Kindred and Affinity

KEITH PRESTON 1884–1927

14 Of all the literary scenes
    Saddest this sight to me:
    The graves of little magazines
    Who died to make verse free.
    The Liberators

JACQUES PRÉVERT 1900–1977

15   *Notre Père qui êtes aux cieux*
                Restez-y
   Et nous nous resterons sur la terre.
   Our Father which art in heaven, stay there; and as for
   us, we shall stay on the earth.
   Paroles (1946), **Pater Noster**

16 *Je suis comme je suis*
   Je suis faite comme ça.
   I am the way I am. That's the way I'm made.
   Je suis comme je suis

17 *Il a mis le café*
   Dans la tasse
   Il a mis le lait
   Dans la tasse de café
   Il a mis le sucre
   Dans le café au lait
   Avec la petite cuiller
   Il a tourné
   Il a bu le café au lait
   Et il a reposé la tasse
   Sans me parler.
   He put the coffee in the cup. He put the milk in the cup
      of coffee. He put the sugar in the white coffee, with
      the tea-spoon, he stirred. He drank the white coffee
      and he put the cup down. Without speaking to me.
   Déjeuner du Matin

MATTHEW PRIOR 1664–1721

18 He's half absolv'd who has confess'd.
    Alma, c.ii, 1.22

19 Dear Cloe, how blubber'd is that pretty face!
    A Better Answer [to Cloe Jealous]

20 Odds life! must one swear to the truth of a song?

21 I court others in verse: but I love thee in prose:
    And they have my whimsies, but thou hast my heart.

22 The song too daring, and the theme too great!
    Carmen Seculare, 1.308

23 Be to her virtues very kind;
    Be to her faults a little blind;
    Let all her ways be unconfin'd;
    And clap your padlock—on her mind.
    An English Padlock, 1.79

24 To John I ow'd great obligation;
       But John, unhappily, thought fit
    To publish it to all the nation:
       Sure John and I are more than quit.
    Epigram

25 Nobles and heralds, by your leave,
       Here lies what once was Matthew Prior;
    The son of Adam and of Eve,
       Can Bourbon or Nassau go higher?
    Epitaph

26 And oft the pangs of absence to remove
    By letters, soft interpreters of love.
    Henry and Emma, 1.147

27 For the idiom of words very little she heeded,
    Provided the matter she drove at succeeded,
    She took and gave languages just as she needed.
    Jinny the Just

28 Venus, take my votive glass;
       Since I am not what I was,

What from this day I shall be,
Venus, let me never see.
The Lady who Offers her Looking-Glass to Venus

1 The merchant, to secure his treasure,
  Conveys it in a borrowed name:
Euphelia serves to grace my measure;
  But Chloe is my real flame.
An Ode

2 He rang'd his tropes, and preach'd up patience;
Back'd his opinion with quotations.
Paulo Purganti and his Wife, l.138

3 Entire and sure the monarch's rule must prove,
Who founds her greatness on her subjects' love.
Prologue Spoken...on Her Majesty's Birthday, 1704, l.17

4 Cur'd yesterday of my disease,
I died last night of my physician.
The Remedy Worse than the Disease

5 Abra was ready ere I call'd her name;
And, though I call'd another, Abra came.
Solomon (1718), bk.ii, l.362

6 What is a King?—a man condemn'd to bear
The public burden of the nation's care.
bk.iii, l.275

7 For as our diff'rent ages move,
  'Tis so ordained, would Fate but mend it,
That I shall be past making love,
  When she begins to comprehend it.
To a Child of Quality of Five Years Old

8 From ignorance our comfort flows,
The only wretched are the wise.
To the Hon. Charles Montague, l.35

9 No, no; for my virginity,
When I lose that, says Rose, I'll die:
Behind the elms last night, cried Dick,
Rose, were you not extremely sick?
A True Mind

10 I never strove to rule the roast,
She ne'er refus'd to pledge my toast.
The Turtle and the Sparrow, l.334

11 They never taste who always drink;
They always talk, who never think.
Upon this Passage in Scaligerana

ALEXANDRE PRIVAT D'ANGLEMONT
1820?–1859

12 *Je les ai épatés, les bourgeois.*
I flabbergasted them, the *bourgeois*.
Attr. Also attr. to Baudelaire, in the form *Il faut épater le bourgeois*.

ADELAIDE ANN PROCTER 1825–1864

13 Seated one day at the organ,
  I was weary and ill at ease,
And my fingers wandered idly
  Over the noisy keys.
Legends and Lyrics (1858). A Lost Chord

14 But I struck one chord of music,
Like the sound of a great Amen.

PROPERTIUS b. c.51 B.C.

15 *Navita de ventis, de tauris narrat arator,*
  Enumerat miles vulnera, pastor oves.

The seaman tells stories of winds, the ploughman of
  bulls; the soldier details his wounds, the shepherd
  his sheep.
Elegies, II.i.43

16 *Quod si deficiant vires, audacia certe*
  Laus erit: in magnis et voluisse sat est.
Even if strength fail, boldness at least will deserve
  praise: in great endeavours even to have had the
  will is enough.
x.5

17 *Cedite Romani scriptores, cedite Grai!*
  Nescioquid maius nascitur Iliade.
Make way, you Roman writers, make way, Greeks!
  Something greater than the Iliad is born.
xxxiv.65. Of Virgil's *Aeneid*

PROTAGORAS c.481–411 B.C.

18 Man is the measure of all things.
Plato, *Theaetetus*, 160d

PIERRE-JOSEPH PROUDHON 1809–1865

19 *La propriété c'est le vol.*
Property is theft.
Qu'est-ce que la Propriété? (1840), ch.1

MARCEL PROUST 1871–1922

20 *Longtemps je me suis couché de bonne heure.*
For a long time I used to go to bed early.
A la Recherche du Temps Perdu, tr. C.K. Scott-Moncrieff and
S. Hudson (1922–1931), *Du côté de chez Swann*, opening
sentence

21 *Et il ne fut plus question de Swann chez les Verdurin.*
After which there was no more talk of Swann at the
Verdurins'.
pt.II

22 Une dame prétentieuse: *Que pensez-vous de l'amour?*
Mme Leroi: *L'amour? Je le fais souvent, mais je n'en
parle jamais.*
A pushing lady: What are your views on love?
Mme Leroi: Love? I make it constantly but I never talk
about it.
Le Côté de Guermantes, vol.I, ch.3. G.D. Painter, in *Marcel
Proust*, vol.I, ch.7, traces this exchange to a conversation between
Mme Lydie Aubernon and Mme Laure Baignères, at a *soirée* held
by the former.

23 *On l'enterra, mais toute la nuit funèbre, aux vitrines
éclairées, ses livres disposés trois par trois veillaient
commes des anges aux ailes éployées et semblaient,
pour celui qui n'était plus, le symbole de sa
résurrection.*
They buried him, but all through the night of
mourning, in the lighted windows, his books arranged
three by three kept watch like angels with outspread
wings and seemed, for him who was no more, the
symbol of his resurrection.
La Prisonnière, vol. I, ch. 1

24 *Ces dépêches dont M. de Guermantes avait
spirituellement fixé le modèle: 'Impossible venir,
mensonge suit.'*
One of those telegrams of which M. de Guermantes
had wittily fixed the formula: 'Cannot come, lie
follows'.
Le Temps Retrouvé, vol.I, ch.1. See 41:17

1 *Les vrais paradis sont les paradis qu'on a perdus.*
The true paradises are paradises we have lost.
vol.II, ch.3

WILLIAM JEFFREY PROWSE 1836–1870

2 Though the latitude's rather uncertain,
And the longitude also is vague,
The persons I pity who know not the city,
The beautiful city of Prague.
The City of Prague

PUBLILIUS SYRUS 1st cent. B.C.

3 *Inopi beneficium bis dat qui dat celeriter.*
He gives the poor man twice as much good who gives
quickly.
Sententiae, 274. J.W. and A.M. Duff, *Minor Latin Poets*, Loeb edn.
(1934). Proverbially *Bis dat qui cito dat* (He gives twice who gives soon.)

4 *Formosa facies muta commendatio est.*
A beautiful face is a mute recommendation.
199. Tr. Bacon, *Apophthegms*, 12

5 *Iudex damnatur ubi nocens absolvitur.*
The judge is condemned when the guilty party is
acquitted.
296

6 *Necessitas dat legem non ipsa accipit.*
Necessity gives the law without itself acknowledging
one.
444. Proverbially *Necessitas non habet legem* (Necessity has no
law.)

JOHN PUDNEY 1909–1977

7 Do not despair
For Johnny head-in-air;
He sleeps as sound
As Johnny underground.
For Johnny

8 Better by far
For Johnny-the-bright-star,
To keep your head
And see his children fed.

WILLIAM PULTENEY, EARL OF BATH
1684–1764

9 Since twelve honest men have decided the cause,
And were judges of fact, tho' not judges of laws.
The Honest Jury, iii. In *The Craftsman*, 1731, vol.5, 337. Refers
to Sir Philip Yorke's unsuccessful prosecution of *The Craftsman*
(1729)

PUNCH

10 Advice to persons about to marry.—'Don't.'
vol.viii, p.1. 1845

11 The Half-Way House to Rome, Oxford.
vol.xvi, p.36. 1849

12 What is better than presence of mind in a railway
accident? Absence of body.
p.231. 1849

13 Never do to-day what you can put off till to-morrow.
vol.xvii, p.241. 1849

14 Who's 'im, Bill?
A stranger!

'Eave 'arf a brick at 'im.
vol.xxvi, p.82. 1854

15 What is Matter?—Never mind.
What is Mind?—No matter.
vol.xxix, p.19. 1855

16 'Peccavi—I've Scinde' wrote Lord Ellen so proud.
More briefly Dalhousie wrote—'Vovi—I've Oude'.
vol.xxx, p.118. 1856. See 575:8

17 It ain't the 'unting as 'urts 'im, it's the 'ammer,
'ammer, 'ammer along the 'ard 'igh road.
p.218. 1856

18 Mun, a had na' been the-erre abune two hours
when—*bang*—went saxpence!!!
vol.liv, p.235. 1868

19 Cats is 'dogs' and rabbits is 'dogs' and so's Parrats,
but this 'ere 'Tortis' is a insect, and there ain't no
charge for it.
vol.lvi, p.96. 1869

20 Nothink for nothink 'ere, and precious little for
sixpence.
vol.lvii, p.152. 1869

21 Sure, the next train has gone ten minutes ago.
vol.lx, p.206. 1871

22 It appears the Americans have taken umbrage.
The deuce they have! Whereabouts is that?
vol.lxiii, p.189. 1872

23 Go directly—see what she's doing, and tell her she
mustn't.
p.202. 1872

24 There was one poor tiger that hadn't *got* a Christian.
vol.lxviii, p.143. 1875

25 There was an old owl liv'd in an oak
The more he heard, the less he spoke;
The less he spoke, the more he heard
O, if men were all like that wise bird!
p.155. 1875

26 It's worse than wicked, my dear, it's vulgar.
Almanac. 1876

27 What did you take out of the bag, Mamma? *I* only got
sixpence.
vol.lxx, p.139. 1876

28 I never read books—I *write* them.
vol.lxxiv, p.210. 1878

29 I am not hungry; but thank goodness, I am greedy.
vol.lxxv, p.290. 1878

30 *Bishop:*
Who is it that sees and hears all we do, and before
whom even I am but as a crushed worm?
Page:
The Missus my Lord.
vol.lxxix, p.63. 1880

31 Ah whiles hae ma doobts aboot the meenister.
p.275. 1880

32 What sort of a doctor is he?
Oh, well, I don't know very much about his ability;
but he's got a very good bedside manner!
vol.lxxxvi, p.121. 1884

33 I used your soap two years ago; since then I have used
no other.
p.197. 1884

34 Don't look at me, Sir, with—ah—in that tone of

voice.
vol.lxxxvii, p.38. 1884

1 Oh yes! I'm sure he's not so fond of me as at first. He's away so much, neglects me dreadfully, and he's so cross when he comes home. What *shall* I do? Feed the brute!
vol.lxxxix, p.206. 1885

2 Nearly all our best men are dead! Carlyle, Tennyson, Browning, George Eliot!—I'm not feeling very well myself.
vol.civ, p.210. 1893

3 Botticelli isn't a wine, you Juggins! Botticelli's a *cheese!*
vol.cvi, p.270. 1894

4 I'm afraid you've got a bad egg, Mr Jones. Oh no, my Lord, I assure you! Parts of it are excellent!
vol.cix, p.222. 1895

5 Look here, Steward, if this is coffee, I want tea; but if this is tea, then I wish for coffee.
vol.cxxiii, p.44. 1902

ISRAEL PUTNAM 1718–1790

6 Men, you are all marksmen—don't one of you fire until you see the whites of their eyes.
Bunker Hill, 1775. Frothingham, *History of the Siege of Boston* (1873), ch.5, note. Also attributed to William Prescott (1726-95)

PYRRHUS 319–272 B.C

7 One more such victory and we are lost.
Plutarch, *Pyrrhus*. After defeating the Romans at Asculum, 279 B.C.

FRANCIS QUARLES 1592–1644

8 I wish thee as much pleasure in the reading, as I had in the writing.
Emblems (1643). To the Reader

9 The heart is a small thing, but desireth great matters. It is not sufficient for a kite's dinner, yet the whole world is not sufficient for it.
bk.i, No.12. **Hugo de Anima**

10 We spend our midday sweat, our midnight oil; We tire the night in thought, the day in toil.
bk.ii, No.2, 1.33

11 Be wisely worldly, be not worldly wise.
1.46

12 Man is Heaven's masterpiece.
No.6, Epig.6

13 Thou art my way; I wander, if thou fly;
Thou art my light; if hid, how blind am I!
Thou art my life; if thou withdraw, I die.
bk.iii, No.7

14 Our God and soldiers we alike adore
Ev'n at the brink of danger; not before:
After deliverance, both alike requited,
Our God's forgotten, and our soldiers slighted.
Epigram

15 My soul, sit thou a patient looker-on;
Judge not the play before the play is done:
Her plot hath many changes; every day
Speaks a new scene; the last act crowns the play.
Epigram. Respice Finem

16 No man is born unto himself alone;
Who lives unto himself, he lives to none.
Esther, Sect.1, Medit.1

17 He teaches to deny that faintly prays.
A Feast for Worms (1620), Sect.7, Medit.7, 1.2

18 Man is man's A.B.C. There is none that can
Read God aright, unless he first spell Man.
Hieroglyphics of the Life of Man (1638), i, 1.1

19 He that begins to live, begins to die.
Epig.1

20 Physicians of all men are most happy; what good success soever they have, the world proclaimeth, and what faults they commit, the earth covereth.
iv. **Nicocles**

21 We'll cry both arts and learning down,
And hey! then up go we!
The Shepherd's Oracles (1646). Eclogue xi. **Song of Anarchus,** iv

FRANÇOIS QUESNAY 1694–1774

22 *Vous ne connaissez qu'une seule règle du commerce; c'est (pour me servir de vos propres termes) de laisser passer et de laisser faire tous les acheteurs et tous les vendeurs quelconques.*
You recognize but one rule of commerce; that is (to avail myself of your own terms) to allow free passage and freedom of action to all buyers and sellers whoever they may be.
Letter from M. Alpha: see Salleron, *François Quesnay et la Physiocratie* (1958), II.940. Also attr. Marquis d'Argenson, *Mémoires* (1736). See 9:10, 11:25

SIR ARTHUR QUILLER-COUCH 1863–1944

23 The best is the best, though a hundred judges have declared it so.
Oxford Book of English Verse (1900), Preface

JOSIAH QUINCY 1772–1864

24 As it will be the right of all, so it will be the duty of some, definitely to prepare for a separation, amicably if they can, violently if they must.
Abridgement of Debates of Congress, 14 Jan. 1811, vol.iv, p.327

QUINTILIAN A.D.c.35–c.100

25 *Satura quidem tota nostra est.*
Verse satire indeed is entirely our own.
Institutio Oratoria, 10.1.93. Meaning Roman as opposed to Greek.

FRANÇOIS RABELAIS 1494?–c.1553

26 *L'appétit vient en mangeant.*
The appetite grows by eating.
Gargantua (1534), I.v

27 *Natura vacuum abhorret.*
Nature abhors a vacuum.
Quoting, in Latin, article of ancient wisdom. Compare Plutarch, *Moralia,* 'De placitis philosophorum', I. xviii

28 *Fay ce que vouldras.*
Do what you like.
lvii

29 *Quaestio subtilissima, utrum chimera in vacuo bombinans possit comedere secundas intentiones.*

A most subtle question: whether a chimera
bombinating in a vacuum can devour second
intentions.
Pantagruel, II.vii

1 *Il aurait répondu à un page...'Je vais quérir un grand
peut-être...' Puis il avait expiré en disant 'Tirez le
rideau, la farce est jouée'.*
He answered a page...'I am going to seek a great
perhaps...' Then he died, saying 'Bring down the
curtain, the farce is played out.'
Attr. last words. See Jean Fleury, *Rabelais et ses oeuvres* (1877),
vol.I, ch.3, pt.15, p.130. Fleury adds, *'Rien, dans les
contemporains, m'autorise ces récits...Tout cela fait partie de la
légende rabelaisienne.'*

JEAN RACINE 1639–1699

2 *C'était pendant l'horreur d'une profonde nuit.*
It was during the horror of a deep night.
Athalie (1691), ii.5

3 *Elle flotte, elle hésite; en un mot, elle est femme.*
She floats, she hesitates; in a word, she's a woman.
iii.3

4 *Ce n'est plus une ardeur dans mes veines cachée:
C'est Vénus tout entière à sa proie attachée.*
It's no longer a warmth hidden in my veins: it's Venus
    entire and whole fastening on her prey.
Phèdre (1677), I.iii

5 *Point d'argent, point de Suisse, et ma porte était
close.*
No money, no service, and my door stayed shut.
Les Plaideurs (1668), I.i

6 *Sans argent l'honneur n'est qu'une maladie.*
Honour, without money, is just a disease.

VICE-ADMIRAL THOMAS RAINBOROWE
d. 1648

7 The poorest he that is in England hath a life to live as
the greatest he.
In the Army debates at Putney, 29 Oct. 1647. Peacock, *Life of
Rainborowe.*

SIR WALTER RALEGH 1552?–1618

8 Now what is love? I pray thee, tell.
It is that fountain and that well,
Where pleasure and repentance dwell.
It is perhaps that sauncing bell,
That tolls all in to heaven or hell:
And this is love, as I hear tell.
A Description of Love

9 If all the world and love were young,
And truth in every shepherd's tongue,
These pretty pleasures might me move
To live with thee, and be thy love.
Answer to Marlow. See 187:24, 329:23, 495:16

10 Go, Soul, the body's guest,
    Upon a thankless arrant:
Fear not to touch the best;
    The truth shall be thy warrant:
        Go, since I needs must die,
        And give the world the lie.
The Lie, i

11 Only we die in earnest, that's no jest.
On the Life of Man

12 Give me my scallop-shell of quiet,
My staff of faith to walk upon,
My scrip of joy, immortal diet,
My bottle of salvation,
My gown of glory, hope's true gage,
And thus I'll take my pilgrimage.
The Passionate Man's Pilgrimage

13 'As you came from the holy land
    Of Walsinghame,
Met you not with my true love
    By the way as you came?'

'How shall I know your true love,
    That have met many one
As I went to the holy land,
    That have come, that have gone?'
Walsingham

14 Fain would I climb, yet fear I to fall.
Line written on a Window-Pane. Fuller, *Worthies of England,*
vol.i, p.419. See 206:1

15 Even such is Time, which takes in trust
Our youth, our joys, and all we have,
And pays us but with age and dust;
Who in the dark and silent grave,
When we have wandered all our ways,
Shuts up the story of our days:
And from which earth, and grave, and dust,
The Lord shall raise me up, I trust.
Written the night before his death. Found in his Bible in the
Gate-house at Westminster

16 O eloquent, just, and mighty Death!...thou hast drawn
together all the farstretched greatness, all the pride,
cruelty, and ambition of man, and covered it all over
with these two narrow words, *Hic jacet.*
A History of the World (1614), bk.v, ch.vi, 12

17 [Feeling the edge of the axe before his execution:]
'Tis a sharp remedy, but a sure one for all ills.
David Hume, *History of Great Britain* (1754), vol.i, ch.iv, p.72

18 [When asked which way he preferred to lay his head
on the block:]
So the heart be right, it is no matter which way the
head lies.
W. Stebbing, *Sir Walter Raleigh,* ch.xxx

19 I have a long journey to take, and must bid the
company farewell.
Edward Thompson, *Sir Walter Raleigh,* ch.26

SIR WALTER RALEIGH 1861–1922

20 I wish I loved the Human Race;
I wish I loved its silly face;
I wish I liked the way it walks;
I wish I liked the way it talks;
And when I'm introduced to one
I wish I thought *What Jolly Fun!*
Laughter from a Cloud (1923), p.228. **Wishes of an Elderly
Man**

JULIAN RALPH 1853–1903

21 News value.
Lecture to Brander Matthews's English Class, Columbia, 1892.
Thomas Beer, *Mauve Decade*

SRINIVASA RAMANUJAN 1887–1920

22 No, it is a very interesting number; it is the smallest

number expressible as a sum of two cubes in two different ways.
Hardy had referred to a cab's number—1729—as 'dull'. The cube roots for the two sums are 1 and 12, and 9 and 10. *Collected Papers of Srinivasa Ramanujan* (1927), Notice by G.H. Hardy, iv

TERENCE RATTIGAN 1911–1977

1 A nice respectable, middle-class, middle-aged maiden lady, with time on her hands and the money to help her pass it...Let us call her Aunt Edna...Aunt Edna is universal, and to those who feel that all the problems of the modern theatre might be saved by her liquidation, let me add that...She is also immortal.
Collected Plays (1953), Vol.II, Preface

2 *Brian:* Elle a des idées au-dessus de sa gare. *Kenneth:* You can't do it like that. You can't say au-dessus de sa gare. It isn't that sort of station.
French Without Tears (1937), Act I

CHARLES READE 1814–1884

3 *Courage, mon ami, le diable est mort!*
The Cloister and the Hearth (1861), ch.24, and *passim*

4 Sow an act, and you reap a habit. Sow a habit, and you reap a character. Sow a character, and you reap a destiny.
Attr. See N. & Q., 9th series, vol.12, p.377

HENRY REED 1914–

5 To-day we have naming of parts. Yesterday
We had daily cleaning. And tomorrow morning,
We shall have what to do after firing. But to-day,
To-day we have naming of parts.
Naming of Parts (1946)

6 And this you can see is the bolt. The purpose of this
Is to open the breech, as you see. We can slide it
Rapidly backwards and forwards: we call this
Easing the spring. And rapidly backwards and
     forwards
The early bees are assaulting and fumbling the
     flowers:
They call it easing the Spring.

7 And the various holds and rolls and throws and
     breakfalls
Somehow or other I always seemed to put
In the wrong place. And as for war, my wars
     Were global from the start.
Unarmed Combat

JOHN REED 1887–1920

8 Ten Days that Shook the World.
Book title, 1919

GENERAL JOSEPH REED 1741–1785

9 I am not worth purchasing, but such as I am, the King of Great Britain is not rich enough to do it.
U.S. Congress, 11 Aug. 1878. Reed understood himself to have been offered a bribe on behalf of the British Crown.

JULES RENARD 1864–1910

10 *Les bourgeois, ce sont les autres.*
The bourgeois are other people.
Journal, 28 Jan. 1890

DR. MONTAGUE JOHN RENDALL 1862–1950

11 Nation shall speak peace unto nation.
Written as the motto of the BBC in 1927 by Dr. Rendall, one of the first Governors of the Corporation

JEAN RENOIR 1894–1979

12 Is it possible to succeed without any act of betrayal?
My Life and My Films (1974), 'Nana', p.86

PIERRE RENOIR 1841–1919

13 *C'étaient des fous, mais ils avaient cette petite flamme qui ne s'éteint pas.*
They were madmen; but they had in them that little flame which is not to be snuffed out. [The men of the French Commune.]
Jean Renoir, *Renoir*, pt.II, 1962 edn., p.136

FREDERIC REYNOLDS 1764–1841

14 How goes the enemy? [Said by Mr. Ennui, 'the timekiller'.]
The Dramatist (1789), I.i

15 Now do take my advice, and write a play—if any incident happens, remember, it is better to have written a damned play, than no play at all—it snatches a man from obscurity.

SIR JOSHUA REYNOLDS 1723–1792

16 If you have great talents, industry will improve them: if you have but moderate abilities, industry will supply their deficiency.
Discourse to Students of the Royal Academy, 11 Dec. 1769

17 A mere copier of nature can never produce anything great.
14 Dec. 1770

18 He who resolves never to ransack any mind but his own, will be soon reduced, from mere barrenness, to the poorest of all imitations; he will be obliged to imitate himself, and to repeat what he has before often repeated.
10 Dec. 1774

19 I should desire that the last words which I should pronounce in this Academy, and from this place, might be the name of—Michael Angelo.
10 Dec. 1790

20 He [Dr. Johnson] has no formal preparation, no flourishing with his sword; he is through your body in an instant.
Boswell's *Johnson* (ed. 1934), vol.ii, p.365, 18 Apr. 1775

21 He [Johnson] qualified my mind to think justly.
vol.iii, p.369, n.3; and Northcote, *Reynolds*, vol.ii, p.282

22 Taste does not come by chance: it is a long and laborious task to acquire it.
James Northcote, *Life of Sir Joshua Reynolds* (1818), 2nd edn. (revised and augmented) of *Memoirs of Sir Joshua Reynolds* (1813-15), vol.i, p.264

GRANTLAND RICE 1880–1954

23 For when the One Great Scorer comes

To write against your name,
He marks—not that you won or lost—
But how you played the game.
Alumnus Football

SIR STEPHEN RICE 1637–1715

1 I will drive a coach and six horses through the Act of
Settlement.
W. King, *State of the Protestants of Ireland* (1672), ch.3, sect.8,
p.6

MANDY RICE-DAVIES 1944–

2 He would, wouldn't he?
When told that Lord Astor had denied her allegations. Trial of
Stephen Ward, 29 June, 1963

BISHOP GEORGE RIDDING 1828–1904

3 I feel a feeling which I feel you all feel.
Sermon in the London Mission of 1885. G.W.E. Russell,
Collections and Recollections, ch.29

RAINER MARIA RILKE 1875–1926

4 *So leben wir und nehmen immer Abschied.*
Thus we live, forever taking leave.
Duineser Elegien, VIII

5 One day (for this there are now already, especially in
northern lands, reliable signs, eloquent and
illuminating), one day there will be the girl, and the
woman, whose character will no longer provide a mere
contrast for masculinity, but something self-justifying,
something in connection with which one thinks not of
a complement and a limitation, but of life and
existence: the womanly person…[This will provide a
basis for a new kind of love.] The love which consists
in this, that two solitudes protect and limit and greet
each other.
Briefe an einem jungen Dichter (1929), 14 May 1904

MARTIN RINKART 1586–1649

6 *Nun danket alle Gott.*
Now thank you all your God.
Das Danklied (1636). Sung as a hymn to the tune by Johann
Crüger (1598–1662) composed in 1649

ARTHUR RIMBAUD 1854–1891

7 *Je m'en allais, les poings dans mes poches crevées;*
Mon paletot aussi devenait idéal.
I was walking along, hands in holey pockets; my
overcoat also was entering the realms of the ideal.
Ma Bohème

8 *Ô saisons, ô châteaux!*
Quelle âme est sans défauts?
O seasons, O castles! What soul is without fault?
Ô saisons, ô châteaux

9 *A noir, E blanc, I rouge, U vert, O bleu: voyelles,*
Je dirais quelque jour vos naissances latentes…
I, pourpres, sang craché, rire des lèvres belles
Dans la colère ou les ivresses pénitentes.
A black, E white, I red, U green, O blue: vowels,
some day I will tell of the births that may be yours.
I, purples, coughed-up blood, laughter of beautiful

lips in anger or penitent drunkennesses.
Voyelles

ANTOINE DE RIVAROL 1753–1801

10 *Ce qui n'est pas clair n'est pas français.*
What is not clear is not French.
Discours sur l'Universalité de la Langue Française (1784)

MAXIMILIEN ROBESPIERRE 1758–1794

11 *Toute loi qui viole les droits imprescriptibles de*
l'homme, est essentiellement injuste et tyrannique; elle
n'est point une loi.
Any law which violates the indefeasible rights of man
is essentially unjust and tyrannical; it is not a law at
all.
Déclaration des Droits de l'homme, 24 Apr. 1793, XVIII. This
article, in slightly different form, is recorded as having figured in
Robespierre's *Projet* of 21 Apr. 1793.

12 *Toute institution qui ne suppose pas le peuple bon, et*
le magistrat corruptible, est vicieuse.
Any institution which does not suppose the people
good, and the magistrate corruptible, is evil.
XIX

SIR BOYLE ROCHE 1743–1807

13 He regretted that he was not a bird, and could not be in
two places at once.
Attr.

14 Mr Speaker, I smell a rat; I see him forming in the air
and darkening the sky; but I'll nip him in the bud.
Attr.

JOHN WILMOT, EARL OF ROCHESTER
1647–1680

15 Since 'tis Nature's law to change,
Constancy alone is strange.
A Dialogue between Strephon and Daphne, l.31

16 What vain, unnecessary things are men!
How well we do without 'em!
Fragment

17   'Is there then no more?'
She cries. 'All this to love and rapture's due;
Must we not pay a debt to pleasure too?'
The Imperfect Enjoyment

18 Here lies a great and mighty king
   Whose promise none relies on;
He never said a foolish thing,
   Nor ever did a wise one.
The King's Epitaph. An alternative version of the first line is:
'Here lies our sovereign lord the King.' For Charles II's answer
see 140:23

19 Love…
That cordial drop heaven in our cup has thrown
To make the nauseous draught of life go down.
A Letter from Artemisia in the Town to Chloe in the Country

20 An age in her embraces past,
Would seem a winter's day.
The Mistress

21 Reason, an *ignis fatuus* of the mind,
Which leaves the light of nature, sense, behind.
A Satire Against Mankind, l.11

22 Then Old Age, and Experience, hand in hand,

Lead him to Death, and make him understand,
After a search so painful, and so long
That all his life he has been in the wrong.
Huddled in dirt the reasoning engine lies,
Who was so proud, so witty and so wise.
l.25

1 For all men would be cowards if they durst.
l.158

2 A merry monarch, scandalous and poor.
A Satire on King Charles II for which he was banished from the Court, l.19

3 Ancient person, for whom I
All the flattering youth defy,
Long be it ere thou grow old,
Aching, shaking, crazy, cold;
     But still continue as thou art,
     Ancient person of my heart.
A Song of a Young Lady to her Ancient Lover

4 The best good man, with the worst-natur'd muse.
To Lord Buckhurst

5 French truth, Dutch prowess, British policy,
Hibernian learning, Scotch civility,
Spaniards' Dispatch, Danes' Wit, are mainly seen in thee.
Upon Nothing

THEODORE ROETHKE 1908–1963

6 I wake to sleep, and take my waking slow.
I feel my fate in what I cannot fear.
I learn by going where I have to go.
The Waking

SAMUEL ROGERS 1763–1855

7 Think nothing done while aught remains to do.
Human Life (1819), l.49. See 319:24

8 But there are moments which he calls his own,
Then, never less alone than when alone,
Those whom he loved so long and sees no more,
Loved and still loves—not dead—but gone before,
He gathers round him.
l.755

9 By many a temple half as old as Time.
Italy. A Farewell (1828), ii.5

10 Go—you may call it madness, folly;
    You shall not chase my gloom away.
There's such a charm in melancholy,
    I would not, if I could, be gay.
To—, 1814

11 It doesn't much signify whom one marries, for one is sure to find next morning that it was someone else.
Table Talk (ed. Alexander Dyce, 1860)

12 When a new book is published, read an old one.
Attr.

THOROLD ROGERS 1823–1890

13 Sir, to be facetious it is not necessary to be indecent.
In imitation of Samuel Johnson. Also attributed to Birkbeck Hill.
John Bailey, *Dr. Johnson and his Circle*

14 While ladling butter from alternate tubs
Stubbs butters Freeman, Freeman butters Stubbs.
Attr. in W.H. Hutton, *Letters of Bishop Stubbs*

MME ROLAND 1754–1793

15 *O liberté! O liberté! que de crimes on commet en ton nom!*
O liberty! O liberty! what crimes are committed in thy name!
Lamartine, *Histoire des Girondins* (1847), livre li, ch.8

16 The more I see of men, the better I like dogs.
Attr.

FR. ROLFE, BARON CORVO 1860–1913

17 Pray for the repose of His soul. He was so tired.
Hadrian VII (1904), last words

PIERRE DE RONSARD 1524–1585

18 *Quand vous serez bien vieille, au soir, à la chandelle,
Assise auprès du feu, dévidant et filant,
Direz, chantant mes vers, en vous émerveillant,
Ronsard me célébrait du temps que j'étais belle.*
When you are very old, and sit in the candle-light at
    evening spinning by the fire, you will say, as you
    murmur my verses, a wonder in your eyes, 'Ronsard
    sang of me in the days when I was fair.'
Sonnets pour Hélène (1578), ii.43

PRESIDENT FRANKLIN D. ROOSEVELT 1882–1945

19 I pledge you—I pledge myself—to a new deal for the American people.
Chicago Convention, 2 July 1932. (See also N. & Q., cxciv, p.529.)

20 Let me assert my firm belief that the only thing we have to fear is fear itself.
First Inaugural Address, 4 Mar. 1933

21 In the field of world policy; I would dedicate this nation to the policy of the good neighbour.

22 I see one-third of a nation ill-housed, ill-clad, ill-nourished.
Second Inaugural Address, 20 Jan. 1937

23 When peace has been broken anywhere, the peace of all countries everywhere is in danger.
Fireside Chat, 3 Sept. 1939

24 A radical is a man with both feet firmly planted in the air.
Broadcast address to Forum on Current Problems, 26 Oct. 1939

25 We must be the great arsenal of democracy.
29 Dec. 1940

26 In the future days, which we seek to make secure, we look forward to a world founded upon four essential human freedoms.
The first is freedom of speech and expression—everywhere in the world.
The second is freedom of every person to worship God in his own way—everywhere in the world.
The third is freedom from want…
The fourth is freedom from fear.
Address to Congress, 6 Jan. 1941

PRESIDENT THEODORE ROOSEVELT 1858–1919

27 I wish to preach, not the doctrine of ignoble ease, but

the doctrine of the strenuous life.
Hamilton Club, Chicago, 10 Apr. 1899

1 There is a homely adage which runs 'Speak softly and carry a big stick; you will go far.'
Minnesota State Fair, 2 Sept. 1901

2 The first requisite of a good citizen in this Republic of ours is that he shall be able and willing to pull his weight.
New York, 11 Nov. 1902

3 A man who is good enough to shed his blood for the country is good enough to be given a square deal afterwards. More than that no man is entitled to, and less than that no man shall have.
At the Lincoln Monument, Springfield (Illinois), 4 June 1903

4 The men with the muck-rakes are often indispensable to the well-being of society; but only if they know when to stop raking the muck:
At the laying of the corner-stone of the Office Building of House of Representatives, 14 Apr. 1906

5 Every reform movement has a lunatic fringe.
Speaking of the Progressive Party, in 1913

6 There can be no fifty-fifty Americanism in this country. There is room here for only 100 per cent Americanism, only for those who are Americans and nothing else.
Republican Convention, Saratoga

7 We demand that big business give the people a square deal; in return we must insist that when any one engaged in big business honestly endeavors to do right he shall himself be given a square deal.
Autobiography (1913), p.615

8 Hyphenated Americans.
Metropolitan Magazine, Oct. 1915, p.7

WENTWORTH DILLON, EARL OF ROSCOMMON 1633?–1685

9 But words once spoke can never be recall'd.
Art of Poetry (1680), 1.438. See 258:22

10 Choose an author as you choose a friend.
Essay on Translated Verse (1684), 1.96

11 Immodest words admit of no defence,
For want of decency is want of sense.
1.113

12 The multitude is always in the wrong.
1.183

LORD ROSEBERY 1847–1929

13 Before Irish Home Rule is conceded by the Imperial Parliament, England as the predominant member of the three kingdoms will have to be convinced of its justice and equity.
House of Lords, 11 Mar. 1894

14 Imperialism, sane Imperialism, as distinguished from what I may call wild-cat Imperialism, is nothing but this—a larger patriotism.
Speech at a City Liberal Club dinner, 5 May 1899

15 It is beginning to be hinted that we are a nation of amateurs.
Rectorial Address, Glasgow, 16 Nov. 1900

16 I must plough my furrow alone.
City of London Liberal Club, 19 July 1901

17 The fly-blown phylacteries of the Liberal Party.
Chesterfield, 16 Dec. 1901

PILOT OFFICER V.A. ROSEWARNE 1916–1940

18 The universe is so vast and so ageless that the life of one man can only be justified by the measure of his sacrifice.
Last letter to his mother, published in *The Times* 18 June 1940, and inscribed on the portrait of the 'Young Airman' by Frank Salisbury in the R.A.F. Museum, Hendon

ALAN C. ROSS 1907–

19 'U' and 'Non-U'.
Upper Class English Usage, *Bulletin de la Société Neo-Philologique de Helsinki* 1954. Reprinted in *Noblesse Oblige* (1956), ed. Nancy Mitford

SIR RONALD ROSS 1857–1932

20 This day relenting God
  Hath placed within my hand
A wondrous thing; and God
  Be praised. At His command,

Seeking His secret deeds
  With tears and toiling breath,
I find thy cunning seeds,
  O million-murdering Death.

I know this little thing
  A myriad men may save.
O Death, where is thy sting?
  Thy victory, O Grave?
In Exile, VI. **Reply**, i. See 77:1. Of his part in the discovery of the life-cycle of the malaria parasite.

CHRISTINA ROSSETTI 1830–1894

21 Oh where are you going with your love-locks flowing?
Amor Mundi, i

22 This downhill path is easy, but there's no turning back.
v

23 My heart is like a singing bird
Whose nest is in a watered shoot;
My heart is like an apple-tree
Whose boughs are bent with thickset fruit;
My heart is like a rainbow shell
That paddles in a halcyon sea;
My heart is gladder than all these
Because my love is come to me.
A Birthday

24 Because the birthday of my life
Is come, my love is come to me.

25 'Come cheer up, my lads, 'tis to glory we steer'—
As the soldier remarked whose post lay in the rear.
Couplet

26 Come to me in the silence of the night;
  Come in the speaking silence of a dream;
Come with soft rounded cheeks and eyes as bright
  As sunlight on a stream;
    Come back in tears,
O memory, hope, love of finished years.
Echo

27 For there is no friend like a sister
In calm or stormy weather;

To cheer one on the tedious way,
To fetch one if one goes astray,
To lift one if one totters down,
To strengthen whilst one stands.
Goblin Market (1862)

1 In the bleak mid-winter
    Frosty wind made moan,
Earth stood hard as iron,
    Water like a stone;
Snow had fallen, snow on snow,
    Snow on snow,
In the bleak mid-winter,
    Long ago.
Mid-Winter

2 The hope I dreamed of was a dream,
    Was but a dream; and now I wake,
Exceeding comfortless, and worn, and old,
    For a dream's sake.
Mirage

3 Remember me when I am gone away,
    Gone far away into the silent land.
Remember

4 Better by far you should forget and smile
Than that you should remember and be sad.

5 O Earth, lie heavily upon her eyes;
Seal her sweet eyes weary of watching, Earth.
Rest

6 Silence more musical than any song.

7 Oh roses for the flush of youth,
    And laurel for the perfect prime;
But pluck an ivy branch for me
    Grown old before my time.
Song: 'Oh Roses for the Flush'

8 When I am dead, my dearest,
    Sing no sad songs for me;
Plant thou no roses at my head,
    Nor shady cypress tree:
Be the green grass above me
    With showers and dewdrops wet;
And if thou wilt, remember,
    And if thou wilt, forget.
Song: 'When I am Dead'

9 And dreaming through the twilight
    That doth not rise nor set,
Haply I may remember,
    And haply may forget.

10 Gone were but the Winter,
    Come were but the Spring,
I would go to a covert
    Where the birds sing.
Spring Quiet

11 Does the road wind up-hill all the way?
    Yes, to the very end.
Will the day's journey take the whole long day?
    From morn to night, my friend.
Up-Hill

12 Will there be beds for me and all who seek?
    Yea, beds for all who come.

DANTE GABRIEL ROSSETTI 1828–1882

13 Like the sweet apple which reddens upon the topmost
    bough,

A-top on the topmost twig,—which the pluckers
    forgot, somehow,—
Forgot it not, nay, but got it not, for none could get it
    till now.
Beauty: A Combination from Sappho. See 414:7

14 The blessed damozel leaned out
    From the gold bar of Heaven;
Her eyes were deeper than the depth
    Of waters stilled at even;
She had three lilies in her hand,
    And the stars in her hair were seven.
The Blessed Damozel (1850), i

15 Her hair that lay along her back
    Was yellow like ripe corn.
ii

16 So high, that looking downward thence,
    She scarce could see the sun.
v

17   As low as where this earth
Spins like a fretful midge.
vi

18 And the souls mounting up to God
    Went by her like thin flames.
vii

19 'We two,' she said, 'will seek the groves
    Where the lady Mary is,
With her five handmaidens, whose names
    Are five sweet symphonies,
Cecily, Gertrude, Magdalen,
    Margaret and Rosalys.'
xviii

20 Was it a friend or foe that spread these lies?
Nay, who but infants question in such wise?
'Twas one of my most intimate enemies.
Fragment

21 A sonnet is a moment's monument,—
Memorial from the Soul's eternity
To one dead deathless hour.
The House of Life (1881), pt.I. Introd.

22 I was a child beneath her touch,—a man
When breast to breast we clung, even I and she,—
A spirit when her spirit looked through me,—
A god when all our life-breath met to fan
Our life-blood, till love's emulous ardours ran,
Fire within fire, desire in deity.
vi. **The Kiss**

23 'Tis visible silence, still as the hour-glass.
xix. **Silent Noon**

24 Deep in the sun-searched growths the dragon-fly
Hangs like a blue thread loosened from the sky:—
So this wing'd hour is dropt to us from above.
Oh! clasp we to our hearts, for deathless dower,
This close-companioned inarticulate hour
When twofold silence was the song of love.

25 They die not,—for their life was death,—but cease;
And round their narrow lips the mould falls close.
pt.II. lxxi. **The Choice,** i

26 Nay, come up hither. From this wave-washed mound
Unto the furthest flood-brim look with me;
Then reach on with thy thought till it be drown'd.
Miles and miles distant though the last line be,
And though thy soul sail leagues and leagues beyond,—

Still, leagues beyond those leagues, there is more sea.
iii

1 Give honour unto Luke Evangelist;
For he it was (the aged legends say)
Who first taught Art to fold her hands and pray.
lxxiv. **Old and New Art,** i

2 Lo! as that youth's eyes burned at thine, so went
Thy spell through him, and left his straight neck bent
And round his heart one strangling golden hair.
lxxviii. **Body's Beauty**

3 I do not see them here; but after death
God knows I know the faces I shall see,
Each one a murdered self, with low last breath.
'I am thyself,—what hast thou done to me?'
'And I—and I—thyself', (lo! each one saith,)
'And thou thyself to all eternity!'
lxxxvi. **Lost Days**

4 Look in my face; my name is Might-have-been;
I am also called No-more, Too-late, Farewell.
xcvii. **A Superscription**

5 Sleepless with cold commemorative eyes.

6 When vain desire at last and vain regret
Go hand in hand to death, and all is vain,
What shall assuage the unforgotten pain
And teach the unforgetful to forget?
ci. **The One Hope**

7 Unto the man of yearning thought
And aspiration, to do nought
Is in itself almost an act.
Soothsay, x

8 I have been here before,
    But when or how I cannot tell:
I know the grass beyond the door,
    The sweet keen smell,
The sighing sound, the lights around the shore.
Sudden Light, i

9 From perfect grief there need not be
Wisdom or even memory:
One thing then learnt remains to me,—
The woodspurge has a cup of three.
The Woodspurge

10 Conception, my boy, *fundamental brainwork*, is what
makes the difference in all art.
Letter to Hall Caine, in Caine's *Recollections of Rossetti* (1882)

GIOACCHINO ROSSINI 1792–1868

11 *Monsieur Wagner a de beaux moments, mais de
mauvais quart d'heures.*
Wagner has lovely moments but awful quarters of an
hour.
Said to Emile Naumann, April 1867. Naumann, *Italienische
Tondichter* (1883), IV, 541

EDMOND ROSTAND 1868–1918

12 Cyrano: *Il y a malgré vous quelque chose
Que j'emporte, et ce soir, quand j'entrerai chez Dieu,
Mon salut balaiera largement le seuil bleu,
Quelque chose que sans un pli, sans une tache,
J'emporte malgré vous...et c'est...*
Roxane: *C'est?...*
Cyrano: *Mon panache!*
Cyrano: There is, in spite of you, something which I
    shall take with me. And tonight, when I go into

God's house, my bow will make a wide sweep
across the blue threshold. Something which, with
not a crease, not a mark, I'm taking away in spite of
you...and it's...
Roxane: It's...
Cyrano: My panache!
Cyrano de Bergerac, V.iv

13 *Le seul rêve intéresse,
Vivre sans rêve, qu'est-ce?
Et j'aime la Princesse
    Lointaine.*
The dream, alone, is of interest. What is life, without
a dream? And I love the Distant Princess.
La Princesse Lointaine, I.iv

LEO C. ROSTEN 1908–

14 Any man who hates dogs and babies can't be all bad.
Of W.C. Fields, and often attributed to him. Speech at Masquers'
Club dinner, 16 Feb. 1939. See letter, *T.L.S.* 24 Jan. 1975

NORMAN ROSTEN

15 And there's the outhouse poet, anonymous:
        Soldiers who wish to be a hero
        Are practically zero
    But those who wish to be civilians
        Jesus they run into millions.
The Big Road (1946), pt.V

CLAUDE-JOSEPH ROUGET DE LISLE 1760–1836

16 *Allons, enfants de la patrie,
Le jour de gloire est arrivé.*
Come, children of our country, the day of glory has
arrived.
La Marseillaise (25 Apr. 1792)

JEAN-JACQUES ROUSSEAU 1712–1778

17 *L'homme est né libre, et partout il est dans les fers.*
Man was born free, and everywhere he is in chains.
Du Contrat Social, ch.1

DR. ROUTH 1755–1854

18 You will find it a very good practice always to verify
your references, sir!
Burgon, *Quarterly Review,* July 1878, vol.cxlvi, p.30, and *Lives
of Twelve Good Men* (1888 edn.), vol I, p.73

NICHOLAS ROWE 1674–1718

19 That false Lothario!
The Fair Penitent (1703), II.i

20 The evening of my age.
IV.i

21 I feel the pangs of disappointed love.

22 Is this that haughty, gallant, gay Lothario?
V.i

23 Like Helen, in the night when Troy was sack'd,
Spectatress of the mischief which she made.

24 Death is the privilege of human nature,
And life without it were not worth our taking.

25 Think on the sacred dictates of thy faith,
And let that arm thy virtue, to perform

What Cato's daughter durst not,—live Aspasia,
And dare to be unhappy.
Tamerlane (1702), IV.i

WILLIAM ROWLEY 1585?–1642?

1 Art thou gone in haste?
    I'll not forsake thee;
Run'st thou ne'er so fast,
    I'll o'ertake thee:
O'er the dales, o'er the downs,
Through the green meadows,
From the fields through the towns,
To the dim shadows.
The Thracian Wonder (1661), ascribed to Rowley and,
improbably, John Webster, I.i

MATTHEW ROYDON fl. 1580–1622

2 A sweet attractive kind of grace,
    A full assurance given by looks,
Continual comfort in a face,
    The lineaments of Gospel books;
    I trow that countenance cannot lie,
    Whose thoughts are legible in the eye.
An Elegy, or Friend's Passion, for his Astrophill (i.e. Sir Philip
Sidney) (1593), xviii

3 Was never eye, did see that face,
    Was never ear, did hear that tongue,
Was never mind, did mind his grace,
    That ever thought the travel long—
    But eyes, and ears, and ev'ry thought,
    Were with his sweet perfections caught.
xix

DAMON RUNYON 1884–1946

4 More than somewhat.
P. rase used frequently in Runyon's work, and adopted as
book-title in 1937.

JOHN RUSKIN 1819–1900

5 You know there are a great many odd styles of
architecture about; you don't want to do anything
ridiculous; you hear of me, among others, as a
respectable architectural man-milliner; and you send
for me, that I may tell you the leading fashion.
The Crown of Wild Olive (1866), 53, lecture ii. **Traffic**

6 Thackeray settled like a meat-fly on whatever one had
got for dinner, and made one sick of it.
Fors Clavigera (1871-84), letter xxxi

7 I have seen, and heard, much of Cockney impudence
before now; but never expected to hear a coxcomb ask
two hundred guineas for flinging a pot of paint in the
public's face.
[On Whistler's 'Nocturne in Black and Gold'] letter lxxix, 18 June
1877. See 569:23

8 No person who is not a great sculptor or painter can be
an architect. If he is not a sculptor or painter, he can
only be a *builder*.
Lectures on Architecture and Painting (1853), 61, Addenda

9 Life without industry is guilt, and industry without art
is brutality.
Lectures on Art, 3. **The Relation of Art to Morals,** 23 Feb.
1870

10 What is poetry? The suggestion, by the imagination,

of noble grounds for the noble emotions.
Modern Painters (1888), vol.iii

11 All violent feelings…produce in us a falseness in all
our impressions of external things, which I would
generally characterize as the 'Pathetic Fallacy'.

12 Mountains are the beginning and the end of all natural
scenery.
vol.iv, pt.v, ch.20, 1

13 There was a rocky valley between Buxton and
Bakewell,…divine as the vale of Tempe; you might
have seen the gods there morning and
evening,—Apollo and the sweet Muses of the
Light…You enterprised a railroad,…you blasted its
rocks away…And now, every fool in Buxton can be at
Bakewell in half-an-hour, and every fool in Bakewell
at Buxton.
Praeterita (1885-9), III.iv. **Joanna's Cave,** 84, note

14 All books are divisible into two classes: the books of
the hour, and the books of all time.
Sesame and Lilies (1865), Lecture i. **Of Kings' Treasuries,** 8

15 But whether thus submissively or not, at least be sure
that you go to the author to get at his meaning, not to
find yours.
13

16 Which of us…is to do the hard and dirty work for the
rest—and for what pay? Who is to do the pleasant and
clean work, and for what pay?
30, note

17 What do we, as a nation, care about books? How
much do you think we spend altogether on our
libraries, public or private, as compared with what we
spend on our horses?
32

18 How long most people would look at the best book
before they would give the price of a large turbot for
it!

19 We call ourselves a rich nation, and we are filthy and
foolish enough to thumb each other's books out of
circulating libraries!

20 I believe the right question to ask, respecting all
ornament, is simply this: Was it done with
enjoyment—was the carver happy while he was about
it?
The Seven Lamps of Architecture (1849), ch.5. **The Lamp of
Life**

21 Better the rudest work that tells a story or records a
fact, than the richest without meaning. There should
not be a single ornament put upon great civic
buildings, without some intellectual intention.
ch.6. **The Lamp of Memory,** 7

22 When we build, let us think that we build for ever.
10

23 Remember that the most beautiful things in the world
are the most useless; peacocks and lilies for instance.
The Stones of Venice (1851-3), vol.i, ch.2, 17

24 The purest and most thoughtful minds are those which
love colour the most.
vol.ii, ch.5, 30

25 Fine art is that in which the hand, the head, and the
heart of man go together.
The Two Paths (1859), Lecture ii

26 Not only is there but one way of *doing* things rightly,

but there is only one way of *seeing* them, and that is, seeing the whole of them.

1 Nobody cares much at heart about Titian; only there is a strange undercurrent of everlasting murmur about his name, which means the deep consent of all great men that he is greater than they.

2 No human being, however great, or powerful, was ever so free as a fish.
Lecture v

3 Labour without joy is base. Labour without sorrow is base. Sorrow without labour is base. Joy without labour is base.
Time and Tide (1867), letter v

4 Your honesty is *not* to be based either on religion or policy. Both your religion and policy must be based on *it*. Your honesty must be based, as the sun is, in vacant heaven; poised, as the lights in the firmament, which have rule over the day and over the night.
letter viii

5 To make your children *capable of honesty* is the beginning of education.

6 I hold it for indisputable, that the first duty of a State is to see that every child born therein shall be well housed, clothed, fed and educated, till it attain years of discretion. But in order to the effecting this the Government must have an authority over the people of which we now do not so much as dream.
letter xiii

7 It ought to be quite as natural and straightforward a matter for a labourer to take his pension from his parish, because he has deserved well of his parish, as for a man in higher rank to take his pension from his country, because he has deserved well of his country.
Unto this Last (1862), preface, 6 (4)

8 The force of the guinea you have in your pocket depends wholly on the default of a guinea in your neighbour's pocket. If he did not want it, it would be of no use to you.
Essay ii, 27

9 Soldiers of the ploughshare as well as soldiers of the sword.
Essay iii, 54

10 Government and co-operation are in all things the laws of life; anarchy and competition the laws of death.

11 Whereas it has long been known and declared that the poor have no right to the property of the rich, I wish it also to be known and declared that the rich have no right to the property of the poor.

12 There is no wealth but life.
Essay iv, 77

13 Each book that a young girl touches should be bound in white vellum.
Said to Jane E. Harrison. *Reminiscences of a Student's Life*, ch.2

14 There is really no such thing as bad weather, only different kinds of good weather.
Quoted by Lord Avebury

BERTRAND RUSSELL 1872–1970

15 Mathematics, rightly viewed, possesses not only truth, but supreme beauty—a beauty cold and austere, like

that of sculpture.
Mysticism and Logic (1918), ch.4

16 This method is, to define as the number of a class the class of all classes similar to the given class.
Principles of Mathematics, pt.II, ch.11, sect.iii (1903)

17 It is undesirable to believe a proposition when there is no ground whatever for supposing it true.
Sceptical Essays (1928), p.1

LORD JOHN RUSSELL 1792–1878

18 It is impossible that the whisper of a faction should prevail against the voice of a nation.
Letter to T. Attwood, Oct. 1831, after the rejection in the House of Lords of the Reform Bill (7 Oct. 1831)

19 If peace cannot be maintained with honour, it is no longer peace.
Greenock, 19 Sept. 1853

20 Among the defects of the Bill, which were numerous, one provision was conspicuous by its presence and another by its absence.
Speech to the electors of the City of London, Apr. 1859

21 A proverb is one man's wit and all men's wisdom.
Ascribed

JOHN RUSSELL 1919–

22 Certain phrases stick in the throat, even if they offer nothing that is analytically improbable. 'A dashing Swiss officer' is one such.
Paris (1960), ch.11

SIR WILLIAM HOWARD RUSSELL 1820–1907

23 They dashed on towards that *thin red line tipped with steel*.
The British Expedition to the Crimea (1877), p.156. Of the Russians charging the British. Russell's original dispatch to *The Times*, 25 Oct. 1854, read 'This thin red streak tipped with a line of steel', *The War* (1855)

LORD RUTHERFORD 1871–1937

24 We haven't the money, so we've got to think.
Attr. in Prof. R.V. Jones, 1962 Brunel Lecture, 14 Feb. 1962

GILBERT RYLE 1900–1976

25 The dogma of the Ghost in the machine.
The Concept of Mind (1949), passim

VICTORIA SACKVILLE-WEST 1892–1962

26 The greater cats with golden eyes
Stare out between the bars.
King's Daughter, II.i

WARHAM ST. LEGER 1850–c.1915

27 There is a fine stuffed chavender,
A chavender, or chub,
That decks the rural pavender,
The pavender, or pub,
Wherein I eat my gravender,
My gravender, or grub.
The Chavender, or Chub, st.1

CHARLES-AUGUSTIN SAINTE-BEUVE
1804–1869

1   *Et Vigny plus secret,*
Comme en sa tour d'ivoire, avant midi rentrait.
And Vigny more reserved,
Returned ere noon, within his ivory tower.
Les Pensées d'Août, à M. Villemain, p.152

'SAKI' (H.H. MUNRO) 1870–1916

2   'The man is a common murderer.'
'A common murderer, possibly, but a very uncommon cook.'
Beasts and Super-Beasts (1914). **The Blind Spot**

3   When she inveighed eloquently against the evils of capitalism at drawing-room meetings and Fabian conferences she was conscious of a comfortable feeling that the system, with all its inequalities and iniquities, would probably last her time. It is one of the consolations of middle-aged reformers that the good they inculcate must live after them if it is to live at all.
The Byzantine Omelette

4   Waldo is one of those people who would be enormously improved by death.
The Feast of Nemesis

5   Romance at short notice was her speciality.
The Open Window

6   He's simply got the instinct for being unhappy highly developed.
The Chronicles of Clovis (1911). **The Match-Maker**

7   Oysters are more beautiful than any religion…There's nothing in Christianity or Buddhism that quite matches the sympathetic unselfishness of an oyster.

8   There are so many things to complain of in this household that it would never have occurred to me to complain of rheumatism.
The Quest

9   Never be a pioneer. It's the Early Christian that gets the fattest lion.
Reginald (1904), **Reginald's Choir Treat**

10 The cook was a good cook, as cooks go; and as cooks go she went.
Reginald on Besetting Sins

11 Women and elephants never forget an injury.

12 Addresses are given to us to conceal our whereabouts.
Reginald in Russia (1910). **Cross Currents**

13 The Western custom of one wife and hardly any mistresses.
A Young Turkish Catastrophe

14 But, good gracious, you've got to educate him first. You can't expect a boy to be vicious till he's been to a good school.
The Baker's Dozen

15 In baiting a mouse-trap with cheese, always leave room for the mouse.
The Square Egg (1924). **The Infernal Parliament**

16 Children with Hyacinth's temperament don't know better as they grow older; they merely know more.
The Toys of Peace (1919). **Hyacinth**

GEORGE AUGUSTUS SALA 1828–1896

17 And now, Sir, we will take a walk down Fleet Street.

Motto of the *Temple Bar* magazine (1860). Ascribed to Dr. Johnson.

LORD SALISBURY 1830–1903

18 No lesson seems to be so deeply inculcated by the experience of life as that you never should trust experts. If you believe the doctors, nothing is wholesome: if you believe the theologians, nothing is innocent: if you believe the soldiers, nothing is safe. They all require to have their strong wine diluted by a very large admixture of insipid common sense.
Letter to Lord Lytton, 15 June 1877. Lady Gwendolen Cecil, *Life of Robert, Marquis of Salisbury*, vol.II, ch.4

19 We are part of the community of Europe and we must do our duty as such.
Speech at Caernarvon, 11 Apr. 1888. Lady Gwendolen Cecil, *Life of Robert, Marquis of Salisbury*, vol.IV, ch.4

20 I cannot help thinking that in discussions of this kind, a great deal of misapprehension arises from the popular use of maps on a small scale. As with such maps you are able to put a thumb on India and a finger on Russia, some persons at once think that the political situation is alarming and that India must be looked to. If the noble Lord would use a larger map—say one on the scale of the Ordnance Map of England—he would find that the distance between Russia and British India is not to be measured by the finger and thumb, but by a rule.
House of Commons, 11 June 1877

21 By office boys for office boys.
Of the Daily Mail. See H. Hamilton Fyfe, *Northcliffe, an Intimate Biography*, ch.4

SALLUST c.86–c.35 B.C.

22 *Alieni appetens, sui profusus.*
Greedy for the property of others, extravagant with his own.
Catiline, 5

23 *Quieta movere magna merces videbatur.*
Just to stir things up seemed a great reward in itself.
21

24 *Esse quam videri bonus malebat.*
He preferred to be rather than to seem good.
54. Of Cato

25 *Punica fide.*
With Carthaginian trustworthiness.
Jugurtha, 108, 3. Meaning treachery.

CARL SANDBURG 1878–1967

26 The fog comes
on little cat feet.

It sits looking
over harbor and city
on silent haunches
and then moves on.
Fog

27 Pile the bodies high at Austerlitz and Waterloo.
Shovel them under and let me work—
I am the grass; I cover all.
Grass

GEORGE SANTAYANA 1863–1952

1 Progress, far from consisting in change, depends on retentiveness...Those who cannot remember the past are condemned to fulfil it.
Life of Reason (1905-6), vol.I, ch.xii. **Flux and Constancy in Human Nature**

2 Reason is not come to repeat the universe but to fulfil it.
vol.V, ch.ii. **History**

3 Music is essentially useless, as life is: but both lend utility to their conditions.
Little Essays (1920), pt.iii, no.54

4 Never since the heroic days of Greece has the world had such a sweet, just, boyish master. It will be a black day for the human race when scientific blackguards, conspirators, churls, and fanatics manage to supplant him.
Soliloquies in England (1922), 9. **The British Character**

5 For an idea ever to be fashionable is ominous, since it must afterwards be always old-fashioned.
Winds of Doctrine (1913). **Modernism and Christianity**

SAPPHO b. c.612 B.C.

6 φαίνεταί μοι κῆνος ἴσος θέοισιν
ἔμμεν' ὤνηρ, ὄττις ἐνάντιός τοι
ἰσδάνει καὶ πλάσιον ἆδυ φωνεί-
σας ὐπακούει
καὶ γελαίσας ἰμέροεν, τό μ' ἦ μὰν
καρδίαν ἐν στήθεσιν ἐπτόαισεν,
ὡς γὰρ ἔς σ' ἴδω βρόχε', ὤς με φώναι-
σ' οὐδ' ἔν ἔτ' εἴκει,
ἀλλ' ἄκαν μεν γλῶσσα πέπαγε, λέπτον
δ' αὔτικα χρῶι πῦρ ὐπαδεδρόμηκεν,
ὀππάτεσσι δ' οὐδ' ἔν ὄρημμ', ἐπιρρόμ-
βεισι δ' ἄκουαι,
κὰδ δέ μ' ἴδρως κακχέεται, τρόμος δὲ
παῖσαν ἄγρει, χλωροτέρα δὲ ποίας
ἔμμι, τεθνάκην δ' ὀλίγω 'πιδεύης
φαίνομ' ἔμ' αὔται.
That man seems to me on a par with the gods who sits in your company and listens to you so close to him speaking sweetly and laughing sexily, such a thing makes my heart flutter in my breast, for when I see you even for a moment, then power to speak another word fails me, instead my tongue freezes into silence, and at once a gentle fire has caught throughout my flesh, and I see nothing with my eyes, and there's a drumming in my ears, and sweat pours down me, and trembling seizes all of me, and I become paler than grass, and I seem to fail almost to the point of death in my very self.
D.L. Page, *Lyrica Selecta Graeca* (1968)

7 οἶον τὸ γλυκύμαλον ἐρεύθεται ἄκρῳ ἐπ' ὔσδῳ,
ἄκρον ἐπ' ἀκροτάτῳ, λελάθοντο δὲ μαλοδρόπηες,
οὐ μὰν ἐκλελάθοντ', ἀλλ' οὐκ ἐδύναντ' ἐπίκεσθαι.
Just as the sweet-apple reddens on the high branch,
high on the highest, and the apple-pickers missed it,
or rather did not miss it out, but dared not reach it.
105(a). Of a girl before her marriage

JEAN-PAUL SARTRE 1905–

8 *Alors, c'est ça l'Enfer. Je n'aurais jamais cru...Vous vous rappelez: le soufre, le bûcher, le gril...Ah! quelle plaisanterie. Pas besoin de gril, l'Enfer, c'est les Autres.*
So that's what Hell is. I'd never have believed it...Do you remember, brimstone, the stake, the gridiron?...What a joke! No need of a gridiron, [when it come to] Hell, it's other people.
Huis Clos, sc.v

9 *Trois heures, c'est toujours trop tard ou trop tôt pour tout ce qu'on veut faire.*
Three o'clock is always too late or too early for anything you want to do.
La Nausée, Vendredi

SIEGFRIED SASSOON 1886–1967

10 If I were fierce and bald and short of breath,
    I'd live with scarlet Majors at the Base,
And speed glum heroes up the line to death.
Base Details

11 And when the war is done and youth stone dead
I'd toddle safely home and die—in bed.

12 I'd like to see a Tank come down the stalls,
Lurching to rag-time tunes, or 'Home, sweet Home,'—
And there'd be no more jokes in Music-halls
To mock the riddled corpses round Bapaume.
'Blighters'

13 Does it matter?—losing your legs?...
For people will always be kind,
And you need not show that you mind
When others come in after hunting
To gobble their muffins and eggs.

Does it matter?—losing your sight?...
There's such splendid work for the blind;
And people will always be kind,
As you sit on the terrace remembering
And turning your face to the light.
Does it Matter?

14 Why do you lie with your legs ungainly huddled,
And one arm bent across your sullen, cold
Exhausted face?
The Dug-Out

15 You are too young to fall asleep for ever;
And when you sleep you remind me of the dead.

16 Everyone suddenly burst out singing.
Everyone Sang

17   The song was wordless;
The singing will never be done.

18 'Good morning; good morning!' the general said
When we met him last week on our way to the line.
Now the soldiers he smiled at are most of 'em dead,
And we're cursing his staff for incompetent swine.
'He's a cheery old card,' grunted Harry to Jack
As they slogged up to Arras with rifle and pack...
But he did for them both with his plan of attack.
The General

19 They have spoken lightly of my deathless friends,
(Lamps for my gloom, hands guiding where I
    stumble,)
Quoting, for shallow conversational ends,
What Shelley shrilled, what Blake once wildly

muttered...

How can they use such names and not be humble?
I have sat silent; angry at what they uttered.
The Grandeur of Ghosts

1 In me the tiger sniffs the rose.
The Heart's Journey, VIII

2 *Alone...the word is life endured and known.*
XII

3 Here sleeps the Silurist; the loved physician;
The face that left no portraiture behind;
The skull that housed white angels and had vision
Of daybreak through the gateways of the mind.
XXIII. **At the Grave of Henry Vaughan**

4 A sallow waiter brings me beans and pork...
Outside there's fury in the firmament.
Ice-cream, of course, will follow; and I'm content.
O Babylon! O Carthage! O New York!
Storm on Fifth Avenue

RICHARD SAVAGE d. 1743

5 Perhaps been poorly rich, and meanly great,
The slave of pomp, a cipher in the state.
The Bastard (1728), l.39

GEORGE SAVILE, MARQUIS OF HALIFAX
see HALIFAX

DOROTHY L. SAYERS 1893–1957

6 I admit it is more fun to punt than to be punted, and
that a desire to have all the fun is nine-tenths of the law
of chivalry.
Gaudy Night, ch.14

7 As I grow older and older,
And totter towards the tomb,
I find that I care less and less
Who goes to bed with whom.
That's why I never read modern novels

FRIEDRICH VON SCHELLING 1775–1854

8 Architecture in general is frozen music.
Philosophie der Kunst (1809)

FRIEDRICH VON SCHILLER 1759–1805

9 *Freude, schöner Götterfunken,*
Tochter aus Elysium,
Wir betreten feuertrunken,
Himmlische, dein Heiligtum.
Deine Zauber binden wieder,
Was die Mode streng geteilt,
Alle Menschen werden Brüder
Wo dein sanfter Flügel weilt.
Joy, beautiful radiance of the gods, daughter of
Elysium, we set foot in your heavenly shrine dazzled
by your brilliance. Your charms re-unite what
common use has harshly divided: all men become
brothers under your tender wing.
An die Freude (1786)

10 *Mit der Dummheit kämpfen Götter selbst vergebens.*
With stupidity the gods themselves struggle in vain.
Die Jungfrau von Orleans (1801), III.vi

11 *Die Weltgeschichte ist das Weltgericht.*

The world's history is the world's judgement.
First lecture as Prof. of History, Jena. 26 May 1789

PROFESSOR E.F. SCHUMACHER 1911–1977

12 Small is beautiful.
Title of book (1973)

CARL SCHURZ 1829–1906

13 Our country, right or wrong! When right, to be kept
right; when wrong, to be put right!
Speech, U.S. Senate, 1872. See 173:1

ALEXANDER SCOTT 1525?–1584?

14 Love is ane fervent fire,
Kindled without desire,
Short pleasure, long displeasure;
Repentance is the hire;
And pure treasure without measure.
Love is ane fervent fire.
Lo, What it is to Love (c. 1568)

C.P. SCOTT 1846–1932

15 The newspaper is of necessity something of a
monopoly, and its first duty is to shun the temptations
of monopoly. Its primary office is the gathering of
news. At the peril of its soul it must see that the supply
is not tainted. Neither in what it gives, nor in what it
does not give, nor in the mode of presentation, must
the unclouded face of truth suffer wrong. Comment is
free but facts are sacred.
Manchester Guardian, 6 May 1926

16 Television? The word is half Latin and half Greek. No
good can come of it.
Attr.

CAPTAIN ROBERT FALCON SCOTT 1868–1912

17 Great God! this is an awful place. [The South Pole.]
Journal, 17 Jan. 1912

18 For God's sake look after our people.
25 Mar. 1912

19 Had we lived, I should have had a tale to tell of the
hardihood, endurance, and courage of my companions
which would have stirred the heart of every
Englishman. These rough notes and our dead bodies
must tell the tale.
Message to the Public

SIR WALTER SCOTT 1771–1832

20 To the Lords of Convention 'twas Claver'se who
spoke,
'Ere the King's crown shall fall there are crowns to be
broke;
So let each cavalier who loves honour and me,
Come follow the bonnet of Bonny Dundee.
Come fill up my cup, come fill up my can,
Come saddle your horses, and call up your men;
Come open the West Port, and let me gang free,
And it's room for the bonnets of Bonny Dundee!'
Bonny Dundee. (*The Doom of Devorgoil*, 1830, Act II, sc.ii).
See 418:30

21 The valiant Knight of Triermain

Rung forth his challenge-blast again,
    But answer came there none.
The Bridal of Triermain (1813), c.III.x

1 The stag at eve had drunk his fill,
Where danced the moon on Monan's rill,
And deep his midnight lair had made
In lone Glenartney's hazel shade.
The Lady of the Lake (1810), c.I.i

2 His ready speech flow'd fair and free,
In phrase of gentlest courtesy;
Yet seem'd that tone, and gesture bland,
Less used to sue than to command.
xxi

3 Huntsman, rest! thy chase is done.
xxxii

4 Hail to the Chief who in triumph advances!
c.II.xix

5 He is gone on the mountain,
    He is lost to the forest,
Like a summer-dried fountain,
    When our need was the sorest.
c.III.xvi

6 Respect was mingled with surprise,
And the stern joy which warriors feel
In foemen worthy of their steel.
c.V.x

7   Where, where was Roderick then?
One blast upon his bugle-horn
    Were worth a thousand men!
c.VI.xviii

8 The way was long, the wind was cold,
The Minstrel was infirm and old;
His wither'd cheek and tresses grey,
Seem'd to have known a better day.
The Lay of the Last Minstrel (1805), introd. l.1

9 The last of all the Bards was he,
Who sung of Border chivalry;
For, welladay! their date was fled,
His tuneful brethren all were dead;
And he, neglected and oppress'd,
Wish'd to be with them, and at rest.
l.7

10 The unpremeditated lay.
l.18

11 Vengeance, deep-brooding o'er the slain,
    Had lock'd the source of softer woe;
And burning pride and high disdain
    Forbade the rising tear to flow.
c.I.ix

12 What shall be the maiden's fate?
Who shall be the maiden's mate?
xvi

13 If thou would'st view fair Melrose aright,
Go visit it by the pale moonlight;
For the gay beams of lightsome day
Gild, but to flout, the ruins grey.
c.II.i

14 Strange sounds along the chancel pass'd,
The banner wav'd without a blast.
xvi

15 Yet somewhat was he chill'd with dread,
And his hair did bristle upon his head.

16 I cannot tell how the truth may be;

I say the tale as 'twas said to me.
xxii

17 In peace, Love tunes the shepherd's reed;
In war, he mounts the warrior's steed;
In halls, in gay attire is seen;
In hamlets, dances on the green.
Love rules the court, the camp, the grove,
And men below, and saints above;
For love is heaven, and heaven is love.
c.III.ii

18   For ne'er
Was flattery lost on poet's ear:
A simple race! they waste their toil
For the vain tribute of a smile.
c.IV, conclusion

19 Call it not vain; they do not err,
    Who say, that when the Poet dies,
Mute Nature mourns her worshipper,
    And celebrates his obsequies.
c.V.i

20 It is the secret sympathy,
The silver link, the silken tie,
Which heart to heart, and mind to mind,
In body and in soul can bind.
xiii

21 Breathes there the man, with soul so dead,
Who never to himself hath said,
    This is my own, my native land!
Whose heart hath ne'er within him burn'd,
As home his footsteps he hath turn'd
    From wandering on a foreign strand!
c.VI.i

22 Despite those titles, power, and pelf,
The wretch, concentred all in self,
Living, shall forfeit fair renown,
And, doubly dying, shall go down
To the vile dust, from whence he sprung,
Unwept, unhonour'd, and unsung.

O Caledonia! stern and wild,
Meet nurse for a poetic child!
Land of brown heath and shaggy wood,
Land of the mountain and the flood,
Land of my sires! what mortal hand
Can e'er untie the filial band
That knits me to thy rugged strand!

23 O! many a shaft, at random sent,
Finds mark the archer little meant!
And many a word, at random spoken,
May soothe or wound a heart that's broken.
The Lord of the Isles (1813), c.V.xviii

24 O hush thee, my babie, thy sire was a knight,
Thy mother a lady, both lovely and bright.
Lullaby of an Infant Chief

25 Then hush thee, my darling, take rest while you may,
For strife comes with manhood, and waking with day.

26 O lovers' eyes are sharp to see,
    And lovers' ears in hearing.
The Maid of Neidpath

27 November's sky is chill and drear,
November's leaf is red and sear.
Marmion (1808), c.I, introd. i

28 To him, as to the burning levin,

Short, bright, resistless course was given.
vi

1 Had'st thou but liv'd, though stripp'd of power,
A watchman on the lonely tower. [On Pitt.]
viii

2 Now is the stately column broke,
The beacon-light is quench'd in smoke,
The trumpet's silver sound is still,
The warder silent on the hill! [On Pitt.]

3 Drop upon Fox's grave the tear,
'Twill trickle to his rival's bier;
O'er Pitt's the mournful requiem sound,
And Fox's shall the notes rebound.
xi

4 But search the land of living men,
Where wilt thou find their like agen?

5 His square-turn'd joints, and strength of limb,
Show'd him no carpet knight so trim,
But in close fight a champion grim,
In camps a leader sage.
c.I.v

6 And come he slow, or come he fast,
It is but Death who comes at last.
c.II.xxx

7 Still is thy name in high account,
And still thy verse has charms,
Sir David Lindesay of the Mount,
Lord Lion King-at-arms!
c.IV.vii

8 O, young Lochinvar is come out of the west,
Through all the wide Border his steed was the best.
c.V.xii

9 So faithful in love, and so dauntless in war,
There never was knight like the young Lochinvar.

10 For a laggard in love, and a dastard in war,
Was to wed the fair Ellen of brave Lochinvar.

11 'O come ye in peace here, or come ye in war,
Or to dance at our bridal, young Lord Lochinvar?'

12 'To lead but one measure, drink one cup of wine.'

13 She look'd down to blush, and she look'd up to sigh,
With a smile on her lips and a tear in her eye,
He took her soft hand, ere her mother could bar,—
'Now tread we a measure!' said young Lochinvar.

14 'She is won! we are gone, over bank, bush, and scaur;
They'll have fleet steeds that follow' quoth young
Lochinvar.

15 Heap on more wood!—the wind is chill;
But let it whistle as it will,
We'll keep our Christmas merry still.
c.VI, introd. i

16 England was merry England, when
Old Christmas brought his sports again.
'Twas Christmas broach'd the mightiest ale;
'Twas Christmas told the merriest tale;
A Christmas gambol oft could cheer
The poor man's heart through half the year.
iii

17 My castles are my King's alone,
From turret to foundation-stone—
The hand of Douglas is his own.
xiii

18 'And dar'st thou then
To beard the lion in his den,
The Douglas in his hall?
And hop'st thou thence unscathed to go?
No, by Saint Bride of Bothwell, no!
Up drawbridge, grooms—what, warder, ho!
Let the portcullis fall.'
xiv

19 O what a tangled web we weave,
When first we practise to deceive!
xvii

20 And such a yell was there,
Of sudden and portentous birth,
As if men fought upon the earth,
And fiends in upper air.
xxv

21 O Woman! in our hours of ease,
Uncertain, coy, and hard to please,
And variable as the shade
By the light quivering aspen made;
When pain and anguish wring the brow,
A ministering angel thou!
xxx

22 'Charge, Chester, charge! On, Stanley, on!'
Were the last words of Marmion.
xxxii

23 O, for a blast of that dread horn,
On Fontarabian echoes borne!
xxxiii

24 The stubborn spear-men still made good
Their dark impenetrable wood,
Each stepping where his comrade stood,
The instant that he fell.
xxxiv

25 Still from the sire the son shall hear
Of the stern strife, and carnage drear,
Of Flodden's fatal field,
Where shiver'd was fair Scotland's spear,
And broken was her shield!

26 To all, to each, a fair good-night,
And pleasing dreams, and slumbers light!
L'envoy

27 Pibroch of Donuil Dhu,
Pibroch of Donuil,
Wake thy wild voice anew,
Summon Clan-Conuil.
Come away, come away,
Hark to the summons!
Come in your war array,
Gentles and commons.
Pibroch of Donuil Dhu

28 Leave untended the herd,
The flock without shelter;
Leave the corpse uninterr'd,
The bride at the altar.

29 See yon pale stripling! when a boy,
A mother's pride, a father's joy!
Rokeby (1813), c.III.xv

30 O, Brignal banks are wild and fair,
And Greta woods are green,
And you may gather garlands there
Would grace a summer queen.
xvi

1 You...whirl'd them to the back o' beyont.
   The Antiquary (1816), ch.2

2 It's no fish ye're buying—it's men's lives.
   ch.11

3 Widow'd wife, and married maid,
   Betrothed, betrayer, and betray'd!
   The Betrothed (1825), ch.15

4 Woman's faith, and woman's trust—
   Write the characters in dust.
   ch.20

5 Look not thou on beauty's charming,—
   Sit thou still when kings are arming,—
   Taste not when the wine-cup glistens,—
   Speak not when the people listens,—
   Stop thine ear against the singer,—
   From the red gold keep thy finger;—
   Vacant heart and hand, and eye,—
   Easy live and quiet die.
   The Bride of Lammermoor (1819), ch.3

6 I live by twa trades, sir,...fiddle, sir, and spade; filling
   the world, and emptying of it.
   ch.24

7 Her winding-sheet is up as high as her throat already.
   ch.34

8 An ower true tale.

9 Touch not the cat but a glove.
   The Fair Maid of Perth (1828), ch.34. but ; without.

10 But no one shall find me rowing against the stream. I
   care not who knows it—I write for the general
   amusement.
   The Fortunes of Nigel (1822), introductory epistle

11 It's ill taking the breeks aff a wild Highlandman.
   ch.5

12 For a con-si-de-ra-tion.
   ch.22

13 O Geordie, Jingling Geordie, it was grand to hear
   Baby Charles laying down the guilt of dissimulation,
   and Steenie lecturing on the turpitude of incontinence.
   ch.31

14 *Mrs. Bertram:* That sounds like nonsense, my dear.
   Mr. Bertram: May be so, my dear; but it may be very
   good law for all that.
   Guy Mannering (1815), ch.9

15 Sophia, as you well know, followed me to India. She
   was as innocent as gay; but, unfortunately for us both,
   as gay as innocent.
   ch.12. See 588:7

16 Gin by pailfuls, wine in rivers,
   Dash the window-glass to shivers!
   For three wild lads were we, brave boys,
   And three wild lads were we;
   Thou on the land, and I on the sand,
   And Jack on the gallows-tree!
   ch.34

17 The ancient and now forgotten pastime of high jinks.
   ch.36

18 The hour is come, but not the man.
   The Heart of Midlothian (1818), ch.4, heading

19 The passive resistance of the Tolbooth-gate.
   ch.6

20 Jock, when ye hae naething else to do, ye may be ay
   sticking in a tree; it will be growing, Jock, when ye're

sleeping.
   ch.8

21 Proud Maisie is in the wood,
      Walking so early,
   Sweet Robin sits in the bush,
      Singing so rarely.
   ch.40

22 'Pax vobiscum' will answer all queries.
   Ivanhoe (1819), ch.26

23 His morning walk was beneath the elms in the
   churchyard; 'for death,' he said, 'had been his
   next-door neighbour for so many years, that he had no
   apology for dropping the acquaintance.'
   A Legend of Montrose (1819), introd.

24 March, march, Ettrick and Teviotdale,
   Why the deil dinna ye march forward in order?
   March, march, Eskdale and Liddesdale,
   All the Blue Bonnets are bound for the Border.
   The Monastery (1820), ch.25

25 Ah! County Guy, the hour is nigh,
      The sun has left the lea,
   The orange flower perfumes the bower,
      The breeze is on the sea.
   Quentin Durward (1823), ch.4

26 And it's ill speaking between a fou man and a fasting.
   Redgauntlet (1824), Letter 11, **Wandering Willie's Tale**

27 Better a finger off, as ay wagging.
   ch.2

28 The ae half of the warld thinks the tither daft.
   ch.7

29 But with the morning cool repentance came.
   Rob Roy (1817), ch.12

30 Come fill up my cup, come fill up my cann,
   Come saddle my horses, and call up my man;
   Come open your gates, and let me gae free,
   I daurna stay langer in bonny Dundee.
   ch.23. See 415:20

31 There's a gude time coming.
   ch.32

32 Speak out, sir, and do not Maister or Campbell
   me— my foot is on my native heath, and my name is
   MacGregor!
   ch.34

33 Fair, fat, and forty.
   St. Ronan's Well (1823), ch.7

34 The play-bill, which is said to have announced the
   tragedy of Hamlet, the character of the Prince of
   Denmark being left out.
   The Talisman (1825), introd. For an earlier report of this anecdote
   see *T.L.S.* 3 June 1939

35 Rouse the lion from his lair.
   ch.6

36 But I must say to the Muse of fiction, as the Earl of
   Pembroke said to the ejected nun of Wilton, 'Go spin,
   you jade, go spin!'
   Journal, 9 Feb. 1826. See 371:10

37 The Big Bow-Wow strain I can do myself like any now
   going; but the exquisite touch, which renders ordinary
   commonplace things and characters interesting, from
   the truth of the description and the sentiment, is denied
   to me. [On Jane Austen.]
   14 Mar. 1826. See 371:12

38 I would like to be there, were it but to see how the cat

jumps.
7 Oct. 1826

1 The blockheads talk of my being like
Shakespeare—not fit to tie his brogues.
11 Dec. 1826

2 I never saw a richer country or to speak my mind a
finer people. The worst of them is the bitter and
envenomed dislike which they have to each other their
factions have been so long envenomed and having so
little ground to fight their battle in that they are like
people fighting with daggers in a hogshead.
Letter to Joanna Baillie, 12 Oct. 1825

3 All men who have turned out worth anything have had
the chief hand in their own education.
Letter to J.G. Lockhart, c.16 June 1830

4 We shall never learn to feel and respect our real calling
and destiny, unless we have taught ourselves to
consider every thing as moonshine, compared with the
education of the heart.
To J.G. Lockhart (Aug. 1825), quoted in Lockhart's *Life of Sir
Walter Scott*, vol. 6 (1837), ch.2

SCOTTISH METRICAL PSALMS 1650

5 The Lord's my shepherd, I'll not want.
　　He makes me down to lie
In pastures green: he leadeth me
　　the quiet waters by.
My soul he doth restore again;
　　and me to walk doth make
Within the paths of righteousness,
　　ev'n for his own name's sake.

Yea, though I walk in death's dark vale,
　　yet will I fear none ill:
For thou art with me; and thy rod
　　and staff me comfort still.
My table thou hast furnished
　　in presence of my foes;
My head thou dost with oil anoint,
　　and my cup overflows.
Psalm xxiii.1. See 390:22

6 I to the hills will lift mine eyes
　　from whence doth come mine aid.
Psalm cxxi.1. See 398:9

7 The race that long in darkness pin'd
　　have seen a glorious light.
Paraphrase 19. Isaiah ix.2

SIR CHARLES SEDLEY 1639?–1701

8 Ah, Chloris! that I now could sit
　　As unconcerned as when
Your infant beauty could beget
　　No pleasure, nor no pain!
Child and Maiden

9 Love still has something of the sea
　　From whence his mother rose.
Love still has Something

10 Phyllis is my only joy,
　　Faithless as the winds or seas;
Sometimes coming, sometimes coy,
　　Yet she never fails to please.
Song

11 　　She deceiving,
　　　　I believing;
What need lovers wish for more?

12 Phyllis, without frown or smile,
Sat and knotted all the while.
Song [Phyllis Knotting]

13 Not, Celia, that I juster am
　　Or better than the rest,
For I would change each hour like them,
　　Were not my heart at rest.
Song [To Celia]

14 Why then should I seek farther store,
　　And still make love anew;
When change itself can give no more,
　　'Tis easy to be true.

ALAN SEEGER 1888–1916

15 I have a rendezvous with Death
At some disputed barricade.
I Have a Rendezvous with Death (*North American Review*, Oct.
1916)

SIR JOHN SEELEY 1834–1895

16 We [the English] seem, as it were, to have conquered
and peopled half the world in a fit of absence of mind.
The Expansion of England (1883), Lecture I

17 History is past politics, and politics present history.
The Growth of British Policy (1895)

JOHN SELDEN 1584–1654

18 *Scrutamini scripturas.* These two words have undone
the world.
Table Talk (1689), 1892 edn. p.10. **Bible Scripture.** See 72:3

19 Old friends are best. King James used to call for his
old shoes; they were easiest for his feet.
p.71. **Friends**

20 'Tis not the drinking that is to be blamed, but the
excess.
p.78. **Humility**

21 Ignorance of the law excuses no man; not that all men
know the law, but because 'tis an excuse every man
will plead, and no man can tell how to confute him.
p.99. **Law**

22 Take a straw and throw it up into the air, you shall see
by that which way the wind is.
p.105. **Libels**

23 Marriage is nothing but a civil contract.
p.109. **Marriage**

24 There never was a merry world since the fairies left
off dancing, and the Parson left conjuring.
p.130. **Parson**

25 There is not anything in the world so much abused as
this sentence, *Salus populi suprema lex esto.*
p.131. **People.** See 151:19

26 Pleasure is nothing else but the intermission of pain,
the enjoying of something I am in great trouble for till
I have it.
p.132. **Pleasure**

1 Preachers say, Do as I say, not as I do.
p.147. **Preaching**

W.C. SELLAR 1898–1951
and R.J. YEATMAN 1898?–1968

2 The Roman Conquest was, however, a *Good Thing*.
1066, And All That (1930), ch.1

3 The memorable epitaph: *'Honi soie qui mal y pense'*
('Honey, your silk stocking's hanging down').
ch.25

4 The Cavaliers (Wrong but Wromantic) and the
Roundheads (Right but Repulsive).
ch.35

5 Charles II was always very merry and was therefore
not so much a king as a Monarch.
ch.36

6 The National Debt is a very Good Thing and it would
be dangerous to pay it off for fear of Political
Economy.
ch.38

7 Napoleon's armies always used to march on their
stomachs, shouting: 'Vive l'Intérieur!'
ch.48

8 A Bad Thing, America was thus clearly top nation,
and History came to a .
ch. 62

SENECA 4 B.C./A.D. 1–65

9 Eternal law has arranged nothing better than this, that
it has given us one way in to life, but many ways out.
Epistulae Morales, 70.14

10 *Homines dum docent discunt.*
Even while they teach, men learn.
Letters, 7.8

11 Anyone can stop a man's life, but no one his death; a
thousand doors open on to it.
Phoenissae, 152

ROBERT W. SERVICE 1874–1958

12 Ah! the clock is always slow;
It is later than you think.
Ballads of a Bohemian. **Spring**, ii

13 This is the Law of the Yukon, that only the Strong
shall thrive;
That surely the Weak shall perish, and only the Fit
survive.
Dissolute, damned, and despairful, crippled and
palsied and slain,
This is the Will of the Yukon,—Lo! how she makes it
plain!
Songs of a Sourdough (1907). **The Law of the Yukon**

14 Back of the bar, in a solo game, sat Dangerous Dan
McGrew,
And watching his luck was his light-o'-love, the lady
that's known as Lou.
The Shooting of Dan McGrew

WILLIAM SEWARD 1801–1872

15 The Constitution devotes the domain to union, to
justice, to defence, to welfare, and to liberty. But there

is a higher law than the Constitution.
U.S. Senate, 11 Mar. 1850

16 I know, and all the world knows, that revolutions
never go backward.
At Rochester on the Irrepressible Conflict, Oct. 1858

EDWARD SEXBY d. 1658

17 Killing no Murder Briefly Discourst in Three
Questions.
Title of Pamphlet, 1657

ANNE SEXTON 1928–1974

18 In a dream you are never eighty.
Old

THOMAS SHADWELL 1642?–1692

19 Words may be false and full of art,
Sighs are the natural language of the heart.
Psyche (1674), Act III

20 And wit's the noblest frailty of the mind.
A True Widow (1678-9), II.i. See 196:23

21 The haste of a fool is the slowest thing in the world.
III.i

22 Every man loves what he is good at.
V.i

23 Instantly, in the twinkling of a bed-staff.
Virtuoso (1676), I.i

**ANTHONY ASHLEY COOPER, 1ST EARL OF
SHAFTESBURY** 1621–1683

24 'People differ in their discourse and profession about
these matters, but men of sense are really but of one
religion.'…'Pray, my lord, what religion is that which
men of sense agree in?' 'Madam,' says the earl
immediately, 'men of sense never tell it.'
Bishop Burnet, *History of My Own Time*, vol.I, bk.ii, ch.1, note
by Onslow

WILLIAM SHAKESPEARE 1564–1616

The line number is given without brackets where the scene is all
verse up to the quotation and the line number is certain, and in
square brackets where prose makes it variable. All references are
to the Oxford Standard Authors Shakespeare in one volume.

ALL'S WELL THAT ENDS WELL

25   It were all one
That I should love a bright particular star
And think to wed it, he is so above me.
I.i.[97]

26 The hind that would be mated with the lion
Must die of love.
[103]

27 Your virginity, your old virginity, is like one of our
French withered pears; it looks ill, it eats drily.
[176]

28 Our remedies oft in ourselves do lie
Which we ascribe to heaven.
[235]

29 It is like a barber's chair that fits all buttocks.
II.ii.[18]

1 A young man married is a man that's marred.
iii.[315]

2 I know a man that had this trick of melancholy sold a
goodly manor for a song.
III.ii.[8]

3 The web of our life is of a mingled yarn, good and ill
together: our virtues would be proud if our faults
whipped them not; and our crimes would despair if
they were not cherished by our own virtues.
IV.iii.[83]

4 The flowery way that leads to the broad gate and the
great fire.
v.[58]. See 460:17

5   Praising what is lost
Makes the remembrance dear.
V.iii.19

ANTONY AND CLEOPATRA

6 The triple pillar of the world transform'd
Into a strumpet's fool.
I.i.12

7 *Cleopatra:* If it be love indeed, tell me how much.
Antony: There's beggary in the love that can be
reckoned.
Cleopatra: I'll set a bourn how far to be belov'd.
Antony: Then must thou needs find out new heaven,
new earth.
14

8 Kingdoms are clay; our dungy earth alike
Feeds beast as man; the nobleness of life
Is to do thus; when such a mutual pair
And such a twain can do't.
35

9 In Nature's infinite book of secrecy
A little I can read.
ii.[11]

10 You shall be yet far fairer than you are.
[18]

11 You shall be more beloving than belov'd.
[24]

12 O excellent! I love long life better than figs.
[34]

13 Mine, and most of our fortunes, to-night, shall
be,—drunk to bed.
[47]

14 But a worky-day fortune.
[57]

15   On the sudden
A Roman thought hath struck him.
[90]

16 The nature of bad news infects the teller.
[103]

17 These strong Egyptian fetters I must break,
Or lose myself in dotage.
[125]

18 There's a great spirit gone!
[131]

19 I must from this enchanting queen break off;
Ten thousand harms, more than the ills I know,
My idleness doth hatch.
[137]

20 I have seen her die twenty times upon far poorer

moment. I do think there is mettle in death which
commits some loving act upon her, she hath such a
celerity in dying.
[150]

21 O sir! you had then left unseen a wonderful piece of
work which not to have been blessed withal would
have discredited your travel.
[164]

22 Indeed the tears live in an onion that should water this
sorrow.
[181]

23   If you find him sad,
Say I am dancing; if in mirth, report
That I am sudden sick.
iii.3

24 *Charmian:* In each thing give him way, cross him in
nothing.
Cleopatra: Thou teachest like a fool; the way to lose
him.
9

25 In time we hate that which we often fear.
12

26 Eternity was in our lips and eyes,
Bliss in our brows bent.
35

27 Though age from folly could not give me freedom,
It does from childishness.
57

28   Courteous lord, one word.
Sir, you and I must part, but that's not it:
Sir, you and I have lov'd, but there's not it;
That you know well: something it is I would,—
O! my oblivion is a very Antony,
And I am all forgotten.
86

29   On the Alps
It is reported thou didst eat strange flesh,
Which some did die to look on.
iv.66

30 Give me to drink mandragora...
That I might sleep out this great gap of time
My Antony is away.
v.4

31 O happy horse, to bear the weight of Antony!
Do bravely, horse, for wot'st thou whom thou mov'st?
The demi-Atlas of this earth, the arm
And burgonet of men. He's speaking now,
Or murmuring 'Where's my serpent of old Nile?'
21

32   Think on me,
That am with Phoebus' amorous pinches black,
And wrinkled deep in time? Broad-fronted Caesar,
When thou wast here above the ground I was
A morsel for a monarch, and great Pompey
Would stand and make his eyes grow in my brow;
There would he anchor his aspect and die
With looking on his life.
27

33   My salad days,
When I was green in judgment, cold in blood,
To say as I said then!
73

34 I do not much dislike the matter, but

The manner of his speech.
II.ii.117

1   Take Antony
Octavia to his wife; whose beauty claims
No worse a husband than the best of men.
133

2 The barge she sat in, like a burnish'd throne,
Burn'd on the water; the poop was beaten gold,
Purple the sails, and so perfumed, that
The winds were love-sick with them, the oars were
    silver,
Which to the tune of flutes kept stroke, and made
The water which they beat to follow faster,
As amorous of their strokes. For her own person,
It beggar'd all description; she did lie
In her pavilion,—cloth-of-gold of tissue,—
O'er-picturing that Venus where we see
The fancy outwork nature; on each side her
Stood pretty-dimpled boys, like smiling Cupids,
With divers-colour'd fans, whose wind did seem
To glow the delicate cheeks which they did cool,
And what they undid did.
[199]

3 Her gentlewomen, like the Nereides,
So many mermaids, tended her i' the eyes,
And made their bends adornings; at the helm
A seeming mermaid steers; the silken tackle
Swell with the touches of those flower-soft hands,
That yarely frame the office. From the barge
A strange invisible perfume hits the sense
Of the adjacent wharfs. The city cast
Her people out upon her, and Antony,
Enthron'd i' the market-place, did sit alone,
Whistling to the air; which, but for vacancy,
Had gone to gaze on Cleopatra too
And made a gap in nature.
[214]

4   I saw her once
Hop forty paces through the public street;
And having lost her breath, she spoke, and panted
That she did make defect perfection,
And, breathless, power breathe forth.
[236]

5 Age cannot wither her, nor custom stale
Her infinite variety; other women cloy
The appetites they feed, but she makes hungry
Where most she satisfies; for vilest things
Become themselves in her, that the holy priests
Bless her when she is riggish.
[243]

6 I have not kept the square, but that to come
Shall all be done by the rule.
iii.6

7 I' the east my pleasure lies.
40

8 *Attendants:* The music, ho!
Cleopatra: Let it alone; let's to billiards: come,
   Charmian.
v.2

9 Give me mine angle; we'll to the river: there—
My music playing far off—I will betray
Tawny-finn'd fishes; my bended hook shall pierce
Their slimy jaws; and, as I draw them up,
I'll think them every one an Antony,

And say, 'Ah, ha!' you're caught.
10

10 I laugh'd him out of patience; and that night
I laugh'd him into patience: and next morn,
Ere the ninth hour, I drunk him to his bed.
19

11   There is gold, and here
My bluest veins to kiss; a hand that kings
Have lipp'd, and trembled kissing.
28

12 Though it be honest, it is never good
To bring bad news; give to a gracious message
A host of tongues, but let ill tidings tell
Themselves when they be felt.
85

13 I will praise any man that will praise me.
vi.[88]

14 *Lepidus:* What manner o' thing is your crocodile?
Antony: It is shaped, sir, like itself, and it is as broad
as it hath breadth; it is just so high as it is, and moves
with its own organs; it lives by that which nourisheth
it; and the elements once out of it, it transmigrates.
Lepidus: What colour is it of?
Antony: Of its own colour too.
Lepidus: 'Tis a strange serpent.
Antony: 'Tis so; and the tears of it are wet.
vii.[47]

15 He sends so poor a pinion of his wing,
Which had superfluous kings for messengers
Not many moons gone by.
III.x.4

16   He wears the rose
Of youth upon him.
xi.20

17 Against the blown rose may they stop their nose,
That kneel'd unto the buds.
39

18   Yet he that can endure
To follow with allegiance a fall'n lord,
Does conquer him that did his master conquer,
And earns a place i' the story.
43

19   Your Caesar's father oft,
When he hath mus'd of taking kingdoms in,
Bestow'd his lips on that unworthy place,
As it rain'd kisses.
82

20 I found you as a morsel, cold upon
Dead Caesar's trencher.
116

21 To let a fellow that will take rewards
And say 'God quit you!' be familiar with
My playfellow, your hand; this kingly seal
And plighter of high hearts.
123

22 Let's have one other gaudy night: call to me
All my sad captains; fill our bowls once more;
Let's mock the midnight bell.
182

23   Since my lord
Is Antony again, I will be Cleopatra.
185

24 To business that we love we rise betime,

And go to 't with delight.
IV.iv.20

1　　　O! my fortunes have
Corrupted honest men.
v.16

2 I am alone the villain of the earth,
And feel I am so most.
vi.30

3 *Cleopatra:* Lord of lords!
O infinite virtue! com'st thou smiling from
The world's great snare uncaught?
Antony: My nightingale,
We have beat them to their beds.
viii.16

4 O sovereign mistress of true melancholy,
The poisonous damp of night dísponge upon me,
That life, a very rebel to my will,
May hang no longer on me.
ix.12

5　　　The hearts
That spaniel'd me at heels, to whom I gave
Their wishes, do discandy, melt their sweets
On blossoming Caesar.
x.33

6 The soul and body rive not more in parting
Than greatness going off.
xi.5

7 Sometimes we see a cloud that's dragonish;
A vapour sometime like a bear or lion,
A tower'd citadel, a pendant rock,
A forked mountain, or blue promontory
With trees upon 't, that nod unto the world
And mock our eyes with air: thou hast seen these
　　　signs;
They are black vesper's pageants.
xii.2

8 That which is now a horse, even with a thought
The rack dislimns, and makes it indistinct,
As water is in water.
9

9 Unarm, Eros; the long day's task is done,
And we must sleep.
35

10 Lie down, and stray no further. Now all labour
Mars what it does; yea, very force entangles
Itself with strength...
　　　Stay for me:
Where souls do couch on flowers, we'll hand in hand,
And with our sprightly port make the ghosts gaze;
Dido and her Aeneas shall want troops,
And all the haunt be ours.
47

11　　　I will be
A bridegroom in my death, and run into 't
As to a lover's bed.
99

12 All strange and terrible events are welcome,
But comforts we despise.
xiii.3

13 *Antony:* Not Caesar's valour hath o'erthrown Antony
But Antony's hath triumphed on itself.
Cleopatra: So it should be, that none but Antony

Should conquer Antony.
14

14 I am dying, Egypt, dying; only
I here importune death awhile, until
Of many thousand kisses the poor last
I lay upon thy lips.
18

15 The miserable change now at my end
Lament nor sorrow at; but please your thoughts
In feeding them with those my former fortunes
Wherein I liv'd, the greatest prince o' the world,
The noblest; and do now not basely die,
Not cowardly put off my helmet to
My countryman; a Roman by a Roman
Valiantly vanquished.
51

16 Hast thou no care of me? shall I abide
In this dull world, which in thy absence is
No better than a sty? O! see my women,
The crown o' the earth doth melt. My lord!
O! wither'd is the garland of the war,
The soldier's pole is fall'n; young boys and girls
Are level now with men; the odds is gone,
And there is nothing left remarkable
Beneath the visiting moon.
60

17 No more, but e'en a woman and commanded
By such poor passion as the maid that milks
And does the meanest chares.
73

18　　　What's brave, what's noble,
Let's do it after the high Roman fashion,
And make death proud to take us.
86

19　　　A rarer spirit never
Did steer humanity; but you, gods, will give us
Some faults to make us men.
V.i.31

20 My desolation does begin to make
A better life. 'Tis paltry to be Caesar;
Not being Fortune, he's but Fortune's knave,
A minister of her will; and it is great
To do that thing that ends all other deeds,
Which shackles accidents, and bolts up change,
Which sleeps, and never palates more the dug,
The beggar's nurse and Caesar's.
ii.1

21 Nor once be chastis'd with the sober eye
Of dull Octavia. Shall they hoist me up
And show me to the shouting varletry
Of censuring Rome? Rather a ditch in Egypt
Be gentle grave unto me! rather on Nilus' mud
Lay me stark naked, and let the water-flies
Blow me into abhorring!
54

22 His legs bestrid the ocean; his rear'd arm
Crested the world; his voice was propertied
As all the tuned spheres, and that to friends;
But when he meant to quail and shake the orb,
He was as rattling thunder. For his bounty,
There was no winter in't; an autumn was
That grew the more by reaping; his delights
Were dolphin-like, they show'd his back above
The element they liv'd in; in his livery

Walk'd crowns and crownets, realms and islands were
As plates dropp'd from his pocket.
82

1 He words me, girls, he words me, that I should not
Be noble to myself.
190

2 Finish, good lady; the bright day is done,
And we are for the dark.
192

3   Antony
Shall be brought drunken forth, and I shall see
Some squeaking Cleopatra boy my greatness
I' the posture of a whore.
217

4 My resolution's plac'd, and I have nothing
Of woman in me; now from head to foot
I am marble-constant, now the fleeting moon
No planet is of mine.
237

5 His biting is immortal; those that do die of it do seldom
or never recover.
[246]

6 A very honest woman, but something given to lie.
[251]

7 I wish you all joy of the worm.
[260]

8 Indeed there is no goodness in the worm.
[267]

9 I know that a woman is a dish for the gods, if the
devil dress her not.
[274]

10 Give me my robe, put on my crown; I have
Immortal longings in me.
[282]

11   Husband, I come:
Now to that name my courage prove my title!
I am fire and air; my other elements
I give to baser life.
[289]

12 If thou and nature can so gently part,
The stroke of death is as a lover's pinch,
Which hurts, and is desir'd.
[296]

13 If thus thou vanishest, thou tell'st the world
It is not worth leave-taking.
[299]

14 *Cleopatra:* If she first meet the curled Antony,
He'll make demand of her, and spend that kiss
Which is my heaven to have. Come, thou mortal
   wretch,
With thy sharp teeth this knot intrinsicate
Of life at once untie; poor venomous fool,
Be angry, and dispatch. O! couldst thou speak,
That I might hear thee call great Caesar ass
Unpolicied.
Charmian: O eastern star!
Cleopatra: Peace! peace!
Dost thou not see my baby at my breast,
That sucks the nurse asleep?
[303]

15 Now boast thee, death, in thy possession lies
A lass unparallel'd.
[317]

16 It is well done, and fitting for a princess
Descended of so many royal kings.
[328]

17   She looks like sleep,
As she would catch a second Antony
In her strong toil of grace.
[347]

18 She hath pursu'd conclusions infinite
Of easy ways to die.
[356]

19 She shall be buried by her Antony:
No grave upon the earth shall clip in it
A pair so famous.
[359]

AS YOU LIKE IT

20 Fleet the time carelessly, as they did in the golden
world.
I.i.[126]

21 Let us sit and mock the good housewife Fortune from
her wheel, that her gifts may henceforth be bestowed
equally.
ii.[35]

22 How now, wit! whither wander you?
[60]

23 Thus men may grow wiser every day: it is the first
time that I ever heard breaking of ribs was sport for
ladies.
[146]

24 Only in the world I fill up a place, which may be
better supplied when I have made it empty.
[206]

25 Wear this for me, one out of suits with fortune,
That could give more, but that her hand lacks means.
[263]

26 Sir, you have wrestled well, and overthrown
More than your enemies.
[271]

27 Hereafter, in a better world than this,
I shall desire more love and knowledge of you.
[301]

28 Thus must I from the smoke into the smother;
From tyrant duke unto a tyrant brother.
[304]

29 O, how full of briers is this working-day world!
iii.[12]

30 We'll have a swashing and a martial outside,
As many other mannish cowards have
That do outface it with their semblances.
[123]

31 Hath not old custom made this life more sweet
Than that of painted pomp? Are not these woods
More free from peril than the envious court?
Here feel we but the penalty of Adam,
The seasons' difference; as, the icy fang
And churlish chiding of the winter's wind,
Which, when it bites and blows upon my body,
Even till I shrink with cold, I smile and say,
'This is no flattery.'
II.i.2

32 Sweet are the uses of adversity,
Which like the toad, ugly and venomous,

Wears yet a precious jewel in his head;
And this our life, exempt from public haunt,
Finds tongues in trees, books in the running brooks,
Sermons in stones, and good in everything.
12

1   The big round tears
Cours'd one another down his innocent nose,
In piteous chase.
38

2 Sweep on, you fat and greasy citizens!
55

3 I love to cope him in these sullen fits,
For then he's full of matter.
67

4 Unregarded age in corners thrown.
iii.42

5   Though I look old, yet I am strong and lusty;
For in my youth I never did apply
Hot and rebellious liquors in my blood.
47

6 Therefore my age is as a lusty winter,
Frosty, but kindly.
52

7 O good old man! how well in thee appears
The constant service of the antique world,
When service sweat for duty, not for meed!
Thou art not for the fashion of these times,
Where none will sweat but for promotion,
And having that, do choke their service up
Even with the having.
56

8 Ay, now am I in Arden; the more fool I. When I was
at home I was in a better place; but travellers must be
content.
iv.[16]

9 In thy youth thou wast as true a lover
As ever sigh'd upon a midnight pillow.
[26]

10 If thou remember'st not the slightest folly
That ever love did make thee run into,
Thou hast not lov'd.
[34]

11 We that are true lovers run into strange capers.
[53]

12 Thou speakest wiser than thou art ware of.
[57]

13 I shall ne'er be ware of mine own wit till I break my
shins against it.
[59]

14 Under the greenwood tree
Who loves to lie with me,
And turn his merry note
Unto the sweet bird's throat,
Come hither, come hither, come hither:
       Here shall he see
       No enemy
But winter and rough weather.
v.1

15 I can suck melancholy out of a song as a weasel sucks
eggs.
[12]

16 Who doth ambition shun
And loves to live i' the sun,

Seeking the food he eats,
And pleas'd with what he gets.
[38]

17 I'll go to sleep if I can; if I cannot, I'll rail against all
the first-born of Egypt.
[60]

18 A fool, a fool! I met a fool i' the forest,
A motley fool; a miserable world!
As I do live by food, I met a fool;
Who laid him down and bask'd him in the sun,
And rail'd on Lady Fortune in good terms,
In good set terms, and yet a motley fool.
'Good morrow, fool,' quoth I. 'No, sir,' quoth he,
'Call me not fool till heaven hath sent me fortune.'
vii.12

19 And so, from hour to hour, we ripe and ripe,
And then from hour to hour, we rot and rot:
And thereby hangs a tale.
26

20 My lungs began to crow like chanticleer,
That fools should be so deep-contemplative,
And I did laugh sans intermission
An hour by his dial. O noble fool!
A worthy fool! Motley's the only wear.
30

21 O worthy fool! One that hath been a courtier,
And says, if ladies be but young and fair,
They have the gift to know it: and in his brain,—
Which is as dry as the remainder biscuit
After a voyage,—he hath strange places cramm'd
With observation, the which he vents
In mangled forms.
36

22   I must have liberty
Withal, as large a charter as the wind,
To blow on whom I please.
47

23 If ever you have look'd on better days,
If ever been where bells have knoll'd to church,
If ever sat at any good man's feast,
If ever from your eyelids wip'd a tear,
And know what 'tis to pity, and be pitied,
Let gentleness my strong enforcement be.
113

24   All the world's a stage,
And all the men and women merely players:
They have their exits and their entrances;
And one man in his time plays many parts,
His acts being seven ages. At first the infant,
Mewling and puking in the nurse's arms.
And then the whining schoolboy, with his satchel,
And shining morning face, creeping like snail
Unwillingly to school. And then the lover,
Sighing like furnace, with a woful ballad
Made to his mistress' eyebrow. Then a soldier,
Full of strange oaths, and bearded like the pard,
Jealous in honour, sudden and quick in quarrel,
Seeking the bubble reputation
Even in the cannon's mouth. And then the justice,
In fair round belly with good capon lin'd,
With eyes severe, and beard of formal cut,
Full of wise saws and modern instances;
And so he plays his part. The sixth age shifts
Into the lean and slipper'd pantaloon,

With spectacles on nose and pouch on side,
His youthful hose well sav'd a world too wide
For his shrunk shank; and his big manly voice,
Turning again towards childish treble, pipes
And whistles in his sound. Last scene of all,
That ends this strange eventful history,
Is second childishness, and mere oblivion,
Sans teeth, sans eyes, sans taste, sans everything.
139

1 Blow, blow, thou winter wind,
Thou art not so unkind
As man's ingratitude:
Thy tooth is not so keen,
Because thou art not seen,
Although thy breath be rude.
Heigh-ho! sing, heigh-ho! unto the green holly:
Most friendship is feigning, most loving mere folly.
Then heigh-ho! the holly!
This life is most jolly.

Freeze, freeze, thou bitter sky,
That dost not bite so nigh
As benefits forgot:
Though thou the waters warp,
Thy sting is not so sharp
As friend remember'd not.
174

2 Run, run, Orlando: carve on every tree
The fair, the chaste, and unexpressive she.
III.ii.9

3 He that wants money, means, and content is without
three good friends.
[25]

4 I earn that I eat, get that I wear, owe no man hate,
envy no man's happiness, glad of other men's good,
content with my harm.
[78]

5 From the east to western Ind,
No jewel is like Rosalind.
[94]

6 Let us make an honourable retreat; though not with
bag and baggage, yet with scrip and scrippage.
[170]

7 O wonderful, wonderful, and most wonderful
wonderful! and yet again wonderful, and after that,
out of all whooping!
[202]

8 It is as easy to count atomies as to resolve the
propositions of a lover.
[246]

9 Do you not know I am a woman? when I think, I must
speak.
[265]

10 I do desire we may be better strangers.
[276]

11 You have a nimble wit; I think 'twas made of
Atalanta's heels.
[294]

12 *Jaques:* I do not like her name.
Orlando: There was no thought of pleasing you when
she was christened.
[283]

13 *Jaques:* Time travels in divers paces with divers
persons...

Orlando: Who stays it still withal?
Jaques: With lawyers in the vacation; for they sleep
between term and term.
[328]

14 There were none principal; they were all like one
another as half-pence are; every one fault seeming
monstrous till his fellow fault came to match it.
[376]. Of women's offences.

15 Truly, I would the gods had made thee poetical.
iii.[16]

16 I am not a slut, though I thank the gods I am foul.
[40]

17 Down on your knees,
And thank heaven, fasting, for a good man's love.
v.57

18 I pray you, do not fall in love with me,
For I am falser than vows made in wine.
[72]

19 Dead shepherd, now I find thy saw of might:
'Who ever lov'd that lov'd not at first sight?'
[81]. See 329:18

20 *Jaques:* Nay then, God be wi' you, an you talk in
blank verse. *(Exit)*
Rosalind: Farewell, Monsieur Traveller: look you lisp
and wear strange suits, disable all the benefits of your
own country, be out of love with your nativity, and
almost chide God for making you the countenance you
are, or I will scarce think you have swam in a
gondola.
IV.i.[33]

21 Come, woo me, woo me; for now I am in a holiday
humour, and like enough to consent.
[70]

22 You were better speak first, and when you were
gravelled for lack of matter, you might take occasion
to kiss.
[75]

23 Men are April when they woo, December when they
wed: maids are May when they are maids, but the sky
changes when they are wives.
[153]

24 O coz, coz, coz, my pretty little coz, that thou didst
know how many fathom deep I am in love!
[217]

25 The horn, the horn, the lusty horn
Is not a thing to laugh to scorn.
IV.ii.[17]

26 Chewing the food of sweet and bitter fancy.
iii.[103]

27 Your brother and my sister no sooner met, but they
looked; no sooner looked but they loved; no sooner
loved but they sighed; no sooner sighed but they asked
one another the reason; no sooner knew the reason but
they sought the remedy: and in these degrees have they
made a pair of stairs to marriage which they will climb
incontinent, or else be incontinent before marriage.
V.ii.[36]

28 Oh! how bitter a thing it is to look into happiness
through another man's eyes.
[48]

29 *Phebe:* Good shepherd, tell this youth what 'tis to
love.
Silvius: It is to be all made of sighs and tears...

It is to be all made of faith and service...
It is to be all made of fantasy,
All made of passion, and all made of wishes;
All adoration, duty, and observance;
All humbleness, all patience, and impatience;
All purity, all trial, all obeisance.
[90]

1 'Tis like the howling of Irish wolves against the
moon.
[120]

2 It was a lover and his lass,
   With a hey, and a ho, and a hey nonino,
That o'er the green cornfield did pass,
   In the spring time, the only pretty ring time,
When birds do sing, hey ding a ding, ding;
Sweet lovers love the spring.

Between the acres of the rye,
   With a hey, and a ho, and a hey nonino,
These pretty country folks would lie,
   In the spring time, &c.

This carol they began that hour,
   With a hey, and a ho, and a hey nonino,
How that a life was but a flower,
   In the spring time, &c.

And therefore take the present time,
   With a hey, and a ho, and a hey nonino;
For love is crowned with the prime
   In the spring time, &c.
iii.[18]

3 Here comes a pair of very strange beasts, which in all
tongues are called fools.
iv.[36]

4 A poor virgin, sir, an ill-favoured thing, sir, but mine
own: a poor humour of mine, sir, to take that that no
man else will. Rich honesty dwells like a miser, sir, in
a poor house, as your pearl in your foul oyster.
[60]

5 The retort courteous...the quip modest...the reply
churlish...the reproof valiant...the countercheck
quarrelsome...the lie circumstantial...the lie direct.
[96]. Of the degrees of the lie.

6 Your 'if' is the only peace-maker; much virtue in 'if'
[108]

7 He uses his folly like a stalking-horse, and under the
presentation of that he shoots his wit.
[112]

8 If it be true that 'good wine needs no bush', 'tis true
that a good play needs no epilogue.
Epilogue [3]

THE COMEDY OF ERRORS

9 They brought one Pinch, a hungry, lean-fac'd villain,
A mere anatomy, a mountebank,
A threadbare juggler, and a fortune-teller,
A needy, hollow-ey'd, sharp-looking wretch,
A living-dead man.
V.i.238

CORIOLANUS

10 He's a very dog to the commonalty.
I.i.[29]

11 The kingly crowned head, the vigilant eye,
  The counsellor heart, the arm our soldier,

Our steed the leg, the tongue our trumpeter.
[121]

12 What's the matter, you dissentious rogues,
That, rubbing the poor itch of your opinion,
Make yourselves scabs?
[170]

13   They threw their caps
As they would hang them on the horns o' the moon,
Shouting their emulation.
[218]

14 I am known to be...one that loves a cup of hot wine
with not a drop of allaying Tiber in't.
II.i.[52]

15   Bid them wash their faces,
And keep their teeth clean.
[65]

16 My gracious silence, hail!
[194]

17   Custom calls me to 't:
What custom wills, in all things should we do't,
The dust on antique time would lie unswept,
And mountainous error be too highly heap'd
For truth to o'erpeer.
II.iii.[124]

18 I thank you for your voices, thank you,
Your most sweet voices.
[179]

19 How youngly he began to serve his country,
How long continu'd.
[244]

20 For the mutable, rank-scented many, let them
Regard me as I do not flatter, and
Therein behold themselves.
III.i.65

21 Hear you this Triton of the minnows? mark you
His absolute 'shall'?
88

22 On both sides more respect.
180

23 You common cry of curs! whose breath I hate
As reek o' the rotten fens, whose loves I prize
As the dead carcases of unburied men
That do corrupt my air,—I banish you.
iii.118

24   Despising,
For you, the city, thus I turn my back:
There is a world elsewhere.
131

25   The beast
With many heads butts me away.
IV.i.1

26 Thou hast a grim appearance, and thy face
Bears a command in't; though thy tackle's torn,
Thou show'st a noble vessel. What's thy name?
v.[66]

27 Let me have war, say I; it exceeds peace as far as day
does night; it's spritely, waking, audible, and full of
vent. Peace is a very apoplexy, lethargy: mulled, deaf,
sleepy, insensible; a getter of more bastard children
than war's a destroyer of men.
[237]

28   I'll never
Be such a gosling to obey instinct, but stand

As if a man were author of himself
And knew no other kin.
V.iii.34

1   Like a dull actor now,
I have forgot my part, and I am out,
Even to a full disgrace.
40

2   O! a kiss
Long as my exile, sweet as my revenge!
Now, by the jealous queen of heaven, that kiss
I carried from thee, dear, and my true lip
Hath virgin'd it e'er since.
44

3   Chaste as the icicle
That's curdied by the frost from purest snow,
And hangs on Dian's temple.
65

4   The god of soldiers,
With the consent of supreme Jove, inform
Thy thoughts with nobleness; that thou mayst prove
To shame unvulnerable, and stick i' the wars
Like a great sea-mark, standing every flaw,
And saving those that eye thee!
70

5   Thou hast never in thy life
Show'd thy dear mother any courtesy;
When she—poor hen! fond of no second brood—
Has cluck'd thee to the wars, and safely home,
Loaden with honour.
160

6 If you have writ your annals true, 'tis there,
That, like an eagle in a dove-cote, I
Flutter'd your Volscians in Corioli:
Alone I did it.
v.114

CYMBELINE

7 If she be furnish'd with a mind so rare,
She is alone the Arabian bird, and I
Have lost the wager. Boldness be my friend!
Arm me, audacity.
I.vi.16

8   Cytherea,
How bravely thou becom'st thy bed! fresh lily,
And whiter than the sheets! That I might touch!
But kiss: one kiss! Rubies unparagon'd,
How dearly they do't! 'Tis her breathing that
Perfumes the chamber thus; the flame of the taper
Bows toward her, and would under-peep her lids
To see the enclosed lights, now canopied
Under these windows, white and azure lac'd
With blue of heaven's own tinct.
II.ii.14

9   On her left breast
A mole cinque-spotted, like the crimson drops
I' the bottom of a cowslip.
37

10 Hark! hark! the lark at heaven's gate sings,
   And Phoebus 'gins arise,
His steeds to water at those springs
   On chalic'd flowers that lies;
And winking Mary-buds begin

To ope their golden eyes:
With everything that pretty is,
   My lady sweet, arise!
iii.[22]

11 Is there no way for men to be, but women
Must be half-workers?
v.1

12   I thought her
As chaste as unsunn'd snow.
12

13 The natural bravery of your isle, which stands
As Neptune's park, ribbed and paled in
With rocks unscalable, and roaring waters.
III.i.18

14 O, for a horse with wings!
ii.[49]

15   What should we speak of
When we are old as you? when we shall hear
The rain and wind beat dark December, how,
In this our pinching cave, shall we discourse
The freezing hours away? We have seen nothing.
iii.35

16   Some jay of Italy,
Whose mother was her painting, hath betray'd him:
Poor I am stale, a garment out of fashion.
iv.[51]

17 Hath Britain all the sun that shines?
[139]

18   Weariness
Can snore upon the flint when resty sloth
Finds the down pillow hard.
vi.33

19 Great griefs, I see, medicine the less.
IV.ii.243

20   Though mean and mighty rotting
Together, have one dust, yet reverence—
That angel of the world—doth make distinction
Of place 'tween high and low.
246

21 Thersites' body is as good as Ajax'
When neither are alive.
252

22 Fear no more the heat o' the sun,
   Nor the furious winter's rages;
Thou thy worldly task hast done,
   Home art gone and ta'en thy wages:
Golden lads and girls all must,
As chimney-sweepers, come to dust.

Fear no more the frown o' the great,
   Thou art past the tyrant's stroke:
Care no more to clothe and eat;
   To thee the reed is as the oak:
The sceptre, learning, physic, must
All follow this, and come to dust.

Fear no more the lightning flash,
   Nor the all-dreaded thunder-stone;
Fear not slander, censure rash;
   Thou hast finish'd joy and moan:
All lovers young, all lovers must
Consign to thee, and come to dust.

No exorciser harm thee!
   Nor no witchcraft charm thee!

Ghost unlaid forbear thee!
 Nothing ill come near thee!
Quiet consummation have:
And renowned be thy grave!
258

1 Every good servant does not all commands.
V.i.6

2 He that sleeps feels not the toothache.
iv.[176]

3 He spake of her as Dian had hot dreams,
And she alone were cold.
v.181

HAMLET

4 You come most carefully upon your hour.
I.i.6

5 For this relief much thanks; 'tis bitter cold
And I am sick at heart.
8

6 Not a mouse stirring.
10

7 *Bernardo:* What! is Horatio there?
Horatio: A piece of him.
19

8 What! has this thing appear'd again to-night?
21

9 Look, where it comes again!
40

10 But in the gross and scope of my opinion,
This bodes some strange eruption to our state.
68

11   This sweaty haste
Doth make the night joint-labourer with the day.
77

12 In the most high and palmy state of Rome,
A little ere the mightiest Julius fell,
The graves stood tenantless and the sheeted dead
Did squeak and gibber in the Roman streets.
113

13   The moist star
Upon whose influence Neptune's empire stands
Was sick almost to doomsday with eclipse.
118

14 I'll cross it, though it blast me.
127

15 We do it wrong, being so majestical,
To offer it the show of violence;
For it is, as the air, invulnerable,
And our vain blows malicious mockery.
143

16 And then it started like a guilty thing
Upon a fearful summons.
148

17 It faded on the crowing of the cock.
Some say that ever 'gainst that season comes
Wherein our Saviour's birth is celebrated,
The bird of dawning singeth all night long;
And then, they say, no spirit can walk abroad;
The nights are wholesome; then no planets strike,
No fairy takes, nor witch hath power to charm,
So hallow'd and so gracious is the time.
157

18 But, look, the morn, in russet mantle clad,
Walks o'er the dew of yon high eastern hill.
166

19 Though yet of Hamlet our dear brother's death
The memory be green...
Therefore our sometime sister, now our queen,...
Have we, as 'twere with a defeated joy,
With one auspicious and one dropping eye,
With mirth in funeral and with dirge in marriage,
In equal scale weighing delight and dole,
Taken to wife.
ii.1

20 The head is not more native to the heart,
The hand more instrumental to the brain,
Than is the throne of Denmark to thy father.
47

21 A little more than kin, and less than kind.
65

22 Not so, my lord; I am too much i' the sun.
67

23 Good Hamlet, cast thy nighted colour off,
And let thine eye look like a friend on Denmark.
68

24 *Queen:* Thou know'st 'tis common; all that live must
  die,
Passing through nature to eternity.
Hamlet: Ay, madam, it is common.
72

25 Seems, madam! Nay, it is; I know not 'seems'.
'Tis not alone my inky cloak, good mother,
Nor customary suits of solemn black,
Nor windy suspiration of forc'd breath,
No, nor the fruitful river in the eye,
Nor the dejected 'haviour of the visage,
Together with all forms, modes, shows of grief,
That can denote me truly; these indeed seem,
For they are actions that a man might play:
But I have that within which passeth show;
These but the trappings and the suits of woe.
76

26   But to persever
In obstinate condolement is a course
Of impious stubbornness; 'tis unmanly grief;
It shows a will most incorrect to heaven,
A heart unfortified, a mind impatient.
92

27 *Hamlet:* I shall in all my best obey you, madam.
King: Why, 'tis a loving and a fair reply.
120

28 O! that this too too solid flesh would melt,
Thaw, and resolve itself into a dew;
Or that the Everlasting had not fix'd
His canon 'gainst self-slaughter! O God! O God!
How weary, stale, flat, and unprofitable
Seem to me all the uses of this world.
Fie on't! O fie! 'tis an unweeded garden,
That grows to seed; things rank and gross in nature
Possess it merely. That it should come to this!
But two months dead: nay, not so much, not two:
So excellent a king; that was, to this,
Hyperion to a satyr: so loving to my mother,
That he might not beteem the winds of heaven
Visit her face too roughly. Heaven and earth!
Must I remember? Why, she would hang on him,

As if increase of appetite had grown
By what it fed on; and yet, within a month,
Let me not think on't: Frailty, thy name is woman!
A little month; or ere those shoes were old
With which she follow'd my poor father's body,
Like Niobe, all tears; why she, even she,—
O God! a beast, that wants discourse of reason,
Would have mourn'd longer,—married with mine
   uncle,
My father's brother, but no more like my father
Than I to Hercules.
129

1 It is not, nor it cannot come to good;
  But break, my heart, for I must hold my tongue!
  158

2 A truant disposition, good my lord.
  169

3 We'll teach you to drink deep ere you depart.
  175

4 Thrift, thrift, Horatio! the funeral bak'd meats
  Did coldly furnish forth the marriage tables.
  Would I had met my dearest foe in heaven
  Ere I had ever seen that day, Horatio!
  180

5 He was a man, take him for all in all,
  I shall not look upon his like again.
  187

6 In the dead vast and middle of the night.
  198

7 Armed at points exactly, cap-a-pe.
  200

8   Distill'd
  Almost to jelly with the act of fear.
  204

9 These hands are not more like.
  212

10 But answer made it none.
  215

11 A countenance more in sorrow than in anger.
  231

12 While one with moderate haste might tell a hundred.
  237

13 *Hamlet:* His beard was grizzled, no?
  Horatio: It was, as I have seen it in his life,
  A sable silver'd.
  239

14 Give it an understanding, but no tongue.
  249

15   All is not well;
  I doubt some foul play.
  254

16   Foul deeds will rise,
  Though all the earth o'erwhelm them, to men's eyes.
  256

17 And keep you in the rear of your affection,
  Out of the shot and danger of desire.
  The chariest maid is prodigal enough
  If she unmask her beauty to the moon.
  iii.34

18 Do not, as some ungracious pastors do,
  Show me the steep and thorny way to heaven,
  Whiles, like a puff'd and reckless libertine,

Himself the primrose path of dalliance treads,
And recks not his own rede.
47

19 And these few precepts in thy memory
  Look thou character. Give thy thoughts no tongue,
  Nor any unproportion'd thought his act.
  Be thou familiar, but by no means vulgar;
  The friends thou hast, and their adoption tried,
  Grapple them to thy soul with hoops of steel;
  But do not dull thy palm with entertainment
  Of each new-hatch'd, unfledg'd comrade. Beware
  Of entrance to a quarrel; but, being in,
  Bear't that th' opposed may beware of thee.
  Give every man thine ear, but few thy voice;
  Take each man's censure, but reserve thy judgment.
  Costly thy habit as thy purse can buy,
  But not express'd in fancy; rich, not gaudy;
  For the apparel oft proclaims the man,
  And they in France of the best rank and station
  Are most select and generous, chief in that.
  Neither a borrower, nor a lender be;
  For loan oft loses both itself and friend,
  And borrowing dulls the edge of husbandry,
  This above all: to thine own self be true,
  And it must follow, as the night the day,
  Thou canst not then be false to any man.
  58

20   You speak like a green girl,
  Unsifted in such perilous circumstance.
  101

21 Ay, springes to catch woodcocks. I do know,
  When the blood burns, how prodigal the soul
  Lends the tongue vows: these blazes, daughter,
  Giving more light than heat, extinct in both,
  Even in their promise, as it is a-making,
  You must not take for fire.
  115

22 *Hamlet:* The air bites shrewdly; it is very cold.
  Horatio: It is a nipping and an eager air.
  iv.1

23 But to my mind,—though I am native here,
  And to the manner born,—it is a custom
  More honour'd in the breach than the observance.
  14

24 Angels and ministers of grace defend us!
  Be thou a spirit of health or goblin damn'd,
  Bring with thee airs from heaven or blasts from hell,
  Be thy intents wicked or charitable,
  Thou com'st in such a questionable shape
  That I will speak to thee: I'll call thee Hamlet,
  King, father; royal Dane, O! answer me:
  Let me not burst in ignorance; but tell
  Why thy canoniz'd bones hearsed in death,
  Have burst their cerements; why the sepulchre,
  Wherein we saw thee quietly inurn'd,
  Hath op'd his ponderous and marble jaws,
  To cast thee up again. What may this mean,
  That thou, dead corse again in complete steel
  Revisit'st thus the glimpses of the moon,
  Making night hideous; and we fools of nature
  So horridly to shake our disposition
  With thoughts beyond the reaches of our souls?
  39

25 I do not set my life at a pin's fee;

And for my soul, what can it do to that,
Being a thing immortal as itself?
65

1   Unhand me, gentlemen,
By heaven! I'll make a ghost of him that lets me.
84

2 Something is rotten in the state of Denmark.
90

3 Alas! poor ghost.
v.4

4 I am thy father's spirit;
Doom'd for a certain term to walk the night.
9

5   But that I am forbid
To tell the secrets of my prison-house,
I could a tale unfold whose lightest word
Would harrow up thy soul, freeze thy young blood,
Make thy two eyes, like stars, start from their spheres,
Thy knotted and combined locks to part,
And each particular hair to stand an end,
Like quills upon the fretful porpentine:
But this eternal blazon must not be
To ears of flesh and blood. List, list, O, list!
13

6 Revenge his foul and most unnatural murder.
25

7 Murder most foul, as in the best it is;
But this most foul, strange, and unnatural.
27

8 And duller shouldst thou be than the fat weed
That rots itself in ease on Lethe wharf,
Wouldst thou not stir in this.
32

9 O my prophetic soul!
My uncle!
40

10 But, soft! methinks I scent the morning air.
58

11 In the porches of mine ears.
63

12 Thus was I, sleeping, by a brother's hand,
Of life, of crown, of queen, at once dispatch'd;
Cut off even in the blossoms of my sin,
Unhousel'd, disappointed, unanel'd,
No reckoning made, but sent to my account
With all my imperfections on my head:
O, horrible! O, horrible! most horrible!
If thou hast nature in thee, bear it not.
74

13   Leave her to heaven,
And to those thorns that in her bosom lodge,
To prick and sting her.
86

14 The glow-worm shows the matin to be near,
And 'gins to pale his uneffectual fire.
89

15   Remember thee!
Ay, thou poor ghost, while memory holds a seat
In this distracted globe. Remember thee!
Yea, from the table of my memory
I'll wipe away all trivial fond records,
All saws of books, all forms, all pressures past,

That youth and observation copied there.
95

16 O most pernicious woman!
O villain, villain, smiling, damned villain!
My tables,—meet it is I set it down,
That one may smile, and smile, and be a villain;
At least I'm sure it may be so in Denmark.
105

17 *Hamlet:* There's ne'er a villain dwelling in all
   Denmark,
But he's an arrant knave.
Horatio: There needs no ghost, my lord, come from
   the grave,
To tell us this.
123

18 These are but wild and whirling words, my lord.
133

19 It is an honest ghost, that let me tell you.
138

20 *Hic et ubique?* then we'll shift our ground.
156

21 Well said, old mole! canst work i' the earth so fast?
162

22 O day and night, but this is wondrous strange!
164

23 There are more things in heaven and earth, Horatio,
Than are dreamt of in your philosophy.
166

24 To put an antic disposition on.
172

25 Rest, rest, perturbed spirit.
182

26 The time is out of joint; O cursed spite,
That ever I was born to set it right!
188

27 By indirections find directions out.
II.i.66

28 Lord Hamlet, with his doublet all unbrac'd;
No hat upon his head; his stockings foul'd,
Ungarter'd, and down-gyved to his ancle.
78

29 This is the very ecstasy of love.
101

30 Brevity is the soul of wit.
ii.90

31   To define true madness,
What is't but to be nothing else but mad?
93

32 More matter with less art.
95

33 That he is mad, 'tis true; 'tis true 'tis pity;
And pity 'tis 'tis true: a foolish figure;
But farewell it, for I will use no art.
97

34 That's an ill phrase, a vile phrase; 'beautified' is a vile
phrase.
[110]

35 Doubt thou the stars are fire;
   Doubt that the sun doth move;
Doubt truth to be a liar;
   But never doubt I love.
[115]

1 Lord Hamlet is a prince, out of thy star.
[141]

2 And he, repulsed,—a short tale to make,—
Fell into a sadness, then into a fast,
Thence to a watch, thence into a weakness,
Thence to a lightness; and by this declension
Into the madness wherein now he raves,
And all we wail for.
[146]

3 Let me be no assistant for a state,
But keep a farm, and carters.
[166]

4 *Polonius:* Do you know me, my lord?
Hamlet: Excellent well; you are a fishmonger.
[173]

5 Ay, sir; to be honest, as this world goes, is to be one
man picked out of ten thousand.
[179]

6 Still harping on my daughter.
[190]

7 *Polonius:* What do you read, my lord?
Hamlet: Words, words, words.
[195]

8 The satirical rogue says here that old men have grey
beards, that their faces are wrinkled, their eyes purging
thick amber and plum-tree gum, and that they have a
plentiful lack of wit, together with most weak hams:
all of which, sir, though I most potently and
powerfully believe, yet I hold it not honesty to have it
thus set down.
[201]

9 Though this be madness, yet there is method in't.
[211]

10 *Polonius:* My honourable lord, I will most humbly
take my leave of you.
Hamlet: You cannot, sir, take from me any thing that I
will more willingly part withal; except my life, except
my life, except my life.
[221]

11 *Guildenstern:* On Fortune's cap we are not the very
button.
Hamlet: Nor the soles of her shoe?
Rosencrantz: Neither, my lord.
Hamlet: Then you live about her waist, or in the
middle of her favours?
Guildenstern: Faith, her privates, we.
Hamlet: In the secret parts of Fortune? O! most true;
she is a strumpet. What news?
Rosencrantz: None, my lord, but that the world's
grown honest.
Hamlet: Then is doomsday near.
[237]

12 There is nothing either good or bad, but thinking
makes it so.
[259]

13 O God! I could be bounded in a nut-shell, and count
myself a king of infinite space, were it not that I have
bad dreams.
[263]

14 Beggar that I am, I am poor even in thanks.
[286]

15 It goes so heavily with my disposition that this goodly
frame, the earth, seems to me a sterile promontory;
this most excellent canopy, the air, look you, this
brave o'erhanging firmament, this majestical roof
fretted with golden fire, why, it appears no other thing
to me but a foul and pestilent congregation of vapours.
What a piece of work is a man! How noble in reason!
how infinite in faculty! in form, in moving, how
express and admirable! in action how like an angel! in
apprehension how like a god! the beauty of the world!
the paragon of animals! And yet, to me, what is this
quintessence of dust? man delights not me; no, nor
woman neither, though, by your smiling, you seem to
say so.
[316]

16 He that plays the king shall be welcome; his majesty
shall have tribute of me.
[341]

17 There is something in this more than natural, if
philosophy could find it out.
[392]

18 I am but mad north-north-west; when the wind is
southerly, I know a hawk from a handsaw.
[405]

19 The great baby you see there is not yet out of his
swaddling-clouts.
[410]

20 The best actors in the world, either for tragedy,
comedy, history, pastoral, pastoral-comical,
historical-pastoral, tragical-historical,
tragical-comical-historical-pastoral, scene individable,
or poem unlimited. Seneca cannot be too heavy, nor
Plautus too light.
[424]

21 One fair daughter and no more,
The which he loved passing well.
[435]

22 Come, give us a taste of your quality.
[460]

23 The play, I remember, pleased not the million; 'twas
caviare to the general.
[465]

24 But who, O! who had seen the mobled queen.
[533]

25 Good my lord, will you see the players well bestowed?
Do you hear, let them be well used; for they are the
abstracts and brief chronicles of the time: after your
death you were better have a bad epitaph than their ill
report while you live.
[553]

26 Use every man after his desert, and who should 'scape
whipping?
[561]

27 O, what a rogue and peasant slave am I:
Is it not monstrous that this player here,
But in a fiction, in a dream of passion,
Could force his soul so to his own conceit
That from her working all his visage wann'd,
Tears in his eyes, distraction in 's aspect,
A broken voice, and his whole function suiting
With forms to his conceit? and all for nothing!
For Hecuba!
What's Hecuba to him or he to Hecuba
That he should weep for her?
[584]

1   He would drown the stage with tears,
And cleave the general ear with horrid speech,
Make mad the guilty, and appal the free,
Confound the ignorant, and amaze, indeed,
The very faculties of eyes and ears.
[596]

2   I,
A dull and muddy-mettled rascal, peak,
Like John-a-dreams, unpregnant of my cause,
And can say nothing.
[601]

3   Am I a coward?
Who calls me villain? breaks my pate across?
Plucks off my beard and blows it in my face?
Tweaks me by the nose? gives me the lie i' the throat,
As deep as to the lungs?
[606]

4 But I am pigeon-liver'd, and lack gall
To make oppression bitter, or ere this
I should have fatted all the region kites
With this slave's offal. Bloody, bawdy villain!
Remorseless, treacherous, lecherous, kindless villain!
[613]

5   I have heard,
That guilty creatures sitting at a play
Have by the very cunning of the scene
Been struck so to the soul that presently
They have proclaim'd their malefactions;
For murder, though it have no tongue, will speak
With most miraculous organ.
[625]

6   The play's the thing
Wherein I'll catch the conscience of the king.
[641]

7 'Tis too much prov'd—that with devotion's visage
And pious action, we do sugar o'er
The devil himself.
III.i.47

8 To be, or not to be: that is the question:
Whether 'tis nobler in the mind to suffer
The slings and arrows of outrageous fortune,
Or to take arms against a sea of troubles,
And by opposing end them? To die: to sleep;
No more; and, by a sleep to say we end
The heart-ache and the thousand natural shocks
That flesh is heir to, 'tis a consummation
Devoutly to be wish'd. To die, to sleep;
To sleep: perchance to dream: ay, there's the rub;
For in that sleep of death what dreams may come
When we have shuffled off this mortal coil,
Must give us pause. There's the respect
That makes calamity of so long life;
For who would bear the whips and scorns of time,
The oppressor's wrong, the proud man's contumely,
The pangs of dispriz'd love, the law's delay,
The insolence of office, and the spurns
That patient merit of the unworthy takes,
When he himself might his quietus make
With a bare bodkin? Who would fardels bear,
To grunt and sweat under a weary life,
But that the dread of something after death,
The undiscover'd country from whose bourn
No traveller returns, puzzles the will,
And makes us rather bear those ills we have,

Than fly to others that we know not of?
Thus conscience doth make cowards of us all;
And thus the native hue of resolution
Is sicklied o'er with the pale cast of thought,
And enterprises of great pith and moment
With this regard their currents turn awry,
And lose the name of action.
56

9   Nymph, in thy orisons
Be all my sins remember'd.
89

10   For, to the noble mind,
Rich gifts wax poor when givers prove unkind.
100

11 Get thee to a nunnery: why wouldst thou be a breeder
of sinners? I am myself indifferent honest; but yet I
could accuse me of such things that it were better my
mother had not borne me. I am very proud,
revengeful, ambitious; with more offences at my beck
than I have thoughts to put them in, imagination to
give them shape, or time to act them in. What should
such fellows as I do crawling between heaven and
earth? We are arrant knaves, all; believe none of us.
[124]

12 Be thou as chaste as ice, as pure as snow, thou shalt
not escape calumny. Get thee to a nunnery, go;
farewell.
[142]

13 I have heard of your paintings too, well enough. God
hath given you one face and you make yourselves
another.
[150]

14 I say, we will have no more marriages.
[156]

15 O! what a noble mind is here o'erthrown:
The courtier's, soldier's, scholar's, eye, tongue,
    sword;
The expectancy and rose of the fair state,
The glass of fashion, and the mould of form,
The observed of all observers, quite, quite, down!
And I, of ladies most deject and wretched,
That suck'd the honey of his music vows,
Now see that noble and most sovereign reason,
Like sweet bells jangled, out of tune and harsh;
That unmatch'd form and figure of blown youth,
Blasted with ecstasy: O! woe is me,
To have seen what I have seen, see what I see!
[159]

16 Speak the speech, I pray you, as I pronounced it to
you, trippingly on the tongue; but if you mouth it, as
many of your players do, I had as lief the town-crier
spoke my lines. Nor do not saw the air too much with
your hand, thus; but use all gently: for in the very
torrent, tempest, and—as I may say—whirlwind of
passion, you must acquire and beget a temperance,
that may give it smoothness. O! it offends me to the
soul to hear a robustious periwig-pated fellow tear a
passion to tatters, to very rags, to split the ears of the
groundlings, who for the most part are capable of
nothing but inexplicable dumb-shows and noise: I
would have such a fellow whipped for o'erdoing
Termagant; it out-herods Herod: pray you, avoid it.
ii.1

17 Be not too tame neither, but let your own discretion be

your tutor: suit the action to the word, the word to the action; with this special observance, that you o'erstep not the modesty of nature; for anything so overdone is from the purpose of playing, whose end, both at the first and now, was and is, to hold, as 'twere, the mirror up to nature; to show virtue her own feature, scorn her own image, and the very age and body of the time his form and pressure. Now, this overdone, or come tardy off, though it make the unskilful laugh, cannot but make the judicious grieve; the censure of which one must in your allowance o'erweigh a whole theatre of others. O! there be players that I have seen play, and heard others praise, and that highly, not to speak it profanely, that, neither having the accent of Christians nor the gait of Christian, pagan, nor man, have so strutted and bellowed that I have thought some of nature's journeymen had made men and not made them well, they imitated humanity so abominably.
[19]

1 Since my dear soul was mistress of her choice
And could of men distinguish, her election
Hath seal'd thee for herself.
[68]

2   Give me that man
That is not passion's slave, and I will wear him
In my heart's core, ay, in my heart of heart,
As I do thee.
[76]

3 It is a damned ghost we have seen,
And my imaginations are as foul
As Vulcan's stithy.
[87]

4 The chameleon's dish: I eat the air,
promise-crammed; you cannot feed capons so.
[98]

5 Here's metal more attractive.
[117]

6 That's a fair thought to lie between maids' legs.
[126]

7 Die two months ago, and not forgotten yet? Then there's hope a great man's memory may outlive his life half a year; but, by'r lady, he must build churches then.
[140]

8 For, O! for, O! the hobby-horse is forgot.
[145]

9 Marry, this is miching mallecho; it means mischief.
[148]

10 *Ophelia:* 'Tis brief, my lord.
Hamlet: As woman's love.
[165]

11 The lady doth protest too much, methinks.
[242]

12 *Hamlet:* No, no, they do but jest, poison in jest; no offence i' the world.
King: What do you call the play?
Hamlet: The Mouse-trap.
[247]

13 We that have free souls, it touches us not: let the galled jade wince, our withers are unwrung.
[255]

14 The story is extant, and writ in very choice Italian.
[277]

15 What! frighted with false fire?
[282]

16 Why, let the stricken deer go weep,
    The hart ungalled play;
For some must watch, while some must sleep:
    So runs the world away.
[287]

17 O wonderful son, that can so astonish a mother!
[347]

18 The proverb is something musty.
[366]

19 It will discourse most eloquent music.
[381]

20 You would play upon me; you would seem to know my stops; you would pluck out the heart of my mystery; you would sound me from my lowest note to the top of my compass.
[387]

21 Do you think I am easier to be played on than a pipe? Call me what instrument you will, though you can fret me, you cannot play upon me.
[393]

22 *Hamlet:* Do you see yonder cloud that's almost in shape of a camel?
Polonius: By the mass, and 'tis like a camel, indeed.
Hamlet: Methinks it is like a weasel.
Polonius: It is backed like a weasel.
Hamlet: Or like a whale?
Polonius: Very like a whale.
[400]

23 They fool me to the top of my bent.
[408]

24 By and by is easily said.
[411]

25 'Tis now the very witching time of night,
When churchyards yawn and hell itself breathes out
Contagion to this world: now could I drink hot blood,
And do such bitter business as the day
Would quake to look on.
[413]

26 Let me be cruel, not unnatural;
I will speak daggers to her, but use none.
[420]

27 O! my offence is rank, it smells to heaven.
iii.36

28 O wretched state! O bosom black as death!
O limed soul, that struggling to be free
Art more engaged!
67

29 Now might I do it pat, now he is praying.
73

30 He took my father grossly, full of bread,
With all his crimes broad blown, as flush as May;
And how his audit stands who knows save heaven?
80

31 My words fly up, my thoughts remain below:
Words without thoughts never to heaven go.
97

32 Tell him his pranks have been too broad to bear with.
iv.2

33 You go not, till I set you up a glass

Where you may see the inmost part of you.
19

1 How now! a rat? Dead, for a ducat, dead!
23

2 A bloody deed! almost as bad, good mother,
As kill a king, and marry with his brother.
28

3 Thou wretched, rash, intruding fool, farewell!
I took thee for thy better.
31

4   Such an act
... makes marriage vows
As false as dicers' oaths; O! such a deed
As from the body of contraction plucks
The very soul, and sweet religion makes
A rhapsody of words.
40

5   Ay me! what act,
That roars so loud, and thunders in the index?
51

6 Look here, upon this picture, and on this.
53

7 Could you on this fair mountain leave to feed,
And batten on this moor?
66

8 You cannot call it love, for at your age
The hey-day in the blood is tame, it's humble,
And waits upon the judgment.
68

9   Speak no more;
Thou turn'st mine eyes into my very soul.
88

10   Nay, but to live
In the rank sweat of an enseamed bed,
Stew'd in corruption, honeying and making love
Over the nasty sty.
91

11 A cut-purse of the empire and the rule,
That from a shelf the precious diadem stole,
And put it in his pocket!
99

12 A king of shreds and patches.
102

13 Conceit in weakest bodies strongest works.
113

14   Mother, for love of grace,
Lay not that flattering unction to your soul.
142

15   Confess yourself to heaven;
Repent what's past; avoid what is to come.
149

16 For in the fatness of these pursy times,
Virtue itself of vice must pardon beg.
153

17 *Queen:* O Hamlet! thou hast cleft my heart in twain.
Hamlet: O! throw away the worser part of it,
And live the purer with the other half.
156

18 Assume a virtue, if you have it not.
That monster, custom, who all sense doth eat,
Of habits devil, is angel yet in this.
160

19 And when you are desirous to be bless'd,
I'll blessing beg of you.
171

20 I must be cruel only to be kind.
178

21 For 'tis the sport to have the enginer
Hoist with his own petar: and it shall go hard
But I will delve one yard below their mines,
And blow them at the moon.
206

22 I'll lug the guts into the neighbour room.
212

23   Indeed this counsellor
Is now most still, most secret, and most grave,
Who was in life a foolish prating knave.
213

24 He keeps them, like an ape doth nuts, in the corner of
his jaw; first mouthed, to be last swallowed.
IV.ii.[19]

25   Diseases desperate grown,
By desperate appliances are reliev'd,
Or not at all.
iii.9

26 A certain convocation of politic worms are e'en at
him. Your worm is your only emperor for diet.
[21]

27 A man may fish with the worm that hath eat of a king,
and eat of the fish that hath fed of that worm.
[29]

28 We go to gain a little patch of ground,
That hath in it no profit but the name.
iv.18

29 How all occasions do inform against me,
And spur my dull revenge! What is a man,
If his chief good and market of his time
Be but to sleep and feed? a beast, no more.
Sure he that made us with such large discourse,
Looking before and after, gave us not
That capability and god-like reason
To fust in us unus'd.
32

30   Some craven scruple
Of thinking too precisely on the event.
40

31   Rightly to be great
Is not to stir without great argument,
But greatly to find quarrel in a straw
When honour's at the stake.
53

32 How should I your true love know
From another one?
By his cockle hat and staff,
And his sandal shoon.
v.[23]

33 He is dead and gone, lady,
He is dead and gone,
At his head a grass-green turf;
At his heels a stone.
[29]

34 White his shroud as the mountain snow...
Larded with sweet flowers;
Which bewept to the grave did go

With true-love showers.
[36]

1 Lord! we know what we are, but know not what we may be.
[43]

2 Then up he rose, and donn'd his clothes.
[53]

3 Come, my coach! Good-night, ladies; good-night, sweet ladies; good night, good-night.
[72]

4 When sorrows come, they come not single spies, But in battalions.
[78]

5   We have done but greenly In hugger-mugger to inter him.
[83]

6 There's such divinity doth hedge a king, That treason can but peep to what it would.
[123]

7 To hell, allegiance! vows, to the blackest devil! Conscience and grace, to the profoundest pit! I dare damnation.
[130]

8 Nature is fine in love, and where 'tis fine It sends some precious instance of itself After the thing it loves.
[160]

9 They bore him barefac'd on the bier; Hey non nonny, nonny, hey nonny; And in his grave rain'd many a tear.
[163]

10 There's rosemary, that's for remembrance; pray, love, remember: and there is pansies, that's for thoughts.
[174]

11 There's fennel for you, and columbines; there's rue for you; and here's some for me; we may call it herb of grace o' Sundays. O! you must wear your rue with a difference. There's a daisy; I would give you some violets, but they withered all when my father died. They say he made a good end,— For bonny sweet Robin is all my joy.
[179]

12 No, no, he is dead; Go to thy death-bed, He never will come again.
[191]

13 He is gone, he is gone, And we cast away moan; God ha' mercy on his soul!
[196]

14 His means of death, his obscure burial, No trophy, sword, nor hatchment o'er his bones, No noble rite nor formal ostentation.
[213]

15 And where the offence is let the great axe fall.
[218]

16 It warms the very sickness in my heart, That I shall live and tell him to his teeth, 'Thus diddest thou.'
vii.55

17 A very riband in the cap of youth, Yet needful too; for youth no less becomes The light and careless livery that it wears

Than settled age his sables and his weeds, Importing health and graveness.
77

18 No place, indeed should murder sanctuarize.
127

19 There is a willow grows aslant a brook, That shows his hoar leaves in the glassy stream; There with fantastic garlands did she come, Of crow-flowers, nettles, daisies, and long purples, That liberal shepherds give a grosser name, But our cold maids do dead men's fingers call them: There, on the pendent boughs her coronet weeds Clambering to hang, an envious sliver broke, When down her weedy trophies and herself Fell in the weeping brook. Her clothes spread wide, And, mermaid-like, awhile they bore her up; Which time she chanted snatches of old tunes, As one incapable of her own distress.
167

20 Too much of water hast thou, poor Ophelia, And therefore I forbid my tears; but yet It is our trick, nature her custom holds, Let shame say what it will.
186

21 Is she to be buried in Christian burial that wilfully seeks her own salvation?
V.i.1

22 There is no ancient gentlemen but gardeners, ditchers and grave-makers; they hold up Adam's profession.
[32]

23 *First Clown:* What is he that builds stronger than either the mason, the shipwright, or the carpenter? *Second Clown:* The gallows-maker; for that frame outlives a thousand tenants.
[44]

24 Cudgel thy brains no more about it, for your dull ass will not mend his pace with beating.
[61]

25 The houses that he makes last till doomsday.
[64]

26 Has this fellow no feeling of his business?
[71]

27 This might be the pate of a politician...one that would circumvent God, might it not?
[84]

28 How absolute the knave is! we must speak by the card, or equivocation will undo us.
[147]

29 The age is grown so picked that the toe of the peasant comes so near the heel of the courtier, he galls his kibe.
[150]

30 *First Clown:* He that is mad, and sent into England. *Hamlet:* Ay, marry; why was he sent into England? *First Clown:* Why, because he was mad; he shall recover his wits there; or, if he do not, 'tis no great matter there. *Hamlet:* Why? *First Clown:* 'Twill not be seen in him there; there the men are as mad as he.
[160]

31 Alas, poor Yorick. I knew him, Horatio; a fellow of infinite jest, of most excellent fancy; he hath borne me

on his back a thousand times; and now, how abhorred in my imagination it is! my gorge rises at it. Here hung those lips that I have kissed I know not how oft. Where be your gibes now? your gambols? your songs? your flashes of merriment, that were wont to set the table on a roar? Not one now, to mock your own grinning? quite chap-fallen? Now get you to my lady's chamber, and tell her, let her paint an inch thick, to this favour she must come; make her laugh at that.
[201]

1 To what base uses we may return, Horatio!
[222]

2 Imperious Caesar, dead, and turn'd to clay,
Might stop a hole to keep the wind away.
[235]

3 We should profane the service of the dead,
To sing a requiem, and such rest to her
As to peace-parted souls.
[258]

4   Lay her i' the earth;
And from her fair and unpolluted flesh
May violets spring! I tell thee, churlish priest,
A ministering angel shall my sister be,
When thou liest howling.
[260]

5 Sweets to the sweet: farewell!
[265]

6 I thought thy bride-bed to have deck'd, sweet maid,
And not have strewed thy grave.
[267]

7 For, though I am not splenetive and rash
Yet have I in me something dangerous.
[283]

8 I lov'd Ophelia: forty thousand brothers
Could not, with all their quantity of love,
Make up my sum.
[291]

9 And thus a while the fit will work on him;
Anon, as patient as the female dove,
When that her golden couplets are disclos'd,
His silence will sit drooping.
[307]

10 This grave shall have a living monument.
[319]

11 There's a divinity that shapes our ends,
Rough-hew them how we will.
ii.10

12 I once did hold it, as our statists do,
A baseness to write fair, and labour'd much
How to forget that learning; but, sir, now
It did me yeoman's service.
33

13 But, sure, the bravery of his grief did put me
Into a towering passion.
79

14 But thou wouldst not think how ill all's here about my heart.
[222]

15 Not a whit, we defy augury; there's a special providence in the fall of a sparrow. If it be now, 'tis not to come; if it be not to come, it will be now; if it be not now, yet it will come: the readiness is all.
[232]

16 I have shot mine arrow o'er the house,
And hurt my brother.
[257]

17 Now the king drinks to Hamlet!
[292]

18 A hit, a very palpable hit.
[295]

19 Why, as a woodcock to mine own springe, Osric;
I am justly kill'd with my own treachery.
[320]

20 O villany! Ho! let the door be lock'd:
Treachery! seek it out.
[325]

21 The point envenom'd too!—
Then, venom, to thy work.
[335]

22   This fell sergeant, death,
Is swift in his arrest.
[350]

23   Report me and my cause aright
To the unsatisfied.
[353]

24 I am more an antique Roman than a Dane.
[355]

25 If thou didst ever hold me in thy heart,
Absent thee from felicity awhile,
And in this harsh world draw thy breath in pain,
To tell my story.
[360]

26 The potent poison quite o'ercrows my spirit.
[367]

27 The rest is silence.
[372]

28 Now cracks a noble heart. Good-night, sweet prince,
And flights of angels sing thee to thy rest!
[373]

29 The ears are senseless that should give us hearing,
To tell him his commandment is fulfill'd,
That Rosencrantz and Guildenstern are dead.
[383]

30   Let four captains
Bear Hamlet, like a soldier, to the stage;
For he was likely, had he been put on,
To have prov'd most royally.
[409]

31 Go, bid the soldiers shoot.
[417]

HENRY IV, Part 1

32 So shaken as we are, so wan with care.
I.i.1

33   In those holy fields
Over whose acres walk'd those blessed feet,
Which fourteen hundred years ago were nail'd
For our advantage, on the bitter cross.
24

34 Unless hours were cups of sack, and minutes capons, and clocks the tongues of bawds, and dials the signs of leaping-houses, and the blessed sun himself a fair hot wench in flame-colour'd taffeta, I see no reason why thou shouldst be so superfluous to demand the time of

day.
ii.[7]

1 Let us be Diana's foresters, gentlemen of the shade, minions of the moon.
[28]

2 *Falstaff:* And is not my hostess of the tavern a most sweet wench?
Prince: As the honey of Hybla, my old lad of the castle.
[44]

3 What, in thy quips and thy quiddities?
[50]

4 Shall there be gallows standing in England when thou art king, and resolution thus fobbed as it is with the rusty curb of old father antick, the law?
[66]

5 Thou hast the most unsavoury similes.
[89]

6 I would to God thou and I knew where a commodity of good names were to be bought.
[92]

7 O! thou hast damnable iteration, and art, indeed, able to corrupt a saint.
[101]

8 Now am I, if a man should speak truly, little better than one of the wicked.
[105]

9 I'll be damned for never a king's son in Christendom.
[108]

10 Why, Hal, 'tis my vocation, Hal; 'tis no sin for a man to labour in his vocation.
[116]. Of stealing.

11 How agrees the devil and thee about thy soul, that thou soldest him on Good Friday last for a cup of Madeira and a cold capon's leg?
[126]

12 If he fight longer than he sees reason, I'll forswear arms.
[206]

13 If all the year were playing holidays,
To sport would be as tedious as to work;
But when they seldom come, they wish'd for come.
[226]

14 And as the soldiers bore dead bodies by,
He call'd them untaught knaves, unmannerly,
To bring a slovenly, unhandsome corpse
Betwixt the wind and his nobility.
With many holiday and lady terms
He question'd me.
iii.42

15 So pester'd with a popinjay.
50

16 It was great pity, so it was,
This villainous saltpetre should be digg'd
Out of the bowels of the harmless earth,
Which many a good tall fellow had destroy'd
So cowardly; and but for these vile guns,
He would himself have been a soldier.
59

17 To put down Richard, that sweet lovely rose,
And plant this thorn, this canker, Bolingbroke.
175

18 O! the blood more stirs
To rouse a lion than to start a hare.
197

19 By heaven methinks it were an easy leap
To pluck bright honour from the pale-fac'd moon,
Or dive into the bottom of the deep,
Where fathom-line could never touch the ground,
And pluck up drowned honour by the locks.
201

20 Why, what a candy deal of courtesy
This fawning greyhound then did proffer me!
251

21 I know a trick worth two of that.
II.i.[40]

22 At hand, quoth pick-purse.
[53]

23 We have the receipt of fern-seed, we walk invisible.
[95]

24 I am bewitched with the rogue's company. If the rascal have not given me medicines to make me love him, I'll be hanged.
ii.[19]

25 Go hang thyself in thine own heir-apparent garters!
[49]

26 On, bacons, on!
[99]

27 It would be argument for a week, laughter for a month, and a good jest for ever.
[104]

28 Falstaff sweats to death
And lards the lean earth as he walks along.
[119]

29 Out of this nettle, danger, we pluck this flower, safety.
iii.[11]

30 A good plot, good friends, and full of expectation; an excellent plot, very good friends.
[21]

31 Away, you trifler! Love! I love thee not,
I care not for thee, Kate: this is no world
To play with mammets and to tilt with lips:
We must have bloody noses and crack'd crowns.
[95]

32 Constant you are,
But yet a woman: and for secrecy,
No lady closer; for I well believe
Thou wilt not utter what thou dost not know.
[113]

33 I am not yet of Percy's mind, the Hotspur of the North; he that kills me some six or seven dozen of Scots at a breakfast, washes his hands, and says to his wife, 'Fie upon this quiet life! I want work.'
iv.[116]

34 There live not three good men unhanged in England, and one of them is fat and grows old.
[146]

35 Call you that backing of your friends? A plague upon such backing! give me them that will face me.
[168]

36 A plague of all cowards, still say I.
[175]

1 I am a Jew else; an Ebrew Jew.
[201]

2 Nay that's past praying for: I have peppered two of them: two I am sure I have paid, two rogues in buckram suits. I tell thee what, Hal, if I tell thee a lie, spit in my face, call me horse. Thou knowest my old ward; here I lay, and thus I bore my point. Four rogues in buckram let drive at me,—
[214]

3 O monstrous! eleven buckram men grown out of two.
[247]

4 These lies are like the father that begets them; gross as a mountain, open, palpable.
[253]

5 Give you a reason on compulsion! if reasons were as plentiful as blackberries I would give no man a reason upon compulsion, I.
[267]

6 Mark now, how a plain tale shall put you down.
[285]

7 What a slave art thou, to hack thy sword as thou hast done, and then say it was in fight!
[292]

8 Instinct is a great matter, I was a coward on instinct.
[304]

9 Ah! no more of that, Hal, an thou lovest me.
[316]

10 What doth gravity out of his bed at midnight?
[328]

11 A plague of sighing and grief! it blows a man up like a bladder.
[370]

12 I will do it in King Cambyses' vein.
[430]

13 Peace, good pint-pot!
[443]

14 Shall the blessed sun of heaven prove a micher and eat blackberries? a question not to be asked.
[454]

15 There is a devil haunts thee in the likeness of a fat old man; a tun of man is thy companion.
[498]

16 That roasted Manningtree ox with the pudding in his belly, that reverend vice, that grey iniquity, that father ruffian, that vanity in years.
[504]

17 If sack and sugar be a fault, God help the wicked!
[524]

18 No, my good lord; banish Peto, banish Bardolph, banish Poins; but for sweet Jack Falstaff, kind Jack Falstaff, true Jack Falstaff, valiant Jack Falstaff, and therefore more valiant, being, as he is, old Jack Falstaff, banish not him thy Harry's company: banish not him thy Harry's company: banish plump Jack and banish all the world.
[528]

19 Play out the play.
[539]

20 O monstrous! but one half-pennyworth of bread to this intolerable deal of sack!
[598]

21 *Glendower:* At my nativity

The front of heaven was full of fiery shapes,
Of burning cressets; and at my birth
The frame and huge foundation of the earth
Shak'd like a coward.
Hotspur: Why, so it would have done at the same
  season, if your mother's cat had but kittened.
III.i.13

22 And all the courses of my life do show
I am not in the roll of common men.
[42]

23 *Glendower:* I can call spirits from the vasty deep.
Hotspur: Why, so can I, or so can any man;
But will they come when you do call for them?
[53]

24 I'll have the current in this place damm'd up,
And here the smug and silver Trent shall run
In a new channel, fair and evenly.
[102]

25 I had rather be a kitten and cry mew
Than one of these same metre ballad-mongers.
[128]

26 That would set my teeth nothing on edge,
Nothing so much as mincing poetry:
'Tis like the forc'd gait of a shuffling nag.
[132]

27 And such a deal of skimble-skamble stuff
As puts me from my faith.
[153]

28   O! he's as tedious
As a tired horse, a railing wife;
Worse than a smoky house. I had rather live
With cheese and garlic in a windmill, far,
Than feed on cates and have him talk to me
In any summer-house in Christendom.
[158]

29 I understand thy kisses, and thou mine,
And that's a feeling disputation.
[204]

30   Thy tongue
Makes Welsh as sweet as ditties highly penn'd,
Sung by a fair queen in a summer's bower,
With ravishing division, to her lute.
[207]

31 Now I perceive the devil understands Welsh.
[233]

32 You swear like a comfit-maker's wife.
[252]

33 Swear me, Kate, like a lady as thou art,
A good mouth-filling oath.
[257]

34 The skipping king, he ambled up and down
With shallow jesters and rash bavin wits.
ii.60

35   Being daily swallow'd by men's eyes,
They surfeited with honey and began
To loathe the taste of sweetness, whereof a little
More than a little is by much too much.
So, when he had occasion to be seen,
He was but as the cuckoo is in June,
Heard, not regarded.
70

36 My near'st and dearest enemy.
123

1 Well, I'll repent, and that suddenly, while I am in some liking; I shall be out of heart shortly, and then I shall have no strength to repent.
iii.[5]

2 Company, villanous company, hath been the spoil of me.
[10]

3 Come, sing me a bawdy song; make me merry.
[15]

4 Shall I not take mine ease in mine inn but I shall have my pocket picked?
[91]

5 Thou knowest in the state of innocency Adam fell; and what should poor Jack Falstaff do in the days of villany. Thou seest I have more flesh than another man, and therefore more frailty.
[184]

6   Where is his son,
That nimble-footed madcap Prince of Wales,
And his comrades, that daff'd the world aside,
And bid it pass?
IV.i.94

7 I saw young Harry, with his beaver on,
His cushes on his thighs, gallantly arm'd,
Rise from the ground like feather'd Mercury,
And vaulted with such ease into his seat,
As if an angel dropp'd down from the clouds,
To turn and wind a fiery Pegasus,
And witch the world with noble horsemanship.
104

8 Doomsday is near; die all, die merrily.
134

9 I have misus'd the king's press damnably.
ii.[13]

10 The cankers of a calm world and a long peace.
[32]

11 I am as vigilant as a cat to steal cream.
[64]

12 Tut, tut; good enough to toss; food for powder, food for powder; they'll fill a pit as well as better: tush, man, mortal men, mortal men.
[72]

13 Greatness knows itself.
iii.74

14 For mine own part, I could be well content
To entertain the lag-end of my life
With quiet hours.
V.i.23

15 Rebellion lay in his way, and he found it.
28

16 I do not think a braver gentleman,
More active-valiant or more valiant-young,
More daring or more bold, is now alive
To grace this latter age with noble deeds.
For my part, I may speak it to my shame,
I have a truant been to chivalry.
89

17 *Falstaff:* I would it were bed-time, Hal, and all well.
Prince: Why, thou owest God a death.
[125]. See 442:7

18 Honour pricks me on. Yea, but how if honour prick me off when I come on? how then? Can honour set-to a leg? No. Or an arm? No. Or take away the grief of a wound? No. Honour hath no skill in surgery, then? No. What is honour? A word. What is that word, honour? Air. A trim reckoning! Who hath it? He that died o' Wednesday. Doth he feel it? No. Doth he hear it? No. It is insensible then? Yea, to the dead. But will it not live with the living? No. Why? Detraction will not suffer it. Therefore I'll none of it: honour is a mere scutcheon: and so ends my catechism.
[131]

19 O gentlemen! the time of life is short;
To spend that shortness basely were too long.
ii.81

20 Now, *Esperance!* Percy! and set on.
96

21 I like not such grinning honour as Sir Walter hath: give me life; which if I can save, so; if not, honour comes unlooked for, and there's an end.
iii.[61]

22 Two stars keep not their motion in one sphere.
iv.65

23 But thought's the slave of life, and life time's fool;
And time, that takes survey of all the world,
Must have a stop.
[81]

24   Fare thee well, great heart!
Ill-weav'd ambition, how much art thou shrunk!
When that this body did contain a spirit,
A kingdom for it was too small a bound;
But now two paces of the vilest earth
Is room enough: this earth, that bears thee dead,
Bears not alive so stout a gentleman.
[87]

25 Thy ignominy sleep with thee in the grave,
But not remember'd in thy epitaph!
What! old acquaintance! could not all this flesh
Keep in a little life? Poor Jack, farewell!
I could have better spar'd a better man.
[100]

26   Full bravely hast thou flesh'd
Thy maiden sword.
[132]

27 Lord, Lord, how this world is given to lying! I grant you I was down and out of breath; and so was he; but we rose both at an instant, and fought a long hour by Shrewsbury clock.
[148]

28 For my part, if a lie may do thee grace,
I'll gild it with the happiest terms I have.
[161]

29 I'll purge, and leave sack, and live cleanly, as a nobleman should do.
[168]

HENRY IV, Part 2

30 I speak of peace, while covert enmity
Under the smile of safety wounds the world.
Induction, 9

31   Rumour is a pipe
Blown by surmises, jealousies, conjectures,
And of so easy and so plain a stop
That the blunt monster with uncounted heads,
The still-discordant wavering multitude,

Can play upon it.
15

1 Even such a man, so faint, so spiritless,
So dull, so dead in look, so woe-begone,
Drew Priam's curtain in the dead of night,
And would have told him, half his Troy was burn'd.
I.i.70

2 Yet the first bringer of unwelcome news
Hath but a losing office, and his tongue
Sounds ever after as a sullen bell,
Remember'd knolling a departed friend.
100

3 The brain of this foolish-compounded clay, man, is
not able to invent anything that tends to laughter, more
than I invent or is invented on me: I am not only witty
in myself, but the cause that wit is in other men. I do
here walk before thee like a sow that hath
overwhelmed all her litter but one.
ii.[7]

4 A rascally yea-forsooth knave.
[40]

5 Your lordship, though not clean past your youth, hath
yet some smack of age in you, some relish of the
saltness of time.
[111]

6 This apoplexy is, as I take it, a kind of lethargy, an't
please your lordship; a kind of sleeping in the blood, a
whoreson tingling.
[127]

7 It is the disease of not listening, the malady of not
marking, that I am troubled withal.
[139]

8 I am as poor as Job, my lord, but not so patient.
[145]

9 Well, I am loath to gall a new-healed wound.
[169]

10 Have you not a moist eye, a dry hand, a yellow cheek,
a white beard, a decreasing leg, an increasing belly? Is
not your voice broken, your wind short, your chin
double, your wit single, and every part about you
blasted with antiquity, and will you yet call yourself
young? Fie, fie, fie, Sir John!
[206]

11 My lord, I was born about three of the clock in the
afternoon, with a white head, and something of a
round belly. For my voice, I have lost it with hollaing,
and singing of anthems.
[213]

12 *Chief Justice:* God send the prince a better companion!
Falstaff: God send the companion a better prince! I
cannot rid my hands of him.
[227]

13 All you that kiss our lady Peace at home.
[236]

14 It was always yet the trick of our English nation, if
they have a good thing, to make it too common.
[244]

15 I would to God my name were not so terrible to the
enemy as it is: I were better to be eaten to death with
rust than to be scoured to nothing with perpetual
motion.
[247]

16 I can get no remedy against this consumption of the

purse: borrowing only lingers and lingers it out, but
the disease is incurable.
[268]

17   When we mean to build,
We first survey the plot, then draw the model;
And when we see the figure of the house,
Then we must rate the cost of the erection;
Which if we find outweighs ability,
What do we then but draw anew the model
In fewer offices, or at last desist
To build at all?
iii.[41]

18 A hundred mark is a long one for a poor lone woman
to bear; and I have borne, and borne, and borne; and
have been fubbed off, and fubbed off, and fubbed off,
from this day to that day, that it is a shame to be
thought on.
II.i.[36]

19 Away, you scullion! you rampallion! you fustilarian!
I'll tickle your catastrophe.
[67]

20 Thou didst swear to me upon a parcel-gilt goblet,
sitting in my Dolphin-chamber, at the round table, by
a sea-coal fire, upon Wednesday in Wheeson week.
[97]

21 Doth it not show vilely in me to desire small beer?
ii.[7]

22 I do now remember the poor creature, small beer.
[12]

23 Let the end try the man.
[52]

24   He was indeed the glass
Wherein the noble youth did dress themselves.
iii.21

25   Shall pack-horses,
And hollow pamper'd jades of Asia,
Which cannot go but thirty miles a day,
Compare with Caesars, and with Cannibals,
And Trojan Greeks? nay, rather damn them with
King Cerberus; and let the welkin roar.
iv. [176]. See 330:16

26 By my troth, captain, these are very bitter words.
[183]

27 Thou whoreson little tidy Bartholomew boar-pig, when
wilt thou leave fighting o' days, and foining o' nights,
and begin to patch up thine old body for heaven?
[249]

28 Is it not strange that desire should so many years
outlive performance?
[283]

29   O sleep! O gentle sleep!
Nature's soft nurse, how have I frighted thee,
That thou no more wilt weigh mine eyelids down
And steep my senses in forgetfulness?
Why rather, sleep, liest thou in smoky cribs,
Upon uneasy pallets stretching thee,
And hush'd with buzzing night-flies to thy slumber,
Than in the perfum'd chambers of the great,
Under the canopies of costly state,
And lull'd with sound of sweetest melody?
III.i.5

30   Then, happy low, lie down!

Uneasy lies the head that wears a crown.
30

1 O God! that one might read the book of fate,
And see the revolution of the times
Make mountains level, and the continent,—
Weary of solid firmness,—melt itself
Into the sea!
45

2   O! if this were seen,
The happiest youth, viewing his progress through,
What perils past, what crosses to ensue,
Would shut the book, and sit him down and die.
54

3 There is a history in all men's lives,
Figuring the nature of the times deceas'd,
The which observ'd, a man may prophesy,
With a near aim, of the main chance of things
As yet not come to life, which in their seeds
And weak beginnings lie intreasured.
80

4 A soldier is better accommodated than with a wife.
ii.[73]

5 Most forcible Feeble.
[181]

6 We have heard the chimes at midnight.
[231]

7 I care not; a man can die but once; we owe God a
death.
[253]. See 440:17

8 He that dies this year is quit for the next.
[257]

9 Lord, Lord! how subject we old men are to this vice
of lying.
[329]

10 When a' was naked, he was, for all the world, like a
forked radish, with a head fantastically carved upon it
with a knife.
[335]

11 Talks as familiarly of John a Gaunt as if he had been
sworn brother to him.
[348]

12 Against ill chances men are ever merry,
But heaviness foreruns the good event.
IV.ii.81

13 That I may justly say with the hook-nosed fellow of
Rome, 'I came, saw, and overcame.'
iii.[44]

14 A man cannot make him laugh; but that's no marvel;
he drinks no wine.
[95]

15 A good sherris-sack hath a two-fold operation in it. It
ascends me into the brain; dries me there all the foolish
and dull and crudy vapours which environ it; makes it
apprehensive, quick, forgetive, full of nimble fiery and
delectable shapes; which, deliver'd o'er to the voice,
the tongue, which is the birth, becomes excellent wit.
The second property of your excellent sherris is, the
warming of the blood; which, before cold and settled,
left the liver white and pale, which is the badge of
pusillanimity and cowardice: but the sherris warms it
and makes it course from the inwards to the parts
extreme. It illumineth the face, which, as a beacon,
gives warning to all the rest of this little kingdom,

man, to arm; and then the vital commoners and inland
petty spirits muster me all to their captain, the heart,
who, great and puffed up with this retinue, doth any
deed of courage; and this valour comes of sherris. So
that skill in the weapon is nothing without sack, for
that sets it a-work; and learning, a mere hoard of gold
kept by a devil till sack commences it and sets it in act
and use.
[103]

16 If I had a thousand sons, the first human principle I
would teach them should be, to forswear thin
potations.
[133]

17 O polish'd perturbation! golden care!
That keep'st the ports of slumber open wide
To many a watchful night! Sleep with it now!
Yet not so sound, and half so deeply sweet
As he whose brow with homely biggin bound
Snores out the watch of night.
v.22

18 This sleep is sound indeed; this is a sleep
That from this golden rigol hath divorc'd
So many English kings.
34

19 Thy wish was father, Harry, to that thought.
91

20   Commit
The oldest sins the newest kind of ways.
124

21 It hath been prophesied to me many years
I should not die but in Jerusalem,
Which vainly I suppos'd the Holy Land.
But bear me to that chamber; there I'll lie:
In that Jerusalem shall Harry die.
235

22 Any pretty little tiny kickshaws, tell William cook.
V.i.[29]

23 This is the English, not the Turkish court;
Not Amurath an Amurath succeeds,
But Harry, Harry.
ii.47

24 Sorrow so royally in you appears,
That I will deeply put the fashion on.
51

25 My father is gone wild into his grave.
123

26 'Tis merry in hall when beards wag all.
iii.[35]

27 A foutra for the world, and worldlings base!
I speak of Africa and golden joys.
[100]

28 Under which king, Bezonian? speak, or die!
[116]

29 Let us take any man's horses; the laws of England are
at my commandment.
[139]

30 I know thee not, old man: fall to thy prayers;
How ill white hairs become a fool and jester!
I have long dream'd of such a kind of man,
So surfeit-swell'd, so old, and so profane.
v.[52]

31 Make less thy body hence, and more thy grace;
Leave gormandising; know the grave doth gape

For thee thrice wider than for other men.
[57]

1 Presume not that I am the thing I was.
[61]

2 Where, for anything I know, Falstaff shall die of a
sweat, unless already a' be killed with your hard
opinions; for Oldcastle died a martyr, and this is not
the man.
Epilogue, [32]

HENRY V

3 O! for a Muse of fire, that would ascend
The brightest heaven of invention;
A kingdom for a stage, princes to act
And monarchs to behold the swelling scene.
Chorus, 1

4   Can this cockpit hold
The vasty fields of France? or may we cram
Within this wooden O the very casques
That did affright the air at Agincourt?
11

5 Consideration like an angel came,
And whipp'd the offending Adam out of him.
I.i.28

6   When he speaks,
The air, a charter'd libertine, is still.
47

7 O noble English! that could entertain
With half their forces the full pride of France,
And let another half stand laughing by,
All out of work, and cold for action.
ii.111

8 And make your chronicle as rich with praise
As is the owse and bottom of the sea
With sunken wrack and sumless treasuries.
163

9   For so work the honey-bees,
Creatures that by a rule in nature teach
The act of order to a peopled kingdom.
They have a king and officers of sorts;
Where some, like magistrates, correct at home,
Others, like merchants, venture trade abroad,
Others, like soldiers, armed in their stings,
Make boot upon the summer's velvet buds;
Which pillage they with merry march bring home
To the tent-royal of their emperor:
Who, busied in his majesty, surveys
The singing masons building roofs of gold,
The civil citizens kneading up the honey,
The poor mechanic porters crowding in
Their heavy burdens at his narrow gate,
The sad-ey'd justice, with his surly hum,
Delivering o'er to executors pale
The lazy yawning drone.
187

10 *King Henry:* What treasure, uncle?
Exeter: Tennis-balls, my liege.
258

11 His present and your pains we thank you for:
When we have match'd our rackets to these balls,
We will in France, by God's grace, play a set
Shall strike his father's crown into the hazard.
260

12 Now all the youth of England are on fire,
And silken dalliance in the wardrobe lies;
Now thrive the armourers, and honour's thought
Reigns solely in the breast of every man:
They sell the pasture now to buy the horse,
Following the mirror of all Christian kings,
With winged heels, as English Mercuries.
For now sits Expectation in the air
And hides a sword from hilts unto the point
With crowns imperial, crowns and coronets,
Promis'd to Harry and his followers.
II. Chorus, 1

13 O England! model to thy inward greatness,
Like little body with a mighty heart,
What might'st thou do, that honour would thee do,
Were all thy children kind and natural!
But see thy fault!
16

14 I dare not fight; but I will wink and hold out mine
iron.
i.[7]

15 For, lambkins, we will live.
[134]

16 Would I were with him, wheresome'er he is, either in
heaven or in hell.
iii.[7]

17 He's in Arthur's bosom, if ever man went to Arthur's
bosom. A' made a finer end, and went away an it had
been any christom child; a' parted even just between
twelve and one, even at the turning o' the tide: for
after I saw him fumble with the sheets and play with
flowers and smile upon his fingers' ends, I knew there
was but one way; for his nose was as sharp as a pen,
and a' babbled of green fields.
[9]

18 So a' cried out 'God, God, God!' three or four times:
now I, to comfort him, bid him a' should not think of
God, I hoped there was no need to trouble himself with
any such thoughts yet. So a' bade me lay more clothes
on his feet: I put my hand into the bed and felt them,
and they were as cold as any stone; then I felt to his
knees, and so upward, and upward, and all was as cold
as any stone.
[19]

19 *Boy:* Yes, that a' did; and said they were devils
incarnate.
Hostess: A' never could abide carnation; 'twas a
colour he never liked.
Boy: A' said once, the devil would have him about
women.
[33]

20   Trust none;
For oaths are straws, men's faiths are wafer-cakes,
And hold-fast is the only dog, my duck.
[53]

21 Once more unto the breach, dear friends, once more;
Or close the wall up with our English dead!
In peace there's nothing so becomes a man
As modest stillness and humility:
But when the blast of war blows in our ears,
Then imitate the action of the tiger;
Stiffen the sinews, summon up the blood,
Disguise fair nature with hard-favour'd rage;

Then lend the eye a terrible aspect.
III.i.1

1   On, on you noblest English!
Whose blood is fet from fathers of war-proof;
Fathers that, like so many Alexanders,
Have in these parts from morn till even fought,
And sheath'd their swords for lack of argument.
17

2   And you, good yeomen,
Whose limbs were made in England, show us here
The mettle of your pasture.
25

3 I see you stand like greyhounds in the slips,
Straining upon the start. The game's afoot:
Follow your spirit; and, upon this charge
Cry 'God for Harry! England and Saint George!'
31

4 Would I were in an alehouse in London! I would give
all my fame for a pot of ale, and safety.
ii.[13]

5 Men of few words are the best men.
[40]

6 A' never broke any man's head but his own, and that
was against a post when he was drunk.
[43]

7 One Bardolph, if your majesty know the man: his face
is all bubukles, and whelks, and knobs, and flames o'
fire.
vi.[110]

8 Give them great meals of beef and iron and steel, they
will eat like wolves and fight like devils.
vii.[166]

9 Now entertain conjecture of a time
When creeping murmur and the poring dark
Fills the wide vessel of the universe.
From camp to camp, through the foul womb of night,
The hum of either army stilly sounds,
That the fix'd sentinels almost receive
The secret whispers of each other's watch.
Fire answers fire, and through their paly flames
Each battle sees the other's umber'd face:
Steed threatens steed, in high and boastful neighs
Piercing the night's dull ear; and from the tents
The armourers, accomplishing the knights,
With busy hammers closing rivets up,
Give dreadful note of preparation.
IV. Chorus, 1

10 The royal captain of this ruin'd band.
29

11 A largess universal, like the sun
His liberal eye doth give to every one,
Thawing cold fear.
43

12 A little touch of Harry in the night.
47

13   Yet sit and see;
Minding true things by what their mockeries be.
52

14 Gloucester, 'tis true that we are in great danger;
The greater therefore should our courage be.
i.1

15 Thus may we gather honey from the weed,

And make a moral of the devil himself.
11

16 Discuss unto me; art thou officer?
Or art thou base, common and popular?
37

17 The king's a bawcock, and a heart of gold,
A lad of life, an imp of fame,
Of parents good, of fist most valiant:
I kiss his dirty shoe, and from my heart-string
I love the lovely bully.
44

18 If you would take the pains but to examine the wars of
Pompey the Great, you shall find, I warrant you, that
there is no tiddle-taddle nor pibble-pabble in Pompey's
camp.
[69]

19 Though it appear a little out of fashion,
There is much care and valour in this Welshman.
[86]

20 I think the king is but a man, as I am: the violet smells
to him as it doth to me.
[106]

21 I am afeard there are few die well that die in a battle;
for how can they charitably dispose of any thing when
blood is their argument?
[149]

22 Every subject's duty is the king's; but every subject's
soul is his own.
[189]

23 Upon the king! let us our lives, our souls,
Our debts, our careful wives,
Our children, and our sins lay on the king!
We must bear all. O hard condition!
[250]

24   What infinite heart's ease
Must kings neglect, that private men enjoy!
And what have kings that privates have not too,
Save ceremony, save general ceremony?
[256]

25 'Tis not the balm, the sceptre and the ball,
The sword, the mace, the crown imperial,
The intertissued robe of gold and pearl,
The farced title running 'fore the king,
The throne he sits on, nor the tide of pomp
That beats upon the high shore of this world,
No, not all these, thrice-gorgeous ceremony,
Not all these, laid in bed majestical,
Can sleep so soundly as the wretched slave,
Who with a body fill'd and vacant mind
Gets him to rest, cramm'd with distressful bread;
Never sees horrid night, the child of hell,
But, like a lackey, from the rise to set
Sweats in the eye of Phoebus, and all night
Sleeps in Elysium.
[280]

26 O God of battles! steel my soldiers' hearts;
Possess them not with fear; take from them now
The sense of reckoning, if the opposed numbers
Pluck their hearts from them.
[309]

27   O! that we now had here
But one ten thousand of those men in England

That do no work to-day.
iii.16

1 If we are mark'd to die, we are enow
To do our country loss; and if to live,
The fewer men, the greater share of honour.
20

2 If it be a sin to covet honour
I am the most offending soul alive.
31

3 He which hath no stomach to this fight,
Let him depart; his passport shall be made,
And crowns for convoy put into his purse:
We would not die in that man's company
That fears his fellowship to die with us.
This day is called the feast of Crispian:
He that outlives this day and comes safe home,
Will stand a tip-toe when this day is nam'd,
And rouse him at the name of Crispian.
He that shall live this day, and see old age,
Will yearly on the vigil feast his neighbours,
And say, 'To-morrow is Saint Crispian:'
Then will he strip his sleeve and show his scars,
And say, 'These wounds I had on Crispin's day.'
Old men forget: yet all shall be forgot,
But he'll remember with advantages
What feats he did that day. Then shall our names,
Familiar in his mouth as household words,
Harry the King, Bedford and Exeter,
Warwick and Talbot, Salisbury and Gloucester,
Be in their flowing cups freshly remember'd.
This story shall the good man teach his son;
And Crispin Crispian shall ne'er go by,
From this day to the ending of the world,
But we in it shall be remembered;
We few, we happy few, we band of brothers;
For he to-day that sheds his blood with me
Shall be my brother; be he ne'er so vile
This day shall gentle his condition:
And gentlemen in England, now a-bed
Shall think themselves accurs'd they were not here,
And hold their manhoods cheap whiles any speaks
That fought with us upon Saint Crispin's day.
35

4 Thou damned and luxurious mountain goat.
iv.[20]

5 There is a river in Macedon, and there is also
moreover a river at Monmouth: it is called Wye at
Monmouth; but it is out of my prains what is the name
of the other river; but 'tis all one, 'tis alike as my
fingers is to my fingers, and there is salmons in both.
vii.[28]

6   But now behold,
In the quick forge and working-house of thought,
How London doth pour out her citizens.
V. Chorus, 22

7 Were now the general of our gracious empress,—
As in good time he may,—from Ireland coming,
Bringing rebellion broached on his sword.
30

8 There is occasions and causes why and wherefore in
all things.
i.[3]

9 Not for Cadwallader and all his goats.
[29]

10 By this leek, I will most horribly revenge.
[49]

11   Let it not disgrace me
If I demand before this royal view,
What rub or what impediment there is,
Why that the naked, poor, and mangled Peace,
Dear nurse of arts, plenties, and joyful births,
Should not in this best garden of the world,
Our fertile France, put up her lovely visage?
ii.31

12   Her fallow leas
The darnel, hemlock and rank fumitory
Doth root upon, while that the coulter rusts
That should deracinate such savagery;
The even mead, that erst brought sweetly forth
The freckled cowslip, burnet, and green clover,
Wanting the scythe, all uncorrected, rank,
Conceives by idleness, and nothing teems
But hateful docks, rough thistles, kecksies, burs,
Losing both beauty and utility.
44

13 For these fellows of infinite tongue, that can rhyme
themselves into ladies' favours, they do always reason
themselves out again.
[162]

14 Shall not thou and I, between Saint Denis and Saint
George, compound a boy, half-French, half-English,
that shall go to Constantinople and take the Turk by
the beard?
[218]

15 It is not a fashion for the maids in France to kiss
before they are married.
[287]

16 God, the best maker of all marriages,
Combine your hearts in one.
[387]

HENRY VI, Part 1

17 Hung be the heavens with black, yield day to night!
I.i.1

18 Expect Saint Martin's summer, halcyon days.
ii.131

19   Unbidden guests
Are often welcomest when they are gone.
II.ii.55

20 But in these nice sharp quillets of the law,
Good faith, I am no wiser than a daw.
iv.17

21 *Plantagenet:* Let him that is a true-born gentleman,
And stands upon the honour of his birth,
If he suppose that I have pleaded truth,
From off this brier pluck a white rose with me.
Somerset: Let him that is no coward nor no flatterer,
But dare maintain the party of the truth,
Pluck a red rose from off this thorn with me.
27

22 Delays have dangerous ends.
III.ii.33

23 I owe him little duty and less love.
IV.iv.34

24 So doth the swan her downy cygnets save,

Keeping them prisoners underneath her wings.
V.iii.56

1 She's beautiful and therefore to be woo'd;
She is a woman, therefore to be won.
78. See 486:15

HENRY VI, Part 2

2 Put forth thy hand, reach at the glorious gold.
I.ii.11

3 Is this the fashion of the court of England?
Is this the government of Britain's isle,
And this the royalty of Albion's king?
iii.[46]

4 She bears a duke's revenues on her back,
And in her heart she scorns our poverty.
[83]

5 Could I come near your beauty with my nails
I'd set my ten commandments in your face.
[144]

6 What stronger breastplate than a heart untainted!
Thrice is he arm'd that hath his quarrel just,
And he but naked, though lock'd up in steel,
Whose conscience with injustice is corrupted.
III.ii.232

7 Forbear to judge, for we are sinners all.
Close up his eyes, and draw the curtain close;
And let us all to meditation.
iii.31

8 The gaudy, blabbing, and remorseful day
Is crept into the bosom of the sea.
IV.i.1

9 True nobility is exempt from fear:
More can I bear than you dare execute.
129

10 I say it was never merry world in England since
gentlemen came up.
ii.[10]

11 *Cade:* There shall be in England seven halfpenny
loaves sold for a penny; the three-hooped pot shall
have ten hoops; and I will make it felony to drink
small beer. All the realm shall be in common, and in
Cheapside shall my palfrey go to grass. And when I am
king,—as king I will be,—...there shall be no money;
all shall eat and drink on my score; and I will apparel
them all in one livery, that they may agree like
brothers, and worship me their lord.
Dick: The first thing we do, let's kill all the lawyers.
[73]

12 Is not this a lamentable thing, that of the skin of an
innocent lamb should be made parchment? that
parchment, being scribbled o'er, should undo a man?
[88]

13 And Adam was a gardener.
[146]

14 Thou hast most traitorously corrupted the youth of the
realm in erecting a grammar school: and whereas,
before, our forefathers had no other books but the
score and the tally, thou hast caused printing to be
used; and, contrary to the king, his crown and dignity,
thou hast built a paper-mill.
vii.[35]

15 Away with him! away with him! he speaks Latin.
[62]

HENRY VI, Part 3

16 O tiger's heart wrapp'd in a woman's hide!
I.iv.137

17 This battle fares like to the morning's war,
When dying clouds contend with growing light,
What time the shepherd, blowing of his nails,
Can neither call it perfect day nor night.
II.v.1

18 O God! methinks it were a happy life,
To be no better than a homely swain;
To sit upon a hill, as I do now,
To carve out dials, quaintly, point by point,
Thereby to see the minutes how they run,
How many make the hour full complete;
How many hours bring about the day;
How many days will finish up the year;
How many years a mortal man may live.
21

19 Gives not the hawthorn bush a sweeter shade
To shepherds, looking on their silly sheep,
Than doth a rich embroider'd canopy
To kings that fear their subjects' treachery?
42

20 Peace! impudent and shameless Warwick, peace;
Proud setter up and puller down of kings.
III.iii.156

21 A little fire is quickly trodden out,
Which, being suffer'd, rivers cannot quench.
IV.viii.7

22 Lo! now my glory smear'd in dust and blood;
My parks, my walks, my manors that I had,
Even now forsake me; and, of all my lands
Is nothing left me but my body's length.
Why, what is pomp, rule, reign, but earth and dust?
And, live we how we can, yet die we must.
V.ii.23

23 Suspicion always haunts the guilty mind;
The thief doth fear each bush an officer.
vi.11

24 Down, down to hell; and say I sent thee thither.
67

HENRY VIII

25 Heat not a furnace for your foe so hot
That it do singe yourself.
I.i.140

26 If I chance to talk a little wild, forgive me;
I had it from my father.
iv.26

27 Go with me, like good angels, to my end;
And, as the long divorce of steel falls on me,
Make of your prayers one sweet sacrifice,
And lift my soul to heaven.
II.i.75

28 *Chamberlain:* It seems the marriage with his brother's
wife
Has crept too near his conscience.
Suffolk: No; his conscience

Has crept too near another lady.
ii.[17]

1   Heaven will one day open
The king's eyes, that so long have slept upon
This bold bad man.
[42]. See 516:1

2   I would not be a queen
For all the world.
45

3 Orpheus with his lute made trees,
And the mountain-tops that freeze,
   Bow themselves when he did sing:
To his music plants and flowers
Ever sprung; as sun and showers
   There had made a lasting spring.

Everything that heard him play,
Even the billows of the sea,
   Hung their heads, and then lay by.
In sweet music is such art,
Killing care and grief of heart
   Fall asleep, or hearing die.
III.i.3

4 Heaven is above all yet; there sits a judge,
That no king can corrupt.
99

5 A spleeny Lutheran.
ii.100

6   Then to breakfast with
What appetite you have.
203

7   I shall fall
Like a bright exhalation in the evening,
And no man see me more.
226

8   In all you writ to Rome, or else
To foreign princes, *Ego et Rex meus*
Was still inscrib'd; in which you brought the king
To be your servant.
313

9 Farewell! a long farewell, to all my greatness!
This is the state of man: to-day he puts forth
The tender leaves of hope; to-morrow blossoms,
And bears his blushing honours thick upon him;
The third day comes a frost, a killing frost;
And, when he thinks, good easy man, full surely
His greatness is a-ripening, nips his root,
And then he falls, as I do. I have ventur'd,
Like little wanton boys that swim on bladders,
This many summers in a sea of glory,
But far beyond my depth: my high-blown pride
At length broke under me, and now has left me
Weary and old with service, to the mercy
Of a rude stream that must for ever hide me.
Vain pomp and glory of this world, I hate ye:
I feel my heart new open'd. O how wretched
Is that poor man that hangs on princes' favours!
There is, betwixt that smile we would aspire to,
That sweet aspect of princes, and their ruin,
More pangs and fears than wars or women have;
And when he falls, he falls like Lucifer,
Never to hope again.
352

10 A peace above all earthly dignities,

A still and quiet conscience.
380

11 A load would sink a navy.
384

12 Cromwell, I charge thee, fling away ambition:
By that sin fell the angels; how can man then,
The image of his Maker, hope to win by't?
Love thyself last: cherish those hearts that hate thee;
Corruption wins not more than honesty.
Still in thy right hand carry gentle peace,
To silence envious tongues: be just, and fear not.
Let all the ends thou aim'st at be thy country's,
Thy God's, and truth's: then if thou fall'st, O
   Cromwell!
Thou fall'st a blessed martyr.
441

13 Had I but serv'd my God with half the zeal
I serv'd my king, he would not in mine age
Have left me naked to mine enemies.
456

14 She had all the royal makings of a queen.
IV.i.87

15 An old man, broken with the storms of state
Is come to lay his weary bones among ye;
Give him a little earth for charity.
ii.21

16 He gave his honours to the world again,
His blessed part to Heaven, and slept in peace.
29

17 So may he rest; his faults lie gently on him!
31

18   He was a man
Of an unbounded stomach.
33

19 His promises were, as he then was, mighty;
But his performance, as he is now, nothing.
41

20 Men's evil manners live in brass; their virtues
We write in water.
45

21 He was a scholar, and a ripe and good one;
Exceeding wise, fair-spoken, and persuading:
Lofty and sour to them that lov'd him not;
But, to those men that sought him, sweet as summer.
51

22 Those twins of learning that he rais'd in you,
Ipswich and Oxford!
58

23 After my death I wish no other herald,
No other speaker of my living actions,
To keep mine honour from corruption,
Than such an honest chronicler as Griffith.
69

24   I had thought
They had parted so much honesty among 'em,—
At least, good manners,—as not thus to suffer
A man of his place, and so near our favour,
To dance attendance on their lordships' pleasures,
And at the door too, like a post with packets.
V.ii.26

25   'Tis a cruelty
To load a falling man.
76

1   In her days every man shall eat in safety
    Under his own vine what he plants; and sing
    The merry songs of peace to all his neighbours.
    v.34

2   Those about her
    From her shall read the perfect ways of honour.
    37

3   Nor shall this peace sleep with her; but as when
    The bird of wonder dies, the maiden phoenix,
    Her ashes new-create another heir
    As great in admiration as herself.
    40

4   Some come to take their ease
    And sleep an act or two.
    Epilogue, 2

JULIUS CAESAR

5   Hence! home, you idle creatures, get you home:
    Is this a holiday?
    I.i.1

6   You blocks, you stones, you worse than senseless
        things!
    O you hard hearts, you cruel men of Rome,
    Knew you not Pompey?
    [39]

7   *Caesar:* Who is it in the press that calls on me?
    I hear a tongue, shriller than all the music,
    Cry 'Caesar'. Speak; Caesar is turn'd to hear.
    Soothsayer: Beware the ides of March.
    ii.15

8   He is a dreamer; let us leave him: pass.
    24

9   I am not gamesome: I do lack some part
    Of that quick spirit that is in Antony.
    28

10 Brutus, I do observe you now of late:
    I have not from your eyes that gentleness
    And show of love as I was wont to have:
    You bear too stubborn and too strange a hand
    Over your friend that loves you.
    32

11   Poor Brutus, with himself at war,
    Forgets the shows of love to other men.
    46

12 Set honour in one eye and death i' the other,
    And I will look on both indifferently.
    86

13 Well, honour is the subject of my story.
    I cannot tell what you and other men
    Think of this life: but, for my single self,
    I had as lief not be as live to be
    In awe of such a thing as I myself.
    92

14 I was born free as Caesar; so were you:
    We both have fed as well, and we can both
    Endure the winter's cold as well as he:
    For once, upon a raw and gusty day,
    The troubl'd Tiber chafing with her shores,
    Caesar said to me, 'Dar'st thou, Cassius, now,
    Leap in with me into this angry flood,
    And swim to yonder point?' Upon the word,
    Accoutred as I was, I plunged in,
    And bade him follow...

But ere we could arrive the point propos'd,
Caesar cried, 'Help me, Cassius, or I sink!'
I, as Aeneas, our great ancestor,
Did from the flames of Troy upon his shoulder
The old Anchises bear, so from the waves of Tiber
Did I the tired Caesar. And this man
Is now become a god.
97

15 He had a fever when he was in Spain,
    And when the fit was on him, I did mark
    How he did shake; 'tis true, this god did shake;
    His coward lips did from their colour fly,
    And that same eye whose bend doth awe the world
    Did lose his lustre.
    119

16   Ye gods, it doth amaze me,
    A man of such a feeble temper should
    So get the start of the majestic world,
    And bear the palm alone.
    128

17 Why, man, he doth bestride the narrow world
    Like a Colossus; and we petty men
    Walk under his huge legs, and peep about
    To find ourselves dishonourable graves.
    Men at some time are masters of their fates:
    The fault, dear Brutus, is not in our stars,
    But in ourselves, that we are underlings.
    134

18 'Brutus' will start a spirit as soon as 'Caesar'.
    Now in the names of all the gods at once,
    Upon what meat doth this our Caesar feed,
    That he is grown so great?
    146

19 When could they say, till now, that talk'd of Rome,
    That her wide walls encompass'd but one man?
    Now is it Rome indeed and room enough,
    When there is in it but one only man.
    153

20 Let me have men about me that are fat;
    Sleek-headed men and such as sleep o' nights;
    Yond' Cassius has a lean and hungry look;
    He thinks too much: such men are dangerous.
    191

21 Would he were fatter! but I fear him not:
    Yet if my name were liable to fear,
    I do not know the man I should avoid
    So soon as that spare Cassius. He reads much;
    He is a great observer, and he looks
    Quite through the deeds of men; he loves no plays,
    As thou dost, Antony; he hears no music;
    Seldom he smiles, and smiles in such a sort
    As if he mock'd himself, and scorn'd his spirit,
    That could be mov'd to smile at anything.
    Such men as he be never at heart's ease,
    Whiles they behold a greater than themselves,
    And therefore are they very dangerous.
    I rather tell thee what is to be fear'd
    Than what I fear, for always I am Caesar.
    197

22 'Tis very like: he hath the falling sickness.
    [255]

23 *Cassius:* Did Cicero say any thing?
    Casca: Ay, he spoke Greek.
    Cassius: To what effect?

Casca: Nay, an I tell you that, I'll ne'er look you i' the face again; but those that understood him smiled at one another and shook their heads; but, for mine own part, it was Greek to me.
[282]

1   Yesterday the bird of night did sit,
Even at noon-day, upon the market-place,
Hooting and shrieking.
iii.26

2 Cassius from bondage will deliver Cassius.
90

3 Nor stony tower, nor walls of beaten brass,
Nor airless dungeon, nor strong links of iron,
Can be retentive to the strength of spirit;
But life, being weary of these worldly bars,
Never lacks power to dismiss itself.
93

4 It is the bright day that brings forth the adder;
And that craves wary walking.
II.i.14

5   'Tis a common proof,
That lowliness is young ambition's ladder,
Whereto the climber-upward turns his face;
But when he once attains the upmost round,
He then unto the ladder turns his back,
Looks in the clouds, scorning the base degrees
By which he did ascend.
21

6 Between the acting of a dreadful thing
And the first motion, all the interim is
Like a phantasma, or a hideous dream:
The genius and the mortal instruments
Are then in council; and the state of man,
Like to a little kingdom, suffers then
The nature of an insurrection.
63

7   O conspiracy!
Sham'st thou to show thy dangerous brow by night,
When evils are most free?
77

8 Let us be sacrificers, but not butchers, Caius.
166

9 Let's carve him as a dish fit for the gods,
Not hew him as a carcass fit for hounds.
173

10 For he is superstitious grown of late,
Quite from the main opinion he held once
Of fantasy, of dreams, and ceremonies.
195

11 But when I tell him he hates flatterers,
He says he does, being then most flattered.
207

12 Enjoy the honey-heavy dew of slumber.
230

13   What! is Brutus sick,
And will he steal out of his wholesome bed
To dare the vile contagion of the night?
263

14   That great vow
Which did incorporate and make us one.
272

15 *Portia:* Dwell I but in the suburbs
Of your good pleasure? If it be no more,

Portia is Brutus' harlot, not his wife.
Brutus: You are my true and honourable wife,
As dear to me as are the ruddy drops
That visit my sad heart.
285

16 I grant I am a woman, but, withal,
A woman that Lord Brutus took to wife;
I grant I am a woman, but, withal,
A woman well-reputed, Cato's daughter.
Think you I am no stronger than my sex,
Being so fathered and so husbanded?
292

17 Nor heaven nor earth have been at peace to-night.
ii.1

18 *Calphurnia:* When beggars die, there are no comets seen;
The heavens themselves blaze forth the death of princes.
Caesar: Cowards die many times before their deaths;
The valiant never taste of death but once.
Of all the wonders that I yet have heard,
It seems to me most strange that men should fear;
Seeing that death, a necessary end,
Will come when it will come.
30

19   Danger knows full well
That Caesar is more dangerous than he:
We are two lions litter'd in one day,
And I the elder and more terrible:
And Caesar shall go forth.
44

20 The cause is in my will: I will not come.
71

21 See! Antony, that revels long o' nights,
Is notwithstanding up.
116

22 O constancy! be strong upon my side;
Set a huge mountain 'tween my heart and tongue;
I have a man's mind, but a woman's might.
How hard it is for women to keep counsel!
iv.6

23 *Caesar:* The ides of March are come.
Soothsayer: Ay, Caesar; but not gone.
III.i.1

24   Be not fond,
To think that Caesar bears such rebel blood
That will be thaw'd from the true quality
With that which melted fools; I mean sweet words,
Low-crooked curtsies, and base spaniel fawning.
Thy brother by decree is banished:
If thou dost bend and pray and fawn for him,
I spurn thee like a cur out of my way.
39

25 If I could pray to move, prayers would move me;
But I am constant as the northern star,
Of whose true-fix'd and resting quality
There is no fellow in the firmament.
The skies are painted with unnumber'd sparks,
They are all fire and every one doth shine,
But there's but one in all doth hold his place:
So, in the world; 'tis furnish'd well with men,
And men are flesh and blood, and apprehensive;
Yet in the number I do know but one
That unassailable holds on his rank,

Unshak'd of motion: and that I am he,
Let me a little show it, even in this,
That I was constant Cimber should be banish'd,
And constant do remain to keep him so.
59

1 *Et tu, Brute?* Then fall, Caesar!
77. See 126:28

2 Ambition's debt is paid.
83

3 That we shall die, we know; 'tis but the time
And drawing days out, that men stand upon.
99

4 He that cuts off twenty years of life
Cuts off so many years of fearing death.
101

5 *Cassius:* How many ages hence
Shall this our lofty scene be acted o'er,
In states unborn, and accents yet unknown!
Brutus: How many times shall Caesar bleed in sport.
111

6 O mighty Caesar! dost thou lie so low?
Are all thy conquests, glories, triumphs, spoils,
Shrunk to this little measure?
148

7   Your swords, made rich
With the most noble blood of all this world.
155

8   Live a thousand years,
I shall not find myself so apt to die:
No place will please me so, no mean of death,
As here by Caesar, and by you cut off,
The choice and master spirits of this age.
159

9 Had I as many eyes as thou hast wounds,
Weeping as fast as they stream forth thy blood,
It would become me better than to close
In terms of friendship with thine enemies.
200

10 The enemies of Caesar shall say this;
Then, in a friend, it is cold modesty.
212

11 O! pardon me, thou bleeding piece of earth,
That I am meek and gentle with these butchers;
Thou art the ruins of the noblest man
That ever lived in the tide of times.
254

12   Caesar's spirit, ranging for revenge,
With Ate by his side, come hot from hell,
Shall in these confines, with a monarch's voice
Cry, 'Havoc!' and let slip the dogs of war;
That this foul deed shall smell above the earth
With carrion men, groaning for burial.
270

13 Passion, I see, is catching.
283

14 Not that I loved Caesar less, but that I loved Rome
more.
ii.[22]

15 As he was valiant, I honour him: but, as he was
ambitious, I slew him.
[27]

16 Who is here so base that would be a bondman? If any,
speak; for him have I offended. Who is here so rude

that would not be a Roman? If any, speak; for him
have I offended. Who is here so vile that will not love
his country? If any, speak; for him have I offended. I
pause for a reply.
[31]

17 Friends, Romans, countrymen, lend me your ears;
I come to bury Caesar, not to praise him.
The evil that men do lives after them,
The good is oft interred with their bones;
So let it be with Caesar. The noble Brutus
Hath told you Caesar was ambitious;
If it were so, it was a grievous fault;
And grievously hath Caesar answer'd it.
Here, under leave of Brutus and the rest,—
For Brutus is an honourable man;
So are they all, all honourable men,—
Come I to speak in Caesar's funeral.
[79]

18 He was my friend, faithful and just to me:
But Brutus says he was ambitious;
And Brutus is an honourable man.
[91]

19 When that the poor have cried, Caesar hath wept;
Ambition should be made of sterner stuff.
[97]

20   On the Lupercal
I thrice presented him a kingly crown
Which he did thrice refuse: was this ambition?
[101]

21 You all did love him once, not without cause.
[108]

22 O judgment! thou art fled to brutish beasts,
And men have lost their reason.
[110]

23 But yesterday the word of Caesar might
Have stood against the world; now lies he there,
And none so poor to do him reverence.
[124]

24 The will, the will! we will hear Caesar's will.
[145]

25 You are not wood, you are not stones, but men;
And, being men, hearing the will of Caesar,
It will inflame you, it will make you mad.
[148]

26 If you have tears, prepare to shed them now.
You all do know this mantle: I remember
The first time ever Caesar put it on;
'Twas on a summer's evening, in his tent,
That day he overcame the Nervii.
[174]

27 See what a rent the envious Casca made.
[180]

28 This was the most unkindest cut of all;
For when the noble Caesar saw him stab,
Ingratitude, more strong than traitors' arms,
Quite vanquish'd him: then burst his mighty heart;
And, in his mantle muffling up his face,
Even at the base of Pompey's statua,
Which all the while ran blood, great Caesar fell.
O! what a fall was there, my countrymen;
Then I, and you, and all of us fell down,
Whilst bloody treason flourish'd over us.
O! now you weep, and I perceive you feel

The dint of pity; these are gracious drops.
[188]

1 I come not, friends, to steal away your hearts:
I am no orator, as Brutus is;
But, as you know me all, a plain, blunt man,
That love my friend.
[220]

2 For I have neither wit, nor words, nor worth,
Action, nor utterance, nor power of speech,
To stir men's blood; I only speak right on;
I tell you that which you yourselves do know.
[225]

3   But were I Brutus,
And Brutus Antony, there were an Antony
Would ruffle up your spirits, and put a tongue
In every wound of Caesar, that should move
The stones of Rome to rise and mutiny.
[230]

4   He hath left you all his walks,
His private arbours, and new-planted orchards,
On this side Tiber; he hath left them you,
And to your heirs for ever; common pleasures,
To walk abroad, and recreate yourselves.
[252]

5 Here was a Caesar! when comes such another?
[257]

6 Now let it work; mischief, thou art afoot,
Take thou what course thou wilt!
[265]

7   Fortune is merry,
And in this mood will give us anything.
[271]

8 Tear him for his bad verses, tear him for his bad
verses.
iii.[34]

9 He shall not live; look, with a spot I damn him.
IV.i.6

10 This is a slight unmeritable man,
Meet to be sent on errands.
12

11 When love begins to sicken and decay,
It useth an enforced ceremony.
There are no tricks in plain and simple faith.
ii.20

12 Let me tell you, Cassius, you yourself
Are much condemn'd to have an itching palm.
iii.7

13   Shall we now
Contaminate our fingers with base bribes?
23

14 I had rather be a dog, and bay the moon,
Than such a Roman.
27

15 Away, slight man!
37

16 I'll use you for my mirth, yea, for my laughter,
When you are waspish.
49

17   For mine own part,
I shall be glad to learn of noble men.
53

18 You wrong me every way; you wrong me, Brutus;

I said an elder soldier, not a better:
Did I say 'better'?
55

19 Do not presume too much upon my love;
I may do that I shall be sorry for.
63

20 There is no terror, Cassius, in your threats;
For I am arm'd so strong in honesty
That they pass by me as the idle wind,
Which I respect not.
66

21 By heaven, I had rather coin my heart,
And drop my blood for drachmas, than to wring
From the hard hands of peasants their vile trash
By any indirection.
72

22 A friend should bear his friend's infirmities,
But Brutus makes mine greater than they are.
85

23 Cassius is aweary of the world;
Hated by one he loves; brav'd by his brother;
Check'd like a bondman; all his faults observ'd,
Set in a note-book, learn'd, and conn'd by rote,
To cast into my teeth.
94

24 O Cassius! you are yoked with a lamb
That carries anger as the flint bears fire;
Who, much enforced, shows a hasty spark,
And straight is cold again.
109

25 O Cassius! I am sick of many griefs.
143

26 Good reasons must, of force, give place to better.
202

27 The enemy increaseth every day;
We, at the height, are ready to decline.
There is a tide in the affairs of men,
Which, taken at the flood, leads on to fortune;
Omitted, all the voyage of their life
Is bound in shallows and in miseries.
On such a full sea are we now afloat,
And we must take the current when it serves,
Or lose our ventures.
215

28 The deep of night is crept upon our talk,
And nature must obey necessity.
225

29 This was an ill beginning of the night:
Never come such division 'tween our souls!
233

30 *Brutus:* Then I shall see thee again?
Ghost: Ay, at Philippi.
Brutus: Why, I will see thee at Philippi, then.
283

31 But for your words, they rob the Hybla bees,
And leave them honeyless.
V.i.34

32 If we do meet again, why, we shall smile!
If not, why then, this parting was well made.
118

33   O! that a man might know
The end of this day's business, ere it come;
But it sufficeth that the day will end,

And then the end is known.
123

1   This day I breathed first: time is come round,
And where I did begin, there shall I end;
My life is run his compass.
iii.23

2   O hateful error, melancholy's child!
Why dost thou show, to the apt thoughts of men,
The things that are not?
67

3   O Julius Caesar! thou art mighty yet!
Thy spirit walks abroad, and turns our swords
In our own proper entrails.
94

4   I had rather have
Such men my friends than enemies.
iv.28

5   Thou seest the world, Volumnius, how it goes;
Our enemies have beat us to the pit:
It is more worthy to leap in ourselves,
Than tarry till they push us.
v.22

6   Thou art a fellow of a good respect;
Thy life hath had some smatch of honour in it.
Hold then my sword, and turn away thy face,
While I do run upon it.
45

7   This was the noblest Roman of them all;
All the conspirators save only he
Did that they did in envy of great Caesar;
He, only, in a general honest thought
And common good to all, made one of them.
His life was gentle, and the elements
So mix'd in him that Nature might stand up
And say to all the world, 'This was a man!'
68

KING JOHN

8   Hadst thou rather be a Faulconbridge
And like thy brother, to enjoy thy land,
Or the reputed son of Coeur-de-Lion,
Lord of thy presence and no land beside.
I.i.134

9   And if his name be George, I'll call him Peter;
For new-made honour doth forget men's names.
186

10 Sweet, sweet, sweet poison for the age's tooth.
213

11 Courage mounteth with occasion.
II.i.82

12 Saint George, that swinged the dragon and e'er since
Sits on his horse back at mine hostess' door.
288

13 Mad world! mad kings! mad composition!
561

14 That smooth-fac'd gentleman, tickling Commodity,
Commodity, the bias of the world.
573

15 Well, whiles I am a beggar, I will rail,
And say there is no sin, but to be rich;
And, being rich, my virtue then shall be,

To say there is no vice, but beggary.
593

16 Thou wear a lion's hide! doff it for shame,
And hang a calf's-skin on those recreant limbs!
III.i.128

17   No Italian priest
Shall tithe or toll in our dominions.
153

18 Old Time the clock-setter, that bald sexton, Time.
324

19 Bell, book, and candle shall not drive me back,
When gold and silver becks me to come on.
iii.12

20 Grief fills the room up of my absent child,
Lies in his bed, walks up and down with me,
Puts on his pretty looks, repeats his words,
Remembers me of all his gracious parts,
Stuffs out his vacant garments with his form:
Then have I reason to be fond of grief.
iv.93

21 Life is as tedious as a twice-told tale,
Vexing the dull ear of a drowsy man.
108

22 Heat me these irons hot.
IV.i.1

23 Methinks nobody should be sad but I:
Yet I remember, when I was in France,
Young gentlemen would be as sad as night,
Only for wantonness.
13

24   Will you put out mine eyes?
These eyes that never did nor never shall
So much as frown on you?
56

25   To be possess'd with double pomp,
To guard a title that was rich before,
To gild refined gold, to paint the lily,
To throw a perfume on the violet,
To smooth the ice, or add another hue
Unto the rainbow, or with taper light
To seek the beauteous eye of heaven to garnish,
Is wasteful and ridiculous excess.
ii.9

26 The spirit of the time shall teach me speed.
176

27 Another lean unwash'd artificer
Cuts off his tale and talks of Arthur's death.
201

28 How oft the sight of means to do ill deeds
Makes ill deeds done!
219

29 Heaven take my soul, and England keep my bones!
iii.10

30 Whate'er you think, good words, I think, were best.
28

31   None of you will bid the winter come
To thrust his icy fingers in my maw;
Nor let my kingdom's rivers take their course
Through my burn'd bosom; nor entreat the north
To make his bleak winds kiss my parched lips
And comfort me with cold. I do not ask you much:
I beg cold comfort; and you are so strait

And so ingrateful you deny me that.
V.vii.36

1 This England never did, nor never shall,
Lie at the proud foot of a conqueror,
But when it first did help to wound itself.
Now these her princes are come home again,
Come the three corners of the world in arms,
And we shall shock them: nought shall make us rue,
If England to itself do rest but true.
112

KING LEAR

2 Nothing will come of nothing: speak again.
I.i.[92]

3 *Lear:* So young, and so untender?
Cordelia: So young, my lord, and true.
Lear: Let it be so; thy truth then be thy dower:
For, by the sacred radiance of the sun,
The mysteries of Hecate and the night,
By all the operation of the orbs
From whom we do exist and cease to be,
Here I disclaim all my paternal care,
Propinquity and property of blood,
And as a stranger to my heart and me
Hold thee from this for ever.
[108]

4 Come not between the dragon and his wrath.
[124]

5 I want that glib and oily art
To speak and purpose not; since what I well intend,
I'll do't before I speak.
[227]

6 It is no vicious blot nor other foulness,
No unchaste action, or dishonour'd step,
That hath depriv'd me of your grace and favour,
But even for want of that for which I am richer,
A still-soliciting eye, and such a tongue
That I am glad I have not, though not to have it
Hath lost me in your liking.
[230]

7 Love is not love
When it is mingled with regards that stand
Aloof from the entire point.
[241]

8 Fairest Cordelia, that art most rich, being poor;
Most choice, forsaken; and most lov'd, despis'd!
[253]

9 Why bastard? wherefore base?
When my dimensions are as well compact,
My mind as generous, and my shape as true,
As honest madam's issue? Why brand they us
With base? with baseness? bastardy? base, base?
Who in the lusty stealth of nature take
More composition and fierce quality
Than doth, within a dull, stale, tired bed,
Go to creating a whole tribe of fops,
Got 'tween asleep and wake?
ii.6

10 I grow, I prosper;
Now, gods, stand up for bastards!
21

11 This is the excellent foppery of the world, that, when we are sick in fortune,—often the surfeit of our own behaviour,— we make guilty of our own disasters the sun, the moon, and the stars; as if we were villains by necessity, fools by heavenly compulsion, knaves, thieves, and treachers by spherical predominance, drunkards, liars, and adulterers by an enforced obedience of planetary influence; and all that we are evil in, by a divine thrusting on: an admirable evasion of whoremaster man, to lay his goatish disposition to the charge of a star! My father compounded with my mother under the dragon's tail, and my nativity was under *ursa major,* so that it follows I am rough and lecherous. 'Sfoot! I should have been that I am had the maidenliest star in the firmament twinkled on my bastardizing.
[132]

12 Pat he comes, like the catastrophe of the old comedy; my cue is villanous melancholy, with a sigh like Tom o' Bedlam.
[150]

13 *Lear:* Dost thou know me, fellow?
Kent: No, sir; but you have that in your countenance which I would fain call master.
Lear: What's that?
Kent: Authority.
iv.[28]

14 Not so young, sir, to love a woman for singing, nor so old to dote on her for any thing.
[40]

15 Have more than thou showest,
Speak less than thou knowest,
Lend less than thou owest.
[132]

16 *Lear:* Dost thou call me fool, boy?
Fool: All thy other titles thou hast given away; that thou wast born with.
[163]

17 Ingratitude, thou marble-hearted fiend,
More hideous, when thou show'st thee in a child,
Than the sea-monster.
[283]

18 Into her womb convey sterility!
Dry up in her the organs of increase.
[302]

19 How sharper than a serpent's tooth it is
To have a thankless child!
[312]

20 O! let me not be mad, not mad, sweet heaven;
Keep me in temper; I would not be mad!
v.[51]

21 Thou whoreson zed! thou unnecessary letter!
II.ii.[68]

22 Goose, if I had you upon Sarum plain,
I'd drive ye cackling home to Camelot.
[88]

23 Sir, 'tis my occupation to be plain:
I have seen better faces in my time
Than stands on any shoulder that I see
Before me at this instant.
[98]

24 Down, thou climbing sorrow!
Thy element's below.
iv.[57]

25 O, sir! you are old;

Nature in you stands on the very verge
Of her confine.
[148]

1 You see me here, you gods, a poor old man,
As full of grief as age; wretched in both!
[275]

2   Touch me with noble anger,
And let not women's weapons, water-drops,
Stain my man's cheeks! No, you unnatural hags,
I will have such revenges on you both
That all the world shall—I will do such things,—
What they are yet I know not,—but they shall be
The terrors of the earth. You think I'll weep;
No, I'll not weep:
I have full cause of weeping, but this heart
Shall break into a hundred thousand flaws
Or ere I'll weep. O fool! I shall go mad.
[279]

3 Contending with the fretful elements;
Bids the wind blow the earth into the sea,
Or swell the curled waters 'bove the main,
That things might change or cease.
III.i.4

4 Blow, winds, and crack your cheeks! rage! blow!
You cataracts and hurricanoes, spout
Till you have drench'd our steeples, drown'd the
  cocks!
You sulphurous and thought-executing fires,
Vaunt-couriers to oak-cleaving thunderbolts,
Singe my white head! And thou, all-shaking thunder,
Strike flat the thick rotundity o' the world!
Crack nature's moulds, all germens spill at once
That make ingrateful man!
ii.1

5 Rumble thy bellyful! Spit, fire! Spout, rain!
Nor rain, wind, thunder, fire, are my daughters:
I tax not you, you elements, with unkindness;
I never gave you kingdom, call'd you children,
You owe me no subscription: then, let fall
Your horrible pleasure; here I stand, your slave,
A poor, infirm, weak, and despis'd old man.
14

6 There was never yet fair woman but she made mouths
in a glass.
[35]

7 No, I will be the pattern of all patience; I will say
nothing.
[37]

8 Marry, here's grace and a cod-piece; that's a wise man
and a fool.
[40]

9   Things that love night
Love not such nights as these.
[42]

10   Close pent-up guilts,
Rive your concealing continents, and cry
These dreadful summoners grace. I am a man
More sinned against than sinning.
[57]

11 The art of our necessities is strange,
That can make vile things precious.
[70]

12 He that has a little tiny wit,

With hey, ho, the wind and the rain,
Must make content with his fortunes fit,
Though the rain it raineth every day.
[74]

13   When the mind's free,
The body's delicate.
iv.11

14 O! that way madness lies; let me shun that.
21

15 Poor naked wretches, wheresoe'er you are,
That bide the pelting of this pitiless storm,
How shall your houseless heads and unfed sides,
Your looped and window'd raggedness, defend you
From seasons such as these?
28

16   Take physic, pomp;
Expose thyself to feel what wretches feel.
33

17 Pillicock sat on Pillicock-hill:
Halloo, halloo, loo, loo!
[75]

18 A serving-man, proud in heart and mind: that curled
my hair, wore gloves in my cap, served the lust of my
mistress's heart, and did the act of darkness with her;
swore as many oaths as I spake words, and broke them
in the sweet face of heaven; one that slept in the
contriving of lust, and waked to do it. Wine loved I
deeply, dice dearly, and in woman out-paramoured the
Turk.
[84]

19 Keep thy foot out of brothels, thy hand out of
plackets, thy pen from lenders' books, and defy the
foul fiend.
[96]

20 Thou art the thing itself; unaccommodated man is no
more but such a poor, bare, forked animal as thou art.
Off, off, you lendings! Come; unbutton here.
[109]

21 'Tis a naughty night to swim in.
[113]

22 This is the foul fiend Flibbertigibbet: he begins at
curfew, and walks till the first cock; he gives the web
and the pin, squints the eye, and makes the harelip;
mildews the white wheat, and hurts the poor creatures
of earth.
[118]

23 The green mantle of the standing pool.
[136]

24 The prince of darkness is a gentleman.
[148]

25 Poor Tom's a-cold.
[151]

26 I will keep still with my philosopher.
[180]

27 Child Roland to the dark tower came,
His word was still, Fie, foh, and fum,
I smell the blood of a British man.
[185]. See 360:6

28 He's mad that trusts in the tameness of a wolf, a
horse's health, a boy's love, or a whore's oath.
vi.[20]

29   The little dogs and all,

Tray, Blanch, and Sweet-heart, see, they bark at me.
[65]

1 Mastiff, greyhound, mongrel grim,
Hound or spaniel, brach or lym;
Or bobtail tike, or trundle-tail;
Tom will make them weep and wail.
[71]

2 By the kind gods, 'tis most ignobly done
To pluck me by the beard.
vii.[35]

3 I am tied to the stake, and I must stand the course.
[54]

4 *Cornwall:* Out, vile jelly!
Where is thy lustre now?
Gloucester: All dark and comfortless.
[83]

5 Yet better thus, and known to be contemn'd,
Than still contemn'd and flatter'd. To be worst,
The lowest and most dejected thing of fortune,
Stands still in esperance, lives not in fear:
The lamentable change is from the best;
The worst returns to laughter.
IV.i.1

6 I have no way, and therefore want no eyes;
I stumbled when I saw.
18

7 Might I but live to see thee in my touch,
I'd say I had eyes again.
23

8   The worst is not,
So long as we can say, 'This is the worst.'
27

9 As flies to wanton boys, are we to the gods;
They kill us for their sport.
36

10 You are not worth the dust which the rude wind
Blows in your face.
ii.30

11 Wisdom and goodness to the vile seem vile;
Filths savour but themselves.
38

12   It is the stars,
The stars above us, govern our conditions.
iii.[34]

13   He was met even now
As mad as the vex'd sea; singing aloud;
Crown'd with rank fumitor and furrow weeds,
With burdocks, hemlock, nettles, cuckoo-flowers,
Darnel, and all the idle weeds that grow
In our sustaining corn.
iv.1

14 How fearful
And dizzy 'tis to cast one's eyes so low!
The crows and choughs that wing the midway air
Show scarce so gross as beetles; half-way down
Hangs one that gathers samphire, dreadful trade!
Methinks he seems no bigger than his head.
The fishermen that walk upon the beach
Appear like mice, and yond tall anchoring bark
Diminish'd to her cock, her cock a buoy
Almost too small for sight. The murmuring surge,
That on the unnumber'd idle pebbles chafes,

Cannot be heard so high.
vi.12

15 They told me I was every thing; 'tis a lie, I am not
ague-proof.
[107]

16 *Gloucester:* Is't not the king?
Lear: Ay, every inch a king:
When I do stare, see how the subject quakes.
I pardon that man's life. What was thy cause?
Adultery?
Thou shalt not die: die for adultery! No:
The wren goes to't, and the small gilded fly
Does lecher in my sight.
Let copulation thrive.
[110]

17 *Lear:* The fitchew nor the soiled horse goes to't
With a more riotous appetite.
Down from the waist they are Centaurs,
Though women all above:
But to the girdle do the Gods inherit,
Beneath is all the fiends':
There's hell, there's darkness, there is the sulphurous
    pit,
Burning, scalding, stench, consumption; fie, fie, fie!
    pah, pah! Give me an ounce of civet, good
    apothecary, to sweeten my imagination; there's
    money for thee.
Gloucester: O! let me kiss that hand!
Lear: Let me wipe it first; it smells of mortality.
Gloucester: O ruin'd piece of nature! This great world
Should so wear out to nought.
[125]

18 A man may see how this world goes with no eyes.
Look with thine ears: see how yond justice rails upon
yond simple thief. Hark, in thine ear: change places;
and, handy-dandy, which is the justice, which is the
thief?
[154]

19 Thou rascal beadle, hold thy bloody hand!
Why dost thou lash that whore? Strip thine own back;
Thou hotly lust'st to use her in that kind
For which thou whipp'st her.
[165]

20   Plate sin with gold,
And the strong lance of justice hurtless breaks;
Arm it in rags, a pigmy's straw doth pierce it.
[170]

21   Get thee glass eyes;
And, like a scurvy politician, seem
To see the things thou dost not.
[175]

22 I know thee well enough; thy name is Gloucester:
Thou must be patient; we came crying hither:
Thou know'st the first time that we smell the air
We waul and cry.
[182]

23 When we are born we cry that we are come
To this great stage of fools.
[187]

24   Mine enemy's dog,
Though he had bit me, should have stood that night
Against my fire.
vii.36

25 Thou art a soul in bliss; but I am bound

Upon a wheel of fire, that mine own tears
Do scald like molten lead.
46

1   I am a very foolish, fond old man,
Fourscore and upward, not an hour more or less;
And, to deal plainly,
I fear I am not in my perfect mind.
60

2   Men must endure
Their going hence, even as their coming hither:
Ripeness is all.
V.ii.9

3   Come, let's away to prison;
We two alone will sing like birds i' the cage:
When thou dost ask me blessing, I'll kneel down,
And ask of thee forgiveness: and we'll live,
And pray, and sing, and tell old tales, and laugh
At gilded butterflies, and hear poor rogues
Talk of court news; and we'll talk with them too,
Who loses, and who wins; who's in, who's out;
And take upon 's the mystery of things,
As if we were God's spies; and we'll wear out,
In a wall'd prison, packs and sets of great ones
That ebb and flow by the moon.
iii.8

4   Upon such sacrifices, my Cordelia,
The gods themselves throw incense.
20

5   The gods are just, and of our pleasant vices
Make instruments to plague us.
[172]

6   The wheel is come full circle.
[176]

7   His flaw'd heart,—
Alack! too weak the conflict to support;
'Twixt two extremes of passion, joy and grief,
Burst smilingly.
[198]

8   Howl, howl, howl, howl! O! you are men of stones:
Had I your tongue and eyes, I'd use them so
That heaven's vaults should crack. She's gone for
    ever!
[259]

9   *Kent:* Is this the promis'd end?
Edgar: Or image of that horror?
Albion: Fall and cease?
[265]

10   Her voice was ever soft,
Gentle and low, an excellent thing in woman.
[274]

11 And my poor fool is hang'd! No, no, no life!
Why should a dog, a horse, a rat, have life,
And thou no breath at all? Thou'lt come no more,
Never, never, never, never, never!
Pray you, undo this button.
[307]

12 Vex not his ghost: O! let him pass; he hates him
That would upon the rack of this tough world
Stretch him out longer.
[314]

13 The weight of this sad time we must obey,
Speak what we feel; not what we ought to say.
The oldest hath borne most: we that are young,

Shall never see so much, nor live so long.
[325]

LOVE'S LABOUR'S LOST

14 Let fame, that all hunt after in their lives,
Live register'd upon our brazen tombs,
And then grace us in the disgrace of death;
When, spite of cormorant devouring Time,
The endeavour of this present breath may buy
That honour which shall bate his scythe's keen edge,
And make us heirs of all eternity.
I.i.1

15 Study is like the heaven's glorious sun,
    That will not be deep-search'd with saucy looks;
Small have continual plodders ever won,
    Save base authority from others' books.
These earthly godfathers of Heaven's lights
    That give a name to every fixed star,
Have no more profit of their shining nights
    Than those that walk and wot not what they are.
84

16   At Christmas I no more desire a rose
Than wish a snow in May's new-fangled mirth;
    But like of each thing that in season grows.
˙105

17 If I break faith, this word shall speak for me,—
I am forsworn 'on mere necessity'.
[152]

18 The world was very guilty of such a ballad some three
ages since; but, I think, now 'tis not to be found.
ii.[117]

19 Assist me some extemporal god of rime, for I am sure
I shall turn sonneter. Devise, wit; write, pen; for I am
for whole volumes in folio.
[192]

20 Beauty is bought by judgment of the eye,
Not utter'd by base sale of chapmen's tongues.
II.i.15

21   A merrier man,
Within the limit of becoming mirth,
I never spent an hour's talk withal.
66

22 Did not I dance with you in Brabant once?
[114]

23 Your wit's too hot, it speeds too fast, 'twill tire.
[119]

24 Thy own wish wish I thee in every place!
[178]

25 Warble, child; make passionate my sense of hearing.
III.i.1

26 This wimpled, whining, purblind, wayward boy,
This senior-junior, giant-dwarf, Dan Cupid;
Regent of love rhymes, lord of folded arms,
The anointed sovereign of sighs and groans,
Liege of all loiterers and malecontents,
Dread prince of plackets, king of codpieces,
Sole imperator and great general
Of trotting 'paritors: O my little heart!
[189]

27 A wightly wanton with a velvet brow,
With two pitch balls stuck in her face for eyes;
Ay, and, by heaven, one that will do the deed
Though Argus were her eunuch and her guard:

And I to sigh for her! to watch for her!
To pray for her!
[206]

1 He hath not fed of the dainties that are bred in a book;
he hath not eat paper, as it were; he hath not drunk
ink.
IV.ii.[25]

2 Old Mantuan! old Mantuan! Who understandeth thee
not, loves thee not.
[102]

3 Here are only numbers ratified; but, for the elegancy,
facility, and golden cadence of poesy, *caret*. Ovidius
Naso was the man: and why, indeed, Naso, but for
smelling out the odoriferous flowers of fancy, the jerks
of invention?
[126]

4 Did not the heavenly rhetoric of thine eye,
  'Gainst whom the world cannot hold argument,
Persuade my heart to this false perjury?
  Vows for thee broke deserve not punishment.
iii.[60]

5 Thou for whom e'en Jove would swear
Juno but an Ethiop were;
And deny himself for Jove,
Turning mortal for thy love.
[117]

6 From women's eyes this doctrine I derive:
They are the ground, the books, the academes,
From whence doth spring the true Promethean fire.
[302]

7 For where is any author in the world
Teaches such beauty as a woman's eye?
[312]

8 But love, first learned in a lady's eyes,
Lives not alone immured in the brain,
But, with the motion of all elements,
Courses as swift as thought in every power,
And gives to every power a double power,
Above their functions and their offices.
It adds a precious seeing to the eye;
A lover's eyes will gaze an eagle blind;
A lover's ears will hear the lowest sound,
When the suspicious head of theft is stopp'd:
Love's feeling is more soft and sensible
Than are the tender horns of cockled snails:
Love's tongue proves dainty Bacchus gross in taste.
For valour, is not love a Hercules,
Still climbing trees in the Hesperides?
Subtle as Sphinx; as sweet and musical
As bright Apollo's lute, strung with his hair;
And when Love speaks, the voice of all the gods
Makes heaven drowsy with the harmony.
Never durst poet touch a pen to write
Until his ink were temper'd with Love's sighs.
[327]

9 From women's eyes this doctrine I derive:
They sparkle still the right Promethean fire;
They are the books, the arts, the academes,
That show, contain, and nourish all the world.
[350]

10 He draweth out the thread of his verbosity finer than
the staple of his argument.
V.i.[18]

11 *Bone? bone,* for *bene:* Priscian a little scratched;

'twill serve.
[31]

12 *Moth:* They have been at a great feast of languages,
and stolen the scraps.
Costard: O! they have lived long on the alms-basket of
words. I marvel thy master hath not eaten thee for a
word; for thou art not so long by the head as
honorificabilitudinitatibus: thou art easier swallowed
than a flap-dragon.
[39]

13 The posteriors of this day; which the rude multitude
call the afternoon.
[96]

14   Had she been light, like you,
Of such a merry, nimble, stirring spirit,
She might ha' been a grandam ere she died;
And so may you; for a light heart lives long.
ii.15

15 Taffeta phrases, silken terms precise,
  Three-pil'd hyperboles, spruce affectation,
Figures pedantical; these summer flies
  Have blown me full of maggot ostentation:
I do forswear them.
407

16 Henceforth my wooing mind shall be express'd
  In russet yeas and honest kersey noes:
And, to begin, wench,—so God help me, la!—
My love to thee is sound, sans crack or flaw.
413

17 A jest's prosperity lies in the ear
Of him that hears it, never in the tongue
Of him that makes it.
[869]

18 When daisies pied and violets blue
  And lady-smocks all silver-white
And cuckoo-buds of yellow hue
  Do paint the meadows with delight,
The cuckoo then, on every tree,
Mocks married men; for thus sings he,
      Cuckoo;
Cuckoo, cuckoo; O, word of fear,
Unpleasing to a married ear!
[902]

19 When icicles hang by the wall,
  And Dick the shepherd, blows his nail,
And Tom bears logs into the hall,
  And milk comes frozen home in pail,
When blood is nipp'd and ways be foul,
Then nightly sings the staring owl,
      Tu-who;
Tu-whit, tu-who—a merry note,
While greasy Joan doth keel the pot.

When all aloud the wind doth blow,
And coughing drowns the parson's saw;
And birds sit brooding in the snow,
And Marion's nose looks red and raw,
When roasted crabs hiss in the bowl.
[920]

20 The words of Mercury are harsh after the songs of
Apollo. You, that way: we, this way.
[938]

MACBETH

1 *First Witch:* When shall we three meet again
In thunder, lightning, or in rain?
Second Witch: When the hurly-burly's done,
When the battle's lost and won.
Third Witch: That will be ere the set of sun.
First Witch: Where the place?
Second Witch: Upon the heath.
Third Witch: There to meet with Macbeth.
First Witch: I come, Graymalkin!
Second Witch: Paddock calls.
Third Witch: Anon!
All: Fair is foul, and foul is fair:
Hover through the fog and filthy air.
I.i.1

2 What bloody man is that?
ii.1

3 Brave Macbeth,— well he deserves that name,—
Disdaining fortune, with his brandish'd steel,
Which smok'd with bloody execution,
Like valour's minion carv'd out his passage
Till he fac'd the slave;
Which ne'er shook hands, nor bade farewell to him,
Till he unseam'd him from the nave to the chaps,
And fix'd his head upon our battlements.
16

4   They
Doubly redoubled strokes upon the foe:
Except they meant to bathe in reeking wounds,
Or memorize another Golgotha,
I cannot tell.
38

5   Bellona's bridegroom, lapp'd in proof,
Confronted him with self-comparisons,
Point against point, rebellious arm 'gainst arm,
Curbing his lavish spirit.
55

6 A sailor's wife had chestnuts in her lap,
And munch'd, and munch'd, and munch'd: 'Give
   me,' quoth I:
'Aroint thee, witch!' the rump-fed ronyon cries.
Her husband's to Aleppo gone, master o' the Tiger:
But in a sieve I'll thither sail,
And, like a rat without a tail,
I'll do, I'll do, and I'll do.
iii.4

7 Sleep shall neither night nor day
Hang upon his pent-house lid.
He shall live a man forbid.
Weary se'nnights nine times nine
Shall he dwindle, peak, and pine:
Though his bark cannot be lost,
Yet it shall be tempest-tost.
19

8 *Third Witch:* A drum! a drum!
Macbeth doth come.
All: The weird sisters, hand in hand,
Posters of the sea and land,
Thus do go about, about.
30

9 So foul and fair a day I have not seen.
38

10   What are these,
So withered, and so wild in their attire,

That look not like th' inhabitants o' the earth,
And yet are on 't? Live you? or are you aught
That man may question? You seem to understand me,
By each at once her choppy finger laying
Upon her skinny lips: you should be women,
And yet your beards forbid me to interpret
That you are so.
39

11 If you can look into the seeds of time,
And say which grain will grow and which will not,
Speak then to me, who neither beg nor fear
Your favours nor your hate.
58

12 Stay, you imperfect speakers, tell me more.
70

13   Say, from whence
You owe this strange intelligence? or why
Upon this blasted heath you stop our way
With such prophetic greeting?
72

14 The earth hath bubbles, as the water has,
And these are of them.
79

15 Were such things here as we do speak about?
Or have we eaten on the insane root
That takes the reason prisoner?
83

16 What! can the devil speak true?
107

17 The Thane of Cawdor lives: why do you dress me
In borrow'd robes?
108

18 Oftentimes, to win us to our harm,
The instruments of darkness tell us truths;
Win us with honest trifles, to betray's
In deepest consequence.
123

19   Two truths are told,
As happy prologues to the swelling act
Of the imperial theme.
127

20 This supernatural soliciting
Cannot be ill, cannot be good; if ill,
Why hath it given me earnest of success,
Commencing in a truth? I am Thane of Cawdor:
If good, why do I yield to that suggestion
Whose horrid image doth unfix my hair
And make my seated heart knock at my ribs,
Against the use of nature? Present fears
Are less than horrible imaginings;
My thought, whose murder yet is but fantastical,
Shakes so my single state of man that function
Is smother'd in surmise, and nothing is
But what is not.
130

21   Come what come may,
Time and the hour runs through the roughest day.
146

22 *Malcolm:* Nothing in his life
Became him like the leaving it: he died
As one that had been studied in his death
To throw away the dearest thing he owed
As 'twere a careless trifle.

Duncan: There's no art
To find the mind's construction in the face;
He was a gentleman on whom I built
An absolute trust.
iv.7

1 Glamis thou art, and Cawdor; and shalt be
What thou art promis'd. Yet I do fear thy nature;
It is too full o' the milk of human kindness
To catch the nearest way; thou wouldst be great,
Art not without ambition; but without
The illness should attend it; what thou wouldst highly,
That thou wouldst holily; wouldst not play false,
And yet wouldst wrongly win; thou'dst have, great
   Glamis,
That which cries, 'Thus thou must do, if thou have it';
And that which rather thou dost fear to do
Than wishest should be undone. Hie thee hither
That I may pour my spirits in thine ear,
And chastise with the valour of my tongue
All that impedes thee from the golden round,
Which fate and metaphysical aid doth seem
To have thee crown'd withal.
v.[16]

2   The raven himself is hoarse
That croaks the fatal entrance of Duncan
Under my battlements. Come, you spirits
That tend on mortal thoughts! unsex me here,
And fill me from the crown to the toe top full
Of direst cruelty; make thick my blood,
Stop up the access and passage to remorse,
That no compunctious visitings of nature
Shake my fell purpose, nor keep peace between
The effect and it! Come to my woman's breasts,
And take my milk for gall, you murdering ministers,
Wherever in your sightless substances
You wait on nature's mischief! Come, thick night,
And pall thee in the dunnest smoke of hell,
That my keen knife see not the wound it makes,
Nor heaven peep through the blanket of the dark,
To cry 'Hold, hold!'
[38]

3 Your face, my thane, is as a book where men
May read strange matters. To beguile the time,
Look like the time; bear welcome in your eye,
Your hand, your tongue: look like the innocent flower,
But be the serpent under't.
[63]

4 *Duncan:* This castle hath a pleasant seat; the air
Nimbly and sweetly recommends itself
Unto our gentle senses.
Banquo: This guest of summer,
The temple-haunting martlet, does approve
By his lov'd mansionry that the heaven's breath
Smells wooingly here: no jutty, frieze,
Buttress, nor coign of vantage, but this bird
Hath made his pendent bed and procreant cradle:
Where they most breed and haunt, I have observ'd,
The air is delicate.
vi.1

5 If it were done when 'tis done, then 'twere well
It were done quickly: if the assassination
Could trammel up the consequence, and catch
With his surcease success; that but this blow
Might be the be-all and the end-all here,
But here, upon this bank and shoal of time,

We'd jump the life to come. But in these cases
We still have judgment here; that we but teach
Bloody instructions, which, being taught, return,
To plague the inventor; this even-handed justice
Commends the ingredients of our poison'd chalice
To our own lips.
vii.1

6   Besides, this Duncan
Hath borne his faculties so meek, hath been
So clear in his great office, that his virtues
Will plead like angels trumpet-tongu'd, against
The deep damnation of his taking-off;
And pity, like a naked new-born babe,
Striding the blast, or heaven's cherubim, hors'd
Upon the sightless couriers of the air,
Shall blow the horrid deed in every eye,
That tears shall drown the wind. I have no spur
To prick the sides of my intent, but only
Vaulting ambition, which o'erleaps itself,
And falls on the other.
16

7 We will proceed no further in this business:
He hath honour'd me of late; and I have bought
Golden opinions from all sorts of people.
31

8   Was the hope drunk,
Wherein you dress'd yourself? hath it slept since,
And wakes it now, to look so green and pale
At what it did so freely? From this time
Such I account thy love. Art thou afeard
To be the same in thine own act and valour
As thou art in desire? Wouldst thou have that
Which thou esteem'st the ornament of life,
And live a coward in thine own esteem,
Letting 'I dare not' wait upon 'I would,'
Like the poor cat i' the adage?
35

9 I dare do all that may become a man;
Who dares do more is none.
46

10 *Lady Macbeth:* I have given suck, and know
How tender 'tis to love the babe that milks me:
I would, while it was smiling in my face,
Have plucked my nipple from his boneless gums,
And dash'd the brains out, had I so sworn as you
Have done to this.
Macbeth: If we should fail,—
Lady Macbeth: We fail!
But screw your courage to the sticking-place,
And we'll not fail.
54

11   Bring forth men-children only;
For thy undaunted mettle should compose
Nothing but males.
72

12 False face must hide what the false heart doth know.
82

13   There's husbandry in heaven;
Their candles are all out.
II.i.4

14 A heavy summons lies like lead upon me,
And yet I would not sleep.
6

15 Is this a dagger which I see before me,

The handle toward my hand? Come, let me clutch
    thee:
I have thee not, and yet I see thee still.
Art thou not, fatal vision, sensible
To feeling as to sight? or art thou but
A dagger of the mind, a false creation,
Proceeding·from the heat-oppressed brain?
33

1   Now o'er the one half-world
Nature seems dead, and wicked dreams abuse
The curtain'd sleep; witchcraft celebrates
Pale Hecate's offerings; and wither'd murder,
Alarum'd by his sentinel, the wolf,
Whose howl's his watch, thus with his stealthy pace,
With Tarquin's ravishing strides, toward his design
Moves like a ghost. Thou sure and firm-set earth,
Hear not my steps, which way they walk, for fear
The very stones prate of my whereabout,
And take the present horror from the time,
Which now suits with it. Whiles I threat he lives:
Words to the heat of deeds too cold breath gives.
I go, and it is done; the bell invites me.
Hear it not, Duncan; for it is a knell
That summons thee to heaven or to hell.
49

2 That which hath made them drunk hath made me bold,
What hath quench'd them hath given me fire.
ii.1

3 It was the owl that shriek'd, the fatal bellman,
Which gives the stern'st good-night.
4

4   The attempt and not the deed,
Confounds us.
12

5   Had he not resembled
My father as he slept I had done't.
14

6 I have done the deed. Didst thou not hear a noise?
16

7   Wherefore could not I pronounce 'Amen'?
I had most need of blessing, and 'Amen'
Stuck in my throat.
32

8 Methought I heard a voice cry, 'Sleep no more!
Macbeth does murder sleep,' the innocent sleep,
Sleep that knits up the ravell'd sleave of care,
The death of each day's life, sore labour's bath,
Balm of hurt minds, great nature's second course,
Chief nourisher in life's feast.
36

9 Glamis hath murder'd sleep, and therefore Cawdor
Shall sleep no more, Macbeth shall sleep no more!
43

10 You do unbend your noble strength to think
So brainsickly of things.
46

11 *Macbeth:* I am afraid to think what I have done;
Look on't again I dare not.
Lady Macbeth: Infirm of purpose!
Give me the daggers. The sleeping and the dead
Are but as pictures; 'tis the eye of childhood
That fears a painted devil. If he do bleed
I'll gild the faces of the grooms withal;

For it must seem their guilt.
52

12   Whence is that knocking?
How is't with me, when every noise appals me?
58

13 Will all great Neptune's ocean wash this blood
Clean from my hand? No, this my hand will rather
The multitudinous seas incarnadine,
Making the green one red.
61

14 A little water clears us of this deed.
68

15 Here's a knocking, indeed! If a man were porter of
hell-gate he should have old turning the key. Knock,
knock, knock! Who's there i' the name of Beelzebub?
Here's a farmer that hanged himself on the expectation
of plenty.
iii.1

16 Who's there i' the other devil's name! Faith, here's an
equivocator, that could swear in both the scales
against either scale; who committed treason enough
for God's sake, yet could not equivocate to heaven: O!
come in, equivocator.
[9]

17 This place is too cold for hell. I'll devil-porter it no
further: I had thought to have let in some of all
professions, that go the primrose way to the everlasting
bonfire.
[19]. See 421:4

18 *Porter:* Drink, sir, is a great provoker of three things.
Macduff: What three things does drink especially
provoke?
Porter: Marry, sir, nose-painting, sleep, and urine.
Lechery, sir, it provokes, and unprovokes; it provokes
the desire, but it takes away the performance.
[28]

19 The labour we delight in physics pain.
[56]

20 The night has been unruly: where we lay
Our chimneys were blown down; and, as they say,
Lamentings heard i' the air; strange screams of death,
And prophesying with accents terrible
Of dire combustion and confus'd events
New-hatch'd to the woeful time. The obscure bird
Clamour'd the live-long night: some say the earth
Was feverous and did shake.
[60]

21 O horror! horror! horror! Tongue nor heart
Cannot conceive nor name thee!
[70]

22 Confusion now hath made his masterpiece!
Most sacrilegious murder hath broke ope
The Lord's anointed temple, and stole thence
The life o' the building!
[72]

23 Shake off this downy sleep, death's counterfeit,
And look on death itself! up, up, and see
The great doom's image!
[83]

24 *Macduff:* Our royal master's murder'd!
Lady Macbeth: Woe, alas!
What! in our house?
[95]

1 Had I but died an hour before this chance,
I had liv'd a blessed time; for, from this instant,
There's nothing serious in mortality:
All is but toys; renown and grace is dead,
The wine of life is drawn, and the mere lees
Is left this vault to brag of.
[98]

2 Who can be wise, amazed, temperate, and furious,
Loyal and neutral, in a moment? No man.
[115]

3 *Lady Macbeth:* Help me hence, ho!
Macduff: Look to the lady.
[125]

4   Where we are,
There's daggers in men's smiles: the near in blood,
The nearer bloody.
[146]

5 A falcon, towering in her pride of place,
Was by a mousing owl hawk'd at and kill'd.
iv.12

6 Thou hast it now: King, Cawdor, Glamis, all,
As the weird women promis'd; and, I fear,
Thou play'dst most foully for't.
III.i.1

7 *Banquo:* Go not my horse the better,
I must become a borrower of the night
For a dark hour or twain.
Macbeth: Fail not our feast.
26

8   To be thus is nothing;
But to be safely thus.
48

9 *First Murderer:* We are men, my liege.
Macbeth: Ay, in the catalogue ye go for men.
91

10 *Second Murderer:* I am one, my liege,
Whom the vile blows and buffets of the world
Have so incens'd, that I am reckless what
I do to spite the world.
First Murderer: I another,
So weary with disasters, tugg'd with fortune,
That I would set my life on any chance,
To mend it or be rid on't.
108

11 Leave no rubs nor botches in the work.
134

12 *Lady Macbeth:* Things without all remedy
Should be without regard: what's done is done.
Macbeth: We have scotch'd the snake, not killed it:
She'll close and be herself, whilst our poor malice
Remains in danger of her former tooth.
But let the frame of things disjoint, both the worlds
  suffer,
Ere we will eat our meal in fear, and sleep
In the affliction of these terrible dreams
That shake us nightly. Better be with the dead,
Whom we, to gain our peace, have sent to peace,
Than on the torture of the mind to lie
In restless ecstasy. Duncan is in his grave;
After life's fitful fever he sleeps well;
Treason has done his worst: nor steel, nor poison,
Malice domestic, foreign levy, nothing,

Can touch him further.
ii.11

13   Ere the bat hath flown
His cloister'd flight, ere, to black Hecate's summons
The shard-borne beetle with his drowsy hums
Hath rung night's yawning peal, there shall be done
A deed of dreadful note.
40

14 Be innocent of the knowledge, dearest chuck,
Till thou applaud the deed. Come, seeling night,
Scarf up the tender eye of pitiful day,
And with thy bloody and invisible hand,
Cancel and tear to pieces that great bond
Which keeps me pale! Light thickens, and the crow
Makes wing to the rooky wood;
Good things of day begin to droop and drowse,
Whiles night's black agents to their preys do rouse.
45

15 The west yet glimmers with some streaks of day:
Now spurs the lated traveller apace
To gain the timely inn.
iii.5

16 Ourself will mingle with society
And play the humble host.
iv.3

17   Now I am cabin'd, cribb'd, confin'd, bound in
To saucy doubts and fears.
24

18 Now good digestion wait on appetite,
And health on both!
38

19 Which of you have done this?
49

20 Thou canst not say I did it: never shake
Thy gory locks at me.
50

21 What man dare, I dare;
Approach thou like the rugged Russian bear,
The arm'd rhinoceros or the Hyrcan tiger,
Take any shape but that, and my firm nerves
Shall never tremble.
99

22   Hence, horrible shadow!
Unreal mockery, hence!
106

23 Stand not upon the order of your going,
But go at once.
119

24 *Macbeth:* It will have blood, they say; blood will have
  blood:
Stones have been known to move and trees to speak;
Augurs and understood relations have
By maggot-pies and choughs and rooks brought forth
The secret'st man of blood. What is the night?
Lady Macbeth: Almost at odds with morning, which is
  which.
122

25   I am in blood
Stepp'd in so far that, should I wade no more,
Returning were as tedious as go o'er.
136

26 You lack the season of all natures, sleep.
141

1   Security
   Is mortals' chiefest enemy.
   v.32

2 Round about the cauldron go;
   In the poison'd entrails throw.
   Toad, that under cold stone
   Days and nights hast thirty-one
   Swelter'd venom sleeping got,
   Boil thou first i' the charmed pot.
   Double, double toil and trouble;
   Fire burn and cauldron bubble.
   IV.i.4

3 Eye of newt, and toe of frog,
   Wool of bat, and tongue of dog,
   Adder's fork, and blind-worm's sting,
   Lizard's leg, and howlet's wing,
   For a charm of powerful trouble,
   Like a hell-broth boil and bubble.
   14

4 Liver of blaspheming Jew,
   Gall of goat, and slips of yew
   Sliver'd in the moon's eclipse,
   Nose of Turk, and Tartar's lips,
   Finger of birth-strangled babe
   Ditch-deliver'd by a drab,
   Make the gruel thick and slab.
   26

5 *Second Witch:* By the pricking of my thumbs,
   Something wicked this way comes.
                  Open, locks,
                  Whoever knocks.
   Macbeth: How now, you secret, black, and midnight
      hags!
   What is't you do?
   Witches: A deed without a name.
   44

6 Be bloody, bold, and resolute; laugh to scorn
   The power of man, for none of woman born
   Shall harm Macbeth.
   79

7 But yet, I'll make assurance double sure,
   And take a bond of fate.
   83

8 Macbeth shall never vanquish'd be until
   Great Birnam wood to high Dunsinane hill
   Shall come against him.
   92

9 Show his eyes, and grieve his heart;
   Come like shadows, so depart!
   110

10 What! will the line stretch out to the crack of doom?
   117

11 His flight was madness: when our actions do not,
   Our fears do make us traitors.
   ii.3

12   He loves us not;
   He wants the natural touch; for the poor wren,
   The most diminutive of birds, will fight—
   Her young ones in her nest—against the owl.
   8

13 *Son:* And must they all be hanged that swear and lie?
   Lady Macduff: Every one.
   Son: Who must hang them?

Lady Macduff: Why, the honest men.
Son: Then the liars and swearers are fools, for there
are liars and swearers enow to beat the honest men and
hang up them.
[51]

14 Angels are bright still, though the brightest fell.
   iii.22

15 Stands Scotland where it did?
   164

16 What! man; ne'er pull your hat upon your brows;
   Give sorrow words: the grief that does not speak
   Whispers the o'er-fraught heart, and bids it break.
   208

17 *Malcolm:* Let's make us medicine of our great
      revenge,
   To cure this deadly grief.
   Macduff: He has no children. All my pretty ones?
   Did you say all? O hell-kite! All?
   What! all my pretty chickens and their dam,
   At one fell swoop?
   216

18 *Malcolm:* Dispute it like a man.
   Macduff: I shall do so;
   But I must also feel it as a man.
   219

19 *Doctor:* You see her eyes are open.
   Gentlewoman: Ay, but their sense is shut.
   V.i.[27]

20 Out, damned spot! out, I say! One; two: why then, 'tis
   time to do't. Hell is murky! Fie, my lord, fie! a
   soldier, and afeard? What need we fear who knows it,
   when none can call our power to account? Yet who
   would have thought the old man to have had so much
   blood in him?
   [38]

21 The Thane of Fife had a wife: where is she now?
   What! will these hands ne'er be clean? No more o'
   that, my lord, no more o' that: you mar all with this
   starting.
   [46]

22 Here's the smell of the blood still: all the perfumes of
   Arabia will not sweeten this little hand. Oh! oh! oh!
   [55]

23 I would not have such a heart in my bosom for the
   dignity of the whole body.
   [60]

24 Wash your hands, put on your night-gown; look not so
   pale.
   [67]

25 What's done cannot be undone. To bed, to bed, to
   bed.
   [74]

26 Foul whisperings are abroad. Unnatural deeds
   Do breed unnatural troubles; infected minds
   To their deaf pillows will discharge their secrets;
   More needs she the divine than the physician.
   [78]

27 Those he commands move only in command,
   Nothing in love; now does he feel his title
   Hang loose about him, like a giant's robe
   Upon a dwarfish thief.
   ii.19

28 Bring me no more reports; let them fly all:

Till Birnam wood remove to Dunsinane
I cannot taint with fear.
iii.1

1 The devil damn thee black, thou cream-faced loon!
Where gott'st thou that goose look?
11

2 I have lived long enough: my way of life
Is fall'n into the sear, the yellow leaf;
And that which should accompany old age,
As honour, love, obedience, troops of friends,
I must not look to have; but, in their stead,
Curses, not loud but deep, mouth-honour, breath,
Which the poor heart would fain deny, and dare not.
22

3 *Macbeth:* Canst thou not minister to a mind diseas'd,
Pluck from the memory a rooted sorrow,
Raze out the written troubles of the brain,
And with some sweet oblivious antidote
Cleanse the stuff'd bosom of that perilous stuff
Which weighs upon the heart?
Doctor: Therein the patient
Must minister to himself.
Macbeth: Throw physic to the dogs; I'll none of it.
37

4 Hang out our banners on the outward walls;
The cry is still, 'They come'; our castle's strength
Will laugh a siege to scorn.
v.1

5 I have almost forgot the taste of fears.
The time has been my senses would have cool'd
To hear a night-shriek, and my fell of hair
Would at a dismal treatise rouse and stir
As life were in't. I have supp'd full with horrors;
Direness, familiar to my slaughterous thoughts,
Cannot once start me.
9

6 She should have died hereafter;
There would have been a time for such a word,
To-morrow, and to-morrow, and to-morrow,
Creeps in this petty pace from day to day,
To the last syllable of recorded time;
And all our yesterdays have lighted fools
The way to dusty death. Out, out, brief candle!
Life's but a walking shadow, a poor player,
That struts and frets his hour upon the stage,
And then is heard no more; it is a tale
Told by an idiot, full of sound and fury,
Signifying nothing.
16

7 If that which he avouches does appear,
There is nor flying hence, nor tarrying here.
I 'gin to be aweary of the sun,
And wish the estate o' the world were now undone.
Ring the alarum-bell! Blow, wind! come, wrack!
At least we'll die with harness on our back.
47

8 *Macbeth:* I bear a charmed life, which must not yield
To one of woman born.
Macduff: Despair thy charm;
And let the angel who thou still hast serv'd
Tell thee, Macduff was from his mother's womb
Untimely ripp'd.
vii.41

9   Lay on, Macduff;

And damn'd be him that first cries, 'Hold, enough!'
62

10 *Siward:* Had he his hurts before?
Ross: Ay, on the front.
Siward: Why, then, God's soldier be he!
Had I as many sons as I have hairs,
I would not wish them to a fairer death.
75

MEASURE FOR MEASURE

11   Now, as fond fathers,
Having bound up the threat'ning twigs of birch,
Only to stick it in their children's sight
For terror, not to use, in time the rod
Becomes more mock'd than fear'd; so our decrees,
Dead to infliction, to themselves are dead,
And liberty plucks justice by the nose;
The baby beats the nurse, and quite athwart
Goes all decorum.
I.iii.23

12 I hold you as a thing ensky'd and sainted;
By your renouncement an immortal spirit,
And to be talk'd with in sincerity,
As with a saint.
iv.34

13 Your brother and his lover have embrac'd:
As those that feed grow full, as blossoming time
That from the seedness the bare fallow brings
To teeming foison, even so her plenteous womb
Expresseth his full tilth and husbandry.
40

14   A man whose blood
Is very snow-broth; one who never feels
The wanton stings and motions of the sense,
But doth rebate and blunt his natural edge
With profits of the mind, study and fast.
57

15 We must not make a scarecrow of the law,
Setting it up to fear the birds of prey,
And let it keep one shape, till custom make it
Their perch and not their terror.
II.i.1

16 'Tis one thing to be tempted, Escalus,
Another thing to fall. I not deny,
The jury, passing on the prisoner's life,
May in the sworn twelve have a thief or two
Guiltier than him they try.
17

17 This will last out a night in Russia,
When nights are longest there.
[144]

18 There is a vice that most I do abhor,
And most desire should meet the blow of justice,
For which I would not plead, but that I must;
For which I must not plead, but that I am
At war 'twixt will and will not.
ii.29

19 Condemn the fault and not the actor of it?
37

20 No ceremony that to great ones 'longs,
Not the king's crown, nor the deputed sword,
The marshal's truncheon, nor the judge's robe,
Become them with one half so good a grace

As mercy does.
59

1   O! it is excellent
To have a giant's strength, but it is tyrannous
To use it like a giant.
107

2   Man, proud man,
Drest in a little brief authority,
Most ignorant of what he's most assur'd,
His glassy essence, like an angry ape,
Plays such fantastic tricks before high heaven,
As make the angels weep.
117

3 Great men may jest with saints; 'tis wit in them,
But, in the less foul profanation.
127

4 That in the captain's but a choleric word,
Which in the soldier is flat blasphemy.
130

5   Is this her fault or mine?
The tempter or the tempted, who sins most?
162

6 O cunning enemy, that, to catch a saint,
With saints dost bait thy hook! Most dangerous
Is that temptation that doth goad us on
To sin in loving virtue; never could the strumpet,
With all her double vigour, art and nature,
Once stir my temper; but this virtuous maid
Subdues me quite. Ever till now
When men were fond, I smil'd and wonder'd how.
180

7 Might there not be a charity in sin
To save this brother's life?
iv.64

8 *Claudio:* The miserable have no other medicine
But only hope:
I have hope to live, and am prepar'd to die.
Duke: Be absolute for death; either death or life
Shall thereby be the sweeter. Reason thus with life:
If I do lose thee, I do lose a thing
That none but fools would keep: a breath thou art
Servile to all the skyey influences,
That dost this habitation, where thou keep'st,
Hourly afflict. Merely, thou art death's fool;
For him thou labour'st by thy flight to shun,
And yet run'st toward him still.
III.i.2

9   If thou art rich, thou'rt poor;
For, like an ass whose back with ingots bows,
Thou bear'st thy heavy riches but a journey,
And death unloads thee.
25

10   Thou hast nor youth nor age;
But, as it were, an after-dinner's sleep,
Dreaming on both; for all thy blessed youth
Becomes as aged, and doth beg the alms
Of palsied eld.
32

11   Dar'st thou die?
The sense of death is most in apprehension,
And the poor beetle, that we tread upon,
In corporal sufferance finds a pang as great

As when a giant dies.
75

12   If I must die,
I will encounter darkness as a bride,
And hug it in mine arms.
81

13   Sure, it is no sin;
Or of the deadly seven it is the least.
108

14 *Claudio:* Death is a fearful thing.
Isabella: And shamed life a hateful.
Claudio: Ay, but to die, and go we know not where;
To lie in cold obstruction and to rot;
This sensible warm motion to become
A kneaded clod; and the delighted spirit
To bathe in fiery floods or to reside
In thrilling region of thick-ribbed ice;
To be imprisoned in the viewless winds,
And blown with restless violence round about
The pendant world; or to be worse than worst
Of those that lawless and incertain thoughts
Imagine howling: 'tis too horrible!
The weariest and most loathed worldly life
That age, ache, penury, and imprisonment
Can lay on nature, is a paradise
To what we fear of death.
114

15   O, fie, fie, fie!
Thy sin's not accidental, but a trade.
146

16 The hand that hath made you fair hath made you
good.
[182]

17 Virtue is bold, and goodness never fearful.
[214]

18 There, at the moated grange, resides this dejected
Mariana.
[279]

19 Some report a sea-maid spawn'd him; some that he
was begot between two stock-fishes. But it is certain
that when he makes water his urine is congealed ice.
ii.[117]

20 A very superficial, ignorant, unweighing fellow.
[151]

21 Take, O take those lips away,
    That so sweetly were forsworn;
And those eyes, the break of day,
    Lights that do mislead the morn:
But my kisses bring again, bring again;
Seals of love, but seal'd in vain, seal'd in vain.
IV.i.1

22   Though music oft hath such a charm
To make bad good, and good provoke to harm.
16

23 He will discredit our mystery.
ii.[29]

24 Every true man's apparel fits your thief.
[46]

25 A man that apprehends death no more dreadfully but
as a drunken sleep; careless, reckless, and fearless of
what's past, present, or to come; insensible of
mortality, and desperately mortal.
[148]

1 O! death's a great disguiser.
[185]

2 I am a kind of burr; I shall stick.
iii.[193]

3 O! your desert speaks loud; and I should wrong it,
To lock it in the wards of covert bosom,
When it deserves, with characters of brass,
A forted residence 'gainst the tooth of time,
And razure of oblivion.
V.i.12

4   Let the devil
Be sometime honour'd for his burning throne.
[289]

5 Haste still pays haste, and leisure answers leisure;
Like doth quit like, and Measure still for Measure.
[411]

6 They say best men are moulded out of faults,
And, for the most, become much more the better
For being a little bad: so may my husband.
[440]

THE MERCHANT OF VENICE

7 *Antonio:* In sooth I know not why I am so sad:
It wearies me; you say it wearies you;
But how I caught it, found it, or came by it,
What stuff 'tis made of, whereof it is born,
I am to learn;
And such a want-wit sadness makes of me,
That I have much ado to know myself.
Salarino: Your mind is tossing on the ocean;
There, where your argosies with portly sail,—
Like signiors and rich burghers on the flood,
Or, as it were, the pageants of the sea,—
Do overpeer the petty traffickers,
That curtsy to them, do them reverence,
As they fly by them with their woven wings.
I.i.1

8   Now, by two-headed Janus,
Nature hath fram'd strange fellows in her time.
50

9 You have too much respect upon the world:
They lose it that do buy it with much care.
74

10 I hold the world but as the world, Gratiano;
A stage where every man must play a part,
And mine a sad one.
77

11 Why should a man, whose blood is warm within,
Sit like his grandsire cut in alabaster?
83

12 There are a sort of men whose visages
Do cream and mantle like a standing pond,
And do a wilful stillness entertain,
With purpose to be dress'd in an opinion
Of wisdom, gravity, profound conceit;
As who should say, 'I am Sir Oracle,
And when I ope my lips let no dog bark!'
O, my Antonio, I do know of these,
That therefore only are reputed wise,
For saying nothing.
88

13   Fish not, with this melancholy bait,
For this fool gudgeon, this opinion.
101

14   Silence is only commendable
In a neat's tongue dried and a maid not vendible.
111

15 Gratiano speaks an infinite deal of nothing, more than
any man in all Venice. His reasons are as two grains
of wheat, hid in two bushels of chaff: you shall seek
all day ere you find them; and, when you have them,
they are not worth the search.
114

16 My purse, my person, my extremest means
Lie all unlock'd to your occasions.
[139]

17 In Belmont is a lady richly left,
And she is fair, and fairer than the word,
Of wondrous virtues; sometimes from her eyes
I did receive fair speechless messages.
[162]

18 By my troth, Nerissa, my little body is aweary of this
great world.
ii.1

19 They are as sick that surfeit with too much, as they
that starve with nothing. It is no mean happiness,
therefore, to be seated in the mean: superfluity comes
sooner by white hairs, but competency lives longer.
[5]

20 If to do were as easy as to know what were good to
do, chapels had been churches, and poor men's
cottages princes' palaces. It is a good divine that
follows his own instructions; I can easier teach twenty
what were good to be done, than be one of the twenty
to follow mine own teaching.
[13]

21 He doth nothing but talk of his horse.
[43]

22 God made him, and therefore let him pass for a man.
[59]

23 If I should marry him, I should marry twenty
husbands.
[66]

24 I think he bought his doublet in Italy, his round hose in
France, his bonnet in Germany, and his behaviour
everywhere.
[78]

25 I will do anything, Nerissa, ere I will be married to a
sponge.
[105]

26 There is not one among them but I dote on his very
absence.
[117]

27 Ships are but boards, sailors but men; there be
land-rats and water-rats, land-thieves and
water-thieves.
iii.[22]

28 I will buy with you, sell with you, talk with you, walk
with you, and so so following; but I will not eat with
you, drink with you, nor pray with you. What news on
the Rialto?
[36]

29 How like a fawning publican he looks!
I hate him for he is a Christian;
But more for that in low simplicity

He lends out money gratis, and brings down
The rate of usance here with us in Venice.
If I can catch him once upon the hip,
I will feed fat the ancient grudge I bear him.
He hates our sacred nation, and he rails,
Even there where merchants most do congregate,
On me, my bargains, and my well-won thrift,
Which he calls interest.
[42]

1 The devil can cite Scripture for his purpose.
An evil soul, producing holy witness,
Is like a villain with a smiling cheek,
A goodly apple rotten at the heart.
O, what a goodly outside falsehood hath!
[99]

2 Signior Antonio, many a time and oft
In the Rialto you have rated me
About my moneys and my usances:
Still have I borne it with a patient shrug,
For sufferance is the badge of all our tribe.
You call me misbeliever, cut-throat dog,
And spet upon my Jewish gabardine,
And all for use of that which is mine own.
[107]

3 You that did void your rheum upon my beard,
And foot me as you spurn a stranger cur
Over your threshold: moneys is your suit.
What should I say to you? Should I not say,
'Hath a dog money? Is it possible
A cur can lend three thousand ducats?' or
Shall I bend low, and in a bondman's key,
With bated breath, and whispering humbleness,
Say this:—
'Fair sir, you spat on me Wednesday last;
You spurn'd me such a day; another time
You call'd me dog; and for these courtesies
I'll lend you thus much moneys?'
[118]

4 O father Abram! what these Christians are,
Whose own hard dealing teaches them suspect
The thoughts of others!
[161]

5 *Antonio:* This Hebrew will turn Christian, he grows
kind.
Bassanio: I like not fair terms and a villain's mind.
[179]

6 Mislike me not for my complexion,
The shadow'd livery of the burnish'd sun,
To whom I am a neighbour and near bred.
II.i.1

7 My conscience, hanging about the neck of my heart,
says very wisely to me, 'my honest friend Launcelot,
being an honest man's son,'—or rather an honest
woman's son;—for, indeed, my father did something
smack, something grow to, he had a kind of
taste;—well, my conscience says, 'Launcelot, budge
not.' 'Budge.' says the fiend. 'Budge not,' says my
conscience. 'Conscience,' say I, 'you counsel well;'
'fiend,' say I, 'you counsel well.'
ii.[13]

8 The boy was the very staff of my age, my very prop.
[71]

9 It is a wise father that knows his own child.
[83]

10 Truth will come to light; murder cannot be hid long.
[86]

11 There is some ill a-brewing towards my rest.
For I did dream of money-bags to-night.
v.17

12 Then it was not for nothing that my nose fell
a-bleeding on Black-Monday.
[24]

13 Lock up my doors; and when you hear the drum,
And the vile squealing of the wry-neck'd fife,
Clamber not you up to the casements then,
Nor thrust your head into the public street
To gaze on Christian fools with varnish'd faces,
But stop my house's ears, I mean my casements;
Let not the sound of shallow foppery enter
My sober house.
[29]

14 Love is blind, and lovers cannot see
The pretty follies that themselves commit.
vi.36

15 What! must I hold a candle to my shames?
41

16   Men that hazard all
Do it in hope of fair advantages:
A golden mind stoops not to shows of dross.
vii.18

17 Had you been as wise as bold,
Young in limbs, in judgment old,
Your answer had not been inscroll'd.
70

18 My daughter! O my ducats! O my daughter!
Fled with a Christian! O my Christian ducats!
Justice! the law! my ducats, and my daughter!
viii.15

19 What many men desire! that 'many' may be meant
By the fool multitude, that choose by show,
Not learning more than the fond eye doth teach;
Which pries not to the interior; but, like the martlet,
Builds in the weather on the outward wall,
Even in the force and road of casualty.
I will not choose what many men desire,
Because I will not jump with common spirits
And rank me with the barbarous multitude.
ix.25

20   Let none presume
To wear an undeserved dignity.
O! that estates, degrees, and offices
Were not deriv'd corruptly, and that clear honour
Were purchased by the merit of the wearer.
How many then should cover that stand bare;
How many be commanded that command;
How much low peasantry would then be glean'd
From the true seed of honour; and how much honour
Pick'd from the chaff and ruin of the times
To be new varnish'd!
39

21 The portrait of a blinking idiot.
54

22 The fire seven times tried this:
Seven times tried that judgment is
That did never choose amiss.
Some there be that shadows kiss;

Such have but a shadow's bliss.
63

1 Thus hath the candle sing'd the moth.
O, these deliberate fools!
79

2 The Goodwins, I think they call the place; a very
dangerous flat, and fatal, where the carcasses of many
a tall ship lie buried, as they say, if my gossip Report
be an honest woman of her word.
III.i.[4]

3 Let him look to his bond.
[51, 52, 54]

4 Hath not a Jew eyes? hath not a Jew hands, organs,
dimensions, senses, affections, passions? fed with the
same food, hurt with the same weapons, subject to the
same diseases, healed by the same means, warmed and
cooled by the same winter and summer, as a Christian
is? If you prick us, do we not bleed? if you tickle us,
do we not laugh? if you poison us, do we not die? and
if you wrong us, shall we not revenge? If we are like
you in the rest, we will resemble you in that.
63

5 The villany you teach me I will execute, and it shall go
hard but I will better the instruction.
[76]

6 Thou stick'st a dagger in me.
[118]

7 *Tubal:* One of them showed me a ring that he had of
your daughter for a monkey.
Shylock: Out upon her! Thou torturest me, Tubal: it
was my turquoise; I had it of Leah when I was a
bachelor: I would not have given it for a wilderness of
monkeys.
[126]

8   He makes a swan-like end
Fading in music.
ii.44

9 Tell me where is fancy bred.
Or in the heart or in the head?
How begot, how nourished?
Reply, reply.

It is engender'd in the eyes,
With gazing fed; and fancy dies
In the cradle where it lies.
Let us all ring fancy's knell:
I'll begin it,—Ding, dong, bell.
63

10 So may the outward shows be least themselves:
The world is still deceived with ornament.
In law, what plea so tainted and corrupt
But, being season'd with a gracious voice,
Obscures the show of evil? In religion,
What damned error, but some sober brow
Will bless it and approve it with a text,
Hiding the grossness with fair ornament?
There is no vice so simple but assumes
Some mark of virtue on his outward parts.
73

11   Ornament is but the guiled shore
To a most dangerous sea; the beauteous scarf
Veiling an Indian beauty; in a word,
The seeming truth which cunning times put on

To entrap the wisest.
97

12 How all the other passions fleet to air,
As doubtful thoughts, and rash-embrac'd despair,
And shuddering fear, and green-ey'd jealousy.
108

13 You see me, Lord Bassanio, where I stand,
Such as I am: though for myself alone
I would not be ambitious in my wish,
To wish myself much better; yet, for you
I would be trebled twenty times myself;
A thousand times more fair, ten thousand times
More rich;
That only to stand high in your account,
I might in virtues, beauties, livings, friends,
Exceed account: but the full sum of me
Is sum of nothing; which, to term in gross,
Is an unlesson'd girl, unschool'd, unpractis'd;
Happy in this, she is not yet so old
But she may learn; happier than this,
She is not bred so dull but she can learn.
149

14 I wish you all the joy that you can wish.
191

15 Here are a few of the unpleasant'st words
That ever blotted paper!
252

16 I will have my bond.
iii.17

17 This comes too near the praising of myself.
iv.22

18 How every fool can play upon the word!
v.[48]

19 Wilt thou show the whole wealth of thy wit in an
instant? I pray thee, understand a plain man in his
plain meaning.
[62]

20 You'll ask me, why I rather choose to have
A weight of carrion flesh than to receive
Three thousand ducats: I'll not answer that:
But say it is my humour: is it answer'd?
IV.i.40

21 Some men there are love not a gaping pig;
Some, that are mad if they behold a cat;
And others, when the bagpipe sings i' the nose,
Cannot contain their urine.
47

22 There is no firm reason to be render'd,
Why he cannot abide a gaping pig;
Why he, a harmless necessary cat;
Why he, a wauling bagpipe.
53

23 I am not bound to please thee with my answer.
65

24 What judgment shall I dread, doing no wrong?
89

25 I am a tainted wether of the flock,
Meetest for death: the weakest kind of fruit
Drops earliest to the ground.
114

26 I never knew so young a body with so old a head.
[163]

27 *Portia:* Then must the Jew be merciful.

Shylock: On what compulsion must I? tell me that.
Portia: The quality of mercy is not strain'd,
It droppeth as the gentle rain from heaven
Upon the place beneath: it is twice bless'd;
It blesseth him that gives and him that takes:
'Tis mightiest in the mightiest: it becomes
The throned monarch better than his crown;
His sceptre shows the force of temporal power,
The attribute to awe and majesty,
Wherein doth sit the dread and fear of kings;
But mercy is above this sceptred sway,
It is enthroned in the hearts of kings,
It is an attribute to God himself,
And earthly power doth then show likest God's
When mercy seasons justice. Therefore, Jew,
Though justice be thy plea, consider this,
That in the course of justice none of us
Should see salvation: we do pray for mercy,
And that same prayer doth teach us all to render
The deeds of mercy.
[182]

1 My deeds upon my head! I crave the law.
[206]

2 Wrest once the law to your authority:
To do a great right, do a little wrong.
[215]

3 *Portia:* There is no power in Venice
Can alter a decree established:
'Twill be recorded for a precedent,
And many an error by the same example
Will rush into the state.
Shylock: A Daniel come to judgment! yea, a Daniel!
O wise young judge, how I do honour thee!
[218]

4 An oath, an oath, I have an oath in heaven:
Shall I lay perjury upon my soul?
No, not for Venice.
[228]

5   I charge you by the law,
Whereof you are a well-deserving pillar,
Proceed to judgment.
[238]

6 The court awards it, and the law doth give it.
[301]

7   Thyself shalt see the act;
For, as thou urgest justice, be assur'd
Thou shalt have justice, more than thou desir'st.
[315]

8 A second Daniel, a Daniel, Jew!
Now, infidel, I have thee on the hip.
[334]

9 I thank thee, Jew, for teaching me that word.
[342]

10 Nay, take my life and all; pardon not that:
You take my house when you do take the prop
That doth sustain my house; you take my life
When you do take the means whereby I live.
[375]

11 He is well paid that is well satisfied.
[416]

12 I see, sir, you are liberal in offers:
You taught me first to beg, and now methinks

You teach me how a beggar should be answer'd.
[439]

13 The moon shines bright: in such a night as this,
When the sweet wind did gently kiss the trees
And they did make no noise, in such a night
Troilus methinks mounted the Troyan walls,
And sigh'd his soul toward the Grecian tents,
Where Cressid lay that night.
V.i.1

14   In such a night
Stood Dido with a willow in her hand
Upon the wild sea-banks, and waft her love
To come again to Carthage.
9

15 How sweet the moonlight sleeps upon this bank!
Here will we sit, and let the sounds of music
Creep in our ears; soft stillness and the night
Become the touches of sweet harmony.
Sit, Jessica: look, how the floor of heaven
Is thick inlaid with patines of bright gold:
There's not the smallest orb which thou behold'st
But in this motion like an angel sings
Still quiring to the young-eyed cherubins;
Such harmony is in immortal souls;
But, whilst this muddy vesture of decay
Doth grossly close it in, we cannot hear it.
54

16 I am never merry when I hear sweet music.
69

17 The man that hath no music in himself,
Nor is not mov'd with concord of sweet sounds,
Is fit for treasons, stratagems, and spoils;
The motions of his spirit are dull as night,
And his affections dark as Erebus:
Let no such man be trusted.
79

18 *Portia:* How far that little candle throws his beams!
So shines a good deed in a naughty world.
Nerissa: When the moon shone, we did not see the
candle.
Portia: So doth the greater glory dim the less:
A substitute shines brightly as a king
Until a king be by, and then his state
Empties itself, as doth an inland brook
Into the main of waters.
90

19 The crow doth sing as sweetly as the lark
When neither is attended, and I think
The nightingale, if she should sing by day,
When every goose is cackling, would be thought
No better a musician than the wren.
How many things by season season'd are
To their right praise and true perfection!
Peace, ho! the moon sleeps with Endymion,
And would not be awak'd!
102

20 This night methinks is but the daylight sick.
124

21 Let me give light, but let me not be light:
For a light wife doth make a heavy husband.
129

22 These blessed candles of the night.
220

THE MERRY WIVES OF WINDSOR

1 I will make a Star-Chamber matter of it.
I.i.1

2 She has brown hair, and speaks small like a woman.
[48]

3 I had rather than forty shillings I had my Book of
Songs and Sonnets here.
[205]

4 'Convey,' the wise it call. 'Steal!' foh! a fico for the
phrase!
iii.[30]

5 Here will be an old abusing of God's patience, and the
king's English.
iv.[5]

6 We burn daylight.
II.i.[54]

7 Faith, thou hast some crotchets in thy head now.
[158]

8 Why, then the world's mine oyster,
Which I with sword will open.
ii.2

9 *Falstaff:* Of what quality was your love, then?
Ford: Like a fair house built upon another man's
ground; so that I have lost my edifice by mistaking the
place where I erected it.
[228]

10 He capers, he dances, he has eyes of youth, he writes
verses, he speaks holiday, he smells April and May.
III.ii.[71]

11 O, what a world of vile ill-favour'd faults
Looks handsome in three hundred pounds a year!
iv.[32]

12 If I be served such another trick, I'll have my brains
ta'en out, and buttered, and give them to a dog for a
new year's gift.
v.[7]

13 You may know by my size that I have a kind of
alacrity in sinking.
[12]

14 He so takes on yonder with my husband; so rails
against all married mankind; so curses all Eve's
daughters, of what complexion soever; and so buffets
himself on the forehead, crying, 'Peer out, peer out!'
that any madness I ever yet beheld seemed but
tameness, civility and patience, to this his distemper he
is in now.
IV.ii.[22]

15 This is the third time; I hope good luck lies in odd
numbers...There is divinity in odd numbers, either in
nativity, chance or death.
V.i.2

16 Fairies, black, grey, green, and white,
You moonshine revellers, and shades of night,
You orphan heirs of fixed destiny,
Attend your office and your quality.
v.43

A MIDSUMMER NIGHT'S DREAM

17   Question your desires;
Know of your youth, examine well your blood,
Whether, if you yield not to your father's choice,
You can endure the livery of a nun,
For aye to be in shady cloister mew'd,
To live a barren sister all your life,
Chanting faint hymns to the cold fruitless moon.
Thrice blessed they that master so their blood,
To undergo such maiden pilgrimage;
But earthlier happy is the rose distill'd,
Than that which withering on the virgin thorn
Grows, lives, and dies, in single blessedness.
I.i.67

18 Ay me! for aught that ever I could read,
Could ever hear by tale or history,
The course of true love never did run smooth.
132

19 O hell! to choose love by another's eye.
140

20   If there were a sympathy in choice,
War, death, or sickness did lay siege to it,
Making it momentany as a sound,
Swift as a shadow, short as any dream,
Brief as the lightning in the collied night,
That, in a spleen, unfolds both heaven and earth,
And ere a man hath power to say, 'Behold!'
The jaws of darkness do devour it up:
So quick bright things come to confusion.
141

21 Your eyes are lodestars! and your tongue's sweet air
More tuneable than lark to shepherd's ear,
When wheat is green, when hawthorn buds appear.
183

22 How happy some o'er other some can be!
Through Athens I am thought as fair as she;
But what of that? Demetrius thinks not so;
He will not know what all but he do know;
And as he errs, doting on Helen's eyes,
So I, admiring of his qualities.
Things base and vile, holding no quantity,
Love can transpose to form and dignity.
Love looks not with the eyes, but with the mind,
And therefore is wing'd Cupid painted blind.
226

23 The most lamentable comedy, and most cruel death of
Pyramus and Thisby.
ii.[11]

24 Masters, spread yourselves.
[16]

25 If I do it, let the audience look to their eyes.
[28]

26 I could play Ercles rarely, or a part to tear a cat in, to
make all split.
[31]

27 This is Ercles' vein, a tyrant's vein.
[43]

28 Nay, faith, let me not play a woman; I have a beard
coming.
[50]

29 I will roar, that I will do any man's heart good to hear
me; I will roar, that I will make the duke say, 'Let him
roar again, let him roar again.'
[73]

30 I will roar you as gently as any sucking dove; I will
roar you as 'twere any nightingale.
[85]

31 Pyramus is a sweet-faced man; a proper man, as one

shall see in a summer's day.
[89]

1 Hold, or cut bow-strings.
[115]

2 *Puck:* How now, spirit! whither wander you?
Fairy: Over hill, over dale,
   Thorough bush, thorough brier,
Over park, over pale,
   Thorough flood, thorough fire,
I do wander everywhere,
Swifter than the moone's sphere;
And I serve the fairy queen,
To dew her orbs upon the green:
The cowslips tall her pensioners be;
In their gold coats spots you see;
Those be rubies, fairy favours,
In those freckles live their savours:
I must go seek some dew-drops here,
And hang a pearl in every cowslip's ear.
II.i.1

3 The wisest aunt, telling the saddest tale,
Sometime for three-foot stool mistaketh me;
Then slip I from her bum, down topples she,
And 'tailor' cries, and falls into a cough;
And then the whole quire hold their hips and loff.
51

4 Ill met by moonlight, proud Titania.
60

5 The fold stands empty in the drowned field,
And crows are fatted with the murrion flock;
The nine men's morris is filled up with mud.
96

6 Therefore the moon, the governess of floods,
Pale in her anger, washes all the air,
That rheumatic diseases do abound:
And thorough this distemperature we see
The seasons alter: hoary-headed frosts
Fall in the fresh lap of the crimson rose.
103

7 Since once I sat upon a promontory,
And heard a mermaid on a dolphin's back
Uttering such dulcet and harmonious breath,
That the rude sea grew civil at her song,
And certain stars shot madly from their spheres,
To hear the sea-maid's music.
149

8 But I might see young Cupid's fiery shaft
Quench'd in the chaste beams of the wat'ry moon,
And the imperial votaress passed on,
In maiden meditation, fancy-free.
Yet mark'd I where the bolt of Cupid fell:
It fell upon a little western flower,
Before milk-white, now purple with love's wound,
And maidens call it, Love-in-idleness.
161

9 I'll put a girdle round about the earth
In forty minutes.
175

10 I know a bank whereon the wild thyme blows,
Where oxlips and the nodding violet grows
Quite over-canopied with luscious woodbine,
With sweet musk-roses, and with eglantine:
There sleeps Titania some time of the night,
Lull'd in these flowers with dances and delight;

And there the snake throws her enamell'd skin,
Weed wide enough to wrap a fairy in.
249

11 You spotted snakes with double tongue,
Thorny hedge-hogs, be not seen;
Newts, and blind-worms, do no wrong;
Come not near our fairy queen.
ii.9

12 Weaving spiders come not here;
Hence you long-legg'd spinners, hence!
Beetles black, approach not near;
Worm nor snail, do no offence.
20

13 Night and silence! who is here?
Weeds of Athens he doth wear.
70

14 God shield us!—a lion among ladies, is a most
dreadful thing; for there is not a more fearful
wild-fowl than your lion living.
III.i.[32]

15 Look in the almanack; find out moonshine, find out
moonshine.
[55]

16 What hempen home-spuns have we swaggering here,
So near the cradle of the fairy queen?
[82]

17 Bless thee, Bottom! bless thee! thou art translated.
[124]

18 *Bottom:* The ousel-cock, so black of hue,
   With orange-tawny bill,
The throstle with his note so true,
   The wren with little quill.
Titania: What angel wakes me from my flowery bed?
[131]

19 Out of this wood do not desire to go.
[159]

20 As wild geese that the creeping fowler eye,
Or russet-pated choughs, many in sort,
Rising and cawing at the gun's report,
Sever themselves, and madly sweep the sky;
So, at his sight, away his fellows fly.
ii.20

21 Lord, what fools these mortals be!
115

22   So we grew together,
Like to a double cherry, seeming parted,
But yet an union in partition;
Two lovely berries moulded on one stem;
So, with two seeming bodies, but one heart.
208

23 Ay, do, persever, counterfeit sad looks,
Make mouths upon me when I turn my back.
237

24 O! when she's angry she is keen and shrewd.
She was a vixen when she went to school:
And though she be but little, she is fierce.
323

25   Night's swift dragons cut the clouds full fast,
And yonder shines Aurora's harbinger;
At whose approach, ghosts, wandering here and there,
Troop home to churchyards.
379

26 Cupid is a knavish lad,

Thus to make poor females mad.
440

1   Jack shall have Jill;
         Nought shall go ill;
The man shall have his mare again,
And all shall be well.
461

2 I must to the barber's, mounsieur, for methinks I am
marvellous hairy about the face.
IV.i.[25]

3 I have a reasonable good ear in music: let us have the
tongs and the bones.
[32]

4 Methinks I have a great desire to a bottle of hay: good
hay, sweet hay, hath no fellow.
[37]

5 I pray you, let none of your people stir me: I have an
exposition of sleep come upon me.
[43]

6 My Oberon! what visions have I seen!
Methought I was enamour'd of an ass.
[82]

7 I was with Hercules and Cadmus once,
When in a wood of Crete they bay'd the bear
With hounds of Sparta: never did I hear…
So musical a discord, such sweet thunder.
[118]

8   Saint Valentine is past:
Begin these wood-birds but to couple now?
[145]

9 I have had a dream, past the wit of man to say what
dream it was.
[211]

10 The eye of man hath not heard, the ear of man hath
not seen, man's hand is not able to taste, his tongue to
conceive, nor his heart to report, what my dream was.
[218]

11 The lunatic, the lover, and the poet,
Are of imagination all compact:
One sees more devils than vast hell can hold,
That is, the madman; the lover, all as frantic,
Sees Helen's beauty in a brow of Egypt:
The poet's eye, in a fine frenzy rolling,
Doth glance from heaven to earth, from earth to
   heaven;
And, as imagination bodies forth
The forms of things unknown, the poet's pen
Turns them to shapes, and gives to airy nothing
A local habitation and a name.
Such tricks hath strong imagination,
That, if it would but apprehend some joy,
It comprehends some bringer of that joy;
Or in the night, imagining some fear,
How easy is a bush suppos'd a bear!
V.i.7

12 What revels are in hand? Is there no play,
To ease the anguish of a torturing hour?
36

13 *A tedious brief scene of young Pyramus*
And his love Thisbe: very tragical mirth.
Merry and tragical! tedious and brief!
That is, hot ice and wondrous strange snow.
56

14 For never anything can be amiss,
When simpleness and duty tender it.
82

15 Out of this silence yet I pick'd a welcome;
And in the modesty of fearful duty
I read as much as from the rattling tongue
Of saucy and audacious eloquence.
100

16 If we offend, it is with our good will.
   That you should think, we come not to offend,
But with good will. To show our simple skill,
   That is the true beginning of our end.
Consider then we come but in despite.
   We do not come as minding to content you,
Our true intent is. All for your delight,
   We are not here.
[108]

17 Whereat, with blade, with bloody blameful blade,
He bravely broach'd his boiling bloody breast.
[148]

18 I see a voice: now will I to the chink,
To spy an I can hear my Thisby's face.
[195]

19 The best in this kind are but shadows, and the worst
are no worse, if imagination amend them.
[215]

20 The iron tongue of midnight hath told twelve;
Lovers, to bed; 'tis almost fairy time.
[372]

21 Now the hungry lion roars,
   And the wolf behowls the moon;
Whilst the heavy ploughman snores,
   All with weary task fordone.
ii.1

22   Not a mouse
Shall disturb this hallow'd house:
I am sent with broom before,
To sweep the dust behind the door.
17

23 If we shadows have offended,
Think but this, and all is mended,
That you have but slumber'd here
While these visions did appear.
54

MUCH ADO ABOUT NOTHING

24 A victory is twice itself when the achiever brings
home full numbers.
I.i.[8]

25 He hath indeed better bettered expectation than you
must expect of me to tell you how.
[15]

26 He is a very valiant trencher-man.
[52]

27 I see, lady, the gentleman is not in your books.
[79]

28 *Beatrice:* I wonder that you will still be talking,
Signior Benedick: nobody marks you.
Benedick: What! my dear Lady Disdain, are you yet
living?
[121]

1 Shall I never see a bachelor of three-score again?
[209]

2 In time the savage bull doth bear the yoke.
[271]

3 Lord! I could not endure a husband with a beard on his face: I had rather lie in the woollen.
II.i.[31]

4 Would it not grieve a woman to be over-mastered with a piece of valiant dust? to make an account of her life to a clod of wayward marl?
[64]

5 I have a good eye, uncle: I can see a church by daylight.
[86]

6 Speak low, if you speak love.
[104]

7 Friendship is constant in all other things
Save in the office and affairs of love.
[184]

8 She speaks poniards, and every word stabs: if her breath were as terrible as her terminations, there were no living near her; she would infect to the north star.
[257]

9 I will go on the slightest errand now to the Antipodes that you can devise to send me on; I will fetch you a toothpicker now from the furthest inch of Asia; bring you the length of Prester John's foot; fetch you a hair off the Great Cham's beard; do you any embassage to the Pigmies, rather than hold three words' conference with this harpy.
[274]

10 Silence is the perfectest herald of joy: I were but little happy, if I could say how much.
[319]

11 Speak, cousin, or, if you cannot, stop his mouth with a kiss.
[322]

12 *Don Pedro:* Out of question, you were born in a merry hour.
Beatrice: No, sure, my lord, my mother cried; but then there was a star danced, and under that was I born.
[348]

13 She is never sad but when she sleeps; and not ever sad then, for I have heard my daughter say, she hath often dreamed of unhappiness and waked herself with laughing.
[360]

14 I have known, when he would have walked ten miles afoot to see a good armour; and now will he lie ten nights awake, carving the fashion of a new doublet.
iii.[16]

15 Is it not strange, that sheeps' guts should hale souls out of men's bodies?
[62]

16 Sigh no more, ladies, sigh no more,
   Men were deceivers ever;
One foot in sea, and one on shore,
To one thing constant never.
      Then sigh not so,
      But let them go,
   And be you blithe and bonny,
Converting all your sounds of woe

Into Hey nonny, nonny.
[65]

17 Sits the wind in that corner?
[108]

18 Doth not the appetite alter? A man loves the meat in his youth that he cannot endure in his age.
[258]

19 The world must be peopled. When I said I would die a bachelor, I did not think I should live till I were married.
[262]

20   Now begin;
For look where Beatrice, like a lapwing, runs
Close by the ground, to hear our counsel.
III.1.23

21 Disdain and scorn ride sparkling in her eyes.
51

22 Contempt, farewell! and maiden pride, adieu!
   No glory lives behind the back of such.
And, Benedick, love on; I will requite thee,
   Taming my wild heart to thy loving hand.
109

23 He hath a heart as sound as a bell, and his tongue is the clapper; for what his heart thinks his tongue speaks.
ii.[12]

24 Well, every one can master a grief but he that has it.
[28]

25 A' brushes his hat a mornings; what should that bode?
[41]

26 The barber's man hath been seen with him; and the old ornament of his cheek hath already stuffed tennis-balls.
[45]

27 To be a well-favoured man is the gift of fortune; but to write and read comes by nature
iii.[14]

28 Well, for your favour, sir, why, give God thanks, and make no boast of it; and for your writing and reading, let that appear when there is no need of such vanity. You are thought here to be the most senseless and fit man for the constable of the watch.
[19]

29 You shall comprehend all vagrom men.
[25]

30 For the watch to babble and to talk is most tolerable and not to be endured.
[36]

31 The most peaceable way for you, if you do take a thief, is, to let him show himself what he is and steal out of your company.
[61]

32 I thank God, I am as honest as any man living, that is an old man and no honester than I.
v.[15]

33 Comparisons are odorous.
[18]

34 A good old man, sir; he will be talking: as they say, 'when the age is in, the wit is out.'
[36]

35 Well, God's a good man.
[39]

1 O! what men dare do! what men may do! what men daily do, not knowing what they do!
IV.i.[19]

2 I do love nothing in the world so well as you: is not that strange?
[271]

3 O God, that I were a man! I would eat his heart in the market-place.
[311]

4 Flat burglary as ever was committed.
ii.[54]

5 O that he were here to write me down an ass! but, masters, remember that I am an ass; though it be not written down, yet forget not that I am an ass.
[80]

6 Patch grief with proverbs.
V.i.17

7   There was never yet philosopher
That could endure the toothache patiently.
35

8 In a false quarrel there is no true valour.
[121]

9 What though care killed a cat, thou hast mettle enough in thee to kill care.
[135]

10 No, I was not born under a riming planet.
ii.[40]

11 Good morrow, masters: put your torches out,
The wolves have prey'd; and look, the gentle day,
Before the wheels of Phoebus, round about
Dapples the drowsy east with spots of grey.
iii.24

OTHELLO

12   'Tis the curse of the service,
Preferment goes by letter and affection,
Not by the old gradation, where each second
Stood heir to the first.
I.i.35

13   You shall mark
Many a duteous and knee-crooking knave,
That, doting on his own obsequious bondage,
Wears out his time, much like his master's ass,
For nought but provender.
44

14 In following him, I follow but myself.
58

15 But I will wear my heart upon my sleeve
For daws to peck at: I am not what I am.
64

16 Even now, now, very now, an old black ram
Is tupping your white ewe.
88

17 'Zounds! sir, you are one of those that will not serve God if the devil bid you.
108

18 Your daughter and the Moor are now making the beast with two backs.
[117]

19 Though I do hate him as I do hell-pains,
Yet, for necessity of present life,
I must show out a flag and sign of love,

Which is indeed but sign.
[155]

20 Though in the trade of war I have slain men,
Yet do I hold it very stuff o' the conscience
To do no contriv'd murder: I lack iniquity
Sometimes to do me service.
ii.1

21 Keep up your bright swords, for the dew will rust them.
59

22 I'll refer me to all things of sense,
Whether a maid so tender, fair, and happy,
So opposite to marriage that she shunn'd
The wealthy curled darlings of our nation,
Would ever have, to incur a general mock,
Run from her guardage to the sooty bosom
Of such a thing as thou.
64

23   My particular grief
Is of so flood-gate and o'bearing nature
That it engluts and swallows other sorrows
And it is still itself.
iii.55

24 *Othello:* Most potent, grave, and reverend signiors,
My very noble and approv'd good masters,
That I have ta'en away this old man's daughter,
It is most true; true, I have married her:
The very head and front of my offending
Hath this extent, no more. Rude am I in my speech,
And little bless'd with the soft phrase of peace;
For since these arms of mine had seven years' pith,
Till now some nine moons wasted, they have us'd
Their dearest action in the tented field;
And little of this great world can I speak,
More than pertains to feats of broil and battle;
And therefore little shall I grace my cause
In speaking for myself. Yet, by your gracious patience,
I will a round unvarnish'd tale deliver
Of my whole course of love; what drugs, what charms,
What conjuration, and what mighty magic,
For such proceeding I am charg'd withal,
I won his daughter.
Brabantio: A maiden never bold;
Of spirit so still and quiet, that her motion
Blush'd at herself.
76

25 Her father lov'd me; oft invited me;
Still question'd me the story of my life
From year to year, the battles, sieges, fortunes
That I have pass'd.
I ran it through, even from my boyish days
To the very moment that he bade me tell it;
Wherein I spake of most disastrous chances,
Of moving accidents by flood and field,
Of hair-breadth 'scapes i' the imminent deadly breach,
Of being taken by the insolent foe
And sold to slavery, of my redemption thence
And portance in my travel's history;
Wherein of antres vast and desarts idle,
Rough quarries, rocks and hills whose heads touch heaven,
It was my hint to speak, such was the process;

And of the Cannibals that each other eat,
The Anthropophagi, and men whose heads
Do grow beneath their shoulders. This to hear
Would Desdemona seriously incline.
128

1 And often did beguile her of her tears,
When I did speak of some distressful stroke
That my youth suffer'd. My story being done,
She gave me for my pains a world of sighs:
She swore, in faith, 'twas strange, 'twas passing
    strange;
'Twas pitiful, 'twas wondrous pitiful:
She wish'd she had not heard it, yet she wish'd
That heaven had made her such a man; she thank'd
    me,
And bade me, if I had a friend that lov'd her,
I should but teach him how to tell my story,
And that would woo her. Upon this hint I spake:
She lov'd me for the dangers I had pass'd,
And I lov'd her that she did pity them.
This only is the witchcraft I have us'd.
156

2 I do perceive here a divided duty.
181

3 The robb'd that smiles steals something from the thief.
208

4 But words are words; I never yet did hear
That the bruis'd heart was pierced through the ear.
218

5 The tyrant custom, most grave senators,
Hath made the flinty and steel couch of war
My thrice-driven bed of down.
[230]

6   If I be left behind,
A moth of peace, and he go to the war,
The rites for which I love him are bereft me,
And I a heavy interim shall support
By his dear absence. Let me go with him.
[257]

7 *Roderigo:* I will incontinently drown myself.
Iago: Well, if thou dost, I shall never love thee after.
Why, thou silly gentleman!
Roderigo: It is silliness to live when to live is torment;
and then have we a prescription to die when death is
our physician.
[307]

8 Virtue! a fig! 'tis in ourselves that we are thus, or
thus. Our bodies are our gardens, to the which our
wills are gardeners.
[323]

9 Put money in thy purse.
[345]

10 These Moors are changeable in their wills;—fill thy
purse with money:—the food that to him now is as
luscious as locusts, shall be to him shortly as bitter as
coloquintida.
[352]

11 There are many events in the womb of time which
will be delivered.
[377]

12 He hath a person and a smooth dispose
Fram'd to make women false.
The Moor is of a free and open nature,

That thinks men honest that but seem to be so.
[403]

13 I have't; it is engender'd; hell and night
Must bring this monstrous birth to the world's light.
[409]

14 Our great captain's captain.
II.i.74

15   You are pictures out of doors,
Bells in your parlours, wild cats in your kitchens,
Saints in your injuries, devils being offended,
Players in your housewifery, and housewives in your
    beds.
109

16   Do not put me to't,
For I am nothing if not critical.
118

17 I am not merry, but I do beguile
The thing I am by seeming otherwise.
122

18 *Iago:* She that was ever fair and never proud,
Had tongue at will and yet was never loud,
Never lack'd gold and yet went never gay,
Fled from her wish and yet said 'Now I may,'
She that being anger'd, her revenge being nigh,
Bade her wrong stay and her displeasure fly,
She that in wisdom never was so frail
To change the cod's head for the salmon's tail,
She that could think and ne'er disclose her mind,
See suitors following and not look behind,
She was a wight, if ever such wight were,—
Desdemona: To do what?
Iago: To suckle fools and chronicle small beer.
Desdemona: O most lame and impotent conclusion!
148

19 With as little a web as this will I ensnare as great a fly
as Cassio.
[169]

20 *Othello:* If it were now to die,
'Twere now to be most happy, for I fear
My soul hath her content so absolute
That not another comfort like to this
Succeeds in unknown fate.
Desdemona: The heavens forbid
But that our loves and comforts should increase
Even as our days do grow!
[192]

21 A slipper and subtle knave, a finder-out of occasions,
that has an eye can stamp and counterfeit advantages,
though true advantage never present itself; a devilish
knave! Besides, the knave is handsome, young, and
hath all those requisites in him that folly and green
minds look after; a pestilent complete knave! and the
woman hath found him already.
[247]

22 Make the Moor thank me, love me, and reward me
For making him egregiously an ass
And practising upon his peace and quiet
Even to madness.
[320]

23 I have very poor and unhappy brains for drinking: I
could well wish courtesy would invent some other
custom of entertainment.
iii.[34]

1 My boat sails freely, both with wind and stream.
[66]

2 *Cassio:* 'Fore God, an excellent song.
Iago: I learned it in England, where indeed they are
most potent in potting; your Dane, your German, and
your swag-bellied Hollander,—drink, ho!—are nothing
to your English.
[78]

3 'Tis pride that pulls the country down.
[99]

4 Silence that dreadful bell! it frights the isle
From her propriety.
[177]

5 But men are men; the best sometimes forget.
[243]

6 Thy honesty and love doth mince this matter.
[249]

7 Reputation, reputation, reputation! O! I have lost my
reputation. I have lost the immortal part of myself, and
what remains is bestial. My reputation, Iago, my
reputation!
[264]

8 O thou invisible spirit of wine! if thou hast no name to
be known by, let us call thee devil!
[285]

9 O God! that men should put an enemy in their mouths
to steal away their brains; that we should, with joy,
pleasance, revel, and applause, transform ourselves
into beasts.
[293]

10 Come, come; good wine is a good familiar creature if
it be well used; exclaim no more against it.
[315]

11 How poor are they that have not patience!
What wound did ever heal but by degrees?
[379]

12 O! thereby hangs a tail.
III.i.[8]

13   My lord shall never rest;
I'll watch him tame, and talk him out of patience;
His bed shall seem a school, his board a shrift;
I'll intermingle every thing he does
With Cassio's suit.
iii.22

14 Excellent wretch! Perdition catch my soul
But I do love thee! and when I love thee not,
Chaos is come again.
90

15 By heaven, he echoes me,
As if there were some monster in his thought
Too hideous to be shown.
106

16 Good name in man and woman, dear my lord,
Is the immediate jewel of their souls;
Who steals my purse steals trash; 'tis something,
       nothing;
'Twas mine, 'tis his, and has been slave to thousands;
But he that filches from me my good name
Robs me of that which not enriches him,
And makes me poor indeed.
155

17   O! beware, my lord, of jealousy;
It is the green-ey'd monster which doth mock

The meat it feeds on.
165

18 In Venice they do let heaven see the pranks
They dare not show their husbands; their best
       conscience
Is not to leave't undone, but keep't unknown.
202

19 I humbly do beseech you of your pardon
For too much loving you.
212

20 Not to affect many proposed matches
Of her own clime, complexion, and degree,
Whereto, we see, in all things nature tends;
Foh! one may smell in such, a will most rank,
Foul disposition, thoughts unnatural.
229

21   If I do prove her haggard,
Though that her jesses were my dear heart-strings,
I'd whistle her off and let her down the wind,
To prey at fortune. Haply, for I am black,
And have not those soft parts of conversation
That chamberers have, or, for I am declin'd
Into the vale of years—yet that's not much—
She's gone, I am abus'd; and my relief
Must be to loathe her. O curse of marriage!
That we can call these delicate creatures ours,
And not their appetites. I had rather be a toad,
And live upon the vapour of a dungeon,
Than keep a corner in the thing I love
For others' uses.
260

22 If she be false, O! then heaven mocks itself.
I'll not believe it.
278

23   Trifles light as air
Are to the jealous confirmations strong
As proofs of holy writ.
323

24   Not poppy, nor mandragora,
Nor all the drowsy syrups of the world,
Shall ever medicine thee to that sweet sleep
Which thou ow'dst yesterday.
331

25 I had been happy, if the general camp,
Pioners and all, had tasted her sweet body,
So I had nothing known. O! now, for ever
Farewell the tranquil mind; farewell content!
Farewell the plumed troop and the big wars
That make ambition virtue! O, farewell!
Farewell the neighing steed and the shrill trump,
The spirit-stirring drum, the ear-piercing fife,
The royal banner, and all quality,
Pride, pomp, and circumstance of glorious war!
And, O you mortal engines, whose rude throats
The immortal Jove's dread clamours counterfeit,
Farewell! Othello's occupation's gone!
346

26   O wretched fool!
That liv'st to make thine honesty a vice.
O monstrous world! Take note, take note, O world!
To be direct and honest is not safe.
376

27 This denoted a foregone conclusion.
429

1   Like to the Pontick sea,
Whose icy current and compulsive course
Ne'er feels retiring ebb, but keeps due on
To the Propontic and the Hellespont,
Even so my bloody thoughts, with violent pace,
Shall ne'er look back, ne'er ebb to humble love,
Till that a capable and wide revenge
Swallow them up.
454

2 For here's a young and sweating devil here,
That commonly rebels. 'Tis a good hand,
A frank one.
iv.43

3 That handkerchief
Did an Egyptian to my mother give.
56

4 'Tis true; there's magic in the web of it;
A sibyl, that had number'd in the world
The sun to course two hundred compasses,
In her prophetic fury sew'd the work;
The worms were hallow'd that did breed the silk,
And it was dy'd in mummy which the skilful
Conserv'd of maidens' hearts.
70

5   Jealous souls will not be answer'd so;
They are not ever jealous for the cause,
But jealous for they are jealous.
158

6 What! keep a week away? seven days and nights?
Eight score eight hours? and lovers' absent hours,
More tedious than the dial eight score times?
O, weary reckoning!
172

7   O! it comes o'er my memory,
As doth the raven o'er the infected house,
Boding to all.
IV.i.20

8 Work on,
My medicine, work! Thus credulous fools are caught.
45

9   'Tis the strumpet's plague
To beguile many and be beguil'd by one.
97

10 I would have him nine years a-killing.
[186]

11 My heart is turned to stone; I strike it, and it hurts my
hand. O! the world hath not a sweeter creature; she
might lie by an emperor's side and command him
tasks.
[190]

12 An admirable musician! O, she will sing the
savageness out of a bear.
[197]

13 But yet the pity of it, Iago! O! Iago, the pity of it,
Iago!
[205]

14 O well-painted passion!
[268]

15 Goats and monkeys!
[274]

16   Is this the noble nature
Whom passion could not shake? whose solid virtue
The shot of accident nor dart of chance

Could neither graze nor pierce?
[277]

17 Your mystery, your mystery; nay, dispatch.
ii.29

18   Had it pleas'd heaven
To try me with affliction, had he rain'd
All kinds of sores, and shames, on my bare head,
Steep'd me in poverty to the very lips,
Given to captivity me and my utmost hopes,
I should have found in some part of my soul
A drop of patience; but, alas! to make me
The fixed figure for the time of scorn
To point his slow and moving finger at;
Yet could I bear that too; well, very well.
But there, where I have garner'd up my heart,
Where either I must live or bear no life,
The fountain from the which my current runs
Or else dries up; to be discarded thence!
Or keep it as a cistern for foul toads
To knot and gender in! Turn thy complexion there,
Patience, thou young and rose-lipp'd cherubin;
Ay, there, look grim as hell!
46

19   O thou weed!
Who art so lovely fair and smell'st so sweet
That the sense aches at thee, would thou hadst ne'er
    been born!
66

20 Heaven stops the nose at it and the moon winks.
76

21   I cry you mercy, then;
I took you for that cunning whore of Venice
That married with Othello. You, mistress,
That have the office opposite to Saint Peter,
And keep the gate of hell!
87

22 Those that do teach young babes
Do it with gentle means and easy tasks;
He might have chid me so; for, in good faith,
I am a child to chiding.
111

23 I will be hang'd, if some eternal villain,
Some busy and insinuating rogue,
Some cogging cozening slave, to get some office,
Have not devis'd this slander.
130

24   Unkindness may do much;
And his unkindness may defeat my life,
But never taint my love.
159

25 *Emilia:* I would you had never seen him.
Desdemona: So would not I; my love doth so approve
    him,
That even his stubbornness, his checks and frowns...
Have grace and favour in them.
iii.18

26 My mother had a maid call'd Barbara;
She was in love, and he she lov'd proved mad
And did forsake her; she had a song of 'willow;'
An old thing 'twas, but it express'd her fortune,
And she died singing it; that song to-night
Will not go from my mind.
26

27 The poor soul sat sighing by a sycamore tree,

Sing all a green willow;
Her hand on her bosom, her head on her knee,
Sing willow, willow, willow:
The fresh streams ran by her, and murmur'd her
    moans;
Sing willow, willow, willow:
Her salt tears fell from her, and soften'd the stones;—
Sing willow, willow, willow:
Sing all a green willow must be my garland.
[41]. See 250:21

1 *Desdemona:* Mine eyes do itch;
Doth that bode weeping?
Emilia: 'Tis neither here nor there.
[59]

2 Who would not make her husband a cuckold to make
him a monarch?
[76]

3 He hath a daily beauty in his life.
That makes me ugly.
V.i.19

4   This is the night
That either makes me or fordoes me quite.
128

5 It is the cause, it is the cause, my soul;
Let me not name it to you, you chaste stars!
It is the cause. Yet I'll not shed her blood,
Nor scar that whiter skin of hers than snow,
And smooth as monumental alabaster.
Yet she must die, else she'll betray more men.
Put out the light, and then put out the light:
If I quench thee, thou flaming minister,
I can again thy former light restore,
Should I repent me; but once put out thy light,
Thou cunning'st pattern of excelling nature,
I know not where is that Promethean heat
That can thy light relume. When I have pluck'd the
    rose,
I cannot give it vital growth again,
It needs must wither: I'll smell it on the tree.
O balmy breath, that dost almost persuade
Justice to break her sword! One more, one more.
Be thus when thou art dead, and I will kill thee,
And love thee after. One more, and this the last:
So sweet was ne'er so fatal. I must weep,
But they are cruel tears; this sorrow's heavenly,
It strikes where it doth love.
ii.1

6 Alas! why gnaw you so your nether lip?
Some bloody passion shakes your very frame;
These are portents, but yet, I hope, I hope
They do not point on me.
43

7 Kill me to-morrow; let me live to-night!
80

8 It is the very error of the moon;
She comes more near the earth than she was wont,
And makes men mad.
107

9   Murder's out of tune,
And sweet revenge grows harsh.
113

10 *Emilia:* O! who hath done this deed?
Desdemona: Nobody; I myself; farewell.
121

11 *Othello:* She's like a liar gone to burning hell;
'Twas I that kill'd her.
Emilia: O! the more angel she,
And you the blacker devil.
127

12   Nay, had she been true,
If heaven would make me such another world
Of one entire and perfect chrysolite,
I'd not have sold her for it.
141

13   May his pernicious soul
Rot half a grain a day! he lies to the heart:
She was too fond of her most filthy bargain.
153

14 Thou hast not half the power to do me harm
As I have to be hurt.
160

15 You told a lie, an odious damned lie;
Upon my soul, a lie, a wicked lie.
178

16   Are there no stones in heaven
But what serve for the thunder?
232

17 Every puny whipster gets my sword.
242

18   I will play the swan,
And die in music.
245

19 Who can control his fate?
264

20 Be not afraid, though you do see me weapon'd;
Here is my journey's end, here is my butt,
And very sea-mark of my utmost sail.
265

21   O ill-starr'd wench!
Pale as thy smock! when we shall meet at compt,
This look of thine will hurl my soul from heaven,
And fiends will snatch at it. Cold, cold, my girl!
Even like thy chastity.
O! cursed, cursed slave. Whip me, ye devils,
From the possession of this heavenly sight!
Blow me about in winds! roast me in sulphur!
Wash me in steep-down gulfs of liquid fire!
O Desdemona! Desdemona! dead!
271

22 An honourable murderer, if you will;
For nought did I in hate, but all in honour.
293

23 I have done the state some service, and they know 't;
No more of that. I pray you, in your letters,
When you shall these unlucky deeds relate,
Speak of me as I am; nothing extenuate,
Nor set down aught in malice: then, must you speak
Of one that lov'd not wisely but too well;
Of one not easily jealous, but, being wrought,
Perplex'd in the extreme; of one whose hand,
Like the base Indian, threw a pearl away
Richer than all his tribe; of one whose subdu'd eyes
Albeit unused to the melting mood,
Drop tears as fast as the Arabian trees
Their med'cinable gum. Set you down this;
And say besides, that in Aleppo once,
Where a malignant and a turban'd Turk

Beat a Venetian and traduc'd the state,
I took by the throat the circumcised dog,
And smote him thus.
338

1 *Gratiano:* All that's spoke is marred.
Othello: I kiss'd thee ere I kill'd thee, no way but this,
Killing myself to die upon a kiss.
356

PERICLES, PRINCE OF TYRE

2 See where she comes apparell'd like the spring.
I.i.12

3 Few love to hear the sins they love to act.
92

4 *Third Fisherman:* Master, I marvel how the fishes live
in the sea.
First Fisherman: Why, as men do a-land: the great
ones eat up the little ones.
II.i.[29]

5   O you gods!
Why do you make us love your goodly gifts,
And snatch them straight away?
III.i.22

RICHARD II

6 Old John of Gaunt, time-honour'd Lancaster.
I.i.1

7 Let's purge this choler without letting blood.
153

8 The purest treasure mortal times afford
Is spotless reputation; that away,
Men are but gilded loam or painted clay.
A jewel in a ten-times-barr'd-up chest
Is a bold spirit in a loyal breast.
Mine honour is my life; both grow in one;
Take honour from me, and my life is done.
177

9 We were not born to sue, but to command.
196

10 The language I have learn'd these forty years,
My native English, now I must forego;
And now my tongue's use is to me no more
Than an unstringed viol or a harp.
iii.159

11 I am too old to fawn upon a nurse,
Too far in years to be a pupil now.
170

12 But what thou art, God, thou, and I do know;
And all too soon, I fear, the king shall rue.
204

13 How long a time lies in one little word!
Four lagging winters and four wanton springs
End in a word; such is the breath of kings.
213

14 Things sweet to taste prove in digestion sour.
236

15 Must I not serve a long apprenticehood
To foreign passages, and in the end,
Having my freedom, boast of nothing else
But that I was a journeyman to grief?
271

16 All places that the eye of heaven visits

Are to a wise man ports and happy havens.
Teach thy necessity to reason thus;
There is no virtue like necessity.
275

17 O! who can hold a fire in his hand
By thinking on the frosty Caucasus?
Or cloy the hungry edge of appetite,
By bare imagination of a feast?
Or wallow naked in December snow
By thinking on fantastic summer's heat?
O, no! the apprehension of the good
Gives but the greater feeling to the worse.
294

18 More are men's ends mark'd than their lives before:
The setting sun, and music at the close,
As the last taste of sweets, is sweetest last,
Writ in remembrance more than things long past.
II.i.11

19 Methinks I am a prophet new inspir'd,
And thus expiring do foretell of him:
His rash fierce blaze of riot cannot last,
For violent fires soon burn out themselves;
Small showers last long, but sudden storms are short;
He tires betimes that spurs too fast betimes.
31

20 This royal throne of kings, this scepter'd isle,
This earth of majesty, this seat of Mars,
This other Eden, demi-paradise,
This fortress built by Nature for herself
Against infection and the hand of war,
This happy breed of men, this little world,
This precious stone set in the silver sea,
Which serves it in the office of a wall,
Or as a moat defensive to a house,
Against the envy of less happier lands,
This blessed plot, this earth, this realm, this England,
This nurse, this teeming womb of royal kings,
Fear'd by their breed and famous by their birth,
Renowned for their deeds as far from home,—
For Christian service and true chivalry,—
As is the sepulchre in stubborn Jewry
Of the world's ransom, blessed Mary's Son:
This land of such dear souls, this dear, dear land,
Dear for her reputation through the world,
Is now leas'd out,—I die pronouncing it,—
Like to a tenement or pelting farm:
England, bound in with the triumphant sea,
Whose rocky shore beats back the envious siege
Of watery Neptune, is now bound in with shame,
With inky blots, and rotten parchment bonds:
That England, that was wont to conquer others,
Hath made a shameful conquest of itself.
40

21 These words hereafter thy tormentors be!
136

22   Lay aside life-harming heaviness,
And entertain a cheerful disposition.
ii.3

23 I am a stranger here in Gloucestershire:
These high wild hills and rough uneven ways
Draw out our miles and make them wearisome.
iii.2

24 I count myself in nothing else so happy

As in a soul remembering my good friends.
46

1 Grace me no grace, nor uncle me no uncle.
87

2 The caterpillars of the commonwealth.
166

3 Things past redress are now with me past care.
171

4 Eating the bitter bread of banishment.
III.i.21

5 Not all the water in the rough rude sea
Can wash the balm from an anointed king;
The breath of worldly men cannot depose
The deputy elected by the Lord.
For every man that Bolingbroke hath press'd
To lift shrewd steel against our golden crown,
God for his Richard hath in heavenly pay
A glorious angel; then, if angels fight,
Weak men must fall, for heaven still guards the right.
ii.54

6 O! call back yesterday, bid time return.
69

7 Is not the king's name twenty thousand names?
Arm, arm, my name! A puny subject strikes
At thy great glory.
85

8 The worst is death, and death will have his day.
103

9 O villains, vipers, damn'd without redemption!
Dogs, easily won to fawn on any man!
Snakes, in my heart-blood warm'd, that sting my
  heart!
Three Judases, each one thrice worse than Judas!
Would they make peace? terrible hell make war
Upon their spotted souls for this offence!
129

10   Of comfort no man speak:
Let's talk of graves, of worms, and epitaphs;
Make dust our paper, and with rainy eyes
Write sorrow on the bosom of the earth.
Let's choose executors, and talk of wills.
144

11 For God's sake, let us sit upon the ground
And tell sad stories of the death of kings:
How some have been depos'd, some slain in war,
Some haunted by the ghosts they have depos'd,
Some poison'd by their wives, some sleeping kill'd;
All murder'd: for within the hollow crown
That rounds the mortal temples of a king
Keeps Death his court, and there the antick sits,
Scoffing his state and grinning at his pomp;
Allowing him a breath, a little scene,
To monarchize, be fear'd, and kill with looks,
Infusing him with self and vain conceit
As if this flesh which walls about our life
Were brass impregnable; and humour'd thus
Comes at the last, and with a little pin
Bores through his castle wall, and farewell king!
155

12 See, see, King Richard doth himself appear,
As doth the blushing discontented sun
From out the fiery portal of the east.
iii.62

13 The purple testament of bleeding war.
94

14   O! that I were as great
As is my grief, or lesser than my name,
Or that I could forget what I have been,
Or not remember what I must be now.
136

15 What must the king do now? Must he submit?
The king shall do it: must he be depos'd?
The king shall be contented: must he lose
The name of king? o' God's name, let it go.
I'll give my jewels for a set of beads,
My gorgeous palace for a hermitage,
My gay apparel for an almsman's gown,
My figur'd goblets for a dish of wood,
My sceptre for a palmer's walking staff,
My subjects for a pair of carved saints,
And my large kingdom for a little grave,
A little little grave, an obscure grave;
Or I'll be buried in the king's highway,
Some way of common trade, where subjects' feet
May hourly trample on their sovereign's head;
For on my heart they tread now whilst I live;
And buried once, why not upon my head?
143

16 Shall we play the wantons with our woes,
And make some pretty match with shedding tears?
164

17 Go, bind thou up yon dangling apricocks,
Which, like unruly children, make their sire
Stoop with oppression of their prodigal weight.
iv.29

18 Old Adam's likeness, set to dress this garden.
73

19 Here did she fall a tear; here, in this place,
I'll set a bank of rue, sour herb of grace;
Rue, even for ruth, here shortly shall be seen,
In the remembrance of a weeping queen.
104

20 Peace shall go sleep with Turks and infidels,
And in this seat of peace tumultuous wars
Shall kin with kin and kind with kind confound;
Disorder, horror, fear and mutiny
Shall here inhabit, and this land be call'd
The field of Golgotha and dead men's skulls.
IV.i.139

21 God save the king! Will no man say, amen?
Am I both priest and clerk? Well then, amen.
172

22 Give me the crown. Here, cousin, seize the crown;
Here cousin,
On this side my hand and on that side thine.
Now is this golden crown like a deep well
That owes two buckets filling one another;
The emptier ever dancing in the air,
The other down, unseen, and full of water:
That bucket down and full of tears am I,
Drinking my griefs, whilst you mount up on high.
181

23 You may my glories and my state depose,
But not my griefs; still am I king of those.
192

1 Now mark me how I will undo myself.
203

2 With mine own tears I wash away my balm,
With mine own hands I give away my crown.
207

3 God pardon all oaths that are broke to me!
God keep all vows unbroke are made to thee!
214

4 Mine eyes are full of tears, I cannot see:
And yet salt water blinds them not so much
But they can see a sort of traitors here.
Nay, if I turn my eyes upon myself,
I find myself a traitor with the rest.
244

5 A brittle glory shineth in this face:
As brittle as the glory is the face.
287

6   This is the way
To Julius Caesar's ill-erected tower.
V.i.1

7   I am sworn brother, sweet,
To grim Necessity, and he and I
Will keep a league till death.
20

8 In winter's tedious nights sit by the fire
With good old folks, and let them tell thee tales
Of woeful ages, long ago betid;
And ere thou bid good night, to quit their grief,
Tell thou the lamentable tale of me,
And send the hearers weeping to their beds.
40

9 That were some love but little policy.
84

10 As in a theatre, the eyes of men,
After a well-grac'd actor leaves the stage,
Are idly bent on him that enters next,
Thinking his prattle to be tedious;
Even so, or with much more contempt, men's eyes
Did scowl on Richard.
ii.23

11   Who are the violets now
That strew the green lap of the new come spring?
46

12 He prays but faintly and would be denied.
iii.103

13 I have been studying how I may compare
This prison where I live unto the world.
v.1

14   How sour sweet music is,
When time is broke, and no proportion kept!
So is it in the music of men's lives.
42

15 I wasted time, and now doth time waste me.
49

16 Mount, mount, my soul! thy seat is up on high,
Whilst my gross flesh sinks downwards here to die.
112

RICHARD III

17 Now is the winter of our discontent
Made glorious summer by this sun of York.
I.i.1

18 Grim-visag'd war hath smooth'd his wrinkl'd front;
And now, instead of mounting barbed steeds,
To fright the souls of fearful adversaries,—
He capers nimbly in a lady's chamber
To the lascivious pleasing of a lute.
But I, that am not shap'd for sportive tricks,
Nor made to court an amorous looking-glass;
I, that am rudely stamp'd, and want love's majesty
To strut before a wanton ambling nymph;
I, that am curtail'd of this fair proportion,
Cheated of feature by dissembling nature,
Deform'd, unfinish'd, sent before my time
Into this breathing world, scarce half made up,
And that so lamely and unfashionable
That dogs bark at me, as I halt by them;
Why, I, in this weak piping time of peace,
Have no delight to pass away the time.
9

19 And therefore, since I cannot prove a lover,
To entertain these fair well-spoken days,
I am determined to prove a villain,
And hate the idle pleasures of these days.
28

20 No beast so fierce but knows some touch of pity.
ii.71

21 Teach not thy lip such scorn, for it was made
For kissing, lady, not for such contempt.
172

22 Was ever woman in this humour woo'd?
Was ever woman in this humour won?
229

23 Cannot a plain man live and think no harm,
But that his simple truth must be abus'd
By silken, sly, insinuating Jacks?
iii.51

24 Since every Jack became a gentleman
There's many a gentle person made a Jack.
72

25 And thus I clothe my naked villany
With odd old ends stol'n forth of holy writ,
And seem a saint when most I play the devil.
336

26 O, I have pass'd a miserable night,
So full of ugly sights, of ghastly dreams,
That, as I am a Christian faithful man,
I would not spend another such a night,
Though 'twere to buy a world of happy days,
So full of dismal terror was the time!
iv.2

27 Lord, Lord! methought what pain it was to drown:
What dreadful noise of water in mine ears!
What sights of ugly death within mine eyes!
Methought I saw a thousand fearful wracks;
A thousand men that fishes gnaw'd upon;
Wedges of gold, great anchors, heaps of pearl,
Inestimable stones, unvalu'd jewels,
All scatter'd in the bottom of the sea.
Some lay in dead men's skulls; and in those holes
Where eyes did once inhabit, there were crept
As 'twere in scorn of eyes, reflecting gems,
That woo'd the slimy bottom of the deep,
And mock'd the dead bones that lay scatter'd by.
21

1 Clarence is come,—false, fleeting, perjur'd Clarence.
55

2 Woe to the land that's govern'd by a child!
II.iii.11. See 56:3

3 So wise so young, they say, do never live long.
III.i.79

4 My Lord of Ely, when I was last in Holborn,
I saw good strawberries in your garden there.
iv.31

5 Talk'st thou to me of 'ifs'? Thou art a traitor:
Off with his head!
74

6 I am not in the giving vein to-day.
IV.ii.115

7 The sons of Edward sleep in Abraham's bosom.
iii.38

8 Thou cam'st on earth to make the earth my hell.
A grievous burden was thy birth to me;
Tetchy and wayward was thy infancy;
Thy school-days frightful, desperate, wild and furious;
Thy prime of manhood daring, bold, and venturous;
Thy age confirm'd, proud, subtle, sly, and bloody,
More mild, but yet more harmful, kind in hatred;
What comfortable hour canst thou name
That ever grac'd me in thy company?
iv.167

9 An honest tale speeds best being plainly told.
359

10 Harp not on that string.
365

11 True hope is swift, and flies with swallow's wings;
Kings it makes gods, and meaner creatures kings.
V.ii.23

12 The king's name is a tower of strength.
iii.12

13 Give me another horse! bind up my wounds!
Have mercy, Jesu! Soft! I did but dream.
O coward conscience, how dost thou afflict me!
178

14 My conscience hath a thousand several tongues,
And every tongue brings in a several tale,
And every tale condemns me for a villain.
194

15 I shall despair. There is no creature loves me;
And if I die, no soul will pity me:
Nay, wherefore should they, since that I myself
Find in myself no pity to myself?
201

16 By the apostle Paul, shadows to-night
Have struck more terror to the soul of Richard
Than can the substance of ten thousand soldiers.
217

17 Conscience is but a word that cowards use,
Devis'd at first to keep the strong in awe.
310

18 A horse! a horse! my kingdom for a horse!
iv.7

19 Slave! I have set my life upon a cast,
And I will stand the hazard of the die.
9

ROMEO AND JULIET

20 From forth the fatal loins of these two foes
A pair of star-cross'd lovers take their life.
Prologue

21 The fearful passage of their death-mark'd love,
And the continuance of their parents' rage,
Which, but their children's end, nought could remove,
Is now the two hours' traffick of our stage.

22 Do you bite your thumb at us, sir?
I.i.[50]

23 I do not bite my thumb at you, sir; but I bite my
thumb, sir.
[56]

24 She will not stay the siege of loving terms,
Nor bide the encounter of assailing eyes,
Nor ope her lap to saint-seducing gold.
[218]

25   'Tis not hard, I think,
For men so old as we to keep the peace.
ii.2

26 *Paris:* Younger than she are happy mothers made.
Capulet: And too soon marr'd are those so early made.
12

27 And then my husband—God be with his soul!
A' was a merry man—took up the child:
'Yea,' quoth he, 'dost thou fall upon thy face?
Thou wilt fall backward when thou hast more wit;
Wilt thou not, Jule?' and, by my halidom,
The pretty wretch left crying, and said 'Ay'…
Pretty fool, it stinted and said 'Ay.'
iii.39

28 O! then, I see, Queen Mab hath been with you…
She is the fairies' midwife, and she comes
In shape no bigger than an agate-stone
On the forefinger of an alderman,
Drawn with a team of little atomies
Athwart men's noses as they lie asleep:
Her waggon-spokes made of long spinners' legs;
The cover, of the wings of grasshoppers;
The traces, of the smallest spider's web;
The collars, of the moonshine's watery beams;
Her whip, of cricket's bone; the lash, of film;
Her waggoner, a small grey-coated gnat,
Not half so big as a round little worm
Prick'd from the lazy finger of a maid;
Her chariot is an empty hazel-nut,
Made by the joiner squirrel or old grub,
Time out o' mind the fairies' coach-makers.
And in this state she gallops night by night
Through lovers' brains, and then they dream of love;
O'er courtiers' knees, that dream on curtsies straight;
O'er lawyers' fingers, who straight dream on fees;
O'er ladies' lips, who straight on kisses dream;
Which oft the angry Mab with blisters plagues,
Because their breaths with sweetmeats tainted are.
Sometimes she gallops o'er a courtier's nose,
And then dreams he of smelling out a suit;
And sometimes comes she with a tithe-pig's tail,
Tickling a parson's nose as a' lies asleep,
Then dreams he of another benefice;
Sometimes she driveth o'er a soldier's neck,
And then dreams he of cutting foreign throats,
Of breaches, ambuscadoes, Spanish blades,
Of healths five fathom deep; and then anon

Drums in his ear, at which he starts and wakes;
And, being thus frighted, swears a prayer or two,
And sleeps again. This is that very Mab
That plats the manes of horses in the night;
And bakes the elf-locks in foul sluttish hairs,
Which once untangled much misfortune bodes;
This is the hag, when maids lie on their backs,
That presses them and learns them first to bear,
Making them women of good carriage.
iv.53

1 You and I are past our dancing days.
v.[35]

2 O! she doth teach the torches to burn bright.
It seems she hangs upon the cheek of night
Like a rich jewel in an Ethiop's ear;
Beauty too rich for use, for earth too dear.
[48]

3   Gentlemen, prepare not to be gone;
We have a trifling foolish banquet towards.
[125]

4 My only love sprung from my only hate!
Too early seen unknown, and known too late!
[142]

5 He jests at scars, that never felt a wound.
But, soft! what light through yonder window breaks?
It is the east, and Juliet is the sun.
II.ii.1

6 It is my lady; O! it is my love:
O! that she knew she were.
10

7 See! how she leans her cheek upon her hand:
O! that I were a glove upon that hand,
That I might touch that cheek.
23

8 O Romeo, Romeo! wherefore art thou Romeo?
Deny thy father, and refuse thy name;
Or, if thou wilt not, be but sworn my love,
And I'll no longer be a Capulet.
33

9 What's in a name? that which we call a rose
By any other name would smell as sweet.
43

10 With love's light wings did I o'er-perch these walls;
For stony limits cannot hold love out,
And what love can do that dares love attempt.
66

11 Thou know'st the mask of night is on my face,
Else would a maiden blush bepaint my cheek
For that which thou hast heard me speak tonight.
85

12 Fain would I dwell on form, fain, fain deny
What I have spoke: but farewell compliment!
88

13   At lovers' perjuries,
They say, Jove laughs. O gentle Romeo!
If thou dost love, pronounce it faithfully:
Or if thou think'st I am too quickly won,
I'll frown and be perverse and say thee nay,
So thou wilt woo; but else, not for the world.
In truth, fair Montague, I am too fond.
92. See 366:11

14   I'll prove more true

Than those that have more cunning to be strange.
100

15 *Romeo:* Lady, by yonder blessed moon I swear
That tips with silver all these fruit-tree tops,—
Juliet: O! swear not by the moon, the inconstant moon,
That monthly changes in her circled orb,
Lest that thy love prove likewise variable.
Romeo: What shall I swear by?
Juliet: Do not swear at all;
Or, if thou wilt, swear by thy gracious self,
Which is the god of my idolatry.
107

16 It is too rash, too unadvis'd, too sudden;
Too like the lightning, which doth cease to be
Ere one can say it lightens. Sweet, good-night!
This bud of love, by summer's ripening breath,
May prove a beauteous flower when next we meet.
118

17 My bounty is as boundless as the sea,
My love as deep; the more I give to thee,
The more I have, for both are infinite.
133

18 Love goes toward love, as schoolboys from their books;
But love from love, toward school with heavy looks.
156

19 *Juliet:* O! for a falconer's voice,
To lure this tassel-gentle back again.
Bondage is hoarse, and may not speak aloud,
Else would I tear the cave where Echo lies,
And make her airy tongue more hoarse than mine,
With repetition of my Romeo's name.
Romeo: It is my soul that calls upon my name:
How silver-sweet sound lovers' tongues by night,
Like softest music to attending ears!
158

20 *Juliet:* 'Tis almost morning; I would have thee gone;
And yet no further than a wanton's bird,
Who lets it hop a little from her hand,
Like a poor prisoner in his twisted gyves,
And with a silk thread plucks it back again,
So loving-jealous of his liberty.
Romeo: I would I were thy bird.
Juliet: Sweet, so would I:
Yet I should kill thee with much cherishing.
Good-night, good-night! parting is such sweet sorrow
That I shall say good-night till it be morrow.
Romeo: Sleep dwell upon thine eyes, peace in thy breast!
Would I were sleep and peace, so sweet to rest!
176

21 One, two, and the third in your bosom.
iv.[24]

22 O flesh, flesh, how art thou fishified!
[41]

23 I am the very pink of courtesy.
[63]

24 A gentleman, nurse, that loves to hear himself talk,
and will speak more in a minute than he will stand to
in a month.
[156]

25   O! so light a foot

Will ne'er wear out the everlasting flint.
vi.16

1 Thy head is as full of quarrels as an egg is full of
meat.
III.i.[23]

2 Men's eyes were made to look, and let them gaze;
I will not budge for no man's pleasure, I.
[59]

3 No, 'tis not so deep as a well, nor so wide as a church
door; but 'tis enough, 'twill serve.
[100]

4   A plague o' both your houses!
They have made worms' meat of me.
[112]

5 O! I am Fortune's fool.
[142]

6 Gallop apace, you fiery-footed steeds,
Towards Phoebus' lodging; such a waggoner
As Phaethon would whip you to the west,
And bring in cloudy night immediately.
Spread thy close curtain, love-performing night!
That runaway's eyes may wink, and Romeo
Leap to these arms, untalk'd of and unseen!
Lovers can see to do their amorous rites
By their own beauties; or, if love be blind,
It best agrees with night. Come, civil night,
Thou sober-suited matron, all in black.
ii.1

7 Come, night! come, Romeo! come, thou day in night!
For thou wilt lie upon the wings of night,
Whiter than new snow on a raven's back.
Come, gentle night; come, loving, black-brow'd
   night,
Give me my Romeo: and, when he shall die,
Take him and cut him out in little stars,
And he will make the face of heaven so fine
That all the world will be in love with night,
And pay no worship to the garish sun.
17

8   He was not born to shame:
Upon his brow shame is ashamed to sit.
91

9 Romeo, come forth; come forth, thou fearful man:
Affliction is enamour'd of thy parts,
And thou art wedded to calamity.
iii.1

10 Thou cutt'st my head off with a golden axe,
And smil'st upon the stroke that murders me.
22

11 Adversity's sweet milk, philosophy.
54

12   Hang up philosophy!
Unless philosophy can make a Juliet.
56

13 Wilt thou be gone? it is not yet near day:
It was the nightingale, and not the lark,
That pierc'd the fearful hollow of thine ear;
Nightly she sings on yon pomegranate tree:
Believe me, love, it was the nightingale.
v.1

14 Night's candles are burnt out, and jocund day
Stands tiptoe on the misty mountain tops.
9

15 I have more care to stay than will to go.
23

16 Villain and he be many miles asunder.
82

17 Thank me no thankings, nor proud me no prouds.
153

18 Is there no pity sitting in the clouds,
That sees into the bottom of my grief?
198

19 Romeo's a dishclout to him.
221

20 Sirrah, go hire me twenty cunning cooks.
IV.ii.2

21 Farewell! God knows when we shall meet again.
I have a faint cold fear thrills through my veins,
That almost freezes up the heat of life.
iii.14

22   Out, alas! she's cold;
Her blood is settled, and her joints are stiff;
Life and these lips have long been separated:
Death lies on her like an untimely frost
Upon the sweetest flower of all the field.
v.25

23 My bosom's lord sits lightly on his throne;
And all this day an unaccustom'd spirit
Lifts me above the ground with cheerful thoughts.
V.i.3

24 Is it even so? then I defy you, stars.
24

25 Being holiday, the beggar's shop is shut.
56

26 *Romeo:* The world is not thy friend nor the world's
   law:
The world affords no law to make thee rich;
Then be not poor, but break it, and take this.
Apothecary: My poverty, but not my will, consents.
Romeo: I pay thy poverty, and not thy will.
72

27 Tempt not a desperate man.
iii.59

28 One writ with me in sour misfortune's book.
82

29 How oft when men are at the point of death
Have they been merry! which their keepers call
A lightning before death.
88

30   Beauty's ensign yet
Is crimson in thy lips and in thy cheeks,
And death's pale flag is not advanced there.
94

31   Shall I believe
That unsubstantial Death is amorous,
And that the lean abhorred monster keeps
Thee here in dark to be his paramour?
For fear of that I still will stay with thee,
And never from this palace of dim night
Depart again: here, here will I remain
With worms that are thy chambermaids; O! here
Will I set up my everlasting rest,
And shake the yoke of inauspicious stars
From this world-wearied flesh. Eyes, look your last!
Arms, take your last embrace! and, lips, O you
The doors of breath, seal with a righteous kiss

A dateless bargain to engrossing death!
102

1 Seal up the mouth of outrage for a while,
Till we can clear these ambiguities.
216

THE TAMING OF THE SHREW

2 Look in the chronicles; we came in with Richard
Conqueror.
Induction i.[4]

3 As Stephen Sly, and old John Naps of Greece,
And Peter Turf, and Henry Pimpernell,
And twenty more such names and men as these,
Which never were nor no man ever saw.
ii.[95]

4 No profit grows where is no pleasure ta'en;
In brief, sir, study what you most affect.
I.i.39

5 Nothing comes amiss, so money comes withal.
ii.[82]

6 O! this learning, what a thing it is.
[163]

7 She is your treasure, she must have a husband;
I must dance bare-foot on her wedding day,
And, for your love to her, lead apes in hell.
II.i.32

8 Say that she rail; why then I'll tell her plain
She sings as sweetly as a nightingale:
Say that she frown; I'll say she looks as clear
As morning roses newly wash'd with dew:
Say she be mute and will not speak a word;
Then I'll commend her volubility,
And say she uttereth piercing eloquence.
171

9   You are call'd plain Kate,
And bonny Kate, and sometimes Kate the curst;
But, Kate, the prettiest Kate in Christendom;
Kate of Kate-Hall, my super-dainty Kate,
For dainties are all cates: and therefore, Kate,
Take this of me, Kate of my consolation.
186

10 Kiss me Kate, we will be married o' Sunday.
318

11   She shall watch all night:
And if she chance to nod I'll rail and brawl,
And with the clamour keep her still awake.
This is the way to kill a wife with kindness.
IV.i.[208]

12 What say you to a piece of beef and mustard?
iii.[23]

13 *Petruchio:* It shall be what o'clock I say it is.
Hortensio: Why, so this gallant will command the sun.
[197]

14   O vile,
Intolerable, not to be endur'd!
V.ii.93

15 Fie, fie! unknit that threatening unkind brow,
And dart not scornful glances from those eyes,
To wound thy lord, thy king, thy governor.
137

16 A woman mov'd is like a fountain troubled,

Muddy, ill-seeming, thick, bereft of beauty.
143

17 Thy husband is thy lord, thy life, thy keeper,
Thy head, thy sovereign; one that cares for thee,
And for thy maintenance commits his body
To painful labour both by sea and land.
147

18 Such duty as the subject owes the prince,
Even such a woman oweth to her husband.
156

19 I am asham'd that women are so simple
To offer war where they should kneel for peace.
162

THE TEMPEST

20 What cares these roarers for the name of king?
I.i.[18]

21 He hath no drowning mark upon him; his complexion
is perfect gallows.
[33]

22 Now would I give a thousand furlongs of sea for an
acre of barren ground; long heath, brown furze, any
thing. The wills above be done! but I would fain die a
dry death.
[70]

23   O! I have suffer'd
With those that I saw suffer: a brave vessel,
Who had, no doubt, some noble creatures in her,
Dash'd all to pieces. O! the cry did knock
Against my very heart. Poor souls, they perish'd.
ii.5

24   What seest thou else
In the dark backward and abysm of time?
49

25 Your tale, sir, would cure deafness.
106

26   My library
Was dukedom large enough.
109

27 The still-vexed Bermoothes.
229

28 For this, be sure, tonight thou shalt have cramps.
325

29 You taught me language; and my profit on't
Is, I know how to curse: the red plague rid you,
For learning me your language!
363

30 Come unto these yellow sands,
    And then take hands:
Curtsied when you have, and kiss'd,—
    The wild waves whist,—
Foot it featly here and there;
And, sweet sprites, the burden bear.
375

31 This music crept by me upon the waters,
Allaying both their fury, and my passion,
With its sweet air.
389

32 Full fathom five thy father lies;
    Of his bones are coral made:
Those are pearls that were his eyes:
    Nothing of him that doth fade,

But doth suffer a sea-change
Into something rich and strange.
Sea-nymphs hourly ring his knell:
       Ding-dong.
Hark! now I hear them,—ding-dong, bell.
394

1 The fringed curtains of thine eye advance,
And say what thou seest yond.
405

2   At the first sight
They have changed eyes.
437

3 He receives comfort like cold porridge.
II.1.10

4 Look, he's winding up the watch of his wit, by and by
it will strike.
[12]

5 What's past is prologue.
[261]

6 They'll take suggestion as a cat laps milk.
[296]

7 A very ancient and fish-like smell.
ii.[27]

8 When they will not give a doit to relieve a lame
beggar, they will lay out ten to see a dead Indian.
[33]

9 Misery acquaints a man with strange bedfellows.
[42]

10 Well, here's my comfort. [*Drinks.*]
The master, the swabber, the boatswain and I,
    The gunner and his mate,
Lov'd Mall, Meg, and Marian and Margery,
      But none of us car'd for Kate;
For she had a tongue with a tang,
    Would cry to a sailor, 'Go hang!'
[48]

11 'Ban, 'Ban, Ca-Caliban,
Has a new master—Get a new man.
[197]

12 *Ferdinand:* Wherefore weep you?
Miranda: At mine unworthiness, that dare not offer
What I desire to give; and much less take
What I shall die to want.
III.i.76

13 *Miranda:* I am your wife, if you will marry me;
If not, I'll die your maid: to be your fellow
You may deny me; but I'll be your servant
Whether you will or no.
Ferdinand: My mistress, dearest;
And thus I humble ever.
Miranda: My husband then?
Ferdinand: Ay, with a heart as willing
As bondage e'er of freedom: here's my hand.
Miranda: And mine, with my heart in't.
83

14 Thou deboshed fish thou.
ii.[30]

15 Flout 'em, and scout 'em; and scout 'em, and flout
   'em;
Thought is free.
[133]

16 He that dies pays all debts.
[143]

17 Be not afeard: the isle is full of noises,
Sounds and sweet airs, that give delight, and hurt not.
[147]

18   In dreaming,
The clouds methought would open and show riches
Ready to drop upon me; that, when I wak'd
I cried to dream again.
[152]

19 Thy banks with pioned and twilled brims,
Which spongy April at thy hest betrims,
To make cold nymphs chaste crowns.
IV.i.64

20 Our revels now are ended. These our actors,
As I foretold you, were all spirits and
Are melted into air, into thin air:
And, like the baseless fabric of this vision,
The cloud-capp'd towers, the gorgeous palaces,
The solemn temples, the great globe itself,
Yea, all which it inherit, shall dissolve
And, like this insubstantial pageant faded,
Leave not a rack behind. We are such stuff
As dreams are made on, and our little life
Is rounded with a sleep.
148

21 I do begin to have bloody thoughts.
[221]

22   We shall lose our time,
And all be turn'd to barnacles, or to apes
With foreheads villanous low.
[250]

23 Ye elves of hills, brooks, standing lakes, and groves;
And ye, that on the sands with printless foot
Do chase the ebbing Neptune and do fly him
When he comes back; you demi-puppets, that
By moonshine do the green sour ringlets make
Whereof the ewe not bites.
V.i.33

24   This rough magic
I here abjure...
      I'll break my staff,
Bury it certain fathoms in the earth,
And, deeper than did ever plummet sound,
I'll drown my book.
50

25 Where the bee sucks, there suck I
In a cowslip's bell I lie;
There I couch when owls do cry.
On the bat's back I do fly
After summer merrily:
Merrily, merrily shall I live now
Under the blossom that hangs on the bough.
88

26 How may goodly creatures are there here!
How beauteous mankind is! O brave new world,
That has such people in't.
182

TIMON OF ATHENS

27 'Tis not enough to help the feeble up,
But to support him after.
I.i.108

28 He that loves to be flattered is worthy o' the flatterer.
[233]

1   The strain of man's bred out
Into baboon and monkey.
[260]

2 I wonder men dare trust themselves with men.
ii.[45]

3 Immortal gods, I crave no pelf;
I pray for no man but myself.
[64]

4 Like madness is the glory of this life.
[141]

5 Men shut their doors against a setting sun.
[152]

6 Nothing emboldens sin so much as mercy.
III.v.3

7 Uncover, dogs, and lap.
vi.[96]

8 You fools of fortune, trencher-friends, time's flies.
[107]

9 We have seen better days.
   IV.ii.27

10 O! the fierce wretchedness that glory brings us.
30

11 He has almost charmed me from my profession, by
persuading me to it.
iii.[457]

12   My long sickness
Of health and living now begins to mend,
And nothing brings me all things.
V.i.[191]

13 Tell them, that, to ease them of their griefs,
Their fears of hostile strokes, their aches, losses,
Their pangs of love, with other incident throes
That nature's fragile vessel doth sustain
In life's uncertain voyage, I will some kindness do
   them.
[203]

14 Timon hath made his everlasting mansion
Upon the beached verge of the salt flood;
Who once a day with his embossed froth
The turbulent surge shall cover.
[220]

TITUS ANDRONICUS

15 She is a woman, therefore may be woo'd;
She is a woman, therefore may be won;
She is Lavinia, therefore must be lov'd.
What, man! more water glideth by the mill
Than wots the miller of; and easy it is
Of a cut loaf to steal a shive, we know.
II.i.82. See 446:1

16 Come, and take choice of all my library,
And so beguile thy sorrow.
IV.i.34

17 The eagle suffers little birds to sing,
And is not careful what they mean thereby.
iv.[82]

18 If one good deed in all my life I did,
I do repent it from my very soul.
V.iii.[189]

TROILUS AND CRESSIDA

19   O! that her hand,

In whose comparison all whites are ink,
Writing their own reproach; to whose soft seizure
The cygnet's down is harsh, and spirit of sense
Hard as the palm of ploughman.
I.i.[57]

20 I have had my labour for my travail.
[73]

21   Women are angels, wooing:
Things won are done; joy's soul lies in the doing;
That she belov'd knows nought that knows not this:
Men prize the thing ungain'd more than it is.
ii.[310]

22 The heavens themselves, the planets, and this centre
Observe degree, priority, and place,
Insisture, course, proportion, season, form,
Office, and custom, in all line of order.
iii.85

23   O! when degree is shak'd,
Which is the ladder to all high designs,
The enterprise is sick.
101

24 Take but degree away, untune that string,
And, hark! what discord follows; each thing meets
In mere oppugnancy.
109

25   The general's disdain'd
By him one step below, he by the next,
That next by him beneath; so every step,
Exampled by the first pace that is sick
Of his superior, grows to an envious fever
Of pale and bloodless emulation.
129

26   We are soldiers;
And may that soldier a mere recreant prove,
That means not, hath not, or is not in love!
286

27 And in such indexes, although small pricks
To their subsequent volumes, there is seen
The baby figure of the giant mass
Of things to come at large.
343

28 The plague of Greece upon thee, thou mongrel
beef-witted lord!
II.i.[13]

29 Achilles...who wears his wit in his belly, and his guts
in his head, I'll tell you what I say of him.
[78]

30   You have both said well;
And on the cause and question now in hand
Have gloz'd but superficially; not much
Unlike young men, whom Aristotle thought
Unfit to hear moral philosophy.
ii.163

31   Thus to persist
In doing wrong extenuates not wrong,
But makes it much more heavy.
186

32 I am giddy, expectation whirls me round.
The imaginary relish is so sweet
That it enchants my sense.
III.ii.[17]

33 This is the monstruosity in love, lady, that the will is
infinite, and the execution confined; that the desire is

boundless, and the act a slave to limit.
[85]

1   To be wise, and love,
Exceeds man's might.
[163]

2 I am as true as truth's simplicity,
And simpler than the infancy of truth.
[176]

3 Time hath, my lord, a wallet at his back,
Wherein he puts alms for oblivion,
A great-siz'd monster of ingratitudes:
Those scraps are good deeds past; which are devour'd
As fast as they are made, forgot as soon
As done.
iii.145

4   Perseverance, dear my lord,
Keeps honour bright: to have done, is to hang
Quite out of fashion, like a rusty mail
In monumental mockery.
150

5   Time is like a fashionable host
That slightly shakes his parting guest by the hand,
And with his arms outstretch'd, as he would fly,
Grasps in the comer: welcome ever smiles,
And farewell goes out sighing.
165

6   Beauty, wit,
High birth, vigour of bone, desert in service,
Love, friendship, charity, are subjects all
To envious and calumniating time.
One touch of nature makes the whole world kin,
That all with one consent praise new-born gawds,
Though they are made and moulded of things past,
And give to dust that is a little gilt
More laud than gilt o'er-dusted.
171

7 A plague of opinion! a man may wear it on both sides,
like a leather jerkin.
[267]

8 How my achievements mock me!
IV.ii.[72]

9 You smile, and mock me, as if I meant naughtily.
iii.38

10 My love admits no qualifying dross.
iv.9

11 What a pair of spectacles is here!
[Pandarus, of the lovers] [13]

12 We two, that with so many thousand sighs
Did buy each other, must poorly sell ourselves
With the rude brevity and discharge of one.
Injurious time now with a robber's haste
Crams his rich thievery up, he knows not how:
As many farewells as be stars in heaven,
With distinct breath and consign'd kisses to them,
He fumbles up into a loose adieu,
And scants us with a single famish'd kiss,
Distasted with the salt of broken tears.
[39]

13   Fie, fie upon her!
There's language in her eye, her cheek, her lip,
Nay, her foot speaks; her wanton spirits look out
At every joint and motive of her body.
v.54

14 What's past, and what's to come is strew'd with husks
And formless ruin of oblivion.
165

15   The end crowns all,
And that old common arbitrator, Time,
Will one day end it.
223

16 Lechery, lechery; still, wars and lechery: nothing else
holds fashion.
V.ii.192

17 Words, words, mere words, no matter from the heart.
iii.[109]

18 Hector is dead; there is no more to say.
x.22

19 O world! world! world! thus is the poor agent
despised. O traitors and bawds, how earnestly are you
set a-work, and how ill requited! why should our
endeavour be so loved, and the performance so
loathed?
[36]

TWELFTH NIGHT

20 If music be the food of love, play on;
Give me excess of it, that, surfeiting,
The appetite may sicken, and so die.
That strain again! it had a dying fall:
O! it came o'er my ear like the sweet sound
That breathes upon a bank of violets,
Stealing and giving odour! Enough! no more:
'Tis not so sweet now as it was before.
O spirit of love! how quick and fresh art thou,
That notwithstanding thy capacity
Receiveth as the sea, nought enters there,
Of what validity and pitch soe'er,
But falls into abatement and low price,
Even in a minute: so full of shapes is fancy,
That it alone is high fantastical.
I.i.1

21 O! when mine eyes did see Olivia first,
Methought she purg'd the air of pestilence.
That instant was I turn'd into a hart,
And my desires, like fell and cruel hounds,
E'er since pursue me.
19

22 And what should I do in Illyria?
My brother he is in Elysium.
ii.2

23 He's as tall a man as any's in Illyria.
iii.[21]

24 He plays o' the viol-de-gamboys, and speaks three or
four languages word for word without book, and hath
all the good gifts of nature.
[27]

25 Methinks sometimes I have no more wit than a
Christian or an ordinary man has; but I am a great
eater of beef, and I believe that does harm to my wit.
[90]

26 *Sir Andrew:* I would I had bestowed that time in the
tongues that I have in fencing, dancing, and
bear-baiting. O! had I but followed the arts!
Sir Toby: Then hadst thou had an excellent head of
hair.
[99]

1 Wherefore are these things hid? wherefore have these
gifts a curtain before 'em? are they like to take dust,
like Mistress Mall's picture? why dost thou not go to
church in a galliard, and come home in a coranto? My
very walk should be a jig.
[135]

2 Is it a world to hide virtues in?
[142]

3   They shall yet belie thy happy years
That say thou art a man: Diana's lip
Is not more smooth and rubious; thy small pipe
Is as the maiden's organ, shrill and sound;
And all is semblative a woman's part.
iv.30

4 Many a good hanging prevents a bad marriage.
v.[20]

5 What says Quinapalus? 'Better a witty fool than a
foolish wit.'
[37]

6 Virtue that transgresses is but patched with sin; and sin
that amends is but patched with virtue.
[52]

7 Good my mouse of virtue, answer me.
[68]

8 A plague o' these pickle herring!
[127]

9 Not yet old enough for a man, nor young enough for a
boy; as a squash is before 'tis a peascod, or a codling
when 'tis almost an apple: 'tis with him in standing
water, between boy and man. He is very
well-favoured, and he speaks very shrewishly: one
would think his mother's milk were scarce out of him.
[166]

10 I would be loath to cast away my speech, for besides
that it is excellently well penned, I have taken great
pains to con it.
[184]

11 I can say little more than I have studied, and that
question's out of my part.
[191]

12 *Olivia:* 'Tis in grain, sir; 'twill endure wind and
       weather.
Viola: 'Tis beauty truly blent, whose red and white
Nature's own sweet and cunning hand laid on:
Lady, you are the cruell'st she alive
If you will lead these graces to the grave
And leave the world no copy.
Olivia: O! sir I will not be so hard-hearted; I will give
out divers schedules of my beauty: it shall be
inventoried, and every particle and utensil labelled
to my will: as *Item*, Two lips, indifferent red; *Item*,
Two grey eyes with lids to them; *Item*, One neck,
one chin, and so forth.
[257]

13 Make me a willow cabin at your gate,
And call upon my soul within the house;
Write loyal cantons of contemned love,
And sing them loud even in the dead of night;
Halloo your name to the reverberate hills,
And make the babbling gossip of the air
Cry out, 'Olivia!' O! you should not rest
Between the elements of air and earth,

But you should pity me!
[289]

14   'What is your parentage?'
'Above my fortune, yet my state is well:
I am a gentleman.'
[310]

15 She is drowned already, sir, with salt water, though I
seem to drown her remembrance again with more.
II.i.[31]

16 Not to be a-bed after midnight is to be up betimes.
iii.1

17 O mistress mine! where are you roaming?
O! stay and hear; your true love's coming,
   That can sing both high and low.
Trip no further, pretty sweeting;
Journeys end in lovers meeting,
   Every wise man's son doth know...

What is love? 'tis not hereafter;
Present mirth hath present laughter;
   What's to come is still unsure:
In delay there lies no plenty;
Then come kiss me, sweet and twenty,
   Youth's a stuff will not endure.
[42]

18 Am not I consanguineous? am I not of her blood?
Tillyvally, lady.
[85]

19 He does it with a better grace, but I do it more natural.
[91]

20 Is there no respect of place, persons, nor time, in you?
[100]

21 Dost thou think, because thou art virtuous, there shall
be no more cakes and ale?
[124]

22 *Maria:* Marry, sir, sometimes he is a kind of puritan.
Sir Andrew: O, if I thought that, I'd beat him like a
dog!
[153]

23 I will drop in his way some obscure epistles of love;
wherein by the colour of his beard, the shape of his
leg, the manner of his gait, the expressure of his eye,
forehead, and complexion, he shall find himself most
feelingly personated.
[171]

24 I was adored once too.
[200]

25 My purpose is, indeed, a horse of that colour.
[184]

26 Now, good Cesario, but that piece of song,
That old and antique song we heard last night;
Methought it did relieve my passion much,
More than light airs and recollected terms
Of these most brisk and giddy-paced times:
Come, but one verse.
iv.2

27 *Duke:* If ever thou shalt love,
In the sweet pangs of it remember me;
For such as I am all true lovers are:
Unstaid and skittish in all motions else,
Save in the constant image of the creature
That is belov'd. How dost thou like this tune?
Viola: It gives a very echo to the seat

Where love is enthron'd.
15

1   Let still the woman take
An elder than herself, so wears she to him,
So sways she level in her husband's heart:
For, boy, however we do praise ourselves,
Our fancies are more giddy and unfirm,
More longing, wavering, sooner lost and worn,
Than women's are.
29

2 Then let thy love be younger than thyself,
Or thy affection cannot hold the bent.
36

3 Mark it, Cesario; it is old and plain.
The spinsters and the knitters in the sun
And the free maids that weave their thread with bones
Do use to chant it: it is silly sooth,
And dallies with the innocence of love,
Like the old age.
43

4 Come away, come away, death,
    And in sad cypress let me be laid;
Fly away, fly away, breath:
    I am slain by a fair cruel maid.
My shroud of white, stuck all with yew,
    O! prepare it.
My part of death no one so true
    Did share it.
51

5 Now, the melancholy god protect thee, and the tailor
make thy doublet of changeable taffeta, for thy mind is
a very opal.
[74]

6   There is no woman's sides
Can bide the beating of so strong a passion
As love doth give my heart; no woman's heart
So big, to hold so much; they lack retention.
Alas! their love may be call'd appetite,
No motion of the liver, but the palate,
That suffer surfeit, cloyment, and revolt;
But mine is all as hungry as the sea,
And can digest so much.
[95]

7 *Viola:* My father had a daughter lov'd a man,
As it might be, perhaps, were I a woman,
I should your lordship.
Duke: And what's her history?
Viola: A blank, my lord. She never told her love,
But let concealment, like a worm i' the bud,
Feed on her damask cheek: she pin'd in thought;
And with a green and yellow melancholy,
She sat like patience on a monument,
Smiling at grief. Was not this love indeed?
We men may say more, swear more; but, indeed,
Our shows are more than will; for still we prove
Much in our vows, but little in our love.
[108]

8 I am all the daughters of my father's house,
And all the brothers too.
[122]

9 How now, my metal of India!
v.[17]

10 Here comes the trout that must be caught with
tickling.
[25]

11 Contemplation makes a rare turkey-cock of him: how
he jets under his advanced plumes!
[35]

12 Now is the woodcock near the gin.
[93]

13 I may command where I adore.
[117]

14 But be not afraid of greatness: some men are born
great, some achieve greatness, and some have
greatness thrust upon them.
[158]

15 Let thy tongue tang arguments of state; put thyself into
the trick of singularity. She thus advises thee that sighs
for thee. Remember who commended thy yellow
stockings, and wished to see thee ever cross-gartered.
[165]

16 Jove and my stars be praised! Here is yet a postscript.
[190]

17 He will come to her in yellow stockings, and 'tis a
colour she abhors; and cross-gartered, a fashion she
detests.
[220]

18 Now Jove, in his next commodity of hair, send thee a
beard.
III.i.[51]

19 This fellow's wise enough to play the fool,
And to do that well craves a kind of wit.
[68]

20 Taste your legs, sir; put them to motion.
[88]

21 Most excellent accomplished lady, the heavens rain
odours on you!
[96]

22   'Twas never merry world
Since lowly feigning was called compliment.
[110]

23 O world! how apt the poor are to be proud.
[141]

24 O! what a deal of scorn looks beautiful
In the contempt and anger of his lip.
[159]

25 Love sought is good, but giv'n unsought is better.
[170]

26 They have been grand-jurymen since before Noah was
a sailor.
ii.[18]

27 You should then have accosted her, and with some
excellent jests, fire-new from the mint, you should
have banged the youth into dumbness.
[23]

28 You are now sailed into the north of my lady's
opinion; where you will hang like an icicle on a
Dutchman's beard.
[29]

29 I had as lief be a Brownist as a politician.
[35]

30 As many lies as will lie in thy sheet of paper, although
the sheet were big enough for the bed of Ware in
England, set 'em down.
[51]

1 If he were opened, and you find so much blood in his liver as will clog the foot of a flea, I'll eat the rest of the anatomy.
[68]

2 Look, where the youngest wren of nine comes.
[73]

3 He does smile his face into more lines than are in the new map with the augmentation of the Indies.
[85]

4 In the south suburbs, at the Elephant,
Is best to lodge.
iii.39

5 I think we do know the sweet Roman hand.
iv.[31]

6 Why, this is very midsummer madness.
[62]

7 What, man! defy the devil: consider, he's an enemy to mankind.
[109]

8 Go, hang yourselves all! you are idle shallow things: I am not of your element.
[138]

9 If this were played upon a stage now, I could condemn it as an improbable fiction.
[142]

10 More matter for a May morning.
[158]

11 Still you keep o' the windy side of the law.
[183]

12 Fare thee well; and God have mercy upon one of our souls! He may have mercy upon mine, but my hope is better; and so look to thyself.
[185]

13 Nay, let me alone for swearing.
[204]

14 He is knight dubbed with unhatched rapier, and on carpet consideration.
[260]

15 I am one that had rather go with sir priest than sir knight; I care not who knows so much of my mettle.
[300]

16 Out of my lean and low ability
I'll lend you something.
[380]

17 I hate ingratitude more in a man
Than lying, vainness, babbling drunkenness,
Or any taint of vice whose strong corruption
Inhabits our frail blood.
[390]

18 In nature there's no blemish but the mind;
None can be call'd deform'd but the unkind.
[403]

19 Out, hyperbolical fiend!
IV.ii.[29]

20 For I am one of those gentle ones that will use the devil himself with courtesy.
[37]

21 *Clown:* What is the opinion of Pythagoras concerning wild fowl?
Malvolio: That the soul of our grandam might haply inhabit a bird.
Clown: What thinkest thou of his opinion?

Malvolio: I think nobly of the soul, and no way approve his opinion.
[55]

22 Leave thy vain bibble-babble.
[106]

23 We took him for a coward, but he's the very devil incardinate.
V.i.[185]

24 Why have you suffer'd me to be imprison'd,
Kept in a dark house, visited by the priest,
And made the most notorious geck and gull
That e'er invention played on? Tell me why.
[353]

25 Thus the whirligig of time brings in his revenges.
[388]

26 I'll be revenged on the whole pack of you.
[390]

27 When that I was and a little tiny boy,
    With hey, ho, the wind and the rain;
A foolish thing was but a toy,
    For the rain it raineth every day.

But when I came to man's estate,
    With hey, ho, the wind and the rain;
'Gainst knaves and thieves men shut their gates,
    For the rain it raineth every day.

But when I came, alas! to wive,
    With hey, ho, the wind and the rain;
By swaggering could I never thrive,
    For the rain it raineth every day.

But when I came unto my beds,
    With hey, ho, the wind and the rain;
With toss-pots still had drunken heads,
    For the rain it raineth every day.

A great while ago the world begun,
    With hey, ho, the wind and the rain;
But that's all one, our play is done,
    And we'll strive to please you every day.
[401]

THE TWO GENTLEMEN OF VERONA

28 Home-keeping youth have ever homely wits.
I.i.2

29 He was more than over shoes in love.
24

30 I have no other but a woman's reason:
I think him so, because I think him so.
ii.23

31 Fie, fie! how wayward is this foolish love
That, like a testy babe, will scratch the nurse
And presently all humbled kiss the rod!
55

32 Poor wounded name! my bosom, as a bed
Shall lodge thee till thy wound be throughly heal'd.
111

33 O! how this spring of love resembleth
    The uncertain glory of an April day,
Which now shows all the beauty of the sun,
    And by and by a cloud takes all away!
iii.84

34 Or as one nail by strength drives out another,
So the remembrance of my former love

Is by a newer object quite forgotten.
II.iv.194

1 Except I be by Silvia in the night,
There is no music in the nightingale;
Unless I look on Silvia in the day,
There is no day for me to look upon.
III.i.178

2 Much is the force of heaven-bred poesy.
ii.71

3 A man I am cross'd with adversity.
IV.i.12

4 Who is Sylvia? what is she,
    That all our swains commend her?
Holy, fair, and wise is she;
    The heaven such grace did lend her,
That she might admired be.

Is she kind as she is fair?
    For beauty lives with kindness:
Love doth to her eyes repair,
    To help him of his blindness;
And, being help'd, inhabits there.

Then to Silvia let us sing,
    That Silvia is excelling;
She excels each mortal thing
    Upon the dull earth dwelling;
To her let us garlands bring.
ii.40

5 How use doth breed a habit in man!
V.iv.1

6   O heaven! were man
But constant, he were perfect.
110

THE WINTER'S TALE

7   We were, fair queen,
Two lads that thought there was no more behind
But such a day to-morrow as to-day,
And to be boy eternal.
I.ii.62

8 We were as twinn'd lambs that did frisk i' the sun,
And bleat the one at the other: what we chang'd
Was innocence for innocence; we knew not
The doctrine of ill-doing, no, nor dream'd
That any did.
67

9 But to be paddling palms and pinching fingers,
As now they are, and making practis'd smiles,
As in a looking-glass.
116

10 How like, methought, I then was to this kernel,
This squash, this gentleman.
160

11 Make that thy question, and go rot!
324

12   A sad tale's best for winter.
I have one of sprites and goblins.
II.i.24

13 It is a heretic that makes the fire,
Not she which burns in 't.
iii.114

14 I am a feather for each wind that blows.
153

15   What's gone and what's past help
Should be past grief.
III.ii.[223]

16 *Exit, pursued by a bear*. iii. Stage Direction.

17 When daffodils begin to peer,
    With heigh! the doxy, over the dale,
Why, then comes in the sweet o' the year;
    For the red blood reigns in the winter's pale.

The white sheet bleaching on the hedge,
    With heigh! the sweet birds, O, how they sing!
Doth set my pugging tooth on edge;
    For a quart of ale is a dish for a king.

The lark, that tirra-lirra chants,
    With, heigh! with, heigh! the thrush and the jay,
Are summer songs for me and my aunts,
    While we lie tumbling in the hay.
IV.ii.1

18 My father named me Autolycus; who being, as I am,
littered under Mercury, was likewise a snapper-up of
unconsidered trifles.
[24]

19 For the life to come, I sleep out the thought of it.
[30]

20 Prig, for my life, prig; he haunts wakes, fairs, and
bear-baitings.
[109]

21 Jog on, jog on the foot-path way,
    And merrily hent the stile-a:
A merry heart goes all the day,
    Your sad tires in a mile-a.
[133]

22 For you there's rosemary and rue; these keep
Seeming and savour all the winter long.
iii.74

23   The fairest flowers o' the season
Are our carnations and streak'd gillyvors,
Which some call nature's bastards.
81

24   I'll not put
The dibble in earth to set one slip of them.
99

25   Here's flowers for you;
Hot lavender, mints, savory, marjoram;
The marigold, that goes to bed wi' the sun,
And with him rises weeping.
103

26   O Proserpina!
For the flowers now that frighted thou let'st fall
From Dis's waggon! daffodils,
That come before the swallow dares, and take
The winds of March with beauty; violets dim,
But sweeter than the lids of Juno's eyes
Or Cytherea's breath; pale prime-roses,
That die unmarried, ere they can behold
Bright Phoebus in his strength,—a malady
Most incident to maids; bold oxlips and
The crown imperial; lilies of all kinds,
The flower-de-luce being one.
116

27 *Perdita:* Sure this robe of mine
Doth change my disposition.
Florizel: What you do
Still betters what is done. When you speak, sweet,

I'd have you do it ever: when you sing,
I'd have you buy and sell so; so give alms;
Pray so; and, for the ordering your affairs,
To sing them too: when you do dance, I wish you
A wave o' the sea, that you might ever do
Nothing but that; move still, still so,
And own no other function: each your doing,
So singular in each particular,
Crowns what you are doing in the present deed,
That all your acts are queens.
134

1   Good sooth, she is
The queen of curds and cream.
160

2 Lawn as white as driven snow.
[220]

3 I love a ballad in print, a-life, for then we are sure they are true.
[262]

4 The self-same sun that shines upon his court
Hides not his visage from our cottage, but
Looks on alike.
[457]

5 Being now awake, I'll queen it no inch further,
But milk my ewes and weep.
[462]

6 Prosperity's the very bond of love,
Whose fresh complexion and whose heart together
Affliction alters.
[586]

7 Ha, ha! what a fool Honesty is! and Trust his sworn brother, a very simple gentleman!
[608]

8 Though I am not naturally honest, I am so sometimes by chance.
[734]

9 I will but look upon the hedge and follow you.
[862]

10   Stars, stars!
And all eyes else dead coals.
V.i.67

11   Still, methinks,
There is an air comes from her: what fine chisel
Could ever yet cut breath?
iii.77

12   O! she's warm.
If this be magic, let it be an art
Lawful as eating.
109

THE PASSIONATE PILGRIM

13 Crabbed age and youth cannot live together:
Youth is full of pleasance, age is full of care.
xii

14 Age, I do abhor thee, youth, I do adore thee.

THE PHOENIX AND THE TURTLE

15 Let the bird of loudest lay,
On the sole Arabian tree,
Herald sad and trumpet be,

To whose sound chaste wings obey.
l.1.

THE RAPE OF LUCRECE

16 What I have done is yours; what I have to do is yours;
being part in all I have, devoted yours.
Dedication

17 Beauty itself doth of itself persuade
The eyes of men without an orator.
l.29

18 Who buys a minute's mirth to wail a week?
Or sells eternity to get a toy?
For one sweet grape who will the vine destroy?
l.213

19 Time's glory is to calm contending kings,
To unmask falsehood, and bring truth to light.
l.939

20 And now this pale swan in her watery nest
Begins the sad dirge of her certain ending.
l.1611

SONNETS

21 To the onlie begetter of these insuing sonnets, Mr. W.H.
Dedication (also attr. Thomas Thorpe)

22 From fairest creatures we desire increase,
That thereby beauty's rose might never die.
1

23 When forty winters shall besiege thy brow,
And dig deep trenches in thy beauty's field.
2

24 Thou art thy mother's glass, and she in thee
Calls back the lovely April of her prime.
3

25 Music to hear, why hear'st thou music sadly?
Sweets with sweets war not, joy delights in joy:
Why lov'st thou that which thou receiv'st not gladly,
Or else receiv'st with pleasure thine annoy?
If the true concord of well-tuned sounds,
By unions married, do offend thine ear,
They do but sweetly chide thee.
8

26 When lofty trees I see barren of leaves,
Which erst from heat did canopy the herd,
And summer's green all girded up in sheaves,
Borne on the bier with white and bristly beard.
12

27 If I could write the beauty of your eyes
And in fresh numbers number all your graces,
The age to come would say, 'This poet lies;
Such heavenly touches ne'er touch'd earthly faces.'
So should my papers, yellow'd with their age,
Be scorn'd, like old men of less truth than tongue,
And your true rights be term'd a poet's rage
And stretched metre of an antique song.
17

28 Shall I compare thee to a summer's day?
Thou art more lovely and more temperate:
Rough winds do shake the darling buds of May,
And summer's lease hath all too short a date:
Sometimes too hot the eye of heaven shines,
And often is his gold complexion dimm'd;

And every fair from fair sometime declines,
By chance, or nature's changing course untrimm'd;
But thy eternal summer shall not fade,
Nor lose possession of that fair thou ow'st,
Nor shall death brag thou wander'st in his shade,
When in eternal lines to time thou grow'st;
   So long as men can breathe, or eyes can see,
   So long lives this, and this gives life to thee.
18

1 My glass shall not persuade me I am old,
So long as youth and thou are of one date;
But when in thee time's furrows I behold,
Then look I death my days should expiate.
22

2 As an unperfect actor on the stage,
Who with his fear is put beside his part,
Or some fierce thing replete with too much rage,
Whose strength's abundance weakens his own heart;
So I, for fear of trust, forget to say
The perfect ceremony of love's rite.
23

3 O! let my books be then the eloquence
And dumb presagers of my speaking breast.

4 The painful warrior famoused for fight,
After a thousand victories once foil'd,
Is from the book of honour razed quite,
And all the rest forgot for which he toil'd.
25

5 Weary with toil, I haste me to my bed,
The dear repose for limbs with travel tired;
But then begins a journey in my head
To work my mind, when body's work's expired.
27

6 When in disgrace with fortune and men's eyes
I all alone beweep my outcast state,
And trouble deaf heaven with my bootless cries,
And look upon myself and curse my fate,
Wishing me like to one more rich in hope,
Featur'd like him, like him with friends possess'd,
Desiring this man's art, and that man's scope,
With what I most enjoy contented least;
Yet in these thoughts myself almost despising,
Haply I think on thee,—and then my state,
Like to the lark at break of day arising
From sullen earth, sings hymns at heaven's gate;
   For thy sweet love remember'd such wealth brings
   That then I scorn to change my state with kings.
29

7 When to the sessions of sweet silent thought
I summon up remembrance of things past,
I sigh the lack of many a thing I sought,
And with old woes new wail my dear times' waste:
Then can I drown an eye, unus'd to flow,
For precious friends hid in death's dateless night,
And weep afresh love's long since cancell'd woe,
And moan the expense of many a vanish'd sight:
Then can I grieve at grievances foregone,
And heavily from woe to woe tell o'er
The sad account of fore-bemoaned moan,
Which I new pay as if not paid before.
   But if the while I think on thee, dear friend,
   All losses are restor'd and sorrows end.
30

8   Since he died, and poets better prove,

Theirs for their style I'll read, his for his love.
32

9 Full many a glorious morning have I seen
Flatter the mountain-tops with sovereign eye,
Kissing with golden face the meadows green,
Gilding pale streams with heavenly alchemy.
33

10 But, out! alack! he was but one hour mine,
The region cloud hath mask'd him from me now.
   Yet him for this my love no whit disdaineth;
   Suns of the world may stain when heaven's sun
      staineth.

11 Why didst thou promise such a beauteous day,
And make me travel forth without my cloak
To let base clouds o'ertake me in my way,
Hiding thy bravery in their rotten smoke?
34

12 Roses have thorns, and silver fountains mud;
Clouds and eclipses stain both moon and sun,
And loathsome canker lives in sweetest bud.
All men make faults.
35

13 As a decrepit father takes delight
To see his active child do deeds of youth,
So I, made lame by fortune's dearest spite,
Take all my comfort of thy worth and truth.
37

14 Against that time when thou shalt strangely pass,
And scarely greet me with that sun, thine eye,
When love, converted from the thing it was,
Shall reasons find of settled gravity.
49

15 What is your substance, whereof are you made,
That millions of strange shadows on you tend?
53

16 O! how much more doth beauty beauteous seem
By that sweet ornament which truth doth give!
54

17 Not marble, nor the gilded monuments
Of princes, shall outlive this powerful rime;
But you shall shine more bright in these contents
Than unswept stone, besmear'd with sluttish time.
55

18 Being your slave, what should I do but tend
Upon the hours and times of your desire?
I have no precious time at all to spend,
Nor services to do, till you require.
Nor dare I chide the world-without-end hour
Whilst I, my sovereign, watch the clock for you,
Nor think the bitterness of absence sour
When you have bid your servant once adieu;
Nor dare I question with my jealous thought
Where you may be, or your affairs suppose,
But like a sad slave, stay and think of nought
Save, where you are, how happy you make those.
   So true a fool is love that in your will,
   Though you do anything, he thinks no ill.
57

19 Like as the waves make towards the pebbled shore,
So do our minutes hasten to their end.
60

20 Time doth transfix the flourish set on youth
And delves the parallels in beauty's brow.

1 Sin of self-love possesseth all mine eye.
62

2 When I have seen by Time's fell hand defac'd
The rich-proud cost of outworn buried age.
64

3 When I have seen the hungry ocean gain
Advantage on the kingdom of the shore.

4 Since brass, nor stone, nor earth, nor boundless sea,
But sad mortality o'ersways their power,
How with this rage shall beauty hold a plea,
Whose action is no stronger than a flower?
65

5 Tir'd with all these, for restful death I cry,
As to behold desert a beggar born,
And needy nothing trimm'd in jollity,
And purest faith unhappily forsworn,
And gilded honour shamefully misplac'd,
And maiden virtue rudely strumpeted,
And right perfection wrongfully disgrac'd,
And strength by limping sway disabled,
And art made tongue-tied by authority,
And folly—doctor-like—controlling skill,
And simple truth miscall'd simplicity,
And captive good attending captain ill:
    Tir'd with all these, from these I would be gone,
    Save that, to die, I leave my love alone.
66

6 No longer mourn for me when I am dead
Than you shall hear the surly sullen bell
Give warning to the world that I am fled
From this vile world, with vilest worms to dwell.
71

7 That time of year thou mayst in me behold
When yellow leaves, or none, or few, do hang
Upon those boughs which shake against the cold,
Bare ruin'd choirs, where late the sweet birds sang.
In me thou see'st the twilight of such day
As after sunset fadeth in the west;
Which by and by black night doth take away,
Death's second self, that seals up all in rest.
73

8 This thou perceiv'st, which makes thy love more
    strong,
To love that well which thou must leave ere long.

9 O! know, sweet love, I always write of you,
And you and love are still my argument;
So all my best is dressing old words new,
Spending again what is already spent.
76

10 Time's thievish progress to eternity.
77

11 Was it the proud full sail of his great verse,
Bound for the prize of all too precious you,
That did my ripe thoughts in my brain inhearse,
Making their tomb the womb wherein they grew?
86

12   That affable familiar ghost
Which nightly gulls him with intelligence.

13 Farewell! thou art too dear for my possessing,
And like enough thou know'st thy estimate:
The charter of thy worth gives thee releasing;
My bonds in thee are all determinate.
For how do I hold thee but by thy granting?

And for that riches where is my deserving?
The cause of this fair gift in me is wanting,
And so my patent back again is swerving.
Thyself thou gav'st, thy own worth then not knowing,
Or me, to whom thou gav'st it, else mistaking;
So thy great gift, upon misprision growing,
Comes home again, on better judgment making.
    Thus have I had thee, as a dream doth flatter,
    In sleep a king, but, waking, no such matter.
87

14 Ah, do not, when my heart hath 'scap'd this sorrow,
Come in the rearward of a conquer'd woe;
Give not a windy night a rainy morrow,
To linger out a purpos'd overthrow.
90

15 They that have power to hurt and will do none,
That do not do the thing they most do show,
Who, moving others, are themselves as stone,
Unmoved, cold, and to temptation slow;
They rightly do inherit heaven's graces,
And husband nature's riches from expense;
They are the lords and owners of their faces,
Others but stewards of their excellence.
The summer's flower is to the summer sweet,
Though to itself it only live and die,
But if that flower with base infection meet,
The basest weed outbraves his dignity:
    For sweetest things turn sourest by their deeds;
    Lilies that fester smell far worse than weeds.
94

16 How like a winter hath my absence been
From thee, the pleasure of the fleeting year!
What freezings have I felt, what dark days seen!
What old December's bareness every where!
97

17 From you have I been absent in the spring,
When proud-pied April, dress'd in all his trim,
Hath put a spirit of youth in everything.
98

18 To me, fair friend, you never can be old,
For as you were when first your eye I ey'd,
Such seems your beauty still. Three winters cold
Have from the forests shook three summers' pride,
Three beauteous springs to yellow autumn turn'd
In process of the seasons have I seen,
Three April perfumes in three hot Junes burn'd,
Since first I saw you fresh, which yet are green.
Ah! yet doth beauty, like a dial-hand,
Steal from his figure, and no pace perceiv'd;
So your sweet hue, which methinks still doth stand,
Hath motion, and mine eye may be deceiv'd:
    For fear of which, hear this, thou age unbred:
    Ere you were born was beauty's summer dead.
104

19 When in the chronicle of wasted time
I see descriptions of the fairest wights,
And beauty making beautiful old rime,
In praise of ladies dead and lovely knights.
106

20 For we, which now behold these present days,
Have eyes to wonder, but lack tongues to praise.

21 Not mine own fears, nor the prophetic soul
Of the wide world dreaming on things to come,
Can yet the lease of my true love control,

Suppos'd as forfeit to a confin'd doom.
The mortal moon hath her eclipse endur'd,
And the sad augurs mock their own presage.
107

1 And thou in this shalt find thy monument,
When tyrants' crests and tombs of brass are spent.

2 O! never say that I was false of heart,
Though absence seem'd my flame to qualify.
109

3 Alas! 'tis true I have gone here and there,
And made myself a motley to the view,
Gor'd mine own thoughts, sold cheap what is most
    dear,
Made old offences of affections new;
Most true it is that I have look'd on truth
Askance and strangely; but, by all above,
These blenches gave my heart another youth,
And worse essays prov'd thee my best of love.
110

4   My nature is subdu'd
To what it works in, like the dyer's hand;
Pity me, then, and wish I were renew'd.
111

5 Let me not to the marriage of true minds
Admit impediments. Love is not love
Which alters when it alteration finds,
Or bends with the remover to remove:
O, no! it is an ever-fixed mark,
That looks on tempests and is never shaken;
It is the star to every wandering bark,
Whose worth's unknown, although his height be
    taken.
Love's not Time's fool, though rosy lips and cheeks
Within his bending sickle's compass come;
Love alters not with his brief hours and weeks,
But bears it out even to the edge of doom.
    If this be error, and upon me prov'd,
    I never writ, nor no man ever lov'd.
116

6 What potions have I drunk of Siren tears,
Distill'd from limbecks foul as hell within,
Applying fears to hopes, and hopes to fears,
Still losing when I saw myself to win!
119

7 The expense of spirit in a waste of shame
Is lust in action; and till action, lust
Is perjur'd, murderous, bloody, full of blame,
Savage, extreme, rude, cruel, not to trust;
Enjoyed no sooner but despised straight;
Past reason hunted; and no sooner had,
Past reason hated, as a swallow'd bait,
On purpose laid to make the taker mad:
Mad in pursuit, and in possession so;
Had, having, and in quest to have, extreme;
A bliss in proof,—and prov'd, a very woe;
Before, a joy propos'd; behind, a dream.
    All this the world well knows; yet none knows well:
    To shun the heaven that leads men to this hell.
129

8 My mistress' eyes are nothing like the sun;
Coral is far more red than her lips' red:
If snow be white, why then her breasts are dun;
If hairs be wires, black wires grow on her head.
130

9 And yet, by heaven, I think my love as rare
As any she belied with false compare.

10 Whoever hath her wish, thou hast thy *Will*,
And *Will* to boot, and *Will* in over-plus.
135

11 When my love swears that she is made of truth,
I do believe her, though I know she lies.
138

12 Two loves I have of comfort and despair,
Which like two spirits do suggest me still:
The better angel is a man right fair,
The worser spirit a woman colour'd ill.
144

13 Poor soul, the centre of my sinful earth,
[Fool'd by] these rebel powers that thee array,
Why dost thou pine within and suffer dearth,
Painting thy outward walls so costly gay?
Why so large cost, having so short a lease,
Dost thou upon thy fading mansion spend?
146

14 So shalt thou feed on Death, that feeds on men,
And Death once dead, there's no more dying then.

15 Past cure I am, now Reason is past care,
And frantic-mad with evermore unrest;
My thoughts and my discourse as madmen's are,
At random from the truth vainly express'd;
    For I have sworn thee fair, and thought thee bright,
    Who art as black as hell, as dark as night.
147

SONNETS TO SUNDRY NOTES OF MUSIC

16 Live with me and be my love,
And we will all the pleasures prove.
That hills and valleys, dales and fields,
And all the craggy mountains yields.
v. See 187:24, 329:23, 404:9

VENUS AND ADONIS

17 If the first heir of my invention prove deformed, I
shall be sorry it had so noble a godfather.
Dedication

18 Hunting he lov'd, but love he laugh'd to scorn.
1.4

19 Bid me discourse, I will enchant thine ear,
Or like a fairy trip upon the green,
Or, like a nymph, with long dishevell'd hair,
Dance on the sands, and yet no footing seen:
    Love is a spirit all compact of fire,
    Not gross to sink, but light, and will aspire.
1.145

20 Round-hoof'd, short-jointed, fetlocks shag and long,
Broad breast, full eye, small head and nostril wide,
High crest, short ears, straight legs and passing strong,
Thin mane, thick tail, broad buttock, tender hide:
    Look, what a horse should have he did not lack,
    Save a proud rider on so proud a back.
1.295

21 By this, poor Wat, far off upon a hill,
Stands on his hinder legs with listening ear,
To hearken if his foes pursue him still.
1.697

22 Good friend, for Jesu's sake forbear

To dig the dust enclosed here.
Blest be the man that spares these stones,
And curst be he that moves my bones.
Epitaph on his tomb at Stratford-on-Avon, supposed to have been chosen by himself.

1 Item, I give unto my wife my second best bed, with the furniture.
Will, 1616

GEORGE BERNARD SHAW 1856–1950

2 All great truths begin as blasphemies.
Annajanska (1917), p.262

3 One man that has a mind and knows it, can always beat ten men who havnt and dont.
The Apple Cart (1929), Act I

4 What Englishman will give his mind to politics as long as he can afford to keep a motor car?

5 I never resist temptation, because I have found that things that are bad for me do not tempt me.
Act II

6 You can always tell an old soldier by the inside of his holsters and cartridge boxes. The young ones carry pistols and cartridges: the old ones, grub.
Arms and the Man (1898), Act I

7 I never apologise.
Act III

8 You're not a man, you're a machine.

9 He is a barbarian, and thinks that the customs of his tribe and island are the laws of nature.
Caesar and Cleopatra (1898), Act II

10 When a stupid man is doing something he is ashamed of, he always declares that it is his duty.
Act III

11 He who has never hoped can never despair.
Act IV

12 A man of great common sense and good taste,—meaning thereby a man without originality or moral courage.
Notes. Julius Caesar

13 We have no more right to consume happiness without producing it than to comsume wealth without producing it.
Candida (1898), Act I

14 Do you think that the things people make fools of themselves about are any less real and true than the things they behave sensibly about?

15 It is easy—terribly easy—to shake a man's faith in himself. To take advantage of that to break a man's spirit is devil's work.

16 I'm only a beer teetotaller, not a champagne teetotaller.
Act III

17 The worst sin towards our fellow creatures is not to hate them, but to be indifferent to them: that's the essence of inhumanity.
The Devil's Disciple, (1897), Act II

18 I never expect a soldier to think.
Act III

19 The British soldier can stand up to anything except the British War Office.

20 Stimulate the phagocytes.
The Doctor's Dilemma (1906), Act I

21 All professions are conspiracies against the laity.

22 I believe in Michael Angelo, Velasquez, and Rembrandt; in the might of design, the mystery of color, the redemption of all things by Beauty everlasting, and the message of Art that has made these hands blessed.

23 With the single exception of Homer, there is no eminent writer, not even Sir Walter Scott, whom I can despise so entirely as I despise Shakespeare when I measure my mind against his...It would positively be a relief to me to dig him up and throw stones at him.
Dramatic Opinions and Essays (1907), vol.II, p.52

24 Parentage is a very important profession; but no test of fitness for it is ever imposed in the interest of children.
Everybody's Political What's What (1944),ch.ix, p.74

25 It's all that the young can do for the old, to shock them and keep them up to date.
Fanny's First Play (1911), Induction

26 You don't expect me to know what to say about a play when I don't know who the author is, do you?...If it's by a good author, it's a good play, naturally. That stands to reason.
Epilogue

27 The one point on which all women are in furious secret rebellion against the existing law is the saddling of the right to a child with the obligation to become the servant of a man.
Getting Married (1908), Preface

28 What God hath joined together no man ever shall put asunder: God will take care of that.
p.216

29 When you loved me I gave you the whole sun and stars to play with. I gave you eternity in a single moment, strength of the mountains in one clasp of your arms, and the volume of all the seas in one impulse of your soul.
p.278

30 We possessed all the universe together; and you ask me to give you my scanty wages as well. I have given you the greatest of all things; and you ask me to give you little things. I gave you your own soul: you ask me for my body as a plaything. Was it not enough? Was it not enough?

31 I am a woman of the world, Hector; and I can assure you that if you will only take the trouble always to do the perfectly correct thing, and to say the perfectly correct thing, you can do just what you like.
Heartbreak House (1917), Act I

32 Go anywhere in England, where there are natural, wholesome, contented, and really nice English people; and what do you always find? That the stables are the real centre of the household.
Act III

33 The captain is in his bunk, drinking bottled ditchwater; and the crew is gambling in the forecastle. She will strike and sink and split. Do you think the laws of God will be suspended in favour of England because you were born in it?

34 Money is indeed the most important thing in the world; and all sound and successful personal and

national morality should have this fact for its basis.
The Irrational Knot (1905), Preface, p.xiv

1 Though the Life Force supplies us with its own purpose, it has no other brains to work with than those it has painfully and imperfectly evolved in our heads.
p.xxv

2 Reminiscences make one feel so deliciously aged and sad.
ch.14

3 A man who has no office to go to—I don't care who he is—is a trial of which you can have no conception.
ch.18

4 What really flatters a man is that you think him worth flattering.
John Bull's Other Island (1907), Act IV

5 There are only two qualities in the world: efficiency and inefficiency; and only two sorts of people: the efficient and the inefficient.

6 The greatest of evils and the worst of crimes is poverty.
Major Barbara (1907), Preface

7 The universal regard for money is the one hopeful fact in our civilization, the one sound spot in our social conscience. Money is the most important thing in the world. It represents health, strength, honour, generosity, and beauty as conspicuously as the want of it represents illness, weakness, disgrace, meanness, and ugliness.

8 Cusins is a very nice fellow, certainly: nobody would ever guess that he was born in Australia.
Act I

9 Nobody can say a word against Greek: it stamps a man at once as an educated gentleman.

10 Wot prawce Selvytion nah?
Act II

11 I am a Millionaire. That is my religion.

12 I am a sort of collector of religions: and the curious thing is that I find I can believe in them all.

13 I cant talk religion to a man with bodily hunger in his eyes.

14 You darent handle high explosives; but youre all ready to handle honesty and truth and justice and the whole duty of man, and kill one another at that game. What a country! What a world!
Act III

15 Nothing is ever done in this world until men are prepared to kill one another if it is not done.

16 Our political experiment of democracy, the last refuge of cheap misgovernment.
Man and Superman (1903), Epistle Dedicatory, p.xxi

17 A lifetime of happiness! No man alive could bear it: it would be hell on earth.
Act I

18 We are ashamed of everything that is real about us; ashamed of ourselves, of our relatives, of our incomes, of our accents, of our opinions, of our experience, just as we are ashamed of our naked skins.

19 The more things a man is ashamed of, the more respectable he is.

20 Vitality in a woman is a blind fury of creation.

21 The true artist will let his wife starve, his children go barefoot, his mother drudge for his living at seventy, sooner than work at anything but his art.

22 Is the devil to have all the passions as well as all the good tunes?
See 251:4

23 Very nice sort of place, Oxford, I should think, for people that like that sort of place.
Act II

24 You think that you are Ann's suitor; that you are the pursuer and she the pursued; that it is your part to woo, to persuade, to prevail, to overcome. Fool: it is you who are the pursued, the marked down quarry, the destined prey.

25 It is a woman's business to get married as soon as possible, and a man's to keep unmarried as long as he can.

26 You can be as romantic as you please about love, Hector; but you mustnt be romantic about money.

27 Hell is full of musical amateurs: music is the brandy of the damned.
Act III

28 An Englishman thinks he is moral when he is only uncomfortable.

29 As an old soldier I admit the cowardice: it's as universal as seasickness, and matters just as little.

30 When the military man approaches, the world locks up its spoons and packs off its womankind.

31 What is virtue but the Trade Unionism of the married?

32 Those who talk most about the blessings of marriage and the constancy of its vows are the very people who delare that if the chain were broken and the prisoners left free to choose, the whole social fabric would fly asunder. You cannot have the argument both ways. If the prisoner is happy, why lock him in? If he is not, why pretend that he is?

33 There are two tragedies in life. One is not to get your heart's desire. The other is to get it.
Act IV. See 555:2

34 Do not do unto others as you would they should do unto you. Their tastes may not be the same.
Maxims for Revolutionists (by 'John Tanner'): **'The Golden Rule'.**

35 The Golden Rule is that there are no golden rules.

36 Democracy substitutes election by the incompetent many for appointment by the corrupt few.
'Democracy'

37 Liberty means responsibility. That is why most men dread it.
'Liberty'

38 He who can, does. He who cannot teaches.
'Education'

39 Marriage is popular because it combines the maximum of temptation with the maximum of opportunity.
'Marriage'

40 When domestic servants are treated as human beings it is not worth while to keep them.
'Servants'

41 If you strike a child, take care that you strike it in anger, even at the risk of maiming it for life. A blow in

cold blood neither can nor should be forgiven.
'How to Beat Children'

1 The reasonable man adapts himself to the world: the
unreasonable one persists in trying to adapt the world
to himself. Therefore all progress depends on the
unreasonable man.
'Reason'

2 The man who listens to Reason is lost: Reason
enslaves all whose minds are not strong enough to
master her.

3 Home is the girl's prison and the woman's workhouse.
'Women in the Home'

4 Every man over forty is a scoundrel.
'Stray Sayings'

5 Youth, which is forgiven everything, forgives itself
nothing: age, which forgives itself anything, is
forgiven nothing.

6 There is nothing so bad or so good that you will not
find Englishmen doing it; but you will never find an
Englishman in the wrong. He does everything on
principle. He fights you on patriotic principles; he robs
you on business principles; he enslaves you on
imperial principles.
The Man of Destiny (1897)

7 An English army led by an Irish general: that might be
a match for a French army led by an Italian general.

8 A great devotee of the Gospel of Getting On.
Mrs. Warren's Profession (1893), Act IV

9 The fickleness of the women I love is only equalled by
the infernal constancy of the women who love me.
The Philanderer (1893), Act II

10 It is clear that a novel cannot be too bad to be worth
publishing...It certainly is possible for a novel to be
too good to be worth publishing.
Plays Pleasant and Unpleasant (1898), vol.1, Preface, p.vi

11 There is only one religion, though there are a hundred
versions of it.
vol.2, Preface, p.vii

12 The English have no respect for their language, and
will not teach their children to speak it...It is
impossible for an Englishman to open his mouth,
without making some other Englishman despise him.
Pygmalion (1912), Preface

13 *Pickering:* Have you no morals, man?
Doolittle: Can't afford them, Governor.
Act II

14 I'm one of the undeserving poor: that's what I am.
Think of what that means to a man. It means that he's
up agen middle class morality all the time...What is
middle class morality? Just an excuse for never giving
me anything.

15 Gin was mother's milk to her.
Act III

16 Walk! Not bloody likely. I am going in a taxi.

17 Assassination is the extreme form of censorship.
The Rejected Statement, Pt.I

18 If ever I utter an oath again may my soul be blasted to
eternal damnation!
St. Joan (1923), Sc.ii

19 How can what an Englishman believes be heresy? It is

a contradiction in terms.
Sc.iv

20 Must then a Christ perish in torment in every age to
save those that have no imagination?
Epilogue

21 Well, sir, you never can tell. That's a principle in life
with me, sir, if you'll excuse my having such a thing.
You Never Can Tell (1897), Act II

22 If you are going to have doctors you had better have
doctors well off; just as if you are going to have a
landlord you had better have a rich landlord. Taking
all the round of professions and occupations, you will
find that every man is the worse for being poor; and
the doctor is a specially dangerous man when poor.
The Socialist Criticism of the Medical Profession. Paper read to
the Medico-Legal Society, 16 Feb. 1909

23 England is still governed from Langar Rectory, from
Shrewsbury School, from Cambridge, with their
annexes of the Stock Exchange and the solicitors'
offices; and even if the human products of these
institutions were all geniuses, they would finally wreck
any modern civilized country after maintaining
themselves according to their own notions at the cost
of the squalor and slavery of four-fifths of its
inhabitants.
Introductory essay to S. Butler's *The Way of All Flesh*, World's
Classics edn. (1936)

THOMAS SHAW 1694–1751

24 I hate a *cui bono* man.
Attr. Boswell's *Life of Johnson*, IV, 112. May 1781

LORD SHAWCROSS 1902–

25 'The question is,' said Humpty Dumpty, 'which is to
be master—that's all.'
We are the masters at the moment, and not only at the
moment, but for a very long time to come.
House of Commons, 2 Apr. 1946. Often misquoted as 'We are the
masters now.' See 135:22

CHARLES SHAW-LEFEVRE, VISCOUNT EVERSLEY 1794–1888

26 What is that fat gentleman in such a passion about?
Remark as a child on hearing Mr. Fox speak in Parliament.
G.W.E. Russell, *Collections and Recollections*, ch.11

PATRICK SHAW STEWART 1888–1917

27 I saw a man this morning
   Who did not wish to die;
I ask, and cannot answer
   If otherwise wish I.
Written during the Gallipoli expedition, 1915. N. Mosley, *Julian
Grenfell* (1976), ch.31

28 I will go back this morning
   From Imbros over the sea;
Stand in the trench, Achilles,
   Flame-capped, and shout for me.

RICHARD SHEALE sixteenth century

29 For Witherington needs must I wail,
   As one in doleful dumps;
For when his legs were smitten off,

He fought upon his stumps.
Ballad of Chevy Chase, Pt. II, x

JOHN SHEFFIELD, DUKE OF BUCKINGHAM
see BUCKINGHAM

MARY WOLLSTONECRAFT SHELLEY
1797–1851

1 Mrs Shelley was choosing a school for her son, and asked the advice of this lady, who gave for advice—to use her own words to me—'Just the sort of banality, you know, one does come out with: "Oh, send him somewhere where they will teach him to think for himself!"'…Mrs Shelley answered: 'Teach him to think for himself? Oh, my God, teach him rather to think like other people!'
Matthew Arnold, *Essays in Criticism, Second Series; Shelley*

PERCY BYSSHE SHELLEY 1792–1822

2 The cemetery is an open space among the ruins, covered in winter with violets and daisies. It might make one in love with death, to think that one should be buried in so sweet a place.
Adonais (1821). Preface

3 I weep for Adonais—he is dead!
O, weep for Adonais! though our tears
Thaw not the frost which binds so dear a head!
I

4 Most musical of mourners, weep again!
Lament anew, Urania!—He died,
Who was the Sire of an immortal strain,
Blind, old and lonely.
IV

5   He went, unterrified,
Into the gulf of death; but his clear Sprite
Yet reigns o'er earth; the third among the sons of
   light.
V

6 To that high Capital, where kingly Death
Keeps his pale court in beauty and decay,
He came.
VII

7   The quick Dreams,
The passion-winged Ministers of thought.
IX

8 Lost Angel of a ruin'd Paradise!
She knew not 'twas her own; as with no stain
She faded, like a cloud which had outwept its rain.
X

9   Desires and Adorations,
Wingèd Persuasions and veiled Destinies,
Splendours, and Glooms, and glimmering Incarnations
Of hopes and fears, and twilight Phantasies;
And Sorrow, with her family of Sighs,
And Pleasure, blind with tears, led by the gleam
Of her own dying smile instead of eyes,
Came in slow pomp.
XIII

10 Ah, woe is me! Winter is come and gone,
But grief returns with the revolving year.
XVIII

11 The great morning of the world when first

God dawned on Chaos.
XIX

12 Alas! that all we loved of him should be,
But for our grief, as if it had not been,
And grief itself be mortal!
XXI

13 Whence are we, and why are we? Of what scene
The actors or spectators?

14 As long as skies are blue, and fields are green,
Evening must usher night, night urge the morrow,
Month follow month with woe, and year wake year to
   sorrow.

15 Why didst thou leave the trodden paths of men
Too soon, and with weak hands though mighty heart
Dare the unpastured dragon in his den?
XXVII

16 The herded wolves, bold only to pursue;
The obscene ravens, clamorous o'er the dead.
XXVIII

17 A pard-like Spirit, beautiful and swift—
A Love in desolation masked;—a Power
Girt round with weakness;—it can scarce uplift
The weight of the superincumbent hour;
It is a dying lamp, a falling shower,
A breaking billow;—even whilst we speak
Is it not broken?
XXXII

18 Our Adonais has drunk poison—oh!
What deaf and viperous murderer could crown
Life's early cup with such a draught of woe?
XXXVI

19 He wakes or sleeps with the enduring dead;
Thou canst not soar where he is sitting now—
Dust to the dust! but the pure spirit shall flow
Back to the burning fountain whence it came,
A portion of the Eternal.
XXXVIII

20 He hath awakened from the dream of life—
'Tis we, who lost in stormy visions, keep
With phantoms an unprofitable strife,
And in mad trance, strike with our spirit's knife
Invulnerable nothings.
XXXIX

21 He has out-soared the shadow of our night;
Envy and calumny and hate and pain,
And that unrest which men miscall delight,
Can touch him not and torture not again;
From the contagion of the world's slow stain
He is secure, and now can never mourn
A heart grown cold, a head grown grey in vain.
XL

22 He lives, he wakes,—'tis Death is dead, not he.
XLI

23 He is made one with Nature: there is heard
His voice in all her music, from the moan
Of thunder, to the song of night's sweet bird.
XLII

24 He is a portion of the loveliness
Which once he made more lovely.
XLIII

25 What Adonais is, why fear we to become?
LI

26 The One remains, the many change and pass;

Heaven's light forever shines, Earth's shadows fly;
Life, like a dome of many-coloured glass,
Stains the white radiance of Eternity,
Until Death tramples it to fragments.
LII

1 The soul of Adonais, like a star,
Beacons from the abode where the Eternal are.
LV

2   Arethusa arose
   From her couch of snows
In the Acroceraunian mountains,—
   From cloud and from crag,
   With many a jag,
Shepherding her bright fountains.
Arethusa

3 A widow bird sate mourning for her love
   Upon a wintry bough;
The frozen wind crept on above,
   The freezing stream below.

There was no leaf upon the forest bare,
   No flower upon the ground,
And little motion in the air
   Except the mill-wheel's sound.
Charles the First (1822), sc.v, l.10

4 I wield the flail of the lashing hail,
   And whiten the green plains under,
And then again I dissolve it in rain,
   And laugh as I pass in thunder.
The Cloud (1819)

5 And I all the while bask in Heaven's blue smile,
   Whilst he is dissolving in rains.

6 That orbèd maiden, with white fire laden,
   Whom mortals call the Moon,
Glides glimmering o'er my fleece-like floor,
   By the midnight breezes strewn;
And wherever the beat of her unseen feet,
   Which only the angels hear,
May have broken the woof of my tent's thin roof,
   The stars peep behind her and peer;
And I laugh to see them whirl and flee
   Like a swarm of golden bees,
When I widen the rent in my wind-built tent,
   Till the calm rivers, lakes, and seas,
Like strips of the sky fallen through me on high,
   Are each paved with the moon and these.

7 I am the daughter of Earth and Water,
   And the nursling of the Sky;
I pass through the pores of the ocean and shores;
   I change, but I cannot die,
For after the rain when with never a stain
   The pavilion of Heaven is bare,
And the winds and sunbeams with their convex gleams
   Build up the blue dome of air,
I silently laugh at my own cenotaph,
   And out of the caverns of rain,
Like a child from the womb, like a ghost from the
   tomb,
   I arise and unbuild it again.

8   How wonderful is Death,
   Death and his brother Sleep!
One pale as the yonder wan and horned moon,
   With lips of lurid blue,
The other glowing like the vital morn,

When throned on ocean's wave
   It breathes over the world:
Yet both so passing strange and wonderful!
The Daemon of the World, Part I, 1,1. See also **Queen Mab,**
opening lines.

9 I never was attached to that great sect,
Whose doctrine is that each one should select
Out of the crowd a mistress or a friend,
And all the rest, though fair and wise, commend
To cold oblivion.
Epipsychidion (1821), l.149

10   The beaten road
Which those poor slaves with weary footsteps tread,
Who travel to their home among the dead
By the broad highway of the world, and so
With one chained friend, perhaps a jealous foe,
The dreariest and the longest journey go.
l.154

11 True Love in this differs from gold and clay,
That to divide is not to take away.
l.160

12   An isle under Ionian skies,
Beautiful as a wreck of Paradise.
l.422

13 I pant, I sink, I tremble, I expire!
l.591

14 Chameleons feed on light and air:
Poets' food is love and fame.
An Exhortation

15   Time's printless torrent grew
A scroll of crystal, blazoning the name
Of Adonais!
Fragment on Keats

16 My spirit like a charmed bark doth swim
   Upon the liquid waves of thy sweet singing.
Fragment: To One Singing. See 503:11

17 Good-night? ah! no; the hour is ill
   Which severs those it should unite;
Let us remain together still,
   Then it will be *good* night.
Good Night

18 Life may change, but it may fly not;
Hope may vanish, but can die not;
Truth be veiled, but still it burneth;
Love repulsed,—but it returneth!
Hellas (1822), l.34

19 Let there be light! said Liberty,
And like sunrise from the sea,
Athens arose!
l.682

20 The world's great age begins anew,
The golden years return,
The earth doth like a snake renew
Her winter weeds outworn;
Heaven smiles, and faiths and empires gleam,
Like wrecks of a dissolving dream.
l.1060

21 A loftier Argo cleaves the main,
Fraught with a later prize;
Another Orpheus sings again,
And loves, and weeps, and dies.
A new Ulysses leaves once more

Calypso for his native shore.
1.1072

1 Although a subtler Sphinx renew
Riddles of death Thebes never knew.
1.1082

2 Another Athens shall arise,
And to remoter time
Bequeath, like sunset to the skies,
The splendour of its prime;
And leave, if nought so bright may live,
All earth can take or Heaven can give.
1.1090

3 O cease! must hate and death return?
Cease! must men kill and die?
Cease! drain not to its dregs the urn
Of bitter prophecy.
The world is weary of the past,
Oh, might it die or rest at last!
1.1102

4 I pursued a maiden and clasped a reed.
Gods and men, we are all deluded thus!
It breaks in our bosom and then we bleed.
Hymn of Pan

5 The awful shadow of some unseen Power
Floats though unseen among us,—visiting
This various world with as inconstant wing
As summer winds that creep from flower to flower.
Hymn to Intellectual Beauty (1816)

6 While yet a boy I sought for ghosts, and sped
Through many a listening chamber, cave and ruin,
And starlight wood, with fearful steps pursuing
Hopes of high talk with the departed dead.

7 The day becomes more solemn and serene
When noon is past—there is a harmony
In autumn, and a lustre in its sky,
Which through the summer is not heard or seen,
As if it could not be, as if it had not been!

8 I arise from dreams of thee
In the first sweet sleep of night.
When the winds are breathing low,
And the stars are shining bright.
The Indian Serenade

9 Oh lift me from the grass!
I die! I faint! I fail!
Let thy love in kisses rain
On my lips and eyelids pale.

10   I love all waste
And solitary places; where we taste
The pleasure of believing what we see
Is boundless, as we wish our souls to be.
Julian and Maddalo (1818), 1.14

11 Thou Paradise of exiles, Italy!
1.57

12 Me—who am as a nerve o'er which do creep
The else unfelt oppressions of this earth.
1.449

13   Most wretched men
Are cradled into poetry by wrong:
They learn in suffering what they teach in song.
1.543

14 O world! O life! O time!
On whose last steps I climb,
Trembling at that where I had stood before;

When will return the glory of your prime?
No more—Oh, never more!
A Lament

15 Fresh spring, and summer, and winter hoar,
Move my faint heart with grief, but with delight
No more—Oh, never more!

16 We watched the ocean and the sky together,
Under the roof of blue Italian weather.
Letter to Maria Gisborne (1820), 1.146

17   London, that great sea, whose ebb and flow
At once is deaf and loud, and on the shore
Vomits its wrecks, and still howls on for more.
1.193

18 You will see Coleridge—he who sits obscure
In the exceeding lustre and the pure
Intense irradiation of a mind,
Which, through its own internal lightning blind,
Flags wearily through darkness and despair—
A cloud-encircled meteor of the air,
A hooded eagle among blinking owls.
You will see Hunt—one of those happy souls
Which are the salt of the earth, and without whom
This world would smell like what it is—a tomb.
1.202

19   Have you not heard
When a man marries, dies, or turns Hindoo,
His best friends hear no more of him?
1.235

20   His fine wit
Makes such a wound, the knife is lost in it. [T.L.
Peacock]
1.240

21 When the lamp is shattered
The light in the dust lies dead—
When the cloud is scattered
The rainbow's glory is shed.
When the lute is broken,
Sweet tones are remembered not;
When the lips have spoken,
Loved accents are soon forgot.
Lines: When the Lamp

22 When hearts have once mingled
Love first leaves the well-built nest;
The weak one is singled
To endure what it once possessed.
O Love! who bewailest
The frailty of things here,
Why choose you the frailest
For your cradle, your home, and your bier?

23 Beneath is spread like a green sea
The waveless plain of Lombardy,
Bounded by the vaporous air,
Islanded by cities fair;
Underneath Day's azure eyes
Ocean's nursling, Venice lies,
A peopled labyrinth of walls,
Amphitrite's destined halls.
Lines written amongst the Euganean Hills (1818), 1.90

24 Sun-girt city, thou hast been
Ocean's child, and then his queen;
Now is come a darker day,
And thou soon must be his prey.
1.115

1 The fountains mingle with the river,
      And the rivers with the ocean;
  The winds of heaven mix for ever
      With a sweet emotion;
  Nothing in the world is single;
      All things, by a law divine,
  In one another's being mingle.
      Why not I with thine?
  Love's Philosophy

2 I met Murder in the way—
  He had a mask like Castlereagh.
  The Mask of Anarchy (1819), II

3 His big tears, for he wept full well,
  Turned to mill-stones as they fell.

  And the little children, who
  Round his feet played to and fro,
  Thinking every tear a gem,
  Had their brains knocked out by them.
  IV. Of 'Fraud' (Lord Eldon)

4 Rise like Lions after slumber
  In unvanquishable number—
  Shake your chains to earth like dew
  Which in sleep had fallen on you—
  Ye are many—they are few.
  XXXVIII and XCI

5 Its horror and its beauty are divine.
  The 'Medusa' of Leonardo da Vinci

6 Nought may endure but Mutability.
  Mutability

7 I stood within the City disinterred;
  And heard the autumnal leaves like light footfalls
  Of spirits passing through the streets; and heard
  The Mountain's slumbrous voice at intervals
  Thrill through those roofless halls.
  Ode to Naples (1820), l.1

8 O wild West Wind, thou breath of Autumn's being,
  Thou, from whose unseen presence the leaves dead
  Are driven, like ghosts from an enchanter fleeing,

  Yellow, and black, and pale, and hectic red,
  Pestilence-stricken multitudes: O thou,
  Who chariotest to their dark wintry bed

  The winged seeds, where they lie cold and low,
  Each like a corpse within its grave, until
  Thine azure sister of the spring shall blow

  Her clarion o'er the dreaming earth, and fill
  (Driving sweet buds like flocks to feed in air)
  With living hues and odours plain and hill:

  Wild Spirit, which art moving everywhere;
  Destroyer and preserver; hear, oh, hear!
  Ode to the West Wind (1819), l.1

9   There are spread
  On the blue suface of thine aëry surge,
  Like the bright hair uplifted from the head

  Of some fierce Maenad, even from the dim verge
  Of the horizon to the zenith's height,
  The locks of the approaching storm.
  l.18

10 Thou who didst waken from his summer dreams
  The blue Mediterranean, where he lay,
  Lulled by the coil of his crystalline streams

  Beside a pumice isle in Baiae's bay,

And saw in sleep old palaces and towers
Quivering within the wave's intenser day,

All overgrown with azure moss and flowers
    So sweet, the sense faints picturing them.
l.29

11   Far below
The sea-blooms and the oozy woods which wear
The sapless foliage of the ocean, know

Thy voice, and suddenly grow gray with fear,
And tremble and despoil themselves.
l.38

12 If I were a dead leaf thou mightest bear;
If I were a swift cloud to fly with thee;
A wave to pant beneath thy power, and share

The impulse of thy strength, only less free
Than thou, O uncontrollable!
l.43

13 Oh, lift me as a wave, a leaf, a cloud!
I fall upon the thorns of life! I bleed!

A heavy weight of hours has chained and bowed
One too like thee: tameless, and swift, and proud.

Make me thy lyre, even as the forest is:
What if my leaves are falling like its own?
The tumult of thy mighty harmonies

Will take from both a deep, autumnal tone,
Sweet though in sadness.
l.53

14 And, by the incantation of this verse,

Scatter, as from an unextinguished hearth
Ashes and sparks, my words among mankind!
Be through my lips to unawakened earth

The trumpet of a prophecy! O, Wind,
If Winter comes, can Spring be far behind?
l.65

15 I met a traveller from an antique land
Who said: Two vast and trunkless legs of stone
Stand in the desert.
Ozymandias

16 'My name is Ozymandias, king of kings:
Look on my works, ye Mighty, and despair!'
Nothing beside remains. Round the decay
Of that colossal wreck, boundless and bare
The lone and level sands stretch far away.

17 Hell is a city much like London—
A populous and smoky city.
Peter Bell the Third (1819), pt.3. **Hell**, i

18 But from the first 'twas Peter's drift
    To be a kind of moral eunuch,
He touched the hem of Nature's shift,
    Felt faint—and never dared uplift
    The closest, all-concealing tunic.
pt.4. **Sin**, xi

19   Ere Babylon was dust,
The Magus Zoroaster, my dead child,
Met his own image walking in the garden,
That apparition, sole of men, he saw.
Prometheus Unbound (1819), I.191

20 Cruel he looks, but calm and strong,
Like one who does, not suffers wrong.
238

21 It doth repent me: words are quick and vain;

Grief for awhile is blind, and so was mine.
I wish no living thing to suffer pain.
303

1 Kingly conclaves stern and cold
Where blood with guilt is bought and sold.
530

2 The good want power, but to weep barren tears.
The powerful goodness want: worse need for them.
The wise want love; and those who love want wisdom.
625

3   Peace is in the grave.
The grave hides all things beautiful and good:
I am a God and cannot find it there.
638

4 The dust of creeds outworn.
697

5 On a poet's lips I slept
Dreaming like a love-adept
In the sound his breathing kept.
737

6 He will watch from dawn to gloom
The lake-reflected sun illume
The yellow bees in the ivy-bloom,
Nor heed, nor see, what things they be;
But from these create he can
Forms more real than living man,
Nurslings of immortality!
743

7   To be
Omnipotent but friendless is to reign.
II.iv.47

8 He gave man speech, and speech created thought,
Which is the measure of the universe.
73

9 All spirits are enslaved which serve things evil.
110

10 Fate, Time, Occasion, Chance, and Change? To these
All things are subject but eternal Love.
119

11   My soul is an enchanted boat,
      Which, like a sleeping swan, doth float
Upon the silver waves of thy sweet singing.
v.72. See 500:16

12 The loathsome mask has fallen, the man remains
Sceptreless, free, uncircumscribed, but man
Equal, unclassed, tribeless, and nationless,
Exempt from awe, worship, degree, the king
Over himself; just, gentle, wise: but man
Passionless?—no, yet free from guilt or pain,
Which were, for his will made or suffered them,
Nor yet exempt, though ruling them like slaves,
From chance, and death, and mutability,
The clogs of that which else might oversoar
The loftiest star of unascended heaven,
Pinnacled dim in the intense inane.
III.iii.193

13 Familiar acts are beautiful through love.
IV.403

14 A traveller from the cradle to the grave
Through the dim night of this immortal day.
551

15 To suffer woes which Hope thinks infinite;
To forgive wrongs darker than death or night;

To defy Power, which seems omnipotent;
To love, and bear; to hope till Hope creates
From its own wreck the thing it contemplates;
  Neither to change, nor falter, nor repent;
This, like thy glory, Titan, is to be
Good, great and joyous, beautiful and free;
This is alone Life, Joy, Empire and Victory.
570

16 That sweet bondage which is freedom's self.
Queen Mab (1813), c.9, l.76

17 I dreamed that, as I wandered by the way,
  Bare Winter suddenly was changed to Spring,
And gentle odours led my steps astray,
  Mixed with a sound of water's murmuring
Along a shelving bank of turf, which lay
  Under a copse, and hardly dared to fling
Its green arms round the bosom of the stream,
  But kissed it and then fled, as thou mightst in
    dream.
The Question

18 There grew pied wind-flowers and violets,
  Daisies, those pearled Arcturi of the earth,
The constellated flower that never sets.

19 And in the warm hedge grew lush eglantine,
  Green cowbind and the moonlight-coloured may,
And cherry-blossoms, and white cups, whose wine
  Was the bright dew, yet drained not by the day;
And wild roses, and ivy serpentine,
  With its dark buds and leaves, wandering astray;
And flowers azure, black, and streaked with gold,
  Fairer than any wakened eyes behold.

20 And nearer to the river's trembling edge
  There grew broad flag-flowers, purple, pranked with
    white,
And starry river buds among the sedge,
  And floating water-lilies, broad and bright.

21 With hue like that when some great painter dips
His pencil in the gloom of earthquake and eclipse.
The Revolt of Islam (1818), c.5. xxiii

22 A Sensitive Plant in a garden grew.
The Sensitive Plant (1820), pt.I, l.1

23 And the rose like a nymph to the bath addressed,
Which unveiled the depth of her glowing breast,
Till, fold after fold, to the fainting air
The soul of her beauty and love lay bare.
l.29

24 And the jessamine faint, and the sweet tuberose,
The sweetest flower for scent that blows.
l.37

25 Rarely, rarely, comest thou,
Spirit of Delight!
Song

26 I love all that thou lovest,
  Spirit of Delight:
The fresh Earth in new leaves dressed,
  And the starry night;
Autumn evening, and the morn
When the golden mists are born.

27 I love snow, and all the forms
Of the radiant frost.

28   Everything almost
Which is Nature's, and may be

Untainted by man's misery.

1 I love tranquil solitude,
 And such society
As is quiet, wise, and good;
 Between thee and me
What difference? but thou dost possess
The things I seek, not love them less.

2 Men of England, wherefore plough
For the lords who lay you low?
Song to the Men of England

3 The seed ye sow, another reaps;
The wealth ye find, another keeps;
The robes ye weave, another wears;
The arms ye forge, another bears.

Sow seed—but let no tyrant reap;
Find wealth—let no impostor heap;
Weave robes—let not the idle wear;
Forge arms, in your defence to bear.

4 Lift not the painted veil which those who live
Call Life.
Sonnet

5   He sought,
For his lost heart was tender, things to love,
But found them not, alas! nor was there aught
The world contains, the which he could approve.
Through the unheeding many he did move,
A splendour among shadows, a bright blot
Upon this gloomy scene, a Spirit that strove
For truth, and like the Preacher found it not.

6 An old, mad, blind, despised, and dying king.
Sonnet: England in 1819

7 Away! the moor is dark beneath the moon,
Rapid clouds have drank the last pale beam of even:
Away! the gathering winds will call the darkness soon,
And profoundest midnight shroud the serene lights of
 heaven.
Stanzas.—April 1814

8 The City's voice itself is soft like Solitude's.
Stanzas Written in Dejection, near Naples (1818)

9 I see the waves upon the shore,
Like light dissolved in star-showers, thrown.

10 Alas! I have nor hope nor health,
 Nor peace within nor calm around,
Nor that content surpassing wealth
 The sage in meditation found,
 And walked with inward glory crowned.

11 I could lie down like a tired child,
 And weep away the life of care
Which I have borne and yet must bear,
 Till death like sleep might steal on me.

12 Music, when soft voices die,
 Vibrates in the memory—
Odours, when sweet violets sicken,
 Live within the sense they quicken.

Rose leaves, when the rose is dead,
 Are heaped for the beloved's bed;
And so thy thoughts, when thou art gone,
 Love itself shall slumber on.
To—

13 One word is too often profaned
 For me to profane it,

One feeling too falsely disdained
 For thee to disdain it.
To—

14 The desire of the moth for the star,
 Of the night for the morrow,
The devotion to something afar
 From the sphere of our sorrow.

15 Hail to thee, blithe Spirit!
 Bird thou never wert,
That from Heaven, or near it,
 Pourest thy full heart
In profuse strains of unpremeditated art.
To a Skylark (1819)

16 And singing still dost soar, and soaring ever singest.

17 Like an unbodied joy whose race is just begun.

18 Thou art unseen, but yet I hear thy shrill delight.

19 Like a Poet hidden
 In the light of thought,
Singing hymns unbidden,
 Till the world is wrought
To sympathy with hopes and fears it heeded not.

20 Chorus Hymeneal,
 Or triumphal chant,
Matched with thine would be all
 But an empty vaunt,
A thing wherein we feel there is some hidden want.

21 What objects are the fountains
 Of thy happy strain?
What fields, or waves, or mountains?
 What shapes of sky or plain?
What love of thine own kind? what ignorance of pain?

22 With thy clear keen joyance
 Languor cannot be:
Shadow of annoyance
 Never came near thee:
Thou lovest—but ne'er knew love's sad satiety.

23 We look before and after;
 We pine for what is not;
Our sincerest laughter
 With some pain is fraught;
Our sweetest songs are those that tell of saddest
 thought.

24 Better than all measures
 Of delightful sound,
Better than all treasures
 That in books are found,
Thy skill to poet were, thou scorner of the ground!

Teach me half the gladness
 That thy brain must know,
Such harmonious madness
 From my lips would flow
The world should listen then—as I am listening now.

25 I am gone into the fields
To take what this sweet hour yields;—
Reflection, you may come to-morrow,
Sit by the fireside with Sorrow.—
You with the unpaid bill, Despair,—
You, tiresome verse-reciter, Care,—
I will pay you in the grave,—
Death will listen to your stave.
To Jane: The Invitation

1 Less oft is peace in Shelley's mind,
   Than calm in waters, seen.
   To Jane: The Recollection

2 Swiftly walk over the western wave,
        Spirit of Night!
   Out of the misty eastern cave,
   Where, all the long and lone daylight,
   Thou wovest dreams of joy and fear,
   Which make thee terrible and dear,—
        Swift be thy flight!
   To Night

3 Blind with thine hair the eyes of Day;
   Kiss her until she be wearied out,
   Then wander o'er city, and sea, and land,
   Touching all with thine opiate wand—
        Come, long-sought!

4 Death will come when thou art dead,
        Soon, too soon—
   Sleep will come when thou art fled;
   Of neither would I ask the boon
   I ask of thee, beloved Night—
   Swift be thine approaching flight,
        Come soon, soon!

5   Art thou pale for weariness
   Of climbing heaven, and gazing on the earth,
        Wandering companionless
   Among the stars that have a different birth,—
   And ever changing, like a joyless eye
   That finds no object worth its constancy?
   To the Moon

6 In honoured poverty thy voice did weave
   Songs consecrate to truth and liberty,—
   Deserting these, thou leavest me to grieve,
   Thus having been, that thou shouldst cease to be.
   To Wordsworth

7 And like a dying lady, lean and pale,
   Who totters forth, wrapped in a gauzy veil.
   The Waning Moon

8 A lovely lady, garmented in light
      From her own beauty.
   The Witch of Atlas (1820, pub.1824), v

9 For she was beautiful—her beauty made
   The bright world dim, and everything beside
   Seemed like the fleeting image of a shade.
   xii

10 A single word even may be a spark of inextinguishable
   thought.
   A Defence of Poetry (1821)

11 The rich have become richer, and the poor have
   become poorer; and the vessel of the state is driven
   between the Scylla and Charybdis of anarchy and
   despotism.

12 Poetry is the record of the best and happiest moments
   of the happiest and best minds.

13 Poets are...the trumpets which sing to battle and feel
   not what they inspire...Poets are the unacknowledged
   legislators of the world.
   See 282:7

14 When it was a matter of wonder how Keats, who was
   ignorant of Greek, could have written his 'Hyperion',
   Shelley, whom envy never touched, gave as a reason,

'Because he *was* a Greek'.
W.S. Landor, *Imaginary Conversations. Southey and Landor,* ii

WILLIAM SHENSTONE 1714–1763

15 Whoe'er has travell'd life's dull round,
        Where'er his stages may have been,
   May sigh to think he still has found
        The warmest welcome, at an inn.
   At an Inn at Henley

16 Laws are generally found to be nets of such a texture,
   as the little creep through, the great break through, and
   the middle-sized are alone entangled in.
   Essays on Men, Manners, and Things (vol.ii of **Works,**
   1764-9), **On Politics.** See 512:23

17 A Fool and his words are soon parted; a man of genius
   and his money.
   On Reserve

PHILIP HENRY SHERIDAN 1831–1888

18 The only good Indian is a dead Indian.
   Attr., at Fort Cobb, Jan. 1869

RICHARD BRINSLEY SHERIDAN 1751–1816

19 Not a translation—only *taken from the French*.
   The Critic (1779), I.i

20 The newspapers! Sir, they are the most
   villainous—licentious—abominable—infernal—Not
   that I ever read them—no—I make it a rule never to
   look into a newspaper.

21 If it is abuse—why one is always sure to hear of it from
   one damned good-natured friend or other!

22 Egad, I think the interpreter is the hardest to be
   understood of the two!
   ii

23 Yes, sir, puffing is of various sorts; the principal are,
   the puff direct, the puff preliminary, the puff
   collateral, the puff collusive, and the puff oblique, or
   puff by implication.

24 No scandal about Queen Elizabeth, I hope?
   II.i

25 I open with a clock striking, to beget an awful
   attention in the audience: it also marks the time, which
   is four o'clock in the morning, and saves a description
   of the rising sun, and a great deal about gilding the
   eastern hemisphere.
   ii

26 Inconsolable to the minuet in Ariadne!

27 The Spanish fleet thou *canst* not see because—
   It is not yet in sight!

28 All that can be said is, that two people happened to hit
   on the same thought—and Shakespeare made use of it
   first, that's all.
   III.i

29 *Burleigh comes forward, shakes his head, and exit.*
   Sneer: He is very perfect indeed. Now pray, what did
   he mean by that?
   Puff: Why, by that shake of the head, he gave you to
   understand that even though they had more justice in
   their cause and wisdom in their measures, yet, if there
   was not a greater spirit shown on the part of the
   people, the country would at last fall a sacrifice to the

hostile ambition of the Spanish monarchy.
Sneer: The devil!—did he mean all that by shaking his head?
Puff: Every word of it. If he shook his head as I taught him.

1 *Whiskerandos:* And Whiskerandos quits this bustling scene
For all eter—
Beefeater: —nity—he would have added, but stern death
Cut short his being, and the noun at once!

2 I wish sir, you would practise this without me. I can't stay dying here all night.

3 O Lord, sir, when a heroine goes mad she always goes into white satin.

4 An oyster may be crossed in love.

5 I was struck all of a heap.
The Duenna (1775), II.ii

6 Conscience has no more to do with gallantry than it has with politics.
iv

7 The throne *we* honour is the *people's choice.*
Pizarro (1799), II.i

8 Illiterate him, I say, quite from your memory.
The Rivals (1775), I.ii

9 'Tis safest in matrimony to begin with a little aversion.

10 Madam, a circulating library in a town is as an evergreen tree of diabolical knowledge! It blossoms through the year! And depend on it, Mrs Malaprop, that they who are so fond of handling the leaves, will long for the fruit at last.

11 You gentlemen's gentlemen are so hasty.
II.ii

12 He is the very pine-apple of politeness!
III.iii

13 An aspersion upon my parts of speech!

14 If I reprehend any thing in this world, it is the use of my oracular tongue, and a nice derangement of epitaphs!

15 She's as headstrong as an allegory on the banks of the Nile.

16 Too civil by half.
iv

17 Our ancestors are very good kind of folks; but they are the last people I should choose to have a visiting acquaintance with.
IV.i

18 No caparisons, miss, if you please. Caparisons don't become a young woman.
ii

19 You are not like Cerberus, three gentlemen at once, are you?

20 The quarrel is a very pretty quarrel as it stands; we should only spoil it by trying to explain it.
iii

21 There's nothing like being used to a thing.
V.iii

22 My valour is certainly going!—it is sneaking off! I feel it oozing out as it were at the palms of my hands!

23 I own the soft impeachment.

24 Thro' all the drama—whether damned or not—
Love gilds the scene, and women guide the plot.
Epilogue

25 Tale-bearers are as bad as the tale-makers.
The School for Scandal (1777), I.i

26 You shall see them on a beautiful quarto page, where a neat rivulet of text shall meander through a meadow of margin.

27 You had no taste when you married me.
ii

28 *Mrs. Candour:* I'll swear her colour is natural: I have seen it come and go.
Lady Teazle: I dare swear you have ma'am; it goes off at night, and comes again in the morning.
II.ii

29 Here is the whole set! a character dead at every word.

30 I'm called away by particular business. But I leave my character behind me.

31 Here's to the maiden of bashful fifteen;
        Here's to the widow of fifty;
Here's to the flaunting, extravagant quean;
        And here's to the housewife that's thrifty.
                Let the toast pass,—
                Drink to the lass,
I'll warrant she'll prove an excuse for the glass.
III.iii. Song

32 Here's to the charmer whose dimples we prize;
        Now to the maid who has none, sir;
Here's to the girl with a pair of blue eyes,
        And here's to the nymph with but one, sir.

33 An unforgiving eye, and a damned disinheriting countenance.
IV.i

34 *Rowley:* I believe there is no sentiment he has such faith in as that 'charity begins at home'.
Sir Oliver Surface: And his, I presume, is of that domestic sort which never stirs abroad at all.
V.i

35 There is no trusting appearances.
ii

36 The Right Honourable gentleman is indebted to his memory for his jests, and to his imagination for his facts.
Speech in Reply to Mr. Dundas. T. Moore, *Life of Sheridan* (1825), II.471

37 You write with ease, to show your breeding,
But easy writing's vile hard reading.
Clio's Protest. See T. Moore, *Life of Sheridan*, I.55

38 A man may surely be allowed to take a glass of wine by his own fireside.
On being encountered drinking a glass of wine in the street, while watching his theatre, the Drury Lane, burn down. II.20

39 Won't you come into the garden? I would like my roses to see you.
To a young lady. Attr. in *The Perfect Hostess*

GENERAL SHERMAN 1820–1891

40 There is many a boy here to-day who looks on war as all glory, but, boys, it is all hell.
Speech, Columbus, Ohio, 11 Aug. 1880. Lewis, *Sherman, Fighting Prophet*

1 I will not accept if nominated, and will not serve if
elected.
*Telegram to General Henderson on being urged to stand as
Republican candidate in the U.S. Presidential election of 1884.
Memoirs,* 4th edition (to which his children had added a new
chapter, XXVII, in which this text appears as the memory of
Sherman's son who was present at its drafting).

JAMES SHIRLEY 1596–1666

2 The glories of our blood and state
    Are shadows, not substantial things;
There is no armour against fate;
    Death lays his icy hand on kings:
        Sceptre and crown
        Must tumble down,
And in the dust be equal made
With the poor crooked scythe and spade.
The Contention of Ajax and Ulysses (1659), I.iii

3 The garlands wither on your brow;
    Then boast no more your mighty deeds!

4 Only the actions of the just
Smell sweet, and blossom in their dust.

5 I presume you're mortal, and may err.
The Lady of Pleasure (1635), II.ii

6   How little room
Do we take up in death, that, living know
No bounds?
The Wedding, (1626), IV.iv

THE SHORTER CATECHISM

7 'What is the chief end of man?'
'To glorify God and to enjoy him for ever'

J.H. SHORTHOUSE 1834–1903

8 'The Church of England,' I said, seeing that Mr
Inglesant paused, 'is no doubt a compromise.'
John Inglesant (1880), ch.40

9 In all probability 'Wordsworth's standard of
intoxication was miserably low'
*Remark to some Wordsworthians who were deploring W.'s
confession that he got drunk at Cambridge. G.W.E. Russell,
Collections and Recollections,* ch.8

HENRY SIDGWICK 1838–1900

10 We think so because other people all think so,
Or because—or because—after all we do think so,
Or because we were told so, and think we must think
    so,
Or because we once thought so, and think we still
    think so,
Or because having thought so, we think we *will* think
    so.
Arthur Sidgwick and Mrs. E.M. Sidgwick, Henry Sidgwick
(1906), end of ch.11

ALGERNON SIDNEY 1622–1683

11 Liars ought to have good memories.
Discourses concerning Government (1698), ch.II, xv

12 Men lived like fishes; the great ones devour'd the
small.
xviii

13 'Tis not necessary to light a candle to the sun.
xxiii

SIR PHILIP SIDNEY 1554–1586

14 Shallow brooks murmur most, deep silent slide away.
The Arcadia (1590), bk.i, **First Eclogues, Lalus and Dorus,**
st.ii

15 Who shoots at the mid-day sun, though he be sure he
shall never hit the mark; yet as sure he is he shall
shoot higher than who aims but at a bush.
bk.ii

16 My true love hath my heart and I have his,
By just exchange one for the other giv'n;
I hold his dear, and mine he cannot miss,
There never was a better bargain driv'n.
bk.iii

17 Biting my truant pen, beating myself for spite,
'Fool,' said my Muse to me, 'look in thy heart and
    write'.
Astrophel and Stella (1591), Sonnet 1

18 With how sad steps, O Moon, thou climb'st the skies!
How silently, and with how wan a face!
What! may it be that even in heavenly place
That busy archer his sharp arrows tries?
Sonnet 31

19 Do they call virtue there ungratefulness?

20 Come, Sleep! O Sleep, the certain knot of peace,
    The baiting-place of wit, the balm of woe,
The poor man's wealth, the prisoner's release,
    Th' indifferent judge between the high and low.
Sonnet 39

21 Take thou of me smooth pillows, sweetest bed;
    A chamber deaf to noise and blind to light,
A rosy garland and a weary head.

22 That sweet enemy, France.
Sonnet 41

23 They love indeed who quake to say they love.
Sonnet 54

24 Doubt you to whom my Muse these notes intendeth,
    Which now my breast o'ercharged to music lendeth?
To you, to you, all song of praise is due;
    Only in you my song begins and endeth.
First song

25 Oh heav'nly fool, thy most kiss-worthy face
Anger invests with such a lovely grace,
That Anger's self I needs must kiss again.
Sonnet 73

26 I never drank of Aganippe well,
    Nor ever did in shade of Tempe sit,
And Muses scorn with vulgar brains to dwell;
    Poor layman I, for sacred rites unfit...
I am no pick-purse of another's wit.
Sonnet 74

27 Highway, since you my chief Parnassus be,
    And that my Muse, to some ears not unsweet,
Tempers her words to trampling horses' feet
    More oft than to a chamber melody,
Now blessed you, bear onward blessed me
    To her, where I my heart, safe-left, shall meet.
Sonnet 84

28 Leave me, O Love, which reacheth but to dust;
    And thou, my mind, aspire to higher things;

Grow rich in that which never taketh rust;
    Whatever fades, but fading pleasure brings.
Certain Sonnets

1 O fair! O sweet! When I do look on thee,
    In whom all joys so well agree,
Heart and soul do sing in me,
    Just accord all music makes.
To the Tune of a Spanish Song

2 With a tale forsooth he cometh unto you, with a tale
which holdeth children from play, and old men from
the chimney corner. [The poet.]
Defence of Poesie (1579-80, pub. 1595)

3 Certainly I must confess mine own barbarousness, I
never heard the old song of Percy and Douglas, that I
found not my heart moved more than with a trumpet.

4 Philip of Macedon reckoned a horse-race won at
Olympus among his three fearful felicities.

5 I will not wish unto you the ass's ears of Midas, nor to
be driven by a poet's verses, as Bubonax was, to hang
himself, nor to be rhymed to death, as is said to be
done in Ireland.

6 Thy necessity is yet greater than mine.
On giving his water-bottle to a dying soldier on the battle-field of
Zutphen, 1586. Sir Fulke Greville, *Life* (1652). The word
'necessity' is more often quoted as 'need'

ABBÉ EMMANUEL JOSEPH SIEYÈS 1748-1836

7 *La mort, sans phrases.*
Death, without rhetoric.
Attr. to Sieyès on voting in the French Convention for the death of
Louis XVI, 19 Jan. 1793. Afterwards repudiated by him

8 *J'ai vécu.*
I survived.
When asked what he had done during the French Revolution. V.
Mignet, 'Notice Historique sur la Vie et les Travaux de M. le
Comte de Sieyès'. *Recueil des Lectures...28 Déc. 1836.* He
afterwards stated he could not recall having said it.

SIMONIDES c.556–468 B.C.

9 ὦ ξεῖν', ἀγγέλλειν Λακεδαιμονίοις ὅτι τῆδε
    κείμεθα τοῖς κείνων ῥήμασι πειθόμενοι.

Go, tell the Spartans, thou who passest by,
    That here obedient to their laws we lie.
Herodotus, *Histories*, vii, 228.

GEORGE R. SIMS 1847–1922

10 It is Christmas Day in the Workhouse.
The Dagonet and Other Poems (1903)

EDITH SITWELL 1887–1964

11 Jane Jane
    Tall as a crane
    The morning light creaks down again.
Aubade

12 Daisy and Lily
Lazy and silly
Walk by the shore of the wan grassy sea
Talking once more 'neath a swan-bosomed tree.
Façade. Waltz

13 Still falls the Rain—
Dark as the world of man, black as our loss—

Blind as the nineteen hundred and forty nails
Upon the Cross.
The Raids 1940. Still falls the Rain

SIR OSBERT SITWELL 1892–1969

14 The British Bourgeoisie
Is not born,
And does not die,
But, if it is ill,
It has a frightened look in its eyes.
At the House of Mrs. Kinfoot

15 *Educ:* during the holidays from Eton.
Who's Who

JOHN SKELTON 1460?–1529

16 Far may be sought
Erst ye can find
So courteous, so kind,
As Merry Margaret, the midsummer flower,
Gentle as falcon or hawk of the tower.
To Mistress Margaret Hussey

17 With solace and gladness,
Much mirth and no madness,
All good and no badness;
So joyously,
So maidenly,
So womanly,
Her demeaning.

18 She is the violet,
The daisy delectable,
The columbine commendable,
The jelofer amiable;
For this most goodly flower,
This blossom of fresh colour,
So Jupiter me succour,
She flourisheth new and new
In beauty and virtue.
The Commendations of Mistress Jane Scrope

19 For the soul of Philip Sparrow,
That was late slain at Carrow
Among the Nunnes Black,
For that sweet soul's sake
And for all sparrows' souls
Set in our bead-rolls,
Pater noster qui
With an *Ave Mari.*
The Sparrow's Dirge

B.F. SKINNER 1904–

20 Education is what survives when what has been learnt
has been forgotten.
Education in 1984. *New Scientist,* 21 May 1964, p.484

CHRISTOPHER SMART 1722–1771

21 For I will consider my Cat Jeoffry.
For he is the servant of the Living God, duly and daily
    serving Him.
Jubilate Agno, XIX.51

22 For he counteracts the powers of darkness by his
    electrical skin and glaring eyes,
For he counteracts the Devil, who is death, by brisking

about the Life.
XX.15

1 He sung of God—the mighty source
Of all things—the stupendous force
    On which all strength depends;
From whose right arm, beneath whose eyes,
All period, pow'r, and enterprize
    Commences, reigns, and ends.
Song to David (1763), st.18

2 For Adoration all the ranks
Of angels yield eternal thanks,
    And David in the midst.
st.51

3 Strong is the horse upon his speed;
Strong in pursuit the rapid glede,
    Which makes at once his game:
Strong the tall ostrich on the ground;
Strong thro' the turbulent profound
    Shoots xiphias to his aim.

Strong is the lion—like a coal
His eye-ball—like a bastion's mole
    His chest against his foes:
Strong, the gier-eagle on his sail,
Strong against tide, th' enormous whale
    Emerges as he goes.

Where ask is have, where seek is find,
    Where knock is open wide.
st.75

4 Glorious the sun in mid-career;
Glorious th' assembled fires appear;
    Glorious the comet's train:
Glorious the trumpet and alarm;
Glorious th' almighty stretch'd-out arm;
    Glorious th' enraptur'd main.

Glorious the northern lights astream;
Glorious the song, when God's the theme;
    Glorious the thunder's roar:
Glorious hosanna from the den;
Glorious the catholic amen;
    Glorious the martyr's gore.

Glorious—more glorious is the crown
Of Him that brought salvation down
    By meekness, call'd thy Son;
Thou that stupendous truth believ'd,
And now the matchless deed's achiev'd,
    Determined, dared, and done.
st.84

SAMUEL SMILES 1812–1904

5 His [Dr. Priestley's] appointment [to act as astronomer to Captain Cook's expedition to the southern seas] had been cancelled, as the Board of Longitude objected to his theology.
Men of Invention and Industry (1904), ch.3

6 Cecil's despatch of business was extraordinary, his maxim being, 'The shortest way to do many things is to do only one thing at once.'
Self-Help (1859), ch.9

7 A place for everything, and everything in its place.
Thrift (1875), ch.5

ADAM SMITH 1723–1790

8 And thus, *Place*, that great object which divides the wives of aldermen, is the end of half the labours of human life; and is the cause of all the tumult and bustle, all the rapine and injustice, which avarice and ambition have introduced into this world.
The Theory of Moral Sentiments, I.iii.2.8

9 The rich only select from the heap what is most precious and agreeable. They consume little more than the poor, and in spite of their natural selfishness and rapacity...they divide with the poor the produce of all their improvements. They are led by an invisible hand to make nearly the same distribution of the necessaries of life which would have been made, had the earth been divided into equal portions among all its inhabitants.
IV.i.10

10 People of the same trade seldom meet together, even for merriment and diversion, but the conversation ends in a conspiracy against the public, or in some contrivance to raise prices.
Wealth of Nations (ed. Todd, 1976), I.x.c.27

11 With the greater part of rich people, the chief enjoyment of riches consists in the parade of riches, which in their eyes is never so complete as when they appear to possess those decisive marks of opulence which nobody can possess but themselves.
xi.c.31

12 To found a great empire for the sole purpose of raising up a people of customers, may at first sight appear a project fit only for a nation of shopkeepers. It is, however, a project altogether unfit for a nation of shopkeepers; but extremely fit for a nation whose government is influenced by shopkeepers.
IV.vii.c.63. See 1:9, 359:15

13 It is the interest of every man to live as much at his ease as he can; and if his emoluments are to be precisely the same, whether he does, or does not perform some very laborious duty, it is certainly his interest, at least as interest is vulgarly understood, either to neglect it altogether, or, if he is subject to some authority which will not suffer him to do this, to perform it in as careless and slovenly a manner as that authority will permit.
V.i.f.7

14 The discipline of colleges and universities is in general contrived, not for the benefit of the students, but for the interest, or more properly speaking, for the ease of the masters.
15

15 There is no art which one government sooner learns of another than that of draining money from the pockets of the people.
ii. h. 12

16 Without a union with Great Britain, the inhabitants of Ireland are not likely for many ages to consider themselves as one people.
iii.89

17 If any of the provinces of the British empire cannot be made to contribute towards the support of the whole empire, it is surely time that Great Britain should free herself from the expense of defending those provinces in time of war, and of supporting any part of their civil or military establishments in time of peace, and endeavour to accommodate her future views and designs to the real mediocrity of her circumstances. 92

1 Be assured, my young friend, that there is a great deal of *ruin* in a nation.
Correspondence of Sir John Sinclair (1831), i.390-91

ALEXANDER SMITH 1830–1867

2 Like a pale martyr in his shirt of fire.
A Life Drama (1853), ii

ALFRED EMANUEL SMITH 1873–1944

3 No matter how thin you slice it, it's still baloney.
Speech, 1936

4 The kiss of death.
Speech, 1926, referring to William Randolph Hearst's support of Ogden Mills

F.E. SMITH
see BIRKENHEAD

JAMES SMITH 1775–1839
and 'HORACE' [HORATIO] SMITH 1779–1849

5 In Craven-street, Strand, ten attorneys find place,
And ten dark coal-barges are moor'd at its base.
Fly, honesty, fly! seek some safer retreat;
For there's craft in the river, and craft in the street.
Craven Street, Strand

6 Hail, glorious edifice, stupendous work!
God bless the Regent and the Duke of York!
Rejected Addresses (1812). No.1. **Loyal Effusion**, l.1

7 Who makes the quartern loaf and Luddites rise?
Who fills the butcher's shops with large blue flies?
l.48

8 What stately vision mocks my waking sense?
Hence, dear delusion, sweet enchantment, hence!
No.3. **An Address Without a Phoenix**

9 In the name of the Prophet—figs!
No.10. **Johnson's Ghost**

LANGDON SMITH 1858–1918

10 When you were a tadpole, and I was a fish,
In the Palaeozoic time,
And side by side in the ebbing tide
We sprawled through the ooze and slime.
A Toast to a Lady. (*The Scrap-Book,* April 1906)

LOGAN PEARSALL SMITH 1865–1946

11 There are two things to aim at in life: first, to get what you want; and after that, to enjoy it. Only the wisest of mankind achieve the second.
Afterthoughts (1931), ch.1. **Life and Human Nature**

12 There are few sorrows, however poignant, in which a good income is of no avail.

13 There is more felicity on the far side of baldness than young men can possibly imagine.
ch.2. **Age and Death**

14 Most people sell their souls, and live with a good conscience on the proceeds.
ch.3. **Other People**

15 When people come and talk to you of their aspirations, before they leave you had better count your spoons.
See 207:8, 275:1

16 Married women are kept women, and they are beginning to find it out.

17 It is the wretchedness of being rich that you have to live with rich people.
ch.4. **In the World**

18 Eat with the rich, but go to the play with the poor, who are capable of joy.
See 355:7

19 To suppose, as we all suppose, that we could be rich and not behave as the rich behave, is like supposing that we could drink all day and keep absolutely sober.

20 A best-seller is the gilded tomb of a mediocre talent.
ch.5. **Art and Letters**

21 People say that life is the thing, but I prefer reading.
ch.6. **Myself**

22 The old know what they want; the young are sad and bewildered.
Last Words (1933)

23 Thank heavens, the sun has gone in, and I don't have to go out and enjoy it.

SAMUEL FRANCIS SMITH 1808–1895

24 My country, 'tis of thee,
Sweet land of liberty,
    Of thee I sing:
Land where my fathers died,
Land of the pilgrims' pride,
From every mountain-side
    Let freedom ring.
America (1831)

STEVIE SMITH 1902–1971

25 Oh I am a cat that likes to
Gallop about doing good.
The Galloping Cat

26 Nobody heard him, the dead man,
But still he lay moaning:
I was much further out than you thought
And not waving but drowning.
Not Waving But Drowning

27 This Englishwoman is so refined
She has no bosom and no behind.
This Englishwoman

REVD. SYDNEY SMITH 1771–1845

28 It requires a surgical operation to get a joke well into a Scotch understanding. Their only idea of wit…is laughing immoderately at stated intervals.
Lady Holland, *Memoir* (1st ed. 1855), vol.I, ch.2, p.15

29 I heard him [Jeffrey] speak disrespectfully of the Equator!
p.17

30 That knuckle-end of England—that land of Calvin, oat-cakes, and sulphur.

31 Take short views, hope for the best, and trust in God.
ch.6, p.48

1 Looked as if she had walked straight out of the Ark.
ch.7, p.157

2 No furniture so charming as books.
ch.9, p.240

3 Madam, I have been looking for a person who disliked gravy all my life; let us swear eternal friendship.
p.257

4 How can a bishop marry? How can he flirt? The most he can say is, 'I will see you in the vestry after service.'
p.258

5 Not body enough to cover his mind decently with; his intellect is improperly exposed.

6 I have, alas, only one illusion left, and that is the Archbishop of Canterbury.
p.259

7 You find people ready enough to do the Samaritan, without the oil and twopence.
p.261

8 As the French say, there are three sexes—men, women, and clergymen.
p.262

9 Praise is the best diet for us, after all.
p.265

10 Daniel Webster struck me much like a steam-engine in trousers.
p.267

11 My definition of marriage:...it resembles a pair of shears, so joined that they cannot be separated; often moving in opposite directions, yet always punishing anyone who comes between them.
ch.11, p.363

12 He [Macaulay] is like a book in breeches.

13 He [Macaulay] has occasional flashes of silence, that make his conversation perfectly delightful.

14 Let onion atoms lurk within the bowl,
And, scarce-suspected, animate the whole.
Recipe for Salad, p.373

15 Serenely full, the epicure would say,
Fate cannot harm me, I have dined to-day.

16 Deserves to be preached to death by wild curates.
p.384

17 I never read a book before reviewing it; it prejudices a man so.
H. Pearson, *The Smith of Smiths* (1934), ch.iii, p.54

18 It is a place with only one post a day...In the country I always fear that creation will expire before tea-time.
ch.5, p.92

19 Minorities...are almost always in the right.
ch.9, p.220

20 —'s idea of heaven is, eating *pâtés de foie gras* to the sound of trumpets.
ch.10, p.236

21 What a pity it is that we have no amusements in England but vice and religion!

22 Let the Dean and Canons lay their heads together and the thing will be done. (It being proposed to surround St Paul's with a wooden pavement.)
p.237

23 Death must be distinguished from dying, with which it is often confused.
ch.11, p.271

24 The only way to deal with such a man as O'Connell is to hang him up and erect a statue to him under the gallows.
p.272

25 What two ideas are more inseparable than Beer and Britannia?

26 I am just going to pray for you at St Paul's, but with no very lively hope of success.
ch.13, p.308

27 Poverty is no disgrace to a man, but it is confoundedly inconvenient.
His Wit and Wisdom (1900), p.89

28 One of the greatest pleasures of life is conversation.
Essays (1877). **Female Education,** p.103

29 This great spectacle of human happiness.
Waterton's Wanderings, p.465

30 The moment the very name of Ireland is mentioned, the English seem to bid adieu to common feeling, common prudence, and common sense, and to act with the barbarity of tyrants, and the fatuity of idiots.
Peter Plymley's Letters (1929), p.9

31 A Curate—there is something which excites compassion in the very name of a Curate!!!
p.127. **Persecuting Bishops**

32 Dame Partington...was seen...with mop and pattens...vigorously pushing away the Atlantic Ocean. The Atlantic Ocean beat Mrs Partington.
p.228

33 Bishop Berkeley destroyed this world in one volume octavo; and nothing remained, after his time, but mind; which experienced a similar fate from the hand of Mr Hume in 1739.
Sketches of Moral Philosophy. Introd.

34 We shall generally find that the triangular person has got into the square hole, the oblong into the triangular, and a square person has squeezed himself into the round hole. The officer and the office, the doer and the thing done, seldom fit so exactly that we can say they were almost made for each other.
Lect.ix

35 I never could find any man who could think for two minutes together.
Lect.xix

36 The motto I proposed for the [*Edinburgh*] *Review* was: *Tenui musam meditamur avena*—'We cultivate literature upon a little oatmeal.'
Works (1859), vol.i, Preface, p.v

37 We can inform Jonathan what are the inevitable consequences of being too fond of glory;—Taxes upon every article which enters into the mouth, or covers the back, or is placed under the foot...taxes on everything on earth, and the waters under the earth.
vol.i. **Review of Seybert's** *Statistical Annals of the United States,* p.291

38 The schoolboy whips his taxed top—the beardless youth manages his taxed horse, with a taxed bridle, on a taxed road;—and the dying Englishman, pouring his medicine, which has paid seven per cent, into a spoon that has paid fifteen per cent—flings himself back upon his chintz bed, which has paid twenty-two per cent—and expires in the arms of an apothecary who has paid a licence of a hundred pounds for the privilege of putting him to death.

1 What bishops like best in their clergy is a dropping-down-deadness of manner.
vol.ii, **First Letter to Archdeacon Singleton**, p.271. Note

2 There is not a better man in England than Lord John Russell; but his worst failure is, that he is utterly ignorant of all moral fear; there is nothing he would not undertake. I believe he would perform the operation for the stone—build St Peter's—or assume (with or without ten minutes' notice) the command of the Channel Fleet; and no one would discover by his manner that the patient had died—the church tumbled down—and the Channel Fleet been knocked to atoms.
Second letter to Archdeacon Singleton, 1838, p.275

3 I like, my dear Lord, the road you are travelling, but I don't like the pace you are driving; too similar to that of the son of Nimshi. I always feel myself inclined to cry out, Gently, John, gently down hill. Put on the drag.
Letter to Lord John Russell, p.300

4 Where etiquette prevents me from doing things disagreeable to myself, I am a perfect martinet.
Letters. To Lady Holland, 6 Nov. 1842

5 I look upon Switzerland as an inferior sort of Scotland.
To Lord Holland, 1815

6 Tory and Whig in turns shall be my host,
I taste no politics in boil'd and roast.
To John Murray. Nov. 1834

7 What would life be without arithmetic, but a scene of horrors?
To Miss —, 22 July 1835

8 I am convinced digestion is the great secret of life.
To Arthur Kinglake, 30 Sept. 1837

9 I have no relish for the country; it is a kind of healthy grave.
To Miss G. Harcourt, 1838

10 I have seen nobody since I saw you, but persons in orders. My only varieties are vicars, rectors, curates, and every now and then (by way of turbot) an archdeacon.
To Miss Berry, 28 Jan. 1843

11 Science is his forte, and omniscience his foible.
[William Whewell.]
Isaac Todhunter, *William Whewell* (1876), i.410

TOBIAS SMOLLETT 1721–1771

12 I think for my part one half of the nation is mad—and the other not very sound.
The Adventures of Sir Launcelot Greaves (1760–2), ch.6

13 He was formed for the ruin of our sex.
Roderick Random (1748), ch.22

14 That great Cham of literature, Samuel Johnson.
Letter to John Wilkes, 16 Mar. 1759. Boswell's *Johnson* (1934), vol.i, p.348

C.P. SNOW 1905–

15 The official world, the corridors of power, the dilemmas of conscience and egotism—she disliked

them all.
Homecomings (1956), ch.22. See also ch.14 'those powerful anonymous *couloirs*'. Snow used the phrase as the title of a subsequent novel: *Corridors of Power* (1964).

16 A good many times I have been present at gatherings of people who, by the standards of the traditional culture, are thought highly educated and who have with considerable gusto been expressing their incredulity at the illiteracy of scientists. Once or twice I have been provoked and have asked the company how many of them could describe the Second Law of Thermodynamics. The response was cold: it was also negative.
The Two Cultures, Rede Lecture, 1959, ch.1

SOCRATES 469–399 B.C.

17 ὁ δὲ ἀνεξέταστος βίος οὐ βιωτὸς ἀνθρώπῳ.
The unexamined life is not worth living.
Plato, *Apology*, 38a

18 But already it is time to depart, for me to die, for you to go on living; which of us takes the better course, is concealed from anyone except God.
42a

19 A man should feel confident concerning his soul, who has renounced those pleasures and fineries that go with the body, as being alien to him, and considering them to result more in harm than in good, but has pursued the pleasures that go with learning and made the soul fine with no alien but rather its own proper refinements, moderation and justice and courage and freedom and truth; thus it is ready for the journey to the world below.
Plato, *Phaedo*, 114d

20 'What do you say about pouring a libation to some god from this cup? Is it allowed or not?'
'We only prepare just the right amount to drink, Socrates,' he said [the jailor.]
'I understand,' he went on; 'but it is allowed and necessary to pray to the gods, that my moving from hence to there may be blessed; thus I pray, and so be it.'
117b

21 ὦ Κρίτων, τῷ Ἀσκληπιῷ ὀφείλομεν ἀλεκτρυόνα. ἀλλὰ ἀπόδοτε καὶ μὴ ἀμελήσητε.
Crito, we owe a cock to Aesculapius; please pay it and don't let it pass.
118. Last words

22 πόσων ἐγὼ χρείαν οὐκ ἔχω.
How many things I can do without!
On looking at a multitude of wares exposed for sale. Diogenes Laertius, *Lives of the Eminent Philosophers*, II.25

SOLON c.630–c.555 B.C.

23 Laws are like spider's webs: if some poor weak creature come up against them, it is caught; but a bigger one can break through and get away.
Diogenes Laertius, *Lives of the Eminent Philosophers*, I.58

24 γηράσκω δ' αἰεὶ πολλὰ διδασκόμενος.
I grow old ever learning many things.
Poetae Lyrici Graeci (ed. Bergk), Solon, 18

25 πρὶν δ' ἂν τελευτήσῃ, ἐπισχεῖν μηδὲ καλέειν κω ὄλβιον, ἀλλ' εὐτυχέα.
Call no man happy till he dies, he is at best but

fortunate.
Herodotus, *Histories*, i.32

ALEXANDER SOLZHENITSYN 1918–

1 The salvation of mankind lies only in making
everything the concern of all.
Nobel Lecture, 1970

WILLIAM SOMERVILLE 1675–1742

2   My hoarse-sounding horn
Invites thee to the chase, the sport of kings;
Image of war, without its guilt.
The Chace (1735), bk.i, l.13. See 172:7

3 Hail, happy Britain! highly favoured isle,
And Heaven's peculiar care!
l.84

SOPHOCLES 496–406 B.C.

4 ὦ παῖ, γένοιο πατρὸς εὐτυχέστερος.
My son, may you be happier than your father.
Ajax, 550

5 ἐχθρῶν ἄδωρα δῶρα κοὐκ ὀνήσιμα.
Enemies' gifts are no gifts and do no good.
665

6 θεοῖς τέθνηκεν οὗτος, οὐ κείνοισιν, οὔ.
His death concerns the gods, not those men, no!
970. Of Ajax's enemies, the Greek leaders

7 πολλὰ τὰ δεινὰ κοὐδὲν ἀν-
θρώπου δεινότερον πέλει.
There are many wonderful things, and nothing is more
   wonderful than man.
Antigone, 332

8 μὴ φῦναι τὸν ἅπαντα νι-
κᾷ λόγον.
Not to be born is, past all prizing, best.
Oedipus Coloneus, 1224. Tr. R.W. Jebb

9 "πῶς," ἔφη, "ὦ Σοφόκλεις, ἔχεις πρὸς τἀφροδίσια;
ἔτι οἷός τε εἶ γυναικὶ συγγίγνεσθαι;" καὶ ὅς,
"εὐφήμει," ἔφη, "ὦ ἄνθρωπε. ἀσμενέστατα μέντοι
αὐτὸ ἀπέφυγον, ὥσπερ λυττῶντά τινα καὶ ἄγριον
δεσπότην ἀποδράς."

Someone asked Sophocles, 'How do you feel now
about sex? Are you still able to have a woman?' He
replied, 'Hush, man; most gladly indeed am I rid of it
all, as though I had escaped from a mad and savage
master.'
Plato, *Republic*, I, 329b

CHARLES HAMILTON SORLEY 1895–1915

10 We swing ungirded hips,
And lightened are our eyes,
The rain is on our lips,
We do not run for prize.
The Song of the Ungirt Runners

JOHN L.B. SOULE 1815–1891

11 Go West, young man, go West!
Editorial, *Terre Haute* (Indiana) *Express* (1851). See 235:26

REVD. ROBERT SOUTH 1634–1716

12 An Aristotle was but the rubbish of an Adam, and
Athens but the rudiments of Paradise.
Sermons, vol.I.ii

THOMAS SOUTHERNE 1660–1746

13   And when we're worn,
Hack'd hewn with constant service, thrown aside
To rust in peace, or rot in hospitals.
The Loyal Brother (1682), Act I

ROBERT SOUTHEY 1774–1843
See also under Coleridge

14 It was a summer evening,
   Old Kaspar's work was done,
And he before his cottage door
   Was sitting in the sun,
And by him sported on the green
His little grandchild Wilhelmine.
The Battle of Blenheim

15 He came to ask what he had found,
That was so large, and smooth, and round.

16 Now tell us all about the war,
And what they fought each other for.

17 But what they fought each other for,
   I could not well make out.

18 But things like that, you know, must be
   At every famous victory.

19 Great praise the Duke of Marlbro' won,
   And our good Prince Eugene.

20 'And everybody praised the Duke,
   Who this great fight did win.'
'But what good came of it at last?'
   Quoth little Peterkin.
'Why that I cannot tell,' said he,
'But 'twas a famous victory.'

21 My name is Death: the last best friend am I.
Carmen Nuptiale. The Lay of the Laureate. The Dream,
lxxxvii

22 And this way the water comes down at Lodore.
The Cataract of Lodore

23 Curses are like young chickens, they always come
   home to roost.
The Curse of Kehama (1810). Motto

24 And Sleep shall obey me,
   And visit thee never,
And the Curse shall be on thee
   For ever and ever.
II.14

25 Hark! at the Golden Palaces
The Brahmin strikes the hour.
V.1

26 They sin who tell us love can die.
With life all other passions fly,
   All others are but vanity.
X.10

27 Thou hast been call'd, O Sleep! the friend of Woe,
But 'tis the happy who have called thee so.
XV.12

28 No stir in the air, no stir in the sea,

The ship was still as she could be.
The Inchcape Rock

1 And then they knew the perilous rock,
And blest the Abbot of Aberbrothok.

2 O Christ! It is the Inchcape Rock!

3 Sir Ralph the Rover tore his hair;
He curst himself in his despair.

4 Blue, darkly, deeply, beautifully blue.
Madoc (1805). Pt.I, **Madoc in Wales**. V, **Lincoya**, l.102

5 We wage no war with women nor with priests.
XV, **The Excommunication**, l.65

6 What will not woman, gentle woman dare,
When strong affection stirs her spirit up?
Pt.II, **Madoc in Aztlan**. II, **The Tidings**, l.125

7 You are old, Father William, the young man cried,
The few locks which are left you are grey;
You are hale, Father William, a hearty old man,
Now tell me the reason, I pray.
The Old Man's Comforts, and how he Gained them

8 You are old, Father William, the young man cried
And pleasures with youth pass away,
And yet you lament not the days that are gone,
Now tell me the reason, I pray.

9 In the days of my youth I remembered my God!
And He hath not forgotten my age.

10 The Monk my son, and my daughter the Nun.
The Old Woman of Berkeley

11 A vague, a dizzy, a tumultuous joy.
Thalaba the Destroyer (1801), bk.III.xix

12 The arts babblative and scribblative.
Colloquies on the Progress and Prospects of Society (1829).
Coll.x. Pt.ii

13 The march of intellect.
Coll.xiv

14 Your true lover of literature is never fastidious.
The Doctor (1812), ch.17

15 Show me a man who cares no more for one place than
another, and I will show you in that same person one
who loves nothing but himself. Beware of those who
are homeless by choice.
ch.34

16 Live as long as you may, the first twenty years are the
longest half of your life.
ch.130

17 The death of Nelson was felt in England as something
more than a public calamity; men started at the
intelligence, and turned pale, as if they had heard of
the loss of a dear friend.
The Life of Nelson (1813), ch.9

18 She has made me half in love with a cold climate.
Letter to his brother Thomas, 28 Apr. 1797

ROBERT SOUTHWELL 1561?–1595

19 As I in hoary winter's night stood shivering in the
snow,
Surprised I was with sudden heat which made my
heart to glow;
And lifting up a fearful eye to view what fire was
near,
A pretty Babe all burning bright did in the air appear.
The Burning Babe (1595)

20 Times go by turns, and chances change by course,
From foul to fair, from better hap to worse.
Times go by Turns. See 11:5

21 Before my face the picture hangs,
That daily should put me in mind
Of those cold qualms, and bitter pangs,
That shortly I am like to find:
But yet alas full little I
Do think hereon that I must die.
Upon the Image of Death

JOHN SPARROW 1906–

22 Chill on the brow and in the breast
The frost of years is spread—
Soon we shall take our endless rest
With the unfeeling dead.

Insensibly, ere we depart,
We grow more cold, more kind:
Age makes a winter in the heart,
An autumn in the mind.
Grave Epigrams (1974), viii

23 That indefatigable and unsavoury engine of pollution,
the dog.
Letter to *The Times*, 30 Sept. 1975

HERBERT SPENCER 1820–1903

24 Science is organized knowledge.
Education (1861), ch.2

25 People are beginning to see that the first requisite to
success in life is to be a good animal.

26 Absolute morality is the regulation of conduct in such
a way that pain shall not be inflicted.
Essays (1891), vol.iii, p.152. **Prison Ethics**

27 The ultimate result of shielding men from the effects
of folly, is to fill the world with fools.
p.354. **State Tamperings with Money and Banks**

28 The Republican form of Government is the highest
form of government; but because of this it requires the
highest type of human nature—a type nowhere at
present existing.
p.478. **The Americans**

29 Evolution…is—a change from an indefinite,
incoherent homogeneity, to a definite coherent
heterogeneity.
First Principles (1862), ch.16, 138

30 It cannot but happen…that those will survive whose
functions happen to be most nearly in equilibrium with
the modified aggregate of external forces…This
survival of the fittest implies multiplication of the
fittest.
Principles of Biology (1865), pt.iii, ch.12, **Indirect
Equilibration**, 164

31 How often misused words generate misleading
thoughts.
Principles of Ethics, bk.I, pt.ii, ch.8, 152

32 Progress, therefore, is not an accident, but a
necessity…It is a part of nature.
Social Statics (1850), pt.i, ch.2, 4

33 A clever theft was praiseworthy amongst the Spartans;
and it is equally so amongst Christians, provided it be
on a sufficiently large scale.
pt.ii, ch.16, 3

1 Education has for its object the formation of character.
  ch.17, 4

2 Opinion is ultimately determined by the feelings, and not by the intellect.
  pt.iv, ch.30, 8

3 No one can be perfectly free till all are free; no one can be perfectly moral till all are moral; no one can be perfectly happy till all are happy.
  16

4 It was remarked to me by the late Mr Charles Roupell...that to play billards well was a sign of an ill-spent youth.
  Duncan, *Life and Letters of Spencer* (1908), ch.20, p.298

5 French art, if not sanguinary, is usually obscene.
  'Two', *Home Life with Herbert Spencer* (1906), ch.IV, p.115

STEPHEN SPENDER 1909–

6 As she will live who, candle-lit
  Floats upon her final breath
  The ceiling of the frosty night
  And her white room beneath
  Wearing not like destruction, but
  Like a white dress, her death.
  Elegy for Margaret, vi

7 I think continually of those who were truly great—
  The names of those who in their lives fought for life,
  Who wore at their hearts the fire's centre.
  I Think Continually of Those

8 Born of the sun they travelled a short while towards the sun,
  And left the vivid air signed with their honour.

9   Their collected
  Hearts wound up with love, like little watch springs.
  The Living Values

10 Never being, but always at the edge of Being.
  Preludes, 10. (*Collected Poems,* 1955)

11 My parents kept me from children who were rough
  Who threw words like stones and who wore torn clothes.
  11

12 What I had not foreseen
  Was the gradual day
  Weakening the will
  Leaking the brightness away.
  12

13 After the first powerful, plain manifesto
  The black statement of pistons, without more fuss
  But gliding like a queen, she leaves the station.
  29. **The Express**

14 Eye, gazelle, delicate wanderer,
  Drinker of horizon's fluid line.
  35

15 The word bites like a fish.
  Shall I throw it back free
  Arrowing to that sea
  Where thoughts lash tail and fin?
  Or shall I pull it in
  To rhyme upon a dish?
  Word

EDMUND SPENSER 1552?–1599

16 The merry cuckoo, messenger of Spring,
  His trumpet shrill hath thrice already sounded.
  Amoretti (1595). Sonnet xix

17 Most glorious Lord of life, that on this day
  Didst make thy triumph over death and sin:
  And, having harrow'd hell, didst bring away
  Captivity thence captive, us to win.
  lxviii

18 So let us love, dear Love, like as we ought,
  —Love is the lesson which the Lord us taught.

19 Fresh spring the herald of love's mighty king,
  In whose coat armour richly are display'd
  All sorts of flowers the which on earth do spring
  In goodly colours gloriously array'd.
  lxx

20 One day I wrote her name upon the strand,
  But came the waves and washed it away:
  Again I wrote it with a second hand,
  But came the tide, and made my pains his prey.
  Vain man, said she, that dost in vain assay,
  A mortal thing so to immortalize,
  For I myself shall like to this decay,
  And eke my name be wiped out likewise.
  Not so, quoth I, let baser things devise
  To die in dust, but you shall live by fame:
  My verse your virtues rare shall eternize,
  And in the heavens write your glorious name,
  Where when as death shall all the world subdue,
  Our love shall live, and later life renew.
  lxxv

21 Triton blowing loud his wreathed horn.
  Colin Clout's Come Home Again (1595), l.245

22 So love is Lord of all the world by right.
  l.883

23 What more felicity can fall to creature,
  Than to enjoy delight with liberty.
  Complaints (1591). Muiopotmos, l.209

24 Of such deep learning little had he need,
  Ne yet of Latin, ne of Greek that breed
  Doubts 'mongst Divines, and difference of texts,
  From whence arise diversity of sects,
  and hateful heresies.
  Prosopopoia or Mother Hubbard's Tale, l.385

25 Open the temple gates unto my love,
  Open them wide that she may enter in.
  Epithalamion (1595), l.204

26 Ah! when will this long weary day have end,
  And lend me leave to come unto my love?
  l.278

27 Song made in lieu of many ornaments,
  With which my love should duly have been deck'd.
  l.427

28 The generall end therefore of all the book is to fashion a gentleman or noble person in vertuous and gentle discipline.
  The Faerie Queen (1596), preface

29 Fierce wars and faithful loves shall moralize my song.
  bk.I, introd. i.1

30 A gentle knight was pricking on the plain.
  c.I.i

31 But on his breast a bloody cross he bore,
  The dear remembrance of his dying Lord.
  ii

32 But of his cheer did seem too solemn sad;

Yet nothing did he dread, but ever was ydrad.

1 A bold bad man, that dar'd to call by name
Great Gorgon, Prince of darkness and dead night.
xxxvii. See 447:1

2   Her angel's face
As the great eye of heaven shined bright,
And made a sunshine in the shady place;
Did never mortal eye behold such heavenly grace.
c.III.vi

3 And all the hinder parts, that few could spy,
Were ruinous and old, but painted cunningly.
c.IV.v

4 The Noble heart, that harbours virtuous thought,
And is with child of glorious great intent,
Can never rest, until it forth have brought
Th' eternal brood of glory excellent.
c.V.i

5   A cruel crafty Crocodile,
Which in false grief hiding his harmful guile,
Doth weep full sore, and sheddeth tender tears.
xviii

6 Still as he fled, his eye was backward cast,
As if his fear still followed him behind.
c.IX.xxi

7 That darksome cave they enter, where they find
That cursed man, low sitting on the ground,
Musing full sadly in his sullen mind.
xxxv

8 Sleep after toil, port after stormy seas,
Ease after war, death after life does greatly please.
xl

9 Death is the end of woes: die soon, O fairy's son.
xlvii

10 So double was his pains, so double be his praise.
bk.II, c.II.xxv

11 Upon her eyelids many Graces sate,
Under the shadow of her even brows.
c.III.xxv

12 And all for love, and nothing for reward.
c.VIII.ii

13 So passeth, in the passing of a day,
Of mortal life the leaf, the bud, the flower,
No more doth flourish after first decay,
That erst was sought to deck both bed and bower,
Of many a Lady, and many a Paramour:
Gather therefore the Rose, whilst yet is prime,
For soon comes age, that will her pride deflower:
Gather the Rose of love, whilst yet is time,
Whilst loving thou mayst loved be with equal crime.
c.XII.lxxv

14   The dunghill kind
Delights in filth and foul incontinence:
Let Grill be Grill, and have his hoggish mind.
lxxxvii

15 Whether it divine tobacco were,
Or Panachaea, or Polygony,
She found, and brought it to her patient dear.
bk.III, c.V.xxxii

16 Hard is to teach an old horse amble true.
c.VIII.xxvi

17 And painful pleasure turns to pleasing pain.
c.X.lx

18 And as she look'd about, she did behold,
How over that same door was likewise writ,
Be bold, be bold, and everywhere Be bold…
At last she spied at that room's upper end
Another iron door, on which was writ
Be not too bold.
c.XI.liv

19 Dan Chaucer, well of English undefiled,
On Fame's eternal beadroll worthy to be filed.
bk.IV, c.II.xxxii

20 For all that nature by her mother wit
Could frame in earth.
c.X.xxi

21 O sacred hunger of ambitious minds.
bk.V, c.XII.i

22 A monster, which the Blatant beast men call,
A dreadful fiend of gods and men ydrad.
xxxvii

23 The gentle mind by gentle deeds is known.
For a man by nothing is so well bewray'd,
As by his manners.
bk.VI, c.III.i

24 What man that sees the ever-whirling wheel
Of Change, the which all mortal things doth sway,
But that thereby doth find, and plainly feel,
How Mutability in them doth play
Her cruel sports, to many men's decay?
bk.VII, c.VI.i

25 For all that moveth doth in Change delight:
But thenceforth all shall rest eternally
With Him that is the God of Sabbaoth hight:
O that great Sabbaoth God, grant me that Sabbaoth's
     sight.
c.VIII.ii

26 So you great Lord, that with your counsel sway
The burden of this kingdom mightily,
With like delights sometimes may eke delay,
The rugged brow of careful Policy.
[Dedicatory Sonnets] **To Sir Christopher Hatton**

27 That beauty is not, as fond men misdeem,
An outward show of things, that only seem.
An Hymn in Honour of Beauty (1596), l.90

28 For of the soul the body form doth take;
For soul is form, and doth the body make.
l.132

29 I was promis'd on a time,
To have reason for my rhyme;
From that time unto this season,
I received nor rhyme nor reason.
Lines on his Pension. Attr.

30 Calm was the day, and through the trembling air,
Sweet breathing Zephyrus did softly play.
Prothalamion (1596), l.1

31 With that, I saw two Swans of goodly hue,
Come softly swimming down along the Lee;
Two fairer Birds I yet did never see:
The Snow which doth the top of Pindus strew,
Did never whiter show,
Nor Jove himself when he a Swan would be
For love of Leda, whiter did appear.
l.37

32 So purely white they were,
That even the gentle stream, the which them bare,

Seem'd foul to them, and bade his billows spare
To wet their silken feathers, lest they might
Soil their fair plumes with water not so fair
And mar their beauties bright,
That shone as Heaven's light,
Against their Bridal day, which was not long:
Sweet Thames, run softly, till I end my Song.
l.46

1 At length they all to merry London came,
To merry London, my most kindly nurse,
That to me gave this life's first native source.
l.127

2 To be wise and eke to love,
Is granted scarce to God above.
The Shepherd's Calendar (1579), **March. Willy's Emblem**

3 Bring hither the Pink and purple Columbine,
  With Gillyflowers:
Bring Coronation, and Sops in wine,
  Worn of paramours.
Strew me the ground with Daffadowndillies,
And Cowslips, and Kingcups, and loved Lilies:
  The pretty Pawnce,
  And the Chevisaunce,
Shall match with the fair flower Delice.
April, l.136

4 And he that strives to touch the stars,
Oft stumbles at a straw.
July, l.99

5 Uncouth unkist, said the old famous Poet Chaucer.
The Shepherd's Calendar. **Letter to Gabriel Harvey**

6 So now they have made our English tongue a
gallimaufry or hodgepodge of all other speeches.

BARUCH SPINOZA 1632–1677

7 *Sedula curavi, humanas actiones non ridere, non
lugere, neque detestare, sed intelligere.*
I have striven not to laugh at human actions, not to
weep at them, nor to hate them, but to understand
them.
Tractatus Politicus 1, iv

REVD. WILLIAM ARCHIBALD SPOONER
1844–1930

8 You will find as you grow older that the weight of
rages will press harder and harder on the employer.
Sir W. Hayter, *Spooner* (1977), ch.6. Many other Spoonerisms,
such as those given in the previous editions of O.D.Q., are now
known to be apocryphal.

9 Poor soul, very sad; her late husband, you know, a
very sad death—eaten by missionaries—poor soul!

SIR CECIL ARTHUR SPRING-RICE 1858–1918

10 I vow to thee, my country—all earthly things above—
Entire and whole and perfect, the service of my love.
Last Poem

11 I am the Dean of Christ Church, Sir:
There's my wife; look well at her.
She's the Broad and I'm the High;
We are the University.
The Masque of Balliol, composed by and current among members
of Balliol College, Oxford, in the late 1870s. This first couplet
(identified as by C.A. Spring-Rice) was unofficially altered to:

12 I am the Dean, and this is Mrs Liddell;

She is the first and I the second fiddle.
See also 7:1, 37:8

J.C. (SIR JOHN) SQUIRE 1884–1958

13 God heard the embattled nations sing and shout
'Gott strafe England!' and 'God save the King!'
God this, God that, and God the other thing—
'Good God', said God, 'I've got my work cut out.'
Epigrams, no.1, **'The Dilemma'**

14 It did not last: the Devil howling 'Ho!
Let Einstein be!' restored the status quo.
Answer to 378:7

MME DE STAEL 1766–1817

15 *Tout comprendre rend très indulgent.*
To be totally understanding makes one very indulgent.
Corinne (1807), lib.iv, ch.2

JOSEPH STALIN 1879–1953

16 The Pope! How many divisions has *he* got?
When asked by Laval to encourage Catholicism in Russia to
conciliate the Pope, 13 May 1935. Churchill, *The Second World
War,* vol.i, 'The Gathering Storm', ch.8

SIR HENRY MORTON STANLEY 1841–1904

17 Dr Livingstone, I presume?
How I found Livingstone (1872), ch.11

COLONEL C.E. STANTON 1859–1933

18 Lafayette, we are here!
Address delivered at the grave of Lafayette, Paris, 4 July 1917.
Often attr. to General John J. Pershing, but disclaimed by him

EDWIN McMASTERS STANTON 1814–1869

19 Now he belongs to the ages.
Of Abraham Lincoln, after his assassination, 15 Apr. 1865. I.M.
Tarbell, *Life of Abraham Lincoln* (1900), vol.II, p.244

JOHN STARK 1728–1822

20 We beat them to-day or Molly Stark's a widow.
Before Battle of Bennington, 16 Aug. 1777. Appleton,
Cyclopaedia of American Biography, vol.v

ENID STARKIE d. 1970

21 Unhurt people are not much good in the world.
Joanna Richardson, *Enid Starkie,* ch.18

SIR RICHARD STEELE 1672–1729

22 I have often thought that a story-teller is born, as well
as a poet.
The Guardian, No.24

23 Gained universal applause by explaining a passage in
the game-act.
The Spectator, No.2

24 I have heard Will Honeycomb say, A Woman seldom
Writes her Mind but in her Postscript.
No.79

25 We were in some little time fixed in our seats, and sat
with that dislike which people not too good-natured

usually conceive of each other at first sight.
No.132

1 The noblest motive is the public good.
No.200. Motto in Ed. 1744

2 There are so few who can grow old with a good grace.
No.263

3 Will Honeycomb calls these over-offended ladies the outrageously virtuous.
No.266

4 Fashion, the arbiter, and rule of right.
No.478. Motto in Ed.1744

5 It is to be noted that when any part of this paper appears dull there is a design in it.
The Tatler, No.38

6 Though her mien carries much more invitation than command, to behold her is an immediate check to loose behaviour; to love her is a liberal education.
No.49

7 Every man is the maker of his own fortune.
No.52

8 The insupportable labour of doing nothing.
No.54

9 Reading is to the mind what exercise is to the body.
No.147

10 The truth of it is, the first rudiments of education are given very indiscreetly by most parents.
No.173

11 Let your precept be, Be easy.
No.196

12 It was very prettily said, that we may learn the little value of fortune by the persons on whom heaven is pleased to bestow it.
No.203. See 320:14

13 These ladies of irresistible modesty are those who make virtue unamiable.
No.217

14 I fared like a distressed Prince who calls in a powerful Neighbour to his Aid; I was undone by my Auxiliary; when I had once called him in, I could not subsist without Dependance on him.
Preface of vol.iv (1711). On his co-editorship, with Addison, of *The Spectator*

LINCOLN STEFFENS 1866–1936

15 I have seen the future, and it works.
After visiting Moscow in 1919, Steffens said to Bernard Baruch 'I have been over into the future, and it works.' He later improved the expression, and used it frequently in the shorter form. William C. Bullitt, the U.S. diplomat with whom Steffens was travelling, claimed he was rehearsing this formula long before seeing Lenin's Russia. J. Kaplan, *Lincoln Steffens* (1975), ch.13, ii

GERTRUDE STEIN 1874–1946

16 Pigeons on the grass alas.
Four Saints in 3 Acts, III.ii

17 Rose is a rose is a rose is a rose.
Sacred Emily

18 You're all a lost generation.
Quoting (in translation), in a particular reference to 'all of you young people who served in the war', a mechanic's rebuke (in French) to his apprentice, who had made a shoddy repair to her car. E. Hemingway, *A Moveable Feast*, ch.3. Used as the epigraph to Hemingway's *The Sun Also Rises* (1926).

19 What *is* the answer?…In that case, what is the question?
Last words. Donald Sutherland, *Gertrude Stein, A Biography of her Work* (1951), ch.6

SIR JAMES FITZJAMES STEPHEN 1829–1894

20 The way in which the man of genius rules is by persuading an efficient minority to coerce an indifferent and self-indulgent majority.
Liberty, Equality and Fraternity (1873), ch.II

21 Progress has its drawbacks and they are great and serious.

J.K. STEPHEN 1859–1892

22 Two voices are there: one is of the deep;
It learns the storm-cloud's thunderous melody,
Now roars, now murmurs with the changing sea,
Now bird-like pipes, now closes soft in sleep:
And one is of an old half-witted sheep
Which bleats articulate monotony,
And indicates that two and one are three,
That grass is green, lakes damp, and mountains steep
And, Wordsworth, both are thine.
Lapsus Calami (1896). **A Sonnet**. See 582:18

23   Good Lord! I'd rather be
Quite unacquainted with the A.B.C.
Than write such hopeless rubbish as thy worst.

24 Will there never come a season
Which shall rid us from the curse
Of a prose which knows no reason
And an unmelodious verse…
When there stands a muzzled stripling,
Mute, beside a muzzled bore:
When the Rudyards cease from kipling
And the Haggards Ride no more.
To R.K.

25 Ah! Matt.: old age has brought to me
Thy wisdom, less thy certainty:
The world's a jest, and joy's a trinket:
I knew that once: but now—I think it.
Senex to Matt. Prior

JAMES STEPHENS 1882–1950

26 I heard a sudden cry of pain!
There is a rabbit in a snare.
The Snare

27 Little One! Oh, Little One!
I am searching everywhere!

LAURENCE STERNE 1713–1768

28 They order, said I, this matter better in France.
A Sentimental Journey (1768), I.1

29 I had had an affair with the moon, in which there was neither sin nor shame.
The Monk. Calais

30 The Sentimental Traveller (meaning thereby myself) who have travell'd, and of which I am now sitting down to give an account—as much out of necessity, and the *besoin de voyager,* as any one in the class.
Preface. In the Desobligeant

31 As an English man does not travel to see English men,

I retired to my room.

1 —You need not tell me what the proposal was, said she, laying her hand upon both mine, as she interrupted me.—A man, my good Sir, has seldom an offer of kindness to make to a woman, but she has a presentiment of it some moments before.
The Remise. Calais

2 I pity the man who can travel from Dan to Beersheba, and cry, 'tis all barren.
In the Street. Calais

3 Having been in love with one princess or another, almost all my life, and I hope I shall go on so, till I die, being firmly persuaded, that if I ever do a mean action, it must be in some interval betwixt one passion and another.
Montriul

4 Vive l'amour! et vive la bagatelle!
The letter

5 Hail ye small sweet courtesies of life.
The Pulse. Paris

6 There are worse occupations in this world than feeling a woman's pulse.

7 'I can't get out,—I can't get out,' said the starling.
The Passport. The Hotel at Paris

8 He gave a deep sigh—I saw the iron enter into his soul!
The Captive. Paris

9 I think there is a fatality in it—I seldom go to the place I set out for.
The Address. Versailles

10 They [the French] are a loyal, a gallant, a generous, an ingenious, and good-temper'd people as is under heaven—if they have a fault, they are too *serious*.
The Character. Versailles

11 God tempers the wind, said Maria, to the shorn lamb.
Maria. From a French proverb, but familiar in Sterne's form of words

12 Dear sensibility! source inexhausted of all that's precious in our joys, or costly in our sorrows!
The Bourbonnois

13 If the supper was to my taste—the grace which followed it was much more so.
The Supper

14 But the fille de chambre hearing there were words between us, and fearing that hostilities would ensue in due course, had crept silently out of her closet, and it being totally dark, had stolen so close to our beds, that she had got herself into the narrow passage which separated them, and had advanced so far up as to be in a line betwixt her mistress and me—
So that when I stretched out my hand, I caught hold of the fille de chambre's
The Case of Delicacy

15 I live in a constant endeavour to fence against the infirmities of ill health, and other evils of life, by mirth; being firmly persuaded that every time a man smiles,—but much more so, when he laughs, that it adds something to this Fragment of Life.
Tristram Shandy (1760–67). Dedication

16 I wish either my father or my mother, or indeed both of them, as they were in duty both equally bound to it, had minded what they were about when they begot me.
bk.I, ch.1, opening words

17 'Pray, my dear,' quoth my mother, 'have you not forgot to wind up the clock?'—'Good G—!' cried my father, making an exclamation, but taking care to moderate his voice at the same time,—'Did ever woman, since the creation of the world, interrupt a man with such a silly question?'

18 As we jog on, either laugh with me, or at me, or in short do anything,—only keep your temper.
ch.6

19 'Tis known by the name of perseverance in a good cause,—and of obstinacy in a bad one.
ch.17

20 What is the character of a family to an hypothesis? my father would reply.
ch.21

21 My uncle Toby would never offer to answer this by any other kind of argument, than that of whistling half a dozen bars of Lillabullero.

22 Digressions, incontestably, are the sunshine;—they are the life, the soul of reading;—take them out of this book for instance,—you might as well take the book along with them.
ch.22

23 I should have no objection to this method, but that I think it must smell too strong of the lamp.
ch.23

24 'I'll not hurt thee,' says my uncle Toby, rising from his chair, and going across the room, with the fly in his hand,—'I'll not hurt a hair of thy head:—Go,' says he, lifting up the sash, and opening his hand as he spoke, to let it escape;—'go, poor devil, get thee gone, why should I hurt thee?—This world surely is wide enough to hold both thee and me.'
bk.ii, ch.12

25 Whenever a man talks loudly against religion,—always suspect that it is not his reason, but his passions which have got the better of his creed.
ch.17

26 'Sir,' replied Dr Slop, 'it would astonish you to know what improvements we have made of late years in all branches of obstetrical knowledge, but particularly in that one single point of the safe and expeditious extraction of the foetus,—which has received such lights, that, for my part (holding up his hands) I declare I wonder how the world has—.'
'I wish,' quoth my uncle Toby, 'you had seen what prodigious armies we had in Flanders.'
ch.18

27 It is the nature of an hypothesis, when once a man has conceived it, that it assimilates every thing to itself, as proper nourishment; and, from the first moment of your begetting it, it generally grows the stronger by every thing you see, hear, read, or understand. This is of great use.
bk.ii, ch.19

28 'Our armies swore terribly in Flanders,' cried my uncle Toby,—'but nothing to this.'
bk.iii, ch.11

29 The corregiescity of Corregio.
ch.12. See 131:19

30 Of all the cants which are canted in this canting

world,—though the cant of hypocrites may be the worst,—the cant of criticism is the most tormenting!

1 Is this a fit time, said my father to himself, to talk of Pensions and Grenadiers?
bk.iv, ch.5 (complete)

2 There is a North-west passage to the intellectual World.
ch.42

3 'There is no terror, brother Toby, in its looks, but what it borrows from groans and convulsions—and the blowing of noses, and the wiping away of tears with the bottoms of curtains, in a dying man's room—Strip it of these, what is it?'—''Tis better in battle than in bed', said my uncle Toby.
bk.v, ch.3. Of death

4 Prejudice of education, he would say, is the devil,—and the multitudes of them which we suck in with our mother's milk—are the devil and all.—We are haunted with them, brother Toby, in all our lucubrations and researches; and was a man fool enough to submit tamely to what they obtruded upon him,—what would his book be?...nothing but a farrago of the clack of nurses, and of the nonsense of the old women (of both sexes) throughout the kingdom.
ch.16

5 'The poor soul will die:—'
'He shall not die, by G—', cried my uncle Toby.—The Accusing Spirit, which flew up to heaven's chancery with the oath, blush'd as he gave it in;—and the Recording Angel, as he wrote it down, dropp'd a tear upon the word, and blotted it out for ever.
bk.vi, ch.8

6 To say a man is fallen in love,—or that he is deeply in love,—or up to the ears in love,—and sometimes even over head and ears in it,—carries an idiomatical kind of implication, that love is a thing below a man:—this is recurring again to Plato's opinion, which, with all his divinityship,—I hold to be damnable and heretical:—and so much for that.
Let love therefore be what it will,—my uncle Toby fell into it.
ch.37

7 My brother Toby, quoth she, is going to be married to Mrs Wadman.
Then he will never, quoth my father, lie *diagonally* in his bed again as long as he lives.
ch.39

8 'A soldier,' cried my Uncle Toby, interrupting the corporal, 'is no more exempt from saying a foolish thing, Trim, than a man of letters.'—'But not so often, an' please your honour,' replied the corporal.
bk.viii, ch.19

9 An eye full of gentle salutations—and soft responses—...whispering soft—like the last low accents of an expiring saint...It did my uncle Toby's business.
ch.25

10 'I am half distracted, Captain Shandy,' said Mrs Wadman,...'a mote—or sand—or something—I know not what, has got into this eye of mine—do look into it.'...In saying which, Mrs Wadman edged herself close in beside my uncle Toby,...'Do look into

it'—said she....
If thou lookest, uncle Toby,...thou art undone.

11 Every time I kiss thy hand to bid adieu, and every absence which follows it, are preludes to that eternal separation which we are shortly to make.
bk.ix, ch.8

12 Said my mother, 'what is all this story about?'—'A Cock and a Bull,' said Yorick.
ch.33

13 This sad vicissitude of things.
Sermon xv

WALLACE STEVENS 1879–1955

14 The only emperor is the emperor of ice-cream.
The Emperor of Ice-Cream

15 Poetry is the supreme fiction, madame.
A High-Toned old Christian Woman

16 Just as my fingers on these keys
Make music, so the selfsame sounds
On my spirit make a music, too.

Music is feeling, then, not sound.
Peter Quince at the Clavier, I

17 Beauty is momentary in the mind—
The fitful tracing of a portal;
But in the flesh it is immortal.
The body dies; the body's beauty lives.
IV

18 Complacencies of the peignoir, and late
Coffee and oranges in a sunny chair.
And the green freedom of a cockatoo
Upon a rug mingle to dissipate
The holy hush of ancient sacrifice.
Sunday Morning, I

ADLAI STEVENSON 1900–1965

19 Someone asked me...how I felt, and I was reminded of a story that a fellow-townsman of ours used to tell—Abraham Lincoln...He [a boy in Mr. Lincoln's story] said that he was too old to cry, but it hurt too much to laugh.
Speech, after electoral defeat, 5 Nov. 1942

20 As the girl said, 'A kiss on the wrist feels good, but, a diamond bracelet lasts forever.'
Address given to Chicago Council on Foreign Relations, 22 Mar. 1946. See 318:3

21 Making peace is harder than making war.

22 He [Mr. Stevenson], derided the Secretary [of State] for boasting of his brinkmanship—the art of bringing up to the edge of the nuclear abyss.
New York Times, 26 Feb. 1956

ROBERT LOUIS STEVENSON 1850–1894

23 The harmless art of knucklebones has seen the fall of the Roman empire and the rise of the United States.
Across the Plains (1892). VII. *The Lantern-Bearers,* i

24 The bright face of danger.
iv

25 Every one lives by selling something.
IX. *Beggars,* iii

26 Our frailties are invincible, our virtues barren; the battle goes sore against us to the going down of the

sun.
XI. Pulvis et Umbra, i

1 Surely we should find it both touching and inspiriting, that in a field from which success is banished, our race should not cease to labour.
ii

2 Still obscurely fighting the lost fight of virtue, still clinging, in the brothel or on the scaffold, to some rag of honour, the poor jewel of their souls!

3 A mortified appetite is never a wise companion.
XII. A Christmas Sermon, i

4 To be honest, to be kind—to earn a little and to spend a little less, to make upon the whole a family happier for his presence, to renounce when that shall be necessary and not be embittered, to keep a few friends, but these without capitulation—above all, on the same grim condition, to keep friends with himself—here is a task for all that a man has of fortitude and delicacy.

5 Here lies one who meant well, tried a little, failed much:—surely that may be his epitaph, of which he need not be ashamed.
iv

6 Politics is perhaps the only profession for which no preparation is thought necessary.
Familiar Studies of Men and Books (1882). **'Yoshida-Torajiro'**

7 Am I no a bonny fighter? [Alan Breck.]
Kidnapped (1886), ch.10

8 I've a grand memory for forgetting, David. [Alan Breck.]
ch.18

9 I have thus played the sedulous ape to Hazlitt, to Lamb, to Wordsworth, to Sir Thomas Browne, to Defoe, to Hawthorne, to Montaigne, to Baudelaire and to Obermann.
Memories and Portraits (1887), ch.4

10 Each has his own tree of ancestors, but at the top of all sits Probably Arboreal.
ch.6, **Pastoral.** See 171:23

11 Lamplough was genteel, Eno was omnipresent; Lamplough was trite, Eno original and abominably vulgar...Am I, then, to sink with Lamplough, or to soar with Eno?
More New Arabian Nights: The Dynamiter (1885). **The Superfluous Mansion**

12 He who was prepared to help the escaping murderer or to embrace the impenitent thief, found, to the overthrow of all his logic, that he objected to the use of dynamite.

13 'Or Opulent Rotunda Strike the Sky,' said the shopman to himself, in the tone of one considering a verse. 'I suppose it would be too much to say "orotunda", and yet how noble it were! "Or Opulent Orotunda Strike the Sky." But that is the bitterness of arts; you see a good effect, and some nonsense about sense continually intervenes.'
Epilogue of the Cigar Divan

14 These are my politics: to change what we can; to better what we can; but still to bear in mind that man is but a devil weakly fettered by some generous beliefs and impositions; and for no word however sounding, and no cause however just and pious, to relax the stricture of these bonds.

15 The devil, depend upon it, can sometimes do a very gentlemanly thing.
The New Arabian Nights (1882). **The Suicide Club. Story of the Young Man with the Cream Tarts**

16 Is there anything in life so disenchanting as attainment?
The Adventure of the Hansom Cab

17 I regard you with an indifference closely bordering on aversion.
The Rajah's Diamond. Story of the Bandbox

18 For my part, I travel not to go anywhere, but to go. I travel for travel's sake. The great affair is to move.
Travels with a Donkey (1879). **Cheylard and Luc**

19 I own I like definite form in what my eyes are to rest upon; and if landscapes were sold, like the sheets of characters of my boyhood, one penny plain and twopence coloured, I should go the length of twopence every day of my life.
Father Apollinaris

20 A faddling hedonist.
The Boarders

21 Fifteen men on the dead man's chest
Yo-ho-ho, and a bottle of rum!
Drink and the devil had done for the rest—
Yo-ho-ho, and a bottle of rum!
Treasure Island (1883), ch.1

22 Tip me the black spot.
ch.3

23 Many's the long night I've dreamed of cheese—toasted, mostly. [Ben Gunn.]
ch.15

24 In marriage, a man becomes slack and selfish, and undergoes a fatty degeneration of his moral being.
Virginibus Puerisque (1881), I.i

25 Acidulous vestals.

26 They have never been in love, or in hate.

27 Even if we take matrimony at its lowest, even if we regard it as no more than a sort of friendship recognised by the police.

28 A little amateur painting in water-colours shows the innocent and quiet mind.

29 Lastly (and this is, perhaps, the golden rule), no woman should marry a teetotaller, or a man who does not smoke.

30 Marriage is a step so grave and decisive that it attracts light-headed, variable men by its very awfulness.

31 Marriage is like life in this—that it is a field of battle, and not a bed of roses.

32 Times are changed with him who marries; there are no more by-path meadows, where you may innocently linger, but the road lies long and straight and dusty to the grave.
ii

33 To marry is to domesticate the Recording Angel. Once you are married, there is nothing left for you, not even suicide, but to be good.

34 Man is a creature who lives not upon bread alone, but principally by catchwords.

35 The cruellest lies are often told in silence.
iv. **Truth of Intercourse**

1 Old and young, we are all on our last cruise.
Crabbed Age and Youth

2 Youth is the time to go flashing from one end of the
world to the other both in mind and body; to try the
manners of different nations; to hear the chimes at
midnight; to see sunrise in town and country; to be
converted at a revival; to circumnavigate the
metaphysics, write halting verses, run a mile to see a
fire, and wait all day long in the theatre to applaud
'Hernani'
See 442:6

3 It is better to be a fool than to be dead.

4 There is no duty we so much underrate as the duty of
being happy.
III. **An Apology for Idlers**

5 He sows hurry and reaps indigestion.

6 By the time a man gets well into the seventies his
continued existence is a mere miracle.
V. **Aes Triplex**

7 Philosophy, in its more rigid sense, has been at the
same work for ages; and...has the honour of laying
before us...her contribution towards the subject: that
life is a Permanent Possibility of Sensation.

8 Even if the doctor does not give you a year, even if he
hesitates about a month, make one brave push and see
what can be accomplished in a week.

9 To travel hopefully is a better thing than to arrive, and
the true success is to labour.
VI. **El Dorado**

10 Though we are mighty fine fellows nowadays, we
cannot write like Hazlitt.
X. **Walking Tours**

11 What hangs people...is the unfortunate circumstance
of guilt.
The Wrong Box (with Lloyd Osbourne, 1889), ch.7

12 Nothing like a little judicious levity.

13 Between the possibility of being hanged in all
innocence, and the certainty of a public and merited
disgrace, no gentleman of spirit could long hesitate.
ch.10

14 'The "Athaeneum", that was the name! Golly, what a
paper!' '"Athenaeum", you mean,' said Morris.
ch.15

15 I believe in an ultimate decency of things.
Letter, 23 Aug. 1893

16 In winter I get up at night
And dress by yellow candle-light.
In summer, quite the other way,—
I have to go to bed by day.

I have to go to bed and see
The birds still hopping on the tree,
Or hear the grown-up people's feet
Still going past me in the street.
A Child's Garden of Verses (1885). I. **Bed in Summmer**

17 A child should always say what's true,
And speak when he is spoken to,
And behave mannerly at table:
At least as far as he is able.
V. **Whole Duty of Children**

18 Whenever the moon and stars are set,
Whenever the wind is high,

All night long in the dark and wet,
A man goes riding by.
Late in the night when the fires are out,
Why does he gallop and gallop about?
IX. **Windy Nights**

19 When I am grown to man's estate
I shall be very proud and great,
And tell the other girls and boys
Not to meddle with my toys.
XII. **Looking Forward**

20 When I was sick and lay a-bed,
I had two pillows at my head,
And all my toys beside me lay
To keep me happy all the day...

I was the giant great and still
That sits upon the pillow-hill,
And sees before him, dale and plain,
The pleasant land of counterpane.
XVI. **The Land of Counterpane**

21 The child that is not clean and neat,
With lots of toys and things to eat,
He is a naughty child, I'm sure—
Or else his dear papa is poor.
XIX. **System**

22 The world is so full of a number of things,
I'm sure we should all be as happy as kings.
XXIV. **Happy Thought**

23 If you would grow great and stately,
You must try to walk sedately.
XXVII. **Good and Bad Children**

24 A birdie with a yellow bill
Hopped upon the window-sill,
Cocked his shining eye and said:
'Ain't you 'shamed, you sleepy-head?'
XXXIV. **Time to Rise**

25 Must we to bed indeed? Well then,
Let us arise and go like men,
And face with an undaunted tread
The long black passage up to bed.
XLI. **North-West Passage. I. Good-Night**

26 But all that I could think of, in the darkness and the
cold,
Was that I was leaving home and my folks were
growing old.
Christmas at Sea

27 Give to me the life I love,
Let the lave go by me,
Give the jolly heaven above
And the byway nigh me.
Bed in the bush with stars to see,
Bread I dip in the river—
There's the life for a man like me,
There's the life for ever.
Songs of Travel (1896). I. **The Vagabond**

28 Let the blow fall soon or late,
Let what will be o'er me;
Give the face of earth around
And the road before me.
Wealth I seek not, hope nor love,
Nor a friend to know me;
All I seek, the heaven above
And the road below me.

29 I will make you brooches and toys for your delight

Of bird-song at morning and star-shine at night.
I will make a palace fit for you and me
Of green days in forests and blue days at sea.
I will make my kitchen, and you shall keep your
   room,
Where white flows the river and bright blows the
   broom,
And you shall wash your linen and keep your body
   white
In rainfall at morning and dewfall at night.
XI

1 Bright is the ring of words
   When the right man rings them,
Fair the fall of songs
   When the singer sings them.
Still they are carolled and said—
   On wings they are carried—
After the singer is dead
   And the maker buried.
XIV

2 In the highlands, in the country places,
Where the old plain men have rosy faces,
And the young fair maidens
      Quiet eyes.
XV

3 Trusty, dusky, vivid, true,
With eyes of gold and bramble-dew,
Steel-true and blade-straight,
The great artificer
Made my mate.
XXV. **My Wife**

4 Sing me a song of a lad that is gone,
   Say, could that lad be I?
Merry of soul he sailed on a day
   Over the sea to Skye.
XLII

5 Be it granted to me to behold you again in dying,
   Hills of home! and to hear again the call;
Hear about the graves of the martyrs the peewees
   crying,
   And hear no more at all.
XLV. **To S.R. Crockett**

6 Of all my verse, like not a single line;
But like my title, for it is not mine.
That title from a better man I stole;
Ah, how much better, had I stol'n the whole!
Underwoods (1887). Foreword. See 285:4

7 Go, little book, and wish to all
Flowers in the garden, meat in the hall,
A bin of wine, a spice of wit,
A house with lawns enclosing it,
A living river by the door,
A nightingale in the sycamore!
bk.I.i. **Envoy.** See 144:17

8 The gauger walked with willing foot,
And aye the gauger played the flute;
And what should Master Gauger play
But 'Over the hills and far away'?
ii. **A Song of the Road**

9 There's nothing under Heav'n so blue
That's fairly worth the travelling to.
iv

10 Under the wide and starry sky
Dig the grave and let me lie.

Glad did I live and gladly die,
   And I laid me down with a will.
This be the verse you grave for me:
'Here he lies where he longed to be;
Home is the sailor, home from sea,
   And the hunter home from the hill.'
xxi. **Requiem**

11 If I have faltered more or less
In my great task of happiness;
If I have moved among my race
And shown no glorious morning face;
If beams from happy human eyes
Have moved me not; if morning skies,
Books, and my food, and summer rain
Knocked on my sullen heart in vain:—
Lord, thy most pointed pleasure take
And stab my spirit broad awake;
Or, Lord, if too obdurate I,
Choose thou, before that spirit die,
A piercing pain, a killing sin,
And to my dead heart run them in!
xxii. **The Celestial Surgeon**

12 Unfrowning caryatides.
xxiii. **Our Lady of the Snows**

13 I am a kind of farthing dip,
   Unfriendly to the nose and eyes;
A blue-behinded ape, I skip
   Upon the trees of Paradise.
xxx. **A Portrait**

EDWARD STILLINGFLEET 1635–1699

14 'My Lord,' a certain nobleman is said to have
observed, after sitting next to [Richard] Bentley at
dinner, 'that chaplain of yours is a very extraordinary
man.' Stillingfleet agreed, adding, 'Had he but the gift
of humility, he would be the most extraordinary man in
Europe.'
R.J. White, *Dr. Bentley* (1965), ch.4

TOM STOPPARD 1937–

15 *Guildenstern:* …Maidens aspiring to godheads—
Rosenkrantz: And vice versa.
Rosenkrantz and Guildenstern Are Dead (1967), Act I

16 I can do you blood and love without the rhetoric, and
I can do you blood and rhetoric without the love and I
can do you all three concurrent or consecutive but I
can't do you love and rhetoric without the blood.
Blood is compulsory—they're all blood you see.

17 To sum up: your father, whom you love, dies, you are
his heir, you come back to find that hardly was the
corpse cold before his younger brother popped on to
his throne and into his sheets, thereby offending both
legal and natural practice. Now why exactly are you
behaving in this extraordinary manner.

18 The bad end unhappily, the good unluckily. That is
what tragedy means.
Act II. See 573:3

HARRIET BEECHER STOWE 1811–1896

19 'Who was your mother?' 'Never had none!' said the
child, with another grin. 'Never had any mother?
What do you mean? Where were you born?' 'Never

was born!' persisted Topsy.
Uncle Tom's Cabin (1852), ch.20

1 'Do you know who made you?' 'Nobody, as I knows on,' said the child, with a short laugh…'I 'spect I grow'd.'

LORD STOWELL 1745–1836

2 The elegant simplicity of the three per cents.
Lord Campbell, *Lives of the Lord Chancellors* (1857), vol.x, ch.212, p.218

3 A precedent embalms a principle.
An Opinion, while Advocate-General, 1788. Attr.

LYTTON STRACHEY 1880–1932

4 The time was out of joint, and he was only too delighted to have been born to set it right.
Of Hurrell Froude. **Eminent Victorians**, I. Cardinal Manning, ii. See 431:26

BISHOP WILLIAM STUBBS 1825–1901

5 Froude informs the Scottish youth
That parsons do not care for truth.
The Reverend Canon Kingsley cries
History is a pack of lies.
What cause for judgments so malign?
A brief reflection solves the mystery—
Froude believes Kingsley a divine,
And Kingsley goes to Froude for history.
Letter to J.R. Green, 17 Dec. 1871. **Letters of Stubbs** (1904), p.162

SIR JOHN SUCKLING 1609–1642

6 Why so pale and wan, fond lover?
    Prithee, why so pale?
Will, when looking well can't move her,
    Looking ill prevail?
Prithee, why so pale?
Aglaura (1637), IV.i. Song

7 Quit, quit, for shame, this will not move:
    This cannot take her.
If of herself she will not love,
    Nothing can make her:
    The devil take her!

8 Her feet beneath her petticoat,
Like little mice, stole in and out,
    As if they fear'd the light.
A Ballad upon a Wedding (1646), viii

9 For streaks of red were mingled there,
Such as are on a Catherine pear
    (The side that's next the sun).

10 Her lips were red, and one was thin,
Compar'd to that was next her chin
    (Some bee had stung it newly).
xi

11 At length the candle's out, and now
All that they had not done they do:
    What that is, who can tell?
But I believe it was no more
Than thou and I have done before
    With Bridget, and with Nell.

12 I prithee send me back my heart,
    Since I cannot have thine:

For if from yours you will not part,
    Why then shouldst thou have mine?
Song. I Prithee Send me Back

13 But love is such a mystery,
    I cannot find it out:
For when I think I'm best resolv'd,
    I then am in most doubt.

14 Out upon it, I have loved
    Three whole days together;
And am like to love three more,
    If it prove fair weather.

Time shall moult away his wings,
    Ere he shall discover
In the whole wide world again
    Such a constant lover.
A Poem with the Answer

15 Had it any been but she,
    And that very face,
There had been at least ere this
    A dozen dozen in her place.

SUETONIUS c.A.D. 69–c. 130

16 *Festina lente.* [σπεῦδε βραδέως.]
Make haste slowly.
Augustus, 25

17 *Ita feri ut se mori sentiat.*
Strike him so that he can feel that he is dying.
Caligula, 30

MAXIMILIEN DE BETHUNE, DUC DE SULLY 1559–1641

18 *Les anglais s'amusent tristement selon l'usage de leur pays.*
The English take their pleasures sadly after the fashion of their country.
Memoirs, c.1630

SU TUNG-P'O 1036–1101

19 Families, when a child is born
Want it to be intelligent.
I, through intelligence,
Having wrecked my whole life,
Only hope the baby will prove
Ignorant and stupid.
Then he will crown a tranquil life
By becoming a Cabinet Minister.
On the Birth of his Son, tr. Arthur Waley, *170 Chinese Poems* (1918), p.98

HENRY HOWARD, EARL OF SURREY 1517?–1547

20 Martial, the things for to attain
The happy life be these, I find:
The riches left, not got with pain;
The fruitful ground, the quiet mind;

The equal friend; no grudge nor strife;
No charge or rule nor governance;
Without disease the healthful life;
The household of continuance.
The Happy Life

21 The chaste wife wise, without debate;

Such sleeps as may beguile the night;
Content thyself with thine estate;
Neither wish death, nor fear his might.

R.S. SURTEES 1803–1864

1 More people are flattered into virtue than bullied out
of vice.
The Analysis of the Hunting Field (1846), ch.1

2 The only infallible rule we know is, that the man who
is always talking about being a gentleman never is
one.
Ask Mamma (1858), ch.1

3 Major Yammerton was rather a peculiar man,
inasmuch as he was an ass, without being a fool.
ch.25

4 'Unting is all that's worth living for—all time is lost
wot is not spent in 'unting—it is like the hair we
breathe—if we have it not we die—it's the sport of
kings, the image of war without its guilt, and only
five-and-twenty per cent of its danger.
Handley Cross (1843), ch.7. See 172:7

5 'Unting fills my thoughts by day, and many a good run
I have in my sleep. Many a dig in the ribs I gives Mrs
J when I think they're running into the warmint
(renewed cheers). No man is fit to be called a
sportsman wot doesn't kick his wife out of bed on a
haverage once in three weeks!
ch.11

6 Tell me a man's a fox-hunter, and I loves him at once.

7 He will bring his nightcap with him, for where the
M.F.H. dines he sleeps, and where the M.F.H. sleeps
he breakfasts.
ch.15

8 I'll fill hup the chinks wi' cheese.

9 Well did that great man, I think it was Sir Walter
Scott, but if it warn't, 'twas little Bartley, the
bootmaker, say, that there was no young man wot
would not rather have a himputation on his morality
than on his 'ossmanship.
ch.16

10 It ar'n't that I loves the fox less, but that I loves the
'ound more.

11 I can stand a wast of praise.
ch.24

12 Unless a man has a good many servants, he had better
have them cleanin' his 'oss than cleanin' his breeches.
ch.27

13 Paid for catching my 'oss, 6d.
ch.29

14 Con-found all presents wot eat!
ch.37

15 Hellish dark, and smells of cheese!
ch.50

16 'Hurrah! blister my kidneys!' exclaimed he in delight,
'it is a frost!—the dahlias are dead!'
ch.59

17 Three things I never lends—my 'oss, my wife, and my
name.
Hillingdon Hall (1845), ch.33

18 Every man shouting in proportion to the amount of his
subscription.
Jorrocks's Jaunts and Jollities (1838). No.1. **Swell and the
Surrey**

19 Jorrocks, who is not afraid of 'the pace' so long as
there is no leaping.

20 Champagne certainly gives one werry gentlemanly
ideas, but for a continuance, I don't know but I should
prefer mild hale.
No.9. **Mr. Jorrocks in Paris**

21 No one knows how ungentlemanly he can look, until
he has seen himself in a shocking bad hat.
Mr. Facey Romford's Hounds (1865), ch.9

22 Better be killed than frightened to death.
ch.32

23 Thinking that life would be very pleasant if it were not
for its enjoyments.
See 314:10

24 These sort of boobies think that people come to balls
to do nothing but dance; whereas everyone knows that
the real business of a ball is either to look out for a
wife, to look after a wife, or to look after somebody
else's wife.
ch.56

25 The young ladies entered the drawing-room in the full
fervour of sisterly animosity.
Mr. Sponge's Sporting Tour (1853), ch.17

26 Women never look so well as when one comes in wet
and dirty from hunting.
ch.21

27 He was a gentleman who was generally spoken of as
having nothing a-year, paid quarterly.
ch.24

28 There is no secret so close as that between a rider and
his horse.
ch.31

29 When at length they rose to go to bed, it struck each
man as he followed his neighbour upstairs that the one
before him walked very crookedly.
ch.35

HANNEN SWAFFER 1879–1962

30 Freedom of the press in Britain is freedom to print
such of the proprietor's prejudices as the advertisers
don't object to.
In conversation with Tom Driberg, c.1928

JONATHAN SWIFT 1667–1745

31 I conceive some scattered notions about a superior
power to be of singular use for the common people, as
furnishing excellent materials to keep children quiet
when they grow peevish, and providing topics of
amusement in a tedious winter-night.
An Argument Against Abolishing Christianity (1708)

32 Satire is a sort of glass, wherein beholders do
generally discover everybody's face but their own.
The Battle of the Books (1704), preface

33 Instead of dirt and poison we have rather chosen to fill
our hives with honey and wax; thus furnishing
mankind with the two noblest of things, which are
sweetness and light.

34 I have heard of a man who had a mind to sell his
house, and therefore carried a piece of brick in his

pocket, which he shewed as a pattern to encourage purchasers.
The Drapier's Letters, No. 2 (4 Aug. 1724)

1 He [the emperor] is taller by almost the breadth of my nail than any of his court, which alone is enough to strike an awe into the beholders.
Gulliver's Travels (1726). **Voyage to Lilliput,** ch.2

2 The colonel and his officers were in much pain, especially when they saw me take out my penknife.

3 He put this engine [a watch] to our ears, which made an incessant noise like that of a water-mill; and we conjecture it is either some unknown animal, or the god that he worships; but we are more inclined to the latter opinion.

4 It is alleged indeed, that the high heels are most agreeable to our ancient constitution: but however this be, his Majesty hath determined to make use of only low heels in the administration of the government.
ch.4

5 I cannot but conclude the bulk of your natives to be the most pernicious race of little odious vermin that nature ever suffered to crawl upon the surface of the earth.
Voyage to Brobdingnag, ch.6

6 And he gave it for his opinion, that whoever could make two ears of corn or two blades of grass to grow upon a spot of ground where only one grew before, would deserve better of mankind, and do more essential service to his country than the whole race of politicians put together.
ch.7

7 He had been eight years upon a project for extracting sun-beams out of cucumbers, which were to be put into vials hermetically sealed, and let out to warm the air in raw inclement summers.
Voyage to Laputa, etc., ch.5

8 These unhappy people were proposing schemes for persuading monarchs to choose favourites upon the score of their wisdom, capacity and virtue; of teaching ministers to consult the public good; of rewarding merit, great abilities and eminent services; of instructing princes to know their true interest by placing it on the same foundation with that of their people: of choosing for employment persons qualified to exercise them; with many other wild impossible chimeras, that never entered before into the heart of man to conceive, and confirmed in me the old observation, that there is nothing so extravagant and irrational which some philosophers have not maintained for truth.
ch.6

9 I said the thing which was not.
A Voyage to the Houyhnhnms, ch.3

10 I told him...that we ate when we were not hungry, and drank without the provocation of thirst.
ch.6

11 Plaguy twelvepenny weather.
Journal to Stella, 26 Oct. 1710

12 'Tis very warm weather when one's in bed.
8 Nov. 1710

13 We are so fond of one another, because our ailments are the same.
1 Feb. 1711

14 Will she pass in a crowd? Will she make a figure in a country church?
9 Feb. 1711

15 I love good creditable acquaintance; I love to be the worst of the company.
17 May 1711

16 He was a fiddler, and consequently a rogue.
25 July 1711

17 He showed me his bill of fare to tempt me to dine with him; poh, said I, I value not your bill of fare, give me your bill of company.
2 Sept. 1711

18 We were to do more business after dinner; but after dinner is after dinner—an old saying and a true, 'much drinking, little thinking'.
26 Feb. 1712

19 Monday is parson's holiday.
3 Mar. 1712

20 Proper words in proper places, make the true definition of a style.
Letter to a Young Clergyman, 9 Jan. 1720

21 If Heaven had looked upon riches to be a valuable thing, it would not have given them to such a scoundrel.
Letter to Miss Vanhomrigh, 12-13 Aug. 1720

22 You have but a very few years to be young and handsome in the eyes of the world; and as few months to be so in the eyes of a husband, who is not a fool.
Letter to a Young Lady on her Marriage (1723)

23 I have ever hated all nations, professions and communities, and all my love is towards individuals...But principally I hate and detest that animal called man; although I heartily love John, Peter, Thomas, and so forth.
Letter to Pope, 29 Sept. 1725

24 Not die here in a rage, like a poisoned rat in a hole.
Letter to Bolingbroke, 21 Mar. 1729

25 Surely man is a broomstick!
A Meditation upon a Broomstick (1710)

26 I have been assured by a very knowing American of my acquaintance in London, that a young healthy child well nursed is at a year old a most delicious, nourishing, and wholesome food, whether stewed, roasted, baked, or boiled, and I make no doubt that it will equally serve in a fricassee, or a ragout.
A Modest Proposal for Preventing the Children of Ireland from being a Burden to their Parents or Country (1729)

27 I mean, you lie—under a mistake.
Polite Conversation (1738). Dialogue 1

28 Why every one as they like; as the good woman said when she kissed her cow.

29 She wears her clothes, as if they were thrown on her with a pitchfork.

30 Faith, that's as well said, as if I had said it myself.
Dialogue 2

31 Lord, I wonder what fool it was that first invented kissing!

32 I'll give you leave to call me anything, if you don't call me spade.

33 I always love to begin a journey on Sundays, because I shall have the prayers of the church, to preserve all that travel by land, or by water.

1 It is a maxim, that those to whom everybody allows the second place, have an undoubted title to the first.
A Tale of a Tub, (1704), Dedication

2 Books, like men their authors, have no more than one way of coming into the world, but there are ten thousand to go out of it, and return no more.

3 Satire, being levelled at all, is never resented for an offence by any.
Preface

4 What though his head be empty, provided his commonplace book be full.
Digression in Praise of Digression

5 Last week I saw a woman flayed, and you will hardly believe, how much it altered her person for the worse.
ch.IX

6 I never saw, heard, nor read, that the clergy were beloved in any nation where Christianity was the religion of the country. Nothing can render them popular, but some degree of persecution.
Thoughts on Religion (1768)

7 We have just enough religion to make us hate, but not enough to make us love one another.
Thoughts on Various Subjects (1706)

8 When a true genius appears in the world, you may know him by this sign, that the dunces are all in confederacy against him.

9 What they do in heaven we are ignorant of; what they do *not* we are told expressly, that they neither marry, nor are given in marriage.
See 67:21

10 The reasons why so few marriages are happy, is, because young ladies spend their time in making nets, not in making cages.

11 Few are qualified to shine in company; but it is in most men's power to be agreeable.

12 Every man desires to live long; but no man would be old.

13 A nice man is a man of nasty ideas.

14 Old men and comets have been reverenced for the same reason; their long beards, and pretences to foretell events.

15 I never wonder to see men wicked, but I often wonder to see them not ashamed.

16 Laws are like cobwebs, which may catch small flies, but let wasps and hornets break through.
A Tritical Essay upon the Faculties of the Mind (1709). See 512:23

17 There is nothing in this world constant, but inconstancy.

18 Good God! what a genius I had when I wrote that book. *[The Tale of a Tub.]*
Sir Walter Scott, *Life of Swift. Works of Swift* (1824), vol.i, p.89

19 I shall be like that tree, I shall die at the top.
Sir Walter Scott, *Memoirs of Swift*

20 How haughtily he cocks his nose,
To tell what every schoolboy knows.
The Country Life, l.81

21 Only take this rule along,
Always to advise her wrong;
And reprove her when she's right;

She may then grow wise for spite.
Daphne (1730), l.35

22 In all distresses of our friends,
We first consult our private ends;
While nature, kindly bent to ease us,
Points out some circumstance to please us.
Verses on the Death of Dr. Swift (1731), l.7

23 Poor Pope will grieve a month, and Gay
A week, and Arbuthnot a day.
St John himself will scarce forbear
To bite his pen, and drop a tear.
The rest will give a shrug, and cry,
'I'm sorry—but we all must die!'
l.207

24 Yet malice never was his aim;
He lash'd the vice, but spared the name;
No individual could resent,
Where thousands equally were meant.
l.512

25 He gave the little wealth he had
To build a house for fools and mad;
And show'd, by one satiric touch,
No nation wanted it so much.
l.538

26 A coming shower your shooting corns presage.
A Description of a City Shower (1710), l.9

27 They never would hear,
But turn the deaf ear,
As a matter they had no concern in.
Dingley and Brent (1724), ii

28 I often wish'd that I had clear,
For life, six hundred pounds a-year,
A handsome house to lodge a friend,
A river at my garden's end,
A terrace walk, and half a rood
Of land, set out to plant a wood.
Imitation of Horace (1714), bk.II, sat.vi, l.1. See 262:9

29 Nor do they trust their tongue alone,
But speak a language of their own;
Can read a nod, a shrug, a look,
Far better than a printed book;
Convey a libel in a frown,
And wink a reputation down.
The Journal of a Modern Lady (1729), l.188

30 Hail, fellow, well met,
All dirty and wet:
Find out, if you can,
Who's master, who's man.
My Lady's Lamentation (1728), l.171

31 Th' artillery of words.
Ode to...Sancroft (1692), i

32 Philosophy! the lumber of the schools.
Ode to Sir W. Temple (1692), ii

33 Say, Britain, could you ever boast,—
Three poets in an age at most?
Our chilling climate hardly bears
A sprig of bays in fifty years.
On Poetry (1733), l.5

34 Then, rising with Aurora's light,
The Muse invoked, sit down to write;
Blot out, correct, insert, refine,
Enlarge, diminish, interline.
l.85

1 As learned commentators view
  In Homer more than Homer knew.
  1.103

2 So geographers, in Afric-maps,
  With savage-pictures fill their gaps;
  And o'er unhabitable downs
  Place elephants for want of towns.
  1.177

3 He gives directions to the town,
  To cry it up, or run it down.
  1.269

4 Hobbes clearly proves, that every creature
  Lives in a state of war by nature.
  1.319

5 So, naturalists observe, a flea
  Hath smaller fleas that on him prey;
  And these have smaller fleas to bite 'em,
  And so proceed *ad infinitum*.
  Thus every poet, in his kind,
  Is bit by him that comes behind.
  1.337

6 Walls have tongues, and hedges ears.
  **A Pastoral Dialogue between Richmond Lodge and Marble
  Hill** (1727), 1.8

7 Humour is odd, grotesque, and wild,
  Only by affectation spoil'd;
  'Tis never by invention got,
  Men have it when they know it not.
  To Mr. Delany (1718), 1.25

8 Hated by fools, and fools to hate,
  Be that my motto and my fate.
  1.171

9 In Church your grandsire cut his throat;
    To do the job too long he tarry'd,
  He should have had my hearty vote,
    To cut his throat before he marry'd.
  Verses on the Upright Judge

10 'Libertas et natale solum':
   Fine words! I wonder where you stole 'em.
   Whitshed's Motto on his Coach (1724)

11 A beggarly people!
   A church and no steeple! [Of St Ann's Church,
     Dublin.]
   Attr. to Swift by Malone. See Prior, *Life of Malone* (1860), p.381

12 *Ubi saeva indignatio ulterius cor lacerare nequit.*
   Where fierce indignation can no longer tear his heart.
   Swift's Epitaph

ALGERNON CHARLES SWINBURNE 1837–1909

13 Superflux of pain.
   Anactoria, 1.27

14 Maiden, and mistress of the months and stars
   Now folded in the flowerless fields of heaven.
   Atalanta in Calydon (1865). **Collected Poetical Works** (1924),
   vol.ii, p.247, l.1

15 When the hounds of spring are on winter's traces,
     The mother of months in meadow or plain
   Fills the shadows and windy places
     With lisp of leaves and ripple of rain;
   And the brown bright nightingale amorous
   Is half assuaged for Itylus,
   For the Thracian ships and the foreign faces,

The tongueless vigil and all the pain.
Chorus, p.249

16 Bind on thy sandals, O thou most fleet,
   Over the splendour and speed of thy feet;
   For the faint east quickens, the wan west shivers,
     Round the feet of the day and the feet of the night.

   Where shall we find her, how shall we sing to her,
     Fold our hands round her knees, and cling?
   O that man's heart were as fire and could spring to
     her,
     Fire, or the strength of the streams that spring!

17 For winter's rains and ruins are over,
     And all the season of snows and sins;
   The days dividing lover and lover,
     The light that loses, the night that wins;
   And time remembered is grief forgotten,
   And frosts are slain and flowers begotten,
   And in green underwood and cover
     Blossom by blossom the spring begins.

18 And Pan by noon and Bacchus by night,
     Fleeter of foot than the fleet-foot kid,
   Follows with dancing and fills with delight
     The Maenad and the Bassarid;
   And soft as lips that laugh and hide
   The laughing leaves of the tree divide,
   And screen from seeing and leave in sight
     The god pursuing, the maiden hid.
   p.250

19 The wolf that follows, the fawn that flies.

20 Before the beginning of years
     There came to the making of man
   Time with a gift of tears,
     Grief with a glass that ran.
   p.258

21 Strength without hands to smite,
     Love that endures for a breath;
   Night, the shadow of light,
     And Life, the shadow of death.

22 We have seen thee, O love, thou art fair; thou art
     goodly, O Love.
   p.273

23 For words divide and rend;
   But silence is most noble till the end.
   p.299

24 For a day and a night Love sang to us, played with us,
     Folded us round from the dark and the light;
   And our hearts were fulfilled with the music he made
       with us,
   Made with our hands and our lips while he stayed with
       us,
     Stayed in mid passage his pinions from flight
       For a day and a night.
   At Parting

25 Shall I strew on thee rose or rue or laurel,
     Brother, on this that was the veil of thee?
     Or quiet sea-flower moulded by the sea,
   Or simplest growth of meadow-sweet or sorrel?
   Ave atque Vale, i

26 Now all strange hours and all strange loves are over,
     Dreams and desires and sombre songs and sweet,
     Hast thou found place at the great knees and feet
   Of some pale Titan-woman like a lover
     Such as thy vision here solicited,

Under the shadow of her fair vast head,
The deep division of prodigious breasts,
The solemn slope of mighty limbs asleep?
vi

1 Sleep; and if life was bitter to thee, pardon,
If sweet, give thanks; thou hast no more to live;
And to give thanks is good, and to forgive.
xvii

2 Villon, our sad bad glad mad brother's name.
Ballad of François Villon

3 O slain and spent and sacrificed
People, the grey-grown speechless Christ.
Before a Crucifix. Poetical Works (1924), vol.i, p.744

4 We shift and bedeck and bedrape us,
Thou art noble and nude and antique.
Dolores (1866), vii

5 Change in a trice
The lilies and languors of virtue
For the raptures and roses of vice.
ix

6 O splendid and sterile Dolores,
Our Lady of Pain.

7 Ah beautiful passionate body
That never has ached with a heart!
xi

8 But sweet as the rind was the core is;
We are fain of thee still, we are fain,
O sanguine and subtle Dolores,
Our Lady of Pain.
xiii

9 The delight that consumes the desire,
The desire that outruns the delight.
xiv

10 For the crown of our life as it closes
Is darkness, the fruit thereof dust;
No thorns go as deep as a rose's,
And love is more cruel than lust.
Time turns the old days to derision,
Our loves into corpses or wives;
And marriage and death and division
Make barren our lives.
xx

11 What ailed us, O gods, to desert you
For creeds that refuse and restrain?
Come down and redeem us from virtue,
Our Lady of Pain.
xxxv

12 I shall remember while the light lives yet
And in the night time I shall not forget.
Erotion

13 There was a poor poet named Clough,
Whom his friends all united to puff,
But the public, though dull,
Had not such a skull
As belonged to believers in Clough.
Essays and Studies (1875), **Matthew Arnold** (printed as prose)

14 Bright with names that men remember, loud with
names that men forget.
Eton: An Ode

15 What adders came to shed their coats?
What coiled obscene
Small serpents with soft stretching throats

Caressed Faustine?
Faustine (1862)

16 Those eyes the greenest of things blue,
The bluest of things grey.
Félise

17 In a coign of the cliff between lowland and highland,
At the sea-down's edge between windward and lee,
Walled round with rocks as an inland island,
The ghost of a garden fronts the sea.
A Forsaken Garden

18 The fields fall southward, abrupt and broken,
To the low last edge of the long lone land.
If a step should sound or a word be spoken,
Would a ghost not rise at the strange guest's hand?
So long have the grey bare walls lain guestless,
Through branches and briars if a man make way,
He shall find no life but the sea-wind's, restless
Night and day.

19 'For the foam-flowers endure when the rose-blossoms
wither
And men that love lightly may die—but we?'
And the same wind sang and the same waves
whitened,
And or ever the garden's last petals were shed,
In the lips that had whispered, the eyes that had
lightened,
Love was dead.

20 Stretched out on the spoils that his own hand spread.
As a god self-slain on his own strange altar,
Death lies dead.

21 Here, where the world is quiet;
Here, where all trouble seems
Dead winds' and spent waves' riot
In doubtful dreams of dreams.
The Garden of Proserpine

22 Pale, beyond porch and portal,
Crowned with calm leaves, she stands
Who gathers all things mortal
With cold immortal hands.

23 Dead dreams of days forsaken,
Blind buds that snows have shaken,
Wild leaves that winds have taken,
Red strays of ruined springs.

24 We are not sure of sorrow,
And joy was never sure.

25 From too much love of living,
From hope and fear set free,
We thank with brief thanksgiving
Whatever gods may be
That no man lives forever,
That dead men rise up never;
That even the weariest river
Winds somewhere safe to sea.

26 Calling a crowned man royal
That was no more than a king.
The Halt before Rome

27 Fiddle, we know, is diddle: and diddle, we take it, is
dee.
The Heptalogia. **The Higher Pantheism in a Nutshell.** See
533:29

28 Green leaves of thy labour, white flowers of thy

thought, and red fruit of thy death.
Hertha

1 But God, if a God there be, is the substance of men
 which is man.
Hymn of Man

2 Glory to Man in the highest! for Man is the master of
 things.

3 Yea, is not even Apollo, with hair and harpstring of
 gold,
 A bitter God to follow, a beautiful God to behold?
 I am sick of singing: the bays burn deep and chafe: I
 am fain
 To rest a little from praise and grievous pleasure and
 pain.
Hymn to Proserpine

4 Wilt thou yet take all, Galilean? but these thou shalt
 not take,
 The laurel, the palms and the paean, the breasts of the
 nymphs in the brake;
 Breasts more soft than a dove's, that tremble with
 tenderer breath;
 And all the wings of the Loves, and all the joy before
 death.

5 Thou hast conquered, O pale Galilean; the world has
 grown grey from Thy breath;
 We have drunken of things Lethean, and fed on the
 fullness of death.
 Laurel is green for a season, and love is sweet for a
 day;
 But love grows bitter with treason, and laurel outlives
 not May.
 See 286:31

6 For the old faiths loosen and fall, the new years ruin
 and rend.

7 Though the feet of thine high priests tread where thy
 lords and our forefathers trod,
 Though these that were Gods are dead, and thou being
 dead art a God,
 Though before thee the throned Cytherean be fallen,
 and hidden her head,
 Yet thy kingdom shall pass, Galilean, thy dead shall go
 down to thee dead.

8 As the deep dim soul of a star.

9 A little soul for a little bears up this corpse which is
 man.

10 I remember the way we parted,
 The day and the way we met;
 You hoped we were both broken-hearted,
 And knew we should both forget.
An Interlude

11 And the best and the worst of this is
 That neither is most to blame,
 If you have forgotten my kisses
 And I have forgotten your name.

12 Swallow, my sister, O sister swallow,
 How can thine heart be full of the spring?
 A thousand summers are over and dead.
 What hast thou found in the spring to follow?
 What hast thou found in thine heart to sing?
 What wilt thou do when the summer is shed?
Itylus (1864)

13 Sister, my sister, O fleet sweet swallow,

Thy way is long to the sun and the south;
 But I, fulfilled of my heart's desire,
 Shedding my song upon height, upon hollow,
 From tawny body and sweet small mouth
 Feed the heart of the night with fire.

I the nightingale all spring through,
 O swallow, sister, O changing swallow,
 All spring through till the spring be done,
 Clothed with the light of the night on the dew,
 Sing, while the hours and the wild birds follow,
 Take flight and follow and find the sun.

14 Till life forget and death remember,
 Till thou remember and I forget.

15 The small slain body, the flower-like face,
 Can I remember if thou forget?

16 Thou hast forgotten, O summer swallow,
 But the world shall end when I forget.

17 Apples of gold for the king's daughter.
The King's Daughter

18 Ah, yet would God this flesh of mine might be
 Where air might wash and long leaves cover me;
 Where tides of grass break into foam of flowers,
 Or where the wind's feet shine along the sea.
Laus Veneris (1866)

19 Until God loosen over sea and land
 The thunder of the trumpets of the night.

20 But you would have felt my soul in a kiss,
 And known that once if I loved you well;
 And I would have given my soul for this
 To burn for ever in burning hell.
Les Noyades

21 If love were what the rose is,
 And I were like the leaf,
 Our lives would grow together
 In sad or singing weather,
 Blown fields or flowerful closes,
 Green pleasure or grey grief.
A Match

22 Ask nothing more of me, sweet;
 All I can give you I give.
 Heart of my heart, were it more,
 More would be laid at your feet:
 Love that should help you to live,
 Song that should spur you to soar.
The Oblation

23 They have tied the world in a tether,
 They have bought over God with a fee.
A Song in Time of Order (1852)

24 The strong sea-daisies feast on the sun.
The Triumph of Time

25 A broken blossom, a ruined rhyme.

26   Content you;
 The gate is strait; I shall not be there.

27 I will go back to the great sweet mother,
 Mother and lover of men, the sea.
 I will go down to her, I and no other,
 Close with her, kiss her and mix her with me.

28 I shall sleep, and move with the moving ships,
 Change as the winds change, veer in the tide.

29 There lived a singer in France of old
 By the tideless dolorous midland sea.

In a land of sand and ruin and gold
There shone one woman, and none but she.

1 Sweet red splendid kissing mouth.
Translations from Villon. **Complaint of the fair Armouress**

2 There's no good girl's lip out of Paris.
Ballad of the Women of Paris

JOHN ADDINGTON SYMONDS 1840–1893

3 These things shall be! A loftier race
Than e'er the world hath known shall rise,
With flame of freedom in their souls,
And light of knowledge in their eyes.
Hymn

JOHN MILLINGTON SYNGE 1871–1909

4 A man who is not afraid of the sea will soon be
drownded for he will be going out on a day he
shouldn't. But we do be afraid of the sea, and we do
only be drownded now and again.
The Aran Islands, Pt.II

5 I've lost the only playboy of the western world.
The Playboy of the Western World, III, closing words

TACITUS A.D. 55 or 56–c.120

6 *Nunc terminus Britanniae patet, atque omne ignotum
pro magnifico est.*
Now the boundary of Britain is revealed, and
everything unknown is held to be glorious.
Agricola, 30. Allegedly reporting a British leader, 'Calgacus'.

7 *Solitudinem faciunt pacem appellant.*
They make a wilderness and call it peace.

8 *Proprium humani ingenii est odisse quem laeseris.*
It is part of human nature to hate the man you have
hurt.
42

9 *Tu vero felix, Agricola, non vitae tantum claritate, sed
etiam opportunitate mortis.*
You were indeed fortunate, Agricola, not only in the
distinction of your life, but also in the lucky timing of
your death.
45

10 *Sine ira et studio.*
Without either anger or zealousness.
Annals, i.1

11 *Elegantiae arbiter.*
The authority on taste.
xvi.18. Of Petronius

12 *Rara temporum felicitate ubi sentire quae velis et quae
sentias dicere licet.*
These times having the rare good fortune that you may
think what you like and say what you think.
Histories, i.1

13 *Maior privato visus dum privatus fuit, et omnium
consensu capax imperii nisi imperasset.*
He seemed much greater than a private citizen while he
still was a private citizen, and had he never become
emperor everyone would have agreed that he had the
capacity to reign.
49. Of the Emperor Galba

14 *Etiam sapientibus cupido gloriae novissima exuitur.*
Love of fame is the last thing even learned men can

bear to be parted from.
iv.6

CHARLES-MAURICE DE TALLEYRAND
1754–1838

15 *Surtout, Messieurs, point de zèle.*
Above all, gentlemen, not the slightest zeal.
P. Chasles, *Voyages d'un critique à travers la vie et les livres*
(1868), vol.2, p.407

16 *Qui n'a pas vécu dans les années voisines de 1789 ne
sait pas ce que c'est que le plaisir de vivre.*
He who has not lived during the years around 1789 can
not know what is meant by the pleasure of life.
M. Guizot, *Mémoires pour servir à l'histoire de mon temps*
(1858), I, 6

17 *Ils n'ont rien appris, ni rien oublié.*
They have learnt nothing, and forgotten nothing.
Attributed to Talleyrand by the Chevalier de Panat in a letter to
Mallet du Pan, Jan. 1796, 'Personne n'est corrigé, personne n'a su
ni rien oublier ni rien apprendre.' *Mémoires et correspondance de
Mallet du Pan* (1851), II.196. See 199:7

18 *Quelle triste vieillesse vous vous préparez.*
What a sad old-age you are preparing for yourself.
J.J.M.C. Amédée Pichot, *Souvenirs Intimes sur M. de
Talleyrand*, 'Le Pour et le Contre.' A young diplomat had prided
himself, in front of Talleyrand, on his ignorance of whist.

19 *Voilà le commencement de la fin.*
This is the beginning of the end.
Attr. On the announcement of Napoleon's defeat at Borodino,
1812. Sainte-Beuve, *M. de Talleyrand* (1870), ch.3

NAHUM TATE 1652–1715
and NICHOLAS BRADY 1659–1726

20 As pants the hart for cooling streams
When heated in the chase.
New Version of the Psalms (1696). **As Pants the Hart**

21 Through all the changing scenes of life.
Through all the Changing

22 While shepherds watch'd their flocks by night,
All seated on the ground,
The Angel of the Lord came down,
And glory shone around.
Supplement to the New Version of the Psalms (1700). **While
Shepherds Watched**

ANN TAYLOR 1782–1866
and JANE TAYLOR 1783–1824

23 I thank the goodness and the grace
Which on my birth have smiled,
And made me, in these Christian days,
A happy English child.
Hymns for Infant Minds, I. **A Child's Hymn of Praise**

24 'Tis a *credit* to any good girl to be neat,
But quite a *disgrace* to be fine.
Hymns for Sunday Schools. **The Folly of Finery**

25 Who ran to help me when I fell,
And would some pretty story tell,
Or kiss the place to make it well?
My Mother.
Original Poems. **My Mother.** (By Ann Taylor)

26 How pleasant it is, at the end of the day,
No follies to have to repent;
But reflect on the past, and be able to say,

That my time has been properly spent.
Rhymes for the Nursery. The Way to be Happy. (By Jane Taylor)

1 Twinkle, twinkle, little star,
How I wonder what you are!
Up above the world so high,
Like a diamond in the sky!
The Star. (By Jane Taylor)

BAYARD TAYLOR 1825–1878

2 Till the sun grows cold,
And the stars are old,
And the leaves of the Judgment Book unfold.
Bedouin Song. Refrain

BISHOP JEREMY TAYLOR 1613–1667

3 As our life is very short, so it is very miserable, and therefore it is well it is short.
The Rule and Exercise of Holy Dying (1651), ch.i, sect.4

4 Too quick a sense of a constant infelicity.
5

5 Every school-boy knows it.
On the Real Presence, V, par.I

6 The union of hands and hearts.
Sermons. The Marriage Ring, pt.i

TOM TAYLOR 1817–1880

7 Hawkshaw, the detective.
The Ticket-of-leave Man, IV.i. Commonly remembered, and delivered, in the form 'I am Hawkshaw, the detective'.

ARCHBISHOP FREDERICK TEMPLE 1821–1902

8 'My aunt was suddenly prevented from going a voyage in a ship what went down—would you call that a case of Providential interference?'
'Can't tell: didn't know your aunt.'
Sandford, *Memoirs of Archbishop Temple*, (1906), vol. II, p. 705

9 There is a certain class of clergyman whose mendicity is only equalled by their mendacity.
Remark at a meeting of the Ecclesiastical Commissioners quoted by Sir George Leveson Gower, *Years of Endeavour* (1942)

SIR WILLIAM TEMPLE 1628–1699

10 When all is done, human life is, at the greatest and the best, but like a froward child, that must be play'd with and humoured a little to keep it quiet till it falls asleep, and then the care is over.
Essay on Poetry, ad fin.

ARCHBISHOP WILLIAM TEMPLE 1881–1944

11 In place of the conception of the Power-State we are led to that of the Welfare-State.
Citizen and Churchman (1941), ch.II

12 Christianity is the most materialistic of all great religions.
Reading in St John's Gospel, vol.I (1939), Introduction

13 'Are you not,' a Rugby master had asked him in discussing one of his [schoolboy] essays, 'a little out of your depth here?' 'Perhaps, Sir,' was the confident

reply, 'but I can swim.'
F.A. Iremonger, *William Temple*

SIR JOHN TENNIEL 1820–1914

14 Dropping the pilot.
Caption of a cartoon and title of a poem in *Punch*, 29 March 1890, referring to the departure from office of Bismark

ALFRED, LORD TENNYSON 1809–1892

15 For nothing worthy proving can be proven,
Nor yet disproven: wherefore thou be wise,
Cleave ever to the sunnier side of doubt.
The Ancient Sage (1885), l.66

16 Her arms across her breast she laid;
She was more fair than words can say:
Bare-footed came the beggar maid
Before the king Cophetua.
In robe and crown the king stept down,
To meet and greet her on her way;
'It is no wonder,' said the lords,
'She is more beautiful than day.'

As shines the moon in clouded skies,
She in her poor attire was seen:
One praised her ankles, one her eyes,
One her dark hair and lovesome mien.
So sweet a face, such angel grace,
In all that land had never been:
Cophetua sware a royal oath:
'This beggar maid shall be my queen!'
The Beggar Maid (1842)

17 Break, break, break,
On thy cold gray stones, O Sea!
And I would that my tongue could utter
The thoughts that arise in me.
Break, Break, Break (1842)

18 And the stately ships go on
To their haven under the hill;
But O for the touch of a vanish'd hand,
And the sound of a voice that is still!

19 A happy bridesmaid makes a happy bride.
The Bridesmaid (1830), l.4

20 I come from haunts of coot and hern,
I make a sudden sally
And sparkle out among the fern,
To bicker down a valley.
The Brook (1864), l.23

21 For men may come and men may go,
But I go on for ever.
l.33

22 The Lord let the house of a brute to the soul of a man,
And the man said, 'Am I your debtor?'
And the Lord—'Not yet: but make it as clean as you can,
And then I will let you a better.'
By an Evolutionist (1889)

23 Half a league, half a league,
Half a league onward,
All in the valley of Death
Rode the six hundred.
The Charge of the Light Brigade (1854)

24 'Forward the Light Brigade!'
Was there a man dismay'd?

Not tho' the soldier knew
   Some one had blunder'd:
Their's not to make reply,
Their's not to reason why,
Their's but to do and die:
Into the valley of Death
   Rode the six hundred.

Cannon to right of them
Cannon to left of them,
Cannon in front of them
   Volley'd and thunder'd.

1 Into the jaws of Death,
Into the mouth of Hell.

2 Come not, when I am dead,
   To drop thy foolish tears upon my grave,
To trample round my fallen head,
   And vex the unhappy dust thou wouldst not save.
Come Not, When I Am Dead (1842), i

3 Sunset and evening star,
   And one clear call for me!
And may there be no moaning of the bar
   When I put out to sea.
Crossing the Bar (1889)

4 Twilight and evening bell,
   And after that the dark!
And may there be no sadness of farewell,
   When I embark;

For tho' from out our bourne of Time and Place
   The flood may bear me far,
I hope to see my Pilot face to face
   When I have crost the bar.

5 O Love what hours were thine and mine,
In lands of palm and southern pine;
   In lands of palm, of orange-blossom,
Of olive, aloe, and maize and vine.
The Daisy (1847), i

6 A daughter of the gods, divinely tall
   And most divinely fair. [Iphigenia.]
A Dream of Fair Women (1833), l.87

7 He clasps the crag with crooked hands;
Close to the sun in lonely lands,
Ring'd with the azure world, he stands.
The wrinkled sea beneath him crawls;
He watches from his mountain walls,
And like a thunderbolt he falls.
The Eagle (1842)

8 The curate; he was fatter than his cure.
Edwin Morris (1842), l.15

9 God made the woman for the man,
   And for the good and increase of the world.
l.50

10   Slight Sir Robert with his watery smile
And educated whisker.
l.128

11 And when they buried him the little port
Had seldom seen a costlier funeral.
Enoch Arden (1864)

12 O mighty-mouth'd inventor of harmonies,
   O skill'd to sing of Time or Eternity,
     God-gifted organ-voice of England,
     Milton, a name to resound for ages.
Experiments. Milton: Alcaics

13   All that bowery loneliness,
The brooks of Eden mazily murmuring.

14 O you chorus of indolent reviewers.
Milton: Hendecasyllabics

15 The mellow lin-lan-lone of evening bells.
Far-Far-Away (1889)

16 O Love, O fire! once he drew
With one long kiss my whole soul thro'
My lips, as sunlight drinketh dew.
Fatima (1833), iii

17 Row us out from Desenzano, to your Sirmione row!
Frater Ave atque Vale

18 Tenderest of Roman poets nineteen-hundred years
    ago,
'Frater Ave atque Vale'—as we wander'd to and fro
Gazing at the Lydian laughter of the Garda lake below
Sweet Catullus' all-but-island, olive-silvery Sirmio!
See 136:28

19 More black than ashbuds in the front of March.
The Gardener's Daughter (1842), l.28

20 A sight to make an old man young.
l.140

21 Then she rode forth, clothed on with chastity.
Godiva (1842), l.53

22 With twelve great shocks of sound, the shameless
    noon
Was clash'd and hammer'd from a hundred towers.
l.74

23   Ah! when shall all men's good
Be each man's rule, and universal Peace
Lie like a shaft of light across the land?
The Golden Year (1842), l.47

24 Thro' all the circle of the golden year.
l.51

25 That a lie which is all a lie may be met and fought
    with outright,
But a lie which is part a truth is a harder matter to
    fight.
The Grandmother (1847), viii

26 That man's the true Conservative
Who lops the moulder'd branch away.
Hands All Round (1885), i

27 Pray God our greatness may not fail
Thro' craven fears of being great.
iii

28 Gigantic daughter of the West,
We drink to thee across the flood...
For art thou not of British blood?
iv. In original version, published in *The Examiner*, 7 Feb. 1852

29 Speak to Him thou for He hears, and Spirit with Spirit
    can meet—
Closer is He than breathing, and nearer than hands and
    feet.
The Higher Pantheism (1847), vi

30 Wearing the white flower of a blameless life,
Before a thousand peering littlenesses,
In that fierce light which beats upon a throne,
And blackens every blot.
The Idylls of the King (1842–1885), Dedication, l.24

31 Man's word is God in man.
The Coming of Arthur, l.132

1 Clothed in white samite, mystic, wonderful.
l.284, and **The Passing of Arthur**, l.199

2 Rain, rain, and sun! a rainbow in the sky!
A young man will be wiser by and by;
An old man's wit may wander ere he die.
l.402

3 From the great deep to the great deep he goes.
l.410

4 Blow trumpet, for the world is white with May.
l.481

5 Live pure, speak true, right wrong, follow the King—
Else, wherefore born?
Gareth and Lynette, l.117

6   The city is built
To music, therefore never built at all,
And therefore built for ever.
l.272

7 Lightly was her slender nose
Tip-tilted like the petal of a flower.
l.576

8 Too late, too late! ye cannot enter now.
Guinevere, l.168

9 For manners are not idle, but the fruit
Of loyal nature, and of noble mind.
l.333

10 The children born of thee are sword and fire,
Red ruin, and the breaking up of laws.
l.422

11 To reverence the King, as if he were
Their conscience, and their conscience as their King,
To break the heathen and uphold the Christ,
To ride abroad redressing human wrongs,
To speak no slander, no, nor listen to it,
To honour his own word as if his God's.
l.465

12 To love one maiden only, cleave to her,
And worship her by years of noble deeds,
Until they won her; for indeed I knew
Of no more subtle master under heaven
Than is the maiden passion for a maid,
Not only to keep down the base in man,
But teach high thought, and amiable words
And courtliness, and the desire of fame,
And love of truth, and all that makes a man.
l.472

13   He never mocks,
For mockery is the fume of little hearts.
l.627

14 I thought I could not breathe in that fine air
That pure severity of perfect light—
I yearn'd for warmth and colour which I found
In Lancelot.
l.640

15 It was my duty to have loved the highest:
It surely was my profit had I known:
It would have been my pleasure had I seen.
We needs must love the highest when we see it,
Not Lancelot, nor another.
l.652

16 To where beyond these voices there is peace.
l.692

17 For good ye are and bad, and like to coins,
Some true, some light, but every one of you

Stamp'd with the image of the King.
The Holy Grail, l.25

18 The cup, the cup itself, from which our Lord
Drank at the last sad supper with his own.
l.46

19 God make thee good as thou art beautiful.
l.136

20 For when was Lancelot wanderingly lewd?
l.148

21 I, maiden, round thee, maiden, bind my belt.
l.159

22   Ye follow wandering fires
Lost in the quagmire!
l.319

23 I will be deafer than the blue-eyed cat,
And thrice as blind as any noon-tide owl,
To holy virgins in their ecstasies,
Henceforward.
l.865

24 So spake the King: I knew not all he meant.
l.919

25 Elaine the fair, Elaine the loveable,
Elaine, the lily maid of Astolat.
Lancelot and Elaine, l.1

26   To me
He is all fault who hath no fault at all:
For who loves me must have a touch of earth.
l.131

27   In me there dwells
No greatness, save it be some far-off touch
Of greatness to know well I am not great.
l.447

28 I know not if I know what true love is,
But if I know, then, if I love not him,
I know there is none other I can love.
l.672

29 The shackles of an old love straiten'd him,
His honour rooted in dishonour stood,
And faith unfaithful kept him falsely true.
l.870

30 Sweet is true love tho' given in vain, in vain;
And sweet is death who puts an end to pain.
l.1000

31   Never yet
Was noble man but made ignoble talk.
He makes no friend who never made a foe.
l.1080

32 Our bond is not the bond of man and wife.
l.1199

33 'Forgive me; mine was jealousy in love.'
He answer'd with his eyes upon the ground,
'That is love's curse; pass on, my Queen, forgiven.'
l.1340

34 Free love—free field—we love but while we may.
The Last Tournament, l.281

35 The dirty nurse, Experience, in her kind
Hath foul'd me.
l.317

36 The greater man, the greater courtesy.
l.628

37 The ptarmigan that whitens ere his hour

Woos his own end.
l.692

1 Our hoard is little, but our hearts are great.
The Marriage of Geraint, l.352

2 For man is man and master of his fate.
l.355

3 Hark, by the bird's song ye may learn the nest.
l.359

4 They take the rustic murmur of their bourg
For the great wave that echoes round the world.
l.419

5 Brave hearts and clean! and yet—God guide
them—young.
Merlin and Vivien, l.29

6 Unfaith in aught is want of faith in all.
l.387

7 It is the little rift within the lute,
That by and by will make the music mute,
And ever widening slowly silence all.
l.388

8 And trust me not at all or all in all.
l.396

9 Man dreams of fame while woman wakes to love.
l.458

10 With this for motto, 'Rather use than fame'.
l.478

11 Where blind and naked Ignorance
Delivers brawling judgments, unashamed,
On all things all day long.
l.662

12 But every page having an ample marge,
And every marge enclosing in the midst
A square of text that looks a little blot.
l.667

13 And none can read the text, not even I;
And none can read the comment but myself.
l.679

14 O selfless man and stainless gentleman!
l.790

15 Defaming and defacing, till she left
Not even Lancelot brave, nor Galahad clean.
l.802

16 For men at most differ as Heaven and Earth,
But women, worst and best, as Heaven and Hell.
l.812

17 Face-flatterer and backbiter are the same.
l.822

18 O great and sane and simple race of brutes
That own no lust because they have no law!
Pelleas and Ettarre, l.471

19 I found Him in the shining of the stars,
I mark'd Him in the flowering of His fields,
But in His ways with men I find Him not.
The Passing of Arthur, l.9

20 So all day long the noise of battle roll'd
Among the mountains by the winter sea.
l.170

21 On one side lay the Ocean, and on one
Lay a great water, and the moon was full.
l.179

22 Authority forgets a dying king.
l.289

23 Clothed with his breath, and looking, as he walk'd,
Larger than human on the frozen hills.
He heard the deep behind him, and a cry
Before.
l.350

24 The days darken round me, and the years,
Among new men, strange faces, other minds.
l.405

25 And slowly answer'd Arthur from the barge:
'The old order changeth, yielding place to new,
And God fulfils himself in many ways,
Lest one good custom should corrupt the world.'
l.407

26 If thou shouldst never see my face again,
Pray for my soul. More things are wrought by prayer
Than this world dreams of. Wherefore, let thy voice
Rise like a fountain for me night and day.
For what are men better than sheep or goats
That nourish a blind life within the brain,
If, knowing God, they lift not hands of prayer
Both for themselves and those who call them friend?
For so the whole round earth is every way
Bound by gold chains about the feet of God.
l.414

27   I am going a long way
With these thou seest—if indeed I go
(For all my mind is clouded with a doubt)—
To the island-valley of Avilion;
Where falls not hail, or rain, or any snow,
Nor ever wind blows loudly; but it lies
Deep-meadow'd, happy, fair with orchard lawns
And bowery hollows crown'd with summer sea,
Where I will heal me of my grievous wound.
l.424

28   Like some full-breasted swan
That, fluting a wild carol ere her death,
Ruffles her pure cold plume, and takes the flood
With swarthy webs.
l.434

29 Believing where we cannot prove.
In Memoriam A.H.H. (1850), prologue. (The numbering of the
Cantos includes the additional Canto No. xxxix, first published in
1869)

30 Thou madest man, he knows not why,
He thinks he was not made to die;
And thou hast made him: thou art just.

31 Our little systems have their day;
They have their day and cease to be:
They are but broken lights of thee,
And thou, O Lord, art more than they.

32 Let knowledge grow from more to more,
But more of reverence in us dwell;
That mind and soul, according well,
May make one music as before.

33 I held it truth, with him who sings
To one clear harp in divers tones,
That men may rise on stepping-stones
Of their dead selves to higher things.
i

34   For words, like Nature, half reveal

And half conceal the Soul within.

v

1 But, for the unquiet heart and brain,
    A use in measured language lies;
    The sad mechanic exercise,
Like dull narcotics, numbing pain.

2   And common is the commonplace,
And vacant chaff well meant for grain.

vi

3   Never morning wore
To evening, but some heart did break.

4   His heavy-shotted hammock-shroud
Drops in his vast and wandering grave.

5 Dark house, by which once more I stand
    Here in the long unlovely street,
    Doors, where my heart was used to beat
So quickly, waiting for a hand.

vii

6 And ghastly thro' the drizzling rain
    On the bald street breaks the blank day.

7   Or where the kneeling hamlet drains
The chalice of the grapes of God.

x

8   The last red leaf is whirl'd away,
The rooks are blown about the skies.

xv

9 Thou comest, much wept for: such a breeze
    Compell'd thy canvas.

xvii

10   And from his ashes may be made
The violet of his native land.

xviii

11 There twice a day the Severn fills;
    The salt sea-water passes by,
    And hushes half the babbling Wye,
And makes a silence in the hills.

xix

12   I do but sing because I must,
And pipe but as the linnets sing.

xxi

13 The Shadow cloak'd from head to foot,
    Who keeps the keys of all the creeds.

xxiii

14   And Thought leapt out to wed with Thought
Ere Thought could wed itself with Speech.

15 I envy not in any moods
    The captive void of noble rage,
    The linnet born within the cage,
That never knew the summer woods.

xxvii

16   'Tis better to have loved and lost
Than never to have loved at all.

17 The time draws near the birth of Christ.

xxviii

18 From every house the neighbours met,
    The streets were fill'd with joyful sound,
    A solemn gladness even crown'd
The purple brows of Olivet.

Behold a man raised up by Christ!
    The rest remaineth unreveal'd;
    He told it not; or something seal'd

The lips of that Evangelist.

xxxi.

19 Her eyes are homes of silent prayer.

xxxii

20 Short swallow-flights of song, that dip
    Their wings in tears, and skim away.

xlviii

21 Be near me when my light is low,
    When the blood creeps, and the nerves prick
    And tingle; and the heart is sick,
And all the wheels of Being slow.

Be near me when the sensuous frame
    Is rack'd with pains that conquer trust;
    And Time, a maniac scattering dust,
And Life, a Fury slinging flame.

l

22 How many a father have I seen,
    A sober man, among his boys,
    Whose youth was full of foolish noise.

liii

23 Hold thou the good: define it well:
    For fear divine Philosophy
    Should push beyond her mark, and be
Procuress to the Lords of Hell.

24 Oh yet we trust that somehow good
    Will be the final goal of ill.

liv

25 That nothing walks with aimless feet;
    That not one life shall be destroy'd,
    Or cast as rubbish to the void,
When God hath made the pile complete.

26 Behold, we know not anything;
    I can but trust that good shall fall
    At last—far off—at last, to all,
And every winter change to spring.

So runs my dream: but what am I?
    An infant crying in the night:
    An infant crying for the light:
And with no language but a cry.

27   So careful of the type she seems,
So careless of the single life.

lv

28   The great world's altar-stairs
That slope thro' darkness up to God.

29 Man...
    Who trusted God was love indeed
    And love Creation's final law—
    Tho' Nature, red in tooth and claw
With ravine, shriek'd against his creed.

lvi

30   Dragons of the prime,
    That tare each other in their slime,
Were mellow music match'd with him.

31 Peace; come away: the song of woe
    Is after all an earthly song:
    Peace; come away: we do him wrong
To sing so wildly: let us go.

lvii

32   The passing of the sweetest soul
That ever look'd with human eyes.

33 O Sorrow, wilt thou live with me

No casual mistress, but a wife.
lix

1   As some divinely gifted man,
     Whose life in low estate began
And on a simple village green;

Who breaks his birth's invidious bar,
     And grasps the skirts of happy chance,
     And breasts the blows of circumstance,
And grapples with his evil star.
lxiv

2   So many worlds, so much to do,
     So little done, such things to be.
lxxiii

3   Death has made
His darkness beautiful with thee.
lxxiv

4   And round thee with the breeze of song
To stir a little dust of praise.
lxxv

5   O last regret, regret can die!
lxxviii

6   Laburnums, dropping-wells of fire.
lxxxiii

7   God's finger touch'd him, and he slept.
lxxxv

8   He brought an eye for all he saw;
     He mixt in all our simple sports;
     They pleased him, fresh from brawling courts
And dusty purlieus of the law.
lxxxix. See 208:28

9   When rosy plumelets tuft the larch,
     And rarely pipes the mounted thrush:
     Or underneath the barren bush
Flits by the sea-blue bird of March.
xci

10   You tell me, doubt is Devil-born.
xcvi

11   There lives more faith in honest doubt,
Believe me, than in half the creeds.

12   Their meetings made December June,
Their every parting was to die.
xcvii

13   He seems so near and yet so far.

14   Ring out, wild bells, to the wild sky,
     The flying cloud, the frosty light:
     The year is dying in the night;
Ring out, wild bells, and let him die.

Ring out the old, ring in the new,
     Ring, happy bells, across the snow:
     The year is going, let him go;
Ring out the false, ring in the true.
cvi

15   Ring out a slowly dying cause,
     And ancient forms of party strife;
     Ring in the nobler modes of life,
With sweeter manners, purer laws.

Ring out the want, the care, the sin,
     The faithless coldness of the times;
     Ring out, ring out my mournful rhymes,
But ring the fuller minstrel in.

Ring out false pride in place and blood,
     The civic slander and the spite;
     Ring in the love of truth and right,
Ring in the common love of good.

Ring out old shapes of foul disease;
     Ring out the narrowing lust of gold;
     Ring out the thousand wars of old,
Ring in the thousand years of peace.

Ring in the valiant man and free,
     The larger heart, the kindlier hand;
     Ring out the darkness of the land;
Ring in the Christ that is to be.

16   Not the schoolboy heat,
The blind hysterics of the Celt.
cix

17   And thus he bore without abuse
     The grand old name of gentleman,
     Defamed by every charlatan,
And soil'd with all ignoble use.
cxi

18   Now fades the last long streak of snow
     Now burgeons every maze of quick
     About the flowering squares and thick
By ashen roots the violets blow.
cxv

19   And drown'd in yonder living blue
The lark becomes a sightless song.

20   There, where the long street roars, hath been
The stillness of the central sea.
cxxiii

21   And thou art worthy; full of power;
     As gentle; liberal-minded, great,
     Consistent; wearing all that weight
Of learning lightly like a flower.
cxxxi, st.13

22   One God, one law, one element,
     And one far-off divine event,
     To which the whole creation moves.
st.37

23   The voice of the dead was a living voice to me.
In the Valley of Cauteretz (1847)

24   Below the thunders of the upper deep;
     Far, far beneath in the abysmal sea,
     His ancient, dreamless, uninvaded sleep
The Kraken sleepeth.
The Kraken

25   There hath he lain for ages and will lie
     Battening upon huge seaworms in his sleep,
Until the latter fire shall heat the deep.

26   At me you smiled, but unbeguiled
     I saw the snare, and I retired:
     The daughter of a hundred Earls,
     You are not one to be desired.
Lady Clara Vere de Vere (1833), i

27   A simple maiden in her flower
     Is worth a hundred coats-of-arms.
ii

28   Her manners had not that repose
     Which stamps the caste of Vere-de-Vere.
v

29   From yon blue heavens above us bent
     The gardener Adam and his wife
     Smile at the claims of long descent.

Howe'er it be, it seems to me,
  'Tis only noble to be good.
Kind hearts are more than coronets,
  And simple faith than Norman blood.
vi

1 Oh! teach the orphan-boy to read,
  Or teach the orphan-girl to sew.

2 On either side the river lie
Long fields of barley and of rye,
That clothe the wold and meet the sky;
And thro' the field the road runs by
  To many-tower'd Camelot.
The Lady of Shalott (1833), pt.i

3 Willows whiten, aspens quiver,
Little breezes dusk and shiver.

4 But who hath seen her wave her hand?
Or at the casement seen her stand?
Or is she known in all the land,
  The Lady of Shalott?

5 Only reapers, reaping early
In among the bearded barley,
Hear a song that echoes cheerly
From the river winding clearly
  Down to tower'd Camelot.

6 She hath no loyal knight and true,
  The Lady of Shalott.
pt.ii

7 Or when the moon was overhead,
Came two young lovers lately wed;
'I am half sick of shadows,' said
  The Lady of Shalott.

8 A bow-shot from her bower-eaves,
He rode between the barley-sheaves,
The sun came dazzling thro' the leaves
And flamed upon the brazen greaves
  Of bold Sir Lancelot.
A red-cross knight for ever kneel'd
To a lady in his shield,
That sparkled on the yellow field,
  Beside remote Shalott.
pt.iii

9 All in the blue unclouded weather
Thick-jewell'd shone the saddle-leather,
The helmet and the helmet-feather
Burn'd like one burning flame together,
  As he rode down to Camelot.

10 'Tirra lirra,' by the river
  Sang Sir Lancelot.

11 She left the web, she left the loom,
She made three paces thro' the room
She saw the water-lily bloom,
She saw the helmet and the plume,
  She look'd down to Camelot.
Out flew the web and floated wide;
The mirror crack'd from side to side;
'The curse is come upon me,' cried
  The Lady of Shalott.

12 Who is this? and what is here?
And in the lighted palace near
Died the sound of royal cheer;
And they cross'd themselves for fear,
  All the knights at Camelot:

But Lancelot mused a little space;
He said, 'She has a lovely face;
God in his mercy lend her grace,
  The Lady of Shalott.'
pt.iv

13 Slander, meanest spawn of Hell.
The Letters (1842)

14 Airy, fairy Lilian.
Lilian (1830)

15 Comrades, leave me here a little, while as yet 'tis early
  morn:
Leave me here, and when you want me, sound upon
  the bugle-horn.
Locksley Hall (1842), l.1

16 Here about the beach I wander'd, nourishing a youth
  sublime
With the fairy tales of science, and the long result of
  Time.
l.11

17 In the Spring a livelier iris changes on the burnish'd
  dove;
In the Spring a young man's fancy lightly turns to
  thoughts of love.
l.19

18 And our spirits rush'd together at the touching of the
  lips.
l.38

19 As the husband is, the wife is: thou art mated with a
  clown,
And the grossness of his nature will have weight to
  drag thee down.

He will hold thee, when his passion shall have spent
  its novel force,
Something better than his dog, a little dearer than his
  horse.
l.47

20   This is truth the poet sings,
That a sorrow's crown of sorrow is remembering
  happier things.
l.75. See 89:6, 171:8

21 Like a dog, he hunts in dreams.
l.79

22 O, I see thee old and formal, fitted to thy petty part,
With a little hoard of maxims preaching down a
  daughter's heart.
l.93

23 But the jingling of the guinea helps the hurt that
  Honour feels.
l.105

24 Men, my brothers, men the workers, ever reaping
  something new:
That which they have done but earnest of the things
  that they shall do:

For I dipt into the future, far as human eye could see,
Saw the Vision of the world, and all the wonder that
  would be;

Saw the heavens fill with commerce, argosies of magic
  sails,
Pilots of the purple twilight, dropping down with
  costly bales;

Heard the heavens fill with shouting, and there rain'd a
  ghastly dew

From the nations' airy navies grappling in the central blue;

Far along the world-wide whisper of the south-wind rushing warm,
With the standards of the peoples plunging thro' the thunder-storm;

Till the war-drum throbb'd no longer, and the battle-flags were furl'd
In the Parliament of man, the Federation of the world.
l.117

1 Science moves, but slowly slowly, creeping on from point to point.
l.134

2 Yet I doubt not thro' the ages one increasing purpose runs,
And the thoughts of men are widen'd with the process of the suns.
l.137

3 Knowledge comes, but wisdom lingers.
l.143

4 I am shamed thro' all my nature to have loved so slight a thing.
l.148

5 Woman is the lesser man, and all thy passions match'd with mine,
Are as moonlight unto sunlight, and as water unto wine.
l.151

6 I will take some savage woman, she shall rear my dusky race.
l.168

7 I the heir of all the ages, in the foremost files of time.
l.178

8 　　　　Forward, forward let us range,
Let the great world spin for ever down the ringing grooves of change.
l.181

9 Better fifty years of Europe than a cycle of Cathay.
l.184

10 He is but a landscape-painter,
And a village maiden she.
The Lord of Burleigh (1842), l.7

11 Weeping, weeping late and early,
Walking up and pacing down,
Deeply mourn'd the Lord of Burleigh,
Burleigh-house by Stamford-town.
l.89

12 'Courage!' he said, and pointed toward the land,
'This mounting wave will roll us shoreward soon.'
In the afternoon they came unto a land
In which it seemed always afternoon.
The Lotos-Eaters (1833)

13 Music that gentlier on the spirit lies,
Than tir'd eyelids upon tir'd eyes.
Choric Song, i

14 There is no joy but calm!
ii

15 Death is the end of life; ah, why
Should life all labour be?
iv

16 　　　　　　Live and lie reclined
On the hills like Gods together, careless of mankind.

For they lie beside their nectar, and the bolts are hurl'd
Far below them in the valleys, and the clouds are lightly curl'd
Round their golden houses, girdled with the gleaming world.

17 Surely, surely, slumber is more sweet than toil, the shore
Than labour in the deep mid-ocean, wind and wave and oar;
Oh rest ye, brother mariners, we will not wander more.

18 The long mechanic pacings to and fro,
The set gray life, and apathetic end.
Love and Duty (1842), l.17

19 Earn well the thrifty months, nor wed
Raw Haste, half-sister to Delay.
Love thou thy Land (1833), xxiv

20 I saw the flaring atom-streams
And torrents of her myriad universe,
Ruining along the illimitable inane.
Lucretius (1868), l.38

21 　　　　Nor at all can tell
Whether I mean this day to end myself,
Or lend an ear to Plato where he says,
That men like soldiers may not quit the post
Allotted by the Gods.
l.145

22 Passionless bride, divine Tranquillity,
Yearn'd after by the wisest of the wise,
Who fail to find thee, being as thou art
Without one pleasure and without one pain.
l.265

23 Weeded and worn the ancient thatch
Upon the lonely moated grange.

She only said, 'My life is dreary,
He cometh not,' she said;
She said, 'I am aweary, aweary.
I would that I were dead!'

Her tears fell with the dews at even;
Her tears fell ere the dews were dried.
Mariana (1830). See 464:18

24 She wept, 'I am aweary, aweary,
O God, that I were dead!'

25 I hate that dreadful hollow behind the little wood.
Maud (1855), Pt.I.i.1

26 For I trust if an enemy's fleet came yonder round by the hill,
And the rushing battle-bolt sang from the three-decker out of the foam,
That the smooth-faced snubnosed rogue would leap from his counter and till,
And strike, if he could, were it but with his cheating yardwand, home.
13

27 Faultily faultless, icily regular, splendidly null,
Dead perfection, no more.
ii

28 The passionate heart of the poet is whirl'd into folly and vice.
iv.7

29 And most of all would I flee from the cruel madness of love—

The honey of poison-flowers and all the measureless
   ill.
  10

1 That jewell'd mass of millinery,
That oil'd and curl'd Assyrian Bull.
vi.6

2 She came to the village church,
And sat by a pillar alone;
An angel watching an urn
Wept over her, carved in stone.
viii

3   I heard no longer
The snowy-banded, dilettante,
Delicate-handed priest intone.

4 Ah God, for a man with heart, head, hand,
Like some of the simple great ones gone
For ever and ever by,
One still strong man in a blatant land,
Whatever they call him, what care I,
Aristocrat, democrat, autocrat—one
Who can rule and dare not lie.

And ah for a man to arise in me,
That the man I am may cease to be!
x.5

5 Birds in the high Hall-garden
When twilight was falling,
Maud, Maud, Maud, Maud,
They were crying and calling.
xii.1

6 I kiss'd her slender hand,
She took the kiss sedately;
Maud is not seventeen,
But she is tall and stately.
4

7 Gorgonised me from head to foot
With a stony British stare.
xiii.2

8 A livelier emerald twinkles in the grass,
A purer sapphire melts into the sea.
xviii.6

9 Come into the garden, Maud,
  For the black bat, night, has flown
Come into the garden, Maud,
  I am here at the gate alone;
And the woodbine spices are wafted abroad,
  And the musk of the rose is blown.

For a breeze of morning moves,
  And the planet of Love is on high,
Beginning to faint in the light that she loves
  On a bed of daffodil sky.
xxii.1

10 All night has the casement jessamine stirr'd
  To the dancers dancing in tune;
Till a silence fell with the waking bird,
  And a hush with the setting moon.
3

11 Queen rose of the rosebud garden of girls.
9

12 There has fallen a splendid tear
  From the passion-flower at the gate.
She is coming, my dove, my dear;
She is coming, my life, my fate;
The red rose cries, 'She is near, she is near;'

And the white rose weeps, 'She is late;'
The larkspur listens, 'I hear, I hear;'
And the lily whispers, 'I wait.'

She is coming, my own, my sweet;
  Were it ever so airy a tread,
My heart would hear her and beat,
  Were it earth in an earthy bed;
My dust would hear her and beat,
  Had I lain for a century dead;
Would start and tremble under her feet,
  And blossom in purple and red.
10

13 O that 'twere possible
After long grief and pain
To find the arms of my true love
Round me once again!
Pt.II.iv.1

14 But the churchmen fain would kill their church,
As the churches have kill'd their Christ.
v.2

15 O me, why have they not buried me deep enough?
Is it kind to have made me a grave so rough,
Me, that was never a quiet sleeper?
11

16 My life has crept so long on a broken wing
Thro' cells of madness, haunts of horror and fear,
That I come to be grateful at last for a little thing.
Pt.III.vi.1

17 When the face of night is fair on the dewy downs,
And the shining daffodil dies.

18 The blood-red blossom of war with a heart of fire.
4

19 It is better to fight for the good, than to rail at the ill;
I have felt with my native land, I am one with my
  kind,
I embrace the purpose of God, and the doom assign'd.
5

20 You must wake and call me early, call me early,
  mother dear;
To-morrow 'ill be the happiest time of all the glad
  New-year;
Of all the glad New-year, mother, the maddest
  merriest day;
For I'm to be Queen o' the May, mother, I'm to be
  Queen o' the May.
The May Queen (1833)

21 Launch your vessel,
And crowd your canvas,
And, ere it vanishes
Over the margin,
After it, follow it,
Follow The Gleam.
Merlin and The Gleam (1886)

22   What, it's you,
The padded man—that wears the stays.
The New Timon and the Poets (1846)

23 What profits now to understand
  The merits of a spotless shirt—
A dapper boot—a little hand—
  If half the little soul is dirt?

24 Dosn't thou 'ear my 'erse's legs, as they canters
  awaäy?
Proputty, proputty, proputty—that's what I 'ears 'em

saäy.
Northern Farmer. New Style (1847)

1 But l knaw'd a Quaäker feller as often 'as towd me this:
'Doänt thou marry for munny, but goä wheer munny is!'

2 Taäke my word for it, Sammy, the poor in a loomp is bad.

3 An' I thowt a said whot a owt to 'a said an' I coom'd awaäy.
Northern Farmer. Old Style (1847)

4 Do godamoighty knaw what a's doing a-taäkin' o' meä?

5 Bury the Great Duke
With an empire's lamentation,
Let us bury the Great Duke
To the noise of the mourning of a mighty nation.
Ode on the Death of the Duke of Wellington (1854), i

6 The last great Englishman is low.
iii

7 Foremost captain of his time,
Rich in saving common-sense,
And, as the greatest only are,
In his simplicity sublime.
O good grey head which all men knew!
iv

8 O fall'n at length that tower of strength
Which stood four-square to all the winds that blew!

9 For this is England's greatest son,
He that gain'd a hundred fights,
Nor ever lost an English gun.
vi

10 In that world-earthquake, Waterloo!

11 That sober freedom out of which there springs
Our loyal passion for our temperate kings.
vii

12 Who never sold the truth to serve the hour,
Nor palter'd with Eternal God for power.

13 Truth-teller was our England's Alfred named.

14 Not once or twice in our rough island-story,
The path of duty was the way to glory.
viii

15 Speak no more of his renown,
Lay your earthly fancies down,
And in the vast cathedral leave him,
God accept him, Christ receive him.
ix

16 There lies a vale in Ida, lovelier
Than all the valleys of Ionian hills.
Oenone (1833), l.1

17 O mother Ida, many-fountain'd Ida.
l.22

18   Then to the bower they came,
Naked they came to that smooth-swarded bower,
And at their feet the crocus brake like fire,
Violet, amaracus, and asphodel,
Lotos and lilies.
l.92

19   Because right is right, to follow right
Were wisdom in the scorn of consequence.
l.147

20 I built my soul a lordly pleasure-house,
Wherein at ease for aye to dwell.
The Palace of Art (1833), i

21 Still as, while Saturn whirls, his stedfast shade
Sleeps on his luminous ring.
iv

22   An English home—gray twilight pour'd
On dewy pasture, dewy trees,
Softer than sleep—all things in order stored,
A haunt of ancient Peace.
xxii

23   Two godlike faces gazed below;
Plato the wise, and large-brow'd Verulam,
The first of those who know.
xli

24 Vex not thou the poet's mind
With thy shallow wit;
Vex not thou the poet's mind;
For thou canst not fathom it.
The Poet's Mind (1830)

25 Dark-brow'd sophist, come not anear:
All the place is holy ground.

26 For some cry 'Quick' and some cry 'Slow ,
But, while the hills remain,
Up hill 'Too-slow' will need the whip,
Down hill 'Too-quick', the chain.
Politics (1889)

27 With prudes for proctors, dowagers for deans,
And sweet girl-graduates in their golden hair.
The Princess (1847), prologue, l.141

28 As thro' the land at eve we went,
And pluck'd the ripen'd ears,
We fell out, my wife and I,
O we fell out I know not why,
And kiss'd again with tears.
And blessings on the falling out
That all the more endears,
When we fall out with those we love
And kiss again with tears!
ii. Song

29 O hard, when love and duty clash!
ii, l.273

30   Follow'd then
A classic lecture, rich in sentiment,
With scraps of thundrous Epic lilted out
By violet-hooded Doctors, elegies
And quoted odes, and jewels five-words long,
That on the stretch'd forefinger of all Time
Sparkle for ever.
l.351

31 Sweet and low, sweet and low,
Wind of the western sea,
Low, low, breathe and blow,
Wind of the western sea!
Over the rolling waters go,
Come from the dying moon, and blow,
Blow him again to me;
While my little one, while my pretty one, sleeps.
iii. Song

32 The splendour falls on castle walls
And snowy summits old in story:
The long light shakes across the lakes,
And the wild cataract leaps in glory.

Blow, bugle, blow, set the wild echoes flying,
Blow, bugle; answer, echoes, dying, dying, dying.

O hark, O hear! how thin and clear,
   And thinner, clearer, farther going!
O sweet and far from cliff and scar
   The horns of Elfland faintly blowing!
iv. Song (1)

1 O love, they die in yon rich sky,
   They faint on hill or field or river:
Our echoes roll from soul to soul,
   And grow for ever and for ever.

2 Tears, idle tears, I know not what they mean,
Tears from the depth of some divine despair
Rise in the heart, and gather to the eyes,
In looking on the happy Autumn-fields,
And thinking of the days that are no more.
Song (2)

3 So sad, so fresh, the days that are no more.

4 Ah, sad and strange as in dark summer dawns
The earliest pipe of half-awaken'd birds
To dying ears, when unto dying eyes
The casement slowly grows a glimmering square;
So sad, so strange, the days that are no more.

Dear as remembered kisses after death,
And sweet as those by hopeless fancy feign'd
On lips that are for others: deep as love,
Deep as first love, and wild with all regret;
O Death in Life, the days that are no more.

5 O Swallow, Swallow, flying, flying South,
Fly to her, and fall upon her gilded eaves,
And tell her, tell her, what I tell to thee.

O tell her, Swallow, thou that knowest each,
That bright and fierce and fickle is the South,
And dark and true and tender is the North.
Song (3)

6 O tell her, Swallow, that thy brood is flown:
Say to her, I do but wanton in the South,
But in the North long since my nest is made.

7 Thy voice is heard thro' rolling drums,
   That beat to battle where he stands;
Thy face across his fancy comes,
   And gives the battle to his hands:
A moment, while the trumpets blow,
   He sees his brood about thy knee;
The next, like fire he meets the foe,
   And strikes him dead for thine and thee.
Song (4)

8 Man is the hunter; woman is his game:
The sleek and shining creatures of the chase,
We hunt them for the beauty of their skins;
They love us for it, and we ride them down.
v, 1.147

9 Man for the field and woman for the hearth:
Man for the sword and for the needle she:
Man with the head and woman with the heart:
Man to command and woman to obey;
All else confusion.
1.427

10 Home they brought her warrior dead.
She nor swoon'd, nor utter'd cry:
All her maidens, watching said,

'She must weep or she will die.'
vi. Song

11 Rose a nurse of ninety years,
   Set his child upon her knee—
Like summer tempest came her tears—
   'Sweet my child, I live for thee.'

12   The woman is so hard
Upon the woman.
1.205

13 Ask me no more: what answer should I give?
I love not hollow cheek or faded eye:
Yet, O my friend, I will not have thee die!
Ask me no more, lest I should bid thee live;
               Ask me no more.
vii. Song (1)

14 Now sleeps the crimson petal, now the white;
Nor waves the cypress in the palace walk;
Nor winks the gold fin in the porphyry font:
The fire-fly wakens: waken thou with me.

Now droops the milk-white peacock like a ghost,
And like a ghost she glimmers on to me.

Now lies the Earth all Danaë to the stars,
And all thy heart lies open unto me.

Now slides the silent meteor on, and leaves
A shining furrow, as thy thoughts in me.

Now folds the lily all her sweetness up,
And slips into the bosom of the lake:
So fold thyself, my dearest, thou, and slip
Into my bosom and be lost in me.
Song (2)

15 Come down, O maid, from yonder mountain height:
What pleasure lives in height?
Song (3)

16 For Love is of the valley, come thou down
And find him; by the happy threshold, he,
Or hand in hand with Plenty in the maize,
Or red with spirted purple of the vats,
Or foxlike in the vine; nor cares to walk
With Death and Morning on the silver horns.

17   Sweet is every sound,
Sweeter thy voice, but every sound is sweet;
Myriads of rivulets hurrying thro' the lawn,
The moan of doves in immemorial elms,
And murmuring of innumerable bees.

18 The woman's cause is man's: they rise or sink
Together.
1.243

19   Happy he
With such a mother! faith in womankind
Beats with his blood, and trust in all things high
Comes easy to him, and tho' he trip and fall
He shall not blind his soul with clay.
1.308

20 No little lily-handed Baronet he,
A great broad-shoulder'd genial Englishman,
A lord of fat prize-oxen and of sheep,
A raiser of huge melons and of pine,
A patron of some thirty charities,
A pamphleteer on guano and on grain.
Conclusion, 1.84

21   At Flores in the Azores Sir Richard Grenville lay,
And a pinnace, like a fluttered bird, came flying from

far away:
'Spanish ships of war at sea! we have sighted
  fifty-three!'
Then sware Lord Thomas Howard: ''Fore God I am no
  coward;
But I cannot meet them here, for my ships are out of
  gear,
And the half my men are sick. I must fly, but follow
  quick.
We are six ships of the line; can we fight with
  fifty-three?'

Then spake Sir Richard Grenville: 'I know you are no
  coward;
You fly them for a moment to fight with them again.
But I've ninety men and more that are lying sick
  ashore.
I should count myself the coward if I left them, my
  Lord Howard,
To these Inquisition dogs and the devildoms of Spain.'

So Lord Howard past away with five ships of war that
  day,
Till he melted like a cloud in the silent summer
  heaven.
The Revenge (1880), i

1 And Sir Richard said again: 'We be all good English
     men.
   Let us bang these dogs of Seville, the children of the
     devil,
   For I never turn'd my back upon Don or devil yet.'
   iv

2 And the sun went down, and the stars came out far
     over the summer sea,
   But never a moment ceased the fight of the one and the
     fifty-three.
   ix

3 'Sink me the ship, Master Gunner—sink her, split her
     in twain!
   Fall into the hands of God, not into the hands of
     Spain!'

   And the gunner said 'Ay, ay', but the seamen made
     reply:
   'We have children, we have wives,
   And the Lord hath spared our lives.'
   xi

4 And they praised him to his face with their courtly
     foreign grace;
   But he rose upon their decks, and he cried:
   'I have fought for Queen and Faith like a valiant man
     and true;
   I have only done my duty as a man is bound to do:
   With a joyful spirit I Sir Richard Grenville die!'
   And he fell upon their decks, and he died.
   xiii

5 And the little Revenge herself went down by the island
     crags
   To be lost evermore in the main.
   xiv

6 Form, Form, Riflemen Form!
   Riflemen Form! (1892)

7 What does little birdie say
   In her nest at peep of day?
   Sea Dreams (1864), l.281

8 My strength is as the strength of ten,

Because my heart is pure.
Sir Galahad (1842)

9 A man had given all other bliss,
   And all his worldly worth for this,
   To waste his whole heart in one kiss
     Upon her perfect lips.
   Sir Launcelot and Queen Guinevere (1842)

10 Alone and warming his five wits,
    The white owl in the belfry sits.
    Song. The Owl (1830)

11 The woods decay, the woods decay and fall,
    The vapours weep their burthen to the ground,
    Man comes and tills the field and lies beneath,
    And after many a summer dies the swan.
    Me only cruel immortality
    Consumes: I wither slowly in thine arms,
    Here at the quiet limit of the world.
    Tithonus (c.1833, pub.1860), l.1

12 Why wilt thou ever scare me with thy tears,
    And make me tremble lest a saying learnt,
    In days far-off, on that dark earth, be true?
    'The gods themselves cannot recall their gifts.'
    l.46

13 Of happy men that have the power to die,
    And grassy barrows of the happier dead.
    l.70

14 God gives us love. Something to love
      He lends us; but, when love is grown
    To ripeness, that on which it throve
      Falls off, and love is left alone.
    To J.S., iv

15 Her court was pure; her life serene;
      God gave her peace; her land reposed;
      A thousand claims to reverence closed
    In her as Mother, Wife, and Queen.
    To the Queen (1851)

16 You'll have no scandal while you dine,
    But honest talk and wholesome wine.
    To the Revd. F.D. Maurice, v

17 All the charm of all the Muses often flowering in a
      lonely word.
    To Virgil (1889), iii

18   I salute thee, Mantovano,
    I that loved thee since my day began,
    Wielder of the stateliest measure ever moulded by the
      lips of man.
    x

19 This truth within thy mind rehearse,
    That in a boundless universe
    Is boundless better, boundless worse.
    The Two Voices (1833), ix

20 No life that breathes with human breath
    Has ever truly long'd for death.
    cxxxii

21 It little profits that an idle king,
    By this still hearth, among these barren crags,
    Match'd with an aged wife, I mete and dole
    Unequal laws unto a savage race.
    Ulysses (1842), l.1

22   I will drink
    Life to the lees: all times I have enjoy'd
    Greatly, have suffer'd greatly, both with those
    That loved me, and alone; on shore, and when

Thro' scudding drifts the rainy Hyades
Vext the dim sea: I am become a name;
For always roaming with a hungry heart
Much have I seen and known; cities of men
And manners, climates, councils, governments,
Myself not least, but honour'd of them all;
And drunk delight of battle with my peers,
Far on the ringing plains of windy Troy.
I am a part of all that I have met;
Yet all experience is an arch wherethro'
Gleams that untravell'd world, whose margin fades
For ever and for ever when I move.
How dull it is to pause, to make an end,
To rust unburnish'd, not to shine in use!
As tho' to breathe were life.
l.6

1   This gray spirit yearning in desire
To follow knowledge like a sinking star,
Beyond the utmost bound of human thought.
l.30

2 This is my son, mine own Telemachus.
l.33

3 There lies the port; the vessel puffs her sail:
There gloom the dark broad seas. My mariners
Souls that have toil'd, and wrought, and thought with
    me—
That ever with a frolic welcome took
The thunder and the sunshine, and opposed
Free hearts, free foreheads—you and I are old;
Old age hath yet his honour and his toil;
Death closes all: but something ere the end,
Some work of noble note, may yet be done,
Not unbecoming men that strove with gods.
The lights begin to twinkle from the rocks:
The long day wanes: the slow moon climbs: the deep
Moans round with many voices. Come, my friends,
'Tis not too late to seek a newer world.
Push off, and sitting well in order smite
The sounding furrows; for my purpose holds
To sail beyond the sunset, and the baths
Of all the western stars, until I die.
It may be that the gulfs will wash us down:
It may be we shall touch the Happy Isles,
And see the great Achilles, whom we knew.
Tho' much is taken, much abides; and tho'
We are not now that strength which in old days
Moved earth and heaven; that which we are, we are;
One equal temper of heroic hearts,
Made weak by time and fate, but strong in will
To strive, to seek, to find, and not to yield.
l.44

4 What is it all but a trouble of ants in the gleam of a
    million million of suns?
Vastness (1889)

5 Fur hoffens we talkt o' my darter es died o' the fever
    at fall:
An' I thowt 'twur the will o' the Lord, but Miss Annie
    she said it wur draäins.
The Village Wife (1880), ii

6 Bitter barmaid, waning fast!
The Vision of Sin (1842), IV.ii

7 Let us have a quiet hour,
    Let us hob-and-nob with Death.
iii

8 Every moment dies a man,
    Every moment one is born.
ix

9 O plump head-waiter at the Cock,
    To which I must resort,
How goes the time? 'Tis five o'clock.
    Go fetch a pint of port.
Will Waterproof's Lyrical Monologue (1842), i

10 I grow in worth, and wit, and sense,
    Unboding critic-pen,
Or that eternal want of pence,
    Which vexes public men.
vi

11 A land of settled government,
    A land of just and old renown,
Where Freedom slowly broadens down
From precedent to precedent.
'You ask me, why' (1833), iii

12 While I live, the owls!
When I die, the GHOULS!!!
Written in 1869 in Hallam Tennyson's commonplace book by the
side of an epigram on a poet's fate by Thomas Hood. H.
Tennyson, *Alfred, Lord Tennyson* (1898), ii, ch.3. See 255:14

13 A louse in the locks of literature.
Said of Churton Collins to Edmund Gosse. Evan Charteris, *Life
and Letters of Sir Edmund Gosse* (1931), ch.xiv

TERENCE c.190–159 B.C.

14 *Hinc illae lacrimae.*
Hence all those tears shed.
Andria, 126

15 *Amantium irae amoris integratio est.*
Lovers' rows make love whole again.
555

16 *Nullumst iam dictum quod non dictum sit prius.*
Nothing has yet been said that's not been said before.
Eunuchus. Prolog. 41

17 *Homo sum; humani nil a me alienum puto.*
I am a man, I count nothing human foreign to me.
Heauton Timorumenos, 77

18 *Fortis fortuna adiuvat.*
Fortune aids the brave.
Phormio, 203

19 *Quot homines tot sententiae: suo' quoique mos.*
There are as many opinions as there are people: each
has his own correct way.
454

ST. TERESA OF ÁVILA 1512–1582

20 *Oh, válame Dios, Señor cómo apretáis a vestros
amadores!*
Alas, O Lord, to what a state dost Thou bring those
who love Thee!
Interior Castles (Mansions), trans. by the Benedictines of
Stanbrook, 1921, VI, xi, 6

TERTULLIAN A.D. c.160–c.225

21 *O testimonium animae naturaliter Christianae.*
O evidence of a naturally Christian soul!
Apologeticus, 17

22 *Plures efficimus quoties metimur a vobis, semen est
sanguis Christianorum.*
As often as we are mown down by you, the more we

grow in numbers; the blood of Christians is the seed.
50,13. Traditionally cited as, The blood of the martyrs is the seed of the Church.

1 *Certum est quia impossibile est.*
It is certain because it is impossible.
De Carne Christi, 5. Often quoted as, *Credo quia impossibile.*

EDWARD TESCHEMACHER nineteenth century

2 Where my caravan has rested,
Flowers I leave you on the grass.
Where My Caravan Has Rested

A.S.J. TESSIMOND 1902–1962

3 Cats, no less liquid than their shadows,
Offer no angles to the wind.
They slip, diminished, neat, through loopholes
Less than themselves.
Cats, II

WILLIAM MAKEPEACE THACKERAY 1811–1863

4 He who meanly admires mean things is a Snob.
The Book of Snobs (1848), ch.2

5 It is impossible, in our condition of Society, not to be sometimes a Snob.
ch.3

6 'Tis not the dying for a faith that's so hard, Master Harry—every man of every nation has done that—'tis the living up to it that is difficult.
The History of Henry Esmond (1852), bk.i, ch.6

7 'Tis strange what a man may do, and a woman yet think him an angel.
ch.7

8 We love being in love, that's the truth on't.
bk.ii, ch.15

9 Why do they always put mud into coffee on board steamers? Why does the tea generally taste of boiled boots?
The Kickleburys on the Rhine (1850)

10 Kind, cheerful, merry Dr Brighton.
The Newcomes (1853-5), bk.i, ch.9

11 What money is better bestowed than that of a school-boy's tip?
ch.16

12 As the last bell struck, a peculiar sweet smile shone over his face, and he lifted up his head a little, and quickly said, 'Adsum!' and fell back. It was the word we used at school, when names were called; and lo, he, whose heart was as that of a little child, had answered to his name, and stood in the presence of The Master.
ch.80

13 Yes, I am a fatal man, Madame Fribsbi. To inspire hopeless passion is my destiny. [Mirobolant.]
Pendennis (1848-50), ch.23

14 Remember, it is as easy to marry a rich woman as a poor woman.
ch.28

15 For a slashing article, sir, there's nobody like the Capting.
ch.32

16 The *Pall Mall Gazette* is written by gentlemen for

gentlemen.

17 Business first; pleasure afterwards. [Queen of Paflagonia.]
The Rose and the Ring (1855), ch.1

18 Runs not a river by my palace wall? Have I not sacks to sew up wives withal? [Valoroso.]
ch.9

19 'No business before breakfast, Glum!' says the King. 'Breakfast first, business next.' [Valoroso.]
ch.11

20 My bold, my beautiful, my Bulbo! [Angelica.]

21 This I set down as a positive truth. A woman with fair opportunities and without a positive hump, may marry whom she likes.
Vanity Fair (1847-8), ch.4

22 [Miss Crawley] had been in France—and loved, ever after, French novels, French cookery, and French wines.
ch.10

23 Whenever he met a great man he grovelled before him, and my-lorded him as only a free-born Briton can do.
ch.13

24 If a man's character is to be abused, say what you will, there's nobody like a relation to do the business.
ch.19

25 Them's my sentiments! [Fred Bullock.]
ch.21

26 Darkness came down on the field and city: and Amelia was praying for George, who was lying on his face, dead, with a bullet through his heart.
ch.32

27 Nothing like blood, sir, in hosses, dawgs, and men. [James Crawley.]
ch.35

28 How to live well on nothing a year.
Title of ch.36

29 Ah! *Vanitas Vanitatum!* Which of us is happy in this world? Which of us has his desire? or, having it, is satisfied?—Come, children, let us shut up the box and the puppets, for our play is played out.
ch.67

30 There's no sweeter tobacco comes from Virginia, and no better brand than the Three Castles.
The Virginians (1857-59), ch.1

31 Ho, pretty page, with the dimpled chin
That never has known the barber's shear,
All your wish is woman to win,
This is the way that boys begin.
    Wait till you come to Forty Year.
The Age of Wisdom

32 There were three sailors of Bristol City
Who took a boat and went to sea.
But first with beef and captain's biscuits
And pickled pork they loaded she.
There was gorging Jack and guzzling Jimmy,
And the youngest he was little Billee.
Now when they got as far as the Equator
They'd nothing left but one split pea.
Little Billee

33 Says gorging Jim to guzzling Jacky,
We have no wittles, so we must eat *we*.

1   There's little Bill as is young and tender,
    We're old and tough—so let's eat *he*.

2   He scarce had said his Cathechism,
    When up he jumps: 'There's land I see!
    There's Jerusalem and Madagascar,
    And North and South Amerikey.
    There's the British Fleet a-riding at anchor,
    With Admiral Napier, K.C.B.'

3   Werther had a love for Charlotte
        Such as words could never utter;
    Would you know how first he met her?
        She was cutting bread and butter.

    Charlotte was a married lady,
        And a moral man was Werther,
    And for all the wealth of Indies,
        Would do nothing for to hurt her.

    So he sighed and pined and ogled,
        And his passion boiled and bubbled,
    Till he blew his silly brains out
        And no more was by it troubled.

    Charlotte, having seen his body
        Borne before her on a shutter,
    Like a well-conducted person,
        Went on cutting bread and butter.
    Sorrows of Werther

4   Oh, Vanity of vanities!
        How wayward the decrees of Fate are;
    How very weak the very wise,
        How very small the very great are!
    Vanitas Vanitatum

LOUIS ADOLPHE THIERS 1797–1877

5   [Le roi] *règne et le peuple se gouverne.*
    The king reigns, and the people govern themselves.
    Le National, 20 Jan. 1830. The article in which this appears was
    unsigned. In *Le National*, 4 Feb. 1830, a signed article by Thiers
    states *'Le roi n'administre pas, ne gouverne pas, il règne.'*

THOMAS À KEMPIS c.1380–1471

6   I would far rather feel remorse than know how to
    define it.
    Of the Imitation of Christ, I.i.3

7   *O quam cito transit gloria mundi.*
    Oh how quickly the world's glory passes away!
    iii.6. See 11:1

8   Seek not to know who said this or that, but take note
    of what has been said.
    v.1

9   It is much safer to be in a subordinate position than in
    one of authority.
    ix.1

10 *Nam homo proponit, sed Deus disponit.*
    For man plans, but God arranges.
    xix.2

11 *Numquam sis ex toto otiosus, sed aut legens, aut
    scribens, aut orans, aut meditans, aut aliquid utilitatis
    pro communi laborans.*
    Never to be completely idle, but either reading, or
    writing, or praying, or meditating, or working at
    something useful for all in common.
    4

12 Would that we had spent one whole day well in this

world!
xxiii.2

13 We are sometimes stirred by emotion and take it for
    zeal.
    II.v.i

14 *Si libenter crucem portas portabit te.*
    If you bear the cross gladly, it will bear you.
    xii.5

15 *De duobus malis minus est semper eligendum.*
    Of the two evils the lesser is always to be chosen.
    III.xii.2

ST. THOMAS AQUINAS c.1225–1274

16 *Pange, lingua, gloriosi*
        Corporis mysterium,
    Sanguinisque pretiosi,
        Quem in mundi pretium
    Fructus ventris generosi
        Rex effudit gentium.
    Sing, my tongue, of the mystery of the glorious Body,
        and of the precious Blood shed to redeem the world
        by the King of all peoples, the fruit of a noble womb.
    Pange Lingua Gloriosi. Corpus Christi hymn

17 *Tantum ergo sacramentum*
        Veneremur cernui;
    Et antiquum documentum
        Novo cedat ritui.
    Therefore we, before him bending,
        This great Sacrament revere;
    Types and shadows have their ending,
        For the newer rite is here.
    Tr. J.M. Neale, E. Caswall, and others. *English Hymnal*, 326

BRANDON THOMAS 1856–1914

18 I'm Charley's aunt from Brazil—where the nuts come
    from.
    Charley's Aunt (1892), Act 1

DYLAN THOMAS 1914–1953

19 Though they go mad they shall be sane,
    Though they sink through the sea they shall rise again;
    Though lovers be lost love shall not;
    And death shall have no dominion.
    And death shall have no dominion. See 75:2

20 I can never remember whether it snowed for six days
    and six nights when I was twelve or whether it snowed
    for twelve days and twelve nights when I was six.
    A Child's Christmas in Wales (1954)

21 The gong was bombilating, and Mrs Prothero was
    announcing ruin like a town crier in Pompeii.

22 Years and years and years ago, when I was a boy,
    when there were wolves in Wales, and birds the colour
    of red-flannel petticoats whisked past the harp-shaped
    hills...when we rode the daft and happy hills
    bareback, it snowed and it snowed.

23 Do not go gentle into that good night,
    Old age should burn and rave at close of day;
    Rage, rage against the dying of the light.
    Do not go gentle into that good night

24 And you, my father, there on that sad height,
    Curse, bless, me now with your fierce tears I pray.

1 Now as I was young and easy under the apple boughs
About the lilting house and happy as the grass was
green.
Fern Hill

2 Oh as I was young and easy in the mercy of his
means,
Time held me green and dying
Though I sang in my chains like the sea.

3 The force that through the green fuse drives the flower
Drives my green age; that blasts the roots of trees
Is my destroyer.
And I am dumb to tell the crooked rose
My youth is bent by the same wintry fever.
The force that through the green fuse drives the flower

4 The hand that signed the paper felled a city;
Five sovereign fingers taxed the breath,
Doubled the globe of death and halved a country;
These five kings did a king to death.
The hand that signed the paper

5 The hand that signed the treaty bred a fever,
And famine grew, and locusts came;
Great is the hand that holds dominion over
Man by a scribbled name.

6 It was my thirtieth year to heaven
Woke to my hearing from harbour and neighbour wood
And the mussel pooled and the heron
Priested shore.
Poem in October

7 Pale rain over the dwindling harbour
And over the sea wet church the size of a snail
With its horns through mist and the castle
Brown as owls
But all the gardens
Of spring and summer were blooming in the tall tales
Beyond the border and under the lark full cloud.
There could I marvel
My birthday
Away but the weather turned around.

8 After the first death, there is no other.
A refusal to mourn the death, by fire, of a child in London

9 It is spring, moonless night in the small town, starless
and bible-black, the cobblestreets silent and the
hunched, courters'-and-rabbits' wood limping invisible
down to the sloeblack, slow, black, crowblack,
fishingboat-bobbing sea.
Under Milk Wood (1954)

10 *Mr Pritchard:* I must dust the blinds and then I must
raise them.
Mrs Ogmore-Pritchard: And before you let the sun in,
mind it wipes its shoes.

11 Gomer Owen who kissed her once by the pig-sty when
she wasn't looking and never kissed her again although
she was looking all the time.

12 Nothing grows in our garden, only washing. And
babies.

13 Oh, what can I do? I'll *never* be refined if I twitch.

14 You just wait. I'll sin till I blow up!

15 Dylan talked copiously, then stopped.
'Somebody's boring me,' he said, 'I think it's me.'
Rayner Heppenstall, *Four Absentees* (1960), xvi

EDWARD THOMAS 1878–1917

16 Yes. I remember Adlestrop—
The name, because one afternoon
Of heat the express train drew up there
Unwontedly. It was late June.
Adlestrop

17 The past is the only dead thing that smells sweet.
Early One Morning

18 If I should ever by chance grow rich
I'll buy Codham, Cockridden, and Childerditch,
Roses, Pyrgo, and Lapwater,
And let them all to my elder daughter.
If I should ever by chance

19 I have come to the borders of sleep,
The unfathomable deep
Forest where all must lose
Their way, however straight,
Or winding, soon or late;
They cannot choose.
Lights Out

20 Out in the dark over the snow
The fallow fawns invisible go
With the fallow doe;
And the winds blow
Fast as the stars are slow.
Out in the Dark

21 As well as any bloom upon a flower
I like the dust on the nettles, never lost
Except to prove the sweetness of a shower.
Tall Nettles

FRANCIS THOMPSON 1859–1907

22 Pontifical Death, that doth the crevasse bridge
To the steep and trifid God.
Anthem of Earth

23 And thou—what needest with thy tribe's black tents
Who hast the red pavilion of my heart?
Arab Love Song

24 It is little I repair to the matches of the Southron folk,
Though my own red roses there may blow;
It is little I repair to the matches of the Southron folk,
Though the red roses crest the caps I know.
For the field is full of shades as I near the shadowy
coast,
And a ghostly batsman plays to the bowling of a
ghost,
And I look through my tears on a soundless-clapping
host
As the run-stealers flicker to and fro,
To and fro:—
O my Hornby and my Barlow long ago!
At Lord's

25 The fairest things have fleetest end,
Their scent survives their close:
But the rose's scent is bitterness
To him that loved the rose.
Daisy

26 She went her unremembering way,
She went and left in me
The pang of all the partings gone,
And partings yet to be.

She left me marvelling why my soul
Was sad that she was glad;

At all the sadness in the sweet,
    The sweetness in the sad.

1 Nothing begins and nothing ends
    That is not paid with moan;
For we are born in other's pain,
    And perish in our own.

2 Ah, for a heart less native to high Heaven,
A hooded eye, for jesses and restraint,
Or for a will accipitrine to pursue!
The Dread of Height

3 Go, songs, for ended is our brief sweet play;
    Go, children of swift joy and tardy sorrow:
And some are sung, and that was yesterday,
    And some unsung, and that may be to-morrow.
Envoy

4 Spring is come home with her world-wandering feet.
And all things are made young with young desires.
The Night of Forebeing. Ode to Easter

5 Let even the slug-abed snail upon the thorn
Put forth a conscious horn!

6 Look for me in the nurseries of Heaven.
To My Godchild

7 And all man's Babylons strive but to impart
The grandeurs of his Babylonian heart.
The Heart, ii

8 I fled Him, down the nights and down the days;
    I fled Him, down the arches of the years;
I fled Him, down the labyrinthine ways
    Of my own mind; and in the mist of tears
I hid from Him, and under running laughter.
The Hound of Heaven

9 But with unhurrying chase,
    And unperturbèd pace,
Deliberate speed, majestic instancy,
    They beat—and a Voice beat
More instant than the Feet—
'All things betray thee, who betrayest Me.'

10 (For, though I knew His love Who followed,
        Yet was I sore adread
Lest, having Him, I must have naught beside.)

11 Fear wist not to evade, as Love wist to pursue.

12 I said to Dawn: Be sudden—to Eve: Be soon.

13 To all swift things for swiftness did I sue;
Clung to the whistling mane of every wind.

14 Came on the following Feet,
And a Voice above their beat—
'Naught shelters thee, who wilt not shelter Me.'

15 I was heavy with the even
When she lit her glimmering tapers
Round the day's dead sanctities.

16 My harness piece by piece Thou hast hewn from me
And smitten me to my knee.

17 Yea, faileth now even dream
    The dreamer, and the lute the lutanist;
Even the linked fantasies, in whose blossomy twist
I swung the earth a trinket at my wrist.

18   Ah! must—
        Designer infinite!—
Ah! must Thou char the wood ere Thou canst limn
    with it?

19   Such is; what is to be?
The pulp so bitter, how shall taste the rind?

20 Yet ever and anon a trumpet sounds
From the hid battlements of Eternity;
Those shaken mists a space unsettle, then
Round the half-glimpsèd turrets slowly wash again.

21   Now of that long pursuit
    Comes on at hand the bruit;
That Voice is round me like a bursting sea:
    'And is thy earth so marred,
    Shattered in shard on shard?
Lo, all things fly thee, for thou fliest Me!'

22 All which I took from thee I did but take,
    Not for thy harms,
But just that thou might'st seek it in My arms.

23   Halts by me that footfall:
    Is my gloom, after all,
Shade of His hand, outstretched caressingly?
    'Ah, fondest, blindest, weakest,
    I am He whom thou seekest!
Thou dravest love from thee, who dravest Me.'

24 O world invisible, we view thee,
O world intangible, we touch thee,
O world unknowable, we know thee,
Inapprehensible, we clutch thee!
In No Strange Land

25 'Tis ye, 'tis your estrangèd faces,
That miss the many-splendoured thing.

But (when so sad thou canst not sadder)
Cry;—and upon thy so sore loss
Shall shine the traffic of Jacob's ladder
Pitched betwixt Heaven and Charing Cross.

Yea, in the night, my Soul, my daughter,
Cry,—clinging Heaven by the hems;
And lo, Christ walking on the water
Not of Gennesareth, but Thames!

26 There is no expeditious road
To pack and label men for God,
And save them by the barrel-load.
A Judgment in Heaven, epilogue

27 Summer set lip to earth's bosom bare,
And left the flushed print in a poppy there.
The Poppy

28 The sleep-flower sways in the wheat its head,
Heavy with dreams, as that with bread:
The goodly grain and the sun-flushed sleeper
The reaper reaps, and Time the reaper.

I hang 'mid men my needless head,
And my fruit is dreams, as theirs is bread:
The goodly men and the sun-hazed sleeper
Time shall reap, but after the reaper
The world shall glean of me, me the sleeper.

29 What heart could have thought you?—
Past our devisal
(O filigree petal!)
Fashioned so purely,
Fragilely, surely,
From what Paradisal
Imagineless metal,
Too costly for cost?
To a Snowflake

1   His hammer of wind,
And His graver of frost.

2   Wake! for the Ruddy Ball has taken flight
That scatters the slow Wicket of the Night;
    And the swift Batsman of the Dawn has driven
Against the Star-spiked Rails a fiery Smite.
Wake! for the Ruddy Ball has Taken Flight. J.C. Squire, *Apes
and Parrots.* See 212:5

3   And, while she feels the heavens lie bare,
She only talks about her hair.
The Way of a Maid

WILLIAM HEPWORTH THOMPSON 1810–1886

4   I never could have supposed that we should have had
so soon to regret the departure of our dear friend the
late Professor.
On Seeley's inaugural lecture as Professor of History at
Cambridge, following Charles Kingsley. A.J. Balfour, *Chapters
of Autobiography* (1930), ch.4

5   We are none of us infallible—not even the youngest of
us.
Remark referring to G.W. Balfour, then Junior Fellow of Trinity.
G.W.E. Russell, *Collections and Recollections,* ch.18

6   What time he can spare from the adornment of his
person he devotes to the neglect of his duties.
Of Sir Richard Jebb, afterwards Professor of Greek at Cambridge.
M.R. Bobbit, *With Dearest Love to All,* ch.7

JAMES THOMSON 1700–1748

7   When Britain first, at heaven's command,
Arose from out the azure main,
This was the charter of the land,
And guardian angels sung this strain:
    'Rule, Britannia, rule the waves;
    Britons never will be slaves.'
Alfred: a Masque (1740), Act II, Scene the last

8   A pleasing land of drowsyhead it was.
The Castle of Indolence (1748), c.I.vi

9   A bard here dwelt, more fat than bard beseems
Who, void of envy, guile, and lust of gain,
On virtue still, and nature's pleasing themes,
Poured forth his unpremeditating strain.
lxviii

10 Delightful task! to rear the tender thought,
To teach the young idea how to shoot.
The Seasons (1728), **Spring,** l.1152

11 An elegant sufficiency, content,
Retirement, rural quiet, friendship, books.
l.1161

12 The sober-suited songstress. [The nightingale.]
Summer, l.746

13 Ships, dim-discovered, dropping from the clouds.
l.946

14 Or sighed and looked unutterable things.
l.1188

15 Autumn nodding o'er the yellow plain
Comes jovial on.
Autumn, l.2

16 While listening senates hang upon thy tongue.
l.15

17   For loveliness
Needs not the foreign aid of ornament,

But is when unadorned adorned the most.
l.204

18 Poor is the triumph o'er the timid hare!
l.401

19   He stands at bay,
And puts his last weak refuge in despair.
The big round tears run down his dappled face;
He groans in anguish; while the growling pack,
Blood-happy, hang at his fair jutting chest,
And mark his beauteous chequered sides with gore.
l.452. Of a stag. See 425:1

20 Find other lands beneath another sun.
l.1286

21 See, Winter comes to rule the varied year,
Sullen and sad.
Winter, l.1

22   Welcome, kindred glooms!
Congenial horrors, hail!
l.5

23 The redbreast, sacred to the household gods,
Wisely regardful of the embroiling sky,
In joyless fields and thorny thickets leaves
His shivering mates, and pays to trusted man
His annual visit.
l.246

24   Studious let me sit,
And hold high converse with the mighty dead.
l.431

25 Oh! Sophonisba! Sophonisba! oh!
Sophonisba (1730), III.ii

26 How the heart listened while he pleading spoke!
While on the enlightened mind, with winning art,
His gentle reason so persuasive stole
That the charmed hearer thought it was his own.
To the Memory of the Lord Talbot (1737), l.103

JAMES THOMSON 1834–1882

27 The City is of Night; perchance of Death,
But certainly of Night.
The City of Dreadful Night

28 As we rush, as we rush in the train,
The trees and the houses go wheeling back,
But the starry heavens above that plain
Come flying on our track.
Sunday at Hampstead, x

29 Give a man a horse he can ride,
Give a man a boat he can sail.
Sunday up the River, xv

LORD THOMSON OF FLEET 1894–1977

30 It's just like having a licence to print your own
money.
(After the opening of Scottish commercial television.) Braddon,
Roy Thomson of Fleet Street, p.240

HENRY DAVID THOREAU 1817–1862

31 I heartily accept the motto, 'That government is best
which governs least'; and I should like to see it acted
up to more rapidly and systematically. Carried out, it
finally amounts to this, which I also believe,— 'That
government is best which governs not at all.'
Civil Disobedience (1849). See 365:22

1 Under a government which imprisons any unjustly, the true place for a just man is also a prison.

2 I have travelled a good deal in Concord.
Walden (1854). **Economy**

3 As if you could kill time without injuring eternity.

4 The mass of men lead lives of quiet desperation.

5 It is a characteristic of wisdom not to do desperate things.

6 I have lived some thirty years on this planet, and I have yet to hear the first syllable of valuable or even earnest advice from my seniors.

7 There are now-a-days professors of philosophy but not philosophers.

8 I long ago lost a hound, a bay horse, and a turtle-dove, and am still on their trail.

9 In any weather, at any hour of the day or night, I have been anxious to improve the nick of time, and notch it on my stick too; to stand on the meeting of two eternities, the past and the future, which is precisely the present moment; to toe that line.

10 It is true, I never assisted the sun materially in his rising, but, doubt not, it was of the last importance only to be present at it.

11 Tall arrowy white pines.

12 The owner of the axe, as he released his hold on it, said that it was the apple of his eye; but I returned it sharper than I received it.

13 For more than five years I maintained myself thus solely by the labor of my hands, and I found, that by working about six weeks in a year, I could meet all the expenses of living.

14 As for Doing-good, that is one of the professions which are full. Moreover, I have tried it fairly, and, strange as it may seem, am satisfied that it does not agree with my constitution.

15 The government of the world I live in was not framed, like that of Britain, in after-dinner conversations over the wine.
conclusion

16 I wanted to live deep and suck out all the marrow of life...to drive life into a corner, and reduce it to its lowest terms, and, if it proved to be mean, why then to get the whole and genuine meanness of it, and publish its meanness to the world; or if it were sublime, to know it by experience, and be able to give a true account of it in my next excursion.
Where I lived, and what I lived for

17 Our life is frittered away by detail...Simplify, simplify.

18 The three-o'-clock in the morning courage, which Bonaparte thought was the rarest.
Sounds. See 359:12

19 Wherever a man goes, men will pursue him and paw him with their dirty institutions, and, if they can, constrain him to belong to their desperate oddfellow society.
The Village

20 I frequently tramped eight or ten miles through the deepest snow to keep an appointment with a beech-tree, or a yellow birch, or an old acquaintance among the pines.
Winter Visitors

21 I once had a sparrow alight upon my shoulder for a moment while I was hoeing in a village garden, and I felt that I was more distinguished by that circumstance than I should have been by any epaulet I could have worn.

22 It has been proposed that the town should adopt for its coat of arms a field verdant, with the Concord circling nine times round.
A Week on the Concord and Merrimack Rivers (1849).
Concord River

23 It takes two to speak the truth,—one to speak, and another to hear.
Wednesday

24 Some circumstantial evidence is very strong, as when you find a trout in the milk.
Journal, 11 Nov. 1850 (pub. 1903)

25 I do not perceive the poetic and dramatic capabilities of an anecdote or story which is told me, its significance, till some time afterwards...We do not enjoy poetry unless we know it to be poetry.
1 Oct. 1856

26 Not that the story need be long, but it will take a long while to make it short.
Letter to Mr. B., 16 Nov. 1857. See 369:14

27 *Emerson:* Why are you here?
Thoreau: Why are you not here?
Thoreau was in prison for failure to pay taxes. Oral tradition in Emerson family, discounted for lack of documentary evidence. Harding, *A Thoreau Handbook* (1959), p.8

28 It were treason to our love
And a sin to God above
One iota to abate
Of a pure impartial hate.
Indeed, Indeed I Cannot Tell (1852)

JAMES THURBER 1894–1961

29 It's a Naïve Domestic Burgundy, Without Any Breeding, But I Think You'll Be Amused by its Presumption.
Men, Women and Dogs. Cartoon caption

30 Well, if I Called the Wrong Number, Why Did You Answer the Phone?

31 All Right, Have It Your Way—You Heard a Seal Bark.
The Seal in the Bedroom. Cartoon caption

EDWARD, FIRST BARON THURLOW 1731–1806

32 Corporations have neither bodies to be punished, nor souls to be condemned, they therefore do as they like.
Poynder, *Literary Extracts* (1844), vol.I. Usually quoted as 'Did you ever expect a corporation to have a conscience, when it has no soul to be damned, and no body to be kicked?'

EDWARD, SECOND BARON THURLOW 1781–1829

33 Nature is always wise in every part.
To a Bird, that haunted the Waters of Lacken, in the Winter

TIBULLUS c.50–19 B.C.

34 *Te spectem, suprema mihi cum venerit hora,*

Et teneam moriens deficiente manu.
May I be looking at you when my last hour has come,
    and dying may I hold you with my weakening hand.
I.i.59

1 *Te propter nullos tellus tua postulat imbres,*
    Arida nec pluvio supplicat herba Iovi.
Because of you your land never pleads for showers,
    nor does its parched grass pray to Jupiter the
    Rain-giver.
vii.25. Of the Nile in Egypt

CHIDIOCK TICHBORNE 1558?–1586

2 My prime of youth is but a frost of cares;
My feast of joy is but a dish of pain;
My crop of corn is but a field of tares;
And all my good is but vain hope of gain.
The day is past, and yet I saw no sun;
And now I live, and now my life is done.
Elegy. (Written in the Tower before his execution)

THOMAS TICKELL 1686–1740

3 There taught us how to live; and (oh! too high
The price for knowledge) taught us how to die.
Epitaph. On the Death of Mr. Addison, 1.81. In Tickell's
edition of Addison's *Works* (1721), preface, p.xx

PAUL TILLICH 1886–1965

4 He who knows about depth knows about God.
The Shaking of the Foundations (1962 ed.), p.64

MATTHEW TINDAL 1657–1733

5 Matters of fact, which as Mr Budgell somewhere
observes, are very stubborn things.
Will of Matthew Tindal (1733), p.23

EMPEROR TITUS A.D. 39–81

6 *Recordatus quondam super cenam, quod nihil cuiquam*
toto die praestitisset, memorabilem illam meritoque
laudatam vocem edidit: 'Amici, diem perdidi.'
On reflecting at dinner that he had done nothing to help
anybody all day, he uttered those memorable and
praiseworthy words: 'Friends, I have lost a day.'
Suetonius, *Titus,* 8, i

JOHN TOBIN 1770–1804

7 The man that lays his hand upon a woman,
Save in the way of kindness, is a wretch
Whom 't were gross flattery to name a coward.
The Honeymoon, II.i

ALEXIS DE TOCQUEVILLE 1805–1859

8 *L'esprit français est de ne pas vouloir de* supérieur.
L'esprit anglais de vouloir des inférieurs. *Le Français*
lève les yeux sans cesse au-dessus de lui avec
inquiétude. L'Anglais les baisse au-dessous de lui
avec complaisance. C'est de part et d'autre de
l'orgueil, mais entendu de manière différente.
The French want no-one to be their *superior.* The
English want *inferiors.* The Frenchman constantly
raises his eyes above him with anxiety. The
Englishman lowers his beneath him with satisfaction.

On either side it is pride, but understood in a different
way.
Voyage en Angleterre et en Irlande de 1835, 18 May

9 *C'est au milieu de ce cloaque infect que la plus grande*
fleuve de l'industrie humaine prend sa source et va
féconder l'univers. De cet égout immonde, l'or pur
s'écoule. C'est là que l'esprit humain se perfectionne
et s'abrutit; que la civilisation produit ses merveilles
et que l'homme civilisée redevient presque sauvage.
It is from the midst of this putrid sewer that the
greatest river of human industry springs up and carries
fertility to the whole world. From this foul drain pure
gold flows forth. Here it is that humanity achieves for
itself both perfection and brutalization, that civilization
produces its wonders, and that civilized man becomes
again almost a savage.
Of Manchester. 2 July

LEO TOLSTOY 1828–1910

10 All happy families resemble one another, but each
unhappy family is unhappy in its own way.
Anna Karenina (1875-7), pt.i, ch.1. Tr. Maude

11 It is amazing how complete is the delusion that beauty
is goodness.
The Kreutzer Sonata, 5. Tr. Maude

12 Our body is a machine for living. It is organized for
that, it is its nature. Let life go on in it unhindered and
let it defend itself, it will do more than if you paralyse
it by encumbering it with remedies.
War and Peace (1868-9), bk.X, ch.29. Tr. A. and L. Maude

13 Pure and complete sorrow is as impossible as pure and
complete joy.
bk.XV, ch.1

14 Art is not a handicraft, it is the transmission of feeling
the artist has experienced.
What is Art? (1898), ch.19. Tr. Maude

15 I sit on a man's back, choking him and making him
carry me, and yet assure myself and others that I am
very sorry for him and wish to ease his lot by all
possible means—except by getting off his back.
What Then Must We Do? (1886), ch.16. Tr. Maude

CYRIL TOURNEUR c.1575–1626

16 Does the silk-worm expend her yellow labours
For thee? for thee does she undo herself?
The Revenger's Tragedy (1607), III.v.71

THOMAS TRAHERNE 1637?–1674

17 You never enjoy the world aright, till the sea itself
floweth in your veins, till you are clothed with the
heavens, and crowned with the stars: and perceive
yourself to be the sole heir of the whole world, and
more than so, because men are in it who are every one
sole heirs as well as you. Till you can sing and rejoice
and delight in God, as misers do in gold, and kings in
sceptres, you never enjoy the world.
Centuries of Meditations. Cent.i, 29

18 The corn was orient and immortal wheat, which never
should be reaped, nor was ever sown. I thought it had
stood from everlasting to everlasting.
Cent.iii, 3

19 The Men! O what venerable and reverend creatures did

the aged seem! Immortal Cherubims! And young men glittering and sparkling Angels, and maids strange seraphic pieces of life and beauty! Boys and girls tumbling in the street, and playing, were moving jewels. I knew not that they were born or should die; but all things abided eternally as they were in their proper places.

1 The hands are a sort of feet, which serve us in our passage towards Heaven, curiously distinguished into joints and fingers, and fit to be applied to any thing which reason can imagine or desire.
Meditations on the Six Days of Creation (1717), vi, p.78

2 Contentment is a sleepy thing
  If it in death alone must die;
A quiet mind is worse than poverty,
  Unless it from enjoyment spring!
That's blessedness alone that makes a King!
Of Contentment

3   I within did flow
With seas of life, like wine.
Wonder, iii

HENRY DUFF TRAILL 1842–1900

4 Look in my face. My name is Used-to-was;
  I am also called Played-out and Done-to-death,
  And It-will-wash-no-more.
After Dilettante Concetti [i.e. Dante Gabriel Rossetti], viii. See 410:4

JOSEPH TRAPP 1679–1747

5 The King, observing with judicious eyes
The state of both his universities,
To Oxford sent a troop of horse, and why?
That learned body wanted loyalty;
To Cambridge books, as very well discerning
How much that loyal body wanted learning.
On George I's Donation of the Bishop of Ely's Library to Cambridge University. Nichols, *Literary Anecdotes*, vol.iii, p.330. For the reply see 97:26

BEN TRAVERS 1886–

6 One night Mr and Mrs Reginald Bingham went to Ciro's. They had been married only about six months. Mr Bingham had never been to Ciro's before in his life. His surprise, therefore, upon seeing his wife there, was considerable.
Mischief (1926), ch.1

HERBERT TRENCH 1865–1923

7 Come, let us make love deathless, thou and I.
To Arolilia, No.2

RICHARD TRENCH, ARCHBISHOP OF DUBLIN 1807–1886

8 England, we love thee better than we know.
Gibraltar

G.M. TREVELYAN 1876–1962

9 Disinterested intellectual curiosity is the life blood of real civilisation.
English Social History (1942), preface, viii

10 Education...has produced a vast population able to read but unable to distinguish what is worth reading.
ch.18

ANTHONY TROLLOPE 1815–1882

11 He must have known me had he seen me as he was wont to see me, for he was in the habit of flogging me constantly. Perhaps he did not recognize me by my face.
Autobiography (1883), ch.1

12 Take away from English authors their copyrights, and you would very soon take away from England her authors.
ch.6

13 Three hours a day will produce as much as a man ought to write.
ch.15

14 Of all the needs a book has the chief need is that it be readable.
ch.19

15 I think that Plantagenet Palliser, Duke of Omnium, is a perfect gentleman. If he be not, then I am unable to describe a gentleman.
ch.20

16 She [Mrs. Stanhope] was rich in apparel, but not bedizened with finery...she well knew the great architectural secret of decorating her constructions, and never descended to construct a decoration.
Barchester Towers (1857), ch.9

17 'Unhand it, sir!' said Mrs Proudie. From what scrap of dramatic poetry she had extracted the word cannot be said; but it must have rested on her memory, and now seemed opportunely dignified for the occasion.
ch.11

18 No man thinks there is much ado about nothing when the ado is about himself.
The Bertrams (1859), ch.27

19 Those who have courage to love should have courage to suffer.

20 How I did respect you when you dared to speak the truth to me! Men don't know women, or they would be harder to them.
The Claverings (1867), ch.15

21 The comic almanacs give us dreadful pictures of January and February; but, in truth, the months which should be made to look gloomy in England are March and April. Let no man boast himself that he has got through the perils of winter till at least the seventh of May.
Doctor Thorne (1858), ch.47

22 For the most of us, if we do not talk of ourselves, or at any rate of the individual circles of which we are the centres, we can talk of nothing. I cannot hold with those who wish to put down the insignificant chatter of the world.
Framley Parsonage (1860), ch.10

23 It's dogged as does it. It ain't thinking about it.
The Last Chronicle of Barset (1867), ch.61

24 With many women I doubt whether there be any more effectual way of touching their hearts than ill-using them and then confessing it. If you wish to get the sweetest fragrance from the herb at your feet, tread on

it and bruise it.
Miss Mackenzie (1865), ch.10

1 We cannot bring ourselves to believe it possible that a foreigner should in any respect be wiser than ourselves. If any such point out to us our follies, we at once claim those follies as the special evidences of our wisdom.
Orley Farm (1862), ch.18

2 It is because we put up with bad things that hotel-keepers continue to give them to us.

3 As for conceit, what man will do any good who is not conceited? Nobody holds a good opinion of a man who has a low opinion of himself.
ch.22

4 A fainéant government is not the worst government that England can have. It has been the great fault of our politicians that they have all wanted to do something.
Phineas Finn (1869), ch.13

5 Mr Turnbull had predicted evil consequences...and was now doing the best in his power to bring about the verification of his own prophecies.
ch.25

6 Perhaps there is no position more perilous to a man's honesty than that...of knowing himself to be quite loved by a girl whom he almost loves himself.
ch.50

7 Men are so seldom really good. They are so little sympathetic. What man thinks of changing himself so as to suit his wife? And yet men expect that women shall put on altogether new characters when they are married, and girls think that they can do so.
Phineas Redux (1874), ch.3

8 It is the necessary nature of a political party in this country to avoid, as long as it can be avoided, the consideration of any question which involves a great change...The best carriage horses are those which can most steadily hold back against the coach as it trundles down the hill.
ch.4

9 To think of one's absent love is very sweet; but it becomes monotonous after a mile or two of a towing-path, and the mind will turn away to Aunt Sally, the Cremorne Gardens, and financial questions. I doubt whether any girl would be satisfied with her lover's mind if she knew the whole of it.
The Small House at Allington (1864), ch.4

10 Why is it that girls so constantly do this,—so frequently ask men who have loved them to be present at their marriages with other men? There is no triumph in it. It is done in sheer kindness and affection. They intend to offer something which shall soften and not aggravate the sorrow that they have caused...I fully appreciate the intention, but in honest truth, I doubt the eligibility of the proffered entertainment.
ch.9

11 It may almost be a question whether such wisdom as many of us have in our mature years has not come from the dying out of the power of temptation, rather than as the results of thought and resolution.
ch.14

12 And, above all things, never think that you're not good enough yourself. A man should never think that. My

belief is that in life people will take you very much at your own reckoning.
ch.32

13 The tenth Muse, who now governs the periodical press.
The Warden (1855), ch.14

14 Is it not singular how some men continue to obtain the reputation of popular authorship without adding a word to the literature of their country worthy of note?...To puff and to get one's self puffed have become different branches of a new profession.
The Way We Live Now (1875), ch.1

15 Love is like any other luxury. You have no right to it unless you can afford it.
ch.84

LEV TROTSKY 1879–1940

16 Old age is the most unexpected of all the things that happen to a man.
Diary in Exile, 8 May 1935

17 In a serious struggle there is no worse cruelty than to be magnanimous at an inopportune time.
The History of the Russian Revolution, tr. M. Eastman (1933), vol.IV, ch.7

18 Where force is necessary, one should make use of it boldly, resolutely, and right to the end. But it is as well to know the limitations of force; to know where to blend force with manoeuvre, assault with conciliation.
Was nun? (1932), p.106

HARRY S. TRUMAN 1884–1972

19 The buck stops here.
Hand-lettered sign on President Truman's desk. Phillips, *The Truman Presidency*, ch.12

20 If you can't stand the heat, get out of the kitchen.
Mr. Citizen, ch.15. Perhaps proverbial in origin, possibly echoing the expression 'kitchen cabinet'.

MARTIN TUPPER 1810–1889

21 A good book is the best of friends, the same to-day and for ever.
Proverbial Philosophy, Series I (1838). **Of Reading**

A.-R.-J. TURGOT 1727–1781

22 *Eripuit coelo fulmen, sceptrumque tyrannis.*
He snatched the lightning shaft from heaven, and the sceptre from tyrants.
A.N. de Condorcet, *Vie de Turgot* (1786), *Oeuvres Complètes* (Paris, 1804), 5, p.230. Inscription composed for a bust of Benjamin Franklin, inventor of the lightning conductor. See 328:11

WALTER JAMES REDFERN TURNER 1889–1946

23 Chimborazo, Cotopaxi,
They had stolen my soul away!
Romance, vii

MARK TWAIN 1835–1910

24 There was things which he stretched, but mainly he told the truth.
The Adventures of Huckleberry Finn (1884), ch.1

1 There was some books...One was *Pilgrim's Progress*,
about a man that left his family, it didn't say why. I
read considerable in it now and then. The statements
was interesting, but tough. Another was *Friendship's
Offering*, full of beautiful stuff and poetry; but I didn't
read the poetry.
ch.17

2 All kings is mostly rapscallions.
ch.23

3 Hain't we got all the fools in town on our side? and
ain't that a big enough majority in any town?
ch.26

4 If there was two birds sitting on a fence, he would bet
you which one would fly first.
The Celebrated Jumping Frog (1865), p.17

5 I don't see no p'ints about that frog that's any better'n
any other frog.
p.20

6 Soap and education are not as sudden as a massacre,
but they are more deadly in the long run.
*The Facts concerning the Recent Resignation. Sketches New &
Old* (1900), p.350

7 It is by the goodness of God that in our country we
have those three unspeakably precious things: freedom
of speech, freedom of conscience, and the prudence
never to practise either of them.
Following the Equator (1897), heading of ch.20

8 Man is the only animal that blushes. Or needs to.
heading of ch.27

9 They spell it Vinci and pronounce it Vinchy;
foreigners always spell better than they pronounce.
The Innocents Abroad (1869), ch.19

10 I do not want Michael Angelo for breakfast...for
luncheon—for dinner—for tea—for supper—for
between meals.
ch.27

11 Lump the whole thing! say that the Creator made Italy
from designs by Michael Angelo!

12 Guides cannot master the subtleties of the American
joke.

13 If you've got a nice *fresh* corpse, fetch him out!

14 At bottom he was probably fond of them, but he was
always able to conceal it. [On Thomas Carlyle and
Americans.]
My First Lie

15 An experienced, industrious, ambitious, and often
quite picturesque liar.
Private History of a Campaign that Failed

16 When angry, count a hundred; when very angry,
swear.
Pudd'nhead Wilson's Calendar, March

17 There's plenty of boys that will come hankering and
gruvvelling around when you've got an apple, and beg
the core off you; but when *they've* got one, and you
beg for the core and remind them how you give them a
core one time, they make a mouth at you and say thank
you 'most to death, but there ain't-a-going to be no
core.
Tom Sawyer Abroad (1894), ch.1

18 There ain't no way to find out why a snorer can't hear
himself snore.
ch.10

19 Adam was but human—this explains it all. He did not
want the apple for the apple's sake, he wanted it only
because it was forbidden.
The Tragedy of Pudd'nhead Wilson (1894), heading of ch.2

20 Whoever has lived long enough to find out what life
is, knows how deep a debt of gratitude we owe to
Adam, the first great benefactor of our race. He
brought death into the world.
heading of ch.3. See 344:20

21 The cross of the Legion of Honour has been conferred
upon me. However, few escape that distinction.
A Tramp Abroad (1880), ch.8

22 The report of my death was an exaggeration.
Cable from Europe to the Associated Press

23 There is a sumptuous variety about the New England
weather that compels the stranger's admiration—and
regret. The weather is always doing something there;
always attending strictly to business; always getting up
new designs and trying them on the people to see how
they will go. But it gets through more business in
spring than in any other season. In the spring I have
counted one hundred and thirty-six different kinds of
weather inside of four-and-twenty hours.
The Weather. Speech at dinner of New England Society, New
York, 22 Dec. 1876. *Speeches* (1910), p.59

24 A verb has a hard time enough of it in this world when
its all together. It's downright inhuman to split it up.
But that's just what those Germans do. They take part
of a verb and put it down here, like a stake, and they
take the other part of it and put it away over yonder
like another stake, and between these two limits they
just shovel in German.
Address at dinner of the Nineteenth Century Club, New York, 20
Nov. 1900, to the toast, 'The Disappearance of Literature'

25 Something that everybody wants to have read and
nobody wants to read. [A classic.]

DOMITIUS ULPIAN d. 228

26 *Nulla iniuria est, quae in volentem fiat.*
No injustice is done to someone who wants that thing
done.
Corpus Iuris Civilis, Digests 47, X.i.5. Usually cited in the form
Volenti non fit iniuria, To someone who wants it no injustice
occurs.

MIGUEL DE UNAMUNO 1864–1937

27 *Fe que no duda es fe muerta.*
Faith which does not doubt is dead faith.
La Agonía del Cristianismo, p.34

28 Cure yourself of the condition of bothering about how
you look to other people. Be concerned only...with the
idea God has of you.
Vida de D. Quijote y Sancho, p.27

ARCHBISHOP JAMES USSHER 1581–1656

29 Which beginning of time [the Creation] according to
our Chronologie, fell upon the entrance of the night
preceding the twenty third day of *Octob.* in the year of
the Julian Calendar, 710 [i.e. B.C. 4004].
The Annals of the World (1658), p.1

PAUL VALÉRY 1871–1945

1 *Il faut n'appeler* Science: *que* l'ensemble des recettes qui réussissent toujours.—*Tout le reste est* littérature.
The term *Science* should not be given to anything but *the aggregate of the recipes that are always successful.* All the rest is *literature.*
Moralités (1932), p.41. See 556:9

SIR JOHN VANBRUGH 1664–1726

2 The want of a thing is perplexing enough, but the possession of it is intolerable.
The Confederacy (1705), I.ii

3 Much of a muchness.
The Provok'd Husband (1728), I.i

4 *Belinda:* Ay, but you know we must return good for evil.
Lady Brute: That may be a mistake in the translation.
The Provok'd Wife (1697), I.i

5 Thinking is to me the greatest fatigue in the world.
The Relapse (1696), II.i

6 No man worth having is true to his wife, or can be true to his wife, or ever was, or ever will be so.
III.ii

WILLIAM HENRY VANDERBILT 1821–1885

7 The public be damned!
Reply to a question whether the public should be consulted about luxury trains. A.W. Cole, Letter, *New York Times,* 25 Aug. 1918

BARTOLOMEO VANZETTI 1888–1927

8 Sacco's name will live in the hearts of the people and in their gratitude when Katzmann's and yours bones will be dispersed by time, when your name, your laws, institutions, and your false god are but a deem remomoring of a cursed past in which man was wolf to the man.
Statement disallowed by Judge Thayer in the Dedham, Massachusetts, court which convicted Sacco and Vanzetti of murder and robbery. Both were sentenced to death on 9 Apr. 1927, the eulogy was written down by Vanzetti on the following day, and both men were executed on 23 August. Katzmann was the prosecuting attorney. F. Russell, *Tragedy in Dedham* (1963), ch.17. See 374:13

CHARLES JOHN VAUGHAN 1816–1897

9 Must you go? Can't you stay?
Remark with which he broke up awkward breakfast parties of schoolboys who were too shy to go. Story retold with the words transposed, 'Can't you go? Must you stay?' G.W.E. Russell, *Collections and Recollections,* ch.24

HENRY VAUGHAN 1622–1695

10 Man is the shuttle, to whose winding quest
And passage through these looms
God order'd motion, but ordain'd no rest.
Silex Scintillans (1650-55), *Man*

11 Wise Nicodemus saw such light
As made him know his God by night.

Most blest believer he!
Who in that land of darkness and blind eyes
Thy long expected healing wings could see
When Thou didst rise!
And, what can never more be done,

Did at midnight speak with the Sun!
The Night, l.5

12 Dear Night! this world's defeat;
The stop to busy fools; care's check and curb;
The day of spirits; my soul's calm retreat
Which none disturb!
l.25

13 My soul, there is a country
Far beyond the stars,
Where stands a wingèd sentry
All skilful in the wars;
There, above noise and danger,
Sweet Peace is crown'd with smiles,
And One born in a manger
Commands the beauteous files.
Peace

14 Happy those early days, when I
Shin'd in my angel-infancy.
Before I understood this place
Appointed for my second race,
Or taught my soul to fancy aught
But a white, celestial thought;
When yet I had not walked above
A mile or two from my first love,
And looking back—at that short space—
Could see a glimpse of His bright face.
The Retreat, l.1

15 And in those weaker glories spy
Some shadows of eternity.
l.13

16 But felt through all this fleshly dress
Bright shoots of everlastingness.
l.19

17 Some men a forward motion love,
But I by backward steps would move,
And when this dust falls to the urn,
In that state I came, return.
l.29

18 They are all gone into the world of light,
And I alone sit lingering here;
Their very memory is fair and bright,
And my sad thoughts doth clear.
They Are All Gone

19 I see them walking in an air of glory,
Whose light doth trample on my days:
My days, which are at best but dull and hoary,
Mere glimmering and decays.

20 Dear, beauteous death! the jewel of the just,
Shining nowhere but in the dark;
What mysteries do lie beyond thy dust,
Could man outlook that mark!

21 And yet, as angels in some brighter dreams
Call to the soul when man doth sleep,
So some strange thoughts transcend our wonted themes,
And into glory peep.

22 I saw Eternity the other night,
Like a great ring of pure and endless light,
All calm, as it was bright;
And round beneath it, Time in hours, days, years,
Driv'n by the spheres
Like a vast shadow mov'd; in which the world

And all her train were hurl'd.
The World

THORSTEIN VEBLEN 1857–1929

1 Conspicuous consumption of valuable goods is a
means of reputability to the gentleman of leisure.
The Theory of the Leisure Class (1899), ch.iv

2 From the foregoing survey of the growth of
conspicuous leisure and consumption, it appears that
the utility of both alike for the purposes of reputability
lies in the element of waste that is common to both. In
the one case it is a waste of time and effort, in the
other it is a waste of goods.

VEGETIUS 4th–5th cent. A.D.

3 *Qui desiderat pacem, praeparet bellum.*
Let him who desires peace, prepare for war.
De Re Mil. 3, prol. Usually cited in the form *Si vis pacem, para
bellum* (If you want peace, prepare for war.)

VENANTIUS FORTUNATUS c.530–c.610

4 *Pange, lingua, gloriosi*
Proelium certaminis.
Sing, my tongue, of the battle in the glorious struggle.
Pange lingua gloriosi. Passiontide hymn, see J.P. Migne,
Patrologia Latina, 88

5 *Vexilla regis prodeunt,*
Fulget crucis mysterium;
Qua vita mortem pertulit,
Et morte vitam protulit.
The banners of the king advance, the mystery of the
cross shines bright; where his life went through with
death, and from death brought forth life.
Vexilla Regis. Analecta Hymnica, 50, No.67, p.74

6 *Regnavit a ligno Deus.*
God reigned from the wood.

PIERRE VERGNIAUD 1753–1793

7 *Il a été permis de craindre que la Révolution, comme
Saturne, dévorât successivement tous ses enfants.*
There was reason to fear that the Revolution, like
Saturn, might devour in turn each one of her children.
Lamartine, *Histoire des Girondins* (1847), bk.xxxviii, ch.20

PAUL VERLAINE 1844–1896

8 *Les sanglots longs*
Des violons
      De l'automne
Blessent mon coeur
D'une langueur
      Monotone.
The drawn-out sobs of the violins of autumn wound
my heart with a monotonous languor.
Chanson de l'automne

9 *Et tout le reste est littérature.*
All the rest is mere fine writing.
Jadis et Naguère (1885). **L'art poétique**

10 *Et, Ô ces voix d'enfants chantants dans la coupole!*
And oh those children's voices, singing beneath the
dome!
Parsifal, A Jules Tellier

EMPEROR VESPASIAN A.D. 9–79

11 *Pecunia non olet.*
Money has no smell.
Traditional summary of Suetonius, *Vespasian*, 23,3. Vespasian
was answering Titus's objection to his tax on public lavatories;
holding a coin to Titus's nose and being told it didn't smell, he
replied:
Atqui e lotio est.
Yet that's made from urine.

12 *Vae, puto deus fio.*
Woe is me, I think I am becoming a god.
Suetonius, *Vespasian*, 23,4. Said when fatally ill

QUEEN VICTORIA 1819–1901

13 I will be good.
To Baroness Lehzen, 11 Mar. 1830. Martin, *The Prince Consort*
(1875), vol.i, p.13

14 The Queen is most anxious to enlist every one who can
speak or write to join in checking this mad, wicked
folly of 'Woman's Rights', with all its attendant
horrors, on which her poor feeble sex is bent,
forgetting every sense of womanly feeling and
propriety. Lady— ought to get a *good whipping.*
It is a subject which makes the Queen so furious that
she cannot contain herself. God created men and
women different—then let them remain each in their
own position.
Letter to Sir Theodore Martin, 29 May 1870

15 The danger to the country, to Europe, to her vast
Empire, which is involved in having all these great
interests entrusted to the shaking hand of an old, wild,
and incomprehensible man of $82\frac{1}{2}$, is very great!
On Gladstone's last appointment as Prime Minister. Letter to Lord
Lansdowne, 12 Aug. 1892

16 Move Queen Anne? Most certainly not! Why it might
some day be suggested that *my* statue should be
moved, which I should much dislike.
When it was suggested that the statue of Queen Anne outside St.
Paul's should be moved, on the occasion of the Diamond Jubilee
in 1887. Duke of Portland, *Men, Women and Things*, ch.5

17 We are not amused.
Attr. *Notebooks of a Spinster Lady*, 2 Jan. 1900

18 We are not interested in the possibilities of defeat; they
do not exist.
To A.J. Balfour, in 'Black Week', Dec. 1899

19 He [Mr Gladstone] speaks to Me as if I was a public
meeting.
G.W.E. Russell, *Collections and Recollections*, ch.14

GORE VIDAL 1925–

20 It is not enough to succeed. Others must fail.
Revd. G. Irvine, *Antipanegyric for Tom Driberg*, 8 Dec. 1976

JOSÉ ANTONIO VIERA GALLO 1943–

21 *El socialismo puede llegar solo en bicicleta.*
Socialism can only arrive by bicycle.
Ivan Illich, *Energy & Equity* (1974), quoting the Under Secretary
of Justice in the Chilean Government of Salvador Allende

ALFRED DE VIGNY 1797–1863

1 *J'aime la majesté des souffrances humaines.*
I love the majesty of human suffering.
La Maison du Berger (1844)

2 *Seul le silence est grand; tout le reste est faiblesse...*
Fais énergiquement ta longue et lourde tâche...
Puis, après, comme moi, souffre et meurs sans parler.
Silence alone is great; all else is feebleness...
Perform with all your heart your long and heavy task...
Then as do I, say naught, but suffer and die.
La Mort du Loup (1838)

PHILIPPE-AUGUSTE VILLIERS DE L'ISLE-ADAM 1838–1889

3 *Vivre? les serviteurs feront cela pour nous.*
Living? The servants will do that for us.
Axël (1890), IV, sect 2

FRANÇOIS VILLON b. 1431

4 *Frères humains qui après nous vivez,*
N'ayez les cuers contre nous endurcis,
Car, se pitié de nous povres avez,
Dieu en aura plus tost de vous mercis...
Mais priez Dieu que tous nous veuille absouldre!
Brothers in humanity who live after us, let not your
  hearts be hardened against us, for, if you take pity
  on us poor ones, God will be more likely to have
  mercy on you. But pray God that he may be willing
  to absolve us all.
Ballade des pendus

5 *Mais où sont les neiges d'antan?*
But where are the snows of yesteryear?
Le Grand Testament (1461). **Ballade des Dames du Temps
Jadis.** Tr. D.G. Rossetti

6 *En ceste foy je veuil vivre et mourir.*
In this faith I wish to live and to die.
Ballade pour prier Nostre Dame

ST. VINCENT OF LERINS d. c.450

7 *Quod semper, quod ubique, quod ab omnibus creditum
est.*
What is always, what is everywhere, what is by all
people believed.
Commonitorium, ii

VIRGIL 70–19 B.C.

8 *Arma virumque cano, Troiae qui primus ab oris
Italiam fato profugus Laviniaque venit
Litora, multum ille et terris iactatus et alto
Vi superum, saevae memorem Iunonis ob iram.*
I sing of arms and the man who first from the shores
  of Troy came destined an exile to Italy and the
  Lavinian beaches, much buffeted he on land and on
  the deep by force of the gods because of fierce
  Juno's never-forgetting anger.
Aeneid, i.1

9 *Tantaene animis caelestibus irae?*
Why such great anger in those heavenly minds?
11

10 *Tantae molis erat Romanam condere gentem.*
So massive was the effort to found the Roman nation.
33

11 *Apparent rari nantes in gurgite vasto.*
Odd figures swimming were glimpsed in the waste of
  waters.
118

12 *Constitit hic arcumque manu celerisque sagittas
Corripuit fidus quae tela gerebat Achates.*
Hereupon he stopped and took up in his hand a bow
  and swift arrows, the weapons that trusty Achates
  carried.
187

13 *O passi graviora, dabit deus his quoque finem.*
O you who have borne even heavier things, God will
  grant an end to these too.
199

14 *Forsan et haec olim meminisse iuvabit.*
Maybe one day we shall be glad to remember even
  these things.
203

15 *Dux femina facti.*
The leader of the enterprise a woman.
364

16 *Dixit et avertens rosea cervice refulsit,
Ambrosiaeque comae divinum vertice odorem
Spiravere; pedes vestis defluxit ad imos,
Et vera incessu patuit dea.*
She said no more and as she turned away there was a
  bright glimpse of the rosy glow of her neck, and
  from her ambrosial head of hair a heavenly
  fragrance wafted; her dress flowed down right to her
  feet, and in her walk it showed, she was in truth a
  goddess.
402

17 *'En Priamus. Sunt hic etiam sua praemia laudi,
Sunt lacrimae rerum et mentem mortalia tangunt.
Solve metus; feret haec aliquam tibi fama salutem.'
Sic ait atque animum pictura pascit inani.*
'Look, there's Priam! Even here prowess has its due
  rewards, there are tears shed for things even here
  and mortality touches the heart. Abandon your
  fears; I tell you, this fame will stand us somehow in
  good stead.' So he spoke, and fed his thoughts on
  the unreal painting.
461

18 *Di tibi, si qua pios respectant numina, si quid
Usquam iustitiae est et mens sibi conscia recti,
Praemia digna ferant.*
Surely as the divine powers take note of the dutiful,
  surely as there is any justice anywhere and a mind
  recognizing in itself what is right, may the gods
  bring you your earned rewards.
603

19 *Non ignara mali miseris succurrere disco.*
No stranger to trouble myself I am learning to care for
  the unhappy.
630

20 *Infandum, regina, iubes renovare dolorem.*
A grief too much to be told, O queen, you bid me
  renew.
ii.3

21   *Quaeque ipse miserrima vidi
Et quorum pars magna fui.*
And the most miserable things which I myself saw and
  of which I was a major part.
5

1 *Equo ne credite, Teucri.*
Quidquid id est, timeo Danaos et dona ferentis.
Do not trust the horse, Trojans. Whatever it is, I fear
the Greeks even when they bring gifts.
48

2 *Crimine ab uno*
Disce omnis.
From the one crime recognize them all as culprits.
65

3 *Tacitae per amica silentia lunae.*
Through the friendly silence of the soundless
moonlight.
255

4 *Tempus erat quo prima quies mortalibus aegris*
Incipit et dono divum gratissima serpit.
It was the time when first sleep begins for weary
mortals and by the gift of the gods creeps over them
most welcomely.
268

5 *Quantum mutatus ab illo*
Hectore qui redit exuvias indutus Achilli.
How greatly changed from that Hector who comes
home wearing the armour stripped from Achilles!
274

6 *Fuimus Troes, fuit Ilium et ingens*
Gloria Teucrorum.
We Trojans are at an end, Ilium has ended and the
vast glory of the Teucrians.
325

7 *Moriamur et in media arma ruamus.*
Una salus victis nullam sperare salutem.
Let us die even as we rush into the midst of the battle.
The only safe course for the defeated is to expect no
safety.
353

8 *Dis aliter visum.*
The gods thought otherwise.
428

9 *Non tali auxilio nec defensoribus istis*
Tempus eget.
Now is not the hour that requires such help, nor those
defenders.
521

10 *Quid non mortalia pectora cogis,*
Auri sacra fames!
What do you not drive human hearts into, cursed
craving for gold!
iii.56

11 *Monstrum horrendum, informe, ingens, cui lumen*
ademptum.
A monster horrendous, hideous and vast, deprived of
sight.
658

12 *Quis fallere possit amantem?*
Who could deceive a lover?
iv.296

13 *Nec me meminisse pigebit Elissae*
Dum memor ipse mei, dum spiritus hos regit artus.
Nor will it ever upset me to remember Elissa so long
as I can remember who I am, so long as the breath
of life controls these limbs.
335. Aeneas, of Dido

14 *Varium et mutabile semper*
Femina.
Fickle and changeable always is woman.
569. Richard Stanyhurst's translation (1582):
     A windfane changabil huf puffe
Always is a woomman.

15 *Exoriare aliquis nostris ex ossibus ultor.*
Arise, you avenger someone, from my bones.
625

16 *Hos successus alit: possunt, quia posse videntur.*
These success encourages: they can because they think
they can.
v.231

17 *Bella, horrida bella,*
Et Thybrim multo spumantem sanguine cerno.
I see wars, horrible wars, and the Tiber foaming with
much blood.
vi.86

18 *Facilis descensus Averno:*
Noctes atque dies patet atri ianua Ditis;
Sed revocare gradum superasque evadere ad auras,
Hoc opus, hic labor est.
Easy is the way down to the Underworld: by night and
by day dark Dis's door stands open; but to withdraw
one's steps and to make a way out to the upper air,
that's the task, that is the labour.
126

19 *Procul, o procul este, profani.*
Far off, Oh keep far off, you uninitiated ones.
258

20 *Ibant obscuri sola sub nocte per umbram*
Perque domos Ditis vacuas et inania regna.
Darkling they went under the lonely night through the
shadow and through the empty dwellings and
unsubstantial realms of Dis.
268

21 *Vestibulum ante ipsum primisque in faucibus Orci*
Luctus et ultrices posuere cubilia Curae,
Pallentesque habitant Morbi tristisque Senectus,
Et Metus et malesuada Fames ac turpis Egestas,
Terribiles visu formae, Letumque Labosque.
Before the very forecourt and in the opening of the
jaws of hell Grief and avenging Cares have placed
their beds, and wan Diseases and sad Old Age live
there, and Fear and Hunger that urges to
wrongdoing, and shaming Destitution, figures
terrible to see, and Death and Toil.
273

22 *Stabant orantes primi transmittere cursum*
Tendebantque manus ripae ulterioris amore.
They stood begging to be the first to make the voyage
over and they reached out their hands in longing for
the further shore.
313

23 *Inventas aut qui vitam excoluere per artis*
Quique sui memores aliquos fecere merendo:
Omnibus his nivea cinguntur tempora vitta.
Or those who have improved life by the knowledge
they have found out, and those who have made
themselves remembered by some for their services:
round the brows of all these is worn a snow-white
band.
663

24 *Spiritus intus alit, totamque infusa per artus*
Mens agitat molem et magno se corpore miscet.

The spirit within nourishes, and mind instilled
  throughout the living parts activates the whole mass
  and mingles with the vast frame.
726

1 *Excudent alii spirantia mollius aera*
  (Credo equidem), vivos ducent de marmore vultus,
  Orabunt causas melius, caelique meatus
  Describent radio et surgentia sidera dicent:
  Tu regere imperio populos, Romane, memento
  (Hae tibi erunt artes), pacique imponere morem,
  Parcere subiectis et debellare superbos.
  Others shall shape bronzes more smoothly so that they
    seem alive (yes, I believe it), shall mould from
    marble living faces, shall better plead their cases in
    court, and shall demonstrate with a pointer the
    motions of the heavenly bodies and tell the stars as
    they rise: you, Roman, make your task to rule
    nations by your government (these shall be your
    skills), to impose ordered ways upon a state of
    peace, to spare those who have submitted and to
    subdue the arrogant.
  847

2 *Heu, miserande puer, si qua fata aspera rumpas,*
  Tu Marcellus eris. Manibus date lilia plenis.
  Alas, pitiable boy—if only you might break your cruel
    fate!—you are to be Marcellus. Give me lilies in
    armfuls.
  882

3 *Sunt geminae Somni portae, quarum altera fertur*
  Cornea, qua veris facilis datur exitus umbris,
  Altera candenti perfecta nitens elephanto,
  Sed falsa ad caelum mittunt insomnia Manes.
  There are two gates of Sleep, one of which it is held is
    made of horn and by it real ghosts have easy egress;
    the other shining fashioned of gleaming white ivory,
    but deceptive are the visions the Underworld sends
    that way to the light.
  893

4   *Geniumque loci primamque deorum*
  Tellurem Nymphasque et adhuc ignota precatur
  Flumina.
  He prays to the spirit of the place and to Earth the first
    of the gods and to the Nymphs and as yet unknown
    rivers.
  vii.136

5 *Flectere si nequeo superos, Acheronta movebo.*
  If I am unable to make the gods above relent, I shall
    move Hell.
  312

6 *O mihi praeteritos referat si Iuppiter annos.*
  Oh if only Jupiter would give me back my past years.
  viii. 560

7 *Quadripedante putrem sonitu quatit ungula campum.*
  Hooves with a galloping sound are shaking the
    powdery plain.
  596

8 *Macte nova virtute, puer, sic itur ad astra.*
  Blessings on your young courage, boy; that's the way
    to the stars.
  ix.641

9 *Audentis Fortuna iuvat.*
  Fortune assists the bold.
  x.284

10 *Experto credite.*

Trust one who has gone through it.
xi.283

11 *Tityre, tu patulae recubans sub tegmine fagi*
  Silvestrem tenui Musam meditaris avena.
  Tityrus, you who lie under cover of the spreading
    beech-tree, you are practising your pastoral music on
    a thin stalk.
  Eclogue, i.1

12 *O Meliboee, deus nobis haec otia fecit.*
  O Meliboeus, it is a god that has made this peaceful
    life for us.
  6

13 *At nos hinc alii sitientis ibimus Afros,*
  Pars Scythiam et rapidum cretae veniemus Oaxen
  Et penitus toto divisos orbe Britannos.
  But we from here are to go some to arid Africa,
    another group to Scythia and others of us shall come
    to the Oaxes swirling with clay, and amongst the
    Britons who are kept far away from the whole
    world.
  64

14 *Formosum pastor Corydon ardebat Alexin,*
  Delicias domini, nec quid speraret habebat.
  The shepherd Corydon was in hot love with handsome
    Alexis, his master's favourite, but he was not getting
    anything he hoped for.
  ii.1

15 *O formose puer, nimium ne crede colori.*
  O handsome lad, don't trust too much in your
    complexion.
  17

16 *Quem fugis, a! demens? Habitarunt di quoque silvas.*
  Ah, madman! Whom are you running away from?
    Gods too have lived in the woods.
  60

17 *Trahit sua quemque voluptas.*
  Everyone is dragged on by their favourite pleasure.
  65

18 *Malo me Galatea petit, lasciva puella,*
  Et fugit ad salices et se cupit ante videri.
  Galatea throws an apple at me, sexy girl, and runs
    away into the willows and wants to have been
    spotted.
  iii.64

19 *Latet anguis in herba.*
  There's a snake hidden in the grass.
  93

20 *Non nostrum inter vos tantas componere lites.*
  It's not in my power to decide such a great dispute
    between you.
  108

21 *Claudite iam rivos, pueri; sat prata biberunt.*
  Close the sluices now, lads; the fields have drunk
    enough.
  111

22 *Sicelides Musae, paulo maiora canamus!*
  Non omnis arbusta iuvant humilesque myricae;
  Si canimus silvas, silvae sint consule dignae.
  * Ultima Cumaei venit iam carminis aetas;*
  Magnus ab integro saeclorum nascitur ordo.
  Iam redit et virgo, redeunt Saturnia regna,
  Iam nova progenies caelo demittitur alto.
  Sicilian Muses, let us sing of rather greater things. Not

everyone likes bushes and low tamarisks; if we sing
of the woods, let them be woods of consular
dignity.
Now has come the last age according to the oracle at
Cumae; the great series of lifetimes starts anew. Now
too the virgin goddess returns, the golden days of
Saturn's reign return, now a new race descends from
high heaven.
iv.1

1 *Incipe, parve puer, risu cognoscere matrem.*
Begin, baby boy, to recognize your mother with a
smile.
60

2 *Incipe, parve puer: qui non risere parenti,*
Nec deus hunc mensa, dea nec dignata cubili est.
Begin, baby boy: if you haven't had a smile for your
parent, then neither will a god think you worth
inviting to dinner, nor a goddess to bed.
62

3 *Ambo florentes aetatibus, Arcades ambo,*
Et cantare pares et respondere parati.
Both in the flower of their youth, Arcadians both, and
matched and ready alike to start a song and to
respond.
vii.4

4 *Saepibus in nostris parvam te roscida mala*
(Dux ego vester eram) vidi cum matre legentem.
Alter ab undecimo tum me iam acceperat annus,
Iam fragilis poteram a terra contingere ramos:
Ut vidi, ut perii, ut me malus abstulit error!
In our orchard I saw you picking dewy apples with
your mother (I was showing you the way). I had
just turned twelve years old, I could reach the brittle
branches even from the ground: how I saw you! how
I fell in love! how an awful madness swept me
away!
viii.37

5 *Nunc scio quid sit Amor.*
Now I know what Love is.
43

6 *Non omnia possumus omnes.*
We can't all do everything.
63. Attributed to Lucilius, Macrobius, *Saturnalia*, vi.1.35

7   *Et me fecere poetam*
Pierides, sunt et mihi carmina, me quoque dicunt
Vatem pastores; sed non ego credulus illis.
Nam neque adhuc Vario videor nec dicere Cinna
Digna, sed argutos inter strepere anser olores.
Me too the Muses made write verse. I have songs of
my own, the shepherds call me also a poet; but I'm
not inclined to trust them. For I don't seem yet to
write things as good either as Varius or as Cinna,
but to be a goose honking amongst tuneful swans.
ix.32

8 *Omnia vincit Amor: et nos cedamus Amori.*
Love conquers all things: let us too give in to Love.
x.69

9 *Ite domum saturae, venit Hesperus, ite capellae.*
Go on home, you have fed full, the evening star is
coming, go on, my she-goats.
77

10 *Ultima Thule.*
Farthest Thule.
Georgics, i.30

11 *Nosque ubi primus equis Oriens adflavit anhelis*
Illic sera rubens accendit lumina Vesper.
And when the rising sun has first breathed on us with
his panting horses, over there the red evening-star is
lighting his late lamps.
250

12 *Ter sunt conati imponere Pelio Ossam*
Scilicet atque Ossae frondosum involvere Olympum;
Ter pater exstructos disiecit fulmine montis.
Three times they endeavoured to pile Ossa on Pelion,
no less, and to roll leafy Olympus on top of Ossa;
three times our Father scattered the heaped-up
mountains with a thunderbolt.
281

13 *O fortunatos nimium, sua si bona norint,*
Agricolas!
O farmers excessively fortunate if only they recognized
their blessings!
ii.458

14 *Felix qui potuit rerum cognoscere causas.*
Lucky is he who has been able to understand the
causes of things.
490

15 *Fortunatus et ille deos qui novit agrestis.*
Fortunate too is the man who has come to know the
gods of the countryside.
493

16 *Optima quaeque dies miseris mortalibus aevi*
Prima fugit; subeunt morbi tristisque senectus
Et labor, et durae rapit inclementia mortis.
All the best days of life slip away from us poor mortals
first; illnesses and dreary old age and pain sneak up,
and the fierceness of harsh death snatches away.
iii.66

17 *Sed fugit interea, fugit inreparabile tempus.*
But meanwhile it is flying, irretrievable time is flying.
284

18 *Hi motus animorum atque haec certamina tanta*
Pulveris exigui iactu compressa quiescent.
All these spirited movements and such great contests
as these will be contained and quieten down by the
throwing of a little dust.
iv.86. Of the battle of the bees

19 *Non aliter, si parva licet componere magnis,*
Cecropias innatus apes amor urget habendi
Munere quamque suo.
Just so, if one may compare small things with great, an
innate love of getting drives these Attic bees each
with his own function.
176

20 *Sic vos non vobis mellificatis apes.*
Sic vos non vobis nidificatis aves.
Sic vos non vobis vellera fertis oves.
Thus you bees make honey not for yourselves. Thus
you birds build nests not for yourselves. Thus you
sheep bear fleeces not for yourselves.
Attr. On Bathyllus' claiming the authorship of certain lines by
Virgil

VOLTAIRE 1694–1778

21 *Si nous ne trouvons pas des choses agréables, nous*
trouverons du moins des choses nouvelles.
If we do not find anything pleasant, at least we shall

find something new.
Candide (1759), ch.17

1 *Dans ce pays-ci il est bon de tuer de temps en temps
un amiral pour encourager les autres.*
In this country [England] it is thought well to kill an
admiral from time to time to encourage the others.
ch.23

2 *Tout est pour le mieux dans le meilleur des mondes
possibles.*
All is for the best in the best of possible worlds.
ch.30

3 *Cela est bien dit, répondit Candide, mais il faut
cultiver notre jardin.*
'That is well said,' replied Candide, 'but we must
cultivate our garden.' (We must attend to our own
affairs.)

4 *Ils ne se servent de la pensée que pour autoriser leurs
injustices, et n'emploient les paroles que pour
déguiser leurs pensées.*
[Men] use thought only to justify their injustices, and
speech only to conceal their thoughts.
Dialogue xiv. **Le Chapon et la Poularde**

5 *Le mieux est l'ennemi du bien.*
The best is the enemy of the good.
Dict. Philosophique (1764). **Art Dramatique**

6 *La superstition met le monde entier en flammes; la
philosophie les éteint.*
Superstition sets the whole world in flames; philosophy
quenches them.
Superstition

7 *Tous les genres sont bons hors le genre ennuyeux.*
All styles are good save the tiresome kind.
L'Enfant Prodigue (1736), preface

8 *Si Dieu n'existait pas, il faudrait l'inventer.*
If God did not exist, it would be necessary to invent
him.
Épîtres, xcvi. **A l'Auteur du Livre des Trois Imposteurs**

9 *Ce corps qui s'appelait et qui s'appelle encore le saint
empire romain n'était en aucune manière ni saint, ni
romain, ni empire.*
This agglomeration which was called and which still
calls itself the Holy Roman Empire was neither holy,
nor Roman, nor an empire.
Essai sur les Moeurs et l'Esprit des Nations (1769), lxx

10 *En effet, l'histoire n'est que le tableau des crimes et
des malheurs.*
Indeed, history is nothing more than a tableau of
crimes and misfortunes.
L'Ingénu (1767), ch.10

11 *Quoi que vous fassiez, écrasez l'infâme, et aimez qui
vous aime.*
Whatever you do, stamp out abuses, and love those
who love you.
Letter to M. d'Alembert, 28 Nov. 1762

12 *Il est plaisant qu'on fait une vertu du vice de chasteté;
et voilà encore une drôle de chasteté que celle qui
mène tout droit les hommes au péché d'Onan, et les
filles aux pâles couleurs!*
It is amusing that a virtue is made of the vice of
chastity; and it's a pretty odd sort of chastity at that,
which leads men straight into the sin of Onan, and
girls to the waning of their colour.
Letter to M. Mariott, 28 Mar. 1766

13 *Je ne suis pas comme une dame de la cour de
Versailles, qui disait: c'est bien dommage que
l'aventure de la tour de Babel ait produit la confusion
des langues; sans cela tout le monde aurait toujours
parlé français.*
I am not like a lady at the court of Versailles, who
said: 'What a dreadful pity that the bother at the tower
of Babel should have got language all mixed up; but
for that, everyone would always have spoken French.'
Letter to Catherine the Great, 26 May 1767

14 *Le superflu, chose très nécessaire.*
The superfluous is very necessary.
Le Mondain (1736), v.22

15 *C'est une des superstitions de l'esprit humain d'avoir
imaginé que la virginité pouvait être une vertu.*
It is one of the superstitions of the human mind to have
imagined that virginity could be a virtue.
Notebooks, ed. T. Besterman, 2nd edn. (1968), vol.II, **The
Leningrad Notebooks** (c.1735–c.1750), p.455

16 *Il faut qu'il y ait des moments tranquilles dans les
grands ouvrages, comme dans la vie après les instants
de passions, mais non pas des moments de dégoût.*
There ought to be moments of tranquillity in great
works, as in life after the experience of passions, but
not moments of disgust.
The Piccini Notebooks, p.500

17 *Il faut, dans le gouvernement, des bergers et des
bouchers.*
Governments need to have both shepherds and
butchers.
p.517

18 *Dieu n'est pas pour les gros bataillons, mais pour
ceux qui tirent le mieux.*
God is on the side not of the heavy batallions, but of
the best shots.
p.547. See 117:7

19 *On doit des égards aux vivants; on ne doit aux morts
que la vérité.*
We owe respect to the living; to the dead we owe only
truth.
Oeuvres (1785), vol.I, p.15n. (**Première Lettre sur Oedipe**)

20 *La foi consiste à croire ce que la raison ne croit
pas...Il ne suffit pas qu'une chose soit possible pour la
croire.*
Faith consists in believing when it is beyond the power
of reason to believe. It is not enough that a thing be
possible for it to be believed.
Questions sur l'Encyclopédie

21 *Le secret d'ennuyer est...de tout dire.*
The way to be a bore is to say everything.
Sept Discours en vers sur l'Homme, VI. **Sur la Nature de
l'Homme.** v.174-5

22 When Voltaire was asked why no woman has ever
written a tolerable tragedy, 'Ah (said the Patriarch) the
composition of a tragedy requires *testicles.*'
Letter from Byron to John Murray, 2 Apr. 1817

23 *Habacuc était capable de tout.*
Habakkuk was capable of anything.
Attr. See N. & Q., clxxxi.46

24 I disapprove of what you say, but I will defend to the
death your right to say it.
Attr. in S.G. Tallentyre, *The Friends of Voltaire* (1907), p.199

RICHARD WAGNER 1813–1883

1 *Frisch weht der Wind*
der Heimat zu:—
mein irisch Kind,
wo weilest du?
Freshly blows the wind to the homeland: my Irish
child, where are you staying?
Tristan und Isolde, I.i

ARTHUR WALEY 1889–1966

2 What is hard today is to censor one's own thoughts—
To sit by and see the blind man
On the sightless horse, riding into the bottomless
abyss.
Censorship

HENRY WALLACE 1888–1965

3 The century on which we are entering—the century
which will come out of this war—can be and must be
the century of the common man.
Address: **The Price of Free World Victory,** 8 May 1942

WILLIAM ROSS WALLACE d. 1881

4 The hand that rocks the cradle
Is the hand that rules the world.
John o'London's Treasure Trove

GRAHAM WALLAS 1858–1932

5 The little girl had the making of a poet in her who,
being told to be sure of her meaning before she spoke,
said: 'How can I know what I think till I see what I
say?'
The Art of Thought

EDMUND WALLER 1606–1687

6 So was the huntsman by the bear oppress'd,
Whose hide he sold—before he caught the beast!
Battle of the Summer Islands, ii, l.111

7 Poets that lasting marble seek
Must carve in Latin or in Greek.
Of English Verse

8 Others may use the ocean as their road,
Only the English make it their abode.
Of a War with Spain, l.25

9 The soul's dark cottage, batter'd and decay'd
Lets in new light through chinks that time has made;
Stronger by weakness, wiser men become,
As they draw near to their eternal home.
Leaving the old, both worlds at once they view,
That stand upon the threshold of the new.
On the Foregoing Divine Poems, l.18

10 That which her slender waist confin'd
Shall now my joyful temples bind;
No monarch but would give his crown
His arms might do what this has done.
On a Girdle

11 Rome, though her eagle through the world had flown,
Could never make this island all her own.
Panegyric to My Lord Protector, xvii

12 Illustrious acts high raptures do infuse,

And every conqueror creates a Muse.
xlvi

13 Go, lovely Rose!
Tell her, that wastes her time and me,
    That now she knows,
When I resemble her to thee,
How sweet and fair she seems to be.
Song: 'Go Lovely Rose!'

14 Small is the worth
    Of beauty from the light retir'd;
Bid her come forth,
    Suffer herself to be desir'd,
And not blush so to be admir'd.

15 Why came I so untimely forth
Into a world which, wanting thee,
Could entertain us with no worth,
Or shadow of felicity?
To My Young Lady Lucy Sidney

16   So all we know
Of what they do above,
Is that they happy are, and that they love.
Upon the Death of My Lady Rich, l.75

17 Under the tropic is our language spoke,
And part of Flanders hath receiv'd our yoke.
Upon the Death of the Lord Protector, l.21

HORACE WALPOLE, FOURTH EARL OF ORFORD 1717–1797

18 Alexander at the head of the world never tasted the
true pleasure that boys of his own age have enjoyed at
the head of a school.
Letters. To Montagu, 6 May 1736

19 Our supreme governors, the mob.
To Mann, 7 Sept. 1743

20 [Lovat] was beheaded yesterday, and died extremely
well, without passion, affectation, buffoonery or
timidity: his behaviour was natural and intrepid.
To Mann, 10 Apr. 1747

21 [Strawberry Hill] is a little plaything-house that I got
out of Mrs Chenevix's shop, and is the prettiest bauble
you ever saw. It is set in enamelled meadows, with
filigree hedges.
To Conway, 8 June 1747

22 But, thank God! the Thames is between me and the
Duchess of Queensberry.

23 Every drop of ink in my pen ran cold.
To Montagu, 3 July 1752

24 It has the true rust of the Barons' Wars.
To Bentley, Sept. 1753

25 At present, nothing is talked of, nothing admired, but
what I cannot help calling a very insipid and tedious
performance: it is a kind of novel, called *The Life and
Opinions of Tristram Shandy;* the great humour of
which consists in the whole narration always going
backwards.
To Dalrymple, 4 Apr. 1760

26 One of the greatest geniuses that ever existed,
Shakespeare, undoubtedly wanted taste.
To Wren, 9 Aug. 1764

27 The works of Richardson...which are pictures of high
life as conceived by a bookseller, and romances as they

would be spiritualized by a Methodist preacher.
To Mann, 20 Dec. 1764

1 At Madame du Deffand's, an old blind *débauchée* of
wit.
To Conway, 6 Oct. 1765

2 What has one to do, when one grows tired of the
world, as we both do, but to draw nearer and nearer,
and gently waste the remains of life with friends with
whom one began it?
To Montagu, 21 Nov. 1765

3 It is charming to totter into vogue.
To Selwyn, 2 Dec. 1765

4 Yes, like Queen Eleanor in the ballad, I sunk at
Charing Cross, and have risen in the Faubourg St
Germain.
To Gray, 25 Jan. 1766

5 The best sun we have is made of Newcastle coal.
To Montagu, 15 June 1768

6 Everybody talks of the constitution, but all sides
forget that the constitution is extremely well, and
would do very well, if they would but let it alone.
To Mann, 18-19 Jan. 1770

7 It was easier to conquer it [the East] than to know
what to do with it.
To Mann, 27 Mar. 1772

8 The way to ensure summer in England is to have it
framed and glazed in a comfortable room.
To Cole, 28 May 1774

9 The next Augustan age will dawn on the other side of
the Atlantic. There will, perhaps, be a Thucydides at
Boston, a Xenophon at New York, and, in time, a
Virgil at Mexico, and a Newton at Peru. At last, some
curious traveller from Lima will visit England and give
a description of the ruins of St Paul's, like the editions
of Balbec and Palmyra.
To Mann, 24 Nov. 1774

10 By the waters of Babylon we sit down and weep, when
we think of thee, O America!
To Mason, 12 June 1775

11 This world is a comedy to those that think, a tragedy
to those that feel.
To the Countess of Upper Ossory, 16 Aug. 1776

12 Tell me, ye divines, which is the most virtuous man,
he who begets twenty bastards, or he who sacrifices an
hundred thousand lives?
To Mann, 7 July 1778

13 When will the world know that peace and propagation
are the two most delightful things in it?

14 The life of any man written under the direction of his
family, did nobody honour.
To Cole, 1 Sept. 1778

15 When men write for profit, they are not very delicate.

16 Easy I am so far, that the ill success of the American
war has saved us from slavery—in truth, I am content
that liberty will exist anywhere, and amongst
Englishmen, even cross the Atlantic.
To Mann, 25 Feb. 1779

17 When people will not weed their own minds, they are
apt to be overrun with nettles.
To Lady Ailesbury, 10 July 1779

18 Prognostics do not always prove prophecies,—at least

the wisest prophets make sure of the event first.
To Thos. Walpole, 19 Feb. 1785

19 It is the story of a mountebank and his zany.
Of Boswell's *Tour to the Hebrides*. To Conway, 6 Oct. 1785

20 All his [Sir Joshua Reynolds's] own geese are swans,
as the swans of others are geese.
To the Countess of Upper Ossory, 1 Dec. 1786

21 I do not dislike the French from the vulgar antipathy
between neighbouring nations, but for their insolent
and unfounded airs of superiority.
To Hannah More, 14 Oct. 1787

22 Virtue knows to a farthing what it has lost by not
having been vice.
L. Kronenberger, *The extraordinary Mr. Wilkes* (1974), Part 3,
ch.2, 'The Ruling Class'

SIR HUGH WALPOLE 1884–1941

23 'Tisn't life that matters! 'Tis the courage you bring to
it.
Fortitude (1913), opening sentence

SIR ROBERT WALPOLE, FIRST EARL OF ORFORD 1676–1745

24 They now *ring* the bells, but they will soon *wring*
their hands.
On the declaration of war with Spain, 1739. W. Coxe, *Memoirs
of Sir Robert Walpole* (1798), vol.i, p.618

25 Madam, there are fifty thousand men slain this year in
Europe, and not one Englishman.
To Queen Caroline, 1734. Hervey, *Memoirs* (1848), vol.i, p.398

26 My Lord Bath, you and I are now two as insignificant
men as any in England.
To Pulteney, Earl of Bath, on their promotion to the House of
Lords. W. King, *Political & Literary Anecdotes* (1819), p.43

27 The balance of power.
House of Commons, 13 Feb. 1741

WILLIAM WALSH 1663–1708

28 And sadly reflecting,
That a lover forsaken
    A new love may get,
But a neck when once broken
    Can never be set.
The Despairing Lover, l.17

29 By partners, in each other kind,
Afflictions easier grow;
In love alone we hate to find
Companions of our woe.
Song, Of All the Torments

30 I can endure my own despair,
But not another's hope.

IZAAK WALTON 1593–1683

31 Angling may be said to be so like the mathematics,
that it can never be fully learnt.
The Compleat Angler (1653), Epistle to the Reader

32 And for winter fly-fishing it is as useful as an almanac
out of date.

33 As no man is born an artist, so no man is born an
angler.

34 I shall stay him no longer than to wish him a rainy

evening to read this following discourse; and that if he
be an honest angler, the east wind may never blow
when he goes a-fishing.

1 I am, Sir, a Brother of the Angle.
pt.i, ch.1

2 Angling is somewhat like poetry, men are to be born
so.

3 Sir Henry Wotton...was also a most dear lover, and a
frequent practiser of the art of angling; of which he
would say, 'it was an employment for his idle time,
which was then not idly spent...a rest to his mind, a
cheerer of his spirits, a diverter of sadness, a calmer of
unquiet thoughts, a moderator of passions, a procurer
of contentedness; and that it begat habits of peace and
patience in those that professed and practised it.'

4 Good company and good discourse are the very sinews
of virtue.
ch.2

5 An excellent angler, and now with God.
ch.4

6 I love such mirth as does not make friends ashamed to
look upon one another next morning.
ch.5

7 A good, honest, wholesome, hungry breakfast.

8 No man can lose what he never had.

9 In so doing, use him as though you loved him.
ch.8. Instructions for baiting a hook with a live frog.

10 This dish of meat is too good for any but anglers, or
very honest men.

11 I love any discourse of rivers, and fish and fishing.
ch.18

12 Look to your health; and if you have it, praise God,
and value it next to a good conscience; for health is the
second blessing that we mortals are capable of; a
blessing that money cannot buy.
ch.21

13 Let the blessing of St Peter's Master be...upon all that
are lovers of virtue; and dare trust in His providence;
and be quiet; and go a-Angling.

14 But God, who is able to prevail, wrestled with him, as
the Angel did with Jacob, and marked him; marked him
for his own.
Life of Donne

15 The great Secretary of Nature and all learning, Sir
Francis Bacon.
Life of Herbert

16 Of this blest man, let his just praise be given,
Heaven was in him, before he was in heaven.
Written in Dr. Richard Sibbes's *Returning Backslider*, now
preserved in Salisbury Cathedral Library

BISHOP WILLIAM WARBURTON 1698–1779

17 Orthodoxy is my doxy; heterodoxy is another man's
doxy.
To Lord Sandwich. Priestley, *Memoirs* (1807), vol.i, p.372

ARTEMUS WARD (CHARLES FARRAR BROWNE) 1834–1867

18 I now bid you a welcome adoo.
Artemus Ward His Book. The Shakers

19 'Mister Ward, don't yur blud bile at the thawt that
three million and a half of your culled brethren air a
clanking their chains in the South?' Sez I, 'not a bile!
Let 'em clank!'
Oberlin

20 If you mean gettin hitched, I'M IN!
The Showman's Courtship

21 My pollertics, like my religion, bein of a exceedin
accommodatin character.
The Crisis

22 Shall we sell our birthrite for a mess of potash?

23 N.B. This is rote Sarcasticul.
A Visit to Brigham Young

24 I girdid up my Lions & fled the Seen.

25 Did you ever hav the measels, and if so how many?
The Census

26 The female woman is one of the greatest institooshuns
of which this land can boste.
Woman's Rights

27 By a sudden and adroit movement I placed my left eye
agin the Secesher's fist.
Thrilling Scenes in Dixie

28 The ground flew up and hit me in the hed.

29 I presunted myself at Betty's bedside late at nite, with
considerbul licker koncealed about my persun.
Betsy-Jain Re-orgunised

30 The happy marrid man dies in good stile at home,
surrounded by his weeping wife and children. The old
batchelor don't die at all—he sort of rots away, like a
polly-wog's tail.
Draft in Baldinsville

31 It is a pity that Chawcer, who had geneyus, was so
unedicated. He's the wuss speller I know of.
Artemus Ward in London, ch.4. **At the Tomb of Shakespeare**

32 He [Brigham Young] is dreadfully married. He's the
most married man I ever saw in my life.
Artemus Ward's Lecture

33 Why is this thus? What is the reason of this thusness?

34 I am happiest when I am idle. I could live for months
without performing any kind of labour, and at the
expiration of that time I should feel fresh and vigorous
enough to go right on in the same way for numerous
more months.
Pyrotechny. III. **Pettingill**

35 Why care for grammar as long as we are good?
V

36 Let us all be happy, and live within our means, even if
we have to borrer the money to do it with.
Science and Natural History

MRS. HUMPHRY WARD 1851–1920

37 'Propinquity does it'—as Mrs Thornburgh is always
reminding us.
Robert Elsmere (1888), bk.i, ch.2

REVD. NATHANIEL WARD 1578–1652

38 The world is full of care, much like unto a bubble;
Woman and care, and care and women, and women
and care and trouble.
Epigram. Attr. by Ward to a lady at the Court of the Queen of
Bohemia. *Simple Cobler's Boy* (1648), p.25

GEORGE WASHINGTON 1732–1799

1 Father, I cannot tell a lie, I did it with my little
hatchet.
Attr. Mark Twain, *Mark Twain as George Washington*. Another
version is: I can't tell a lie, Pa; you know I can't tell a lie. I did
cut it with my hatchet. Weems, *Washington*, (Fifth edition, 1806)

2 It is our true policy to steer clear of permanent alliance
with any portion of the foreign world.
Farewell Address to the People of the United States, 17 Sept. 1796

3 Labour to keep alive in your breast that little spark of
celestial fire, called conscience.
Rules of Civility and Decent Behaviour. Sparks, *Life of
Washington* (1839), vol.ii, p.109

4 We must consult Brother Jonathan.
Said to have been a frequent remark of his during the American
Revolution, referring to Jonathan Trumbull, 1710-85, Governor of
Connecticut. *Publications of the Colonial Society of
Massachusetts* (1905), vol.vii, p.94

5 Put none but Americans on guard to-night.
Attr. based on his circular letter to regimental commanders, 30
Apr. 1777

ROWLAND WATKYNS fl. 1662

6 I love him not, but shew no reason can
Wherefore, but this, *I do not love* the man.
Flamma sine fumo. Antipathy. See 331:9

7 For every marriage then is best in tune,
When that the wife is May, the husband June.
**To the most Courteous and Fair Gentlewoman, Mrs. Elinor
Williams**

WILLIAM WATSON 1559?–1603

8 *Fiat justitia et ruant coeli.*
Let justice be done though the heavens fall.
**A Decacordon of Ten Quodlibeticall Questions Concerning
Religion and State** (1602). First citation in an English work of a
famous maxim. See 210:33

SIR WILLIAM WATSON 1858–1936

9 April, April,
Laugh thy girlish laughter;
Then, the moment after,
Weep thy girlish tears!
April

10 O be less beautiful, or be less brief.
Autumn

11 How all her care was but to be fair,
And all her task to be sweet.
The Heart of the Rose

12 Who never negligently yet
Fashioned an April violet,
Nor would forgive, did June disclose
Unceremoniously the rose.
Nature's Way

13 The staid, conservative,
Came-over-with-the-Conqueror type of mind.
A Study in Contrasts, i, I.42

ISAAC WATTS 1674–1748

14 Lord, I ascribe it to Thy grace,
And not to chance, as others do,
That I was born of Christian race,

And not a Heathen, or a Jew.
Divine Songs for Children, vi. **Praise for the Gospel**

15 There's no repentance in the grave.
x. **Solemn Thoughts of God and Death**

16 There is a dreadful Hell,
And everlasting pains;
There sinners must with devils dwell
In darkness, fire, and chains.
xi. **Heaven and Hell**

17 Let dogs delight to bark and bite,
For God hath made them so;
Let bears and lions growl and fight,
For 'tis their nature too.
xvi. **Against Quarrelling**

18 But, children, you should never let
Such angry passions rise;
Your little hands were never made
To tear each other's eyes.

19 Whatever brawls disturb the street,
There should be peace at home.
xvii. **Love between Brothers and Sisters**

20 Birds in their little nests agree
And 'tis a shameful sight,
When children of one family
Fall out, and chide, and fight.

21 How doth the little busy bee
Improve each shining hour,
And gather honey all the day
From every opening flower!
xx. **Against Idleness and Mischief**

22 In works of labour, or of skill,
I would be busy too;
For Satan finds some mischief still
For idle hands to do.

23 One sickly sheep infects the flock,
And poisons all the rest.
xxi. **Against Evil Company**

24 Let me be dress'd fine as I will,
Flies, worms, and flowers, exceed me still.
xxii. **Against Pride in Clothes**

25 'Tis the voice of the sluggard; I heard him complain,
'You have wak'd me too soon, I must slumber again'.
As the door on its hinges, so he on his bed,
Turns his sides and his shoulders and his heavy head.
Moral Songs, i. **The Sluggard**

26 How rude are the boys that throw pebbles and mire.
ii. **Innocent Play**

27 I'll not willingly offend,
Nor be easily offended;
What's amiss I'll strive to mend,
And endure what can't be mended.
vi. **Good Resolution**

28 Hark! from the tombs a doleful sound.
Hymns and Spiritual Songs, bk.ii, No.63. **Hark! from the
Tombs**

EVELYN WAUGH 1903–1966

29 The sound of the English county families baying for
broken glass.
Decline and Fall (1928), Prelude

30 'We class schools, you see, into four grades: Leading
School, First-rate School, Good School, and School.

Frankly', said Mr Levy, 'School is pretty bad.'
Pt.I. ch.1

1 You can't get into the soup in Ireland, do what you like.
ch.3

2 For generations the British bourgeoisie have spoken of themselves as gentlemen, and by that they have meant, among other things, a self-respecting scorn of irregular perquisites. It is the quality that distinguishes the gentleman from both the artist and the aristocrat.
ch.6

3 Feather-footed through the plashy fen passes the questing vole.
Scoop (1938), bk.I, ch.1

4 Up to a point, Lord Copper.
Meaning 'No'. *passim*

5 Lady Peabury was in the morning room reading a novel; early training gave a guilty spice to this recreation, for she had been brought up to believe that to read a novel before luncheon was one of the gravest sins it was possible for a gentlewoman to commit.
Work Suspended (1942), **An Englishman's Home** [1939]

BEATRICE WEBB 1848–1943

6 If I ever felt inclined to be timid as I was going into a room full of people, I would say to myself, 'You're the cleverest member of one of the cleverest families in the cleverest class of the cleverest nation in the world, why should you be frightened?'
Bertrand Russell, *Portraits from Memory* (1956), VIII. Sidney and Beatrice Webb

SIDNEY WEBB 1859–1947

7 The inevitability of gradualness.
Presidential address to the annual conference of the Labour Party, 1920

8 Marriage is the waste-paper basket of the emotions.
Attr. by Beatrice Webb. Bertrand Russell, *Portraits from Memory* (1956), VIII. Sidney and Beatrice Webb

DANIEL WEBSTER 1782–1852

9 There is always room at the top.
When advised not to become a lawyer as the profession was overcrowded

10 The people's government, made for the people, made by the people, and answerable to the people.
Second Speech in the Senate on Foot's Resolution, 26 Jan. 1830

11 Liberty and Union, now and forever, one and inseparable!

12 On this question of principle, while actual suffering was yet afar off, they [the Colonies] raised their flag against a power, to which, for purposes of foreign conquest and subjugation, Rome, in the height of her glory, is not to be compared; a power which has dotted over the surface of the whole globe with her possessions and military posts, whose morning drum-beat, following the sun, and keeping company with the hours, circles the earth with one continuous and unbroken strain of the martial airs of England.
Speech in the Senate on the President's Protest, 7 May 1834

13 Thank God, I—I also—am an American!
Speech on the Completion of Bunker Hill Monument, 17 June 1843

14 The Law: It has honoured us, may we honour it.

15 I was born an American; I will live an American; I shall die an American.
Speech in the Senate on 'The Compromise Bill', 17 July 1850

16 Fearful concatenation of circumstances.
Argument on the Murder of Captain Joseph White

JOHN WEBSTER 1580?–1625?

17 Vain the ambition of kings
Who seek by trophies and dead things,
To leave a living name behind,
And weave but nets to catch the wind.
The Devil's Law-Case, V.iv

18 *Ferdinand:* And women like that part which, like the lamprey,
Hath never a bone in't.
Duchess: Fie, sir!
Ferdinand: Nay,
I mean the tongue; variety of courtship:
What cannot a neat knave with a smooth tale
Make a woman believe?
The Duchess of Malfi (1623), ed. C.B. Wheeler (1915), I.ii.43

19 Unequal nature, to place women's hearts
So far upon the left side.
II.v.33

20   Why should only I...
Be cas'd up, like a holy relic? I have youth
And a little beauty.
III.ii.135

21 Raised by that curious engine, your white hand.
297

22   O, that it were possible,
We might but hold some two days' conference
With the dead!
IV.ii.18

23 I have made a soap-boiler costive.
117

24 I am Duchess of Malfi still.
146

25 Glories, like glow-worms, afar off shine bright,
But looked to near, have neither heat nor light.
148

26 I know death hath ten thousand several doors
For men to take their exits.
222. See 215:11, 336:1, 420:11

27 *Ferdinand:* Cover her face; mine eyes dazzle: she died young.
Bosola: I think not so; her infelicity
Seem'd to have years too many.
267

28 Physicians are like kings,—they brook no contradiction.
V.ii.72

29 We are merely the stars' tennis-balls, struck and bandied
Which way please them.
iv.53

30 Is not old wine wholesomest, old pippins toothsomest, old wood burn brightest, old linen wash whitest? Old

soldiers, sweethearts, are surest, and old lovers are soundest.
Westward Hoe (1607), II.ii

1   Fortune's a right whore:
If she give aught, she deals it in small parcels,
That she may take away all at one swoop.
The White Devil (1612), I.i.4

2 'Tis just like a summer birdcage in a garden; the birds that are without despair to get in, and the birds that are within despair, and are in a consumption, for fear they shall never get out.
ii.47

3 A mere tale of a tub, my words are idle.
II.i.92

4 Only the deep sense of some deathless shame.
ii.67

5 Cowardly dogs bark loudest.
III.i.163

6 A rape! a rape!...
Yes, you have ravish'd justice;
Forced her to do your pleasure.
271

7 There's nothing sooner dry than women's tears.
V.iii.192

8 Call for the robin-red-breast and the wren,
Since o'er shady groves they hover,
And with leaves and flowers do cover
The friendless bodies of unburied men.
iv.100

9 But keep the wolf far thence that's foe to men,
For with his nails he'll dig them up again.
108

10 We think caged birds sing, when indeed they cry.
128

11 And of all axioms this shall win the prize,—
'Tis better to be fortunate than wise.
vi.183

12 There's nothing of so infinite vexation
As man's own thoughts.
206

13 My soul, like to a ship in a black storm,
Is driven, I know not whither.
248

14 Prosperity doth bewitch men, seeming clear;
But seas do laugh, show white, when rocks are near.
250

15   I have caught
An everlasting cold; I have lost my voice
Most irrecoverably.
270

JOSIAH WEDGWOOD 1730–1795

16 Am I not a man and a brother.
Legend on Wedgwood cameo depicting a kneeling negro slave in chains, reproduced in facsimile in E. Darwin, *The Botanic Garden* pt.1 (1791), facing p.87

THOMAS EARLE WELBY 1881–1933

17 'Turbot, Sir,' said the waiter, placing before me two fishbones, two eyeballs, and a bit of black

mackintosh.
The Dinner Knell

DUKE OF WELLINGTON 1769–1852

18 Not upon a man from the colonel to the private in a regiment—both inclusive. We may pick up a marshal or two perhaps; but not worth a damn.
On being asked whether he calculated upon any desertion in Buonaparte's army. *Creevey Papers*, ch.x, p.228

19 It has been a damned serious business—Blücher and I have lost 30,000 men. It has been a damned nice thing—the nearest run thing you ever saw in your life...By God! I don't think it would have done if I had not been there.
p.236

20 All the business of war, and indeed all the business of life, is to endeavour to find out what you don't know by what you do; that's what I called 'guessing what was at the other side of the hill'.
Croker Papers (1885), vol.iii, p.276

21 I believe I forgot to tell you I was made a Duke.
Postscript to a letter to his nephew Henry Wellesley, 22 May 1814

22 I never saw so many shocking bad hats in my life.
On seeing the first Reformed Parliament. Sir William Fraser, *Words on Wellington* (1889), p.12

23 You must build your House of Parliament upon the river: so...that the populace cannot exact their demands by sitting down round you.
p.163

24 The battle of Waterloo was won on the playing fields of Eton.
See Montalembert, *De l'Avenir Politique de l'Angleterre* (1856). The attribution was refuted by the 7th Duke.

25 The next greatest misfortune to losing a battle is to gain such a victory as this.
S. Rogers, *Recollections* (1859), p.215

26 'What a glorious thing must be a victory, Sir.' 'The greatest tragedy in the world, Madam, except a defeat.'
footnote

27 I always say that, next to a battle lost, the greatest misery is a battle gained.
Frances, Lady Shelley, *Diary,* p.102

28 So he is a fool, and a d—d fool; but he can take Rangoon.
G.W.E. Russell, *Collections and Recollections*, ch.2. On its being objected that he had always spoken of Lord Combermere as a fool, and yet had proposed him as commander of an expedition to take Rangoon. The story is probably apocryphal: Wellington thought highly of Combermere, who, moreover, was never involved in the Rangoon campaign.

29 In my situation as Chancellor of the University of Oxford, I have been much exposed to authors.

30 Not half so surprised as I am now, Mum!
On being asked by Mrs. Arbuthnot if he had not been surprised at Waterloo

31 I have no small talk and Peel has no manners.
ch.14

32 Hard pounding this, gentlemen; let's see who will pound longest.
At Waterloo. Sir W. Scott, *Paul's Letters* (1815)

33 I used to say of him [Napoleon] that his presence on

the field made the difference of forty thousand men.
Stanhope, *Notes of Conversations with the Duke of Wellington*, 2 Nov. 1831

1 Ours [our army] is composed of the scum of the earth—the mere scum of the earth.
4 Nov. 1831

2 My rule always was to do the business of the day in the day.
2 Nov. 1835

3 What is the best to be done for the country? How can the Government be carried on?
18 May 1839

4 Beginning reform is beginning revolution.
Mrs. Arbuthnot's Journal, 7 Nov. 1830

5 I hate the whole race…There is no believing a word they say—your professional poets, I mean—there never existed a more worthless set than Byron and his friends for example.
Noted in Lady Salisbury's diary, 26 Oct. 1833. C. Oman, *The Gascoyne Heiress* (1968), III

6 When I reflect upon the characters and attainments of some of the general officers of this army, and consider that these are the persons on whom I am to rely to lead columns against the French, I tremble; and as Lord Chesterfield said of the generals of his day, 'I only hope that when the enemy reads the list of their names, he trembles as I do.'
Dispatch to Torrens, 29 Aug. 1810. Usually quoted as 'I don't know what effect these men will have upon the enemy, but, by God, they frighten me.' Also attributed to George III.

7 [To a gentleman who accosted him in the street saying, 'Mr. Jones, I believe?']
If you believe that you will believe anything.
Attr.

8 There is no mistake; there has been no mistake; and there shall be no mistake.
Wellingtoniana (1852), p.78

9 Up Guards and at them again!
Letter from Captain Batty 22 June 1815. Booth, *Battle of Waterloo*. See also Croker, *Correspondence and Diaries* (1884), III, 280

10 Publish and be damned.
Attr. According to legend, Wellington wrote these words across a blackmailing letter from Stockdale, publisher of Harriette Wilson's *Memoirs*, and posted it back to him. See Elizabeth Pakenham, *Wellington: The Years of the Sword* (1969), ch.10

H.G. WELLS 1866–1946

11 The thing his novel is *about* is always there. It is like a church lit but without a congregation to distract you, with every light and line focused on the high altar. And on the altar, very reverently placed, intensely there, is a dead kitten, an egg-shell, a bit of string. [Of Henry James.]
Boon, ch.4, sect.3

12 In the Country of the Blind the One-eyed Man is King.
The Country of the Blind

13 'I'm a Norfan, both sides,' he would explain, with the air of one who had seen trouble.
Kipps, bk.i, ch.6, I

14 'I expect,' he said, 'I was thinking jest what a Rum Go everything is. I expect it was something like that.'
bk.iii, ch.3, 8

15 The Social Contract is nothing more or less than a vast conspiracy of human beings to lie to and humbug themselves and one another for the general Good. Lies are the mortar that bind the savage individual man into the social masonry.
Love and Mr. Lewisham, ch.23

16 Human history becomes more and more a race between education and catastrophe.
The Outline of History, ch.40 of the 1951 edn.

CHARLES WESLEY 1707–1788

17 Gentle Jesus, meek and mild,
    Look upon a little child;
Pity my simplicity,
    Suffer me to come to thee.
Hymns and Sacred Poems (1742), **Gentle Jesus, Meek and Mild**

JOHN WESLEY 1703–1791

18 I look upon all the world as my parish.
Journal, 11 June 1739

19 Once in seven years I burn all my sermons; for it is a shame if I cannot write better sermons now than I did seven years ago.
1 Sept. 1778

20 Though I am always in haste, I am never in a hurry.
Select Letters (1837). Letter to a member of the Society. 10 Dec. 1777

21 Do all the good you can,
By all the means you can,
In all the ways you can,
In all the places you can,
At all the times you can,
To all the people you can,
As long as ever you can.
Letters (1915). **Rule of Conduct**

22 Let it be observed, that slovenliness is no part of religion; that neither this, nor any text of Scripture, condemns neatness of apparel. Certainly this is a duty, not a sin. 'Cleanliness is, indeed, next to godliness.'
Sermons, No. xciii. **On Dress**

23 Beware you be not swallowed up in books! An ounce of love is worth a pound of knowledge.
R. Southey, *Life of Wesley* (1820), ch.16

24 We should constantly use the most common, little, easy words (so they are pure and proper) which our language affords.
Of preaching to 'plain people'

REVD. SAMUEL WESLEY 1662–1735

25 Style is the dress of thought; a modest dress, Neat, but not gaudy, will true critics please.
An Epistle to a Friend concerning Poetry (1700)

MAE WEST 1892?–

26 'Goodness, what beautiful diamonds.'
'Goodness had nothing to do with it, dearie.'
Night After Night (1932), script by Vincent Lawrence

27 Why don't you come up sometime, see me?
She Done Him Wrong (1933). Commonly misquoted as 'Come up and see me sometime'.

DAME REBECCA WEST 1892–

1 A life of immorality which involves posing as a page-boy in an Italian hotel must have been something so rich and strange that few of us could forebear to pause and inquire.
The Strange Necessity (1928). **The Tosh Horse**

2 God forbid that any book should be banned. The practice is as indefensible as infanticide.

RICHARD BETHELL, LORD WESTBURY 1800–1873

3 Then, sir, you will turn it over once more in what you are pleased to call your mind.
Related by Jowett and denied, not very convincingly, by Westbury. T.A. Nash, *Life of Lord Westbury* (1888), bk.2, ch.12

EDWARD NOYES WESTCOTT 1846–1898

4 They say a reasonable amount o' fleas is good fer a dog—keeps him from broodin' over bein' a dog, mebbe.
David Harum, ch.32

JOHN FANE, LORD WESTMORLAND 1759–1841

5 *Merit,* indeed!...We are come to a pretty pass if they talk of *merit* for a bishopric.
Noted in Lady Salisbury's diary, 9 Dec. 1835. C. Oman, *The Gascoyne Heiress* (1968), V

SIR CHARLES WETHERELL 1770–1846

6 Then there is my noble and biographical friend who has added a new terror to death.
Of Lord Campbell. Lord St. Leonards, *Misrepresentations in Campbell's Lives of Lyndhurst and Brougham* (1869), p.3. See 321:17

ROBERT WEVER fl. 1550

7 In a harbour grene aslepe whereas I lay,
The byrdes sang swete in the middes of the day,
I dreamèd fast of mirth and play:
    In youth is pleasure, in youth is pleasure.
Lusty Juventus

EDITH WHARTON 1862–1937

8 Mrs Ballinger is one of the ladies who pursue Culture in bands, as though it were dangerous to meet it alone.
Xingu (1916), ch.1

9 Another unsettling element in modern art is that common symptom of immaturity, the dread of doing what has been done before.
The Writing of Fiction, ch.1, pt.iii

THOMAS, 1st MARQUIS OF WHARTON 1648–1715

10 Ho, Brother *Teague,* dost hear de Decree?
    Lilli Burlero Bullena-la.
Dat we shall have a new Debity,
    Lilli Burlero Bullena-la.
A New Song. Written 1687; published on a single sheet 1688; first collected, in the above form, as 'Song' in *Poems on Affairs of State* (1704), vol.III, p.231

RICHARD WHATELY, ARCHBISHOP OF DUBLIN 1787–1863

11 Preach not because you have to say something, but because you have something to say.
Apophthegms

12 Happiness is no laughing matter.
p.218

13 It is a folly to expect men to do all that they may reasonably be expected to do.
p.219

14 Honesty is the best policy; but he who is governed by that maxim is not an honest man.

15 'Never forget, gentlemen,' he said, to his astonished hearers, as he held up a copy of the 'Authorized Version' of the Bible, 'never forget that this is *not* the Bible,' then, after a moment's pause, he continued, 'This, gentlemen, is only a *translation* of the Bible.'
To a meeting of his diocesan clergy. H. Solly, *These Eighty Years* (1893), vol.II. ch.ii, p.81

WILLIAM WHEWELL 1794–1866

16 Hence no force however great can stretch a cord however fine into an horizontal line which is accurately straight: there will always be a bending downwards.
Elementary Treatise on Mechanics, (1819), ch.IV, prob.ii. Often cited as an example of accidental metre and rhyme, and changed in later editions.

JAMES McNEILL WHISTLER 1834–1903

17 I am not arguing with you—I am telling you.
The Gentle Art of Making Enemies (1890)

18 Art is upon the Town!
'Ten O'Clock' (1885)

19 Listen! There never was an artistic period. There never was an Art-loving nation.

20 Nature is usually wrong.

21 'I only know of two painters in the world,' said a newly introduced feminine enthusiast to Whistler, 'yourself and Velasquez.' 'Why,' answered Whistler in dulcet tones, 'why drag in Velasquez?'
D.C. Seitz, *Whistler Stories* (1913), p.27

22 [In answer to a lady who said that a landscape reminded her of his work]
Yes madam, Nature is creeping up.
p.9

23 [In answer to the question 'For two days' labour, you ask two hundred guineas?']
No, I ask it for the knowledge of a lifetime.
p.40

24 You shouldn't say it is not good. You should say you do not like it; and then, you know, you're perfectly safe.
p.35

25 [Answering Oscar Wilde's 'I wish I had said that']
You will, Oscar, you will.
L.C. Ingleby, *Oscar Wilde,* p.67

WILLIAM WHITING 1825–1878

26 O hear us when we cry to Thee

For those in peril on the sea.
Eternal Father Strong to Save

WALT WHITMAN 1819–1892

1 Silent and amazed even when a little boy,
  I remember I heard the preacher every Sunday put God
    in his statements,
  As contending against some being or influence.
  A Child's Amaze

2 Full of life now, compact, visible,
  I, forty year old the eighty-third year of the States,
  To one a century hence or any number of centuries
    hence,
  To you yet unborn these, seeking you.
  Full of life now

3 Give me the splendid silent sun with all his beams
    full-dazzling!
  Give Me the Splendid Silent Sun

4 I dream'd in a dream I saw a city invincible to the
    attacks of the whole of the rest of the earth,
  I dream'd that was the new city of Friends.
  I Dream'd in a Dream

5 The institution of the dear love of comrades.
  I Hear it was Charged against Me

6 Me imperturbe, standing at ease in Nature.
  Me Imperturbe

7 O Captain! my Captain! our fearful trip is done,
  The ship has weather'd every rack, the prize we
    sought is won,
  The port is near, the bells I hear, the people all
    exulting.
  O Captain! My Captain! (1865-6), i

8 The ship is anchor'd safe and sound, its voyage closed
    and done.
  From fearful trip the victor ship comes in with object
    won;
  Exult O shores, and ring O bells! But I with mournful
    tread
  Walk the deck my Captain lies, Fallen cold and dead.
  iii

9 Out of the cradle endlessly rocking,
  Out of the mocking-bird's throat, the musical shuttle...
  A reminiscence sing.
  Out of the Cradle endlessly Rocking (1860)

10 Come my tan-faced children,
  Follow well in order, get your weapons ready,
  Have you your pistols? have you your sharp-edged
    axes?
      Pioneers! O pioneers!
  Pioneers! O Pioneers! (1865)

11 Beautiful that war and all its deeds of carnage must in
    time be utterly lost,
  That the hands of the sisters Death and Night
    incessantly softly wash again, and ever again, this
    soil'd world;
  For my enemy is dead, a man as divine as myself is
    dead,
  I look where he lies white-faced and still in the
    coffin—I draw near,
  Bend down and touch lightly with my lips the white
    face in the coffin.
  Reconciliation

12 What do you see Walt Whitman?

Who are they you salute, and that one after another
    salute you?
  Salut au monde

13 Camerado, this is no book,
  Who touches this touches a man,
  (Is it night? Are we here together alone?)
  It is I you hold and who holds you.
  I spring from the pages into your arms—decease calls
    me forth.
  So Long!

14 Where the populace rise at once against the
    never-ending audacity of elected persons.
  Song of the Broad Axe (1856), 5, l.12

15 Where women walk in public processions in the streets
    the same as the men,
  Where they enter the public assembly and take places
    the same as the men;
  Where the city of the faithfullest friends stands,
  Where the city of the cleanliness of the sexes stands,
  Where the city of the healthiest fathers stands,
  Where the city of the best-bodied mothers stands,
  There the great city stands.
  l.20

16 I celebrate myself, and sing myself.
  Song of Myself (1855), 1

17 Urge and urge and urge,
  Always the procreant urge of the world.
  3

18 A child said *What is the grass?* fetching it to one with
    full hands
  How could I answer the child? I do not know what it is
    any more than he.

  I guess it must be the flag of my disposition, out of the
    hopeful green stuff woven.

  Or I guess it is the handkerchief of the Lord,
  A scented gift and remembrancer designedly dropt,
  Bearing the owner's name someway in the corners,
    that we may see and remark, and say *Whose?*...
  And now it seems to me the beautiful uncut hair of
    graves.
  6

19 Has any one supposed it lucky to be born?
  I hasten to inform him or her, it is just as lucky to die
    and I know it.
  7

20 I also say it is good to fall, battles are lost in the same
    spirit in which they are won.
  18

21 I believe a leaf of grass is no less than the
    journey-work of the stars,
  And the pismire is equally perfect, and a grain of
    sand, and the egg of the wren,
  And the tree toad is a chef-d'oeuvre for the highest,
  And the running blackberry would adorn the parlors of
    heaven.
  31

22 I think I could turn and live with animals, they are so
    placid and self-contain'd,
  I stand and look at them long and long.
  They do not sweat and whine about their condition,
  They do not lie awake in the dark and weep for their
    sins,
  They do not make me sick discussing their duty to

God,
Not one is dissatisfied, not one is demented with the
mania of owning things,
Not one kneels to another, nor to his kind that lived
thousands of years ago,
Not one is respectable or unhappy over the whole
earth.
32

1 Behold, I do not give lectures or a little charity,
When I give I give myself.
39

2 My rendezvous is appointed, it is certain,
The Lord will be there and wait till I come on perfect
terms,
The great Camerado, the lover true for whom I pine
will be there.
44

3 I have said that the soul is not more than the body,
And I have said that the body is not more than the
soul,
And nothing, not God, is greater to one than one's self
is.
47

4 In the faces of men and women I see God, and in my
own face in the glass,
I find letters from God dropt in the street, and every
one is sign'd by God's name,
And I leave them where they are, for I know that
wheresoe'er I go,
Others will punctually come for ever and ever.

5 Do I contradict myself?
Very well then I contradict myself,
(I am large, I contain multitudes.)
50

6 I sound my barbaric yawp over the roofs of the world.
51

7 Afoot and light-hearted I take to the open road,
Healthy, free, the world before me,
The long brown path before me leading wherever I
choose.
Song of the Open Road, I, l.1

8 The earth, that is sufficient,
I do not want the constellations any nearer,
I know they are very well where they are,
I know they suffice for those who belong to them.
l.8

9 I will put in my poems that with you is heroism upon
land and sea,
And I will report all heroism from an American point
of view.
Starting from Paumanok (1860), 6

10 This dust was once the man,
Gentle, plain, just and resolute, under whose cautious
hand,
Against the foulest crime in history known in any land
or age,
Was saved the Union of these States.
This Dust was Once a Man

11 The earth does not argue,
Is not pathetic, has no arrangements,
Does not scream, haste, persuade, threaten, promise,
Makes no discriminations, has no conceivable failures,

Closes nothing, refuses nothing, shuts none out.
To the sayers of words, 2

12 When lilacs last in the dooryard bloom'd,
And the great star early droop'd in the western sky in
the night,
I mourn'd, and yet shall mourn with ever-returning
spring.
When Lilacs Last in the Dooryard Bloom'd (1865-6), 1

13 Come lovely and soothing death,
Undulate round the world, serenely arriving, arriving,
In the day, in the night, to all, to each,
Sooner or later, delicate death.
Prais'd be the fathomless universe,
For life and joy, and for objects and knowledge
curious,
And for love, sweet love—but praise! praise! praise!
For the sure-enwinding arms of cool-enfolding death.
14

14 These United States.
A Backward Glance O'er Travell'd Roads (1888), 'These
States' is *passim* in Whitman's verse

JOHN GREENLEAF WHITTIER 1807–1892

15 Up from the meadows rich with corn,
Clear in the cool September morn,

The clustered spires of Frederick stand
Green-walled by the hills of Maryland.
Barbara Frietchie, l.1

16 Up the street came the rebel tread,
Stonewall Jackson riding ahead.
l.23

17 'Shoot, if you must, this old gray head,
But spare your country's flag,' she said.

A shade of sadness, a blush of shame,
Over the face of the leader came.
l.35

18 'Who touches a hair of yon gray head
Dies like a dog! March on!' he said.
l.41

19 For all sad words of tongue or pen,
The saddest are these: 'It might have been!'
Maud Muller, l.105

20 The Indian Summer of the heart!
Memories, ix

21 O brother man! fold to thy heart thy brother.
Worship, l.49

ROBERT WHITTINGTON fl.1520

22 As time requireth, a man of marvellous mirth and
pastimes, and sometime of as sad gravity, as who say:
a man for all seasons.
[Of Sir Thomas More.] **Vulgaria** (1521). pt.II, **De constructione
nominum.** Erasmus famously applied the idea to More, writing in
his prefatory letter to *In Praise of Folly* (1509), in Latin, that he
played *'omnium horarum hominem.'*

BENJAMIN WHORF 1897–1941

23 We dissect nature along lines laid down by our native
language...Language is not simply a reporting device
for experience but a defining framework for it.
Thinking in Primitive Communities, in Hoyer (ed.), *New
Directions in the Study of Language,* 1964

CORNELIUS WHURR c.1845

1 What lasting joys the man attend
Who has a polished female friend.
The Accomplished Female Friend

GEORGE JOHN WHYTE-MELVILLE 1821–1878

2 Then drink, puppy, drink, and let ev'ry puppy drink,
That is old enough to lap and to swallow;
For he'll grow into a hound, so we'll pass the bottle
    round,
And merrily we'll whoop and we'll holloa.
Drink, Puppy, Drink, chorus

BISHOP SAMUEL WILBERFORCE 1805–1873

3 If I were a cassowary
On the plains of Timbuctoo,
I would eat a missionary,
Cassock, band, and hymn-book too.
Impromptu verse, ascribed also to W.M. Thackeray

RICHARD WILBUR 1921–

4 We milk the cow of the world, and as we do
We whisper in her ear, 'You are not true.'
Epistemology, ii

ELLA WHEELER WILCOX 1855–1919

5 Laugh and the world laughs with you;
Weep, and you weep alone;
For the sad old earth must borrow its mirth,
    But has trouble enough of its own.
Solitude

6 So many gods, so many creeds,
    So many paths that wind and wind,
While just the art of being kind
Is all the sad world needs.
The World's Need

OSCAR WILDE 1854–1900

7 He did not wear his scarlet coat,
    For blood and wine are red,
And blood and wine were on his hands
When they found him with the dead.
The Ballad of Reading Gaol (1898), pt.I.i

8 I never saw a man who looked
    With such a wistful eye
Upon that little tent of blue
    Which prisoners call the sky.
iii

9 When a voice behind me whispered low,
    'That fellow's got to swing.'
iv

10 Yet each man kills the thing he loves,
    By each let this be heard,
Some do it with a bitter look,
    Some with a flattering word.
The coward does it with a kiss,
    The brave man with a sword!
vii

11 Like two doomed ships that pass in storm
    We had crossed each other's way:
But we made no sign, we said no word,

We had no word to say.
II.xii

12 The Governor was strong upon
    The Regulations Act:
The Doctor said that Death was but
    A scientific fact:
And twice a day the Chaplain called,
    And left a little tract.
III.iii

13 Something was dead in each of us,
    And what was dead was Hope.
xxxi

14 And the wild regrets, and the bloody sweats,
    None knew so well as I:
For he who lives more lives than one
    More deaths than one must die.
xxxvii

15 I know not whether Laws be right,
    Or whether Laws be wrong;
All that we know who lie in gaol
    Is that the wall is strong;
And that each day is like a year,
    A year whose days are long.
V.i

16 How else but through a broken heart
    May Lord Christ enter in?
xiv

17   And yet, and yet,
These Christs that die upon the barricades,
God knows it I am with them, in some things.
Sonnet to Liberty: Not that I Love Thy Children

18 All her bright golden hair
    Tarnished with rust,
She that was young and fair
    Fallen to dust.
Requiescat

19 O Singer of Persephone!
In the dim meadows desolate
Dost thou remember Sicily?
Theocritus

20 A little sincerity is a dangerous thing, and a great deal
of it is absolutely fatal.
The Critic as Artist, Part 2

21 Ah! don't say that you agree with me. When people
agree with me I always feel that I must be wrong.

22 As long as war is regarded as wicked, it will always
have its fascination. When it is looked upon as vulgar,
it will cease to be popular.

23 There is no sin except stupidity.

24 Art never expresses anything but itself.
The Decay of Lying (1891), p.43

25 Really, if the lower orders don't set us a good
example, what on earth is the use of them?
The Importance of Being Earnest (1895), Act I

26 It is very vulgar to talk like a dentist when one isn't a
dentist. It produces a false impression.

27 The truth is rarely pure, and never simple.

28 In married life three is company and two none.

29 I have invented an invaluable permanent invalid called
Bunbury, in order that I may be able to go down into
the country whenever I choose.

1 To lose one parent, Mr Worthing, may be regarded as a misfortune; to lose both looks like carelessness.

2 All women become like their mothers. That is their tragedy. No man does. That's his.

3 The good ended happily, and the bad unhappily. That is what Fiction means. [Miss Prism on her novel.]
Act II

4 The chapter on the Fall of the Rupee you may omit. It is somewhat too sensational.

5 I hope you have not been leading a double life, pretending to be wicked and being really good all the time. That would be hypocrisy.

6 Charity, dear Miss Prism, charity! None of us are perfect. I myself am peculiarly susceptible to draughts.

7 On an occasion of this kind it becomes more than a moral duty to speak one's mind. It becomes a pleasure.

8 I couldn't help it. I can resist everything except temptation.
Lady Windermere's Fan (1891), Act I

9 Many a woman has a past, but I am told that she has a least a dozen, and that they all fit.

10 Do you know, Mr Hopper, dear Agatha and I are so much interested in Australia. It must be so pretty with all the dear little kangaroos flying about. [Duchess of Berwick.]
Act II

11 We are all in the gutter, but some of us are looking at the stars.
Act III

12 There is nothing in the whole world so unbecoming to a woman as a Nonconformist conscience.

13 A man who knows the price of everything and the value of nothing.
Definition of a cynic

14 *Dumby:* Experience is the name every one gives to their mistakes.
Cecil Graham: One shouldn't commit any.
Dumby: Life would be very dull without them.

15 There is no such thing as a moral or an immoral book. Books are well written, or badly written.
The Picture of Dorian Gray (1891), preface

16 The nineteenth century dislike of Realism is the rage of Caliban seeing his own face in the glass.

17 The moral life of man forms part of the subject matter of the artist, but the morality of art consists in the perfect use of an imperfect medium.

18 There is only one thing in the world worse than being talked about, and that is not being talked about.
ch.1

19 A man cannot be too careful in the choice of his enemies.

20 A cigarette is the perfect type of a perfect pleasure. It is exquisite, and it leaves one unsatisfied. What more can one want?
ch.6

21 It is better to be beautiful than to be good. But...it is better to be good than to be ugly.
ch.17

22 Anybody can be good in the country.
ch.19

23 As for the virtuous poor, one can pity them, of course, but one cannot possibly admire them.
The Soul of Man under Socialism

24 Democracy means simply the bludgeoning of the people by the people for the people.

25 *Mrs Allonby:* They say, Lady Hunstanton, that when good Americans die they go to Paris.
Lady Hunstanton: Indeed? And when bad Americans die, where do they go to?
Lord Illingworth: Oh, they go to America.
A Woman of No Importance (1893), Act I. See 11:13

26 The youth of America is their oldest tradition. It has been going on now for three hundred years.

27 The English country gentleman galloping after a fox—the unspeakable in full pursuit of the uneatable.

28 One should never trust a woman who tells one her real age. A woman who would tell one that, would tell one anything.

29 *Lord Illingworth:* The Book of Life begins with a man and a woman in a garden.
Mrs Allonby: It ends with Revelations.

30 Children begin by loving their parents; after a time they judge them; rarely, if ever, do they forgive them.

31 To be in it [society] is merely a bore. But to be out of it is simply a tragedy.
Act III

32 You should study the Peerage, Gerald...It is the best thing in fiction the English have ever done.

33 No publisher should ever express an opinion of the value of what he publishes. That is a matter entirely for the literary critic to decide...A publisher is simply a useful middle-man. It is not for him to anticipate the verdict of criticism.
Letter in *St. James's Gazette*, 28 June 1890

34 A thing is not necessarily true because a man dies for it.
Sebastian Melmoth (1904), p.12. *Oscariana* (1910), p.8

35 *Voulez-vous savoir le grand drame de ma vie? C'est que j'ai mis mon génie dans ma vie; je n'ai mis que mon talent dans mes ouvres.*
Do you want to know the great drama of my life? It's that I have put my genius into my life; all I've put into my works is my talent.
Spoken to André Gide. Gide, *Oscar Wilde: In Memoriam*

36 [At the New York Custom House]
I have nothing to declare except my genius.
F. Harris, *Oscar Wilde* (1918), p.75

37 'Will you very kindly tell me, Mr Wilde, in your own words, your viewpoint of George Meredith?'
'George Meredith is a prose Browning, and so is Browning.'
'Thank you. His style?'
'Chaos, illumined by flashes of lightning.'
Ada Leverson, *Letters to the Sphinx* (1930), 'Reminiscences', 1

38 There seems to be some curious connection between piety and poor rhymes.
E.V. Lucas (ed.), *A Critic in Pall Mall* (1919), 'Sententiae'

39 Work is the curse of the drinking classes.
H. Pearson, *Life of Oscar Wilde* (1946), ch.12

1 He has fought a good fight and has had to face every difficulty except popularity.
Unpublished character sketch of W.E. Henley written for Rothenstein's *English Portraits*. See W. Rothenstein, *Men and Memories*, vol. I, ch.25

2 He [Bernard Shaw] hasn't an enemy in the world, and none of his friends like him.
Shaw, *Sixteen Self Sketches*, ch.17

3 [A huge fee for an operation was mentioned] 'Ah, well, then, I suppose that I shall have to die beyond my means.'
R.H. Sherard, *Life of Oscar Wilde* (1906), p.421

KAISER WILHELM II 1859–1941

4 It is my Royal and Imperial Command that you concentrate your energies, for the immediate present, upon one single purpose, and that is that you address all your skill and all the valour of my soldiers to exterminate first the treacherous English, and to walk over General French's contemptible little Army.
Of the British Expeditionary Force. Order dated Headquarters, Aix-la-Chapelle, 19 Aug. 1914, as reported in *The Times*, 1 Oct. 1914

JOHN WILKES 1727–1797

5 The chapter of accidents is the longest chapter in the book.
Attr. by Southey in *The Doctor* (1837), vol.iv, p.166

6 'Wilkes,' said Lord Sandwich, 'you will die either on the gallows, or of the pox.'
'That,' replied Wilkes blandly, 'must depend on whether I embrace your lordship's principles or your mistress.'
Charles Chenevix-Trench, *Portrait of a Patriot* (1962)., ch 3. But see H. Brougham, *Statesmen of George III*, third series (1843), p. 189. Also attr. Samuel Foote.

EMMA HART WILLARD 1787–1870

7 Rocked in the cradle of the deep.
Song

KING WILLIAM III 1650–1702

8 'Do you not see your country is lost?' asked the Duke of Buckingham. 'There is one way never to see it lost' replied William, 'and that is to die in the last ditch.'
Burnet, *History of his own Times* (1715), i.457

9 Every bullet has its billet.
John Wesley, *Journal*, 6 June 1765

WILLIAM CARLOS WILLIAMS 1883–1963

10 so much depends
upon

a red wheel
barrow

glazed with rain
water

beside the white
chickens.
The Red Wheelbarrow

11 Is it any better in Heaven, my friend Ford,
Than you found it in Provence?
To Ford Madox Ford in Heaven

12 I will teach you my townspeople how to perform a funeral
for you have it over a troop of artists—
unless one should scour the world—
you have the ground sense necessary.
Tract

NATHANIEL PARKER WILLIS 1806–1867

13 At present there is no distinction among the upper ten thousand of the city.
Necessity for a Promenade Drive

WENDELL WILLKIE 1892–1944

14 The Constitution does not provide for first and second class citizens.
New York Herald Tribune, 13 June 1944

CHARLES ERWIN WILSON 1890–1961

15 For many years I thought what was good for our country was good for General Motors, and vice versa.
Testimony before the Senate Armed Services Committee, Jan. 1953

SIR HAROLD WILSON 1916–

16 That doesn't mean, of course, that the pound here in Britain—in your pocket or purse or in your bank—has been devalued.
Ministerial Broadcast, 19 Nov. 1967

17 The Britain that is going to be forged in the white heat of this revolution.
Speech at the Labour Party conference, Scarborough, 1 Oct. 1963. Usually quoted as 'the white heat of the technological revolution.'

18 A week is a long time in politics.
Phrase used a number of times in 1965-6

HARRIETTE WILSON 1789–1846

19 I shall not say why and how I became, at the age of fifteen, the mistress of the Earl of Craven.
Memoirs, First sentence

JOHN WILSON
see CHRISTOPHER NORTH

PRESIDENT WOODROW WILSON 1856–1924

20 There is such a thing as a man being too proud to fight.
Address at Philadelphia, 10 May 1915

21 We have stood apart, studiously neutral.
Message to Congress, 7 Dec. 1915

22 Armed neutrality.
26 Feb. 1917

23 A little group of wilful men reflecting no opinion but their own have rendered the great Government of the United States helpless and contemptible.
Statement made on 4 Mar. 1917 after a successful filibuster against his bill to arm American merchant ships against German submarine attacks

24 The world must be made safe for democracy.
Address to Congress, 2 Apr. 1917

1 Open covenants of peace openly arrived at.
Address to Congress, 8 Jan. 1918. First of *Fourteen Points.*

2 It is indispensable that the governments associated against Germany should know beyond a peradventure with whom they are dealing.
Note to Germany, 14 Oct. 1918

3 Sometimes people call me an idealist. Well, that is the way I know I am an American. America is the only idealistic nation in the world.
Address at Sioux Falls, 8 Sept. 1919

ANNE FINCH, LADY WINCHILSEA 1661–1720

4   For see! where on the Bier before ye lies
The pale, the fall'n, th' untimely Sacrifice
To your mistaken Shrine, to your false Idol Honour.
All is Vanity, iii

5 Nor will in fading silks compose
Faintly the inimitable rose.
The Spleen

6 Now the Jonquille o'ercomes the feeble brain;
We faint beneath the aromatic pain.

WILLIAM WINDHAM 1750–1810

7 Those entrusted with arms…should be persons of some substance and stake in the country.
House of Commons, 22 July 1807

CATHERINE WINKWORTH 1827–1878

8 *Peccavi*—I have Sindh.
Of Sir Charles Napier's conquest of Sind (1843). Pun sent to *Punch,* 13 May 1844, and printed as 'the most laconic despatch ever issued', supposedly sent by Napier to Lord Ellenborough, *Punch,* vi, p.209, 18 May 1844. See N.M. Billimoria, *Proceedings of the Sind Historical Society,* II (1938) and N. & Q., cxcix (1954), p.219.

ROBERT CHARLES WINTHROP 1809–1894

9 A Star for every State, and a State for every Star.
Speech on Boston Common, 27 Aug. 1862

CARDINAL WISEMAN 1802–1865

10 Dr Wiseman was particularly pleased by the conversion of a Mr Morris, who, as he said, was 'the author of the essay…on the best method of prooving Christianity to the Hindoos.'
Lytton Strachey, *Eminent Victorians,* I.iii

OWEN WISTER 1860–1938

11 When you call me that, *smile.*
The Virginian (1902), ch.2

GEORGE WITHER 1588–1667

12 Shall I, wasting in despair,
   Die because a woman's fair?
Or make pale my cheeks with care,
   'Cause another's rosy are?
Be she fairer than the day,
Or the flow'ry meads in May;
   If she think not well of me,
   What care I how fair she be?
Sonnet

13 I loved a lass, a fair one,
   As fair as e'er was seen;
She was indeed a rare one,
   Another Sheba queen.
I Loved a Lass, a Fair One

LUDWIG WITTGENSTEIN 1889–1951

14 *Die Welt ist alles, was der Fall ist.*
The world is everything that is the case.
Tractatus Logico-Philosophicus (1922), 1

15 *Die Logik muss für sich selber sorgen.*
Logic must take care of itself.
5.473

16 *Die Welt des Glücklichen ist eine andere als die des Unglücklichen.*
The world of the happy is quite another than the world of the unhappy.
6.43

17 *Wovon man nicht sprechen kann, darüber muss man schweigen.*
Whereof one cannot speak, thereon one must remain silent.
7

P.G. WODEHOUSE 1881–1975

18 There was another ring at the front door. Jeeves shimmered out and came back with a telegram.
Carry on Jeeves (1925). **Jeeves Takes Charge**

19 He spoke with a certain what-is-it in his voice, and I could see that, if not actually disgruntled, he was far from being gruntled.
The Code of the Woosters (1938)

20 Slice him where you like, a hellhound is always a hellhound.

21 To my daughter Leonora without whose never-failing sympathy and encouragement this book would have been finished in half the time.
The Heart of a Goof (1926), dedication

22 Her hair was a deep chestnut, her eyes blue, her nose small and laid back with about as much loft as a light iron.
Chester Forgets Himself

23 The lunches of fifty-seven years had caused his chest to slip down to the mezzanine floor.

24 While they were content to peck cautiously at the ball, he never spared himself in his efforts to do it a violent injury.

25 She fitted into my biggest arm-chair as if it had been built round her by someone who knew they were wearing arm-chairs tight about the hips that season.
My Man Jeeves (1919). **Jeeves and the Unbidden Guest**

26 What with excellent browsing and sluicing and cheery conversation and what-not the afternoon passed quite happily.

27 Ice formed on the butler's upper slopes.
Pigs Have Wings (1952), ch.5. pt.i

28 The Right Hon was a tubby little chap who looked as if he had been poured into his clothes and had forgotten to say 'When!'
Very Good Jeeves (1930). **Jeeves and the Impending Doom**

1 ...the unpleasant, acrid smell of burned poetry...
Young Men in Spats (1936). **The Fiery Wooing of Mordred**

CHARLES WOLFE 1791–1823

2 Not a drum was heard, not a funeral note,
As his corse to the rampart we hurried.
The Burial of Sir John Moore at Corunna, i

3 We buried him darkly at dead of night,
The sods with our bayonets turning.
ii

4 But he lay like a warrior taking his rest,
With his martial cloak around him.
iii

5 We carved not a line, and we raised not a stone—
But we left him alone with his glory.
viii

HUMBERT WOLFE 1886–1940

6 You cannot hope
to bribe or twist,
thank God! the
British journalist.

But, seeing what
the man will do
unbribed, there's
no occasion to.
The Uncelestial City, Bk.I. ii.2. **Over the Fire**

JAMES WOLFE 1727–1759

7 The General...repeated nearly the whole of Gray's
Elegy...adding, as he concluded, that he would prefer
being the author of that poem to the glory of beating
the French to-morrow.
J. Playfair, *Biogr. Acc. of J. Robinson* in *Transactions R. Soc.
Edinb.* (1814), vii. 499

8 Now God be praised, I will die in peace.
Dying words. J. Knox, *Historical Journal of Campaigns,
1757-60* (1769), ed. 1914, vol.ii, p.114

MARY WOLLSTONECRAFT 1759–1797

9 The *divine right* of husbands, like the divine right of
kings, may, it is hoped, in this enlightened age, be
contested without danger.
A Vindication of the Rights of Woman (1792), ch.3

10 A king is always a king—and a woman always a
woman: his authority and her sex ever stand between
them and rational converse.
ch.4

11 I do not wish them [women] to have power over men;
but over themselves.

12 When a man seduces a woman, it should, I think, be
termed a *left-handed* marriage.

CARDINAL WOLSEY 1475?–1530

13 Father Abbot, I am come to lay my bones amongst
you.
Cavendish, *Negotiations of Thomas Woolsey* (1641), p.108

14 Had I but served God as diligently as I have served the
King, he would not have given me over in my gray
hairs.
p.113

MRS. HENRY WOOD 1814–1887

15 Dead! and...never called me mother.
East Lynne (dramatized version by T.A. Palmer, 1874). These
words do not occur in the novel

LIEUT.-COMMANDER THOMAS WOODROOFE 1899–1978

16 The Fleet is all lit up.
First live outside broadcast, Coronation Spithead review, May
1937. See A. Briggs, *A History of Broadcasting in the United
Kingdom,* vol.II (1965), pt.ii, 2

VIRGINIA WOOLF 1882–1941

17 It is vain and foolish to talk of knowing Greek.
The Common Reader (1925), **On Not Knowing Greek**

18 She bore about with her, she could not help knowing
it, the torch of her beauty; she carried it erect into any
room that she entered; and after all, veil it as she
might, and shrink from the monotony of bearing that it
imposed on her, her beauty was apparent. She had
been admired. She had been loved.
To the Lighthouse (1927), I.8

19 So that is marriage, Lily thought, a man and a woman
looking at a girl throwing a ball.
13

20 I have lost friends, some by death...others through
sheer inability to cross the street.
The Waves (1931), p.202

DOROTHY WORDSWORTH 1771–1855

21 When we were in the woods beyond Gowbarrow park
we saw a few daffodils close to the waterside...But as
we went along there were more and yet more and at
last under the boughs of the trees, we saw that there
was a long belt of them along the shore, about the
breadth of a country turnpike road. I never saw
daffodils so beautiful they grew among the mossy
stones about and about them, some rested their heads
upon these stones as on pillow for weariness and the
rest tossed and reeled and danced and seemed as if they
verily laughed with the wind that blew upon them over
the lake.
The Grasmere Journals, 15 Apr. 1802

ELIZABETH WORDSWORTH 1840–1932

22 If all the good people were clever,
And all clever people were good,
The world would be nicer than ever
We thought that it possibly could.

But somehow, 'tis seldom or never
The two hit it off as they should;
The good are so harsh to the clever,
The clever so rude to the good!
St. Christopher and Other Poems: **Good and Clever**

WILLIAM WORDSWORTH 1770–1850

23 My apprehensions come in crowds;
I dread the rustling of the grass;
The very shadows of the clouds

Have power to shake me as they pass.
The Affliction of Margaret — (1807)

1 And three times to the child I said,
'Why, Edward, tell me why?'
Anecdote for Fathers (1798)

2 Action is transitory,—a step, a blow,
The motion of a muscle, this way or that—
'Tis done, and in the after-vacancy
We wonder at ourselves like men betrayed:
Suffering is permanent, obscure and dark,
And shares the nature of infinity.
The Borderers (1842), III.1539

3 Who is the happy Warrior? Who is he
That every man in arms should wish to be?
It is the generous spirit, who, when brought
Among the tasks of real life, hath wrought
Upon the plan that pleased his childish thought:
Whose high endeavours are an inward light
That makes the path before him always bright:
Who, with a natural instinct to discern
What knowledge can perform, is diligent to learn.
Character of the Happy Warrior (1807)

4 Ah! then, if mine had been the Painter's hand,
To express what then I saw; and add the gleam,
The light that never was, on sea or land,
The consecration, and the Poet's dream.
Elegiac Stanzas (on a picture of Peele Castle in a storm, 1807)

5 Not in the lucid intervals of life
That come but as a curse to party strife...
Is Nature felt, or can be.
Evening Voluntaries (1835), iv

6 By grace divine,
Not otherwise, O Nature, we are thine.

7 On Man, on Nature, and on Human Life,
Musing in solitude.
The Excursion (1814), preface, l.1

8 The Mind of Man—
My haunt, and the main region of my song.
l.40

9 Oh! many are the Poets that are sown
By Nature; men endowed with highest gifts,
The vision and the faculty divine;
Yet wanting the accomplishment of verse.
bk.i, l.77

10 What soul was his, when from the naked top
Of some bold headland, he beheld the sun
Rise up, and bathe the world in light!
l.198

11 The good die first,
And they whose hearts are dry as summer dust
Burn to the socket.
l.500

12 This dull product of a scoffer's pen.
bk.ii, l.484. Of *Candide*

13 The intellectual power, through words and things,
Went sounding on, a dim and perilous way!
bk.iii, l.700

14 Society became my glittering bride,
And airy hopes my children.
l.735

15 'Tis a thing impossible, to frame
Conceptions equal to the soul's desires;
And the most difficult of tasks to *keep*

Heights which the soul is competent to gain.
bk.iv, l.136

16 I have seen
A curious child, who dwelt upon a tract
Of inland ground applying to his ear
The convolutions of a smooth-lipped shell;
To which, in silence hushed, his very soul
Listened intensely; and his countenance soon
Brightened with joy; for from within were heard
Murmurings, whereby the monitor expressed
Mysterious union with its native sea.
l.1132

17 'To every Form of being is assigned',
Thus calmly spoke the venerable Sage,
'An *active* Principle.'
bk.ix, l.1

18 The rapt one, of the godlike forehead,
The heaven-eyed creature sleeps in earth:
And Lamb, the frolic and the gentle,
Has vanished from his lonely hearth.
Extempore Effusion upon the Death of James Hogg (1835)

19 How fast has brother followed brother,
From sunshine to the sunless land!

20 The wiser mind
Mourns less for what age takes away
Than what it leaves behind.
The Fountain (1800)

21 Bliss was it in that dawn to be alive,
But to be young was very heaven!
French Revolution, as it Appeared to Enthusiasts (1809), and
The Prelude, bk.xi, l.108

22 The moving accident is not my trade;
To freeze the blood I have no ready arts:
'Tis my delight, alone in summer shade,
To pipe a simple song for thinking hearts.
Hart-leap Well (1800), pt.2, l.1

23 'Tis he whom you so long have lost,
He whom you love, your Idiot Boy.
The Idiot Boy (1798), l.370

24 As her mind grew worse and worse,
Her body—it grew better.
l.415

25 All shod with steel
We hissed along the polished ice, in games
Confederate.
Influence of Natural Objects (1809) and *The Prelude,* bk.i, l.414

26 Leaving the tumultuous throng
To cut across the reflex of a star;
Image, that flying still before me, gleamed
Upon the glassy plain.

27 Yet still the solitary cliffs
Wheeled by me—even as if the earth had rolled
With visible motion her diurnal round!
(also *The Prelude,* bk.i, l.458)

28 I travelled among unknown men
In lands beyond the sea;
Nor, England! did I know till then
What love I bore to thee.
I Travelled among Unknown Men (1807)

29 I wandered lonely as a cloud
That floats on high o'er vales and hills,
When all at once I saw a crowd,
A host, of golden daffodils;

Beside the lake, beneath the trees,
Fluttering and dancing in the breeze.
I Wandered Lonely as a Cloud (1807)

1 A poet could not but be gay,
In such a jocund company:
I gazed—and gazed—but little thought
What wealth to me the show had brought:

For oft, when on my couch I lie
In vacant or in pensive mood,
They flash upon that inward eye
Which is the bliss of solitude;
And then my heart with pleasure fills,
And dances with the daffodils.

2   The gods approve
The depth, and not the tumult, of the soul.
Laodamia (1815), 1.74

3 Of all that is most beauteous—imaged there
In happier beauty; more pellucid streams,
An ampler ether, a diviner air,
And fields invested with purpureal gleams.
1.103

4   I have owed to them,
In hours of weariness, sensations sweet,
Felt in the blood, and felt along the heart;
And passing even into my purer mind,
With tranquil restoration:—feelings too
Of unremembered pleasure: such, perhaps,
As have no slight or trivial influence
On that best portion of a good man's life,
His little, nameless, unremembered, acts
Of kindness and of love.
Lines composed a few miles above Tintern Abbey (1798), 1.26

5   That blessed mood,
In which the burthen of the mystery,
In which the heavy and the weary weight
Of all this unintelligible world,
Is lightened.
1.37

6   For nature then
(The coarser pleasures of my boyish days,
And their glad animal movements all gone by)
To me was all in all.—I cannot paint
What then I was. The sounding cataract
Haunted me like a passion: the tall rock,
The mountain, and the deep and gloomy wood,
Their colours and their forms, were then to me
An appetite; a feeling and a love,
That had no need of a remoter charm,
By thought supplied, nor any interest
Unborrowed from the eye.
1.72

7   I have learned
To look on nature, not as in the hour
Of thoughtless youth; but hearing often-times
The still, sad music of humanity,
Nor harsh nor grating, though of ample power
To chasten and subdue. And I have felt
A presence that disturbs me with the joy
Of elevated thoughts; a sense sublime
Of something far more deeply interfused,
Whose dwelling is the light of setting suns,
And the round ocean and the living air,
And the blue sky, and in the mind of man.
1.88

8 A power is passing from the earth
To breathless Nature's dark abyss;
But when the great and good depart,
What is it more than this—

That Man who is from God sent forth,
Doth yet again to God return?—
Such ebb and flow must ever be,
Then wherefore should we mourn?
Lines on the Expected Dissolution of Mr. Fox (1807)

9 And much it grieved my heart to think
What man has made of man.
Lines Written in Early Spring (1798)

10 I chanced to see at break of day
The solitary child.
Lucy Gray (1800)

11 Sweet Highland Girl, a very shower
Of beauty is thy earthly dower.
Memorials of a Tour in Scotland, 1803. vi. **To a Highland Girl**

12 What, you are stepping westward?
viii. **Stepping Westward**

13 Behold her, single in the field,
    Yon solitary Highland lass!
ix. **The Solitary Reaper**

14 Will no one tell me what she sings?—
Perhaps the plaintive numbers flow
For old, unhappy, far-off things,
And battles long ago.

15 Some natural sorrow, loss, or pain
That has been, and may be again.

16 The music in my heart I bore,
Long after it was heard no more.

17   The good old rule
Sufficeth them, the simple plan,
That they should take, who have the power,
    And they should keep who can.
xi. **Rob Roy's Grave**

18 Degenerate Douglas! Oh, the unworthy lord!
xii. **Sonnet**

19 My heart leaps up when I behold
    A rainbow in the sky:
So was it when my life began;
So is it now I am a man;
So be it when I shall grow old,
    Or let me die!
The Child is father of the Man;
And I could wish my days to be
Bound each to each by natural piety.
My Heart Leaps Up (1807)

20   Move along these shades
In gentleness of heart; with gentle hand
Touch—for there is a spirit in the woods.
Nutting (1800)

21 But Thy most dreaded instrument
In working out a pure intent,
Is man,—arrayed for mutual slaughter,
Yea, Carnage is Thy daughter.
Ode, 1815 (Imagination—ne'er before content, 1816)

22 There was a time when meadow, grove, and stream,
The earth, and every common sight,
    To me did seem
    Apparelled in celestial light,
The glory and the freshness of a dream.

It is not now as it hath been of yore;—
　Turn wheresoe'er I may,
　By night or day,
The things which I have seen I now can see no more.

　　The rainbow comes and goes,
　　And lovely is the rose,
　　The moon doth with delight
Look round her when the heavens are bare,
　　Waters on a starry night
　　Are beautiful and fair;
　　The sunshine is a glorious birth:
　　But yet I know, where'er I go,
That there hath passed away a glory from the earth.
Ode. Intimations of Immortality (1807), i

1　A timely utterance gave that thought relief,
　And I again am strong.
　iii

2　The winds come to me from the fields of sleep.

3　Shout round me, let me hear thy shouts, thou happy
　　Shepherd-boy.

4　　　　　　The sun shines warm,
　And the Babe leaps up on his Mother's arm.
　iv

5　—But there's a tree of many, one,
　A single field which I have looked upon,
　Both of them speak of something that is gone:
　　The pansy at my feet
　　Doth the same tale repeat:
　Whither is fled the visionary gleam?
　Where is it now, the glory and the dream?

　Our birth is but a sleep and a forgetting:
　　The Soul that rises with us, our life's Star,
　　Hath had elsewhere its setting,
　　And cometh from afar;
　Not in entire forgetfulness,
　And not in utter nakedness,
　But trailing clouds of glory do we come
　　From God, who is our home:
　Heaven lies about us in our infancy!
　Shades of the prison-house begin to close
　　Upon the growing boy,
　But he beholds the light, and whence it flows,
　　He sees it in his joy;
　The youth, who daily farther from the east
　　Must travel, still is Nature's priest,
　　And by the vision splendid
　　Is on his way attended;
　At length the man perceives it die away,
　And fade into the light of common day.

6　As if his whole vocation
　Were endless imitation.
　vii

7　　　　　Thou Eye among the blind,
　That, deaf and silent, read'st the eternal deep
　Haunted for ever by the eternal mind.
　viii

8　Why with such earnest pains dost thou provoke
　The years to bring the inevitable yoke,
　Thus blindly with thy blessedness at strife?
　Full soon thy Soul shall have her earthly freight,
　And custom lie upon thee with a weight,
　Heavy as frost, and deep almost as life!

9　O joy! that in our embers

　Is something that doth live,
　That nature yet remembers
　What was so fugitive!
The thought of our past years in me doth breed
Perpetual benediction.
　ix

10　Not for these I raise
　The song of thanks and praise;
　　But for those obstinate questionings
　　Of sense and outward things,
　　Fallings from us, vanishings;
　　Blank misgivings of a creature
　Moving about in worlds not realised,
　High instincts before which our mortal nature
　Did tremble like a guilty thing suprised.

11　Our noisy years seem moments in the being
　Of the eternal Silence: truths that wake,
　　To perish never.

12　Hence in a season of calm weather
　　Though inland far we be,
　Our souls have sight of that immortal sea
　　Which brought us hither,
　　Can in a moment travel thither,
　And see the children sport upon the shore,
　And hear the mighty waters rolling evermore.

13　Though nothing can bring back the hour
　Of splendour in the grass, of glory in the flower;
　We will grieve not, rather find
　Strength in what remains behind…
　In the faith that looks through death,
　In years that bring the philosophic mind.

　And O, ye fountains, meadows, hills and groves,
　Forbode not any severing of our loves!
　Yet in my heart of hearts I feel your might;
　I only have relinquished one delight
　To live beneath your more habitual sway.

14　Another race hath been, and other palms are won.
　Thanks to the human heart by which we live,
　Thanks to its tenderness, its joys and fears,
　To me the meanest flower that blows can give
　Thoughts that do often lie too deep for tears.

15　Stern daughter of the voice of God!
　O Duty! if that name thou love
　Who art a light to guide, a rod
　To check the erring and reprove.
　Ode to Duty (1807)

16　Thou dost preserve the stars from wrong;
　And the most ancient heavens, through Thee, are fresh
　　and strong.

17　　　　　Sweetest melodies
　Are those by distance made more sweet.
　Personal Talk (1807), ii. See 158:21

18　There's something in a flying horse,
　There's something in a huge balloon;
　But through the clouds I'll never float
　Until I have a little Boat,
　Shaped like the crescent moon.
　Peter Bell (1819), prologue, l.1

19　A primrose by a river's brim
　A yellow primrose was to him,
　And it was nothing more.
　pt.i, l.249

1 He gave a groan, and then another,
Of that which went before the brother,
And then he gave a third.
l.443

2 Is it a party in a parlour?
Cramm'd just as they on earth were cramm'd—
Some sipping punch, some sipping tea,
But, as you by their faces see,
All silent and all damn'd!
(pt.i, st.66 in MS of 1819, later omitted)

3 Physician art thou?—one, all eyes,
Philosopher!—a fingering slave,
One that would peep and botanize
Upon his mother's grave?
A Poet's Epitaph (1800)

4 A reasoning, self-sufficing thing,
An intellectual All-in-all!

5 In common things that round us lie
Some random truths he can impart,—
The harvest of a quiet eye,
That broods and sleeps on his own heart.

But he is weak; both Man and Boy,
Hath been an idler in the land;
Contented if he might enjoy
The things which others understand.

—Come hither in thy hour of strength;
Come, weak as is a breaking wave.

6 I recoil and droop, and seek repose
In listlessness from vain perplexity,
Unprofitably travelling toward the grave.
The Prelude (1850), bk.i, l.265

7 Made one long bathing of a summer's day.
l.290

8 Fair seed-time had my soul, and I grew up
Fostered alike by beauty and by fear.
l.301

9 When the deed was done
I heard among the solitary hills
Low breathings coming after me, and sounds
Of undistinguishable motion, steps
Almost as silent as the turf they trod.
l.321

10 Though mean
Our object and inglorious, yet the end
Was not ignoble.
l.328

11 Dust as we are, the immortal spirit grows
Like harmony in music; there is a dark
Inscrutable workmanship that reconciles
Discordant elements, makes them cling together
In one society.
l.340

12 The grim shape
Towered up between me and the stars, and still,
For so it seemed, with purpose of its own
And measured motion like a living thing,
Strode after me.
l.382

13 For many days, my brain
Worked with a dim and undetermined sense
Of unknown modes of being.
l.391

14 Huge and mighty forms that do not live
Like living men, moved slowly through the mind
By day, and were a trouble to my dreams.
l.398

15 I was taught to feel, perhaps too much,
The self-sufficing power of Solitude.
bk.ii, l.76

16 To thee
Science appears but, what in truth she is,
Not as our glory and our absolute boast,
But as a succedaneum, and a prop
To our infirmity.
l.211

17 Where the statue stood
Of Newton, with his prism and silent face,
The marble index of a mind for ever
Voyaging through strange seas of Thought, alone.
bk.iii, l.61

18 Spirits overwrought
Were making night do penance for a day
Spent in a round of strenuous idleness.
bk.iv, l.376

19 Even forms and substances are circumfused
By that transparent veil with light divine,
And, through the turnings intricate of verse,
Present themselves as objects recognised,
In flashes, and with glory not their own.
bk.v, l.601

20 We were brothers all
In honour, as in one community,
Scholars and gentlemen.
bk.ix, l.227

21 All things have second birth;
The earthquake is not satisfied at once.
bk.x, l.83

22 In the People was my trust,
And in the virtues which mine eyes had seen.
bk.xi, l.11

23 Not in Utopia—subterranean fields,—
Or some secreted island, Heaven knows where!
But in the very world, which is the world
Of all of us,—the place where, in the end
We find our happiness, or not at all!
l.140

24 There is
One great society alone on earth:
The noble Living and the noble Dead.
l.393

25 I shook the habit off
Entirely and for ever, and again
In Nature's presence stood, as now I stand,
A sensitive being, a *creative* soul.
bk.xii, l.204

26 Imagination, which, in truth,
Is but another name for absolute power
And clearest insight, amplitude of mind,
And Reason in her most exalted mood.
bk.xiv, l.190

27 There was a roaring in the wind all night;
The rain came heavily and fell in floods;
But now the sun is rising, calm and bright.
Resolution and Independence (1807), i

28 I thought of Chatterton, the marvellous boy,

The sleepless soul, that perished in his pride;
Of him who walked in glory and in joy,
Following his plough, along the mountain side:
By our own spirits are we deified:
We poets in our youth begin in gladness;
But thereof comes in the end despondency and
    madness.
    vii

1 His words came feebly, from a feeble chest,
But each in solemn order followed each,
With something of a lofty utterance drest—
Choice words, and measured phrase, above the reach
Of ordinary men; a stately speech;
Such as grave Livers do in Scotland use.
    xiv

2   The fear that kills;
And hope that is unwilling to be fed;
Cold, pain, and labour, and all fleshly ills;
And mighty Poets in their misery dead.
—Perplexed, and longing to be comforted,
My question eagerly I did renew.
'How is it that you live, and what is it you do?'
    xvii

3 At the corner of Wood Street, when daylight appears,
Hangs a Thrush that sings loud, it has sung for three
    years:
Poor Susan has passed by the spot, and has heard
In the silence of morning the song of the Bird.

'Tis a note of enchantment; what ails her? She sees
A mountain ascending, a vision of trees;
Bright volumes of vapour through Lothbury glide,
And a river flows on through the vale of Cheapside.
The Reverie of Poor Susan

4 I thought of Thee, my partner and my guide,
As being past away—Vain sympathies!
For, backward, Duddon! as I cast my eyes,
I see what was, and is, and will abide;
Still glides the Stream, and shall for ever glide;
The Form remains, the Function never dies.
The River Duddon (1820), xxxiv. **After-Thought**

5 Enough, if something from our hands have power
To live, and act, and serve the future hour;
And if, as toward the silent tomb we go,
Through love, through hope, and faith's transcendent
    dower,
We feel that we are greater than we know.

6 She dwelt among the untrodden ways
    Beside the springs of Dove,
A maid whom there were none to praise
    And very few to love:

A violet by a mossy stone
    Half hidden from the eye!
Fair as a star, when only one
    Is shining in the sky.

She lived unknown, and few could know
    When Lucy ceased to be;
But she is in her grave, and, oh,
    The difference to me!
She Dwelt Among the Untrodden Ways (1800)

7 She was a phantom of delight
When first she gleamed upon my sight.
She was a Phantom of Delight (1807)

8 I saw her upon nearer view,

A spirit, yet a woman too!
Her household motions light and free,
And steps of virgin liberty;
A countenance in which did meet
Sweet records, promises as sweet;
A creature not too bright or good
For human nature's daily food;
For transient sorrows, simple wiles,
Praise, blame, love, kisses, tears, and smiles.

And now I see with eye serene,
The very pulse of the machine;
A being breathing thoughtful breath,
A traveller betwixt life and death;
The reason firm, the temperate will,
Endurance, foresight, strength, and skill;
A perfect woman, nobly planned,
To warn, to comfort, and command;
And yet a spirit still, and bright
With something of angelic light.

9 For still, the more he works, the more
    Do his weak ankles swell.
Simon Lee (1798)

10 A slumber did my spirit seal;
    I had no human fears:
She seemed a thing that could not feel
    The touch of earthly years.

No motion has she now, no force;
    She neither hears nor sees;
Rolled round in earth's diurnal course,
    With rocks, and stones, and trees.
A Slumber did My Spirit Seal (1800)

11 Love had he found in huts where poor men lie;
His daily teachers had been woods and rills,
The silence that is in the starry sky,
The sleep that is among the lonely hills.
Song at the Feast of Brougham Castle (1807)

12 O Man, that from thy fair and shining youth
Age might but take the things Youth needed not!
The Small Celandine (There is a flower, 1807)

13 Another year!—another deadly blow!
Another mighty Empire overthrown!
And we are left, or shall be left, alone.
Sonnets. **Another year!** (1807)

14 Earth has not anything to show more fair;
Dull would he be of soul who could pass by
A sight so touching in its majesty:
This City now doth, like a garment, wear
The beauty of the morning; silent, bare,
Ships, towers, domes, theatres, and temples lie
Open unto the fields, and to the sky;
All bright and glittering in the smokeless air.
Composed upon Westminster Bridge (1807)

15 Dear God! the very houses seem asleep;
And all that mighty heart is lying still!

16 A genial hearth, a hospitable board,
And a refined rusticity.
A genial hearth (1822)

17   Not choice
But habit rules the unreflecting herd.
Grant that by this (1822)

18 It is a beauteous evening, calm and free,
The holy time is quiet as a nun,

Breathless with adoration.
It is a beauteous evening (1807)

1 Dear Child! dear Girl! that walkest with me here
If thou appear untouched by solemn thought,
Thy nature is not therefore less divine.
Thou liest in Abraham's bosom all the year;
And worshipp'st at the temple's inner shrine,
God being with thee when we know it not.

2 It is not to be thought of that the Flood
Of British freedom, which, to the open sea
Of the world's praise, from dark antiquity
Hath flowed, 'with pomp of waters, unwithstood'...
Should perish.
It is not to be thought of (1807)

3   In our halls is hung
Armoury of the invincible Knights of old:
We must be free or die, who speak the tongue
That Shakespeare spake; the faith and morals hold
Which Milton held.—In everything we are sprung
Of Earth's first blood, have titles manifold.

4 Jones! as from Calais southward you and I
Went pacing side by side, this public Way
Streamed with the pomp of a too-credulous day.
Jones! as from Calais (1807). Referring to 14 July 1790.

5 Milton! thou shouldst be living at this hour:
England hath need of thee; she is a fen
Of stagnant waters: altar, sword, and pen,
Fireside, the heroic wealth of hall and bower,
Have forfeited their ancient English dower
Of inward happiness.
Milton! thou shouldst (1807)

6   Some happy tone
Of meditation, slipping in between
The beauty coming and the beauty gone.
Most sweet it is (1835)

7 Nuns fret not at their convent's narrow room;
And hermits are contented with their cells.
Nuns fret not (1807)

8 In sundry moods, 'twas pastime to be bound
Within the Sonnet's scanty plot of ground;
Pleased if some souls (for such there needs must be)
Who have felt the weight of too much liberty,
Should find some solace there, as I have found.

9 Plain living and high thinking are no more:
The homely beauty of the good old cause
Is gone; our peace, our fearful innocence,
And pure religion breathing household laws.
O friend! I know not (1807)

10 Once did she hold the gorgeous East in fee,
And was the safeguard of the West.
Once did she hold (1807)

11 Venice, the eldest Child of Liberty.
She was a maiden City, bright and free.

12 Isis and Cam, to patient Science dear!
Open your gates (1822)

13 A Poet!—He hath put his heart to school,
Nor dares to move unpropped upon the staff
Which Art hath lodged within his hand—must laugh
By precept only, and shed tears by rule.
A Poet! He hath put his heart (1842)

14 Scorn not the Sonnet; Critic, you have frowned,
Mindless of its just honours; with this key

Shakespeare unlocked his heart.
Scorn not the Sonnet (1827)

15 Surprised by joy—impatient as the Wind
I turned to share the transport—Oh! with whom
But Thee, deep buried in the silent tomb.
Surprised by joy (1815)

16 Tax not the royal Saint with vain expense,
With ill-matched aims the Architect who planned—
Albeit labouring for a scanty band
Of white-robed Scholars only—this immense
And glorious work of fine intelligence!
Give all thou canst; high Heaven rejects the lore
Of nicely-calculated less or more.
Tax not the royal Saint (1822). Of King's College Chapel, Cambridge.

17 Though fallen thyself, never to rise again,
Live, and take comfort. Thou hast left behind
Powers that will work for thee; air, earth, and skies;
There's not a breathing of the common wind
That will forget thee; thou hast great allies;
Thy friends are exultations, agonies,
And love, and man's unconquerable mind.
Toussaint, the most unhappy man (1803)

18 Two Voices are there; one is of the sea,
One of the mountains; each a mighty Voice,
In both from age to age thou didst rejoice,
They were thy chosen music, Liberty!
Two Voices are there (1807)

19 The world is too much with us; late and soon,
Getting and spending, we lay waste our powers:
Little we see in Nature that is ours.
The world is too much with us (1807)

20   Great God! I'd rather be
A Pagan suckled in a creed outworn,
So might I, standing on this pleasant lea,
Have glimpses that would make me less forlorn;
Have sight of Proteus rising from the sea,
Or hear old Triton blow his wreathed horn.
See 515:21

21 What fond and wayward thoughts will slide
Into a Lover's head!
'O mercy!' to myself I cried,
'If Lucy should be dead!'
Strange Fits of Passion (1800)

22 Up! up! my friend, and quit your books;
Or surely you'll grow double.
The Tables Turned (1798)

23   Our meddling intellect
Misshapes the beauteous forms of things:—
We murder to dissect.

Enough of science and of art;
Close up these barren leaves.
Come forth, and bring with you a heart
That watches and receives.

24 I've measured it from side to side:
'Tis three feet long and two feet wide.
The Thorn (1798), iii [early reading]

25 O blithe new-comer! I have heard,
I hear thee and rejoice.
O Cuckoo! Shall I call thee bird,
Or but a wandering voice?
To the Cuckoo (O blithe new-comer!, 1807)

26 Oft on the dappled turf at ease

I sit, and play with similes,
Loose types of things through all degrees.
To the Same Flower [Daisy] (With little here to do, 1807)

1 Type of the wise who soar, but never roam;
True to the kindred points of heaven and home!
To a Skylark (Ethereal minstrel!, 1827)

2 There's a flower that shall be mine,
'Tis the little celandine.
To the Small Celandine (Pansies, lilies, 1807)

3 Spade! with which Wilkinson hath tilled his lands,
And shaped these pleasant walks by Emont's side,
Thou art a tool of honour in my hands;
I press thee, through the yielding soil, with pride.
To the Spade of a Friend (1807)

4 But an old age, serene and bright,
And lovely as a Lapland night,
Shall lead thee to thy grave.
To a Young Lady (1802)

5   A simple child, dear brother Jim
That lightly draws its breath,
And feels its life in every limb,
What should it know of death?
We are Seven (1798). The words 'dear brother Jim' were omitted
in the 1815 edition of his poems.

6 I take my little porringer
And eat my supper there.

7 'But they are dead; those two are dead!
Their spirits are in Heaven!'
'Twas throwing words away; for still
The little Maid would have her will,
And said, 'Nay, we are seven!'

8 The Poet writes under one restriction only, namely,
that of the necessity of giving pleasure to a human
Being possessed of that information which may be
expected from him, not as a lawyer, a physician, a
mariner, an astronomer or a natural philosopher, but as
a Man.
Lyrical Ballads, preface to 2nd edn. (1802)

9 Poetry is the breath and finer spirit of all knowledge;
it is the impassioned expression which is in the
countenance of all science.

10 Poetry is the spontaneous overflow of powerful
feelings: it takes its origin from emotion recollected in
tranquillity.

11 Never forget what I believe was observed to you by
Coleridge, that every great and original writer, in
proportion as he is great and original, must himself
create the taste by which he is to be relished.
Letter to Lady Beaumont, 21 May 1807

SIR HENRY WOTTON 1568–1639

12 How happy is he born and taught
That serveth not another's will;
Whose armour is his honest thought,
And simple truth his utmost skill!
The Character of a Happy Life, i

13 Who God doth late and early pray
More of his grace than gifts to lend;
And entertains the harmless day
With a religious book, or friend.

This man is freed from servile bands,
Of hope to rise, or fear to fall:—

Lord of himself, though not of lands,
And having nothing, yet hath all.
v

14 He first deceas'd; she for a little tri'd
To live without him: lik'd it not, and di'd.
Death of Sir Albertus Moreton's Wife

15 You meaner beauties of the night,
That poorly satisfy our eyes,
More by your number, than your light;
You common people of the skies,
What are you when the moon shall rise?
On His Mistress, the Queen of Bohemia

16 In *Architecture* as in all other *Operative* Arts, the *end*
must direct the *Operation*. The *end* is to build well.
Well building hath three Conditions. *Commodity,
Firmness,* and *Delight.*
Elements of Architecture (1624), pt.I

17 Take heed of thinking, *The farther you go from the
church of Rome, the nearer you are to God.*
Izaak Walton, *Sir Henry Wotton,* in Christopher Wordsworth,
Ecclesiastical Biography (1810), vol.V, p.44; first published in
Walton's first edition of *Reliquiae Wottonianae* (1651)

18 An ambassador is an honest man sent to lie abroad for
the good of his country.
Written in the Album of Christopher Fleckmore (1604). Izaak
Walton, *Life*

SIR THOMAS WYATT 1503?–1542

19 And wilt thou leave me thus?
Say nay, say nay, for shame.
An Appeal

20 What should I say,
Since faith is dead,
And Truth away
From you is fled?
Farewell

21 They flee from me, that sometime did me seek
With naked foot, stalking in my chamber.
I have seen them gentle, tame, and meek,
That now are wild, and do not remember
That sometime they put themselves in danger
To take bread at my hand.
Remembrance

22 When her loose gown from her shoulders did fall,
And she me caught in her arms long and small,
Therewith all sweetly did me kiss
And softly said, 'Dear heart how like you this?'

23 My lute, awake! perform the last
Labour that thou and I shall waste,
An end that I have now begun;
For when this song is sung and past,
My lute, be still, for I have done.
To his Lute

WILLIAM WYCHERLEY 1640?–1716

24 A mistress should be like a little country retreat near
the town, not to dwell in constantly, but only for a
night and away.
The Country Wife (1672-3), Act I.i

25 Go to your business, I say, pleasure, whilst I go to my
pleasure, business.
Act II

26 Nay, you had both felt his desperate deadly daunting

dagger:—there are your d's for you!
The Gentleman Dancing-Master (1671-2), Act V

1 Fy! madam, do you think me so ill bred as to love a husband?
Love in a Wood (1671), III.iv

2 You [drama critics] who scribble, yet hate all who write…
And with faint praises one another damn.
The Plain Dealer (1677), prologue

GEORGE WYNDHAM 1863–1913

3 Over the construction of Dreadnoughts…What the people said was, 'We want eight, and we won't wait.'
Wigan, 27 Mar. 1909

ANDREW OF WYNTOUN 1350?–1420?

4 Quhen Alysander oure kyng wes dede,
   That Scotland led in luve and le,
Away wes sons of ale and brede,
   Of wyne and wax, of gamyn and gle;
Oure gold wes changyd into lede,
   Cryst, borne into virgynyte,
Succour Scotland, and remede,
   That stad is in perplexyte.
The Orygynale Cronykil, vol.i, p.401, edn. 1795

XENOPHON c.428/7–c.354 B.C.

5 θάλαττα θάλαττα.
The sea! the sea!
Anabasis, IV.vii.24

AUGUSTIN, MARQUIS DE XIMÉNÈZ 1726–1817

6 *Attaquons dans ses eaux*
La perfide Albion!
Let us attack in her own waters perfidious Albion!
L'Ère des Français (Oct. 1793). *Poésies Révolutionnaires et contre-révolutionnaires* (Paris, 1821), I, p.160. See 90:14

THOMAS RUSSELL YBARRA b. 1880

7 A Christian is a man who feels
Repentance on a Sunday
For what he did on Saturday
And is going to do on Monday.
The Christian (1909)

W.F. YEAMES R.A. 1835–1918

8 And when did you last see your father?
Title of painting (1878) now in the Walker Art Gallery, Liverpool

W.B. YEATS 1865–1939

9   A line will take us hours maybe;
Yet if it does not seem a moment's thought,
Our stitching and unstitching has been naught.
Adam's Curse

10   When I was young,
I had not given a penny for a song
Did not the poet sing it with such airs
That one believed he had a sword upstairs.
All Things can Tempt me

11 O body swayed to music, O brightening glance,

How can we know the dancer from the dance?
Among School Children, VIII

12 A starlit or a moonlit dome disdains
All that man is,
All mere complexities,
The fury and the mire of human veins.
Byzantium

13 That dolphin-torn, that gong-tormented sea.

14 The intellect of man is forced to choose
Perfection of the life, or of the work.
The Choice

15   Now that my ladder's gone,
I must lie down where all the ladders start,
In the foul rag-and-bone shop of the heart.
The Circus Animals' Desertion, III

16 I made my song a coat
Covered with embroideries
Out of old mythologies
From heel to throat;
But the fools caught it,
Wore it in the world's eyes
As though they'd wrought it.
Song, let them take it,
For there's more enterprise
In walking naked.
A Coat

17 The years like great black oxen tread the world,
And God the herdsman goads them on behind,
And I am broken by their passing feet.
The Countess Cathleen, Act IV

18   The Light of Lights
Looks always on the motive, not the deed,
The Shadow of Shadows on the deed alone.

19 A woman can be proud and stiff
When on love intent;
But Love has pitched his mansion in
The place of excrement;
For nothing can be sole or whole
That has not been rent.
Crazy Jane talks to the Bishop

20 Nor dread nor hope attend
A dying animal;
A man awaits his end
Dreading and hoping all.
Death

21 He knows death to the bone—
Man has created death.

22 Down by the salley gardens my love and I did meet;
She passed the salley gardens with little snow-white feet.
She bid me take love easy, as the leaves grow on the tree;
But I, being young and foolish, with her would not agree.

In a field by the river my love and I did stand,
And on my leaning shoulder she laid her snow-white hand.
She bid me take life easy, as the grass grows on the weirs;
But I was young and foolish, and now am full of tears.
Down by the Salley Gardens

23 She was more beautiful than thy first love,

This lady by the trees.
A Dream of Death, early version

1 I have met them at close of day
Coming with vivid faces
From counter or desk among grey
Eighteenth-century houses.
I have passed with a nod of the head
Or polite meaningless words,
And thought before I had done
Of a mocking tale or a gibe
To please a companion
Around the fire at the club,
Being certain that they and I
But lived where motley is worn:
All changed, changed utterly:
A terrible beauty is born.
Easter 1916

2 Too long a sacrifice
Can make a stone of the heart.

3 I see a schoolboy when I think of him,
With face and nose pressed to a sweet-shop window,
For certainly he sank into his grave
His senses and his heart unsatisfied,
And made—being poor, ailing and ignorant,
Shut out from all the luxury of the world,
The coarse-bred son of a livery-stable keeper—
Luxuriant song.
Ego Dominus Tuus. Of Keats.

4 Those great honey-coloured
Ramparts at your ear.
For Anne Gregory

5 Only God, my dear,
Could love you for yourself alone
And not your yellow hair.

6 Never to have lived is best, ancient writers say;
Never to have drawn the breath of life, never to have
    looked into the eye of day;
The second best's a gay goodnight and quickly turn
    away.
From 'Oedipus at Colonus'

7 The ghost of Roger Casement
Is beating on the door.
The Ghost of Roger Casement

8 But weigh this song with the great and their pride;
I made it out of a mouthful of air,
Their children's children shall say they have lied.
He thinks of those who have Spoken Evil of his Beloved

9 Had I the heavens' embroidered cloths,
Enwrought with golden and silver light,
The blue and the dim and the dark cloths
Of night and light and the half-light,
I would spread the cloths under your feet:
But I, being poor, have only my dreams;
I have spread my dreams under your feet;
Tread softly because you tread on my dreams.
He wishes for the Cloths of Heaven

10 I mourn for that most lonely thing; and yet God's will
    be done:
I knew a phoenix in my youth, so let them have their
    day.
His Phoenix

11 The light of evening, Lissadell,
Great windows open to the south

Two girls in silk kimonos, both
Beautiful, one a gazelle.
In Memory of Eva Gore-Booth and Con Markiewicz

12 The innocent and the beautiful
Have no enemy but time.

13 I am accustomed to their lack of breath,
But not that my dear friend's dear son,
Our Sidney and our perfect man,
Could share in that discourtesy of death.
In Memory of Major Robert Gregory, VI

14 Out-worn heart, in a time out-worn,
Come clear of the nets of wrong and right;
Laugh, heart, again in the grey twilight,
Sigh, heart, again in the dew of the morn.
Into the Twilight

15 Nor law, nor duty bade me fight,
Nor public men, nor cheering crowds,
A lonely impulse of delight
Drove to this tumult in the clouds;
I balanced all, brought all to mind,
The years to come seemed waste of breath,
A waste of breath the years behind
In balance with this life, this death.
An Irish Airman Forsees his Death

16 None other knows what pleasures man
    At table or in bed.
What shall I do for pretty girls
    Now my old bawd is dead?
John Kinsella's Lament for Mrs. Mary Moore

17 I will arise and go now, and go to Innisfree,
And a small cabin build there, of clay and wattles
    made:
Nine bean-rows will I have there, a hive for the
    honey-bee,
And live alone in the bee-loud glade.

And I shall have some peace there, for peace comes
    dropping slow,
Dropping from the veils of the morning to where the
    cricket sings;
There midnight's all a-glimmer, and noon a purple
    glow,
And evening full of the linnet's wings.

I will arise and go now, for always night and day
I hear lake water lapping with low sounds by the
    shore;
While I stand on the roadway, or on the pavements
    gray,
I hear it in the deep heart's core.
The Lake Isle of Innisfree

18 Of a land where even the old are fair,
And even the wise are merry of tongue.
The Land of Heart's Desire

19   Land of Heart's Desire,
Where beauty has no ebb, decay no flood,
But joy is wisdom, Time an endless song.

20 What lively lad most pleasured me
Of all that with me lay?
I answer that I gave my soul
And loved in misery,
But had great pleasure with a lad
That I loved bodily.

Flinging from his arms I laughed
To think his passion such

He fancied that I gave a soul
Did but our bodies touch,
And laughed upon his breast to think
Beast gave beast as much.
A Last Confession

1 A sudden blow: the great wings beating still
Above the staggering girl, her thighs caressed
By the dark webs, her nape caught in his bill,
He holds her hapless breast upon his breast.

How can those terrified vague fingers push
The feathered glory from her loosening thighs?
Leda and the Swan

2 A shudder in the loins engenders there
The broken wall, the burning roof and tower
And Agamemnon dead.

3 Our master Caesar is in the tent,
Where the maps are spread,
His eyes fixed upon nothing,
A hand under his head.
Like a long-legged fly upon the stream
His mind moves upon silence.
Long-legged Fly

4 What were all the world's alarms
To mighty Paris when he found
Sleep upon a golden bed
That first dawn in Helen's arms?
Lullaby

5 In the Junes that were warmer than these are, the
    waves were more gay,
When I was a boy with never a crack in my heart.
The Meditation of the Old Fisherman

6 Think where man's glory most begins and ends,
And say my glory was I had such friends.
The Municipal Gallery Revisited, VII

7 Why, what could she have done, being what she is?
Was there another Troy for her to burn?
No Second Troy

8 Where, where but here have Pride and Truth,
That long to give themselves for wage,
To shake their wicked sides at youth
Restraining reckless middle age?
On hearing that the Students of our New University have joined
the Agitation against Immoral Literature

9 A pity beyond all telling
Is hid in the heart of love.
The Pity of Love

10 Rose of all Roses, Rose of all the World!
The Rose of Battle

11 That is no country for old men. The young
In one another's arms, birds in the trees
—Those dying generations—at their song,
The salmon-falls, the mackerel-crowded seas,
Fish, flesh, or fowl, commend all summer long
Whatever is begotten, born, and dies.
Sailing to Byzantium, I

12 An aged man is but a paltry thing,
A tattered coat upon a stick, unless
Soul clap its hands and sing, and louder sing
For every tatter in its mortal dress.
II

13 And therefore I have sailed the seas and come
To the holy city of Byzantium.

14 Bald heads, forgetful of their sins,

Old, learned, respectable bald heads
Edit and annotate the lines
That young men tossing on their beds,
Rhymed out in love's despair
To flatter beauty's ignorant ear.

All shuffle there; all cough in ink;
All wear the carpet with their shoes;
All think what other people think;
All know the man their neighbour knows.
Lord, what would they say
Did their Catullus walk that way?
The Scholars

15 Turning and turning in the widening gyre
The falcon cannot hear the falconer;
Things fall apart; the centre cannot hold;
Mere anarchy is loosed upon the world,
The blood-dimmed tide is loosed, and everywhere
The ceremony of innocence is drowned;
The best lack all conviction, while the worst
Are full of passionate intensity.
The Second Coming

16 And what rough beast, its hour come round at last,
Slouches towards Bethlehem to be born?

17 A woman of so shining loveliness
That men threshed corn at midnight by a tress.
The Secret Rose

18 When shall the stars be blown about the sky,
Like the sparks blown out of a smithy, and die?
Surely thine hour has come, thy great wind blows,
Far-off, most secret, and inviolate Rose?

19 Was it for this the wild geese spread
The grey wing upon every tide;
For this that all that blood was shed,
For this Edward Fitzgerald died,
And Robert Emmet and Wolfe Tone,
All that delirium of the brave?
Romantic Ireland's dead and gone,
It's with O'Leary in the grave.
September 1913

20 I thought no more was needed
Youth to prolong
Than dumb-bell and foil
To keep the body young.
O who could have foretold
That the heart grows old?
A Song

21 And pluck till time and times are done
The silver apples of the moon
The golden apples of the sun.
The Song of Wandering Aengus

22 A girl arose that had red mournful lips
And seemed the greatness of the world in tears,
Doomed like Odysseus and the labouring ships
And proud as Priam murdered with his peers;

Arose, and on the instant clamorous eaves,
A climbing moon upon an empty sky,
And all that lamentation of the leaves,
Could but compose man's image and his cry.
The Sorrow of Love

23 You think it horrible that lust and rage
Should dance attention upon my old age;
They were not such a plague when I was young;

What else have I to spur me into song?
The Spur

1 Pythagoras planned it. Why did the people stare?
His numbers, though they moved or seemed to move
In marble or in bronze, lacked character.
But boys and girls, pale from the imagined love
Of solitary beds, knew what they were,
That passion could bring character enough,
And pressed at midnight in some public place
Live lips upon a plummet-measured face.

No! Greater than Pythagoras, for the men
That with a mallet or a chisel modelled these
Calculations that look but casual flesh, put down
All Asiatic vague immensities,
And not the banks of oars that swam upon
The many-headed foam at Salamis.
Europe put off that foam when Phidias
Gave women dreams and dreams their looking-glass.
The Statues

2 When Pearse summoned Cuchulain to his side,
What stalked through the Post Office? What intellect,
What calculation, number, measurement, replied?
We Irish, born into that ancient sect
But thrown upon this filthy modern tide
And by its formless spawning fury wrecked,
Climb to our proper dark, that we may trace
The lineaments of a plummet-measured face.

3 Swift has sailed into his rest;
Savage indignation there
Cannot lacerate his breast.
Imitate him if you dare,
World-besotted traveller; he
Served human liberty.
Swift's Epitaph. See 528:12

4 But was there ever dog that praised his fleas?
*To a Poet, who would have me Praise certain Bad Poets,
Imitators of His and Mine*

5 I know what wages beauty gives,
How hard a life her servant lives,
Yet praise the winters gone:
There is not a fool can call me friend,
And I may dine at journey's end
With Landor and with Donne.
To a Young Beauty

6 Red Rose, proud Rose, sad Rose of all my days!
To the Rose upon the Rood of Time

7 Measurement began our might.
Under Ben Bulben, IV

8 Irish poets, learn your trade,
Sing whatever is well made,
Scorn the sort now growing up
All out of shape from toe to top,
Their unremembering hearts and heads
Base-born products of base beds.
Sing the peasantry, and then
Hard-riding country gentlemen,
The holiness of monks, and after
Porter-drinkers' randy laughter.
V

9 Cast your mind on other days
That we in coming days may be
Still the indomitable Irishry.

10 Under bare Ben Bulben's head

In Drumcliff churchyard Yeats is laid...
On limestone quarried near the spot
By his command these words are cut:

*Cast a cold eye
On life, on death.
Horseman, pass by!*
VI

11 While on the shop and street I gazed
My body of a sudden blazed;
And twenty minutes more or less
It seemed, so great my happiness,
That I was blessèd and could bless.
Vacillation

12 When you are old and gray and full of sleep,
And nodding by the fire, take down this book,
And slowly read, and dream of the soft look
Your eyes had once, and of their shadows deep;

How many loved your moments of glad grace,
And loved your beauty with love false or true,
But one man loved the pilgrim soul in you,
And loved the sorrows of your changing face;

And bending down beside the glowing bars,
Murmur, a little sadly, how Love fled
And paced upon the mountains overhead
And hid his face amid a crowd of stars.
When you are Old

13 My son is now between nine and ten and should begin
Greek at once...Do not teach him one word of Latin.
The Roman people were the classical decadence, their
literature form without matter. They destroyed Milton,
the French seventeenth and our eighteenth century, and
our schoolmasters even today read Greek with Latin
eyes.
Explorations, sel. Mrs. W.B. Yeats (1962), II.iv. **A Letter to
Michael's schoolmaster**

14 Greece, could we but approach it with eyes as young
as its own, might renew our youth.

EDWARD YOUNG 1683–1765

15   Be wise with speed;
A fool at forty is a fool indeed.
Love of Fame: The Universal Passion (1725-8), Sat.ii, l.281

16 For who does nothing with a better grace?
Sat.iv, l.86

17 With skill she vibrates her eternal tongue,
For ever most divinely in the wrong.
Sat.vi, l.106

18 For her own breakfast she'll project a scheme,
Nor take her tea without a stratagem.
l.187

19 One to destroy, is murder by the law;
And gibbets keep the lifted hand in awe;
To murder thousands, takes a specious name,
War's glorious art, and gives immortal fame.
Sat.vii, l.55

20 How commentators each dark passage shun,
And hold their farthing candle to the sun.
l.97

21 Tir'd Nature's sweet restorer, balmy sleep!
He, like the world, his ready visit pays
Where fortune smiles; the wretched he forsakes.
The Complaint: Night Thoughts (1742-5), Night i, l.1

1 Night, sable goddess! from her ebon throne
In rayless majesty, now stretches forth
Her leaden sceptre o'er a slumb'ring world.
l.18

2   We take no note of Time
But from its Loss.
l.55

3 Be wise to-day; 'tis madness to defer.
l.390

4 Procrastination is the thief of time.
l.393

5 At thirty a man suspects himself a fool;
Knows it at forty, and reforms his plan;
At fifty chides his infamous delay,
Pushes his prudent purpose to resolve;
In all the magnanimity of thought
Resolves; and re-resolves; then dies the same.
l.417

6 All men think all men mortal, but themselves.
l.424

7   Beautiful as sweet!
And young as beautiful! and soft as young!
And gay as soft! and innocent as gay.
Night iii, l.81

8 Shall our pale, wither'd hands be still stretch'd out,
Trembling, at once, with Eagerness and Age?
With Avarice, and Convulsions grasping hand?
Grasping at Air! for what has Earth beside?
Man wants but little; nor that little, long.
Night iv, l.118

9 A God all mercy is a God unjust.
l.233

10 By night an atheist half believes a God.
Night v, l.176

11 To know the world, not love her, is thy point,
She gives but little, nor that little, long.
Night viii, l.1276

12 Devotion! daughter of astronomy!
An undevout astronomer is mad.
Night ix, l.769

13 Life is the desert, life the solitude;
Death joins us to the great majority.
The Revenge (1721), Act IV

14 You are so witty, profligate, and thin,
At once we think thee Milton, Death, and Sin.
Epigram on Voltaire

GEORGE W. YOUNG 1846–1919

15 Your lips, on my own, when they printed 'Farewell',
Had never been soiled by the 'beverage of hell';
But they come to me now with the bacchanal sign,
And the lips that touch liquor must never touch mine.
The Lips That Touch Liquor Must Never Touch Mine; also
attr., in a different form, to Harriet A. Glazebrook

ISRAEL ZANGWILL 1864–1926

16 Scratch the Christian and you find the pagan—spoiled.
Children of the Ghetto (1892), bk.ii, ch.6

17 America is God's Crucible, the great Melting-Pot
where all the races of Europe are melting and
re-forming!
The Melting Pot (1908), Act I

EMILIANO ZAPATA 1879?–1919

18 *Muchos de ellos, por complacer a tiranos, por un
puñado de monedas, o por cohecho o soborno, están
derramando la sangre de sus hermanos.*
Many of them, so as to curry favour with tyrants, for a
fistful of coins, or through bribery or corruption, are
making the blood of their brothers spurt forth.
Of the *maderistas* who, in Zapata's view, had betrayed the
revolutionary cause. *Plan de Ayala*, 28 Nov. 1911, para.10

ÉMILE ZOLA 1840–1902

19 *Ne me regardez plus comme ça, parce que vous allez
vous user les yeux.*
Don't go on looking at me like that, because you'll
wear your eyes out.
La Bête Humaine (1889–90), ch.5

20 *J'accuse.*
I accuse.
Title of an open letter to the President of the French Republic, in
connection with the Dreyfus case, published in *L'Aurore*, 13 Jan.
1898

INDEX

NOTE. The order of the index both in the keywords and in the entries following each keyword is strictly alphabetical. Singular and plural nouns (including their possessive forms) are grouped separately: for 'with some old lover's ghost' see 'lover'; for 'at lovers' perjuries' see 'lovers'. All spellings and word forms appear in the index precisely as they do in the main text.

Foreign words are included in the general alphabetical scheme. A separate Greek index follows the main index.

The references show the author's name, usually in an abbreviated form, followed by the page and item numbers: 163:15 = quotation 15 on page 163.

To save space, the definite and indefinite articles, and the words Oh, O, but, and, for, as, have been dropped from the beginning of most entries, and the alphabetical order is thus decided by more significant words: 'And is it true' is shown as 'is it true'.

Les a. ont toujours tort　　　　　DEST 175:14
Absolute: A. across the hall　　　BELL 39:28
a. power corrupts　　　　　　　ACTON 1:5
A. rule　　　　　　　　　　MILT 347:22
Be a. for death　　　　　　　SHAK 464:8
foreknowledge a.　　　　　　MILT 346:19
hath her content so a.　　　　SHAK 474:20
So a. she seems　　　　　　　MILT 349:7
yet how peremptory and a.　　ELIOT 201:30
absolutism: a. moderated by assassination
　　　　　　　　　　　　　ANON 5:5
absolv'd: half a. who has confess'd
　　　　　　　　　　　　　PRIOR 400:18
absolve: be willing to a. us all　　VILL 557:4
absolved: a. from all duty to his PEAC 370:18
absolvitur: damnatur ubi nocens a.
　　　　　　　　　　　　　PUBL 402:5
absouldre: que tous nous veuille a.
　　　　　　　　　　　　　VILL 557:4
Abstain: A. from fleshly lusts　　BIBLE 80:24
Abstinence: A. is as easy to me JOHN 280:22
A. sows sand all over　　　　BLAKE 86:20
lean and sallow A.　　　　　MILT 341:16
made almost a sin of a.　　　DRYD 195:28
total a. is easier than　　　　AUG 21:22
abstinent: Multi quidem facilius se a.
　　　　　　　　　　　　　AUG 21:22
Abstract: A. liberty　　　　　BURKE 109:21
abstracted: disposed to a. meditation
　　　　　　　　　　　　　JOHN 281:40
abstracts: a. and brief chronicles
　　　　　　　　　　　　　SHAK 432:25
abstulit: ut me malus a. error　　VIRG 560:4
absurd: a. but some philosopher CIC 151:17
It is as a. to argue men　　　NEWM 362:8
Proving a. all written　　　　BROW 100:5
rather a. about the past　　　BEER 37:12
scientific faith's a.　　　　　BROW 100:21
thing becomes a.　　　　　　HOPE 255:27
absurdity: dull without a single a.
　　　　　　　　　　　　　GOLD 232:31
abundance: a. of the heart the mouth
　　　　　　　　　　　　　BIBLE 66:9
he shall have a.　　　　　　BIBLE 68:4
sound of a. of rain　　　　　BIBLE 51:10
upon us the a. of thy mercy　PRAY 386:20
were promised a. for all　　　KIPL 299:16
Whose strength's a. weakens SHAK 493:2
abuse: a. in public and to read　BORR 89:26
If it is a.　　　　　　　　　SHER 505:21
more dangerous the a.　　　BURKE 109:1
will you a. our patience　　　CIC 151:25
abused: a. it more　　　　　BYRON 123:26
man's character is to be a.　THAC 545:24
much a. as this sentence　　SELD 419:25
abuses: attended with considerable a.
　　　　　　　　　　　　　BURKE 109:3
stamp out a.　　　　　　　VOLT 561:11
abusing: old a. of God's patience SHAK 469:5
Abydos: Sestos and A. of her breasts
　　　　　　　　　　　　　DONNE 188:14
abysm: backward and a. of time SHAK 484:24
abyss: a. gazes also into you　NIET 363:10
breathless Nature's dark a.　WORD 578:8
edge of the nuclear a.　　　STEV 520:22
into the bottomless a.　　　WALEY 562:2
secrets of th' a. to spy　　　GRAY 235:19
abysses: a. are all so shallow　JAMES 271:32
in its a. of ineptitude　　　　HOUS 266:15
Abyssinian: It was an A. maid　COL 156:30
Academe: there the olive grove of A.
　　　　　　　　　　　　　MILT 350:8
truth in the groves of A.　　HOR 259:4
academes: ground, the books, the a.
　　　　　　　　　　　　　SHAK 457:6
academy: groves of *their* a.　BURKE 111:12
Mr Wackford Squeers's A.　DICK 179:34
accent: a. of a coming Foot　DICK 183:18
L'a. du pays où l'on est　　LA R 310:17
with a shrill and sad a.　　　CLAR 152:20

accents: a. of an expiring saint　STER 520:9
A. uncertain　　　　　　　BROW 100:35
a. yet unknown　　　　　　SHAK 450:5
caught his clear a.　　　　　BROW 102:5
come refin'd with th'a.　　　DAN 170:23
follow with a. sweet　　　　CAMP 129:18
Loved a. are soon forgot　　SHEL 501:21
acceptable: a. unto God　　　BIBLE 75:15
a. year of the Lord　　　　　BIBLE 60:8
be alway a. in thy sight　　　PRAY 390:13
this is a. with God　　　　　BIBLE 80:26
accepted: a. wit has but to say 'Pass
　　　　　　　　　　　　　GILB 229:10
accepteth: God now a. thy works BIBLE 55:28
accepting: Charms by a.　　　POPE 377:27
accepts: Man a. the compromise KIPL 299:5
accident: By many a happy a.　MIDD 338:19
disqualified by the a. of death CHES 148:5
have it found out by a.　　　LAMB 308:2
of a. nor dart of chance　　　SHAK 476:16
Accidents: A. will occur in the
　　best-regulated　　　　　DICK 177:15
chapter of a.　　　　　　　CHES 146:2
chapter of a. is the longest　WILK 574:5
Of moving a. by flood　　　SHAK 473:25
that he runs into a.　　　　MARQ 331:2
Which shackles a.　　　　　SHAK 423:20
accipitrine: will a. to pursue　THOM 548:2
accommodatin: exceedin a. character
　　　　　　　　　　　　　WARD 564:21
*accommodements: trouve avec lui des
　a.*　　　　　　　　　　　MOL 353:26
accompany: a. me with a pure heart
　　　　　　　　　　　　　PRAY 384:10
accomplice: signifies a ready-made a.
　　　　　　　　　　　　　PEAC 370:14
accomplished: a. man to his finger-tips
　　　　　　　　　　　　　HOR 262:4
desire a. is sweet　　　　　BIBLE 53:37
material creation is a.　　　JOYCE 286:18
what can be a. in a week　　STEV 522:8
accomplishments: a. give lustre CHES 145:31
accord: a. to make our common
　supplications　　　　　　PRAY 385:8
Should of his own a.　　　　ANON 8:24
according: each a. to his abilities MARX 333:5
accosted: should then have a. her
　　　　　　　　　　　　　SHAK 489:27
account: a. wife and children　BACON 26:32
accurate and exhaustive a.　BEER 37:13
sent to my a.　　　　　　　SHAK 431:12
Such I a. thy love　　　　　SHAK 459:8
they shall give a. thereof　　BIBLE 66:10
accuracy: of a. must be sacrificed JOHN 281:4
accurate: a. and exhaustive account
　　　　　　　　　　　　　BEER 37:13
accurs'd: themselves a. they were not
　here　　　　　　　　　　SHAK 445:3
accursed: a. power which stands BELL 39:21
Accurst: A. be he that first invented
　　　　　　　　　　　　　MARL 330:6
accuse: J'a.　　　　　　　ZOLA 588:20
yet I could a. me of such　　SHAK 433:11
accused: apology before you be a.
　　　　　　　　　　　　　CHAR 140:17
security to persons who are a. DENM 174:22
than a. of deficiency　　　　JOHN 277:9
Accuser: not my A., but my judges
　　　　　　　　　　　　　NEWM 361:15
accustomed: a. to their lack of breath
　　　　　　　　　　　　　YEATS 585:13
ace: a. of trumps up his sleeve　LAB 306:10
was about to play the a.　　FIELD 211:3
aces: hands that hold the a.　BETJ 42:13
Achaeans: A. have suffered for so
　　　　　　　　　　　　　HOMER 253:28
myriad sufferings for the A.　HOMER 253:26
Achates: fidus quae tela gerebat A.
　　　　　　　　　　　　　VIRG 557:12
ache: has made my heart to a.　BLAKE 87:7

ached: never has a. with a heart　SWIN 529:7
Acheronta: A. movebo　　　VIRG 559:5
aches: That the sense a. at thee SHAK 476:19
achieve: a. of, the mastery of　HOPK 257:5
I shall a. in time　　　　　　GILB 227:5
Our patience will a. more　　BURKE 111:24
to a. that I have done　　　MAL 327:20
achieved: It is a.　　　　　BIBLE 83:23
achievements: How my a. mock me
　　　　　　　　　　　　　SHAK 487:8
achieving: Still a., still pursuing LONG 317:5
Achilles: A.' cursed anger sing HOMER 253:26
A. wears his wit in his　　　SHAK 486:29
armour stripped from A.　　VIRG 558:5
I've stood upon A.' tomb　　BYRON 123:13
name A. assumed　　　　　BROW 97:14
see the great A.　　　　　　TENN 544:3
Stand in the trench, A.　　　SHAW 498:28
to work out A. his armour　BROW 95:18
Aching: A., shaking　　　　ROCH 407:3
Achitophel: these the false A. was first
　　　　　　　　　　　　　DRYD 194:6
Achivi: reges plectuntur A.　HOR 258:12
Acids: A. stain you　　　　PARK 368:18
Acidulous: A. vestals　　　STEV 521:25
Ackney Marshes: You could see to 'A.
　　　　　　　　　　　　　BAT 35:3
acknowledge: a. thee to be the Lord
　　　　　　　　　　　　　PRAY 384:16
I a. my faults　　　　　　　PRAY 393:4
acorns: Tall oaks from little a.　EVER 209:10
wringing lilies from the a.　POUND 383:2
Acquaintance: A. I would have COWL 164:14
first an a., next a mistress　CHEK 145:5
have a visiting a. with　　　SHER 506:17
hope our a. may be a long　DICK 182:5
I do not make a new a.　　JOHN 279:25
love good creditable a.　　　SWIFT 526:15
man does not make new a.　JOHN 274:15
Should auld a. be forgot　　BURNS 112:30
acquainted: a. with grief　　BIBLE 59:21
been one a. with the night　FROST 218:27
Love and I were well a.　　GILB 228:38
Sentiment is what I am not a. FLEM 215:2
she and I were long a.　　　HOUS 265:8
acquent: When we were first a.
　　　　　　　　　　　　　BURNS 114:12
acquiesce: remains but to a. with silence
　　　　　　　　　　　　　JOHN 281:9
acquitted: guilty party is a.　PUBL 402:5
acre: furlongs of sea for an a. SHAK 484:22
acres: few paternal a. bound　POPE 380:23
lass that has a. o' charms　BURNS 114:6
Three a. and a cow　　　　COLL 158:11
acrimonious: a. and surly republican
　　　　　　　　　　　　　JOHN 281:33
Acroceraunian: In the A. mountains
　　　　　　　　　　　　　SHEL 500:2
Acrostic: peaceful province in A. Land
　　　　　　　　　　　　　DRYD 196:35
act: a. in the living Present　LONG 317:3
a. of darkness with her　　SHAK 454:18
a. of dying is not of importance JOHN 275:31
A. of God was defined　　　HERB 246:19
A. upon it　　　　　　　　GILB 225:27
I could a. as well as he　　FIEL 211:32
in any A. of Parliament　　HERB 246:14
in itself almost an a.　　　ROSS 410:7
it is the foolishest a.　　　BROW 96:33
made honest by an a.　　　JONS 283:25
motion And the a.　　　　ELIOT 203:10
nobility is the a. of time　BACON 26:39
princes to a.　　　　　　SHAK 443:3
prologues to the swelling a. SHAK 458:19
Regulations A.　　　　　　WILDE 572:12
same in thine own a.　　　SHAK 459:8
sins they love to a.　　　　SHAK 478:3
sleep an a. or two　　　　SHAK 448:4
To see him a.　　　　　　COL 157:31
what a., That roars so　　SHAK 435:5

adversitate: Nam in omni a. fortunae
BOET 89:6
adversité: Dans l'a. de nos meilleurs
LA R 310:8
adversities: all our troubles and a.
PRAY 385:22
adversity: a. doth best discover virtue
BACON 25:21
a. is the blessing BACON 25:18
a. is not without comforts BACON 25:20
A. is sometimes hard upon CARL 131:36
A.'s sweet milk SHAK 483:11
any other a. PRAY 387:16
bread of a. BIBLE 58:28
brother is born for a. BIBLE 54:11
in the day of a. consider BIBLE 55:21
Like old companions in a. BRY 106:9
man I am cross'd with a. SHAK 491:3
men contending with a. BURT 116:24
Sweet are the uses of a. SHAK 424:32
advertise: shall call him and a. him
PRAY 387:5
advertisement: is the soul of an a.
JOHN 281:19
advertisers: a. don't object SWAF 525:30
Advice: A. is seldom welcome CHES 145:19
earnest a. from my seniors THOR 550:6
Love be controll'd by a. GAY 222:14
matrimony I never give any a. CHES 146:3
tea and comfortable a. KEATS 294:5
To ask a. is in nine cases COLL 158:14
woman seldom asks a. before ADD 2:23
advise: would a. no man to marry
JOHN 280:13
advises: It's my old girl that a. DICK 176:18
thus a. thee that sighs SHAK 489:15
advocate: intellect of an a. BAG 29:17
our Mediator and A. PRAY 385:23
advocates: a. of peace upon earth GEOR 224:4
you of a. the best CAT 137:3
aedificaverit: Nisi Dominus a. domum
BIBLE 83:12
Aeneas: as A., our great ancestor
SHAK 448:14
Dido and her A. shall want SHAK 423:10
down to join our father A. HOR 261:16
Quo pater A. HOR 261:16
aeneus: Hic murus a. esto HOR 258:9
Aequam: A. memento rebus in arduis
HOR 260:6
aequo: Pallida Mors a. HOR 259:13
aequor: Cras ingens iterabimus a.
HOR 259:17
aequus: animus si te non deficit a. HOR 258:19
aere: monumentum a. perennius HOR 259:12
aery: execute their a. purposes MILT 345:15
aes: robur et a. triplex HOR 259:12
Aeschylus: I was fondest of A. COL 158:6
Aesculapius: we owe a cock to A.
SOCR 512:21
aesthetic: high a. line GILB 227:20
high a. band GILB 227:23
aestimemus: Omnes unius a. assis CAT 136:25
Aetas: A. parentum peior avis HOR 260:26
fugerit invida A. HOR 259:20
Aetolian: Through Europe to the A. shore
ARN 13:9
afar: peace to you which were a. BIBLE 77:22
afeard: Be not a. SHAK 485:17
soldier, and a. SHAK 462:20
affair: had an a. with the moon STER 518:29
affaire: then quelle a. BLUC 89:1
affairs: tide in the a. of women
BYRON 123:20
tide in the a. of men SHAK 451:27
affectation: have been so used to a.
ETH 208:26
spruce a. SHAK 457:15
They are the a. of affectation FIEL 211:15
wits to sophistry and a. BACON 28:12

affected: His accent was a. HARE 242:7
Really I believe I'm so a. BEAR 35:11
Affecting: A. to seem unaffected
CONG 159:18
affection: heard Of any true a. MIDD 338:18
in the rear of your a. SHAK 430:17
still he fills a.'s eye JOHN 278:35
thy a. cannot hold SHAK 489:2
When strong a. stirs her SOUT 514:6
With a. beaming in one DICK 179:5
your a. on things above BIBLE 78:25
affections: his a. dark as Erebus SHAK 468:17
holiness of the heart's a. and the truth
KEATS 293:15
is a history of the a. IRV 270:20
offences of a. new SHAK 495:3
our young a. run to waste BYRON 121:12
souls descend T'a. DONNE 188:25
unruly wills and a. PRAY 386:12
Affects: A. to nod DRYD 194:24
afflicted: he was a. BIBLE 59:22
afflicting: most a. to a parent's mind
AUST 23:18
Affliction: A. alters SHAK 492:6
A. is enamour'd of thy SHAK 483:9
all a. taught a lover yet POPE 376:12
bread of a. and with water BIBLE 51:20
Remembering mine a. and my misery
BIBLE 60:29
saveth in time of a. BIBLE 62:21
thee in the furnace of a. BIBLE 59:14
To try me with a. SHAK 476:18
waters of a. BIBLE 58:28
Afflictions: A. sorted HERB 248:10
A. easier grow WALSH 563:29
describing the a. of Job BACON 25:19
affluent: a. society no useful distinction
GALB 220:28
afford: can a. to keep a motor car
SHAW 496:4
Can't a. them SHAW 498:13
parties could any way a. it EDG 199:21
unless you can a. it TROL 553:15
Whether we can a. it or no GAY 223:24
Afield: A. for palms the girls HOUS 262:19
afire: bush a. with God BROW 97:33
afloat: full sea are we now a. SHAK 451:27
afraid: a. of me POPE 380:20
a. of the sea will soon SYNGE 531:4
a. to look upon God BIBLE 47:5
a. to speak evil of dignities BIBLE 81:1
do what you are a. to do EMER 207:23
I am a. to think what SHAK 460:11
I am devilishly a. DRYD 195:18
in short, I was a. ELIOT 203:23
keep myself from being a. DRYD 195:19
many are a. of God LOCK 315:20
not so much a. of death BROW 96:20
of his near approach a. GARR 221:16
see all, nor be a. BROW 104:2
stranger and a. HOUS 264:25
that he is a. of his enemy PLUT 374:20
they were sore a. BIBLE 69:9
we do be a. of the sea SYNGE 531:4
whereof our conscience is a. PRAY 386:20
whom then shall I be a. PRAY 391:7
yet a. of death CHUR 148:32
yet a. to strike POPE 376:26
Afric: geographers, in A.-maps SWIFT 528:2
Africa: all A. and her prodigies BROW 96:12
are to go some to arid A. VIRG 559:13
silent over A. BROW 101:9
speak of A. and golden joys SHAK 442:27
Till China and A. meet AUDEN 18:9
African: strength of this A. national
MACM 326:1
after: a. many a summer dies TENN 543:11
'A. sharpest shoures LANG 309:28
A. such knowledge ELIOT 203:5
A. the first death THOM 547:8

tell them that come a. PRAY 392:27
you who come a. me HOR 260:12
aftermaths: In a. of soft September
HOUS 265:8
afternoon: rude multitude call the a.
SHAK 457:13
Summer a. JAMES 271:30
which it seemed always a. TENN 539:12
aftersight: mind to a. and foresight
ELIOT 202:25
after-silence: in the a. on the shore
BYRON 125:10
after-times: something so written to a.
MILT 352:14
after-tram-ride: a. quiet BETJ 43:19
Afton: sweet A. BURNS 113:27
Agag: A. came unto him delicately
BIBLE 50:5
again: Come a., with the feet HARDY 238:22
comfort of thy help a. PRAY 393:6
hang the man over a. BARH 33:9
I do it again and a. CARR 133:22
Against: A. my fire SHAK 455:24
A. thee only have I sinned PRAY 393:4
hand will be a. every man BIBLE 46:5
He said he was a. it COOL 162:10
I have somewhat a. thee BIBLE 81:16
is not with me is a. me BIBLE 66:6
Shall come a. him SHAK 462:8
who can be a. us BIBLE 75:12
Agamemnon: A. dead YEATS 586:2
When A. cried aloud ELIOT 204:16
Agamemnona: Vixere fortes ante A.
HOR 261:18
Aganippe: I never drank of A. well
SIDN 507:26
agate-stone: shape no bigger than an
a. SHAK 481:28
age: a. are threescore years PRAY 395:19
A. cannot wither her SHAK 422:5
a. fatal to Revolutionists DESM 175:13
a. from folly could not SHAK 421:27
A., I do abhor thee SHAK 492:14
a. in her embraces past ROCH 406:20
a. is a dream that is dying OSH 365:21
a. is as a lusty winter SHAK 425:6
A. is deformed BAST 35:2
A. makes a winter SPAR 514:22
A. might but take the things WORD 581:12
a. of chivalry is gone BURKE 111:9
a. of chivalry is never KING 297:18
a. shall be able to destroy OVID 366:19
A. shall not weary them BINY 84:10
a., which forgives itself SHAW 498:5
A. will not be defied BACON 27:6
all the faults of the a. BALF 30:5
arrogance of a. must submit BURKE 110:23
Athens in his riper a. DRYD 197:14
away in the time of a. PRAY 394:17
buried in a good old a. BIBLE 46:4
companions for middle a. BACON 26:34
Crabbed a. and youth SHAK 492:13
Diseases and sad Old A. VIRG 558:21
evening of my a. ROWE 410:20
Every a. has a kind DRYD 197:39
fetch the a. of gold MILT 344:11
flower of thee a. BIBLE 49:33
full of grief as a. SHAK 454:1
governed their rude a. BAG 28:28
hath yet some smack of a. SHAK 441:5
He died in a good old a. BIBLE 51:40
He is of a. BIBLE 72:15
He is of no a. COL 158:8
He was not of an a. JONS 284:23
if a. could EST 208:25
invention of a barbarous a. MILT 344:17
Is common at your a. BELL 38:25
labour with an a. of ease GOLD 230:19
less for what a. takes away WORD 577:20
Let a. approve of youth BROW 104:13

592

now enjoys his a.   DRYD 196:3
Now has come the last a.   VIRG 559:22
now in a. I bud again   HERB 247:22
Old A. a regret   DISR 185:40
Old a. brings along with   EMER 207:45
Old a. is the most unexpected   TROT 553:16
old a. of cards   POPE 377:26
pays us but with a.   RAL 404:15
poison for the a.'s tooth   SHAK 452:10
soon comes a.   SPEN 516:13
tell a woman's a.   GILB 228:27
Than settled a. his sables   SHAK 436:17
That men call a.   BROO 94:7
this a. best pleaseth me   HERR 249:17
thou a. unbred   SHAK 494:18
Thou hast nor youth nor a.   SHAK 464:10
tiresomeness of old a.   ANON 10:13
To complain of the a. we   BURKE 108:17
Towards the a. of twenty-six   BELL 39:5
To youth and a. in common   ARN 15:13
very staff of my a.   SHAK 466:8
vice and follies of the a.   CENT 138:10
wealth a well-spent a.   CAMP 129:19
well stricken in a.   BIBLE 46:6
'when the a. is   SHAK 472:34
who tells one her real a.   WILDE 573:28
with Eagerness and A.   YOUNG 588:8
With leaden a. o'ercargoed   FLEC 214:16
worth an a. without a name   MORD 357:6
aged: a. man is but a paltry   YEATS 586:1
don't object to an a. parent   DICK 178:12
I saw an a., aged man   CARR 136:5
reverend creatures did the a.   TRAH 551:19
ageless-ancient: mother-naked and a.
    DAY-L 172:21
agendum: dum quid superesset a.
    LUCAN 319:24
agent: is the poor a. despised   SHAK 487:19
agents: night's black a.   SHAK 461:14
ages: acts being seven a.   SHAK 425:24
A. of hopeless end   MILT 346:11
a. of imagination this   BLAKE 88:26
heir of all the a.   TENN 539:7
next a.   BACON 28:14
Now he belongs to the a.   STAN 517:19
our diff'rent a. move   PRIOR 401:7
ageth: Earthly glory a. and seareth
    POUND 383:19
aggravating: She was an a. child   BELL 39:12
aggregate: From the large a. of little
    MORE 357:11
aghast: stared a. to watch him eat
    HOUS 264:15
Agincourt: affright the air at A.   SHAK 443:4
a-gley: Gang aft a.   BURNS 115:22
a-glimmer: There midnight's all a.
    YEATS 585:17
Agnes: St A.' Eve   KEATS 289:9
agnostic: appropriate title of 'a.'   HUXL 269:4
Agnus: A. Dei   MASS 335:7
agonies: exultations, a., And love
    WORD 582:17
Agony: A. and bloody Sweat   PRAY 385:17
a. and spoil   KIPL 300:6
a. is abated   MAC 324:24
Hard and bitter a. for us   ELIOT 203:15
intense the a.   BRON 93:21
it happen and am in a.   CAT 137:14
strong swimmer in his a.   BYRON 122:18
agree: a. in the truth of thy   PRAY 387:13
a. the kettle and the earthen   BIBLE 63:3
A. with thine adversary   BIBLE 64:13
colours will a. in the dark   BACON 27:32
does not a. with my constitution   THOR 550:14
in their little nests a.   BELL 40:6
Music and sweet Poetry a.   BARN 34:2
they may a. like brothers   SHAK 446:11
When people a. with me   WILDE 572:21
whom all joys so well a.   SIDN 508:1
world and I shall ne'er a.   COWL 164:11

agreeable: himself a most a. fellow
    AUST 22:10
Is the old min a.   DICK 180:24
most men's power to be a.   SWIFT 527:11
'My idea of an a. person   DISR 186:24
agreement: death and an a. with hell'
    GARR 221:19
with hell are we at a.   BIBLE 58:22
agrestis: ille deos qui novit a.   VIRG 560:15
agri: modus a. non ita magnus   HOR 262:9
agriculture: fall upon a.   GIBB 224:26
agua: a. que ahuyenta la sed   CERV 138:20
ague-proof: I am not a.   SHAK 455:15
Ahab: ran before A.   BIBLE 51:12
a-hunting: a. we will go   FIEL 211:36
We daren't go a.   ALL 3:20
Aid: Summoned the Immediate A.   BELL 39:8
Their a. they yield   COWP 168:9
Aide-toi: A., le ciel t'aidera   LA F 306:17
aik: lean'd my back unto an a.   BALL 32:10
ail: what can a. thee   KEATS 290:15
ailes: a. de géant l'empêchent   BAUD 35:6
ailing: poor, a. and ignorant   YEATS 585:3
ailments: because our a. are the same
    SWIFT 526:13
aim: at which all things a.   ARIS 12:6
you must a. a little above   LONG 316:11
aimai: plus j'a. ma patrie   BELL 40:17
aime: C'est mourir à ce qu'on a.   HAR 238:20
Et j'a. la Princesse   ROST 410:13
aimeth: Who a. at the sky   HERB 247:8
aimez: et a. qui vous aime   VOLT 561:11
aiming: a. at a million   BROW 100:38
aimless: nothing walks with a. feet
    TENN 536:25
obscure them by an a. rhetoric   HUXL 269:13
aims: a. his heart had learned   GOLD 230:22
other a. than my delight   HARDY 240:6
aim'st: Let all the ends thou a.   SHAK 447:12
ain't: she a.   KIPL 302:11
You a. heard nothin' yet   JOLS 283:9
air: a., a charter'd libertine   SHAK 443:6
a. a live tradition   POUND 382:14
a. a solemn stillness holds   GRAY 234:18
a. broke into a mist with   BROW 103:11
a. is delicate   SHAK 459:4
a. might wash and long   SWIN 530:18
a. Nimbly and sweetly   SHAK 459:4
a. shall note her soft   DONNE 188:9
a. signed with their honour   SPEN 515:8
are built with a.   JONS 283:26
Behold the fowls of the a.   BIBLE 64:28
breathing English a.   BROO 94:30
burning fills the startled a.   BELL 40:7
diviner a.   WORD 578:3
excellent canopy, the a.   SHAK 432:15
fair and floral a.   FLEC 214:6
firmly planted in the a.   ROOS 407:24
I am fire and a.   SHAK 424:11
into thin a.   SHAK 485:20
Leaving a blacker a.   HARDY 240:11
let out to warm the a.   SWIFT 526:7
merely vans to beat the a.   ELIOT 202:1
morning to take the a.   FRY 219:21
my heart an a. that kills   HOUS 263:22
nipping and an eager a.   SHAK 430:22
ocean and the living a.   WORD 578:7
one that beateth the a.   BIBLE 76:9
Only to kiss that a.   HERR 250:3
other passions fleet to a.   SHAK 467:12
out of a mouthful of a.   YEATS 585:8
Out of the a. a voice   AUDEN 20:10
over the fowl of the a.   BIBLE 45:4
parching a. Burns frore   MILT 346:21
There is an a. comes from   SHAK 492:11
through the trembling a.   SPEN 516:30
To a. the ditty   HOUS 265:12
'twixt a. and Angels' purity   DONNE 187:22
with pinions skim the a.   FRERE 218:25
world-mothering a.   HOPK 256:6

airly: you've gut to git up a.   LOW 319:1
Airly Beacon: Shires and towns from
A.   KING 296:16
airman: most intrepid a.   CHUR 150:16
airports: a. almost deserted   AUDEN 19:2
airs: a. from heaven or blasts   SHAK 430:24
'don't give yourself a.   CARR 133:23
poet sing it with such a.   YEATS 584:10
Sounds and sweet a.   SHAK 485:17
Airy: A., fairy Lilian   TENN 538:14
a. subtleties in religion   BROW 96:8
Ajalon: in the valley of A.   BIBLE 49:4
Ajax: Thersites' body is as good as A.
    SHAK 428:21
a-killing: have him nine years a.   SHAK 476:10
Akond: Is the A. of Swat   LEAR 312:25
al: nat kepe me chaast in a.   CHAU 143:17
alabaster: a. box of very precious BIBLE 68:8
his grandsire cut in a.   SHAK 465:11
smooth as monumental a.   SHAK 477:5
alacrity: kind of a. in sinking   SHAK 469:13
ALARM: A. and DESPONDENCY
    PEN 371:13
Glorious the trumpet and a.   SMART 509:4
alarms: Swept with confused a. of struggle
    ARN 12:23
were all the world's a.   YEATS 586:4
alarum: At once the wild a. clashed
    MAC 322:2
Alas: A. but cannot help nor   AUDEN 20:17
Albatross: I shot the A.   COL 155:10
Albion: La perfide A.   XIM 584:6
Alcestis: me like A. from the grave
    MILT 351:12
alchemy: By happy a. of mind   GREEN 236:2
aldermen: divides the wives of a.
    SMITH 509:8
Aldershot: Furnish'd and burnish'd by
A.   BETJ 44:6
ale: a. is a dish for a king   SHAK 491:17
be no more cakes and a.   SHAK 488:21
broach'd the mightiest a.   SCOTT 417:16
drink your a.   HOUS 264:22
Good a.   BORR 90:8
have fed purely upon a.   FARQ 209:23
my fame for a pot of a.   SHAK 444:4
Of jolly good a. and old   ANON 5:21
...ordered a glass of this a.   DICK 176:22
spicy nut-brown a.   MILT 342:23
wes sons of a. and brede   WYNT 584:4
while England talked of a.   CHES 147:13
alehouse: were in an a. in London
    SHAK 444:4
Aleppo: Her husband's to A. gone
    SHAK 458:6
Alexander: A. at the head of the world
    WALP 562:18
A. women   LEE 313:13
If I were not A.   ALEX 3:12
Alexandrine: needless A. ends the song
    POPE 378:21
Alexin: pastor Corydon ardebat A.
    VIRG 559:14
Alfred: high tide!' King A.   CHES 146:20
Truth-teller was our England's A.
    TENN 541:13
alget: Probitas laudatur et a.   JUV 287:10
alibi: He always has an a.   ELIOT 203:26
Alice: A., where art thou   BUNN 107:8
don't you remember sweet A.   ENGL 208:19
Alien: A. they seemed to be   HARDY 239:6
tears amid the a. corn   KEATS 291:23
With an a. people clutching   ELIOT 203:15
Alieni: A. appetens   SALL 413:22
alienum: humani nil a me a. puto TER 544:17
alights: Daintily a. Elaine   BETJ 43:13
alike: light to thee are both a.   PRAY 399:5
Looks on a.   SHAK 492:4
there should be none a.   BROW 96:31

aliquid: *Meas esse a. putare nugas*
      CAT 136:20

aliquo: *aut a. modo destruator*   MAGN 327:2

aliter: *Dis a. visum*   VIRG 558:8

Alive: A. like patterns a murmuration
      AUDEN 20:6
a. so stout a gentleman   SHAK 440:24
A. with sparkles   KEATS 289:4
Christ shall all be made a.   BIBLE 76:22
I am a. for evermore   BIBLE 81:15
if I am a. I shall be delighted   HOLL 253:3
is a. again   BIBLE 70:21
it in that dawn to be a.   WORD 577:21
Life's not just being a.   MART 331:12
living which are yet a.   BIBLE 55:14
Looking as if she were a.   BROW 102:21
noise and tumult when a.   EDW 200:6
Officiously to keep a.   CLOU 153:26
show that one's a.   BURN 112:22
still a. at twenty-two   KING 297:19
that he is no longer a.   BENT 41:5
When I was man a.   HOUS 263:9

all: a. for love   SPEN 516:12
A. for one   DUMAS 199:3
A. for your delight   SHAK 471:16
a. goes right and nothing   GILB 228:29
a. hell broke loose   MILT 348:11
A. is for the best   VOLT 561:2
A. men make faults   SHAK 493:12
a. our yesterdays have   SHAK 463:6
A.'s right with the world   BROW 103:21
A. that a man hath will   BIBLE 52:8
a. that's best of dark   BYRON 125:21
a. the rest forgot   SHAK 493:4
a. the silent manliness   GOLD 231:6
A. things are lawful   BIBLE 76:10
A. things bright and beautiful   ALEX 3:13
a. things to all men'   ANON 6:11
A. things to all men   BIBLE 76:7
A. things were made   BIBLE 71:22
A. this and heaven too   HENRY 245:22
a. to Heaven   JONES 283:13
a. we have and are   KIPL 299:6
A. we have willed or hoped   BROW 98:19
always is A. everywhere   DONNE 188:32
are a. gone out of the way   PRAY 390:3
because not a. was right   COWP 168:20
everything the concern of a.   SOLZ 513:1
Her a. on earth   BYRON 121:35
man for a. seasons   WHIT 571:22
not at all or all in a.   TENN 535:8
nothing brings me a. things   SHAK 486:12
Then a. were for the state   MAC 322:18
this is a. that is known   NEWM 362:5
to have his a. neglected   JOHN 274:5
upholdeth a. such as fall   PRAY 399:14
When a. night long a chap   GILB 226:8
When a. the world is young   KING 297:5

Allah: A. created the English   KIPL 300:14
A. is great   CLOU 153:11

Allaying: A. both their fury   SHAK 484:31
drop of a. Tiber   SHAK 427:14

allegiance: Any victim demands a.
      GREE 236:5
religious a.   BAG 28:21
To hell, a.   SHAK 436:7
to swear a. to any master   HOR 258:7

allegorical: a. paintings they can shew
      JOHN 280:19

allegory: headstrong as an a.   SHER 506:15
Shakespeare led a life of a.   KEATS 294:13
Which things are an a.   BIBLE 77:16
worth is a continual a.   KEATS 294:12

allemand: *hommes et a. à mon cheval*
      CHAR 140:31

alles: *Die Welt ist a.*   WITT 575:14

alleviate: a. so severe a misfortune
      AUST 23:18

alley: she lives in our a.   CAREY 130:26

alleybi: governor don't prove a a.
      DICK 182:15
vy won't there a a.   DICK 182:24

alleys: a. of London do not present
      DOYLE 192:1

alleyways: crossroads and in the a. CAT 137:5

allgemeines: *Maxime solle ein a. Gesetz*
      KANT 288:9

alliance: clear of permanent a.   WASH 565:2
rumours of a morganatic a.   HARD 238:21

alliances: entangling a. with none JEFF 272:8

allied: nearly a. to excellence   GOLD 232:8

allies: thou hast great a.   WORD 582:17

All-in-all: intellectual A.   WORD 580:4

Alliteration: apt A.'s artful aid   CHUR 149:2

allotted: a. death and hell   MARL 329:13

allow: a. their names to be mentioned
      AUST 23:19

all-round: he was a wonderful a. man
      BEER 38:6

Allsopp: Guinness, A., Bass   CALV 127:12

All-Souls: at Christ-Church and A.
      JOHN 275:22

alluring: little scorn is a.   CONG 161:2
more a. than a levee from   CONG 161:4

Almack: to A.'s too   ANST 11:8

Alma Mater: A. lie dissolv'd in port
      POPE 375:21

almanac: useful as an a. out of date
      WALT 563:21

Almighty: A.'s orders to perform   ADD 1:14
arrow from the A.'s bow   BLAKE 86:6

almond: a. tree shall flourish   BIBLE 56:11

alms: accept our a. and oblations PRAY 387:13
a. Of palsied eld   SHAK 464:10
a. of thy superfluous praise   DRAY 193:20
he puts a. for oblivion   SHAK 487:3
When thou doest a.   BIBLE 64:22

alms-basket: long on the a. of words
      SHAK 457:12

aloe: olive, a.   TENN 533:5

aloft: now he's gone a.   DIBD 175:22

alone: all a. went she   KING 296:25
A. he rides   JOHN 273:23
A. I did it   SHAK 428:6
a. on a hill during a clear   HARDY 241:9
A. on a wide wide sea   COL 155:20
A., poor maid   MEW 338:12
alone than when wholly a.   CIC 151:23
A. word is   SASS 415:2
Are we here together a.   WHIT 570:13
be a. on earth   BYRON 120:16
bear the palm a.   SHAK 448:16
down a. bent on his prey   MILT 347:10
experienced at being a. together LA B 306:13
I feel I am a.   LAND 308:24
I lie down a.   HOUS 265:17
Ill fortune seldom comes a.   DRYD 195:36
In leafy dells a.   HOUS 265:7
is the man who stands a.   IBSEN 269:20
it a. is high fantastical   SHAK 487:20
I want to be a.   GARBO 221:3
leaves her too much a.   POUND 382:5
left him a. with his glory   WOLFE 576:5
let me a. for swearing   SHAK 490:13
Let me a.   BIBLE 52:20
Lives not a.   BLAKE 85:20
love is left a.   TENN 543:14
mortal millions live *a.*   ARN 13:12
most unfit to be a.   CONG 159:17
never less a. than when   ROG 407:8
One is one and all a.   ANON 6:5
shall be left, a.   WORD 581:13
shalt be, art, a.   ARN 13:11
sparrow: that sitteth a.   PRAY 396:12
that the man should be a.   BIBLE 45:10
they would but let it a.   WALP 563:6
things were a. with theirs   BETJ 42:9
To live in Paradise a.   MARV 332:8
trodden the winepress a.   BIBLE 60:11

we ask is to be let a.   DAVIS 172:19
we were a. and completely   DANTE 171:9
Will he not let us a.   DONNE 190:5

Aloof: A. from the entire point   SHAK 453:7

aloud: thee all Angels cry a.   PRAY 384:16

Alpes: *et saevas curre per A.*   JUV 288:2

Alph: A., the sacred river   COL 156:26

Alpha: 'I am A. and Omega   AUDEN 21:7
I am A. and Omega   BIBLE 81:10

alphabet: got to the end of the a.   DICK 182:7
struggled through the a.   DICK 178:6

Alpheus: A., the dread voice is   MILT 343:14

Alpine: on the A. mountains cold   MILT 351:9

Alps: A. on Alps arise   POPE 378:14
A. shaping like a backbone   HARDY 239:13
beneath some snow-deep A.   ELIOT 202:5
fading a. and archipelagoes   ALDR 3:11
O'er the white A. alone   DONNE 188:12

also: hell, thou art there a.   PRAY 399:5

altar: a. with this inscription   BIBLE 74:12
self-slain on his own strange a.   SWIN 529:20
so will I go to thine a.   PRAY 391:5
that I may go unto the a.   PRAY 391:7
To what green a.   KEATS 291:8

altars: even thy a., O Lord   PRAY 395:11
shining a. of Japan they raise   POPE 381:6
threw our a. to the ground   JORD 285:18

altar-stairs: great world's a.   TENN 536:28

alter: a. the past, historians can BUTL 118:21
not a. in my faith of him   JONS 283:25
Will it a. my life altogether   AUDEN 21:2

alteram: *Audi partem a.*   AUG 21:20

alteration: alters when it a. finds SHAK 495:2

altered: how much it a. her person
      SWIFT 527:5

alternative: unhappy a. is before you
      AUST 23:15

alternatives: more a., the more difficult
      ALL 3:19

Althea: my divine A. brings   LOV 318:15

Altior: *A. Italiae ruinis*   HOR 260:24

altissimo: *Onorate l'a. poeta*   DANTE 171:6

Altogether: A. elsewhere   AUDEN 18:16
I shall not a. die   HOR 261:9
righteous a.   PRAY 390:12

altrui: *Lo pane a.*   DANTE 171:17

alway: He will not a. be chiding PRAY 396:16
I am with you a.   BIBLE 68:25

always: a. with us, or we die   KEATS 289:2
It wasn't a. like this   AUDEN 19:15
man with God is a.   KNOX 305:18
research is a. incomplete   PATT 370:8
third who walks a. beside   ELIOT 205:8

Alysander: Quhen A. oure kyng wes
      WYNT 584:4

am: grace of God I am what I a. BIBLE 76:19
Here I a., and here I stay   MACM 325:17
I AM THAT I A.   BIBLE 47:7
I am the way I a.   PREV 400:16
therefore I a.   DESC 175:10
what I a., none cares   CLARE 152:12

amabam: *Nondum a.*   AUG 21:12

amantem: *Quis fallere possit a.*   VIRG 558:12

amanti: *mulier cupido quod dicit a.*
      CAT 137:7

Amantium: *A. irae amoris integratio*
      TER 544:15

amantum: *alto periuria ridet a.*   OVID 366:11

amaracus: Violet, a., and asphodel
      TENN 541:18

amaranth: Of a. lie   DE L 173:25

amaranthus: Bid a. all his beauty shed
      MILT 343:15

amare: *amans a.*   AUG 21:12

amari: *Surgit a. aliquid quod*   LUCR 320:11

Amaryllis: To sport with A.   MILT 343:8

amateur: a. painting in water-colours
      STEV 521:28
Eavy-sterned a. old men   KIPL 303:11

amateurs: disease that afflicts a.   CHES 148:1

that we are a nation of a.   ROS 408:15
amavi: Sero te a.   AUG 21:16
amavit: Cras amet qui nunquam a.
   ANON 10:11
amaz'd: a., and curious   BURNS 115:10
Amaze: A. th' unlearn'd   POPE 378:18
these cogitations still a.   ELIOT 202:11
vainly men themselves a.   MARV 331:21
amazed: a., temperate, and furious
   SHAK 461:2
Silent and a. even when   WHIT 570:1
ambassador: a. is an honest man sent
   WOTT 583:18
Ambassadors: A. cropped up like hay
   GILB 225:29
amber: be prepared gold and a.   JONS 285:14
ceiling of a.   ARN 13:7
in a. to observe the forms   POPE 376:24
to lutes of a.   HERR 250:9
ambergris: Proclaim the a. on shore
   MARV 331:16
ambiguities: Till we can clear these a.
   SHAK 484:1
Ambition: A., Distraction   CARR 134:10
A. first sprung from your   POPE 376:8
A., in a private man   MASS 335:13
a. mock their useful toil   GRAY 234:21
A.'s debt is paid   SHAK 450:2
A. should be made of sterner   SHAK 450:19
a. to be a wag   JOHN 281:2
Art not without a.   SHAK 459:1
Cromwell was a man in whom a.
   BURKE 111:29
fling away a.   SHAK 447:12
Ill-weav'd a.   SHAK 440:24
lowliness is young a.'s ladder   SHAK 449:5
specimens, the lilies of a.   DOUG 191:8
that a. can creep as well   BURKE 112:9
That make a. virtue   SHAK 475:25
'tis not with a. join'd   CONG 161:3
To low a.   POPE 379:1
Vaulting a.   SHAK 459:6
was this a.   SHAK 450:20
Who doth a. shun   SHAK 425:16
Your heart's supreme a.   LYTT 321:20
ambitious: Brutus says he was a.
   SHAK 450:18
he was a.   SHAK 450:15
hunger of a. minds   SPEN 516:21
told you Caesar was a.   SHAK 450:17
would not be a. in my wish   SHAK 467:13
ambo: Arcades a.   VIRG 560:3
Amboss: *A. oder Hammer sein*   GOET 230:7
âme: grands n'ont point d'â.   LA B 306:14
Quelle â. est sans défauts   RIMB 406:8
Amelia: A. was praying for George
   THAC 545:24
amemus: atque a.   CAT 136:25
Amen: A.' Stuck in my throat   SHAK 460:7
Glorious the catholic a.   SMART 509:4
sound of a great A.   PROC 401:14
Will no man say, a.   SHAK 479:21
amenable: should be a.   MOL 353:18
amenities: meaning 'a.'   CAT 137:13
America: America! A.   BATES 35:4
A. is a country of young   EMER 208:11
A. is God's Crucible   ZANG 588:17
A. is just ourselves   ARN 15:14
A. is the only idealistic   WILS 575:3
A., thou half-brother   BAIL 29:22
A. was thus clearly top   SELL 420:8
ask not what A. will do   KENN 295:10
business of A. is business   COOL 162:11
'next to of course god a.   CUMM 170:10
O my A.   DONNE 188:16
than *whole A.*   BURKE 109:20
there is A.   BURKE 109:15
think of thee, O A.   WALP 563:10
to the discovery of A.   HELPS 244:17
You cannot conquer A.   PITT 373:27

youth of A. is their oldest   WILDE 573:26
American: A. girls turn into American
   HAMP 238:17
A. system of rugged individualism
   HOOV 255:23
except an A.   JOHN 277:30
fallen in love with A. names   BENET 40:19
I also—am an A.   WEBS 566:13
I am A. bred   MILL 340:2
I shall die an A.   WEBS 566:15
new deal for the A.   ROOS 407:19
real A. is all right   CHES 148:6
subtleties of the A. joke   TWAIN 554:12
Virginian, but an A.   HENRY 245:26
what I call the A. idea   PARK 368:26
Americanism: can be no fifty-fifty A.
   ROOS 408:6
Americans: A. on guard to-night   WASH 565:5
are A. and nothing else   ROOS 408:6
Good A.   APPL 11:13
Hyphenated A.   ROOS 408:8
when bad A. die   WILDE 573:25
worse Than ignorant A.   MASS 335:15
Amerikey: North and South A.   THAC 546:2
amet: Cras a. qui nunquam amavit
   ANON 10:11
amethyst: last an a.   BROW 97:34
amiability: found to have gained in a.
   BUTL 118:28
amiable: a. weakness   FIEL 211:28
a. words   TENN 534:12
how a. are thy dwellings   PRAY 395:11
with any thing that is a.   CONG 159:28
amiably-disposed: You're a a. young
man   DICK 182:29
amicably: a. if they can   QUIN 403:24
Amicus: A. Plato   ARIS 12:12
amiral: a. pour encourager les   VOLT 561:1
amis: de se défier de ses a.   LA R 310:10
Nos a., les ennemis   BER 41:15
amiss: All is a.   BARN 34:4
Nothing comes a.   SHAK 484:5
Nothing shall come a.   BUCK 106:18
to mark what is done a.   PRAY 398:23
amitié: L'a. de la connaissance   BUSS 117:5
l'a. ferme les yeux   ANON 9:11
ammer: 'a. along the 'ard 'igh   PUNCH 402:17
ammiral: mast Of some great A.   MILT 345:12
ammunition: pass the a.   FORGY 216:21
Amo: A., amas   OKEE 364:23
Non a. te, Sabidi   MART 331:9
Odi et a.   CAT 137:14
among: a. the English Poets after
   KEATS 294:9
how a. so many millions   BROW 96:31
What are they a. so many   BIBLE 72:4
amongst: a. you and remain with   PRAY 388:4
Amor: A. vincit omnia   CHAU 141:17
Cedet a. rebus   OVID 366:21
come a. lo strinse   DANTE 171:9
L'a. che muove il sole   DANTE 171:18
Nunc scio quid sit A.   VIRG 560:5
Omnia vincit A.   VIRG 560:8
Suprema citius solvet a.   HOR 259:21
amorem: longum subito deponere a.
   CAT 137:10
Amorites: Sehon king of the A.   PRAY 399:1
amorous: a. ditties all a summer's
   MILT 345:17
a. of their strokes   SHAK 422:2
be a., but be chaste   BYRON 124:22
court an a. looking-glass   SHAK 480:18
excite my a. propensities   JOHN 274:2
sweet reluctant a. delay   MILT 347:23
unsubstantial Death is a.   SHAK 483:31
Amour: beginning of an A.   BEHN 38:10
commencement et le déclin de l'a.
   LA B 306:13
faire l'a. en tout temps   BEAU 35:17
L'a. est aveugle   ANON 9:11

L'a.? Je le fais souvent   PROU 401:22
L'a., tel qu'il existe   CHAM 139:15
L'a. vient de l'aveuglement   BUSS 117:5
quitter L'a. de ma mie   ANON 9:17
Vive l'a.   STER 519:4
amphibii: These rational a. go   MARV 332:23
amphibious: this a. ill-born mob began
   DEFOE 173:12
Amphitrite: A.'s destined halls   SHEL 501:23
ample: cabin'd a. Spirit   ARN 14:6
from an a. nation   DICK 183:22
ampulla: meis vidi in a. pendere   PETR 373:2
ampullas: a. et sesquipedalia verba
   HOR 257:16
Amurath: Not A. an Amurath succeeds
   SHAK 442:23
amuse: is just a talent to a.   COW 163:17
Amused: be A. by its Presumption
   THUR 550:29
We are not a.   VICT 556:17
amusement: not cough for my own a.
   AUST 23:12
providing topics of a.   SWIFT 525:31
write for the general a.   SCOTT 418:10
amusements: his a., like his politics
   CHUR 149:20
tolerable but for its a.   LEWIS 314:10
amusent: anglais s'a. tristement
   SULLY 524:18
amusing: a. herself with me more
   MONT 355:2
book may be a. with numerous   GOLD 232:31
Anabaptists: A. do falsely boast   PRAY 400:12
anagram: mild a.   DRYD 196:35
Anak: sons of A.   BIBLE 48:11
Analytics: Sweet A.   MARL 329:3
anapaestic: rolling a.   BROW 98:16
Anapaests: bound the swift A. throng
   COL 157:4
anarchy: a. and competition   RUSK 412:10
a. and despotism   SHEL 505:11
a. prevails in my kitchen   JOHN 281:1
Mere a. is loosed upon   YEATS 586:15
servitude was the cure of a.   BURKE 109:30
Anathema: Let him be A. Maran-atha
   BIBLE 77:3
anatomy: eat the rest of the a.   SHAK 490:1
mere a.   SHAK 427:9
ancestors: from the wisdom of our a.
   BURKE 108:21
has his own tree of a.   STEV 521:10
look backward to what a.   BURKE 111:7
Our a. are very good kind   SHER 506:17
ancestral: a. fields with his own   HOR 259:7
ancestry: I can trace my a. back   GILB 226:20
without pride of a.   POWER 384:3
Anchises: old A. bear   SHAK 448:14
anchor: a. his aspect and die   SHAK 421:32
anchor'd: ship is a. safe and sound
   WHIT 570:8
anchored: stars is a. and the young
   FLEC 214:7
ancient: a. grudge I bear him   SHAK 465:29
a. nobility is the act   BACON 26:39
A. of days did sit   BIBLE 61:8
a. permanence which   HARDY 241:21
A. person of my heart   ROCH 407:3
A. times were the youth   BACON 25:10
ape an a. rage   CHES 147:12
both so a. and so fresh   AUG 21:16
From a. melody have ceas'd...   BLAKE 88:10
intruders on his a. home   ARN 14:21
It is an a. Mariner   COL 155:5
Time makes a. good uncouth   LOW 319:14
very a. and fish-like smell   SHAK 485:7
With the a. is wisdom   BIBLE 52:24
worlds revolve like a.   ELIOT 204:8
ancients: a. dreaded death   HARE 242:3
a. without idolatry   CHES 145:20
anders: Ich kann nicht a.   LUTH 320:16

Anderson: John A. my jo   BURNS 114:12
Andrea del Sarto: A. apears for a moment
    BEER 37:25
anecdotage: man fell into his a. it
    DISR 186:19
anfractuosities: Among the a. of the
human   JOHN 278:13
anfractuous: Paint me the bold a. rocks
    ELIOT 204:11
angat: quod in ipsis floribus a.   LUCR 320:11
Angel: A. did with Jacob   WALT 564:14
   A. of a ruin'd Paradise   SHEL 499:8
   A. of the Lord came upon   BIBLE 69:9
   A. of the Lord came down   TATE 531:22
   a. satyr walks these hills   KILV 296:7
   a. took up a stone like   BIBLE 82:24
   a. to pass, flying slowly   FIRB 212:1
   a. watching an urn   TENN 540:2
   a. writing in a book   HUNT 268:4
   beautiful and ineffectual a.   ARN 16:10
   better a. is a man right fair   SHAK 495:12
   domesticate the Recording A.   STEV 521:33
   drive an a. from your door   BLAKE 88:4
   Her a.'s face   SPEN 516:2
   in action how like an a.   SHAK 432:15
   Is man an ape or an a.   DISR 185:2
   ministering a. thou   SCOTT 417:21
   ministering a. shall my   SHAK 437:4
   more a. she   SHAK 477:11
   'ooman a Wenus or a a.   DICK 182:13
   prepared to paint an a.   BROW 102:30
   Recording A., as he wrote   STER 520:5
   reverence— That a.   SHAK 428:20
   She drew an a. down   DRYD 195:9
   sigh is the sword of an A.   BLAKE 86:6
   Though an a. should write   MOORE 356:1
   What a. wakes me from my   SHAK 470:18
   White as an a. is the English   BLAKE 88:2
   Who wrote like an a.   GARR 221:13
   woman yet think him an a.   THAC 545:7
Angeli: Non Angli sed A.   GREG 236:13
angelic: With something of a. light
    WORD 581:8
angel-infancy: Shin'd in my a.   VAUG 555:14
angel of death: a. has been abroad
throughout   BRIG 93:1
   A. spread his wings   BYRON 122:2
Angelorum: A. chori   ANON 10:14
angels: all the a. stood round   BIBLE 81:32
   A. affect us oft   DONNE 187:18
   a. all were singing out   BYRON 126:5
   A. alone, that soar above   LOV 318:18
   A. and ministers of grace   SHAK 430:24
   A. are bright still   SHAK 462:14
   A. are painted fair   OTWAY 366:4
   A. came and ministered   BIBLE 64:4
   a. heave up Sir Launcelot   MAL 328:7
   a. in some brighter dreams   VAUG 555:21
   a. of God ascending   BIBLE 46:18
   a. with outspread wings   PROU 401:23
   a. would be gods   POPE 379:7
   By that sin fell the a.   SHAK 447:12
   entertained a. unawares   BIBLE 80:3
   flights of a. sing thee   SHAK 437:28
   fools rush in where a.   POPE 378:31
   Four a. to my bed   ANON 6:15
   glittering and sparkling A.   TRAH 551:19
   God and a. to be lookers on   BACON 24:24
   Hear all ye A.   MILT 348:22
   He maketh his a. spirits   PRAY 396:18
   his a. charge over thee   PRAY 395:22
   if a. fight   SHAK 479:5
   little lower than the a.   BETJ 43:4
   madest him lower than the a.   PRAY 389:28
   make the a. weep   SHAK 464:2
   Michael and his a. fought   BIBLE 82:11
   neglect God and his A.   DONNE 191:1
   nor life, nor a.   BIBLE 75:13
   nothing to what the a. know   NEWM 362:5
   Now walk the a.   MARL 330:12

Our acts our a. are   FLET 215:13
So man did eat a.' food   PRAY 395:6
Therefore with A. and Archangels
    PRAY 387:23
   this smell of cooped-up a.   FRY 220:4
   tongues of men and of a.   BIBLE 76:14
   To thee all A. cry aloud   PRAY 384:16
   '-triumph and sorrow for a.   BROW 102:7
   'twixt air and A.' purity   DONNE 187:22
   Where a. tremble   GRAY 235:19
angel-visits: Like a.   CAMP 129:10
anger: Achilles' cursed a. sing   HOMER 253:26
   a. as the flint bears fire   SHAK 451:24
   a. in those heavenly minds   VIRG 557:9
   A. invests with such   SIDN 507:25
   A. is a short madness   HOR 258:15
   A. is never without   HAL 238:1
   A. is one of the sinews   FULL 220:17
   A. makes dull men witty   ELIZ 205:21
   either a. or zealousness   TAC 531:10
   He that is slow to a. is   BIBLE 54:9
   his a. is not turned away   BIBLE 57:27
   In the contempt and a.   SHAK 489:24
   Juno's never-forgetting a.   VIRG 557:8
   keepeth he his a. for ever   PRAY 396:16
   life of telegrams and a.   FORS 217:1
   more in sorrow than in a.   SHAK 430:11
   that you strike it in a.   SHAW 497:41
   thy mistress some rich a.   KEATS 291:15
   Touch me with noble a.   SHAK 454:2
anges: *a. aux ailes éployées*   PROU 401:23
Angevin: *l'air marin la douceur A.*
    DU B 198:27
angiportis: *Nunc in quadriviis et a.*
    CAT 137:5
anglais: *a. s'amusent tristement* SULLY 524:18
   L'A. les baisse au-dessous   TOCQ 551:8
   Les A. sont occupés   MONT 355:8
Angle: Brother of the A.   WALT 564:1
   Give me mine a.   SHAK 422:9
   Themselves in every a. greet   MARV 331:19
angler: excellent a., and now with God
    WALT 564:5
   so no man is born an a.   WALT 563:33
   that if he an honest a.   WALT 563:34
anglers: too good for any but a.   WALT 564:10
Angles: not A. but Angels   GREG 236:13
   Offer no a. to the wind   TESS 545:3
Angleterre: *L'A. est une nation de*
boutiquiers   NAP 359:15
   la perfide A.   BOSS 90:14
Anglicana: *A. ecclesia libera*   MAGN 327:1
Angling: A. is somewhat like poetry
    WALT 564:2
   A. may be said to be so   WALT 563:31
   a. or float fishing I can   JOHN 280:28
   be quiet; and go a-A.   WALT 564:13
   practiser of the art of a.   WALT 564:3
Anglo-Saxon: natural idol of the A. BAG 29:4
   those are A. attitudes   CARR 135:29
   vigour of our old A. breed   ARN 15:27
angry: a. and poor and happy   CHES 147:22
   a. at a slander makes it   JONS 283:20
   a. with a man for loving   BACON 27:8
   'a. young men' of England   FEAR 210:32
   be a. with his judgment   BROW 96:4
   Be ye a. and sin not   BIBLE 78:1
   I was a. with my friend   BLAKE 87:21
   not an a. father   CAMP 129:3
   proud and a. dust   HOUS 264:22
   that's a. with me   BROW 96:7
   When he was a.   BECK 36:19
   when she's a. she is keen   SHAK 470:24
   when very a., swear   TWAIN 554:16
anguis: *Latet a. in herba*   VIRG 559:19
anguish: a. of all sizes   HERB 248:10
   gay modulating a.   FRY 220:1
   of a solitary hidden a.   ELIOT 201:16
   To ease the a. of a torturing   SHAK 471:12
   With a. moist and fever   KEATS 290:16

Angulus: *A. ridet*   HOR 260:8
angusta: *Res a. domi*   JUV 287:18
anheling: cive, a., wipes   HOLM 253:18
anhelis: *equis Oriens adflavit a.*   VIRG 560:11
Animae: *A. dimidium meae*   HOR 259:11
   a. naturaliter Christianae   TERT 544:21
animal: a., and mineral   GILB 228:16
   Be a good a.   LAWR 311:4
   being a social a. and created
    DEM 174:19
   by nature a political a.   ARIS 12:7
   Cet a. est très méchant   ANON 9:4
   coitum omne a. triste   ANON 10:17
   constitution a religious a.   BURKE 111:18
   doubt as to a. magnetism   COL 157:34
   either some unknown a.   SWIFT 526:3
   err is human, not to, a.   FROST 219:13
   life is to be a good a.   SPEN 514:25
   Man is a noble a.   BROW 97:23
   only a. that blushes   TWAIN 554:8
   their glad a. movements   WORD 578:6
   This a. is very bad   ANON 9:4
animalculous: scientific names of beings
a.   GILB 228:16
Animals: A. are such agreeable friends
    ELIOT 201:24
   a. were created solely   PEAC 370:15
   a. will not look   AUDEN 20:17
   could turn and live with a.   WHIT 570:22
   Man didn't find the a.   NIET 363:3
animam: *Liberavi a. meam*   BERN 41:24
animate: scarce-suspected, a. the whole
    SMITH 511:14
Animosities: A. are mortal   NORTH 364:5
   dissensions and a. of mankind   BURKE 111:3
animosity: fervour of sisterly a.   SURT 525:25
animosus: *Non sine dis a. infans* HOR 260:21
Animula: *A. vagula blandula*   HADR 237:9
animum: *Caelum non a. mutant*   HOR 258:19
anise: mint and a. and cummin   BIBLE 67:24
Anjou: air the sweetness of A.   DU B 198:27
ankles: Do his weak a. swell   WORD 581:9
   One praised her a.   TENN 532:16
Ann: A., Ann   DE L 173:23
   we all know A. Livia   JOYCE 286:6
Anna: we all know A. Livia   JOYCE 286:6
Annabel Lee: I and my A.   POE 374:22
annals: a. are blank in history-books
    CARL 131:20
   simple a. of the poor   GRAY 234:21
Anne: *ma soeur A.*   PERR 372:25
   Move Queen A.   VICT 556:16
annabaptist: a. is a thing I am not FLEM 215:1
annihilate: a. but space and time POPE 380:22
Annihilating: A. all that's made MARV 332:5
Annihilation: Oblivion is a kind of A.
    BROW 95:14
anniversaries: secret a. of the heart
    LONG 317:15
Anno Domini: you shall taste my A.
    FARQ 209:22
annotate: Edit and a. the lines YEATS 586:14
announcing: a. ruin like a town crier
    THOM 546:21
annoy: He only does it to a.   CARR 133:26
annoyance: Shadow of a.   SHEL 504:22
annuity: a. is a very serious business
    AUST 23:24
annus: *monet a. et almum*   HOR 261:15
anointed: a. Solomon   BIBLE 50:30
   hast a. my head with oil   PRAY 390:22
   wash the balm from an a.   SHAK 479:5
anointing: Thou the a. Spirit art   PRAY 400:5
another: a. shall gird thee   BIBLE 73:17
   a. Troy for her to burn   YEATS 586:7
   censure or condemn a.   BROW 96:32
   fair house built upon a.   SHAK 469:9
   happiness through a. man's eyes SHAK 426:28
   love one a. or die   AUDEN 20:9
   members one of a.   BIBLE 77:29
   not spend a. such a night   SHAK 480:26
   setteth up a.   PRAY 394:26

Of candied a.   KEATS 289:20
there over me the a. tree   BARN 33:28
trees of small green a.   BETJ 43:7
when 'tis almost an a.   SHAK 488:9
With a. pie and cheese   FIELD 211:1
young and easy under the a.   THOM 547:1
apple-dumplings: pure mind who refuses
a.   LAMB 307:6
apple-pie: to make an a.   FOOTE 216:7
was an a.   ANON 4:25
apples: a., cherries   DICK 181:27
A. of gold for the king's   SWIN 530:17
comfort me with a.   BIBLE 56:21
Like to the a. on the Dead   BYRON 120:28
Moon-washed a. of wonder   DRIN 193:23
Ripe a. drop about my head   MARV 332:3
saw you picking dewy a.   VIRG 560:4
silver a. of the moon   YEATS 586:21
spoken is like a. of gold   BIBLE 54:26
stolen, be your a.   HUNT 268:11
apple-tree: My heart is like an a. ROSS 408:23
Swing up into the a.   ELIOT 203:16
applications: a. for situations   AUDEN 20:2
seulement des a. de la science   PAST 369:17
applied: such things as a. sciences
                                       PAST 369:17
apply: a. new remedies must expect
                                       BACON 26:28
a. our hearts unto wisdom   PRAY 395:20
appointed: even in the time a.   PRAY 395:9
house a. for all living   BIBLE 52:36
appointment: a. by the corrupt few
                                       SHAW 497:36
a. with a beech-tree   THOR 550:20
Every time I make an a.   LOUI 318:9
apprehend: it would but a. some joy
                                       SHAK 471:11
apprehension: a. of the good   SHAK 478:17
of death is most in a.   SHAK 464:11
apprehensions: My a. come in crowds
                                       WORD 576:23
apprentice: a. for to bind   BALL 30:8
appris: Ils n'ont rien a.   TALL 531:17
oublié et n'ont rien a.   DUM 199:7
sans avoir jamais rien a.   MOL 353:23
approach: Much of his near a. afraid
                                       GARR 221:16
snuff the a. of tyranny   BURKE 109:23
Approbation: A. from Sir Hubert Stanley
                                       MORT 358:16
approve: I do not a.   MILL 339:23
it and a. it with a text   SHAK 467:10
men of sense a.   POPE 378:24
my love doth so a. him   SHAK 476:25
which he could a.   SHEL 504:5
apricocks: thou up yon dangling a.
                                       SHAK 479:17
April: A., April   WATS 565:9
A. is the cruellest month   ELIOT 204:17
A. of your youth adorns   HERB 246:20
A.'s in the west wind   MAS 334:9
blossoming boughs of A.   BRID 92:8
Calls back the lovely A.   SHAK 492:24
England are March and A.   TROL 552:21
green hill in an A. shroud   KEATS 291:15
I've an A. blindness   FRY 219:26
Men are A. when they woo   SHAK 426:23
Now that A.'s there   BROW 101:5
sweet love seemed that A.   BRID 92:20
Three A. perfumes in three   SHAK 494:18
uncertain glory of an A. day   SHAK 490:33
When proud-pied A.   SHAK 494:18
Which spongy A. at thy   SHAK 485:19
April-fools: One of love's A.   CONG 160:18
Aprill: Whan that A. with his shoures
                                       CHAU 141:7
aprons: made themselves a.   BIBLE 45:15
apt: find myself so a. to die   SHAK 450:8
aptitude: grande a. à la patience   BUFF 106:21
greater a. for patience   BUFF 106:21

aquae: scribuntur a. potoribus   HOR 258:25
Aquitaine: prince d'A. à la tour   NERV 360:26
Arabia: all the perfumes of A.   SHAK 462:22
A. and Saba shall bring   PRAY 394:20
given of the gold of A.   PRAY 394:21
with the spell of far A.   DE L 173:26
Arabian: On the sole A. tree   SHAK 492:15
She is alone the A. bird   SHAK 428:7
wish the A. Tales were true   NEWM 361:16
Arabians: Cretes and A.   BIBLE 73:23
Arabs: like the A.   LONG 316:10
Araby: Of A. the Blest   MILT 347:17
That burns in glorious A.   DARL 171:21
Aral Sea: shine upon the A.   ARN 15:1
Aram: Eugene A. walked between
                                       HOOD 254:12
Araminta: A., say 'No   PRAED 384:4
aratro: nullo contusus a.   CAT 137:6
Arbiter: A. of others' fate   BYRON 125:8
Elegantiae a.   TAC 531:11
high a. Chance governs   MILT 347:4
arbitrary: supreme power must be a.
                                       HAL 237:19
arbitrate: Does a. th' event   MILT 341:9
who shall a.   BROW 104:7
arbitrator: that old common a.   SHAK 487:15
Arboreal: of all sits Probably A. STEV 521:10
probably a. in its habits   DARW 171:23
arbour: a. where the rain beat   ELIOT 202:16
arbours: His private a.   SHAK 451:4
arbusta: Non omnis a. iuvant humilesque
                                       VIRG 559:22
Arcades: A. ambo   VIRG 560:3
'A. ambo.' *id est*   BYRON 123:12
Arcadia: Et in A. ego   ANON 10:12
Arcadians: A. both   VIRG 560:3
arceo: Odi profanum vulgus et a.   HOR 260:13
Archangel: A. a little damaged   LAMB 307:29
Archangels: Therefore with Angels and
A.   PRAY 387:23
Archbishop: is the A. of Canterbury
                                       SMITH 511:6
Lord A. of Rheims   BARH 33:11
archdeacon: (by way of turbot) an a.
                                       SMITH 512:10
archer: a. his sharp arrows tries SIDN 507:18
mark the a. little meant   SCOTT 416:23
arches: down the a. of the years   THOM 548:8
archewyves: a., stondeth at defense
                                       CHAU 142:10
arch-flatterer: well said that 'the a.
                                       BACON 26:30
archipelagoes: fading alps and a. ALDR 3:11
Architect: aims the A. who planned
                                       WORD 582:16
a., one of the greatest   BARH 33:7
painter can be an a.   RUSK 411:8
architectooralooral: it is there drawd
too a.   DICK 178:13
architectural: respectable a. man-milliner
                                       RUSK 411:5
well knew the great a.   TROL 552:16
Architecture: A. in general is frozen
                                       SCH 415:8
frolic a. of the snow   EMER 206:24
many odd styles of a. about   RUSK 411:5
New styles of a.   AUDEN 20:7
wondrous A. of the world   MARL 330:8
archways: Of a ripple under a.   HARDY 239:18
archy: jamais triste a.   MARQ 330:21
arcs: earth the broken a.   BROW 98:18
Arcturi: pearled A. of the earth   SHEL 503:18
Arden: now am I in A.   SHAK 425:8
ardet: paries cum proximus a.   HOR 258:23
ardeur: a. dans mes veines cachée   RAC 404:4
ardor: *frío que templa el a.*   CERV 138:20
ardour: a. of my zeal repress'd   CHUR 148:22
ardua: Per a. ad astra   ANON 10:16
arduis: Aequam memento rebus in a.
                                       HOR 260:6

are: actions a. what they are   BUTL 117:10
a. strangers before thee   BIBLE 51:39
know that which we a.   BYRON 124:9
Let them be as they a.   CLEM 153:1
so very indubitably *a.*   BEER 37:23
we know what we a.   SHAK 436:1
will tell you what you a.   BRIL 93:9
arena: a. swims around him   BYRON 121:15
Arethusa: A. arose   SHEL 500:2
argent: l'a. ou de la petite monnaie
                                       CHAM 139:14
Sans a. l'honneur n'est   RAC 404:6
argifying: What's the good of a.   KIPL 304:26
Argo: loftier A. cleaves   SHEL 500:21
argosies: of magic sails   TENN 538:24
your a. with portly sail   SHAK 465:7
argue: earth does not a.   WHIT 571:11
he could a. still   GOLD 231:3
It is as absurd to a. men   NEWM 362:8
argues: heart a., not the mind   ARN 13:20
It a. an insensibility   LAMB 307:4
argufies: a. sniv'ling and piping DIBD 175:19
arguing: Be calm in a.   HERB 247:6
I am not a. with you   WHIS 569:17
in a. with the inevitable   LOW 319:18
necessity will be much a.   MILT 352:2
There is no a. with Johnson   GOLD 232:40
argument: All a. is against it   JOHN 277:21
A.'s hot to the close   BROW 102:11
heard great a.   FITZ 212:20
highth of this great a.   MILT 344:22
I have found you an a.   JOHN 279:21
is never without an a.   HAL 238:1
It is the a. of tyrants   PITT 374:3
It would be a. for a week   SHAK 438:27
love are still my a.   SHAK 494:9
nice knock-down a. for you   CARR 135:21
than the staple of his a.   SHAK 457:10
their swords for lack of a.   SHAK 444:1
This is a rotten a.   ANON 8:8
Tories own no a. but force   BROW 97:26
to stir without great a.   SHAK 435:31
Whigs admit no force but a.   BROW 97:26
argumentative: be of a studious or a.
                                       JOHN 278:21
arguments: No a. shall be wanting
                                       AUST 23:18
tongue tang a. of state   SHAK 489:15
Argus: Though A. were her eunuch
                                       SHAK 456:27
argutos: a. inter strepere anser   VIRG 560:7
Ariadne: Inconsolable to the minuet in
A.   SHER 505:26
Since A. was a vintager   KEATS 289:4
Arian: three sips the A. frustrate BROW 105:6
Ariel: Caliban casts out A.   POUND 383:6
deal of A.   HENL 245:12
aright: sought the Lord a.   BURNS 113:6
Ariosto: A. of the North   BYRON 121:5
arise: ah for a man to a. in me   TENN 540:4
a. and unbuild it again   SHEL 500:7
A. from their graves   BLAKE 87:22
A., shine   BIBLE 60:7
I will a. and go now   YEATS 585:17
Let God a.   PRAY 394:6
My lady sweet, a.   SHAK 428:10
ariseth: sun a.   PRAY 397:1
Aristocracy: A. of the Moneybag
                                       CARL 131:27
a. to what is decent   HOPE 255:29
a. the most democratic   MAC 324:16
Aristocrat: A. who banks with Coutts
                                       GILB 225:23
aristocratic: a. class from the Philistines
                                       ARN 15:19
Aristotle: A. was but the rubbish
                                       SOUTH 513:12
follow this counsel of A.   ASCH 17:4
Of A. and his philosophie   CHAU 141:24
whom A. thought   SHAK 486:30

Though a.'s hid causes   JONS 283:27
trade and half an a.   INGE 270:8
unsettling element in modern a.   WHAR 569:9
when A. Is too precise   HERR 249:2
Who first taught A.   ROSS 410:1
without a. is brutality   RUSK 411:9
works of a.   ALB 3:7
artes: a. *Intulit agresti*   HOR 259:2
didicisse fideliter a.   OVID 366:25
(Hae tibi erunt a.)   VIRG 559:1
artful: He's a.   ELIOT 202:8
Arthur: He's in A.'s bosom   SHAK 443:17
talks of A.'s death   SHAK 452:27
article: be snuff'd out by an a.   BYRON 123:32
of being the correct a.   ASHF 17:12
'What's the next a.   GILB 227:28
artifex: *Qualis a. pereo*   NERO 360:24
artificer: Another lean unwash'd a.   SHAK 452:27
great a. Made my mate   STEV 523:3
Old father, old a.   JOYCE 286:19
artificial: All things are a.   BROW 96:13
artificially: people hang together a.   BUTL 118:29
artillery: Th' a. of words   SWIFT 527:31
With the self-same a.   LOV 318:12
artisan: give employment to the a.   BELL 39:29
artist: a., like the God   JOYCE 286:18
a. never dies   LONG 316:24
a. writes his own autobiography ELLIS 206:14
grant the a. his subject   JAMES 271:13
Never trust the a.   LAWR 311:10
no man is born an a.   WALT 563:33
true a. will let his wife   SHAW 497:11
West and from now on an a.   CONN 161:16
What an a. dies with me   NERO 360:24
artistic: a. performance requires   JAMES 271:29
a. temperament is a disease   CHES 148:1
give a. verisimilitude   GILB 227:12
artistries: Eternal a. in Circumstance   HARDY 239:11
artistry: scaled invention or true a.   POUND 382:13
Art-loving: There never was an A. nation   WHIS 569:19
arts: a. into rustic Latium   HOR 259:2
cry both a. and learning   QUAR 403:21
Dear nurse of a.   SHAK 445:11
fam'd in all great a.   ARN 15:11
gentle a. which refine   DICK 177:29
had I but followed the a.   SHAK 487:26
hate for a. that caus'd   POPE 376:26
His virtues were his a.   BURKE 112:13
is the bitterness of a.   STEV 521:13
liberal a. refines behaviour   OVID 366:25
mechanical a. and merchandise   BACON 27:34
mother of a. And eloquence   MILT 350:8
No a.; no letters   HOBB 251:18
our a. with laughters low   JOYCE 286:10
therefore the lowest of the a.   MOORE 355:17
Where grew the a. of war   BYRON 122:32
artus: *dum spiritus hos regit a.*   VIRG 558:13
totamque infusa per a.   VIRG 558:24
Aryan: health to hustle the A.   KIPL 301:18
ascendant: became lord of the a.   BURKE 109:6
ascended: He a. into heaven   PRAY 384:26
ascendeth: smoke of their torment a.   BIBLE 82:17
ascending: angels of God a. and descending   BIBLE 46:18
Ascension: glorious Resurrection and A.   PRAY 385:17
ascetic: a. rocks and the sensual   MER 337:27
ascribe: a. to an opponent motives   BARR 34:9
A. unto the Lord the honour   PRAY 396:5
Ash: Oak, and A., and Thorn   KIPL 303:25
Only the A.   DE L 174:18

ashamed: are a. of our naked skins   SHAW 497:18
a. thereof   BROW 96:20
be a. to own he has been   POPE 381:19
does not make friends a.   WALT 564:6
doing something he is a.   SHAW 496:10
Hope maketh not a.   BIBLE 74:41
Let them be a. and confounded   PRAY 394:15
more things a man is a.   SHAW 497:19
Nor ever once a.   ARN 12:19
to be a. with the noble   KING 297:6
to beg I am a.   BIBLE 70:23
wonder to see them not a.   SWIFT 527:15
ashbuds: More black than a.   TENN 533:19
ashes: All a. to the taste   BYRON 120:28
Are a. under Uricon   HOUS 263:15
a. new-create another heir   SHAK 448:3
a. of an Oak in the Chimney   DONNE 190:23
a. of his fathers   MAC 322:15
a. where once I was fire   PRAY 389:13
a. where once I was fire   BYRON 125:31
from his a. may be made   TENN 536:10
into a. all my lust   MARV 332:19
little monograph on the a.   DOYLE 191:16
Scatter my a.   GRAH 233:16
sour grapes and a.   ASHF 17:14
turn the universe to a.   CEL 138:5
turn to a. on the lips   MOORE 356:26
unto them beauty for a.   BIBLE 60:9
Asia: army on the mainland of A.   MONT 355:9
churches which are in A.   BIBLE 81:9
churches which are in A.   BIBLE 81:12
It dawns in A.   HOUS 262:13
much A. and she is too old   KIPL 304:27
ye pampered Jades of A.   MARL 330:16
Asiatic: A. vague immensities   YEATS 587:1
aside: turned a. and wept   AYT 24:8
ask: all that we a. or think   BIBLE 77:26
a. amid the dews of morning   HOUS 265:10
A., and it shall be given   BIBLE 65:2
A. me no more where Jove   CAREW 130:18
A. me no more   TENN 542:13
A. the booksellers of London   BURKE 111:17
blindness we cannot a.   PRAY 388:7
greatest fool may a. more   COLT 159:9
things which we a. faithfully   PRAY 387:1
Where a. is have   SMART 509:3
you a. me for my body   SHAW 496:30
asked: I have a. to be   HOPK 256:17
Oliver Twist has a. for more   DICK 180:32
You a. for it   MOL 353:15
Askelon: not in the streets of A.   BIBLE 50:16
asketh: Every one that a. receiveth   BIBLE 65:3
asking: is the first time of a.   PRAY 388:23
offering too little and a.   CANN 129:25
asks: a. no questions isn't told   KIPL 302:22
asleep: are too young to fall a.   SASS 414:15
Fall a., or hearing die   SHAK 447:3
Got 'tween a. and wake   SHAK 453:9
he lies fast a.   FITZ 212:14
men were all a. the snow   BRID 92:12
sucks the nurse a.   SHAK 424:14
those that are a. to speak   BIBLE 57:10
very houses seem a.   WORD 581:15
Where the winds are all a.   ARN 13:6
asp: play on the hole of the a.   BIBLE 58:11
asparagus: Grew like a. in May   GILB 225:29
mention A. and it appeared   DICK 178:25
Aspect: A. anything but bland   CALV 127:14
aspens: a. quiver   TENN 538:3
Asperges: A. me   MASS 334:10
A. me hyssopo   BIBLE 83:6
aspersion: a. upon my parts of speech   SHER 506:13
aspes: a. leef she gan to quake   CHAU 144:9
asphodel: Violet, amaracus, and a.   TENN 541:18

aspiration: yearning thought And a.   ROSS 410:7
aspirations: talk to you of their a.   SMITH 510:15
aspire: be that by due steps a.   MILT 340:24
crouch whom the rest bade a.   BROW 102:6
from their graves and a.   BLAKE 87:22
light, and will a.   SHAK 495:19
aspired: I am he that a. to KNOW   BROW 103:3
aspires: All art constantly a. towards   PATER 369:20
Aspiring: A. to be angels men rebel   POPE 379:7
us all to have a. minds   MARL 330:8
ass: ashamed the law is such an a.   CHAP 140:12
a. his master's crib   BIBLE 57:15
a.'s ears of Midas   SIDN 508:5
a. when thou art present   CONG 160:22
a. will not mend his pace   SHAK 436:24
a., without being a fool   SURT 525:3
Bumble…'the law is a a.   DICK 181:2
Caesar a. Unpoliced   SHAK 424:14
jaw of an a. have I slain   BIBLE 49:24
making him egregiously an a.   SHAK 474:22
nor his a.   BIBLE 47:24
to write me down an a.   SHAK 473:5
was enamour'd of an a.   SHAK 471:6
Wild A.   FITZ 212:14
Assailant: A. on the perched roosts   MILT 350:29
assaille: a. His wyves pacience   CHAU 142:9
assassination: absolutism moderated by a.   ANON 5:5
A. has never changed   DISR 185:3
A. is the quickest way   MOL 353:24
A. is the extreme form   SHAW 498:17
if the a. Could trammel   SHAK 459:5
Assassiner: A. *c'est le plus court* MOL 353:24
assassins: *que MM les a. commencent*   KARR 288:16
assault: thoughts which may a. and hurt   PRAY 386:9
assaults: crafts and a. of the devil   PRAY 385:16
in all a. of our enemies   PRAY 385:2
assay: a. ther may no man it preve   CHAU 143:28
Th' a. so hard   CHAU 143:32
assembled: Once again a. here   BUCK 106:16
assemblies: calling of a.   BIBLE 57:17
assembly: parliament is a *deliberative* a.   BURKE 109:12
assent: a. with civil leer   POPE 376:26
asses: Death hath a.' ears   BEDD 36:27
Mankind are the a. who pull   BYRON 124:32
riches to those gross a.   LUTH 320:14
seeking a.   MILT 350:6
wild a. quench their thirst   PRAY 396:19
asshen: Yet in oure a. olde is   CHAU 143:10
assis: *Omnes unius aestimemus a.*   CAT 136:25
assistant: learned British Museum a.   POUND 383:14
me be no a. for a state   SHAK 432:3
assisted: never a. the sun   THOR 550:10
assuage: a. the unforgotten pain   ROSS 410:6
Assume: A. a virtue   SHAK 435:18
We must never a. that which   LEWES 314:7
assumed: name Achilles a.   BROW 97:14
Assumes: A. the god   DRYD 194:24
assuming: a. that he's got any   GILB 226:8
assurance: full a. given by looks   ROYD 411:2
I'll make a. double sure   SHAK 462:7
laws is the a. of incorruption   BIBLE 62:19
One of the low on whom a.   ELIOT 205:1
Assyrian: A. came down like the wolf   BYRON 122:1
oil'd and curl'd A. Bull   TENN 540:1

Assyrians: She doted upon the A. her
　　　　　　　　　　　BIBLE 60:37
Astarte: A., Queen of Heav'n　MILT 345:16
Astolat: lily maid of A.　TENN 534:25
astonish: of things that would a.　GILB 226:8
that can so a. a mother　SHAK 434:17
astonished: a. at my own moderation
　　　　　　　　　　　CLIVE 153:5
astonishment: Your a.'s odd　ANON 4:29
astra: Per ardua ad a.　ANON 10:16
sic itur ad a.　VIRG 559:8
astray: like sheep have gone a.　BIBLE 59:22
odours led my steps a.　SHEL 503:17
one that had been led a.　MILT 342:3
were as sheep going a.　BIBLE 80:27
astronomer: undeserv'd a. is mad
　　　　　　　　　　　YOUNG 588:12
astronomers: Confounding her a.
　　　　　　　　　　　HODG 252:5
astronomy: daughter of a.　YOUNG 588:12
asunder: bones are smitten a.　PRAY 392:9
let not man put a.　BIBLE 67:8
together let no man put a.　PRAY 389:6
asure: Lyk a. were his legges　CHAU 142:32
Atahualpa: who strangled A.　MAC 323:14
Atalanta: 'twas made of A.'s heels
　　　　　　　　　　　SHAK 426:11
ate: a. a good supper at night　ANST 11:7
a. his bread in sorrow　GOET 230:12
a. when we were not hungry　SWIFT 526:10
never after a. but little　MAL 328:6
With A. by his side　SHAK 450:12
Athalus: Than A.　CHAU 141:6
Athanasian: A. Creed is the most splendid
　　　　　　　　　　　DISR 186:7
atheism: honest a. for my money
　　　　　　　　　　　OTWAY 365:26
inclineth man's mind to a.　BACON 25:24
miracle to convince a.　BACON 25:23
owlet A.　COL 156:19
atheist: a. brooding and blaspheming
　　　　　　　　　　　CHES 148:7
a.-laugh's a poor exchange　BURNS 113:18
By night an a. half believes　YOUNG 588:10
here a female a. talks　JOHN 282:22
he was no a.　CHAR 140:4
is the Turk, and the A.　CHES 146:27
Rebel and A. too　DONNE 189:26
Athenaeum: A. with jugs of stout
　　　　　　　　　　　HERB 246:15
A.'', you mean　STEV 522:14
Athenians: A. and strangers which
　　　　　　　　　　　BIBLE 74:11
Athens: Another A. shall arise　SHEL 501:2
A. arose　SHEL 500:19
A. but the rudiments　SOUTH 513:12
A., Florence　INGE 270:10
A., the eye of Greece　MILT 350:8
Truths as refin'd as ever A.　ARMS 12:16
Ye men of A.　BIBLE 74:12
athirst: that is a. of the fountain　BIBLE 82:32
Atkins: Thank you, Mister A.　KIPL 303:22
Atlantic: A. Ocean beat Mrs Partington
　　　　　　　　　　　SMITH 511:32
In the steep A. stream　MILT 340:27
other side of the A.　WALP 563:9
To where the A. raves　ARN 14:21
Atlas: demi-A. of this earth　SHAK 421:31
disencumber'd A. of the state　COWP 166:16
atomic: a. bomb is a paper tiger　MAO 328:20
primordial a. globule　GILB 226:20
atomies: easy to count a.　SHAK 426:8
Atoms: A. of Democritus　BLAKE 86:24
A. or systems into ruin　POPE 379:4
fortuitous concurrence of a.　PALM 368:11
atom-streams: I saw the flaring a.
　　　　　　　　　　　TENN 539:20
atrabilious: bowl with a. liquor　HUXL 269:2
attach: Where people wish to a.　AUST 23:5

attachment: a. à la Plato for a bashful
　　　　　　　　　　　GILB 227:23
attack: dared a. my Chesterton　BELL 39:27
I shall a.　FOCH 216:3
attacked: when a. it defends itself　ANON 9:4
attain: I cannot a. unto it　PRAY 399:5
attained: Were not a. by sudden flight
　　　　　　　　　　　LONG 316:19
attainment: so disenchanting as a.
　　　　　　　　　　　STEV 521:16
attaque: Quand on l'a. il se défend ANON 9:4
attempt: a. and not the deed　SHAK 460:4
A. the end　HERR 249:19
can do that dares love a.　SHAK 482:10
fond a. to give a deathless　COWP 165:32
attempted: Something a., something
done　LONG 317:19
attend: Another to a. him　HERB 248:3
attendance: To dance a. on their lordships'
　　　　　　　　　　　SHAK 447:24
attendant: Am an a. lord　ELIOT 203:24
attendants: countenances of the a.
　　　　　　　　　　　DICK 176:11
attended: Is on his way a.　WORD 579:5
attendre: J'ai failli a.　LOUI 318:10
attention: a. of the nation is concentrated
　　　　　　　　　　　BAG 28:30
awful a. in the audience　SHER 505:25
close the Valves of her a.　DICK 183:22
serious a. than history　ARIS 12:10
attentions: a. proceed from the impulse
　　　　　　　　　　　AUST 23:13
attentive: a. and favourable hearers
　　　　　　　　　　　HOOK 255:19
sit a. to his own applause　POPE 376:27
Attic: A. shape　KEATS 291:9
A. warbler pours her throat　GRAY 235:16
A. wit　PLINY 374:17
glory of the A. stage　ARN 15:10
sleeps up in the a. there　MEW 338:12
where the A. bird　MILT 350:8
Atticus: if A. were he　POPE 376:28
attire: bride her a.　BIBLE 60:15
My Love in her a. doth　ANON 6:20
attired: suitably a. in leather　HOUS 266:9
attitudes: those are Anglo-Saxon a.
　　　　　　　　　　　CARR 135:29
attorney: gentleman was an a.　JOHN 275:35
in love with a rich a.'s　GILB 229:3
office boy to an A.'s　GILB 228:4
attorneys: ten a. find place　SMITH 510:5
Attract: A. a Silver Churn　GILB 227:24
attraction: flies feels the a. of earth
　　　　　　　　　　　LONG 316:11
attracts: commerce which now a. the
envy　BURKE 109:15
attribute: grandest moral a.　BARR 34:20
is an a. to God himself　SHAK 467:27
attributes: False are a. of speech
　　　　　　　　　　　HOBB 251:1
Auburn: Sweet A.　GOLD 230:16
auctioneer: saleroom and varnishing
a.　CARL 131:19
auctoritee: Experience though noon a.
　　　　　　　　　　　CHAU 143:16
audace: et toujours de l'a.　DANT 171:19
audacia: a. certe Laus erit　PROP 401:31
audacious: saucy and a. eloquence
　　　　　　　　　　　SHAK 471:15
audacity: Arm me, a.　SHAK 428:7
a. of elected persons　WHIT 570:14
aude: sapere a.　HOR 258:14
audendi: Quidlibet a. semper fuit　HOR 257:10
Audi: A. partem alteram　AUG 21:20
audible: a., and full of vent　SHAK 427:27
audience: a. into the middle of thi HOR 257:20
a. look to their eyes　SHAK 469:25
audit: a. The accounts later　MACN 326:6
how his a. stands who knows　SHAK 434:30

auditorem: secus ac notas a. rapit
　　　　　　　　　　　HOR 257:20
Augescunt: A. aliae gentes　LUCR 320:7
augmentation: with the a. of the Indies
　　　　　　　　　　　SHAK 490:3
augur: a. misgovernment　BURKE 109:23
He bored with his a.　BALL 31:3
Augurs: A. and understood relations
　　　　　　　　　　　SHAK 461:24
a. mock their own presage　SHAK 494:21
augury: we defy a.　SHAK 437:15
August: already yellow with A.
　　　　　　　　　　　POUND 383:17
A. for the people and their　AUDEN 18:12
To recommence in A.　BYRON 124:3
Augustan: next A. age will dawn WALP 563:9
Augustus: A. was a chubby lad　HOFF 252:11
aujourd'hui: le vivace et le bel a.
　　　　　　　　　　　MALL 327:10
auld: 'tis a. it waxeth cauld　BALL 32:10
aunt: didn't know your a.　TEMP 532:8
I had an a. in Yucatan　BELL 40:4
Until Matilda's A. succeeded　BELL 39:9
Aunt Edna: A. is universal　RATT 405:1
aunts: a., who are not married　CHES 147:26
his cousins and his a.　GILB 228:3
Auream: A. quisquis mediocritatem
　　　　　　　　　　　HOR 260:9
Auri: A. sacra fames　VIRG 558:10
Aurora: yonder shines A.'s harbinger
　　　　　　　　　　　SHAK 470:25
Aurum: A. irrepertum et sic melius
　　　　　　　　　　　HOR 260:20
ausrechnen: nicht a., was es kostet
　　　　　　　　　　　BREC 91:21
Austen: great favourite, Miss A., MITF 352:22
austere: beauty cold and a.　RUSS 412:15
knewest that I was an a. man　BIBLE 71:1
Australia: so much interested in A.
　　　　　　　　　　　WILDE 573:10
that he was born in A.　SHAW 497:5
Austria: Don John of A. is going　CHES 147:2
Don John of A. Is riding　CHES 147:3
auteur: l'esprit pour être a.　LA B 306:12
s'attendait de voir un a.　PASC 369:4
author: a. and giver of all good　PRAY 386:19
a. is concealed behind　JOHN 274:23
a. of peace and lover　PRAY 385:2
a. to get at his meaning　RUSK 411:17
a. who speaks about his　DISR 185:11
be but a shrimp of an a.　GRAY 235:25
Choose an a. as you choose　ROOS 408:10
four qualities of his a.　ARN 16:11
If it's by a good a.　SHAW 496:26
Jesus the a. and finisher　BIBLE 79:35
man were a. of himself　SHAK 427:28
next in merit to the a.　LAND 309:9
No a. ever spar'd a brother　GAY 223:12
ruin half an a.'s graces　MORE 357:9
sole a. of his own disgrace　COWP 165:13
store Of the first a.　MARV 332:17
than wit to become an a.　LA B 306:12
This is indeed to be an a.　HAZL 243:12
where is any a. in the world　SHAK 457:7
authoress: ever dared to be an a.　AUST 24:2
authorities: poison imposed by the a.
　　　　　　　　　　　PLATO 374:9
authority: are put in a. under her
　　　　　　　　　　　PRAY 387:14
A. forgets a dying king　TENN 535:22
base a. from others' books　SHAK 456:15
by the a. of an Aristotle　HOBB 251:15
Drest in a little brief a.　SHAK 464:2
Even reproofs from a. ought　BACON 26:25
Government must have an a.　RUSK 412:6
I am a man under a.　BIBLE 65:15
nor to usurp a. over　BIBLE 79:9
position than in one of a.　THOM 546:6
Rulers have no a. from　MAYH 336:6
taught them as one having a.　BIBLE 65:13

601

Authorized: 'A. Version' of the Bible
                                            WHAT 569:15
authors: been much exposed to a.
                                            WELL 567:29
English a. their copyrights   TROL 552:12
people arises from its a.   JOHN 281:10
reciprocal civility of a.   JOHN 281:29
So let great a. have their   BACON 24:15
They damn those a. whom   CHUR 148:19
We a.   DISR 185:24
authorship: reputation of popular a.
                                            TROL 553:14
autobiography: artist writes his own
a.   ELLIS 206:14
autocrate: je serai a.   CATH 136:17
Autolycus: My father named me A.
                                            SHAK 491:18
automne: violons De l'a.   VERL 556:8
autres: ce sont les a.   REN 405:10
l'Enfer, c'est les A.   SART 414:8
pour encourager les a.   VOLT 561:1
autumn: a. and of winter cometh
                                            CLARE 152:16
a. and the falling fruit   LAWR 311:8
a. evening   ARN 14:8
A. evening   SHEL 503:26
a. in the mind   SPAR 514:22
A. nodding o'er the yellow   THOM 549:15
A. sunsets exquisitely   HUXL 269:1
a. was That grew the more   SHAK 423:22
a., what our golden harvests   DONNE 188:9
I saw old A. in the misty   HOOD 255:1
leaves fall early this a.   POUND 383:17
melancholy A. comes to Wembley
                                            BETJ 42:16
springs to yellow a. turn'd   SHAK 494:18
there is a harmony In a.   SHEL 501:7
This a. morning   BROW 101:20
thou breath of A.'s being   SHEL 502:8
traveller's joy beguiles in a.   HOUS 265:9
when the mists in a.   KING 297:21
autumnal: deep, a. tone   SHEL 502:13
have seen in one A. face   DONNE 188:7
autumn-evenings: When the long dark
a. come   BROW 99:17
Autumn-fields: looking on the happy
A.   TENN 542:2
Auxiliary: I was undone by my A.
                                            STEE 518:14
avails: a. the sceptred race   LAND 308:26
Avarice: A., the spur of industry
                                            HUME 267:16
beyond the dreams of a.   JOHN 278:27
beyond the dreams of a.   MOORE 355:14
I must take up with a.   BYRON 122:15
low drudgery of a.   BURKE 108:7
Avatar: In Vishnu-land what A. BROW 105:33
avaunt: Conscience a.   CIBB 151:13
ave: a. atque vale   CAT 137:15
A. Caesar   ANON 10:7
A. Maria   ANON 10:8
A. verum corpus   ANON 10:9
With an *A. Mari*   SKEL 508:19
Ave Maria: A.! 'tis the hour of prayer
                                            BYRON 123:8
Avenge: A., O Lord   MILT 351:9
avenger: enemy, and the a.   PRAY 389:28
you a. someone   VIRG 558:15
averages: fugitive from th' law of a.
                                            MAUL 336:5
Averno: Facilis descensus A.   VIRG 558:18
aversion: begin with a little a. SHER 506:9
closely bordering on a.   STEV 521:17
manner which is my a.   BYRON 123:6
avert: May the gods a. this omen CIC 151:29
aveugle: L'amour est a.   ANON 9:11
aveuglement: L'amour vient de l'a.
                                            BUSS 117:5
Avilion: island-valley of A.   TENN 535:27
avis: Rara a. in terris nigroque   JUV 287:20

avoid: a. what is to come   SHAK 435:15
avoiding: superstition in a. superstition
                                            BACON 27:22
Avon: Sweet Swan of A.   JONS 284:25
where lucid A. stray'd   GRAY 235:18
awaÿ: 'a said an' I coom'd a.   TENN 541:3
awaiting: a. instructions Jellings BEER 38:2
A. the sensation of a short   GILB 226:31
Awake: A., beloved   LONG 317:13
A., my heart   BRID 92:7
A., O north wind   BIBLE 56:29
Being now a.   SHAK 492:5
clamour keep her still a.   SHAK 484:11
England!   BLAKE 86:11
myself will a. right early   PRAY 393:16
They shall a. as *Jacob* did   DONNE 191:3
use its guard staying a.   BIBLE 83:12
We're very wide a.   GILB 226:32
which I am trying to a.   JOYCE 286:23
will he lie ten nights a.   SHAK 472:14
awaked: must be a.   BIBLE 51:9
So the Lord a. as one out   PRAY 395:7
aware: infant child is not a.   HOUS 266:11
made a.   BROO 94:30
away: a.! for I will fly   KEATS 291:20
A. from me   PRAY 389:27
a. his fellows fly   SHAK 470:20
A. we both must hie   HOUS 265:12
black night doth take a.   SHAK 494:7
get a. from earth awhile   FROST 219:1
keep a week a.   SHAK 476:6
kiss, a sigh, and so a.   CRAS 169:14
they get them a. together   PRAY 397:1
To get the Men to go a.   BELL 39:9
awe: a. into the beholders   SWIFT 526:1
Exempt from a.   SHEL 503:12
eye whose bend doth a.   SHAK 448:15
in a., and sin not   PRAY 389:20
In a. of such a thing   SHAK 448:13
increasing wonder and a.   KANT 288:8
pity and mournful a.   ARN 13:8
to keep the strong in a.   SHAK 481:17
aweary: Cassius is a. of the world
                                            SHAK 451:23
'gin to be a. of the sun   SHAK 463:7
'I am a.   TENN 539:24
my little body is a.   SHAK 465:18
awf'lly: It's a. bad luck on Diana BETJ 42:21
awful: this is an a. place   SCOTT 415:17
awkward: a. squad fire over me   BURNS 116:9
awry: at me for leaning all a.   FITZ 213:10
be gone as one shaped a.   HARDY 240:3
axe: a. is laid unto the root   BIBLE 63:39
a.'s edge did try   MARV 332:9
head off with a golden a.   SHAK 483:10
Lizzie Borden took an a.   ANON 6:12
offence is let the great a.   SHAK 436:15
owner of the a.   THOR 550:4
then the a. to the root   PAINE 368:4
axes: you your sharp-edged a.   WHIT 570:10
Axioms: A. in philosophy are not
                                            KEATS 293:30
axis: a. of the earth sticks   HOLM 253:16
soft under-belly of the A.   CHUR 150:13
axle: His glowing a. doth allay MILT 340:27
axletree: a. of the chariot-wheel BACON 27:33
Ay: it stinted and said 'A.   SHAK 481:27
Aye: Charybdis of A. and No   NEWM 361:21
Ayr: Auld A.   BURNS 115:4
Azores: At Flores in the A. Sir TENN 542:21
Azure: A. hath a canker by usura
                                            POUND 382:11
a. sister of the spring   SHEL 502:8
outdares Stokes in a. feats   BROW 103:27
azure-lidded: still she slept an a. sleep
                                            KEATS 289:20
B: B. bit it   ANON 4:25
Baa: B.! Baa   KIPL 299:10
babblative: arts b. and scribblative
                                            SOUT 514:12

babble: learned b. of the saleroom
                                            CARL 131:19
babbled: a' b. of green fields   SHAK 443:17
babbler: What will this b. say   BIBLE 74:10
Babe: B. all burning bright did SOUT 514:19
B. leaps up on his Mother's   WORD 579:4
Come little b.   BRET 92:6
Finger of birth-strangled b.   SHAK 462:4
Hath laid her B. to rest   MILT 344:15
if my young b. were born   BALL 32:11
like a naked new-born b.   SHAK 459:6
love the b. that milks   SHAK 459:10
to bring the b. to rest   EDW 200:5
Babel: bother at the tower of B. VOLT 561:13
babes: mouth of very b. and sucklings
                                            PRAY 389:28
newborn b.   BIBLE 80:22
babies: bit the b. in the cradles BROW 103:15
hates dogs and b.   ROST 410:14
than putting milk into b.   CHUR 150:15
Bab-lock-hithe: stripling Thames at B.
                                            ARN 14:14
baboon: Into b. and monkey   SHAK 486:1
baby: b. beats the nurse   SHAK 463:11
b. boy   VIRG 560:1
b. fell a-thinking   HARDY 241:1
b. figure of the giant   SHAK 486:27
B. in an ox's stall   BETJ 42:8
first b. laughed   BARR 34:13
great b. you see there   SHAK 432:19
not see my b. at my breast   SHAK 424:14
till he was showed the b.   DICK 179:27
With his b. on my knee   KING 296:17
Babylon: B. in all its desolation DAV 172:13
B. is fallen   BIBLE 82:16
B.! O Carthage   SASS 415:4
B. THE GREAT   BIBLE 82:23
B. we sit down and weep   WALP 563:10
Ere B. was dust   SHEL 502:19
great city B. be thrown down   BIBLE 82:24
I was a King in B.   HENL 245:10
waters of B. we sat   PRAY 399:3
Babylonian: jargon of their B. pulpits
                                            BURKE 111:6
Babylons: all man's B. strive   THOM 548:7
bacchanal: me now with the b. sign
                                            YOUNG 588:5
Bacchus: B. ever fair   DRYD 194:25
dainty B. gross in taste   SHAK 457:8
Not charioted by B.   KEATS 291:20
Of B. and his revellers   MILT 348:29
Pan by noon and B. by night   SWIN 528:18
Baccy: 'B. for the Clerk   KIPL 302:22
Bach: By B.   GILB 227:6
bachelor: b. of three-score again SHAK 472:1
facts that you are a b.   DOYLE 192:14
I said I would die a b.   SHAK 472:19
pleasant dining with a b.   GASK 222:2
bachelors: All reformers are b.
                                            MOORE 355:15
reasons for b. to go out   ELIOT 201:20
Two old B. were living   LEAR 312:23
back: at my b. from time to time
                                            ELIOT 204:27
B. and side go bare   ANON 5:21
b. to the shop Mr John   LOCK 315:22
bolt is shot b.   ARN 12:22
borne me on his b.   SHAK 436:31
by thumps upon your b.   COWP 165:9
come b., Horatius   MAC 322:20
I sit on a man's b.   TOLS 551:15
lean'd my b. unto an aik   BALL 32:10
looking b.   BIBLE 69:25
never turned his b.   BROW 98:32
one by one b. in the Closet   FITZ 213:5
plowers plowed upon my b.   PRAY 398:22
rider on so proud a b.   SHAK 495:20
stamp me b. to common   FITZ 213:12
them to the b. o' beyont   SCOTT 418:1
there's no turning b.   ROSS 408:22

think that he'll come b. KIPL 301:15
wife looked b. BIBLE 46:8
will b. the masses against GLAD 229:17
backbiter: Face-flatterer and b. are
TENN 535:17
backbone: Alps shaping like a b.
HARDY 239:13
b. of the Army is the Non-commissioned
KIPL 298:22
backgammon: I ever mastered was b.
JERR 273:13
background: landscape but a b. AUDEN 19:16
backing: always b. into the limelight
BERN 42:1
plague upon such b. SHAK 438:35
backs: making the beast with two b.
SHAK 473:18
Our b. is easy ris DICK 179:18
when maids lie on their b. SHAK 481:28
With our b. to the wall HAIG 237:11
backward: drew me b. by the hair
BROW 98:9
I by b. steps would move VAUG 555:17
let them be turned b. PRAY 394:15
look b. to their ancestors BURKE 111:7
Thames flowed b. to its PLOM 374:19
Thou wilt fall b. when SHAK 481:27
backwards: memory that only works
b. CARR 135:16
bacon: b.'s not the only thing KING 297:20
b. was nat fet for hem CHAU 143:18
Unless you give him b. CHES 146:26
bacons: On, b., on SHAK 438:26
bad: b., and dangerous to know LAMB 306:25
b. die late DEFOE 173:2
b. end unhappily STOP 523:18
B. laws are the worst sort BURKE 110:20
b. news infects the teller SHAK 421:16
b.'s the best of us FLET 215:10
B. Thing SELL 420:8
because we put up with b. TROL 553:2
being a little b. SHAK 465:6
bold b. man SHAK 447:1
bold b. man SPEN 516:1
Defend the b. against DAY-L 172:23
find the world ugly and b. NIET 363:8
good ye are and b. TENN 534:17
her badness when she's b. BARR 34:17
it's always a b. sign MITF 352:25
never so good or so b. MACK 325:11
nothing either good or b. SHAK 432:12
Persecution is a b. BROW 96:16
sad and b. and mad BROW 100:8
sad b. glad SWIN 529:2
shocking b. hats in my life WELL 567:22
so much b. in the best ANON 8:2
such thing as b. weather RUSK 412:14
This animal is very b. ANON 9:4
To bring b. news SHAK 422:12
To make b. good SHAK 464:22
was not really b. at heart BELL 39:12
When b. men combine BURKE 108:22
bade: b. betwixt their shores ARN 13:13
crouch whom the rest b. aspire BROW 102:6
badge: b. of pusillanimity SHAK 442:15
sufferance is the b. SHAK 466:2
badgers: When b. fight then everyone's
CLARE 152:3
badly: it is worth doing b. CHES 148:10
badness: To the b. of her badness BARR 34:17
baffled: b., get up and begin again
BROW 102:1
matter is not easily b. BAG 28:31
bag: b. and baggage GLAD 229:13
eggs inside a paper b. ISH 270:27
not with b. and baggage SHAK 426:6
wages to put it into a b. BIBLE 62:2
bagatelle: et vive la b. STER 519:4
baggage: believe the b. loves me
CONG 160:17

bagpipe: when the b. sings i' SHAK 467:21
Baiae: Beside a pumice isle in B.'s
SHEL 502:10
bailiff: b.'s daughter of Islington BALL 30:9
loved the b.'s daughter BALL 30:7
baille: Le désespoir b. HUGO 267:12
Bainters: hate all Boets and B. GEOR 223:34
bait: swallow'd b. SHAK 495:7
trout for factitious b. POUND 383:2
baits: while good news b. MILT 350:28
baked: 'You have b. me too brown
CARR 134:16
baker: b. rhymes for his pursuit BROW 105:4
Bakers: B. and brewers LANG 309:26
Baker Street: B. irregulars DOYLE 192:32
Bakewell: valley between Buxton and
B. RUSK 411:13
balaiera: salut b. largement le seuil
ROST 410:12
balance: at the b. let's be mute BURNS 112:26
b. of power WALP 563:27
In b. with this life YEATS 585:15
small dust of the b. BIBLE 59:8
uncertain b. of proud time GREE 236:9
weigh thy words in a b. BIBLE 63:12
balanced: I b. all YEATS 585:15
balances: Thou art weighed in the b.
BIBLE 61:6
balanza: b. y peso que iguala al CERV 138:20
Balbec: editions of B. and Palmyra
WALP 563:9
bald: b. and unconvincing narrative
GILB 227:12
bare mountain tops are b. ARN 16:7
If I were fierce and b. SASS 414:10
respectable b. heads YEATS 586:14
thou b. head BIBLE 51:24
we found him b. too BROW 100:35
baldheaded: Go into it b. LOW 319:5
baldness: felicity on the far side of b.
SMITH 510:13
with a b. full of grandeur ARN 16:7
bales: beach undid his corded b. ARN 14:21
dropping down with costly b. TENN 538:24
Balkans: damned silly thing in the B.
BISM 84:26
ball: at a girl throwing a b. WOOLF 576:19
B. no question makes FITZ 213:6
Only wind it into a b. BLAKE 86:8
peck cautiously at the b. WOD 575:24
real business of a b. SURT 525:24
Ruddy B. has taken flight THOM 549:2
Urge the flying b. GRAY 235:10
ballad: b. of Sir Patrick Spence COL 156:6
I love a b. in print SHAK 492:3
I met with a b. CALV 127:10
very guilty of such a b. SHAK 456:18
ballad-mongers: of these same metre
b. SHAK 439:25
ballads: b., songs and snatches GILB 226:18
better than all the b. LONG 316:8
permitted to make all the b. FLET 215:6
ballet: b. of bloodless categories BRAD 91:10
Balliol: B. made me BELL 40:14
balloon: moon's a b. CUMM 170:8
something in a huge b. WORD 579:18
balloons: Are light as b. FROST 219:4
ballot: b. is stronger than LINC 314:13
balls: elliptical billiard b. GILB 227:7
our rackets to these b. SHAK 443:11
two pitch b. SHAK 456:27
Ballyhoo: variants from Builth to B.
KIPL 302:4
Balm: B. of hurt minds SHAK 460:8
b. th'hydroptic earth hath DONNE 189:28
Can wash the b. from SHAK 479:5
Is there no b. in Gilead BIBLE 60:21
our calm is in that b. NORT 364:8
out a b. upon the world KEATS 289:28
wept odorous gums and b. MILT 347:19

baloney: it's still b. SMITH 510:3
Balzac: All B.'s novels occupy BROW 99:3
bamboo: *Under the b. tree* ELIOT 204:13
bamboozle: to understand I would b.
GREE 236:7
banal: *Eldorado b. de tous les vieux*
BAUD 35:8
Banbury: To B. came BRAT 91:24
band: captain of this ruin'd b. SHAK 444:10
heaven-born b. HOPK 257:8
high aesthetic b. GILB 227:23
stormy sturdy b. HARDY 240:16
we b. of brothers SHAK 445:3
when the wearied B. HUXL 268:22
bandaged: death b. my eyes BROW 103:32
bands: drew them...with b. of love
BIBLE 61:12
loose the b. of Orion BIBLE 53:5
loose the b. of wickedness BIBLE 60:4
Bandusiae: *fons B. splendidior vitro*
HOR 261:3
bandy: b. civilities with my Sovereign
JOHN 275:20
Would not have b. children BLAKE 87:20
bane: Deserve the precious b. MILT 346:1
thou b. of the most generous GRAN 234:7
bang: b. these dogs of Seville TENN 543:1
b.—went sixpence PUNCH 387:6
with a b. but a whimper ELIOT 203:11
banged: b. the youth into dumbness
SHAK 489:18
banish: b. not him thy Harry's SHAK 439:18
b. plump Jack and banish SHAK 439:18
Everything did b. moan BARN 33:32
I b. you SHAK 427:23
banish'd: constant Cimber should be
b. SHAK 449:25
banished: b. man BALL 31:10
brother by decree is b. SHAK 449:24
from which success is b. STEV 521:1
my wilful crime art b. hence MILT 349:28
banishing: worst effect is b. for hours
COWP 165:4
banishment: bitter bread of b. SHAK 479:4
bank: Along a shelving b. of turf SHEL 503:17
b. and shoal of time SHAK 459:5
contemplate an entangled b. DARW 171:28
cried all the way to the b. LIB 314:11
George goes to sleep at a b. JER 272:24
moonlight sleeps upon this b. SHAK 468:15
pregnant b. swelled up DONNE 188:21
Banker: thought he saw a B.'s Clerk
CARR 133:13
Bankrupt: B. of life DRYD 194:7
banks: b. and braes o' bonny Doon
BURNS 116:6
letters from b. AUDEN 20:2
Thy b. with pioned SHAK 485:19
banned: that any book should be b.
WEST 569:2
banner: b. wav'd without a blast
SCOTT 416:14
b. with the strange device LONG 316:14
Freedom's b. streaming DRAKE 193:5
His b. over me was love BIBLE 56:20
'Tis the star-spangled b. KEY 295:14
yet thy b. BYRON 121:11
banners: all thy b. wave CAMP 128:22
b. of the king advance VEN 556:5
Hang out our b. SHAK 463:4
terrible as an army with b. BIBLE 57:5
banquet: Corpses are set to b. POUND 382:11
trifling foolish b. towards SHAK 482:3
banqueting: beggar by b. upon borrowing
BIBLE 63:6
banter: how does fortune b. us BOL 89:13
Baptism: B., and the Supper PRAY 388:19
Godmothers in my B. PRAY 388:12
that B. be administered PRAY 388:8
baptize: I b. with water BIBLE 71:29

bar: Back of the b.   SERV 420:14
  b. in Lower Thames Street   ELIOT 205:4
  b. of the Black Badger   DICK 177:29
  be no moaning of the b.   TENN 533:3
  door and b. for thy mouth   BIBLE 63:12
  Get up and b. the door   BALL 31:1
  his birth's invidious b.   TENN 537:1
  Mute at the b.   CHUR 149:5
  When I have crost the b.   TENN 533:4
  When I went to the B.   GILB 226:6
Barabbas: At least we withstand B.
      BROW 101:4
  Now B. was a robber   BIBLE 72:45
  Now B. was a publisher   CAMP 129:15
barajar: paciencia y b.   CERV 138:18
Barbara: mother had a maid call'd B.
      SHAK 476:26
Barbara Allen: Her name was B.   BALL 30:10
barbares: temps b. et gothiques   FRAN 217:27
Barbarian: B., Scythian   BIBLE 78:26
  He is a b.   SHAW 496:9
barbarians: become of us without any
  b.   CAV 137:17
  Greeks, and to the B.   BIBLE 74:30
  his young b. all at play   BYRON 121:16
  in my own mind *the B.*   ARN 15:19
  with the B. quite left   ARN 15:14
barbaric: b. yawp over the roofs   WHIT 571:6
barbarisms: clear it from colloquial b.
      JOHN 282:5
barbarity: act with the b. of tyrants
      SMITH 511:30
barbarous: air with b. dissonance
      MILT 341:13
  invention of a b. age   MILT 344:18
  me with the b. multitude   SHAK 466:19
  This b. philosophy   BURKE 111:11
barbarousness: must confess mine own
  b.   SIDN 508:3
barbe: laisserons pousser notre b.
      FLAU 214:2
barber: b.'s chair that fits all   SHAK 420:29
  has known the b.'s shear   THAC 545:31
  I must to the b.'s   SHAK 471:2
Barbiton: B. hic paries habebit   HOR 261:6
bard: blame not the b.   MOORE 356:14
  Hear the voice of the B.   BLAKE 87:13
  he was the wisest b.   BEHN 38:11
  If the B. was weatherwise   COL 156:6
  more fat than b. beseems   THOM 549:9
Bardolph: banish B.   SHAK 439:18
Bards: B. of Passion and of Mirth
      KEATS 290:31
  last of all the B. was he   SCOTT 416:9
  worst of b. confessed   CAT 137:9
bare: Back and side go b.   ANON 5:21
  b. mountain tops are bald   ARN 16:7
  B. ruin'd choirs   SHAK 494:9
  beauty and love lay b.   SHEL 503:23
  they b. children to them   BIBLE 45:33
  Though I go b.   ANON 5:21
barefac'd: bore him b. on the bier
      SHAK 436:9
barefoot: b. friars were singing   GIBB 224:16
  makes shoes go b. himself   BURT 116:16
bareness: old December's b.   SHAK 494:16
bargain: b. dog never bites   NASH 360:3
  dateless b. to engrossing death   SHAK 483:31
  fond of her most filthy b.   SHAK 477:13
  Necessity never made a good b.   FRAN 218:8
  never was a better b. driv'n   SIDN 507:16
bargains: b., and my well-won thrift
      SHAK 465:29
barge: b. she sat   SHAK 422:2
Baring: taken by Rothschild and B.
      GILB 226:16
bark: come out as I do, and *b.*   JOHN 279:3
  fatal and perfidious b.   MILT 343:10
  my b. is on the sea   BYRON 125:32
  spirit like a charmed b.   SHEL 500:16

star to every wandering b.   SHAK 495:5
  That dogs b. at me   SHAK 480:18
  they b. at me   SHAK 454:29
  they don't b.   NERV 361:1
  Though his b. cannot be   SHAK 458:7
  yond tall anchoring b.   SHAK 455:14
  You Heard a Seal B.   THUR 550:31
Barkis: B. is willin'   DICK 176:31
barley: fields of b. and of rye   TENN 538:2
  In among the bearded b.   TENN 538:5
  Sitting on a heap of B.   LEAR 312:5
Barleycorn: John B. should die
      BURNS 114:13
Barlow: my Hornby and my B.   THOM 547:24
barmaid: Bitter b., waning fast   TENN 544:6
barmie: b. noddle's working prime
      BURNS 113:23
barn: from the b. and the forge   HOUS 263:6
barnacles: b., or to apes   SHAK 485:22
barn-cocks: Ere the b. say   HARDY 240:8
barns: nor gather into b.   BIBLE 64:28
Baronetage: up any book but the B.
      AUST 23:7
baronets: All b. are bad   GILB 228:30
  there were b. by dozens   GILB 225:10
Barons: rust of the B.' Wars   WALP 562:24
barouche-landau: They will have their
  b.   AUST 22:16
Barrack: B. and bivouac shall be
      AUDEN 19:11
barred: spot that's always b.   GILB 227:7
barrel: b. of Malmesey wine within
      FABY 209:17
  handful of meal in a b.   BIBLE 51:7
barrel-load: save them by the b.
      THOM 548:26
barrel-organ: was a kind of human b.
      DICK 177:24
barreltone: base b. voice   JOYCE 286:26
barren: b. and dry land where no
      PRAY 393:21
  b. sister all your life   SHAK 469:17
  b. superfluity of words   GARTH 221:21
  b. woman to keep house   PRAY 397:15
  city is b.   DICK 176:17
  Close up these b. leaves   WORD 582:23
  I am but a b. stock   ELIZ 205:20
  Make b. our lives   SWIN 529:10
  none is b. among them   BIBLE 56:26
  'tis all b.   STER 519:2
  underneath the b. bush   TENN 537:9
barricade: At some disputed b.   SEEG 419:15
barricades: Christs that die upon the
  b.   WILDE 572:17
barrier: b. against matrimony which
      KEATS 294:10
barring: b. of the door   BALL 30:21
barrow: b. and the camp abide   KIPL 303:12
  red wheel b.   WILL 574:10
barrows: grassy b. of the happier dead
      TENN 543:13
bars: Between their silver b.   FLEC 214:21
  out through the same b.   LANG 309:21
  weary of these worldly b.   SHAK 449:3
barton: lonely b. by yonder coomb
      HARDY 240:14
barty: Hans Breitmann gife a b.   LEL 313:16
Basan: fat bulls of B.   PRAY 390:18
  Og the king of B.   PRAY 399:1
base: b. and ignoble creature   BACON 25:25
  b. barreltone voice   JOYCE 286:26
  b., common and popular   SHAK 444:16
  b. old man   FRY 219:28
  keep down the b. in man   TENN 534:12
  Labour without joy is b.   RUSK 412:3
  scarlet Majors at the B.   SASS 414:10
  scorning the b. degrees   SHAK 449:5
  Things b. and vile   SHAK 469:22
  To what b. uses we may   SHAK 437:1
  wherefore b.   SHAK 453:9

Base-born: B. products of base beds
      YEATS 587:8
baseless: b. fabric of this vision   SHAK 485:20
basely: To spend that shortness b.
      SHAK 440:19
baseness: child of ignorance and b.
      BACON 25:31
baser: I give to b. life   SHAK 424:11
  lewd fellows of the b.   BIBLE 74:8
bashful: never laughed, being b.
      POUND 383:16
  Plato for a b. young potato   GILB 227:23
bashfulness: England a particular b.
      ADD 2:21
basia: Da mi b. mille   CAT 136:26
basically: b. I'm viable from ten   BETJ 42:14
Basil: over her sweet B. evermore
      KEATS 290:11
basilisk: That b. is sure to kill   GAY 222:30
Basil-pot: 'To steal my B. away from
      KEATS 290:12
basin: Holding the b. to gowned   MACN 326:9
  stare in the b.   AUDEN 18:10
Basingstoke: hidden meaning—like B.
      GILB 228:36
bask: b. in Heaven's blue smile   SHEL 500:5
baskets: that remained twelve b.   BIBLE 66:24
basking: loves to lie a-b. in the sun
      GILB 228:21
bason: tip up b. and a hose   ASHF 17:8
Basques: Scalinger used to say of the
  B.   CHAM 139:16
Bass: Guinness, Allsopp, B.   CALV 127:12
Bassarid: Maenad and the B.   SWIN 528:18
bassoon: he heard the loud b.   COL 155:8
bass-viol: Ye mid burn the old b.
      HARDY 239:19
bastard: getter of more b. children
      SHAK 427:27
  Why b.   SHAK 453:9
bastardizing: firmament twinkled on
  my b.   SHAK 453:11
bastards: he who begets twenty b.
      WALP 563:12
  stand up for b.   SHAK 453:10
  Which some call nature's b.   SHAK 491:23
bastion: like a b.'s mole   SMART 509:3
bat: b. that flits at close   BLAKE 85:11
  black b., night   TENN 540:9
  Ere the b. hath flown   SHAK 461:13
  I march with b. and pad   HOUS 262:22
  On the b.'s back I do   SHAK 485:25
  squeak of a b.   FORS 217:8
  where the weak-ey'd b.   COLL 158:1
  Wool of b.   SHAK 462:3
batailled: b. as it were a castle   CHAU 142:32
bataillons: n'est pas pour les gros b.
      VOLT 561:18
batallions: side not of the heavy b.
      VOLT 561:18
batchelor: old b. don't die at all
      WARD 564:30
bated: With b. breath   SHAK 466:3
bath: b. room has got a tip up   ASHF 17:8
  can ever be tired of the b.   AUST 23:3
  nymph to the b. addressed   SHEL 503:23
  soaping her breasts in the b.   EWART 209:11
  sore labour's b.   SHAK 460:8
bathe: b. those beauteous feet   FLET 215:29
  to b. in reeking wounds   SHAK 458:4
bathing: b. machine and a very small
      GILB 226:13
  b. of a summer's day   WORD 580:7
  Gentleman caught the Whigs b.   DISR 184:14
Bath-rabbim: by the gate of B.   BIBLE 57:9
baths: b. Of all the western stars   TENN 544:3
  Having b. in Camden Town   BETJ 42:6
  Two walking b.   CRAS 169:12
bâtir: c'est b. la mort   MONT 354:15
baton: b. of a marshal of France   NAP 359:9

bats: are like b. amongst birds BACON 27:23
...Do b. eat cats CARR 133:15
Flittering b. JOYCE 286:8
batsman: b. plays to the bowling THOM 547:24
if the b. thinks he's bowled LANG 309:19
swift B. of the Dawn has THOM 549:2
battaglie: b. e morte GAR 221:10
batten: b. on this moor SHAK 435:7
Battening: B. upon huge seaworms TENN 537:25
Batter: B. my heart DONNE 189:8
battle: Agreed to have a b. CARR 134:33
at Sheriffmuir A b. there was MCL 325:15
b., a big one LIVY 315:12
B., and the loves of men HOUS 265:4
b. fares like to the morning's SHAK 446:17
b. goes sore against us STEV 520:26
better in b. than in bed STER 520:3
brave that die in the b. CLOU 153:13
day long the noise of b. TENN 535:20
die well that die in a b. SHAK 444:21
drunk delight of b. with TENN 543:22
Each b. sees the other's SHAK 444:9
first blow is half the b. GOLD 232:27
forefront of the hottest b. BIBLE 50:19
foremost in b. was Mary Ambree BALL 31:8
from b. and murder PRAY 385:16
he smelleth the b. afar BIBLE 53:7
into the midst of the b. VIRG 558:7
Lord mighty in b. PRAY 390:24
misfortune to losing a b. WELL 567:25
next to a b. lost WELL 567:27
nor the b. to the strong BIBLE 55:30
Nor war, nor b.'s sound MILT 344:6
of the b. in the glorious VEN 556:4
prepare himself to the b. BIBLE 76:15
See the front o' b. lour BURNS 114:34
That beat to b. where he TENN 542:7
that it is a field of b. STEV 521:31
they make them ready to b. PRAY 398:8
to feats of broil and b. SHAK 473:24
trumpets which sing to b. SHEL 505:13
When the b.'s lost SHAK 458:1
battle-bolt: rushing b. sang from TENN 539:26
Battledore: B. and shuttlecock's DICK 181:34
battle-flags: b. were furl'd TENN 538:24
battlements: b. it sees MILT 342:20
came and perched on b. BEER 38:2
fix'd his head upon our b. SHAK 458:3
From the hid b. of Eternity THOM 548:20
battles: b. and death GAR 221:10
b. are lost in the same WHIT 570:20
b. long ago WORD 578:14
b., sieges, fortunes SHAK 473:25
God of b. SHAK 444:26
that I have fought his b. BUNY 107:38
three pitched b. in India MAC 324:23
bauble: Pleas'd with this b. still POPE 379:19
Take away that fool's b. CROM 169:25
Baum: grün des Lebens goldner B. GOET 230:3
bavin: shallow jesters and rash b. SHAK 439:34
bawcock: king's a b. SHAK 444:17
bawd: Now my old b. is dead YEATS 585:16
bawdy: Bloody, b. villain SHAK 433:4
bawdy-house: pretence of keeping a b. JOHN 278:18
bawl: bang and roar and b. BELL 39:28
bawling: b. what it likes ARN 15:20
bay: b. the moon SHAK 451:14
He stands at b. THOM 549:19
baying: families b. for broken WAUGH 565:29
bayonets: Chains are worse than b. JERR 273:11
himself a throne of b. INGE 270:9
sods with our b. turning WOLFE 576:3
bays: b. burn deep and chafe SWIN 530:3
Have I no b. to crown it HERB 247:14

sprig of b. in fifty years SWIFT 527:33
bay-tree: flourishing like a green b. PRAY 391:29
be: b. rather than to seem SALL 413:24
b. the people never so PRAY 396:10
b. what they behold POPE 375:11
is that which shall b. BIBLE 55:7
Let them b. as they are CLEM 153:1
To b., or not to be SHAK 433:8
beach: about the b. I wander'd TENN 538:16
all left behind on the b. CARR 133:2
b. undid his corded bales ARN 14:21
only pebble on the b. BRAI 91:17
beached: b. verge of the salt flood SHAK 486:14
Beachy Head: Birmingham by way of B. CHES 147:11
beacon: face, which, as a b. SHAK 442:15
From Clee to heaven the b. HOUS 262:12
beacon-light: b. is quench'd in smoke SCOTT 417:2
Beacons: B. from the abode where SHEL 500:1
b. of wise men HUXL 269:10
beaded: With b. bubbles winking KEATS 291:18
beadroll: On Fame's eternal b. worthy SPEN 516:19
bead-rolls: Set in our b. SKEL 508:19
Beadsman: B., after thousand aves KEATS 289:24
b. now that was your knight PEELE 371:8
beak: He can take in his b. MERR 338:8
thy b. from out my heart POE 375:6
beaker: b. full of the warm South KEATS 291:18
Beale: Miss Buss and Miss B. ANON 6:16
be-all: b. and the end-all here SHAK 459:5
beam: b. that is in thine own BIBLE 64:34
b. upon my inward view ARN 13:4
beameth: one knows for whom it b. MOORE 356:11
beamish: b. nephew CARR 133:7
my b. boy CARR 134:29
beams: b. of his chambers PRAY 396:18
moonshine's watery b. SHAK 481:28
tricks his b. MILT 343:17
bean: dined on one pea and one b. LEAR 313:2
home of the b. and the cod BOSS 90:13
not too French French b. GILB 227:23
bean-flowers: b.' boon BROW 100:13
bean-rows: Nine b. will I have there YEATS 585:17
beans: You must not give him b. CHES 146:26
Bear: B. of Very Little Brain MILNE 340:13
b. onward blessed me SIDN 507:27
B. them we can HOUS 264:22
b. the palm alone SHAK 448:16
b. the yoke in his youth BIBLE 60:30
b. up the pillars of it PRAY 394:25
b. with a sore head MARR 331:4
has been eaten by the b. HOUS 266:11
How a b. likes honey MILNE 340:12
huntsman by the b. oppress'd WALL 562:6
is a bush suppos'd a b. SHAK 471:11
like the rugged Russian b. SHAK 461:21
makes us rather b. those SHAK 433:8
Moppsikon Floppsikon b. LEAR 313:1
More can I b. than you SHAK 446:9
my safe old b. BETJ 44:9
No dancing b. was so genteel COWP 165:22
pursued by a b. SHAK 491:16
rode on the back of a b. LEAR 313:1
still bless the b. FRERE 218:25
Their habits from the B. BELL 38:26
there's no mortal can b. GAY 222:36
They shall b. thee in their PRAY 395:22
To pardon or to b. it COWP 165:9
We must b. all SHAK 444:23

We've fought the B. before HUNT 268:3
which we b. to live POPE 379:21
wounded spirit who can b. BIBLE 54:13
ye cannot b. them now BIBLE 72:39
bear-baiting: Puritan hated b. MAC 324:19
bear-baitings: fairs, and b. SHAK 491:20
beard: b. of formal cut SHAK 425:24
brave b. curled CHES 147:3
by the colour of his b. SHAK 488:23
endure a husband with a b. SHAK 472:3
grey b. and glittering eye COL 155:5
His b. was grizzled SHAK 430:13
icicle on a Dutchman's b. SHAK 489:18
I have a b. coming SHAK 469:28
King of Spain's B. DRAKE 193:3
Plucks off my b. and blows SHAK 433:3
send thee a b. SHAK 489:18
To b. the lion in his den SCOTT 417:18
To pluck me by the b. SHAK 455:2
void your rheum upon my b. SHAK 466:3
was an Old Man with a b. LEAR 311:15
with white and bristly b. SHAK 492:26
bearded: b. like the pard SHAK 425:24
beards: their long b. SWIFT 527:14
'Tis merry in hall when b. SHAK 442:26
We'll grow b. FLAU 214:2
your b. forbid me to interpret SHAK 458:10
Beardsley: belong to the B. period BEER 37:11
Beareth: B. all things BIBLE 76:14
that b. up things light BACON 27:5
bearing: from the monotony of b. WOOLF 576:18
bearings: b. of this observation DICK 177:31
bears: dancing dogs and b. HODG 252:2
Let b. and lions growl WATTS 565:17
wandering b. may come with buns ISH 270:27
beast: be a b. or a fool alone KILV 296:8
B. gave beast as much YEATS 585:20
b. who is always spoiling MAC 324:26
b. With many heads SHAK 427:25
count the number of the b. BIBLE 82:14
doubt the maw-crammed b. BROW 104:3
evil b. hath devoured him BIBLE 46:29
Feeds b. as man SHAK 421:8
following the questing b. MAL 327:18
I have a b. on my back DOUG 191:7
just b. ANON 4:9
making the b. with two backs SHAK 473:18
name of the b. BIBLE 82:13
No b. so fierce but knows SHAK 480:20
noise in the b.'s belly MAL 327:15
preeminence above a b. BIBLE 55:13
regardeth the life of his b. BIBLE 53:34
solitude is either a wild b. BACON 26:14
splendorous blond b. NIET 363:14
terrible marks of the b. HARDY 241:17
what rough b. YEATS 586:16
Who is like unto the b. BIBLE 82:12
worship the b. and his image BIBLE 82:17
beastie: tim'rous b. BURNS 115:20
beasties: ghosties and long-leggety b. ANON 5:8
beastly: let's be b. to the Germans COW 163:15
Beasts: B. did leap and birds did BARN 33:32
b. of the forest are mine PRAY 393:2
b. of the field drink thereof PRAY 396:19
b. of the forest do move PRAY 397:1
b. that have no understanding PRAY 388:25
be compared unto the b. PRAY 392:28
charming as the b. AUDEN 19:12
elders and the four b. BIBLE 81:32
fought with b. at Ephesus BIBLE 76:24
four b. and four and twenty BIBLE 81:27
four b. full of eyes BIBLE 81:23
man is of kin to the b. BACON 25:25
manner of four-footed b. BIBLE 73:37
beat: b. down Satan under our PRAY 385:19
b. him when he sneezes CARR 133:26

B. its straight path along COL 157:11
b. of a horse's feet KIPL 304:1
b. of her unseen feet SHEL 500:6
b. of the off-shore wind KIPL 300:23
b. the ground MILT 340:29
b. their swords into plowshares BIBLE 57:19
b. them to their beds SHAK 423:3
b. upon that house BIBLE 65:12
can always b. ten men who SHAW 496:3
could b. three *Frenchmen* ADD 2:19
enemies have b. us to the pit SHAK 452:5
I'd b. him like a dog SHAK 488:22
though Miss Jenkyns b. time GASK 222:1
Voice above their b. THOM 548:14
waves that b. on Heaven's BLAKE 85:15
We b. them to-day or Molly STARK 517:20
when thy heart began to b. BLAKE 87:15
ye b. my people to pieces BIBLE 57:20
beaten: b. by a piece of timber FRY 219:22
Thrice was I b. with rods BIBLE 77:12
beateth: not as one that b. the air BIBLE 76:9
beating: b. in the void his luminous
ARN 16:10
b. myself for spite SIDN 507:17
Charity and b. begins at home FLET 215:25
daily the b. of man's heart AUDEN 20:6
glory of b. the French WOLFE 576:7
Greeks who take the b. HOR 258:12
hear the b. of his wings BRIG 93:1
hearts b. each to each BROW 102:14
Is b. on the door YEATS 585:7
not mend his pace with b. SHAK 436:24
than driven by b. ASCH 17:1
Beatrice: You whisper 'B.' BROW 102:30
Beats: B. all the lies you can BLAKE 85:14
light which b. upon a throne TENN 533:30
beatum: *Parte b.* HOR 260:11
possit facere et servare b. HOR 258:17
vocaveris Recte b. HOR 261:19
Beatus: *B. ille* HOR 259:7
B. vir qui timet Dominum BIBLE 83:9
beau: *l'art pour l'art...le b.* COUS 163:9
Beaumont: rare B. lie BASSE 35:1
beauté: *tout n'est qu'ordre et b.* BAUD 35:7
beauteous: b. chequered sides with
THOM 549:16
b. flower when next we SHAK 482:16
How b. mankind is SHAK 485:26
love all b. things BRID 92:10
Of all that is most b. WORD 578:3
Beauties: B. in vain their pretty POPE 381:11
By their own b. SHAK 483:6
Of common b. liv'd unknown CAREW 130:13
proportions we just b. see JONS 285:8
sav'd by b. not his own POPE 375:16
unripened b. of the north ADD 1:19
You meaner b. of the night WOTT 583:15
beautified: adorned and b. with his
presence PRAY 388:25
'b.' is a vile phrase SHAK 431:34
b. with our feathers GREE 236:12
beautiful: acts are b. through love
SHEL 503:13
Against the b. GREE 236:3
All things bright and b. ALEX 3:13
art for art's sake...the b. COUS 163:9
b. and ineffectual angel ARN 16:10
b. and death-struck year HOUS 264:1
b. are thy feet with shoes BIBLE 57:7
B. as a wreck of Paradise SHEL 500:12
B. as sweet YOUNG 588:7
b. face is a mute PUBL 402:4
b. God to behold SWIN 530:3
B. must be the mountains BRID 92:17
B. Railway Bridge MCG 325:6
b., the tender, the kind MILL 339:23
b. things in the world RUSK 411:23
b. than any religion SAKI 413:7
B. that war and all its WHIT 570:11
B. than thy first love YEATS 584:23

b. woman on top HOR 257:9
b. words in the English JAMES 271:30
be less b. WATS 565:10
believe to be b. MORR 358:14
deal of scorn looks b. SHAK 489:24
entirely b. AUDEN 19:17
has made His darkness b. TENN 537:3
Here lies a most b. lady DE L 173:27
How b. upon the mountains BIBLE 59:18
how b. they are COL 156:7
how b. KIPL 299:14
indeed appear b. outward BIBLE 67:25
innocent and the b. YEATS 585:12
it comes up more b. HOR 261:12
one was b. BYRON 124:12
Our love of what is b. PER 372:22
'She is more b. than day TENN 532:16
She's b. and therefore SHAK 446:1
she was b. SHEL 505:9
Small is b. SCH 415:12
thee good as thou art b. TENN 534:19
they're too b. to live DICK 180:7
to be b. than to be good WILDE 573:21
when a woman isn't b. CHEK 145:6
will always make it b. CONS 162:2
world over to find the b. EMER 207:12
yet more b. daughter HOR 259:22
beautifully: Print it as it stands—b.
JAMES 271:26
beauty: After the wildest b. OWEN 367:10
alike by b. and by fear WORD 580:8
alone has looked on B. bare MILL 339:28
b. beat on his conceits MARL 330:11
B. by constraint GAY 222:9
b. calls and glory leads LEE 313:10
b. cold and austere RUSS 412:15
b. coming and the beauty WORD 582:6
b. draws us with a single POPE 381:1
b. faded has no second PHIL 373:9
B. for some provides escape HUXL 269:1
b. from the light retir'd WALL 562:14
B. in things exists HUME 267:17
B. is bought by judgment SHAK 456:20
B. is momentary STEV 520:17
B. is Nature's coin MILT 341:17
B. is Nature's brag MILT 341:18
b. is the mind diseased BYRON 121:13
B. is the lover's gift CONG 161:1
'B. is truth KEATS 291:11
B. itself doth of itself SHAK 492:17
b. like slow old tunes MAS 333:17
B. lives though lilies FLEC 214:9
b. lives with kindness SHAK 491:4
b. making beautiful old SHAK 494:19
b. of Israel is slain BIBLE 50:16
b. of the good old cause WORD 582:9
B.'s conquest of your AUDEN 20:21
B.'s ensign yet SHAK 483:30
B. she was statue cold FLEC 214:6
b.'s rose might never SHAK 492:22
b.'s self she is ANON 6:20
b. that hath not some strangeness
BACON 25:28
B. that must die KEATS 291:15
b. that we should desire BIBLE 59:21
b., though injurious MILT 350:25
b. to delight DAV 172:12
B. took from those who DE L 174:3
B. too rich for use SHAK 482:2
B. unadorn'd BEHN 38:19
b. vanishes DE L 173:27
B., wit, High birth SHAK 487:6
bereft of b. SHAK 484:16
body's b. lives STEV 520:17
born was b.'s summer dead SHAK 494:18
Christian b. Defects POUND 383:8
clear perception of its b. KEATS 294:11
close relationship with b. KEATS 293:18
deep trenches in thy b.'s SHAK 492:23
delusion that b. is goodness TOLS 551:11

delves the parallels in b.'s SHAK 493:20
dreamed that life was B. HOOP 255:22
fatal gift of b. BYRON 121:6
fathers-forth whose b. HOPK 256:23
force and b. of its process JAMES 272:2
give unto them b. for ashes BIBLE 60:9
He hath a daily b. in his SHAK 477:3
Her b. fed my common earth MAS 333:22
her b. was apparent WOOLF 576:18
home and b. BRAH 91:16
horror and its b. are divine SHEL 502:5
I know what wages b. gives YEATS 587:5
In b. and virtue SKEL 508:18
in your b.'s orient deep CAREW 130:18
is simply order and b. BAUD 35:7
is the best part of b. BACON 25:27
June for whose b. ARN 15:4
Lord in the b. of holiness PRAY 396:5
Losing both b. and utility SHAK 445:12
loved the principle of b. KEATS 294:28
more doth b. beauteous seem SHAK 493:16
much b. as could die JONS 284:3
near your b. with my nails SHAK 446:5
No b. she doth miss ANON 6:20
No woman can be a b. without FARQ 210:2
power of b. I remember DRYD 195:32
principal b. in building FULL 220:16
rarest gift To B. MER 337:11
redemption of all things by B. SHAW 496:22
round the ghosts of b. glide POPE 377:26
seizes as b. must be truth KEATS 293:15
She walks in b. BYRON 125:21
shower Of b. WORD 578:11
simple b. and nought else BROW 100:29
soul of her b. and love SHEL 503:23
straight her b. to my sense DONNE 188:9
such b. as a woman's eye SHAK 457:7
Such seems your b. still SHAK 494:18
terrible b. is born YEATS 585:1
That b. is not SPEN 516:27
their b. shall consume PRAY 393:1
thing of b. GILB 228:13
thing of b. is a joy KEATS 288:20
thou B. both so ancient AUG 21:16
thought that where B. was GALS 220:30
thy b. is to me POE 375:7
Thy b. shall no more be MARV 332:19
'Tis b. truly blent SHAK 488:12
To flatter b.'s ignorant YEATS 586:14
unmask her b. to the moon SHAK 430:17
What ills from b. spring JOHN 283:4
What is b. saith my sufferings MARL 330:11
When b. fires the blood DRYD 195:33
Where b. has no ebb YEATS 585:19
Where perhaps some b. lies MILT 342:20
whose b. claims SHAK 422:1
winds of March with b. SHAK 491:26
with this rage shall b. SHAK 494:4
write the b. of your eyes SHAK 492:7
Your infant b. could beget SEDL 419:8
your world of b.'s gone HERR 250:2
youth And a little b. WEBS 566:20
beaux: Where none are b. LYTT 321:2
beaver: Cock up your b. HOGG 253:2
Harry, with his b. on SHAK 440:7
became: he b. his admirers AUDEN 19:3
because: B. I think him so SHAK 490:30
B. it is there MALL 327:13
'B. it was he MONT 354:4
becks: b., and wreathed smiles MILT 342:14
become: do all that may b. a man SHAK 459:9
becomes: b. his coffin prodigiously
GOLD 232:14
peace there's nothing so b. SHAK 443:21
becometh: holiness b. thine house
PRAY 396:1
bed: able to have a spare b. PEPYS 372:17
Are the weans in their b. MILL 340:3
b. after the hurly-burly CAMP 128:9
b. and procreant cradle SHAK 459:4

b. at night	GOLD 231:4	**beech:** appointment with a b.-tree				PRAY 399:4
B. be blest that I lie	ANON 6:15		THOR 550:20	Was nothin' much b.		KIPL 299:17
B. in the bush with stars	STEV 522:27	yonder b.-tree single	MER 337:1	**beforehand:** so good as it seems b.		
b. I sought him whom my	BIBLE 56:25	**beech-tree:** cover of the spreading b.				ELIOT 201:25
b. of Ware in England	SHAK 489:30		VIRG 559:11	**beg:** to b. I am ashamed		BIBLE 70:23
better in battle than in b.	STER 520:3	**beef:** am a great eater of b.	SHAK 487:25	to b. in the streets		FRAN 217:26
bounced out of b.	MILNE 340:9	b. and captain's biscuits	THAC 545:32	We cannot b. for pardon		MACN 326:15
die—in b.	SASS 414:11	piece of b. and mustard	SHAK 484:12	you b. for the core		TWAIN 554:17
drunk to b.	SHAK 421:13	roast b. of England	FIEL 211:10	You taught me first to b.		SHAK 468:12
dull, stale, tired b.	SHAK 453:9	**beefsteak:** English an article as a b.		**began:** All things b. in order		BROW 95:20
earth in an earthy b.	TENN 540:12		HAWT 243:5	dark womb where I b.		MAS 333:22
ever on her pensive b.	POPE 381:9	**beef-witted:** thou mongrel b. lord		first the human race b.		BURNS 113:21
Every b. is narrow	MILL 339:29		SHAK 486:28	left off before you b.		CONG 160:24
every night wash I my b.	PRAY 389:26	**beefy:** b. ATS	BETJ 42:18	that's how it all b.		KIPL 300:22
go to b. in another world	HENS 246:4	**bee-loud:** live alone in the b. glade		was it when my life b.		WORD 578:19
grave as little as my b.	KEN 295:9		YEATS 585:17	**begetter:** To the onlie b. of these		
have to go to b. by day	STEV 522:16	**bee-mouth:** to Poison while the b.				SHAK 492:21
heaped for the beloved's b.	SHEL 504:12		KEATS 291:15	**beggar:** Bare-footed came the b. maid		
His b. shall seem a school	SHAK 475:13	**been:** b. and gone and done	GILB 225:12			TENN 532:16
I drunk him to his b.	SHAK 422:10	if it had not b.	SHEL 499:12	b. by banqueting upon borrowing		BIBLE 63:6
I haste me to my b.	SHAK 493:5	'Thou hast b.	ARN 13:11	b. should be answer'd		SHAK 468:12
I in my b. again	ANON 8:16	**Beer:** B.! O Hodgson	CALV 127:12	b.'s nurse and Caesar's		SHAK 423:20
In going to my naked b.	EDW 200:5	chronicle small b.	SHAK 474:18	B. that I am		SHAK 432:14
in thy cold b.	KING 296:11	'Did you ever taste b.	DICK 180:30	behold desert a b. born		SHAK 494:5
I put my hand into the b.	SHAK 443:18	drink beer will think b.	IRV 270:22	certain b. named Lazarus		BIBLE 70:28
I toward thy b.	FLEC 214:12	drink some b.	JOHN 277:14	He's an absent-minded b.		KIPL 297:23
I used to go to b. early	PROU 401:20	felony to drink small b.	SHAK 446:11	whiles I am a b.		SHAK 452:15
kick his wife out of b.	SURT 525:5	I'm only a b. teetotaller	SHAW 496:16	**beggar'd:** It b. all description		SHAK 422:2
lawn I lie in b.	AUDEN 20:18	in me to desire small b.	SHAK 441:21	**beggarly:** b. people		SWIFT 528:11
lie *diagonally* in his b.	STER 520:7	inseparable than B. and Britannia		**Beggars:** B., fleas		KING 296:20
Lord Tomnoddy went home to b.	BARH 33:9		SMITH 511:25	B. invention and makes		COWP 166:20
make my b.	BALL 30:12	Life ain't all b. and skittles	DU M 199:4	When b. die		SHAK 449:18
make my b. soon	BALL 31:5	like thine inspirer, b.	POPE 375:20	**beggary:** b. in the love that can		SHAK 421:7
me he mostly sent to b.	LAND 309:2	muddy ecstasies of b.	COWP 168:8	no vice, but b.		SHAK 452:15
migrations from the blue b.	GOLD 232:34	parson, much bemus'd in b.	POPE 376:19	they knew b.		MAC 324:6
Must we to b. indeed	STEV 522:25	poor creature, small b.	SHAK 441:22	**begged:** HOMER b. his Bread		ANON 7:14
newly gone to b.	MILT 344:16	quarts of Ludlow b.	HOUS 264:12	**beggere:** beste b. in his hous		CHAU 141:21
nor a goddess to b.	VIRG 560:2	rate you drink your b.	HOUS 264:11	**begging:** his seed b. their bread		PRAY 391:28
not a b. of roses	STEV 521:31	such all b. and skittles	CALV 127:19	**Begin:** 'B. at the beginning		CARR 134:19
ought to come to b. in boots	HERB 246:12	**Beer-sheba:** From Dan even to B.		b. charges which once begun		BACON 26:10
pluck me from my naked b.	KYD 306:2		BIBLE 49:30	B. these wood-birds		SHAK 471:8
so to b.	PEPYS 371:19	travel from Dan to B.	STER 519:2	get up and b. again		BROW 102:1
sweat of an enseamed b.	SHAK 435:10	**bees:** b. are stirring	COL 157:14	My way is to b. with		BYRON 122:5
take up thy b.	BIBLE 72:1	b. each with his own function	VIRG 560:19	Then I'll b.		LANG 309:20
This b. thy centre is	DONNE 190:13	b. make honey not for yourselves		where I did b.		SHAK 452:1
thy b. Of crimson joy	BLAKE 87:12		VIRG 560:20	will b. with certainties		BACON 24:16
To b., to bed, to bed	SHAK 462:5	b. who have lost their	FRY 220:7	**beginning:** been told you from the b.		
to deck both b. and bower	SPEN 516:13	early b. are assaulting	REED 405:6			BIBLE 59:9
weather when one's in b.	SWIFT 526:5	forest b. are humming near	CLARE 152:14	Before the b. of years		SWIN 528:20
When boyes go first to b.	HERB 248:4	hive of silvery B.	LEAR 312:9	b. and the ending		BIBLE 81:10
Who goes to b. with whom	SAY 415:7	Like a swarm of golden b.	SHEL 500:6	b. God created the heaven		BIBLE 44:22
whole world out of b.	MAS 333:24	murmuring of innumerable b.	TENN 542:17	b. is often the end		ELIOT 203:1
wife my second best b.	SHAK 496:1	of half a number of b.	LONG 317:23	b. of any great matter		DRAKE 193:1
bedes: peire of b.	CHAU 141:17	rob the Hybla b.	SHAK 451:31	B. reform is beginning		WELL 568:4
bedfellows: acquaints a man with strange		yellow b. in the ivy-bloom	SHEL 503:6	Each venture Is a new b.		ELIOT 202:23
b.	SHAK 485:9	**beest:** b. is deed he hath no peyne		end of the b.		CHUR 150:11
Poverty has strange b.	BULW 107:6		CHAU 142:17	In my b. is my end		ELIOT 202:18
Bedlam: with a sigh like Tom o' B.		**bees-winged:** was it his b. eyes	BETJ 42:4	In the b. was the Word		BIBLE 71:21
	SHAK 453:12	**Beethoven:** With Spohr and B.	GILB 227:6	it was in the b.		PRAY 384:15
Bedonebyasyoudid: Mrs B. is coming		**beetle:** Nor let the b.	KEATS 291:14	Lord is the b. of wisdom		PRAY 397:13
	KING 297:11	poor b.	SHAK 464:11	That is the true b.		SHAK 471:16
beds: beat them to their b.	SHAK 423:3	Save where the b. wheels	GRAY 234:18	that was the b. of fairies		BARR 34:13
hearers weeping to their b.	SHAK 480:8	shard-borne b. with his	SHAK 461:13	thing is the b. of an Amour		BEHN 38:10
them rejoice in their b.	PRAY 399:24	where the b. winds	COLL 158:18	This is the b. of the end		TALL 531:19
when I came unto my b.	SHAK 490:27	**Beetles:** B. black	SHAK 470:12	Thou, Lord, in the b.		PRAY 396:13
Will there be b. for me	ROSS 409:12	Show scarce so gross as b.	SHAK 455:14	Which b. of time according		USSH 554:29
bedside: Betty's b. late at nite	WARD 564:29	**befall:** it must b.	GILB 229:7	**beginnings:** may our ends by our b.		
got a very good b. manner	PUNCH 402:32	**beflagged:** b. jam pots	JAMES 271:34			DENH 174:20
bed-staff: in the twinkling of a b.		**before:** art not what thou wast b.	AYT 24:4	mighty things from small b.		DRYD 195:22
	SHAD 420:23	B., behind	DONNE 188:16	**begins:** He that b. to live		QUAR 403:19
bed-time: I would it were b.	SHAK 440:18	b. the flood they were	BIBLE 67:32	she b. to comprehend it		PRIOR 401:7
bee: b. has quit the clover	KIPL 300:23	doing what has been done b.	WHAR 569:9	world's great age b. anew		SHEL 500:20
b.'s kiss	BROW 101:15	I have been here b.	ROSS 410:8	**begot:** b. Within a pair of minutes		KYD 306:6
b. with honied thigh	MILT 342:8	large a trunk b.	BELL 38:28	mother on his father him b.		BLAKE 87:2
brisk as a b. in conversation	JOHN 274:1	said our remarks b.	DON 187:17	some that he was b. between		SHAK 464:19
doth the little busy b.	WATTS 565:21	Saviour Christ is gone b.	PRAY 384:9	were about when they b. me		STER 519:16
horribly bored by a b.	LEAR 311:16	sent b. my time	SHAK 480:18	**Begotten:** B., not made		PRAY 387:10
like a b.	LODGE 316:3	that's not been said b.	TER 544:16	hath b. the drops of dew		BIBLE 53:4
(Some b. had stung it newly)	SUCK 524:10	those b. cried 'Back	MAC 322:19	only b. of the Father		BIBLE 71:27
Where the b. sucks	SHAK 485:25	those things which are b.	BIBLE 78:18			

Whatever is b.   YEATS 586:11
Begriffes: Gemüt Namen eines B.   NOV 364:9
beguile: kiaugh and care b.   BURNS 113:5
so b. thy sorrow   SHAK 486:16
To b. many and be beguil'd   SHAK 476:9
To b. the time   SHAK 459:3
beguiled: serpent b. me   BIBLE 45:19
beguiles: traveller's joy b. in autumn
   HOUS 265:9
Beguine: refused to begin the 'B.'
   COW 163:22
begun: have not yet b. to fight   JONES 283:11
To have b. is half   HOR 258:14
works, b., continued   PRAY 388:6
behave: b. as the rich behave   SMITH 510:19
How well did I b.   HOUS 263:1
behaving: b. in this extraordinary
language and ways of b.   STOP 523:17
   JUV 287:15
behaviour: himself upon his good b.
   BYRON 123:16
immediate check to loose b.   STEE 518:6
liberal arts refines b.   OVID 366:25
of good b.   BIBLE 79:12
there we'll teach better b.   HOGG 253:2
beheaded: was b. yesterday   WALP 562:20
beheld: Where I b. what never was
   BYRON 123:15
behemoth: Behold now b.   BIBLE 53:8
behind: At such a little tail b.   BELL 38:28
b., between   DONNE 188:16
B. the cloud-topp'd hill   POPE 379:5
b. the throne greater than   PITT 373:24
B. you swiftly the figure   AUDEN 18:10
Broad before and broad b.   BETJ 44:14
come no more b. your scenes   JOHN 274:2
dusk with a light b.   GILB 229:4
has no bosom and no b.   SMITH 510:27
Scratches its innocent b.   AUDEN 19:19
those b. cried 'Forward   MAC 322:19
those things which are b.   BIBLE 78:18
turn thee b. me   BIBLE 51:32
whatever he put b. him   DICK 181:10
Behold: B. an Israelite indeed   BIBLE 71:32
b. a pale horse   BIBLE 81:29
b. a white horse   BIBLE 82:25
B. my mother and my brethren   BIBLE 66:15
B. the man   BIBLE 83:22
b. us with Thy blessing   BUCK 106:16
b. with prejudice the French   BROW 96:28
be what they b.   POPE 375:11
to b. you again in dying   STEV 523:5
beholden: b. to Machiavel and others
   BACON 24:25
be'ind: less than 'arf o' that b.   KIPL 299:17
Being: always at the edge of B.   SPEN 515:10
B., erect upon two legs   DICK 182:18
have our b.   BIBLE 74:14
in the middle of my b.   LAWR 311:3
Of unknown modes of b.   WORD 580:13
selfish b. all my life   AUST 23:21
will call no b. good   MILL 339:5
beings: human b. are born free   ANON 4:14
bekke: west upon the peple I b.   CHAU 143:5
Belbroughton: B. Road is bonny   BETJ 43:12
Belgium: lightly drawn until B.   ASQ 17:17
Belgrave Square: May beat in B.   GILB 226:5
Belial: B., in act more graceful   MILT 346:9
thou son of B.   BIBLE 50:24
wander forth the sons Of B.   MILT 345:18
belie: shall yet b. thy happy years   SHAK 488:3
belied: she b. with false compare   SHAK 495:9
belief: all b. is for it   JOHN 277:21
bamboozle myself into b.   GREE 236:7
b. of truth   BACON 27:31
believe in B. I disbelieve   FORS 217:10
loved each other beyond b.   HEINE 244:10
beliefs: dust of exploded b.   MADAN 326:18
generous b. and impositions   STEV 521:14
sorts of old defunct b.   IBSEN 269:21

two contradictory b.   ORW 365:13
believe: b. also in me   BIBLE 72:30
b. and take for granted   BACON 27:18
B. a woman or an epitaph   BYRON 124:18
b. everything a *young* man   JOW 285:22
b. in God in spite of what   JOW 286:1
b. in God the Father   PRAY 384:26
b. what one does not believe   PAINE 367:20
brain that won't b.   BLAKE 85:11
Corrected *I b.* to *One does feel*   KNOX 305:20
Do you b. in fairies   BARR 34:16
Firmly I b. and truly   NEWM 362:11
him a determination to b.   HUME 267:21
I b. in Michael Angelo   SHAW 496:22
I b. it was no more   SUCK 524:11
I do b. her   SHAK 495:11
I do not b.   BUTL 119:11
I don't b. a word of it   CHAM 139:16
If you b. that you will   WELL 568:7
If you'll b. in me   CARR 136:2
is a being born to b.   DISR 184:30
I will not b.   BIBLE 73:10
Let Apella the Jew b. it   HOR 262:5
little ones which b. in me   BIBLE 67:3
Lord, I b.   BIBLE 68:35
potently and powerfully b.   SHAK 432:8
power of reason to b.   VOLT 561:20
preaching to save them that b.   BIBLE 75:29
Though ye b. not me   BIBLE 72:21
to b. of my own stories   IRV 270:24
To b. only possibilities   BROW 96:24
To b. your own thought   EMER 207:34
undesirable to b. a proposition   RUSS 412:17
We can b. what we choose   NEWM 362:16
whom shall my soul b.   BROW 104:7
willingly b. what they wish   CAES 126:27
Will ne'er b.   BLAKE 85:17
ye will not b.   BIBLE 71:43
you must b. what you ought   NEWM 362:17
believed: against hope b. in hope   BIBLE 74:40
all that b. were together   BIBLE 73:24
seen, and yet have b.   BIBLE 73:12
what is by all people b.   VINC 557:7
Who hath b. our report   BIBLE 59:20
believer: Most blest b. he   VAUG 555:11
believers: belonged to b. in Clough
   SWIN 529:13
Kingdom of Heaven to all b.   PRAY 384:17
believes: that he more readily b.   BACON 28:7
believeth: b. all things   BIBLE 76:14
b. he that it is the sound   BIBLE 53:7
b. in him should not perish   BIBLE 71:38
b. on me hath everlasting   BIBLE 72:7
Believing: B. where we cannot prove
   TENN 535:29
Be not faithless, but b.   BIBLE 73:11
heads of parties against b.   ARB 11:19
She deceiving, I b.   SEDL 419:11
torture them, into b.   NEWM 362:8
bell: be asked to toll the b.   HARDY 241:18
B., book, and candle   SHAK 452:19
b. invites me   SHAK 460:1
b.-swarmed   HOPK 256:10
ever after as a sullen b.   SHAK 441:2
heart as sound as a b.   SHAK 472:23
hear the surly sullen b.   SHAK 494:6
mock the midnight b.   SHAK 422:22
sexton toll'd the b.   HOOD 254:16
Silence that dreadful b.   SHAK 475:4
they rang a b.   ELIOT 202:7
Thrice rung the b.   POPE 380:29
tinkledy-binkledy-winkled a b.   LEAR 312:19
to know for whom the *b.*   DONNE 190:20
Twilight and evening b.   TENN 533:4
very word is like a b.   KEATS 291:23
Bella: B., horrida bella   VIRG 558:17
belle: Garde bien ta b. folie   BANV 33:1
'La b. dame sans merci'   KEATS 289:21
belles: b. ringeth to evensonge   HAWES 243:3
belli: Nervos b.   CIC 151:30

bellies: Such as for their b.' sake   MILT 343:12
Bellman: B., perplexed and distressed
   CARR 133:6
fatal b.   SHAK 460:3
I stayed up till the b.   PEPYS 371:18
Bellona: B.'s bridegroom   SHAK 458:5
bellows: My b. too have lost their   ANON 6:19
bell-rope: swam to the b. and grasped
   BEER 37:14
Bells: B. are booming down   BETJ 43:7
b., bells, bells   POE 375:1
b. have knoll'd to church   SHAK 425:23
b. justle in the tower   HOUS 266:6
b. of Hell go ting-a-ling-a-ling   ANON 7:4
b. they sound so clear   HOUS 263:4
broke into a mist with b.   BROW 103:11
Down in the b. and grass   HODG 252:4
I heard the church b. hollowing   BETJ 44:9
Like sweet b. jangled   SHAK 433:15
lin-lan-lone of evening b.   TENN 533:15
noisy b., be dumb   HOUS 263:5
sad b. brings back her   JOHN 273:20
'Twould ring the b. of Heaven   HODG 252:2
bellum: praeparet b.   VEG 556:3
belly: b. God send thee good ale   ANON 5:21
b. is as bright ivory overlaid   BIBLE 57:4
b. is like an heap of wheat   BIBLE 57:8
b. of the fish three days   BIBLE 61:22
b. will hardly mind anything   JOHN 275:11
filled his b. with the husks   BIBLE 70:19
increasing b.   SHAK 441:10
individual b. and orders   AUDEN 20:15
its slimy b. on the bank   ELIOT 204:26
it was in Jonadge's b.   DICK 179:23
meat best fits a little b.   HERR 249:21
my b. was bitter   BIBLE 82:9
noise in the beast's b.   MAL 327:15
something of a round b.   SHAK 441:11
wears his wit in his b.   SHAK 486:29
Whose God is their b.   BIBLE 78:19
belly-ache: It gives a chap the b.   HOUS 264:11
bellyful: Rumble thy b.   SHAK 454:5
belly-tension: bitter b. between a man
   GIBB 225:4
Belmont: B. is a lady richly left   SHAK 465:17
belong: suffice for those who b.   WHIT 571:8
To b. to other nations   GILB 228:10
belongs: it b. to Him   CHAP 140:1
belov'd: be more beloving than b.
   SHAK 421:11
bourn how far to be b.   SHAK 421:7
Shall never be b. by men   BLAKE 85:12
That she b. knows nought   SHAK 486:21
beloved: b. come into his garden   BIBLE 56:29
b. is white and ruddy   BIBLE 57:3
beloved more than another b.   BIBLE 57:2
Dearly b.   PRAY 388:24
man greatly b.   BIBLE 61:9
My b. is mine   BIBLE 56:24
This is my b.   BIBLE 57:4
This is my b. Son   BIBLE 63:40
voice of my b. that knocketh   BIBLE 57:1
beloving: be more b. than belov'd
   SHAK 421:11
below: above, b.   DONNE 188:16
By him one step b.   SHAK 486:25
journey to the world b.   SOCR 512:19
love is a thing b. a man   STER 520:6
Thy element's b.   SHAK 453:24
belt: bind my b.   TENN 534:21
belted: Though I've b. you an'   KIPL 299:20
belts: They braced their b. about   HOUS 265:6
Belvoir: Till B.'s lordly terraces   MAC 322:4
bely: O wombe! O b.   CHAU 143:6
Ben: Saint B., to aid me   HERR 249:6
Ben Bolt: remember sweet Alice, B.
   ENGL 208:19
Bench: hand a drowsy B. protect
   COWP 168:28
suppose I am on the B.   BIRK 84:16

bend: I b. and I break not   LA F 306:18
Bends: B. to the grave with unperceiv'd
    GOLD 230:20
made their b. adornings   SHAK 422:3
That b. not as I tread   MILT 341:21
Though she b. him   LONG 317:12
bene: bone, for *b.*   SHAK 457:11
Beneath: B. is all the fiends'   SHAK 455:17
some springing from b.   BACON 24:20
that is in the earth b.   BIBLE 47:24
Benedicite: B., omnia opera Domini
    BIBLE 83:16
benediction: Perpetual b.   WORD 579:9
Benedictus: B. qui venit in nomine
    MASS 335:4
benefacta: Siqua recordanti b. priora
    CAT 137:5
benefactor: first great b. of our race
    TWAIN 554:20
benefice: dreams he of another b.
    SHAK 481:28
beneficial: hands even for b. purposes
    MILL 339:15
benefit: b. of a people whom he
    BURKE 110:26
b. of the students   SMITH 509:14
without the b. o' the Clergy   CONG 160:4
benefits: bite so nigh As b. forgot SHAK 426:1
forget not all his b.   PRAY 396:14
benevolence: b. of mankind does most
    BAG 29:18
b. of the passive order   MER 338:4
Bengal: In B., to move at all   COW 163:20
benight: selves b. our happiest day
    DONNE 188:20
their shafts b. the air   HOUS 265:3
Benighted: B. walks under the midday
    MILT 341:18
benign: By stars b.   HOUS 265:14
under that b. sky   BRON 94:1
benison: b. of hot water   BROO 94:9
b. to fall On our meat   HERR 250:10
Benjamin: of the tribe of B.   BIBLE 78:16
bent: b. to make some port he   ARN 15:2
Just as the twig is b.   POPE 377:12
My youth is b. by the same   THOM 547:3
They are not our b.   GILB 228:25
Bentley: B. or Elias Stoeber was HOUS 266:15
Bequeath: B., like sunset   SHEL 501:2
bereav'd: if b. of light   BLAKE 88:2
bereft: b. Of wet and wildness   HOPK 256:18
bergers: des b. et des bouchers VOLT 561:17
Berkeley: B. destroyed this world
    SMITH 511:33
When Bishop B. said 'there   BYRON 123:28
Berliner: words Ich bin ein B.   KENN 295:11
Bermoothes: still-vexed B.   SHAK 484:27
Bermudas: Where the remote B. ride
    MARV 331:15
Bernard: B. the monk ne saugh nat
    CHAU 143:28
berries: cometh beauty of b. POUND 383:18
I come to pluck your b.   MILT 343:2
Two lovely b. moulded   SHAK 470:22
berry: could have made a better b.
    BUTL 119:23
sweeter than the b.   GAY 222:8
berth: which happen'd in his b. HOOD 254:16
beryl: gold rings set with the b. BIBLE 57:4
beschränken: sich zu b. und zu isolieren
    GOET 229:27
beseech: I pray and b. you   PRAY 384:10
We b. thee to hear us   PRAY 385:18
beside: thou art b. thyself   BIBLE 74:25
thousand shall fall b.   PRAY 395:21
besiege: forty winters shall b. SHAK 492:23
besoin: b. de voyager   STER 518:30
besought: Tho' they b. her   COW 163:22
bespake: their Lord himself b.   MILT 344:7

Bessere: grössere das B. zu empfinden
    GOET 230:8
best: ae b. dance e'er cam   BURNS 113:13
All is b.   MILT 351:3
All is for the b.   VOLT 561:2
all our b. men are dead   PUNCH 403:2
Always to be b.   HOMER 253:30
bad's the b. of us   FLET 215:10
b. administer'd is best   POPE 379:20
b. and happiest moments   SHEL 505:12
b. and the worst of this   SWIN 530:11
b. and worst, and parted   BROO 94:6
b. be still   ARN 13:14
b. chosen language   AUST 22:31
b. days of life   VIRG 560:16
b. government is that which   OSUL 365:22
b. in this kind are   SHAK 471:19
b. is like the worst   KIPL 301:8
b. is the best   QUIL 403:23
b. is the enemy   VOLT 561:5
b. is yet to be   BROW 104:2
b. lack all conviction   YEATS 586:15
b. of all possible worlds   CAB 126:25
b. that has been known   ARN 16:17
B., to forget   BROW 104:35
b. trousers on when you   IBSEN 269:19
b. words in the best order   COL 157:32
ears the low-voiced B.   HARDY 240:3
Fear not to touch the b.   RAL 404:10
he made the b. of this   BURNS 113:26
in art the b. is good   GOET 230:8
is the b. of all trades   BELL 40:15
is the b. part of beauty   BACON 25:27
It was the b. of times   DICK 183:5
lamentable change is from the b. SHAK 455:5
loveliest and the b.   BELL 39:20
loveliest and b.   FITZ 212:17
one another's b.   DONNE 188:21
On that b. portion   WORD 578:4
past all prizing, b.   SOPH 513:8
propagate the b. that is known   ARN 16:1
Send forth the b. ye breed   KIPL 304:6
strongest is always the b.   LA F 306:21
Than any other person's b.   HAZL 243:11
To seek out the b. through   JEFF 272:13
wisest and justest and b.   PLATO 374:10
beste: b., out of they stal   CHAU 144:22
in der Kunst ist das B.   GOET 230:8
Bestie: lüstern schweifende blonde B.
    NIET 363:14
bestow: Let them b. on every airth
    GRAH 233:16
Bestows: B. her gifts on such JONS 284:10
bestride: doth b. the narrow world
    SHAK 448:17
best-seller: b. is the gilded tomb
    SMITH 510:20
b. was a book which somehow BOOR 89:21
bet: he would b. you which one TWAIN 554:4
betake: b. myself to that course PEPYS 372:21
Bethel: God of B.   DODD 187:15
Bethlehem: come ye to B.   ANON 10:4
Slouches towards B.   YEATS 586:16
venite in B.   ANON 10:4
betimes: that spurs too fast b. SHAK 478:19
betray: 'All things b. thee   THOM 548:9
b.'s In deepest consequence SHAK 458:18
B. sweet Jenny's unsuspecting BURNS 113:7
b. Tawny-finn'd fishes   SHAK 422:9
else she'll b. more men   SHAK 477:5
encourage those who b.   GAY 222:33
finds too late that men b. GOLD 231:31
guts to b. my country   FORS 217:12
betrayal: succeed without any act of b.
    REN 405:12
betray'd: Betrothed, betrayer, and b.
    SCOTT 418:3
betrayed: at ourselves like men b.
    WORD 577:2
b. by what is false within   MER 337:14

b. him by their adulation   BURKE 109:5
by ourselves, b.   CONG 160:20
same night that he was b.   PRAY 388:1
betrayer: Betrothed, b., and betray'd
    SCOTT 418:3
betrayeth: which is he that b. thee
    BIBLE 73:18
Betrothed: B., betrayer, and betray'd
    SCOTT 418:3
Betsey: B. and I are out   CARL 130:28
Bette: Auf seinem B. weinen sass
    GOET 230:12
better: am getting better and b. COUE 163:8
B. be courted and jilted   CAMP 128:23
B. by far you should forget ROSS 409:4
b. day   HENRY 245:17
b. for worse   PRAY 389:4
B. is the end of a thing   BIBLE 55:19
b. supplied when I have   SHAK 424:24
b. than all the ballads   LONG 316:8
B. than all measures   SHEL 504:24
b. than light and safer   HASK 243:1
b. to be left than never   CONG 160:35
b. to have loved and lost   BUTL 119:16
b. to have loved and lost   TENN 536:16
b. to marry than to burn   BIBLE 76:2
blame of those ye b.   KIPL 304:8
did it b. than any other   JOHN 277:25
far, far b. thing   DICK 183:12
from b. hap to worse   SOUT 514:20
have better spar'd a b.   SHAK 440:25
He is not b.   ANON 4:17
holds that if way to the B. HARDY 240:3
home I was in a b. place   SHAK 425:8
in a b. world than this   SHAK 424:27
is b. than a thousand   PRAY 395:13
is b. to be a fool than   STEV 522:3
I see the b. way   OVID 366:17
It is b. that some should   JOHN 277:5
it is much b. than likely   BRON 94:2
I took thee for thy b.   SHAK 435:3
knows of a b. 'ole   BAIR 29:23
loves him still the b.   GOLD 232:9
made b. by their presence ELIOT 201:27
make a b. mouse-trap   EMER 208:15
nae b. than he should be BURNS 113:12
never b. than when I am mad KYD 306:5
party breaks up the b.   AUST 22:13
render our fellow-men b.   MOL 353:19
say there was nothing b.   CARR 135:31
see b. days   BEHN 38:15
Seem'd to have known a b. day SCOTT 416:8
seen b. faces in my time   SHAK 453:23
she'd b.   CARL 132:30
Something b. than his dog TENN 538:19
talk I'm kent the b.   BURNS 114:32
that which is truly b.   MILT 351:24
to b. what we can   STEV 521:14
We have seen b. days   SHAK 486:9
which of us takes the b.   SOCR 512:18
will b. it in Scripture   OVER 366:7
will b. the instruction   SHAK 467:5
You are no b. than you   BEAU 36:2
you have look'd on b. days SHAK 425:23
You're a b. man than   KIPL 299:20
bettered: b. expectation than you
    SHAK 471:25
betters: Still b. what is done SHAK 491:27
between: anyone who comes b. them
    SMITH 511:11
b., above   DONNE 188:16
b. France and England   JERR 273:4
b. his Darkness and his   BYRON 126:8
B. the dark and the daylight LONG 316:9
B. two worlds life hovers BYRON 124:9
something b. compliments AUST 22:27
wasn't for the 'ouses in b.   BAT 35:3
betwixt: b. and between   HOUS 266:18
that's the day that comes b. CAREY 130:27

BEVERAGE BIRTHRIGHT

beverage: soiled by the 'b. of hell' YOUNG 588:15
Beware: B. of the scribes BIBLE 68:37
B. of the dog PETR 372:30
B. the ides of March SHAK 448:7
beweep: alone b. my outcast state SHAK 493:6
bewept: Which b. to the grave did SHAK 435:34
bewildered: young are sad and b. SMITH 510:22
bewitch: Do more b. me HERR 249:2
bewitched: I am b. with the rogue's SHAK 438:24
Bewrapt: B. past knowing to what HARDY 240:9
bewrayeth: Thy speech b. thee BIBLE 68:19
beye: our soules for to b. CHAU 144:19
beyond: are not b. all conjecture BROW 97:14
b. the knowledge of a man BEAU 35:16
is there anything b. BROO 94:10
loved each other b. belief HEINE 244:10
organism to live b. its income BUTL 118:27
beyont: them to the back o' b. SCOTT 418:1
Bezonian: B. speak SHAK 442:28
bias: b. of the world SHAK 452:14
bibble-babble: Leave thy vain b. SHAK 490:22
bibendum: *Nunc est b.* HOR 260:3
bibisti: *edisti satis atque b.* HOR 259:6
Bible: are only fit for the B. FRY 219:30
B. as if it was a constable's KING 297:7
B. clash and contradict DOW 191:11
B. only is the religion CHIL 148:12
big ha'-B. BURNS 113:9
English B. MAC 323:4
knows even his B. ARN 15:22
read the B. day and night BLAKE 85:22
that book is the B. ARN 16:13
to be hanged with the B. AUBR 17:23
translation of the B. WHAT 569:15
was but litel on the B. CHAU 141:30
bible-black: starless and b. THOM 547:9
bibles: b., billet-doux POPE 380:31
B. laid open HERB 248:10
Bible-Society: B. found CARL 131:6
bicicleta: *puede llegar solo en b.* VIER 556:21
bicker: To b. down a valley TENN 532:20
bicycle: Salisbury Plain on a b. GILB 226:15
Socialism can only arrive by b. VIER 556:21
bid: b. the soldiers shoot SHAK 437:31
bide: b. by the buff BURNS 114:5
Bidst: B. them avaunt CALV 127:28
bien: *mieux est l'ennemi du b.* VOLT 561:5
mon b. où je le trouve MOL 354:3
bienfaits: *recevoir de plus grands b.* LA R 310:16
bier: float upon his watery b. MILT 343:2
him barefac'd on the b. SHAK 436:9
big: b. business give the people ROOS 408:7
b. enough majority in any TWAIN 554:3
b. squadrons against BUSS 117:7
b. words for little JOHN 275:14
die will be an awfully b. adventure BARR 34:15
fear those b. words JOYCE 286:22
letters in a b. round hand GILB 228:5
Big Brother: B. is watching you ORW 365:12
bigger: b. they come FITZ 214:1
seems no b. than his head SHAK 455:14
biggin: whose brow with homely b. SHAK 442:17
Big-Sea-Water: By the shining B. LONG 317:10
Bilbo: B.'s the word CONG 160:21
bill: b. of fare to tempt me SWIFT 526:17
b. of indemnity...for raid KRUG 306:1
b. of my Divorce to all DONNE 189:11
birdie with a yellow b. STEV 522:24
Half-a-crown in the b. DICK 181:25
Take thy b. BIBLE 70:24
There's little B. as is THAC 546:1
billards: play b. well SPEN 515:4
billboard: b. lovely as a tree NASH 360:2
Billee: youngest he was little B. THAC 545:32
billet: Every bullet has its b. WILL 574:9
billiard: b. sharp whom any one catches GILB 227:7
elliptical b. balls GILB 227:7
billiards: let's to b. SHAK 422:8
billing: fond, and b. BUTL 118:7
billion: this a b. dollar country FOST 217:16
billow: breaking b. SHEL 499:17
billowing: sail in amply b. gown BELL 39:28
billows: b. smooth and bright CARR 135:3
Even the b. of the sea SHAK 447:3
billowy: plunged himself into the b. GILB 227:17
bills: children but as b. of charges BACON 26:32
inflammation of his weekly b. BYRON 122:29
Billy: heart to poke poor B. GRAH 233:13
Who's Silly B. now GLOU 229:23
bin: have gone to stall and b. FROST 219:11
bind: apprentice for to b. BALL 30:8
b. another to its delight BLAKE 87:19
b. their kings in chains PRAY 399:24
b. the sweet influences BIBLE 53:5
b. up the nation's wounds LINC 315:3
b. your sons to exile KIPL 304:6
body and in soul can b. SCOTT 416:20
ever sure to b. POPE 375:24
Rob me, but b. me not DONNE 189:16
binds: who b. to himself a Joy BLAKE 86:18
Bingham: B. had never been to Ciro's TRAV 552:6
Binnorie: *bonnie milldams o' B.* BALL 30:14
binomial: b. theorems I'm teeming GILB 228:17
Biographers: B., translators MAC 323:10
Boswell is the first of b. MAC 324:5
biographical: b. friend who has added WETH 569:6
biographies: essence of innumerable b. CARL 131:9
Biography: B. is about chaps BENT 41:3
b. of great men CARL 131:31
no history; only b. EMER 207:24
nothing but b. DISR 186:4
birch: nor fasting, nor b. BLAKE 87:20
to go by climbing a b. FROST 219:1
bird: at the voice of the b. BIBLE 56:11
b. forlorn HOOD 255:2
b. of dawning singeth all SHAK 429:17
b. of night did sit SHAK 449:1
b. of wonder dies SHAK 448:3
b.'s song ye may learn TENN 535:3
b. That flutters least COWP 167:29
b. that thinks two notes DAV 172:14
B. thou never wert SHEL 504:15
b. would trust Her household HERB 246:23
Dromedary is a cheerful b. BELL 38:27
fell with the waking b. TENN 540:10
forgets the dying b. PAINE 368:3
further than a wanton's b. SHAK 482:20
heart is like a singing b. ROSS 408:23
household b. DONNE 188:19
in the sight of any b. BIBLE 53:14
is escaped even as a b. PRAY 398:14
I would I were thy b. SHAK 482:20
Let the b. of loudest lay SHAK 492:15
Like that self-begotten b. MILT 350:30
obscure b. SHAK 460:20
rare b. on this earth JUV 287:20
regretted that he was not a b. ROCHE 406:13
sea-blue b. of March TENN 537:9
secular b. MILT 350:31
Shall I call thee b. WORD 582:25
Stirred for a b. HOPK 257:5
Sweet b., that shunn'st MILT 342:2
Unto the sweet b.'s throat SHAK 425:14
wakeful b. Sings darkling MILT 347:8
were all like that wise b. PUNCH 402:25
widow b. sate mourning SHEL 500:3
young b. in this bush LEAR 311:18
birdcage: summer b. in a garden WEBS 567:2
bird-haunted: b. English lawn ARN 14:1
birdie: b. with a yellow bill STEV 522:24
What does little b. say TENN 543:7
birds: are like bats amongst b. BACON 27:23
Beasts did leap and b. BARN 33:32
b. are on the wing COL 157:14
B. build HOPK 257:3
B. in the high Hall-garden TENN 540:5
B. in their little nests BELL 40:6
B. in their little nests WATTS 565:20
b. of the air have nests BIBLE 65:18
b. sit brooding SHAK 457:19
b. still hopping STEV 522:16
b. the colour of red-flannel THOM 546:22
children casual as b. AUDEN 18:5
diminutive of b., will fight SHAK 462:12
happy as b. in the spring BLAKE 87:20
I envy b. their wings CLARE 152:7
If b. confabulate or no COWP 166:5
Melodious b. sing madrigals MARL 330:1
nest of singing b. JOHN 273:28
no b. sing KEATS 290:15
pipe of half-awaken'd b. TENN 542:4
see all the b. are flown CHAR 140:18
sing like b. i' the cage SHAK 456:3
song of the b. for mirth GURN 237:7
so that the b. of the air BIBLE 66:20
suffers little b. to sing SHAK 486:17
time of the singing of b. BIBLE 56:22
Two fairer B. I yet did SPEN 516:31
very merciful to the b. ANON 8:15
We think caged b. sing WEBS 567:10
what these unobservant b. ISH 270:27
where late the sweet b. sang SHAK 494:7
With charm of earliest b. MILT 348:4
you b. build nests not VIRG 560:20
bird-song: b. at morning and star-shine STEV 522:29
Birmingham: B. by way of Beachy Head CHES 147:11
no great hopes from B. AUST 22:18
Birnam wood: B. to high Dunsinane hill SHAK 462:8
Till B. remove to Dunsinane SHAK 462:28
birth: at my b. SHAK 439:21
Beauty, wit, High b. SHAK 487:6
bed for this huge b. CRAS 169:7
B., and copulation ELIOT 204:12
bring this monstrous b. SHAK 474:13
draws near the b. of Christ TENN 536:17
grievous burden was thy b. SHAK 481:8
his b.'s invidious bar TENN 537:1
I had seen b. and death ELIOT 203:15
laid us as we lay at b. ARN 13:17
Nobility of b. commonly BACON 27:1
one that is coming to b. OSH 365:21
Our b. is but a sleep WORD 579:5
Saviour's b. is celebrated SHAK 429:17
she who gives a baby b. MAS 333:25
sudden and portentous b. SCOTT 417:20
Terms like grace, new b. ARN 16:18
that have a different b. SHEL 505:5
There was a B. ELIOT 203:15
to say as a sorrowful b. MAL 327:17
virtue, and not b. FLET 215:18
birthday: Because the b. of my life ROSS 408:24
marvel My b. Away THOM 547:7
birth-pangs: shorten and lessen the b. MARX 333:8
birth-place: b. of valour BURNS 114:26
birth-rate: Into a rising b. FRY 219:32
birthright: Esau selleth his b. for a mess BIBLE 46:12
sold his b. unto Jacob BIBLE 46:14

birthrite: b. for a mess of potash WARD 564:22
births: b. of living creatures BACON 26:27
joyful b. SHAK 445:11
which are the b. of time BACON 26:27
birth-strangled: Finger of b. babe SHAK 462:4
bis: b. dat qui dat celeriter PUBL 402:3
biscuit: b., or confectionary plum COWP 166:3
dry as the remainder b. SHAK 425:21
he took a captain's b. DICK 179:4
biscuit box: didn't look like a b. did it COW 163:13
biscuits: eat and the b. you nibble KIPL 298:5
with beef and captain's b. THAC 545:32
Bishop: another B. dead MELB 336:19
B.-Elect of Vermont KNOX 305:23
B. of Rome hath no jurisdiction PRAY 400:10
b. then must be blameless BIBLE 79:12
desire the office of a b. BIBLE 79:11
How can a b. marry SMITH 511:4
Shepherd and B. of your souls BIBLE 80:27
think of contradicting a B. JOHN 279:14
bishopric: talk of *merit* for a b. WEST 569:5
bishops: b. like best in their clergy SMITH 512:1
If elderly b. were seen HERB 246:15
Send down upon our B. PRAY 385:7
thee to illuminate all B. PRAY 385:18
to all B. and Curates PRAY 387:15
bisier: he semed b. than he was CHAU 141:26
bisy: Nowher so b. a man as he CHAU 141:26
bit: b. by him that comes behind SWIFT 528:5
b. him till he bled HOFF 252:13
b. the babies in the cradles BROW 103:15
held with b. and bridle PRAY 391:18
requital b. his fingers CHIL 148:13
Though he had b. me SHAK 455:24
Went mad and b. the man GOLD 231:13
Bitch: called John a Impudent B. FLEM 214:27
old b. gone in the teeth POUND 383:10
why b. FIEL 211:12
bitch-goddess: flabbiness born of the b. SUCCESS JAMES 272:3
bite: b. some of my other generals GEOR 223:36
b. so nigh As benefits forgot SHAK 426:1
b. the hand that fed BURKE 112:10
forbear To b. his pen SWIFT 527:23
man recover'd of the b. GOLD 231:14
you b. your thumb at us SHAK 481:22
bites: bargain dog never b. NASH 360:3
dog b. a man BOG 89:9
biteth: last it b. like a serpent BIBLE 54:24
biting: His b. is immortal SHAK 424:5
more than b. Time can sever ELIOT 204:3
bitter: be not b. against them BIBLE 78:27
b. belly-tension between GIBB 225:4
b. bread of banishment SHAK 479:4
b. God to follow SWIN 530:3
does truth sound b. BROW 102:9
do such b. business SHAK 434:25
end is b. as wormwood BIBLE 53:20
life unto the b. in soul BIBLE 52:14
love groans b. with treason SWIN 530:5
make misfortunes more b. BACON 27:3
mirth that has no b. springs KIPL 298:12
my belly was b. BIBLE 82:9
pulp so b. THOM 548:19
shortly as b. as coloquintida SHAK 474:10
Some do it with a b. look WILDE 572:10
something b. that chokes LUCR 320:11
sweet water and b. BIBLE 80:15
these are very b. words SHAK 441:26
bitterness: b. of death is past BIBLE 50:5
must have no hatred or b. CAV 137:18
rose's scent is b. THOM 547:25
scorn in the b. of his soul BIBLE 62:26

think the b. of absence sour SHAK 493:18
years in the b. of my soul BIBLE 59:3
bivouac: Barrack and b. shall be AUDEN 19:11
blabbing: b., and remorseful day SHAK 446:8
black: be a b. man or a fair man ADD 2:7
be the heavens with b. SHAK 445:17
b. and merciless things JAMES 271:23
B. as the Pit from pole HENL 245:4
b., but comely BIBLE 56:16
b. eyes and lemonade MOORE 356:3
b. it stood as night MILT 346:24
b. men fought on the coast MAC 323:21
b. piano appassionato LAWR 311:7
b. ram Is tupping SHAK 473:16
Black's not so b. CANN 129:29
b. *sun* of *melancholy* NERV 360:26
b. vesper's pageants SHAK 423:7
customary suits of solemn b. SHAK 429:25
devil damn thee b. SHAK 463:1
I am b. SHAK 475:21
I am b. BLAKE 88:2
it here in b. and white JONS 284:7
More b. than ashbuds TENN 533:19
night's b. agents SHAK 461:14
read'st b. where I read white BLAKE 85:22
shall not neutralize the b. BROW 104:31
sloeblack, slow, b., crowblack THOM 547:9
They were as b. as they BALL 32:7
Tip me the b. spot STEV 521:22
velvet that is b. and soft CHES 147:5
vexed not his fantasy B. DONNE 190:3
Who art as b. as hell SHAK 495:15
worse for wearing a b. gown CHES 145:11
you wear b. all the time CHEK 144:25
blackberries: plentiful as b. SHAK 439:5
prove a micher and eat b. SHAK 439:14
sit round it and pluck b. BROW 97:33
blackberry: running b. would adorn WHIT 570:21
blackbird: b.'s tune BROW 100:13
b., what a boy you are BROWN 95:11
blackbirds: full of b. than of cherries ADD 2:25
blackens: b. all the water about ADD 2:24
b. every blot TENN 533:30
blacker: Leaving a b. air HARDY 240:11
blackguard: brute and b. made the world HOUS 264:21
Sesquipedalian b. CLOU 153:17
That man's a b. HOR 262:3
blackguards: b. both BYRON 123:12
ever done to you young b. FARR 210:28
Blackheath: from wild B. MAC 322:3
blacking: drink and b. the Corporal's KIPL 298:7
blacksmith: Never was a b. like our KIPL 297:26
Black Widow: This is the B. LOW 319:19
bladder: blows a man up like a b. SHAK 439:11
bladders: boys that swim on b. SHAK 447:9
blade: b. is layed low POUND 383:19
cling round the sickly b. COWP 168:26
destroy a b. of grass BOTT 90:17
His b. struck the water COKE 154:15
vorpal b. went snicker-snack CARR 134:29
with bloody blameful b. SHAK 471:17
blade-straight: Steel-true and b. STEV 523:3
blains: breaking forth with b. BIBLE 47:14
Blake: B. is damned good to steal FUS 220:22
B. was no good BUTL 118:35
B. went dotty as he sang AUDEN 18:20
what B. once wildly muttered... SASS 414:19
blame: Alike reserv'd to b. POPE 376:27
am not disposed to b. him BURKE 109:5
b. of those ye better KIPL 304:8
only The Master shall b. KIPL 304:3
That neither is most to b. SWIN 530:11

blameless: bishop then must be b. BIBLE 79:12
white flower of a b. life TENN 533:30
blanch: plain when counsellors b. BACON 25:39
Tray, B., and Sweet-heart SHAK 454:29
blanching: under b. mays HOUS 265:8
bland: Aspect anything but b. CALV 127:14
composed and b. ARN 14:4
lines mellifluously b. BYRON 123:14
tone, and gesture b. SCOTT 416:2
blandula: Animula vagula b. HADR 237:9
Blank: B. to Zoroaster on his BROW 102:35
political b. cheque GOSC 233:2
Presented with a universal b. MILT 347:8
you talk in b. verse SHAK 426:20
blanket: right side of the b. ASHF 17:12
through the b. of the dark SHAK 459:2
blankets: rough male kiss of b. BROO 94:8
blasphemies: great truths begin as b. SHAW 496:2
blaspheming: brooding and b. over the village CHES 148:7
Liver of b. Jew SHAK 462:4
blasphemous: were b. fables PRAY 400:9
blasphemy: b. against the Holy Ghost BIBLE 66:7
soldier is flat b. SHAK 464:4
blast: banner wav'd without a b. SCOTT 416:14
B. of the Desert cried LONG 317:8
b. of war blows in our SHAK 443:21
every b. of vain doctrine PRAY 387:3
in the trances of the b. COL 156:23
One b. upon his bugle-horn SCOTT 416:7
though it b. me SHAK 429:14
blasted: about you b. with antiquity SHAK 441:10
b. heath you stop our way SHAK 458:13
b. with excess of light GRAY 235:19
B. with ecstasy SHAK 433:15
no sooner blown but b. MILT 344:2
you b. its rocks away RUSK 411:13
blasts: airs from heaven or b. SHAK 430:24
Blatant: which the B. beast men SPEN 516:22
blaze: broader still became the b. MAC 322:3
heavens themselves b. forth the death SHAK 449:18
that brighten at the b. GOLD 231:26
unclouded b. of living light BYRON 121:37
blazed: My body of a sudden b. YEATS 587:11
blazes: b., and expires BYRON 124:30
blazing: you b. ass CALV 127:18
blazon: this eternal b. must not be SHAK 431:5
Bleach: B. the bones of comrades HOUS 263:19
bleaching: white sheet b. on the hedge SHAK 491:17
bleak: In the b. mid-winter ROSS 409:1
bleat: b. the one at the other SHAK 491:8
bled: bit him till he b. HOFF 252:13
knew that marble b. FLEC 214:15
bleed: Caesar b. in sport SHAK 450:5
do we not b. SHAK 467:4
I b. SHEL 502:13
If he do b. SHAK 460:11
mee downe and b. a while BALL 31:15
our bosom and then we b. SHEL 501:4
'Twill b. because of it HOUS 264:9
bleeding: pageant of his b. heart ARN 13:9
testament of his b. war SHAK 479:13
thou b. piece of earth SHAK 450:11
blemish: lamb shall be without b. BIBLE 47:16
there's no b. but the mind SHAK 490:18
without fear and without b. ANON 9:5
blenches: These b. gave my heart SHAK 495:3
Bless: B. her when she is riggish SHAK 422:5

b. the hand that gave — DRYD 197:27
B. the Lord — BIBLE 83:16
B. the squire and his relations — DICK 176:23
b. ye the Lord — PRAY 384:19
Curse, b., me now — THOM 546:24
except thou b. me — BIBLE 46:24
'God b. us every one — DICK 176:24
him how to load and b. — KEATS 293:5
was blessèd and could b. — YEATS 587:11
Blessed: B. are the poor in spirit — BIBLE 64:6
B. are the eyes which see — BIBLE 69:29
B. are the dead which die — BIBLE 82:18
b. are the horny hands — LOW 319:9
B. art thou among women — ANON 10:8
b. art thou among women — BIBLE 69:4
B. be he that cometh — PRAY 398:3
b. be the name of the Lord — BIBLE 52:7
b. damozel leaned out — ROSS 409:14
B. is he who has found — CARL 132:10
B. is the man that endureth — BIBLE 80:8
B. is the man that hath — PRAY 389:14
B. is the man unto whom — PRAY 391:16
b. is the man that trusteth — PRAY 391:21
B. is the man whose strength — PRAY 395:12
b. mutter of the mass — BROW 99:14
b. the latter end of Job — BIBLE 53:13
b. they that master so — SHAK 469:17
B. to give than to receive — BIBLE 74:19
buttercup Had b. with gold — OWEN 367:8
call her b. — BIBLE 55:4
generations shall call me b. — BIBLE 69:5
hence to there may be b. — SOCR 512:20
His b. part to Heaven — SHAK 447:16
How b. is he — DRYD 196:3
I b. them unaware — COL 155:22
I was b. and could bless — YEATS 587:11
Judge none b. before his — BIBLE 63:1
That b. mood — WORD 578:5
This b. plot — SHAK 478:20
Thou fall'st a b. martyr — SHAK 447:12
thou hast altogether b. — BIBLE 48:16
what all the b. Evil's — BROW 99:8
whom thou blessest is b. — BIBLE 48:13
blessedness: b. alone that makes a King — TRAH 552:2
blindly with thy b. at strife — WORD 579:8
in single b. — SHAK 469:17
Blesses: B. his stars — ADD 1:17
blessest: visitest the earth, and b. — PRAY 394:2
blesseth: It b. him that gives — SHAK 467:27
blessing: behold us with Thy b. — BUCK 106:16
b. of God Almighty — PRAY 388:4
b. of the Old Testament — BACON 25:18
b. that money cannot buy — WALT 564:21
come as a boon and a b. — ANON 8:5
continual dew of thy b. — PRAY 389:5
contrariwise b. — BIBLE 80:30
daughter would have been a b. — AUST 23:18
hath taken away thy b. — BIBLE 46:17
I'll b. beg of you — SHAK 435:19
in the pursuit of the b. — AUST 22:30
shall give us his b. — PRAY 394:5
When thou dost ask me b. — SHAK 456:3
You enjoy but half the b. — GAY 222:9
blessings: Are b. in disguise — HERV 250:17
b. on the falling out — TENN 541:28
Having a glass of b. standing — HERB 248:6
In b. on your head — COWP 165:27
they recognized their b. — VIRG 560:13
blest: always To be b. — POPE 379:5
Bed be b. that I lie — ANON 6:15
B. pair of Sirens — MILT 340:20
last promotion of the b. — DRYD 197:32
their country's wishes b. — COLL 158:19
blew: b. his silly brains out — THAC 546:3
hotched an' b. wi' might — BURNS 115:11
blight: is the b. man was born — HOPK 256:27
Blimber: nonsense about Miss B. — DICK 177:23
blind: Altho' a poor b. boy — CIBB 151:8

b. as any noon-tide owl — TENN 534:23
b. his soul with clay — TENN 542:19
b. Homer sing — MARL 329:9
b. man in a dark room — BOWEN 90:23
b. man On the sightless — WALEY 562:2
b., now I see — BIBLE 72:16
b. old man of Scio's rocky — BYRON 120:3
B. to Galileo on his turret — BROW 102:35
B. with thine hair — SHEL 505:3
Country of the B. the One-eyed — WELLS 568:12
Cupid b. did rise — LYLY 321:11
eyes were b. with stars — HODG 252:8
eyes will gaze an eagle b. — SHAK 457:8
giveth sight to the b. — PRAY 399:17
go drawing back the b. — KIPL 302:22
halt, and the b. — BIBLE 70:12
her faults a little b. — PRIOR 400:23
if the blind lead the b. — BIBLE 66:29
I was eyes to the b. — BIBLE 52:35
Love is b. — ANON 9:11
man to a b. woman — COL 157:19
of darkness and b. eyes — VAUG 555:11
old, mad, b. — SHEL 504:6
old Maeonides the b. — FLEC 214:22
own internal lightning b. — SHEL 501:18
passion and party b. — COL 157:20
splendid work for the b. — SASS 414:13
That myself am b. — POPE 381:12
That nourish a b. life — TENN 535:26
Thou Eye among the b. — WORD 579:7
though she be b. — BACON 26:13
though she's painted b. — BUTL 118:14
unbelief is b. — MILT 341:12
will accompany my being b. — PEPYS 372:21
wing'd Cupid painted b. — SHAK 469:22
Ye b. guides — BIBLE 67:24
blinded: dulness of our b. sight — PRAY 400:5
blindfold: b. and alone — KIPL 298:25
blindly: nor b. right — POPE 378:32
blindness: From all b. of heart — PRAY 385:16
is a triple sight in b. — KEATS 292:5
I've an April b. — FRY 219:26
our b. we cannot ask — PRAY 388:7
To help him of his b. — SHAK 491:4
blinds: b. let through the day — HOUS 265:2
dusk a drawing-down of b. — OWEN 367:3
blind-worm: b.'s sting — SHAK 462:3
blind-worms: b., do no wrong — SHAK 470:11
blinking: b. sort o' place — HARDY 241:22
portrait of a b. idiot — SHAK 466:21
blisfully: His lighte goost ful b. — CHAU 144:18
Bliss: B. in our brows bent — SHAK 421:26
b. in proof — SHAK 495:7
B. was it in that dawn — WORD 577:21
certainty of waking b. — MILT 341:5
deprived of everlasting b. — MARL 329:7
each to his point of b. — BROW 105:20
had given all other b. — TENN 543:9
highest b. of human-kind — KEATS 292:20
it will be b. — BETJ 43:15
Milk-soup men call domestic b. — PATM 370:4
mutual and partaken b. — MILT 341:17
Of bliss on b. — MILT 348:1
promise of pneumatic b. — ELIOT 205:14
Thou art a soul in b. — SHAK 455:25
where ignorance is b. — GRAY 235:13
Which is the b. of solitude — WORD 578:1
with hopes of earthly b. — COWP 167:17
blister: b. my kidneys — SURT 525:16
blithe: be you b. and bonny — SHAK 472:16
buxom, b., and debonair — MILT 342:13
Hail to thee, b. Spirit — SHEL 504:15
No b. Irish lad was so — CAMP 128:20
No lark more b. than he — BICK 83:28
block: chopper on a big black b. — GILB 226:31
each b. cut smooth — POUND 382:8
old b. itself — BURKE 110:22
blockhead: bookful b. — POPE 378:30
if I had not been a b. — ADD 2:17

man but a b. ever wrote — JOHN 277:4
when a b.'s insult points — JOHN 282:23
blocks: You b., you stones — SHAK 448:6
Blond: B. comme un soleil d'Italie — BANV 33:1
blonde: b. Bestie nicht zu verkennen — NIET 363:14
blood: am I not of her b. — SHAK 488:18
b. and smoke and flame — HOUS 266:4
b. and wine are red — WILDE 572:7
B., as all men know — HUXL 269:2
b. be the price of admiralty — KIPL 303:4
b. in his liver as will — SHAK 490:1
B. is compulsory — STOP 523:16
b. is fet from fathers — SHAK 444:1
b. Is very snow-broth — SHAK 463:14
b. more stirs — SHAK 438:18
b. of all the Howards — POPE 379:23
b. Of human sacrifice — MILT 345:14
B. of Jesus whispers — BICK 84:4
b. of patriots and tyrants — JEFF 272:10
B. of the New Testament — PRAY 388:1
b. ran down the stairs — AUDEN 21:7
b. reigns in the winter's — SHAK 491:11
b.'s a rover — HOUS 262:15
b. will have blood — SHAK 461:24
b. with guilt is bought — SHEL 503:1
blow in cold b. — SHAW 497:41
by crikey b. will tell — MARQ 330:20
choler without letting b. — SHAK 478:7
drink the b. of goats — PRAY 393:3
drop my b. for drachmas — SHAK 451:21
examine well your b. — SHAK 469:17
flesh and b. so cheap — HOOD 255:8
fountain fill'd with b. — COWP 165:24
from kindred b. — BURKE 110:2
getting b. out of a turnip — MARR 331:3
give me B. — DICK 177:13
good enough to shed his b. — ROOS 408:3
guiltless of his country's b. — GRAY 234:23
have had so much b. in him — SHAK 462:20
Her b. is settled — SHAK 483:22
Here's the smell of the b. — SHAK 462:22
His b. be on us — BIBLE 68:22
I am innocent of the b. — BIBLE 68:21
in b. Stepp'd in so far — SHAK 461:25
Inhabits our frail b. — SHAK 490:2
kind of sleeping in the b. — SHAK 441:6
'Let there be b. — BYRON 123:3
make thick my b. — SHAK 459:2
Man of B. was there — MAC 322:7
man shall his b. be shed — BIBLE 45:39
men are flesh and b. — SHAK 449:25
moment when the moon was b. — CHES 146:22
most noble b. — SHAK 450:7
near in b. — SHAK 461:4
Neptune's ocean wash this b. — SHAK 460:13
not against flesh and b. — BIBLE 78:10
Nothing like b. — THAC 545:27
nothing to offer but b. — CHUR 149:29
now could I drink hot b. — SHAK 434:25
out through b. and iron — BISM 84:25
pride in place and b. — TENN 537:15
Propinquity and property of b. — SHAK 453:3
pure and eloquent b. — DONNE 189:31
rivers of b. must yet flow — JEFF 272:14
See see where Christ's b. — MARL 329:11
shedding of b. is no remission — BIBLE 79:29
shed innocent b. — BIBLE 60:6
smear'd in dust and b. — SHAK 446:22
smell the b. of a British — SHAK 454:27
summon up the b. — SHAK 443:21
Sweat ran and b. sprang — HOUS 264:24
that all that b. was shed — YEATS 586:19
that sheds his b. with me — SHAK 445:3
there's b. upon her gown — FLEC 214:6
they stream forth thy b. — SHAK 450:9
thicks man's b. with cold — COL 155:15
this tincture in the b. — DEFOE 173:4
Tiber foaming with much b. — VIRG 558:17
voice of thy brother's b. — BIBLE 45:26

In the name of the B. — BIRR 84:18
body: Absent in b. — BIBLE 75:34
anger at the clog of his b. — FULL 220:19
b. and material substance — CARL 131:34
b. did contain a spirit — SHAK 440:24
b. fill'd and vacant mind — SHAK 444:25
b. form doth take — SPEN 516:28
b. is a machine for living — TOLS 551:12
b. is aweary of this great — SHAK 465:18
b. is even like melting — PRAY 390:19
b. is perfectly spherical — LEAR 311:23
b.—it grew better — WORD 577:24
b.'s beauty lives — STEV 520:17
b.'s delicate — SHAK 454:13
b. than raiment — BIBLE 64:28
change our vile b. — PRAY 389:13
commit his b. to the ground — PRAY 389:13
commit his b. to the deep — PRAY 400:4
edifying of the b. of Christ — BIBLE 77:28
education of the b. I admire — DISR 186:21
Find thy b. by the wall — ARN 13:15
from the b. of this death — BIBLE 75:6
gigantic b. — MAC 324:7
Gin a body meet a b. — BURNS 113:3
give my b. to be burned — BIBLE 76:14
had tasted her sweet b. — SHAK 475:25
Hail the true b. — ANON 10:9
her b. thought — DONNE 189:31
I had the use of my b. — BECK 36:17
I keep under my b. — BIBLE 76:9
I know I have the b. — ELIZ 206:4
In doubt his mind or b. — POPE 379:12
is not more than the b. — WHIT 571:3
joint and motive of her b. — SHAK 487:13
left me but my b.'s length — SHAK 446:22
linen and keep your b. — STEV 522:29
Make less thy b. hence — SHAK 442:31
mind, b., or estate — PRAY 386:1
mind in a sound b. — JUV 288:4
My b. of a sudden blazed — YEATS 587:11
mystery of the glorious b. — THOM 546:16
Naught broken save this b. — BROO 94:28
nothing the b. suffers — MER 337:28
provinces of his b. revolted — AUDEN 19:3
Resurrection of the b. — PRAY 384:26
softness of my b. will — LOW 318:25
Take, eat; this is my b. — BIBLE 68:11
Thersites' b. is as good — SHAK 428:1
Thy b. is all vice — JOHN 274:4
To keep the b. young — YEATS 586:20
unacquainted with your b. — BACON 26:17
Upon my buried b. lay — BEAU 36:8
when b.'s work's expired — SHAK 493:5
Whose b. Nature is — POPE 379:10
with my b. I thee worship — PRAY 389:5
yet the b. is more capable — CAB 126:24
you ask me for my b. — SHAW 496:30
young a b. with so old — SHAK 467:26
Your b. is the temple — BIBLE 76:1
Boets: hate all B. and Bainters — GEOR 223:34
boil: b. at different degrees — EMER 208:9
b. breaking forth with — BIBLE 47:14
B. thou first i' the charmed — SHAK 462:2
discontent, b. bloody — OWEN 367:11
To b. eggs in your shoes — LEAR 313:3
boil'd: eels b. in broo' — BALL 31:5
politics in b. and roast — SMITH 512:6
boilers: parcel of b. and vats — JOHN 278:27
boiling: broach'd his b. bloody breast — SHAK 471:17
with b. oil in it — GILB 227:11
Boire: B. sans soif et faire l'amour — BEAU 35:17
bois: Nous n'irons plus aux b. — ANON 9:15
bok: Farewell my b., and my devocioun — CHAU 143:29
Go, litel b. — CHAU 144:17
bokes: On b. for to rede I me — CHAU 143:29
bold: be b. and be sensible — HOR 258:14
Be bold, be b. — SPEN 516:18

Be not too b. — SPEN 516:18
b. bad man — SHAK 447:1
b. bad man — SPEN 516:1
b. only to pursue — SHEL 499:16
b. spirit in a loyal breast — SHAK 478:8
Fortune assists the b. — VIRG 559:9
Modestly b. — POPE 378:32
righteous are b. as a lion — BIBLE 54:41
them drunk hath made me b. — SHAK 460:2
you been as wise as b. — SHAK 466:17
boldest: b. held his breath — CAMP 128:15
Boldness: B., and again boldness — DANT 171:19
b. at least will deserve — PROP 401:16
B. be my friend — SHAK 428:7
b. is a child of ignorance — BACON 25:31
B. is an ill keeper — BACON 25:32
Familiarity begets b. — MARM 330:18
Bolingbroke: canker, B. — SHAK 438:17
Who now reads B. — BURKE 111:17
bolt: b. is shot back — ARN 12:22
this you can see is the b. — REED 405:6
bolts: b. are hurl'd — TENN 539:16
bomb: atomic b. is a paper tiger — MAO 328:20
b. the Germans — BETJ 43:5
merely a climber with a b. — ORW 365:16
Bombazine: B. would have shown a deeper — GASK 222:3
bomber: b. will always get through — BALD 29:27
bombilating: gong was b. — THOM 546:21
bombinating: b. in a vacuum can devour — RAB 403:29
bombs: b., and fall on Slough — BETJ 44:5
bona: sua si b. norint — VIRG 560:13
Bonaparte: which B. thought was — THOR 550:18
bond: b. nor free — BIBLE 78:26
b. Which keeps me pale — SHAK 461:14
I will have my b. — SHAK 467:16
Let him look to his b. — SHAK 467:3
not the b. of man and wife — TENN 534:32
take a b. of fate — SHAK 462:7
you break that sole b. — BURKE 110:4
Bondage: B. is hoarse — SHAK 482:19
b. which is freedom's self — SHEL 503:16
Cassius from b. will deliver — SHAK 449:2
Disguise our b. as we will — MOORE 357:1
modern b. of Rhyming — MILT 344:19
on his own obsequious b. — SHAK 473:13
out of the house of b. — BIBLE 47:24
spirit of b. again to fear — BIBLE 75:8
bondmaid: one by a b. — BIBLE 77:16
bondman: base that would be a b. — SHAK 450:16
Check'd like a b. — SHAK 451:23
bonds: except these b. — BIBLE 74:28
He loves his b. — HERR 250:4
Let us break their b. asunder — PRAY 389:16
My b. in thee are all determinate — SHAK 494:13
bondsmen: Hereditary b. — BYRON 120:14
bone: ball of feather and b. — HARDY 240:20
b., for bene — SHAK 457:11
B. of my bone thou art — MILT 349:19
bright hair about the b. — DONNE 190:5
curs mouth a b. — CHUR 149:8
hardened into the b. of manhood — BURKE 109:17
Hath never a b. in't — WEBS 566:18
He knows death to the b. — YEATS 584:21
his every b. a-stare — BROW 99:28
rag and a b. and a hank — KIPL 303:29
This is now b. of my bones — BIBLE 45:12
vigour of b. — SHAK 487:6
boneless: see the b. wonder sitting — CHUR 149:27
bones: all my b. are out of joint — PRAY 390:19
be he that moves my b. — SHAK 495:22
Bleach the b. of comrades — HOUS 263:19

b. are smitten asunder — PRAY 392:9
b. consumed away through — PRAY 391:16
b. which thou hast broken — PRAY 393:5
canoniz'd b. hearsed in death — SHAK 430:24
Can these b. live — BIBLE 61:1
England keep my b. — SHAK 452:29
glas he hadde pigges b. — CHAU 142:7
have the tongs and the b. — SHAK 471:3
healthy b. of a single — BISM 84:22
I may tell all my b. — PRAY 390:20
lay his weary b. among ye — SHAK 447:15
mock'd the dead b. that — SHAK 480:27
nor hatchment o'er his b. — SHAK 436:14
Of his b. are coral made — SHAK 484:32
Rattle his b. over — NOEL 363:19
sure my b. would not rest — BYRON 126:20
their b. and soul's delivery — DONNE 189:5
to lay my b. amongst you — WOLS 576:13
to subsist in b. — BROW 97:15
valley which was full of b. — BIBLE 60:38
weave their thread with b. — SHAK 489:3
whose b. Lie scattered — MILT 351:9
within full of dead men's b. — BIBLE 67:25
ye dry b. — BIBLE 61:2
bonfire: way to the everlasting b. — SHAK 460:17
Bong-tree: To the land where the B. — LEAR 312:12
bonhomie: Overcame his natural b. — BENT 41:8
bon-mots: By plucking b. from their — MORE 357:9
bonnet: follow the b. of Bonny Dundee — SCOTT 415:20
in antique ruff and b. — JOHN 280:9
Bonnets: All the Blue B. are bound — SCOTT 418:24
Bonnie: B. wee thing — BURNS 113:1
honest men and b. lasses — BURNS 115:4
Bonnivard: By B. — BYRON 125:15
bonny: Am I no a b. fighter — STEV 521:7
Belbroughton Road is b. — BETJ 43:12
be you blithe and b. — SHAK 472:16
bono: Cui b. — CIC 151:32
bonum: Summum b. — CIC 151:21
bonus: Give me the b. of laughter — BETJ 43:10
booby: Who'd give her b. for another — GAY 223:11
Boojum: If your Snark be a B. — CARR 133:7
book: adversary had written a b. — BIBLE 52:38
all the needs a b. has — TROL 552:14
any b. but the Baronetage — AUST 23:7
any b. should be banned — WEST 569:2
be a man behind the b. — EMER 208:5
Bell, b., and candle — SHAK 452:19
b. a devil's chaplain might — DARW 172:1
b. comes into my mouth — POUND 382:15
b. is the best of friends — TUPP 553:21
b. is the precious life-blood — MILT 351:23
b. is the purest essence — CARL 132:29
b. it is written of me — PRAY 392:2
b. may be amusing with — GOLD 232:31
b. of honour razed quite — SHAK 493:4
B. of Life begins with — WILDE 573:29
B. of Verse — FITZ 212:11
book's a b. — BYRON 124:16
b. that a young girl touches — RUSK 412:13
b. that furnishes no quotations — PEAC 370:12
b. that is not a year old — EMER 208:7
Charlotte has been writing a b. — BRON 94:2
cover of an old b. — FRAN 218:20
dainties that are bred in a b. — SHAK 457:1
Death put down his b. — AUDEN 20:19
for to print My b. — HERR 250:15
Go, little b. — STEV 523:7
Here's my small b. out — CAT 136:19
his picture, but his b. — JONS 284:17
hotch-potch of my little b. — JUV 287:12
I'll drown my b. — SHAK 485:24
is as a b. where men — SHAK 459:3

borne: b. away with every breath
BYRON 125:20
b. it with a patient shrug SHAK 466:2
b. me a man of strife BIBLE 60:23
Had b. my breath away HOOD 254:17
I have b., and borne SHAK 441:18
my mother had not b. me SHAK 433:11
who have b. even heavier VIRG 557:13
borogoves: All mimsy were the b.
CARR 134:28
boroughs: bright b. HOPK 256:28
fresh eggs to rotten b. MAC 323:15
borrer: b. the money to do it with
WARD 564:36
borrow: earth must b. its mirth WILC 572:5
men who b. LAMB 307:12
borrow'd: dress me In b. robes SHAK 458:17
borrowed: Conveys it in a b. name
PRIOR 401:1
borrower: become a b. of the night
SHAK 461:7
b., nor a lender be SHAK 430:19
borrowers: I mean your *b. of books*
LAMB 307:12
borrowing: beggar by banqueting upon
b. BIBLE 63:6
b. only lingers and lingers SHAK 441:16
bosom: b. beats not in his country's
POPE 375:12
b. black as death SHAK 434:28
b. of the urgent West BRID 92:19
carried into Abraham's b. BIBLE 70:28
carry them in his b. BIBLE 59:7
Cleanse the stuff'd b. SHAK 463:3
guardage to the sooty b. SHAK 473:22
has no b. and no behind SMITH 510:27
in your fragrant b. dies CAREW 130:20
leaning on Jesus' b. BIBLE 72:28
little son into his b. FLET 215:28
man take fire in his b. BIBLE 53:23
my b., as a bed SHAK 490:32
My b.'s lord sits lightly SHAK 483:23
sleep in Abraham's b. SHAK 481:7
third in your b. SHAK 482:21
those thorns that in her b. SHAK 431:13
Through my burn'd b. SHAK 452:31
wring his b. GOLD 231:31
bosoms: b. of your actresses excite
JOHN 274:2
hang and brush their b. BROW 105:26
Quiet to quick b. is a hell BYRON 120:30
Bosque: B. taketh blossom POUND 383:18
Bossuet: excite the horror of B. MAC 324:9
Boston: B. bells ING 270:12
B. man is the east wind APPL 11:12
B.'s a hole BROW 102:20
say the cows laid out B. EMER 207:7
solid man of B. LONG 316:23
this is good old B. BOSS 90:13
bo'sun: b. tight GILB 225:16
Boswell: B. is the first of biographers
MAC 324:5
Boswelliana: exposed to the *Lues B.*
MAC 323:10
botanist: I am not a b. JOHN 274:19
botanize: down to b. in the swamp
CHES 148:7
that would peep and b. WORD 580:3
botched: b. civilization POUND 383:10
botches: Leave no rubs nor b. SHAK 461:11
both: a Norfan, b. sides WELLS 568:13
b. were faiths ARN 13:8
gentlemen b. ELIZ 205:23
long as ye b. shall live PRAY 389:3
may wear it on b. sides SHAK 487:7
bother: 'Oh b. the flowers that GILB 227:14
Though 'B. it' I may GILB 228:2
botom: I now sit down on my b. FLEM 215:3
botté: *toujours b. et prêt à partir*
MONT 354:13

Botticelli: B.'s a *cheese* PUNCH 403:3
bottle: crack a b. with a friend CHES 147:21
farthest b. labelled 'Ether' BROW 100:7
great desire to a b. of hay SHAK 471:4
'leave the b. on the chimley-piece
DICK 179:10
little for the b. DIBD 175:16
My b. of salvation RAL 404:12
nor a b. to give him DICK 177:26
put my tears into thy b. PRAY 393:13
we'll pass the b. round WHYT 572:2
bottles: forty b. of Ring-Bo-Ree LEAR 312:9
new wine into old b. BIBLE 65:25
bottom: b. of the monstrous world
MILT 343:16
scatter'd in the b. of the sea SHAK 480:27
Which will reach the b. GRAH 233:10
woman had a b. of good sense JOHN 278:28
bottomless: after them to the b. pit
MILT 348:27
Law is a b. pit ARB 11:20
riding into the b. abyss WALEY 562:2
smoke of the pit that is b. JAM 271:3
bouchers: *des bergers et des b.* VOLT 561:17
boue: *La nostalgie de la b.* AUG 21:11
bough: blossom that hangs on the b.
SHAK 485:25
of Bread beneath the b. FITZ 212:11
Touch not a single b. MORR 358:6
with bloom along the b. HOUS 262:14
boughs: b. and the brushwood sheaf
BROW 101:5
b. which shake against SHAK 494:7
I got me b. off many HERB 247:17
bought: b. over God with a fee SWIN 530:7
guilt is b. and sold SHEL 503:1
have b. it at any price CLAR 152:21
knowledge is b. in the market CLOU 153:18
bougies: *le vent éteint les b.* LA R 310:15
boum: all produce 'b.' FORS 217:8
bounced: b. out of bed MILNE 340:9
bound: b. him a thousand years BIBLE 82:27
b. in the spirit unto Jerusalem BIBLE 74:18
fast b. in misery PRAY 397:7
Fresh-b. CAT 136:19
my duty as a man is b. TENN 543:4
tied and b. by the chain PRAY 385:23
to another b. GREV 236:16
utmost b. of human thought TENN 544:1
boundary: has a right to fix the b.
PARN 369:2
of smouldering b. stones POUND 382:7
bounded: could be b. in a nut-shell
SHAK 432:13
bounden: b. duty and service PRAY 388:2
our b. duty PRAY 387:23
bounding: heart less b. at emotion ARN 15:9
boundless: believing what we see Is b.
SHEL 501:10
b. better, boundless worse TENN 543:19
b., endless BYRON 121:26
bounty is as b. as the sea SHAK 482:17
that the desire is b. SHAK 486:33
bounds: flaming b. of place and time
GRAY 235:19
hast set them their b. PRAY 396:19
bounties: Thy morning b. ere I left
COWP 166:3
bounty: his b., There was no winter
SHAK 423:22
lust of the goat is the b. BLAKE 88:21
My b. is as boundless SHAK 482:17
those his former b. fed DRYD 195:3
bour: twa sisters sat in a b. BALL 30:14
Bourbon: Can B. or Nassau go higher
PRIOR 400:25
bourg: rustic murmur of their b. TENN 535:4
bourgeois: b. are other people REN 405:10
'*B.*,' I observed, 'is an epithet' HOPE 255:29
How beastly the b. is LAWR 311:6

pissent au bas et les b. montent FLAU 214:3
proletarian for the b. LENIN 313:21
Bourgeoisie: British B. SITW 508:14
generations the British b. WAUGH 566:2
bourn: bound for the same b. HOUS 264:1
b. how far to be belov'd SHAK 421:7
to see beyond our b. KEATS 289:8
bousing: While we sit b. at the nappy
BURNS 115:3
boutique: *arrière b. toute notre* MONT 354:20
boutiquiers: *L'Angleterre est une nation
de b.* NAP 359:15
bow: all griefs which b. ARN 14:24
b. my knees unto the Father BIBLE 77:24
b. myself in the house BIBLE 51:29
b. of burning gold BLAKE 86:16
B. themselves when he did SHAK 447:3
b., ye tradesmen GILB 225:35
certain man drew a b. BIBLE 51:21
do set my b. in the cloud BIBLE 45:40
fascination in his very b. BYRON 123:36
from the Almighty's b. BLAKE 86:6
he breaketh the b. PRAY 392:21
Jesus every knee should b. BIBLE 78:14
like an unbent b. DONNE 190:3
Lord of the unerring b. BYRON 121:19
my b. will make a wide ROST 410:12
reason doth buckle and b. BACON 24:19
strong men shall b. themselves BIBLE 56:11
Thou shalt not b. down BIBLE 47:24
To draw the b. BYRON 124:10
two strings to my b. FIEL 211:19
unto the b. the cord is LONG 317:12
bow'd: it b. and syne it brake BALL 32:10
We b. our head and held ARN 13:16
bowed: At her feet he b. BIBLE 49:11
hours has chained and b. SHEL 502:13
bowels: Have you no b. GAY 222:31
in the b. of Christ CROM 169:21
shutteth up his b. of compassion BIBLE 81:4
bower: b. quiet for us KEATS 288:20
lime-tree b. my prison COL 157:10
queen in a summer's b. SHAK 439:30
that smooth-swarded b. TENN 541:18
to deck both bed and b. SPEN 516:13
bower-eaves: bow-shot from her b.
TENN 538:8
bowers: green and pleasant b. BLAKE 86:12
bowery: All that b. loneliness TENN 533:13
b. hollows crown'd with TENN 535:27
bowl: b. to sea went wise men PEAC 371:3
golden b. be broken BIBLE 56:11
inverted B. we call The Sky FITZ 213:8
Love in a golden b. BLAKE 85:19
Morning in the B. of Night FITZ 212:5
bowler: If the wild b. thinks he LANG 309:19
Bowling: lies poor Tom B. DIBD 175:21
plays to the b. of a ghost THOM 547:24
Some recommend the b. green GREEN 235:28
bow'r: b. of wanton Shrewsbury POPE 378:1
Bows: B. toward her SHAK 428:8
wood of English b. DOYLE 191:14
bow-shot: b. from her bower-eaves
TENN 538:8
bowsprit: b. got mixed with the rudder
CARR 133:5
bow-strings: cut b. SHAK 470:1
bow-windows: putting b. to the house
DICK 177:2
Bow-Wow: Big B. strain I can do
SCOTT 418:37
were it not for his *b. way* PEMB 371:12
bow-wows: gone to the demnition b.
DICK 180:23
box: b. where sweets compacted HERB 248:16
having an alabaster b. BIBLE 68:8
to him and said 'B. about AUBR 17:26
twelve good men into a b. BROU 95:4
boxes: He had forty-two b. CARR 133:2
holsters and cartridge b. SHAW 496:6

boy: Alas, pitiable b.	VIRG 559:2	b. to think again	BRON 93:21	Fortune aids the b.	TER 544:18
Altho' a poor blind b.	CIBB 151:8	b. Worked with a dim	WORD 580:13	home of the b.	KEY 295:14
b.'s love	SHAK 454:28	Chimera in my b.	DONNE 191:2	How sleep the b.	COLL 158:19
b. stood on the burning	HEM 244:20	draughts intoxicate the b.	POPE 378:13	'I'm very b. generally	CARR 135:14
b.'s will is the wind's	LONG 316:22	fibre from the b. does tear	BLAKE 85:10	intelligent, the witty, the b.	MILL 339:23
b. to be vicious till he's	SAKI 413:14	from the heat-oppressed b.	SHAK 459:15	In the b. days of old	MAC 322:18
b. with never a crack	YEATS 586:5	glean'd my teeming b.	KEATS 292:30	late to-morrow to be b.	ARMS 12:17
compound a b.	SHAK 445:14	harmful to the b.	JAM 271:3	make one b. push	STEV 522:8
good-humoured b.	BEER 37:21	instrumental to the b.	SHAK 429:20	None but the b.	DRYD 194:23
hood-wink'd b. I call'd	GARR 221:16	it might injure the b.	CARR 133:22	Of the b. and innocent	AUDEN 19:7
like any other b.	FLEC 214:20	let my b. lie also	BROW 102:34	passing b. to be a King	MARL 330:7
Mad about the b.	COW 163:18	petrifactions of a plodding b.	BYRON 124:25	posterity as a b. bad man	CLAR 152:22
more who would not be a b.	BYRON 120:11	schoolmasters puzzle their b.	GOLD 231:22	souls of the b. that die in the battle	
nor young enough for a b.	SHAK 488:9	stars, Which are the b.	MER 337:5		CLOU 153:13
only b.	KIPL 305:5	tares of mine own b.	BROW 96:18	straight, the b.	HOUS 265:6
purblind, wayward b.	SHAK 456:26	through which the b. explores	DOUG 191:7	that delirium of the b.	YEATS 586:19
roughly to your little b.	CARR 133:26	to leave that b. outside	GILB 226:9	that was b.	HOUS 264:2
saw a little vulgar B.	BARH 33:19	What hand and b. went ever	BROW 101:26	Then I was clean and b.	HOUS 263:1
seat sat the journeying b.	HARDY 240:9	**brained:** large-b. woman	BROW 98:15	Toll for the b.	COWP 165:30
Smiling the b. fell dead	BROW 101:16	**brain-pan:** weak is their b.	BLAKE 87:1	What's b., what's noble	SHAK 423:18
squeaking Cleopatra b.	SHAK 424:3	**brains:** Blows out his b. upon	BROW 105:4	with what a b. Carouse	FITZ 213:1
Take the thanks of a b.	BEEC 37:9	b. in my head and the heart	HOUS 266:7	*would not sleep with the b.*	HOUS 264:19
that were when he was a b.	HOR 257:21	b. out of a brass knob	DICK 178:23	**braver:** I have done one b. thing	
To be a soaring human b.	DICK 176:14	b. ta'en out, and buttered	SHAK 469:12		DONNE 190:16
to be b. eternal	SHAK 491:7	Cudgel thy b. no more about	SHAK 436:24	not think a b. gentleman	SHAK 440:16
Upon the growing b.	WORD 579:5	dash'd the b. out	SHAK 459:10	**bravery:** b. of his grief did put	SHAK 437:13
was and a little tiny b.	SHAK 490:27	Had their b. knocked out	SHEL 502:3	Hiding thy b. in their	SHAK 493:11
what a b. you are	BROWN 95:11	He exercises of his b.	GILB 226:8	natural b. of your isle	SHAK 428:13
When I was a little b.	ANON 8:19	I mix them with my b.	OPIE 365:6	**braw:** He was a b. gallant	BALL 30:16
boyaux: étranglés avec les b.	MESL 338:9	no other b. to work with	SHAW 497:1	**brawler:** not a b., not covetous	BIBLE 79:12
boyes: When b. go first to bed	HERB 248:4	not maggots in your b.	FLET 215:26	**brawling:** b. woman in a wide house	
boys: among his b.	TENN 536:22	Till he blew his silly b.	THAC 546:3		BIBLE 54:20
B. and girls tumbling	TRAH 551:19	to steal away their b.	SHAK 475:9	**brawls:** Whatever b. disturb	WATTS 565:19
b. get at one end they	JOHN 276:32	**brainsickly:** So b. of things	SHAK 460:10	**Brazil:** B.—where the nuts	THOM 546:18
b. that swim on bladders	SHAK 447:9	*brainwork: fundamental b.*	ROSS 410:10	**breach:** More honour'd in the b.	SHAK 430:23
'B. will be boys	HOPE 255:28	**brake:** he b. that gallant ship	BALL 30:19	Once more unto the b.	SHAK 443:21
Christian b. I can scarcely	ARN 16:27	his neck b.	BIBLE 49:39	**bread:** ate his b. in sorrow	GOET 230:12
Deceive b. with toys	LYS 321:18	it bow'd and syne it b.	BALL 32:10	bit of butter to my b.	MILNE 340:8
flies to wanton b.	SHAK 455:9	**brakes:** rove the b. and thorns	COWP 165:12	bitter b. of banishment	SHAK 479:4
is the way that b. begin	THAC 545:31	**bramble-bush:** if it had been a b.	DICK 178:6	b. and butter that feels	MACK 325:10
men that were b. when	BELL 40:11	**bramble-dew:** With eyes of gold and		b. and flesh in the morning	BIBLE 51:6
of children (except b.	CARR 136:12	b.	STEV 523:3	b. and the big match	JUV 287:28
office boys for office b.	SAL 413:21	**brambles:** nettles and b. in the fortresses		b. eaten in secret is pleasant	BIBLE 53:28
only know two sorts of b.	DICK 180:37		BIBLE 58:31	b. enough and to spare	BIBLE 70:19
three merry b. are we	FLET 215:9	**bran:** this the Plebeian b.	DONNE 190:23	B. I dip in the river	STEV 522:27
to virgin girls and b.	HOR 260:13	**Branch:** B. shall grow out of his	BIBLE 58:9	b. of adversity	BIBLE 58:28
Bozrah: dyed garments from B.	BIBLE 60:10	Cut is the b. that might	MARL 329:16	b. of affliction and with	BIBLE 51:20
Brabant: I dance with you in B.	SHAK 456:22	Every b. big with it	HARDY 240:21	b. to strengthen man's	PRAY 396:21
brace: b. ourselves to our duties	CHUR 150:1	lops the moulder'd b.	TENN 533:26	Cast thy b. upon the waters	BIBLE 56:5
b. their belts about them	HOUS 265:6	reddens on the high b.	SAPP 414:7	cramm'd with distressful b.	SHAK 444:25
bracelet: b. of bright hair about	DONNE 190:5	**branches:** b. of the frankincense	BIBLE 63:27	eat thy b. with joy	BIBLE 55:28
diamond b. lasts forever	STEV 520:20	lodge in the b. thereof	BIBLE 66:20	face shalt thou eat b.	BIBLE 45:22
bracelets: b. and bright feathers		sing among the b.	PRAY 396:19	'For the b. that you eat	KIPL 298:5
	HARDY 240:19	Thy b. ne'er remember	KEATS 293:3	half-pennyworth of b.	SHAK 439:20
braces: Damn b.	BLAKE 88:23	**branchy:** city and b. between towers		Here with a Loaf of B.	FITZ 212:11
brach: b. or lym	SHAK 455:1		HOPK 256:9	HOMER begged his B.	ANON 7:14
Bracing: B. brain and sinew	KING 296:24	**brand:** over by that flaming b.	MILT 350:1	Honest b. is very well	JERR 272:27
bracken: through b. turning brown		**brandy:** be a hero must drink b.	JOHN 278:7	Jesus took b.	BIBLE 68:11
	BRAD 91:8	B. for the Parson	KIPL 302:22	lives not upon b. alone	STEV 521:34
Bradford: silk hat on a B. millionaire		is the b. of the damned	SHAW 497:27	loaf of b.	CARR 135:8
	ELIOT 205:1	pray get me a glass of b.	GEOR 224:3	Man doth not live by b.	BIBLE 48:22
Bradshaw: vocabulary of 'B.' is		There's some are fou o' b.	BURNS 114:9	Man shall not live by b.	BIBLE 64:1
	DOYLE 192:37	**brass:** am become as sounding b.	BIBLE 76:14	Royal slice of b.	MILNE 340:7
braes: among thy green b.	BURNS 113:27	b., nor stone	SHAK 494:4	smell of b. and butter	BYRON 119:32
banks and b. o' bonny Doon	BURNS 116:6	evil manners live in b.	SHAK 447:20	taste of another man's b.	DANTE 171:17
brag: Beauty is Nature's b.	MILT 341:18	feet like unto fine b.	BIBLE 81:14	that b. should be so dear	HOOD 255:8
Is left this vault to b.	SHAK 461:1	that was ever writ in b.	JONS 284:17	that makes the holy b.	MAS 333:26
Nor shall death b. thou	SHAK 492:28	this be your wall of b.	HOR 258:9	that which is not b.	BIBLE 59:25
Brahmin: B. strikes the hour	SOUT 513:25	wall all Germany with b.	MARL 329:5	Their learning is like b.	JOHN 276:27
I the hymn the B. sings	EMER 206:18	**brav'd:** b. by his brother	SHAK 451:23	theirs is b.	THOM 548:28
braided: she has b. her yellow hair	BALL 32:1	**brave:** adventure b. and new	BROW 104:5	them in breaking of b.	BIBLE 71:19
braids: twisted b. of lilies knitting		b. beard curled	CHES 147:3	took B.	PRAY 388:1
	MILT 341:20	B. hearts and clean	TENN 535:5	took the B. and brake it	ELIZ 205:19
brain: alone immured in the b.	SHAK 457:8	B. Macbeth	SHAK 458:3	to steal b.	FRAN 217:26
ascends me into the b.	SHAK 442:15	b. man with a sword	WILDE 572:10	To take b. at my hand	WYATT 583:21
Bear of Very Little B.	MILNE 340:13	b. men lived before Agamemnon's		unleavened b.	BIBLE 47:17
b. attic stocked with all	DOYLE 192:2		HOR 261:18	unleavened b. of sincerity	BIBLE 75:36
b. of feathers	POPE 375:18	b. Music of a *distant*	FITZ 212:12	us this day our daily b.	BIBLE 64:24
b. perplexes and retards	KEATS 291:20	b. new world	SHAK 485:26	was cutting b. and butter	THAC 546:3
b. that won't believe	BLAKE 85:11	b. old Scottish Cavalier	AYT 24:11	who did also eat of my b.	PRAY 392:5

whom if his son ask b.	BIBLE 65:4
With the b. eaten up	CERV 138:14
breadfruit: *Where the b. fall*	ELIOT 204:13
breadth: 'Let me have length and b.	
	BALL 31:14
whole b. of the way	BUNY 107:15
break: b. a man's spirit is devil's	
	SHAW 496:15
B., break, break	TENN 532:17
b. faith with us who die	MCCR 324:31
b., my heart	SHAK 430:1
b. the ice by some whose	BACON 25:41
bruised reed shall he not b.	BIBLE 59:11
chanced to see at b. of day	WORD 578:10
I bend and I b. not	LA F 306:18
I'll b. my staff	SHAK 485:24
lark at b. of day	SHAK 493:6
of nature round him b.	ADD 2:30
sighs the strings do b.	CAMP 129:17
that ye b. every yoke	BIBLE 60:4
thyself must b. at last	ARN 13:14
us b. their bonds asunder	PRAY 389:16
ye b. my best blue china	HARDY 239:20
you b. the bloody glass	MACN 326:8
breakers: I wanton'd with thy b.	
	BYRON 121:27
breaketh: he b. the bow	PRAY 392:21
Lord b. the cedar-trees	PRAY 391:10
breakfalls: rolls and throws and b.	
	REED 405:7
breakfast: All too soon the tiny b.	BETJ 42:7
b. she'll project a scheme	YOUNG 587:18
Hope is a good b.	BACON 25:8
impossible things before b.	CARR 135:18
'No business before b.	THAC 545:19
One doth but b. here	HENS 246:4
period in matrimony is b.-time	HERB 246:16
That b.	BELL 39:2
Then to b. with	SHAK 447:6
twin that I b. on gin	HERB 246:8
want Michael Angelo for b.	TWAIN 554:10
'Where shall we our b. take	BALL 32:7
wholesome, hungry b.	WALT 564:7
breakfasted: b. with you and shall sup	
	BRUCE 106:2
breakfasts: sleeps he b.	SURT 525:7
breaking: b. of ribs was sport	SHAK 424:23
b. up of laws	TENN 534:10
b. what it likes	ARN 15:20
By b. of windows	MORE 357:7
England take pleasure in b.	ANON 7:22
known of them in b. of bread	BIBLE 71:19
breaks: b. a butterfly upon a wheel	
	POPE 376:30
day b. not	DONNE 188:3
It b. in our bosom	SHEL 501:4
some heart indignant b.	MOORE 356:10
where Helicon b. down	ARN 13:2
breast: back somewhere in our b.	ARN 12:22
b. o'ercharged to music	SIDN 507:24
broach'd his boiling bloody b.	SHAK 471:17
charms to sooth a savage b.	CONG 160:14
depth of her glowing b.	SHEL 503:23
eternal in the human b.	POPE 379:5
God within my b.	BRON 93:19
hapless b. upon his breast	YEATS 586:1
heart out of your b.	HOUS 264:18
in my b.	GOET 229:30
laughed upon his b.	YEATS 585:20
render back from out thy b.	BYRON 123:2
soft hand, and softer b.	KEATS 292:13
stood b. high amid the corn	HOOD 255:4
That singeth with her b.	HOOD 255:2
unwonted calm pervades his b.	ARN 12:22
When breast to b. we clung	ROSS 409:22
World broods with warm b.	HOPK 256:13
breastie: what a panic's in thy b.	
	BURNS 115:20
breastless: b. creatures under ground	
	ELIOT 205:13

breastplate: b. of judgment the Urim	
	BIBLE 48:1
b. of righteousness	BIBLE 78:10
b. of faith and love	BIBLE 79:2
b. than a heart untainted	SHAK 446:6
breasts: all night betwixt my b.	BIBLE 56:18
b. are like two young roes	BIBLE 56:26
b. of the nymphs	SWIN 530:4
b. the blows of circumstance	TENN 537:1
division of prodigious b.	SWIN 528:26
feel my b all perfume	JOYCE 286:30
Sestos and Abydos of her b.	DONNE 188:14
she hath no b.	BIBLE 57:13
soaping her b. in the bath	EWART 209:11
why then her b. are dun	SHAK 495:8
within their b. the grief	AYT 24:5
breath: accustomed to their lack of b.	
	YEATS 585:13
All the b. and the bloom	BROW 98:30
Although thy b. be rude	SHAK 426:1
are but the b. of kings	BURNS 113:10
bald and short of b.	SASS 414:10
b. can make them	GOLD 230:18
breathing thoughtful b.	WORD 581:8
b. of worldly men cannot	SHAK 479:5
B.'s a ware that will	HOUS 262:15
b. thou art	SHAK 464:8
Clothed with his b.	TENN 535:23
Could ever yet cut b.	SHAK 492:11
deeds too cold b. gives	SHAK 460:1
down and out of b.	SHAK 440:27
dust expend an idle b.	CAT 137:15
every thing that hath b.	PRAY 400:1
flutter'd and fail'd for b.	ARN 14:6
fly away, b.	SHAK 449:4
from the healthy b. of morn	KEATS 289:33
Had borne my b. away	HOOD 254:17
having lost her b.	SHAK 422:4
hear her tender-taken b.	KEATS 292:12
heaven's b. Smells wooingly	SHAK 459:4
last b. he drew in	LAMB 308:11
mansion call the fleeting b.	GRAY 234:22
our head and held our b.	ARN 13:16
sweeter woman ne'er drew b.	ING 270:16
Sweet is the b. of morn	MILT 348:4
sweetness of man's b.	JAM 271:4
tears and toiling b.	ROSS 408:20
That lightly draws its b.	WORD 583:5
this present b. may buy	SHAK 456:14
thou no b. at all	SHAK 456:11
waste of b. the years behind	YEATS 585:15
world draw thy b. in pain	SHAK 437:25
year with toil of b.	COL 156:17
you have it use your b.	FLET 215:7
breathe: b. not his name	MOORE 356:15
b. the air of the Enchanted	MER 337:37
like the hair we b.	SURT 525:4
So long as men can b.	SHAK 492:28
tho' to b. were life	TENN 543:22
breathed: b. into his nostrils	BIBLE 45:7
This day I b. first	SHAK 452:1
Breathes: B. there the man	SCOTT 416:21
breathing: b. English air	BROO 94:30
B. out threatenings	BIBLE 73:32
Closer is He than b.	TENN 533:29
In the sound his b. kept	SHEL 503:5
quiet b.	KEATS 288:20
rifle all the b. spring	COLL 158:16
breathings: Low b. coming after me	
	WORD 580:9
breathless: b. hush in the Close to-night	
	NEWB 361:8
B. with adoration	WORD 581:18
breaths: b. with sweetmeats tainted	
	SHAK 481:18
bred: strain of man's b.	SHAK 486:1
brede: wes sons of ale and b.	WYNT 584:4
Bredon: In summertime on B.	HOUS 263:4
bree: little abune her b.	BALL 32:1

breeches: He is like a book in b.	
	SMITH 511:12
jacket was red and his b.	COL 156:11
'oss than cleanin' his b.	SURT 525:12
So have your b.	CANN 129:26
breed: b. of their horses	PENN 371:15
b. one work that wakes	HOPK 257:3
endless war still b.	MILT 351:16
Fear'd by their b.	SHAK 478:20
This happy b.	SHAK 478:20
Where they most b. and haunt	SHAK 459:4
breeder: thou be a b. of sinners	SHAK 433:11
breedeth: Severity b. fear	BACON 26:25
breeding: such true b. of a gentleman	
	BYRON 122:30
though spoiled i' the b.	BROME 93:12
Breeds: B. hard English men	KING 296:23
lesser b. without the Law	KIPL 302:9
breeks: b. aff a wild Highlandman	
	SCOTT 418:11
breeze: b. is on the sea	SCOTT 418:25
b. of morning moves	TENN 540:9
such a b.	TENN 536:9
'the cooling western b.'	POPE 378:21
thee with the b. of song	TENN 537:4
volleying rain and tossing b.	ARN 15:5
breezes: Little b. dusk and shiver	TENN 538:3
other b. than are blown	KEATS 292:15
Breezy: B., Sneezy	ELLIS 206:13
breite: b. Masse eines Volkes	HITL 251:9
Brekekekex: B. koax koax	ARIS 12:5
Bremen: being a foreigner of B.	DEFOE 173:5
brent: Your bonny brow was b.	
	BURNS 114:12
brethren: Behold my mother and my	
b.	BIBLE 66:15
b. and companions' sakes	PRAY 398:12
Dearly beloved b.	PRAY 384:9
joyful a thing it is: b.	PRAY 398:26
least of these my b.	BIBLE 68:7
thee and me…for we be b.	BIBLE 46:2
tuneful b. all were dead	SCOTT 416:9
breuis: *uita b., sensus hebes*	JOHN 273:17
Brevis: *B. esse laboro*	HOR 257:12
Vitae summa b. spem	HOR 259:14
Brevity: B. is the soul of wit	SHAK 431:30
Its body b.	COL 156:15
brewer: not a b.'s servant	BLAKE 87:8
brewers: Bakers and b.	LANG 309:26
brewery: take me to a b.	ANON 6:1
brews: many a peer of England b.	
	HOUS 264:12
Bribe: Taking of a B. or Gratuity PENN 371:16
to b. or twist	WOLFE 576:6
Too poor for a b.	GRAY 235:21
very considerable b.	GILB 226:26
bribes: man open to b. was to be GREE 236:4
our fingers with base b.	SHAK 451:13
brick: 'Eave 'arf a b. at 'im	PUNCH 402:14
I inherited it b. and left	AUG 22:5
piece of b. in his pocket	SWIFT 525:34
bricks: carried the b. to Lawley	BETJ 44:2
Bridal: Against their B. day	SPEN 516:32
b. of the earth and sky	HERB 248:16
to dance at our b.	SCOTT 417:11
bride: barren b.	POPE 377:20
became my glittering b.	WORD 577:14
b. adorned for her husband	BIBLE 82:30
b. at the altar	SCOTT 417:28
b. her attire	BIBLE 60:15
bridesmaid makes a happy b.	TENN 532:19
darling, my life and my b.	POE 374:23
encounter darkness as a b.	SHAK 464:12
I drew my b.	PATM 370:2
is ready to be thy b.	BALL 30:9
like a blooming Eastern b.	DRYD 194:23
Passionless b.	TENN 539:22
proud b. of a ducal coronet	DICK 179:32
unravish'd b. of quietness	KEATS 291:2

virgin-widow and a *Mourning B.*
　　　　　　　　　　　　　　DRYD 197:11
yet a b.　　　　　　　　　　　CAREW 130:15
young b. and her bridegroom　POUND 382:11
bride-bed: thought thy b. to have deck'd
　　　　　　　　　　　　　　SHAK 437:6
bridegroom: Bellona's b.　　SHAK 458:5
b. in my death　　　　　　　　SHAK 423:11
b. out of his chamber　　　　　PRAY 390:11
funeral train which the b.　　　CLOU 153:10
Like a b. from his room　　　　AYT 24:9
young bride and her b.　　　　POUND 382:11
bride-grooms: Of b.　　　　HERR 248:18
brides: b., and of their bridal-cakes
　　　　　　　　　　　　　　HERR 248:18
uppe 'The B. of Enderby'　　　ING 270:13
bridesmaid: happy b. makes a happy
bride　　　　　　　　　　　　TENN 532:19
Bridge: Beautiful Railway B.　MCG 325:6
keep b. with me　　　　　　　MAC 322:17
well Horatius kept the b.　　　MAC 322:23
when thy b. I crost　　　　　　CLOU 154:2
(Which goes with B.　　　　　BELL 39:21
Bridge of Sighs: on the B.　　BYRON 121:1
bridle: be held with bit and b.　PRAY 391:18
with a taxed b.　　　　　　　SMITH 511:38
bridle-ring: took him by the b.　BALL 30:9
bridles: She heard the b. ring　BALL 32:2
bridleth: b. not his tongue　　BIBLE 80:11
brief: be less b.　　　　　　WATS 565:10
B. as the lightning　　　　　　SHAK 469:20
Drest in a little b. authority　　SHAK 464:2
I strive to be b.　　　　　　　HOR 257:12
lust is gross and b.　　　　　PETR 373:5
tedious and b.　　　　　　　SHAK 471:13
'Tis b., my lord　　　　　　　SHAK 434:10
briefer: garland b. than a girl's　HOUS 263:3
brier: b. shall come up the myrtle
　　　　　　　　　　　　　　BIBLE 59:28
thorough b.　　　　　　　　　SHAK 470:2
brier-patch: Bred en bawn in a b.
　　　　　　　　　　　　　　HARR 242:20
briers: b. is this working-day　SHAK 424:29
bright: All things b. and beautiful　ALEX 3:13
Behold the b. original appear　GAY 223:19
b. and fierce and fickle　　　　TENN 542:5
B. as the day　　　　　　　　GRAN 234:6
b. blot　　　　　　　　　　　SHEL 504:5
b., broken Maginn　　　　　　LOCK 315:23
b. day is done　　　　　　　SHAK 424:2
b. face of danger　　　　　　STEV 520:24
b. girdle furl'd　　　　　　　ARN 12:23
b. in the fruitful valleys　　　BRID 92:17
B. is the ring of words　　　　STEV 523:1
b. things come to confusion　SHAK 469:20
b. to the coiner　　　　　　　HOUS 263:8
burning b.　　　　　　　　　BLAKE 87:14
creature not too b. or good　　WORD 581:8
Dark with excessive b.　　　　MILT 347:9
garden of b. images　　　　　BRAM 91:22
It is the b. day that brings　　SHAK 449:4
Keep up your b. swords　　　SHAK 473:21
obscurely b.　　　　　　　　BYRON 121:37
on earth your fame is b.　　　BRID 92:18
purpose and his eyes are b.　KEATS 294:17
thought thee b.　　　　　　　SHAK 495:15
was a young lady named B.　　BULL 106:22
you shall shine more b.　　　SHAK 493:17
brightness: being the b. of his glory
　　　　　　　　　　　　　　BIBLE 79:28
b. didst outshine Myriads　　MILT 344:26
B. falls from the air　　　　　NASHE 360:7
b. in their failing eyes　　　　BLUN 89:2
b. of his presence his　　　　PRAY 390:9
b., purity, and truth　　　　　OTWAY 366:4
his Darkness and his B.　　　BYRON 126:8
Leaking the b. away　　　　　SPEN 515:12
Brighton: cheerful, merry Dr B.　THAC 545:10
Brignal: B. banks are wild and fair
　　　　　　　　　　　　　　SCOTT 417:30

Brig o' Dread: From B. when thou may'st
　　　　　　　　　　　　　　BALL 31:7
brilliant: envy of b. men　　BEER 37:28
less b. pen　　　　　　　　　BEER 37:13
brillig: 'Twas b.　　　　　CARR 134:28
brim: bubbles winking at the b. KEATS 291:18
sparkles near the b.　　　　　BYRON 120:19
brimstone: From his b. bed at break
　　　　　　　　　　　　　　COL 156:10
rain snares, fire and b.　　　PRAY 389:31
bring: b. in cloudy night immediately
　　　　　　　　　　　　　　SHAK 483:6
B. me my arrows of desire　　BLAKE 86:16
B. out number　　　　　　　BLAKE 88:18
b. up the rear in heaven　　　BROW 96:26
knowest not what a day may b.　BIBLE 54:36
would b. home knowledge　　JOHN 277:31
bringer: first b. of unwelcome news
　　　　　　　　　　　　　　SHAK 441:2
bringeth: him that b. good tidings
　　　　　　　　　　　　　　BIBLE 59:18
bringing: that her b. me up by hand
　　　　　　　　　　　　　　DICK 178:9
brinkmanship: boasting of his b.
　　　　　　　　　　　　　　STEV 520:22
brioche: Qu'ils mangent de la b.　MAR 328:22
brisk: b. as a bee in conversation　JOHN 274:1
b. fond lackey to fetch　　　　HOUS 265:18
spoke a b. little somebody　　BROW 99:1
brisker: land fares b.　　　POUND 383:18
brisking: by b. about the Life　SMART 508:22
bristle: his hair did b. upon his　SCOTT 416:15
bristles: memory, my skin b.　HOUS 266:17
Bristol: he is not member of B.　BURKE 109:12
were three sailors of B.　　　THAC 545:32
Britain: boundary of B. is revealed　TAC 531:6
B. all the sun that shines　　SHAK 428:17
B., could you ever boast　　　SWIFT 527:33
Hail, happy B.　　　　　　　SOM 513:3
I've lost B.　　　　　　　　KIPL 302:13
Yet B. set the world ablaze　GILB 226:11
Britannia: B., rule the waves　THOM 549:7
inseparable than Beer and B.　SMITH 511:25
brither: lo'ed him like a vera b.　BURNS 115:5
British: art thou not of B. blood　TENN 533:28
B. Bourgeoisie　　　　　　　SITW 508:14
B. bourgeoisie have spoken　WAUGH 566:2
B. Fleet a-riding at anchor　　THAC 546:2
B. journalist　　　　　　　WOLFE 576:6
B. manhood was put together　CARL 131:14
B. policy　　　　　　　　　ROCH 407:5
B. soldier can stand up　　　SHAW 496:19
dismissed by the B. electorate　CHUR 150:26
Flood Of B. freedom　　　　WORD 582:2
greatness of the *B.* Nation　ADD 2:19
majesty the B. soldier fights　NAP 359:7
provinces of the B. empire　SMITH 509:17
smell the blood of a B.　　　SHAK 454:27
so ridiculous as the B.　　　MAC 324:1
With a stony B. stare　　　　TENN 540:7
with B. and Armoric knights　MILT 345:23
world less known by the B.　BORR 90:3
British Empire: B. and the United States
　　　　　　　　　　　　　　CHUR 150:3
destinies of the B.　　　　　DISR 184:27
liquidation of the B.　　　　CHUR 150:12
British Islands: than these selfsame B.
　　　　　　　　　　　　　　BORR 90:3
British Museum: keep my books at the
B.　　　　　　　　　　　　BUTL 118:22
very learned B. assistant　　POUND 383:14
British Public: B., ye who like me not
　　　　　　　　　　　　　　BROW 104:16
Briton: glory in the name of B.　GEOR 224:1
only a free-born B. can do　THAC 545:23
Britons: amongst the B. who are　VIRG 559:1
B. never will be slaves　　　THOM 549:7
brittle: arms you bear are b.　HOUS 264:3
b. glory shineth in this　　　SHAK 480:5
broached: Bringing rebellion b.　SHAK 445:7

Broad: B. and I'm the High　SPR 517:11
b. is the way　　　　　　　BIBLE 65:6
B. of Church and broad　　BETJ 44:14
b. on the roots of things　BROW 98:17
b. sunshine of life　　　　JOHN 278:6
brooks too b. for leaping　HOUS 264:10
make b. their phylacteries　BIBLE 67:22
broader: b. lands and better days　CHUR 150:3
brogues: not fit to tie his b.　SCOTT 419:1
broiled: piece of a b. fish　BIBLE 71:20
broke: b. any man's head but his　SHAK 444:6
he b. forth　　　　　　　　CIC 151:27
Vows for thee b. deserve　SHAK 457:4
Who b. the laws of God　LOCK 316:1
you b. a British square　KIPL 299:8
you that b. the new wood　POUND 383:12
broken: baying for b. glass　WAUGH 565:29
bright, b. Maginn　　　　　LOCK 315:23
b. and castaway wine-pots　CLOU 153:7
b. and contrite heart　　　PRAY 393:8
b. head in Cold Bath Fields　MAC 324:23
b. open on the most scientific　PEAC 370:13
b. the lock and splintered　AUDEN 20:5
b. with the storms of state　SHAK 447:15
charm they have b.　　　　BRID 92:15
cord is not quickly b.　　　BIBLE 55:15
earth the b. arcs　　　　　BROW 98:18
else but through a b. heart　WILDE 572:16
healeth those that are b.　PRAY 399:19
I am b. by their passing　YEATS 584:17
Is it not b.　　　　　　　SHEL 499:17
Laws were made to be b.　NORTH 364:3
Naught b. save this body　BROO 94:28
neck when once b.　　　　WALSH 563:28
Nor a b. thing mend　　　BELL 40:10
pitcher be b. at the fountain　BIBLE 56:11
sound of b. glass　　　　　BELL 40:5
thou hast b. may rejoice　PRAY 393:5
touched a b. girl　　　　　FLEC 214:15
When the lute is b.　　　　SHEL 501:21
brokenhearted: To bind up the b.　BIBLE 60:8
We had ne'er been b.　　　BURNS 112:29
You hoped we were both b.　SWIN 530:10
broker: honest b.　　　　BISM 84:23
bronze: gold and lungs of b.　BELL 39:28
longer lasting than b.　　　HOR 261:8
with oak and three-ply b.　HOR 259:12
bronzes: Others shall shape b. more
　　　　　　　　　　　　VIRG 559:1
broo: eels boil'd in b.'　BALL 31:5
brooch: theron heng a b. of gold　CHAU 141:17
brooches: b. and toys for your delight
　　　　　　　　　　　　STEV 522:29
brood: eternal b. of glory excellent
　　　　　　　　　　　　SPEN 516:4
fond of no second b.　　　SHAK 428:5
He sees his b. about thy　TENN 542:7
that thy b. is flown　　　　TENN 542:6
brooding: atheist b. and blaspheming
　　　　　　　　　　　　CHES 148:7
broods: b. and sleeps on his own　WORD 580:5
World b. with warm breast　HOPK 256:13
brook: b. and river meet　LONG 316:20
b. Into the main　　　　　SHAK 468:18
dwelt by the b. Cherith　BIBLE 51:6
Fell in the weeping b.　　SHAK 436:19
noise like of a hidden b.　COL 155:26
brooks: b. are Thames's tributaries　ARN 15:8
b. of Eden mazily murmuring　TENN 533:13
b. too broad for leaping　HOUS 264:10
'Only b. of Sheffield　　　DICK 176:26
Shallow b. murmur most　SIDN 507:14
broom: bright blows the b.　STEV 522:29
I am sent with b. before　SHAK 471:22
broomstick: Surely man is a b.　SWIFT 526:25
Brot: sein B. mit Tränen ass　GOET 230:12
brothels: b. with bricks of Religion
　　　　　　　　　　　　BLAKE 88:20
Keep thy foot out of b.　SHAK 454:19
brother: Am I my b.'s keeper　BIBLE 45:25

Lord has b. the house	BIBLE 83:12	Half-b. in the snow was	LONG 316:16	Burton: why was B. built on Trent	
Prisons are b. with stones	BLAKE 88:20	I'll be b. in the king's	SHAK 479:15		HOUS 264:12
therefore b. for ever	TENN 534:6	rich-proud cost of outworn b.	SHAK 494:2	Bury: B. it certain fathoms	SHAK 485:24
we have b. do we discern	ARN 13:23	Rose as where some b. Caesar	FITZ 212:15	B. my heart at Wounded Knee	BENET 40:20
Builth: variants from B. to Ballyhoo		shall be b. by her Antony	SHAK 424:19	b. whom he help'd to starve	POPE 376:29
	KIPL 302:4	They b. him	PROU 401:23	disposed to b. for nothing	DICK 179:13
Bulbo: my beautiful, my B.	THAC 545:20	they b. him the little port	TENN 533:11	I b. some of you	DONNE 188:28
bull: are gone to milk the b.	JOHN 275:3	they not b. me deep enough	TENN 540:15	I come to b. Caesar	SHAK 450:17
blaring b. went wading	HARDY 240:22	This living b. man	DONNE 190:1	Let the dead b. their dead	BIBLE 65:19
Cock and a B.	STER 520:12	twenty generations lie b.	MAC 323:20	Past b. its dead	LONG 317:3
curl'd Assyrian B.	TENN 540:1	Upon my b. body lay	BEAU 36:8	they'll meet to b.	BROO 94:16
Irish b. is always pregnant	MAH 327:4	We b. him darkly at dead	WOLFE 576:3	bus: Descending from the b.	CARR 133:13
savage b. doth bear the yoke	SHAK 472:2	Burke: only specimen of B. is	HAZL 243:9	I'm not even a b.	HARE 242:8
See an old unhappy b.	HODG 252:3	time with B. under a shed	JOHN 279:15	She tumbled off a b.	GRAH 233:11
bullet: Every b. has its billet	WILL 574:9	Burleigh: mourn'd the Lord of B.		bush: Bed in the b. with stars	STEV 522:27
is stronger than the b.	LINC 314:13		TENN 539:11	b. burned with fire	BIBLE 47:3
with a b. through his heart	THAC 545:26	burn: beacons b. again	HOUS 262:12	B., the dusty loam	HARDY 239:8
bullets: With b. made of platinum	BELL 38:30	better to marry than to b.	BIBLE 76:2	every common b. afire	BROW 97:33
bull-fighters: b. of Spain	BORR 90:6	b. the old bass-viol that	HARDY 239:19	fear each b. an officer	SHAK 446:23
bullied: b. out of vice	SURT 525:1	B. to the socket	WORD 577:11	flame? The B. is bare	BROW 98:29
bullocks: wisdom…whose talk is of b.		B. upward each to his point	BROW 105:20	is a b. suppos'd a bear	SHAK 471:11
	BIBLE 63:20	Did not our heart b. within	BIBLE 71:18	Thorough b.	SHAK 470:2
young b. upon thine altar	PRAY 393:9	I rage, I melt, I b.	GAY 222:6	young bird in this b.	LEAR 311:18
bulls: eat b.' flesh	PRAY 393:3	Old age should b. and rave	THOM 546:23	bushel: neither under a b.	BIBLE 70:1
fat b. of Basan	PRAY 390:18	shall not b. thee by day	PRAY 398:9	bushes: discovereth the thick b.	PRAY 391:11
ploughman of b.	PROP 401:15	To b. always with th	PATER 369:21	likes b. and low tamarisks	VIRG 559:22
two chairs like mad b.	DICK 178:18	To b. for ever in burning	SWIN 530:20	busied: b. in his majesty	SHAK 443:9
bully: I love the lovely b.	SHAK 444:17	violent fires soon b. out	SHAK 478:19	business: annuity is a very serious b.	
Like a tall b.	POPE 378:2	We b. daylight	SHAK 469:6		AUST 23:24
mentality, too, is b.	BEER 38:1	years I b. all my sermons	WESL 568:19	be about my Father's b.	BIBLE 69:13
bulrushes: took for him an ark of b.		Burn'd: B. on the water	SHAK 422:2	B. first	THAC 545:17
	BIBLE 46:41	Through my b. bosom	SHAK 452:31	b. of America is business	COOL 162:11
bulwark: floating b. of the island	BLAC 85:4	burnèd: b. is Apollo's laurel	MARL 329:16	b. of everybody is	MAC 323:6
bulwarks: b. of Mark	PRAY 392:27	bush b. with fire	BIBLE 47:3	b. of the wealthy man	BELL 39:29
bum: Then slip I from her b.	SHAK 470:3	his clothes not be b.	BIBLE 53:23	b. of the day	DRYD 195:37
bumbast: to b. out a blank verse	GREE 236:12	I give my body to be b.	BIBLE 76:14	b. of the day in the day	WELL 568:2
bump: that go b. in the night	ANON 5:8	smell of b. poetry	WOD 576:1	b. that we love we rise	SHAK 422:24
Bunbury: permanent invalid called B.		Wherever books are b. men	HEINE 244:14	B. was his aversion	EDG 199:24
	WILDE 572:29	burneth: b. the chariots	PRAY 392:21	did my uncle Toby's b.	STER 520:9
bunch: b. of other men's flowers	MONT 355:6	burning: bow of b. gold	BLAKE 86:16	everybody minded their own b.	CARR 133:25
Buncombe: through reporters to B.		b. and a shining light	BIBLE 72:2	far away from b.	HOR 259:7
	CARL 132:4	b. bright	BLAKE 87:14	If it's b. of consequence	BARH 33:10
bundle: b. of prejudices	LAMB 307:7	b. fiery furnace	BIBLE 61:3	importunity Of b.	LAMB 307:33
buns: bears may come with b.	ISH 270:27	B. for burning	BIBLE 47:25	In civil b.	BACON 25:31
Bunyan: genius in literature—B.	ARN 16:23	b. of a Pope	DRYD 197:5	it is your b.	HOR 258:23
buona: b. imagine paterna	DANTE 171:12	b. of the leaves	BINY 84:8	know your own foolish b.	CHES 146:8
burbled: b. as it came	CARR 134:29	b. Sappho loved and sung	BYRON 122:32	lucrative b. of mystery	BURKE 108:12
burd: arms b. Helen dropt	BALL 31:4	b. witches when we're only	CHES 147:7	my b. is to Create	BLAKE 86:2
burden: bear the b. and the heat	ARN 13:23	firebrand plucked out of the b.	BIBLE 61:20	my pleasure, b.	WYCH 583:25
b. and heat of the day	BIBLE 67:15	pretty Babe all b. bright	SOUT 514:19	'No b. before breakfast	THAC 545:19
b. of them is intolerable	PRAY 387:19	smell of b. fills the startled	BELL 40:7	occupy their b. in great	PRAY 397:9
b. of the nation's care	PRIOR 401:6	their eyes are b.	AUDEN 20:5	On a thousand b. women	BETJ 42:6
grievous b. was thy birth to me	SHAK 481:8	your lights b.	BIBLE 70:6	our b. to lose innocence	BOWEN 91:6
Is the b. of my song	ANON 6:13	burnish'd: Furnish'd and b. by Aldershot		people is 'B. as usual'	CHUR 149:26
my b. is light	BIBLE 66:5		BETJ 44:6	person on b. from Porlock	COL 156:25
Take up the White Man's b.	KIPL 304:6	Burns: B., Shelley, were with us	BROW 102:5	praying, it spoils b.	OTWAY 366:5
They have cast their b.	KIPL 303:10	Lovely B. has charms	BURNS 114:16	proceed no further in this b.	SHAK 459:7
burdens: to undo the heavy b.	BIBLE 60:4	Not she which b. in 't	SHAK 491:13	projects than for settled b.	BACON 27:39
Burg: Ein' feste B. ist unser	LUTH 321:2	burnt-offerings: thou delightest not in		requisite in b. than dispatch	ADD 1:12
burghers: Like signiors and rich b.		b.	PRAY 393:8	rest is not our b.	ELIOT 202:24
	SHAK 465:7	burnt-out: b. ends of smoky days		robs you on b. principles	SHAW 498:6
roused the b. of Carlisle	MAC 322:4		ELIOT 204:7	servants of b.	BACON 26:21
burglar: When the enterprising b.'s		burr: I am a kind of b.	SHAK 465:2	That's the true b. precept	DICK 179:9
	GILB 228:20	Burrow: B. awhile and build	BROW 98:17	to do your own b.	BIBLE 79:11
burglary: Flat b. as ever was committed		is always so near his b.	MEYN 338:16	Treasury is the spring of b.	BAG 28:22
	SHAK 473:4	burrows: b. of the Nightmare	AUDEN 18:10	We demand that big b. give	ROOS 408:7
burgonet: arm And b. of men	SHAK 421:31	burrs: Do roses stick like b.	BROW 105:27	woman's b. to get married	SHAW 497:25
Burgundy: It's a Naïve Domestic B.		burst: b. Joy's grape	KEATS 291:15	busk: wherefore should I b. my heid	
	THUR 550:29	B. smilingly	SHAK 456:7		BALL 32:10
burial: buried in Christian b.	SHAK 436:21	first that ever b.	COL 155:12	bus'ness: some to b.	POPE 377:25
groaning for b.	SHAK 450:12	Let me not b. in ignorance	SHAK 430:24	Buss: Miss B. and Miss Beale	ANON 6:16
his obscure b.	SHAK 436:14	mast b. open with a rose	FLEC 214:19	bust: her friendly b.	ELIOT 205:14
in one red b. blent	BYRON 120:27	moonlit cedar what a b.	ARN 14:2	merit raise the tardy b.	JOHN 282:29
thy precious Death and B.	PRAY 385:17	suddenly b. out singing	SASS 414:14	only give a b. of marriages	BYRON 122:27
burial-ground: b. God's-Acre	LONG 316:18	then b. his mighty heart	SHAK 450:28	storied urn or animated b.	GRAY 234:22
buried: be b. in a good old age	BIBLE 46:4	words or I shall b.	FARQ 210:12	Bustle: B. in a House	DICK 183:17
be b. in so sweet a place	SHEL 499:2	bursts: b. come crowding through	ARN 14:3	of all the tumult and b.	SMITH 509:8
being b. with Christ	PRAY 388:10	b. of open day between	FRY 220:5	busts: picture plac'd the b. between	
B. beneath some snow-deep	ELIOT 202:5	burthen: vapours weep their b.	TENN 543:11		CHES 145:8
b., He descended into	PRAY 384:26	which the b. of the mystery	WORD 578:5	busy: b., and you will be safe	OVID 366:21

B. old fool, unruly Sun   DONNE 190:11
thou knowest how b. I must   ASTL 17:20
but: tout b. dénature l'art   CONS 162:5
butcher: b. tells you that *his heart*
                                JOHN 274:21
son of a first rate b.   ASHF 17:12
want to know a b. paints   BROW 105:4
Butcher'd: B. to make a Roman holiday
                                BYRON 121:16
butchers: Even b. weep   GAY 222:20
gentle with these b.   SHAK 450:11
have both shepherds and b.   VOLT 561:17
sacrificers, but not b.   SHAK 449:8
butler: on the b.'s upper slopes WOD 575:27
Butlers: In my opinion B. ought BELL 39:4
butt: here is my b.   SHAK 477:20
knocks you down with the b.   GOLD 232:40
butt-end: knock me down with the b.
                                CIBB 151:11
Butter: (B. and eggs and a pound
                                CALV 127:10
B. and honey shall he eat   BIBLE 58:3
'B., eh?'   MILNE 340:9
b.'s spread too thick   CARR 135:9
b. will only make us fat   GOER 229:25
'Could we have some b.   MILNE 340:7
forth b. in a lordly dish   BIBLE 49:10
it's the b. that makes   JERR 272:27
'It was the *best* b.   CARR 134:1
little bit of b. to my bread   MILNE 340:8
mouth were softer than b.   PRAY 393:12
piece of bread and b. th   MACK 325:10
smell of bread and b.   BYRON 119:32
was cutting bread and b.   THAC 546:3
While ladling b. from alternate ROG 407:14

buttercup: b. Had blessed with gold
                                OWEN 367:8
I'm called Little B.   GILB 227:29
Buttercups: B. and daisies   HOW 267:2
b., the little children's   BROW 101:7
eggs and b. fried with fish   LEAR 312:21
buttered: always on the b. side PAYN 370:9
brains ta'en out, and b.   SHAK 469:12
b. scones and crumpets   ELIOT 202:5
butterflies: b. and cockyolybirds would
                                KING 297:13
b. are already yellow with   POUND 383:17
'I look for b.   CARR 136:6
laugh At gilded b.   SHAK 456:3
what it concedes to the b.   DICK 176:6
butterfly: b. dreaming I am a man
                                CHUA 148:17
b. upon the road   KIPL 302:1
Kill not the moth nor b.   BLAKE 85:13
Who breaks a b. upon   POPE 376:30
buttock: by boiling his b.   AUBR 17:25
buttocks: chair that fits all b. SHAK 420:29
gorgeous b. of the ape   HUXL 269:1
button: little round b. at top FOOTE 216:7
undo this b.   SHAK 456:11
we are not the very b.   SHAK 432:11
we don't care a b.   LEAR 312:8
buttoning: All this b. and unbuttoning
                                ANON 4:16
buttons: I had a soul above b. COLM 159:4
button-stick: I've a tongue like a b.
                                KIPL 298:7
buttress: regarded as a b. of the church
                                MELB 336:22
butts: beast With many heads b. SHAK 427:25
buxom: b., blithe, and debonair MILT 342:13
Buxton: every fool in B. can be RUSK 411:13
buy: b. a world of happy days   SHAK 480:26
b. it first   HEM 245:1
b. wine and milk   BIBLE 59:25
Did b. each other   SHAK 487:12
I will b. with you   SHAK 465:28
no man might b. or sell   BIBLE 82:13
pasture now to b. the horse   SHAK 443:12
They lose it that do b.   SHAK 465:9

wonder what the Vintners b.   FITZ 213:14
buyer: naught, saith the b.   BIBLE 54:19
buying: It's no fish ye're b.   SCOTT 418:2
ruined by b. good pennyworths   FRAN 218:12
buys: Civility costs nothing and b.
                                MONT 354:10
public b. its opinions   BUTL 119:4
Who b. a minute's mirth   SHAK 492:18
buzz: 'Does it b.   LEAR 311:16
uncertain stumbling B.   DICK 183:19
buzzing: What is he b. in my ears
                                BROW 100:6
By: B. and by is easily said   SHAK 434:24
B. thy cold breast   BYRON 125:4
shall hear it by and b.   BROW 98:20
byle: b. was blak   CHAU 142:32
bymatter: if it had been a b.   BACON 25:42
byrdes: b. sang swete in the middes
                                WEVER 569:7
When the lytle b. swetely   HAWES 243:2
Byron: B. is only great as a poet GOET 229:26
Close thy B.   CARL 132:20
From the poetry of Lord B.   MAC 324:3
Goethe's sage mind and B.'s   ARN 13:18
that B. bore   ARN 13:9
When B.'s eyes were shut   ARN 13:16
bystanders: b. are animated with EMER 207:5
byword: shall be a proverb and a b.
                                BIBLE 50:31
Byzantium: Soldan of B. is smiling
                                CHES 146:28
To the holy city of B.   YEATS 586:13
C: C. cut it   ANON 4:25
caballería: Religión es la c. CERV 138:15
Caballero: C. de la Triste Figura
                                CERV 138:12
cabbage: That c. hashed up again JUV 287:24
cabbage-leaf: garden to cut a c. FOOTE 216:7
cabbages: c.—and kings   CARR 135:7
c. are coming now   BETJ 44:5
find me planting my c.   MONT 354:14
cabin: small c. build there   YEATS 585:17
willow c. at your gate   SHAK 488:13
Cabin-boy: So the C. did swim all BALL 31:3
cabin'd: c. ample Spirit   ARN 14:6
c., cribb'd, confin'd   SHAK 461:17
cabinet: c. of pleasure   HERB 248:2
consequence of c. government   BAG 28:23
this C. of Mediocrities   DISR 185:36
Cabinet Minister: By becoming a C.
                                SU T 524:19
cable: c. can so forcibly draw BURT 116:33
Cabots: Lowells talk only to C. BOSS 90:13
cachée: ardeur dans mes veines c. RAC 404:4
cacher: savoir c. son habileté LA R 310:13
*cachinnorum: Ridete quidquid est domi
c.*   CAT 136:28
cackling: drive ye c. home to Camelot
                                SHAK 453:22
cacoethes: Scribendi c. et aegro JUV 287:23
cadence: dans les vers une juste c. BOIL 89:10
harsh c. of a rugged line   DRYD 197:33
reverent c. and subtle   AUDEN 18:3
cadendo: non vi sed saepe c.   LAT 310:20
Cadiz Bay: reeking into C.   BROW 101:8
Cadogan: One-eighty-nine C. Square
                                BETJ 43:6
Cadwallader: C. and all his goats
                                SHAK 445:9
caelestibus: Tantaene animis c. irae
                                VIRG 557:9
Caelum: C. non animum mutant HOR 258:19
ruat c.   MANS 328:16
Caesar: always I am C.   SHAK 448:21
Aut C., aut nihil   BORG 89:25
Ave C.   ANON 10:7
be 'like C.'s wife   ANON 6:11
Broad-fronted C.   SHAK 421:32
C. and his fortune with   CAES 127:2
C. ass Unpoliced   SHAK 424:14

C. bears such rebel blood   SHAK 449:24
C. bleed in sport   SHAK 450:5
C. hath wept   SHAK 450:19
C. is turn'd to hear   SHAK 448:7
C.'s laurel crown   BLAKE 85:16
C.'s wife must be above   CAES 127:1
contrary to the decrees of C.   BIBLE 74:9
Dead C.'s trencher   SHAK 422:20
did in envy of great C.   SHAK 452:7
Did I the tired C.   SHAK 448:14
enemies of C. shall say   SHAK 450:10
first time ever C. put it   SHAK 450:26
Hail C.   ANON 10:7
Here was a C.   SHAK 451:5
I appeal unto C.   BIBLE 74:23
Imperious C., dead   SHAK 437:2
long as C.'s self is God's   CRAS 169:13
meat doth this our C. feed   SHAK 448:18
Not C.'s valour hath o'erthrown SHAK 423:13
Not that I loved C. less   SHAK 450:14
On blossoming C.   SHAK 423:5
Our master C. is   YEATS 586:3
Regions C. never knew   COWP 164:24
Render therefore unto C.   BIBLE 67:20
speak in C.'s funeral   SHAK 450:17
That C. is more dangerous   SHAK 449:19
that C. might be great   CAMP 129:8
Then fall, C.   SHAK 450:1
'Tis paltry to be C.   SHAK 423:20
unto C. shalt thou go   BIBLE 74:24
we will hear C.'s will   SHAK 450:24
where some buried C. bled   FITZ 212:15
yesterday the word of C.   SHAK 450:23
Caesar Augustus: went out a decree
from C.   BIBLE 69:8
Caesars: come now no Kings nor C.
                                POUND 383:19
with C., and with Cannibals   SHAK 441:25
cage: He keeps a lady in a c.   CHES 147:19
linnet born within the c.   TENN 536:15
Nor iron bars a c.   LOV 318:18
Robin Redbreast in a C.   BLAKE 85:9
sing like birds i' the c.   SHAK 456:3
We cannot c. the minute   MACN 326:15
caged: We think c. birds sing   WEBS 567:10
cages: not in making c.   SWIFT 527:10
Cain: by thy brotherhood of C. BYRON 125:4
C. went out from the presence   BIBLE 45:29
Had C. been Scot   CLEV 153:4
Lord set a mark upon C.   BIBLE 45:28
Of C. and his brother   COL 156:12
caitiff: c. smite the other   HOLM 253:11
cake: geological home-made c.   DICK 179:3
Let them eat c.   MAR 328:22
cakes: of their bridal-c.   HERR 248:18
shall be no more c. and ale   SHAK 488:21
tea and c. and ices   ELIOT 203:22
Calais: 'C.' lying in my heart MARY 339:13
from C. southward you   WORD 582:4
to shew light at C.   JOHN 275:8
calamities: new perturbations and c.
                                BACON 27:44
calamity: power of no c. while death
                                BROW 96:22
something more than a public c. SOUT 514:17
That makes c. of so long   SHAK 433:8
thou art wedded to c.   SHAK 483:9
calamus: sit c. saevior ense patet
                                BURT 116:22
calculate: c. the stars   MILT 349:3
you are calculating, c.   JOHN 277:8
calculated: Of nicely-c. less or more
                                WORD 582:16
calculation: c. shining out of the other
                                DICK 179:5
it scarcely admits of c.   HUME 267:16
Calculations: C. that look but casual
                                YEATS 587:1
calculus: integral and differential c.
                                GILB 228:16

cantie: Contented wi' little and c.
                 BURNS 113:4
canton: establish the robin's plucky c.
                 AUDEN 20:15
cantons: loyal c. of contemned love
                 SHAK 488:13
canvas: Compell'd thy c.   TENN 536:9
   crowd your c.   TENN 540:21
canvassers: c. whom they do not know
                 HURST 268:17
canvasses: good in c. and factions
                 BACON 25:40
cap: riband in the c. of youth   SHAK 436:17
   Stuck a *i*eather in his c.   BANGS 32:16
capa: *c. que cubre todos los*   CERV 138:20
Capability: Negative C.   KEATS 293:19
   That c. and god-like reason   SHAK 435:29
capable: *Habacuc était c. de tout*
                 VOLT 561:23
capacious: pipe for my c. mouth   GAY 222:7
capacity: described as a supreme c.
                 BUTL 118:34
   that he had the c. to reign   TAC 531:13
   transcendent c. of taking trouble CARL 131:18
   wisdom, c. and virtue   SWIFT 526:8
cap-a-pe: Armed at points exactly, c.
                 SHAK 430:7
caparisons: No c., miss   SHER 506:18
capax: *c. imperii nisi imperasset* TAC 531:13
Cape: Beyond the C. of Hope   MILT 347:17
   Round the c. of a sudden   BROW 103:9
Capella: star called C. was yellow
                 HARDY 241:9
caper: Till first ae c.   BURNS 115:11
capers: c. nimbly in a lady's chamber
                 SHAK 480:18
   He c., he dances   SHAK 469:10
   lovers run into strange c.   SHAK 425:11
capiatur: *Nullus liber homo c.*   MAGN 327:2
capitaine: *c. de vingt-quatre soldats*
                 ANON 9:8
Capital: shall not want C. in Heaven
                 ELIOT 202:4
   To that high C.   SHEL 499:6
Capitalism: C., wisely managed KEYN 295:18
   definition of c.   HAMP 238:17
   unacceptable face of c.   HEATH 244:5
capitulate: I will not c.   JOHN 279:26
capon: of Madeira and a cold c.'s
                 SHAK 438:11
capons: you cannot feed c. so   SHAK 434:4
Capri: wordy letter came from C.   JUV 287:27
caprice: ev'ry meteor of c. must play
                 JOHN 282:26
caprices: which has her c.   BURKE 110:15
caps: roses crest the c. I know   THOM 547:24
   They threw their c.   SHAK 427:13
capta: *Graecia c. ferum victorem* HOR 259:2
Captain: c. is a good travelling FARQ 210:5
   c. is in his bunk   SHAW 496:3
   c. of the Hampshire grenadiers…has
                 GIBB 224:15
   c.'s but a choleric word   SHAK 464:4
   C. Webb from Dawley   BETJ 44:2
   crew of the c.'s gig   GILB 225:16
   Foremost c. of his time   TENN 541:7
   I am a cook and a c. bold   GILB 225:16
   I am the C. of the *Pinafore*   GILB 227:30
   I am the c. of my soul   HENL 245:5
   O Captain! my C.   WHIT 570:7
   Our great captain's c.   SHAK 474:14
   plain russet-coated c.   CROM 169:20
   royal c. of this ruin'd band   SHAK 444:10
   Saying 'C.   BALL 31:3
   their c., the heart   SHAK 442:15
   Walk the deck my C. lies   WHIT 570:8
captains: All my sad c.   SHAK 422:22
   c. and rulers clothed   BIBLE 60:37
   C. and the Kings depart   KIPL 302:7
   c. couragious whom death   BALL 31:8

   C. of industry   CARL 132:11
   There were c. by the hundred   GILB 225:10
   thunder of the c.   BIBLE 53:7
Capting: there's nobody like the C.
                 THAC 545:15
captive: Captivity thence c.   SPEN 515:17
   From the foes they c. make   CHAN 139:19
   they that led us away c.   PRAY 399:3
   thou hast led captivity c.   PRAY 394:10
   when I am thy c.   MILT 348:12
captives: proclaim liberty to the c. BIBLE 60:8
   To serve your c.' need   KIPL 304:6
   upon all prisoners and c.   PRAY 385:20
captivity: no leading into c.   PRAY 399:3
   prisoners out of c.   PRAY 394:7
   turned again the c. of Sion   PRAY 398:16
   Turn our c.   PRAY 398:17
Capulets: than in the tomb of the C.
                 BURKE 108:6
caput: *c. pedibus supposuisse*   OVID 366:22
car: afford to keep a motor c.   SHAW 496:4
   gilded c. of day   MILT 340:27
   Put the c. away   AUDEN 19:15
cara: *c. e buona imagine*   DANTE 171:12
caravan: Put up your c.   HODG 252:9
   Where my c. has rested   TESC 545:2
Caravanserai: in this batter'd C. FITZ 212:13
Carboniferous: In the C. Epoch we were
                 KIPL 299:16
carbuncular: young man c.   ELIOT 205:1
carcase: Wheresoever the c. is   BIBLE 67:30
carcases: dead c. of unburied men
                 SHAK 427:23
carcass: him as a c. fit for hounds
                 SHAK 449:9
card: 'He's a cheery old c.   SASS 414:18
   we must speak by the c.   SHAK 436:28
Cardinal: Jackdaw sat on the C.'s chair
                 BARH 33:11
cards: be that can pack the c.   BACON 25:40
   not learned to play at c.   JOHN 280:6
   play'd At c. for kisses   LYLY 321:10
   shuffle the c.   CERV 138:18
   some were playing c.   BALL 31:3
care: absolute paternal c.   ELIOT 202:22
   age is full of c.   SHAK 492:13
   are now with me past c.   SHAK 479:3
   beneath Thy special c.   BETJ 43:6
   c. and valour in this Welshman SHAK 444:19
   C., at the horseman's   CALV 127:28
   c. fifty times more   BAG 28:29
   Careless she is with artful c.   CONG 159:18
   c. of all the churches   BIBLE 77:12
   c.'s check and curb   VAUG 555:12
   c. to stay than will   SHAK 483:15
   c. where the water goes   CHES 147:28
   Deliberation sat and public c.   MILT 346:14
   disclaim all my paternal c.   SHAK 453:3
   do buy it with much c.   SHAK 465:9
   enough in thee to kill c.   SHAK 473:9
   forgather wi' Sorrow and C.   BURNS 113:4
   Hast thou no c. of me   SHAK 423:16
   Have closed our anxious c.   PEAC 370:20
   Heaven's peculiar c.   SOM 513:3
   her c. was but to be fair   WATS 565:11
   Hippocleides doesn't c.   HILL 251:7
   I c. for nobody   BICK 84:1
   I c. not two-pence   BEAU 36:3
   I shan't c. or ho   HARDY 239:20
   is past my c.   FLET 215:12
   kiaugh and c. beguile   BURNS 113:5
   Killing c. and grief of heart   SHAK 447:3
   learning to c. for the unhappy VIRG 557:19
   least as feeling her c.   HOOK 255:20
   nipt With c.   MIDD 338:18
   Nor c. beyond to-day   GRAY 235:12
   now Reason is past c.   SHAK 495:15
   ravell'd sleave of c.   SHAK 460:8
   Sport that wrinkled C.   MILT 342:15
   Take c. of the pence   LOWN 319:21

   then the c. is over   TEMP 532:9
   things beyond our c.   DRYD 197:10
   tiresome verse-reciter, C.   SHEL 504:25
   to take c. of the minutes   CHES 145:18
   us to care and not to c.   ELIOT 202:1
   we don't c. a button   LEAR 312:8
   weep away the life of c.   SHEL 504:11
   Will neither c. nor know   HOUS 265:10
   With middle-ageing c.   POUND 383:20
   with what c. Thou hast   HERB 248:10
   women and c. and trouble   WARD 564:38
   Young ladies should take c.   AUST 22:17
Cared: C. not to be at all   MILT 346:7
   Gallio c. for none of those   BIBLE 74:15
career: boy's ideal of a manly c.   DISR 186:28
   which might damage his c.   BARR 34:20
careful: c. of the type she seems TENN 536:27
carefully: come most c. upon your hour
                 SHAK 429:4
Careless: C. folly done and said HOUS 265:4
   C. she is with artful care   CONG 159:18
   first fine c. rapture   BROW 101:6
   So c. of the single life   TENN 536:27
   'twere a c. trifle   SHAK 458:22
carelessly: unbent bow, c.   DONNE 190:3
carelessness: lose both looks like c.
                 WILDE 573:1
   With carefullest c.   BETJ 44:6
carent: *c. quia vate sacro*   HOR 261:18
cares: blessed than to put c. away CAT 136:28
   c. that infest the day   LONG 316:10
   c. were to increase his   HOME 253:22
   devil has ended his c.   BROW 102:13
   ever against eating c.   MILT 342:26
   hell Grief and avenging C.   VIRG 558:21
   Hush, hush, Nobody c.   MORT 358:15
   kings have c. that wait   GREE 236:11
   one c. for none of them   AUST 24:1
   these small c. of daughter   MORE 357:11
   youth is but a frost of c.   TICH 551:2
caret: golden cadence of poesy, c.
                 SHAK 457:3
careth: c. not for the sheep   BIBLE 72:19
Carew: tends the grave of Mad C.
                 HAYES 243:7
carf: c. biforn his fader   CHAU 141:13
cargo: With a c. of ivory   MAS 333:31
caribous: c. lie around and snooze
                 COW 163:20
caricature: With a c. of a face   GILB 227:14
carl: c., with sory grace   CHAU 143:7
carl-hemp: Thou stalk o' c. in man
                 BURNS 115:14
Carlisle: You may go to C.'s   ANST 11:8
Carlyle: C. and Mrs Carlyle marry
                 BUTL 119:22
   C. has led us all out into   CLOU 154:6
carmina: *placere diu nec vivere c.*
                 HOR 258:25
   sunt et mihi c.   VIRG 560:7
carnage: all its deeds of c.   WHIT 570:11
   c. and his conquests cease   BYRON 120:4
   C. is Thy daughter   WORD 578:21
carnal: men's c. lusts and appetites
                 PRAY 388:25
carnally: to be c. minded is death BIBLE 75:7
carnation: A' never could abide c.
                 SHAK 443:19
carnations: Are our c. and streak'd
                 SHAK 491:23
   Of bright c. did o'erspread   DRUM 193:28
   Soon will the musk c. break   ARN 15:6
CARO: VERBUM C. FACTUM EST
                 MASS 335:12
carol: This c. they began that   SHAK 427:2
   wild c. ere her death   TENN 535:28
carolled: Still they are c. and said STEV 523:1
Carouse: with what a brave C.   FITZ 213:1
carpe: *c. diem*   HOR 259:20
carpenter: Is not this the c.'s son BIBLE 66:22

understood Christ was a c.   BLAKE 87:8
Walrus and the C.   CARR 135:5
You may scold a c. who   JOHN 274:26
carpet: All wear the c. with their
                               YEATS 586:14
colours in the Turkey c.   MAC 323:30
figure in the c.   JAMES 271:22
him no c. knight so trim   SCOTT 417:5
on c. consideration   SHAK 490:14
carpets: c. rose along the gusty KEATS 289:22
Over thick c. with a deadened BETJ 42:12
carping: obnoxious to each c. tongue
                               BRAD 91:13
Carrets: Sowe C. in your Gardens
                               GARD 221:8
Carriage: C. held but just Ourselves
                               DICK 183:15
very small second class c.   GILB 226:13
women of good c.   SHAK 481:28
carried: being not like children c. PRAY 387:3
carrion: c. comfort, Despair HOPK 256:7
With c. men   SHAK 450:12
Carrow: That was late slain at C.
                               SKEL 508:19
carry: Books that you may c. JOHN 280:17
c. a letter to my love   BALL 30:20
c. everything before me   DISR 185:31
c. the buckler unto Samson   BROW 96:14
c. their comfort about   ELIOT 201:17
c. them in his bosom   BIBLE 59:7
c. the moon in my pocket   BROW 102:13
c. within us the wonders   BROW 96:12
certain we can c. nothing out BIBLE 79:17
choking him and making him c. TOLS 551:15
man must c. knowledge with   JOHN 277:31
softly and c. a big stick   ROOS 408:1
cart: horse is drawn by the c. KIPL 298:16
useful C.   LEAR 312:9
carters: keep a farm, and c. SHAK 432:3
Carthage: C. must be destroyed CATO 136:18
O C.! O New York   SASS 415:4
Carthaginian: With C. trustworthiness
                               SALL 413:25
Carthago: Delenda est C.   CATO 136:18
magna C.   HOR 260:24
cartridge: holsters and c. boxes SHAW 496:6
carve: c. heads upon cherry-stones
                               JOHN 279:18
c. on every tree   SHAK 426:2
Let's c. him as a dish fit   SHAK 449:9
To c. out dials   SHAK 446:14
ye c. my epitaph aright   BROW 99:13
carved: c. names the rain-drop HARDY 239:10
head fantastically c.   SHAK 442:10
carving: Now is a time for c. POUND 383:12
caryatides: Unfrowning c.   STEV 523:11
Casca: what a rent the envious C.
                               SHAK 450:27
cas'd: c. up, like a holy relic WEBS 566:20
case: c. is concluded   AUG 22:2
c. will be dismissed with   HOR 262:7
Clutching a little c.   AUDEN 18:9
corpse in the c. with a sad   BARH 33:16
everything that is the c.   WITT 575:14
nothing to do with the c.   GILB 227:13
this c. is that case   ARAB 11:16
when a lady's in the c.   GAY 223:16
casement: c. high and triple-arch'd
                               KEATS 289:10
c. ope at night   KEATS 292:4
c. slowly grows a glimmering   TENN 542:4
ghost of Roger C.   YEATS 585:7
casements: Charm'd magic c. KEATS 291:23
cash: c. that goes therewith CHES 146:11
In epochs when c. payment   CARL 131:17
takes your c.   CHUR 148:30
take the C. in hand   FITZ 212:12
with the squalid c. interpretation JAMES 272:3
Casket: hushed C. of my Soul KEATS 292:29
casse: tout c.   ANON 9:20

Cassius: C. from bondage will deliver
                               SHAK 449:2
C. is aweary of the world   SHAK 451:23
Dar'st thou, C.   SHAK 448:14
cassock'd: c. huntsman and a fiddling
                               COWP 166:7
cassowary: If I were a c.   WILB 572:3
Cast: *C. a cold eye*   YEATS 587:10
c. away the works of darkness PRAY 386:4
C. me not away from thy   PRAY 393:6
c. off the works of darkness   BIBLE 75:24
C. thy bread upon the waters   BIBLE 56:5
c. ye your pearls before   BIBLE 65:1
first c. a stone at her   BIBLE 72:10
have c. their burden upon   KIPL 303:10
have set my life upon a c.   SHAK 481:19
he c. into the sea   BIBLE 70:30
I will in no wise c. out   BIBLE 72:6
loath to c. away my speech   SHAK 488:10
more he c. away   BUNY 107:34
Nor c. one longing ling'ring   GRAY 235:2
over Edom will I c.   PRAY 393:18
suddenly c. down   PRAY 392:25
trouble me c. me in the teeth PRAY 392:9
Tush, I shall never be c.   PRAY 389:30
will I c. out of my sight   BIBLE 50:31
castaway: I myself should be a c. BIBLE 76:9
mighty is vilely c.   BIBLE 50:16
castels: make c. thanne in Spayne
                               CHAU 144:1
casteth: He c. out devils through BIBLE 65:28
Castilian: might an old C.   BYRON 126:9
castitatem: Da mihi c. et continentiam
                               AUG 21:14
castle: c., called Doubting-Castle
                               BUNY 107:20
c. or building not in decay   BACON 26:38
him as his c. and fortress   COKE 154:23
man's house is his c.   COKE 154:21
my old lad of the c.   SHAK 438:2
rich man in his c.   ALEX 3:14
splendour falls on c. walls   TENN 541:32
This c. hath a pleasant   SHAK 459:4
castled: c. crag of Drachenfels BYRON 120:31
Castle Downe: Look owre the C. BALL 30:17
Castlereagh: He had a mask like C.
                               SHEL 502:2
intellectual eunuch C.   BYRON 122:4
castles: all the c. I have   JONS 283:26
C. in the air   IBSEN 270:3
My c. are my King's alone   SCOTT 417:17
casual: children c. as birds AUDEN 18:5
half-believers in our c. creeds ARN 14:17
casualty: first c. when war JOHN 273:18
force and road of c.   SHAK 466:19
casuistry: Mountains of c. heap'd
                               POPE 375:26
casuists: soundest c. doubt POPE 377:30
cat: c. in profound meditation ELIOT 204:6
c.'s mew rise to a scream   AUDEN 20:8
C., the Rat, and Lovell   COLL 158:10
deafer than the blue-eyed c.   TENN 534:23
Foss is the name of his c.   LEAR 311:23
Had Tiberius been a c.   ARN 14:4
Hanging of his c. on Monday   BRAT 91:24
harmless necessary c.   SHAK 467:22
I am a c. that likes   SMITH 510:25
it might have been c.   BARH 33:6
I will consider my C. Jeoffry SMART 508:21
killing a c. than choking   KING 297:15
Lat take a c.   CHAU 142:25
mother's c. had but kittened   SHAK 439:21
part to tear a c.   SHAK 469:26
pavilion c.   LANG 309:19
poor c. i' the adage   SHAK 459:8
room to swing a c.   DICK 177:18
Runcible C. with crimson   LEAR 312:20
see the c. i' the dairy   ELIOT 200:18
Self-reliant like the c.   MOORE 355:22
suggestion as a c. laps milk   SHAK 485:6

to see how the c. jumps   SCOTT 418:38
Touch not the c.   SCOTT 418:9
very fine c. indeed   JOHN 279:9
vigilant as a c. to steal cream SHAK 440:11
What c.'s averse to fish   GRAY 235:6
When I play with my c.   MONT 355:2
catalogue: dull c. of common things
                               KEATS 290:27
in the c. ye go for men   SHAK 461:9
cataract: sounding c.   WORD 578:6
wild c. leaps in glory   TENN 541:32
cataracts: You c. and hurricanoes
                               SHAK 454:4
catastrophe: between education and c.
                               WELLS 568:16
c. of the old comedy   SHAK 453:12
I'll tickle your c.   SHAK 441:19
catch: c. my flying soul   POPE 376:14
game of catch as c. can   FOOTE 216:7
hard to c. and conquer   MER 337:2
Perdition c. my soul   SHAK 475:14
usual to c. a mouse or two   GRAY 235:23
catched: not be c.   PEPYS 372:12
catching: c. a train is to miss CHES 148:11
Passion, I see, is c.   SHAK 450:13
poverty's c.   BEHN 38:17
catchwords: principally by c. STEV 521:34
catechism: so ends my c.   SHAK 440:18
Catechist: something of the Shorter-C.
                               HENL 245:12
Categorical: This imperative is C.
imperative   KANT 288:10
categories: ballet of bloodless c. BRAD 91:10
caterpillar: c., and the palmerworm
                               BIBLE 61:14
c. on the leaf   BLAKE 85:13
caterpillars: c. of the commonwealth
                               SHAK 479:2
cates: Than feed on c. and have SHAK 439:28
Cathay: Europe than a cycle of C.
                               TENN 539:9
Cathechism: scarce had said his C.
                               THAC 546:2
Cathedral: Heft Of C. Tunes DICK 184:1
in the vast c. leave him   TENN 541:15
Catherine: Such as are on a C. pear
                               SUCK 524:9
catherine-wheels: in a cloud of crimson
c.   FRY 219:26
Catholic: Druse and the C. CHES 146:27
I cannot be a good C.   NORF 364:1
Catholick: C. and Apostolick Church
                               PRAY 387:11
holy C. Church   PRAY 384:26
that he hold the C. Faith   PRAY 385:11
Catiline: abuse our patience, C. CIC 151:25
Cato: C.'s daughter durst not ROWE 410:25
C.'s daughter   SHAK 449:16
Like C.   POPE 376:27
losing one pleased C.   LUCAN 319:22
What C. did   BUDG 106:19
Cats: C. is 'dogs' and rabbits PUNCH 402:19
C., no less liquid than   TESS 545:3
Do c. eat bats   CARR 133:15
dogs and killed the c.   BROW 103:15
greater c. with golden eyes   SACK 412:26
Mill his three black c.   DE L 174:4
monkeys and c.   JAMES 271:24
Naming of C. is a difficult   ELIOT 204:5
where cats are c.   MARQ 330:23
cattle: are mostly troublesome c.
                               LOVER 318:22
c. rise and listen   KING 297:21
c. upon a thousand hills   PRAY 393:2
forth grass for the c.   PRAY 396:20
go and call the c. home   KING 296:25
over the c.   BIBLE 45:4
these who die as c.   OWEN 367:2
unknown to the c.   CAT 137:6

Catullus: C. gives you warmest thanks
                               CAT 137:3
Did their C. walk that   YEATS 586:14
Poor C.   CAT 136:27
caught: 'Ah, ha!' you're c.   SHAK 422:9
before he c. the beast   WALL 562:6
c. at God's skirts   BROW 101:18
c. his clear accents   BROW 102:5
c. in her arms long   WYATT 583:22
his sweet perfections c.   ROYD 411:3
if he be c. young   JOHN 276:10
must be c. with tickling   SHAK 489:10
ram c. in a thicket   BIBLE 46:11
cauld: 'tis auld it waxeth c. BALL 32:10
cauldron: Fire burn and c. bubble
                           SHAK 462:2
Round about the c. go   SHAK 462:2
causa: c. finita est
                           AUG 22:2
Victrix c. deis placuit LUCAN 319:22
causas: vitam vivendi perdere c. JUV 287:25
cause: beauty of the good old c. WORD 582:9
between c. and effect   LA B 306:15
called amiss *The good old C.* MILT 352:11
c. is in my will   SHAK 449:20
c. of dullness in others FOOTE 216:9
c. of Freedom is the cause BOWL 91:7
c., or just impediment   PRAY 388:23
c. that perishes with them CLOU 153:13
c. that wit is in other   SHAK 441:3
c. this evil is upon us   BIBLE 61:21
defendeth the c. of widows PRAY 394:7
defend my c. against   PRAY 392:10
final c. of the human nose COL 157:30
Freedom is the c. of God BOWL 91:7
have full c. of weeping   SHAK 454:2
increased devotion to that c. LINC 314:23
in the justice of our c.   HAIG 237:11
it is the c., my soul   SHAK 477:5
judge thou my c.   BIBLE 60:32
man can shew any just c. PRAY 389:2
no c. however just   STEV 521:14
Our c. is just   DICK 184:4
perseverance in a good c. STER 519:19
Report me and my c. aright SHAK 437:23
Ring out a slowly dying c. TENN 537:15
So little c. for carollings HARDY 239:7
support Caledonia's c. BURNS 114:5
Thou Great First C.   POPE 381:12
unites it with the secret c. JOYCE 286:17
unpregnant of my c.   SHAK 433:2
Causer: C. of this   BARN 34:4
causes: c. that they represent FORS 217:15
is in its c. just   DRYD 197:4
is the knowledge of c.   BACON 28:6
understand the c. of things VIRG 560:14
cautiously: do c.   ANON 10:18
Cavalier: brave old Scottish C. AYT 24:11
So let each c. who loves SCOTT 415:20
cavaliero: he was a perfect c. BYRON 119:30
Cavaliers: C. (Wrong but Wromantic)
                           SELL 420:4
cavat: Gutta c. lapidem OVID 366:27
cave: burst stomach like a c. DOUG 191:10
echo in a Marabar c.   FORS 217:8
her vacant interlunar c. MILT 350:16
In this our pinching c.   SHAK 428:15
littera scriptum 'C. canem PETR 372:30
lone c.'s stillicide   HARDY 239:18
tear the c. where Echo SHAK 482:19
That darksome c. they enter SPEN 516:7
Caveant: C. consules ne quid res publica
                           ANON 10:10
Cave of Adullam: called his political
  C.   BRIG 93:5
cavern: skulking Truth to her old c.
                         POPE 375:26
Caverns: Gluts twice ten thousand C.
                        KEATS 292:22
out of the c. of rain   SHEL 500:7
Sand-strewn c.   ARN 13:6

caves: unfathom'd c. of ocean bear
                        GRAY 234:23
woods and desert c.   MILT 343:6
caveto: tu, Romane, c. HOR 262:3
caviare: 'twas c. to the general SHAK 432:23
Cawdor: Glamis thou art, and C. SHAK 459:1
Thane of C. lives   SHAK 458:17
cawing: Rising and c. at the gun's
                        SHAK 470:20
Cease: C.! must men kill SHEL 501:3
c. upon the midnight with KEATS 291:22
C., ye prudes   BURNS 114:16
Fall and c.   SHAK 456:9
have fears that I may c. KEATS 292:30
He did not c. while he HAZL 243:13
He maketh wars to c.   PRAY 392:21
maketh the storm to c.   PRAY 397:10
night shall not c.   BIBLE 45:37
not c. from Mental Fight BLAKE 86:16
that thou shouldst c. to be SHEL 505:6
things might change or c. SHAK 454:3
to see me c. to live   ARN 15:12
whom we do exist and c. SHAK 453:3
ceased: it c. to be with Sarah BIBLE 46:6
ceases: Love c. to be a pleasure BEHN 38:12
ceasing: Remembering without c.
                        BIBLE 78:30
Without c. I make mention BIBLE 74:29
Cecilia: Blessed C.   AUDEN 18:4
'It is only C.   AUST 22:31
cedar: moonlit c. what a burst ARN 14:2
cedars: brambles like tall c. show COTT 163:7
c. of Libanus which he PRAY 396:20
devour the c. of Lebanon BIBLE 49:19
excellent as the c.   BIBLE 57:4
cedar-trees: Lord breaketh the c.
                        PRAY 391:10
Cedite: C. Romani scriptores PROP 401:17
ceiling: c. of amber   ARN 13:7
in the lines of the c.   ELUA 206:16
celandine: 'Tis the little c. WORD 583:2
celebrat: semper c. superna curia ABEL 1:1
celebrate: just to c. the event JERR 273:12
celebrated: Saviour's birth is c. SHAK 429:17
celebrates: c. his obsequies SCOTT 416:19
heavenly court for ever c. ABEL 1:1
celebrity: c. is a person who is known
                        BOOR 89:20
celerity: hath such a c. in dying SHAK 421:20
celestial: Apparelled in c. light WORD 578:22
lighten with c. fire   PRAY 400:5
that c. light   MILT 345:9
Celia: C. (since thou art so proud
                        CAREW 130:13
celibacy: c. has no pleasures JOHN 282:9
cell: Each in his narrow c. GRAY 234:20
solitary c.   COL 156:14
Thou hast given me a c. HERR 250:14
cellar: Born in a c.   FOOTE 216:6
I was born in a c.   CONG 160:5
Cellarer: Old Simon the C. keeps BELL 38:22
cells: c. and gibbets for 'the man' ELIZ 162:8
contented with their c. WORD 582:7
Celt: blind hysterics of the C. TENN 537:16
C. in all his variants KIPL 302:4
Celtic: enchanted woods of C. antiquity
                        KEYN 295:19
cement: With the same c. POPE 375:24
cemetery: c. is an open space among
                        SHEL 499:2
Help me down C. Road LARK 310:7
cenotaph: laugh at my own c. SHEL 500:7
censor: to c. one's own thoughts
                        WALEY 562:2
censorship: extreme form of c. SHAW 498:17
censure: All c. of a man's self JOHN 277:33
c. freely who have written POPE 378:10
c. or condemn another BROW 96:32
c. this mysterious writ DRYD 196:17
I do not presume to c. BURKE 109:5

Take each man's c.   SHAK 430:19
to read, and c.   HEM 245:1
censured: behold is c. by our eyes
                        MARL 329:18
censuring: varletry Of c. Rome SHAK 423:21
centaur: c. in his dragon world POUND 382:13
c., man and wife   BYRON 123:19
Centaurs: from the waist they are C.
                        SHAK 455:17
centre: c. cannot hold YEATS 586:15
earth is the c.   DONNE 190:22
Mon c. cède   FOCH 216:3
My c. is giving way   FOCH 216:3
now in the c. of politics MOSL 358:19
poor c. of a man's actions BACON 27:36
which the c. is everywhere ANON 7:27
centres: of which we are the c. TROL 552:22
centric: c. and eccentric scribbled MILT 349:3
centum: deinde c.   CAT 136:26
centuries: All c. but this GILB 226:25
forty c. look down upon NAP 359:8
I shall lie through c.   BROW 99:14
century: c. of the common man WALL 562:3
intellectual life of our c. ARN 15:25
last for more than a c.   CAT 136:21
Rafael made a c. of sonnets BROW 102:28
seventeenth c. a dissociation ELIOT 205:17
To one a c. hence or any WHIT 570:2
Cerberus: damn them with King C.
                        SHAK 441:25
loathed Melancholy, Of C. MILT 342:12
You are not like C.   SHER 506:19
cerebration: well of unconscious c.
                        JAMES 271:17
cerements: Have burst their c. SHAK 430:24
ceremonial: any c. purposes the otherwise
                        HERB 246:18
ceremonies: of dreams, and c. SHAK 449:10
ceremony: c. of innocence is drowned
                        YEATS 586:15
It useth an enforced c. SHAK 451:11
No c. that to great ones SHAK 463:20
perfect c. of love's rite SHAK 493:2
save general c.   SHAK 444:24
thrice-gorgeous c.   SHAK 444:25
Ceres: laughing C. re-assume the land
                        POPE 378:5
which cost C. all that pain MILT 347:21
certain: c. because it is impossible
                        TERT 545:1
c. hope of the Resurrection PRAY 389:13
dirge of her c. ending   SHAK 492:20
more c. than incertainties BARN 34:3
one thing is c.   FITZ 212:19
To c. death by certain KIPL 302:6
certain age: lady of a 'c. BYRON 123:21
Certainly: C. the growth of the fore-brain
                        AUDEN 19:10
certain place: receive your reward in
  a c.   BROWN 95:8
certainties: man will begin with c.
                        BACON 24:16
When hot for c. in this MER 337:18
certainty: c. for an uncertainty JOHN 281:20
sober c. of waking bliss MILT 341:5
certamina: animorum atque haec c. tanta
                        VIRG 560:18
etiam belli c. magna tueri LUCR 320:6
Certare: C. ingenio   LUCR 320:6
certezza: Di doman non c'è c. MED 336:9
certified: c. how long I have to live
                        PRAY 391:30
certifieth: one night c. another PRAY 390:11
certitude: Nor c.   ARN 12:23
Cervantes: C. is never petulant MAC 324:9
C. on his galley sets   CHES 147:6
C. smiled Spain's chivalry BYRON 124:1
cervicem: populus Romanus unam c.
                        CAL 127:6

cesspool: that great c. into which
DOYLE 192:33
Ceylon: Blow soft o'er C.'s isle HEBER 244:6
Cézanne: All C.'s apples I would
AUDEN 19:16
chaast: wol nat kepe me c. in al CHAU 143:17
chacals: c. pissent au bas et les FLAU 214:3
Chadband: C. style of oratory is DICK 176:13
chafe: Champ and c. and toss ARN 13:5
he that lets Another c. HERB 247:7
chaff: c. well meant for grain TENN 536:2
chaffinch: c. sings on the orchard
BROW 101:5
Chagrin: C. d'amour dure toute la
FLOR 215:34
chain: bound by the c. of our sins
PRAY 385:23
broke at once the vital c. JOHN 279:1
c. that is round us now CORY 163:3
flesh to feel the c. BRON 93:21
hill 'Too-quick', the c. TENN 541:26
remove a lengthening c. GOLD 231:24
that Homer's golden c. BURT 116:31
chained: hours has c. and bowed SHEL 502:13
chains: adamantine c. and penal fire
MILT 344:24
am thy captive talk of c. MILT 348:12
bind their kings in c. PRAY 399:24
c. about the feet of God TENN 535:26
C. and slaverie BURNS 114:34
C. are worse than bayonets JERR 273:11
clanking their c. WARD 564:19
everywhere he is in c. ROUS 410:17
sang in my c. like the sea THOM 547:2
Shake your c. to earth SHEL 502:4
since a woman must wear c. FARQ 210:1
Chair: C. she sat ELIOT 204:23
Give Dayrolles a c. CHES 146:9
has one vacant c. LONG 317:6
He fills a c. JOHN 278:26
It is like a barber's c. SHAK 420:29
La c. est triste MALL 327:9
sat on the Cardinal's c. BARH 33:11
Seated in thy silver c. JONS 283:24
to his father's c. JONS 285:7
chairs: next suggested elbow-c. COWP 166:28
two glasses and two c. MACN 326:11
chaise-longue: hurly-burly of the c.
CAMP 128:9
chalcedony: third c. BROW 97:34
chalice: c. of the grapes of God TENN 536:7
chalices: treen priests and golden c.
JEWEL 273:14
Cham: That great C. of literature
SMOL 512:14
chamber: bridegroom out of his c.
PRAY 390:11
cannot find a c. in the inn ANON 9:1
c. deaf to noise SIDN 507:21
heart, and in your c. PRAY 389:20
into the conference c. BEVAN 44:17
stalking in my c. WYATT 583:21
chambermaid: of a c. as of a Duchess
JOHN 278:4
chambermaids: With worms that are
thy c. SHAK 483:31
chambers: in the c. of the East BLAKE 88:10
of his c. in the waters PRAY 396:16
perfum'd c. of the great SHAK 441:29
chambre: demeurer en repos dans une
PASC 369:5
chameleon: c.'s dish SHAK 434:4
Chameleons: C. feed on light and air
SHEL 500:14
Champ: C. and chafe and toss ARN 13:5
Champagne: C. certainly gives one
SURT 525:20
not a c. teetotaller SHAW 496:16
with c. and a chicken MONT 354:8
Women and C. BELL 39:21

champion: in close fight a c. grim
SCOTT 417:5
chance: accident nor dart of c. SHAK 476:16
bludgeonings of c. HENL 245:4
C., and Change SHEL 503:10
c., and death, and mutability SHEL 503:12
c. favours only the prepared PAST 369:16
high arbiter C. governs MILT 347:4
it was by c. BRAD 91:13
law, c., hath slain DONNE 189:4
of the main c. of things SHAK 442:3
skirts of happy c. TENN 537:1
various turns of c. below DRYD 195:4
voice to come in as by c. BACON 25:41
Which erring man call c. MILT 341:15
will never eliminate c. MALL 327:11
would set my life on any c. SHAK 461:10
Chancellor: C. of the Exchequer is
LOWE 318:24
C. of the University WELL 567:29
England's high C. JONS 285:7
rather susceptible C. GILB 226:2
Chancery: pretty young wards in C.
GILB 226:2
chances: c. change by course SOUT 514:20
changes and c. of this mortal PRAY 388:5
choose Between the c. AUDEN 21:6
spake of most disastrous c. SHAK 473:25
chang'd: man but c. his mind POPE 377:10
Change: all that moveth doth in C.
SPEN 516:15
bolts up c. SHAK 423:20
certain relief in c. IRV 270:25
Chance, and C. SHEL 503:10
C. and decay in all around LYTE 321:19
C. as the winds change SWIN 530:28
c., but I cannot die SHEL 500:7
C. came o'er the spirit BYRON 124:13
C. is not made without HOOK 255:21
c. of heart AUDEN 20:7
c. our vile body PRAY 389:13
c. best carriage horses TROL 553:8
C. the name and it's about HOR 261:22
c. th'expiring flame renews GAY 223:23
dead there is no c. MAC 324:9
did you c. your stockings AUST 22:11
Doth c. my disposition SHAK 491:27
ever-whirling wheel Of C. SPEN 516:24
extremes by c. more fierce MILT 346:22
fill my pockets with c. DICK 180:19
God cannot c. the past AGAT 3:4
heavy c. MILT 343:5
How will the c. strike BROW 99:20
is necessary not to c. FALK 209:19
I would c. each hour like SEDL 419:13
I would not c. for thine JONS 284:12
lamentable c. is from the best SHAK 455:5
like a c. in the weather AUDEN 21:2
love will c. in growing old BRID 92:20
miserable c. now at my SHAK 423:15
more things c. KARR 288:15
Neither to c. SHEL 503:15
nor wished to c. GOLD 230:22
nous avons c. tout cela MOL 353:17
point is to c. MARX 333:1
progressive country c. DISR 185:4
ringing grooves of c. TENN 539:24
scorn to c. my state SHAK 493:6
take silver or small c. CHAM 139:14
that love could never c. BRID 92:20
That we must c. for Heav'n MILT 345:9
things might c. or cease SHAK 454:3
thou ever c. Kate into Nan BLAKE 86:1
To c. the cod's head SHAK 474:10
to c. what we can STEV 521:14
To know the c. and feel KEATS 293:4
vesture shalt thou c. them PRAY 396:13
we c. with them ANON 11:5
When c. itself can give SEDL 419:14
wind of c. is blowing MACM 326:1

with fear of c. MILT 345:24
without the means of some c. BURKE 111:4
changeable: Moors are c. in their wills
SHAK 474:10
changed: c. from that Hector who VIRG 558:5
c. into little water drops MARL 329:15
c. that my oldest creditors FOX 217:24
c. utterly YEATS 585:1
that it be not c. BIBLE 61:7
they shall be c. PRAY 396:13
Though c. in outward lustre MILT 345:2
we shall all be c. BIBLE 76:29
changefu: seen sae mony c.' years
BURNS 114:15
changeless: would fain keep her c. MER 337:4
changes: c. and chances of this PRAY 388:5
Her plot hath many c. QUAR 403:15
If the c. that we fear JOHN 281:9
Play all your c. ING 270:12
sundry and manifold c. PRAY 386:12
changest: who c. not LYTE 321:19
changing: c. guard at Buckingham Palace
MILNE 340:4
c. scenes of life TATE 531:21
What man thinks of c. TROL 553:7
Chankly Bore: Of the Hills of the C.
LEAR 312:2
Channel: Butting through the C. MAS 333:19
new c., fair and evenly SHAK 439:24
you are crossing the C. GILB 226:13
channels: through the c. of the ear
AUDEN 20:3
chant: triumphal c. SHEL 504:20
chantants: O ces voix d'enfants c.
VERL 556:10
chante: on le c. BEAU 35:14
chanted: c. snatches of old tunes
SHAK 436:19
chanticleer: lungs began to crow like
c. SHAK 425:20
Chanting: C. faint hymns to the cold
SHAK 469:17
Chaos: C. illumined WILDE 573:37
C. is come again SHAK 475:14
C.! is restor'd POPE 376:2
C., rudis indigestaque OVID 366:5
C. umpire sits MILT 347:4
God dawned on C. SHEL 499:11
reign of C. and old Night MILT 345:20
chap: c. that did not kill me HOUS 266:4
second eleven sort of c. BARR 34:8
chapel: decent whitewashed c. BETJ 43:7
There is the empty c. ELIOT 205:10
chapels: Stolen looks are nice in c.
HUNT 268:11
Chaplain: twice a day the C. called
WILDE 572:12
Chapman: Mr C.'s yea was yea BENT 41:4
chapmen: base sale of c.'s tongues
SHAK 456:20
chaps: from the nave to the c. SHAK 458:3
several c. out of the City CHES 147:16
chapter: c. of accidents CHES 146:2
c. of accidents is WILK 574:7
c. of 'The Natural History JOHN 277:28
char: c. the wood ere Thou canst
THOM 548:18
character: belongs not to the female c.
KNOX 305:24
c. dead at every word SHER 506:29
c. in the full current GOET 230:10
'c. is destiny ELIOT 201:21
c. of a family to an hypothesis STER 519:20
entailing Divergence of C. DARW 171:28
I leave my c. behind me SHER 506:30
man's c. is to be abused THAC 545:24
object the formation of c. SPEN 515:1
passion could bring c. YEATS 587:1
personal c. and relations NAP 359:10
regaining my c. I despare FLEM 214:29

She gave me a good c. CARR 134:22
short c. when he was page CHAR 140:27
Sow a c. READE 405:4
that fate and c. are NOV 364:9
What is c. but the determination JAMES 271:12
characteristic: c. of the English Monarchy BAG 28:28
characters: c. of hell to trace GRAY 234:15
from high life high c. POPE 377:11
Most women have no c. POPE 377:17
Who have c. to lose BURNS 114:20
Charakter: *Sich ein C. in dem Strom* GOET 230:10
Charge: 'C., Chester, charge! SCOTT 417:22
c. is prepar'd GAY 223:1
c. or rule nor governance SURR 524:20
c. with all thy chivalry CAMP 128:22
C. you more if you dine DICK 181:25
shall give his angels c. PRAY 395:22
charged: c. the troops of error BROW 96:5
is c. with the grandeur HOPK 256:12
charges: children but as bills of c. BACON 26:32
ought warily to begin c. BACON 26:10
chariest: c. maid is prodigal enough SHAK 430:17
Charing-Cross: human existence is at C. JOHN 276:21
I sunk at C. WALP 563:4
Pitched betwixt Heaven and C. THOM 548:25
chariot: Bring me my c. of fire BLAKE 86:16
c. of Israel BIBLE 51:22
maketh the clouds his c. PRAY 396:18
slap-up gal in a bang-up c. DICK 181:15
charioted: c. by Bacchus and his pards KEATS 291:20
chariotest: c. to their dark wintry SHEL 502:8
chariots: burneth the c. in the fire PRAY 392:21
c., and some in horses PRAY 390:14
tarry the wheels of his c. BIBLE 49:12
chariot-wheel: axletree of the c. BACON 27:33
charitably: how can they c. dispose SHAK 444:21
charitie: doughterly loue and deere c. MORE 357:20
charities: cold c. of man to man COWP 168:27
patron of some thirty c. TENN 542:20
charity: Candour, who, with the c. CHUR 148:22
C. and beating begins FLET 215:25
C. and Mercy DICK 179:6
C., dear Miss Prism WILDE 573:6
c. edifieth BIBLE 76:5
c. envieth not BIBLE 76:14
C. never faileth BIBLE 76:14
C. shall cover the multitude BIBLE 80:32
C. suffereth long BIBLE 76:14
c. vaunteth not itself BIBLE 76:14
c. will hardly water BACON 26:33
c. with your neighbours PRAY 387:18
faith, hope, c. BIBLE 76:14
greatest of these is c. BIBLE 76:14
have not c. BIBLE 76:14
healing voice of Christian c. BURKE 111:2
him a little earth for c. SHAK 447:15
lectures or a little c. WHIT 571:1
living need c. ARN 12:20
Love, friendship, c. SHAK 487:6
mankind's concern is c. POPE 379:20
spent in so-called c. today CARN 132:31
that 'c. begins at home' SHER 506:34
there not be a c. in sin SHAK 464:7
with c. for all LINC 315:3
charlatan: Defamed by every c. TENN 537:17
Charlemain: When C. with all his peerage MILT 345:23
Charles: my gentle-hearted C. COL 157:12
used by C. the First COW 164:4
Charles II: C. was always very merry SELL 420:5
Charles the First: King C. out of the Memorial DICK 177:5
Charlie: We'll o'er the water to C. HOGG 253:1
charlock: shoot the c. throws a shade COWP 168:26
Charlotte: C. has been writing a book BRON 94:2
Werther had a love for C. THAC 546:3
charm: c. can soothe her melancholy GOLD 231:31
c. he never so wisely PRAY 393:17
c. of all the Muses often TENN 543:17
c. of powerful trouble SHAK 462:3
c. they have broken BRID 92:15
Completing the c. ELIOT 202:10
powers of C. and Desire CAT 136:22
such a c. in melancholy ROG 407:10
charmed: Boil thou first i' the c. SHAK 462:2
c. it with smiles and soap CARR 133:8
c. me from my profession SHAK 486:11
I bear a c. life SHAK 463:8
charmer: hear the voice of the c. PRAY 393:17
perils Of cheat and c. HOUS 265:14
Were t'other dear c. away GAY 222:35
charming: c. is divine philosophy MILT 341:11
Every thing that is c. AUST 23:23
innocent and c. as the beasts AUDEN 19:12
So smoothes her c. tones MILT 348:24
charmingly: How c. sweet you sing LEAR 312:12
Charms: C. strike the sight POPE 381:11
c. the town with humour CHUR 149:12
lass that has acres o' c. BURNS 114:6
Music has c. to sooth CONG 160:14
those endearing young c. MOORE 356:4
what drugs, what c. SHAK 473:24
Charrington: Outside C.'s we waited BETJ 43:18
charter: c. of thy worth gives thee SHAK 494:13
This was the c. of the land THOM 549:7
charts: busied in c. BAG 29:11
Charybdis: Scylla and C. NEWM 361:21
Scylla and C. SHEL 505:11
chase: c. of honours and distinction BURKE 108:7
c. the glowing Hours with BYRON 120:21
In piteous c. SHAK 425:1
shining creatures of the c. TENN 542:8
Thy c. had a beast in view DRYD 197:19
thy c. is done SCOTT 416:3
When heated in the c. TATE 531:20
Wherein he doth forever c. ARN 12:22
with unhurrying c. THOM 548:9
chasing: he was always c. Rimbauds PARK 368:20
chasm: romantic c. which slanted COL 156:27
chasse: *souvenirs sont cors de c.* APOL 11:10
chassis: counthry's in a state of c. OCAS 364:16
chaste: Be thou as c. as ice SHAK 433:12
C. as the icicle SHAK 428:3
c. as unsunn'd snow SHAK 428:12
c. polygamy CAREW 130:15
C. to her husband POPE 377:20
cold nymphs c. crowns SHAK 485:19
If I pronounce it c. GILB 227:25
married, charming, c. BYRON 122:8
My English text is c. GIBB 224:19
Nor ever c. DONNE 189:9
nunnery Of thy c. breast LOV 318:20
chasten: power To c. and subdue WORD 578:7
chasteneth: Lord loveth he c. BIBLE 80:1
chasteté: *une vertu du vice de c.* VOLT 561:12
chastis'd: Nor once be c. with SHAK 423:21
chastise: c. with the valour of my SHAK 459:1
chastised: father hath c. you with whips BIBLE 51:3
having been a little c. BIBLE 62:13
chastisement: c. of our peace was upon BIBLE 59:22
chastity: clothed on with c. TENN 533:21
Even like thy c. SHAK 477:21
Give me c. and continency AUG 21:14
made of the vice of c. VOLT 561:12
that c. of honour BURKE 111:10
'Tis C., my brother MILT 341:10
chasuble: He wore, I think, a c. HARTE 242:31
châteaux: *Ô saisons, ô c.* RIMB 406:8
Chatham: C. with his sabre drawn ANON 5:10
everyday politics than a C. BAG 28:25
chats: spoiled the women's c. BROW 103:15
chatte: *Quand je me joue à ma c.* MONT 355:2
chatter: c. about Shelley FREE 218:24
insignificant c. of the world TROL 552:22
matter if it's only idle c. GILB 227:21
chatters: science and logic he c. PRAED 384:5
Chatterton: C.! how very sad thy fate KEATS 292:23
C., the marvellous boy WORD 580:28
Chaucer: C., well of English undefiled SPEN 516:19
mean Master Geoffrey C. CAXT 138:2
old famous Poet C. SPEN 517:5
To learned C. BASSE 35:1
chavender: There is a fine stuffed c. ST L 412:27
Chawcer: It is a pity that C. WARD 564:31
cheap: c. and chippy chopper GILB 226:31
done as c. as other men PEPYS 372:6
flesh and blood so c. HOOD 255:8
hold their manhoods c. SHAK 445:3
maketh himself c. BACON 25:37
sold c. what is most dear SHAK 495:3
cheaper: principle that it is c. BUTL 119:4
cheaply: put him c. off DRYD 195:13
cheapness: tawdry c. Shall outlast POUND 383:7
Cheapside: in C. shall my palfrey SHAK 446:11
through the vale of C. WORD 581:3
cheat: detecting what I think a c. JOHN 276:16
he may c. at cards genteelly BOSW 90:16
it's so lucrative to c. CLOU 153:28
perils Of c. and charmer HOUS 265:14
so monosyllabic as to c. FRY 220:6
sweet c. gone DE L 174:5
To c. a man is nothing GAY 222:29
Cheated: C. of feature by dissembling SHAK 480:18
enthusiasm I have been c. KEATS 294:15
Of being c. BUTL 118:6
Old men who never c. BETJ 42:12
quality to be exceedingly c. EVEL 209:7
cheating: Forbids the c. of our friends CHUR 148:30
cheats: c. with an oath acknowledges PLUT 374:20
check: dreadful is the c. BRON 93:21
immediate c. to loose behaviour STEE 518:6
I would not c. LAND 308:24
To c. the erring and reprove WORD 579:15
Check'd: C. like a bondman SHAK 451:23
cheek: bring a blush into the c. DICK 181:11
C. of hers to incarnadine FITZ 212:7
c. to him that smiteth BIBLE 60:31
Feed on her damask c. SHAK 489:7
give this c. a little red POPE 377:16
hangs upon the c. of night SHAK 482:2
Her c. was soft as silk PAIN 367:19
He that loves a rosy c. CAREW 130:12
iron tears down Pluto's c. MILT 342:6

kissed each other's c.   GILB 228:31
leans her c. upon her hand   SHAK 482:7
old ornament of his c.   SHAK 472:26
on thy c. a fading rose   KEATS 290:16
smite thee on thy right c.   BIBLE 64:17
Where's the c. that doth   KEATS 289:31
yellow c.   SHAK 441:10
cheeks: c. of sorry grain wi   MILT 341:18
crack your c.   SHAK 454:4
Fat ruddy c. Augustus had   HOFF 252:11
Her c. were so red   KING 297:4
Spoke in her c.   DONNE 189:31
cheer: Be of good c..   BIBLE 66:26
be of good c.   BIBLE 72:41
c. us when we recover   BURKE 110:19
Could scarce forbear to c.   MAC 322:22
Died the sound of royal c.   TENN 538:12
Don't c.   PHIL 373:8
Greet the unseen with a c.   BROW 98:33
let thy heart c. thee   BIBLE 56:10
That c. but not inebriate   COWP 167:11
to c. but not inebriate   BERK 41:21
Cheer'd: C. up himself with ends   BUTL 117:31
cheerer: c. of his spirits   WALT 564:3
cheerful: c. countenance, and bread   PRAY 396:20
c. noise unto the God   PRAY 395:9
Dromedary is a c. bird   BELL 38:27
entertain a c. disposition   SHAK 478:22
ground with c. thoughts   SHAK 483:23
heart maketh a c. countenance   BIBLE 54:5
he looking as c. as any   PEPYS 372:1
loveth a c. giver   BIBLE 77:9
more c. and hopeful than   HOLM 253:14
cheerfulness: c. was always breaking   EDW 200:8
cheerioh: 'c.' and 'cheeri-bye'   BETJ 42:18
cheers: sounds no worse than c.   HOUS 263:2
cheese: baiting a mouse-trap with c.   SAKI 413:15
Botticelli's a c.   PUNCH 403:3
c. and garlic in a windmill   SHAK 439:28
fill hup the chinks wi' c.   SURT 525:8
like some valley c.   AUDEN 20:14
night I've dreamed of c.   STEV 521:23
smells of c.   SURT 525:15
swiss c. would think   MARQ 330:25
that has 265 kinds of c.   DE G 173:17
With apple pie and c.   FIELD 211:1
cheeses: ate the c. out of the vats   BROW 103:15
chef: je suis leur c.   LEDR 313:6
chef-d'oeuvre: tree toad is a c.   WHIT 570:21
chemin: c'est le plus court c.   MOL 353:24
chemist: c., fiddler, statesman   DRYD 194:11
cheque: c. and the postal order   AUDEN 20:1
political blank c.   GOSC 233:2
Chequer-board: C. of Nights and Days   FITZ 213:5
chequered: beauteous c. sides with gore   THOM 549:19
chercherais: c. pas si tu ne me possédais   PASC 369:13
cherish: c. those hearts that hate   SHAK 447:12
love, c., and to obey   PRAY 389:4
Then c. pity   BLAKE 88:4
cherishing: kill thee with much c.   SHAK 482:20
Cherith: dwelt by the brook C.   BIBLE 51:6
cheroot: of a whackin' white c.   KIPL 301:6
cherries: c., hops   DICK 181:27
There c. grow   ALIS 3:18
There c. grow   CAMP 129:22
cherry: c. now   HOUS 262:14
C. Orchard is now mine…I've   CHEK 144:24
C.-ripe   HERR 248:21
Like to a double c.   SHAK 470:22
ruddier than the c.   GAY 222:8
see the c. hung with snow   HOUS 262:14

Till c. ripe themselves   ALIS 3:18
Till 'C. ripe' themselves   CAMP 129:22
cherry-blossoms: c., and white cups   SHEL 503:19
cherry-isle: There's the land, or c.   HERR 248:15
cherry-stones: not carve heads upon c.   JOHN 279:18
Chertsey: There was an old Lady of C.   LEAR 311:17
cherub: c.'s face   POPE 377:4
Cherubic: C. Creatures— These Gentlewomen   DICK 184:3
cherubim: c. does cease to sing   BLAKE 85:10
heaven's c.   SHAK 459:6
helmed C.   MILT 344:9
That the C. may cry   ANON 10:14
cherubims: He rode upon the c.   PRAY 390:8
Immortal C.   TRAH 551:19
sitteth between the c.   PRAY 396:10
Cherubin: To thee C.   PRAY 384:16
cherubins: quiring to the young-eyed   SHAK 468:15
cherubynnes: fyr-reed c. face   CHAU 142:4
ches: First of the c.   CHAU 141:6
chess: Life's too short for c.   BYRON 126:23
chess-board: called the c. white   BROW 99:5
c. is the world   HUXL 269:6
chest: caused his c. to slip down   WOD 575:23
c. of drawers by day   GOLD 231:4
His c. against his foes   SMART 509:3
men on the dead man's c.   STEV 521:21
Chester: 'Charge, C., charge!   SCOTT 417:22
Chesterton: dared attack my C.   BELL 39:27
chestnut: c. casts his flambeaux   HOUS 264:20
dogwood and c.   ELIOT 203:4
showers betumble the c.   HARDY 241:2
Under the spreading c. tree   LONG 317:18
chestnuts: sailor's wife had c.   SHAK 458:6
cheval: hommes et allemand à mon c.   CHAR 140:31
Chevalier: C. sans peur et sans reproche   ANON 9:5
chew: savoury pulp they c.   MILT 347:25
chewed: few to be c. and digested   BACON 27:19
cheweth: yet he c. not the cud   BIBLE 48:6
chewing: c. little bits of string   BELL 38:34
Chicken: character called the Game C.   DICK 177:29
c. in his pot every Sunday   HENR 245:13
Some c.   CHUR 150:10
with champagne and a c.   MONT 354:8
chickens: Curses are like young c.   SOUT 513:23
gathereth her c. under her wings   BIBLE 67:26
pretty c. and their dam   SHAK 462:11
chid: He c. their wand'rings   GOLD 230:23
chide: the world-without-end   SHAK 493:18
They do but sweetly c.   SHAK 492:25
chiding: c. of the winter's wind   SHAK 424:31
He will not alway be c.   PRAY 396:16
I am a child to c.   SHAK 476:22
chief: c. of the ways of God   BIBLE 53:9
Hail to the C. who in triumph   SCOTT 416:4
I'm the c. of Ulva's isle   CAMP 129:2
Sinners; of whom I am c.   BIBLE 79:8
chiefest: c. among ten thousand   BIBLE 57:3
Chief Justice: C. was rich   MAC 323:18
chieftain: c. to the Highlands bound   CAMP 129:1
Great a. o' the puddin'-race   BURNS 115:16
Sate Brunswick's fated c.   BYRON 120:23
chiels: Facts are c. that winna ding   BURNS 113:14
chiens: monade des gens comme les c.   NERV 361:1
Chiesa: Libera C. in libero Stato   CAV 138:1
child: adventurous c.   HOR 260:21
angel is the English c.   BLAKE 88:2

Around the c. bend all   LAND 308:17
Behold the c.   POPE 379:18
care for the c.'s rattle   JOHN 275:19
c. deserves the maximum   JUV 288:7
C.! do not throw this   BELL 38:23
c. imposes on the man   DRYD 196:19
c. in the street I could   CLOU 153:9
c. is afraid of being whipped   JOHN 273:25
C. is father of the Man   WORD 578:19
c. is known by his doings   BIBLE 54:17
c. may joy to hear   BLAKE 87:25
c. of glorious great intent   SPEN 516:4
c. of God   PRAY 388:12
c.'s a plaything   LAMB 304:11
c. should always say what's   STEV 522:17
c. that is not clean   STEV 522:21
Defend, O Lord, this thy C.   PRAY 388:22
father that knows his own c.   SHAK 466:9
friend or c. I speak   ARN 13:8
had been any christom c.   SHAK 443:17
happy English c.   TAYL 531:23
healthy c. well nursed is   SWIFT 526:26
heard one calling, 'C.'   HERB 247:15
He never spoils the c.   HOOD 254:19
he who gives a c. a treat   MAS 333:25
I am a c. to chiding   SHAK 476:22
If you strike a c.   SHAW 497:41
Is it well with the c.   BIBLE 51:25
is to see that every c.   RUSK 412:6
It was a crime in a c.   MAC 324:18
I was a c. and she was   POE 374:22
leave a c. alone   BROW 104:22
lie down like a tired c.   SHEL 504:11
like a froward c.   TEMP 532:9
little c. shall lead them   BIBLE 58:10
making love is c.'s play   MITF 352:26
mother's sake the c. was dear   COL 157:9
my Irish c.   WAGN 562:1
named the c. I-chabod   BIBLE 49:40
nicest c. I ever knew   BELL 38:32
On a cloud I saw a c.   BLAKE 87:7
receive one such little c.   BIBLE 67:3
room up of my absent c.   SHAK 452:20
saddling of the right to a c.   SHAW 496:27
seen A curious c.   WORD 577:16
Set his c. upon her knee   TENN 542:11
She was an aggravating c.   BELL 39:12
sing to the c. on thy knee   BRID 92:21
slayeth the c. in the womb   POUND 382:10
solitary c.   WORD 578:10
spoil the c.   BUTL 118:2
sucking c. shall play   BIBLE 58:11
that's govern'd by a c.   SHAK 481:2
This painted c. of dirt   POPE 377:1
thou show'st thee in a c.   SHAK 453:17
To have a thankless c.   SHAK 453:19
To see his active c. do   SHAK 493:13
Train up a c. in the way   BIBLE 54:22
'Twas a c. that so did   JONS 284:2
unto us a c. is born   BIBLE 58:7
use of a new-born c.   FRAN 218:19
was a c. beneath her touch   ROSS 409:22
waters wild went o'er his c.   CAMP 129:5
when a c. is born   SU T 524:19
When I was a c.   BIBLE 76:14
when thy king is a c.   BIBLE 56:3
While the c. was yet alive   BIBLE 50:22
woman forget her sucking c.   BIBLE 59:17
would not *coddle* the c.   JOHN 275:28
wretched c. expires   BELL 39:2
yet a c.   POPE 376:23
childbirth: Mountains will heave in c.   HOR 257:18
Childe Roland: 'C. to the Dark Tower came   BROW 99:30
Childhood: C. is the kingdom where   MILL 339:24
c. shows the man   MILT 350:7
From his c. onward this   HARD 238:21
Our c. used to know'   HARDY 240:14

that oft in c. solac'd me | COWP 166:2
'tis the eye of c. | SHAK 460:11
Womanhood and c. fleet | LONG 316:20
childish: again towards c. treble | SHAK 425:24
are either knavish or c. | JOHN 278:9
c. valourous than manly | MARL 330:15
glamour Of c. days | LAWR 311:7
I put away c. things | BIBLE 76:14
It was a c. ignorance | HOOD 254:18
my c. wave of pity | BETJ 43:19
Wordsworth chime his c. | BYRON 124:29
childishness: Is second c. | SHAK 425:24
It does from c. | SHAK 421:27
childless: have proceeded from c. men | BACON 27:4
children: Accustom your c. constantly | JOHN 277:20
airy hopes my c. | WORD 577:14
all our c.'s fate | KIPL 299:6
be called the c. of God | BIBLE 64:6
become as little c. | BIBLE 67:2
becometh the c. of light | PRAY 388:11
call'd you c. | SHAK 454:5
c. at play are not playing | MONT 354:17
C. begin by loving their | WILDE 573:30
c. born of thee are sword | TENN 534:10
c. capable of honesty is | RUSK 412:5
c. carried away with every | PRAY 387:3
c. casual as birds | AUDEN 18:5
c. cried in the streets | MOTL 358:20
c. died in the streets | AUDEN 18:15
c. follow'd with endearing | GOLD 231:1
c. in England take pleasure | ANON 7:22
c. in Holland take pleasure | ANON 7:22
c. innocent and charming | AUDEN 19:12
c. in whom is no faith | BIBLE 48:31
c. like the olive-branches | PRAY 398:20
C. of the future age | BLAKE 87:17
c., quietly talking alone | BOWEN 91:3
c.'s teeth are set | BIBLE 60:34
c. stood watching them | KING 297:2
C. sweeten labours | BACON 27:3
C. with Hyacinth's temperament | SAKI 413:16
c., you should never let | WATTS 565:18
Come my tan-faced c. | WHIT 570:10
committed by c. on children | BOWEN 91:3
doeth for the c. of men | PRAY 397:7
dogs than of their c. | PENN 371:15
even so are the young c. | PRAY 398:19
father pitieth his own c. | PRAY 396:17
fathers, provoke not your c. | BIBLE 78:7
fathers upon the c. unto | BIBLE 47:24
fear death as c. | BACON 26:1
fond of c. (except boys) | CARR 136:12
He has no c. | SHAK 462:17
Her c. arise up | BIBLE 55:4
her c. came from school | BURT 116:34
His c.'s looks | GOLD 231:26
I have gathered thy c. | BIBLE 67:26
imposed in the interest of c. | SHAW 496:24
I never knows the c. | MARR 331:7
keep c. quiet | SWIFT 525:31
kept from c. and from fools | DRYD 197:20
kitchen and their c. | FITZ 213:19
known as the C.'s Hour | LONG 316:9
little c.'s dower | BROW 101:7
many c. | JOHN 274:22
me from c. who were rough | SPEN 515:11
Men are but c. of a larger | DRYD 195:15
neither c. nor Gods | KIPL 298:23
Nourish thy c. | BIBLE 62:6
of the c. of the light | ARN 16:3
old men and c. | PRAY 399:23
procreation of c. | PRAY 389:1
Rachel weeping for her c. | BIBLE 63:34
see his c. fed | PUDN 402:8
see the c. sport upon | WORD 579:10
shall return us the c. | KIPL 298:9
Suffer the little c. | BIBLE 68:36
Their children's c. shall | YEATS 585:8

they bare c. to them | BIBLE 45:33
those c.'s voices | VERL 556:10
thou shalt bring forth c. | BIBLE 45:21
thou shalt have c. | PRAY 392:18
We are the c. of God | BIBLE 75:9
'We have c. | TENN 543:3
Were all thy c. kind | SHAK 443:13
When c. of one family | WATTS 565:20
When the voices of c. are | BLAKE 88:3
which holdeth c. from play | SIDN 508:2
who appear to me as c. | KEATS 294:10
wife and c. hath given hostages | BACON 26:31
wife and c. but as bills | BACON 26:32
wiser than the c. of light | BIBLE 70:25
Women, then, are only c. | CHES 145:25
Would not have bandy c. | BLAKE 87:20
young c. | PRAY 385:20
child-wife: It's only my c. | DICK 177:19
chill: bitter c. it was | KEATS 289:9
C. on the brow | SPAR 514:22
First—C.—then Stupor | DICK 183:14
So haunt thy days and c. | KEATS 290:30
Chillon: C.! thy prison is a holy | BYRON 125:15
chilly: c. stars I can forgo | CORY 163:5
I feel c. and grown old | BROW 105:26
Chiltern Hundreds: take the C. while you can | CHES 146:13
Chimborazo: C., Cotopaxi | TURN 553:23
chime: let your silver c. | MILT 344:10
some soft c. had stroked | JONS 285:10
Chimera: C. in my brain | DONNE 191:2
utrum c. in vacuo bombinans | RAB 403:29
chimeras: dire c. and enchanted isles | MILT 341:12
other wild impossible c. | SWIFT 526:8
chimes: heard the c. at midnight | SHAK 442:6
hear the c. at midnight | STEV 522:2
chimney: Who smoked like a c. | BARH 33:17
chimney-piece: Buffalo Upon the c. | CARR 133:11
chimneys: good grove of c. for me | MORR 358:4
Our c. were blown down | SHAK 460:20
So your c. I sweep | BLAKE 88:5
chimney-sweepers: c., come to dust | SHAK 428:22
chin: rye reach to the c. | PEELE 371:9
China: from C. to Peru | JOHN 282:28
infusion of a C. plant | ADD 2:11
though C. fall | POPE 377:28
Till C. and Africa meet | AUDEN 18:9
treads the Wall Of C. | PATM 370:7
ye break my best blue c. | HARDY 239:20
Chinamen: With C. | BELL 40:6
Chinee: heathen C. is peculiar | HARTE 242:29
Chinese: ruined by C. cheap labour | HARTE 242:30
chinks: fill hup the c. wi' cheese | SURT 525:8
chintzy: c. cheeriness | BETJ 42:10
chip: Not merely a c. | BURKE 110:22
chipping: c. at the countenances | DICK 176:11
chippy: cheap and c. chopper | GILB 226:31
chips: given them nothing but c. | CHUR 149:21
chirche: Housbondes at c. dore she | CHAU 141:31
chisel: Usura rusteth the c. | POUND 382:10
chitchat: home of iridescent c. | NASH 360:3
chivalrie: He loved c. | CHAU 141:9
chivalry: age of c. is gone | BURKE 111:9
age of c. is never past | KING 297:18
age of c. is past | DISR 187:3
Cervantes smiled Spain's c. | BYRON 124:1
Christian service and true c. | SHAK 478:20
forgetful of his c. | HOMER 254:3
have a truant been to c. | SHAK 440:16
learn the noble acts of c. | CAXT 138:4
nine-tenths of the law of c. | SAY 415:6
Who sung of Border c. | SCOTT 416:9
choice: being just the terrible c. | BROW 104:31

c. and master spirits | SHAK 450:8
c. dishes the Doctor has | GARR 221:12
c. of friends | COWL 164:14
C. words | WORD 581:1
decision or reason or c. | CHOM 148:16
Each to his c. | KIPL 303:16
honour is the *people's c.* | SHER 506:7
in the worth and c. | JONS 283:23
money and you takes your c. | ANON 9:2
more difficult the c. | ALL 3:19
take c. of all my library | SHAK 486:16
there were a sympathy in c. | SHAK 469:20
was mistress of her c. | SHAK 434:1
choir: c. of heaven and furniture | BERK 41:19
c. the small gnats mourn | KEATS 293:8
I join the c. invisible | ELIOT 201:27
choirs: Bare ruin'd c. | SHAK 494:7
choisir: c'est c. | LEVIS 314:5
choke: c. the word | BIBLE 66:17
do c. their service up | SHAK 425:7
nothing but to c. a man | JONS 284:5
choked: thorns sprang up and c. them | BIBLE 66:16
chokes: something bitter that c. | LUCR 320:11
choking: cat than c. her with cream | KING 297:15
c. him and making him carry | TOLS 551:15
choleric: captain's but a c. word | SHAK 464:4
Chommoda: C. dicebat | CAT 137:13
choose: can believe what we c. | NEWM 362:16
can believe what you c. | NEWM 362:17
c. A Jewish God | BROW 95:13
C. an author as you choose | ROOS 408:10
c. life that both thou | BIBLE 48:29
c. love by another's eye | SHAK 469:19
c. the good | BIBLE 58:3
c. Their place of rest | MILT 350:1
C. thou whatever suits | COL 157:5
c. time is to save time | BACON 26:7
I lie as lads would c. | HOUS 263:11
leading wherever I c. | WHIT 571:7
Let's c. executors | SHAK 479:10
not c. not to be | HOPK 256:7
that c. by show | SHAK 466:19
They cannot c. | THOM 547:19
To c. The Jews | EWER 209:13
Choosing: C. each stone | MARV 331:20
just c. so | BROW 99:25
chop: day you'll eat a pork c. | CAMP 128:7
chopcherry: c. ripe within | PEELE 371:9
chopper: cheap and chippy c. | GILB 226:31
Chops: C. and Tomata sauce | DICK 182:19
chord: feel for the common c. | BROW 98:22
I struck one c. of music | PROC 401:14
chords: *are* c. in the human mind | DICK 176:15
choristers: go the chanting c. | LAWR 311:5
chortled: He c. in his joy | CARR 134:29
Chorus: C. Hymeneal | SHEL 504:20
chose: c. him five smooth stones | BIBLE 50:11
chosen: best c. language | AUST 22:31
c. thee in the furnace | BIBLE 59:14
fast that I have c. | BIBLE 60:4
few are c. | BIBLE 67:18
hath c. the weak things | BIBLE 75:30
Mary hath c. that good part | BIBLE 69:35
name is rather to be c. | BIBLE 54:21
opponent of the c. people | ARN 16:3
ye are a c. generation | BIBLE 80:23
Ye have not c. me | BIBLE 72:37
choughs: c. and rooks brought forth | SHAK 461:24
crows and c. that wing | SHAK 455:14
choux: *trouve plantant mes c.* | MONT 354:14
Christ: am all at once what C. is | HOPK 257:1
Are they ministers of C. | BIBLE 77:11
Came C. the tiger | ELIOT 203:4
C. and his mother and all | HOPK 256:29
C. being raised from | BIBLE 75:2
C. came and preached peace | BIBLE 77:22

C. cannot find a chamber ANON 9:1
C. erecteth his Church BANC 32:14
C. follows Dionysus POUND 383:6
C. is all BIBLE 78:26
C. our passover is sacrificed BIBLE 75:36
C. perish in torment SHAW 498:20
C. receive him TENN 541:15
C. shall all be made alive BIBLE 76:22
C.'s particular love's BROW 104:22
C.'s stamp to boot HERB 247:9
C. walking on the water THOM 548:25
C. which strengtheneth BIBLE 78:23
churches have kill'd their C. TENN 540:14
counted loss for C. BIBLE 78:17
draws near the birth of C. TENN 536:17
edifying of the body of C. BIBLE 77:28
estate C. adorned PRAY 388:25
grey-grown speechless C. SWIN 529:3
heathen and uphold the C. TENN 534:11
in the bowels of C. CROM 169:21
is C. risen from the dead BIBLE 76:22
joint-heirs with C. BIBLE 75:9
last kind word to C. BROW 104:25
love of C. BIBLE 77:25
May Lord C. enter WILDE 572:16
me to live is C. BIBLE 78:11
now by Baptism put on C. PRAY 388:11
only we have hope in C. BIBLE 76:21
Priest did offer C. PRAY 400:9
Ring in the C. that is TENN 537:15
Saviour C. again to Earth MAS 333:26
stature of the fulness of C. BIBLE 77:28
Thy everlasting mercy, C. MAS 333:26
to be with C. BIBLE 78:12
understood C. was a carpenter BLAKE 87:8
unsearchable riches of C. BIBLE 77:23
Vision of C. that thou BLAKE 85:21
We withstood C. then BROW 101:4
where C.'s blood streams MARL 329:11
Christ-Church: festal light in C. ARN 14:16
I am the Dean of C. SPR 517:11
study at C. and All-Souls JOHN 275:22
Christe: C. eleison MASS 334:16
C. receive thy saule BALL 31:6
christened: pleasing you when she was
c. SHAK 426:12
Christiad: C. than a Pauliad to his
HARDY 241:24
Christian: Because it is only C. men
CHES 146:19
buried in C. burial SHAK 436:21
C. beauty Defects POUND 383:5
C. boys I can scarcely ARN 16:27
C. can only fear dying HARE 242:3
C. hold for me the glass ANON 10:14
C. ideal has not been tried CHES 148:9
C. is a man who feels YBAR 584:7
C. religion doubted BUTL 119:13
C. religion not only was HUME 267:21
C. resolution to find NIET 363:8
C. service and true chivalry SHAK 478:20
C.'s health to hustle KIPL 301:18
darkness fell upon C. BUNY 107:25
evidence of a naturally C. soul TERT 544:21
good C. at her heart POPE 377:19
hate him for he is a C. SHAK 465:29
he is the only early C. CHES 148:3
honourable style of a C. BROW 96:2
I die a C. CHAR 140:20
I mean the C. religion FIEL 211:23
is the true wayfaring C. MILT 351:24
It's the Early C. that SAKI 413:9
Let every C. BLAKE 86:10
little as a C. can DOYLE 192:40
of his C. name a synonym MAC 323:27
peace a C. can die ADD 2:29
persuadest me to be a C. BIBLE 74:27
Scratch the C. and you ZANG 588:16
souls of C. peoples… CHES 146:11
That I was born of C. race WATTS 565:14

This Hebrew will turn C. SHAK 466:5
three C. men CAXT 138:3
tiger that hadn't *got* a C. PUNCH 402:24
to forgive them as a c. AUST 23:19
to form C. men ARN 16:27
you were a C. Slave HENL 245:10
Christianity: age come from C. and
journalism BALF 30:5
C. better than Truth will COL 157:18
C. is part of the Common HALE 237:13
C. is the most materialistic TEMP 532:11
His C. was muscular DISR 186:6
local cult called C. HARDY 239:14
prooving C. to the Hindoos WIS 575:10
that C. is not so much BUTL 117:8
where C. was the religion SWIFT 527:6
Christian name: superfluous C. lopped
off ARN 15:27
Christians: blood of C. is the seed
TERT 544:22
call themselves C. may PRAY 385:25
C. all behave so badly BAYL 35:9
C. have burnt each other BYRON 122:10
what these C. are SHAK 466:4
Christ Jesus: glory in the church by C.
BIBLE 77:26
Christmas: C. gambol oft could cheer
SCOTT 417:16
C. I no more desire a rose SHAK 456:16
C. morning bells say 'Come BETJ 42:8
insulting C. card GROS 237:3
keep our C. merry still SCOTT 417:15
that C. should fall out ADD 2:16
'Twas the night before C. MOORE 355:12
Christmas Day: at Home the C. is breaking
KIPL 298:13
It is C. in the Workhouse SIMS 508:10
Christmas Eve: C., and twelve
HARDY 240:13
Christopher Robin: C. went down with
Alice MILNE 340:4
C. is saying his prayers MILNE 340:11
Christs: C. that die upon the barricades
WILDE 572:17
chronic: It is c. DICK 179:7
chronicle: in the c. of wasted time
SHAK 494:19
it is the c. of a solitary ELIOT 201:16
make your c. as rich with SHAK 443:8
chronicler: honest as Griffith SHAK 447:23
chronicles: abstracts and brief c. SHAK 432:25
Look in the c. SHAK 484:2
Chrononhotonthologos: Where left you
C. CAREY 130:21
chub: chavender, or c. ST L 412:27
Chuck: C. it, Smith CHES 146:11
church: because I persecuted the c.
BIBLE 76:19
bells have knoll'd to c. SHAK 425:23
best harmony in a c. MILT 351:26
Broad of C. and broad BETJ 44:14
buttress of the c. MELB 336:22
came to the village c. TENN 540:2
Catholick and Apostolick C. PRAY 387:11
Christ erecteth his C. BANC 32:14
c. and no steeple SWIFT 528:11
C. is said to want NEWM 361:21
c. lit but without a congregation
WELLS 568:11
C. militant here in earth PRAY 387:12
C.'s Restoration BETJ 43:2
C. with psalms must shout HERB 246:26
'Come all to c. HOUS 263:5
English C. shall be free MAGN 327:1
equal are within the C.'s HERB 247:10
estate of the Catholick C. PRAY 385:25
ever was the c. for peace BROW 99:12
fain would kill their c. TENN 540:14
free c. in a free state CAV 138:1
glory in the c. by Christ Jesus BIBLE 77:26

he never passes a c. without JOHN 274:27
Here's a c. DICK 178:14
I like a c. EMER 206:22
I like the silent c. before EMER 207:40
keep thy household the C. PRAY 386:23
nearer the C. the further ANDR 4:8
not the c. for his mother CYPR 170:19
other c. has ever understood MAC 323:17
parish c. of Kentish Town BETJ 43:18
publick Prayer in the C. PRAY 400:8
rock I will build my c. BIBLE 66:33
salvation outside the c. AUG 21:19
see a c. by daylight SHAK 472:5
some to c. repair POPE 378:20
there must be the C. AMBR 4:1
took young Cyril to c. ELIOT 202:7
wet c. the size of a snail THOM 547:7
What is a c. COWP 168:4
who is always at c. BLAKE 87:20
women to speak in the c. BIBLE 76:17
churches: care of all the c. BIBLE 77:12
C. built to please BURNS 114:19
Down c. praise KIPL 303:14
he must build c. then SHAK 434:7
keep silence in the c. BIBLE 76:16
seven c. which are in Asia BIBLE 81:9
seven c. which are in Asia BIBLE 81:12
churchmen: c. fain would kill their
TENN 540:14
life doth well with c. BACON 26:33
Church of England: been the wisdom
of the C. PRAY 384:7
'C.,' I said SHOR 507:8
Profession of the C. CHAR 140:20
Protestant religion but the C. FIEL 211:23
churchyard: beneath the elms in the c.
SCOTT 418:23
blown the dust of the C. DONNE 190:23
c. thing KEATS 289:14
devil in the same c. will BANC 32:14
lie in Mellstock c. now HARDY 239:17
of a little country c. BURKE 108:6
worse taste, than in a c. JOW 285:23
churchyards: Troop home to c. SHAK 470:25
When c. yawn and hell itself SHAK 434:7
Churn: Attract a Silver C. GILB 227:24
chute: Vivre est une c. horizontale
COCT 154:12
Cicero: If I could have known C. DICK 177:25
opinion can alienate C. MAC 324:9
ciel: montez au c. FIRM 212:2
cielo: Que el c. exista BORG 89:23
cieux: Père qui êtes aux c. PREV 400:15
cigar: c., and cigarette tobacco DOYLE 191:16
good c. is a Smoke KIPL 298:3
sweet post-prandial c. BUCH 106:11
cigarette: c. is the perfect type WILDE 573:20
Cilicia: city in C. BIBLE 74:20
Cimber: constant Cimber should be banish'd
SHAK 449:25
Cinara: when dear C. was my queen
HOR 261:10
Cinarae: Sub regno C. HOR 261:10
Cincinnatus: C. of the West BYRON 125:9
cinco: c. en punto de la tarde GARC 221:5
cinder: dry a c. this world DONNE 187:20
cinders: I've made the c. fly KIPL 298:7
cinerem: nequiquam alloquerer c. CAT 137:15
cinguntur: his nivea c. tempora vitta
VIRG 558:23
cinnamon: c. and cloves BEAU 36:5
tinct with c. KEATS 289:20
cipher: c. in the state SAV 415:5
Circe: elegance of C.'s hair POUND 383:3
circenses: Panem et c. JUV 287:28
circle: God is a c. of which the centre
ANON 7:27
Love is a c. that doth HERR 249:9
Round and round the c. ELIOT 202:10
Weave a c. round him thrice COL 157:1

wheel is come full c.　SHAK 456:6
circles: Conversation is a game of c.
　　　　EMER 207:14
individual c. of which we are　TROL 552:22
circuitous: foil'd c. wanderer　ARN 15:1
Circumcised: C. the eighth day　BIBLE 78:16
circumcision: c. nor uncircumcision
　　　　BIBLE 78:26
circumference: everywhere and the c.
　is nowhere　ANON 7:27
circumfused: forms and substances are
　c.　WORD 580:19
Circumlocution: C. Office was beforehand
　　　　DICK 178:16
circumspectly: that ye walk c.　BIBLE 78:4
Circumspice: C., si Monumentum
　　　　BARH 33:7
monumentum requiris, c.　ANON 11:2
Nisi monumentum requiris, c.　INGE 270:11
circumstance: am the very slave of c.
　　　　BYRON 125:20
breasts the blows of c.　TENN 537:1
Eternal artistries in C.　HARDY 239:11
ignorant of this remarkable c.　MAC 324:12
In the fell clutch of c.　HENL 245:4
Of plastic c.　BROW 104:1
pomp, and c.　SHAK 475:25
To a philosopher no c.　GOLD 232:3
Circumstances: C. beyond my individual
　　　　DICK 177:20
Fearful concatenation of c.　WEBS 566:16
see a husband in these c.　GAY 222:31
circumstantial: c. evidence is very strong
　　　　THOR 550:24
circumvent: politician...one that would
　c. God　SHAK 436:27
Ciro: Bingham had never been to C.'s
　　　　TRAV 552:6
cirque: always like a c. of mountains
　　　　AUDEN 19:12
citadel: mountain-built with peaceful
　c.　KEATS 291:8
citadels: circle-c. there　HOPK 256:28
Cities: C. and their civilities　PATM 370:7
C. entered　HOUS 265:4
c. hostile and the towns　ELIOT 203:13
hell in the c.　AESC 3:1
Of human c. torture　BYRON 120:35
citizen: c. of no mean city　BIBLE 74:20
greater than a private c.　TAC 531:13
he is a c. of the world　BACON 26:20
humblest c. of all　BRYAN 106:7
requisite of a good c.　ROOS 408:2
citizens: Before Man made us c.　LOW 319:11
c. kneading up the honey　SHAK 443:9
first and second class c.　WILL 574:14
you fat and greasy c.　SHAK 425:2
CITTÀ: PER ME SI VA NELLA C.
　DOLENTE　DANTE 171:3
city: all the c. on an uproar　BIBLE 74:8
Back from the C. of Sleep　KIPL 298:14
Behold now this vast c.　MILT 352:1
briskly to infect a c.　AUDEN 18:19
citizen of no mean c.　BIBLE 74:20
c. and I see a man hurrying　KEATS 294:17
c. consists in its men　NIC 362:25
c., I can sometimes hear　ELIOT 205:4
c. is barren　DICK 176:17
c. is built To music　TENN 534:6
C. is of Night　THOM 549:27
c. state of the sponge　AUDEN 20:15
C.'s voice itself is soft　SHEL 504:8
c.: that is at unity　PRAY 398:11
c. that is set on an hill　BIBLE 64:8
C. with her dreaming spires　ARN 15:4
crowning c.　BIBLE 58:16
Despising, For you, the c.　SHAK 427:24
doth the c. sit solitary　BIBLE 60:27
dream'd in a dream I saw a c. invincible
　　　　WHIT 570:4

each and every town or c.　HOLM 253:16
Except the Lord keep the c.　PRAY 398:18
first c. Cain　COWL 164:9
Happy is that c. which　ANON 5:12
have we no continuing c.　BIBLE 80:5
he looked for a c. which　BIBLE 79:32
holy c., new Jerusalem　BIBLE 82:30
in perils of the c.　BIBLE 77:12
live in a c.　COLT 159:10
long in populous c. pent　MILT 349:13
looking over harbor and c.　SAND 413:26
Lord guards the c.　BIBLE 83:12
people went up into the c.　BIBLE 49:2
pity who know not the c.　PROW 402:2
possession of truth as of a c.　BROW 96:6
rose-red c. 'half as old　BURG 108:4
several chaps out of the C.　CHES 147:16
Shall there be evil in a c.　BIBLE 61:19
She was a maiden C.　WORD 582:11
Soft morning, c.　JOYCE 286:14
street of the c. was pure gold　BIBLE 82:33
streets and lanes of the c.　BIBLE 70:12
Sun-girt c.　SHEL 501:24
than he that taketh a c.　BIBLE 54:9
that great c.　BIBLE 82:16
This C. now doth　WORD 581:14
this great hive, the c.　COWL 164:11
thou c. of God　PRAY 395:16
to the oppressing c.　BIBLE 61:27
We build the Perfect C.　AUDEN 19:12
went about the c. found me　BIBLE 57:2
Where the c. of the faithfullest　WHIT 570:15
who has been long in c.　KEATS 292:27
why not their c. too　BYRON 121:32
within the C. disinterred　SHEL 502:7
Woe to the bloody c.　BIBLE 61:26
City of London: C. remains as it is
　　　　CHAM 139:4
city-square: day in the c.　BROW 105:31
cive: c., anheling, wipes　HOLM 253:18
civet: Give me an ounce of c.　SHAK 455:17
civic: ornament put upon great c. buildings
　　　　RUSK 411:21
Civics: talk on 'Sex and C.　BETJ 43:1
civil: 'Always be c. to the girls　MITF 352:23
c. to folk he ne'er saw　ANST 11:8
effects from c. discord　ADD 1:25
good people, be c.　GWYN 237:8
In c. business　BACON 25:31
That the rude sea grew c.　SHAK 470:7
Too c. by half　SHER 506:16
civilian: meet a mushroom rich c.
　　　　BYRON 126:9
civilians: those who wish to be c.
　　　　ROST 410:15
civilisation: brutal in the history of c.
　　　　BEEC 37:5
douceur de la c. actuelle　HUGO 267:13
life blood of real c.　TREV 552:9
civilities: bandy c. with my Sovereign
　　　　JOHN 275:20
Cities and their c.　PATM 370:7
Civility: C. costs nothing and buys
　　　　MONT 354:10
I see a wild c.　HERR 249:2
reciprocal c. of authors　JOHN 281:29
to use the c. of my knee　BROW 96:3
civilization: botched c.　POUND 383:10
c. advances　MAC 323:22
great elements of modern c.　CARL 131:3
resources of c. are not　GLAD 229:14
civilized: c. man cannot live without
　　　　MER 338:6
last thing c. by Man　MER 337:34
civilizers: leisure are the two c.　DISR 185:9
civilizes: sex whose presence c. ours
　　　　COWP 165:4
Civis: C. Romanus sum　CIC 151:28
could say C. Romanus sum　PALM 368:10

civium: Non c. ardor prava iubentium
　　　　HOR 260:18
clad: naked every day he c.　GOLD 231:11
claes: An' some upo' their c.　BURNS 114:7
claim: last territorial c. which　HITL 251:12
claim: c. crowns his cup which　BIBLE 83:13
clair: pas c. n'est pas français　RIV 406:10
claith: web o' the silken c.　BALL 31:18
clamavi: De profundis c. ad te　BIBLE 83:13
clan: Against the c. M'Tavish　AYT 24:6
Clan-Conuil: Summon C.　SCOTT 417:27
clank: Let 'em c.　WARD 564:19
Clap: C. her broad wings　FRERE 218:26
c. your hands　BARR 34:16
c. your hands together　PRAY 392:22
doors c.　HOUS 264:20
Soul c. its hands and sing　YEATS 586:12
clappeth: Ay c. as a mille　CHAU 142:10
clapping: tears on a soundless-c.
　　　　THOM 547:24
clapte: c. the wyndow　CHAU 142:28
Clarence: perjur'd C.　SHAK 481:1
claret: c. crowns his cup　BROW 103:27
C. is the liquor for boys　JOHN 278:7
c. that 'it would be port　BENT 41:11
dozen of C. on my Tomb　KEATS 294:22
was his mutton and his c.　HOME 253:25
clarion: Her c. o'er the dreaming　SHEL 502:8
Clash: sun and the rain C.　FRY 219:26
clash'd: Was c. and hammer'd from
　　　　TENN 533:22
clasp: reason why I c. them　CORY 163:6
clasps: c. the crag with crooked　TENN 533:7
class: c. distinction　BETJ 43:6
c. struggle necessarily leads　MARX 333:11
c. the class of all classes　RUSS 412:16
Englishman of our upper c.　ARN 15:17
history of c. struggle　MARX 333:3
Like many of the upper c.　BELL 40:5
Philistines proper, or middle c.　ARN 15:19
someone of the middle c.　BELL 39:30
this c. we have a designation　ARN 15:18
classes: divisible into two great c.　BEER 37:17
masses against the c.　GLAD 229:17
ye lower middle c.　GILB 225:35
classic: happen to have an Elzevir c.
　　　　CHES 145:22
tread on c. ground　ADD 2:4
What avails the c. bent　KIPL 298:2
classical: c. Monday Pops　GILB 227:6
C. quotation is the parole　JOHN 278:29
classics: Than the c. in paraphrase
　　　　POUND 383:4
clatter: c. and a chatter from within
　　　　ELIOT 205:4
Claudel: will pardon Paul C.　AUDEN 19:8
Claudite: C. iam rivos　VIRG 559:21
claw: Nature, red in tooth and c.　TENN 536:29
claws: been a pair of ragged c.　ELIOT 204:21
c. that catch　CARR 134:28
How neatly spreads his c.　CARR 133:18
to see her stick her c.　LOW 319:3
clay: associate of this c.　HADR 237:9
blind his soul with c.　TENN 542:19
C. lies still　HOUS 262:15
c. say to him that fashioneth　BIBLE 59:13
cover'd thick with other c.　BYRON 120:27
knowest Who hast made the C.　KIPL 301:16
Making a woman of c.　AUDEN 21:7
of c. and wattles made　YEATS 585:17
out of the mire and c.　PRAY 392:1
Potter and c. endure　BROW 104:10
potter power over the c.　BIBLE 75:14
this the c. grew tall　OWEN 367:5
thousand scatter'd into C.　FITZ 212:8
clean: All c. and comfortable　KEATS 294:25
Brave hearts and c.　TENN 535:5
c., verb active　DICK 180:4
fear of the Lord is c.　PRAY 390:12
He did not love c. linen　JOHN 274:25
I shall be c.　PRAY 393:5

keep their teeth c.   SHAK 427:15
make it as c. as you can   TENN 532:22
Make me a c. heart   PRAY 393:6
nor Galahad c.   TENN 535:15
one more thing to keep c.   FRY 219:27
small and white and c.   MORR 358:10
so c. an ending   HOUS 264:2
that is not c. and neat   STEV 522:21
Then I was c. and brave   HOUS 263:1
these hands ne'er be c.   SHAK 462:21
cleaned: c. the windows and I swept
    GILB 228:4
cleanin: c.' his 'oss than cleanin' SURT 525:12
cleaning: We had daily c.   REED 405:5
Cleanliness: C. is, indeed   WESL 568:22
c. of the sexes stands   WHIT 570:15
Who of late for c.   CORB 162:14
cleanse: c. me from my sin   PRAY 393:4
C. the stuff'd bosom   SHAK 463:3
C. the thoughts of our   PRAY 387:7
c. thou me from my secret   PRAY 390:13
Wherewithal shall a young man c.
    PRAY 398:4
cleansed: doors of perception were c.
    BLAKE 88:28
What God hath c.   BIBLE 74:1
Clear: C. the land of evil   KIPL 303:6
c. your *mind* of cant   JOHN 279:11
is not c. is not French   RIV 406:10
night is as c. as the day   PRAY 399:5
sad road lies so c.   PATM 370:6
So c. in his great office   SHAK 459:6
clearing: very best means of c. up
    HUXL 269:7
clearing-house: c. of the world CHAM 139:4
clears: little water c. us of this SHAK 460:14
cleave: c. the general ear with SHAK 433:1
c. the wood and there am   ANON 7:11
shall c. unto his wife   BIBLE 45:13
tongue c. to the roof   PRAY 399:3
cleaveth: whose spirit c. not stedfastly
    PRAY 395:4
cleaving: c. the grass, gazelles MOORE 355:23
Clee: C. to heaven the beacon HOUS 262:12
clemens: O c., o pia   ANON 10:19
Cleopatra: C.'s nose been shorter PASC 369:6
every man's C.   DRYD 195:16
Had gone to gaze on C. too SHAK 422:3
I will be C.   SHAK 422:23
pleased with less than C.   DRYD 195:13
squeaking C. boy   SHAK 424:3
clercs: *La trahison des c.*   BENDA 40:18
clergy: bishops like best in their c.
    SMITH 512:1
of what the c. tell you   JOW 286:1
that the c. were beloved   SWIFT 527:6
without the benefit o' the C. CONG 160:4
clergyman: c. whose mendicity is only
    TEMP 532:8
good enough to be a c.   JOHN 276:7
Mr Wilkinson, a c.   FITZ 213:21
than a proud c.   FIEL 211:8
clergymen: men, women, and c. SMITH 511:8
To have with c. to do   DOYLE 192:40
Cleric: C. before   BUTL 117:32
Clerk: C. ther was of Oxenford CHAU 141:23
less illustrious, goes the c. COWP 166:1
small house agent's c.   ELIOT 205:1
thought he saw a Banker's C. CARR 133:13
clerkes: c. been noght wisest men
    CHAU 143:11
clever: c., but is it Art   KIPL 298:16
c. theft was praiseworthy SPEN 514:33
c. to a fault   BROW 99:7
c. woman to manage a fool KIPL 304:35
good people were c.   WORD 576:22
let who can be c.   KING 296:19
Some parts were c.   ANON 8:12
we are all c. here   FOAK 216:2
cleverest: 'You're the c. member WEBB 566:6

cleverness: c. is to be able to conceal
    LA R 310:13
cliff: In a coign of the c. between SWIN 529:17
In c. to the sea   ARN 13:2
cliffs: of the chalk c. of Dover BALD 29:28
where down cloudy c.   ARN 14:21
white c. I never more   MAC 322:10
Yet still the solitary c.   WORD 577:27
climate: chilling c. hardly bears SWIFT 527:33
c. more uncertain than   CONG 159:17
C., or years dampy my intended MILT 349:10
in the c. or the company   JOHN 280:12
love with a cold c.   SOUT 514:18
climax: that c. of all human ills
    BYRON 122:29
climb: can teach ye how to c. MILT 341:22
church lewd hirelings c. MILT 347:18
c. not at all   ELIZ 206:1
Fain would I c.   RAL 404:14
I c. up into the heaven   PRAY 399:5
should I c. the look out   POUND 383:16
climb'd: While my love c. up to me
    KING 296:16
climbed: Meredith c. towards the sun
    CHES 148:7
climber: c. with a bomb in his pocket
    ORW 365:16
climber-upward: Whereto the c. turns
his   SHAK 449:5
climbing: weariness Of c. heaven SHEL 505:5
clime: after that sweet golden c. BLAKE 87:22
marvel save in Eastern c.   BURG 108:4
They change their c.   HOR 258:19
this the soil, the c.   MILT 345:9
climes: Of cloudless c. and starry
    BYRON 125:21
Cling: C., swing   ELIOT 203:16
clinging: blood-thirsty c. to life ARN 15:24
clings: heart c. to and confides LUTH 320:18
Clive: What I like about C.   BENT 41:5
Cliveden: in C.'s proud alcove POPE 378:1
cloak: travel forth without my c. SHAK 493:11
With his martial c. around WOLFE 576:4
cloaque: *c. infect que la plus grande*
    TOCQ 551:9
clock: c. collected in the tower HOUS 264:28
c. has stopped in the dark ELIOT 202:9
c. is always slow   SERV 420:12
Court the slow c.   POPE 377:7
forgot to wind up the c.   STER 519:17
is making a c.   LA B 306:12
open with a c. striking   SHER 505:25
to stop the church c.   KILV 296:6
turned into a sort of c.   HUXL 269:8
varnish'd c. that click'd GOLD 231:4
watch the c. for you   SHAK 493:18
clocks: c. the tongues of bawds SHAK 437:34
morning c. will ring   HOUS 262:17
clock-setter: Old Time the c. SHAK 452:18
clod: to a c. of wayward marl SHAK 472:4
clogs: age to quit their c.   MILT 351:9
c. of that which else might SHEL 503:12
cloister: to be in shady c. mew'd
    SHAK 469:17
To walk the studious c.'s   MILT 342:9
cloistered: fugitive and c. virtue MILT 351:24
cloisters: in quiet collegiate c. CLOU 153:12
cloke: not dissemble nor c. them PRAY 384:9
with the knyf under the c. CHAU 142:20
close: c. the drama with the day BERK 41:20
c. the wall up with our   SHAK 443:21
C. to the sun in lonely   TENN 533:7
C. with her, kiss her   SWIN 530:27
c. your eyes with holy   COL 157:1
Doth c. behind him tread   COL 155:27
ever best found in the c.   MILT 351:3
I have met them at c.   YEATS 585:1
still hasten to a c.   COWP 165:1
Closed: C. his eyes in endless GRAY 235:19
c. up the flesh instead   BIBLE 45:11

close-lipp'd: c. Patience for our only
    ARN 14:18
Closer: C. is He than breathing TENN 533:29
friend that sticketh c.   BIBLE 54:14
Closes: C. nothing, refuses nothing
    WHIT 571:11
fields or flowerful c.   SWIN 530:21
closet: not in a c.   CHES 145:12
one by one back in the C. FITZ 213:5
closing time: c. in the gardens CONN 161:16
cloth: fair white linen c.   PRAY 387:6
On a c. untrue   GILB 227:7
clothe: c. my naked villany SHAK 480:25
clothed: captains and rulers c. BIBLE 60:37
C., and in his right mind BIBLE 68:31
c., fed and educated   RUSK 412:6
c. on with chastity   TENN 533:21
C. with transcendent brightness MILT 344:26
C. with his breath   TENN 535:23
man c. in soft raiment   BIBLE 66:2
who c. you in scarlet   BIBLE 50:17
woman c. with the sun   BIBLE 82:10
words c. in reason's   MILT 346:12
ye c. me   BIBLE 68:6
clothes: donn'd his c.   SHAK 436:2
Her c. spread wide   SHAK 436:19
his c. and had forgotten WOD 575:28
his c. not be burned   BIBLE 53:9
Kindles in c. a wantonness HERR 249:2
lay more c. on his feet   SHAK 443:18
liquefaction of her c.   HERR 250:8
walked away with their c. DISR 184:14
When he put on his c.   GOLD 231:11
Who touched my c.   BIBLE 68:32
witnesses laid down their c. BIBLE 73:28
clothing: c. for the soul divine BLAKE 85:14
come to you in sheep's c. BIBLE 65:8
Gave thee c. of delight BLAKE 87:26
her c. is of wrought gold PRAY 392:17
Things in books' c.   LAMB 307:1
which love to go in long c. BIBLE 68:37
cloth of gold: c. you cease to care
    GILB 225:30
cloths: heavens' embroidered c. YEATS 585:9
cloud: by and by a c. takes all SHAK 490:33
Choose a firm c.   POPE 377:18
c. of crimson catherine-wheels FRY 219:26
day in a pillar of a c.   BIBLE 47:21
did a skew c.   MILT 341:2
do set my bow in the c. BIBLE 45:40
Do you see yonder c. that's SHAK 434:22
entrails of yon labouring c. MARL 329:1
great a c. of witnesses BIBLE 79:35
like a c. which had outwept SHEL 499:8
Like a fiend hid in a c. BLAKE 87:23
little c. out of the sea   BIBLE 51:11
On a c. I saw a child   BLAKE 87:24
region c. hath mask'd him SHAK 493:10
see a c. that's dragonish SHAK 423:7
Stooping through a fleecy c. MILT 342:3
swift c. to fly with thee SHEL 502:12
Till he melted like a c. TENN 542:21
wandered lonely as a c. WORD 577:29
When the c. is scattered SHEL 501:11
cloud-continents: great c. of sunset-seas
    ALDR 3:11
Cloudcuckooland: How about 'C.' ARIS 12:3
clouded: mind is c. with a doubt)
    TENN 535:27
Clouds: C. and eclipses stain both
    SHAK 493:12
c. and wind without rain BIBLE 54:27
c. blew off from a high   BRID 92:13
c. drop fatness   PRAY 394:3
c. I'll never float   WORD 579:18
c. methought would open SHAK 485:18
c. return after the rain   BIBLE 56:11
clouds the c. chase   MER 336:26
c. ye so much dread   COWP 165:27
dropping from the c.   THOM 549:13

he cometh with c.   BIBLE 81:10
Looks in the c.   SHAK 449:5
maketh the c. his chariot   PRAY 396:18
O c., unfold   BLAKE 86:16
of his presence his c.   PRAY 390:9
Rapid c. have drank   SHEL 504:7
regardeth the c. shall not reap   BIBLE 56:7
Sees God in c.   POPE 379:5
To let base c. o'ertake   SHAK 493:11
to this tumult in the c.   YEATS 585:15
trailing c. of glory   WORD 579:5
When dying c. contend with   SHAK 446:17
White c. on the wing   ALL 3:21
Clough: was a poor poet named C.   SWIN 529:13
clouts: stones and c. make martyrs   BROW 97:9
cloven-footed: be c.   BIBLE 48:6
clover: bee has quit the c.   KIPL 300:23
c. and corn lay sleeping   KING 296:18
You are knee deep in c.   LAMB 307:36
cloves: cinnamon and c.   BEAU 36:5
clown: thou art mated with a c.   TENN 538:19
club: is the best c. in London   DICK 181:13
Legion and Social C.   BETJ 42:13
rose politely in the c.   CHES 146:12
savage wields his c.   HUXL 269:3
clubable: Boswell is a very c. man   JOHN 279:13
clubs: c. typical of strife   COWP 167:16
cluck'd: Has c. thee to the wars   SHAK 428:5
clue: almost invariably a c.   DOYLE 191:15
Clun: quieter place than C.   HOUS 264:8
Clunton: C. and Clunbury   HOUS 264:7
clutch: either hand may rightly c.   KIPL 298:8
clutching: c. the inviolable shade   ARN 14:20
C Major: C. of this life   BROW 98:22
Cnut: C., King, rowed   CAN 130:9
coach: drive a c. and six horses   RICE 406:1
hold back against the c.   TROL 553:8
rattling of a c.   DONNE 191:1
coach and six: me indifference and a c.   COLM 158:24
coach-house: cottage with a double c.   COL 156:13
coach-makers: o' mind the fairies' c.   SHAK 481:28
coachman: c.'s a privileged indiwidual   DICK 183:2
coal: having a live c. in his   BIBLE 57:30
is made of Newcastle c.   WALP 563:5
like a c. His eye-ball   SMART 509:3
whole world turn to c.   HERB 248:17
With a cargo of Tyne c.   MAS 333:19
With England's own c.   KIPL 298:4
coal-barges: ten dark c. are moor'd   SMITH 510:5
coalition: You may call it c.   PALM 368:11
coalitions: England does not love c.   DISR 184:21
coals: all eyes else dead c.   SHAK 492:10
c. of fire upon his head   BIBLE 54:29
c. of fire   PRAY 390:9
I sleep on the c.   DICK 176:33
My c. are spent   ANON 6:19
coarse: c. complexions   MILT 341:18
coarse-bred: c. son of a livery-stable   YEATS 585:3
coast: Gospel's pearls upon our c.   MARV 331:16
I near the shadowy c.   THOM 547:24
coaster: c. with a salt-caked smoke   MAS 333:19
merry Grecian c.   ARN 14:21
coat: him a c. of many colours   BIBLE 46:26
hold my c., and snicker   ELIOT 203:23
I made my song a c.   YEATS 584:16
riband to stick in his c.   BROW 102:4
tattered c. upon a stick   YEATS 586:12
that loves a scarlet c.   HOOD 254:15

coats: Their c. were brushed   CARR 135:6
coats-of-arms: Is worth a hundred c.   TENN 537:27
cobweb: that c. of the brain   BUTL 117:33
cobwebs: Laws are like c.   SWIFT 527:16
cock: before the c. crow   BIBLE 68:12
C. and a Bull   STER 520:12
c.'s shrill clarion   GRAY 234:20
Diminish'd to her c.   SHAK 455:14
He was like a c. who thought   ELIOT 200:16
immediately the c. crew   BIBLE 68:19
on the crowing of the c.   SHAK 429:17
Our c. won't fight   BEAV 36:14
owe c. to Aesculapius   SOCR 512:21
plump head-waiter at the C.   TENN 544:9
walks till the first c.   SHAK 454:22
While the c. with lively   MILT 342:17
cockatrice: hand on the c.' den   BIBLE 58:11
cockle: By his c. hat and staff   SHAK 435:32
Cockney: C. impudence before now   RUSK 411:7
cockpit: Can this c. hold   SHAK 443:4
cocks: drown'd the c.   SHAK 454:4
cocksure: c. of anything as Tom Macaulay   MELB 336:10
cockyolybirds: butterflies and c. would   KING 297:13
Cocoa: C. is a vulgar beast   CHES 147:27
cocotte: Normande c.   POUND 383:14
Cocqcigrues: Till the coming of the C.   KING 297:14
cod: of the bean and the c.   BOSS 90:13
stynkyng c. Fulfilled   CHAU 143:6
To change the c.'s head   SHAK 474:18
coddle: I would not c. the child   JOHN 275:28
Codlin: C.'s the friend   DICK 180:27
codling: c. when 'tis almost   SHAK 488:9
cod-piece: here's grace and a c.   SHAK 454:8
codpieces: king of c.   SHAK 456:26
coelitus: Et emitte c.   LANG 309:29
coepit: Dimidium facti qui c.   HOR 258:14
coerce: minority to c. an indifferent   STEP 518:20
coeur: c. a ses raisons que la l'esprit et dans le c.   PASC 369:10
   LA R 310:17
que le c. est du côté   MOL 353:17
Coeur-de-Lion: reputed son of C.   SHAK 452:8
co-exist: master-passions cannot c.   CAMP 129:11
coffee: always put mud into c.   THAC 545:9
C. and oranges in a sunny   STEV 520:18
C., (which makes the politician   POPE 381:7
He put the c. in the cup   PREV 400:17
if this is c.   PUNCH 403:5
slavery of the tea and c.   COBB 154:7
coffee-house: to some c. I stray   GREEN 235:29
coffee spoons: measured out my life with c.   ELIOT 203:20
coffin: becomes his c. prodigiously   GOLD 232:14
like a c. clapt in a canoe   BYRON 119:29
silver plate on a c.   OCON 364:22
white-faced and still in the c.   WHIT 570:11
cofre: he but litel gold in c.   CHAU 141:24
cog: c. o' gude swats   BURNS 113:4
make me a c. in a machine   MACN 326:15
cogimur: Omnes eodem c.   HOR 260:7
cogitation: In cogibundity of c.   CAREY 130:22
cogitations: Sometimes these c. still amaze   ELIOT 202:11
Cogito: C., ergo sum   DESC 175:10
cognizance: c. of men and things   BROW 101:11
cognoscere: potuit rerum c. causas   VIRG 560:14
coherence: all c. gone   DONNE 187:19
cohorts: c. were gleaming in purple   BYRON 122:1
coign: c. of the cliff between   SWIN 529:17

nor c. of vantage   SHAK 459:4
coil: c. of his crystalline streams   SHEL 502:10
coin: Beauty is Nature's c.   MILT 341:17
I had rather c. my heart   SHAK 451:21
With the one c. for fee   HOUS 265:18
coincidence: long arm of c.   CHAM 139:12
'strange c.'   BYRON 123:22
coincident: bent By paths c.   HARDY 239:6
coiner: bright to the c.   HOUS 263:8
c. of sweet words   ARN 14:25
coins: like to c.   TENN 534:17
coition: trivial and vulgar way of c.   BROW 96:33
coitu: Foeda est in c. et brevis   PETR 373:5
coitum: Post c. omne animal   ANON 10:17
cok: c. hadde in his governaunce   CHAU 142:32
cold: all was as c. as any stone   SHAK 443:18
blow in c. blood   SHAW 497:41
Cast a c. eye   YEATS 587:10
caught An everlasting c.   WEBS 567:15
c. and heat   BIBLE 45:37
c. Christ and tangled Trinities   KIPL 302:2
c. coming they had of it   ANDR 4:7
c. commemorative eyes   ROSS 410:5
c., frosty, windy morning   PEPYS 371:18
c. grave she was lain   BALL 32:9
c. hearts and muddy   BURKE 111:11
c. in blood   SHAK 421:33
C. in the earth   BRON 93:22
c., my girl   SHAK 477:15
c. nymphs chaste crowns   SHAK 485:19
c. performs th' effect   MILT 346:17
c. that moderates heat   CERV 138:20
comfort like c. porridge   SHAK 485:3
crazy, c.   ROCH 407:3
darkness and the c.   STEV 522:26
Dick would hate the c.   HOUS 265:1
dwelleth i' the c. o' the moon   BROW 99:24
Even till I shrink with c.   SHAK 424:31
grow more c., more kind   SPAR 514:22
I beg c. comfort   SHAK 452:31
in the midst of a c. war   BAR 34:25
love with a c. climate   SOUT 514:18
of ink in my pen ran c.   WALP 562:23
Of those c. qualms   SOUT 514:21
place is too c. for hell   SHAK 460:17
Poor Tom's a-c.   SHAK 454:24
she alone were c.   SHAK 429:3
shelter me from the c.   BELL 40:11
she's c.   SHAK 483:22
straight is c. again   SHAK 451:24
thicks man's blood with c.   COL 155:15
thou art neither c. nor hot   BIBLE 81:20
'tis bitter c.   SHAK 429:5
To lie in c. obstruction   SHAK 464:14
warm what is c.   LANG 310:1
We called a cold a c.   BENN 40:21
ye Frost and C.   PRAY 384:22
colder: proves the pleasanter the c.   BUTL 118:21
seas c. than the Hebrides   FLEC 214:7
Coldly: C., sadly descends   ARN 14:8
coldness: faithless c. of the times   TENN 537:15
Coleridge: brother C. lull the babe   BYRON 124:29
observed to you by C.   WORD 583:11
You will see C.   SHEL 501:18
Coliseum: While stands the C.   BYRON 121:18
Collapse: 'C. of Stout Party'   ANON 8:10
collar: braw brass c.   BURNS 115:25
collarbone: my silly old c.'s bust   BETJ 42:22
collector: sort of c. of religions   SHAW 497:12
collectors: great c. before me   DOUG 191:8
collects: beautiful c. which had soothed   MAC 324:18
college: Than either school or c.   BURNS 114:8
colleges: a' their c. and schools   BURNS 115:27
discipline of c. and universities   SMITH 509:14

inquiry to the other c.   GIBB 224:8
collegiate: faces in quiet c. cloisters
                                       CLOU 153:12
Cologne: Doth wash your city of C.
                                       COL 156:5
Colonel: C.'s Lady an' Judy O'Grady
                                       KIPL 300:18
Colonies: C. do not cease to be colonies
                                       DISR 184:26
commerce with our c.   BURKE 109:16
My hold of the c. is   BURKE 110:2
Colonus: Singer of sweet C.   ARN 15:10
color: mystery of c.   SHAW 496:22
colori: nimium ne crede c.   VIRG 559:15
colors: c. dont quite match your   ASHF 17:7
Colossus: genius that could cut a C.
                                       JOHN 279:18
Like a C.   SHAK 448:17
colour: are those which love c.   RUSK 411:24
cast thy nighted c. off   SHAK 429:23
c. I think of little moment   BECK 36:18
c. which I found In Lancelot   TENN 534:14
giveth his c. in the cup   BIBLE 54:24
Her c. comes and goes   DOBS 187:12
life is c. and warmth   GREN 236:15
prison for the c. of his hair   HOUS 266:8
swear her c. is natural   SHER 506:28
'tis a c. she abhors   SHAK 489:17
'twas a c. he never liked   SHAK 443:19
coloured: see the c. counties   HOUS 263:4
Colourless: C. green ideas   CHOM 148:15
colours: c. in the Turkey carpet   MAC 323:30
C. seen by candle-light   BROW 98:5
c. will agree in the dark   BACON 27:32
His c. laid so thick   DRYD 196:7
In goodly c. gloriously   SPEN 515:19
made him a coat of many c.   BIBLE 46:26
run The c. from my   BROW 98:10
Their c. and their forms   WORD 578:6
wrought about with divers c.   PRAY 392:16
Colour-Sergeant: She's C. of the Nonpareil
                                       DICK 176:22
coltes: I hadde alwey a c. tooth   CHAU 143:21
Columbia: C.! happy land   HOPK 257:8
columbine: c. commendable   SKEL 508:10
Pink and purple C.   SPEN 517:3
columbines: fennel for you, and c.
                                       SHAK 436:11
column: is the stately c. broke   SCOTT 417:2
tower like a public c.   AUDEN 19:15
Where London's c.   POPE 378:2
columna: La quinta c.   MOLA 352:29
columnae: non concessere c.   HOR 258:4
comae: Arboribusque c.   HOR 261:14
comam: Cui flavam religas c.   HOR 259:15
combat: c. deepens   CAMP 128:22
him that can win the c.   BACON 26:2
To c. may be glorious   COWP 167:10
combatants: Involves the c.   COWP 167:3
combattu: nous avons c. à Arques
                                       HENR 245:14
combed: rock sat down and c. their hair
                                       HOUS 265:3
combine: nations c. each cry   AUDEN 20:15
When bad men c.   BURKE 108:22
combustion: Of dire c. and confus'd
                                       SHAK 460:20
With hideous ruin and c.   MILT 344:24
come: beds for all who c.   ROSS 409:12
Cannot c., lie follows   PROU 401:24
C. again, with the feet   HARDY 238:22
'C. all to church   HOUS 263:5
C., and he cometh   BIBLE 65:15
C., friendly bombs   BETJ 44:4
c. he slow   SCOTT 417:6
C., Holy Spirit   LANG 309:29
C. in the speaking silence   ROSS 408:26
C. into the garden   TENN 540:9
c. is strew'd with husks   SHAK 487:14
c., let us sing   PRAY 396:3

C. like shadows   SHAK 462:9
C. little babe   BRET 92:6
C., little cottage girl   PAIN 367:19
C., my Celia   JONS 285:12
C. not between the dragon   SHAK 453:4
c. now no Kings nor Caesars   POUND 383:19
c. out, thou bloody man   BIBLE 50:24
C. over into Macedonia   BIBLE 74:6
c. to make a show themselves   OVID 366:10
C. unto me   BIBLE 66:5
C. unto these yellow sands   SHAK 484:30
C. up sometime, see me   WEST 568:27
C. up to us and we will   BIBLE 50:2
C. were but the Spring   ROSS 409:10
C. what come may   SHAK 458:21
C. when you're called   EDG 199:23
c. with old Khayyám   FITZ 212:9
c. with old Khayyám   FITZ 212:19
c. without warning   DAVIS 172:20
dreaming on things to c.   SHAK 494:21
Even so, c., Lord Jesus   BIBLE 83:4
He never will c. again   SHAK 436:12
hour your Lord doth c.   BIBLE 68:1
I c. quickly   BIBLE 83:2
it needn't c. to that   CARR 135:24
I will c.   HOUS 263:5
I will not c.   SHAK 449:20
jump the life to c.   SHAK 459:5
King of glory shall c.   PRAY 390:24
leave to c. unto my love   SPEN 515:26
Lo, I c.   PRAY 392:2
men c. for Mary or Kitty   AUST 23:22
men may c. and men may   TENN 532:21
mine hour is not yet c.   BIBLE 71:33
my love is c. to me   ROSS 408:24
O c., all ye faithful   ANON 10:4
Of things to c. at large   SHAK 486:27
One to c., and one to go   CARR 135:30
Suffer me to c. to thee   WESL 568:17
tells thee I c.   KING 296:12
That it should c. to this   SHAK 429:28
they c. when you do call   SHAK 439:23
'tis not to c.   SHAK 437:15
'twill to my father anon'   AUBR 13:21
ve must all c. to it   DICK 183:1
Very sorry can't c.   BER 41:17
What's to c. is still unsure   SHAK 488:17
wheel is c. full circle   SHAK 456:6
Where did you c. from   MACD 325:2
wherefore art thou c.   BIBLE 68:17
which is to c.   BIBLE 81:9
whistle, and I'll c. to you   BURNS 116:4
Will come when it will c.   SHAK 449:18
will it c. without warning   AUDEN 21:2
comédie: soit la c. en tout le reste PASC 369:8
comedies: c. are ended by a marriage
                                       BYRON 122:28
comedy: catastrophe of the old c.
                                       SHAK 453:12
most lamentable c.   SHAK 469:23
This world is a c. to those   WALP 563:11
tragedy, c., history   SHAK 432:20
comedye: myght to make in som c.
                                       CHAU 144:17
comeliness: He hath no form nor c.
                                       BIBLE 59:21
comely: black, but c.   BIBLE 56:16
c., but not costly   LYLY 321:14
perpetual hyperbole is c.   BACON 26:29
thy speech is c.   BIBLE 56:26
comer: Grasps in the c.   SHAK 487:5
comes: all c. to the same thing   BROW 98:25
book c. into my mouth   POUND 382:15
c. again in the morning   SHER 506:28
consummation c.   HARDY 239:6
late c. round by Rome   BROW 104:24
Look, where it c. again   SHAK 429:9
comest: thou c. into thy kingdom   BIBLE 71:12
Thou c., much wept   TENN 536:9
comet: Glorious the c.'s train   SMART 509:4

cometh: Blessed be he that c. in the Name
                                       PRAY 398:3
canst not tell whence it c.   BIBLE 71:36
c. beauty of berries   POUND 383:18
He c. not   TENN 539:23
he c. with clouds   BIBLE 81:10
Him that c. to me I will   BIBLE 72:6
master of the house c.   BIBLE 69:1
no man c. unto the Father   BIBLE 72:32
comets: Old men and c. have been
                                       SWIFT 527:14
there are no c. seen   SHAK 449:18
Ye country c.   MARV 332:12
comfit-maker: You swear like a c.'s
                                       SHAK 439:32
comfort: another c. like to this   SHAK 474:20
a' the c. we're to got   BURNS 115:24
beside the waters of c.   PRAY 390:21
carrion c., Despair   HOPK 256:7
c. and help the weak-hearted   PRAY 385:19
c. her   PRAY 389:3
c. like cold porridge   SHAK 485:3
c. of thy help again   PRAY 393:6
C.'s a cripple and comes   DRAY 193:6
c. serves in a whirlwind   HOPK 256:21
c. ye my people   BIBLE 59:4
Continual c. in a face   ROYD 411:2
here's my c.   SHAK 485:10
holy Sacrament to your c.   PRAY 387:18
I beg cold c.   SHAK 452:31
I have of c. and despair   SHAK 495:12
Man seeketh in society c.   BACON 25:1
neither found I any to c. me   PRAY 394:12
not ecstasy but it was c.   DICK 178:25
Of c. no man speak   SHAK 479:10
requireth further c. or counsel   PRAY 387:17
sober c.   MORE 357:11
staff me c. still   SCOT 419:5
Take all my c. of thy worth   SHAK 493:13
that I may take c. a little   BIBLE 52:20
they never knew c.   MAC 324:6
think they carry their c.   ELIOT 201:17
to c. all that mourn   BIBLE 60:8
What would c. the one   GAY 222:30
you naught for your c.   CHES 146:16
comfortable: Christians have a c. creed
                                       BYRON 122:19
c. estate of widowhood   GAY 222:18
c. man, with dividends   LONG 316:23
c. words our Saviour Christ   PRAY 387:20
c. hour canst thou name   SHAK 481:8
Progress is a c. disease   CUMM 170:11
comfortably: liv'd c. so long together
                                       GAY 222:13
lot of money to die c.   BUTL 118:30
Speak ye c. to Jerusalem   BIBLE 59:4
comforted: longing to be c.   WORD 581:2
Lord hath c. his people   BIBLE 59:19
they shall be c.   BIBLE 64:6
would not be c.   BIBLE 63:34
Comforter: C. will not come unto you
                                       BIBLE 72:38
comforters: Miserable c. are ye all
                                       BIBLE 52:27
comforting: where is your c.   HOPK 256:19
comfortless: All dark and c.   SHAK 455:4
c., and worn, and old   ROSS 409:2
leave us not c.   PRAY 386:13
comforts: c. we despise   SHAK 423:12
loves and c. should increase   SHAK 474:20
not without c. and hopes   BACON 25:20
Which c. while it mocks   BROW 104:4
comical: I often think it's c.   GILB 226:8
coming: cold c. we had of it   ELIOT 203:12
c. after me is preferred   BIBLE 71:29
c. events cast their shadows   CAMP 128:24
c. of the King of Heaven   ANON 9:1
c. of the Son of Man   BIBLE 67:32
c. of the Cocqcigrues   KING 297:14
do you see nothing c.   PERR 372:25

even as their c. hither   SHAK 456:2
good both going and c.   FROST 219:1
'He is c.   AYT 24:9
it is on the road and c.   DICK 183:9
She is c., my dove   TENN 540:12
There's a gude time c.   SCOTT 418:31
way of c. into the world   SWIFT 527:2
command: commands move only in c.
    SHAK 462:27
c. what you will   AUG 21:17
face Bears a c.   SHAK 427:26
gallant will c. the sun   SHAK 484:13
hast c. of every part   HERR 249:27
I may c. where I adore   SHAK 489:13
Man to c.   TENN 542:9
more invitation than c.   STEE 518:6
mortals to c. success   ADD 1:16
not be able to c. the rain   PEPYS 372:5
That shall c. my heart   CRAS 169:15
used to sue than to c.   SCOTT 416:2
why people c. rather badly   COMP 159:14
commanded: God so c.   MILT 349:15
many be c. that command   SHAK 466:20
commandest: thing which thou c.
    PRAY 386:12
commandment: c. of the Lord is pure
    PRAY 390:12
Commandments: chiefly learn by these
C.   PRAY 388:14
Fear God, and keep his c.   BIBLE 56:14
following the c. of God   PRAY 387:18
hadst hearkened to my c.   BIBLE 59:15
in keeping of thy c.   PRAY 386:15
keep my c.   BIBLE 47:24
set my ten c. in your face   SHAK 446:5
Ten for the ten c.   ANON 6:5
there aren't no Ten C.   KIPL 301:8
Commands: C. the beauteous files
    VAUG 555:13
servant does not all c.   SHAK 429:1
commemorative: cold c. eyes   ROSS 410:5
commencement: c. et le déclin de l'amour
    LA B 306:13
Voilà le c. de la fin   TALL 531:19
commend: c., A tim'rous foe   POPE 376:27
forced to c. her highly   PEPYS 372:9
hands I c. my spirit   BIBLE 71:14
hands I c. my spirit   PRAY 391:15
That doth best c. a book   HEM 245:1
Then I'll c. her volubility   SHAK 484:8
virtue to c.   CONG 160:31
commendable: Silence is only c.
    SHAK 465:14
commendatio: Formosa facies muta c.
    PUBL 402:4
commendation: Small matters win great
c.   BACON 25:36
commendeth: discommendeth others
obliquely c.   BROW 95:15
commends: me most who lavishly c.
    CHUR 148:18
comment: can read the c. but myself
    TENN 535:13
C. is free but facts are   SCOTT 415:15
commentators: c. each dark passage
shun   YOUNG 587:20
comments: his works are the c. KEATS 294:13
commerce: c., and honest friendship
    JEFF 272:8
c. the fault of the Dutch   CANN 129:25
c. with our colonies   BURKE 109:16
disinterested c. between equals   GOLD 232:11
heavens fill with c.   TENN 538:24
Let there be c. between us   POUND 383:12
that c. which now attracts   BURKE 109:15
commit: c. A social science   AUDEN 21:5
c. his body to the ground   PRAY 389:13
c. his body to the deep   PRAY 400:4
Committee: therefore got on a C.
    CHES 147:16

Commodity: C., Firmness, and Delight
    WOTT 583:16
c. of good names were   SHAK 438:6
distributed c. in the world   DESC 175:11
tickling C.   SHAK 452:14
common: are no members of the c.
    GILB 228:22
Ay, madam, it is c.   SHAK 429:24
base, c. and popular   SHAK 444:16
be the century of the c.   WALL 562:3
Cloe is…and c. as the air   GRAN 234:6
c. antipathies that I can   BROW 96:28
c. enemy and oppressor   BURKE 110:33
c. of silence on every   EMER 207:14
c. opinion and uncommon   BAG 29:15
c. pursuit of true judgement   ELIOT 205:15
c. sense and observation   BROW 96:18
c. sense and good taste   SHAW 496:12
c. task   KEBLE 295:4
concur with the c. reader   JOHN 281:39
dull catalogue of c. things   KEATS 290:27
feel for the c. chord   BROW 98:22
grazed the c. of literature   JOHN 274:28
had all things c.   BIBLE 73:24
He nothing c. did or mean   MARV 332:9
In c. things that round   WORD 580:5
Is much more c. where   BYRON 122:9
jump with c. spirits   SHAK 466:19
loathe all things held in c.   CALL 127:7
man is a c. murderer   SAKI 413:2
nor lose the c. touch   KIPL 300:2
not in the roll of c. men   SHAK 439:22
of Christians are not c.   PRAY 400:21
saw nought c. on Thy Earth   KIPL 301:17
stamp me back to c.   FITZ 213:12
steals a goose from off a c.   ANON 7:24
that call not thou c.   BIBLE 74:1
they are not already c.   LOCKE 315:13
things they have in c.   BLUN 89:2
to make it too c.   SHAK 441:14
to speak as the c. people   ASCH 17:4
You c. people of the skies   WOTT 583:15
commonalty: He's a very dog to the c.
    SHAK 427:10
common-looking: Lord prefers c. people
    LINC 315:5
commonplace: common is the c. TENN 536:2
'C.,' said Holmes   DOYLE 192:34
c. things and characters   SCOTT 418:37
provided his c. book be full   SWIFT 527:4
Common Prayer: Because they hated
C.   JORD 285:18
Commons: C., faithful to their   MACK 325:12
common sense: admixture of insipid c.
    SAL 413:18
C. is the best distributed   DESC 175:11
c. and plain dealing   EMER 207:11
gift To Beauty, C.   MER 337:11
Rich in saving c.   TENN 541:7
trained and organized c.   HUXL 269:3
commonwealth: caterpillars of the c.
    SHAK 479:2
c. is fixed and stable   BURKE 110:17
ever despaired of the C.   DISR 185:34
service and conduct of the c.   BURKE 108:24
commonwealths: raise up c. and ruin
kings   DRYD 194:5
commune: c. with your own heart
    PRAY 389:20
communi: utilitatis pro c. laborans
    THOM 546:11
communia: Difficile est proprie c.
    HOR 257:17
communicate: good and to c. forget
    BIBLE 80:6
communication: Let your c. be Yea
    BIBLE 64:16
communications: Evil c. corrupt good
manners   BIBLE 76:25
Communion: C. of Saints   PRAY 384:26

one equal c. and Identity   DONNE 191:3
partakers of the holy C.   PRAY 387:5
should come to the holy C.   PRAY 387:17
They pluck't c. tables down   JORD 285:18
Communion-time: C. having a fair white
    PRAY 387:6
Communism: C. is Soviet power plus
    LENIN 313:22
C. with a human face   DUBC 198:24
spectre of C.   MARX 333:2
Communist: C. must grasp the truth
    MAO 328:19
What is a c.   ELL 206:11
community: c. of Europe and we must
    SAL 413:19
part of the c. of Europe   GLAD 229:18
compact: Are of imagination all c.
    SHAK 471:11
c. which exists between   GARR 221:19
life now, c., visible   WHIT 570:2
compañía: El pan comido y la c. deshecha
    CERV 138:14
companion: appetite is never a wise c.
    STEV 521:3
c. to owls   BIBLE 52:37
earth-born c. An' fellow-mortal
    BURNS 115:21
last C.   BELL 40:8
my c.: my guide   PRAY 393:11
only fit c. is his horse   COWP 165:6
prince a better c.   SHAK 441:12
companioned: close-c. inarticulate hour
    ROSS 409:24
companionless: c. Among the stars
    SHEL 505:5
companions: c. for middle age BACON 26:34
C. of our woe   WALSH 563:29
His best c.   GOLD 230:18
I have had c.   LAMB 308:6
Like old c. in adversity   BRY 106:9
my brethren and c.' sakes   PRAY 398:12
company: before God and this c. PRAY 389:7
be the worst of the c.   SWIFT 526:15
c. and good discourse are   WALT 564:4
c. below your ambition   EMER 207:45
C. for carrying on an undertaking ANON 4:11
c., hath been the spoil   SHAK 440:2
c. of all faithful people   PRAY 388:3
c. of the heavenly host   BLAKE 88:29
c. of the preachers   PRAY 394:8
crowd is not c.   BACON 26:15
except the present c.   OKEE 365:2
fellows shall bear her c.   PRAY 392:17
give me your bill of c.   SWIFT 526:17
in the climate or the c.   JOHN 280:12
is what I call good c.   AUST 23:8
little love and good c.   FARQ 210:8
married life three is c.   WILDE 572:28
Punctual Delivery C.   DICK 179:33
qualified to shine in c.   SWIFT 527:11
steal out of your c.   SHAK 472:31
Take the tone of the c.   CHES 145:16
up breaks the c.   CERV 138:14
very good c.   AUBR 18:1
whose c. I delight myself   BUNY 107:39
with all the c. of heaven   PRAY 387:23
comparable: nothing c. for shortness
all   BORR 90:11
compare: been studying how I may c.
    SHAK 480:13
c. small things with great   VIRG 560:19
c. thee to a summer's day   SHAK 492:28
she belied with false c.   SHAK 495:9
will not Reason and C.   BLAKE 86:2
compared: c. unto the beasts that
    PRAY 392:28
comparison: by c. with the infirmity
    HOBB 251:22
high the heaven is in c.   PRAY 396:17
Comparisons: C. are odorous   SHAK 472:33

Confronted him with self-c.   SHAK 458:5
Comparisouns: C. doon offte gret
  greuaunce   LYDG 321:7
compass: c. of the notes it ran   DRYD 197:21
c. of the world   PRAY 390:23
My life is run his c.   SHAK 452:1
note to the top of my c.   SHAK 434:20
compassed: snares of death c.   PRAY 397:19
compassion: is full of c. and mercy
  BIBLE 62:21
is full of c. and mercy   PRAY 396:16
she should not have c.   BIBLE 59:17
shutteth up his bowels of c.   BIBLE 81:4
something which excites c.   SMITH 511:31
compel: c. them to come   BIBLE 70:13
c. us to be equal upstairs   BARR 34:7
shall c. thee to go a mile   BIBLE 64:18
competency: c. lives longer   SHAK 465:19
competition: anarchy and c. the laws
  RUSK 412:10
Approves all forms of c.   CLOU 154:1
Complacencies: C. of the peignoir
  STEV 520:18
complain: farmers, flourish and c.
  COWP 168:16
Never c. and never explain   DISR 185:30
raised a dust and then c.   BERK 41:18
To c. of the age we live   BURKE 108:17
to me to c. of rheumatism   SAKI 413:8
complainers: c. for the public to be
  BURKE 108:15
complaining: away through my daily
  c.   PRAY 391:16
no c. in our streets   PRAY 399:13
complaint: from the words of my c.
  PRAY 390:16
voice of my c.   PRAY 398:23
Complaints: 'C. is many and various
  GRAV 234:12
c. of ill-usage contemptible   MELB 336:18
when c. are freely heard   MILT 351:20
complete: c. with hat and gloves CALV 127:16
in herself c.   MILT 349:7
completed: c. labours are pleasant CIC 151:18
complexion: clime, c., and degree
  SHAK 475:20
Mislike me not for my c.   SHAK 466:6
often is his gold c. dimm'd   SHAK 492:28
their health and their c.   AUST 22:17
trust too much in your c.   VIRG 559:15
compliance: by a timely c.   FIEL 211:11
to join c. with reason   BURKE 111:26
complicated: c. state of mind   GILB 227:21
complies: He that c. against his   BUTL 118:13
compliment: farewell c.   SHAK 482:12
feigning was called c.   SHAK 489:22
To return the c.   GILB 228:1
compliments: c. and—and love   AUST 22:27
componere: inter vos tantas c. lites
  VIRG 559:20
parva licet c. magnis   VIRG 560:19
composed: c. and bland   ARN 14:4
conceived and c. in their wits   ARN 16:9
Composer: contemplation of the first
  C.   BROW 97:1
Composing: startle C. mortals   AUDEN 18:4
composition: mad c.   SHAK 452:13
compound: c. a boy   SHAK 445:14
comprehend: built to c. a lie   KIPL 302:17
c. the richness and variety   HOUS 266:15
shall c. all vagrom men   SHAK 472:29
Time we may c.   BROW 96:10
When she begins to c. it   PRIOR 401:7
comprehended: darkness c. it not
  BIBLE 71:23
comprehends: It c. some bringer of that
  SHAK 471:11
comprendre: Tout c. rend très indulgent
  STAEL 517:15

compromise: Give me the Brown c. when
  HUGH 267:7
'is no doubt a c.   SHOR 507:8
compulsion: fools by heavenly c.
  SHAK 453:11
Give you a reason on c.   SHAK 439:5
Made happy by c.   COL 157:13
On what c. must   SHAK 467:27
sweet c. doth in music lie   MILT 340:19
compulsive: Whose icy current and c.
  SHAK 476:1
compunctious: That no c. visitings
  SHAK 459:2
compute: What's done we partly may
  c.   BURNS 112:26
Comrade: C., look not on the west
  HOUS 264:18
comrades: Bleach the bones of c.
  HOUS 263:19
C., leave me here a little   TENN 538:15
of the dear love of c.   WHIT 570:5
Your c. chase e'en now   CLOU 154:4
con: taken great pains to c.   SHAK 488:10
conati: Ter sunt c. imponere   VIRG 560:12
concatenation: Fearful c. of circumstances
  WEBS 566:16
In a c. accordingly   GOLD 232:23
concave: shout that tore hell's c.   MILT 345:20
conceal: cleverness is to be able to c.
  LA R 310:13
express our wants as to c.   GOLD 232:5
Fate tried to c. him   HOLM 253:7
should c. it as well   AUST 23:5
us to c. our whereabouts   SAKI 413:12
yet cannot all c.   BYRON 121:22
concealed: book when the author is c.
  JOHN 274:23
flower grows c. in an enclosed   CAT 137:6
concealing: all-c. tunic   SHEL 502:18
hazard of c.   BURNS 113:17
Rive your c. continents   SHAK 454:10
concealment: c., like a worm   SHAK 489:7
Conceit: C. in weakest bodies strongest
  SHAK 435:13
c., what man will do any   TROL 553:3
c. which came in his way   DRYD 198:10
he be wise in his own c.   BIBLE 54:41
him with self and vain c.   SHAK 479:11
is wiser in his own c.   BIBLE 54:35
man wise in his own c.   BIBLE 54:33
suiting With forms to his c.   SHAK 432:27
conceited: never any pity for c. people
  ELIOT 201:17
conceits: current and accepted for c.
  BACON 24:22
have beauty beat on his c.   MARL 330:11
not wise in you own c.   BIBLE 75:17
Our best c. do prove   DRAY 193:9
such c. as clownage keeps   MARL 330:2
conceive: c. you may use any language
  GILB 226:12
virgin shall c.   BIBLE 58:3
Whether it be the heart to c.   JUN 287:5
conceived: poetry is c. and composed
  ARN 16:9
sin hath my mother c. me   PRAY 393:5
There is a man child c.   BIBLE 52:11
was c. by the Holy Ghost   PRAY 384:26
Conceives: C. by idleness   SHAK 445:12
conceiving: delight in c. an Iago KEATS 294:7
thus c. and subduing both   MARL 330:11
concentrated: more and more c. in you
  KEATS 294:30
concentrates: it c. his mind wonderfully
  JOHN 277:16
Conceptions: C. equal to the soul's
  WORD 577:15
concern: life and its largest c.   ARN 16:21
matter they had no c.   SWIFT 527:27
concerns: Think only what c. thee MILT 349:4

concert: persons acting in c. together
  ARAB 11:16
concertina: I've a head like a c.   KIPL 298:7
concessions: c. of the weak are BURKE 109:14
conciseness: must be sacrificed to c.
  JOHN 281:4
conclave: In stately c. met   CHES 146:24
conclaves: Kingly c. stern and cold
  SHEL 503:1
concluded: case is c.   AUG 22:2
conclusion: most lame and impotent c.
  SHAK 474:18
other is a c.   JOHN 274:11
ultimate c. in unmitigated act   KIPL 299:5
conclusions: c.—largely inarticulate
  KIPL 302:5
draw from it narrow c.   MILL 339:1
hath pursu'd c. infinite   SHAK 424:18
sufficient c. from insufficient   BUTL 118:26
conclusive: verdict of the world is c.
  AUG 21:18
concord: c. of well-tuned sounds
  SHAK 492:25
Love-quarrels oft in pleasing c.   MILT 350:26
of peace and lover of c.   PRAY 385:2
travelled a good deal in C.   THOR 550:2
truth, unity, and c.   PRAY 387:13
with c. of sweet sounds   SHAK 468:17
with the C. circling nine   THOR 550:22
Concordia: C. discors   HOR 258:20
concubines: Twenty-two acknowledged
  c.   GIBB 224:25
concupiscite: sine dolo lac c.   BIBLE 83:25
concurrence: fortuitous c. of atoms
  PALM 368:11
sweet c. of the heart   HERR 250:11
condamner: de songer à c. les gens
  MOL 353:20
condemn: censure or c. another BROW 96:32
C. the fault and not   SHAK 463:19
c. you to death   CARR 133:19
does some delights c.   MOL 353:26
Neither do I c. thee   BIBLE 72:11
nor the years c.   BINY 84:10
they c. recourse to war   KELL 295:8
Condemn'd: C. alike to groan   GRAY 235:13
c. to have an itching palm   SHAK 451:12
condemned: c. cells of Newgate BUTL 119:12
C. to do the flitting   MER 337:17
condemns: with which Dr Johnson c.
  BURN 112:20
*condere: Tantae molis erat Romanam
  c.*   VIRG 557:10
condescend: c. to men of low estate
  BIBLE 75:17
condition: devils in life and c.   ASCH 17:3
hard c.   SHAK 444:23
man could do in that c.   PEPYS 372:1
primordial c. of liberty   BAK 29:25
conditions: c. for its solution already
  MARX 333:7
c. That seem unpropitious   ELIOT 202:24
govern our c.   SHAK 455:12
sorts and c. of men   PRAY 385:24
condolement: obstinate c. is a course
  SHAK 429:26
Conduct: C. is three-fourths   ARN 16:21
c. of a losing party   BURKE 111:27
C. the prejudice of good   ANON 4:28
gentlemanly c.   ARN 16:26
into the service and c.   BURKE 108:24
nice c. of a clouded cane   POPE 381:10
regulation of c.   SPEN 514:26
right way to c. our lives   PLATO 374:11
rottenness begins in his c.   JEFF 272:11
what is c.   ARN 16:19
cones: eat the c. under his pines FROST 219:9
firs with c. upon them   LONG 317:10
confederacy: dunces are all in c. against
  SWIFT 527:8

console: c. us when we fall   BURKE 110:19
consolidates: kindness and c. society   JOHN 280:6
consonant: Nature is very c. and conformable   NEWT 362:18
consort: such c. as they keep   MILT 342:8
Conspicuous: C. consumption of valuable   VEBL 556:1
was c. by its presence   RUSS 412:20
conspiracies: All professions are c.   SHAW 496:21
conspiracy: c. against the manhood   EMER 207:36
c. against the public   SMITH 509:10
'c. of silence' concerning   COMTE 159:15
less than a vast c.   WELLS 568:15
O c.! Sham'st thou   SHAK 452:7
conspirators: All the c.   SHAK 452:7
conspire: thou and I with Fate c.   FITZ 213:16
Conspired: C. against our God with   MARL 329:6
conspires: world c. to praise her   POPE 380:26
Conspiring: C. with him how to load   KEATS 293:5
constable: it was a c.'s handbook   KING 297:7
constabulary: When c. duty's to be done   GILB 228:19
constancy: blessings of marriage and the c.   SHAW 497:32
C. alone is strange   ROCH 406:15
c. lives in realms above   COL 156:4
c. of the women who love   SHAW 498:9
is but c. in a good   BROW 96:15
no object worth its c.   SHEL 505:5
O c.! be strong   SHAK 449:22
Of c. to a bad   BYRON 126:6
to stablish dangerous c.   DONNE 189:18
constant: c. as the northern star   SHAK 449:25
c. do remain to keep him   SHAK 449:25
c. image of the creature   SHAK 488:27
C. in nothing but inconstancy   BARN 34:3
C., in Nature were inconstancy   COWL 164:10
c. service of the antique   SHAK 425:7
C. you are   SHAK 438:32
Friendship is c. in all   SHAK 472:7
if thou wilt be c. then   GRAH 233:15
in a c. course of nature   DONNE 190:24
Like to a c. woman   FORD 216:14
nothing in this world c.   SWIFT 527:17
One here will c. be   BUNY 107:36
sense of a c. infelicity   TAYL 532:4
She is so c. to me   KEATS 289:5
Such a c. lover   SUCK 524:14
To one thing c. never   SHAK 472:16
were man But c.   SHAK 491:6
whatsoever is grave and c.   JOYCE 286:17
Constantinople: Russians shall not have C.   HUNT 268:3
constellated: c. flower that never sets   SHEL 503:18
constellations: c. of feeling   DOUG 191:7
not want the c. any nearer   WHIT 571:8
strange-eyed c. reign   HARDY 239:9
Constitution: C., in all its provisions   CHASE 141:3
country has its own c.   ANON 5:5
Everybody talks of the c.   WALP 563:6
higher law than the C.   SEW 420:15
I am of a c. so general   BROW 96:27
invoke the genius of the C.   PITT 373:28
principle of the English c.   BLAC 85:5
principles of a free c.   GIBB 224:22
proportioned to the human c.   BERK 41:21
purpose to construe the C.   LINC 314:18
very essence of the c.   JUN 287:2
constitutional: c. guardian   GILB 226:2
c. right of amending it   LINC 314:19
no eyes but c. eyes   LINC 315:7
constitutions: c. of later Greece ruled   BAG 28:28

constrained: c. to dwell with Mesech   PRAY 398:7
violence c. to do anything   ELIZ 205:25
constreyned: nat been c. by maistrye   CHAU 142:12
constructed: defences of peace must be c.   ANON 7:16
constructing: last thing one knows in c.   PASC 369:3
construction: mind's c. in the face   SHAK 458:22
constructions: secret of decorating her c.   TROL 552:16
constructs: worse. It c. it   COMP 159:13
construe: to c. the Constitution   LINC 314:18
consul: born when I was c.   CIC 152:2
consule: natam me c. Romam   CIC 152:2
consules: Caveant c. ne quid res publica   ANON 10:10
consuls: c. see to it that no harm   ANON 10:10
consulted: right to be c.   BAG 29:3
consults: he neither c. them about   CHES 145:26
consume: born to c. resources   HOR 258:13
c. happiness without producing   SHAW 496:13
their beauty shall c.   PRAY 393:1
They c. little more than   SMITH 509:9
consumed: bush was not c.   BIBLE 47:3
my bones c. away through   PRAY 391:16
consumer: In a c. society there are   ILL 270:5
consumere: numerus sumus et fruges c.   HOR 258:13
Consumes: cruel immortality C.   TENN 543:11
consummation: c. comes   HARDY 239:6
c. Devoutly to be wish'd   SHAK 433:8
Quiet c. have   SHAK 428:22
consummatum: 'c. est   BEDE 37:2
C. est   BIBLE 83:23
consumption: against this c. of the purse   SHAK 441:16
Conspicuous c. of valuable   VEBL 556:1
contact: deux fantaisies et le c.   CHAM 139:15
contagion: c. of the world's slow   SHEL 499:21
C. to this world   SHAK 434:25
Rot inwardly and foul c.   MILT 343:13
vile c. of the night   SHAK 449:13
Contaminate: C. our fingers with base   SHAK 451:13
contemn'd: Than still c. and flatter'd   SHAK 455:5
contemned: it would utterly be c.   BIBLE 57:12
contemneth: c. small things shall fall   BIBLE 63:7
contemplates: in the mind which c. them   HUME 267:17
contemplation: c. of the first Composer   BROW 97:1
c. he and valour formed   MILT 347:22
C. makes a rare turkey-cock   SHAK 489:11
Has left for c.   BETJ 43:2
is engaged in a rapt c.   ELIOT 204:6
mind serene for c.   GAY 223:17
with her best nurse C.   MILT 341:8
contemplative: fools should be so deep-c.   SHAK 425:20
contempt: c. and anger of his lip   SHAK 489:24
C., farewell   SHAK 472:22
c. of God's good gifts   JAM 271:4
c. too high   COWL 164:13
moderns without c.   CHES 145:20
religion when in rags and c.   BUNY 107:19
they looked down with c.   MAC 323:26
was only an Object of C.   AUST 22:25
contemptible: complaints of ill-usage c.   MELB 336:18
c. little Army   WILH 574·4
sacrifice in a c. struggle   BURKE 108:·2
those poor c. men   CROM 170:3

contend: Let's c. no more   BROW 105:35
thought c. is the policy   MAO 328:18
contending: c. against some being   WHIT 570:1
C. with the fretful elements   SHAK 454:3
let fierce c. nations know   ADD 1:25
content: Be c. with your wages   BIBLE 69:15
c. surpassing wealth   SHEL 504:10
C. thyself with thine estate   SURR 524:21
C. to breathe his native   POPE 380:23
c.! whate'er thy name   POPE 379:21
c. with six foot   BROW 97:24
c. with a vegetable love   GILB 227:23
c. with what we spoiled   OWEN 367:11
c. with my harm   SHAK 426:4
c. with his fortunes fit   SHAK 454:12
hath her c. so absolute   SHAK 474:20
land of lost c.   HOUS 263:22
money, means, and c.   SHAK 426:3
Nothing less will c. me   BURKE 109:20
remaining c. with half-knowledge   KEATS 293:19
sweet C.   BARN 33:27
sweet c.   DEKK 173:20
Contented: C. if he might enjoy   WORD 580:5
C. wi' little and cantie   BURNS 113:4
he was c. there   ARIS 12:4
king shall be c.   SHAK 479:15
no one lives c.   HOR 261:21
With what I most enjoy c.   SHAK 493:6
contentedness: procurer of c.   WALT 564:3
contention: Let the long c. cease   ARN 13:14
strife and a man of c.   BIBLE 60:23
swears he will have no c.   LAND 308:21
contentious: day and a c. woman   BIBLE 54:39
Contentment: C. is a sleepy thing   TRAH 552:2
Preaches c. to that toad   KIPL 302:1
what c. find   MILT 349:6
contents: Its c. worn out   FRAN 218:20
Contentus: C. vivat   HOR 261:21
contest: Great c. follows   COWP 167:3
contests: such great c. as these   VIRG 560:18
continency: c.—but not yet   AUG 21:14
You impose c. upon us   AUG 21:17
continent: c.,— Weary of solid firmness   SHAK 442:1
C. will not suffer England   DISR 184:11
destiny to overspread the c.   OSUL 365:23
man is a piece of the C.   DONNE 190:20
continentiam: Imperas nobis c.   AUG 21:17
continents: nations and three separate c.   DOYLE 192:29
continual: c. dew of thy blessing   PRAY 385:7
continuance: c., I don't know   SURT 525:20
household of c.   SURT 524:20
Patient c. in well doing   BIBLE 74:33
which in c. of time hath   PRAY 384:8
continue: c. thine for ever   PRAY 388:22
runagates c. in scarceness   PRAY 394:7
which once begun will c.   BACON 26:10
continued: works, begun, c.   PRAY 388:6
continueth: Here c. to rot   ARB 11:21
continuing: c. unto the end until it   DRAKE 193:1
here have we no c. city   BIBLE 80:5
contortions: c. of the Sibyl without   BURKE 112:14
contract: every c. to make the terms   EMER 207:4
healthy or proper c.   CHUR 152:3
nothing but a civil c.   SELD 419:23
Social C. is nothing more   WELLS 568:15
contradict: Do I c. myself   WHIT 571:5
I never c.   DISR 187:5
Read not to c. and confute   BACON 27:18
truth which you cannot c.   PLATO 374:12
contradicted: I dogmatise and am c.   JOHN 280:21

contradicting: soon think of c. a Bishop
JOHN 279:14
contradiction: It is a c. in terms SHAW 498:19
they brook no c. WEBS 566:28
Woman's at best a c. still POPE 377:29
contradictions: bundle of c. COLT 159:11
hath been one chain of c. CLARE 152:5
contrairy: everythink goes c. with me
DICK 176:27
contrariwise: c. blessing BIBLE 80:30
'C.,' continued Tweedledee CARR 135:2
contrary: c. to custom and experience
HUME 267:21
c. to the decrees of Caesar BIBLE 74:9
trial is by what is c. MILT 351:24
contrast: mere c. for masculinity RILKE 406:5
contree: Know thy c. CHAU 144:22
contrite: broken and c. heart PRAY 393:8
sighing of a c. heart PRAY 385:22
contrivance: Government is a c. of human
wisdom BURKE 111:8
contrivances: wisdom of human c.
BURKE 109:18
contrive: c. To save appearances MILT 349:3
How Nature always does c. GILB 226:8
control: Who can c. his fate SHAK 477:19
controlled: plainly that events have c.
LINC 315:1
controversy: c. is either superfluous
NEWM 362:10
contumely: proud man's c. SHAK 433:8
convenience: c. of the business BURKE 108:16
C. next suggested elbow-chairs COWP 166:28
convenient: feed me with food c. BIBLE 54:45
convent: c. of the Sacred Heart ELIOT 204:16
high up in the c. wall AUDEN 21:1
Nuns fret not at their c.'s WORD 582:7
Convention: To the Lords of C. 'twas
SCOTT 415:20
Conventionality: C. is not morality
BRON 93:14
conversant: is always c. in himself
DONNE 190:22
conversation: brisk as a bee in c. JOHN 274:1
C. is a game of circles EMER 207:14
c. perfectly delightful SMITH 511:13
have a great deal of c. AUST 23:8
ignorance cramps my c. HOPE 255:30
pleasures of life is c. SMITH 511:28
proper subject of c. CHES 146:4
Questioning is not the mode of c.
JOHN 276:37
That is the happiest c. JOHN 276:26
those soft parts of c. SHAK 475:21
who is always spoiling c. MAC 324:26
you stick on c.'s burrs HOLM 253:12
conversations: after-dinner c. over the
wine THOR 550:15
'without pictures or c. CARR 133:14
converse: between them and rational
c. WOLL 576:10
c. with the mighty dead THOM 549:24
Form'd by thy c. POPE 380:3
sweet c. of an innocent mind KEATS 292:20
Converses: C. at the door apart ELIOT 204:16
conversing: c. with W.H.'s forehead
HAZL 243:14
conversion: Till the c. of the Jews
MARV 332:18
converted: Except ye be c. BIBLE 67:2
to be c. at a revival STEV 522:2
When love, c. SHAK 493:14
converting: c. the soul PRAY 390:12
Convey: 'C.,' the wise call it SHAK 469:4
conviction: best lack all c. YEATS 586:15
triumphant c. of strength CONR 161:24
Convictions: Such Dimity C. DICK 184:3
convince: people labouring to c. JOHN 275:2
we c. ourselves JUN 287:4

convincing: c. myself that I am right
AUST 23:27
not for the sake of c. BLAKE 87:11
thought of c. GOLD 231:17
too c.—dangerously dear BYRON 121:34
convoy: crowns for c. put into SHAK 445:3
convulsions: gall'ry in c. hurl'd POPE 376:21
conwiviality: kindled at the taper of c.
DICK 180:25
Coodle: Lord C. would go out DICK 176:21
cook: c. and a captain bold GILB 225:16
C. is a little unnerved BETJ 42:19
tell William c. SHAK 442:22
very uncommon c. SAKI 413:2
Cookery: C. is become an art BURT 116:19
Kissing don't last: c. do MER 338:1
cooking: tragedy of English c. MORP 358:2
cooks: as c. go she went SAKI 413:10
cannot live without c. MER 338:6
c. are gentlemen BURT 116:19
Devil sends c. GARR 221:12
entrusted to 'plain' c. MORP 358:2
hire me twenty cunning c. SHAK 483:20
lik'd those literary c. MORE 357:9
praise it, not the c. HAR 242:9
there been a *Synod of C.* JOHN 275:13
With a legion of c. BYRON 124:41
cool: garden in the c. of the day BIBLE 45:16
So c. a purple KEATS 289:4
Cool'd: C. a long age in the deep-delved
KEATS 291:18
cool-hair'd: Lifting the c. creepers ARN 14:21
coolness: of c. plays upon his face ARN 12:22
coomb: His c. was redder than CHAU 142:32
lonely barton by yonder c. HARDY 240:14
co-operation: Government and c. are
RUSK 412:10
coot: haunts of c. and hern TENN 532:20
cope: c. him in these sullen SHAK 425:3
Cophetua: Before the king C. TENN 532:16
copia: Inopem me c. fecit OVID 366:15
copier: I c. all the letters GILB 228:5
copier: c. of nature can never REYN 405:17
copies: I find I must keep c. CONG 160:37
Copper: C. for the craftsman cunning
KIPL 298:15
copse: Under a c. SHEL 503:17
copula: Quos irrupta tenet c. HOR 259:21
copulation: c. and death ELIOT 204:12
Let c. thrive SHAK 455:16
copy: according to my c. CAXT 138:4
leave the world no c. SHAK 488:17
statuaries loved to c. MAC 323:33
Copybook: Gods of the C. Headings
KIPL 299:16
copyrights: English authors their c.
TROL 552:12
coquetry: c. of public opinion BURKE 110:15
Cor: C. ad cor loquitur NEWM 362:7
corages: priketh hem nature in hir c.)
CHAU 141:8
coral: c. aboute hire arm she CHAU 141:17
C. is far more red than SHAK 495:8
Of his bones are c. made SHAK 484:32
redder than the fyn c. CHAU 142:32
coranto: come home in a c. SHAK 488:1
corbies: I heard twa c. making BALL 32:8
cord: c. however fine into WHEW 569:16
ever the silver c. be loosed BIBLE 56:11
threefold c. is not quickly BIBLE 55:15
triple c. BURKE 112:5
unto the bow the c. is LONG 317:12
corda: Sursum c. MASS 335:2
cords: cast away their c. from us PRAY 389:16
made a scourge of small c. BIBLE 71:35
core: ain't-a-going to be no c. TWAIN 554:17
sweet as the rind was the c. SWIN 529:8
Corinth: lucky enough to get to C.
HOR 258:21

Corinthum: homini contingit adire C.
HOR 258:21
cork-heel'd: wat their c. shoon BALL 31:19
corking-pin: c. stuck through his tail
BARH 33:5
corkscrew: clean tumbler, and a c.
DICK 180:20
corkscrews: heart are as crooked as c.
AUDEN 18:13
cormorant: common c. or shag ISH 270:27
Sat like a c. MILT 347:18
spite of c. devouring Time SHAK 456:14
corn: better stop raising c. LEASE 313:4
breast high amid the c. HOOD 255:4
c. is but a field of tares TICH 551:2
c. that makes the holy MAS 333:26
c. was orient and immortal TRAH 551:18
he treadeth out the c. BIBLE 48:25
In our sustaining c. SHAK 455:13
meadows rich with c. WHIT 571:15
raise the price of c. BYRON 119:26
stand so thick with c. PRAY 394:3
tears amid the alien c. KEATS 291:23
that there was c. in Egypt BIBLE 46:33
there was c. HERB 247:14
two ears of c. SWIFT 526:6
Was yellow like ripe c. ROSS 409:15
Where the clover and c. KING 296:18
Cornea: C., qua veris facilis VIRG 559:3
Corneille: C. is to Shakespeare JOHN 280:3
corner: c. in the thing I love SHAK 475:21
c. of a foreign field BROO 94:30
c. of the world smiles HOR 260:8
drive life into a c. THOR 550:16
head-stone in the c. PRAY 398:2
Sits the wind in that c. SHAK 472:17
thing was not done in a c. BIBLE 74:26
corners: all the c. of the earth PRAY 396:4
polished c. of the temple PRAY 399:12
round earth's imagined c. DONNE 189:3
sheet knit at the four c. BIBLE 73:37
three c. of the world SHAK 453:1
Unregarded age in c. thrown SHAK 425:4
cornet: hear the sound of the c. BIBLE 61:3
cornfield: o'er the green c. did pass
SHAK 427:2
Cornish: Here's twenty thousand C. men
HAWK 243:4
corns: shower your shooting c. SWIFT 527:26
Coromandel: On the coast of C. LEAR 311:25
Coronation: Bring C. SPEN 517:3
reject a petrarchal c. KEATS 293:32
coronet: proud bride of a ducal c.
DICK 179:32
coronets: hearts are more than c. TENN 537:29
Corporal: drink and blacking the C.'s
KIPL 298:7
Corporations: C. have neither bodies
THUR 550:32
corpore: mens sana in c. sano JUV 288:4
Corporis: C. mysterium THOM 546:16
corpse: begin and carry up this c.
BROW 100:32
c. in the case with a sad BARH 33:16
Each like a c. within its SHEL 502:8
frozen c. was he LONG 317:21
He'd make a lovely c. DICK 179:14
Leave the c. uninterr'd SCOTT 417:28
makes a very handsome c. GOLD 232:14
slovenly, unhandsome c. SHAK 438:14
this c. which is man SWIN 530:9
you've got a nice *fresh* c. TWAIN 554:13
Corpses: C. are set to banquet POUND 382:11
loves into c. or wives SWIN 529:10
To mock the riddled c. SASS 414:12
corpus: Ave verum c. ANON 10:9
corpuscula: Quantula sint hominum c.
JUV 288:3
correct: All present and c. ANON 4:15
c., insert, refine SWIFT 527:34

critical than to be c. DISR 184:23
each has his own c. way TER 544:19
with Plato than be c. with CIC 152:1
correcteth: whom the Lord loveth he
c. BIBLE 53:15
Correggio: correggiosity of C. CARL 131:19
Correggios: C., and stuff GOLD 231:21
corregiescity: c. of Corregio STER 519:29
Corregio: corregiescity of C. STER 519:29
correlative: finding an 'objective c.
ELIOT 205:16
corridors: c. into the mind DOUG 191:7
c. of power SNOW 512:15
corriger: se mêler à c. le monde MOL 353:19
corroboration: particular c. of this
aphorism BIRK 84:12
corroborative: Merely c. detail GILB 227:12
corrupcioun: Fulfilled of dong and of
c. CHAU 143:6
corrupt: able to c. a saint SHAK 438:7
Among a people generally c. BURKE 110:14
appointment by the c. few SHAW 497:36
Away with a c. world MER 337:37
be equally wicked and c. BURKE 108:20
c., and become abominable PRAY 390:2
c. government on the earth JEFF 272:12
C. influence BURKE 110:16
c. the souls of those they ARN 13:2
moth and rust doth c. BIBLE 64:25
one good custom should c. TENN 535:25
Peace to c. no less than MILT 349:27
sanguinary punishments which c.
PAINE 368:4
That do c. my air SHAK 427:23
That no king can c. SHAK 447:4
Unlimited power is apt to c. PITT 373:23
corrupted: conscience with injustice
is c. SHAK 446:6
c. by this stinking smoke JAM 271:4
c. the youth of the realm SHAK 446:14
had been c. by sentiment GREE 236:4
my fortunes have C. SHAK 423:1
of time hath not been c. PRAY 384:8
corruptible: c. must put on incorruption
BIBLE 76:29
it to obtain a c. crown BIBLE 76:9
corrupting: c. the young men and not
PLATO 374:8
corruption: are in danger of great c.
KNOX 305:25
C., the most infallible GIBB 224:27
C. wins not more than honesty SHAK 447:12
It is sown in c. BIBLE 76:27
of vice whose strong c. SHAK 490:17
Stew'd in c. SHAK 435:10
thy Holy One to see c. PRAY 390:7
to be turned into c. PRAY 400:4
corruptions: man's c. made him wretched
OTWAY 365:27
corruptly: Were not deriv'd c. SHAK 466:20
corrupts: absolute power c. ACTON 1:5
cors: souvenirs sont c. de chasse APOL 11:10
corse: c. again in complete steel SHAK 430:24
his c. to the rampart we WOLFE 576:2
Cortez: like stout C. when with KEATS 292:10
coruscations: c. of summer lightning
GOUL 233:5
Corydon: Formosum pastor C. ardebat
VIRG 559:14
For Time, not C. ARN 15:7
Cos: she goes in a gleam of C. POUND 382:15
Supplants the mousseline of C. POUND 383:5
cosmogeny: blot out c. BROW 99:9
cosmopolitan: to become c. in the end
MOORE 355:16
Cosmos: too much Ego in your C.
KIPL 304:31
cost: c. of the squalor and slavery
SHAW 498:23
counteth the c. BIBLE 70:14

not wish to count the c. BREC 91:26
rate the c. of the erection SHAK 441:17
Too costly for c. THOM 548:29
Why so large c. SHAK 495:13
coster: c.'s finished jumping GILB 228:21
costive: have made a soap-boiler c.
WEBS 566:23
costly: comely, but not c. LYLY 321:14
c. in our sorrows STER 519:12
C. thy habit as thy purse SHAK 430:19
cot: c. with a pot of pink geraniums
MACN 326:8
Cotopaxi: Chimborazo, C. TURN 553:23
cottage: c. of gentility COL 156:13
court to c. he depart PEELE 371:8
his visage from our c. SHAK 492:4
left as a c. in a vineyard BIBLE 57:16
Love and a c. COLM 158:24
soul's dark c. WALL 562:9
cottages: march in c. of strowed reeds
MARL 330:11
cottage-smell: Sweet-William with his
homely c. ARN 15:6
Cottle: Amos C. BYRON 124:24
couch: all my frowzy c. in sorrow
BURNS 113:22
flinty and steel c. of war SHAK 474:5
home and rest on the c. CAT 136:28
than a levee from a c. CONG 161:4
There I c. when owls do cry SHAK 485:25
water my c. with my tears PRAY 389:26
when on my c. I lie WORD 578:1
couché: Longtemps je me suis c. PROU 401:20
make his c. of silk CHAU 142:25
Couched: C. with her arms behind MER 337:1
coucher: pauvre de c. sous les ponts
FRAN 217:26
couches: stilly c. she HARDY 239:4
cough: all c. in ink YEATS 586:14
falls into a c. SHAK 470:3
Keep a c. by them ready CHUR 148:27
coughing: c. drowns the parson's
SHAK 457:19
coughs: c. when you would kiss AUDEN 18:10
no discretion in her c. AUST 23:12
could: I c. not look on Death KIPL 298:25
coulter: while that the c. rusts SHAK 445:12
Councillor: C. to King James GREV 236:18
counsel: darkeneth c. by words BIBLE 52:41
Dost sometimes c. take POPE 381:2
execution than for c. BACON 27:39
follow this c. of Aristotle ASCH 17:4
his c. was not followed BIBLE 50:25
in the c. of the ungodly PRAY 389:14
is for women to keep c. SHAK 449:22
keep my own c. I will venture GLAD 229:16
lightly regarded the c. PRAY 397:7
princely c. in his face MILT 346:14
requireth further comfort or c. PRAY 387:17
spirit of c. and might GILB 225:27
Take my c. PRAY 393:11
We took sweet c. together BURT 116:26
Who cannot give good c. POPE 378:32
who c. can bestow SHAK 466:7
'you c. well KIPL 300:2
Counsellor: C., The mighty God BIBLE 58:7
this c. Is now most still SHAK 435:23
counsellors: plain when c. blanch
BACON 25:39
With kings and c. BIBLE 52:12
counsels: all good c. PRAY 385:9
designs and crooked c. fit DRYD 194:6
United thoughts and c. MILT 345:1
count: c. five-and-twenty DICK 178:21
c. the number of the beast BIBLE 82:14
had better c. your spoons SMITH 510:15
her c. and calls her 'Miss' CHES 147:19
I c. it not an inn BROW 97:3
I c. myself in nothing SHAK 478:24
If all men c. with you KIPL 300:2

Let me c. the ways BROW 98:13
let us c. our spoons JOHN 275:1
We should c. time BAIL 29:21
counted: are c. as the small dust BIBLE 59:8
c. loss for Christ BIBLE 78:17
c. them and cursed his HOUS 264:28
faster we c. our spoons EMER 207:8
countenance: c. was as the sun shineth
BIBLE 81:14
damned disinheriting c. SHER 506:33
did the C. Divine BLAKE 86:16
grim grew his c. BALL 30:18
heart maketh a cheerful c. BIBLE 54:5
his c. is as Lebanon BIBLE 57:4
Knight of the Doleful C. CERV 138:12
lift up his c. upon thee BIBLE 48:9
light of thy c. upon us PRAY 389:27
make him a cheerful c. PRAY 396:20
making you the c. you are SHAK 426:20
sharpenth the c. of his friend BIBLE 54:40
shew the light of thy c. PRAY 395:8
trow that c. cannot lie ROYD 411:2
us the light of his c. PRAY 394:4
which is the help of my c. PRAY 392:12
withal of a beautiful c. BIBLE 50:7
counter: All things c., original HOPK 256:23
From c. or desk among grey YEATS 585:1
counteracts: he c. the Devil SMART 508:22
countercheck: c. quarrelsome SHAK 427:5
Counterfeit: C. values always resemble
AUDEN 19:20
c. sad looks SHAK 470:23
light to c. a gloom MILT 342:5
stamp and c. advantages SHAK 474:21
counterfeited: well they laugh'd with
c. GOLD 231:2
counterpane: pleasant land of c. STEV 522:20
counterpoint: Too much c. BEEC 37:4
counters: Words are wise men's c.
HOBB 251:15
countest: c. the steps of the Sun BLAKE 87:22
counties: Forget six c. overhung MORR 358:10
see the coloured c. HOUS 263:4
counting: c. votes instead of weighing
INGE 270:7
countrey: I will into some far c. BALL 30:9
countries: c. where he came his own
DRYD 195:25
preferreth all c. before his own OVER 366:6
country: airs make unto me one c.
BROW 96:29
all these c. patriots born BYRON 119:26
always zealous for his c.'s GAY 223:21
America is a c. of young EMER 208:11
Anybody can be good in the c. WILDE 573:22
benefits of your own c. SHAK 426:20
best c. ever is GOLD 231:25
bosom beats not in his c.'s POPE 375:12
c. and they only saved CHES 146:25
c. folks who live beneath CLOU 155:9
country for our c.'s good BARR 34:23
c. has its own constitution ANON 5:5
C. in the town MART 331:14
C. of the Blind the One-eyed WELLS 568:12
c. retreat near the town WYCH 583:24
c. that has 265 kinds DE G 173:17
c. 'tis of centuries come CUMM 170:10
c. was good for General WILS 574:15
departed into their own c. BIBLE 63:33
ever exist in a free c. BURKE 110:1
every c. but his own GILB 226:25
fate of this c. depends DISR 185:12
Father of his C. ANON 5:7
fight for its King and c. ANON 7:19
fit c. for heroes to live GEOR 223:33
friends of every c. save DISR 185:14
From yon far c. blows HOUS 263:9
God made the c. COWP 166:31
good news from a far c. BIBLE 54:30
good of one's c. FARQ 210:4

good to be had in the c. HAZL 243:21
great deal of unmapped c. ELIOT 200:22
guts to betray my c. FORS 217:12
have no relish for the c. SMITH 512:9
heart bleeds for his c. JOHN 274:21
he began to serve his c. SHAK 427:19
He likes the c. COWP 166:17
his journey into a far c. BIBLE 70:18
his pension from his c. RUSK 412:7
his power to leave his c. COBB 154:9
how I leave my c. PITT 374:7
I loathe the c. CONG 161:5
Indeed I tremble for my c. JEFF 272:16
in defence of one's c. HOMER 254:2
In the c. of the free BROW 97:36
in the c. places STEV 523:2
is to die for one's c. HOR 260:17
I vow to thee, my c. SPR 517:10
Leaving his c. for his FITZ 212:4
life to lose for my c. HALE 237:14
Love thy c. DOD 187:16
My c. is the world PAINE 368:5
My c., 'tis of thee SMITH 510:24
not see your c. is lost WILL 574:8
of every c. but his own CANN 129:28
once to serve our c. ADD 1:22
Our c. is the world GARR 221:18
our c., right or wrong DEC 173:1
Our c., right or wrong SCH 415:13
prepare the mind of the c. DISR 185:5
pride that pulls the c. SHAK 475:3
senators and I pray for the c. HALE 237:12
shed his blood for the c. ROOS 408:3
she is my c. still CHUR 148:24
That is no c. for old men YEATS 586:11
that was in another c. MARL 329:22
that will not love his c. SHAK 450:16
their c.'s wishes blest COLL 158:19
they've undone his c. ADD 1:21
this a billion dollar c. FOST 217:16
thou aim'st at be thy c.'s SHAK 447:21
to vegetate like the c. HAZL 243:31
What a c. SHAW 497:14
what your c. can do for you KENN 295:10
who leads a c. life DRYD 196:3
whose c. he has turned BURKE 110:33
countrymen: Friends, Romans, c.
SHAK 450:17
in perils by mine own c. BIBLE 77:12
our c. are all mankind GARR 221:18
countryside: know the gods of the c.
VIRG 560:15
smiling and beautiful c. DOYLE 192:1
county: English c. families WAUGH 565:29
coupés: les lauriers sont c. ANON 9:15
couple: c. whose ties are unbroken
HOR 259:21
wood-birds but to c. now SHAK 471:8
coupler-flange: c. to spindle-guide I see
KIPL 301:2
couplets: creaking c. in a tavern
BYRON 124:14
Shovel your c. to their CAMP 128:11
courage: Blessings on your young c.
VIRG 559:8
'C!' he said TENN 539:12
C. in your own GORD 233:1
C. is the thing BARR 34:10
C., mon ami READE 405:3
C. mounteth with occasion SHAK 452:11
c. never to submit or yield MILT 345:3
c. the greater ANON 8:9
fearful saints fresh c. take COWP 165:27
I mean instantaneous c. NAP 359:12
originality or moral c. SHAW 496:12
screw your c. to the sticking-place
SHAK 459:10
should have c. to suffer TROL 552:19
strong and of a good c. BIBLE 48:36
therefore should our c. be SHAK 444:14

three-o'-clock in the morning c. THOR 550:18
'Tis the c. you bring WALP 563:23
unto him with a good c. PRAY 391:19
vain faith, and c. vain MAC 322:8
which inspired c. whilst BURKE 111:10
couragious: captains c. whom death
BALL 31:8
couriers: sightless c. of the air SHAK 459:6
Vaunt-c. to oak-cleaving thunderbolts
SHAK 454:4
cours: c. of hire withholde CHAU 142:29
course: betake myself to that c. PEPYS 372:21
c. of true love never did SHAK 469:18
forgot his c. FLEC 214:18
giant to run his c. PRAY 390:11
I have finished my c. BIBLE 79:26
I must stand the c. SHAK 455:3
in the c. of human events JEFF 272:5
regular c. different branches CARR 134:10
Take thou what c. thou wilt SHAK 451:6
court: *Assassiner c'est le plus c. chemin*
MOL 353:24
c. an amorous looking-glass SHAK 480:18
c. awards it SHAK 468:6
c. for owls BIBLE 58:31
C. the slow clock POPE 377:7
c. to cottage he depart PEELE 371:8
cultivated c. of the Empress GILB 227:22
heavenly c. for ever celebrates ABEL 1:1
Her c. was pure TENN 543:15
I c. others in verse PRIOR 400:21
peril than the envious c. SHAK 424:31
plead their cases in c. VIRG 559:1
she will c. you JONS 284:11
Talk of c. news SHAK 456:3
that shines upon his c. SHAK 492:4
what a c. ABEL 1:2
courte: *loisir de la faire plus c.* PASC 369:14
courted: Better be c. and jilted CAMP 128:23
courteous: gracious and c. to strangers
BACON 26:20
greeting be c. or rough AUDEN 21:2
courteoust: thou wert the c. knight MAL 328:8
courtesies: these c. SHAK 466:3
ye small sweet c. of life STER 519:5
courtesy: all women with perfect c.
KITC 305:14
am the very pink of c. SHAK 482:23
devil himself with c. SHAK 490:20
Grace of God is in C. BELL 39:14
greater man, the greater c. TENN 534:36
In phrase of gentlest c. SCOTT 416:2
thy dear mother any c. SHAK 428:5
trust thy honest offer'd c. MILT 341:6
what a candy deal of c. SHAK 438:20
courtezan: she was a c. in the old
POUND 382:5
courtier: near the heel of the c. SHAK 436:29
courting: stayeth the young man's c.
POUND 382:11
courtly: with their c. foreign grace
TENN 543:4
Courts: C. and camps are the only
CHES 145:14
C. for cowards were erected BURNS 114:19
founts falling in the c. CHES 146:28
fresh from brawling c. TENN 537:8
is still before the c. HOR 257:15
longing to enter into the c. PRAY 395:11
one day in thy c. PRAY 395:13
Courtship: C. to marriage CONG 160:29
cousins: His sisters and his c. GILB 228:3
Coutts: Aristocrat who banks with C.
GILB 225:23
couvre: les c., les nourrit, les incite
MONT 355:1
cove: c. with pushing prow BROW 102:14
covenant: be for a token of a c. BIBLE 45:40
c. with death and an agreement GARR 221:19
have made a c. with death BIBLE 58:22

covenanted: c. with him for thirty BIBLE 68:9
covenants: Open c. of peace openly
WILS 575:1
Cover: C. her face WEBS 566:27
jewels c. ev'ry part POPE 378:16
leaves and flowers do c. WEBS 567:8
(Like the c. of an old book FRAN 218:20
neither turn again to c. PRAY 396:19
should c. that stand bare SHAK 466:20
covered: twain he c. his face BIBLE 57:28
covert: c. from the tempest BIBLE 58:30
I would go to a c. ROSS 409:10
covet: c. thy neighbour's house BIBLE 47:24
sin to c. honour SHAK 445:2
Thou shalt not c. CLOU 154:1
coveted: Englishman as ever c. his
KING 297:9
covetous: not a brawler, not c. BIBLE 79:12
covetousness: all uncleanness, or c.
BIBLE 78:2
cow: c. is kept for every three MILL 339:16
I never saw a Purple C. BURG 108:2
isn't grass to graze a c. BETJ 44:4
Kiss till the c. comes home BEAU 36:11
milk the c. of the world WILB 572:4
Three acres and a c. COLL 158:11
to keep a c. BUTL 119:4
Truth, Sir, is a c. JOHN 275:3
when she kissed her c. SWIFT 526:28
coward: Am I a c. SHAK 433:3
c. does it with a kiss WILDE 572:10
c. lips did from their SHAK 448:15
c.'s castle CHAP 140:9
c. shame distain his name BURNS 114:21
c.'s weapon FLET 215:32
"Fore God I am no c. TENN 542:21
gross flattery to name a c. TOBIN 551:7
I was a c. on instinct SHAK 439:8
live a c. in thine own SHAK 459:8
may call me c. if you will FIEL 211:31
No c. soul is mine BRON 93:18
Shak'd like a c. SHAK 439:21
We took him for a c. SHAK 490:23
cowardice: mutual c. keeps us in peace
JOHN 278:3
of pusillanimity and c. SHAK 442:15
soldier I admit the c. SHAW 497:29
cowardly: Not c. put off my helmet
SHAK 423:15
cowards: being all c. JOHN 278:3
conscience doth make c. SHAK 434:3
Conscience is but a word that c. SHAK 481:17
Courts for c. were erected BURNS 114:19
C. die many times before SHAK 449:18
c. flinch and traitors CONN 161:10
C. in scarlet pass GRAN 234:9
many other mannish c. have SHAK 424:30
Nonconformist Conscience makes c.
BEER 37:19
plague of all c. SHAK 438:36
would be c. if they durst ROCH 407:1
cowbind: Green c. and the
moonlight-coloured SHEL 503:19
cowcumber: she wouldn't have a c.
DICK 179:25
cowl: I like a c. EMER 206:22
Cows: C. are my passion DICK 177:28
say the c. laid out Boston EMER 207:7
cowslip: In a c.'s bell I lie SHAK 485:25
I' the bottom of a c. SHAK 428:9
O'er the c.'s velvet head MILT 341:21
Cowslips: C., and Kingcups SPEN 517:3
c. in boys' hats appear... CLARE 152:14
c. tall her pensioners SHAK 470:2
c. wan that hang the pensive MILT 343:15
coxcombs: c. nature meant but fools
POPE 378:11
coy: c. and tender to offend HERB 248:14
Then be not c. HERR 250:6

coyness: c., Lady, were no crime
    MARV 332:18
coz: my pretty little c.   SHAK 426:24
Crabbed: C. age and youth   SHAK 492:13
crabs: When roasted c. hiss   SHAK 457:19
Crab-spawn: Mars to C. found in my
    GRAV 234:12
crab-tree: grievous c. cudgel   BUNY 107:22
crack: canst hear the mighty c.   POPE 376:21
  c. in the tea-cup opens   AUDEN 18:10
  C. nature's moulds   SHAK 454:4
  heaven's vaults should c.   SHAK 456:8
  sans c. or flaw   SHAK 457:16
  snarls…You'd better c. up   DICK 179:18
  with never a c. in my heart   YEATS 586:5
  would hear the mighty c.   ADD 2:30
crack'd: have bloody noses and c.
    SHAK 438:31
cracked: c. lookingglass of a servant
    JOYCE 286:21
cracker: those lovely c. mottoes GILB 225:11
crackling: c. of thorns under a pot
    BIBLE 55:18
cracks: Now c. a noble heart   SHAK 437:28
cradle: bed and procreant c.   SHAK 459:4
  Between the c.   DYER 199:18
  frailest For your c.   SHEL 501:22
  from the c. to the grave   SHEL 503:14
  In his soft c.   JONS 285:7
  mountain c. in Pamere   ARN 15:1
  Out of the c. endlessly   WHIT 570:9
  Rocked in the c. of the deep   WILL 574:7
  rocking a grown man in the c. BURKE 110:13
craft: Between c. and credulity BURKE 110:10
  c. so long to lerne   CHAU 143:32
  c. so long to learn   HIPP 251:8
  there's c. in the river   SMITH 510:5
craftier: Ful c. to pley she was CHAU 141:6
crafts: from the c. and assaults PRAY 385:16
craftsman: Copper for the c. cunning
    KIPL 298:15
  rusteth the craft and the c. POUND 382:10
crag: He clasps the c. with crooked
    TENN 533:7
crags: among these barren c.   TENN 543:21
crambe: miseros c. repetita magistros
    JUV 287:24
cramm'd: they on earth were c. WORD 580:2
cramoisi: c. is unbroidered   POUND 382:11
cramped: delicate growth c. by
  crookedness   HARDY 240:3
cramps: tonight thou shalt have c.
    SHAK 484:28
crams: c. with cans of poisoned CHES 147:20
Cranberry: C. Tart   LEAR 312:9
crane: Jane Jane Tall as a c.   SITW 508:11
cranes: Warred on by c.   MILT 345:22
crank: steersmen when the vessel's c.
    MER 337:20
cranks: personal prejudices and c.
    ELIOT 205:15
  Quips and c.   MILT 342:14
crape: saint in c. is twice   POPE 377:11
Cras: C. amet qui nunquam amavit
    ANON 10:11
  C. ingens iterabimus aequor HOR 259:17
crastina: Sera nimis vita est c. MART 331:8
cratère: raison tonne en son c. POTT 382:3
Cratinus: If you believe C. from HOR 258:25
craved: who c. no crumb   GILB 229:9
craven: c. fears of being great TENN 533:27
Craven-street: In C.   SMITH 510:5
craving: full as c. too   DRYD 195:15
crawl: slimy things did c. with COL 155:14
crawling: such fellows as I do c. SHAK 433:11
craze: stands In a careworn c. HARDY 240:15
crazed: He is c. with the spell DE L 173:26
crazier: World is c. and more MACN 326:14
crazy: c., cold   ROCH 407:3

creaking: c. couplets in a tavern
    BYRON 124:14
cream: c. and mantle like a standing
    SHAK 465:12
  milk masquerades as c.   GILB 228:8
  queen of curds and c.   SHAK 492:1
  than choking her with c.   KING 297:15
  vigilant as a cat to steal c. SHAK 440:11
  will you take a little c.   PAIN 367:19
cream-faced: thou c. loon   SHAK 463:1
crease: with not a c.   ROST 410:12
create: ashes new-c. another heir SHAK 448:3
  c. new heavens and a new   BIBLE 60:14
  from these c. he can   SHEL 503:6
  I must C. a System   BLAKE 86:2
  must himself c. the taste   WORD 583:11
  strains that might c. a soul   MILT 341:14
  time to murder and c.   ELIOT 203:19
  well to c. good precedents   BACON 26:24
created: beginning God c. the heaven
    BIBLE 44:22
  c. equal…In a larger sense   LINC 314:23
  C. half to rise   POPE 379:13
  he immediately c. other   NIET 363:3
  image of him that c. him   BIBLE 78:26
  Male and female c.   BIBLE 45:5
  Man has c. death   YEATS 584:21
  men are c. equal   JEFF 272:6
  that all men are c. equal   ANON 8:14
  Thou hast c. all things   BIBLE 81:25
  why was it not c. sooner   JOHN 278:5
  written or c. unless Minerva   HOR 258:5
creating: c. a whole tribe of fops SHAK 453:9
Creation: been present at the C. ALF 3:16
  c. groaneth and travaileth   BIBLE 75:10
  c. will expire before tea-time SMITH 511:18
  like the God of the c.   JOYCE 286:18
  love C.'s primal law   TENN 536:29
  mars c.'s plan   CANN 130:3
  Such as c.'s dawn beheld   BYRON 121:25
  We bless thee for our c.   PRAY 384:6
  when c. rises again   CEL 138:6
  which the whole c. moves   TENN 537:22
  woman is a blind fury of c.   SHAW 497:20
creations: person acts his own c. BROW 103:4
creative: c. soul   WORD 580:25
  destruction is also a c.   BAK 29:24
Creator: C. and Preserver of all PRAY 385:24
  creature more than the C.   BIBLE 74:32
  depends on his C.   BURT 116:31
  glory of the C. and the relief BACON 24:17
  great C. from his work   MILT 349:2
  marvellous work of the C. HOUS 266:15
  now he hasn't been a c.   CHEK 145:4
  Remember now thy C.   BIBLE 56:11
creatura: Cum resurget c.   CEL 138:6
creature: base and ignoble c. BACON 25:25
  c. hath a purpose and its   KEATS 294:17
  c.'s at his dirty work   POPE 376:22
  God's first C.   BACON 28:5
  kill the young c. at once   GASK 221:24
  Let the living c. lie   AUDEN 19:17
  served the c. more than the Creator
    BIBLE 74:32
creatures: births of living c. BACON 26:27
  c. great and small   ALEX 3:13
  generations of living c.   LUCR 320:7
  goodly c. are there here   SHAK 485:26
  Hugest of living c.   MILT 349:1
  meanest of his c.   BROW 102:36
  other c. have gone to stall FROST 219:11
  perverse c. in the world   ADD 2:18
  take unto other living c.   BACON 26:19
  than c. set upon tables   JOHN 276:30
Credat: C. Iudaeus Apella   HOR 262:5
credence: gave no c. to his word PRAY 397:5
  yive I feyth and ful c.   CHAU 143:29
credit: c. in this World much wrong
    FITZ 213:13
  it's greatly to his c.   GILB 228:9

  Not to thy c.   CALV 128:1
  There an't much c. in that   DICK 179:1
  'Tis a c. to any good girl   TAYL 531:24
creditable: love good c. acquaintance
    SWIFT 526:15
credite: Experto c.   VIRG 559:10
creditor: trembling at a c.   JOHN 281:40
creditors: c. would hardly know me
    FOX 217:24
Credo: C. in unum Deum   MASS 334:20
credulity: Between craft and c. BURKE 110:10
  c. below the milkiness   BURKE 108:20
  c. increases his impudence HUME 267:19
  present age is craving c.   DISR 184:29
credulous: positive men are the most
  c.   POPE 381:22
  with the pomp of a too-c.   WORD 582:4
credulus: sed non ego c. illis VIRG 560:7
credunt: homines id quod volunt c.
    CAES 126:27
creed: Christians have a comfortable
  c.   BYRON 122:19
  c. of a second-rate man   BAG 29:16
  got the better of his c.   STER 519:25
  His c. no parson ever knew DOYLE 192:40
  it is the c. of slaves   PITT 374:3
  Pagan suckled in a c. outworn WORD 582:20
  shrieked against his c.   TENN 536:29
  solemn c. with solemn sneer BYRON 120:37
creeds: c. that refuse and restrain SWIN 529:11
  dust of c. outworn   SHEL 503:4
  half-believers in our casual c. ARN 14:17
  keys of all the c.   TENN 536:13
  so many c.   WILC 572:6
  Vain are the thousand c.   BRON 93:20
creep: ambition can c. as well as soar
    BURKE 112:9
  bade me c. past   BROW 103:32
  C. in our ears   SHAK 468:15
  C. into thy narrow bed   ARN 13:14
  it and little dwarfs to c.   CHES 147:5
  'with pleasing murmurs c.' POPE 378:21
creepers: Lifting the cool-hair'd c. ARN 14:21
creeping: are c. things innumerable
    PRAY 397:1
  c. thing that creepeth   BIBLE 45:4
  c. things, and fowls   BIBLE 73:37
Creeps: C. in this petty pace   SHAK 463:6
  c. rustling to her knees   KEATS 289:17
creetur: 'I am a lone lorn c.   DICK 176:27
Cremorne: C. Gardens   TROL 553:9
crept: c. too near his conscience SHAK 446:28
  one c. silently to Rest   FITZ 212:17
Cretes: C. and Arabians   BIBLE 73:23
crevasse: like a scream from a c. GREE 236:6
  that doth the c. bridge   THOM 547:22
crew: admit me of thy c.   MILT 342:16
  c. is gambling in the forecastle SHAW 496:13
  c. of the Captain's gig   CHES 146:27
  c. of the captain's gig   GILB 225:16
  darling of our c.   DIBD 175:21
  immediately the cock c.   BIBLE 68:19
  Set the c. laughing   FLEC 214:18
  We were a ghastly c.   COL 155:25
  With his industrious c.   MILT 346:4
crib: ass his master's c.   BIBLE 57:15
cribs: liest thou in smoky c.   SHAK 441:29
Cricket: his nose there was a C. LEAR 312:5
  Save the c. on the hearth   MILT 342:5
  son of grief at c.   HOUS 262:22
Cricklewood: bound for C.   BETJ 43:17
cried: c. all the way to the bank LIB 314:11
  c. the little children   AUDEN 18:15
  from the depths I have c.   BIBLE 83:13
  I c. to dream again   SHAK 485:18
  little children c.   MOTL 358:20
  still she c.   ELIOT 204:24
  When that the poor have c. SHAK 450:19
Crier: when the C. cried   BARH 33:22
cries: heaven with my bootless c. SHAK 493:6

Night and day on me she c.   BALL 31:4
'tailor' c.   SHAK 470:3
crieth: that c. in the wilderness   BIBLE 59:5
crikey: always game by c. blood will tell
   MARQ 330:20
Crillon: brave C.   HENR 245:14
crime: C'est pire qu'un c.   BOUL 90:19
commonplace a c. is   DOYLE 191:15
c. in a child to read   MAC 324:18
c. of being a young man...I   PITT 373:20
c. so shameful as poverty   FARQ 209:26
c. to love too well   POPE 376:6
foulest c. in history   WHIT 571:10
Godlike c. was to be kind   BYRON 125:18
He is the Napoleon of c.   DOYLE 192:11
It is worse than a c.   BOUL 90:19
jury for a capital c.   JOHN 277:2
loved be with equal c.   SPEN 516:13
love, was thought a c.   BLAKE 87:17
No c.'s so great as daring   CHUR 148:21
that's the c.   GRAN 234:8
Who for my wilful c.   MILT 349:28
Crimes: C., like virtues   FARQ 210:14
our c. would despair   SHAK 421:3
reach the dignity of c.   MORE 357:8
register of the c.   GIBB 224:23
Successful c. alone are   DRYD 197:3
tableau des c. et des malheurs   VOLT 561:10
their c. confin'd   GRAY 234:24
thousand c.   BYRON 121:36
what c. are committed   ROL 407:15
With all his c. broad blown   SHAK 434:30
with reiterated c. he might   MILT 345:8
worst of c. is poverty   SHAW 497:6
Crimine: C. ab uno   VIRG 558:2
crimson: in that c. lake   GRAH 233:16
Is c. in thy lips   SHAK 483:30
crisis: force the moment to its c.   ELIOT 203:22
in this c.   PAINE 368:1
Crispian: called the feast of C.   SHAK 445:3
Crispin: C. Crispian shall ne'er   SHAK 445:3
Crist: C.! whan that it remembreth
   CHAU 143:19
Cristen: C. man shall wedde   CHAU 143:17
Cristes: C. loore and his apostles   CHAU 142:3
criterion: infallible c. of wisdom
   BURKE 111:27
critic: attribute of a good c.   LOW 319:16
C. and whippersnapper   BROW 99:1
c., one would suppose   ELIOT 205:15
c. spits on what is done   HOOD 255:14
c. to decide...A publisher   WILDE 573:33
nicely Jonson knew the c.'s   COLL 158:23
critical: be c. than to be correct   DISR 184:23
c. judgement is so exquisite   FRY 219:24
c. period in matrimony   HERB 246:16
I am nothing if not c.   SHAK 474:16
criticism: anticipate the verdict of c.
   WILDE 573:33
c. is the most tormenting   STER 519:30
c. of administration   BAG 28:23
father of English c.   JOHN 281:35
I do not resent c.   CHUR 150:5
my own definition of c.   ARN 16:1
our c. is applied only   JAMES 271:13
People ask you for c.   MAUG 336:3
two because it permits c.   FORS 217:13
wreathed the rod of c.   DISR 187:8
criticizing: spite of all the c. elves
   CHUR 149:13
critic-pen: Unboding c.   TENN 544:10
critics: Cosmopolitan c.   DISR 185:14
c. all are ready made   BYRON 124:17
therefore they turn c.   COL 157:26
Turn'd c. next   POPE 378:12
You know who the c. are   DISR 186:23
You trust in c.   BYRON 124:18
croaks: That c. the fatal entrance   SHAK 459:2
Crocodile: cruel crafty C.   SPEN 516:5
How doth the little c.   CARR 133:17

manner o' thing is your c.   SHAK 422:14
To these c.'s tears   BURT 116:35
crocodiles: is the wisdom of the c.
   BACON 27:38
crocus: feet the c. brake like fire   TENN 541:18
Croesus: not an intellectual C.   DISR 186:20
crois: for love Upon a c.   CHAU 144:19
mais je n'en c. rien   CHAM 139:16
croit: ce que la raison ne c.   VOLT 561:20
Cromwell: C. guiltless of his country's
   GRAY 234:23
C.; the Philistine   ARN 16:23
C. was a man in whom ambition
   BURKE 111:29
They set up C. and his heir   JORD 285:18
crony: drouthy c.   BURNS 115:5
crook: such a thumping c.   BETJ 43:4
crooked: c. shall be made straight   BIBLE 59:5
c. timber of humanity   KANT 288:14
dumb to tell the c. rose   THOM 547:3
heart are as c. as corkscrews   AUDEN 18:13
With your c. heart   AUDEN 18:11
crookedly: before him walked very c.
   SURT 525:29
crookedness: delicate growth cramped
by c.   HARDY 240:3
crop-full: Irks care the c. bird   BROW 104:3
crop-headed: c. Parliament swing
   BROW 99:26
Croppy: C., Droppy   ELLIS 206:13
croquet: c. matches in summer   AUDEN 21:1
cross: before him endured the c.   BIBLE 79:35
beside the c. weeping while   JAC 270:31
by thy C. and Passion   PRAY 385:17
c. him in nothing   SHAK 421:24
his breast a bloody c.   SPEN 515:31
I am getting c.   HOFF 252:15
If you bear the c. gladly   THOM 546:14
I'll c. it   SHAK 429:14
mankind upon a c. of gold   BRYAN 106:8
mystery of the c. shines   VEN 556:5
suffer death upon the c.   PRAY 387:24
cross-bow: With my c.   COL 155:10
cross'd: they c. themselves for fear
   TENN 538:12
crossed: c. be uncrossed   ELIOT 202:10
oyster may be c. in love   SHER 506:4
We had c. each other's   WILDE 572:11
crosses: c., row on row   MCCR 324:30
E'en c. from his sov'reign   HERV 250:17
they clinging to their c.   CHES 146:10
tumbled down the c.   JORD 285:18
what c. to ensue   SHAK 442:2
cross-gartered: wished to see thee ever
c.   SHAK 489:15
cross-grained: there ever such a c. brute
   GOLD 232:28
Crossing: C. alone the nighted ferry
   HOUS 265:18
C. the stripling Thames   ARN 14:14
crossroads: c. and in the alleyways   CAT 137:5
crossways: Things at home are c.
   CARL 130:28
crotchets: some c. in thy head now
   SHAK 469:7
crouch: c. whom the rest bade aspire
   BROW 102:6
crow: before the cock c.   BIBLE 68:12
c. doth sing as sweetly   SHAK 468:19
c. Makes wing   SHAK 461:14
flew down a monstrous c.   CARR 134:33
had risen to hear him c.   ELIOT 200:16
Old Adam, the carrion c.   BEDD 36:26
there is an upstart c.   GREE 236:12
crowd: c. flowed over London Bridge
   ELIOT 204:20
c. is not company   BACON 26:15
fear or favour of the c.   KIPL 298:11
I hate the c.   LAND 309:5
madding c.'s ignoble strife   GRAY 235:1

not feel the c.   COWP 167:12
of these faces in the c.   POUND 383:11
riotousness of the c. is   ALC 3:9
crowding: come c. in so fast upon
   DRYD 198:7
thick the bursts come c.   ARN 14:3
Crowds: C. without company   GIBB 224:14
Frail c. that a delicate   MOORE 355:23
If you can talk with c.   KIPL 300:2
crowe: thenk upon the c.   CHAU 142:26
crowes feet: Til c. be growen under
   CHAU 144:5
crown: both divide the c.   DRYD 195:9
Caesar's laurel c.   BLAKE 85:16
c. him with glory and worship   PRAY 389:28
C. is according   BAG 28:22
c. of our life as it closes   SWIN 529:10
c. o' the earth doth melt   SHAK 423:16
c. ourselves with rosebuds   BIBLE 62:11
c. thy good with brotherhood   BATES 35:4
'Ere the King's c. shall   SCOTT 415:20
fruition of an earthly c.   MARL 330:8
Give me the c.   SHAK 479:22
hairy gold c. on 'er 'ead   KIPL 304:9
head a c. of twelve stars   BIBLE 82:10
head that wears a c.   SHAK 441:30
influence of the C. has   DUNN 199:14
labour this c. of thorns   BRYAN 106:8
likeness of a kingly c.   MILT 346:24
mace, the c. imperial   SHAK 444:25
monarch but would give his c.   WALL 562:10
more glorious is the c.   SMART 509:4
Not the king's c.   SHAK 463:20
obtain a corruptible c.   BIBLE 76:9
Of life, of c., of queen   SHAK 431:12
power of the c.   BURKE 108:19
presented him a kingly c.   SHAK 450:20
put on my c.   SHAK 424:10
shall receive the c. of life   BIBLE 80:8
strike his father's c.   SHAK 443:11
That c. the wat'ry glade   GRAY 235:9
thought of hath worn the c.   BIBLE 62:31
will give thee a c. of life   BIBLE 81:17
wished to restore the c.   JOHN 276:22
within the hollow c.   SHAK 479:11
Crown'd: C., and again discrown'd
   JOHN 273:22
C. with rank fumitor   SHAK 455:13
crowned: Calling a c. man royal   SWIN 529:26
Crowner: Medical C.'s a queer   BARH 33:16
crownest: c. the year with thy goodness
   PRAY 394:3
crown imperial: oxlips and The c.
   SHAK 491:26
crowning: c. mercy   CROM 169:22
crowns: cold nymphs chaste c.   SHAK 485:19
c. are empty things   DEFOE 173:16
c. for convoy put into   SHAK 445:3
'Give c. and pounds   HOUS 262:20
happy he who c. in shades   GOLD 230:19
I'd c. resign to call thee   MACN 326:2
It is the end that c. us   HERR 249:4
last act c. the play   QUAR 403:15
With c. imperial   SHAK 443:12
crows: c. and choughs that wing   SHAK 455:14
crow-toe: tufted c.   MILT 343:15
croyait: c. Victor Hugo   COCT 154:13
croys: c. of latoun ful of stones   CHAU 142:7
crucem: *libenter c. portas portabit te*
   THOM 546:14
Crucible: America is God's C.   ZANG 588:17
crucified: Was c.   PRAY 384:26
Crucifixus: C. etiam pro nobis   MASS 334:20
crucify: c. mankind upon a cross
   BRYAN 106:8
c. the old man   PRAY 388:10
people would not even c. him   CARL 132:26
Cruel: C., but composed and bland   ARN 14:4
C. he looks   SHEL 502:20
c., not unnatural   SHAK 434:26

Yet at mothy c.-tide | HARDY 239:18
curia: quae c. | ABEL 1:2
 semper celebrat superna c. | ABEL 1:1
curing: Morrison's Pill for c. | CARL 132:9
curiosa: Horatii c. felicitas | PETR 373:3
curiosities: c. would be quite forgot | AUBR 17:22
curiosity: c., freckles | PARK 368:15
 Disinterested intellectual c. | TREV 552:9
 eminent degree of c. | JOHN 282:19
curious: amaz'd, and c. | BURNS 115:10
 Be not c. in unnecessary | BIBLE 62:23
 c. engine, your white hand | WEBS 566:21
 objects and knowledge c. | WHIT 571:13
Curiouser: 'C. and curiouser | CARR 133:16
curiously: others to be read but not c. | BACON 27:19

curis: solutis est beatius c. | CAT 136:28
curl: Who had a little c. | LONG 317:22
 would make your hair c. | GILB 228:34
Curl'd: C. minion | ARN 14:25
curled: brave beard c. | CHES 147:3
 C. like vapour over shrines | BROW 98:16
 that c. my hair | SHAK 454:18
 wealthy c. darlings | SHAK 473:22
curls: find unwithered on its c. | HOUS 263:3
 Frocks and C. | DICK 184:2
currency: common c. that buys all | CERV 138:20
 Debasing the moral c. | ELIOT 201:26
current: c. and compulsive course | SHAK 476:1
 c. in this place damm'd | SHAK 439:24
 smooth c. of domestic joy | JOHN 282:21
 take the c. when it serves | SHAK 451:27
 works have been most c. | BACON 25:17
currents: regard their c. turn awry | SHAK 433:8
curs: c. mouth a bone | CHUR 149:8
 c. of low degree | GOLD 231:12
 You common cry of c. | SHAK 427:23
curs'd: by Nature c. | CHUR 148:32
 She c. Cole Porter too | COW 163:22
curse: began he to c. and to swear | BIBLE 68:19
 c. be ended | ELIOT 202:10
 C., bless, me now | THOM 546:24
 C. God | BIBLE 52:10
 c. of this country is eloquent | EMER 208:10
 C. on his virtues | ADD 1:21
 C. shall be on thee | SOUT 513:24
 c. to party strife | WORD 577:5
 c. with their heart | PRAY 393:19
 heard such a terrible c. | BARH 33:14
 I know how to c. | SHAK 484:29
 is to me a c. | MASS 335:17
 look upon myself and c. | SHAK 493:6
 open foe may prove a c. | GAY 223:13
 'That is love's c. | TENN 534:33
 'The c. is come upon me | TENN 538:11
 thee to c. mine enemies | BIBLE 48:16
 'Tis the c. of the service | SHAK 473:12
 Work is the c. of the drinking | WILDE 573:39
cursed: counted them and c. his | HOUS 264:28
 c. Whatever brute | HOUS 264:21
 He c. him in sleeping | BARH 33:13
 That c. man | SPEN 516:7
 whom thou cursest is c. | BIBLE 48:13
Curses: C. are like young chickens | SOUT 513:23
 C., not loud but deep | SHAK 463:2
 so c. all Eve's daughters | SHAK 469:14
 with c. from pole to pole | BLAKE 85:24
curst: all succeeding ages c. | DRYD 194:6
 c. be he that moves my | SHAK 495:22
curtail: we c. the already curtail'd | CALV 127:15
curtain: draw the c. close | SHAK 446:7
 Drew Priam's c. | SHAK 441:1
 iron c. has descended across | CHUR 150:18

saying 'Bring down the c. | RAB 404:1
 these gifts a c. before 'em | SHAK 488:1
 'Up with the c. | BROW 100:35
 when she drew the c. | BALL 30:11
Curtain'd: C. with cloudy red | MILT 344:14
curtains: c. of Solomon | BIBLE 56:16
 fringed c. of thine eye | SHAK 485:1
Curteis: C. he was | CHAU 141:13
curteisie: freedom and c. | CHAU 141:9
curteisye: She is mirour of alle c. | CHAU 142:23
curtiosity: was full of 'satiable c. | KIPL 304:20
Curtsey: C. while you're thinking | CARR 134:30
 Who made a remarkable c. | LEAR 311:17
curtsies: Low-crooked c. | SHAK 449:24
 that dream on c. straight | SHAK 481:28
curveship: c. lend a myth to God | CRANE 168:29
Curzon: is George Nathaniel C. | ANON 7:1
Cusha: C.!' calling | ING 270:14
cushes: His c. on his thighs | SHAK 440:7
cushion: c. and soft Dean invite | POPE 378:4
custard pie: joke is ultimately a c. | ORW 365:10
Custodes: custodiet ipsos C. | JUV 287:22
custodierit: Nisi Dominus c. civitatem | BIBLE 83:12
custodiet: c. ipsos Custodes | JUV 287:22
custom: contrary to c. and experience | HUME 267:21
 c., and fear | HARDY 240:3
 C. calls me to 't | SHAK 427:17
 c. lie upon thee with | WORD 579:8
 c. loathsome to the eye | JAM 271:3
 C. reconciles us to everything | BURKE 108:10
 c. should corrupt the world | TENN 535:25
 C. that is before all law | DAN 170:22
 C., that unwritten law | DAV 172:4
 C., then | HUME 267:14
 custom to whom c. | BIBLE 75:22
 Hath not old c. made this | SHAK 424:31
 nor c. stale | SHAK 422:5
 sitting at the receipt of c. | BIBLE 65:21
 That monster, c. | SHAK 435:18
customer: tough c. in argeyment | DICK 175:24
customers: raising up a people of c. | SMITH 509:12
customs: ancient c. and its manhood | ENN 208:23
 c. of his tribe and island | SHAW 496:9
cut: an' c. 'is stripes away | KIPL 298:20
 Cannot see the record c. | HOUS 263:2
 cheerful ways of men C. off | MILT 347:8
 c. his throat before he | SWIFT 528:9
 C. is the branch that might | MARL 329:16
 c. my conscience to fit | HELL 244:15
 c. off out of the land | BIBLE 59:23
 C. short his being | SHER 506:1
 guardsman's c. and thrust | HUXL 269:3
 in the evening it is c. | PRAY 395:18
 Nor c. each other's throats | GOLD 231:15
 scuttled ship or c. a throat | BYRON 122:30
 unkindest c. of all | SHAK 450:28
 will I c. off Israel out | BIBLE 50:31
 you can c. that right out | AUDEN 19:14
cute: nitidum bene curata c. vises | HOR 258:16
Cutlets: suggested we should play 'C.' | GROS 237:1
cut-purse: c. of the empire | SHAK 435:11
Cuts: C. off so many years | SHAK 450:4
cutting: c. all the pictures out | BELL 38:23
 he of c. foreign throats | SHAK 481:28
 Went on c. bread and butter | THAC 546:3
Cutty-sark: Weel done, C. | BURNS 115:11
cygnes: un lac au milieu des c. | AUG 21:11
cygnet: c.'s down is harsh | SHAK 486:19
cygnets: doth the swan her downy c. | SHAK 445:24
cymbal: talk but a tinkling c. | BACON 26:15

 tinkling c. | BIBLE 76:14
cymbals: upon the well-tuned c. | PRAY 400:1
Cynara: faithful to thee, C. | DOWS 191:12
Cynic: precepts from the C. tub | MILT 341:16
cynical: of a melancholy nor a c. | CHES 145:23
Cynicism: C. is intellectual dandyism | MER 337:31
cynosure: c. of neighbouring eyes | MILT 342:20
Cynthia: C. of this minute | POPE 377:18
cypress: in sad c. let me be laid | SHAK 489:4
 Nor waves the c. | TENN 542:14
 shall see the c. spread | PEAC 371:1
cypresses: Along the avenue of c. | LAWR 311:5
Cyprus: That rings black C. with | FLEC 214:16
Cyrano: C.: Mon panache | ROST 410:12
Cyrene: parts of Libya about C. | BIBLE 73:23
Cyril: took young C. to church | ELIOT 202:7
Cythera: It's C. | BAUD 35:8
Cytherean: throned C. be fallen | SWIN 530:7
D: big D. | GILB 228:2
 there are your d.'s for you | WYCH 583:26
Da: D. mi basia mille | CAT 136:26
 D. mihi castitatem et continentiam | AUG 21:14
 D. quod iubes et iube quod | AUG 21:17
Dad: To meet their D. | BURNS 113:5
dada: mama of d. | FAD 209:18
daffadillies: d. fill their cups with | MILT 343:15
Daffadowndillies: Strew me the ground with D. | SPEN 517:3
daff'd: that d. the world aside | SHAK 440:6
daffodil: On a bed of d. sky | TENN 540:9
 shining d. dies | TENN 540:17
daffodils: d., That come before | SHAK 491:26
 dances with the d. | WORD 578:1
 Fair d. | HERR 249:28
 host, of golden d. | WORD 577:29
 I never saw d. so beautiful | WORD 576:21
 in the west wind, and d. | MAS 334:9
 When d. begin to peer | SHAK 491:17
daft: d. and happy hills | THOM 546:22
 warld thinks the d. | SCOTT 418:28
dagger: d. of the mind | SHAK 459:15
 desperate deadly daunting d. | WYCH 583:26
 Is this a d. which I see | SHAK 459:15
 Thou stick'st a d. in me | SHAK 467:6
daggers: fighting with d. in a hogshead | SCOTT 419:2
 Give me the d. | SHAK 460:11
 I will speak d. to her | SHAK 434:26
 There's d. in men's smiles | SHAK 461:4
Dahin: D.! Dahin | GOET 230:13
dahlias: d. are dead | SURT 525:16
daily: consumed away through my d. complaining | PRAY 391:16
 d. beauty in his life | SHAK 477:3
 d. increase in thy holy | PRAY 388:22
 Give us this day our d. bread | BIBLE 64:24
 which cometh upon me d. | BIBLE 77:12
Daily Telegraph: young lions of the D. | ARN 15:23
dainties: d. are all cates | SHAK 484:9
 hath not fed of the d. | SHAK 457:1
 spiced d. | KEATS 289:20
daintily: must have things d. served | BETJ 42:19
dairies: now foul sluts in d. | CORB 162:13
dairy: doth nightly rob the d. | JONS 284:15
daisies: Buttercups and d. | HOW 267:2
 d. growing over me | KEATS 295:2
 d. pied and violets blue | SHAK 457:18
 D. smell-less | FLET 215:21
 D., those pearled Arcturi | SHEL 503:18
 lie upon the d. and discourse | GILB 227:21
 Meadows trim with d. pied | MILT 342:20
 sea-d. feast on the sun | SWIN 530:24
Daisy: D. and Lily | SITW 508:12
 d. delectable | SKEL 508:18

thou who mourn'st the D.'s   BURNS 115:19
Dalhousie: Lady D. are dead   MCG 325:5
dalliance: d. in the wardrobe lies
                                SHAK 443:12
primrose path of d. treads   SHAK 430:18
dallies: d. with the innocence   SHAK 489:3
dam: did not give a singel d.   FLEM 214:25
pretty chickens and their d.   SHAK 462:17
damage: moral or intellectual d.   KRUG 306:1
which might d. his career   BARR 34:20
You might d. the trees   LEAR 312:26
damaged: Archangel a little d.   LAMB 307:29
damages: He first d. his mind   ANON 10:1
Damascus: rivers of D.   BIBLE 51:28
dame: 'La belle d. sans mercy'   KEATS 289:21
'La belle D. sans Merci   KEATS 290:21
sits our sulky sullen d.   BURNS 115:3
Dame Lurch: modest D.   BLAKE 87:20
dames: Stoutly struts his d. before
                                MILT 342:17
damm'd: current in this place d.   SHAK 439:24
dammed: only saved by being d.
                                HOOD 255:18
damn: d. by rule   OTWAY 366:3
d. her at a venture   LAMB 308:10
'D. the age   LAMB 307:37
D. the torpedoes   FARR 210:24
d. those authors whom they   CHUR 148:19
D. with faint praise   POPE 376:26
D. you, Jack   BONE 89:19
He doesn't give a d.   ANON 7:13
like a parson's d.   HARDY 241:14
not worth a d.   WELL 567:18
praises one another d.   WYCH 584:2
to d. the consequences   MILN 340:18
with a spot I d. him   SHAK 451:9
Damna: D. tamen celeres reparant
                                HOR 261:16
damnation: be blasted to eternal d.
                                SHAW 498:18
deep d. of his taking-off   SHAK 459:6
from everlasting d.   PRAY 385:16
Heap on himself d.   MILT 345:8
I dare d.   SHAK 436:7
damnations: Twenty-nine distinct d.
                                BROW 105:7
damn'd: All silent and all d.   WORD 580:2
d. to everlasting fame   POPE 380:1
foremost shall be d. to fame   POPE 375:19
health or goblin d.   SHAK 430:24
damned: d. and luxurious mountain
                                SHAK 445:4
D. from here to Eternity   KIPL 304:9
d. lies and statistics   DISR 187:7
ever d. with Lucifer   MARL 329:6
has been a d. nice thing   WELL 567:19
I'll be d. for never   SHAK 438:9
is the brandy of the d.   SHAW 497:27
one d. thing   OMAL 365:5
public be d.   VAND 555:7
Publish and be d.   WELL 568:10
those who shall be d.   JOHN 279:17
thou must be d. perpetually   MARL 329:11
to have written a d. play   REYN 405:15
Water your d. flower-pots   BROW 105:5
what those d. dots meant   CHUR 149:24
will be d. if you don't   DOW 191:11
damnés: les d. de la terre   POTT 382:3
damning: always had a taste for d.
                                MOORE 357:4
By d. those they have no   BUTL 117:23
careless of the d. sin   COWP 165:8
Damnosa: D. hereditas   GAIUS 220:27
D. quid non imminuit dies   HOR 260:26
damoysele: cleped fair d. Pertelote
                                CHAU 142:32
damozel: blessed d. leaned out   ROSS 409:14
damp: d. souls of housemaids   ELIOT 203:27
poisonous d. of night disponge   SHAK 423:4
damsel: d. with a dulcimer   COL 156:30

to every man a d. or two   BIBLE 49:13
Dan: Dangerous D. McGrew   SERV 420:14
From D. even to Beer-sheba   BIBLE 49:30
travel from D. to Beersheba   STER 519:2
Danaë: Now lies the Earth all D.   TENN 542:14
Danaos: timeo D. et dona   VIRG 558:1
dance: ae best d. e'er cam   BURNS 113:13
at least before they d.   POPE 380:8
d. an antic hay   MARL 329:17
d. attendance on their   SHAK 447:24
d. is a measured pace   BACON 24:23
D. on the sands   SHAK 495:19
dancer from the d.   YEATS 584:11
d. while you can   AUDEN 18:13
d. with you in Brabant   SHAK 456:22
departs too far from the d.   POUND 383:21
fixed thee mid this d.   BROW 104:11
On with the d.   BYRON 120:21
there the d. is   ELIOT 202:15
time to d.   BIBLE 55:12
to d. at our bridal   SCOTT 417:11
when you do d.   SHAK 491:27
who have learn'd to d.   POPE 378:22
will you join the d.   CARR 134:14
danced: David d. before the Lord
                                BIBLE 50:18
They d. by the light   LEAR 312:14
ye have not d.   BIBLE 66:3
dancer: d., coiner of sweet words   ARN 14:25
in measure, like a d.   ELIOT 202:26
know the d. from the dance   YEATS 584:11
dancers: To the d. dancing in tune
                                TENN 540:10
dances: breaks the threaded d.   AUDEN 18:10
He capers, he d.   SHAK 469:10
In hamlets, d. on the green   SCOTT 416:17
makes no progress; it d.   LIGNE 314:12
shall have no time for d.   MACN 326:16
Their d. were procession   CORB 162:15
danceth: in hope d. without musick
                                HERB 246:22
Dan Chaucer: D., mighty Shakespeare
                                BRID 92:9
Dancing: D. in the chequered shade
                                MILT 342:22
Fluttering and d.   WORD 577:29
Follows with d. and fills   SWIN 528:10
manners of a d. master   JOHN 274:10
now for some d. with   HOR 260:3
Say I am d.   SHAK 421:23
You and I are past our d.   SHAK 482:1
dandelions: Sheaves of drooping d.
                                BETJ 43:19
dandyism: Cynicism is intellectual d.
                                MER 337:31
Dane: antique Roman than a D.   SHAK 437:24
never get rid of the D.   KIPL 298:18
Dane-geld: is called paying the D.
                                KIPL 298:18
Danes: D.' Wit   ROCH 407:5
danger: bright face of d.   STEV 520:24
d. chiefly lies in acting   CHUR 148:21
D. knows full well   SHAK 449:19
d. o'er   OWEN 366:28
d. of hell fire   BIBLE 64:12
D., the spur of all great   CHAP 140:15
d. to the country   VICT 556:15
everything is in d.   NIET 363:5
having any share in the d.   LUCR 320:6
in d. of her former tooth   SHAK 461:12
in d. of Popery so long   ADD 2:19
much as to be out of d.   HUXL 269:9
One would be in less d.   NASH 359:18
Out of this nettle, d.   SHAK 438:29
run into any kind of d.   PRAY 385:3
that we are in great d.   SHAK 444:14
There is no d. to a man   CHAP 140:8
they put themselves in d.   WYATT 583:21
dangerous: Beware, I am d.   BAG 28:20
D. Dan McGrew   SERV 420:14

d. to sit to Sargent   ANON 6:8
d. to know   LAMB 306:25
fables, and d. deceits   PRAY 400:9
have I in me something d.   SHAK 437:7
Into the d. world I leapt   BLAKE 87:23
is a d. precedent   CORN 162:23
little knowledge is d.   HUXL 269:9
such men are d.   SHAK 448:20
though it were d. to meet   WHAR 569:8
To a most d. sea   SHAK 467:11
dangerously: from life is to live d.   NIET 363:9
Dangers: D. by being despised grow
                                BURKE 111:33
d. fright him and no labours   JOHN 282:30
d. I had pass'd   SHAK 474:1
fear of tomorrow's d.   DONNE 191:2
of so many and great d.   PRAY 386:8
perils and d. of this night   PRAY 385:10
What d. thou canst make   BURNS 115:9
dangling: thou up yon d. apricocks
                                SHAK 479:17
Daniel: D. come to judgment   SHAK 468:3
second D.   SHAK 468:8
danket: Nun d. alle Gott   RINK 406:6
Danny Deever: 'For they're hangin' D.
                                KIPL 298:20
danse: marche pas, il d.   LIGNE 314:12
Dant: That highte D.   CHAU 142:31
Dante: D.—known to that gentleman
                                DICK 178:27
D. never stays too long   MAC 324:9
D. of the dread Inferno   BROW 103:1
D. once prepared to paint   BROW 102:30
D., who loved well because   BROW 102:31
we knew D. was no good   BUTL 118:35
Daphne: Apollo hunted D. so   MARV 332:2
dapper: d. boot   TENN 540:23
dappled: Glory be to God for d.   HOPK 256:22
round tears run down his d.   THOM 549:19
dapple-dawn-drawn: d. Falcon   HOPK 257:4
Dapples: D. the drowsy east   SHAK 473:11
dare: always had licence to d.   HOR 257:10
d. not trust it without   BROW 97:5
D. the unpastured dragon   SHEL 499:15
D. to be true   HERB 247:2
d. to be unhappy   ROWE 410:25
d. to die   POPE 379:21
d. to do our duty as we   LINC 314:17
do menace heaven and d.   MARL 330:5
gentle woman d.   SOUT 514:6
I can d. to be poor   GAY 223:25
Letting 'I d. not' wait   SHAK 459:8
none d. call it treason   HAR 242:10
our unworthiness we d.   PRAY 388:7
What man dare, I d.   SHAK 461:21
what men d. do   SHAK 473:1
You who d.   MER 337:21
dared: d. attack my Chesterton   BELL 39:27
Determined, d., and done   SMART 509:4
dares: do that d. love attempt   SHAK 482:10
Who d. do more is none   SHAK 459:9
Darien: upon a peak in D.   KEATS 292:18
daring: d. of a moment's surrender
                                ELIOT 205:11
song too d.   PRIOR 400:22
dark: All d. and comfortless   SHAK 455:4
Between the d.   LONG 316:9
blind man in a d. room   BOWEN 90:23
children fear to go in the d.   BACON 26:1
Climb to our proper d.   YEATS 587:2
clock has stopped in the d.   ELIOT 202:9
colours will agree in the d.   BACON 27:32
d., amid the blaze   MILT 350:15
D. and terrible beyond   MAC 324:22
d. and true and tender   TENN 542:5
d. as night   SHAK 495:15
d. backward and abysm   SHAK 484:24
d., boggy   GOLD 232:25
d. horse   DISR 187:2

'D. lowers the tempest overhead
    LONG 316:15
d. night of the soul   FITZ 213:22
d. sanctuary of incapacity   CHES 146:5
d. Satanic mills   BLAKE 86:16
D. with excessive bright   MILT 347:9
d. womb where I began   MAS 333:22
d. world of sin   BICK 84:4
dim and the d. cloths   YEATS 585:9
ever-during d.   MILT 347:8
great leap in the d.   HOBB 251:24
Hellish d.   SURT 525:15
hides a d. soul   MILT 341:8
Kept in a d. house   SHAK 490:24
Lady is as good i' th' d.   HERR 249:12
made a leap into the d.   BROWN 95:9
murmur and the poring d.   SHAK 444:9
one stride comes the d.   COL 155:16
Out in the d. over   THOM 547:20
saturnine, d., and melancholic   CONG 159:17
That for ways that are d.   HARTE 242:29
through the blanket of the d.   SHAK 459:2
through the spaces of the d.   ELIOT 204:9
us i' the d. to rise   BROW 104:27
want to go home in the d.   HENRY 245:24
we are for the d.   SHAK 424:2
darken: days d. round me   TENN 535:24
darkeneth: d. counsel by words   BIBLE 52:41
darkening: sky is d. like a stain   AUDEN 21:10
darker: let us speak of d. days   CHUR 150:8
Save that the sky grows d.   CHES 146:16
world was at least not d.   ELIOT 201:12
darkling: are here as on a d. plain   ARN 12:23
D. I listen   KEATS 291:22
darkly: d. looked he at the wall   MAC 322:14
through a glass, d.   BIBLE 76:14
darkness: Aye on the shores of d.
    KEATS 292:25
cast away the works of d.   PRAY 386:4
cast off the works of d.   BIBLE 75:24
cast out into outer d.   BIBLE 65:17
d., and in the shadow   PRAY 397:7
D. came down on the field   THAC 545:26
d. comprehended it not   BIBLE 71:23
d. had to a great extent   HARDY 241:19
darkness is no d. with thee   PRAY 399:5
d. over the land of Egypt   BIBLE 47:15
d. that it may be night   PRAY 397:1
d. was upon the face   BIBLE 44:22
Death hath made His d.   TENN 537:3
did the act of d. with   SHAK 454:18
encounter d. as a bride   SHAK 464:12
far as light excelleth d.   BIBLE 55:10
great d. falling on my   PAIN 367:18
Great Gorgon, Prince of d.   SPEN 516:1
great horror and d. fell   BUNY 107:25
horror of great d. fell   BIBLE 46:3
instruments of d. tell us truths   SHAK 458:18
in the d. and the cold   STEV 522:26
jaws of d. do devour it   SHAK 469:20
land of d. and the shadow   BIBLE 52:20
land…where the light is as d.   BIBLE 52:21
leaves the world to d.   GRAY 234:18
lie where shades of d.   DE L 174:1
Lighten our d.   PRAY 385:10
lump bred up in d.   KYD 306:6
Men loved d. rather than   BIBLE 71:39
pass'd the door of D.   FITZ 213:4
people that walked in d.   BIBLE 58:6
Peradventure the d. shall   PRAY 399:5
pestilence that walketh in d.   PRAY 395:21
prince of d. is a gentleman   SHAK 454:24
race that long in d. pin'd   SCOT 419:7
rather d. visible   MILT 344:25
Ring out the d. of the land   TENN 537:15
Scatters the rear of d.   MILT 342:17
slope thro' d. up to God   TENN 536:28
Swaddled with d.   ELIOT 203:4
talks of d. at noon-day   COWP 166:12
Terror of d.   CHAP 140:7

To sit in d. here   MILT 346:15
to them that sit in d.   BIBLE 69:7
universal d. buries all   POPE 376:2
When awful d. and silence   LEAR 312:2
winds will call the d.   SHEL 504:7
Yet still between his D.   BYRON 126:8
darksome: he goes along the d. road
    CAT 136:23
spent the d. hours   GOET 230:12
Dark Tower: 'Childe Roland to the D.
    BROW 99:30
darling: d. buds of May   SHAK 492:28
D. Mr Discobbolos   LEAR 312:10
d., my life and my bride   POE 374:23
my d. from the lions   PRAY 391:25
She is the d. of my heart   CAREY 130:26
which was my lady's d.   CAT 136:22
darlings: wealthy curled d.   SHAK 473:22
Dar'st: D. thou, Cassius   SHAK 448:14
dart: Time shall throw a d.   BROW 97:25
darter: d. es died o' the fever   TENN 544:5
darts: fiery d. of the wicked   BIBLE 78:10
Dasein: grössten Genuss vom D.   NIET 363:9
Dash: D. down yon cup of Samian
    BYRON 123:4
dashing: d. Swiss officer'   RUSS 412:22
dastard: d. in war   SCOTT 417:10
dastards: commands, and d. me   BROW 96:7
dat: Inopi beneficium bis d.   PUBL 402:3
data: theorize before one has d.   DOYLE 192:7
date: keep them up to d.   SHAW 496:25
dated: music should never be d.   GOLD 232:29
dateless: d. bargain to engrossing
    SHAK 483:31
dates: Manna and d.   KEATS 289:20
three d. on their slates   CARR 134:18
very few D. in this History   AUST 22:19
daubed: d. it with slime   BIBLE 46:41
daughter: alive will ever rear a d.   GAY 222:12
all to my elder d.   THOM 547:18
bailiff's d. of Islington   BALL 30:9
Carnage is Thy d.   WORD 578:21
Cato's d.   SHAK 449:16
'D. am I in my mother's   KIPL 301:20
d. of a hundred Earls   TENN 537:26
d. of debate   ELIZ 205:27
D. of the Vine to Spouse   FITZ 213:1
d. of the gods   TENN 533:6
d. of Zion is left   BIBLE 57:16
d. went through the river   BUNY 107:37
death of your d. would   AUST 23:18
Duke-and-a-Duchess's d.   BARH 33:26
Elderly ugly d.   GILB 229:2
farmer's d. hath soft brown   CALV 127:10
Gigantic d. of the West   TENN 533:28
gold for the king's d.   SWIN 530:17
had taken his little d.   LONG 317:20
I am the d. of Earth   SHEL 500:7
King's d. is all glorious   PRAY 392:17
landlord's d.   NOYES 364:13
loved the bailiff's d.   BALL 30:7
maxims preaching down a d.'s   TENN 538:22
my ducats! O my d.   SHAK 466:18
My father had a d. lov'd   SHAK 489:7
One fair d. and no more   SHAK 432:21
put your d. on the stage   COW 163:21
so is her d.   BIBLE 60:33
sole d. of my house   BYRON 120:17
Stern d. of the voice of God   WORD 579:15
Still harping on my d.   SHAK 432:6
this Lord Ullin's d.   CAMP 129:2
Translated D.   AUDEN 18:4
What Cato's d. durst not   ROWE 410:25
Who married Noah's d.   AYT 24:7
yet more beautiful d.   HOR 259:22
youngest virgin-d. of the skies   DRYD 197:32
daughters: be none of Beauty's d.
    BYRON 125:27
came in unto the d. of men   BIBLE 45:33
d. may be as the polished   PRAY 399:12

d. of musick shall be brought   BIBLE 56:11
I am all the d. of my father's   SHAK 489:8
Kings' d. were among thy   PRAY 392:16
so curses all Eve's d.   SHAK 469:14
sweet her artless d.   KEATS 292:16
Words are men's d.   MADD 326:19
words are the d. of earth   JOHN 281:6
ye d. of Jerusalem   BIBLE 56:16
your d. shall prophesy   BIBLE 61:15
Daumier: one small Goya or a D.
    AUDEN 19:16
daunte: whom death could not d.   BALL 31:8
dauntless: d. child   GRAY 235:18
D. the slug-horn to my   BROW 99:30
so d. in war   SCOTT 417:9
dauphin: kingdom of daylight's d.
    HOPK 257:4
David: D. his ten thousands   BIBLE 50:13
D. in the midst   SMART 509:2
D. wrote the Psalms   NAYL 360:10
Teste D. cum Sibylla   CEL 138:5
Though D. had his Jonathan   HERB 247:5
Davy: D. Abominated gravy   BENT 41:6
Davy Jones: if D. were after you   DICK 176:10
daw: I am no wiser than a d.   SHAK 445:20
dawn: catch and to reflect the d.   MAC 323:11
d. comes up like thunder   KIPL 301:5
D. shall over Lethe break   BELL 39:22
Dreaming when D.'s Left   FITZ 212:6
dusk and d. many a head   MULL 359:1
face and a grey d. breaking   MAS 334:4
I said to d.: Be sudden   THOM 548:12
moon on my left and the d.   BELL 39:16
music of its trees at d.   ARN 14:1
Rosy-fingered d.   HOMER 254:5
through night hooting at d.   BEER 38:2
We'd see truth d. together   BROW 99:2
Will sing at d.   BROW 97:27
dawns: It d. in Asia   HOUS 262:13
strange as in dark summer d.   TENN 542:4
day: all in one d.   BOIL 89:11
alternate Night and D.   FITZ 212:13
arrow that flieth by d.   PRAY 395:21
at least in this thy d.   BIBLE 71:3
Believe each d. that has   HOR 258:16
benight our happiest d.   DONNE 188:20
blinds let through the d.   HOUS 265:2
breaks the blank d.   TENN 536:6
bright d. is done   SHAK 424:2
burden and heat of the d.   BIBLE 67:15
bursts of open d. between   FRY 220:5
business of the day in the d.   WELL 568:2
close the drama with the d.   BERK 41:20
compare thee to a summer's d.   SHAK 492:28
d. and a night Love sang   SWIN 528:24
d. and night shall not   BIBLE 45:37
d. becomes more solemn   SHEL 501:7
d. be never so longe   HAWES 243:3
d. brought back my night   MILT 351:14
D. by day   PRAY 384:18
d. in a pillar of a cloud   BIBLE 47:21
d. in which he was taken   BIBLE 73:20
d. is at hand   BIBLE 75:24
d. is gone   KEATS 292:13
d. joins the past Eternity   BYRON 121:4
d. of his wrath is come   BIBLE 81:30
d. of small nations has   CHAM 139:6
d. of the Lord is near   BIBLE 61:17
d. of vengeance of our   BIBLE 60:8
d. perish wherein I was   BIBLE 52:11
d. returns too soon   BYRON 125:26
d. Rose with delight   KING 296:13
d.'s at the morn   BROW 103:21
d.'s dead sanctities   THOM 548:15
d.'s disasters in his   GOLD 231:2
d. star arise in your hearts   BIBLE 80:34
d. that comes betwixt   CAREY 130:27
d. Thou gavest   ELL 206:7
d. which the Lord hath   PRAY 398:2
death of each d.'s life   SHAK 460:8

death was a dark cold d.	AUDEN 19:2
each d. dies with sleep	HOPK 256:21
encounter such a d. as this	AUST 22:10
end of this d.'s business	SHAK 451:33
everlasting d.	DONNE 187:23
Farewell night, welcome d.	BUNY 107:37
foul and fair a d.	SHAK 458:9
from d.'s detested glare	POPE 381:9
garden in the cool of the d.	BIBLE 45:16
Good things of d. begin	SHAK 461:14
go w'en de great d. comes	HARR 242:17
greater light to rule the d.	BIBLE 45:3
guest that tarrieth but a d.	BIBLE 62:18
hair the eyes of D.	SHEL 505:3
have known a better d.	SCOTT 416:8
I have lost a d.	TITUS 551:6
it is not yet near d.	SHAK 483:13
It was Thy d.	CRAS 169:6
joint-labourer with the d.	SHAK 429:11
Joy ruľ'd the d.	DRYD 197:18
lark at break of d.	SHAK 493:6
left alone with our d.	AUDEN 20:17
long d. wanes	TENN 544:3
more unto the perfect d.	BIBLE 53:19
morning were the first d.	BIBLE 45:1
mouth of the dying d.	AUDEN 19:2
murmur of a summer's d.	ARN 14:11
my arms till break of d.	AUDEN 19:17
night be turned to d.	PRAY 399:5
night do penance for a d.	WORD 580:18
night of this immortal d.	SHEL 503:14
no proper time of d.	HOOD 254:27
Now's the d.	BURNS 114:34
ofte a myrie someris d.	CHAU 144:8
one d. in thy courts	PRAY 395:13
One d. telleth another	PRAY 390:11
'Our d. is our loss	AUDEN 20:15
perfect d. nor night	SHAK 446:17
posteriors of this d.	SHAK 457:13
profit every d. that Fate	HOR 259:18
rainy d. and a contentious	BIBLE 54:39
Round the feet of the d.	SWIN 528:16
shall not burn thee by d.	PRAY 398:9
singer of an empty d.	MORR 358:9
snatches a nice d. away	HOR 261:15
Spirit on the Lord's d.	BIBLE 81:11
stand at the latter d.	BIBLE 52:31
succeeds thy little d.	PEAC 370:20
Sufficient unto the d.	BIBLE 64:32
take the whole long d.	ROSS 409:11
that each d. is like a year	WILDE 572:15
There is no d. for me	SHAK 491:1
There's night and d.	BORR 90:4
this long weary d. have end	SPEN 515:26
thou d. in night	SHAK 483:7
thousand Blossoms with the D.	FITZ 212:8
Underneath D.'s azure	SHEL 501:23
Until the d. break	BIBLE 56:24
what a d. may bring forth	BIBLE 54:36
while d. stood distinct	HARDY 241:19
who dwell in realms of D.	BLAKE 85:18
Without all hope of d.	MILT 350:15
with some streaks of d.	SHAK 461:15
withstand in the evil d.	BIBLE 78:10
Would seem a winter's d.	ROCH 406:20
daybreak: vision Of d.	SASS 415:3
white tremendous d.	BROO 94:29
day-dreams: Like the d. of melancholy	
	DRYD 197:16
daye: d. very meete and conveniente	
	MORE 357:20
dayeseye: it calle may the 'd.'	CHAU 143:31
day-labour: 'Doth God exact d.	MILT 351:10
daylight: abed and d. slumber	HOUS 262:15
all the long and lone d.	SHEL 505:2
Between the dark and the d.	LONG 316:9
kingdom of d.'s dauphin	HOPK 257:4
methinks is but the d. sick	SHAK 468:20
see a church by d.	SHAK 472:5
We burn d.	SHAK 469:6

Dayrolles: Give D. a chair	CHES 146:9
days: all the d. of my life	PRAY 390:22
all the works and d.	ELIOT 203:19
because the d. are evil	BIBLE 78:4
behold these present d.	SHAK 494:20
best d. of life	VIRG 560:16
broader lands and better d.	CHUR 150:3
burnt-out ends of smoky d.	ELIOT 204:7
cause that the former d.	BIBLE 55:20
Chequer-board of Nights and D.	FITZ 213:5
d. are in the yellow leaf	BYRON 125:11
d. are swifter than a weaver's	BIBLE 52:18
d. dividing lover and lover	SWIN 528:17
d. of golden dreams	BRON 93:24
d. of his pilgrimage vanish	LEAR 311:24
d. of Methuselah were nine	BIBLE 45:31
d. of our youth are	BYRON 125:29
d. of wine and roses	DOWS 191:13
d. seem lank and long	GILB 228:29
d. that are no more	TENN 542:2
d. will finish up the year	SHAK 446:18
drawing d. out	SHAK 450:3
dream of the d. when work	CHES 147:22
end my d. in a tavern	ANON 10:14
fair d. will shine	GILB 228:15
fall'n on evil d.	MILT 348:28
from the d. that have been	BULW 107:1
good d. speed and depart	MART 331:11
I am but two d. old	BLAKE 88:1
In the d. ere I was born	BLUNT 89:5
in the midst of his d.	BIBLE 60:25
length of d. understanding	BIBLE 52:24
Length of d. is in her	BIBLE 53:16
life with multitude of d.	JOHN 283:1
man in his hasty d.	BRID 92:10
number of my d.	PRAY 391:30
of a woman is of few d.	BIBLE 52:26
of d. in goodness spent	BYRON 125:22
our d. on the earth are	BIBLE 51:39
O ye Nights, and D.	PRAY 384:22
see better d.	BEHN 38:15
see good d.	PRAY 391:23
seemed unto him but a few d.	BIBLE 46:21
Six d. shalt thou labour	BIBLE 47:24
teach us to number our d.	PRAY 395:20
that thy d. may be long	BIBLE 47:24
These are not dark d.	CHUR 150:8
these fair well-spoken d.	SHAK 480:19
up the story of our d.	RAL 404:15
We have seen better d.	SHAK 486:9
What are d.	LARK 310:3
day-star: So sinks the d.	MILT 343:17
daysyes: men callen d. in our toun	
	CHAU 143:30
day-time: I cry in the d.	PRAY 390:16
dazzled: flowed in it d. their eyes	BALL 31:3
shrine d. by your brilliance	SCH 415:9
De: doctrine of the enclitic D.	BROW 101:1
Deacons: D., with true knowledge	
	PRAY 385:18
dead: act as if we were d.	POUND 383:15
After the singer is d.	STEV 523:1
all our best men are d.	PUNCH 403:2
all the rest are d.	LONG 316:8
another Bishop d.	MELB 336:19
any man fears to be d.	BACON 27:41
barrows of the happier d.	TENN 543:13
be a fool than to be d.	STEV 522:3
being d. unto sin	PRAY 388:10
Beside the Severn's d.	HOUS 262:13
Better be with the d.	SHAK 461:12
Blessed are the d. which	BIBLE 82:18
character d. at every word	SHER 506:29
charity more than the d.	ARN 12:20
cheer a d. man's sweetheart	HOUS 263:11
Christ risen from the d.	BIBLE 76:22
clamorous o'er her d.	SHEL 499:16
Come not, when I am d.	TENN 533:2
conference With the d.	WEBS 566:22
converse with the mighty d.	THOM 549:24

d., and buried	PRAY 384:26
d. Are but as pictures	SHAK 460:11
dead bury their d.	BIBLE 65:19
d., but in the Elysian	DISR 185:25
d. Did squeak and gibber	SHAK 429:12
D. flies cause the ointment	BIBLE 56:1
D., for a ducat	SHAK 435:1
D. from the waist down	BROW 101:1
d. hour of the night	BALL 32:2
d. leaf thou mightest bear	SHEL 502:12
d. or my watch has stopped	MARX 333:1
d. shall be raised incorruptible	BIBLE 76:29
d. shall live	DRYD 197:25
d. there is no rivalry	MAC 324:9
d., the sweet musician	LONG 317:14
d. thing that smells sweet	THOM 547:17
d. we owe only truth	VOLT 561:19
d. which he slew at his	BIBLE 49:28
d. whose pupils we have	BUTL 119:21
d., who will not fight	GREN 236:15
d. woman bites not	GRAY 234:13
democracy of the d.	CHES 148:5
dew on the face of the d.	BEERS 36:3
England mourns for her d.	BINY 84:9
Evelyn Hope is d.	BROW 100:25
Faith without works is d.	BIBLE 80:12
famous, calm, and d.	BROW 100:34
fell at his feet as d.	BIBLE 81:14
fortnight d.	ELIOT 205:6
frightful when one's d.	POPE 377:16
gaze the strengthless d.	HOUS 263:3
generally shammin' when 'e's d.	KIPL 299:9
God is d.	NIET 363:6
God is d.	NERV 360:25
Harrow the house of the d.	AUDEN 20:7
Hector is d.	SHAK 487:18
He is d. and gone	SHAK 435:33
Here d. lie we because	HOUS 266:3
himself must be d.	AUST 23:29
his brother is d.	BIBLE 46:35
if I am d. he would like	HOLL 253:3
'If Lucy should be d.	WORD 582:10
if the d. rise not	BIBLE 76:24
I lain for a century d.	TENN 540:12
imagined for the mighty d.	KEATS 289:1
immortal d. who live again	ELIOT 201:27
I should be d. of joy	BROW 101:21
It struck him d.	BELL 39:29
I would that I were d.	TENN 539:23
judge the quick and the d.	PRAY 384:26
King of all these the d.	HOMER 254:6
King of Spain is d.	FARQ 210:23
kissed by the English d.	OWEN 367:6
ladies d. and lovely knights	SHAK 494:19
Lady Dalhousie are d.	MCG 325:5
lane to the land of the d.	AUDEN 18:10
lasting mansions of the d.	COWP 168:10
living among the d.	BIBLE 71:16
Living and the noble D.	WORD 580:24
Lovely lads and d. and rotten	HOUS 263:19
Lycidas is d.	MILT 343:2
maid is not d., but sleepeth	BIBLE 65:27
Mistah Kurtz—he d.	CONR 161:1
much less when he's d.	DICK 178:23
my enemy is d.	WHIT 570:11
My lady's sparrow is d.	CAT 136:22
mysel' were d. and gane	BALL 32:11
Nobody heard him, the d. man	SMITH 510:26
not d.—but gone before	ROG 407:8
once d. by fate	BEAU 36:1
out ten to see a d. Indian	SHAK 485:8
over the rich D.	BROO 94:7
Past bury its d.	LONG 317:3
profane the service of the d.	SHAK 437:3
quite for ever d.	CONG 160:16
Rejoice ye d.	BRID 92:18
resurrection of the d.	BIBLE 76:22
resurrection of the d.	BIBLE 76:27
resuscitate the d. art Of poetry	POUND 383:1
sculptur'd d. on each side	KEATS 289:10

sea gave up the d. which	BIBLE 82:29	
Sea shall give up her d.	PRAY 400:4	
she has been d. many times	PATER 369:19	
she's d.	DONNE 187:20	
simplify me when I'm d.	DOUG 191:9	
Since faith is d.	WYATT 583:20	
sleeps with the enduring d.	SHEL 499:19	
Smiling the boy fell d.	BROW 101:16	
stepping-stones Of their d. selves		
	TENN 535:33	
strikes him d. for thine	TENN 542:7	
talk with the departed d.	SHEL 501:6	
'thanked God my wife was d.	BROW 106:1	
that are d. to sin	BIBLE 74:43	
That d. men rise up never	SWIN 529:25	
that's a d. donkey	DICK 182:38	
their home among the d.	SHEL 500:10	
their wages and are d.	HOUS 265:7	
There are no d.	MAET 326:20	
they found him with the d.	WILDE 572:7	
they told me you were d.	CORY 163:4	
This my son was d.	BIBLE 70:21	
thou being d. art a God	SWIN 530:7	
though d. with frost ere now	GREV 236:17	
'tis Death is d.	SHEL 499:22	
to my d. heart run them	STEV 523:11	
Towns contend for HOMER D.	ANON 7:14	
tuneful brethren all were d.	SCOTT 416:9	
two months d.	SHAK 429:28	
Tyrawley and I have been d.	CHES 146:7	
up with our English d.	SHAK 443:21	
very d. of Winter	ANDR 4:7	
voice of the d. was a living	TENN 537:23	
was beauty's summer d.	SHAK 494:18	
'we are all d.'	KEYN 296:2	
wench is d.	MARL 329:22	
what was d. was Hope	WILDE 572:13	
when she was d.	GOLD 231:8	
Where d. men meet on lips	BUTL 119:17	
Wherefore I praised the d.	BIBLE 55:14	
where there was not one d.	BIBLE 47:19	
Who was alive and is d.	ANON 5:15	
wished to see my d. body	HARDY 241:18	
within full of d. men's bones	BIBLE 67:25	
your remind me of the d.	SASS 414:15	
youth stone d.	SASS 414:11	
deadly: all other d. sin	PRAY 385:16	
species is more d. than	KIPL 299:4	
Dead March: you can hear the D. play		
	KIPL 298:20	
Deadwood: Tucson and D. and Lost		
	BENET 40:19	
deaf: chamber d. to noise	SIDN 507:21	
happen to be d. and dumb	HOUS 266:9	
He is as d. as a door	BRET 92:4	
To their d. pillows	SHAK 462:26	
turn the d. ear	SWIFT 527:27	
union of a d. man	COL 157:19	
woman's d.	POPE 380:26	
deafen'd: loudest wit I e'er was d.		
	BYRON 124:11	
deafer: d. than the blue-eyed cat	TENN 534:23	
deafness: mother's d. is very trifling		
	AUST 22:12	
tale, sir, would cure d.	SHAK 484:25	
deal: d. by speech than by letter	BACON 26:37	
d. with life as children	COWP 165:11	
don't d. in lies	KIPL 299:22	
great d. of gold	JAMES 271:33	
himself be given a square d.	ROOS 408:7	
is a great d. to be said	BENT 41:5	
new d. for the American	ROOS 407:17	
to be given a square d.	ROOS 408:3	
dealbabor: et super nivem d.	BIBLE 83:6	
dealer: d. in magic and spells	GILB 229:2	
dealing: common-sense and plain d.		
	EMER 207:11	
peradventure with whom they are d.		
	WILS 575:2	
Whose own hard d. teaches	SHAK 466:4	

Dean: cushion and soft D. invite	POPE 378:4	
D. of Christ Church	SPR 517:11	
may clothe an English d.	COWP 167:35	
no dogma, no D.	DISR 185:23	
not do as the d. pleases	AUDEN 21:4	
was an old person of D.	LEAR 313:2	
deans: dowagers for d.	TENN 541:27	
dear: days when I was d. to you	HOR 260:27	
d. and kindly paternal	DANTE 171:12	
d. Brutus	SHAK 448:17	
d., deluding Woman	BURNS 113:25	
D. heart how like you	WYATT 583:22	
d. to me as are the rud	SHAK 449:15	
d. to me in the middle	LAWR 311:3	
make thee terrible and d.	SHEL 505:2	
Plato is d. to me	ARIS 12:12	
right d. in the sight	PRAY 397:22	
sold cheap what is most d.	SHAK 495:3	
that bread should be so d.	HOOD 255:8	
this dear, d. land	SHAK 478:20	
too convincing—dangerously d.		
	BYRON 121:34	
too d. for my possessing	SHAK 494:13	
was to all the country d.	GOLD 230:22	
dearer: d. still is truth	ARIS 12:12	
D. than self	BYRON 120:12	
d. was the mother	COL 157:9	
law of thy mouth is d.	PRAY 398:5	
little d. than his horse	TENN 538:19	
dearest: assure you she's the d. girl		
	DICK 177:14	
d., you're a dunce	JOHN 278:30	
near'st and d. enemy	SHAK 439:36	
To throw away the d. thing	SHAK 458:22	
dearie: thinking on my d.	BURNS 112:36	
Dearly: D. beloved brethren	PRAY 384:9	
D. beloved	PRAY 388:24	
dearth: measure in a year of d.	BLAKE 88:18	
pine within and suffer d.	SHAK 495:13	
death: added a new terror to d.	WETH 569:6	
added another terror to d.	LYND 321:17	
After the first d.	THOM 547:8	
All in the valley of D.	TENN 532:23	
allotted d. and hell	MARL 329:13	
ancients dreaded d.	HARE 242:3	
any man's d. diminishes	DONNE 190:20	
apprehends d. no more dreadfully		
	SHAK 464:25	
are at the point of d.	SHAK 483:29	
arms of cool-enfolding d.	WHIT 571:13	
back resounded, D.	MILT 347:2	
bargain to engrossing d.	SHAK 483:31	
battles and d.	GAR 221:10	
Be absolute for d.	SHAK 464:8	
beauteous d.	VAUG 555:20	
be carnally minded is d.	BIBLE 75:7	
been studied in his d.	SHAK 458:22	
Be thou faithful unto d.	BIBLE 81:17	
bitterness of d. is past	BIBLE 50:5	
blaze forth the d. of princes	SHAK 449:18	
bosom black as d.	SHAK 434:28	
bridegroom in my d.	SHAK 423:11	
brother of d. exacteth	BROW 95:24	
brother of d. exacteth	BROW 96:1	
Brother to D.	FLET 215:22	
Brought d. into the world	MILT 344:20	
build your ship of d.	LAWR 311:8	
canoniz'd bones hearsed in d.	SHAK 430:24	
can this be d.	POPE 376:4	
chance, and d., and mutability	SHEL 503:2	
come away, d.	SHAK 489:4	
competition the laws of d.	RUSK 412:10	
consenting unto his d.	BIBLE 73:29	
copulation and d.	ELIOT 204:12	
couragious whom d. could not daunte		
	BALL 31:8	
cry'd out, D.	MILT 347:2	
darkness and the shadow of d.	BIBLE 52:20	
days shall men seek d.	BIBLE 82:7	
d. after life does greatly	SPEN 516:8	

D. alone reveals how small	JUV 288:3	
D. and his brother Sleep	SHEL 500:8	
D. and Morning on the silver	TENN 542:16	
D. and Night incessantly	WHIT 570:11	
D. and Toil	VIRG 558:21	
d., a necessary end	SHAK 449:18	
d.; a thousand doors	SEN 420:11	
d. bandaged my eyes	BROW 103:32	
D. be not proud	DONNE 189:5	
d. brag thou wander'st	SHAK 492:28	
D. broke at once the vital	JOHN 279:1	
d. came with friendly care	COL 156:18	
d. canonizes and sanctifies	BURKE 109:5	
D. closes all	TENN 544:3	
d. complete the same	BROW 104:13	
D. devours all lovely things	MILL 339:29	
D.! ere thou hast slain	BROW 97:25	
d. gnaweth upon them	PRAY 393:1	
D. goes dogging everywhere	HENL 245:6	
D. has a thousand doors	MASS 336:1	
D. has made His darkness	TENN 537:3	
D. hath asses' ears	BEDD 36:27	
d. hath no more dominion	BIBLE 75:2	
D. hath so many doors	FLET 215:11	
D. hath this also	BACON 26:4	
d.,' he said	SCOTT 418:23	
D., I do conceive myself	BROW 96:19	
D., in itself	DRYD 195:26	
D. is a fearful thing	SHAK 464:14	
d. is as a lover's pinch	SHAK 424:12	
d. is most in apprehension	SHAK 464:11	
D. is still working like	HERB 247:23	
d. is the cure of all diseases	BROW 97:2	
D. is the end of life	TENN 539:15	
D. is the privilege	ROWE 410:24	
D. joins us to the great	YOUNG 588:13	
D. kicks his way equally	HOR 259:13	
D. lays his icy hand	SHIR 507:2	
D. lies dead	SWIN 529:20	
D. lies on her like	SHAK 483:22	
D. must be distinguished	SMITH 511:23	
d. my days should expiate	SHAK 493:1	
D. never takes the wise	LA F 306:22	
d. no one so true Did share	SHAK 489:4	
d. of a political economist	BAG 29:12	
d. of each day's life	SHAK 460:8	
d. of your daughter would	AUST 23:18	
D. opens unknown doors	MAS 334:1	
D. put down his book	AUDEN 20:19	
d.'s a great disguiser	SHAK 465:1	
d.'s counterfeit	SHAK 460:23	
d. shall have no dominion	THOM 546:19	
d.'s pale flag is not	SHAK 483:30	
D.'s second self	SHAK 494:7	
D.'s self is sorry	JONS 284:2	
D.'s shadow at the door	BLUN 89:2	
D. stands above me	LAND 308:19	
d. that is immortal has	LUCR 320:9	
d. the journey's end	DRYD 197:10	
D., the poor man's dearest	BURNS 114:24	
D. therefore is nothing	LUCR 320:8	
d. they were not divided	BIBLE 50:17	
d., thou shalt die	DONNE 189:6	
D. tramples it to fragments	SHEL 499:26	
d. unloads thee	SHAK 464:9	
D. was but A scientific	WILDE 572:12	
D., whene'er he call	GILB 229:7	
D., where is thy sting-a-ling-a-ling	ANON 7:4	
d., where is thy sting	BIBLE 77:1	
D., where is thy sting	ROSS 408:20	
d. who had the soldier	DOUG 191:10	
D. will be aghast and so	CEL 138:6	
D. will come when thou	SHEL 505:4	
d. will have his day	SHAK 479:8	
D. will listen to your	SHEL 504:25	
D., without rhetoric	SIEY 508:7	
decent hall of d.	CHES 147:12	
direful d. indeed they	FLEM 214:25	
disqualified by the accident of d.	CHES 148:5	
Doubled the globe of d.	THOM 547:4	

decayed: d. hole among the mountains
ELIOT 205:10
you are sufficiently d. GILB 227:18
decaying: we are but d. HERR 248:26
decays: Mere glimmering and d. VAUG 555:19
decease: d. calls me forth WHIT 570:13
decede: d. peritis HOR 259:6
deceit: d., and lust DONNE 190:4
I am not up to small d. HARTE 242:32
used no d. in his tongue PRAY 390:4
deceitful: bloodthirsty and d. man
PRAY 389:23
children of men are d. PRAY 393:20
d. and a virgin renowned HOR 261:2
from the d. and wicked man PRAY 392:10
heart is d. above all things BIBLE 60:24
deceitfulness: Cat of such d. and suavity
ELIOT 203:26
deceits: all the d. of the world PRAY 385:16
fables, and dangerous d. PRAY 400:9
prophesy d. BIBLE 58:26
Deceive: D. boys with toys LYS 321:18
d. you with vain words BIBLE 78:3
don't d. me ANON 5:3
first we practise to d. SCOTT 417:19
let not Time d. you AUDEN 18:10
they lie in wait to d. BIBLE 77:28
we d. ourselves BIBLE 81:3
Who could d. a lover VIRG 558:12
deceived: Adam was not d. BIBLE 79:10
d. the mother of mankind MILT 344:23
is still d. with ornament SHAK 467:10
should we desire to be d. BUTL 117:10
woman being d. was BIBLE 79:10
deceiver: I'm a gay d. COLM 159:2
thou kind d. DRYD 195:17
deceivers: Men were d. ever SHAK 472:16
deceiveth: d. his own heart BIBLE 80:11
deceiving: arched roof in words d.
MILT 344:13
d., could no longer harm ELIOT 202:20
d. mirror of self-love MASS 335:22
d. your own selves BIBLE 80:10
She d., I believing SEDL 419:11
December: D. when they wed SHAK 426:23
In a drear-nighted D. KEATS 293:3
old D.'s bareness SHAK 494:16
rain and wind beat dark D. SHAK 428:15
Their meetings made D. June TENN 537:12
Tomorrow comes D. HOUS 265:1
Decembers: fifteen wild D. BRON 93:22
decencies: to dwell in d. for ever POPE 377:23
decency: believe in an ultimate d.
STEV 522:15
want of d. is want of sense ROOS 408:11
decent: aristocracy to what is d. HOPE 255:29
d. hall of death CHES 147:12
d. obscurity of a learned GIBB 224:19
decently: be done d. and in order BIBLE 76:13
deceptive: d. are the visions VIRG 559:3
decerated: d. dark red as I have somber
ASHF 17:8
decide: comes the moment to d. LOW 319:12
d. such a great dispute VIRG 559:20
decidimus: Nos ubi d. HOR 261:10
decimal: adapted to them the d. system
NAP 359:13
decision: multitudes in the valley of d.
BIBLE 61:17
will or d. or reason CHOM 148:16
deck: d. put on its leaves again FLEC 214:19
stood on the burning d. HEM 244:20
to d. her mistress' head BYRON 125:24
Walk the d. my Captain lies WHIT 570:8
deck'd: should duly have been d. SPEN 515:27
thy bride-bed to have d. SHAK 437:6
decks: he fell upon their d. TENN 543:4
declaim: d.; and when you are calculating
JOHN 277:8
declamatio: Ut pueris placeas et d. JUV 288:2

declare: d., if thou hast understanding
BIBLE 53:2
d. the wonders that he PRAY 397:7
heavens d. the glory PRAY 390:11
nothing to d. WILDE 573:36
ye are to d. it PRAY 388:23
declension: by this d. SHAK 432:2
déclin: d. de l'amour se font sentir
LA B 306:13
decline: are ready to d. SHAK 451:27
D.-and-Fall-Off DICK 181:6
idea of writing the d. GIBB 224:16
Morn in weary Night's d. BLAKE 86:1
declined: dear Carrie rightly d. GROS 237:1
decoration: descended to construct a
d. TROL 552:16
decorum: athwart Goes all d. SHAK 463:11
Dulce et d. est pro patria HOR 260:17
hunt D. down BYRON 124:26
Let them cant about d. BURNS 114:20
decree: Can alter a d. established SHAK 468:3
d. from Caesar Augustus BIBLE 69:8
dost hear de D. WHAR 569:10
establish the d. BIBLE 61:7
Decreed: D. in the market place POUND 383:8
own soul has to itself d. KEATS 292:7
decrees: contrary to the d. of Caesar
BIBLE 74:9
decrepitude: their d., their decay
LAND 309:13
decus: praesidium et dulce d. HOR 259:8
dede: leff woord and tak the d. LYDG 321:4
dedicate: larger sense we cannot d.
LINC 314:23
dedicated: dreariness in d. spirits FRY 219:23
dedication: d. of his life to me ELIOT 201:29
dedis: gentil that dooth gentil d. CHAU 143:25
deductions: long train of d. DOYLE 192:35
Dee: Across the sands of D. KING 296:25
Lived on the river D. BICK 83:28
deed: attempt and not the d. SHAK 460:4
beest is d. he hath no peyne CHAU 142:17
bloody d. SHAK 435:2
blow the horrid d. SHAK 459:6
both in will and d. PRAY 386:15
d. is all GOET 230:5
d. of dreadful note SHAK 461:13
d. without a name SHAK 462:5
Fit for the d. I had to do CARR 135:26
good d. in a naughty SHAK 468:5
Grisilde is d. CHAU 142:9
If one good d. in all my SHAK 486:18
I have done the d. SHAK 460:6
Shadow of Shadows on the d. YEATS 584:18
she if oon of hem were d. CHAU 141:16
To do the right d. ELIOT 204:4
whatever time the d. took place ELIOT 203:26
When the d. was done WORD 580:9
worse d. HENRY 245:17
deeds: because their d. were evil BIBLE 71:39
D., not words shall speak FLET 215:15
d. that some knights used CAXT 138:4
d. which should not pass BYRON 120:32
Foul d. will rise SHAK 430:16
My d. upon my head SHAK 468:1
nameless in worthy d. BROW 97:17
Our d. determine us ELIOT 200:12
Our d. still travel with ELIOT 201:14
sager sort our d. reprove CAT 136:25
Seeking His secret d. ROSS 408:20
deem: In doubt to d. himself POPE 379:12
deep: commit his body to the d. PRAY 400:4
day have I been in the d. BIBLE 77:12
d. almost as life WORD 579:8
D. as first love TENN 542:4
D. in the shady sadness KEATS 289:33
d. like as with a garment PRAY 396:18
d. sense of some deathless WEBS 567:4
d. upon her peerless eyes KEATS 291:15
D. versed in books MILT 350:10

d. where Holland lies GOLD 231:27
great deep to the great d. TENN 534:3
hath made the d. as dry KIPL 303:5
have they not buried me d. TENN 540:15
heard the d. behind him TENN 535:23
her arms along the d. proudly CAMP 128:14
himself in terms too d. GILB 227:21
his wonders in the d. PRAY 397:9
house with d. thatch BELL 40:11
in the cradle of the d. WILL 574:7
lowest d. a lower deep MILT 347:15
Not d. the Poet sees ARN 14:7
often lie too d. for tears WORD 579:14
One d. calleth another PRAY 392:8
one is of the d. STEP 518:22
Out of the d. have I called PRAY 398:23
sea my love is d. LEAR 311:26
singularly d. young man GILB 227:21
'tis not so d. as a well SHAK 483:3
too d. for his hearers GOLD 231:17
unadornèd bosom of the d. MILT 340:25
upon the face of the d. BIBLE 44:22
when the remorseless d. MILT 343:7
deeper: d. than did ever plummet
SHAK 485:24
Her eyes were d. than ROSS 409:14
shown a d. sense of her loss GASK 222:3
Deep-hearted: D. man BROW 98:8
Deep-meadow'd: D., happy TENN 535:27
deer: Around the dying d. AYT 24:10
hunting the beautiful d. AUDEN 18:8
I was a stricken d. COWP 167:1
let the stricken d. go SHAK 434:16
deeth: be lad Toward his d. CHAU 142:24
man after his d. moot wepe CHAU 142:17
defaced: Antiquities are history d.
BACON 24:18
defacing: Defaming and d. TENN 535:15
Defamed: D. by every charlatan TENN 537:17
Defaming: D. and defacing TENN 535:15
défauts: Quelle âme est sans d. RIMB 406:8
defeat: are triumph and d. LONG 316:27
in d., defiance CHUR 150:25
possibilities of d. VICT 556:18
this world's d. VAUG 555:12
defeated: d. were us LIVY 315:12
Down with the d. LIVY 315:11
safe course for the d. VIRG 558:7
defect: chief of Henry King BELL 38:34
this fair d. Of Nature MILT 349:23
Defects: Christian beauty D. POUND 383:8
In our plain d. FRY 219:25
defence: at one gate to make d. MILT 350:22
cant in d. of savages JOHN 279:19
D., not defiance ANON 5:1
d. of England you no longer BALD 29:28
d. or apology before you CHAR 140:17
fight in d. of one's country HOMER 254:2
house of d. very high PRAY 395:22
Lord is thy d. upon thy PRAY 398:9
ready in d. BURKE 109:23
defences: d. of peace must be constructed
ANON 7:16
defend: d. my cause against PRAY 392:10
D., O Lord, this thy Child PRAY 388:22
D. the bad against DAY-L 172:23
d. to the death your right VOLT 561:24
D. us thy humble servants PRAY 385:2
foremost to d. BYRON 124:40
Le ciel d. MOL 353:26
mercy d. us from all perils PRAY 385:10
Quand on l'attaque il se d. ANON 9:4
we shall d. our island CHUR 149:31
whom he had promised to d. MAC 323:21
defended: these d. HOUS 265:7
defending: sake of d. those who do
BLAKE 87:11
defends: when attacked it d. itself ANON 9:4
defensoribus: Non tali auxilio nec d.
VIRG 558:9

defer: 'tis madness to d. YOUNG 588:3
deference: d. due to me GILB 227:9
deferred: Hope d. maketh the heart
BIBLE 53:35
defiance: Defence, not d. ANON 5:1
d. in their eye GOLD 231:28
deficiant: Quod si d. vires PROP 401:16
deficiente: Et teneam moriens d. manu
TIB 550:34
defied: Age will not be d. BACON 27:6
défier: honteux de se d. de ses amis
LA R 310:10
defiled: toucheth pitch shall be d. BIBLE 63:2
defileth: into the mouth d. a man BIBLE 66:28
define: know how to d. it THOM 546:6
To d. true madness SHAK 431:31
definition: by my own d. of criticism
ARN 16:1
d. of a gentleman to say NEWM 362:3
definitions: I hate d. DISR 186:40
deflower: that will her pride d. SPEN 516:13
deform'd: None can be call'd d. SHAK 490:18
deformed: of my invention prove d.
SHAK 495:17
deformity: foot the d. of which MAC 323:33
defrauding: Penalties as the d. of the
State PENN 371:16
defy: d. the devil SHAK 490:7
d. the foul fiend SHAK 454:19
d. th' Omnipotent to arms MILT 344:24
then I d. you SHAK 483:24
dégagé: half so d. COWP 165:22
Degenerate: D. Douglas WORD 578:18
degeneration: fatty d. of his moral being
STEV 521:24
dégoût: non pas des moments de d.
VOLT 561:16
degraded: wouldn't be sufficiently d.
GILB 226:26
degree: d., priority, and place SHAK 486:22
exalted them of low d. BIBLE 69:6
when d. is shak'd SHAK 486:23
Dei: Ad majorem D. gloriam ANON 10:6
vox D. ALC 3:9
deid: y'er a lang time d. ANON 4:27
deified: our own spirits are we d.
WORD 580:28
de'il: d.'s awa wi' th'Exciseman
BURNS 113:13
Deity: D. offended BURNS 113:18
desire in d. ROSS 409:22
deject: ladies most d. and wretched
SHAK 433:15
dejected: lowest and most d. thing
SHAK 455:5
Nor the d. 'haviour SHAK 429:25
delay: chides his infamous d. YOUNG 588:5
d. there lies no plenty SHAK 488:17
half-sister to D. TENN 539:19
sell, or deny, or d. MAGN 327:3
delayed: d. till I am indifferent JOHN 274:7
delaying: d. put the state to rights ENN 208:22
delays: d. are dangerous in war DRYD 197:35
D. have dangerous ends SHAK 445:22
strong through long d. OVID 366:20
Delectable: came to the D. Mountains
BUNY 107:23
delectando: Lectorem d. pariterque
monendo HOR 258:1
Delenda: D. est Carthago CATO 136:18
Delia: While D. is away JAGO 271:1
deliberate: these d. fools SHAK 467:1
Where both d. MARL 329:18
deliberates: woman that d. is lost ADD 1:20
Deliberation: D. sat and public care
MILT 346:14
delicacy: has of fortitude and d. STEV 521:4
delicate: body's d. SHAK 454:13
d. death WHIT 571:13
delight is a d. growth cramped HARDY 240:3

these d. creatures ours SHAK 475:21
they are not very d. WALP 563:15
Young ladies are d. plants AUST 22:17
Delice: with the fair flower D. SPEN 517:3
deliciae: d. meae puellae CAT 136:22
Delicias: D. domini VIRG 559:14
délicieux: il n'y en a point de d. LA R 310:11
delicious: d. story is ripe to tell AUDEN 20:22
'tis d. to hate you MOORE 356:24
deliciously: Reminiscences make one
feel so d. SHAW 497:2
Delicta: D. maiorum immeritus lues
HOR 260:25
delight: All for your d. SHAK 471:16
bind another to its d. BLAKE 87:19
By thy d. in others' pain BYRON 125:4
Commodity, Firmness, and *D.* WOTT 583:16
day Rose with d. KING 296:13
d. in conceiving an Iago KEATS 294:7
d. is a delicate growth HARDY 240:3
d. in proper young BURNS 114:17
d. of battle with my peers TENN 543:22
D. of lust is gross PETR 373:5
desire that outruns the d. SWIN 529:9
Energy is Eternal D. BLAKE 88:11
go to 't with d. SHAK 422:24
Had other aims than my d. HARDY 240:6
have relinquished one d. WORD 579:13
Him in whose company I d. BUNY 107:39
in the very temple of d. KEATS 291:15
labour we d. in physics SHAK 460:19
Let dogs d. to bark WATTS 565:17
lonely impulse of d. YEATS 585:15
Moon of my D. who know'st FITZ 213:17
My d. and thy delight BRID 92:16
my ever new d. MILT 348:14
our d. or as our treasure HERB 248:2
rejoice and d. in God TRAH 551:17
sentiments I find d. JOHN 280:21
She was a phantom of d. WORD 581:7
source of little visible d. BRON 93:25
Spirit of D. SHEL 503:25
Studies serve for d. BACON 27:15
sweetest d. of gardens BROW 95:21
Teach us d. in simple things KIPL 298:12
that give d. SHAK 485:17
Their d. is in lies PRAY 393:19
There is in d. LAND 309:1
thing met conceives d. MILT 349:13
thought that lurks in all d. MEYN 338:13
'Tis never too late for d. MOORE 356:21
to d. at once and lash POPE 378:8
to do ill our sole d. MILT 345:5
to enjoy d. with liberty SPEN 515:23
turn d. into a sacrifice HERB 246:27
unrest which men miscall d. SHEL 499:21
we have a degree of d. BURKE 108:8
with d. No more SHEL 501:15
yet I hear thy shrill d. SHEL 504:18
delighted: d. in solitude is either
BACON 26:14
d. with any thing that CONG 159:28
You have d. us long enough AUST 23:14
delightest: d. not in burnt-offerings
PRAY 393:8
delighteth: d. he in any man's legs
PRAY 399:20
king d. to honour BIBLE 52:3
delightful: all that is d. to man MILT 351:25
almost as d. LOCK 315:19
two most d. things WALP 563:13
delighting: d. the reader at the same
HOR 258:1
Delights: D. in filth and foul incontinence
SPEN 516:19
does some d. condemn MOL 353:26
his d. Were dolphin-like SHAK 423:22
midst of the fountain of d. LUCR 320:11
thee king of intimate d. COWP 167:13

delineation: happiest d. of its varieties
AUST 22:31
delinquencies: naturally indulge in a
few d. ELIOT 201:23
delinquent: condemns a less d. for't
BUTL 118:19
delirant: d. reges plectuntur HOR 258:12
delirium: All that d. of the brave
YEATS 586:19
delitabill: Storys to rede ar d. BARB 33:3
Deliver: D. Israel PRAY 391:3
d. me from the deceitful PRAY 392:1
d. my soul from the calamities PRAY 391:25
d. us PRAY 385:16
d. us from evil BIBLE 64:24
I will d. him unto you BIBLE 68:9
let him d. him PRAY 390:17
neither shall he d. any PRAY 391:20
shall d. me from the body BIBLE 75:6
delivered: God hath d. him into mine
BIBLE 50:14
hast d. my soul from death PRAY 397:20
delivereth: d. them out of their distress
PRAY 397:10
dells: In leafy d. alone HOUS 265:9
Delphos: hollow shriek the steep of D.
MILT 344:13
deluded: kind of Heaven to be d. LEE 313:9
we are all d. thus SHEL 501:4
déluge: Après nous le d. POMP 375:9
delusion: announce but that addled d.
ELIOT 201:2
d., a mockery, and a snare DENM 174:22
d. that beauty is goodness TOLS 551:11
Hence, dear d. SMITH 510:8
delusive: d. seduction of martial BURN 112:21
demand: He'll make d. of her SHAK 424:14
superfluous to d. the time of day
SHAK 437:34
Demas: D., greet you BIBLE 78:29
demd: What's the d. total DICK 180:15
demens: d.? Habitarunt di quoque
VIRG 559:16
dementat: d. prius DUP 199:15
demented: d. with the mania of owning
WHIT 570:22
demerit: preacher's merit or d. BROW 100:4
demeure: Les jours s'en vont je d.
APOL 11:11
demeurer: d. en repos dans une chambre
PASC 369:5
demi-paradise: other Eden, d. SHAK 478:20
demi-puppets: you d. SHAK 485:23
democracy: capacity for justice makes
d. NIEB 362:26
D. and proper drains BETJ 43:6
D. is only an experiment INGE 270:7
D. means simply the bludgeoning
WILDE 573:24
d. or absolute oligarchy ARIS 12:8
D. resumed her reign BELL 39:21
D. substitutes election SHAW 497:36
great arsenal of d. ROOS 407:25
idea demands...a d. PARK 368:26
It is the d. of the dead CHES 148:5
must be made safe for d. WILS 574:24
perfect d. is therefore BURKE 111:19
political experiment of d. SHAW 497:16
So Two cheers for D. FORS 217:13
thanks to wine-lees and d. BROW 98:28
that d. is the worst form CHUR 150:19
that of our Author's D. BENT 40:26
themselves grieved under a d. HOBB 251:20
democratic: aristocracy the most d.
MAC 324:16
Democritus: rideret D. HOR 259:3
demon-lover: woman wailing for her
d. COL 156:27
demonstrandum: Quod erat d. EUCL 209:1

Demosthenes: D. never comes
  unseasonably   MAC 324:9
den: hand on the cockatrice' d.   BIBLE 58:11
  made it a d. of thieves   BIBLE 67:17
denial: d. vain, and coy excuse   MILT 343:3
denied: faintly and would be d.   SHAK 480:12
  if it be but half d.   BUTL 118:11
  in my dreams you have d.   POUND 383:13
  to our moist vows d.   MILT 343:16
denies: spirit that always d.   GOET 230:1
deniges: 'Who d. of it   DICK 179:26
denk: d.' ich Heut und morgen   LESS 313:26
Denmark: All the might of D.'s CAMP 128:14
  Prince of D. being left out   SCOTT 418:34
  rotten in the state of D.   SHAK 431:2
  sure it may be so in D.   SHAK 431:16
  Than is the throne of D.   SHAK 429:20
dens: d. and in the rocks   BIBLE 81:30
  lay them down in their d.   PRAY 397:1
dentist: vulgar to talk like a d. WILDE 572:26
dents longues: le temps d'avoir les d.
         MOL 353:16
deny: d. a God destroy   BACON 25:25
  I never d.   DISR 187:5
  Life offers—to d.   HARDY 241:8
  Room to us ourselves   KEBLE 295:4
  sell, or d., or delay   MAGN 327:3
  so ingrateful you d. me   SHAK 452:31
  thou shalt d. me thrice   BIBLE 68:12
  yet will I not d. thee   BIBLE 68:13
  You must d. yourself   GOET 230:2
Deo: D. gratias   MASS 334:19
  Ille mi par esse d. videtur   CAT 137:4
deorum: Parcus d. cultor et infrequens
        HOR 260:2
depart: already it is time to d. SOCR 512:18
  court to cottage he d.   PEELE 371:8
  D.,—be off   HOLM 253:19
  d. the souls of the brave   CLOU 153:13
  Having a desire to d.   BIBLE 78:12
  he will not d. from it   BIBLE 54:22
  I am ready to d.   LAND 308:20
  servant d. in peace   BIBLE 69:12
  when the great and good d. WORD 578:8
departed: Dead he is not, but d. LONG 316:24
  d. into their own country   BIBLE 63:33
  D. never to return   BURNS 116:7
  d. this life in thy faith   PRAY 387:16
  glory is d. from Israel   BIBLE 49:40
  He d., he withdrew   CIC 151:27
  knolling a d. friend   SHAK 441:2
  Lord was d. from him   BIBLE 49:26
  our dear brother here d.   PRAY 389:13
departing: flood-ways to be far d.
        POUND 383:18
departure: so soon to regret the d.
        THOM 549:4
  their d. is taken for misery BIBLE 62:13
depend: joys of home d.   MORE 357:11
Dependance: not subsist without D.
        STEE 518:14
depends: so much d.   WILL 574:10
dépeuplé: et tout est d.   LAM 306:24
déplaît: chose qui ne nous d. pas LA R 310:8
deponere: Difficile est longum subito
  d. amorem   CAT 137:10
depopulating: d. his dominions and making
        BECK 36:19
Deportment: his D.   DICK 176:9
depose: glories and my state d. SHAK 479:23
depositary: d. of power is always
  unpopular   DISR 185:43
depraved: ever suddenly became d.
        JUV 287:14
  In d. May   ELIOT 203:4
depravity: proof of stupidity than d.
        JOHN 275:33
  total d. of inanimate things HAM 238:14
deprest: heart of a man is d. GAY 222:26
deprived: d. of everlasting bliss MARL 329:7

depth: d., and not the tumult WORD 578:2
  d. in philosophy bringeth   BACON 25:24
  d. in that study brings   FULL 220:14
  far beyond my d.   SHAK 447:9
  He who knows about d. knows TILL 551:4
  little out of your d. here   TEMP 532:12
depths: d. I have cried to thee BIBLE 83:13
  his d. and his shallows   BURNS 115:2
  of the unfathomable d.   COL 158:8
deputy: also may be read by d. BACON 27:19
  d. elected by the Lord   SHAK 479:5
deracinate: That should d. such savagery
        SHAK 445:12
derangement: nice d. of epitaphs
        SHER 506:14
derision: Lord shall have them in d.
        PRAY 389:17
  turns the old days to d.   SWIN 529:10
  Uglification and D.   CARR 134:10
dernière: La d. chose qu'on trouve
        PASC 369:3
Dertemouthe: he was of D. CHAU 141:29
dés: Un coup de d. jamais n'abolira
        MALL 327:11
desart: beyond High-Park's a d. ETH 208:31
descend: Intervene. O d. as a dove
        AUDEN 20:15
  into the Dust d.   FITZ 212:18
Descended: D. of so many royal kings
        SHAK 424:16
descending: island d. incontinently
        CHUR 151:4
  of God ascending and d.   BIBLE 46:18
descensus: Facilis d. Averno VIRG 558:18
descent: at the claims of long d. TENN 537:29
described: d. as a supreme capacity
        BUTL 118:34
describing: d. the afflictions of Job
        BACON 25:19
Descried: D. at sunrise an emerging
        ARN 14:21
description: He answered the d. FARQ 210:18
descriptions: d. of the fairest wights
        SHAK 494:19
deseo: término que pide un buen d.
        CERV 138:19
Desert: Blast of the D. cried aloud
        LONG 317:8
  d. shall rejoice   BIBLE 58:32
  d. sighs in the bed   AUDEN 18:10
  d. were a paradise   BURNS 114:31
  every man after his d.   SHAK 432:26
  Life is the d.   YOUNG 588:13
  never will d. Mr Micawber DICK 177:3
  owl that is in the d.   PRAY 396:12
  pain'd d. lion   ARN 14:26
  scare myself with my own d. FROST 219:3
  Stand in the d.   SHEL 502:15
  straight in the d. a highway BIBLE 59:5
  streams in the d.   BIBLE 58:34
  that the d. were my dwelling-place
        BYRON 121:21
  us all out into the d.   CLOU 154:6
  water but the d.   BYRON 121:12
  your d. speaks loud   SHAK 465:3
Deserted: D. at his utmost need DRYD 195:3
Deserts: D. of vast eternity MARV 332:19
  his d. are small   GRAH 233:14
  In the d. of the heart   AUDEN 19:9
  When she d. the night   MILT 350:16
deserve: d. any thanks from anyone
        CAT 137:8
  those who really d. them   FIEL 211:20
  we'll d. it   ADD 1:16
  wicked to d. such pain   BROW 99:29
  would d. better of mankind SWIFT 526:6
  you somehow haven't to d. FROST 219:2
deserves: everyone has the face he d.
        ORW 365:18
  has the government it d.   MAIS 327:8

deserving: that riches where is my d.
        SHAK 494:13
désespoir: Le d. baîlle   HUGO 267:12
design: appears dull there is a d. STEE 518:5
  in the might of d.   SHAW 496:22
  that d. might cover their   POUND 382:8
Designer: D. infinite   THOM 548:18
designing: Say I am d. St Paul's BENT 41:9
designs: His d. were strictly honourable
        FIEL 211:29
  Immanent Will and its d. HARDY 239:11
  ladder to all high d.   SHAK 486:23
  large to his own dark d.   MILT 345:8
  Lofty d. must close   BROW 101:2
Desinat: D. in piscem mulier HOR 257:9
Desine: D. de quoquam quicquam CAT 137:8
desint: Ut d. vires   OVID 366:26
desipere: Dulce est d. in loco HOR 261:20
  Dulce et decorum est d.   BUTL 119:9
desirable: all of them d. young men
        BIBLE 60:37
desir'd: hurts, and is d.   SHAK 424:12
  Suffer herself to be d.   WALL 562:14
desire: beauty that we should d. BIBLE 59:21
  bloom of young d. and purple GRAY 235:17
  Bring me my arrows of d. BLAKE 86:16
  depth and dream of my d. KIPL 301:16
  d. accomplished is sweet BIBLE 53:37
  d. and longing to enter   PRAY 395:11
  d. at last and vain regret ROSS 410:6
  D. gratified   BLAKE 86:20
  d. in deity   ROSS 409:32
  d. of the moth   SHEL 504:14
  d. on the part of every   BUTL 118:27
  d. other men's goods   PRAY 388:18
  d. should so many years   SHAK 441:28
  d. that outruns the delight SWIN 529:9
  d. the office of a bishop BIBLE 79:11
  exceed all that we can d. PRAY 386:18
  few things to d. and many BACON 26:8
  fulfilled of my heart's d. SWIN 530:13
  hours and times of your d. SHAK 493:18
  it provokes the d.   SHAK 460:18
  kindle soft d.   DRYD 195:8
  Land of Heart's D.   YEATS 585:19
  lineaments of gratified d. BLAKE 86:17
  man's d. is for the woman COL 157:33
  mixing Memory and d.   ELIOT 204:17
  naught for your d.   CHES 146:16
  nearer to the Heart's D. FITZ 213:16
  powers of Charm and D. CAT 136:22
  shall d. to die   BIBLE 82:7
  shot and danger of d.   SHAK 430:17
  that the d. is boundless   SHAK 486:33
  this fond d.   ADD 1:24
  thou art in d.   SHAK 459:8
  to get your heart's d.   SHAW 497:33
  tongue has its d.   AUDEN 20:22
  weariness treads on d.   PETR 373:5
  What many men d.   SHAK 466:19
  what you can d. or hope   DRYD 197:5
  when the d. cometh   BIBLE 53:35
  Which of us has his d.   THAC 545:29
  wonder and a wild d.   BROW 104:19
  Youth pined away with d. BLAKE 87:22
desired: d. by all healthy and good CIC 151:33
  d. to know nothing   JOHN 276:22
  I have d. to go   HOPK 256:17
  kings have d. to see   BIBLE 69:29
  More to be d. are they   PRAY 390:12
  You are not one to be d. TENN 537:26
desiren: 'Wommen d. to have sovereynetee
        CHAU 143:24
desires: all d. known   PRAY 387:7
  By all d. which thereof   DONNE 188:10
  consists in doing what one d. MILL 339:13
  D. and Adorations   SHEL 499:9
  d. and other hopes beset BRON 93:23
  d., like fell and cruel   SHAK 487:21
  d. of the heart are   AUDEN 18:13

Dreams and d. and sombre SWIN 528:26
enough to answer back to d. HOR 262:10
from whom all holy d. PRAY 385:9
Fulfil now, O Lord, the d. PRAY 385:8
He who d. but acts not BLAKE 88:15
into our minds good d. PRAY 386:10
much the devices and d. PRAY 384:11
nurse unacted d. BLAKE 88:24
Question your d. SHAK 469:17
shows of things to the d. BACON 24:19
was winged with vain d. DRYD 196:13
we fondly flatter our d. DRAY 193:9
whilst his d. were as warm BURKE 110:21

desirest: thou d. no sacrifice PRAY 393:8
desireth: hart the water-brooks PRAY 392:6
Desiring: D. this man's art SHAK 493:6
is to admire without d. BRAD 91:11
desist: d. To build at all SHAK 441:17
desk: dry drudgery of the d.'s LAMB 307:33
From counter or d. among YEATS 585:1
Is but a d. to write upon BUTL 118:1
votary of the d. LAMB 307:11
desks: Stick close to your d. and never GILB 228:7

desnuda: Verte d. es recordar GARC 221:4
desolate: d. places for themselves BIBLE 52:12
making his palace d. BECK 36:19
that are d. and oppressed PRAY 385:20
desolated: they have d. and profaned GLAD 229:13
desolation: Love in d. masked SHEL 499:17
My d. does begin to make SHAK 423:20
see the abomination of d. BIBLE 67:29
years of d. pass over JEFF 272:14

despair: begotten by d. Upon impossibility MARV 331:18
Bid me d. HERR 249:27
carrion comfort, D. HOPK 256:7
curst himself in his d. SOUT 514:3
depth of some divine d. TENN 542:2
d. to the regeneration CONR 161:21
D. was powerless to destroy BRON 93:24
D. yawns HUGO 267:12
Do not d. PUDN 402:7
from d. Thus high uplifted MILT 346:6
have of comfort and d. SHAK 495:12
Heaven in Hell's d. BLAKE 87:18
I can endure my own d. WALSH 563:30
I shall d. SHAK 481:15
last weak refuge in d. THOM 549:19
near neighbour to D. ARN 14:18
never hoped can never d. SHAW 496:11
No cause for d. HOR 259:16
now fiercer by d. MILT 346:7
owner whereof was Giant D. BUNY 107:20
quality of his d. CONN 161:16
racked with deep d. MILT 345:4
rash-embrac'd d. SHAK 467:12
unpaid bill, D. SHEL 504:25
what resolution from d. MILT 345:7
despaired: ever d. of the Commonwealth DISR 185:34
despairer: Too quick d. ARN 15:6
despairs: leaden-eyed d. KEATS 291:19
despare: regaining my character I d. FLEM 214:29
despatchful: with d. looks in haste MILT 348:18
desperandum: Nil d. Teucro duce et auspice HOR 259:16
desperate: characteristic of wisdom not to do d. THOR 550:5
d. strait and cannot steer MASS 335:18
Diseases d. grown SHAK 435:25
Tempt not a d. man SHAK 483:27
desperately: d. mortal SHAK 464:25
desperation: lives of quiet d. THOR 550:4
Despicere: D. unde queas alios passimque LUCR 320:6

despis'd: d. old man SHAK 454:5
despise: d. Shakespeare when I measure SHAW 496:23
d. them most BURNS 114:29
d. the skylark's song BRON 93:13
ere you d. the other DRYD 198:5
other Englishman d. him SHAW 498:12
pretend to d. Art BLAKE 86:9
reason to hate and to d. HAZL 243:18
shalt thou not d. PRAY 393:8
despised: Dangers by being d. grow BURKE 111:33
d. and rejected of men BIBLE 59:21
d., and dying king SHEL 504:6
d. as well as served it BUTL 119:6
Enjoyed no sooner but d. SHAK 495:7
my part I always d. Mr CONG 160:13
despises: is the thing that she d. CONG 159:19
despising: d. all manner of éclat BAG 29:11
d. the shame BIBLE 79:35
thoughts myself almost d. SHAK 493:6
despite: builds a Hell in Heaven's d. BLAKE 87:19
D. of all your generals LAND 308:18
despoil: tremble and d. themselves SHEL 502:11
Despond: name of the slough was D. BUNY 107:11
despondency: in the end d. and madness WORD 580:28
last words of Mr D. BUNY 107:37
said 'SPREAD ALARM and D. PEN 371:13
despot: country governed by a d. JOHN 277:29
despotism: anarchy and d. SHEL 505:11
d. tempered by epigrams CARL 131:21
d. will come from either ARIS 12:8
desp'rate: Beware of d. steps COWP 165:20
dessin: Le d. est la probité de INGR 270:19
destinies: d. of the British Empire DISR 184:27
Persuasions and veiled D. SHEL 499:9
destiny: 'character is d. ELIOT 201:21
D. the Commissary of God DONNE 189:35
D. with Men for Pieces FITZ 213:5
His own funereal d. BYRON 125:19
In shady leaves of d. CRAS 169:15
orphan heirs of fixed d. SHAK 469:16
Our manifest d. to overspread OSUL 365:23
you reap a d. READE 405:4
destitute: worst solitude is to be d. BACON 25:14
Destitution: shaming D. VIRG 558:21
destroy: after my skin worms d. BIBLE 52:31
age shall be able to d. OVID 366:19
Despair was powerless to d. BRON 93:24
d. a blade of grass BOTT 90:17
D. his fib or sophistry POPE 376:22
Doth the winged life d. BLAKE 86:18
God d. man's nobility BACON 25:25
impatient to d. JOHN 283:1
not to d., but to fulfil BIBLE 64:10
sin will d. a sinner BUNY 107:29
They shall not hurt nor d. BIBLE 58:11
Whom God would d. He first DUP 199:15
destroy'd: d. by Time's devouring BRAM 91:23
not one life shall be d. TENN 536:25
destroyed: Berkeley d. this world SMITH 511:33
D. by subtleties these MER 337:16
made great is a name d. HILL 251:5
that shall be d. is death BIBLE 76:23
Destroyer: D. and preserver SHEL 502:8
only a d. CHEK 154:4
destroyeth: sickness that d. PRAY 395:21
destroys: Death d. a man FORS 217:3
first d. their mind DRYD 196:12
he who d. a good book MILT 351:22
destruator: aut aliquo modo d. MAGN 327:2

destruction: d. of the poor is their BIBLE 53:30
from us to be utter d. BIBLE 62:13
Pride goeth before d. BIBLE 54:8
startles at d. ADD 1:24
that leadeth to d. BIBLE 65:6
to their d. draw DONNE 187:23
urge for d. is also a creative BAK 29:24
destructive: d. forest laments in order CHUR 149:20
d. of the manhood JERR 273:11
d. man LEE 313:14
In the d. element immerse CONR 161:19
desuper: d., et nubes pluant Justum BIBLE 83:15
detail: frittered away by d. Simplify THOR 550:17
Merely corroborative d. GILB 227:12
occupied in trivial d. BAG 29:11
detect: in the moment you d. POPE 377:9
Detection: D. is, or ought to be DOYLE 192:28
detective: Hawkshaw, the d. TAYL 532:7
Deteriora: D. sequor OVID 366:17
determination: d. to believe what is most HUME 267:21
determine: Let us d. to die here BEE 37:3
Our deeds d. us ELIOT 200:12
determined: am d. to prove a villain SHAK 480:19
D., dared, and done SMART 509:4
determining: d. a point of law BURKE 109:28
detest: hate and d. that animal SWIFT 526:23
they d. at leisure BYRON 123:38
yet d. th'offence POPE 376:12
detestare: non lugere, neque d. SPIN 517:7
detested: I have d. you long enough... POUND 383:12
Detraction: D. is but baseness' varlet JONS 284:14
D. will not suffer it SHAK 440:18
detrimenti: ne quid res publica d. ANON 10:10
Deum: D. de Deo MASS 334:20
D. patrem qui ecclesiam CYPR 170:19
deus: d. nobis haec otia fecit VIRG 559:12
Nec d. hunc mensa VIRG 560:2
puto d. fio VESP 556:12
'Sit D. propitius ANON 10:14
devant: Présentez toujours le d. MOL 353:1
development: contributions to human d. ARN 15:21
De Vere: why not of D. CREWE 169:18
deviates: Shadwell never d. into sense DRYD 196:34
deviation: where d. from truth will end JOHN 277:20
device: imagined such a d. as they PRAY 390:15
reporting d. for experience WHORF 571:23
devices: d. and desires of our own PRAY 384:11
Devil: Apology for the D. BUTL 119:1
are of your father the d. BIBLE 72:13
assaults of the d. PRAY 385:16
because your adversary the d. BIBLE 80:33
can the d. speak true SHAK 458:16
children of the d. TENN 543:1
defy the d. SHAK 490:7
D. always builds a chapel DEFOE 173:11
d. a monk wou'd be MOTT 358:22
d. Be sometime honour'd SHAK 465:4
d. can cite Scripture SHAK 466:1
d. damn thee black SHAK 463:1
d., depend upon it STEV 521:15
d. finds some mischief MADAN 326:17
D. fly away with the fine arts CARL 132:5
d. haunts thee in the likeness SHAK 439:15
D., having nothing else BELL 39:24
d. himself with courtesy SHAK 490:20

Fall asleep, or hearing d.   SHAK 447:3
few d. well   SHAK 444:21
find myself so apt to d.   SHAK 450:8
forgets that he can d.   BROW 96:22
go away is to d. a little   HAR 238:20
have to d. beyond my means   WILDE 574:3
how can man d. better   MAC 322:15
How often are we to d.   POPE 381:17
how to d.   PORT 381:33
I d. a Christian   CHAR 140:20
I d. happy   FOX 217:22
I d. pronouncing it   SHAK 478:20
If I should d.   BROO 94:30
If it were now to d.   SHAK 474:20
If we are mark'd to d.   SHAK 445:1
I have seen her d. twenty   SHAK 421:20
I'll d. for him to-morrow   BALL 30:12
I must d.   BIBLE 50:3
in Adam all d.   BIBLE 76:22
I shall d. at the top   SWIFT 527:19
Is not to d.   CAMP 128:19
It is most grand to d.   MAS 334:1
it was sure to d.   MOORE 356:25
I will d. in peace   WOLFE 576:8
I will not have thee d.   TENN 542:10
''I would d.   PETR 373:2
Jerusalem shall Harry d.   SHAK 442:21
kiss my Lord before I d.   MARL 330:13
Let me d. eating ortolans   DISR 187:1
Let us determine to d.   BEE 37:3
Let us d. even as we rush   VIRG 558:7
live or d. wi' Charlie   HOGG 253:1
look about us and to d.   POPE 379:1
love one another or d.   AUDEN 20:9
lucky to d. and I know it   WHIT 570:19
man can d. but once   SHAK 442:7
may be smitten, and d.   BIBLE 50:19
might it d. or rest at last   SHEL 501:3
money to d. comfortably   BUTL 118:30
much beauty as could d.   JONS 284:3
Muse forbids to d.   HOR 261:17
Must d. of love   SHAK 420:26
must weep or she will d.   TENN 542:10
myself to d. upon a kiss   SHAK 478:1
natural to d. as to be born   BACON 26:3
night to d. upon the sand   ARN 14:26
Not d. here in a rage   SWIFT 526:24
not so difficult to d.   BYRON 125:5
not to live, but to d.   BROW 97:3
not willingly let it d.   MILT 352:14
'Now that I come to d.   BROW 100:6
Of easy ways to d.   SHAK 424:18
of king should ever d.   BROW 103:23
Only we d. in earnest   RAL 404:11
peace a Christian can d.   ADD 2:29
'People can't d.   DICK 177:17
persons d. before they sing   COL 156:16
shall break it must d.   KIPL 300:20
shall desire to d.   BIBLE 82:7
shall not altogether d.   HOR 261:9
shall Trelawny d.   HAWK 243:4
should d. before I wake   ANON 7:3
should d. for the people   BIBLE 72:24
since I needs must d.   RAL 404:10
Sir Richard Grenville d.   TENN 543:4
sit him down and d.   SHAK 442:2
stand the hazard of the d.   SHAK 481:19
suffer and d.   VIGNY 557:2
taught us how to d.   TICK 551:3
that have the power to d.   TENN 543:13
that I shall d. to-day   MORE 357:13
that love lightly may d.   SWIN 529:19
that must fight and d.   HOOV 255:25
That we shall d., we know   SHAK 450:3
Their's but to do and d.   TENN 532:24
thereof thou shalt surely d.   BIBLE 45:9
These Christs that d. upon   WILDE 572:17
these who d. as cattle   OWEN 367:2
they d. in yon rich sky   TENN 542:1
They must conquer or d.   GAY 223:27

think hereon that I must d.   SOUT 514:21
thinks he was not made to d.   TENN 535:30
Though I should d. with thee   BIBLE 68:13
time to d.   BIBLE 55:12
to d. for one's country   HOR 260:17
to d. in the last dyke   BURKE 110:31
to d. in the last ditch   WILL 574:8
to d. is gain   BIBLE 78:11
To live and d. for thee   HERR 249:27
to make a malefactor d.   DRYD 198:13
To men that d. at morn   HOUS 262:16
To-morrow let us do or d.   CAMP 128:18
to morrow we d.   BIBLE 76:24
to morrow we shall d.   BIBLE 58:15
unwise they seemed to d.   BIBLE 62:13
we all must d.   SWIFT 527:23
we needs must d.   BIBLE 50:23
We shall d. alone   PASC 369:9
What I shall d. to want   SHAK 485:12
What 'tis to d.   BEAU 36:10
When beggars d.   SHAK 449:18
When I d., the GHOULS   TENN 544:12
when they d.   APPL 11:13
when they d. by thousands   CHES 147:20
when you have to d.   MOL 353:21
Which some did d. to look   SHAK 421:29
Who did not wish to d.   SHAW 498:27
who lives is born to d.   DRYD 197:10
who would wish to d.   BORR 90:4
wisdom shall d. with you   BIBLE 52:23
Wise men also d.   PRAY 392:28
wish to live and to d.   VILL 557:6
with you be ready to d.   HOR 261:1
work till we d.   LEWIS 314:9
Would do any thing but d.   LAMB 308:5
wretch that dares not d.   BURNS 114:21
ye shall d. like men   PRAY 395:10
yet cannot choose but d.   DONNE 188:32
yet d. we must   SHAK 446:22
yet I love her till I d.   ANON 8:1
Yet she must d.   SHAK 477:5
you don't work, you d.   KIPL 299:16
Dieb: *er war ein D.*   HEINE 244:10
died: been a grandam ere she d.   SHAK 457:14
been the same since God d.   MILL 339:25
beggar d.   BIBLE 70:28
children d. in the streets   AUDEN 18:15
children who d. for our lands   KIPL 298:9
could have d. contented   DICK 177:25
darter es d. o' the fever   TENN 544:5
d. by the hand of the Lord   BIBLE 47:23
d. extremely well   WALP 562:20
d. last night of my physician   PRIOR 401:4
d. like a Duke-and-a-Duchess's   BARH 33:26
d. to save their country   CHES 146:25
d. to succour me   BALL 31:4
dog it was that d.   GOLD 231:14
Had I but d. an hour before   SHAK 461:1
He d. in a good old age   BIBLE 51:40
he d. unto sin once   BIBLE 75:2
Helen d.   LAND 309:7
He that d. o' Wednesday   SHAK 440:18
should have d. hereafter   SHAK 463:6
There d. a myriad   POUND 383:10
there they d. for me   HOUS 265:6
These all d. in faith   BIBLE 79:33
thought it d. of grieving   KEATS 292:10
When I d. last   DONNE 189:21
would God I had d. for thee   BIBLE 50:26
diem: *carpe d.*   HOR 259:20
d. perdidi   TITUS 551:6
d. tibi diluxisse supremum   HOR 258:16
dienen: *Oder d. und verlieren*   GOET 230:7
dies: artist never d.   LONG 316:24
d. fighting has increase   GREN 236:15
D. irae   CEL 138:5
D. like a dog   WHIT 571:18
d., or turns Hindoo   SHEL 501:19
Every moment d. a man   BABB 24:13
Every moment d. a man   TENN 544:8

gods love d. young   MEN 336:25
hath blown for ever d.   FITZ 212:19
He that d. pays all debts   SHAK 485:16
kingdom where nobody d.   MILL 339:24
king never d.   BLAC 85:3
marrid man d. in good stile   WARD 564:30
matters not how a man d.   JOHN 275:31
necessarily true because a man d.   WILDE 573:34
One d. only once   MOL 353:8
Optima quaeque d. miseris   VIRG 560:16
primrose that forsaken d.   MILT 343:15
summer d. the swan   TENN 543:11
that d. this year is quit   SHAK 442:8
Where all life d.   MILT 346:23
Who d. if England live   KIPL 299:7
who d.rich dies disgraced   CARN 132:32
worm that never d.   BROO 94:14
diest: Where thou d.   BIBLE 49:32
diet: d., humour, air   BROW 96:27
d. unparalleled   DICK 179:34
Praise is the best d.   SMITH 511:9
that oft with gods doth d.   MILT 341:27
Dieu: *D. en aura plus tost de*   VILL 557:4
D. d'ordinaire pour   BUSS 117:7
D. est mort   NERV 360:25
D. n'est pas pour les gros   VOLT 561:18
Je parle espagnol à D.   CHAR 140:2
Le bon D. n'a que dix   CLEM 152:30
le Verbe, c'est D.   HUGO 267:9
Si D. n'existait pas   VOLT 561:8
differemus: *nulli negabimus aut d.*   MAGN 327:3
difference: d. between genuine poetry   ARN 16:9
d. of taste in jokes   ELIOT 200:21
d. of texts   SPEN 515:24
d. to me   WORD 581:6
evil that makes racial d.   CONR 161:23
find much d.   JOHN 280:12
Strange the d. of men's   PEPYS 371:17
that has made all the d.   FROST 219:10
that the d. is best postponed   DICK 181:9
upon the d. of an opinion   BROW 96:4
different: d. methods different men   CHUR 148:23
from those who have a d.   CONR 161:17
How d. from us   ANON 6:16
other naturs thinks d.   DICK 179:11
They are d. from you   FITZ 213:24
very d. from the home life   ANON 5:20
We boil at d. degrees   EMER 208:9
who follow d. paths   HOR 261:21
will show you something d.   ELIOT 204:19
differential: integral and d. calculus   GILB 228:16
differently: they do things d. there   HART 242:34
differeth: One star d. from another   BIBLE 76:26
Difficile: *D. est longum subito deponere*   CAT 137:10
D. est saturam non   JUV 287:9
Difficult: D. do you call it   JOHN 280:24
It has been found d.   CHES 148:9
more alternatives, the more d.   ALL 3:19
'tis not so d. to die   BYRON 125:5
which it is d. to speak   BURKE 110:30
difficulties: d. do not make one doubt   NEWM 362:1
little local d.   MACM 325:19
that somebody is in d.   LUCR 320:6
difficulty: great d. I am got hither   BUNY 107:38
has had to face every d.   WILDE 574:1
with d. and labour he   MILT 347:7
Diffidence: her name was D.   BUNY 107:21
in the d. that faltered   POUND 382:14
Diffugere: *D. nives*   HOR 261:14
diffused: appeals to d. feeling   BAG 28:30

dig: d. him up and throw stones SHAW 496:23
d. in the ribs I gives SURT 525:5
D. the grave and let me STEV 523:10
d. till you gently perspire KIPL 300:11
I cannot d. BIBLE 70:23
nails he'll d. it up again ELIOT 204:22
with his nails he'll d. WEBS 567:9
digest: can d. so much SHAK 489:6
inwardly d. them PRAY 386:5
digested: few to be chewed and d.
BACON 27:19
digestion: d. is the great secret SMITH 512:8
from pure d. bred MILT 348:13
good d. wait on appetite SHAK 461:18
sweet to taste prove in d. SHAK 478:14
digestions: Few radicals have good d.
BUTL 118:31
diggeth: d. a pit shall fall BIBLE 56:2
digne: *tabac n'est pas d. de vivre* MOL 353:9
dignitate: *cum d. otium* CIC 151:33
dignities: afraid to speak evil of d. BIBLE 81:1
indignities men come to d. BACON 26:23
dignity: accessions of d. from the king
LAMB 307:25
below the d. of history MAC 324:15
d. compos'd and high exploit MILT 346:9
d. of this high calling BURKE 110:7
d. of thinking beings JOHN 281:24
d. of the whole body SHAK 462:23
equal in d. and rights ANON 4:14
maintained the d. of history BOL 89:18
May reach the d. of crimes MORE 357:8
room with silent d. GROS 237:2
There's no d. in it FRY 220:8
To wear an undeserved d. SHAK 466:20
write trifles with d. JOHN 278:23
Dignum: *D. et justum est* MASS 335:3
D. laude virum Musa vetat HOR 261:17
dignus: *Domine, non sum d.* MASS 335:8
digression: there began a lang d.
BURNS 115:26
Digressions: D., incontestably STER 519:22
digs: d. my grave at each remove
HERB 247:23
dilectione: *d. hominum et odio vitiorum*
AUG 22:1
dilettante: snowy-banded, d. TENN 540:3
Dilige: *D. et quod vis fac* AUG 21:21
Diligence: D. is the mother of good
CERV 138:19
diligencia: *La d. es madre de la buena*
CERV 138:19
dim: d. and perilous way WORD 577:13
d. and the dark cloths YEATS 585:9
doth the greater glory d. SHAK 468:18
Not when the sense is d. BEEC 37:9
with every year grows d. CORN 161:24
dimanches: *tous les d. sa poule au pot*
HENR 245:13
dimensions: d. of this mercy are above
CROM 169:22
my d. are as well compact SHAK 453:9
dimidium: *Animae d. meae* HOR 259:11
D. facti qui coepit HOR 258:14
diminish: Enlarge, d., interline SWIFT 527:34
Diminish'd: D. to her cock SHAK 455:14
diminished: ought to be d. DUNN 199:14
dimittimus: *sicut et nos d. debitoribus*
MASS 335:5
dimittis: *Nunc d. servum tuum* BIBLE 83:19
Dimity: Such D. Convictions DICK 184:3
dimmed: glory of the sun will be d.
BALF 30:3
di'mond: quadrangular of d. form
COWP 167:16
dimpled: Stood pretty-d. boys SHAK 422:2
dimples: charmer whose d. we prize
SHER 506:32
dimpling: shallow streams run d. POPE 377:2
din: wealth and d. of Rome HOR 261:7

din'd: had not d. POPE 377:10
dine: d. somewhere among JERR 273:12
go to inns to d. CHES 147:18
hang that jury-men may d. POPE 381:4
I'd as soon d. with Jack JOHN 277:11
I d. at Blenheim once ANON 7:2
I may d. at journey's end YEATS 587:5
no scandal while you d. TENN 543:16
this should stay to d. CARR 133:13
'Where sall we gang and d. BALL 32:8
dined: 'I d. last night with BEER 37:18
I have d. to-day SMITH 511:15
diner-out: philosophic d. BROW 102:18
dines: d. he sleeps SURT 525:7
ding: are chiels that winna d. BURNS 113:14
Dingo: Yellow-Dog D. behind KIPL 300:13
dining: d. late with peers BETJ 44:12
that can live without d. MER 338:7
while they thought of d. GOLD 231:17
dinner: d. and feasting reconciles
PEPYS 372:14
d. of herbs where love BIBLE 54:6
doubtful of his d. JOHN 281:40
expect if we haven't any d. LEAR 312:24
good d. upon his table JOHN 280:18
if you'd watch a d. out BROW 99:2
more business after d. SWIFT 526:18
not have had a better d. JOHN 275:13
They would ask him to d. CARL 132:26
three hours' march to d. HAZL 243:32
was not a d. to *ask* a man JOHN 275:12
'What gat ye to your d. BALL 31:5
you worth inviting to d. VIRG 560:2
dinner-bell: tocsin of the soul—the d.
BYRON 123:17
dinner-knives: gravel paths with broken
d. KIPL 299:14
Dinted: D. with the silver-pointed
BROW 102:28
Diocese: All the air is thy D. DONNE 188:18
Diogenes: I would be D. ALEX 3:12
Dionysus: Christ follows D. POUND 383:6
dip: am a kind of farthing d. STEV 523:13
Diplomacy: Dollar D. ANON 5:2
dire: d. offence from am'rous POPE 380:28
direct: d. and honest is not safe SHAK 475:26
House is pleased to d. LENT 313:23
puff d. SHER 505:23
things d. and rule our hearts PRAY 386:21
were all going d. to Heaven DICK 183:5
directe: this book I d. CHAU 144:20
directed: all d. your way HOR 258:11
direction: d. which thou canst not
POPE 379:11
directions: By indirections find d.
SHAK 431:27
He gives d. to the town SWIFT 528:3
rode madly off in all d. LEAC 311:14
direful: d. death indeed they had FLEM 214:25
something d. in the sound AUST 22:18
dirge: d. of her certain ending SHAK 492:20
unseen their d. is sung COLL 158:20
with d. in marriage SHAK 429:19
dirt: d. the reasoning engine ROCH 406:22
half the little soul is d. TENN 540:23
if d. were trumps LAMB 308:9
poverty, hunger, and d. HOOD 255:6
dirty: An' for all 'is d. 'ide KIPL 299:18
creature's at his d. work POPE 376:22
d., dangerous way GOLD 232:25
d. nurse, Experience TENN 534:35
d. work for the rest RUSK 411:16
their d. songs and dreary BROO 94:27
Wash what is d. LANG 310:1
Dis: by gloomy D. Was gathered MILT 347:21
dark D.'s door stands open VIRG 558:18
D. aliter visum VIRG 558:8
unsubstantial realms of D. VIRG 558:20
disagree: men only d. MILT 346:18

disagreeable: doing things d. to myself
SMITH 512:4
enough to tell him d. truths BULW 107:7
everybody says I'm such a d. GILB 228:26
disagreeables: making all d. evaporate
KEATS 293:18
disappeared: He d. in the dead of winter
AUDEN 19:2
disappears: that nothing really d.
BACON 25:15
disappoint: can't abide to d. myself
GOLD 232:20
disappointed: feel the pangs of d. love
ROWE 410:21
I am d. by that stroke JOHN 281:36
disappointeth: d. him not PRAY 390:5
Disappointment: D. all I endeavour end
HOPK 257:2
disapprove: I d. of what you say VOLT 561:24
disapproves: condemns whatever he d.
BURN 112:20
Disaster: meet with Triumph and D.
KIPL 299:22
disasters: day's d. in his morning GOLD 231:2
make guilty of our own d. SHAK 453:11
So weary with d. SHAK 461:10
disbelief: d. in great men CARL 131:30
willing suspension of d. COL 157:22
discandy: d., melt their sweets SHAK 423:5
Disce: *D. omnis* VIRG 558:2
discept: Two must d. BROW 102:12
discern: that now you can never d.
HOUS 263:7
we have built do we d. ARN 13:23
discharge: responsibility and to d. EDW 200:4
there is no d. in that war BIBLE 55:25
There's no d. in the war KIPL 298:6
discharged: d. from the war HOR 261:6
disciple: d. is not above his master
BIBLE 65:34
d. whom Jesus loved BIBLE 73:18
only in the name of a d. BIBLE 65:41
other d. did outrun Peter BIBLE 73:6
disciples: d., whom Jesus loved BIBLE 72:28
discipline: d. and perfect steadiness
KITC 305:14
D. must be maintained DICK 176:18
d. of colleges and universities SMITH 509:14
order and military d. ANON 4:28
disclaim: d. all my paternal care SHAK 453:3
willing to d. her for a mother GIBB 224:7
disclose: more and more to d. truth
BACON 25:5
disco: *mali miseris succurrere d.* VIRG 557:19
Discobbolos: Till Mrs D. said LEAR 312:10
Discobolus: to the gospel of the D.
BUTL 119:20
discomfort: great d. of my soul PRAY 391:24
discommendeth: d. others obliquely
commendeth BROW 95:15
disconsolate: gate Of Eden stood, d.
MOORE 356:27
discontent: d., boil bloody OWEN 367:11
is the winter of our d. SHAK 480:12
pale contented sort of d. KEATS 290:26
prone to d. HERR 249:16
youth and age in common—d. ARN 15:13
discontented: blushing d. sun SHAK 479:12
that are d. under *monarchy* HOBB 251:20
To be d. with the divine KING 289:7
discontents: More d. I never had HERR 249:3
discord: effects from civil d. ADD 1:25
Harmony in d. HOR 258:20
that eke d. doth sow ELIZ 205:27
what d. follows SHAK 486:24
Discordant: reconciles D. elements
WORD 580:11
still-d. wavering multitude SHAK 440:31
Discords: D. make the sweetest airs
BUTL 118:9

discors: Concordia d.   HOR 258:20
discountenance: Religious, d. every
   BLAKE 86:9
discouragement: There's no d.   BUNY 107:36
discourse: came in to punctuate my d.
   COL 158:5
d. and nearest prose   DRYD 197:15
d. The freezing hours   SHAK 428:15
Good company and good d.   WALT 564:4
I love any d. of rivers   WALT 564:11
nor to find talk and d.   BACON 27:18
not the d. of the elders   BIBLE 62:27
upon the daisies and d.   GILB 227:21
discourtesy: fault and truth d.   HERB 247:6
share in that d. of death   YEATS 585:13
discover: further to d. truth   BACON 24:15
discoverers: They are ill d. that think
   BACON 24:21
discovereth: d. the thick bushes PRAY 391:11
discoveries: not much wish well to d.
   JOHN 281:25
virtue and consequence of d.   BACON 28:9
discovering: d. in the eyes of the very
   POUND 383:14
discovery: are the portals of d. JOYCE 286:27
discredit: He will d. our mystery
   SHAK 464:23
discredited: would have d. your travel
   SHAK 421:21
discreet: d. and learned Minister PRAY 387:17
discretion: guide his words with d.
   PRAY 397:14
has no d. in her coughs   AUST 23:12
till it attain years of d.   RUSK 412:6
woman which is without d.   BIBLE 53:32
your own d. be your tutor   SHAK 433:17
discreto: rey y al simple con el d.
   CERV 138:20
discriminate: Not to d. every moment
   PATER 369:22
discriminations: Makes no d.   WHIT 571:11
discunt: Homines dum docent d. SEN 420:10
disdain: burning pride and high d.
   SCOTT 416:11
D. and scorn ride sparkling SHAK 472:21
fixed mind And high d.   MILT 345:2
little d. is not amiss   CONG 161:2
me more love or more d.   CAREW 130:16
my dear Lady D.   SHAK 471:28
disdain'd: general's d.   SHAK 486:25
disdained: feeling too falsely d. SHEL 504:13
If now I be d.   ANON 7:15
disdaineth: this my love no whit d.
   SHAK 493:10
disdains: He d. all things above OVER 366:6
diseas'd: minister to a mind d. SHAK 463:3
disease: almost hath his favourite d.
   FIEL 211:22
are suggested for a d.   CHEK 144:23
Confront d. at its onset   PERS 372:28
Cur'd yesterday of my d.   PRIOR 401:4
cure the d. and kill   BACON 26:17
desperate d. requires   FAWK 210:31
d. has grown strong through OVID 366:20
d. is incurable   SHAK 441:16
d. of admiration   MAC 323:10
d. of modern life   ARN 14:19
d. of not listening   SHAK 441:7
d. that afflicts amateurs   CHES 148:1
is just a d.   RAC 404:6
is no cure for this d.   BELL 39:1
long d., my life   POPE 376:23
out old shapes of foul d.   TENN 537:15
Progress is a comfortable d. CUMM 170:11
remedy is worse than the d. BACON 27:13
Without d. the healthful life SURR 524:20
your skin is a shocking d.   AUDEN 18:18
diseased: beauty is the mind d. BYRON 121:13
diseases: death is the cure of all d.
   BROW 97:2

D. and sad Old Age live   VIRG 558:21
D. desperate grown   SHAK 435:25
subject to the same d.   SHAK 467:4
disenchanting: life so d. as attainment
   STEV 521:16
disencumber'd: d. Atlas of the state
   COWP 166:16
disentangle: cannot d.   ANON 7:15
disfigure: that in a moment can so d.
   BROW 96:20
disfigured: snow d. the public statues
   AUDEN 19:2
Disfigures: D. earth   COWP 166:30
disgrace: and ignominy of our BROW 96:20
d. with fortune and men's SHAK 493:6
Even to a full d.   SHAK 428:1
grace us in the d. of death SHAK 456:14
public and merited d.   STEV 522:13
quite a *d.* to be fine   TAYL 531:24
sharp antidote against d.   BURKE 111:9
sole author of his own d.   COWP 165:13
disgraced: who dies...rich dies d.
   CARN 132:32
disgraceful: something d.   JUV 288:7
disguise: Are blessings in d. HERV 250:17
D. fair nature with hard-favour'd
   SHAK 443:21
go naked is the best d.   CONG 159:27
disguiser: death's a great d. SHAK 465:1
disguises: troublesome d. which we wear
   MILT 348:1
disgust: began to d. this refined age
   EVEL 209:9
not moments of d.   VOLT 561:16
disgusted: quite d. with literary men
   KEATS 293:12
dish: forth butter in a lordly d. BIBLE 49:10
Let's carve him as a d.   SHAK 449:9
woman is a d. for the gods SHAK 424:9
dishabilly: cannot be devout in d.
   FARQ 210:21
dishclout: Romeo's a d. to him SHAK 483:19
dishcover: d. the riddle   CARR 136:11
dishes: Are these the choice d. GARR 221:12
d. were ill-sorted   DRYD 198:10
Home-made d. that drive HOOD 254:26
there's no washing of d.   ANON 5:13
were the d. wherein to me   AUG 21:13
dishonour: another unto d. BIBLE 75:14
who fears d.   HOR 261:19
dishonourable: find ourselves d. graves
   SHAK 448:17
dishonour'd: d. step   SHAK 453:6
dislecti: d. membra poetae HOR 262:2
disinclination: d. to inflict pain upon
   MER 338:4
disinheriting: damned d. countenance
   SHER 506:33
disintegration: rapine to d. and
dismemberment   GLAD 229:15
disinterested: d. endeavour to learn ARN 16:1
d. commerce between equals GOLD 232:1
dislike: do not much d. the matter
   SHAK 421:34
sat with that d. which   STEE 517:25
dislikings: made up of likings and d.
   LAMB 307:7
dismal: d. headache, and repose GILB 226:12
d. tidings when he frown'd GOLD 231:2
of d. terror was the time   SHAK 480:26
Professors of the D. Science CARL 131:40
that d. cry rose slowly   BROW 98:2
dismay'd: Was there a man d. TENN 532:24
dismemberment: disintegration and d.
of the Empire   GLAD 229:15
dismiss: d. us with Thy blessing BUCK 106:17
lacks power to d. itself   SHAK 449:3
dismissed: d. by the British electorate
   CHUR 150:26
will be d. with a laugh   HOR 262:7

disobedience: Of Man's first d. MILT 344:20
upon the children of d.   BIBLE 78:3
Disorder: D., horror   SHAK 479:20
sweet d. in the dress   HERR 249:2
disparity: Just such d.   DONNE 187:22
dispatch: requisite in business than d.
   ADD 1:12
dispensation: in the old d. ELIOT 203:15
display: does a Human Form d. BLAKE 85:18
displeased: were so wrathfully d. at us
   PRAY 398:13
displeasing: something which is not d.
to us   LA R 310:8
displeasure: her wrong stay and her d.
   SHAK 474:18
dispoged: lips to it when I am so d.
   DICK 179:10
disponit: sed Deus d.   THOM 546:10
dispose: d. the way of thy servants
   PRAY 388:5
disposition: Doth change my d. SHAK 491:27
entertain a cheerful d.   SHAK 478:22
free have d. to be truthful AUDEN 19:13
horridly to shake our d.   SHAK 430:24
must be the flag of my d. WHIT 570:18
of a mild or choleric d.   ADD 2:7
to lay his goatish d.   SHAK 453:11
To put an antic d.   SHAK 431:24
dispraised: d. were no small praise
   MILT 350:4
To be d.   JONS 283:22
disputants: Our d. put me in mind ADD 2:24
disputation: that's a feeling d. SHAK 439:29
disputations: Doubtful d.   BIBLE 75:26
dispute: decide such a great d. VIRG 559:20
D. it like a man   SHAK 462:18
right there is none to d.   COWP 167:38
disputes: Hath left to their d. MILT 349:3
disquieted: art thou so d. within me
   PRAY 392:7
Never to be d.   KING 296:11
disquieteth: d. himself in vain PRAY 391:31
disrespectfully: speak d. of the Equator
   SMITH 510:29
Diss: with you by train to D. BETJ 43:15
dissaisiatur: imprisonetur, aut d. MAGN 327:2
dissatisfied: Not one is d.   WHIT 570:22
dissect: thro' creatures you d. POPE 377:9
We d. nature along lines WHORF 571:23
We murder to d.   WORD 582:23
dissemble: d. in their double heart
   PRAY 389:32
d. sometimes your knowledge BACON 26:5
not d. nor cloke them   PRAY 384:9
right to d. your love   BICK 83:27
dissembling: Cheated of feature by d.
   SHAK 480:18
dissensions: d. and animosities of mankind
   BURKE 111:3
dissent: is the dissidence of d. BURKE 109:22
dissentious: you d. rogues   SHAK 427:12
dissertates: One d.   BROW 102:12
dissidence: it is the d. of dissent
   BURKE 109:22
dissimulate: to d. their instability
   HOUS 266:14
dissimulation: defined by one word—d.
   DISR 186:5
laying down the guilt of d. SCOTT 418:13
dissipation: d. without pleasure GIBB 224:14
dissociation: century a d. of sensibility
   ELIOT 205:17
Dissolute: D., damned, and despairful
   SERV 420:13
dissolve: d., and quite forget KEATS 291:18
D. me into ecstasies   MILT 342:10
dissolved: tabernacle of this house were
d.   BIBLE 77:6
dissonance: air with barbarous d. MILT 341:13
far off the barb'rous d.   MILT 348:29

dissonant: No sound is d. which tells
COL 157:12
distain: coward shame d. his name
BURNS 114:21
distance: by d. made more sweet
WORD 579:17
d. is nothing
DU D 198:28
La d. n'y fait rien
DU D 198:28
notes by d. made more sweet
COLL 158:21
sixty seconds' worth of d.
KIPL 300:2
'Tis d. lends enchantment
CAMP 128:9
distant: All places are d. from
BURT 116:28
dull prospect of a d. good
DRYD 196:18
Music of a d. Drum
FITZ 212:12
Ye d. spires
GRAY 235:9
Distasted: D. with the salt of broken
SHAK 487:12
distastes: without many fears and d.
BACON 25:20
distemperature: thorough this d. we
see
SHAK 470:6
distempered: That questions the d. part
ELIOT 202:21
Distilled: D. by the sun
HARDY 241:21
distinction: chase of honours and d.
BURKE 108:7
d. between virtue and vice
JOHN 275:1
few escape that d.
TWAIN 554:21
no d. among
WILL 574:13
preference and d. of excelling
CONG 159:29
distinctions: d. of meum and tuum
LAMB 307:13
to despise d.
HOR 262:10
distinctive: man's d. mark alone
BROW 100:11
distinguish: could of men d.
SHAK 434:1
distinguished: at last, the d. thing
JAMES 271:31
discept,—has d.
BROW 102:12
d. by that circumstance
THOR 550:21
d. into joints and fingers
TRAH 552:1
man is d. from all other
ADD 2:26
to be d. above the rest
HOMER 253:30
distinguishes: it d. nothing
DONNE 190:23
Distorts: D. the Heavens from pole
BLAKE 85:23
distracted: I shall go d.
AUST 23:23
Distraction: D., Uglification and Derision
CARR 134:10
d. in 's aspect
SHAK 432:27
distress: All pray in their d.
BLAKE 88:6
could foretell this sore d.
BRID 92:22
delivereth them out of their d.
PRAY 397:10
incapable of her own d.
SHAK 436:19
open to d.
CHUR 149:3
distress'd: quite vacant is a mind d.
COWP 166:19
distressed: afflicted, or d.
PRAY 386:1
distresses: In all d. of our friends
SWIFT 527:22
distressful: speak of some d. stroke
SHAK 474:1
distribution: same d. of the necessaries
SMITH 509:9
disturb: me to d. your season due MILT 343:2
Which none d.
VAUG 555:12
disturbed: moment d. its solitude BALF 30:3
disturbs: he d. the order here HARDY 240:3
dit: d. et l'on vient trop tard LA B 306:11
la peine d'être d.
BEAU 35:14
ditch: environed with a great d. CROM 170:4
is to die in the last d.
WILL 574:8
Rather a d. in Egypt
SHAK 423:21
shall fall into the d.
BIBLE 66:29
Ditch-deliver'd: D. by a drab SHAK 462:4
ditchers: d. and grave-makers SHAK 436:22
ditches: water-land of Dutchmen and
of d.
BYRON 123:27
ditchwater: drinking bottled d. SHAW 496:33

ditties: In amorous d. all a summer's
MILT 345:17
Pipe to the spirit d.
KEATS 291:4
Ditto: D. ditto my song
GILB 226:17
ditty: He play'd an ancient d.
KEATS 289:21
To air the d.
HOUS 265:12
diurnal: With visible motion her d.
WORD 577:27
Diuturnity: D. is a dream and a folly
BROW 97:21
divan: Enacted on this same d.
ELIOT 205:2
dive: Heav'n's great lamps do d.
CAT 136:25
search for pearls must d.
DRYD 195:10
diver: d.'s brilliant bow
AUDEN 18:10
has been a d. in deep seas
PATER 369:19
Divergence: entailing D. of Character
DARW 171:28
divers: led away with d. lusts
BIBLE 79:24
diversa: laudet d. sequentis
HOR 261:21
diversion: 'tis a country d.
CONG 161:5
diversite: ther is so gret d.
CHAU 144:17
diversities: Now there are d. of gifts
BIBLE 76:13
diversity: whence arise d. of sects
SPEN 515:24
Divert: D. her eyes with pictures POPE 377:7
dives: quo Tullus d. et Ancus HOR 261:16
divide: d. is not to take away SHEL 500:11
d. with the poor the produce SMITH 509:9
rejoice when they d. the spoil BIBLE 58:6
though he d. the hoof BIBLE 48:6
divided: common use has harshly d.
SCH 415:9
death they were not d.
BIBLE 50:17
Have they not d. the prey BIBLE 49:13
He d. the sea
PRAY 395:5
household d. the spoil PRAY 394:8
If a house be d. against BIBLE 68:27
perceive here a d. duty SHAK 474:2
Thy kingdom is d.
BIBLE 61:6
whole is d. into three parts CAES 126:26
dividends: comfortable man, with d.
LONG 316:23
divideth: d. his spoils BIBLE 69:36
dividing: by d. we fall DICK 184:5
days d. lover and lover SWIN 528:17
their gifts some tragic d. PATER 369:22
divine: all are d.
ARN 13:3
arsenals of d. vengeance HOUS 266:13
believes Kingsley a d. STUB 524:5
by a d. thrusting SHAK 453:11
by a law d.
SHEL 502:1
could d. his real thought BYRON 122:30
depth of some d. despair TENN 542:2
did the Countenance D. BLAKE 86:16
d. enchanting ravishment MILT 341:4
D. of Kings to govern wrong POPE 375:23
d. right of husbands WOLL 576:9
d. than the physician SHAK 462:26
Door— To her d. Majority DICK 183:21
energy d.
POPE 380:15
Fanny Kelly's d. plain face LAMB 307:31
heavy, but no less d. BYRON 123:5
horror and its beauty are d. SHEL 502:5
human form d.
BLAKE 88:7
inspired by d. revelation BACON 24:20
is not therefore less d. WORD 582:1
It is a good d. that follows SHAK 465:20
one far-off d. event TENN 537:22
some are fou o' love d. BURNS 114:9
Terror the human form d. BLAKE 88:9
their motions harmony d. MILT 348:24
to forgive, d.
POPE 378:27
vision and the faculty d. WORD 577:9
what the form d.
LAND 308:26
Whether it d. tobacco were SPEN 516:15
worshipp'd by the names d. BLAKE 86:1
wrote that monarchs were d. KIPL 300:5
You look d. as you advance NASH 360:5

divinely: ever most d. in the wrong
YOUNG 587:17
most d. fair
TENN 533:6
divineness: people hath some d. BACON 25:11
some participation of d. BACON 24:19
divines: eternal reproach of the d.
MILT 352:12
divinest: two d. things this world
HUNT 268:13
divinity: d. doth hedge a king SHAK 436:6
d. in odd numbers SHAK 469:15
d. or school metaphysics HUME 267:15
d. that shapes our ends SHAK 437:11
doctors of law or d. BURKE 108:12
is something in it of d. BROW 97:1
is surely a piece of d. BROW 97:4
'Tis the d. that stirs ADD 1:24
wingy mysteries in d. BROW 96:8
divisible: Mankind is d. into two BEER 37:17
Division: D. is as bad ANON 6:18
such d. 'tween our souls SHAK 451:29
divisions: Pope! How many d. STAL 517:16
divisos: Et penitus toto d. orbe VIRG 559:13
Divitias: D. operosiores HOR 260:16
divorc'd: d. So many English kings
SHAK 442:18
divorce: long d. of steel SHAK 446:27
then this bill of my D. DONNE 189:11
divorced: Demand to be d. CHES 147:26
D. old barren Reason from FITZ 213:1
Dixeris: D. egregie notum si callida
HOR 257:13
dixerunt: qui ante nos nostra d. DON 187:17
dixit: 'Ipse d.
CIC 151:20
dizzy: d., a tumultuous joy SOUT 514:11
d. 'tis to cast one's eyes SHAK 455:14
do: can't all d. everything VIRG 560:6
d. any man's heart good SHAK 469:29
d. anything well till we HAZL 243:25
D. as I say
SELD 420:1
d. as much for my true-love BALL 32:9
d. as you would be done CHES 145:17
d. for pretty girls YEATS 585:16
d. it yourself
BARH 33:10
D. lovely things KING 296:19
D. not do unto others SHAW 497:34
d. nothing and get something DISR 186:28
d. only one thing SMIL 509:6
'D. other men
DICK 179:9
d. something today which COLL 158:12
d. were as easy as to know SHAK 465:20
D. what you like RAB 403:28
d. ye even so to them BIBLE 65:5
having too little to d. KIPL 300:9
How many things I can d. SOCR 512:22
HOW NOT TO D. IT DICK 178:16
I am to d. what I please FRED 218:22
I can d. no other LUTH 320:16
I'll do, and I'll d. SHAK 458:6
I'll d. 't before I speak SHAK 453:5
'I should d. so DOYLE 192:36
It revolts me, but I d. it GILB 226:21
I will d. such things SHAK 454:2
I would they should d. PRAY 388:15
Let us d. or die BURNS 115:1
Love and d. what you will AUG 21:21
my girl...it won't d. JOHN 275:9
not knowing what they d. SHAK 473:1
one that will d. the deed SHAK 456:27
out what you cannot d. BLAKE 87:6
People don't d. such things IBSEN 270:1
Their's but to d. and die TENN 532:24
they know not what they d. BIBLE 71:11
things we cannot all d. LUC 320:2
This will never d. JEFF 272:19
to d. those things which KEYN 295:17
To-morrow let us d. or die CAMP 128:18
trouble always to d. SHAW 496:31
true and d. what is right HUXL 269:9
'We cannot d. it CARR 135:25

What are we going to d.	AUDEN 19:14	living d. is better than	BIBLE 55:27	**Doleful:** Knight of the D. Countenance	
Whatever you d.	ANON 10:18	Lovell our d.	COLL 158:10		CERV 138:12
what I d. in any thing	HERB 247:18	Mine enemy's d.	SHAK 455:24	**dolefull'st:** there sung the d. ditty	BARN 33:32
what is it you d.	WORD 581:2	my poor d. Tray	CAMP 128:20	*DOLENTE: ME SI VA NELLA CITTÀ*	
What must I d. to be saved	BIBLE 74:7	'O keep the D. far hence	ELIOT 204:22	D.	DANTE 171:3
what you are afraid to d.	EMER 207:23	ope my lips let no d.	SHAK 465:12	**doll:** doll in the d.'s house	DICK 181:19
who can d. all things well	CHUR 148:23	Orion and the D. Are veiled	ELIOT 204:15	once had a sweet little d.	KING 297:4
Doasyouwouldbedoneby: her name is		poor d.	BYRON 124:40	**dollar:** almighty d. is the only	ANON 7:21
Mrs D.	KING 297:12	preaching is like a d.'s	JOHN 275:10	almighty d.	IRV 270:26
docent: Homines dum d. discunt	SEN 420:10	see the portrait of a d.	JOHN 280:19	D. Diplomacy	ANON 5:2
doceri: fas est et ab hoste d.	OVID 366:16	Something better than his d.	TENN 538:19	**dolor:** sanguine and subtle D.	SWIN 529:8
docile: that they may be more d.	MILL 339:15	tail must wag the d.	KIPL 298:16	splendid and sterile D.	SWIN 529:9
docks: hateful d.	SHAK 445:12	that town a d. was found	GOLD 231:12	**dolour:** have wept to see the d.	MAL 328:4
spudding up d.	HARDY 240:19	'The d. did nothing	DOYLE 192:16	**dolphin:** heard a mermaid on a d.'s	
doctor: d. found	GOLD 231:8	tongue of d.	SHAK 462:3		SHAK 470:7
d. full of phrase and fame	ARN 15:12	very d. to the commonalty	SHAK 427:10	his delights Were d.-like	SHAK 423:22
d. is a specially dangerous	SHAW 498:22	very flea of his d.	JONS 284:6	That d.-torn	YEATS 584:13
d.'s thesis On education	AUDEN 21:4	whose d. are you	POPE 376:16	**Dolphin-chamber:** sitting in my D.	
God and the d. we alike	OWEN 366:28	You call'd me d.	SHAK 466:3		SHAK 441:20
man therein d. but himself	MILT 350:21	young man's d. with them	BIBLE 62:9	**dolphins:** d. of kindlier waves	MOORE 355:23
outliv'd the d.'s pill	GAY 222:30	**dogfight:** We were regaled by a d.		**Dolphin-scales:** 'There's Venus objects	
Than fee the d. for a nauseous	DRYD 196:5		MAC 324:26	to D.	GRAV 234:12
When the artless d. sees	HERR 250:12	**dogged:** It's d. as does it	TROL 552:23	**dome:** Build up the blue d.	SHEL 500:7
doctors: better have d. well off	SHAW 498:22	**doggy:** on with their d. life	AUDEN 19:19	starlit or a moonlit d.	YEATS 584:12
budge d. of the Stoic	MILT 341:16	**dog-kennel:** his ears in a empty d.		**domestic:** d. as a plate	MILL 339:27
d. cocking their medical	DICK 183:11		DICK 179:27	d. business is no less	MONT 354:19
d. of law or divinity	BURKE 108:12	**dogma:** d. has been the fundamental		d. servants are treated	SHAW 497:40
If you believe the d.	SAL 413:18		NEWM 361:20	Milk-soup men call d. bliss	PATM 370:4
when d. disagree	POPE 377:30	d. of the Ghost	RYLE 412:25	minute d. happiness	KEATS 294:10
doctrine: about with every wind of d.		no d., no Dean	DISR 185:23	smooth current of d. joy	JOHN 282:21
	BIBLE 77:28	**dogmatise:** I d. and am contradicted		**domesticate:** d. the Recording Angel	
d. of the enclitic *De*	BROW 101:1		JOHN 280:21		STEV 521:33
d. of the strenuous life	ROOS 407:27	**dogs:** attentive to the feelings of d.		*domi: Res angusta d.*	JUV 287:18
d. set forth thy true	PRAY 387:15		ELIOT 201:11	**dominant:** d.'s persistence till	BROW 105:24
d. so illogical and so	KEYN 295:16	bang these d. of Seville	TENN 543:1	**domination:** d. over them in the morning	
every blast of vain d.	PRAY 387:3	barking d. by Highgate Pond	BETJ 43:19		PRAY 393:1
Not for the d.	POPE 378:20	better I like d.	ROL 407:16	military d. of Prussia	ASQ 17:17
doctrines: By d. fashion'd	GOLD 230:22	Cowardly d. bark loudest	WEBS 567:5	**dominion:** death hath no more d. over	
d. of devils	BIBLE 79:13	dancing d. and bears	HODG 252:2		BIBLE 75:2
makes all d. plain and clear	BUTL 118:10	D., easily won to fawn	SHAK 479:9	death shall have no d.	THOM 546:19
documents: England are ready to sign		d. eat of the crumbs which	BIBLE 66:30	d. of the sea	COV 163:10
d.	HURST 268:17	d. licked his sores	BIBLE 70:28	d. of the world	MAHAN 327:5
wants more d. than he can	JAMES 271:18	Goethe had an aversion to d.	NERV 361:1	D. over palm and pine	KIPL 302:7
Dodger: *sobriquet* of 'The artful D.		hates d. and babies	ROST 410:14	His d. shall be also from	PRAY 394:20
	DICK 180:33	Lame d. over stiles	KING 296:21	I'm truly sorry Man's d.	BURNS 115:21
dodgers: dodgerest of the d.	DICK 181:20	Let d. delight to bark	WATTS 565:17	inglorious period of our d.	BURKE 110:24
d. as these old men are	JOW 285:22	let's go to the d. to-night	HERB 246:7	them have d. over the fish	BIBLE 45:4
Dodo: D. never had a chance	CUPPY 170:15	let slip the d. of war	SHAK 450:12	they get the d. over me	PRAY 390:13
doers: be ye d. of the word	BIBLE 80:10	like dancing d.	JOHN 276:30	**dominions:** of depopulating his d.	BECK 36:19
does: d.—nothing at all	FARQ 209:25	little d. and all	SHAK 454:29	tithe or toll in our d.	SHAK 452:17
d., not suffers wrong	SHEL 502:20	Mad d. and Englishmen	COW 163:19	*Dominus: D. custodierit civitatem*	
doest: That thou d., do quickly	BIBLE 72:29	Now for the d. and apes	BROW 100:37		BIBLE 83:12
doeth: Whoso d. these things	PRAY 390:5	of their horses and d.	PENN 371:15	D. *illuminatio mea*	BIBLE 83:5
doff't: Had d. her gawdy trim	MILT 344:5	That d. bark at me	SHAK 480:18	D. *vobiscum*	MASS 334:11
dog: Am I a d.	BIBLE 50:12	They fought the d.	BROW 103:15	*domum: Ite d. saturae*	VIRG 560:9
bargain he. never bites	NASH 360:3	they were na men but d.	BURNS 116:1	**Don:** D. different from those	BELL 39:28
Beware of the d.	PETR 372:30	Things are but as straw d.	LAO 310:2	Remote and ineffectual D.	BELL 39:27
call a d. *Hervey*	JOHN 273:30	Throw physic to the d.	SHAK 463:3	turn'd my back upon D.	TENN 543:1
courtesy help a lame d.	CHIL 148:13	Uncover, d., and lap	SHAK 486:7	*dona: d. nobis pacem*	MASS 335:7
cut-throat d.	SHAK 466:2	Unmiss'd but by his d.	COWP 166:6	*Requiem aeternam d. eis*	MASS 334:17
Dies like a d.	WHIT 571:18	without are d.	BIBLE 83:3	*timeo Danaos et d.*	VIRG 558:1
d. bites a man	BOG 89:9	**Dog-star:** D. rages	POPE 376:18	**done:** anything remained to be d.	
d. is turned to his own	BIBLE 81:2	**dogwood:** d. and chestnut	ELIOT 203:4		LUCAN 319:24
d. it was that died	GOLD 231:14	**doileys:** I'm soiling the d.	BETJ 42:20	Apostles would have d.	BYRON 122:10
d. returneth to his vomit	BIBLE 54:32	**doing:** be up and d.	LONG 317:5	been and gone and d.	GILB 225:12
d. starv'd at his master's	BLAKE 85:10	continuance in well d.	BIBLE 74:33	consider it d.	CAL 127:9
d. that praised his fleas	YEATS 587:4	done instead of not d.	POUND 382:14	Determined, dared, and d.	SMART 509:4
d., to gain some private	GOLD 231:13	dread of d. what has been done	WHAR 569:9	doing what has been d. before	WHAR 569:9
engine of pollution, the d.	SPAR 514:23	heaven-born privilege of d.	ARN 15:20	d. anything that could	DISR 186:27
every d. his day	KING 297:5	joy's soul lies in the d.	SHAK 486:21	D. because we are too menny	HARDY 241:15
fleas is good fer a d.	WEST 569:4	labour of d. nothing	STEE 518:8	d. instead of not doing	POUND 382:14
giving your heart to a d.	KIPL 302:3	not be weary in well d.	BIBLE 77:20	d. the state some service	SHAK 477:23
good d., like a good candidate	BECK 36:18	see what she's d.	PUNCH 402:23	d. to you young blackguards	FARR 210:28
'Hath a d. money	SHAK 466:3	still be d.	BUTL 117:22	d. with Hope and Honour	KIPL 299:11
His faithful d. shall bear	POPE 379:6	This is the Lord's d.	PRAY 398:2	he has d. it all himself	BARR 34:22
I'd beat him like a d.	SHAK 488:22	way of d. things rightly	RUSK 411:26	he might have d. with us	CLOU 153:22
I had rather be a d.	SHAK 451:14	what everyone is d.	HERB 246:9		
infidel as a d. is an infidel	JOHN 275:26	What was he d.	BROW 98:6		
Is thy servant a d.	BIBLE 51:31	**Doing-good:** D., that is one	THOR 550:14		
Like a d.	TENN 538:21	**doings:** child is known by his d.	BIBLE 54:17		

DOWNCAST DREAMS

levellers wish to level *d.* JOHN 275:5
quite, quite, d. SHAK 433:15
sloth Finds the d. pillow SHAK 428:18
soft young d. of her MEW 338:12
they must be kept d. MARL 329:2
way d. to the Underworld VIRG 558:18
you don't go d. with me MILNE 340:6
downcast: people to feel a little d. MCG 325:5
downfall: regress is either a d. BACON 26:23
down-gyved: d. to his ancle SHAK 431:28
downhearted: Are we d. ANON 4:23
We are not d. CHAM 139:7
downhill: This d. path is easy ROSS 408:22
Downs: D. the fleet was moor'd GAY 223:28
is fair on the dewy d. TENN 540:17
that looks on Ilsley d. ARN 15:3
down-sitting: d., and mine up-rising PRAY 399:4
downstairs: why did you kick me d. BICK 83:27
downward: Were always d. bent MILT 345:26
downwards: could look no way but d. BUNY 107:28
my gross flesh sinks d. SHAK 480:16
dozen: d. dozen in her place SUCK 524:15
dozens: Whom he reckons up by d. GILB 228:3
draäins: Annie she said it wur d. TENN 544:5
drab: Ditch-deliver'd by a d. SHAK 462:4
Drachenfels: castled crag of D. BYRON 120:31
drachmas: drop my blood for d. SHAK 451:21
drag: have weight to d. thee down TENN 538:19
Put on the d. SMITH 512:3
dragg'd: have d. to three-and-thirty BYRON 126:15
dragon: angels fought against the d. BIBLE 82:11
between the d. and his wrath SHAK 453:4
centaur in his d. world POUND 382:13
Dare the unpastured d. SHEL 499:15
d.-green FLEC 214:8
d. shalt thou tread under PRAY 395:22
ev'ning d. came MILT 350:29
he laid hold on the d. BIBLE 82:27
my mother under the d.'s SHAK 453:11
swinged the d. and e'er since SHAK 452:12
to be a d. MOORE 355:18
dragon-fly: sun-searched growths the d. ROSS 409:24
dragons: be an habitation of d. BIBLE 58:31
D. in their pleasant palaces BIBLE 58:12
D. of the prime TENN 536:30
I am a brother to d. BIBLE 52:37
ye d., and all deeps PRAY 399:22
drags: d. at each remove a lengthening GOLD 231:24
d. its slow length along POPE 378:21
draiglet: She d. a' her petticoatie BURNS 113:2
drain: d. pure gold flows forth TOCQ 551:9
have put it down the d. HERB 246:11
drained: yet d. not by the day SHEL 503:19
drains: Democracy and proper d. BETJ 43:6
Drake: D. he's in his hammock NEWB 361:7
drama: close the d. with the day BERK 41:20
d.'s laws the drama's JOHN 282:27
Dramatise: D., dramatise JAMES 271:14
dramatist: d. only wants more liberties JAMES 271:18
drame: *savoir le grand d. de ma vie* WILDE 573:35
Drang: *Sturm und D.* KAUF 288:17
drank: d. my ale FARQ 209:23
d. Prussic acid without BARH 33:26
d. without the provocation SWIFT 526:10
he d. of the brook BIBLE 51:6
Jamshyd gloried and d. FITZ 212:14
They all d. his health FARR 210:29
went to the well and d. MAL 327:15
drapery: with the d. of his figures COL 158:8
Drastic: D. measures is Latin ANST 11:9
draught: cup with such a d. of woe SHEL 499:18
does not think of the d. AUST 22:14
draughts: peculiarly susceptible to d. WILDE 573:6
draughty: d. church at smokefall ELIOT 202:16
dravest: Thou d. love from thee THOM 548:23
draw: began to d. to our end BIBLE 62:17
cable can so forcibly d. BURT 116:33
Can d. you to her *with* DRYD 198:21
d. Hearts after them MILT 350:2
D. near with faith PRAY 387:18
d. the Thing as he sees KIPL 304:3
is to d. a full face DRYD 198:11
only used to d. Madonnas BROW 102:28
thou d. out leviathan with BIBLE 53:11
drawbacks: everything has its d. JER 272:25
drawers: waistcoat and flannel d. GASK 221:24
wood and d. of water BIBLE 49:3
drawing: d. days out SHAK 450:3
D. is the true test INGR 270:19
I meant it for d.' CONS 162:3
no d. back BRON 94:3
think that I am d. to an end PAIN 367:18
Drawling: *he* taught us D. CARR 134:11
drawn: It oughtn't to be d. DICK 176:32
drayhorse: fettle for the great grey d. HOPK 256:11
Dr Busby: D., a great man ADD 2:17
dread: d. and fear of kings SHAK 467:27
d. of doing what has been WHAR 569:9
let him be your d. BIBLE 58:4
Nor d. nor hope attend YEATS 584:20
was he chill'd with d. SCOTT 416:15
What d. hand BLAKE 87:15
whence this secret d. ADD 1:24
Yet nothing did he d. SPEN 515:32
your eyes with holy d. COL 157:1
dreaded: Thy most d. instrument WORD 578:21
dreadful: Between the acting of a d. SHAK 449:6
deed of d. note SHAK 461:13
d. fiend of gods and men SPEN 516:22
d. is the check BRON 93:21
Give d. note of preparation SHAK 444:9
silences Of d. things AUDEN 18:5
Dreading: D. and hoping all YEATS 584:20
dreads: Greatly his foes he d. CHUR 148:18
dream: altogether vanished like a d. CARL 131:34
awakened from the d. of life SHEL 499:20
behold it was a d. BUNY 107:27
Diuturnity is a d. and a folly BROW 97:21
d. doth flatter SHAK 494:13
D. of Loveliness descending LEL 313:18
d. of money-bags to-night SHAK 466:11
d. of the days when work CHES 147:22
d. of the soft look YEATS 587:12
d.'s sake ROSS 409:2
d. that I am home again FLEC 214:5
each age is a d. that is OSH 365:21
empty words of a d. BRID 92:10
faileth now even d. THOM 548:17
freshness of a d. WORD 578:22
from a deep d. of peace HUNT 268:4
glory and the d. WORD 579:5
He should d. of the devil BARH 33:13
hope I dreamed of was a d. ROSS 409:2
I cried to d. again SHAK 485:18
I did but d. SHAK 481:13
if I d. I have you DONNE 188:8
If you can d. KIPL 299:22
I have a d. KING 296:15
In a d. you are never SEXT 420:18
Is but a d. within a dream POE 375:2
Life is but an empty d. LONG 317:1
life, that insane d. BROW 100:22
life, without a d. ROST 410:13
likened our life to a d. MONT 355:5
like unto them that d. PRAY 398:16
lost traveller's d. BLAKE 86:1
love's young d. MOORE 356:12
My d. thou brok'st not DONNE 188:5
not d. them KING 296:19
o'er the spirit of my d. BYRON 124:13
perceived they had dreamed a d. BROW 105:19
perchance to d. SHAK 433:8
perfectibility as a d. MILL 339:17
phantasma, or a hideous d. SHAK 449:6
pleasures in a long immortal d. KEATS 290:23
quiet sleep and a sweet d. MAS 334:6
short as any d. SHAK 469:20
sights as youthful poets d. MILT 342:26
sight to d. COL 156:3
smiling face a d. of Spring COL 157:14
so d. all night without KEATS 290:5
So runs my d. TENN 536:26
That children d. not BROW 95:23
then they d. of love SHAK 481:28
thou mightst in d. SHEL 503:17
vision and the old men's d. DRYD 194:9
waking d. KEATS 291:23
With the first d. that MEYN 338:14
wit of man to say what d. SHAK 471:9
wrecks of a dissolving d. SHEL 500:20
you d. you are crossing GILB 226:13
dream'd: d. in a dream I saw a city WHIT 570:4
d. that Greece might still BYRON 122:33
I d. of the devil ANST 11:7
dreamed: child I d. CHES 147:8
d. that life was Beauty HOOP 255:22
he d., and behold a ladder BIBLE 46:18
I d. fast of mirth WEVER 569:7
night I've d. of cheese STEV 521:23
perceived they had d. a dream BROW 105:19
dreamer: d. of dreams...Thou shalt BIBLE 48:23
D. of dreams MORR 358:9
He is a d. SHAK 448:8
poet and the d. are distinct KEATS 289:28
this d. cometh BIBLE 46:28
dreamers: We are the d. of dreams OSH 365:20
dreaming: City with her d. spires ARN 15:4
d. through the twilight ROSS 409:9
I am now a butterfly d. CHUA 148:17
dreams: affliction of these terrible d. SHAK 461:12
angels in some brighter d. VAUG 555:21
because you tread on my d. YEATS 585:9
before us like a land of d. ARN 12:23
beyond the d. of avarice JOHN 278:27
days of golden d. BRON 93:24
Dead d. of days forsaken SWIN 529:23
dream'd his white Platonic d. JOHN 273:19
D. and desires and sombre SWIN 528:26
d. are dreams CALD 127:5
d. happy as her day BROO 94:30
d. their children dreamed COL 155:3
d. you have denied yourself POUND 383:13
dreamt of in d. BARH 33:11
Drumming like a noise in d. HOUS 263:18
Even in d. good works are CALD 127:4
fantasy Black d. DONNE 190:3
Heavy with d. THOM 548:28
he hunts in d. TENN 538:21
her as Dian had hot d. SHAK 429:3
I arise from d. of thee SHEL 501:8
If there were d. to sell BEDD 36:28
In doubtful d. of dreams SWIN 529:21
not make d. your master KIPL 299:22
not that I have bad d. SHAK 432:13

of d., and ceremonies   SHAK 449:10
old men shall dream d.   BIBLE 61:15
Our d. are tales   DE L 173:25
Phidias Gave women d.   YEATS 587:1
pleasing d.   SCOTT 417:26
quick D.   SHEL 499:7
Real are the d. of Gods   KEATS 290:23
rich beyond the d. of avarice   MOORE 355:14
sick men's d.   BROW 95:23
stuff As d. are made on   SHAK 485:20
Than this world d.   TENN 535:26
thousand such enchanting d.   HERR 249:1
Thou wovest d. of joy   SHEL 505:2
were a trouble to my d.   WORD 580:14
we see it in our d.   CHEK 144:26
who lived by honest d.   DAY-L 172:23
wicked d. abuse   SHAK 460:1
dreamt: d. of in your philosophy
   SHAK 431:23
Drear: D. all this excellence   POUND 383:19
vast edges d.   ARN 12:23
dreariness: d. in dedicated spirits   FRY 219:23
dregs: among the d. of Romulus   CIC 151:16
from the d. of life   DRYD 195:27
dreme: d. of joye   CHAU 144:1
drench: then a strong horse d.   LAMB 307:30
drench'd: you have d. our steeples
   SHAK 454:4
Drene: Delicately drowns in D.   BETJ 43:14
dress: does it signify how we d.   GASK 221:23
d. by yellow candle-light   STEV 522:16
more value than their d.   HAZL 243:20
noble youth did d. themselves   SHAK 441:24
Peace, the human d.   BLAKE 88:7
sweet disorder in the d.   HERR 249:2
through all this fleshly d.   VAUG 555:16
we d. when we're ruined   HARDY 240:19
dress'd: Let me be d. fine   WATTS 565:24
dressed: temper when he's well d.   DICK 179:1
dresses: neat-handed Phyllis d.   MILT 342:21
dressing: d. old words   SHAK 494:9
dressings: every season she hath d.
   ANON 6:20
Drest: D. in a little brief authority
   SHAK 464:2
drew: I d. my snickersnee   GILB 227:8
man a bow at a venture   BIBLE 51:11
Dr Fell: I do not love you, D.   BROWN 95:10
Dr Froyd: So then D. said that all   LOOS 318:6
dried: d. up, and withered   PRAY 395:18
Drift: D. across the window-panes
   ELIOT 204:1
drifting: I am d. with the tide   BALL 31:3
drifts: with its dank yellow d.   ARN 14:8
drills: double d. and no canteen   KIPL 299:19
drink: Aunt Jobiska made him d.
   LEAR 312:17
Barring d. and the girls   LOCK 315:23
beasts of the field d.   PRAY 396:19
be their portion to d.   PRAY 389:31
can d. till all look blue   FORD 216:17
Doth ask a d. divine   JONS 284:12
d., and be merry   BIBLE 70:4
d. and blacking the Corporal's   KIPL 298:7
d., and forget his poverty   BIBLE 55:25
D. and the devil had done   STEV 521:21
d. cold brandy and water   LAMB 308:7
D. fair   DICK 179:28
D.! for you know not whence   FITZ 213:9
D. no longer water   BIBLE 79:16
D. not the third glass   HERB 247:1
d. shall be prepared gold   JONS 285:14
D., sir, is a great provoker   SHAK 460:18
d. some beer   JOHN 277:14
d. that slakes thirst   CERV 138:20
d. the blood of goats   PRAY 393:3
d. thy wine with a merry   BIBLE 55:28
D. to me only with thine   JONS 284:12
d. unto one of these little   BIBLE 65:41
d. with you   SHAK 465:28

D. ye all of this   PRAY 388:1
d. your ale   HOUS 264:22
eat, and to d.   BIBLE 55:26
felony to d. small beer   SHAK 446:11
five reasons we should d.   ALDR 3:10
Givin' d. to poor damned   KIPL 299:19
I d. well   MORT 358:17
in debt, and in d.   BROME 93:10
Leeze me on d.   BURNS 114:8
Let us eat and d.   BIBLE 58:15
let us eat and d.   BIBLE 76:24
man may d. and no be drunk   BURNS 115:13
Man wants but little d.   HOLM 253:13
meaning is my meat and d.   BROW 90:31
never taste who always d.   PRIOR 401:11
Nor any drop to d.   COL 155:14
now could I d. hot blood   SHAK 434:25
proper d. of Englishmen   BORR 90:8
sat down to eat and to d.   BIBLE 48:3
Shall sit and d. with me   BELL 40:11
shook to see him d. it up   HOUS 264:15
Should every creature d.   COWL 164:8
strong d. is raging   BIBLE 54:15
taste for d.   GILB 225:21
that I can d.   ANON 5:21
Then d., puppy   WHYT 572:2
they may follow strong d.   BIBLE 57:25
They will d. our healths   KIPL 298:13
thirsty and ye gave me d.   BIBLE 68:6
thou gavest meat or d.   BALL 31:7
We'll teach you to d. deep   SHAK 430:3
drinkers: is written by d. of water
   HOR 258:25
drinketh: he d. up a river   BIBLE 53:10
sunlight d. dew   TENN 533:16
drinking: constant d. fresh and fair
   COWL 164:7
dancing, d.   DRYD 197:12
days in a tavern d.   ANON 10:14
d. at somebody else's expense   LEIGH 313:15
d. bottled ditchwater   SHAW 496:33
D. is the soldier's pleasure   DRYD 195:1
d. largely sobers us again   POPE 378:13
D. my griefs   SHAK 479:22
D. the blude-red wine   BALL 31:16
d. too much of Mr Weston's   AUST 22:11
D. watered orange-pulp   BROW 105:6
D. when we are not thirsty   BEAU 35:17
is the curse of the d.   WILDE 573:39
much d., little thinking   SWIFT 526:18
There is no d. after death   FLET 215:7
they were eating and d.   BIBLE 67:32
thought surpass eating and d.   CLOU 153:21
'Tis not the d. that is   SELD 419:20
unhappy brains for d.   SHAK 474:23
drinks: king d. to Hamlet   SHAK 437:17
Now for d.   HOR 260:3
drip: That long d. of human tears
   HARDY 240:12
Dripping: D. along   BETJ 44:3
drive: difficult to d.   BROU 95:6
d. a coach and six horses   RICE 406:1
d. an angel from your door   BLAKE 88:4
d. me mad on my deathbed   BYRON 126:20
driven: towns all Inns have been d.
   BELL 40:16
drives: d. fat oxen should himself
   JOHN 279:20
D. my green age   THOM 547:3
one nail by strength d.   SHAK 490:34
driving: d. briskly in a post-chaise
   JOHN 277:15
driving is like the d. of Jehu   BIBLE 51:33
drizzle: blasted English d. wakes   KIPL 301:7
Dr Johnson: D. condemns whatever he
   BURN 112:20
D.'s morality was as English   HAWT 243:5
droghte: d. of March hath perced   CHAU 141:7
droits: *Toute loi qui viole les d.*   ROB 406:11
drollery: That fatal d. called   DISR 186:34

dromedary: Donne, whose muse on d.
   COL 157:6
D. is a cheerful bird   BELL 38:27
drone: lazy yawning d.   SHAK 443:9
droon: I d. twa'   ANON 7:12
Droop: D. in a hundred A.B.C.'s
   ELIOT 202:5
Droops: D. on the little hands   MILNE 340:11
drop: are as a d. of a bucket   BIBLE 59:8
clouds d. fatness   PRAY 394:3
dance till you d.   AUDEN 18:13
d. of allaying Tiber   SHAK 427:14
d. of rain maketh a hole   LAT 310:20
d., slow tears   FLET 215:29
One d. would save my soul   MARL 329:11
should like very well to d.   JOHN 278:24
Then d. into thyself   POPE 379:14
To d. a limb on the head   KIPL 303:26
we d. like the fruits   MER 336:26
dropped: glory d. from their youth
   BROW 105:19
heavens d. at the presence   PRAY 394:7
would not wish to be d.   JOHN 278:24
dropping: d. down the ladder rung
   KIPL 299:11
d. in a very rainy day   BIBLE 54:39
D. the pilot   TENN 532:14
peace comes d. slow   YEATS 585:17
dropping-down-deadness: d. of manner
   SMITH 512:1
drops: changed into little water d.
   MARL 329:15
D. earliest to the ground   SHAK 467:25
d. on gate-bars hang   HARDY 241:4
d. That visit my sad heart   SHAK 449:15
soft with the d. of rain   PRAY 394:3
these are gracious d.   SHAK 450:28
dropsies: were people who died of d.
   JOHN 280:2
dropt: arms burd Helen d.   BALL 31:4
D. from the ruin'd sides   BEAU 36:1
D. from the zenith like   MILT 346:3
dross: admits no qualifying d.   SHAK 487:10
is d. that is not Helena   MARL 329:10
stoops not to shows of d.   SHAK 466:16
drove: he d. them all out   BIBLE 71:35
Drown: D. all my faults and fears
   FLET 215:30
d. myself in the Thames…I   DICK 180:19
I'll d. my book   SHAK 485:24
I will incontinently d.   SHAK 474:7
tears shall d. the wind   SHAK 459:6
what pain it was to d.   SHAK 480:27
drown'd: d. in yonder living blue
   TENN 537:19
d. my Glory in a Shallow   FITZ 213:13
d. the cocks   SHAK 454:4
thy thought till it be d.   ROSS 409:26
drownded: d. now and again   SYNGE 531:4
drowned: he were d. in the depth   BIBLE 67:3
She is d. already   SHAK 488:15
drowning: By d. their speaking   BROW 103:15
hath no d. mark upon him   SHAK 484:21
not waving but d.   SMITH 510:26
drowns: Delicately d. in Drene   BETJ 43:14
d. things weighty and solid   BACON 27:5
drowsy: Dapples the d. east   SHAK 473:11
d. numbness pains   KEATS 291:16
Nor all the d. syrups   SHAK 475:24
these d. approaches of sleep   BROW 95:22
Vexing the dull ear of a d.   SHAK 452:21
drowsyhead: pleasing land of d. it was
   THOM 549:8
drudge: harmless d.   JOHN 274:13
drudgery: d. of the desk's dead wood
   LAMB 307:33
in the low d. of avarice   BURKE 108:7
Makes d. divine   HERB 247:19
drug: literature is a d.   BORR 90:7
drugs: d. cause cramp   PARK 368:18

drum: An' d. them up the Channel
    NEWB 361:6
Bang-whang-whang goes the d. BROW 105:31
Beats like a fatalistic d. ELIOT 204:9
d.! a drum SHAK 458:8
Dumb as a d. with a hole DICK 182:4
follow an antique d. ELIOT 202:27
melancholy as an unbrac'd d. CENT 138:11
Music of a distant D. FITZ 212:12
My pulse like a soft d. KING 296:12
Not a d. was heard WOLFE 576:2
spirit-stirring d. SHAK 475:25
when you hear the d. SHAK 466:13
drum-beat: whose morning d. WEBS 566:12
drummer: Far I hear the steady d.
    HOUS 263:18
Hodge the D. never knew HARDY 239:8
drumming: Down in the valley d.
    AUDEN 20:4
drums: beat the d. DRYD 194:26
beat the d. MOR 357:21
en de bangin' er de d. HARR 242:17
heard thro' rolling d. TENN 542:7
like muffled d. LONG 317:2
when the d. begin to roll KIPL 303:24
drunk: against a post when he was d.
    SHAK 444:6
Be not d. with wine BIBLE 78:5
contracted in trying to get d. JOHN 280:2
d. deep of the Pierian DRAY 193:15
d. old wine straightway BIBLE 69:19
d. to bed SHAK 421:13
d. with sight of power KIPL 302:9
eaten and d. enough HOR 259:6
fields have d. enough VIRG 559:21
genteel when he gets d. BOSW 90:16
got d. PORS 381:29
Have d. their Cup a Round FITZ 212:17
he hath not d. ink SHAK 457:1
I d. him to his bed SHAK 422:10
if it be d. moderately BIBLE 63:15
may drink and no be d. BURNS 115:13
must get d. BYRON 122:22
not the art of getting d. JOHN 278:8
once saw Wordsworth d. HOUS 266:18
partly she was d. BURNS 114:18
Philip to Philip sober ANON 4:22
that this meeting is d. DICK 182:17
Then hasten to be d. DRYD 195:37
th'hydroptic earth hath d. DONNE 189:28
Was the hope d. SHAK 459:8
when men have well d. BIBLE 71:34
which hath made them d. SHAK 460:2
drunkard: English d. made the rolling
    CHES 147:10
Reel in a d. CHUR 149:1
drunkards: MSS as d. use lamp-posts
    HOUS 266:14
drunken: dreadfully but as a d. sleep
    SHAK 464:25
got more d. PORS 381:29
Shall be brought d. forth SHAK 424:3
stagger like a d. man PRAY 397:10
Sure I had d. in my dreams COL 155:24
They are d. BIBLE 58:23
drunkenly: Who now goes d. out
    POUND 382:5
drunkenness: branch of the sin of d.
    JAM 271:2
drunkennesses: in anger or penitent d.
    RIMB 406:9
Druse: D. and the Catholic CHES 146:27
dry: being d. ALDR 3:10
d. a cinder this world DONNE 187:20
d. as the remainder biscuit SHAK 425:21
d. one's eyes BROW 102:1
d. place, as the shadow BIBLE 58:30
d. the starting tear GILB 225:8
d. your eyes KEATS 289:25
I am so d. ANON 6:1

in a barren and d. land PRAY 393:21
nothing sooner d. WEBS 567:7
old man in a d. month ELIOT 203:3
Rabelais dwelling in a d. place COL 158:2
refresh it when it was d. PRAY 386:3
shall be done in the d. BIBLE 71:10
they whose hearts are d. WORD 577:11
thoroughly small and d. ELIOT 202:1
tones as d. and level AUDEN 20:10
water what is d. LANG 310:1
would fain die a d. death SHAK 484:22
ye d. bones BIBLE 61:2
Dryad: light-winged D. of the trees
    KEATS 291:17
Dryden: D. fails to render him ARN 16:12
poetry and the poetry of D. ARN 16:9
drynke: his hous of mete and d. CHAU 141:28
Dublin: D., though a place much JOHN 279:23
ducats: my d.! O my daughter SHAK 466:18
duce: quot libras in d. summo JUV 288:1
Duchess: chambermaid as of a D. JOHN 278:4
D. of Malfi still WEBS 566:24
D. painted on the wall BROW 102:21
D.! The Duchess CARR 133:20
may not blossom into a D. AIL 3:5
Duck: D. and the Kangaroo LEAR 312:4
Put a d. on a lake AUG 21:11
ducks: country stealing d. ARAB 11:18
Four d. on a pond ALL 3:21
duda: Fe que no d. es fe muerta UNAM 554:27
Duddon: backward, D. WORD 581:4
due: season we shall reap BIBLE 77:20
d. time we may enjoy them PRAY 385:21
render to every one his d. JUST 287:8
dues: simple d. of fellowship BROW 97:30
therefore to all their d. BIBLE 75:22
dug: never palates more the d. SHAK 423:20
dugs: old man with wrinkled d. ELIOT 205:1
Duke: D. of Plaza Toro GILB 225:18
d.'s revenues on her back SHAK 446:4
everybody praised the D. SOUT 513:20
From tyrant d. unto a tyrant SHAK 424:28
knows enough who knows a d. COWP 167:31
Let us bury the Great D. TENN 541:5
tell you I was made a D. WELL 567:21
dukedom: library Was d. SHAK 484:26
dukes: d. were three a penny GILB 225:29
Dulce: D. est desipere in loco HOR 261:20
D. et decorum est desipere BUTL 119:9
D. et decorum est pro patria HOR 260:17
D. ridentem CAT 137:4
D. ridentem Lalagen amabo HOR 259:24
dulcet: and harmonious breath SHAK 470:7
dulci: miscuit utile d. HOR 258:1
dulcimer: damsel with a d. COL 156:30
d., and all kinds of musick BIBLE 61:3
dulcis: d. virgo Maria ANON 10:19
dull: at best but d. and hoary VAUG 555:19
be very d. without them WILDE 573:14
can be d. in Fleet Street LAMB 307:23
d. and deep potations excused GIBB 224:9
d. and muddy-mettled rascal SHAK 433:2
d. cold ear of death GRAY 234:22
d. product of a scoffer's WORD 577:12
d. without a single absurdity GOLD 232:31
D. would he be of soul WORD 581:4
He was d. in a new way JOHN 276:19
How d. it is to pause TENN 543:22
is not only d. in himself FOOTE 216:9
make dictionaries is d. JOHN 281:11
Of his d. life BEAU 35:19
of this paper appears d. STEE 518:5
Sherry is d. JOHN 275:7
so d. but she can learn SHAK 467:13
so illogical and so d. KEYN 295:16
so smoothly d. POPE 375:20
Though it's d. at whiles KING 296:21
venerably d. CHUR 149:11
wasn't as d. as ditch water DICK 181:17
What's this d. town to me KEPP 295:12

words oft creep in one d. line POPE 378:20
young Woman her name was D. BUNY 107:30
dullard: d.'s envy of brilliant BEER 37:28
duller: d. shouldst thou be than SHAK 431:8
d. spectacle this earth DE Q 175:1
dullness: cause of d. in others FOOTE 216:9
d. of our senses JOHN 273:17
dully: just walking d. along AUDEN 19:18
dulness: d. of our blinded sight PRAY 400:5
dumb: before her shearers is d. BIBLE 59:22
D. as a drum with a hole DICK 182:4
D., inscrutable and grand ARN 14:4
d. presagers of my speaking SHAK 493:3
D. to Homer BROW 102:35
happen to be deaf and d. HOUS 266:9
noisy bells, be d. HOUS 263:5
otherwise I shall be d. KEATS 294:14
swell is in the havens d. HOPK 256:17
tongue of the d. sing BIBLE 58:34
dumb-bell: Than d. and foil YEATS 586:20
dumbness: banged the youth into d.
    SHAK 489:27
dumbs: now he is one of the d. LEAR 311:21
dumb-shows: inexplicable d. and noise
    SHAK 433:16
Dummheit: Mit der D. kämpfen Götter
    SCH 415:10
dun: then her breasts are d. SHAK 495:8
Duncan: fatal entrance of D. SHAK 459:2
dunce: dearest, you're a d. JOHN 278:30
d. with wits POPE 375:22
Excels a d. that has been COWP 166:11
thou art but a d. BLAKE 86:1
duncery: inquisitorious and tyrannical
    d. MILT 352:15
dunces: d. are all in confederacy SWIFT 527:8
Dundee: bonnet of Bonny D. SCOTT 415:20
stay langer in bonny D. SCOTT 418:30
Dunfermline: king sits in D. town
    BALL 31:16
dungeon: d. horrible MILT 344:25
D., that I'm rotting in CANN 130:5
In a d. cell GILB 227:7
dungeons: Brightest in d., Liberty
    BYRON 125:14
dunghill: d. kind SPEN 516:14
Dunmowe: men han in Essex at D.
    CHAU 143:18
dunnest: in the d. smoke of hell SHAK 459:2
Dunsinane: Birnam wood remove to
    D. SHAK 462:28
Birnam wood to high D. SHAK 462:8
duodecimos: humbler band of d.
    COWP 168:11
dupe: d. of friendship HAZL 243:18
durance: d. vile here must I wake
    BURNS 113:22
duration: is a fallacy in d. BROW 97:15
durst: more mischief than they d.
    HOUS 263:13
dusk: d. and dawn many a head MULL 359:1
d. with a light behind GILB 229:4
dusky: she shall rear my d. race TENN 539:6
straight path along the d. COL 157:11
dust: All valiant d. that builds KIPL 302:10
are they like to take d. SHAK 488:1
chimney-sweepers, come to d. SHAK 428:22
d. and a shadow HOR 261:16
D. as we are WORD 580:11
d. expend an idle breath CAT 137:15
d. of exploded beliefs MADAN 326:18
d. of great persons' graves DONNE 190:23
d. on antique time would SHAK 427:17
d. return to the earth BIBLE 56:11
d. that is a little gilt SHAK 487:6
d. thou art BIBLE 45:23
D. thou art LONG 317:1
d. to be mingled with yours POUND 383:16
d. to dust PRAY 389:13
D. was Gentlemen and Ladies DICK 184:2

earn: I e. that I eat   SHAK 426:4
there's little to e.   KING 297:3
to e. a monumental pile   COWP 166:30
Earned: E. a precarious living   ANON 5:4
Has e. a night's repose   LONG 317:19
earnest: e. of the things that they
  TENN 538:24
I am in e.   GARR 221:17
it is time to be in e.   JOHN 281:23
steadily e. in the pursuit   AUST 22:30
earnestly: e. repent you of your sins
  PRAY 387:18
earns: e. a place i' the story   SHAK 422:18
ears: adder that stoppeth her e.   PRAY 393:17
ass's e. of Midas   SIDN 508:5
Creep in our e.   SHAK 468:15
Death hath asses' e.   BEDD 36:27
devoured the seven good e.   BIBLE 46:32
e., and hear not   PRAY 397:18
e. are senseless that should   SHAK 437:29
e. in an empty dog-kennel   DICK 179:27
e. like errant wings   CHES 146:22
e. of every one that heareth   BIBLE 49:37
earth has stopped the e.   HOUS 263:2
Enemy e. are listening   ANON 9:18
have heard with our e.   PRAY 392:13
hedges e.   SWIFT 528:6
He that hath e. to hear   BIBLE 68:28
is he buzzing in my e.   BROW 100:6
lend me your e.   SHAK 450:17
let thine e. consider well   PRAY 398:23
Look with thine e.   SHAK 455:18
lovers' e. in hearing   SCOTT 416:26
lover's e. will hear   SHAK 457:8
my e. yielding like swinging   DOUG 191:7
Once bless our human e.   MILT 344:10
pluck'd the ripen'd e.   TENN 541:28
porches of mine e.   SHAK 431:11
sets all nations by the e.   LAND 308:21
stop my house's e.   SHAK 466:13
there's a drumming in my e.   SAPP 414:6
to split the e.   SHAK 433:16
was a shout about my e.   CHES 146:23
With ravish'd e.   DRYD 194:24
earth: all the corners of the e.   PRAY 396:4
all the ends of the e.   PRAY 394:1
'And is thy e. so marred   THOM 548:21
are the daughters of e.   JOHN 281:6
are the salt of the e.   BIBLE 64:7
blow the e. into the sea   SHAK 454:3
bowels of the harmless e.   SHAK 438:16
bring food out of the e.   PRAY 396:20
canst work i' the e. so   SHAK 431:21
Cold in the e.   BRON 93:22
composed of the scum of the e.   WELL 568:1
Could frame in e.   SPEN 516:20
created the heaven and the e.   BIBLE 44:22
differ as Heaven and E.   TENN 535:16
dust return to the e.   BIBLE 56:11
E. all Danaë to the stars   TENN 542:14
E. and high heaven are   HOUS 264:3
e. a richer dust concealed   BROO 94:30
e. a trinket at my wrist   THOM 548:17
e. Be but the shadow   MILT 348:21
e. breaks up and heaven   BROW 99:20
e. can take or Heaven can   SHEL 501:2
e. covereth   QUAR 403:20
e. does not argue   WHIT 571:11
e. doth like a snake renew   SHEL 500:20
e. exhales   BETJ 44:5
E. felt the wound   MILT 349:16
e. has not anything   WORD 581:14
e. has stopped the ears   HOUS 263:2
e. his sober inn   CAMP 129:19
e. in an earthy bed   TENN 540:12
e. is all the home I have   AYT 24:12
E. is but a star   FLEC 214:10
e. is cover'd thick with   BYRON 120:27
e. is not too low   HERB 246:26
e. is the Lord's   BIBLE 76:11

e. is the Lord's   PRAY 390:23
e. is weak   PRAY 394:25
e. I wait forlorn   ARN 13:8
E., receive an honoured   AUDEN 19:7
E.'s crammed with heaven   BROW 97:33
e.'s foundations stay   HOUS 265:7
e. shall be full   BIBLE 58:11
e. shall melt away   PRAY 392:20
e. shall wail because   BIBLE 81:10
e. shook   PRAY 394:7
E.'s shadows fly   SHEL 499:26
E.'s the right place   FROST 219:1
E. stood hard as iron   ROSS 409:1
e. sure   DONNE 188:9
e. that is not filled with   BIBLE 54:46
e., that is sufficient   WHIT 571:8
e. the broken arcs   BROW 98:18
E. the first of the gods   VIRG 559:4
e., tideless and inert   BALF 30:3
e. to earth   PRAY 389:13
earth to make the e. my hell   SHAK 481:8
e. Was feverous   SHAK 460:20
e. were paper white   LYLY 321:16
E. will hold us   ANON 10:13
even as if the e. had rolled   WORD 577:27
feels the attraction of e.   LONG 316:11
feel the e. move   HEM 245:3
flowery lap of e.   ARN 13:17
foundation of the e.   PRAY 396:13
foundations of the e.   BIBLE 53:2
fresh E. in new leaves   SHEL 503:26
from which e.   RAL 404:15
girdle round about the e.   SHAK 470:9
gives all men all e. to love   KIPL 303:16
going the way of all the e.   BIBLE 49:5
going to and fro in the e.   BIBLE 52:5
hath made heaven and e.   PRAY 398:14
heaven and e. is named   BIBLE 77:24
Heaven and E. are not ruthful   LAO 310:2
Her all on e.   BYRON 121:35
heroic for e. too hard   BROW 98:20
huge foundation of the e.   SHAK 439:21
I find e. not grey   BROW 98:34
It fell to e.   LONG 316:6
I will move the e.   ARCH 11:24
Lay her i' the e.   SHAK 437:4
Lay that e. upon thy heart   KIPL 298:8
let the E. bless the Lord   PRAY 384:23
Lie heavy on him, E.   EVANS 209:5
life from the glowing e.   GREN 236:15
life of men on e.   BEDE 37:1
Lightly gently e.   BEAU 36:8
like to get away from e.   FROST 219:1
little e. for charity   SHAK 447:15
low as where this e.   ROSS 409:17
made heaven and e.   PRAY 388:20
Man is but e.   DONNE 190:22
Man marks the e. with ruin   BYRON 121:23
meek-spirited shall possess the e.
  PRAY 391:27
must have a touch of e.   TENN 534:26
naked e. is warm with Spring   GREN 236:15
new heaven and a new e.   BIBLE 82:20
new heaven, new e.   SHAK 421:7
new heavens and a new e.   BIBLE 60:14
Nor heaven nor e. have   SHAK 449:17
nought common on Thy E.   KIPL 301:17
O E., lie heavily   ROSS 409:5
Of E.'s first blood   WORD 582:3
on e. peace   BIBLE 69:11
our days on the e. are   BIBLE 51:39
our dungy e. alike   SHAK 421:8
pilgrims on the e.   BIBLE 79:33
poetry of e. is never dead   KEATS 292:21
pure ablution round e.'s   KEATS 292:11
replenish the e.   BIBLE 45:6
Rolled round in e.'s diurnal   WORD 581:10
round e.'s shore   ARN 12:23
round e.'s imagined corners   DONNE 189:3
sleepers in that quiet e.   BRON 94:1

smile o' the brown old e.   BROW 101:20
so much too good for e.   JONS 284:2
Standing on e.   MILT 348:28
Substance from the common E.   FITZ 213:12
Take of English e. as much   KIPL 298:8
that creepeth upon the e.   BIBLE 45:4
there is our e. here   BROW 105:23
There were giants in the e.   BIBLE 45:33
they shall inherit the e.   BIBLE 64:6
th'hydroptic e. hath drunk   DONNE 189:28
th' inhabitants o' the e.   SHAK 458:10
This e. of majesty   SHAK 478:20
this e., this realm   SHAK 478:20
this goodly frame, the e.   SHAK 432:15
thou bleeding piece of e.   SHAK 450:11
though the e. be moved   PRAY 392:19
to e. I   HOUS 265:12
tread on E. unguess'd   ARN 14:24
vilest e. Is room enough   SHAK 440:24
visitest the e., and blessest   PRAY 394:2
water under the e.   BIBLE 47:24
Which men call E.   MILT 340:23
While the e. remaineth   BIBLE 45:37
whole e. as their memorial   PER 372:23
whole e. is our hospital   ELIOT 202:22
whole round e. is every way   TENN 535:26
Yours is the E. and everything   KIPL 300:2
earth-born: e. companion An'
fellow-mortal   BURNS 115:21
earthly: any e. thing   BALL 32:2
e. godfathers of Heaven's   SHAK 456:15
earthquake: e. is not satisfied   WORD 580:21
gloom of e. and eclipse   SHEL 503:21
If an e. were to engulf   JERR 273:12
Lord was not in the e.   BIBLE 51:14
very good against an e.   ADD 2:28
earthy: man is of the earth, e.   BIBLE 76:28
ease: another gives its e.   BLAKE 87:18
be never at heart's e.   SHAK 448:4
Bring equal e. unto my pain   CAREW 130:16
doctrine of ignoble e.   ROOS 407:27
E. after war   SPEN 516:8
e. in mine inn but I shall   SHAK 440:4
e. in writing comes from   POPE 378:22
e. my breast of melodies   KEATS 289:25
e. of the masters   SMITH 509:14
e. the anguish of a torturing   SHAK 471:12
e. them of their griefs   SHAK 486:13
embers in hearthside e.   HARDY 240:13
in another's loss of e.   BLAKE 87:19
labour with an age of e.   GOLD 230:19
much at his e. as he can   SMITH 509:13
nature, kindly bent to e.   SWIFT 527:22
Some come to take their e.   SHAK 448:4
standing at e. in Nature   WHIT 570:6
Studious of elegance and e.   GAY 223:18
Studious of laborious e.   COWP 167:8
take thine e.   BIBLE 70:4
thou wilt e. thine heart   BEDD 36:23
To e. my weary limb   BALL 30:9
Virtue shuns e. as a companion   MONT 354:24
Wherein at e. for aye   TENN 541:20
Who live at home at e.   PARK 368:25
easer: thou e. of all woes   FLET 215:22
easier: e. for a camel to go through
  BIBLE 67:11
easing: They call it e. the Spring   REED 405:6
East: chambers of the E.   BLAKE 88:10
Dapples the drowsy e.   SHAK 473:11
E. all the way into Mississippi Bay
  KIPL 300:24
E. and west on fields forgotten   HOUS 263:19
E. at heel is marched from   HOUS 265:3
E. is a career   DISR 186:37
E. is East   KIPL 297:27
e. my pleasure lies   SHAK 422:7
e., nor from the west   PRAY 394:26
e. wind made flesh   APPL 11:12
e. wind may never blow   WALT 563:34
faint e. quickens   SWIN 528:16

fiery portal of the e. SHAK 479:12
from the e. to Jerusalem BIBLE 63:31
gorgeous E. with richest hand MILT 346:6
hold the gorgeous E. in fee WORD 582:10
It is the e. SHAK 482:5
Look how wide also the e. PRAY 396:17
me somewheres e. of Suez KIPL 301:8
on the e. of Eden BIBLE 45:29
practice of politics in the E. DISR 186:5
three kings into the e. BURNS 114:13
wind's in the e. DICK 176:5
eastern: gilding the e. hemisphere
SHER 505:25
marvel save in E. clime BURG 108:4
Out of the misty e. cave SHEL 505:2
Right against the e. gate MILT 342:18
Eastertide: Wearing white for E.
HOUS 262:14
eastward: garden e. in Eden BIBLE 45:7
east-wind: through the e. PRAY 392:26
easy: e. as one's discourse OSB 365:19
E. is the way down VIRG 558:18
E. live and quiet die SCOTT 418:5
e. writing's vile hard SHER 506:37
How e. it is to call rogue DRYD 198:11
If to do were as e. SHAK 465:20
I lie e. HOUS 263:11
Now as I was young and e. THOM 547:1
Of e. ways to die SHAK 424:18
on the rack of a too e. POPE 375:25
precept be, Be e. STEE 518:11
She bid me take love e. YEATS 584:22
type of the normal and e. JAMES 271:15
eat: aghast to watch him e. HOUS 264:15
Butter and honey shall he e. BIBLE 58:3
can not e. but little meat ANON 5:21
Con-found all presents wot e. SURT 525:14
did also e. of my bread PRAY 392:5
down to e. and to drink BIBLE 48:3
e., and to drink BIBLE 55:26
e. bulls' flesh PRAY 393:3
e. but ye have not enough BIBLE 62:2
e., drink BIBLE 70:4
e. his heart in the market-place SHAK 473:3
e. like wolves SHAK 444:8
E. not of it raw BIBLE 47:17
e. our pot of honey MER 337:10
e. the fat of the land BIBLE 46:36
e. the rest of the anatomy SHAK 490:1
e. your victuals fast enough HOUS 264:11
every man shall e. in safety SHAK 448:1
face shalt thou e. bread BIBLE 45:22
great ones e. up the little SHAK 478:4
have meat and cannot e. BURNS 114:14
he hath not e. paper SHAK 457:1
I did e. BIBLE 45:17
I e. well MORT 358:17
I have e. my ale FARQ 209:23
I'll e. my head DICK 180:36
I will e. exceedingly JONS 283:16
I will not e. with you SHAK 465:28
I would e. a missionary WILB 572:3
Let us e. and drink BIBLE 58:15
let us e. and drink BIBLE 76:24
neither should he e. BIBLE 79:5
of toys and things to e. STEV 522:21
One should e. to live MOL 353:2
so we must e. we THAC 545:33
Take, e., this is my Body PRAY 388:1
Tell me what you e. BRIL 93:9
that "I see what I e." CARR 133:29
thou didst e. strange flesh SHAK 421:29
thou shalt not e. of it BIBLE 45:9
thy princes e. in the morning BIBLE 56:3
will e. our meal in fear SHAK 461:12
ye shall e. it in haste BIBLE 47:18
eaten: e. and drunk enough HOR 259:6
e. by missionaries SPOO 517:9
e. on the insane root SHAK 458:15
e. to death with rust SHAK 441:15

He was e. of worms BIBLE 74:3
see God made and e. BROW 99:14
They'd e. every one CARR 135:11
to have been e. by lions CHES 148:3
eater: I am a great e. of beef SHAK 487:25
of the e. came forth meat BIBLE 49:21
eaters: so small e. MORE 357:19
eateth: e. grass as an ox BIBLE 53:8
e. not of the fruit thereof BIBLE 76:6
e. your Master with publicans BIBLE 65:22
eathen: 'e. in 'is blindness bows KIPL 298:21
You're a pore benighted 'e. KIPL 299:8
eating: appetite grows by e. RAB 403:26
e. or opening a window AUDEN 19:18
e. pâtés de foie gras SMITH 511:20
they were e. and drinking BIBLE 67:32
thought surpass e. and drinking CLOU 153:21
eats: Man is what he e. FEUE 210:35
That whatever Miss T e. DE L 174:11
Eave: E. 'arf a brick at 'im PUNCH 402:14
eaves: fall upon her gilded e. TENN 542:5
instant clamorous e. YEATS 586:22
ebb: e. and flow must ever be WORD 578:8
ne'er e. to humble love SHAK 476:1
ebbing: steady than an e. sea FORD 216:20
ebony: in e. as if done in ivory FULL 220:15
Ecce: E. homo BIBLE 83:22
Eccentric: intricate, E., intervolved
MILT 348:24
With centric and e. scribbled MILT 349:3
ecclesia: Anglicana e. libera MAGN 327:1
ibi ergo e. AMBR 4:1
ecclesiam: patrem qui e. non habet matrem
CYPR 170:19
Salus extra e. non est AUG 21:19
Ecclesiastes: dixit E. BIBLE 83:14
Ecclesiaste: E. tyranny's the worst
DEFOE 173:15
ecclesiastical: e. lyric ever poured forth
DISR 186:7
ecclesiologist: keen e. BETJ 44:14
echo: e. arose from the suicide's GILB 227:17
E. beyond the Mexique Bay MARV 331:17
e. in a Marabar cave FORS 217:8
e. is not faint at last LAND 309:8
gives a very e. to the seat SHAK 488:27
left an e. in the sense JONS 285:10
My words e. Thus ELIOT 202:13
seem an e. to the sense POPE 378:22
Sweet E., sweetest nymph MILT 341:3
tear the cave where E. SHAK 482:19
echoes: e., dying TENN 541:32
great wave that e. round TENN 535:4
he e. me SHAK 475:15
Only the e. which he made DRUM 193:25
Our e. roll from soul TENN 542:1
stage but e. back the public JOHN 282:27
echoing: e. straits between us thrown
ARN 13:12
éclat: manner of é. and eloquence BAG 29:11
eclipse: almost to doomsday with e.
SHAK 429:13
at least an e. BACON 26:23
E. first OKEL 365:3
gloom of earthquake and e. SHEL 503:21
In a merciful e. GILB 225:26
mortal moon hath her e. SHAK 494:21
Sliver'd in the moon's e. SHAK 462:4
sun... In dim e. MILT 345:24
total e. MILT 350:15
eclipsed: e. the gaiety of nations JOHN 281:36
eclipses: Clouds and e. stain both
SHAK 493:12
écoles: toutes les é. de théologie DID 184:7
economic: attaining e. ends KEYN 295:18
e. law of motion of modern MARX 333:8
social and e. experiment HOOV 255:24
economist: death of a political e. BAG 29:12
slaves of some defunct e. KEYN 295:20

Economy: E. is going without something
HOPE 255:26
e. where there is no efficiency DISR 185:33
fear of Political E. SELL 420:6
'Principles of Political E.' BENT 41:8
écrivain: L'é. original n'est pas celui
CHAT 141:5
ecstasies: Dissolve me into e. MILT 342:10
holy virgins in their e. TENN 534:23
ecstasy: Blasted with e. SHAK 433:15
e., is success in life PATER 369:21
In restless e. SHAK 461:12
In such an e. KEATS 291:22
in the e. of being ever BROW 97:24
seraph-wings of e. GRAY 235:19
think thereof without an e. BROW 96:10
This is the very e. of love SHAK 431:29
What wild e. KEATS 291:3
edax: Tempus e. rerum OVID 366:18
Eden: attempt a picnic in E. BOWEN 91:6
E.'s dread probationary COWP 166:13
E. took their solitary MILT 350:1
garden eastward in E. BIBLE 45:7
happier E. MILT 348:1
on the east of E. BIBLE 45:29
This other E. SHAK 478:20
voice that breathed o'er E. KEBLE 295:6
edge: always at the e. of Being SPEN 515:10
blunt his natural e. SHAK 463:14
children's teeth are set on e. BIBLE 60:34
my teeth nothing on e. SHAK 439:26
your 'e. of cultivation' KIPL 299:3
edges: vast e. drear ARN 12:23
edideris: Quod non e. HOR 258:6
edification: than the e. of the hearers
BURKE 108:14
edifice: Hail, glorious e. SMITH 510:6
edifieth: charity e. BIBLE 76:5
edifying: e. of the body of Christ BIBLE 77:28
edisti: e. satis atque bibisti HOR 259:6
Edit: E. and annotate the lines YEATS 586:14
edition: more beautiful e. FRAN 218:20
new e. fifty volumes long BROW 99:3
new e. of human nature HAZL 243:12
Edom: over E. will I cast PRAY 393:18
this that cometh from E. BIBLE 60:10
Educ: E.: during the holidays SITW 508:15
educated: e. man's BROW 104:32
e. whisker TENN 533:10
fed and e. RUSK 412:6
once as an e. gentleman SHAW 497:9
than he is now to an e. man COL 158:8
Educating: E. the natives of
Borrioboola-Gha DICK 176:4
education: all this fuss about e. MELB 336:21
between e. and catastrophe WELLS 568:16
chief hand in their own e. SCOTT 419:3
complete and generous e. MILT 352:8
doctor's thesis On e. AUDEN 21:4
E. has for its object SPEN 515:1
E. produced a vast population TREV 552:10
E. is what survives when SKIN 508:20
E. makes a people easy BROU 95:6
E. makes us what we are HELV 244:19
e. most have been misled DRYD 196:19
e. of the body...What I admire DISR 186:6
first rudiments of e. are STEE 518:10
highest e. since the Greek DISR 186:21
is a part of e. BACON 27:27
is the beginning of e. RUSK 412:5
learning and a liberal e. HENRY 245:21
love her is a liberal e. STEE 518:6
Prejudice of e. STER 520:4
Printing has destroyed e. DISR 186:21
Soap and e. are not TWAIN 554:6
(thank your e. JONS 285:15
'Tis E. forms the common POPE 377:12
Upon the e. of the people DISR 185:12
with the e. of the heart SCOTT 419:4
eel: I have seen but an e. DICK 176:17

eels: e. boil'd in broo'   BALL 31:5
efface: May none those marks e.
                                   BYRON 125:15
effacerai: j'en e. trois   BOIL 89:12
Effanineffable: ineffable effable E.
                                   ELIOT 204:6
effect: between cause and e.   LA B 306:15
bring the same to good e.   PRAY 386:10
rod produces an e. which   JOHN 273:25
effecting: e. of all things possible
                                   BACON 28:6
effects: e. from civil discord   ADD 1:25
effectually: faithfully we may obtain
e.   PRAY 387:1
effeminate: harbour thoughts e. and faint
                                   MARL 330:11
efficiency: economy where there is no
e.   DISR 185:33
e. and inefficiency   SHAW 497:5
efficient: e. and the inefficient SHAW 497:5
e. minority to coerce   STEP 518:20
effort: e. very nearly killed her BELL 39:7
if that e. be too great   ANON 6:17
What is written without e.   JOHN 280:25
effraie: ces espaces infinis m'e. PASC 369:7
effugere: Soles e. atque abire sentit
                                   MART 331:11
effugies: At non e. meos iambos   CAT 137:16
effusions: e. of wit and humour   AUST 22:31
these were not common e.   BRON 93:17
égalité: majestueuse é. des lois FRAN 217:26
égards: doit des é. aux vivants   VOLT 561:19
Egdon: glory of the E. waste began
                                   HARDY 241:20
yet E. remained   HARDY 241:21
Egestas: malesuada Fames ac turpis E.
                                   VIRG 558:21
egg: afraid you've got a bad e.   PUNCH 403:4
e. boiled very soft is   AUST 22:7
e. of the wren   WHIT 570:21
fatal e. by pleasure laid   COWP 166:9
full of quarrels as an e.   SHAK 483:1
is eating a demnition e.   DICK 180:14
radish and an e.   COWP 167:14
See this e.   DID 184:7
sitting on one addled e.   ELIOT 201:2
that a hen is only an e.'s   BUTL 118:24
white and hairless as an e.   HERR 249:15
eggs: e. and buttercups fried   LEAR 312:21
eighty-five ways to dress e.   MOORE 356:2
fresh e. to rotten boroughs   MAC 323:15
Lays e. inside a paper bag   ISH 270:27
partridge sitteth on e.   BIBLE 60:25
weasel sucks e.   SHAK 425:15
were but to roast their e.   BACON 27:37
egg-shell: dead kitten, an e.   WELLS 568:11
eglantine: warm hedge grew lush e.
                                   SHEL 503:19
with e.   SHAK 470:10
Ego: E. et Rex meus   SHAK 447:8
Et in Arcadia e.   ANON 10:12
too much E. in your Cosmos   KIPL 304:31
egotist: engendered in the whims of an
e.   KEATS 293:22
egotistical: Wordsworthian or e. sublime
                                   KEATS 294:7
égout: De cet é. immonde   TOCQ 551:9
egregiously: making him e. an ass
                                   SHAK 474:22
Egypt: all the first-born of E.   SHAK 425:17
arose up a new king over E.   BIBLE 46:40
darkness over the land of E.   BIBLE 47:15
E.'s might is tumbled   COL 155:3
firstborn in the land of E.   BIBLE 47:18
servant in the land of E.   BIBLE 48:19
that there was corn in E.   BIBLE 46:33
thee out of the land of E.   BIBLE 47:24
there was a great cry in E.   BIBLE 47:19
When Israel came out of E.   PRAY 397:16
wonders in the land of E.   BIBLE 47:11

Egyptian: E. fetters I must break
                                   SHAK 421:17
handkerchief Did an E.   SHAK 476:3
Egyptians: they spoiled the E.   BIBLE 47:20
Eheu: E. fugaces   HOR 260:10
Ehrlicher: E. Makler   BISM 84:23
eight: 'We want e.   WYND 584:3
will hear the stroke of e.   HOUS 262:18
eighthe: holughnesse of the e. spere
                                   CHAU 144:18
eighty: dream you are never e.   SEXT 420:18
Einbildung: sondern der E. ist   KANT 288:12
Einstein: Let E. be   SQUI 517:14
Eisen: sich nur durch Blut und E. BISM 84:25
either: e. reading   THOM 546:11
happy could I be with e.   GAY 222:35
their troth e. to other   PRAY 389:7
Elaine: Daintily alights E.   BETJ 43:13
E., the lily maid of Astolat   TENN 534:25
elbow: e. has a fascination that   GILB 227:10
elbows: with her e. on the table   JAMES 271:21
eld: alms Of palsied e.   SHAK 464:10
elder: e. and more terrible   SHAK 449:19
e. man not at all   BACON 26:35
five days e. than ourselves   BROW 96:10
I said an e. soldier   SHAK 451:18
scent of e. bushes   AUDEN 21:1
woman take An e.   SHAK 489:1
elderly: Mr Salteena was an e. man
                                   ASHF 17:5
elders: discourse of the e.   BIBLE 62:27
e. and the four beasts   BIBLE 81:32
four and twenty e. fell   BIBLE 81:27
eldest: e. of things   MILT 347:5
eldest son: Earl of Fitzdotterel's e. BROU 95:3
Eldorado: E. banal de tous les vieux
                                   BAUD 35:8
Eleanor: like Queen E. in the ballad
                                   WALP 563:4
elect: knit together thine e.   PRAY 387:4
elected: audacity of e. persons   WHIT 570:14
will not serve if e.   SHER 507:1
election: e. by the incompetent many
                                   SHAW 497:36
e. is coming   ELIOT 200:25
right of e. is the very   JUN 287:2
elections: it's no go the   MACN 326:8
electorate: dismissed by the British e.
                                   CHUR 150:26
Electric: mend the E. Light   BELL 39:29
Runs the red e. train   BETJ 43:13
electrical: e. skin and glaring eyes
                                   SMART 508:22
Electrician: E. is no longer there BELL 40:7
electrification: e. of the whole country
                                   LENIN 313:22
elegance: casque has outdone your e.
                                   POUND 382:13
e. of female friendship   JOHN 282:12
Studious of e. and ease   GAY 223:18
elegant: e. but not ostentatious   JOHN 281:38
It's so e.   ELIOT 204:25
elegies: e. And quoted odes   TENN 541:30
elegy: e., and sonnet   JOHN 280:9
eleison: Kyrie e.   MASS 334:16
element: e. of fire is quite put   DONNE 187:9
I am not of your e.   SHAK 490:8
Thy e.'s below   SHAK 453:24
Elementary: 'E.,' said he   DOYLE 192:9
elements: Become our e.   MILT 346:13
Contending with the fretful e.   SHAK 454:3
e. of modern civilization   CARL 131:3
e. once out of it   SHAK 422:14
e. So mix'd in him   SHAK 452:7
with the motion of all e.   SHAK 457:8
world made cunningly Of e.   DONNE 189:2
elephant: Appears a monstrous e.   COTT 163:7
E., Is best to lodge   SHAK 490:4
E., The only harmless   DONNE 190:3
He thought he saw an E.   CARR 133:10

th' unwieldy e.   MILT 347:26
elephanto: candenti perfecta nitens e.
                                   VIRG 559:3
elephants: Place e. for want of towns
                                   SWIFT 528:2
Women and e. never forget   SAKI 413:11
Eleusis: have brought whores for E.
                                   POUND 382:11
elevated: generous and e. mind   JOHN 282:19
joy Of e. thoughts   WORD 578:7
elevates: e. above the vulgar herd GAIS 220:25
elevating: wild, melancholy, and e.
                                   BRON 93:17
elevation: emotion that e. and that fall
                                   BURKE 111:9
eleven: e. buckram men grown out
                                   SHAK 439:3
second e. sort of chap   BARR 34:8
tells you he's only e.   GILB 226:14
elf: deceiving e.   KEATS 291:23
not a modest maiden e.   HARDY 240:7
too often a negligent e.   BARH 33:10
Elfland: horns of E. faintly blowing
                                   TENN 541:32
Elginbrodde: Here lie I, Martin E.
                                   MACD 325:3
Eli: E., lama sabachthani   BIBLE 68:24
eligendum: malis minus est semper e.
                                   THOM 546:15
Elijah: E. passed by him   BIBLE 51:15
E. went up by a whirlwind   BIBLE 51:22
spirit of E. doth rest   BIBLE 51:23
Elisha: Elijah doth rest on E.   BIBLE 51:23
E. saw it   BIBLE 51:22
Elizabeth: Than my sonne's wife, E.
                                   ING 270:16
Ellen: fair E. of brave Lochinvar
                                   SCOTT 417:10
ELLIOT: E. OF KELLYNCH-HALL
                                   AUST 23:7
elliptical: e. billiard balls   GILB 227:7
Ellum: E. she hateth mankind   KIPL 303:26
elm: green buds hang in the e.   HOUS 265:15
elms: Behind the e. last night   PRIOR 401:9
Beneath those rugged e.   GRAY 234:20
doves in immemorial e.   TENN 542:17
e., Fade into dimness   ARN 14:8
elm-tree: Round the e. bole are   BROW 101:5
elope: must be methodically   GOLD 232:17
Eloquence: Bag of Parliamentary E.
                                   CARL 132:1
embellisher of ornate e.   CAXT 138:2
gift of graceful e.   HOR 257:23
his superior e.   BURKE 109:5
intoxicated with my own e.   DISR 186:3
manner of *éclat* and e.   BAG 29:11
mother of arts And e.   MILT 350:8
my books be then the e.   SHAK 493:3
saucy and audacious e.   SHAK 471:15
should say that e. is *heard*   MILL 339:20
eloquent: curse of this country is e.
                                   EMER 208:10
e. in some sublime language   MAC 323:26
e., just, and mighty Death   RAL 404:16
pure and e. blood   DONNE 189:31
soft, so calm, yet e.   BYRON 125:22
else: e. would I give it thee   PRAY 393:8
elsewhere: Altogether e.   AUDEN 18:16
elsewhere live as they live e.   AMBR 4:2
not be e. for thousands   NELS 360:16
ELUCESCEBAT: E. quoth our friend
                                   BROW 99:15
elusive: flying and e. shadow   ARN 12:22
elves: all the criticizing e.   CHUR 149:13
e. also   HERR 249:11
Ye e. of hills   SHAK 485:23
Ely: Merrily sang the monks in E. CAN 130:9
Elysian: in the E. fields   DISR 185:25
Elysium: daughter of E.   SCH 415:9
My brother he is in E.   SHAK 487:22

Enderby: uppe 'The Brides of E. ING 270:13
ending: beginning and the e. BIBLE 81:10
dirge of her certain e. SHAK 492:20
profession an unhappy e. JAMES 272:1
so clean an e. HOUS 264:2
endless: I take my e. way HOUS 263:17
Endlich: E. fortissimo MAHL 327:6
endow: e. a college POPE 377:31
worldly goods I thee e. PRAY 389:5
Endowed: E. by the ruined millionaire ELIOT 202:22
ends: all the e. of the earth PRAY 394:1
best e. by the best means HUTC 268:19
divinity that shapes our e. SHAK 437:11
E. all our month-long love BRID 92:11
e. by our beginnings know DENH 174:20
e. thou aim'st at be thy SHAK 447:12
into the e. of the world PRAY 390:11
make both e. meet FULL 220:12
More are men's e. mark'd SHAK 478:18
To do that thing that e. SHAK 423:20
worthy e. and expectations BACON 26:4
Endue: E. her plenteously with PRAY 385:5
endurance: patient e. is godlike LONG 316:13
endurcis: les cuers contre nous e. VILL 557:4
endure: all that human hearts e. GOLD 231:30
all that human hearts e. JOHN 282:21
days wear on but I e. APOL 11:11
e. an hour and see injustice HOUS 264:5
e. Their going hence SHAK 456:2
e. the toothache patiently SHAK 473:7
E. the winter's cold SHAK 448:14
e. what can't be mended WATTS 565:27
e. what it once possessed SHEL 501:22
heaviness may e. for a night PRAY 391:13
I can e. my own despair WALSH 563:30
if I continue to e. you CONG 161:8
immortal spirit must e. ARN 14:24
nature itselfe cant e. FLEM 214:26
Potter and clay e. BROW 104:10
thou shalt e. PRAY 396:13
We first e. POPE 379:16
Youth's a stuff will not e. SHAK 488:17
endured: life e. and known SASS 415:2
tolerable and not to be e. SHAK 472:30
which much is to be e. JOHN 282:8
endureth: e. all things BIBLE 76:14
mercy e. for ever PRAY 399:2
the praise of it e. PRAY 397:13
enemies: all assaults of our e. PRAY 385:2
called thee to curse mine e. BIBLE 48:16
E.' gifts are no gifts SOPH 513:5
e. having surrendered unconditionally CHUR 150:26
e. of Caesar shall say SHAK 450:10
e. shall lick the dust PRAY 394:20
friendship with thine e. SHAK 450:9
in the choice of his e. WILDE 573:19
left me naked to mine e. SHAK 447:13
let his e. be scattered PRAY 394:6
Love your e. BIBLE 69:21
make thine e. thy footstool PRAY 397:11
men my friends than e. SHAK 452:4
of my most intimate e. ROSS 409:20
open society and its e. POPP 381:24
Our e. have beat us SHAK 452:5
overthrown More than your e. SHAK 424:26
People wish their e. dead MONT 354:11
To forgive e. H BLAKE 87:5
trophies unto the e. of truth BROW 96:5
with their e. in the gate PRAY 398:19
enemy: common e. and oppressor BURKE 110:33
Do be my e. BLAKE 87:7
e., and the avenger PRAY 389:28
e. came and sowed tares BIBLE 66:18
E. ears are listening ANON 7:8
e. hath done this BIBLE 66:19
e. increaseth every day SHAK 451:27
e. in their mouths to steal SHAK 475:9

e. of truth and freedom IBSEN 269:17
e. who speaks ill of your NELS 360:12
friend and e. is but Death BROO 94:28
hasn't an e. in the world WILDE 574:2
Have no e. but time YEATS 585:12
he is afraid of his e. PLUT 374:20
Here comes the e. CONDE 159:16
he's an e. to mankind SHAK 490:7
How goes the e. REYN 405:14
I am the e. you killed OWEN 367:12
If thine e. be hungry BIBLE 54:29
Is mortals' chiefest e. SHAK 462:1
is no such terrible e. BACON 26:2
last e. that shall be destroyed BIBLE 76:23
mine e. BIBLE 51:18
Mine e.'s dog SHAK 455:24
my e. is dead WHIT 570:11
my vision's greatest e. BLAKE 85:21
near'st and dearest e. SHAK 439:36
No e. But winter SHAK 425:14
Our friends, the e. BER 41:15
that great e. of reason BROW 96:30
that old e. the gout HOOD 254:21
That sweet e. SIDN 507:22
to be taught by the e. OVID 366:16
while the e. oppresseth me PRAY 392:9
energies: e. of our system will decay BALF 30:3
energy: e. divine POPE 380:15
E. is Eternal Delight BLAKE 88:11
enfants: e. de la patrie ROUG 410:16
Les e. terribles GAV 222:5
que les jeux d'e. ne sont MONT 354:17
se font pas comme les e. FLAU 214:3
Enfer: l'E., c'est les Autres SART 414:8
Enfin: E. Malherbe vint BOIL 89:10
enflamment: feux qui s'e. au vent FRAN 218:2
enforced: It useth an e. ceremony SHAK 451:11
engage: e. himself openly and publicly BLAKE 86:10
engagement: from every honourable e. BURKE 108:23
engine: curious e., your white hand WEBS 566:21
e. that moves HARE 242:8
put this e. to our ears SWIFT 526:3
that two-handed e. MILT 343:13
Wit's an unruly e. HERB 247:4
engineer: furious papa or a mild e. AUDEN 20:15
engineering: Piecemeal social e. POPP 381:25
engineer: sport to have the e. SHAK 435:21
engines: e. to play a little BURKE 111:1
scape By all his e. MILT 346:4
England: about the defence of E. BALD 29:28
away from E. her authors TROL 552:12
Be E. what she will CHUR 148:24
between France and E. JERR 273:4
children in E. take pleasure ANON 7:22
cold queen of E. is looking CHES 147:1
Common Law of E. has been HERB 246:13
Elizabethan E. INGE 270:10
E.—a happy land we know CHUR 148:26
E. and Saint George SHAK 444:3
E. a particular bashfulness ADD 2:21
E.! awake BLAKE 86:11
E. breed again DRAY 193:11
E. expects that every man NELS 360:20
E., full of sin HERB 247:3
E. hath need of thee WORD 582:5
E., home and beauty BRAH 91:16
E. invented the phrase BAG 28:25
E. is a garden that is KIPL 299:12
E. is a nation of shopkeepers NAP 359:15
E. is finished and dead MILL 340:2
E. is still governed from SHAW 498:23
E. is the paradise of women FLOR 216:1
E. keep my bones SHAK 452:29
E. mourns for her dead BINY 84:9

E., my England HENL 245:11
E.'s green and pleasant BLAKE 86:12
E.'s green & pleasant BLAKE 86:16
E. shall bide till Judgement KIPL 303:27
E. should be free than MAGEE 326:21
E.'s on the anvil KIPL 297:26
E.'s winding sheet BLAKE 85:17
E. was merry England SCOTT 417:16
E. was too pure an Air ANON 7:7
England was what E. seems KIPL 302:11
E., we love thee better TREN 552:8
E., with all thy faults COWP 166:33
ere E.'s griefs began GOLD 230:18
faithless E. BOSS 90:14
fashion of the court of E. SHAK 446:3
get me to E. once again BROO 94:22
gloomy in E. are March TROL 552:21
Happy is E. KEATS 292:15
hear our noble E.'s praise MAC 321:25
heart of E. well may call DRAY 193:18
here did E. help me BROW 101:9
history of E. is emphatically MAC 323:12
in E.'s song for ever NEWB 361:10
influenced manners in E. BURKE 111:15
Ireland gives E. her soldiers MER 337:24
jurisdiction in this Realm of E. PRAY 400:10
lamented that Old E. is lost JOHN 277:12
Let not E. forget her precedence MILT 352:6
lost the last of E. BELL 40:16
mad, and sent into E. SHAK 436:30
martial airs of E. WEBS 566:12
men that worked for E. CHES 146:24
Noon strikes on E. FLEC 214:6
Nor, E.! did I know WORD 577:28
O E.! model to thy inward SHAK 443:13
of a king of E. too ELIZ 206:4
Old E. to adorn KIPL 303:25
only seeing a worse E. JOHN 277:24
poison E. at her roots BOTT 90:17
road that leads him to E. JOHN 274:30
royal navy of E. hath ever BLAC 85:4
should they know of E. KIPL 298:24
Slaves cannot breathe in E. COWP 166:32
sneer at the bruisers of E. BORR 90:6
Stately Homes of E. COW 164:3
stately homes of E. HEM 244:21
strong arm of E. will protect PALM 368:10
suffer E. to be the workshop DISR 184:11
suspended in favour of E. SHAW 496:33
That is for ever E. BROO 94:30
The further off from E. CARR 134:15
This aged E. upon by transitions EMER 207:10
This E. never did SHAK 453:1
this E. SHAK 478:20
this is E.'s greatest TENN 541:9
to be in E. BROW 101:5
to ensure summer in E. WALP 563:8
to the landscape of E. AUST 22:22
Walk upon E.'s mountains BLAKE 86:16
we are the people of E. CHES 147:15
while E. talked of ale CHES 147:13
Who dies if E. live KIPL 299:7
With E.'s own coal KIPL 298:4
worst government that E. TROL 553:4
youth of E. are on fire SHAK 443:12
English: Allah created the E. mad KIPL 300:14
angel is the E. child BLAKE 88:2
are nothing to your E. SHAK 475:2
be the second E. satirist HALL 238:6
bird-haunted E. lawn ARN 14:1
Breeds hard E. men KING 296:23
characteristic of the E. Monarchy BAG 28:28
Dr Johnson's morality was as E. HAWT 243:5
E. are busy MONT 355:8
E. are perhaps the least BAG 29:2
E. are very little indeed NORTH 364:2
E. army led by an Irish SHAW 498:7
E. Bible MAC 323:4

E. Church shall be free — MAGN 327:1
E. county families — WAUGH 565:29
E. drunkard made the rolling — CHES 147:10
E. home — TENN 541:22
E. (it must be owned) a — HAZL 244:1
E. make it their abode — WALL 562:8
E. man does not travel — STER 518:31
E., not the Turkish court — SHAK 442:23
E., now I must forego — SHAK 478:10
E. subject's sole prerogative — DRYD 197:31
E. take their pleasures — SULLY 524:18
E. tongue a gallimaufry — SPEN 517:6
E. would manage to meet — JERR 273:12
favour of boys learning E. — CHUR 150:23
feet of E. ground — HAR 242:11
fine old E. gentleman — ANON 6:10
forfeited their ancient E. dower — WORD 582:5
half-French, half-E. — SHAK 445:14
happy E. child — TAYL 531:23
if he went among the E. — BARR 34:19
I hope we E. will long — CARL 131:37
In an E. lane — BROW 100:12
I shall be among the E. — KEATS 294:9
king's E. — SHAK 469:5
kissed by the E. dead — OWEN 367:6
marks our E. dead — KIPL 303:3
noble E. — SHAK 443:7
not the expression in E. — ARN 16:4
one E. book and one only — ARN 16:13
on that grave where E. — HARTE 242:26
on you noblest E. — SHAK 444:1
principle of the E. constitution — BLAC 85:5
really nice E. people — SHAW 496:32
Roman-Saxon-Danish-Norman E. — DEFOE 173:13
sagacity of E. enterprise — BURKE 109:17
sort of E. up with which — CHUR 151:6
Take of E. earth as much — KIPL 298:8
'tis the talent of our E. — DRYD 197:12
to the E. that of the sea — JEAN 272:4
trick of our E. nation — SHAK 441:14
under an E. heaven — BROO 94:30
When the E. began to hate — KIPL 298:1
wishes to attain an E. style — JOHN 281:38
your E. summer's done — KIPL 300:23
Englishman: broad-shoulder'd genial E. — TENN 542:20
Either for E. or Jew — BLAKE 85:25
E. a combination of qualities — DICK 181:12
E., Being flatter'd — CHAP 140:3
E. believes be heresy — SHAW 498:19
E. could beat three Frenchmen — ADD 2:19
E. is content to say nothing — JOHN 278:17
E. never enjoys himself — HERB 246:17
E. of our upper class — ARN 15:17
E.'s heaven-born privilege — ARN 15:20
E. thinks he is moral when — SHAW 497:28
E. to open his mouth — SHAW 498:12
E. unmoved that statement — GILB 228:3
E. whose heart is — BAG 28:31
find an E. in the wrong — SHAW 498:6
heart of a true *E.* — ADD 2:19
He is an E. — GILB 228:9
He remains an E. — GILB 228:10
ill-natur'd thing, an E. — DEFOE 173:12
last great E. is low — TENN 541:6
not one E. — WALP 563:25
religious rights of an E. — JUN 287:1
smell the bloud of an E. — NASHE 360:6
stirred the heart of every E. — SCOTT 415:19
thorough an E. as ever coveted — KING 297:9
What E. will give his mind — SHAW 496:4
Englishmen: absurd nature of E. — PEPYS 372:7
first to His E. — MILT 351:27
Honest E. — KING 296:21
Mad dogs and E. — COW 163:19
our very name as E. — PITT 374:4
proper drink of E. — BORR 90:8
Englishwoman: This E. is so refined — SMITH 510:27

Englissh: E. and in writyng of oure — CHAU 144:17
E. sweete upon his tonge — CHAU 141:22
engrafted: meekness the e. word — BIBLE 80:10
engross: when he should e. — POPE 376:19
enigma: mystery inside an e. — CHUR 149:28
Resolving the e. — ELIOT 202:21
enjoy: Contented if he might e. — WORD 580:5
e. but half the blessing — GAY 222:9
e. her while she's kind — DRYD 198:17
e. idling thoroughly unless — JER 272:22
e. paradise in the next — BECK 36:20
e. poetry unless we know — THOR 550:25
glorify God and to e. — SHOR 507:7
have to go out and e. it — SMITH 510:23
in due time we may e. them — PRAY 385:21
Let me e. the earth no — HARDY 240:6
most e. contented least — SHAK 493:6
never e. the world aright — TRAH 551:17
that private men e. — SHAK 444:24
to e. it — SMITH 510:11
to e. thy land — SHAK 452:8
enjoy'd: all times I have e. — TENN 543:22
warm and still to be e. — KEATS 291:7
Enjoyed: E. no sooner but despised — SHAK 495:7
e. the gifts of the founder — GIBB 224:8
little to be e. — JOHN 282:8
enjoyment: chief e. of riches consists — SMITH 509:11
e. as the greatest orator — HUME 267:22
Was it done with e. — RUSK 411:20
enjoyments: Fire-side e. — COWP 167:13
it were not for its e. — SURT 525:23
enjoys: now e. his age — DRYD 196:3
Enlarge: E., diminish, interline — SWIFT 527:34
enlargement: stability or e. of the language — JOHN 281:7
enlightened: While on the e. mind — THOM 549:26
enmities: reconciliation where the e. — MAC 323:20
enmity: while covert e. — SHAK 440:30
Enna: fair field Of E. — MILT 347:21
ennemi: *Voilà l'e.* — CONDE 159:16
ennemies: *Les oreilles e. vous écoutent* — ANON 9:18
ennemis: *Nos amis, les e.* — BER 41:15
ennoble: What can e. sots — POPE 379:23
ennobled: which e. whatever it touched — BURKE 111:10
ennui: *symétrie, c'est l'e.* — HUGO 267:12
ennuyer: *Le secret d'e. est...de tout* — VOLT 561:21
ennuyeux: *sont bons hors le genre e.* — VOLT 561:7
Eno: to soar with E. — STEV 521:11
Enoch: E. walked with God — BIBLE 45:30
Enormous: E. through the Sacred Town — BELL 39:28
enough: best is good e. — GOET 230:8
eaten and drunk e. — HOR 259:6
e. for fifty hopes — BROW 99:4
e., for nature's ends — MALL 327:12
E. of science and of art — WORD 582:23
E. that he heard it once — BROW 98:20
had never had e. — GILB 225:9
It is e. — BIBLE 54:46
Once is more than e. — BIRCH 84:11
'tis e., 'twill serve — SHAK 483:3
Was it not e. — SHAW 496:30
When thou hast e. — BIBLE 63:5
enquiries: remote e. — JOHN 281:40
enquiring: My object in e. is to know — HOUS 266:9
enraptur'd: Glorious th' e. main — SMART 509:4
enrich: T'e. unknowing nations — DAN 170:23
enrichment: e. of our native language — DRYD 197:38

ensample: noble e. to his sheep — CHAU 142:1
ense: *sit calamus saevior e.* — BURT 116:22
Ensham: Above by E. — ARN 15:8
ensign: Th' imperial e. — MILT 345:19
ensky'd: thing e. and sainted — SHAK 463:12
enslave: impossible to e. — BROU 95:6
superstition to e. a philosophy — INGE 270:6
enslaved: All spirits are e. which — SHEL 503:9
ensnare: web as this will I e. — SHAK 474:19
ensue: peace, and e. it — PRAY 391:23
entangled: middle-sized are alone e. — SHEN 505:15
to contemplate an e. bank — DARW 171:28
Entbehren: *E. sollst Du* — GOET 230:2
entente: Th' e. is al — CHAU 144:16
enter: Abandon all hope, you who e. — DANTE 171:3
e. into the kingdom of heaven — BIBLE 64:11
e. into the kingdom of heaven — BIBLE 67:2
E. not into judgement with — PRAY 399:11
E. these enchanted woods — MER 337:21
e. who does not know geometry — ANON 10:2
King of England cannot e. — PITT 373:29
than for a rich man to e. — BIBLE 67:11
they that have riches e. — BIBLE 70:36
ye cannot e. now — TENN 534:8
entered: e. are. into their labours — BIBLE 71:42
iron e. into his soul — PRAY 397:3
enterprise: e. is sick — SHAK 486:23
e. In walking naked — YEATS 584:16
hazard in the glorious e. — MILT 345:1
enterprised: e., nor taken in hand — PRAY 388:25
enterprises: e. of great pith and moment — SHAK 433:8
impediments to great e. — BACON 26:31
enterprising: e. burglar's not a-burgling — GILB 228:20
enterprize: period, pow'r, and e. — SMART 509:1
entertain: Could e. us with no worth — WALL 562:15
e. a cheerful disposition — SHAK 478:22
e. the lag-end of my life — SHAK 440:14
e. With half their forces — SHAK 443:7
forgetful to e. strangers — BIBLE 80:3
There e. him all the saints — MILT 343:18
To e. divine Zenocrate — MARL 330:12
entertained: e. angels unawares — BIBLE 80:3
entertaining: grown very e. to my self — CONG 160:22
entertainment: eligibility of the proffered e. — TROL 553:10
e. this week cost me above — PEPYS 372:20
not dull thy palm with e. — SHAK 430:19
some other custom of e. — SHAK 474:23
entertainments: delightful and most improving e. — ADD 2:9
entertains: e. the harmless day — WOTT 583:13
enthrall: Except you me — DONNE 189:3
enthroned: e. in the hearts of kings — SHAK 467:27
enthusiasm: e. I have been cheated — KEATS 294:15
ever achieved without e. — EMER 207:16
enthusiasts: e. can be trusted to speak — BALF 30:4
how to deal with e. — MAC 323:17
Entia: *E. non sunt multiplicanda* — OCCAM 364:19
entice: e. thee secretly...Thou shalt — BIBLE 48:24
enticing: Mirth can do with her e. — ANON 6:7
Entire: E. and sure the monarch's — PRIOR 401:3
entirely: e. beautiful — AUDEN 19:17
entirety: who would dissipate my e. — MACN 326:13
entrails: In our own proper e. — SHAK 452:3
In the poison'd e. throw — SHAK 462:2

entrañas: y en guerra con mis e. MACH 325:7
entrance: some e. into the language
    BACON 27:27
entrances: their exits and their e.
    SHAK 425:24
entrap: To e. the wisest   SHAK 467:11
entrusted: e. with arms…should WIND 575:7
Entschluss: Der christliche E.   NIET 363:8
entsichere: e. ich meinen Browning
    JOHST 283:8
Entuned: E. in hir nose ful semely
    CHAU 141:15
entwine: Would e. itself verdantly
    MOORE 356:4
Enumerat: E. miles vulnera   PROP 401:15
envie: no makyng thow n'e.   CHAU 144:17
envious: e. siege Of watery Neptune
    SHAK 478:20
  e. Time   MILT 344:17
grows to an e. fever   SHAK 486:25
prudes, your e. railing   BURNS 114:16
To silence e. tongues   SHAK 447:12
environed: e. with a great ditch from
    CROM 170:4
envy: attracts the e. of the world
    BURKE 109:15
did in e. of great Caesar   SHAK 452:7
do not e. me   DOUG 191:7
E. and wrath shorten   BIBLE 63:13
e. is a kind of praise   GAY 223:15
e. of brilliant men   BEER 37:28
e. of less happier lands   SHAK 478:20
e. of the devil came death   BIBLE 62:12
E.'s a sharper spur than   GAY 223:12
extinguisheth e.   BACON 26:4
from e., hatred, and malice   PRAY 385:16
I e. birds their wings   CLARE 152:7
I e. not in any moods   TENN 536:15
moved with e.   BIBLE 74:8
Pride, E., Malice   LAND 308:17
prisoners of e.   MILT 344:23
Stirr'd up with e. and revenge   MILT 344:23
through e. of thy happy lot   KEATS 291:17
void of e.   THOM 549:9
whom e. never touched   SHEL 505:14
épatés: é., les bourgeois   PRIV 401:12
ephemeral: grave Proves the child e.
    AUDEN 19:17
Ephesians: Great is Diana of the E.
    BIBLE 74:17
Ephesus: fought with beasts at E.
    BIBLE 76:24
Ephraim: E. also is the strength PRAY 393:18
grapes of E. better than the vintage
    BIBLE 49:17
epic: legend of an e. hour   CHES 147:8
thundrous E. lilted out   TENN 541:30
epicure: e. would say   SMITH 511:15
Epicuri: Cum ridere voles E. de   HOR 258:16
Epicurus: he was E. owene sone
    CHAU 141:27
one of E.' herd of pigs   HOR 258:16
épidermes: et le contact de deux é.
    CHAM 139:15
Epigram: What is an E.   COL 156:15
Epigramm: Witz ist das E. auf den Tod
    NIET 363:13
epigrams: despotism tempered by e.
    CARL 131:21
epilogue: good play needs no e.   SHAK 427:8
epistles: some obscure e. of love SHAK 488:23
epistula: Verbosa et grandis e. venit
    JUV 287:27
epitaph: are no e. of that Oak DONNE 190:23
Believe a woman or an e.   BYRON 124:18
better have a bad e.   SHAK 432:25
e. drear   KIPL 301:18
memorable e.   SELL 420:3
not remember'd in thy e.   SHAK 440:25
surely that may be his e.   STEV 521:5

That's if ye carve my e.   BROW 99:13
Wit is the e. of an emotion   NIET 363:13
epitaphs: nice derangement of e. SHER 506:14
of worms, and e.   SHAK 479:10
epithet: coined an e. for a knave MAC 323:27
Fair is too foul an e.   MARL 330:10
epithets: To e. like these   BELL 38:29
epitome: all mankind's e.   DRYD 194:13
Eppur: E. si muove   GAL 220:29
equal: admitted to that e. sky   POPE 379:6
all men are created e.   LINC 314:23
All men are e.   FORS 216:26
All shall e. be   GILB 225:23
are more e. than others   ORW 365:9
compel us to be e. upstairs   BARR 34:7
earth the separate and e.   JEFF 272:5
e. are within the Church's   HERB 247:10
e. division of unequal   ELL 206:11
e. in dignity and rights   ANON 4:14
E. in strength   MILT 346:7
e. poise of hope and fear   MILT 341:9
E., unclassed   SHEL 503:12
faith shines e.   BRON 93:18
hast made them e. unto us   BIBLE 67:15
in the dust be e. made   SHIR 507:2
men are created e.   JEFF 272:6
one e. eternity   DONNE 191:3
robbery to be e. with God   BIBLE 78:13
them as if they were e.   FROU 219:18
Though e. to all things   GOLD 231:17
under the rule of e. justice   MILL 339:19
equalises: weight that e. the shepherd
    CERV 138:20
equality: e. in fact as corollary   BAK 29:25
e. in the servants' hall   BARR 34:7
in a general state of e.   JOHN 277:5
principle of perfect e.   MILL 339:18
true apostles of e.   ARN 15:16
without the idea of e.   HUGH 267:6
equally: Death kicks his way e.   HOR 259:13
henceforth be bestowed e.   SHAK 424:21
It comes e. to us all   DONNE 190:23
equals: disinterested commerce between
  e.   GOLD 232:11
least of all between e.   BACON 26:11
equanimity: No man can face with e.
    GILB 226:10
equation: e. will come out at last MACN 326:6
Equator: disrespectfully of the E.
    SMITH 510:29
they got as far as the E.   THAC 545:32
equi: lente currite noctis e.   MARL 329:11
equinox: who knows when was the e.
    BROW 97:20
equipment: shabby e. always deteriorating
    ELIOT 202:23
equitem: Post e. sedet atra Cura HOR 260:15
equity: people with e.   PRAY 396:9
equivocate: I will not e.   GARR 221:17
equivocation: e. will undo us   SHAK 436:28
equivocator: here's an e.   SHAK 460:16
Equo: E. ne credite   VIRG 558:1
eradicating: fault without e. the virtue
    GOLD 232:8
Erasmus: law-givers are E. and Montaigne
    FORS 217:11
Erastian: E. Whig   CHES 146:27
ere: Oon e. it herde, at tothir CHAU 144:12
erect: e. and manly foe   CANN 130:1
erected: met each other with e. DRYD 197:30
erecteth: Christ e. his Church   BANC 32:14
erection: rate the cost of the e. SHAK 441:17
Eremite: sleepless E.   KEATS 292:11
Erickin': to have any beastly E. KIPL 305:6
err: Better to e. with Pope   BYRON 124:19
e. is human, not to, animal FROST 219:13
is a people that do e.   PRAY 396:4
most may e. as grossly   DRYD 194:18
reas'ning but to e.   POPE 379:12

To e. is human   POPE 378:27
errand: Blackheath the warlike e. MAC 322:3
e. now to the Antipodes   SHAK 472:9
in thy joyous E. reach   FITZ 213:18
errands: little e. for the Ministers
    GILB 225:24
Meet to be sent on e.   SHAK 451:10
erred: have e. exceedingly   BIBLE 50:15
We have e.   PRAY 384:11
erreur: L'e. n'a jamais approché
    METT 338:10
erring: e. on ventiferous ripes HOLM 253:18
error: All men are liable to e. LOCKE 315:17
charged the troops of e.   BROW 96:5
e. be too highly heap'd   SHAK 427:17
e. by the same example   SHAK 468:3
e. is all in the not done   POUND 382:14
e. is immense   BOL 89:15
fierceness makes E. a fault   HERB 247:6
hateful e.   SHAK 452:2
If this be e.   SHAK 495:5
in endless e. hurl'd   POPE 379:13
Man is in e. throughout   GOET 229:29
man that he is in an e.   LOCKE 315:16
stalking-horse to e.   BOL 89:16
than all the hosts of e.   BRYAN 106:7
ut me malus abstulit e.   VIRG 560:4
very e. of the moon   SHAK 477:8
errors: amusing with numerous e.
    GOLD 232:31
e. are volitional and are   JOYCE 286:27
E., like straws   DRYD 195:10
E. look so very ugly   ELIOT 201:23
e. of a wise man   BLAKE 87:9
harmful than reasoned e.   HUXL 269:11
her share some female e.   POPE 380:33
errs: He seldom e.   HOME 253:23
Erst: E. kommt das Fressen   BREC 91:25
erstwhile: my e. dear   MILL 340:1
erthe: This litel spot of e.   CHAU 144:18
erubuit: et e.   CRAS 169:2
erudite: e. Verger translated   BARH 33:7
erump: evade,—e.   HOLM 253:19
erupit: evasit, e.   CIC 151:27
eruption: This bodes some strange e.
    SHAK 429:10
es: je te dirai ce que tu e.   BRIL 93:9
Esau: E. my brother is a hairy BIBLE 46:15
E. selleth his birthright   BIBLE 46:12
E. was a cunning hunter   BIBLE 46:13
hands are the hands of E.   BIBLE 46:16
escadrons: gros e. contre les petits
    BUSS 117:7
escalier: L'esprit de l'e.   DID 184:6
escape: Beauty for some provides e.
    HUXL 269:1
e. from emotion   ELIOT 205:18
E. me? Never   BROW 101:30
guilty persons e. than one innocent
    BLAC 85:6
help those we love to e.   HUGEL 267:5
let me ever e. them   PRAY 399:10
Let no guilty man e.   GRANT 234:3
make our e. into the calm   HUME 268:2
Man e. from rope   GAY 222:30
What struggle to e.   KEATS 291:3
escaped: e. the shipwreck of time
    BACON 24:18
e. with the skin of my   BIBLE 52:29
is e. even as a bird out   PRAY 398:14
that out of battle I e.   OWEN 367:9
through language and e.   BROW 104:8
Eschew: E. evil   PRAY 391:23
escondida: la e. senda   LUIS 320:12
Eseln: Reichtum den grossen E. LUTH 320:14
Eskdale: E. and Liddesdale SCOTT 418:24
espaces: ces e. infinis m'effraie PASC 369:7
espagnol: Je parle e. à Dieu CHAR 140:31
Esperance: E.! Percy   SHAK 440:20
Stands still in e.   SHAK 455:5

espousèd: Methought I saw my late e. Saint　MILT 351:12
My fairest, my e.　MILT 348:14
esprit: de l'e. pour être auteur　LA B 306:12
d'e. et les grands n'ont　LA B 306:14
jamais approché de mon e.　METT 338:10
L'e. de l'escalier　DID 184:6
l'e. et dans le coeur comme　LA R 310:17
esprits: favorise que les e. préparés　PAST 369:16
essays: My e.　BACON 25:17
worse e. prov'd thee my　SHAK 495:3
Esse: E. quam videri bonus malebat　SALL 413:24
essence: e. of war is violence　MAC 323:8
History is the e. of innumerable　CARL 131:9
purest e. of a human soul　CARL 132:29
uncompounded is their e. pure…　MILT 345:15
Essene: E., Erastian Whig　CHES 146:27
Essentially: E. I integrate the current　BETJ 42:14
Music is e. useless　SANT 414:3
established: e. injustices are sanctioned　FRAN 217:25
so sure e.　PRAY 384:8
estate: condescend to men of low e.　BIBLE 75:17
e. by the same occupation　BUNY 107:18
e. Christ adorned　PRAY 388:25
e. of the Catholick Church　PRAY 385:25
e. o' the world were now　SHAK 463:7
has become a fourth e.　MAC 323:7
low e. of his handmaiden　BIBLE 69:5
mind, body, or e.　PRAY 386:1
order'd their e.　ALEX 3:14
relief of man's e.　BACON 24:17
esteemed: they e. themselves rich　MAC 323:26
we e. him not　BIBLE 59:21
esthetic: mystery of e. like that　JOYCE 286:18
estimate: enough thou know'st thy e.　SHAK 494:13
larger than Man can ever e.　AUDEN 18:8
estranging: e. sea　ARN 13:13
estribo: Puesto ya el pie en el e.　CERV 139:2
esuriens: Graeculus e.　JUV 287:16
Esurientes: E. implevit bonis　BIBLE 83:18
esurienti: e. te inferebatur sol et　AUG 21:13
établies: sanction des injustices é.　FRAN 217:25
État: L'É. c'est moi　LOU 318:8
ete: appetit hath he to e. a mous　CHAU 142:25
éteint: petite flamme qui ne s'é.　REN 405:13
eternal: draw near to their e. home　WALL 562:9
e. in the heavens　BIBLE 77:6
E. Passion　ARN 14:3
e. separation which we　STER 520:11
e. silence of these infinite　PASC 369:7
E. summer gilds them yet　BYRON 122:32
e. summer shall not fade　SHAK 492:28
Grant them e. rest　MASS 334:17
Hope springs e.　POPE 379:5
keeps e. whisperings around　KEATS 292:22
lose not the things e.　PRAY 386:16
portion of the E.　SHEL 499:19
swear an e. friendship　CANN 130:4
think ye have e. life　BIBLE 72:3
This way for e. suffering　DANTE 171:3
to be boy e.　SHAK 491:7
eternally: all things abided e.　TRAH 551:19
eternities: on the meeting of two e.　THOR 550:9
Seasons; not E.　MER 337:9
eternity: ages Of e.　CARN 132:33
day joins the past E.　BYRON 121:4
E. in an hour　BLAKE 85:8
E. is in love with　BLAKE 88:17
E. shut in a span　CRAS 169:8
E.'s too short　ADD 2:20
E.! thou pleasing　ADD 1:24

E. was in that moment　CONG 160:23
E. was in our lips　SHAK 421:26
from here to E.　KIPL 299:10
Heads Were toward E.　DICK 183:16
hid battlements of E.　THOM 548:20
I gave you e. in a single　SHAW 496:29
image of e.　BYRON 121:26
intimates e. to man　ADD 1:24
I saw E. the other night　VAUG 555:22
Lives in E.'s sunrise　BLAKE 86:18
make us heirs of all e.　SHAK 456:14
one equal e.　DONNE 191:3
Passing through nature to e.　SHAK 429:24
same sweet e. of love　HERR 249:9
sells e. to get a toy　SHAK 492:18
Silence is deep as E.　CARL 131:13
Silence is of E.　CARL 132:3
skill'd to sing of Time or E.　TENN 533:12
Some shadows of e.　VAUG 555:15
That opes the palace of E.　MILT 340:24
thievish progress to e.　SHAK 494:10
time without injuring e.　THOR 550:3
white radiance of E.　SHEL 499:26
Who can speak of e. without　BROW 96:10
yet this great wink of e.　CRANE 168:31
eternize: your virtues rare shall e.　SPEN 515:20
ETERNO: ME SI VA NELL' E. DOLORE　DANTE 171:3
ether: ampler e.　WORD 578:3
farthest bottle labelled 'E.　BROW 100:7
etherized: Like a patient e. upon　ELIOT 203:17
ethics: they drew a system of e.　MAC 324:3
Ethiop: Juno but an E. were　SHAK 457:5
Ethiopian: Can the E. change his skin　BIBLE 60:22
ethnology: e., what not…　BROW 99:9
etiquette: It isn't e. to cut any　CARR 136:10
Where e. prevents me from　SMITH 512:4
étoile: Ma seule é. est morte　NERV 360:26
Eton: during the holidays from E.　SITW 508:15
playing fields of E.　WELL 567:24
étrange: C'est une é. entreprise　MOL 353:7
étrangers: Plus je vis d'é.　BELL 40:17
étranglés: é. avec les boyaux des　MESL 338:9
Etrurian: where th' E. shades　MILT 345:13
Ettrick: E. and Teviotdale　SCOTT 418:24
Euclid: E. alone has looked　MILL 339:28
fifth proposition of E.　DOYLE 192:28
Eugene: our good Prince E.　SOUT 513:19
Eugene Aram: E., though a thief　CALV 127:27
Eugenia: Listen, E.　ARN 14:3
eunuch: intellectual e. Castlereagh　BYRON 122:4
Though Argus were her e.　SHAK 456:27
Time's e.　HOPK 257:3
To be a kind of moral e.　SHEL 502:18
euonymus: Her father's e. shines　BETJ 44:7
Eureka: E.! (I've got it　ARCH 11:23
Euripides: middle-age I preferred E.　COL 158:6
Europe: are going out all over E.　GREY 236:19
Better fifty years of E.　TENN 539:9
E. is disclosed as a prone　HARDY 239:13
E. is the less　DONNE 190:20
E. made his woe then own　ARN 13:9
glory of E. is extinguished　BURKE 111:9
noblest river in *E.*　ADD 2:19
of the community of E.　GLAD 229:18
of the community of E.　SAL 413:19
where will E.'s latter hour　ARN 13:18
Europeans: You are learned E.　MASS 335:15
Eurydice: His half regain'd E.　MILT 343:1
Euston: flushpots of E. and the hanging　JOYCE 286:5
three in E. waiting-room　CORN 162:20

evade: Fear wist not to e.　THOM 548:11
Evae: clamamus exsules filii E.　ANON 10:19
Evangelist: lips of that E.　TENN 536:18
evangelists: prophets; and some, e.　BIBLE 77:28
evaporate: making all disagreeables e.　KEATS 293:18
evasion: admirable e. of whoremaster man　SHAK 453:11
evasit: e., erupit　CIC 151:27
Eve: banished children of E.　ANON 10:19
close at the ear of E.　MILT 348:12
E. from his side arose　ANON 8:21
E., with her basket　HODG 252:4
fairest of her daughters E.　MILT 347:24
fallen sons of E.　CHES 147:23
from e. and morning　HOUS 263:16
past E. and Adam's　JOYCE 286:2
pensive E.　COLL 158:17
thro' the land at e. we　TENN 541:28
to E.: Be soon　THOM 548:12
When E. upon the first　HOOD 255:3
eve-jar: spins the brown e.　MER 337:3
Evelyn: E. Hope is dead　BROW 100:25
Even: (E. as you and I)　KIPL 303:29
last pale beam of e.　SHEL 504:7
my heart in summer's e.　HOUS 266:4
When the grey-hooded E.　MILT 340:30
Would God it were e.　BIBLE 48:27
evening: autumn e.　ARN 14:8
bright exhalation in the e.　SHAK 447:7
e. and the morning were　BIBLE 45:1
e. full of the linnet's　YEATS 585:17
E. must usher night　SHEL 499:14
e. of my age　ROWE 410:20
e. star is coming　VIRG 560:9
e. withhold not thine hand　BIBLE 56:8
ever went with e. dress　KIPL 303:2
hands be an e. sacrifice　PRAY 399:9
in the e. it is cut down　PRAY 395:18
into the corners of the e.　ELIOT 203:18
It is a beauteous e.　WORD 581:18
Of grateful e. mild　MILT 348:5
undrugged in e. light the decent　CHES 147:12
When e. shuts　BROW 104:6
When it is e.　BIBLE 66:31
When the e. is spread out　ELIOT 203:17
winter e. settles down　ELIOT 204:7
worse at arriving in the e.　CONN 161:14
yet the E. listens　KEATS 292:5
evenings: still recall those e. when　AUDEN 20:19
evening-star: over there the red e. is　VIRG 560:11
evensong: e. Of joy illimited　HARDY 239:7
evensonge: belles ringeth to e.　HAWES 243:3
event: had over-prepared the e.　POUND 383:20
halves of one august e.　HARDY 239:6
How much the greatest e.　FOX 217:19
hurries to the main e.　HOR 257:20
One e. happeneth to them　BIBLE 55:11
events: coming e. cast their shadows　CAMP 128:24
e. in the womb of time　SHAK 474:11
that e. have controlled me　LINC 315:1
ever: beauty is a joy for e.　KEATS 288:20
continue thine for e.　FRAY 388:22
e. thus with simple folk　GILB 229:10
e. wilt thou love　KEATS 291:5
hereafter for e. hold his peace　PRAY 389:2
houses shall continue for e.　PRAY 392:28
Is seldom, if e. done　COW 163:20
Mary e. Virgin　MASS 334:15
mercy endureth for e.　PRAY 399:2
not be destroyed for e.　ANON 11:4
punctually come for e. and ever　WHIT 571:4
Round the world for e.　ARN 13:6
that I could last for e.　CONR 161:24
things to last for e.　HOR 261:15
ever-burning: Berenice's e. hair　CHAP 140:4

Executioner: yet I am mine own *E.*
DONNE 190:19
executive: is nominated by the e. GIBB 224:22
executors: Delivering o'er to e. pale
SHAK 443:9
Let's choose e. SHAK 479:10
exegi: Iamque opus e. OVID 366:19
exemplaria: Vos e. Graeca HOR 257:22
exemplars: pages of your Greek e.
HOR 257:22
Exempt: E. from awe SHEL 503:12
exercise: e. myself in great matters
PRAY 398:25
mind what e. is to the body STEE 518:9
on e. depend DRYD 196:5
sad mechanic e. TENN 536:1
exercises: He e. of his brains GILB 226:8
exertions: saved herself by her e. PITT 374:5
exhalation: fall Like a bright e. SHAK 447:7
Rose like an e. MILT 346:2
exhaled: through a pipe and e. in a pun'
LAMB 308:11
exhaust: e. the realm of the possible
PIND 373:15
exhibited: by being publicly e. ALB 3:7
exile: bind your sons to e. KIPL 304:6
journey to endless e. HOR 260:7
Troy came destined an e. VIRG 557:8
exiles: we are e. from our fathers' GALT 221:2
Which none save e. feel AYT 24:5
exist: Art and Science cannot e. BLAKE 86:7
dreamed of good shall e. BROW 98:19
impression that we e. BECK 36:16
She may still e. in undiminished MAC 323:16
should be presumed to e. OCCAM 364:19
we do e. and cease to be SHAK 453:3
Why do you and I e. JOHN 278:5
existence: detail the struggle for e.
DARW 171:26
E. saw him spurn her bounded JOHN 282:25
Let us contemplate e. DICK 179:8
loving longest, when e. AUST 23:10
our e. as a nation PITT 374:4
prefer mere e. to honour JUV 287:25
'Tis woman's whole e. BYRON 122:14
Exit: E., pursued by a bear SHAK 491:16
exits: men to take their e. WEBS 566:26
their e. and their entrances SHAK 442:6
exorciser: No e. harm thee SHAK 428:22
Exoriare: E. aliquis nostris ex ossibus
VIRG 558:15
expands: Work e. so as to fill PARK 369:1
expatiates: Rests and e. in a life POPE 379:5
Expect: E. him not in the just HOUS 265:14
know more of mankind I e. JOHN 279:12
expectancy: e. and rose of the fair
SHAK 433:15
expectation: dream and a folly of e.
BROW 97:21
e. whirls me round SHAK 486:32
indeed better bettered e. SHAK 471:25
now sits E. in the air SHAK 443:12
expectations: worthy ends and e. BACON 26:4
expected: reasonable man could have
e. HERB 246:19
they may reasonably be e. WHAT 569:13
what we least e. generally DISR 186:10
expecto: e. resurrectionem mortuorum
MASS 334:20
expects: e. his evening prey GRAY 234:16
expedient: all things are not e. BIBLE 76:10
consider that it is e. for us BIBLE 72:24
e. for you that I go away BIBLE 72:38
may be most e. for them PRAY 385:8
principle, but an e. DISR 184:15
expéditif: C'est une homme e. MOL 353:21
expedition: abandoning the e. DOUG 191:8
expeditious: He's an e. man MOL 353:21
expellas: Naturam e. furca HOR 258:18
Expende: E. Hannibalem JUV 288:1

expenditure: annual e. nineteen nineteen
DICK 177:4
expense: drinking at somebody else's
e. LEIGH 313:15
e. of spirit in a waste SHAK 495:7
Would be at the e. of two CLOU 153:25
expenses: meet all the e. of living
THOR 550:13
expensive: Everything in Rome is e.
JUV 287:19
love fruit when it's e. PIN 373:17
experience: acquist Of true e. MILT 351:4
are perfected by e. BACON 27:17
contrary to custom and e. HUME 267:21
dirty nurse, E. TENN 534:35
e. find those words mis-plac'd CONG 160:27
E. is the child of Thought DISR 186:41
E. is never limited JAMES 271:11
E. is the name every one WILDE 573:14
E. though noon auctoritee CHAU 143:16
E. teaches slowly FROU 219:19
here can go beyond his e. LOCKE 315:15
I have e. CONG 160:33
knowledge too but recorded e. CARL 131:8
light which e. gives COL 157:20
of trying every e. once ANON 4:24
part of e. BACON 27:27
reality of e. JOYCE 286:19
reporting device for e. WHORF 571:23
sometimes worth a life's e. HOLM 253:21
Then Old Age, and E. ROCH 406:22
Till old e. do attain MILT 342:11
To a great e. one thing BAG 29:14
triumph of hope over e. JOHN 275:36
Yet all e. is an arch wherethro' Gleams
TENN 543:22
experienced: becomes real till it is e.
KEATS 294:18
Experientia: E. does it DICK 177:1
experiment: full tide of successful e.
JEFF 272:7
social and economic e. HOOV 255:24
tried an e. in his life DARW 172:2
expers: Vis consili e. mole ruit HOR 260:23
expert: e. is one who knows more
BUTL 117:13
to those who are e. at it HOR 259:6
Experto: E. credite VIRG 559:10
experts: you never should trust e. SAL 413:18
expiate: death my days should e. SHAK 493:1
expire: I tremble, I e. SHEL 500:13
expires: e., too soon, too soon CONR 161:24
wretched child e. BELL 39:2
expiring: accents of an e. saint STER 520:9
thus e. do foretell SHAK 478:19
explain: e. all the poems that ever
CARR 135:23
'I can't e. *myself* CARR 133:21
Never complain and never e. DISR 185:30
spoil it by trying to e. SHER 506:20
unwilling to e. FROST 218:27
would e. his explanation BYRON 122:3
explaining: e. a passage in the game-act
STEE 517:23
explanations: I do loathe e. BARR 34:12
expletives: While e. their feeble aid
POPE 378:20
exploded: dust of e. beliefs MADAN 326:18
exploding: poets e. like bombs AUDEN 20:16
exploit: dignity compos'd and high e.
MILT 346:9
exploration: shall not cease from e.
ELIOT 203:2
explorers: endeavours are unlucky e.
DOUG 191:8
Explosionsstoff: als einen furchtbaren
E. NIET 363:5
explosive: terrible e. in the presence
NIET 363:5

explosives: You darent handle high e.
SHAW 497:14
export: integrate the current e. BETJ 42:14
exposed: been much e. to authors
WELL 567:29
intellect is improperly e. SMITH 511:5
exposes: e. himself when he is intoxicated
JOHN 278:8
exposition: e. of sleep come upon me
SHAK 471:5
exposure: unseemly e. of the mind
HAZL 243:26
express: e. image of his person BIBLE 79:28
e. our wants as to conceal GOLD 232:5
e. the images of their BACON 27:4
e. train drew up there THOM 547:16
To e. what then I saw WORD 577:4
What I can ne'er e. BYRON 121:22
which a picture cannot e. BACON 25:27
express'd: ne'er so well e. POPE 378:17
expresser: was a most gentle e. of it
HEM 245:2
expresses: 'If this young man e. himself
GILB 227:21
expressible: e. as a sum of two cubes
RAM 404:22
expression: e. of no-encouragement
BRAM 91:19
have not the e. in English ARN 16:4
His e. may often be called ARN 16:7
impassioned e. WORD 583:9
indolent e. and an undulating BELL 40:2
not the e. of personality ELIOT 205:18
vulgar e. of the passion CONG 159:22
expressive: Eyes too e. to be blue ARN 13:4
expressure: e. of his eye SHAK 488:23
expung'd: works to me e. and raz'd
MILT 347:8
exquisite: e. touch SCOTT 418:37
Exsilium: E. impositura cumbae HOR 260:7
extant: be but pyramidally e. BROW 97:15
story is e. SHAK 434:14
extend: let e. thy mind o'er all MILT 350:7
extension: L'e. des privilèges des
FOUR 217:18
extenuate: nothing e. SHAK 477:23
extenuates: e. not wrong SHAK 486:31
extinct: purpose of becoming e. CUPPY 170:15
Extinction: of Character and the E.
DARW 171:28
extinguished: glory of Europe is e.
BURKE 111:9
One e. family waits BETJ 43:9
sometimes overcome, seldom e.
BACON 26:36
extinguishes: wind e. candles LA R 310:15
extirpate: To e. the vipers AYT 24:6
extol: e. Him first, him last MILT 348:16
extracts: e. made of them by others
BACON 27:19
extraordinary: behaving in this e. manner
STOP 523:17
most e. man in Europe STIL 523:14
'this is an e. man JOHN 279:15
extravagance: beautiful does not lead
to e. PER 372:22
extravagancies: undisgraced by those
e. CHES 145:24
extravagant: e. with his own SALL 413:22
e. and irrational which SWIFT 526:8
extreme: e. to mark what is done
PRAY 398:23
where th' e. of vice POPE 379:16
extremes: e. by change more fierce
MILT 346:22
'E. meet' HOOD 255:17
mean between the two e. PRAY 384:7
show his judgement) in e. DRYD 194:14
toil in other men's e. KYD 306:4
two e. appear like man CHUR 149:14

extricate: is unable to e. himself ADD 2:24
exuitur: cupido gloriae novissima e.
TAC 531:14
exuletur: utlagetur, aut e. MAGN 327:2
Exult: E. O shores WHIT 570:8
Our souls e. BLAKE 86:12
exultations: e., agonies, And love
WORD 582:17
exulting: people all e. WHIT 570:7
exuvias: redit e. indutus Achilli VIRG 558:5
eye: apple of his e. BIBLE 48:30
auspicious and one dropping e. SHAK 429:19
beard and glittering e. COL 155:5
bought by judgment of the e. SHAK 456:20
brought an e. for all he saw TENN 537:8
Cast a cold e. YEATS 587:10
custom loathsome to the e. JAM 271:3
every e. shall see him BIBLE 81:10
e. begins to see BRON 93:21
E. for eye BIBLE 47:25
e. full of gentle salutations STER 520:9
E., gazelle SPEN 515:14
e. is not satisfied with BIBLE 55:7
e. of heaven to garnish SHAK 452:25
e. of man hath not heard SHAK 471:10
e. of peninsulas and islands CAT 136:28
e. sinks inward ARN 12:22
e. the unconquered flame POUND 382:14
e. whose bend doth awe SHAK 448:15
fettered to her e. LOV 318:15
fringed curtains of thine e. SHAK 485:1
glass to his sightless e. NEWB 361:4
got into this e. of mine STER 520:10
great e. of heaven shined SPEN 516:2
harvest of a quiet e. WORD 580:5
heavenly rhetoric of thine e. SHAK 457:4
He had but one e. DICK 179:35
he that made the e. PRAY 396:2
his e. was backward cast SPEN 516:6
hooded e. THOM 548:2
hot the e. of heaven SHAK 492:28
If thine e. offend thee BIBLE 67:5
I have neither e. to see LENT 313:23
immortal hand or e. BLAKE 87:14
inward e. 'tis an old Man BLAKE 86:14
is in thy brother's e. BIBLE 64:34
learning more than the fond e. SHAK 466:19
Lesbia hath a beaming e. MOORE 356:11
Lock'd up from mortal e. CRAS 169:15
man has cast a longing e. JEFF 272:11
mild and magnificent e. BROW 102:5
mine e. may be deceiv'd SHAK 494:18
neither a wit in his own e. CONG 160:11
not thro', the e. BLAKE 85:23
now may her e. seeth thee BIBLE 53:12
On it may stay his e. HERB 247:18
Russian e. Is underlined ELIOT 205:14
saving those that e. thee SHAK 428:4
seeing e. BIBLE 54:18
sniv'ling and piping your e. DIBD 175:19
still-soliciting e. SHAK 453:6
Then can I drown an e. SHAK 493:7
There's language in her e. SHAK 487:13
they shall see eye to e. BIBLE 59:19
Thou E. among the blind WORD 579:7
thoughts are legible in the e. ROYD 411:2
through the e. of a needle BIBLE 67:11
turned his blindest e. CHES 146:21
twinkling of an e. BIBLE 76:29
twinkling of an e. PRAY 391:13
Was never e. ROYD 411:3
watchful e. and the strong arm PALM 368:10
Who sees with equal e. POPE 379:4
'with his e. on the object' ARN 16:12
with his glittering e. COL 155:6
with its soft black e. MOORE 356:25
eyeball: e. owns the mystic rod BROW 105:14
like a coal His e. SMART 509:3
eye-balls: my e. roll POPE 376:14

eyebrow: Made to his mistress' e.
SHAK 425:24
eyelashes: lose our teeth and e. LEAR 312:24
Eyeless: E. in Gaza MILT 350:14
eyelids: e. are a little weary PATER 369:18
her e. many Graces sate SPEN 516:11
marble e. are not wet BROW 98:8
Than tir'd e. upon tir'd TENN 539:13
wilt weigh mine e. down SHAK 441:29
With e. heavy and red HOOD 255:6
eyes: approach it with e. YEATS 587:14
asked him with my e. JOYCE 286:30
at times my e. are lenses DOUG 191:7
audience look to their e. SHAK 469:25
beams from happy human e. STEV 523:11
because you'll wear your e. ZOLA 588:19
bein' only e. DICK 182:23
black e. and lemonade MOORE 356:3
Blessed are the e. which BIBLE 69:29
bright e. Rain influence MILT 342:25
brightness in their failing e. BLUN 89:2
brown of her—her e. MEW 338:12
Closed his e. in endless GRAY 235:19
close your e. with holy COL 157:1
cocking their medical e. DICK 183:11
cold commemorative e. ROSS 410:5
cynosure of neighbouring e. MILT 342:20
death bandaged my e. BROW 103:32
deep upon her peerless e. KEATS 291:15
dry one's e. BROW 102:1
electrical skin and glaring e. SMART 508:22
e. above him with anxiety TOCQ 551:8
e. are quickened so with GRAV 234:11
e. did see Olivia first SHAK 487:21
e. have they PRAY 397:18
e. like lead BROW 100:35
E., look your last SHAK 483:31
e. of gold and bramble-dew STEV 523:3
E. of most unholy blue MOORE 356:6
e. purging thick amber SHAK 432:8
e. that had lightened SWIN 529:19
e., the break of day SHAK 464:21
e. the glow-worm lend thee HERR 249:11
e. the greenest of things SWIN 529:16
E. the shady night has HOUS 263:2
e. to behold the sun BIBLE 56:9
E. too expressive to be ARN 13:4
e. were as a flame of fire BIBLE 81:14
e. were blind with stars HODG 252:8
fair maidens Quiet e. STEV 523:2
four beasts full of e. BIBLE 81:23
friend to close his e. DRYD 195:3
from star-like e. CAREW 130:12
From women's e. this doctrine SHAK 457:6
From women's e. this doctrine SHAK 457:9
Gasp and Stretch one's E. BELL 39:7
gaze not in my e. HOUS 262:21
Get thee glass e. SHAK 455:21
God be in my e. ANON 5:9
greater cats with golden e. SACK 412:26
hair the e. of Day SHEL 505:3
Hath not a Jew e. SHAK 467:4
Have e. to wonder SHAK 494:20
Her e. are homes of silent TENN 536:19
her e. the gazers strike POPE 380:32
her e. were blind KEATS 290:16
Her e. were deeper than ROSS 409:14
he set her both his e. LYLY 321:11
his e. are bright with it KEATS 294:17
his e. became so terrible BECK 36:19
His e. drop out LOCK 315:18
I'd say I had e. again SHAK 455:7
I gave her e. my own eyes BROW 102:2
in it dazzled their e. BALL 31:3
is engender'd in the e. SHAK 467:9
is marvellous in our e. PRAY 398:2
I was e. to the blind BIBLE 52:25
lightened are our e. SORL 513:10
Look not in my e. HOUS 262:21
Love-darting e. MILT 341:18

Love in her sunny e. does COWL 164:6
Love looks not with the e. SHAK 469:22
lovers' e. are sharp SCOTT 416:26
lover's e. will gaze an eagle SHAK 457:8
make his e. grow in my brow SHAK 421:32
many e. as thou hast wounds SHAK 450:9
Men's e. were made to look SHAK 483:2
Mine e. are full of tears SHAK 480:4
Mine e. do itch SHAK 477:1
Mine e. have seen the glory HOWE 266:19
mock our e. with air SHAK 423:7
My mistress' e. are nothing SHAK 495:8
night has a thousand e. BOUR 90:21
Night hath a thousand e. LYLY 321:15
no eyes but constitutional e. LINC 315:7
no e., but fountains KYD 306:3
not proud of those two e. HERR 250:1
of one whose subdu'd e. SHAK 477:23
one, all e. WORD 580:3
open The king's e. SHAK 447:1
optics of these e. to behold BROW 96:21
Our gloom-pleas'd e. KEATS 292:28
pair of sparkling e. GILB 225:26
pearls that were his e. SHAK 484:32
scornful, yet with jealous e. POPE 376:26
see nothing with my e. SAPP 414:6
shut her wild, wild e. KEATS 290:20
Soft e. look'd love BYRON 120:20
stars! And all e. else SHAK 492:10
stuck in her face for e. SHAK 456:27
Suddenly discovering in the e. POUND 383:14
that your e. might be shining LAWR 311:12
that youth's e. burned ROSS 410:2
their e. are burning AUDEN 20:5
Their five e. smouldering DE L 174:4
therefore want no e. SHAK 455:6
they are hid from thy e. BIBLE 71:3
They have changed e. SHAK 485:2
They strike mine e. JONS 283:27
They were full of e. within BIBLE 81:24
thine e. like the fishpools BIBLE 57:9
things with his half-shut e. POPE 381:7
thou hast doves' e. within BIBLE 56:26
Thou turn'st mine e. SHAK 435:9
through another man's e. SHAK 426:28
to me only with thine e. JONS 284:12
Two grey e. with lids SHAK 488:12
We fix our e. upon his JOHN 282:16
what her e. enthral'd CONG 160:2
when unto dying e. TENN 542:4
wheresoe'er I turn my ravished e. ADD 2:4
Whose woollen e. looked BETJ 44:9
will trouble thine e. DONNE 190:23
Will you put out mine e. SHAK 452:24
With e. up-rais'd COLL 158:21
with fortune and men's e. SHAK 493:6
world to turn thine e. JOHN 282:29
write the beauty of your e. SHAK 492:27
Your e. are lodestars SHAK 469:21
You see her e. are open SHAK 462:19
eyeservice: with e., as menpleasers
BIBLE 78:8

Faber: F. est suae quisque fortunae
CLAU 152:26
fabill: that thai be nocht bot f. BARB 33:3
fables: all the f. in the legend BACON 25:22
f., and dangerous deceits PRAY 400:9
F. and endless genealogies BIBLE 79:6
Hesperian f. true MILT 347:19
Than f. yet have feigned MILT 346:23
fabric: baseless f. of this vision SHAK 485:20
out of the earth a f. huge MILT 346:2
Fabula: F. narratur HOR 261:22
fac: Dilige et quod vis f. AUG 21:21
face: Am I in f. to-day GOLD 232:21
beautiful f. is a mute PUBL 402:4
Beauty's conquest of your f. AUDEN 20:21
blubber'd is that pretty f. PRIOR 400:19
born with a different f. BLAKE 86:15
can hear my Thisby's f. SHAK 471:18

She was more f. than words TENN 532:16
these f. well-spoken days SHAK 480:19
this f. defect Of Nature MILT 349:23
'This isn't f. dealing KIPL 301:19
thou art f. BIBLE 56:26
thousand times more f. SHAK 467:13
To be f. LYTT 321:20
What care I how f. she be WITH 575:12
what's right and f. HUGH 267:7
where even the old are f. YEATS 585:18
will spit on all things f. CHAP 140:9
you f. hath made you good SHAK 464:16
fairer: f. person lost not Heav'n MILT 346:9
F. than any wakened eyes SHEL 503:19
F. than feign'd of old MILT 350:3
f. than the word SHAK 465:17
Is f. far in May JONS 285:8
surely the f. way is not BACON 25:4
yet far f. than you are SHAK 421:10
fairest: f. of creation MILT 349:17
f. shepherd on our green PEELE 371:6
f. things have fleetest THOM 547:25
From f. creatures we desire SHAK 492:22
thou f. among women BIBLE 56:17
faireste: f. hewed on hir throte CHAU 142:32
fairies: Do you believe in f. BARR 34:16
F., black SHAK 469:16
I don't believe in f. BARR 34:14
merry world since the f. SELD 419:24
She is the f.' midwife SHAK 481:28
There are f. at the bottom FYL 220:23
was the beginning of f. BARR 34:13
fairs: f., and bear-baitings SHAK 491:20
fairy: Come not near our f. queen
                                      SHAK 470:11
die soon, O f.'s son SPEN 516:9
f. hands their knell is COLL 158:20
f. kind of writing which DRYD 196:26
f. tales of science TENN 538:16
Like f. gifts fading away MOORE 356:4
Lilly believes it was a f. AUBR 18:2
'tis almost f. time SHAK 471:20
fairy-tale: head a f. of olden times
                                      HEINE 244:9
fais: L'amour? Je le f. souvent PROU 401:22
faisaient: soldats f. la haie ELIOT 202:8
fait: un seul f. accompli BOIL 89:11
faite: Je suis f. comme ça PREV 400:16
faith: aught is want of f. in all TENN 535:6
break f. with us who die MCCR 324:31
breastplate of f. and love BIBLE 79:2
children in whom is no f. BIBLE 48:31
confidence and f. of the heart LUTH 320:17
doubt diversified by f. BROW 99:5
Draw near with f. PRAY 387:18
f. and fire within us HARDY 240:8
f. and hope the world will POPE 379:20
f. and labour of love BIBLE 78:30
f. as a grain of mustard BIBLE 67:1
F. consists in believing VOLT 561:20
f. hath made thee whole BIBLE 65:26
f., hope, charity BIBLE 76:14
f. in a nation of sectaries DISR 186:1
F. is the substance BIBLE 79:31
F.'s defying BARN 34:4
f. shines equal BRON 93:18
f.'s transcendent dower WORD 581:5
f. that looks through death WORD 579:13
f.: these ought ye BIBLE 67:24
f. unfaithful kept him TENN 534:29
F. which does not doubt UNAM 554:27
F. without works is dead BIBLE 80:12
fanatic f. MOORE 356:28
Fight the good fight of f. BIBLE 79:19
finisher of our f. BIBLE 79:35
fought for Queen and F. TENN 534:8
have not found so great f. BIBLE 65:16
he hold the Catholick F. PRAY 385:11
If I break f. SHAK 456:17
I have kept the f. BIBLE 79:26

in plain and simple f. SHAK 451:11
in the unity of the f. BIBLE 77:28
just shall live by f. BIBLE 74:31
Kept f. with me HARDY 239:21
life in thy f. and fear PRAY 387:16
made of f. and service SHAK 426:29
more could fright my f. DRYD 196:13
more f. in honest doubt TENN 537:11
more strongly have f. LUTH 320:15
moved by f. to assent to it HUME 267:21
My staff of f. to walk RAL 404:12
not for all his f. can see EMER 206:22
not the dying for a f. THAC 545:6
purest f. unhappily forsworn SHAK 494:5
puts me from my f. SHAK 439:27
sacred dictates of thy f. ROWE 410:25
scientific f.'s absurd BROW 100:21
Sea of F. ARN 12:23
shake a man's f. in himself SHAW 496:15
should not alter in my f. JONS 283:25
simple f. than Norman blood TENN 537:29
Since f. is dead WYATT 583:20
taking the shield of f. BIBLE 78:10
that do not have the f. CHES 147:25
These all died in f. BIBLE 79:33
this f. I wish to live VILL 557:6
though I have all f. BIBLE 76:14
thou of little f. BIBLE 66:27
vain f., and courage vain MAC 322:8
which constitutes poetic f. COL 157:22
with a stronger f. embrace LOV 318:20
Woman's f. SCOTT 418:4
faithful: be mentally f. to himself
                                      PAINE 367:20
Be thou f. unto death BIBLE 81:17
blessed company of all f. PRAY 388:3
f. and just to me SHAK 450:18
F. are the wounds BIBLE 54:38
F., below DIBD 175:22
f. friend is the medicine BIBLE 62:25
f. in that which is least BIBLE 70:27
f. of thy word GRAH 233:15
f. to thee, Cynara DOWS 191:12
for the f. are minished PRAY 389:32
good and f. servant BIBLE 68:2
him was called F. and True BIBLE 82:25
O come, all ye f. ANON 10:4
So f. in love SCOTT 417:9
words are true and f. BIBLE 82:31
faithfully: things which we ask f. PRAY 387:1
faithless: Be not f. BIBLE 73:11
f. and stubborn generation PRAY 395:4
F. as the winds or seas SEDL 419:10
f. was she ARN 13:7
Human on my f. arm AUDEN 19:17
faiths: both were f. ARN 13:8
men's f. are wafer-cakes SHAK 443:20
old f. loosen and fall SWIN 530:6
Falcon: dapple-dawn-drawn F. HOPK 257:4
f. cannot hear the falconer YEATS 586:15
f., towering in her pride SHAK 461:5
Gentle as f. or hawk SKEL 508:16
falconer: f.'s voice SHAK 482:19
falcons: were rapid f. in a snare MER 337:17
fall: also say it is good to f. WHIT 570:20
Another thing to f. SHAK 463:16
by dividing we f. DICK 184:5
come and f. on me MARL 329:12
contemneth small things shall f. BIBLE 63:7
dew shall weep thy f. to-night HERB 248:16
diggeth a pit shall f. BIBLE 56:2
else they will f. BURKE 108:22
F. and cease SHAK 456:9
f. backward when thou hast SHAK 481:27
f. into the ocean MARL 329:15
F. into the hands of God TENN 543:3
f. in with the marriage-procession
                                      CLOU 153:10
f. Like a bright exhalation SHAK 447:7
F. of the Rupee you may WILDE 573:4

f. on the ground without BIBLE 65:35
f. upon the thorns of life SHEL 502:13
fearful thing to f. into BIBLE 79:30
forts of folly f. ARN 13:15
great was the f. of it BIBLE 65:12
haughty spirit before a f. BIBLE 54:8
Held we f. to rise BROW 98:32
his f. from power BURKE 109:5
I meditated on the F. BETJ 43:1
in this we stand or f. MILT 348:20
is down needs fear no f. BUNY 107:32
Is less likely to f. GAY 223:4
it had a dying f. SHAK 487:20
laugh at a f. BROW 102:1
let us worship and f. down PRAY 396:4
rocks, F. on us BIBLE 81:30
See that ye f. not out BIBLE 46:37
shall f. into the ditch BIBLE 66:29
shall never f. PRAY 390:5
Soar not too high to f. MASS 335:16
Something is going to f. AUDEN 21:10
take warning by the f. BALL 30:13
that can f. without shaking MONT 354:7
that elevation and that f. BURKE 111:9
Then f., Caesar SHAK 450:1
Therefore f. the people PRAY 394:22
Things f. apart YEATS 586:15
thousand shall f. beside PRAY 395:21
to raise up them that f. PRAY 385:19
upholdeth all such as f. PRAY 399:14
was der F. ist WITT 575:14
Weak men must f. SHAK 479:5
we should happen to f. LEAR 312:10
what a f. was there SHAK 450:28
Why do ye f. so fast HERR 248:20
will f. into the hands BIBLE 62:22
yet fear I for f. RAL 404:14
Fallacy: characterize as the 'Pathetic
F. RUSK 411:11
fallen: All our hope is f. HOR 261:13
art thou f. from heaven BIBLE 58:13
Babylon is f. BIBLE 82:16
F. from his high estate DRYD 195:3
f. into the midst of it PRAY 393:15
how are the mighty f. BIBLE 50:16
How are the mighty f. BIBLE 50:17
keeps their f. day about PATER 369:19
lay great and greatly f. HOMER 254:3
lot is f. unto me PRAY 390:6
many have f. by the edge of the sword
                                      BIBLE 63:11
say a man is f. in love STER 520:6
Though f. thyself WORD 582:17
Fallentis: F. semita vitae HOR 258:24
fallere: Quis f. possit amantem VIRG 558:12
falling: by oft f. LAT 310:20
cruelty To load a f. man SHAK 447:25
day when heaven was f. HOUS 265:7
f. out of faithful friends EDW 200:5
f. with a falling state POPE 375:12
he hath the f. sickness SHAK 448:22
my feet from f. PRAY 397:20
stand secure amidst a f. world ADD 2:30
Fallings: F. from us WORD 579:10
fall'n: f. on evil days MILT 348:28
follow with allegiance a f. SHAK 422:18
fallow: f. fawns invisible go THOM 547:20
Falls: F. with the leaf still FLET 215:8
then he f., as I do SHAK 447:9
Where he f. short CHUR 149:15
false: all was f. and hollow MILT 346:9
betrayed by what is f. MER 337:14
Beware of f. prophets BIBLE 65:8
f. creation SHAK 459:15
F., ere I come DONNE 190:10
f. face must hide what SHAK 459:12
f. grief hiding his harmful SPEN 516:5
f. Idol Honour WINC 575:4
f. impossible shore ARN 15:2
f. philosophy MILT 346:20

f. quantities | DRYD 198:20
f. teeth and hurling them | DOYLE 191:17
f. witness against thy | BIBLE 47:24
Fram'd to make women f. | SHAK 474:12
If she be f. | SHAK 475:22
men would be f. | LYLY 321:9
not then be f. to any man | SHAK 430:19
perils among f. brethren | BIBLE 77:12
produces a f. impression | WILDE 572:26
Ring out the f. | TENN 537:14
Round numbers are always f. | JOHN 277:19
save them from f. Sextus | MAC 322:16
say that I was f. of heart | SHAK 495:2
thou be not f. to others | BACON 27:35
wouldst not play f. | SHAK 459:1

Falsehood: F. has a perennial spring | BURKE 109:4
goodly outside f. hath | SHAK 466:1
Let her and F. grapple | MILT 352:5
strife of Truth with F. | LOW 319:12

falsely: Anabaptists do f. boast | PRAY 400:12
prophets prophesy f. | BIBLE 60:18
Science f. so called | BIBLE 79:21

falseness: f. in all our impressions | RUSK 411:11

falser: f. than vows made in wine | SHAK 426:18

Falstaff: F. shall die of a sweat | SHAK 443:2
sweet Jack F. | SHAK 439:18

Falter: F., are lost in the storm | ARN 14:9
nor f., nor repent | SHEL 503:15
Who hesitate and f. life | ARN 14:17

faltered: diffidence that f. | POUND 382:14
If I have f. more or less | STEV 523:11

fam'd: f. in all great arts | ARN 15:11

fame: all my f. for a pot of ale | SHAK 444:4
blush to find it f. | POPE 380:18
damn'd to everlasting f. | POPE 380:1
desire of f. | TENN 534:12
doctor full of phrase and f. | ARN 15:12
earth your f. is bright | BRID 92:18
Enough my meed of f. | HOLL 253:4
establishment of my f. | GIBB 224:18
fair f. inspires | POPE 376:26
F. and tranquillity can | MONT 354:22
F. is a food that dead | DOBS 187:11
F. is like a river | BACON 27:5
F. is no plant that grows | MILT 343:9
f. is the last thing even | TAC 531:14
F. is the spur that | MILT 343:8
f., sete, marcie forzate | GAR 221:10
F.'s eternal beadroll | SPEN 516:19
f., that all hunt after | SHAK 456:14
foremost shall be damn'd to f. | POPE 375:19
gives immortal f. | YOUNG 587:19
her f. survives | MILT 350:31
his f. the ocean sea | BARN 34:5
immoderate passion for f. | BURKE 109:8
love and f. to nothingness | KEATS 293:2
Man dreams of f. | TENN 535:9
no one shall work for f. | KIPL 304:3
nor yet a fool to f. | POPE 376:23
not to purchase f. | DRYD 196:35
openeth the gate to good f. | BACON 26:4
Physicians of the utmost f. | BELL 39:1
Poets' food is love and f. | SHEL 500:14
'Rather use than f. | TENN 535:10
selfish hope of a season's f. | NEWB 361:8
servants of f. | BACON 26:21
speaking trump of future f. | BYRON 124:24
That f. can never heal | AYT 24:5
What is f. | GRAI 233:20
while f. elates thee | MOORE 356:8
you shall live by f. | SPEN 515:20

fames: Auri sacra f. | VIRG 558:10
malesuada F. ac turpis Egestas | VIRG 558:21

familiar: Be thou f. | SHAK 430:19
Don't let us be f. or fond | CONG 161:7
F. acts are beautiful through | SHEL 503:13
f. friend, whom I trusted | PRAY 392:5

F. in his mouth as household | SHAK 445:3
f. with her face | POPE 379:16
mine own f. friend | PRAY 393:11
once f. word | BAYLY 35:10

Familiarity: F. begets boldness | MARM 330:18

familiarly: Talks as f. of John a Gaunt | SHAK 442:11

families: All happy f. resemble one | TOLS 551:10
English county f. | WAUGH 565:29
f. last not three oaks | BROW 97:16
Good f. are generally worse | HOPE 256:1
Great f. of yesterday we | DEFOE 173:14
in the best-regulated f. | DICK 177:15
Mothers of large f. | BELL 38:31
of your antediluvian f. | CONG 160:10
There are secrets in all f. | FARQ 210:7

famille: au gouvernement d'une f. | MONT 354:19

family: brought up a large f. | GOLD 232:32
direction of his f. | WALP 563:14
f. happier for his presence | STEV 521:4
f. in heaven and earth | BIBLE 77:24
f. pride is something in-conceivable | GILB 226:20
F. Pride | GILB 227:4
his f. was not unworthy | DISR 186:14
I am the f. face | HARDY 240:1
in the running of a f. | MONT 354:19
is the character of a f. | STER 519:20
of a good f. | DEFOE 173:5
One extinguished f. waits | BETJ 43:9
prolong f. connection | BUTL 118:29

famine: die by f. die by inches | HENRY 245:20
f.; from battle and murder | PRAY 385:16
f. in his face | CHUR 149:5

famous: At every f. victory | SOUT 513:18
f. by my sword | GRAH 233:15
f. by their birth | SHAK 478:20
f., calm, and dead | BROW 100:34
f. men have the whole earth | PER 372:23
f. then By wisdom | MILT 350:7
found myself f. | BYRON 126:22
Let us now praise f. men | BIBLE 63:21
thrice f. deeds she wrought | MAC 321:25

fan: f. spread and streamers | CONG 160:36
F. the sinking flame | DICK 180:26

Fanatics: F. have their dreams | KEATS 289:26

fancies: drop your silly f. | CAT 136:27
f. are more giddy and unfirm | SHAK 489:1
F. that broke through language | BROW 104:8
full of f. | KEATS 293:10
Lay your earthly f. down | TENN 541:15
When you set your f. free | BROW 98:31

fancy: Did your f. never stray | GAY 222:21
dorgs is some men's f. | DICK 177:9
Ever let the f. roam | KEATS 289:29
f. cannot cheat so well | KEATS 291:23
f. is the sails | KEATS 293:13
f. outwork nature | SHAK 422:2
from f. to the heart | POPE 380:4
invention and makes f. lame | COWP 166:2
keep your f. free | HOUS 262:20
now the f. passes | HOUS 263:1
odoriferous flowers of f. | SHAK 457:3
of most excellent f. | SHAK 436:31
of sweet and bitter f. | SHAK 426:26
So fair a f. few would | HARDY 240:14
so full of shapes is f. | SHAK 487:20
Tell me where is f. bred | SHAK 467:9
those by hopeless f. feign'd | TENN 542:4
young man's f. | TENN 538:17

fancy-free: In maiden meditation, f. | SHAK 470:8

fans: With divers-colour'd f. | SHAK 422:2
Wi' their f. into their | BALL 31:20

fantaisies: f. et le contact de deux | CHAM 139:15

fantasies: Even the linked f. | THOM 548:17
exchange of two f. | CHAM 139:15

fantastic: horrible, f., incredible | CHAM 139:9
In a light f. round | MILT 340:29
On the light f. toe | MILT 342:15
thinking on f. summer's heat | SHAK 478:17

fantastical: That it alone is high f. | SHAK 487:20

fantasy: is to be all made of f. | SHAK 426:29
opinion he held once Of f. | SHAK 449:10
vexed not his f. Black | DONNE 190:3

Far: F. and few | LEAR 312:6
F. be that fate from us | OVID 366:8
f., far better thing | DICK 183:12
f. from the lips we love | MOORE 356:19
F. from the madding crowd's | GRAY 235:1
few and f. between | CAMP 129:10
He's happy who, f. away | HOR 259:7
keep f. from me | OVID 366:9
keep f. off, you uninitiated | VIRG 558:19
more felicity on the f. | SMITH 510:13
quarrel in a f.-away country | CHAM 139:9
seems so near and yet so f. | TENN 537:13
She is f. from the land | MOORE 356:17
so f. as it goes | DICK 180:11
whole is f. from gay | LEAR 312:22

Faraday: remain plain Michael F. | FAR 209:20

farce: la f. est jouée' | RAB 404:1
second as f. | MARX 333:9

fardels: Who would f. bear | SHAK 433:8

Fare: F. thee well! and if for ever | BYRON 124:33
showed me his bill of f. | SWIFT 526:17
to f. forth on the water | POUND 383:18

fareweel: Ae f. | BURNS 112:27

fare wel: f. al the snow of ferne | CHAU 144:15
F. my bok, and my devocioun | CHAU 143:29

Farewell: F.! a long farewell | SHAK 447:9
f. compliment | SHAK 482:12
f. content | SHAK 475:25
f. goes out sighing | SHAK 487:5
F. happy fields | MILT 345:10
f. king | SHAK 479:11
F. night, welcome day | BUNY 107:37
F., rewards and Fairies | CORB 162:13
F. to the Highlands | BURNS 114:26
hail, and f. evermore | CAT 137:15
life than waving me f. | HOPE 256:4
must bid the company f. | RAL 404:19
nor bade f. to him | SHAK 458:3
there be no sadness of f. | TENN 533:4
Too-late, F. | ROSS 410:4
with hope f. fear | MILT 347:16

farewells: Everlasting f. | DE Q 175:3
many f. as be stars | SHAK 487:12

far-flung: Lord of our f. battle-line | KIPL 302:7

farm: fields to cross till a f. | BROW 102:14
keep a f. | SHAK 432:3
snug little f. the earth | COL 156:10

farmer: f. that hanged himself | SHAK 460:15

farmers: f. excessively fortunate | VIRG 560:13
f., flourish and complain | COWP 168:16
now the f. swear | KING 297:21
once the embattled f. stood | EMER 206:19
Three jolly F. | DE L 174:14

farms: pleasant villages and f. | MILT 349:13
what f. are those | HOUS 263:22
wi' the weel-stockit f. | BURNS 114:6

far-off: old, unhappy, f. things | WORD 578:14

farrago: discursus nostri f. libelli est | JUV 287:12

farrow: old sow that eats her f. | JOYCE 286:16

farther: f. you go from the church | WOTT 583:17
know I'm f. off from heav'n | HOOD 254:18

Farthest: F. Thule | VIRG 560:10

farthing: f. less | ADD 2:2
hast paid the uttermost f. | BIBLE 64:14
I am a kind of f. dip | STEV 523:13
sparrows sold for a f. | BIBLE 65:35
Virtue knows to a f. what | WALP 563:22

FARTHINGS FATHOM

farthings: sparrows sold for two f. BIBLE 70:3
fascination: My right elbow has a f. GILB 227:10
There's a f. frantic GILB 227:18
With f. in his very bow BYRON 123:36
fashion: appear a little out of f. SHAK 444:19
carving the f. of a new SHAK 472:14
f. a gentleman or noble SPEN 515:28
F.—a word which knaves CHUR 149:9
f. of this world passeth BIBLE 76:4
f. of these times SHAK 425:7
f. she detests SHAK 489:17
F., the arbiter STEE 518:4
F., though Folly's child COWP 168:12
garment out of f. SHAK 428:16
glass of f. SHAK 433:15
in my f. DOWS 191:12
in the first style of f. AUST 23:28
'is a highflyer at F. DICK 181:7
laws of markets and f. ALB 3:7
marriage ever out of f. BUTL 118:8
men in shape and f. ASCH 17:3
nothing else holds f. SHAK 487:16
out of the f. CIBB 151:10
tell you the leading f. RUSK 411:5
vegetable f. must excite GILB 227:23
very independent of f. GASK 221:23
will deeply put the f. SHAK 442:24
fashionable: idea ever to be f. is ominous SANT 414:5
With other f. topics GOLD 232:36
Fashion'd: F. so slenderly HOOD 254:9
Fashioned: F. so purely THOM 548:29
Which day by day were f. PRAY 399:7
fashioneth: clay say to him that f. BIBLE 59:13
fashions: conscience to fit this year's f. HELL 244:15
fast: can never be done too f. GOLD 232:17
f. bound in misery PRAY 397:7
f. that I have chosen BIBLE 60:4
fun grew f. and furious BURNS 115:10
he talks it so very f. FARQ 210:6
my heart is f. ANON 7:15
Spare F. MILT 341:27
study and f. SHAK 463:14
then into a f. SHAK 432:2
who will not f. in peace COWP 168:14
Fasten: F. your seatbelts DAVIS 172:18
faster: speed was far f. than light BULL 106:22
travel f. than a stagecoach GOLD 232:18
fastest: He travels the f. who travels KIPL 304:11
fastidious: literature is never f. SOUT 514:14
fasting: Apollo turned f. friar MER 337:29
between a fou man and a f. SCOTT 418:26
lives upon hope will die f. FRAN 218:13
nor f., nor birch BLAKE 87:20
thank heaven, f. SHAK 426:17
fasts: that come in f. divine HOPK 256:15
fat: eat the f. of the land BIBLE 46:36
Fair, f., and forty SCOTT 418:33
f. bulls of Basan PRAY 390:18
F., fair and forty OKEE 365:1
f. man a thin one is wildly CONN 161:15
f. of others' works BURT 116:13
f. white woman whom nobody CORN 162:22
find me f. and sleek HOR 258:16
fresher, and more f. DONNE 188:2
grow f. and look young DRYD 196:36
he nas nat right f. CHAU 141:23
men about me that are f. SHAK 448:20
oxen should himself be f. JOHN 279:20
seven f. kine BIBLE 46:31
she help'd him to f. BARH 33:6
them is f. and grows old SHAK 438:34
thin man inside every f. ORW 365:11
What is that f. gentleman SHAW 498:26
Who's your f. friend BRUM 106:3
you f. and greasy citizens SHAK 425:2
fatal: fair and f. king JOHN 273:23
f. and perfidious bark MILT 343:10
f. bellman SHAK 460:3
f. facility of the octo-syllabic BYRON 121:29
f. gift of beauty BYRON 121:6
f. to religion as indifference BURKE 111:35
I am a f. man THAC 545:13
Our f. shadows that walk FLET 215:13
So f. to my suit before GARR 221:16
So sweet was ne'er so f. SHAK 477:5
Their f. hands MILT 347:1
fatalistic: Beats like a f. drum ELIOT 204:9
fatality: think there is a f. in it STER 519:9
fate: am the master of my f. HENL 245:5
build that nation's f. BLAKE 85:17
cannot suspend their f. DEFOE 173:2
Far be that f. from us OVID 366:8
f. and metaphysical aid SHAK 459:1
F. cannot harm me SMITH 511:15
f. has torn your living CAT 137:15
F. is not an eagle BOWEN 91:5
F. keeps on happening LOOS 318:2
F. never wounds more deep JOHN 282:23
f. of a nation was riding LONG 316:26
f. of the great wen COBB 154:10
F. so enviously debars MARV 331:19
F.'s Urn shakes HOR 260:7
F., Time, Occasion SHEL 503:10
F. tried to conceal him HOLM 253:7
F. wrote her a most tremendous BEER 37:20
hanging breathless on thy f. LONG 316:7
He either fears his f. GRAH 233:14
how very sad thy f. KEATS 292:23
I feel my f. in what ROET 407:6
I hold f. FORD 216:20
is he that knows not F. CHES 147:4
is no armour against f. SHIR 507:2
I thy f. shall overtake KING 296:11
man and master of his f. TENN 535:2
might read the book of f. SHAK 442:1
now at length my f. I know BROW 101:22
once dead by f. BEAU 36:1
our f. but our business BOWEN 91:6
our folly, or our f. DENH 174:21
profit every day that F. HOR 259:18
shall be the maiden's f. SCOTT 416:12
should they know their f. GRAY 235:13
struggling in the storms of f. POPE 375:12
take a bond of f. SHAK 462:7
that f. and character are NOV 364:9
That Time and F. of all FITZ 212:17
thou and I with F. conspire FITZ 213:16
triumph'd over f. BYRON 124:28
us is over-rul'd by f. MARL 329:18
wayward the decrees of F. are THAC 546:4
what I will is f. MILT 348:30
when f. summons DRYD 196:33
Who can control his f. SHAK 477:19
With the severity of f. FORD 216:12
would F. but mend it PRIOR 401:7
fated: though f. not to die DRYD 196:11
fates: are masters of their f. SHAK 448:17
Father: about my F.'s business BIBLE 69:13
ance his f.'s pride BURNS 113:9
are of your f. the devil BIBLE 72:13
because I go to the F. BIBLE 72:40
become the f. of many nations BIBLE 74:40
be happier than your f. SOPH 513:4
believe in God the F. PRAY 384:26
bow my knees unto the F. BIBLE 77:24
brood of Folly without f. MILT 341:23
cannot have God for his f. CYPR 170:19
decrepit f. takes delight SHAK 493:13
did you last see your f. YEAM 584:8
Diogenes struck the f. BURT 116:36
down from the F. of lights BIBLE 80:9
either my f. or my mother STER 519:16
even as your F. which is BIBLE 64:21
everlasting F. BIBLE 58:7
f. answered never a word LONG 317:21
f. compounded with my mother SHAK 453:11
f. had a daughter lov'd SHAK 489:7
f., Harry, to that thought SHAK 442:19
F., I have sinned against BIBLE 70:19
f. is gone wild into his SHAK 442:25
F. is rather vulgar DICK 178:26
F. of his Country ANON 5:7
f. pitieth his own children PRAY 396:17
f.'s helm is far too big FLEM 215:5
F.'s house are many mansions BIBLE 72:31
f.'s joy SCOTT 417:29
F., that I have sinned MASS 334:15
F. which seeth in secret BIBLE 64:22
features of my f.'s face BYRON 125:13
Glory be to the F. PRAY 384:15
Had it been his f. ANON 5:15
Hath the rain a f. BIBLE 53:4
Have a turnip than his f. JOHN 280:10
He took my f. grossly SHAK 434:30
hired servants of my f.'s BIBLE 70:19
Honour thy f. and thy mother BIBLE 47:24
How many a f. have I seen TENN 536:22
I am thy f.'s spirit SHAK 431:4
I had it from my f. SHAK 446:26
It is a wise f. that knows SHAK 466:9
leave his f. and his mother BIBLE 45:13
lively picture of his f.'s FLET 215:28
man cometh unto the F. BIBLE 72:32
mother on his f. him begot BLAKE 87:2
My f. feeds his flocks HOME 253:22
My f. was an eminent button COLM 159:4
my f. wept BLAKE 87:23
no more like my f. SHAK 429:28
not an angry f. CAMP 129:3
one God the F. Almighty PRAY 387:10
only begotten of the F. BIBLE 71:27
only f. GOLD 232:13
Our F. which art in heaven BIBLE 64:24
Our F. which art in heaven PREV 400:15
resembled My f. SHAK 460:5
She gave her f. forty-one ANON 6:12
son maketh a glad f. BIBLE 53:29
thicker than my f.'s loins BIBLE 51:2
Thy f.'s shame BRET 92:6
'twill come to my f. anon' AUBR 17:26
withered all when my f. died SHAK 436:11
worshipful f. and first founder CAXT 138:2
your F. had an accident POTT 382:1
fathered: Are f. by our heroism ELIOT 203:6
Being so f. and so husbanded SHAK 449:16
fatherless: defendeth the f. and widow PRAY 399:18
f. children PRAY 385:20
He is a Father of the f. PRAY 394:7
visit the f. and widows BIBLE 80:11
fatherly: thy f. goodness all those PRAY 386:1
fathers: f.-forth whose beauty HOPK 256:23
f. have eaten sour grapes BIBLE 60:34
f., provoke not your children BIBLE 78:7
fet from f. of war-proof SHAK 444:1
healthiest f. stands WHIT 570:15
He slept with his f. BIBLE 51:5
I like to be as my f. were BLUNT 89:5
iniquity of the f. upon BIBLE 47:24
Instead of thy f. PRAY 392:18
Lord God of your f. BIBLE 47:8
our f. have told us PRAY 392:13
past unto the f. by the prophets BIBLE 79:28
sins of your f. HOR 260:25
sojourners, as were all our f. BIBLE 51:39
such as our f. have told us PRAY 395:3
When your f. tempted me PRAY 396:4
which thy f. have set BIBLE 54:23
Father William: You are old, F. CARR 133:22
You are old, F. SOUT 514:7
fathom: Full f. five SHAK 484:32
Full many a f. deep CAMP 128:16

To wet their silken f.   SPEN 516:32
featly: Foot it f. here and there   SHAK 484:30
feats: outdares Stokes in azure f.
   BROW 103:27
to f. of broil and battle   SHAK 473:24
''Twas one of my f.   BYRON 125:1
What f. he did that day   SHAK 445:3
Featur'd: F. like him   SHAK 493:6
feature: every f. works   AUST 22:9
fed: bite the hand that f.   BURKE 112:10
f. and educated   RUSK 412:6
f. horses in the morning   BIBLE 60:16
f. of the dainties that   SHAK 457:1
f. on the fullness of death   SWIN 530:5
f. with the same food   SHAK 467:4
souls most f. with Shakespeare's   CHES 147:17
We both have f. as well   SHAK 448:14
you have f. full   VIRG 560:9
Federal: F. Union: it must be preserved
   JACK 270:30
Federation: F. of the world   TENN 538:24
fee: bought over God with a f.   SWIN 530:23
gorgeous East in f.   WORD 582:10
feeble: confirm the f. knees   BIBLE 58:33
f. God has stabb'd me   GAY 222:6
Most forcible F.   SHAK 442:5
not enough to help the f.   SHAK 485:27
poor f. sex   VICT 556:14
such a f. temper should   SHAK 448:16
feebly: His words came f.   WORD 581:1
feed: bid thee f.   BLAKE 87:26
doth this our Caesar f.   SHAK 448:18
f. his flock like a shepherd   BIBLE 59:7
F. in the ooze of their   ARN 13:6
f. me in a green pasture   PRAY 390:21
...F. my lambs   BIBLE 73:14
F. the brute   PUNCH 403:1
f. thee out of my own vitals   CONG 160:6
f. with the rich   JOHN 275:23
So shalt thou f. on Death   SHAK 495:14
Then f. on thoughts   MILT 347:8
feedeth: he f. among the lilies   BIBLE 56:24
Feeds: F. beast as man   SHAK 421:8
ruin that it f. upon   COWP 166:10
feel: believe to *One does* f.   KNOX 305:20
can f. that he is dying   SUET 524:17
feel a feeling which I f.   RIDD 406:3
f. for the common chord   BROW 98:22
f. my breasts all perfume   JOYCE 286:30
f. not what they inspire   SHEL 505:13
f. the earth move   HEM 245:3
f. what wretches feel   SHAK 454:16
'I f. it more than other   DICK 176:28
mean or more than they f.   CONN 161:11
must also f. it as a man   SHAK 462:18
Of making figments f.   HARDY 239:16
Speak what we f.   SHAK 456:13
thing that could not f.   WORD 581:10
Those who would make us f.   CHUR 149:13
to f. so small and sweet   PATM 370:5
tragedy to those that f.   WALP 563:11
feeling: appeals to diffused f.   BAG 28:30
constellations of f.   DOUG 191:7
f. that I could last   CONR 161:24
f. too falsely disdained   SHEL 504:13
f. which I feel you all   RIDD 406:3
fellow no f. of his business   SHAK 436:26
formal f. comes   DICK 183:13
generous and honest f.   BURKE 108:24
Had fed the f. past   MARL 330:11
I'm not f. very well myself   PUNCH 403:2
Love's f. is more soft   SHAK 457:8
man is as old as he's f.   COLL 158:15
mess of imprecision of f.   ELIOT 202:23
petrifies the f.   BURNS 113:17
probably is there more true f.   JOW 285:23
pulse of f. stirs   ARN 12:22
sensible To f. as to sight   SHAK 459:15
transmission of f.   TOLS 551:14
feelings: on what we call our f.   DICK 179:21

out of the f. of humanity   BLAC 85:2
overflow of powerful f.   WORD 583:10
ultimately determined by the f.   SPEN 515:2
fees: hope, but of his f.   HERR 250:12
they took their f.   BELL 39:1
who straight dream on f.   SHAK 481:28
feet: aching hands and bleeding f.   ARN 13:23
At her f. he bowed   BIBLE 49:11
bathe those beauteous f.   FLET 215:29
beat of her unseen f.   SHEL 500:6
beautiful are thy f. with shoes   BIBLE 57:7
better to die on your f.   IBAR 269:16
Came on the following F.   THOM 548:14
clothes at a young man's f.   BIBLE 73:28
dost thou wash my f.   BIBLE 72:27
down Satan under our f.   PRAY 385:19
f., and the palms of her   BIBLE 51:37
f. are always in the water   AMES 4:3
f. have they   PRAY 397:18
f. like unto fine brass   BIBLE 81:14
f. of him that bringeth   BIBLE 59:18
f. of the day and the feet   SWIN 528:16
f. of thine high priests   SWIN 530:7
f. shall stand in thy gates   PRAY 398:11
f. shod with the preparation   BIBLE 78:10
f. they hurt in the stocks   PRAY 397:3
f. was I to the lame   BIBLE 52:35
fell at his f. as dead   BIBLE 81:14
great knees and f.   SWIN 528:26
hands are a sort of f.   TRAH 552:1
Her f. beneath her petticoat   SUCK 524:8
Her f. go down to death   BIBLE 53:20
Her pretty f.   HERR 250:7
is a lantern unto my f.   PRAY 398:6
Its f. were tied   KEATS 292:10
let my due f. never fail   MILT 342:9
moon under her f.   BIBLE 82:10
more clothes on his f.   SHAK 443:18
my dreams under your f.   YEATS 585:9
my f. from falling   PRAY 397:20
nations under our f.   PRAY 392:23
nearer than hands and f.   TENN 533:29
off the dust of your f.   BIBLE 65:32
pierced my hands and my f.   PRAY 390:20
radical is a man with both f.   ROOS 407:24
Scots lords at his f.   BALL 31:20
set my f. upon the rock   PRAY 392:1
seven f. of English   HAR 242:11
slipping underneath our F.   FITZ 212:22
splendour and speed of thy f.   SWIN 528:16
They hadn't any f.   CARR 135:6
those f. in ancient time   BLAKE 86:16
Thus I set my printless f.   MILT 341:21
thy shoes from off thy f.   BIBLE 47:4
to guide our f. into   BIBLE 69:7
tremble under her f.   TENN 540:12
twain he covered his f.   BIBLE 57:28
walk'd those blessed f.   SHAK 437:33
wash their f. in soda water   ELIOT 204:27
what dread f.   BLAKE 87:15
white f. of laughing girls   MAC 322:12
world with their f. forward   BROW 97:10
Fehlgriff: Erste F. Gottes   NIET 363:3
war der zweite F. Gottes   NIET 363:4
feigned: Than fables yet have f.   MILT 346:23
feigning: f. was called compliment
   SHAK 489:22
felde: faire f. ful of folke fonde   LANG 309:23
fele: that thow shalt nat f.   CHAU 144:3
felice: *ricordarsi del tempo f.*   DANTE 171:8
felicem: *fuisse f.*   BOET 89:6
Felices: *F. ter et amplius*   HOR 259:21
felicitas: *Horatii curiosa f.*   PETR 373:3
felicite: respect of the pleyn f.   CHAU 144:18
felicities: Job than the f. of Solomon
   BACON 25:19
three fearful f.   SIDN 508:4
felicity: Absent thee from f. awhile
   SHAK 437:25
f. on the far side of baldness   SMITH 510:13

none can boast sincere f.   DRYD 197:10
Our own f. we make or find   JOHN 282:21
possessed approaches f.   MER 337:32
shadow of f.   WALL 562:15
Their green f.   KEATS 293:3
these eyes to behold f.   BROW 96:21
throne of human f.   JOHN 280:20
What more f. can fall   SPEN 515:23
Felix: F. qui potuit rerum cognoscere
   VIRG 560:14
fell: f. among thieves   BIBLE 69:30
f. at his feet as dead   BIBLE 81:14
f. before the throne   BIBLE 81:32
F. in the weeping brook   SHAK 436:19
f. into his anecdotage   DISR 186:19
Firefrorefiddle, the Fiend of the F.
   ELIOT 203:7
From morn To noon he f.   MILT 346:3
it f. not   BIBLE 65:11
my uncle Toby f. into it   STER 520:6
ran to help me when I f.   TAYL 531:25
So I f. in love with   GILB 229:3
that the wall f. down flat   BIBLE 49:2
though the brightest f.   SHAK 462:14
We f. out   TENN 541:28
where the dead leaf f.   KEATS 290:1
fellow: f. that will take rewards   SHAK 422:21
himself a most agreeable f.   AUST 22:10
His f. traveller   ANON 8:4
take a f. eight years old   BROW 100:30
touchy, testy, pleasant f.   ADD 2:10
want of it, the f.   POPE 379:22
'you're a f.   DICK 181:32
fellow-citizens: heated passions of his
f.   HOR 260:18
fellow-creatures: apply that epithet to
my f.   MILL 339:5
fellow-feeling: f. makes one wond'rous
   GARR 221:15
fellow-men: one that loves his f.   HUNT 268:5
fellow-mortal: earth-born companion
An' f.   BURNS 115:21
fellows: fortunate f. that now you   HOUS 263:7
hath fram'd strange f.   SHAK 465:8
these f. of infinite tongue   SHAK 445:13
fellowship: in one communion and f.
   PRAY 387:4
right hands of f.   BIBLE 77:15
simple dues of f.   BROW 97:30
felonious: some f. end   MILT 341:1
felony: f. to drink small beer   SHAK 446:11
felt: darkness which may be f.   BIBLE 47:15
f. along the heart   WORD 578:4
f. him like the thunder's   * ARN 13:16
pity who has f. the woe   GAY 223:7
female: despight they cast on f. wits
   BRAD 91:13
elegance of f. friendship   JOHN 282:12
f. atheist talks you dead   JOHN 282:22
f. mind is not capable   KNOX 305:24
f. of the species is more   KIPL 299:4
f. woman is one   WARD 564:26
life for the British f.   CLOU 153:9
Male and f. created   BIBLE 45:5
male and the f.   BIBLE 45:34
share some f. errors fall   POPE 380:33
unlearned and uninformed f.   AUST 24:2
What f. heart can gold   GRAY 235:6
Who has a polished f. friend   WHURR 572:1
females: with eighty mile o' f.   DICK 183:2
femina: *Dux f. facti*   VIRG 557:15
Nemo magis gaudet quam f.   JUV 288:6
feminine: Purity is the f.   HARE 242:5
she's of the f. gender   OKEE 364:23
femme: *Cherchons la f.*   DUMAS 199:2
elle est f.   RAC 404:3
femmes: *des privilèges des f.*   FOUR 217:18
fen: through the plashy f.   WAUGH 566:3
fences: f. make good neighbours   FROST 219:9
Yet all these f. and their   HERB 248:11

fire-folk: look at all the f. sitting HOPK 256:28
Firefrorefiddle: F., the Fiend of the Fell
   ELIOT 203:7
fires: arose the answering f. MAC 322:2
Big f. flare up in a wind FRAN 218:2
f. soon burn out themselves SHAK 478:19
Fuel to maintain his f. CAREW 130:12
misled by wandering f. DRYD 196:13
th' assembled f. appear SMART 509:4
thought-executing f. SHAK 454:4
fire-side: adventures were by the f.
   GOLD 232:34
glass of wine by his own f. SHER 506:38
no f., howsoe'er defended LONG 317:6
people to leave their own f. AUST 22:10
To make a happy f. clime BURNS 115:15
firing: have what to do after f. REED 405:5
Firm: F. Resolve BURNS 115:14
firmament: f. sheweth his handy-work
   PRAY 390:11
is no fellow in the f. SHAK 449:25
spacious f. on high ADD 2:22
there's fury in the f. SASS 415:4
this brave o'erhanging f. SHAK 432:15
Waters that be above the F. PRAY 384:20
Firmly: F. I believe and truly NEWM 362:11
Firmness: Commodity, F., and Delight
   WOTT 583:16
little objects with like f. BYRON 120:29
Thy f. makes my circle DONNE 190:18
first: beautiful than thy f. love YEATS 584:23
be done for the f. time CORN 162:23
by the clash of the F. HARDY 240:3
certainty are not the f. HOUS 264:21
Ever since afore her F. DICK 179:27
extol Him f., him last MILT 348:16
f. and second class citizens WILL 574:14
f. baby laughed BARR 34:13
f. blow is half the battle GOLD 232:27
f. by whom the new are POPE 378:19
f. casualty when war JOHN 273:18
f. destroys their mind DRYD 196:22
f. duty of a State RUSK 412:6
f. impulse was never CORN 162:18
f. impulses as they are MONT 355:11
f. in a village than second CAES 127:3
f. in war LEE 313:7
f., last, everlasting DONNE 187:23
f. man is of the earth BIBLE 76:28
f. of earthly blessings GIBB 224:17
f. of those who know TENN 541:23
f. step that is difficult DU D 198:28
F. time he kissed me BROW 98:12
f. true gentleman that DEKK 173:19
God's f. Creature BACON 28:5
he'd have been here f. CARR 135:32
I am not the f. HOUS 263:11
in the very f. line GOLD 231:19
last shall be f. BIBLE 67:13
loved not at f. sight MARL 329:18
morning were the f. day BIBLE 45:1
Since f. I saw you fresh SHAK 494:18
there is no last nor f. BROW 103:25
Thou know'st the f. time SHAK 455:22
undoubted title to the f. SWIFT 527:1
used by Charles the f. COW 164:4
were the f. that ever burst COL 155:12
when f. your eye I ey'd SHAK 494:18
work is what to put f. PASC 369:3
first-born: against all the f. of Egypt
   SHAK 425:17
brought forth her f. son BIBLE 69:9
will smite all the f. BIBLE 47:18
first day: f. of our Jubilee is death
   BROW 96:21
firstfruits: f. of them that slept BIBLE 76:22
First-rate: F. School WAUGH 565:30
powers of a f. man BAG 29:16
firsts: f. in some less favoured BETJ 44:11
fish: buttercups fried with f. LEAR 312:21

f. and fishing WALT 564:11
F. is plentiful and cheap LEAR 311:26
f. with the worm that hath SHAK 435:27
have dominion over the f. BIBLE 45:4
in a black and ugly f. HOR 257:9
in the belly of the f. BIBLE 61:22
is a pretty kettle of f. MARY 333:14
It's no f. ye're buying SCOTT 418:2
I was a f. SMITH 510:10
littlest f. may enter BROO 94:13
mind of the skuttle f. ADD 2:24
piece of a broiled f. BIBLE 71:20
said the small 'stute F. KIPL 304:14
seem older than the f. FRY 219:23
St Ives says the smell of f. KILV 296:6
stranded f. gaped among PLOM 374:19
subject to rape like f. DONNE 190:2
that f. would have bright KEATS 289:3
There's a f. that talks DE L 173:23
Thou deboshed f. thou SHAK 485:14
Un-dish-cover the f. CARR 136:11
was ever so free as a f. RUSK 412:2
What cat's averse to f. GRAY 235:6
word bites like a f. SPEN 515:15
worms to torture f. COLM 159:6
fished: He f. by obstinate isles POUND 383:3
fishermen: f. that walk upon the beach
   SHAK 455:14
Where f. lounge at noon ELIOT 205:4
fishers: Three f. went sailing away
   KING 297:2
will make you f. of men BIBLE 64:5
fishes: betray Tawny-finn'd f. SHAK 422:9
Dim moon-eyed f. near HARDY 239:5
f. first to shipping did DRYD 195:22
f. flew and forests walked CHES 146:22
f. leap in silver stream CLARE 152:14
F., that tipple LOV 318:17
how the f. live in the sea SHAK 478:4
little f. of the sea CARR 135:25
Men lived like f. SIDN 507:12
men that f. gnaw'd upon SHAK 480:27
of the loaves and the f. PEAC 370:16
So are the f. CHUR 150:4
uncommunicating muteness of f. LAMB 308:4
welcomes little f. CARR 133:18
fishified: flesh, how art thou f. SHAK 482:18
fishing: angling or float f. I can JOHN 280:28
blow when he goes a-f. WALT 563:34
I go a f. BIBLE 73:15
On f. up the moon PEAC 371:3
was f. in the dull canal ELIOT 204:26
fish-knives: Phone for the f. BETJ 42:19
fish-like: very ancient and f. smell
   SHAK 485:7
fishmonger: you are a f. SHAK 432:4
fishpond: That great f. (the sea) DEKK 173:18
fishpools: eyes like the f. in Heshbon
   BIBLE 57:9
fishy: f. form and mind BROO 94:13
Fissures: F. appeared in football PLOM 374:19
fist: agin the Secesher's f. WARD 564:27
of f. most valiant SHAK 444:17
fistful: f. of coins ZAP 588:18
fists: groan and shake their f. HOUS 266:8
fit: become f. for this world KEATS 293:14
f. for the kingdom of God BIBLE 69:25
f. to use their freedom MAC 323:25
f. will work on him SHAK 437:9
isn't f. for humans now BETJ 44:4
most senseless and f. man SHAK 472:28
taen the f. o' rhyme BURNS 113:23
they are not f. to live JOHN 276:33
when the f. was on him SHAK 448:15
when the melancholy f. KEATS 291:15
Why then I'll f. you KYD 306:8
fitchew: f. nor the soiled horse SHAK 455:17
fitful: life's f. fever SHAK 461:12
fitless: In f. finger-stalls GILB 227:7
fitly: word f. spoken BIBLE 54:26

fits: wen bein' took with f. DICK 179:27
fitter: Young men are f. to invent
   BACON 27:39
Fittest: Survival of the F. is more
   DARW 171:27
survival of the f. SPEN 514:30
fitting: f. for a princess SHAK 424:16
It is right and f. MASS 335:3
Fitzgerald: shall hoarse F. bawl
   BYRON 124:14
this Edward F. died YEATS 586:19
five: At exactly f. in the afternoon
   GARC 221:5
f. days elder than ourselves BROW 96:10
f. minutes too late all COWL 164:21
Full fathom f. SHAK 484:32
Must rise at f. CLAR 152:24
Not f. in five score PORS 381:27
These f. kings did a king THOM 547:4
five-and-twenty: reputation of f.
   DRYD 196:36
five per cent: f. is the natural interest
   MAC 323:29
five-pound: Wrapped up in a f. note
   LEAR 312:11
fix: right to f. the boundary PARN 369:2
such a f. to be so fertile NASH 360:4
fixed: great gulf f. BIBLE 70:29
He f. thee mid this dance BROW 104:11
may surely there be f. PRAY 386:12
You are the one f. point DOYLE 192:23
fizz: sheer necessity of f. BELL 39:31
flabbiness: f. born of the bitch-goddess
   JAMES 272:3
flag: death's pale f. is not SHAK 483:30
debt, an' a f. LOW 319:7
f. of all the free CHES 147:3
f. of my disposition WHIT 570:14
out a f. and sign of love SHAK 473:19
spare your country's f. WHIT 571:17
their f. against a power WEBS 566:12
We'll keep the red f. flying CONN 161:10
Whose f. has braved CAMP 129:12
Flag-flapper: Jelly-bellied F. KIPL 305:8
flag-flowers: There grew broad f.
   SHEL 503:26
flagitium: Peiusque leto f. timet HOR 261:19
flagons: Stay me with f. BIBLE 56:21
flakes: Some f. have lost their HARDY 240:21
flambeaux: chestnut casts his f. HOUS 264:20
flame: blood and smoke and f. HOUS 266:4
Chloe is my real f. PRIOR 401:1
eye the unconquered f. POUND 382:14
f. of the taper SHAK 428:8
f. out like shining from HOPK 256:12
f.? The Bush is bare BROW 98:29
full of subtil f. BEAU 35:19
hard, gemlike f. PATER 369:21
his eyes were as a f. BIBLE 81:14
in them that little f. REN 405:31
Kindled a f. I still deplore GARR 221:16
one burning f. together TENN 538:9
only change th'expiring f. GAY 223:23
seem'd my f. to qualify SHAK 495:2
so in a shapeless f. DONNE 187:18
Still plays about the f. GAY 222:11
throne was like the fiery f. BIBLE 61:8
Whose f. creeps in at every PEELE 371:7
flamed: f. upon the brazen greaves
   TENN 538:8
flames: Commit it then to the f. HUME 267:15
F. in the forehead MILT 343:17
So his f. must waste away CAREW 130:12
thou king of f. CHAP 140:7
warmth of shepherds' f. MARL 330:11
Went by her like thin f. ROSS 409:18
With rich f. BROW 97:8
flaming: ministers a f. fire PRAY 396:18
thou f. minister SHAK 477:5
Wav'd over by that f. brand MILT 350:1

flammantia: f. moenia mundi | LUCR 320:3
flamme: f. qui ne s'éteint pas | REN 405:13
flammes: met le monde entier en f. | VOLT 561:6
Flanders: F. fields the poppies blow | MCCR 324:30
F. hath receiv'd our yoke | WALL 562:17
had brought him a F. mare | HENR 246:2
prodigious armies we had in F. | STER 519:26
flanks: silken f. with garlands drest | KEATS 291:8
flannel: waistcoat and f. drawers | GASK 221:24
flannelled: f. fools at the wicket | KIPL 300:4
flap-dragon: easier swallowed than a f. | SHAK 457:12
flashes: objects recognised, In f. | WORD 580:19
occasional f. of silence | SMITH 511:13
Flask: F. of Wine | FITZ 212:11
Flat: F. and flexible truths | BROW 95:18
half so f. as Walter Scott | ANON 7:8
very dangerous f. | SHAK 467:2
your life extremely f. | GILB 228:29
flaterye: feyned f. and japes | CHAU 142:7
flats: different sharps and f. | BROW 103:15
flatten: His hide is sure to f. | BELL 38:30
flatter: before you f. a man so | JOHN 280:29
do but f. with their lips | PRAY 389:32
f. beauty's ignorant ear | YEATS 586:14
F. the mountain-tops with | SHAK 493:9
I am afraid to f. him | BURKE 109:5
Regard me as I do not f. | SHAK 427:20
flatter'd: Englishman, Being f. | CHAP 140:3
I have not f. its rank | BYRON 120:38
still contemn'd and f. | SHAK 455:5
flattered: being then most f. | SHAK 449:11
f. into virtue | SURT 525:1
He that loves to be f. | SHAK 485:28
who neither feared nor f. | DOUG 191:6
flatterer: flattered is worthy o' the f. | SHAK 485:28
hypocrite, and f. | BLAKE 86:7
flatterers: by f. besieged | POPE 376:27
I tell him he hates f. | SHAK 449:11
surrounded by sycophants and f. | HARD 238:21
flattering: f. unction to your soul | SHAK 435:14
Some with a f. word | WILDE 572:10
flatters: humours and f. them | CHES 145:26
What really f. a man is | SHAW 497:4
flattery: Everyone likes f. | DISR 185:28
f. is worth his having | JOHN 280:29
gained by every sort of f. | CHES 146:1
is paid with f. | JOHN 281:15
'This is no f. | SHAK 424:31
tout for f. | COLL 158:14
Was f. lost on poet's ear | SCOTT 416:18
Flaubert: His true Penelope was F. | POUND 383:3
flavour: from its high celestial f. | BYRON 122:26
flaw: no kind of fault or f. | GILB 226:1
sans crack or f. | SHAK 457:16
flaws: wished the f. were fewer | BROW 100:4
flax: smoking f. shall he not quench | BIBLE 59:11
flayed: Last week I saw a woman f. | SWIFT 527:5
flaying: f. would be fair | HOUS 266:8
flea: between a louse and a f. | JOHN 279:8
f. Hath smaller fleas | SWIFT 528:5
honour the very f. of his dog | JONS 284:6
will clog the foot of a f. | SHAK 490:1
fleas: dog that praised his f. | YEATS 587:4
F. know not whether they | LAND 309:15
f. that tease in the high | BELL 40:13
o' f. is good fer a dog | WEST 569:4
flebilis: Multis ille bonis f. occidit | HOR 260:1
Flecte: F. quod est rigidum | LANG 310:1

Flectere: F. si nequeo superos | VIRG 559:5
fled: earth's foundations f. | HOUS 265:7
F. is that music | KEATS 291:23
I f. Him | THOM 548:8
kissed it and then f. | SHEL 503:17
sea saw that, and f. | PRAY 397:16
Still as he f. | SPEN 516:6
Truth away From you is f. | WYATT 583:20
Whence all but he had f. | HEM 244:20
world that I am f. | SHAK 494:6
flee: death shall f. from them | BIBLE 82:7
f. away, and be at rest | PRAY 393:10
f. from the wrath to come | BIBLE 63:38
sorrow and sighing shall f. | BIBLE 59:1
that Fortune list to f. | CHAU 142:29
They f. from me | WYATT 583:21
wicked f. when no man pursueth | BIBLE 54:41
with their armies did f. | PRAY 394:8
fleece: forest f. the Wrekin | HOUS 263:14
fleeces: Thus you sheep bear f. | VIRG 560:20
fleet: All in the Downs the f. | GAY 223:28
command of the Channel F. | SMITH 512:2
enemy's f. came yonder | TENN 539:26
Fire and f. and candle-lighte | BALL 31:6
F. in which we serve | PRAY 400:2
F. is all lit up | WOOD 576:16
f. of stars is anchored | FLEC 214:7
F. the time carelessly | SHAK 424:20
Spanish f. thou canst not | SHER 505:27
There's the British F. | THAC 546:2
toward the Japanese f. | HALS 238:11
we took care of our f. | ADD 2:19
fleeth: hireling f. | BIBLE 72:19
My soul f. unto the Lord | PRAY 398:24
fleets: interested in armies and f. | AUDEN 18:15
Fleet Street: who can be dull in F. | LAMB 307:23
will take a walk down F. | SALA 413:17
flesh: All f. is as grass | BIBLE 80:21
All f. is grass | BIBLE 59:6
all f. shall see it together | BIBLE 59:5
bondwoman was born after the f. | BIBLE 77:16
brought him bread and f. | BIBLE 51:6
carrion f. than to receive | SHAK 467:20
closed up the f. instead | BIBLE 45:11
could not all this f. | SHAK 440:25
delicate white human f. | FIEL 211:25
east wind made f. | APPL 11:12
eat bulls' f. | PRAY 393:3
eat the f. in that night | BIBLE 47:17
fair and unpolluted f. | SHAK 437:4
f., alas, is wearied | MALL 327:9
f. and blood so cheap | HOOD 255:8
f., and the devil | PRAY 385:16
f., how art thou fishified | SHAK 482:22
f. of my flesh | BIBLE 45:12
F. perishes, I live on | HARDY 240:1
f. sinks downwards here | SHAK 480:16
f. to feel the chain | BRON 93:31
From this world-wearied f. | SHAK 483:31
he might trust in the f. | BIBLE 78:16
if this f. which walls | SHAK 479:11
in my f. shall I see God | BIBLE 52:31
men are f. and blood | SHAK 449:25
mind the things of the f. | BIBLE 75:7
more f. than another man | SHAK 440:5
my heart and my f. rejoice | PRAY 395:11
not against f. and blood | BIBLE 78:10
not provision for the f. | BIBLE 75:25
reasonable soul and human f. subsisting | PRAY 385:14
since f. must live | BROW 105:3
sinful lusts of the f. | PRAY 388:13
soul to feel the f. | BRON 93:21
ta'en out thy heart o' f. | BALL 32:3
that look but casual f. | YEATS 587:1
these our f. upright | DONNE 188:15
they shall be one f. | BIBLE 45:13
to me a thorn in the f. | BIBLE 77:13

too solid f. would melt | SHAK 429:28
unto thee shall all f. come | PRAY 393:23
wants to make your f. creep | DICK 181:29
willing but the f. is weak | BIBLE 68:16
Word was made f. | BIBLE 71:27
WORD WAS MADE F. | MASS 335:12
would I could subdue the f. | BETJ 44:1
yet would God this f. | SWIN 530:18
flesh'd: f. Thy maiden sword | SHAK 440:26
fleshly: through all this f. dress | VAUG 555:16
flesh pots: when we sat by the f. | BIBLE 47:23
fletu: fraterno multum manantia f. | CAT 137:15
fleurs: amas de f. étrangères | MONT 355:6
flew: f. the web and floated | TENN 538:11
sparrows from outside f. | BEDE 37:1
flexible: Flat and f. truths | BROW 95:18
Flibbertigibbet: This is the foul fiend F. | SHAK 454:22
flichterin: wi' f.' noise an' glee | BURNS 113:5
flies: Dead f. cause the ointment | BIBLE 56:1
f. to wanton boys | SHAK 455:9
F., worms, and flowers | WATTS 565:2
his skin the swart f. move | DOUG 191:10
kisses the Joy as it f. | BLAKE 86:18
murmurous haunt of f. | KEATS 291:21
shops with large blue f. | SMITH 510:7
these summer f. | SHAK 457:15
which may catch small f. | SWIFT 527:16
flight: alarms of struggle and f. | ARN 12:23
His cloister'd f. | SHAK 461:13
His f. was madness | SHAK 462:11
now wing thy distant f. | HADR 237:9
Swift be thy f. | SHEL 505:2
that puts the Stars to F. | FITZ 212:5
will not take their f. | MILT 344:7
flights: f. upon the banks of Thames | JONS 284:25
flim-flam: This is a pretty f. | BEAU 36:6
flinch: cowards f. and traitors | CONN 161:10
facts are facts and f. | BROW 104:21
Fling: F. but a stone | GREEN 235:28
f. the ringleaders from | ARN 16:28
I'll have a f. | FLET 215:20
Flinging: F. from his arms I laughed | YEATS 585:20
flint: anger as the f. bears fire | SHAK 451:24
flirtation: Merely innocent f. | BYRON 123:35
flits: bat that f. at close | BLAKE 85:11
flittings: Thou tellest my f. | PRAY 393:13
float: clouds I'll never f. | WORD 579:18
floated: Out flew the web and f. | TENN 538:11
floating: f. bulwark of the island | BLAC 85:4
flock: feed his f. like a shepherd | BIBLE 59:7
f. to gaze the strengthless | HOUS 263:3
hair is as a f. of goats | BIBLE 56:26
have seen the ravens f. | AYT 24:10
keeping watch over their f. | BIBLE 69:9
said as we sat in f. | HARDY 240:13
tainted wether of the f. | SHAK 467:25
was the f. in woolly fold | KEATS 289:9
flocks: My father feeds his f. | HOME 253:22
My f. feed not | BARN 34:4
shepherds watch'd their f. | TATE 531:21
Flodden: Of F.'s fatal field | SCOTT 417:25
flog: f. the rank and file | ARN 16:28
flogging: habit of f. me constantly | TROL 552:11
There is now less f. | JOHN 276:32
flood: beached verge of the salt f. | SHAK 486:14
f. could not wash away | CONG 160:10
f. may bear me far | TENN 533:4
F. Of British freedom | WORD 582:2
f. unto the world's end | PRAY 394:20
giant race before the f. | DRYD 196:1
nearly spoiled ta F. | AYT 24:7
no wave Of a great f. | MER 337:10
taken at the f. | SHAK 451:27
that were before the f. | BIBLE 67:32
Thorough f. | SHAK 470:2

with me into this angry f. SHAK 448:14
flood-brim: furthest f. look with me
  ROSS 409:26
Floodgate: F. of the deeper heart FLEC 214:24
Is of so f. and o'bearing SHAK 473:23
floods: f. are risen PRAY 396:1
f. came BIBLE 65:12
haystack in the f. MORR 358:11
heavily and fell in f. WORD 580:27
moon, the governess of f. SHAK 470:6
neither can the f. drown it BIBLE 57:12
She quells the f. below CAMP 129:13
flood-ways: On f. to be far departing
  POUND 383:18
floor: fell upon the sanded f. PAYN 370:9
how the f. of heaven SHAK 468:15
I could f. them all DISR 185:31
nicely sanded f. GOLD 231:4
floors: across the f. of silent seas
  ELIOT 203:21
flop: An' f. round the earth KIPL 304:10
flopping: must go f. yourself down
  DICK 183:8
Flora: Tasting of F. and the country
  KEATS 291:18
floral: fair and f. air FLEC 214:6
Florence: F., Elizabethan England
  INGE 270:10
lily of F. blossoming LONG 316:17
Rode past fair F. KEATS 290:10
sporting prints of Aunt F.'s COW 164:2
Flores: F. in the Azores Sir Richard
  TENN 542:21
floribus: aliquid quod in ipsis f. angat
  LUCR 320:11
florid: Let a f. music praise AUDEN 20:21
flos: Ut f. in saeptis secretus CAT 137:6
flotte: Elle f. RAC 404:3
flour: whitter than the lylye f. CHAU 142:32
floures: emperice and flour of f. CHAU 143:31
that passeth soone as f. CHAU 144:19
that the f. gynnen CHAU 143:29
thise f. white and rede CHAU 143:30
flourish: No more doth f. SPEN 516:13
peculiar f. of his right arm DICK 181:10
Princes and lords may f. GOLD 230:18
swoop, a swing, a f. JAMES 271:34
transfix the f. set on youth SHAK 493:20
Truth shall f. out PRAY 395:15
youth of a state arms do f. BACON 27:34
flourisheth: f. as a flower of a field
  PRAY 396:17
She f. new and new SKEL 508:18
flourishing: f. like a green bay-tree
  PRAY 391:29
no f. with his sword REYN 405:20
flours: f. be planted on my grave
  HARDY 241:18
flout: Gild, but to f. SCOTT 416:13
scout 'em, and f. 'em SHAK 485:15
Flow: F. gently BURNS 113:27
foolish tears would f. CLAR 152:23
I within did f. TRAH 562:3
rivers of blood must yet f. JEFF 272:14
salt tides seaward f. ARN 13:5
Such ebb and f. must ever WORD 578:8
unus'd to f. SHAK 493:7
What need you f. so fast ANON 8:13
Flowed: F. up the hill and down ELIOT 204:21
flower: art the f. of cities all DUNB 199:10
cometh forth like a f. BIBLE 52:26
constellated f. that never SHEL 503:18
creep from flower to f. SHEL 501:5
die in the f. of their age BIBLE 49:33
every f. that sad embroidery MILT 343:15
f. fadeth BIBLE 59:6
f. grows concealed CAT 137:6
f. is born to blush unseen GRAY 234:23
f. of roses in the spring BIBLE 63:27
F. that once hath blown FITZ 212:19

f. that shall be mine WORD 583:2
f. thereof falleth away BIBLE 80:21
f. with base infection SHAK 494:15
From every opening f. WATTS 565:21
glory of man as the f. BIBLE 80:21
Heaven in a Wild F. BLAKE 85:8
he flourisheth as a f. PRAY 396:17
is no stronger than a f. SHAK 494:4
leaf, the bud, the f. SPEN 516:13
learning lightly like a f. TENN 537:21
look like the innocent f. SHAK 459:3
May prove a beauteous f. SHAK 482:16
meanest f. that blows WORD 579:14
of glory in the f. WORD 579:13
plant and f. of light JONS 285:8
pluck this f., safety SHAK 438:29
saw the water-flags in f. PATM 370:2
simple maiden in her f. TENN 537:27
summer's f. is to the summer SHAK 494:15
sweetest f. for scent SHEL 503:24
that a life was but a f. SHAK 427:2
this is the noble f. DONNE 190:23
this most goodly f. SKEL 508:18
this same f. that smiles HERR 250:5
upon a little western f. SHAK 470:8
white f. of a blameless life TENN 533:30
flower-de-luce: f. being one SHAK 491:26
flowering: About the f. squares TENN 537:18
f. judas ELIOT 203:4
in the f. of His fields TENN 535:19
flower-pots: Water your damned f.
  BROW 105:5
flowers: All sorts of f. the which SPEN 515:19
are f. but fading seen PEELE 371:8
bunch of other men's f. MONT 355:6
cool-rooted f. KEATS 292:1
fairest f. o' the season SHAK 491:23
Flies, worms, and f. WATTS 565:24
f. and fruits of love BYRON 125:11
f. appear on the earth BIBLE 56:22
f. azure, black SHEL 503:19
f. growing over him KEATS 295:1
F. I leave you on the grass TESC 545:2
F. in the garden STEV 523:7
f. now that frighted thou SHAK 491:26
F. of all hue MILT 347:20
f. of the forest are a' ELL 206:8
f. that bloom in the spring GILB 227:13
f. were dead PEAC 371:1
frosts are slain and f. SWIN 528:17
gathered f. are dead FLEC 214:13
got me f. to strew Thy way HERB 247:1
grass break into foam of f. SWIN 530:18
I have seen f. come MAS 333:23
it won't be f. AUDEN 21:10
Larded with sweet f. SHAK 435:34
Letting a hundred f. blossom MAO 328:18
No f., by request AING 3:6
odoriferous f. of fancy SHAK 457:3
plants and f. Ever sprung SHAK 447:3
play with f. and smile SHAK 443:17
Proserpin gathering f. MILT 347:21
see what f. are at my feet KEATS 291:24
swath and all its twined f. KEATS 293:6
That f. would bloom KEATS 289:3
took the f. to fair HOUS 264:17
were but as a bed of f. DONNE 190:26
Where souls do couch on f. SHAK 423:10
Who gave them f. OWEN 367:7
with azure moss and f. SHEL 502:10
You shall pick f. AUDEN 18:8
flowery: at her f. work doth sing MILT 342:8
f. lap of earth ARN 13:17
f. way that leads SHAK 421:4
you walk your f. way GILB 227:23
flowing: All things are a f. POUND 383:7
land f. with milk BIBLE 47:6
Robes loosely f. JONS 283:27
flown: whither f. again FITZ 213:15
flowret: meanest f. of the vale GRAY 235:15

flow'rs: Insnar'd with f. MARV 332:3
Time did beckon to the f. HERB 247:24
flows: Everything f. and nothing stays
  HER 246:5
fluent: f. talkers or most plausible
  HAZL 243:24
flummoxed: Italians call reg'larly f.
  DICK 182:15
flung: f. us on the windy hill BROO 94:15
flush: f. the man HOPK 257:7
roses for the f. of youth ROSS 409:7
flushed: f. print in a poppy there
  THOM 548:27
flushing: constant sound of f. runneth
  BETJ 43:12
flushpots: f. of Euston and the hanging
  JOYCE 286:5
flute: f. and the trumpet AUDEN 20:21
f., harp BIBLE 61:3
gauger played the f. STEV 523:8
his brains upon the f. BROW 105:4
Shepherds shall f. their AUDEN 18:8
soft complaining f. DRYD 197:24
flutes: Of f. and soft recorders MILT 345:21
sound of lyres and f. PATER 369:19
tune of f. kept stroke SHAK 422:2
Flutter: F. and bear him up BETJ 42:11
flutter'd: f. and fail'd for breath ARN 14:6
fluttered: On f. folk and wild KIPL 304:6
Fluttering: F. and dancing in the breeze
  WORD 577:29
fly: all things f. thee THOM 548:21
are no longer wings to f. ELIOT 202:1
'as pigs have to f. CARR 134:9
blue-bottle f. on a rather large BARH 33:5
F. fishing may be a very JOHN 280:28
F., honesty, f. SMITH 510:5
f. sat upon the axletree BACON 27:33
f., Sir, may sting JOHN 274:8
f. that sips treacle is GAY 222:30
F. to her TENN 542:5
f. to India for gold MARL 329:4
fur F. 'bout the ears BUTL 117:30
I heard a F. buzz DICK 183:19
I will f. to thee KEATS 291:20
Like a long-legged f. upon YEATS 586:3
man is not a f. POPE 379:8
never f. conceals a hook BROO 94:13
noise of a f. DONNE 191:1
Often have seen spiders f. EDW 200:7
said a spider to a f. HOW 267:3
small gilded f. SHAK 455:16
sparks f. upward BIBLE 52:17
they ever f. by twilight BACON 27:23
thirsty f. OLDYS 365:4
those that f. BUTL 118:12
To f. from BYRON 120:34
to f. is safe COWP 167:10
which way shall I f. MILT 347:15
with the f. in his hand STER 519:24
with twain he did f. BIBLE 57:28
You f. them for a moment TENN 542:17
flyer: no high f. PEPYS 372:10
fly-fishing: winter f. it is as useful
  WALT 563:32
flyin'-fishes: Where the f. play KIPL 301:5
flying: asleep the snow came f. BRID 92:12
came f. upon the wings PRAY 390:8
dear little kangaroos f. WILDE 573:10
f. and elusive shadow ARN 12:22
irretrievable time is f. VIRG 560:11
lead was f. HOUS 266:4
There is nor f. hence SHAK 463:7
Foal: F. of an oppressed race COL 157:16
foam: opening on the f. KEATS 291:23
through sheets of f. ARN 14:21
was wild and dank with f. KING 296:25
foam-flowers: f. endure when the
  rose-blossoms SWIN 529:19
foe: commend, A tim'rous f. POPE 376:27

darkly at the f.	MAC 322:14
erect and manly f.	CANN 130:1
f. but falls before us	DRAKE 193:5
f. of tyrants	CAMP 129:9
f.! they come	BYRON 120:25
f. was folly and his weapon	HOPE 256:2
Forbids the robbing of a f.	CHUR 148:30
friend who never made a f.	TENN 534:31
I was angry with my f.	BLAKE 87:21
like fire he meets the f.	TENN 542:7
met my dearest f. in heaven	SHAK 430:4
nor shuns his f.	DRYD 195:21
not a furnace for your f.	SHAK 446:25
open f. may prove a curse	GAY 223:13
perhaps a jealous f.	SHEL 500:10
praise the merit of a f.	POPE 378:32
redoubled strokes upon the f.	SHAK 458:4
willing f. and sea room	ANON 4:26
wolf far thence that's f.	WEBS 567:9
ye sail to meet the f.	NEWB 361:7
Foeda: F. est in coitu et brevis	PETR 373:5
foeman: it to a soldier and a f.	HOUS 266:4
When the f. bares his steel	GILB 228:18
foes: art in the midst of f.	ELL 206:9
f. nor loving friends can	KIPL 300:2
f. they captive make	CHAN 139:19
Greatly his f. he dreads	CHUR 148:18
his f. pursue him still	SHAK 495:21
Keep far our f.	PRAY 400:5
long inveterate f. saluted	DRYD 197:30
man's f. shall be they	BIBLE 65:39
thrice he routed all his f.	DRYD 195:2
whom we have held as f.	BUTL 119:21
foetus: expeditious extraction of the f.	STER 519:26
fog: brown f. of a winter dawn	ELIOT 204:20
Fear death?—to feel the f.	BROW 103:31
f. comes on little cat	SAND 413:26
f. of the good man's mind	BROW 100:1
f. that rubs its back upon	ELIOT 203:18
London particular...A f.	DICK 176:3
through the f. and filthy air	SHAK 458:1
fog-blathering: You bubble-mouthing, f.	FRY 219:28
fogs: His rising f. prevail upon	DRYD 196:34
foi: *La f. consiste à croire*	VOLT 561:20
foible: omniscience his f.	SMITH 512:11
foie: *et le f. du côté droit*	MOL 353:17
foil: like shining from shook f.	HOPK 256:12
Than dumb-bell and f.	YEATS 586:20
foil'd: f. circuitous wanderer	ARN 15:1
foining: f. o' nights	SHAK 441:27
fold: f. his legs and have out	JOHN 277:22
f. stands empty	SHAK 470:5
like the wolf on the f.	BYRON 122:1
mill and the f.	HOUS 263:6
Shall f. their tents	LONG 316:10
which are not of this f.	BIBLE 72:20
Folded: F. us round from the dark	SWIN 528:24
Knees and tresses f.	MER 337:1
ocean Is f. and hung	AUDEN 18:9
Quiet takes back her f. fields	JOYCE 286:9
sweetest leaves yet f.	BYRON 124:8
folding: f. of the hands to sleep	BIBLE 53:22
folds: f. shall be full of sheep	PRAY 394:3
tinklings lull the distant f.	GRAY 234:18
foliage: sapless f. of the ocean	SHEL 502:11
folie: *C'est une f. à nulle autre*	MOL 353:19
Garde bien ta belle f.	BANV 33:1
folio: whole volumes in f.	SHAK 456:19
folios: mighty f. first	COWP 168:11
folk: how civil to f. he ne'er	ANST 11:8
Of lusty f.	CHAU 143:20
On fluttered f. and wild	KIPL 304:6
folk-dancing: excepting incest and f.	ANON 4:24
folke: faire felde ful of f. fonde	LANG 309:23
folks: f. git ole en strucken	HARR 242:13
F. *prefer* in fact a hovel	CALV 127:22

folks rail against other f.	FIEL 211:17
was leaving home and my f.	STEV 522:26
follies: f., and misfortunes	GIBB 224:23
f. of the town crept slowly	GOLD 232:18
f. of the wise	JOHN 283:3
No f. to have to repent	TAYL 531:26
Of all human f. there's	MOL 353:19
point out to us our f.	TROL 553:1
pretty f. that themselves	SHAK 466:14
vice and f. of the age	CENT 138:10
vices and f. of human kind	CONG 159:20
Where f. naturally grow	CHUR 148:26
follow: expect to see when I f. you	DOYLE 192:22
f. and find the sun	SWIN 530:13
F. me	BIBLE 64:5
F. The Gleam	TENN 540:21
F. well in order	WHIT 570:10
f. with allegiance a fall'n	SHAK 422:18
F. your Saint	CAMP 129:18
F. your spirit	SHAK 444:3
I f. but myself	SHAK 473:14
I f. the worse	OVID 366:17
Pay, pack, and f.	BURT 116:11
really ought to f. them	LEDR 313:6
their works do f. them	BIBLE 82:18
To f. in their train	HEBER 244:7
to f. mine own teaching	SHAK 465:20
Ye f. wandering fires	TENN 534:22
followed: he arose and f. him	BIBLE 65:21
following: with a mighty f.	MAC 322:13
Follow up: F.! Follow up	BOWEN 90:25
folly: all a too presumptuous f.	HARTE 242:26
Careless f. done and said	HOUS 265:4
dream and a f. of expectation	BROW 97:21
fear usually ends in f.	COL 158:3
foe was f. and his weapon	HOPE 256:2
f.—doctor-like	SHAK 494:5
f. like a stalking-horse	SHAK 427:7
f. of our youth to be	CHES 147:12
f. of the wise	JOHN 280:27
f.'s all they've taught	MOORE 356:18
F.'s at full length	CHES 145:8
fool according to his f.	BIBLE 54:31
fool according to his f.	BIBLE 54:31
fool returneth to his f.	BIBLE 54:32
forts of f. fall	ARN 13:15
from the effects of f.	SPEN 514:27
God calleth preaching f.	HERB 247:12
harmless f. of the time	HERR 248:25
He knew human f. like	AUDEN 18:15
her coral lips such f.	CONG 160:2
knavery and f. to excuse	CHUR 149:9
lovely woman stoops to f.	ELIOT 205:3
lovely woman stoops to f.	GOLD 231:31
of F. without father bred	MILT 341:23
our f., or our fate	DENH 174:21
remember'st not the slightest f.	SHAK 425:10
shoot f. as it flies	POPE 379:2
shunn'st the noise of f.	MILT 342:2
this mad, wicked f.	VICT 556:14
Though age from f. could	SHAK 421:27
'Tis f. to be wise	GRAY 235:13
unworthy piece of f.	BROW 96:33
whirl'd into f. and vice	TENN 539:28
Wisdom excelleth f.	BIBLE 55:10
would be due to human f.	LAW 311:1
would persist in his f.	BLAKE 88:19
folwed: first he f. it hymselve	CHAU 142:3
fond: be fair and yet not f.	OXF 367:14
f. and foolish mind	BALL 30:8
f. of her most filthy bargain	SHAK 477:13
f. of ill-luck that they	JERR 273:8
f. of pets that must be	ELIOT 201:11
f. to live or fear to die	ELIZ 206:3
learning more than the f. eye	SHAK 466:19
let us be familiar or f.	CONG 161:7
men would be f.	LYLY 321:9
over-f. of resisting temptation	BECK 36:21
reason to be f. of grief	SHAK 452:20

too f. to rule alone	POPE 376:26
was probably f. of them	TWAIN 554:14
We are so f. of one another	SWIFT 526:13
When men were f.	SHAK 464:6
fonder: makes the heart grow f.	ANON 4:10
fons: *f. Bandusiae splendidior*	HOR 261:3
vicinus iugis aquae f.	HOR 262:9
font: fin in the porphyry f.	TENN 542:14
portable second-hand f.	KNOX 305:23
Fontarabian: On F. echoes borne	SCOTT 417:23
fonte: *Medio de f. leporum*	LUCR 320:11
food: Books, and my f.	STEV 523:11
bring f. out of the earth	PRAY 396:20
chief of Scotia's f.	BURNS 113:8
either our cupboard of f.	HERB 248:2
fed with the same f.	SHAK 467:4
f. and not fine words	MOL 353:19
F. enough for a week	MERR 338:8
f. for powder	SHAK 440:12
f. that satisfies hunger	CERV 138:20
f. unpriced	MAS 333:26
gave them f. from heaven	PRAY 395:6
good for f.	BIBLE 45:8
homely was their f.	GARTH 221:20
human nature's daily f.	WORD 581:8
nourishing, and wholesome f.	SWIFT 526:26
with f. convenient for me	BIBLE 54:45
fool: Answer not a f. according	BIBLE 54:31
ass, without being a f.	SURT 525:3
be a f.	POPE 379:14
Better a witty f.	SHAK 488:5
By the f. multitude	SHAK 466:19
'Call me not f. till heaven	SHAK 425:18
clever woman to manage a f.	KIPL 304:35
Dost thou call me f.	SHAK 453:16
every f. in Buxton can be	RUSK 411:13
every f. is not a poet	POPE 376:17
Every f. will be meddling	BIBLE 54:16
f. according to his folly	BIBLE 54:31
F. and his words are soon	SHEN 505:17
f. at forty is a fool indeed	YOUNG 587:15
f. can call me friend	YEATS 587:5
f. can play upon the word	SHAK 467:18
f. consistent	POPE 377:13
F. had stuck himself up	BENT 40:26
f. hath said in his heart	PRAY 390:2
f. in the eye of the world	CONG 160:11
f. a man who never	DARW 172:2
f. is happy that he knows	POPE 379:17
f. is love that in your	SHAK 493:18
F. lies here who tried	KIPL 301:18
f. of love	HAZL 243:18
f. returneth to his folly	BIBLE 54:32
f. sees not the same tree	BLAKE 88:16
f. than of the wise	BACON 25:29
f. there was and he made	KIPL 303:29
f., this night thy soul	BIBLE 70:5
f. uttereth all his mind	BIBLE 54:43
f. would persist in his	BLAKE 88:19
greatest f. may ask more than	COLT 159:9
hardly be a beast or a f.	KILV 296:8
haste of a f. is the slowest	SHAD 420:21
heart of the f.	MILT 350:21
he is a Wise man or a F.	BLAKE 86:13
He's a muddle-headed f.	CERV 138:16
he's become the golden f.	BLAKE 87:4
I hate a f.	DICK 178:20
I have played the f.	BIBLE 50:15
I met a f. i' the forest	SHAK 425:18
is the laughter of a f.	BIBLE 55:18
It is better to be a f.	STEV 522:3
knowledgeable f. is a greater	MOL 353:12
life time's f.	SHAK 440:23
longer I live the more f.	ANON 8:19
make a man appear a f.	DRYD 198:11
man suspects himself a f.	YOUNG 588:4
nor yet a f. to fame	POPE 376:23
of wisdom is made a f.	EMER 207:18

forfeit: deadly f. should release MILT 344:3
f. to a confin'd doom SHAK 494:21
shall f. fair renown SCOTT 416:22
forfended: music of f. spheres PATM 370:7
forgather: f. wi' Sorrow and Care
　　　　　　　　　　　　　　　BURNS 113:4
forgave: f. th' offence DRYD 195:35
kindness and f. the theft BROW 104:25
forge: f. and the mill HOUS 263:6
f. *des Dieux à douzaines* MONT 355:4
man can't f. his own will GILB 228:35
my f. decayed ANON 6:19
quick f. and working-house SHAK 445:6
forget: best sometimes f. SHAK 475:5
conversing I f. all time MILT 348:3
do not quite f. CHES 147:15
do not thou f. me ASTL 17:20
elephants never f. an injury SAKI 413:11
f. not all his benefits PRAY 396:14
F. six counties overhung MORR 358:10
f. thee, O Jerusalem PRAY 399:3
f. the human race BYRON 121:21
f. the source that keeps MER 337:3
f. us till another year KIPL 298:13
good and to communicate f. BIBLE 80:6
Half to f. the wandering FLEC 214:5
hardest science to f. POPE 376:12
honour doth f. men's names SHAK 452:9
How long wilt thou f. PRAY 390:1
how to f. KING 296:13
if I f. thee BRON 93:23
if thou wilt, f. ROSS 409:8
I sometimes f. DISR 187:5
knew we should both f. SWIN 530:10
learn so little and f. DAV 172:10
Lest we f. KIPL 302:7
never f. CARR 134:26
night time I shall not f. SWIN 529:12
nor worms f. DICK 179:30
not to f. we are gentlemen BURKE 108:24
Old men f. SHAK 445:3
Sun himself cannot f. ANON 8:4
teach the unforgetful to f. ROSS 410:6
that I could f. what SHAK 479:14
thou remember and I f. SWIN 530:14
we f. because we must ARN 12:21
with names that men f. SWIN 529:14
words shall ye f. your tears MORR 358:8
yet will I not f. thee BIBLE 59:17
you'll f. 'em all POPE 380:33
you should f. and smile ROSS 409:4
forgetful: Earth in f. snow ELIOT 204:17
f. of their sins YEATS 586:14
forgetfulness: Not in entire f. WORD 579:5
steep my senses in f. SHAK 441:29
who to dumb F. a prey GRAY 235:2
Forgets: F. the shows of love SHAK 448:11
forgetteth: f. what manner of man he
　　　　　　　　　　　　　　　BIBLE 80:10
forgetting: f. the bright speed he ARN 15:1
F. those things which are BIBLE 78:18
if f. could be willed MER 337:3
is but a sleep and a f. WORD 579:5
I've a grand memory for f. STEV 521:8
With dark f. of my care DAN 171:1
world f. POPE 376:13
forgive: Father, f. them BIBLE 71:11
f., if I forget thee BRON 93:23
f. us our debts BIBLE 64:24
f. us our trespasses PRAY 384:14
good Lord will f. me CATH 136:17
I f. him? till seven times BIBLE 67:7
I'll f. Thy great big one FROST 219:7
lambs could not f. DICK 179:30
love nor pity nor f. KIPL 302:17
mercy to f. DRYD 196:14
ought to f. our friends MED 336:8
rarely, if ever, do they f. WILDE 573:30
To f. enemies H BLAKE 87:5
to f. them as a christian AUST 23:19

To f. wrongs darker than SHEL 503:15
Wilt thou f. those sins DONNE 189:13
woman can f. another GAY 222:15
Women can't f. failure CHEK 145:1
forgiven: f.; for she loved much BIBLE 69:24
forgiveness: ask of thee f. SHAK 456:3
F. to the injured does DRYD 195:30
F. free of evil done KIPL 298:12
F. of sins PRAY 384:26
Mutual F. of each vice BLAKE 85:26
what f. ELIOT 203:5
forgives: which f. itself anything SHAW 498:5
forgo: chilly stars I can f. CORY 163:5
forgot: all the rest f. for which SHAK 493:4
by the world f. POPE 376:13
curiosities would be quite f. AUBR 17:22
f. as soon As done SHAK 487:3
f. his course FLEC 214:18
f. the taste of fears SHAK 463:5
giver is f. CONG 159:30
God f. me BROW 99:16
I believe I f. to tell WELL 567:21
I f. Goschen CHUR 149:23
I have f. my part SHAK 428:1
she f. the stars KEATS 290:11
soul that God f. HOUS 264:27
unknown propos'd as things f. POPE 378:29
forgotten: been learnt has been f. SKIN 508:20
East and west on fields f. HOUS 263:19
f. nothing and learnt nothing DUM 199:7
f. nothing TALL 531:17
God is f. OWEN 366:28
had f. to say 'When WOD 575:28
have f. his own sentiments CLAY 152:29
He hath not f. my age SOUT 514:9
Homer and Virgil are f. PORS 381:28
I am all f. SHAK 421:28
newer object quite f. SHAK 490:34
of them is f. before God BIBLE 70:3
ruins of f. times BROW 97:7
sooner f. than an insult CHES 145:13
want to be f. even by God BROW 103:6
foris: ecce intus eras et ego f. AUG 21:16
forked: f. animal as thou art SHAK 454:20
forks: pursued it with f. and hope CARR 133:8
forlorn: cheerless, and f. HADR 237:7
earth I wait f. ARN 13:8
F.! the very word is like KEATS 291:23
in these wild woods f. MILT 349:18
form: earth was without f. BIBLE 44:22
ev'ry respect but the f. GAY 222:31
Fain would I dwell on f. SHAK 482:12
fishy f. and mind BROO 94:13
f. of a servant and was BIBLE 78:13
f. of government rather JOHN 276:4
f. of sound words BIBLE 79:23
F. remains WORD 581:4
F., Riflemen Form TENN 543:6
hath no f. nor comeliness BIBLE 59:21
I like definite f. STEV 521:19
mould of f. SHAK 433:15
take thy f. from off my POE 375:6
time to lick it into f. BURT 116:14
'To every F. of being is WORD 577:17
what the f. divine LAND 308:26
formal: f. feeling comes DICK 183:13
second-best is a f. order AUDEN 18:13
formed: formed say to him that f. it
　　　　　　　　　　　　　　　BIBLE 75:14
Man was f. for society BLAC 85:1
former: again thy f. light restore SHAK 477:5
f. and the latter rain PRAY 386:3
f. days were better than BIBLE 55:20
f. things are passed away BIBLE 82:31
with those my f. fortunes SHAK 423:15
formless: f. spawning fury YEATS 587:2
Formosa: *F. facies muta commendatio*
　　　　　　　　　　　　　　　PUBL 402:4
Formosum: *F. pastor Corydon ardebat*
　　　　　　　　　　　　　　　VIRG 559:14

forms: f. and substances are circumfused
　　　　　　　　　　　　　　　WORD 580:19
F. more real than living SHEL 503:6
f. of government let fools POPE 379:20
f. of things unknown SHAK 471:11
mighty f. that do not live WORD 580:14
formula: f. of that *particular* emotion
　　　　　　　　　　　　　　　ELIOT 205:16
Fornication: F., and all uncleanness
　　　　　　　　　　　　　　　BIBLE 78:2
F. But that was in another MARL 329:22
From f. PRAY 385:16
Fors: *Quem F. dierum cumque dabit*
　　　　　　　　　　　　　　　HOR 259:18
forsake: f. me not when my strength
　　　　　　　　　　　　　　　PRAY 394:17
F. not an old friend BIBLE 62:30
I'll not f. thee ROWL 411:1
is a woman that you f. KIPL 299:21
nor f. thee BIBLE 48:35
forsaken: f. beliefs ARN 15:25
never the righteous f. PRAY 391:28
primrose that f. dies MILT 343:15
why hast thou f. me BIBLE 68:24
why hast thou f. me PRAY 390:16
forsaking: f. all other PRAY 389:3
F. even military men GILB 228:39
Forsan: *F. et haec olim meminisse*
　　　　　　　　　　　　　　　VIRG 557:14
forsook: my true Love has me f. BALL 32:10
forsworn: That so sweetly were f.
　　　　　　　　　　　　　　　SHAK 464:21
forsythia: Of prunus and f. across BETJ 43:12
fort: Hold the f. BLISS 88:31
La raison du plus f. est LA F 306:21
fortes: *Vixere f. ante Agamemnona*
　　　　　　　　　　　　　　　HOR 261:18
Fortescue: Was Charles Augustus F.
　　　　　　　　　　　　　　　BELL 38:32
forth: f. I must HOUS 265:15
Man goeth f. to his work PRAY 397:1
My road leads me f. MAS 334:3
Fortis: *F. fortuna adiuvat* TER 544:18
fortissimo: *Endlich f.* MAHL 327:6
fortiter: *Esto peccator et pecca f.*
　　　　　　　　　　　　　　　LUTH 320:15
fortitude: man has of f. and delicacy
　　　　　　　　　　　　　　　STEV 521:4
What f. the Soul contains DICK 183:18
fortress: him as his castle and f. COKE 154:23
This f. built by Nature SHAK 478:20
fortresses: brambles in the f. thereof
　　　　　　　　　　　　　　　BIBLE 58:31
forts: f. of folly fall ARN 13:15
Fortuna: *Audentis F. iuvat* VIRG 559:9
Fortis f. adiuvat TER 544:18
Quandoquidem f. mihi tete CAT 137:15
fortunae: *Faber est suae quisque f.*
　　　　　　　　　　　　　　　CLAU 152:26
fortunatam: *f. natam me consule* CIC 152:2
fortunate: better to be f. than wise
　　　　　　　　　　　　　　　WEBS 567:11
f. fellows that now you HOUS 263:7
he is at best but f. SOLON 512:25
f. is merry SHAK 451:7
fortunatos: *f. nimium* VIRG 560:13
fortune: arrows of outrageous f. SHAK 433:8
be a beauty without a f. FARQ 210:2
Disdaining f. SHAK 458:3
disgrace with f. and men's eyes SHAK 493:6
ere f. made him so DRYD 196:9
F. aids the brave TER 544:18
F. is full of fresh variety BARN 34:3
F. is merry SHAK 451:7
F.'s a right whore WEBS 567:1
F., that favours fools JONS 283:14
good f. where I find it MOL 354:3
happily upon a plentiful f. JOHN 275:2
hast Caesar and his f. CAES 127:2
hath given hostages to f. BACON 26:31
heaven hath sent me f. SHAK 425:18

her f. by way of marriage FIEL 211:29	F. deeds will rise SHAK 430:16	It is f. times as big LEAR 311:18
he's but F.'s knave SHAK 423:20	f. is fair SHAK 458:1	**four-footed:** of f. beasts of the earth
he shall see F. BACON 26:13	however f. within CHUR 148:33	BIBLE 73:37
how does f. banter us BOL 89:13	I doubt some f. play SHAK 430:15	**four hundred:** f. people in New York
I am F.'s fool SHAK 483:5	Is f. in the ending thereof PAIN 367:17	society MCAL 321:23
is the mother of good f. CERV 138:19	less f. profanation SHAK 464:3	**four-in-hand:** with the fiery f. COL 158:7
leads on to f. SHAK 451:27	portress f. to see HOUS 265:5	**fours:** make a simile go on all f. MAC 324:4
little value of f. STEE 518:12	thank the gods I am f. SHAK 426:16	**fourscore:** strong that they come to f.
made lame by f.'s dearest SHAK 493:13	too f. an epithet for thee MARL 330:10	PRAY 395:19
maker of his own f. STEE 518:7	**foules:** that I here the f. synge CHAU 143:29	**four-square:** Which stood f. to all
method of making a f. GRAY 235:21	**foulest:** way is commonly the f. BACON 25:4	TENN 541:8
mock the good housewife F. SHAK 424:21	**foully:** Thou play'dst most f. for't SHAK 461:6	**fourteen:** f. I married My Lord POUND 383:16
mould of a man's f. is BACON 26:12	**foul-mouthed:** rather a f. nation HAZL 244:1	F. The good Lord has CLEM 152:30
one out of suits with f. SHAK 424:25	**found:** country as good as he had f.	**fourth:** reporters sit has become a f. estate
On F.'s cap we are not SHAK 432:11	COBB 154:9	MAC 323:7
possession of a good f. AUST 23:11	f. a kingdom MILT 350:6	*fous: C'étaient des f.* REN 405:13
secret parts of F. SHAK 432:11	f. and lost again and again ELIOT 202:24	*Le monde est plein de f.* ANON 9:12
smith of his own f. CLAU 152:26	f. in lowly sheds With MILT 341:6	**foutra:** f. for the world SHAK 442:27
so many men of large f. AUST 22:26	f. me here KEATS 290:21	*Fove: F. quod est frigidum* LANG 310:1
visit pays Where f. smiles YOUNG 587:21	f. myself famous BYRON 126:22	**foweles:** smale f. maken melodye CHAU 141:8
whan that F. list to flee CHAU 142:29	f. my sheep which was lost BIBLE 70:16	**fowl:** broiled f. and mushrooms DICK 181:26
when we are sick in f. SHAK 453:11	f. out musical tunes BIBLE 63:23	Of tame villatic f. MILT 350:24
whereas people of f. may ELIOT 201:23	f. the Roman nation VIRG 557:10	over the f. of the air BIBLE 45:4
worky-day f. SHAK 421:14	Hast thou f. me BIBLE 51:18	Pythagoras concerning wild f. SHAK 490:21
You fools of f. SHAK 486:8	have it f. out by accident LAMB 308:2	'You elegant f. LEAR 312:12
Fortunes: F. tumbling into some men's	less often sought than f. BYRON 125:12	**fowler:** of the snare of the f. PRAY 398:14
BACON 25:3	lost, and is f. BIBLE 70:21	**fowls:** Behold the f. of the air BIBLE 64:28
make content with his f. SHAK 454:12	not yet f. a role ACH 1:4	Beside them shall the f. PRAY 396:19
my f. have Corrupted SHAK 423:1	place could no where be f. PRAY 391:29	creeping things, and f. BIBLE 73:37
of f. sharpe adversitee CHAU 144:11	shall be f. by the fire BROW 99:18	f. came and devoured them BIBLE 66:16
with those my former f. SHAK 423:15	They f. no more of her BIBLE 51:37	**fowlys:** all small f. singis DOUG 191:5
forty: at f., the judgement FRAN 218:10	When f., make a note DICK 177:26	**fox:** ar'n't that I loves the f. SURT 525:10
Fair, fat, and f. SCOTT 418:33	when thou mayest be f. PRAY 391:17	daun Russell the f. stirte CHAU 143:2
Fat, fair and f. OKEE 365:1	**foundation:** Good order is the f.	f. knows many things ARCH 11:22
fool at f. is a fool indeed YOUNG 587:15	BURKE 111:25	f. said once upon a time HOR 258:11
f. winters shall besiege SHAK 492:23	laid the f. of the earth PRAY 396:13	from the f. and the lion MACH 325:8
F. years long was I grieved PRAY 396:4	number is the f. of morals BENT 40:25	galloping after a f. WILDE 573:27
F. years on BOWEN 90:24	**foundations:** city which hath f. BIBLE 79:32	upon F.'s grave the tear SCOTT 417:3
have f. million reasons KIPL 300:21	hour when earth's f. fled HOUS 265:7	**foxed:** ever I was f. it was now PEPYS 372:4
hopeful than to be f. years HOLM 253:14	laid the f. of the earth BIBLE 53:2	**foxes:** f. have a sincere interest ELIOT 200:25
look young till f. DRYD 196:36	laid the f. of the earth PRAY 396:18	f. have holes BIBLE 65:18
man over f. is a scoundrel SHAW 498:4	noblest works and f. BACON 27:4	little f. BIBLE 56:23
passing rich with f. pounds GOLD 230:22	**founded:** fixt of old and f. strong HOUS 264:3	may be a portion for f. PRAY 393:22
till you come to F. Year THAC 545:31	**founder:** father and first f. and embellisher	**fox-hunter:** Tell me a man's a f. SURT 525:6
forty-three: may very well pass for f.	CAXT 138:2	**foxlike:** f. in the vine TENN 542:16
GILB 229:4	**Founding:** F. a firm state by proportions	**foy:** *f. je veuil vivre et mourir* VILL 557:6
forward: f. let us range TENN 539:8	MARV 331:20	**frabjous:** f. day CARR 134:29
marched breast f. BROW 98:32	**fount:** fresh f. JONS 283:21	**fragile:** That nature's f. vessel SHAK 486:13
not look f. to posterity BURKE 111:7	**fountain:** athirst of the f. of the water	**Fragment:** something to this F. of Life
Some men a f. motion love VAUG 555:17	BIBLE 82:32	STER 519:15
to hold from this day f. PRAY 389:4	burning f. whence it came SHEL 499:19	**fragments:** Death tramples it to f.
world with their feet f. BROW 97:10	Doth a f. send forth BIBLE 80:15	SHEL 499:26
Foss: F. is the name of his cat LEAR 311:23	f. from the which my current SHAK 476:18	f. have I shored against ELIOT 205:13
fossil: Language is f. poetry EMER 207:31	f. is choked up and polluted BURKE 111:15	f. that remained twelve BIBLE 66:24
foster-child: f. of silence and slow	f. of all goodness PRAY 385:6	Gather up the f. that remain BIBLE 72:5
KEATS 291:2	f. of delights rises something LUCR 320:11	**fragrance:** sweetest f. from the herb
Fostered: F. alike by beauty WORD 580:8	'f. of honour' BAG 28:22	TROL 552:24
fou: between a f. man and a fasting	f. sealed BIBLE 56:28	**Frail:** F. as thy love PEAC 371:1
SCOTT 418:26	He is the f. of honour BACON 27:43	F. crowds that a delicate MOORE 355:23
f. qui se croyait Victor COCT 154:13	Here at the f.'s sliding MARV 332:6	f. mortality shall trust BACON 28:16
I wasna f. BURNS 113:11	hexameter rises the f.'s COL 157:7	*frailes: f. y muchos son los caminos*
There's some are f. o' brandy BURNS 114:9	Let the healing f. start AUDEN 19:9	CERV 138:15
fought: angels f. against the dragon	Like a summer-dried f. SCOTT 416:5	**frailties:** Our f. are invincible STEV 520:26
BIBLE 82:11	mighty f. momently was COL 156:27	**frailty:** but a f. of the mind CONG 161:3
better to have f. and lost CLOU 154:2	perpetual f. of good sense DRYD 198:9	f. of things here SHEL 501:22
courses f. against Sisera BIBLE 49:9	Rise like a f. for me night TENN 535:26	F., thy name is woman SHAK 429:28
f. against me from my youth PRAY 398:21	woman mov'd is like a f. SHAK 484:16	love's the noblest f. DRYD 196:23
f. a long hour by Shrewsbury SHAK 440:27	**fountain'd:** many-f. Ida TENN 541:17	noblest f. of the mind SHAD 420:20
f. at Arques and you were HENR 245:14	**fountains:** f. mingle with the river SHEL 502:1	that by reason of the f. PRAY 386:8
f. the dogs and killed BROW 103:15	sad f. ANON 8:13	therefore more f. SHAK 440:5
f. with beasts at Ephesus BIBLE 76:24	Shepherding her bright f. SHEL 500:2	**frame:** Could f. in earth SPEN 516:20
He f. upon his stumps SHEA 498:29	silver f. mud SHAK 493:12	f. of nature round him ADD 2:30
if men f. upon the earth SCOTT 417:20	What objects are the f. SHEL 504:21	f. thy fearful symmetry BLAKE 87:14
I have f. a good fight BIBLE 79:26	whose f. are within COL 156:8	mighty f. of the world BERK 41:19
Philip f. men LEE 313:13	**founts:** f. falling in the courts CHES 146:28	sensuous f. Is rack'd TENN 536:21
their lives f. for life SPEN 515:7	**four:** f. beasts full of eyes BIBLE 81:23	shakes this fragile f. HARDY 240:2
what they f. each other SOUT 513:16	f. essential human freedoms ROOS 407:26	That yarely f. the office SHAK 422:3
foul: f. and fair a day SHAK 458:9	F. lagging winters SHAK 478:13	universal f. is without a mind BACON 25:22
f. and midnight murther GRAY 234:17	f. pillars of government BACON 27:10	Whatever stirs this mortal f. COL 157:2
f. deed shall smell above SHAK 450:12	F. things greater than KIPL 297:28	**framed:** England is to have it f. WALP 563:8

framework: experience but a defining
f. WHORF 571:23
français: *aurait toujours parlé f.* VOLT 561:13
f. aux hommes et allemand CHAR 140:31
F. lève les yeux sans TOCQ 551:8
pas clair n'est pas f. RIV 406:10
Tout soldat f. porte dans NAP 359:9
France: baton of a marshal of F. NAP 359:9
between F. and England JERR 273:4
England the nearer is to F. CARR 134:15
Fair stood the wind for F. DRAY 193:10
fashion for the maids in F. SHAK 445:13
forces the full pride of F. SHAK 443:7
F., fam'd in all great ARN 15:11
F. has always more or less BURKE 111:15
F., mère des arts DU B 198:25
F., mother of arts DU B 198:25
F. With all her vines COWP 166:34
his round hose in F. SHAK 465:24
nor the activity of F. BURKE 109:17
Our fertile F. SHAK 445:11
That sweet enemy, F. SIDN 507:22
There lived a singer in F. SWIN 530:29
this matter better in F. STER 518:28
until F. is adequately ASQ 17:17
vasty fields of F. SHAK 443:4
Frankfort: I went to F. PORS 381:29
frankincense: branches of the f. tree
BIBLE 63:27
f., and myrrh BIBLE 63:32
frantic: There's a fascination f. GILB 227:18
frantic-mad: f. with evermore unrest
SHAK 495:15
frater: f., *ad inferias* CAT 137:15
f., ave atque vale CAT 137:15
Fratresque: F. *tendentes opaco* HOR 260:22
fratrum: Par nobile f. HOR 262:8
fraud: f., are in war the two HOBB 251:19
Grown old in f. CHUR 149:5
May is a pious f. LOW 319:15
this pious f. GAY 223:3
fraudatrix: auellit *ab animo f. scientiae*
JOHN 273:17
frauds: well stored with pious f.
BURKE 108:14
fray: eager for the f. CIBB 151:13
freckled: fickle, f. HOPK 256:23
f. like a pard KEATS 290:22
Of f. Human Nature DICK 184:3
freckles: f., and doubt PARK 368:15
In those f. live their SHAK 470:2
Fred: Here lies F. ANON 5:15
Frederick: clustered spires of F. stand
WHIT 571:15
Here is cruel F. HOFF 252:12
fredome: f. is a noble thing BARB 33:4
free: appal the f. SHAK 433:1
assure freedom to the f. LINC 314:22
bond nor f. BIBLE 78:26
English Church shall be f. MAGN 327:1
ever exist in a f. country BURKE 110:1
fain have her f. MER 337:4
flag of all the f. CHES 147:3
f. as nature first made DRYD 195:29
f. behave much as the respectable
AUDEN 19:20
f. church in a free state CAV 138:1
f. have disposition AUDEN 19:13
f. land of the grave HOUS 265:18
F. love TENN 534:34
F. speech, free passes BETJ 43:6
f., uncircumscribed SHEL 503:12
f. verse is like playing FROST 219:15
Greece might still be f. BYRON 122:33
half slave and half f. LINC 314:14
happy and handsome and f. AUDEN 18:7
human beings are born f. ANON 4:14
In the country of the f. BROW 97:36
I only ask to be f. DICK 176:6
Italia shall be f. MER 338:3

I was born f. as Caesar SHAK 448:14
I was f. born BIBLE 74:21
leaves f. to all MILT 348:7
leaves soul f. BROW 99:2
let the oppressed go f. BIBLE 60:4
lines and life are f. HERB 247:14
Man was born f. ROUS 410:17
More f. from peril than SHAK 424:31
naturally were born f. MILT 352:18
noble that was born most f. OTWAY 365:27
O'er the land of the f. KEY 295:14
only less f. Than thou SHEL 502:12
people let him go f. PRAY 397:4
perfectly free till all are f. SPEN 515:3
should themselves be f. BROO 94:4
So f. we seem BROW 98:23
Teach the f. man how AUDEN 19:9
that England should be f. MAGEE 326:21
Thou art f. ARN 14:23
truth shall make you f. BIBLE 72:12
valiant man and f. TENN 537:15
was ever so f. as a fish RUSK 412:2
We must be f. or die WORD 582:3
what a f. government is BURKE 110:11
When the mind's f. SHAK 454:13
Who died to make verse f. PRES 400:14
wholly slaves or wholly f. DRYD 196:16
whom the truth makes f. COWP 167:22
Who would be f. themselves BYRON 120:14
freed: drowsy at that hour which f.
BROW 95:22
f. his soul the nearest JOHN 279:1
I have f. my soul BERN 41:24
thousands He hath f. CHAN 139:19
freedom: are fit to use their f. MAC 323:25
call it the idea of f. PARK 368:26
can do for the f. of man KENN 295:10
cause of F. is the cause BOWL 91:7
desire their Liberty and F. CHAR 140:19
du believe in F.'s cause LOW 319:3
enemy of truth and f. IBSEN 269:17
establishes his true f. MONT 354:20
few men talked of f. CHES 147:13
fight for f. and truth IBSEN 269:19
flame of f. in their souls SYM 531:3
Flood Of British f. WORD 582:2
f. and curteisie CHAU 141:9
F. and not servitude is BURKE 109:30
F. and Whisky gang thegither BURNS 113:9
F. has a thousand charms COWP 166:25
f. of speech TWAIN 554:7
F. of the press in Britain SWAF 525:30
F. shrieked CAMP 129:7
F., the seven pillared LAWR 311:12
F. which in no other land DRYD 197:31
If I have f. in my love LOV 318:18
if Man will give up F. AUDEN 19:11
I gave my life for f. EWER 209:12
In giving f. to the slave LINC 314:22
Let f. ring SMITH 510:24
newly acquired f. produces MAC 323:24
None can love f. heartily MILT 352:17
on the principles of f. BURKE 109:27
Our f. as free lances MACN 326:16
Perfect f. is reserved COLL 158:13
Regain'd my f. with a sigh BYRON 125:17
service is perfect f. PRAY 385:2
speak with the f. of history BURKE 109:5
sum obtained I this f. BIBLE 74:21
sweet bondage which is f.'s SHEL 503:16
That sober f. out of which TENN 541:11
this participation of f. BURKE 110:4
Thus f. now so seldom wakes MOORE 356:10
what is f. COL 154:25
What stands if F. fall KIPL 299:7
Where F. slowly broadens TENN 544:11
With F.'s soil beneath DRAKE 193:5
freedoms: four essential human f.
ROOS 407:26
freehold: life is given to none f. LUCR 320:10

free lances: Our freedom as f. MACN 326:16
Free-livers: F. on a small scale IRV 270:23
Freeman: Stubbs butters F. ROG 407:14
Freemason: F., and an asthmatic
DOYLE 192:14
freemen: f., are the only slaves MASS 335:17
To rule o'er f. BROO 94:4
freendes: That f. everych oother CHAU 142:12
freewoman: other by a f. BIBLE 77:16
freeze: f., thou bitter sky SHAK 426:1
f. thy young blood SHAK 431:5
To f. the blood I have WORD 577:22
Freezing: F. persons, recollect DICK 183:14
night is f. fast HOUS 265:1
freezings: What f. have I felt SHAK 494:16
freight: shall have her earthly f. WORD 579:8
Freighted: F. with amber grapes ARN 14:21
French: dislike the F. WALP 563:21
F. are wiser than they BACON 27:14
F. are with equal advantage CANN 129:25
F. army led by an Italian SHAW 498:7
F. art, if not sanguinary SPEN 515:5
F. novels, French cookery THAC 545:22
F., or Turk, or Proosian GILB 228:10
F. the empire of the land JEAN 272:4
F. truth ROCH 407:5
glory of beating the F. WOLFE 576:7
half-F., half-English SHAK 445:14
how it's improved her F. GRAH 233:9
I hate the F. because they GOLD 232:6
is not clear is not F. RIV 406:10
much all he knew of F. BLUC 89:1
not too French F. bean GILB 227:23
scrofulous F. novel BROW 105:8
some are fond of F. MAS 333:20
Speak in F. when you can't CARR 134:31
to men F. CHAR 140:31
would always have spoken F. VOLT 561:13
Frenchies: Those F. seek him everywhere
ORCZY 365:7
Frenchman: F., easy COWP 166:24
F. must be always talking JOHN 278:17
hate a F. NELS 360:12
Frenchmen: *Englishman* could beat three
F. ADD 2:19
million F. can't be wrong GUIN 237:6
Frenssh: F. of Parys was to hire CHAU 141:15
F. she spak ful faire CHAU 141:15
frenzy: in a fine f. rolling SHAK 471:11
frequent: f. cups prolong the rich POPE 381:6
f. hearses shall besiege POPE 376:9
f. tears have run BROW 98:10
when young did eagerly f. FITZ 212:20
Frere: F. there was CHAU 141:19
mon semblable,—mon f. BAUD 35:5
Sois mon f. CHAM 139:18
Frères: F. humains qui après nous VILL 557:4
fresh: both so ancient and so f. AUG 21:16
f. lap of the crimson rose SHAK 470:6
f. revolving pleasures GAY 223:23
f. woods, and pastures MILT 349:7
Since first I saw you f. SHAK 494:18
So sad, so f. TENN 542:3
you've got a nice f. corpse TWAIN 554:13
fresher: f., and more fat DONNE 188:2
Fressen: Erst kommt das F. BREC 91:25
fressh: f. as is the month of May
CHAU 141:11
fret: fever, and the f. KEATS 291:18
f. a passage through it FULL 220:19
f. not after knowledge KEATS 292:7
F. not thyself because PRAY 391:26
though you can f. me SHAK 434:21
Frets: F. doubt the maw-crammed
BROW 104:3
f. the saints in heaven BROW 97:14
struts and f. his hour SHAK 463:6
Fretted: F. the pigmy body to decay
DRYD 194:6
Freude: F., *schöner Götterfunken* SCH 415:9

friar: Apollo turned fasting f.   MER 337:29
friars: We cannot all be f.   CERV 138:15
   while the barefoot f. were   GIBB 224:16
fricassee: will equally serve in a f.
     SWIFT 526:26
Friday: F. fil al this meschaunce   CHAU 143:3
   takes my man F. with me   DEFOE 173:8
Friede: ewige F. ist ein Traum   MOLT 354:4
friend: are the wounds of a f.   BIBLE 54:38
   author as you choose a f.   ROOS 408:10
   could not see my little f.   BARH 33:21
   countenance of his f.   BIBLE 54:40
   country and betraying my f.   FORS 217:12
   crack a bottle with a f.   CHES 147:21
   equal f.   SURR 524:20
   every mess I finds a f.   DIBD 175:18
   faithful f. is the medicine   BIBLE 62:25
   familiar f., whom I trusted   PRAY 392:5
   fav'rite has no f.   GRAY 235:7
   Forsake not an old f.   BIBLE 62:30
   F. and associate of this   HADR 237:9
   F., go up higher   BIBLE 70:8
   f. in power is a friend   ADAMS 1:7
   friendless name the f.   JOHN 278:35
   f. loveth at all times   BIBLE 54:11
   f. may spit upon my curious   HERB 248:15
   f. may well be reckoned   EMER 207:20
   f. of every country   CANN 129:28
   f. of Grey   HOLL 253:4
   F. of my better days   HALL 238:9
   f. or child I speak   ARN 13:8
   f. remember'd not   SHAK 426:1
   f. should bear his friend's   SHAK 451:22
   f. that sticketh closer   BIBLE 54:14
   F. to Sir Philip Sidney   GREV 236:18
   f. unseen   FLEC 214:23
   F., wherefore art thou   BIBLE 68:17
   from the candid f.   CANN 130:1
   good-natured f. or other   SHER 505:21
   handsome house to lodge a f.   SWIFT 527:28
   He makes no f.   TENN 534:31
   He was my f.   SHAK 450:18
   I can merely be your f.   LEAR 312:1
   In every f. we lose a part   POPE 381:17
   in his life forgave a f.   BLAKE 87:5
   in life the firmest f.   BYRON 124:40
   I was angry with my f.   BLAKE 87:21
   last best f. am   SOUT 513:21
   look like a f. on Denmark   SHAK 429:23
   marry your old f.'s love   BROW 105:17
   mine own familiar f.   PRAY 393:11
   never want a f. in need   DICK 177:26
   not a fool can call me f.   YEATS 587:5
   not a f. to close his eyes   DRYD 195:3
   not use a f. as I use Thee   HERB 248:14
   of the loss of a dear f.   SOUT 514:17
   Over your f. that loves   SHAK 448:10
   Patience for our only f.   ARN 14:18
   pretended f. is worse   GAY 223:13
   religious book, or f.   WOTT 583:13
   still a f. in my retreat   COWP 166:21
   suspicious f.   POPE 376:27
   That love my f.   SHAK 451:1
   there is no f. like a sister   ROSS 408:27
   Thou art not my f.   EMER 206:20
   to have a f. is to be one   EMER 207:21
   truest f. to thy lover   MAL 328:8
   ('twas all he wish'd) a f.   GRAY 235:5
   very much his f. indeed   COWP 165:9
   what he can find a f. sincere   BULW 107:7
   who lost no f.   POPE 378:6
   Who's your fat f.   BRUM 106:3
   With one chained f.   SHEL 500:10
   woman can become a man's f.   CHEK 145:5
   world can countervail a f.   GRIM 236:20
   world is not thy f. nor   SHAK 483:26
   worst f. and enemy   BROO 94:28
   yet f. to truth   POPE 378:6
friendless: every f. name the friend
     JOHN 278:35

Omnipotent but f. is to reign   SHEL 503:7
friendliness: Of more than common f.
     BRID 92:22
friendly: f. seas they softly run   FLEC 214:17
friends: all distresses of our f.   SWIFT 527:22
   book is the best of f.   TUPP 553:21
   cheating of our f.   CHUR 148:30
   choice of f.   COWL 164:14
   comes to meet one's f.   BURN 112:22
   down his life for his f.   BIBLE 72:36
   enter on my list of f.   COWP 167:28
   excellent plot, very good f.   SHAK 438:30
   faithfullest f. stands   WHIT 570:15
   F. and loves we have none   MAS 334:7
   f. are lapp'd in lead   BARN 34:1
   f. hear no more of him   SHEL 501:19
   f. hid in death's dateless   SHAK 493:7
   f. of every country save   DISR 185:14
   f. of the mammon of unrighteousness
     BIBLE 70:26
   F., Romans, countrymen   SHAK 450:17
   f. thou hast   SHAK 430:19
   F. to congratulate their   DRYD 197:30
   F. who set forth at our   ARN 14:9
   glory was I had such f.   YEATS 586:6
   golden f. I had   HOUS 264:10
   Good thoughts his only f.   CAMP 129:19
   hath f. in the garrison   HAL 237:17
   house of God as f.   PRAY 393:11
   How few of his f.' houses   JOHN 279:5
   I have lost f.   WOOLF 576:20
   In spite of all their f.   LEAR 312:4
   in the multitude of f.   JONS 283:23
   is without three good f.   SHAK 426:3
   laughter and the love of f.   BELL 39:15
   like him with f. possess'd   SHAK 493:6
   matter separateth very f.   BIBLE 54:10
   misfortune of our best f.   LA R 310:8
   My f. forsake me like   CLARE 152:12
   neither foes nor loving f.   KIPL 300:2
   old f.   GOLD 232:19
   ought to forgive our f.   MED 336:8
   Our f., the enemy   BER 41:15
   remembering my good f.   SHAK 478:24
   shameful to spurn one's f.   LA R 310:10
   something left to treat my f.   MALL 327:12
   Such men my f. than enemies   SHAK 452:4
   Than want of f.   BRET 92:3
   they had been f. in youth   COL 156:4
   Thy f. are exultations   WORD 582:17
   to all thy f.   BIBLE 60:26
   to keep f. with himself   STEV 521:4
   was the new city of F.   WHIT 570:4
   We may live without f.   MER 338:8
   when his f. did   BALL 30:8
   wretched have no f.   DRYD 195:14
friendship: destitute of sincere f.
     BACON 25:14
   dupe of f.   HAZL 243:18
   elegance of female f.   JOHN 282:12
   f. closes its eyes   ANON 9:11
   f. from knowledge   BUSS 117:5
   F. is Love without his   BYRON 124:37
   F. is a disinterested commerce   GOLD 232:11
   F. is not always the sequel   JOHN 282:3
   F. is constant in all other   SHAK 472:7
   f. never moults a feather   DICK 180:25
   f. oft has made my heart   BLAKE 87:7
   f. recognised by the police   STEV 521:27
   F. should be more than   ELIOT 204:3
   him to cultivate your f.   JOHN 278:33
   honest f. with all nations   JEFF 272:8
   let us swear eternal f.   SMITH 511:3
   Love, f., charity   SHAK 487:6
   Most f. is feigning   SHAK 426:1
   of f. with thine enemies   SHAK 450:9
   scene where genial f. plays   HOLM 253:6
   should keep his f. in constant   JOHN 274:15
   swear an eternal f.   CANN 130:4
   There is little f.   BACON 26:11

to f. clear   CAREW 130:14
   way of f.'s gone   HERB 247:5
   woman's f. ever ends   GAY 223:9
Friendships: F. begin with liking
     ELIOT 200:23
fright: f. my faith than Three   DRYD 196:13
   To f. the souls of fearful   SHAK 480:18
   wake in a f.   BARH 33:13
frighted: flowers now that f. thou
     SHAK 491:26
   F. the reign of Chaos   MILT 345:20
   f. with false fire   SHAK 434:15
frighten: street and f. the horses   CAMP 128:8
frightened: It has a f. look in its   SITW 508:14
   killed than f. to death   SURT 525:22
   upon the stage is not f.   FIEL 211:31
   why should you be f.   WEBB 566:6
fringe: movement has a lunatic f.   ROOS 408:5
fringed: f. curtains of thine eye   SHAK 485:1
fringes: f. of a southward-facing   ARN 14:21
frío: f. que templa el ardor   CERV 138:20
Frisch: F. weht der Wind   WAGN 562:1
fritillaries: what purple f.   ARN 15:8
Fritter-my-wig: Fry me!' or 'F.   CARR 133:3
fritters: best f. that ever I eat   PEPYS 372:2
frivolity: chatter of irresponsible f.
     DISR 185:18
Frocks: F. and Curls   DICK 184:2
frog: any better'n any other f.   TWAIN 554:5
   Expiring f.   DICK 181:31
   F. is justly sensitive   BELL 38:29
   toe of f.   SHAK 462:3
from: f. here to Eternity   KIPL 299:10
   f. the Sublime To the Ridiculous
     GRAH 233:11
   gamut of the emotions f.   PARK 368:21
fromages: 265 spécialités de f.   DE G 173:17
front: Always show your f.   MOL 353:1
   in f. of one's nose   ORW 365:17
   which f. these were sent   OWEN 367:7
frontier: f.-grave is far away   NEWB 361:1
   where our f. lies to-day   BALD 29:28
frost: forms Of the radiant f.   SHEL 503:27
   f. performs its secret   COL 156:21
   is able to abide his f.   PRAY 399:21
   'it is a f.   SURT 525:16
   Terror like a f. shall   AUDEN 19:11
   Thaw not the f. which binds   SHEL 499:3
   third day comes a f.   SHAK 447:9
   though dead with f. ere   GREV 236:17
frosts: f. are slain and flowers   SWIN 528:17
   hoary-headed f.   SHAK 470:6
   O ye Dews, and F.   PRAY 384:22
frosty: cold, f., windy morning   PEPYS 371:18
   F., but kindly   SHAK 425:6
   Into the f. starlight   ARN 14:28
froth: f. amid the boundless main   BRON 93:20
   Life is mostly f. and bubble   GORD 233:1
Froude: Kingsley goes to F. for history
     STUB 524:5
froward: are a very f. generation   BIBLE 48:31
frown: Convey a libel in a f.   SWIFT 527:29
   I'll f. and be perverse   SHAK 482:13
   more the f. o' the great   SHAK 428:22
   Say that she f.   SHAK 484:8
   So much as f. on you   SHAK 452:24
   trembled with fear at your f.   ENGL 208:19
frown'd: dismal tidings when he f.
     GOLD 231:2
frowned: is not true to say I f.   CHES 146:12
Frowns: F. o'er the wide and winding
     BYRON 120:31
   Her very f. are fairer   COL 155:1
frowst: f. with a book by the fire   KIPL 300:11
frowzy: f. couch in sorrow steep
     BURNS 113:22
frozen: Architecture in general is f. music
     SCH 415:8
   milk comes f. home in pail   SHAK 457:19
   pump has f. to-night   GRAV 234:12

greatest misery is a battle g.   WELL 567:27
gains: Light g. make heavy purses
    BACON 25:35
Gainsboroughs: G. and Lawrences
    COW 164:2
gait: forc'd g. of a shuffling nag SHAK 439:26
manner of his g.   SHAK 488:23
Galatea: *Malo me G. petit*   VIRG 559:18
Galatians: There's a great text in G.
    BROW 105:7
gale: g., it plies the saplings   HOUS 263:14
Midland waters with the g.   ARN 14:21
note that swells the g.   GRAY 235:15
Galeotto: G. was the book and writer
    DANTE 171:10
galère: allait-il faire dans cette g. MOL 353:14
Galice: In G. at Seint-Jame   CHAU 141:31
Galilean: Pilot of the G. lake   MILT 343:11
thou yet take all, G.   SWIN 530:4
You have won, G.   JUL 286:31
Galilee: rolls nightly on deep G.
    BYRON 122:1
Galileo: Blind to G. on his turret
    BROW 102:35
gall: take my milk for g.   SHAK 459:2
They gave me g. to eat   PRAY 394:12
to g. a new-healed wound   SHAK 441:9
wormwood and the g.   BIBLE 60:29
gallant: died a very g. gentleman ATK 17:21
G. and gay   POPE 378:1
He was a braw g.   BALL 30:16
We were a g. company   BYRON 125:23
gallantry: more to do with g.   SHER 506:6
What men call g.   BYRON 122:9
galleon: moon was a ghostly g. tossed
    NOYES 364:12
galleons: where are the g. of Spain
    DOBS 187:10
gallery: faces are but a g. of pictures
    BACON 26:15
g. in which the reporters   MAC 323:7
galleys: Their g. blaze   BYRON 121:32
Gallia: G. est omnis divisa   CAES 126:26
galliard: not go to church in a g. SHAK 488:1
galligaskins: Donn'd g.   CALV 127:16
gallimaufry: g. or hodgepodge of all
    SPEN 517:6
Gallio: G. cared for none of those
    BIBLE 74:15
gallop: does he gallop and g. about
    STEV 522:18
G. about doing good   SMITH 510:25
G. apace   SHAK 483:6
galloped: old white horse g. away
    ELIOT 203:14
we g. all three   BROW 101:12
galloping: Hooves with a g. sound
    VIRG 559:7
gallows: complexion is perfect g.
    SHAK 484:21
g. fifty cubits high   BIBLE 52:4
It grew a g. and did bear   KYD 306:7
on the g., or of the pox   WILK 574:6
see nothing but the g.   BURKE 111:12
Shall there be g. standing   SHAK 438:4
statue to him under the g.   SMITH 511:24
Under the G.-Tree   FLET 215:9
gallows-foot: To the g.   KIPL 303:18
gallows-maker: g.; for that frame outlives
    SHAK 436:23
gallows-tree: Jack on the g.   SCOTT 418:16
galumphing: He went g. back   CARR 134:29
gambler: whore and g.   BLAKE 85:17
gambling: crew is g. in the forecastle
    SHAW 496:33
gambol: Christmas g. oft could SCOTT 417:16
game: Conversation is a g. of circles
    EMER 207:14
g. of the few   BERK 41:22
g. on these lone heaths   HAZL 243:32

g.'s afoot   SHAK 444:3
g., That must be lost   BEAU 36:10
how you played the g.   RICE 405:23
of time to win this g.   DRAKE 193:2
once a lady always g.   MARQ 330:20
silly g. where nobody wins   FULL 220:20
Socratic manner is not a g.   BEER 38:4
game-act: explaining a passage in the
g.   STEE 517:23
gamecocks: Wits are g. to one another
    GAY 223:12
games: their g. should be seen MONT 354:17
gamesome: I am not g.   SHAK 448:9
gammon: of g. and spinnage it is DICK 177:12
gamut: of the emotions from PARK 368:21
gamyn: of g. and gle   WYNT 584:4
Gang: G. aft a-gley   BURNS 115:22
he be doing in this g.   MOL 353:14
old g.   CHUR 149:19
sall we g. and dine the day   BALL 32:8
they may g. a kennin wrang BURNS 112:25
Ganges: by the Indian G.' side MARV 332:18
gaol: that we know who lie in g.
    WILDE 572:15
world's thy g.   DONNE 189:23
gap: made a g. in nature   SHAK 422:3
sleep out this great g.   SHAK 421:30
That g. is the grave where   AUDEN 18:17
gaped: stranded fish g. among PLOM 374:19
gaping: g. wretches of the sea HUNT 268:7
Garda: Lydian laughter of the G.
    TENN 533:18
Garde: La G. meurt   CAMB 128:2
garden: at the bottom of our g. FYL 220:23
beloved come into his g.   BIBLE 56:29
Come into the g.   TENN 540:9
concealed in an enclosed g.   CAT 137:6
g. and a spring   HOR 262:9
g. inclosed is my sister   BIBLE 56:28
g. is a lovesome thing   BROWN 95:12
g. loves a greenhouse too   COWP 167:9
g. of bright images   BRAM 91:22
g. of your face   HERB 246:20
g. shady this holy lady   AUDEN 18:3
g.'s last petals were   SWIN 529:19
g., That grows to seed   SHAK 429:28
g. with your pen   CAMP 128:11
ghost of a g. fronts   SWIN 529:17
Glory of the G. lies   KIPL 299:12
God Almighty first planted a g. BACON 26:18
God the first g. made   COWL 164:9
I have a g. of my own   MARV 332:14
I value my g. more   ADD 2:25
lodge in a g. of cucumbers BIBLE 57:16
man and a woman in a g. WILDE 573:29
nearer God's Heart in a g.   GURN 237:7
Nothing grows in our g. THOM 547:12
Our England is a g. that   KIPL 299:12
planted a g. eastward   BIBLE 45:7
potter round the g.   AUDEN 21:9
rosebud g. of girls   TENN 540:11
set to dress this g.   SHAK 479:18
summer birdcage in a g.   WEBS 567:2
That every Hyacinth the G. FITZ 212:15
There is in her face   CAMP 129:22
this best g. of the world   SHAK 445:11
through his g. walketh God BROW 105:14
Through this same G. after me FITZ 213:17
walking in the g. in the cool BIBLE 45:16
gardener: Adam was a g.   KIPL 299:15
Adam was a g.   SHAK 446:13
g. Adam and his wife   TENN 537:29
supposing him to be the g. BIBLE 73:8
That half a proper g.'s   KIPL 299:15
Will come the G. in white FLEC 214:13
gardeners: ancient gentlemen but g.
    SHAK 436:22
gardens: closing time in the g. CONN 161:16
Down by the salley g.   YEATS 584:22
g. Of spring and summer   THOM 547:7

'imaginary g. with real toads MOORE 355:20
In the g. of the night   BRID 92:16
Our bodies are our g.   SHAK 474:8
Sowe Carrets in your G.   GARD 221:8
sweetest delight of g.   BROW 95:21
Thames bordered by its g. MORR 358:10
trim g. takes his pleasure   MILT 342:1
garden-state: Such was that happy g.
    MARV 332:7
garden-trees: through the vext g. ARN 15:5
gare: say au-dessus de sa g.   RATT 405:2
garish: no worship to the g. sun SHAK 483:7
garland: g. briefer than a girl's HOUS 263:3
green willow is my g.   HEYW 250:21
rosy g. and a weary head   SIDN 507:21
that immortal g.   MILT 351:24
wither'd is the g. of the war SHAK 423:16
garlanded: All g. with carven imag'ries
    KEATS 289:16
garlands: fantastic g. did she come
    SHAK 436:19
g. wither on your brow   SHIR 507:3
her silken flanks with g. KEATS 291:8
To her let us g. bring   SHAK 491:4
To weave the g. of repose MARV 331:21
you may gather g. there   SCOTT 417:30
garleek: Wel loved he g.   CHAU 142:5
garlic: cheese and g. in a windmill
    SHAK 439:28
garment: deep like as with a g. PRAY 396:18
g. of praise for the spirit   BIBLE 60:9
g. was white as snow   BIBLE 61:8
know the g. from the man BLAKE 86:1
left his g. in her hand   BIBLE 46:30
wax old as doth a g.   PRAY 396:13
garments: borders of their g. BIBLE 67:22
dyed g. from Bozrah   BIBLE 60:10
Reasons are not like g.   ESSEX 208:24
Stuffs out his vacant g.   SHAK 452:20
They part my g. among them PRAY 390:20
garnished: swept, and g.   BIBLE 66:13
garret: Born in the g.   BYRON 125:24
jewels into a g. four stories BACON 25:7
living in a g.   FOOTE 216:6
Garrick: Here lies David G. GOLD 231:18
Our G.'s a salad   GOLD 231:16
garrison: hath friends in the g. HAL 237:17
gars: g. ye rin sae still   ANON 7:12
Garsington: Here is Hey for G. KETT 295:13
Garter: George and G. dangling POPE 377:33
I like the G.   MELB 336:12
garters: thine own heir-apparent g.
    SHAK 438:25
gas: All is g. and gaiters   DICK 180:21
G. smells awful   PARK 368:18
g. was on in the Institute   BETJ 44:2
gashouse: evening round behind the g.
    ELIOT 204:26
gas-lamps: his g. seven   KING 296:20
Gasp: G. and Stretch one's Eyes BELL 39:7
sudden came a g. for breath PAIN 367:18
When he was at the last g. BIBLE 63:30
gat: g. me to my Lord right PRAY 391:14
gate: A-sitting on a g.   CARR 136:5
broad g. and the great fire SHAK 421:4
g. is strait   SWIN 530:26
G. With dreadful faces   MILT 350:1
into that g. they shall   DONNE 191:3
keep the g. of hell   SHAK 476:21
latch ter de golden g.   HARR 242:17
lead you in at Heaven's g. BLAKE 86:8
matters not how strait the g. HENL 245:5
openeth the g. to good fame BACON 26:4
poor man at his g.   ALEX 3:14
their enemies in the g.   PRAY 398:19
this is the g. of heaven   BIBLE 46:20
which was laid at his g.   BIBLE 70:28
Wide is the g.   BIBLE 65:6
gate-bars: drops on g. hang in a row
    HARDY 241:4

gates: feet shall stand in thy g.   PRAY 398:11
g., and be ye lift up   PRAY 390:24
g. are mine to open   KIPL 301:20
g. of heaven opened against   MAL 328:7
g. of hell shall not prevail   BIBLE 66:33
g. of it shall not be shut   BIBLE 82:34
shut the g. of mercy   GRAY 234:24
stranger that is within thy g.   BIBLE 47:24
temple g. unto my love   SPEN 515:25
There are two g. of Sleep   VIRG 559:3
Gath: Tell it not in G.   BIBLE 50:16
gather: cannot tell who shall g. them
   PRAY 391:31
g. the lambs with his arm   BIBLE 59:7
G. ye rosebuds while ye   HERR 250:5
gathered: by gloomy Dis Was g.   MILT 347:21
g. from the air a live   POUND 382:14
g. thy children together   BIBLE 67:26
some g. at six   DONNE 190:26
two or three are g.   PRAY 385:8
where two or three are g.   BIBLE 67:6
which cannot be g. up again   BIBLE 50:23
Gathering: G. her brows like gathering
   BURNS 115:3
g. where thou hast not   BIBLE 68:3
gathers: Who g. all things mortal
   SWIN 529:22
Gat-tothed: G. I was   CHAU 143:21
Gaudeamus: G. igitur   ANON 10:13
gaudium: quod illud g.   ABEL 1:2
gaudy: g., blabbing   SHAK 446:8
have one other g. night   SHAK 422:22
Neat, but not g.   WESL 568:25
rich, not g.   SHAK 430:19
than this g. melon-flower   BROW 101:7
gauger: g. walked with willing   STEV 523:8
Gaul: G. as a whole is divided   CAES 126:26
I've lost G.   KIPL 302:13
Gaunt: on G.'s embattled pile   MAC 322:4
seige of the city of G.   BALL 31:8
gauntlet: g. with a gift in't   BROW 97:28
gave: his only begotten Son   BIBLE 71:38
G. thee life   BLAKE 87:26
g. thee thy renown   CAREW 130:13
I g. you your own soul   SHAW 496:30
Lord g.   BIBLE 52:7
she g. me of the tree   BIBLE 45:17
That we g.   ANON 7:20
then he g. a third   WORD 580:1
What wee g.   ANON 8:17
gawds: consent praise new-born g.
   SHAK 487:6
gay: g. as innocent   SCOTT 418:15
g. as soft   YOUNG 588:7
I'm a g. deceiver   COLM 159:2
making Gay *rich* and Rich *g.*   JOHN 282:1
outward walls so costly g.   SHAK 495:13
second best's a g. goodnight   YEATS 585:6
So g. against the great   AUDEN 18:5
steer From grave to g.   POPE 380:3
whole is far from g.   LEAR 312:22
Gaza: Eyeless in G.   MILT 350:14
gaze: g. not in my eyes   HOUS 262:21
g. on Christian fools with   SHAK 466:13
moveless hands And face and g.
   HARDY 240:15
Stand fixt in stedfast g.   MILT 344:7
to g. out from the land   LUCR 320:6
gazelle: both Beautiful, one a g.
   YEATS 585:11
g., delicate wanderer   SPEN 515:14
never nurs'd a dear g.   MOORE 356:25
never nursed a dear G.   DICK 180:29
gazelles: cleaving the grass, g.   MOORE 355:23
gazes: does he see when he g.   HARDY 240:15
gazing: stand ye g. up into heaven
   BIBLE 73:21
géant: Ses ailes de g. l'empêchent   BAUD 35:6
gear: Gaze at the gilded g.   HARDY 239:5
hate all that Persian g.   HOR 260:4

my ships are out of g.   TENN 542:21
Gebet: ist das vollkommenste G.   LESS 314:1
geck: most notorious g. and gull   SHAK 490:24
Gedanke: Ein einziger dankbarer G.
   LESS 314:1
'Zwei Seelen und ein G.   HALM 238:10
Geese: G. are swans   ARN 13:14
it for this the wild g.   YEATS 586:19
Like g. about the sky   AUDEN 18:9
still famous for its g.   HOUS 266:15
swans of others are g.   WALP 563:20
Gefahr: vor dem Alles in G. ist   NIET 363:5
gefährlich: g. leben   NIET 363:9
*Gefühls: Epigramm auf den Tod eines
G.*   NIET 363:13
Gehazi: Whence comest thou, G.   BIBLE 51:30
Gehenna: to G. or up to the Throne
   KIPL 304:11
Geist: der G. der stets verneint   GOET 230:1
gem: Full many a g. of purest   GRAY 234:23
Thinking every tear a g.   SHEL 502:3
geminae: Sunt g. Somni portae   VIRG 559:3
gemlike: hard, g. flame   PATER 369:21
gems: prow-promoted g. again   BETJ 42:18
Rich and various g. inlay   MILT 340:25
these the g. of Heav'n   MILT 348:5
Gemüt: Schicksal und G. Namen   NOV 364:9
gender: she's of the feminine g.   OKEE 364:23
genealogies: Fables and endless g.   BIBLE 79:6
general: army led by an Irish g.   SHAW 498:7
country was good for G.   WILS 574:15
feet of the great g.   OVID 366:22
G. Good is the plea   BLAKE 86:7
G. notions are generally   MONT 354:9
g. of our gracious empress   SHAK 445:7
g. Of trotting 'paritors   SHAK 456:26
g.'s disdain'd   SHAK 486:25
good morning!' the g.   SASS 414:18
governed too much by g. maxims
   BURKE 109:5
'twas caviare to the g.   SHAK 432:23
useless as a g. maxim   MAC 323:28
you find in that great g.   JUV 288:1
generalities: g. of natural right which
   CHOA 148:14
Glittering g.   EMER 208:14
generally: g. necessary to salvation
   PRAY 388:19
generals: *bite* some of my other g.
   GEOR 223:36
Despite of all your g.   LAND 308:18
Russia has two g. in whom   NICH 362:23
generation: censor of the young g.
   HOR 257:21
evil and adulterous g.   BIBLE 66:11
faithless and stubborn g.   PRAY 395:4
g. of them that hate me   BIBLE 47:24
g. of vipers   BIBLE 63:38
g. that set not   PRAY 395:4
g. wiser than the children   BIBLE 70:25
Had it been the whole g.   ANON 5:15
I grieved with this g.   PRAY 396:4
leaves is a g. of men   HOMER 253:29
One g. passeth away   BIBLE 55:5
they are a very froward g.   BIBLE 48:31
to a yet more vicious g.   HOR 260:26
ye are a chosen g.   BIBLE 80:23
You're all a lost g.   STEIN 518:18
generations: g. shall call me blessed
   BIBLE 69:5
G. pass while some tree   BROW 97:16
g. 'from shirt-sleeves   BUTL 117:12
G. have trod   HOPK 256:12
g. of living creatures   LUCR 320:7
No hungry g. tread thee   KEATS 291:23
Ten g. failed to alter   HARDY 241:13
generous: g. and honest feeling that
   BURKE 108:24
g. and elevated mind   JOHN 282:19
impulses as they are always g.   MONT 355:11

It is the g. spirit   WORD 577:3
My mind as g.   SHAK 453:9
they have more g. sentiments   JOHN 275:4
Genesis: set you square with G.   BROW 99:9
Geneva: grim G. ministers   AYT 24:10
génie: j'ai mis mon g. dans ma vie
   WILDE 573:35
Le g. n'est qu'une plus   BUFF 106:21
vous croyez un grand g.   BEAU 35:18
Geniumque: G. loci primamque deorum
   VIRG 559:4
genius: Consult the g. of the place   POPE 378:3
'Eccentricities of g.   DICK 182:8
g. and the mortal instruments   SHAK 449:6
g. are the first things   KEATS 293:21
G. does what it must   MER 338:5
G. been defined as a supreme   BUTL 118:34
g. is no more than a girl   POUND 382:15
G. is of no country   CHUR 149:7
G. is one per cent inspiration   EDIS 199:25
G. is only a greater aptitude   BUFF 106:21
g. of the Constitution   PITT 373:28
g. rules is by persuading   STEP 518:20
g. that could cut a Colossus   JOHN 279:18
'G.' (which means transcendent   CARL 131:18
Gives g. a better discerning   GOLD 231:22
good g. presiding over you   KEATS 293:11
have put my g. into my life   WILDE 573:35
If Shakespeare's g. had   CHES 145:24
instantly recognizes g.   DOYLE 192:38
kind of universal g.   DRYD 197:39
man of g. makes no mistakes   JOYCE 286:27
man of g. and his money   SHEN 505:17
models destroy g. and art   HAZL 243:28
only on its heights of g.   HOUS 266:15
Philistine of g. in religion   ARN 16:23
Ramp up my g.   JONS 284:13
she creates a g. to do it   EMER 208:3
sphere for Shelley's g.   ARN 16:2
stupendous g.! damned fool   BYRON 126:17
that is g.   EMER 207:34
Three-fifths of him g.   LOW 319:8
to declare except my g.   WILDE 573:36
To raise the g.   POPE 375:11
true g. is a mind of large   JOHN 281:30
True g. kindles   POPE 376:26
was g. found respectable   BROW 97:31
what a g. I had when   SWIFT 527:18
When a true g. appears   SWIFT 527:8
yourself to be a great g.   BEAU 35:18
Gennesareth: Not of G.   THOM 548:25
genres: Tous les g. sont bons hors
   VOLT 561:7
gens: g. de qualité savent   MOL 353:23
*GENTE: SI VA TRA LA PERDUTA
G.*   DANTE 171:3
genteel: beast to the truly g.   HARDY 241:17
not g. when he gets drunk   BOSW 90:16
gentes: Augescunt aliae g.   LUCR 320:7
gentil: g. that dooth gentil dedis   CHAU 143:25
parfit g. knyght   CHAU 141:10
Gentiles: should preach among the G.
   BIBLE 77:23
gentle: day shall g. his condition   SHAK 445:3
Do not go g. into that   THOM 546:23
G. as falcon or hawk   SKEL 508:16
G. Jesus   WESL 568:17
g. mind by gentle deeds   SPEN 516:23
g. rain from heaven   SHAK 467:27
His life was g.   SHAK 452:7
I have seen them g.   WYATT 583:21
person in vertuous and g.   SPEN 515:28
gentleman: almost a definition of a g.
   NEWM 362:4
Be a little g.   HOFF 252:14
being a g. never is one   SURT 525:2
book is to fashion a g.   SPEN 515:28
died a very gallant g.   ATK 17:21
every Jack became a g.   SHAK 480:24
finish'd g. from top   BYRON 123:37

bug with g. wings POPE 377:1
g. loam or painted clay SHAK 478:8
trim the g. vessel goes GRAY 234:16
Gilding: G. pale streams with heavenly
SHAK 493:9
g. the eastern hemisphere SHER 505:25
Gilead: G. is mine PRAY 393:18
Is there no balm in G. BIBLE 60:21
that appear from mount G. BIBLE 56:26
Gillyflowers: With G. SPEN 517:3
Gilpin: John G. was a citizen COWP 165:15
gilt: dust that is a little g. SHAK 487:6
Gin: G. by pailfuls SCOTT 418:16
G. was mother's milk SHAW 498:15
that I breakfast on g. HERB 246:8
woodcock near the g. SHAK 489:12
ginger: Nutmegs and g. BEAU 36:5
'ot sand an' g. when alive KIPL 299:9
ginger-beer: He cannot abide it LEAR 311:24
Giotto: G.'s tower LONG 316:17
giovinezza: *Quant' è bella g.* MED 336:9
Gipfeln: *Über allen G. Ist Ruh'* GOET 230:11
gipseying: lass that were to go a-g.
LAMB 308:3
Gipsies: same the G. wore ARN 14:13
gipsy: g. by Reynolds to his Majesty's
MAC 324:2
giraffe: Swelling to maculate g. ELIOT 204:14
Giraffes: G.! —a People CAMP 128:10
Gird: G. up now thy loins like BIBLE 53:1
girded: g. himself with strength PRAY 395:24
He g. up his loins BIBLE 51:12
is g. about with power PRAY 394:1
Let your loins be g. about BIBLE 70:6
With your loins g. BIBLE 47:18
girdedst: thou g. thyself BIBLE 73:17
girdeth: g. on his harness boast BIBLE 51:16
girdid: I g. up my Lions & fled WARD 564:24
girdle: bright g. furl'd ARN 12:23
g. do the Gods inherit SHAK 455:17
g. round about the earth SHAK 470:9
leathern g. about his loins BIBLE 63:37
girdled: g. with the gleaming world
TENN 539:16
girl: Above the staggering g. YEATS 586:16
at a g. throwing a ball WOOLF 576:19
Each book that a young g. RUSK 412:13
garland briefer than a g.'s HOUS 263:3
genius is no more than a g. POUND 382:15
g. arose that had red mournful YEATS 586:22
g. like I LOOS 318:1
g.'s lip out of Paris SWIN 531:2
Home is the g.'s prison SHAW 498:3
Is an unlesson'd g. SHAK 467:13
little cottage g. PAIN 367:19
mountainous sports g. BETJ 43:20
no g. wants to laugh all LOOS 318:5
There was a little g. LONG 317:2
to any good g. to be neat TAYL 531:24
touched a broken g. FLEC 214:15
We all love a pretty g. BICK 84:2
You speak like a green g. SHAK 430:10
girl-graduates: sweet g. in their golden
TENN 541:27
girlish: to the brim with g. glee GILB 226:27
girls: Afield for palms the g. HOUS 262:19
All very agreeable g. GILB 226:2
'Always be civil to the g. MITF 352:23
At g. who wear glasses PARK 368:16
Barring drink and the g. LOCK 315:23
before to virgin g. and boys HOR 260:13
Boys and g. tumbling TRAH 551:19
do for pretty g. YEATS 585:16
g. we was all of us ladies we was
MARQ 330:20
lads for the g. HOUS 263:6
My life with g. has ended HOR 261:6
Of all the g. that are CAREY 130:26
pallor of g.' brows OWEN 367:3
prevent girls from being g. HOPE 255:28

process whereby American g. HAMP 238:17
rosebud garden of g. TENN 540:11
rose-lipt g. are sleeping HOUS 264:10
swear to never kiss the g. BROW 100:30
white feet of laughing g. MAC 322:12
girt: loins g. about with truth BIBLE 78:10
git: you've gut to g. up airly LOW 319:1
Gitche Gumee: By the shore of G.
LONG 317:10
Gitche Manito: G., the mighty LONG 317:9
give: All I can g. you I give SWIN 530:22
all other things g. place GAY 223:16
blessed to g. than to receive BIBLE 74:19
did not g. a singel dam FLEM 214:25
freely g. BIBLE 65:31
G. all thou canst WORD 582:16
G., and it shall be given BIBLE 69:23
'G. crowns and pounds HOUS 262:20
G. every man thine ear SHAK 430:19
g. her booby for another GAY 223:11
g. me back my legions AUG 22:4
g. me back my heart BYRON 125:3
g. me back my heart again GRAN 234:4
G. me more love or more CAREW 130:16
G. me,' quoth I SHAK 458:6
G. me your tired LAZ 311:13
g. them a core one time TWAIN 554:17
g. the world the lie RAL 404:10
G. this man place BIBLE 70:7
G. to me the life I love STEV 522:27
g. to the poor BIBLE 67:9
G. us the tools CHUR 150:6
G. us this day our daily BIBLE 64:24
G. what you command AUG 21:17
honourable alike in what we g. LINC 314:22
never g. up their liberties BURKE 110:27
receive but what we g. COL 156:9
such as I have g. I thee BIBLE 73:25
What I desire to g. SHAK 485:12
What will ye g. me BIBLE 68:9
which the world cannot g. PRAY 385:9
given: he would not have g. me WOLS 576:14
one that hath shall be g. BIBLE 68:4
sister is g. to government DICK 178:7
Something g. that way FLET 215:14
unto us a son is g. BIBLE 58:7
giver: author and g. of all good PRAY 386:19
g. is forgot CONG 159:30
Lord and g. of life PRAY 387:11
loveth a cheerful g. BIBLE 77:9
givers: poor when g. prove unkind
SHAK 433:10
gives: g. to airy nothing SHAK 471:11
much good who g. quickly PUBL 402:3
giving: g. and receiving of a Ring PRAY 389:7
Godlike in g. MOORE 357:5
not in the g. vein to-day SHAK 481:6
Stealing and g. odour SHAK 487:20
glacier: g. knocks in the cupboard
AUDEN 18:10
glad: bad g. mad SWIN 530:2
G. did I live and gladly STEV 523:10
gladness when she's g. BARR 34:17
g. of other men's good SHAK 426:4
g. that you won BETJ 44:6
I was g. when they said PRAY 398:11
maketh g. the heart of man PRAY 396:20
moments of g. grace YEATS 587:12
shew ourselves g. in him PRAY 396:3
solitary place shall be g. BIBLE 58:32
son maketh a g. father BIBLE 53:29
To g. me with its soft MOORE 356:25
Trying to be g. HOUS 262:22
was made to make men g. BIBLE 63:15
will rejoice and be g. PRAY 398:2
yea g. with all my heart DRAY 193:21
gladder: My heart is g. than all ROSS 408:23
glade: alone in the bee-loud g. YEATS 585:17
gladiators: What were the g. of Rome
BORR 90:6

gladness: g. of her gladness when BARR 34:17
serve the Lord with g. PRAY 396:11
shall obtain joy and g. BIBLE 59:1
solemn g. even crown'd TENN 536:18
Teach me half the g. SHEL 504:24
thee with the oil of g. PRAY 392:15
Gladstone: G.'s always having LAB 306:10
Glamis: G. hath murder'd sleep SHAK 460:9
G. thou art, and Cawdor SHAK 459:1
glamour: g. Of childish days LAWR 311:7
glance: Doth g. from heaven SHAK 471:11
g. of supernatural hate BYRON 126:7
mutual g. of great politeness BYRON 126:8
whose g. was glum GILB 229:9
glare: from day's detested g. POPE 381:9
strange unheavenly g. BRID 92:13
There is a g. in some men's BAG 28:20
glass: baying for broken g. WAUGH 565:29
dome of many-coloured g. SHEL 499:26
double g. o' the invariable DICK 182:11
Drink not the third g. HERB 247:1
England is looking in the g. CHES 147:1
Get thee g. eyes SHAK 455:21
g. I drink from is not MUSS 359:2
g. is falling hour by hour MACN 326:8
g. of blessings standing HERB 248:6
g. when I am shrinking ANON 10:14
Grief with a g. that ran SWIN 528:20
He was indeed the g. SHAK 441:24
his natural face in a g. BIBLE 80:10
his own face in the g. WILDE 573:16
it were a sea of g. mingled BIBLE 82:19
like it out of a thin g. PINT 373:18
man that looks on g. HERB 247:18
My g. shall not persuade SHAK 493:1
Over the g.'s edge when BROW 99:2
prove an excuse for the g. SHER 506:31
Satire is a sort of g. SWIFT 525:32
she made mouths in a g. SHAK 454:6
sound of broken g. BELL 40:5
throne there was a sea of g. BIBLE 81:23
through a g., darkly BIBLE 76:14
till I set you up a g. SHAK 434:33
turn down an empty G. FITZ 213:18
when he looked into the g. DISR 186:14
you break the bloody g. MACN 326:8
glasses: At girls who wear g. PARK 368:16
broke our painted g. JORD 285:18
Fill all the g. there COWL 164:8
were two g. and two chairs MACN 326:11
with plenty of looking g. ASHF 17:10
Wiv a ladder and some g. BAT 35:3
gle: of gamyn and g. WYNT 584:4
gleam: add the g. WORD 577:4
Follow The G. TENN 540:21
g. on the years that shall BULW 107:1
spent lights quiver and g. ARN 13:6
gleamed: first she g. upon my sight
WORD 581:7
g. Upon the glassy plain WORD 577:26
gleams: sunbeams with their convex g.
SHEL 500:7
glean: reap thou shouldst but g. HOOD 255:5
world shall g. of me THOM 548:28
glean'd: pen has g. my teeming KEATS 292:30
gleaning: g. of the grapes of Ephraim
BIBLE 49:17
glede: in pursuit the rapid g. SMART 509:3
glee: At their tempestuous g. LONG 317:8
brim with girlish g. GILB 226:27
Piping songs of pleasant g. BLAKE 87:24
glen: Down the rushy g. ALL 3:20
Glenartney: In lone G.'s hazel shade
SCOTT 416:1
Glenlivet: Only half G. AYT 24:7
glib: g. and oily art SHAK 453:5
glides: meadows where it g. ARN 12:22
glimmering: Mere g. and decays
VAUG 555:19
glimpse: g. of His bright face VAUG 555:14

glimpses: thus the g. of the moon
   SHAK 430:24
glisters: Nor all, that g., gold   GRAY 235:8
glittering: g. and sounding generalities
   CHOA 148:14
  g. prizes to those who   BIRK 84:14
how that g. taketh me   HERR 250:8
gloat: Hear me g.   KIPL 305:4
global: my wars Were g.   REED 405:7
globe: g. of death and halved   THOM 547:4
great g. itself   SHAK 485:20
rattle of a g. to play   DRYD 195:13
wears the turning g.   HOUS 265:1
globule: primordial atomic g.   GILB 226:20
Glöckchen: Höhr ihr das G. klingeln
   HEINE 244:11
gloire: g. et le repos sont choses MONT 354:22
Le jour de g. est arrivé   ROUG 410:16
gloom: Brooding o'er the g.   MER 337:3
g. of earthquake and eclipse   SHEL 503:21
Inspissated g.   JOHN 275:25
Is my g.   THOM 548:23
(Lamps for my g.   SASS 414:19
light to counterfeit a g.   MILT 342:5
Our g.-pleas'd eyes   KEATS 292:28
There g. the dark broad seas   TENN 544:3
tunnel of green g.   BROO 94:17
Upon the growing g.   HARDY 239:7
glooms: Through verdurous g.   KEATS 291:20
Welcome, kindred g.   THOM 549:22
gloomy: g. in England are March
   TROL 552:21
way to such g. thoughts   AUST 23:17
Gloria: G. in excelsis Deo   MASS 334:18
G. Patri   MASS 334:14
gloriam: Ad majorem Dei g.   ANON 10:6
sed nomini tuo da g.   BIBLE 83:10
gloried: Jamshyd g. and drank deep
   FITZ 212:14
glories: g. and my state depose   SHAK 479:23
G., like glow-worms   WEBS 566:25
g. of our blood and state   SHIR 507:2
in those weaker g. spy   VAUG 555:15
glorify: g. God and to enjoy   SHOR 507:7
glorious: all g. within   PRAY 392:17
g. are those sabbaths which   ABEL 1:1
g. fault of angels   POPE 376:8
G. the sun in mid-career   SMART 509:4
g. thing must be a victory   WELL 567:26
how g.   BETJ 43:3
I'll make thee g. by my pen   GRAH 233:15
reach at the g. gold   SHAK 446:2
shown no g. morning face   STEV 523:11
Sing the g. day's renown   CAMP 128:14
Tam was g.   BURNS 115:6
'tis a g. thing   GILB 225:22
glory: are the days of our g.   BYRON 125:29
Be Thine the g.   DRYD 196:13
brightness of his g.   BIBLE 79:28
brittle g. shineth in this   SHAK 480:5
calls the g. from the grey   BROW 104:6
chief g. of every people   JOHN 281:10
count the g. of my crown   ELIZ 206:5
day of g. has arrived   ROUG 410:16
drown'd my G. in a Shallow Cup FITZ 213:13
duty was the way to g.   TENN 541:14
earth are full of thy g.   PRAY 387:23
earth is full of his g.   BIBLE 57:28
eternal brood of g. excellent   SPEN 516:4
feathered g. from her loosening YEATS 586:1
fierce wretchedness that g.   SHAK 486:10
fill thy breast with g.   HERB 247:3
finished yields the true g.   DRAKE 193:1
from another star in g.   BIBLE 76:26
G. and loveliness have   KEATS 292:26
g. and our absolute boast   WORD 580:16
g. and the nothing   BYRON 121:28
g. and the dream   WORD 579:5
g. as of the only begotten   BIBLE 71:27
G. be to God for dappled   HOPK 256:22

G. be to the Father   PRAY 384:15
g. dropped from their youth   BROW 105:19
g. in the church by Christ Jesus BIBLE 77:26
g. in the name of Briton   GEOR 224:1
g. is departed from Israel   BIBLE 49:40
g., jest, and riddle   POPE 379:13
G., like the phoenix 'midst   BYRON 124:30
g. of Europe is extinguished   BURKE 111:9
g. of man as the flower   BIBLE 80:21
g. of the Attic stage   ARN 15:10
g. of the Creator   BACON 24:17
G. of the Garden lies   KIPL 299:12
g. of the Lord shall be   BIBLE 59:5
g. of the Lord is risen   BIBLE 60:7
g. of the Lord shone round   BIBLE 69:9
g. of the sun will be dimmed   BALF 30:3
g. of the winning were   MER 337:2
g., or the grave   CAMP 128:22
g. shone around   TATE 531:22
G. to God in the highest   BIBLE 69:11
G. to Man in the highest   SWIN 530:2
g. was I had such friends   YEATS 586:6
g. was not arrayed like   BIBLE 64:30
Go where g. waits thee   MOORE 356:8
has ended and the vast g.   VIRG 558:6
heavens declare the g.   PRAY 390:11
hope of g.   PRAY 386:2
I felt it was g.   BYRON 125:30
infirm g. of the positive   ELIOT 201:33
into g. peep   VAUG 555:21
King of g. shall come   PRAY 390:24
Land of Hope and G.   BENS 40:24
left him alone with his g.   WOLFE 576:5
long hair, it is a g.   BIBLE 76:12
looks on war as all g.   SHER 506:40
madness is the g. of this life   SHAK 486:4
Majesty: of thy G.   PRAY 384:16
much g. and so much shame   MAC 324:11
My gown of g.   RAL 404:12
nothing else but sudden g.   HOBB 251:22
not the g.   GOET 230:5
now my g. smear'd in dust   SHAK 446:22
of being too fond of g.   SMITH 511:37
of g. in the flower   WORD 579:13
of the peacock is the g.   BLAKE 88:21
passed away a g.   WORD 578:22
passes the g. of the world   ANON 11:1
paths of g. lead   GRAY 234:21
quickly the world's g.   THOM 546:7
return the g. of your prime   SHEL 501:14
sea Of g. streams along   BYRON 121:4
short of the g. of God   BIBLE 74:38
solely is the sum of g.   MARL 330:11
that will die in their g.   HOUS 263:8
'There's g. for you   CARR 135:21
'Tis beauty calls and g.   LEE 313:10
'tis to g. we steer'   ROSS 408:25
to crown him with g.   PRAY 389:28
To the g. that was Greece   POE 377:7
To the greater g. of God   ANON 10:6
to thy name give g.   BIBLE 83:10
trailing clouds of g.   WORD 579:5
unspeakable and full of g.   BIBLE 80:20
Vain pomp and g. of this   SHAK 447:9
walked in g. and in joy   WORD 580:28
walked with inward g. crowned SHEL 504:10
walking in an air of g.   VAUG 555:9
what g. is it   BIBLE 80:26
When gout and g. seat me   BROW 100:19
whose g. is their shame   BIBLE 78:19
Why in the name of G. were   KEATS 290:9
with g. not their own   WORD 580:19
glotoun: g. of wordes   LANG 309:24
Gloucester: thy name is G.   SHAK 455:22
Gloucestershire: am a stranger here in
G.   SHAK 478:23
glove: were a g. upon that hand   SHAK 482:7
gloves: complete with hat and g.   CALV 127:16
through the fields in g.   CORN 162:22
wore g. in my cap   SHAK 454:18

glow: that g. in the heart that   CONR 161:24
glowing: other g. like the vital   SHEL 500:8
glow-worm: g. shows the matin to be
   SHAK 431:14
Her eyes the g. lend thee   HERR 249:11
glow-worms: Glories, like g.   WEBS 566:25
gloz'd: g. but superficially   SHAK 486:30
Glubit: G. magnanimos Remi nepotes
   CAT 137:5
Glücklichen: Die Welt des G. ist eine
   WITT 575:16
Glückseligkeit: G. nicht ein Ideal der
   KANT 288:12
glut: g. thy sorrow on a morning
   KEATS 291:15
glutinous: turtle green and g.   BROW 103:16
gluve: he play'd at the g.   BALL 30:17
Glyn: With Elinor G.   ANON 8:23
gnashing: weeping and g. of teeth
   BIBLE 65:17
gnat: small grey-coated g.   SHAK 481:28
which strain at a g.   BIBLE 67:24
gnats: wailful choir the small g.   KEATS 293:8
gnaw: g. you so your nether lip   SHAK 477:6
gnaweth: death g. upon them   PRAY 393:1
go: because I g. to the Father   BIBLE 72:40
expedient for you that I g.   BIBLE 72:38
G., and do thou likewise   BIBLE 69:33
G. and find it   KIPL 299:2
G., and he goeth   BIBLE 65:15
G. and look behind   KIPL 299:2
G., and the Lord be with   BIBLE 50:10
g. at once   SHAK 461:23
g. by climbing a birch   FROST 219:1
G., for they call you   ARN 14:10
g. gentle into that good   THOM 546:23
going where I have to g.   ROET 407:6
G., litel bok   CHAU 144:17
G. out into the highways   BIBLE 70:13
G. to the ant thou sluggard   BIBLE 53:21
g. to the devil where he   JOHN 279:31
g. to 't with delight   SHAK 422:24
g. unto the altar of God   PRAY 392:11
g. we know not where   SHAK 464:14
G. West   GREE 235:26
G. ye into all the world   BIBLE 69:2
How you do g. it   BROWN 95:11
I g. on for ever   TENN 532:21
I like to g. by myself   HAZL 243:30
In the name of God,   CROM 169:26
I shall g. to him but he   BIBLE 50:22
Is to g. hence unwilling   MILT 349:28
it's no g. the rickshaw   MACN 326:7
I will arise and g. now   YEATS 585:17
I will not let thee g.   BIBLE 46:24
I will not let thee g.   BRID 92:11
Let my people g.   BIBLE 47:13
Let us g. then   ELIOT 203:17
Must you g.   VAUG 555:9
not g., For weariness   DONNE 190:7
therefore pay you cash to g.   KIPL 298:12
There g. the ships   PRAY 397:1
to g. with the man I love   BREC 91:26
to hell I will g.   MILL 339:5
unto Caesar shalt thou g.   BIBLE 74:24
Victoria Station and g.   BEVIN 44:18
we'll g. no more a roving   BYRON 125:25
Whither shall I g. then   PRAY 399:5
will g. into the house   PRAY 398:11
will g. onward the same   HARDY 240:5
Will g. with you along   HERR 249:28
will neither g. nor hang   BIGOD 84:5
goads: words of the wise are as g.
   BIBLE 56:12
goal: g. stands up   HOUS 263:10
grave is not its g.   LONG 317:1
stood I to keep the g.   HOUS 262:22
Will be the final g. of ill   TENN 536:24
goals: They live by positive g.   BERL 41:23
goat: Gall of g.   SHAK 462:4

maker and builder is G.	BIBLE 79:32
mammon than a bogus g.	MACN 326:4
man be more just than G.	BIBLE 52:16
man hath seen G.	BIBLE 71:28
Man is G.'s image	HERB 247:9
man Is now become a g.	SHAK 448:14
man sent from G.	BIBLE 71:24
man's the noblest work of G.	BURNS 113:10
Man's word is G. in man	TENN 533:31
many are afraid of G.	LOCK 315:20
men as had the fear of G.	CROM 169:20
men that G. made mad	CHES 146:17
mighty G.	BIBLE 58:7
mills of G. grind slowly	LOGAU 316:5
morowe longe I to goe to G.	MORE 357:20
my duty towards G.	PRAY 388:14
my flesh shall I see G.	BIBLE 52:31
my G.	HOPK 256:8
My G., I love Thee	CASW 136:16
my G., look upon me	PRAY 390:16
my King and my G.	PRAY 395:11
nature is the art of G.	BROW 96:13
nature of G. is a circle	ANON 7:27
Nearer, my G., to thee	ADAMS 1:10
nearer you are to G.	WOTT 583:17
neglect G. and his Angels	DONNE 191:1
not tempt the Lord thy G.	BIBLE 64:2
not the G. of Nature	HERB 248:7
now G. alone knows	KLOP 305:16
Now G. be praised	WOLFE 576:8
of the mysteries of G.	BIBLE 75:32
Of what I call G.	BROW 104:29
One G., one law, one element	TENN 537:22
one more insult to G.	BROW 102:7
Only G. can tell the saintly	AUDEN 19:20
only...with the idea G. has of you	
	UNAM 554:28
other but the house of G.	BIBLE 46:20
Our G.'s forgotten	QUAR 403:14
Our sufficiency is of G.	BIBLE 77:4
out of the mouth of G.	BIBLE 64:1
owe G. a death	SHAK 442:7
pack and label men for G.	THOM 548:26
peace of G.	BIBLE 78:21
people is the voice of G.	ALC 3:9
Perfect G.	PRAY 385:14
power belongeth unto G.	PRAY 393:20
presents the g. unshorn	HERR 248:22
put G. in his statements	WHIT 570:1
put thy trust in G.	PRAY 392:12
ranks the same with G.	BROW 103:25
reader of the works of G.	COWP 167:5
reason and the will of G.	ARN 15:15
reflect that G. is just	JEFF 272:16
rejoice and delight in G.	TRAH 551:17
relenting G. Hath placed	ROSS 408:20
reserved only for G. and angels	BACON 24:24
respect of persons with G.	BIBLE 74:34
righteousness of G.	BIBLE 80:10
robbery to be equal with G.	BIBLE 78:13
sacraments to a dying g.	HEINE 244:11
safe stronghold our G.	LUTH 321:2
searching find out G.	BIBLE 52:22
seek their meat from G.	PRAY 397:1
seen G. face to face	BIBLE 46:25
servant of the Living G.	SMART 508:21
she for G. in him	MILT 347:22
short of the glory of G.	BIBLE 74:38
should not think of G.	SHAK 443:18
soul and G. stand sure	BROW 104:9
Spirit of the Lord G. is	BIBLE 60:8
spirit shall return unto G.	BIBLE 56:11
Standeth G. within	LOW 319:10
steep and trifid G.	THOM 547:22
Strong Brother in G.	BELL 40:8
such is the kingdom of G.	BIBLE 68:36
Teach me, my G. and King	HERB 247:18
thank G. of al	CHAU 144:22
that be are ordained of G.	BIBLE 75:20
that G. had put it there	LAB 306:10

that G. made the thunder	MAC 323:32
that is really your G.	LUTH 320:18
That Man who is from G.	WORD 578:8
that would circumvent G.	SHAK 436:27
'There is no G.	CLOU 153:22
There is no G.	PRAY 390:2
They believe G. to be there	JOHN 275:30
they shall see G.	BIBLE 64:6
think I am becoming a g.	VESP 556:12
this g. did shake	SHAK 448:15
this is acceptable with G.	BIBLE 80:26
this is G.'s hill	PRAY 394:9
thou being dead art a G.	SWIN 530:7
thou city of G.	PRAY 395:16
thought that the gift of G.	BIBLE 73:30
Thou, my G., art in't	HERR 250:15
Thou shalt have one G. only	CLOU 153:25
three person'd G.	DONNE 189:8
thro' darkness up to G.	TENN 536:28
through his garden walketh G.	BROW 105:14
throws himself on G.	BROW 100:38
thy God is a jealous G.	BIBLE 48:21
thy God my G.	BIBLE 49:32
To G. I speak Spanish	CHAR 140:31
To justify G.'s ways	HOUS 264:12
To see G. only	DONNE 189:12
TO THE UNKNOWN G.	BIBLE 74:12
to think there is a G.	CLOU 153:23
trust in G.	AUDEN 21:6
unto the G. of gods appeareth	PRAY 395:12
us from the love of G.	BIBLE 75:13
Verb is G.	HUGO 267:9
Very God of very G.	PRAY 387:10
walk humbly with thy G.	BIBLE 61:25
was G. or Devil	DRYD 194:14
was the holy Lamb of G.	BLAKE 86:16
We give thanks to G. always	BIBLE 78:30
we have a building of G.	BIBLE 77:6
were I Lord G.	MACD 325:3
What G. abandoned	HOUS 265:7
What G. hath cleansed	BIBLE 74:1
What g., man, or hero	POUND 383:9
What hath G. wrought	BIBLE 48:15
Whenever G. prepares evil	ANON 10:1
When G. at first made man	HERB 248:6
when G.'s the theme	SMART 509:4
when the sons of G. came	BIBLE 45:33
Where is now thy G.	PRAY 392:9
Wherever G. erects a house	DEFOE 173:11
Who G. doth late and early	WOTT 583:13
whole armour of G.	BIBLE 78:9
whole armour of G.	BIBLE 78:10
who saw the face of G.	MARL 329:7
Whose G. is their belly	BIBLE 78:19
who think not G. at all	MILT 350:20
Who trusted G. was love	TENN 536:29
with Eternal G. for power	TENN 541:12
with the grandeur of G.	HOPK 256:12
woman is the work of G.	BLAKE 88:21
Woman was G.'s second	NIET 363:4
Word was with G.	BIBLE 71:21
worship one G. in Trinity	PRAY 385:12
Yblessed be g. that I have wedded	
	CHAU 143:17
ye believe in G.	BIBLE 72:30
Yellow G. forever gazes	HAYES 243:7
yet G. has not said a word	BROW 103:30
you must believe in G.	JOW 286:1
you think the laws of G.	SHAW 496:33
youth I remembered my G.	SOUT 514:9
you want to take in G.	LOW 319:1
God Almighty: G. first planted a garden	
	BACON 26:18
Hey for G.	KETT 295:13
godamoighty: Do g. knaw what a's doing	
	TENN 541:4
Goddamm: Lhude sing G.	POUND 382:4
goddes: alle hire g. may availle	CHAU 144:19
Goddess: G., excellently bright	JONS 283:24

goddesses: wondrously like the immortal	
g.	HOMER 253:28
godfather: sorry it had so noble a g.	
	SHAK 495:17
Godfathers: G. and Godmothers in my	
	PRAY 388:12
These earthly g. of Heaven's	SHAK 456:15
Godhead: touching his G.	PRAY 385:14
godheads: ...Maidens aspiring to g.	
	STOP 523:15
godlike: dictates of his g. mind	
	OTWAY 365:27
patient endurance is g.	LONG 316:13
godliness: Church in continual g.	
	PRAY 386:23
godly: g. love	PRAY 387:13
may hereafter live a g.	PRAY 384:13
ran his g. race	GOLD 230:22
That still a g. race he ran	GOLD 231:10
there is not one g. man left	PRAY 389:32
Godmothers: Godfathers and G. in my	
Baptism	PRAY 388:12
Godolphin Horne: G. was nobly born	
	BELL 38:33
Godot: We're waiting for G.	BECK 36:15
gods: daughter of the g.	TENN 533:6
dish fit for the g.	SHAK 449:9
first in the world made g.	JONS 284:16
fit love for G.	MILT 349:14
g. are come down to us	BIBLE 74:4
g. love dies young	MEN 336:25
gods that made the g.	CHES 146:15
g. themselves cannot recall	TENN 543:12
g. thought otherwise	VIRG 558:8
G. who live for ever	MAC 323:2
he creates G. by the dozen	MONT 355:4
hills like G. together	TENN 539:16
His death concerns the g.	SOPH 513:6
Kings it makes g.	SHAK 481:11
May the g. avert this omen	CIC 151:29
neither children nor G.	KIPL 298:23
not recognizing the g.	PLATO 374:8
on a par with the g.	SAPP 414:6
people clutching their g.	ELIOT 203:15
shalt have no other g.	BIBLE 47:24
So many g.	WILC 572:6
These be thy g., O Israel	BIBLE 48:2
Thinking of his own G.	ARN 13:8
to be g. if angels fell	POPE 379:7
to the girdle do the G.	SHAK 455:17
utterance of the early G.	KEATS 290:3
Whatever g. may be	SWIN 529:25
What men or g. are these	KEATS 291:3
winning cause pleased the g.	LUCAN 319:22
woman is a dish for the g.	SHAK 424:9
Ye are g.	PRAY 395:10
Ye shall be as g.	BIBLE 45:15
God's-Acre: burial-ground G.	LONG 316:18
goes: grace of God there g.	BRAD 91:9
it g. off at night	SHER 506:28
goest: whithersoever thou g.	BIBLE 48:36
whither thou g.	BIBLE 49:32
goeth: now g. on his way weeping	
	PRAY 398:17
whither it g.	BIBLE 71:36
Goethe: G. had an aversion to dogs	
	NERV 361:1
G.'s sage mind and Byron's	ARN 13:18
open thy G.	CARL 132:20
going: endure Their g. hence	SHAK 456:2
g. down of the sun	BINY 84:10
g. one knows not where	MAS 334:8
g. to and fro in the earth	BIBLE 52:5
good both g. and coming	FROST 219:1
knowing to what he was g.	HARDY 240:9
their g. from us to be	BIBLE 62:13
you were g. to a feast	JONS 283:27
goings: ordered my g.	PRAY 392:1
gold: apples of g. in pictures	BIBLE 54:26
be prepared g. and amber	JONS 285:14

bow of burning g. — BLAKE 86:16
bringing g. — BIBLE 50:34
burned g. was his colour — CHAU 142:32
buttercup Had blessed with g. — OWEN 367:8
by suicide, a bag of g. — BRAM 91:21
clothing is of wrought g. — PRAY 392:17
cursed craving for g. — VIRG 558:10
desired are they than g. — PRAY 390:12
fetch the age of g. — MILT 344:11
fetters, though of g. — BACON 27:42
fly to India for g. — MARL 329:4
From the red g. keep thy — SCOTT 418:5
given of the g. of Arabia — PRAY 394:21
gleaming in purple and g. — BYRON 122:1
glistering g. but more to shine — BRAD 91:15
g. and flowing serpent — LAWR 311:3
g., and frankincense — BIBLE 63:32
g. and silver becks me — SHAK 452:19
G. a transient — GRAI 233:20
G. is for the mistress — KIPL 298:25
g. kept by a devil till — SHAK 442:15
G. undiscovered (and all — HOR 260:20
g. wes changyd into lede — WYNT 584:4
great deal of g. — JAMES 271:33
hair and harpstring of g. — SWIN 530:3
hands are as g. rings — BIBLE 57:4
hearts of g. and lungs — BELL 39:28
he but litel g. in cofre — CHAU 141:24
her feathers like g. — PRAY 394:8
If g. ruste — CHAU 142:2
Ionian white and g. — ELIOT 205:4
Is she not pure g. — BROW 105:10
jewel of g. in a swine's — BIBLE 53:32
lap to saint-seducing g. — SHAK 481:24
mankind upon a cross of g. — BRYAN 106:8
Nor all, that glisters, is g. — GRAY 235:8
over with pillars of g. — BLAKE 86:4
Plate sin with g. — SHAK 455:20
queen in a vesture of g. — PRAY 392:16
reach at the glorious g. — SHAK 446:2
religion of g. — BAG 29:4
sand and ruin and g. — SWIN 530:29
street of the city was pure g. — BIBLE 82:33
streets are paved with g. — COLM 158:25
this foul drain pure g. — TOCQ 551:9
thousands of g. and silver — PRAY 398:5
'To gild refined g. — BYRON 122:31
To gild refined g. — SHAK 452:25
travell'd in the realms of g. — KEATS 292:17
truth with g. she weighs — POPE 375:13
us rarer gifts than g. — BROO 94:7
vine and grapes in g. — FLEC 214:17
with patines of bright g. — SHAK 468:15
Would he have g. — HERB 248:15
gold-dusted: shall we have g. snapdragon — ARN 15:6
golden: after that sweet g. clime — BLAKE 87:22
circle of the g. year — TENN 533:24
days of g. dreams — BRON 93:24
g. apples of the sun — YEATS 586:21
g. bowl be broken — BIBLE 56:11
'g.-calf of Self-love — CARL 131:4
g. days of Saturn's reign — VIRG 559:19
G. lads and girls all must — SHAK 428:22
g. lamps in a green night… — MARV 331:16
G. lie the meadows — MER 337:37
g. locks time hath to silver — PEELE 371:8
g. mind stoops not to shows — SHAK 466:16
G. opinions from all sorts — SHAK 459:7
G. Road to Samarkand — FLEC 214:14
g. vials full of odours — BIBLE 81:27
g. years return — SHEL 500:20
Happy the g. mean — MASS 335:17
Love in a g. bowl — BLAKE 85:19
observ'd the g. rule — BLAKE 87:4
safe in a g. ewer — BROW 100:4
seven g. candlesticks — BIBLE 81:13
Someone who loves the g. mean — HOR 260:9
that there are no g. rules — SHAW 497:35
they did in the g. world — SHAK 424:20

wander in that g. maze — DRYD 197:16
with g. and silver light — YEATS 585:9
you the end of a g. string — BLAKE 86:8
Golden Gate: West to the G. — KIPL 300:24
Goldengrove: Over G. unleaving — HOPK 256:25
Golden Vanity: goes by the name of the G. — BALL 31:2
gold-giving: Nor g. lords like those — POUND 383:19
Goldsmith: Here lies Nolly G. — GARR 221:13
To Oliver G. — JOHN 277:13
golf: When ye come to play g. — MACD 325:1
Golgotha: field of G. and dead men's — SHAK 479:20
memorize another G. — SHAK 458:4
Gomorrah: overthrew Sodom and G. — BIBLE 61:20
gondola: g. of London — DISR 186:18
think you have swam in a g. — SHAK 426:20
What else is like the g. — CLOU 153:20
gone: all are g. — LAMB 308:6
Art thou g. in haste — ROWL 411:1
been and g. and done — GILB 225:12
both are g. — ARN 13:8
from these I would be g. — SHAK 494:5
G. far away into the silent — ROSS 409:3
g. into the world of light — VAUG 555:18
g. over to the majority — CARL 131:11
g. to-morrow — BEHN 38:13
g. to the demnition bow-wows — DICK 180:23
g. up with a merry noise — PRAY 392:24
g. with the wind — DOWS 191:12
great spirit g. — SHAK 421:18
He is g. on the mountain — SCOTT 416:5
I have g. here and there — SHAK 495:3
I would have thee g. — SHAK 482:20
lo, he was g. — PRAY 391:29
Man is very far g. — PRAY 400:7
not dead—but g. before — ROG 407:8
Not lost but g. before — NORT 364:8
not the days that are g. — SOUT 514:8
Now thou art g. — MILT 343:5
of something that is g. — WORD 579:5
prepare not to be g. — SHAK 482:3
She's g. for ever — SHAK 456:8
song of a lad that is g. — STEV 523:4
they are g. — KEATS 289:23
they are g. forever — MANN 328:14
those Lords I had g. so far — MORE 357:12
welcomest when they are g. — SHAK 445:19
what haste I can to be g. — CROM 170:5
What's g. and what's past — SHAK 491:15
Wilt thou be g. — SHAK 483:13
yet now he is g. — THOM 546:21
gong: g. was bombilating — YEATS 584:13
that g.-tormented sea — CHES 147:2
gongs: g. groaning as the guns — COW 163:14
struck regularly, like g. — MILL 339:12
good: All g. things which exist — TICH 551:2
all my g. is but vain hope — GREL 236:14
any g. thing therefore — SHAK 478:17
apprehension of the g. — LOCK 315:21
are not a terror to g. — BIBLE 75:21
author and giver of all g. — PRAY 386:19
Be g., sweet maid — KING 296:19
Beneath the g. how far — GRAY 235:20
best g. man — ROCH 407:4
better to fight for the g. — TENN 540:19
Blake was no g. — BUTL 118:35
can be g. in the country — WILDE 573:22
captive g. attending captain — SHAK 494:5
choose the g. — BIBLE 58:3
common g. to all — SHAK 452:7
country for our country's g. — BARR 34:23
country was g. for General — WILS 574:15
course only too g. for him — AUST 22:30
creature not too bright or g. — WORD 581:8
crown thy g. with brotherhood — BATES 35:4

do a g. action by stealth — LAMB 308:2
Do all the g. you can — WESL 568:21
doeth g., no not one — PRAY 390:2
dreamed of g. shall exist — BROW 98:19
everything in the world is g. — DRYD 197:28
evil and on the g. — BIBLE 64:19
Evil be thou my G. — MILT 347:16
evil, that g. may come — BIBLE 74:37
for the public g. — COWP 164:28
General G. is the plea — BLAKE 86:7
Ghastly G. Taste — BETJ 44:15
God saw that it was g. — BIBLE 45:2
g. and faithful servant — BIBLE 68:2
g. and increase of the world — TENN 533:9
g. and to communicate forget — BIBLE 80:6
g. as thou art beautiful — TENN 534:19
g. both going and coming — FROST 219:1
G., but not religious-good — HARDY 241:26
g. deed in a naughty — SHAK 468:18
g. deed in all my life — SHAK 486:18
g. die early — DEFOE 173:2
g. die first — WORD 577:11
g. divine that follows — SHAK 465:20
g. ended happily — WILDE 573:3
g. enough to be a clergyman — JOHN 276:7
g. face is a letter — ADD 2:15
g. in canvasses and factions — BACON 25:40
g. income is of no avail — SMITH 510:12
g. Indian is a dead Indian — SHER 505:18
g. in everything — SHAK 424:32
g. is oft interred with — SHAK 450:17
g. man, and did good — HARDY 242:1
g. man is merciful — PRAY 397:14
g. man was ther of religioun — CHAU 141:32
G. men must not obey — EMER 207:32
g. name is rather to be — BIBLE 54:21
g. of one's country — FARQ 210:4
g. of subjects is the end — DEFOE 173:16
g. of the people is — CIC 151:19
g. opinion of a man who — TROL 553:3
g. people's wery scarce — DICK 183:4
g. people were clever — WORD 576:22
g. provoke to harm — SHAK 464:22
g. Shall come out of water — BROO 94:11
g. societies say — FORS 217:4
g. that I would I do not — BIBLE 75:5
g. they inculcate — SAKI 413:3
G. Thing — SELL 420:2
g. thing come out of Nazareth — BIBLE 71:31
G. things of day begin — SHAK 461:14
g. to be out on the road — MAS 334:8
G., to forgive — BROW 104:35
g. to them which hate you — BIBLE 69:21
g. unluckily — STOP 523:18
g. want power — SHEL 503:2
g. will toward men — BIBLE 69:11
G. without effort — BYRON 121:20
g. without pretence — POPE 378:9
g. words — SHAK 452:30
g. ye are and bad — TENN 534:17
great who are truly g. — CHAP 140:13
happiness makes them g. — LAND 309:12
have never had it so g. — MACM 325:18
heaviness foreruns the g. — SHAK 442:12
He was g. man — BIBLE 71:15
He who would do g. to another — BLAKE 86:7
He wos wery g. to me — DICK 176:8
highest g. — CIC 151:21
hold fast that which is g. — BIBLE 79:4
Hold thou the g. — TENN 536:23
if they have a g. thing — SHAK 441:14
in art the best is g. — GOET 230:8
I never saw any g. that — DRYD 195:20
in the common love of g. — TENN 537:15
is the enemy of the g. — VOLT 561:5
is what I call g. company — AUST 23:8
it is for the g. of all — PEDR 371:4
I will be g. — VICT 556:13
kept the g. wine until now — BIBLE 71:34
knowing g. and evil — BIBLE 45:15

knowledge of g. and evil   BIBLE 45:8
Know their own g.   DRYD 198:18
likes that little g.   BUTL 119:8
love, Fool, for the g.   PATM 370:1
luxury of doing g.   COWP 168:21
mankind does most g. or harm   BAG 29:18
man loves what he is g.   SHAD 420:22
Men are never so g. or so bad   MACK 325:11
motive is the public g.   STEE 518:1
must return g. for evil   VANB 555:4
never led to g. intention's   CERV 138:19
noble type of g.   LONG 317:7
nor it cannot come to g.   SHAK 430:1
nothing either g. or bad   SHAK 432:12
now to call a man a g. man   JOHN 279:12
only g. thing left to me   MUSS 359:3
out of g. still to find   MILT 345:6
overcome evil with g.   BIBLE 75:19
passions as well as all the g. tunes
                                  SHAW 497:22
perseverance in a g. cause   STER 519:19
policy of the g. neighbour   ROOS 407:21
rather than to seem g.   SALL 413:24
rewarded me evil for g.   PRAY 391:24
satisfieth my mouth with g.   PRAY 396:15
scraps are g. deeds past   SHAK 487:3
see g. days   PRAY 391:23
seek their subjects' g.   HERR 249:8
so g. for a Pobble's toes   LEAR 312:17
so much too g. for earth   JONS 284:2
So the g. has been well   ARIS 12:6
sovereign g. of human nature   BACON 27:31
success in life is to be a g. animal
                                  SPEN 514:25
that doeth g. is of God   BIBLE 81:8
that Thou art g.   POPE 381:12
that to the public g.   MILT 350:24
their luxury was doing g.   GARTH 221:20
them that call evil g.   BIBLE 57:26
Then it will be g. night   SHEL 500:17
Then the g. minute goes   BROW 105:29
There is so much g.   ANON 8:2
There's a g. time coming   MACK 325:9
They love the G.   BROO 94:24
they may see your g. works   BIBLE 64:9
they want but what is g.   CROM 169:23
things are of g. report   BIBLE 78:22
this woman was full of g.   BIBLE 73:36
those who go about doing g.   CREI 169:17
thyself to be obscurely g.   ADD 1:23
we know the G.   AUDEN 19:12
we see but means our g.   HERB 248:2
we trust that somehow g.   TENN 536:24
what g. came of it   SOUT 513:20
when shall all men's g.   TENN 533:23
When she was g.   LONG 317:22
while g. news baits   MILT 350:28
whoso hath this world's g.   BIBLE 81:4
will call no being g.   MILL 339:5
work for g. to them that love   BIBLE 75:11
world has still Much g.   HOUS 264:14
worst speaks something g.   HERB 247:12
yet don't look too g.   KIPL 299:22
you fair hath made you g.   SHAK 464:16
Goodbye: G. is not worth while HARDY 241:7
G., moralitee   HERB 246:10
G., proud world   EMER 206:20
kissed his sad Andromache g.   CORN 162:20
nod g. to La Rochefoucauld   ELIOT 202:2
goodliest: thou wert the g. person MAL 328:8
goodly: art fair; thou art g. SWIN 528:22
g. fellowship of the Prophets   PRAY 384:16
g. to look   BIBLE 50:7
I have a g. heritage   PRAY 390:6
goodman: g. is not at home   BIBLE 53:24
Good morrow: G. to the day so fair
                                  HERR 249:10
I bade g.   KEATS 289:5
now g. to our waking souls   DONNE 188:30

goodness: delusion that beauty is g.
                                  TOLS 551:11
fountain of all g.   PRAY 385:6
G. does not more certainly   LAND 309:12
'G. had nothing to do with   WEST 568:26
g. never fearful   SHAK 464:17
If g. lead him not   HERB 248:8
inclination to g. is imprinted   BACON 26:19
long-suffering, and of great g.   PRAY 396:16
Love, sweetness, g.   MILT 351:13
praise the Lord for his g.   PRAY 397:7
tell of days in g. spent   BYRON 125:22
there is no g. in the worm   SHAK 424:8
verily to see the g.   PRAY 391:9
Wisdom and g. to the vile   SHAK 455:11
Good-night: bid the world G. HERR 249:5
fair g.   SCOTT 417:26
gay g. and quickly turn   YEATS 585:6
G.; ensured release   HOUS 266:5
g., sweet ladies   SHAK 436:3
G., sweet prince   SHAK 437:28
say g. till it be morrow   SHAK 482:20
so, g.   DU M 199:6
Which gives the stern'st g.   SHAK 460:3
goods: desire other men's g. PRAY 388:18
g. and services can be   NOCK 363:18
G. may be most their own   CHAR 140:19
his g. are in peace   BIBLE 69:36
precious as the G. they sell   FITZ 213:14
Riches and G. of Christians   PRAY 400:12
worldly g. I thee endow   PRAY 389:5
good-sense: reasoning g.   CHES 145:25
Goodwins: G., I think they call SHAK 467:2
goose: every g. a swan   KING 297:5
g. honking amongst tuneful   VIRG 560:7
G., if I had you upon   SHAK 453:22
gott'st thou that g. look   SHAK 463:1
steals a g. from off a common   ANON 7:24
gooseberries: g. which makes my teeth
                                  FLEM 214:28
goost: g. ful blisfully is went CHAU 144:18
Gor'd: G. mine own thoughts   SHAK 495:3
gordian: She was a g. shape of dazzling
                                  KEATS 290:22
gore: chequered sides with g. THOM 549:19
Glorious the martyr's g.   SMART 509:4
hope it mayn't be human g.   DICK 175:25
gored: you tossed and g. several BOSW 90:15
gorge: my g. rises at it   SHAK 436:31
gorging: g. Jack and guzzling Jimmy
                                  THAC 545:32
Gorgon: Great G., Prince of darkness
                                  SPEN 516:1
Gorgonised: G. me from head to foot
                                  TENN 540:7
Gorgonzola: Been trotting out the G.
                                  KIPL 305:2
gormandising: Leave g.   SHAK 442:31
Gormed: I'm G.   DICK 177:21
gory: never shake Thy g. locks SHAK 461:20
Welcome to your g. bed   BURNS 114:34
gosling: such a g. to obey instinct
                                  SHAK 427:28
Gospel: devotee of the G. of Getting
                                  SHAW 498:8
Four for the G. makers   ANON 6:5
g. according to Jean Jacques   CARL 131:24
G. of Silence is now effectively MORL 357:24
G.'s pearls upon our coast   MARV 331:16
lineaments of G. books   ROYD 411:2
music of the G. leads us   FABER 209:14
preach the g. to every   BIBLE 69:2
Preferrest thou the g.   BUTL 119:20
truth of thy holy G.   PRAY 387:3
goss-hawk: well's me o' my gay g.
                                  BALL 30:20
gossip: babbling g. of the air SHAK 488:13
g. from all the nations   AUDEN 20:2
G. is a sort of smoke that   ELIOT 200:20
g. Report be an honest   SHAK 467:2

gost: lat thy g. thee lede   CHAU 144:22
Got: G. 'tween asleep and wake SHAK 453:9
I've g. a little list   GILB 226:24
Gothic: more than G. ignorance FIEL 211:26
gothiques: *temps barbares et g.* FRAN 217:27
Gott: *G. ist tot*   NIET 363:6
G. würfelt nicht   EINS 200:10
Nun danket alle G.   RINK 406:6
Gotte: *Sakramente einem sterbenden*
G.   HEINE 244:11
gotten: he g. himself the victory PRAY 396:7
Gottes: *der zweite Fehlgriff G.* NIET 363:4
Krieg ein Glied in G. Weltordnung
                                  MOLT 354:4
Gottesmühlen: *G. mahlen langsam*
                                  LOGAU 316:5
GOTTINGEN: -NIVERSITY OF G.
                                  CANN 130:5
gout: combined with g.   GILB 225:21
g. and glory seat me there   BROW 100:19
I say give them the g.   MONT 354:11
le bon sens et le bon g.   LA B 306:15
that old enemy the g.   HOOD 254:21
gouverne: *règne et le peuple se g.* THIE 546:5
gouvernement: *g. d'une famille que d'un*
                                  MONT 354:19
le g. qu'elle mérite   MAIS 327:8
Gouverner: *G., c'est choisir* LEVIS 314:5
govern: easy to g.   BROU 95:6
G. two millions of men   BURKE 109:27
He that would g. others   MASS 335:14
I will g. according   JAM 271:5
out and g. New South Wales   BELL 39:6
people g. themselves   THIE 546:5
stars above us, g.   SHAK 455:12
such should g.   FLET 215:18
To g. is to make choices   LEVIS 314:5
governance: charge or rule nor g.
                                  SURR 524:20
peaceably ordered by thy g.   PRAY 386:17
governaunce: gentil cok hadde in his
                                  CHAU 142:32
governed: England is still g. from
                                  SHAW 498:23
g. by a despot is an inverted   JOHN 277:29
g. by thy good Spirit   PRAY 385:25
has always been g.   CHES 146:6
kings g. their rude age   BAG 28:28
nation is not g.   BURKE 109:19
well g. as they ought to be   HOOK 255:19
wisdom the world is g.   OXEN 367:13
governing: right of g. was not property
                                  FOX 217:20
totally incapable of g.   CHES 146:6
government: administration of the g.
                                  SWIFT 526:4
all g. is evil   OSUL 365:22
any ask me what a free g.   BURKE 110:11
become the most corrupt g.   JEFF 272:12
best g. is that which   OSUL 365:22
called a representative g.   DISR 186:34
consequence of cabinet g.   BAG 28:23
country has the g. it deserves   MAIS 327:8
erected into a system of G.   GLAD 229:19
fainéant g. is not   TROL 553:4
fit for a nation whose g.   SMITH 509:12
forms of g. let fools contest   POPE 379:20
four pillars of g.   BACON 27:10
giving money to the G.   HERB 246:11
G. at Washington lives   GARF 221:9
G. and co-operation are   RUSK 412:10
G., even in its best state   PAINE 367:22
G. is a contrivance   BURKE 111:8
G. must have an authority   RUSK 412:6
g. of all the people   PARK 368:26
g. of men and morning newspapers
                                  PHIL 373:12
g. of the world I live   THOR 550:15
G. of the United States   WILS 574:23
g. shall be upon his shoulder   BIBLE 58:7

g. without a king BANC 32:13
having share in G. that is nothing
CHAR 140:19
highest form of g. SPEN 514:28
How can the G. be carried WELL 568:3
important thing for G. KEYN 295:17
increase of his g. BIBLE 58:7
indispensable duty of g. PAINE 367:23
is no art which one g. SMITH 509:15
is the worst form of G. CHUR 150:19
Is this the g. of Britain's SHAK 446:3
land of settled g. TENN 544:11
live under one form of g. JOHN 276:4
Monarchy is a strong g. BAG 28:27
No G. can be long secure DISR 185:35
only an experiment in g. INGE 270:7
party Parliamentary g. DISR 185:7
people's g. WEBS 566:10
rule nations by your g. VIRG 559:1
still loathe the present G. HERR 249:16
that g. of the people LINC 314:23
'That g. is best which THOR 549:31
there has been no G. DICK 176:21
Under a g. which imprisons THOR 550:1
under every form of g. JOHN 276:6
virtue of paper g. BURKE 109:13
want of g., is any new HOBB 251:20
Your sister is given to g. DICK 178:7
Governments: G. need to have both
shepherds VOLT 561:17
teach g. humanity PAINE 368:4
Governor: Can't afford them, G.
SHAW 498:13
G. was strong upon WILDE 572:12
lord, thy king, thy g. SHAK 484:15
T'other g. DICK 181:18
governors: Our supreme g. WALP 562:19
submit myself to all my g. PRAY 388:16
governs: g. the passions and resolutions
HUME 267:22
gowd: g. kames in their hair BALL 31:20
man's the g. for a' that BURNS 113:28
Gower: moral G. CHAU 144:20
gown: loose g. from her shoulders
WYATT 583:22
My g. of glory RAL 404:12
sail in amply billowing g. BELL 39:28
wearing a black g. CHES 145:11
who preaches in her g. HOOD 255:12
Goya: one small G. or a Daumier
AUDEN 19:16
Gracchos: *G. de seditione querentes*
JUV 287:13
grace: Angels and ministers of g.
SHAK 430:24
behold such heavenly g. SPEN 516:2
does it with a better g. SHAK 488:19
full of g. and truth BIBLE 71:27
God shed His g. on thee BATES 35:4
g. before Shakspeare LAMB 307:5
G. be unto you BIBLE 81:9
g. did much more abound BIBLE 74:42
G. is given of God CLOU 153:18
G. me no grace SHAK 479:1
G. of God is in Courtesy BELL 39:14
g. of God I am what I am BIBLE 76:19
g. of God there goes BRAD 91:9
g. which followed it was STER 519:13
grow old with a good g. STEE 518:2
Have g. and favour in them SHAK 476:25
heaven such g. did lend her SHAK 491:4
here's g. and a cod-piece SHAK 454:8
him was the peculiar g. BROW 100:36
I ascribe it to Thy g. WATTS 565:14
In her strong toil of g. SHAK 424:17
in his mercy lend her g. TENN 538:12
inward and spiritual g. PRAY 388:19
means of g. PRAY 386:2
meek and unaffected g. GOLD 230:24
me of your g. and favour SHAK 453:6

moments of glad g. YEATS 587:12
nothing with a better g. YOUNG 587:16
serves to g. my measure PRIOR 401:1
special g. preventing PRAY 386:10
speech be alway with g. BIBLE 78:28
sweet attractive g. MILT 347:22
sweet attractive kind of g. ROYD 411:2
Take heart of g. GILB 228:14
Terms like g., new birth ARN 16:18
their courtly foreign g. TENN 543:4
then g. us in the disgrace SHAK 456:14
throne of the heavenly g. PRAY 384:10
To g. this latter age with SHAK 440:16
unbought g. of life BURKE 111:10
Weel are ye wordy o' a g. BURNS 115:16
what a pretty skipping g. MARV 332:13
wi' patriarchal g. BURNS 113:9
with sory g. CHAU 143:7
womanly discovering g. DONNE 188:11
Ye are fallen from g. BIBLE 77:17
graceful: g. air and heavenly mug FLEM 215:4
Gracehoper: G. was always jigging ajog
JOYCE 286:13
grace-proud: g. faces BURNS 115:23
graces: do inherit heaven's g. SHAK 494:15
g. slighted COWP 168:5
half-mile g. BURNS 115:23
of deficiency in *the g.* JOHN 277:9
that the G. do not seem CHES 145:27
to sacrifice to the g. BURKE 111:26
Upon her eyelids many G. SPEN 516:11
gracilis: multa g. te puer in rosa HOR 259:15
gracious: favourable and g. unto Sion
PRAY 393:8
g. and courteous to strangers BACON 26:20
how g. the Lord is PRAY 391:21
Lord, for he is g. PRAY 399:2
Remembers me of all his g. SHAK 452:20
So hallow'd and so g. is SHAK 429:17
tasted that the Lord is g. BIBLE 80:22
these are g. drops SHAK 450:28
gradation: Not by the old g. SHAK 473:12
gradations: No cold g. of decay JOHN 279:1
gradient: g.'s against her AUDEN 20:1
gradual: Was the g. day SPEN 515:21
gradualness: inevitability of g. WEBB 566:7
Graeca: Vos exemplaria G. HOR 257:22
Graecia: G. capta ferum victorem HOR 259:2
Graeculus: G. esuriens JUV 287:16
Graft: G. in our hearts the love PRAY 386:19
grain: chaff well meant for g. TENN 536:2
faith as a g. of mustard BIBLE 67:1
goodly as the sun-flushed THOM 548:28
pamphleteer on guano and on g. TENN 542:20
say which g. will grow SHAK 458:11
to a g. of mustard seed BIBLE 66:20
World in a G. of Sand BLAKE 85:8
Grais: G. ingenium HOR 257:23
gramina: redeunt iam g. campis HOR 261:14
grammar: g., and nonsense, and learning
GOLD 231:22
Heedless of g. BARH 33:15
in erecting a g. school SHAK 446:14
posterity talking bad g. DISR 187:6
Why care for g. as long WARD 564:35
grammars: What sairs your g. BURNS 113:19
Grammatici: G. certant et adhuc sub
HOR 257:15
Grammaticus: G., rhetor JUV 287:16
granary: sitting careless on a g. floor
KEATS 293:6
grand: g. Perhaps BROW 99:4
g. style arises in poetry ARN 16:14
inscrutable and g. ARN 14:4
It is most g. to die MAS 334:1
Seul le silence est g. VIGNY 557:2
that g. old man NORT 364:7
grandam: ha' been a g. ere she died
SHAK 457:14
grandes: des choses g. et hautes MONT 354:12

grandest: g. moral attribute BARR 34:20
grandeur: charged with the g. of God
HOPK 256:12
g. of the dooms KEATS 289:1
g. that was Rome POE 375:7
Scotia's g. springs BURNS 113:10
with a baldness full of g. ARN 16:7
grandeurs: g. of his Babylonian heart
THOM 548:7
grandfather: having an ape for his g.
HUXL 269:1
he whipped my g. ADD 2:17
grand-jurymen: g. since before Noah
was SHAK 489:26
grandparents: worse than our g.' HOR 260:26
grands: g. n'ont point d'âme LA B 306:14
grandsire: Church your g. cut his throat
SWIFT 528:9
his g. cut in alabaster SHAK 465:11
grange: at the moated g. SHAK 464:18
Upon the lonely moated g. TENN 539:23
granites: g. which titanic wars had
OWEN 367:9
Grantchester: would I were In G.
BROO 94:20
granted: believe and take for g. BACON 27:18
Never take anything for g. DISR 184:28
granting: hold thee but by thy g.
SHAK 494:13
grants: no go the Government g. MACN 326:8
grape: burst Joy's g. KEATS 291:15
G. that can with Logic FITZ 213:2
g. who will the vine destroy SHAK 492:18
grapes: chalice of the g. of God TENN 536:7
fathers have eaten sour g. BIBLE 60:34
gleaning of the g. of Ephraim BIBLE 49:17
g. of the wine-press which MAC 322:6
g. of wrath are stored HOWE 266:19
it brought forth wild g. BIBLE 57:22
men gather g. of thorns BIBLE 65:9
sour g. and ashes ASHF 17:14
vine and g. in gold FLEC 214:17
grapeshot: whiff of g. CARL 131:22
Grapple: G. them to thy soul with
SHAK 430:19
grapples: g. with his evil star TENN 537:1
Grasp: G. it like a man of mettle HILL 251:2
G. not at much HERB 248:12
reach should exceed his g. BROW 98:24
grasped: bell-rope and g. it for a tinkle
BEER 37:14
Grasping: G. at Air YOUNG 588:8
shadow of an idea without g. BOWEN 91:1
Grasps: G. in the comer SHAK 487:5
grass: away suddenly like the g. PRAY 395:18
blue is the g. about POUND 382:5
child said *What is the g.* WHIT 570:18
cleaving the g., gazelles MOORE 355:23
days of man are but as g. PRAY 396:17
destroy a blade of g. BOTT 90:17
Down in the bells and g. HODG 252:4
eateth g. as an ox BIBLE 53:8
emerald twinkles in the g. TENN 540:8
forth g. for the cattle PRAY 396:20
From the heaps of couch g. HARDY 240:5
g. below CLARE 152:13
g. break into foam of flowers SWIN 530:18
g. grows on the weirs YEATS 584:22
g. is singing ELIOT 205:10
g. returns to the fields HOR 261:14
g. withereth BIBLE 59:6
g. withereth BIBLE 80:21
green g. growing over me BALL 32:11
happy as the g. was green THOM 547:1
I am the g. SAND 413:27
I become paler than g. SAPP 414:6
I fall on g. MARV 332:3
isn't g. to graze a cow BETJ 44:4
kissed the lovely g. BROO 94:15
leaf of g. is no less than WHIT 570:21

One of the g.   DRYD 198:6
than not be among the g.   KEATS 294:6
There sunk the g.   BYRON 120:29
time is the g. innovator   BACON 26:28
you the g. of all things   SHAW 496:30
Great-heart: One G.   BUNY 107:31
Great-hearted: G. gentlemen   BROW 99:26
greatly: it's g. to his credit   GILB 228:9
must do so who would g. win   BYRON 125:6
greatness: farewell, to all my g. SHAK 447:9
far-off touch Of g.   TENN 534:27
G. knows itself   SHAK 440:13
g. of the *British* Nation   ADD 2:19
g. of the world in tears   YEATS 586:22
G., with private men   MASS 335:17
having intended g. for men   ELIOT 201:10
is the nature of all g.   BURKE 109:3
seen the moment of my g.   ELIOT 203:23
some have g. thrust upon   SHAK 489:14
Than g. going off   SHAK 423:6
greaves: flamed upon the brazen g.
                                       TENN 538:8
Grecian: merry G. coaster   ARN 14:21
Greece: constitutions of later G. BAG 28:28
Fair G.   BYRON 120:13
G. a tear   BYRON 123:1
G., could we but approach   YEATS 587:14
G. is fallen and Troy town   COL 155:3
G., once overcome   HOR 259:2
I dream'd that G. might   BYRON 122:33
insolent G. or haughty   JONS 284:22
isles of G.   BYRON 122:32
plague of G. upon thee   SHAK 486:28
To the glory that was G.   POE 375:7
Greedy: G. for the property   SALL 413:22
I am g.   PUNCH 402:29
not g. of filthy lucre   BIBLE 79:12
Greek: 'Because he *was* a G.'   SHEL 505:14
brown G. manuscripts   BROW 99:13
can say a word against G.   SHAW 497:9
carve in Latin or in G.   WALL 562:7
foolish to talk of knowing G.   WOOLF 576:17
Germans in G.   PORS 381:27
G. as a treat   CHUR 150:23
G. can do everything   JUV 287:16
G. was free from rhyme's   JONS 285:6
is not G. in its origin   MAINE 327:7
it was G. to me   SHAK 448:23
mentioned as reading G.   AUST 22:23
me whisky's name in G.   BURNS 112:34
natural, and G.   BYRON 122:23
schoolmasters even today read G.
                                       YEATS 587:13
small Latin, and less G.   JONS 284:21
That questioned him in G.   CARR 133:12
there is neither G. nor Jew   BIBLE 78:26
understand G. and Latin   DRYD 198:14
upon you the study of G.   GAIS 220:25
when his wife talks G.   JOHN 280:18
will be paid at the G.   AUG 22:6
your G. exemplars by night   HOR 257:22
Greeks: G. a blush   BYRON 123:1
G., and to the Barbarians   BIBLE 74:30
G. or the Romans   DISR 185:27
G. who take the beating   HOR 258:12
I fear the G. even when   VIRG 558:1
Let *G.* be *Greeks*   BRAD 91:14
make way, G.   PROP 401:17
To the G. the Muse gave   HOR 257:23
When G. joined Greeks   LEE 313:12
green: actual life springs ever g. GOET 230:3
blue or the shore-sea g.   FLEC 214:17
children are heard on the g.   BLAKE 88:3
Colourless g. ideas   CHOM 148:15
dry smooth-shaven g.   MILT 342:3
England's g. and pleasant   BLAKE 86:12
England's g. & pleasant Land   BLAKE 86:16
feed me in a g. pasture   PRAY 390:21
force that through the g. fuse   THOM 547:3
g. arms round the bosom   SHEL 503:17

g. banks of Shannon   CAMP 128:20
g. buds they were swellin'   BALL 30:10
g. days in forests   STEV 522:29
G. grow the rushes   ANON 6:5
G. grow the rashes   BURNS 114:1
g. herb for the service   PRAY 396:20
G. I love you green   GARC 221:7
g. lap of the new come   SHAK 480:11
g. mantle of the standing   SHAK 454:23
G. Things upon the Earth   PRAY 384:24
g. thought in a green shade   MARV 332:5
hae laid him on the g.   BALL 30:15
In the morning it is g.   PRAY 395:18
keeps his own wounds g.   BACON 27:9
Learn of the g. world   POUND 382:13
Like golden lamps in a g.   MARV 331:16
Making the g. one red   SHAK 460:13
on a simple village g.   TENN 537:1
out of the hopeful g. stuff   WHIT 570:18
summer's g. all girded   SHAK 492:26
these things in a g. tree   BIBLE 71:10
Time held me g. and dying   THOM 547:2
to look so g. and pale   SHAK 459:8
tunnel of g. gloom   BROO 94:17
turtle g. and glutinous   BROW 103:16
wearin' o' the G.   ANON 6:6
When I was g. in judgment   SHAK 421:33
when the trees were g.   CLARE 152:4
When wheat is g.   SHAK 469:21
Where the g. swell is   HOPK 256:17
green-coat: shoot the sleepy, g.   HOFF 252:21
greenery-yallery: g., Grosvenor Galley
                                       GILB 227:27
greenest: Those eyes the g. of things
                                       SWIN 529:16
green-ey'd: g. monster which doth mock
                                       SHAK 475:17
greenhouse: loves a garden loves a g.
                                       COWP 167:9
greenly: We have done but g.   SHAK 436:5
greenness: Could have recovered g.
                                       HERB 247:21
greens: plain water and raw g.   AUDEN 21:6
Greensleeves: G. was all my joy   ANON 5:11
greensward: beech-tree single on the
g.   MER 337:1
greenwood: I must to the g. go   BALL 31:10
Under the g. tree   SHAK 425:14
Greet: G. the unseen with a cheer
                                       BROW 98:33
How should I g. thee   BYRON 126:14
scarely g. me with that   SHAK 493:14
Greise: Ward mancher Kopf zum G.
                                       MULL 359:1
grenadier: single Pomeranian g.   BISM 84:22
Grenadiers: talk of Pensions and G.
                                       STER 520:1
grene: In a harbour g. aslepe   WEVER 569:7
Grenville: Azores Sir Richard G. lay
                                       TENN 542:21
Greta: G. woods are green   SCOTT 417:30
greuaunce: Comparisouns doon offte
gret g.   LYDG 321:7
grew: distance g. the Iceberg too
                                       HARDY 239:6
g. a gallows and did bear   KYD 306:7
So we g. together   SHAK 470:22
Grex: G. rather than sex   FROST 219:14
grey: calls the glory from the g. BROW 104:6
eye 'tis an old Man g.   BLAKE 86:14
head grown g. in vain   SHEL 499:21
lend me your g. mare   BALL 32:12
Too lovely to be g.   ARN 13:4
wither'd cheek and tresses g.   SCOTT 416:8
world has grown g. from   SWIN 530:5
grey-grown: g. speechless Christ   SWIN 529:3
greyhound: g., mongrel grim   SHAK 455:1
This fawning g. then did   SHAK 438:20
greyhounds: stand like g. in the slips
                                       SHAK 444:3

grief: acquainted with g.   BIBLE 59:21
After long g. and pain   TENN 540:13
are quickened so with g.   GRAV 234:11
bravery of his g. did put   SHAK 437:13
Can I see another's g.   BLAKE 88:8
every one can master a g.   SHAK 472:24
From perfect g. there need   ROSS 410:9
full of g. as age   SHAK 454:1
great As is my g.   SHAK 479:14
Green pleasure or grey g.   SWIN 530:21
G. fills the room up   SHAK 452:20
g. flieth to it   BACON 26:2
G. for awhile is blind   SHEL 502:21
G. for thy dead in silence   BROW 98:8
G. is a species of idleness   JOHN 281:26
G. is itself a med'cine   COWP 164:25
g. itself be mortal   SHEL 499:12
G. never mended no broken   DICK 183:4
g. returns with the revolving   SHEL 499:10
g. that does not speak   SHAK 462:16
g. too much to be told   VIRG 557:20
G. with a glass that ran   SWIN 528:20
hell A. and avenging Cares   VIRG 558:21
hopeless g. is passionless   BROW 98:7
into the bottom of my g.   SHAK 483:18
it was pain and g. to me   PRAY 391:30
Killing care and g.   SHAK 447:3
my faint heart with g.   SHEL 501:15
My particular g.   SHAK 473:23
only time for g.   HOOD 255:9
open his g.   PRAY 387:17
Patch g. with proverbs   SHAK 473:6
Pitched past pitch of g.   HOPK 256:19
plague of sighing and g.   SHAK 439:11
Should be past g.   SHAK 491:15
shows of g.   SHAK 429:25
Silence augmenteth g.   GREV 236:17
silent manliness of g.   GOLD 231:6
Smiling at g.   SHAK 489:7
son of g. at cricket   HOUS 262:22
still sad when others' g.   BYRON 124:35
Thine be the g.   AYT 24:4
thirsty g. in wine we steep   LOV 318:17
Thus g. still treads upon   CONG 160:27
thy mother's g.   BRET 92:6
time remembered is g. forgotten   SWIN 528:17
'tis unmanly g.   SHAK 429:26
To cure this deadly g.   SHAK 462:17
to thee thy mother's g.   BLAKE 85:13
was a journeyman to g.   SHAK 478:15
Was there g. once   NICH 362:24
Which in false g. hiding   SPEN 516:5
within their breasts the g.   AYT 24:5
griefs: all g. which bow   ARN 14:24
cutteth g. in halves   BACON 26:16
Drinking my g.   SHAK 479:22
ere England's g. began   GOLD 230:18
Great g., I see   SHAK 428:19
g. that harrass the distress'd   JOHN 282:23
I am sick of many g.   SHAK 451:25
lion g. loped from   AUDEN 20:19
not my g.   SHAK 479:23
so are their g. and fears   BACON 27:2
solitary g.   JOHN 273:21
Surely he hath borne our g.   BIBLE 59:21
to ease them of their g.   SHAK 486:13
which had soothed the g.   MAC 324:18
grievance: hundred with a g.   LOUI 318:9
grieve: g. his heart   SHAK 462:9
g. or triumph   GOET 230:7
made to g. on account   HARDY 241:18
make the judicious g.   SHAK 433:17
Nor joy nor g. too much   DRYD 197:10
Poor Pope will g. a month   SWIFT 527:23
than a nation g.   DRYD 194:11
Then can I g. at grievances   SHAK 493:7
thou leavest me to g.   SHEL 505:6
what could it g.   KEATS 292:10
grieved: g. with this generation   PRAY 396:4

grieves: aught inanimate e'er g. BYRON 120:26
grieving: are you g. HOPK 256:25
grievous: g. crab-tree cudgel BUNY 107:22
  remembrance of them is g. PRAY 387:19
  through my most g. fault MASS 334:15
Griffith: honest chronicler as G. SHAK 447:23
Grill: Let Grill be G. SPEN 516:14
grim: g. grew his countenance BALL 30:18
  g. shape Towered up WORD 580:12
  look g. as hell SHAK 476:18
  Thou hast a g. appearance SHAK 427:26
grimness: what an element of g. ARN 15:27
grin: cheerfully he seems to g. CARR 133:18
  ending with the g. CARR 133:27
  opens on her like a g. ELIOT 204:9
  Relax'd into a universal g. COWP 167:15
  wears one universal g. FIEL 211:33
  woodland g. PAIN 367:19
grind: did g. in the prison house BIBLE 49:27
  g. the faces of the poor BIBLE 57:20
  Laws g. the poor GOLD 231:29
  life is one demd horrid g. DICK 180:22
  mills of God g. slowly LOGAU 316:5
Grinder: G., who serenely grindest CALV 127:23
grinders: divided into incisors and g. BAG 29:13
  g. cease because they are BIBLE 56:11
grinning: g. honour as Sir Walter SHAK 440:21
  to mock your own g. SHAK 436:31
Grishkin: G. is nice ELIOT 205:14
Grisilde: G. is deed CHAU 142:9
gristle: g. and not yet hardened BURKE 109:17
grizzled: His beard was g. SHAK 430:13
groan: Condemn'd alike to g. GRAY 235:13
  depths with bubbling g. BYRON 121:24
  g. of the martyr's woe BLAKE 86:6
  hear each other g. KEATS 291:18
  He gave a g. WORD 580:1
groan'd: My mother g. BLAKE 87:23
groaneth: creation g. and travaileth BIBLE 75:10
groaning: g. for burial SHAK 450:12
  I am weary of my g. PRAY 389:26
groans: sovereign of sighs and g. SHAK 456:26
  with everlasting g. MILT 346:11
Grocer: God made the wicked G. CHES 147:18
Gromboolian: Over the great G. plain LEAR 312:2
groom: by his dogs and by his g. COWP 166:6
  that death is but a g. DONNE 189:30
grooms: gild the faces of the g. SHAK 460:11
grooves: In predestinate g. HARE 242:8
  ringing g. of change TENN 539:8
gros: g. escadrons contre les BUSS 117:7
gross: g. as a mountain SHAK 439:4
  lust is g. and brief PETR 373:5
  Not g. to sink SHAK 495:19
  things rank and g. in nature SHAK 429:28
grossen: Volkes...einer g. Lüge HITL 251:9
grossness: Hiding the g. with fair SHAK 467:10
  touch of g. in our race ARN 15:26
Grosvenor Galley: greenery-yallery, G. GILB 227:27
grotesque: At so g. a blunder BENT 41:10
  from the g. to the horrible DOYLE 192:25
  G. Art in English Poetry BAG 29:20
ground: acre of barren g. SHAK 484:22
  commit his body to the g. PRAY 389:13
  crieth unto me from the g. BIBLE 45:26
  fallen unto me in a fair g. PRAY 390:6
  feet of English g. HAR 242:11
  five miles of fertile g. COL 156:26
  found six feet of g. HOUS 265:6
  gain a little patch of g. SHAK 435:28

g. flew up and hit me WARD 564:28
g., the books, the academes SHAK 457:6
  having so little g. SCOTT 419:2
  He swalloweth the g. with BIBLE 53:7
  In a fair g. KIPL 303:16
  In his own g. POPE 380:23
  Israelites passed over on dry g. BIBLE 49:1
  let us sit upon the g. SHAK 479:11
  lose to-morrow the g. won ARN 14:17
  man of the dust of the g. BIBLE 45:7
  other fell into good g. BIBLE 66:16
  seek the g. of my heart PRAY 399:8
  stirrup and the g. CAMD 128:5
  thou standest is holy g. BIBLE 47:4
  tread on classic g. ADD 2:4
  upon the g. I se thee stare CHAU 143:13
  water spilt on the g. BIBLE 50:23
  When every rood of g. maintain'd GOLD 230:18
  will hardly water the g. BACON 26:33
grounde: that g. is of alle LANG 309:27
grove: good g. of chimneys for me MORR 358:4
  olive g. of Academe MILT 350:8
grovelled: he met a great man he g. THAC 545:23
groves: g. of their academy BURKE 111:12
  truth in the g. of Academe HOR 259:4
grow: g. every tree that is pleasant BIBLE 45:8
  g. for ever and for ever TENN 542:1
  hand wrought to make it g. FITZ 212:21
  I g. in worth TENN 544:10
  resolved to g. fat DRYD 196:36
  shelter to g. ripe ARN 13:10
  that ye may g. thereby BIBLE 80:22
grow'd: short laugh...'I 'spect I g. STOWE 524:1
growing: g., Jock, when ye're sleeping SCOTT 418:20
  It is not g. like a tree JONS 285:8
growl: sit and g. JOHN 279:3
grown: I am g. to man's estate STEV 522:19
  When we are g. and take KIPL 298:10
grown-up: hear the g. people's feet STEV 522:16
grows: Nothing g. in our garden THOM 547:12
growth: children of a larger g. DRYD 195:15
  g. of the fore-brain AUDEN 19:10
  'G. the only evidence NEWM 361:18
  mushroom of a night's g. DONNE 190:5
  quick a g. to meet decay HERR 249:28
grub: My gravender, or g. ST L 412:27
  old ones, g. SHAW 496:6
grudge: feed fat the ancient g. SHAK 465:29
gruel: Make the g. thick and slab SHAK 462:4
grumble: nothing whatever to g. GILB 228:29
  we g. a little now GOLD 232:30
Grundy: more of Mrs G. LOCK 315:20
  What will Mrs G. think MORT 358:18
gruntled: he was far from being g. WOD 575:19
guano: pamphleteer on g. and on grain TENN 542:20
guarantee: g. success in war CHUR 151:1
guard: Be on your g. ANON 9:18
  calls not Thee to g. KIPL 302:10
  g. a title that was rich SHAK 452:25
  hate of those ye g. KIPL 304:6
  marrying one of the g. MILNE 340:4
  none but Americans on g. WASH 565:5
  They're changing g. MILNE 340:4
  use its g. staying awake BIBLE 83:12
guarda: g., e passa DANTE 171:4
guarded: ever g. is scarcely worth GOLD 232:35
guardian: constitutional g. GILB 226:2
Guards: G. die but do not surrender CAMB 128:2
  Lord g. the city BIBLE 83:12
  to guard the g. JUV 287:22

Up G. and at them again WELL 568:9
guardsman: g.'s cut and thrust HUXL 269:3
gude: cog o' g. swats BURNS 113:4
  There's a g. time coming SCOTT 418:31
gudeman: When our g.'s awa' ANON 8:3
gude-willie: We'll tak' a right g. waught BURNS 112:31
gudgeon: fool g., this opinion SHAK 465:13
guenille: ma g. m'est chère MOL 353:11
guerdon: fair g. when we hope MILT 343:8
guerra: en g. con mis entrañas MACH 325:7
guerre: g. est l'industrie nationale MIR 352:19
  la g. NAP 359:10
  mais ce n'est pas la g. BOSQ 90:12
guess: first we met we did not g. BRID 92:22
  'G. now who holds thee BROW 98:9
guessing: 'g. what was at the other WELL 567:20
guest: at the strange g.'s hand SWIN 529:18
  awaited the expected g. ELIOT 205:1
  away the worthy bidden g. MILT 343:12
  built by the g. DONNE 190:1
  receive an honoured g. AUDEN 19:7
  remembrance of a g. that tarrieth BIBLE 62:18
  shakes his parting g. SHAK 487:1
  some poor nigh-related g. COL 157:17
  Soul, the body's g. RAL 404:10
  speed the going g. POPE 380:6
  your g. tomorrow night' ANON 8:24
guests: hosts and g. BEER 37:17
  I would my g. should praise HAR 242:9
  Unbidden g. SHAK 445:19
guid: g. to be merry and wise BURNS 114:5
guide: being our ruler and g. PRAY 386:16
  great g. of human life HUME 267:14
  g. our feet into the way BIBLE 69:7
  g., philosopher, and friend POPE 380:4
  Have God to be thy g. BUNY 107:32
  Who art a light to g. WORD 579:15
guided: man to be g. by the wiser CARL 131:16
Guides: G. cannot master the subtleties TWAIN 554:12
  Ye blind g. BIBLE 67:24
guiding-star: he was the g. of a whole MOTL 358:20
Guildenstern: That Rosencrantz and G. SHAK 437:29
guile: grief hiding his harmful g. SPEN 516:5
  in whom is no g. BIBLE 71:32
  packed with g. BROO 94:23
  that they speak no g. PRAY 391:23
  unfathom'd gulfs of g. BYRON 125:4
  whose spirit there is no g. PRAY 391:16
guilt: art can wash her g. GOLD 231:31
  blood with g. is bought SHEL 503:1
  Calls g., in first confusion CLOU 153:23
  closely connected with g. CONN 161:14
  G. in his heart CHUR 149:5
  g. of dissimulation SCOTT 418:13
  it must seem their g. SHAK 460:11
  no g. to make you turn HOR 258:9
  pens dwell on g. and misery AUST 22:29
  sign of g., or of ill breeding CONG 160:34
  unfortunate circumstance of g. STEV 522:11
  war, without its g. SOM 513:2
  without industry is g. RUSK 411:9
  yet free from g. or pain SHEL 503:12
Guiltier: G. than him they try SHAK 463:16
guiltless: g. that taketh his name BIBLE 47:24
  Some Cromwell g. of his GRAY 234:23
guilts: Close pent-up g. SHAK 454:10
guilty: g., but to me AUDEN 19:17
  g. of our own disasters SHAK 453:11
  g. of such a ballad some SHAK 456:18
  g. party is acquitted PUBL 402:5
  g. persons escape than BLAC 85:6
  In g. splendour COWP 166:37
  Let no g. man escape GRANT 234:3
  like a g. thing suprised WORD 579:10

Lose all their g. stains | COWP 165:24
Make mad the g. | SHAK 433:1
no g. man is acquitted | JUV 288:5
strength of g. kings | ARN 13:22
Suspicion always haunts the g. | SHAK 446:23
That g. creatures sitting | SHAK 433:5
then it started like a g. | SHAK 429:16
guinea: fire somewhat like a g. | BLAKE 88:29
force of the g. you have | RUSK 412:8
jingling of the g. | TENN 538:23
rank is but the g.'s stamp | BURNS 113:28
sixpences you know to one g. | JOHN 280:14
within the compass of a g. | IRV 270:23
guinea-pig: lift a g. up by the tail | LOCK 315:18
guineas: crowns and pounds and g. | HOUS 262:20
Guinness: drink G. from a thick mug | PINT 373:18
G., Allsopp, Bass | CALV 127:12
guitar: sang to a small g. | LEAR 312:11
gulf: great g. fixed | BIBLE 70:29
gulfs: g. will wash us down | TENN 544:3
steep-down g. of liquid fire | SHAK 477:21
gull: g.'s way and the whale's | MAS 334:6
most notorious geck and g. | SHAK 490:24
gulls: Forgot the cry of g. | ELIOT 205:6
g. him with intelligence | SHAK 494:12
gulp: he drains his at one g. | BROW 105:6
gum: thick amber and plum-tree g. | SHAK 432:8
gums: wept odorous g. and balm | MILT 347:19
gun: bare-legg'd beggarly son of a g. | CALV 127:17
escape from rope and g. | GAY 222:30
ever lost an English g. | TENN 541:9
got The Maxim G. | BELL 40:1
out of the barrel of a g. | MAO 328:19
through a door with a g. | CHAN 139:21
Gunga Din: better man than I am, G. | KIPL 299:20
Gunpowder: G., Printing | CARL 131:3
printing, g. and the magnet | BACON 28:9
reason why g. treason | ANON 7:10
such as g. and sealing-wax | CARR 136:4
till the g. ran out | FOOTE 216:7
guns: don't get away from the g. | KIPL 302:16
gongs groaning as the g. | CHES 147:2
G. aren't lawful | PARK 368:18
G. will make us powerful | GOER 229:25
monstrous anger of the g. | OWEN 367:2
these vile g. | SHAK 438:16
when the g. begin to shoot | KIPL 303:23
gurgite: Apparent rari nantes in g. | VIRG 557:14
gurgle: g. he gave | GILB 227:17
gurly: g. grew the sea | BALL 30:18
gusts: g. shake the door | ARN 13:7
gusty: carpets rose along the g. | KEATS 289:22
Gute: ist das G. zu geniessen | GOET 230:8
guts: are modified in the g. | AUDEN 19:4
g. should hale souls | SHAK 472:15
his g. in his head | SHAK 486:29
I'll lug the g. into | SHAK 435:22
strangled in the g. of priests | MESL 338:9
Gutta: G. cavat lapidem | LAT 310:20
G. cavat lapidem | OVID 366:27
gutter: We are all in the g. | WILDE 573:11
Guy: Ah! County G. | SCOTT 418:25
guzzling: was gorging Jack and g. | THAC 545:32
gym: flare was up in the g. | BETJ 44:2
gypsy: to the vagrant g. life | MAS 334:6
you old g. man | HODG 252:9
gyre: g. and gimble in the wabe | CARR 134:28
gyves: With g. upon his wrist | HOOD 254:12
habendi: innatus apes amor urget in. | VIRG 560:19
haberdasher: brother-in-law is h. to Mr Spurgeon | BUTL 119:20

habile: h. pour connaître tout | LA R 310:14
habileté: de savoir cacher son h. | LA R 310:13
habit: h. of living indisposeth | BROW 97:13
h. rules the unreflecting | WORD 581:17
H. with him was all | COWP 168:7
How use doth breed a h. | SHAK 491:5
I shook the h. off | WORD 580:25
Sow a h. | READE 405:4
habita: Tecum h. | PERS 372:29
Habitarunt: H. di quoque silvas | VIRG 559:16
habitation: even God in his holy h. | PRAY 394:7
h. among the tents of Kedar | PRAY 398:7
Let their h. be void | PRAY 394:13
local h. and a name | SHAK 471:11
of the air have their h. | PRAY 396:19
shall be an h. of dragons | BIBLE 58:31
habitations: you into everlasting h. | BIBLE 70:26
habiter: maison est une machine à h. | LE C 313:5
habits: Of h. devil | SHAK 435:18
Small h., well pursued | MORE 357:8
Their h. from the Bear | BELL 38:26
habitual: live beneath your more h. | WORD 579:13
hack: Do not h. me as you did | MONM 354:5
had: all knew you h. it in you | PARK 368:22
h. my world as in my tyme | CHAU 143:19
haedis: Et ab h. me sequestra | CEL 138:8
haggard: If I do prove her h. | SHAK 475:21
Whene'er with h. eyes I view | CANN 130:5
Haggards: H. Ride no more | STEP 518:24
hag-ridden: h. magic and enchanted | KEYN 295:19
hags: midnight h. | SHAK 462:5
haie: soldats faisaient la h. | ELIOT 202:8
hail: Fire and h. | PRAY 399:22
flail of the lashing h. | SHEL 500:4
flies no sharp and quick h. | HOPK 256:17
h., and farewell evermore | CAT 137:15
H. Caesar | ANON 10:7
H., fellow, well met | SWIFT 527:30
H., glorious edifice | SMITH 510:6
H. holy queen | ANON 10:19
H. Mary | ANON 10:8
H., thou art highly favoured | BIBLE 69:4
H. to the Chief who | SCOTT 416:4
H. to thee, blithe Spirit | SHEL 504:15
indomitable heroes, h. | LAND 308:18
Where falls not h. | TENN 535:27
Hails: H. me so solemnly to yonder | JONS 285:9
hailstones: h., and coals of fire | PRAY 390:9
hair: All her bright golden h. | WILDE 572:18
All her h. | BROW 103:29
beautiful uncut h. of graves | WHIT 570:18
Berenice's ever-burning h. | CHAP 140:4
Blind with thine h. the eyes | SHEL 505:3
bright h. about the bone | DONNE 190:5
colour of his h. | HOUS 266:8
down and combed their h. | HOUS 265:3
do you pin up your h. with | CONG 160:37
draws us with a single h. | POPE 381:1
dressing your golden h. | HOR 259:15
drew me backward by the h. | BROW 98:9
excellent head of h. | SHAK 487:26
from his horrid h. | MILT 346:26
gowd kames in their h. | BALL 31:20
h. as free | JONS 283:27
h. did bristle upon his | SCOTT 416:15
h. has become very white | CARR 133:22
h. is as a flock of goats | BIBLE 56:26
h. is mussed on her forehead | POUND 382:15
h. of a woman can draw | HOW 266:21
h. of his head like | BIBLE 61:8
h. of my flesh stood up | BIBLE 52:15
h. soft-lifted by the winnowing | KEATS 293:6
h. to stand an end | SHAK 431:5
has braided her yellow h. | BALL 32:1

heart one strangling golden h. | ROSS 410:2
her h., her hair | MEW 338:12
Her h. that lay along her | ROSS 409:15
Her h. was long | KEATS 290:16
her h. was so charmingly | KING 297:4
his next commodity of h. | SHAK 489:18
image doth unfix my h. | SHAK 458:20
I must sugar my h. | CARR 134:16
lie tangled in her h. | LOV 318:15
Like the bright h. uplifted | SHEL 502:9
like the h. we breathe | SURT 525:4
long black h. out tight | ELIOT 205:9
long h., it is a glory | BIBLE 76:12
man have long h. | BIBLE 76:12
morrow to mine own torn h. | HERR 249:10
mother bids me bind my h. | HUNT 268:15
My h. is grey | BYRON 125:16
my h. is sleek | ANON 7:2
never brush their h. | BELL 38:26
not your yellow h. | YEATS 585:5
of thy amber-dropping h. | MILT 341:20
only talks about her h. | THOM 549:3
raiment of camel's h. | BIBLE 63:37
ruddy limbs and flaming h. | BLAKE 86:20
Shall I part my h. behind | ELIOT 203:25
She smoothes her h. | ELIOT 205:3
stars in her h. were seven | ROSS 409:14
strung with his h. | SHAK 457:8
That subtle wreath of h. | DONNE 188:27
to her with a single h. | DRYD 198:21
touches a h. of yon gray head | WHIT 571:18
wherefore should I kame my h. | BALL 32:10
with his long essenced h. | MAC 322:7
with long dishevell'd h. | SHAK 495:19
with such h. | BROW 105:26
With vine leaves in his h. | IBSEN 269:23
would make your h. curl | GILB 228:34
hairless: white and h. as an egg | HERR 249:15
hairs: elf-locks in foul sluttish h. | SHAK 481:28
gray h. with sorrow | BIBLE 46:35
h. of your head are all | BIBLE 65:36
head and his h. were white | BIBLE 81:14
If h. be wires | SHAK 495:8
Those set our h. | DONNE 188:15
hairy: Esau my brother is a h. | BIBLE 46:15
marvellous h. about the face | SHAK 471:2
haïssable: Le moi est h. | PASC 369:12
halcyon: h. days | SHAK 445:18
hale: guts should h. souls | SHAK 472:15
I should prefer mild h. | SURT 525:20
You are h. | SOUT 514:7
half: ae h. of the warld thinks | SCOTT 418:28
h. a library to make one | JOHN 276:24
h. as good as justified | BUTL 118:11
H. as sober as a judge | LAMB 308:1
H. dead and half alive | BETJ 42:10
h. in love with easeful | KEATS 291:22
h. is greater than | HES 250:19
h. Latin and half Greek | SCOTT 415:16
h. of my own life | HOR 259:11
H. our days we pass | BROW 95:24
H. our days we pass | BROW 96:1
h. slave and half free | LINC 314:14
h. some sturdy strumpet | HARDY 240:7
h. that's got my keys | GRAH 233:12
h. the power to do me harm | SHAK 477:14
h. to fall | POPE 379:13
H. to forget the wandering | FLEC 214:5
h. was not told me | BIBLE 50:33
have been finished in h. | WOD 575:21
of myself and dearer h. | MILT 348:15
One h. of the world cannot | AUST 22:8
overcome but h. his foe | MILT 345:25
temple h. as old as Time | ROG 407:9
half-a-dozen: h. of the other | MARR 331:7
half-and-half: No h. affair | GILB 225:22
half-believers: h. in our casual creeds | ARN 14:17
half-brother: thou h. of the world | BAIL 29:22

half-child: Half-devil and h.　KIPL 304:6
Half-devil: H. and half-child　KIPL 304:6
half-human: this h. visitor to our
　　KEYN 295:19
half-knowledge: remaining content with
　h.　KEATS 293:19
half-light: night and light and the h.
　　YEATS 585:9
Half-past: H. one, The street-lamp
　　ELIOT 204:9
half-pence: like one another as h.
　　SHAK 426:14
half-shut: things with his h. eyes　POPE 381:7
half-way: ill-luck that they run h.　JERR 273:8
hall: decent h. of death　CHES 147:12
　equality in the servants' h.　BARR 34:7
　H. or Terrace or lofty　LEAR 312:3
　Meet her in the h.　COW 164:5
　Mr H.'s nay was nay　BENT 41:4
　than the pram in the h.　CONN 161:12
　vasty h. of death　ARN 14:6
　window'd niche of that high h.
　　BYRON 120:23
hallow'd: So h. and so gracious is
　　SHAK 429:17
Hallowed: H. be thy name　BIBLE 64:24
halls: Amphitrite's destined h.　SHEL 501:23
　dwelt in marble h.　BUNN 107:9
　In h., in gay attire　SCOTT 416:17
　In our h. is hung　WORD 582:3
　through those roofless h.　SHEL 502:7
halo: What, after all, Is a h.　FRY 219:27
halt: h., and the blind　BIBLE 70:12
　H. by the headstone naming　HOUS 266:2
　h. ye between two opinions　BIBLE 51:8
halves: twin h. of one august event
　　HARDY 239:6
ham: case when there's h.　DICK 181:8
　Shem, H., and Japheth　BIBLE 45:32
hambre: manjar que quita la h.　CERV 138:20
　salsa del mundo es el h.　CERV 138:13
hame: It's hame and it's h.　CUNN 170:14
　thou must bring her h.　BALL 31:17
Hamelin: H. Town's in Brunswick
　　BROW 103:14
Hamlet: announced the tragedy of H.
　　SCOTT 418:34
　I am not Prince H.　ELIOT 203:24
　I'll call thee H.　SHAK 430:24
　king drinks to H.　SHAK 437:17
　Lord H. is a prince　SHAK 432:1
　of H. most of all　HENL 245:12
　rude forefathers of the h.　GRAY 234:20
　where the kneeling h. drains　TENN 536:7
hamlets: In h., dances on the green
　　SCOTT 416:17
Hammer: Amboss oder H. sein　GOET 230:7
　be the anvil or the h.　GOET 230:7
　His h. of wind　THOM 549:1
　little h. under the pillow　DICK 176:11
　took an h. in her hand　BIBLE 49:7
hammer'd: Was clash'd and h. from
　　TENN 533:22
hammered: h. into line　KIPL 297:26
hammers: busy h. closing rivets up
　　SHAK 444:9
hammock: Drake he's in his h. till
　　NEWB 361:7
hammock-shroud: His heavy-shotted
　h.　TENN 536:4
hams: together with most weak h.
　　SHAK 432:8
Ha'nacker Hill: Sally is gone from H.
　　BELL 39:26
hand: adorable tennis-girl's h.　BETJ 44:8
　Beneath whose awful H. we hold　KIPL 302:7
　bite the h. that fed　BURKE 112:10
　bloody and invisible h.　SHAK 461:14
　bloody h. that drew from　HEINE 244:12
　by Time's devouring h.　BRAM 91:23

Clean from my h.　SHAK 460:13
curious engine, your white h.　WEBS 566:21
died by the h. of the Lord　BIBLE 47:23
either h. may rightly clutch　KIPL 298:8
Emprison her soft h.　KEATS 291:15
evening withhold not thine h.　BIBLE 56:8
fingers of this h. wherewith　BROW 98:12
Great is the h. that holds　THOM 547:5
h. and brain went ever　BROW 101:26
h. a needle better fits　BRAD 91:13
h. are all the corners　PRAY 396:4
h. dare seize the fire　BLAKE 87:15
h. for hand　BIBLE 47:25
h. into the hand of God　HASK 243:1
h. is stretched out still　BIBLE 57:27
h. more instrumental　SHAK 429:20
h. of Douglas is his own　SCOTT 417:17
h. of every man's brother　BIBLE 45:38
h. of the physician　BIBLE 63:18
h. on the cockatrice' den　BIBLE 58:11
h. that fired the shot　BALL 31:4
h. that hath made you fair　SHAK 464:16
h. that kings Have lipp'd　SHAK 422:21
h. that rocks the cradle　WALL 562:4
h. that signed the paper　THOM 547:4
H. then of the Potter shake　FITZ 213:10
h. to bless　CHUR 149:3
h. to execute any mischief　CLAR 152:19
h. to execute　GIBB 224:28
h. to execute　JUN 287:5
h. will be against every　BIBLE 46:5
Heaving up my either h.　HERR 250:10
here's my h.　SHAK 485:13
her h., In whose comparison　SHAK 486:19
Her h. on her bosom　SHAK 476:27
him with his skinny h.　COL 155:6
His mind and h. went together　HEM 245:2
his right h. seven stars　BIBLE 81:14
I fear thy skinny h.　COL 155:19
I kiss'd her slender h.　TENN 540:6
immortal h. or eye　BLAKE 87:14
imposition of a mightier h.　MAC 323:24
In a bold determined h.　CAMP 128:14
I put my h. into the bed　SHAK 443:18
it hurts my h.　SHAK 476:11
it will go into his h.　BIBLE 51:38
kingdom of heaven is at h.　BIBLE 63:35
know the sweet Roman h.　SHAK 490:5
lays his h. upon a woman　TOBIN 551:7
led by an invisible h.　SMITH 509:9
left h. is under my head　BIBLE 56:21
left his garment in her h.　BIBLE 46:30
let me kiss that h.　SHAK 455:17
let not thy left h. know　BIBLE 64:22
letters in a big round h.　GILB 228:5
lily in your medieval h.　GILB 227:23
man's h. is not able　SHAK 471:10
mighty h. and by a stretched　BIBLE 48:19
My h. sought hers　BROW 102:2
my knee, my hat, and h.　BROW 96:3
My playfellow, your h.　SHAK 422:21
My times be in Thy h.　BROW 104:13
One lovely h. she stretched　CAMP 129:4
On this side my h.　SHAK 479:22
onward lend thy guiding h.　MILT 350:13
other h. held a weapon　BIBLE 52:1
Our times are in His h.　BROW 104:2
right h. forget her cunning　PRAY 399:3
right h. of the Majesty　BIBLE 79:28
seen by Time's fell h.　SHAK 494:2
Shade of His h.　THOM 548:23
sheep of his h.　PRAY 396:4
she waves her little h.　HARDY 240:16
sitteth on the right h.　PRAY 384:26
soft h., and softer breast　KEATS 292:13
spirit-small h. propping it　BROW 99:19
Sword sleep in my h.　BLAKE 86:16
take the pen out of his h.　ARN 16:8
there's a h.　BURNS 112:33
This living h.　KEATS 290:30

thousand at thy right h.　PRAY 395:21
thrust my h. into his side　BIBLE 73:10
'Tis a good h.　SHAK 476:2
top-mast wi' his h.　BALL 30:19
touch of a vanish'd h.　TENN 532:18
tricks by slight of h.　CONG 160:9
unto you with mine own h.　BIBLE 77:21
waiting for a h.　TENN 536:5
was the h. that wrote it　CRAN 169:1
wav'd her lily h.　GAY 223:30
were a glove upon that h.　SHAK 482:7
Whatsoever thy h. findeth to do　BIBLE 55:29
when I stretched out my h.　STER 519:14
white h. a warm wet cheek　LAND 308:25
whose h. is ever at his　KEATS 291:15
With his own right h.　PRAY 396:7
Your h., your tongue　SHAK 459:3
handbook: it was a constable's h.　KING 297:7
handclasp: Out where the h.'s a little
　　CHAP 140:2
handcuffs: young sinner with the h.
　　HOUS 266:8
Handel: Compar'd to H.'s a mere
　　BYROM 119:24
handful: fear in a h. of dust　ELIOT 204:19
　h. of meal in a barrel　BIBLE 51:7
　life in the h. of dust　CONR 161:2
handiwork: beyond or above his h.
　　JOYCE 286:18
　not-incurious in God's h.　BROW 100:24
handkerchief: feels like a damp h.
　　MACK 325:10
　h. Did an Egyptian　SHAK 476:3
　Holding his pocket-h.　CARR 135:10
　it is the h. of the Lord　WHIT 570:18
　snuffle and sniff and h.　BROO 94:16
handkerchiefs: waistcoats and moral
　pocket h.　DICK 182:6
handle: h. not　BIBLE 78:24
　I polished up the h.　GILB 228:4
　One old jug without a h.　LEAR 311:25
　to h. honesty and truth　SHAW 497:14
handles: hath two h.　BURT 116:25
handling: make a slip in h. us　KIPL 302:17
handmaid: nature's h. art　DRYD 195:22
　our h. unheeding　PAIN 367:17
　Riches are a good h.　BACON 25:9
handmaiden: low estate of his h.　BIBLE 69:5
handmaidens: With her five h.　ROSS 409:19
handmaids: sent me only your h.
　　POUND 383:13
hands: accept refreshment at any h.
　　GILB 226:22
　aching h. and bleeding feet　ARN 13:23
　All h. to work　ANON 8:24
　are the horny h. of toil　LOW 319:9
　Before rude h. have touch'd　JONS 285:4
　by joining of h.　PRAY 389:7
　caught the world's great h.　HUNT 268:9
　clap your h.　BARR 34:6
　crag with crooked h.　TENN 533:7
　dirty h.　MAC 324:7
　Fall into the h. of God　TENN 543:3
　folding of the h. to sleep　BIBLE 53:22
　Fold our h. round her knees　SWIN 528:16
　fortune is in his own h.　BACON 26:12
　h., and handle not　PRAY 397:18
　h. are as gold rings　BIBLE 57:4
　h. are a sort of feet　TRAH 552:1
　h. are the hands of Esau　BIBLE 46:16
　h. be an evening sacrifice　PRAY 399:9
　h. from picking and stealing　PRAY 388:17
　h. guiding where I stumble　SASS 414:19
　h. I commend my spirit　BIBLE 71:14
　h. I commend my spirit　PRAY 391:1
　h. of peasants their vile　SHAK 451:21
　h. of the living God　BIBLE 79:30
　h. that hold the aces which　BETJ 42:13
　h. wrought in the work　BIBLE 52:1
　hath not a Jew h.　SHAK 467:4

house not made with h.   BIBLE 77:6
house not made with h.   BROW 99:20
in temples made with h.   BIBLE 74:13
into the h. of spoilers   BIBLE 49:6
into the h. of the Lord   BIBLE 62:22
I warmed both h. before   LAND 308:20
Let us hold h. and look   BETJ 43:4
Licence my roving h.   DONNE 188:16
Lift not thy h. to *It*   FITZ 213:8
Made with our h. and our   SWIN 528:24
nearer than h. and feet   TENN 533:29
of those flower-soft h.   SHAK 422:3
Our h. will never meet   HOOD 255:13
Pale h. I loved   HOPE 256:3
pierced my h. and my feet   PRAY 390:20
plunge your h. in water   AUDEN 18:10
right h. of fellowship   BIBLE 77:15
Seem'd washing his h. with   HOOD 254:23
Shake h. for ever   DRAY 193:21
shook h. with time   FORD 216:16
some mischief still for h.   MADAN 326:17
So to'entergraft our h.   DONNE 188:22
Strengthen ye the weak h.   BIBLE 58:33
stretching of the h.   PAIN 367:18
Their fatal h.   MILT 347:1
their h. are blue   LEAR 312:6
Their h. upon their hearts   HOUS 264:23
These h. are not more like   SHAK 430:9
these h. ne'er be clean   SHAK 462:21
they reached out their h.   VIRG 558:22
union of h. and hearts   TAYL 532:6
violent h. upon themselves   PRAY 389:10
washed his h. before   BIBLE 68:21
wash my h. in innocency   PRAY 391:5
Wash your h.   SHAK 462:24
With cold immortal h.   SWIN 529:22
wither'd h. be still stretch'd   YOUNG 588:8
With mine own h. I give   SHAK 480:2
Your little h. were made   BELL 38:24
Your little h. were never   WATTS 565:18

handsaw: I know a hawk from a h.
   SHAK 432:18

handshake: h., the cough, the kiss
   AUDEN 21:1

handsome: h. in three hundred pounds
   SHAK 469:11

h. lad   VIRG 559:15
happy and h. and free   AUDEN 18:7
knave is h.   SHAK 474:21
my h. young man   BALL 31:5
who was once h. and tall   ELIOT 205:7
years to be young and h.   SWIFT 526:22

handy: It'll come in h.   ELIOT 202:8

handy-work: firmament sheweth his
   PRAY 390:11

hang: Go h. thyself in thine   SHAK 438:25
h. a calf's-skin on those   SHAK 452:16
h. and brush their bosoms   BROW 105:26
h. a pearl in every cowslip's   SHAK 470:2
H. it all, Robert Browning   POUND 382:6
h. the man over again   BARH 33:9
h. us now in Shrewsbury   HOUS 262:16
h. your hat on a pension   MACN 326:8
H. your husband and be   GAY 222:19
H. yourself   HENR 245:14
Here they h. a man first   MOL 353:22
man as O'Connell is to h.   SMITH 511:24
must indeed all h. together   FRAN 218:14
people h. together artificially   BUTL 118:29
power to h. one another   FARQ 210:9
shall all h. separately   FRAN 218:14
she would h. on him   SHAK 429:28
will neither go nor h.   BIGOD 84:5
will not h. myself to-day   CHES 146:14

hang'd: my poor fool is h.   SHAK 456:11

hanged: being h. in all innocence
   STEV 522:13

h. for stealing horses   HAL 237:22
h. himself   BIBLE 50:25
h. with the Bible under   AUBR 17:23

harps, we h. them up   PRAY 399:3
Here's a farmer that h.   SHAK 460:15
If I were h. on the highest   KIPL 301:14
must they all be h. that   SHAK 462:13
to be h. in a fortnight   JOHN 277:16

hangin: they're h.' men an' women ANON 6:6
they're h.' Danny Deever   KIPL 298:20

hanging: bare h.   DRYD 198:13
H. and marriage   FARQ 210:19
h. garments of Marylebone   JOYCE 286:5
h. isn't bad enough   HOUS 266:8
H. is too good for him   BUNY 107:17
h.-look to me   CONG 160:4
H. of his cat on Monday   BRAT 91:24
h. prevents a bad marriage   SHAK 488:4
That's cured by h. from   KING 297:20
your silk stocking's h.   SELL 420:3

hangman: even a h.   JERR 273:6
louse for the h.   JONS 284:4
naked to the h.'s noose   HOUS 262:17

Hangs: H. in the uncertain balance
   GREE 236:9
that h. on princes' favours   SHAK 447:9
thereby h. a tale   SHAK 425:19
What h. people…is the unfortunate
   STEV 522:11

hank: rag and a bone and a h.   KIPL 303:29
Hannibalem: Expende H.   JUV 288:1
Hanover: By famous H. city   BROW 103:14
Hans: H.' old Mill his three   DE L 174:4
Hans Breitmann: H. gife a barty   LEL 313:16
Haply: H. I may remember   ROSS 409:9
happen: accidents which started out to h.
   MARQ 331:2
poetry makes nothing h.   AUDEN 19:6
There shall no evil h.   PRAY 395:22

happened: I wonder what h. to him
   COW 163:16

happens: dependent on what h. to her
   ELIOT 201:3
h. anywhere   LARK 310:4

happier: is remembering h. things
   TENN 538:20
seek No h. state   MILT 348:9
that I am h. than I know   MILT 349:5
That Pobbles are h. without   LEAR 312:21
upon the whole a family h.   STEV 521:4
you be h. than your father   SOPH 513:4

happiest: gild it with the h. terms
   SHAK 440:28
h. time of all the glad   TENN 540:20
record of the best and h.   SHEL 505:12

happily: h. upon a plentiful fortune
   JOHN 275:2

happiness: all the h. mankind can
   DRYD 196:25
away you take away his h.   IBSEN 270:4
being too happy in thine h.   KEATS 291:17
Doesn't h. issue from pain   APOL 11:11
general h. of the nation   PEDR 371:4
great spectacle of human h.   SMITH 511:29
H. consists in the multiplicity   JOHN 275:17
h. for the greatest numbers   HUTC 268:20
h. in boats and carriage   HOR 258:19
h. is not an ideal of reason   KANT 288:12
H. is no laughing matter   WHAT 569:12
h. of the greatest number   BENT 40:25
h. of the next world   BROW 97:11
h. of the human race   BURKE 110:7
H.! our being's end   POPE 379:21
h. through another man's   SHAK 426:28
h. too swiftly flies   GRAY 235:13
home-born h.   COWP 167:13
In my great task of h.   STEV 523:11
It is a flaw In h.   KEATS 289:8
lifetime of h.   SHAW 497:17
makes the h. she does not   JOHN 283:6
more right to consume h.   SHAW 496:13
'Our unrivalled h.'   ARN 15:27
pursuit of h.   JEFF 272:6

recall a time of h. in misery   DANTE 171:8
recipe for h. I ever heard   AUST 22:28
secret of h. is to admire   BRAD 91:11
so great my h.   YEATS 587:11
so much h. is produced   JOHN 276:35
than h. makes them good   LAND 309:12
Travelling is the ruin of all h.   BURN 112:17
was the only thing for h.   EDG 199:21
We find our h.   WORD 580:23
Who gain a h. in eyeing   HUXL 269:1
Withdraws into its h.   MARV 332:4

happy: angry and poor and h.   CHES 147:22
Are you all h. now   LAND 308:21
Be h. while y'er leevin   ANON 4:27
Call no man h.   SOLON 512:25
daft and h. hills   THOM 546:22
duty of being h.   STEV 522:4
h. and handsome and free   AUDEN 18:7
h. as birds in the spring   BLAKE 87:20
h. as the grass was green   THOM 547:1
h. could I be with either   GAY 222:35
h. families resemble one   TOLS 551:10
h. he who crowns in shades   GOLD 230:19
H. he who like Ulysses   DU B 198:26
h. in *three wives* as Mr   LAMB 308:13
h. issue out of all their   PRAY 386:1
H. is that city which   ANON 5:12
H. is the man who fears   BIBLE 83:9
H. is the man that hath   PRAY 398:19
h. is the rose distill'd   SHAK 469:17
h. life be these   SURR 524:20
h. low, lie down   SHAK 441:30
h. men that have the power   TENN 543:13
h. noise to hear   HOUS 263:4
h., pair   DRYD 194:23
H. the hare at morning   AUDEN 18:14
H. the man   POPE 380:23
H. the people whose annals   CARL 131:20
H. those early days   VAUG 555:14
He's h. who, far away   HOR 259:7
How h. is he born and taught   WOTT 583:12
How h. some o'er other   SHAK 469:22
how h. you make those   SHAK 493:18
I die h.   FOX 217:22
is h. nature to explore   POPE 379:17
Is that they h. are   WALL 562:16
I've had a h. life   HAZL 244:4
Made h. by compulsion   COL 157:13
make a h. fire-side clime   BURNS 115:15
make two lovers h.   POPE 380:22
making of an old woman h.   FRAN 218:5
me at all h. without you   KEATS 294:30
methinks it were a h. life   SHAK 446:18
More h., if less wise   BYRON 124:42
must be regarded as h.   CAMUS 129:24
myself in nothing else so h.   SHAK 478:24
no chance to be very h.   GAY 223:26
nor as h. as one hopes   LA R 310:18
of us is h. in this world   THAC 545:29
one thing to make me h.   HAZL 243:15
perfectly happy till all are h.   SPEN 515:3
should all be as h. as kings   STEV 522:22
so late their h. seat   MILT 350:1
so long as you're h.   DU M 199:4
splendid and a h. land   GOLD 231:5
that can make a man h.   HOR 258:17
that none should be h.   JOHN 277:5
think no birds so h. as we   LEAR 312:15
This h. breed   SHAK 478:20
Thrice h. he who   MARV 332:2
To keep me h. all the day…   STEV 522:20
To make men h.   POPE 380:10
too h. in thine happiness   KEATS 291:17
'Twere now to be most h.   SHAK 474:20
was most h. and prosperous   GIBB 224:24
was the carver h. while   RUSK 411:20
What makes a nation h.   MILT 350:11
whether you are h.   MILL 338:21
Whoever wants to be h.   MED 336:9
who so h.   LEAR 312:4

world of the h. is quite WITT 575:16
you be right to call h. HOR 261:19
Happy Isles: be we shall touch the H.
TENN 544:3
haps: neutral-tinted h. and such
HARDY 239:22
harbor: looking over h. and city SAND 413:26
harbour: h. grene aslepe whereas
WEVER 569:7
Though the h. bar be moaning KING 297:3
where doth thine h. hold BARN 33:27
Which in life did h. give JONS 284:3
Hard: H. as the palm of ploughman
SHAK 486:19
h. dealing teaches th SHAK 466:4
H.,' replied the Dodger DICK 180:34
h. sentences of old PRAY 395:3
h. to catch and conquer MER 337:2
H. was their lodging GARTH 221:20
how h. to make a man appear DRYD 198:11
it was too h. for me PRAY 394:23
Long is the way And h. MILT 346:17
never think I have hit h. JOHN 276:20
Nothing's so h. HERR 249:19
that thou art an h. man BIBLE 68:3
harden: h. not your hearts PRAY 396:4
h. Pharaoh's heart BIBLE 47:11
hardened: gristle and not yet h. into the
bone BURKE 109:17
harder: h. they fall FITZ 214:1
they would be h. to them TROL 552:20
hard-faced: lot of h. men who look
BALD 29:26
hardly: He's h. ever sick at sea GILB 227:31
Hardy: H. went down to botanize CHES 148:7
hare: Happy the h. at morning AUDEN 18:14
h. limp'd trembling through KEATS 289:9
h. sits snug in leaves HOFF 252:20
it look'd like h. BARH 33:6
like the hunting of the h. BLUNT 89:4
lion than to start a h. SHAK 438:18
outcry of the hunted h. BLAKE 85:10
Take your h. when it is GLAS 229:21
thou woldest fynde an h. CHAU 143:13
triumph o'er the timid h. THOM 549:18
hare-brained: h. chatter of irresponsible
DISR 185:18
harelip: makes the h. SHAK 454:22
hares: little hunted h. HODG 252:2
merry brown h. came leaping KING 296:18
Hark: H., my soul COWP 165:25
H., the dominant's persistence BROW 105:24
harlot: Every h. was a virgin once
BLAKE 86:1
h.'s cry from street BLAKE 85:17
Portia is Brutus' h. SHAK 449:15
prerogative of the h. throughout KIPL 305:13
harlots: devoured thy living with h.
BIBLE 70:22
MOTHER OF H. AND ABOMINATIONS
BIBLE 82:23
harm: believe that does h. to my wit
SHAK 487:20
content with my h. SHAK 426:4
deceiving, could no longer h. ELIOT 202:20
I fear we'll come to h. BALL 31:18
mankind does most good or h. BAG 29:18
no h. come to the state ANON 10:10
no h. happen unto me PRAY 389:30
No people do so much h. CREI 169:17
prevent h. to others MILL 339:7
Shall h. Macbeth SHAK 462:18
to win us to our h. SHAK 458:18
harme: most h. to the mene puple
LANG 309:26
harmless: Elephant, The only h.
DONNE 190:3
h. as doves BIBLE 65:33
h. necessary cat SHAK 467:22

harmonies: mighty-mouth'd inventor
of h. TENN 533:12
tumult of thy mighty h. SHEL 502:13
harmonious: Such h. madness SHEL 504:24
Uttering such dulcet and h. SHAK 470:7
harmony: best h. in a church MILT 351:26
from heavenly h. DRYD 197:21
H. in discord HOR 258:20
h. is in immortal souls SHAK 468:15
h. not understood POPE 379:11
heaven drowsy with the h. SHAK 457:8
Like h. in music WORD 580:11
sentimentally I am disposed to h. LAMB 307:2
their motions h. divine MILT 348:24
them the other h. of prose DRYD 198:7
there is a h. In autumn SHEL 501:7
touches of sweet h. SHAK 468:15
voice the h. of the world HOOK 255:20
wherever there is a h. BROW 96:34
with your ninefold h. MILT 344:10
harms: Ten thousand h. SHAK 421:19
harness: between the joints of the h.
BIBLE 51:21
girdeth on his h. boast BIBLE 51:16
h. and not the horses that CANN 130:7
hear the h. jingle HOUS 263:9
least we'll die with h. SHAK 463:7
My h. piece by piece Thou THOM 548:16
To wait in heavy h. KIPL 304:6
harp: awake, lute and h. PRAY 393:16
H. not on that string SHAK 481:10
h., sackbut BIBLE 61:3
h. that once through Tara's MOORE 356:9
h. will I give thanks unto PRAY 392:11
his wild h. slung behind MOORE 356:13
merry h. with the lute PRAY 395:9
No h. like my own could CAMP 128:20
sing to the h. with a psalm PRAY 396:8
To one clear h. in divers TENN 535:33
harpers: h. harping with their harps
BIBLE 82:15
harping: harpers h. with their harps
BIBLE 82:15
He hath not heart for h. POUND 383:18
Still h. on my daughter SHAK 432:6
harps: harpers harping with their h.
BIBLE 82:15
h., we hanged them up PRAY 399:3
having every one of them h. BIBLE 81:27
harp-shaped: whisked past the h. hills
THOM 546:22
harpy: conference with this h. SHAK 432:9
harrass: all the griefs that h. JOHN 282:23
Harriet: 'treatment of the H. problem'
FREE 218:24
Harris: 'Bother Mrs H. DICK 179:29
Harrow: H. the house of the dead
AUDEN 20:7
toad beneath the h. knows KIPL 302:1
Would h. up thy soul SHAK 431:5
harrow'd: having h. hell SPEN 515:17
Harry: banish not him thy H.'s SHAK 439:18
Cry 'God for H. SHAK 444:3
H., Harry SHAK 442:23
Jerusalem shall H. die SHAK 442:21
little touch of H. SHAK 444:12
Promis'd to H. and his SHAK 443:12
Such a King H. DRAY 193:11
harshness: enough no h. gives offence
POPE 378:22
hart: h. desireth the water-brooks PRAY 392:6
h. ungalled play SHAK 434:16
lame man leap as an h. BIBLE 58:34
pants the h. for cooling TATE 531:20
roe or to a young h. upon BIBLE 57:14
was I turn'd into a h. SHAK 487:21
harumfrodite: 'E's a kind of a giddy
h. KIPL 302:23
harvest: according to the joy in h. BIBLE 58:6
all the H. that I reap'd FITZ 212:21

are white already to h. BIBLE 71:41
grassy h. of the river-fields ARN 15:8
h. is past BIBLE 60:20
h. of a quiet eye WORD 580:5
h. truly is plenteous BIBLE 65:29
Have I no h. but a thorn HERB 247:14
if the h. is over BETJ 43:10
seedtime and h. BIBLE 45:37
Share my h. and my home HOOD 255:5
she laughs with a h. JERR 273:7
Where the thin h. waves COWP 168:26
harvests: Deep h. bury all his pride
POPE 378:5
h. of Arretium MAC 322:12
Harwich: about in a steamer from H.
GILB 226:13
has: 'one of the h. beens HONE 254:7
hasard: de l'observation le h. PAST 369:16
jamais n'abolira le h. MALL 327:11
Hasdrubal: of our name lost with H.
HOR 261:13
Hasdrubale: Nominis H. interempto
HOR 261:13
hässlich: Welt h. und schlecht NIET 363:8
Hast: Ohne H. GOET 230:15
haste: h. of a fool is the slowest SHAD 420:21
h., persuade WHIT 571:11
H. still pays haste SHAK 465:5
h. to be rich shall not BIBLE 54:42
I h. me to my bed SHAK 493:5
I said in my h. PRAY 397:21
Make h. slowly SUET 524:16
Men love in h. BYRON 123:38
Raw H. TENN 539:19
This sweaty h. SHAK 429:11
Though I am always in h. WESL 568:20
Without h. GOET 230:15
ye shall eat it in h. BIBLE 47:18
hasten: So do our minutes h. SHAK 493:19
hasty: man in his h. days BRID 92:10
hat: A' brushes his h. a mornings
SHAK 472:25
Antichrist in that lewd h. JONS 283:15
away with a h. like that LOOS 318:4
complete with h. and gloves CALV 127:16
hang your h. on a pension MACN 326:8
h. of antique shape ARN 14:13
himself in a shocking bad h. SURT 525:21
my knee, my h., and hand BROW 96:3
No h. upon his head SHAK 431:28
with my h. upon my head JOHN 280:26
without pulling off his h. JOHN 274:27
your h. has got a hole in't CANN 129:26
your h. upon your brows SHAK 462:16
hatch'd: new-h., unfledg'd comrade
SHAK 430:19
hatched: an' h. different ELIOT 200:11
hatches: is continually under h. KEATS 293:16
hatchet: did it with my little h. WASH 565:1
hatcheth: h. them not BIBLE 60:25
Hatching: H. vain empires MILT 346:15
hate: away this murdherin' h. OCAS 364:17
cherish those hearts that h. SHAK 447:12
do good to them which h. BIBLE 69:21
English began to h. KIPL 298:1
generation of them that h. BIBLE 47:24
glance of supernatural h. BYRON 126:7
h. a Frenchman NELS 360:12
h. all Boets and Bainters GEOR 223:34
h. all that don't love FARQ 210:11
h. and detest that animal SWIFT 526:23
h. and to despise myself HAZL 243:18
h. any one that we know HAZL 244:2
h. for arts that caus'd POPE 376:26
h. him as I do hell-pains SHAK 473:19
h. him for he is a Christian SHAK 465:29
h. of those ye guard KIPL 304:8
h. that dreadful hollow TENN 539:25
h. the French because they GOLD 232:6
h. the idle pleasures SHAK 480:19

h. the man you have hurt	TAC 531:8	I h. thee not	SHAK 459:15	Majesty's h. on a sign-post	MAC 324:2
have seen much to h. here	MILL 340:2	long as you h. your life	JAMES 271:20	make you shorter by the h.	ELIZ 205:26
I h. and I love	CAT 137:14	they will not let you h. it	HAZL 243:21	Man with the h.	TENN 542:9
I h. false words	LAND 309:11	have-his-carcase: h., next to the perpetual		Megrim at her h.	POPE 381:9
I h. the crowd	LAND 309:5		DICK 182:33	My deeds upon my h.	SHAK 468:1
I h. the unholy masses	HOR 260:13	haven: their h. under the hill	TENN 532:18	my h. is a map	FIEL 211:21
I h. the whole race…There	WELL 568:5	have-nots: haves and the have-nots	CERV 138:17	My h. is bloody	HENL 245:4
immortal h.)	MILT 345:3	haves: h. and the have-nots	CERV 138:17	My ho h. halls	JOYCE 286:8
in love, or in h.	STEV 521:26	Havoc: Cry, 'H.!'	SHAK 450:12	never broke any man's h.	SHAK 444:6
In time we h. that which	SHAK 421:25	hawk: Gentle as falcon or h.	SKEL 508:16	not where to lay his h.	BIBLE 65:18
large the h.	AUDEN 18:8	h. at eagles with a dove	HERB 248:9	nowhere yet to rest my h.	ARN 13:8
Let them h.	ACC 1:3	His h. to fetch the wild-fowl	BALL 32:8	Off with his h.	CIBB 151:12
must h. and death return	SHEL 501:3	know a h. from a handsaw	SHAK 432:18	out of King Charles's h.	DICK 177:7
need not be to h.	BYRON 120:34	hawks: …Dark h. hear us	JOYCE 286:8	parboiled h. upon a stake	GRAH 233:16
nought did I in h.	SHAK 477:22	h. favoured an air strike	BART 34:24	plateau of Spain forming a h.	HARDY 239:13
Of a pure impartial h.	THOR 550:28	Hawkshaw: H., the detective	TAYL 532:7	poured it on his h.	BIBLE 68:8
present day is that men h.	MELB 336:20	hawthorn: h. bush a sweeter shade		repairs his drooping h.	MILT 343:17
religion to make us h.	SWIFT 527:7		SHAK 446:19	rolling his h.	MAC 324:14
roughness breedeth h.	BACON 26:25	Stream from the h.	HOUS 264:20	seems no bigger than his h.	SHAK 455:14
sprung from my only h.	SHAK 482:4	Under the h. in the dale	MILT 342:19	shadow of her fair vast h.	SWIN 528:26
Ten men love what I h.	BROW 104:7	hay: dance an antic h.	MARL 329:17	shake his sapient h.	ARN 15:12
that h. him flee before him	PRAY 394:6	desire to a bottle of h.	SHAK 471:4	shake of his poor little h.	GILB 227:16
There's no h. lost	MIDD 338:20	eating h. when you're faint	CARR 135:31	stand. ''On my h.	DISR 185:32
Those fellows h. us	LAMB 307:34	I made h. while the sun	BETJ 43:10	star with my exalted h.	HERR 248:19
time to h.	BIBLE 55:12	lie tumbling in the h.	SHAK 491:17	that by shaking his h.	SHER 505:29
'tis delicious to h. you	MOORE 356:24	that's what h. looks like	MARY 333:16	thou bald h.	BIBLE 51:24
to h. your neighbour	MAC 324:3	world is a bundle of h.	BYRON 124:32	Thou wilt show my h.	DANT 171:20
hated: being h., don't give way	KIPL 299:22	haystack: Beside the h. in the floods		to get one's h. cut off	CARR 135:13
H. by fools	SWIFT 528:8		MORR 358:11	touches a hair of yon gray h.	WHIT 571:18
H. by one he loves	SHAK 451:23	hazard: h. in the glorious enterprise		under my h. a sod	BALL 31:14
h. the ruling few than	BENT 41:1		MILT 345:1	Uneasy lies the h. that	SHAK 441:30
never saw a brute I h.	BROW 99:29	He has put to h. his ease	BURKE 110:26	what seem'd his h.	MILT 346:24
Past reason h.	SHAK 495:7	Men that h. all	SHAK 466:16	What though his h. be empty	SWIFT 527:4
She might have h.	BROW 101:24	stand the h. of the die	SHAK 481:19	which binds so dear a h.	SHEL 499:3
hateful: Must learn the h. art	KING 296:13	haze: seaward h.	HARDY 240:15	your h. are all numbered	BIBLE 65:36
shamed life a h.	SHAK 464:14	hazel-nut: chariot is an empty h.	SHAK 481:28	headache: awake with a dismal h.	
hater: he was a very good h.	JOHN 280:11	Hazlitt: we cannot write like H.	STEV 522:10		GILB 226:12
hates: h. dogs and babies	ROST 410:14	he: Art thou h. that should	BIBLE 66:1	to-day I happen to have a h.	CARR 135:14
He h. our sacred nation	SHAK 465:29	H. that hath with child	BACON 26:31	headaches: In h. and in worry	AUDEN 18:10
just heaven now h.	ANON 5:14	poorest h. that is in England	RAIN 404:7	head-in-air: Johnny h.	PUDN 402:7
hateth: h. his brother	BIBLE 81:7	head: bear with a sore h.	MARR 331:4	headland: naked top Of some bold h.	
rod h. his son	BIBLE 53:38	begins a journey in my h.	SHAK 493:5		WORD 577:10
hath: one that h. shall be given	BIBLE 68:4	body with so old a h.	SHAK 467:26	Headlong: H. themselves they threw	
hating: don't give way to h.	KIPL 299:22	bowed his comely h.	MARV 332:10		MILT 348:27
in h. all other nations	GASK 222:4	broken h. in Cold Bath	MAC 324:23	was h. sent	MILT 346:4
special reason for h. school	BEER 37:21	cuts the wrong man's h. off	DICK 182:3	Headmasters: H. have powers at their	
hatless: young man lands h.	BETJ 42:12	dawn many a h. has turned white	MULL 359:1		CHUR 150:22
hatred: from envy, h., and malice		enjoyed at the h. of a school	WALP 562:18	Headpiece: H. filled with straw	ELIOT 203:8
	PRAY 385:16	gently lay my h.	BROW 97:6	Prompt hand and h. clever	HOUS 265:1
h. for the Tory Party	BEVAN 44:16	God be in my h.	ANON 5:9	heads: had ever very empty h.	BACON 25:7
h. or bitterness towards	CAV 137:18	good grey h.	TENN 541:7	H. Were toward Eternity	DICK 183:16
like love to h. turn'd	CONG 160:15	h. and front of my offending	SHAK 473:24	Hide their diminished h.	MILT 347:13
stalled ox and h.	BIBLE 54:6	h. and his hairs were white	BIBLE 81:14	Hung their h.	SHAK 447:3
hats: inside men's Sunday h.	BROW 103:15	h. and which was the tail	BRIG 93:6	lay their h. together	SMITH 511:22
so many shocking bad h.	WELL 567:22	h. could carry all he knew	GOLD 231:3	Lift up your h.	PRAY 390:24
They wat their h. aboon	BALL 31:19	h. is as full of quarrels	SHAK 483:1	stood them on their h.	BARR 34:11
haughtiness: h. of soul	ADD 1:18	h. is not more native	SHAK 429:20	Their h. are green	LEAR 312:6
haughty: Greece or h. Rome	JONS 284:22	h. of a family of	DICK 181:23	head-stone: become the h. in the corner	
h. spirit before a fall	BIBLE 54:8	H. of a traveller	HOUS 266:9		PRAY 398:2
haunches: on silent h.	SAND 413:18	h. off with a golden axe	SHAK 483:10	Halt by the h. naming	HOUS 266:2
haunt: all the h. be ours	SHAK 423:10	h. thou dost with oil anoint	SCOT 419:5	headstrong: She's as h. as an allegory	
h. of flies on summer eves	KEATS 291:21	h. to contrive	GIBB 224:28		SHER 506:15
h. thy days and chill thy	KEATS 290:30	h. upon our battlements	SHAK 458:3	head-waiter: plump h. at the Cock	
Haunted: H. for ever by the eternal		h. which statuaries loved	MAC 323:33		TENN 544:9
	WORD 579:7	heart or in the h.	SHAK 467:9	Heady: H., not strong	POPE 375:20
shape of a woman has h.	KEATS 294:3	heart runs away with his h.	COLM 159:5	heal: h. me of my grievous wound	
summer eves by h. stream	MILT 342:26	He had a h. to contrive	CLAR 152:19		TENN 535:27
That is a h. town to me	LANG 309:17	her h. on her knee	SHAK 476:27	That fame can never h.	AYT 24:5
haunts: Are h. meet for thee	ARN 13:2	Hers is the h. upon which	PATER 369:18	What wound did ever h.	SHAK 475:11
h. of coot and hern	TENN 532:20	hidden her h.	SWIN 530:7	When there is none to h.	KEATS 293:4
he h. wakes	SHAK 491:20	his guts in his h.	SHAK 486:29	heal'd: thy wound be throughly h.	
mothers and fathers that h. us	IBSEN 269:21	If you can keep your h.	KIPL 299:22		SHAK 490:32
hause-bane: 'Ye'll sit on his white h.		I'll hold my h. so high	HOR 259:10	healed: They have h. also the hurt	
	BALL 32:8	incessantly stand on your h.	CARR 133:22		BIBLE 60:19
haute: h. la tempête et se rit	BAUD 35:6	It shall bruise thy h.	BIBLE 45:20	with his stripes we are h.	BIBLE 59:22
hautes: des choses grandes et h.	MONT 354:12	I've a h. like a concertina	KIPL 298:7	healer: compassion of the h.'s art	
have: because other folks h.	FIEL 211:17	Lay your sleeping h.	AUDEN 19:17		ELIOT 202:21
h. and to hold from this	PRAY 389:4	left hand is under my h.	BIBLE 56:21	It is not a great h.	COMP 159:12
H. more than thou showest	SHAK 453:15	like God's own h.	COL 155:11	healeth: h. those that are broken	PRAY 399:19
if he will h. him	PRAY 390:17	madness was not of the h.	BYRON 125:2	healing: arise with h. in his wings	BIBLE 62:3

expected h. wings could see   VAUG 555:11
h. of the nations   BIBLE 83:1
h. voice of Christian charity   BURKE 111:2
no h. has been necessary   COMP 159:12
Wordsworth's h. power   ARN 13:18
health: art so far from my h.   PRAY 390:16
h. and living now begins   SHAK 486:12
h., and quiet breathing   KEATS 288:20
h. and their complexion   AUST 22:17
h. and wealth have missed   HUNT 268:10
h. and wealth long to live   PRAY 385:5
h. unbought   DRYD 196:5
Here's a double h. to thee   BYRON 125:32
he that will this h. deny   DYER 199:19
horse's h.   SHAK 454:28
Importing h. and graveness   SHAK 436:17
innocence and h.   GOLD 230:18
in sickness and in h.   PRAY 389:4
Look to your h.   WALT 564:12
overthroweth your h.   BACON 26:17
spirit of h. or goblin   SHAK 430:24
there is no h. in us   PRAY 384:12
thine h. shall spring forth   BIBLE 60:5
thy saving h. among all   PRAY 394:4
Where h. and plenty cheered   GOLD 230:16
healthful: h. Spirit of thy grace   PRAY 385:7
Without disease the h.   SURR 524:20
healthy: h. bones of a single Pomeranian   BISM 84:22
H. by temp'rance   POPE 377:5
h. state of political life   MILL 339:10
h. stomach is nothing   BUTL 118:31
heap: h. of all your winnings   KIPL 300:1
was struck all of a h.   SHER 506:5
waters to stand on an h.   PRAY 395:5
heap'd: error be too highly h.   SHAK 427:17
heapeth: h. up riches   PRAY 391:31
hear: Be swift to h.   BIBLE 80:10
can h. my Thisby's face   SHAK 471:18
child may joy to h.   BLAKE 87:25
h. it in the deep heart's   YEATS 585:17
H. my law, O my people   PRAY 395:3
h. no more at all   STEV 523:5
H. not my steps   SHAK 460:1
H., O Israel   BIBLE 48:20
H. the other side   AUG 21:20
h. the word of the Lord   BIBLE 61:2
He cannot choose but h.   COL 155:6
He that hath ears to h.   BIBLE 68:28
houses h. clocks ticking   BETJ 42:12
I h. thy shrill delight   SHEL 504:18
I h. you   HOUS 263:5
in such wise h. them read   PRAY 386:5
Lord, h. our prayers   PRAY 388:21
shall he not h.   PRAY 396:2
she is sure to h.   AUST 22:12
They never would h.   SWIFT 527:27
to h. the sins they love   SHAK 439:35
to h. those things which   BIBLE 69:29
We beseech thee to h. us   PRAY 385:18
we can always h. them   AUDEN 19:13
we shall h. it   BROW 98:20
would h. the mighty crack   ADD 2:30
you will h. me   DISR 184:10
You will h. more good things   HAZL 243:16
heard: after it was h. no more   WORD 578:16
Cannot be h. so high   SHAK 455:14
Enough that he h. it once   BROW 98:20
ever h. Any good   LAND 309:6
have ye not h.   BIBLE 59:9
h. for their much speaking   BIBLE 64:23
H. melodies are sweet   KEATS 291:4
H., not regarded   SHAK 439:35
I have h. of thee   BIBLE 53:12
I will be h.   GARR 221:17
more he h.   PUNCH 402:25
only tell us what he h.   GRAY 235:24
then is h. no more   SHAK 463:6
twice I have also h.   PRAY 393:20
Which we have h. and known   PRAY 395:3

You ain't h. nothin' yet   JOLS 283:9
hearers: attentive and favourable h.   HOOK 255:19
edification of the h.   BURKE 108:14
not h. only   BIBLE 80:10
too deep for his h.   GOLD 231:17
heareth: thy servant h.   BIBLE 49:36
hearing: Fall asleep, or h. die   SHAK 447:3
passionate my sense of h.   SHAK 456:25
thought he was within h.   JOHN 278:22
hearken: h. than the fat of rams   BIBLE 50:4
hearkened: hadst h. to my commandments   BIBLE 59:15
h. not unto the voice   PRAY 397:5
hears: h. its winding murmur   ARN 12:22
She neither h. nor sees   WORD 581:10
hearsay: have formerly lived by h.   BUNY 107:39
walls have h.   FONS 216:4
hearse: laureate h. where Lycid lies   MILT 343:15
Underneath this sable h.   BROW 97:25
walk before the h.   GARR 221:11
hearses: frequent h. shall besiege   POPE 376:9
heart: abundance of the h.   BIBLE 66:9
abundance weakens his own h.   SHAK 493:2
accompany me with a pure h.   PRAY 384:10
all's here about my h.   SHAK 437:14
Batter my h.   DONNE 189:8
beating of man's h.   AUDEN 20:6
Blessed are the pure in h.   BIBLE 64:6
blind side of the h.   CHES 146:18
brains in my head and the h.   HOUS 266:7
break, my h.   SHAK 430:1
broken h. lies here   MAC 322:10
Bury my h. at Wounded Knee   BENET 40:20
Calais' lying in my h.   MARY 333:13
calm sunshine of the h.   CONS 162:4
can no longer tear his h.   SWIFT 528:12
consenting language of the h.   GAY 223:5
curse with their h.   PRAY 393:19
Dear h. how like you   WYATT 583:22
deceiveth his own h.   BIBLE 80:10
desires of the h. are as crooked   AUDEN 18:13
do any man's h. good   SHAK 469:29
drops That visit my sad h.   SHAK 449:15
education of the h.   SCOTT 419:4
Englishman whose h. is   BAG 28:31
faint h. ne'er wan   BURNS 115:14
faith of the h. alone make both God   LUTH 320:17
Far other aims his h. had   GOLD 230:22
felt along the h.   WORD 578:4
Floodgate of the deeper h.   FLEC 214:24
give me back my h. again   GRAN 234:4
God be in my h.   ANON 5:9
good Christian at her h.   POPE 377:19
great no h. I had to choose   LA B 306:14
harden Pharaoh's h.   BIBLE 47:11
has stabb'd me to the h.   GAY 222:6
hast cleft my h. in twain   SHAK 435:17
have garner'd up my h.   SHAK 476:18
having war in his h.   PRAY 393:12
head and woman with the h.   TENN 542:9
hear it in the deep h.'s   YEATS 585:17
h. and my flesh rejoice   PRAY 395:11
H. and soul do sing   SIDN 508:1
h. and stomach of a king   ELIZ 206:4
h. and voice would fail   CLAR 152:23
h. argues, not the mind   ARN 13:20
h. as sound as a bell   SHAK 472:14
h. bleeds for his country   JOHN 274:21
h. cheer thee in the days   BIBLE 56:10
h. clings to and confides   LUTH 320:18
h. doth need a language   COL 157:8
h. fail because of him   BIBLE 50:9
h. grows older   HOPK 256:26
h. has felt the tender   GAY 223:3
h. has its reasons which   PASC 369:10
h. hath 'scap'd this sorrow   SHAK 494:14

h. high-sorrowful and cloy'd   KEATS 291:7
h.—how shall I say   BROW 102:22
h. in his grave is lying   MOORE 356:17
h. is a small thing   QUAR 403:9
h. is deceitful above all   BIBLE 60:24
h. is Highland   GALT 221:2
h. is inditing of a good   PRAY 392:14
h. is like a singing bird   ROSS 408:23
h. is on the left   MOL 353:17
h. is sick   TENN 536:21
h. is strong and the human   BAG 28:30
h. keeps empty in thy tomb   KING 296:11
h. less bounding at emotion   ARN 15:9
h. lies plain   ARN 12:22
h. no longer stirred   HOUS 266:2
h. of a man is deprest   GAY 222:26
h. of a true *Englishman*   ADD 2:19
h. of kings is unsearchable   BIBLE 54:25
h. of lead   POPE 375:18
h. one strangling golden hair   ROSS 410:2
h. out of your breast   HOUS 264:18
h. runs away with his head   COLM 159:5
H.'s denying   BARN 34:4
H. speaks to heart   NEWM 362:7
h. that has truly lov'd   MOORE 356:5
h. the keener   ANON 8:9
h. to pity   CHUR 149:3
h. unfortified   SHAK 429:26
h. untravell'd fondly turns   GOLD 231:24
h. were as fire and could   SWIN 528:16
h. within blood-tinctured   BROW 98:3
H. within, and God o'erhead   LONG 317:3
Here's a h. for every fate   BYRON 126:1
He sought, For his lost h.   SHEL 504:5
he tears out the h.   KNOW 305:17
His flaw'd h.   SHAK 456:7
home the h. you gave me   DRAY 193:16
How the h. listened while   THOM 549:26
human h. by which we live   WORD 579:14
humble and a contrite h.   KIPL 302:7
I am gathered to thy h.   MEYN 338:14
I am sick at h.   SHAK 429:1
I feel my h. new open'd   SHAK 447:9
If thy h. fails thee   ELIZ 206:1
I had lock'd my h.   BALL 32:11
I had rather coin my h.   SHAK 451:21
in the h. or in the head   SHAK 467:9
I said to H.   BELL 39:17
is the darling of my h.   CAREY 130:26
Is your h. at rest   FLET 215:19
it be the h. to conceive   JUN 287:5
I wish my h. had never   ANON 7:15
I would eat his h.   SHAK 473:3
Land of H.'s Desire   YEATS 585:19
laughter the h. is sorrowful   BIBLE 54:1
lent out my h. with usury   LAMB 307:24
light h. lives long   SHAK 457:14
little body with a mighty h.   SHAK 443:13
look in thy h. and write   SIDN 507:17
loos'd our h. in tears   ARN 13:17
Lord looketh on the h.   BIBLE 50:6
make a stone of the h.   YEATS 585:2
Make me a clean h.   PRAY 393:6
make my seated h. knock   SHAK 458:20
Makes my h. go pit-a-pat   BROW 103:17
makes the h. grow fonder   ANON 4:10
making melody in your h.   BIBLE 78:5
man after his own h.   BIBLE 50:1
Mercy has a human h.   BLAKE 88:7
merry h. doeth good like   BIBLE 54:12
merry h. maketh a cheerful   BIBLE 54:5
mighty h. is lying still   WORD 581:15
My h. aches   KEATS 291:16
my h. also in the midst   PRAY 390:19
My h. at some noonday   BROW 101:15
My h. in hiding   HOPK 257:5
My h. is heavy   GOET 230:4
My h. is turned to stone   SHAK 476:11
My h. leaps up when I behold   WORD 578:19
my h. puts forth its pain   BROO 94:5

My h.'s in the Highlands BURNS 114:25
my h. waketh BIBLE 57:1
My h. was hot within me PRAY 391:30
My h. would hear her TENN 540:12
my little h. SHAK 456:26
my poor h. doth think LYLY 321:16
naked thinking h. DONNE 188:1
natural language of the h. SHAD 420:19
naughtiness of thine h. BIBLE 50:8
nearer to the H.'s Desire FITZ 213:16
never a crack in my h. YEATS 586:5
never has ached with a h. SWIN 529:7
no man layeth it to h. BIBLE 60:2
no matter from the h. SHAK 487:17
nor his h. to report SHAK 471:10
not more native to the h. SHAK 429:20
not of the head, but h. BYRON 125:2
not our h. burn within us BIBLE 71:18
not your h. be troubled BIBLE 72:30
not your h. away HOUS 262:20
now from the h. of joy BEEC 37:9
no woman's h. So big SHAK 489:6
of mischief he had a h. GIBB 224:28
oft has made my h. to ache BLAKE 87:7
on my h. they tread now SHAK 479:15
Open my h. and you will BROW 100:14
Open not thine h. to every BIBLE 62:28
out my reins and my h. PRAY 391:4
Out-worn h. YEATS 585:14
pageant of his bleeding h. ARN 13:9
Possess thy h. BRID 92:21
prithee send me back my h. SUCK 524:12
rag-and-bone shop of the h. YEATS 584:15
rebuke hath broken my h. PRAY 394:12
red pavilion of my h. THOM 547:23
revolting and a rebellious h. BIBLE 60:17
seal upon thine h. BIBLE 57:11
Shakespeare unlocked his h. BROW 101:10
She wants a h. POPE 377:22
sighing of a contrite h. PRAY 385:22
since man's h. is small KIPL 303:16
smoke and flame I lost my h. HOUS 266:4
softer pillow than my h. BYRON 126:16
some h. did break TENN 536:3
some h. indignant breaks MOORE 356:10
So the h. be right RAL 404:18
sure of his unspotted h. PEELE 371:8
Sweeping up the H. DICK 183:17
sweet concurrence of the h. HERR 250:11
ta'en out thy h. o' flesh BALL 32:3
Take any h. GILB 228:15
Take h. of grace GILB 228:14
Taming my wild h. to thy SHAK 472:22
that earth upon thy h. KIPL 298:8
that had the lion's h. CHUR 150:21
that maketh glad the h. PRAY 396:20
that sting my h. SHAK 475:9
That the bruis'd h. was SHAK 474:4
That the h. grows old YEATS 586:20
their captain, the h. SHAK 442:15
then burst his mighty h. SHAK 450:28
there will your h. be also BIBLE 64:26
this h. Shall break SHAK 454:2
thought my shrivel'd h. HERB 247:21
thou hast my h. PRIOR 400:21
thou wilt ease thine h. BEDD 36:23
thy beak from out my h. POE 375:6
thy h. lies open TENN 542:14
thy wine with a merry h. BIBLE 55:28
tiger's h. wrapp'd SHAK 446:16
to get your h.'s desire SHAW 497:33
to mend the h. POPE 375:11
to my dead h. run them STEV 523:11
'tween my h. and tongue SHAK 449:22
twist the sinews of thy h. BLAKE 87:15
warmth about my h. like a load KEATS 294:4
wear him In my h.'s core SHAK 434:2
wear my h. upon my sleeve SHAK 473:15
well as want of h. HOOD 254:20
Were not my h. at rest SEDL 419:13

Were with his h. BYRON 121:16
where I my h., safe-left SIDN 507:27
Where my h. lies BROW 102:34
Whispers the o'er-fraught h. SHAK 462:16
With a h. for any fate LONG 317:5
with my h. in't SHAK 485:13
without the h. GAY 222:9
With your crooked h. AUDEN 18:11
would not have such a h. SHAK 462:23
wouldst wish thine own h. KEATS 290:30
your h. to a dog to tear KIPL 302:3
heart-ache: sleep to say we end The h.
  SHAK 433:8
heart-break: h. in the heart of things
  GIBS 225:5
heart-easing: most h. things KEATS 292:9
heart-throbs: count time by h. BAIL 29:21
hearth: By this still h. TENN 543:21
  from an unextinguished h. SHEL 502:14
  genial h. WORD 581:16
  Save the cricket on the h. MILT 342:5
  woman for the h. TENN 542:9
hearth-fire: h. and the home-acre KIPL 299:21
hearth-stane: His clean h. BURNS 113:5
heartily: h. rejoice in the strength PRAY 396:3
heartless: h., witless nature HOUS 265:10
hearts: cold h. and muddy BURKE 111:11
  Combine your h. in one SHAK 445:16
  day star arise in your h. BIBLE 80:34
  draw H. after them MILT 350:2
  Ensanguin'd h. COWP 167:16
  finite h. that yearn BROW 105:30
  first in the h. of his LEE 313:7
  harden not your h. PRAY 396:4
  h. and intellects like MILL 339:22
  h. are dry as summer dust WORD 577:11
  h. are more than coronets TENN 537:29
  h. beating each to each BROW 102:14
  h. I lost my own HOUS 265:6
  H. just as pure and fair GILB 226:5
  h. of gold and lungs BELL 39:28
  h. that honour could not BROO 94:27
  H. that have lost their HOUS 265:9
  h. That spaniel'd me SHAK 423:5
  h. were fulfilled with SWIN 528:24
  H. wound up with love SPEN 515:9
  hidden in each other's h. DICK 179:17
  is enthroned in the h. SHAK 467:27
  keep your h. and minds BIBLE 78:21
  let not your h. be hardened VILL 557:4
  Lift up your h. PRAY 387:21
  met, but not our h. HOOD 255:13
  opportunity for a jining of h. DICK 181:1
  our h. are great TENN 535:1
  our h., though stout LONG 317:2
  Pluck their h. from them SHAK 444:26
  sleepless children's h. are glad BETJ 42:8
  stout h. and sharp swords BIRK 84:14
  take away our h. o' stone OCAS 364:17
  Their hands upon their h. HOUS 264:23
  their h. are in the right DISR 186:12
  thousand h. beat happily BYRON 120:20
  To live in h. we leave CAMP 128:19
  to place women's h. WEBS 566:19
  to steal away your h. SHAK 451:1
  Two h. that beat as one HALM 238:10
  undeveloped h. FORS 216:22
  union of hands and h. TAYL 532:6
  unto whom all h. be open PRAY 387:7
  When h. have once mingled SHEL 501:22
  Who sing to find your h. FLEC 214:9
  wins more h. ANON 6:7
  You are high in our h. BETJ 42:15
  you hard h. SHAK 448:6
heart-strings: jesses were my dear h.
  SHAK 475:21
heat: bear the burden and the h. ARN 13:23
  burden and h. of the day BIBLE 67:15
  cold and h. BIBLE 45:37
  Fear no more the h. o' SHAK 428:22

Giving more light than h. SHAK 430:21
have neither h. nor light WEBS 566:25
H. me these irons hot SHAK 452:22
H. not a furnace for your SHAK 446:25
h. of life in the handful CONR 161:24
Lap your loneliness in h. BETJ 42:7
nor any h. BIBLE 82:3
not without dust and h. MILT 351:24
Surprised I was with sudden h. SOUT 514:19
white h. of this revolution WILS 574:17
you can't stand the h. TRUM 553:20
heated: When h. in the chase TATE 531:20
heath: h., with withering brake COWP 168:26
  h. wore the appearance HARDY 241:19
  said to understand the h. HARDY 241:20
  sword sung on the barren h. BLAKE 86:19
  There's the wind on the h. BORR 90:5
  Upon the h. SHAK 458:1
  Upon this blasted h. you SHAK 458:13
heathen: be exalted among the h.
  PRAY 392:21
  Guard even h. things CHES 146:19
  h. heart that puts her KIPL 302:10
  h. in his blindness HEBER 244:6
  h. make much ado PRAY 392:20
  h. so furiously rage PRAY 389:15
  in perils by the h. BIBLE 77:12
  machine for converting the H. CARL 131:6
  repetitions, as the h. do BIBLE 64:23
  To be avenged of the h. PRAY 399:24
  To break the h. TENN 534:11
  very h. in the carnal part POPE 377:19
heather: red h. we dance together
  CALV 127:25
heaths: some game on these lone h.
  HAZL 243:32
heat-oppressed: Proceeding from the
  h. brain SHAK 459:15
heave: angels h. up Sir Launcelot MAL 328:7
Heaven: All earth can take or H. SHEL 501:2
  All I seek, the h. above STEV 522:28
  all of h. we have below ADD 2:6
  All this and h. too HENRY 245:22
  all to H. JONES 283:13
  appeared a great wonder in h. BIBLE 82:10
  art thou fallen from h. BIBLE 58:13
  ascend to h. FIRM 212:2
  bask in H.'s blue smile SHEL 500:5
  beat on H.'s shore BLAKE 85:15
  Be but the shadow of H. MILT 348:21
  become the hoped-for h. MILL 339:22
  be hell that are not h. MARL 329:8
  betwixt H. and Charing Cross THOM 548:25
  bring all H. before mine MILT 342:10
  bring up the rear in h. BROW 96:26
  by a whirlwind into h. BIBLE 51:22
  call it the Road to H. BALL 32:5
  coming of the King of H. ANON 9:1
  created the h. and the earth BIBLE 44:22
  day when h. was falling HOUS 265:7
  do in h. we are ignorant SWIFT 527:9
  Down from the verge of H. MILT 348:27
  Earth and high h. are fixt HOUS 264:3
  earth breaks up and h. BROW 99:20
  Earth's crammed with h. BROW 97:33
  eleven who went to h. ANON 6:5
  enter into the kingdom of h. BIBLE 64:11
  eye of h. to garnish SHAK 452:25
  family in h. and earth BIBLE 77:24
  Father which art in h. BIBLE 64:24
  flowerless fields of h. SWIN 528:14
  from a high and frosty h. BRID 92:13
  gave them food from h. PRAY 395:6
  Give the jolly h. above STEV 522:27
  God's in his h. BROW 103:21
  God we know the way to h. ELST 206:15
  have sinned against h. BIBLE 70:19
  h. above me and the moral KANT 288:8
  H. and earth shall pass BIBLE 67:31
  H. and Earth are not ruthful LAO 310:2

Hermon: little hill of H. PRAY 392:8
hern: haunts of coot and h. TENN 532:20
Hernani: theatre to applaud 'H.' STEV 522:2
hero: Came the h. from his prison AYT 24:9
conquering h. comes MOR 357:21
god-like h. sate DRYD 194:23
h. becomes a bore at last EMER 208:4
H. can be Poet CARL 131:33
h. perish POPE 379:4
man is a h. to his valet CORN 162:24
Soldiers who wish to be a h. ROST 410:15
very valet seem'd a h. BYRON 119:30
What god, man, or h. POUND 383:9
Herod: it out-herods H. SHAK 433:16
heroes: Britain a fit country for h.
  GEOR 223:33
frightened both the h. so CARR 134:33
h. of old BROW 104:1
h. up the line to death SASS 414:10
land that needs h. BREC 92:1
Thoughts of h. were MER 337:22
heroic: finish'd A life h. MILT 351:1
h. for earth too hard BROW 98:20
is a h. poem of its sort CARL 131:12
heroically: h. mad DRYD 194:21
heroine: h. goes mad she always SHER 506:3
heroism: Are fathered by our h. ELIOT 203:6
heron: h. Priested shore THOM 547:6
héros: h. pour son valet de chambre
  CORN 162:24
Herostatus: H. lives that burnt BROW 97:19
Herren-Moral: H. und Sklaven-Moral
  NIET 363:12
herrin: they'll roast thee like a h.
  BURNS 115:12
herring: plague o' these pickle h. SHAK 488:3
herring-pond: h. is wide BROW 102:20
herrschen: Du musst h. und gewinnen
  GOET 230:7
Hers: lips once sanctified by H. BROW 106:1
herself: gave me h. indeed BROW 102:2
half of her should rise h. HARDY 240:7
herte: h. have hem in reverence CHAU 143:29
renneth soone in gentil h. CHAU 142:19
tikleth me aboute myn h. roote CHAU 143:19
Hervey: call a dog *H.* JOHN 273:30
Herveys: men, women, and H. MONT 354:6
Herz: Mein H. ist schwer GOET 230:4
Herzen: Zwei H. und ein Schlag
  HALM 238:10
Heshbon: like the fishpools in H. BIBLE 57:9
hesitate: Do not h. to shoot BALF 30:1
h. and falter life away ARN 14:17
of spirit could long h. STEV 522:13
hesitates: Who h. toward you ELIOT 204:9
hésite: elle h. RAC 404:3
Hesper: slippered H. BROO 94:19
Hesperian: H. fables true MILT 347:19
Hesperides: climbing trees in the H.
  SHAK 457:8
Ladies of th' H. MILT 350:3
Hesperus: H. entreats thy light JONS 283:24
It was the schooner H. LONG 317:20
venit H. VIRG 560:9
heterodoxy: h. is another man's doxy
  WARB 564:17
My-doxy and H. or Thy-doxy CARL 131:25
heterogeneity: definite coherent h.
  SPEN 514:29
Heu: H., *miserande puer* VIRG 559:2
heures: Trois h., c'est toujours trop tard
  SART 414:9
heureux: faut imaginer Sisyphe h.
  CAMUS 129:24
H. qui comme Ulysse a fait DU B 198:26
ni si h. qu'on espère LA R 310:18
Heut: denk' ich H. und morgen LESS 313:26
Heute: H. leid' ich LESS 313:26
hevene: hath in h. or helle ybe CHAU 143:28
sit in h. above CHAU 144:19

hevenyssh: sownes ful of h. melodie
  CHAU 144:18
hew: h. him as a carcass fit SHAK 449:9
hewers: h. of wood and drawers BIBLE 49:3
hexameter: h. rises the fountain's COL 157:7
Hey: H. for God Almighty KETT 295:13
Then h. for boot and horse KING 297:5
hey-day: h. in the blood is tame SHAK 435:8
heye wey: Hold the h. CHAU 144:22
Hi: He would answer to 'H. CARR 133:3
Hibernian: H. learning ROCH 407:5
hic: Quod petis h. est HOR 258:19
Hic et ubique: H. then we'll shift our
  SHAK 431:20
Hic jacet: these two narrow words, H.
  RAL 404:16
hid: assumed when he h. himself among
  women BROW 97:14
h. as it were our faces BIBLE 59:21
h. his face amid a crowd YEATS 587:12
h. in the heart of love YEATS 586:9
h. themselves in the dens BIBLE 81:30
maiden h. SWIN 528:18
Moses h. his face BIBLE 47:5
on an hill cannot be h. BIBLE 64:8
they are h. from thy eyes BIBLE 71:3
to keep that h. DONNE 190:16
Wherefore are these things h. SHAK 488:1
hidden: Half h. from the eye WORD 581:6
h. her head SWIN 530:7
h. in each other's hearts DICK 179:17
h. meaning—like Basingstoke GILB 228:36
h. path down which have LUIS 320:12
Nature is often h. BACON 26:36
'Something h. KIPL 299:2
hide: h. is sure to flatten 'em BELL 38:30
H. their diminished heads MILT 347:13
h. us from the face BIBLE 81:30
h. with ornaments their POPE 378:16
it a world to h. virtues SHAK 488:2
thou h. thy face from me PRAY 390:1
Thou wear a lion's h. SHAK 452:16
Whose h. he sold WALL 562:6
wrapp'd in a woman's h. SHAK 446:16
hideous: h. notes of woe BYRON 124:6
Making night h. SHAK 430:24
hides: h. a dark soul MILT 341:8
H. from himself its state JOHN 283:1
H. not his visage from SHAK 492:4
h. the ruin that it feeds COWP 166:10
hiding: h. place from the wind BIBLE 58:30
H. the grossness with fair SHAK 467:10
H. thy bravery in their SHAK 493:11
My heart in h. HOPK 257:5
hie: Away we both must h. HOUS 265:12
Hier: H. stehe ich LUTH 320:16
Hierusalem: H., my happy home ANON 5:19
Higginbottom: such hideous names as
  H. ARN 15:26
high: Altogether upon the h. horse
  BROWN 95:7
are h. in our hearts today BETJ 42:15
Broad and I'm the H. SPR 517:11
Cannot be heard so h. SHAK 455:14
Every man who is h. up BARR 34:22
from a h. and frosty heaven BRID 92:13
h. aesthetic line GILB 227:20
h. aesthetic band GILB 227:23
h. contracting parties KELL 295:8
'H. diddle diddle' GILB 227:25
h. heels are most agreeable SWIFT 526:4
h. life high characters POPE 377:11
h. road that leads him JOHN 274:30
h. that proved too high BROW 98:20
h. the heaven is in comparison PRAY 396:17
h. tide and the turn CHES 146:20
house of defence very h. PRAY 395:22
is h. time to awake out BIBLE 75:24
judgements about great and h. MONT 354:12
knowledge in the most H. PRAY 394:22

Lord most H. PRAY 387:23
slain in thine h. places BIBLE 50:17
So h., that looking downward ROSS 409:16
teach h. thought TENN 534:12
That only to stand h. SHAK 467:13
This h. man BROW 100:38
which are too h. for me PRAY 398:25
Highbury: H. bore me ELIOT 205:5
higher: find my own the h. CORN 162:19
go up h. BIBLE 70:8
man in h. rank to take RUSK 412:7
shoot h. than who aims SIDN 507:15
subject unto the h. powers BIBLE 75:20
Highest: children of the most H. PRAY 395:10
Glory to God in the h. BIBLE 69:11
h. reaches of a human wit MARL 330:11
invariably from the h. principles FARR 210:25
needs must love the h. TENN 534:15
sit not down in the h. room BIBLE 70:7
Highgate: barking dogs by H. Pond
  BETJ 43:19
high jinks: forgotten pastime of h.
  SCOTT 418:19
Highland: heart is H. GALT 221:2
Sweet H. Girl WORD 578:11
Highlandman: breeks aff a wild H.
  SCOTT 418:11
Highlands: chieftain to the H. bound
  CAMP 129:1
Farewell to the H. BURNS 114:26
In the h. STEV 523:2
My heart's in the H. BURNS 114:25
Ye H. and ye Lawlands BALL 30:15
highly: From a h. impossible tree GILB 225:13
what thou wouldst h. SHAK 459:1
high-minded: I am not h. PRAY 398:24
high-mindedness: joss-sticks and
honourable h. BRAM 91:21
High-Park: beyond H.'s a desart to you
  ETH 208:31
high-sorrowful: That leaves a heart h.
  KEATS 291:7
highway: h. of the world SHEL 500:10
H., since you my chief SIDN 507:27
straight in the desert a h. BIBLE 59:5
highwayman: h. came riding NOYES 364:12
highways: happy h. where I went
  HOUS 263:22
out into the h. and hedges BIBLE 70:13
hilarity: h. was like a scream from
  GREE 236:6
sinking flame of h. with DICK 180:26
hill: every mountain and h. shall BIBLE 59:5
flung us on the windy h. BROO 94:15
holy h., and to thy dwelling PRAY 392:11
hunter home from the h. STEV 523:10
I climbed a h. as light HODG 252:6
idle h. of summer HOUS 263:18
laughing is heard on the h. BLAKE 88:3
little h. of Hermon PRAY 392:8
Mahomet will go to the h. BACON 25:33
nursed upon the self-same h. MILT 343:4
other side of the h. WELL 567:20
set on an h. cannot be hid BIBLE 64:8
shall rest upon thy holy h. PRAY 390:4
standing alone on a h. HARDY 241:9
stood upon that silent h. HODG 252:8
their haven under the h. TENN 532:18
this is God's h. PRAY 394:9
vineyard in a very fruitful h. BIBLE 57:21
hills: angel satyr walks these h. KILV 296:7
blue remembered h. HOUS 263:22
cattle upon a thousand h. PRAY 393:2
daft and happy h. THOM 546:22
forth upon our clouded h. BLAKE 86:1
high h. are a refuge PRAY 397:1
H. of home STEV 523:5
H. of the Chankly Bore LEAR 312:2
h. of the South Country BELL 40:9
H. peep o'er hills POPE 378:14

h. shall rejoice on every PRAY 394:3
h. stand about Jerusalem PRAY 398:15
h., they shall smoke PRAY 397:2
h. where his life rose ARN 12:22
hop ye so, ye high h. PRAY 394:9
immutable as the H. KIPL 304:32
I to the h. will lift SCOT 419:6
little h. righteousness PRAY 394:19
little h. like young sheep PRAY 397:16
Lord who made the h. KIPL 303:14
name to the reverberate h. SHAK 488:13
old brown h. MAS 334:9
Over the h. and far away GAY 222:22
'Over the h. and far away' STEV 523:8
rocks and h. whose heads SHAK 473:25
strength of the h. is his PRAY 396:4
though the h. be carried PRAY 392:19
to be out on the h. alone KILV 296:8
up mine eyes unto the h. PRAY 398:9
waters stand in the h. PRAY 396:18
while the h. remain TENN 541:26
yon are the h. o' Heaven BALL 30:18
hill-side: h.'s dew-pearled BROW 103:21
Him: H. that walked the waves MILT 343:17
I hid from H. THOM 548:8
I would remember H. BEEC 37:9
'That's h. BARH 33:15
ways with men I find H. TENN 535:19
Himalayan: H. peasant meets the he-bear KIPL 299:4
himputation: h. on his morality than SURT 525:9
himself: end by loving h. better COL 157:18
'He h. said it' CIC 151:20
he shall speak for h. BIBLE 72:15
man for loving h. BACON 27:8
of a man's actions, h. BACON 27:36
shake a man's faith in h. SHAW 496:15
subdue all things to h. PRAY 389:13
that he has done it all h. BARR 34:22
when the ado is about h. TROL 552:18
with h. at war SHAK 448:11
hinan: Ewig-Weibliche zieht uns h. GOET 230:6
Hinc: H. illae lacrimae TER 544:14
hind: h. that would be mated SHAK 420:26
hinder: all the h. parts SPEN 516:3
dog's walking on his h. JOHN 275:10
she's helpless to h. that HARDY 241:16
Stands on his h. legs with SHAK 495:21
hindered: sore let and h. PRAY 386:6
hinders: wickedness that h. loving BROW 102:31
Hindoo: turns H. SHEL 501:19
Hindoos: Christianity to the H. WIS 575:10
hindrance: though it were to his own h. PRAY 390:5
hindrances: h. to human improvement MILL 339:18
hinds: h. to bring forth young PRAY 391:11
Soft maids and village h. COLL 158:16
hinges: door on its h. WATTS 565:25
on their h. grate MILT 347:3
hint: Just h. a fault POPE 376:26
hip: catch him once upon the h. SHAK 465:29
I have thee on the h. SHAK 468:8
smote them h. and thigh BIBLE 49:23
Hippocrene: blushful H. KEATS 291:18
Hippopotamus: found it was A H. CARR 133:13
I shoot the H. BELL 38:30
hips: We swing ungirded h. SORL 513:10
whole quire hold their h. SHAK 470:3
hire: labourer is worthy of his h. BIBLE 69:27
hired: h. tears BROW 97:8
I'm sick of the h. women KIPL 301:10
hireling: h. fleeth BIBLE 72:19
his: we are h. people PRAY 396:11
hiss: dismal universal h. MILT 349:22
hissed: h. along the polished ice WORD 577:25

histoire: l'h. n'est que le tableau VOLT 561:10
Peu connu dans l'h. BER 41:14
historian: h., essentially JAMES 271:18
H.Imagination is not required JOHN 274:29
h. of the Roman empire GIBB 224:15
life of the h. must be GIBB 224:18
historians: alter the past, h. can BUTL 118:21
remain a portent to the h. KEYN 295:16
These gentle h. BURKE 112:3
Histories: H. make men wise BACON 27:21
history: Antiquities are h. defaced BACON 24:18
art is the h. of revivals BUTL 118:33
below the dignity of h. MAC 324:15
brutal in the h. of civilisation BEEC 37:5
fix the period in the h. GIBB 224:24
great dust-heap called 'h. BIRR 84:17
great h. of the land LONG 317:7
have no h. ELIOT 201:18
H., abounding with kings MAC 324:21
H. a distillation of rumour CARL 131:23
H. came SELL 420:8
H. is a nightmare from JOYCE 286:23
H. is a pack of lies STUB 524:5
H. is more or less bunk FORD 216:11
h. is nothing more than VOLT 561:10
H. is past politics SEEL 419:17
H. is philosophy from examples DION 184:9
H. is the essence of innumerable CARL 131:9
h. of all hitherto existing MARX 333:3
h. of England is emphatically MAC 323:12
h. of the human spirit ARN 16:17
h. of the world is CARL 131:31
H. the operator AUDEN 20:15
h. to produce a little JAMES 271:8
H. to the defeated AUDEN 20:17
Human h. becomes more WELLS 568:16
is a h. of the affections IRV 270:20
learned anything from h. HEGEL 244:8
Little known to h. BER 41:14
maintained the dignity of h. BOL 89:18
makes rattling good h. HARDY 239:15
memorable in the h. of our race CHUR 150:8
men could learn from h. COL 157:20
no h.; only biography EMER 207:24
product of h. CARL 131:8
Real solemn h. AUST 23:4
serious attention than h. ARIS 12:10
Thames is liquid h. BURNS 112:23
There is a h. in all men's SHAK 442:3
this strange eventful h. SHAK 425:24
tragedy, comedy, h. SHAK 432:20
very few Dates in this H. AUST 22:19
welding of their later h. HARDY 239:6
When I made h. ELIOT 203:7
with the freedom of h. BURKE 109:5
world's h. is the world's SCH 415:11
history-books: annals are blank in h. CARL 131:20
hit: can h. from far HERB 247:16
If you would h. the mark LONG 316:11
never think I have h. hard JOHN 276:20
two h. it off as they should WORD 576:22
up and h. me in the hed WARD 564:28
very palpable h. SHAK 437:18
Hitch: H. your wagon to a star EMER 208:8
hitch'd: then he h. his trousers up BARH 33:23
hitched: If you mean gettin h. WARD 564:20
hither: come h. SHAK 425:14
Hitler: H. has missed the bus CHAM 139:11
vassal state of H.'s Empire CHUR 150:7
hive: helmet now shall make a h. PEELE 371:8
h. for the honey-bee YEATS 585:17
h. of silvery Bees LEAR 312:9
ho: music, h. SHAK 422:8
hoard: Our h. is little TENN 535:1
hoar-frost: scattereth the h. like ashes PRAY 399:21
hoarse: Bondage is h. SHAK 482:19

raven himself is h. SHAK 459:2
hoary: at best but dull and h. VAUG 555:19
hob-and-nob: Let us h. with Death TENN 544:7
Hobbes: H. clearly proves SWIFT 528:4
hobby-horse: h. is forgot SHAK 434:8
hobgoblin: consistency is the h. of little minds EMER 207:38
Hoc: H. erat in votis HOR 262:9
H. opus VIRG 558:18
hock: at a weak h. and seltzer BETJ 42:4
Hock-carts: H., wassails HERR 248:18
Hockley: Hey H. KETT 295:13
Hodge: Will H. for ever be HARDY 239:9
hodgepodge: tongue a gallimaufry or h. SPEN 517:6
hodmen: unconscious h. of the men HEINE 244:12
hoe: darned long row to h. LOW 319:2
h. and she laughs with JERR 273:7
large h. and a shovel also KIPL 300:11
hoed: h. and trenched and weeded HOUS 264:17
hog: all England under a h. COLL 158:10
hoggish: have his h. mind SPEN 516:14
hogshead: fighting with daggers in a h. SCOTT 419:2
Höhere: warte ich...auf H. NIET 363:2
Höhlen: jahrtausendlang H. geben NIET 363:6
hoi polloi: h., 'tis no matter what DRYD 198:4
Hoist: H. with his own petar SHAK 435:21
Holborn: when I was last in H. SHAK 481:4
hold: does it h. good measure BROW 100:4
Earth will h. us ANON 10:13
hell gat h. upon me PRAY 397:19
He will h. thee TENN 538:19
h. a candle to my shames SHAK 466:15
H., enough! SHAK 463:9
h. fast that which is good BIBLE 79:4
H. Infinity in the palm BLAKE 85:8
H., or cut bow-strings SHAK 470:1
h. readily in your hand JOHN 280:17
h. thee but by thy granting SHAK 494:13
H. the fort BLISS 88:31
H. thou the good TENN 536:23
I h. it towards you KEATS 290:30
It is I you h. WHIT 570:13
keep a h. of Nurse BELL 39:3
quire h. their hips and loff SHAK 470:3
she h. the gorgeous East WORD 582:10
these should h. their peace BIBLE 71:2
To cry 'H., hold SHAK 459:2
to have and to h. from PRAY 389:4
hold-fast: h. is the only dog SHAK 443:20
Holding: H. the basin to gowned MACN 326:9
holds: h. and rolls and throws REED 405:7
h. him with his skinny COL 155:6
hole: decayed h. among the mountains ELIOT 205:10
h. where the tail came COL 156:11
play on the h. of the asp BIBLE 58:11
poisoned rat in a h. SWIFT 526:24
your hat has got a h. in't CANN 129:26
holes: foxes have h. BIBLE 65:18
holiday: Being h. SHAK 483:25
Butcher'd to make a Roman h. BYRON 121:16
he speaks h. SHAK 469:10
Is this a h. SHAK 448:5
it's a regular h. to them DICK 182:17
Monday is parson's h. SWIFT 526:19
now I am in a h. humour SHAK 426:21
On a sunshine h. MILT 342:22
With many h. and lady terms SHAK 438:14
holidays: during the h. from Eton SITW 508:15
h., till we leave school LEWIS 314:9
year were playing h. SHAK 438:13
holier: I am h. than thou BIBLE 60:13
holiest: of the truest and the h. MAL 327:22
to the H. in the height NEWM 362:12

honey-bees: so work the h.   SHAK 443:9
honey-coloured: great h. Ramparts
  YEATS 585:4
honeycomb: of an h.   BIBLE 71:20
strange woman drop as an h.   BIBLE 53:20
than honey, and the h.   PRAY 390:12
honey'd: h. middle of the night KEATS 289:12
honey-dew: he on h. hath fed   COL 157:1
honey-heavy: Enjoy the h. dew of slumber
  SHAK 449:12
honeyless: leave them h.   SHAK 451:31
Hongry: H. rooster don't cackle HARR 242:24
Honi: H. soit qui mal y pense   ANON 9:6
honking: to be a goose h. amongst
  VIRG 560:7
honores: contemnere h.   HOR 262:10
honour: air signed with their h. SPEN 515:8
all in h.   SHAK 477:22
cannot be maintained with h.   RUSS 412:19
did nobody h.   WALP 563:14
done with Hope and H.   KIPL 299:11
drowned h. by the locks   SHAK 438:19
false Idol H.   WINC 575:4
Fear God. H. the King   KITC 305:14
'fountain of h.   BAG 28:22
fount whence h. springs   MARL 330:9
gilded h. shamefully misplac'd SHAK 494:5
Giving h. unto the wife   BIBLE 80:29
greater share of h.   SHAK 445:1
hath had some smatch of h.   SHAK 452:6
hearts that h. could not move BROO 94:27
He is the fountain of h.   BACON 27:43
helps the hurt that H.   TENN 538:23
his end to be without h.   BIBLE 62:16
His h. rooted in dishonour   TENN 534:29
H. all men   BIBLE 80:25
h. and his quality taken   BLUN 89:3
h., and keep her in sickness   PRAY 389:3
h. and life have been spared   FRAN 218:1
H. a physician with   BIBLE 63:17
h. aspireth to it   BACON 26:2
H. be yours   NEWB 361:3
H. but an empty bubble   DRYD 195:5
h. doth forget men's names   SHAK 452:9
h. due unto his Name   PRAY 396:5
H. hath no skill in surgery   SHAK 440:18
h. his own word as if his   TENN 534:11
H. in one eye and death   SHAK 448:12
h. is the subject of my   SHAK 448:13
h. Pick'd from the chaff   SHAK 466:20
H. pricks me   SHAK 440:18
h. the very flea of his   JONS 284:6
H. thy father and thy mother BIBLE 47:24
honour to whom h.   BIBLE 75:22
H., without money   RAC 404:6
idiot race to h.   BURNS 114:29
I h. him   SHAK 450:15
In dignitye or h. goeth   DUNB 199:12
in h. clear   POPE 378:6
In h. I gained them   NELS 360:18
Is from the book of h.   SHAK 493:4
is leisure with h.   CIC 151:33
Keeps h. bright   SHAK 487:4
king delighteth to h.   BIBLE 52:3
learn Latin as an h.   CHUR 150:23
left hand riches and h.   BIBLE 53:16
Let us h. if we can   AUDEN 20:11
like not such grinning h.   SHAK 440:21
loss of h. was a wrench   GRAH 233:9
louder he talked of his h.   EMER 207:8
Lov'd I not h. more   LOV 318:20
make one vessel unto h.   BIBLE 75:14
man will not abide in h.   PRAY 392:28
Mine h. is my life   SHAK 478:8
not a stain in thine h.   BIBLE 63:16
peace I hope with h.   DISR 185:15
peace with h.   CHAM 139:10
perfect ways of h.   SHAK 448:2
places where their h. died POPE 377:26
post of h. is a private   ADD 1:23

prefer mere existence to h.   JUV 287:25
prophet is not without h.   BIBLE 66:23
republic a roll of h.   CLEV 153:2
resolved to h. and renown ye ANON 7:15
sin to covet h.   SHAK 445:2
that chastity of h.   BURKE 111:10
That h. which shall bate   SHAK 456:14
Thou art a tool of h.   WORD 583:3
throne we h. is the people's SHER 506:7
tide is ready her to h.   BEST 42:2
To keep mine h. from corruption
  SHAK 447:23
To pluck bright h. from   SHAK 438:19
to some rag of h.   STEV 521:2
Trouthe and h.   CHAU 141:9
Truth the masculine, of H. HARE 242:5
When h.'s at the stake   SHAK 435:31
Ye take mine h. from me   KIPL 300:19
your quaint h. turn to dust MARV 332:19
honourable: Brutus is an h. man SHAK 450:17
Brutus is an h. man   SHAK 450:18
daughters were among thy h. PRAY 392:16
h. style of a Christian   BROW 96:2
joss-sticks and h. high-mindedness
  BRAM 91:20
lest a more h. man than   BIBLE 70:7
Let us make an h. retreat   SHAK 426:6
Paul to be h. among all men PRAY 388:25
honour'd: By strangers h.   POPE 376:10
He hath h. me of late   SHAK 459:7
h. of them all   TENN 543:22
More h. in the breach than SHAK 430:23
honoured: It has h. us   WEBS 566:14
honouring: Not so much h. thee JONS 284:12
honours: am stripped of all my h.
  BURKE 112:4
bears his blushing h. thick   SHAK 447:9
chase of h. and distinction BURKE 108:7
He gave his h. to the world SHAK 447:16
held the patent for his h.   BURNS 113:15
offer you either h. or wages GAR 221:10
With all his h.   AUDEN 21:9
honteux: h. de se défier de ses
  LA R 310:10
Hood: Here lies bold Robin H. BALL 31:14
hood-wink'd: h. boy I call'd in aid
  GARR 221:16
hoof: though he divide the h.   BIBLE 48:6
hoofs: h. of a swinish multitude
  BURKE 111:14
hurry of h. in a village   LONG 316:26
plunging h. were gone   DE L 174:10
hook: great h. nose like thine BLAKE 85:21
my bended h. shall pierce   SHAK 422:9
never fly conceals a h.   BROO 94:13
out leviathan with an h.   BIBLE 53:11
subscribers baits his h.   CHUR 148:30
hookah-mouth: sliding puffs from the
h.   KIPL 297:28
hook-nosed: with the h. fellow of Rome
  SHAK 442:13
Hooly: H. writ is the scripture JER 272:21
Hooting: H. and shrieking   SHAK 449:1
h. at dawn flew away none   BEER 38:2
h. at the glorious sun   COL 156:19
life to shunting and h.   BURR 116:10
Hop: H. forty paces through   SHAK 422:4
h. ye so, ye high hills   PRAY 394:9
hope: Abandon all h., you who enter
  DANTE 171:3
against hope believed in h.   BIBLE 74:40
All our h. is fallen   HOR 261:13
are also heirs through h.   PRAY 388:3
Can something, h.,   HOPK 256:7
done with H. and Honour KIPL 299:11
do not h. to turn again   ELIOT 201:32
equal h.   MILT 345:1
equal poise of h. and fear MILT 341:9
Evelyn H. is dead   BROW 100:25
failure of h.   GIBB 224:20
faith, h., charity   BIBLE 76:14

From h. and fear set free   SWIN 529:25
God is our h. and strength PRAY 392:19
He that lives upon h. will   FRAN 218:13
h. again for aught that   MORR 358:8
H. deferred maketh   BIBLE 53:35
H., for a season   CAMP 129:7
h. for the best   SMITH 510:31
h. I dreamed of was a dream ROSS 409:2
H. is a good breakfast   BACON 25:8
h. I will be religious   FLEM 214:29
Hopeless h. hopes   CLARE 152:9
H. maketh not ashamed   BIBLE 74:41
H. may vanish   SHEL 500:18
h. never comes   MILT 344:25
h. of a fool than of him   BIBLE 54:33
h. of all the ends   PRAY 394:1
h. of glory   PRAY 386:2
h. of the City of God   MAS 334:7
h. of the ungodly   BIBLE 62:18
h., once crushed   ARN 15:9
h. our acquaintance may   DICK 182:5
H., politeness, the blowing FORS 217:8
H. springs eternal   POPE 379:5
h. that is unwilling   WORD 581:2
h. that keeps up a wife's   GAY 222:18
h. who never had a fear   COWP 167:36
h. without an object cannot COL 157:15
I have h. to live   SHAK 464:8
In faith and h. the world POPE 379:20
in sure and certain h.   PRAY 389:13
Land of H. and Glory   BENS 40:24
leisure for love or h.   HOOD 255:9
Let us h. for better things AUST 23:17
my h. is better   SHAK 490:12
Never to h. again   SHAK 447:9
Nor dread nor h. attend   YEATS 584:20
not another's h.   WALSH 563:30
Not to h. for things   HOR 261:15
nursing the unconquerable h. ARN 14:20
only we have h. in Christ   BIBLE 76:21
patience of h. in our Lord BIBLE 78:30
poet's h.   AUDEN 20:14
reinforcement we may gain from h.
  MILT 345:7
secret h. for greater favours LA R 310:16
Some blessed H.   HARDY 239:7
strength and my h. is perished BIBLE 60:29
tender leaves of h.   SHAK 447:9
their h. full of immortality BIBLE 62:13
Through love, through h. WORD 581:2
to hope till H. creates   SHEL 503:15
to one more rich in h.   SHAK 493:6
triumph of h. over experience JOHN 275:36
True h. is swift   SHAK 481:11
unsettled is there any h.   EMER 207:15
Was the h. drunk   SHAK 459:8
what is h. but deceiving   MER 338:7
what was dead was H.   WILDE 572:13
what you can desire or h. DRYD 197:5
whence this pleasing h.   ADD 1:24
when existence or when h. AUST 23:10
Where feeble H. could ne'er MARV 331:18
wish for what I faintly h. DRYD 197:16
with h. farewell fear   MILT 347:16
hoped: getting anything he h. VIRG 559:14
never h. can never despair SHAW 496:11
substance of things h.   BIBLE 79:31
hoped-for: already become the h. heaven
  MILL 339:22
hopeful: far more cheerful and h.
  HOLM 253:14
h. green stuff woven   WHIT 570:18
h. thou'lt recover once   GRAH 233:16
theirs with the h. past   BROW 101:25
hopefully: To travel h. is a better STEV 522:9
hopeless: Ages of h. end   MILT 346:11
either superfluous or h.   NEWM 362:10
h. grief is passionless   BROW 98:7
h. passion is my destiny   THAC 545:13
h. than a scheme of merriment JOHN 281:21

Terror the h. form divine — BLAKE 88:9
think the full tide of h. — JOHN 276:21
thorough knowledge of h. — AUST 22:31
'Tis a shame to h. nature — HOUS 266:8
To be a soaring h. boy — DICK 176:14
To err is h. — POPE 378:27
To step aside is h. — BURNS 112:25
Treatise of H. Nature — HUME 268:1
When in the course of h. — JEFF 272:5
wisdom of h. contrivances — BURKE 109:18
wish I loved the H. Race — RAL 404:20
would be due to h. folly — LAW 311:1
humani: h. nil a me alienum puto — TER 544:17
Humanities: H. live for ever — NORTH 364:5
humanity: crooked timber of h. — KANT 288:14
h., reason, and justice — BURKE 109:26
H. with all its fears — LONG 316:7
law of h. — BURKE 110:32
out of the feelings of h. — BLAC 85:2
popular h. is treason — ADD 1:21
religion of h. — PAINE 368:7
So act as to treat h. — KANT 288:13
spirit never Did steer h. — SHAK 423:19
still, sad music of h. — WORD 578:7
strait jacket for h. — MER 337:23
teach governments h. — PAINE 368:4
they imitated h. so abominably — SHAK 433:17
wearisome condition of h. — GREV 236:16
human kind: vices and follies of h. — CONG 159:20
human race: h., to which so many — CHES 148:2
humans: It isn't fit for h. now — BETJ 44:4
Humber: Of H. would complain — MARV 332:18
humble: Be it ever so h. — PAYNE 370:10
confess them with an h. — PRAY 384:9
He that is h. ever shall — BUNY 107:32
he that shall h. himself — BIBLE 67:23
h. and a contrite heart — KIPL 302:7
such names and not be h. — SASS 414:19
humbled: maintains that I am h. now — CORN 162:19
humbleness: All h. — SHAK 426:29
whispering h. — SHAK 466:3
humbler: h. heav'n — POPE 379:5
humblest: h. citizen of all the land — BRYAN 106:7
humbleth: he that h. himself shall — BIBLE 70:9
humbly: me to my Lord right h. — PRAY 391:14
walk h. with thy God — BIBLE 61:25
humbug: h. in a Pickwickian point — DICK 181:22
Hume: hand of Mr H. in 1739 — SMITH 511:33
humid: h. nightblue fruit — JOYCE 286:29
Humiliation: valley of H. — BUNY 107:13
humility: 'Had he but the gift of h. — STIL 523:14
H. may clothe an English — COWP 167:35
modest stillness and h. — SHAK 443:21
pride that apes h. — COL 156:13
to visit us in great h. — PRAY 386:4
humour: effusions of wit and h. — AUST 22:31
ever woman in this h. won — SHAK 480:22
H. is odd, grotesque — SWIFT 528:7
h. just, yet new — CHUR 149:12
h. temp'ring virtuous rage — POPE 378:8
most perfect h. and irony — BUTL 118:23
say it is my h. — SHAK 467:20
humoured: must be play'd with and h. — TEMP 532:9
humours: h. and flatters them — CHES 145:26
In all thy h. — ADD 2:10
hump: Camel's h. is an ugly lump — KIPL 300:9
H. that is black and blue — KIPL 300:10
uglier yet is the H. we get — KIPL 300:9
without a positive h. — THAC 545:21
humphed: Camel h. himself — KIPL 304:18
humus: Nos habebit h. — ANON 10:13
Hun: H. is at the gate — KIPL 299:6

Huncamunca: To sun my self in H.'s — FIEL 211:34
hundred: His h.'s soon hit — BROW 100:38
moderate haste might tell a h. — SHAK 430:12
hundreds: h. to Ludlow come — HOUS 263:6
Hundredth: At my door the H. Psalm — CALV 127:23
left him practising the h. — BYRON 126:10
Hung: H. be the heavens with — SHAK 445:17
ocean Is folded and h. — AUDEN 18:9
Hungarian: It's not enough to be H. — KORDA 305:27
Hunger: H. allows no choice — AUDEN 20:9
h. and thirst after righteousness — BIBLE 64:6
H. is the best sauce — CERV 138:13
h. of ambitious minds — SPEN 516:21
H. that urges to wrongdoing — VIRG 558:21
h., thirst, forced marches — GAR 221:10
I perish with h. — BIBLE 70:19
lack, and suffer h. — PRAY 391:22
poverty, h., and dirt — HOOD 255:6
remember the time of h. — BIBLE 63:5
They shall h. no more — BIBLE 82:3
with bodily h. in his eyes — SHAW 497:13
Yet fed your h. like — CRANE 168:30
hungred: I was an h. — BIBLE 68:6
hungry: ate when we were not h. — SWIFT 526:10
Cassius has a lean and h. — SHAK 448:20
fierce, weeping, h. man — CARL 132:24
filleth the h. soul with — PRAY 397:7
have seen the h. ocean gain — SHAK 494:3
He hath filled the h. with — BIBLE 69:6
h. with good things — BIBLE 83:18
I am not h. — PUNCH 402:29
If thine enemy be h. — BIBLE 54:29
is all as h. as the sea — SHAK 489:6
roaming with a h. heart — TENN 543:22
she makes h. — SHAK 422:5
tigers are getting h. — CHUR 151:3
You've time to get h. — MOL 353:16
hunt: can h. a poetaster down — BYRON 124:31
We h. them for the beauty — TENN 542:8
You will see H. — SHEL 501:18
hunted: others by their h. expression — LEWIS 314:8
Past reason h. — SHAK 495:7
hunter: Esau was a cunning h. — BIBLE 46:13
from the snare of the h. — PRAY 395:21
h. home from the hill — STEV 523:10
H. of the East has caught — FITZ 212:5
Nimrod the mighty h. before — BIBLE 46:1
trail'd the h.'s javelin — ARN 14:26
Hunter Dunn: Joan H. — BETJ 44:6
hunters: That seith that h. ben — CHAU 141:18
hunting: discourse was about h. — PEPYS 372:11
ever to call h. one of them — JOHN 280:15
go h. the beautiful deer — AUDEN 18:8
H. he lov'd — SHAK 495:18
I'm weary wi' h. — BALL 31:5
in wet and dirty from h. — SURT 525:26
I went h. wild — OWEN 367:10
like the h. of the hare — BLUNT 89:4
than to h. and shooting — BURR 116:10
There is a passion for h. — DICK 180:35
huntress: Queen and h. — JONS 283:24
hunts: he h. in dreams — TENN 538:21
huntsman: cassock'd h. and a fiddling — COWP 166:7
h. by the bear oppress'd — WALL 562:6
H., rest — SCOTT 416:3
hurl: h. my soul from heaven — SHAK 477:21
hurl'd: Swift to be h. — HOOD 254:10
Hurled: H. headlong flaming from — MILT 344:24
hurly-burly: h. of the chaise-longue — CAMP 128:9
When the h.'s done — SHAK 458:1
hurricanoes: You cataracts and h. — SHAK 454:4

hurried: who was h. hence — CLEV 153:3
hurry: h. of hoofs in a village — LONG 316:26
I am never in a h. — WESL 568:20
old man in a h. — CHUR 149:12
sows h. and reaps — STEV 522:5
hurt: assault and h. the soul — PRAY 386:9
done the lover mortal h. — DOUG 191:10
do nothing for to h. her — THAC 546:3
hate the man you have h. — TAC 531:8
have healed also the h. — BIBLE 60:19
Heavenly H., it gives — DICK 184:1
h. in a state than th — BACON 25:43
h. nor destroy in all my — BIBLE 58:11
h. not thy foot against — PRAY 395:22
h. that Honour feels — TENN 538:23
h. the truest knight — MAL 327:16
h. with the same weapons — SHAK 467:4
I have to be h. — SHAK 477:14
'I'll not h. thee — STER 519:24
it h. too much to laugh — STEV 520:19
shall h. the little wren — BLAKE 85:12
that doth the h. — BACON 27:30
that seek the h. of my soul — PRAY 393:22
that they mayn't h. you — LAMB 307:30
They that have power to h. — SHAK 494:15
Those have most power to h. — BEAU 36:9
hurtig: You are h. be — KIPL 304:22
hurting: once it has stopped h. — BOWEN 91:2
hurts: He h. me most who lavishly — CHUR 148:18
h., and is desir'd — SHAK 424:12
h. the poor creatures — SHAK 454:22
husband: answers till a h. cools — POPE 377:27
bride adorned for her h. — BIBLE 82:30
Chaste to her h. — POPE 377:20
comes my h. from his whist — BROW 100:20
good h., little ant — LOV 318:14
Hang your h. and be dutiful — GAY 222:19
h. a cuckold to make him — SHAK 477:2
h. could have made me like — CONG 160:13
H., I come — SHAK 424:11
h. in these circumstances — GAY 222:31
h. is a whole-time job — BENN 40:22
h. is, the wife is — TENN 538:19
h. nature's riches from — SHAK 494:15
h. of one wife — BIBLE 79:12
h. with a beard on his — SHAK 472:3
ill bred as to love a h. — WYCH 584:1
life her h. makes for her — ELIOT 201:9
man and most indulgent h. — DICK 178:25
monstrous animal a h. and wife — FIEL 211:30
much for one h. to hear — GAY 222:36
My h. then — SHAK 485:13
No worse a h. than — SHAK 422:1
she must have a h. — SHAK 484:7
so in the eyes of a h. — SWIFT 526:22
so may my h. — SHAK 465:6
sways she level in her h.'s — SHAK 489:1
Thy h. is thy lord — SHAK 484:17
unbelieving h. is sanctified — BIBLE 76:3
wife doth make a heavy h. — SHAK 468:21
woman is a crown to her h. — BIBLE 53:33
woman oweth to her h. — SHAK 484:18
husbanded: Being so fathered and so h. — SHAK 449:16
husband-hunting: h. butterfly she ever remembers — MITF 352:22
husbandry: Expresseth his full tilth and h. — SHAK 463:13
There's h. in heaven — SHAK 459:13
husbands: dare not show their h. — SHAK 475:18
divine right of h. — WOLL 576:9
H., love your wives — BIBLE 78:27
reasons for h. to stay at home — ELIOT 201:20
them ask their h. at home — BIBLE 76:17
yourselves to your own h. — BIBLE 78:6
hush: holy h. of ancient sacrifice — STEV 520:18
H.! Here comes the enemy — CONDE 159:14
H., hush, Nobody cares — MORT 358:15

h. with the setting moon TENN 540:10
H. your tongues HOR 260:13
old man who said 'H. LEAR 311:18
There's a breathless h. NEWB 361:8
hush'd: Now air is h. COLL 158:18
hush'd: h. the shrunken seas ELIOT 204:15
Hushing: H. the latest traffic BRID 92:12
husks: come is strew'd with h. SHAK 487:14
filled his belly with the h. BIBLE 70:19
hustle: health to h. the Aryan brown KIPL 301:18
who tried to h. the East KIPL 301:18
hut: Love in a h. KEATS 290:24
huts: Love had he found in h. WORD 581:11
Hyacinth: Children with H.'s temperament SAKI 413:16
every H. the Garden wears FITZ 212:15
Hyades: scudding drifts the rainy H. TENN 543:22
Hybla: rob the H. bees SHAK 451:31
Hymeneal: Chorus H. SHEL 504:20
hymns: Chanting faint h. SHAK 469:17
happy h. of farmers KING 297:21
Singing h. unbidden SHEL 504:19
sings h. at heaven's gate SHAK 493:6
with h. uproarious BETJ 43:3
yourselves in psalms and h. BIBLE 78:5
hyperbole: perpetual h. is comely BACON 26:29
hyperboles: Three-pil'd h. SHAK 457:15
hyperbolical: h. fiend SHAK 490:19
hypercritical: Constitution or laws by any h. LINC 314:18
Hyperion: H. to a satyr SHAK 429:28
Hyphenated: H. Americans ROOS 408:8
hypocrisie: L'h. est un hommage que le LA R 310:12
hypocrisy: By thy shut soul's h. BYRON 125:4
Government is an organized h. DISR 184:16
h.; from envy PRAY 385:16
H., the only evil that MILT 347:12
organized h. BAG 29:8
That would be h. WILDE 573:5
hypocrite: h., and flatterer BLAKE 86:7
H. lecteur BAUD 35:5
h. lecteur ELIOT 204:22
is a h. in his pleasures JOHN 279:22
hypocrites: h.! for ye pay tithe BIBLE 67:24
though the cant of h. may STER 519:30
hypoteneuse: about the square on the h. GILB 228:17
hypothesis: beautiful h. by an ugly fact HUXL 269:5
character of a family to an h. STER 519:20
is the nature of an h. STER 519:27
hyssop: shalt purge me with h. PRAY 393:5
will sprinkle me with h. BIBLE 83:6
hysterics: blind h. of the Celt TENN 537:16
I: altogether such as I am BIBLE 74:23
A noir, E blanc, I. rouge RIMB 406:9
Here am I., here are you AUDEN 19:14
I. am fearfully and wonderfully PRAY 399:6
I. am the batsman LANG 309:19
'I. am thyself ROSS 410:3
if I. had not been there WELL 567:19
'I. is hateful PASC 369:12
to earth I. HOUS 265:12
Tush, I. shall never be cast PRAY 389:30
were I. Lord God MACD 325:3
Why not I. with thine SHEL 502:1
iactu: Pulveris exigui i. compressa VIRG 560:18
Iago: conceiving an I. as an Imogen KEATS 294:7
Iam: I. redit et virgo VIRG 559:22
Iambics: I. march from short COL 157:4
iambos: At non effugies meos i. CAT 137:16
ianua: dies patet atri i. Ditis VIRG 558:18
Ibant: I. obscuri sola sub nocte VIRG 558:20
Iberians: dark I. come ARN 14:21

ibit: in caelum iusseris i. JUV 287:16
ice: forth his i. like morsels PRAY 399:21
hissed along the polished i. WORD 577:25
his urine is congealed i. SHAK 464:19
hot i. and wondrous strange SHAK 471:13
I. formed on the butler's WOD 575:27
i., mast-high COL 155:9
In skating over thin i. EMER 207:33
is good to break the i. BACON 25:41
penny i. and cold meat GILB 226:14
To smooth the i. SHAK 452:25
ye I. and Snow PRAY 384:22
Iceberg: silent distance grew the I. HARDY 239:6
ice-cream: emperor is the emperor of i. STEV 520:14
I., of course SASS 415:4
iced: three parts i. over ARN 16:24
Iceland: is not so bad as I. JOHN 279:23
ices: tea and cakes and i. ELIOT 203:22
I-chabod: named the child I. BIBLE 49:40
ichor: perspiration was but i. BYRON 126:7
icicle: Chaste as the i. SHAK 428:3
i. on a Dutchman's beard SHAK 489:28
icicles: hang them up in silent i. COL 156:43
When i. hang by the wall SHAK 457:19
icumen: Sumer is i. ANON 7:18
Ida: There lies a vale in I. TENN 541:16
Whether on I.'s shady brow BLAKE 88:10
idea: against invasion by an i. HUGO 267:11
Between the i. And the reality ELIOT 203:10
call it the i. of freedom PARK 368:26
he had only one i. DISR 186:31
i. ever to be fashionable SANT 414:5
i. of Death saves FORS 217:3
is the pain of a new i. BAG 29:19
me to possess but one i. JOHN 275:34
politician does get an i. MARQ 331:1
simplicity of his i. calling CONR 161:21
young i. how to shoot THOM 549:10
ideal: happiness is not an i. of reason KANT 288:12
i. reader suffering from JOYCE 286:3
it is the i. American who CHES 148:6
nicht ein I. der Vernunft KANT 288:12
paletot aussi devenait i. RIMB 406:7
softly sleeps the calm I. DICK 179:22
idealistic: America is the only i. WILS 575:3
idealize: they i. love too much JOW 285:24
ideas: are but the signs of i. JOHN 281:6
green i. sleep CHOM 148:15
idées: Elle a des i. au-dessus RATT 405:2
pas à l'invasion des i. HUGO 267:11
identity: because he has no i. KEATS 294:8
equal communion and I. DONNE 191:3
His i. presses upon me KEATS 294:2
ides: Beware the i. of March SHAK 448:7
i. of March are come SHAK 449:23
idiom: i. of words very little PRIOR 400:27
idioms: licentious i. JOHN 282:5
idiosyncrasy: rather i. BROW 96:27
idiot: blaspheming over the village i. CHES 148:7
e'er the beauteous i. spoke CONG 160:2
i. race to honour BURNS 114:29
i. who praises GILB 226:25
portrait of a blinking i. SHAK 466:21
tale Told by an i. SHAK 463:6
your I. Boy WORD 577:23
idiots: fatuity of i. SMITH 511:30
idle: am happiest when I am i. WARD 564:34
be not i. BURT 117:3
calling for this i. trade POPE 376:23
employment for his i. time WALT 564:3
have not been i.' ANON 6:9
home, you i. creatures SHAK 448:5
i. as a painted ship COL 155:13
i. chatter of a transcendental GILB 227:21
i. hands to do WATTS 565:22
i. hill of summer HOUS 263:18

i. spear and shield MILT 344:6
idle than when wholly i. CIC 151:23
i. word that men shall BIBLE 66:10
most i. and unprofitable GIBB 224:7
Most 'scruciating i. KIPL 304:17
Never to be completely i. THOM 546:11
not learnt how to be i. MADAN 326:17
solitary, be not i. JOHN 278:11
whom the world Calls i. COWP 167:7
would all be i. if we could JOHN 277:3
ye here all the day i. BIBLE 67:14
you are i. shallow things SHAK 490:8
idleness: Conceives by i. SHAK 445:12
Grief is a species of i. JOHN 281:26
I. is only the refuge CHES 145:28
i., its opposite CERV 138:19
My i. doth hatch SHAK 421:19
pains and penalties of i. POPE 375:25
round of strenuous i. WORD 580:18
idler: Hath been an i. in the land WORD 580:5
hopes to be, an i. JOHN 281:17
idling: impossible to enjoy i. JER 272:22
Idol: false I. Honour WINC 575:4
make both God and an i. LUTH 320:17
natural i. of the Anglo-Saxon BAG 29:4
on an 'eathen i.'s foot KIPL 301:6
idolaters: i., and whosoever loveth BIBLE 83:3
idolatries: To its i. a patient knee BYRON 120:38
idolatry: ancients without i. CHES 145:20
on this side i. JONS 285:1
There is no i. in the Mass JOHN 275:30
Which is the god of my i. SHAK 482:15
Idols: I. I have loved so long FITZ 213:13
idoneus: Vixi puellis nuper i. HOR 261:6
idyll: Will rank as an i. GILB 227:25
If: I. I am not for myself HILL 251:6
i. I said so GOLD 232:4
I. thou must love me BROW 98:11
i. thou wert there BURNS 114:31
I. you can keep your head KIPL 299:22
much virtue in 'i.' SHAK 427:6
ifs: Talk'st thou to me of 'i.' SHAK 481:5
ignara: i. mali miseris succurrere VIRG 557:19
ignoble: base and i. creature BACON 25:25
end Was not i. WORD 580:10
soil'd with all i. use TENN 537:17
ignominy: disgrace and i. of our natures BROW 96:20
Thy i. sleep with thee SHAK 440:25
ignorance: Alike in i. POPE 379:12
child of i. and baseness BACON 25:31
From i. our comfort flows PRIOR 401:8
from knowledge i. BROW 100:10
i. cramps my conversation HOPE 255:30
I. is not innocence BROW 101:17
i. of wealth GOLD 230:18
I. of the law excuses no SELD 419:21
I pity his i. and despise DICK 180:10
more than Gothic i. FIEL 211:26
pure i. JOHN 274:17
putting us to i. again BROW 100:5
smallest allowance for i. HUXL 269:6
there is no sin but i. MARL 329:19
was distinguished for i. DISR 186:31
what i. of pain SHEL 504:21
Where blind and naked I. TENN 535:11
where i. is bliss GRAY 235:13
women in a state of i. KNOX 305:26
ignorant: Be not i. of any thing BIBLE 62:24
Confound the i. SHAK 433:1
i. armies clash by night ARN 12:23
i. of his understanding COL 157:21
i. of their Mother Tongue DRYD 198:14
i., unweighing fellow SHAK 464:20
In language, the i. DUPPA 199:16
poor, ailing and i. YEATS 585:19
schoolboy of fourteen is i. MAC 324:12

they should always be i.   AUST 23:5
this right of the i. man   CARL 131:16
utterly i. of all moral fear   SMITH 512:2
well as the i. and foolish   PRAY 392:28
ignorantly: I did it i. in unbelief   BIBLE 79:7
therefore ye i. worship   BIBLE 74:12
ignore: qu'un homme comme vous i.
   BEAU 35:16
ignotique: Urgentur i. longa   HOR 261:18
ignotum: omne i. pro magnifico est TAC 531:6
Ignotus: I. *pecori*   CAT 137:6
iguala: balanza y peso que i. al pastor
   CERV 138:20
île: î. triste et noire   BAUD 35:8
Iliad: greater than the I. is born PROP 401:17
Ilium: fuit I. et ingens   VIRG 558:6
ill: all the measureless i.   TENN 539:29
bad epitaph than their i.   SHAK 432:25
be the final goal of i.   TENN 536:24
he thinks no i.   SHAK 493:18
i. all's here about my   SHAK 437:14
i. beginning of the night   SHAK 451:29
i. bred as to love a husband   WYCH 584:1
i. discoverers that think   BACON 24:21
I. fares the land   GOLD 230:18
i. he cannot cure a name   ARN 15:12
i. keeper of promise   BACON 25:32
I. met by moonlight   SHAK 470:4
let i. tidings tell Themselves   SHAK 422:12
much less good than i.   HOUS 264:14
no i. can come   PRAY 400:5
old and i. and terrified   BETJ 44:13
sight of means to do i.   SHAK 452:28
than to rail at the i.   TENN 540:19
There is some i. a-brewing   SHAK 466:11
to do i. our sole delight   MILT 345:5
train for i. and not   HOUS 264:14
illacrimabiles: sed omnes i.   HOR 261:18
ill-bred: so illiberal and so i.   CHES 145:10
ill breeding: sign of guilt, or of i.
   CONG 160:34
ill-clad: i., ill-nourished   ROOS 407:22
ill-contrived: is a singularly i. world
   BALF 30:6
ill-doing: doctrine of i.   SHAK 493:18
Ille: I. *mi par esse deo videtur*   CAT 137:4
ill-fed: it is i.   JOHN 279:16
Ill fortune: I. seldom comes alone
   DRYD 195:36
ill-housed: one-third of a nation i.
   ROOS 407:22
illiberal: nothing so i. and so ill-bred
   CHES 145:10
illiteracy: at the i. of scientists SNOW 512:16
Illiterate: I. him   SHER 506:8
ill-luck: fond of i. that they run   JERR 273:8
way upon the singular i.   CHES 146:6
illness: i. should attend it   SHAK 459:1
Living is an i. to which   CHAM 139:13
illnesses: i. and dreary old age   VIRG 560:16
ill-nourished: ill-clad, i.   ROOS 407:22
illogical: doctrine so i. and so dull
   KEYN 295:16
ills: climax of all human i.   BYRON 122:29
have they i. to come   GRAY 235:12
i. enow To be a woman   DONNE 190:4
i. o' life victorious   BURNS 115:6
i. the scholar's life assail   JOHN 282:29
sure one for all i.   RAL 404:17
What i. from beauty spring   JOHN 283:4
ill-shapen: creatures at first are i.
   BACON 26:27
ill-spent: was a sign of an i. youth SPEN 515:4
ill-tempered: Some think him i. and queer
   LEAR 311:20
ill-treated: This is for all i. fellows
   HOUS 265:13
illuminate: please thee to i. all Bishops
   PRAY 385:18
illuminatio: Dominus i. mea   BIBLE 83:5

Illumine: What in me is dark I.   MILT 344:22
illumined: i. by flashes of lightning
   WILDE 573:37
illumineth: It i. the face   SHAK 442:15
ill-usage: complaints of i. contemptible
   MELB 336:18
illusion: i. that it is the other   GOW 233:7
nothing but sophistry and i.   HUME 267:15
only one i. left   SMITH 511:6
So thankful for i.   CLOU 153:23
illustrate: I the Trinity i.   BROW 105:6
Illustrious: I. acts high raptures do
   WALL 562:12
less i., goes the clerk   COWP 166:1
One of my i. predecessors   FIEL 211:9
Illyria: what should I do in I.   SHAK 487:22
image: Best i. of myself and dearer
   MILT 348:15
compose man's i. and his cry YEATS 586:22
express i. of his person   BIBLE 79:28
fleeting i. of a shade   SHEL 505:9
God nevertheless his i.   FULL 220:15
i. of eternity   BYRON 121:26
i. of his Maker   SHAK 447:12
I., that flying still   WORD 577:26
i. that Nebuchadnezzar   BIBLE 61:3
knowledge after the i.   BIBLE 78:26
Let us make man in our i.   BIBLE 45:4
Man is God's i.   HERB 247:9
Save in the constant i.   SHAK 488:27
Scatter'd his Maker's i.   DRYD 194:2
this i. and superscription   BIBLE 67:19
unto thee any graven i.   BIBLE 47:24
where name and i. meet   AUDEN 20:6
with the i. of the King   TENN 534:17
worship the beast and his i.   BIBLE 82:17
images: express the i. of their minds
   BACON 27:4
garden of bright i.   BRAM 91:22
imaginary: Don't let us make i. evils
   GOLD 232:12
'i. gardens with real toads MOORE 355:20
i. relish is so sweet   SHAK 486:32
imagination: abhorred in my i. it is
   SHAK 436:31
affections and the truth of i. KEATS 293:15
Are of i. all compact   SHAK 471:11
hunting-grounds for the poetic i. ELIOT 201:7
ideal of reason but of i.   KANT 288:12
if i. amend them   SHAK 471:19
i. of man's heart is evil   BIBLE 45:36
I. cold and barren   BURKE 109:16
I. droops her pinion   BYRON 123:9
i. of a boy is healthy   KEATS 288:19
i. the rudder   KEATS 293:13
i. resembled the wings   MAC 323:5
i. bodies forth   SHAK 471:11
I., which, in truth   WORD 580:26
in ages of i. this firm   BLAKE 88:26
only upon the force of i.   DRYD 196:26
refined play of the i.   BURKE 108:7
requisite for an Historian…I. JOHN 274:29
save those that have no i.   SHAW 498:20
scattered the proud in the i. BIBLE 69:6
to his i. for his facts   SHER 506:36
to sweeten my i.   SHAK 455:17
Were it not for i.   JOHN 278:4
whispering chambers of I.   DICK 179:22
imaginations: my i. are as foul SHAK 434:3
perish through their own i. PRAY 389:25
imagine: buona i. paterna DANTE 171:12
may as well i. the scene   COMP 159:13
people i. a vain   PRAY 389:15
imagined: i. such a device as they
   PRAY 390:15
imaginibus: umbris et i. in veritatem
   NEWM 362:6
imaginings: Are less than horrible i.
   SHAK 458:20
imbecility: moderation in war is i. MAC 323:8

imitan: pintores i. la naturaleza CERV 139:1
imitate: be obliged to i. himself REYN 405:18
I. him if you dare   YEATS 587:3
i. the action of the tiger   SHAK 443:21
painters i. nature   CERV 139:1
imitated: he who can be i. by none
   CHAT 141:5
i. humanity so abominably SHAK 433:17
imitation: not a good i. of Johnson
   BURKE 112:14
Were endless i.   WORD 579:6
imitator: was a happy i. of Nature HEM 245:2
imitatores: i., servum pecus   HOR 259:1
imiter: que personne ne peut i.   CHAT 141:5
Immanuel: shall call his name I.   BIBLE 58:3
immaturity: that common symptom of
i.   WHAR 569:9
immense: error is i.   BOL 89:15
immensities: Asiatic vague i. YEATS 587:1
Immensity: I. cloistered in thy dear
   DONNE 189:1
swift into the vortex of i.   DICK 179:22
imminuit: Damnosa quid non i. dies
   HOR 260:26
immonde: De cet égout i.   TOCQ 551:9
immoral: people looked on it as i.
   GALS 220:30
immorality: i. which involves posing
   WEST 569:1
immortal: Being a thing i. as itself
   SHAK 430:25
do not seek i. life   PIND 373:15
grew i. in his own despite   POPE 380:12
i. hand or eye   BLAKE 87:14
I. longings in me   SHAK 424:10
i. spirit grows   WORD 580:11
I., though no more   BYRON 120:13
I. youth to mortal maids LAND 308:22
lost the i. part of myself   SHAK 475:7
make me i. with a kiss   MARL 329:10
pleasures in a long i. dream KEATS 290:23
Sire of an i. strain   SHEL 499:4
souls have sight of that i. sea WORD 579:12
when death that is i. has   LUCR 320:9
With cold i. hands   SWIN 529:22
Immortalia: I. *ne speres*   HOR 261:15
immortalis: Mortalem vitam mors cum
i.   LUCR 320:9
immortality: cruel i. Consumes TENN 543:11
earthly i.   FORD 216:14
God, I., Duty   ELIOT 201:30
heart like a load of i.   KEATS 294:4
If I. unveil   DICK 183:20
is their hope full of i.   BIBLE 62:13
long to believe in i.   KEATS 294:29
Nurslings of i.   SHEL 503:6
This longing after i.   ADD 1:24
this mortal must put on i.   BIBLE 76:29
immortalize: mortal thing so to i.
   SPEN 515:20
Immortals: President of the I. (in
   HARDY 241:25
immured: not alone i. in the brain
   SHAK 457:8
Immutable: I. as my regret   PEAC 371:1
She was as i. as the Hills   KIPL 304:32
Imogen: conceiving an Iago as an I.
   KEATS 294:7
imp: i. of fame   SHAK 444:17
impairs: All weakness which i.   ARN 14:24
Impaling: I. worms to torture   COLM 159:6
Imparadised: I. in one another's arms
   MILT 348:1
impartial: neutrality of an i. judge
   BURKE 111:34
Of a pure i. hate   THOR 550:28
security for its i. administration PEEL 371:5
impatience: all patience, and i. SHAK 426:29
impatient: i. of servitude   BURKE 109:27
people never so i.   PRAY 396:10

Impavidum: I. ferient ruinae HOR 260:19
impeach: I i. him in the name BURKE 110:33
impeachment: I own the soft i. SHER 506:23
impedes: All that i. thee from SHAK 459:1
impediment: cause, or just i. PRAY 388:23
impediments: i. to great enterprises
BACON 26:31
imperasset: consensu capax imperii nisi
i. TAC 531:13
Imperativ: I. ist kategorisch KANT 288:10
imperative: i. is Categorical KANT 288:10
imperator: Sole i. and great general
SHAK 456:26
imperatur: Naturae enim non i. BACON 28:10
imperfect: perfect use of an i. medium
WILDE 573:17
substance, yet being i. PRAY 399:7
you i. speakers SHAK 458:12
imperfections: With all my i. on my
head SHAK 431:12
imperial: enslaves you on i. principles
SHAW 498:6
'I. fiddlestick CARR 134:27
Of the i. theme SHAK 458:19
We have had an I. lesson KIPL 300:21
Imperialism: sane I. ROS 408:14
Imperially: Learn to think I. CHAM 139:5
imperio: Tu regere i. populos VIRG 559:1
Imperishable: I. peace HOUS 266:5
Imperium: I. et Libertas DISR 185:19
impertinent: don't ask i. questions
DARW 172:3
privileg'd to be very i. FARQ 210:22
imperturbe: Me i. WHIT 570:6
impious: i. hand to the Crown BRON 93:14
i. men bear sway ADD 1:23
impiously: i. gay COWP 168:13
implore: we these i. ANON 6:17
imponere: Ter sunt conati i. VIRG 560:12
import: works and ones of great i.
HOR 257:11
importance: subject of almost equal i.
BRAM 91:22
important: importunate for being less
i. MONT 354:19
puff and look i. and to say KIPL 298:18
importantes: occupations domestiques
moins i. MONT 354:19
importune: I here i. death awhile
SHAK 423:14
too proud to i. GRAY 235:21
importunes: n'en sont pas moins i.
MONT 354:19
importunity: i. Of business LAMB 307:33
impose: You i. continency upon us AUG 21:17
imposition: priests by the i. of a mightier
MAC 323:26
impositions: generous beliefs and i.
STEV 521:14
impossibile: Certum est quia i. est
TERT 545:1
impossibilities: not i. enough in Religion
BROW 96:8
Probable i. are to be preferred ARIS 12:11
impossibility: begotten by despair Upon
i. MARV 331:18
impossible: believed as many as six i.
CARR 135:18
certain because it is i. TERT 545:1
false i. shore ARN 15:2
have eliminated the i. DOYLE 192:30
i.? cela se fera CAL 127:9
i. loyalties ARN 15:25
i. to be silent BURKE 110:30
i.? that will be done CAL 127:9
In two words: i. GOLD 232:42
I wish it were i. JOHN 280:24
Patently I. and Vain KIPL 303:1
'tis more than i. CONG 161:6
With men this is i. BIBLE 67:12

impostor: let no i. heap SHEL 504:3
impostors: those two i. just the same
KIPL 299:22
imposuisse: Pelion i. Olympo HOR 260:22
impotently: Rolls i. on as Thou FITZ 213:8
imprecision: Decay with i. ELIOT 202:17
general mess of i. of feeling ELIOT 202:23
impression: i. of pleasure in itself
BACON 24:14
us the i. that we exist BECK 36:16
impressive: i. sights in the world BARR 34:21
impressiveness: i. on what we call our
DICK 179:21
Imprimendi: Artis nimirum I. BACON 28:9
imprint: have done set it in i. CAXT 138:4
imprison'd: you suffer'd me to be i.
SHAK 490:24
Imprisoned: I. in every fat man a thin
CONN 161:5
i. in the viewless winds SHAK 464:14
imprisonetur: i., aut dissaisiatur MAGN 327:2
imprisonment: leaves his well belov'd
i. DONNE 189:1
improbable: preferred to i. possibilites
ARIS 12:11
improper: only hope it is not i. GASK 222:2
proper or i. FULL 220:10
impropriety: without i. GILB 226:12
improve: anxious to i. the nick of time
THOR 550:9
I. each shining hour WATTS 565:21
Man can i. himself AUDEN 19:13
improved: be enormously i. by death
SAKI 413:4
i. life by the knowledge VIRG 558:23
improvement: hindrances to human i.
MILL 339:18
political i. are very laughable JOHN 275:29
improvements: No great i. in the lot
MILL 338:22
imprudent: Nobody could be so i.
AUST 22:15
impudence: credulity increases his i.
HUME 267:19
men starve for want of i. DRYD 195:38
much of Cockney i. before RUSK 411:7
impulse: first i. was never a crime
CORN 162:18
from the i. of the moment AUST 23:13
lonely i. of delight YEATS 585:15
seas in one i. of your soul SHAW 496:29
impulses: no truck with first i. MONT 355:11
impune: Nemo me i. lacessit ANON 10:15
impunity: one provokes me with i.
ANON 10:15
impure: Puritan all things are i. LAWR 311:2
impurity: we bring i. much rather
MILT 351:24
imputantur: Qui nobis pereunt et i.
MART 331:11
impute: sin I i. to each frustrate BROW 105:21
imputeth: whom the Lord i. no sin
PRAY 391:16
in: are out wish to get i. EMER 208:6
i. it is merely a bore WILDE 573:31
profanation to keep i. HERR 248:24
that the one is i. CHUR 148:20
Thou, my God, art i.'t HERR 250:15
thy coming i. PRAY 398:10
who's i., who's out SHAK 456:3
inaccuracy: hate i. BUTL 119:5
inactivity: wise and masterly i. MACK 325:12
inane: along the illimitable i. TENN 539:20
Pinnacled dim in the intense i. SHEL 503:12
inania: Ditis vacuas et i. regna VIRG 558:20
inanimate: if aught i. e'er grieves
BYRON 120:26
total depravity of i. things HAM 238:14
Inapprehensible: I., we clutch thee
THOM 548:24

inarticulate: close-companioned i. hour
ROSS 409:24
conclusions—largely i. KIPL 302:5
raid on the i. ELIOT 202:23
inaudible: Am I i. FRY 219:29
incantation: by the i. of this verse
SHEL 502:14
incapable: one i. of her own distress
SHAK 436:19
organically I am i. of a tune LAMB 307:2
totally i. of governing CHES 146:6
incapacity: dark sanctuary of i. CHES 146:5
incardinate: he's the very devil i.
SHAK 490:23
incarnadine: multitudinous seas i.
SHAK 460:13
yellow Cheek of hers to i. FITZ 212:7
Incarnations: glimmering I. SHEL 499:9
incarnatus: et i. est de Spiritu Sancto
MASS 334:20
Incens'd: I. with indignation Satan
MILT 346:26
Incense: blest unfabled I. Tree DARL 171:21
call of i.-breathing Morn GRAY 234:20
gods themselves throw i. SHAK 456:4
i. is an abomination unto BIBLE 57:17
Nor what soft i. hangs KEATS 291:20
strong thick stupefying i.-smoke BROW 99:14
incertainties: Nothing more certain than
i. BARN 34:3
incest: excepting i. and folk-dancing'
ANON 4:24
inch: every i. a king SHAK 455:16
Inchcape: It is the I. Rock SOUT 514:2
inches: die by famine die by i. HENRY 245:20
when full i. seven BRID 92:13
incident: curious i. of the dog DOYLE 192:16
determination of i. JAMES 271:12
Incipe: I., parve puer VIRG 560:1
incisive: lady of i. features MER 337:26
incisors: divided into i. and grinders
BAG 29:13
incite: les couvre, les nourrit, les i.
MONT 355:1
incivility: to i. and procrastination DE Q 175:5
inclementia: et durae rapit i. mortis
VIRG 560:16
inclination: i. to goodness is imprinted
BACON 26:19
ought to read just as i. JOHN 274:31
inclin'd: tree's i. POPE 377:12
Incline: I. our hearts to keep this PRAY 387:8
i. your ears unto the words PRAY 395:3
inclined: he i. unto me PRAY 392:1
of them i. to the landed ADD 2:14
Include: known for saying 'I. me out'
GOLD 232:44
You can i. me out GOLD 232:45
income: Annual i. twenty pounds DICK 177:4
£40,000 a year a moderate i. LAMB 308:15
in which a good i. is SMITH 510:2
large i. is the best recipe AUST 22:28
organism to live beyond its i. BUTL 118:27
incommunicable: burden of the i.
DE Q 174:26
incompetent: cursing his staff for i. swine
SASS 414:18
substitutes election by the i. SHAW 497:36
incomplete: research is always i. PATT 370:8
incomprehensible: old, wild, and i.
VICT 556:15
There are not three i. PRAY 385:13
in-conceivable: family pride is something
GILB 226:20
Inconsolable: I. to the minuet in Ariadne
SHER 505:26
inconstancy: Constant in nothing but
i. BARN 34:3
world constant, but i. SWIFT 527:17
Yet this i. is such LOV 318:20

Inconstant: I., childish KEATS 293:10
i. woman GAY 223:26
various world with as i. wing SHEL 501:5
incontinence: Delights in filth and foul
i. SPEN 516:14
on the turpitude of i. SCOTT 418:13
incontinent: else be i. before marriage
SHAK 426:27
incontinently: island descending i.
CHUR 151:4
I will i. drown myself SHAK 474:7
inconvenient: it is confoundedly i.
SMITH 511:27
incorporate: members i. in the mystical
PRAY 388:3
incorruptible: dead shall be raised i.
BIBLE 76:29
seagreen I. CARL 131:26
incorruption: corruptible must put on
i. BIBLE 76:29
is the assurance of i. BIBLE 62:19
it is raised in i. BIBLE 76:27
increase: blessest the i. of it PRAY 394:3
cares were to i. his store HOME 253:22
comforts should i. SHAK 474:20
creatures we desire i. SHAK 492:22
dies fighting has i. GREN 236:15
earth bring forth her i. PRAY 394:5
God gave the i. BIBLE 75:31
good and i. of the world TENN 533:9
I. and multiply upon us PRAY 386:16
i. in thy holy Spirit PRAY 388:22
i. of his government BIBLE 58:7
in her the organs of i. SHAK 453:18
increased: not i. the joy BIBLE 58:6
incredible: horrible, fantastic, i. CHAM 139:9
incredulity: i.! the wit of fools CHAP 140:9
increment: Unearned i. MILL 339:4
indecent: not necessary to be i. ROG 407:13
indefatigable: That i. and unsavoury
engine SPAR 514:23
indemnity: bill of i. raid KRUG 306:1
independence: of earthly blessings, i.
GIBB 224:17
inderpendunt: Ain't to be i. LOW 319:7
index: face the i. of a feeling COWP 168:24
publishes a book without an I. CAMP 128:6
thunders in the i. SHAK 435:5
indexes: He writes i. to perfection
GOLD 232:2
in such i. SHAK 486:27
India: driven out of I. this day BURKE 110:24
final message of I. FORS 217:9
fly to I. for gold MARL 329:4
I.'s spicy shores COWP 164:27
key of I. is London DISR 185:20
my metal of I. SHAK 489:9
treasures of I. GIBB 224:6
Indian: good Indian is a dead I. SHER 505:18
I. Summer of the heart WHIT 571:20
Like the base I. SHAK 477:23
out ten to see a dead I. SHAK 485:8
pith of an I. cane ADD 2:11
poor I.'s sleep KEATS 292:6
poor I. POPE 379:5
Veiling an I. beauty SHAK 467:11
Indicat: I. Motorem Bum... GODL 229:24
indices: are full of i. and surds CARR 134:25
indictment: i. against an whole people
BURKE 109:25
Indies: augmentation of the I. SHAK 490:3
indifference: fatal to religion as i.
BURKE 111:35
i. closely bordering STEV 521:17
me i. and a coach and six COLM 158:24
torpor of our i. JOHN 273:17
indifferent: been delayed till I am i.
JOHN 274:7
coerce an i. and self-indulgent STEP 518:20
i. in a week AUDEN 19:7

It is simply i. HOLM 253:5
to be i. to them SHAW 496:17
indifferently: i. minister justice PRAY 387:14
I will look on both i. SHAK 448:12
indigestion: hurry and reaps i. STEV 522:5
indignantly: day and night held on i.
ARN 14:21
indignatio: facit i. versum JUV 287:11
I. principis mors MORE 357:13
indignation: Savage i. there YEATS 587:3
they had i. saying BIBLE 68:8
Where fierce i. can no SWIFT 528:12
indignities: i. men come to dignities
BACON 26:23
indirection: By any i. SHAK 451:21
indirections: By i. find directions out
SHAK 431:27
indiscretion: one blazing i. MORL 358:1
indispensable: eloquence are i. to them
MAC 323:13
indisposeth: living i. us for dying
BROW 97:13
indistinct: host with someone i. ELIOT 204:16
makes it i. SHAK 423:8
inditing: heart is i. of a good matter
PRAY 392:14
individual: common notions in an i.
HOR 257:17
I. is wicked AUDEN 19:11
injustice done to an i. JUN 287:6
liberty of the i. must MILL 339:11
No i. could resent SWIFT 527:24
not the i. JOHN 282:6
individualism: American system of rugged
i. HOOV 255:23
individuals: all my love is towards i.
SWIFT 526:23
worth of the i. composing it MILL 339:14
Indocilis: I. pauperiem pati HOR 259:9
indolent: i. expression and an undulating
BELL 40:2
readers to become more i. GOLD 232:1
you chorus of i. reviewers TENN 533:14
indomitable: Still the i. Irishry YEATS 587:9
indubitably: They so very i. *are* BEER 37:23
inducas: et ne nos i. in tentationem
MASS 335:5
induce: wrong could religion i. LUCR 320:4
indulgence: might expect more i.
GOLD 232:13
others in their turn this i. HOR 257:10
industrie: La guerre est l'i. nationale
MIR 352:19
industrious: i. crew to build in hell
MILT 346:4
industry: birth commonly abateth i.
BACON 27:1
Captains of i. CARL 132:11
greatest river of human i. TOCQ 551:9
i. only, but his judgement BURKE 109:11
i. will improve them REYN 405:16
i. without art is brutality RUSK 411:9
national i. of Prussia MIR 352:19
perilous mode of hard i. BURKE 109:17
spur of i. HUME 267:16
indutus: Hectore qui redit exuvias i.
VIRG 558:5
inebriate: That cheer but not i. COWP 167:11
to cheer but not i. BERK 41:21
ineffectual: beautiful and i. angel ARN 16:10
Remote and i. Don BELL 39:27
inefficiency: efficiency and i. SHAW 497:5
inefficient: efficient and the i. SHAW 497:5
ineptior: Nam risu inepto res i. CAT 137:1
ineptire: desinas i. CAT 136:27
ineptitude: in its abysses of i. HOUS 266:15
inertia: Strenua nos exercet i. HOR 258:9
inestimable: thine i. love in the redemption
PRAY 386:2
inevitability: i. of gradualness WEBB 566:7

inevitable: Awaits alike th' i. hour
GRAY 234:21
in arguing with the i. LOW 319:18
inexactitude: risk of terminological i.
CHUR 149:25
inextinguishable: spark of i. thought
SHEL 505:10
infallible: i. criterion of wisdom
BURKE 111:27
only i. rule we know is SURT 525:2
We are none of us i. THOM 549:5
infâme: écrasez l'i. VOLT 561:11
infamous: quiet, and i. MAC 323:18
infancy: have their i. BOL 89:17
lies about us in our i. WORD 579:5
simpler than the i. SHAK 487:1
wayward was thy i. SHAK 481:8
Infandum: I., regina VIRG 557:20
infans: Non sine dis animosus i. HOR 260:21
infant: At first the i. SHAK 425:24
describe the i. phenomenon DICK 180:16
Has gobbled up the i. child HOUS 266:11
i. crying in the night TENN 536:26
i. prattling on his knee BURNS 113:5
Sooner murder an i. BLAKE 88:24
to a little i. BACON 26:3
Where the noble I. lay CRAS 169:6
Your i. beauty could beget SEDL 419:8
infanticide: is as indefensible as i.
WEST 569:2
infantry: That small i. MILT 345:22
infants: i. question in such wise ROSS 409:20
infect: milieu de ce cloaque i. TOCQ 551:9
out briskly to i. a city AUDEN 18:19
infected: All seems i. that th'infected
POPE 378:28
i. minds SHAK 462:26
infection: Against i. and the hand of war
SHAK 478:20
that flower with base i. SHAK 494:15
was free from rhyme's i. JONS 285:6
infects: bad news i. the teller SHAK 421:16
infelicity: i. Seem'd to have years
WEBS 566:27
sense of a constant i. TAYL 532:4
inferias: ad i. CAT 137:15
inferior: knowing myself i. to myself
MILT 352:13
pleasure of pleasing i. CLOU 153:8
inferiority: always conscious of an i.
JOHN 277:6
i. that their gratitude JOHN 282:4
inferiors: English want i. TOCQ 551:8
Infernal: hail I. world MILT 345:10
Inferno: their Dante of the dread I.
BROW 103:1
infidel: infidel as a dog is an i. JOHN 275:26
i., I have thee SHAK 468:8
Wine has play'd the I. FITZ 213:14
infidelity: half i. BURKE 111:35
I. does not consist PAINE 367:20
infierno: nuestro lugar sea el i. BORG 89:23
infini: Malgré moi l'i. me tourmente
MUSS 359:4
Infinite: because there is an I. in him
CARL 132:19
both are i. SHAK 482:17
dark unbottom'd i. abyss MILT 346:16
eternal silence of these i. PASC 369:7
idea of the i. torments MUSS 359:4
speaks an i. deal of nothing SHAK 465:15
that the will is i. SHAK 486:33
Infinity: Hold I. in the palm BLAKE 85:8
shares the nature of i. WORD 577:2
infirm: i. glory of the positive ELIOT 201:33
infirmi: i. est animi exiguique JUV 288:6
infirmitie: feblit with i. DUNB 199:8
infirmities: against the i. of ill health
STER 519:15
sake and thine often i. BIBLE 79:16

should bear his friend's i.   SHAK 451:22
infirmity: comparison with the i.
   HOBB 251:22
last i. of noble mind   MILT 343:8
prop To our i.   WORD 580:16
inflame: It will i. you   SHAK 450:25
inflammation: i. of his weekly bills
   BYRON 122:29
inflicted: that pain shall not be i. SPEN 514:26
inflicts: is one who never i. pain NEWM 362:3
influence: bright eyes Rain i.   MILT 342:5
Corrupt i.   BURKE 110:16
i. of the Crown has increased   DUNN 199:14
i. them till they ask   HUGEL 267:5
no slight or trivial i.   WORD 578:4
obedience of planetary i.   SHAK 453:11
one way their precious i.   MILT 344:7
Spheres of i.   ANON 7:17
under the name of I.   BURKE 108:19
influences: bind the sweet i. of Pleiades
   BIBLE 53:5
influenza: 'There was no i. in my BENN 40:21
inform: How all occasions do i. SHAK 435:29
i. his princes after his   PRAY 397:4
I will i. thee   PRAY 391:18
informally: Quite i.   COW 164:4
information: I only ask for i.   DICK 177:10
knowledge we have lost in i. ELIOT 202:3
know where we can find i.   JOHN 276:28
must resort to other i.   JEFF 272:13
informed: i. by the light of nature
   BACON 24:20
infortune: worst kynde of i. is this
   CHAU 144:11
infrequens: Parcus deorum cultor et i.
   HOR 260:2
infusion: i. of a China plant sweetened
   ADD 2:11
ingeminate: i. the word *Peace* CLAR 152:20
ingenio: Certare i.   LUCR 320:6
ingenium: Grais i.   HOR 257:23
ingenuas: Adde quod i. didicisse OVID 366:25
ingle: His wee bit i.   BURNS 113:5
Inglese: I. Italianato   ASCH 17:3
Inglissh: Sithe he off I. in makyng
   LYDG 321:6
inglorious: i. period of our dominion
   BURKE 110:24
mean Our object and i.   WORD 580:10
ingots: take i. with us to market CHAM 139:14
ingrat: cent mécontents et un i. LOUI 318:9
ingrateful: so i. you deny me   SHAK 452:31
That make i. man   SHAK 454:4
ingratitude: I hate i. more in a man
   SHAK 490:15
I., more strong than traitors' SHAK 450:28
I., thou marble-hearted   SHAK 453:17
unkind As man's i.   SHAK 426:1
ingratitudes: great-siz'd monster of i.
   SHAK 487:3
Ingres: I.'s the modern man who
   BROW 100:17
inhabitants: like th' i. o' the earth
   SHAK 458:10
inhearse: thoughts in my brain i.
   SHAK 494:11
inherit: rightly do i. heaven's graces
   SHAK 494:15
they shall i. the earth   BIBLE 64:6
To-night it doth i.   ARN 14:6
inheritance: Ruinous i.   GAIUS 220:27
inherited: i. it brick and left it   AUG 22:5
inheritor: i. of the kingdom of heaven
   PRAY 388:12
inhibitions: was to cultivate a few i.
   LOOS 318:6
inhuman: i. shout which hail'd
   BYRON 121:15
inhumanity: Man's i. to man   BURNS 114:23
that's the essence of i.   SHAW 496:17

iniquities: was bruised for our i. BIBLE 59:22
iniquity: hand is a right hand of i.
   PRAY 399:12
I lack i.   SHAK 473:20
i. of oblivion blindly   BROW 97:18
Rejoiceth not in i.   BIBLE 76:14
righteousness, and hated i.   PRAY 392:15
that grey i.   SHAK 439:16
visiting the i. of the fathers   BIBLE 47:24
iniuria: Nulla i. est   ULP 554:26
injur'd: I i. neither name   HOLL 253:4
injure: feared it might i. the brain
   CARR 133:22
injured: Forgiveness to the i. does
   DRYD 195:30
from sense of i. merit   MILT 345:2
i. lover's hell   MILT 348:19
injuries: is adding insult to i. MOORE 355:13
injury: efforts to do it a violent i. WOD 575:24
i. and sullenness against   MILT 352:10
i. is much sooner forgotten   CHES 145:13
least i. you can do him   JAMES 271:27
injustice: all the rapine and i.   SMITH 509:8
conscience with i. is corrupted SHAK 446:6
endure an hour and see i.   HOUS 264:5
him against i. and wrong   PALM 368:10
i. done to an individual   JUN 287:6
justice or i. of the cause   JOHN 279:30
man's inclination to i.   NIEB 362:26
No i. is done to someone   ULP 554:26
injustices: only to justify their i. VOLT 561:4
sanction des i. établies   FRAN 217:25
ink: all cough in i.   YEATS 586:14
all the sea were i.   LYLY 321:16
comparison all whites are i. SHAK 486:19
he hath not drunk i.   SHAK 457:1
of i. in my pen ran cold   WALP 562:23
Until his i. were temper'd   SHAK 457:8
inky: 'Tis not alone my i. cloak SHAK 429:25
inlaid: i. with patines of bright SHAK 468:15
inland: Though i. far we be WORD 579:12
tract Of i. ground   WORD 577:16
inmost: may see the i. part of you
   SHAK 434:33
inn: by a good tavern or i.   JOHN 276:35
Did this soul's second i.   DONNE 190:1
Do you remember an I.   BELL 40:12
earth his sober i.   CAMP 129:19
find a chamber in the i.   ANON 9:1
life at best is but an i.   HOW 267:1
not an i., but an hospital   BROW 97:3
old i., and the lights   MORR 358:12
room for them in the i.   BIBLE 69:9
take mine ease in mine i.   SHAK 440:4
To gain the timely i.   SHAK 461:15
warmest welcome, at an i. SHEN 505:15
world's an i.   DRYD 197:10
innatus: i. apes amor urget habendi
   VIRG 560:19
inner: Spirit in the i. man   BIBLE 77:24
Innisfree: go to I.   YEATS 585:17
settle down on I.   NASH 360:3
innkeepers: righteous minds of i.
   CHES 147:21
innocence: being hanged in all i. STEV 522:13
ceremony of i. is drowned YEATS 586:15
dallies with the i. of love   SHAK 489:3
Ignorance is not i. but sin BROW 101:17
i. and health   GOLD 230:18
I. is closing up his eyes   DRAY 193:21
I. thy Sister dear   MARV 331:22
is the badge of lost i.   PAINE 367:22
our business to lose i.   BOWEN 91:6
ou. 'earful i.   WORD 582:9
to know we sinn'd is i.   DAV 172:5
Valour and I.   KIPL 302:6
Was innocence for i.   SHAK 491:8
innocency: Keep i.   PRAY 391:29
wash my hands in i.   PRAY 391:5

innocent: another down his i. nose
   SHAK 425:1
Be i. of the knowledge   SHAK 461:14
be rich shall not be i.   BIBLE 54:42
children i. and charming   AUDEN 19:12
escape than one i. suffer   BLAC 85:6
gay as i.   SCOTT 418:15
heart whose love is i.   BYRON 125:22
i. and quiet mind   STEV 521:28
i. and the beautiful   YEATS 585:12
i. as gay   YOUNG 588:7
i. from the great offence   PRAY 390:13
i. of the blood of this   BIBLE 68:21
'Men are not i. as beasts   AUDEN 19:13
Of the brave and i.   AUDEN 19:7
shed i. blood   BIBLE 60:6
source of i. merriment   GILB 227:5
sweet converse of an i.   KEATS 292:20
taken reward against the i.   PRAY 390:5
innocuous: lambent but i.   GOUL 233:5
innovate: To i. is not to reform BURKE 112:2
innovations: so are all i.   BACON 26:27
innovator: time is the greatest i.
   BACON 26:28
Inns: all I. have been driven   BELL 40:16
go to i. to dine   CHES 147:18
innumerable: are creeping things i.
   PRAY 397:1
Inopem: I. me copia fecit   OVID 366:15
inopportune: be magnanimous at an i.
   TROT 553:17
inquest: i. of the nation has begun
   BURKE 110:28
together like the Coroner's I. CONG 160:32
inquiète: Ne t'i. donc pas   PASC 369:13
Inquisition: I. dogs and the devildoms
   TENN 542:21
inreparabile: fugit i. tempus VIRG 560:17
insane: eaten on the i. root SHAK 458:15
hereditary monarch was i.   BAG 29:9
Only the i. take themselves   BEER 38:7
insaniae: tumultuositas vulgi semper i.
   ALC 3:9
inscription: found an altar with this i.
   BIBLE 74:12
inscriptions: In lapidary i. a man is
   JOHN 276:31
inscrutable: Deep and i. singular Name
   ELIOT 204:6
i. and grand   ARN 14:4
i. workings of Providence   BIRK 84:16
insect: one is but an i.   JOHN 274:8
this 'ere 'Tortis' is a i.   PUNCH 402:19
insects: loud and troublesome i.
   BURKE 111:16
insensibility: It argues an i. LAMB 307:4
stark i.   JOHN 273:27
insensible: It is i. then   SHAK 440:18
inseparable: i. propriety of time BACON 25:5
one and i.   WEBS 566:11
insert: correct, i., refine   SWIFT 527:34
inside: mortal blow right i.   AESC 3:2
insight: clearest i.   WORD 580:26
moment's i. is sometimes   HOLM 253:21
insignificance: sterling i.   AUST 23:28
insignificant: I are now two as i. men
   WALP 563:26
insincerity: mark of i. of purpose BRAM 91:18
insinuating: i. Jacks   SHAK 480:23
Some busy and i. rogue   SHAK 476:23
insipid: i. and tedious performance
   WALP 562:25
insisted: He i. on people praying JOHN 274:24
insolence: flown with i. and wine MILT 345:18
i. of wealth will creep   JOHN 277:32
that i. is not invective   DISR 184:20
wretch who supports with i. JOHN 281:15
insolent: i. Greece or haughty JONS 284:22
insomnia: caelum mittunt i. Manes
   VIRG 559:3

suffering from an ideal i.   JOYCE 286:3
inspiration: Genius is one per cent i.
                              EDIS 199:25
is not drawing, but *i.*   CONS 162:3
Sibyl without the i.   BURKE 112:14
inspir'd: one i.   COLL 158:21
inspire: feel not what they i.   SHEL 505:13
our souls i.   PRAY 400:5
inspired: i. by divine revelation   BACON 24:20
inspirit: Songs may i. us   BROW 102:6
Inspissated: I. gloom   JOHN 275:25
instability: to dissimulate their i.
                              HOUS 266:14
instance: some precious i. of itself
                              SHAK 436:8
instances: wise saws and modern i.
                              SHAK 425:24
instancy: majestic i.   THOM 548:9
instant: Be i. in season   BIBLE 79:25
wealth of thy wit in an i.   SHAK 467:19
instantaneous: I mean i. courage   NAP 359:12
instinct: all healthy i. for it   BUTL 119:3
i. bring back the old names   COL 157:8
i. for being unhappy highly   SAKI 413:6
i. of all great souls   BURKE 109:8
I was a coward on i.   SHAK 439:8
masterful like an i.   CONR 161:23
natural i. to discern   WORD 577:3
such a gosling to obey i.   SHAK 427:28
With whose i. the soul   MARL 330:11
instincts: High i. before which our
                              WORD 579:10
true to your animal i.   LAWR 311:4
institooshuns: one of the greatest i.
                              WARD 564:26
Institute: I., Legion and Social   BETJ 42:13
institution: i. of the dear love   WHIT 570:5
It's an i.   HUGH 267:8
Toute i. qui ne suppose   ROB 406:12
institutions: him with their dirty i.
                              THOR 550:19
these i. were all geniuses   SHAW 498:23
instructing: same time as i. him   HOR 258:1
instruction: I will better the i.   SHAK 467:5
wiser than the horses of i.   BLAKE 88:22
instructions: knows whither awaiting
i.   BEER 38:2
Instructor: grand I.   BURKE 112:1
instrument: Call me what i. you will
                              SHAK 434:21
is only the i. of science   JOHN 281:6
instrumental: hand more i. to the brain
                              SHAK 429:20
instruments: genius and the mortal i.
                              SHAK 449:6
What i. we have agree   AUDEN 19:2
insubstantial: like this i. pageant faded
                              SHAK 485:20
insufferable: Oxford that has made me
i.   BEER 37:21
insufficient: conclusions from i. premises
                              BUTL 118:26
insularum: Paene i.   CAT 136:28
insult: is adding i. to injuries   MOORE 355:13
one more i. to God   BROW 102:7
sooner forgotten than an i.   CHES 145:13
Than when a blockhead's i.   JOHN 282:23
insulted: i. by a very considerable
                              GILB 226:26
Insultin: I. the sun   NORTH 364:4
insulting: i. Christmas card   GROS 237:3
insults: i. the victim whom he kills
                              COWP 168:28
insured: they were heavily i.   GILB 225:8
insurrection: nature of an i.   SHAK 449:6
intabescant: Virtutem videant i.que
                              PERS 372:27
intangible: world i.   THOM 548:24
Integer: I. vitae scelerisque   HOR 259:23

integral: i. and differential calculus
                              GILB 228:16
integrate: Essentially I i. the current
                              BETJ 42:14
integratio: Amantium irae amoris i.
                              TER 544:15
integrity: i. of my intellect   FAR 209:20
knowledge without i. is   JOHN 282:11
virgin white i.   DONNE 187:21
intellect: integrity of my i.   FAR 209:20
i. is improperly exposed   SMITH 511:5
i. not only on its heights   HOUS 266:15
i. of man is forced   YEATS 584:14
'Is it weakness of i.   GILB 227:16
living i. that bred them   MILT 351:21
march of i.   SOUT 514:13
not by the i.   SPEN 515:2
Our meddling i.   WORD 582:23
put on I.   BLAKE 86:13
restless and versatile i.   HUXL 269:13
with the i. of an advocate   BAG 29:17
intellects: few hearts and i. like   MILL 339:22
highest i.   MAC 323:11
intellectual: All i. improvement arises
                              JOHN 276:12
being i.   CALV 127:27
I am an i. chap   GILB 226:8
i. life of our century   ARN 15:25
i. ability   ARN 16:26
i. eunuch Castlereagh   BYRON 122:4
i. World   STER 520:2
i. power   WORD 577:13
i. All-in-all   WORD 580:4
moral or i. damage   KRUG 306:1
tear in an i. thing   BLAKE 86:6
this i. being   MILT 346:10
with i. nature is necessary   JOHN 281:32
without some i. intention   RUSK 411:21
word 'I.' suggests straight   AUDEN 20:13
intelligence: glorious work of fine i.
                              WORD 582:16
nightly gulls him with i.   SHAK 494:12
people have little i.   LA B 306:14
intelligencies: we are The i.   DONNE 188:24
intelligent: i. anticipation of facts
                              CURZ 170:17
i., the witty, the brave   MILL 339:23
Not i.   GILB 228:25
Want it to be i.   SU T 524:19
intelligere: sed i.   SPIN 517:7
intelligible: i. in his own day than   COL 158:8
that it is an i. government   BAG 28:27
intemperance: potations excused the
brisk i.   GIBB 224:9
intend: i. to lead a new life   PRAY 387:18
since what I well i.   SHAK 453:5
intended: years damp my i. wing MILT 349:10
intense: i. the agony   BRON 93:21
intensity: Are full of passionate i.
                              YEATS 586:15
of every art is its i.   KEATS 293:18
intent: child of glorious great i.   SPEN 516:4
His first avow'd i.   BUNY 107:36
Our true i. is   SHAK 471:16
pier it is my fixed i.   BARH 33:20
prick the sides of my i.   SHAK 459:6
that's told with bad i.   BLAKE 85:14
When on love i.   YEATS 584:19
intention: i. to keep my own counsel
                              GLAD 229:16
intentions: firm grasp of his i.   HOR 260:18
intents: Be thy i. wicked or charitable
                              SHAK 430:24
inter: In hugger-mugger to i.   SHAK 436:5
intercession: made i. for the transgressors
                              BIBLE 59:24
interchange: calm quiet i. of sentiments
                              JOHN 276:26
interchanging: pleasing game of i. praise
                              HOLM 253:6

intercourse: abject i. between tyrants
                              GOLD 232:11
interest: common i. always will prevail
                              DRYD 194:17
five per cent is the natural i.   MAC 323:29
I *du* in i.   LOW 319:4
i. to a twice-told tale   BYRON 124:36
i. Unborrowed from the eye   WORD 578:6
O Love, the i.   AUDEN 20:6
unbound by any i. to pay   HOR 259:7
interested: subsequent proceedings i.
                              HARTE 242:33
interesting: is that it be i.   JAMES 271:10
person doing i. actions   BAG 28:30
statements was i.   TWAIN 554:1
interference: case of Providential i.
                              TEMP 532:8
interfering: in i. with the liberty   MILL 339:6
interfused: something far more deeply
i.   WORD 578:7
Intérieur: 'Vive l'I.   SELL 420:7
interior: Which pries not to the i.
                              SHAK 466:19
interline: Enlarge, diminish, i.   SWIFT 527:34
International: I. will encompass the human
                              POTT 382:3
interpose: Those who in quarrels i.
                              GAY 223:14
interpretation: of bearing some other
i.   DOYLE 192:35
interpreted: i. the world in various
                              MARX 333:10
interpreter: God is his own i.   COWP 165:29
I think the i. is the hardest   SHER 505:22
interpreters: in general they need i.
                              PIND 373:14
letters, soft i.   PRIOR 400:26
interred: good is oft i. with their
                              SHAK 450:17
interstices: with i. between the intersections
                              JOHN 281:13
interval: through and make a lucid i.
                              DRYD 196:34
intervalos: lleno de lúcidos i.   CERV 138:16
intervals: lucid i. and happy pauses
                              BACON 27:44
Not in the lucid i.   WORD 577:5
with frequent lucid i.   CERV 138:16
Intervene: I.. O descend as a dove
                              AUDEN 20:15
intervention: No i.   LAND 308:21
interview: first strange and fatal i.
                              DONNE 188:10
intervolved: intricate, Eccentric, i.
                              MILT 348:24
interwoven: By Bach, i.   GILB 227:6
intestines: product of the smaller i.
                              CARL 131:7
intimate: one of my most i. enemies
                              ROSS 409:20
into: i. the Dust descend   FITZ 212:18
intolerable: burden of them is i.   PRAY 387:19
O vile, I.   SHAK 484:14
intolerant: Time that is i.   AUDEN 19:7
intoxicated: been once i. with power
                              BURKE 111:28
exposes himself when he is i.   JOHN 278:8
God-i. man   NOV 364:10
i. with my own eloquence   DISR 186:3
intoxication: best of life is but i.
                              BYRON 122:22
Wordsworth's standard of i.   SHOR 507:9
intreasured: weak beginnings lie i.
                              SHAK 442:3
Intreat: I. me not to leave thee   BIBLE 49:32
intrepid: behaviour was natural and i.
                              WALP 562:20
intricate: i., Eccentric, intervolved
                              MILT 348:24
intricated: Poor i. soul   DONNE 190:25

than all the waters of I. BIBLE 51:28
Then I.'s monarch DRYD 194:2
Then will I cut off I. BIBLE 50:31
there is a prophet in I. BIBLE 51:27
These be thy gods, O I. BIBLE 48:2
together the out-casts of I. PRAY 399:19
When I. came out of Egypt PRAY 397:16
Israelite: Behold an I. indeed BIBLE 71:32
Israelites: Are they I. BIBLE 77:11
I. passed over on dry ground BIBLE 49:1
isst: was er i. FEUE 210:35
issue: happy i. out of all their PRAY 386:1
honest madam's i. SHAK 453:9
ist: Der Mensch i. FEUE 210:35
isthmus: Plac'd on this i. POPE 379:12
it: i. shall not come nigh PRAY 395:21
It's just I. KIPL 305:9
knew what i. meant once KLOP 305:16
Italia: I.! oh Italia BYRON 121:6
I. shall be free MER 338:3
Italiam: I. fato profugus Laviniaque
VIRG 557:8
Italian: French army led by an I. SHAW 498:7
good because he learnt I. BUTL 118:35
No I. priest SHAK 452:17
perhaps I. GILB 228:10
roof of blue I. weather SHEL 501:16
to women I. CHAR 140:31
writ in very choice I. SHAK 434:14
Italians: I. call reg'larly flummoxed
DICK 182:15
Italie: Blond comme un soleil d'I. BANV 33:1
italien: i. aux femmes CHAR 140:31
Italy: bought his doublet in I. SHAK 465:24
building here after seeing I. BURN 112:17
I.. my Italy BROW 100:14
I. a vassal state of Hitler's CHUR 150:7
I. from designs by Michael Angelo
TWAIN 554:11
I. is a geographical expression METT 338:11
Paradise of exiles, I. SHEL 501:11
proclaim throughout I. CAV 138:1
shocking collapse of I. HOR 260:24
Some jay of I. SHAK 428:16
who has not been in I. JOHN 277:6
itch: i. of literature comes LOVER 318:21
poor i. of your opinion SHAK 427:12
itching: condemn'd to have an i. palm
SHAK 451:12
Ite: I. domum saturae VIRG 560:9
I. missa est MASS 335:9
iteration: thou hast damnable i. SHAK 438:7
itur: sic i. ad astra VIRG 559:8
Itylus: Is half assuaged for I. SWIN 528:15
iubeo: Hoc volo, sic i. JUV 287:21
iubes: Da quod i. et iube quod AUG 21:17
i. renovare dolorem VIRG 557:20
Iudaeus: Credat I. Apella HOR 262:5
iudicat: Securus i. orbis AUG 21:18
iudice: et adhuc sub i. lis est HOR 257:15
magno se I. quisque tuetur LUCAN 319:22
se I. nemo nocens JUV 288:5
iudicetur: Unde mundus i. CEL 138:6
iunctura: Reddiderit i. novum HOR 257:13
Iuppiter: I. ex alto periuria ridet OVID 366:11
iurare: Nullius addictus i. in verba HOR 258:7
iustis: Quis i. induit arma LUCAN 319:22
iuvabit: haec olim meminisse i. VIRG 557:14
iuventa: ego hoc ferrem calidus i. HOR 261:4
ivoire: Comme en sa tour d'I. SAIN 413:1
ivory: ebony as if done in i. FULL 220:15
fashioned of gleaming white i. VIRG 559:3
his belly is as bright i. BIBLE 57:4
i., and apes BIBLE 50:34
i. fingers drive a tune POUND 382:15
i. on which I work with AUST 24:3
neck is as a tower of i. BIBLE 57:9
With a cargo of i. MAS 333:18
within his i. tower SAIN 413:1
ivory gate: dreams out of the i. BROW 95:23

ivy: creeping i. clings to wood COWP 166:10
pluck an i. branch ROSS 409:7
yellow bees in the i.-bloom SHEL 503:6
ivy-mantled: that from yonder i. tow'r
GRAY 234:19
Jabberwock: 'Beware the J. CARR 134:28
Jack: Damn you, J. BONE 89:19
every J. became a gentleman SHAK 480:24
J. shall have Jill SHAK 471:1
This J., joke HOPK 257:1
jackal: This whipped j. CHUR 150:7
Jackals: ...J. piss at their foot FLAU 214:3
Jackdaw: J. sat on the Cardinal's BARH 33:11
Jack-daws: some green J. LEAR 312:9
jacket: could thresh his old j. COWP 168:1
j. was red and his breeches COL 156:11
short j. is always worn EDW 200:2
Jack Ketch: J.'s wife said of his DRYD 198:13
Jack Nastys: J. or fine ladies' maids
HUGH 267:6
Jacks: He calls the knaves, J. DICK 178:8
Jackson: J. standing like a stone wall
BEE 37:3
Stonewall J. riding ahead WHIT 571:16
Jacksonian: name for the J. vulgarity
POTT 382:2
Jacky: gorging Jim to guzzling J.
THAC 545:33
Jacob: Angel did with J. WALT 564:14
God of J. BIBLE 47:8
God of J. is our refuge PRAY 392:20
his birthright unto J. BIBLE 46:14
J. from among the strange PRAY 397:16
J. served seven years BIBLE 46:21
J. was a plain man BIBLE 46:13
Lord will have mercy on J. BROW 101:3
of J.'s thigh was out BIBLE 46:23
Talk to him of J.'s ladder JERR 273:10
They shall awake as J. DONNE 191:3
traffic of J.'s ladder THOM 548:25
voice is J.'s voice BIBLE 46:16
Jacqmar: J. scarf of mauve and green
BETJ 43:14
jade: arrant j. on a journey GOLD 232:7
let the galled j. wince SHAK 434:13
jades: hollow pamper'd j. of Asia
SHAK 441:25
ye pampered J. of Asia MARL 330:16
Jael: J. Heber's wife BIBLE 49:7
Jaguar: I've never seen a J. KIPL 300:8
JAH: praise him in his name J. PRAY 394:7
jail: patron, and the j. JOHN 282:29
ship is being in a j. JOHN 274:18
jam: beflagged j. pots JAMES 271:34
never j. to-day CARR 135:15
jamais: j. triste archy MARQ 330:21
mais je n'en parle j. PROU 401:22
James: J. James Morrison Morrison
MILNE 340:5
work of Henry J. has always GUED 237:5
James Lee: dead of joy, J. BROW 101:21
Jameson: indemnity...for raid by Dr
J. KRUG 306:1
Jane: J. Jane Tall as a crane SITW 508:11
Janus: is the very J. of poets DRYD 198:5
Janvier: Generals J. and Février NICH 362:23
Japan: On shining altars of J. POPE 381:6
Japanese: speed toward the J. fleet
HALS 238:11
jape: Indulge the loud unseemly j. BELL 38:26
japes: feyned flaterye and j. CHAU 142:7
Japheth: Shem, Ham, and J. BIBLE 45:32
jargon: j. of their Babylonian BURKE 111:6
your j. o' your schools BURNS 113:19
Jarndyce: J. and Jarndyce still drags
DICK 176:2
jasmines: alighted on the j. LONG 317:23
Jason: Whom J. hath received BIBLE 74:9
jasper: j. and a sardine stone BIBLE 81:22
'J. first BROW 97:34

jaundic'd: looks yellow to the j. eye
POPE 378:28
javelin: trail'd the hunter's j. ARN 14:26
jaw: j. of an ass have I slain BIBLE 49:24
jaw-jaw: j. is better than to war-war
CHUR 150:20
jaws: Into the j. of Death TENN 533:1
j. of darkness do devour SHAK 469:20
j. that bite CARR 134:28
opening of the j. of hell VIRG 558:21
ponderous and marble j. SHAK 430:24
With gently smiling j. CARR 133:18
jay: Some j. of Italy SHAK 428:16
thrush and the j. SHAK 491:17
jay-bird: j. say ter der squinch-owl
HARR 242:16
jealous: Are to the j. confirmations
SHAK 475:23
Art is a j. mistress EMER 207:6
jealous for they are j. SHAK 476:5
J. in honour SHAK 425:24
Lord thy God am a j. God BIBLE 47:24
Lord thy God is a j. God BIBLE 48:21
Of one not easily j. SHAK 477:23
question with my j. thought SHAK 493:18
so I am j. now DONNE 189:10
wit with j. eye surveys CHUR 148:28
jealousy: beware, my lord, of j. SHAK 475:17
ear of j. heareth all things BIBLE 62:10
green-ey'd j. SHAK 467:12
J. a human face BLAKE 88:9
j. is cruel as the grave BIBLE 57:11
mine was j. in love TENN 534:33
Nor j. Was understood MILT 348:19
quiet resting from all j. BEAU 36:10
tyrant J. DRYD 196:32
Jean Jacques: gospel according to J.
CARL 131:24
jeering: forbear laughing and j. PEPYS 372:7
jeers: gibes and flouts and j. DISR 185:13
jeet: j. it shoon CHAU 142:32
Jeffersonian: Washingtonian dignity
for the J. POTT 382:2
Jehu: like the driving of J. BIBLE 51:33
jellies: With j. soother than KEATS 289:20
jelly: j. with the act of fear SHAK 430:8
Meaty j. DICK 181:8
pipkin fits this little j. HERR 249:21
vile j. SHAK 455:4
Jelly-bellied: J. Flag-flapper KIPL 305:8
jelofer: j. amiable SKEL 508:18
Jemmy Grove: J. on his death-bed lay
BALL 30:10
Je-ne-sais-quoi: J. young man GILB 227:26
Jenny: Betray sweet J.'s unsuspecting
BURNS 113:7
J. kissed me when we met HUNT 268:10
jeopardy: Went in j. of their lives
BIBLE 50:29
Jericho: down from Jerusalem to J.
BIBLE 69:30
jerks: j. of invention SHAK 457:3
right to bring me up by j. DICK 178:9
Jerusalem: Building up of J. BLAKE 86:10
build thou the walls of J. PRAY 393:8
Built in J.'s wall BLAKE 86:8
down from J. to Jericho BIBLE 69:30
he hath redeemed J. BIBLE 59:19
hills stand about J. PRAY 398:15
holy city, new J. BIBLE 82:30
if I prefer not J. in my PRAY 399:3
J. is built as a city PRAY 398:11
J. shall Harry die SHAK 442:21
J., thou that killest BIBLE 67:26
J. thy sister calls BLAKE 86:11
Lord doth build up J. PRAY 399:19
men from the east to J. BIBLE 63:31
pray for the peace of J. PRAY 398:12
Speak ye comfortably to J. BIBLE 59:4
there J.'s pillars stood BLAKE 86:4

There's J. and Madagascar — THAC 546:2
thries hadde she been at J. — CHAU 141:31
vow be performed in J. — PRAY 393:23
was J. builded here — BLAKE 86:16
ye daughters of J. — BIBLE 56:16
jessamine: casement j. stirr'd — TENN 540:10
j. faint — SHEL 503:24
Jesse: rod out of the stem of J. — BIBLE 58:9
jesses: j. and restraint — THOM 548:2
j. were my dear heart-strings — SHAK 475:13
jest: bitter is a scornful j. — JOHN 282:23
fellow of infinite j. — SHAK 436:31
glory, j., and riddle — POPE 379:13
good j. for ever — SHAK 438:27
Great men may j. with saints — SHAK 464:3
J. and youthful jollity — MILT 342:14
j.'s prosperity lies — SHAK 457:17
j. without the smile — COL 157:17
Life is a j. — GAY 223:22
poison in j. — SHAK 434:12
To use my self in j. — DONNE 190:7
whole wit in a j. — BEAU 35:19
world's a j. — STEP 518:25
jesters: shallow j. and rash bavin wits — SHAK 439:34
jesting: nor j. — BIBLE 78:2
jests: He j. at scars — SHAK 482:5
to his memory for his j. — SHER 506:36
Jesu: J., by a nobler deed — CHAN 139:19
J., the very thought — CASW 136:15
Jesuit: tool, a J. — KING 297:16
Jesus: another king, one J. — BIBLE 74:9
Blood of J. whispers — BICK 84:4
bon Sansculotte J. — DESM 175:13
disciple whom J. loved — BIBLE 73:18
Gentle J. — WESL 568:17
J. a pleuré — HUGO 267:13
J. Christ his only Son — PRAY 384:26
J. increased in wisdom — BIBLE 69:14
J. the author and finisher — BIBLE 79:35
J. they run into millions — ROST 410:15
J. wept — BIBLE 72:23
J. wept; Voltaire smiled — HUGO 267:13
J.! with all thy faults — BUTL 119:10
leaning on J.' bosom — BIBLE 72:28
name of J. every knee — BIBLE 78:14
sound of J.' breath — BLAKE 85:24
sure this J. will not do — BLAKE 85:25
sweet reasonableness of J. — ARN 16:22
Jesus Christ: If J. were to come to-day — CARL 132:26
J. the same yesterday — BIBLE 80:4
jets: j. under his advanced plumes — SHAK 489:11
Jetty: J., to the milking shed — ING 270:15
jeunesse: Si j. savoit — EST 208:25
jeux: j. d'enfants ne sont pas — MONT 354:17
Jew: Ebrew J. — SHAK 439:1
Either for Englishman or J. — BLAKE 85:25
Hath not a J. eyes — SHAK 467:4
is neither Greek nor J. — BIBLE 78:26
Liver of blaspheming J. — SHAK 462:4
must the J. be merciful — SHAK 467:27
This is the J. — POPE 381:15
which am a J. of Tarsus — BIBLE 74:20
jewel: immediate j. of their souls — SHAK 475:16
j. of gold in a swine's — BIBLE 53:32
j. of the just — VAUG 555:20
Lest my j. it should tine — BURNS 113:1
Like a rich j. in an Ethiop's — SHAK 482:2
No j. is like Rosalind — SHAK 426:5
poor j. of their souls — STEV 521:2
precious j. in his head — SHAK 424:32
jewels: are my j. — BURT 116:34
j. five-words long — TENN 541:30
j. into a garret four stories — BACON 25:7
were moving j. — TRAH 551:19
Jewry: In J. is God known — PRAY 395:1
Jews: born King of the J. — BIBLE 63:31

conversion of the J. — MARV 332:18
J., a headstrong — DRYD 194:4
J. stink naturally…is — BROW 95:25
J. which believed not — BIBLE 74:8
like to see the J. coming — BAYL 35:9
Of the J. five times received — BIBLE 77:12
spurn the J. — BROW 95:13
three J. — CAXT 138:3
To choose The J. — EWER 209:13
jig: very walk should be a j. — SHAK 488:1
jilted: Better be courted and j. — CAMP 128:23
Jim: dear brother J. — WORD 583:5
gorging J. to guzzling Jacky — THAC 545:33
they called him Sunny J. — HANFF 238:19
jingle: hear the harness j. — HOUS 263:9
jingo: by j. if we do — HUNT 268:3
jining: j. of hearts and house-keepings — DICK 181:1
Joan: J. doth keel the pot — SHAK 457:19
Miss J. Hunter Dunn — BETJ 44:8
Job: afflictions of J. than the felicities — BACON 25:19
blessed the latter end of J. — BIBLE 53:13
Doth J. fear God for naught — BIBLE 52:6
good j. too — GILB 229:6
heard of the patience of J. — BIBLE 80:17
husband is a whole-time j. — BENN 40:22
I am as poor as J. — SHAK 441:8
Living is my j. and my art — MONT 354:23
we will finish the j. — CHUR 150:6
jobs: little j. about the house — AUDEN 21:9
jocund: In such a j. company — WORD 578:1
jocunditie: jasper of j. — DUNB 199:10
jog: j. on the foot-path way — SHAK 491:21
man might j. on with — LAMB 308:15
John: back to the shop Mr J. — LOCK 315:22
J. to the seven churches — BIBLE 81:9
to blessed J. the Baptist — MASS 334:15
John-a-dreams: Like J. — SHAK 433:2
John a Gaunt: Talks as familiarly of J. — SHAK 442:11
John Barleycorn: Inspiring bold J. — BURNS 115:9
John Bull: greatest of all is J. — BYRON 124:32
John Grubby: J., who was short — CHES 147:9
Johnny: J. head-in-air — PUDN 402:7
Little J. Head-In-Air — HOFF 252:16
John of Gaunt: Old J. — SHAK 478:6
Johnson: good imitation of J. — BURKE 112:14
J. marched to kettle-drums — COLM 159:3
Samuel J. — SMOL 512:14
There is no arguing with J. — GOLD 232:40
joie: La j. venait toujours après — APOL 11:11
le peuple a de la j. — MONT 355:7
join: If two lives j. — BROW 99:23
them that j. house to house — BIBLE 57:24
To j. the muster came — MAC 322:13
join'd: third she j. the former two — DRYD 196:30
joined: persons should not be j. — PRAY 388:23
Those whom God hath j. — PRAY 389:6
What God hath j. together — SHAW 496:28
What therefore God hath j. — BIBLE 67:8
joint: Jacob's thigh was out of j. — BIBLE 46:23
j. and motive of her body — SHAK 487:13
my bones are out of j. — PRAY 390:19
Remove the j. — CARR 136:10
time is out of j. — SHAK 431:26
time was out of j. — STR 524:4
joint-heirs: j. with Christ — BIBLE 75:9
joint-labourer: night j. with the day — SHAK 429:11
joints: distinguished into j. and fingers — TRAH 552:1
His square-turn'd j. — SCOTT 417:5
j. that you carve — KIPL 298:5
joke: custard pie… A dirty j. — ORW 365:10
dullness ever loves a j. — POPE 375:17
It's our only j. — BARR 34:22
j.'s a very serious thing — CHUR 148:31

j. well into a Scotch understanding — SMITH 510:28
Life is a j. that's just — GILB 226:28
many a j. had he — GOLD 231:2
subtleties of the American j. — TWAIN 554:12
This Jack, j. — HOPK 257:1
jokes: difference of taste in j. — ELIOT 200:21
hackney'd j. from Miller — BYRON 124:17
my little j. on Thee — FROST 219:7
Wooden-shoes are standing j. — ADD 2:1
jolitee: on my j. — CHAU 143:19
jollity: Jest and youthful j. — MILT 342:14
needy nothing trimm'd in j. — SHAK 494:5
jolly: '…For he's a j. good fe-el-low — FARR 210:29
J. boating weather — CORY 163:2
Some credit in being j. — DICK 179:2
There was a j. miller once — BICK 83:28
This life is most j. — SHAK 426:1
Jonadage: wish it was in J.'s belly — DICK 179:23
Jonah: lot fell upon J. — BIBLE 61:21
Jonathan: must consult Brother J. — WASH 565:4
Saul and J. were lovely — BIBLE 50:17
Though David had his J. — HERB 247:5
Jones: J.! as from Calais southward — WORD 582:4
Jonquille: Now the J. o'ercomes — WINC 575:6
jonquils: land-locked pools of J. — BETJ 43:12
Jonson: J. knew the critic's part — COLL 158:23
J.'s learnèd sock be — MILT 342:26
learn'd J. — DRAY 193:15
Jordan: concerning the land of J. — PRAY 392:8
J. was driven back — PRAY 397:16
Joseph: Israel loved J. — BIBLE 46:26
J., who was sold — PRAY 397:3
which knew not J. — BIBLE 46:40
joss-sticks: odour of j. and honourable — BRAM 91:20
jostle: Philistines may j. — GILB 227:23
jostling: done by j. in the street — BLAKE 87:10
jour: qu'en un j. — BOIL 89:11
journalism: from Christianity and j. — BALF 30:5
journalist: British j. — WOLFE 576:6
of the modern j. may be — CURZ 170:17
Journalists: J. say a thing that they — BENN 40:23
journey: death the j.'s end — DRYD 197:10
dreariest and the longest j. — SHEL 500:10
he is gone a long j. — BIBLE 53:24
Here is my j.'s end — SHAK 477:20
his j. into a far country — BIBLE 70:18
I have a long j. to take — RAL 404:19
j. to the world below — SOCR 512:19
such a long j. — ELIOT 203:12
then begins a j. in my head — SHAK 493:5
to begin a j. on Sundays — SWIFT 526:33
to take a j. — ANDR 4:7
traveller's j. is done — BLAKE 87:22
when the j.'s over — HOUS 262:15
Will the day's j. take — ROSS 409:11
world is going on a j. — HAZL 243:30
journeying: third-class seat sat the j. boy — HARDY 240:9
journeyman: that I was a j. to grief — SHAK 478:15
Journeys: J. end in lovers meeting — SHAK 488:17
jours: j. s'en vont je demeure — APOL 11:11
Jousted: J. in Aspramont or Montalban — MILT 345:23
Jove: J.'s planet rises — BROW 101:9
lovelier than the Love of J. — MARL 330:3
Nor J. himself when he — SPEN 516:31
whom e'en J. would swear — SHAK 457:5
Jowett: my name is J. — BEEC 37:8
joy: all the j. before death — SWIN 530:4
all the passages of j. — JOHN 283:1

beauty is a j. for ever   KEATS 288:20
Break forth into j.   BIBLE 59:19
Brightened with j.   WORD 577:16
burst J.'s grape   KEATS 291:15
child may j. to hear   BLAKE 87:25
evensong Of j. illimited   HARDY 239:7
ever in j.   BROW 105:1
fed without the aid of j.   BRON 93:24
Gaudium, what j. is in it   ANDR 4:6
Gemme of all j.   DUNB 199:10
good tidings of great j.   BIBLE 69:10
Hath really neither j.   ARN 12:23
headlong j. is ever on the wing   MILT 350:12
He sees it in his j.   WORD 579:5
I should be dead of j.   BROW 101:21
J. and woe are woven fine   BLAKE 85:14
J., beautiful radiance   SCH 415:9
j. cometh in the morning   PRAY 391:13
j. delights in joy   SHAK 492:25
J., Empire and Victory   SHEL 503:15
j. for it worth worlds   HERB 247:11
j. in hevene and peyne   CHAU 143:28
j. in the making   BRID 92:10
j. is but a dish of pain   TICH 551:2
J. is my name   BLAKE 88:1
j. is wisdom   YEATS 585:19
j. nor grieve too much   DRYD 197:10
j. of love is too short   MAL 327:19
j. of the working   KIPL 304:3
J. rul'd the day   DRYD 197:10
j.'s a trinket   STEP 518:25
j.'s soul lies   SHAK 486:21
j. that you can wish   SHAK 467:14
j. unspeakable and full   BIBLE 80:20
j. was never sure   SWIN 529:24
J., whose hand is ever   KEATS 291:15
Labour without j. is base   RUSK 412:3
let j. be unconfined   BYRON 120:21
Like an unbodied j.   SHEL 504:17
My scrip of j.   RAL 404:12
not increased the j.   BIBLE 58:6
now from the heart of j.   BEEC 37:9
oil of j. for mourning   BIBLE 60:9
O j.! that in our embers   WORD 579:9
perfectest herald of j.   SHAK 472:10
purchase pain with all that j.   POPE 377:21
pure and complete j.   TOLS 551:13
Rising in j. over wolds   AUDEN 20:6
shall obtain j. and gladness   BIBLE 59:1
shall reap in j.   PRAY 398:17
snatch a fearful j.   GRAY 235:11
sons of God shouted for j.   BIBLE 53:3
stern j. which warriors feel   SCOTT 416:6
Surprised by j.   WORD 582:15
swift j. and tardy sorrow   THOM 548:3
There is no j. but calm   TENN 539:14
There's not a j. the world   BYRON 125:28
thy bed Of crimson j.   BLAKE 87:12
tumultuous j.   SOUT 514:11
'twere with a defeated j.   SHAK 429:19
Variety's the source of j.   GAY 223:23
walked in glory and in j.   WORD 580:28
Where j. for ever dwells   MILT 345:10
Where's all the j. and mirth   KEPP 295:12
who are capable of j.   SMITH 510:18
who binds to himself a J.   BLAKE 86:18
who for the j. that was   BIBLE 79:35
wish you all j. of the worm   SHAK 424:7
would but apprehend some j.   SHAK 471:11
Writh'd not at passing j.   KEATS 293:4
joyance: With thy clear keen j.   SHEL 504:22
joye: dreme of j.   CHAU 144:1
joyful: be j. in the Lord   PRAY 396:11
   day of prosperity be j.   BIBLE 55:21
J. and triumphant   ANON 10:4
j. a thing it is: brethren   PRAY 398:26
j. mother of children   PRAY 397:15
j. rain upon thine inheritance   PRAY 386:3
Let the saints be j.   PRAY 399:24
joyfully: Sing j. to God   BIBLE 83:8

joyicity: hoppy on akkant of his j.   JOYCE 286:13
joyous: j. Errand reach the Spot   FITZ 213:18
   rout send forth a j. shout   MAC 322:6
joyously: So j., So maidenly   SKEL 508:17
joys: all our j. are but fantastical   DONNE 188:8
eternal j. of heaven   MARL 329:7
It redoubleth j.   BACON 26:16
J. in another's loss   BLAKE 87:19
j., like griefs, are silent   MARM 330:19
j. of home depend   MORE 357:11
j. of marriage are   FORD 216:14
j. of parents are secret   BACON 27:2
minds me o' departed j.   BURNS 116:7
of Africa and golden j.   SHAK 442:27
present j. are more   DRYD 196:18
season made for j.   GAY 222:28
that's precious in our j.   STER 519:12
Thy j. when shall I see   ANON 5:19
vain deluding j.   MILT 341:23
What lasting j. the man   WHURR 572:1
where true j. are to be   PRAY 386:12
who lived for j. in vain   CLARE 152:8
whom all j. so well agree   SIDN 508:1
Jubilate: J. Deo   BIBLE 83:8
Jubilee: first day of our J. is death   BROW 96:21
Judah: J. is my law-giver   PRAY 393:18
   J. was his sanctuary   PRAY 397:16
judas: flowering j.   ELIOT 203:4
   J. saith unto him   BIBLE 72:34
one thrice worse than J.   SHAK 479:9
judge: after a time they j. them   WILDE 573:30
am no j. of such matters   PRAED 384:5
cause before a great j.   LUCAN 319:22
fitter to invent than to j.   BACON 27:39
Forbear to j.   SHAK 446:7
God is the J.   PRAY 394:26
'I'll be j.   CARR 133:19
j. is condemned when   PUBL 402:5
J. none blessed before   BIBLE 63:1
J. not   BIBLE 69:22
J. not   BIBLE 64:33
J. not the preacher   HERB 247:12
J. not the play before   QUAR 403:15
j. the prize   MILT 342:25
j. the quick and the dead   PRAY 384:26
j. thou my cause   BIBLE 60:32
neutrality of an impartial j.   BURKE 111:34
nor the j.'s robe   SHAK 463:20
now I am j.   GILB 229:5
own mouth will I j. thee   BIBLE 71:1
righteousness shall he j.   PRAY 396:9
Shall not the J. of all   BIBLE 46:7
Sole j. of truth   POPE 379:13
thee a prince and a j.   BIBLE 47:1
there sits a j.   SHAK 447:4
Th' indifferent j. between   SIDN 507:20
to be decided by the j.   JOHN 279:30
To j. the earth one day   AUDEN 21:7
to make answer to the j.   CEL 138:6
You wags that j. by rote   OTWAY 361:1
judged: guilty man is acquitted if j.   JUV 288:5
they were j. every man   BIBLE 82:29
whereby the world will be j.   CEL 138:6
judgement: at forty, the j.   FRAN 218:10
before we pass j. on others   MOL 353:20
common pursuit of true j.   ELIOT 205:15
His critical j. is so exquisite   FRY 219:24
history is the world's j.   SCH 415:11
if unassisted by j.   HOR 260:23
industry only, but his j.   BURKE 109:11
in the day of j.   PRAY 385:17
into j. with thy servant   PRAY 399:11
Last J. draweth nigh   BLAKE 85:13
people's j. always true   DRYD 194:18
right j. in all things   PRAY 386:14
their j. is a mere lottery   DRYD 198:4
will replace reasoned j.   JUV 287:21

judgements: diff'ring j. serve   COWP 165:14
Give the King thy j.   PRAY 394:18
j. about great and high   MONT 354:12
j. of the Lord are true   PRAY 390:12
judges: hungry j. soon the sentence   POPE 381:4
J. all rang'd (a terrible   GAY 223:1
not my Accuser, but my j.   NEWM 361:15
were j. of fact   PULT 402:9
judgment: be angry with his j.   BROW 96:4
breastplate of j. the Urim   BIBLE 48:1
bring every work into j.   BIBLE 56:14
he looked for j.   BIBLE 57:23
J. drunk   COWP 166:12
j., mercy   BIBLE 67:24
j. of the great whore that   BIBLE 82:8
j. was set   BIBLE 61:8
leaves of the J. Book unfold   TAYL 532:2
O j.! thou art fled   SHAK 450:12
on better j. making   SHAK 494:13
reserve thy j.   SHAK 430:19
thereof in the day of j.   BIBLE 66:10
vulgarize the day of j.   JERR 273:5
waits upon the j.   SHAK 435:8
What j. I had increases   DRYD 198:7
What j. shall I dread   SHAK 467:24
would not give his j. rashly   ADD 2:13
judgments: Delivers brawling j.   TENN 535:11
reasons of state to influence our j.   MANS 328:16
What cause for j. so malign   STUB 524:5
judicious: cannot but make the j. grieve   SHAK 433:17
like a little j. levity   STEV 522:12
Judy O'Grady: Colonel's Lady an' J.   KIPL 300:18
jug: it git loose fum de j.   HARR 242:23
j., jug, tereu   LYLY 321:12
old j. without a handle   LEAR 311:25
juger: j. des choses grandes et   MONT 354:12
juggler: perceive a j.'s sleight   BUTL 118:6
threadbare j.   SHAK 427:9
Jug Jug: 'J.' to dirty ears   ELIOT 204:14
Julia: Whenas in silks my J. goes   HERR 250:8
Julias: J., Maeves and Maureens   BETJ 43:7
Juliet: philosophy can make a J.   SHAK 483:12
Julius Caesar: J.'s ill-erected tower   SHAK 480:6
Jumblies: lands where the J. live   LEAR 312:6
jump: j. the life to come   SHAK 459:5
j. with common spirits   SHAK 466:19
To j.   BARH 33:20
jumping: finished j. on his mother   GILB 228:21
June: husband J.   WATK 565:7
In the leafy month of J.   COL 155:26
meetings made December J.   TENN 537:12
needs not J. for beauty's   ARN 15:4
serves for the old J. weather   BROW 100:7
When J. is past   CAREW 130:7
Junes: J. that were warmer than   YEATS 586:5
perfumes in three hot J. burn'd   SHAK 494:18
Jungle: keep the J. Law   KIPL 301:13
this is the Law of the J.   KIPL 300:20
juniper: sat down under a j. tree   BIBLE 51:13
Juno: J. but an Ethiop were   SHAK 457:5
J.'s never-forgetting   VIRG 567:5
she's J. when she walks   JONS 285:5
Jupiter: J. est quodcumque vides   LUCAN 320:1
J. the Rain-giver   TIB 551:1
Quem J. vult perdere   DUP 199:15
So J. me succour   SKEL 508:18
jurisdiction: Rome hath no j. in this Realm of England   PRAY 400:10
Jurisprudence: gladsome light of J.   COKE 154:19
jury: I'll be j.   CARR 133:19
j. eagerly wrote down all   CARR 134:18
j., passing on the prisoner's   SHAK 463:16

just: all j. works do proceed PRAY 385:9
be j., and fear not SHAK 447:12
Expect him not in the j. HOUS 265:18
faithful and j. to me SHAK 450:18
gods are j. SHAK 456:5
have the interest to be j. AUDEN 19:13
is in its causes j. DRYD 197:4
jewel of the j. VAUG 555:20
j. and lasting peace among LINC 315:3
J. are the ways of God MILT 350:20
J. as I am ELL 206:10
j. man is also a prison THOR 550:1
j. shall live by faith BIBLE 74:31
J. when we're safest BROW 99:4
land of j. and old renown TENN 544:11
meanly j. JOHN 282:29
nothing to do with that j. man BIBLE 68:20
Only the actions of the j. SHIR 507:4
over ninety and nine j. BIBLE 70:17
path of the j. is BIBLE 53:19
rain it raineth on the j. BOWEN 90:22
reflect that God is j. JEFF 272:16
scrupulous and the j. CONR 161:22
sendeth rain on the j. BIBLE 64:19
spirits of j. men BIBLE 80:2
that hath his quarrel j. BILL 84:6
that hath his quarrel j. SHAK 446:6
that some cause was j. AUDEN 20:10
Thou art indeed j., Lord HOPK 257:2
thou art j. TENN 535:30
thou'lt raise me with the j. GRAH 233:16
whatsoever things are j. BIBLE 78:22
With j. enough of learning BYRON 124:17
juster: that I j. am SEDL 419:13
justest: reasoners are not always the j.
  thinkers HAZL 243:24
wisest and j. and best PLATO 374:10
justice: has j. enough to accuse GOLD 232:38
humanity, reason, and j. BURKE 109:26
indifferently minister j. PRAY 387:14
j. anywhere and a mind VIRG 557:18
j. est la sanction des FRAN 217:25
j., In fair round belly SHAK 425:24
J. is open to all MATH 336:2
J. is the constant JUST 287:8
J. is truth in action DISR 184:18
j. makes democracy possible NIEB 362:26
j. of my quarrel ANON 6:4
j. or injustice JOHN 279:30
j. should not only be done HEW 250:20
J., though she's painted BUTL 118:14
'J.' was done HARDY 241:25
Let j. be done FERD 210:33
Let j. be done though WATS 565:8
liberty plucks j. by the nose SHAK 463:11
moderator and equal piece of j. BROW 96:19
mystery begins, j. ends BURKE 108:12
Poetic J. POPE 375:19
Revenge is a kind of wild j. BACON 27:7
right or j. MAGN 327:3
sad-ey'd j. SHAK 443:9
strong lance of j. hurtless SHAK 455:20
sword of j. first lay down DEFOE 173:16
talks about j. and right KIPL 301:19
temper so J. with mercy. MILT 349:21
this even-handed j. SHAK 459:5
Thou shalt have j. SHAK 468:7
Thwackum was for doing j. FIEL 211:24
under the rule of equal j. MILL 339:19
what you think j. requires MANS 328:17
When mercy seasons j. SHAK 467:27
Where J. naked is AUDEN 18:10
which is the j. SHAK 455:18
With sword of j. thee ruleth DUNB 199:12
you have ravish'd j. WEBS 567:6
justification: j., in short ARN 16:18
justified: man can only be j. ROS 408:18
shall no man living be j. PRAY 399:11
'Tis half as good as j. BUTL 118:11
Wisdom is j. of her children BIBLE 66:4

justifies: An' j. th' ill opinion BURNS 115:21
end j. the means BUS 117:4
justify: j. the ways of God to Men
  MILT 344:22
To j. God's ways to man HOUS 264:12
yet men j. him BIBLE 63:4
justitia: are bound to say '*fiat j.* MANS 328:16
Fiat j. et pereat FERD 210:33
justitian: rectum aut j. MAGN 327:3
justle: When the bells j. HOUS 266:6
justly: fits a man to perform j. MILT 352:8
to do j. BIBLE 61:25
justum: Dignum et j. est MASS 335:3
et nubes pluant J. BIBLE 83:15
Juvenes: J. dum sumus ANON 10:13
juventus: Antiquitas saeculi j. mundi
  BACON 25:10
juventutem: Post jucundam j. ANON 10:13

juvescence: in the j. of the year ELIOT 203:4
Juxtaposition: J. his prophet CLOU 153:11
kame: wherefore should I k. my hair
  BALL 32:10
Kamerad: exclaiming *Mein lieber K.*
  BLUC 89:1
kames: gowd k. in their hair BALL 31:20
Kangaroo: Duck and the K. LEAR 312:4
Old Man K. first KIPL 300:13
kangaroos: dear little k. flying about
  WILDE 573:10
kann: Ich k. nicht anders LUTH 320:16
Wovon man nicht sprechen k. WITT 575:17
Kant: K. on the handle-bars BETJ 43:16
Karoo: meaning of the broad K.
  HARDY 239:8
Karshish: K., the picker-up of learning's
  BROW 100:24
Kaspar: Old K.'s work was done
  SOUT 513:14
Kate: K. of my consolation SHAK 484:9
none of us car'd for K. SHAK 485:10
kategorisch: Dieser Imperativ ist k.
  KANT 288:10
Keats: dumb to K. BROW 102:35
K., who was kill'd off BYRON 123:32
matter of wonder how K. SHEL 505:14
Prancing Nigger, Blunden, K. BETJ 44:10
What porridge had John K. BROW 103:27
whether Mister John K. KEATS 294:1
Who killed John K. BYRON 125:1
Wordsworth and out-glittering K.
  BULW 107:3
Kedar: habitation among the tents of
  K. PRAY 398:7
tents of K. BIBLE 56:16
keel: Joan doth k. the pot SHAK 457:19
keen: be swayed by quite as k. GILB 228:13
keener: grows k. with constant use IRV 270:21
with his k. eye MARV 332:9
keep: Except the Lord k. the city PRAY 398:18
He may k. that will HOUS 264:24
If you can k. your head KIPL 299:22
k. a hold of Nurse BELL 39:3
k. her in sickness PRAY 389:3
k. his friendship in constant JOHN 274:15
k. on saying it long enough BENN 40:23
k. the bridge with me MAC 322:17
k. thee in all thy ways PRAY 395:22
k. the gate of hell SHAK 476:21
k. the Jungle Law KIPL 301:13
k. the wolf far thence WEBS 567:9
k. your hearts and minds BIBLE 78:21
many to k. KING 297:3
mercy k. us in the same PRAY 386:19
my own intention to k. GLAD 229:16
need k. the shutters up DICK 179:17
'O k. the Dog far hence ELIOT 204:22
sufficient to k. them together JOHN 276:2
they should k. who can WORD 578:17
to *k.* Heights WORD 577:15

To k. your head PUDN 402:8
ware that will not k. HOUS 262:15
keeper: Am I my brother's k. BIBLE 45:25
ill k. of promise BACON 25:32
k. Stands up HOUS 263:10
Lord himself is thy k. PRAY 398:9
poacher a k. turned inside KING 297:8
keepers: k. of the walls took away BIBLE 57:2
keepeth: he that k. thee PRAY 398:9
Kempenfelt: When K. went down
  COWP 165:31
kenne: Ich k. mich auch nicht GOET 229:28
Kennst: K. du das Land GOET 230:13
K. du es wohl GOET 230:13
kennt: Der k. euch nicht GOET 230:12
Kensal Green: to Paradise by way of
  K. CHES 147:12
Kent: everybody knows K. DICK 181:27
talk I'm k. the better BURNS 114:32
Kentish: K. Sir Byng stood for his
  BROW 99:26
Kentish Town: Anglo-Norman parish
  church of K. BETJ 43:18
dandelions to the courts of K. BETJ 43:19
Pancras and K. repose BLAKE 86:5
Kenton: to the westward over K. BETJ 42:17
kept: I have k. the faith BIBLE 79:26
I k. them in thy name BIBLE 72:42
What wee k. ANON 8:17
kerchief: fetch the county k. HOUS 264:27
kernel: I then was to this k. SHAK 491:10
kettle: always back to the tea-k. DISR 184:17
how agree the k. BIBLE 63:3
I took a k. large and new CARR 135:26
merry k. boils away PAIN 367:15
this is a pretty k. of fish MARY 333:14
Kew: down to K. in lilac-time NOYES 364:11
his Highness' dog at K. POPE 376:16
Richmond and K. Undid me ELIOT 205:5
key: away the k. of knowledge BIBLE 70:2
got the k. of the street DICK 182:37
hands on that golden k. MILT 340:24
k. of India is London DISR 185:20
Turn the k. deftly KEATS 292:29
with an easy k. DRYD 195:17
keys: half that's got my k. GRAH 233:12
k. of all the creeds TENN 536:13
k. of hell and of death BIBLE 81:15
my fingers on these k. STEV 520:16
Over the noisy k. PROC 401:13
Two massy k. he bore MILT 343:11
Khatmandu: idol to the north of K.
  HAYES 243:7
Khayyám: come with old K. and leave
  FITZ 212:9
come with old K. FITZ 212:19
kiaugh: k. and care beguile BURNS 113:5
kibe: he galls his k. SHAK 436:29
kick: did you k. me downstairs BICK 83:27
I'll k. you downstairs CARR 133:23
scarcely k. to come to the top KEATS 293:31
sportsman wot doesn't k. his wife SURT 525:5
to k. against the pricks BIBLE 73:34
who dies of an ass's k. BROW 102:25
kicked: any k. up stairs before HAL 238:5
cursed and k. the stairs MILL 339:27
Kicking: K. you seems the common
  BROW 106:1
kickshaws: Any pretty little tiny k.
  SHAK 442:22
kid: shall lie down with the k. BIBLE 58:10
Thou shalt not seethe a k. BIBLE 47:27
kiddies: k. have crumpled the serviettes
  BETJ 42:19
kidneys: blister my k. SURT 525:16
kill: animals never k. for sport FROU 219:17
chap that did not k. me HOUS 266:4
disease and k. the patient BACON 26:17
enough in thee to k. care SHAK 473:9
fain would k. their church TENN 540:14

I k. you	CHAM 139:18	thus musing the fire k.	PRAY 391:30	**K. OF KINGS**	BIBLE 82:26
I'll k. you if you quote it	BURG 108:3	**kindles:** k. fire	LA R 310:15	k. of shreds and patches	SHAK 435:12
I will k. thee	SHAK 477:5	**kindleth:** matter a little fire k.	BIBLE 80:13	K. of tremendous majesty	CEL 138:7
I will k. you	BALL 31:3	**kindliness:** cool k. of sheets	BROO 94:8	k. Over himself	SHEL 503:12
k. a king	SHAK 435:2	**kindly:** k. treat her	GAY 222:9	K. over the Water	ANON 7:25
k. a man as kill a good	MILT 351:22	preserve to our use the k. fruits	PRAY 385:21	k. reigns	THIE 546:5
k. a wife with kindness	SHAK 484:11	**kindness:** I will some k. do them		k.'s a bawcock	SHAK 444:17
K. me to-morrow	SHAK 477:7		SHAK 486:13	King's a K.	DRAY 193:8
K. not the moth nor butterfly	BLAKE 85:13	kill a wife with k.	SHAK 484:11	k. sate on the rocky brow	BYRON 122:34
k. sick people groaning	MARL 329:21	k. and consolidates society	JOHN 280:6	K.'s crown shall fall	SCOTT 415:20
k. thee with much cherishing	SHAK 482:20	K. in another's trouble	GORD 233:1	K.'s daughter is all glorious	PRAY 392:17
k. the poor creature	GASK 221:24	milk of human k.	CHUR 148:22	k.'s English	SHAK 469:5
k. with looks	SHAK 479:11	milk of human k.	SHAK 459:1	K.'s First Minister	CHUR 150:12
let's k. all the lawyers	SHAK 446:11	Of k. and of love	WORD 578:4	k. sits in Dunfermline	BALL 31:16
nor yet canst thou k. me	DONNE 189:5	still the great have k.	POPE 376:29	k.'s name is a tower	SHAK 481:12
Otherwise k. me	MACN 326:13	think it k. to his Majesty	HALL 238:8	k.'s name twenty thousand	SHAK 479:7
prepared to k. one another	SHAW 497:15	value on spontaneous k.	JOHN 278:30	K. thought mair o' Marie	BALL 31:11
They k. us for their sport	SHAK 455:9	We'll tak a cup o' k. yet	BURNS 112:32	K. To be your servant	SHAK 447:8
Thou shalt not k.	BIBLE 47:24	**kindnesses:** recalling the thought of k.		K. to have things done	PEPYS 372:6
Thou shalt not k.	CLOU 153:26	done	CAT 137:9	K. to Oxford sent a troop	BROW 97:26
time to k.	BIBLE 55:12	**kindred:** haunts two k. spirits flee		k. was much moved	BIBLE 50:26
To k. a human being is	JAMES 271:27		KEATS 292:20	*K. with half the East*	HOUS 265:3
When you have to k. a man	CHUR 151:2	to k. dear	CAREW 130:14	Lord is K.	PRAY 395:24
kill'd: I kiss'd thee ere I k.	SHAK 478:1	**kindreds:** k. of the earth shall wail		lord, thy k., thy governor	SHAK 484:15
k. with my own treachery	SHAK 437:19		BIBLE 81:10	My castles are my K.'s	SCOTT 417:1
killed: Better be k.	SURT 525:22	**kine:** seven fat k.	BIBLE 46:31	My dead K.	JOYCE 286:15
effort very nearly k. her	BELL 39:7	**King:** a' for our rightfu' K.	BURNS 114:10	My God and K.	HERB 246:26
have so many people k.	AUST 24:1	against Heav'n's matchless K.	MILT 347:14	my K. and my God	PRAY 395:11
I am the enemy you k.	OWEN 367:12	ale is a dish for a k.	SHAK 491:17	my life to make you K.	CHAR 140:29
k. a calf he would do it	AUBR 17:27	all were looking for a k.	MACD 325:4	myself a k. of infinite space	SHAK 432:13
k. hisself on principle	DICK 182:19	another k., one Jesus	BIBLE 74:9	no k. in Israel	BIBLE 49:29
k. with your hard opinions	SHAK 443:2	apples of gold for the k.'s daughter		Og the k. of Basan	PRAY 399:1
killer: here the lover and k. are	DOUG 191:10		SWIN 530:17	open The k.'s eyes	SHAK 447:1
killest: thou that k. the prophets	BIBLE 67:26	arose up a new k. over Egypt	BIBLE 46:40	Our k. has written a braid	BALL 31:17
killeth: letter k.	BIBLE 77:4	Authority forgets a dying k.	TENN 535:22	our sins lay on the k.	SHAK 444:23
killing: k. a cat than choking	KING 297:15	banners of the k. advance	VEN 556:5	passing brave to be a K.	MARL 330:7
k. Kruger with your mouth	KIPL 297:22	blessedness alone that makes a K.		shepherd and the k.	CERV 138:20
K. myself to die upon	SHAK 478:1		TRAH 552:2	shines brightly as a k.	SHAK 468:18
K. no Murder Briefly Discourst		born K. of the Jews	BIBLE 63:31	Sir Byng stood for his K.	BROW 99:26
	SEXBY 420:17	coming of the K. of Heaven	ANON 9:1	skipping k.	SHAK 439:34
k. of a mouse on Sunday	BRAT 91:24	conscience as their K.	TENN 534:11	so much a k. as a Monarch	SELL 420:5
kills: man k. the thing he loves	WILDE 572:10	despised, and dying k.	SHEL 504:6	sort of k. should ever die	BROW 103:23
my heart an air that k.	HOUS 263:22	discharge my duties as K.	EDW 200:4	still am I k. of those	SHAK 479:23
waste remains and k.	EMPS 208:17	divinity doth hedge a k.	SHAK 436:6	subject's duty is the k.'s	SHAK 444:22
kilted: has k. her green kirtle	BALL 32:1	every inch a k.	SHAK 455:16	That the k. can do no wrong	BLAC 85:5
kimonos: Two girls in silk k.	YEATS 585:11	Fear God. Honour the k.	BIBLE 80:25	That was no more than a k.	SWIN 529:26
kin: certainly man is of k.	BACON 25:25	fight for its K. and country	ANON 7:19	There was a k. of Yvetot	BER 41:14
If one's own k. and kith	NASH 359:18	First Moloch, horrid k.	MILT 345:14	think the k. is but a man	SHAK 444:20
k. with kin and kind with	SHAK 479:20	follow the k.	TENN 534:5	To be a Pirate K.	GILB 228:12
little less than 'k.'	BARH 33:25	Give the K. thy judgements	PRAY 394:18	To my true k. I offer'd	MAC 322:8
little more than k.	SHAK 429:21	God bless the K.	BYROM 119:25	Under which k.	SHAK 442:28
makes the whole world k.	SHAK 487:6	God save our gracious k.	CAREY 130:24	What a k.	ABEL 1:2
kind: beautiful, the tender, the k.	MILL 339:23	God save the k.	BIBLE 49:42	What is a K.	PRIOR 401:6
be cruel only to be k.	SHAK 435:20	God save the k.	HOGG 252:24	What must the k. do now	SHAK 479:15
be honest, to be k.	STEV 521:4	God save the k.	SHAK 479:21	when I am k.	SHAK 446:11
coarsely k.	JOHN 278:35	government without a k.	BANC 32:13	who speaks ill of your k.	NELS 360:12
enjoy her while she's k.	DRYD 198:17	hath not offended the k.	MORE 357:18	with the image of the K.	TENN 534:17
Godlike crime was to be k.	BYRON 125:18	heart and stomach of a k.	ELIZ 206:4	worm that hath eat of a k.	SHAK 435:27
grow more cold, more k.	SPAR 514:22	he might hae been a k.	BALL 30:16	Would shake hands with a k.	HALL 238:8
had been k.	JOHN 274:7	He played the K. as though	FIELD 211:3	yesterday a K.	BYRON 125:7
he grows k.	SHAK 466:5	herald of love's mighty k.	SPEN 515:19	**King Charles:** trouble out of K.'s head	
Is she k. as she is fair	SHAK 491:4	He that plays the k. shall	SHAK 432:16		DICK 177:7
just the art of being k.	WILC 572:6	I have made unto the K.	PRAY 392:14	**Kingcups:** K., and loved Lilies	SPEN 517:3
just try to be *k.*	FOAK 216:2	I serv'd my k.	SHAK 447:13	**kingdom:** Advantage on the k. of the	
K. are her answers	CAMP 129:21	I was a K. in Babylon	HENL 245:10	shore	SHAK 494:3
k. of people do they think	CHUR 150:9	kill a k.	SHAK 435:2	enter into the k. of heaven	BIBLE 64:11
k. things done by men with	MAS 333:23	k. and officers of sorts	SHAK 443:9	found a k.	MILT 350:6
k. William Maginn	LOCK 315:23	k. delighteth to honour	BIBLE 52:3	God hath numbered thy k.	BIBLE 61:6
k. with kind confound	SHAK 479:20	k. drinks to Hamlet	SHAK 437:17	I never gave you k.	SHAK 454:5
less than k.	SHAK 429:21	k. for my money	FIEL 211:32	inheritor of the k.	PRAY 388:12
makes one wond'rous k.	GARR 221:15	k. is always a king	WOLL 576:10	In this k. by the sea	POE 374:22
mein irisch K.	WAGN 562:1	k. is strongest	BIBLE 62:4	k. against kingdom	BIBLE 67:28
people will always be k.	SASS 414:13	k. may make a nobleman	BURKE 111:37	k. for a stage	SHAK 443:3
rather more than 'k.'	BARH 33:25	k. my brother's wreck	ELIOT 204:26	k. for it was too small	SHAK 440:24
to her virtues very k.	PRIOR 400:23	k. never dies	BLAC 85:3	k. of heaven is at hand	BIBLE 63:35
Too kind—too k.	NIGH 363:15	K., observing with judicious	TRAPP 552:5	k. where nobody dies	MILL 339:24
Yet he was k.	GOLD 231:2	K. of all these the dead	HOMER 254:6	large k. for a little grave	SHAK 479:15
kindest: k. and the best	BURNS 114:24	k. of codpieces	SHAK 456:26	Like to a little k.	SHAK 449:6
thou wert the k. man that	MAL 328:8	K. of glory shall come	PRAY 390:24	man to enter into the k.	BIBLE 67:11
kindled: k., (yea, but a little	PRAY 389:19	K. of Great Britain is	REED 405:9	my k. for a horse	SHAK 481:18

My mind to me a k. is	DYER 199:17
of such is the k. of God	BIBLE 68:36
Seek ye first the k. of God	BIBLE 64:31
theirs is the k. of heaven	BIBLE 64:6
thou comest into thy k.	BIBLE 71:12
Thy k. come	BIBLE 64:24
Thy k. is divided	BIBLE 61:6
Yet thy k. shall pass	SWIN 530:7

kingdom of God: k. is within you BIBLE 70:31
riches enter into the k. BIBLE 70:36

kingdom of heaven: k. is like to a grain BIBLE 66:20
shall not enter into the k. BIBLE 67:2

kingdoms: all the k. of the world BIBLE 64:3
hath mus'd of taking k. SHAK 422:19
K. are clay SHAK 421:8
many goodly states and k. KEATS 292:17

King George: In good K.'s glorious GILB 226:11
K. will be able to read HANC 238:18

Kingly: K. conclaves stern SHEL 503:1
this k. seal SHAK 422:21

king of Israel: smote the k. between BIBLE 51:21

King Pandion: K., he is dead BARN 34:1

kings: abounding with k. thirty MAC 324:21
All k. shall fall down PRAY 394:20
all the powerful K. DONNE 190:26
any madness of their k. HOR 258:12
are but the breath of k. BURNS 113:10
bind their k. in chains PRAY 399:24
cabbages—and k. CARR 135:7
Captains and the K. depart KIPL 302:7
come now no K. nor Caesars POUND 383:19
commonwealths and ruin k. DRYD 194:5
Conquering k. their titles CHAN 139:19
divorc'd So many English k. SHAK 442:18
dread and fear of k. SHAK 467:27
godly k. had built her FLEC 214:6
heart of k. is unsearchable BIBLE 54:25
heart's ease Must k. neglect SHAK 444:24
it's the sport of k. SURT 525:4
k. crept out again to feel BROW 97:35
K.' daughters were among PRAY 392:16
k. governed their rude BAG 28:28
k. have cares that wait GREE 236:11
k. is mostly rapscallions TWAIN 554:2
k. of the earth: are gathered PRAY 392:25
k. of the sea ARN 13:7
K. seek their subjects' HERR 249:8
k. that fear their subjects' SHAK 446:19
K. will be tyrants from BURKE 111:13
K. with their armies did PRAY 394:8
mad k. SHAK 452:13
Many k. have sat down upon BIBLE 62:31
meaner creatures k. SHAK 481:11
passion for our temperate k. TENN 541:11
Physicians are like k. WEBS 566:28
poor and the castles of k. HOR 259:13
prophets and k. have desired BIBLE 69:29
ruin'd sides of K. BEAU 36:1
saddest of all K. JOHN 273:22
shall be accounted poet k. KEATS 292:9
should all be as happy as k. STEV 522:22
sport of k. SOM 513:2
stories of the death of k. SHAK 479:11
strength of guilty k. ARN 13:22
subjects is the end of k. DEFOE 173:16
superfluous k. for messengers SHAK 422:15
That part which laws or k. GOLD 231:30
That part which laws or k. JOHN 282:21
These five k. did a king THOM 547:4
three k. into the east BURNS 114:13
up and puller down of k. SHAK 446:20
walk with k. KIPL 300:2
With k. and counsellors BIBLE 52:13

Kingsley: Froude believes K. a divine STUB 524:5
kinship: any k. with the stars MER 337:7

Kipling: Pardoned K. and his views AUDEN 19:8
Rudyards cease from k. STEP 518:24
kirk: Marie Hamilton's to the k. BALL 31:11
Kirkconnell: On fair K. lea BALL 31:4
kirtle: has kilted her green k. BALL 32:1
kis: k. the steppes CHAU 144:17
Kismet: is he that saith not 'K.' CHES 147:4
kiss: add to that k. a score HERR 249:22
Ae fond k. BURNS 112:27
another with an holy k. BIBLE 75:28
Close with her, k. her SWIN 530:27
Colder thy k. BYRON 126:13
coughs when you would k. AUDEN 18:10
coward does it with a k. WILDE 572:10
drew With one long k. TENN 533:16
handshake, the cough, the k. AUDEN 21:1
have felt my soul in a k. SWIN 530:20
his whole heart in one k. TENN 543:9
human souls did never k. KEATS 289:3
I dare not ask a k. HERR 250:3
I k. his dirty shoe SHAK 444:17
I'll k. my girl on her KIPL 301:10
'I saw you take his k. PATM 370:3
k., a sigh, and so away CRAS 169:14
k. before they are married SHAK 445:15
K. her until she be wearied SHEL 505:3
k. is but a kiss now MER 337:10
k. Long as my exile SHAK 428:2
k. me and never no more MAL 328:4
K. me as if you made believe BROW 101:15
K. me, Hardy NELS 360:23
K. me Kate SHAK 484:10
k. my Julia's dainty leg HERR 249:15
k. my Lord before I die MARL 330:13
k. of death SMITH 510:4
k. on the wrist STEV 520:20
k. our lady Peace at home SHAK 441:13
K. the book's outside who COWP 165:8
k. the place to make it TAYL 531:25
K. the Son PRAY 389:19
K. till the cow comes home BEAU 36:11
leave a k. but in the cup JONS 284:12
let me k. that hand SHAK 455:17
make me immortal with a k. MARL 329:10
man may k. a bonnie lass BURNS 115:13
many a glowing k. had won HOOD 255:4
might take occasion to k. SHAK 426:22
My bluest veins to k. SHAK 422:11
myself to die upon a k. SHAK 478:1
Only to k. that air HERR 250:3
part at last without a k. MORR 358:11
presently all humbled k. the rod SHAK 490:31
Quit in a single k. BRID 92:11
self I needs must k. again SIDN 507:25
spend that k. SHAK 424:14
stop his mouth with a k. SHAK 472:11
swear to never k. the girls BROW 100:30
Then come k. me SHAK 488:17
this last lamenting k. DONNE 188:20
with a single famish'd k. SHAK 487:12

kiss'd: I k. her slender hand TENN 540:6
k. again with tears TENN 541:28
k. thee ere I kill'd thee SHAK 478:1

kissed: Being k. by a man who didn't KIPL 304:37
First time he k. me BROW 98:12
first we k. beside the thorn BRID 92:20
k. by the English dead OWEN 367:6
k. her once by the pig-sty THOM 547:11
k. it and then fled SHEL 503:17
k. the lovely grass BROO 94:15
laughed and k. his hand HOUS 266:4
righteousness and peace have k. PRAY 395:15
said when she k. her cow SWIFT 526:28
they k. each other's cheek GILB 228:31

kisses: consign'd k. to them SHAK 487:12
Give me a thousand k. CAT 136:26
it rain'd k. SHAK 422:19
I understand thy k. SHAK 439:29

Let thy love in k. rain	SHEL 501:9
littered with remembered k.	MACN 326:3
more than k.	DONNE 189:22
my k. bring again	SHAK 464:21
play'd At cards for k.	LYLY 321:10
poor half-k. kill me quite	DRAY 193:17
remembered k. after death	TENN 542:4
Stolen k. much completer	HUNT 268:11
thousand k. the poor last	SHAK 423:14
who k. the Joy as it flies	BLAKE 86:18
who straight on k. dream	SHAK 481:28
With k. four	KEATS 290:20
with the k. of his mouth	BIBLE 56:15
you have forgotten my k.	SWIN 530:11

Kissing: K. don't last: cookery do MER 338:1
k., kind-hearted gentleman COWP 168:3
K. with golden face SHAK 493:9
K. your hand may make you LOOS 318:3
made For k. SHAK 480:21
Sweet red splendid k. mouth SWIN 531:1
that first invented k. SWIFT 526:31
trembled k. SHAK 422:11
when the k. had to stop BROW 105:25

kiss-worthy: thy most k. face SIDN 507:25
kitchen: anarchy prevails in my k. JOHN 281:1
get out of the k. TRUM 553:20
in the k. bred BYRON 125:24
I will make my k. STEV 522:29
k. and their children FITZ 213:19

Kitchen-cabals: K., and nursery-mishaps COWP 168:6
Kitchener: if K. was not a great man ASQ 17:19
kitchens: wild cats in your k. SHAK 474:15
Kite: Ere Chil the K. swoops KIPL 303:7
kites: fatted all the region k. SHAK 433:4
kith: If one's own kin and k. NASH 359:18
kitten: dead k., an egg-shell WELLS 568:11
My imperial k. CARR 134:27
rather be a k. and cry mew SHAK 439:25
kittened: mother's cat had but k. SHAK 439:21

Kitty: K., a fair GARR 221:16
kleinen: Opfer fällt als einer k. HITL 251:9
knappeth: k. the spear in sunder PRAY 392:21
knave: coined an epithet for a k. MAC 323:27
duteous and knee-crooking k. SHAK 473:13
he's an arrant k. SHAK 431:17
he's but Fortune's k. SHAK 423:20
How absolute the k. is SHAK 436:28
life a foolish prating k. SHAK 435:23
neat k. with a smooth tale WEBS 566:18
petty sneaking k. I knew BLAKE 87:3
rascally yea-forsooth k. SHAK 441:4
slipper and subtle k. SHAK 474:21
To feed the titled k. BURNS 115:24

knavery: k. and folly to excuse CHUR 149:9
knaves: call'd them untaught k. SHAK 438:14
He calls the k., Jacks DICK 178:8
k. and thieves men shut SHAK 490:27
most part of fools and k. BUCH 106:12
We are arrant k. SHAK 433:14

knavish: are either k. or childish JOHN 278:9
kneaded: k. by the moon HARDY 241:21
knee: fore-mast wi' his k. BALL 30:19
infant prattling on his k. BURNS 113:5
Jesus every k. should bow BIBLE 78:14
little abune her k. BALL 32:1
Lord Primate on bended k. BARH 33:11
my k., my hat, and hand BROW 96:3
set upon the nurse's k. BALL 32:11
sit upon the curate's k. CHES 147:9
straw under my k. DONNE 191:2
to the child on thy k. BRID 92:3

kneel: k. before the Lord our PRAY 396:4
see the oxen k. HARDY 240:14
they should k. for peace SHAK 484:19
wilderness shall k. before him PRAY 394:20
kneel'd: That k. unto the buds SHAK 422:17

Kneeling: K. ne'er spoil'd silk stocking
    HERB 247:10
  meekly k. upon your knees PRAY 387:18
kneels: Not one k. to another WHIT 570:22
knees: at the great k. and feet SWIN 528:26
  bow my k. unto the Father BIBLE 77:24
  confirm the feeble k. BIBLE 58:33
  creeps rustling to her k. KEATS 289:17
  K. and tresses folded MER 337:1
  our hands round her k. SWIN 528:16
  Petticoats up to the k. CLOU 153:15
  rest on his k. DICK 178:24
  Richmond I raised my k. ELIOT 205:5
  Sweeney spreads his k. ELIOT 204:14
  than to live on your k. IBAR 269:16
  then I felt to his k. SHAK 443:18
  they are all on their k. HARDY 240:13
  to sit on Sweeney's k. ELIOT 204:15
  work is done upon his k. KIPL 299:15
knell: By fairy hands their k. COLL 158:20
  it is a k. SHAK 460:1
  Sea-nymphs hourly ring his k. SHAK 484:32
  strikes like a rising k. BYRON 120:20
knew: George the First k. nothing
    JOHN 276:22
  head could carry all he k. GOLD 231:3
  he k. not what to say BYRON 124:43
  I k. all her ways HOUS 265:8
  I k. not all he meant TENN 534:24
  I k. not where LONG 316:6
  I k. that once STEP 518:25
  I k. you once BROW 105:36
  k. it all before you KIPL 301:11
  k. me, and was Ned HOUS 265:5
  much righter than one k. POUND 383:22
  said it that k. it best BACON 25:30
  that he k. nothing yet BEHN 38:11
  that I k. almost as much JOHN 273:26
  that she k. she were SHAK 482:6
  we k. the worst too young KIPL 299:11
  world k. him not BIBLE 71:26
knife: k. has slit The throat HOUS 264:9
  k. is lost in it SHEL 501:20
  k. see not the wound it SHAK 459:2
  stood there holding the k. AUDEN 21:7
  strike with our spirit's k. SHEL 499:20
  'War even to the k. BYRON 120:8
  War to the k. PAL 368:4
  wind's like a whetted k. MAS 334:6
Knife-grinder: Needy K. CANN 129:26
knight: beadsman now that was your
  k. PEELE 371:8
  came a k. to be their wooer BALL 30:14
  gentle k. was pricking SPEN 515:30
  hath no loyal k. and true TENN 538:6
  He is k. dubbed with unhatched SHAK 490:14
  K. at arms KEATS 290:15
  K. of the Doleful Countenance CERV 138:12
  k. shall not be whole MAL 327:16
  K. without fear and without ANON 9:5
  red-cross k. for ever kneel'd TENN 538:8
  Show'd him no carpet k. SCOTT 417:5
  sir priest than sir k. SHAK 490:15
  there lies a new-slain k. BALL 32:8
  There never was k. like SCOTT 417:9
  This k. was indeed a valiant EVEL 209:6
  thy sire was a k. SCOTT 416:24
knight-errantry: Religion *is* k. CERV 138:15
Knightly: ever the K. years were gone
    HENL 245:10
Knighton: long way further than K.
    HOUS 264:8
knights: accomplishing the k. SHAK 444:9
  Armoury of the invincible K. WORD 582:3
  By k. of Logres MILT 350:3
  ladies dead and lovely k. SHAK 494:19
  virtuous deeds that some k. CAXT 138:4
knit: k. together thine elect PRAY 387:4
  sheet k. at the four corners BIBLE 73:37
  stuff of life to k. me HOUS 263:16

knits: k. me to thy rugged strand
    SCOTT 416:22
  Sleep that k. up the ravell'd SHAK 460:8
knitter: Like a k. drowsed HARDY 239:12
knitters: spinsters and the k. SHAK 489:3
knitting: twisted braids of lilies k.
    MILT 341:20
knob: brains out of a brass k. DICK 178:23
knobs: k., and flames o' fire SHAK 444:7
Knochen: *Die gesunden K. eines einzigen*
    BISM 84:22
knock: k., and it shall be opened BIBLE 65:2
  K. as you please POPE 376:15
  K. at a star with my exalted HERR 248:19
  k. me down with the butt-end CIBB 151:11
  k. on my door in the morning AUDEN 21:2
  right to k. him down for it JOHN 278:15
  stand at the door, and k. BIBLE 81:21
  We should k. him down first JOHN 277:1
  Where k. is open wide SMART 509:3
knocked: have k. the factious dogs
    JOHN 279:10
  k. Mr Toots about the head DICK 177:29
  K. on my sullen heart STEV 523:11
  with decency, k. POUND 382:14
knocker: Tie up the k. POPE 376:18
knocketh: voice of my beloved that k.
    BIBLE 57:1
knocking: Here's a k. SHAK 460:15
  k. at Preferment's door ARN 14:12
  K. on the moonlit door DE L 174:7
  Whence is that k. SHAK 460:12
knocks: k. you down with the butt
    GOLD 232:40
knoll'd: bells have k. to church SHAK 425:23
knolling: k. a departed friend SHAK 441:2
knot: k. intrinsicate Of life SHAK 424:14
  So the k. be unknotted ELIOT 202:10
knot-grass: bunches of k. KEATS 289:16
knots: pokers into true-love k. COL 157:6
knotted: Sat and k. all the while SEDL 419:12
know: 'All that we k. is BYRON 120:10
  all ye need to k. KEATS 291:11
  am he that aspired to K. BROW 103:3
  canvassers whom they do not k.
    HURST 268:17
  creditors would hardly k. FOX 217:24
  does not k. himself LA F 306:20
  from what we k. POPE 379:2
  God, thou, and I do k. SHAK 478:12
  God we might k. as much KIPL 298:17
  go we k. not where SHAK 464:14
  hate any one that we k. HAZL 244:2
  have it when they k. it not SWIFT 528:7
  have much ado to k. myself SHAK 465:7
  He will not k. what all SHAK 469:22
  'How shall I k. your true RAL 404:13
  I do not k. myself GOET 229:28
  I k. nothing whatever about DOYLE 192:14
  I k. not the Lord BIBLE 47:10
  I k. not the man BIBLE 68:19
  I k. what I like BEER 38:5
  k. more of mankind I expect JOHN 279:12
  K. most of the rooms FULL 220:13
  k. of England who only KIPL 298:24
  k. so much that ain't so BILL 84:7
  k. that I am God PRAY 392:21
  k. that my redeemer liveth BIBLE 52:31
  k. that which we are BYRON 124:9
  k. the change and feel KEATS 293:4
  k. thee not, old man SHAK 442:30
  K. their own good DRYD 198:18
  k. the man their neighbour YEATS 586:14
  K. then thyself POPE 379:12
  k. the place for the first ELIOT 203:2
  K. thyself ANON 9:21
  'K. thyself' CARL 132:18
  k. to know no more MILT 348:9
  'K. what thou canst work CARL 132:18
  K. ye the land where BYRON 120:1

  K. you the land where GOET 230:13
  let me k. mine end PRAY 391:30
  master of them that k. DANTE 171:7
  more than to k. little BACON 27:24
  neither shall his place k. BIBLE 52:19
  no one to k. what it is ANON 4:11
  now I k. it GAY 223:22
  People of quality k. everything MOL 353:23
  place saying you want to k. DICK 178:17
  searching what we k. not MILT 351:26
  suffer us to k. but little JOHN 273:17
  they k. not what they do BIBLE 71:11
  they merely k. more SAKI 413:16
  To be we k. not what DRYD 195:26
  to k. a thing or two MOL 353:5
  To k. but this POPE 381:12
  to k. that you know not BACON 26:5
  To k. the world YOUNG 588:11
  To k. this only MILT 350:9
  to others that we k. not SHAK 433:8
  unless we k. it to be poetry THOR 550:25
  We k. a subject ourselves JOHN 276:23
  we k. in part BIBLE 76:14
  we k. not anything TENN 536:26
  We *k.* our will is free JOHN 275:24
  we *k. the Good* AUDEN 19:12
  What do I k. MONT 355:3
  What they are yet I k. not SHAK 454:2
  when it came to k. me well MOORE 356:25
  which you yourselves do k. SHAK 451:2
  Who k. them best BURNS 114:29
Know-All: Ole man K. died las' year
    HARR 242:22
knowe: he that kan hymselven k.
    CHAU 142:30
knowed: 'e knew they k. KIPL 304:5
  that there is to be k. GRAH 233:19
knowest: k. not what a day may bring
    BIBLE 54:36
  Speak less than thou k. SHAK 453:15
  thou k. that I love thee BIBLE 73:16
  thou k. my down-sitting PRAY 399:4
knoweth: He that loveth not k. not
    BIBLE 81:5
knowing: foolish to talk of k. Greek
    WOOLF 576:17
  lust of k. what should FLEC 214:14
  misfortune of k. any thing AUST 23:5
  With a k. ignorance JOHN 273:16
knowledge: After such k. ELIOT 203:5
  all k. to be my province BACON 28:1
  anything be beyond the k. BEAU 35:16
  climbing after k. infinite MARL 330:8
  close the five ports of k. BROW 95:19
  counsel by words without k. BIBLE 52:41
  desire more love and k. SHAK 424:27
  dissemble sometimes your k. BACON 26:5
  finer spirit of all k. WORD 583:9
  first the literature of *k.* DE Q 175:6
  foundation is the k. of causes BACON 28:6
  fret not after k. KEATS 292:5
  from k. ignorance BROW 100:10
  full of the k. of the Lord BIBLE 58:11
  he would bring home k. JOHN 277:31
  if he wants any *k.* COL 158:9
  improved life by the k. VIRG 558:23
  increaseth k. increaseth sorrow BIBLE 55:9
  is worth a pound of k. WESL 568:23
  K. advances by steps MAC 323:3
  K. and wonder (which is BACON 24:14
  K. comes TENN 539:3
  K. dwells COWP 167:3
  K. enormous makes a God KEATS 290:8
  K. gained and virtue lost HOUS 265:4
  k. in the making MILT 352:2
  K. is bought in the market CLOU 153:18
  K. is proud that he has COWP 167:24
  K. is of two kinds JOHN 276:28
  k. is, ourselves to know POPE 380:4
  K. itself is power BACON 28:11

k., it shall vanish BIBLE 76:14
K. may give weight CHES 145:31
k. of man is as the waters BACON 24:20
k. of truth BACON 27:31
k. of the Son of God BIBLE 77:28
k. of the ancient languages BRIG 93:8
k. of the world is only CHES 145:12
k. of London was extensive DICK 181:35
k. of nothing DICK 183:3
k. of a lifetime WHIS 569:23
K. puffeth up BIBLE 76:5
k. shall be increased BIBLE 61:10
k. too but recorded experience CARL 131:8
k. without integrity is JOHN 282:11
Let k. grow from more TENN 535:32
light of k. in their eyes SYM 531:3
little k. is dangerous HUXL 269:9
multiplieth words without k. BIBLE 52:40
No man's k. here can go LOCKE 315:15
Out-topping k. ARN 14:23
price for k. TICK 551:3
province of k. to speak HOLM 253:20
Pursuit of k. under difficulties DICK 182:10
renewed in k. after the image BIBLE 78:26
Science is organized k. SPEN 514:24
spirit of k. and of the fear BIBLE 58:9
Such k. is too wonderful PRAY 399:5
taken away the key of k. BIBLE 70:2
There is more k. JOHN 276:8
there k. in the most High PRAY 394:22
thorough k. of human nature AUST 22:31
to communicate k. DE Q 175:7
To follow k. like a sinking TENN 544:1
to follow virtue and k. DANTE 171:13
tree of diabolical k. SHER 506:10
tree of k. of good BIBLE 45:8
Unto this k. to aspire DONNE 188:26
What I don't know isn't k. BEEC 37:8
what is k. but grieving MER 338:7
What k. can perform WORD 577:3
which passeth k. BIBLE 77:25
wisdom we have lost in k. ELIOT 202:3
With too much k. POPE 379:12
known: best that is k. and thought ARN 16:1
child is k. by his doings BIBLE 54:17
devil where he is k. JOHN 279:31
done and little to be k. JOHN 280:7
don't choose to have it k. CHES 146:7
Have ye not k. BIBLE 59:9
he should have k. no more HOBB 251:23
If you would be k. COLT 159:10
In Jewry is God k. PRAY 395:1
is she k. in all the land TENN 538:4
know even as also I am k. BIBLE 76:14
knowing what should not be k. FLEC 214:14
k. and said in the world ARN 16:17
k. by the British than BORR 90:3
k. for his well-knownness BOOR 89:20
k. of old KIPL 302:7
k. of them in breaking BIBLE 71:19
k. too late SHAK 482:4
life endured and k. SASS 415:2
light and safer than a k. HASK 243:1
needs only to be k. DRYD 196:3
not be k. to do anything EMER 207:41
So I had nothing k. SHAK 475:25
Soldier of the Great War K. KIPL 305:12
That thy way may be k. PRAY 394:4
then the end is k. SHAK 451:33
this is all that is k. NEWM 362:5
till I am k. JOHN 274:7
Which we have heard and k. PRAY 395:3
yet hast thou not k. me BIBLE 72:33
knows: HE k.—HE knows FITZ 213:6
He k. ye not GOET 230:12
k. about depth knows about TILL 551:4
k. even his Bible ARN 15:22
k. nothing whatever about KNOX 305:21
k. of a better 'ole BAIR 29:23
no man truly k. another BROW 96:32

now God alone k. KLOP 305:16
'She k. wot's wot DICK 182:27
that has a mind and k. SHAW 496:3
knowses: goodness only k. CHES 147:24
knucklebones: harmless art of k. has STEV 520:23
knuckle-end: That k. of England SMITH 510:30
knyf: smylere with the k. under CHAU 142:20
knyght: parfit gentil k. CHAU 141:10
kotched: sinners'll be k. out late HARR 242:17
Kraken: K. sleepeth TENN 537:24
Krieg: Der K. ist nichts als eine CLAU 152:27
K. ein Glied in Gottes MOLT 354:4
Krorluppia: Nasticreechia K. LEAR 311:19
Kruger: you've finished killing K. KIPL 297:22
krummen: Aus so k. Holze KANT 288:14
Kubla: 'mid this tumult K. heard COL 156:29
Kubla Khan: In Xanadu did K. COL 156:26
Kultur: Wenn ich K. höre JOHST 283:8
kummervollen: Wer nie die k. Nächte GOET 230:12
Kunst: in der K. ist das Beste GOET 230:8
zuletzt die grösste K. GOET 229:27
Kurd: say the same about the K. BELL 38:27
Kurtz: Mistah K.—he dead CONR 161:18
Kyrie: K. eleison MASS 334:16
label: l. to cover himself with HUXL 269:4
pack and l. men for God THOM 548:26
labelled: utensil l. to my will SHAK 488:12
labor: hic l. est VIRG 558:18
solely by the l. of my hands THOR 550:13
laborans: utilitatis pro communi l. THOM 546:11
laboraverunt: in vanum l. qui aedificant BIBLE 83:12
labore: dies niti praestante l. LUCR 320:6
labores: Iucundi acti l. CIC 151:18
laboribus: quod unum est pro l. tantis CAT 136:28
laborious: perform some very l. duty SMITH 509:13
labour: all l. Mars what it does SHAK 423:10
All things are full of l. BIBLE 55:7
brow of l. this crown BRYAN 106:8
Endless l. to be wrong JOHN 280:9
every l. sped GOLD 231:26
faith and l. of love BIBLE 78:30
forget his l. an' his toil BURNS 113:5
Green leaves of thy l. SWIN 529:28
had my l. for my travail SHAK 486:20
Honest l. bears a lovely DEKK 173:20
I l. for peace PRAY 398:8
In all l. there is profit BIBLE 54:2
l. against our own cure BROW 97:2
l. for that which satisfieth BIBLE 59:25
l. of doing nothing STEE 518:8
l. of your life is to build MONT 354:15
l. spread her wholesome GOLD 230:18
l. we delight in physics SHAK 460:19
l. which he taketh under BIBLE 55:5
L. without joy is base RUSK 412:3
Learn to l. and to wait LONG 317:5
man to l. in his vocation SHAK 438:10
many still must l. BYRON 121:30
ruined by Chinese cheap l. HARTE 242:30
Should life all l. be TENN 539:15
should not cease to l. STEV 521:1
Six days shalt thou l. BIBLE 47:24
sore l.'s bath SHAK 460:8
strength then but l. and sorrow PRAY 395:19
that l. and are heavy laden BIBLE 66:5
their l. is but lost that PRAY 398:18
to his l. PRAY 397:1
To painful l. both by sea SHAK 484:17
true success is to l. STEV 522:9
We l. soon BURNS 115:24
with difficulty and l. MILT 347:7
youth of l. with an age GOLD 230:19

laboured: builders have l. in vain BIBLE 83:12
I l. more abundantly than BIBLE 76:20
labourer: l. is worthy of his hire BIBLE 69:27
l. to take his pension RUSK 412:7
labourers: l. are few BIBLE 65:29
labouring: Albeit l. for a scanty WORD 582:16
all women l. of child PRAY 385:20
l. man, and know but little HARDY 240:4
sleep of a l. man is sweet BIBLE 55:17
labours: are entered into their l. BIBLE 71:42
Children sweeten l. BACON 27:3
completed l. are pleasant CIC 151:18
dangers fright him and no l. JOHN 282:30
l. of a servile state BYRON 124:28
line too l. POPE 378:23
may rest from their l. BIBLE 82:18
their uncessant l. MARV 331:21
Laburnums: L., dropping-wells TENN 537:6
labyrinth: peopled l. of walls SHEL 501:23
labyrinthical: l. soul DONNE 190:25
labyrinthine: l. ways Of my own mind THOM 548:8
Still more l. buds the rose BROW 105:13
lac: sine dolo l. concupiscite BIBLE 83:25
lace: l. my bodice blue HUNT 268:15
Through the Nottingham l. BETJ 42:4
Laces: L. for a lady KIPL 302:22
lacessit: Nemo me impune l. ANON 10:15
lachende: l. Löwen müssen kommen NIET 363:2
lack: accustomed to their l. of breath YEATS 585:13
I sigh the l. of many SHAK 493:7
l., and suffer hunger PRAY 391:22
l. of love from love made BROW 100:10
should have he did not l. SHAK 495:20
therefore can I l. nothing PRAY 390:21
they l. their sacred poet HOR 261:18
lack'd: If I l. any thing HERB 247:25
lackey: brisk fond l. to fetch HOUS 265:18
lacrimae: Hinc illae l. TER 544:14
Sunt l. rerum VIRG 557:17
lad: l. does not care JOHN 275:19
l. That I loved bodily YEATS 585:20
song of a l. that is gone STEV 523:4
was a l. I served a term GILB 228:4
ladder: are dropping down the l. KIPL 299:11
he dreamed, and behold a l. BIBLE 46:18
is young ambition's l. SHAK 449:5
l. out of our vices AUG 22:3
l. to all high designs SHAK 486:23
Now that my l.'s gone YEATS 584:15
Wiv a l. and some glasses BAT 35:3
laden: labour and are heavy l. BIBLE 66:5
ladies: Come from a l.' seminary GILB 226:29
Dust was Gentlemen and L. DICK 184:2
girls we was all of us l. we was MARQ 330:20
l. dead and lovely knights SHAK 494:19
l. most deject and wretched SHAK 433:15
l. of St James's DOBS 187:3
L. of th' Hesperides MILT 350:3
lion among l. SHAK 470:3
lords of l. intellectual BYRON 122:7
rhyme themselves into l.' SHAK 445:13
ribs was sport for l. SHAK 424:23
seminaries of young l. KNOX 305:25
Store of l. MILT 342:25
when he has l. to please AUST 22:9
you...I am parshial to l. ASHF 17:6
Young l. should take care AUST 22:17
lads: I lie as l. would choose HOUS 263:11
l. in their hundreds HOUS 263:6
lightfoot l. are laid HOUS 264:10
lady: Gaping at the l. in the swing ELIOT 203:28
He capers nimbly in a l.'s SHAK 480:18
He keeps a l. in a cage CHES 147:21
His l.'s ta'en anither BALL 32:8

his strange l. all I know — LAND 308:19
in every l. even deafanddumb — CUMM 170:10
In l., the ignorant — DUPPA 199:16
in our l. should perish — MAC 323:4
is neither speech nor l. — PRAY 390:11
is never the l. of poetry — GRAY 235:22
laboured to refine our l. — JOHN 282:5
l. and ways of behaving — JUV 287:15
l. convey more than they — CONN 161:11
l. he was the lodesterre — LYDG 321:5
l. I have learn'd these — SHAK 478:10
L. is called the garment — CARL 132:15
L. is only the instrument — JOHN 281:6
L. is the dress of thought — JOHN 281:31
language...L. is not simply a reporting — WHORF 571:23
l. of the heart — POPE 377:5
l. that would make your — GILB 228:34
L. was not powerful enough — DICK 180:16
Learned his great l. — BROW 102:5
literature is simply l. — POUND 384:1
Money speaks sense in a l. — BEHN 38:18
...My l. fails — BELL 39:6
natural l. of the heart — SHAD 420:19
no respect for their l. — SHAW 498:12
persuasive l. of a tear — CHUR 149:17
primitive l. of the law — BURKE 111:6
some entrance into the l. — BACON 27:27
speak a l. of their own — SWIFT 527:29
spoken in their own l. — BIBLE 62:20
sure in l. strange she — KEATS 290:19
There's l. in her eye — SHAK 487:13
they can only speak one l. — DISR 186:21
think anything of that l. — DICK 180:13
Under the tropic is our l. — WALL 562:17
with no l. but a cry — TENN 536:26
Worships l. and forgives — AUDEN 19:7
You taught me l. — SHAK 484:29
languages: ancient l. is mainly a luxury — BRIG 93:8
at a great feast of l. — SHAK 457:12
because l. are the pedigree — JOHN 280:1
gave l. just as she needed — PRIOR 400:27
graves of deceased l. — DICK 177:23
Playing among the ruined l. — AUDEN 18:5
said will be wit in all l. — DRYD 198:1
'silent in seven l. — BAG 29:11
speaks three or four l. — SHAK 487:24
langueur: une l. Monotone — VERL 556:8
languid: excite your l. spleen — GILB 227:23
l. patience of thy face — COL 157:16
through the music of the l. — LANG 309:18
languish: Relieve my l. — DAN 171:1
languished: l. in a foreign clime — MAC 322:9
Languor: L. cannot be — SHEL 504:22
languors: lilies and l. of virtue — SWIN 529:5
lank: days seem l. and long — GILB 228:29
lantern: gives is a l. on the stern — COL 157:20
word is a l. unto my feet — PRAY 398:6
lap: Carrie to sit on his l. — GROS 237:1
flowery l. of earth — ARN 13:17
fresh l. of the crimson rose — SHAK 470:9
l. to saint-seducing gold — SHAK 481:24
L. your loneliness in heat — BETJ 42:7
That strew the green l. — SHAK 480:11
Uncover, dogs, and l. — SHAK 486:7
lapdogs: when l. breathe their last — POPE 381:8
lapidary: l. inscriptions a man is — JOHN 276:31
Lapland: lovely as a L. night — WORD 583:4
lapp'd: friends are l. in lead — BARN 34:1
laps: tumbling into some men's l. — BACON 25:3
lapwing: like a l. — SHAK 472:20
larboard: did swim all to the l. — BALL 31:3
larch: rosy plumelets tuft the l. — TENN 537:9
lard: l. their lean books with — BURT 116:13
lards: l. the lean earth as he — SHAK 438:28
larem: Labore fessi venimus l. — CAT 136:28
large: fly on a rather l. scale — BARH 33:5
It's as l. as life — CARR 136:1

l. a letter I have written — BIBLE 77:21
l., and smooth, and round — SOUT 513:15
l. a trunk before — BELL 38:28
l.-brained woman — BROW 98:15
live in and too l. to hang on a watch-chain — ANON 8:11
Mothers of l. families — BELL 38:31
Priest writ l. — MILT 351:15
sufficiently l. scale — SPEN 514:33
large-hearted: woman and l. man — BROW 98:15
largely: drinking l. sobers us again — POPE 378:13
Larger: L. than human on the frozen — TENN 535:23
l. than Man can ever estimate — AUDEN 18:8
Lord would use a l. map — SAL 413:20
largess: l. universal — SHAK 444:11
largest: l. lamp is lit — MAC 322:23
lark: l. at break of day — SHAK 493:6
l. at heaven's gate sings — SHAK 428:10
l. becomes a sightless — TENN 537:19
l.-charmèd — HOPK 256:10
l. from her light wing — CRAW 169:16
l. soars — BROW 103:21
l.'s on the wing — BROW 97:29
l., that tirra-lirra chants — SHAK 491:17
late l. twitters from — HENL 245:7
More tuneable than l. — SHAK 469:21
No l. more blithe than he — BICK 83:28
sing as sweetly as the l. — SHAK 468:19
Some late l. singing — HENL 245:9
swallow for the holy l. — BROW 97:27
under the l. full cloud — THOM 547:7
We rise with the l. — BRET 92:2
larke: bisy l. — CHAU 142:18
Larks: Four L. and a Wren — LEAR 311:15
hear the l. so high — HOUS 263:4
larkspur: l. listens, 'I hear — TENN 540:12
larme: l. divine et de ce sourire — HUGO 267:13
Lars: L. Porsena of Clusium — MAC 322:11
LASCIATE: L. OGNI SPERANZA VOI CH'ENTRATE — DANTE 171:3
lascivious: l. pleasing of a lute — SHAK 480:18
lash: delight at once and l. — POPE 378:5
dost thou l. that whore — SHAK 455:19
rum, sodomy and the l. — CHUR 151:7
lass: every l. a queen — KING 297:5
It cam' wi' a l. — JAM 271:7
l. that has acres o' charms — BURNS 114:6
l. that loves a sailor — DIBD 175:20
l. that were to go a-gipseying — LAMB 308:3
l. unparallel'd — SHAK 424:15
lordliest l. of earth — BROO 94:16
Met again, my l. — HOUS 265:5
Sweet l. of Richmond Hill — MACN 326:2
was a lover and his l. — SHAK 427:2
lasse: tout l. — ANON 9:20
lasses: An' then she made the l. — BURNS 114:4
He dearly lov'd the l. — BURNS 114:3
lassie: young l. do wi' an auld man — BURNS 116:3
last: bring a man peace at the l. — PRAY 391:29
families l. not three oaks — BROW 97:16
'It will l. my time — CARL 131:10
l. act crowns the play — QUAR 403:15
l. act is bloody — PASC 369:8
l. and best — MILT 349:17
l. breath he drew in — LAMB 308:11
l. enemy that shall be — BIBLE 76:23
l. great Englishman is — TENN 541:6
l. have wrought but one — BIBLE 67:15
L. Judgement draweth nigh — BLAKE 85:13
l. red leaf is whirl'd — TENN 536:8
L. scene of all — SHAK 425:24
l. shall be first — BIBLE 67:13
l. state of that man is — BIBLE 66:11
l. syllable of recorded — SHAK 463:6
l. taste of sweets — SHAK 478:18

l. thing one knows in constructing — PASC 369:3
l. to lay the old aside — POPE 378:19
L. week in Babylon — HODG 252:10
l. words of Mr Despondency — BUNY 107:37
l. words of Marmion — SCOTT 417:22
l. words which I should — REYN 405:19
lost the l. of England — BELL 40:16
Love of fame is the l. — TAC 531:14
My l. good night — KING 296:11
present were the world's l. night — DONNE 189:7
that has dawned is your l. — HOR 258:16
that I could l. for ever — CONR 161:24
that's the l. thing I shall — PALM 368:13
there is no l. nor first — BROW 103:25
thief said the l. kind word — BROW 104:25
this day may be the l. — NELS 360:16
Tristram Shandy did not l. — JOHN 276:34
When he was at the l. gasp — BIBLE 63:30
will give unto this l. — BIBLE 67:16
with low l. breath — ROSS 410:3
lasting: memorial longer l. than bronze — HOR 261:8
latch: no l. ter de golden gate — HARR 242:17
latchet: shoe's l. I am not worthy — BIBLE 71:29
late: damned fella will be l. — MITF 352:24
It came to them very l. — KIPL 298:1
l. for medicine to be prepared — OVID 366:20
l. or too early for anything — SART 414:9
l. to-morrow to be brave — ARMS 12:17
offering even that too l. — NEV 361:2
of human thought too l. — LA B 306:11
sinners'll be kotched out l. — HARR 242:17
So l. into the night — BYRON 125:25
that leaves him out so l. — FROST 219:11
Too l. came I to love thee — AUG 21:16
Too late, too l. — TENN 534:8
later: It is l. than you think — SERV 420:12
there will be sunlight l. — MACN 326:6
Latet: L. anguis in herba — VIRG 559:19
lath: l. of wood painted — BISM 84:27
Latin: carve in L. or in Greek — WALL 562:7
half L. and half Greek — SCOTT 415:10
he speaks L. — SHAK 446:15
L., queen of tongues, — JONS 285:6
learn L. as an honour — CHUR 150:23
measures is L. for a whopping — ANST 11:9
small L., and less Greek — JONS 284:21
teach him one word of L. — YEATS 587:13
understand Greek and L. — DRYD 198:14
Your L. names for horns — BURNS 113:19
Latio: *artes Intulit agresti L.* — HOR 259:2
latitude: Though the l.'s rather — PROW 402:2
Latium: arts into rustic L. — HOR 259:2
latoun: croys of l. ful of stones — CHAU 142:7
latrone: Cantabit vacuus coram l. viator — JUV 287:26
Lattenzaun: Es war einmal ein L. — MORG 357:22
latter: former and the l. rain — PRAY 386:3
stand at the l. day — BIBLE 52:31
To carry off the l. — PEAC 371:2
laud: l. and magnify thy glorious — PRAY 387:23
More l. than gilt o'er-dusted — SHAK 487:6
Laudamus: L. te — MASS 334:18
Te Deum l. — ANON 11:3
Laudant: L. illa sed ista legunt — MART 331:10
Laudate: L. Dominum — BIBLE 83:11
laudator: l. temporis acti — HOR 257:21
Laudes: L. to their maker early — HAWES 243:2
laudi: concedant laurea l. — CIC 151:22
laugh: Anything awful makes me l. — LAMB 307:27
be dismissed with a l. — HOR 20. 7
behind her a meaning l. — EWART 209:1
Democritus would l. — HOR 259:3
do we not l. — SHAK 467:4
his arms hang down to l. — ELIOT 204:14

men must not obey the l.	EMER 207:32	l., the bud, the flower	SPEN 516:13	words of l. length	GOLD 231:3
not whether L. be right	WILDE 572:15	November's l. is red	SCOTT 416:27	learning: cry both arts and l.	QUAR 403:21
of bad or obnoxious l.	GRANT 233:22	we all do fade as a l.	BIBLE 60:12	encourage a will to l.	ASCH 17:2
purer l.	TENN 537:15	league: Half a l. onward	TENN 532:23	Get l. with a great sum	BIBLE 63:28
schoolmasters Deliver us to l.	HERB 248:10	She hadna sail'd a l.	BALL 30:18	grammar, and nonsense, and l.	GOLD 231:22
sweeps a room as for Thy l.	HERB 247:19	Will keep a l. till death	SHAK 480:7	I grow old ever l.	SOLON 512:24
tho' not judges of l.	PULT 402:9	leagues: l. beyond those leagues	ROSS 409:26	just enough of l. to misquote	BYRON 124:17
Unequal l. unto a savage race	TENN 543:21	scarce long l. apart descried	CLOU 154:3	l., a mere hoard of gold	SHAK 442:15
which l. or kings can cause	GOLD 231:30	leak: One l. will sink a ship	BUNY 107:29	l.; and then both of them	BACON 27:34
which l. or kings can cause	JOHN 282:21	Leaking: L. the brightness away	SPEN 515:12	L. hath gained most	FULL 220:18
Who broke the l. of God	LOCK 316:1	leaks: Vaguely life l. away	AUDEN 18:10	l. is like bread in a besieged	JOHN 276:27
lawyer: (as a l. knows how)	COWP 166:15	lean: another would make it l.	HAL 237:18	l. lightly like a flower	TENN 537:21
l. has no business with	JOHN 279:30	has a l. and hungry look	SHAK 448:20	l. more than the fond eye	SHAK 466:19
saw a L. killing a viper	COL 156:12	l. on one another	BURKE 112:11	l.'s triumph o'er her	JOHN 282:25
what a l. tells me I may do	BURKE 109:26	on which if a man l.	BIBLE 51:38	L., that cobweb	BUTL 117:33
lawyers: l. are met	GAY 223:1	She help'd him to l.	BARH 33:6	l., what a thing it is	SHAK 484:6
l.! for ye have taken	BIBLE 70:2	sideways would she l.	KEATS 290:17	L. will be cast into	BURKE 111:14
let's kill all the l.	SHAK 446:11	study had made him very l.	HOOD 254:11	liberty, and of l.	DISR 185:10
With l. in the vacation	SHAK 426:13	Lean'd: L. her breast up-till	BARN 33:32	little l. is a dang'rous	POPE 378:13
lay: bird of loudest l.	SHAK 492:15	l. my back unto an aik	BALL 32:10	love he bore to l. was	GOLD 231:2
difficult suddenly to l.	CAT 137:10	Leaned: L. backward with a lipless		mind by that traitor to l.	JOHN 273:17
laid us as we l. at birth	ARN 13:17		ELIOT 205:13	much l. doth make thee mad	BIBLE 74:25
l. erewhile a holocaust	MILT 350:30	leaning: sneer at me for l. all awry		Of such deep l. little	SPEN 515:24
L. her i' the earth	SHAK 437:4		FITZ 213:10	picker-up of l.'s crumbs	BROW 100:24
L. on, Macduff	SHAK 463:9	leans: Where the broad ocean l.	GOLD 231:7	pleasures that go with l.	SOCR 512:19
L. your sleeping head	AUDEN 18:7	leap: great l. in the dark	HOBB 251:24	polite l. and a liberal	HENRY 245:21
man l. down his wife	JOYCE 286:28	I shall l. over the wall	PRAY 390:10	that loyal body wanted l.	TRAPP 552:5
oneself is that one can l.	BUTL 119:14	lame man l. as an hart	BIBLE 58:34	That's a' the l. I desire	BURNS 113:20
our sins l. on the king	SHAK 444:23	L. to these arms	SHAK 483:6	Then l. is most excellent	FOOTE 216:8
prepared to l. down my life	CLOU 153:9	made a l. into the dark	BROWN 95:9	Those twins of l. that	SHAK 447:22
unpremeditated l.	SCOTT 416:10	methinks it were an easy l.	SHAK 438:19	'till l. fly the shore	POPE 375:21
will l. me down in peace	PRAY 389:22	worthy to l. in ourselves	SHAK 452:5	to attain good l.	ASCH 17:1
lays: constructing tribal l.	KIPL 300:3	leaped: God have I l. over a wall BIBLE 50:27		to be written for our l.	PRAY 386:5
She l. it on with a trowel	CONG 159:24	I l. headlong into	KEATS 294:5	Wear your l.	CHES 145:21
we know wot l. afore us	DICK 179:24	thousand swords must have l.	BURKE 111:9	Whence is thy l.	GAY 223:10
Lazarus: certain beggar named L.		leaping: brooks too broad for l.	HOUS 264:10	learnt: been l. has been forgotten SKIN 508:20	
	BIBLE 70:28	l., and praising God	BIBLE 73:26	easiest l.	MILT 350:11
lead: Do scald like molten l.	SHAK 455:25	l. light for you discovers	AUDEN 20:3	forgotten nothing and l.	DUM 199:7
friends are lapp'd in l.	BARN 34:1	long as there is no l.	SURT 525:19	it can never be fully l.	WALT 563:31
if the blind l. the blind	BIBLE 66:29	one's horse as he is l.	HARE 242:4	They have l. nothing	TALL 531:17
L., kindly Light	NEWM 362:14	leapt: dangerous world I l.	BLAKE 87:23	lease: having so short a l.	SHAK 495:13
l. me in the right way	PRAY 391:8	Lear: pleasant to know Mr L.	LEAR 311:20	l. of my true love control	SHAK 494:21
L. us, Heavenly Father	EDM 199:26	learn: An' l. about women from me		summer's l. hath all too	SHAK 492:28
l. us not into temptation	BIBLE 64:24		KIPL 300:17	least: am the l. of the apostles	BIBLE 76:19
l. was flying	HOUS 266:4	cannot l. men from books	DISR 186:41	faithful in that which is l.	BIBLE 70:27
l. you in at Heaven's gate	BLAKE 86:8	craft so long to l.	HIPP 251:8	find it the l. of all evils	BACON 27:40
little child shall l. them	BIBLE 58:10	endeavour to l. and propagate	ARN 16:1	indeed is the l. of all seeds	BIBLE 66:20
makes a people easy to l.	BROU 95:6	glad to l. of noble men	SHAK 451:17	is best which governs l.'	THOR 549:31
shall gently l. those that	BIBLE 59:7	If they will l. any thing	BIBLE 76:17	l. injury you can do him	JAMES 271:27
This is the Hour of L.	DICK 183:14	I l. two things	PRAY 388:14	l. of these my brethren	BIBLE 68:7
'To l. but one measure	SCOTT 417:12	is diligent to l.	WORD 577:3	leather: attired in l. boots	HOUS 266:9
To l. such dire attack	MAC 322:19	l., and inwardly digest	PRAY 386:5	is all but l. or prunella	POPE 379:22
to l. them the way	BIBLE 47:21	l. from the Yellow an'	KIPL 300:15	l. on these gritty pavin'-stones	KIPL 301:7
when we think we l.	BYRON 126:4	l. in suffering what they	SHEL 501:13	leathern: l. girdle about his loins BIBLE 63:37	
leaden: Because if I use l. ones	BELL 38:30	l. Latin as an honour	CHUR 150:23	leave: be ready to l.	MONT 354:13
Her voice revives the l.	CAMP 129:17	l. so little and forget	DAV 172:10	forever taking l.	RILKE 406:4
l. foot time creeps along	JAGO 271:1	l. the noble acts of chivalry	CAXT 138:4	I l. my love alone	SHAK 494:5
leaden-stepping: Call on the lazy l. hours		L. to labour and to wait	LONG 317:5	I l. them where they are	WHIT 571:4
	MILT 344:17	L. to write well	BUCH 106:15	Intreat me not to l. thee	BIBLE 49:32
leader: I am their l.	LEDR 313:6	men could l. from history	COL 157:20	l. a child alone	BROW 104:22
In camps a l. sage	SCOTT 417:5	men l.	SEN 420:10	l. a living name behind	WEBS 566:17
l. is fairest	ARN 13:3	so dull but she can l.	SHAK 467:13	L. her to heaven	SHAK 431:13
l. whose experience	MAC 323:13	so much to l. so little	DICK 182:7	l. his country as good	COBB 154:9
Over the face of the l.	WHIT 571:17	song we may l. the nest	TENN 535:3	l. his father and his mother	BIBLE 45:13
leaders: not the l. of a revolution		therefore we must l. both arts	CARL 131:39	l. me here a little	TENN 538:15
	CONR 161:22	there is much desire to l.	MILT 352:2	l. me there to die	ANON 6:1
leader-writers: God exists only for l.		We live and l.	POMF 375:8	l. my soul in hell	PRAY 390:7
	GREE 236:7	Learn'd: L. without sense	CHUR 149:11	L. not a rack behind	SHAK 485:20
leading: I owe no light or l. received		learned: decent obscurity of a l.	GIBB 224:19	L. not a stain in thine	BIBLE 63:16
	MILT 352:7	discreet and l. Minister	PRAY 387:17	L. off first for manners'	BIBLE 63:14
l. wherever I choose	WHIT 571:7	grew within this l. man	MARL 329:16	l. something so written	MILT 352:14
no l. into captivity	PRAY 399:13	last thing even l. men	TAC 531:14	l. the future to the divine	BACON 24:26
of light and l. in England	BURKE 111:20	l. about women from 'er	KIPL 300:16	l. their riches for other	PRAY 392:28
praise to have pleased l.	HOR 258:21	l. anything from history	HEGEL 244:8	l. the issue to the Gods	CORN 162:17
leaf: caterpillar on the l.	BLAKE 85:13	L. his great language	BROW 102:5	l. the word of God	BIBLE 73:27
days are in the yellow l.	BYRON 125:11	loads of l. lumber	POPE 378:30	l. the world unseen	KEATS 291:10
Falls with the l. still	FLET 215:8	make the l. smile	POPE 378:18	l. to Heaven the measure	JOHN 283:5
If I were a dead l. thou	SHEL 502:12	opinion with the l.	CONG 160:1	'L. Truth to the police	AUDEN 19:12
I were like the l.	SWIN 530:21	prescribed laws to the l.	DUPPA 199:16	L. untended the herd	SCOTT 417:28
last red l. is whirl'd	TENN 536:8	Things l. on earth	BROW 102:26	L. writing plays	DRYD 196:35

never l. me	ANON 5:3
shall l. them in the midst	BIBLE 60:25
thought to l. her far away	KEATS 289:5
under l. of Brutus	SHAK 450:17
which thou must l. ere long	SHAK 494:8
wilt thou l. me thus	WYATT 583:19
with old Khayyám and l.	FITZ 212:9
leaven: l. leaveneth the whole	BIBLE 75:35
l. of malice and wickedness	BIBLE 75:36
l. of malice and wickedness	PRAY 386:11
leaves: bags full of l.	FROST 219:4
burning of the l.	BINY 84:8
Close up these barren l.	WORD 582:23
crowding through the l.	ARN 14:3
Crowned with calm l.	SWIN 529:22
fields and l. to the trees	HOR 261:14
heard the autumnal l.	SHEL 502:8
laughing l. of the tree	SWIN 528:18
l. dead Are driven	SHEL 502:8
l. fall early this autumn	POUND 383:17
l. grow on the tree	YEATS 584:22
l. His shivering mates	THOM 549:23
l. is a generation of men	HOMER 253:29
l. it as fast as they can	LOCK 316:2
l. of the tree were	BIBLE 83:1
l. soul free	BROW 99:2
l. the world to darkness	GRAY 234:18
long l. cover me	SWIN 530:18
noiseless noise among the l.	KEATS 290:13
Of wither'd l.	ARN 14:8
one l. behind a part	HAR 238:20
pond edged with grayish l.	HARDY 240:10
sewed fig l.	BIBLE 45:16
Shatter your l. before	MILT 343:2
tender l. of hope	SHAK 447:9
that lamentation of the l.	YEATS 586:22
Thick as autumnal l.	MILT 345:13
thick on Severn snow the l.	HOUS 263:14
to put l. round his head	DICK 178:27
trees I see barren of l.	SHAK 492:26
What if my l. are falling	SHEL 502:13
When yellow l.	SHAK 494:7
whole deck put on its l.	FLEC 214:19
Wild l. that winds have	SWIN 529:23
leave-taking: It is not worth l.	SHAK 424:13
leaving: Became him like the l. it	
	SHAK 458:22
L. a blacker air	HARDY 240:11
L. his country for his	FITZ 212:4
Lebanon: devour the cedars of L.	
	BIBLE 49:19
his countenance is as L.	BIBLE 57:4
nose is as the tower of L.	BIBLE 57:9
Samarcand to cedar'd L.	KEATS 289:20
leben: gefährlich l.	NIET 363:9
l. wir und nehmen immer	RILKE 406:4
wollt ihr ewig l.	FRED 218:23
Lebens: grün des L. goldner Baum	
	GOET 230:3
lecher: Does l. in my sight	SHAK 455:16
lecherous: follows I am rough and l.	
	SHAK 453:11
he was and l. as a sparwe	CHAU 142:4
Lechery: L., sir, it provokes	SHAK 460:18
wars and l.	SHAK 487:16
lecto: Desideratoque acquiescimus l.	
	CAT 136:28
Lectorem: L. delectando pariterque	
	HOR 258:1
lecture: classic l.	TENN 541:30
lectures: give l. or a little charity	WHIT 571:1
l. in her night-dress	HOOD 255:12
lecturing: l. had convinced me that	
	HUXL 269:7
led: Carlyle has l. us all out	CLOU 154:6
l. his regiment from behind	GILB 225:17
we are most l.	BYRON 126:4
Leda: love of L.	SPEN 516:31
lede: gold wes changyd into l.	WYNT 584:4
lat thy gost thee l.	CHAU 144:22

Lee: swimming down along the L.	
	SPEN 516:31
leef: aspes l. she gan to quake	CHAU 144:9
light as l. on lynde	CHAU 142:11
leek: By this l.	SHAK 445:10
leene: l. was his hors as is	CHAU 141:23
lees: drink Life to the l.	TENN 543:22
feast of wine on the l.	BIBLE 58:18
left: all l. behind on the beach	CARR 133:2
are l. alone with our day	AUDEN 20:17
hath l. you all his walks	SHAK 451:4
have l. a name behind them	BIBLE 63:24
he has l. us there	CLOU 154:6
he l. the thorn wi' me	BURNS 116:8
he was l. lamenting	CAMP 129:5
l. and is now in the centre	MOSL 358:19
l. fair Scotland's strand	BURNS 114:10
l. off before you began	CONG 160:24
of my l. hand	MILT 352:13
other l.	BIBLE 67:33
So far upon the l. side	WEBS 566:19
That we l.	ANON 7:20
thou hast l. thy first love	BIBLE 81:16
Thou hast l. behind	WORD 582:17
'tis better to be l. than	CONG 160:35
We l. our country for our	BARR 34:23
Ye have l. your souls	KEATS 290:31
'You l. us in tatters	HARDY 240:19
left-handed: be termed a l. marriage	
	WOLL 576:12
leg: decreasing l.	SHAK 441:10
here I leave my second l.	HOOD 254:14
kiss my Julia's dainty l.	HERR 249:15
shape of his l.	SHAK 488:23
with a wooden l.	DICK 181:3
legacy: l. from a rich relative	BIRK 84:13
lege: Tolle l.	AUG 21:15
legem: Necessitas dat l. non ipsa	PUBL 402:6
legend: all the fables in the l.	BACON 25:22
l. of an epic hour	CHES 147:8
legens: sed aut l.	THOM 546:11
leges: Silent enim l. inter arma	CIC 151:31
leggemmo: giorno più non vi l. avante	
	DANTE 171:10
legges: were his l. and his toon	CHAU 142:32
leggiavamo: Noi l. un giorno per diletto	
	DANTE 171:9
legible: thoughts are l. in the eye	ROYD 411:2
Legion: My name is L.	BIBLE 68:30
Legion of Honour: cross of the L. has	
been	TWAIN 554:21
legions: give me back my l.	AUG 22:4
legislation: foundation of morals and	
l.	BENT 40:25
legislator: l. of mankind	JOHN 282:7
people is the true l.	BURKE 112:12
legislators: are the unacknowledged l.	
	SHEL 505:13
legislature: l. can manufacture in any	
	BAG 28:21
legitimate: such a thing as l. warfare	
	NEWM 361:14
legs: cannon-ball took off his l.	HOOD 254:13
delighteth he in any man's l.	PRAY 399:20
Four l. good	ORW 365:8
His l. bestrid the ocean	SHAK 423:22
l. are as pillars of marble	BIBLE 57:4
l. when I take my boots	DICK 178:2
losing your l.	SASS 414:13
Matching their lily-white l.	CLOU 153:15
recuvver the use of his l.	DICK 180:8
Taste your l.	SHAK 489:20
thou 'ear my 'erse's l.	TENN 540:24
to lie between maids' l.	SHAK 434:6
vast and trunkless l.	SHEL 502:15
Walk under his huge l.	SHAK 448:17
when his l. were smitten	SHEA 498:29
your l. ungainly huddled	SASS 414:14
legunt: Laudant illa sed ista l.	MART 331:10
Leicester: Here lies the Earl of L.	ANON 5:14

leid: Heute l.' ich	LESS 313:26
Leiden: L. oder triumphieren	GOET 230:7
Leisure: add to these retired L.	MILT 342:1
cometh by opportunity of l.	BIBLE 63:19
conspicuous l. and consumption	VEBL 556:2
I am quite at l.	AUST 23:22
improvement arises from l.	JOHN 276:12
is l. with honour	CIC 151:33
l. answers leisure	SHAK 465:5
l. are the two civilizers	DISR 185:9
l. for love or hope	HOOD 255:9
they detest at l.	BYRON 123:38
we may polish it at l.	DRYD 197:37
What l. to grow wise	ARN 13:10
lekes: oynons, and eek l.	CHAU 142:5
lemon: in the squeezing of a l.	GOLD 232:24
l. is squeezed	GEDD 223:32
lemonade: black eyes and l.	MOORE 356:3
lemon-trees: land where the l. bloom	
	GOET 230:13
lend: l l. it instantly	HERB 248:15
I'll l. you something	SHAK 490:16
I'll l. you thus much moneys	SHAK 466:3
L. less than thou owest	SHAK 453:15
l. me your ears	SHAK 450:17
men who l.	LAMB 307:12
onward l. thy guiding hand	MILT 350:13
lender: borrower, nor a l. be	SHAK 430:19
lenders: thy pen from l.' books	SHAK 454:19
lendeth: merciful, and l.	PRAY 397:14
lendings: you l.	SHAK 454:20
lends: Three things I never l.	SURT 525:17
length: have l. and breadth enough	
	BALL 31:14
l. of days understanding	BIBLE 52:24
L. of days is in her right	BIBLE 53:16
l. of time which is unknowable	BEDE 37:1
words of learned l.	GOLD 231:33
lengthen: To l. our days	MOORE 356:21
lengthening: drags at each remove a l.	
chain	GOLD 231:24
lenses: at times my eyes are l.	DOUG 191:7
lent: l. out my heart with usury	LAMB 307:24
thing only has been l.	ARN 15:13
lente: Festina l.	SUET 524:16
l. currite noctis equi	MARL 329:11
leoni: vulpes aegroto cauta l.	HOR 258:11
Léonie: Weep not for little L.	GRAH 233:9
leopard: l. his spots	BIBLE 60:22
l. shall lie down with	BIBLE 58:10
leporum: Medio de fonte l.	LUCR 320:11
lerne: craft so long to l.	CHAU 143:32
wolde he l. and gladly teche	CHAU 141:25
Lesbia: L. hath a beaming eye	MOORE 356:11
L. let us live and love	CAT 136:25
L. whom Catullus once loved	CAT 137:5
L. with her sparrow	MILL 339:29
mea L.	CAT 136:25
Lesley: saw ye bonnie L.	BURNS 112:37
less: Even l. am	HOPE 256:5
had he pleas'd us l.	ADD 2:3
Is l. likely to fall	GAY 223:4
l. brilliant pen	BEER 37:13
l. often sought than found	BYRON 125:12
L. than a span	BACON 28:15
L. than the dust beneath	HOPE 256:5
Make l. thy body hence	SHAK 442:31
more about less and l.	BUTL 117:13
rather than be l.	MILT 346:7
small Latin, and l. Greek	JONS 284:21
then l. is learned there	JOHN 276:32
lessen: 'because they l. from day	CARR 134:12
lesser: Of the two evils the l.	THOM 546:15
lesson: have had an Imperial l.	KIPL 300:21
still harder l.	PORT 381:33
lessons: reason they're called l.	CARR 134:12
Lest: L. we forget	KIPL 302:7
let: another to l. in the foe	MILT 350:22
before you l. the sun	THOM 547:10
L. her alone	JONS 284:11

L. justice be done	FERD 210:33	often quite picturesque l.	TWAIN 554:15
L. my people go	ANON 8:18	only answered 'Little L.	BELL 39:11
L. there be light	BIBLE 44:22	She's like a l. gone	SHAK 477:11
l. the sounds of music	SHAK 468:15	liars: All men are l.	PRAY 397:21
L. the words of my mouth	PRAY 390:13	do prove the greatest l.	DRAY 193:9
L. us make man in our image	BIBLE 45:4	l. and swearers are fools	SHAK 462:13
L. what will be o'er me	STEV 522:28	L. ought to have good memories	SIDN 507:11
sore l. and hindered	PRAY 386:6	Libanus: breaketh the cedars of L.	
then I will l. you a better	TENN 532:22		PRAY 391:10
they would but l. it alone	WALP 563:6	even the cedars of L. which	PRAY 396:20
lethargy: kind of l.	SHAK 441:6	libation: say about pouring a l.	SOCR 512:20
Lethe: Dawn shall over L. break	BELL 39:22	libbaty: l.'s a kind o' thing	LOW 319:3
go not to L.	KEATS 291:13	libel: Convey a l. in a frown	SWIFT 527:29
itself in ease on L. wharf	SHAK 431:8	libellum: Cui dono lepidum novum l.	
on the wharf of L. waiting	HOUS 265:18		CAT 136:19
Lethean: have drunken of things L.		Liber: L. scriptus proferetur	CEL 138:6
	SWIN 530:5	Nullus l. homo capiatur	MAGN 327:2
letrres: nat the l. space	CHAU 144:16	libera: Anglicana ecclesia l.	MAGN 327:1
lets: l. loose a thinker on this	EMER 207:13	L. Chiesa in libero Stato	CAV 138:1
letter: carry a l. to my love	BALL 30:20	Sed l. nos a malo	MASS 335:5
deal by speech than by l.	BACON 26:37	Liberal: Is either a little L.	GILB 226:8
face is a l. of recommendation	ADD 2:15	learning and a l. education	HENRY 245:21
Give 'im a l.	KIPL 302:20	panted for a l. profession	COLM 159:4
great art o' l. writin'	DICK 182:14	phylacteries of the L. Party	ROS 408:17
has written a braid l.	BALL 31:17	When a l. is abused	LENIN 313:19
in one l. of Richardson's	JOHN 276:8	you are l. in offers	SHAK 468:12
large a l. I have written	BIBLE 77:21	Liberator: 'Europe's L.'	BYRON 123:25
l. from his wife	CARR 133:10	Liberavi: L. animam meam	BERN 41:24
l. killeth	BIBLE 77:4	Libertas: Imperium et L.	DISR 185:19
that when he wrote a l.	BACON 25:42	'L. et natale solum'	SWIFT 528:10
this l. longer than usual	PASC 369:14	Liberté: L.! Égalité	ANON 9:13
thou unnecessary l.	SHAK 453:21	l. et principale retraite	MONT 354:20
till you write your l.	DONNE 190:10	libertee: desiren l.	CHAU 142:12
wordy l. came from Capri	JUV 287:27	liberties: dramatist only wants more l.	
letters: All l., methinks	OSB 365:19		JAMES 271:18
find l. from God dropt	WHIT 571:4	never give up their l.	BURKE 110:27
generally like women's l.	HAZL 243:8	libertine: air, a charter'd l.	SHAK 443:6
his long marvellous l.	AUDEN 21:9	puff'd and reckless l.	SHAK 430:18
I am persecuted with l.	CONG 160:37	liberty: Abstract l.	BURKE 109:21
l. for a spy	KIPL 302:22	all the feelings of l.	PITT 373:21
L. for the rich	AUDEN 20:1	Brightest in dungeons, L.	BYRON 125:14
l. mingle souls	DONNE 189:22	conceived in l.	LINC 314:23
L. of thanks	AUDEN 20:2	consecrate to truth and l.	SHEL 505:6
l., soft interpreters	PRIOR 400:26	desire their L. and Freedom	CHAR 140:19
make in the republic of l.	ADD 1:11	distinction between l. and slavery	
No arts; no l.	HOBB 251:18		CAMD 128:4
receive no l. in the grave	JOHN 279:29	eldest Child of L.	WORD 582:11
than a man of l.	STER 520:8	give me l.	HENRY 245:27
your hair with all your l.	CONG 160:37	Give me the l. to know	MILT 352:4
letting: then the l. go	DICK 183:14	he Served human l.	YEATS 587:3
levee: l. from a couch in some	CONG 161:4	I am content that l. will	WALP 563:16
level: Are l. now with men	SHAK 423:16	I must have l.	SHAK 425:22
low life was the l.'s	BROW 100:33	insolent and L. to be saucy	HAL 237:21
tones as dry and l.	AUDEN 20:10	it certainly destroys l.	JOHN 279:2
to one dead l. ev'ry mind	POPE 375:24	Know no such l.	LOV 318:15
level-headed: remember to stay l.	HOR 260:6	known rules of ancient l.	MILT 351:7
levellers: Your l. wish to level down		l., and of learning	DISR 185:10
	JOHN 275:5	L. and Union	WEBS 566:11
leviathan: draw out l. with an hook		l. cannot long exist	BURKE 110:14
	BIBLE 53:11	l. connected with order	BURKE 109:10
there is that L.	PRAY 397:1	L. consists in doing what	MILL 339:13
There L.	MILT 349:1	L. means responsibility	SHAW 497:37
levin: to the burning l.	SCOTT 416:28	l. of action of any	MILL 339:6
levity: like a little judicious l.	STEV 522:12	l. of the press is	JUN 287:1
lewd: church l. hirelings climb	MILT 347:18	l. of the individual must	MILL 339:11
Lancelot wanderingly l.	TENN 534:20	l. plucks justice	SHAK 463:11
l. fellows of the baser	BIBLE 74:8	L.'s a glorious feast	BURNS 114:19
lex: populi suprema est l.	CIC 151:19	l., shall I leave thee	CONG 161:6
Salus populi suprema l.	SELD 419:25	L.'s in every blow	BURNS 115:1
lexicographer: doomed at last to wake		l. still more	BROW 102:20
a l.	JOHN 281:8	l. to man is eternal vigilance	CURR 170:16
L.: a writer of dictionaries	JOHN 274:13	L., too, must be limited	BURKE 110:12
l. can only hope to escape	JOHN 281:5	life, and l.	JEFF 272:6
lexicography: am not yet so lost in l.		life, l.	ANON 8:14
	JOHN 281:6	light! said l.	SHEL 500:19
lexicon: In the l. of youth	BULW 107:5	loudest yelps for l. among	JOHN 282:18
Two men wrote a l.	ANON 8:12	love of l. is the love	HAZL 243:19
liaison: l. man and partly P.R.O.	BETJ 42:14	loving-jealous of his l.	SHAK 482:20
liar: every man a l.	BIBLE 74:36	mansion-house of l.	MILT 352:1
he is a l.	BIBLE 72:13	men are to wait for l.	MAC 323:25

mountain nymph, sweet L.	MILT 342:15
notion of l. amuses	JOHN 274:21
O liberty! O l.	ROL 407:15
On Naples and on l.	CHES 146:21
People contend for their L.	HAL 237:20
power and to lose l.	BACON 26:22
primordial condition of l.	BAK 29:25
proclaim l. to the captives	BIBLE 60:8
regulated l. as well	BURKE 110:34
something to the spirit of l.	BURKE 109:18
spirit of divinest L.	COL 156:20
such refreshing airs of l.	BURKE 108:11
Sweet land of l.	SMITH 510:24
symptom of constitutional l.	GIBB 224:27
then shall the voice of l.	CUMM 170:10
they mean when they cry L.	MILT 351:8
to enjoy delight with l.	SPEN 515:23
tree of l. must be refreshed	JEFF 272:10
utmost bound of civil l.	MILT 351:20
weight of too much l.	WORD 582:8
were thy chosen music, L.	WORD 582:18
woman l. to gad abroad	BIBLE 63:9
Liberty-Hall: This is L.	GOLD 232:26
libraries: books out of circulating l.	
	RUSK 411:19
spend altogether on our l.	RUSK 411:17
library: circulating l. in a town	SHER 506:10
half a l. to make one book	JOHN 276:24
l. of sixty-two thousand	GIBB 224:25
l. Was dukedom	SHAK 484:26
lumber room of his l.	DOYLE 192:2
take choice of all my l.	SHAK 486:16
libre: L'homme est né l.	ROUS 410:17
libro: Galeotto fu il l. e chi	DANTE 171:10
licence: apothecary who has paid a l.	
	SMITH 511:38
had l. to dare anything	HOR 257:10
L. they mean when they	MILT 351:8
l. to print your own money	THOM 549:30
love not freedom, but l.	MILT 352:17
universal l. to be good	COL 154:25
Licences: L. poétiques. Il n'y en	BANV 33:2
Licensed: L., build that nation's	BLAKE 85:17
licensers: work of twenty l.	MILT 351:25
licentious: all l. passages are left	GIBB 224:19
rapacious and l. soldiery	BURKE 110:25
Licht: Mehr L.	GOET 230:14
lick: enemies shall l. the dust	PRAY 394:20
time to l. it into form	BURT 116:14
Licked: L. its tongue into	ELIOT 203:18
l. the soup from the cooks'	BROW 103:15
moreover the dogs l. his	BIBLE 70:28
Licker: L. talks mighty loud w'en	
	HARR 242:23
with considerbul l. koncealed	WARD 564:29
Liddell: right part wrote L.	ANON 8:12
this is Mrs L.	SPR 517:17
Liddesdale: Eskdale and L.	SCOTT 418:24
lids: with eternal l. apart	KEATS 292:11
lie: big l. than to a small	HITL 251:9
built to comprehend a l.	KIPL 302:17
Cannot come, l. follows	PROU 401:24
can rule and dare not l.	TENN 540:4
compulsion doth in music l.	MILT 340:19
country folks would l.	SHAK 427:2
dost thou l. so low	SHAK 450:6
fain wald l. down	BALL 31:5
give the world the l.	RAL 404:10
God's own name upon a l.	COWP 166:26
He makes me down to l.	SCOT 419:5
I cannot tell a l.	WASH 565:1
if a l. may do thee grace	SHAK 440:28
I l. down alone	HOUS 265:17
I l. even among the children	PRAY 393:15
lawn I l. in bed	AUDEN 20:18
leads you to believe a l.	BLAKE 85:23
l. as quietly among	EDW 200:6
l. circumstantial	SHAK 427:5
l. diagonally in his bed	STER 520:7
l. direct	SHAK 427:5

745

L. follows by post — BER 41:17
L. heavy on him, Earth — EVANS 209:5
l. in cold obstruction — SHAK 464:14
l. tangled in her hair — LOV 318:15
l. that flatters I abhor — COWP 166:22
l. that sinketh — BACON 27:30
l.—under a mistake — SWIFT 526:27
l. where shades of darkness — DE L 174:1
l. which is all a lie — TENN 533:25
L. with me — BIBLE 46:30
Live and l. reclined — TENN 539:16
long night through must l. — HOUS 262:21
loveth and maketh a l. — BIBLE 83:3
me the l. i' the throat — SHAK 433:3
mixture of a l. doth ever — BACON 27:29
must l. upon the daisies — GILB 227:21
My love and I would l. — HOUS 263:4
Nature admits no l. — CARL 132:3
nothing can need a l. — HERB 247:2
not l. easy at Winchelsea — BENET 40:20
obedient to their laws we l. — SIM 508:9
odious damned l. — SHAK 477:15
sent to l. abroad — WOTT 583:18
shall l. through centuries — BROW 99:14
she might l. by an emperor's — SHAK 476:11
something given to l. — SHAK 424:6
that he should l. — BIBLE 48:14
They l. — FORS 217:4
to l. between maids' legs — SHAK 434:6
what is a l. — BYRON 123:30
When he speaketh a l. — BIBLE 72:31
Whoever would l. usefully — HERV 250:18
Who loves to l. with me — SHAK 425:14
will he l. ten nights awake — SHAK 472:14
lieb: *sich beide so herzlich l.* — HEINE 244:10
liebe: *ihm gehen, den ich l.* — BREC 91:26
Was ist denn L. — HALM 238:10
liebt: *Gestern l.' ich* — LESS 313:26
lied: being l. about — KIPL 299:22
shall say they have l. — YEATS 585:8
Liege: L. of all loiterers — SHAK 456:26
lien: ye have l. among the pots — PRAY 394:8
lies: all full of l. and robbery — BIBLE 61:26
bare earth expos'd he l. — DRYD 195:3
Beats all the l. you can — BLAKE 85:14
believing their own l. — ARB 11:19
cruellest l. are often — STEV 521:35
ever-bubbling spring of endless l. — COWP 166:13

foe that spread these l. — ROSS 409:20
he l. to the heart — SHAK 477:13
History is a pack of l. — STUB 524:5
is where our frontier l. — BALD 29:28
l. about his wooden horse — FLEC 214:18
L. are the mortar that — WELLS 568:15
L. in his bed — SHAK 452:20
lifts the head, and l. — POPE 378:2
many l. as will lie — SHAK 489:30
Matilda told such Dreadful L. — BELL 39:7
matter which way the head l. — RAL 404:18
open truth to cover l. — CONG 159:27
Rest is L. — FITZ 212:19
Their delight is in l. — PRAY 393:19
There are three kinds of l. — DISR 187:7
These l. are like the father — SHAK 439:4
though I know she l. — SHAK 495:11
white l. to ice a cake — ASQ 17:18
wish I were where Helen l. — BALL 31:4
lieto: *Chi vuol esser l.* — MED 336:9
lieu: *Qu'en un l.* — BOIL 89:11
life: accounted his l. madness — BIBLE 62:16
all human l. is there — JAMES 271:24
all the days of my l. — PRAY 390:22
all things the laws of l. — RUSK 412:10
amended his former naughty l. — PRAY 387:5
Anythin' for a quiet l. — DICK 182:34
are few situations in l. — BRAM 91:21
awakened from the dream of l. — SHEL 499:20
aware of his l.'s flow — ARN 12:22
away my l. to make you King — CHAR 140:29

best days of l. — VIRG 560:16
bitterness of l. — CARR 133:10
blood-thirsty clinging to l. — ARN 15:24
Book of L. begins with — WILDE 573:29
brevity of our l. — JOHN 273:17
broad sunshine of l. — JOHN 278:6
busy scenes of crowded l. — JOHN 282:28
by brisking about the L. — SMART 508:22
careless of the single l. — TENN 536:27
changing scenes of l. — TATE 531:21
C Major of this l. — BROW 98:22
crowded hour of glorious l. — MORD 357:6
Crushing out l. than waving — HOPE 256:4
days of the years of my l. — BIBLE 46:38
day-to-day business l. is — LAF 306:23
dedication of my l. — ELIOT 201:29
desert where no l. is found — HOOD 255:11
devils in l. and condition — ASCH 17:3
disease of modern l. — ARN 14:19
dissonant which tells of L. — COL 157:12
doctrine of the strenuous l. — ROOS 407:27
Does thy l. destroy — BLAKE 87:12
down his l. for his friends — BIBLE 72:36
dreamed that l. was Beauty — HOOP 255:22
drink L. to the lees — TENN 543:22
drink of l. again — HOUS 265:15
entertain the lag-end of my l. — SHAK 440:14
except a little l. — BYRON 125:10
except my l. — SHAK 432:10
experiment in his l. — DARW 172:2
fall upon the thorns of l. — SHEL 502:13
feels its l. in every limb — WORD 583:5
findeth his l. shall lose — BIBLE 65:40
finish'd A l. heroic — MILT 351:1
fountain of the water of l. — BIBLE 82:32
freezes up the heat of l. — SHAK 483:21
friend is the medicine of l. — BIBLE 62:25
Gave thee l. — BLAKE 87:26
give thee a crown of l. — BIBLE 81:17
giveth his l. for the sheep — BIBLE 72:18
Give to me the l. I love — STEV 522:27
going to turn over a new l. — FLEM 214:28
golden tree of actual l. — GOET 230:3
great guide of human l. — HUME 267:14
half of my own l. — HOR 259:11
hands before the fire of l. — LAND 308:20
have everlasting l. — BIBLE 71:38
have set my l. upon a cast — SHAK 481:19
heat of l. in the handful — CONR 161:24
he ne'er saw in his l. — ANST 11:8
He still loves l. — AUDEN 20:20
he studied from the l. — ARMS 12:15
hills where his l. rose — ARN 12:22
His l. was gentle — SHAK 452:7
How good is man's l. — BROW 105:1
human l. is — TEMP 532:9
I bear a charmed l. — SHAK 463:8
if l. was bitter to thee — SWIN 529:1
I know my l.'s a pain — DAV 172:11
I love long l. better than — SHAK 421:12
I'm in mourning for my l. — CHEK 144:25
In balance with this l. — YEATS 585:15
in his pleasure is l. — PRAY 391:13
In l.'s uncertain voyage — SHAK 486:13
intellectual l. of our century — ARN 15:25
in the sea of l. enisled — ARN 13:12
I pass my whole l. — DICK 183:6
I require the l. of man — BIBLE 45:38
Is l. a boon — GILB 229:7
isn't your l. extremely flat — GILB 228:29
is the glory of this l. — SHAK 486:4
It is art that *makes* l. — JAMES 272:2
it is a tree of l. — BIBLE 53:35
It is in l. as it is — BACON 25:4
I've had a happy l. — HAZL 244:4
jump the l. to come — SHAK 459:5
Just gave what l. requir'd — GOLD 230:18
lad of l. — SHAK 444:17
last of l. — BROW 104:2
later l. renew — SPEN 515:20

lay hold on eternal l. — BIBLE 79:19
lead to a Struggle for L. — DARW 171:28
Let us (since L. can little — POPE 379:1
L., a Fury slinging flame — TENN 536:21
L. ain't all beer and skittles — DU M 199:4
l., and liberty — JEFF 272:6
l. and power that took — FOX 217:23
L. and these lips have — SHAK 483:22
l. at best is but an inn — HOW 267:1
l., a very rebel — SHAK 423:4
l., being weary of these — SHAK 449:3
l. closed twice before — DICK 183:20
L. death does end and each — HOPK 256:21
l. endured and known — SASS 415:2
L. Force supplies us with — SHAW 497:1
l. forget and death remember — SWIN 530:14
L. for life — BIBLE 47:25
l. from the glowing earth — GREN 236:15
L. is a jest — GAY 223:22
L. is a joke that's just — GILB 226:28
L. is all a variorum — BURNS 114:20
L. is an incurable disease — COWL 164:19
L. is as tedious as a twice-told — SHAK 452:21
l. is but a day — KEATS 292:6
L. is but an empty dream — LONG 317:1
l. is colour and warmth — GREN 236:15
L. is falling sideways — COCT 154:12
l. is given to none freehold — LUCR 320:10
L. is just one damned — OMAL 365:5
L. is made up of sobs — HENRY 245:23
L. is mostly froth — GORD 233:1
l. is of a mingled yarn — SHAK 421:3
L. is one long process — BUTL 118:25
L. is real — LONG 317:1
L. is the desert — YOUNG 588:13
l. it is reserved only — BACON 24:24
l., liberty — ANON 8:14
L., like a dome of many-coloured — SHEL 499:26
L. may change — SHEL 500:18
l. may perfect be — JONS 285:8
l.: no man cometh unto — BIBLE 72:32
l. now, compact, visible — WHIT 570:2
l. of any man written under — WALP 563:14
l. of doubt diversified — BROW 99:5
L. offers—to deny — HARDY 241:11
l. of man — BACON 28:15
l. of man — HOBB 251:18
l. of men on earth — BEDE 37:1
l. of sensations rather — KEATS 293:17
l. of the historian must — GIBB 224:18
l. protracted is protracted — JOHN 283:1
L.'s but a walking shadow — SHAK 463:6
l.'s cool ev'ning satiate — POPE 380:7
l.'s fitful fever — SHAK 461:12
L.'s last scene what prodigies — JOHN 283:3
L.'s Liquor in its Cup — FITZ 212:6
l. so fast doth fly — DAV 172:10
l. so short — HIPP 251:8
l.'s poor play is o'er — POPE 379:19
L.'s too short for chess — BYRON 126:23
l. succeed in that it seems — BROW 104:4
l., that insane dream — BROW 100:22
L., the shadow of death — SWIN 528:21
l. time's fool — SHAK 440:23
l. to come — SHAK 491:19
l. to lose for my country — HALE 237:14
l. unto the bitter in soul — BIBLE 52:14
L. we have lost in living — ELIOT 202:3
l. went through with death — VEN 556:5
L. will suit Itself — BYRON 120:28
l. with girls has ended — HOR 261:3
l., without a dream — ROST 410:13
l. without it were not — ROWE 410:24
L. without industry is — RUSK 411:9
L. would be tolerable — LEWIS 314:10
l. would be very pleasant — SURT 525:23
Like following l. thro' — POPE 377:9
likened our l. to a dream — MONT 355:5
lines and l. are free — HERB 247:14

little l. Is rounded	SHAK 485:20	sweet is this human l.	CORY 163:5
little l. with dried tubers	ELIOT 204:17	take my l. and all	SHAK 468:10
living sepulchre of l.	CLARE 152:15	Tenants of l.'s middle state	COWP 167:33
Lolita, light of my l.	NAB 359:5	that a l. was but a flower	SHAK 427:2
London all that l. can afford	JOHN 277:17	that is l. without theory	DISR 186:4
long as you have your l.	JAMES 271:20	that L. flies	FITZ 212:19
long disease, my l.	POPE 376:23	That to me gave this l.'s	SPEN 517:1
long l. will I satisfy	PRAY 395:23	their l. was death	ROSS 409:25
long littleness of l.	CORN 162:21	their lives fought for l.	SPEN 515:7
Lord and giver of l.	PRAY 387:11	therefore choose l. that	BIBLE 48:29
low l. was the level's	BROW 100:33	there is a space of l.	KEATS 288:19
Madam L.'s a piece in bloom	HENL 245:6	There is no l. of a man	CARL 131:12
Mad from l.'s history	HOOD 254:10	There is no wealth but l.	RUSK 412:12
man's l. of any worth is	KEATS 294:12	There's the l. for ever	STEV 522:27
many doors to let out l.	FLET 215:11	think ye have eternal l.	BIBLE 72:3
may here find l. in death	COL 156:17	this gives l. to thee	SHAK 492:28
me hath everlasting l.	BIBLE 72:7	This is alone L.	SHEL 503:15
Men deal with l. as children	COWP 165:11	This l. is most jolly	SHAK 426:1
middle of the road of our l.	DANTE 171:2	Thorough the iron gates of l.	MARV 332:20
midst of l. we are in death	PRAY 389:12	those who live Call L.	SHEL 504:4
most loathed worldly l.	SHAK 464:14	Thou art my l.	QUAR 403:13
My l. has crept so long	TENN 540:16	thousand doors to let out l.	MASS 336:1
My l. is run his compass	SHAK 452:1	Three-fourths of l.	ARN 16:19
my l. seemed meant	BROW 101:22	Through l.'s road	BYRON 126:15
my l. with coffee spoons	ELIOT 203:20	time of l. is short	SHAK 440:19
My l. within this band	HERB 247:24	'Time to taste l.	BROW 100:35
name out of the book of l.	BIBLE 81:18	'Tisn't l. that matters	WALP 563:23
nauseous draught of l.	ROCH 406:19	'Tis the sunset of l. gives	CAMP 128:24
need thou hast in l.	HOPE 256:5	to this Fragment of L.	STER 519:15
Nobody can write the l.	JOHN 276:3	travell'd l.'s dull round	SHEN 505:15
no l. but the sea-wind	SWIN 529:18	traveller betwixt l. and death	WORD 581:8
No l. that breathes with	TENN 543:20	tree of l. also	BIBLE 45:8
No, no, no l.	SHAK 456:11	unblemished l. and spotless record	
nostrils the breath of l.	BIBLE 45:7		HOR 259:23
Not so much l.	KEATS 290:1	undying L.	BRON 93:19
not the l. more than meat	BIBLE 64:28	Vaguely l. leaks away	AUDEN 18:10
nourisher in l.'s feast	SHAK 460:8	value of l. lies not	MONT 354:16
now my l. is done	TICH 551:2	voyage of their l.	SHAK 451:27
off twenty years of l.	SHAK 450:4	walk in newness of l.	BIBLE 75:1
Of his dull l.	BEAU 35:19	well-written L. is almost	CARL 131:2
Of l., of crown, of queen	SHAK 431:12	We should show l. neither	CHEK 144:26
of man's l. a thing apart	BYRON 122:14	What a minefield L. is	FRY 220:8
one l. and one death	BROW 101:13	What is this l.	DAV 172:17
One l. for each to give	KIPL 299:7	what is your l.	BIBLE 80:16
one l. shall be destroy'd	TENN 536:25	What l. and death is	CHAP 140:8
one way in to l.	SEN 420:9	what l. is then to a man	BIBLE 63:15
only evidence of l.'	NEWM 361:18	When I consider how my l.	NASH 360:1
only honour and l. have	FRAN 218:1	when l.'s sweet fable	CRAS 169:14
our l. is very short	TAYL 532:3	Where all l. dies	MILT 346:23
O world! O l.! O time	SHEL 501:14	which he slew in his l.	BIBLE 49:28
passion and the l.	COL 156:8	which leadeth unto l.	BIBLE 65:7
pay glad l.'s arrears	BROW 104:1	Who saw l. steadily	ARN 15:19
prepared to lay down my l.	CLOU 153:9	will he give for his l.	BIBLE 52:8
purpose to a life beyond l.	MILT 351:23	wine of l. is drawn	SHAK 461:1
put my genius into my l.	WILDE 573:25	With seas of l.	TRAH 552:3
R.ailing at l.	CHUR 148:32	Women and wine should l.	GAY 222:25
:eceive the crown of l.	BIBLE 80:8	worth a l.'s experience	HOLM 253:21
regardeth l. of his beast	BIBLE 53:34	yet not come to l.	SHAK 442:3
Resurrection and the L.	AUDEN 21:7	life-blood: book is the precious l.	MILT 351:23
river of water of l.	BIBLE 82:35	LIFE-IN-DEATH: Night-mare L. was	
runners relay the torch of l.	LUCR 320:7	she	COL 155:15
run The colours from my l.	BROW 98:10	Lifeless: L. charms	GAY 222:9
Rushes l. in a race	MER 336:26	life-lie: Take the l. away from	IBSEN 270:4
say that l. is the thing	SMITH 510:21	lifetime: knowledge of a l.	WHIS 569:23
'sech is l.	DICK 179:16	lift: floods l. up their waves	PRAY 396:1
selfish being all my l.	AUST 23:21	L. her with care	HOOD 254:9
set my l. at a pin's fee	SHAK 430:25	L. me as a wave	SHEL 502:13
set my l. on any chance	SHAK 461:10	l. mine eyes	SCOT 419:6
shade the evening of l.	GIBB 224:20	L. not thy hands to *It*	FITZ 213:8
She bid me take l. easy	YEATS 584:22	l. thou up: the light	PRAY 389:21
shilling l. will give you	AUDEN 21:8	l. up mine eyes	PRAY 398:9
single l. doth well with	BACON 26:33	L. up your hearts	PRAY 387:21
slits the thin-spun l.	MILT 343:8	L. up your heads	PRAY 390:24
So have I loitered my l.	HAZL 243:15	Lifting: L. the cool-hair'd creepers ARN 14:21	
So in my veins red l. might	KEATS 290:30	l. up of my hands be	PRAY 399:9
So on the ocean of l. we	LONG 317:17	light: against the dying of the l.	THOM 546:23
sphere of private l.	MELB 336:13	are the l. of the world	BIBLE 64:8
spirit giveth l.	BIBLE 77:4	bathe the world in l.	WORD 577:10
Squat on my l.	LARK 310:6	bear witness of that L.	BIBLE 71:25
such is L.	DICK 178:10	becometh the children of l.	PRAY 388:11

Be near me when my l. is	TENN 536:21
blasted with excess of l.	GRAY 235:19
burning and a shining l.	BIBLE 72:2
can again thy former l.	SHAK 477:5
Casting a dim religious l.	MILT 342:10
children of the l.	ARN 16:3
come in may see the l.	BIBLE 70:1
contend with growing l.	SHAK 446:17
darkness have seen a great l.	BIBLE 58:6
darkness rather than l.	BIBLE 71:39
dusk with a l. behind	GILB 229:4
Enable with perpetual l.	PRAY 400:5
endeavours are an inward l.	WORD 577:3
festal l. in Christ-Church	ARN 14:16
garmented in l.	SHEL 505:8
give l. to them that sit	BIBLE 69:7
giveth l. unto the eyes	PRAY 390:12
Give us a l.	ELIOT 202:8
Giving more l. than heat	SHAK 430:21
God is L.	BLAKE 85:18
gone into the world of l.	VAUG 555:18
growing or full constant l.	DONNE 189:20
Had she been l.	SHAK 457:14
happy realms of l.	MILT 344:26
have neither heat nor l.	WEBS 566:21
have seen a glorious l.	SCOT 419:7
heaven the beam of your l.	LANG 309:29
he beholds the l.	WORD 579:5
here there is no l.	KEATS 291:20
He that has l. within his	MILT 341:8
hours of l. return	ARN 13:23
if bereav'd of l.	BLAKE 88:2
if once we lose this l.	JONS 285:13
if they fear'd the l.	SUCK 524:8
In a l. fantastic round	MILT 340:29
infant crying for the l.	TENN 536:26
informed by the l. of nature	BACON 24:20
It gives a lovely l.	MILL 339:26
It is the l. of Terewth	DICK 176:16
just is as the shining l.	BIBLE 53:19
land is scattered with l.	BRID 92:8
land…where the l. is as darkness BIBLE 52:21	
leaping l. for you discovers	AUDEN 20:3
let me not be l.	SHAK 468:21
let perpetual l. shine	MASS 334:17
Lets in new l. through	WALL 562:9
Let there be l.	BIBLE 44:22
'Let there be l.' said God	BYRON 123:23
levell'd rule of streaming l.	MILT 341:7
lift thou up: the l.	PRAY 389:21
l. and leading in England	BURKE 111:20
L. and Mrs Humphry Ward	CHES 146:12
l., and will aspire	SHAK 495:19
l. as leef on lynde	CHAU 142:11
l. but the shadow of God	BROW 95:17
l. dissolved in star-showers	SHEL 504:9
l. emerging from the smoke	HOR 257:19
L. (God's eldest daughter)	FULL 220:16
l. heart lives long	SHAK 457:14
lighthouse without any l.	HOOD 254:24
l. in mine eye	DONNE 191:2
l. in the dust lies dead	SHEL 501:21
l. of his countenance	PRAY 394:4
L. of Lights	YEATS 584:18
L. of step and heart was	DE L 173:27
l. of thy Holy Spirit	PRAY 386:14
L. or leading received	MILT 352:7
l.! said Liberty	SHEL 500:19
l., shade, and perspective	CONS 162:2
l. shineth in darkness	BIBLE 71:23
l. such a candle by God's	LAT 310:21
l. that I may tread safely	HASK 243:1
l. that loses	SWIN 528:17
l. that never was	WORD 577:4
l. to counterfeit a gloom	MILT 342:5
l. to shine upon the road	COWP 165:23
l. to thee are both alike	PRAY 399:5
l. unto my paths	PRAY 398:6
little l. Of love's bestowing	DU M 199:6

heroes up the l. to death SASS 414:10
high aesthetic l. GILB 227:20
in the very first l. GOLD 231:19
l. is length without breadth EUCL 209:2
l. of scarlet thread BIBLE 48:37
l. too labours POPE 378:23
l. upon line BIBLE 58:21
l. will take us hours maybe YEATS 584:9
lives along the l. POPE 379:9
oft creep in one dull l. POPE 378:20
thin red l. RUSS 412:23
thou whatever suits the l. COL 157:5
We carved not a l. WOLFE 576:5
will the l. stretch out SHAK 462:10
lineage: Poets of the proud old l. FLEC 214:9
lineaments: l. of gratified desire BLAKE 86:17
l. of Gospel books ROYD 411:2
Yet in my l. they trace BYRON 125:13
linen: clothed in purple and fine l.
BIBLE 70:28
fair white l. cloth PRAY 387:6
In blanched l. KEATS 289:20
Love is like l. often chang'd FLET 215:31
not l. you're wearing HOOD 255:7
old l. wash whitest WEBS 566:30
very fine l. BRUM 106:5
you shall wash your l. STEV 522:29
lines: consisted of l. like these CALV 127:10
l. and life are free HERB 247:14
l. so loves oblique may MARV 331:19
liquid l. mellifluously bland BYRON 123:14
Prose is when all the l. BENT 41:2
smile his face into more l. SHAK 490:3
town-crier spoke my l. SHAK 433:16
linger: late rose may yet l. HOR 260:5
To l. out a purpos'd overthrow SHAK 494:14
lingered: I l. round them BRON 94:1
lingering: I alone sit l. here VAUG 555:18
Something l. GILB 227:11
lingots: au marché avec des l. CHAM 139:14
lingring: l. and consumptive passion
ETH 208:29
lingua: l., gloriosi THOM 546:16
l., gloriosi VEN 556:4
linguam: Et l. et mores JUV 287:15
lining: Turn forth her silver l. MILT 341:2
link: silver l. SCOTT 416:20
linked: my name too will be l. OVID 366:12
links: strong as l. of iron BURKE 110:2
lin-lan-lone: mellow l. of evening bells
TENN 533:15
linnet: evening full of the l.'s YEATS 585:17
l. born within the cage TENN 536:15
linnets: pipe but as the l. sing TENN 536:12
linsy-woolsy: lawless l. brother BUTL 117:32
lion: from the fox and the l. MACH 325:8
go upon the l. and adder PRAY 395:22
is better than a dead l. BIBLE 55:27
l. among ladies SHAK 470:14
l. and the fatling together BIBLE 58:10
L. and the Lizard keep FITZ 212:14
l. griefs loped from AUDEN 20:19
l. is the wisdom of God BLAKE 88:21
l. shall eat straw like BIBLE 58:11
l. who dies of an ass's BROW 102:25
Lord L. King-at-arms SCOTT 417:7
Now the hungry l. roars SHAK 471:21
pain'd desert l. ARN 14:26
righteous are bold as a l. BIBLE 54:41
roaring l. BIBLE 80:33
Rouse the l. from his lair SCOTT 418:35
Sporting the l. ramped MILT 347:26
Strong is the l. SMART 509:3
that gets the fattest l. SAKI 413:9
that had the l.'s heart CHUR 150:21
There is a l. in the way BIBLE 54:34
Thou wear a l.'s hide SHAK 452:16
To beard the l. in his SCOTT 417:18
To rouse a l. than to start SHAK 438:18
upon a time to the sick l. HOR 258:11

would be mated with the l. SHAK 420:26
Lions: I girdid up my L. & fled WARD 564:24
laughing l. must come NIET 363:2
Let bears and l. growl WATTS 565:17
l. do lack PRAY 391:22
l. of the Daily Telegraph ARN 15:23
L., or Vanity-Fair he feared not BUNY 107:33
l. roaring after their PRAY 397:1
my darling from the l. PRAY 391:25
my soul is among l. PRAY 393:15
on the other, l. PATM 370:7
Rise like L. after slumber SHEL 502:4
they were stronger than l. BIBLE 50:17
to have been eaten by l. CHES 148:3
We are two l. litter'd SHAK 449:19
lip: girl's l. out of Paris SWIN 531:2
gnaw you so your nether l. SHAK 477:6
'Keep a stiff upper l. CARY 136:14
Teach not thy l. such scorn SHAK 480:21
Whose l. mature is ever KEATS 289:31
lipless: Leaned backward with a l.
ELIOT 205:13
lips: Bestow'd his l. on that SHAK 422:19
Be through my l. to unawakened SHEL 502:14
coral l. such folly broke CONG 160:2
far from the l. we love MOORE 356:19
flatter with their l. PRAY 389:32
heaven be in these l. MARL 329:10
Here hung those l. that SHAK 436:31
Her l. were red SUCK 524:10
His coward l. did from SHAK 448:15
In prayer the l. ne'er HERR 250:11
In the l. that had whispered SWIN 529:19
keep the door of my l. PRAY 399:9
Life and these l. have SHAK 483:22
l. are not yet unsealed BALD 29:29
l. are now forbid to speak BAYLY 35:10
l. cannot fail of taking BURG 108:5
l. of a strange woman drop BIBLE 53:20
l. of dying men ARN 14:27
l. of those that are asleep BIBLE 57:10
l. of those who love you BRID 92:18
l. once sanctified by Hers BROW 106:1
l., that they speak no PRAY 391:23
l. that touch liquor must YOUNG 588:15
l. to it when I am so dispoged DICK 179:10
Live l. upon a plummet-measured
YEATS 587:1
mammets and to tilt with l. SHAK 438:31
meet on l. of living men BUTL 119:17
On l. that are for others TENN 542:4
ope my l. let no dog SHAK 465:12
people of unclean l. BIBLE 57:29
rain is on our l. SORL 513:10
Red l. are not so red OWEN 367:6
round their narrow l. ROSS 409:25
See my l. tremble POPE 376:14
soft as l. that laugh SWIN 528:18
starv'd l. in the gloam KEATS 290:21
sweet l. KEATS 292:13
take those l. away SHAK 464:21
that had red mournful l. YEATS 586:22
that those l. had language COWP 166:2
they shoot out their l. PRAY 390:17
this hath touched thy l. BIBLE 57:30
Thou shalt open my l. PRAY 393:8
Thy l. are like a thread BIBLE 56:26
To part her l. HERR 249:18
touching of the l. TENN 538:18
touch lightly with my l. WHIT 570:11
turn to ashes on the l. MOORE 356:26
Two l., indifferent red SHAK 488:12
Upon her perfect l. TENN 543:9
very good words for the l. DICK 178:26
When the l. have spoken SHEL 501:21
Where my Julia's l. do smile HERR 248:21
winds kiss my parched l. SHAK 452:31
lipsed: Somwhat he l. CHAU 141:32
liquefaction: That l. of her clothes
HERR 250:8

liquid: let their l. siftings fall ELIOT 204:16
l. lines mellifluously BYRON 123:14
otherwise excellent l. HERB 246:18
Thames is l. history BURNS 112:23
liquidation: l. of the British Empire
CHUR 150:12
liquidity: purpose in l. BROO 94:11
liquor: bowl with atrabilious l. HUXL 269:2
Good l. GOLD 231:22
lads for the l. HOUS 263:6
Life's L. in its Cup FITZ 212:6
lips that touch l. must YOUNG 588:15
l. Is quicker NASH 359:19
Livelier l. than the Muse HOUS 264:12
such other spiritual l. BYRON 126:7
which wanteth not l. BIBLE 57:8
liquors: spouts the grateful l. POPE 381:6
lisp'd: I l. in numbers POPE 376:23
list: I've got a little l. GILB 226:24
list, O, l.! SHAK 431:5
listed: 'l. at home for a lancer HOUS 264:19
listen: Darkling I l. KEATS 291:22
Do you think I can l. all CARR 133:23
if we care to l. AUDEN 19:13
L., Eugenia ARN 14:3
privilege of wisdom to l. HOLM 253:20
silence is wonderful to l. HARDY 241:27
world should l. then SHEL 504:24
Listened: soul L. intensely WORD 577:16
We l. and looked sideways COL 155:17
listeners: least stir made the l. DE L 174:9
listening: Enemy ears are l. ANON 9:18
is the disease of not l. SHAK 441:7
listens: who l. to Reason is lost SHAW 498:2
yet the Evening l. KEATS 292:5
listeth: wind bloweth where it l. BIBLE 71:36
listlessness: seek repose In l. WORD 580:6
lit: Fleet is all l. up WOOD 576:16
literary: head of the l. profession DISR 185:29
He lik'd those l. cooks MORE 357:9
Like an unsuccessful l. BELL 40:2
l. and scientific opinion ARN 16:5
l. man DICK 181:3
lowest class is l. footmen HAZL 243:29
Never l. attempt was more HUME 268:1
quite disgusted with l. KEATS 293:12
which with St Paul are l. ARN 16:18
literature: All that is l. seeks DE Q 175:7
All the rest is l. VAL 555:1
grazed the common of l. JOHN 274:28
have failed in l. and art DISR 186:23
L. flourishes best when INGE 270:8
l. is a drug BORR 90:7
L. is news that STAYS news POUND 383:23
l. is simply language charged POUND 384:1
l. of power DE Q 175:6
louse in the locks of l. TENN 544:13
must wash l. off ourselves ART 16:29
Philistine of genius in l. ARN 16:23
That great Cham of l. SMOL 512:14
to produce a little l. JAMES 271:8
'We cultivate l. upon SMITH 511:36
When once the itch of l. LOVER 318:21
Your true lover of l. is SOUT 514:14
lites: vos tantas componere l. VIRG 559:20
litter: all her l. but one SHAK 441:3
Like l. that a riot leaves PLOM 374:19
littérature: Et tout le reste est l. VERL 556:9
faut nous laver de la l. ART 16:29
littered: l. under Mercury SHAK 491:18
l. with remembered kisses MACN 326:3
little: contemptible l. Army WILH 574:4
done and l. to be known JOHN 280:7
drink unto one of these l. BIBLE 65:41
grateful at last for a l. TENN 540:16
great ones eat up the l. SHAK 478:4
he only knew a l. of law ANON 6:3
here a l. BIBLE 58:21
it was a very l. one MARR 331:5
l. creep through SHEN 505:16

l. drops of water — CARN 132:33
l. dwarfs creep out — CHES 147:5
l. emptiness of love — BROO 94:27
l. finger shall be thicker — BIBLE 51:2
l. friendship in the world — BACON 26:11
l. hill of Hermon — PRAY 392:8
l. in our love — SHAK 489:7
l. learning is a dang'rous — POPE 378:13
l. life Is rounded — SHAK 485:20
little l. grave — SHAK 479:15
l. local difficulties — MACM 325:19
l. more — BROW 99:22
l. More than a little — SHAK 439:35
l. objects with like firmness — BYRON 120:29
l. philosophy inclineth — BACON 25:24
l. saint best fits a little — HERR 249:20
l. the mind is actually — JOHN 276:23
L. things affect little — DISR 186:30
l. things are infinitely — DOYLE 191:18
'L. to do — DICK 182:22
'Man wants but l. here — BUTL 119:8
Man wants but l. — GOLD 231:7
Man wants but l. — YOUNG 588:8
mockery is the fume of l. — TENN 534:13
offering Germany too l. — NEV 361:2
Our hoard is l. — TENN 535:1
So l. done — TENN 537:2
this l. world — SHAK 478:30
though she be but l. — SHAK 470:24
was l. seemed to him great — MAC 324:8
words for l. matters — JOHN 275:14
littleness: l. than disbelief in great
 — CARL 131:30
long l. of life — CORN 162:21
littlenesses: Before a thousand peering
 l. — TENN 533:30
liturgical: l., Turgidical — FRY 219:28
Liturgy: compiling of her Publick L.
 — PRAY 384:7
liv'd: has never l. — GAY 223:2
 l., in Settle's numbers — POPE 375:14
live: always getting ready to l. — EMER 207:43
Bid me to l. — HERR 249:25
cannot l. without cooks — MER 338:6
Can these bones l. — BIBLE 61:1
certified how long I have to l. — PRAY 391:30
Come l. with me — DONNE 187:24
Come l. with me — MARL 329:23
Days are where we l. — LARK 310:3
don't know how to l. right — HOR 259:6
doth not l. by bread only — BIBLE 48:22
Every man desires to l. long — SWIFT 527:12
Glad did I l. and gladly — STEV 523:10
good they inculcate must l. — SAKI 413:3
health and wealth long to l. — PRAY 385:5
He shall l. — PRAY 394:21
He shall not l. — SHAK 451:9
He that begins to l. — QUAR 403:19
How can I l. without thee — MILT 349:18
'How is it that you l. — WORD 581:2
human heart by which we l. — WORD 579:14
I cannot l. with you — MART 331:13
I do not wish to l. — MILL 340:2
I have hope to l. — SHAK 464:8
I l. not in myself — BYRON 120:35
ill report while you l. — SHAK 432:25
I must l. — ARG 12:1
in him we l., and move — BIBLE 74:14
'I shall l. to do that' — MART 331:8
is he that lusteth to l. — PRAY 391:23
It is silliness to l. when — SHAK 474:7
I wanted to l. deep — THOR 550:14
I wish to l. with you — KEATS 294:29
I wish to l. and to die — VILL 557:6
I would l. to study — BACON 28:4
just shall l. by faith — BIBLE 74:31
Law by which we l. — KIPL 302:17
Lesbia let us l. and love — CAT 136:25
lest I should bid thee l. — TENN 542:13
let me l. to-night — SHAK 477:7

lief not be as l. to be — SHAK 448:13
life is to l. dangerously — NIET 363:9
L. all you can — JAMES 271:20
l. alone and smash his — ANON 9:12
L. and lie reclined — TENN 539:16
l. and shame the land from — HOUS 266:3
L., and take comfort — WORD 582:17
l. any longer in sin — BIBLE 74:43
l. as they live elsewhere — AMBR 4:2
L. a thousand years — SHAK 450:8
l. beneath your more habitual — WORD 579:13
l. cleanly, as a nobleman — SHAK 440:29
l. in hearts we leave behind — CAMP 128:19
L. lips upon a plummet-measured
 — YEATS 587:1
l. only by fighting evils — BERL 41:23
l. or die wi' Charlie — HOGG 253:1
(L. till tomorrow) will — COWP 165:20
l. too long — DAN 170:24
l. well on nothing a year — THAC 545:28
L. with me and be my love — SHAK 495:16
L. with yourself — PERS 372:29
L. you — SHAK 458:10
living he'd learn how to l. — BROW 100:36
long as ye both shall l. — PRAY 389:3
longer I l. the more fool — ANON 8:19
May it l. and last — CAT 136:21
means whereby I l. — SHAK 468:10
me to l. is Christ — BIBLE 78:11
must l. or bear no life — SHAK 476:18
my child, I l. for thee — TENN 542:11
None would l. past years — DRYD 195:27
nor l. so long — SHAK 456:13
nothing but a rage to l. — POPE 377:21
not l. within thy means — AUDEN 21:6
not to l., but to die — BROW 97:3
one bare hour to l. — MARL 329:11
One should eat to l. — MOL 353:2
resolv'd to l. a fool — BEAU 35:19
Sacco's name will l. — VANZ 555:8
shall no man see me and l. — BIBLE 48:5
shall not l. by bread alone — BIBLE 64:1
short time to l. — PRAY 389:11
suffer a witch to l. — BIBLE 47:26
teaching nations how to l. — MILT 352:6
Teach me to l. — KEN 295:9
Tell me whom you l. with — CHES 145:15
than to l. on your knees — IBAR 269:16
That we come to l. — HARDY 241:8
Then you l. about her waist — SHAK 432:11
There taught us how to l. — TICK 551:3
things for which we l. — CORY 163:6
thou hast no more to l. — SWIN 529:1
Thus let me l. — POPE 380:24
To l. and die for thee — HERR 249:27
To l. is like to love — BUTL 119:3
To l. with thee — RAL 404:9
Too small to l. in — ANON 8:11
to see me cease to l. — ARN 15:12
tri'd To l. without him — WOTT 583:14
turn and l. with animals — WHIT 570:21
We l. and learn — POMF 375:8
were a martyrdom to l. — BROW 97:11
we that l. to please — JOHN 282:27
which we bear to l. — POPE 379:21
While I l., the owls — TENN 544:12
would gladly l. for ever — BORR 90:5
wouldn't l. under Niagara — CARL 132:28
would you l. for ever — FRED 218:23
years a mortal man may l. — SHAK 446:18
you I should love to l. — HOR 261:1
You might as well l. — PARK 368:18
you shall l. by fame — SPEN 515:20
lived: have formerly l. by hearsay
 — BUNY 107:39
He who has not l. during — TALL 531:16
I have l. long enough — SHAK 463:2
l. better than I have done — MAL 327:20
L. in his mild and magnificent — BROW 102:5
l. in social intercourse — JOHN 276:3

l. where motley is worn — YEATS 585:1
Many brave men l. before — HOR 261:18
Never to have l. is best — YEATS 585:6
Livelier: L. liquor than the Muse
 — HOUS 264:12
lively: forth thy true and l. Word PRAY 387:15
from l. to severe — POPE 380:3
l. form of death — KYD 306:3
liver: left the l. white and pale — SHAK 442:15
l. is on the right — MOL 353:17
L. of blaspheming Jew — SHAK 462:4
No motion of the l. — SHAK 489:6
notorious evil l. — PRAY 387:5
so much blood in his l. — SHAK 490:1
liver'd: I am pigeon-l. — SHAK 433:4
Liverpool: Lord L. is better in everyday
 — BAG 28:25
Liverpool Street: meet, my sweet, at
 L. — BETJ 43:15
Livers: grave L. do in Scotland use
 — WORD 581:1
livery: apparel them all in one l. SHAK 446:11
light and careless l. — SHAK 436:17
l. of the burnish'd sun — SHAK 466:6
this party-coloured l. — CONG 160:22
livery-stable: coarse-bred son of a l.
 — YEATS 585:3
lives: ends mark'd than their l. — SHAK 478:18
Everything that l. — BLAKE 85:20
evil that men do l. after — SHAK 450:17
he l. in bliss — BURNS 113:26
Herostatus l. that burnt — BROW 97:19
how he l. — JOHN 275:31
in jeopardy of their l. — BIBLE 50:29
it l. by that which nourisheth — SHAK 422:14
L. in Eternity's sunrise — BLAKE 86:18
l. in hope danceth without — HERB 246:22
L. of great men all remind — LONG 317:4
l. of quiet desperation — THOR 550:4
l. upon hope will die fasting — FRAN 218:13
l. without tobacco is not — MOL 353:9
Lord hath spared our l. — TENN 543:3
man who l. by his own work — COLL 158:13
'one really l. no where — BURN 112:18
Our l. would grow together — SWIN 530:21
pleasant in their l. — BIBLE 50:17
right way to conduct our l. — PLATO 374:11
sort of woman who l. for — LEWIS 314:8
That no man l. forever — SWIN 529:25
Weep for the l. your wishes — AUDEN 18:6
who lives more l. than one — WILDE 572:14
Who l. unto himself — QUAR 403:16
liveth: he l. unto God — BIBLE 75:2
I am he that l. — BIBLE 81:15
know that my redeemer l. — BIBLE 52:31
l. longest doth but sup — HENS 246:4
name l. for evermore — BIBLE 63:26
Livia: we all know Anna L. — JOYCE 286:6
living: are you yet l. — SHAK 471:28
bodies a l. sacrifice — BIBLE 75:15
body is a machine for l. — TOLS 551:2
devoured thy l. with harlots — BIBLE 70:22
Earned a precarious l. — ANON 5:4
fever call'd 'L. — POE 375:3
From too much love of l. — SWIN 529:25
habit of l. indisposeth — BROW 97:13
hands of the l. God — BIBLE 79:30
house appointed for all l. — BIBLE 52:36
I am l. in the Midlands — BELL 40:9
Let the l. creature lie — AUDEN 19:17
Life we have lost in l. — ELIOT 202:3
Living and partly l. — ELIOT 204:2
l. death — MILT 350:17
l. dog is better than — BIBLE 55:27
L. is an illness to which — CHAM 139:13
L. is my job and my art — MONT 354:23
l. know No bounds — SHIR 507:6
l. need charity — ARN 12:20
l. peaceably in their habitations BIBLE 63:23
L. The servants will — VILL 557:3

l. unto righteousness PRAY 388:10
L., we fret BROW 104:35
l. which are yet alive BIBLE 55:14
man became a l. soul BIBLE 45:7
men meet on lips of l. BUTL 119:17
mere l. BROW 105:1
mother of all l. BIBLE 45:24
my mother I'm l. in sin HERB 246:8
noble L. and the noble Dead WORD 580:24
Of health and l. now begins SHAK 486:12
out of the book of the l. PRAY 394:14
out of the land of the l. BIBLE 59:23
Plain l. and high thinking WORD 582:9
reasons for l. JUV 287:25
shadows of the l. BROW 95:17
shall no man l. be justified PRAY 399:11
someone's death to get a l. MOL 353:16
substance with riotous l. BIBLE 70:18
their preaching and l. PRAY 385:18
there are no l. people in it CHEK 144:26
There is no l. with thee ADD 2:10
things l. with plenteousness PRAY 399:15
This l. buried man DONNE 190:1
'tis the l. up to it that THAC 545:6
truly to get mine own l. PRAY 388:18
unexamined life is not worth l. SOCR 512:17
Why seek ye the l. among BIBLE 71:16
ye are l. poems LONG 316:8
you to go on l. SOCR 512:18
living-dead: l. man SHAK 427:9
living-machine: house is a l. LE C 313:5
Livingstone: Dr L., I presume STAN 517:17
livre: métier que de faire un l. LA B 306:12
livres: et j'ai lu tous les l. MALL 327:9
Les l. cadrent mal avec MOL 353:12
Les l. ne se font pas comme FLAU 214:3
ses l. disposés PROU 401:23
liv'st: what thou l. Live well MILT 349:25
Lizard: L.'s leg SHAK 462:3
say the Lion and the L. FITZ 212:14
Lizzie Borden: L. took an axe ANON 6:12
Llama: L. is a woolly sort BELL 40:2
Lo: L., I come PRAY 392:2
load: cruelty To l. a falling man SHAK 447:25
heart like a l. of immortality KEATS 294:4
him how to l. and bless KEATS 293:5
l. every rift of your subject KEATS 294:31
l. would sink a navy SHAK 447:11
loads: of learned lumber POPE 378:30
loaf: cut l. to steal a shive SHAK 486:15
quartern l. and Luddites rise SMITH 510:7
with a L. of Bread beneath FITZ 212:11
loan: brief l. of his own body CAB 126:24
l. oft loses both itself SHAK 430:19
loathe: I do l. explanations BARR 34:12
I l. the country CONG 161:5
l. the taste of sweetness SHAK 439:35
relief Must be to l. her SHAK 475:21
loathed: performance so l. SHAK 487:19
loaves: of the l. and the fishes PEAC 370:16
seven halfpenny l. SHAK 446:11
lobster: has seen the mailed l. FRERE 218:26
like a l. boil'd BUTL 118:3
still the l. held KING 297:10
'Tis the voice of the l. CARR 134:16
lobsters: I have a liking for l. NERV 361:1
local: little l. difficulties MACM 325:19
l., but prized elsewhere AUDEN 20:14
l. habitation and a name SHAK 471:11
not l. prejudices ought BURKE 109:12
localism: genuine spirit of l. BORR 90:2
Lochinvar: young L. is come out
SCOTT 417:8
loci: Geniumque l. primamque VIRG 559:4
lock: it's broken the l. AUDEN 20:5
why l. him SHAW 497:27
Wi' ae l. o' his gowden BALL 32:8
lock'd: Had l. the source of softer
SCOTT 416:11
l. my heart in a case o' BALL 32:11

locks: combined l. to part SHAK 431:5
few l. which are left you SOUT 514:7
l. of the approaching storm SHEL 502:9
l. up his spoons and packs SHAW 497:30
louse in the l. of literature TENN 544:13
never shake Thy gory l. SHAK 461:20
Open, l. SHAK 462:5
shaking her invincible l. MILT 352:3
turn those amber l. to grey DRAY 193:12
Your l. were like the raven BURNS 114:12
locust: palmerworm hath left hath the
l. BIBLE 61:13
locusts: meat was l. and wild honey
BIBLE 63:37
locuta: Roma l. est AUG 22:2
lodesterre: language he was the l.
LYDG 321:5
lodge: Elephant, Is best to l. SHAK 490:4
l. in a garden of cucumbers BIBLE 57:16
still l. Him in the manger ANON 9:1
lodger: mere l. in my own house
GOLD 232:10
lodgest: where thou l. BIBLE 49:32
lodging: Hard was their l. GARTH 221:20
lodgings: poor in their fireless l. AUDEN 20:15
Such as take l. in a head BUTL 117:21
Lodore: water comes down at L. SOUT 513:22
lo'ed: l. him like a vera brither BURNS 115:5
l'offense: monde est ce qui fait l. MOL 354:1
loft: much l. as a light iron WOD 575:22
loftier: l. race SYM 531:3
Loftily: L. lying BROW 101:2
Lofty: L. and sour to them that SHAK 447:21
L. designs must close BROW 101:2
of a l. utterance drest WORD 581:1
Logic: Common Room stank of L.'
NEWM 361:22
Grape that can with L. FITZ 213:2
It is the l. of our times DAY-L 172:23
l. and rhetoric BACON 27:21
L., of course CLOU 153:16
overthrow of all his l. STEV 521:12
push the l. of a fact KIPL 299:5
That's l. CARR 135:2
Logical: L. consequences are HUXL 269:10
logically: l. predicate his finish KIPL 302:4
logicians: If we may believe our l. ADD 2:26
Logik: Die L. muss für sich selber
WITT 575:15
logs: Tom bears l. into the hall SHAK 457:19
logyk: That unto l. hadde longe CHAU 141:23
loi: l. qui viole les droits ROB 406:11
loin: lamp and the ungirt l. BROW 105:21
loins: fire of my l. NAB 359:5
He girded up his l. BIBLE 51:12
l. girt about with truth BIBLE 78:10
shudder in the l. engenders YEATS 586:2
thicker than my father's l. BIBLE 51:2
up now thy l. like a man BIBLE 53:1
With your l. girded BIBLE 47:18
your l. be girded about BIBLE 70:6
Loire: my Gallic L. more than DU B 198:27
lois: majestueuse égalité des l. FRAN 217:26
loiter: do l l. round these chartered
MACN 326:9
loitered: So have I l. my life away
HAZL 243:15
loiterers: Liege of all l. and malecontents
SHAK 456:26
loitering: Alone and palely l. KEATS 290:15
Lolita: L., light of my life NAB 359:5
lollipop: lovely Monkey with l. paws
LEAR 312:9
Lombardy: waveless plain of L. SHEL 501:23
London: Ask the booksellers of L.
BURKE 111:17
chief advantage of L. is MEYN 338:16
dream of L. MORR 358:10
in L. only is a trade DRYD 197:13
is a city much like L. SHEL 502:17

L.; a nation DISR 186:17
L. doth pour out her citizens SHAK 445:6
L. is a fine town COLM 158:25
L. is a modern Babylon DISR 186:38
L. is the epitome of our EMER 207:9
L. particular…A fog DICK 176:3
L.'s lasting shame GRAY 234:17
L.'s Noble Fire Brigade BELL 39:8
L.'s towers BLAKE 86:12
L. streets the Shropshire HOUS 263:21
L., that great cesspool DOYLE 192:33
L., that great sea SHEL 501:17
L., thou art of townes DUNB 199:9
L., thou art the flower DUNB 199:10
lungs of L. PITT 374:2
Meet me at L. DONNE 188:2
Of famous L. town COWP 165:15
One road leads to L. MAS 334:2
sent him up to fair L. BALL 30:8
than a rainy Sunday in L. DE Q 175:1
they all to merry L. came SPEN 517:1
vilest alleys of L. do DOYLE 192:1
Weller's knowledge of L. DICK 181:35
When a man is tired of L. JOHN 277:17
Where L.'s column POPE 378:2
London Bridge: broken arch of L.
MAC 323:16
crowd flowed over L. ELIOT 204:20
that L. was a greater piece ADD 2:19
lone: 'I am a l. lorn creetur' DICK 176:27
l. shieling of the misty GALT 221:2
l. unhaunted place possesst DONNE 190:1
three l. weirs ARN 15:3
loneliness: All that bowery l. TENN 533:13
Lap your l. in heat BETJ 42:7
lonely: is troubled with her l. PEPYS 372:8
l. impulse of delight YEATS 586:9
rapture on the l. shore BYRON 121:22
to the l. sea and the sky MAS 334:4
lonesomeness: starlight lit my l. HARDY 241:5
long: appear most l. and terrible LEE 313:8
arms l. and small WYATT 583:22
certified how l. I have to live PRAY 391:30
craft so l. to lerne CHAU 143:32
days seem lank and l. GILB 228:29
feet l. and two feet wide WORD 582:24
foolish thing to make a l. prologue
BIBLE 63:29
fulfilled a l. time BIBLE 62:15
has been l. in city pent KEATS 292:27
How l. a time lies in one SHAK 478:13
How l. wilt thou forget PRAY 390:1
I am going a l. way TENN 535:27
It cannot hold you l. GOLD 231:9
it hath very l. arms HAL 238:2
l. as ye both shall live PRAY 389:3
l. day's task is done SHAK 423:9
l. for the fruit at last SHER 506:10
L. is the way And hard MILT 346:17
l. life will I satisfy PRAY 395:23
Lord, how l. BIBLE 58:2
man goeth to his l. home BIBLE 56:11
many girls l. for it CAT 137:6
nor that little, l. YOUNG 588:8
Nor wants that little l. GOLD 231:7
So l. as men can breathe SHAK 492:28
that the story need be l. THOR 550:26
to keep unmarried as l. SHAW 497:25
week is a l. time in politics WILS 574:18
witty and it sha'n't be l. CHES 145:7
words a foot and a half l. HOR 257:16
You l. for simple pewter GILB 225:30
long-cramped: l. scroll BROW 101:24
long'd-for: l. dash of waves is heard
ARN 15:1
longe: day be never so l. HAWES 243:3
morowe l. I to goe to God MORE 357:20
longer: l. I live the more fool ANON 8:19
man that was wished l. JOHN 280:16

longest: dreariest and the l. journey go
SHEL 500:10
longeth: flesh also l. after thee PRAY 393:21
so l. my soul after thee PRAY 392:6
longing: has cast a l. eye on them JEFF 272:11
l. comes upon him to fare POUND 383:18
l. to be at 'em ANON 5:10
soul hath a desire and l. PRAY 395:11
This l. after immortality ADD 1:24
longings: Immortal l. in me SHAK 424:10
longitude: l. also is vague PROW 402:2
L. objected to his theology SMIL 509:5
long-legged: *l. fly upon the stream*
YEATS 586:3
Long Melford: then tip them to L.
BORR 90:11
long-suffering: l., and very pitiful
BIBLE 62:21
l., and of great goodness PRAY 396:16
longtemps: *et c'est pour si l.* MOL 353:8
L. je me suis couché de PROU 401:20
longue: *l. que parce que je n'ai* PASC 369:14
look: afraid to l. upon God BIBLE 47:5
...'Do l. into it' STER 520:10
do we l. for another BIBLE 66:1
Hit l. lak sparrer-grass HARR 242:14
how you l. to other people UNAM 554:28
I l. at the senators HALE 237:12
Let him l. to his bond SHAK 467:3
longing ling'ring l. behind GRAY 235:2
l., and pass on DANTE 171:4
l. grim as hell SHAK 476:18
l. in my face TRAI 552:4
l. not in my eyes HOUS 262:21
L. not thou upon the wine BIBLE 54:24
L. not thou down but up BROW 104:12
L..not thou on beauty's SCOTT 418:5
l. no way but downwards BUNY 107:28
l. on both indifferently SHAK 448:12
L., stranger AUDEN 20:3
L. thy last on all things DE L 174:3
l. to the end ANON 10:18
L. to the lady SHAK 461:3
L. to your Moat HAL 238:4
l. upon myself and curse SHAK 493:6
l. upon the hedge and follow SHAK 492:9
L. with thine ears SHAK 455:18
Men's eyes were made to l. SHAK 483:2
not l. upon his like again SHAK 430:5
'O l. at the trees BRID 92:14
read a nod, a shrug, a l. SWIFT 527:29
sake l. after our people SCOTT 415:18
shall tremble at the l. PRAY 397:2
so l. to thyself SHAK 490:12
sweet to l. into the fair KEATS 292:27
that we may l. upon thee BIBLE 57:6
to l. about us and to die) POPE 379:1
to l. at things in bloom HOUS 262:14
We l. before and after SHEL 504:23
When I do l. on thee SIDN 508:1
looked: be l. upon by posterity CLAR 152:22
be so wise as Thurlow l. FOX 217:21
l. for a city which hath BIBLE 79:32
l. upon Peter BIBLE 71:9
wife l. back BIBLE 46:8
lookers on: God and angels to be l.
BACON 24:24
looketh: l. on the outward appearance
BIBLE 50:6
looking: Here's l. at you BOG 89:8
l. back BIBLE 69:25
l. for a man's foot-print BEER 37:27
l. for the sacred Emperor BRAM 91:18
l. one way BUNY 107:18
May I be l. at you TIB 550:34
she was l. all the time THOM 547:11
They all were l. for a king MACD 325:4
With l. on his life SHAK 421:32
would not be l. for Me PASC 369:13

looking forward: have not been l.
HOR 258:16
looking-glass: court an amorous l.
SHAK 480:18
cracked l. of a servant JOYCE 286:21
dreams and dreams their l. YEATS 587:1
smiles, As in a l. SHAK 491:9
looks: full assurance given by l. ROYD 411:2
her l. went everywhere BROW 102:22
His l. adorn'd the venerable GOLD 230:24
I have no proud l. PRAY 398:25
Stolen l. are nice in chapels HUNT 268:11
that would those l. reprove GOLD 230:17
woman as old as she l. COLL 158:15
loom: she left the l. TENN 538:11
loomp: poor in a l. is bad TENN 541:2
looms: passage through these l. VAUG 555:10
loon: grey-beard l. COL 155:6
thou cream-faced l. SHAK 463:1
loo paper: When the l. gets thicker
MITF 352:25
loopholes: through l. Less than themselves
TESS 545:3
through the l. of retreat COWP 167:12
loore: Cristes l. and his apostles CHAU 142:3
loos'd: l. our heart in tears ARN 13:17
loose: all hell broke l. MILT 348:11
l. from every honourable BURKE 108:23
l. gown from her shoulders WYATT 583:22
l. the bands of Orion BIBLE 53:5
l. the bands of wickedness BIBLE 60:4
L. types of things through WORD 582:26
Put me into something l. PIN 373:16
to l. the seals thereof BIBLE 81:26
wear those things so l. BARH 33:23
loosen: Until God l. over sea SWIN 530:19
lops: l. the moulder'd branch TENN 533:26
loquendi: *est et ius et norma l.* HOR 257:14
Lord: acceptable year of the L. BIBLE 60:8
became l. of the ascendant BURKE 109:6
Because you are a great l. BEAU 35:18
cometh in the Name of the L. PRAY 398:3
day of the L. is near BIBLE 61:17
day which the L. hath made PRAY 398:2
died by the hand of the L. BIBLE 47:23
doth the L. require of thee BIBLE 61:25
earth is the L.'s BIBLE 76:11
earth is the L.'s PRAY 390:23
Even the L. of hosts PRAY 391:1
fear and nurture of the L. PRAY 389:1
Forgive, O L. FROST 219:7
glory of the L. shall be BIBLE 59:5
Good L. PRAY 385:16
Great l. of all things POPE 379:13
in the house of the L. PRAY 390:22
into the hands of the L. BIBLE 62:22
into the house of the L. PRAY 398:11
In whom the 'L. of Hosts' HERB 246:25
kiss my L. before I die MARL 330:13
knowed the L. was nigher LOW 319:6
knowledge of the L. BIBLE 58:11
lesson which the L. us taught SPEN 515:18
let a l. once own the happy POPE 378:25
L. and Lady Dalhousie MCG 325:5
L. Archbishop of Rheims BARH 33:11
L., art more than they TENN 535:31
L., behold us with Thy BUCK 106:16
L. be with thee BIBLE 50:10
L., dismiss us with Thy BUCK 106:17
L., dost thou wash my BIBLE 72:27
L. guards the city BIBLE 83:12
L. has built the house BIBLE 83:12
L. hath not spoken by me BIBLE 51:20
L., have mercy upon us PRAY 384:18
L., how long BIBLE 58:2
L. is a man of war BIBLE 47:22
L. is King PRAY 395:24
L. is my light PRAY 391:7
L. is my shepherd PRAY 390:21
L. is the source of my BIBLE 83:5

L. let the house of a brute TENN 532:22
L. looketh on the heart BIBLE 50:6
L. loveth he chasteneth BIBLE 80:1
L. make his face shine BIBLE 48:9
L., make me coy and tender HERB 248:14
L. mighty in battle PRAY 390:24
L. No Zoo DICK 178:29
l. of folded arms SHAK 456:26
L. of himself WOTT 583:13
L. OF LORDS BIBLE 82:26
L. of our far-flung battle-line KIPL 302:7
L. of thy presence SHAK 452:8
Lord our God is one L. BIBLE 48:20
L. prefers common-looking LINC 315:5
L., remember me when thou BIBLE 71:12
L. said unto my Lord PRAY 397:11
L.'s anointed temple SHAK 460:22
L. set a mark upon Cain BIBLE 45:28
L. shall bring again Zion BIBLE 59:19
L.'s my shepherd SCOT 419:5
l., thy king, thy governor SHAK 484:15
L. turned BIBLE 71:9
L. watch between me BIBLE 46:22
L., what fools these mortals SHAK 470:31
L. will be there and wait WHIT 571:2
L., with what care Thou HERB 248:10
Love is our L.'s meaning JUL 286:33
married My L. you POUND 383:16
mouth of the L. hath spoken BIBLE 59:5
of the coming of the L. HOWE 266:19
of the mouth of the L. BIBLE 48:22
of those who love the L. HUNT 268:4
O L., to what a state TER 544:20
patience of hope in our L. BIBLE 78:30
Prepare ye the way of the L. BIBLE 59:5
Prepare ye the way of the L. BIBLE 63:36
Rejoice in the L. alway BIBLE 78:20
remembrance of his dying L. SPEN 515:31
Sae let the L. be thankit BURNS 114:14
sapient sutlers of the L. ELIOT 204:1
Seek ye the L. while he BIBLE 59:26
servant above his l. BIBLE 65:34
shall we sing the L.'s song PRAY 399:3
So love is L. of all SPEN 515:22
sought the L. aright BURNS 113:6
soul doth magnify the L. BIBLE 69:5
Spirit on the L.'s day BIBLE 81:11
tasted that the L. is gracious BIBLE 80:22
They have taken away my L. BIBLE 73:7
'twur the will o' the L. TENN 544:5
unhouse and house the L. HOPK 256:16
wait upon the L. shall renew BIBLE 59:10
Welcum the l. of lycht DOUG 191:5
we own thee L. ANON 11:3
what hour your L. doth come BIBLE 68:1
Lord Jesus: Even so, come, L. BIBLE 83:4
lordliest: l. lass of earth BROO 94:16
Whoe'er lived in life most l. POUND 383:19
Lord Lilac: L. thought it rather rotten
CHES 147:16
Lord Primate: served the L. on bended
knee BARH 33:11
Lord Randal: L., my Son BALL 31:5
lords: About the l. of the creation
BURNS 115:26
is only a wit among L. JOHN 274:9
l. and our forefathers SWIN 530:7
L. are lordliest in their MILT 350:27
l. have their pleasures MONT 355:7
L. of Convention 'twas SCOTT 415:20
l. of human kind pass GOLD 231:28
L. too are bards BYRON 124:27
l. who lay you low SHEL 504:2
l. whose parents were DEFOE 173:14
Scots l. at his feet BALL 31:20
They are the l. and owners SHAK 494:15
thither from the House of L. NORF 364:1
lordships: good enough for their l. ANON 8:8
Lord Tomnoddy: my L. went home to
bed BARH 33:9

lore: all the l. its scholars — KEBLE 295:5
lose: day you may l. them all' — LEAR 312:17
findeth his life shall l. — BIBLE 65:40
hope and nothing to l. — BURKE 110:8
I love to l. myself — LAMB 307:16
is nothing much to l. — HOUS 266:3
l., and start again — KIPL 300:1
l. a volume to C carries — LAMB 307:15
l. his own soul — BIBLE 66:35
l. his own soul — BIBLE 68:34
l. it that do buy it with — SHAK 465:9
l. my heart in summer's — HOUS 266:4
l. myself in dotage — SHAK 421:17
l. our teeth and eyelashes — LEAR 312:24
l. our ventures — SHAK 451:27
l. the name of action — SHAK 433:8
l., Though full of pain — MILT 346:10
l. to-morrow the ground — ARN 14:17
No man can l. what he never — WALT 564:8
power and to l. liberty — BACON 26:22
to l. itself in the sky — BROW 98:20
to l. myself in a mystery — BROW 96:9
To l. one parent — WILDE 573:1
to l. thee were to lose — MILT 349:20
To win or l. it all — GRAH 233:14
way to l. him — SHAK 421:24
losers: all are l. — CHAM 139:8
So both should l. be — HERB 248:7
loses: l. his misery — ARN 14:22
Who l., and who wins — SHAK 456:3
losest: fear thou l. all — HERB 248:12
losing: conduct of a l. party — BURKE 111:27
Hath but a l. office — SHAK 441:2
l. a battle is to gain — WELL 567:25
L. both beauty and utility — SHAK 445:12
l. one pleased Cato — LUCAN 319:22
Still l. when I saw myself — SHAK 495:6
loss: black as our l. — SITW 508:13
breathe a word about your l. — KIPL 300:1
counted l. for Christ — BIBLE 78:17
deeper sense of her l. — GASK 222:3
enow To do our country l. — SHAK 445:1
'Our day is our l. — AUDEN 20:15
perhaps neither gain nor l. — ELIOT 202:24
profit and l. — ELIOT 205:6
upon thy so sore l. — THOM 548:25
When a man's l. comes — BROW 100:10
losses: l. are restor'd and sorrows — SHAK 493:7
lost: All is not l. — MILT 345:3
are l. in the storm — ARN 14:9
are paradises we have l. — PROU 402:1
battles are l. in the same — WHIT 570:20
better to have fought and l. — CLOU 154:2
better to have loved and l. — TENN 536:16
found my sheep which was l. — BIBLE 70:16
Hath l. me in your liking — SHAK 453:6
having l. but once your prime — HERR 250:6
Hearts that have l. their — HOUS 265:9
He is l. to the forest — SCOTT 416:5
He sought, For his l. heart — SHEL 504:5
him was almost l. in Art — COLL 158:23
Home of l. causes — ARN 15:25
horse the rider was l. — FRAN 218:6
I have l. a day — TITUS 551:6
I have l. all the names — JOHN 278:31
I long ago l. a hound — THOR 550:8
Is the year only l. — HERB 247:14
itself shall not be l. — FRAN 218:20
Life we have l. in living — ELIOT 202:3
l., and is found — BIBLE 70:21
l. an Empire and has not — ACH 1:4
l. but the son of perdition — BIBLE 72:42
l. evermore in the main — TENN 543:5
L. in the quagmire — TENN 534:22
l. sheep of the house — BIBLE 65:30
l., that is unsought — CHAU 144:3
l. the last of England — BELL 40:16
l. thing could I never — BELL 40:10
l. to love and truth — BURNS 113:7
l. to me — BARH 33:8

l. traveller's dream — BLAKE 86:1
love it and be l. like — HOUS 262:21
make wherever we're l. — FRY 220:3
my bosom and be l. in me — TENN 542:14
next to a battle l. — WELL 567:27
Not l. but gone before — NORT 364:8
Praising what is l. — SHAK 421:5
recover what has been l. — ELIOT 202:24
see is lost let it be l. — CAT 136:27
see your country is l. — WILL 574:8
Something l. behind — KIPL 299:2
so that I have l. my edifice — SHAK 469:9
than never to have l. — BUTL 119:16
That all was l. — MILT 349:16
that deliberates is l. — ADD 1:20
that nothing be l. — BIBLE 72:5
that Old England is l. — JOHN 277:12
they're l. to us and counted — MART 331:11
Though lovers be l. love — THOM 546:19
treacle is l. in the sweets — GAY 222:30
we are l. to Love and Truth — KIPL 299:11
When all is l. — BYRON 125:10
who have l. their queen — FRY 220:7
who l. in stormy visions — SHEL 499:20
who l. the world for love — DRYD 197:8
whom you so long have l. — WORD 577:23
yet so l. in lexicography — JOHN 281:6
You're all a l. generation — STEIN 518:18
lot: cast my l. in an island — DICK 183:7
l. has fallen to me — KIPL 303:16
l. is fallen unto me — PRAY 390:6
Our loving l. was cast — HOOD 254:8
policeman's l. is not — GILB 228:19
Remember L.'s wife — BIBLE 70:32
Lothario: gay L. — ROWE 410:22
That false L. — ROWE 410:19
Lothbury: vapour through L. glide — WORD 581:3
Lotos: L. and lilies — TENN 541:18
lots: cast l. upon my vesture — PRAY 390:20
Gathering fuel in vacant l. — ELIOT 204:8
So they cast l. — BIBLE 61:21
lotus: like l.-buds that float — HOPE 256:4
Lou: lady that's known as L. — SERV 420:14
loud: him upon the l. cymbals — PRAY 400:1
in the senate l. — CHUR 149:5
l. and troublesome *insects* — BURKE 111:16
will and yet was never l. — SHAK 474:18
louder: l. he talked of his honour — EMER 207:8
loue: doughterly l. and deere charitie — MORE 357:20
Louis Philippe: L. far better than a Napoleon — BAG 28:25
Lounjun: L. 'roun' en suffer'n' — HARR 242:21
louse: between a l. and a flea — JOHN 279:8
l. for the hangman — JONS 284:4
l. in the locks of literature — TENN 544:13
louts: oafish l. remember Mum — BETJ 42:8
lov'd: Had we never l. sae kindly — BURNS 112:29
heart that has truly l. — MOORE 356:5
He dearly l. the lasses — BURNS 114:3
I l. Ophelia — SHAK 437:8
l. not at first sight — SHAK 426:19
most l., despis'd — SHAK 453:8
nor no man ever l. — SHAK 495:5
Shall never be by woman l. — BLAKE 85:12
She who has never l. — GAY 223:2
sour to them that l. him — SHAK 447:21
therefore must be l. — SHAK 486:15
Thou hast not l. — SHAK 425:10
till we l. — DONNE 188:29
We l. the doctrine — DEFOE 173:3
who never l. before — ANON 10:11
love: all for l. and a little all for l. — DIBD 175:16
All l. at first — BUTL 118:17
All l. is lost but upon — DUNB 199:13
all men all earth to l. — KIPL 303:16
All who deserve his l. — DRYD 196:3

ape the magnanimity of l. — MER 337:6
are beautiful through l. — SHEL 503:13
are but ministers of L. — COL 157:2
are l. not a gaping pig — SHAK 467:21
arms of my true l. — TENN 540:13
aside a long-cherished l. — CAT 137:10
As woman's l. — SHAK 434:10
beautiful than thy first l. — YEATS 584:23
beauty and l. lay bare — SHEL 503:23
Because my l. is come — ROSS 408:23
Because we freely l. — MILT 348:20
be in l. with his fetters — BACON 27:42
be my l. — DONNE 187:24
be my l. — MARL 329:23
be wroth with one we l. — COL 156:4
bid me l. — HERR 249:25
boy's l. — SHAK 454:28
breastplate of faith and l. — BIBLE 79:2
bring those who l. Thee — TER 544:20
can l. freedom heartily — MILT 352:17
cantons of contemned l. — SHAK 488:13
carry a letter to my l. — BALL 30:20
comely in nothing but in l. — BACON 26:29
compliments and—and l. — AUST 22:27
constancy of the women who l. — SHAW 498:9
content with a vegetable l. — GILB 227:23
corner in the thing I l. — SHAK 475:21
cruel madness of l. — TENN 539:29
day and a night L. sang — SWIN 528:24
Deep as first l. — TENN 542:4
dinner of herbs where l. — BIBLE 54:6
do not fall in l. with me — SHAK 426:18
Dreaming like a l.-adept — SHEL 503:5
drew them…with bands of l. — BIBLE 61:12
earth could never living l. — ANON 5:14
Ends all our month-long l. — BRID 92:11
Eternity is l. with — BLAKE 88:17
ever wilt thou l. — KEATS 291:5
Except for l.'s sake only — BROW 98:11
faith and labour of l. — BIBLE 78:30
far from the lips we l. — MOORE 356:19
fathom deep I am in l. — SHAK 426:24
fickleness of the women I l. — SHAW 498:9
fit l. for Gods — MILT 349:14
fitter L. for me — DONNE 190:7
flowers and fruits of l. — BYRON 125:11
fool of l. — HAZL 243:18
Forgets the shows of l. — SHAK 448:11
Frail as thy l. — PEAC 371:1
Friendship is L. without — BYRON 124:37
From too much l. of living — SWIN 529:25
fruit of the Spirit is l. — BIBLE 77:18
gasp of L.'s latest breath — DRAY 193:21
Gather the Rose of l. — SPEN 516:13
gin l. be bonnie — BALL 32:10
Give to me the life I l. — STEV 522:27
give up my darling's l. — ANON 9:17
God gives us l. — TENN 543:14
godly l. — PRAY 387:13
God of l. my Shepherd — HERB 248:13
God si L. — FORS 217:9
good man's l. — SHAK 426:17
good to them that l. God — BIBLE 75:11
Greater l. hath no man — BIBLE 72:36
greatness on her subjects' l. — PRIOR 401:3
green and happy in first l. — CLOU 153:23
Hail wedded l. — MILT 348:8
hast left thy first l. — BIBLE 81:16
hate all that don't l. — FARQ 210:11
hearts such l. toward thee — PRAY 386:18
help those we l. to escape — HUGEL 267:5
herald of l.'s mighty king — SPEN 515:19
herself she will not l. — SUCK 524:7
hid in the heart of l. — YEATS 586:9
His banner over me was l. — BIBLE 56:20
his dark secret l. — BLAKE 87:12
his for his l. — SHAK 493:8
honeying and making l. — SHAK 435:10
How do I l. thee — BROW 98:13
how I fell in l. — VIRG 560:4

how l. and murder will out	CONG 159:26	l. all waste And solitary	SHEL 501:10
how l. constrained him	DANTE 171:9	l., an abject intercourse	GOLD 232:11
how this spring of l. resembleth	SHAK 490:33	L. and a cottage	COLM 158:24
human l. will be seen	FORS 217:2	L. and do what you will	AUG 21:21
I am sick of l.	BIBLE 56:21	l. and fame to nothingness	KEATS 293:2
I could not l. thee (Dear)	LOV 318:20	l. and good company improves	FARQ 210:8
I do l. nothing	SHAK 473:2	L. and I were well acquainted	GILB 228:38
I do not l. the man	WATK 565:6	l. and knowledge of you	SHAK 424:27
I do not l. you	BROWN 95:10	l. and rhetoric without	STOP 523:16
I don't l. you	MART 331:9	l. and scandal are	FIEL 211:18
If ever thou shalt l.	SHAK 488:27	l. and thanks of men	PAINE 368:1
If it be l. indeed	SHAK 421:7	l. and toil in the years	KIPL 298:10
If l. were all	COW 163:17	l. a woman for singing	SHAK 453:14
if my l. were in my arms	ANON 8:16	l. a woman so well when	ELIOT 201:10
If this be not l.	CONG 160:22	l. a womman that she woot	CHAU 144:3
I hae parted frae my L.	BURNS 114:11	L. bade me welcome	HERB 247:25
I hate and I l.	CAT 137:14	L. be controll'd by advice	GAY 222:14
I have been half in l.	KEATS 291:22	l. betwixt us two	COWL 164:17
I have been in l.	BROME 93:10	l. be younger than thyself	SHAK 489:2
I have freedom in my l.	LOV 318:18	L. built on beauty	DONNE 188:6
I knew it was l.	BYRON 125:30	l. but only her	BYRON 121:21
I know whose l. would follow	KIPL 301:14	l. can do with a twined	BURT 116:33
ill bred as to l. a husband	WYCH 584:1	L. can transpose to form	SHAK 469:22
I l. a lass	OKEE 364:23	L. ceases to be a pleasure	BEHN 38:12
I l. but you alone	BALL 31:9	l., cherish, and to obey	PRAY 389:4
I l. not man the less	BYRON 121:22	L. comes from blindness	BUSS 117:5
I l. thee in prose	PRIOR 400:21	L. conquers all things	VIRG 560:8
'I l. thee true	KEATS 290:19	l. Creation's final law	TENN 536:29
I l. the lovely bully	SHAK 444:17	L., curiosity	PARK 368:15
I l. to be the worst	SWIFT 526:15	l., devoid of art	GAY 223:5
I'm tired of L.	BELL 39:18	L. doth to her eyes repair	SHAK 491:4
In books and l.	GAY 223:23	l. every thing that's old	GOLD 232:19
In l. alone we hate	WALSH 563:29	L. finally is great	AUDEN 18:8
in l., or in hate	STEV 521:26	l., first learned	SHAK 457:8
in l. with loving	AUG 21:12	L. first leaves the well-built	SHEL 501:2
in l. with one princess	STER 519:3	l., Fool, for the good	PATM 370:1
invincible l. of reading	GIBB 224:6	l. for any lady	PEELE 371:6
is better than secret l.	BIBLE 54:37	L., forgive us	KEATS 290:24
is none other I can l.	TENN 534:28	L., friendship, charity	SHAK 487:6
is not in l.	SHAK 486:26	L. gilds the scene	SHER 506:24
is the l. of the people	BURKE 110:5	l. God whom he hath not	BIBLE 81:7
I think my l. as rare	SHAK 495:9	L. goes toward love	SHAK 482:18
It is l.'s great artillery	CRAS 169:11	L. had he found in huts	WORD 581:11
it is my l.	SHAK 482:6	L. has pitched his mansion	YEATS 584:19
It's no go my honey l.	MACN 326:8	l. he bore to learning	GOLD 231:2
it's the general l.	AUDEN 20:8	l. he had to her	BIBLE 46:21
I would L. infinitely	BROW 103:3	l. he laugh'd to scorn	SHAK 495:18
joy of l. is too short	MAL 327:19	l. her is a liberal education	STEE 518:6
knew His l. Who followed	THOM 548:10	L.! I love thee not	SHAK 438:31
knew thee but to l. thee	HALL 238:9	L. I make it constantly	PROU 401:22
know that l. endures no tie	DRYD 197:7	L. in a golden bowl	BLAKE 85:19
lack of l. from love made	BROW 100:10	L. in a hut	KEATS 290:24
ladies' l. unfit	DRYD 195:32	L. in a palace is perhaps	KEATS 290:24
lady would not l. a shepherd	GREE 236:11	L. in desolation masked	SHEL 499:17
last acquainted with L.	JOHN 274:6	L. in her attire doth show	ANON 6:20
laughter and the l. of friends	BELL 39:15	L. in her sunny eyes does	COWL 164:6
lease of my true l. control	SHAK 494:21	L., in love's philosophy	DONNE 189:19
Leave me, O L.	SIDN 507:28	L. in my bosom	LODGE 316:3
leave to come unto my l.	SPEN 515:26	L. in this part	BYRON 126:18
leisure for l. or hope	HOOD 255:9	L. is a boy	BUTL 118:2
Lesbia let us live and l.	CAT 136:25	L. is a circle that doth	HERR 249:9
Let brotherly l. continue	BIBLE 80:3	L. is a growing or full	DONNE 189:20
Let l. therefore be what	STER 520:6	L. is ane fervent fire	SCOTT 415:14
let me l.	DONNE 188:4	L. is a passion that hath	HAL 237:17
Let me not l. Thee	HERB 246:24	L. is a spirit all compact	SHAK 495:19
Let those l. now	ANON 10:11	l. is a thing that can	PARK 368:14
let us make l. deathless	TREN 552:7	L. is crowned with	SHAK 427:2
like l. to hatred turn'd	CONG 160:15	L. is dying	BARN 34:4
lips of those who l. you	BRID 92:18	L. is lame at fifty years	HARDY 240:18
little duty and less l.	SHAK 445:23	L. is like any other luxury	TROL 553:15
little emptiness of l.	BROO 94:27	L. is like linen often	FLET 215:31
little in our l.	SHAK 489:7	L. is like the measles	JER 272:23
little light Of l.'s bestowing	DU M 199:6	l. is Lord of all the world	SPEN 515:22
Live with me and be my l.	SHAK 495:16	l. is lost	HERB 247:5
look'd at me as she did l.	KEATS 290:18	l. is maister wher he wile	GOWER 233:6
lost to l. and truth	BURNS 113:7	l. is more cruel than lust	SWIN 529:10
l. admits no qualifying	SHAK 487:2	L. is mor than gold	LYDG 321:8
L., all alike	DONNE 190:12	L. is not love	SHAK 453:7
l. all beauteous things	BRID 92:10	L. is not love	SHAK 495:5
l. all that thou lovest	SHEL 503:26	L. is not secure	CHES 146:18

l. is of man's life a thing	BYRON 122:14		
L. is of the valley	TENN 542:16		
L. is our Lord's meaning	JUL 286:33		
l. is slight	MARL 329:18		
l. is strong as death	BIBLE 57:11		
l. is such a mystery	SUCK 524:13		
l. is sweet for a day	SWIN 530:5		
L. is the fulfilling	BIBLE 75:23		
l. is the keeping of her	BIBLE 62:19		
L. is the lesson which	SPEN 515:18		
l. is then our duty	GAY 222:28		
L. is the wisdom	JOHN 280:27		
l. is towards individuals	SWIFT 526:23		
L. it and be lost like	HOUS 262:21		
L. it more than tongue	BROW 105:29		
L. itself shall slumber	SHEL 504:12		
l., let us be gay	ARN 12:23		
l. long life better than	SHAK 421:12		
L. looks not with the eyes	SHAK 469:22		
L. made him weep his pints	AUDEN 21:9		
l. make themselves felt	LA B 306:13		
l. may be call'd appetite	SHAK 489:6		
L. me little	ANON 6:13		
l. me long	ANON 6:13		
l. nor pity nor forgive	KIPL 302:17		
L. not such nights as these	SHAK 454:9		
l. o'ercome sae sair	BURNS 114:18		
l. of Christ	BIBLE 77:25		
l. of finished years	ROSS 408:26		
l. of God is shed abroad	BIBLE 74:41		
l. of liberty is the love	HAZL 243:19		
l. of money is the root	BIBLE 79:18		
l. of pleasure	POPE 377:24		
l. one another or die	AUDEN 20:9		
L. repulsed,—but it returneth	SHEL 500:18		
l. rules the court	SCOTT 416:17		
l.'s a malady without	DRYD 197:6		
L.'s a man of war	HERB 247:16		
L.'s but a frailty	CONG 161:3		
l. Scotland better than	JOHN 281:22		
L. seeketh not itself	BLAKE 87:18		
L. seeketh only Self	BLAKE 87:19		
L.'s harbinger	MILT 349:26		
l. slights it	BACON 26:2		
L.'s like the measles	JERR 273:3		
L.'s martyr	DONNE 188:28		
l. so dearly joined	MILT 349:18		
L. sought is good	SHAK 489:25		
L. sounds the alarm	GAY 222:10		
L.'s passives are his	CRAS 169:3		
L.'s pleasure lasts	FLOR 215:34		
L.'s sweetest part, Variety	DONNE 189:17		
l.'s the noblest frailty	DRYD 196:23		
L. still has something	SEDL 419:9		
L.'s tongue is	FLET 215:33		
l., sweet love	WHIT 571:13		
L., sweetness, goodness	MILT 351:12		
l.'s young dream	MOORE 356:12		
L. That cordial drop	ROCH 406:19		
L. that dare not speak	DOUG 191:4		
L. that endures for a breath	SWIN 528:21		
L., that had robbed us	MER 337:1		
l. that loves a scarlet	HOOD 254:15		
l. that moves the sun	DANTE 171:18		
L. that never told can	BLAKE 86:21		
L. that should help you	SWIN 530:2		
L. that so desires would	MER 337:4		
l. the babe that milks	SHAK 459:10		
L. the Beloved Republic	FORS 217:13		
L. the brotherhood	BIBLE 80:25		
l. thee after	SHAK 477:5		
l. thee better after death	BROW 98:14		
l. the highest when we	TENN 534:15		
L., the human form divine	BLAKE 88:7		
l. their land because it	HALL 238:8		
L. the night	DRYD 197:18		
l. the offender	POPE 376:12		
l. the uppermost rooms	BIBLE 67:22		
l. tho' given in vain	TENN 534:30		

I l. a lass WITH 575:13
I l. thee once AYT 24:4
I l. you, so I drew LAWR 311:12
Indeed the Idols I have l. FITZ 213:13
I saw and l. GIBB 224:12
Israel l. Joseph BIBLE 46:26
lad That I l. bodily YEATS 585:20
Lesbia whom Catullus once l. CAT 137:5
l. each other beyond belief HEINE 244:10
l. not at first sight MARL 329:18
l. one all together BROW 102:24
l., sir—used to meet BROW 100:8
l. so slight a thing TENN 539:4
l. the bailiff's daughter BALL 30:7
l. Three whole days together SUCK 524:14
men who have l. them TROL 553:10
Might she have l. me BROW 101:24
more I l. my homeland BELL 40:17
no sooner l. but they sighed SHAK 426:27
Not that I l. Caesar less SHAK 450:14
only know we l. in vain BYRON 124:34
our endeavour be so l. SHAK 487:19
Pale hands I l. HOPE 256:5
pressed to say why I l. him MONT 354:18
say the lad that l. you HOUS 266:2
She had been l. WOOLF 576:18
Solomon l. many strange women BIBLE 51:1
so young, I l. him so BROW 99:16
than never to have been l. CONG 160:35
that all we l. of him should SHEL 499:12
that once if I l. you well SWIN 530:20
thrice had I l. thee DONNE 187:18
'Tis better to have l. BUTL 119:16
use him as though you l. WALT 564:9
Wel l. he garleek CHAU 142:5
We that had l. him so BROW 102:5
When you l. me I gave you SHAW 496:29
which he l. passing well SHAK 432:21
Which I have l. long since NEWM 362:15
Whilst loving thou mayst l. SPEN 516:13

love-forty: l., oh! weakness of joy BETJ 44:6
Love-in-idleness: maidens call it, L.
SHAK 470:8
love-knot: Plaiting a dark red l. NOYES 364:13
loveliest: l. and best FITZ 212:17
l. fairy in the world KING 297:12
L. of trees HOUS 262:14
world the l. and the best BELL 39:20
Love-light: L. of Spain CHES 147:3
loveliness: Enough their simple l. for
me KEATS 292:16
Glory and l. have pass'd KEATS 292:26
Her l. I never knew COL 154:26
I am weak from your l. BETJ 44:6
is a portion of the l. SHEL 499:24
Its l. increases KEATS 288:20
l. and the hour of my death KEATS 294:21
l. Needs not THOM 549:17
They saw a Dream of L. LEL 313:18
woman of so shining l. YEATS 586:17
Lovell: Cat, the Rat, and L. COLL 158:10
love-locks: going with your l. flowing
ROSS 408:21
lovely: down in l. muck I've lain HOUS 264:13
it's a l. thing MOL 353:5
Lap from some once l. Head FITZ 212:15
l. and a fearful thing BYRON 122:24
l. April of her prime SHAK 492:24
L. are the curves MER 337:3
l. is the rose WORD 578:22
L. lads and dead and rotten HOUS 263:19
l. rice pudding for dinner MILNE 340:10
l. way that led HOUS 265:4
l. woman stoops to folly ELIOT 205:3
l. woman stoops to folly GOLD 231:31
more l. and more temperate SHAK 492:28
whatsoever things are l. BIBLE 78:22
Which once he made more l. SHEL 499:24
you have l. hair CHEK 145:6

love-lyrics: account I write so many l.
POUND 382:15
love-making: which is the l. BACON 27:31
Love Powders: rogue gives you L.
LAMB 307:30
Love-quarrels: L. oft in pleasing concord
MILT 350:26
lover: affliction taught a l. POPE 376:12
days dividing lover and l. SWIN 528:17
give repentance to her l. GOLD 231:31
injured l.'s hell MILT 348:19
Into a L.'s head WORD 582:21
I sighed as a l. GIBB 224:13
It was a l. and his lass SHAK 427:2
lived she was a true l. MAL 328:2
l. and killer are mingled DOUG 191:10
l. and sensuality HENL 245:12
l., and the poet SHAK 471:11
l. of literature is never SOUT 514:14
l.'s eyes will gaze SHAK 457:8
l., Sighing like furnace SHAK 425:24
l. true for whom I pine WHIT 571:2
magnetic, Peripatetic L. GILB 227:24
my fause l. stole my rose BURNS 116:8
one was round her l. CAMP 129:4
passion woman loves her l. BYRON 122:25
propositions of a l. SHAK 426:8
roaming l. CALL 127:7
says to her lusting l. CAT 137:7
searching for a new l. CONN 161:13
since I cannot prove a l. SHAK 480:19
Such a constant l. SUCK 524:14
Suff'ring is the l.'s part GAY 222:9
that is in any manner a l. MAL 328:1
thou wast as true a l. SHAK 425:9
Titan-woman like a l. SWIN 528:26
Who could deceive a l. VIRG 558:12
with some old l.'s ghost DONNE 189:25
you l. of trees BROW 100:12
Your brother and his l. SHAK 463:13
lovers: All but the pieties of l.' CRANE 168:31
Almighty l. in the spring CHES 146:18
At l.' perjuries SHAK 482:13
even l. find their peace FLEC 214:10
I am all true l. are SHAK 488:27
Journeys end in l. meeting SHAK 488:17
laughs at l.' perjury DRYD 197:7
laughs at l.' perjuries OVID 366:11
l.' absent hours SHAK 476:6
l. be lost love shall not THOM 546:19
l. cannot see SHAK 466:14
L. can see to do their SHAK 483:6
l.' ears in hearing SCOTT 416:26
l.' eyes are sharp SCOTT 416:26
l. fled away into the storm KEATS 289:23
l.' hours be full eternity DONNE 189:21
l., just at twelve, awake POPE 380:29
l. must Consign to thee SHAK 428:22
L.' rows make love whole TER 544:15
L., to bed SHAK 471:20
make two l. happy POPE 380:29
motions l.' seasons run DONNE 190:11
old l. are soundest WEBS 566:30
pair of star-cross'd l. SHAK 481:20
Thy l. were all untrue DRYD 197:19
timid l.' declarations AUDEN 20:2
two young l. lately wed TENN 538:7
We that are true l. SHAK 425:11
What need I wish for more SEDL 419:11
Loves: all the wings of the L. SWIN 530:4
any severing of our l. WORD 579:13
ar'n't that I l. the fox less SURT 525:10
A-waiting for their ain dear l. BALL 31:20
believe the baggage l. CONG 160:17
Fierce wars and faithful l. SPEN 515:29
Friends and l. we have MAS 334:7
girl whom he almost l. TROL 553:6
grete god of L. name CHAU 143:26
Hated by one he l. SHAK 451:23
He l. us not SHAK 462:12

He that l. a rosy cheek CAREW 130:12
hours and all strange l. SWIN 528:26
I l. him at once SURT 525:6
lines so l. oblique may MARV 331:19
l. and comforts should SHAK 474:20
l. him still the better GOLD 232:9
l. into corpses or wives SWIN 529:10
l. of men HOUS 265:4
l. the meat in his youth SHAK 472:18
l. to be flattered is worthy SHAK 485:28
l. to hear himself talk SHAK 482:24
man kills the thing he l. WILDE 572:10
man l. what he is good SHAD 420:22
one l. His world so much BROW 103:22
one that l. his fellow-men HUNT 268:5
others all the l. is love BYRON 122:25
She l. me dearly KEATS 289:5
That l. and saves her soul BROW 99:6
There is no creature l. me SHAK 481:15
truly l. on to the close MOORE 356:5
who l. me must have a touch TENN 534:26
Who l. not woman LUTH 321:1
who l. nothing but himself SOUT 514:15
Love-sick: L. all against our will GILB 227:19
winds were l. with them SHAK 422:2
lovesome: garden is a l. thing BROWN 95:12
lovest: I love all that thou l. SHEL 503:26
l. thou me more that these BIBLE 73:14
What thou l. well POUND 382:12
loveth: He made and l. all COL 155:30
he that l. another hath BIBLE 75:22
Lord l. he correcteth BIBLE 53:1
Lord l. he chasteneth BIBLE 80:1
l. a cheerful giver BIBLE 77:9
l. and maketh a lie BIBLE 83:3
sought him whom my soul l. BIBLE 56:25
that l. not knoweth not God BIBLE 81:5
loving: heart be still as l. BYRON 125:25
in love with l. AUG 21:12
l. himself better than COL 157:18
l. longest, when existence AUST 23:10
l. thou mayst loved be SPEN 516:13
man for l. himself BACON 27:8
most l. mere folly SHAK 426:1
night was made for l. BYRON 125:26
not stay the siege of l. SHAK 481:24
perfectly sore with l. DICK 178:1
so l. to my mother SHAK 429:28
too much l. you SHAK 475:19
who can help l. the land MOORE 356:2
wickedness that hinders l. BROW 102:31
loving-kindness: thy l. and mercy shall
PRAY 390:22
lov'st: Because thou l. the one BARN 34:2
low: condescend to men of l. estate
BIBLE 75:17
dost thou lie so l. SHAK 450:6
exalted them of l. degree BIBLE 69:6
hum of that l. land ARN 14:28
life in l. estate began TENN 537:1
l. estate of his handmaiden BIBLE 69:5
l. life was the level's BROW 100:33
l. on whom assurance sits ELIOT 205:1
Malice is of a l. stature HAL 238:2
Sweet and l. TENN 541:31
That l. man seeks a little BROW 100:38
to cast one's eyes so l. SHAK 455:14
Too l. for envy COWL 164:15
Lowells: L. talk only to Cabots BOSS 90:13
lowely: l., and servysable CHAU 141:13
Löwen: lachende L. müssen kommen
NIET 363:2
lower: if the l. orders don't WILDE 572:25
madest him l. than the angels PRAY 389:28
lowest: l. and most dejected thing SHAK 455:5
shame to take the l. room BIBLE 70:7
therefore the l. of the arts MOORE 355:17
Low-lands: she sails by the L. low BALL 31:2
lowliness: l. is young ambition's SHAK 449:5
lowly: I am meek and l. in heart BIBLE 66:5

in the l. air GILB 226:5
low-voiced: ears the l. Best is killed
HARDY 240:3
loyal: fruit Of l. nature TENN 534:9
L. and neutral, in a moment SHAK 461:2
loyalties: impossible l. ARN 15:25
l. which centre upon number one
CHUR 150:27
loyalty: learned body wanted l. TRAPP 552:5
Lucan: L., and Stace CHAU 144:17
Lucasta: L. that bright northern LOV 318:13
Then my L. might I crave LOV 318:19
lucem: sed ex fumo dare l. HOR 257:19
lucid: l. intervals and happy BACON 27:44
l. intervals of life WORD 577:5
l. intervals and make a l. interval DRYD 196:34
with frequent l. intervals CERV 138:16
lúcidos: lleno de l. intervalos CERV 138:16
Lucifer: he falls like L. SHAK 447:9
L., son of the morning BIBLE 58:13
L. that often warned them MILT 344:7
spirits that fell with L. MARL 329:6
starred night Prince L. uprose MER 337:5
luck: Has he l. NAP 359:16
have wished you good l. PRAY 398:3
light in ragged l. HENL 245:12
l. of our name lost with HOR 261:13
L.'s a chance HOUS 264:14
There's nae l. about the house ANON 8:3
watching his l. was his SERV 420:14
luckless: l. man CAT 137:4
Lucky: L. to touch it KIPL 302:19
supposed it l. to be born WHIT 570:19
lucrative: l. business of mystery
BURKE 108:12
lucre: not greedy of filthy l. BIBLE 79:12
lucro: dierum cumque dabit l. HOR 259:18
Lucy: 'If L. should be dead WORD 582:21
When L. ceased to be WORD 581:6
Luddites: quartern loaf and L. rise
SMITH 510:7
Ludlow: hundreds to L. come HOUS 263:6
I have been to L. fair HOUS 264:13
lug: l. the guts into the neighbour
SHAK 435:22
Lüge: Volkes...einer grossen L. HITL 251:9
lugere: non l., neque detestare SPIN 517:7
Lugete: L., O Veneres Cupidinesque
CAT 136:22
lugger: forcing her on board the l. JOHN 283:7
Luke: honour unto L. Evangelist ROSS 410:1
L., the beloved physician BIBLE 78:29
lukewarm: then because thou art l.
BIBLE 81:20
Lukewarmness: L. I account a sin
COWL 164:18
lull: l. in the hot race ARN 12:22
lullaby: dreamy l. GILB 226:18
I will sing a l. DEKK 173:22
lull'd: l. with sound of sweetest SHAK 441:29
Lulled: L. by the singer MORR 358:9
lumber: loads of learned l. POPE 378:30
l. of the schools SWIFT 527:32
lumen: l. de lumine MASS 334:20
luminous: beating in the void his l. wings
ARN 16:10
l. home of waters ARN 15:1
lump: leaveneth the whole l. BIBLE 75:35
l. bred up in darkness KYD 306:6
luna: te inferebatur sol et l. AUG 21:13
lunae: celeres reparant caelestia l.
HOR 261:16
Tacitae per amica silentia l. VIRG 558:3
lunar: l. world securely pry DRYD 195:23
lunatic: l., the lover SHAK 471:11
reform movement has a l. fringe ROOS 408:5
luncheon: dinner, l. BROW 103:19
gentleman has soup at l. CURZ 170:18
read a novel before l. WAUGH 566:5
Lunching: L. with poets BETJ 44:12

lune: l. ne garde aucune rancune ELIOT 204:10
lungs: dangerous to the l. JAM 271:3
even my l. are affected BEAR 35:11
gold and l. of bronze BELL 39:28
l. began to crow like chanticleer SHAK 425:20
l. of London PITT 374:2
Lupercal: On the L. SHAK 450:20
Lupus: L. est homo homini PLAU 374:13
lurcher: half l. and half cur COWP 167:18
lure: l. it back to cancel half FITZ 213:7
l. this tassel-gentle back SHAK 482:19
lurid: It is l. and melodramatic LAWR 311:11
luscious: now is as l. as locusts SHAK 474:10
over-canopied with l. woodbine SHAK 470:10
Lusisti: L. satis HOR 259:6
lust: commanded l. PETR 373:5
Delight of l. is gross YEATS 586:23
horrible that l. and rage HOPK 256:15
hutch of tasty l. MARV 332:19
into ashes all my l. SHAK 495:7
Is l. in action SWIN 520:10
love is more cruel than l. BAK 29:24
L. der Zerstörung ist FLEC 214:14
l. of knowing what should SHAK 454:18
l. of my mistress's heart BLAKE 88:21
l. of the goat is the bounty TENN 537:15
narrowing l. of gold TENN 535:18
That own no l. because PRAY 391:23
lusteth: man is he that l. to live PRAY 391:19
lustily: sing praises l. unto him PRAY 391:19
lusting: woman says to her l. lover CAT 137:7
lustre: accomplishments give l. CHES 145:31
Though changed in outward l. MILT 345:2
Where is thy l. now SHAK 455:4
lustres: six l. almost now outwore
DONNE 189:36
lusts: Abstain from fleshly l. BIBLE 80:24
led away with divers l. BIBLE 79:24
l. of your father ye will BIBLE 72:13
sinful l. of the flesh PRAY 388:13
to fulfil the l. thereof BIBLE 75:25
lust'st: hotly l. to use her SHAK 455:19
lusty: flourisheth in l. deeds MAL 328:1
l. stealth of nature SHAK 453:9
Of l. folk CHAU 143:20
young and l. as an eagle PRAY 396:15
lute: awake, l. and harp PRAY 393:16
bright Apollo's l. SHAK 457:8
lasciviousing of a l. SHAK 480:18
little rift within the l. TENN 535:7
l. its tones KEATS 289:3
merry harp with the l. PRAY 395:9
My l., awake WYATT 583:23
Orpheus with his l. made trees SHAK 447:3
When the l. is broken SHEL 501:21
When to her l. Corinna CAMP 129:17
lutes: to l. of amber HERR 250:9
Luther: Grand rough old Martin L.
BROW 105:27
L.; the Philistine ARN 16:23
Lutheran: spleeny L. SHAK 447:5
luve: he was the Queen's l. BALL 30:17
L.'s like a red red rose BURNS 114:27
L. will venture BURNS 114:33
lux: l. perpetua luceat eis MASS 334:17
Luxe: L., calme et volupté BAUD 35:7
luxuries: between l. and necessaries
GALB 220:28
Give us the l. of life MOTL 358:21
luxurious: damned and l. mountain goat
SHAK 445:4
exquisite sense of the l. KEATS 293:29
luxury: languages is mainly a l. BRIG 93:8
Love is like any other l. TROL 553:15
l., peace BAUD 35:7
their l. was doing good GARTH 221:20
They knew l. MAC 324:6
thinks it l. ADD 1:17
Lycid: laureate hearse where L. MILT 343:15
Lycidas: L. is dead MILT 343:2

So L. sunk low MILT 343:17
Lydian: Lap me in soft L. airs MILT 342:26
L. laughter of the Garda TENN 533:18
waters of the L. lake CAT 136:28
lye: wenen every thing a l. CHAU 143:28
lyf: That l. so short CHAU 143:32
lyght: hath reft the sonne his l. CHAU 142:13
lying: are to this vice of l. SHAK 442:9
l., and slandering PRAY 388:17
l. awake with a dismal GILB 226:12
not mind l. BUTL 119:5
One of you is l. PARK 368:19
this world is given to l. SHAK 440:27
lym: brach or l. SHAK 455:1
lynde: light as leef on l. CHAU 142:11
Lynn: stern-faced men set out from L.
HOOD 254:12
Lyonnesse: When I set out for L.
HARDY 241:5
lyre: drive a tune through the l. POUND 382:15
hang my weapons and my l. HOR 261:6
Make me thy l. SHEL 502:13
'Omer smote 'is bloomin' l. KIPL 304:4
lyres: sound of l. and flutes PATER 369:19
turn to rhythmic tidal l. HARDY 239:4
lyric: splendid ecclesiastical l. DISR 186:7
lyricis: Quodsi me l. vatibus inseres
HOR 259:10
lyve: worthy womman al hir l. CHAU 141:31
M: N or M. PRAY 388:12
Mab: This is M. JONS 284:15
Macaroni: called it M. BANGS 32:16
Macaulay: cocksure of anything as Tom
M. MELB 336:10
Lord M. ARN 16:6
M. is well for a while CARL 132:28
Macavity: there's no one like M.
ELIOT 203:26
Macbeth: Brave M. SHAK 458:3
M. does murder sleep SHAK 460:8
M. shall sleep no more SHAK 460:9
M. shall never vanquish'd SHAK 462:8
Shall harm M. SHAK 462:6
There to meet with M. SHAK 458:1
Macduff: Lay on, M. SHAK 463:8
M. was from his mother's SHAK 463:8
mace: that fool's bauble, the m. CROM 169:25
Macedon: There is a river in M. SHAK 445:5
Macedonia: Come over into M. BIBLE 74:6
MacGregor: my name is M. SCOTT 418:32
Machiavel: are much beholden to M.
BACON 24:25
machine: body is a m. for living TOLS 551:12
less of a taxing m. LOWE 318:24
m. for converting the Heathen CARL 131:6
maison est une m. à habiter LE C 313:5
of the Ghost in the m. RYLE 412:25
very pulse of the m. WORD 581:8
you're a m. SHAW 496:8
Machinery: It is the Age of M. CARL 131:5
whole m. of the State BROU 95:4
Mächte: ihr himmlischen M. GOET 230:12
mackerel: m.-crowded seas YEATS 586:11
Not so the m. FRERE 218:25
mackintosh: bit of black m. WELBY 567:17
mack'rel: blew a m. gale DRYD 196:20
maculate: Swelling to m. giraffe
ELIOT 204:14
mad: better than when I am m. KYD 306:5
created the English m. KIPL 300:10
destroy He first sends m. DUP 199:15
drive me m. on my deathbed BYRON 126:20
glad m. brother's SWIN 529:2
half of the nation is m. SMOL 512:12
has made me m. all my life JOHN 279:33
heroically m. DRYD 194:21
house for fools and m. SWIFT 527:25
How m. I am BETJ 44:6
I am but m. north-north-west SHAK 432:18
I shall go m. SHAK 454:2

it will make you m.   SHAK 450:25
laid to make the taker m.   SHAK 495:7
learning doth make thee m.   BIBLE 74:25
less m. on one point   KIPL 304:33
let me not be m.   SHAK 453:20
M. about the boy   COW 163:18
m. all are in God's keeping   KIPL 304:25
m. and savage master   SOPH 513:9
m., and sent into England   SHAK 436:30
m. as the vex'd sea   SHAK 455:13
M., bad   LAMB 306:25
M. dogs and Englishmen   COW 163:19
m. that trusts in the tameness   SHAK 454:28
m., 'tis true   SHAK 431:33
M. world   SHAK 452:13
Make m. the guilty   SHAK 433:1
makes men m.   SHAK 477:8
men that God made m.   CHES 146:17
nobly wild, not m.   HERR 249:13
old, m., blind   SHEL 504:6
sad and bad and m.   BROW 100:8
tends the grave of M. Carew   HAYES 243:7
this m., wicked folly   VICT 556:14
tho' some did count him m.   BUNY 107:34
to make poor females m.   SHAK 470:26
Went m. and bit the man   GOLD 231:13
when a heroine goes m.   SHER 506:3
Madagascar: There's Jerusalem and M.
    THAC 546:2
Madam: M. I may not call you   ELIZ 205:28
madden: midden whose odours will m.
    AUDEN 18:17
now m. to crime   BYRON 120:1
maddest: m. merriest day   TENN 540:30
m. of all mankind   KIPL 300:14
madding: Far from the m. crowd's
    GRAY 235:1
made: All things were m. by him BIBLE 71:22
almost m. for each other   SMITH 511:34
Begotten, not m.   PRAY 387:10
Dost thou know who m. thee   BLAKE 87:26
earth and the world were m.   PRAY 395:17
fearfully and wonderfully m.   PRAY 399:6
He m. and loveth all   COL 155:30
he m. the best of this   BURNS 113:26
In a world I never m.   HOUS 264:25
it is he that hath m. us   PRAY 396:11
knoweth whereof we are m.   PRAY 396:17
m. by the Lord Chancellor   JOHN 276:36
m. heaven and earth   PRAY 388:20
m. honest by an act   JONS 283:25
M. with our hands and our   SWIN 528:24
man was m. to mourn   BURNS 114:22
night was m. for loving   BYRON 125:26
see God m. and eaten   BROW 99:14
thinks he was not m. to die   TENN 535:30
which the Lord hath m.   PRAY 398:2
who m. the Lamb make thee   BLAKE 87:16
Why hast thou m. me thus   BIBLE 75:14
Madeira: M. and a cold capon's leg
    SHAK 438:11
Madhouse: I am in a M. and quite
    CLARE 152:17
in a m. there exists no   CLARE 152:7
Madhouses: M., prisons, whore-shops
    CLARE 152:5
madman: If a m. were to come into
    JOHN 277:1
m. shakes a dead geranium   ELIOT 204:9
Madmen: M. in authority   KEYN 295:20
of m. is a saint run mad   POPE 380:11
They were m.   REN 405:13
which none but m. know   DRYD 197:26
madness: always very close to m.   ALC 3:9
Anger is a short m.   HOR 258:15
any m. of their kings   HOR 258:12
cure for this sort of m.   BIRK 84:13
end despondency and m.   WORD 580:28
Even to m.   SHAK 474:22
fools accounted his life m.   BIBLE 62:16

from the cruel m. of love   TENN 539:29
Great wits are sure to m.   DRYD 194:6
His flight was m.   SHAK 462:11
His m. was not of the head   BYRON 125:2
it is m.   CONG 160:22
Love watching M. with unalterable
    BYRON 121:7
m. and her weather still   AUDEN 19:6
m. is the glory of this   SHAK 486:4
m. of many for the gain   POPE 381:16
m. of the people   PRAY 394:1
m. wherein now he raves   SHAK 432:2
moon-struck m.   MILT 349:24
My love's a noble m.   DRYD 195:11
Such harmonious m.   SHEL 504:24
that any m. I ever yet   SHAK 469:14
that fine m. still he did   DRAY 193:14
that way m. lies   SHAK 454:14
this is very midsummer m.   SHAK 490:6
Though this be m.   SHAK 432:9
Thro' cells of m.   TENN 540:16
To define true m.   SHAK 431:31
work like m. in the brain   COL 156:4
Madoc: M. will be read   PORS 381:28
Madonnas: he only used to draw M.
    BROW 102:28
their Rafael of the dear M.   BROW 103:1
madrigal: Sing a merry m.   GILB 227:1
What woeful stuff this m.   POPE 378:25
madrigals: Melodious birds sing m.
    MARL 330:1
silence all the airs and m.   MILT 351:25
Maecenas: M. atavis edite regibus HOR 259:8
Maenad: M. and the Bassarid   SWIN 528:18
Of some fierce M.   SHEL 502:9
Maeonides: old M. the blind   FLEC 214:22
maestro: Il m. di color che sanno
    DANTE 171:7
Maeves: Julias, M. and Maureens BETJ 43:7
magazines: graves of little m.   PRES 400:14
Magdalen: fourteen months at M. College
    GIBB 224:7
manufactures of the monks of M. GIBB 224:8
maggot: m. must be born i'   ELIOT 200:15
me full of m. ostentation   SHAK 457:15
maggot-pies: m. and choughs and rooks
    SHAK 461:24
maggots: you not m. in your brains
    FLET 215:26
magic: If this be m.   SHAK 492:12
I'm a dealer in m.   GILB 229:2
nothing but a M. Shadow-show   FITZ 213:3
rough m. I here abjure   SHAK 485:24
secret m. of numbers   BROW 96:11
there's m. in the web of it   SHAK 476:4
what mighty m.   SHAK 473:24
With a m. like thee   BYRON 125:27
With m. in my eyes   HARDY 241:6
Maginn: kind William M.   LOCK 315:23
magistrate: m. corruptible   ROB 406:12
magistrates: like m., correct at home
    SHAK 443:9
magistri: iurare in verba m.   HOR 258:7
magna: Et quorum pars m. fui   VIRG 557:21
M. est veritas   BIBLE 83:26
Magna Carta: Bible under one arm and
M.   AUBR 17:23
Magna Charta: M. is such a fellow
    COKE 154:16
magnanimity: In all the m. of thought
    YOUNG 588:5
in victory, m.   CHUR 150:25
M. in politics is not seldom   BURKE 110:6
you might curb your m.   KEATS 294:31
magnanimos: Glubit m. Remi nepotes
    CAT 137:5
magnanimous: m. at an inopportune
time   TROT 553:17
magnanimously: skilfully and m. all
    MILT 352:8

magnet: Can m. ever   GILB 227:24
printing, gunpowder and the m.   BACON 28:9
magnetic: m., Peripatetic Lover   GILB 227:24
magnetism: doubt as to animal m.
    COL 157:34
Magnificat: M. anima mea Dominum
    BIBLE 83:17
magnificent: It is m.   BOSQ 90:12
mild and m. eye   BROW 102:5
Mute and m.   DRYD 197:29
magnifico: atque omne ignotum pro m.
    TAC 531:6
magnifique: C'est m.   BOSQ 90:12
magnify: My soul doth m. the Lord
    BIBLE 83:17
praise him, and m.   PRAY 384:21
soul doth m. the Lord   BIBLE 69:5
we laud and m. thy glorious   PRAY 387:23
we m. thee   PRAY 384:18
worthily m. thy holy Name   PRAY 387:7
magnis: parva licet componere m.
    VIRG 560:19
Magnus: M. ab integro saeclorum
    VIRG 559:22
walls Of M. Martyr   ELIOT 205:4
Magus: M. Zoroaster   SHEL 502:19
Mahomet: M. will go to the hill BACON 25:33
maid: Bare-footed came the beggar m.
    TENN 532:16
dried and a m. not vendible   SHAK 465:14
frozen m.   GARR 221:16
had a m. call'd Barbara   SHAK 476:26
I once was a m.   BURNS 114:17
is the m. ov all maïdens   BARN 33:30
lazy finger of a m.   SHAK 481:28
m. forget her ornaments   BIBLE 60:15
m. is not dead, but sleepeth   BIBLE 65:27
M. of Athens   BYRON 125:3
m. sing in the valley   ANON 5:3
m. Subdues me   SHAK 464:6
m. whom there were none   WORD 581:6
She could not live a m.   PEELE 371:9
There was a fair m. dwellin'   BALL 30:10
way of a man with a m.   BIBLE 55:1
way of a man with a m.   KIPL 301:1
Whether a m. so tender   SHAK 473:24
Yonder a m. and her wight   HARDY 240:5
maiden: Else would a m. blush bepaint
    SHAK 482:11
flesh'd Thy m. sword   SHAK 440:26
Here's not a modest m. elf   HARDY 240:7
In m. meditation   SHAK 470:8
I pursued a m. and clasped   SHEL 501:4
Is as the m.'s organ   SHAK 488:3
m. hid   SWIN 528:18
m. modesty would float   HUXL 268:23
m. never bold   SHAK 473:24
m. of bashful fifteen   SHER 506:31
rare and radiant m. whom   POE 375:5
shall be the m.'s fate   SCOTT 416:12
simple m. in her flower   TENN 537:27
sweeter m. in a cleaner   KIPL 301:7
This m. she lived with   POE 374:21
undergo such m. pilgrimage   SHAK 469:12
village m. she   TENN 539:10
maidenly: So joyously, So m.   SKEL 508:12
maidens: all the m. pretty   COLM 158:25
Conserv'd of m.' hearts   SHAK 476:4
is the maïd ov all m.   BARN 33:30
...M. aspiring to godheads   STOP 523:15
Twenty love-sick m. we   GILB 227:19
What m. loth   KEATS 291:3
Young men and m.   PRAY 399:23
maids: Immortal youth to mortal m.
    LAND 308:22
m. and village hinds shall   COLL 158:16
m. are May when they are   SHAK 426:23
m. strange seraphic pieces   TRAH 551:19
Most incident to m.   SHAK 491:26
seven m. with seven mops   CARR 135:5

Three little m. from school	GILB 226:27
when m. lie on their backs	SHAK 481:28
maidservant: nor thy m.	BIBLE 47:24
Maid-servants: M., I hear people complaining	CARL 131:38
mail: like a rusty m.	SHAK 487:4
This is the Night M. crossing	AUDEN 20:1
mailed: seen the m. lobster rise	FRERE 218:26
maimed: m., and the halt	BIBLE 70:12
main: brook Into the m.	SHAK 468:18
flooding in, the m.	CLOU 154:4
froth amid the boundless m.	BRON 93:20
Glorious th' enraptur'd m.	SMART 509:4
lost evermore in the m.	TENN 543:5
maintain: m. mine own ways before	BIBLE 52:25
maintained: I m. myself thus solely	THOR 550:13
Maior: M. privato visus dum privatus	TAC 531:13
maiorum: Delicta m. immeritus lues	HOR 260:25
mair: m. they talk I'm kent	BURNS 114:32
Maire: Thy famous M.	DUNB 199:12
Maisie: Proud M. is in the wood	SCOTT 418:21
maison: m. est une machine à habiter	LE C 313:5
Maister: do not M. or Campbell me	SCOTT 418:32
That love is m. wher he	GOWER 233:6
maistrye: been constreyned by m.	CHAU 142:12
maîtresses: j'aurai des m.	GEOR 223:35
maize: hand with Plenty in the m.	TENN 542:16
	TENN 533:5
m. and vine	ARN 14:28
majestic: m. River floated	MILT 346:14
M. though in ruin	SHAK 444:25
majestical: laid in bed m.	
majestueuse: m. égalité des lois	FRAN 217:26
Majesty: appearance of Your M.	BIBLE 44:21
his m. is	BIBLE 62:22
if his m. our sovereign	ANON 8:24
m. of human suffering	VIGNY 557:1
M.: of thy Glory	PRAY 384:16
Reynolds to his M.'s head	MAC 324:2
right hand of the M.	BIBLE 79:28
sight so touching in its m.	WORD 581:14
This earth of m.	SHAK 478:20
want love's m.	SHAK 480:18
Major-General: model of a modern M.	GILB 228:16
majorité: est toujours dans la m.	KNOX 305:18
majorities: action Wisdom goes by m.	MER 337:35
majority: ain't that a big enough m.	TWAIN 554:3
damned, compact, liberal m.	IBSEN 269:17
Door— To her divine M.	DICK 183:21
has gone over to the m.	CARL 131:11
He's gone to join the m.	PETR 373:1
indifferent and self-indulgent m.	STEP 518:20
joins us to the great m.	YOUNG 588:13
m. has the might	IBSEN 269:18
m. is always the best repartee	DISR 186:35
Majors: with scarlet M. at the Base	SASS 414:10
make: I could not well m. out	SOUT 513:17
I m. it constantly	PROU 401:22
I too will something m.	BRID 92:10
joint stools to m. faces	JOHN 276:30
king may m. a nobleman	BURKE 111:37
lest he should m. an end	JONS 285:2
m. a better mouse-trap	EMER 208:5
m. an end the sooner	BACON 26:6
m. both ends meet	FULL 220:12
m. his sword to approach	BIBLE 53:9
M. me a clean heart	PRAY 393:6

M. mouths upon me when	SHAK 470:23
m. myself laugh at everything	BEAU 35:15
m. the most of what we	FITZ 212:18
m. thine own	ARN 13:11
M. yourself necessary	EMER 207:3
man will m. more opportunities	BACON 25:38
not m. a new acquaintance	JOHN 279:25
not m. new acquaintance	JOHN 274:15
than a Scotsman on the m.	BARR 34:21
To m. bad good	SHAK 464:22
maked: God first m. man	CHAU 143:1
Maker: before the Lord our M.	PRAY 396:4
be more pure than his m.	BIBLE 52:16
his M.'s image through	DRYD 194:2
Laudes to their m. early	HAWES 243:2
m. and builder is God	BIBLE 79:32
m. buried	STEV 523:1
m. is hymself ybeten	CHAU 144:2
M. of heaven and earth	PRAY 384:26
M. of heaven and earth	PRAY 387:10
m. of his own fortune	STEE 518:7
meet my M. brow to brow	CORN 162:19
that sinneth before his M.	BIBLE 63:18
that striveth with his m.	BIBLE 59:13
makes: He m. a solitude	BYRON 120:4
m. no mistakes does not	PHEL 373:7
m. the happiness she does	JOHN 283:6
night That either m. me	SHAK 477:4
makest: What m. thou	BIBLE 59:13
maketh: loveth and m. a lie	BIBLE 83:3
making: Holland take pleasure in m.	ANON 7:22
joy in the m.	BRID 92:10
M. peace is harder than	STEV 520:21
That I shall be past m.	PRIOR 401:7
There came to the m. of man	SWIN 528:20
makings: royal m. of a queen	SHAK 447:14
Makler: Ehrlicher M.	BISM 84:23
mal: connaître tout le m. qu'il fait	LA R 310:14
mala: Usque ad m.	HOR 262:1
malade: sur les bras un homme m.	NICH 362:22
malades: aime à dépêcher ses m.	MOL 353:21
maladie: l'honneur n'est qu'une m.	RAC 404:6
m. dont le sommeil nous	CHAM 139:13
malady: love's a m. without a cure	DRYD 197:6
m. of not marking	SHAK 441:7
medicine worse than the m.	FLET 215:16
male: especially the m. of the species	LAWR 311:6
M. and female created	BIBLE 45:5
m. and the female	BIBLE 45:34
more deadly than the m.	KIPL 299:4
rough m. kiss of blankets	BROO 94:8
malecontents: of all loiterers and m.	SHAK 456:26
malefactions: have proclaim'd their m.	SHAK 433:5
males: Nothing but m.	SHAK 459:11
malesuada: Metus et m. Fames	VIRG 558:21
Malfi: Duchess of M. still	WEBS 566:24
Malherbe: At last came M.	BOIL 89:10
malheur: Tout le m. des hommes vient	PASC 369:5
malheureux: jamais si m. qu'on croit	LA R 310:18
malheurs: tableau des crimes et des m.	VOLT 561:10
mali: Non ignara m. miseris succurrere	VIRG 557:19
malice: from envy, hatred, and m.	PRAY 385:16
leaven of m. and wickedness	BIBLE 75:36
leaven of m. and wickedness	PRAY 386:11
M. is of a low stature	HAL 238:2
m., to breed causes	JONS 285:15
Much m. mingled with	DRYD 196:17

Nor set down aught in m.	SHAK 477:23
Pride, Envy, M.	LAND 308:17
With m. toward none	LINC 315:3
Yet m. never was his aim	SWIFT 527:24
malignity: motive-hunting of motiveless m.	COL 157:28
with a m. truly diabolical	BURKE 108:20
Mall: like Mistress M.'s picture	SHAK 488:1
mallard: swapping, swapping m.	ANON 7:28
mallecho: this is miching m.	SHAK 434:9
mallow: slimy m. waves her silky	COWP 168:26
Malmesey: drowned in a barrel of M.	FABY 209:17
Malmsey: Of M. and Malvoisie	BELL 38:22
Malo: M. me Galatea petit	VIRG 559:18
Sed libera nos a m.	MASS 335:5
malorum: religio potuit suadere m.	LUCR 320:4
malt: m. does more than Milton	HOUS 264:12
Maluerne: on a May morwenyng on M.	LANG 309:25
Malvoisie: Of Malmsey and M.	BELL 38:22
Mama: M. came and made a scene	DICK 178:18
m. of dada	FAD 209:18
mammets: play with m.	SHAK 438:31
mammon: authentic m. than a bogus god	MACN 326:4
cannot serve God and m.	BIBLE 64:27
friends of the m. of unrighteousness	BIBLE 70:26
M. led them	MILT 345:26
man: All know the m. their neighbour	YEATS 586:14
all that makes a m.	TENN 534:12
All that m. is	YEATS 584:12
all that may become a m.	SHAK 459:9
ambition of m.	RAL 404:16
apparel oft proclaims the m.	SHAK 430:19
Arms, and the m.	DRYD 198:22
Around the m. bend other	LAND 308:17
be a m.	ARN 13:1
become a m.'s friend only	CHEK 145:5
become the servant of a m.	SHAW 496:27
Before M. made us citizens	LOW 319:11
be M. and Wife together	PRAY 389:7
better angel is a m. right	SHAK 495:12
between a m. and a woman	GIBB 225:4
Blessed is the m. that	PRAY 389:14
Blessed is the m. unto	PRAY 391:16
bold bad m.	SHAK 447:1
bold bad m.	SPEN 516:1
borne me a m. of strife	BIBLE 60:23
came to the making of m.	SWIN 528:20
Cannot a plain m. live	SHAK 480:23
centaur, m. and wife	BYRON 123:19
childhood shows the m.	MILT 350:7
Child is father of the M.	WORD 578:19
coiner the mintage of m.	HOUS 263:8
coming of the Son of M.	BIBLE 67:32
Cristen m. shall wedde	CHAU 143:17
crucify the old m.	PRAY 388:10
cruelty To load a falling m.	SHAK 447:25
deaf m. to a blind	COL 157:19
delighteth he in any m.'s legs	PRAY 399:20
detest that animal called m.	SWIFT 526:21
dog bites a m.	BOG 89:9
Ech m. for hymself	CHAU 142:16
encompass'd but one m.	SHAK 448:19
end try the m.	SHAK 441:23
Eustace is a m. no longer	KING 297:16
exclusively for the use of m.	PEAC 370:15
eye 'tis an old M. grey	BLAKE 86:14
Feeds beast as m.	SHAK 421:8
figure of 'The Reasonable M.	HERB 246:13
first m. is of the earth	BIBLE 76:28
forgetteth what manner of m.	BIBLE 80:10
garment from the m.	BLAKE 86:1
get out the m.	POPE 375:24

manger: laid him in a m.   BIBLE 69:9
m. pour vivre et non pas   MOL 353:2
not too cleanly, m.   CRAS 169:7
One born in a m.   VAUG 555:13
still lodge Him in the m.   ANON 9:1
manges: *Dis-moi ce que tu m.*   BRIL 93:9
Mangle: immense pecuniary M.   DICK 183:6
mangled: vents In m. forms   SHAK 425:21
mangler: m. in a million million   DICK 181:16
mangrove: m. swamps where the python   COW 163:20
manhood: ancient customs and its m.   ENN 208:23
conspiracy against the m.   EMER 207:36
hardened into the bone of m.   BURKE 109:17
M. a struggle   DISR 185:40
M. taken by the Son   NEWM 362:11
sounder piece of British m.   CARL 131:14
strife comes with m.   SCOTT 416:25
touching his M.   PRAY 385:14
manhoods: m. cheap whiles any speaks   SHAK 445:3
maniac: m. scattering dust   TENN 536:21
manifest: love from love made m.   BROW 100:10
m. destiny to overspread   OSUL 365:23
manifesto: plain m.   SPEN 515:13
manifold: how m. are thy works   PRAY 397:1
our m. sins and wickedness   PRAY 384:9
sundry and m. changes   PRAY 386:12
man-in-the-street: To the m.   AUDEN 20:13
manjar: *m. que quita la hambre*   CERV 138:20
mankind: apple damn'd m.   OTWAY 366:2
careless of m.   TENN 539:16
crucify m. upon a cross   BRYAN 106:8
dissensions and animosities of m.   BURKE 111:3
Ellum she hateth m.   KIPL 303:26
Example is the school of m.   BURKE 112:7
How beauteous m. is   SHAK 485:26
legislator of m.   JOHN 282:7
M. always sets itself on   MARX 333:7
M. is divisible into two   BEER 37:17
misfortunes of m.   GIBB 224:23
need not be to hate, m.   BYRON 120:34
of all m.   BALL 31:9
one giant leap for m.   ARMS 12:18
our countrymen are all m.   GARR 221:18
put m. and posterity most   INGE 270:10
rather as a spectator of m.   ADD 2:8
ride m.   EMER 206:21
superfluities of m.   GAY 222:24
th'original perus'd m.   ARMS 12:15
which m. are warranted   MILL 339:6
willing to love all m.   JOHN 277:30
manliness: silent m. of grief   GOLD 231:6
Manlio: *nata mecum consule M.*   HOR 261:5
manly: childish valourous than m.   MARL 330:15
full likely to be a m.   MAL 327:17
man-milliner: respectable architectural m.   RUSK 411:5
manna: He rained down m. also   PRAY 395:6
his tongue Dropt m.   MILT 346:9
news, the m. of a day   GREEN 235:29
We loathe our m.   DRYD 197:2
manned: m. by Manning and new-manned   BROW 104:17
manner: in this extraordinary m.   STOP 523:17
m. of his speech   SHAK 421:34
m. rude and wild   BELL 38:25
m. which is my aversion   BYRON 123:6
shall be well and all m.   JUL 286:32
Socratic m. is not a game   BEER 38:4
stolzer M. der Tat   HEINE 244:12
This m. of writing where   MILT 352:13
to the m. born   SHAK 430:23
manners: by his m.   SPEN 516:23
catch the m. living   POPE 379:2
communications corrupt good m.   BIBLE 76:25

evil m. live in brass   SHAK 447:20
good m. to mention here   BROWN 95:8
Her m. had not that repose   TENN 537:28
His m. are not so polite   KIPL 301:19
influenced m. in England   BURKE 111:15
Leave off first for m.'   BIBLE 63:14
m. are not idle   TENN 534:9
m. of a dancing master   JOHN 274:10
m. of a Marquis with   GILB 228:33
not men, but m.   FIEL 211:14
Of m. gentle   POPE 378:8
old m.   GOLD 232:19
polish'd m. and fine sense   COWP 167:28
printing thereby to rectify m.   MILT 351:25
take their m. from the Ape   BELL 38:26
talk and Peel has no m.   WELL 567:31
times! Oh, the m.   CIC 151:26
uncouth m.   BURKE 109:15
With sweeter m.   TENN 537:15
Manning: manned by M. and new-manned   BROW 104:17
Manningtree: M. ox with the pudding   SHAK 439:16
manque: *Un seul être vous m.*   LAM 306:24
manservant: thy m.   BIBLE 47:24
mansion: Love has pitched his m.   YEATS 584:19
made his everlasting m.   SHAK 486:14
m. call the fleeting breath   GRAY 234:22
My m. is   MILT 340:22
upon thy fading m. spend   SHAK 495:13
mansions: Father's house are many m.   BIBLE 72:31
lasting m. of the dead   COWP 168:10
mantle: cast his m. upon him   BIBLE 51:15
dark her silver m. threw   MILT 348:2
Do cream and m. like   SHAK 465:12
in russet m. clad   SHAK 429:18
m. muffling up his face   SHAK 450:28
You all do know this m.   SHAK 450:26
Mantovano: I salute thee, M.   TENN 543:18
Mantuan: old M.   SHAK 457:2
manufacture: that no legislature can m.   BAG 28:21
manunkind: busy monster, m.   CUMM 170:11
manure: It is its natural m.   JEFF 272:10
manuscript: m. put away at home   HOR 258:6
Youth's sweet-scented M.   FITZ 213:15
manuscripts: brown Greek m.   BROW 99:13
many: 'Complaints is m. and various   GRAV 234:12
desire and m. things to fear   BACON 26:8
m. are called   BIBLE 67:18
m. for the remission   PRAY 388:1
m. (questionless) canonized   BROW 96:17
m. still must labour   BYRON 121:30
M. things I thought   HOUS 265:4
m. ways out   SEN 420:9
owed by so m. to so few   CHUR 150:2
So m. worlds   TENN 537:2
There's m. a good tune played   BUTL 119:15
we are m.   BIBLE 68:30
What are they among so m.   BIBLE 72:4
What m. men desire   SHAK 466:17
why he makes so m. of them   LINC 315:5
Ye are m.—they are few   SHEL 502:4
many-colour'd: change of m. life he drew   JOHN 282:25
many-splendoured: That miss the m. thing   THOM 548:25
map: Lord would use a larger m.   SAL 413:20
M. me no maps   FIEL 211:21
m. with the augmentation   SHAK 490:3
Roll up that m.   PITT 374:6
maps: geographers, in Afric-m.   SWIFT 528:2
Geography is about m.   BENT 41:3
mar: m. all with this starting   SHAK 462:21
Marabar: echo in a M. cave   FORS 217:8
Maran-atha: Let him be Anathema M.   BIBLE 77:3

Marathon: M. looks on the sea   BYRON 122:33
marble: dwelt in m. halls   BUNN 107:9
Glowed on the m.   ELIOT 204:23
hovel to your dreary m.   CALV 127:22
I am m.-constant   SHAK 424:4
it brick and left it m.   AUG 22:5
knew that m. bled   FLEC 214:15
legs are as pillars of m.   BIBLE 57:4
m. eyelids are not wet   BROW 98:8
m. index of a mind   WORD 580:17
m. to retain   BYRON 119:31
mould from m. living faces   VIRG 559:1
need of all this m. crust   MARV 332:21
Not m.   SHAK 493:17
slate more than hard m.   DU B 198:27
marbled: Place me on Sunium's m.   BYRON 123:4
marbly: mistresses with great smooth m. limbs   BROW 99:13
marbre: *Plus que le m. dur me plaist*   DU B 198:27
Marcellus: *Tu M. eris*   VIRG 559:2
March: ashbuds in the front of M.   TENN 533:19
Beware the ides of M.   SHAK 448:7
Did m. to the seige   BALL 31:8
dinna ye m. forward in order   SCOTT 418:24
droghte of M. hath perced   CHAU 141:7
England are M. and April   TROL 552:21
ides of M. are come   SHAK 449:23
m. of intellect   SOUT 514:13
m. of mind has marched   PEAC 370:13
m. of the human mind is   BURKE 109:29
m. through rapine to disintegration   GLAD 229:15
Men who m. away   HARDY 240:8
sea-blue bird of M.   TENN 537:9
That highte M.   CHAU 143:1
three hours' m. to dinner   HAZL 243:32
We shall m. prospering   BROW 102:6
winds of M. with beauty   SHAK 491:26
March-bloom: Look! M.   HOPK 256:29
marched: Around the ancient track m.   MER 337:5
East at heel is m. from   HOUS 265:3
m. breast forward   BROW 98:32
M. into their land   AYT 24:6
M. them along   BROW 99:26
Märchen: *Ein M. aus alten Zeiten*   HEINE 244:9
marches: army m. on its stomach   ANON 9:3
Funeral m. to the grave   LONG 317:2
hunger, thirst, forced m.   GAR 221:10
marching: 'Tis the people m.   MORR 358:7
us by m. where it likes   ARN 15:20
marcie: *fame, sete, m. forzate*   GAR 221:10
mare: *animum mutant qui trans m.*   HOR 258:19
brought him a Flanders m.   HENR 246:2
lend me your grey m.   BALL 32:12
man shall have his m. again   SHAK 471:1
Marengo: this is our M.   DOYLE 192:17
Margaret: It is M. you mourn   HOPK 256:27
so kind, As Merry M.   SKEL 508:16
Margate: 'Twas in M. last July   BARH 33:19
marge: page having an ample m.   TENN 535:12
margin: through a meadow of m.   SHER 506:26
mari: *m. magno turbantibus aequora*   LUCR 320:21
With an *Ave M.*   SKEL 508:19
Maria: *Ave M.*   ANON 10:8
dulcis virgo M.   ANON 10:19
ex M. Virgine   MASS 334:20
mariage: *cadrent mal avec le m.*   MOL 353:13
speke of wo that is in m.   CHAU 143:16
mariages: *Il y a de bons m.*   LA R 310:11

Mariana: resides this dejected M.
　　　　　　　　　　　　　　SHAK 464:18
Marie Hamilton: M.'s to the kirk gane
　　　　　　　　　　　　　　BALL 31:11
Maries: Yestreen the Queen had four
　　M.　　　　　　　　　　BALL 31:12
Marie Seaton: There was M.　BALL 31:12
marigold: m., that goes to bed wi'
　　　　　　　　　　　　　　SHAK 491:25
marijuana: of m. in his hair　LOW 319:20
mariner: haul and draw with the m.
　　　　　　　　　　　　　　DRAKE 193:4
It is an ancient M.　　　　　COL 155:5
mariners: My m.　　　　　TENN 544:3
rest ye, brother m.　　　　　TENN 539:17
Ye M. of England　　　　　CAMP 129:12
Marion: M.'s nose looks red　SHAK 457:19
marjoram: savory, m.　　　SHAK 491:25
mark: He hath no drowning m.　SHAK 484:21
hundred m. is a long one　　SHAK 441:18
I press toward the m.　　　　BIBLE 78:18
Lord set a m. upon Cain　　BIBLE 45:28
man's distinctive m. alone　BROW 100:11
m., learn　　　　　　　　　PRAY 386:5
m. me how I will undo myself　SHAK 480:1
m. of insincerity of purpose　BRAM 91:18
M. well her bulwarks　　　PRAY 392:27
not a m.　　　　　　　　　ROST 410:12
That M. our place　　　　　MCCR 324:30
wilt be extreme to m. what　PRAY 398:23
market: knowledge is bought in the m.
　　　　　　　　　　　　　　CLOU 153:18
love salutations in the m.places　BIBLE 68:37
take ingots with us to m.　　CHAM 139:14
market-place: Antony, Enthron'd i' the
　　m.　　　　　　　　　　SHAK 422:3
Decreed in the m.　　　　　POUND 383:8
eat his heart in the m.　　　SHAK 473:3
markets: laws of m. and fashion　ALB 3:7
When the great m.　　　　FLEC 214:10
marking: malady of not m.　SHAK 441:7
marks: m. and scars I carry with
　　　　　　　　　　　　　　BUNY 107:38
terrible m. of the beast　　HARDY 241:17
marl: to a clod of wayward m.　SHAK 472:4
Marlbro: M.'s mighty soul was prov'd
　　　　　　　　　　　　　　ADD 1:13
praise the Duke of M. won　SOUT 513:19
Marlb'rough: M.'s eyes the streams
　　　　　　　　　　　　　　JOHN 283:3
marle: Over the burning m.　MILT 345:12
Marlowe: M.'s mighty line　JONS 284:20
marmasyte: Call Tullia's ape a m.
　　　　　　　　　　　　　　ANON 5:18
Marmion: Were the last words of M.
　　　　　　　　　　　　　　SCOTT 417:22
Marquis: combines the manners of a
　　M.　　　　　　　　　　GILB 228:33
marred: All that's spoke is m.　SHAK 478:1
married is a man that's m.　SHAK 421:1
marriage: be incontinent before m.
　　　　　　　　　　　　　　SHAK 426:27
blessings of m.　　　　　SHAW 497:32
comedies are ended by a m.　BYRON 122:28
Courtship to m.　　　　　CONG 160:29
curse of m.　　　　　　　SHAK 475:21
every m. then is best　　　WATK 565:7
fall in with the m.-procession　CLOU 153:10
funeral and with dirge in m.　SHAK 429:19
furnish forth the m. tables　SHAK 430:4
Hanging and m.　　　　　FARQ 210:19
hanging prevents a bad m.　SHAK 488:4
her fortune by way of m.　FIEL 211:29
In m., a man becomes slack　STEV 521:24
Is not m. an open question　EMER 208:6
joys of m. are the heaven　FORD 216:14
long monotony of m.　　　GIBB 225:4
m. and death and division　SWIN 529:10
M. from love, like vinegar　BYRON 122:26
M. has many pains　　　　JOHN 282:9

M. is a step so grave　　　STEV 521:30
M. is like life in this　　　STEV 521:31
M. is nothing but a civil　SELD 419:23
M. is popular because it　SHAW 497:39
M. is the result　　　　　CAMP 128:9
M. is the waste-paper basket　WEBB 566:8
m. than a ministry　　　　BAG 28:29
m. vows As false　　　　　SHAK 435:4
m. with his brother's wife　SHAK 446:28
most happy m. I can picture　COL 157:19
My definition of m.　　　SMITH 511:11
nor are given in m.　　　BIBLE 67:21
nor are given in m.　　　SWIFT 527:9
of m. that we find all　　JOHN 276:2
Second M. in my house　FITZ 213:1
termed a *left-handed*.　WOLL 576:12
that is m., Lily thought　WOOLF 576:19
think there is any in m.　GAY 222:32
Tho' m. makes man and wife　CONG 159:23
to the m. of true minds　SHAK 495:5
Was m. ever out of fashion　BUTL 118:8
woman dictates before m.　ELIOT 201:6
marriages: best maker of all m.　SHAK 445:14
M. would in general be　JOHN 276:36
taste for m. and public executions
　　　　　　　　　　　　　　DISR 186:25
their m. with other men　TROL 553:10
There are good m.　　　　LA R 310:11
we will have no more m.　SHAK 433:14
why so few m. are happy　SWIFT 527:10
marrid: m. man dies in good stile
　　　　　　　　　　　　　　WARD 564:30
married: Charlotte was a m. lady　THAC 546:3
fool at least in every m.　FIEL 211:7
fourteen I m. My Lord　POUND 383:16
had no taste when you m.　SHER 506:27
He's the most m. man　WARD 564:32
if ever we had been m.　GAY 222:13
if we were not m. at all　CONG 161:7
I m. him　　　　　　　　BRON 93:15
imprudently m. the barber　FOOTE 216:7
I'm to be m. to-day　　　GILB 225:33
I would be m. to a single　CRAS 169:9
kiss before they are m.　SHAK 445:15
let us be m.　　　　　　LEAR 312:12
like to be m. to a poem　KEATS 294:20
m. and brought up a large　GOLD 232:32
m., charming, chaste　BYRON 122:8
m. is a man that's marred　SHAK 421:1
m. life three is company　WILDE 572:28
m. past redemption　　　DRYD 197:1
M. to immortal verse　　MILT 342:26
m. with mine uncle　　　SHAK 429:28
M. women are kept women　SMITH 510:16
Mocks m. men　　　　　SHAK 457:18
mostly m. people　　　　CLOU 153:23
One was never m.　　　BURT 116:23
Reading goes ill with the m.　MOL 353:13
say what delight we m.　PEPYS 372:15
she has m. a sot　　　　POUND 382:5
should live till I were m.　SHAK 472:19
Some were m.　　　　　KIPL 304:30
so rails against all m.　SHAK 469:14
So they were m.　　　　MACN 326:12
that are going to be m.　GOLD 232:17
They are m.　　　　　　CLOU 153:19
Three daughters m.　　AUST 23:23
Trade Unionism of the m.　SHAW 497:31
Unpleasing to a m. ear　SHAK 457:18
wench who is just m.　GAY 222:9
Wen you're a m. man　DICK 182:7
woman's business to get m.　SHAW 497:25
marries: changed with him who m.
　　　　　　　　　　　　　　STEV 521:32
much signify whom one m.　ROG 407:11
When a man m.　　　　SHEL 501:19
marrow: of fat things full of m.　BIBLE 58:18
suck out all the m.　　　THOR 550:16
marry: better to m. than to burn　BIBLE 76:2
Carlyle and Mrs Carlyle m.　BUTL 119:22

'Doänt thou m. for munny　TENN 541:1
Every woman should m.　DISR 186:22
How can a bishop m.　SMITH 511:4
I should m. twenty husbands　SHAK 465:23
it in my heart to m. thee　CONG 160:28
it was sure to m. a market-gardener
　　　　　　　　　　　　　　DICK 180:29
Man may not m. his Mother　PRAY 400:13
m. a landlord's daughter　LAMB 308:7
m. a rich woman as a poor　THAC 545:14
M. my body to that dust　KING 296:11
m. with his brother　　　SHAK 435:2
m. your old friend's love　BROW 105:17
may m. whom she likes　THAC 545:21
men that women m.　　LONG 316:21
never know who they may m.　MITF 352:23
persons about to m..—'Don't　PUNCH 402:10
quite prepared to m. again　GILB 226:3
resurrection they neither m.　BIBLE 67:21
that they neither m.　　SWIFT 527:9
to m. any vun among them　DICK 183:2
To m. is to domesticate　STEV 521:33
when a man should m.　BACON 26:35
Where I m., cannot love　MOORE 356:22
while ye may, go m.　　HERR 250:6
woman should m. a teetotaller　STEV 521:29
would advise no man to m.　JOHN 280:13
you do *not* m. Mr Collins　AUST 23:15
marry'd: At leisure m.　CONG 160:27
his throat before he m.　SWIFT 528:9
M. in haste　　　　　　CONG 160:27
marrying: Alice is m. one of the guard
　　　　　　　　　　　　　　MILNE 340:4
m. and giving in marriage　BIBLE 67:32
they aren't the m. brand　KIPL 301:9
mars: m. creation's plan　CANN 130:3
M. to Crab-spawn found　GRAV 234:12
Marsala: drinks a good deal of M.
　　　　　　　　　　　　　　LEAR 311:22
marshal: baton of a m. of France　NAP 359:9
We may pick up a m.　WELL 567:18
Martha: He lays it on M.'s Sons　KIPL 303:10
M. was cumbered about much　BIBLE 69:34
martial: ever become valiant and m.
　　　　　　　　　　　　　　BACON 27:26
have a swashing and a m.　SHAK 424:30
his m. cloak around him　WOLFE 576:4
Sonorous metal blowing m.　MILT 345:20
martinet: I am a perfect m.　SMITH 512:4
martlet: like the m.　SHAK 466:19
temple-haunting m.　SHAK 459:4
Martyr: am the M. of the People
　　　　　　　　　　　　　　CHAR 140:19
Glorious the m.'s gore　SMART 509:4
groan of the m.'s woe　BLAKE 86:6
he has the soul of a m.　BAG 29:17
if thou goe a m.　　　　CHAU 144:13
m. in his shirt of fire　SMITH 510:2
Oldcastle died a m.　SHAK 443:2
Thou fall'st a blessed m.　SHAK 447:12
martyrdom: dreadful m. must run its
　　course　　　　　　AUDEN 19:19
have not the gift of m.　DRYD 196:15
it were a m. to live　BROW 97:11
M. is the test　　　　JOHN 278:15
martyred: ghosts to be m. over and over
　　　　　　　　　　　　　　MACN 326:9
martyrs: graves of the m. the peewees
　　　　　　　　　　　　　　STEV 523:5
noble army of M.　PRAY 384:16
stones and clouts make m.　BROW 97:9
marvel: m. and a mystery　LONG 316:21
m. My birthday Away　THOM 547:7
m. save in Eastern clime　BURG 108:4
To m. at nothing is just　HOR 258:17
marvelled: They m. to see such things
　　　　　　　　　　　　　　PRAY 392:25
marvelling: She left me m. why my soul
　　　　　　　　　　　　　　THOM 547:26

marvellous: because he has done m. things BIBLE 83:7
Chatterton, the m. boy WORD 580:28
he hath done m. things PRAY 396:7
it is m. in our eyes PRAY 398:2
mankind towards the m. HUME 267:20
marvels: alone workest great m. PRAY 385:7
Marx: M. in the saddlebag BETJ 43:16
Marxist: know is that I am not a M.
MARX 333:12
Mary: Born of the Virgin M. PRAY 384:26
Hail M. ANON 10:8
M. ever Virgin MASS 334:15
M. had a little lamb HALE 237:15
M. hath chosen that good BIBLE 69:35
(M., pity women!) KIPL 301:11
My M.'s name to give CLARE 152:10
passion for the name of 'M.' BYRON 123:15
Philip and M. on a shilling BUTL 118:7
Where the lady M. is ROSS 409:19
Mary Ambree: foremost in battle was
M. BALL 31:8
Marybone: fields from Islington to M.
BLAKE 86:4
Mary-buds: winking M. begin SHAK 428:10
Mary Jane: What *is* the matter with M.
MILNE 340:10
Maryland: Green-walled by the hills
of M. WHIT 571:15
Marylebone: hanging garments of M.
JOYCE 286:5
Mary Magdalene: week cometh M. early
BIBLE 73:5
masculine: Truth the m., of Honour
HARE 242:5
With Spirits m. MILT 349:23
masculinity: mere contrast for m.
RILKE 406:5
Masefield: To M. something more
BEER 37:15
mask: had a m. like Castlereagh SHEL 502:2
loathsome m. has fallen SHEL 503:12
m. like open truth to cover CONG 159:27
m. of night is on my face SHAK 482:11
To pluck the m. from BRON 93:14
masons: singing m. building roofs
SHAK 443:9
masquerade: truth in m. BYRON 123:30
masquerades: Skim milk m. as cream
GILB 228:8
mass: activates the whole m. VIRG 558:24
between the fields to M. BETJ 43:7
blessed mutter of the m. BROW 99:14
is no idolatry in the M. JOHN 275:30
m. of public wrongs KYD 306:3
Paris is well worth a m. HENR 245:15
rough and unordered m. OVID 366:13
two thousand years of m. HARDY 239:3
massacre: are not as sudden as a m.
TWAIN 554:6
Masse: breite M. eines Volkes HITL 251:9
masses: huddled m. yearning LAZ 311:13
I hate the unholy m. HOR 260:13
I will back the m. against GLAD 229:17
m. and fugues and 'ops' GILB 227:6
sacrifices of M. PRAY 400:9
massive: m. paws of elder persons
BELL 38:24
mast: m. burst open with a rose FLEC 214:19
m. Of some great ammiral MILT 345:12
master: ass his m.'s crib BIBLE 57:15
choice and m. spirits SHAK 450:8
Cold Iron—is m. KIPL 298:15
disciple is not above his m. BIBLE 65:34
eateth your M. with publicans BIBLE 65:22
great soul of an ancient M. BROW 102:25
Has a new m. SHAK 485:11
I am M. of this college BEEC 37:8
I am the m. of my fate HENL 245:5
is man and m. of his fate TENN 535:2

mad and savage m. SOPH 513:9
Man is the m. of things SWIN 530:2
m. a grief but he that SHAK 472:24
m. of himself MASS 335:14
m. of the house cometh BIBLE 69:1
m. of them that know DANTE 171:7
M., we have toiled all BIBLE 69:18
more subtle m. under heaven TENN 534:12
only The M. shall praise us KIPL 304:3
presence of The M. THAC 545:12
swear allegiance to any m. HOR 258:7
sweet, just, boyish m. SANT 414:4
This is our m. BROW 100:34
Thrice blessed they that m. SHAK 469:17
'which is to be m. CARR 135:22
which I would fain call m. SHAK 453:13
who slew his m. BIBLE 51:35
Who's m., who's man SWIFT 527:30
would prove so hard a m. BRID 92:22
You must be m. and win GOET 230:7
masterly: wise and m. inactivity
MACK 325:12
masterpiece: Man is Heaven's m.
QUAR 403:12
Nature's great m. DONNE 190:3
reckoned the m. of Nature EMER 207:20
masters: ease of the m. SMITH 509:14
it mates and m. the fear BACON 26:2
light-hearted M. of the waves ARN 14:21
noble and approv'd good m. SHAK 473:24
Old M. AUDEN 19:18
people are the m. BURKE 110:18
prevail on our future m. LOWE 318:23
serve two m. BIBLE 64:27
spiritual pastors and m. PRAY 388:16
their Victory but new m. HAL 237:20
time are m. of their fates SHAK 448:17
We are the m. at the moment SHAW 498:25
mastery: achieve of, the m. of HOPK 257:5
voice said in m. while BROW 98:9
Mastiff: M., greyhound SHAK 455:1
match: Almighty made 'em to m. the
men ELIOT 200:19
blue spurt of a lighted m. BROW 102:14
bread and the big m. JUV 287:28
dont quite m. your face ASHF 17:7
love m. was the only thing EDG 199:21
to make and the m. to win NEWB 361:8
matched: has m. us with His hour
BROO 94:26
m. of earthly knight's MAL 328:8
matches: he plays extravagant m. GILB 227:7
m. of the Southron folk THOM 547:24
Matching: M. their lily-white legs
CLOU 153:15
matchless: now the m. deed's achiev'd
SMART 509:4
matchwood: m., immortal diamond
HOPK 257:1
mate: bold m. of Henry Morgan MAS 333:21
great artificer Made my m. STEV 523:3
m. of the *Nancy* brig GILB 225:16
shall be the maiden's m. SCOTT 416:12
there walk'd without a m. MARV 332:7
mated: thou art m. with a clown TENN 538:19
would be m. with the lion SHAK 420:26
mater: Magna ista scientiarum m.
BACON 28:8
M. saeva Cupidinum HOR 261:10
Stabat M. dolorosa JAC 270:31
Materialismus: *Krieg wurde die Welt*
in M. MOLT 354:4
materialistic: Christianity is the most
m. TEMP 532:11
mates: leaves His shivering m. THOM 549:23
m. and masters the fear BACON 26:2
mathematics: m., subtile BACON 27:21
M., rightly viewed RUSS 412:15
order and mystical m. BROW 95:20
said to be so like the m. WALT 563:31

Matilda: M. told such Dreadful Lies
BELL 39:7
matin: glow-worm shows the m. SHAK 431:14
matre: m. pulchra filia pulchrior HOR 259:22
matrem: ecclesiam non habet m. CYPR 170:19
Matrimonial: M. devotion GILB 227:3
one cares for m. cooings BYRON 122:27
matrimony: forms a barrier against m.
KEATS 294:10
in m. is breakfast-time HERB 246:16
joined together in holy M. PRAY 388:23
matters of religion and m. CHES 146:3
more of love than m. GOLD 232:39
'Tis safest in m. to begin SHER 506:9
we take m. at its lowest STEV 521:27
matron: m.'s glance that would GOLD 230:17
Thou sober-suited m. SHAK 483:6
matter: beginning of any great m.
DRAKE 193:1
Does it m. SASS 414:13
if it is it doesn't m. GILB 228:37
is inditing of a good m. PRAY 392:14
is to take away the m. BACON 27:11
little 'twill m. to one HOUS 264:8
m. she drove at succeeded PRIOR 400:27
More m. with less art SHAK 431:32
order, said I, this m. STER 518:28
part nor lot in this m. BIBLE 73:31
proverb is much m. decocted FULL 220:11
seeing the root of the m. BIBLE 52:32
speculations upon m. are voluntary
JOHN 281:32
that the sum of m. remains BACON 25:15
There is a volume in the m. POUND 382:15
What is M. PUNCH 402:15
What *is* the m. with Mary Jane MILNE 340:10
whose heart is in a m. BAG 28:31
wretched m. and lame metre MILT 344:18
mattering: m. once it has stopped
BOWEN 91:2
matters: exercise myself in great m.
PRAY 398:25
m. win great commendation BACON 25:36
words for little m. JOHN 275:14
Matthew: M., Mark ANON 6:15
mature: have in our m. years TROL 553:11
maturing: bosom-friend of the m. sun
KEATS 293:5
Maud: Come into the garden, M. TENN 540:9
maugree: m. hir heed CHAU 143:23
Maureens: Julias, Maeves and M. BETJ 43:7
mausoleum: Whose fantastic m. BETJ 43:9
mavult: enim m. homo verum esse
BACON 28:7
maw: his icy fingers in my m. SHAK 452:31
maw-crammed: Frets doubt the m. beast
BROW 104:3
mawkish: So sweetly m. POPE 375:20
mawkishness: thence proceeds m.
KEATS 288:19
maxim: could also will that my m.
KANT 288:9
got The M. Gun BELL 40:1
useless as a general m. MAC 323:28
maxima: *mea m. culpa* MASS 334:15
Maxime: M. solle ein allgemeines
KANT 288:9
maxims: m. in office ready made
BURKE 108:16
m. preaching down a daughter's TENN 538:22
too much by general m. BURKE 109:5
maximum: m. of temptation with
SHAW 497:39
May: darling buds of M. SHAK 492:28
fayr as is the rose in M. CHAU 143:24
fressh as is the month of M. CHAU 141:11
fruit and flourish in M. MAL 328:1
How less what we m. be BYRON 124:9
In depraved M. ELIOT 203:4
Is fairer far in M. JONS 285:8

know not what we m. be   SHAK 436:1
laurel outlives not M.   SWIN 530:5
lawyer tells me I *m.* do   BURKE 109:26
least the seventh of M.   TROL 552:21
maids are M. when they   SHAK 426:23
matter for a M. morning   SHAK 490:10
M. is a pious fraud   LOW 319:15
M. morwenyng on Maluerne   LANG 309:25
may say that M. is come   CLARE 152:14
merry month of M.   BALL 30:10
merry month of M.   BALL 31:13
merry month of M.   BARN 33:32
merry month of M.   BRET 92:5
mid-M.'s eldest child   KEATS 291:21
month of M. Is comen   CHAU 143:29
moonlight-coloured m.   SHEL 503:19
Pink m., double may   BETJ 43:16
Than wish a snow in M.'s   SHAK 456:16
there's an end of M.   HOUS 264:20
Whenas M. was in his pride   BRET 92:5
When that the wife is M.   WATK 565:7
world is white with M.   TENN 534:4
maydenhed: he rafte hire m.   CHAU 143:23
Maying: let's go a-M.   HERR 248:26
May-mess: look: a M.   HOPK 256:29
maypole: organ and the m.   JORD 285:18
  where's the M. in the Strand   BRAM 91:23
May-poles: I sing of M.   HERR 248:18
mays: under blanching m.   HOUS 265:8
Maytime: Now in M. to the wicket
    HOUS 262:22
maze: burgeons every m. of quick
    TENN 537:18
mighty m.   POPE 379:1
wander in that golden m.   DRYD 197:16
mazes: in wand'ring m. lost   MILT 346:19
mazily: brooks of Eden m. murmuring
    TENN 533:13
McGregor: Mr M.'s garden   POTT 382:1
McGrew: Dangerous Dan M.   SERV 420:14
me: let m. ever escape them   PRAY 399:10
M. too the Muses made write   VIRG 560:7
no harm happen unto m.   PRAY 389:30
queer wench thee and m.   OWEN 366:29
there they died for m.   HOUS 265:6
'This man loved *m.*   LAND 308:25
mead: stream and o'er the m.   BLAKE 87:26
meadow: meander through a m. of margin
    SHER 506:26
painted m.   ADD 2:5
stranger's feet may find the m.   HOUS 265:10
meadows: are no more by-path m.
    STEV 521:32
Do paint the m. with delight   SHAK 457:18
from the m. rich with corn   WHIT 571:15
golden face the m. green   SHAK 493:9
is set in enamelled m.   WALP 562:21
m. runnels   KEATS 289:3
M. trim with daisies pied   MILT 342:20
m. where it glides   ARN 12:22
meadow-sweet: simplest growth of m.
  or sorrel   SWIN 528:25
meal: handful of m. in a barrel   BIBLE 51:7
no man gets a full m.   JOHN 276:27
mean: admires m. things is a Snob
    THAC 545:4
careful what they m. thereby   SHAK 486:17
convey more than they m.   CONN 161:11
Down these m. streets   CHAN 139:22
Happy the golden m.   MASS 335:17
if I ever do a m. action   STER 519:3
m. Our object and inglorious   WORD 580:10
no m. of death   SHAK 450:8
nothing common did or m.   MARV 332:9
should say what you m.   CARR 133:29
They m. well   DISR 186:12
Though m. and mighty rotting   SHAK 428:20
to be seated in the m.   SHAK 465:19
what did he m. by that   SHER 505:29
what does it m.   AUDEN 19:14

what I choose it to m.   CARR 135:21
what we m.   ARN 12:22
who loves the golden m.   HOR 260:9
Meander: By slow M.'s margent green
    MILT 341:3
meandering: Meeting those m. down
  they   HARDY 240:21
miles m. with a mazy motion   COL 156:28
meaner: because only m. things   ELIOT 201:3
leave all m. things   POPE 379:1
opponent motives m.   BARR 34:9
meanest: m. flowret of the vale   GRAY 235:15
m. of his creatures   BROW 102:36
m. of mankind   POPE 380:1
meaning: another-while m. for meaning
    ALFR 3:17
author to get at his m.   RUSK 411:15
hidden m.—like Basingstoke   GILB 228:36
language charged with m.   POUND 384:1
Love is our Lord's m.   JUL 286:33
m. doesn't matter if it's   GILB 227:21
M., however   CALV 127:24
m. is my meat and drink   BROW 100:31
m. of religion is thus   ARN 16:20
plain man in his plain m.   SHAK 467:19
times when words had a m.   FRAN 217:27
to the m.   CALV 127:11
within the m. of the Act   ANON 4:21
meaningless: polite m. words   YEATS 585:1
meanings: His mind with m. that he
    COWP 167:2
there are two m. packed   CARR 135:28
Where the M., are   DICK 184:1
wrestle With words and m.   ELIOT 202:19
meanly: m. great   SAV 415:5
means: as an end withal, never as m.
    KANT 288:13
best ends by the best m.   HUTC 268:19
By all the m. you can   WESL 568:21
end justifies the m.   BUS 117:4
have to die beyond my m.   WILDE 574:3
I don't know what it m.   GILB 225:14
in persons of small m.   ELIOT 201:23
knew what England m.   CHES 146:26
live within our m.   WARD 564:36
m. and increased leisure   DISR 185:9
m. in his power which are   KANT 288:11
m. of grace   PRAY 386:2
m. of rising in the world   JOHN 276:29
m. of some change is without   BURKE 111:4
money, m., and content   SHAK 426:3
not live within thy m.   AUDEN 21:6
sight of m. to do ill   SHAK 452:28
take the m. whereby I live   SHAK 468:10
that her hand lacks m.   SHAK 424:25
meant: I knew not all he m.   TENN 534:24
my life seemed m.   BROW 101:22
measels: Did you ever hav the m.
    WARD 564:25
measles: Love is like the m.   JER 272:23
Love's like the m.   JERR 273:3
measure: does it hold good m.   BROW 100:4
fill the m. of the year   KEATS 292:14
good m., pressed down   BIBLE 69:23
in m., like a dancer   ELIOT 202:26
is the m. of the universe   SHEL 503:8
Man is the m. of all things   PROT 401:18
m. of our torment is   KIPL 299:11
M. still for Measure   SHAK 465:5
M. your mind's height   BROW 103:5
narrow m. spans   HOUS 265:13
'Now tread we a m.   SCOTT 417:13
Shrunk to this little m.   SHAK 450:6
Things have their due m.   HOR 261:23
'To lead but one m.   SCOTT 417:12
With what m. ye mete   BIBLE 68:29
measured: dance is a m. pace   BACON 24:23
I've m. it from side   WORD 582:24
m. out my life with coffee spoons
    ELIOT 203:20

m. phrase   WORD 581:1
use in m. language lies   TENN 536:1
Measurement: M. began our might
    YEATS 587:7
Measures: cant of 'M. not men'   CANN 130:7
in short m.   JONS 285:8
system of weights and m.   NAP 359:13
meat: abhorred all manner of m.   PRAY 397:8
benison to fall On our m.   HERR 250:10
can not eat but little m.   ANON 5:21
do seek their m. from God   PRAY 397:1
eater came forth m.   BIBLE 49:21
egg is full of m.   SHAK 483:1
give them m. in due season   PRAY 397:1
Heaven sends us good m.   GARR 221:12
he sent them m. enough   PRAY 395:6
little of solid m. for men   DRYD 198:10
meaning is my m. and drink   BROW 100:31
m. doth this our Caesar   SHAK 448:18
m. in the hall   STEV 523:7
not the life more than m.   BIBLE 64:28
Out-did the m.   HERR 249:14
penny ice and cold m.   GILB 226:14
Some have m. and cannot eat   BURNS 114:14
taste My m.   HERB 248:1
them their m. in due season   PRAY 399:15
They put arsenic in his m.   HOUS 264:15
This dish of m. is too   WALT 564:10
thou gavest m. or drink   BALL 31:7
with cans of poisoned m.   CHES 147:20
ye gave me m.   BIBLE 68:6
meat-fly: Thackeray settled like a m.
    RUSK 411:6
meat-offering: m., thou wouldest not
    PRAY 392:2
meatus: *caelique m. Describent radio*
    VIRG 559:1
Meccah: some to M. turn to pray FLEC 214:12
mechanic: m. part of wit   ETH 208:30
mechanical: m. arts and merchandise
    BACON 27:34
méchant: Cet animal est très m.   ANON 9:4
un m. animal   MOL 354:2
mécontents: fais cent m. et un ingrat
    LOUI 318:9
meddle: 'm. and muddle'   DERBY 175:9
Not to m. with my toys   STEV 522:19
meddling: Every fool will be m.   BIBLE 54:16
mede: al the floures in the m.   CHAU 143:30
médecine: m. d'une méthode toute
    MOL 353:17
Medes: given to the M. and Persians
    BIBLE 61:6
law of the M. and Persians   BIBLE 61:7
medias: eventum festinat et in m. res
    HOR 257:20
Mediator: our M. and Advocate PRAY 385:23
Medical: M. Crowner's a queer   BARH 33:16
medicina: sero m. paratur   OVID 366:20
medicine: friend is the m. of life BIBLE 62:25
heart doeth good like a m.   BIBLE 54:12
it's late for m. to be   OVID 366:20
m. of our great revenge   SHAK 462:17
m. the less   SHAK 428:19
m. thee to that sweet sleep   SHAK 475:24
m. to heal their sickness   PRAY 399:19
m. worse than the malady   FLET 215:16
miserable have no other m.   SHAK 464:8
My m., work   SHAK 476:8
we now practise m.   MOL 353:17
Medicine Hat: plumed war-bonnet of
M.   BENET 40:19
medicines: me m. to make me love him
    SHAK 438:24
medicus: littera plus sum quam m.
    PLAU 374:15
medieval: lily in your m. hand   GILB 227:23
Medio: M. tutissimus ibis   OVID 366:14
mediocre: tomb of a m. talent   SMITH 510:20

médiocres: L'absence diminue les m.
passions   LA R 310:15
Mediocribus: M. esse poetis   HOR 258:4
mediocritatem: Auream quisquis m.
    HOR 260:9
Mediocrities: over this Cabinet of M.
    DISR 185:36
Mediocrity: M. knows nothing higher
    DOYLE 192:38
m. of her circumstances   SMITH 509:17
meditaris: Silvestrem tenui Musam m.
avena   VIRG 559:11
meditate: matchless songs does m.
    MARV 332:12
m. the thankless Muse   MILT 343:8
meditated: I m. on the Fall   BETJ 43:1
meditating: m., or working at something
    THOM 546:11
meditation: disposed to abstracted m.
    JOHN 281:40
let us all to m.   SHAK 446:7
m. of my heart   PRAY 390:13
notice a cat in profound m.   ELIOT 204:6
sage in m. found   SHEL 504:10
Some happy tone Of m.   WORD 582:6
Mediterranean: blue M.   SHEL 502:10
see the shores of the M.   JOHN 277:6
medium: m. is the message   MCL 325:16
meed: m. of some melodious tear   MILT 343:2
meek: am m. and lowly in heart   BIBLE 66:5
believing that the m. shall   BIRK 84:12
Blessed are the m.   BIBLE 64:6
borne his faculties so m.   SHAK 459:6
m. and quiet spirit   BIBLE 80:28
m. and unaffected grace   GOLD 230:24
meekest: m. man and the gentlest   MAL 328:8
meekly: m. kneeling upon your knees
    PRAY 387:18
meekness: brought salvation down By
m.   SMART 509:4
m. the engrafted word   BIBLE 80:10
meek-spirited: m. shall possess the earth
    PRAY 391:27
meenister: ma doobts aboot the m.
    PUNCH 402:31
meet: brook and river m.   LONG 316:20
comes to m. one's friends   BURN 112:22
'Extremes m.   HOOD 255:17
goeth on to m. the armed men   BIBLE 53:6
If I should m. thee   BYRON 126:14
If we do m. again   SHAK 451:32
It is m. and right so   PRAY 387:22
loved, sir—used to m.   BROW 100:8
make both ends m.   FULL 220:12
M. me at London   DONNE 188:2
m. the raging of the skies   CAMP 129:3
men and mountains m.   BLAKE 87:10
One would m. in every place   KEATS 289:32
shall we three m. again   SHAK 458:1
So I'll m. 'im later   KIPL 299:19
Though infinite can never m.   MARV 331:19
will come out to m. you   POUND 383:17
will make him an help m.   BIBLE 45:10
Yet m. we shall   BUTL 119:17
meete: it were a daye very m.   MORE 357:20
meeter: therefore deemed it m.   PEAC 371:2
meeting: if I was a public m.   VICT 556:14
Journeys end in lovers m.   SHAK 488:17
m. where it likes   ARN 15:20
neither overtaking nor m.   CONG 159:25
meets: is meant than m. the ear   MILT 342:7
Méfiez-vous: M.! Les oreilles ennemies
    ANON 9:18
Megrim: M. at her head   POPE 381:9
melancholic: saturnine, dark, and m.
    CONG 159:17
melancholy: black sun of m.   NERV 360:26
charm can soothe her m.   GOLD 231:31
had this trick of m.   SHAK 421:2
Hail divinest M.   MILT 341:25

have a rare recipe for m.   LAMB 307:23
loathed M., Of Cerberus   MILT 342:12
lovely m.   FLET 215:17
m. as an unbrac'd drum   CENT 138:11
m. god protect thee   SHAK 489:5
m., long, withdrawing   ARN 12:23
M. mark'd him for her own   GRAY 235:4
m. nor a cynical disposition   CHES 145:23
m. of human reflections   BAG 29:18
m. out of a song as a weasel   SHAK 425:15
m.'s child   SHAK 452:2
m. when thou art absent   CONG 160:22
moping m.   MILT 349:24
most m.   MILT 342:2
my cue is villanous m.   SHAK 453:12
Naught so sweet as M.   BURT 116:12
Pale M. sate retir'd   COLL 158:21
sovereign mistress of true m.   SHAK 423:4
There's such a charm in m.   ROG 407:10
This m. is   FORD 216:18
Veil'd M. has her sovran   KEATS 291:15
vile m. from my father   JOHN 279:33
when the m. fit shall fall   KEATS 291:15
wild, m., and elevating   BRON 93:17
with a green and yellow m.   SHAK 489:7
Young man untroubled by m.   BANV 33:1
mélancolie: Jeune homme sans m.   BANV 33:1
Melchisedech: ever after the order of
M.   PRAY 397:12
meliora: Video m.   OVID 366:17
meliorist: not an optimist but a m.
    ELIOT 201:31
melius: Aurum irrepertum et sic m.
    HOR 260:20
mellificatis: Sic vos non vobis m. apes
    VIRG 560:20
mellow: Indeed is too m. for me   MONT 354:7
m., like good wine   PHIL 373:10
mellows: tart temper never m. with
    IRV 270:21
Mellstock: lie in M. churchyard now
    BETJ 42:13
lie in M. churchyard now   HARDY 239:17
melodie: sownes ful of hevenyssh m.
    CHAU 144:18
melodies: Heard m. are sweet   KEATS 291:4
Sweetest m.   WORD 579:17
To ease my breast of m.   KEATS 289:25
melodious: divine m. truth   KEATS 291:1
In some m. plot   KEATS 291:17
Melting m. words   HERR 250:9
Move in m. time   MILT 344:10
melodramatic: It is lurid and m.
    LAWR 311:11
melody: blund'ring kind of m.   DRYD 194:21
From ancient m. have ceas'd…   BLAKE 88:10
God with the voice of m.   PRAY 392:22
making m. in your heart   BIBLE 78:5
m., in our heaviness   PRAY 399:3
Moved to delight by the m.   AUDEN 18:3
oft than to a chamber m.   SIDN 507:27
pentameter aye falling in m.   COL 157:7
with sound of sweetest m.   SHAK 441:29
melodye: smale foweles maken m.
    CHAU 141:8
melon-flower: brighter than this gaudy
m.   BROW 101:7
melons: raiser of huge m. and of pine
    TENN 542:20
Stumbling on m.   MARV 332:3
Melrose: would'st view fair M. aright
    SCOTT 416:13
melt: crown o' the earth doth m.   SHAK 423:16
discandy, m. their sweets   SHAK 423:5
earth shall m. away   PRAY 392:20
I rage, I m., I burn   GAY 222:6
m. itself Into the sea   SHAK 442:1
m. with ruth   MILT 343:16
Now m. into sorrow   BYRON 120:1
So let us m.   DONNE 190:17

too solid flesh would m.   SHAK 429:28
melted: Are m. into air   SHAK 485:20
M. to one vast Iris   BYRON 121:4
Till he m. like a cloud   TENN 542:21
With that which m. fools   SHAK 449:24
melting: body is even like m. wax
    PRAY 390:19
Melting-Pot: great M. where all   ZANG 588:17
melts: then m. for ever   BURNS 115:7
member: Distinguishable in m.   MILT 346:24
he is a m. of *parliament*   BURKE 109:12
he is not m. of Bristol   BURKE 109:12
is a thing I am not a m.   FLEM 215:1
was made a m. of Christ   PRAY 388:12
members: book were all my m. written
    PRAY 399:7
m. incorporate in the mystical   PRAY 388:3
m. of the common throng   GILB 228:22
m. one of another   BIBLE 77:29
membra: disiecti m. poetae   HOR 262:2
Membranis: M. intus positis   HOR 258:6
meminisse: Forsan et haec olim m. iuvabit
    VIRG 557:14

Nec me m. pigebit Elissae   VIRG 558:13
Memling: Emerald findeth no M.
    POUND 382:11
memor: Dum m. ipse mei   VIRG 558:13
memorable: m. in the history of our
    CHUR 150:8
memorandum: you don't make a m.
of it   CARR 134:26
memores: m. aliquos fecere merendo
    VIRG 558:23
Memorial: Charles the First out of the
M.   DICK 177:5
m. longer lasting than   HOR 261:8
Perhaps a frail m.   COWP 166:4
which have no m.   BIBLE 63:25
whole earth as their m.   PER 372:23
Memories: M. are hunting horns whose
    APOL 11:10
memorize: m. another Golgotha   SHAK 458:4
Memory: Fond M. brings the light
    MOORE 357:2
Footfalls echo in the m.   ELIOT 202:13
from the m. a rooted sorrow   SHAK 463:3
from the table of my m.   SHAK 431:15
grand m. for forgetting   STEV 521:8
'His m. is going   JOHN 279:6
it comes o'er my m.   SHAK 476:7
M. fades   DE L 174:2
m. of men without distinction   BROW 97:18
m. of yesterday's pleasures   DONNE 191:2
m. that only works backwards   CARR 135:16
Midnight shakes the m.   ELIOT 204:9
mixing M. and desire   ELIOT 204:17
my name and m.   BACON 28:14
Only a m. of the same   BROW 101:22
poetry strays into my m.   HOUS 266:17
Queen *Elizabeth* of most happy m.
    BIBLE 44:20
Their very m. is fair   VAUG 555:18
there's hope a great man's m.   SHAK 434:7
thy tablets, M.   ARN 13:19
to his m. for his jests   SHER 506:36
while m. holds a seat   SHAK 431:15
men: all m. are created equal   ANON 8:14
all things to all m.   ANON 6:11
all things to all m.   BIBLE 76:7
catalogue ye go for m.   SHAK 461:9
clerkes been noght wisest m.   CHAU 143:11
cognizance of m. and things   BROW 101:11
could of m. distinguish   SHAK 434:1
created m. and women different   VICT 556:14
days shall m. seek death   BIBLE 82:7
deals with the memory of m.   BROW 97:18
despised and rejected of m.   BIBLE 59:21
fashions m. with true nobility   MARL 330:11
fear of little m.   ALL 3:20
finds too late that m. betray   GOLD 231:31

furnish'd well with m. SHAK 449:25
great Nature made us m. LOW 319:11
hell to m. AESC 3:1
herb for the service of m. PRAY 396:20
I drew these tides of m. LAWR 311:12
indignities m. come to dignities
BACON 26:23
I see m. as trees BIBLE 68:33
it issue not towards m. BACON 26:19
it's m.'s lives SCOTT 418:2
justify the ways of God to M. MILT 344:22
just m. made perfect BIBLE 80:2
least talked about by m. PER 372:24
leaves is a generation of m. HOMER 253:29
life of m. on earth BEDE 37:1
lips of dying m. ARN 14:27
make you fishers of m. BIBLE 64:5
many m. JOHN 274:22
many m. of large fortune AUST 22:26
m. all so good for nothing AUST 23:4
m. and mountains meet BLAKE 87:10
m. and women with our race KIPL 298:10
M. are April when they SHAK 426:23
M. are but children DRYD 195:15
m. are created equal JEFF 272:6
M. are everything CANN 130:7
M. are never so good MACK 325:11
M. are suspicious HERR 249:16
m. at most differ as Heaven TENN 535:16
m. decay GOLD 230:18
M. don't know women TROL 552:20
M. fear death BACON 26:1
m. fought under the earth SCOTT 417:20
m. hate one another so MELB 336:20
m. have precedency BRAD 91:14
m. in a world of men KIPL 298:23
M. in great place are thrice BACON 26:21
M. in shape and fashion ASCH 17:3
m. in women do require BLAKE 86:17
M. lived like fishes SIDN 507:12
m. loved darkness rather BIBLE 71:39
m. may come and men may TENN 532:21
M. move unhoming FRY 220:7
m. must work KING 297:3
M., my brothers TENN 538:24
m. naturally were born MILT 352:18
m. of like passions with BIBLE 74:5
m. of other minds my fancy GOLD 231:27
m. only disagree MILT 346:18
M. seldom make passes PARK 368:16
m., that are set on fire PRAY 393:15
m. that were boys when BELL 40:11
m. that women marry LONG 316:21
M. were deceivers ever SHAK 472:16
M. who have loved them TROL 553:10
M. who march away HARDY 240:8
m. who will support me MELB 336:17
m., women, and Herveys MONT 354:6
m., women, and clergymen SMITH 511:8
M. would be angels POPE 379:7
m. would be false LYLY 321:9
m. would weep upon your HUXL 268:23
Mocks married m. SHAK 457:18
need of a world of m. BROW 103:9
not m., but manners FIEL 211:14
not stones, but m. SHAK 450:25
of m. are deceitful upon PRAY 393:20
proceeded from childless m. BACON 27:4
proper young m. BURNS 114:17
punished in the sight of m. BIBLE 62:13
purgatory of m. FLOR 216:1
schemes o' mice an' m. BURNS 115:22
seasons in the mind of m. KEATS 292:14
sick m.'s dreams BROW 95:23
Some faults to make us m. SHAK 423:19
sorts and conditions of m. PRAY 385:24
stamp is the cant of Not m. BURKE 108:23
State which dwarfs its m. MILL 339:15
streets the same as the m. WHIT 570:15
studied books than m. BACON 28:13

them to have power over m. WOLL 576:11
therefore…exceeding tall m. BACON 25:7
there no way for m. to be SHAK 428:11
thousand of those m. in England SHAK 444:27
to form Christian m. ARN 16:27
tongues of m. and of angels BIBLE 76:14
trust themselves with m. SHAK 486:2
unnecessary things are m. ROCH 406:16
unto the daughters of m. BIBLE 45:33
us arise and go like m. STEV 522:25
us in the likeness of m. BIBLE 74:4
wander in the ways of m. BURNS 114:15
ways with m. I find Him not TENN 535:19
What m. or gods are these KEATS 291:3
When m. were all asleep BRID 92:12
When m. were fond SHAK 464:6
Where Destiny with M. FITZ 213:5
With four-and-twenty m. AYT 24:6
With m. he can be rational AUST 22:9
Words are m.'s daughters MADD 326:19
ye shall die like m. PRAY 395:10
menace: become a m. to all mankind
NEV 361:2
looks do m. heaven and dare MARL 330:5
men-children: Bring forth m. only
SHAK 459:11
mend: m. the Electric Light BELL 39:29
Nor a broken thing m. BELL 40:10
To m. it or be rid on't SHAK 461:10
mendacities: Better m. POUND 383:4
mendacity: only equalled by their m.
TEMP 532:8
mendax: Splendide m. et in omne virgo
HOR 261:2
mended: all is m. SHAK 471:23
endure what can't be m. WATTS 565:27
nothing else but to be m. BUTL 117:22
mendicity: class of clergyman whose
m. TEMP 532:8
Mendicus: M. es PLAU 374:15
mendier: de m. dans les rues et FRAN 217:26
MENE: M.; God hath numbered BIBLE 61:6
menny: Done because we are too m.
HARDY 241:15
menpleasers: with eyeservice, as m.
BIBLE 78:8
Mens: M. agitat molem et magno VIRG 558:24
M. cuiusque is est quisque CIC 151:24
m. sana in corpore sano JUV 288:4
m. sibi conscia recti VIRG 557:18
mensa: Nec deus hunc m. VIRG 560:2
Mensch: Es irrt der M. GOET 229:29
M. fand die Tiere nicht NIET 363:3
Menschen: Alle M. werden Brüder SCH 415:9
verbrennt man am Ende auch M.
HEINE 244:14
mental: m. pursuit for the Building
BLAKE 86:10
m. suffering had been undergone
BUTL 119:12
will not cease from M. BLAKE 86:16
mention: m. of you in our prayers
BIBLE 78:30
we never m. her BAYLY 35:10
Without ceasing I make m. BIBLE 74:29
mentioned: allow their names to be m.
AUST 23:19
mer: savent les secrets de la m. NERV 361:1
mercenary: Followed their m. calling
HOUS 265:7
merchandise: mechanical arts and m.
BACON 27:34
Mummy is become m. BROW 97:22
merchant: heaven is like unto a m. man
BIBLE 66:21
m. shall hardly keep himself BIBLE 63:10
m., to secure his treasure PRIOR 401:1
merchantman: monarchy is a m. which
AMES 4:3
merchants: like m., venture trade SHAK 443:9

whose m. are princes BIBLE 58:16
mercies: tender m. of the wicked BIBLE 53:34
Thanks for m. past receive BUCK 106:17
merciful: Blessed are the m. BIBLE 64:6
'God be m. to a soul ANON 10:14
God be m. to me a sinner BIBLE 70:35
God be m. unto us PRAY 394:9
In a m. eclipse GILB 225:26
Then must the Jew be m. SHAK 467:27
was very m. to the birds ANON 8:15
merciless: black and m. things JAMES 271:23
mercis: aura plus tost de vous m. VILL 557:4
Mercuries: English M. SHAK 443:12
Mercury: ground like feather'd M.
SHAK 440:7
littered under M. SHAK 491:18
m. sank in the mouth AUDEN 19:2
To Saturn nor to M. HOUS 264:26
words of M. are harsh after SHAK 457:20
Mercy: Charity and M. DICK 179:6
dimensions of this m. are CROM 169:22
easy in the m. of his means THOM 547:2
emboldens sin so much as m. SHAK 486:6
folks over to God's m. ELIOT 200:17
full of compassion and m. BIBLE 62:21
God all m. is a God unjust YOUNG 588:9
God ha' m. on such as we KIPL 299:10
God have m. upon one SHAK 490:12
gracious m. and protection PRAY 389:9
leaving m. to heaven FIEL 211:24
likely to have m. on you VILL 557:4
Lord, have m. upon us PRAY 384:18
m., and faith BIBLE 67:24
M. and truth are met PRAY 395:15
m. does SHAK 463:20
m. embraceth him on every PRAY 391:18
m. endureth for ever PRAY 399:2
M. has a human heart BLAKE 88:7
M. I asked CAMD 128:5
m. Of a rude stream SHAK 447:9
m. to forgive DRYD 196:14
m. unto thousands of them BIBLE 47:24
m. upon us miserable sinners PRAY 385:15
property is ever to have m. PRAY 385:23
quality of m. is not strain'd SHAK 467:27
shut the gates of m. GRAY 234:24
so is his m. BIBLE 62:22
temper so Justice with m. MILT 349:21
That m. I to others show POPE 381:13
they shall obtain m. BIBLE 64:6
Thy m. on Thy People KIPL 302:10
to love m. BIBLE 61:25
When m. seasons justice SHAK 467:27
will have m. on Jacob yet BROW 101:3
Meredith: M. is a prose Browning
WILDE 573:37
while M. climbed towards CHES 148:7
merely: I can m. be your friend LEAR 312:1
merendo: memores aliquos fecere m.
VIRG 558:23
mereri: quicquam bene velle m. CAT 137:8
meridian: under any m. BROW 96:29
merit: by the m. of the wearer SHAK 466:21
from sense of injured m. MILT 345:2
his m. handsomely allowed JOHN 278:32
m. raise the tardy bust JOHN 282:29
m.'s all his own CHUR 149:15
m. wins the soul POPE 381:11
praise the m. of a foe POPE 378:32
preacher's m. or demerit BROW 100:4
talk of m. for a bishopric WEST 569:5
there is no damned m. in it MELB 336:12
What is m. PALM 368:12
mérite: gouvernement qu'elle m. MAIS 327:8
merits: m. of a spotless shirt TENN 540:23
not weighing our m. PRAY 388:2
Mermaid: Choicer than the M. Tavern
KEATS 290:28
Done at the M. BEAU 35:19
M. in the Zodiac KEATS 290:29

m. on a dolphin's back | SHAK 470:7
Which is the M.'s now | JONS 284:1
mermaids: have heard the m. singing | ELIOT 203:25
So many m. | SHAK 422:3
merrier: m. man | SHAK 456:21
merrily: die all, die m. | SHAK 440:8
m. hent the stile-a | SHAK 491:21
M. sang the monks in Ely | CAN 130:9
m. shall I live now | SHAK 485:25
Sing we m. unto God our | PRAY 395:9
we went m. | BYRON 125:23
merriment: hopeless than a scheme of m. | JOHN 281:21
m. of parsons is mighty | JOHN 278:25
source of innocent m. | GILB 227:5
merry: all went m. as a marriage | BYRON 120:20
be m. | BIBLE 70:4
chances men are ever m. | SHAK 442:12
even the wise are m. | YEATS 585:18
gone up with a m. noise | PRAY 392:24
Have they been m. | SHAK 483:29
I am not m. | SHAK 474:17
It's guid to be m. | BURNS 114:5
M. and tragical | SHAK 471:13
m. Grecian coaster | ARN 14:21
m. heart doeth good like | BIBLE 54:12
m. heart goes all the day | SHAK 491:21
m. heart maketh a cheerful | BIBLE 54:5
m. in hall when beards | SHAK 442:26
m. misery | BETJ 44:1
m. monarch | ROCH 407:2
m. month of May | BALL 30:10
m. month of May | BALL 31:13
m. month of May | BARN 33:32
m. month of May | BRET 92:5
m. when I hear sweet music | SHAK 468:16
m. world since the fairies | SELD 419:24
never m. world in England | SHAK 446:10
to be m. | BIBLE 55:26
to have such a m. day once | PEPYS 372:20
you were born in a m. hour | SHAK 472:12
merrygoround: It's no go the m. | MACN 326:7
merryman: It's a song of a m. | GILB 229:9
Merses: M. profundo | HOR 261:12
meruit: Palmam qui m. | JORT 285:19
merye: wantowne and a m. | CHAU 141:19
meschaunce: Friday fil al this m. | CHAU 143:3
Mesech: constrained to dwell with M. | PRAY 398:7
Meshach: Shadrach, M., and Abed-nego | BIBLE 61:4
mess: birthright for a m. of potage | BIBLE 46:12
birthrite for a m. of potash | WARD 564:22
every m. I finds a friend | DIBD 175:18
message: give to a gracious m. | SHAK 422:15
medium is the m. | MCL 325:16
simple m. to the world of man | AUDEN 19:11
messager: m. of day | CHAU 142:18
messages: receive fair speechless m. | SHAK 465:17
messe: Paris vaut bien une m. | HENR 245:15
other M.'s called Hatta | CARR 135:30
messengers: bade his m. ride forth | MAC 322:11
superfluous kings for m. | SHAK 422:15
messes: other country m. | MILT 342:21
messing: simply m. about in boats | GRAH 233:18
mesures: système de poids et m. | NAP 359:13
met: day and the way we m. | SWIN 530:10
Hail, fellow, well m. | SWIFT 527:30
He was m. even now | SHAK 455:13
know how first he m. her | THAC 546:3
Mercy and truth are m. | PRAY 395:15
M. again, my lass | HOUS 265:5

m. each other with erected | DRYD 197:30
m. my dearest foe in heaven | SHAK 430:4
m. them at close of day | YEATS 585:1
M. you not with my true | RAL 404:13
never be m. with again | CARR 133:7
That have m. many one | RAL 404:13
When first we m. we did | BRID 92:22
metal: Here's m. more attractive | SHAK 434:5
my m. of India | SHAK 489:9
metaphor: All slang is m. | CHES 147:29
to hunt down a tired m. | BYRON 124:2
Metaphysic: M. calls for aid on Sense | POPE 375:26
m. wit can fly | BUTL 117:20
metaphysical: fate and m. aid | SHAK 459:1
métaphysiciens: dirais volontiers des m. | CHAM 139:16
metaphysics: of divinity or school m. | HUME 267:15
to circumnavigate the m. | STEV 522:2
mete: his hous of m. and drynke | CHAU 141:28
With what measure ye m. | BIBLE 68:29
metempsychosis: Pythagoras' m. | MARL 329:14
meteor: cloud-encircled m. of the air | SHEL 501:18
Now slides the silent m. | TENN 542:14
Shone like a m. streaming | MILT 345:19
method: by a completely new m. | MOL 353:17
m. and secret and sweet | ARN 16:22
m. of making a fortune | GRAY 235:21
yet there is m. in't | SHAK 432:9
méthode: d'une m. toute nouvelle | MOL 353:17
methodically: must elope m. | GOLD 232:17
Methodist: spiritualized by a M. preacher | WALP 562:27
with the morals of a M. | GILB 228:33
methods: different m. different men excel | CHUR 148:23
You know my m. | DOYLE 192:8
You know my m. | DOYLE 192:31
Methought: M. I heard a voice cry | SHAK 460:8
m. what pain it was | SHAK 480:27
Methuselah: all the days of M. were | BIBLE 45:31
métier: c'est son m. | CATH 136:17
m. et mon art c'est vivre | MONT 354:23
m. que de faire un livre | LA B 306:12
metre: laws of God and man and m. | LOCK 316:1
m.-making argument | EMER 207:29
stretched m. of an antique | SHAK 492:27
these same m. ballad-mongers | SHAK 439:25
understanding what m. is | COL 158:4
wretched matter and lame m. | MILT 344:18
metropolis: called…'the m. of the empire' | COBB 154:10
mettle: m. in death which commits | SHAK 421:20
m. of your pasture | SHAK 444:2
undaunted m. should compose | SHAK 459:11
metuant: dum m. | ACC 1:3
Metus: M. et malesuada Fames | VIRG 558:21
meum: distinctions of m. and tuum | LAMB 307:13
M. est propositum | ANON 10:14
meurs: souffre et m. sans parler | VIGNY 557:2
meurt: m. le bruit parmi le vent | APOL 11:10
On ne m. qu'une fois | MOL 353:8
mew: be a kitten and cry m. | SHAK 439:25
Let cat's m. rise | AUDEN 20:8
Mewling: M. and puking in the nurse's | SHAK 425:24
Mexique Bay: Echo beyond the M. | MARV 331:17
mezzanine: to slip down to the m. | WOD 575:23
mezzo: m. del cammin di nostra | DANTE 171:2
mice: Appear like m. | SHAK 455:14

Like little m. | SUCK 524:8
schemes o' m. an' men | BURNS 115:22
Michael: M. and his angels fought | BIBLE 82:11
to blessed M. the Archangel | MASS 334:15
Michael Angelo: Enter M. | BEER 37:25
I believe in M. | SHAW 496:22
Italy from designs by M. | TWAIN 554:11
M. for breakfast…for luncheon | TWAIN 554:10
might be the name of—M. | REYN 405:19
Michelangelo: Talking of M. | ELIOT 203:18
micher: m. and eat blackberries | SHAK 439:14
miching: this is m. mallecho | SHAK 434:9
microscopes: magnifyin' gas m. of hextra power | DICK 182:23
microscopic: Why has not man a m. eye | POPE 379:8
Midas: ass's ears of M. | SIDN 508:5
mid-career: Glorious the sun in m. | SMART 509:4
mid-day: more clear, than our m. | DONNE 189:32
midden: m. whose odours will madden | AUDEN 18:17
middle: cannot steer A m. course | MASS 335:18
companions for m. age | BACON 26:34
into the m. of things | HOR 257:20
me in the m. of my being | LAWR 311:3
m. course is the safest | OVID 366:14
M. of Next Week | CARR 133:12
m. of the road of our life | DANTE 171:2
m. state | MALL 327:12
someone of the m. class | BELL 39:30
Tenants of life's m. state | COWP 167:33
Middle Age: enchantments of the M. Home | ARN 15:25
last enchantment of the M. | BEER 37:26
m. is to find out that | POUND 383:22
Restraining reckless m. | YEATS 586:8
middle-ageing: With m. care | POUND 383:20
Middle Class: M. was quite prepared | BELL 39:6
What is m. morality | SHAW 498:14
Middlesex: acre in M. is better than | MAC 324:10
middle-sized: m. are alone entangled | SHEN 505:16
midge: lightly skims the m. | BETJ 42:18
Spins like a fretful m. | ROSS 409:17
Midian: host of M. was beneath | BIBLE 49:16
Midland: M. waters with the gale | ARN 14:21
Midlands: When I am living in the M. | BELL 40:9
midnight: at m. speak with the Sun | VAUG 555:11
At the m. in the silence | BROW 98:31
blackest M. born | MILT 342:12
books consum'd the m. oil | GAY 223:10
budding morrow in m. | KEATS 292:25
embalmer of the still m. | KEATS 292:28
heard the chimes at m. | SHAK 442:6
hill during a clear m. | HARDY 241:9
iron tongue of m. hath | SHAK 471:20
m. never come | MARL 329:11
M. shakes the memory | ELIOT 204:9
m. shroud the serene lights | SHEL 504:7
m. when the noon-heat breathes | HARDY 239:18
mock the m. bell | SHAK 422:22
Not to be a-bed after m. | SHAK 488:16
Once upon a m. dreary | POE 375:4
our m. oil | QUAR 403:10
sigh'd upon a m. pillow | SHAK 425:9
stroke of m. ceases | HOUS 265:17
There m.'s all a-glimmer | YEATS 585:17
threshed corn at m. by a tress | YEATS 585:17
'Tis the year's m. | DONNE 189:27
to hear the chimes at m. | STEV 522:2

troubled m. and the noon's ELIOT 202:11
upon the m. with no pain KEATS 291:22
Upon the m. hour KEATS 292:2
visions before m. BROW 95:23
mid-sea: Painted the m. blue FLEC 214:17
midshipmite: bo'sun tight, and a m.
GILB 225:16
midst: God is in the m. of her PRAY 392:20
m. of life we are in death PRAY 389:12
them in the m. of his days BIBLE 60:25
Midsummer: high M. pomps come ARN 15:6
this is very m. madness SHAK 490:6
midwife: She is the fairies' m. SHAK 481:28
mid-winter: In the bleak m. ROSS 409:1
mie: *J'aime mieux ma m.* ANON 9:17
mien: dark hair and lovesome m.
TENN 532:16
mieux: *je vais de mieux en m.* COUE 163:8
m. est l'ennemi du bien VOLT 561:5
Tout est pour le m. dans VOLT 561:2
Might: Because the all-enacting M.
HARDY 240:6
do it with thy m. BIBLE 55:29
Exceeds man's m. SHAK 487:1
faith that right makes m. LINC 314:17
'It m. have been HARTE 242:28
'It m. have been WHIT 571:19
Lord of all power and m. PRAY 386:19
majority has the m. IBSEN 269:18
Measurement began our m. YEATS 587:7
m. of Denmark's crown CAMP 128:14
of hearts I feel your m. WORD 579:13
our m. lessens ANON 8:9
spirit of counsel and m. BIBLE 58:9
them mirth us'd all his m. MILT 347:26
woman's m. SHAK 449:22
You m. as well live PARK 368:18
Might-have-been: my name is M. ROSS 410:4
mightier: imposition of a m. hand
MAC 323:26
pen is m. than the sword BULW 107:4
word m. than they in arms MILT 348:26
mightiest: 'Tis m. in the mightiest
SHAK 467:27
mighty: according to the m. working
PRAY 389:13
bringeth m. things to pass PRAY 398:1
God who made thee m. BENS 40:24
how are the m. fallen BIBLE 50:16
How are the m. fallen BIBLE 50:17
Lord m. in battle PRAY 390:24
m. from their seats BIBLE 60:6
m. hand and by a stretched BIBLE 48:19
m. things from small beginnings
DRYD 195:22
same became m. men which BIBLE 45:33
there the shield of the m. BIBLE 50:16
things which are m. BIBLE 75:30
thou art m. yet SHAK 452:3
Though mean and m. rotting SHAK 428:20
migrations: our m. from the blue bed
GOLD 232:34
mild: brought reg'lar and draw'd m.
DICK 179:12
m. and magnificent eye BROW 102:5
m. as she is seeming so GREE 236:10
mildest: He was the m. manner'd
BYRON 122:30
mildews: m. the white wheat SHAK 454:22
mile: compel thee to go a m. BIBLE 64:18
Miles: M. and miles distant though
ROSS 409:26
m. around the wonder grew HOUS 263:1
m. to go before I sleep FROST 219:12
na on the lang Scots m. BURNS 115:3
People come m. to see it GILB 227:10
Sed m., sed pro patria NEWB 361:5
milestones: There's m. on the Dover
Road DICK 178:22
Militant: Poets M. below COWL 164:16

state of Christ's Church m. PRAY 387:12
military: Forsaking even m. men GILB 228:39
m. domination of Prussia ASQ 17:17
m. empires of the shark AUDEN 20:15
order and m. discipline ANON 4:28
thing to be left to the m. CLEM 152:31
When the m. man approaches SHAW 497:30
militavi: *Et m. non sine gloria* HOR 261:6
militi: are gone to m. the bull JOHN 275:3
buy value and m. BIBLE 59:25
drunk the m. of Paradise COL 157:1
find a trout in the m. THOR 550:24
flowing with m. and honey BIBLE 47:6
forstre hym wel with m. CHAU 142:25
Gin was mother's m. SHAW 498:15
…Kindly pass the m. PAIN 367:18
little drop of m. PAIN 367:19
M. and then just as it BETJ 42:20
m. comes frozen home SHAK 457:19
m. is more likely to be BUTL 119:4
m. my ewes and weep SHAK 492:5
m. of human kindness BURKE 112:3
m. of human kindness CHUR 148:22
m. of human kindness SHAK 459:1
m. the cow of the world WILB 572:4
m. were scarce out of him SHAK 488:9
she gave him m. BIBLE 49:10
sincere m. of the word BIBLE 80:22
sincere m. of the word BIBLE 83:25
suggestion as a cat laps m. SHAK 485:6
take my m. for gall SHAK 459:2
than putting m. into babies CHUR 150:15
white curd of ass's m. POPE 376:30
milking: to the m. shed ING 270:15
Milk-soup: M. men call domestic bliss
PATM 370:4
milk-white: mounted on her m. steed
BALL 32:4
Mill: In Hans' old M. his three DE L 174:4
John Stuart M. BENT 41:8
m. and the fold HOUS 263:6
m. turns round POPE 381:6
water glideth by the m. SHAK 486:15
mille: Ay clappeth as a m. CHAU 142:10
Da mi basia m. CAT 136:26
Miller: hackney'd jokes from M.
BYRON 124:17
Than wots the m. SHAK 486:15
There was a jolly m. once BICK 83:28
millinery: That jewell'd mass of m.
TENN 540:1
million: Treble that m. HERR 249:22
millionaire: Endowed by the ruined m.
ELIOT 202:22
I am a M. SHAW 497:11
silk hat on a Bradford m. ELIOT 205:1
million-murdering: m. Death ROSS 408:20
millions: among so many m. of faces
BROW 96:31
Jesus they run into m. ROST 410:15
m. of strange shadows SHAK 493:15
mortal m. live *alone* ARN 13:12
our yearly multiplying m. OSUL 365:23
What m. died CAMP 129:8
mills: dark Satanic m. BLAKE 86:16
m. of God grind slowly LOGAU 316:5
millstone: m. were hanged abut his
BIBLE 67:3
m. were hanged about his BIBLE 70:30
mill-stones: Turned to m as they fell
SHEL 502:3
mill-wheel: Except the m.'s sound
SHEL 500:3
Milton: classic M. BRID 92:9
England's M. equals both COWP 167:34
malt does more than M. HOUS 264:12
M. almost requires a solemn LAMB 307:19
M., a name to resound TENN 533:12
M., Death, and Sin YOUNG 588:14
M.'s the prince of poets BYRON 123:5

M.! thou shouldst be living WORD 582:5
M. was for us BROW 102:5
M. wrote in fetters when BLAKE 88:12
morals hold Which M. held WORD 582:3
Some mute inglorious M. GRAY 234:23
mimicked: beggars in the street m.
MAC 323:33
mimsy: All m. were the borogoves
CARR 134:28
mince: honesty and love doth m. SHAK 475:6
They dined on m. LEAR 312:14
mind: am not in my perfect m. SHAK 456:1
amplitude of m. WORD 580:26
autumn in the m. SPAR 514:22
beauty is the m. diseased BYRON 121:13
be of one m. in an house PRAY 394:7
body fill'd and vacant m. SHAK 444:25
calm the troubled m. CONG 159:31
certain unsoundness of m. MAC 323:23
chords in the human m. DICK 176:15
Church and broad of m. BETJ 44:14
Come back into my m. BELL 40:9
complicated state of m. GILB 227:21
conjunction of the m. MARV 331:19
corridors into the m. DOUG 191:7
dagger of the m. SHAK 459:15
depths of his own oceanic m. COL 158:8
dictates of his godlike. OTWAY 365:27
effectually robs the m. BURKE 108:9
ever by the eternal m. WORD 579:7
excursions in my own m. COL 157:29
feeling which arrests the m. JOYCE 286:17
find the m.'s construction SHAK 458:22
fishy form and m. BROO 94:13
fit of absence of m. SEEL 419:16
fixed m. And high disdain MILT 345:2
fog of the good man's m. BROW 100:1
fond and foolish m. BALL 30:8
fool uttereth all his m. BIBLE 54:43
frailty of the m. CONG 161:3
furnish'd with a m. so rare SHAK 428:7
generous and elevated m. JOHN 282:19
golden m. stoops not SHAK 466:16
heart argues, not the m. ARN 13:20
He first damages his m. ANON 10:1
Henceforth my wooing m. SHAK 457:16
her m. grew worse and worse WORD 577:24
his belly will hardly m. JOHN 275:11
His m. his kingdom COWP 167:37
His m. moves upon silence YEATS 586:3
his m. or body to prefer POPE 379:12
how little the m. is actually JOHN 276:23
how love exalts the m. DRYD 195:33
human m. in ruins DAV 172:13
I have a man's m. SHAK 449:22
index of a feeling m. COWP 168:24
in his right m. BIBLE 68:31
Intense irradiation of a m. SHEL 501:18
in the m. of man WORD 578:7
is no passion in the m. BACON 26:2
is nothing great but m. HAM 238:16
labyrinthine ways Of my own m. THOM 548:8
Let this m. be in you BIBLE 78:13
man but chang'd his m. POPE 377:10
man's unconquerable m. WORD 582:17
man that has a m. and knows SHAW 496:3
marble index of a m. WORD 580:17
march of m. has marched PEAC 370:13
Measure your m.'s height BROW 103:5
men agree to be of one m. BACON 25:11
m. and hand went together HEM 245:2
m. and soul, according TENN 535:32
m. be a thoroughfare KEATS 294:26
m., body, or estate PRAY 386:1
m. does not make us soft PER 372:22
m., from pleasure less MARV 332:4
m. has a thousand eyes BOUR 90:21
m. has mountains HOPK 256:20
m. impatient SHAK 429:26
m. in a sound body JUV 288:4

m. instilled throughout VIRG 558:24
m. is free DRAY 193:8
m. not to be changed MILT 345:10
M. of Man WORD 577:8
m. quite vacant is a mind COWP 166:19
m. serene for contemplation GAY 223:17
m. the things of the flesh BIBLE 75:7
m.; which experienced SMITH 511:33
minister to a m. diseas'd SHAK 463:3
moved slowly through the m. WORD 580:14
my m. baulks at it COMP 159:13
my m.'s unsworn EUR 209:4
My m. to me a kingdom is DYER 199:17
noblest frailty of the m. SHAD 420:20
not their frame of m. HOR 258:19
of a sound m. BIBLE 79:22
of m. to have few things BACON 26:8
of the human m. is slow BURKE 109:29
one dead level ev'ry m. POPE 375:24
out of sight is out of m. CLOU 154:5
padlock—on her m. PRIOR 400:23
perfect presence of m. JAMES 271:29
persuaded in his own m. BIBLE 75:27
pleased to call your m. WEST 569:3
raise and erect the m. BACON 24:19
seasons in the m. of men KEATS 292:14
serve thee with a quiet m. PRAY 386:22
She had a frugal m. COWP 165:17
She unbent her m. afterwards LAMB 307:9
So let extend thy m. o'er MILT 350:7
squares of his m. were AUDEN 19:5
subsistence without a m. BERK 41:19
that the female m. is not KNOX 305:24
there's no blemish but the m. SHAK 490:18
thy m. all virtue JOHN 274:4
thy m. is a very opal SHAK 489:5
To cure the m.'s wrong GREEN 235:28
To work my m. SHAK 493:5
universal frame is without a m. BACON 25:22
unseemly exposure of the m. HAZL 243:26
untrodden region of my m. KEATS 292:3
want to light up my own m. BROW 102:19
Was never m. ROYD 411:3
what a noble m. is here SHAK 433:15
What is M. PUNCH 402:15
when the m. lays by its CAT 136:28
When the m.'s free SHAK 454:13
whose untutor'd m. POPE 379:5
Will not go from my m. SHAK 476:26
with a well-informed m. AUST 23:5
With profits of the m. SHAK 463:14
minded: had m. what they were about STER 519:16

Mindful: M. of th' unhonour'd dead GRAY 235:3
that thou art m. of him PRAY 389:28
minds: actions speak great m. FLET 215:18
cultivated by narrow m. MILL 339:1
fairly developed m. FORS 216:22
great empire and little m. BURKE 110:6
hobgoblin of little m. EMER 207:38
hunger of ambitious m. SPEN 516:21
images of their m. where BACON 27:4
keep your hearts and m. BIBLE 78:21
marriage of true m. SHAK 495:5
M. innocent and quiet take LOV 318:18
only the refuge of weak m. CHES 145:28
Since wars begin in the m. ANON 7:16
spur of all great m. CHAP 140:15
things affect little m. DISR 186:10
Thou m. me o' departed joys BURNS 116:7
To men of other m. my fancy GOLD 231:27
will not weed their own m. WALP 563:17
mine: be m. the shame DRYD 196:13
but m. own SHAK 427:4
he was but one hour m. SHAK 493:10
Manasses is m. PRAY 393:14
m. own familiar friend PRAY 393:11
shall be m. JONS 284:1
then shouldst thou have m. SUCK 524:12

'Twas m., 'tis his SHAK 475:16
would she were m. LODGE 316:4
minefield: What a m. Life is FRY 220:8
mineral: animal, and m. GILB 228:16
miners: rugged m. poured to war MAC 321:27
Minerva: dices faciesve M. HOR 258:5
M. when she talks JONS 285:5
written or created unless M. HOR 258:5
mines: Like plants in m. which BROW 103:7
M. reported in the fairway KIPL 301:12
one yard below their m. SHAK 435:21
mingle: one another's being m. SHEL 502:1
To m. with the Universe BYRON 121:22
mingled: desired my dust to be m. POUND 383:16
When hearts have once m. SHEL 501:22
mining-claims: snakeskin-titles of m. BENET 40:19
minion: Like valour's m. carv'd SHAK 458:3
this morning morning's m. HOPK 257:4
minished: for the faithful are m. PRAY 389:32
Minister: become the King's First M. CHUR 150:12
discreet and learned M. PRAY 387:17
God help the M. that meddles MELB 336:16
m. kiss'd the fiddler's BURNS 114:28
m. to a mind diseas'd SHAK 463:3
one fair spirit for my m. BYRON 121:21
patient Must m. to himself SHAK 463:3
wisdom of a great m. JUN 287:3
ministered: Angels came and m. unto BIBLE 64:4
thousand thousands m. unto him BIBLE 61:8
ministering: m. angel thou SCOTT 417:21
m. angel shall my sister SHAK 437:4
ministers: Angels and m. of grace SHAK 430:24
Are they m. of Christ BIBLE 77:1
grim Geneva m. AYT 24:10
little errands for the M. GILB 225:24
m. a flaming fire PRAY 396:18
m. of the new testament BIBLE 77:4
m. to consult the public SWIFT 526:8
my actions are my m. CHAR 140:23
passion-winged M. of thought SHEL 499:7
you murdering m. SHAK 459:2
ministrations: m. to one and to all HARDY 238:22
ministries: Times has made many m. BAG 28:24
ministry: if the secret m. of frost COL 156:23
marriage than a m. BAG 28:29
m. of all the talents ANON 7:26
work of the m. BIBLE 77:28
Minnehaha: M., Laughing Water LONG 317:11
minnows: you this Triton of the m. SHAK 427:21
minor: spared these m. monuments BROW 97:12
Minorities: M. almost always SMITH 511:19
minority: efficient m. to coerce STEP 518:20
m. is always right IBSEN 269:18
Minstrel: M. Boy to the war is gone MOORE 356:13
M. was infirm and old SCOTT 416:8
ring the fuller m. TENN 537:15
wandering m. GILB 226:18
mint: pockets the mark of the m. CHES 147:22
tithe of m. and anise BIBLE 67:24
mintage: coiner the m. of man HOUS 263:8
mints: m., savory SHAK 491:25
minuet: Inconsolable to the m. in Ariadne SHER 505:26
minute: Cynthia of this m. POPE 377:18
do it in M. Particulars BLAKE 86:7
fill the unforgiving m. KIPL 300:2
is too m. GOLD 232:3
m. domestic happiness KEATS 294:10
m.'s success pays BROW 98:27

sucker born every m. BARN 34:6
Then the good m. goes BROW 105:29
minutes: I have been five m. too COWL 164:21
m. capons SHAK 437:34
our m. hasten to their end SHAK 493:19
see the m. how they run SHAK 446:18
set with sixty diamond m. MANN 328:14
think for two m. together SMITH 511:35
three m. is a long time HOUS 266:12
to take care of the m. CHES 145:18
Minx: I am a M., or a Sphinx DICK 181:14
Mirabeau: Sous le pont M. coule la APOL 11:11
mirabilia: quia m. fecit BIBLE 83:7
miracle: any m. attested by a sufficient HUME 267:18
existence is a mere m. STEV 522:6
first m. that he wrought PRAY 388:25
shoulder-blade that is a m. GILB 227:10
Take the m. of our age CAREW 130:11
That m. of a youth EVEL 209:8
would seem a M. DONNE 190:24
wrought m. to convince atheism BACON 25:23
miracles: first attended with m. HUME 267:21
M. do not happen ARN 16:16
miraculous: With most m. organ SHAK 433:5
mire: fury and the m. of human YEATS 584:12
out of the m. and clay PRAY 392:1
slimepit and the m. HOUS 265:4
that throw pebbles and m. WATTS 565:26
mirk: It was m. BALL 32:6
miroir: et casser son m. ANON 9:12
mirror: alone and smash his m. ANON 9:12
Following the m. of all SHAK 443:12
for fear They m. true HOUS 262:21
m. crack'd from side TENN 538:11
m. up to nature SHAK 433:17
use of a m. MAC 323:31
mirrors: m. of the sea are strewn FLEC 214:21
Over the m. meant HARDY 239:4
Mirth: Bards of Passion and of M. KEATS 290:31
buys a minute's m. to wail SHAK 492:18
dim and decorous m. BROO 94:16
Far from all resort of m. MILT 342:5
Howe'er in m. most magnified POUND 383:19
I'll use you for my m. SHAK 451:16
I love such m. as does WALT 564:6
In m., that after no repenting MILT 351:11
limit of becoming m. SHAK 456:21
M., admit me of thy crew MILT 342:16
M. can do with her enticing ANON 6:7
m. hath present laughter SHAK 488:17
m. in funeral and with SHAK 429:19
m. that has no bitter springs KIPL 298:12
them m. us'd all his might MILT 347:26
Where's all the joy and m. KEPP 295:12
misbehaved: I m. once at a funeral LAMB 307:27
misbeliever: You call me m. SHAK 466:2
miscarriage: success and m. are empty JOHN 274:1
to be disgraced by m. JOHN 281:5
miscarriages: pregnancies and at least four m. BEEC 37:7
Misce: M. stultitiam consiliis HOR 261:20
miscet: et magno se corpore m. VIRG 558:24
mischief: All punishment is m. BENT 40:27
either of virtue or m. BACON 26:31
From all evil and m. PRAY 385:16
hand to execute any m. CLAR 152:19
Have willed more m. than HOUS 263:13
if m. befell him BIBLE 46:35
intended m. against thee PRAY 390:15
it means m. SHAK 434:9
little knowest the m. NEWT 362:21
little neglect may breed m. FRAN 218:5
m. he had a heart to resolve GIBB 224:28

m. still for hands that　　　MADAN 326:17
m., thou art afoot　　　　　SHAK 451:6
Satan finds some m. still　WATTS 565:21
Spectatress of the m. which　ROWE 410:23
To m. trained　　　　　　　CHUR 149:5
mischiefs: I will heap m. upon them
　　　　　　　　　　　　　　BIBLE 48:32
M. feed Like beasts　　　　JONS 285:6
record the m. he has done　COWP 166:30
mischievous: m. excitability is　BAG 28:20
m. devil Love　　　　　　　BUTL 119:2
miscuit: m. utile dulci　　HOR 258:1
misdoings: sorry for these our m.
　　　　　　　　　　　　　　PRAY 387:19
miserable: are of all men most m.
　　　　　　　　　　　　　　BIBLE 76:21
God would make a man m.　CHAR 140:24
having made a young girl m.　FRAN 218:5
I have pass'd a m. night　SHAK 480:26
make only two people m.　BUTL 119:22
Me m.　　　　　　　　　　MILT 347:15
mercy upon us m. sinners　PRAY 385:15
M. comforters are ye all　BIBLE 52:27
m. have no other medicine　SHAK 464:8
m. state of mind to have　BACON 26:8
most m. things which　VIRG 557:21
so it is very m.　　　　　TAYL 532:3
miserande: m. puer　　　VIRG 559:2
miserere: m. nobis　　　MASS 335:7
miseria: Nella m.　　　　DANTE 171:8
miseries: bound in shallows and in m.
　　　　　　　　　　　　　　SHAK 451:27
heap m. upon us yet entwine　JOYCE 286:10
whom the m. of the world　KEATS 289:27
misery: bound in m. and iron　PRAY 397:7
certain amount of m. which　LOWE 318:24
departure is taken for m.　BIBLE 62:13
given to him that is in m.　BIBLE 52:14
greatest m. is a battle gained　WELL 567:27
happiness and final m.　MILT 346:20
is full of m.　　　　　　　PRAY 389:11
loses his m.　　　　　　　ARN 14:22
loved in m.　　　　　　　YEATS 585:20
merry m.　　　　　　　　BETJ 44:1
mine affliction and my m.　BIBLE 60:29
M. acquaints a man with　SHAK 485:9
pens dwell on guilt and m.　AUST 22:29
remember his m. no more　BIBLE 55:2
result m.　　　　　　　　DICK 177:4
through the vale of m.　PRAY 395:12
time of happiness in m.　DANTE 171:8
Untainted by man's m.　SHEL 503:28
misfortune: alleviate so severe a m.
　　　　　　　　　　　　　　AUST 23:18
m. of our best friends　LA R 310:8
sort of m. is to have been　BOET 89:6
writ with me in sour m.'s　SHAK 483:28
misfortunes: All the m. of men derive
　　　　　　　　　　　　　　PASC 369:5
if a man talks of his m.　JOHN 278:20
m. and pains of others　BURKE 108:8
m. hardest to bear are　LOW 319:17
strong enough to bear the m.　LA R 310:9
tableau of crimes and m.　VOLT 561:10
they make m. more bitter　BACON 27:3
misgivings: Blank m. of a creature
　　　　　　　　　　　　　　WORD 579:10
misgovernment: augur m.　BURKE 109:23
last refuge of cheap m.　SHAW 497:16
misleading: words generate m. thoughts
　　　　　　　　　　　　　　SPEN 514:31
misled: education most have been m.
　　　　　　　　　　　　　　DRYD 196:19
long m. by wandering fires　DRYD 196:13
Mislike: M. me not for my complexion
　　　　　　　　　　　　　　SHAK 466:6
misquote: enough of learning to m.
　　　　　　　　　　　　　　BYRON 124:17
Mis'ry: He gave to M. all he had　GRAY 235:5
laughs the sense of m.　COWP 166:24

miss: catching a train is to m.　CHES 148:11
count and calls her 'M.　CHES 147:19
m. for pleasure　　　　　GAY 223:31
M. not the discourse　　　BIBLE 62:27
so might I m.　　　　　　BROW 101:24
missa: Ite m. est　　　　MASS 335:9
vox m. reverti　　　　　　HOR 258:6
missed: No one would have m. her
　　　　　　　　　　　　　　ANON 5:15
who never would be m.　GILB 226:24
Missing: M. so much and so much
　　　　　　　　　　　　　　CORN 162:22
mission: Never have a m.　DICK 176:20
missionaries: eaten by m.　SPOO 517:9
missionary: I would eat a m.　WILB 572:3
Mississippi: I have seen the M.　BURNS 112:23
Mississippi Bay: East all the way into
　　M.　　　　　　　　　　KIPL 300:24
Miss T: That whatever M. eats　DE L 174:11
Missus: M. my Lord　　　PUNCH 402:30
mist: broke into a m. with bells　BROW 103:11
Faustus like a foggy m.　MARL 329:13
grey m. on the sea's face　MAS 334:4
m. and hum of that low　ARN 14:28
m. in my face　　　　　　BROW 103:31
m. is dispell'd when　　GAY 222:26
rolling m. came down　KING 297:1
mistake: Among all forms of m.　ELIOT 201:8
he never overlooks a m.　HUXL 269:6
it's a m. not　　　　　　JAMES 271:20
lie—under a m.　　　　　SWIFT 526:27
Man is Nature's sole m.　GILB 228:28
m. in the translation　　VANB 555:4
m. to theorize before one　DOYLE 192:7
There is no m.　　　　　WELL 568:8
We will pardon Thy M.　BETJ 43:5
when she made any such m.　DICK 180:5
mistaken: here, unless I am m.　DOYLE 192:24
possible you may be m.　CROM 169:21
To your m. Shrine　　　WINC 575:4
mistakes: All great men make m.
　　　　　　　　　　　　　　CHUR 149:23
at the cost of m.　　　　FROU 219:19
every one gives to their m.　WILDE 573:14
If he makes m. they must　CHUR 150:27
I hope will excuse m.　DICK 180:9
man of genius makes no m.　JOYCE 286:27
man who makes no m. does　PHEL 373:7
there are few m. they have　CHUR 150:17
mistress: Art is a jealous m.　EMER 207:6
ever be m. of this house　AUST 23:17
first an acquaintance, next a m.　CHEK 145:5
In ev'ry port a m. find　GAY 223:29
Like m., like maid　　　FARQ 210:15
lordship's principles or your m.　WILK 574:6
make me m. to the man　POPE 376:11
m. I am ashamed to call　ELIZ 205:28
m. in my own　　　　　　KIPL 301:20
m., in the midmost　　　POUND 382:5
m. mine　　　　　　　　SHAK 488:17
m. of herself　　　　　　POPE 377:20
m. of the months and stars　SWIN 528:14
m. of the Earl of Craven　WILS 574:19
m. should be like a little　WYCH 583:24
m. some rich anger shows　KEATS 291:15
new m. now I chase　　LOV 318:20
No casual m.　　　　　　TENN 536:33
served the lust of my m.'s　SHAK 454:18
So court a m.　　　　　　JONS 284:11
teeming m.　　　　　　　POPE 377:20
worst m.　　　　　　　　BACON 25:9
mistresses: I shall have m.　GEOR 223:35
m. with great smooth marbly　BROW 99:13
one wife and hardly any m.　SAKI 413:13
Wives are young men's m.　BACON 26:34
mists: Season of m. and mellow　KEATS 293:5
Those shaken m. a space　THOM 548:20
When the golden m. are born　SHEL 503:26
when the m. in autumn　KING 297:21
misty: of a ful m. morwe　CHAU 144:8

misunderstood: To be great is to be m.
　　　　　　　　　　　　　　EMER 207:39
misus'd: m. the king's press damnably
　　　　　　　　　　　　　　SHAK 440:9
misused: m. words generate misleading
　　　　　　　　　　　　　　SPEN 514:31
mites: she threw in two m.　BIBLE 68:38
Mithras: M., God of the Morning　KIPL 303:9
Mithridates: M., he died old　HOUS 264:16
mitigation: some m. of the criminal law
　　　　　　　　　　　　　　PEEL 371:5
Mittel: Einmischung anderer M.　CLAU 152:27
niemals bloss als M. brachest　KANT 288:13
unentbehrlich notwendige M.　KANT 288:11
mix: I m. them with my brains　OPIE 365:6
kiss her and m. her with　SWIN 530:27
M. a little foolishness　HOR 261:20
winds of heaven m.　　　SHEL 502:1
mixing: m. it with other things　CARR 136:4
mixture: Had the m. peen　AYT 24:7
m. of a lie doth ever add　BACON 27:29
Moab: M. is my wash-pot　PRAY 393:18
moan: Everything did banish m.　BARN 33:32
made sweet m.　　　　　KEATS 290:18
m. the expense of many　SHAK 493:7
That is not paid with m.　THOM 548:1
virgin-choir to make delicious m.
　　　　　　　　　　　　　　KEATS 292:2
we cast away m.　　　　SHAK 436:13
moanday: All m̃., tearsday, wailsday
　　　　　　　　　　　　　　JOYCE 286:11
moaning: still he lay m.　SMITH 510:26
there be no m. of the bar　TENN 533:3
Moat: Look to your M.　HAL 238:4
moated: at the m. grange　SHAK 464:18
mob: amphibious ill-born m.　DEFOE 173:12
M., Parliament, Rabble　COBB 154:8
occasions to do what the m. do　DICK 181:30
supreme governors, the m.　WALP 562:19
mobled: who had seen the m. queen
　　　　　　　　　　　　　　SHAK 432:24
mock: augurs m. their own presage
　　　　　　　　　　　　　　SHAK 494:21
How my achievements m.　SHAK 487:8
if they yet m. what women　OWEN 367:7
m. on, Voltaire, Rousseau　BLAKE 86:23
m. our eyes with air　SHAK 423:7
m. the midnight bell　SHAK 422:22
m. the riddled corpses　SASS 414:12
They m. the air with idle　GRAY 234:14
to m. your own grinning　SHAK 436:31
When I m. poorness　JONS 283:18
You smile, and m. me　SHAK 487:9
mock'd: if he m. himself　SHAK 448:21
scorn which m. the smart　ARN 13:9
mocked: God is not m.　BIBLE 77:19
mocker: Wine is a m.　BIBLE 54:15
mockeries: things by what their m. be
　　　　　　　　　　　　　　SHAK 444:13
mockery: In monumental m.　SHAK 487:4
m. is the fume of little　TENN 534:13
Unreal m., hence　SHAK 461:12
vain blows malicious m.　SHAK 429:15
mocking-bird: Out of the m.'s throat
　　　　　　　　　　　　　　WHIT 570:9
Mocks: M. married men　SHAK 457:18
Which comforts while it m.　BROW 104:4
model: fellow-countryman is a m. of
　　a man　　　　　　　　DICK 179:19
m. of a modern Major-General　GILB 228:16
when they come to m. Heaven　MILT 349:3
models: Rules and m. destroy genius
　　　　　　　　　　　　　　HAZL 243:28
moderate: £40,000 a year a m.
income　　　　　　　　LAMB 308:15
Read that m. man Voltaire　HARDY 240:17
moderated: absolutism m. by assassination
　　　　　　　　　　　　　　ANON 5:5
moderately: if it be drunk m.　BIBLE 63:15

methinks I scent the m.	SHAK 431:10
M. in the Bowl of Night	FITZ 212:5
M.'s at seven	BROW 103:21
m. stars sang	BIBLE 53:3
m. well-aired before	BRUM 106:4
Never glad confident m.	BROW 102:8
Never m. wore To evening	TENN 536:3
private view in the m.	EDW 200:2
rise up early in the m.	BIBLE 57:25
shown no glorious m. face	STEV 523:11
started that m. from Devon	GILB 226:14
take the wings of the m.	PRAY 399:5
this morning m.'s minion	HOPK 257:4
three o'clock in the m.	FITZ 213:22
Up in the m. early	BURNS 116:2
vanish in the m.	FRY 219:31
we won't go home till m.	BUCK 106:18
With Death and M.	TENN 542:16
Would God it were m.	BIBLE 48:27
mornings: *always* had m. like this	
	MILNE 340:17
Morns: M. abed and daylight	HOUS 262:15
moron: See the happy m.	ANON 7:13
morris: nine men's m. is filled	SHAK 470:5
Morrison's Pill: M. for curing the maladies	
	CARL 132:9
morrow: Eagerly I wished the m.	POE 375:5
therefore no thought for the m.	BIBLE 64:32
watching for the m.	GOET 230:12
mors: Indignatio principis m.	MORE 357:13
M. stupebit et natura	CEL 138:6
Nil igitur m. est ad nos	LUCR 320:8
Pallida M. aequo	HOR 259:13
morsel: I found you as a m.	SHAK 422:20
m. for a monarch	SHAK 421:32
morsels: casteth forth his ice like m.	
	PRAY 399:21
mort: c'est bâtir la m.	MONT 354:15
Dieu est m.	NERV 360:25
Je veux...que la m. me trouve	MONT 354:14
La m. est le remède	CHAM 139:13
La m., sans phrases	SIEY 508:7
m. ne surprend point le	LA F 306:22
veut abolir la peine de m.	KARR 288:16
mortal: all men m., but themselves	
	YOUNG 588:6
chances of this m. life	PRAY 388:5
desperately m.	SHAK 464:25
genius and the m. instruments	SHAK 449:6
'Here came a m.	ARN 13:7
Her last disorder m.	GOLD 231:8
if I laugh at any m. thing	BYRON 121:18
I presume you're m.	SHIR 507:5
M., guilty	AUDEN 19:17
m. millions live *alone*	ARN 13:12
m. mixture of earth's mould	MILT 341:4
m. must put on immortality	BIBLE 76:29
m. thing so to immortalize	SPEN 515:20
rais'd a m. to the skies	DRYD 195:9
shuffled off this m. coil	SHAK 433:8
struck a m. blow right inside	AESC 3:2
time of this m. life	PRAY 386:4
Turning m. for thy love	SHAK 457:5
tush, man, m. men	SHAK 440:12
'twas beyond a m.'s share	MARV 332:8
Who gathers all things m.	SWIN 529:22
Mortalem: M. vitam mors cum immortalis	
	LUCR 320:9
mortalia: mentem m. tangunt	VIRG 557:17
mortality: frail m. shall trust	BACON 28:16
insensible of m.	SHAK 464:25
it smells of m.	SHAK 455:17
m. touches the heart	VIRG 557:17
M. Weighs heavily	KEATS 292:19
Old m.	BROW 97:7
sad m. o'ersways their	SHAK 494:4
There's nothing serious in m.	SHAK 461:1
urns and sepulchres of m.	CREWE 169:18
mortals: greatest good that m. know	ADD 2:6
m. to command success	ADD 1:16

Security Is m.' chiefest	SHAK 462:1
what fools these m. be	SHAK 470:21
morte: battaglie e m.	GAR 221:10
mortified: m. appetite is never	STEV 521:3
mortifying: without very m. reflections	
	CONG 160:3
mortis: etiam opportunitate m.	TAC 531:9
postremo donarem munere m.	CAT 137:15
morts: doit aux m. que la vérité	VOLT 561:19
Il n'y a pas de m.	MAET 326:20
mortuus: Passer m. est meae puellae	
	CAT 136:22
Moscow: If I lived in M. I don't	CHEK 145:3
One is don't march on M.	MONT 355:9
Moses: I was with M.	BIBLE 48:35
M. hid his face	BIBLE 47:5
was sitting in M.' chair	BLAKE 85:24
which M. sent to spy out	BIBLE 48:10
moss: miles of golden m.	AUDEN 18:16
with azure m. and flowers	SHEL 502:10
most: m. material in the postscript	
	BACON 25:42
mot: Le m., c'est le Verbe	HUGO 267:9
mote: Why beholdest thou the m.	BIBLE 64:34
motes: m. that people the sunbeams	
	MILT 341:24
moth: candle sing'd the m.	SHAK 467:1
desire of the m.	SHEL 504:14
Kill not the m. nor butterfly	BLAKE 85:13
like a m.	GAY 222:11
m. and rust doth corrupt	BIBLE 64:25
m. of peace	SHAK 474:6
m.'s kiss	BROW 101:15
mother: and...never called me m.	
	WOOD 576:15
back to the great sweet m.	SWIN 530:27
Behold my m. and my brethren	BIBLE 66:15
Behold thy m.	BIBLE 73:2
Christ and his m. and all	HOPK 256:29
'Daughter am I in my m.'s	KIPL 301:20
dearer was the m.	COL 157:9
deceived The m. of mankind	MILT 344:23
either my father or my m.	STER 519:16
finished jumping on his m.	GILB 228:21
gave her m. forty whacks	ANON 6:12
Happy he With such a m.	TENN 542:19
heaviness of his m.	BIBLE 53:29
Honour thy father and thy m.	BIBLE 47:24
I arose a m. in Israel	BIBLE 49:8
ignorant of their M. Tongue	DRYD 198:14
I had No m.	BROW 99:16
is the m.	BIBLE 60:33
is the m. of Parliaments	BRIG 93:4
leave his father and his m.	BIBLE 45:13
mighty M. did unveil	GRAY 235:18
m. bids me bind my hair	HUNT 268:15
m., do not cry	FARM 209:21
m. Ida	TENN 541:17
m. know that you are out	BARH 33:24
m., make my bed	BALL 30:12
m. of all living	BIBLE 45:24
M. OF HARLOTS AND ABOMINATIONS	BIBLE 82:23
m. of months in meadow	SWIN 528:15
M. of the Free	BENS 40:24
m. of the lovely Cupids	HOR 261:10
m. o' mine	KIPL 301:14
m. on his father him begot	BLAKE 87:2
m.'s head off	DICK 181:23
m.'s life made me a man	MAS 333:22
m.'s pride	SCOTT 417:29
m. under the dragon's tail	SHAK 453:11
m. who talks about her	DISR 185:11
M., Wife, and Queen	TENN 543:15
m. will be there	HERB 246:7
My M.	TAYL 531:25
my m. cried	SHAK 472:1
My m. groan'd	BLAKE 87:23
'Never had any m.	STOWE 523:19
not the church for his m.	CYPR 170:19

recognize your m. with a smile	VIRG 560:1
standing the sorrowing M.	JAC 270:31
that can so astonish a m.	SHAK 434:17
That great m. of sciences	BACON 28:8
There was their Dacian m.	BYRON 121:16
Thou art thy m.'s glass	SHAK 492:24
thou hast murdered thy m.	MAL 327:17
thy dear m. any courtesy	SHAK 428:5
Thy m. a lady	SCOTT 416:24
thy m.'s grief	BRET 92:6
to be a joyful m. of children	PRAY 397:15
Took great Care of his M.	MILNE 340:5
Upon his m.'s grave	WORD 580:3
What a beautiful m.	HOR 259:22
when the m. that bore you	KIPL 301:11
Whose m. was her painting	SHAK 428:16
yet was ever found a m.	GAY 223:11
Your m. will never see	AUST 23:15
mother-in-law: man said when his m. died	
	JER 272:25
mother-naked: m. and ageless-ancient	
	DAY-L 172:21
mothers: best-bodied m. stands	WHIT 570:15
M. of large families	BELL 38:31
women become like their m.	WILDE 573:2
Younger than she are happy m.	SHAK 481:26
mother-wits: jigging veins of rhyming m.	
	MARL 330:2
mothy: m. and warm	HARDY 239:2
Yet at m. curfew-tide	HARDY 239:18
motion: Devoid of sense and m.	MILT 346:10
God order'd m.	VAUG 555:10
her m. Blush'd	SHAK 473:24
little m. in the air	SHEL 500:3
meandering with a mazy m.	COL 156:28
measured m. like a living	WORD 580:12
m. And the act	ELIOT 203:10
next to the perpetual m.	DICK 182:33
No m. has she now	WORD 581:10
Of time's eternal m.	FORD 216:20
Of undistinguishable m.	WORD 580:9
put them to m.	SHAK 489:20
rolled With visible m.	WORD 577:27
this m. like an angel sings	SHAK 468:15
motions: m. of his spirit are dull	SHAK 468:17
secret m. of things	BACON 28:6
two weeping m.	CRAS 169:12
motive: joint and m. of her body	SHAK 487:13
m., not the deed	YEATS 584:18
noblest m.	STEE 518:1
motiveless: motive-hunting of m. malignity	
	COL 157:28
motives: opponent m. meaner	BARR 34:9
reasons and for m. not of State	KIPL 302:5
motley: lived where m. is worn	YEATS 585:1
m. fool	SHAK 425:18
M.'s the only wear	SHAK 425:20
myself a m. to the view	SHAK 495:3
Motor Bus: Can it be a M.	GODL 229:24
Motoribus: Cincti Bis M.	GODL 229:24
motors: sound of horns and m.	ELIOT 204:27
mots: m. avaient un sens	FRAN 217:27
motto: Be that my m. and my fate	
	SWIFT 528:8
With this for m.	TENN 535:10
mottoes: than the m. on sun-dials	
	POUND 383:3
those lovely cracker m.	GILB 225:11
motus: Hi m. animorum atque haec	
	VIRG 560:18
mould: mortal mixture of earth's m.	
	MILT 341:4
m. falls close	ROSS 409:25
m. of a man's fortune is	BACON 26:12
then broke the m.	ARIO 12:2
moulded: made and m. of things past	
	SHAK 487:6
men are m. out of faults	SHAK 465:6
moulder'd: lops the m. branch	TENN 533:26
moulds: Crack nature's m.	SHAK 454:4

Moulmein: By the old M. Pagoda KIPL 301:5
moulted: m. feather BROW 102:16
mound: From this wave-washed m.
                                         ROSS 409:26
mount: m., my soul SHAK 480:16
m. up with wings as eagles BIBLE 59:10
Singing of M. Abora COL 156:30
mountain: bare m. tops are bald ARN 16:7
destroy in all my holy m. BIBLE 58:11
fool alone on a great m. KILV 296:8
from yonder m. height TENN 542:15
gross as a m. SHAK 439:4
He watches from his m. TENN 533:7
huge m. 'tween my heart SHAK 449:22
'If the m. will not...') BACON 25:33
I never see another m. LAMB 307:22
into an exceeding high m. BIBLE 64:3
m. and hill shall be made BIBLE 59:5
m. cradle in Pamere ARN 15:1
m. sheep are sweeter PEAC 371:2
M.'s slumbrous voice SHEL 502:7
shall say unto this m. BIBLE 67:1
sun looked over the m.'s BROW 103:9
taking him up into a high m. BIBLE 69:16
this fair m. leave to feed SHAK 435:7
tiptoe on the misty m. SHAK 483:14
Up the airy m. ALL 3:20
mountainous: m. sports girl BETJ 43:20
mountains: Beautiful must be the m.
                                         BRID 92:17
Before the m. were brought PRAY 395:17
came to the Delectable M. BUNY 107:23
decayed hole among the m. ELIOT 205:10
heaped-up m. with a thunderbolt VIRG 560:12
High m. are a feeling BYRON 120:35
in the rocks of the m. BIBLE 81:30
Make m. level SHAK 442:1
men and m. meet BLAKE 87:10
Molehills seem m. COTT 163:7
m. also shall bring peace PRAY 394:19
M. are the beginning RUSK 411:12
m. by the winter sea TENN 535:20
m. look on Marathon BYRON 122:33
m. skipped like rams PRAY 397:16
M. will heave in childbirth HOR 257:18
One of the m. WORD 582:18
paced upon the m. overhead YEATS 587:12
strength setteth fast the m. PRAY 394:1
that I could remove m. BIBLE 76:14
Ye m. of Gilboa BIBLE 50:16
mountain-tops: Flatter the m. with
  sovereign SHAK 493:9
m. that freeze SHAK 447:3
mountebank: m. who sold pills which
                                         ADD 2:28
story of a m. and his zany WALP 563:19
mounted: m. on her milk-white steed
                                         BALL 32:4
mounts: now he m. above me DRYD 195:12
mourir: et quand on a à m. MOL 353:21
foy je veuil vivre et m. VILL 557:6
Partir c'est m. un peu HAR 238:20
mourn: Blessed are they that m. BIBLE 64:6
countless thousands m. BURNS 114:23
day be time enough to m. DAN 171:1
don't m. for me never ANON 5:13
each will m. her own (she ING 270:16
I did not m. HOUS 264:4
I'll sit and m. all BALL 32:9
I m. for that most lonely YEATS 585:10
It is Margaret you m. HOPK 256:27
man was made to m. BURNS 114:22
M., you powers of Charm CAT 136:22
No longer m. for me when SHAK 494:6
now can never m. SHEL 499:21
time to m. BIBLE 55:12
to comfort all that m. BIBLE 60:8
us in summer skies to m. KEATS 289:8
wherefore should we m. WORD 578:8
yet shall m. with ever-returning WHIT 571:12

mourn'd: m. the Lord of Burleigh
                                         TENN 539:11
Would have m. longer SHAK 429:28
mourned: we have m. unto you BIBLE 66:3
mourner: constant m. o'er the dead
                                         BYRON 124:35
mourners: Most musical of m. SHEL 499:4
mournful: girl arose that had red m. lips
                                         YEATS 586:22
pity and m. awe ARN 13:8
mourning: great m. BIBLE 63:34
I'm in m. for my life CHEK 144:25
m. that either his mother AUST 23:29
oil of joy for m. BIBLE 60:9
To the noise of the m. TENN 541:5
widow bird sate m. SHEL 500:3
mourns: England m. for her dead BINY 84:9
Nature m. her worshipper SCOTT 416:19
mourn'st: who m. the Daisy's fate
                                         BURNS 115:19
mourra: On m. seul PASC 369:9
mous: appetit hath he to ete a m.
                                         CHAU 142:25
if that she saugh a m. CHAU 141:16
mouse: always leave room for the m.
                                         SAKI 413:15
Good my m. of virtue SHAK 488:7
killing of a m. on Sunday BRAT 91:24
m.'s limp tail hanging MOORE 355:22
Not a m. Shall disturb SHAK 471:22
Not a m. stirring SHAK 429:6
other caught a M. LEAR 312:23
silly little m. will be born HOR 257:18
usual to catch a m. or two GRAY 235:23
mouse-trap: baiting a m. with cheese
                                         SAKI 413:15
Hamlet: The M. SHAK 434:12
make a better m. EMER 208:15
mousseline: Supplants the m. of Cos
                                         POUND 383:5
moustache: who didn't wax his m. was
                                         KIPL 304:37
mouth: body and sweet small m. SWIN 530:13
book comes into my m. POUND 382:15
cleave to the roof of my m. PRAY 399:3
door and bar for thy m. BIBLE 63:12
Englishman to open his m. SHAW 498:12
God be in my m. ANON 5:9
His m. is most sweet BIBLE 57:4
Keep your m. shut ANON 9:18
Let the words of my m. PRAY 390:13
m. filled with laughter PRAY 398:16
m. is smoother than oil BIBLE 53:20
m. like an old potato KIPL 298:7
m. of the Lord doth man BIBLE 48:22
m. of the Lord hath spoken BIBLE 59:5
m. of very babes and sucklings PRAY 389:28
mouths are one with M. BROO 95:1
m. shall shew thy praise PRAY 393:8
m. sweet as honey BIBLE 82:9
m. went a sharp twoedged BIBLE 81:14
own m. will I judge thee BIBLE 71:1
pipe for my capacious m. GAY 222:7
praises of God be in their m. PRAY 399:24
proceedeth out of the m. of God BIBLE 64:1
purple-stained m. KEATS 291:18
red splendid kissing m. SWIN 531:1
slap-dash down in the m. CONG 160:25
so he openeth not his m. BIBLE 59:22
spue thee out of my m. BIBLE 81:20
which cometh out of the m. BIBLE 66:28
with the kisses of his m. BIBLE 56:15
yet he opened not his m. BIBLE 59:22
mouthed: first m. SHAK 435:24
m. to flesh-burst HOPK 257:7
mouthful: made it out of a m. of air
                                         YEATS 585:8
mouths: Blind m. MILT 343:12
enemy in their m. to steal SHAK 475:9
issue from your smoky m. MARL 329:13

Make m. upon me when SHAK 470:23
m., and speak not PRAY 397:18
m. were made for tankards MAS 333:21
she made m. in a glass SHAK 454:6
moutons: Revenons à ces m. ANON 9:16
mouvement: Un premier m. ne fut jamais
                                         CORN 162:18
mouvements: Défiez-vous des premiers
  m. MONT 355:11
Movable: M. Types was disbanding
                                         CARL 132:12
move: feel the earth m. HEM 245:3
If I could pray to m. SHAK 449:25
in him we live, and m. BIBLE 74:11
I propose to m. immediately GRANT 234:1
I shall m. Hell VIRG 559:5
it does m. GAL 220:29
I will m. the earth ARCH 11:24
Let's all m. one place CARR 134:4
M. him into the sun OWEN 367:4
M. my faint heart with SHEL 501:15
M. Queen Anne VICT 556:16
m. with the moving ships SWIN 530:28
that honour could not m. BROO 94:27
that it never should m. PRAY 396:11
this will not m. SUCK 524:7
whichever way you m. LUCAN 320:1
moved: king was much m. BIBLE 50:26
M. earth and heaven TENN 544:3
m. more than with a trumpet SIDN 508:3
Spirit of God m. upon BIBLE 44:22
suffer thy foot to be m. PRAY 398:9
though the earth be m. PRAY 392:19
moveless: m. hands And face and gaze
                                         HARDY 240:15
watch and m. woe BROW 98:8
movement: intelligent may begin a m.
                                         CONR 161:22
is almost a palpable m. HARDY 241:9
neither arrest nor m. ELIOT 202:15
movere: Quieta m. magna merces
                                         SALL 413:23
moveris: quocumque m. LUCAN 320:1
movers: We are the m. and shakers
                                         OSH 365:20
moves: m. with its own organs SHAK 422:14
nothing m. in this world MAINE 327:7
moveth: all that m. SPEN 516:25
moving: always m. as the restless
                                         MARL 330:8
m. accident is not my trade WORD 577:22
M. Finger writes FITZ 213:7
m. from hence to there SOCR 512:20
m. Toyshop of their heart POPE 380:30
mower: m. whets his scythe MILT 342:19
Mozambic: M., off at sea north-east
                                         MILT 347:17
MPs: in that House M. divide GILB 226:9
Of dull M. in close proximity GILB 226:10
Mr Collins: if you do not marry M.
                                         AUST 23:15
Mr Slateena: M. was an elderly man
                                         ASHF 17:5
MSS: M. as drunkards use lamp-posts
                                         HOUS 266:14
M'Tavish: Against the clan M. AYT 24:6
much: do as m. for my true-love BALL 32:9
just so m., no more BROW 105:28
M. hath been done BYRON 121:32
M. have I seen and known TENN 543:22
M. in our vows SHAK 489:7
m. is to be done and little JOHN 280:7
so m. to do TENN 537:2
tell me how m. SHAK 421:7
that is too m. in anything BACON 25:37
'There won't be m. for us CARR 133:13
muchness: Much of a m. VANB 555:3
muck: down in lovely m. I've HOUS 264:13
Money is like m. BACON 27:12
when to stop raking the m. ROOS 408:4

muckrake: with a m. in his hand
BUNY 107:28
muck-rakes: men with the m. are often
ROOS 408:4
mud: come of water and of m. BROO 94:11
inhabitants of m. moving FORS 217:5
Longing to be back in the m. AUG 21:11
Me name is M. DENN 174:23
morris is filled up with m. SHAK 470:5
m., celestially fair BROO 94:13
m. into coffee on board THAC 545:9
M.'s sister, not himself HOUS 266:10
One sees the m. LANG 309:21
muddied: m. oafs at the goals KIPL 300:4
muddle: manage somehow to m. through
BRIG 93:3
'meddle and m. DERBY 175:9
muddy: are tickled best in m. BUTL 118:20
hearts and m. understandings BURKE 111:11
m. ecstasies of beer COWP 168:8
M., ill-seeming SHAK 484:16
m. vesture of decay SHAK 468:15
muero: Muero porque no m. JOHN 273:15
Muffin: Hot M. and Crumpet Baking
DICK 179:33
One caught a M. LEAR 312:23
muffling: in his mantle m. up his
SHAK 450:28
mug: graceful air and heavenly m.
FLEM 215:4
Guinness from a thick m. PINT 373:18
mule: m. of politics that engenders
DISR 185:41
not like to horse and m. PRAY 391:18
mules: m. of politics POWER 384:3
mulier: Desinat in piscem m. HOR 257:9
m. cupido quod dicit amanti CAT 137:7
Multas: M. per gentes et multa CAT 137:15
multiplicanda: Entia non sunt m. praeter
OCCAM 364:19
Multiplication: M. is vexation ANON 6:18
multiplicity: m. of agreeable consciousness
JOHN 275:17
multiplied: Thou hast m. the nation
BIBLE 58:6
multiplieth: m. words without knowledge
BIBLE 52:40
multiply: Increase and m. upon us
PRAY 386:16
m., and replenish BIBLE 45:6
m. my signs and my wonders BIBLE 47:11
multiplying: of our yearly m. millions
OSUL 365:23
multitude: By the fool m. SHAK 466:19
giddy m. MASS 335:25
great m. BIBLE 81:31
hoofs of a swinish m. BURKE 111:14
me with the barbarous m. SHAK 466:19
m. is always in the wrong ROOS 408:12
m. of the isles may be PRAY 396:6
m.; that numerous piece BROW 96:30
my life with m. of days JOHN 283:1
not in the m. of friends JONS 283:23
multitudes: I contain m. WHIT 571:5
m. in the valley of decision BIBLE 61:17
weeping m. ELIOT 202:5
mummy: dy'd in m. SHAK 476:4
M. is become merchandise BROW 97:22
munch: m. on, crunch on BROW 103:19
munch'd: m., and munch'd SHAK 458:6
mundanal: del que huye el m. ruido
LUIS 320:12
mundi: Antiquitas saeculi juventus m.
BACON 25:10
cito transit gloria m. THOM 546:7
flammantia moenia m. LUCR 320:3
Sic transit gloria m. ANON 11:1
tollis peccata m. MASS 335:7
munditiis: Simplex m. HOR 259:15
mundus: justitia et pereat m. FERD 210:33

Unde m. iudicetur CEL 138:6
munere: sunt tristi m. ad inferias CAT 137:15
Muneribus: M. sapienter uti HOR 261:19
munny: 'Doänt thou marry for m. TENN 541:1
muove: Eppur si m. GAL 220:29
L'amor che m. il sole DANTE 171:18
murals: with its m. on the wall BETJ 43:1
murder: foul and most unnatural m.
SHAK 431:6
from battle and m. PRAY 385:16
I met M. in the way SHEL 502:2
indeed should m. sanctuarize SHAK 436:18
indulges himself in m. DE Q 175:5
is m. by the law YOUNG 587:19
Killing no M. Briefly Discourst
SEXBY 420:17
Macbeth does m. sleep SHAK 460:8
Most sacrilegious m. hath SHAK 460:22
m. an infant in its cradle BLAKE 88:24
m. cannot be hid long SHAK 466:10
M. Considered as One DE Q 175:4
M., like talent LEWES 314:6
M. most foul SHAK 431:7
M.'s out of tune SHAK 477:9
m., though it have no SHAK 433:5
One m. made a villain PORT 381:31
See how love and m. will CONG 159:26
Thou shalt do no m. PRAY 387:9
time to m. and create ELIOT 203:19
To do no contriv'd m. SHAK 473:20
To m. and to rafish AYT 24:6
We m. to dissect WORD 582:23
whose m. yet is but fantastical SHAK 458:20
wither'd m. SHAK 460:1
murder'd: Our royal master's m.
SHAK 460:24
Who m. in Thirteen Fifty-One COW 164:5
murdered: Each one a m. self ROSS 410:3
m. reputations of the week CONG 160:32
thou hast m. thy mother MAL 327:17
murderer: deaf and viperous m. SHEL 499:18
He was a m. from the beginning BIBLE 72:13
honourable m. SHAK 477:22
man is a common m. SAKI 413:2
m. or to embrace the impenitent STEV 521:12
murderers: m., and idolaters BIBLE 83:3
taken by our friends the m. KARR 288:16
murders: upon the stroke that m.
SHAK 483:10
murd'rer: was the first m.'s son
COWP 167:21
murex: Who fished the m. up BROW 103:27
murmur: creeping m. and the poring
dark SHAK 444:9
hears its winding m. ARN 12:22
m. of a summer's day ARN 14:11
rustic m. of their bourg TENN 535:4
murmuration: patterns a m. of starlings
AUDEN 20:6
murmured: m. in their tents PRAY 397:5
murmuring: brooks of Eden mazily m.
TENN 533:13
m. of innumerable bees TENN 542:17
murmurs: hear our mutual m. sweep
BYRON 123:4
In hollow m. died away COLL 158:22
murners: & that no m. walk behind
HARDY 241:18
murrain: Usura is a m. POUND 382:9
Murray: hae slain the Earl of M. BALL 30:15
My M. BYRON 126:2
murther: foul and midnight m. fed
GRAY 234:17
mus: nascetur ridiculus m. HOR 257:18
Musa: laude virum M. vetat mori HOR 261:17
M. loqui HOR 257:23
Musarum: Audita M. sacerdos HOR 260:13
muscle: motion of a m. WORD 577:2
muscles: m. of his brawny arms LONG 317:18
Muse: conqueror creates a M. WALL 562:12

Donne, whose m. on dromedary COL 157:6
Livelier liquor than the M. HOUS 264:12
M. but serv'd to ease some POPE 376:23
m. in silence sings aloud CLARE 152:10
M. invoked SWIFT 527:34
M. of fire SHAK 443:3
praise the M. forbids to die | HOR 261:17
talked shop like a tenth m. ANON 5:17
tenth M. TROL 553:13
this the Tragic M. first POPE 375:11
with the worst-natur'd m. ROCH 407:4
Muses: charm of all the M. often
TENN 543:17
Me too the M. made write VIRG 560:7
M. scorn with vulgar brains SIDN 507:26
priest of the M. HOR 260:13
mushroom: meet a m. rich civilian
BYRON 126:9
m. of a night's growth DONNE 190:26
m. On whom the dew FORD 216:13
mushrooms: broiled fowl and m. DICK 181:26
Music: brave M. of a distant FITZ 212:12
breast o'ercharged to m. SIDN 507:24
by will make the m. mute TENN 535:7
chief m. of our May DRAY 193:19
city is built To m. TENN 534:6
deep sea and m. in its roar BYRON 121:22
die in m. SHAK 477:18
discourse most eloquent m. SHAK 434:19
Extraordinary how potent cheap m.
COW 163:12
Fading in m. SHAK 467:8
fiddled whisper m. ELIOT 205:9
Fled is that m. KEATS 291:23
genius was the sphere of m. ARN 16:2
had also a peculiar m. BRON 93:17
he hears no m. SHAK 448:21
His voice in all her m. SHEL 499:23
How sour sweet m. is SHAK 480:14
If m. be the food of love SHAK 487:20
in general is frozen m. SCH 415:8
In sweet m. is such art SHAK 447:3
in the m. of men's lives SHAK 480:14
I shall be made thy M. DONNE 189:14
Just accord all m. makes SIDN 508:1
Let a florid m. praise AUDEN 20:21
let the sounds of m. SHAK 468:15
Like m. on my heart COL 155:28
Like softest m. to attending SHAK 482:19
little m. out of doors KEATS 294:24
maintain the m. of the spheres BROW 96:34
man that hath no m. SHAK 468:17
May make one m. as before TENN 535:32
mellow m. match'd with him TENN 536:30
merry when I hear sweet m. SHAK 468:16
M. alone with sudden charms CONG 159:31
M. and sweet Poetry agree BARN 34:2
M. and women I cannot PEPYS 372:16
m. at the close SHAK 478:18
M. begins to atrophy when POUND 383:21
m. for to lilt upon MAS 333:21
M. has charms to sooth CONG 160:14
m., ho SHAK 422:8
m. in my heart I bore WORD 578:16
M. is essentially useless SANT 414:3
M. is feeling STEV 520:16
m. is the brandy SHAW 497:27
m. of forfended spheres PATM 370:7
m. of its trees at dawn ARN 14:1
m. of the Gospel leads FABER 209:14
m. of the languid hours LANG 309:18
m. plants and flowers SHAK 447:3
M. shall untune the sky DRYD 197:25
m. soars within the little BROW 97:29
M. that gentlier TENN 539:13
m. that I care to hear HOPK 256:14
M., the greatest good ADD 2:6
M., when soft voices die SHEL 504:12
m., yearning like a God KEATS 289:13
My m. playing far off SHAK 422:9

no m. in the nightingale	SHAK 491:1
Of m. Dr Johnson used	JOHN 280:23
one equal m.	DONNE 191:3
practising your pastoral m.	VIRG 559:11
rather like m.	FRY 220:1
reasonable good ear in m.	SHAK 471:3
seduction of martial m.	BURN 112:21
Shelley with liquid m.	BRID 92:9
shriller than all the m.	SHAK 448:7
solemn service of m.	LAMB 307:19
soul of m. shed	MOORE 356:9
still, sad m. of humanity	WORD 578:7
struck one chord of m.	PROC 401:14
that vulgar and tavern m.	BROW 97:1
their own M. when they stray	CAMP 129:21
This m. crept by me upon	SHAK 484:31
Though m. oft hath such	SHAK 464:22
thou hast thy m. too	KEATS 293:7
to the heavy part the m.	JONS 283:21
To the Master of all m.	LONG 317:14
to the sound of soft m.	DISR 187:1
towards the condition of m.	PATER 369:20
We are the m. makers	OSH 365:20
were fulfilled with the m.	SWIN 528:24
What passion cannot M.	DRYD 197:22
why hear'st thou m. sadly	SHAK 492:25
Women and m. should never	GOLD 232:29
'Your voice is m.	BEER 38:5
musical: found out m. tunes	BIBLE 63:23
his m. finesse was such	COWP 166:27
Most m.	MILT 342:2
Most m. of mourners	SHEL 499:4
m. as is Apollo's lute	MILT 341:11
m. glasses	GOLD 232:36
Silence more m. than any	ROSS 409:6
So m. a discord	SHAK 471:7
We were none of us m.	GASK 222:1
music-hall: m. singer attends a series	GILB 227:6
Music-halls: be no more jokes in M.	SASS 414:12
musician: better a m. than the wren	SHAK 468:19
lady is a m.	DOYLE 192:20
only a poet and not a m.	BUTL 118:32
musicians: 'tis we m. know	BROW 98:21
To all m., appear	AUDEN 18:4
musick: all kinds of m.	BIBLE 61:3
all the daughters of m.	BIBLE 56:11
hope daunceth without m.	HERB 246:22
music-maker: Schumann's our m. now	BROW 100:16
musicologist: m. is a man who can read	BEEC 37:6
Musing: M. full sadly in his sullen	SPEN 516:7
M. in solitude	WORD 577:7
thus m. the fire kindled	PRAY 391:30
musk: m. carnations break	ARN 15:6
musk-rose: coming m.	KEATS 291:21
musk-roses: With sweet m.	SHAK 470:10
muss: darüber m. man schweigen	WITT 575:17
M. es sein	BEET 38:9
mussed: if hair is m. on her forehead	POUND 382:15
mussel: m. pooled and the heron	THOM 547:6
must: forth I m.	HOUS 265:15
if we can we m.	HOUS 264:22
Is m. a word to be addressed	ELIZ 206:6
It m. be	BEET 38:9
It m. be so	ADD 1:24
m. shall foam	MAC 322:12
Something m. be done	EDW 200:3
Thou m.	EMER 207:2
we forget because we m.	ARN 12:21
mustard: faith as a grain of m.	BIBLE 67:1
mustard seed: is like to a grain of m.	BIBLE 66:20
mustered: m. their soldiers by two	BALL 31:8

musty: proverb is something m.	SHAK 434:18
mutabile: Varium et m. semper	VIRG 558:14
mutability: chance, and death, and m.	SHEL 503:12
How M. in them doth play	SPEN 516:24
Nought may endure but M.	SHEL 502:6
mutable: m., rank-scented many	SHAK 427:20
mutamur: et nos m. in illis	ANON 11:5
mutant: animum m. qui trans mare	HOR 258:19
Mutato: M. nomine de te	HOR 261:22
mutatus: Quantum m. ab illo	VIRG 558:5
mute: balance let's be m.	BURNS 112:26
face is a m. recommendation	PUBL 402:4
long since m.	KEATS 289:21
M. and magnificent	DRYD 197:29
m. inglorious Milton here	GRAY 234:23
m. ministrations to one	HARDY 238:22
of natures that are m.	MER 337:12
street and pavement m.	HARDY 240:21
will make the music m.	TENN 535:7
muteness: uncommunicating m. of fishes	LAMB 308:4
mutiny: fear and m.	SHAK 479:20
of Rome to rise and m.	SHAK 451:3
mutter: blessed m. of the mass	BROW 99:14
Wizards that peep and that m.	BIBLE 58:5
mutton: his m. and his claret good	HOME 253:25
m. with the usual trimmings	DICK 182:26
mutton-pies: I make them into m.	CARR 136:6
mutual: that m. cowardice keeps us	JOHN 278:3
muzzle: m. the ox when he treadeth	BIBLE 48:25
smoke that rubs its m.	ELIOT 203:18
my: m. Hornby and my Barlow	THOM 547:24
My-doxy: Orthodoxy or M. and Heterodoxy	CARL 131:25
Myfanwy: my staunch M.	BETJ 43:16
myriad: There died a m.	POUND 383:10
myriad-minded: Our m. Shakespeare	COL 157:23
myrrh: frankincense, and m.	BIBLE 63:32
m. is my wellbeloved unto	BIBLE 56:18
myrtle: brier shall come up the m.	BIBLE 59:28
m. and turkey part of it	AUST 22:28
myrtles: Which a grove of m. made	BARN 33:32
myself: Am quite m. again	HOUS 263:1
'because I'm not m.	CARR 133:21
I celebrate m.	WHIT 570:16
I do not know m.	GOET 229:28
If I am not for m.	HILL 251:6
I m. a sterling lad	HOUS 264:13
is to love him as m.	PRAY 388:15
M. alone I seek to please	GAY 223:18
m. a traitor with the rest	SHAK 480:4
M. when young did eagerly	FITZ 212:20
near the praising of m.	SHAK 467:17
of such a thing as I m.	SHAK 448:13
pray for no man but m.	SHAK 486:3
thought of thinking for m.	GILB 228:6
When I give I give m.	WHIT 571:1
mysmetre: m. for defaute of tonge	CHAU 144:17
mysteries: m. of Hecate and the night	SHAK 453:3
Stewards of the m. of God	BIBLE 75:32
understand all m.	BIBLE 76:14
What m. do lie beyond thy	VAUG 555:20
wingy m. in divinity	BROW 96:8
mysterious: nothing m. or supernatural	HUME 267:20
mystery: from the Penetralium of m.	KEATS 293:19
He will discredit our m.	SHAK 464:23
in a m. inside an enigma	CHUR 149:28

I shew you a m.	BIBLE 76:29
love is such a m.	SUCK 524:13
lucrative business of m.	BURKE 108:12
marvel and a m.	LONG 316:21
M., BABYLON THE GREAT	BIBLE 82:23
m. of the glorious Body	THOM 546:16
m. of the cross shines	VEN 556:5
out the heart of my m.	SHAK 434:20
reflection solves the m.	STUB 524:5
That moment of m.	ELIOT 203:7
that where m. begins	BURKE 108:12
to lose myself in a m.	BROW 96:9
upon 's the m. of things	SHAK 456:3
which the burthen of the m.	WORD 578:5
your m.; nay, dispatch	SHAK 476:17
mystic: eyeball owns the m. rod	BROW 105:14
m. reverence	BAG 28:21
you walk your m. way	GILB 227:21
mystical: members incorporate in the m.	PRAY 388:3
m. body of thy Son	PRAY 387:4
m. way of Pythagoras	BROW 96:11
order and m. mathematics	BROW 95:20
myswrite: prey I God that non m.	CHAU 144:17
myth: curveship lend a m.	CRANE 168:29
mythical: built about a m. figure	HERB 246:13
mythologies: Out of old m.	YEATS 584:16
N: N. or M	PRAY 388:12
Naboth: N. the Jezreelite had	BIBLE 51:17
nachdenken: nicht n., ob es gut ist	BREC 91:26
Nächte: nie die kummervollen N.	GOET 230:12
nag: gait of a shuffling n.	SHAK 439:26
Naiad: N. 'mid her reeds	KEATS 290:2
nail: blows his n.	SHAK 457:19
…for want of a n.	FRAN 218:6
n. by strength drives out	SHAK 490:34
smote the n. into his temples	BIBLE 49:7
nail'd: n. For our advantage	SHAK 437:33
nails: 'As n.	DICK 180:34
blowing of his n.	SHAK 446:17
into the print of the n.	BIBLE 73:10
My N. are Drove	ANON 6:19
n. bitten and pared	MAC 324:7
n. he'll dig them up again	WEBS 567:9
nineteen hundred and forty n.	SITW 508:13
your beauty with n.	SHAK 446:5
naître: êtes donné la peine de n.	BEAU 35:18
Naïve: It's a N. Domestic Burgundy	THUR 550:29
naked: clothe my n. villany	SHAK 480:25
enterprise In walking n.	YEATS 584:16
Half n., loving	BYRON 122:23
left me n. to mine enemies	SHAK 447:13
N., and ye clothed me	BIBLE 68:6
n. ape self-named Homo	MORR 358:5
n. every day he clad	GOLD 231:11
n. into the conference	BEVAN 44:11
n. is the best disguise	CONG 159:27
n. shingles of the world	ARN 12:24
N. they came to that smooth-swarded	TENN 541:18
n. to the hangman's noose	HOUS 262:17
Nilus' mud Lay me stark n.	SHAK 423:21
orchid she rode quite n.	AUDEN 18:3
outcries pluck me from my n. bed	KYD 306:2
To see you n. is to recall	GARC 221:4
we are ashamed of our n.	SHAW 497:18
When a' was n.	SHAK 442:10
With n. foot	WYATT 583:21
nakedness: n. of the land ye are come	BIBLE 46:34
n. of woman is the work	BLAKE 88:21
not in utter n.	WORD 579:5
name: Bearing the owner's n.	WHIT 570:10
Ben Adhem's n. led all	HUNT 268:6
blot out his n. out of the book	BIBLE 81:18
breathe not his n.	MOORE 356:15

natura: Mors stupebit et n. CEL 138:6
N. il fece ARIO 12:2
N. vacuum abhorret RAB 403:27
Naturae: N. enim non imperatur
BACON 28:10
natural: behaviour was n. and intrepid
WALP 562:20
five per cent is the n. interest MAC 323:29
He wants the n. touch SHAK 462:12
I do it more n. SHAK 488:19
n. for a man and woman JOHN 276:2
n. idol of the Anglo-Saxon BAG 29:4
n. to die as to be born BACON 26:3
On the stage he was n. GOLD 231:20
Some n. sorrow WORD 578:15
something in this more than n. SHAK 432:17
sorrow enough in the n. KIPL 302:3
swear her colour is n. SHER 506:28
term of N. Selection DARW 171:25
that n. fear in children BACON 26:1
twice as n. CARR 136:1
what is n. cannot touch me ETH 208:26
When we see a n. style PASC 369:4
naturaleza: pintores imitan la n. CERV 139:1
naturaliter: testimonium animae n.
Christianae TERT 544:21
naturally: poetry comes not as n.
KEATS 293:25
Naturam: N. expellas furca HOR 258:18
nature: All n. is but art unknown POPE 379:11
All N. seems at work COL 157:14
All N. was degraded BLAKE 85:7
art and n. SHAK 464:6
be aghast and so will n. CEL 138:6
Beauty is N.'s brag MILT 341:18
blind forces of N. MAINE 327:7
breathless N.'s dark abyss WORD 578:8
by N. curs'd CHUR 148:32
constant course of n. DONNE 190:24
Everything almost Which is N.'s
SHEL 503:28
experiencing n. BAG 29:14
fancy outwork n. SHAK 422:2
fault was N.'s fault not BYRON 126:3
fools call N. BROW 104:29
force of n. could no farther DRYD 196:30
frame of n. round him break ADD 2:30
fulfils great N.'s plan BURNS 113:21
great N. made us men LOW 319:11
great n.'s second course SHAK 460:8
great Secretary of N. WALT 564:15
happy imitator of N. HEM 245:2
Has broken N.'s social BURNS 115:21
Hath read in N.'s mystic MARV 332:22
Heaven and N. seem'd JONS 284:2
He is made one with N. SHEL 499:23
he paid the debt of n. FABY 209:15
horribly cruel works of n. DARW 172:1
I am as free as n. first DRYD 195:29
If honest N. made you fools BURNS 113:19
informed by the light of n. BACON 24:20
In N.'s infinite book SHAK 421:9
In n. there are neither ING 270:18
interpreter of n. JOHN 282:7
Is N. felt WORD 577:5
It can't be N. CHUR 148:25
lap was N.'s darling laid GRAY 235:18
law of n. BURKE 110:32
learn'd is happy n. POPE 379:17
learned To look on n. WORD 578:7
life alone does N. live COL 156:9
looks through N. POPE 380:2
lusty stealth of n. SHAK 453:9
made a gap in n. SHAK 422:3
Man is N.'s sole mistake GILB 228:28
mere copier of n. can never REYN 405:17
mirror held up n.'s light POPE 380:4
mirror up to n. SHAK 433:17
My n. is subdu'd SHAK 495:4
N. abhors a vacuum RAB 403:27

N. admits no lie CARL 132:3
N. always does contrive GILB 226:8
N., and Nature's laws POPE 378:7
N. breeds MILT 346:23
N. cannot be ordered about BACON 28:10
N. gave thee CHUR 149:3
N. hath fram'd strange SHAK 465:8
n. her custom holds SHAK 436:20
N. herself seems ARN 16:8
N. in awe to him MILT 344:5
N. in him was almost lost COLL 158:23
N. in you stands SHAK 453:25
N. is always wise in every THUR 550:33
N. is but a name COWP 167:26
N. is creeping up WHIS 569:22
N. is fine in love SHAK 436:8
N. is often hidden BACON 26:36
n. is the art of God BROW 96:13
n. is tugging at every EMER 207:4
N. is usually wrong WHIS 569:20
N. is very consonant NEWT 362:18
n., kindly bent to ease SWIFT 527:22
N. made him ARIO 12:2
N. made her what she is BURNS 112:37
N. mourns her worshipper SCOTT 416:19
n. must obey necessity SHAK 451:28
N. never makes excellent LOCKE 315:14
n. of all greatness not BURKE 109:3
n. of God is a circle ANON 7:27
N., red in tooth and claw TENN 536:29
N. say one thing and Wisdom BURKE 112:8
n.'s changing course untrimm'd SHAK 492:28
N. seems dead SHAK 460:1
n.'s fragile vessel doth SHAK 486:13
N.'s great masterpiece DONNE 190:3
n.'s handmaid art DRYD 195:22
N. that is above all art DAN 170:7
n. then WORD 578:6
n. to advantage dress'd POPE 378:17
N., we are thine WORD 577:6
N. wears one universal FIEL 211:33
necessity...It is a part of n. SPEN 514:32
new edition of human n. HAZL 243:12
next to N. LAND 308:20
nice I suppose it is my n. ASHF 17:6
One touch of n. makes SHAK 487:6
out n. with a pitchfork HOR 258:18
painters imitate n. CERV 139:1
Passing through n. to eternity SHAK 429:24
pattern of excelling n. SHAK 477:5
perfect n. and are perfected BACON 27:17
priketh hem n. in hir corages) CHAU 141:8
production of human n. ADD 2:9
rest in N. HERB 248:7
rest on N. fix COKE 154:22
seem'd when N. him began DRAY 193:7
Since 'tis N.'s law ROCH 406:15
sovereign good of human n. BACON 27:31
spark o' N.'s fire BURNS 113:20
spectacles of books to read N. DRYD 198:2
standing at ease in N. WHIT 570:6
still is N.'s priest WORD 579:5
sullenness against N. not MILT 352:10
that n. by her mother wit SPEN 516:20
That n. yet remembers WORD 579:9
Then n. rul'd GAY 223:5
'tis N.'s fault alone CHUR 149:15
'tis their n. too WATTS 565:17
touched the hem of N.'s shift SHEL 502:18
Treatise of Human N. HUME 268:1
weakness of our mortal n. PRAY 386:15
what n. itselfe cant endure FLEM 214:26
When N. has work to be done EMER 208:3
Whose body N. is POPE 379:10
Wise n. did never put her BACON 25:7
With N.'s pride MARL 330:5
witless n. HOUS 265:10
Yet simple N. to his hope POPE 379:5
yet to N. true CHUR 149:12

natures: humane, and devoted n.
CONR 161:22
ignominy of our n. BROW 96:20
naught: I must have n. beside THOM 548:10
let it be for n. BROW 98:11
N. broken save this body BROO 94:28
n., saith the buyer BIBLE 54:1
naughtily: if I meant n. SHAK 487:9
naughtiness: filthiness and superfluity
of n. BIBLE 80:10
n. of thine heart BIBLE 50:8
naughty: amended his former n. life
PRAY 387:5
deed in a n. world SHAK 468:18
He is a n. child STEV 522:21
n. night to swim SHAK 454:21
nauseated: intolerably dull that it n. me
DARW 171:24
nauseous: n. draught of life ROCH 406:19
Nauticae: et Acus N. BACON 28:9
naval: his figurative n. manner DICK 176:10
to me about n. tradition CHUR 151:7
nave: from the n. to the chaps SHAK 458:3
navel: n. is like a round goblet BIBLE 57:8
navibus: n. atque Quadrigis HOR 258:19
navies: From the nations' airy n. TENN 538:24
Navita: N. de ventis PROP 401:15
navy: came the n. of Tharshish BIBLE 50:34
It is upon the n. under CHAR 140:21
load would sink a n. SHAK 447:11
n. nothing but rotten timber BURKE 110:5
n. of England hath ever BLAC 85:4
nay: and your n., nay BIBLE 80:18
say n., for shame WYATT 583:19
nayles: His n. whitter than CHAU 142:32
Nazareth: good thing come out of N.
BIBLE 71:31
Nazi: until finally N. Germany NEV 361:2
né: L'homme est n. libre ROUS 410:17
Neaera: with the tangles of N.'s MILT 343:8
near: come not n. to me BIBLE 60:13
n. in blood SHAK 461:4
n. me when my light is TENN 536:21
n. neighbour to Despair ARN 14:18
seems so n. and yet so far TENN 537:13
Nearer: N., my God, to thee ADAMS 1:10
n. than hands and feet TENN 533:29
n. the Church the further ANDR 4:8
n. to the Heart's Desire FITZ 213:16
n. you are to God WOTT 583:17
near'st: n. and dearest enemy SHAK 439:36
neat: any good girl to be n. TAYL 531:21
N., but not gaudy WESL 568:25
Still to be n. JONS 283:27
that is not clean and n. STEV 522:21
Nebuchadnezzar: golden image that
N. BIBLE 61:3
necessaries: between luxuries and n.
GALB 220:28
necessary: all things n. to salvation
PRAY 400:6
intellectual nature is n. JOHN 281:32
is but a n. evil PAINE 367:22
it is n. not to change FALK 209:19
Make yourself n. to someone EMER 207:3
they are n. evils JOHN 282:14
Necessitas: N. dat legem non ipsa accipit
PUBL 402:6
nécessité: Je n'en vois pas la n. ARG 12:1
necessities: art of our n. is strange
SHAK 454:11
will dispense with its n. MOTL 358:21
necessity: am forsworn 'on mere n.'
SHAK 456:17
first n. invented stools COWP 166:28
I do not see the n. ARG 12:1
nature must obey n. SHAK 451:28
N. and chance MILT 348:30
N. gives the law without PUBL 402:6
N. hath no law CROM 170:2

N. is the plea for every | PITT 374:3
N. makes an honest man | DEFOE 173:10
N. never made a good bargain | FRAN 218:8
n. of being *ready* increases | LINC 314:20
n., The tyrant's plea | MILT 347:27
sheer n. of fizz | BELL 39:31
There is no virtue like n. | SHAK 478:11
Thy n. is yet greater than | SIDN 508:6
To grim N. | SHAK 480:7
we were villains by n. | SHAK 453:11
world to see that n. is | FIEL 211:20
neck: his n. brake | BIBLE 49:39
his n. unto a second yoke | HERR 250:4
left his straight n. bent | ROSS 410:2
my n. is very short | MORE 357:17
n. God made for other use | HOUS 262:17
n. is as a tower of ivory | BIBLE 57:9
n. when once broken | WALSH 563:28
Roman people had but one n. | CAL 127:6
Some n. | CHUR 150:10
Thy n. is like the tower | BIBLE 56:26
were hanged abut his n. | BIBLE 67:3
necktie: left my n. God knows where | HOUS 264:13
nectar: hope draws n. in a sieve | COL 157:15
might I of Jove's n. sup | JONS 284:12
they lie beside their n. | TENN 539:16
To comprehend a n. | DICK 183:23
nectarine: n. and curious peach | MARV 332:3
Ned: knew me, and was N. | HOUS 265:5
need: all ye n. to know | KEATS 291:11
living in. charity | ARN 12:20
n. of a world of men | BROW 103:9
n., sickness | PRAY 387:16
n. the other women know | BROW 98:26
n. thou hast in life | HOPE 256:5
seeth his brother have n. | BIBLE 81:4
To suit and serve his n. | HERB 247:15
What can I want or n. | HERB 248:13
When our n. was the sorest | SCOTT 416:5
needed: showing them they were not n. | BELL 39:9
needful: one thing is n. | BIBLE 69:35
needle: blunteth the n. | POUND 382:9
for the n. she | TENN 542:9
Hinders n. and thread | HOOD 255:10
Plying her n. and thread | HOOD 255:6
through the eye of a n. | BIBLE 67:11
Who sayes my hand a n. | BRAD 91:13
needlework: King in raiment of n. | PRAY 392:17
needs: each according to his n. | BAK 29:25
each according to his n. | MARX 333:5
n. not June for beauty's | ARN 15:4
needy: considereth the poor and n. | PRAY 392:4
n. nothing trimm'd in jollity | SHAK 494:5
Ne'er: N. a verse to thee | KING 296:22
nefas: scire n. | HOR 259:19
negabimus: nulli n. aut differemus | MAGN 327:3
negation: This is the n. of God erected | GLAD 229:19
Negative: N. Capability | KEATS 293:19
neglect: little n. may breed mischief | FRAN 218:6
most tender mercy is n. | COWP 168:28
punished for n. these unhappy | JOHN 281:5
Such sweet n. more taketh | JONS 283:27
to the n. of his duties | THOM 549:6
wise and salutary n. | BURKE 109:18
neglected: pleased to have his all n. | JOHN 274:5
negligent: servant's too often a n. elf | BARH 33:10
negotiis: qui procul n. | HOR 259:7
nègres: Les pauvres sont les n. | CHAM 139:1
negro: respecting his n. friend | BECK 36:18
negroes: among the drivers of n. | JOHN 282:18
providing the infant n. | DICK 182:6

nehmen: wir und n. immer Abschied | RILKE 406:4
neiges: où sont les n. d'antan | VILL 557:5
neighbour: guinea in your n.'s pocket | RUSK 412:8
have an accommodating n. | DOYLE 192:12
I am a n. and near bred | SHAK 466:6
know the man their n. | YEATS 586:14
lug the guts into the n. | SHAK 435:22
my duty to my N. | PRAY 388:14
My duty towards my N. | PRAY 388:15
Narrows the world to my n.'s | MER 337:19
near n. to Despair | ARN 14:18
neighed after his n.'s wife | BIBLE 60:16
next-door n. for so many years | SCOTT 418:23
nor done evil to his n. | PRAY 390:4
our n.'s house is on fire | BURKE 111:1
policy of the good n. | ROOS 407:21
removeth his n.'s landmark | BIBLE 48:26
shall love your crooked n. | AUDEN 18:11
shalt not covet thy n.'s | BIBLE 47:24
that he might rob a n. | MAC 323:21
Thou shalt love thy n. | BIBLE 48:8
to hate your n. | MAC 324:3
Withdraw thy foot from thy n.'s | BIBLE 54:28
neighbouring: cynosure of n. eyes | MILT 342:20
neighbours: charity with your n. | PRAY 387:18
From every house the n. met | TENN 536:18
'Good fences make good n. | FROST 219:9
is happening to our n. | CHAM 139:7
songs of peace to all his n. | SHAK 448:1
to make sport for our n. | AUST 23:20
vigil feast his n. | SHAK 445:3
neighed: n. after his neighbour's | BIBLE 60:16
neighs: in high and boastful n. | SHAK 444:9
neither: n. children nor Gods | KIPL 298:23
'Tis n. here nor there | SHAK 477:1
nekke: to strecche forth the n. | CHAU 143:5
Nell: Pretty witty N. | PEPYS 372:13
Nelly: Let not poor N. starve | CHAR 140:28
Nelson: death of N. was felt | SOUT 514:17
N. turned his blindest | CHES 146:21
Of N. and the North | CAMP 128:14
To N.'s peerless name | NEWB 361:3
Nelson touch: explain to them the 'N.' | NELS 360:19
keep the N. | NEWB 361:12
Nemo: N. me impune lacessit | ANON 10:15
Nephew: N. of Fox | HOLL 253:4
Neptune: influence N.'s empire stands | SHAK 429:13
N.'s park | SHAK 428:13
nequiores: Nos n. | HOR 260:26
nerve: who am as a n. o'er which | SHEL 501:12
nerves: expredge my n. this night | DICK 179:31
my firm n. | SHAK 461:21
n. prick | TENN 536:21
N. sit ceremonious | DICK 183:13
N. that steeled themselves | AUDEN 21:3
nobody feels for my poor n. | AUST 23:16
to keep the n. at strain | BROW 102:1
with us strengthens our n. | BURKE 111:23
Nervii: day he overcame the N. | SHAK 450:26
nescit: n. vox missa | HOR 258:6
nest: Her soft and chilly n. | KEATS 289:18
her warm n. of renaissance | DAY-L 172:21
leaves the well-built n. | SHEL 501:22
long since my n. is made | TENN 542:6
n. of singing birds | JOHN 273:28
song ye may learn the n. | TENN 535:3
swallow a n. where she | PRAY 395:11
We'll theek our n. when | BALL 32:8
Nestling: N. me everywhere | HOPK 256:6
nests: Birds in their little n. agree | BELL 40:6
birds of the air have n. | BIBLE 65:18
built their n. in my beard | LEAR 311:15
Thus you birds build n. | VIRG 560:20

net: Fain would fling the n. | MER 337:4
have laid a n. for my feet | PRAY 393:15
I will let down the n. | BIBLE 69:18
vain the n. is spread | BIBLE 53:14
Whizzing them over the n. | BETJ 43:20
nets: be n. of such a texture | SHEN 505:16
into their own n. together | PRAY 399:10
n. and stratagems to catch | HERB 248:10
n. of wrong and right | YEATS 585:14
their time in making n. | SWIFT 527:10
them tangled in amorous n. | MILT 350:2
weave but n. to catch | WEBS 566:17
nettle: Out of this n., danger | SHAK 438:29
Tender-handed stroke a n. | HILL 251:2
nettles: apt to be overrun with n. | WALP 563:17
like the dust on the n. | THOM 547:21
n. and brambles | BIBLE 58:31
neutral: Loyal and n., in a moment | SHAK 461:2
studiously n. | WILS 574:21
neutrality: Armed n. | WILS 574:22
for a word—'n.' | BETH 42:3
n. of an impartial judge | BURKE 111:34
neutralize: White shall not n. the black | BROW 104:31
neutral-tinted: n. haps and such | HARDY 239:22
never: be the people n. so impatient | PRAY 396:10
desks and n. go to sea | GILB 228:7
I could n. go back again | MORE 357:12
I n. use a big | GILB 228:2
I n. would lay down my | PITT 373:26
kiss me and n. no more | MAL 328:4
let me n. see | PRIOR 400:28
N. ask me whose | HOUS 263:11
N. do to-day what you can | PUNCH 402:13
n. fly conceals a hook | BROO 94:13
n. home came she | KING 297:1
N., never, never, | SHAK 456:11
n. sad but when she sleeps | SHAK 472:13
n. saw a brute I hated | BROW 99:29
n. see another mountain | LAMB 307:22
n. should move at any time | PRAY 396:18
n. sick at sea | GILB 227:31
n. taste who always drink | PRIOR 401:1
N. the time and the place | BROW 102:24
n. the twain shall meet | KIPL 297:27
n. thought of thinking | GILB 228:6
n. to admit them in your | AUST 23:19
N. to have lived is best | YEATS 585:6
N. trust the artist | LAWR 311:10
n. turned his back | BROW 98:32
N. was born | STOWE 523:19
people have n. had it so good | MACM 325:18
She who has n. lov'd | GAY 223:2
than n. to have lost at all | BUTL 119:16
Which n. were nor no man | SHAK 484:3
who n. would be missed | GILB 226:24
would you had n. seen him | SHAK 476:25
You must n. go down | MILNE 340:6
you n. can tell | SHAW 498:21
Nevermore: 'N.' | POE 375:6
Never-never: your 'N. country' | KIPL 299:3
new: adventure brave and n. | BROW 104:5
against the n. and untried | LINC 314:16
Among n. men | TENN 535:24
blessing of the N. | BACON 25:18
brave n. world | SHAK 485:26
ever reaping something n. | TENN 538:24
first by whom the n. are | POPE 378:19
have put on the n. man | BIBLE 78:26
I make all things n. | BIBLE 82:31
intend to lead a n. life | PRAY 387:18
n. deal for the American | ROOS 407:19
n. friend is as new wine | BIBLE 62:30
n. heaven and a new earth | BIBLE 82:30
n. heaven, new earth | SHAK 421:7
n. man may be raised up | PRAY 388:9

N. nobility is	BACON 26:39	
n. people takes the land	CHES 147:14	
n. race descends from high	VIRG 559:22	
n. song: sing praises lustily	PRAY 391:19	
N. styles of architecture	AUDEN 20:7	
N. Testament was less	HARDY 241:24	
n. wine into old bottles	BIBLE 65:25	
n. years ruin and rend	SWIN 530:6	
no n. thing under the sun	BIBLE 55:7	
offences of affections n.	SHAK 495:3	
old lamps for n.	ARAB 11:14	
piping songs for ever n.	KEATS 291:6	
ring in the n.	TENN 537:14	
shall find something n.	VOLT 560:21	
sing unto the Lord a n. song	PRAY 396:7	
threshold of the n.	WALL 562:9	
to hear some n. thing	BIBLE 74:11	
Whether it be n. or old	ANON 5:21	
write upon him my n. name	BIBLE 81:19	
yielding place to n.	TENN 535:25	

new-bathed: whose floor the n. stars ARN 15:1

new-born: use of a n. child FRAN 218:19

Newcastle: sun we have is made of N. coal WALP 563:5

new-comer: blithe n. WORD 582:25

New England: variety about the N. weather TWAIN 554:23

newer: n. object quite forgotten SHAK 490:34

n. rite is here THOM 546:17

newest: oldest sins the n. SHAK 442:20

new-manned: manned by Manning and n. BROW 104:17

new-moon: up the trumpet in the n. PRAY 395:9

newness: walk in n. of life BIBLE 75:1

news: bites a dog that is n. BOG 89:9

bringer of unwelcome n. SHAK 441:2

evil n. rides post MILT 350:28

good n. from a far country BIBLE 54:30

'Have you n. of my boy KIPL 301:15

Ill n. hath wings DRAY 193:6

Literature is n. that STAYS POUND 383:23

master-passion is the love of n. COWP 168:15

n. and Prince of Peace FLET 215:29

n. that's fit to print OCHS 364:20

n., the manna of a day GREEN 235:29

N. value RALPH 404:21

was any n. in the paper AUST 23:26

What n. on the Rialto SHAK 465:28

newspaper: never to look into a n. SHER 505:20

n. and I seem to see ghosts IBSEN 269:21

n. is of necessity something SCOTT 415:15

newspapers: government of men and morning n. PHIL 373:12

newt: Eye of n. SHAK 462:3

Newton: Let N. be POPE 378:7

N. at Peru WALP 563:9

N., childlike sage COWP 167:5

statue stood Of N. WORD 580:17

Newts: N., and blind-worms SHAK 470:11

New World: I called the N. into existence CANN 130:8

New York: four hundred people in N. society MCAL 321:23

O Carthage! O N. SASS 415:4

O Yorker: Read *The N.* AUDEN 21:6

New Zealand: gone to N. CLOU 153:19

next: n. to a battle lost WELL 567:27

'n. to of course god america CUMM 170:10

n. train has gone ten minutes PUNCH 402:21

next door: wall n. catches fire HOR 258:23

nexus: sole n. of man to man CARL 131:17

nez: Le n. de Cléopâtre PASC 369:6

Niagara: wouldn't *live* under N. CARL 132:28

nice: Cusins is a very n. fellow SHAW 497:8

'N. but nubbly KIPL 304:14

n. man is a man of nasty SWIFT 527:13

n. sort of place, Oxford SHAW 497:23

N. while it lasted	KIPL 301:11	
Too n. for a statesman	GOLD 231:17	

nicer: Are wiser and n. AUDEN 20:12

nicest: n. child I ever knew BELL 38:32

niche: window'd n. of that high hall BYRON 120:23

Nicholas: St N. soon would be there MOORE 355:12

nicht: n. ausrechnen, was es kostet BREC 91:26

nicht-gown: down stairs in his n. MILL 340:3

nick: anxious to improve the n. THOR 550:9

N., or Clootie BURNS 112:24

nickname: n. is the heaviest stone HAZL 243:27

those who invented the n. ARN 16:3

nicknamed: n. Adam CLOU 153:14

Nicodemus: Wise N. saw such light VAUG 555:11

nidificatis: Sic vos non vobis n. aves VIRG 560:20

niger: Hic n. est HOR 262:3

left bank of the N. DICK 176:4

niggers: Thet don't agree with n. LOW 319:3

nigh: shall any plague come n. PRAY 395:22

they shall not come n. him PRAY 391:17

nighing: n. his hour HOUS 264:28

night: acquainted with the n. FROST 218:27

afraid for any terror by n. PRAY 395:21

are alternate N. and Day FITZ 212:13

ask of thee, beloved N. SHEL 505:4

ate a good supper at n. ANST 11:7

be by Silvia in the n. SHAK 491:1

become a borrower of the n. SHAK 461:7

black bat, n. TENN 540:9

black n. doth take away SHAK 494:7

blessed candles of the n. SHAK 468:22

bring in cloudy n. immediately SHAK 483:6

by n. in a pillar of fire BIBLE 47:21

City is of N. THOM 549:27

civil n. SHAK 483:6

covered by the long n. HOR 261:18

dangers of this n. PRAY 385:10

darkness that it may be n. PRAY 397:1

dark n. of the soul FITZ 213:22

day and n. shall not cease BIBLE 45:37

day brought back my n. MILT 351:14

dead hour of the n. BALL 32:2

Dear N. VAUG 555:12

drown'd with us in endless n. HERR 248:26

dusky n. rides down FIEL 211:36

Evening must usher n. SHEL 499:14

everlasting n. DONNE 189:12

Farewell n., welcome day BUNY 107:37

feet of the n. SWIN 528:16

fourth watch of the n. BIBLE 66:25

from this palace of dim n. SHAK 483:31

hangs upon the cheek of n. SHAK 482:2

hath n. to do with sleep MILT 340:28

have toiled all the n. BIBLE 69:18

heart of the n. with fire SWIN 530:13

heaviness may endure for a n. PRAY 391:13

honey'd middle of the n. KEATS 289:12

horror of a deep n. RAC 404:2

ignorant armies clash by n. ARN 12:23

ill beginning of the n. SHAK 451:29

in death's dateless n. SHAK 493:7

in endless n. GRAY 235:19

infant crying in the n. TENN 536:26

in such a n. as this SHAK 468:13

In the forests of the n. BLAKE 87:14

In the gardens of the n. BRID 92:16

Is it n. WHIT 570:13

it goes off at n. SHER 506:28

know'st the mask of n. SHAK 482:11

last out a n. in Russia SHAK 463:17

lesser light to rule the n. BIBLE 45:3

light of the n. on the dew SWIN 530:13

Long n. succeeds thy little PEAC 370:20

lovely n. through the shadow VIRG 558:20

love-performing n.	SHAK 483:6	
Love the n.	DRYD 197:18	
loving, black-brow'd n.	SHAK 483:7	
Making n. hideous	SHAK 430:24	
meaner beauties of the n.	WOTT 583:15	
middle of the n.	CARR 135:3	
Morning in the Bowl of N.	FITZ 212:5	
Morn in weary N.'s decline	BLAKE 86:1	
mysteries of Hecate and the n.	SHAK 453:3	
naughty n. to swim	SHAK 454:21	
neither the moon by n.	PRAY 398:9	
Never sees horrid n.	SHAK 444:25	
n. an atheist half believes	YOUNG 588:10	
n. and light and the half-light	YEATS 585:9	
N. and silence	SHAK 470:13	
n. before Christmas	MOORE 355:12	
n. be turned to day	PRAY 399:5	
n. cometh	BIBLE 72:14	
n. do penance for a day	WORD 580:18	
n. has a thousand eyes	BOUR 90:21	
N. hath a thousand eyes	LYLY 321:15	
n. is crept upon our talk	SHAK 451:28	
n. is far spent	BIBLE 75:24	
n. is freezing fast	HOUS 265:1	
N. is growing gray	HARDY 240:8	
n. joint-labourer with	SHAK 429:11	
N. Mail crossing the Border	AUDEN 20:1	
N. makes no difference	HERR 249:12	
n. of memories and of sighs	LAND 308:26	
n. of this immortal day	SHEL 503:14	
n. of time far surpasseth	BROW 97:20	
N., sable goddess	YOUNG 588:9	
n.'s black agents	SHAK 461:14	
N.'s candles are burnt	SHAK 483:14	
n. she'll hae but three	BALL 31:12	
N.'s swift dragons cut	SHAK 470:25	
n. That either makes me	SHAK 477:4	
n. that he was betrayed	PRAY 388:1	
n. that wins	SWIN 528:17	
N., the shadow of light	SWIN 528:21	
n. time I shall not forget	SWIN 529:12	
n. to die upon the sand	ARN 14:26	
n. was made for loving	BYRON 125:26	
N. with her train of stars	HENL 245:8	
of an instalment of n.	HARDY 241:19	
one n. certifieth another	PRAY 390:11	
One the long n. through	HOUS 262:21	
only for a n. and away	WYCH 583:24	
Out of the n. that covers	HENL 245:4	
past as a watch in the n.	PRAY 395:18	
perfect day nor n.	SHAK 446:17	
poor souls who dwell in N.	BLAKE 85:18	
Queen of the silent n.	BEST 42:2	
read, much of the n.	ELIOT 204:18	
Read out my words at n.	FLEC 214:23	
read the Bible day and n.	BLAKE 85:22	
reign of Chaos and old N.	MILT 345:20	
returned home the previous n.	BULL 106:22	
rung n.'s yawning peal	SHAK 461:13	
Sable-vested N.	MILT 347:5	
sisters Death and N. incessantly	WHIT 570:11	
sleep one ever-during n.	CAT 136:25	
So late into the n.	BYRON 125:25	
sound lovers' tongues by n.	SHAK 482:19	
sound of revelry by n.	BYRON 120:20	
spend another such a n.	SHAK 480:26	
Spirit of N.	SHEL 505:2	
Such n. in England ne'er	MAC 321:26	
tender is the n.	KEATS 291:10	
that go bump in the n.	ANON 5:8	
Then it will be *good* n.	SHEL 500:17	
there shall be no n. there	BIBLE 82:34	
There's n. and day	BORR 90:4	
thievish N.	MILT 341:1	
This n. methinks is	SHAK 468:27	
through the foul womb of n.	SHAK 444:9	
thy dangerous brow by n.	SHAK 449:7	
'Tis with us perpetual n.	JONS 285:13	
toiling upward in the n.	LONG 316:19	
trumpets of the n.	SWIN 530:19	

vast and middle of the n.	SHAK 430:6	have him n. years a-killing	SHAK 476:10	nobleman: king may make a n.	BURKE 111:37	
vile contagion of the n.	SHAK 449:13	His choir, the N.	ARN 13:3	noblemen: all n. who have gone wrong		
were the world's last n.	DONNE 189:7	n. and sixty ways of constructing	KIPL 300:3		GILB 228:22	
What is the n.	SHAK 461:24	N. bean-rows will I have	YEATS 585:17	nobleness: allied with perfect n.	ARN 16:13	
what of the n.	BIBLE 58:14	n. men's morris is filled	SHAK 470:5	n. of life Is to do thus	SHAK 421:8	
When the face of n. is	TENN 540:17	not the stroke of n.	HOUS 262:18	Thy thoughts with n.	SHAK 428:4	
womb of uncreated n.	MILT 346:10	there be n. worthy	CAXT 138:3	nobler: Ring in the n. modes	TENN 537:15	
Yesterday the bird of n.	SHAK 449:1	nine-tenths: n. of the law of chivalry		Whether 'tis n.	SHAK 433:8	
yet it is not n.	BYRON 121:4		SAY 415:6	nobles: n. by the right of an earlier		
nightblue: humid n. fruit	JOYCE 286:29	ninety: n. and nine in the wilderness			MAC 323:26	
night-cap: give me my n.	MOL 353:3		BIBLE 70:15	their n. with links of iron	PRAY 399:24	
night-dress: lectures in her n.	HOOD 255:12	n. and nine just persons	BIBLE 70:17	noblest: amongst the n. of mankind		
nighte: Every n. and alle	BALL 31:6	That n. lives have been	MCG 325:6		CALV 127:27	
nighted: cast thy n. colour off	SHAK 429:23	Nineveh: Is one with N. and Tyre	KIPL 302:8	art the ruins of the n.	SHAK 450:11	
Crossing alone the n. ferry	HOUS 265:18	ninth: be kept till the n. year	HOR 258:6	Her n. work she classes	BURNS 114:4	
night-flies: buzzing n. to thy slumber		Niobe: Like N., all tears	SHAK 429:28	honest God is the n.	ING 270:17	
	SHAK 441:29	N. of nations	BYRON 121:10	honest God's the n.	BUTL 119:7	
night-gown: put on your n.	SHAK 462:24	nip: I'll n. him in the bud	ROCHE 406:14	honest man's the n.	BURNS 113:10	
Nightingale: ah, the N.	ARN 14:2	nipping: is a n. and an eager air	SHAK 430:22	honest man's the n.	POPE 379:24	
all but the wakeful n.	MILT 348:2	nipple: plucked my n.	SHAK 459:10	n. prospect which a Scotchman	JOHN 274:30	
brown bright n. amorous	SWIN 528:15	Nisi: N. Dominus aedificaverit	BIBLE 83:12	n. Roman of them all	SHAK 452:7	
Crave the tuneful n.	DRAY 193:19	niti: dies n. praestante labore	LUCR 320:22	n. works and foundations	BACON 27:4	
I the n. all spring through	SWIN 530:13	nives: Diffugere n.	HOR 261:14	Nobly: N., nobly Cape St Vincent		
It was the n.	SHAK 483:13	No: Araminta, say 'N.	PRAED 384:4		BROW 101:8	
little brown n. bills his	HARDY 241:2	Blake was n. good	BUTL 118:35	Spurn not the n. born	GILB 226:4	
My n.	SHAK 423:3	Charybdis of Aye and N.	NEWM 361:21	Nobody: Hush, hush, N. cares	MORT 358:15	
n. when May is past	CAREW 130:19	everlasting N.	CARL 132:17	kingdom where n. dies	MILL 339:24	
N. cries to the Rose	FITZ 212:7	n. better than you should	BEAU 36:2	Methinks n. should be sad	SHAK 452:23	
N. that in the Branches	FITZ 213:15	n. man gets a full meal	JOHN 276:27	N. heard him, the dead man	SMITH 510:26	
n. does sit so late	MARV 332:12	N. money	RAC 404:5	N.; I myself	SHAK 477:10	
n., that on yon bloomy	MILT 351:5	'n. nothing	BYRON 126:19	N. is on my side	AUST 23:16	
n., if she should sing	SHAK 468:19	'N. sense in going further'	KIPL 299:3	N. speaks the truth when	BOWEN 91:4	
n. in the sycamore	STEV 523:7	N. sun—no moon!	HOOD 254:27	N. tells me anything	GALS 221:1	
roar you as 'twere any n.	SHAK 469:30	not those men, in	SOPH 513:6	there's n. at home	POPE 376:15	
Save the n. alone	BARN 33:32	people cried, 'O N.'	BARH 33:22	wants to have read and n.	TWAIN 554:25	
sings as sweetly as a n.	SHAK 484:8	There is n. God	PRAY 390:2	nocens: damnatur ubi n. absolvitur		
spoils the singing of the n.	KEATS 289:8	there is n. more to say	SHAK 487:18		PUBL 402:5	
There is no music in the n.	SHAK 491:1	there is n. such word	BULW 107:5	Nocturna: N. versate manu	HOR 257:22	
'tis the ravish'd n.	LYLY 321:12	Noah: before N. was a sailor	SHAK 489:26	nocturnal: private n. terror	AUDEN 20:15	
Where the n. doth sing	KEATS 291:1	cataclysm but one poor N.	HUXL 268:21	Some n. blackness	HARDY 239:2	
nightingales: By Eve's n.	DE L 173:25	N. begat Shem	BIBLE 45:32	Nod: dwelt in the land of N.	BIBLE 45:29	
n. are singing near	ELIOT 204:16	N. he often said to his	CHES 147:28	N. with your hand to signify	HOUS 266:9	
nightly: its n. roll into darkness		Who married N.'s daughter	AYT 24:7	read a n., a shrug, a look	SWIFT 527:29	
	HARDY 241:20	nobility: ancient n. is the act	BACON 26:39	noddle: barmie n.'s working prime		
nightmare: History is a n. from which		Betwixt the wind and his n.	SHAK 438:14		BURNS 113:23	
	JOYCE 286:23	fashions men with true n.	MARL 330:11	nodosities: n. of the oak without its		
In the burrows of the N.	AUDEN 18:10	God destroy man's n.	BACON 25:25		BURKE 112:14	
Nights: Chequer-board of N. and Days		leave us still our old n.	MANN 328:15	nods: even excellent Homer n.	HOR 258:2	
	FITZ 213:5	New n. is but the act	BACON 26:39	it n. a little	FARQ 210:20	
Love not such n. as these	SHAK 454:9	N. is a graceful ornament	BURKE 111:21	N., and becks	MILT 342:14	
n. are wholesome	SHAK 429:17	N. of birth commonly abateth	BACON 27:1	Noe: N. entered into the ark	BIBLE 67:32	
open day between the n.	FRY 220:5	order of n. is of great	BAG 29:4	noes: yeas and honest kersey n.	SHAK 457:16	
O ye N., and Days	PRAY 384:22	save N.	BYRON 120:7	noir: Porte le soleil n. de la	NERV 360:26	
night-season: n. also I take no rest		True n. is exempt from fear	SHAK 446:9	noire: île triste et n.	BAUD 35:8	
	PRAY 390:16	nobis: Non n.	BIBLE 83:10	noise: barbarous n. environs me	MILT 351:7	
night-wind: breath Of the n.	ARN 12:3	noble: be glad to learn of n.	SHAK 451:17	chamber deaf to n.	SIDN 507:21	
nihil: Aut Caesar, aut n.	BORG 89:25	except for a n. purpose	HERB 246:17	Didst thou not hear a n.	SHAK 460:6	
Vox et praeterea n.	ANON 11:6	fredome is a n. thing	BARB 33:4	gone up with a merry n.	PRAY 392:24	
Nil: N. admirari prope res est	HOR 258:17	grounds for the n. emotions	RUSK 411:10	happy n. to hear	HOUS 263:4	
N. desperandum Teucro duce	HOR 259:16	Here all were n.	BYRON 120:7	inexplicable dumb-shows and n.	SHAK 433:16	
N. igitur mors est ad nos	LUCR 320:8	Is this the n. nature	SHAK 476:10	make a cheerful n. unto	PRAY 395:9	
N. posse creari De nilo	LUCR 320:5	Man is a n. animal	BROW 97:23	monkeys make sorrowful n.	POUND 383:16	
Nile: N. spills his overflow	HOUS 262:19	may see and learn the n.	CAXT 138:4	n. in mine ear	DONNE 191:2	
on the banks of the N.	SHER 506:15	n. and nude and antique	SWIN 529:4	n. in the beast's belly	MAL 327:15	
pour the waters of the N.	CARR 133:17	n. and puissant nation	MILT 352:3	n. like that of a water-mill	SWIFT 526:3	
We live on the N.	LEAR 312:16	n. ensample to his sheep	CHAU 142:1	n. of battle roll'd	TENN 535:20	
'Where's my serpent of old N.	SHAK 421:31	N. heart	SPEN 516:4	n. of the mourning	TENN 541:5	
nilo: Nil posse creari De n.	LUCR 320:5	n. in motive and far-reaching	HOOV 255:24	n. of water in mine ears	SHAK 480:27	
Nilus: N.' mud Lay me stark naked		n. mind is here o'erthrown	SHAK 433:15	n. they make in pouring	POPE 381:20	
	SHAK 423:21	not Be n. to myself	SHAK 424:1	Nursed amid her n.	LAMB 307:24	
nimble: n. and airy servitors trip	MILT 351:19	not birth that makes us n.	FLET 215:18	pleasant n. till noon	COL 155:26	
nimbler: it was n. much than hinds		pitting their n. birth	LUCR 320:6	that those who make the n.	BURKE 111:16	
	MARV 332:13	quiet us in a death so n.	MILT 351:2	the n. the people	ANON 7:6	
nimini-pimini: pronouncing to yourself		silence is most n. till	SWIN 528:23	valued till they make a n.	COWP 168:22	
n.	BURG 108:5	Some work of n. note	TENN 544:3	was full of foolish n.	TENN 536:22	
Nimrod: N. the mighty hunter before		'Tis only n. to be good	TENN 537:29	when every n. appals me	SHAK 460:12	
	BIBLE 46:1	Was born most n. that was	OTWAY 365:27	noiseless: n. noise among the leaves		
Nimshi: son of N.	BIBLE 51:33	What's brave, what's n.	SHAK 423:18		KEATS 290:13	
to that of the son of N.	SMITH 512:3	when a n. nature	ARN 16:14	n. tenor of their way	GRAY 235:1	
nine: final stroke of n.	ELIOT 204:21	woods she n. savage ran	DRYD 195:29	noises: isle is full of n.	SHAK 485:17	

you are liberal in o.   SHAK 468:12
office: find a set of maxims in o.
   BURKE 108:16
insolence of o.   SHAK 433:8
man who has no o. to go   SHAW 497:3
office boys for o. boys   SAL 413:21
o. boy to an Attorney's   GILB 228:4
o. is a matter of right   JEFF 272:15
officer: art thou o.   SHAK 444:16
dashing Swiss o.'   RUSS 412:22
doth fear each bush an o.   SHAK 446:23
o. and a gentleman shall...be   ANON 4:20
officers: They have a king and o.   SHAK 443:9
offices: functions and their o.   SHAK 457:8
officials: that o. are the servants   GOW 233:7
Officious: O., innocent   JOHN 278:35
Officiously: O. to keep alive   CLOU 153:26
offspring: true source Of human o.
   MILT 348:8
oft: o. as ye shall drink it   PRAY 388:1
tell how o. he offendeth   PRAY 390:13
What o. was thought   POPE 378:17
Og: O. the king of Basan   PRAY 399:1
ogled: sighed and pined and o.   THAC 546:3
oil: anointed my head with o.   PRAY 390:22
consum'd the midnight o.   GAY 223:10
head thou dost with o.   SCOT 419:5
little o. in a cruse   BIBLE 51:7
mouth is smoother than o.   BIBLE 53:20
o. of gladness above thy   PRAY 392:15
o. of joy for mourning   BIBLE 60:9
o. out of the tabernacle   BIBLE 50:30
o. to make him a cheerful   PRAY 396:20
O., vinegar   GOLD 231:16
our midnight o.   QUAR 403:10
thine 'incomparable o.'   BYRON 122:6
with boiling o. in it   GILB 227:11
With everlasting o.   MILT 341:1
without the o. and twopence   SMITH 511:7
words were smoother than o.   PRAY 393:12
oily: glib and o. art   SHAK 453:5
ointment: box of very precious o.   BIBLE 68:8
flies cause the o. of the apothecary
   BIBLE 56:1
o. sold for three hundred   BIBLE 72:25
old: Asia and she is too o.   KIPL 304:27
been young, and now am o.   PRAY 391:28
body with so o. a head   SHAK 467:26
comfortless, and worn, and o.   ROSS 409:2
considered the days of o.   PRAY 395:2
crucify the o. man   PRAY 388:10
dressing o. words   SHAK 494:9
first sign of o. age   HICKS 250:23
foolish, fond o. man   SHAK 456:1
growing o. in drawing nothing   COWP 167:4
Grown o. before my time   ROSS 409:7
Grow o. along with me   BROW 104:2
grow o. with a good grace   STEE 518:2
grow o. virtuous in their o.   POPE 381:21
hard sentences of o.   PRAY 395:3
he died o.   HOUS 264:16
I am too o.   BACON 28:3
I am too o. to fawn upon   SHAK 478:11
I grow o. ever learning   SOLON 512:24
I grow o. grow old...   ELIOT 203:25
I'm not so o.   GILB 226:3
in judgment o.   SHAK 466:17
it is o. and plain   SHAK 489:3
lads that will never be o.   HOUS 263:6
last to lay the o. aside   POPE 378:19
Leaving the o.   WALL 562:9
love every thing that's o.   GOLD 232:19
making of an o. woman happy   FRAN 218:5
man is as o. as he's feeling   COLL 158:15
my folks were growing o.   STEV 522:26
no man would be o.   SWIFT 527:12
not persuade me I am o.   SHAK 493:1
o. Adam in this Child   PRAY 388:9
O. age brings along with   EMER 207:45
O. age hath yet his honour   TENN 544:3

O. age is the most unexpected   TROT 553:16
o. age, serene and bright   WORD 583:4
O. age should burn   THOM 546:23
o. and ill and terrified   BETJ 44:13
O. as I am   DRYD 195:32
o. as we to keep the peace   SHAK 481:25
o. December's bareness   SHAK 494:16
o. faiths loosen and fall   SWIN 530:6
O. friends are best   SELD 419:19
o. is having lighted rooms   LARK 310:5
o. know what they want   SMITH 510:22
o. lamps for new   ARAB 11:14
o. lovers are soundest   WEBS 566:30
o., mad, blind   SHEL 504:6
o. man and no honester   SHAK 472:32
o. man decayed in his intellects   JOHN 279:6
o. man in a dry month   ELIOT 203:3
o. man's wit may wander   TENN 534:2
o. men and children   PRAY 399:23
O. men and comets have   SWIFT 527:14
o. men from the chimney   SIDN 508:2
o. men have grey beards   SHAK 432:8
O. men in country houses   BETJ 42:12
o. men of less truth than   SHAK 492:27
o. men shall dream dreams   BIBLE 61:15
o. men's nurses   BACON 26:34
o. order changeth   TENN 535:25
o. plays began to disgust   EVEL 209:9
o., wild, and incomprehensible   VICT 556:15
o. women (of both sexes)   STER 520:4
read an o. one   ROG 407:12
rebuild it on the o. plan   MILL 339:3
Ring out the o.   TENN 537:14
she is not yet so o.   SHAK 467:13
should accompany o. age   SHAK 463:2
so o., and so profane   SHAK 442:30
sugared about by the o.   KIPL 303:11
teach an o. horse   SPEN 516:16
tell an o. soldier   SHAW 496:6
That is no country for o.   YEATS 586:11
That the heart grows o.   YEATS 586:20
Then O. Age, and Experience   ROCH 406:22
they get to feeling o.   BROO 94:24
They shall grow not o.   BINY 84:10
Though I look o.   SHAK 425:5
times begin to wax o.   BIBLE 62:7
tiresomeness of o. age   ANON 10:13
'Tis well an o. age is out   DRYD 197:19
to make an o. man young   TENN 533:20
Very o. are we men   DE L 173:25
wax o. as doth a garment   PRAY 396:13
Were ruinous and o.   SPEN 516:3
when thou shalt be o.   BIBLE 73:17
When you are o. and gray   YEATS 587:12
When you are very o.   RONS 407:18
where even the o. are fair   YEATS 585:18
Whether it be new or o.   ANON 5:21
will change in growing o.   BRID 92:20
yet o. enough for a man   SHAK 488:9
you are o.   SHAK 453:25
You are o., Father William   CARR 133:22
You are o., Father William   SOUT 514:7
you never can be o.   SHAK 494:18
old age: dance attention upon my o.
   YEATS 586:23
dreary o. and pain sneak up   VIRG 560:16
O., a second child   CHUR 148:32
sad o. you are preparing   TALL 531:18
Oldcastle: O. died a martyr   SHAK 443:2
older: He was o.   LUC 320:2
I grow o. and older   SAY 415:7
O. men declare war   HOOV 255:25
o. than the rocks among   PATER 369:19
richer still the o.   BUTL 118:17
They hurt me. I grow o.   POUND 383:17
oldest: Commit The o. sins   SHAK 442:20
o. hath borne most   SHAK 456:13
When the o. cask is opened   MAC 322:23
old maid: o. courted by Incapacity
   BLAKE 88:14

Old Retainer: O. night and day   BELL 39:4
Old Testament: blessing of the O.
   BACON 25:18
ole: knows of a better 'o.   BAIR 29:23
W'en folks git o. en strucken   HARR 242:13
O'Leary: It's with O. in the grave
   YEATS 586:19
Ole Hundred: when he made O. ring
   LOW 319:6
olet: Pecunia non o.   VESP 556:11
oligarchy: democracy or absolute o.
   ARIS 12:8
olive: o., aloe   TENN 533:5
o.-silvery Sirmio   TENN 533:18
olive-branches: o.: round about thy table
   PRAY 398:20
Olivet: purple brows of O.   TENN 536:18
Olivia: Cry out, 'O.!'   SHAK 488:13
when mine eyes did see O.   SHAK 487:21
ologies: getting instructed in the 'o.'
   CARL 131:38
olores: inter strepere anser o.   VIRG 560:7
Olympian: O. bolts   DISR 184:19
Olympus: horse-race won at O. among
   SIDN 508:4
leafy O. on top of Ossa   VIRG 560:10
Omar: diver O. plucked them from
   LOW 319:10
ombrifuge: o. (Lord love you   CALV 127:16
Omega: 'I am Alpha and O.'   AUDEN 21:7
I am Alpha and O.   BIBLE 81:10
omen: Procul o. abesto   OVID 366:8
Quod di o. avertant   CIC 151:29
This is the one best o.   HOMER 254:2
Omer: O., Lucan   CHAU 144:17
'O. smote 'is bloomin' lyre   KIPL 304:4
omitted: have o. the weightier matters
   BIBLE 67:24
O., all the voyage   SHAK 451:27
Omnes: O. eodem cogimur   HOR 260:7
omnia: Amor vincit o.   CHAU 141:17
non o. possumus omnes   LUC 320:2
Non o. possumus omnes   VIRG 560:6
O. vincit Amor   VIRG 560:8
omnibuses: only ridden more in o.
   HELPS 244:18
Omnipotent: defy th' O. to arms   MILT 344:24
O. but friendless is   SHEL 503:7
omnis: Disce o.   VIRG 558:2
Non o. moriar   HOR 261:9
omniscience: his specialism is o.
   DOYLE 192:21
o. his foible   SMITH 512:11
Omnium: Duke of O.   TROL 552:15
Onan: straight into the sin of O.   VOLT 561:12
Onaway: O.! Awake   LONG 317:13
once: if it were done but o.   DONNE 190:24
I was adored o. too   SHAK 488:24
oblation of himself o.   PRAY 387:24
o. familiar word   BAYLY 35:10
o. in a great while   PEPYS 372:20
O. is more than enough   BIRCH 84:11
O. to every man and nation   LOW 319:12
o. was prodigal before   DRYD 196:2
trying every experience o.   ANON 4:24
was o. handsome and tall   ELIOT 205:7
one: apparel them all in o. livery   SHAK 446:11
doeth good, no not o.   PRAY 390:2
do only o. thing   SMIL 509:6
encompass'd but o. man   SHAK 448:19
had one body and o. heart   DOUG 191:10
heard o. side of the case   BUTL 119:1
he putteth down o.   PRAY 394:26
he sighed for o.   AUDEN 21:9
I am o. with my kind   TENN 540:19
in a procession of o.   DICK 179:20
incorporate and make us o.   SHAK 449:14
is to be o. man picked   SHAK 432:5
Lord our God is o. Lord   BIBLE 48:20
means to make us o.   DONNE 188:22

members o. of another BIBLE 77:29
mouths are o. with Mouth BROO 95:1
o. by one back in the Closet FITZ 213:5
o. damned thing OMAL 365:5
o. day in thy courts PRAY 395:13
O. man shall have one vote CART 136:13
O. man that has a mind SHAW 496:3
O. more such victory PYRR 403:7
O. near one is too far BROW 99:23
o. penny the worse BARH 33:14
o. small step for a man ARMS 12:18
o. that was never thought BIBLE 62:31
O. the long night through HOUS 262:21
O. to destroy YOUNG 587:19
o. way in to life SEN 420:9
stranger to o. of your parents AUST 23:15
they shall be o. flesh BIBLE 45:13
To love o. maiden only TENN 534:12
who but trifles with o. GAY 223:4
one-and-twenty: Long-expected o.
JOHN 279:28
When I was o. HOUS 262:20
One-eyed: Country of the Blind the O.
WELLS 568:12
There's a o. yellow idol HAYES 243:7
onehandled: statue of the o. adulterer
JOYCE 286:25
one-hoss: of the wonderful o. shay
HOLM 253:8
one-third: o. of a nation ill-housed
ROOS 407:22
onion: Let o. atoms lurk within SMITH 511:14
tears live in an o. SHAK 421:22
onlie: o. begetter of these insuing
SHAK 492:21
only: If o. I could get down PINT 373:19
keep thee o. unto her PRAY 389:3
o. begotten of the Father BIBLE 71:27
O. connect the prose FORS 217:2
o. to stand high in your SHAK 467:13
say o. the word MASS 335:8
only-begotten: o. Son of God PRAY 387:10
onori: offrirgli nè o. nè stipendi GAR 221:10
onset: Vain thy o. ARN 13:14
ooth: o. was but by Seinte Loy CHAU 141:14
ooze: Feed in the o. of their ARN 13:6
through the o. and slime SMITH 510:10
oozing: I feel it o. out as it SHER 506:22
oozy: sea-blooms and the o. woods
SHEL 502:11
opal: thy mind is a very o. SHAK 489:5
ope: o. my lips let no dog SHAK 465:12
open: equally o. to the poor ANON 4:13
light-hearted I take to the o. road WHIT 571:7
o. and notorious evil PRAY 387:5
O. covenants of peace openly WILS 575:1
o. his grief PRAY 387:17
O. not thine heart to every BIBLE 62:28
O. rebuke is better than BIBLE 54:37
O. Sesame ARAB 11:15
o. society and its enemies POPP 381:24
o. that Pandora's Box you BEVIN 44:19
o. the Kingdom of Heaven PRAY 384:17
O. the temple gates SPEN 515:25
O. the windows AUST 22:15
O. to me BIBLE 57:1
O. unto the fields WORD 581:14
O., ye everlasting gates MILT 349:2
Secret thoughts and o. ALB 3:8
Thou shalt o. my lips PRAY 393:8
You see her eyes are o. SHAK 462:19
open door: o. for all nations' trade BER 41:16
opened: favourite volume always o.
AUST 23:7
If he were o. SHAK 490:1
o. the seventh seal BIBLE 82:5
Towards the door we never o. ELIOT 202:13
openeth: o. the gate to good fame
BACON 26:4
opening: o. of the prison to them BIBLE 60:8

o. the doors very often AUST 22:14
openly: engage himself o. and publicly
BLAKE 86:10
himself shall reward you o. BIBLE 64:22
opera: omnia o. Domini BIBLE 83:16
operosiores: Divitias o. HOR 260:16
opes: emergere o. rerumque potiri
LUCR 320:6
Fumum et o. strepitumque HOR 261:7
golden o. MILT 343:11
Ophelia: I lov'd O. SHAK 437:8
opinion: An' justifies th' ill o. BURNS 115:21
Back'd his o. with quotations PRIOR 401:2
coquetry of public o. BURKE 110:15
difference of an o. BROW 96:4
fool gudgeon, this o. SHAK 465:13
general a man of common o. BAG 29:15
gross and scope of my o. SHAK 429:10
In vain o.'s waste COWP 165:12
Is of his own o. still BUTL 118:13
literary and scientific o. ARN 16:5
Nobody holds a good o. TROL 553:3
north of my lady's o. SHAK 489:28
o. he held once Of fantasy SHAK 449:10
o. in good men is but knowledge MILT 352:2
o. is about a woman JAMES 271:28
O. is ultimately determined SPEN 515:2
o. one man entertains PALM 368:12
o. we are endeavouring MILL 339:9
o. with the learned CONG 160:1
our own o. from another EMER 207:35
plague of o. SHAK 487:7
poor itch of your o. SHAK 427:12
reflecting no o. but their own WILS 574:23
sacrifices it to your o. BURKE 109:11
scorching world's o. FLET 215:19
that approve a private o. HOBB 251:16
thinkest thou of his o. SHAK 490:21
think the last o. right POPE 378:26
to admire except his o. FRY 219:24
were of one o. MILL 339:8
opinions: don't consult anyone's o.
PERS 372:26
Golden o. from all sorts SHAK 459:7
good or so bad as their o. MACK 325:11
halt ye between two o. BIBLE 51:8
killed with your hard o. SHAK 443:2
moderate o. they abhor MAC 323:13
o. are always suspected LOCKE 315:13
public buys its o. BUTL 119:4
There are as many o. TER 544:19
opium: mighty o. DE Q 175:2
o.-dose for keeping beasts KING 297:7
Religion...is the o. MARX 333:6
opponent: o. motives meaner BARR 34:9
o. of the chosen people ARN 16:3
opportunitate: sed etiam o. mortis TAC 531:9
opportunities: Devil watches all o.
CONG 160:19
man will make more o. BACON 25:38
opportunity: cometh by o. of leisure
BIBLE 63:19
had mortal man such o. BYRON 123:26
man must make his o. BACON 28:2
O. makes a thief BACON 28:2
Thou strong seducer, o. DRYD 195:31
with the maximum of o. SHAW 497:39
oppose: to o. everything DERBY 175:8
opposed: o. paths to persevere PATM 370:6
pretensions may be bravely o. KEYN 296:1
opposing: by o. end them SHAK 433:8
Opposition: 'Her Majesty's O.' BAG 28:23
o. of the stars MARV 331:19
phrase 'His Majesty's O.' HOBH 252:1
that the duty of an O. DERBY 175:8
without a formidable O. DISR 185:35
oppressed: Foal of an o. race COL 157:16
He was o. BIBLE 59:22
to let the o. go free BIBLE 60:4

oppresseth: while the enemy o. me
PRAY 392:9
oppressing: to the o. city BIBLE 61:27
oppression: behold o. BIBLE 57:23
O. makes the wise man mad BROW 102:10
To make o. bitter SHAK 433:4
oppressions: else unfelt o. of this
SHEL 501:12
oppressor: common enemy and o.
BURKE 110:33
o.'s wrong SHAK 433:8
oppugnancy: In mere o. SHAK 486:24
optabile: o. omnibus sanis et bonis CIC 151:33
optavere: multae o. puellae CAT 137:6
optics: o. of these eyes to behold BROW 96:21
Optima: O. quaeque dies miseris VIRG 560:16
optimist: not an o. but a meliorist
ELIOT 201:31
o. proclaims that we live CAB 126:25
opulence: those decisive marks of o.
SMITH 509:11
opulent: To glass the o. HARDY 239:4
opus: Hoc o. VIRG 558:18
Iamque o. exegi OVID 366:19
Orabunt: O. causas melius VIRG 559:1
Oracle: 'I am Sir O. SHAK 465:12
Oracles: are the lively O. of God COR 162:25
o. are dumb MILT 344:13
oracular: use of my o. tongue SHER 506:14
orange: in shades the o. bright MARV 331:16
o. flower perfumes SCOTT 418:25
orange-blossom: lands of palm, of o.
TENN 533:5
orange-pulp: Drinking watered o.
BROW 105:6
oranges: Coffee and o. in a sunny
STEV 520:18
orange-tree: that I were an o. HERB 247:20
orantes: Stabant o. primi transmittere
VIRG 558:22
oration: not studied as an o. OSB 365:19
orator: enjoyment as the greatest o.
HUME 267:22
eyes of men without an o. SHAK 492:17
I am no o. SHAK 451:1
orators: swords shall play the o. MARL 330:4
oratory: Chadband style of o. is DICK 176:13
object of o. MAC 324:20
orb: splendid o. was entirely set BURKE 109:6
orbis: Securus iudicat o. AUG 21:18
Si fractus illabatur o. HOR 260:19
orbs: operation of the o. SHAK 453:3
their glimmering o. and glow MILT 344:7
orchard: chaffinch sings on the o.
BROW 101:5
Cherry O. is now mine...I've CHEK 144:24
orchards: new-planted o. SHAK 451:4
Orci: primisque in faucibus O. VIRG 558:21
ordained: powers that be are o. BIBLE 75:20
'Tis so o. PRIOR 401:7
ordainer: o. of order and mystical
BROW 95:20
order: act of o. to a peopled SHAK 443:2
after the o. of Melchisedech PRAY 397:12
All things began in o. BROW 95:20
along with o. and virtue BURKE 109:10
done decently and in o. BIBLE 76:18
each in solemn o. followed WORD 581:1
Good o. is the foundation BURKE 111:25
he disturbs the o. here HARDY 240:3
in all line of o. SHAK 486:22
is simply o. and beauty BAUD 35:7
liberty connected with o. BURKE 109:10
old o. changeth TENN 535:25
ordainer of o. and mystical BROW 95:20
o. and military discipline ANON 4:28
o. or proportion BROW 96:34
O. reigns in Warsaw ANON 9:14
o., said I, this matter STER 518:28
party of o. or stability MILL 339:10

put his household in o.	BIBLE 50:25
Set thine house in o.	BIBLE 59:2
so I o. it done	JUV 287:21
to possess internal o.	FORS 217:14
upon the o. of your going	SHAK 461:23
order'd: o. their estate	ALEX 3:14
ordered: o. my goings	PRAY 392:1
orders: Almighty's o. to perform	ADD 1:14
ordinance: according to God's holy o.	
	PRAY 389:4
ordinary: Heaven in o.	HERB 248:5
o. one seem original	HOR 257:13
such a very o. little woman	BETJ 43:4
***ordo:** integro saeclorum nascitur o.*	
	VIRG 559:22
***ordre:** ce serait changer l'o.*	FRAN 217:25
L'o. règne à Varsovie	ANON 9:14
tout n'est qu'o. et beauté	BAUD 35:7
ore: of your subject with o.	KEATS 294:31
with new spangled o.	MILT 343:17
***oreilles:** o. ennemies vous écoutent*	
	ANON 9:18
organ: great o. of public opinion	DISR 184:19
Is as the maiden's o.	SHAK 488:3
is mellering to the o.	DICK 181:8
let the pealing o. blow	MILT 342:10
of heav'n's deep o. blow	MILT 344:10
o. and the maypole	JORD 285:18
o. to enlarge her prayer	AUDEN 18:3
Seated one day at the o.	PROC 401:13
organise: o. the theatre	ARN 16:15
organism: o. to live beyond its income	
	BUTL 118:27
organized: o. hypocrisy	BAG 29:8
organs: his owls was o.	DICK 179:27
in her the o. of increase	SHAK 453:18
moves with its own o.	SHAK 422:14
organ-voice: God-gifted o. of England	
	TENN 533:12
Oriel: O. Common Room stank	NEWM 361:22
***Oriens:** equis O. adflavit anhelis*	VIRG 560:11
Oriental: although an O.	CHES 147:27
more-than-o.-splendour	KIPL 304:19
you are an O.	FORS 217:6
origin: indelible stamp of his lowly o.	
	DARW 171:24
original: Behold the bright o. appear	
	GAY 223:19
I have nothing o. in me	CAMP 129:14
is very far gone from o.	PRAY 400:7
L'écrivain o. n'est pas	CHAT 141:5
ordinary one seem o.	HOR 257:13
o. es infiel a la traducción	BORG 89:24
o. is unfaithful	BORG 89:24
o. writer is not he who	CHAT 141:5
th'o. perus'd mankind	ARMS 12:15
originality: exist are the fruits of o.	
	MILL 339:12
without o. or moral courage	SHAW 496:12
originator: Next to the o. of a good	
	EMER 208:2
origins: Consider your o.	DANTE 171:13
Orion: loose the bands of O.	BIBLE 53:5
O. and the Dog Are veiled	ELIOT 204:15
O. plunges prone	HOUS 265:17
orisons: patter out their hasty o.	OWEN 367:2
orisonte: th'o. hath reft the sonne	
	CHAU 142:13
Orlando: Run, run, O.	SHAK 426:2
ornament: esteem'st the o. of life	SHAK 459:8
grossness with fair o.	SHAK 467:10
Nobility is a graceful o.	BURKE 111:21
not the foreign aid of o.	THOM 549:17
O. is but the guiled shore	SHAK 467:11
O. of a meek and quiet	BIBLE 80:28
o. of his cheek hath already	SHAK 472:26
o. put upon great civic	RUSK 411:21
o. to her profession	BUNY 107:35
o. which truth doth give	SHAK 493:16
respecting all o.	RUSK 411:20

still deceived with o.	SHAK 467:10
ornaments: Can a maid forget her o.	
	BIBLE 60:15
hide with o. their want	POPE 378:16
made in lieu of many o.	SPEN 515:27
ornate: embellisher of o. eloquence	
	CAXT 138:2
O., and Grotesque Art	BAG 29:20
***ornavit:** Nullum quod tetigit non o.*	
	JOHN 277:13
***Orontes:** in Tiberim defluxit O.*	JUV 287:15
Orotunda: "Or Opulent O. Strike	
	STEV 521:13
orphan-boy: teach the o. to read	TENN 538:1
orphans: with wrong'd o.' tears	MASS 335:21
Orpheus: Another O. sings again	
	SHEL 500:21
bid the soul of O. sing	MILT 342:6
O. with his lute made trees	SHAK 447:3
Orthodoxy: O. is my doxy	WARB 564:17
O. or My-doxy and Heterodoxy	CARL 131:25
ortolans: Let me die eating o.	DISR 187:1
Oscar: You will, O.	WHIS 569:25
oss: have them cleanin' his 'o.	SURT 525:12
'o., my wife, and my name	SURT 525:17
Paid for catching my 'o.	SURT 525:13
Ossa: pile O. on Pelion	VIRG 560:12
ossmanship: morality than on his 'o.	
	SURT 525:9
ostentation: blown me full of maggot	
o.	SHAK 457:15
use rather than for o.	GIBB 224:25
ostrich: resembled the wings of an o.	
	MAC 323:5
tall o. on the ground	SMART 509:3
Othello: O.'s occupation's gone	SHAK 475:25
other: caitiff smite the o.	HOLM 253:11
desire o. men's goods	PRAY 388:18
forsaking all o.	PRAY 389:3
o. side of the hill'	WELL 567:20
strange faces, o. minds	TENN 535:24
that I am not as o. men are	BIBLE 70:34
their troth either to o.	PRAY 389:7
This o. Eden	SHAK 478:20
turn to him the o. also	BIBLE 64:17
Were t'o. dear charmer away	GAY 222:35
others: liberty is the love of o.	HAZL 243:19
misfortunes and pains of o.	BURKE 108:8
O., I am not the first	HOUS 263:13
playtime of the o.	BROW 97:36
thou be not false to o.	BACON 27:35
we pass judgement on o.	MOL 353:20
otherwise: gods thought o.	VIRG 558:3
***otia:** deus nobis haec o. fecit*	VIRG 559:12
***otiosum:** Numquam se minus o. esse*	
	CIC 151:23
***otiosus:** Numquam sis ex toto o.*	THOM 546:11
***otium:** cum dignitate o.*	CIC 151:33
***oublié:** ni rien o.*	TALL 531:17
o. et n'ont rien appris	DUM 199:7
ought: hadn't o. to be	HARTE 242:28
must believe what you o.	NEWM 362:17
not what they o. to do	BACON 24:25
O. to be told to come	FROST 219:11
tell me I o. to do	BURKE 109:26
what things they o. to do	PRAY 386:7
which we o. to have done	PRAY 384:12
***Oun:** Properly based O.*	BROW 101:1
ounce: o. of love is worth a pound	
	WESL 568:23
ound: that I loves the 'o. more	SURT 525:10
Our: O. Father which art	BIBLE 64:24
ours: see in Nature that is o.	WORD 582:19
They were not o.	OWEN 367:7
ourselves: five days elder than o.	BROW 96:10
in o., are triumph	LONG 316:27
knowledge is, o. to know	POPE 380:4
long and carefully at o.	MOL 353:20
not we o.	PRAY 396:11
of o. to help ourselves	PRAY 386:9

Our remedies oft in o.	SHAK 420:28
power is the love of o.	HAZL 243:19
unsafe to be trusted with o.	CONG 159:17
ousel: o. and the throstlecock	DRAY 193:19
ousel-cock: o., so black of hue	SHAK 470:18
ouses: wasn't for the 'o. in between	BAT 35:3
out: down and o. of breath	SHAK 440:27
I believe they went o.	DISR 186:9
'I can't get o.	STER 519:7
I o. of myself	AUG 21:16
Lord Coodle would go o.	DICK 176:21
many ways o.	SEN 420:9
mother know that you are o.	BARH 33:24
other o.	CHUR 148:20
o., brief candle	SHAK 463:6
o. of sight is out of mind	CLOU 154:5
O. of the deep have I called	PRAY 398:23
O. of this wood do not	SHAK 470:19
O. on the lawn I lie	AUDEN 20:18
shall preserve thy going o.	PRAY 398:10
such as are o. wish to get	EMER 208:6
that o. of battle I escaped	OWEN 367:9
you will soon be o. of it	EMER 207:45
out-argue: out-vote them we will o.	
	JOHN 277:23
outcast: all alone beweep my o.	SHAK 493:6
o. of the people	PRAY 390:17
Spiritless o.	CANN 129:27
out-casts: together the o. of Israel	
	PRAY 399:19
outcries: o. pluck me from my naked	
	KYD 306:2
outcry: Each o. of the hunted hare	
	BLAKE 85:10
outgrabe: mome raths o.	CARR 134:28
outlawed: nor be o., nor excommunicate	
	COKE 154:24
outlive: shall o. this powerful rime	
	SHAK 493:17
outlives: He that o. this day	SHAK 445:3
laurel o. not May	SWIN 530:5
outlook: Could man o. that mark	
	VAUG 555:20
out-paramoured: woman o. the Turk	
	SHAK 454:18
outrage: Seal up the mouth of o.	SHAK 484:1
outrageously: over-offended ladies the	
o. virtuous	STEE 518:3
outshine: o. Myriads though bright	
	MILT 344:26
outside: support it from the o.	MELB 336:22
Out-topping: O. knowledge	ARN 14:23
out-vote: o. them we will out-argue	
	JOHN 277:23
outward: hope from o. forms to win	
	COL 156:8
In all her o. parts Love's	COWL 164:6
looketh on the o. appearance	BIBLE 50:6
mark of virtue on his o.	SHAK 467:10
Of sense and o. things	WORD 579:10
o. and visible sign	PRAY 388:19
o. shows be least themselves	SHAK 467:10
o. show of things	SPEN 516:21
taper to the o. room	DONNE 189:30
weather on the o. wall	SHAK 466:19
outwardly: us both o. in our bodies	
	PRAY 386:9
outweighs: Which if we find o. ability	
	SHAK 441:17
outwore: six lustres almost now o.	
	DONNE 189:36
Out-worn: O. heart	YEATS 585:14
rich-proud cost of o. buried age	SHAK 494:2
***ouvrage:** continuel o. de votre vie*	
	MONT 354:15
***ouvrages:** tranquilles dans les grands*	
o.	VOLT 561:16
***ouvres:** mon talent dans mes o.*	WILDE 573:35
over: All this is o. now	CAT 136:24
O. hill, over dale	SHAK 470:2

in rest from p. DRYD 196:25
intermission of p. SELD 419:26
it was p. and grief to me PRAY 391:30
joy is but a dish of p. TICH 551:2
life's a p. and but a span DAV 172:11
living thing to suffer p. SHEL 502:21
lose, Though full of p. MILT 346:10
methought what p. it was SHAK 480:27
midnight with no p. KEATS 291:22
Never p. to tell thy love BLAKE 86:21
nor help for p. ARN 12:23
numbing p. TENN 536:1
Our Lady of P. SWIN 529:6
P. at her side POPE 381:9
p. shall not be inflicted SPEN 514:26
piercing p. STEV 523:11
pleasure and without one p. TENN 539:22
pleasures to another's p. COWP 167:6
pleasure turns to pleasing p. SPEN 516:17
purchase p. with all that joy POPE 377:21
quite sure she felt no p. BROW 103:29
reliev'd their p. GOLD 230:23
rues et de voler du p. FRAN 217:26
shall there be any more p. BIBLE 82:31
Superflux of p. SWIN 528:13
Sweet is pleasure after p. DRYD 195:1
tender for another's p. GRAY 235:13
thou certain p. GRAN 234:7
thy delight in others' p. BYRON 125:4
tongueless vigil and all the p. SWIN 528:15
wandering and the p. FLEC 214:5
well and she hasn't a p. MILNE 340:10
what ignorance of p. SHEL 504:21
what p. ARN 14:2
what p. it is to part GAY 222:23
When p. and anguish wring SCOTT 417:21
wicked to deserve such p. BROW 99:29
With some p. is fraught SHEL 504:23
yet free from guilt or p. SHEL 503:12
pain'd: p. desert lion ARN 14:26
painful: one is as p. as the other BACON 26:3
p. pleasure turns to pleasing SPEN 516:17
pains: His present and your p. SHAK 443:11
made my p. his prey SPEN 515:20
men come to greater p. BACON 26:23
misfortunes and p. of others BURKE 108:8
One of the greatest p. BAG 29:1
p. of hell gat hold PRAY 397:19
P. of love be sweeter far DRYD 197:36
p. the immortal spirit ARN 14:24
possessors into p. of all kinds BUTL 118:34
So double was his p. SPEN 516:10
stings you for your p. HILL 251:2
taken great p. to con it SHAK 488:10
with p. that conquer trust TENN 536:14
paint: fain would p. a picture BROW 102:32
let her p. an inch thick SHAK 436:31
only showed the p. DRYD 196:7
p. 'em truest praise ADD 1:15
p. in the public's face RUSK 411:7
P. me the bold anfractuous ELIOT 204:11
p. my picture truly like CROM 169:24
p. the lily BYRON 122:31
p. the meadows with delight SHAK 457:18
prepared to p. an angel BROW 102:30
to p. the lily SHAK 452:25
painted: are but gilded loam or p. SHAK 478:8
Duchess p. on the wall BROW 102:34
idle as a p. ship COL 155:13
is not to be p. upon MAC 323:31
lath of wood p. BISM 84:27
p. cunningly SPEN 516:3
p. meadow ADD 2:5
P. the mid-sea blue FLEC 214:17
p. veil which those who SHEL 504:4
She p. her face BIBLE 51:34
so young as they are p. BEER 37:10
That fears a p. devil SHAK 460:11
This p. child of dirt POPE 377:1
was p. on the wall PETR 372:30

painter: am a p. CORR 163:1
great p. dips His pencil SHEL 503:21
great sculptor or p. can RUSK 411:8
had been the P.'s hand WORD 577:4
He is but a landscape-p. TENN 539:10
me a p. and I am grateful CONS 162:1
painters: know of two p. in the world WHIS 569:21
'P. and poets alike have HOR 257:10
p. imitate nature CERV 139:1
p., poets and builders MARL 329:2
painting: amateur p. in water-colours STEV 521:28
knew as much about p. LAND 309:16
P. thy outward walls so SHAK 495:13
poem is like that of a p. HOR 258:3
thoughts on the unreal p. VIRG 557:17
Whose mother was her p. SHAK 428:16
paintings: all the allegorical p. JOHN 280:19
have heard of your p. too SHAK 433:13
paint-pots: p. and his words a foot HOR 257:16
paints: Ingres's the modern man who p. BROW 100:17
want to know a butcher p. BROW 105:4
pair: been a p. of ragged claws ELIOT 203:21
of this ever diverse p. MER 337:17
p. of very strange beasts SHAK 427:3
p. so famous SHAK 424:19
resembles a p. of shears SMITH 511:11
Sleep on, Blest p. MILT 348:9
Take a p. of sparkling eyes GILB 225:26
paired: brain went ever p. BROW 101:26
palace: Be thine own p. DONNE 189:23
dominions and making his p. desolate BECK 36:19
from this p. of dim night SHAK 483:31
gorgeous p. for a hermitage SHAK 479:15
in the lighted p. near TENN 538:12
I will make a p. fit STEV 522:29
leads to the p. of wisdom BLAKE 88:13
Love in a p. is perhaps KEATS 290:24
man armed keepeth his p. BIBLE 69:36
p. and a prison on each BYRON 121:1
P. in smoky light POUND 382:7
p. is more than a house COL 158:1
purple-lined p. of sweet sin KEATS 290:25
palaces: Dragons in their pleasant p. BIBLE 58:12
frail p. ALDR 3:11
gorgeous p. SHAK 485:20
Mid pleasures and p. though PAYNE 370:1
plenteousness with thy p. PRAY 398:12
sleep old p. and towers SHEL 502:10
paladin: starry p. BROW 105:12
Palaeozoic: In the P. time SMITH 510:10
palate: of the liver, but the p. SHAK 489:6
P., the hutch of tasty HOPK 256:15
palates: never p. more the dug SHAK 423:20
palatium: quale p. ABEL 1:2
pale: behold a p. horse BIBLE 81:29
bond Which keeps me p. SHAK 461:14
look not so p. SHAK 462:24
make p. my cheeks with WITH 575:12
One p. as the yonder wan SHEL 500:8
P. as thy smock SHAK 477:21
P., beyond porch and portal SWIN 529:22
p. contented sort of discontent KEATS 290:26
p. from the imagined love YEATS 587:1
P. grew thy cheek and cold BYRON 126:13
P. hands I loved HOPE 256:3
p. prime-roses SHAK 491:26
p., unripened beauties ADD 1:19
to look so green and p. SHAK 459:8
turn not p., beloved snail CARR 134:15
was a p. young curate then GILB 229:1
which the world grew p. JOHN 282:31
Why so p. and wan SUCK 524:6
paler: I become p. than grass SAPP 414:6
paletot: p. aussi devenait idéal RIMB 406:7

paling: p. shuts the spouse Christ HOPK 256:29
pall: brows shall be their p. OWEN 367:3
Palladium: of the press is the P. JUN 287:1
pallescere: nulla p. culpa HOR 258:9
pallets: cumber Sunlit p. HOUS 262:15
Upon uneasy p. stretching SHAK 441:29
palliate: we p. what we cannot cure JOHN 281:9
Pallida: P. Mors aequo HOR 259:13
Pallidula: P. rigida nudula HADR 237:9
Palliser: think that Plantagenet P. TROL 552:15
Pall Mall: sweet shady side of P. MORR 358:3
pallor: p. of girls' brows OWEN 367:3
palls: everthing p. ANON 9:20
palm: bear the p. alone SHAK 448:16
condemn'd to have an itching p. SHAK 451:12
Hard as the p. of ploughman SHAK 486:19
has won it bear the p. JORT 285:19
Hold Infinity in the p. BLAKE 85:8
In lands of p. and southern TENN 533:5
Quietly sweating palm to p. HUXL 268:22
victor's p. without the dust HOR 258:8
palmae: dulcis sine pulvere p. HOR 258:8
palmer: votarist in p.'s weed MILT 340:30
palmerworm: p. hath left hath the locust BIBLE 61:13
palms: Afield for p. the girls HOUS 262:19
other p. are won WORD 579:14
p. and the paean SWIN 530:4
p. before my feet CHES 146:23
Palmyra: editions of Balbec and P. WALP 563:9
palpable: is almost a p. movement HARDY 241:9
palsey: It hath brought p. to bed POUND 382:11
palsied: alms Of p. eld SHAK 464:10
palsy: ole en strucken wid de p. HARR 242:13
palter'd: Nor p. with Eternal God TENN 541:12
paltry: aged man is but a p. thing YEATS 586:12
'Tis p. to be Caesar SHAK 423:20
Pam: P., you great big mountainous BETJ 43:20
Pamere: mountain cradle in P. ARN 15:1
pampered: God's p. people DRYD 194:4
pamphleteer: p. on guano and on grain TENN 542:20
Pan: great god P. BROW 98:6
great P. is dead BROW 98:2
P. by noon and Bacchus SWIN 528:18
p. comido y la compañía CERV 138:14
P. did after Syrinx speed MARV 332:2
Panachaea: Or P., or Polygony SPEN 516:15
panache: Cyrano: *Mon p.* ROST 410:14
Pancras: P. and Kentish Town repose BLAKE 86:5
Pandoemonium: P., the high capitol MILT 346:5
Pandora's Box: If you open that P. you BEVIN 44:19
pane: Lo p. altrui DANTE 171:17
p. is blind with showers HOUS 264:20
tap at the p. BROW 102:14
Panem: P. et circenses JUV 287:28
p. nostrum quotidianum MASS 335:5
panes: diamonded with p. of quaint KEATS 289:16
pang: p. of all the partings THOM 547:26
sufferance finds a p. as great SHAK 464:11
Pange: P., lingua THOM 546:16
P., lingua VEN 556:4
pangs: In the sweet p. of it remember SHAK 488:27
p. and fears than wars SHAK 447:9
Their p. of love SHAK 486:13
panic: it but p. and emptiness FORS 216:25

p.'s in thy breastie BURNS 115:20
Panjandrum: grand P. himself FOOTE 216:7
pansies: p., that's for thoughts SHAK 436:10
pansy: p. at my feet WORD 579:5
p. freakt with jet MILT 343:15
pant: I p., I sink SHEL 500:13
pantaloon: lean and slipper'd p. SHAK 425:24
panting: ever p. and for ever young
KEATS 291:7
pantoufles: *apportez-moi mes p.* MOL 353:3
pants: p. the hart for cooling TATE 531:20
your lower limbs in p. NASH 360:5
papa: else his dear p. is poor STEV 522:21
furious p. or a mild engineer AUDEN 20:15
P., potatoes, poultry DICK 178:26
scene of it with my P. DICK 178:18
Papacy: P. is not other than HOBB 251:21
paper: atomic bomb is a p. tiger MAO 328:20
dust upon the p. eye DOUG 191:10
Golly, what a p. STEV 522:14
grey p. with blunt type BROW 105:8
hand that signed the p. THOM 547:4
he hath not eat p. SHAK 457:1
If all the earth were p. LYLY 321:16
just for a scrap of p. BETH 42:3
p. appears dull there is STEE 518:5
That ever blotted p. SHAK 467:15
virtue of p. government BURKE 109:13
was any news in the p. AUST 23:26
paper-mill: thou hast built a p. SHAK 446:14
Papist: P., yet a *Calvinist* CLEV 153:3
Paquin: P. pull down POUND 382:13
Par: P. *nobile fratrum* HOR 262:8
parable: will open my mouth in a p.
PRAY 395:3
parade: consists in the p. of riches
SMITH 509:11
paradis: sont les p. qu'on a perdus
PROU 402:1
Paradise: All P. opens DISR 187:1
Beautiful as a wreck of P. SHEL 500:14
drunk the milk of P. COL 157:1
eastern side beheld Of P. MILT 350:1
England is a p. for women BURT 116:37
England is the p. of women FLOR 216:1
enjoy p. in the next BECK 36:20
in P., If we meet BROW 105:36
I was taught in P. KEATS 289:25
Life's p. FORD 216:14
Lost Angel of a ruin'd P. SHEL 499:8
P. by way of Kensal Green CHES 147:12
p. for a sect KEATS 289:26
P. of Fools MILT 347:11
rudiments of P. SOUTH 513:12
shalt thou be with me in p. BIBLE 71:13
Such are the Gates of P. BLAKE 85:26
Thou hast the keys of P. DE Q 175:2
Thou P. of exiles SHEL 501:11
To him are opening p. GRAY 235:15
To live in P. alone MARV 332:8
Upon the trees of P. STEV 523:13
Wilderness is P. enow FITZ 212:11
would destroy their p. GRAY 235:9
paradises: paradises are p. we have lost
PROU 402:1
paradox: Man is an embodied p. COLT 159:11
parallel: ours so truly p. MARV 331:19
Parallelograms: Princess of P. BYRON 126:21
parallels: p. in beauty's brow SHAK 493:20
paramours: his sustres and his p.
CHAU 142:32
Worn of p. SPEN 517:3
paraphrase: Than the classics in p.
POUND 383:4
parcels: she deals it in small p. WEBS 567:1
Parce que: 'P. c'était lui MONT 354:18
Parcere: P. *subiectis et debellare* VIRG 559:1
parchment: features bound in stale p.
MER 337:26

innocent lamb should be made p.
SHAK 446:12
rotten p. bonds SHAK 478:20
virtue of wax and p. BURKE 109:24
Parcus: P. *deorum cultor et infrequens*
HOR 260:2
pard: p.-like Spirit SHEL 499:17
pardon: beseech you of your p. SHAK 475:19
cannot help nor p. AUDEN 20:17
faithful people p. and peace PRAY 386:22
God may p. you ELIZ 205:29
God will p. me HEINE 244:13
p. all oaths that are broke SHAK 480:3
they ne'er p. DRYD 195:30
thousand Ta's and P.'s BETJ 43:13
To p. or to bear it COWP 165:9
We cannot beg for p. MACN 326:15
We will p. Thy Mistake BETJ 43:5
pardonable: then it is p. CONG 160:22
Pardoned: P. Kipling and his views
AUDEN 19:8
pardoning: p. our offences PRAY 388:2
pardonnera: Et le bon Dieu me p.
CATH 136:17
pardoun: Bretful of p. CHAU 142:6
parent: don't object to an aged p.
DICK 178:12
Fear is the p. of cruelty FROU 219:20
had a smile for your p. VIRG 560:2
most afflicting to a p.'s AUST 23:18
That would put any p. mad FLEM 214:25
To lose one p. WILDE 573:1
Parentage: P. is a very important
SHAW 496:24
'What is your p. SHAK 488:14
parents: begin by loving their p.
WILDE 573:30
indiscreetly by most p. STEE 518:10
joys of p. are secret BACON 27:2
lords whose p. were DEFOE 173:14
Of p. good SHAK 444:17
Our p.' age (worse than HOR 260:26
P. first season us HERB 248:10
p.' tears MILT 345:14
stranger to one of your p. AUST 23:15
parentum: Aetas p. peior avis tulit
HOR 260:26
parfit: p. gentil knyght CHAU 141:10
paries: Barbiton hic p. habebit HOR 261:6
p. *cum proximus ardet* HOR 258:23
pariete: in p. erat pictus superque
PETR 372:30
Paris: Americans die they go to P.
WILDE 573:25
girl's lip out of P. SWIN 531:2
go to P. APPL 11:13
king had given me P. ANON 9:17
P. is well worth a mass HENR 245:15
should go and live in P. ANON 6:2
To mighty P. when he found YEATS 586:4
parish: all the world as my p. WESL 568:18
his pension from his p. RUSK 412:7
p. of rich women AUDEN 19:5
paritors: general Of trotting 'p. SHAK 456:26
parium: judicium p. suorum MAGN 327:2
parle: mais je n'en p. jamais PROU 401:22
parler: souffre et meurs sans p. VIGNY 557:2
Parliament: Bidding the crop-headed
P. BROW 99:26
In the P. of man TENN 538:24
p. can do any thing PEMB 371:11
p. is a *deliberative* assembly BURKE 109:12
P. speaking through reporters CARL 132:4
to fun in any Act of P. HERB 246:14
Parliamentary: unhappy Bag of P.
Eloquence CARL 132:1
Parliaments: England is the mother of
P. BRIG 93:4
we shall have no more P. JONS 284:26
parlour: Is it a party in a p. WORD 580:2

'Will you walk into my p. HOW 267:3
Parnassus: since you my chief P. be
SIDN 507:27
Parnell: Poor P. JOYCE 286:15
parochial: Art must be p. in the beginning
MOORE 355:16
he was p. JAMES 271:9
parody: devil's walking p. CHES 146:22
parole: Classical quotation is the p.
JOHN 278:29
paroles: et n'emploient les p. que VOLT 561:4
paronomasia: (You catch the p. CALV 127:15
parritch: halesome p. BURNS 113:8
pars: Et *quorum p. magna fui* VIRG 557:21
parshial: p. to ladies if they are ASHF 17:6
parson: coughing drowns the p.'s saw
SHAK 457:19
If P. lost his senses HODG 252:2
like a p.'s damn HARDY 241:14
Monday is the p.'s holiday SWIFT 526:19
parson and the p.'s wife CLOU 153:23
p. knows enough who knows COWP 167:31
P. left conjuring SELD 419:24
p., much bemus'd in beer POPE 376:21
p. own'd his skill GOLD 231:3
Then the P. might preach BLAKE 87:20
There goes the p. COWP 166:1
Tickling a p.'s nose SHAK 481:28
parsons: p. are very like other CHES 145:11
p. do not care for truth STUB 524:5
This merriment of p. is JOHN 278:25
part: come let us kiss and p. DRAY 193:21
death p. thee and me BIBLE 49:32
every man must play a p. SHAK 465:10
ev'ry prudent p. POPE 377:22
forgotten this day we must p. CRAW 169:16
hath chosen that good p. BIBLE 69:35
I am a p. of all TENN 543:22
more willingly p. withal SHAK 432:10
now I know in p. BIBLE 76:14
p. at last without a kiss MORR 358:11
p. my garments among them PRAY 390:20
p. nor lot in this matter BIBLE 73:31
P. steals HARDY 240:2
p. to tear a cat SHAK 469:24
Shall I p. my hair behind ELIOT 203:25
Suff'ring is the lover's p. GAY 222:9
take your own p. BORR 90:11
till death us do p. PRAY 389:4
To p. her time 'twixt reading POPE 377:7
was not p. of their blood KIPL 298:1
We two now p. PATM 370:6
what pain it is to p. GAY 222:23
which I was a major p. VIRG 557:21
you and I must p. SHAK 421:28
partagée: chose du monde la mieux p.
DESC 175:11
partakers: p. of the holy Communion
PRAY 387:5
parted: a' p. even just between SHAK 443:17
best and worst, and p. BROO 94:6
his words are soon p. SHEN 505:17
Mine never shall be p. MILT 349:19
remember the way we p. SWIN 530:10
though p. then AUDEN 20:19
When we two p. BYRON 126:13
Parthenophil: P. is lost FORD 216:19
Parthians: P., and Medes BIBLE 73:23
partial: p. for th' observer's sake POPE 377:8
participation: have some p. of divineness
BACON 24:19
particle: pushing young p. GILB 227:28
Particles: Newtons P. of Light BLAKE 86:24
particular: should love a bright p. star
SHAK 420:25
Particulars: must do it in Minute P.
BLAKE 86:7
parties: high contracting p. solemnly
KELL 295:8
p. against believing their ARB 11:19

P. must ever exist	BURKE 110:1
parting: Ere the p. hour go	ARN 13:19
In every p. there is	ELIOT 201:22
P. is all we know of heaven	DICK 183:20
p. is such sweet sorrow	SHAK 482:20
P.'s well-paid with soon	PATM 370:5
rive not more in p.	SHAK 423:6
stood at the p. of the ways	BIBLE 60:36
Their every p. was to die	TENN 537:12
this p. was well made	SHAK 451:32
partings: pang of all the p. gone	THOM 547:26
Partington: Atlantic Ocean beat Mrs P.	SMITH 511:32
Partir: P. c'est mourir un peu	HAR 238:20
partly: Living and p. living	ELIOT 204:2
p. she was drunk	BURNS 114:18
partner: While his lov'd p.	GOLD 231:26
partridge: Always p.	ANON 9:19
p. sitteth on eggs	BIBLE 60:25
parts: his time plays many p.	SHAK 425:24
P. of it are excellent	PUNCH 403:4
p. of one stupendous whole	POPE 379:10
smaller p.-o'-speech	CALV 127:15
To-day we have naming of p.	REED 405:5
truth in the inward p.	PRAY 393:5
weep upon your hinder p.	HUXL 268:23
Parturient: *P. montes*	HOR 257:18
party: again to save the p. we love	GAIT 220:26
and...to educate our p.	DISR 185:5
'Collapse of Stout P.'	ANON 8:10
conduct of a losing p.	BURKE 111:27
existence the stupidest p.	MILL 339:2
I always voted at my p.'s	GILB 228:6
Is it a p. in a parlour	WORD 580:2
maintain the p. of the truth	SHAK 445:21
nature of a political p.	TROL 553:8
P. is organized opinion	DISR 185:1
p. of friends	GILB 226:14
p. of order or stability	MILL 339:10
p. Parliamentary government	DISR 185:7
passion and p. blind	COL 157:20
phylacteries of the Liberal P.	ROS 408:17
sooner every p. breaks	AUST 22:13
Stick to your p.	DISR 185:21
Then none was for a p.	MAC 322:18
party-coloured: known by this p. livery	CONG 160:22
Party-spirit: P., which at best is	POPE 381:16
parva: p. licet componere magnis	VIRG 560:19
Parys: Frenssh of P. was to hire	CHAU 141:15
pas: n'y a que le premier p.	DU D 198:28
pasarán: No p.	IBAR 269:15
pascit: atque animum pictura p.	VIRG 557:17
pass: bringeth mighty things to p.	PRAY 398:1
cunning men p. for wise	BACON 25:43
deeds which should not p.	BYRON 120:32
Generations p. while some tree	BROW 97:16
Individuals p. like shadows	BURKE 110:17
I shall not p. this way	GREL 236:14
I will p. nor turn my face	BROW 105:36
let him p.	SHAK 456:12
let this cup p. from me	BIBLE 68:14
let us p.	BURKE 110:19
my words shall not p. away	BIBLE 67:31
p., and turn again	EMER 206:17
p. but the end is not yet	BIBLE 67:27
p. by me as the idle wind	SHAK 451:20
P. into nothingness	KEATS 288:20
p. man's understanding	PRAY 386:11
p. the ammunition	FORGY 216:21
P. the hat for your credit's	KIPL 297:25
p. through things temporal	PRAY 386:16
pay us, p. us	CHES 147:15
shining Foot shall p.	FITZ 213:18
that it may not p. away	KIPL 299:15
therefore let him p. for a man	SHAK 465:22
They shall not p.	IBAR 269:15

thou shalt strangely p.	SHAK 493:14
to p. through this world	GREL 236:14
'Try not the P.	LONG 316:15
well p. for forty-three	GILB 229:4
which they shall not p.	PRAY 396:19
Will she p. in a crowd	SWIFT 526:14
passa: guarda, e p.	DANTE 171:4
passage: desired to fret a p. through	FULL 220:19
Down the p. which we did	ELIOT 202:13
ever you meet with a p.	JOHN 276:14
long black p. up to bed	STEV 522:25
minion carv'd out his p.	SHAK 458:3
North-west p.	STER 520:2
p. is what I call the sublime	COL 158:7
passages: cheated into some fine p.	KEATS 294:15
shuts up all the p. of joy	JOHN 283:1
Time shall not lose our p.	DONNE 188:9
passageways: With smell of steaks in p.	ELIOT 204:7
pass'd: p. the door of Darkness	FITZ 213:4
passe: Tout p.	ANON 9:20
passed: I have p. with a nod	YEATS 585:1
p. by on the other side	BIBLE 69:31
passengers: we the p.	HOW 267:1
Passer: P. mortuus est meae puellae	CAT 136:22
passeront: Ils ne p. pas	NIV 363:17
passes: Everything p.	ANON 9:20
Men seldom make p.	PARK 368:16
p. the glory of the world	ANON 11:1
passeth: fashion of this world p.	BIBLE 76:4
which p. all understanding	BIBLE 78:21
world, that p.	CHAU 144:19
passi: p. graviora	VIRG 557:13
passing: Deign on the p. world	JOHN 282:29
I did but see her p.	ANON 8:1
in the p. of a day	SPEN 516:13
p. the love of women	BIBLE 50:17
So be my p.	HENL 245:9
Writh'd not at p. joy	KEATS 293:4
passing-bells: What p. for these who die	OWEN 367:2
passion: All breathing human p.	KEATS 291:7
All made of p.	SHAK 426:29
all p. spent	MILT 351:4
Bards of P. and of Mirth	KEATS 290:31
betwixt one p. and another	STER 519:3
by thy Cross and P.	PRAY 385:17
commanded By such poor p.	SHAK 423:17
connect the prose and the p.	FORS 217:2
desolate and sick of an old p.	DOWS 191:12
Eternal P.	ARN 14:3
gentleman in such a p. about	SHAW 498:26
has felt the tender p.	GAY 223:3
his p. boiled and bubbled	THAC 546:3
I have no p. for it	JOHN 274:25
immoderate p. for fame	BURKE 109:8
in a dream of p.	SHAK 432:27
Infinite p.	BROW 105:30
Into a towering p.	SHAK 437:13
is so obstinate a p.	HUME 267:14
lingring and consumptive p.	ETH 208:29
maiden p. for a maid	TENN 534:12
Methought it did relieve my p.	SHAK 488:26
One p. doth expel another	CHAP 140:11
p. and party blind	COL 157:20
p. and the life	COL 156:16
p. could bring character	YEATS 587:1
p. for hunting something	DICK 180:35
p. for our temperate kings	TENN 541:11
p. in the mind of man so	BACON 26:2
P., I see, is catching	SHAK 450:13
P. speechless lies	DRAY 193:21
p. that left the ground	BROW 98:20
p. woman loves her lover	BYRON 122:25
periwig-pated fellow tear a p.	SHAK 433:16
Queen was in a furious p.	CARR 134:5
ruling p.	DICK 176:11

ruling p. in man is not	FROST 219:14
ruling p. conquers reason	POPE 377:32
Search then the Ruling P.	POPE 377:13
sentimental p. of a vegetable	GILB 227:23
Some bloody p. shakes your	SHAK 477:6
That is not p.'s slave	SHAK 434:2
To be in a p. you good	BLAKE 85:17
To inspire hopeless p.	THAC 545:13
vulgar expression of the p.	CONG 159:22
well-painted p.	SHAK 476:14
what is p. but pining	MER 338:7
What p. cannot Music raise	DRYD 197:22
when his p. shall have	TENN 538:19
Whom p. could not shake	SHAK 476:16
passionate: Ah beautiful p. body	SWIN 529:7
Are full of p. intensity	YEATS 586:15
discriminate every moment some p.	PATER 369:22
passion-flower: From the p. at the gate	TENN 540:12
passionless: hopeless grief is p.	BROW 98:7
man P.—no	SHEL 503:11
passions: also are men of like p.	BIBLE 74:5
après les instants de p.	VOLT 561:16
Desolate p.	JOHN 273:21
devil to have all the p.	SHAW 497:21
diminue les médiocres p.	LA R 310:15
governs the p. and resolutions	HUME 267:22
his p. which have got	STER 519:25
moderator of p.	WALT 564:3
Oft' shifts her p.	GAY 223:8
other p. fleet to air	SHAK 467:12
p. match'd with mine	TENN 539:5
p. of his fellow-citizens	HOR 260:18
Two master-p. cannot co-exist	CAMP 129:11
we various ruling p. find	POPE 377:24
when he acts from the p.	DISR 186:2
With life all other p. fly	SOUT 513:26
passive: benevolence of the p. order	MER 338:4
p., recording, not thinking	ISH 270:28
passover: Christ our p. is sacrificed	BIBLE 75:36
it is the Lord's p.	BIBLE 47:18
p.; his p. shall be made	SHAK 445:3
passport: his p. shall be made	SHAK 445:3
past: alter the p., historians can	BUTL 118:21
are p. our dancing days	SHAK 482:1
bitterness of death is p.	BIBLE 50:5
cannot remember the p.	SANT 414:1
future contained in time p.	ELIOT 202:12
give me back my p. years	VIRG 559:6
God cannot change the p.	AGAT 3:4
is the funeral of the p.	CLARE 152:15
itself upon the p. has pow'r	DRYD 198:16
like a child for the p.	LAWR 311:7
Many a woman has a p.	WILDE 573:9
more than things long p.	SHAK 478:18
moulded of things p.	SHAK 487:6
nothing but the p.	KEYN 295:15
p., and future sees	BLAKE 87:13
p. as a watch in the night	PRAY 395:18
P. bury its dead	LONG 317:3
p. is a foreign country	HART 242:34
p. is the only dead thing	THOM 547:17
P. reason hated	SHAK 495:7
P. redress are now with	SHAK 479:3
P. ruin'd Ilion Helen lives	LAND 308:22
plan the future by the p.	BURKE 111:31
rather absurd about the p.	BEER 37:12
remembrance of things p.	SHAK 493:7
remomoring of a cursed p.	VANZ 555:8
scraps are good deeds p.	SHAK 487:3
shall be p. making love	PRIOR 401:7
soul of the whole P. Time	CARL 131:34
they that will times p.	HERR 249:17
thought of our p. years	WORD 579:9
Time p. and time future	ELIOT 202:16
time p. unto the fathers	BIBLE 79:28
to lament the p.	BURKE 108:17
to remember what is p.	HAL 238:3

what is p. my help — FLET 215:12
What's p. — SHAK 487:14
What's p. is prologue — SHAK 485:5
world is weary of the p. — SHEL 501:3
years that are p. — PRAY 395:2
pastime: made to take his p. therein — PRAY 397:1
'twas p. to be bound — WORD 582:8
pastor: iguala al p. con el rey — CERV 138:20
Pastoral: Cold P. — KEATS 291:10
p. music on a thin stalk — VIRG 559:11
pastors: some ungracious p. do — SHAK 430:18
spiritual p. and masters — PRAY 388:16
pasture: are the people of his p. — PRAY 396:4
feed me in a green p. — PRAY 390:21
mettle of your p. — SHAK 444:2
sheep of his p. — PRAY 396:11
pasture-ground: in the ooze of their p. — ARN 13:6
pastures: fresh woods, and p. — MILT 343:20
On England's pleasant p. — BLAKE 86:16
Over the green p. there — AUDEN 18:8
pat: Now might I do it p. — SHAK 434:29
P. he comes — SHAK 453:12
Patch: P. grief with proverbs — SHAK 473:6
p., matchwood — HOPK 257:1
p. up thine old body — SHAK 441:27
patches: king of shreds and p. — SHAK 435:12
thing of shreds and p. — GILB 226:18
pate: made by an aged old p. — ANON 4:19
p. of a politician — SHAK 436:27
patent: p. for his honours immediately — BURNS 113:15
so my p. back again is — SHAK 494:13
Pater: P. noster — MASS 335:5
paterna: buona imagine p. — DANTE 171:12
P. rura bubus — HOR 259:7
paternal: dear and kindly p. image — DANTE 171:12
Die of the absolute p. care — ELIOT 202:22
disclaim all my p. care — SHAK 453:3
path: beaten p. to his door — EMER 208:15
ears this p. that wandereth — CHES 147:12
follows the hidden p. down — LUIS 320:12
is the P. of Wickedness — BALL 32:5
Our p. emerges for a while — DOWS 191:13
p. before me leading wherever — WHIT 571:7
p. of the just is — BIBLE 53:19
straight p. along the dusky air — COL 157:11
This downhill p. is easy — ROSS 408:22
was a p. of gold for him — BROW 103:9
Pathetic: characterize as the 'P. Fallacy' — RUSK 411:11
Is not p. — WHIT 571:11
It was too p. for the feelings — AUST 22:24
pathless: heav'n's wide p. way — MILT 342:3
pleasure in the p. woods — BYRON 121:22
pathos: true p. and sublime — BURNS 115:15
paths: all her p. are peace — BIBLE 53:17
bitter p. wherein I stray — KIPL 301:16
leave the trodden p. of men — SHEL 499:15
light unto my p. — PRAY 398:6
make his p. straight — BIBLE 63:36
opposed to p. to persevere — PATM 370:6
p. of glory lead — GRAY 234:21
So many p. that wind — WILC 572:6
pathway: p. to the ends of all — KIPL 303:5
patience: all p. — SHAK 426:29
are they that have not p. — SHAK 475:11
be the pattern of all p. — SHAK 454:7
close-lipp'd P. for our only friend — ARN 14:18
drop of p. — SHAK 476:18
grande aptitude à la p. — BUFF 106:21
greater aptitude for p. — BUFF 106:21
habits of peace and p. — WALT 564:3
have heard of the p. of Job — BIBLE 80:17
I laugh'd him into p. — SHAK 422:10
languid p. of thy face — COL 157:16
long will you abuse our p. — CIC 151:25
My p. is now at an end — HITL 251:11

old abusing of God's p. — SHAK 469:5
p., and shuffle the cards — CERV 138:18
p. have her perfect work — BIBLE 80:7
p. of hope in our Lord — BIBLE 78:30
p. possess ye your souls — BIBLE 71:5
P., the beggar's virtue — MASS 335:20
P., thou young and rose-lipp'd — SHAK 476:18
p. under their sufferings — PRAY 386:1
p. will achieve more than — BURKE 111:24
preach'd up p. — PRIOR 401:2
preacheth p. — HERB 247:12
sat like p. on a monument — SHAK 489:7
talk him out of p. — SHAK 475:13
Though with p. He stands — LOGAU 316:5
patient: Beware the fury of a p. — DRYD 194:20
disease and kill the p. — BACON 26:17
not so p. — SHAK 441:8
P. continuance in well — BIBLE 74:33
p. etherized upon a table — ELIOT 203:17
p. Must minister to himself — SHAK 463:3
p., not a brawler — BIBLE 79:12
sit thou a p. looker-on — QUAR 403:15
Thou must be p. — SHAK 455:22
patiently: I waited p. for the Lord — PRAY 392:1
ye shall take it p. — BIBLE 80:26
ye take it p. — BIBLE 80:26
patients: likes to hurry his p. along — MOL 353:21
patines: inlaid with p. of bright gold — SHAK 468:15
patrem: Deum p. qui ecclesiam — CYPR 170:19
patria: decorum est pro p. mori — HOR 260:17
Sed miles, sed pro p. — NEWB 361:5
patriarchal: wi' p. grace — BURNS 113:9
patrician: regular p. — GILB 228:11
This is the P. — DONNE 190:23
patrie: plus j'aimai ma p. — BELL 40:17
patriot: Never was p. yet — DRYD 194:19
soldier and the sunshine p. — PAINE 368:1
steady p. of the world — CANN 129:28
Such is the p.'s boast — GOLD 231:25
patriotic: fights you on p. principles — SHAW 498:6
patriotism: larger p. — ROS 408:14
P. is the last refuge — JOHN 276:25
p. which consists in hating — GASK 222:4
realize that p. is not enough — CAV 137:15
patriots: blood of p. and tyrants — JEFF 272:10
so to be p. — BURKE 108:24
True be p. we — BARR 34:23
Patron: Is not a P. — JOHN 274:7
p., and the jail — JOHN 282:29
p. of some thirty charities — TENN 542:20
patronage: public and even private p. — ALB 3:7
Patroness: My celestial P. — MILT 349:9
patronum: tu optimus omnium's p. — CAT 137:3
patter: unintelligible p. — GILB 228:17
pattern: be the p. of all patience — SHAK 454:7
cunning'st p. of excelling nature — SHAK 477:5
In a p. called a war — LOW 318:25
Made him our p. to live — BROW 102:5
which he shewed as a p. — SWIFT 525:34
patterns: Alive like p. a murmuration — AUDEN 20:6
What are p. — LOW 318:25
paucity: p. of human pleasures should — JOHN 280:15
Paul: crush Under P.'s dome — HODG 252:10
holy Apostles Peter and P. — MASS 334:15
once echoed The voice of P. — HARDY 240:4
to pay for collective P. — KIPL 299:16
with the charity of P. — CHUR 148:22
Pauliad: less a Christiad than a P. — HARDY 241:24
pauper: He's only a p. — NOEL 363:19
pauperiem: Duramque callet p. pati — HOR 261:19
Indocilis p. pati — HOR 259:9
paupertas: Nil habet infelix p. — JUV 287:17

pause: Comes a p. in the day's — LONG 316:9
forebear to p. and inquire — WEST 569:1
How dull it is to p. — TENN 543:22
I p. for a reply — SHAK 450:16
p. awhile from letters — JOHN 282:29
pauses: intervals and happy p. — BACON 27:44
pauvre: p. paysan en mon royaume — HENR 245:13
pauvres: p. sont les nègres de — CHAM 139:17
paved: Are each p. with the moon — SHEL 500:6
streets are p. with gold — COLM 158:25
pavement: p. of pearl — ARN 13:7
street and p. mute — HARDY 240:21
pavements: on the p. gray — YEATS 585:17
p. fang'd with murderous — COL 156:5
pavender: That decks the rural p. — ST L 412:27
pavilion: hast the red p. of my heart — THOM 547:23
paving: horses' heels Over the p. — ELIOT 202:6
pavin'-stones: leather on these gritty p. — KIPL 301:7
paweth: He p. in the valley — BIBLE 53:6
Pawnce: pretty P. — SPEN 517:3
paws: massive p. of elder persons — BELL 38:24
my dear p. — CARR 133:20
pax: et in terra p. hominibus — MASS 334:18
P. Domini sit semper vobiscum — MASS 335:6
P. Vobis — BIBLE 83:20
Pax vobiscum: 'P.' will answer all queries — SCOTT 418:22
pay: called upon to p. the bill — HARD 238:21
devil to p. — MOORE 357:5
even then she had to p. — BELL 39:9
going to p. every penny — GEDD 223:32
I p. thy poverty — SHAK 483:26
make me able to p. for it — PEPYS 371:20
now I must p. for my fun — KIPL 300:17
p. a debt to pleasure — ROCH 406:17
P. every debt — EMER 207:1
p. glad life's arrears — BROW 104:1
P., pack, and follow — BURT 116:11
p.—pay—pay — KIPL 297:25
p. us, pass us — CHES 147:15
Peter to p. for collective Paul — KIPL 299:16
sharper spur than p. — GAY 223:12
sum of things for p. — HOUS 265:7
therefore p. you cash to go away — KIPL 298:18
unbound by any interest to p. — HOR 259:7
wonders what's to p. — HOUS 265:2
ye must p. for one by one — KIPL 303:20
paying: called p. the Dane-geld — KIPL 298:18
payment: p. of half twenty shillings — BURKE 109:2
paynims: That is to wit three p. — CAXT 138:3
Payris: Ez fur away ez P. is — LOW 319:3
pays: I scent wich p. the best — LOW 319:5
p. us but with age — RAL 404:15
p. your money and you takes — ANON 9:2
paz: vivo en p. con los hombres — MACH 325:7
pea: dined on one p. and one bean — LEAR 313:2
nothing left but one split p. — THAC 545:32
peace: all her paths are p. — BIBLE 53:17
alone burns lamps of p. — DE L 174:17
bad p. — FRAN 218:17
bring a man p. at the last — PRAY 391:29
calls it—p. — BYRON 120:4
calm P., and Quiet — MILT 341:27
calm world and a long p. — SHAK 440:10
certain knot of p. — SIDN 507:20
chastisement of our p. — BIBLE 59:22
cherish a just and lasting p. — LINC 315:3
cowardice keeps us in p. — JOHN 278:3
even lovers find their p. — FLEC 214:10
Everlasting p. is a dream — MOLT 354:4
ever was the church for p. — BROW 99:12
faithful people pardon and p. — PRAY 386:22
feet into the way of p. — BIBLE 69:7
first in p. — LEE 313:7
give p. at home — PRAY 400:5

Give p. in our time	PRAY 385:1
give thee p.	BIBLE 48:9
God gave her p.	TENN 543:15
habits of p. and patience	WALT 564:3
had thy p. been as a river	BIBLE 59:15
Had Zimri p.	BIBLE 51:35
hast thou to do with p.	BIBLE 51:32
haunt of ancient P.	TENN 541:22
hereafter for ever hold his p.	PRAY 389:2
his goods are in p.	BIBLE 69:36
I am for 'P.	BRIG 93:2
I came not to send p.	BIBLE 65:38
if only p. of mind doesn't	HOR 258:19
If p. cannot be maintained	RUSS 412:19
I labour for p.	PRAY 398:8
Imperishable p.	HOUS 266:5
I must go where lazy P.	DAV 172:7
ingeminate the word P.	CLAR 152:20
In His will is our p.	DANTE 171:16
in p., goodwill	CHUR 150:25
In p., Love tunes	SCOTT 416:17
interest that keeps p.	CROM 170:1
in the multitude of p.	PRAY 391:27
Let him who desires p.	VEG 556:3
Let us have p.	GRANT 234:2
Let war yield to p.	CIC 151:22
luxury, p.	BAUD 35:7
makes a good p.	HERB 246:21
Making p. is harder than	STEV 520:21
merry songs of p.	SHAK 448:1
mind at p. with all below	BYRON 125:22
moth of p.	SHAK 474:6
mountains also shall bring p.	PRAY 394:19
mountain tops is p.	GOET 230:14
my everlasting p.	HOOD 254:22
My p. is gone	GOET 230:4
my reign is p.	LAND 308:21
Nation shall speak p. unto	REND 405:11
news and Prince of P.	FLET 215:29
nor earth have been at p.	SHAK 449:17
not p. at any price	JERR 273:11
old as we to keep the p.	SHAK 481:25
on earth p.	BIBLE 69:11
p. above all earthly dignities	SHAK 447:12
p. a Christian can die	ADD 2:29
p. among our peoples let	KIPL 303:6
p., and ensue it	PRAY 391:23
p. and propagation are	WALP 563:13
p., and take my rest	PRAY 389:22
p. at the last	NEWM 362:9
P. be to this house	BIBLE 69:26
P. be to this house	PRAY 389:8
P. be unto you	BIBLE 83:20
P.; come away	TENN 536:31
P., comes dropping slow	YEATS 585:11
P., commerce	JEFF 272:2
p. does nothing to relieve	COWP 165:7
p. for our time	CHAM 139:10
p., from him which is	BIBLE 81:9
peaceful sloth, Not p.	MILT 346:12
p. has been broken anywhere	ROOS 407:23
P. hath her victories	MILT 351:17
P. I hope with honour	DISR 185:15
P. I leave with you	BIBLE 72:35
P.! impudent and shameless	SHAK 446:20
p. in Shelley's mind	SHEL 505:1
P. is a very apoplexy	SHAK 427:27
P. is indivisible	LITV 315:10
P. is in the grave	SHEL 503:3
P. is poor reading	HARDY 239:15
P. its ten thousands	PORT 381:32
p. of God	BIBLE 78:21
p. of Jerusalem	PRAY 398:12
p. of the double bed after	CAMP 128:3
P., perfect peace	BICK 84:4
P. shall go sleep with	SHAK 479:20
P., the human dress	BLAKE 88:7
p. there's nothing so becomes	SHAK 443:21
P. to corrupt no less than	MILT 349:27
P. to him that is far off	BIBLE 60:3

p. to you which were afar	BIBLE 77:22
P. upon earth!' was said	HARDY 239:3
p. within nor calm around	SHEL 504:10
p. with men and at war	MACH 325:7
people the blessing of p.	PRAY 391:12
poor, and mangled P.	SHAK 445:11
potent advocates of p.	GEOR 224:4
practising upon his p. and quiet	SHAK 474:22
preparation of the gospel of p.	BIBLE 78:10
Prince of P.	BIBLE 58:7
righteousness and p. have kissed	PRAY 395:15
right hand carry gentle p.	SHAK 447:12
servant depart in p.	BIBLE 69:12
shall this p. sleep with her	SHAK 448:3
slept in p.	SHAK 447:16
So enamoured on p. that	CLAR 152:21
Sweet P. is crown'd with	VAUG 555:13
that publisheth p.	BIBLE 59:18
that the defences of p.	ANON 7:16
There is no p.	BIBLE 59:16
There is p. from twelve	COW 163:20
There should be p. at home	WATTS 565:19
these voices there is p.	TENN 534:16
they are in p.	BIBLE 62:13
they should kneel for p.	SHAK 484:19
thou return at all in p.	BIBLE 51:20
thousand years of p.	TENN 537:15
thy servants that p.	PRAY 385:9
time of p.	BIBLE 55:12
to gain our p.	SHAK 461:12
To rust in p.	SOUT 513:13
universal P.	TENN 533:23
verses are like the p. of God	JAM 271:6
ways upon a state of p.	VIRG 559:1
weak piping time of p.	SHAK 480:18
What is p.? Is it war?	DICK 176:12
when there is no p.	BIBLE 60:19
which belong unto thy p.	BIBLE 71:3
who art the author of p.	PRAY 385:2
wilderness and call it p.	TAC 531:7
with the soft phrase of p.	SHAK 473:24
work us a perpetual p.	MILT 344:3
Would I were sleep and p.	SHAK 482:20
you that kiss our lady P.	SHAK 441:13
peaceably: 'p. if we can	CLAY 152:29
p. ordered by thy governance	PRAY 386:17
peaceful: made this p. life for us	VIRG 559:12
peacemakers: Blessed are the p.	BIBLE 64:6
peach: Do I dare to eat a p.	ELIOT 203:25
nectarine and curious p.	MARV 332:3
Peacock: Ere Mor the P. flutters	KIPL 303:7
Eyed like a p.	KEATS 290:22
milk-white p. like a ghost	TENN 542:14
p. is the glory of God	BLAKE 88:21
peacocks: apes, and p.	BIBLE 50:34
apes and p.	MAS 333:18
p. and lilies for instance	RUSK 411:23
terraces and p. strutting	KIPL 299:12
pea-green: In a beautiful p. boat	LEAR 312:11
peak: small things from the p.	CHES 147:30
peal: rung night's yawning p.	SHAK 461:13
pear: are on a Catherine p.	SUCK 524:9
go round the prickly p.	ELIOT 203:22
pearl: found one p. of great price	BIBLE 66:21
hang a p. in every cowslip's	SHAK 470:2
ocean for orient p.	MARL 329:4
Of orient p. a double row	CAMP 129:23
pavement of p.	ARN 13:7
threw a p. away	SHAK 477:23
your p. in your foul oyster	SHAK 427:4
pearls: are p. that were his eyes	SHAK 484:32
Give p. away and rubies	HOUS 262:20
p. of thought in Persian	LOW 319:10
search for p. must dive	DRYD 195:10
Some ask'd how p. did grow	HERR 249:18
ye your p. before swine	BIBLE 65:1
pears: our French withered p.	SHAK 420:27
Pearse: P. summoned Cuchulain	YEATS 587:2
peartree: glassy p. leaves and blooms	HOPK 256:24

peas: first green p.	LONG 316:23
peasant: that the toe of the p.	SHAK 436:29
what a rogue and p. slave	SHAK 432:27
peasantry: bold p.	GOLD 230:18
Sing the p.	YEATS 587:8
peasants: hands of p. their vile trash	SHAK 451:21
peascod: squash is before 'tis a p.	SHAK 488:9
pebble: only p. on the beach	BRAI 91:17
pebbles: boys that throw p. and mire	WATTS 565:26
unnumber'd idle p. chafes	SHAK 455:14
peccata: tollis p. mundi	MASS 335:7
peccator: Esto p. et pecca fortiter	LUTH 320:15
Peccavi: P.—I have Sindh	WINK 575:8
P.—I've Scinde	PUNCH 402:16
quia p. nimis cogitatione	MASS 334:15
pécher: p. que pécher en silence	MOL 354:1
peck: p. cautiously at the ball	WOD 575:24
peculiar: in him was the p. grace	BROW 100:36
London was extensive and p.	DICK 181:35
p. people	BIBLE 80:23
Pecunia: P. non olet	VESP 556:11
pecuniam: p. infinitam	CIC 151:30
pecuniary: turning an immense p. Mangle	DICK 183:6
Pedant: precious apothegmaticall P.	NASHE 360:6
pedantic: little too p. for a gentleman	CONG 160:12
pedantical: Figures p.	SHAK 457:15
pedants: Which learned p. much affect	BUTL 117:17
pede: nunc p. libero	HOR 260:3
pedestalled: so be p. in triumph	BROW 104:30
pedigree: languages are the p. of nations	JOHN 280:1
Peel: talk and P. has no manners	WELL 567:31
peep: into glory p.	VAUG 555:21
that would p. and botanize	WORD 580:3
Wizards that p. and that	BIBLE 58:5
peepshow: ticket for the p.	MACN 326:7
Peer: About this unimportant P.	BELL 39:30
hath not left his p.	MILT 343:2
many a p. of England brews	HOUS 264:12
rhyming p.	POPE 376:19
peerage: p., or Westminster Abbey	NELS 360:14
You should study the P.	WILDE 573:32
Peers: My Lord in the P. will	BROU 95:3
praise in p. to write at all	BYRON 124:27
peewees: graves of the martyrs the p.	STEV 523:5
Pegasus: thought it P.	KEATS 292:8
turn and wind a fiery P.	SHAK 440:7
peignoir: Complacencies of the p.	STEV 520:18
peine: donné la p. de naître	BEAU 35:18
la p. d'être dit	BEAU 35:14
pelago: Commisit p. ratem	HOR 259:12
pelf: about what they call p.	CLOU 153:21
I crave no p.	SHAK 486:3
pelican: like a p. in the wilderness	PRAY 396:12
Pluffskin, P. jee	LEAR 312:15
wonderful bird is the p.	MERR 338:8
wouldst thou have me turn p.	CONG 160:6
Pelion: P. imposuisse Olympo	HOR 260:22
pile Ossa on P.	VIRG 560:12
pellucid: more p. streams	WORD 578:3
Pelting: P. each other for the public	COWP 164:28
pen: Biting my truant p.	SIDN 507:17
could use the sword and p.	LAND 308:23
foolish when he had not a p.	JOHN 278:19
forbear To bite his p.	SWIFT 527:23
garden with your p.	CAMP 128:11
he take a p. in his hand	JOHN 274:1

His fingers held the p.   COWP 165:31
less brilliant p.   BEER 37:13
nose was as sharp as a p.   SHAK 443:17
p. has glean'd my teeming   KEATS 292:30
p. is mightier than   BULW 107:4
p. is worse than the sword   BURT 116:22
p.: of a ready writer   PRAY 392:14
prevents his holding a p.   DICK 180:8
product of a scoffer's p.   WORD 577:12
scratching of a p.   LOVER 318:21
take the p. out of his hand   ARN 16:8
thee glorious by my p.   GRAH 233:15
Waverley p.   ANON 8:5
With such acts fill a p.   DRAY 193:11
penalty: p. of Adam   SHAK 424:31
penance: night do p. for a day   WORD 580:18
pence: He took out two p.   BIBLE 69:32
Take care of the p.   LOWN 319:21
that eternal want of p.   TENN 544:10
Yet loss of p.   COWP 165:18
pencil: p. of the Holy Ghost hath   BACON 25:19
with the silver-pointed p.   BROW 102:28
pendre: par faire p. un homme   MOL 353:22
Pends-toi: P., brave Crillon   HENR 245:14
pendule: comme de faire une p.   LA B 306:12
pendulum: ominous vibration of a p.   JUN 287:3
pendulums: discontented p. as we are   EMER 207:45
Penelope: His true P. was Flaubert   POUND 383:3
Penetralium: caught from the P. of mystery   KEATS 293:19
penetrating: p. power   ARN 16:8
penguin: *p. call*   ELIOT 204:13
peninsulas: eye of p. and islands   CAT 136:28
penitence: distinguish p. from love   POPE 376:12
penitent: p., and obedient heart   PRAY 384:9
penitus: p. toto divisos orbe Britannos   VIRG 559:13
penknife: they saw me take out my p.   SWIFT 526:2
penned: is excellently well p.   SHAK 488:10
penny: give me one p.   BALL 30:9
one p. plain and twopence   STEV 521:19
one p. the worse   BARH 33:14
To turn a p. in the way   COWP 166:26
pennyworths: ruined by buying good p.   FRAN 218:12
pens: p. dwell on guilt and misery   AUST 22:29
p. that ever poets held   MARL 330:11
Who p. a stanza   POPE 376:19
pensamientos: cubre todos los humanos p.   CERV 138:20
pensant: mais c'est un roseau p.   PASC 369:11
pensées: pour déguiser leurs p.   VOLT 561:4
pensieri: p. stretti ed il viso sciolto   ALB 3:8
pension: hang your hat on a p.   MACN 326:8
p. jingle in his pockets   COWP 168:1
p. list of the republic   CLEV 153:2
take his p. from his parish   RUSK 412:7
Think of 'is p. an'   KIPL 302:20
Pensions: talk of P. and Grenadiers   STER 520:1
pensive: cowslips wan that hang the p.   MILT 343:15
In vacant or in p. mood   WORD 578:1
sighs for ever on her p. bed   POPE 381:9
pentameter: p. aye falling in melody   COL 157:7
pent-house: Hang upon his p. lid   SHAK 458:7
Pentire: P. in a flood of sunset   BETJ 42:17
Pentridge: P. by the river   BARN 33:29
peonies: wealth of globèd p.   KEATS 291:15
people: All the p. like us are We   KIPL 304:2
all the p.   PARK 368:26
am the Martyr of the P.   CHAR 140:19
are the p. of his pasture   PRAY 396:4

August for the p. and their belongs to the p.   AUDEN 18:12
belongs to the p.   LINC 314:19
benefit of a p. whom he   BURKE 110:26
bludgeoning of the p.   WILDE 573:24
bourgeois are other p.   REN 405:10
don't think I understand p.   FORS 217:6
doubt but ye are the p.   BIBLE 52:23
give strength unto his p.   PRAY 391:12
good of the p. is the chief   CIC 151:19
Good p. all   GOLD 231:9
honour is the *p.'s* choice   SHER 506:7
If by the p. you understand   DRYD 198:4
indictment against an whole p.   BURKE 109:25
In the P. was my trust   WORD 580:22
into a room full of p.   WEBB 566:6
is what the p. think so   BURKE 110:11
It is the love of the p.   BURKE 110:5
I would be of the p.   LA B 306:14
Let my p. go   ANON 8:18
Let the p. praise thee   PRAY 394:4
madness of the p.   PRAY 394:1
man should die for the p.   BIBLE 72:24
mean ye that ye beat my p.   BIBLE 57:20
my p. love to have it so   BIBLE 60:18
not suppose the p. good   ROB 406:12
of p. whose loss will be   GILB 226:23
one of the smallest p.   BAG 29:10
only two sorts of p.   SHAW 497:5
opponent of the chosen p.   ARN 16:3
p., all springs   DISR 186:43
p. are never in the wrong   BURKE 108:18
p. are the masters   BURKE 110:18
P. come miles to see it   GILB 227:10
P. crushed by law have   BURKE 110:8
p. govern themselves   THIE 546:5
p. imagine a vain   PRAY 389:15
p. is the true legislator   BURKE 112:12
p. overlaid with taxes   BACON 27:26
p.'s government   WEBS 566:10
p. that do err in their   PRAY 396:4
p. which call upon thee   PRAY 386:7
P. you know   LARK 310:5
Privileged and the P. formed   DISR 186:32
pushed by this recent p.   BURKE 109:17
Roman p. had but one neck   CAL 127:6
sake look after our p.   SCOTT 415:18
saying the voice of the p.   ALC 3:9
surely the p. is grass   BIBLE 59:6
That has such p. in't   SHAK 485:26
that was full of p.   BIBLE 60:27
the noise…and the p.   ANON 7:6
thy people shall be my p.   BIBLE 49:32
'Tis the p. marching   MORR 358:7
trouble with p. is not   BILL 84:7
two p. with the one pulse   MACN 326:11
understanded of the p.   PRAY 400:8
very few p. come this way   LEAR 312:22
voice of the p. hath some   BACON 25:11
we are the p. of England   CHES 147:15
What kind of p. do they   CHUR 150:9
When wilt thou save the p.   ELL 206:12
whole world is bereft of p.   LAM 306:24
peopled: to have conquered and p.   SEEL 419:16
world must be p.   SHAK 472:19
peoples: peace among our p. let   KIPL 303:6
sullen p.   KIPL 304:7
peple: 'O stormy p.   CHAU 142:8
person and the p. his apes   CHAU 142:7
Pepper: P. and vinegar besides   CARR 135:8
peppered: I have p. two of them   SHAK 439:2
PER: P. ME SI VA NELLA CITTÀ   DANTE 171:3
Peradventure: P. the darkness shall cover   PRAY 399:5
peragravit: Atque omne immensum p.   LUCR 320:3
perceive: p. and know what things   PRAY 386:7
unapt to p. how the world   ARN 15:17

perception: doors of p. were cleansed   BLAKE 88:28
perch: p. and not their terror   SHAK 463:15
perchance: p. to dream   SHAK 433:8
perched: owls came and p. on battlements   BEER 38:2
Percy: old song of P. and Douglas   SIDN 508:3
perdere: Quem Jupiter vult p.   DUP 199:15
perdidi: diem p.   TITUS 551:6
perdition: lost but the son of p.   BIBLE 72:42
To bottomless p.   MILT 344:24
perditum: quod vides perisse p. ducas   CAT 136:27
perdrix: Toujours p.   ANON 9:19
perdus: les paradis qu'on a p.   PROU 402:1
PERDUTA: ME SI VA TRA LA P. GENTE…   DANTE 171:3
Père: Notre P. qui êtes aux cieux   PREV 400:15
P., et le Fils, et le Pigeon   ANON 9:7
Pereant: P., inquit   DON 187:17
pereat: justitia et p. mundus   FERD 210:33
peremptory: p. and absolute the third   ELIOT 201:30
perenne: Plus uno maneat p. saeclo   CAT 136:21
perennial: Falsehood has a p. spring   BURKE 109:4
perennius: monumentum aere p.   HOR 261:8
PERES: P.; Thy kingdom is divided   BIBLE 61:6
pereunt: Qui nobis p. et imputantur   MART 331:11
pereza: la buena ventura y la p.   CERV 138:19
perfect: Be ye therefore p.   BIBLE 64:21
He is very p. indeed   SHER 505:29
he were p.   SHAK 491:6
If thou wilt be p.   BIBLE 67:9
just men made p.   BIBLE 80:2
made p. in a short time   BIBLE 62:15
more unto the p. day   BIBLE 53:19
never will himself be p.   AUDEN 19:13
None of us are p.   WILDE 573:6
One p. limousine   PARK 368:17
Our Sidney and our p. man   YEATS 585:13
patience have her p. work   BIBLE 80:7
p. democracy is therefore   BURKE 111:19
P. God   PRAY 385:14
p. in this world   DONNE 191:2
p. nature and are perfected   BACON 27:17
p. presence of mind   JAMES 271:29
p. round   BROW 98:18
P. the cup as planned   BROW 104:13
pismire is equally p.   WHIT 570:21
read the p. ways of honour   SHAK 448:2
service is p. freedom   PRAY 385:2
severity of p. light   TENN 534:14
strength is made p. in weakness   BIBLE 77:14
That p. bliss and sole   MARL 330:8
that which is p. is come   BIBLE 76:14
unto a p. man   BIBLE 77:22
perfected: nature and are p. by experience   BACON 27:17
perfectibility: who speak of p. as a dream   MILL 339:17
perfecting: p. of the saints   BIBLE 77:28
perfection: Dead p.   TENN 539:17
P. is the child of Time   HALL 238:7
P., of a kind   AUDEN 18:15
P. of the life   YEATS 584:14
pursuit of p.   ARN 15:15
right p. wrongfully disgrac'd   SHAK 494:5
right praise and true p.   SHAK 468:19
she did make defect p.   SHAK 422:4
take her own way to p.   BURKE 109:18
top of p. not to know them   CONG 159:32
very pink of p.   GOLD 232:22
What's come to p. perishes   BROW 102:26
perfections: fair eyes where all p. keep   ANON 6:7
Rather than the p. of a fool   BLAKE 87:9

with his sweet p. caught ROYD 411:3
perfectly: She's p. well and she hasn't
MILNE 340:10
that we may p. love thee PRAY 387:7
perfide: La p. Albion XIM 584:6
la p. Angleterre BOSS 90:14
perfidious: fatal and p. bark MILT 343:10
her own waters p. Albion XIM 584:6
perform: Almighty's orders to p. ADD 1:14
they are not able to p. PRAY 390:15
performance: All words, And no p.
MASS 335:24
her p. keeps no day CAMP 129:21
his p., as he is now SHAK 447:19
it takes away the p. SHAK 460:18
p. so loathed SHAK 487:19
so many years outlive p. SHAK 441:28
that any artistic p. requires JAMES 271:29
performed: vow be p. in Jerusalem
PRAY 393:23
perfume: feel my breasts all p. JOYCE 286:30
invisible p. hits the sense SHAK 422:3
p. and most melodious twang AUBR 18:2
throw a p. on the violet SHAK 452:25
perfumes: No p. BRUM 106:5
p. of Arabia will not sweeten SHAK 462:22
P. the chamber thus SHAK 428:8
Perfusus: P. liquidis urget odoribus
HOR 259:6
Perhaps: grand P. BROW 99:4
seek a great p. RAB 404:1
Peri: P. at the gate Of Eden MOORE 356:27
perii: ut p. VIRG 560:4
peril: there is no p. in the fight CORN 162:16
those in p. on the sea WHIT 569:26
vaincre sans p. CORN 162:16
perilous: dim and p. way WORD 577:13
p. mode of hard industry BURKE 109:17
then they knew the p. rock SOUT 514:1
perils: in p. of waters BIBLE 77:12
p. and dangers of this PRAY 385:10
p. Of cheat and charmer HOUS 265:14
what p. do environ BUTL 117:29
What p. past SHAK 442:2
period: belong to the Beardsley p. BEER 37:11
fix the p. in the history GIBB 224:24
inglorious p. of our dominion BURKE 110:24
p., pow'r, and enterprize SMART 509:1
Peripatetic: magnetic, P. Lover GILB 227:24
periphrastic: p. study in a worn-out
ELIOT 202:19
perish: all his thoughts will p. BALF 30:17
believeth in him should not p. BIBLE 71:38
day p. wherein I was born BIBLE 52:11
if I p. BIBLE 52:2
I p. with hunger BIBLE 70:19
Must then a Christ p. SHAW 498:20
people p. BIBLE 54:44
p. than to continue schoolmastering
CARL 132:27
P. the thought CIBB 151:14
p. through their own imaginations
PRAY 389:25
shall p. with the sword BIBLE 68:18
They shall p. PRAY 396:13
though the world p. FERD 210:33
Thy money p. with thee BIBLE 73:30
To p. rather MILT 346:10
whole nation p. not BIBLE 72:24
ye p. from the right way PRAY 389:19
you as well as I P. HOUS 262:21
perished: else p., and he remained
BRON 93:25
Just because it p. MILL 340:1
p. in the waters BIBLE 65:20
strength and my hope is p. BIBLE 60:29
weapons of war p. BIBLE 50:17
perishes: cause that p. with them
CLOU 153:13
everthing p. ANON 9:20

What's come to perfection p. BROW 102:26
perisheth: righteous p. BIBLE 60:2
peritis: decede p. HOR 259:6
periuria: ex alto p. ridet amantum
OVID 366:11
Perivale: of harbour lights at P. BETJ 42:17
periwig-pated: p. fellow tear a passion
SHAK 433:16
perjuries: At lovers' p. SHAK 482:13
high laughs at lovers' p. OVID 366:11
Till p. are common as bad COWP 165:8
perjury: heart to this false p. SHAK 457:4
laughs at lovers' p. DRYD 197:7
Shall I lay p. upon my soul SHAK 468:4
permanence: place had an ancient p.
HARDY 241:21
permanent: Nought's p. among the human
BYRON 123:33
P. Possibility of Sensation STEV 522:7
Suffering is p. WORD 577:2
permission: p. of all-ruling Heaven
MILT 345:8
permitted: not p. unto them to speak
BIBLE 76:16
p. to make all the ballads FLET 215:6
pernicious: most p. woman SHAK 431:16
p. race of little odious SWIFT 526:5
p. soul Rot SHAK 447:13
perpetua: lux p. luceat eis MASS 334:17
Nox est p. una dormienda CAT 136:25
perpetual: have therefore a p. quarrel
BURKE 109:31
let p. light shine on them MASS 334:17
make P. day MARL 329:11
p. hyperbole is comely BACON 26:29
'Tis with us p. night JONS 285:13
perpetually: We are p. moralists JOHN 281:32
which is p. to be conquered BURKE 109:19
perplex: when nae real ills p. them
BURNS 115:27
Perplexes: P. monarchs MILT 345:24
Though the dull brain p. KEATS 291:20
perplexity: listlessness from vain p.
WORD 580:6
perplexyte: That stad is in p. WYNT 584:4
perquisites: self-respecting scorn of
irregular p. WAUGH 566:2
persecute: Why p. we him BIBLE 52:32
persecuted: because I p. the church of
God BIBLE 76:19
persecutest: why p. thou me BIBLE 73:33
Persecution: P. is a bad and indirect
BROW 96:16
P. produced its natural MAC 324:17
Religious p. may shield BURKE 110:29
some degree of p. SWIFT 527:6
Persephone: Singer of P. WILDE 572:19
Persepolis: ride in triumph through P.
MARL 330:7
persever: Ay, do, p. SHAK 470:23
Perseverance: P., dear my lord SHAK 487:4
p. in a good cause STER 519:19
persevere: opposed paths to p. PATM 370:6
Persian: I hate all that P. gear HOR 260:4
P.'s Heaven is easily MOORE 356:3
Persians: given to the Medes and P.
BIBLE 61:6
law of the Medes and P. BIBLE 61:7
Persicos: P. odi HOR 260:4
persist: fool would p. in his folly
BLAKE 88:19
persistence: dominant's p. till it must
BROW 105:24
person: adornment of his p. he THOM 549:6
express image of his p. BIBLE 79:28
I am a most superior p. ANON 7:1
p. and the peple his apes CHAU 142:7
p. in the Spanish cape ELIOT 204:15
p. on business from Porlock COL 156:25
purse, my p. SHAK 465:16

personal: No p. considerations GRANT 234:3
P. relations are the important FORS 217:1
personality: escape from p. ELIOT 205:18
personated: himself most feelingly p.
SHAK 488:23
persons: God is no respecter of p. BIBLE 74:2
massive paws of elder p. BELL 38:24
Neither confounding the P. PRAY 385:12
p. should not be joined PRAY 388:23
respect of p. with God BIBLE 74:34
perspective: light, shade, and p. CONS 162:2
perspiration: course his p. was but ichor
BYRON 126:7
ninety-nine per cent p. EDIS 199:25
perspire: dig till you gently p. KIPL 300:11
that Mr Gladstone may p. CHUR 149:20
persuade: p., threaten WHIT 571:11
persuaded: fully p. in his own mind
BIBLE 75:27
were p. of them BIBLE 79:33
persuadest: p. me to be a Christian
BIBLE 74:27
persuading: By p. others JUN 287:4
by p. me to it SHAK 486:11
persuasion: alone is not truth, but p.
MAC 324:20
firm p. that a thing is so BLAKE 88:26
Persuasions: P. and veiled Destinies
SHEL 499:9
persuasive: His gentle reason so p.
THOM 549:26
p. language of a tear CHUR 149:17
Pert: P. as a schoolgirl well GILB 226:27
Pertelote: cleped fair damoysele P.
CHAU 142:32
Pertness: half P. and half Pout BYRON 119:32
perturbation: polish'd p. SHAK 442:17
perturbations: in new p. and calamities
BACON 27:44
perturbed: Rest, rest, p. spirit SHAK 431:25
Peru: from China to P. JOHN 282:28
perus'd: th'original p. mankind ARMS 12:15
perverse: I'll frown and be p. SHAK 482:13
p. creatures in the world ADD 2:18
Perverts: P. the Prophets BYRON 124:23
Peschiera: P., when thy bridge CLOU 154:2
pessimist: p. fears this is true CAB 126:25
pessimus: Agit p. omnium poeta CAT 137:3
pest: like a p. in the street CONR 161:21
pester'd: So p. with a popinjay SHAK 438:15
pestilence: breeds p. BLAKE 88:15
from the noisome p. PRAY 395:21
p., and famine PRAY 385:16
P.-stricken multitudes SHEL 502:8
p. that walketh in darkness PRAY 395:21
Shakes p. and war MILT 346:26
she purg'd the air of p. SHAK 487:21
winter, plague and p. NASHE 360:8
pestilences: with wars or p. AUST 23:4
Pests: P. of society BOL 89:14
petal: Now sleeps the crimson p. TENN 542:14
(O filigree p. THOM 548:29
Tip-tilted like the p. TENN 534:7
petals: ever the garden's last p. SWIN 529:19
P., on a wet POUND 383:11
petar: Hoist with his own p. SHAK 435:21
Peter: disciple did outrun P. BIBLE 73:6
first 'twas P.'s drift SHEL 502:18
holy Apostles P. and Paul MASS 334:15
I'll call him P. SHAK 452:9
looked upon P. BIBLE 71:9
P. to pay for collective KIPL 299:16
Simon P. saith unto them BIBLE 73:13
Thou art P. BIBLE 66:33
to see Shock-headed P. HOFF 252:22
Where P. is AMBR 4:1
petis: Quod p. hic est HOR 258:19
petitions: desires and p. of thy servants
PRAY 385:8
petits: escadrons contre les p. BUSS 117:7

Peto: banish P.   SHAK 439:18
Petrarch: if Laura had been P.'s
  BYRON 122:27
petrarchal: would reject a p. coronation
  KEATS 293:32
petrifactions: p. of a plodding brain
  BYRON 124:25
petrifies: p. the feeling   BURNS 113:7
pets: she was not fond of p.   ELIOT 201:11
petticoat: I for one venerate a p.
  BYRON 124:5
p. I were able to live   ELIZ 205:25
petticoatie: She draiglet a' her p.
  BURNS 113:2
Petticoats: P. up to the knees   CLOU 153:15
petty: Creeps in this p. pace   SHAK 463:6
we p. men   SHAK 448:17
petulance: learn that p. is not sarcasm
  DISR 184:20
peuple: *je veux être p.*   LA B 306:14
ne suppose pas le p. bon   ROB 406:12
règne et le p. se gouverne   THIE 546:5
peur: *Chevalier sans p. et sans*   ANON 9:5
peut-être: *p. Puis il avait expiré*   RAB 404:1
pews: Talk about the p. and steeples
  CHES 146:11
pewter: You long for simple p.   GILB 225:30
peyne: beest is deed he hath no p.
  CHAU 142:17
p. I me to strecche forth   CHAU 143:5
ys joy in hevene and p.   CHAU 143:28
phagocytes: Stimulate the p.   SHAW 496:20
phalanx: move In perfect p.   MILT 345:21
Phallic: P. and ambrosial   POUND 383:6
Phantasies: twilight P.   SHEL 499:9
phantasma: p., or a hideous dream
  SHAK 449:6
phantom: She was a p. of delight
  WORD 581:7
phantoms: With p. an unprofitable
  SHEL 499:20
Pharaoh: harden P.'s heart   BIBLE 47:11
Pharisee: touching the law, a P.   BIBLE 78:16
Pharisees: P., hypocrites   BIBLE 67:24
righteousness of the scribes and P.
  BIBLE 64:11
scribes and the P. brought   BIBLE 72:9
Phayrisees: In them infarnal P.   LOW 319:3
pheasant: brake the whirring p. springs
  POPE 381:14
phenomenon: describe the infant p.
  DICK 180:16
Phidias: P. Gave women dreams   YEATS 587:1
Phil: fidgety P.   HOFF 252:15
philanthropists: one of those wise p.
who   JERR 273:2
Philip: Appeal from P. drunk   ANON 4:22
hast thou not known me, P.   BIBLE 72:33
Let me see if P. can   HOFF 252:14
P. and Mary on a shilling   BUTL 118:7
P. fought men   LEE 313:13
Philippi: I will see thee at P.   SHAK 451:30
Philistia: P., be thou glad of me   PRAY 393:18
Philistine: P. must have originally   ARN 16:3
P. of genius in religion   ARN 16:23
Philistines: daughters of the P. rejoice
  BIBLE 50:16
designation of P.   ARN 15:18
great apostle of the P.   ARN 16:4
P., and Populace   ARN 15:14
P. proper, or middle class   ARN 15:19
P. be upon thee   BIBLE 49:25
Though the P. may jostle   GILB 227:23
Philistinism: P.!—We have not the
expression   ARN 16:4
Philologists: P. who chase   COWP 166:18
Philosophen: *Wie ich den P. verstehe*
  NIET 363:5
philosopher: any p.-kings in England
  MACN 326:5

guide, p., and friend   POPE 380:4
he was a shrewd p.   BUTL 117:18
nothing so absurd but some p.   CIC 151:17
old p. is still among us   MAC 324:14
P., sir   DICK 181:24
P.!—a fingering slave   WORD 580:3
same time a profound p.   COL 157:24
To a p. no circumstance   GOLD 232:3
too in my time to be a p.   EDW 200:8
What I understand by 'p.'   NIET 363:5
will keep still with my p.   SHAK 454:26
philosophers: nation of pure p.   BAG 29:2
sayings of p.   BUTL 117:31
philosophic: years that bring the p. mind
  WORD 579:13
philosophical: p. and more worthy of
serious   ARIS 12:10
p. doubt as to animal   COL 157:34
philosophie: *la p. les éteint*   VOLT 561:6
philosophre: al be that he was a p.
  CHAU 141:24
philosophy: Adversity's sweet milk, p.
  SHAK 483:11
All good moral p. is   BACON 24:28
are dreamt of in your p.   SHAK 431:23
Axioms in p. are not axioms   KEATS 293:30
bullied into a certain p.   KEATS 293:22
fear divine P.   TENN 536:23
History is p. from examples   DION 184:9
How charming is divine p.   MILT 341:11
if p. could find it out   SHAK 432:17
little p. inclineth man's   BACON 25:24
love for p.   KEATS 293:29
mere P.   BROW 96:24
mere touch of cold p.   KEATS 290:27
natural p., deep   BACON 27:21
new p. calls all in doubt   DONNE 187:19
now-a-days professors of p.   THOR 550:7
P., in its more rigid   STEV 522:7
p. quenches them   VOLT 561:6
P., that lean'd on Heav'n   POPE 375:26
P.! the lumber   SWIFT 527:32
P. will clip an Angel's   KEATS 290:27
regions of p.   HUME 268:2
same p. is a good horse   GOLD 232:7
superstition to enslave a p.   INGE 270:6
This barbarous p.   BURKE 111:11
Unfit to hear moral p.   SHAK 486:30
Unless p. can make a Juliet   SHAK 483:12
phlegm: Spit out thy p.   HERB 247:3
Phoebus: P.' amorous pinches black
  SHAK 421:32
P. Apollo turned fasting   MER 337:29
P., arise   DRUM 193:26
P. 'gins arise   SHAK 428:10
Sweats in the eye of P.   SHAK 444:25
Phoenician: Phlebas the P.   ELIOT 205:6
phoenix: I knew a p. in my youth
  YEATS 585:10
like the p. 'midst her   BYRON 124:30
maiden p.   SHAK 448:3
P. builds her spicy nest   CAREW 130:20
p. moment   DAY-L 172:21
Phone: P. for the fish-knives   BETJ 42:19
Why Did You Answer the P.   THUR 550:30
phrase: doctor full of p. and fame   ARN 15:12
England invented the p.   BAG 28:23
fico for the p.   SHAK 469:4
phrases: Certain p. stick in the throat
  RUSS 412:22
La mort, sans p.   SIEY 508:7
p. of your complicated   GILB 227:21
Taffeta p.   SHAK 457:15
phylacteries: p. of the Liberal Party
  ROS 408:17
They make broad their p.   BIBLE 67:22
Phyllis: neat-handed P. dresses   MILT 342:21
P. is my only joy   SEDL 419:10
physic: Take p., pomp   SHAK 454:16
Throw p. to the dogs   SHAK 463:3

physician: beloved p.   BIBLE 78:29
be whole need not a p.   BIBLE 65:23
died last night of my p.   PRIOR 401:4
die when death is our p.   SHAK 474:7
divine than the p.   SHAK 462:26
Every p. almost hath his   FIEL 211:22
Honour a p. with the honour   BIBLE 63:17
if you would call a p.   BACON 26:17
into the hand of the p.   BIBLE 63:18
Pale death, the grand p.   CLARE 152:8
P. art thou   WORD 580:3
P., heal thyself   BIBLE 69:17
Time is the great p.   DISR 186:11
physicians: It is incident to p.   JOHN 273:29
P. are like kings   WEBS 566:28
P. of the utmost fame   BELL 39:1
P. of all men are most   QUAR 403:20
physics: delight in p. pain   SHAK 460:19
physique: To a beautiful p.   AUDEN 19:7
pia: *O clemens, o p.*   ANON 10:19
pianist: Please do not shoot the p.   ANON 7:9
piano: black p. appassionato   LAWR 311:7
piano-forte: p. is a fine resource   BROW 99:3
pianola: p. 'replaces' Sappho   POUND 383:5
pibble-pabble: no tiddle-taddle nor p.
  SHAK 444:18
Pibroch: P. of Donuil Dhu   SCOTT 417:27
Piccadilly: walk down P. with a poppy
  GILB 227:23
picked: shall have my pocket p.   SHAK 440:4
picker-up: p. of learning's crumbs
  BROW 100:24
picket: p.'s off duty forever   BEERS 38:8
picking: hands from p. and stealing
  PRAY 388:17
Just as I'm p. my nose   AUDEN 21:2
p. dewy apples with your   VIRG 560:14
pick-purse: am no p. of another's wit
  SIDN 507:26
At hand, quoth p.   SHAK 438:21
pickt: not p. from the leaves   BROW 96:18
Pickwick: P., the Owl   ANON 8:5
Pickwickian: used the word in its P.
  DICK 181:22
picnic: to attempt a p. in Eden   BOWEN 91:6
Pictoribus: '*P. atque poetis*   HOR 257:10
pictura: *atque animum p. pascit inani*
  VIRG 557:17
picture: Before my face the p. hangs
  SOUT 514:21
he fain would paint a p.   BROW 102:32
his p., but his book   JONS 284:17
It's no go the p. palace   MACN 326:8
like Mistress Mall's p.   SHAK 488:1
Look here, upon this p.   SHAK 435:6
p. of his father's face   FLET 215:28
p. of somebody reading   KEATS 294:16
p. plac'd the busts between   CHES 145:8
which a p. cannot express   BACON 25:27
your skill to paint my p.   CROM 169:24
pictures: all his p. faded   BLAKE 85:7
dead Are but as p.   SHAK 460:11
gold in p. of silver   BIBLE 54:26
Of cutting all the p. out   BELL 38:23
p. in our eyes to get   DONNE 188:22
they would never buy my p.   LAND 309:16
where the p. for the page   POPE 375:20
'without p. or conversations   CARR 133:14
pie: in a p. by Mrs McGregor   POTT 382:1
p. in the sky when you   HILL 251:3
Puesto ya el p. en el estribo   CERV 139:2
piece: p. of him   SHAK 429:2
surely a p. of divinity in us   BROW 97:4
Piecemeal: P. social engineering   POPP 381:25
pieces: Is broken into p.   HOOD 254:22
p. are the phenomena   HUXL 269:6
p. like a potter's vessel   PRAY 389:18
thirty p. of silver   BIBLE 68:9
'Tis all in p.   DONNE 187:19
pied: p. wind-flowers and violets   SHEL 503:18

pier: I walk'd upon the p.   BARH 33:19
p. it is my fixed intent   BARH 33:20
pierce: p. it   BIBLE 51:38
pierced: p. my hands and my feet   PRAY 390:20
they also which p. him   BIBLE 81:10
Pierian: drunk deep of the P. spring   DRAY 193:15
Pierides: *Et me fecere poetam P.*   VIRG 560:7
pietate: *reddite mi hoc pro p. mea*   CAT 137:12
pietatis: *fons p.*   CEL 138:7
pieties: p. of lovers' hands   CRANE 168:31
piety: between p. and poor rhymes   WILDE 573:38
each to each by natural p.   WORD 578:19
mistaken and over-zealous p.   BURKE 110:29
nor all thy P. nor Wit   FITZ 213:7
this in return for my p.   CAT 137:12
to p. more prone   ALEX 3:15
piffle: are as p. before the wind   ASHF 17:11
pig: are love not a gaping p.   SHAK 467:21
they brought a P.   LEAR 312:9
pigeon: I am p.-liver'd   SHAK 433:4
Père, et le Fils, et le P.   ANON 9:7
Pigeons: P. on the grass alas   STEIN 518:16
pigges: glas he hadde p. bones   CHAU 142:7
Piggy-wig: there in a wood a P. stood   LEAR 312:12
pigmy: p.'s straw doth pierce   SHAK 455:20
pignora: *dedimus tot p. fatis*   LUCAN 319:25
pigs: 'as p. have to fly   CARR 134:9
of Epicurus' herd of p.   HOR 258:16
whether p. have wings   CARR 135:7
pig-sticking: He took to p. in *quite*   COW 163:16
pig-sty: kissed her once by the p.   THOM 547:11
pike: I'll p. out his bonny blue   BALL 32:8
Pilate: P. saith unto him   BIBLE 72:44
Suffered under Pontius P.   PRAY 384:26
Pilates: gowned and spectacled P.   MACN 326:9
pile: hath made the p. complete   TENN 536:25
p. Ossa on Pelion   VIRG 560:12
to earn a monumental p.   COWP 166:30
pilfering: p., unprotected race   CLARE 152:11
pilgrim: loved the p. soul in you   YEATS 587:12
p. borne in heedless hum   COLL 158:18
p., forth   CHAU 144:22
p.'s limbs affected slumber   CAMP 129:20
To be a p.   BUNY 107:36
pilgrimage: Ere the days of his p.   LEAR 311:24
quiet p.   CAMP 129:19
shall succeed me in my p.   BUNY 107:38
thus I'll take my p.   RAL 404:12
undergo such maiden p.   SHAK 469:17
Who through this weary p.   DODD 187:15
with songs beguile your p.   FLEC 214:9
pilgrimages: longen folk to goon on p.   CHAU 141:8
pilgrims: Land of the p.' pride   SMITH 510:24
strangers and p. on the earth   BIBLE 79:33
Robinson Crusoe, and the P.   JOHN 280:16
pill: When his potion and his p.   HERR 250:12
pillage: Which p. they with merry   SHAK 443:9
pillar: are a well-deserving p.   SHAK 468:5
cannot be regarded as a p.   MELB 336:22
day in a p. of a cloud   BIBLE 47:21
p. of state   MILT 346:14
p. of the world transform'd   SHAK 421:6
she became a p. of salt   BIBLE 46:8
pillared: Freedom, the seven p.   LAWR 311:12
pillars: builded over with p. of gold   BLAKE 86:4
four p. of government   BACON 27:10
hath hewn out her seven p.   BIBLE 53:27
I bear up the p. of it   PRAY 394:25

With antique p. massy proof   MILT 342:10
Pillicock: P. sat on Pillicock-hill   SHAK 454:17
pillow: like a p. on a bed   DONNE 188:21
sigh'd upon a midnight p.   SHAK 425:9
softer p. than my heart   BYRON 126:16
pillow-hill: That sits upon the p.   STEV 522:20
pillows: I had two p. at my head   STEV 522:20
P. his chin upon an orient   MILT 344:14
Take thou of me smooth p.   SIDN 507:21
To their deaf p.   SHAK 462:26
pills: mountebank who sold p.   ADD 2:28
pilot: daring p. in extremity   DRYD 194:6
Dropping the p.   TENN 532:14
P. of the Galilean lake   MILT 343:11
to see my P. face to face   TENN 533:4
pilotage: our lives in learning p.   MER 337:20
Pilots: P. of the purple twilight   TENN 538:24
piminy: miminy, p.   GILB 227:26
Pimpernel: demmed, elusive P.   ORCZY 365:7
pin: gives the web and the p.   SHAK 454:22
little p. Bores through   SHAK 479:11
pinn'd it wi' a siller p.   BALL 32:11
p. up your hair with all   CONG 160:37
set my life at a p.'s fee   SHAK 430:25
Stay not for th' other p.   HERB 247:11
pinch: death is as a lover's p.   SHAK 424:12
They brought one P.   SHAK 427:9
pinches: with Phoebus' amorous p.   SHAK 421:32
pinching: be paddling palms and p.   SHAK 491:9
In this our p. cave   SHAK 428:15
pin'd: she p. in thought   SHAK 489:7
pine: lover true for whom I p.   SHAK 571:2
of huge melons and of p.   TENN 542:20
of palm and southern p.   TENN 533:5
p. within and suffer dearth   SHAK 495:13
This spray of Western p.   HARTE 242:26
We p. for what is not   SHEL 504:23
pine-apple: very p. of politeness   SHER 506:12
pined: p. by Arno for my lovelier   MAC 322:9
sighed and p. and ogled   THAC 546:3
Youth p. away with desire   BLAKE 87:22
pines: acquaintance among the p.   THOR 550:3
p. are gossip pines   FLEC 214:4
Tall arrowy white p.   THOR 550:11
pine-trees: black and gloomy p.   LONG 317:10
pinguem: *Me p. et nitidum bene curata*   HOR 258:16
pinion: Imagination droops her p.   BYRON 123:9
so poor a p. of his wing   SHAK 422:15
pinions: race with p. skim the air   FRERE 218:25
Stayed in mid passage his p.   SWIN 528:24
Pink: P. and purple Columbine   SPEN 517:3
very p. of courtesy   SHAK 482:23
very p. of perfection   GOLD 232:22
pinkly: p. bursts the spray   BETJ 43:12
pinko-gray: white races are really p.   FORS 217:7
pinnacled: There in p. protection   BETJ 43:9
pinn'd: p. it wi' a siller pin   BALL 32:11
pins: Here files of p. extend   POPE 380:31
pintores: *p. imitan la naturaleza*   CERV 139:1
pint-pot: Peace, good p.   SHAK 439:13
pints: Love made him weep his p.   AUDEN 21:9
P. and quarts of Ludlow   HOUS 264:13
pioneer: Never be a p.   SAKI 413:9
Pioneers: P.! O pioneers   WHIT 570:10
pios: *si qua p. respectant numina*   VIRG 557:18
pious: p. but Mr Salteena was   ASHF 17:9
this p. fraud   GAY 223:3
this p. morn   KEATS 291:8
well stored with p. frauds   BURKE 108:14
pipe: different varieties of p.   DOYLE 191:16
my small p. best fits my   HERR 249:21
p. a simple song for thinking   WORD 577:22

'P. a song about a Lamb   BLAKE 87:24
p. but as the linnets sing   TENN 536:12
p. for my capacious mouth   GAY 222:7
P. me to pastures still   HOPK 256:14
P. to the spirit ditties   KEATS 291:4
p., with solemn interposing   COWP 165:3
quite a three-p. problem   DOYLE 192:3
Rumour is a p.   SHAK 440:31
So put that in your p.   BARH 33:18
thy small p.   SHAK 488:3
piped: We have p. unto you   BIBLE 66:3
pipers: especially p.   BROW 103:20
five-and-thirty p.   AYT 24:6
pipes: Grate on their scrannel p.   MILT 343:13
Tho' the p. that supply   COW 164:4
What p. and timbrels   KEATS 291:3
piping: p. loud   BLAKE 87:23
P. songs of pleasant glee   BLAKE 87:24
sniv'ling and p. your eye   DIBD 175:19
weak p. time of peace   SHAK 480:18
pipkin: p. fits this little jelly   HERR 249:21
Pippa: P. passes   BEER 37:25
pippins: old p. toothsomest   WEBS 566:30
pips: until the p. squeak   GEDD 223:32
Pirate: To be a P. King   GILB 228:12
pire: *C'est p. qu'un crime*   BOUL 90:19
piscem: *Desinat in p. mulier*   HOR 257:9
pismire: p. is equally perfect   WHIT 570:21
pissent: *...Les chacals p. au bas*   FLAU 214:3
pistol: when his p. misses fire   GOLD 232:40
pistols: Have you your p.   WHIT 570:10
piston: snorting steam and p. stroke   MORR 358:10
pistons: black statement of p.   SPEN 515:13
pit: diggeth a p. shall fall   BIBLE 56:2
have beat us to the p.   SHAK 452:5
have digged a p. before me   PRAY 393:15
know what is in the p.   BLAKE 85:19
Law is a bottomless p.   ARB 11:20
many-headed monster of the p.   POPE 380:17
out of the horrible p.   PRAY 392:1
them to the bottomless p.   MILT 348:27
there is the sulphurous p.   SHAK 455:17
they'll fill a p. as well   SHAK 440:12
will go down into the p.   BALIF 30:3
pit-a-pat: Makes my heart go p.   BROW 103:17
pitch: bumping p. and a blinding   NEWB 361:8
Of what validity and p.   SHAK 487:20
that when you make p. hot   DICK 176:10
toucheth p. shall be defiled   BIBLE 63:2
pitch-and-toss: risk it on one turn of p.   KIPL 300:1
pitched: Love has p. his mansion   YEATS 584:19
pitcher: p. be broken at the fountain   BIBLE 56:11
pitchfork: Can't I use my wit as a p.   LARK 310:6
drive out nature with a p.   HOR 258:18
thrown on her with a p.   SWIFT 526:29
pitee: p. renneth soone in gentil   CHAU 142:19
pith: p. is in the postscript   HAZL 243:8
p. of an Indian cane   ADD 2:11
pitié: *se p. de nous povres avez*   VILL 557:4
pities: He p. the plumage   PAINE 368:3
pitieth: father p. his own children   PRAY 396:17
pitiful: 'God be p.   BROW 98:1
'twas wondrous p.   SHAK 474:1
very p.   BIBLE 62:21
were she p. as she is fair   GREE 236:10
pitifulness: yet let the p. of thy great   PRAY 385:23
Pitt: O'er P.'s the mournful   SCOTT 417:3
P. is to Addington   CANN 130:2
pittore: *Anch' io sono p.*   CORR 163:1
pity: by means of p. and fear   ARIS 12:9
dint of p.   SHAK 450:28
her that she did p. them   SHAK 474:1
in myself no p. to myself   SHAK 481:15

our p. is played out | THAC 545:29
P. all your changes | ING 270:12
P. it | BOG 89:7
P. out the play | SHAK 439:19
p.'s the thing | SHAK 433:6
p. the game | NEWB 361:8
p. the game | NEWB 361:9
p. the man | LAT 310:21
p. the wantons with our | SHAK 479:16
p. without a woman in it | KYD 306:9
prologue to a very dull P. | CONG 160:29
refined p. of the imagination | BURKE 108:7
rest of the p. may be | PASC 369:8
rose up to p. | BIBLE 48:3
see that Interesting P. | BELL 39:10
sheets and p. with flowers | SHAK 443:17
sun and stars to p. with | SHAW 496:29
that his p. is always fair | HUXL 269:6
They will not let my p. run | DENN 174:25
what to say about a p. | SHAW 496:26
When I p. with my cat | MONT 355:2
wouldst not p. false | SHAK 459:1
you cannot p. upon me | SHAK 434:21
Your p.'s hard to act | CHEK 144:26
You would p. upon me | SHAK 434:20

play-bills: have no time to read p. | BURN 112:22

playboy: p. of the western world | SYNGE 531:5

play'd: be p. with and humoured | TEMP 532:9
he p. at the gluve | BALL 30:11
He p. so truly | JONS 284:2
That's sweetly p. in tune | BURNS 114:27

play'dst: Thou p. most foully for't | SHAK 461:6

played: how you p. the game | RICE 405:23
I have p. the fool | BIBLE 50:15
p. the King as though under | FIELD 211:3
she p. it in tights | BEER 37:20
Played-out: called P. and Done-to-death | TRAI 552:4

player: p. on the other side is | HUXL 269:6
poor p., That struts | SHAK 463:6
There as strikes the P. | FITZ 213:6
wrapped in a p.'s hide | GREE 236:12
players: men and women merely p. | SHAK 425:24
see the p. well bestowed | SHAK 432:25
there be p. that I have | SHAK 433:17
playfellow: My p., your hand | SHAK 422:21
playing: from the purpose of p. | SHAK 433:17
on the p. fields of Eton | WELL 567:24
playmates: I have had p. | LAMB 308:6
plays: he loves no p. | SHAK 448:21
he p. extravagant matches | GILB 227:7
p. the king shall be welcome | SHAK 432:16
p. with them | CHES 145:26
plaything: child's a p. for an hour | LAMB 308:14
plaything-house: is a little p. that I got | WALP 562:21
playthings: Great princes have great p. | COWP 167:19
playtime: in the p. of the others | BROW 97:36
plea: Good is the p. of the scoundrel | BLAKE 86:7
necessity, The tyrant's p. | MILT 347:27
Though justice be thy p. | SHAK 467:27
what p. so tainted | SHAK 467:10
plead: p. that man's excuse | ANON 7:24
which I would not p. | SHAK 463:18
pleasance: Youth is full of p. | SHAK 492:13
pleasant: abridgement of all that was p. | GOLD 231:18
do not find anything p. | VOLT 560:21
England's p. pastures seen | BLAKE 86:16
few think him p. enough | LEAR 311:20
gets too excitin' to be p. | DICK 181:34
green and p. bowers | BLAKE 86:12
How p. it is to have money | CLOU 153:21

'How p. to know Mr Lear | LEAR 311:20
life would be very p. | SURT 525:23
p. sight to see | KING 296:16
p. thing it is to be thankful | PRAY 399:19
scorn of that p. land | PRAY 397:5
so many p. things are | GASK 222:2
pleasanter: proves the p. the colder | BUTL 118:17
pleasantness: Her ways are ways of p. | BIBLE 53:17
p. of an employment does | AUST 23:25
pleas'd: He more had p. us | ADD 2:3
p. with what he gets | SHAK 425:16
please: after life does greatly p. | SPEN 516:8
are to say what they p. | FRED 218:22
coy, and hard to p. | SCOTT 417:21
I am to do what I p. | FRED 218:22
Myself alone I seek to p. | GAY 223:18
seeketh only Self to p. | BLAKE 87:19
some circumstance to p. us | SWIFT 527:22
strive to p. you every day | SHAK 490:27
to p. thee with my answer | SHAK 467:23
To tax and to p. | BURKE 109:9
Towered cities p. us then | MILT 342:24
'twas natural to p. | DRYD 194:3
we that live to p. | JOHN 282:27
when he has ladies to p. | AUST 22:9
Yet she never fails to p. | SEDL 419:10
pleased: All seemed well p. | MILT 348:23
apt to be p. as anybody | CHES 145:23
in whom I am well p. | BIBLE 63:40
p. not the million | SHAK 432:23
pleasing consists in being p. | HAZL 243:22
praise to have p. leading men | HOR 258:21
pleases: Though every prospect p. | HEBER 244:6
pleaseth: this age best p. me | HERR 249:17
which it p. him to dwell | PRAY 394:9
pleasing: p. consists in being pleased | HAZL 243:22
pleasure of p. inferior | CLOU 153:8
pleasure turns to p. pain | SPEN 516:17
Pleasure: aching P. nigh | KEATS 291:15
because it gave p. | MAC 324:19
cabinet of p. | HERB 248:2
capable of much curious p. | CAB 126:24
did p. me in his top-boots | MARL 329:1
England take p. in breaking | ANON 7:22
fading p. brings | SIDN 507:28
Forced her to do your p. | WEBS 567:6
general read without p. | JOHN 280:25
Green p. or grey grief | SWIN 530:21
grievous p. and pain | SWIN 530:3
hath no p. in the strength | PRAY 399:20
Holland take p. in making | ANON 7:22
I have no p. in them | BIBLE 56:11
ineffable p. | LEIGH 313:15
in his p. is life | PRAY 391:13
In youth is p. | WEVER 569:7
is an impression of p. | BACON 24:14
Is not in p. | DRYD 196:25
It becomes a p. | WILDE 573:7
I' the east my p. lies | SHAK 422:7
lie doth ever add p. | BACON 27:9
little p. out of the way | CHAR 140:24
Love ceases to be a p. | BEHN 38:12
love of p. | POPE 377:24
make a bait of p. | HERB 246:27
make poetry and give p. | HOR 261:11
meant by the p. of life | TALL 531:16
mind, from p. less | MARV 332:4
mixed practicality with p. | HOR 258:1
Money gives me p. all | BELL 39:18
much p. in the reading | QUAR 403:8
my p., business | WYCH 583:25
necessity of giving p. | WORD 583:8
no p. if it were realized | MILL 339:17
no verse can give p. | HOR 258:25
of all weren't to give p. | MOL 353:6
Of unremembered p. | WORD 578:4

on by their favourite p. | VIRG 559:17
painful p. turns to pleasing | SPEN 516:17
pay a debt to p. | ROCH 406:17
perfect type of a perfect p. | WILDE 573:20
p. afterwards | THAC 545:17
p. and repentance dwell | RAL 404:8
p. and without one pain | TENN 539:22
P. at the helm | GRAY 234:16
P., blind with tears | SHEL 499:9
p. in the pathless woods | BYRON 121:22
P. is labour too | COWP 165:10
P. is nothing else | SELD 419:26
P. never is at home | KEATS 289:29
p. of having it over | HOOD 254:25
p. of pleasing inferior | CLOU 153:8
p. of the fleeting year | SHAK 494:16
P.'s a sin | BYRON 122:13
p. so exquisite as almost | HUNT 268:14
p. was his business | EDG 199:24
public stock of harmless p. | JOHN 281:36
receiv'st with p. thine annoy | SHAK 492:25
Refrain from the unholy p. | BELL 38:23
some to p. take | POPE 377:25
suburbs Of your good p. | SHAK 449:15
Sweet is p. after pain | DRYD 195:1
then my heart with p. fills | WORD 578:1
There is a p. sure | DRYD 197:26
there is no such p. in life | BROW 105:31
Thou doubtful p. | GRAN 234:7
though on p. she was bent | COWP 165:17
thy most pointed p. take | STEV 523:11
thy p. they are and were | BIBLE 81:25
treads upon the heels of p. | CONG 160:27
trim gardens takes his p. | MILT 342:1
turn to p. all they find | GREEN 236:2
Variety is the soul of p. | BEHN 38:16
What p. lives in height | TENN 542:15
when Youth and P. meet | BYRON 120:21
Your horrible p. | SHAK 454:5
pleasured: What lively lad most p. me | YEATS 585:20
pleasure-dome: stately p. decree | COL 156:26
pleasure-house: built my soul a lordly p. | TENN 541:20
pleasures: After the p. of youth | ANON 10:13
coarser p. of my boyish | WORD 578:6
common p. | SHAK 451:4
English take their p. sadly | SULLY 524:18
Great lords have their p. | MONT 355:7
gross and merely sensual p. | BURKE 108:7
has renounced those p. | SOCR 512:19
hate the idle p. of these | SHAK 480:19
In unreproved p. free | MILT 342:16
is a hypocrite in his p. | JOHN 279:22
Look not on p. as they come | HERB 247:13
memory of yesterday's p. | DONNE 191:2
My p. are plenty | HOUS 266:7
other knows what p. man | YEATS 585:16
paucity of human p. should | JOHN 280:15
p. and palaces though we | PAYNE 370:10
p. are like poppies spread | BURNS 115:7
p. in a long immortal dream | KEATS 290:23
p. of thought surpass eating | CLOU 153:23
p. of life is conversation | SMITH 511:28
p. that to verse belong | KEATS 289:7
p. with youth pass away | SOUT 514:8
purest of human p. | BACON 26:18
still fresh revolving p. | GAY 223:23
understand the p. of the other | AUST 22:8
we will all the p. prove | MARL 329:23
we will all the p. prove | SHAK 495:16
we will some new p. prove | DONNE 187:24
with p. too refin'd | POPE 377:21
Plebeian: this the P. bran | DONNE 190:23
plectuntur: reges p. Achivi | HOR 258:12
pledge: I will p. with mine | JONS 284:12
ne'er refus'd to p. my toast | PRIOR 401:10
p. our Empire vast across | HUXL 269:2
we p. to thee | KIPL 298:10
pledged: p. their troth either | PRAY 389:7

799

pledges: Fair p. of a fruitful tree HERR 248:20
Pledging: P. with contented smack
KEATS 290:29
Pleiades: sweet influences of P. BIBLE 53:5
Pleiads: rainy P. wester HOUS 265:17
weeping P. wester HOUS 265:16
Plena gratiä: there's Vespers! P. BROW 105:9
Pleni: P. sunt coeli et terra MASS 335:4
plenteous: harvest truly is p. BIBLE 65:29
thou makest it very p. PRAY 394:2
plenteously: Endue her p. with heavenly
PRAY 385:5
p. bringing forth the fruit PRAY 387:2
plenteousness: all things living with p.
PRAY 399:15
p. with thy palaces PRAY 398:12
plenties: p., and joyful births SHAK 445:11
plentiful: Fish is p. and cheap LEAR 311:26
plenty: As it is, p. AUDEN 19:1
delay there lies no p. SHAK 488:1
hand with P. in the maize TENN 542:16
just had p. BURNS 113:11
on the expectation of p. SHAK 460:15
P. has made me poor OVID 366:15
p. to get DICK 182:22
that here is God's p. DRYD 198:8
Where health and p. cheered GOLD 230:16
plesaunce: hennes for to doon al his p.
CHAU 142:32
pleuré: d'avoir quelquefois p. MUSS 359:3
p., Voltaire a souri HUGO 267:13
pleurer: d'être obligé d'en p. BEAU 35:15
pley: Ful craftier to p. she CHAU 141:6
pleyne: deeth moot wepe and p. CHAU 142:17
pli: Quelque chose que sans un p.
ROST 410:12
plie: fail of taking their p. BURG 108:5
Je p. et ne romps pas LA F 306:18
plies: it p. the saplings double HOUS 263:14
plight: I p. thee my troth PRAY 389:4
plighter: p. of high hearts SHAK 422:21
plodders: have continual p. ever won
SHAK 456:15
plods: ploughman homeward p. his
GRAY 234:18
plot: devil does the p. signify BUCH 106:13
excellent p., very good friends SHAK 438:30
Gunpowder Treason and P. ANON 7:10
Passions upon the p. MER 337:14
p. for a short story CHEK 145:2
p. thickens very much upon BUCH 106:14
This blessed p. SHAK 478:20
We first survey the p. SHAK 441:17
women guide the p. SHER 506:24
Plots: P., true or false DRYD 194:5
plotting: p. in the dark COWP 166:30
p. some new reformation DRYD 197:12
plough: bruised by no p. CAT 137:6
Following his p. WORD 580:28
must p. my furrow alone ROS 408:16
put his hand to the p. BIBLE 69:25
Speed his p. CHAP 140:5
this morning held the p. BETJ 42:13
wherefore p. SHEL 504:2
ploughing: 'Is my team p. HOUS 263:9
ploughman: Hard as the palm of p.
SHAK 486:19
p. homeward plods his weary GRAY 234:18
p. near at hand MILT 342:19
p. of bulls PROP 401:15
Whilst the heavy p. snores SHAK 471:21
ploughs: names the rain-drop p.
HARDY 239:10
ploughshare: Soldiers of the p. as well
RUSK 412:9
Stern Ruin's p. drives BURNS 115:19
plowed: had not p. with my heifer
BIBLE 49:22
plowers: p. plowed upon my back
PRAY 398:22

plowshares: beat their swords into p.
BIBLE 57:19
Beat your p. into swords BIBLE 61:16
pluck: p. it out BIBLE 67:5
To p. me by the beard SHAK 455:2
to p. your berries harsh MILT 343:2
pluck'd: p. the ripen'd ears TENN 541:28
plucked: p. my nipple SHAK 459:10
We p. them as we passed HOOD 254:8
pluckers: which the p. forgot ROSS 409:13
Plucks: P. off my beard and blows
SHAK 433:3
plum: confectionary p. COWP 166:3
plumage: He pities the p. PAINE 368:3
plume: Hector took off his p. CORN 162:20
In blast-beruffled p. HARDY 239:7
Ruffles her pure cold p. TENN 535:28
saw the helmet and the p. TENN 538:11
plumelets: When rosy p. tuft the larch
TENN 537:9
plumes: jets under his advanced p.
SHAK 489:11
Soil their fair p. with SPEN 516:32
When p. were under heel HOUS 266:4
plummet: like a leaden p. FORD 216:15
plunder: Let no man stop to p. MAC 323:2
Take your ill-got p. NEWB 361:11
Was für p. BLUC 88:32
Plunge: P. it in deep water HOR 261:12
p. the struggling sheep MAC 322:12
p. your hands in water AUDEN 18:10
plunged: I p. SHAK 448:14
p. himself into the billowy GILB 227:17
plunges: Orion p. prone HOUS 265:17
plural: Incorrigibly p. MACN 326:14
plures: Abiit ad p. PETR 373:1
Plus: P. ça change KARR 288:15
p. royaliste que le roi ANON 9:9
Plush: would as soon assault a P. DICK 183:3
Pluto: won the ear Of P. MILT 343:1
pluvio: p. supplicat herba Iovi TIB 551:1
Plymouth Hoe: dreamin' arl the time
o' P. NEWB 361:7
pneumatic: Gives promise of p. bliss
ELIOT 205:14
Po: wandering P. GOLD 231:23
poacher: p. a keeper turned inside KING 297:8
Pobble: P. who has no toes LEAR 312:17
Pobbles: P. are happier without LEAR 312:21
poches: poings dans mes p. crevées
RIMB 406:7
pocket: carry the moon in my p.
BROW 102:13
in your neighbour's p. RUSK 412:8
in your p. or purse WILS 574:16
not scruple to pick a p. DENN 174:24
plates dropp'd from his p. SHAK 423:22
put it in his p. SHAK 435:11
shall have my p. picked SHAK 440:4
pockets: hands in holey p. RIMB 406:7
pension jingle in his p. COWP 168:1
rare in our p. the mark CHES 147:22
young man feels his p. HOUS 265:2
Poe: P. with his raven like LOW 319:8
poem: author of that p. WOLFE 576:7
drowsy frowzy p. BYRON 123:6
had made one p.'s period MARL 330:11
he fain would write a p. BROW 102:32
himself to be a true p. MILT 351:18
is a heroic p. of its sort CARL 131:12
It is a pretty p. BENT 41:12
like to be married to a p. KEATS 294:20
long p. is a test of invention KEATS 293:13
p. is like that of a painting HOR 258:3
p. lovely as a tree KILM 296:3
P. should be palpable MACL 325:13
p. should be wordless MACL 325:13
p. should not mean MACL 325:14
p. unlimited SHAK 432:20
p., whose subject is not CHAP 140:14

true ornament of p. MILT 344:18
poems: can explain all the p. CARR 135:23
most sublime p. which either DRYD 198:6
P. are made by fools like KILM 296:4
ye are living p. LONG 316:8
poesy: force of heaven-bred p. SHAK 491:2
golden cadence of p. SHAK 457:3
immortal flowers of P. MARL 330:11
indignation call p. *vinum daemonum*
BACON 24:27
overwhelm Myself in p. KEATS 292:7
P. was ever thought BACON 24:19
Sense and wit with p. allied BYRON 124:20
viewless wings of P. KEATS 291:20
poesye: subgit be to alle p. CHAU 144:17
poet: apothecary than a starved p.
LOCK 315:22
because he was a true P. BLAKE 88:12
better p. than Porson HOUS 266:18
Buffoon and p. HENL 245:11
business of a comic p. CONG 159:20
business of a p. JOHN 282:6
Byron is only great as a p. GOET 229:26
consecration, and the P.'s dream WORD 577:4
driven by a p.'s verses SIDN 508:5
every fool is not a p. POPE 376:17
God is the perfect p. BROW 103:4
good p.'s made JONS 284:24
Hero can be P. CARL 131:33
Honour to the greatest p. DANTE 171:6
I was a p. FLEC 214:23
Like a P. hidden SHEL 504:19
limbs of a p. HOR 262:2
lover, and the p. SHAK 471:11
Never durst p. touch SHAK 457:8
Not deep the P. sees ARN 14:7
On a p.'s lips I slept SHEL 503:5
passionate heart of the p. TENN 539:28
Perhaps no person can be a p. MAC 323:23
p. and not a musician BUTL 118:32
P. and Saint COWL 164:15
p. and the dreamer are KEATS 289:28
p. can do today is to warn OWEN 367:1
p. could not but be gay WORD 578:1
P.!—He hath put his heart WORD 582:13
p. is like the prince BAUD 35:6
p. is the most unpoetical KEATS 294:8
p. like a pale candle guttering MACN 326:10
p. ranks far below LEON 313:24
p.'s eye SHAK 471:11
p. sing it with such airs YEATS 584:10
p.'s inward pride DAY-L 172:22
P.'s Pen BRAD 91:13
P. writes under one restriction WORD 583:8
rights be term'd a p.'s rage SHAK 492:27
shall be accounted p. kings KEATS 292:9
shepherds call me also a p. VIRG 560:7
should possess a p.'s brain DRAY 193:14
Spare the p. for his subject's COWP 164:29
that when the P. dies SCOTT 416:19
They had no p. and they POPE 380:21
they lack their sacred p. HOR 261:18
This is truth the p. sings TENN 538:20
'This p. lies SHAK 492:27
Thus every p. SWIFT 528:5
thy once-loved P. sung POPE 377:6
Thy skill to p. were SHEL 504:24
true p. that you are BROW 103:26
Vex not thou the p.'s TENN 541:24
was a poor p. named Clough SWIN 529:13
was ever yet a great p. COL 157:24
Was flattery lost on p.'s SCOTT 416:18
were the dreams of a p. JOHN 281:8
What is a modern p.'s HOOD 255:14
what is left the p. here BYRON 123:1
you will never be a p. DRYD 198:23
poeta: Agit pessimus omnium p. CAT 137:3
Onorate l'altissimo p. DANTE 171:6
poetae: disiecti membra p. HOR 262:2

poetaster: I too can hunt a p. down
BYRON 124:31

poete: grete p. of Ytaille
CHAU 142:31
Le p. est semblable au
BAUD 35:6

poetess: maudlin p.
POPE 376:19

poetic: is a pleasure in p. pains
COWP 166:35
Meet nurse for a p. child
SCOTT 416:22
P. fields encompass me
ADD 2:4
P. licence
BANV 33:2
putting it was more p.
NASH 360:3
which constitutes p. faith
COL 157:22

poetical: gods had made thee p.
SHAK 426:15
I have heard you are p.
FLET 215:14
study in a worn-out p.
ELIOT 202:19
to the p. character itself
KEATS 294:7

poétiques: Licences p... *Il n'y en*
BANV 33:2

poetis: *Mediocribus esse p.*
HOR 258:4
'Pictoribus atque p.
HOR 257:10

poetrie: Jonson his best piece of p.
JONS 283:28

poetry: all metaphor is p.
CHES 147:29
Angling is somewhat like p.
WALT 564:2
be the Polar star of p.
KEATS 293:13
cradled into p. by wrong
SHEL 501:13
difference between genuine p.
ARN 16:9
friend he drops into p.
DICK 181:4
grand style arises in p.
ARN 16:14
Grotesque Art in English P.
BAG 29:20
has never written any p.
CHES 148:4
'I can repeat p. as well
CARR 135:24
I didn't read the p.
TWAIN 554:1
In p.
ARN 16:10
In whining P.
DONNE 190:15
It is not p.
POPE 376:25
Made to p. a mere mechanic
COWP 166:27
make p. and give pleasure
HOR 261:11
Music and sweet P. agree
BARN 34:2
never the language of p.
GRAY 235:22
Nothing so much as mincing p.
SHAK 439:26
not of p.
ARN 16:2
p. almost necessarily declines
MAC 323:22
...p. begins to atrophy when
POUND 383:21
p. comes not as naturally
KEATS 293:25
p. he invented was easy
AUDEN 18:15
P. is certainly something
COL 158:1
p. is conceived and composed
ARN 16:9
P. is in the pity
OWEN 366:30
P. is not a turning loose
ELIOT 205:18
p. is *overheard*
MILL 339:20
p. is something more philosophical
ARIS 12:10
P. is the record
SHEL 505:12
P. is the supreme fiction
STEV 520:15
P. is the breath and finer
WORD 583:9
P. is the spontaneous overflow
WORD 583:10
P. is what gets lost
FROST 219:16
P. is when some of them
BENT 41:2
p. makes nothing happen
AUDEN 19:6
p. of earth is never dead
KEATS 292:21
p. of Lord Byron they drew
MAC 324:3
P.'s a mere drug
FARQ 210:17
P. should be great
KEATS 293:23
P. should surprise
KEATS 293:24
p. sinks and swoons under
LAND 309:10
p. strays into my memory
HOUS 266:17
P.'s unnat'ral
DICK 182:12
p.; the *best* words
COL 157:32
P. women generally write
BRON 93:17
p. would be made subsequent
MILT 352:9
read a little p. sometimes
HOPE 255:30
resuscitate the dead art Of p.
POUND 383:1
She that with p. is won
BUTL 118:1
smell of burned p.
WOD 576:1
So p.
DRYD 197:13
then P. and Religion
CARL 131:7
unless we know it to be p.
THOR 550:25
was trying to say was p.
OVID 366:23
We may live without p.
MER 338:6
we should drop into p.
DICK 181:5
what is p.
JOHN 277:7

What is p.
RUSK 411:10
will make again, good p.
MAC 323:30
word of true p. anywhere
JOW 285:23

poets: All p. are mad
BURT 116:17
all the pens that ever p.
MARL 330:11
he the worst of p. ranks
CAT 137:3
include me among the lyric p.
HOR 259:10
Irish p.
YEATS 587:8
Lunching with p.
BETJ 44:12
mighty P. in their misery
WORD 581:2
Milton's the prince of p.
BYRON 123:5
'Painters and p. alike
HOR 257:10
painters, p. and builders
MARL 329:2
P. are...the trumpets which
SHEL 505:13
p. better prove
SHAK 493:8
p. exploding like bombs
AUDEN 20:16
P.' food is love and fame
SHEL 500:14
P., like painters
POPE 378:16
P. Militant below
COWL 164:16
P. of the proud old lineage
FLEC 214:9
P. that are sown By Nature
WORD 577:9
P. that lasting marble
WALL 562:7
p., witty
BACON 27:21
sensitive race of p.
HOR 259:5
Souls of p. dead and gone
KEATS 290:28
That the first p. had
DRAY 193:13
Three p.
DRYD 196:30
Three p. in an age at most
SWIFT 527:33
true P. must be truthful
OWEN 367:1
We p. in our youth begin
WORD 580:28
When amatory p. sing their
BYRON 123:14
While pensive p. painful
POPE 375:15
with p.' being second-rate
HOR 258:4
would be theft in other p.
DRYD 198:3
your professional p.
WELL 568:5

Pogram: 'To be presented to a P.
DICK 179:21

poids: système de p. et mesures
NAP 359:13

Poins: banish P.
SHAK 439:18

point: Aloof from the entire p.
SHAK 453:7
determining a p. of law
BURKE 109:28
each to his p. of bliss
BROW 105:20
more or less mad on one p.
KIPL 304:33
'Not to put too fine a p.
DICK 176:7
n'y en a p. de délicieux
LA R 310:11
Point against p.
SHAK 458:5
P. d'argent
RAC 404:5
p. envenom'd too
SHAK 437:21
They do not p. on me
SHAK 477:6
thus I bore my p.
SHAK 439:2
To p. his slow and moving
SHAK 476:18
Up to a p., Lord Copper
WAUGH 566:4
You've hit the p.
PLAU 374:15

poising: p. every weight
MARV 331:20

poison: coward's weapon, p.
FLET 215:32
He drank the p. and his
HOME 253:25
if you p. us
SHAK 467:4
I go about and p. wells
MARL 329:21
Our Adonais has drunk p.
SHEL 499:18
p. England at her roots
BOTT 90:17
p. imposed by the authorities
PLATO 374:9
p. in jest
SHAK 434:12
p. the wells
NEWM 361:14
P. while the bee-mouth
KEATS 291:15
potent p. quite o'ercrows
SHAK 437:26
Slowly the p. the whole
EMPS 208:17
strongest p. ever known
BLAKE 85:16
sweet p. for the age's
SHAK 452:10

poison'd: ingredients of our p. chalice
SHAK 459:5
In the p. entrails throw
SHAK 462:2

poisoned: crams with cans of p. meat
CHES 147:20
p. air and tortured soil
KIPL 300:6
p. rat in a hole
SWIFT 526:24

poison-flowers: honey of p. and all
TENN 539:29

poison-gas: We've got as far as p.
HARDY 239:3

poisonous: its p. wine
KEATS 291:13
p. damp of night dispenge
SHAK 423:4

poisons: p. all the rest
WATTS 565:23

poke: heart to p. poor Billy
GRAH 233:13

Polar: be the P. star of poetry
KEATS 293:13

pole: curses from pole to p.
BLAKE 85:24
Heavens from pole to p.
BLAKE 85:23
not rapt above the P.
MILT 348:28

pole-axed: is no good he must be p.
CHUR 150:27

Poles: few virtues that the P.
CHUR 150:17

police: friendship recognised by the p.
STEV 521:27
'I'll send for the P.
CARR 133:11
'Leave Truth to the p.
AUDEN 19:12

Policeman: must go back with P. Day
KIPL 298:14
p.'s lot is not a happy
GILB 228:19
terrorist and the p. both
CONR 161:20

policemen: first time how young the p.
HICKS 250:23

policies: We cannot restore old p.
ELIOT 202:27

policy: either on religion or p.
RUSK 412:4
foreign p. of the noble
DERBY 175:9
My p. is to be able
BEVIN 44:18
p. of the good neighbour
ROOS 407:21
rugged brow of careful P.
SPEN 516:26
some love but little p.
SHAK 480:9
thought contend is the p.
MAO 328:18
will be tyrants from p.
BURKE 111:13

polis: pas le temps d'être p.
MONT 355:8
P. as Polis
OCAS 364:18

polish: we may p. it at leisure
DRYD 197:37

polish'd: p. perturbation
SHAK 442:17

polished: I p. up the handle
GILB 228:4
p. and well-rounded
HOR 262:10
p. corners of the temple
PRAY 399:12
Who has a p. female friend
WHURR 572:1

polite: costs nothing to be p.
CHUR 151:2
don't have time to be p.
MONT 355:8
His manners are not so p.
KIPL 301:19
p. learning and a liberal
HENRY 245:21
p. meaningless words
YEATS 585:1
till the English grew p.
KIPL 299:1

politeness: Hope, p., the blowing
FORS 217:8
mutual glance of great p.
BYRON 126:8
very pine-apple of p.
SHER 506:12

political: accomplice in any species of
p. villainy
PEAC 370:14
called his p. Cave of Adullam
BRIG 93:5
death of a p. economist
BAG 29:12
healthy state of p. life
MILL 339:10
is by nature a p. animal
ARIS 12:7
nature of a p. party
TROL 553:8
not regard p. consequences
MANS 328:16
off for fear of P. Economy
SELL 420:6
p. blank cheque
GOSC 233:2
'P. power grows out
MAO 328:19
'Principles of P. Economy'
BENT 41:8
remembrance of p. affairs
MAC 324:22
schemes of p. improvement
JOHN 275:29

politician: Every p. ought to sacrifice
BURKE 111:26
lief be a Brownist as a p.
SHAK 489:29
like a scurvy p.
SHAK 455:21
might be the pate of a p.
SHAK 436:27
when a p. does get
MARQ 331:1
(which makes the p. wise
POPE 381:7

politicians: fault of our p.
TROL 553:4
Old p. chew on wisdom past
POPE 377:14
race of p. put together
SWIFT 526:6

politics: Confound their p.
CAREY 130:25
everyday p. than a Chatham
BAG 28:25
From p.
AUST 23:6
gallantry than it has with p.
SHER 506:6
give his mind to p.
SHAW 496:4
his amusements, like his p.
CHUR 149:20
History is past p.
SEEL 419:17
holy mistaken zeal in p.
JUN 287:4
In p.
COL 158:3
Magnanimity in p. is not
BURKE 110:6

mule of p. that engenders   DISR 185:41
not the language of p.   DISR 184:22
now in the centre of p.   MOSL 358:19
Philistine of genius in p.   ARN 16:23
P. and the pulpit are terms   BURKE 111:2
p. and little else beside   CAMP 128:13
P. are now nothing more   JOHN 276:29
p. in boil'd and roast   SMITH 512:6
p. in the East may be defined   DISR 186:5
P. is not an exact science   BISM 84:19
P. is not a science…but   BISM 84:24
P. is perhaps the only   STEV 521:6
P. we bar   GILB 228:25
That p. go by the weather   GREEN 235:29
They p. like ours profess   GREEN 235:27
They shoved him into p.   BELL 39:5
week is a long time in p.   WILS 574:18

Politik: P. ist keine exakte Wissenschaft
  BISM 84:19

pollertics: My p., like my religion
  WARD 564:21
polluted: fountain is choked up and p.
  BURKE 111:15
her that is filthy and p.   BIBLE 61:27
pollution: unsavoury engine of p.
  SPAR 514:23
Polly: Our P. is a sad slut   GAY 222:12
P. put the kettle   DICK 175:26
polly-wog: like a p.'s tail   WARD 564:30
polygamy: Before p. was made a sin
  DRYD 194:1
chaste p.   CAREW 130:15
Polygony: Or Panachaea, or P.   SPEN 516:15
Pomegranate: from Browning some 'P.
  BROW 98:3
of a p. within thy locks   BIBLE 56:26
Pomeranian: bones of a single P. grenadier
  BISM 84:22
Pomp: after Sultan with his P.   FITZ 212:13
all our p. of yesterday   KIPL 302:8
grinning at his p.   SHAK 479:11
it has all his p.   BURKE 112:14
nor the tide of p.   SHAK 444:25
p., and circumstance   SHAK 475:25
p. and glory of this world   SHAK 447:9
p. and plenty   JOHN 279:28
P. ascended jubilant   MILT 349:2
p. of a too-credulous day   WORD 582:4
p. of pow'r   GRAY 234:21
possess'd with double p.   SHAK 452:25
slave of p.   SAV 415:5
Take physic, p.   SHAK 454:16
what is p.   SHAK 446:22
'with p. of waters   WORD 582:2
world of p. and state   BEAU 36:1
Pompeii: like a town crier in P.   THOM 546:21
Pompey: base of P.'s statua   SHAK 450:28
great P. Would stand   SHAK 421:32
Knew you not P.   SHAK 448:6
wars of P. the Great   SHAK 444:18
pompous: p. in the grave   BROW 97:23
pomps: p. and vanity of this wicked
  PRAY 388:13
will the high Midsummer p.   ARN 15:6
pond: Four ducks on a p.   ALL 3:21
have their stream and p.   BROO 94:10
mantle like a standing p.   SHAK 465:12
p. edged with grayish leaves   HARDY 240:10
will find by hedge or p.   HOUS 262:19
ponies: Five and twenty p.   KIPL 302:22
Her p. have swallowed their   BETJ 42:21
wretched, blind, pit p.   HODG 252:2
pont: p. Mirabeau coule la Seine   APOL 11:11
ponts: de coucher sous les p.   FRAN 217:26
pool: it must first fill a p.   BACON 26:33
pooled: mussel p. and the heron   THOM 547:6
pools: p. are filled with water   PRAY 395:12
Where the p. are bright   HOGG 252:23
poop: p. was beaten gold   SHAK 422:2
poor: angry and p. and happy   CHES 147:22

apt the p. are to be proud   SHAK 489:23
Blessed are the p. in spirit   BIBLE 64:6
bring in hither the p.   BIBLE 70:12
congregation of the p.   PRAY 394:24
considereth the p. and needy   PRAY 392:4
cottages of the p.   HOR 259:13
destruction of the p. is   BIBLE 53:30
else his dear papa is p.   STEV 522:21
feel for the p.   LAND 308:16
given to the p.   BIBLE 72:25
give to the p.   BIBLE 67:9
Good to the p.   CAREW 130:14
grind the faces of the p.   BIBLE 57:20
have their p. relations   DICK 176:19
how p. a thing is man   DAN 170:21
I am p. even in thanks   SHAK 432:14
I can dare to be p.   GAY 223:25
I have very p. and unhappy   SHAK 474:23
it inconvenient to be p.   COWP 164:26
Laws grind the p.   GOLD 231:29
letters for the p.   AUDEN 20:1
little more than the p.   SMITH 509:9
makes me p. indeed   SHAK 475:16
marry a rich woman as a p.   THAC 545:14
murmuring p.   COWP 168:14
my goods to feed the p.   BIBLE 76:14
one of the undeserving p.   SHAW 498:14
open to the p. and the rich   ANON 4:13
Plenty has made me p.   OVID 366:15
p., ailing and ignorant   YEATS 585:3
p. always ye have with   BIBLE 72:26
p., And Thou within them   HERB 248:15
p. are Europe's blacks   CHAM 139:17
p. centre of a man's actions   BACON 27:36
p. feeble sex   VICT 556:14
p. have become poorer   SHEL 505:11
p. in a loomp is bad   TENN 541:2
p. in their fireless lodgings   AUDEN 20:15
P. little rich girl   COW 164:1
p. man at his gate   ALEX 3:14
p. man had nothing   BIBLE 50:20
p. man is   HERB 247:9
p. man's dearest friend   BURNS 114:24
p. man slipped   BIBLE 63:4
p. soul sat sighing   SHAK 476:27
P. wandering one   GILB 228:14
Resolve not to be p.   JOHN 279:2
RICH AND THE P.   DISR 186:29
simple annals of the p.   GRAY 234:21
so p. that he is unable   HENR 245:13
specially dangerous man when p.
  SHAW 498:22
that the p. have no right   RUSK 412:11
to the play with the p.   SMITH 510:18
train to accept being p.   HOR 259:9
virtuous p.   WILDE 573:23
When that the p. have cried   SHAK 450:19
which forbids rich and p.   FRAN 217:26
your tired, your p.   LAZ 311:13
poorer: richer for p.   PRAY 389:4
ruined and the land grows p.   CHEK 145:4
poorest: p. he that is in England   RAIN 404:7
p. man may in his cottage   PITT 373:29
Poorly: P. (poor man) he liv'd   FLET 215:27
poorness: When I mock p.   JONS 283:18
Pop: P. goes the weasel   MAND 328:10
Pope: Better to err with P.   BYRON 124:19
burning of a P.   DRYD 197:5
Poor P. will grieve a month   SWIFT 527:23
P., and all their school   ARN 16:9
P. composes with his eye   ARN 16:12
P.! How many divisions   STAL 517:16
Popery: antiquity inclines a man to P.
  FULL 220:14
never be in danger of P.   ADD 2:19
popinjay: So pester'd with a p.   SHAK 438:15
Popish: P. liturgy   PITT 373:25
poppies: Drows'd with the fume of p.
  KEATS 293:6
Flanders fields the p.   MCCR 324:30

pleasures are like p. spread   BURNS 115:7
…'p. was nothing to it   DICK 182:31
poppy: flushed print in a p. there
  THOM 548:27
Piccadilly with a p. or a lily   GILB 227:23
p., nor mandragora   SHAK 475:24
Pops: classical Monday P.   GILB 227:6
Populace: P.; and America is just   ARN 15:14
propriety give the name of P.   ARN 15:20
popular: base, common and p.   SHAK 444:16
p. humanity is treason   ADD 1:21
popularity: even his darling p.   BURKE 110:26
every difficulty except p.   WILDE 574:1
Population: P., when unchecked   MALT 328:9
single and only talked of p.   GOLD 232:32
populi: Salus p. suprema   CIC 151:19
Salus p. suprema lex   SELD 419:25
Vox p.   ALC 3:9
populus: p. Romanus unam cervicem
  CAL 127:6
porcelain: dainty rogue in p.   MER 337:30
porches: In the p. of mine ears   SHAK 431:11
porcum: voles Epicuri de grege p.
  HOR 258:16
pores: I pass through the p.   SHEL 500:7
pork: pickled p. they loaded   THAC 545:32
Porlock: person on business from P.
  COL 156:25
porpentine: quills upon the fretful p.
  SHAK 431:5
porpoise: 'There's a p. close behind
  CARR 134:13
porridge: comfort like cold p.   SHAK 485:3
What p. had John Keats   BROW 103:27
porringer: I take my little p.   WORD 583:6
Porson: better poet than P.   HOUS 266:18
port: Alma Mater lie dissolv'd in p.
  POPE 375:21
buried him the little p.   TENN 533:11
claret that 'it would be p.   BENT 41:11
every p. he finds a wife   BICK 84:3
ev'ry p. a mistress find   GAY 223:29
Go fetch a pint of p.   TENN 544:9
In every p. a wife   DIBD 175:18
Let him drink p.   HOME 253:25
p. after stormy seas   SPEN 516:8
p. for men   JOHN 278:7
p. is near   WHIT 570:7
Still bent to make some p.   ARN 15:2
There lies the p.   TENN 544:3
with our sprightly p.   SHAK 423:10
portabit: libenter crucem portas p.
  THOM 546:14
portable: Get hold of p. property   DICK 178:11
P., and compendious oceans   CRAS 169:12
portae: Sunt geminae Somni p.   VIRG 559:3
portal: fiery p. of the east   SHAK 479:12
portals: are the p. of discovery   JOYCE 286:27
portcullis: Let the p. fall   SCOTT 417:11
portent: p. to the historians   KEYN 295:11
portents: These are p.   SHAK 477:6
porter: all p. and skittles   DICK 182:32
I'll devil-p. it no further   SHAK 460:17
p. of hell-gate he should   SHAK 460:15
She curs'd Cole P. too   COW 163:22
shone bright on Mrs P.   ELIOT 204:27
porters: poor mechanic p. crowding
  SHAK 443:9
Portia: P. is Brutus' harlot   SHAK 449:15
Portion: P. of that around me   BYRON 120:35
p. of that unknown plain   HARDY 239:9
shall be their p. to drink   PRAY 389:31
they may be a p. for foxes   PRAY 393:22
portioned: Then lands were fairly p.
  MAC 322:13
portmanteau: You see it's like a p.
  CARR 135:28
portrait: p. (in frame) of the Bishop-Elect
  KNOX 305:23
p. of a dog that I know   JOHN 280:19

p. of a blinking idiot SHAK 466:21
two styles of p. painting DICK 180:6
portraiture: face that left no p. behind
SASS 415:3
portress: p. foul to see HOUS 265:5
ports: five p. of knowledge BROW 95:19
p. of slumber open wide SHAK 442:17
posing: involves p. as a page-boy WEST 569:1
position: Every p. must be held HAIG 237:11
positions: p. of considerable emolument
GAIS 220:25
positive: p. men are the most credulous
POPE 381:22
They live by p. goals BERL 41:23
possédais: chercherais pas si tu ne me
p. PASC 369:13
possess: meek-spirited shall p. the earth
PRAY 391:27
patience p. ye your souls BIBLE 71:5
P. thy heart BRID 92:21
thou dost p. SHEL 504:1
possess'd: regain Love once p. MILT 350:25
possessed: endure what it once p.
SHEL 501:22
limited in order to be p. BURKE 110:12
p. all the universe together SHAW 496:30
p. his land BIBLE 48:12
Webster was much p. by death ELIOT 205:13
possessing: art too dear for my p.
SHAK 494:13
Beauty by constraint, p. GAY 222:9
yet p. all things BIBLE 77:8
possession: in p. so SHAK 495:7
one equal p. DONNE 191:3
p. of truth as of a city BROW 96:6
p. of the same PRAY 400:12
p. of it is intolerable VANB 555:2
P. without obligation MER 337:32
single man in p. AUST 23:11
possessions: are behind the great p.
JAMES 271:23
he had great p. BIBLE 67:10
many p. will you be right HOR 261:19
possessor: Hell Receive thy new p.
MILT 345:10
possibilites: preferred to improbable p.
ARIS 12:11
possibilities: To believe only p. BROW 96:24
Possibility: Permanent P. of Sensation
STEV 522:7
sceptic to deny the p. HUXL 269:14
possible: effecting of all things p.
BACON 28:6
exhaust the realm of the p. PIND 373:15
if a thing is p. CAL 127:9
Politics is the art of the p. BISM 84:20
si c'est p. CAL 127:9
with God all things are p. BIBLE 67:12
possidentem: Non p. multa vocaveris
HOR 261:19
possumus: non omnia p. omnes LUC 320:2
Non omnia p. omnes VIRG 560:6
possunt: p., *quia posse videntur* VIRG 558:16
post: evil news rides p. MILT 350:28
like a p. with packets SHAK 447:24
place with only one p. SMITH 511:18
P. coitum omne animal ANON 10:17
p. o'er Land and Ocean MILT 351:10
p. of honour is a private ADD 1:23
still as a p. DE L 174:13
whose p. lay in the rear ROSS 408:25
postal order: Bringing the cheque and
the p. AUDEN 20:1
postboy: Never...see...a dead p. DICK 182:38
post-chaise: driving briskly in a p.
JOHN 277:15
poster: great p. ASQ 17:19
posteri: Credite p. HOR 260:12
posteriors: p. of this day SHAK 457:13
Posterity: are the trustees of P. DISR 186:33

have put mankind and p. INGE 270:10
hope of p. POWER 384:3
I would fain see P. do ADD 2:27
looked upon by p. as a brave CLAR 152:22
not look forward to p. BURKE 111:7
that p. is a pack-horse DISR 184:25
Thy p. shall sway COWP 164:24
Posters: P. of the sea and land SHAK 458:8
Post Office: stalked through the P.
YEATS 587:2
post-prandial: sweet p. cigar BUCH 106:11
postscript: all the pith is in the p. HAZL 243:8
Here is yet a p. SHAK 489:16
her Mind but in her P. STEE 517:24
most material in the p. BACON 25:42
Postume: P., *Postume* BARH 33:8
postures: same our p. were DONNE 188:23
posy: I made a p. while the day HERB 247:24
I pluck a p. BROW 98:34
pot: Another for the p. PAIN 367:16
crackling of thorns under a p. BIBLE 55:18
eat our p. of honey MER 337:10
Joan doth keel the p. SHAK 457:19
kettle and the earthen p. BIBLE 63:3
There is death in the p. BIBLE 51:26
three-hooped p. SHAK 446:11
treasures from an earthen p. HERB 247:12
who the P. FITZ 213:11
potage: birthright for a mess of p.
BIBLE 46:12
potash: birthrite for a mess of p.
WARD 564:22
potations: Their dull and deep p. GIBB 224:9
to forswear thin p. SHAK 442:16
potato: bashful young p. GILB 227:23
has a p. in his head HARE 242:6
mouth like an old p. KIPL 298:7
potatoes: small p. and few in the hill
KIPL 304:29
Tired of digging p. HARDY 240:19
potatori: Huic p. ANON 10:14
potency: do contain a p. of life MILT 351:21
potent: Extraordinary how p. cheap music
is COW 163:12
p., grave, and reverend SHAK 473:24
they are most p. in potting SHAK 475:2
potestas: Nam et ipsa scientia p.
BACON 28:11
potion: When his p. and his pill HERR 250:12
potions: p. have I drunk of Siren SHAK 495:6
Potomac: All quiet along the P. BEERS 38:8
All quiet along the P. MCCL 324:29
potoribus: Quae scribuntur aquae p.
HOR 258:25
pots: beflagged jam p. JAMES 271:34
have lien among the p. PRAY 394:8
potsherd: Let the p. strive with BIBLE 59:13
poor p. HOPK 257:1
p. to scrape himself withal BIBLE 52:9
Potter: Hand then of the P. shake FITZ 213:10
pieces like a p.'s vessel PRAY 389:18
P. and clay endure BROW 104:10
p. power over the clay BIBLE 75:14
p. round the garden AUDEN 21:9
'Who *is* the P. FITZ 213:11
potting: they are most potent in p.
SHAK 475:2
pouch: spectacles on nose and p.
SHAK 425:24
poule: tous les dimanches sa p. HENR 245:13
poultry: prolonging the lives of the p.
ELIOT 200:25
pound: love is worth a p. of knowledge
WESL 568:23
that the p. here in Britain WILS 574:16
pounding: Hard p. this WELL 567:32
pounds: About two hundred p. a year
BUTL 118:10
crowns and p. and guineas HOUS 262:20
handsome in three hundred p. SHAK 469:11

how many p. will you find JUV 288:1
p. will take care of themselves LOWN 319:21
six hundred p. a-year SWIFT 527:28
Pour: P. into our hearts such PRAY 386:18
p. out my spirit upon all BIBLE 61:15
That I may p. my spirits SHAK 459:1
poured: been p. into his clothes WOD 575:28
I am p. out like water PRAY 390:19
p. it on his head BIBLE 68:8
pouring: more noise they make in p.
POPE 381:20
p. forth thy soul abroad KEATS 291:22
pourpres: p., *sang craché* RIMB 406:9
poverty: crime so shameful as p. FARQ 209:26
drink, and forget his p. BIBLE 55:2
heart she scorns our p. SHAK 446:4
In honoured p. thy voice SHEL 505:6
me neither p. nor riches BIBLE 54:45
misfortunes of p. carry JUV 287:17
of the poor is their p. BIBLE 53:30
p. and oysters always seem DICK 182:2
p., but not my wealth SHAK 483:26
p. come as one that travelleth BIBLE 53:22
P. has strange bedfellows BULW 107:6
p., hunger, and dirt HOOD 255:6
P. is a great enemy JOHN 279:2
P. is no disgrace SMITH 511:27
p.'s catching BEHN 38:17
quiet mind is worse than p. TRAH 552:2
Slow rises worth by p. JOHN 282:24
suffer so much p. and excess PENN 371:14
to put up with rough p. HOR 261:19
worst of crimes is p. SHAW 497:6
povre: was a p. Persoun of a Toun
CHAU 141:32
powder: food for p. SHAK 440:12
when your p.'s runnin' low NEWB 361:6
powder-blue: I was wearing my p. suit
CHAN 139:20
powder'd: Still to be p. JONS 283:27
powders: p., patches POPE 380:31
power: absolute p. corrupts ACTON 1:5
according to the P. of the Sword
CHAR 140:19
accursed p. which stands BELL 39:21
another name for absolute p. WORD 580:26
balance of p. WALP 563:27
Between his p. and thine JONS 284:16
certainty of p. DAY-L 172:22
chief p. in the State CHUR 150:26
common p. to keep them all HOBB 251:17
defy P., which seems omnipotent
SHEL 503:15
depositary of p. is always DISR 185:43
drunk with sight of p. KIPL 302:9
every power a double p. SHAK 457:8
feel all the pride of p. BURKE 109:18
force of temporal p. SHAK 467:27
friend in p. is a friend ADAMS 1:7
from our hands have p. WORD 581:5
from the p. of our senses JOHN 281:24
good want p. SHEL 503:2
greater the p. BURKE 109:1
have most p. to hurt us BEAU 36:9
have no hopes but from p. BURKE 110:8
Him the Almighty P. MILT 344:24
his fall from p. BURKE 109:5
Horses and P. and War KIPL 297:28
If some great P. would HUXL 269:8
is girded about with p. PRAY 394:1
Knowledge itself is p. BACON 28:11
legislative p. is nominated GIBB 224:21
literature of p. DE Q 175:6
Lord of all p. and might PRAY 386:19
nobility is but the act of p. BACON 26:39
no more than p. in trust DRYD 194:10
not exempted from her p. HOOK 255:20
notions about a superior p. SWIFT 525:31
of the p. of temptation TROL 553:11
once intoxicated with p. BURKE 111:28

when I have p. to others | BIBLE 76:9
preacher: Judge not the p. | HERB 247:12
like the P. found it not | SHEL 504:5
p.'s merit or demerit | BROW 100:4
private advantage of the p. | BURKE 108:14
preachers: was the company of the p.
| PRAY 394:8
preaches: wife who p. in her gown
| HOOD 255:12
preaching: foolishness of p. to save
| BIBLE 75:29
God calleth p. folly | HERB 247:12
p. and living they may | PRAY 385:18
woman's p. is like a dog's | JOHN 275:10
preamble: This is a long p. of a tale
| CHAU 143:22
precedency: point of p. between a louse
| JOHN 279:8
precedent: From precedent to p. | TENN 544:11
is a dangerous p. | CORN 162:23
p. embalms a principle | STOW 524:3
'Twill be recorded for a p. | SHAK 468:3
precedents: well to create good p.
| BACON 26:24
precept: more efficacious than p.
| JOHN 282:10
p. must be upon precept | BIBLE 58:21
precepts: love the p. for the teacher's
| FARQ 210:13
these few p. in thy memory | SHAK 430:19
precincts: Left the warm p. | GRAY 235:2
precious: adds a p. seeing to the eye
| SHAK 457:8
all that's p. in our joys | STER 519:12
can make vile things p. | SHAK 454:11
p. apothegmaticall Pedant | NASHE 360:6
p. as the Goods they sell | FITZ 213:14
p. stone set in the silver | SHAK 478:20
thy p. Death and Burial | PRAY 385:17
precipice: antagonist over the edge of
a p. | BRAM 91:21
precipices: p. show untrodden green
| KEATS 292:25
precisely: thinking too p. on the event
| SHAK 435:30
precisian: devil turned p. | MASS 335:19
predecessors: One of my illustrious p.
| FIEL 211:9
Predestination: P. in the stride o' yon
| KIPL 301:2
predicate: logically p. his finish | KIPL 302:4
we all p. | BEER 38:1
predicted: p. evil consequences | TROL 553:5
predominance: treachers by spherical
p. | SHAK 453:11
preeminence: hath no p. above a beast
| BIBLE 55:13
of the Lord hath the p. | PRAY 398:1
prees: Flee fro the p. | CHAU 144:21
Prefaces: written nothing but his P.
| CONG 159:29
prefer: I should p. mild hale | SURT 525:20
p. not Jerusalem in my | PRAY 399:3
preference: p. and distinction of excelling
| CONG 159:29
Preferment: knocking at P.'s door | ARN 14:12
P. goes by letter and affection | SHAK 473:12
preferred: therefore let use be p.
| BACON 25:34
who coming after me is p. | BIBLE 71:29
pregnancies: p. and at least four
miscarriages | BEEC 37:7
pregnant: Irish bull is always p. | MAH 327:4
prejudice: Conduct...to the p. of good
order | ANON 4:28
nor do I behold with p. | BROW 96:28
popular p. runs in favour | DICK 179:35
P. of education | STER 520:4
result of PRIDE AND P. | BURN 112:19
To everybody's p. I know | GILB 228:27

prejudices: always be above national
p. | NORTH 364:2
bundle of p. | LAMB 307:7
his personal p. and cranks | ELIOT 205:15
it p. a man so | SMITH 511:17
not local p. ought to guide | BURKE 109:12
print such of the proprietor's p.
| SWAF 525:30
prelate: religion without a p. | BANC 32:13
Prelatical: Presbyterial, or P. | MILT 352:12
prelaty: impertinent yoke of p. | MILT 352:15
premier: p. mouvement ne fut jamais
| CORN 162:18
que le p. pas qui coûte | DU D 198:28
première: *qu'il faut mettre la p.* | PASC 369:3
premiers: *p. mouvements parce qu'ils*
| MONT 355:11
premises: conclusions from insufficient
p. | BUTL 118:26
prentice: Her p. han' she tried | BURNS 114:4
preparation: feet shod with the p.
| BIBLE 78:10
Give dreadful note of p. | SHAK 444:9
no p. is thought necessary | STEV 521:6
prepare: good God p. me | PEPYS 372:21
I go to p. a place for you | BIBLE 72:31
p. himself to the battle | BIBLE 76:15
p. to shed them now | SHAK 450:26
P. vault for funeral | BEER 38:3
P. ye the way of the Lord | BIBLE 59:5
P. ye the way of the Lord | BIBLE 63:36
prepared: his hands p. the dry land
| PRAY 396:4
who hast p. for them that | PRAY 386:18
préparés: *favorise que les ésprits p.*
| PAST 369:16
préparez: *vieillesse vous vous p.* | TALL 531:18
preposterousest: To the p. end | BUTL 118:16
Prerogative: almost dead and rotten as
P. | BURKE 108:19
English subject's sole p. | DRYD 197:31
last p. | DRYD 196:14
p. of the harlot throughout | KIPL 305:13
presage: augurs mock their own p.
| SHAK 494:21
presagers: dumb p. of my speaking
| SHAK 493:3
Presbyter: P. is but old Priest writ
| MILT 351:15
Presbyterial: P., or Prelatical | MILT 352:12
presence: beautified with his p. | PRAY 388:25
before his p. with a song | PRAY 396:11
festoon The room with my p. | FRY 219:29
his p. his clouds removed | PRAY 390:9
his p. with thanksgiving | PRAY 396:3
his p. on the field made | WELL 567:33
made better by their p. | ELIOT 201:27
me not away from thy p. | PRAY 393:6
perfect p. of mind | JAMES 271:29
p. that disturbs me with | WORD 578:7
was conspicuous by its p. | RUSS 412:20
What is better than p. | PUNCH 402:12
Present: act in the living P. | LONG 317:3
All p. and correct | ANON 4:15
ass when thou art p. | CONG 160:22
except the p. company | OKEE 365:2
his p. is futurity | HARDY 241:13
importance only to be p. at it | THOR 550:10
It's God's p. to our nation | KIPL 299:3
know nothing but the p. | KEYN 295:15
many as are here p. | PRAY 384:10
mirth hath p. laughter | SHAK 488:17
No time like the p. | MANL 328:12
offers no redress for the p. | DISR 185:37
p. and your pains we thank | SHAK 443:11
p. help in time of trouble | ANON 4:18
p. in spirit | BIBLE 75:34
p. is the funeral | CLARE 152:15
p. joys are more to flesh | DRYD 196:18
p. were the world's last | DONNE 189:7

Such p. joys therein | DYER 199:17
therefore take the p. time | SHAK 427:2
things which are just in p. | BACON 24:26
un-birthday p. | CARR 135:20
very p. help in trouble | PRAY 392:19
When the P. has latched | HARDY 239:1
presented: 'To be p. to a Pogram | DICK 179:21
Présentez: *P. toujours le devant au*
| MOL 353:1
presentiment: she has a p. of it some
| STER 519:1
presents: bring p. | PRAY 396:5
Con-found all p. wot eat | SURT 525:14
isles shall give p. | PRAY 394:20
'P.,' I often say, 'endear | LAMB 307:3
preservation: p., and all the blessings
| PRAY 386:2
preserve: Lord shall p. thy going out
| PRAY 398:10
p. as in a vial the purest | MILT 351:21
P. it as your chiefest | BELL 38:23
p. the unity of the empire | BURKE 110:4
p. the stars from wrong | WORD 579:16
p. to our use the kindly | PRAY 385:21
what we give and what we p. | LINC 314:22
preserved: Federal Union: it must be
p. | JACK 270:30
my life is p. | BIBLE 46:25
Preserver: Creator and P. of all mankind
| PRAY 385:24
Destroyer and p. | SHEL 502:8
President: choose to run for P. in 1928
| COOL 162:9
P. of the Immortals (in | HARDY 241:25
rather be right than be P. | CLAY 152:28
Press: fell *dead-born from the P.* | HUME 268:1
Freedom of the p. in Britain | SWAF 525:30
governs the periodical p. | TROL 553:13
have misus'd the king's p. | SHAK 440:9
I p. toward the mark | BIBLE 78:18
of our idolatry, the p. | COWP 166:13
p. is the *Palladium* | JUN 287:1
P. was squared | BELL 39:6
racket is back in its p. | BETJ 44:6
turned him about in the p. | BIBLE 68:32
pressed: p. at midnight in some | YEATS 587:1
p. down my soul | PRAY 393:15
With face and nose p. | YEATS 585:3
Press-men: P.; Slaves of the Lamp | ARN 12:19
presume: Let none p. | SHAK 466:20
p. not God to scan | POPE 379:12
P. not that I am the thing | SHAK 443:1
p. to censure I may have | BURKE 109:5
p. too much upon my love | SHAK 451:19
Presumption: You'll be Amused by its
P. | THUR 550:29
presumptuous: p. man | CANN 130:3
servant also from p. sins | PRAY 390:13
prêt: *est toujours p. à partir* | LA F 306:22
pretence: p. make long prayers | BIBLE 68:37
p. of keeping a bawdy-house | JOHN 278:18
some faint meaning make p. | DRYD 196:34
pretend: does p. | BLAKE 87:5
p. to despise Art | BLAKE 86:9
pretended: p. friend is worse | GAY 223:13
Pretender: James II, and the Old P.
| GUED 237:5
who P. is | BYROM 119:25
pretending: p. to be wicked and being
| WILDE 573:5
pretexts: Tyrants seldom want p.
| BURKE 111:30
pretio: *Omnia Romae Cum P.* | JUV 287:19
pretty: *do for p. girls* | YEATS 585:16
He is a very p. weoman | FLEM 215:4
It must be so p. with all | WILDE 573:10
p. chickens and their dam | SHAK 462:17
p. follies that themselves | SHAK 466:14
P. fool, it stinted | SHAK 481:27
p. to see what money will | PEPYS 372:19

printed: that they were p. in a book
BIBLE 52:30
printers: those books by which the p.
FULL 220:18
printing: hast caused p. to be used
SHAK 446:14
invented the art of p. CARL 132:12
P., and the Protestant CARL 131:3
p., gunpowder and the magnet BACON 28:9
P. has destroyed education DISR 186:21
p. thereby to rectify manners MILT 351:25
was in a p. house in Hell BLAKE 88:27
printless: that on the sands with p.
SHAK 485:23
prints: sporting p. of Aunt Florence's
COW 164:2
priority: degree, p., and place SHAK 486:22
prisca: Ut p. gens mortalium HOR 259:7
Priscian: P. a little scratched SHAK 457:11
prism: with his p. and silent face
WORD 580:17
prison: Came the hero from his p. AYT 24:9
Else a great Prince in p. DONNE 188:25
girl's p. and the woman's SHAW 498:3
He did grind in the p. BIBLE 49:27
In the p. of his days AUDEN 19:9
I was in p. BIBLE 68:6
just man is also a p. THOR 550:1
let's away to p. SHAK 456:3
lime-tree bower my p. COL 157:10
Lord looseth men out of p. PRAY 399:17
opening of the p. to them BIBLE 60:8
palace and a p. on each BYRON 121:1
p. for the colour of his HOUS 266:8
prison in a p. DICK 182:30
Stone walls do not a p. LOV 318:18
This p. where I live unto SHAK 480:13
prisoner: If the p. is happy SHAW 497:32
Like a poor p. in his twisted SHAK 482:20
make each p. pent GILB 227:5
passing on the p.'s life SHAK 463:16
p. of the Lord BIBLE 77:27
p.'s release SIDN 507:20
That takes the reason p. SHAK 458:15
Your p. admits the crimes PETR 373:4
prisoners: addiction and the p. of envy
ILL 270:5
p. out of captivity PRAY 394:7
p. underneath her wings SHAK 445:24
upon all p. and captives PRAY 385:20
Which p. call the sky WILDE 572:8
prison-house: Shades of the p. begin
WORD 579:5
tell the secrets of my p. SHAK 431:5
prisons: improving his p. in Hell COL 156:14
Madhouses, p., whore-shops CLARE 152:5
P. are built with stones BLAKE 88:20
P. of flesh DONNE 189:37
prius: quod non dictum sit p. TER 544:16
Sed haec p. fuere CAT 136:24
privacy: that takes its prey to p.
MOORE 355:22
private: first consult our p. ends
SWIFT 527:22
grave's a fine and p. place MARV 332:19
honour is a p. station ADD 1:23
invade the sphere of p. life MELB 336:13
P. faces in public AUDEN 20:12
p. reason for this AUDEN 21:1
P. respects must yield MILT 350:24
p. station GAY 223:17
p. view in the morning EDW 200:2
that p. men enjoy SHAK 444:24
to serve our p. ends CHUR 148:30
privates: her p., we SHAK 432:11
privato: Maior p. visus dum privatus
TAC 531:13
privileg'd: p. to be very impertinent
FARQ 210:22

privilege: Death is the p. of human
ROWE 410:24
power which stands on P. BELL 39:21
p. I claim for my own sex AUST 23:10
p. of doing as he likes ARN 15:20
p. of wisdom to listen HOLM 253:20
take the p. o' sitting down ELIOT 201:19
privileged: "Cos a coachman's a p.
DICK 183:2
P. and the People formed DISR 186:32
privilèges: L'extension des p. des femmes
FOUR 217:18
stand for your p. we know HEM 245:1
prize: Bound for the p. of all SHAK 494:11
judge the p. MILT 342:25
one receiveth the p. BIBLE 76:8
p.-oxen and of sheep TENN 542:20
p. the thing ungain'd more SHAK 486:21
Timotheus yield the p. DRYD 195:9
We do not run for p. SORL 513:10
prizes: to offer glittering p. BIRK 84:14
which in herself she p. CONG 159:19
prizing: past all p., best SOPH 513:8
P.R.O.: liaison man and partly P. BETJ 42:14
probability: p. is the very guide BUTL 117:9
Probable: P. impossibilities are ARIS 12:11
Probably: of all sits P. Arboreal STEV 521:10
probationary: Eden's dread p. tree
COWP 166:13
Probitas: P. laudatur et alget JUV 287:10
problem: p. must puzzle the devil
BURNS 115:2
problems: of its most difficult p. DICK 181:10
such p. as it can solve MARX 333:7
proboque: Video meliora, p. OVID 366:17
proboscis: sinewy p. did remissly
DONNE 190:3
wreathed His lithe p. MILT 347:26
proceed: all just works do p. PRAY 385:9
p. no further in this business SHAK 459:7
P. to judgment SHAK 468:5
proceedeth: Who p. from the Father
PRAY 387:11
proceedings: p. interested him no more
HARTE 242:33
process: force and beauty of its p.
JAMES 272:2
long p. of getting tired BUTL 118:25
We look at the p. POUND 382:15
procession: in a p. of one DICK 179:20
torchlight p. marching OSUL 365:24
proclaim: p. throughout Italy this CAV 138:1
proclaims: apparel oft p. the man
SHAK 430:19
proclamation: Thou art the p. DONNE 189:33
Proconsul: great P. MAC 323:19
Procrastination: P. is the thief of time
YOUNG 588:4
that to incivility and p. DE Q 175:3
procreant: bed and p. cradle SHAK 459:4
p. urge of the world WHIT 570:17
procreate: that we might p. like trees
BROW 96:33
procreation: ordained for the p. of children
PRAY 389:1
proctors: With prudes for p. TENN 541:27
procul: o p. este, profani VIRG 558:19
P. hinc OVID 366:9
P. omen abesto OVID 366:8
'Qui p. hinc' NEWB 361:5
qui p. negotiis HOR 259:7
Procures: P. to the Lords of Hell
TENN 536:23
procuring: other means of p. respect
JOHN 276:38
prodigal: chariest maid is p. enough
SHAK 430:17
how p. the soul SHAK 430:21
oppression of their p. weight SHAK 479:17
that but once was p. before DRYD 196:2

who are p. within the compass IRV 270:23
yet p. of ease DRYD 194:7
prodigality: perennial spring of all p.
BURKE 110:16
prodigies: is all Africa and her p.
BROW 96:12
prodigious: p. armies we had in Flanders
STER 519:26
produce: p. it in God's name CARL 132:22
product: infinitesimal fraction of a p.
CARL 132:22
p. of the smaller intestines' CARL 131:7
production: p. of human nature ADD 2:9
productions: love with the p. of time
BLAKE 88:17
These modern p. ELIOT 203:7
Proelium: P. certaminis VEN 556:4
profanation: in the less foul p. SHAK 464:3
p. to keep HERR 248:24
'Twere p. of our joys DONNE 190:17
profane: Coldly p. COWP 168:13
p. one BRAT 91:24
p. the service of the dead SHAK 437:3
so old, and so p. SHAK 442:30
ye p. COWL 164:20
profaned: One word is too often p.
SHEL 504:13
they have desolated and p. GLAD 229:13
profani: o procul este, p. VIRG 558:19
profanum: Odi p. vulgus et arceo HOR 260:13
profess: p. and call themselves PRAY 385:25
p. any religion in name BURKE 111:20
profession: almost charmed me from
SHAK 486:11
my p. SHAK 486:11
ancient p. in the world KIPL 304:36
different branches of a new p. TROL 553:14
discharge of any p. JOHN 276:23
man a debtor to his p. BACON 25:16
ornament to her p. BUNY 107:35
panted for a liberal p. COLM 159:4
Professionally: P. he declines and falls
DICK 181:4
professions: have let in some of all p.
SHAK 460:17
p. are conspiracies against SHAW 496:21
professor: With that more learn'd p.
PORS 381:29
Zarathustra, sometime regius p.
JOYCE 286:28
professors: conscientious p. thereof
PAINE 367:23
P. of the Dismal Science CARL 131:40
p. of philosophy but not THOR 550:7
profit: all labour there is p. BIBLE 54:2
Have no more p. of their SHAK 456:15
in it no p. but the name SHAK 435:28
No p. grows where is no SHAK 484:4
p. and loss ELIOT 205:6
p. every day that Fate HOR 259:18
suffers the soul may not p. MER 337:28
To whose p. CIC 151:32
What p. hath a man of all BIBLE 55:5
what shall it p. a man BIBLE 68:34
When men write for p. WALP 563:15
winds will blow the p. MACN 326:8
profitable: it is not p. MARQ 330:24
profited: What is a man p. BIBLE 66:35
profiteth: it p. me nothing BIBLE 76:14
profits: It little p. that an idle TENN 543:21
nothing p. more Than self-esteem MILT 349:8
With p. of the mind SHAK 463:14
profligate: witty, p., and thin YOUNG 588:14
profonde: l'horreur d'une p. nuit RAC 404:2
profound: thro' the turbulent p. SMART 509:3
turbid look the most p. LAND 309:14
profundis: De p. clamavi ad te BIBLE 83:13
profundo: Merses p. HOR 261:12
profusus: sui p. SALL 413:22
Progeniem: P. vitiosiorem HOR 260:26

progenies: Iam nova p. caelo demittitur VIRG 559:22
progeny: soul was whose p. they are MILT 351:21
Prognostics: P. do not always prove WALP 563:18
progrès: principe général de tous p. FOUR 217:18
progress: emphatically the history of p. MAC 323:12
It was no summer p. ANDR 4:7
nations trek from p. OWEN 367:11
party of p. or reform MILL 339:10
p. depends on the unreasonable SHAW 498:1
P., far from consisting SANT 414:1
P. has its drawbacks STEP 518:21
P. is a comfortable disease CUMM 170:11
P., man's distinctive BROW 100:11
p. of a deathless soul DONNE 189:34
p. of human society CARL 132:8
P., therefore SPEN 514:32
spoke of p. spiring round CHES 146:12
thievish p. to eternity SHAK 494:10
To swell a p. ELIOT 203:24
youth, viewing his p. SHAK 442:2
progressive: p. country change is constant DISR 185:4
proie: entière à sa p. attachée RAC 404:4
projects: p. than for settled business BACON 27:39
proletarian: substitution of the p. LENIN 313:21
proletariat: dictatorship of the p. MARX 333:11
prologue: thing to make a long p. BIBLE 63:29
What's past is p. SHAK 485:5
witty p. to a very dull Play CONG 160:29
Prologues: P. precede the piece GARR 221:11
p. to the swelling act SHAK 458:19
prolong: Youth to p. YEATS 586:20
Promethean: not where is that P. heat SHAK 477:5
spring the true P. fire SHAK 457:6
promis'd: I was p. on a time SPEN 516:29
weird women p. SHAK 461:6
promise: freewoman was by p. BIBLE 77:16
he was a young man of p. BALF 30:2
ill keeper of p. BACON 25:32
p.-crammed SHAK 434:4
P., large promise JOHN 281:19
see how truly the P. runs KIPL 303:10
threaten, p. WHIT 571:11
Who broke no p. POPE 378:6
Why didst thou p. such SHAK 493:11
promised: long-p. invasion CHUR 150:4
p. land seem older than FRY 219:23
whom he had p. to defend MAC 323:21
promises: According to thy p. declared PRAY 384:13
having received the p. BIBLE 79:33
he was a young man of p. BALF 30:2
I have p. to keep FROST 219:12
may obtain thy p. PRAY 386:18
p. as sweet WORD 581:8
p. were, as he then was SHAK 447:19
promontory: like a p. sleeps or swims MILT 349:1
Since once I sat upon a p. SHAK 470:7
Promoted: P. everybody GILB 225:28
promoting: by p. the wealth BURKE 110:7
promotion: last p. of the blest DRYD 197:32
none will sweat but for p. SHAK 425:7
p. cometh neither from PRAY 394:26
prompt: foot less p. to meet ARN 15:9
P. hand and headpiece clever HOUS 265:1
prone: p. and emaciated figure HARDY 239:13
to piety more p. ALEX 3:15
pronounce: If I p. it chaste GILB 227:25
not frame to p. it right BIBLE 49:20

pronouncing: p. to yourself nimini-pimini BURG 108:5
proof: bliss in p. SHAK 495:7
lapp'd in p. SHAK 458:5
p. of stupidity than depravity JOHN 275:33
which is incapable of p. LEWES 314:7
proofs: p. of holy writ SHAK 475:23
Prooshans: others may be P. DICK 179:11
Proosian: French, or Turk, or P. GILB 228:10
prooving: method of p. Christianity WIS 575:10
Prop: P. and Ruin of the State CLEV 153:3
p. To our infirmity WORD 580:16
propagate: learn and p. the best ARN 16:1
likely to p. understanding JOHN 280:13
p., and rot POPE 379:15
propagation: know that peace and p. WALP 563:13
Was all our p. DONNE 188:22
propensities: excite my amorous p. JOHN 274:2
side of their natural p. BURKE 112:6
propensity: usual p. of mankind towards HUME 267:20
proper: always know our p. stations DICK 176:23
Climb to our p. dark YEATS 587:2
p. man SHAK 469:31
p. or improper FULL 220:10
p. study of mankind is POPE 379:12
p. subject of conversation CHES 146:4
P. words in proper places SWIFT 526:20
p. young men BURNS 114:17
properly: my time has been p. spent TAYL 531:26
Who never did anything p. LEAR 313:3
property: consider himself as public p. JEFF 272:17
give me a little snug p. EDG 199:20
Greedy for the p. of others SALL 413:22
P. has its duties as well DRUM 193:24
p. is ever to have mercy PRAY 385:23
P. is theft PROU 401:19
Propinquity and p. of blood SHAK 453:3
right of governing was not p. FOX 217:20
right to the p. of the rich RUSK 412:11
prophecies: p., they shall fail BIBLE 76:14
verification of his own p. TROL 553:5
prophecy: p. is the most gratuitous ELIOT 201:8
though I have the gift of p. BIBLE 76:14
trumpet of a p.! O, Wind SHEL 502:14
urn Of bitter p. SHEL 501:3
prophesy: eat exceedingly, and p. JONS 283:16
man may p. SHAK 442:3
p. deceits BIBLE 58:26
we p. in part BIBLE 76:14
your daughters shall p. BIBLE 61:15
prophesying: p. with accents terrible SHAK 460:20
voices p. war COL 156:29
prophet: I love a p. of the soul EMER 206:22
I'm the P. of the Utterly KIPL 303:1
In the name of the P. SMITH 510:9
Juxtaposition his p. CLOU 153:11
man put off the p. BROW 102:33
Methinks I am a p. new inspir'd SHAK 478:19
more than a p. BIBLE 66:2
p. is not without honour BIBLE 66:23
there arise among you a p. BIBLE 48:23
there is a p. in Israel BIBLE 51:27
What-you-may-call-it is his p. DICK 177:32
prophetic: her p. fury sew'd the work SHAK 476:4
p. soul! My uncle SHAK 431:9
something like p. strain MILT 342:11
With such p. greeting SHAK 458:13
prophets: at least the wisest p. WALP 563:18
Beware of false p. BIBLE 65:8

goodly fellowship of the P. PRAY 384:16
p. and kings have desired BIBLE 69:29
p. prophesy falsely BIBLE 60:18
Saul also among the p. BIBLE 49:41
this is the law and the p. BIBLE 65:5
thou that killest the p. BIBLE 67:26
unto the fathers by the p. BIBLE 79:28
Who spake by the P. PRAY 387:11
Propinquity: P. and property of blood SHAK 453:3
'P. does it' WARD 564:37
propitius: 'Sit Deus p. ANON 10:14
proponit: Nam homo p. THOM 546:10
proportion: Every man shouting in p. SURT 525:18
no p. kept SHAK 480:14
order or p. BROW 96:34
some strangeness in the p. BACON 25:28
proportioned: p. to the human constitution BERK 41:21
proportions: Founding a firm state by p. true MARV 331:22
proposal: 'Your p. comes too late LEAR 311:26
propose: if he do not p. DONNE 188:13
proposed: He p. seven times once DICK 178:24
proposition: undesirable to believe a p. RUSS 412:17
propositions: resolve the p. of a lover SHAK 426:8
propositum: Meum est p. ANON 10:14
propounds: Man p. negotiations KIPL 299:5
propre: moins p. à la société CHAM 139:14
proprie: Difficile est p. communia dicere HOR 257:17
propriété: La p. c'est le vol PROU 401:19
proprietor: of the p.'s prejudices SWAF 525:30
propriety: inseparable p. of time BACON 25:5
not always evince its p. AUST 23:25
Study first p. CALV 127:26
propter: Qui p. nos homines MASS 334:20
Proputty: P., proputty TENN 540:24
prose: connect the p. and the passion FORS 217:2
differs in nothing from p. GRAY 235:22
discourse and nearest p. DRYD 197:15
I love thee in p. PRIOR 400:21
is that p. MOL 353:3
Meredith is a p. Browning WILDE 573:37
only p. BROW 99:18
other harmony of p. DRYD 198:7
pin up my hair with p. CONG 160:37
p. is like a window pane ORW 365:15
P. is when all the lines BENT 41:2
P. on certain occasions LAND 309:10
p. run mad POPE 376:25
p.; words in their best COL 157:32
speaking p. without knowing MOL 353:3
that is not p. is verse MOL 353:4
That p. is verse BYRON 124:21
unattempted yet in p. or rhyme MILT 344:21
Proserpin: where P. gathering flowers MILT 347:21
prospect: dull p. of a distant good DRYD 196:18
noblest p. which a Scotchman JOHN 274:30
Though every p. pleases HEBER 244:6
prospects: all his p. bright'ning GOLD 230:20
gilded scenes and shining p. ADD 2:4
prosper: I grow, I p. SHAK 453:10
that shall keep it may p. KIPL 300:20
Why do sinners' ways p. HOPK 257:2
prospering: We shall march p. BROW 102:6
prosperitee: man to han ben in p. CHAU 144:11
prosperity: day of p. be joyful BIBLE 55:21
I will wish thee p. PRAY 398:12
jest's p. lies in the ear SHAK 457:17

one man who can stand p.	CARL 131:36
P. doth best discover vice	BACON 25:21
P. doth bewitch men	WEBS 567:14
P. is the blessing	BACON 25:18
P. is not without many	BACON 25:20
P.'s the very bond	SHAK 492:6
prosperous: race was most happy and	
p.	GIBB 224:24
prostitute: I puff the p. away	DRYD 198:17
protect: I'll p. it now	MORR 358:6
protection: gracious mercy and p.	
	PRAY 389:9
P. is not a principle	DISR 184:15
P. is not only dead	DISR 185:22
surrounded with His p.	MILT 352:1
use, and p.	BACON 25:1
us such strength and p.	PRAY 386:8
protector: p. of all that trust	PRAY 386:16
protest: lady doth p. too much	SHAK 434:11
Protestant: I am the P. whore	GWYN 237:8
P. counterpoint	BEEC 37:4
protestantism of the P.	BURKE 109:22
P., if he wants aid	DISR 186:16
P. Religion	CARL 131:3
Thy P. to be	HERR 249:25
protestantism: p. of the Protestant religion	
	BURKE 109:22
Protestants: only is the religion of P.	
	CHIL 148:12
Proteus: Have sight of P. rising	WORD 582:20
protoplasmal: p. primordial atomic	
	GILB 226:20
protracted: That life protracted is p.	
	JOHN 283:1
proud: apt the poor are to be p.	SHAK 489:23
Celia (since thou art so p.	CAREW 130:13
ever fair and never p.	SHAK 474:18
he hath scattered the p.	BIBLE 69:6
he was very stiff and p.	CARR 135:27
I have no p. looks	PRAY 398:25
I must be p. to see	POPE 380:20
know not whether I am p.	LAND 309:5
make death p. to take us	SHAK 423:18
man being too p. to fight	WILS 574:20
might grow p. the while	HERR 250:3
nation p. in arms	MILT 340:25
nor p. me no prouds	SHAK 483:17
not p. of those two eyes	HERR 250:1
Poets of the p. old lineage	FLEC 214:9
p. and angry dust	HOUS 264:22
p. and yet a wretched thing	DAV 172:11
p. as Priam murdered with	YEATS 586:22
p. full sail of his great	SHAK 494:11
p. in heart and mind	SHAK 454:18
p. of seeing our names	CHES 147:22
P. word you never spoke	LAND 308:25
tameless, and swift, and p.	SHEL 502:13
too p. for a wit	GOLD 231:17
we ain't p.	DICK 180:12
Who was so p.	ROCH 406:22
Why were they p.	KEATS 290:9
woman can be p. and stiff	YEATS 584:19
yet not p. to know	POPE 378:32
prov'd: Marlbro's mighty soul was p.	
	ADD 1:13
To have p. most royally	SHAK 437:30
prove: Believing where we cannot p.	
	TENN 535:29
I if thou wouldst p. me	CONS 161:25
let us p.	JONS 285:12
might p. anything by figures	CARL 131:15
P. all things	BIBLE 79:4
p. me	PRAY 399:8
p. me	PRAY 391:4
p. the sweetness of a shower	THOM 547:21
since I cannot p. a lover	SHAK 480:19
That Love would p. so hard	BRID 92:22
proved: God p. them	BIBLE 62:13
P. by statistics that some	AUDEN 20:10
p. me, and saw my works	PRAY 396:4

something or other could be p.	FRY 220:2
Which was to be p.	EUCL 209:1
whole you have p. to be	HARDY 239:21
proven: worthy proving can be p.	
	TENN 532:15
Provençal: P. song	KEATS 291:18
Provence: P. and La Palie	CLOU 153:24
Than you found it in P.	WILL 574:11
provender: nought but p.	SHAK 473:13
proverb: even a p. is no proverb	
	KEATS 294:18
p. and a byword among all	BIBLE 50:31
p. is much matter decocted	FULL 220:11
p. is one man's wit	RUSS 412:21
p. is something musty	SHAK 434:18
Proverbs: King Solomon wrote the P.	
	NAYL 360:10
Patch grief with p.	SHAK 473:6
provide: God will p. himself a lamb	
	BIBLE 46:10
wisdom to p. for human	BURKE 111:8
Provided: 'P. for'	DICK 177:16
providence: Behind a frowning p.	
	COWP 165:28
future to the divine P.	BACON 24:26
I go the way that P. dictates	HITL 251:10
I may assert eternal P.	MILT 344:22
inscrutable workings of P.	BIRK 84:16
P. kept it from being any	HARDY 241:11
P. their guide	MILT 350:1
Providential: case of P. interference	
	TEMP 532:8
province: all knowledge to be my p.	
	BACON 28:1
p. of knowledge to speak	HOLM 253:20
p. they have desolated	GLAD 229:13
provinces: obedience of distant p.	MAC 323:9
p. of his body revolted	AUDEN 19:3
provincial: was worse than p.	JAMES 271:9
proving: worthy p. can be proven	
	TENN 532:15
provision: Make not p. for the flesh	
	BIBLE 75:25
provocation: Ask you what p. I have	
had	POPE 380:19
in the p.	PRAY 396:4
provoke: fathers, p. not your children	
	BIBLE 78:7
voice p. the silent dust	GRAY 234:22
provoker: Drink, sir, is a great p.	
	SHAK 460:18
provokes: one p. me with impunity	
	ANON 10:15
prow: cove with pushing p.	BROW 102:14
sunrise an emerging p.	ARN 14:21
proximus: paries cum p. ardet	HOR 258:23
Prudence: P. is a rich	BLAKE 88:14
p. never to practise either	TWAIN 554:7
prudenter: p. agas	ANON 10:18
prudes: p., your envious railing	
	BURNS 114:16
With p. for proctors	TENN 541:27
prunella: is all but leather or p.	POPE 379:22
prunes: especially p. and prism	DICK 178:26
pruninghooks: their spears into p.	
	BIBLE 57:19
your p. into spears	BIBLE 61:16
prunus: p. and forsythia across	BETJ 43:12
Prusse: *l'industrie nationale de la P.*	
	MIR 352:19
Prussia: military domination of P.	ASQ 17:17
national industry of P.	MIR 352:19
Prussic acid: She drank P. without any	
	BARH 33:26
pry: lunar world securely p.	DRYD 195:23
psalm: cadence and subtle p.	AUDEN 18:3
sing to the harp with a p.	PRAY 396:8
Take the p.	PRAY 395:9
psalmist: David...the sweet p. of Israel	
	BIBLE 50:28

psalms: Church with p. must shout	
	HERB 246:26
David wrote the P.	NAYL 360:10
ourselves glad in him with p.	PRAY 396:3
p. and hymns and spiritual	BIBLE 78:5
sonnets turn'd to holy p.	PEELE 371:8
psaltery: p., dulcimer	BIBLE 61:3
Psyche: Your mournful P.	KEATS 291:14
Psychical: P. Research	COW 164:5
ptarmigan: p. that whitens ere his	
	TENN 534:37
pub: pavender, or p.	ST L 412:27
some one take me to a p.	CHES 146:12
public: abuse in p. and to read	BORR 89:26
complainers for the p.	BURKE 108:15
coquetry of p. opinion	BURKE 110:15
exempt from p. haunt	SHAK 424:32
for the p. good	COWP 164:28
man assumes a p. trust	JEFF 272:17
ministers to consult the p.	SWIFT 526:8
motive is the p. good	STEE 518:1
pot of paint in the p.'s	RUSK 411:7
principles of p. morality	BURKE 108:15
Private faces in p.	AUDEN 20:12
p. and merited disgrace	STEV 522:13
p. be damned	VAND 555:7
p. buys its opinions	BUTL 119:4
servants of the p.	GOW 233:7
shake the p. ways	COWP 166:37
things on which the p.	JOHN 281:37
this p. Way Streamed	WORD 582:4
three things which the p.	HOOD 255:15
Where they enter the p.	WHIT 570:15
publican: How like a fawning p. he	
	SHAK 465:29
publicans: Master with p. and sinners	
	BIBLE 65:22
not even the p. the same	BIBLE 64:20
public executions: taste for marriages	
and p.	DISR 186:25
publick: p. Prayer in the Church	PRAY 400:8
publicly: engage himself openly and p.	
	BLAKE 86:10
Public schools: P. 'tis public folly feeds	
	COWP 167:30
P. are the nurseries	FIEL 211:16
publish: I'll p., right or wrong	BYRON 124:15
P. and be damned	WELL 568:10
p. it not in the streets	BIBLE 50:16
p. it to all the nation	PRIOR 400:24
published: whatever you haven't p.	
	HOR 258:6
When a new book is p.	ROG 407:12
publisher: Now Barabbas was a p.	
	CAMP 129:15
p. is simply a useful	WILDE 573:33
publishing: too good to be worth p.	
	SHAW 498:10
Puck: just a streak of P.	HENL 245:12
pudding: Manningtree ox with the p.	
	SHAK 439:16
p. against empty praise	POPE 375:13
p. as well as translate	JOHN 273:31
puellis: Vixi p. nuper idoneus	HOR 261:6
puer: Quis multa gracilis te p.	HOR 259:15
pueris: p. placeas et declamatio	JUV 288:2
puerisque: Virginibus p. canto	HOR 260:13
puero: Maxima debetur p. reverentia	
	JUV 288:7
Se p.	HOR 257:21
puff: friends all united to p.	SWIN 529:13
I p. the prostitute away	DRYD 198:17
with solemn interposing p.	COWP 165:3
puffed: get one's self p.	TROL 553:14
p. up with this retinue	SHAK 442:15
puffeth: Knowledge p. up	BIBLE 76:5
puffing: p. is of various sorts	SHER 505:23
puffs: p. from the hookah-mouth	KIPL 297:28
pug: lovely O most charming p.	FLEM 215:4

pugilist: put in the p. (Lord Palmerston)
BAG 28:26
Pugna: P. magna victi sumus LIVY 315:12
puissant: noble and p. nation MILT 352:3
puking: Mewling and p. in the nurse's
SHAK 425:24
pulchrior: matre pulchra filia p. HOR 259:22
p. evenit HOR 261:12
pulchritudo: p. tam antiqua et tam nova
AUG 21:16
Pull: P. down thy vanity POUND 382:13
willing to p. his weight ROOS 408:2
puller: setter up and p. down SHAK 446:20
pulling: p. in one's horse as he HARE 242:4
pulp: p. so bitter THOM 548:19
pulpit: Politics and the p. are BURKE 111:2
pulpits: of their Babylonian p. BURKE 111:6
P. and Sundays HERB 248:10
Pulsanda: P. tellus HOR 260:3
pulse: My p. like a soft drum KING 296:12
Now feel that p. no more MOORE 356:9
people with the one p. MACN 326:11
p. in the eternal mind BROO 94:30
p. of feeling stirs ARN 12:22
secret vigour and a p. EMER 207:10
than feeling a woman's p. STER 519:6
very p. of the machine WORD 581:8
When the p. begins to throb BRON 93:21
pulses: are proved upon our p. KEATS 293:30
pulvere: dulcis sine p. palmae HOR 258:8
Pulveris: P. exigui iactu compressa
VIRG 560:18
P. Tormentarii, et Acus BACON 28:9
Pulvis: P. et umbra sumus HOR 261:16
pumice: Arido modo p. expolitum CAT 136:19
p. isle in Baiae's bay SHEL 502:10
pump: p. has frozen to-night GRAV 234:12
pumpkins: Where the early p. blow
LEAR 311:25
pun: could make so vile a p. DENN 174:24
pipe and exhaled in a p. LAMB 308:11
puñado: por un p. de monedas ZAP 588:18
punch: Some sipping p. WORD 580:2
punctilio: None of your dam p. MER 337:33
Punctuality: P. is the politeness LOUI 318:11
punctually: p. come for ever and ever
WHIT 571:4
punctuate: came in to p. my discourse
COL 158:5
Punica: P. fide SALL 413:25
Punish: P. a body which he could
DRYD 194:7
punished: p. everlastingly JOHN 279:17
p. in the sight of men BIBLE 62:13
should be p. with as severe PENN 371:16
punishment: All p. is mischief BENT 40:27
deserve not p. SHAK 457:4
My p. is greater than BIBLE 45:27
object of p. is MANN 328:13
power of p. is to silence JOHN 282:13
To let the p. fit the crime GILB 227:5
punishments: charged with p. the scroll
HENL 245:5
sanguinary p. which corrupt PAINE 368:4
punt: admit it is more fun to p. SAY 415:6
slow p. swings round ARN 14:14
story get out of the p. JOYCE 286:7
punto: cinco en p. de la tarde GARC 221:5
pupil: in years to be a p. now SHAK 478:11
pupils: Among the dead whose p.
BUTL 119:21
puplis: is the scripture of p. JER 272:21
puppets: shut up the box and the p.
THAC 545:29
whose p. BROW 103:25
puppy: let ev'ry p. drink WHYT 572:2
purchase: it is all a p. HOPK 256:29
p. pain with all that joy POPE 377:21
purchased: gift of God may be p.
BIBLE 73:30

purchasing: I am not worth p. REED 405:9
pure: Because my heart is p. TENN 543:8
be more p. than his maker BIBLE 52:16
Blessed are the p. in heart BIBLE 64:6
If I have led a p. life CAT 137:11
Is she not p. gold BROW 105:10
Live p. TENN 534:5
most particularly p. young GILB 227:23
nation of p. philosophers BAG 29:2
pure all things are p. BIBLE 79:27
p. and eloquent blood DONNE 189:31
P. and ready to mount DANTE 171:15
p. as snow SHAK 433:12
p. mind who refuses apple-dumplings
LAMB 307:6
P., Ornate BAG 29:20
P. religion and undefiled BIBLE 80:11
so p. as you BUTL 119:18
That England was too p. ANON 7:7
what God declares P. MILT 348:7
whatsoever things are p. BIBLE 78:22
working out a p. intent WORD 578:21
pureness: in p. of living and truth
PRAY 386:11
purer: live the p. with the other SHAK 435:17
purest: p. and most thoughtful RUSK 411:24
p. of human pleasures BACON 26:18
purgatory: no other p. but a woman
BEAU 36:12
p. of men FLOR 216:1
To P. fire thou com'st BALL 31:7
purg'd: p. the air of pestilence SHAK 487:21
purge: I'll p., and leave sack SHAK 440:29
Let's p. this choler without SHAK 478:7
shalt p. me with hyssop PRAY 393:5
purged: had by himself p. our sins
BIBLE 79:28
purified: every creature shall be p.
MARL 329:8
purifies: that which p. us is trial MILT 351:24
purify: p. the dialect of the tribe ELIOT 202:25
Puritan: P. all things are impure LAWR 311:2
P. hated bear-baiting MAC 324:19
sometimes he is a kind of p. SHAK 488:22
Puritane-one: Where I saw a P. BRAT 91:24
puriter: *Si vitam p. egi* CAT 137:11
purity: brightness, p., and truth OTWAY 366:4
p., all trial, all obeisance SHAK 426:29
P. is the feminine HARE 242:5
purlieus: dusty p. of the law TENN 537:8
within the p. of the Law ETH 208:28
purling: p. stream ADD 2:5
purloins: p. the Psalms BYRON 124:23
Puro: P. e disposto a salire DANTE 171:15
purple: clothed in p. and fine linen
BIBLE 70:28
desire and p. light of love GRAY 235:17
gleaming in p. and gold BYRON 122:1
I never saw a P. Cow BURG 108:2
now p. with love's wound SHAK 470:8
p. testament of bleeding SHAK 479:13
So cool a p. KEATS 289:4
some p. patch or other HOR 257:11
what p. fritillaries ARN 15:8
purpose: ages one increasing p. runs
TENN 539:2
any p. perverts art CONS 162:5
are the measure of his p. NIGH 363:16
creature hath a p. KEATS 294:17
far-reaching in p. HOOV 255:24
himself except for a noble p. HERB 246:17
his prudent p. to resolve YOUNG 588:5
I embrace the p. of God TENN 540:19
Infirm of p. SHAK 460:11
mark of insincerity of p. BRAM 91:18
My p. is, indeed SHAK 488:25
p. in liquidity BROO 94:11
Shake my fell p. SHAK 459:2
supplies us with its own p. SHAW 497:1
time to every p. under BIBLE 55:12

To speak and p. not SHAK 453:5
unconquerable p. shall be realized
LAMB 307:28
what if I fail of my p. BROW 102:1
with p. of its own WORD 580:12
purposes: Can execute their aery p.
MILT 345:15
purposing: signify A thwarted p.
HARDY 241:8
purpureal: fields invested with p.
WORD 578:3
Purpureus: P., late qui splendeat HOR 257:11
purse: Costly thy habit as thy p. SHAK 430:19
empty p. BRET 92:3
fill thy p. with money SHAK 474:10
law can take a p. in open BUTL 118:19
p., my person SHAK 465:16
Put money in thy p. SHAK 474:9
this consumption of the p. SHAK 441:16
Who steals my p. steals SHAK 475:1
purses: Light gains make heavy p.
BACON 25:35
pursue: hearken if his foes p. SHAK 495:21
it will p. JONS 284:11
knowing it, p. DRYD 198:18
Love wist to p. THOM 548:11
Men must p. things which BACON 24:26
p. my reason to an *O altitudo* BROW 96:9
thing we all p. BEAU 36:10
what shadows we p. BURKE 110:21
who p. Culture in bands WHAR 569:8
will accipitrine to p. THOM 548:2
pursued: it is you who are the p.
SHAW 497:24
p. a maiden and clasped SHEL 501:4
pursues: still the world p. ELIOT 204:24
pursueth: wicked flee when no man p.
BIBLE 54:41
pursuing: god p. SWIN 528:18
Still achieving, still p. LONG 317:5
yet p. BIBLE 49:18
pursuit: common p. of true judgement
ELIOT 205:15
full p. of the uneatable WILDE 573:27
in the p. of the blessing AUST 22:30
liberty and the p. of happiness ANON 8:14
Mad in p. SHAK 495:7
mental p. for the Building BLAKE 86:10
p. of happiness JEFF 272:6
P. of knowledge under difficulties
DICK 182:10
p. of perfection ARN 15:15
Strong in p. the rapid glede SMART 509:3
What mad p. KEATS 291:3
pursy: fatness of these p. times SHAK 435:16
purtenance: with the p. thereof BIBLE 47:17
purus: vitae scelerisque p. HOR 259:23
push: make one brave p. STEV 522:8
P. off TENN 544:3
p. the logic of a fact KIPL 299:5
Than tarry till they p. us SHAK 452:5
pushing: p. young particle GILB 227:28
pusillanimity: badge of p. and cowardice
SHAK 442:15
Pusset: Used to call his cat P. HARE 242:7
Pussy: What a beautiful P. you are
LEAR 312:11
Pussy-Cat: Owl and the P. went LEAR 312:11
put: by Baptism p. on Christ PRAY 388:11
never be p. out LAT 310:21
p. beneath Thy special BETJ 43:6
p. his hand to the plough BIBLE 69:25
P. it down a we DICK 182:1
P. money in thy purse SHAK 474:9
p. not your trust in princes PRAY 399:16
p. off the old man with BIBLE 78:26
P. off thy shoes from off BIBLE 47:4
P. out the light SHAK 477:5
p. too fine a point upon DICK 176:7
p. upon us the armour PRAY 386:4

p. up with bad things that   TROL 553:2
So p. that in your pipe   BARH 33:18
with which I will not p.   CHUR 151:6
puto: p. deus fio   VESP 556:12
Puts: P. on his pretty looks   SHAK 452:20
putty: p., brass, an' paint   KIPL 302:11
puzzle: problem must p. the devil
   BURNS 115:2
Rule of three doth p. me   ANON 6:18
schoolmasters p. their brain   GOLD 231:22
puzzling: This is a p. world   ELIOT 201:15
Pym: P. and such carles   BROW 99:26
pyramides: mais comme les p. ça ne
   FLAU 214:3
pyramids: p. they're just as useless
   FLAU 214:3
Pyramus: cruel death of P. and Thisby
   SHAK 469:23
Pyrenees: P. have ceased to exist LOUI 318:7
that tease in the high P.   BELL 40:13
Pythagoras: mystical way of P.   BROW 96:11
P. concerning wild fowl   SHAK 490:21
P.' metempsychosis   MARL 329:14
P. planned it   YEATS 587:1
this 'himself' was P.   CIC 151:20
python: mangrove swamps where the
p.   COW 163:20
Who bought a P. from a man   BELL 40:4
Quaäker: I knaw'd a Q. feller   TENN 541:1
quack: potent q.   COWP 168:28
Quad: always about in the Q.   ANON 4:29
no one about in the Q.   KNOX 305:22
Quadrigis: navibus atque Q.   HOR 258:19
Quadripedante: Q. putrem sonitu quatit
   VIRG 559:7
quadriviis: Nunc in q. et angiportis
   CAT 137:5
quadruped: hairy q.   DARW 171:23
quaesiveris: Nec te q. extra   PERS 372:26
Quaestio: Q. subtilissima   RAB 403:29
quaff'd: jested, q., and swore DOYLE 192:39
quaffing: q., and unthinking time
   DRYD 197:17
quagmire: Lost in the q.   TENN 534:22
quailing: No q., Mrs Gaskell   BRON 94:3
quails: we long for q.   DRYD 197:2
quake: aspes leef she gan to q.   CHAU 144:9
Quaker: out the Q. (Lord Aberdeen)
   BAG 28:26
qualify: absence seem'd my flame to
q.   SHAK 495:2
qualifying: love admits no q. dross
   SHAK 487:10
qualis: Non sum q. eram bonae   HOR 261:10
qualité: gens de q. savent   MOL 353:23
qualités: Des q. trop supérieures
   CHAM 139:14
qualities: Englishman a combination
of q.   DICK 181:12
In whom his q. are reigning   BYRON 126:6
of four q. the author   ARN 16:11
only two q. in the world   SHAW 497:5
Q. too elevated often unfit   CHAM 139:14
such q. as would wear well   GOLD 232:33
quality: composition and fierce q.
   SHAK 453:9
give us a taste of your q.   SHAK 432:22
his honour and his q. taken   BLUN 89:3
man of q. than to laugh   CONG 159:22
People of q. know everything   MOL 353:22
q. of his despair   CONN 161:16
q. of mercy is not strain'd   SHAK 467:27
q. to be exceedingly cheated   EVEL 209:7
qualms: Of those cold q.   SOUT 514:21
quanta: q. qualia sunt illa sabbata ABEL 1:1
Quantula: Q. sint hominum corpuscula
   JUV 288:3
quantum: I wave the q. o'the sin
   BURNS 113:17
Q. mutatus ab illo   VIRG 558:5

quarks: Three q. for Muster Mark
   JOYCE 286:12
quarrel: arm'd that hath his q. just
   SHAK 446:6
armed that hath his q. just   BILL 84:6
Beware Of entrance to a q.   SHAK 430:19
greatly to find q. in a straw   SHAK 435:31
justice of my q.   ANON 6:4
q. in a far-away country   CHAM 139:9
q. there is no true valour   SHAK 473:8
therefore a perpetual q.   BURKE 109:31
They quite forgot their q.   CARR 134:33
very pretty q. as it stands   SHER 506:20
quarrelled: I have q. with my wife
   PEAC 370:18
quarrellin: q. wi' the equawtor NORTH 364:4
quarrelling: set them a q.   HUME 268:2
quarrels: never strained by nasty q.
   HOR 259:21
of q. as an egg is full   SHAK 483:1
q. of popes and kings   AUST 23:4
quarry: lightless in the q.   HOUS 264:4
marked down q.   SHAW 497:24
Quarterly: 'I,' says the Q.   BYRON 125:1
quartern: q. loaf and Luddites rise
   SMITH 510:7
quarters: Sprinkle the q.   HOUS 264:28
to the wind's twelve q.   HOUS 263:17
quarto: them on a beautiful q. page
   SHER 506:26
quartos: Then q.   COWP 168:11
quarts: Pints and q. of Ludlow beer
   HOUS 264:13
quatit: Mente q. solida   HOR 260:18
Quatorze: Q. Le bon Dieu n'a que
   CLEM 152:30
quean: flaunting, extravagant q. SHER 506:31
Queen: am the Ruler of the Q.'s   GILB 228:4
Apparent q. unveil'd her   MILT 348:2
beggar maid shall be my q.   TENN 532:16
enchanting q. break off   SHAK 421:19
ev'ry lady would be Q.   POPE 377:25
fair q. in a summer's bower   SHAK 439:30
had seen the mobled q.   SHAK 432:24
Hail holy q.   ANON 10:19
he was the Q.'s luve   BALL 30:17
I'll q. it no inch further   SHAK 492:5
I would not be a q.   SHAK 447:2
laughing q. that caught   HUNT 268:9
life of our own dear Q.   ANON 5:20
Most Gracious Q.   ANON 6:17
Mother, Wife, and Q.   TENN 543:15
Move Q. Anne   VICT 556:16
Of life, of crown, of q.   SHAK 431:12
pale Q. of the silent night   BEST 42:2
Q. and Faith like a valiant   TENN 543:4
Q. and huntress   JONS 283:24
q. in a vesture of gold   PRAY 392:16
q. of curds and cream   SHAK 492:1
q. of England is looking   CHES 147:1
q. of Scots this day   ELIZ 30:17
Q. so furious that she   VICT 556:14
Q. was in a furious passion   CARR 134:5
remembrance of a weeping q.   SHAK 479:19
right-down regular Royal Q.   GILB 225:22
royal makings of a q.   SHAK 447:14
since I saw the Q. of France   BURKE 111:9
sometime sister, now our q.   SHAK 429:19
we love our Q.   GILB 228:24
who have lost their q.   FRY 220:7
Would grace a summer q.   SCOTT 417:30
Yestreen the Q. had four Maries BALL 31:12
Queen Anne: Q. was one of the smallest
   BAG 29:10
Queen Elizabeth: No scandal about Q.
   SHER 505:24
Q. of most happy memory   BIBLE 44:20
Queen Mab: Q. hath been with you...
   SHAK 481:28
Queen o' the May: I'm to be Q. TENN 540:20

Queens: beautiful Q. of this world
   DONNE 190:26
Q. have died young   NASHE 360:7
That all your acts are q.   SHAK 491:27
Queensberry: me and the Duchess of
Q.   WALP 562:22
queer: him ill-tempered and q.   LEAR 311:20
Medical Crowner's a q.   BARH 33:16
Q. are the ways of a man   HARDY 240:15
q. save thee and me   OWEN 366:29
quells: She q. the floods below CAMP 129:13
Quem: Q. fugis   VIRG 559:16
quench: If I q. thee   SHAK 477:5
Many waters cannot q. love   BIBLE 57:12
q. all the fiery darts   BIBLE 78:10
q. its speed i' the slushy   BROW 102:14
smoking flax shall he not q.   BIBLE 59:11
quench'd: What hath q. them hath
   SHAK 460:2
querimoniis: Divulsus q.   HOR 259:21
quest: to whose winding q.   VAUG 555:10
what thy q.   BRID 92:19
questing: fen passes the q. vole WAUGH 566:3
q. beast that had in shape   MAL 327:18
question: drop a q. on your plate
   ELIOT 203:19
Make that thy q.   SHAK 491:11
man with such a silly q.   STER 519:17
Others abide our q.   ARN 14:23
q. de Swann chez les Verdurin PROU 401:21
q. not to be asked   SHAK 439:14
q. with my jealous thought   SHAK 493:18
That man may q.   SHAK 458:10
that q.'s out of my part   SHAK 488:11
what is the q.   STEIN 518:19
who but infants q. in such   ROSS 409:20
questionable: com'st in such a q. shape
   SHAK 430:24
Questioning: Q. is not the mode of
conversation   JOHN 276:37
questionings: those obstinate q. WORD 579:10
questions: have answered three q.
   CARR 133:23
q. of will or decision   CHOM 148:16
q. the distempered part   ELIOT 202:21
Them that asks no q. isn't   KIPL 302:22
There are innumerable q.   JOHN 278:5
qui: Siete voi q.   DANTE 171:11
quia: Certum est q. impossibile est
   TERT 545:1
quibble: q. is to Shakespeare what
   JOHN 282:15
quick: bitten and pared to the q.   MAC 324:7
burgeons every maze of q.   TENN 537:18
judge the q. and the dead   PRAY 384:26
less q. to spring again   ARN 15:9
Q.' and some cry 'Slow'   TENN 541:26
q. spirit that is in Antony   SHAK 448:9
Touched to the q.   BROW 101:16
quicken: turn again, and q.   PRAY 395:14
quickened: eyes are q. so with grief
   GRAV 234:11
quickeneth: It is the spirit that q. BIBLE 72:8
quickens: faint east q.   SWIN 528:16
quickest: that q. in all the world   MOL 353:21
quickly: much good who gives q. PUBL 402:3
That thou doest, do q.   BIBLE 72:29
quickness: With too much q. ever
   POPE 377:21
quick'ning: not look upon the q. sun
   DONNE 188:9
quiddities: in thy quips and thy q.
   SHAK 438:3
Quidquid: Q. agas   ANON 10:18
Q. agunt homines   JUV 287:12
quiero: Que no q. verla   GARC 221:6
quies: prima q. mortalibus aegris VIRG 558:4
quiet: All q. along the Potomac MCCL 324:29
be q.; and go a-Angling   WALT 564:13
by this means cannot q.   PRAY 387:17

calm Peace, and Q.	MILT 341:27
Easy live and q. die	SCOTT 418:5
Fair q.	MARV 331:22
'Fie upon this q. life	SHAK 438:33
He sat as q. as a lump	AUDEN 21:7
In q. she reposes	ARN 14:5
lain still and been q.	BIBLE 52:12
Let us have a q. hour	TENN 544:7
lives of q. desperation	THOR 550:4
meek and q. spirit	BIBLE 80:28
my scallop-shell of q.	RAL 404:12
q. along the Potomac to-night	BEERS 38:8
q., grave man	BAG 29:11
q. mind	SURR 524:20
q. mind is worse than poverty	TRAH 552:2
Q. takes back her folded	JOYCE 286:9
Q. to quick bosoms is	BYRON 120:30
q. us in a death so noble	MILT 351:2
serve thee with a q. mind	PRAY 386:22
Study to be q.	BIBLE 79:1
this q.	KEATS 295:2
With q. hours	SHAK 440:14

Quieta: Q. movere magna merces — SALL 413:23
quieten: q. down by the throwing — VIRG 560:18
quietest: q. places Under the sun — HOUS 264:7
quietly: lie as q. among the graves — EDW 202:6
Q. they go — MILL 339:23
quietness: q. and in confidence shall — BIBLE 58:27
serve thee in all godly q. — PRAY 386:17
unravish'd bride of q. — KEATS 291:2
quietus: himself might his q. make — SHAK 433:8
quill: through a q. — LAMB 307:11
quillets: nice sharp q. of the law — SHAK 445:20
quills: q. upon the fretful porpentine — SHAK 431:5
tender stops of various q. — MILT 343:19
Quinapalus: What says Q. — SHAK 488:5
quince: slices of q. — LEAR 312:14
quincunx: q. of heaven runs low — BROW 95:19
Quinquireme: Q. of Nineveh from distant — MAS 333:18
quinta: La q. columna — MOLA 352:29
quintessence: heavenly q. they still — MARL 330:11
quip: q. modest — SHAK 427:5
quips: thy q. and thy quiddities — SHAK 438:3
quire: full-voiced q. below — MILT 342:10
q. of Saints for evermore — DONNE 189:14
Quires: Q. and Places where they — PRAY 385:4
quiring: q. to the young-eyed cherubins — SHAK 468:15
Quis: Q. rex — ABEL 1:2
quisque: Mens cuiusque is est q. — CIC 151:24
quit: age to q. their clogs — MILT 351:7
I are more than q. — PRIOR 400:24
I'll q. the port o' Heaven — NEWB 361:6
Q. in a single kiss — BRID 92:11
q. this mortal frame — POPE 376:3
Q. you like men — BIBLE 77:2
q. your books — WORD 582:22
Q. yourselves like men — BIBLE 49:38
soldiers may not q. the post — TENN 539:21
that dies this year is q. — SHAK 442:8
quiver: man that hath his q. full — PRAY 398:19
Quivering: Q. within the wave's intenser — SHEL 502:10
Quo: Q. vadis — BIBLE 83:21
quocumque: q. moveris — LUCAN 320:1
quodcumque: Jupiter est q. vides — LUCAN 320:1
Quot: Q. homines tot sententiae — TER 544:19
quotation: Every q. contributes something — JOHN 281:7
quotations: Back'd his opinion with q. — PRIOR 401:2
book that furnishes no q. — PEAC 370:12

I hate q.	EMER 207:44
man to read books of q.	CHUR 150:24

quote: I'll kill you if you q. — BURG 108:3
we all q. — EMER 208:1
quoter: sentence is the first q. of it — EMER 208:2
Quoth: Q. the Raven — POE 375:6
quotidianum: panem nostrum q. da nobis — MASS 335:5
quotidienne: que la vie est q. — LAF 306:23
Quoting: Q., for shallow conversational — SASS 414:19
Quousque: Q. tandem abutere — CIC 151:25
rabbit: There is a r. in a snare — STEP 518:26
rabble: army would be a base r. — BURKE 110:5
Rabelais: soul of R. dwelling in a dry — COL 158:2
race: All is r. — DISR 186:36
Another r. hath been — WORD 579:14
avails the sceptred r. — LAND 308:26
Foal of an oppressed r. — COL 157:16
forget the human r. — BYRON 121:21
giant r. before the flood — DRYD 196:1
happiness of the human r. — BURKE 110:7
hindered in running the r. — PRAY 386:6
idiot r. to honour — BURNS 114:29
in the history of our r. — CHUR 150:8
like the rest of my r. — BLAKE 86:15
loftier r. — SYM 531:3
longer tolerate the r. — BALF 30:3
lovely ere his r. be run — BYRON 121:37
lull in the hot r. — ARN 12:22
men and women with our r. — KIPL 298:10
most pernicious r. of little — SWIFT 526:5
My r. of glory run — MILT 350:23
now a new r. descends from — VIRG 559:22
of Europe's stone age r. — BETJ 43:8
r. is not to the swift — BIBLE 55:30
r. is run by one and one — KIPL 303:19
r. that is set before us — BIBLE 79:35
r. that long in darkness — SCOT 419:7
ran his godly r. — GOLD 230:22
run the r. with Death — JOHN 279:24
Rushes life in a r. — MER 336:26
That still a godly r. he — GOLD 231:10
they which run in a r. — BIBLE 76:8
till thou run out thy r. — MILT 344:17
tree did end their r. — MARV 332:2
unprotected r. — CLARE 152:11
whose r. is just begun — SHEL 504:17
wish I loved the Human R. — RAL 404:20
races: Some r. increase — LUCR 320:7
Rachel: R. weeping for her children — BIBLE 63:34
seven years for R. — BIBLE 46:21
racial: r. pride shall tower like — AUDEN 19:11
that makes r. difference — CONR 161:23
rack: Leave not a r. behind — SHAK 485:20
r. dislimns — SHAK 423:8
r. of a too easy chair — POPE 375:25
r. of this tough world — SHAK 456:12
racked: r. with deep despair — MILT 345:4
racket: r. is back in its press — BETJ 44:6
rackets: match'd our r. to these balls — SHAK 443:11
radiance: beautiful r. of the gods — SCH 415:9
My r. rare and fathomless — HARDY 241:6
radiant: r. maiden whom the angels — POE 375:5
radical: r. is a man with both feet — ROOS 407:24
radicals: r. have good digestions — BUTL 118:31
radio: caelique meatus Describent r. — VIRG 559:1
radish: like a forked r. — SHAK 442:10
r. and an egg — COWP 167:14
Rafael: R. made a century of sonnets — BROW 102:28
R. of the dear Madonnas — BROW 103:1
raft: republic is a r. which — AMES 4:3

rafte: he r. hire maydenhed — CHAU 143:23
rafters: lowly sheds With smoky r. — MILT 341:6
stars come down from the r. — AUDEN 18:13
rag: bloomin' old r. over 'ead — KIPL 304:10
r. and a bone and a hank — KIPL 303:29
rag-and-bone: foul r. shop of the heart — YEATS 584:15
rage: ape an ancient r. — CHES 147:3
captive void of noble r. — TENN 536:15
heathen so furiously r. — PRAY 389:15
Heav'n has no r. — CONG 160:15
horrible that lust and r. — YEATS 586:23
humour temp'ring virtuous r. — POPE 378:8
I r., I melt, I burn — GAY 222:6
nature with hard-favour'd r. — SHAK 443:21
Not die here in a r. — SWIFT 526:24
nothing but a r. to live — POPE 377:21
Puts all Heaven in a R. — BLAKE 85:9
r. against the dying — THOM 546:23
r. of Caliban — WILDE 573:16
replete with too much r. — SHAK 493:2
rights be term'd a poet's r. — SHAK 492:27
this r. shall beauty hold — SHAK 494:4
writing increaseth r. — GREV 236:17
rages: Dog-star r. — POPE 376:18
older that the weight of r. — SPOO 517:8
Sudden she r. — GAY 223:8
raggedness: looped and window'd r. — SHAK 454:15
raging: meet the r. of the skies — CAMP 129:3
r. of the sea — PRAY 394:1
strong drink is r. — BIBLE 54:15
ragioniam: Non r. di lor — DANTE 171:4
rags: Arm it in r. — SHAK 455:20
fond of my r. and tatters — MOL 353:11
righteousnesses are as filthy r. — BIBLE 60:12
when in r. and contempt — BUNY 107:19
which are the r. of time — DONNE 190:12
rag-time: Lurching to r. tunes — SASS 414:12
raid: indemnity...for r. by Dr Jameson — KRUG 306:1
rail: all night groan on the r. — HOUS 262:16
any body else to r. at me — CONG 160:17
folks r. against other folks — FIEL 211:17
her six young on the r. — BROW 101:19
Say that she r. — SHAK 484:8
than to r. at the ill — TENN 540:19
railing: prudes, your envious r. — BURNS 114:16
R. at life — CHUR 148:32
railing for r. — BIBLE 80:30
railroad: You enterprised a r. — RUSK 411:13
rails: purgatorial r. — KEATS 289:10
r. against all married — SHAK 469:14
Star-spiked R. a fiery Smite — THOM 549:2
Railway: Beautiful R. Bridge — MCG 325:6
railway-share: threatened its life with a r. — CARR 133:8
raiment: body than r. — BIBLE 64:28
King in r. of needlework — PRAY 392:17
man clothed in soft r. — BIBLE 66:2
r. of camel's hair — BIBLE 63:37
rain: able to command the r. — PEPYS 372:5
after the r. when with — SHEL 500:7
again I dissolve it in r. — SHEL 500:4
arbour where the r. beat — ELIOT 202:16
clouds and wind without r. — BIBLE 54:27
clouds return after the r. — BIBLE 56:11
droppeth as the gentle r. — SHAK 467:27
Dull roots with spring r. — ELIOT 204:17
former and the latter r. — PRAY 386:3
Hath the r. a father — BIBLE 53:4
Jupiter the R.-giver — TIB 551:1
look of hard wet r. — CHAN 139:20
more smell the dew and r. — HERB 247:22
neither let there be r. — BIBLE 50:16
r., and sun — TENN 534:2
r. came heavily and fell — WORD 580:27
r. descended — BIBLE 65:12
r. into the little valleys — PRAY 394:3

r. is over and gone   BIBLE 56:22
r. it raineth on the just   BOWEN 90:22
r. it raineth every day   SHAK 490:27
r. set early in to-night   BROW 103:28
sendeth r. on the just   BIBLE 64:19
send my roots r.   HOPK 257:3
small rain down can r.   ANON 8:16
sound of abundance of r.   BIBLE 51:10
Still falls the R.   SITW 508:13
sun and the r. Clash   FRY 219:26
thirsty earth soaks up the r.   COWL 164:7
Though the r. it raineth   SHAK 454:12
thresh of the deep-sea r.   KIPL 300:23
thro' the drizzling r.   TENN 536:6
volleying r. and tossing breeze   ARN 15:5
Weather and r. have undone   KIPL 303:31
with ranging in the r.   GREE 236:8
rainbow: another hue Unto the r.
   SHAK 452:25
awful r. once in heaven   KEATS 290:27
heart is like a r. shell   ROSS 408:23
It was the R. gave thee   DAV 172:16
on the r. of the salt sand-wave   KEATS 291:15
r. and a cuckoo's song   DAV 172:15
r. comes and goes   WORD 578:22
r. in the sky   TENN 534:2
r. in the sky   WORD 578:19
r. round about the throne   BIBLE 81:22
r.'s glory is shed   SHEL 501:21
rain'd: it r. kisses   SHAK 422:19
rain-drop: names the r. ploughs
   HARDY 239:10
rained: r. down manna also upon   PRAY 395:6
Raineth: R. drop and staineth slop
   POUND 382:4
rain it r. on the just   BOWEN 90:22
rainfall: r. at morning and dewfall
   STEV 522:29
rains: he is dissolving in r.   SHEL 500:5
rainy: not a windy night a r.   SHAK 494:14
r. day and a contentious   BIBLE 54:39
raise: contrivance to r. prices   SMITH 509:10
Lord shall r. me up   RAL 404:15
r. the price of corn   BYRON 119:26
R. the stone   ANON 7:11
to r. the wretched than   GOLD 230:22
what a dust do I r.   BACON 27:33
raised: Behold a man r. up by Christ
   TENN 536:18
Christ being r. from   BIBLE 75:2
dead shall be r. incorruptible   BIBLE 76:29
it is r. in incorruption   BIBLE 76:27
r. the price of everything   MAC 323:15
raising: r. corn and begin raising LEASE 313:4
raison: r. du plus fort est toujours
   LA F 306:21
r. tonne en son cratère   POTT 382:3
tout le monde a r.   LA C 306:16
raisons: Le coeur a ses r. que la PASC 369:10
rake: thus playing the r.   MOORE 356:29
was his hors as a r.   CHAU 141:23
woman is at heart a r.   POPE 377:25
rakes: scholar among r.   MAC 324:13
raking: when to stop r. the muck ROOS 408:4
rallies: voice of the schoolboy r.   NEWB 361:9
Rally: R. behind the Virginians   BEE 37:3
Ralph: Sir R. the Rover tore his   SOUT 514:3
ram: r. caught in a thicket   BIBLE 46:11
Rama: R. was there a voice heard
   BIBLE 63:34
ramas: Verde r.   GARC 221:7
Rampage: On the R.   DICK 178:10
Ramparts: great honey-coloured R.
   YEATS 585:4
rams: hearken than the fat of r.   BIBLE 50:4
mountains skipped like r.   PRAY 397:16
My r. speed not   BARN 34:4
ran: It r. a hundred years   HOLM 253:8
r. before Ahab   BIBLE 51:12
r. his godly race   GOLD 230:22

R. purple to the sea   MILT 345:17
So they r. both together   BIBLE 73:6
they r. awa'   MCL 325:15
rancune: lune ne garde aucune r.
   ELIOT 204:10
random: r. are afterwards confirmed
   KEATS 293:11
randy: Porter-drinkers' r. laughter
   YEATS 587:8
rangers: Eight for the eight bold r. ANON 6:5
Ranges: look behind the R.   KIPL 299:2
Rangoon: chunkin' from R. to Mandalay
   KIPL 301:5
he can take R.   WELL 567:28
rank: my offence is r.   SHAK 434:27
r. pride   ADD 1:18
r. tongue blossom into   BROW 99:24
that when a man of r. appeared JOHN 278:32
things r. and gross in nature   SHAK 429:28
unassailable holds on his r.   SHAK 449:25
Will r. as an idyll   GILB 227:25
you will r. as an apostle   GILB 227:23
ranks: even the r. of Tuscany   MAC 322:22
seen in glittering r.   MILT 344:9
service r. the same with God   BROW 103:25
rank-scented: mutable, r. many SHAK 427:20
Ransack: R. the ocean for orient MARL 329:4
ransom: Of the world's r.   SHAK 478:20
rap: To r. and knock and enter   BROW 99:4
rapacious: r. and licentious soldiery
   BURKE 110:25
rape: r.! a rape   WEBS 567:6
subject to r. like fish   DONNE 190:2
Raphaels: they talk'd of their R. GOLD 231:21
rapid: This particularly r.   GILB 228:37
rapier: dubbed with unhatched r.
   SHAK 490:14
rapine: all the r. and injustice   SMITH 509:8
march through r. to disintegration
   GLAD 229:15
R., deceit   DONNE 190:4
rapping: r. at my chamber door   POE 375:4
rapscallions: All kings is mostly r.
   TWAIN 554:2
rapt: r. one   WORD 577:18
rapture: first fine careless r.   BROW 101:6
Modified r.   GILB 226:30
r. on the lonely shore   BYRON 121:22
raptures: r. and roses of vice   SWIN 529:5
Rara: R. avis in terris nigroque   JUV 287:20
rare: man of culture r.   GILB 227:20
r. in our pockets the mark   CHES 147:22
r. things will   BROW 102:29
Rich and r. were the gems   MOORE 356:16
raree-show: r. of Peter's successor
   BROW 100:3
rarely: r., comest thou   SHEL 503:25
rarer: made us r. gifts than gold   BROO 94:7
r. spirit never Did steer   SHAK 423:19
rari: r. nantes in gurgite vasto   VIRG 557:11
rascaille: of swich r.   CHAU 144:19
rascal: would rather be called a r. JOHN 277:9
rascally: r. yea-forsooth knave   SHAK 441:4
Rascals: R., would you live   FRED 218:23
there are r. in all countries   JOHN 278:1
rase: slowly r. she up   BALL 30:11
rash: Her r. hand in evil hour   MILT 349:16
He was not r.   GRAH 233:17
It is too r.   SHAK 482:16
rashes: Green grow the r.   BURNS 114:1
rassembler: On ne peut pas r. à froid
   DE G 173:17
Rast: aber ohne R.   GOET 230:15
Rat: Cat, the R., and Lovell   COLL 158:10
giant r. of Sumatra   DOYLE 192:26
How now! a r.   SHAK 435:1
it creeps like a r.   BOWEN 91:5
like a r. without a tail   SHAK 458:6
like the sound of a r.   BROW 103:17
poisoned r. in a hole   SWIFT 526:24

r. crept softly through   ELIOT 204:26
ratem: Commisit pelago r.   HOR 259:12
rather: I had r. than forty shillings
   SHAK 469:3
r. tough worm in your little   GILB 227:16
ratiocination: pay with r.   BUTL 117:14
rationabile: r., sine dolo lac concupiscite
   BIBLE 83:25
rational: between them and r. converse
   WOLL 576:10
men he can be r. and unaffected   AUST 22:9
These r. amphibii go   MARV 332:23
rat-riddled: rotten-runged r. stairs
   BROW 102:13
rats: bins for the thieving r.   DE L 174:4
rattle: hearing 'em r. a little   FARQ 210:1
Pleas'd with a r.   POPE 379:18
R. his bones over the stones   NOEL 363:19
r. of a globe to play withal   DRYD 195:13
spoilt his nice new r.   CARR 134:33
Rattlesnake: He thought he saw a R.
   CARR 133:12
ravage: Any nose May r.   BROW 105:15
rav'd: r. and grew more fierce   HERB 247:15
rave: age should burn and r.   THOM 546:23
soft hand and let her r.   KEATS 291:15
raven: doth the r. o'er the infected
   SHAK 476:7
locks were like the r.   BURNS 114:12
Quoth the R.   POE 375:6
r. himself is hoarse   SHAK 459:2
There comes Poe with his r.   LOW 319:8
ravening: inwardly they are r. wolves
   BIBLE 65:8
ravenous: They're a r. horde   GILB 226:14
ravens: obscene r.   SHEL 499:16
r. brought him bread   BIBLE 51:6
three r. sat on a tree   BALL 32:7
you have seen the r. flock   AYT 24:10
raves: madness wherein now he r.
   SHAK 432:2
To where the Atlantic r.   ARN 14:21
ravish: except you r. me   DONNE 189:9
ravish'd: r. with the whistling   POPE 380:1
you have r. me   WEBS 567:6
ravished: did not seduce, she r.   MER 337:25
have r. me away by a power   KEATS 294:27
least would have r. her   FIEL 211:11
'tis thou hast r. me   MARL 329:3
ravishment: r. its sweet   KEATS 289:3
such divine enchanting r.   MILT 341:4
raw: Eat not of it r.   BIBLE 47:17
ray: genuine night admits no r. DRYD 196:34
rayless: In r. majesty   YOUNG 588:1
raz'd: works to me expung'd and r.
   MILT 347:8
razor: r. ceases to act   HOUS 266:17
to hew blocks with a r.   POPE 381:18
Razors: R. pain you   PARK 368:18
reach: all things above his r.   OVER 366:6
I could r. the brittle   VIRG 560:4
r. should exceed his grasp   BROW 98:24
will r. the bottom first   GRAH 233:10
reached: heights by great men r. LONG 316:19
top of it r. to heaven   BIBLE 46:18
reaching: r. after fact and reason
   KEATS 293:19
r. forth unto those things   BIBLE 78:18
reactionaries: All r. are paper tigers
   MAO 328:20
read: authors whom they never r.
   CHUR 148:19
be r. but not curiously   BACON 27:14
day therein we r. no more   DANTE 171:10
do you r. books through   JOHN 276:13
early years I r. very hard   JOHN 273:26
fast as they can r.   HAZL 243:10
general r. without pleasure   JOHN 280:25
have r. and nobody wants   TWAIN 554:25
I cannot r. it   CHES 147:25

I never r. much — AUST 23:2
King George will be able to r. — HANC 238:18
little I can r. — SHAK 421:9
May r. strange matters — SHAK 459:3
Much had he r. — ARMS 12:15
none can r. the text — TENN 535:13
Not that I ever r. them — SHER 505:20
public and to r. in secret — BORR 89:26
r. a book before reviewing — SMITH 511:17
r. and perhaps understand — KEATS 293:26
r. a nod, a shrug, a look — SWIFT 527:29
r. an old one — ROG 407:12
r. a novel before luncheon — WAUGH 566:5
r. any thing which I call — LAMB 307:17
r. as much as other men — HOBB 251:23
R. God aright — QUAR 403:18
r. just as inclination — JOHN 274:31
r., much of the night — ELIOT 204:18
R. no history — DISR 186:4
R. not to contradict — BACON 27:18
r. Richardson for the story — JOHN 276:9
R. somewhat seldomer — BROW 99:7
r. the Bible day and night — BLAKE 85:22
r. when they're in trouble — HOUS 265:13
such wise hear them r. — PRAY 386:5
Take up and r. — AUG 21:15
teach the orphan-boy to r. — TENN 538:1
that they never r. — DISR 186:21
they're not the ones they r. — MART 331:10
to r., and censure — HEM 245:1
to r. a novel I write one — DISR 185:26
to write and r. comes — SHAK 472:27
Unborn shall r. o'er ocean — LAND 309:4
What do you r. — SHAK 432:7
Who ever r. him through — BURKE 111:17

readable: chief need is that it be r.
— TROL 552:14

reader: by delighting the r. — HOR 258:1
making the r. breathless — KEATS 293:24
R., I married him — BRON 93:15
r. seldom peruses a book — ADD 2:7
Sagacious r. of the works of God — COWP 167:5
said r. to rider — AUDEN 18:17
That ideal r. suffering — JOYCE 286:3
'Tis the good r. that makes — EMER 208:12
readers: common sense of r. uncorrupted
— JOHN 281:39
make your r. suffer so much — JOHN 281:3
r. to become more indolent — GOLD 232:1
so many of my r. belong — CHES 148:2
readeth: that he may run that r. — BIBLE 62:1
readiness: r. is all — SHAK 437:15
reading: distinguish what is worth r.
— TREV 552:10
invincible love of r. — GIBB 224:6
I prefer r. — SMITH 510:21
much pleasure in the r. — QUAR 403:8
Peace is poor r. — HARDY 239:15
picture of somebody r. — KEATS 294:16
R. goes ill with the married — MOL 353:13
r. is right which requires — JOHN 282:17
R. is sometimes an ingenious — HELPS 244:16
r. is to skip judiciously — HAM 238:12
R. is to the mind what — STEE 518:9
R. maketh a full man — BACON 27:20
soul of r. — STER 519:22
therefore not worth r. — AUST 22:21
There is an art of r. — DISP 187:9
writing's vile hard r. — SHER 506:37
your writing and r. — SHAK 472:28
reads: He r. much — SHAK 448:21
R. verse and thinks she — BROW 100:15
Who often r. — COWP 168:17
Who r. Incessantly — MILT 350:10
read'st: r. the eternal deep — WORD 579:7
ready: conference a r. man — BACON 27:20
he is always r. to go — LA F 306:22
I am r. to depart — LAND 308:20
is r. to be thy bride — BALL 30:9
most gracious and r. help — PRAY 388:5

necessity of being r. increases — LINC 314:20
pen: of a r. writer — PRAY 392:14
r. ere I call'd her name — PRIOR 401:5
R. to be any thing — BROW 97:24
r. way to virtue — BROW 96:25
real: any less r. and true — SHAW 496:14
Forms more r. than living — SHEL 503:6
r. till it is experienced — KEATS 294:18
realised: about in worlds not r. — WORD 579:10
Realism: dislike of R. — WILDE 573:16
reality: Between the idea And the r.
— ELIOT 203:10
Cannot bear very much r. — ELIOT 202:14
may always be another r. — FRY 220:9
parts for the time with r. — CHUR 150:5
shadows and types to the r. — NEWM 362:6
realm: this earth, this r. — SHAK 478:20
welfare of this r. do chiefly — CHAR 140:21
realms: calls up the r. of fairy — BYRON 123:15
Napoleon of the r. of rhyme — BYRON 123:31
r. and islands were — SHAK 423:22
travell'd in the r. of gold — KEATS 292:17
reap: clouds shall not r. — BIBLE 56:7
neither do they r. — BIBLE 64:28
r. his old reward — KIPL 304:8
r., if we faint not — BIBLE 77:20
r. thou shouldst but glean — HOOD 255:5
shall r. in joy — PRAY 398:17
that shall he also r. — BIBLE 77:19
they shall r. the whirlwind — BIBLE 61:11
you r. a habit — READE 405:4
reaped: which never should be r.
— TRAH 551:18
reaper: Time the r. — THOM 548:28
reapers: Only r. — TENN 538:5
reaping: ever r. something new — TENN 538:24
r. where thou hast not — BIBLE 68:3
That grew the more by r. — SHAK 423:22
reaps: hurry and r. indigestion — STEV 522:5
seed ye sow, another r. — SHEL 504:3
rear: bring up the r. in heaven — BROW 96:26
she shall r. my dusky race — TENN 539:6
to r. the tender thought — THOM 549:10
whose post lay in the r. — ROSS 408:25
rearward: r. of a conquer'd woe — SHAK 494:14
reason: against the r. of my Love'
— KEATS 294:27
all r. is against it — BUTL 119:3
Blest with plain r. — POPE 378:9
bound To rules of r. — HERB 248:10
capability and god-like r. — SHAK 435:29
decision or r. or choice — CHOM 148:16
Divorced old barren R. — FITZ 213:1
false rules pranked in r.'s — MILT 341:19
feast of r. and the flow — POPE 380:5
gentle r. so persuasive stole — THOM 549:26
Give you a r. on compulsion — SHAK 439:5
had the full use of my r. — CHES 145:23
has been endowed with r. — CHEK 145:4
How noble in r. — SHAK 432:15
humanity, r., and justice — BURKE 109:26
ideal of r. but of imagination — KANT 288:12
if it be against r. — COKE 154:17
in erring r.'s spite — POPE 379:11
join compliance with r. — BURKE 111:26
kills r. itself — MILT 351:22
man who listens to R. is — SHAW 498:2
men have lost their r. — SHAK 450:22
men that can render a r. — BIBLE 54:35
Mere r. is insufficient — HUME 267:21
noble and most sovereign r. — SHAK 433:15
nothing is law that is not r. — POW 384:2
now R. is past care — SHAK 495:15
Now tell me the r. — SOUT 514:8
other but a woman's r. — SHAK 490:30
our r. is our law — MILT 349:15
private r. for this — AUDEN 21:1
pursue my r. to an *O altitudo* — BROW 96:9
r. abuseth me — KYD 306:5
r. and the will of God — ARN 15:15

R., an *ignis fatuus* — ROCH 406:21
r. can imagine or desire — TRAH 552:1
r. doth buckle and bow — BACON 24:19
r. firm — WORD 581:8
R. has moons — HODG 252:5
R. in her most exalted — WORD 580:26
r. I should be the same — AYT 24:4
R. is not come to repeat — SANT 214:2
R. is the life of the law — COKE 154:18
R. to rule — DRYD 196:14
r. why gunpowder treason — ANON 7:10
received nor rhyme nor r. — SPEN 516:29
right deed for the wrong r. — ELIOT 204:4
strong and the human r. weak — BAG 28:30
that great enemy of r. — BROW 96:30
That takes the r. prisoner — SHAK 458:15
that wants discourse of r. — SHAK 429:28
Their's not to r. why — TENN 532:24
they do always r. themselves — SHAK 445:13
voice of r. is stifled — BURKE 110:10
What can we r. — POPE 379:2
will not R. and Compare — BLAKE 86:2
words clothed in r.'s — MILT 346:12
Reasonable: figure of 'The R. Man'
— HERB 246:15
r. moderator and equal — BROW 96:19
r. man could have expected — HERB 246:19
r. man adapts himself — SHAW 498:1
r. soul and human flesh — PRAY 385:21
reasonableness: secret and sweet r.
— ARN 16:22
reasonably: may r. be expected to do
— WHAT 569:13
reason'd: r. high Of providence — MILT 346:19
reasoned: r. or acted consequentially
— CHES 145:25
reasoners: talkers or most plausible r.
— HAZL 243:24
reasoning: r. engine lies — ROCH 406:22
r., self-sufficing thing — WORD 580:4
truth by consecutive r. — KEATS 293:16
reasons: five r. we should drink — ALDR 3:10
Good r. must — SHAK 451:26
His r. are as two grains — SHAK 465:15
never give your r. — MANS 328:17
R. are not like garments — ESSEX 208:24
r. find of settled gravity — SHAK 493:14
r. for living — JUV 287:25
undemocratic r. and for motives — KIPL 302:5
We have forty million r. — KIPL 300:21
reasons of state: r. to influence our
judgments — MANS 328:16
reason'st: thou r. well — ADD 1:24
reave: my two troubles they r. — HOUS 266:7
rebel: life, a very r. — SHAK 423:4
R. and Atheist too — DONNE 189:26
street came the r. tread — WHIT 571:16
rebellatrix: r., tandem — OVID 366:22
rebelled: Because they r. against — PRAY 397:7
rebellion: if r. was the certain consequence
— MANS 328:16
little r. now and then — JEFF 272:9
r. against the existing — SHAW 496:27
r. broached on his sword — SHAK 445:7
r. is as the sin of witchcraft — BIBLE 50:4
R. lay in his way — SHAK 440:15
R. to tyrants is obedience — BRAD 91:12
rum, Romanism, and r. — BURC 108:1
rebellious: Hot and r. liquors in my
— SHAK 425:5
r. arm 'gainst arm — SHAK 458:5
revolting and a r. heart — BIBLE 60:17
rebels: subjects are r. from principle
— BURKE 111:13
rebounds: unless it r. — JOHN 276:20
rebuild: r. it on the old plan — MILL 339:3
rebuke: Open r. is better than — BIBLE 54:37
r. hath broken my heart — PRAY 394:12
· to r. the people — PRAY 399:24
rebus: *Cedet amor r.* — OVID 366:21

recall: greater sorrow than to r.   DANTE 171:8
themselves cannot r. their gifts   TENN 543:12
recall'd: once spoke can never be r.
                                         ROOS 408:9
recalled: anything that could be r.
                                          DISR 186:27
recedes: research the horizon r.   PATT 370:8
receipt: he had a special r.   DU M 199:5
sitting at the r. of custom   BIBLE 65:21
receive: blessed to give than to r.   BIBLE 74:19
r. one such little child   BIBLE 67:3
r. your reward in a certain place   BROWN 95:8
Then r. him as best such   BYRON 124:41
received: by him best r.   MILT 347:23
Freely ye have r.   BIBLE 65:31
his own r. him not   BIBLE 71:26
receiver: r. is always thought   CHES 145:9
receives: heart That watches and r.
                                         WORD 582:23
receiveth: Every one that asketh r.   BIBLE 65:3
receiving: giving and r. of a Ring   PRAY 389:7
recent: pushed by this r. people
                                         BURKE 109:17
recettes: r. qui réussissent toujours   VAL 555:1
Rechten: *seiner R. alle Wahrheit und*
                                          LESS 314:2
rechtwinklig: *die r. gebaut sind ab Leib*
                                         NIET 363:2
recipe: rare r. for melancholy   LAMB 307:23
recipes: *aggregate of the r. that*   VAL 555:1
reciprocal: r. civility of authors   JOHN 281:29
recirculation: commodius vicus of r.
back   JOYCE 286:2
recited: r. verses in writing   BIBLE 63:23
reckless: r. what I do to spite   SHAK 461:10
Restraining r. middle age   YEATS 586:8
reckoned: love that can be r.   SHAK 421:7
reckoning: No r. made   SHAK 431:12
sense of r.   SHAK 444:26
very much at your own r.   TROL 553:12
weary r.   SHAK 476:6
recks: r. not his own rede   SHAK 430:18
recognised: objects r., In flashes
                                         WORD 580:19
recognize: did not r. me by my face
                                          TROL 552:11
r. virtue and rot   PERS 372:27
recognizing: r. the gods that the city
                                          PLATO 374:8
recollect: does not r. where he laid
                                         JOHN 279:6
recommendation: face is a letter of r.
                                           ADD 2:15
face is a mute r.   PUBL 402:4
recompense: not because r. is a pleasure
                                         JOHN 282:4
reconciles: Custom r. us to everything
                                         BURKE 108:10
dinner and feasting r.   PEPYS 372:14
r. Discordant elements   WORD 580:11
reconciliation: silence and r. where the
enmities   MAC 323:20
reconnaissance: *La r. de la plupart des*
                                          LA R 310:1
record: Cannot see the r. cut   HOUS 263:2
puts a r. on the gramophone   ELIOT 205:3
recordanti: *r. benefacta priora voluptas*
                                          CAT 137:9
recorded: knowledge too but r. experience
                                          CARL 131:8
recorders: Of flutes and soft r.   MILT 345:21
Recording: domesticate the R. Angel
                                          STEV 521:33
passive, r., not thinking   ISH 270:28
R. Angel, as he wrote   STER 520:5
records: away all trivial fond r.   SHAK 431:15
recover: it do seldom or never r.   SHAK 424:5
r. what has been lost   ELIOT 202:24
thou'lt r. once my dust   GRAH 233:16
thou might'st him yet r.   DRAY 193:21

recreant: calf's-skin on those r. limbs
                                         SHAK 452:16
that soldier a mere r.   SHAK 486:26
recreate: r. yourselves   SHAK 451:4
recreation: purposes of r. he has
                                         CHUR 149:20
recte: *Si possis r.*   HOR 258:10
Vivere si r. nescis   HOR 259:6
recti: *mens sibi conscia r.*   VIRG 557:18
rectum: *citraque nequit consistere r.*
                                          HOR 261:23
r. aut justitian   MAGN 327:3
recurret: *tamen usque r.*   HOR 258:18
recuvver: r. the use of his legs   DICK 180:8
red: good Tray grew very r.   HOFF 252:13
hectic r.   SHEL 502:8
In coats of r.   DE L 174:6
jolly r. nose   BEAU 36:5
Luve's like a r. red rose   BURNS 114:27
Making the green one r.   SHAK 460:13
more red than her lips' r.   SHAK 495:8
Nature, r. in tooth and claw   TENN 536:29
pays us poor beggars in r.   KIPL 304:9
r. flag flying here   CONN 161:10
Red lips are not so r.   OWEN 367:6
r. men scalped each other   MAC 323:21
r. rose from off this thorn   SHAK 445:21
r. wheel barrow   WILL 574:10
r. wherso thow be   CHAU 144:17
sky is r.   BIBLE 66:31
streaks of r. were mingled   SUCK 524:9
that never blows so r.   FITZ 212:15
thin r. line   RUSS 412:23
this cheek a little r.   POPE 377:16
vindictive scribble of r.   BROW 100:23
your raiment all r.   MAC 322:6
redbreast: r., sacred to the household
                                         THOM 549:23
r. sit and sing   COL 156:23
r. whistles from a garden-croft   KEATS 293:9
redder: His coomb was r. than   CHAU 142:32
rede: recks not his own r.   SHAK 430:18
redeem: down and r. us from virtue
                                         SWIN 529:11
redeemed: he hath r. Jerusalem   BIBLE 59:19
r. his vices   JONS 285:1
which were r. from   BIBLE 82:15
redeemer: know that my r. liveth   BIBLE 52:31
my strength, and my r.   PRAY 390:13
such and so mighty a R.   MISS 352:20
Redeeming: R. the time   BIBLE 78:4
redemption: married past r.   DRYD 197:1
Our great r. from above   MILT 344:3
r. of all things by Beauty   SHAW 496:22
Redemptorem: *tantum meruit habere*
R.   MISS 352:20
redeunt: *r. Saturnia regna*   VIRG 559:22
red-flannel: birds the colour of r.
                                         THOM 546:22
redire: *unde negant r. quemquam*   CAT 136:23
redress: Things past r. are now   SHAK 479:3
to r. the balance   CANN 130:8
redressing: ride abroad r. human wrongs
                                         TENN 534:11
redtape: than a r. Talking-machine
                                         CARL 132:1
reed: bruised r. shall he not break
                                         BIBLE 59:11
he is a thinking r.   PASC 369:11
maiden and clasped a r.   SHEL 501:4
nymph, but for a r.   MARV 332:2
r. shaken with the wind   BIBLE 66:2
staff of this bruised r.   BIBLE 51:38
thee the r. is as the oak   SHAK 428:22
reeds: cottages of strowed r.   MARL 330:11
Down in the r. by the river   BROW 98:6
hundred r. of decent growth   GAY 222:7
My worn r. broken   DE L 174:15
reeking: r. into Cadiz Bay   BROW 101:8
Reel: R. in a drunkard   CHUR 149:1

They r. to and fro   PRAY 397:10
reels: There's threesome r.   BURNS 113:13
references: always to verify your r.
                                         ROUTH 410:18
refin'd: r. with th'accents that   DAN 170:23
refine: correct, insert, r.   SWIFT 527:34
r. our language to grammatical   JOHN 282:5
refined: began to disgust this r.   EVEL 209:9
never be r. if I twitch   THOM 547:13
r. out of existence   JOYCE 286:18
This Englishwoman is so r.   SMITH 510;27
refining: unless restored by the r.
                                         ELIOT 202:26
Reflection: R., you may come to-morrow
                                         SHEL 504:25
reflections: melancholy of human r.
                                          BAG 29:18
without very mortifying r.   CONG 160:3
reflects: soon as he r.   GOET 229:26
reflex: across the r. of a star   WORD 577:26
reform: Beginning r. is beginning
                                         WELL 568:4
cured by r. or revolution   BERL 41:23
party of progress or r.   MILL 339:10
r. movement has a lunatic   ROOS 408:5
r.', the watchword   BRIG 93:2
To innovate is not to r.   BURKE 112:2
reformation: be plotting some new r.
                                         DRYD 197:12
reforming of R. itself   MILT 351:27
reformed: speedily r.   MILT 351:20
reformers: All r. are bachelors MOORE 355:15
consolations of middle-aged r.   SAKI 413:3
Refrain: R. from the unholy pleasure
                                          BELL 38:23
refresh: to r. it when it was dry   PRAY 386:3
refreshed: giant r. with wine   PRAY 395:7
refreshment: I accept r. at any hands
                                          GILB 226:22
reft: th'orisonte hath r.   CHAU 142:13
refuge: eternal God is thy r.   BIBLE 48:33
God of Jacob is our r.   PRAY 392:20
high hills are a r.   PRAY 397:1
last weak r. in despair   THOM 549:19
they're so easy to take r.   IBSEN 270:3
thou hast been our r.   PRAY 395:17
refusal: great r.   DANTE 171:5
refuse: may know to r. the evil   BIBLE 58:3
Which he did thrice r.   SHAK 450:20
Refused: R. about the age of three
                                         CHES 147:9
stone which the builders r.   PRAY 398:2
refuses: Closes nothing, r. nothing
                                         WHIT 571:11
refute: this does not r. my general
                                         JOHN 275:27
Who can r. a sneer   PALEY 368:9
Regain'd: R. my freedom with a sigh
                                         BYRON 125:17
regarder: *On doit se r. soi-même* MOL 353:20
regardeth: r. the clouds shall not   BIBLE 56:7
regardless: r. of their doom   GRAY 235:12
regards: mingled with r. that stand
                                         SHAK 453:7
Rege: *R. quod est devium*   LANG 310:1
regeneration: madness and despair to
the r.   CONR 161:21
Regent: God bless the R.   SMITH 510:6
R. of love rhymes   SHAK 456:26
who revelled with the R.   BEER 37:16
reges: *delirant r. plectuntur*   HOR 258:12
regibus: *Maecenas atavis edite r.*   HOR 259:3
regiment: He led his r. from behind
                                         GILB 225:17
Monstrous R. of Women   KNOX 305:19
R. an' pokes the 'eathen   KIPL 298:21
regina: *r., mater misericordiae*   ANON 10:19
region: untrodden r. of my mind   KEATS 292:3
register: than the r. of the crimes   GIBB 224:23

register'd: r. upon our brazen tombs   SHAK 456:14
reg'lar: brought r. and draw'd mild   DICK 179:12
règle: r. de toutes les règles   MOL 353:6
Regnavit: R. a ligno Deus   VEN 556:6
regni: cuius r. non erit finis   MASS 334:20
regnum: adveniat r. tuum   MASS 335:5
regress: r. is either a downfall   BACON 26:23
regret: desire at last and vain r.   ROSS 410:6
   Immutable as my r.   PEAC 371:1
   I only r. that I have   HALE 237:14
   r. can die   TENN 537:5
   r. the departure of our   THOM 549:4
   wild with all r.   TENN 542:4
Regrets: past R. and Future Fears   FITZ 212:16
   series of congratulatory r.   DISR 185:16
   wild r.   WILDE 572:14
regular: icily r.   TENN 539:7
   r. Then most, when most   MILT 348:24
   right-down r. Royal Queen   GILB 225:22
regulate: we must r. all recreations   MILT 351:25
Regulations: R. Act   WILDE 572:12
Regumque: R. turris   HOR 259:13
Reichtum: gemeiniglich R. den grossen
   Eseln   LUTH 320:14
reign: Better to r. in hell   MILT 345:11
   friendless is to r.   SHEL 503:7
   had the capacity to r.   TAC 531:13
   my r. is peace   LAND 308:21
   Nymphs that r. o'er sewers   COL 156:5
   of the same sort of r.   BENT 40:26
reigned: that I have r. with your   ELIZ 206:5
reigneth: Thy God r.   BIBLE 59:18
reigns: king r.   THIE 546:5
   red blood r. in the winter's   SHAK 491:17
   r. thirty thousand years   MAC 324:21
reindeer: Herds of r. move across   AUDEN 18:16
   R. are coming to drive   AUDEN 18:7
reinforcement: r. we may gain from
   hope   MILT 345:7
reins: try out my r. and my heart   PRAY 391:4
rejected: despised and r. of men   BIBLE 59:21
rejoice: daughters of the Philistines r.
      BIBLE 50:16
   desert shall r.   BIBLE 58:32
   let us heartily r.   PRAY 396:3
   Let us then r.   ANON 10:13
   little hills shall r.   PRAY 394:3
   Making all the vales r.   BLAKE 87:26
   men r. when they divide   BIBLE 58:6
   R. in the Lord alway   BIBLE 78:20
   r. the heart   PRAY 390:12
   R. with them that do rejoice   BIBLE 75:16
   R. ye dead   BRID 92:18
   thou hast broken may r.   PRAY 393:5
   will r. and be glad in it   PRAY 398:2
rejoiced: my spirit hath r. in God   BIBLE 69:5
   R. they were na men   BURNS 116:1
rejoiceth: r. as a giant to run his   PRAY 390:11
   r. in his strength   BIBLE 53:6
rejoicing: what r. is there   ABEL 1:2
relation: just supply and all r.   DONNE 187:19
   nobody like a r.   THAC 545:24
   poor r.   LAMB 307:20
relations: Augurs and understood r.
      SHAK 461:24
   Bless the squire and his r.   DICK 176:23
   men have their poor r.   DICK 176:19
   new stock or to visit r.   AUDEN 20:2
   personal character and r.   NAP 359:10
relationship: r. with beauty and truth
      KEATS 293:18
relaxes: Bless r.   BLAKE 88:23
relearn: Let them r. the Law   KIPL 300:6
release: ensured r.   HOUS 266:5
relent: make the gods above r.   VIRG 559:5
   Shall make him once r.   BUNY 107:36

relenting: r. God Hath placed   ROSS 408:20
relic: cas'd up, like a holy r.   WEBS 566:20
   sad r. of departed worth   BYRON 120:13
relics: hallow'd r. should be hid   MILT 344:1
   other's hands these r. came   DONNE 188:28
   unhonour'd his r. are laid   MOORE 356:15
relief: Creator and the r. of man's
      BACON 24:17
   death is rather a r. to me   FITZ 213:19
   not seek for kind r.   BLAKE 88:8
   r. Must be to loathe her   SHAK 475:21
   this r. much thanks   SHAK 429:5
   utterance gave that thought r.   WORD 579:1
   which sleep provides r.   CHAM 139:13
reliev'd: desperate appliances are r.
      SHAK 435:25
relieve: it did r. my passion much
      SHAK 488:26
   thee to comfort and r. them   PRAY 386:1
religio: Tantum r. potuit suadere   LUCR 320:4
religion: airy subtleties in r.   BROW 96:8
   are really but of one r.   SHAD 420:24
   based either on r. or policy   RUSK 412:4
   brothels with bricks of R.   BLAKE 88:20
   England but vice and r.   SMITH 511:21
   enough r. to make us hate   SWIFT 527:7
   established a r. without a prelate
      BANC 32:13
   every thing that regards r.   ADD 2:21
   fatal to r. as indifference   BURKE 111:35
   fundamental principle of my r.   NEWM 361:20
   him about again to our r.   FULL 220:14
   I cant talk r. to a man   SHAW 497:13
   I count r. but a childish   MARL 329:19
   impossibilities enough in R.   BROW 96:8
   increase in us true r.   PRAY 386:19
   indirect way to plant r.   BROW 96:16
   inward tranquillity which r.   FORB 216:10
   is but an handmaid to r.   BACON 24:28
   is the r. of Protestants   CHIL 148:12
   men's minds about to r.   BACON 25:24
   more beautiful than any r.   SAKI 413:7
   more fierce in its r.   NEWM 361:19
   my r. is to do good   PAINE 368:5
   Notre r. est faite pour   MONT 355:1
   old r.'s sake   HERR 249:6
   One r. is as true as another   BURT 117:2
   Philistine of genius in r.   ARN 16:23
   r. and matrimony I never   CHES 146:3
   R. blushing veils her sacred   POPE 376:1
   r. breathing household   WORD 582:9
   r. ends   BURKE 108:12
   R. es la caballería   CERV 138:15
   r., I hold it to be   PAINE 367:23
   r. is allowed to invade   MELB 336:13
   R. is by no means a proper   CHES 146:4
   R. is knight-errantry   CERV 138:15
   R. the opium of the people   MARX 333:6
   r. most prevalent in our   BURKE 109:22
   r. must still be allowed   CHES 145:30
   r. of cold   BAG 29:4
   r. of humanity   PAINE 368:7
   R.'s in the heart   JERR 273:1
   r. when in rags and contempt   BUNY 107:19
   rum and true r.   BYRON 122:16
   slovenliness is no part of r.   WESL 568:22
   some of r.   EDG 199:20
   some other new r.   PLATO 374:8
   Superstition is the r.   BURKE 111:22
   suspended the sentiments of r.   BURKE 111:29
   sweet r. makes A rhapsody   SHAK 435:4
   take my r. from the priest   GOLD 232:41
   talks loudly against r.   STER 519:25
   that a man's r. is   CARL 131:28
   That is my r.   SHAW 497:11
   then Poetry and R.   CARL 131:7
   There is only one r.   SHAW 498:11
   this man's r. is vain   BIBLE 80:11
   To become a popular r.   INGE 270:6
   to profess any r. in name   BURKE 111:20

   true meaning of r. is thus   ARN 16:20
   was not a r. for gentlemen   CHAR 140:25
   We must have r. for religion's   COUS 163:9
   When I mention r.   FIEL 211:23
religions: are sixty different r.   CAR 130:10
   sort of collector of r.   SHAW 497:12
religioun: good man was ther of r.
      CHAU 141:32
religious: among you seem to be r.
      BIBLE 80:11
   constitution a r. animal   BURKE 111:18
   I hope I will be r. again   FLEM 214:29
   intellect in r. enquiries   NEWM 362:2
   not r.-good   HARDY 241:26
   r. and moral principles   ARN 16:26
   r. book, or friend   WOTT 583:13
   R., discountenance every   BLAKE 86:9
   r. factions are volcanoes   BURKE 111:32
   R. persecution may shield   BURKE 110:29
   that I suspended my r.   GIBB 224:11
   troubled with r. doubt   CHES 147:9
relinquished: only have r. one delight
      WORD 579:13
relish: r. of the saltness of time   SHAK 441:5
reluctance: superstitious r. to sit   JOHN 278:13
reluctant: with r. feet   LONG 316:20
rem: quocumque modo r.   HOR 258:10
remain: be amongst you and r. with
      PRAY 388:4
   up the fragments that r.   BIBLE 72:5
remained: else perished, and he r.
      BRON 93:25
   while anything r. to be done   LUCAN 319:24
remains: look at least on love's r.
      BROW 103:24
   nothing done while aught r.   ROG 407:7
   One r.   SHEL 499:26
   Strength in what r. behind...   WORD 579:13
remark: Which I wish to r.   HARTE 242:29
remarkable: there is nothing left r.
      SHAK 423:16
remarks: said our r. before   DON 187:17
remède: La mort est le r.   CHAM 139:13
remedies: encumbering it with r.   TOLS 551:12
   r. oft in ourselves do   SHAK 420:28
   that will not apply new r.   BACON 26:28
   When a lot of r.   CHEK 144:23
remedy: Force is not a r.   BRIG 93:7
   know not how to r. our own   KYD 306:4
   r. is worse than the disease   BACON 27:13
   requires a dangerous r.   FAWK 210:31
   sovereign r. to all diseases   BURT 116:29
   Things without all r.   SHAK 461:12
   'Tis a sharp r.   RAL 404:17
   true r. for superstition   BURKE 109:30
remember: can't r. how They go
      CALV 127:13
   don't you r. sweet Alice   ENGL 208:19
   Do you r. an Inn   BELL 40:12
   glad to r. even these   VIRG 557:19
   Half to r. days that have   FLEC 214:5
   he'll r. with advantages   SHAK 445:3
   If I do not r. thee   PRAY 399:3
   if thou wilt, r.   ROSS 409:8
   I r., I remember   HOOD 254:17
   I r. the way we parted   SWIN 530:10
   is to r. what is past   HAL 238:3
   I would r. Him   BEEC 37:9
   let not man r.   HOUS 264:27
   like to something I r.   FORD 216:19
   Must I r.   SHAK 429:28
   never r. whether it snowed   THOM 546:30
   not r. what I must be now   SHAK 479:14
   oafish louts r. Mum   BETJ 42:8
   power of beauty I r.   DRYD 195:32
   r. me when thou comest   BIBLE 71:12
   R. me when I am dead   DOUG 191:9
   R. me when I am gone away   ROSS 409:3
   R. now thy Creator   BIBLE 56:11
   r. of this unstable world   MAL 327:21

r. the Fifth of November ANON 7:10
R. the sabbath day BIBLE 47:24
r. the past are condemned SANT 414:1
R. thee SHAK 431:15
r. while the light lives SWIN 529:12
still r. me MOORE 356:8
& that no man r. me HARDY 241:18
Till thou r. and I forget SWIN 530:14
To r. with tears ALL 3:21
Well I r. how you smiled LAND 309:4
We will r. them BINY 84:10
when the iris blooms, R. COL 155:4
with names that men r. SWIN 529:14
you should r. and be sad ROSS 409:4
remember'd: flowing cups freshly r.
SHAK 445:3
r. for a very long time MCG 325:6
r. that he once was young ARMS 12:14
remembered: blue r. hills HOUS 263:22
He r. too late on his thorny PEAC 370:19
of my youth I r. my God SOUT 514:9
r. by some for their services VIRG 558:23
R. on waking BRID 92:10
r. Perishing be DE L 174:2
said anything that was r. DISR 186:27
would have made myself r. KEATS 294:28
Remembering: R. without ceasing your
BIBLE 78:30
R. him like anything CHES 147:17
soul r. my good friends SHAK 478:24
Remembers: R. me of all his gracious
SHAK 452:20
remember'st: r. not the slightest folly
SHAK 425:10
remembrance: appear almost a r.
KEATS 293:24
be had in everlasting r. PRAY 397:14
dear r. of his dying Lord SPEN 515:31
Do this in r. of me PRAY 388:1
Makes the r. dear SHAK 421:5
r. of a guest that tarrieth BIBLE 62:18
r. of them is grievous PRAY 387:19
r. of his holiness PRAY 391:13
r. of a weeping queen SHAK 479:19
r. of my former love SHAK 490:34
rosemary, that's for r. SHAK 436:10
summon up r. of things past SHAK 493:7
Writ in r. more than things SHAK 478:18
remembrancer: scented gift and r.
designedly WHIT 570:18
remembreth: Crist! when that it r.
CHAU 143:19
reminiscence: r. sing WHIT 570:9
Reminiscences: R. make one feel so
deliciously SHAW 497:2
remission: many for the r. of sins PRAY 388:1
shedding of blood is no r. BIBLE 79:29
to have r. of pain or guilt PRAY 400:9
remissly: sinewy proboscis did r.
DONNE 190:3
remnant: r. of our Spartan dead BYRON 123:2
remnants: some r. of history which
BACON 24:18
remomoring: deem r. of a cursed pean
VANZ 555:8
remorse: access and passage to r. SHAK 459:2
far rather feel r. THOM 546:6
R., the fatal egg by pleasure COWP 166:9
remorseful: r. day SHAK 446:8
remorseless: when the r. deep MILT 343:7
Remote: R. and ineffectual Don BELL 39:27
r. enquiries JOHN 281:40
R. from towns he ran his GOLD 230:22
R., unfriended GOLD 231:23
remoter: had no need of a r. charm
WORD 578:6
Remove: R. hence to yonder place BIBLE 67:1
R. not the ancient landmark BIBLE 54:23
remover: bends with the r. to remove
SHAK 495:5

renaissance: in her warm nest of r.
DAY-L 172:21
renascentur: Multa r. quae iam cecidere
HOR 257:14
rend: mais ne se r. pas CAMB 128:2
render: r. back from out thy breast
BYRON 123:2
r. The deeds of mercy SHAK 467:27
R. therefore unto Caesar BIBLE 67:20
R. therefore to all their BIBLE 75:22
rendezvous: I have a r. with Death
SEEG 419:15
My r. is appointed WHIT 571:2
rending: till the r. of the rocks JOYCE 286:4
renew: Although a subtler Sphinx r.
SHEL 501:1
Lord shall r. their strength BIBLE 59:10
r. a right spirit PRAY 393:6
renew'd: wish I were r. SHAK 495:4
r. is r. in knowledge after BIBLE 78:26
renewing: r. is of love EDW 200:5
renounce: r. the devil and all his PRAY 388:13
renovare: iubes r. dolorem VIRG 557:20
renown: land of just and old r. TENN 544:11
men of r. BIBLE 45:33
Speak no more of his r. TENN 541:15
rent: r. the envious Casca made SHAK 450:27
That has not been r. YEATS 584:19
When I widen the r. SHEL 500:6
why? for r. BYRON 119:27
repairs: anon r. his drooping head
MILT 343:17
repast: cups prolong the rich r. POPE 381:6
repay: I will r. BIBLE 75:18
I will r. thee BIBLE 69:32
Will find a Tiger well r. BELL 38:31
repeal: r. of bad or obnoxious GRANT 233:22
r. repeat: come to r. the universe SANT 414:2
repeateth: r. a matter separateth BIBLE 54:10
repeats: r. his words SHAK 452:20
repel: retard what we cannot r. JOHN 281:9
repent: from their marble caves r.
DRUM 193:25
have no strength to r. SHAK 440:1
I do r. it from my very SHAK 486:18
I hardly ever r. NASH 360:1
It doth r. me SHEL 502:21
No follies to have to r. TAYL 531:26
nor falter, nor r. SHEL 503:15
R. what's past SHAK 435:15
R. ye BIBLE 63:35
they r. in haste CONG 160:27
truly and earnestly r. PRAY 387:18
weak alone r. BYRON 121:33
we may r. at leisure CONG 160:27
repentance: morning cool r. came
SCOTT 418:29
R. is the virtue of weak DRYD 196:24
R. is but want of power DRYD 197:9
R. is the hire SCOTT 415:14
R. on a Sunday YBAR 584:7
sinners to r. BIBLE 65:24
There's no r. in the grave WATTS 565:15
To give r. to her lover GOLD 231:31
Where pleasure and r. dwell RAL 404:8
repente: Nemo r. fuit turpissimus JUV 287:14
repented: much r. BYRON 122:11
repenteth: over one sinner that r. BIBLE 70:17
repenting: In mirth, that after no r.
MILT 351:11
repetita: Occidit miseros crambe r.
JUV 287:24
repetitions: r., as the heathen do BIBLE 64:23
repine: 'Do not r.' DICK 179:7
replaces: pianola 'r.' Sappho POUND 383:5
replenish: r. the earth BIBLE 45:6
replete: thing r. with too much rage
SHAK 493:2
reply: I made r. HOUS 265:5
I pause for a r. SHAK 450:16

loving and a fair r. SHAK 429:27
r. churlish SHAK 427:5
Their's not to make r. TENN 532:24
Report: R. me and my cause aright
SHAK 437:23
whatsoever things are of good r. BIBLE 78:22
Who hath believed our r. BIBLE 59:20
reporter: I am a r. GREE 236:7
reporters: gallery in which the r. MAC 323:7
through r. to Buncombe CARL 132:4
reporting: r. device for experience
WHORF 571:23
reports: Bring me no more r. SHAK 462:28
repos: demeurer en r. dans une chambre
PASC 369:5
La gloire et le r. sont MONT 354:22
repose: dear r. for limbs with SHAK 493:5
Has earned a night's r. LONG 317:19
Pray for the r. of His soul ROLFE 407:17
r. is taboo'd by anxiety GILB 226:12
seek r. In listlessness WORD 580:6
sleep should be his last r. ANON 8:21
weave the garlands of r. MARV 331:21
reposes: In quiet she r. ARN 14:5
reprehend: If I r. any thing in this
SHER 506:14
represent: Unwillingly r. GILB 227:5
representation: Taxation and r. CAMD 128:4
Taxation without r. is OTIS 365:25
representative: expressed by himself
CAMD 128:4
or r. BURKE 109:11
Your r. owes you SHAW 497:7
represents: It r. health SHAW 497:7
repress: r. the speech they know
ELIOT 200:24
repress'd: ardour of my zeal r. CHUR 148:22
reproach: eternal r. of the divines
MILT 352:12
It is a r. to religion PENN 371:14
only hope to escape r. JOHN 281:5
Writing their own r. SHAK 486:19
reproche: Chevalier sans peur et sans
r. ANON 9:5
reproof: r. valiant SHAK 427:5
reproofs: r. from authority ought
BACON 26:25
reprove: sager sort our deeds r. CAT 136:25
r. all the rest POPE 377:4
reptile: first turn myself into a r. JOHN 274:19
republic: make in the r. of letters ADD 1:11
Only Love the Beloved R. FORS 217:13
r. a roll of honour CLEV 153:2
r. is a raft which will AMES 4:3
R. is a government in which BAG 28:30
were living in Plato's R. CIC 151:16
republican: acrimonious and surly r.
JOHN 281:33
R. form of Government is SPEN 514:28
Republicans: We are R. and don't propose
BURC 108:1
Republics: R. weak because they appeal
BAG 28:30
Repudiate: R. the repudiators FESS 210:34
repugnances: those national r. do not
BROW 96:28
repugnant: plainly r. to the Word of
God PRAY 400:8
Repugnare: R. ut detur vacuum sive
DESC 175:12
reputability: of r. to the gentleman
VEBL 556:1
reputation: At ev'ry word a r. dies
POPE 381:3
Dear for her r. through SHAK 478:20
ever written out of r. BENT 41:13
I have lost my r. SHAK 475:7
Is spotless r. SHAK 478:8
made himself of no r. BIBLE 78:13
Seeking the bubble r. SHAK 425:14
sold my R. for a Song FITZ 213:13

wink a r. down   SWIFT 527:29
wrinkle and the r. of five-and-twenty
    DRYD 196:36
reputations: large home of ruined r.
    ELIOT 201:5
sit upon the murdered r.   CONG 160:32
true fuller's earth for r.   GAY 222:17
reputed: therefore only are r. wise
    SHAK 465:12
request: be ruined at our own r. MORE 357:10
No flowers, by r.   AING 3:6
Requiem: R. aeternam dona eis MASS 334:17
thy high r. become a sod   KEATS 291:22
To sing a r.   SHAK 437:3
Requiescat: R. in pace   MASS 335:10
require: men in women do r.   BLAKE 86:17
What doth the Lord r.   BIBLE 61:25
required: captive r. of us then a song
    PRAY 399:3
night thy soul shall be r.   BIBLE 70:5
of him can nothing be r.   FIEL 211:13
requisite: first r. of a good citizen ROOS 408:2
r. in business than dispatch   ADD 1:12
requited: how ill r.   SHAK 487:19
rerum: Sunt lacrimae r.   VIRG 557:17
res: festinat et in medias r.   HOR 257:20
r. age   OVID 366:21
R. angusta domi   JUV 287:18
rescue: Thus did Apollo r. me   HOR 262:6
research: r. is always incomplete PATT 370:8
resemble: we will r. you in that   SHAK 467:4
resented: is never r. for an offence
    SWIFT 527:3
Who r. it   COW 164:5
resentment: difficult to get up r.
    NEWM 361:13
reserv'd: Alike r. to blame   POPE 376:27
reserve: r. the more weighty voice
    BACON 25:41
reserved: life it is r. only for God
    BACON 24:24
r. for some end or other   CLIVE 153:6
residuum: to this vast r. we may   ARN 15:20
resignation: by r. none   JEFF 272:15
While r. gently slopes   GOLD 230:20
resigned: I am not r.   MILL 339:23
resist: fascination that few can r. GILB 227:10
I never r. temptation   SHAW 496:5
r. everything except temptation WILDE 573:8
R. not evil   BIBLE 64:17
resistance: r. of the Tolbooth-gate
    SCOTT 418:19
resisted: know not what's r.   BURNS 112:26
resisting: over-fond of r. temptation
    BECK 36:21
resistless: r. course was given SCOTT 416:28
resolution: Certain my r. is to die
    MILT 349:18
In war, r.   CHUR 150:25
r. thus fobbed as it is   SHAK 438:4
results of thought and r.   TROL 553:11
thus the native hue of r.   SHAK 433:8
what r. from despair   MILT 345:7
resolutions: governs the passions and
r.   HUME 267:22
Of great and mighty r.   BUTL 117:28
resolv'd: r. to live a fool   BEAU 35:19
when I think I'm best r.   SUCK 524:13
Resolve: Firm R.   BURNS 115:14
R. not to be poor   JOHN 279:2
R. to be thyself   ARN 14:22
resolved: r. to grow fat   DRYD 196:36
speech they have r. not   ELIOT 200:24
Resolves: R.; and re-resolves   YOUNG 588:5
To dr or r. an' triggers   LOW 319:3
resonance: r. of his solitude   CONN 161:16
resounding: full-r. line   POPE 380:15
resource: infinite-r.-and-sagacity KIPL 304:16
resources: born to consume r.   HOR 258:13
r. of civilization are   GLAD 229:14

respect: art a fellow of a good r.   SHAK 452:6
How I did r. you when you   TROL 552:20
Is there no r. of place   SHAK 488:20
neither doth God r. any   BIBLE 50:23
On both sides more r.   SHAK 427:22
other means of procuring r.   JOHN 276:38
r. of persons with God   BIBLE 74:34
R. was mingled with surprise   SCOTT 416:6
too much r. upon the world   SHAK 465:9
Which I r. not   SHAK 451:20
respectable: consider him as a r. Hottentot
    CHES 145:32
devil's most devilish when r.   BROW 97:32
more r. he is   SHAW 497:19
Not one is r. or unhappy   WHIT 570:22
riff-raff apply to what is r.   HOPE 255:29
when was genius found r.   BROW 97:31
respecter: God is no r. of persons BIBLE 74:2
respects: Private r. must yield   MILT 350:24
respice: et r. finem   ANON 10:18
respond: start a song and to r.   VIRG 560:3
Responsare: R. cupidinibus   HOR 262:10
responsibility: Liberty means r. SHAW 497:37
Power without r.   KIPL 305:13
r. and to discharge my   EDW 200:4
responsible: you know who are r.
    PLATO 374:9
Responsive: R. to the cuckoo's note
    GRAY 235:16
res publica: consules ne quid r. detrimenti
    ANON 10:10
rest: a-brewing towards my r.   SHAK 466:11
all the r. were little   ELIZ 205:22
because they are at r.   PRAY 397:10
choose Their place of r.   MILT 350:1
elusive shadow, r.   ARN 12:22
far better, that I go   DICK 183:12
flee away, and be at r.   PRAY 393:10
From r. and sleep   DONNE 189:5
Good r. to all   KIPL 301:13
Grant them eternal r.   MASS 334:17
have no r. day or night   BIBLE 82:17
holy r.   NEWM 362:9
home and r. on the couch   CAT 136:28
I will give you r.   BIBLE 66:5
may r. from their labours   BIBLE 82:18
might it die or r. at last   SHEL 501:3
needful hours of r.   DRYD 194:7
night-season also I take no r.   PRAY 390:16
nowhere yet to r. my head   ARN 13:8
Now she's at r.   DRYD 196:8
one crept silently to R.   FITZ 212:17
ordain'd no r.   VAUG 555:10
ourselves and never r.   MARL 330:8
peace, and take my r.   PRAY 389:22
r. a little from praise   SWIN 530:3
r. for the sole of her   BIBLE 45:35
R. in soft peace   JONS 283:28
r. is silence   SHAK 437:27
r. may reason and welcome   BROW 98:21
r. on its original plan   BURKE 110:13
r. quiet in Montparnasse   BENET 40:20
R., rest, perturbed spirit   SHAK 431:25
r. to his mind   WALT 564:3
seeking r.   BIBLE 66:13
shall r. upon thy holy hill   PRAY 390:4
shortly be with them that r.   MILT 350:23
should not enter into my r.   PRAY 396:4
sure my bones would not r.   BYRON 126:20
that seals up all in r.   SHAK 494:7
thenceforth all shall r. eternally SPEN 516:25
then had I been at r.   BIBLE 52:12
there did it r.   KEATS 290:1
there the weary be at r.   BIBLE 52:13
they r. not day and night   BIBLE 81:24
who sink to r.   COLL 158:19
will not let them r.   KEATS 289:27
without r.   GOET 230:15
reste: J'y suis, j'y r.   MACM 325:17
tout le r. est littérature   VERL 556:9

rested: r. the seventh day   BIBLE 47:24
restful: r. death I cry   SHAK 494:5
restituit: homo nobis cunctando r. ENN 208:22
restless: r. and versatile intellect HUXL 269:13
restlessness: keep them with repining
r.   HERB 248:8
Restoration: Church's R.   BETJ 43:2
With tranquil r.   WORD 578:4
restore: r. the crown to its hereditary
    JOHN 276:20
R. thou them that are penitent PRAY 384:13
Time may r. us in his course   ARN 13:18
restored: r. by the refining fire ELIOT 202:26
restorer: Tir'd Nature's sweet r.
    YOUNG 587:21
restoring: I am r. tranquillity   BURKE 109:28
restraint: jesses and r.   THOM 548:2
r. with which they write   CAMP 128:12
were free from this r.   CONG 160:30
resume: to resumption is to r.   CHASE 141:4
resurrection: also is the r. of the dead
    BIBLE 76:3
also the r. of the dead   BIBLE 76:22
certain hope of the R.   PRAY 389:13
Church of Ireland r.   BETJ 43:9
glorious R. and Ascension   PRAY 385:17
'I'm the R. and the Life'   AUDEN 21:7
r. they neither marry   BIBLE 67:21
r., and the life.   BIBLE 72:22
R. of the body   PRAY 384:26
symbol of his r.   PROU 401:23
resurrectionem: Et expecto r. mortuorum
    MASS 334:20
resurrexit: Et r. tertia die   MASS 334:20
resuscitate: r. the dead art Of poetry
    POUND 383:1
retain: spirit to r. the spirit   BIBLE 55:25
retard: r. what we cannot repel   JOHN 281:9
retention: they lack r.   SHAK 489:6
retentive: r. to the strength of spirit
    SHAK 449:3
Reticence: R., in three volumes GLAD 229:20
reticulated: Anything r. or decussated
    JOHN 281:13
retinue: puffed up with this r.   SHAK 442:15
retire: him to r. from the world DISR 186:19
r. at half-past eight   MILL 339:27
Skill'd to r.   MILT 350:2
with a blush r.   DICK 178:3
Retired: R. to their tea and scandal
    CONG 159:21
retirement: short r. urges sweet return
    MILT 349:12
retort: r. courteous   SHAK 427:5
retrace: Thy steps r.   GILB 228:14
retraite: liberté et principale r. MONT 354:20
retreat: conquer or die who've no r.
    GAY 223:27
I will not r. a single   GARR 221:17
my soul's calm r.   VAUG 555:12
through the loopholes of r. COWP 167:12
us make an honourable r.   SHAK 426:6
woman's noblest station is r. LYTT 321:21
retreating: Have you seen yourself r.
    NASH 360:5
retrench: We r. the superfluities GAY 222:24
retrenchment: r., and reform'   BRIG 93:2
retrograde: be not r.   JONS 284:13
r. if it does not advance   GIBB 224:29
retrorsum: nulla r.   HOR 258:11
return: be the day of their r.   MAC 324:22
go whence I shall not r.   BIBLE 52:20
he shall not r. to me   BIBLE 50:22
hours of light r.   ARN 13:23
In that state I came, r.   VAUG 555:17
I shall r.   MAC 321:24
Let us r. to our sheep   ANON 9:16
never must r.   MILT 343:5
r. into my house from whence   BIBLE 66:13
r. no more to his house   BIBLE 52:19

r., O Shulamite — BIBLE 57:6
r. Sicilian Muse — MILT 343:14
r. your thanks would pass — BROW 106:1
spirit shall r. unto God — BIBLE 56:11
thou r. at all in peace — BIBLE 51:20
To r. the compliment — GILB 228:1
unto dust shalt thou r. — BIBLE 45:23
returned: r. home the previous night — BULL 106:22
We r. to our places — ELIOT 203:15
returning: *home there's no r.* — HOUS 265:3
R. were as tedious as go — SHAK 461:25
returns: Not one r. to tell us — FITZ 213:4
not to me r. Day — MILT 347:8
whence they say no one r. — CAT 136:23
reum: Habes confitentem r. — PETR 373:4
re-unite: Your charms r. what common — SCH 415:9
réussissent: l'ensemble des recettes qui r. — VAL 555:1
rêve: Vivre sans r., qu'est-ce — ROST 410:13
reveal: What does He then but r. — MILT 351:27
revealed: arm of the Lord r. — BIBLE 59:20
of the Lord shall be r. — BIBLE 59:5
revelation: inspired by divine r. — BACON 24:20
Revelations: It ends with R. — WILDE 573:29
r. and gifts of the Holy Ghost — BUTL 117:11
revelled: all who r. with the Regent — BEER 37:16
revellers: You moonshine r. — SHAK 469:16
revelry: sound of r. by night — BYRON 120:20
revels: Our r. now are ended — SHAK 485:20
that r. long o' nights — SHAK 449:21
What r. are in hand — SHAK 471:12
revenge: I will most horribly r. — SHAK 445:11
little R. herself went — TENN 543:5
man that studieth r. keeps — BACON 27:9
medicine of our great r. — SHAK 462:17
pleasure in r. — JUV 288:6
ranging for r. — SHAK 450:12
R. his foul and most unnatural — SHAK 431:6
R. is a kind of wild justice — BACON 27:7
R. triumphs over death — BACON 26:2
shall we not r. — SHAK 467:4
spur my dull r. — SHAK 435:29
Stirr'd up with envy and r. — MILT 344:23
study of r. — MILT 345:3
Sweet is r. — BYRON 122:12
sweet r. grows harsh — SHAK 477:9
that a capable and wide r. — SHAK 476:1
revenged: be r. on the whole pack — SHAK 490:26
revenges: have such r. on you both — SHAK 454:2
of time brings in his r. — SHAK 490:25
Revenons: R. à ces moutons — ANON 9:16
revenue: Instead of a standing r. — BURKE 109:31
revenues: She bears a duke's r. — SHAK 446:4
Revere: midnight ride of Paul R. — LONG 316:25
reverence: more of r. in us dwell — TENN 535:32
myn herte have hem in r. — CHAU 143:29
mystic r. — BAG 28:21
none so poor to do him r. — SHAK 450:23
r.— That angel — SHAK 428:20
To r. the King — TENN 534:11
reverend: It is a r. thing to see — BACON 26:38
reverent: r. cadence and subtle — AUDEN 18:3
reveries: From r. so airy — COWP 167:4
reversion: no bright r. in the sky — POPE 376:7
reverti: vox missa r. — HOR 258:6
Reviewers: R. are usually people who — COL 157:26
you chorus of indolent r. — TENN 533:14
reviewing: read a book before r. — SMITH 511:17
revivals: art is the history of r. — BUTL 118:33

revocare: Sed r. gradum superasque — VIRG 558:18
revolting: r. and a rebellious heart — BIBLE 60:17
revolts: It r. me, but I do it — GILB 226:21
revolution: be cured by reform or r. — BERL 41:23
c'est une grande r. — LA R 310:19
impossible without a violent r. — LENIN 313:21
is...a sort of mental r. — ORW 365:10
not the leaders of a r. — CONR 161:22
reform is beginning r. — WELL 568:4
R., like Saturn — VERG 556:7
see the r. of the times — SHAK 442:1
what a r. — BURKE 111:9
white heat of this r. — WILS 574:17
revolutionary: r. is merely a climber — ORW 365:16
their r. right to dismember — LINC 314:19
Revolutionists: age fatal to R. — DESM 175:13
revolutions: nursery of future r. — BURKE 111:5
r. are not to be evaded — DISR 185:42
share in two r. is living — PAINE 368:6
that r. never go backward — SEW 420:16
revolve: worlds r. like ancient women — ELIOT 204:8
reward: himself shall r. you openly — BIBLE 64:22
in no wise lose his r. — BIBLE 65:41
nothing for r. — SPEN 516:12
only r. of virtue is virtue — EMER 207:21
reap his old r. — KIPL 304:8
receive your r. in a certain place — BROWN 95:8
r. against the innocent — PRAY 390:5
r. of a thing well done — EMER 207:26
what r. have ye — BIBLE 64:20
rewarded: r. me evil for good — PRAY 391:24
thee be plenteously r. — PRAY 387:2
they shall be greatly r. — BIBLE 62:13
rewarder: be my r. he passed over — BUNY 107:38
rewardest: thou r. every man according — PRAY 393:20
rewards: are their own r. — FARQ 210:14
fellow that will take r. — SHAK 422:21
r. and Fairies — CORB 162:13
Rex: Ego et R. meus — SHAK 447:8
Quis r. — ABEL 1:2
R. tremendae maiestatis — CEL 138:7
rey: pastor con el r. y al simple — CERV 138:20
Reynolds: gipsy by R. to his Majesty's — MAC 324:2
When Sir Joshua R. died — BLAKE 85:7
Rheims: Lord Archbishop of R. — BARH 33:11
rhetoric: can't you love and r. — STOP 523:16
Death, without r. — SIEY 508:7
heavenly r. of thine eye — SHAK 457:4
logic and r. — BACON 27:21
obscure them by an aimless r. — HUXL 269:13
r. he could not ope — BUTL 117:8
rhetorical: sophistical r. — DISR 185:17
rhetorick: Ornate r. taught out — MILT 352:9
rheum: void your r. upon my beard — SHAK 466:3
rheumatic: That r. diseases do abound — SHAK 470:6
rheumatism: to me to complain of r. — SAKI 413:8
Rhine: henceforth wash the river R. — COL 156:5
king-like rolls the R. — CALV 127:20
R. circle fair Wertenberg — MARL 329:5
wide and winding r. — BYRON 120:31
You think of the R. — BALD 29:28
rhinoceros: arm'd r. or the Hyrcan tiger — SHAK 461:31
Rhodope: Brighter than is the silver R. — MARL 330:3
rhyme: build the lofty r. — MILT 343:2

could not get a r. for roman — FLEM 215:4
free from r.'s infection — JONS 285:6
In a sort of Runic r. — POE 375:1
I r. for fun — BURNS 113:24
me that my murmuring r. — MORR 358:9
names in many a mused r. — KEATS 291:22
Napoleon of the realms of r. — BYRON 123:31
received nor r. nor reason — SPEN 516:29
R. being no necessary adjunct — MILT 344:18
R. is the rock on which — DRYD 194:22
R. thee to good — HERB 246:27
r. themselves into ladies' — SHAK 445:13
r. the rudder is of verses — BUTL 117:25
ruined r. — SWIN 530:25
still more tired of R. — BELL 39:18
taen the fit o' r. — BURNS 113:23
To r. upon a dish — SPEN 515:15
unattempted yet in prose or r. — MILT 344:21
Was never said in r. — KEATS 293:4
rhymed: nor to be r. to death — SIDN 508:5
R. out in love's despair — YEATS 586:14
rhymes: between piety and poor r. — WILDE 573:38
pair their r. as Venus — BYRON 123:14
Regent of love r. — SHAK 456:26
R. are so scarce in this — CALV 127:25
ring out my mournful r. — TENN 537:15
These r. I've made — CAT 137:16
Rhyming: modern bondage of R. — MILT 344:19
Rialto: What news on the R. — SHAK 465:28
riband: r. in the cap of youth — SHAK 436:17
r. to stick in his coat — BROW 102:4
ribbon: blue r. of the turf — DISR 186:13
road was a r. of moonlight — NOYES 364:12
ribboned: slake of a r. coat — NEWB 361:8
ribbons: Tie up my sleeves with r. — HUNT 268:15
Wi' r. on her breast — BALL 31:11
ribs: breaking of r. was sport — SHAK 424:23
he took one of his r. — BIBLE 45:11
Many a dig in the r. — SURT 525:5
mountain-chains like r. — HARDY 239:13
Ribstone Pippin: 'Right as a R. — BELL 39:17
rice: *it's lovely r. pudding* — MILNE 340:10
pound of R. — LEAR 312:9
rich: am r. beyond the dreams — MOORE 355:14
behave as the r. behave — SMITH 510:19
Eat with the r. — SMITH 510:18
esteemed themselves r. — MAC 323:26
ever by chance grow r. — THOM 547:18
ever seems it r. to die — KEATS 291:22
feed with the r. — JOHN 275:23
from the r. man's table — BIBLE 70:28
He wished all men as r. — GILB 225:28
is not r. enough to do it — REED 405:9
Let him be r. and weary — HERB 248:8
like to one more r. in hope — SHAK 493:6
making Gay r. and Rich gay — JOHN 282:1
marry a r. woman as a poor — THAC 545:14
most r., being poor — SHAK 453:8
no law to make thee r. — SHAK 483:26
no sin, but to be r. — SHAK 452:15
passing r. with forty pounds — GOLD 230:22
Perhaps been poorly r. — SAV 415:5
Poor little r. girl — COW 164:1
property of the r. — RUSK 412:11
r. and poor alike to sleep — FRAN 217:26
R. and rare were the gems — MOORE 356:16
R. AND THE POOR — DISR 186:29
r. have become richer — SHEL 505:11
r. he hath sent empty away — BIBLE 69:6
R. in good works — BIBLE 79:20
R. in the simple worship — KEATS 291:12
r. man in his castle — ALEX 3:14
r. man to enter into — BIBLE 67:11
R. men furnished with ability — BIBLE 63:23
r. men rule the law — GOLD 231:29
r., not gaudy — SHAK 430:19
r. only select from — SMITH 509:9

Rimmon: myself in the house of R.
                                    BIBLE 51:29
rin: gars ye r. sae still   ANON 7:12
rind: burnished with golden r.   MILT 347:19
how shall taste the r.   THOM 548:19
sweet as the r.   SWIN 529:8
ring: both the shires they r.   HOUS 263:4
Bright is the r. of words   STEV 523:1
giving and receiving of a R.   PRAY 389:7
he rid at the r.   BALL 30:16
only pretty r. time   SHAK 427:2
r. at the end of his nose   LEAR 312:12
r. on her wand she bore   MOORE 356:16
R. out the false   TENN 537:14
R. out, wild bells   TENN 537:14
R. out ye crystal spheres   MILT 344:10
sat unconquered in a r.   CHES 147:17
She heard the bridles r.   BALL 32:2
Sleeps on his luminous r.   TENN 541:21
They now r. the bells   WALP 563:24
what shall we do for a r.   LEAR 312:12
With this R. I thee wed   PRAY 389:5
Ring-Bo-Ree: forty bottles of R.   LEAR 312:9
Ring'd: R. with the azure world   TENN 533:7
ring-having: nor in r.   POUND 383:18
ringleaders: fling the r. from the Tarpeian
                                    ARN 16:28
ringlets: do the green sour r. make
                                    SHAK 485:23
rings: gold r. set with the beryl BIBLE 57:4
Rio: Go rolling down to R.   KIPL 300:7
riot: Like litter that a r. leaves PLOM 374:19
rash fierce blaze of r.   SHAK 478:19
r. is at bottom the language   KING 296:14
winds' and spent waves' r.   SWIN 529:21
rioting: r., the old Roman way   ARN 16:28
riotous: wasted his substance with r.
living   BIBLE 70:18
riotousness: r. of the crowd is always
                                    ALC 3:9
ripe: shelter to grow r.   ARN 13:10
we r. and ripe   SHAK 425:19
Ripeness: R. is all   SHAK 456:2
ripening: His greatness is a-r.   SHAK 447:9
riper: chooses Athens in his r. age
                                    DRYD 197:14
ripes: erring on ventiferous r.   HOLM 253:18
ripple: Of a r. under archways   HARDY 239:18
rire: me presse de r. de tout   BEAU 35:15
r. les honnêtes gens   MOL 353:7
rise: Held we fall to r.   BROW 98:32
if the dead r. not   BIBLE 76:24
may r. on stepping-stones   TENN 535:33
nation shall r. against   BIBLE 67:28
nobody who does not r.   JOHN 279:32
of her should r. herself   HARDY 240:7
populace r. at once against   WHIT 570:14
r. of the United States   STEV 520:23
R., take up thy bed   BIBLE 72:1
r. with the lark and go   BRET 92:2
stoop to r.   MASS 335:16
That dead men r. up never   SWIN 529:25
to r. out of obscurity   JUV 287:18
us i' the dark to r.   BROW 104:27
Woe unto them that r. up   BIBLE 57:25
wretched than to r.   GOLD 230:22
risen: floods are r.   PRAY 396:1
rises: Jove's planet r.   BROW 101:9
Rise up: R., my love   BIBLE 56:22
risible: authors is one of the most r.
                                    JOHN 281:29
rising: All r. to great place is   BACON 26:26
Moon of Heav'n is r. once   FITZ 213:17
more than a means of r.   JOHN 276:29
on a plat of r. ground   MILT 342:4
R. and cawing at the gun's   SHAK 470:20
R. in joy over wolds   AUDEN 20:6
r. unto place is laborious   BACON 26:23
risk: r. it on one turn of pitch-and-toss
                                    KIPL 300:1

risu: r. cognoscere matrem   VIRG 560:1
r. inepto res ineptior   CAT 137:1
Solventur r. tabulae   HOR 262:7
rite: newer r. is here   THOM 546:17
No noble r. nor formal   SHAK 436:14
rites: of payens corsed olde r.   CHAU 144:19
r. for which I love him   SHAK 474:6
ritui: Novo cedat r.   THOM 546:17
Ritz: open to all, like the R.   MATH 336:2
rivalry: dead there is no r.   MAC 324:9
rivals: Three for the r.   ANON 6:5
rive: r. not more in parting   SHAK 423:6
riveder: quindi uscimmo a r. le stelle
                                    DANTE 171:14
river: Alph, the sacred r.   COL 156:26
Among the r. sallows   KEATS 293:8
brook and r. meet   LONG 316:20
dale the sacred r. ran   COL 156:28
daughter went through the r. singing
                                    BUNY 107:37
Fame is like a r.   BACON 27:5
fountains mingle with the r.   SHEL 502:1
fruitful r. in the eye   SHAK 429:25
he drinketh up a r.   BIBLE 53:10
House of Parliament upon the r.   WELL 567:23
in the reeds by the r.   BROW 98:6
living r. by the door   STEV 523:7
majestic R. floated   ARN 14:28
nearer to the r.'s trembling   SHEL 503:20
noblest r. in *Europe*   ADD 2:19
On a tree by a r. a little   GILB 227:15
On either side the r. lie   TENN 538:2
Pentridge by the r.   BARN 33:29
r. at my garden's end   SWIFT 527:28
r. flows on through   WORD 581:3
r. jumps over the mountain   AUDEN 18:9
r. of water of life   BIBLE 82:35
r.-rounded   HOPK 256:10
Runs not a r. by my palace   THAC 545:18
That even the weariest r.   SWIN 529:25
There is a r. in Macedon   SHAK 445:5
thy peace been as a r.   BIBLE 59:15
Time the refreshing r.   AUDEN 20:15
twice into the same r.   HER 246:6
we'll to the r.   SHAK 422:9
white flows the r.   STEV 522:29
river-fields: grassy harvest of the r. ARN 15:8
rivering: Beside the r. waters of JOYCE 286:8
riverrun: r. past Eve and Adam's,
from swerve   JOYCE 286:2
rivers: All the r. run into   BIBLE 55:6
By shallow r.   MARL 330:1
kingdom's r. take their course   SHAK 452:31
lilies by the r. of waters   BIBLE 63:27
love any discourse of r.   WALT 564:11
Nymphs and as yet unknown r.   VIRG 559:4
R. are damp   PARK 368:18
r. cannot quench   SHAK 446:21
r. in the south   PRAY 398:17
r. of blood must yet flow   JEFF 272:14
r. of Damascus   BIBLE 51:28
r. of water in a dry place   BIBLE 58:30
springs into the r.   PRAY 396:19
Their fighters drink the r.   HOUS 265:3
rivets: busy hammers closing r.   SHAK 444:9
rivulet: r. of text shall meander SHER 506:26
rivulets: Myriads of r. hurrying   TENN 542:17
road: along the 'ard 'igh r.   PUNCH 402:17
call it the R. to Heaven   BALL 32:5
free as the r.   HERB 247:14
goes along the darksome r.   CAT 136:23
good to be out on the r.   MAS 334:8
guide what goes off the r.   LANG 310:1
in the moon the long r.   HOUS 263:20
is a long time on the r.   DICK 183:9
is the high r. that leads   JOHN 274:30
light-hearted I take to the open r.   WHIT 571:7
light to shine upon the r.   COWP 165:23
on a taxed r.   SMITH 511:38
One r. leads to London   MAS 334:2

On every r. I wandered   HOUS 264:1
On the r. to Mandalay   KIPL 301:5
r. below me   STEV 522:28
r. is rough and long   BRON 93:13
r. lies long and straight   STEV 521:32
r. of excess leads   BLAKE 88:13
r. through the woods   KIPL 303:31
r. was a ribbon of moonlight   NOYES 364:12
rolling English r.   CHES 147:10
that on a lonesome r.   COL 155:27
who takes no private r.   POPE 380:2
winding r. before me   HAZL 243:32
roads: Two r. diverged in a wood
                                    FROST 219:10
roadway: While I stand on the r.
                                    YEATS 585:17
roam: soar, but never r.   WORD 583:1
that has been sent to r.   COWP 166:11
Where'er I r.   GOLD 231:24
roaming: where are you r.   SHAK 488:17
roar: called upon to give the r.   CHUR 150:21
let him r. again   SHAK 469:29
most like the r.   ARN 14:26
r. you as gently as any   SHAK 469:30
Swinging slow with sullen r.   MILT 342:4
they r. their ribs out   GILB 229:10
withdrawing r.   ARN 12:23
roared: ran about the room and r.
                                    CHES 146:12
roarers: r. for the name of king   SHAK 484:20
roareth: What is this that r. thus GODL 229:24
roaring: lions r. after their prey PRAY 397:1
magnificent r. of the young lions   ARN 15:23
There was a r. in the wind   WORD 580:27
roast: In hell they'll r. thee   BURNS 115:12
never strove to rule the r.   PRIOR 401:10
politics in boil'd and r.   SMITH 512:6
r. me in sulphur   SHAK 477:21
r. with fire   BIBLE 47:17
were but to r. their eggs   BACON 27:37
rob: r. a lady of her fortune   FIEL 211:29
r. a neighbour whom he   MAC 323:21
r. the Hybla bees   SHAK 451:31
robb'd: r. me of my Robe of Honour
                                    FITZ 213:14
robbed: that had r. us of immortal
                                    MER 337:15
robber: can sing in the r.'s face JUV 287:26
Injurious time now with a r.'s   SHAK 487:12
Now Barabbas was a r.   BIBLE 72:45
robbers: in perils of r.   BIBLE 77:12
robbery: all full of lies and r.   BIBLE 61:26
end in conquest and r.   JOHN 281:25
In scandal, as in r.   CHES 145:9
r. to be equal with God   BIBLE 78:13
trust not in wrong and r.   PRAY 393:20
robbing: Forbids the r. of a foe   CHUR 148:30
r. selected Peter to pay   KIPL 299:10
robe: Give me my r.   SHAK 424:10
intertissued r. of gold   SHAK 444:25
like a giant's r.   SHAK 462:27
nor the judge's r.   SHAK 463:20
robes: are arrayed in white r.   BIBLE 82:1
have washed their r.   BIBLE 82:2
R. loosely flowing   JONS 283:27
r. ye weave, another wears   SHEL 504:3
When all her r. are gone   ANON 6:20
Robespierre: R. war nichts als die Hand
                                    HEINE 244:12
Robin: bonny sweet R. is all my   SHAK 436:11
R. Redbreast in a Cage   BLAKE 85:9
r.-red-breast   WEBS 567:8
R.'s not near   KEPP 295:12
r.'s plucky canton   AUDEN 20:15
Sweet R. sits in the bush   SCOTT 418:21
Robinson Crusoe: R., and the *Pilgrim's*
Progress   JOHN 280:16
Robs: R. not one light seed from   KEATS 290:1
r. the mind of all its   BURKE 108:9
robur: r. et aes triplex   HOR 259:12

rock: it was founded upon a r.   BIBLE 65:11
of a serpent upon a r.   BIBLE 55:1
pleasant shade of some r.   HOR 259:15
Rhyme is the r. on which   DRYD 194:22
r. in a weary land   BIBLE 58:30
r. I will build my church   BIBLE 66:33
r. of offence to both   BIBLE 58:4
sea-wet r. sat down and combed   HOUS 265:3
set my feet upon the r.   PRAY 392:1
they knew the perilous r.   SOUT 514:1
Rocked: R. in the cradle   WILL 574:7
She r. it, and rated it   EDW 200:5
rocket: that as he rose like a r.   PAINE 368:2
rocking horse: sway'd about upon a r.
  KEATS 292:8
rocks: hand that r. the cradle   WALL 562:4
him a native of the r.   JOHN 274:6
r. and hills whose heads   SHAK 473:25
r. of the mountains   BIBLE 81:30
She is older than the r.   PATER 369:19
stony r. for the conies   PRAY 397:1
till the rending of the r.   JOYCE 286:4
With r. unscalable   SHAK 428:13
rocky: king sate on the r. brow BYRON 122:34
rod: Aaron's r. swallowed up   BIBLE 47:12
all humbled kiss the r.   SHAK 490:31
bruise them with a r. of iron   PRAY 389:18
child and spares the r.   HOOD 254:19
eyeball owns the mystic r.   BROW 105:14
r. and thy staff comfort   PRAY 390:22
r. Becomes more mock'd   SHAK 463:11
r. out of the stem of Jesse   BIBLE 58:9
r. produces an effect which   JOHN 273:25
spareth his r. hateth   BIBLE 53:38
Then spare the r.   BUTL 118:2
Wisdom be put in a silver r.   BLAKE 85:19
rode: He r. upon the cherubims   PRAY 390:8
r. all that day and all   MAL 328:5
r. madly off in all directions   LEAC 311:14
that r. sublime   GRAY 235:19
Roderick: where was R. then   SCOTT 416:7
rods: Thrice was I beaten with r.   BIBLE 77:12
roe: r. or to a young hart upon   BIBLE 57:14
roes: breasts are like two young r.
  BIBLE 56:26
Roger: R. is landlord to the whole   ADD 2:12
rogue: busy and insinuating r.   SHAK 476:23
consequently a r.   SWIFT 526:16
dainty r. in porcelain   MER 335:8
Has he not a r.'s face   CONG 160:4
r. and peasant slave am   SHAK 432:27
r. gives you Love Powders   LAMB 307:30
r. is married to a whore   KIPL 302:18
smooth-faced snubnosed r.   TENN 539:26
rogues: r. in buckram let drive   SHAK 439:2
see the r. flourish   BROW 99:26
roi: Il était un r. d'Yvetot   BER 41:14
Si le R. m'avait donné   ANON 9:17
Roland: R. to the dark tower came
  SHAK 454:27
roll: All away began to r.   BLAKE 85:24
Let it r. on full flood   CHUR 150:3
r. of the world eastward   HARDY 241:9
R. on, thou deep and dark   BYRON 121:23
R. up that map   PITT 374:6
us r. all our strength   MARV 332:20
rolling: drunkard made the r. English
road   CHES 147:10
Go r. down to Rio   KIPL 300:7
r. anapaestic   BROW 98:16
rolls: holds and r. and throws   REED 405:7
R. impotently on as Thou   FITZ 213:8
r. it under his tongue   HENRY 245:19
Roma: R. locuta est   AUG 22:2
Soldati, io esco da R.   GAR 221:10
Romae: Si fueris R.   AMBR 4:2
romain: ni r., ni empire   VOLT 561:9
Romam: natam me consule R.   CIC 152:2
Roman: after the high R. fashion
  SHAK 423:18

antique R. than a Dane   SHAK 437:24
at Rome live in the R.   AMBR 4:2
been a virtue with the R.   KING 297:17
Butcher'd to make a R. holiday
  BYRON 121:16
by a R. Valiantly vanquished   SHAK 423:15
do know the sweet R. hand   SHAK 490:5
found the R. nation   VIRG 557:10
I am a R. citizen   CIC 151:28
I'm a R. for that   FARQ 210:4
Make way, you R. writers   PROP 401:17
noblest R. of them all   SHAK 452:7
noses cast is of the r.   FLEM 215:4
R. came to Rye or out   CHES 147:10
R. Conquest was   SELL 420:2
R. meal   COWP 167:14
R. people were the classical   YEATS 587:13
R.'s life, a Roman's arms   MAC 322:21
R. thought hath struck   SHAK 421:15
Than such a R.   SHAK 451:14
that would not be a R.   SHAK 450:16
Then 'twas the R.   HOUS 263:15
you, R., make your task   VIRG 559:1
Romana: Moribus antiquis res stat R.
virisque   ENN 208:23
romance: cloudy symbols of a high r.
  KEATS 293:1
not a little given to r.   EVEL 209:6
R. at short notice was   SAKI 413:5
you think steam spoils r.   KIPL 301:4
romances: r. as they would be spiritualized
  WALP 562:27
R. paint at full length   BYRON 122:27
tall woods with high r.   KEATS 292:15
Roman Empire: Ghost of the deceased
R.   HOBB 251:21
Romanism: rum, R., and rebellion
  BURC 108:1
Romans: Friends, R., countrymen
  SHAK 450:17
Greeks or the R.   DISR 185:27
R. call it stoicism   ADD 1:18
R. were like brothers   MAC 322:18
romantic: In a ruin that's r.   GILB 227:18
mustn t be r. about money   SHAW 497:26
Romanus: Civis R. sum   CIC 151:28
when he could say Civis R.   PALM 368:10
Rome: At R. she hadde been   CHAU 141:31
Bishop of R. hath no jurisdiction
  PRAY 400:10
Cato is the voice of R.   JONS 283:19
comen from R. al hoot   CHAU 142:6
Everything in R. is expensive   JUV 287:19
Glorious R. hath lost her   COL 155:3
go from the church of R.   WOTT 583:17
grandeur that was R.   POE 375:7
Greece or haughty R.   JONS 284:22
Half-Way House to R.   PUNCH 402:11
happy R.   CIC 152:2
high and palmy state of R.   SHAK 429:12
hook-nosed fellow of R.   SHAK 442:13
late comes round by R.   BROW 104:24
R., believe me   CLOU 153:7
R. has spoken   AUG 22:2
R. indeed and room enough   SHAK 448:19
'R. is above the Nations   KIPL 303:9
R. live in the Roman style   AMBR 4:2
R.! my country   BYRON 121:9
R. of to-day   EMER 207:9
R., though her eagle through   WALL 562:11
sires have marched to R.   MAC 322:12
that I loved R. more   SHAK 450:14
time will doubt of R.   BYRON 123:13
varletry Of censuring R.   SHAK 423:21
village than second at R.'   CAES 127:3
wealth and din of R.   HOR 261:7
We burn For R. so near   DAY-L 172:21
when R. falls   BYRON 121:18
you cruel men of R.   SHAK 448:6
Romeo: wherefore art thou R.   SHAK 482:8

Romuli: tamquam in R. faece sententiam
  CIC 151:16
Romulus: than among the dregs of R.
  CIC 151:16
Ronsard: 'R. sang of me in the days
  RONS 407:18
rood: half a r. Of land   SWIFT 527:28
roof: cleave to the r. of my mouth PRAY 399:3
had no r. to shroud his   HEYW 250:22
He has restored the r.   BETJ 43:3
humble r. Is weather-proof   HERR 250:14
r. of blue Italian weather   SHEL 501:16
shouldest come under my r.   BIBLE 65:14
shouldst enter under my r.   MASS 335:8
this majestical r. fretted   SHAK 432:15
until my r. whirl around   JONS 285:14
roof-tree: heavens my wide r.   AYT 24:12
rook: r.-racked   HOPK 256:10
When the last r.   COL 157:11
rooks: maggot-pies and choughs and
r.   SHAK 461:24
r. are blown about   TENN 536:8
r. came home in scramble   HODG 252:6
r. in families homeward   HARDY 241:4
room: always leave r. for the mouse
  SAKI 413:16
coming to that holy r.   DONNE 189:14
down in the highest r.   BIBLE 70:7
In ev'ry grave make r.   DAV 172:6
Infinite riches in a little r.   MARL 329:20
into a r. full of people   WEBB 566:6
is always r. at the top   WEBS 566:9
is it Rome indeed and r.   SHAK 448:19
no r. for them in the inn   BIBLE 69:9
r. Do we take up in death   SHIR 507:6
R. to deny ourselves   KEBLE 295:4
r. to swing a cat   DICK 177:18
shame to take the lowest r.   BIBLE 70:7
shew you a large upper r.   BIBLE 71:6
sometimes in a smoking r.   KIPL 302:5
taper to the outward r.   DONNE 189:30
was not sufficient r.   BARN 34:5
you shall keep your r.   STEV 522:29
rooms: Know most of the r.   FULL 220:13
lighted r. Inside your head   LARK 310:5
uppermost r. at feasts   BIBLE 67:22
uppermost r. at feasts   BIBLE 68:37
roos: r., and sit in hevene   CHAU 144:19
Rooshan: 'It is R.   DICK 181:9
Rooshans: Some people…may be R.
  DICK 179:11
Roosian: he might have been a R.
  GILB 228:10
roost: always come home to r.   SOUT 513:23
rooster: Hongry r. don't cackle HARR 242:24
roosts: Assailant on the perched r.
  MILT 350:29
root: because they had no r.   BIBLE 66:16
eaten on the insane r.   SHAK 458:15
money is the r. of all evil   BIBLE 79:18
nips his r.   SHAK 447:9
r. is ever in its grave   HERB 248:16
r. of the matter is found   BIBLE 52:32
square r. of half a number   LONG 317:23
then the axe to the r.   PAINE 368:4
unto the r. of the trees   BIBLE 63:39
roote: me aboute myn herte r.   CHAU 143:19
roots: broad on the r. of things   BROW 98:17
poison England at her r.   BOTT 90:17
r., and ever green   PEELE 371:8
r. that can be pulled up   ELIOT 200:23
send my r. rain   HOPK 257:3
shall grow out of his r.   BIBLE 58:9
stirring Dull r.   ELIOT 204:17
rope: escape from r. and gun   GAY 222:30
to set his hand to a r.   DRAKE 193:4
Rorate: R., coeli   BIBLE 83:15
rosa: r. quo locorum   HOR 260:5
Rosalind: No jewel is like R.   SHAK 426:5
rose: Against the blown r. may   SHAK 422:17

ROSEAU RUDE

blossom as the r. BIBLE 58:32
brier pluck a white r. SHAK 445:21
Christmas I no more desire a r. SHAK 456:16
earthlier happy is the r. SHAK 469:17
English unofficial r. BROO 94:18
expectancy and r. SHAK 433:15
fading r. CAREW 130:18
Faintly the inimitable r. WINC 575:5
fause lover stole my r. BURNS 116:8
fayr as is the r. in May CHAU 143:27
fresh lap of the crimson r. SHAK 470:6
Gather therefore the R. SPEN 516:13
Go, lovely R. WALL 562:13
hills where his life r. ARN 12:22
I am the r. of Sharon BIBLE 56:19
If love were what the r. SWIN 530:21
I pluck the r. BROW 105:29
labyrinthine buds the r. BROW 105:13
late r. may yet linger HOR 260:5
leaves the R. of Yesterday FITZ 212:10
lovely is the r. WORD 578:22
Luve's like a red red r. BURNS 114:27
mast burst open with a r. FLEC 214:19
musk of the r. is blown TENN 540:9
Nightingale cries to the R. FITZ 212:7
One perfect r. PARK 368:17
O R., thou art sick BLAKE 87:12
Pluck a red r. from off SHAK 445:21
raise up the ghost of a r. BROW 95:21
ravage with impunity a r. BROW 105:15
red as any r. BALL 30:9
R. as where some buried FITZ 212:15
r. By any other name SHAK 482:9
R. crossed the road DOBS 187:14
R. is a rose is a rose STEIN 518:17
r. like a nymph SHEL 503:23
R. of all Roses YEATS 586:10
r. of the rosebud garden TENN 540:11
r. Of youth SHAK 422:16
r. o' the wrong side BROME 93:11
r.'s scent is bitterness THOM 547:25
r. the wrong way to-day BEHN 38:20
R., were you not extremely PRIOR 401:9
r. with all its sweetest BYRON 124:8
r. without the thorn HERR 250:13
Roves back the r. DE L 173:24
sad R. of all my days YEATS 587:6
secret, and inviolate R. YEATS 586:18
should vanish with the R. FITZ 213:15
sorrow on a morning r. KEATS 291:15
strew on thee r. or rue SWIN 528:25
supplication to the r. FLEC 214:11
Sweet r., whose hue HERB 248:16
That thereby beauty's r. SHAK 492:22
third day he r. again from PRAY 384:26
though a r. should shut KEATS 289:19
tiger sniffs the r. SASS 415:1
'Tis the last r. of summer MOORE 356:20
to tell the crooked r. THOM 547:3
Unceremoniously the r. WATS 565:12
under the r. BICK 84:2
When I have pluck'd the r. SHAK 477:5
when the r. is dead SHEL 504:12
white r. weeps TENN 540:12
without thorn the r. MILT 347:20
yet a r. full-blown HERR 250:16
***roseau:** mais c'est un r. pensant* PASC 369:11
Rose Aylmer: R., all were thine LAND 308:26
rose-blossoms: foam-flowers endure when the r. SWIN 529:19
rosebuds: crown ourselves with r. BIBLE 62:11
Gather ye r. while ye may HERR 250:5
like r. fill'd with snow CAMP 129:23
rose-garden: can the moment in the r. ELIOT 202:16
Into the r. ELIOT 202:13
rose-lipt: many a r. maiden HOUS 264:10
rosemary: r., that's for remembrance SHAK 436:10
you there's r. and rue SHAK 491:22
Rosencrantz: R. and Guildenstern are SHAK 437:29
rose-petals: on a pile of r. HOR 259:15
rose-red: r. city 'half as old BURG 108:4
r. sissy half as old PLOM 374:18
roses: days of wine and r. DOWS 191:13
Do r. stick like burrs BROW 105:27
Each Morn a thousand R. FITZ 212:10
flower of r. in the spring BIBLE 63:27
In fields where r. fade HOUS 264:10
It was the time of r. HOOD 254:8
Lilies without, r. within MARV 332:15
not a bed of r. STEV 521:31
own red r. there may blow THOM 547:24
Plant thou no r. at my ROSS 409:8
raptures and r. of vice SWIN 529:5
r., all the way BROW 103:10
R. at first were white HERR 249:7
r. for the flush of youth ROSS 409:7
R. have thorns SHAK 493:12
r. to the moonrise burst HOUS 266:4
scent of the r. will hang MOORE 356:7
Seek r. in December BYRON 124:18
Strew on her r. ARN 14:5
'Two red r. across the moon MORR 358:13
virgins are soft as the r. BYRON 120:2
wild r., and ivy serpentine SHEL 503:19
would like my r. to see you SHER 506:39
rose-water: would pour r. over a toad JERR 273:9
rosy: 'Cause another's r. are WITH 575:12
sent thee late a r. wreath JONS 284:12
Rosy-fingered: R. dawn HOMER 254:5
rot: cold obstruction and to r. SHAK 464:14
go r. SHAK 491:11
Here continueth to r. ARB 11:21
I will r. HOUS 264:27
pernicious soul R. SHAK 477:13
recognize virtue and r. PERS 372:27
r. in hospitals SOUT 513:13
R. inwardly and foul contagion MILT 343:13
very deep did r. COL 155:14
we r. and rot SHAK 425:19
rote: conn'd by r. SHAK 451:23
Rothschild: are taken by R. and Baring GILB 226:16
rots: he sort of r. away WARD 564:30
rotten: fresh eggs to r. boroughs MAC 323:15
Lord Lilac thought it rather r. CHES 147:16
Lovely lads and dead and r. HOUS 263:19
r. in the state of Denmark SHAK 431:2
rottenness: r. begins in his conduct JEFF 272:11
rotten-runged: r. rat-riddled stairs BROW 102:13
rotundity: thick r. o' the world SHAK 454:4
***rotundo:** Grais dedit ore r.* HOR 257:23
***rotundus:** teres, atque r.* HOR 262:10
rough: Because the road is r. BRON 93:13
follows I am r. and lecherous SHAK 453:11
from children who were r. SPEN 515:11
greeting be courteous or r. AUDEN 21:2
...R. he may be DICK 179:19
r. magic I here abjure SHAK 485:24
r. male kiss of blankets BROO 94:8
r. places plain BIBLE 59:5
r. than polished diamond CHES 145:27
R. winds do shake the darling SHAK 492:28
Rough-hew: R. them how we will SHAK 437:11
roughness: r. breedeth hate BACON 26:25
roughs: among his fellow r. DOYLE 192:39
Roumania: I am Marie of R. PARK 368:14
this might be R. MARY 333:15
round: act of walking r. him BEER 38:6
himself into the r. hole SMITH 511:34
large, and smooth, and r. SOUT 513:15
one was r. her lover CAMP 129:4
perfect r. BROW 98:18
R. numbers are always false JOHN 277:19
R. the world for ever ARN 13:6
r. the world away KING 297:5
r. unvarnish'd tale deliver SHAK 473:24
r. world so sure PRAY 395:24
roundabouts: What's lost upon the r. CHAL 139:3
rounded: little life Is r. SHAK 485:20
Round-heads: R. and Wooden-shoes are ADD 2:1
R. (Right but Repulsive) SELL 420:4
rouse: anything might r. him now OWEN 367:4
No more shall r. them from GRAY 234:20
r. a lion than to start SHAK 438:18
R. the lion from his lair SCOTT 418:35
roused: r. in many an ancient hall MAC 322:3
***Rousseau:** dessen Seele R. geschaffen* HEINE 244:12
mock on, Voltaire, R. BLAKE 86:23
not ask Jean Jacques R. COWP 166:5
wild R. BYRON 120:36
rout: after all their r. CHUR 148:20
pleasures of having a r. HOOD 254:25
rove: r. the brakes and thorns COWP 165:12
rover: blood's a r. HOUS 262:15
roving: we'll go no more a r. BYRON 125:25
row: to your Sirmione r. TENN 533:17
watermen, that r. one way BURT 116:15
rowing: me r. against the stream SCOTT 418:10
r. another BUNY 107:18
Rowland: Warren's blackin' or R.'s DICK 182:12
rows: Lovers' r. make love whole TER 544:15
royal: Calling a crowned man r. SWIN 529:26
descended from r. forebears HOR 259:8
no 'r. road' to geometry EUCL 209:3
r. captain of this ruin'd SHAK 444:10
r. priesthood BIBLE 80:23
R. slice of bread MILNE 340:7
R. Society desires to confer FAR 209:20
Tax not the r. Saint WORD 582:16
This r. throne of kings SHAK 478:20
royaliste: plus r. que le roi ANON 9:9
royally: Sorrow so r. in you appears SHAK 442:24
To have prov'd most r. SHAK 437:30
Royalty: R. is a government in which BAG 28:30
when you come to R. you DISR 185:28
***ruamus:** Moriamur et in media arma r.* VIRG 558:7
***ruat:** r. caelum'* MANS 328:16
rub: there's the r. SHAK 433:8
What r. or what impediment SHAK 445:11
rubbish: cast as r. to the void TENN 536:25
was but the r. of an Adam SOUTH 513:12
What r. BLUC 88:32
write such hopeless r. STEP 518:23
***rubens:** r. accendit lumina Vesper* VIRG 560:11
rubies: Give pearls away and r. HOUS 262:20
her price is far above r. BIBLE 55:3
price of wisdom is above r. BIBLE 52:34
R. unparagon'd SHAK 428:8
Wisdom is better than r. BIBLE 53:26
rubs: r. nor botches in the work SHAK 461:11
yellow fog that r. its ELIOT 203:18
ruby: That r. which you wear HERR 250:2
rudder: bowsprit got mixed with the r. CARR 133:5
rhyme the r. is of verses BUTL 117:25
snatch'd his r. ARN 14:21
ruddier: r. than the cherry GAY 222:8
ruddy: beloved is white and r. BIBLE 57:3
Now he was r. BIBLE 50:7
R. Ball has taken flight THOM 549:2
rude: How r. are the boys that WATTS 565:26
of which were rather r. COW 164:2

new moons and s.	BIBLE 57:17
Sabean: S. odours from the spicy	MILT 347:17
saber: Con un no s. sabiendo	JOHN 273:16
Sabidi: Non amo te, S.	MART 331:9
sabiendo: Con un no saber s.	JOHN 273:16
Sabina: Cur valle permutem S.	HOR 260:16
sabios: los pocos s. que en el	LUIS 320:12
sable: the lot	SHAK 430:13
Sable-vested: S. Night	MILT 347:5
sabre: Great Chatham with his s.	ANON 5:10
That took the s. straight	HOUS 266:4
Sabrina: S. fair	MILT 341:20
Sacco: S.'s name will live	VANZ 555:8
sack: I'll purge, and leave s.	SHAK 440:29
intolerable deal of s.	SHAK 439:20
s. and sugar be a fault	SHAK 439:17
S. the lot	FISH 212:3
sackbut: s., psaltery	BIBLE 61:3
sacks: s. to sew up wives	THAC 545:18
Sacrament: holy S. to your comfort	PRAY 387:18
Sacraments: How many S. hath Christ	PRAY 388:19
S. in a tongue not understood	PRAY 400:8
Sacred: Enormous through the S. Town	BELL 39:28
is free but facts are s.	SCOTT 415:15
s. head of thine	MILT 343:10
s. rites unfit...	SIDN 507:26
s. to the household gods	THOM 549:23
two most s. names of earth	COWL 164:15
Sacred Heart: convent of the S.	ELIOT 204:16
sacrifice: blood Of human s.	MILT 345:14
bodies a living s.	BIBLE 75:15
Burnt-offerings, and s. for sin	PRAY 392:2
hands be an evening s.	PRAY 399:9
holy hush of ancient s.	STEV 520:18
measure of his s.	ROS 408:18
obey is better than s.	BIBLE 50:4
ought to s. to the graces	BURKE 111:26
perfect, and sufficient s.	PRAY 387:24
s. of God is a troubled	PRAY 393:8
s. to God of the devil's	POPE 381:21
stands Thine ancient s.	KIPL 302:7
these coming to the s.	KEATS 291:8
thou desirest no s.	PRAY 393:8
Too long a s.	YEATS 585:2
turn delight into a s.	HERB 246:27
your prayers one sweet s.	SHAK 446:27
sacrificed: Christ our passover is s.	BIBLE 75:36
must be s. to conciseness	JOHN 281:4
slain and spent and s.	SWIN 529:3
sacrificers: s., but not butchers	SHAK 449:8
sacrifices: he s. it to your opinion	BURKE 109:11
he who s. an hundred thousand	WALP 563:12
Upon such s., my Cordelia	SHAK 456:4
sacrilege: consecrated s.	DISR 185:6
sacrilegious: s. murder hath broke ope	SHAK 460:22
sad: All my s. captains	SHAK 422:22
did seem too solemn s.	SPEN 515:32
her sadness when she's s.	BARR 34:17
If you find him s.	SHAK 421:23
know not why I am so s.	HEINE 244:9
know not why I am so s.	SHAK 465:7
like a s. slave	SHAK 493:18
s. and bad and mad	BROW 100:8
s. bad glad	SWIN 529:2
s. I am	BETJ 44:6
s. mortality o'ersways	SHAK 494:4
s. road lies so clear	PATM 370:6
s. swell'd face	BARH 33:16
s. tale's best for winter	SHAK 491:12
s. vicissitude of things	STER 520:13
s. when others' grief is	BYRON 124:35
She is never s. but when	SHAK 472:13
should remember and be s.	ROSS 409:4
So s., so fresh	TENN 542:3
tell s. stories	SHAK 479:11
there on that s. height	THOM 546:24
would be as s. as night	SHAK 452:23
young as s. and bewildered	SMITH 510:22
Your s. tires in a mile-a	SHAK 491:21
sad-coloured: s. sect	HOOD 255:16
saddens: thought which s. while	BROW 103:13
sadder: s. and a wiser man	COL 156:1
saddest: telling the s. tale	SHAK 470:3
that tell of s. thought	SHEL 504:23
saddle: Come s. my horses	SCOTT 418:30
Things are in the s.	EMER 206:21
up they hang his s.	BEAU 36:7
saddle-leather: Thick-jewell'd shone the s.	TENN 538:9
sadly: take their pleasures s.	SULLY 524:18
sadness: At all the s. in the sweet	THOM 547:26
diverter of s.	WALT 564:3
Fell into a s.	SHAK 432:2
Good day s.	ELUA 206:16
s. of her sadness when	BARR 34:17
shade of s.	WHIT 571:17
soul shall taste the s.	KEATS 291:15
such a want-wit s. makes	SHAK 465:7
Sweet though in s.	SHEL 502:13
saeclorum: integro s. nascitur ordo	VIRG 559:22
saeclum: Solvet s. in favilla	CEL 138:5
saecula: et in s. saeculorum	MASS 334:14
Saepibus: S. in nostris parvam te	VIRG 560:4
safe: He give us a s. lodging	NEWM 362:9
s. course for the defeated	VIRG 558:7
s. in a golden ewer	BROW 100:4
s. I sing with mortal voice	MILT 348:28
see me s. up	MORE 357:16
us s. under every form	JOHN 276:6
Winds somewhere s. to sea	SWIN 529:25
safeguard: was the s. of the West	WORD 582:10
safely: I'd toddle s. home	SASS 414:11
to be s. thus	SHAK 461:8
tread s. into the unknown'	HASK 243:1
safer: s. than a known way	HASK 243:1
s. to be in a subordinate	THOM 546:9
safest: Just when we're s.	BROW 99:4
middle course is the s.	OVID 366:14
safety: every man shall eat in s.	SHAK 448:1
pluck this flower, s.	SHAK 438:29
source of my light and my s.	BIBLE 83:5
Under the smile of s. wounds	SHAK 440:30
safety-catch: s. on my pistol	JOHST 283:8
safire: diamond and s. bracelet	LOOS 318:3
safliest: s. when with one man mann'd	DONNE 188:16
saft: make it s. and narrow	BALL 30:12
sage: simpleton and the s.	CERV 138:20
When the smiling s. reply'd	JOHN 277:14
sager: s. sort our deeds reprove	CAT 136:25
said: Everything has been s.	LA B 306:11
fool hath s. in his heart	PRAY 390:2
He s. true things	BROW 99:11
if I had s. it myself	SWIFT 526:30
if I s. so	GOLD 232:4
is a great deal to be s.	BENT 41:5
might be s. on both sides	ADD 2:13
s. anything that was remembered	DISR 186:27
(S. I to myself	GILB 226:6
s. our remarks before	DON 187:17
S. the Piggy, 'I will.'	LEAR 312:13
s. what a owt to 'a said	TENN 541:3
Seek not to know who s.	THOM 546:8
so very little s.	CHUR 149:10
that has been known and s.	ARN 16:17
that's not been s. before	TER 544:16
they are carolled and s.	STEV 523:1
thought cannot wisely be s.	PEAC 370:19
sail: argosies with portly s.	SHAK 465:7
Never weather-beaten s.	CAMP 129:20
s. in amply billowing gown	BELL 39:28
sea-mark of my utmost s.	SHAK 477:20
shook out more s.	ARN 14:21
sieve I'll thither s.	SHAK 458:6
To s. beyond the sunset	TENN 544:3
towers of s. at dawn of day	CLOU 154:3
vessel puffs her s.	TENN 544:3
Was it the proud full s.	SHAK 494:11
white s.'s shaking	MAS 334:4
sail'd: She hadna a league	BALL 30:18
sailed: have s. the seas and come	YEATS 586:13
Swift has s. into his rest	YEATS 587:3
They s. away for a year	LEAR 312:12
you never s. with *me* before	JACK 270:29
sailing: Come s. to the strand	BALL 31:20
failing occurred in the s.	CARR 133:6
sailor: Home is the s.	STEV 523:10
lass that loves a s.	DIBD 175:20
No man will be a s. who	JOHN 274:18
s. frae the main	BURNS 114:11
s.'s wife had chestnuts	SHAK 458:6
soldier an' s. too	KIPL 302:23
take the most gallant s.	CHUR 150:16
there ever s. free to choose	KIPL 303:30
Sailor-men: It's very odd that S. should	BARH 33:23
sailors: s. but men	SHAK 465:27
s., when away	GAY 223:29
three s. of Bristol City	THAC 545:32
sails: argosies of magic s.	TENN 538:24
Purple the s.	SHAK 422:2
s. by the Low-lands low	BALL 31:2
To the white dipping s.	MAS 334:2
yet still the s. made	COL 155:26
saint: able to corrupt a s.	SHAK 438:7
accents of an expiring s.	STER 520:9
became a S.	NEWM 362:5
en aucune manière ni s.	VOLT 561:9
His s. is sure of his unspotted	PEELE 371:8
in vain the s. adore	DRAY 193:16
little s. best fits a little	HERR 249:20
neither s. nor sophist-led	ARN 13:1
Poet and S.	COWL 164:15
reel out a s.	CHUR 149:1
s. in crape is twice	POPE 377:11
seem a s. when most I play	SHAK 480:25
she cou'd make of me a s.	CONG 160:30
Tax not the royal S.	WORD 582:16
'twould a s. provoke	POPE 377:15
with a s.	SHAK 463:12
worst of madmen is a s.	POPE 380:11
sainted: thing ensky'd and s.	SHAK 463:12
Saint George: England and S.	SHAK 444:3
S., that swinged the dragon	SHAK 452:12
Saint Martin: Expect S.'s summer	SHAK 445:18
Saints: Communion of S.	PRAY 384:26
follow thy blessed S.	PRAY 387:4
Great men may jest with s.	SHAK 464:3
his lot is among the s.	BIBLE 62:16
is the death of his s.	PRAY 397:22
I think it frets the s.	BROW 97:30
Let the s. be joyful	PRAY 399:24
perfecting of the s.	BIBLE 77:28
S. in your injuries	SHAK 474:15
s. may do the same things	BUTL 118:5
shall never be S. in Heaven	BROW 96:17
than the least of all s.	BIBLE 77:23
thy slaughtered s.	MILT 351:9
which are the prayers of s.	BIBLE 81:27
With s. dost bait thy hook	SHAK 464:6
with thy quire of S.	DONNE 189:14
saint-seducing: lap to s. gold	SHAK 481:24
Saint Somebody: Miracles of S.	BROW 104:15
sair: love o'ercome sae s.	BURNS 114:18
saisons: Ô s., ô châteaux	RIMB 406:8
sake: Christ's particular love's s.	BROW 104:22

country for his country's s.   FITZ 212:4
friendship's s.   BLAKE 87:7
my s. shall find it   BIBLE 65:40
partial for th' observer's s.   POPE 377:8
wine for thy stomach's s.   BIBLE 79:16
Sal: S. Atticum   PLINY 374:17
salad: cheap but wholesome s.   COWP 167:27
My s. days   SHAK 421:33
Our Garrick's a s.   GOLD 231:16
primroses make a capital s.   DISR 186:15
s., for which   DU M 199:5
salamandrine: Of her s. fires   HARDY 239:4
salary: that he had a s. to receive   GIBB 224:10
sale: proverai sì come sa di s.   DANTE 171:17
Salem: At S. is his tabernacle   PRAY 395:1
saleroom: learned babble of the s.
                                      CARL 131:19
salire: disposto a s. alle stelle   DANTE 171:15
Salisbury: S. makes a great speech
                                      MORL 358:1
Salisbury Plain: crossing S. on a bicycle
                                      GILB 226:15
salley: Down by the s. gardens   YEATS 584:22
sallow: s. waiter brings me beans   SASS 415:4
sallows: on mealed-with-yellow s.
                                      HOPK 256:29
sally: I make a sudden s.   TENN 532:20
S. is gone from Ha'nacker Hill   BELL 39:26
There's none like pretty S.   CAREY 130:26
salmon: cod's head for the s.'s   SHAK 474:18
first s. and the first   LONG 316:23
'It was the s.   DICK 181:28
s.-falls   YEATS 586:11
s. sing in the street   AUDEN 18:9
salmons: there is s. in both   SHAK 445:5
saloons: Solomon of s.   BROW 102:18
salsa: s. del mundo es el hambre   CERV 138:13
salt: are the s. of the earth   BIBLE 64:7
are the s. of the earth   SHEL 501:18
beached verge of the s. flood   SHAK 486:14
Distasted with the s.   SHAK 487:12
eating an egg without s.   KIPL 304:37
s., estranging sea   ARN 13:13
s. is the taste of another   DANTE 171:17
s. tides seaward flow   ARN 13:5
seasoned with it   BIBLE 78:28
she became a pillar of s.   BIBLE 46:8
saltness: relish of the s. of time   SHAK 441:5
s. agree   GOLD 231:16
saltpetre: villainous s. should be digg'd
                                      SHAK 438:16
Salus: S. extra ecclesiam non   AUG 21:19
S. populi suprema   CIC 151:19
S. populi suprema lex   SELD 419:26
Una s. victis nullam sperare   VIRG 558:7
salut: s. balaiera largement le   ROST 410:12
salutant: morituri te s.   ANON 10:7
salutations: love s. in the marketplaces
                                      BIBLE 68:37
salute: I s. thee, Mantovano   TENN 543:19
S. one another with   BIBLE 75:28
who are about to die s.   ANON 10:7
Who are they you s.   WHIT 570:12
Salva: S. me   CEL 138:7
salvaged: Our ships have been s.   HALS 238:11
salvation: brought s. down By meekness
                                      SMART 509:4
generally necessary to s.   PRAY 388:19
helmet, the hope of s.   BIBLE 79:2
My bottle of s.   RAL 404:12
my light, and my s.   PRAY 391:7
no s. outside the church   AUG 21:19
now is our s. nearer than   BIBLE 75:24
s. of our own souls   JOHN 275:18
s. of mankind lies only   SOLZ 513:1
s. with fear and trembling   BIBLE 78:15
shew him my s.   PRAY 395:23
Should see s.   SHAK 467:27
strength of our s.   PRAY 396:3
that publisheth s.   BIBLE 59:18

things necessary to s.   PRAY 400:6
Salve: S., regina   ANON 10:19
Samarcand: silken S. to cedar'd Lebanon
                                      KEATS 289:20
Samaritan: ready enough to do the S.
                                      SMITH 511:7
Samarkand: take the Golden Road to
S.   FLEC 214:14
same: he is much the s.   ANON 4:17
It all comes to the s.   BROW 98:25
it would be all the s.   DICK 180:5
Jesus Christ the s. yesterday   BIBLE 80:4
more they are the s.   KARR 288:15
reason I should be the s.   AYT 24:4
s. in thine own act   SHAK 459:8
this will go onward the s.   HARDY 240:5
thou art the s.   PRAY 396:13
we must all say *the* s.   MELB 336:14
With the s. cement   POPE 375:24
you are the s. you   MART 331:13
samite: Clothed in white s.   TENN 534:1
samphire: Hangs one that gathers s.
                                      SHAK 455:14
sampler: serve to ply The s.   MILT 341:18
Samson: carry the buckler unto S.
                                      BROW 96:14
S. hath quit himself   MILT 351:1
Samuel: Lord called S.   BIBLE 49:34
Sana: S. quod est saucium   LANG 310:1
sancta: sed s. simplicitas   JER 272:20
sanctam: Et unam s. Catholicam et
                                      MASS 334:20
sanctified: husband is s. by the wife
                                      BIBLE 76:3
lips once s. by Hers   BROW 106:1
sanctifies: death canonizes and s.
                                      BURKE 109:5
Sanctify: S. the Lord of hosts himself
                                      BIBLE 58:4
sanction: s. des injustices établies
                                      FRAN 217:25
sanctioned: established injustices are
s.   FRAN 217:25
sanctities: Round the day's dead s.
                                      THOM 548:15
sanctuaries: round these chartered s.
                                      MACN 326:9
sanctuarize: indeed should murder s.
                                      SHAK 436:18
sanctuary: dark s. of incapacity   CHES 146:5
he shall be for a s.   BIBLE 58:4
Sanctus: S., sanctus, sanctus   MASS 335:4
sand: built his house upon the s.   BIBLE 65:12
grain of s.   WHIT 570:21
islets of yellow s.   LEAR 312:16
land of s. and ruin   SWIN 530:29
name upon The soft sea-s.   LAND 309:4
night to die upon the s.   ARN 14:26
plain to be seen in the s.   DEFOE 173:7
s. against the wind   BLAKE 86:23
S.-strewn caverns   ARN 13:6
speed i' the slushy s.   BROW 102:14
Such quantities of s.   CARR 135:5
tide crept up along the s.   KING 297:1
World in a Grain of S.   BLAKE 85:8
sandal: bright and battering s.   HOPK 256:11
his s. shoon   SHAK 435:32
sandals: Bind on thy s.   SWIN 528:16
still morn went out with s.   MILT 343:19
Sandford: down by S.   ARN 15:8
sands: Across the s. of Dee   KING 296:25
Footprints on the s. of time   LONG 317:4
Here are s.   BEAU 36:1
lone and level s. stretch   SHEL 502:16
looks at the s.   HARDY 240:15
s. with printless foot   SHAK 485:23
sang: auld Scotish s.   BURNS 113:4
I s. in my chains like   THOM 547:2
morning stars s.   BIBLE 53:3
Perhaps it may turn out a s.   BURNS 113:16

s. themselves to sleep   HODG 252:6
s. to a small guitar   LEAR 312:11
song the Syrens s.   BROW 97:14
Thus s. the uncouth swain   MILT 343:19
sanglant: Le dernier acte est s.   PASC 369:8
sanglots: Les s. longs   VERL 556:8
sanguinary: s. punishments which corrupt
                                      PAINE 368:4
sanguis: semen est s. Christianorum
                                      TERT 544:22
Sanitas: S. sanitatum et omnia sanitas
                                      MEN 336:24
sanitatum: Sanitas s. et omnia sanitas
                                      MEN 336:24
sank: s. her in the sea   BALL 30:19
she s. by the Low-lands   BALL 31:3
sanno: maestro di color che s.   DANTE 171:7
sano: mens sana in corpore s.   JUV 288:4
sans: s. End   FITZ 212:18
S. teeth, sans eyes   SHAK 425:24
sanza: e s. alcun sospetto   DANTE 171:9
sap: Lord also are full of s.   PRAY 396:20
world's whole s. is sunk   DONNE 189:28
sapere: s. aude   HOR 258:14
sapient: s. sutlers of the Lord   ELIOT 204:1
shake his s. head   ARN 15:12
sapienti: Dictum s. sat est   PLAU 374:14
saplings: it plies the s. double   HOUS 263:14
sapphire: 'And second s.   BROW 97:34
purer s. melts into the sea   TENN 540:8
sapphires: ivory overlaid with s.   BIBLE 57:4
Sappho: pianola 'replaces' S.   POUND 383:5
Where burning S. loved   BYRON 122:32
Whether my S.'s breast   HERR 249:7
Sarah: Now Abraham and S. were
                                      BIBLE 46:6
Sarcasticul: This is rote S.   WARD 564:23
sardine: jasper and a s. stone   BIBLE 81:22
Sargent: dangerous to sit to S.   ANON 6:8
Sarum: I had you upon S. plain   SHAK 453:22
sassy: 'I'm sickly but s.   HARR 242:16
sat: Babylon we s. down and wept
                                      PRAY 399:3
Dictum sapienti s. est   PLAU 374:14
Many kings have s. down   BIBLE 62:31
once I s. upon a promontory   SHAK 470:7
S. and knotted all   SEDL 419:12
s. prata biberunt   VIRG 559:21
You have s. too long here   CROM 169:26
Satan: beat down S. under our feet
                                      PRAY 385:19
capitol Of S. and his peers   MILT 346:5
Ev'n S. glowr'd   BURNS 115:11
Get thee behind me, S.   BIBLE 66:34
Incens'd with indignation S.   MILT 346:26
messenger of S. to buffet   BIBLE 77:13
my S.   BLAKE 86:1
S. as lightning fall from   BIBLE 69:28
S. came also among them   BIBLE 52:5
S. exalted sat   MILT 346:6
S. finds some mischief   WATTS 565:22
S. met his ancient friend   BYRON 126:9
S., Nick   BURNS 112:24
S., so call him now   MILT 348:5
Satanic: dark S. mills   BLAKE 86:16
satiable: was full of 's. curtiosity KIPL 304:20
satiate: life's cool ev'ning s.   POPE 380:7
satiety: another occasion of s.   BACON 25:37
ne'er knew love's sad s.   SHEL 504:22
satin: always goes into white s.   SHER 506:3
satire: It's hard not to write s.   JUV 287:9
let s. be my song   BYRON 124:15
S., being levelled   SWIFT 527:3
S. is a sort of glass   SWIFT 525:32
S. or satyr   POPE 376:30
Verse s. indeed is entirely   QUIN 403:25
satiric: by one s. touch   SWIFT 527:25
satirical: s. rogue says here that   SHAK 432:8
satirist: be the second English s.   HALL 238:6

satisfaction: own s. in the year 1399
    AUST 22:20
to give you s.   GAY 222:32
satisfied: things that are never s. BIBLE 54:46
well paid that is well s.   SHAK 468:11
satisfies: Where most she s.   SHAK 422:5
satisfieth: he s. the empty soul   PRAY 397:7
labour for that which s.   BIBLE 59:25
s. thy mouth with good   PRAY 396:15
satisfy: long life will I s.   PRAY 395:23
That poorly s. our eyes   WOTT 583:15
satisfying: s. a voracious appetite FIEL 211:25
Satura: S. quidem tota nostra est QUIN 403:25
saturam: s. non scribere   JUV 287:9
Saturday: S. and Monday   CAREY 130:27
what he did on S.   YBAR 584:7
Saturn: Sat gray-hair'd S.   KEATS 289:33
To S. nor to Mercury   HOUS 264:26
while S. whirls   TENN 541:21
Saturnia: redeunt S. regna   VIRG 559:22
saturnine: s., dark, and melancholic
    CONG 159:17
satyr: angel s. walks these hills   KILV 296:7
sauce: et une seule s.   CAR 130:10
Hunger is the best s.   CERV 138:16
only one s.   CAR 130:10
saucefleem: s. he was   CHAU 142:4
saucer: sing the s. and the cup   PAIN 367:15
saucy: deep-search'd with s.   SHAK 456:15
s. and audacious eloquence   SHAK 471:15
saugh: if that she s. a mous   CHAU 141:16
Saul: S. also among the prophets BIBLE 49:41
S. and Jonathan were lovely   BIBLE 50:17
S. hath slain his thousands   BIBLE 50:13
S. was consenting unto   BIBLE 73:29
S., why persecutest thou   BIBLE 73:33
weep over S.   BIBLE 50:17
saule: Christe receive thy s.   BALL 31:6
sausage: Don't throw away that s.
    ELIOT 202:8
savage: mad and s. master   SOPH 513:9
Unequal laws unto a s.   TENN 543:21
which a s. wields his club   HUXL 269:3
wild in woods the noble s.   DRYD 195:29
will take some s. woman   TENN 539:6
you with stories of s.   BURKE 109:15
savageness: she will sing the s. out
    SHAK 476:12
savages: cant in defence of s.   JOHN 279:19
save: choose time is to s. time   BACON 26:7
God s. king Solomon   BIBLE 50:30
God s. the king   HOGG 252:24
himself he cannot s.   BIBLE 68:23
matter enough to s. one's own   BROW 102:3
preaching to s. them that believe BIBLE 75:29
s. my soul   ANON 7:5
s. them by the barrel-load   THOM 548:26
shall s. his soul alive   BIBLE 60:35
souls I could not s.   HOUS 265:6
Themselves they could not s.   HOUS 262:13
vain thing to s. a man   PRAY 391:20
wilt thou s. the people   ELL 206:12
you would s. none of me   DONNE 188:28
saved: do to be s. in this World   HAL 238:4
He s. others   BIBLE 68:23
s. herself by her exertions   PITT 374:5
they only s. the world   CHES 146:25
we are not s.   BIBLE 60:20
What must I do to be s.   BIBLE 74:7
Whosoever will be s.   PRAY 385:11
savent: gens de qualité s.   MOL 353:23
saves: idea of Death s.   FORS 217:3
who freely s. those who   CEL 138:7
saveth: s. in time of affliction   BIBLE 62:21
saving: s. health among all nations
    PRAY 394:4
s. those that eye thee   SHAK 428:4
Saviour: Call'd 'S. of the Nations'
    BYRON 123:25
it's 'S. of 'is country'   KIPL 303:23

S.'s birth is celebrated   SHAK 429:17
saviours: s. come not home tonight
    HOUS 262:13
savoir: c'est de s. être à soi   MONT 354:21
que de s. quelque chose   MOL 353:5
savory: s., marjoram   SHAK 491:25
savour: salt have lost his s.   BIBLE 64:7
Seeming and s. all the winter   SHAK 491:22
send forth a stinking s.   BIBLE 56:1
savoury: s. pulp they chew   MILT 347:25
saw: drowns the parson's s.   SHAK 457:19
I came, s., and overcame   SHAK 442:13
I just s. Virgil   OVID 366:24
I s. and loved   GIBB 224:12
I s. it   BROW 102:23
I stumbled when I s.   SHAK 455:6
I who s. the face of God   MARL 329:7
myself s. and of which I was   VIRG 557:21
Nor do not s. the air too   SHAK 433:16
s., he sigh'd, he lov'd   GAY 223:6
saws: s. and modern instances   SHAK 425:24
Saxon: leave the S. alone   KIPL 301:19
like that ancient S. phrase   LONG 316:18
saxpence: bang—went s.   PUNCH 402:18
say: All I can s. is   BROW 102:23
are to s. what they please   FRED 218:22
Englishman is content to s.   JOHN 278:17
Have something to s.   ARN 16:25
if I could s. how much   SHAK 472:10
I s., before the morning   PRAY 398:24
many things to s. unto you   BIBLE 72:39
nothing to what I could s.   CARR 134:8
Poyser 'has her s. out'   ELIOT 200:13
S. I'm weary   HUNT 268:10
s. it is my humour   SHAK 467:20
S. not the struggle naught   CLOU 154:4
s. what you think   TAC 531:12
should s. what you mean   CARR 133:29
should s. you do not like it   WHIS 569:24
there is no more to s.   SHAK 487:18
They'l s. it's stolne   BRAD 91:13
think till I see what I s.   WALL 562:5
to s. about a play when   SHAW 496:26
To s. as I said then   SHAK 421:33
to s. the perfectly correct   SHAW 496:31
we must all s. the same   MELB 336:14
you have nothing to s.   COLT 159:8
you have something to s.   WHAT 569:11
saying: if something is not worth s.
    BEAU 35:14
rage for s. something   JOHN 274:17
s. anything two or three   AUST 22:12
that if they keep on s.   BENN 40:23
tremble lest a s. learnt   TENN 543:12
sayings: s. are generally like women's
    HAZL 243:8
s. of philosophers   BUTL 117:31
Says: S. little   FARQ 209:25
scabbard: he threw away the s. CLAR 152:18
scabbards: have leaped from their s.
    BURKE 111:9
scabs: Make yourselves s.   SHAK 427:12
scaffold: To the s. and the doom AYT 24:9
Truth forever on the s.   LOW 319:13
scald: mine own tears Do s.   SHAK 455:25
scale: e'l salir per l'altrui s.   DANTE 171:17
fly on a rather large s.   BARH 33:5
sufficiently large s.   SPEN 514:33
would not sink i' the s.   BROW 104:4
scaled: s. invention or true artistry
    POUND 382:13
scales: could swear in both the s.
    SHAK 460:16
Scalinger: S. used to say of the Basques
    CHAM 139:16
scallop-shell: Give me my s. of quiet
    RAL 404:12
scaly: s. horror of his folded   MILT 344:12
scan: Then gently s. your brother
    BURNS 112:25

scandal: have no s. while you dine
    TENN 543:16
In s., as in robbery   CHES 145:9
It is public s. that constitutes   MOL 354:1
Love and s. are the best   FIEL 211:18
Retired to their tea and s.   CONG 159:21
s. about Queen Elizabeth   SHER 505:24
there is no s. like rags   FARQ 209:26
scandale: s. du monde est ce qui   MOL 354:1
scandalous: s. and poor   ROCH 407:2
scapegoat: Let him go for a s. into
    BIBLE 48:7
scar: Nor s. that whiter skin   SHAK 477:5
scarce: good people's wery s.   DICK 183:4
scarcely: I would s. kick to come
    KEATS 293:31
scarceness: runagates continue in s.
    PRAY 394:7
scare: 'Because those footprints s.
    HOR 258:11
ever s. me with thy tears   TENN 543:12
s. myself with my own desert FROST 219:3
scarecrow: not make a s. of the law
    SHAK 463:15
scarecrows: s. of fools and the beacons
    HUXL 269:10
scarely: s. greet me with that sun
    SHAK 493:14
Scarf: S. up the tender eye   SHAK 461:14
scarlet: are like a thread of s.   BIBLE 56:26
Cowards in s. pass   GRAN 234:9
did not wear his s. coat   WILDE 572:7
'His sins were s.   BELL 39:19
In S. town   BALL 30:10
line of s. thread   BIBLE 48:37
love that loves a s. coat   HOOD 254:15
Only the s. soldiers   AUDEN 20:4
though clothed in s.   JONS 284:14
Though your sins be as s.   BIBLE 57:18
who clothed you in s.   BIBLE 50:17
scars: My marks and s. I carry   BUNY 107:38
seamed with the s. of disease   MAC 324:7
sleeve and show his s.   SHAK 445:3
Scatter: S., as from an unextinguished
    SHEL 502:14
scatter'd: thousand s. into Clay   FITZ 212:8
scattered: land is s. with light   BRID 92:8
let his enemies be s.   PRAY 394:6
s. the proud in the imagination   BIBLE 69:6
s. the heaped-up mountains   VIRG 560:12
scatterest: soon as thou s. them they
    PRAY 395:18
Scatters: S. the rear of darkness   MILT 342:17
scelerisque: vitae s. purus   HOR 259:23
scene: behold the swelling s.   SHAK 443:3
highly impossible s.   GILB 225:13
In life's last s. what   JOHN 283:3
Last s. of all   SHAK 425:24
Love gilds the s.   SHER 506:24
o'er all this s. of man   POPE 379:1
our lofty s. be acted o'er   SHAK 450:5
s. individable   SHAK 432:20
s. of it with my Papa   DICK 178:18
start a s. or two   ELIOT 203:24
there I laid the s.   COWP 167:17
scenery: end of all natural s.   RUSK 411:12
S. is fine   KEATS 293:27
s.'s divine   CALV 127:20
scenes: busy s. of crowded life   JOHN 282:28
changing s. of life   TATE 531:21
no more behind your s.   JOHN 274:2
s. and shining prospects   ADD 2:4
scent: dripping with s.   HOR 259:15
methinks I s. the morning air   SHAK 431:10
s. of the roses will hang   MOORE 356:7
sweetest flower for s.   SHEL 503:24
Their s. survives their   THOM 547:25
whose s. the fair annoys   COWP 165:4
scepter'd: this s. isle   SHAK 478:20

sceptic: s. to deny the possibility
HUXL 269:14
What ever s. could inquire BUTL 117:19
scepticism: all-dissolving s. NEWM 362:2
wise s. is the first attribute LOW 319:16
sceptre: His s. shows the force SHAK 467:27
s. and the ball SHAK 444:25
s. o'er a slumb'ring world YOUNG 588:1
sceptred: avails the s. race LAND 308:26
Sceptreless: man remains S. SHEL 503:12
sceptrumque: s. tyrannis TURG 553:22
schaffende: *Zerstörung ist zugleich eine
s.* BAK 29:24
Schatten: *denen man seinen S. zeigt*
NIET 363:6
wollen niemand in den S. BULOW 106:23
schedules: out divers s. of my beauty
SHAK 488:12
Scheldt: by the lazy S. GOLD 231:23
scheme: breakfast she'll project a s.
YOUNG 587:18
sorry S. of Things FITZ 213:16
schemes: s. of political improvement
JOHN 275:29
s. o' mice an' men BURNS 115:22
Scherzando: *S. ma non troppo* GILB 225:15
Schicksal: *S. und Gemüt Namen* NOV 364:9
Schlag: *Zwei Herzen und ein S.* HALM 238:10
schlecht: *Welt hässlich und s.* NIET 363:8
scholar: better s. than Wordsworth
HOUS 266:18
distractions about which, as a s. LIPP 315:9
He was a s. SHAK 447:21
s. all Earth's volumes CHAP 140:16
s. among rakes MAC 324:13
There mark what ills the s.'s JOHN 282:29
scholars: nor its great s. great HOLM 253:17
Of white-robed S. only WORD 582:16
S. and gentlemen WORD 580:20
S. dispute HOR 257:15
school: doctrine never was there a s.
MILT 350:21
enjoyed at the head of a s. WALP 562:18
Example is the s. of mankind BURKE 112:7
hath put his heart to s. WORD 582:13
he's been to a good s. SAKI 413:14
in erecting a grammar s. SHAK 446:14
microcosm of a public s. DISR 186:39
'S. is pretty bad WAUGH 565:30
s. nonsense which was knocked BEER 37:22
special reason for hating s. BEER 37:21
Than either s. or college BURNS 114:8
till we leave s. LEWIS 314:9
Unwillingly to s. SHAK 425:24
vixen when she went to s. SHAK 470:24
was whipt at s. DRYD 198:20
schoolboy: Every s. knows who imprisoned
MAC 323:14
Every s. knows it TAYL 532:5
I see a s. when I think YEATS 585:3
s. of fourteen is ignorant MAC 324:12
s.'s tale BYRON 120:9
tell what every s. knows SWIFT 527:20
than that of a s.'s tip THAC 545:11
then the whining s. SHAK 425:24
schoolboys: duly to delight s. JUV 288:2
s. from their books SHAK 482:18
s. playing in the stream PEELE 371:9
school-days: Thy s. frightful SHAK 481:8
schoolgirl: Pert as a s. well can be
GILB 226:27
schoolman: he knew no s.'s subtle
POPE 377:5
schoolmaster: s. is abroad BROU 95:5
schoolmastering: perish than to continue
s. CARL 132:27
schoolmasters: s. puzzle their brain
GOLD 231:22
s. Deliver us to laws HERB 248:10
s. even today read Greek YEATS 587:13

schoolrooms: Better build s. for 'the
boy' ELIZ 162:8
schools: a' their colleges and s. BURNS 115:27
bewilder'd in the maze of s. POPE 378:11
lumber of the s. SWIFT 527:32
public s. with silk MARL 329:5
rules were not in the s. BUTL 117:34
s. of thought contend MAO 328:18
wrangling s. DONNE 188:26
your jargon o' your s. BURNS 113:19
Schosse: *aus dem S. der Zeit* HEINE 244:12
schuf: *er s. alsbald noch andere* NIET 363:3
Schumann: S.'s our music-maker now
BROW 100:16
schweigen: *darüber muss man s.* WITT 575:17
S. ist golden CARL 132:23
Sciatica: S.: he cured it AUBR 17:25
Science: Art and S. cannot exist BLAKE 86:7
commit A social s. AUDEN 21:5
countenance of all s. WORD 583:9
despise Art and S. BLAKE 86:9
everything that relates to s. LAMB 307:10
Fair S. frown'd not GRAY 235:4
Geometry (which is the only s. HOBB 251:14
great tragedy of S. HUXL 269:5
His soul proud S. never POPE 379:5
human s. is at a loss CHOM 148:16
Il faut n'appeler S. VAL 555:1
La vraye s. et le vray CHAR 141:1
only applications of s. PAST 369:17
only the instrument of S. JOHN 281:6
Politics is not an exact s. BISM 84:19
Professors of the Dismal S. CARL 131:40
S. appears WORD 580:16
S. falsely so called BIBLE 79:21
S. is his forte SMITH 512:11
S. is nothing but trained HUXL 269:3
S. is organized knowledge SPEN 514:24
S. moves TENN 539:1
to patient S. dear WORD 582:12
With the fairy tales of s. TENN 538:16
sciences: Books must follow s. BACON 25:6
That great mother of s. BACON 28:8
scientia: *et ipsa s. potestas est* BACON 28:11
scientiae: *ab animo fraudatrix s.* JOHN 273:17
scientiarum: *Magna ista s. mater*
BACON 28:8
scientific: broken open on the most s.
PEAC 370:13
Death was but A s. WILDE 572:12
if they were s. terms ARN 16:18
literary and s. opinion ARN 16:5
s. faith's absurd BROW 100:21
s. names of beings animalculous GILB 228:16
scientists: at the illiteracy of s. SNOW 512:16
scintillations: s. of your wit be like
GOUL 233:5
scire: s. nefas HOR 259:19
scissor-man: red-legged s. HOFF 252:18
scoff: some that came to s. at him AYT 24:8
who came to s. GOLD 230:24
scoffer: dull product of a s.'s pen
WORD 577:12
Scoffing: S. his state and grinning
SHAK 479:11
scold: 'amper an' 'inder an' s. men
KIPL 303:11
scole: s. of Stratford atte Bowe CHAU 141:15
scones: buttered s. and crumpets ELIOT 202:5
scooped: thirsted s. the brimming stream
MILT 347:25
scope: that man's s. SHAK 493:6
scorched: grey wig with the s. foretop
MAC 324:7
they were s. BIBLE 66:16
Scorer: when the One Great S. comes
RICE 405:23
scorn: deal of s. looks beautiful SHAK 489:24
Disdain and s. ride sparkling SHAK 472:21
figure for the time of s. SHAK 476:18

Fools may our s. GAY 223:15
held the human race in s. BELL 38:33
little s. is alluring CONG 161:2
love he laugh'd to s. SHAK 495:18
S. not the Sonnet WORD 582:14
s. of irregular perquisites WAUGH 566:2
s. of that pleasant land PRAY 397:5
S. the sort now growing YEATS 587:8
s. to change my state SHAK 493:6
s. which mock'd the smart ARN 13:9
sound Of public s. MILT 349:22
Teach not thy lip such s. SHAK 480:21
to s. in the bitterness BIBLE 62:26
treat with virtuous s. GILB 226:4
very s. of men PRAY 390:17
We s. their bodies BAST 35:2
'Where I have had many a s. BALL 30:9
scorn'd: Not s. in heav'n COWP 166:4
s. his spirit SHAK 448:21
was s. and died GAY 223:6
scorner: thou s. of the ground SHEL 504:24
scornful: dart not s. glances from
SHAK 484:15
sat in the seat of the s. PRAY 389:14
s., yet with jealous eyes POPE 376:26
scorning: s. the base degrees SHAK 449:5
time and nonsense s. BUCK 106:18
scorpions: will chastise you with s.
BIBLE 51:3
Scot: Had Cain been S. CLEV 153:4
Scotch: indeed inferior to the S. NORTH 364:2
joke well into a S. understanding
SMITH 510:28
S. civility ROCH 407:5
that the S. have found JOHN 277:12
scotch'd: We have s. the snake SHAK 461:12
Scotchman: is that makes a S. happy
JOHN 280:4
Much may be made of a S. JOHN 276:10
noblest prospect which a S. JOHN 274:30
one S. but what was a man LOCK 316:2
Scotchmen: all my life to like S. LAMB 307:8
scot-free: will get off s. HOR 262:7
Scotia: chief of S.'s food BURNS 113:8
S.'s grandeur springs BURNS 113:4
Scotish: swats and an auld S. sang
BURNS 113:4
Scotland: do indeed come from S.
JOHN 274:20
grave Livers do in S. use WORD 581:1
inferior sort of S. SMITH 512:5
in S. supports the people JOHN 281:14
left fair S.'s strand BURNS 114:10
love S. better than truth JOHN 281:22
Seeing S. JOHN 277:24
shiver'd was fair S.'s spear SCOTT 417:25
Stands S. where it did SHAK 462:15
That S. led in luve WYNT 584:4
Scots: dozen of S. at a breakfast SHAK 438:33
S. lords at his feet BALL 31:20
S., wha hae wi' Wallace BURNS 114:34
Scotsman: moral attribute of a S. BARR 34:20
S. of your ability let BARR 34:19
world than a S. on the make BARR 34:27
Scott: half so flat as Walter S. ANON 7:8
think it was Sir Walter S. SURT 525:9
wrong part wrote S. ANON 8:12
Scottish: brave old S. Cavalier AYT 24:5
Froude informs the S. youth STUB 524:5
scoundrel: given them to such a s.
SWIFT 526:21
Good is the plea of the s. BLAKE 86:5
last refuge of a s. JOHN 276:25
man over forty is a s. SHAW 498:4
scoundrels: healthy hatred of s. CARL 132:2
scoured: with rust than to be s. SHAK 441:15
scourge: made a s. of small cords
BIBLE 71:35
S. of God MARL 330:17
scout: s. 'em, and flout 'em SHAK 485:15

scowl: Did s. on Richard SHAK 480:10
With anxious s. drew near AYT 24:10
scowling: At fifteen I stopped s.
POUND 383:16
scramble: s. at the shearers' feast
MILT 343:12
scrap: just for a s. of paper BETH 42:3
scrape: took him a potsherd to s. BIBLE 52:9
scrappy: days when work was s. CHES 147:22
scraps: stolen the s. SHAK 457:12
scratch: quick sharp s. BROW 102:14
s. his name on the Abbey-stones
BROW 101:27
S. the Christian and you ZANG 588:16
will s. the nurse SHAK 490:31
scratched: considerably worried and s.
DICK 178:6
Priscian a little s. SHAK 457:11
Scratches: S. its innocent behind
AUDEN 19:19
scratching: cure it but the s. of a pen
LOVER 318:21
scream: Does not s. WHIT 571:11
like a s. from a crevasse GREE 236:6
mew rise to a s. on the tool-shed AUDEN 20:8
screaming: I am s. out loud all DICK 180:9
screams: strange s. of death SHAK 460:20
screen: s. from seeing and leave SWIN 528:18
screw: s. your courage SHAK 459:10
scribblative: arts babblative and s.
SOUT 514:12
scribble: Always s. GLOU 229:22
fierce vindictive s. of red BROW 100:23
Scribe: At ille inquit 'S. BEDE 37:2
scribendi: Qui nullum fere s. genus
JOHN 277:13
S. cacoethes et aegro JUV 287:23
scribens: aut s. THOM 546:11
scribere: In vento et rapida s. oportet
CAT 137:7
saturam non s. JUV 287:9
scribes: Beware of the s. BIBLE 68:37
of the s. and Pharisees BIBLE 64:11
s., and Pharisees BIBLE 67:24
s. and the Pharisees brought BIBLE 72:9
scrip: My s. of joy RAL 404:12
yet with s. and scrippage SHAK 426:6
scriptores: Cedite Romani s. PROP 401:17
scripturas: Scrutamini s. SELD 419:18
Scripture: devil can cite S. for his
SHAK 466:1
Holy S. containeth PRAY 400:6
I will better it in S. OVER 366:7
S. moveth us in sundry PRAY 384:9
writ is the s. of puplis JER 272:21
Scriptures: hast caused all holy S.
PRAY 386:5
Search the s. BIBLE 72:3
scrivener: notched and cropt s. LAMB 307:11
scrofulous: s. French novel BROW 105:8
scroll: long-cramped s. BROW 101:24
s. of crystal SHEL 500:10
with punishments the s. HENL 245:5
scrotum: s.tightening sea JOYCE 286:20
scruple: Some craven s. SHAK 435:30
scrupulosity: himself with oriental s.
JOHN 282:2
scrupulous: s. and the just CONR 161:22
Scrutamini: S. scripturas SELD 419:18
scullion: Away, you s. SHAK 441:19
sculptor: great s. or painter can be
RUSK 411:8
sculptur'd: s. dead on each side seem
KEATS 289:10
sculpture: like that of s. RUSS 412:15
scum: composed of the s. of the earth
WELL 568:1
scutcheon: honour is a mere s. SHAK 440:18
scuttled: s. ship or cut a throat BYRON 122:30
Scuttling: S. across the floors ELIOT 203:21

Scylla: S. and Charybdis NEWM 361:21
S. and Charybdis SHEL 505:11
scythe: bate his s.'s keen edge SHAK 456:14
mower whets his s. MILT 342:19
poor crooked s. and spade SHIR 507:2
Wanting the s. SHAK 445:12
Scythia: another group to S. VIRG 559:13
Scythian: whitest snow on S. hills
MARL 330:3
se: s., and eek for to be CHAU 143:20
s. Iudice nemo nocens JUV 288:5
sea: all as hungry as the s. SHAK 489:6
all the s. were ink LYLY 321:16
beneath in the abysmal s. TENN 537:24
blow the earth into the s. SHAK 454:3
blue days at s. STEV 522:29
boundless as the s. SHAK 482:17
cold gray stones, O S. TENN 532:17
crown'd with summer s. TENN 535:27
desks and never go to s. GILB 228:7
do be afraid of the s. SYNGE 531:4
dominion of the s. COV 163:10
estranging s. ARN 13:13
far over the summer s. TENN 543:2
frail boat on the rough s. HOR 259:12
From s. to shining sea BATES 35:4
full s. are we now afloat SHAK 451:27
gaping wretches of the s. HUNT 268:7
great and wide s. also PRAY 397:1
gurly grew the s. BALL 30:18
has something of the s. SEDL 419:9
heaven by s. as by land GILB 225:7
he cast into the s. BIBLE 70:30
He divided the s. PRAY 395:5
his footsteps in the s. COWP 165:26
home from s. STEV 523:10
if we gang to s. master BALL 31:18
if Ye take away the s. KIPL 300:19
In a solitude of the s. HARDY 239:4
In cliff to the s. ARN 13:2
In my chains like the s. THOM 547:2
in perils in the s. BIBLE 77:12
in the bottom of the s. SHAK 480:27
in the midst of the s. BIBLE 55:1
in the s. of life enisled ARN 13:12
Into that silent s. COL 155:5
into the midst of the s. PRAY 392:19
is not afraid of the s. SYNGE 531:4
is the sound of the s. ELIOT 204:13
kings of the s. ARN 13:7
little cloud out of the s. BIBLE 51:11
lover of men, the s. SWIN 530:27
mad as the vex'd s. SHAK 455:13
mirrors of the s. are strewn FLEC 214:21
mountains by the winter s. TENN 535:20
never sick at s. GILB 227:31
not having been at s. JOHN 277:26
of a sudden came the s. BROW 103:9
of the swing of the s. HOPK 256:17
one is of the s. WORD 582:18
one s. to the other PRAY 394:20
on this windy s. of land MILT 347:10
owse and bottom of the s. SHAK 443:8
particular s. that it is old HARDY 241:21
Ran purple to the s. MILT 345:17
Receiveth as the s. SHAK 487:20
remain in the broad s. PRAY 394:1
ride slowly towards the s. CHES 147:14
round me like a bursting s. THOM 548:21
sapphire melts into the s. TENN 540:8
s. for an acre of barren SHAK 484:22
s. gave up the dead which BIBLE 82:29
s. grew civil at her song SHAK 470:7
s. is his PRAY 396:4
S. of Faith ARN 12:23
s. of glass like unto crystal BIBLE 81:23
s. of glass mingled with BIBLE 82:19
s. rises higher CHES 146:16
s. saw that, and fled PRAY 397:16
S. shall give up her dead) PRAY 400:4

s.! the sea XEN 584:5
s. was made his tomb BARN 34:5
s. where it goes ARN 12:22
serpent-haunted s. FLEC 214:8
settle somewhere near the s. KIPL 303:30
sheet and a flowing s. CUNN 170:13
sight of that immortal s. WORD 579:12
snotgreen s. JOYCE 286:20
steady than an ebbing s. FORD 216:20
stillness of the central s. TENN 537:20
stone set in the silver s. SHAK 478:20
summers in a s. of glory SHAK 447:9
sun was shining on the s. CARR 135:3
swaying sound of the s. AUDEN 20:3
that gong-tormented s. YEATS 584:13
that great s. SHEL 501:17
that whirls me to the s. MER 337:10
there was no more s. BIBLE 82:30
they sink through the s. THOM 546:19
those in peril on the s. WHIT 569:26
tideless dolorous midland s. SWIN 530:29
till the s. itself floweth TRAH 551:17
union with its native s. WORD 577:16
uttermost parts of the s. PRAY 399:5
Vext the dim s. TENN 543:22
walking on the s. BIBLE 66:25
water in the rough rude s. SHAK 479:5
waves of the s. BIBLE 59:15
waves of the s. are mighty PRAY 396:1
waves on the great s. LUCR 320:6
Went down into the s. COL 155:7
When I put out to s. TENN 533:3
who rush across the s. HOR 258:19
why the s. is boiling hot CARR 135:7
willing foe and s. room ANON 4:26
Within a walk of the s. BELL 40:11
wrinkled s. beneath him TENN 533:7
yet the s. is not full BIBLE 55:6
sea-beasts: Where the s. rang'd all ARN 13:6
sea-blooms: s. and the oozy woods
SHEL 502:11
sea-change: doth suffer a s. SHAK 484:32
sea-faring: In land-travel or s. BROW 105:34
sea-flower: quiet s. moulded SWIN 528:25
sea-fogs: here the s. lap and cling KIPL 303:13
seagreen: s. Incorruptible CARL 131:26
seagull: Remember you shot a s. CHEK 145:2
seal: opened the seventh s. BIBLE 82:5
S. her sweet eyes weary ROSS 409:5
s. upon thine heart BIBLE 57:11
S. up the mouth of outrage SHAK 484:1
this kingly s. SHAK 422:21
You Heard a S. Bark THUR 550:31
seal'd: Hath s. thee for herself SHAK 434:1
sea-life: When men come to like a s.
JOHN 276:33
sealing wax: shoes—and ships—and
s. CARR 135:7
such as gunpowder and s. CARR 136:4
Seals: S. of love SHAK 464:21
that s. up all in rest SHAK 494:7
to loose the s. thereof BIBLE 81:26
sea-maid: report a s. spawn'd him
SHAK 464:19
seaman: s. tells stories of winds PROP 401:15
sea-mark: Like a great s. SHAK 428:4
very s. of my utmost sail SHAK 477:20
sear: s., the yellow leaf SHAK 463:2
search: active s. for Truth LESS 314:2
s. for pearls must dive DRYD 195:10
S. the scriptures BIBLE 72:3
s. will find it out HERR 249:19
they are not worth the s. SHAK 465:15
where I made s. for thee AUG 21:16
search'd: deep-s. with saucy SHAK 456:15
searched: thou hast s. me out PRAY 399:4
searching: I am s. everywhere STEP 518:27
s. find out God BIBLE 52:22
s. what we know not MILT 351:26

seareth: Earthly glory ageth and s.
POUND 383:19

seas: floors of silent s.   ELIOT 203:21
gloom the dark broad s.   TENN 544:3
hushed the shrunken s.   ELIOT 204:15
multitudinous s. incarnadine   SHAK 460:13
must down to the s. again   MAS 334:4
now through friendly s.   FLEC 214:17
On the dangers of the s.   PARK 368:25
s. are too long   BACON 28:3
s. colder than the Hebrides   FLEC 214:7
s. do laugh   WEBS 567:14
such as pass on the s.   PRAY 400:3
treacle and s. of butter   MAC 324:21
sea-sand: is the ribbed s.   COL 155:19
sea-scented: Then a mile of warm s.
BROW 102:14
sea-shore: boy playing on the s. NEWT 362:20
seasickness: it's as universal as s.
SHAW 497:29

season: Be instant in s.   BIBLE 79:25
Compels me to disturb your s.   MILT 343:2
due s. we shall reap   BIBLE 77:20
each thing that in s. grows   SHAK 456:16
every thing there is a s.   BIBLE 55:12
give them meat in due s.   PRAY 397:1
in a s. of calm weather   WORD 579:12
it is but for a s.   HOUS 264:5
S. of mists and mellow   KEATS 293:5
s. she hath dressings fit   ANON 6:20
them their meat in due s.   PRAY 399:15
things by s. season'd are   SHAK 468:19
word spoken in due s.   BIBLE 54:7
You lack the s. of all   SHAK 461:26
Youth's the s. made   GAY 222:28

season'd: s. with a gracious voice
SHAK 467:10
seasoned: s. with salt   BIBLE 78:28
seasons: From s. such as these   SHAK 454:15
In those vernal s.   MILT 352:10
man for all s.   WHIT 571:22
O s., O castles   RIMB 406:8
s. alter   SHAK 470:6
s.' difference   SHAK 424:31
s. in the mind of men   KEATS 292:14
S.; yet Eternities   MER 337:9
S. return   MILT 347:8
Therefore all s. shall   COL 156:23
We've seen the s. through   KIPL 300:23
seat: in the s. of the scornful   PRAY 389:14
Not a s. but a springboard   CHUR 150:14
this s. of Mars   SHAK 478:20
with such ease into his s.   SHAK 440:7
seatbelts: Fasten your s.   DAVIS 172:18
Seated: S. one day at the organ   PROC 401:13
seats: chief s. in the synagogues BIBLE 67:22
chief s. in the synagogues   BIBLE 68:37
seaward: woods go s. from the town
HUNT 268:12
seawards: My road leads me s.   MAS 334:2
sea-water: salt s. passes   TENN 536:11
sea-wet: Spartans on the s. rock   HOUS 265:3
sea-wind: no life but the s.   SWIN 529:18
sea-worm: s. crawls   HARDY 239:4
seaworms: Battening upon huge s.
TENN 537:25
second: All things have s. birth   WORD 580:21
beauty faded has no s. spring   PHIL 373:9
everybody allows the s. place   SWIFT 527:1
first and s. class citizens   WILL 574:14
grounds for the s. time   PEAC 370:17
Is s. childishness   SHAK 425:24
loudly against s. marriages   FIEL 211:6
No s. stroke intend   MILT 347:1
s. and sober thoughts   HENRY 245:18
s. best's a gay goodnight   YEATS 585:6
s. eleven sort of chap   BARR 34:8
unto my wife my s. best bed   SHAK 496:1
village than s. at Rome'   CAES 127:3

second-best: s. is a formal order
AUDEN 18:13
second-rate: man and the creed of a s.
BAG 29:16
up with poets' being s.   HOR 258:4
secrecy: Nature's infinite book of s.
SHAK 421:9
s., No lady closer   SHAK 438:32
S. the human dress   BLAKE 88:9
secret: At last the s. is out   AUDEN 20:22
bread eaten in s. is pleasant   BIBLE 53:28
cleanse thou me from my s. faults
PRAY 390:13
digestion is the great s.   SMITH 512:8
I know that's a s.   CONG 160:7
joys of parents are s.   BACON 27:2
no s. so close   SURT 525:28
public and to read in s.   BORR 89:26
rebuke is better than s. love   BIBLE 54:37
s., and inviolate Rose   YEATS 586:18
s. and sweet reasonableness   ARN 16:22
s. himself shall reward   BIBLE 64:22
s. magic of numbers   BROW 96:11
s. of happiness is to admire   BRAD 91:11
s. parts of Fortune   SHAK 432:11
s. things belong unto   BIBLE 48:28
S. thoughts and open countenance... ALB 3:8
Seeking His s. deeds   ROSS 408:20
then in s. sin   CHUR 148:33
There is always a wicked s.   AUDEN 21:1
Three may keep a s.   FRAN 218:9
unites it with the s. cause   JOYCE 286:17
when it ceases to be a s.   BEHN 38:12
with every s. thing   BIBLE 56:14
Secretary: S. of Nature and all learning
WALT 564:15
secretly: entice thee s. shalt not BIBLE 48:24
secrets: from whom no s. are hid PRAY 387:7
s. are edged tools   DRYD 197:20
s. of th' abyss to spy   GRAY 235:19
S. with girls   COWP 168:22
There are s. in all families   FARQ 210:7
They know the s. of the sea   NERV 361:1
will discharge their s.   SHAK 462:26
sect: attached to that great s.   SHEL 500:9
It found them a s.   MAC 324:17
paradise for a s.   KEATS 289:26
sad-coloured s.   HOOD 255:16
sectaries: faith in a nation of s.   DISR 186:1
Hence jarring s. may learn   COWP 165:21
sectes: Angleterre soixante s.   CAR 130:10
Sects: Two-and-Seventy jarring S. confute
FITZ 213:2
whence arise diversity of s.   SPEN 515:24
secular: s. bird   MILT 350:31
secure: He is s.   SHEL 499:21
security: allowed to be a collateral s.
CHES 145:30
Our watchword is s.   PITT 374:1
s. for its impartial administration PEEL 371:5
S. Is mortals' chiefest   SHAK 462:1
Securus: S. iudicat orbis   AUG 21:18
sed: agua que ahuyenta la s.   CERV 138:20
Sedan chair: flood of tears and a S.
DICK 182:25
sedens: Qui s. adversus identidem CAT 137:4
sedge: river buds among the s.   SHEL 503:20
s. is wither'd from   KEATS 290:15
seditione: tulerit Gracchos de s.   JUV 287:13
seditions: way to prevent s.   BACON 27:11
seduce: did not s., she ravished   MER 337:25
seducer: Thou strong s.   DRYD 195:31
seducing: Giving heed to s. spirits
BIBLE 79:13
seduction: delusive s. of martial music
BURN 112:21
Seductive: S. Waltz   BYRON 126:11
Sedula: S. curavi   SPIN 517:7
sedulous: played the s. ape to Hazlitt
STEV 521:9

see: blind, now I s.   BIBLE 72:16
Can I s. another's woe   BLAKE 88:8
does he s. when he gazes so   HARDY 240:15
fain s. good   PRAY 391:23
I could not see to s.   DICK 183:19
I don't want to s. it   GARC 221:6
'I'm damned if I s. it'   NEWB 361:4
In all things Thee to s.   HERB 247:16
into the wilderness to s.   BIBLE 66:2
I s. a voice   SHAK 471:18
I s. the better way   OVID 366:17
I s. them all so excellently   COL 156:7
"I s. what I eat" is   CARR 133:29
Jupiter is whatever you s.   LUCAN 320:1
kings have desired to s.   BIBLE 69:29
live to s. them in my touch   SHAK 455:7
Lovers can s. to do their   SHAK 483:6
more I s. of men   ROL 407:16
more people s. than weigh   CHES 145:31
no man s. me more   SHAK 447:7
s. a church by daylight   SHAK 472:5
s. all, nor be afraid   BROW 104:2
s. an author and we find   PASC 369:4
s. better days   BEHN 38:15
s. God made and eaten   BROW 99:14
s. his active child do   SHAK 493:1
seem To s.   SHAK 455:21
s. my own funeral afore   EDG 199:22
S. where she comes apparell'd s. SHAK 478:2
shall he not s.   PRAY 396:2
Shall never s. so much   SHAK 456:13
shall no man s. me and live   BIBLE 48:5
taste and s.   PRAY 391:21
then complain we cannot s.   BERK 41:18
Then I shall s. thee again   SHAK 451:30
things which ye s.   BIBLE 69:29
thing that no man never s.   DICK 182:38
To s. and be seen   DRYD 198:19
to s. beyond our bourn   KEATS 289:8
To s. her is to love her   BURNS 112:37
to s. her was to love her   BURNS 112:28
To s. oursels as others   BURNS 115:18
verily to s. the goodness   PRAY 391:9
ye shall not s. me   BIBLE 72:40
yet I s. thee still   SHAK 459:15
you last s. your father   YEAM 584:8
seed: Are they the s. of Abraham BIBLE 77:11
beareth forth good s.   PRAY 398:17
garden, That grows to s.   SHAK 429:28
morning sow thy s.   BIBLE 56:8
Robs not one light s. from   KEATS 290:1
s. its harvest   KEATS 289:3
s. of ruin in himself   ARN 13:21
S. of Wisdom did I sow   FITZ 212:21
s. ye sow, another reaps   SHEL 504:3
wonder (which is the s.   BACON 24:14
seeds: I find thy cunning s.   ROSS 408:20
is the least of all s.   BIBLE 66:20
look into the s. of time   SHAK 458:13
some s. fell by the wayside   BIBLE 66:16
winged s.   SHEL 502:8
seed-time: Fair s. had my soul   WORD 580:8
s. and harvest   BIBLE 45:37
seeing: is not satisfied with s.   BIBLE 55:7
It adds a precious s.   SHAK 457:8
only one way of s. them   RUSK 411:29
only s. a worse England   JOHN 277:24
seek: All I s., the heaven above   STEV 522:28
confounded that s. after my soul PRAY 394:15
If you s. for a monument   ANON 11:2
might'st s. it in My arms   THOM 548:22
Myself alone I s. to please   GAY 223:18
not s. for kind relief   BLAKE 88:8
s., and ye shall find   BIBLE 65:2
S. not to know who said   THOM 546:8
s. power and to lose   BACON 26:22
s. with care   LAND 309:11
S. ye first the kingdom   BIBLE 64:31
s. ye the living among   BIBLE 71:16
S. ye the Lord while he   BIBLE 59:26

should I s. farther store SEDL 419:14
that sometime did me s. WYATT 583:21
They s. so many new DONNE 187:19
things I s. SHEL 504:1
To strive, to s. TENN 544:3
We s. him here ORCZY 365:7
where s. is find SMART 509:3
you shall s. all day ere SHAK 465:15
seekest: I am He whom thou s. THOM 548:23
seeketh: he that s. findeth BIBLE 65:3
seeking: s. asses MILT 350:6
S. His secret deeds ROSS 408:20
S. shall find Him BROW 100:38
S. the food he eats SHAK 425:16
seeks: one that neither s. DRYD 195:21
s. her own salvation SHAK 436:21
Seele: dessen S. Rousseau geschaffen
HEINE 244:12
Seelen: 'Zwei S. und ein Gedanke
HALM 238:10
Zwei S. wohnen GOET 229:30
seem: be rather than to s. good SALL 413:24
men honest that but s. SHAK 474:12
things are not what they s. LONG 317:1
seemed: All s. well pleased MILT 348:23
sweet love s. that April BRID 92:20
seeming: mild as she is s. so GREE 236:10
S. and savour all the winter SHAK 491:22
that most s. virtuous eye BYRON 125:4
thing I am by s. otherwise SHAK 474:17
seems: I know not 's.' SHAK 429:25
seen: evidence of things not s. BIBLE 79:31
God whom he hath not s. BIBLE 81:7
have seen what I have s. SHAK 433:15
If I have s. further it NEWT 362:19
I have s. dawn and sunset MAS 333:17
lov'd needs only to be s. DRYD 196:12
man hath s. God BIBLE 71:28
Much more had s. ARMS 12:15
my Lions & fled the S. WARD 564:24
s., and yet have believed BIBLE 73:12
s. God face to face BIBLE 46:25
things a' didn't wish s. HARDY 241:16
things which I have s. WORD 578:22
Too early s. unknown SHAK 482:4
To see and be s. DRYD 198:19
undoubtedly be s. to be done HEW 250:20
We have s. thee, O love SWIN 528:22
What things have we s. BEAU 35:19
Whom having not s. BIBLE 80:20
Yet s. too oft POPE 379:16
sees: draw the Thing as he s. KIPL 304:3
dwarf s. farther than COL 157:25
future s. BLAKE 87:13
She neither hears nor s. WORD 581:10
Who is it that s. and hears PUNCH 402:30
Who s. with equal eye POPE 379:4
seeth: yf himself yt s. CHAU 143:28
seethe: s. a kid in his mother's BIBLE 47:27
seethed: spring-tide of blossom s. BETJ 43:12
segashuate: yo' sym'tums seem ter s.
HARR 242:18
seige: Did march to the s. BALL 31:8
seigneur: vous êtes un grand s. BEAU 35:18
Seinte Loy: gretteste ooth was but by
S. CHAU 141:14
seize: hand dare s. the fire BLAKE 87:15
You s. the flow'r BURNS 115:7
Selbstmord: S. ist ein starkes Trostmittel
NIET 363:11
seldom: Is s., if ever done COW 163:20
Things are s. what they GILB 228:8
when they s. come SHAK 438:13
select: that each one should s. SHEL 500:9
Selection: term of Natural S. DARW 171:25
self: concentred all in s. SCOTT 416:22
greater to one than one's s. WHIT 571:3
never to think of one's s. CLOU 153:21
seeketh only S. to please BLAKE 87:19
spirit is the true s. CIC 151:24

with s. and vain conceit SHAK 479:11
self-consumer: I am the s. of my woes
CLARE 152:12
self-esteem: nothing profits more Than
s. MILT 349:8
self-evident: hold these truths to be s.
ANON 8:14
luminously s. beings NEWM 361:17
self-expression: void of s. they confide
KIPL 302:5
self-honour'd: s., self-secure ARN 14:24
self-indulgent: indifferent and s. majority
STEP 518:20
selfish: s. being all my life AUST 23:21
sensible people are s. EMER 207:4
selfless: s. man and stainless gentle
TENN 535:14
self-love: deceiving mirror of s. MASS 335:22
'golden-calf of S. CARL 131:4
Sin of s. possesseth all SHAK 494:1
That true s. and social POPE 380:4
self-lovers: nature of extreme s. BACON 27:37
self-protection: is s. MILL 339:6
Self-reliant: S. like the cat MOORE 355:22
self-revelation: terrible fluidity of s.
JAMES 271:16
Self-righteousness: S. is not religion
BRON 93:14
self-scann'd: s., self-honour'd ARN 14:24
Self-school'd: S., self-scann'd ARN 14:24
self-secure: self-honour'd, s. ARN 14:24
self-slain: god s. on his own strange
SWIN 529:20
self-slaughter: His canon 'gainst s.
SHAK 429:28
self-sufficing: reasoning, s. thing WORD 580:4
s. power of Solitude WORD 580:15
sell: go and s. that thou hast BIBLE 67:9
had a mind to s. his house SWIFT 525:34
Most people s. their souls SMITH 510:14
must poorly s. ourselves SHAK 487:12
no man might buy or s. BIBLE 82:13
precious as the Goods they s. FITZ 213:14
s., or deny, or delay MAGN 327:3
s. them in the street CARR 136:6
s. the pasture now to buy SHAK 443:12
s. with you SHAK 465:28
there were dreams to s. BEDD 36:28
will I s. my goodly steed BALL 30:9
selling: one lives by s. something STEV 520:25
sells: s. eternity to get a toy SHAK 492:18
seltzer: sipped at a weak hock and s.
BETJ 42:4
Selvytion: Wot prawce S. nah SHAW 497:10
semblable: mon s.,—mon frère BAUD 35:5
semblances: outface it with their s.
SHAK 424:30
semen: s. est sanguis Christianorum
TERT 544:22
semenza: Considerate la vostra s.
DANTE 171:13
seminaries: large s. of young ladies
KNOX 305:25
seminary: Come from a ladies' s.
GILB 226:29
semita: Fallentis s. vitae HOR 258:24
semper: et nunc, et s. MASS 334:14
Quod s., quod ubique VINC 557:7
Sempronius: S.; we'll deserve it ADD 1:16
senate: give his little s. laws POPE 376:27
senates: s. hang upon thy tongue
THOM 549:16
senators: green-rob'd s. of mighty woods
KEATS 290:5
laughed, respectable s. AUDEN 18:15
look at the s. and I pray HALE 237:12
teach his s. wisdom PRAY 397:4
send: Here am I; s. me BIBLE 58:1
S. me not this DONNE 190:14
senda: la escondida s. LUIS 320:12

Seneca: S. cannot be too heavy SHAK 432:20
Senectus: habitant Morbi tristisque S.
VIRG 558:21
senectutem: Post molestam s. ANON 10:13
seniors: earnest advice from my s.
THOR 550:6
se'nnights: s. nine times nine SHAK 458:7
sens: Le bon s. est la chose DESC 175:11
s. et le bon goût il y LA B 306:15
sensation: Awaiting the s. of a short
GILB 226:31
Permanent Possibility of S. STEV 522:7
s. among us than three MAC 324:23
sensational: It is somewhat too s.
WILDE 573:4
sensations: life of s. rather than KEATS 293:17
s. sweet WORD 578:4
sense: common s. and observation
BROW 96:18
common s. and good taste SHAW 496:12
deep s. of some deathless WEBS 567:4
Devoid of s. and motion MILT 346:10
exquisite s. of the luxurious KEATS 293:29
it is not s. CHUR 148:25
light of nature, s. ROCH 406:21
man of s. only trifles CHES 145:26
'men of s. never tell it SHAD 420:24
never deviates into s. DRYD 196:34
Nor numbed s. to steel it KEATS 293:4
no s. In gittin' riled HARTE 242:27
Not when the s. is dim BEEC 37:9
of decency is want of s. ROOS 408:11
Of s. and outward things WORD 579:10
perpetual fountain of good s. DRYD 198:5
Satire or s. POPE 376:30
seem an echo to the s. POPE 378:22
s. and good taste there LA B 306:15
S. and wit with poesy allied BYRON 124:20
s. faints picturing them SHEL 502:10
servilely creeps after s. DRYD 197:34
some nonsense about s. STEV 521:13
something more than good s. COL 158:1
stings and motions of the s. SHAK 463:14
Take care of the s. CARR 134:7
That the s. aches at thee SHAK 476:19
Their s. is with their MER 337:16
their s. is shut SHAK 462:19
Through s. and nonsense DRYD 194:21
what was a man of s. LOCK 316:2
who all s. doth eat SHAK 435:18
within the s. they quicken SHEL 504:12
without one grain of s. DRYD 195:38
with sober s. POPE 378:9
senseless: most s. and fit man SHAK 472:28
you worse than s. things SHAK 448:6
senses: from the power of our s. JOHN 281:24
power to touch our s. so) MILT 344:10
Unto our gentle s. SHAK 459:4
sensibility: century a dissociation of s.
ELIOT 205:17
Dear s. STER 519:12
it is an immense s. JAMES 271:11
that s. of principle BURKE 111:10
sensible: All s. people are selfish EMER 207:4
be bold and be s. HOR 258:14
which a s. person would AUST 23:5
woman was fundamentally s. JOHN 278:28
sensibly: things they behave s. about
SHAW 496:14
sensitive: Frog is justly s. BELL 38:29
please the s. race of poets HOR 259:10
s. being WORD 580:25
S. Plant in a garden grew SHEL 503:22
sensual: ascetic rocks and the s. MER 337:27
merely s. pleasures BURKE 108:7
Not to the s. ear KEATS 291:4
s. pleasure without vice JOHN 280:23
sensualist: lover and s. HENL 245:12
sent: man s. from God BIBLE 71:24
say I s. thee thither SHAK 446:24

tongue That S. spake WORD 582:3
To S. gave as much DRYD 196:2
tried lately to read S. DARW 171:22
What needs my S. for his MILT 344:1
Shakespeherian: that S. Rag ELIOT 204:25
shaking: s., crazy ROCH 407:3
that can fall without s. MONT 354:7
to the s. hand of an old VICT 556:15
shall: His absolute 's.' SHAK 427:21
shallow: abysses are all so s. JAMES 271:32
S. brooks murmur most SIDN 507:14
s. in himself MILT 350:10
s. streams run dimpling POPE 377:2
There s. draughts intoxicate POPE 378:13
you are idle s. things SHAK 490:8
shallows: bound in s. and in miseries
　SHAK 451:27
With his depths and his s. BURNS 115:2
Shalott: Lady of S. TENN 538:4
shalt: Thou s. have no other gods BIBLE 47:24
shame: be mine the s. DRYD 196:13
blush of s. WHIT 571:17
despising the s. BIBLE 79:35
doff it for s. SHAK 452:16
I must keep from s. HOUS 263:21
is now bound in with s. SHAK 478:20
much glory and so much s. MAC 324:11
sense of some deathless s. WEBS 567:4
s. for women to speak BIBLE 76:17
s. to take the lowest room BIBLE 70:7
spirit in a waste of s. SHAK 495:7
Thy father's s. BRET 92:6
'Tis a s. to human nature HOUS 266:8
To live and s. the land HOUS 266:3
To s. unvulnerable SHAK 428:4
Upon his brow s. is ashamed SHAK 483:8
whose glory is their s. BIBLE 78:19
wrought the deed of s. MAC 322:16
shamed: Ain't you 's., you sleepy-head
　STEV 522:24
I am s. thro' all my nature TENN 539:4
shameful: s. conquest of itself SHAK 478:20
s. to spurn one's friends LA R 310:10
shameless: most s. thing in the world
　BURKE 111:19
shames: hold a candle to my s. SHAK 466:15
s., on my bare head SHAK 476:18
shammin': generally s. when 'e's dead
　KIPL 299:9
shamming: whate'er their gentle s.
　MOORE 357:4
shank: his shrunk s. SHAK 425:24
spindle s. a guid whip-lash BURNS 115:17
Shannon: On the green banks of S.
　CAMP 128:20
shape: hat of antique s. ARN 14:13
If s. it might be call'd MILT 346:24
in what s. they choose MILT 345:15
men in s. and fashion ASCH 17:3
subtly wrought me into S. FITZ 213:12
such a questionable s. SHAK 430:24
Take any s. but that SHAK 461:21
you might be any s. CARR 135:19
shaped: It is s., sir, like itself SHAK 422:14
s., made aware BROO 94:30
shapen: I was s. in wickedness PRAY 393:5
shapes: fiery and delectable s. SHAK 442:15
heaven was full of fiery s. SHAK 439:21
s. of sky or plain SHEL 504:21
shard: reeking tube and iron s. KIPL 302:10
share: greater s. of honour SHAK 445:1
no one so true Did s. SHAK 489:4
s. in Government that CHAR 140:1
s. in two revolutions is PAINE 368:6
S. my harvest and my home HOOD 255:5
s. the good man's smile GOLD 231:1
Thou its ruin didst not s. DOD 187:16
turned to s. the transport WORD 582:10
shares: s. are a penny GILB 226:16
shark: s. And the tiger AUDEN 20:15

Sharon: I am the rose of S. BIBLE 56:19
sharp: s. antidote against disgrace
　BURKE 111:9
s. as a twoedged sword BIBLE 53:20
'Somebody's s. DICK 176:26
so s. the conquerynge CHAU 143:32
'Tis a s. remedy RAL 404:17
sharpeneth: s. the countenance of his
　BIBLE 54:40
sharper: He'd be s. than a serpent's
　DICK 181:17
I returned it s. than THOR 550:12
s. than a serpent's tooth SHAK 453:19
sharpest: 'After s. shoures LANG 309:28
sharpness: overcome the s. of death
　PRAY 384:17
sharps: fifty different s. and flats
　BROW 103:15
Shatter: S. your leaves before MILT 343:25
you may s. the vase MOORE 356:7
shatterday: thumpsday, frightday, s.
　JOYCE 286:11
Shattered: S. in shard on shard THOM 548:21
When the lamp is s. SHEL 501:21
shaving: when I am s. of a morning
　HOUS 266:17
Shaw: Mr S. is (I suspect) CHES 148:4
shawms: trumpets also, and s. PRAY 396:8
shay: wonderful one-hoss s. HOLM 253:8
she: Had it any been but s. SUCK 524:15
same party was the S. AUST 23:30
s. shall be called Woman BIBLE 45:12
S., she is dead DONNE 187:20
S. that was ever fair SHAK 474:18
S. who trifles with all GAY 223:4
That not impossible s. CRAS 169:15
unexpressive s. SHAK 426:2
you are the cruell'st s. SHAK 488:12
sheaf: made obeisance to my s. BIBLE 46:27
shearers: scramble at the s.' feast
　MILT 343:12
sheep before her s. is dumb BIBLE 59:22
shears: Fury with th' abhorred s. MILT 343:8
resembles a pair of s. SMITH 511:11
sheath: sword back in the s. CHES 147:6
sheath'd: s. their swords for lack SHAK 444:1
sheaves: bring his s. with him PRAY 398:17
rode between the barley-s. TENN 538:8
your s. stood round about BIBLE 46:27
Sheba: Another S. queen WITH 575:13
S. had seen all Solomon's BIBLE 50:32
she-bear: s. thus accosted rends KIPL 299:10
shed: down the monarch of a s. GOLD 231:26
man shall his blood be s. BIBLE 45:39
prepare to s. them now SHAK 450:26
s. for you and for many PRAY 388:1
s. his blood for the country ROOS 408:3
s. innocent blood BIBLE 60:6
with Burke under a s. JOHN 279:15
Yet I'll not s. her blood SHAK 477:5
shedding: s. of blood is no remission
　BIBLE 79:29
sheep: better than s. or goats TENN 535:26
black s. who've gone astray KIPL 299:10
careth not for the s. BIBLE 72:19
else their s. MILT 344:8
Feed my s. BIBLE 73:15
folds shall be full of s. PRAY 394:3
found my s. which was lost BIBLE 70:16
from thy ways like lost s. PRAY 384:11
giveth his life for the s. BIBLE 72:18
Go rather to the lost s. BIBLE 65:30
His silly s. COWP 166:8
hungry s. look up MILT 343:13
Let us return to our s. ANON 9:16
lie in the hell like s. PRAY 393:1
like s. have gone astray BIBLE 59:5
little hills like young s. PRAY 397:16
looking on their silly s. SHAK 446:19
mountain s. are sweeter PEAC 371:2

noble ensample to his s. CHAU 142:1
of an old half-witted s. STEP 518:22
of s. that are even shorn BIBLE 56:26
One sickly s. infects WATTS 565:23
Other s. I have BIBLE 72:20
plunge the struggling s. MAC 322:19
prize-oxen and of s. TENN 542:20
s. before her shearers BIBLE 59:22
s. bringeth no gain with POUND 382:9
s. in sheep's clothing GOSSE 233:4
s. may bring forth thousands PRAY 399:13
s. of his hand PRAY 396:4
s. on his right hand BIBLE 68:5
s. set me a place and separate CEL 138:8
s. that have not a shepherd BIBLE 51:19
to you in s.'s clothing BIBLE 65:8
were as s. going astray BIBLE 80:27
you s. bear fleeces not VIRG 560:20
sheep-bells: s. and the ship-bells ring
　KIPL 303:13
sheep-hook: know how to hold A s.
　MILT 343:12
sheer: s., penetrating power ARN 16:8
sheet: although the s. were big SHAK 489:30
England's winding s. BLAKE 85:17
s. bleaching on the hedge SHAK 491:17
s. knit at the four corners BIBLE 73:37
waters were his winding s. BARN 34:5
wet s. and a flowing sea CUNN 170:13
sheets: cool kindliness of s. BROO 94:8
fumble with the s. SHAK 443:17
Sheffield: 'Only Brooks of S. DICK 176:26
she-goats: go on, my s. VIRG 560:9
shell: convolutions of a smooth-lipped
　WORD 577:16
Shelley: Burns, S., were with us BROW 102:5
did you once see S. plain BROW 102:15
peace in S.'s mind SHEL 505:1
S., whom envy never touched SHEL 505:14
S. with liquid music BRID 92:9
sphere for S.'s genius ARN 16:2
There S. dream'd his white JOHN 273:19
What S. shrilled SASS 414:19
shelter: s. to grow ripe ARN 13:10
To s. me from the cold BELL 40:11
sheltered: In youth it s. me MORR 358:6
shelters: 'Naught's thee THOM 548:14
Shem: done with the Tents of S. KIPL 300:23
S., Ham, and Japheth BIBLE 45:32
Shepherd: call you, S. ARN 14:10
Dick the s. SHAK 457:19
equalises the s. and the king CERV 138:20
every s. tells his tale MILT 342:19
fairest s. on our green PEELE 371:6
feed his flock like a s. BIBLE 59:7
God of love my S. HERB 248:13
good s. giveth his life BIBLE 72:18
lady would not love a s. GREE 236:11
Lord is my s. PRAY 390:2
sheep that have not a s. BIBLE 51:19
S. and Bishop of your souls BIBLE 80:27
s. his sheep PROP 401:17
slighted, s.'s trade MILT 343:8
truth in every s.'s tongue RAL 404:9
weather the s. shuns HARDY 241:3
What time the s. SHAK 446:17
Shepherd-boy: thou happy S. WORD 579:3
shepherdess: s. of sheep MEYN 338:1
Shepherding: S. her bright fountains
　SHEL 500:2
shepherds: have both s. and butchers
　VOLT 561:17
s. abiding in the field BIBLE 69:9
s. call me also a poet VIRG 560:7
S. shall flute their sweetest AUDEN 18:8
s. watch'd their flocks TATE 531:22
That liberal s. give SHAK 436:19
warmth of s.' flames MARL 330:11
Sheriffmuir: at S. A battle there was
　MCL 325:15

sherris: this valour comes of s.　SHAK 442:15
sherris-sack: good s. hath a two-fold
　　　　　　　　　　　　　　　　　　SHAK 442:15
sherry: s. in the cupboard　BETJ 44:10
shew: man can s. any just cause　PRAY 389:2
　mouth shall s. thy praise　PRAY 393:8
　s. him my salvation　PRAY 395:23
　s. ourselves glad in him　PRAY 396:3
　s. the light of thy countenance　PRAY 395:8
　we will s. you a thing　BIBLE 50:2
sheweth: s. him all the kingdoms　BIBLE 64:3
Shibboleth: Say now S.　BIBLE 49:20
shield: idle spear and s.　MILT 344:6
　shall be thy s. and buckler　PRAY 395:21
　s. of the mighty is vilely　BIBLE 50:16
　taking the s. of faith　BIBLE 78:10
　To a lady in his s.　TENN 538:8
shieling: From the lone s.　GALT 221:2
shift: down let me s. for my self　MORE 357:16
　then we'll s. our ground　SHAK 431:20
shifted: He s. his trumpet　GOLD 231:21
shifts: Oft' s. her passions　GAY 223:8
shillin: s.' a day　KIPL 302:19
shilling: Philip and Mary on a s.　BUTL 118:7
　s. life will give you all　AUDEN 21:8
　willing to sell for one s.　LEAR 312:13
shillings: payment of half twenty s.
　　　　　　　　　　　　　　　　　　BURKE 109:2
shimmered: Jeeves s. out and came
　　　　　　　　　　　　　　　　　　WOD 575:18
shine: anxious for to s. in the high
　　　　　　　　　　　　　　　　　　GILB 227:20
　fire and every one doth s.　SHAK 449:25
　glistering gold but more to s.　BRAD 91:15
　Let the hot sun S. on　AUDEN 20:21
　Let your light so s. before　BIBLE 64:9
　Lord make his face s.　BIBLE 48:9
　not to s. in use　TENN 543:22
　qualified to s. in company　SWIFT 527:11
　s.; for thy light is come　BIBLE 60:7
　s. more bright in these　SHAK 493:17
　S. upon the starry sky　BLAKE 86:5
　than s. with Pye　BYRON 124:19
　they s. on all alike　POPE 380:32
　visitation they shall s.　BIBLE 62:14
　where the wind's feet s.　SWIN 530:18
shined: in her person s.　MILT 351:13
　them hath the light s.　BIBLE 58:6
shiners: nine bright s.　ANON 6:5
shines: She s. sae bright to wyle　BURNS 116:5
　s. the moon in clouded　TENN 532:16
　substitute s. brightly as a king　SHAK 468:18
shineth: light s. in darkness　BIBLE 71:23
shingles: naked s. of the world　ARN 12:23
shining: Even to s. ones who dwell　BETJ 42:8
　I see it s. plain　HOUS 263:22
　s. Foot shall pass　FITZ 213:18
　s. morning face　SHAK 425:24
　S. unto no higher end　MARV 332:12
　will flame out like s.　HOPK 256:12
　with the sun not s.　CHAN 139:20
　woman of s. loveliness　YEATS 586:17
shins: own wit till I break my s.　SHAK 425:13
ship: all I ask is a tall s.　MAS 334:4
　build your s. of death　LAWR 311:8
　idle as a painted s.　COL 155:13
　is a s.'s upon the sea　KIPL 301:1
　It was so old a s.　FLEC 214:19
　My soul, like to a s.　WEBS 567:13
　One leak will sink a s.　BUNY 107:29
　s., an isle　FLEC 214:21
　s. has weather'd every　WHIT 570:7
　s. I have got in the North　BALL 31:2
　s. is being in a jail　JOHN 274:18
　S. of State　LONG 316:7
　s. that goes　DIBD 175:20
　s. was still as she could　SOUT 513:28
　s. would *not* travel due　CARR 133:6
　smart s. grew　HARDY 239:6
　splendid s.　BRID 92:19

that gallant s. in twain　BALL 30:19
'There was a s.　COL 155:6
way of a s. in the midst　BIBLE 55:1
What is a s. but a prison　BURT 116:27
ship-bells: sheep-bells and the s.　KIPL 303:13
Shipman: S. was ther　CHAU 141:29
shipping: Thus fishes first to s.　DRYD 195:22
ships: beauty and mystery of the s.
　　　　　　　　　　　　　　　　　　LONG 316:22
go down to the sea in s.　PRAY 397:9
Hell to s.　AESC 3:1
launch'd a thousand s.　MARL 329:10
Like two doomed s.　WILDE 572:11
little s. of England brought　GUED 237:4
mighty s. ten thousand　HODG 252:7
move with the moving s.　SWIN 530:28
my s. are out of gear　TENN 542:21
Our s. have been salvaged　HALS 238:11
s. and stars and isles　FLEC 214:9
s. and the foreign faces　SWIN 528:15
S. are but boards　SHAK 465:27
s., becalmed at eve　CLOU 154:3
s., by thousands　BYRON 122:34
S., dim-discovered　THOM 549:13
s. sail like swans asleep　FLEC 214:16
S. that pass in the night　LONG 317:17
S., towers, domes　WORD 581:14
shoes—and s.—and sealing wax　CARR 135:7
'Spanish s. of war　TENN 542:21
stately s. go　TENN 532:18
storm-beaten s.　MAHAN 327:5
There go the s.　PRAY 397:1
They crossed in s. the sea　HOUS 265:6
thousand s. to Tenedos　MARL 330:14
Thou shalt break the s.　PRAY 392:26
We are six s. of the line　TENN 542:21
When boats or s. came near　LEAR 312:19
When stately s. are twirled　HODG 252:7
wrong with our bloody s.　BEAT 35:12
ye s. of Tarshish　BIBLE 58:17
shipwreck: escaped the s. of time
　　　　　　　　　　　　　　　　　　BACON 24:18
s. of my ill adventured　DAN 171:1
thrice I suffered s.　BIBLE 77:12
shire: That s. which we the heart
　　　　　　　　　　　　　　　　　　DRAY 193:18
shires: both the s. they ring them　HOUS 263:4
s. have seen it plain　HOUS 262:12
shirt: martyr in his s. of fire　SMITH 510:2
till he tucks in his s.　KIPL 304:28
your s. and your socks　GILB 226:15
shirt-sleeves: 'from shirt-sleeves to s.'
　　　　　　　　　　　　　　　　　　BUTL 117:12
shive: cut loaf to steal a s.　SHAK 486:15
shivers: wan west s.　SWIN 528:16
shoal: bank and s. of time　SHAK 459:5
s. of fools for tenders　CONG 160:36
shock: short, sharp s.　GILB 226:31
to s. them and keep them　SHAW 496:25
we shall s. them　SHAK 453:1
shock-headed: my s. victor　BETJ 44:6
Than to see S. Peter　HOFF 252:22
shocks: thousand natural s.　SHAK 433:8
twelve great s. of sound　TENN 533:22
withindoors house The s.　HOPK 256:29
shod: can foot feel, being s.　HOPK 256:12
your feet s. with the preparation　BIBLE 78:10
shoddy: Up goes the price of s.　GILB 225:30
shoe: Edom will I cast out my s.　PRAY 393:18
Finds sixpence in her s.　CORB 162:14
I kiss his dirty s.　SHAK 444:17
Into a left-hand s.　CARR 136:7
s.'s latchet I am not　BIBLE 71:29
s. was lost　FRAN 218:6
shoelace: tail hanging like a s.　MOORE 355:22
shoemaker: take my shoes from the s.
　　　　　　　　　　　　　　　　　　GOLD 232:41
shoes: adorns my s.　HOUS 266:10
beautiful are thy feet with s.　BIBLE 57:7
ere those s. were old　SHAK 429:28

his s. were far too tight　LEAR 312:5
more than over s. in love　SHAK 490:29
most of the s. of his soldiers　BAG 29:11
Put off thy s. from off　BIBLE 47:4
s.—and ships—and sealing wax　CARR 135:7
Their s. were clean　CARR 135:6
To boil eggs in your s.　LEAR 313:3
to call for his old s.　SELD 419:19
your s. on your feet　BIBLE 47:18
shoe-string: careless s.　HERR 249:2
shone: glory of the Lord s. round　BIBLE 69:9
S. like a meteor streaming　MILT 345:19
that once had s.　FLEC 214:10
There s. one woman　SWIN 530:29
shook: earth s.　PRAY 394:7
monk who s. the world　MONT 355:10
s. hands with time　FORD 216:16
Ten Days that S. the World　REED 405:8
Which ne'er s. hands　SHAK 458:3
shoon: night in her silver s.　DE L 174:16
wat their cork-heel'd s.　BALL 31:19
shoot: Do not hesitate to s.　BALF 30:1
I s. the Hippopotamus　BELL 38:30
'I will s. you　BALL 31:3
Please do not s. the pianist　ANON 7:9
s. folly as it flies　POPE 379:2
s. the sleepy, green-coat　HOFF 252:21
they s. out their lips　PRAY 390:17
They up and s. themselves　BROO 94:24
young idea how to s.　THOM 549:10
shooting: than to hunting and s.　BURR 116:10
shooting-stars: s. attend thee　HERR 249:11
Shoots: S. higher much than he　HERB 247:8
Who s. at the mid-day sun　SIDN 507:15
shop: back to the s. Mr John　LOCK 315:22
Because a man has s. to mind　BROW 105:3
beggar's s. is shut　SHAK 483:25
himself a little back s.　MONT 354:20
shopkeepers: England is a nation of s.
　　　　　　　　　　　　　　　　　　NAP 359:15
nation of s. are very seldom　ADAMS 1:9
only for a nation of s.　SMITH 509:12
shopocracy: hear you abuse the s.
　　　　　　　　　　　　　　　　　　NORTH 364:6
shops: might shun the awful s.　CHES 147:18
shore: after-silence on the s.　BYRON 125:10
beat on Heaven's s.　BLAKE 85:15
By the s. of Gitche Gumee　LONG 317:10
false impossible s.　ARN 15:2
high s. of this world　SHAK 444:25
lights around the s.　ROSS 410:8
longing for the further s.　VIRG 558:22
on the kingdom of the s.　SHAK 494:3
Over some wide-watered s.　MILT 342:4
rapture on the lonely s.　BYRON 121:22
Stops with the s.　BYRON 121:23
surges lash the sounding s.　POPE 378:23
shored: These fragments have I s.
　　　　　　　　　　　　　　　　　　ELIOT 205:12
shoreless: s. watery wild　ARN 13:12
shores: bade betwixt their s.　ARN 13:13
s. of darkness there is　KEATS 292:25
s. of the Mediterranean　JOHN 277:6
wilder s. of love　BLAN 88:30
shore-sea: blue or the s. green　FLEC 214:17
shoreward: winds s. blow　ARN 13:5
shorn: sheep that are even s.　BIBLE 56:26
went home s.　BROW 102:17
short: being made perfect in a s.　BIBLE 62:15
be s. in the story itself　BIBLE 63:29
hath but a s. time to live　PRAY 389:11
how s. is the longest life　KEATS 294:29
Life's s. span forbids　HOR 259:14
nasty, brutish, and s.　HOBB 251:18
our life is very s.　TAYL 532:3
s. jacket is always worn　EDW 200:2
s. of the glory of God　BIBLE 74:38
take s. views　AUDEN 21:6
Take s. views　SMITH 510:31
time of life is s.　SHAK 440:19

We have as s. a Spring HERR 249:28
you find it wond'rous s. GOLD 231:9
shorten: s. I the stature of my MER 337:8
shorter: make you s. by the head ELIZ 205:26
s. Poems of Donne AUDEN 21:3
time to make it s. PASC 369:14
shortest: s. way is commonly BACON 25:4
shortness: nothing comparable for s.
BORR 90:11
To spend that s. basely SHAK 440:19
shot: Am not I s. LOV 318:12
be s. at for sixpence a-day DIBD 175:17
bolt is s. back ARN 12:22
hand that fired the s. BALL 31:4
have s. mine arrow o'er SHAK 437:16
s. heard round the world EMER 206:19
S. so quick HOUS 264:2
s. to pieces by the shorter AUDEN 21:3
very long s. DOYLE 192:15
young Sahib s. divinely ANON 8:15
shots: of the best s. VOLT 561:18
shoulder: government shall be upon his
s. BIBLE 58:7
S. the sky HOUS 264:22
white steam over her s. AUDEN 20:1
shoulder-blade: left s. that is a miracle
GILB 227:10
Light my touch on your s. BETJ 43:16
shoulders: Born on our s. BROW 100:34
dwarfs on the s. of giants BERN 41:25
lawn about the s. thrown HERR 249:2
loose gown from her s. WYATT 583:22
standing on the s. of giants NEWT 362:19
shout: Ere ceased the inhuman s.
BYRON 121:15
It's no use raising a s. AUDEN 19:14
shouted with a great s. BIBLE 49:2
s. for me SHAW 498:28
S. round me WORD 579:3
s. that tore hell's concave MILT 345:20
s. to him golden shouts MER 337:37
'S. with the largest DICK 181:30
There was a s. about my ears CHES 146:23
Who s. and bang and roar BELL 39:28
shouted: I went and s. in his ear CARR 135:27
sons of God s. for joy BIBLE 53:3
shouting: Every man s. in proportion
SURT 525:18
heavens fill with s. TENN 538:24
tumult and the s. dies KIPL 302:7
shouts: cuckoo s. all day at nothing
HOUS 265:9
He s. to scare the monster KIPL 299:4
shoved: They s. him into politics BELL 39:5
shovel: limits they just s. in German
TWAIN 554:24
S. your couplets to their CAMP 128:11
take a large hoe and a s. KIPL 300:11
Shovelling: S. white steam over her
AUDEN 20:1
show: all rang'd (a terrible s. GAY 223:1
s. my head to the people DANT 171:20
s. your front to the world MOL 353:1
s. you something different ELIOT 204:19
they come to make a s. OVID 366:10
thing they most do s. SHAK 494:15
To s. our simple skill SHAK 471:16
what they s. to kings COWP 168:9
shower: falling s. SHEL 499:17
prove the sweetness of a s. THOM 547:21
s. of curates has fallen BRON 93:16
s. your shooting corns SWIFT 527:26
showers: pane is blind with s. HOUS 264:20
s. betumble the chestnut HARDY 241:2
Small s. last long SHAK 478:19
With true-love s. SHAK 435:34
ye S. PRAY 384:21
Showery: S., Flowery ELLIS 206:13
showest: Have more than thou s. SHAK 453:15

showing: s. them they were not needed
BELL 39:9
shown: must be s. In courts MILT 341:18
shows: by submitting the s. BACON 24:19
mind stoops not to s. of dross SHAK 466:16
s. sufficient of His light BROW 104:27
So may the outward s. be SHAK 467:10
shreds: king of s. and patches SHAK 435:12
thing of s. and patches GILB 226:18
shrewishly: he speaks very s. SHAK 488:9
Shrewsbury: fought a long hour by S.
SHAK 440:27
High the vanes of S. gleam HOUS 263:12
They hang us now in S. HOUS 262:16
Shrewsbury School: from S., from
Cambridge SHAW 498:23
shriek: solitary s. BYRON 122:18
With hollow s. MILT 344:13
With short shrill s. flits COLL 158:18
shrieked: s. against his creed TENN 536:29
shrieking: Hooting and s. SHAK 449:1
With s. and squeaking BROW 103:15
shrieks: Not louder s. to pitying POPE 381:8
shriller: s. than all the music SHAK 448:7
shrimp: be but a s. of an author GRAY 235:25
shrine: at the temple's inner s. WORD 582:1
To your mistaken S. WINC 575:4
shrines: Curled like vapour over s.
BROW 98:16
shrink: sall never make thee s. BALL 31:7
shrinking: glass when I am s. ANON 10:14
wagtail showed no s. HARDY 240:22
Shropshire: In London streets the S.
HOUS 263:21
S. names are read HOUS 262:13
shroud: green hill in an April s.
KEATS 291:15
My s. of white SHAK 489:4
stiff dishonoured s. ELIOT 204:16
White his s. as the mountain SHAK 435:34
Who ever comes to s. me DONNE 188:27
shrouded: Virgin s. in snow BLAKE 87:22
shrubbery: of Priapus in the s. ELIOT 203:28
shrug: borne it with a patient s. SHAK 466:2
read a nod, as., a look SWIFT 527:29
Shrunk: S. to this little measure SHAK 450:6
That s. thy streams MILT 343:14
shrunken: hushed the s. seas ELIOT 204:15
shudder: s. in the loins engenders
YEATS 586:2
shuffling: tune and the s. of feet MORR 358:12
Shulamite: return, O S. BIBLE 57:6
shun: let me s. that SHAK 454:14
s. the fault I fell BALL 30:13
s. the heaven that leads SHAK 495:7
S. what I follow BROW 104:7
shunn'st: Sweet bird, that s. MILT 342:2
shuns: weather the shepherd s. HARDY 241:3
shunting: to s. and hooting than BURR 116:10
shut: beggar's shop is s. SHAK 483:25
gates of it shall not be s. BIBLE 82:34
shady night has s. HOUS 263:2
s. her wild, wild eyes KEATS 290:20
s. the door POPE 376:18
s. the gates of mercy GRAY 234:34
s. their doors against SHAK 486:5
their sense is s. SHAK 462:19
shuts: s. none out WHIT 571:11
shutter: Borne before her on a s. THAC 546:3
shutters: close the s. fast COWP 167:11
S., shut your shutters BETJ 42:5
we'd need keep the s. up DICK 179:17
shutteth: s. up his bowels of compassion
BIBLE 81:4
shuttle: Man is the s. VAUG 555:10
musical s. WHIT 570:9
swifter than a weaver's s. BIBLE 52:18
shuttlecock: Battledore and s.'s DICK 181:34
shy: We are not s. GILB 226:32
Si: S. possis recte HOR 258:10

Sibyl: contortions of the S. without
BURKE 112:14
S. at Cumae PETR 373:2
Sibylla: Teste David cum S. CEL 138:5
Sicelides: S. Musae VIRG 559:22
sich: believe there's no s. a person
DICK 179:29
Sicily: Dost thou remember S. WILDE 572:19
Syrtes and soft S. ARN 14:21
sick: all s. persons PRAY 385:20
cattle then are s. KING 297:21
enterprise is s. SHAK 486:23
first pace that is s. SHAK 486:25
half my men are s. TENN 542:21
have on our hands a s. man NICH 362:22
hir'd to watch the s. COWP 166:29
I am s. of both JOHN 277:10
I am s. of love BIBLE 56:21
I am s. of many griefs SHAK 451:25
I'm more than a little s. KIPL 298:7
is Brutus s. SHAK 449:13
is but the daylight s. SHAK 468:20
I was s. BIBLE 68:6
kill s. people groaning MARL 329:21
make any man s. to hear her PEPYS 372:9
never s. at sea GILB 227:31
O Rose, thou art s. BLAKE 87:12
person seldom falls s. EMER 207:5
report That I am sudden s. SHAK 421:23
s. men's dreams BROW 95:23
s. that surfeit with too SHAK 465:19
they all make me s. MITF 352:27
They do not make me s. WHIT 570:22
they that are s. BIBLE 65:23
to be at when he is s. JOHN 279:5
Was s. almost to doomsday SHAK 429:13
were you not extremely s. PRIOR 401:9
When I was s. and lay a-bed STEV 522:20
when s. for home KEATS 291:23
when we are s. in fortune SHAK 453:11
you s. or are you sullen JOHN 279:27
sicken: love begins to s. and decay
SHAK 451:11
Will s. soon and die MILT 344:11
sicken'd: He s. at all triumphs CHUR 149:4
sickening: monstrous head and s. cry
CHES 146:22
sickens: s. at another's praise CHUR 148:28
sick-hearted: true, s. slave HOUS 265:18
sickle: bending s.'s compass come
SHAK 495:5
s. in the fruitful field BLAKE 86:19
sickly: 'I'm s. but sassy HARR 242:16
s. sheep infects the flock WATTS 565:23
smiled a kind of s. smile HARTE 242:33
sickness: grief, or s. must KING 296:11
he hath the falling s. SHAK 448:22
in s. and in health PRAY 389:4
medicine to heal their s. PRAY 399:19
My long s. SHAK 486:12
s., or any other adversity PRAY 387:16
s. that destroyeth PRAY 395:21
thy s. shall depart KIPL 298:8
Sidcup: I could get down to S. PINT 373:19
side: Are on our s. to-day MAC 323:2
embraceth him on every s. PRAY 391:18
Eve from his s. arose ANON 8:21
had not been on our s. PRAY 398:13
have only heard one s. BUTL 119:1
Hear the other s. AUG 21:20
on the s. of the angels DISR 185:2
passed by on the other s. BIBLE 69:31
rose o' the wrong s. BROME 93:1
she standeth by thy s. BALL 30:9
shifting his s. COWP 166:15
s. my hand and on that SHAK 479:22
s. that's next the sun SUCK 524:9
thrust my hand into his s. BIBLE 73:10
Who is on my s. BIBLE 51:36
side-arms: 'E keeps 'is s. awful KIPL 298:21

side-long: bashful virgin's s. looks
GOLD 230:17
sidera: *Sublimi feriam s. vertice* HOR 259:10
sides: might be said on both s. ADD 2:13
shake their wicked s. YEATS 586:8
There is no woman's s. SHAK 489:6
Sidney: Our S. and our perfect man
YEATS 585:13
S.'s self BROW 105:12
siècles: quarante s. vous contemplent
NAP 359:8
siege: envious s. Of watery Neptune
SHAK 478:20
stay the s. of loving terms SHAK 481:24
Sleghaftere: Stärkere, S., Wohlgemutere
NIET 363:2
Siesta: Englishmen detest a S. COW 163:19
Slete: *S. voi qui* DANTE 171:11
sieve: hope draws nectar in a s. COL 157:15
in a s. I'll thither sail SHAK 458:6
they went to sea in a S. LEAR 312:6
sift: to s. those dusts again DONNE 190:23
siftings: let their liquid s. fall ELIOT 204:16
sigh: Here's a s. to those who BYRON 126:1
He took her with a s. BLAKE 86:22
I to s. for her SHAK 456:27
prompts th' eternal s. POPE 379:21
she look'd up to s. SCOTT 417:13
S., heart YEATS 585:14
s. is the sword of an Angel BLAKE 86:6
s. like Tom o' Bedlam SHAK 453:12
S. no more SHAK 472:16
s. the lack of many a thing SHAK 493:7
very s. that silence heaves KEATS 290:13
Sigh'd: S. and look'd DRYD 195:6
s. his soul toward SHAK 468:13
sighed: he s. for one AUDEN 21:9
he s. for the love GILB 229:3
He sobbed and he s. GILB 227:17
I s. as a lover GIBB 224:13
She s. sore EDW 200:5
s. and pined and ogled THAC 546:3
Sighing: laughter and ability and S.
DICK 184:2
plague of s. and grief SHAK 439:11
poor soul sat s. by a sycamore SHAK 476:27
s. of a contrite heart PRAY 385:22
sorrow and s. shall flee BIBLE 59:1
sighs: all made of s. and tears SHAK 426:29
my pains a world of s. SHAK 474:1
S. are the natural language SHAD 420:19
s. the strings do break CAMP 129:17
sovereign of s. and groans SHAK 456:26
Spent in star-defeated s. HOUS 262:21
thus advises thee that s. SHAK 489:15
with her family of S. SHEL 499:9
sight: deprived of s. VIRG 558:11
done this evil in thy s. PRAY 393:4
end in s. was a vice BROW 105:2
in thy s. shall no PRAY 399:11
It is not yet in s. SHER 505:27
Lord giveth s. to the blind PRAY 399:17
loved not at first s. MARL 329:18
out of s. is out of mind CLOU 154:5
possession of this heavenly s. SHAK 477:21
punished in the s. of men BIBLE 62:13
right dear in the s. PRAY 397:22
seeing and leave in s. SWIN 528:18
sensible To feeling as to s. SHAK 459:15
s. of means to do ill SHAK 452:28
s. of the unwise they seemed BIBLE 62:13
s. to dream COL 156:3
s. to make an old man young TENN 533:20
spread in the s. of any bird BIBLE 53:14
that is pleasant to the s. BIBLE 45:8
to admit them in your s. AUST 23:9
together here in the s. of God PRAY 388:24
triple s. in blindness keen KEATS 292:25
where I shall live by s. BUNY 107:39
will I cast out of my s. BIBLE 50:31

years in thy s. are but as yesterday
PRAY 395:18
sightless: blind man On the s. WALEY 562:2
lark becomes a s. song TENN 537:19
sights: few more impressive s. BARR 34:21
Her s. and sounds BROO 94:30
s. as youthful poets dream MILT 342:26
sign: generation seeketh after a s. BIBLE 66:11
outward and visible s. PRAY 388:7
s. documents which they HURST 268:17
s. you must not touch DONNE 188:27
signal: Only a s. shown and a distant
LONG 317:17
really do not see the s. NELS 360:17
signal-elm: s., that looks on Ilsley ARN 15:3
signals: fading s. and grey eternal BEER 37:26
sign'd: one is s. by God's name WHIT 571:4
signed: air s. with their honour SPEN 515:8
hand that s. the paper THOM 547:4
signify: devil does the plot s. BUCH 106:13
does it s. how we dress GASK 221:23
Nod with your hand to s. HOUS 266:9
signiors: Like s. and rich burghers
SHAK 465:7
reverend s. SHAK 473:24
signo: In hoc s. vinces CONS 162:6
sign-post: Majesty's head on a s. MAC 324:2
signs: are but the s. of ideas JOHN 281:6
dials the s. of leaping-houses SHAK 437:34
discern the s. of the times BIBLE 66:32
Except ye see s. and wonders BIBLE 71:43
multiply my s. and my wonders BIBLE 47:11
S. are taken for wonders ELIOT 203:4
silence: are answered best with s. JONS 285:11
bound the common of s. EMER 207:14
Elected S., sing to me HOPK 256:14
eternal s. of these infinite PASC 369:7
ever widening slowly s. all TENN 535:7
golden Gospel of S. is MORL 357:24
Grief for thy dead in s. BROW 98:8
His mind moves upon s. YEATS 586:3
His s. will sit drooping SHAK 437:9
how the s. surged softly DE L 174:10
in s. with all subjection BIBLE 79:9
in the icy s. of the tomb KEATS 290:30
Let your women keep s. BIBLE 76:16
maintaining the 'conspiracy of s.'
COMTE 159:15
makes a s. in the hills TENN 536:11
My gracious s., hail SHAK 427:16
Night and s. SHAK 470:13
occasional flashes of s. SMITH 511:13
of punishment is to s. JOHN 282:13
Of the eternal S. WORD 579:11
of the very sigh that s. KEATS 290:13
pêcher que pêcher en s. MOL 354:1
rest is s. SHAK 437:27
S. alone is great VIGNY 557:2
s. also does not necessarily ELIOT 201:2
S. and sleep like fields DE L 173:25
S. augmenteth grief GREV 236:17
S. invaded the suburbs AUDEN 19:3
S. is become his mother GOLD 232:15
S. is deep as Eternity CARL 131:13
s. is divine CARL 131:39
S. is golden CARL 132:23
s. is most noble till SWIN 528:23
S. is only commendable SHAK 465:14
S. is the virtue of fools BACON 25:13
S. is the perfectest herald SHAK 472:10
s. is wonderful to listen HARDY 241:27
S. more musical than any ROSS 409:6
s. of the sleep-time BROW 98:31
s. sank COL 155:28
s. sounds no worse than HOUS 263:2
S. that dreadful bell SHAK 475:4
s. that is in the starry WORD 581:11
S.! Voilà l'ennemi CONDE 159:16
S. was pleas'd MILT 348:2
s. was the song of love ROSS 409:24

s. where hath been no sound HOOD 255:11
s., yea, even from good PRAY 391:30
s. yet I pick'd a welcome SHAK 471:15
small change of s. MER 338:2
Sorrow and s. are strong LONG 316:13
Stand shadowless like S. HOOD 255:1
Still-born S. FLEC 214:24
that s. we the tempest fear DRYD 195:24
That temple of s. and reconciliation
MAC 323:20
There was s. deep as death CAMP 128:15
Thou foster-child of s. KEATS 291:2
thunders of white s. BROW 98:4
Till a s. fell with TENN 540:10
'Tis visible s. ROSS 409:23
to be in s. BIBLE 79:9
was an easy step to s. AUST 23:6
was s. in heaven about BIBLE 82:5
With s. and tears BYRON 126:14
silences: s. Of dreadful things AUDEN 18:5
silencing: justified in s. mankind MILL 339:8
silent: All s. and all damn'd WORD 580:2
all the s. manliness GOLD 231:6
approached unlocked her s. throat GIBB 225:1
beauty's S. music CAMP 129:16
impossible to be s. BURKE 110:30
joys, like griefs, are s. MARM 330:19
on s. haunches SAND 413:26
S. and amazed even when WHIT 570:1
s. church before the service EMER 207:40
S. enim leges inter arma CIC 151:31
's. in seven languages' BAG 29:11
s. over Africa BROW 101:9
s. touches of time BURKE 111:36
S., upon a peak in Darien KEATS 292:18
s. witnesses to the desolation GEOR 224:4
then s. night MILT 348:5
why art thou s. CRAW 169:16
silentia: Tacitae per amica s. lunae
VIRG 558:3
Silently: S. and very fast AUDEN 18:16
silk: hallow'd that did breed the s.
SHAK 476:4
Kneeling ne'er spoil'd s. stocking
HERB 247:10
make his couche of s. CHAU 142:25
public schools with s. MARL 329:5
s. hat on a Bradford millionaire ELIOT 205:1
s. makes the difference FULL 220:21
s. stockings and white JOHN 274:2
s. thread plucks it back SHAK 482:20
that thing of s. POPE 376:30
silken: s. terms precise SHAK 457:15
silks: Whenas in s. my Julia goes HERR 250:8
will in fading s. compose WINC 575:5
silk-worm: Does the s. expend her
TOUR 551:16
siller: pinn'd it wi' a s. pin BALL 32:11
sillier: nothing s. than a silly laugh CAT 137:1
silliness: s. to live when to live SHAK 474:7
silly: it's lovely to be s. HOR 261:20
s. game where nobody wins FULL 220:20
s. thoughts so busy keep MILT 344:8
S. women laden with sins BIBLE 79:24
thou s. gentleman SHAK 474:7
'tis very s. BYRON 122:31
Who's S. Billy now GLOU 229:23
wish I loved its s. face RAL 404:20
with such a s. question STER 519:17
You were s. like us AUDEN 19:5
Silurist: Here sleeps the S. SASS 415:3
silvae: Et paulum s. super his HOR 262:9
s. sint consule dignae VIRG 559:22
silvas: Habitarunt di quoque s. VIRG 559:16
s. Academi quaerere verum HOR 259:4
Silver: Attract a S. Churn GILB 227:24
Between their s. bars FLEC 214:21
Enwrought with golden and s. YEATS 585:9
ever the s. cord be loosed BIBLE 56:11
golden locks time hath to s. PEELE 371:8

gold in pictures of s.	BIBLE 54:26	Burnt-offerings, and sacrifice for s.		sinewy: s. proboscis did remissly	
handful of s. he left us	BROW 102:4		PRAY 392:2		DONNE 190:3
her s. lining on the night	MILT 341:2	commit one single venial s.	NEWM 362:4	sinful: any s. games	HARTE 242:32
is covered with s. wings	PRAY 394:8	dark world of s.	BICK 84:4	sing: blind Homer s.	MARL 329:9
Is made of s.	GILB 225:30	day we fall into no s.	PRAY 385:3	cannot s. the old songs now	CALV 127:13
night in her s. shoon	DE L 174:16	dreadful record of s.	DOYLE 192:1	charmingly sweet you s.	LEAR 312:12
S. and gold have I none	BIBLE 73:25	emboldens s. so much as mercy	SHAK 486:6	come, let us s.	PRAY 396:3
s. answer rang…'Not Death	BROW 98:9	England, full of s.	HERB 247:3	crow doth s. as sweetly	SHAK 468:19
s. apples of the moon	YEATS 586:21	Excepting Original S.	CAMP 129:14	did s. in a hempen string	FLET 215:9
s. for the maid	KIPL 298:15	he bare the s. of many	BIBLE 59:24	Elected Silence, s. to me	HOPK 256:14
s., ivory	BIBLE 50:34	he died unto s. once	BIBLE 75:2	found in thine heart to s.	SWIN 530:12
s. plate on a coffin	OCON 364:22	He that is without s. among	BIBLE 72:10	her flowery work doth s.	MILT 342:8
take s. or small change	CHAM 139:14	How shall I lose the s.	POPE 376:12	how shall we s. to her	SWIN 528:16
thirty pieces of s.	BIBLE 68:9	I'll s. till I blow up	THOM 547:14	I do but s. because I must	TENN 536:12
thousands of gold and s.	PRAY 398:5	in awe, and s. not	PRAY 389:20	I know ye s. well	FLET 215:23
watch return'd a s. sound	POPE 380:29	I ne'er heard of a s.	LOCK 315:23	I s. of brooks	HERR 248:18
When gold and s. becks	SHAK 452:19	is not innocence but s.	BROW 101:17	let me s. and die	BYRON 123:4
Wisdom be put in a s. rod	BLAKE 85:19	it is no s.	SHAK 464:13	maid s. in the valley	ANON 5:3
silver'd: sable s.	SHAK 430:13	killing s.	STEV 523:11	More safe I s. with mortal	MILT 348:28
silver-pointed: Dinted with the s. pencil		known s., but by the law	BIBLE 75:4	persons die before they s.	COL 156:16
	BROW 102:28	Lord imputeth no s.	PRAY 391:16	Places where they s.	PRAY 385:4
silver-sweet: How s. sound lovers' tongues		Lukewarmness I account a s.	COWL 164:18	poet s. it with such airs	YEATS 584:10
	SHAK 482:19	Milton, Death, and S.	YOUNG 588:14	s. A faery's song	KEATS 290:17
silver-tufted: Her waving s. wand		mother I'm living in s.	HERB 246:8	S. a merry madrigal	GILB 227:1
	HOUS 262:19	my brother s. against me	BIBLE 67:7	s. among the branches	PRAY 396:19
Silvia: I be by S. in the night	SHAK 491:1	no s., but to be rich	SHAK 452:15	s. like birds i' the cage	SHAK 456:3
Silv'ry: Bridge of the S. Tay	MCG 325:6	not be a charity in s.	SHAK 464:7	S. me your song	GILB 229:8
simile: make a s. go on all fours	MAC 324:4	Plate s. with gold	SHAK 455:20	s. myself	WHIT 570:16
similes: hast the most unsavoury s.		purple-lined palace of sweet s.	KEATS 290:25	S., my tongue	VEN 556:4
	SHAK 438:5	say that we have no s.	BIBLE 81:3	S. no sad songs for me	ROSS 409:8
play with s.	WORD 582:26	Shall we continue in s.	BIBLE 74:43	s. praises unto his name	PRAY 394:7
Similia: S. similibus curantur	HAHN 237:10	she knew no s.	DRYD 196:10	S., riding's a joy	BROW 101:28
Simon: Old S. the Cellarer keeps	BELL 38:22	s. could blight or sorrow	COL 156:18	s., that I may seem valiant	DRYD 195:18
Simon Pure: real S.	CENT 138:9	S., Death, and Hell	BUNY 107:33	S. the peasantry	YEATS 587:8
simple: asham'd that women are so s.		S. I impute to each frustrate	BROW 105:21	s. the saucer and the cup	PAIN 367:15
	SHAK 484:19	S. is behovely	JUL 286:32	S. thou smoothly with t	CAMP 129:16
giveth wisdom unto the s.	PRAY 390:12	s. is ever before me	PRAY 393:4	S. thy songs of happy cheer	BLAKE 87:24
rey y al s. con el discreto	CERV 138:20	s. no more	BIBLE 72:11	s. to the child on thy	BRID 92:21
s. dues of fellowship	BROW 97:30	S. of self-love possesseth	SHAK 494:1	S. to the harp with a psalm	PRAY 396:8
s. he looks	BURNS 115:2	s. of witchcraft	BIBLE 50:4	S. to the Lord a new song	BIBLE 83:7
s. little rules and few	BELL 40:4	s. that amends is but patched	SHAK 488:6	s. unto God with the voice	PRAY 392:22
s. truth must be abus'd	SHAK 480:23	s. that was sweet	PAIN 367:17	s. unto the Lord a new	PRAY 391:19
Teach us delight in s.	KIPL 298:12	s. to covet honour	SHAK 445:2	s. unto the Lord a new	PRAY 396:7
'Tis ever thus with s.	GILB 229:10	s. to God above	THOR 550:28	S. us one of the songs	PRAY 399:3
very s. gentleman	SHAK 492:7	s. which doth so easily	BIBLE 79:35	S. we merrily unto God	PRAY 395:9
simpleness: When s. and duty tender		s. who tell us love can	SOUT 513:26	S. whatever is well made	YEATS 587:8
it	SHAK 471:14	s. will destroy a sinner	BUNY 107:29	Soul clap its hands and s.	YEATS 586:12
simpler: Make s. daily the beating		s. ye do by two and two	KIPL 303:20	Still wouldst thou s.	KEATS 291:22
	AUDEN 20:6	sometimes s.'s a pleasure	BYRON 122:13	suffers little birds to s.	SHAK 486:17
s. than the infancy	SHAK 487:2	sorrow dogging s.	HERB 248:10	That can s. both high	SHAK 488:17
Simplex: S. munditiis	HOR 259:15	that s. fell the angels	SHAK 447:12	that they will s. to me	ELIOT 203:25
simplicitas: sancta s.	HUSS 268:18	then in secret s.	CHUR 148:33	they shall laugh and s.	PRAY 394:3
sed sancta s.	JER 272:20	there is no s. but ignorance	MARL 329:19	tongue of the dumb s.	BIBLE 58:34
simplicity: Cultivate s.	LAMB 307:21	Thy s.'s not accidental	SHAK 464:15	used to s. in the water	DICK 178:30
holy s.	HUSS 268:18	To go away and s. no more	ANON 6:17	when you s.	SHAK 491:27
holy s.	JER 272:20	To s. in loving virtue	SHAK 464:6	Whilst thus I s.	CIBB 151:8
In his s. sublime	TENN 541:7	to s. in secret is not	MOL 354:1	Who s. to find your hearts	FLEC 214:9
Pity my s.	WESL 568:17	triumph over death and s.	SPEN 515:17	Will s. at dawn	BROW 97:27
simple truth miscall'd s.	SHAK 494:5	us this day without s.	PRAY 384:18	will s. the savageness out	SHAK 476:12
s., a child	POPE 378:8	wages of s. is death	BIBLE 75:3	world in ev'ry corner s.	HERB 246:36
s. or with severity a serious	ARN 16:14	want of power to s.	DRYD 197:9	would not s. for Lycidas	MILT 343:2
s. of his idea calling	CONR 161:21	wave the quantum o'the s.	BURNS 113:17	Singe: S. my white head	SHAK 454:4
s. of the three per cents	DISR 186:8	We wallow in our s.	ANON 9:1	That it do s. yourself	SHAK 446:25
s. of the three per cents	STOW 524:2	Where s. abounded	BIBLE 74:42	singeing: s. of the King of Spain's	
That makes s. a grace	JONS 283:27	which taketh away the s.	BIBLE 71:30		DRAKE 193:3
true as truth's s.	SHAK 487:2	Wilt thou forgive that s.	DONNE 189:13	singer: Beside the s.	LAND 309:1
Simplify: frittered away by detail…S.		worst s. towards our fellow	SHAW 496:17	idle s. of an empty day	MORR 358:8
	THOR 550:17	Would you like to s.	ANON 8:23	lived a s. in France of old	SWIN 530:29
s. me when I'm dead	DOUG 191:9	since: s. 'tis so	BROW 101:22	Lulled by the s.	MORR 358:9
simply: s. but with such style	HOR 259:15	sincere: tho' well-bred, s.	POPE 378:32	sans S.	FITZ 212:18
simulacrum: itself is but the dark s.		very s. in good principles	JOHN 280:5	s. not the song	ANON 8:7
	BROW 95:17	sincerity: bread of s. and truth	BIBLE 75:36	S. of sweet Colonus	ARN 15:10
sin: abolish the whole body of s.	PRAY 388:10	little s. is a dangerous	WILDE 572:20	Thou the s.	GILB 225:34
almost a s. of abstinence	DRYD 195:28	Sindh: I have S.	WINK 575:8	When the s. sings them	STEV 523:1
being dead unto s.	PRAY 388:10	sinecure: part of the world is no s.		singers: ago he was one of the s.	LEAR 311:21
Be sure your s. will find	BIBLE 48:17		BYRON 126:18	Singest: S. of summer in full-throated	
Be ye angry and s. not	BIBLE 78:1	sinews: money the s. of war	BACON 27:25		KEATS 291:17
black and soft as s.	CHES 147:5	S. of concord	FORD 216:14	singeth: milkmaid s. blithe	MILT 342:19
bosom s. blows quite away	HERB 248:11	Stiffen the s.	SHAK 443:21	s. with her breast against	HOOD 255:2
		twist the s. of thy heart	BLAKE 87:15	singing: angels all were s. out	BYRON 126:5

clear voice suddenly s.   AUDEN 21:1
Everyone suddenly burst out s.   SASS 414:16
grass is s.   ELIOT 205:10
have heard the mermaids s.   ELIOT 203:25
I am sick of s.   SWIN 530:3
I see ye have a s. face   FLET 215:23
liquid waves of thy sweet s.   SHEL 500:16
love a woman for s.   SHAK 453:14
me s. in the Wilderness   FITZ 212:11
nest of s. birds   JOHN 273:28
silver waves of thy sweet s.   SHEL 500:16
s. and making melody   BIBLE 78:5
s. beneath the dome   VERL 556:10
S., 'Here came a mortal   ARN 13:7
s. in their glory move   MILT 343:18
S. of Mount Abora   COL 156:30
S. so rarely   SCOTT 418:4
s. still dost soar   SHEL 504:16
s. will never be done   SASS 414:17
There is delight in s.   LAND 309:1
To the Master of all s.   LONG 317:14
went through the river s.   BUNY 107:37
Singing-boys: six little S.   BARH 33:12
single: in s. blessedness   SHAK 469:17
Let a s. completed action   BOIL 89:11
Nothing in the world is s.   SHEL 502:11
s. and only talked of population   GOLD 232:32
s. grateful thought raised   LESS 314:1
s. in the field   WORD 578:13
s. life doth well with   BACON 26:33
s. man in possession   AUST 23:11
they come not s. spies   SHAK 436:4
singles: What strenuous s. we played
    BETJ 44:6
sings: he s. each song twice over   BROW 101:6
motion like an angel s.   SHAK 468:15
one tell me what she s.   WORD 578:14
singular: So s. in each particular SHAK 491:27
Singularity: S. is almost invariably
    DOYLE 191:15
thyself into the trick of s.   SHAK 489:15
singularly: s. deep young man   GILB 227:21
sinister: that of the strange and s.
    JAMES 271:15
sink: Help me, Cassius, or I s.   SHAK 448:14
I pant, I s.   SHEL 500:13
load would s. a navy   SHAK 447:11
Not gross to s.   SHAK 495:10
raft which will never s.   AMES 4:3
'S. me the ship   TENN 543:3
s. through the sea they   THOM 546:19
to s. with Lamplough   STEV 521:11
would not s. i' the scale   BROW 104:4
'You may s. by the Low-lands   BALL 31:3
sinking: kind of alacrity in s.   SHAK 469:13
when they see me s.   ANON 10:14
sinks: He s. into thy depths with
    BYRON 121:24
It s.   LAND 308:20
So s. the day-star   MILT 343:17
Sinn: kommt mir nicht aus dem S.
    HEINE 244:9
sinned: all have s.   BIBLE 74:38
I have s. against heaven   BIBLE 70:19
s. against than sinning   SHAK 454:10
sinner: Be a s. and sin strongly   LUTH 320:15
be merciful to me a s.   BIBLE 70:35
I of her a s.   CONG 160:30
over one s. that repenteth   BIBLE 70:17
poor s.   COWP 165:25
sin will destroy a s.   BUNY 107:29
young s. with the handcuffs   HOUS 266:8
sinners: Master with publicans and s.
    BIBLE 65:22
mercy upon us miserable s.   PRAY 385:15
s.'ll be kotched out late   HARR 242:17
S.; of whom I am chief   BIBLE 79:8
s., plunged beneath that   COWP 165:24
s. to repentance   BIBLE 65:24
stood in the way of s.   PRAY 389:14

There s. must with devils   WATTS 565:16
thou be a breeder of s.   SHAK 433:11
we are s. all   SHAK 446:7
Why do s.' ways prosper   HOPK 257:2
sinning: sinned against than s.   SHAK 454:10
sins: are thinkin' on their s.   BURNS 114:7
Be all my s. remember'd   SHAK 433:9
by himself purged our s.   BIBLE 79:28
by the chain of our s.   PRAY 385:23
Commit The oldest s.   SHAK 442:20
cover the multitude of s.   BIBLE 80:32
dark and weep for their s.   WHIT 570:22
far hath he set our s.   PRAY 396:17
Few love to hear the s.   SHAK 478:3
forgetful of their s.   YEATS 586:14
forgiveth s.   BIBLE 62:21
Her s., which are many   BIBLE 69:24
'His s. were scarlet   BELL 39:19
Silly women laden with s.   BIBLE 79:24
s. and offences of my youth   PRAY 391:2
s. of your fathers   HOR 260:25
s., they are inclin'd   BUTL 117:23
Though your s. be as scarlet   BIBLE 57:18
was one of the gravest s.   WAUGH 566:5
which is the root of all s.   JAM 271:2
yet all s. must bear   DONNE 188:32
Sint: S. ut sunt aut non sint   CLEM 153:1
Sion: again the captivity of S.   PRAY 398:16
favourable and gracious unto S.   PRAY 393:8
God, art praised in S.   PRAY 393:23
his dwelling in S.   PRAY 395:1
one of the songs of S.   PRAY 399:3
praise to Mount S.   BUNY 107:12
Walk about S.   PRAY 392:27
we remembered thee, O S.   PRAY 399:3
sip: can't be tasted in a s.   DICK 180:30
sipped: Who s. no sup   GILB 229:9
Sir-come-spy-see: ask for his Monument,
S.   BARH 33:7
Sire: S. of an immortal strain   SHEL 499:4
thy s. was a knight   SCOTT 416:24
Siren: potions have I drunk of S. tears
    SHAK 495:6
Sirens: Blest pair of S.   MILT 340:20
S.! Dear me   DICK 178:30
sires: s. have marched to Rome   MAC 322:12
Sirion: S., like a young unicorn   PRAY 391:10
Sirius: S. pierced the eye with   HARDY 241:9
Sirmio: olive-silvery S.   TENN 533:18
S., bright rays of peninsulas   CAT 136:28
Sisera: courses fought against S.   BIBLE 49:9
S. looked out at a window   BIBLE 49:12
sissy: rose-red s. half as old   PLOM 374:18
sister: azure s. of the spring   SHEL 502:8
Had it been his s.   ANON 5:15
is no friend like a s.   ROSS 408:27
moon is my s.   BELL 39:16
My s. and my sister's child   COWP 165:16
my s., my spouse   BIBLE 56:28
s. Anne replied   PERR 372:25
s. hath left me to serve   BIBLE 69:34
sometime s., now our queen   SHAK 429:19
To live a barren s. all   SHAK 469:17
We have a little s.   BIBLE 57:13
Your brother and my s.   SHAK 426:27
sisterly: fervour of s. animosity   SURT 525:25
sisters: Are s. under their skins   KIPL 300:18
His s. and his cousins   GILB 228:3
Sphere-born harmonious s.   MILT 340:20
weird s.   SHAK 458:8
were twa s. sat in a bour   BALL 30:14
Sisyphus: S. must be regarded CAMUS 129:24
sit: dangerous s. to Sargent   ANON 6:8
he cannot s. on it   INGE 270:9
he can't S. still   MILL 339:25
I can s. and look at it   JER 272:26
is a good thing to s.   JOHN 278:14
'I shall s. here   CARR 133:24
let us s. upon the ground   SHAK 479:11
May s. i' th' centre   MILT 341:8

now s. down on my botom   FLEM 215:3
Shall s. and drink with me   BELL 40:11
s. and mourn all at her   BALL 32:9
s. down,' says Love   HERB 248:1
s. him down and die   SHAK 442:2
s. not down in the highest   BIBLE 70:7
S. on your arse for fifty   MACN 326:8
S. thou on my right hand   PRAY 397:11
S. thou still when kings   SCOTT 418:5
superstitious reluctance to s.   JOHN 278:13
Teach us to s. still   ELIOT 202:1
Their strength is to s.   BIBLE 58:24
them that s. in darkness   BIBLE 69:7
Though I s. down now   DISR 184:10
To s. still for once   HOFF 252:14
To s. upon a hill   SHAK 446:18
where men s. and hear each   KEATS 291:18
sittin: of it's s.' and thinkin'   KIPL 300:17
sitting: Are you s. comfortably   LANG 309:20
Lord s. upon a throne   BIBLE 57:28
not soar where he is s.   SHEL 499:19
s. in one place rather   ELIOT 201:13
s. in the shade   KIPL 299:14
take the privilege o' s.   ELIOT 201:19
situation: s. excellente   FOCH 216:3
situations: s. in life that cannot   BRAM 91:21
six: All's set at s. and seven   ANON 9:1
found s. feet of ground   HOUS 265:6
his s. days' work   MILT 349:2
Shakespeare never had s.   JOHN 275:27
S. days shalt thou labour   BIBLE 47:24
S. hours in sleep   COKE 154:22
s. hundred threescore and six   BIBLE 82:14
s. impossible things before   CARR 135:18
s. little Singing-boys   BARH 33:12
s. lustres almost now outwore DONNE 189:36
S. o'clock   ELIOT 204:7
s. of one and half-a-dozen   MARR 331:7
whether it snowed for s.   THOM 546:20
world on s. and sevene   CHAU 144:13
six foot: content with s.   BROW 97:24
six hundred: Rode the s.   TENN 532:23
sixpence: *I* give thee s.   CANN 129:27
I only got s.   PUNCH 402:27
precious little for s.   PUNCH 402:20
Whoso has s. is sovereign   CARL 132:14
sixpences: s. you know to one guinea
    JOHN 280:14
sixte: Welcome the s.   CHAU 143:17
sixteen: At s. you departed   POUND 383:16
sixth: s. age shifts   SHAK 425:24
sixty: s. seconds' worth of distance
    KIPL 300:2
size: Those of the largest s.   CARR 135:10
skating: In s. over thin ice   EMER 207:33
skelp: I gie them a s.   BURNS 113:4
sketch: s. the ruins of St Paul's   MAC 323:16
Skiddaw: Till S. saw the fire that   MAC 322:4
skies: common people of the s.   WOTT 583:15
exchange thy sullen s.   COWP 166:34
meet the raging of the s.   CAMP 129:3
paint the sable s.   DRUM 193:26
s. are painted with unnumber'd   SHAK 449:25
soaring claim the s.   FRERE 218:26
some watcher of the s.   KEATS 292:18
virgin-daughter of the s.   DRYD 197:32
skilfully: s. and magnanimously all
    MILT 352:8
skill: All s. to naught   KIPL 301:3
his s. runs on the lees   HERR 250:12
none, or little s.   HERR 250:12
nothing with a deal of s.   COWP 166:23
parson own'd his s.   GOLD 231:3
S. comes so slow   DAV 172:10
s. in antiquity inclines   FULL 220:14
s. in the weapon is nothing   SHAK 442:15
Thy s. to poet were   SHEL 504:24
'Tis God gives s.   ELIOT 201:28
who has the power and s.   ANON 8:20

skilled: fingers play in s. unmindfulness HARDY 239:12
skim: s. away TENN 536:20
S. milk masquerades GILB 228:8
skimble-skamble: such a deal of s. stuff SHAK 439:27
skims: lightly s. the midge BETJ 42:18
skin: Ethiopian change his s. BIBLE 60:22
my s. bristles so that HOUS 266:17
Nor scar that whiter s. SHAK 477:5
s. of an innocent lamb SHAK 446:12
skull beneath the s. ELIOT 205:13
spot on your s. is a shocking AUDEN 18:18
throws her enamell'd s. SHAK 470:10
with the s. of my teeth BIBLE 52:29
skinny: holds him with his s. hand COL 155:6
skins: beauty of their s. TENN 542:8
sisters under their s. KIPL 300:18
skip: art of reading is to s. HAM 238:12
them also to s. like a calf PRAY 391:10
skipped: mountains s. like rams PRAY 397:16
skipper: s. had taken his little LONG 317:20
skipping: s. king SHAK 439:9
With what a pretty s. grace MARV 332:13
skirt: swish of a s. in the dew KIPL 304:1
skirts: caught at God's s. BROW 101:18
grasps the s. of happy chance TENN 537:1
skittish: Unstaid and s. in all motions SHAK 488:27
skittles: all porter and s. DICK 182:32
Life ain't all beer and s. DU M 199:4
Sklaven-Moral: Herren-Moral und S. NIET 363:12
Skugg: Here S. Lies snug FRAN 218:16
skull: more of her than the s. BIBLE 51:37
s. beneath the skin ELIOT 205:13
s. that housed white angels SASS 415:3
skuttle: me in mind of the s. fish ADD 2:24
sky: admitted to that equal s. POPE 379:6
all the blue ethereal s. ADD 2:22
bear him up the Norfolk s. BETJ 42:11
blue s. of spring ALL 3:21
clear blue s. over my head HAZL 243:32
discern the face of the s. BIBLE 66:32
freeze, thou bitter s. SHAK 426:1
inverted Bowl we call The S. FITZ 213:8
Like strips of the s. fallen SHEL 500:6
On a bed of daffodil s. TENN 540:9
shapes of s. or plain SHEL 504:21
Shine upon the starry s. BLAKE 86:5
shoulders held the s. suspended HOUS 265:7
Shoulder the s. HOUS 264:22
s. changes when they are SHAK 426:23
s. grows darker yet CHES 146:16
s₂ is darkening like AUDEN 21:10
s₂ is red BIBLE 66:31
stars be blown about the s. YEATS 586:18
to lose itself in the s. BROW 98:20
vaulted s. CLARE 152:13
watched the ocean and the s. SHEL 501:16
Were close against the s. HOOD 254:18
Which prisoners call the s. WILDE 572:8
Who aimeth at the s. HERB 247:8
wide and starry s. STEV 523:10
wrote my will across the s. LAWR 311:12
You'll get pie in the s. HILL 251:3
Skye: Over the sea to S. STEV 523:4
skylark: despise the s.'s song BRON 93:13
s. wounded in the wing BLAKE 85:10
slacks: girls in s. remember Dad BETJ 42:8
slain: am hurt but I am not s. BALL 31:15
beauty of Israel is s. BIBLE 50:16
ere thou hast s. another BROW 97:25
fifty thousand men s. WALP 563:25
I am s. by a fair cruel SHAK 489:4
if the s. think he is slain EMER 206:17
is my most noble lord s. MAL 328:3
jaw of an ass have I s. BIBLE 49:24
law, chance, hath s. DONNE 189:4
many a gallant man was s. ANON 7:8

may fight and no be s. BURNS 115:13
own eyes might see him s. MORR 358:11
Saul hath s. his thousands BIBLE 50:13
shall himself be s. MAC 323:1
s. in thine high places BIBLE 50:17
small s. body SWIN 530:15
That was late s. at Carrow SKEL 508:19
there lies a new-s. knight BALL 32:8
thrice he slew the s. DRYD 195:2
slander: civic s. and the spite TENN 537:15
Fear not s. SHAK 428:22
Have not devis'd this s. SHAK 476:23
S., meanest spawn of Hell TENN 538:13
To speak no s. TENN 534:11
Who's angry at a s. makes JONS 283:20
slandered: hath not s. his neighbour PRAY 390:4
slandering: lying, and s. PRAY 388:17
slang: All s. is metaphor CHES 147:29
Slant: There's a certain S. of light DICK 184:1
slap-dash: am I s. down in the mouth CONG 160:25
slap-up: s. gal in a bang-up chariot DICK 181:15
slashing: s. article THAC 545:15
slate: his thoughts upon a s. HOOD 255:14
wiping something off a s. KIPL 297:23
slates: out the slipping s. BETJ 43:9
slaughter: arrayed for mutual s. WORD 578:21
brought as a lamb to the s. BIBLE 59:22
Forbad to wade through s. GRAY 234:24
out threatenings and s. BIBLE 73:32
ox goeth to the s. BIBLE 53:25
s. will ensue CONG 160:21
steeled themselves for s. AUDEN 21:3
slaughter'd: 'ye have s. and made NEWB 361:11
slaughtered: thy s. saints MILT 351:9
slaughterous: familiar to my s. thoughts SHAK 463:5
slave: Being your s. SHAK 493:18
fingering s. WORD 580:3
giving freedom to the s. LINC 314:22
half s. and half free LINC 314:14
here I stand, your s. SHAK 454:5
like a sad s. SHAK 493:18
No more s. States CHASE 141:2
S. to no sect POPE 380:2
soundly as the wretched s. SHAK 444:25
Till he fac'd the s. SHAK 458:3
true, sick-hearted s. HOUS 265:18
very s. of circumstance BYRON 125:20
What a s. art thou SHAK 439:7
would have made him a s. BURKE 109:2
you were a Christian s. HENL 245:10
slaverie: Chains and s. BURNS 114:34
slavery: between liberty and s. CAMD 128:4
classified as s. CHUR 149:25
cost of the squalor and s. SHAW 498:23
s. of the tea and coffee COBB 154:7
S. they can have anywhere BURKE 110:3
state is a state of S. GILL 229:11
war has saved us from s. WALP 563:16
slaves: because they are all s. GOLD 232:6
Britons never will be s. THOM 549:7
freemen, are the only s. MASS 335:17
grandfather were s. CHEK 144:24
inevitably two kinds of s. ILL 270:5
land of s. shall ne'er BYRON 123:4
S. cannot breathe in England COWP 166:32
s. of some defunct economist KEYN 295:20
S. of the Lamp ARN 12:19
too pure an Air for S. ANON 7:7
voluntarily to submit to be s. PITT 373:21
Which those poor s. with SHEL 500:10
wholly s. or wholly free DRYD 196:16
slavish: you s. herd HOR 259:1
slay: s., and slay, and slay MAC 323:2
Though he s. me BIBLE 52:25
slayer: priest who slew the s. MAC 323:1

red s. think he slays EMER 206:17
slayeth: s. the child in the womb POUND 382:11
slaying: s. of a beautiful hypothesis HUXL 269:5
slayn: he was s. in this manere CHAU 144:18
slays: red slayer think he s. EMER 206:17
s. A thousand LAND 308:21
sledge: s. and anvil lie declined ANON 6:10
sleek: find me fat and s. HOR 258:16
s. and shining creatures TENN 542:8
Sleek-headed: S. men and such as sleep SHAK 448:20
sleekit: s., cow'rin' BURNS 115:20
sleep: after-dinner's s. SHAK 464:10
Back from the City of S. KIPL 298:14
balmy s. YOUNG 587:21
By night we s. on the cliffs LEAR 312:16
Can s. so soundly SHAK 444:25
Care-charmer S. DAN 171:1
Care-charming S. FLET 215:22
Come, S.! O Sleep SIDN 507:20
comes with the first s. MEYN 338:14
come to the borders of s. THOM 547:19
Death and his brother S. SHEL 500:8
deep s. to fall upon Adam BIBLE 45:11
Do I wake or s. KEATS 291:23
dreadfully but as a drunken s. SHAK 464:25
dreamless, uninvaded s. TENN 537:24
drowsy approaches of s. BROW 95:22
each day dies with s. HOPK 256:21
Entice the dewy-feather'd s. MILT 342:8
first sweet s. of night SHEL 501:8
folding of the hands to s. BIBLE 53:22
From rest and s. DONNE 189:5
gray and full of s. YEATS 587:12
hath night to do with s. MILT 340:28
have an exposition of s. SHAK 471:5
her great gift of s. HENL 245:8
His s. Was aery light MILT 348:13
How long wilt thou s. BIBLE 53:22
How s. the brave COLL 158:19
I always s. upon ale FARQ 209:23
ideas s. furiously CHOM 148:15
I'll go to s. if I can SHAK 425:17
In s. a king SHAK 494:13
in soot I s. BLAKE 88:5
I s. BIBLE 57:1
I s. out the thought SHAK 491:19
I s. well MORT 358:17
I wake to s. ROET 407:6
keepeth thee will not s. PRAY 398:9
life Is rounded with a s. SHAK 485:20
Macbeth does murder s. SHAK 460:8
Macbeth shall s. no more SHAK 460:9
medicine thee to that sweet s. SHAK 475:24
me from the fields of s. WORD 579:2
might s. out this great gap SHAK 421:30
miles to go before I s. FROST 219:12
nose-painting, s., and urine SHAK 460:18
Now I lay me down to s. ANON 7:3
on him who invented s. CERV 138:20
Only s. BROW 105:35
O sleep! O gentle s. SHAK 441:20
O S.! the friend of Woe SOUT 513:27
season of all natures, s. SHAK 461:26
Shake off this downy s. SHAK 460:23
She looks like s. SHAK 424:17
Silence and s. like fields DE L 173:25
Six hours in s. COKE 154:22
Sleek-headed men and such as s. SHAK 448:20
S. after toil SPEN 516:8
s. an act or two SHAK 448:4
s. and a forgetting WORD 579:5
s. and a sweet dream when MASS 334:6
S.; and if life was bitter SWIN 529:1
s. between term and term SHAK 426:13
sleep, dear, s. BEDD 36:23
s. in Abraham's bosom SHAK 481:7

s. in it besides himself ADD 2:12
S. is a death BROW 97:6
S. is sweet to the labouring BUNY 107:24
S.! it is a gentle thing COL 155:23
'S. no more SHAK 460:8
s. not so sound, as sweet HERR 249:1
s. of a labouring man is BIBLE 55:17
s. old palaces and towers SHEL 502:10
s. one ever-during night CAT 136:25
S. on, my Love KING 296:11
s. provides relief every CHAM 139:13
S. shall neither night SHAK 458:7
S. shall obey me SOUT 513:24
s. should be his last repose ANON 8:21
s. that is among the lonely WORD 581:11
S. to wake BROW 98:32
S. will come when thou SHEL 505:4
S. your fill BELL 39:22
slept an azure-lidded s. KEATS 289:20
Sword s. in my hand BLAKE 86:16
them they are even as a s. PRAY 395:18
There are two gates of S. VIRG 559:3
There'll be time enough to s. HOUS 262:15
This s. is sound indeed SHAK 442:18
thou arise out of thy s. BIBLE 53:22
thou s. the sleep of death BLAKE 86:11
time to awake out of s. BIBLE 75:24
time when first s. begins VIRG 558:4
To die: to s. SHAK 433:8
to s. at a bank from ten JER 272:24
to s. at the root of my LAWR 311:3
to s. before evening PATER 369:22
us from everlasting s. BROW 95:22
waking s. MONT 355:5
We shall not all s. BIBLE 76:29
We shall not s. MCCR 324:31
while some must s. SHAK 434:16
Would I were s. and peace SHAK 482:20
would make anyone go to s. DICK 182:31
would not s. with the brave HOUS 264:19
yet I would not s. SHAK 459:14
sleeper: me the s. THOM 548:28
that was never a quiet s. TENN 540:15
sleepers: slumbers for the s. in that quiet
earth BRON 94:1
snorted we in the Seven S. DONNE 188:29
sleepeth: maid is not dead, but s. BIBLE 65:27
peradventure he s. BIBLE 51:9
sleep-flower: s. sways in the wheat its
THOM 548:28
sleeping: growing, Jock, when ye're s.
SCOTT 418:20
He cursed him in s. BARH 33:13
kind of s. in the blood SHAK 441:6
Lay your s. head AUDEN 19:17
s. and the dead Are SHAK 460:11
s., by a brother's hand SHAK 431:12
suddenly he find you s. BIBLE 69:1
wakened us from s. BROO 94:9
young love s. in the shade MER 337:1
Sleepless: S. as the river under thee
CRANE 168:29
s. soul WORD 580:28
S. themselves POPE 375:15
S. with cold commemorative ROSS 410:5
sleeps: dines he s. SURT 525:7
heaven-eyed creature s. WORD 577:18
He wakes or s. with SHEL 499:19
moon s. with Endymion SHAK 468:19
Now s. the crimson petal TENN 542:14
s. feels not the toothache SHAK 429:2
S. in Elysium SHAK 444:25
S. on his luminous ring TENN 541:21
Such s. as may beguile SURR 524:21
That broods and s. on his WORD 580:5
Till tir'd, he s. POPE 379:19
while my pretty one, s. TENN 541:31
sleep-time: in the silence of the s.
BROW 98:31

sleepwalker: with the assurance of a s.
HITL 251:10
Sleepy: S. with the flow of streams
HOUS 263:18
who in the s. region stay MORR 358:9
sleepy-head: Ain't you 'shamed, you
s. STEV 522:24
sleeve: wear my heart upon my s.
SHAK 473:15
sleeves: Tie up my s. with ribbons
HUNT 268:15
sleigh: snow on an ebony s. AUDEN 18:7
sleight: by the s. of men BIBLE 77:28
more th' admire his s. BUTL 118:6
slender: she puts forth a s. hand POUND 382:5
Slept: Edward the Confessor S. under
the dresser BENT 41:7
firstfruits of them that s. BIBLE 76:22
He s. with his fathers BIBLE 51:5
I should have s. BIBLE 52:12
On a poet's lips I s. SHEL 503:5
thought he thought I s. PATM 370:3
while their companions s. LONG 316:19
Whilst Adam s. ANON 8:21
slepyng: s. hound to wake CHAU 144:7
slew: I s. him SHAK 450:15
s. at his death were more BIBLE 49:28
s. mighty kings PRAY 399:1
who s. his master BIBLE 51:35
Slice: S. him where you like WOD 575:20
slight: Away, s. man SHAK 451:15
loved so s. a thing TENN 539:4
s. all that do FARQ 210:11
s. what I receive BROW 104:7
slighted: Doctor s. OWEN 366:28
slim: Who's the s. boy now HOR 259:15
slime: daubed it with s. BIBLE 46:41
slimier s. BROO 94:12
through the ooze and s. SMITH 510:10
slimepit: To the s. and the mire HOUS 265:4
slimier: s. slime BROO 94:12
slimy: s. things did crawl with COL 155:14
thousand thousand s. things COL 155:21
slings: s. and arrows of outrageous
SHAK 433:8
slip: caused his chest to s. WOD 575:23
in earth to set one s. SHAK 491:24
make a s. in handling us KIPL 302:17
Since he gave us all the s. BROW 105:32
s. Into my bosom TENN 542:14
Then s. I from her bum SHAK 470:3
then s. out of the world DRYD 196:36
Under the tension, s. ELIOT 202:17
slipper: s. and subtle knave SHAK 474:21
s. knock'd the ground POPE 380:29
slippered: s. Hesper BROO 94:19
slippers: bring me my s. MOL 353:3
walks in his golden s. BUNY 107:19
slippery: standing is s. BACON 26:23
Slit: S. your girl's KING 297:19
slither: in a s. of dyed stuff POUND 382:15
slits: s. the thin-spun life MILT 343:8
sliver: envious s. broke SHAK 436:19
Sloane Square: S. and South Kensington
GILB 226:14
sloe: lush-kept plush-capped s. HOPK 257:7
slog: foot—s.—slog KIPL 298:6
slop: Raineth drop and staineth s.
POUND 382:4
slopes: on the butler's upper s. WOD 575:27
sloth: most of s. HERB 247:3
much time in studies is s. BACON 27:16
peaceful s., Not peace MILT 346:2
s. Finds the down pillow SHAK 428:18
slothful: s. man saith BIBLE 54:34
Slouches: S. towards Bethlehem
YEATS 586:16
Slough: bombs, and fall on S. BETJ 44:5
name of the s. was Despond BUNY 107:11
was an old person of S. LEAR 312:26

slovenliness: s. is no part of religion
WESL 568:22
slow: I am s. of speech BIBLE 47:9
of the human mind is s. BURKE 109:29
Quick' and some cry 'S. TENN 541:26
sloeblack, s., black, crowblack THOM 547:9
s., fresh fount JONS 283:21
s. to anger is better than BIBLE 54:9
s. to speak BIBLE 80:17
slowest: s. thing in the world SHAD 420:21
slowly: Make haste s. SUET 524:16
Slug-a-bed: Get up, sweet S. HERR 248:23
sluggard: foul s.'s comfort CARL 131:10
Go to the ant thou s. BIBLE 53:21
s. is wiser in his own BIBLE 54:35
s.'s cradle CHAP 140:9
'Tis the voice of the s. WATTS 565:25
slug-horn: Dauntless the s. to my
BROW 99:30
Slugs: S. leave their lair COL 157:14
sluices: Close the s. now VIRG 559:21
sluicing: excellent browsing and s.
WOD 575:26
slum: swear-word in a rustic s. BEER 37:15
slumber: abed and daylight s. HOUS 262:15
Ere S.'s chain has bound MOORE 357:2
honey-heavy dew of s. SHAK 449:12
keep'st the ports of s. SHAK 442:17
little sleep, a little s. BIBLE 53:22
pilgrim's limbs affected s. CAMP 129:20
shall neither s. not sleep PRAY 398:9
s. did my spirit seal WORD 581:10
s. is more sweet than toil TENN 539:7
will start from her s. ARN 13:7
slumber'd: That you have but s. here
SHAK 471:23
slumbered: warm between them s.
HOUS 265:11
slumbers: Golden s. kiss your eyes
DEKK 173:22
s. light SCOTT 417:26
unquiet s. for the sleepers BRON 94:1
yet hast thou golden s. DEKK 173:20
slumb'ring: leaden sceptre o'er a s.
YOUNG 588:1
slut: I am not a s. SHAK 426:16
sluts: now foul s. in dairies CORB 162:13
sluttish: besmear'd with s. time SHAK 493:17
elf-locks in foul s. hairs SHAK 481:28
sly: s., ensnaring art BURNS 113:7
smack: yet some s. of age in you SHAK 441:5
small: Almost too s. for sight SHAK 455:14
arms long and s. WYATT 583:22
compare s. things with great VIRG 560:19
creatures great and s. ALEX 3:13
In s. proportions we just JONS 285:8
my s. cruse best fits my HERR 249:20
she deals it in s. parcels WEBS 567:1
shows how s. the world is GROS 236:22
S. is beautiful SCH 415:12
s. Latin, and less Greek JONS 284:21
s. things from the peak CHES 147:30
so thoroughly s. and dry ELIOT 202:1
speaks s. like a woman SHAK 469:2
squadrons against the s. BUSS 117:7
still s. voice BIBLE 51:14
That s. infantry MILT 345:22
Too s. to live in ANON 8:11
use of maps on a s. scale SAL 413:20
very s. the very great are THAC 546:4
with s. men no great thing MILL 339:15
smaller: flea Hath s. fleas SWIFT 528:5
smallest: Queen Anne was one of the
s. people BAG 29:10
Smart: lief pray with Kit S. JOHN 274:24
Of love and all its s. BEDD 36:23
scorn which mock'd the s. ARN 13:9
smatch: some s. of honour in it SHAK 452:6
smattering: s. of everything DICK 183:3

smell: Cheered with the grateful s.
                                    MILT 347:17
even a s. remembered   GREE 236:4
I s. a rat   ROCHE 406:14
Money has no s.   VESP 556:11
s. and hideous hum   GODL 229:24
s. of bread and butter   BYRON 119:32
s. of burning fills   BELL 40:7
s. of burned poetry   WOD 576:1
s. of fish there is sometimes   KILV 296:6
s. of the blood still   SHAK 462:22
s. the blood of a British   SHAK 454:27
s. too strong of the lamp   STER 519:23
smudge and shares man's s.   HOPK 256:12
sweet keen s.   ROSS 410:8
this foul deed shall s.   SHAK 450:12
this s. of cooped-up angels   FRY 220:4
This world would s. like   SHEL 501:18
smelleth: he s. the battle afar off BIBLE 53:7
smells: dead thing that s. sweet THOM 547:17
he s. April and May   SHAK 469:10
it s. of mortality   SHAK 455:17
it s. to heaven   SHAK 434:27
smile: bask in Heaven's blue s. SHEL 500:5
betwixt that s. we would   SHAK 447:9
Did he s. his work to see   BLAKE 87:16
gigantic s. o' the brown   BROW 101:20
her own dying s.   SHEL 499:9
I dare not beg a s.   HERR 250:3
I hear a s.   CROSS 170:6
jest without the s.   COL 157:17
Let me s. with the wise   JOHN 275:23
morn those Angel faces s.   NEWM 362:15
Out where the s. dwells   CHAP 140:2
recognize your mother with a s. VIRG 560:1
Robert with his watery s.   TENN 533:10
share the good man's s.   GOLD 231:1
s., and be a villain   SHAK 431:16
S. at us   CHES 147:15
smiled a kind of sickly s.   HARTE 242:33
s. his face into more lines   SHAK 490:3
s. of safety wounds   SHAK 440:30
s. to those who hate   BYRON 126:1
s. upon his fingers' ends   SHAK 443:17
vain tribute of the s.   SCOTT 416:18
we shall s.   SHAK 451:32
When you call me that, s.   WIST 575:11
Where my Julia's lips do s.   HERR 248:21
you should forget and s.   ROSS 409:4
You s., and mock me   SHAK 487:9
smiled: At me you s.   TENN 537:26
Has s. and said 'Good Night   BELL 39:20
Jesus wept; Voltaire s.   HUGO 267:13
Until she s. on me   COL 154:26
Well I remember how you s.   LAND 309:4
smiles: charmed it with s. and soap
                                    CARR 133:8
corner of the world s.   HOR 260:8
Seldom he s.   SHAK 448:21
She is Venus when she s.   JONS 285:5
s., As in a looking-glass   SHAK 491:9
S. awake you when you rise   DEKK 173:22
S. by his cheerful fire   GOLD 231:26
s. his emptiness betray   POPE 377:2
s. steals something from   SHAK 474:3
s., with sniffles predominating HENRY 245:23
Than s. of other maidens   COL 155:1
There's daggers in men's s.   SHAK 461:4
thy own sweet s. I see   COWP 166:2
welcome ever s.   SHAK 487:5
wreathed s.   MILT 342:14
smilest: Thou s. and art still   ARN 14:23
smiling: He hides a s. face   COWP 165:28
like patience on a monument s. at
grief   SHAK 489:7
s., destructive man   LEE 313:14
S. the boy fell dead   BROW 101:16
s. through her tears   HOMER 254:1
S., while hurt   HARDY 240:16
smil'st: s. upon the stroke that SHAK 483:10

smite: caitiff s. the other   HOLM 253:11
s. thee on thy right cheek   BIBLE 64:17
Stands ready to s. once   MILT 343:13
Star-spiked Rails a fiery S.   THOM 549:2
Strength without hands to s.   SWIN 528:21
will s. all the firstborn   BIBLE 47:18
smiteth: his cheek to him that s. BIBLE 60:31
Smith: conceal him by naming him S.
                                    HOLM 253:7
s., a mighty man is he   LONG 317:18
s. of his own fortune   CLAU 152:26
s. was the first murd'rer's   COWP 167:21
smithy: to forge in the s. of my JOYCE 286:19
smitten: bones are s. asunder   PRAY 392:9
s. me to my knee   THOM 548:16
smok'd: s. with bloody execution SHAK 458:3
smoke: blood and s. and flame   HOUS 266:4
bravery in their rotten s.   SHAK 493:11
coaster with a salt-caked s.   MAS 333:19
corrupted by this stinking s.   JAM 271:4
counties overhung with s.   MORR 358:10
her beloved s.   LAMB 307:24
hills, they shall s.   PRAY 397:2
him full of s. and embers   JONS 284:5
horrible Stygian s.   JAM 271:3
light emerging from the s.   HOR 257:19
man who does not s.   STEV 521:29
Only thin s. without flame   HARDY 240:5
s. and stir of this dim   MILT 340:23
s. and wealth and din   HOR 261:7
s. into the smother   SHAK 424:28
s. of their torment ascendeth   BIBLE 82:17
s. that rubs its muzzle   ELIOT 203:18
there's never s. without fire   AUDEN 20:22
you gwine do wid de s.   HARR 242:25
smoked: Who s. like a chimney   BARH 33:17
smokefall: draughty church at s. ELIOT 202:16
smokeless: glittering in the s. air
                                    WORD 581:14
smoking: power of s. at such a rate
                                    LAMB 308:12
s. flax shall he not quench   BIBLE 59:11
sometimes in a s. room   KIPL 302:5
What a blessing this s. is   HELPS 244:17
smoky: Palace in s. light   POUND 382:7
Worse than a s. house   SHAK 439:28
smooth: I am a s. man   BIBLE 46:15
large, and s., and round   SOUT 513:15
neat knave with a s. tale   WEBS 566:18
person and a s. dispose   SHAK 474:12
s. as monumental alabaster   SHAK 477:5
Speak unto us s. things   BIBLE 58:26
To s. the ice   SHAK 452:25
true love never did run s.   SHAK 469:18
smoother: his words were s. than oil
                                    PRAY 393:12
mouth is s. than oil   BIBLE 53:20
smooth-fac'd: That s. gentleman
                                    SHAK 452:14
smote: He s. divers nations   PRAY 399:1
Israel s. him with   BIBLE 48:12
s. him thus   SHAK 477:23
s. the king of Israel between   BIBLE 51:21
s. them hip and thigh   BIBLE 49:23
s. the nail into his temples   BIBLE 49:7
smother: from the smoke into the s.
                                    SHAK 424:28
smudge: wears man's s. and shares man's
                                    HOPK 256:12
smut-hounds: was brought down by s.
                                    AUDEN 18:20
smylere: s. with the knyf under CHAU 142:20
snaffle: use the s. and the curb CAMP 128:12
snail: church the size of a s.   THOM 547:7
creeping like s.   SHAK 425:24
is easy paced) this s.   DONNE 189:23
said a whiting to a s.   CARR 134:13
slug-abed s. upon the thorn   THOM 548:5
s.'s on the thorn   BROW 103:21
Worm nor s.   SHAK 470:12

snails: Like s. did creep   HERR 250:7
tender horns of cockled s.   SHAK 457:8
snake: earth doth like a s. renew SHEL 500:20
like a wounded s.   POPE 378:21
of the eagle or the s.   KIPL 301:1
s. hidden in the grass   VIRG 559:19
S. is living yet   BELL 40:4
there the s. throws her   SHAK 470:10
We have scotch'd the s.   SHAK 461:12
Snakes: S., in my heart-blood   SHAK 479:9
There are no s. to be met   JOHN 277:28
You spotted s. with double   SHAK 470:11
snap-dragon: s. growing on the walls
                                    NEWM 361:23
we have gold-dusted s.   ARN 15:6
snapper-up: s. of unconsidered trifles
                                    SHAK 491:18
snare: delusion, a mockery, and a s.
                                    DENM 174:22
from the s. of the hunter   PRAY 395:21
I saw the s.   TENN 537:26
of the s. of the fowler   PRAY 398:14
There is a rabbit in a s.   STEP 518:26
were rapid falcons in a s.   MER 337:17
world's great s. uncaught   SHAK 423:3
snares: rain s., fire and brimstone
                                    PRAY 389:31
s. of death compassed   PRAY 397:19
Snark: If your S. be a Boojum   CARR 133:7
S. was a Boojum   CARR 133:9
snarled: s. and yelping seas   ELIOT 204:11
snatch: s. them straight away   SHAK 478:5
snatch'd: s. his rudder   ARN 14:21
snatched: s. the lightning shaft TURG 553:22
who has been s. from us   BURKE 110:21
snatches: s. a man from obscurity
                                    REYN 405:15
sneaking: petty s. knave I knew BLAKE 87:3
sneer: flinch and traitors s.   CONN 161:10
laughing devil in his s.   BYRON 121:31
s. at me for leaning all   FITZ 213:10
solemn creed with solemn s.   BYRON 120:37
teach the rest to s.   POPE 376:26
Who can refute a s.   PALEY 368:9
witlings s. and rivals rail   JOHN 282:20
sneering: I was born s.   GILB 226:20
sneery: hair and looked very s. ASHF 17:13
sneeze: 'If you s.   LEAR 312:26
sneezed: Not to be s.   COLM 159:1
sneezes: beat him when he s.   CARR 133:26
snicker-snack: vorpal blade went s.
                                    CARR 134:29
snickersnee: I drew my s.   GILB 227:8
sniff: snuffle and s. and handkerchief
                                    BROO 94:16
sniffles: with s. predominating HENRY 245:23
sniffs: tiger s. the rose   SASS 415:1
Snob: admires mean things is a S.
                                    THAC 545:4
not to be sometimes a S.   THAC 545:5
snooze: caribous lie around and s.
                                    COW 163:30
snore: snorer can't hear himself s.
                                    TWAIN 554:18
Weariness Can s.   SHAK 428:18
snored: have simply sat and s.   CHES 146:12
Snores: S. out the watch of night
                                    SHAK 442:18
snoring: s., she disturbs   COWP 166:29
snorted: s. we in the Seven Sleepers
                                    DONNE 188:29
snot: s. green sea   JOYCE 286:20
snout: gold in a swine's s.   BIBLE 53:32
snow: architecture of the s.   EMER 206:24
asleep the s. came flying   BRID 92:1
bloodless lay the untrodden s.   CAMP 128:21
chaste as unsunn'd s.   SHAK 428:12
cherry hung with s.   HOUS 262:14
Drifts the appalling s.   AUDEN 18:10
Earth in forgetful s.   ELIOT 204:17

fall o' the s. JONS 285:4
fare wel al the s. of ferne CHAU 144:15
garment was white as s. BIBLE 61:8
He giveth s. like wool PRAY 399:21
I love s. SHEL 503:27
I, this incessant s. DE L 174:12
last long streak of s. TENN 537:18
Lawn as white as driven s. SHAK 492:2
like the s. falls BURNS 115:7
recollect the S. DICK 183:14
rosebuds fill'd with s. CAMP 129:23
shall be as white as s. BIBLE 57:18
shall be whiter than s. PRAY 393:5
sit brooding in the s. SHAK 457:19
s. and vapours PRAY 399:22
s. disfigured the public AUDEN 19:2
s. in May's new-fangled SHAK 456:16
S. on snow ROSS 409:1
S. which doth the top SPEN 516:31
Virgin shrouded in s. BLAKE 87:22
white as s. BIBLE 81:14
Whiter than new s. SHAK 483:7
wondrous strange s. SHAK 471:13
ye Ice and S. PRAY 384:22
Snowdon: We've the stones of S.
KING 296:20
snowed: s. for six days and six THOM 546:20
snows: are the s. of yesteryear VILL 557:5
From her couch of s. SHEL 500:2
Said our Lady of the S. KIPL 301:20
s. have dispersed HOR 261:14
Snowy: S., Flowy ELLIS 206:13
snub: has a s. nose like to mine BLAKE 85:21
snuff: only took s. GOLD 231:21
s. the approach of tyranny BURKE 109:23
s., tobacker DICK 177:9
You abuse s. COL 157:30
snuff'd: be s. out by an article BYRON 123:32
snuffle: s. and sniff and handkerchief
BROO 94:16
snug: Here Skugg Lies s. FRAN 218:16
what a s. little Island DIBD 175:23
soap: charmed it with smiles and s.
CARR 133:3
hands with invisible s. HOOD 254:23
I used your s. two years PUNCH 402:33
S. and education are not TWAIN 554:6
soap-boiler: I have made a s. costive
WEBS 566:23
soaping: s. her breasts in the bath
EWART 209:11
soar: can creep as well as s. BURKE 112:9
s., but never roam WORD 583:1
S. not too high to fall MASS 335:16
s. where he is sitting SHEL 499:19
that should spur you to s. SWIN 530:22
to s. with Eno STEV 521:11
soared: He has out-s. the shadow SHEL 499:21
soaring: s. ever singest SHEL 504:16
soars: lark s. BROW 97:29
sobbed: He s. and he sighed GILB 227:17
sober: at least not s. JOHN 279:33
Be s., be vigilant BIBLE 80:33
clean, shaved and s. CHAN 139:20
Half a s. as a judge LAMB 308:1
men at whiles are s. HOUS 264:23
once saw Porson s. HOUS 266:18
Philip drunk to Philip s. ANON 4:22
righteous, and s. life PRAY 384:13
second and s. thoughts HENRY 245:18
should be compulsorily s. MAGEE 326:21
s., of good behaviour BIBLE 79:12
that will go to bed s. FLET 215:8
woman s. PEPYS 372:10
sober-suited: s. songstress THOM 549:12
Sobranies: Balkan S. in a wooden box
BETJ 44:10
sobs: Life is made up of s. HENRY 245:23
s. of the violins of aut VERL 556:8
social: commit A s. science AUDEN 21:5

man into the s. masonry WELLS 568:15
Piecemeal s. engineering POPP 381:25
s. and economic experiment HOOV 255:24
s. animal and created DEM 174:19
S. Contract is nothing WELLS 568:15
sociale: ...si s. animal et in commune
DEM 174:19
Socialism: Marxian S. must always
KEYN 295:16
S. can only arrive by bicycle VIER 556:21
socialismo: El s. puede llegar solo
VIER 556:21
socialist: to construct the s. order
LENIN 313:20
société: homme moins propre à la s.
CHAM 139:14
societies: good s. say FORS 217:4
solemn troops and sweet s. MILT 343:18
society: be a distinct gain to s. GILB 226:23
curing the maladies of S. CARL 132:9
first duty to serve s. JOHN 275:18
four hundred people in New York s.
MCAL 321:23
honour which the Royal S. FAR 209:20
in our condition of S. THAC 545:5
In the affluent s. no useful GALB 220:28
kindness and consolidates s. JOHN 280:6
Man seeketh in s. comfort BACON 25:1
Man was formed for s. BLAC 85:1
no s. HOBB 251:18
of motion of modern s. MARX 333:8
often unfit a man for s. CHAM 139:14
One great s. alone on earth WORD 580:24
open s. and its enemies POPP 381:24
Ourself will mingle with s. SHAK 461:16
Our s. distributes itself ARN 15:14
Pests of s. BOL 89:14
S. became my glittering WORD 577:14
S. everywhere is in conspiracy EMER 207:36
S. is all but rude MARV 332:1
solitude sometimes is best s. MILT 349:12
Soul selects her own S. DICK 183:21
such s. As is quiet SHEL 504:1
When s. requires to be MILL 339:3
woman made S. BRAD 91:8
sock: If Jonson's learnèd s. MILT 342:26
socket: Burn to the s. WORD 577:11
sockets: set upon s. of fine gold BIBLE 57:4
socks: when thy s. were JONS 284:22
your shirt and your s. GILB 226:15
Socrates: difficulty contradict S.
PLATO 374:12
S. commits a crime by corrupting
PLATO 374:8
S., I shall not accuse PLATO 374:9
Socratic: S. manner is not a game BEER 38:4
sod: high requiem become a s. KEATS 291:22
under my head a s. BALL 31:14
soda-water: Sermons and s. the day
BYRON 122:21
wash their feet in s. ELIOT 204:27
sodden: nor s. at all with water BIBLE 47:17
That are s. and unkind BELL 40:9
Sodium: Of having discovered S. BENT 41:6
Sodom: overthrew S. and Gomorrah
BIBLE 61:20
sodomy: rum, s. and the lash CHUR 151:7
sods: s. with our bayonets turning
WOLFE 576:3
Sofa: accomplish'd S. last COWP 166:28
wheel the s. round COWP 167:11
soft: black and s. as sin CHES 147:5
mind does not make us s. PER 372:22
seson whan s. was the sonne LANG 309:22
s. answer turneth away BIBLE 54:4
s. as young YOUNG 588:7
S. morning, city JOYCE 286:14
s., unhappy sex BEHN 38:21
so white! O so s. JONS 285:4
with the s. phrase of peace SHAK 473:24

softer: words of his mouth were s.
PRAY 393:12
softly: shall go s. all my years BIBLE 59:3
s. and suddenly vanish CARR 133:7
softness: s. she and sweet attractive
MILT 347:22
that whisper s. in chambers MILT 351:25
soger: s. frae the wars returns BURNS 114:11
Sohne: ist viel zu weit dem S. FLEM 215:5
sol: c'est de savoir être à s. MONT 354:21
soie: Honi s. qui mal y pense SELL 420:3
soil: Before the s. hath smutch'd JONS 285:4
rather be tied to the s. HOMER 254:6
s. Is bare now HOPK 256:12
that grows in every s. BURKE 110:3
this the s., the clime MILT 345:9
soil'd: s. with all ignoble use TENN 537:17
soiled: Anoint and cheer our s. face
PRAY 400:5
sojourners: s., as were all our fathers
BIBLE 51:39
sol: te inferebatur s. et luna AUG 21:13
solace: let us s. ourselves with BIBLE 53:24
Should find some s. there WORD 582:8
sold: book which somehow s. well
BOOR 89:21
guilt is bought and s. SHEL 503:1
I'd not have s. her for it SHAK 477:12
s. a goodly manor SHAK 421:2
s. his birthright unto BIBLE 46:14
s. my Reputation FITZ 213:13
sparrows s. for a farthing BIBLE 65:35
sparrows s. for two farthings BIBLE 70:3
stocks were s. BELL 39:6
Then spoils were fairly s. MAC 322:18
was not this ointment s. BIBLE 72:25
went and s. all that he BIBLE 66:21
Who never s. the truth TENN 541:12
Whose hide he s. WALL 562:6
Soldan: S. of Byzantium is smiling
CHES 146:28
Soldati: S., io esco da Roma GAR 221:10
soldats: capitaine de vingt-quatre s.
ANON 9:8
s. faisaient la haie ELIOT 202:8
soldier: arm our s., Our steed the leg
SHAK 427:11
Ben Battle was a s. bold HOOD 254:13
British s. can stand up SHAW 496:19
death who had the s. singled DOUG 191:10
Drinking is the s.'s pleasure DRYD 195:1
Every French s. carries NAP 359:9
God's s. be he SHAK 463:10
great s. BAG 29:11
himself have been a s. SHAK 438:16
I said an elder s. SHAK 451:18
it to a s. and a foeman HOUS 266:4
majesty the British s. NAP 359:7
most audacious s. CHUR 150:16
never expect a s. to think SHAW 496:18
not having been a s. JOHN 277:26
not tell us what the s. DICK 182:22
s. a mere recreant prove SHAK 486:26
s., and afeard SHAK 462:20
s. an' sailor too KIPL 302:23
s. details his wounds PROP 401:15
s., Full of strange oaths SHAK 425:24
s. I listed DIBD 175:17
s. is better accommodated SHAK 442:4
s. is flat blasphemy SHAK 464:4
S. of the Great War Known KIPL 305:12
s. of the King KITC 305:14
s.'s life is terrible hard MILNE 340:4
s.'s pole is fall'n SHAK 423:16
summer s. and the sunshine PAINE 368:1
tell an old s. SHAW 496:6
soldiers: bid the s. shoot SHAK 437:31
god of s. SHAK 428:4
having s. under me BIBLE 65:15
if you believe the s. SAL 413:18

You have heard the s.   KIPL 300:23
songe: apparié notre vie à un s.   MONT 355:5
elles s.   CHAU 144:17
songes: He koude s. make and wel
    CHAU 141:12
songs: all their s. are sad   CHES 146:17
Are summer s. for me   SHAK 491:17
Book of S. and Sonnets here   SHAK 469:3
cannot sing the old s.   CALV 127:13
cannot sing the old s.   CLAR 152:23
desires and sombre s.   SWIN 528:26
ever piping s. for ever new   KEATS 291:6
Fair the fall of s.   STEV 523:1
Go, s.   THOM 548:3
harsh after the s. of Apollo   SHAK 457:20
Heine for s.   BROW 100:18
hymns and spiritual s.   BIBLE 78:5
I have s. of my own   VIRG 560:7
I wrote my happy s.   BLAKE 87:25
matchless s. does meditate   MARV 332:12
Our sweetest s. are those   SHEL 504:23
Piping of pleasant glee   BLAKE 87:24
Sing no sad s. for me   ROSS 409:8
s. beguile your pilgrimage   FLEC 214:9
S. consecrate to truth   SHEL 505:6
S. may inspirit us   BROW 102:6
s. never heard before   HOR 260:13
s. that I made for thee   BRID 92:21
Sussex s. be sung   BELL 40:11
their dirty s. and dreary   BROO 94:27
Their lean and flashy s.   MILT 343:13
Their s. were Ave Marys   CORB 162:15
them fruit for their s.   ADD 2:25
to make s.   BELL 40:15
us one of the s. of Sion   PRAY 399:3
Where are the s. of Spring   KEATS 293:7
songstress: sober-suited s.   THOM 549:12
sonitu: s. quatit ungula campum
    VIRG 559:7
sonne: brighte s. loste his hewe   CHAU 142:13
'most sheene is the s.   LANG 309:28
seson whan soft was the s.   LANG 309:22
unseren Platz an der S.   BULOW 106:23
Up roos the s.   CHAU 142:21
sonnet: elegy, and s.   JOHN 280:9
it turned to a S.   DOBS 187:14
Scorn not the S.   WORD 582:14
s. is a moment's monument   ROSS 409:21
S.'s scanty plot of ground   WORD 582:8
sonneteer: some starv'd hackney s.
    POPE 378:25
sonneter: am sure I shall turn s.   SHAK 456:19
sonnets: Rafael made a century of s.
    BROW 102:28
s. turn'd to holy psalms   PEELE 371:8
written s. all his life   BYRON 122:27
Sonorous: S. metal blowing martial
    MILT 345:20
sons: God's s. are things   MADD 326:19
Had I as many s. as I have   SHAK 463:10
If I had a thousand s.   SHAK 442:16
patient s. before me stand   GOLD 231:27
s. and your daughters shall   BIBLE 61:15
s. of God came in unto   BIBLE 45:33
s. of God came to present   BIBLE 52:5
s. of God shouted for joy   BIBLE 53:3
that Abraham had two s.   BIBLE 77:16
That our s. may grow up   PRAY 399:12
Their s., they gave   BROO 94:7
things are the s. of heaven   JOHN 281:6
soon: Come s., soon   SHEL 505:4
sooner: make an end the s.   BACON 26:6
no s. looked but they loved   SHAK 426:27
s. every party breaks up   AUST 22:13
soong: s. the service dyvyne   CHAU 141:15
soot: in s. I sleep   BLAKE 88:5
sooth: charms to s. a savage breast
    CONG 160:14
it is silly s.   SHAK 489:3
soothe: s. or wound a heart that's
    SCOTT 416:23

to s. thine ear   COLL 158:17
soothed: s. the griefs of forty   MAC 324:18
sooty: guardage to the s. bosom   SHAK 473:22
sophist: Be neither saint nor s.-led   ARN 13:1
Dark-brow'd s.   TENN 541:25
self-torturing s.   BYRON 120:36
sophistry: nothing but s. and illusion
    HUME 267:15
wits to s. and affectation   BACON 28:12
Sophocles: that S. is the most perfect
    COL 158:6
Sophonisba: S.! Sophonisba   THOM 549:25
Sops: S. in wine   SPEN 517:3
sorcerers: s., and whoremongers   BIBLE 83:3
Sordello: can but be the one 'S.'
    POUND 382:6
may hear S.'s story told   BROW 105:11
Who would has heard S.'s   BROW 105:16
sore: bear with a s. head   MARR 331:4
perfectly s. with loving her   DICK 178:1
s. let and hindered   PRAY 386:6
s. throats are always worse   AUST 23:9
sores: full of s.   BIBLE 70:28
sorrel: growth of meadow-sweet or s.
    SWIN 528:25
sorrow: ate his bread in s.   GOET 230:12
by the fireside with S.   SHEL 504:25
forgather wi' S. and Care   BURNS 113:4
From the sphere of our s.   SHEL 504:14
Give s. words   SHAK 462:16
hairs with s. to the grave   BIBLE 46:35
heart hath 'scap'd this s.   SHAK 494:14
In s. thou shalt bring   BIBLE 45:21
knowledge increaseth s.   BIBLE 55:9
Labour without s. is base   RUSK 412:3
Lycidas your s. is not dead   MILT 343:17
memory a rooted s.   SHAK 463:3
more in s. than in anger   SHAK 430:11
not be in s. too   BLAKE 88:8
Nought but vast s. was there   DE L 174:5
parting is such sweet s.   SHAK 482:20
Pure and complete s.   TOLS 551:13
Regions of s.   MILT 344:25
Since s. never comes too   GRAY 235:13
sin could blight or s.   COL 156:18
so beguile thy s.   SHAK 486:16
Some natural s.   WORD 578:15
s. and sighing shall flee   BIBLE 59:1
S. and silence are strong   LONG 316:13
s. dogging sin   HERB 248:10
s. enough in the natural   KIPL 302:3
sorrow like unto my s.   BIBLE 60:28
s., need   PRAY 387:16
s. Of each day's growing   DU M 199:6
S. proud to be exalted   ANON 6:7
S.'s most detested fruit   BYRON 120:28
S. so royally in you appears   SHAK 442:24
s.'s tribute to the passing   CAT 137:15
s. than to recall a time   DANTE 171:8
S., wilt thou live   TENN 536:33
S., with her family   SHEL 499:9
swift joy and tardy s.   THOM 548:3
That a s.'s crown of sorrow   TENN 538:20
then but labour and s.   PRAY 395:19
Then glut thy s. on a morning   KEATS 291:15
think is to be full of s.   KEATS 291:19
this s.'s heavenly   SHAK 477:5
thou climbing s.   SHAK 453:24
To S., I bade   KEATS 289:5
'-triumph and s. for angels   BROW 102:7
useless and hopeless s.   JOHN 281:27
We are not sure of s.   SWIN 529:24
Write s. on the bosom   SHAK 479:10
sorrowful: desire of such as be s.
    PRAY 385:22
He went away s.   BIBLE 67:10
laughter the heart is s.   BIBLE 54:1
much to say as a s. birth   MAL 327:17
This way for the s. city   DANTE 171:3

sorrowing: was standing the s. Mother
    JAC 270:31
sorrows: carried our s.   BIBLE 59:21
costly in our s.   STER 519:12
engluts and swallows other s.   SHAK 473:23
losses are restor'd and s.   SHAK 493:7
man of s.   BIBLE 59:21
shall my s. have an end   ANON 5:19
s. of women would be averted   ELIOT 200:24
s. of your changing face   YEATS 587:12
Then all my s. are   GAY 222:16
There are few s.   SMITH 510:12
transient s., simple wiles   WORD 581:8
When s. come   SHAK 436:4
sorry: may do that I shall be s.   SHAK 451:19
out and I was never s.   HOUS 264:4
s. for these our misdoings   PRAY 387:19
s. Scheme of Things   FITZ 213:16
sort: all the s. of person you   CARL 131:1
is a s. of treason   BURKE 110:9
see a s. of traitors here   SHAK 480:4
sortem: nemo, quam sibi s.   HOR 261:21
sorts: s. and conditions of men   PRAY 385:24
sory: with s. grace   CHAU 143:7
sospetto: e sanza alcun s.   DANTE 171:9
sot: she has married a s.   POUND 382:5
Un s. savant est sot plus   MOL 353:12
sothfastnesse: dwelle with s.   CHAU 144:21
souffrances: majesté des s. humaines
    VIGNY 557:1
souffre: s. et meurs sans parler   VIGNY 557:2
souffrons: mais s. sur les cimes HUGO 267:10
sought: By night on my bed I s.   BIBLE 56:25
Come, long-s.   SHEL 505:3
He s., For his lost heart   SHEL 504:5
I s. them far and found   HOUS 265:6
lack of many a thing I s.   SHAK 493:7
less often s. than found   BYRON 125:12
Love s. is good   SHAK 489:25
never have s. the world   JOHN 279:4
s. the Lord aright   BURNS 113:6
They s. it with thimbles   CARR 133:8
to those men that s. him   SHAK 447:21
soul: accomplished is sweet to the s.
    BIBLE 53:37
am the captain of my s.   HENL 245:5
art pouring forth thy s.   KEATS 291:22
assault and hurt the s.   PRAY 386:9
Be still, my s.   HOUS 264:3
bit of FIAT in my s.   BEDD 36:25
bitterness of my s.   BIBLE 59:3
bitterness of his s.   BIBLE 62:26
blind his s. with clay   TENN 542:19
Call to the s. when man   VAUG 555:21
call upon my s. within   SHAK 488:13
catch my flying s.   POPE 376:14
chosen thus to fling his s.   HARDY 239:7
city of the s.   BYRON 121:9
clothing for the s. divine   BLAKE 85:14
composed to the s.   ARN 16:9
Conceptions equal to the s.'s   WORD 577:19
confident concerning his s.   SOCR 512:19
Could swell the s. to rage   DRYD 195:8
deep dim s. of a star   SWIN 530:8
Did this s.'s second inn   DONNE 190:1
fancied that I gave a s.   YEATS 585:20
fine point of his s. taken   KEATS 293:14
five windows of the s.   BLAKE 85:23
fool, this night thy s.   BIBLE 70:5
freed his s. the nearest   JOHN 279:1
Full soon thy S. shall   WORD 579:8
God the s.   POPE 379:19
half conceal the S. within   TENN 535:34
half the little s. is dirt   TENN 540:23
haughtiness of his s.   ADD 1:18
have felt my s. in a kiss   SWIN 530:20
have given my s. for this   SWIN 530:20
Heart and s. do sing   SIDN 508:1
Heaven take my s.   SHAK 452:29
he had a little S.   MOORE 357:3

long to the sun and the s. SWIN 530:13
nor yet from the s. PRAY 394:26
rivers in the s. PRAY 398:17
S. to the blind Horn's KIPL 300:24
South Africa: S., renowned both far
CAMP 128:13
Southampton: weekly from S. KIPL 300:7
South Country: great hills of the S.
BELL 40:9
southern: bore me in the s. wild BLAKE 88:2
Grow to some S. tree HARDY 239:9
South Kensington: at Sloane Square
and S. GILB 226:14
Southron: matches of the S. folk
THOM 547:24
southward-facing: fringes of a s. brow
ARN 14:21
south-wind: world-wide whisper of the
s. TENN 538:24
souvent: L'amour? Je le fais s. PROU 401:22
Sovereign: bandy civilities with my S.
JOHN 275:20
servants of the s. or state BACON 26:21
s. good of human nature BACON 27:31
S. has BAG 29:3
s. of sighs and groans SHAK 456:26
Subject and a S. are clean CHAR 140:19
subject and what to be a s. ELIZ 206:3
that he will have no s. COKE 154:16
Whoso has sixpence is s. CARL 132:14
sovereynetee: 'Wommen desiren to have
s. CHAU 143:24
Soviet: Communism is S. power plus
LENIN 313:22
sow: Ireland is the old s. that JOYCE 286:16
observeth the wind shall not s. BIBLE 56:7
right s. by the ear HENR 246:3
S. an act READE 405:4
sower went forth to s. BIBLE 66:16
s. that hath overwhelm SHAK 441:3
they s. not BIBLE 64:28
They that s. in tears PRAY 398:17
sower: s. went forth to sow BIBLE 66:16
soweth: whatsoever a man s. BIBLE 77:19
sown: It is s. in corruption BIBLE 76:27
nor was ever s. TRAH 551:18
Poets that are s. By Nature WORD 577:9
They have s. the wind BIBLE 61:11
where thou hast not s. BIBLE 68:3
Ye have s. much BIBLE 62:2
sownes: s. ful of hevenyssh melodie
CHAU 144:18
sows: s. hurry and reaps STEV 522:5
space: annihilate but s. and time POPE 380:22
is a s. of life between KEATS 288:19
me more than time and s. LAMB 307:26
myself a king of infinite s. SHAK 432:13
vast s. he fills BURKE 109:5
spaces: great open s. MARQ 330:23
me with their empty s. FROST 219:3
spade: boldly nominate a s. JONS 284:13
cultivated entirely by the s. MILL 339:16
fiddle, sir, and s. SCOTT 418:6
if you don't call me s. SWIFT 526:32
poor crooked scythe and s. SHIR 507:2
s. is never so merely FRY 220:6
S.! with which Wilkinson WORD 583:3
Write with your s. CAMP 128:11
Spades: Let S. be trumps POPE 381:5
S. take up leaves FROST 219:4
s., the emblem of untimely COWP 167:16
Spain: are the galleons of S. DOBS 187:10
like slow old tunes of S. MAS 333:17
plateau of S. forming a head HARDY 239:13
spak: carl s. oo thing CHAU 142:15
Frenssh she s. ful faire CHAU 141:15
spake: God s. all these words BIBLE 47:24
God s. once PRAY 393:20
s. in time past BIBLE 79:28
s. wisely, and could have BIBLE 63:4

span: Contract into a s. HERB 248:6
Less than a s. BACON 28:15
life's a pain and but a s. DAV 172:11
Spaniards: S.' Dispatch ROCH 407:5
S. seem wiser than they BACON 27:14
to thrash the S. too DRAKE 193:2
spaniel: base s. fawning SHAK 449:24
Hound or s. SHAK 455:1
spaniel'd: hearts That s. me SHAK 423:5
Spanish: he cannot speak S. LEAR 311:24
I must learn S. BROW 100:28
person in the S. cape ELIOT 204:15
some are fond of S. wine MAS 333:20
S. sailors with bearded LONG 316:22
'S. ships of war TENN 542:21
taken by a S. Ga-la-lee BALL 31:2
To God I speak S. CHAR 140:31
spans: narrow measure s. HOUS 265:13
spar'd: have better s. a better man
SHAK 440:25
spare: bread enough and to s. BIBLE 70:19
S. all I have FARQ 210:10
s. bed for my friends PEPYS 372:17
s. that tree MORR 358:6
s. the beechen tree CAMP 128:17
S. their women for Thy BETJ 43:5
S. the poet for his subject's COWP 164:29
s. time and in his working GILL 229:11
s. your country's flag WHIT 571:17
to s. those who have submitted VIRG 559:1
spared: honour and life have been s.
FRAN 218:1
s. these minor monuments BROW 97:12
troubles you are yourself s. LUCR 320:6
spares: man that s. these stones SHAK 495:22
spareth: s. his rod hateth BIBLE 53:38
spark: shows a hasty s. SHAK 451:24
s. from heaven to fall ARN 14:15
s. of inextinguishable SHEL 505:10
s. o' Nature's fire BURNS 113:20
Vital s. of heav'nly flame POPE 376:3
waitest for the s. from heaven ARN 14:17
Sparkle: S. for ever TENN 541:30
s. out among the fern TENN 532:20
They s. still the right SHAK 457:9
sparkles: cup but s. near the brim
BYRON 120:19
sparks: like s. among the stubble BIBLE 62:14
painted with unnumber'd s. SHAK 449:25
s. fly upward BIBLE 52:17
sparrer-grass: en I bless ef 'taint s.
HARR 242:14
sparrow: I once had a s. alight THOR 550:21
Lesbia with her s. MILL 339:29
My lady's s. is dead CAT 136:22
providence in the fall of a s. SHAK 437:15
soul of Philip S. SKEL 508:19
s. fall POPE 379:4
s. hath found her an house PRAY 395:11
s.: that sitteth alone PRAY 396:12
sparrows: more value than many s.
BIBLE 65:37
s. from outside flew very BEDE 37:1
s. sold for a farthing BIBLE 65:35
s. sold for two farthings BIBLE 70:3
spars: Under the s. of which HERR 250:14
Spartan: remnant of our S. dead
BYRON 123:2
Spartans: praiseworthy amongst the S.
SPEN 514:33
S. on the sea-wet rock HOUS 265:3
tell the S. SIM 508:9
sparwe: was and lecherous as a s.
CHAU 142:4
spat: you s. on me Wednesday SHAK 466:3
spawn: meanest s. of Hell TENN 538:13
spawn'd: Some report a sea-maid s.
SHAK 464:19
spawning: formless s. fury YEATS 587:2

Spayne: make castels thanne in S.
CHAU 144:1
speak: Books will s. plain BACON 25:39
did he stop and s. to you BROW 102:15
duty to s. one's mind WILDE 573:7
friend or child I s. ARN 13:8
grief that does not s. SHAK 462:16
he shall s. for himself BIBLE 72:15
I also could s. as ye do BIBLE 52:28
if they s. first CONG 160:1
I'll do't before I s. SHAK 453:5
I only s. right SHAK 451:2
let him now s. PRAY 389:2
'Let us not s. BETJ 43:4
Let us not s. of them DANTE 171:4
lips are now forbid to s. BAYLY 35:10
men shall s. well of you BIBLE 69:20
mute and will not s. a word SHAK 484:8
neither s. they through PRAY 397:18
one that can s. so well MASS 335:23
permitted unto them to s. BIBLE 76:16
province of knowledge to s. HOLM 253:20
ride, and s. the truth BYRON 124:10
slow to s. BIBLE 80:10
speak, and to s. well JONS 285:3
s. as the common people ASCH 17:4
s. in Caesar's funeral SHAK 450:17
s. in our tongues the wonderful BIBLE 73:23
s. less than thou knowest SHAK 433:15
S., Lord BIBLE 49:36
S. low, if you speak love SHAK 472:6
S. not when the people SCOTT 418:5
S. now HOUS 263:17
s. of eternity without BROW 96:10
S. of the moderns without CHES 145:20
S. roughly to your little CARR 133:26
'S. softly and carry a big ROOS 408:1
S. the speech SHAK 433:16
S. to Him thou for He hears TENN 533:29
s. to the wise PIND 373:14
S. unto us smooth things BIBLE 58:26
s. very well in the House of Commons
DISR 187:4
S. what we feel SHAK 456:13
s. when he is spoken STEV 522:17
'S. when you're spoken CARR 136:8
S. ye comfortably to Jerusalem BIBLE 59:4
that dare not s. its name DOUG 191:4
they never s. well of one JOHN 276:17
they s. with their enemies PRAY 398:19
those that are asleep to s. BIBLE 57:10
To s. and purpose not SHAK 453:5
unable to s. a word ELIOT 203:4
What should we s. SHAK 428:15
when I s. unto them therof PRAY 398:8
when I think, I must s. SHAK 426:9
When you s. SHAK 491:27
Whereof one cannot s. WITT 575:17
which it is difficult to s. BURKE 110:30
women to s. in the church BIBLE 76:17
word wad ane o' them s. BALL 30:21
would not cease to s. COWP 168:18
You were better s. first SHAK 426:22
speaker: No other s. of my living
SHAK 447:23
speakers: you imperfect s. SHAK 458:12
speaketh: heart the mouth s. BIBLE 66:9
he s. of his own BIBLE 72:13
he s. things not to be BIBLE 63:4
speaking: adepts in the s. trade CHUR 148:27
By drowning their s. BROW 103:15
heard for their much s. BIBLE 64:23
In s. for myself SHAK 473:24
s. in a perpetual hyperbole BACON 26:29
S. to yourselves in psalms BIBLE 78:5
Without s. to me PREV 400:17
speaks: her foot s. SHAK 487:13
He s. to Me as if I was VICT 556:19
he s. very shrewishly SHAK 488:9
No man s. concerning another JOHN 278:22

847

she never s. well of me CONG 160:17
She s. poniards SHAK 472:8
s. small like a woman SHAK 469:2
When he s. SHAK 443:6
when Love s. SHAK 457:8
worst s. something good HERB 247:12
spear: Bring me my s. BLAKE 86:16
His s., to equal which MILT 345:12
idle s. and shield MILT 344:6
knappeth the s. in sunder PRAY 392:21
spear-men: stubborn s. still made
SCOTT 417:24
spears: stars threw down their s. BLAKE 87:16
teeth are s. and arrows PRAY 393:15
their s. into pruninghooks BIBLE 57:19
their s. was like stars BYRON 122:1
your pruninghooks into s. BIBLE 61:15
special: s. grace preventing PRAY 386:10
s. receipt of his own DU M 199:5
specialists: All other men are s.
DOYLE 192:21
speciality: short notice was her s. SAKI 413:5
species: female of the s. is more KIPL 299:4
specimen: only s. of Burke is HAZL 243:9
specimens: s., the lilies of ambition
DOUG 191:8
spectacle: great s. of human happiness
SMITH 511:29
s. unto the world BIBLE 75:33
spectacles: s. of books to read Nature
DRYD 198:2
What a pair of s. is here SHAK 487:11
without a pair Of s. HOFF 252:20
With s. on nose and pouch SHAK 425:24
spectantia: Omnia te adversum s. HOR 258:11
spectare: magnum alterius s. laborem
LUCR 320:6
Spectat: S. et audit CAT 137:4
spectator: s. of mankind than as one ADD 2:8
spectators: actors or s. SHEL 499:13
Spectatress: S. of the mischief which
ROWE 410:23
Spectatum: S. veniunt OVID 366:1
spectem: Te s. TIB 550:34
spectre: dancing s. seems the moon
MER 337:13
s. of Communism MARX 333:2
spectre-thin: s., and dies KEATS 291:19
speculations: s. upon matter are voluntary
JOHN 281:32
wrung from s. and subtleties BROW 96:18
speech: aspersion upon my parts of s.
SHER 506:13
Consul's s. was low MAC 322:14
could wed itself with S. TENN 536:16
deal by s. than by letter BACON 26:37
False are attributes of s. HOBB 251:13
freedom of s. and expression ROOS 407:26
freedom of s. TWAIN 554:7
have strange power of s. COL 155:29
I am slow of s. BIBLE 47:9
judgement and the code of s. HOR 257:14
loath to cast away my s. SHAK 488:10
make a s. AUBR 17:27
manner of his s. SHAK 421:34
neither s. nor language PRAY 390:11
nor power of s. SHAK 451:2
Our concern was s. ELIOT 202:25
perfect plainness of s. ARN 16:13
Speak the s. SHAK 433:16
s. created thought SHEL 503:8
s. in that victorious brow ARN 14:24
S. is human CARL 131:39
S. is often barren ELIOT 201:2
s. is shallow as Time CARL 131:13
S. is silvern CARL 132:23
S. is the small change MER 338:2
s. only to conceal their VOLT 561:4
s. than to give evidence HAL 237:23
s. they have resolved not ELIOT 200:24

stately s. WORD 581:1
Thy s. bewrayeth thee BIBLE 68:19
thy s. is comely BIBLE 56:26
tongue blossom into s. BROW 99:24
true use of s. is not so GOLD 232:5
verse is a measured s. BACON 24:23
your s. be alway with grace BIBLE 78:28
speeches: to men's charitable s. BACON 28:14
speechless: great persons' graves is s.
DONNE 190:23
grey-grown s. Christ SWIN 529:3
speech-making: subject for practising
s. JUV 288:2
speed: Deliberate s. THOM 548:9
forgetting the bright s. ARN 15:1
our safety is in our s. EMER 207:33
quench its s. i' the slushy BROW 102:14
s. the going guest POPE 380:6
s. the parting guest POPE 380:25
s. was far faster than BULL 106:22
time shall teach me s. SHAK 452:26
speek: shall s. of the somwhat CHAU 144:6
spell: foreigners always s. better TWAIN 554:9
Thy s. through him ROSS 410:2
Who lies beneath your s. HOPE 256:3
you s. it with a "V DICK 182:20
speller: He's the wussl s. I know
WARD 564:31
taste and fancy of the s. DICK 182:20
spells: seldom talismans and s. COWP 167:25
spem: Vitae summa brevis s. HOR 259:14
Spence: ballad of Sir Patrick S. COL 156:6
spend: most of what we yet may s.
FITZ 212:18
s. too much time in studies BACON 27:16
to s. a little less STEV 521:4
whatever you have, s. less JOHN 279:2
spende: so wol we s. CHAU 143:8
spendeth: whatsoever thou s. more
BIBLE 69:32
spending: Getting and s. WORD 582:19
Riches are for s. BACON 26:9
S. again what is already SHAK 494:9
Spens: sent it to Sir Patrick S. BALL 31:17
Spenser: little nearer S. BASSE 35:1
Renowned S. BASSE 35:1
Thee gentle S. fondly led LAND 309:2
spent: dollars is unwisely s. CARN 132:31
had s. one whole day well THOM 546:12
I have s. all the money JOHN 278:31
s. lights quiver and gleam ARN 13:6
s. the darksome hours GOET 230:12
That we s. ANON 7:20
What wee s. ANON 8:17
sperabitur: superveniet quae non s. hora
HOR 258:16
SPERANZA: LASCIATE OGNI S. VOI
CH'ENTRATE DANTE 171:3
sperare: salus victis nullam s. VIRG 558:7
speraret: nec quid s. habebat VIRG 559:14
speravi: s.: non confundar in aeternum
ANON 11:4
spere: holughnesse of the eighthe s.
CHAU 144:18
spermatozoa: million million s. HUXL 268:21
Spes: occidit S. omnis HOR 261:13
spet: s. upon my Jewish gabardine
SHAK 466:2
spewed: Sure the poet...s. up a good
DRYD 198:12
sphere: s. for Shelley's genius ARN 16:2
their motion in one s. SHAK 440:22
Yonder starry s. MILT 348:24
spheres: all the tuned s. SHAK 423:22
Driv'n by the s. VAUG 555:22
maintain the music of the s. BROW 96:34
music of forfended s. PATM 370:7
seems to shake the s. DRYD 194:24
S. of action GRAN 234:10
S. of influence ANON 7:17

spherical: His body is perfectly s.
LEAR 311:23
treachers by s. predominance SHAK 453:11
Sphinx: Although a subtler S. renew
SHEL 501:1
Subtle as S. SHAK 457:8
Spices: No S. wanting HERR 249:24
that the s. thereof may BIBLE 56:29
upon the mountain of s. BIBLE 57:14
spider: of the smallest s.'s web SHAK 481:28
said a s. to a fly HOW 267:3
s.'s touch POPE 379:9
spiders: I saw the s. marching through
LOW 319:19
they Often have seen s. fly EDW 200:7
Weaving s. come not here SHAK 470:12
spider-web: kind of huge s. JAMES 271:11
spies: if we were God's s. SHAK 456:3
Ye are s. BIBLE 46:34
spill: stone and let them not s. me
MACN 326:13
spilt: water s. on the ground BIBLE 50:23
spin: neither do they s. BIBLE 64:30
you jade, go s. SCOTT 418:36
spindle-guide: From coupler-flange to
s. KIPL 301:2
spinis: iuvat s. de pluribus una HOR 259:6
spinnage: world of gammon and s.
DICK 177:12
spinner: stoppeth the s.'s cunning
POUND 382:9
Till the S. of the Years HARDY 239:6
spinners: Hence you long-legg'd s.
SHAK 470:12
waggon-spokes made of long s.' legs
SHAK 481:28
spinning: candle-light at evening s.
RONS 407:12
Spins: S. like a fretful midge ROSS 409:17
spinsters: and the knitters SHAK 489:3
spirantia: Excudent alii s. mollius VIRG 559:1
spires: City with her dreaming s. ARN 15:4
from all her reeling s. MAC 322:2
Ye distant s. GRAY 235:9
Spirit: be filled with the S. BIBLE 78:5
Blessed are the poor in s. BIBLE 64:6
Brutus' will start a s. SHAK 448:18
cabin'd ample S. ARN 14:6
Curbing his lavish s. SHAK 458:5
day an unaccustom'd s. SHAK 483:23
Eternal s. of the chainless BYRON 125:14
fair s. for my minister BYRON 121:21
fruit of the S. is love BIBLE 77:18
genuine s. of localism BORR 90:2
given us the s. of fear BIBLE 79:22
God is a S. BIBLE 71:40
great s. gone SHAK 421:18
Hail to thee, blithe S. SHEL 504:15
hands I commend my s. BIBLE 71:14
hands I commend my s. PRAY 391:15
haughty s. before a fall BIBLE 54:8
he that ruleth his s. than BIBLE 54:9
history of the human s. ARN 16:17
I go bound in the s. unto BIBLE 74:18
immortal s. must endure ARN 14:24
Is a bold s. in a loyal SHAK 478:8
is the s. that quickeneth BIBLE 72:8
least erected S. that fell MILT 345:24
light of thy Holy S. PRAY 386:14
Love is a s. all compact SHAK 495:19
meek and quiet s. BIBLE 80:28
motions of his s. are dull SHAK 468:17
never approached my s. METT 338:10
nimble, stirring s. SHAK 457:19
no more s. in her BIBLE 50:32
no s. can walk abroad SHAK 429:17
o'er the s. of my dream BYRON 124:13
of God is a troubled s. PRAY 393:3
of kin to God by his s. BACON 25:25
Of s. so still and quiet SHAK 473:24

deep of the Pierian s. DRAY 193:15
every winter change to s. TENN 536:26
faded has no second s. PHIL 373:9
Falsehood has a perennial s. BURKE 109:4
flower of roses in the s. BIBLE 63:27
flowers that bloom in the s. GILB 227:13
Fresh s. SHEL 501:15
garden and a s. HOR 262:9
happy as birds in the s. BLAKE 87:20
heart be full of the s. SWIN 530:12
hounds of s. are on winter's SWIN 528:15
I been absent in the s. SHAK 494:17
lap of the new come s. SHAK 480:11
less quick to s. again ARN 15:9
messenger of S. SPEN 515:16
more business in s. TWAIN 554:23
perennial s. of all prodigality BURKE 110:16
rifle all the breathing s. COLL 158:16
smiling face a dream of S. COL 157:14
S. a young man's fancy lightly TENN 538:17
S. comes slowly up this COL 156:2
s. from the pages into WHIT 570:13
s., full of sweet days HERB 248:16
S. is come home with her THOM 548:4
S., nor Summer beauty DONNE 188:7
s. of Bandusia HOR 261:3
S. restores balmy warmth CAT 137:2
s. shut up BIBLE 56:28
S., sing ELIOT 203:16
s. the herald of love's SPEN 515:19
S., the sweet spring NASHE 360:9
suddenly was changed to S. SHEL 503:17
Sweet lovers love the s. SHAK 427:2
that S. should vanish with FITZ 213:15
There had made a lasting s. SHAK 447:3
They call it easing the S. REED 405:6
this s. of love resembleth SHAK 490:33
through till the s. be done SWIN 530:13
Treasury is the s. of business BAG 28:22
We have as short a S. HERR 249:28
Where are the songs of S. KEATS 293:7
Where smiling s. its earliest GOLD 230:16
with ever-returning s. WHIT 571:12
springboard: Not a seat but a s. CHUR 150:14
springe: woodcock to mine own s.

SHAK 437:19
springes: s. to catch woodcocks SHAK 430:21
springs: from seventy s. a score HOUS 262:14
Red strays of ruined s. SWIN 529:23
Scotia's grandeur s. BURNS 113:10
sendeth the s. into the rivers PRAY 396:19
s. o' that countrie BALL 32:6
Where s. not fail HOPK 256:17
springtide: brings back her old s.

JOHN 273:20
Springtime: Merry S.'s Harbinger

FLET 215:21
Sprinkle: S. the quarters HOUS 264:28
s. the lime like rain HOUS 265:15
You will s. me with hyssop BIBLE 83:6
sprite: fleeting, wav'ring s. HADR 237:9
his clear S. SHEL 499:5
sprites: have one of s. and goblins

SHAK 491:12
Sprouting: S. despondently at area

ELIOT 203:27
spudding: s. up docks HARDY 240:19
spue: s. thee out of my mouth BIBLE 81:20
spumantem: Thybrim multo s. sanguine

VIRG 558:17
spur: Fame is the s. that MILT 343:8
have I to s. me into song YEATS 586:23
I have no s. SHAK 459:6
s. of all great minds CHAP 140:15
Spurgeon: is haberdasher to Mr S.

BUTL 119:20
Spurn: S. not the nobly born GILB 226:4
s. thee like a cur out SHAK 449:24
you s. a stranger cur SHAK 466:3
Spurning: S. of his stirrups like CHES 147:3

spy: sent to s. out the land BIBLE 48:10
squad: Don't let the awkward s. BURNS 116:9
squadrons: big s. against the small

BUSS 117:7
squalor: cost of the s. and slavery

SHAW 498:23
squander: Then do not s. time FRAN 218:11
squandering: s. wealth was his peculiar

DRYD 194:15
square: given a s. deal afterwards ROOS 408:3
himself be given a s. deal ROOS 408:7
I have not kept the s. SHAK 422:6
set you s. with Genesis BROW 99:9
slowly grows a glimmering s. TENN 542:4
s. on the hypoteneuse GILB 228:17
s. person has squeezed SMITH 511:34
s. root of half a number LONG 317:23
you broke a British s. KIPL 299:8
squared: Press was s. BELL 39:6
squares: s. of his mind were empty

AUDEN 19:3
squash: s. is before 'tis a peascod SHAK 488:9
This s., this gentleman SHAK 429:12
squattin: 'E'll be s.' on the coals KIPL 299:19
squawking: seven stars go s. AUDEN 18:9
squeak: dead Did s. and gibber SHAK 429:12
until the pips s. GEDD 223:32
squeaking: s. Cleopatra boy SHAK 424:3
With shrieking and s. BROW 103:15
squealing: s. of the wry-neck'd fife

SHAK 466:13
squeeze: madly s. a right-hand foot

CARR 136:7
squeezed: they are going to be s.

GEDD 223:32
squeezing: you in the s. of a lemon

GOLD 232:24
squinch-owl: jay-bird say ter der s.

HARR 242:16
squint: gladly banish s. suspicion MILT 341:9
squints: s. the eye SHAK 454:22
squire: Bless the s. and his relations

DICK 176:23
squires: hall the gallant s. of Kent MAC 322:3
s. ride slowly towards CHES 147:14
stab: s. my spirit broad awake STEV 523:11
Stabant: S. orantes primi transmittere

VIRG 558:22
Stabat: S. Mater dolorosa JAC 270:31
stabb'd: feeble God has s. me GAY 222:6
stability: party of order or s. MILL 339:10
to the s. or enlargement JOHN 281:7
stable: good horse in the s. GOLD 232:7
stables: That the s. are the real SHAW 496:32
stablish: s. me with thy free Spirit

PRAY 393:6
stabs: every word s. SHAK 472:8
Stace: Lucan, and S. CHAU 144:17
stacher: s. through BURNS 113:5
stad: That s. is in perplexyte WYNT 584:4
stadium: it's no go the s. MACN 326:8
near the S. are trembly BETJ 42:16
staff: By his cockle hat and s. SHAK 435:32
I'll break my s. SHAK 485:24
s. of faith to walk upon RAL 404:12
s. Which Art hath lodged WORD 582:13
thy rod and thy s. comfort PRAY 390:22
trustest upon the s. of this bruised

BIBLE 51:38
was the very s. of my age SHAK 466:8
your s. in your hand BIBLE 47:18
stag: runnable s. DAV 172:8
s. at eve had drunk his SCOTT 416:1
stage: All the world's a s. SHAK 425:24
drown the s. with tears SHAK 433:1
glory of the Attic s. ARN 15:10
kingdom for a s. SHAK 443:3
lags the vet'ran on the s. JOHN 283:2
On the s. he was natural GOLD 231:20
shake a s. JONS 284:22

s. is not frightened FIEL 211:31
s.'s jewel JONS 284:2
s. where every man must SHAK 465:10
to the well-trod s. anon MILT 342:26
To this great s. of fools SHAK 455:23
well-grac'd actor leaves the s. SHAK 480:10
were played upon a s. now SHAK 490:9
wonder of our s. JONS 284:19
your daughter on the s. COW 163:21
stage-coach: found in travelling in a s.

IRV 270:25
s. from London to Oxford HAZL 243:16
travel faster than a s. GOLD 232:18
stagger: s. like a drunken man PRAY 397:10
stagnant: fen Of s. waters WORD 582:5
stain: I offer'd free from s. MAC 322:8
is darkening like a s. AUDEN 21:10
Leave not a s. in thine BIBLE 63:16
of the world's slow s. SHEL 499:21
To s. the stiff dishonoured ELIOT 204:16
which felt a s. like a wound BURKE 111:10
with no s. She faded SHEL 499:8
stained: s. with their own works PRAY 397:6
staineth: stain when heaven's sun s.

SHAK 493:10
stainless: s. gentleman TENN 535:14
stains: of s. and splendid dyes KEATS 289:5
S. the white radiance SHEL 499:26
stair: He's the ruffian on the s. HENL 245:6
I was going up the s. MEAR 336:7
place is by a winding s. BACON 26:26
Staircase: S. wit DID 184:6
stairs: blood ran down the s. AUDEN 21:7
cursed and kicked the s. MILL 339:14
down another man's s. DANTE 171:17
rotten-runged rat-riddled s. BROW 102:13
they made a pair of s. SHAK 426:27
stairway: s. which leads to a dark

CHUR 151:4
stake: deep s. they have in such BURKE 110:5
I am tied to the s. SHAK 455:3
persons of some substance and s. WIND 575:7
recollect...what it is we have at s. PITT 374:4
yonder like another s. TWAIN 554:7
stal: out of they s. CHAU 144:22
stale: Poor I am s. SHAK 428:16
s., not ripe POPE 375:20
stalked: s. through the Post Office

YEATS 587:2
stalking: s. in my chamber WYATT 583:21
stalking-horse: truth serve as a s. to error

BOL 89:16
uses his folly like a s. SHAK 427:7
stall: have gone to s. and bin FROST 219:11
stalled: s. ox and hatred BIBLE 54:6
stalls: Tank come down the s. SASS 414:12
Stamford-town: Burleigh-house by S.

TENN 539:11
stamp: Christ's s. to boot HERB 247:9
is but the guinea's s. BURNS 113:12
s. me back to common FITZ 213:12
stampa: e poi roppe la s. ARIO 12:7
Stamp'd: S. with the image TENN 534:17
stamping: s. his foot with anger FARR 210:28
stand: By uniting we s. DICK 184:5
casement seen her s. TENN 538:4
feet shall s. in thy gates PRAY 398:11
Give me somewhere to s. ARCH 11:24
Here s. LUTH 320:16
in this we s. or fall MILT 348:20
I s. at the door BIBLE 81:21
no time to s. and stare DAV 172:17
serve who only s. and wait MILT 351:10
s. at the latter day BIBLE 52:31
s. at the window AUDEN 18:11
S. by thyself BIBLE 60:13
s. in the holy place BIBLE 67:29
s. me now and ever in good JOYCE 286:19
s.. "On my head DISR 185:32
s. out of my sun a little DIOG 184:8

world of pomp and s. BEAU 36:1
worth of a S. MILL 339:14
wretched s. SHAK 434:28
stateliest: Wielder of the s. measure
TENN 543:18
stately: she is tall and s. TENN 540:6
S. Homes of England COW 164:3
s. homes of England HEM 244:21
s. tents of war MARL 330:2
would grow great and s. STEV 522:23
statement: black s. of pistons SPEN 515:13
Englishman unmoved that s. GILB 228:23
States: composed of indestructible s.
CHASE 141:3
debt have been small s. INGE 270:10
goodly s. and kingdoms seen KEATS 292:17
In s. unborn SHAK 450:5
No more slave S. CHASE 141:2
saved the Union of these S. WHIT 571:10
S., like men LAND 309:13
statesman: chemist, fiddler, s. DRYD 194:13
constitutional s. is BAG 29:15
of a constitutional s. BAG 29:16
S., yet friend to truth POPE 378:6
Too nice for a s. GOLD 231:17
Statesmen: like great S. GAY 222:33
station: honour is a private s. ADD 1:23
It isn't that sort of s. RATT 405:2
walls of that antique s. BEER 37:26
stationer: s. says HEM 245:1
stations: always know our proper s.
DICK 176:23
statisticians: sit With s. AUDEN 21:5
statistics: damned lies and s. DISR 187:17
Proved by s. that some AUDEN 20:10
thoughts we must study s. NIGH 363:16
We are just s. HOR 258:13
Stato: Libera Chiesa in libero S. CAV 138:1
statua: base of Pompey's s. SHAK 450:28
statuaries: head which s. loved to copy
MAC 323:33
statue: Most like a monumental s. BROW 98:8
s. of the onehandled adulterer JOYCE 286:25
s. to him under the gallows SMITH 511:24
that *my* s. should be moved VICT 556:16
statues: disfigured the public s. AUDEN 19:2
towers and tombs and s. FLEC 214:6
We like sepulchral s, lay DONNE 188:23
With s. on the terraces KIPL 299:12
stature: add one cubit unto his s. BIBLE 64:29
increased in wisdom and s. BIBLE 69:14
Malice is of a low s. HAL 238:2
shorten I the s. of my soul MER 337:8
s. of the fulness of Christ BIBLE 77:28
statutes: s. of the Lord are right PRAY 390:12
stave: will listen to your s. SHEL 504:25
staves: thou comest to me with s. BIBLE 50:12
stay: asking peaple to s. with him ASHF 17:5
behind my tremulous s. HARDY 239:1
Can't you s. VAUG 555:9
care to s. than will SHAK 483:15
earth's foundations s. HOUS 265:7
Here I am, and here I s. MACM 325:17
'S. a little BACON 26:6
S. for me SHAK 423:10
will not s. in place ELIOT 202:17
without thee here to s. MILT 349:28
Stayed: S. in mid passage his pinions
SWIN 528:24
s. still with her DONNE 188:2
staying: Tell the people I'm s. PEDR 371:4
stays: Everything flows and nothing s.
HER 246:5
that wears the s. TENN 540:22
stead: now and ever in good s. JOYCE 286:19
soul were in my soul's s. BIBLE 52:28
steadfast: would I were s. as thou art
KEATS 292:11
steadiness: s. under fire but also KITC 305:14
Steady: S. the Buffs KIPL 305:1

thought more s. than an ebbing FORD 216:20
steaks: smell of s. in passageways
ELIOT 204:7
steal: Blake is damned good to s. FUS 220:22
Even s. us from ourselves DRYD 195:17
most cunningly did s. away HERB 247:24
mouths to s. away their brains SHAK 475:9
…or s. one poor farthing NEWM 362:4
silently s. away LONG 316:10
S. from the world POPE 380:24
s. my Basil-pot away from KEATS 290:12
s. out of your company SHAK 472:31
s. the bags to hold ISH 270:27
thieves break through and s. BIBLE 64:25
Thou shalt not s. BIBLE 47:24
Thou shalt not s. CLOU 153:28
to s. a few hours from MOORE 356:21
to s. away your hearts SHAK 451:1
to s. bread FRAN 217:26
will s. the very teeth out ARAB 11:17
stealing: about the country s. ducks
ARAB 11:18
hands from picking and s. PRAY 388:17
hanged for s. horses HAL 237:22
S. and giving odour SHAK 487:20
steals: robb'd that smiles s. something
SHAK 474:3
s. a goose from off a common ANON 7:24
s. my purse steals trash SHAK 475:16
stealth: do a good action by s. LAMB 308:2
Do good by s. POPE 380:18
lusty s. of nature SHAK 453:9
Steam: exceptin' always S. KIPL 301:2
fiery s. issued and came BIBLE 61:8
Shovelling white s. over AUDEN 20:1
snorting s. and piston stroke MORR 358:10
s. spoils romance at sea KIPL 301:4
steam-engine: He traces the s. always
DISR 184:17
much like a s. in trousers SMITH 511:10
steamer: about in a s. from Harwich
GILB 226:13
Steamers: all you Big S. KIPL 298:4
Great s. KIPL 300:7
into coffee on board s. THAC 545:9
steed: Border his s. was the best SCOTT 417:8
from a s. flying fearless LONG 316:26
mounted on her milk-white s. BALL 32:4
Our s. the leg SHAK 427:11
set her on my pacing s. KEATS 290:17
Steed threatens s. SHAK 444:9
sturdy s. now goes to grass BEAU 36:7
will I sell my goodly s. BALL 30:9
steeds: instead of mounting barbed s.
SHAK 480:18
They'll have fleet s. that SCOTT 417:14
steel: All shod with s. WORD 577:25
corse again in complete s. SHAK 430:24
foeman bares his s. GILB 228:18
foemen worthy of their s. SCOTT 416:6
Give them the cold s. ARM 12:13
is clad in complete s. MILT 341:10
long divorce of s. SHAK 446:27
with his brandish'd s. SHAK 458:3
with more than complete s. ANON 6:4
wounded surgeon plies the s. ELIOT 202:21
Steel-true: S. and blade-straight STEV 523:3
steep: hastens to the monstrous s.
KEATS 292:6
s. and trifid God THOM 547:22
s. my senses in forgetfulness SHAK 441:29
When things are s. HOR 260:6
steeple: church and no s. SWIFT 528:11
in his lone religious s. CAMP 128:10
shadow of the s. CLOU 153:23
stood, and heard the s. HOUS 264:28
steeples: In s. far and near HOUS 263:4
Talk about the pews and s. CHES 146:11
you have drench'd our s. SHAK 454:4
steer: ships they s. their courses BUTL 117:25

s. From grave to gay POPE 380:3
steersmen: grow good s. MER 337:20
stehe: Hier s. ich LUTH 320:16
stelle: disposto a salire alle s. DANTE 171:15
muove il sole e l'altre s. DANTE 171:18
uscimmo a riveder le s. DANTE 171:14
Stellenbosch: fear o' S. KIPL 303:11
stem: rod out of the s. of Jesse BIBLE 58:9
s. the torrent of a woman's ANON 8:20
stenches: counted two and seventy s.
COL 156:5
step: it is only the first s. DU D 198:28
one s. enough for me NEWM 362:14
s. should sound or a word SWIN 529:18
That's one small s. ARMS 12:18
To s. aside is human BURNS 112:25
Stephen Sly: S., and old John Naps
SHAK 484:3
Stepp'd: in blood S. in so far SHAK 461:25
steppes: kis the s. CHAU 144:17
stepping: s. where his comrade stood
SCOTT 417:24
you are s. westward WORD 578:12
stepping-stones: s. Of their dead selves
TENN 535:33
steps: countest the s. of the Sun BLAKE 87:22
Hear not my s. BLAKE 460:1
her s. take hold on hell BIBLE 53:20
s. Almost as silent WORD 580:9
s. of virgin liberty WORD 581:8
with to support uneasy s. MILT 345:12
stept: She s. to him BALL 30:9
sterb: Morgen s.' ich LESS 313:26
sterbenden: Sakramente einem s. Gotte
HEINE 244:11
sterile: seems to me a s. promontory
SHAK 432:15
sterility: Into her womb convey s.
SHAK 453:18
sterling: I myself a s. lad HOUS 264:13
stern: is a lantern on the s. COL 157:20
s. to view GOLD 231:2
sterner: Ambition should be made of
s. stuff SHAK 450:19
sternest: thou wert the s. knight MAL 328:8
steward: commended the unjust s.
BIBLE 70:25
stewards: Others but s. of their SHAK 494:15
S. of the mysteries BIBLE 75:32
Stew'd: S. in corruption SHAK 435:10
St George: streets leading from S.'s
BUTL 119:12
stick: he fell like the s. PAINE 368:2
I shall s. SHAK 465:2
notch it on my s. too THOR 550:9
softly and carry a big s. ROOS 408:1
S. close to your desks GILB 228:7
sticketh: friend that s. closer BIBLE 54:14
stiff: Bend what is s. LANG 310:1
'Keep a s. upper lip' CARY 136:14
stiffnecked: thou art a s. people BIBLE 48:4
stiffness: too much s. in refusing PRAY 384:7
stifle: to s. is a false opinion MILL 339:9
Stiggins: S., Bugg ARN 15:26
still: At the s. point ELIOT 202:15
best be s. ARN 13:14
be s. PRAY 389:20
Be s., my soul HOUS 264:3
Be s. then PRAY 392:21
Duchess of Malfi s. WEBS 566:24
gars ye rin sae s. ANON 7:12
he can't Sit s. MILL 339:25
keep s. with my philosopher SHAK 454:26
mighty heart is lying s. WORD 581:15
ship was s. as she could SOUT 513:28
sound of a voice that is s. TENN 532:18
S. glides the Stream WORD 581:4
s., sad music of humanity WORD 578:4
s. small voice BIBLE 51:14
s. the wonder grew GOLD 231:3

S. waters run deep | AUDEN 20:22
thou mightest s. the enemy | PRAY 389:28
Thou wouldst s. be ador'd | MOORE 356:4
waves thereof are s. | PRAY 397:10
Will not stay s. | ELIOT 202:17
Still-born: S. Silence | FLEC 214:24
stilleth: s. the raging of the | PRAY 394:1
stillicide: lone cave's s. | HARDY 239:18
stillness: Achieved that s. ultimately | CRANE 168:30
all the air a solemn s. | GRAY 234:18
do a wilful s. entertain | SHAK 465:12
modest s. and humility | SHAK 443:21
s. first invades the ear | DRYD 195:24
s. of the central sea | TENN 537:20
still-vexed: s. Bermoothes | SHAK 484:27
stilly: in the s. night | MOORE 357:2
s. couches she | HARDY 239:4
Stilton: no end of S. Cheese | LEAR 312:9
Stimulate: S. the phagocytes | SHAW 496:20
sting: death, where is thy s. | BIBLE 77:1
Death, where is thy s. | ROSS 408:20
it is a s. | PEELE 371:7
Thy s. is not so sharp | SHAK 426:1
sting-a-ling-a-ling: where is thy s. | ANON 7:4
stingeth: s. like an adder | BIBLE 54:24
stings: soldiers, armed in their s. | SHAK 443:9
that stings and s. | POPE 377:1
there were s. in their tails | BIBLE 82:8
wanton s. and motions | SHAK 463:14
stink: That the Jews s. naturally…is | BROW 95:25
stinking: apothecary to send forth a s. savour | BIBLE 56:1
stinks: that s. and stings | POPE 377:1
stipendi: offrirgli nè onori nè s. | GAR 221:10
stir: Above the smoke and s. | MILT 340:23
How should we s. ourselves | ANON 8:24
Just to s. things up seemed | SALL 413:23
must s. it and stump it | GILB 228:32
No s. in the air | SOUT 513:28
No s. of air was there | KEATS 290:1
S. up | PRAY 387:2
s. without great argument | SHAK 435:31
To s. men's blood | SHAK 451:2
stirbt: er s. ab | ENG 208:18
stirred: night long we have not s. | BROW 103:30
s. the heart of every Englishman | SCOTT 415:19
stirring: s. times we live | HARDY 241:12
stirrup: Betwixt the s. and the ground | CAMD 128:5
foot already in the s. | CERV 139:2
heard his foot upon the s. | DE L 174:10
I sprang to the s. | BROW 101:12
stirrups: Spurning of his s. like | CHES 147:3
stirs: pulse of feeling s. | ARN 12:22
Stitch: S.! stitch | HOOD 255:6
stitching: s. and unstitching has | YEATS 584:9
stithy: Vulcan's s. | SHAK 434:3
St Ives: S. says the smell of fish | KILV 296:6
St Lawrence: I have seen the S. | BURNS 112:23
stock: see how his s. goes | COL 156:10
Stock Exchange: S. and the solicitors' | SHAW 498:23
stocking: Honey, your silk s.'s | SELL 420:3
Kneeling ne'er spoil'd silk s. | HERB 247:10
stockings: come to her in yellow s. | SHAK 489:17
commended thy yellow s. | SHAK 489:15
did you change your s. | AUST 22:17
his s. foul'd | SHAK 431:28
s. were hung by the chimney | MOORE 355:12
stocks: feet they hurt in the s. | PRAY 397:3
s. in fragrant blow | ARN 15:6
worshipped s. and stones | MILT 351:9
Stoeber: Richard Bentley or Elias S. | HOUS 266:15

Stoic: budge doctors of the S. | MILT 341:16
stoicism: think the Romans call it s. | ADD 1:18
stole: precious diadem s. | SHAK 435:11
They knew 'e s. | KIPL 304:5
wonder where you s. 'em | SWIFT 528:10
stolen: s., be your apples | HUNT 268:11
S. sweets are best | CIBB 151:15
s. the scraps | SHAK 457:12
S. waters are sweet | BIBLE 53:28
They have s. his wits away | DE L 173:26
stoles: nice white s. | BARH 33:12
stol'n: had I s. the whole | STEV 523:6
that has s. the treasure | CONG 160:8
stolzer: s. Männer der Tat | HEINE 244:12
stomach: army marches on its s. | ANON 9:3
army marches on its s. | NAP 359:17
burst s. like a cave | DOUG 191:10
hath no s. to this fight | SHAK 445:3
healthy s. is nothing | BUTL 118:31
heart and s. of a king | ELIZ 206:4
man Of an unbounded s. | SHAK 447:18
My s. is not good | ANON 5:21
s., gentlemen, a *stomach* | HUNT 268:16
s. sets us to work | ELIOT 201:4
wine for thy s.'s sake | BIBLE 79:16
stomacher: with the red s. | DONNE 188:19
stomachs: used to march on their s. | SELL 420:7
stone: all was as cold as any s. | SHAK 443:18
are themselves as s. | SHAK 494:15
At his heels a s. | SHAK 435:33
Before some fallen Runic s. | ARN 13:8
brass, nor s. | SHAK 494:4
Can make a s. of the heart | YEATS 585:2
conscious s. to beauty | EMER 206:23
Fling but a s. | GREEN 235:28
Florence blossoming in s. | LONG 316:17
give them the s. | MONT 354:11
jasper and a sardine s. | BIBLE 81:22
last to be a precious s. | HERR 250:2
lay s. on stone | ARN 13:23
let him first cast a s. | BIBLE 72:10
maketh a hole in the s. | LAT 310:20
man a house of good s. | POUND 382:8
mighty angel took up a s. | BIBLE 82:24
not as s. | POPE 380:24
not thy foot against a s. | PRAY 395:22
One s. the more swings | KIPL 301:17
operation for the s. | SMITH 512:2
quiet as a s. | KEATS 289:33
Raise the s. | ANON 7:11
seeth the s. taken away | BIBLE 73:5
S., bronze | ELIOT 202:6
s. of stumbling | BIBLE 58:4
s. once echoed The voice | HARDY 240:4
S. that puts the Stars | FITZ 212:5
s. the twenty-first | BROW 99:25
S. walls do not a prison | LOV 318:10
s. which the builders refused | PRAY 398:2
sword of this s. and anvil | MAL 327:14
take away our hearts o' s. | OCAS 364:17
This precious s. set | SHAK 478:20
Virtue is like a rich s. | BACON 25:26
water hollows out a s. | OVID 366:27
we raised not a s. | WOLFE 576:5
will he give him a s. | BIBLE 65:4
Stone Age: Where a S. people breeds | BETJ 43:8
stoned: once was I s. | BIBLE 77:12
stones: Are there no s. in heaven | SHAK 477:16
chose him five smooth s. | BIBLE 50:11
croys of latoun ful of s. | CHAU 142:7
man that spares these s. | SHAK 495:22
not s., but men | SHAK 450:25
s. and clouts make martyrs | BROW 97:9
s. of Rome to rise | SHAK 451:3
s. prate of my whereabout | SHAK 460:1
s. would immediately cry | BIBLE 71:2
threw words like s. | SPEN 515:11
worshipped stocks and s. | MILT 351:9

stonest: s. them which are sent | BIBLE 67:26
stone wall: Jackson standing like a s. | BEE 37:3
stony: Some fell upon s. places | BIBLE 66:16
s. limits cannot hold love | SHAK 482:10
stood: had s. them on their heads | BARR 34:11
Have s. against the world | SHAK 450:23
I've s. upon Achilles' tomb | BYRON 123:13
should have s. that night | SHAK 455:24
since he s. for England | CHES 146:26
s., and heard the steeple | HOUS 264:28
s. there holding the knife | AUDEN 21:7
ten thousand s. before him | BIBLE 61:8
stool: sit upon a s. for some | DICK 178:27
three-foot s. mistaketh me | SHAK 470:3
stools: first necessity invented s. | COWP 166:28
stoop: Do I s. | BROW 98:34
Stooping: S. through a fleecy cloud | MILT 342:3
stop: Anyone can s. a man's life | SEN 420:11
did he s. and speak to you | BROW 102:15
easy and so plain a s. | SHAK 440:31
first cries out s. thief | CONG 160:8
I could not s. for Death | DICK 183:15
Might s. a hole to keep | SHAK 437:2
oaten s., or pastoral song | COLL 158:17
s. his mouth with a kiss | SHAK 472:11
S. it at the start | OVID 366:20
s. my house's ears | SHAK 466:13
S. thine ear against | SCOTT 418:5
s. to busy fools | VAUG 555:12
then s. everyone from doing | HERB 246:9
when the kissing had to s. | BROW 105:25
stopp'd: Nor s. till where he had | COWP 165:19
stopped: clock has s. in the dark | ELIOT 202:9
you've said can't be s. | HOR 258:6
stoppeth: he s. one of three | COL 155:5
stops: tender s. of various quills | MILT 343:19
would seem to know my s. | SHAK 434:20
store: seen thee oft amid thy s. | KEATS 293:6
spread her wholesome s. | GOLD 230:18
were to increase his s. | HOME 253:22
storehouse: rich s. for the glory | BACON 24:17
Storied: S. of old in high immortal | MILT 341:12
stories: jewels into a garret four s. | BACON 25:7
seaman tells s. of winds | PROP 401:15
tell sad s. | SHAK 479:11
to believe of my own s. | IRV 270:24
With dismal s. | BUNY 107:36
you with s. of savage men | BURKE 109:15
storm: are lost in the s. | ARN 14:9
directs the s. | ADD 1:14
he maketh the s. to cease | PRAY 397:10
locks of the approaching s. | SHEL 502:9
lovers fled away into the s. | KEATS 289:23
Now sinks the s. | GAY 223:8
pelting of this pitiless s. | SHAK 454:15
rides upon the s. | COWP 165:26
S. and stress | KAUF 288:17
s., fulfilling his word | PRAY 399:22
s. has gone over me | BURKE 112:4
s. is coming on the Chiltern | CHES 146:13
s. nor in the strife | BYRON 125:10
when the s. is drawing near | MORR 358:7
storms: all thy waves and s. are | PRAY 392:8
sudden s. are short | SHAK 478:19
Where no s. come | HOPK 256:1
storm-troubled: trembler in the world's s. | BRON 93:18
stormy: s. sturdy band | HARDY 240:16
to scape s. days | DONNE 189:12
story: about you, that s. | HOR 261:22
delicious s. is ripe | AUDEN 20:2
earns a place i' the s. | SHAK 422:18
endeth the s. of the Sangreal | MAL 327:22
may hear Sordello's s. | BROW 105:11
novel tells a s. | FORS 216:24

plot for a short s. CHEK 145:2
read Richardson for the s. JOHN 276:9
Shuts up the s. of our days RAL 404:15
Still is the s. told MAC 322:23
s. always old and always BROW 104:20
s. for which the world DOYLE 192:26
s. is extant SHAK 434:14
s. of Sussex told BELL 40:11
teach him how to tell my s. SHAK 474:1
that the s. need be long THOR 550:26
to be short in the s. itself BIBLE 63:29
To tell my s. SHAK 437:25
would some pretty s. tell TAYL 531:25
Storys: S. to rede ar delitabill BARB 33:3
story-teller: thought that a s. is born
STEE 517:22
stout: Athenaeum with jugs of s. HERB 246:15
'Collapse of S. Party' ANON 8:10
s. Cortez when with eagle KEATS 292:18
s. hearts and sharp swords BIRK 84:14
stoutness: see no objection to s. GILB 225:32
St Patrick: Wearing, by S.'s bounty
LAND 308:23
St Paul: description of the ruins of S.'s
WALP 563:9
Say I am designing S.'s BENT 41:9
sketch the ruins of S.'s MAC 323:16
with S. are literary terms ARN 16:18
Strachan: waiting for Sir Richard S.
ANON 5:10
strack: s. the top-mast wi' his BALL 30:19
straddled: s. quite over the whole
BUNY 107:15
Stradivari: Antonio S.'s violins ELIOT 201:28
Strafford: S., who was hurried hence
CLEV 153:3
straight: crooked shall be made s. BIBLE 59:5
make his paths s. BIBLE 63:36
might have grown full s. MARL 329:16
nothing ever ran quite s. GALS 220:30
s. in the desert a highway BIBLE 59:5
s., the brave HOUS 265:6
street which is called S. BIBLE 73:35
walked s. out of the Ark SMITH 511:1
straightway: He goeth after her s.
BIBLE 53:25
strain: no, but s. HOPK 257:3
sages drop the drowsy s. COWP 165:3
s. of man's bred SHAK 486:1
That s. again SHAK 487:20
to keep the nerves at s. BROW 102:1
which s. at a gnat BIBLE 67:24
strains: in s. that might create MILT 341:14
s. of unpremeditated art SHEL 504:15
Such s. as would have won MILT 343:1
strait: Into a desperate s. MASS 335:18
S. is the gate BIBLE 65:7
straitened: s. circumstances at home
JUV 287:18
strait jacket: creed a s. for humanity
MER 337:23
Straits: Outside the Western S. ARN 14:21
With echoing s. between ARN 13:12
strand: Come sailing to the s. BALL 30:19
I walk'd along the S. JOHN 280:26
knits me to thy rugged s. SCOTT 416:22
left fair Scotland's s. BURNS 114:10
on some far northern s. ARN 13:8
where's the Maypole in the S. BRAM 91:23
wrote her name upon the s. SPEN 515:20
strands: these last s. of man HOPK 256:7
strange: All is s. JOHN 280:9
be very s. and well-bred CONG 161:7
everything that looks s. PEPYS 372:7
hand of s. children PRAY 399:12
have more cunning to be s. SHAK 482:14
Into something rich and s. SHAK 484:32
is not that s. SHAK 473:2
Jacob from among the s. PRAY 397:16
man with s. bedfellows SHAK 485:9

millions of s. shadows SHAK 493:15
Nature hath fram'd s. fellows SHAK 465:8
owe this s. intelligence SHAK 458:13
pair of very s. beasts SHAK 427:3
passing s. and wonderful SHEL 500:8
Poverty has s. bedfellows BULW 107:6
song: in a s. land PRAY 399:3
s. and sinister embroidered JAMES 271:15
s. and terrible events SHAK 423:12
s., and unnatural SHAK 431:7
s., astonished-looking HUNT 268:7
s. faces, other minds TENN 535:24
s. hours and all strange SWIN 528:26
stranger in a s. land BIBLE 47:2
S. the difference of men's PEPYS 371:17
this is wondrous s. SHAK 431:22
too stubborn and too s. SHAK 448:10
you lisp and wear s. suits SHAK 426:20
strange-eyed: s. constellations reign
HARDY 239:9
strangeness: some s. in the proportion
BACON 25:28
stranger: entertain Him always like a
s. ANON 9:1
entertain this starry s. CRAS 169:7
From the wiles of a s. NASH 359:18
I was a s. BIBLE 68:6
Look, s. AUDEN 20:3
On earth I am a s. grown BURNS 114:15
s. and afraid HOUS 264:25
s. here in Gloucestershire SHAK 478:23
s. in a strange land BIBLE 47:2
s. that is within thy gates BIBLE 47:24
S. than fiction BYRON 124:7
s. to my heart and me SHAK 453:3
s. to one of your parents AUST 23:15
that is surety for a s. BIBLE 53:31
What s.'s feet may find HOUS 265:10
strangers: all the Athenians and s.
BIBLE 74:11
By s. honour'd POPE 376:10
desire we may be better s. SHAK 426:10
forgetful to entertain s. BIBLE 80:3
gracious and courteous to s. BACON 26:20
Lord careth for the s. PRAY 399:18
s. of Rome BIBLE 73:23
they were s. and pilgrims BIBLE 79:33
we are s. before thee BIBLE 51:39
strangest: in did come the s. figure
BROW 103:18
strangled: s. her BROW 103:29
s. illegitimate child ARN 15:27
s. in the guts of priests MESL 338:9
strangling: heart one s. golden hair
ROSS 410:2
Than s. in a string HOUS 262:17
Strapped: S., noosed HOUS 264:28
Strasbourg: S., a city still famous
HOUS 266:15
stratagem: take her tea without a s.
YOUNG 587:18
stratagems: Fine nets and s. to catch
HERB 248:10
strathspeys: There's hornpipes and
BURNS 113:13
straw: Headpiece filled with s. ELIOT 203:8
Oft stumbles at a s. SPEN 517:4
pigmy's s. doth pierce SHAK 455:20
shall eat s. like the ox BIBLE 58:11
s. under my knee DONNE 191:2
Take a s. and throw it SELD 419:22
Things are but as s. dogs LAO 310:2
strawberries: I saw good s. in your garden
SHAK 481:4
s. at the mouth of their ELIZ 205:22
S. swimming in the cream PEELE 371:9
strawed: where thou hast not s. BIBLE 68:3
straws: oaths are s. SHAK 443:20
stray: Did your fancy never s. GAY 222:21
with me you'd fondly s. GAY 222:22

strayed: s. from thy ways like lost
PRAY 384:11
Though thou hast surely s. GILB 228:14
strays: Red s. of ruined springs SWIN 529:23
streaks: glimmers with some s. of day
SHAK 461:15
stream: cool s. thy fingers wet ARN 14:14
fishes leap in silver s. CLARE 152:14
little s. best fits a little HERR 249:21
mercy Of a rude s. SHAK 447:9
me rowing against the s. SCOTT 418:10
purling s. ADD 2:5
salt weed sways in the s. ARN 13:6
schoolboys playing in the s. PEELE 371:9
scooped the brimming s. MILT 347:25
Still glides the S. WORD 581:4
s. and o'er the mead BLAKE 87:26
s. will not run long BURKE 111:15
That even the gentle s. SPEN 516:32
they have their s. and pond BROO 94:10
Streamed: this public Way S. WORD 582:4
streamers: s. waving in the wind GAY 223:28
with her fan spread and s. CONG 160:36
streams: coil of his crystalline s. SHEL 502:10
eyes the s. of dotage flow JOHN 283:3
Gilding pale s. with heavenly SHAK 493:9
gratulations flow in s. CAREY 130:23
hart for cooling s. TATE 531:20
more pellucid s. WORD 578:3
Sleepy with the flow of s. HOUS 263:18
Stillest s. COWP 167:29
s. in the desert BIBLE 58:34
S. like the thunder-storm BYRON 121:11
strength of the s. that SWIN 528:16
strebt: so lang er s. GOET 229:29
strecche: Thanne peyne I me to s.
CHAU 143:5
street: done by jostling in the s. BLAKE 87:10
inability to cross the s. WOOLF 576:20
in the long unlovely s. TENN 536:5
looking in the s. KIPL 302:22
On the bald s. TENN 536:6
salmon sing in the s. AUDEN 18:9
s. and pavement mute HARDY 240:21
s. of the city was pure gold BIBLE 82:33
s. were time and he ELIOT 202:2
s. which is called Straight BIBLE 73:35
where the long s. roars TENN 537:20
You've got the key of the s. DICK 182:37
street-lamp: Half-past one, The s.
ELIOT 204:9
streets: Down these mean s. CHAN 139:22
lion is in the s. BIBLE 54:34
not in the s. of Askelon BIBLE 50:16
s. and lanes of the city BIBLE 70:12
s. are paved with gold COLM 158:25
s. were fill'd with joyful TENN 536:18
s. where the great men FLEC 214:6
ten thousands in our s. PRAY 399:13
when night Darkens the s. MILT 345:18
strength: any man by his great s.
PRAY 391:20
confidence shall be your s. BIBLE 58:27
do unbend your noble s. SHAK 460:10
girded himself with s. PRAY 395:24
give s. unto his people PRAY 391:12
God is our hope and s. PRAY 392:19
hath shewed s. with his arm BIBLE 69:6
His s. the more is BUNY 107:36
hither in thy hour of s. WORD 580:5
impulse of thy s. SHEL 502:12
Its s., and struck HOUS 264:28
length that tower of s. TENN 541:8
Let us roll all our s. MARV 332:20
Lord shall renew their s. BIBLE 59:10
name is a tower of s. SHAK 481:12
of the Sun in his s. BIBLE 44:21
On which all s. depends SMART 509:1
pleasure in the s. of an horse PRAY 399:20
rejoiceth in his s. BIBLE 53:6

Suez: me somewheres east of S.	KIPL 301:8
suffer: Better one s.	DRYD 194:11
doth s. a sea-change	SHAK 484:32
escape than one innocent s.	BLAC 85:6
Hell I s. seems a Heaven	MILT 347:15
If s. we must	HUGO 267:10
living thing to s. pain	SHEL 502:21
should have courage to s.	TROL 552:19
s. A man of his place	SHAK 447:24
s. and die	VIGNY 557:2
s. a witch to live	BIBLE 47:26
s. for it	BIBLE 80:26
S. the little children	BIBLE 68:36
s. thy foot to be moved	PRAY 398:9
s. thy Holy One to see	PRAY 390:7
to make your readers s.	JOHN 281:3
With those that I saw s.	SHAK 484:23
ye s. fools gladly	BIBLE 77:10
sufferance: s. is the badge of all	SHAK 466:2
suffer'd: have s. greatly	TENN 543:22
Suffered: S. under Pontius Pilate	
	PRAY 384:26
well-greaved Achaeans have s.	
	HOMER 253:28
suffering: About s. they were never	
	AUDEN 19:18
learn in s. what they teach	SHEL 501:13
majesty of human s.	VIGNY 557:1
mental s. had been undergone	BUTL 119:12
ruling few than loved the s.	BENT 41:1
S. is permanent	WORD 577:2
sufferings: constant in human s.	
	JOYCE 286:17
myriad s. for the Achaeans	HOMER 253:26
patience under their s.	PRAY 386:1
suffer'n: Lounjun 'roun' en s.	HARR 242:21
suffers: does, not s. wrong	SHEL 502:20
nothing the body s.	MER 337:28
suffice: s. for those who belong	WHIT 571:8
sufficeth: it s. me	MAL 327:20
sufficiency: elegant s.	THOM 549:11
Our s. is of God	BIBLE 77:4
sufficient: he have s. to finish it	BIBLE 70:14
perfect, and s. sacrifice	PRAY 387:24
s. conclusions from insufficient	BUTL 118:26
S. unto the day	BIBLE 64:32
whole world is not s.	QUAR 403:9
sufficiently: s. degraded in their own	
	GILB 226:26
think you are s. decayed	GILB 227:18
sugar: If sack and s. be a fault	SHAK 439:17
I must s. my hair	CARR 134:16
s., and saltness agree	GOLD 231:16
s. o'er The devil himself	SHAK 433:7
sugared: s. about by the old men	KIPL 303:11
suggestion: s. as a cat laps milk	SHAK 485:6
suicide: arose from the s.'s grave	GILB 227:17
by s., a bag of gold	BRAM 91:21
thought of s. is a great	NIET 363:11
suicides: downward lay the huddled s.	
	PLOM 374:19
suis: Je s. comme je suis	PREV 400:16
J'y s., j'y reste	MACM 325:17
Suisse: point de S.	RAC 404:5
suit: Doesn't seem to s. her notion	GILB 227:3
moneys is your s.	SHAK 466:3
suitable: no s. material to work	COMP 159:14
suitably: s. attired in leather	HOUS 266:9
suitor: think that you are Ann's s.	
	SHAW 497:24
suits: Than s. a man to say	HOUS 266:1
thou whatever s. the line	COL 157:5
trappings and the s. of woe	SHAK 429:25
suivre: il fallait bien les s.	LEDR 313:6
sukebind: when the s. hangs heavy	
	GIBB 225:3
sullen: Musing full sadly in his s.	SPEN 516:7
s. from the suppliant crowd	COWP 168:9
to cope him in these s.	SHAK 425:3
you sick or are you s.	JOHN 279:27

sullenness: injury and s. against Nature	
	MILT 352:10
sulphur: oat-cakes, and s.	SMITH 510:30
sulphurous: s. and thought-executing	
	SHAK 454:4
Sultan: Sultan after S. with his Pomp	
	FITZ 212:13
sultry: where the climate's s.	BYRON 122:9
sum: ergo s.	DESC 175:10
Is s. of nothing	SHAK 467:13
s. obtained I this freedom	BIBLE 74:21
s. of human wretchedness	BYRON 125:18
s. of matter remains exactly	BACON 25:15
s. of things for pay	HOUS 265:7
Sumer: S. is icumen	ANON 7:18
summer: After s. merrily	SHAK 485:25
bathing of a s.'s day	WORD 580:7
compare thee to a s.'s day	SHAK 492:28
Expect Saint Martin's s.	SHAK 445:18
first S. month that brings	FITZ 212:10
hollows crown'd with s. sea	TENN 535:27
idle hill of s.	HOUS 263:18
if it takes all s.	GRANT 233:21
Indian S. of the heart	WHIT 571:20
lose my heart in s.'s even	HOUS 266:4
murmur of a s.'s day	ARN 14:11
must have a villa in s.	MORR 358:3
out far over the s. sea	TENN 543:2
parting s.'s lingering	GOLD 230:16
shall see in a s.'s day	SHAK 469:31
Singest of s. in full-throated	KEATS 291:17
Spring, nor S. beauty	DONNE 188:7
S. afternoon	JAMES 271:30
s. and winter	BIBLE 45:37
s., and winter hoar	SHEL 501:15
s. birdcage in a garden	WEBS 567:2
s. dies the swan	TENN 543:11
S. has set in with its	COL 157:27
s. how it ripened	DONNE 188:9
s. in England is to have	WALP 563:8
s. is ended	BIBLE 60:20
s., quite the other way	STEV 522:16
S. set lip to earth's bosom	THOM 548:27
s.'s flower is	SHAK 494:15
s.'s green all girded	SHAK 492:26
S.'s joys are spoilt	KEATS 289:30
s.'s lease hath all too	SHAK 492:28
s. soldier and the sunshine	PAINE 368:1
S.s pleasures they are	CLARE 152:16
sweet as s.	SHAK 447:21
their lordships on a hot s.	ANON 8:8
thinking on fantastic s.'s	SHAK 478:17
This guest of s.	SHAK 459:4
thy eternal s. shall not	SHAK 492:28
'Tis S. Time on Bredon	KING 297:21
'Tis the last rose of s.	MOORE 356:20
tree in the time of s.	BIBLE 63:27
us in s. skies to mourn	KEATS 289:8
waken from his s. dreams	SHEL 502:10
whether it's winter or s.	CHEK 145:3
Whether the s. clothe	COL 156:23
your English s.'s done	KIPL 300:23
summer-night: upon a trancèd s.	
	KEATS 290:5
summers: forests shook three s.'	SHAK 494:18
s. in a sea of glory	SHAK 447:9
thousand s. are over	SWIN 530:12
summertime: In s. on Bredon	HOUS 263:4
summerward: He singeth s.	POUND 383:18
summits: Nations touch at their s.	BAG 29:7
snowy s. old in story	TENN 541:32
summon: To s. his array	MAC 322:11
summoned: Pearse s. Cuchulain	YEATS 587:2
S. the Immediate Aid	BELL 39:8
summoners: These dreadful s. grace	
	SHAK 454:10
summons: heavy s. lies like lead	SHAK 459:14
That s. thee to heaven	SHAK 460:1
Upon a fearful s.	SHAK 429:16
Summum: S. bonum	CIC 151:21

sums: exact in s.	BAG 29:11
sun: all the beauty of the s.	SHAK 490:33
are nothing like the s.	SHAK 495:8
before you let the s.	THOM 547:10
best s. we have	WALP 563:5
black s. of melancholy	NERV 360:26
blushing discontented s.	SHAK 479:12
Born of the s. they travelled	SPEN 515:8
bosom-friend of the maturing s.	KEATS 293:5
Busy old fool, unruly S.	DONNE 190:11
clear as the s.	BIBLE 57:5
climbed towards the s.	CHES 148:7
Close to the s. in lonely	TENN 533:7
common s.	GRAY 235:15
countenance was as the s.	BIBLE 81:14
countest the steps of the S.	BLAKE 87:22
Distilled by the s.	HARDY 241:21
doors against a setting s.	SHAK 486:5
except their s.	BYRON 122:32
eyes to behold the s.	BIBLE 56:9
farthing candle to the s.	YOUNG 587:20
from the s. Take warmth	GREN 236:15
front the s. climbs slow	CLOU 154:4
gallant will command the s.	SHAK 484:13
give me the s.	IBSEN 269:22
glorious S. uprist	COL 155:11
Glorious the s. in mid-career	SMART 509:4
glory of the s. will be	BALF 30:3
God-curst s.	HARDY 240:1
going down of the s.	BINY 84:10
golden apples of the s.	YEATS 586:21
great S. begins his state	MILT 342:18
Hath Britain all the s.	SHAK 428:17
heaven's glorious s.	SHAK 456:15
he beheld the s.	WORD 577:10
he taketh under the s.	BIBLE 55:5
I am too much i' the s.	SHAK 429:22
Juliet is the s.	SHAK 482:5
just as the s. was rising	ANON 5:3
kind old s. will know	OWEN 367:4
kiss of the s. for pardon	GURN 237:7
lands beneath another s.	THOM 549:20
Laughed in the s.	BROO 94:15
Let the hot s. Shine on	AUDEN 20:21
light a candle to the s.	SIDN 507:13
Linden, when the s. was low	CAMP 128:21
livery of the burnish'd s.	SHAK 466:6
loves to live i' the s.	SHAK 425:16
make our s. Stand still	MARV 332:20
midnight speak with the S.	VAUG 555:11
Monday, when the s. is hot	MILNE 340:16
Move him into the s.	OWEN 367:4
name shall the S. of righteousness	BIBLE 62:3
never assisted the s.	THOR 550:10
new thing under the s.	BIBLE 55:5
Now the s. is laid to sleep	JONS 283:24
now the S. is rising	WORD 580:27
of the S. in his strength	BIBLE 44:21
our own place in the s.	BULOW 106:23
out again to feel the s.	BROW 97:35
quietest places Under the s.	HOUS 264:7
rain, and s.	TENN 534:2
run to the rime-ringed s.	KIPL 300:24
sacred radiance of the s.	SHAK 453:3
scarce could see the s.	ROSS 409:16
sea-daisies feast on the s.	SWIN 530:24
self-same s. that shines	SHAK 492:4
served up the s. and moon	AUG 21:13
setting s.	SHAK 478:18
shall the s. light on them	BIBLE 82:3
shoots at the mid-day s.	SIDN 507:15
So when the s. in bed	MILT 344:14
splendid silent s. with	WHIT 570:3
summer by this s. of York	SHAK 480:17
S. and Moon should doubt	BLAKE 85:17
s. and the other stars	DANTE 171:18
s. and the rain Clash	FRY 219:26
s. ariseth	PRAY 397:1
s. came dazzling thro'	TENN 538:8
S. came up upon the left	COL 155:7

surpassed: Man is something to be s.
NIET 363:1
surplice-question: thrilling view of the
s.　　　　　　　　　　　　BROW 100:2
surprend: La mort ne s. point le LA F 306:22
surprise: His s., therefore, upon TRAV 552:6
Respect was mingled with s. SCOTT 416:6
takes the wise man by s. LA F 306:22
surprised: Not half so s. as I am now
WELL 567:30
S. by unjust force MILT 341:15
S. by joy WORD 582:15
surprises: millions of s. HERB 248:10
surrender: daring of a moment's s.
ELIOT 205:11
Guards die but do not s. CAMB 128:2
immediate s. can be accepted GRANT 234:1
we shall never s. CHUR 149:31
surrendered: all our enemies having
s.　　　　　　　　　　　　CHUR 150:26
Surrey: full S. twilight BETJ 44:8
to that S. homestead BETJ 43:11
Sursum: S. corda MASS 335:2
Surtout: S., Messieurs, point de zèle
TALL 531:15
survey: that takes s. of all SHAK 440:23
We first s. the plot SHAK 441:17
surveyors: there are worse s. EMER 207:7
Survival: S. of the Fittest is more
DARW 171:27
s. of the fittest SPEN 514:30
victory there is no s. CHUR 149:30
survived: I s. SIEY 508:8
your gift s. it all AUDEN 19:5
survives: Education is what s. when
SKIN 508:20
survivor: ourselves that I may be the
s.　　　　　　　　　　　　AUST 23:17
Susan: black-ey'd S. came aboard
GAY 223:28
Poor S. has passed WORD 581:3
suspect: 'Always s. everybody DICK 180:31
nothing makes a man s. much BACON 27:24
s. The thoughts of others SHAK 466:4
suspected: opinions are always s.
LOCKE 315:13
suspended: shoulders held the sky s.
HOUS 265:7
s. my religious inquiries GIBB 224:11
s. the sentiments of religion BURKE 111:29
Suspenders: must *not* forget the S.
KIPL 304:15
suspension: willing s. of disbelief COL 157:22
suspicion: Caesar's wife must be above
s.　　　　　　　　　　　　CAES 127:1
gladly banish squint s. MILT 341:9
S. always haunts the guilty SHAK 446:23
Suspicions: S. amongst thoughts are
BACON 27:23
suspicious: Men are s. HERR 249:16
suspiration: Nor windy s. of forc'd
SHAK 429:25
Sussex: No more than S. weed KIPL 303:15
S. by the sea KIPL 303:16
S. men are noted fools BLAKE 87:1
S. songs be sung BELL 40:11
sustaining: In our s. corn SHAK 455:13
sustres: his s. and his paramours CHAU 142:32
sutlers: sapient s. of the Lord ELIOT 204:1
swab: only have to s. a plank DICK 176:10
Swaddled: S. with darkness ELIOT 203:4
swaddling: wrapped him in s. clothes
BIBLE 69:9
swaddling-clouts: is not yet out of his
s.　　　　　　　　　　　　SHAK 432:19
swaggering: By s. could I never thrive
SHAK 490:27
swain: better than a homely s. SHAK 446:18
cheered the labouring s. GOLD 230:16
Thus sang the uncouth s. MILT 343:19

swains: That all our s. commend her
SHAK 491:4
swallow: chaffering s. for the holy lark
BROW 97:27
come before the s. dares SHAK 491:26
sister s. SWIN 530:12
some'll s. tay and stuff MAS 333:20
s. a camel BIBLE 67:24
s. a nest where she may PRAY 395:11
S., flying TENN 542:5
s. has set her six young BROW 101:19
s. twitt'ring from GRAY 234:20
swallowed: easier s. than a flap-dragon
SHAK 457:12
others to be s. BACON 27:19
They had s. us up quick PRAY 398:13
to be last s. SHAK 435:24
you be not s. up in books WESL 568:23
swalloweth: s. the ground with fierceness
BIBLE 53:7
swallow-flights: Short s. of song TENN 536:20
swallowing: s. his tea in oceans MAC 324:14
swallows: engluts and s. other sorrows
SHAK 473:23
gathering s. twitter KEATS 293:9
swam: She s. to the bell-rope BEER 37:14
you have s. in a gondola SHAK 426:20
swamp: down to botanize in the s.
CHES 148:7
swan: I will play the s. SHAK 477:18
Leda's goose a s. ANON 5:18
Like a black s. as death AUDEN 18:3
like a sleeping s. SHEL 503:11
Like some full-breasted s. TENN 535:28
now this pale s. in her SHAK 492:20
silver s. GIBB 225:1
so much as a black s. JUV 287:20
summer dies the s. TENN 543:11
s. her downy cygnets save SHAK 445:24
s. sail with her young MER 337:15
Sweet S. of Avon JONS 284:25
swan-bosomed: once more 'neath a s.
tree SITW 508:12
swan-like: He makes a s. end SHAK 467:8
Swann: fut plus question de S. PROU 401:21
swans: honking amongst tuneful s.
VIRG 560:7
in the midst of some s. AUG 21:11
I saw two S. of goodly SPEN 516:31
old ships sail like s. FLEC 214:16
s. are geese ARN 13:14
s. of others are geese WALP 563:20
S. sing before they die COL 156:16
Very like s. DICK 178:30
swap: s. horses while crossing LINC 315:2
swapping: s., swapping mallard ANON 7:28
sware: Unto whom I s. in my wrath
PRAY 396:4
Swarm: S. over, Death BETJ 44:4
swarry: friendly s. DICK 182:26
swashing: s. and a martial outside
SHAK 424:30
Swat: Is the Akond of S. LEAR 312:25
swath: s. and all its twined flowers
KEATS 293:6
swats: cog o' gude s. BURNS 113:4
sway: above this sceptred s. SHAK 467:27
little s. DYER 199:18
love of s. POPE 377:24
swayed: she be s. by quite as keen
GILB 228:13
swaying: s. sound of the sea AUDEN 20:3
sways: s. she level in her husband's
SHAK 489:1
swear: began he to curse and to s.
BIBLE 68:19
s. an eternal friendship CANN 130:4
s. in both the scales against SHAK 460:16
s. like a comfit-maker's SHAK 439:32
S. not at all BIBLE 64:15

s. not by the moon SHAK 482:15
s. thou think'st I love DONNE 190:14
s. to never kiss the girls BROW 100:30
s. to the truth of a song PRIOR 400:20
time I ever heard you s. FARR 210:27
time you s. you're his PARK 368:19
when very angry, s. TWAIN 554:16
swearers: Then the liars and s. are
SHAK 462:13
sweareth: He that s. unto his neighbour
PRAY 390:5
swearing: let me alone for s. SHAK 490:13
swears: s. with so much grace LEE 313:9
swear-word: s. in a rustic slum BEER 37:15
Sweat: Agony and bloody S. PRAY 385:17
Falstaff shall die of a s. SHAK 443:2
In the s. of thy face shalt BIBLE 45:22
rank s. of an enseamed bed SHAK 435:10
s. and whine about their WHIT 570:22
s. pours down me SAPP 414:6
S. ran and blood sprang HOUS 264:4
tears and s. CHUR 149:29
We spend our midday s. QUAR 403:10
will s. but for promotion SHAK 425:7
sweated: s. through his apostolic
BYRON 126:7
sweating: Quietly s. palm to palm
HUXL 268:22
sweats: bloody s. WILDE 572:14
Falstaff s. to death SHAK 438:28
S. in the eye of Phoebus SHAK 444:25
Sweeney: Apeneck S. spreads his knees
ELIOT 204:14
S. to Mrs Porter ELIOT 204:27
sweep: madly s. the sky SHAK 470:20
So your chimneys I s. BLAKE 88:5
To s. the dust behind SHAK 471:22
Sweeping: S. up the Heart DICK 183:17
sweeps: s. a room as for Thy laws
HERB 247:19
sweet: about them if TO-DAY be s.
FITZ 212:22
all her task to be s. WATS 565:11
All is not s. JONS 283:27
all s. things BORR 90:4
Beyond a man's saying s. HARDY 238:22
by distance made more s. COLL 158:21
comes in the s. o' the year SHAK 491:17
dead thing that smells s. THOM 547:17
fair and smell'st so s. SHAK 476:19
how it was s. BROW 100:8
How s. and fair she seems WALL 562:13
I mean s. words SHAK 449:24
made this life more s. SHAK 424:31
mouth s. as honey BIBLE 82:9
myself that am so s. to you PATM 370:5
of a labouring man is s. BIBLE 55:17
parting is such s. sorrow SHAK 482:20
passing s., is solitude COWP 166:21
should be buried in so s. SHEL 499:2
sin that was s. PAIN 367:17
Sleep is s. to the labouring BUNY 107:24
so s. is she JONS 285:4
So s. was ne'er so fatal SHAK 477:5
Stolen waters are s. BIBLE 53:28
such s. thunder SHAK 471:17
S. and low TENN 541:31
s. and twenty SHAK 488:17
S. are the uses of adversity SHAK 424:32
s. as summer SHAK 447:21
s. cheat gone DE L 174:5
s. is death who puts TENN 534:30
S. is pleasure after pain DRYD 195:1
S. is revenge BYRON 122:12
S. is the breath of morn MILT 348:4
s. is this human life CORY 163:5
s. love remember'd such SHAK 493:6
s. love seemed that April BRID 92:20
s. poison for the age's SHAK 452:10
s. the moonlight sleeps SHAK 468:15

syntax: both in his s. and in his   ARN 16:11
Syrens: song the S. sang   BROW 97:14
Syrian: allur'd The S. damsels   MILT 345:17
S. Orontes has now   JUV 287:15
Syrinx: Pan did after S. speed   MARV 332:2
syrops: lucent s.   KEATS 289:20
Syrtes: Betwixt the S. and soft Sicily   ARN 14:21
system: energies of our s. will decay   BALF 30:3
I must Create a S.   BLAKE 86:2
into a s. of Government   GLAD 229:19
Observe how s. into system   POPE 379:3
to them the decimal s.   NAP 359:13
système: s. de poids et mesures   NAP 359:13
systems: Atoms or s. into ruin hurl'd   POPE 379:4
Away with S.   MER 337:37
Our little s. have their   TENN 535:31
T: description the page gave to a T.   FARQ 210:18
Ta: thousand T.'s and Pardon's   BETJ 43:13
taäkin: a's doing a-t.' o' meä   TENN 541:4
taberna: In t. mori   ANON 10:14
tabernacle: At Salem is his t.   PRAY 395:1
he set a t. for the sun   PRAY 390:11
t. of this house were dissolved   BIBLE 77:6
who shall dwell in thy t.   PRAY 390:4
tabernas: pulsat pede pauperum t.   HOR 259:13
table: behave mannerly at t.   STEV 522:17
from their masters' t.   BIBLE 66:30
from the rich man's t.   BIBLE 70:28
it before them in a t.   BIBLE 58:25
My t. thou hast furnished   SCOT 419:5
olive-branches: round about thy t.   PRAY 398:20
T., at the Communion-time   PRAY 387:6
though you cannot make a t.   JOHN 274:26
Thou shalt prepare a t.   PRAY 390:22
to come to the Lord's T.   PRAY 387:5
tableau: l'histoire n'est que le t. des crimes   VOLT 561:10
Table Bay: horse and foot going to T.   KIPL 297:24
Table Mountain: I reside at T.   HARTE 242:32
tables: make it plain upon t.   BIBLE 62:1
serve t.   BIBLE 73:27
tablets: thy t., Memory   ARN 13:19
taboo: repose is t.'d by anxiety   GILB 226:12
tabret: bring hither the t.   PRAY 395:9
tabulae: Solventur risu t.   HOR 262:7
tache: sans une t.   ROST 410:12
tackle: silken t.   SHAK 422:3
though thy t.'s torn   SHAK 427:26
tactics: master of the art of t.   BAG 29:11
tadpole: When you were a t.   SMITH 510:10
taedium vitae: helps to keep off the t.   JOHN 274:21
taen: t. the fit o' rhyme   BURNS 113:23
taffeta: doublet of changeable t.   SHAK 489:5
T. phrases   SHAK 457:15
tail: corking-pin stuck through his t.   BARH 33:5
guinea-pig up by the t.   LOCK 315:18
head and which was the t.   BRIG 93:6
he's treading on my t.   CARR 134:13
horror of his folded t.   MILT 344:12
Improve his shining t.   CARR 133:17
like a rat without a t.   SHAK 458:6
mouse's limp t. hanging   MOORE 355:22
such a little t. behind   BELL 38:28
t. must wag the dog   KIPL 298:16
Thin mane, thick t.   SHAK 495:20
thy t. hangs down behind   KIPL 302:14
was a hole where the t.   COL 156:11
tailor: my coat from the t.   GOLD 232:41
t. make thy doublet   SHAK 489:5
tails: were stings in their t.   BIBLE 82:8
taint: I cannot t. with fear   SHAK 462:28

never t. my love   SHAK 476:24
tainted: t. wether of the flock   SHAK 467:25
Taisez-vous: T.! Méfiez-vous   ANON 9:18
take: good Lord would t. him   AUDEN 20:20
got to t. under my wing   GILB 227:14
humbly t. my leave of you   SHAK 432:10
Let us t. any man's horses   SHAK 442:29
She bid me t. love easy   YEATS 584:22
T. any heart   GILB 228:15
T. a pair of sparkling   GILB 225:26
t. away all at one swoop   WEBS 567:1
T. away from English authors   TROL 552:12
t. away the matter of them   BACON 27:11
T. care of the pence   LOWN 319:21
T., eat, this is my Body   PRAY 388:1
t. it away   PAIN 367:17
T. me, Lieutenant   BETJ 43:11
t. my life   FARQ 210:10
t. my life and all   SHAK 468:10
t. not thy holy Spirit   PRAY 393:6
t. our fill of love   BIBLE 53:24
t. those lips away   SHAK 464:21
T. your hare when it is   GLAS 229:21
They have to t. you in'   FROST 219:2
thou yet t. all, Galilean   SWIN 530:4
which I shall t. with me   ROST 410:12
taken: because she was t. out of Man   BIBLE 45:12
day in which he was t. up   BIBLE 73:20
Lord hath t. away   BIBLE 52:7
One shall be t.   BIBLE 67:33
only t. from the French   SHER 505:19
They have t. away my Lord   BIBLE 73:7
Tho' much is t.   TENN 544:3
When t., To be well shaken   COLM 159:7
takes: give like that it t. away   BYRON 125:28
if it t. all summer   GRANT 233:21
money and you t. your choice   ANON 9:2
t. a woman must be undone   GAY 222:30
t. two to speak the truth   THOR 550:21
taketh: that t. from the store   MARV 332:17
which t. away the sin   BIBLE 71:30
taking-off: deep damnation of his t.   SHAK 459:6
tale: adorn a t.   JOHN 282:31
bodies must tell the t.   SCOTT 415:19
brings in a several t.   SHAK 481:14
Christmas told the merriest t.   SCOTT 417:16
honest t. speeds best being   SHAK 481:9
how a plain t. shall put   SHAK 439:6
I could a t. unfold whose   SHAK 431:5
I say the t. as 'twas said   SCOTT 416:16
I should have had a t.   SCOTT 415:19
I tell the t. that I heard   HOUS 264:16
long preamble of a t.   CHAU 143:22
mere t. of a tub   WEBS 567:3
ower true t.   SCOTT 418:8
round unvarnish'd t. deliver   SHAK 473:24
t. should be judicious   COWP 165:2
t., sir, would cure deafness   SHAK 484:25
t. Told by an idiot   SHAK 463:6
tedious as a twice-told t.   SHAK 452:21
Telling a t. not too importunate   MORR 358:9
telling the saddest t.   SHAK 470:3
thereby hangs a t.   SHAK 425:19
thou the lamentable t.   SHAK 480:8
Trust the t.   LAWR 311:10
With a t. forsooth he cometh   SIDN 508:2
Tale-bearers: T. are as bad as the tale-makers   SHER 506:25
talent: Blest with each t.   POPE 376:26
Es bildet ein T. sich   GOET 230:10
grand t. pour le silence   CARL 131:37
had is just a t. to amuse   COW 163:17
into my works is my t.   WILDE 573:35
que mon t. dans mes ouvres   WILDE 573:35
T. develops in quiet places   GOET 230:10
T. does what it can   MER 338:5
t. instantly recognizes   DOYLE 192:38
t. of our English nation   DRYD 197:12

T. which is death to hide   MILT 351:10
tomb of a mediocre t.   SMITH 510:20
you must have t. too   KORDA 305:27
talented: I'm sure he's a t. man   PRAED 384:5
talents: career open to t.   NAP 359:14
If you have great t.   REYN 405:16
ministry of all the t.   ANON 7:26
they have tried their t.   COL 157:26
tales: children is increased with t.   BACON 26:1
let them tell thee t.   SHAK 480:8
marvellous t.   FLEC 214:9
tell old t.   SHAK 456:3
tali: t. auxilio nec defensoribus   VIRG 558:9
talismans: not seldom t. and spells   COWP 167:25
talk: by beginning to t.   HAZL 243:13
chance to t. a little wild   SHAK 446:26
How he will t.   LEE 313:11
I have no small t.   WELL 567:31
I never t. about it   PROU 401:22
'It's very easy to t.   DICK 180:14
It would t.   BEAU 36:13
I won't t. of his book   JOHN 275:21
legs and have out his t.   JOHN 277:22
loves to hear himself t.   SHAK 482:24
mair they t. I'm kent   BURNS 114:32
night is crept upon our t.   SHAK 451:28
nothing but t. of his horse   SHAK 465:21
No use to t. to me   HOUS 262:20
should t. so very queer   BARH 33:23
spent an hour's t. withal   SHAK 456:21
T. about the pews and steeples   CHES 146:11
t. but a tinkling cymbal   BACON 26:15
t. him out of patience   SHAK 475:13
t. not to me of a name   BYRON 125:29
t. of wills   SHAK 479:10
t. six times with the same   BYRON 123:34
t. slid north   KIPL 297:28
t. too much   DRYD 194:12
t. with crowds and keep   KIPL 300:2
t. with some old lover's   DONNE 189:25
t. with you   FLEC 214:20
t. with you   SHAK 465:28
They always t.   PRIOR 401:11
'Tis the t.   GRAN 234:8
to find t. and discourse   BACON 27:18
To t. about the rest   ANON 8:2
'To t. of many things   CARR 135:7
we do not t. of ourselves   TROL 552:22
wished him to t. on for ever   HAZL 243:17
world may t. of hereafter   COLL 158:12
talk'd: So much they t.   CHUR 149:10
t. like poor Poll   GARR 221:13
they t. of their Raphaels   GOLD 231:21
talked: he t. with us by the way   BIBLE 71:18
I believe they t. of me   FARQ 210:3
least t. about by men   PER 372:24
single and only t. of population   GOLD 232:32
t. shop like a tenth muse   ANON 5:17
worse than being t. about   WILDE 573:18
talkers: most fluent t. or most   HAZL 243:18
talking: filthiness, nor foolish t.   BIBLE 78:2
Frenchman must be always t.   JOHN 278:17
T. and eloquence are not   JONS 285:3
that you will still be t.   SHAK 471:28
tired the sun with t.   CORY 163:4
Talking-machine: other than a redtape T.   CARL 132:1
talks: Licker t. mighty loud w'en   HARR 242:23
Minerva when she t.   JONS 285:5
She only t. about her hair   THOM 549:3
t. it so very fast that   FARQ 210:6
t. of Arthur's death   SHAK 452:27
t. of darkness at noon-day   COWP 166:2
t. of his misfortunes there   JOHN 278:20
wish I liked the way it t.   RAL 404:20
tall: divinely t.   TENN 533:5
He's as t. a man as any's   SHAK 487:23

she is t. and stately TENN 540:6
t. men had ever very empty BACON 25:7
taller: He is t. by almost SWIFT 526:1
Tam: T. was glorious BURNS 115:6
tamarisks: High noon behind the t.
KIPL 298:13
tambourine: play the t. on her other
DICK 180:18
Tamburlaine: T., the Scourge of God
MARL 330:17
tame: Be not too t. neither SHAK 433:17
hey-day in the blood is t. SHAK 435:8
tongue can no man t. BIBLE 80:14
which thou canst not t. HERB 247:1
tamed: themselves in one year t.
MARV 332:11
tameless: t., and swift, and proud
SHEL 502:13
tameness: trusts in the t. of a wolf
SHAK 454:28
Taming: T. my wild heart to thy SHAK 472:22
Tam Lin: what I ken this night, T. BALL 32:3
Tandy: I met wid Napper T. ANON 6:6
tangere: Noli me t. BAG 28:20
Noli me t. BIBLE 83:24
tangled: cold Christ and t. Trinities
KIPL 302:2
Hearts after them t. in amorous nets
MILT 350:2
lie t. in her hair LOV 318:15
tangles: t. of Neaera's hair MILT 343:8
Tank: T. come down the stalls SASS 414:12
tankards: mouths were made for t.
MAS 333:21
Tantae: T. molis erat Romanam condere
VIRG 557:10
Tantum: T. ergo sacramentum THOM 546:17
T. religio potuit suadere LUCR 320:4
taper: Out went the t. as she KEATS 289:15
t. to the outward room DONNE 189:30
with t. light SHAK 452:25
tapers: she lit her glimmering t. THOM 548:15
tapestry: wrong side of a Turkey t.
HOW 266:20
tapped: They t. Victor on the shoulder
AUDEN 21:7
tapping: suddenly there came a t. POE 375:4
tapsalteerie: May a' gae t. BURNS 114:2
Tara: harp that once through T.'s
MOORE 356:9
when T. rose so high LAND 308:23
taratantara: tuba terribili sonitu t.
ENN 208:21
Tar-baby: T. ain't sayin' nuthin'
HARR 242:19
tar-barrel: black as a t. CARR 134:33
tard: dit et l'on vient trop t. LA B 306:11
Trois heures, c'est toujours trop t.
SART 414:9
tarde: cinco en punto de la t. GARC 221:5
tare: That t. each other in their TENN 536:30
tares: amongst the weeds and t. BROW 96:18
clasping t. cling round COWP 168:26
corn is but a field of t. TICH 551:2
enemy came and sowed t. BIBLE 66:18
t. to which we are all ELIOT 205:15
tarn: dark t. dry DE L 174:15
tarnished: is neither t. nor afraid
CHAN 139:22
Tarquin: T.'s ravishing strides SHAK 460:1
That the great house of T. MAC 322:11
tarried: too long we have t. LEAR 312:12
tarrieth: remembrance of a guest that
t. BIBLE 62:18
tarry: do not t. CAMP 129:1
t. the wheels of his chariots BIBLE 49:12
will that he t. till I come BIBLE 73:19
You may for ever t. HERR 250:6
tarry'd: job too long he t. SWIFT 528:9
tarrying: make no long t. PRAY 392:3

nor t. here SHAK 463:7
Tarshish: ye ships of T. BIBLE 58:17
Tarsus: man which am a Jew of T.
BIBLE 74:20
Tart: T., cathartic virtue EMER 207:22
Tartar: T.'s lips SHAK 462:4
task: all her t. to be sweet WATS 565:11
All with weary t. fordone SHAK 471:21
here is a t. for all that STEV 521:4
long day's t. is done SHAK 423:9
My t. accomplished HENL 245:9
that's the t. VIRG 558:18
There is but one t. for all KIPL 299:7
thy worldly t. hast done SHAK 428:22
vanity, sets love a t. HUNT 268:8
what he reads as a t. will JOHN 274:31
tasks: Among the t. of real life WORD 577:3
tassel-gentle: To lure this t. back again
SHAK 482:19
taste: authority on t. TAC 531:11
bad t. of the smoker ELIOT 200:20
common sense and good t. SHAW 496:12
dainty Bacchus gross in t. SHAK 457:8
difference of t. in jokes ELIOT 200:21
forgot the t. of fears SHAK 463:5
Ghastly Good T. BETJ 44:15
good sense and good t. LA B 306:15
last t. of sweets SHAK 478:18
let me t. the whole BROW 104:1
must himself create the t. WORD 583:11
never t. who always drink PRIOR 401:11
no t. when you married me SHER 506:27
on my tongue the t. HOUS 266:6
shall t. my *Anno Domini* FARQ 209:22
supper was to my t. STER 519:10
t. a little honey with BIBLE 50:3
t. and see PRAY 391:21
T. does not come by chance REYN 405:22
t. for marriages and public executions
DISR 186:25
t. My meat HERB 248:1
t. not BIBLE 78:24
t. not the Pierian spring POPE 378:13
T. not when the wine-cup SCOTT 418:5
T. your legs SHAK 489:20
Things sweet to t. prove SHAK 478:14
undoubtedly wanted t. WALP 562:6
us a t. of your quality SHAK 432:22
wild vicissitudes of t. JOHN 282:26
worse t., than in a churchyard JOW 285:23
tasted: had t. her sweet body SHAK 475:25
it can't be t. in a sip DICK 180:30
Some books are to be t. BACON 27:19
t. that the Lord is gracious BIBLE 80:22
t. the sweets and the bitters BYRON 124:38
tastes: So he that t. woman GAY 222:30
Their t. may not be SHAW 497:34
Tasting: T. of Flora and the country
KEATS 291:18
Tat: Die T. ist alles GOET 230:5
stolzer Männer der T. HEINE 244:12
tattered: t. coat upon a stick YEATS 586:12
tatters: fond of my rags and t. MOL 353:11
'You left us in t. HARDY 240:19
tattle: have an entertaining t. CHES 145:25
taught: having been t. anything MOL 353:23
heeds what we have t. her GAY 222:12
He t. us little ARN 13:16
In them is plainest t. MILT 350:11
right to be t. by the enemy OVID 366:16
t. Art to fold her hands ROSS 410:1
taught as if you t. them not POPE 378:29
t. them as one having authority BIBLE 65:13
t. to think that moderation BURKE 110:9
There t. us how to live TICK 551:3
You t. me first to beg SHAK 468:12
You t. me language SHAK 484:29
taughte: afterward he t. CHAU 142:1
taunting: not t. BACON 26:25

tavern: creaking couplets in a t.
BYRON 124:14
days in a t. drinking ANON 10:14
heard a Voice within the T. FITZ 212:6
not my hostess of the t. SHAK 438:2
produced as by a good t. or inn JOHN 276:35
'So is the London T.' ANON 4:13
t. chair was the throne JOHN 280:20
that vulgar and t. music BROW 97:1
tavernes: He knew the t. well CHAU 141:20
taverns: t. while the tempest hurled
HOUS 264:21
tawdry: t. cheapness Shall outlast
POUND 383:7
tawny: From t. body and sweet SWIN 530:13
tax: hateful t. levied upon JOHN 281:12
T. not the royal Saint WORD 582:16
t. not you, you elements SHAK 454:5
To t. and to please BURKE 109:9
Taxation: T. and representation CAMD 128:4
T. without representation OTIS 365:25
taxed: schoolboy whips his t. top
SMITH 511:38
world should be t. BIBLE 69:8
taxes: All t. must GIBB 224:26
'...as t. is DICK 177:11
except death and t. FRAN 218:18
people overlaid with t. BACON 27:26
T. upon every article which SMITH 511:37
taxing: less of a t. machine LOWE 318:24
Tay: T. Bridge of the Silv'ry T. MCG 325:6
Te: T. Deum laudamus ANON 11:3
tea: best sweeteners of t. FIEL 211:18
her t. without a stratagem YOUNG 587:18
if this is t. PUNCH 403:5
Make me some fresh t. AUDEN 19:14
slavery of the t. and coffee COBB 154:7
some sipping t. WORD 580:2
sometimes t. POPE 381:2
'Take some more t. CARR 134:3
T., although an Oriental CHES 147:27
t. and cakes and ices ELIOT 203:22
t. and comfortable advice KEATS 294:5
there honey still for t. BROO 94:25
to their t. and scandal CONG 159:21
To want my cup of t. PAIN 367:19
was nothing on it but t. CARR 133:28
we'll all have t. DICK 175:26
Why does the t. generally THAC 545:9
with t. solaces the midnight JOHN 281:28
teach: apt to t. BIBLE 79:12
Even while they t. SEN 420:10
I will t. you my townspeople WILL 574:12
Let such t. others who POPE 378:10
She can t. ye how to climb MILT 341:22
Still pleas'd to t. POPE 378:32
suffering what they t. in song SHEL 501:13
t. an old horse SPEN 516:16
t. Bloody instructions SHAK 459:5
t. eternal wisdom how POPE 379:14
T. him how to live PORT 381:33
t. him how to tell my story SHAK 474:1
t. him to think for himself SHEL 499:1
t. his senators wisdom PRAY 397:4
T. me, my God and King HERB 247:1
T. me thy way PRAY 391:8
T. me to feel another's POPE 381:13
T. me to live KEN 295:9
t. thee in the way wherein PRAY 391:18
T. the free man how AUDEN 19:3
t. the torches to burn SHAK 482:2
t. the unforgetful to forget ROSS 410:4
T. us to care and not ELIOT 202:1
t. you to drink deep ere SHAK 430:3
Those that do t. young babes SHAK 476:22
To t. the young idea how THOM 549:10
what you t. them first JOHN 275:6
years t. much which EMER 207:19
teacher: doctrine for the t.'s sake
DEFOE 173:3

solemn t. — SHAK 485:20
t. lie — WORD 581:14
t. of his Gods — MAC 322:15
thy t. are like a piece — BIBLE 56:26
tous les t. de la terre — DID 184:7
Tempora: T. mutantur — ANON 11:5
t., O mores — CIC 151:26
temporal: pass through things t. — PRAY 386:16
temporary: of force alone is but *t.* — BURKE 109:19
tempt: not t. the Lord thy God — DAY-L 172:22
T. me no more — SHAK 483:27
T. not a desperate man — FORD 216:12
T. not the stars — MILT 346:16
t. with wand'ring feet — BELL 39:24
to t. my Lady Poltagrue — OVID 366:23
temptabam: quod t. dicere versus
temptation: combines the maximum of
t. — SHAW 497:39
I never resist t. — SHAW 496:5
insist on their resisting t. — KNOX 305:26
last t. — ELIOT 204:4
lead us not into t. — BIBLE 64:24
man that endureth t. — BIBLE 80:8
of t. is just to yield — GRAH 233:8
of t. in the wilderness — PRAY 396:4
oughtn't to yield to t. — HOPE 255:27
out of the power of t. — TROL 553:11
over-fond of resisting t. — BECK 36:21
resist everything except t. — WILDE 573:8
t. to a rich and lazy nation — KIPL 298:18
that ye enter not into t. — BIBLE 68:16
to t. slow — SHAK 494:15
under t. to it — LOCKE 315:17
Why comes t. but for man — BROW 104:30
temptations: carry us through all t.
PRAY 386:8
in spite of all t. — GILB 228:10
shun the t. of monopoly — SCOTT 415:15
t. both in wine and women — KITC 305:14
tempted: tempter or the t. — SHAK 464:5
'Tis one thing to be t. — SHAK 463:16
When your fathers t. me — PRAY 396:4
Which other men are t. — BUTL 118:5
tempter: t. or the tempted — SHAK 464:5
tempts: Not all that t. your wand'ring
GRAY 235:8
tempus: fugit inreparabile t. — VIRG 560:17
T. abire tibi est — HOR 259:6
T. edax rerum — OVID 366:18
ten: Church clock at t. to three — BROO 94:25
good Lord has only t. — CLEM 152:30
T. Days that Shook — REED 405:8
t. thousands in our streets — PRAY 399:13
tenacem: Iustum et t. propositi — HOR 260:18
tenant: She's the t. of the room — HENL 245:6
tenantless: graves stood t. — SHAK 429:12
tend: t. the wounded under fire — KIPL 299:18
Tendebantque: T. manus ripae ulterioris
VIRG 558:22
tended: however watched and t. — LONG 317:6
tender: beautiful, the t., the kind — MILL 339:23
coy and t. to offend — HERB 248:14
Gave thee such a t. voice — BLAKE 87:26
heart has felt the t. passion — GAY 223:3
t. for another's pain — GRAY 235:3
t. is the night — KEATS 291:20
t. mercies of the wicked — BIBLE 53:34
that are t. and unpleasing — BACON 25:41
true and t. is the North — TENN 542:5
tenderly: Take her up t. — HOOD 254:9
tenderness: Thanks to its t. — WORD 579:14
Want of t. is want of parts — JOHN 275:33
ténébreux: Je suis le t. — NERV 360:26
tenebricosum: Qui nunc it per iter t.
CAT 136:23
tenement: Into a clayey t. — CAREW 130:17
Like to a t. or pelting — SHAK 478:20
tenir: Doit se t. tout seul — ANON 9:12

son el tenir y el no t. — CERV 138:17
tennis-balls: are merely the stars' t.
WEBS 566:29
T., my liege — SHAK 443:10
Tennyson: Lawn T. — JOYCE 286:24
T. and Browning — BAG 29:20
T. goes without saying — BUTL 118:35
T. was not Tennysonian — JAMES 271:25
tenor: They kept the noiseless t. — GRAY 235:1
tent: Hosts' did pitch His t. — HERB 246:25
Upon that little t. of blue — WILDE 572:8
woof of my t.'s thin roof — SHEL 500:6
tenth: talked shop like a t. muse — ANON 5:17
This Submerged T. — BOOTH 89:22
ten thousand: t. times More rich
SHAK 467:13
Tents: done with the T. of Shem — KIPL 300:23
dwelling in t. — BIBLE 46:13
habitation among the t. of Kedar — PRAY 398:7
in the t. of ungodliness — PRAY 395:13
man to dwell in their t. — PRAY 394:13
murmured in their t. — PRAY 397:5
Shall fold their t. — LONG 316:10
stately t. of war — MARL 330:2
t. of Kedar — BIBLE 56:16
To your t. — BIBLE 51:4
Where Israel's t. do shine — BLAKE 86:24
with thy tribe's black t. — THOM 547:23
tepores: ver egelidos refert t. — CAT 137:2
Ter: T. sunt conati imponere — VIRG 560:12
Terence: T. this is stupid — HOUS 264:11
teres: t., atque rotundus — HOR 262:10
Tereu: Tereu, T. — BARN 33:32
Terewth: It is the light of T. — DICK 176:16
term: sleep between term and t. — SHAK 426:13
t., holidays — LEWIS 314:9
was a lad I served a t. — GILB 228:4
Termagant: whipped for o'erdoing T.
SHAK 433:16
terminations: were as terrible as her t.
SHAK 472:8
termini: t. which bound the common
EMER 207:14
terminological: risk of t. inexactitude
CHUR 149:25
terms: hard to come to t. with Him
MOL 353:26
himself in t. too deep for *me* — GILB 227:21
it with the happiest t. — SHAK 440:28
Many t. which have now — HOR 257:14
T. like grace, new birth — ARN 16:18
t. of moderation takes — BACON 25:12
till I come on perfect t. — WHIT 571:2
terra: t. pax hominibus bonae — MASS 334:18
Terrace: Hall or T. or lofty Tower
LEAR 312:3
t. blackish-brown — BETJ 43:18
t. walk — SWIFT 527:28
terrarum: Ille t. mihi praeter omnis
HOR 260:8
terre: nous resterons sur la t. — PREV 400:15
tous les temples de la t. — DID 184:7
terrible: All strange and t. events
SHAK 423:12
being just the t. choice — BROW 104:31
Dark and t. beyond any — MAC 324:22
I the elder and more t. — SHAK 449:19
It would *not* be t. — JOHN 275:14
lend the eye a t. aspect — SHAK 443:21
my name were not so t. — SHAK 441:15
of his eyes became so t. — BECK 36:19
t. as an army with banners — BIBLE 57:5
t. as hell — MILT 346:24
t. as her terminations — SHAK 472:8
t. beauty is born — YEATS 585:1
t. future may have just — AUDEN 18:19
t. in the simplicity — CONR 161:21
which is t. — FIEL 211:5
Which make thee t. and dear — SHEL 505:2
terrified: ill and t. and tight — BETJ 44:13

t. vague fingers — YEATS 586:1
territorial: last t. claim which I have
HITL 251:12
Territories: no slave T. — CHASE 141:2
terror: added a new t. to death — WETH 569:6
added another t. to death — LYND 321:17
afraid for any t. by night — PRAY 395:21
are not a t. to good works — BIBLE 75:21
For t., not to use — SHAK 463:11
Have struck more t. — SHAK 481:16
make thee a t. to thyself — BIBLE 60:26
perch and not their t. — SHAK 463:15
So full of dismal t. was — SHAK 480:26
T. is the feeling which — JOYCE 286:17
T. like a frost shall halt — AUDEN 19:11
T. of darkness — CHAP 140:7
t. of my name — MARL 330:11
T. the human form divine — BLAKE 88:9
There is no t. — SHAK 451:20
Thy t., O Christ — HOPK 257:6
terrorist: t. and the policeman both
CONR 161:20
terrors: t. of the earth — SHAK 454:2
though t. reign — GOLD 231:30
Tertium: his Wife and a T. Quid — KIPL 305:10
test: is the best t. of truth — CHES 145:33
testa: ...pia t. — HOR 261:5
testament: ministers of the new t. — BIBLE 77:4
New T. was less a Christiad — HARDY 241:24
purple t. of bleeding — SHAK 479:13
testicles: of a tragedy requires t. — VOLT 561:22
testify: they are which t. of me — BIBLE 72:3
testimonies: t., O Lord, are very sure
PRAY 396:1
testimony: t. of the Lord is sure — PRAY 390:12
tether: t. time or tide — BURNS 115:8
tied the world in a t. — SWIN 530:23
Tetigisti: T. acu — PLAU 374:15
tetigit: scribendi genus non t. — JOHN 277:13
Teucer: T. shall lead and his star — HOR 259:16
Teviotdale: Ettrick and T. — SCOTT 418:24
text: approve it with a t. — SHAK 467:10
ev'ry t. and gloss over — BUTL 117:18
God takes a t. — HERB 247:12
great t. in Galatians — BROW 105:7
square of t. that looks — TENN 535:12
To your t. — ELIZ 205:24
where a neat rivulet of t. — SHER 506:26
Thackeray: T. settled like a meat-fly
RUSK 411:6
thame: Lat t. say — KEITH 295:7
Thames: brooks are T.'s tributaries — ARN 15:8
flights upon the banks of T. — JONS 284:25
of Gennesareth, but T. — THOM 548:25
On banks of T. they must — HOUS 263:21
shall I see the T. again — BETJ 42:18
stripling T. at Bab-lock-hithe — ARN 14:14
Sweet T., run softly — SPEN 516:3
T. bordered by its gardens — MORR 358:10
T. flowed backward to its — PLOM 374:19
T. is between me — WALP 562:22
T. is liquid history — BURNS 112:3
T. was the noblest river — ADD 2:9
'Till T. see Eaton's sons — POPE 375:21
With no allaying T. — LOV 318:16
youthful T. — ARN 15:3
Thammuz: T. came next behind — MILT 345:17
Thane: T. of Cawdor lives — SHAK 458:17
T. of Fife had a wife — SHAK 462:21
thank: I t. the goodness — TAYL 531:23
Now t. you all your God — RINK 406:6
say t. you 'most to death — TWAIN 554:17
t. heaven, fasting — SHAK 426:11
T. me no thankings — SHAK 483:17
t. thee, Jew — SHAK 468:9
We t. with brief thanksgiving — SWIN 529:25
thank'd: When I'm not t. at all — FIEL 211:35
thanked: 't. God my wife was dead
BROW 106:1

thankful: pleasant thing it is to be t.
PRAY 399:19
thankfulness: name in pride and t.
BROW 101:22
thankit: Sae let the Lord be t.
BURNS 114:14
thankless: To have a t. child
SHAK 453:19
Upon a t. arrant
RAL 404:10
thanks: angels yield eternal t.
SMART 509:2
Catullus gives you warmest t.
CAT 137:3
deserves the love and t.
PAINE 368:1
give t. unto thee
PRAY 387:23
give t. unto the Lord
PRAY 399:2
harp will I give t. unto
PRAY 392:11
How to return your t. would
BROW 106:1
I am poor even in t.
SHAK 432:14
I will give t. unto thee
PRAY 399:6
Letters of t.
AUDEN 20:2
song of t. and praise
WORD 579:10
Take the t. of a boy
BEEC 37:9
T. for mercies past receive
BUCK 106:17
t. to God always for you
BIBLE 78:30
T. to the human heart
WORD 579:14
to give t. is good
SWIN 529:1
wanting to deserve any t.
CAT 137:8
when he had given t.
PRAY 388:1
thanksgiving: before his presence with
t.
PRAY 396:3
may shew the voice of t.
PRAY 391:5
With proud t.
BINY 84:9
Tharshish: years came the navy of T.
BIBLE 50:34
Tharsis: T. and of the isles shall
PRAY 394:20
that: I've t. within
GARR 221:14
Take t., you hound
DOYLE 192:18
thatch: house with deep t.
BELL 40:11
worn the ancient t.
TENN 539:23
thatch-eaves: vines that round the t.
KEATS 293:5
thaw'd: That will be t. from
SHAK 449:24
Thawing: T. cold fear
SHAK 444:11
Theatre: Aunt was off to the T.
BELL 39:10
in a t.
SHAK 480:10
jusqu'à la fin le t. rempli
BOIL 89:11
problems of the modern t.
RATT 405:1
t. is irresistible
ARN 16:15
t. of man's life it is
BACON 24:24
T.'s certainly not what
ELIOT 203:7
theatres: t., and temples lie
WORD 581:14
Thebes: Riddles of death T.
SHEL 501:1
thee: queer save t. and me
OWEN 366:29
theek: t. our nest when it grows
BALL 32:8
theft: clever t. was praiseworthy
SPEN 514:33
kindness and forgave the t.
BROW 104:25
Property is t.
PROU 401:19
suspicious head of t. is stopp'd
SHAK 457:8
would be t. in other poets
DRYD 198:3
thegither: had been fou for weeks t.
BURNS 115:5
them: not of t.
BYRON 120:39
theme: Fools are my t.
BYRON 124:15
t. For reason
DONNE 188:5
t. too great
PRIOR 400:22
themselves: should t. be free
BROO 94:4
T. they could not save
HOUS 262:13
Therein behold t.
SHAK 427:20
These...are a law unto t.
BIBLE 74:35
violent hands upon t.
PRAY 389:10
'women are a sex by t.
BEER 37:24
theologians: if you believe the t.
SAL 413:18
t. have employed
ARN 16:18
théologie: toutes les écoles de t.
DID 184:7
theology: golden rule in t.
MILT 351:26
objected to his t.
SMIL 509:5
Theophilus: thee...most excellent T.
BIBLE 69:3
T., of all that Jesus
BIBLE 73:20
theorems: About binomial t. I'm teeming
GILB 228:17
Theorie: ist alle T.
GOET 230:3
theories: kinds of old defunct t.
IBSEN 269:21

theorize: capital mistake to t. before
DOYLE 192:7
theory: All t.
GOET 230:3
there: because he was not t.
BARH 33:21
Because it is t.
MALL 327:13
cry over me, T., there
PRAY 394:15
heaven, thou art t.
PRAY 399:5
if I had not been t.
WELL 567:19
I shall not be t.
SWIN 530:26
T. go the ships
PRAY 397:1
t. vor me the apple tree
BARN 33:28
thereby: t. hangs a tail
SHAK 475:12
therein: all that t. is
PRAY 390:23
thereof: place t. shall know it
PRAY 396:17
thereout: t. suck they no small advantage
PRAY 394:22
thereto: t. I give thee my troth
PRAY 389:4
Thermodynamics: describe the Second
Law of T.
SNOW 512:16
Thermopylae: There was an old man
of T.
LEAR 313:3
To make a new T.
BYRON 123:2
Thersites: T.' body is as good
SHAK 428:21
thesis: doctor's t. On education
AUDEN 21:4
thews: t. that lie and cumber
HOUS 262:15
They: every one else is T.
KIPL 304:2
thick: dash'd through t. and thin
DRYD 194:21
shall stand so t. with corn
PRAY 394:3
t. and numberless
MILT 341:24
thickens: now the plot t. very much
BUCH 106:14
thicker: finger shall be t. than my father's
BIBLE 51:2
When the loo paper gets t.
MITF 352:25
thicket: ram caught in a t.
BIBLE 46:11
thief: embrace the impenitent t.
STEV 521:12
first cries out stop t.
CONG 160:8
he was a t.
HEINE 244:10
I come as a t.
BIBLE 82:20
if you do take a t.
SHAK 472:31
man's apparel fits your t.
SHAK 464:24
Opportunity makes a t.
BACON 28:2
steals something from the t.
SHAK 474:3
subtle t. of youth
MILT 351:6
t. doth fear each bush
SHAK 446:23
t. said the last kind word
BROW 104:25
this first grand t.
MILT 347:18
thought as bad as the t.
CHES 145:9
which is the t.
SHAK 455:18
thievery: Crams his rich t. up
SHAK 487:12
thieves: boldest t., be Yank
KIPL 302:12
fell among t.
BIBLE 69:30
'Gainst knaves and t. men
SHAK 490:27
have made it a den of t.
BIBLE 67:17
t. break through and steal
BIBLE 64:25
t., the nine figures
DICK 178:6
Thou best of t.
DRYD 195:17
thievish: Time's t. progress
SHAK 494:10
thigh: bee with honied t.
MILT 342:8
his vesture and on his t.
BIBLE 82:26
Jacob's t. was out of joint
BIBLE 46:23
smote them hip and t.
BIBLE 49:23
thighs: glory from her loosening t.
YEATS 586:1
thimbles: They sought it with t.
CARR 133:8
thin: Imprisoned in every fat man a t.
CONN 161:15
into t. air
SHAK 485:20
it's 'T. red line of 'eroes'
KIPL 303:24
like it out of a t. glass
PINT 373:18
t. man inside every fat
ORW 365:11
t. red line
RUSS 412:23
t., yet never clear
POPE 375:20
witty, profligate, and t.
YOUNG 588:14
Thine: Be T. the glory
DRYD 196:13
continue t. for ever
PRAY 388:22
not my will, but t.
BIBLE 71:8
only call me t.
COL 157:5
t. is the kingdom
BIBLE 64:24
Why not I with t.
SHEL 502:1

thing: do only one t.
SMIL 509:6
firm persuasion that a t.
BLAKE 88:26
has this t. appear'd again
SHAK 429:8
man is not quite the t.
AUST 22:14
most unattractive old t.
GILB 227:14
nearest run t.
WELL 567:19
one damned t.
OMAL 365:5
play's the t.
SHAK 433:6
reward of a t. well done
EMER 207:26
said the t. which was not
SWIFT 526:9
t. ensky'd and sainted
SHAK 463:12
t. of beauty is a joy
KEATS 288:20
t. that ends all other
SHAK 423:20
t. they most do show
SHAK 494:15
t. wherein we feel there
SHEL 504:20
thrusts the t. we have prayed
BROW 97:28
very t. he'll set you
BLAKE 87:6
we will shew you a t.
BIBLE 50:2
When every blessed t. you
GILB 225:30
things: all t. to all men
BIBLE 76:7
all ye Green T. upon
PRAY 384:24
black and merciless t.
JAMES 271:23
bright t. come to confusion
SHAK 469:23
cognizance of men and t.
BROW 101:11
done but earnest of the t.
TENN 538:24
excellent t. are spoken
PRAY 395:4
God's sons are t.
MADD 326:19
How can these t. be
BIBLE 71:37
little t. are infinitely
DOYLE 191:18
love all beauteous t.
BRID 92:10
much for t. beyond our care
DRYD 197:10
Of t. to come at large
SHAK 486:27
sorry Scheme of T.
FITZ 213:16
such t. to be
TENN 537:2
there are tears shed for t.
VIRG 557:17
These t. shall be
SYM 531:3
T. are in the saddle
EMER 206:21
t. are not what they seem
LONG 317:1
T. are seldom what they
GILB 228:8
t. are the sons of heaven
JOHN 281:6
T. fall apart
YEATS 586:15
t. in boards that moderns
LAMB 307:38
T. in books' clothing
LAMB 307:12
t. that are not
SHAK 452:2
t. that go bump
ANON 5:8
t. they have in common
BLUN 89:2
t. through Christ which
BIBLE 78:23
t. unknown propos'd
POPE 378:29
think of t. that would
GILB 226:8
think: above all that we ask or t.
BIBLE 77:26
because I have time to t.
DARW 172:3
because I t. him so
SHAK 490:30
because they t. they can
VIRG 558:16
Books t. for me
LAMB 307:16
comedy to those that t.
WALP 563:11
commonly attains to t. right
JOHN 281:37
don't t. foolishly
JOHN 279:11
expect a soldier to t.
SHAW 496:18
Haply I t. on thee
SHAK 493:6
How can I know what I t.
WALL 562:5
'I am inclined to t.
DOYLE 192:36
I can't t. why
GILB 228:26
if the while I t. on thee
SHAK 493:7
If you can t.
KIPL 299:22
infancy to t. all men virtuous
BURKE 108:20
I t. continually of those
SPEN 515:7
I t.
DESC 175:10
It is later than you t.
SERV 420:12
never to t. of one's self
CLOU 153:21
qualified my mind to t. justly
REYN 405:21
She could not t.
COWP 168:18
She that could t. and ne'er
SHAK 474:18
so we've got to t.
RUTH 412:24
swear thou t.'st I love
DONNE 190:14
swiss cheese would t.
MARQ 330:25
t. by fits and starts
HOUS 264:23
t. for two minutes together
SMITH 511:35
t. is to be full of sorrow
KEATS 291:19
T. no more
HOUS 264:6
T. not of them
KEATS 293:7

T. of 'is pension an'   KIPL 302:20
t. of one's absent love   TROL 553:9
t. of things that would   GILB 226:8
T. of your forefathers   ADAMS 1:8
T. only what concerns thee   MILT 349:4
t. on these things   BIBLE 78:22
t. perhaps even less   BROW 99:7
t. too little and who talk   DRYD 194:12
t. what is true and do   HUXL 269:8
t. what you like   TAC 531:12
t. ye have eternal life   BIBLE 72:3
those who greatly t.   POPE 376:7
to t. as wise men do   ASCH 17:4
to t. like other people   SHEL 499:1
We t. so because other   SIDG 507:10
We t. so then   LEAR 312:15
when I t., I must speak   SHAK 426:9
who never t.   PRIOR 401:11

thinker: great God lets loose a t.
   EMER 207:13

thinkers: not always the justest t.
   HAZL 243:24

thinking: All t. for themselves is GILB 226:10
baby fell a-t.   HARDY 241:1
gentleman's way of t.   ANON 10:14
he is a t. reed   PASC 369:11
It ain't t. about it   TROL 552:23
much drinking, little t.   SWIFT 526:18
passive, recording, not t.   ISH 270:28
pipe a simple song for t.   WORD 577:22
Plain living and high t.   WORD 582:9
shall halt the flood of t.   AUDEN 19:11
She's been t. of the old 'un   DICK 176:30
T. is to me the greatest   VANB 555:5
t. Lays lads underground   HOUS 264:6
t. makes it so   SHAK 432:12
T. of his own Gods   ARN 13:8
thought of t. for myself   GILB 228:6
us in the dignity of t.   JOHN 281:24
well as an art of t.   DISR 187:9
With too much t. to have   POPE 377:21

thinks: he t. no ill   SHAK 493:18
He t. too much   SHAK 448:20
t. less   FARQ 209:25
whene'er she t. at all   CHUR 148:22
Whether he t. too little   POPE 379:12

thinner: keep on growing t.   LEAR 312:24
thicker and the writing paper t.   MITF 352:25

third: stood there with never a t. BROW 99:21
t. among the sons of light   SHEL 499:5
t. day he rose again from   PRAY 384:26
t. in your bosom   SHAK 482:21
t. who walks always beside   ELIOT 205:8
twenty t. day of *Octob*   USSH 554:29

third-class: t. seat sat the journeying
   HARDY 240:9

thirst: an' a man can raise a t. KIPL 301:8
hunger, t., forced marches   GAR 221:10
I t.   BIBLE 73:3
neither t. any more   BIBLE 82:3
t. that from the soul doth   JONS 284:12
which do hunger and t.   BIBLE 64:6
without the provocation of t. SWIFT 526:10

thirsteth: every one that t.   BIBLE 59:25
My soul t. for thee   PRAY 393:21

thirsty: if he be t.   BIBLE 54:29
t. and ye gave me drink   BIBLE 68:6
t. they gave me vinegar   PRAY 394:12
waters to a t. soul   BIBLE 54:30

thirteen: Years he number'd scarce t.
   JONS 284:2

thirtieth: was my t. year to heaven
   THOM 547:6

thirty: At t. a man suspects himself
   YOUNG 588:5
I am past t.   ARN 16:24
T. days hath September   ANON 8:6
t. pieces of silver   BIBLE 68:9
t., the wit   FRAN 218:10

thirty-one: Days and nights hast t.
   SHAK 462:2
This: T. happy breed   SHAK 478:20
t. young man expresses   GILB 227:21
Thistle: T. across my way   BLAKE 86:14
thistledown: on the green as a t. ball
   HARDY 238:22
thistles: figs of t.   BIBLE 65:9
There t. stretch their   COWP 168:26
thither: t. the tribes go up   PRAY 398:11
thoghte: he t. another   CHAU 142:15
Thomas: ta'en true T. up behind BALL 32:4
T., because thou hast   BIBLE 73:12
thorn: figs grew upon t.   CHES 146:22
give to be rid of one t.   HOR 259:6
Have I no harvest but a t.   HERB 247:14
he left the t. wi' me   BURNS 116:8
her breast against a t.   HOOD 255:2
her breast up-till a t.   BARN 33:32
Oak, and Ash, and T.   KIPL 303:25
rose without the t.   HERR 250:13
t. shall come up the fir   BIBLE 59:28
to me a t. in the flesh   BIBLE 77:13
we kissed beside the t.   BRID 92:20
without t. the rose   MILT 347:20
thorns: crackling of t. under a pot
   BIBLE 55:18
fall upon the t. of life   SHEL 502:13
labour this crown of t.   BRYAN 106:8
men gather grapes of t.   BIBLE 65:9
No t. go as deep as a rose's SWIN 529:10
rove the brakes and t.   COWP 165:12
some fell among t.   BIBLE 66:16
t. shall come up in her   BIBLE 58:31
t. that in her bosom lodge   SHAK 431:13
thorough: t. an Englishman as ever
   KING 297:9
thoroughfare: to let the mind be a t.
   KEATS 294:26
thou: God, t., and I do know   SHAK 478:12
T. art over all   KIPL 303:9
T. heardst me truer than   HOPK 257:6
T. shalt have no other   BIBLE 47:24
thought: a-down the deeps of t. COL 155:3
all the magnanimity of t.   YOUNG 588:5
An' what 'e t. 'e might   KIPL 304:4
attention and t. about Tom Thumb
   JOHN 278:12
best that is known and t.   ARN 16:1
called the garment of t.   CARL 132:15
constitution of their modes of t. MILL 338:22
device for avoiding t.   HELPS 244:16
dost tease us out of t.   KEATS 291:10
evolution of his t.   ARN 16:11
father, Harry, to that t.   SHAK 442:19
green t. in a green shade   MARV 332:5
happened to hit on the same t. SHER 505:28
have often t. upon death   BACON 27:40
heart could have t. you   THOM 548:29
heart that thought the t.   BALL 31:4
he has never t. upon   JOHN 275:26
her body t.   DONNE 189:31
In the light of t.   SHEL 504:19
is wrought by want of t.   HOOD 254:20
I thought he t. I slept   PATM 370:3
I t. so once   GAY 223:22
knowledge of that you are t.   BACON 26:5
Language is the dress of t.   JOHN 281:31
leapt out to wed with T.   TENN 536:14
lived with no other t.   POE 374:21
loftiness of t. surpass'd   DRYD 196:30
Many things I t. of then   HOUS 265:4
never t. of thinking   GILB 228:6
not seem a moment's t.   YEATS 584:9
of inextinguishable t.   SHEL 505:10
of the t. of his name   ELIOT 204:6
one that was never t.   BIBLE 62:31
One t. more steady than   FORD 216:20
passion-winged Ministers of t.   SHEL 499:7
Perish the t.   CIBB 151:14

pleasures of t. surpass eating   CLOU 153:21
reach on with thy t.   ROSS 409:26
results of t. and resolution   TROL 553:11
Roman t. hath struck him   SHAK 421:15
schools of t. contend   MAO 328:18
sessions of sweet silent t.   SHAK 493:7
souls with but a single t.   HALM 238:10
speech created t.   SHEL 503:8
splendour of a sudden t.   BROW 100:9
Style is the dress of t.   WESL 568:25
sulphurous and t.-executing   SHAK 454:4
That ever t. the travel   ROYD 411:3
that harbours virtuous t.   SPEN 516:4
therefore no t. for the morrow   BIBLE 64:32
These pearls of t. in Persian   LOW 319:10
t. and felt all the time   EMER 207:35
t. can add one cubit unto   BIBLE 64:29
t. cannot wisely be said   PEAC 370:19
T. is free   SHAK 485:15
t. is irksome and three   HOUS 266:12
T. is the child of Action   DISR 186:41
t. of thee   MEYN 338:13
t. on the woman who loved   KING 297:2
T. shall be the harder   ANON 8:9
t.'s the slave of life   SHAK 440:23
t. that love could never   BRID 92:20
t. which saddens while   BROW 103:13
T. would destroy their   GRAY 235:13
through strange seas of T.   WORD 580:17
To believe your own t.   EMER 207:34
to rear the tender t.   THOM 549:10
unmeaning thing they call a t.   POPE 378:21
use t. only to justify   VOLT 561:4
utmost bound of human t.   TENN 544:1
utterance gave that t. relief   WORD 579:1
want of t.   DRYD 195:34
we t. so still   LEAR 312:15
We tire the night in t.   QUAR 403:10
what he t.   HEM 245:2
What oft was t.   POPE 378:17
white, celestial t.   VAUG 555:14
white flowers of thy t.   SWIN 529:28
without a t. of Heaven or Hell   BROW 96:23
with the pale cast of t.   SHAK 433:8
words are images of t.   KEATS 292:20
working-house of t.   SHAK 445:6

thoughtful: purest and most t. minds
   RUSK 411:24

thoughts: all his t. will perish   BALF 30:3
begin to have bloody t.   SHAK 485:19
Cleanse the t. of our hearts   PRAY 387:7
Even so my bloody t.   SHAK 476:1
evil t. which may assault   PRAY 386:9
examine my t.   PRAY 399:8
familiar to my slaughterous t.   SHAK 463:5
generate misleading t.   SPEN 514:31
Give thy t. no tongue   SHAK 430:19
give way to such gloomy t.   AUST 23:17
Good t. his only friends   CAMP 129:19
Gor'd mine own t.   SHAK 495:3
ground with cheerful t.   SHAK 483:23
man's own t.   WEBS 567:12
my sad t. doth clear   VAUG 555:18
not make t. your aim   KIPL 299:22
Of t. which were not their   BYRON 120:39
pansies, that's for t.   SHAK 436:10
replete with t. of other men   COWP 167:23
second and sober t.   HENRY 245:3
So some strange t. transcend   VAUG 555:21
Stal'd are my t.   GREV 236:17
Suspicions amongst t. are   BACON 27:23
that covers all human t.   CERV 138:20
that did them silly t.   MILT 344:8
Then feed on t.   MILT 347:2
thoroughfare for all t.   KEATS 294:26
thoughts are not your t.   BIBLE 59:27
t. are legible in the eye   ROYD 411:2
t. by England given   BROO 94:30
t. in my brain inhearse   SHAK 494:11
T. of heroes were as good   MER 337:22

t. of men are widen'd with | TENN 539:2
t. of youth are long | LONG 316:22
t. that wander through | MILT 346:10
t. that arise in me | TENN 532:17
T. that do often lie too | WORD 579:14
thy t. in me | TENN 542:14
to censor one's own t. | WALEY 562:2
To understand God's t. | NIGH 363:16
United t. and counsels | MILT 345:1
Where branched t. | KEATS 292:3
With t. beyond the reaches | SHAK 430:24
Words without t. never | SHAK 434:31
writers expressed t. | FRAN 217:27
thousand: cattle upon a t. hills | PRAY 393:2
death; a t. doors | SEN 420:11
Death has a t. doors | MASS 336:1
is better than a t. | PRAY 395:13
man picked out of ten t. | SHAK 432:5
night has a t. eyes | BOUR 90:21
One man among a t. have | BIBLE 55:23
t. Blossoms with the Day | FITZ 212:8
t. shall fall beside | PRAY 395:21
t. times more fair | SHAK 467:13
t. years in thy sight | PRAY 395:18
'Would he had blotted a t. | JONS 285:1
thousands: forth t. and ten thousands | PRAY 399:13
Saul hath slain his t. | BIBLE 50:13
showing mercy unto t. | BIBLE 47:24
t. of gold and silver | PRAY 398:5
Where t. equally were meant | SWIFT 527:24
Thousandth: T. Man will stand by you | KIPL 303:18
Thracian: T. ships and the foreign | SWIN 528:15
thral: been constreyned as a t. | CHAU 142:12
thraldom: single t. | BACON 28:17
thrall: Hath thee in t. | KEATS 290:21
thread: can do with a twined t. | BURT 116:33
Feels at each t. | POPE 379:9
Hinders needle and t. | HOOD 255:10
line of scarlet t. | BIBLE 48:37
t. of his verbosity finer | SHAK 457:10
t. of my own hand's weaving | KEATS 292:10
weave their t. with bones | SHAK 489:3
with a silk t. plucks it | SHAK 482:20
threaded: Time breaks the t. dances | AUDEN 18:10
threat: Whiles I t. he lives | SHAK 460:1
threaten: t., promise | WHIT 571:11
threaten'd: reader's t. | POPE 378:21
t., a lion | CHAP 140:3
threatened: t. its life with a railway-share | CARR 133:8
threatenings: Breathing out t. and slaughter | BIBLE 73:32
threats: in your t. | SHAK 451:20
three: Every man at t. years old | LEON 313:25
married life t. is company | WILDE 572:28
rather than hold t. words' | SHAK 472:9
shook t. summers' pride | SHAK 494:18
There are t. kinds of lies | DISR 187:7
thought is irksome and t. minutes | HOUS 266:12
t. corners of the world | SHAK 453:1
t. gentlemen at once | SHER 506:19
T. hours a day will produce | TROL 552:13
T. in One | KIPL 302:2
T. jolly gentlemen | DE L 174:6
t. kings into the east | BURNS 114:13
T. little maids from school | GILB 226:27
t. lone weirs | ARN 15:3
T. may keep a secret | FRAN 218:9
t. merry boys are we | FLET 215:9
T. o'clock is always too | SART 414:9
t. ravens sat on a tree | BALL 32:7
t. things which the public | HOOD 255:15
t. unspeakably precious | TWAIN 554:7
two t. are gathered | PRAY 385:8
whole is divided into t. | CAES 126:26

woodspurge has a cup of t. | ROSS 410:9
three-and-thirty: I have dragg'd to t. | BYRON 126:15
Three Castles: better brand than the T. | THAC 545:30
threefold: t. cord is not quickly | BIBLE 55:15
three-fourths: Conduct is t. of our life | ARN 16:21
three hundred: handsome in t. pounds | SHAK 469:11
three o'clock: always t. in the morning | FITZ 213:22
t. in the morning courage | THOR 550:18
three per cents: elegant simplicity of the t. | STOW 524:2
sweet simplicity of the t. | DISR 186:8
threescore: age are t. years | PRAY 395:19
Now of my t. years | HOUS 262:14
thresh: t. his old jacket till | COWP 168:1
t. of the deep-sea rain | KIPL 300:23
threshold: Across my t. | PATM 370:2
goest over the t. thereof | FULL 220:13
stand upon the t. of the new | WALL 562:9
starry t. of Jove's Court | MILT 340:22
sweep across the blue t. | ROST 410:12
threw: She t. me in front | BETJ 42:22
stars t. down their spears | BLAKE 87:16
thrice: thou shalt deny me t. | BIBLE 68:12
t. he slew the slain | DRYD 195:2
T. is he arm'd that hath | SHAK 446:6
T. was I beaten with rods | BIBLE 77:12
Weave a circle round him t. | COL 157:1
thrid: Cold currents t. | HARDY 239:4
thrift: bargains, and my well-won t. | SHAK 465:29
t., Horatio | SHAK 430:4
thrive: Bold knaves t. without | DRYD 195:38
He that would t. | CLAR 152:24
throat: Amen' Stuck in my t. | SHAK 460:7
down the t. of Old Time | DICK 178:4
expression and an undulating t. | BELL 40:2
gives me the lie i' the t. | SHAK 433:3
if your t. 'tis hard | KING 297:19
knife has slit The t. | HOUS 264:9
phrases stick in the t. | RUSS 412:22
procession marching down your t. | OSUL 365:24
rather felt you round my t. | HOPE 256:4
thy t. is shut and dried | KIPL 303:8
times her little t. around | BROW 103:29
To cut his t. before he | SWIFT 528:9
to feel the fog in my t. | BROW 103:31
unlocked her silent t. | GIBB 225:1
your sweet dividing t. | CAREW 130:19
throats: My sore t. are always worse | AUST 23:9
throb: only t. she gives | MOORE 356:10
throbs: with no t. of fiery pain | JOHN 279:1
throne: everyone before the t. | CEL 138:6
fell before the t. on their | BIBLE 81:32
Gehenna or up to the T. | KIPL 304:11
High on a t. of royal state | MILT 346:6
himself a t. of bayonets | INGE 270:9
honour'd for his burning t. | SHAK 465:4
I saw a great white t. | BIBLE 82:28
it is God's t. | BIBLE 64:15
light which beats upon a t. | TENN 533:30
Lord sitting upon a t. | BIBLE 57:28
rainbow round about the t. | BIBLE 81:22
something behind the t. | PITT 373:24
stood before the t. | BIBLE 81:31
that sitteth upon the t. | BIBLE 81:30
This royal t. of kings | SHAK 478:20
t. he sits | SHAK 444:25
t. of Denmark to thy father | SHAK 429:20
t. of human felicity | JOHN 280:20
t. of the heavenly grace | PRAY 384:10
T. sent word to a Throne | KIPL 301:20
t. was like the fiery flame | BIBLE 61:8
t. we honour is the *people's* | SHER 506:7

Wrong forever on the t. | LOW 319:13
throned: t. on her hundred isles | BYRON 121:2
thrones: his stirrups like the t. | CHES 147:3
Not t. and crowns | ELL 206:12
throng: Leaving the tumultuous t. | WORD 577:26
thronum: *Coget omnes ante t.* | CEL 138:6
throstle: t. with his note so true | SHAK 470:18
throstlecock: ousel and the t. | DRAY 193:19
throte: faireste hewed on hir t. | CHAU 142:32
through: he is t. your body | REYN 405:20
let them go t. | PRAY 395:5
who has gone t. it | VIRG 559:10
wind that blows t. me | LAWR 311:9
throughly: Wash me t. from my wickedness | PRAY 393:4
throw: body I would t. it out of the window | BECK 36:17
I t. myself down in my | DONNE 191:1
me to dig him up and t. | SHAW 496:23
t. away the worser part | SHAK 435:17
t. away the dearest thing | SHAK 458:22
thrown: then t. out | JOHN 280:3
t. on her with a pitchfork | SWIFT 526:29
t. upon this filthy modern | YEATS 587:2
throws: rolls and t. and breakfalls | REED 405:7
t. himself on God | BROW 100:38
thrush: aged t. | HARDY 239:7
Hangs a T. that sings loud | WORD 581:3
rarely pipes the mounted t. | TENN 537:9
That's the wise t. | BROW 101:6
t. and the jay | SHAK 491:17
thrust: guardsman's cut and t. | HUXL 269:3
t. my hand into his side | BIBLE 73:10
thrusting: by a divine t. | SHAK 453:11
Thucydides: be a T. at Boston | WALP 563:9
historical works of T. | COBD 154:11
Thug: T. and the Druse | CHES 146:27
Thule: *Ultima T.* | VIRG 560:10
thumb: Do you bite your t. | SHAK 481:22
t. each other's books out | RUSK 411:19
thumbs: By the pricking of my t. | SHAK 462:5
Leastways if you reckon two t. | LEAR 311:21
Thummin: judgment the Urim and the T. | BIBLE 48:1
thumping: such a t. crook | BETJ 43:4
thunder: dawn comes up like t. outer | KIPL 301:5
Glorious the t.'s roar | SMART 509:4
Had *felt* him like the t.'s | ARN 13:16
Harsh t. | MILT 347:3
Here falling houses t. | JOHN 282:22
He was as rattling t. | SHAK 423:22
laugh as I pass in t. | SHEL 500:4
lightning shaft and power to t. | MAN 328:11
such sweet t. | SHAK 471:7
surge and t. of the Odyssey | LANG 309:18
that God made the t. | MAC 323:32
they steal my t. | DENN 174:25
t. of the captains | BIBLE 53:7
t. of the trumpets | SWIN 530:19
voice of a great t. | BIBLE 82:15
what serve for the t. | SHAK 477:16
thunderbolt: harmless t. | PLINY 374:16
heaped-up mountains with a t. | VIRG 560:12
like a t. he falls | TENN 533:7
thunderbolts: Vaunt-curiers to oak-cleaving t. | SHAK 454:4
thunders: t. from her native oak | CAMP 129:13
t. in the index | SHAK 435:5
t. of white silence | BROW 98:4
thunder-stone: Nor the all-dreaded t. | SHAK 428:22
thunder-storm: peoples plunging thro' the t. | TENN 538:24
Thus: T. have I had thee | SHAK 494:13
T., or words to that | JOYCE 286:28
'T. thou must do | SHAK 459:1
To be t. is nothing | SHAK 461:8
thusness: is the reason of this t. | WARD 564:33

thwarted: signify A t. purposing
HARDY 241:8

Thybrim: *T. multo spumantem sanguine*
VIRG 558:17

Thy-doxy: My-doxy and Heterodoxy or T.
CARL 131:25

thyme: sweet t. true
FLET 215:21
the wild t. blows
SHAK 470:10
t. and the gadding vine
MILT 343:6

thyself: 'And thou t. to all eternity
ROSS 410:3
Be so true to t. as thou
BACON 27:35
thou art beside t.
BIBLE 74:25
T. thou gav'st
SHAK 494:13

Tiber: drop of allaying T.
SHAK 427:14
Tiber! father T.
MAC 322:21
T. foaming with much blood
VIRG 558:17
troubl'd T. chafing with
SHAK 448:14

Tiberim: *Syrus in T. defluxit Orontes*
JUV 287:15

Tiberius: So T. might have sat
ARN 14:4

Ticket: In his hat a Railway-T.
LEAR 312:5
t. at Victoria Station
BEVIN 44:18

tickle: if you t. us
SHAK 467:4
I'll t. your catastrophe
SHAK 441:19
t. her with a hoe and she
JERR 273:7

tickled: t. with a straw
POPE 379:18
trouts are t. best in muddy
BUTL 118:20

tickles: He t. this age that can
ANON 5:18

tickling: must be caught with t.
SHAK 489:10
T. a parson's nose as a'
SHAK 481:28
t. Commodity
SHAK 452:14

tidal: turn to rhythmic t. lyres
HARDY 239:4

tiddle-taddle: no t. nor pibble-pabble
SHAK 444:18

tide: am drifting with the t.
BALL 31:3
call of the running t.
MAS 334:5
came the t.
SPEN 515:20
'except when the t.'s
DICK 177:17
going out with the t.
DICK 177:17
high t.!' King Alfred
CHES 146:20
Not this t.
KIPL 301:15
perhaps under the whelming t.
MILT 343:16
since written what no t.
LAND 309:4
tether time or t.
BURNS 115:8
t. crept up along the sand
KING 297:1
t. in the affairs of women
BYRON 123:20
t. in the affairs of men
SHAK 451:27
t. is ready her to honour
BEST 42:2
upon this filthy modern t.
YEATS 587:2
veer in the t.
SWIN 530:28

tides: salt t. seaward flow
ARN 13:5
t. of men into my hands
LAWR 311:12

tidings: him that bringeth good t.
BIBLE 59:18
let ill t. tell Themselves
SHAK 422:12
you good t. of great joy
BIBLE 69:10

tie: not fit to t. his brogues
SCOTT 419:1
silken t.
SCOTT 416:20
that love endures no t.
DRYD 197:7
T. up my sleeves with ribbons
HUNT 268:15

tied: t. and bound by the chain
PRAY 385:23
t. to the soil as another
HOMER 254:6

Tiere: *der Mensch fand die T.*
NIET 363:3

Tierra: *desnuda es recordar la T.*
GARC 221:4

ties: only the string that t.
MONT 355:6

tiger: atomic bomb is a paper t.
MAO 328:20
Came Christ the t.
ELIOT 203:4
imitate the action of the t.
SHAK 443:21
master o' the T.
SHAK 458:6
orang-outang or the T.
BURKE 110:24
rhinoceros or the Hyrcan t.
SHAK 461:21
shark And the t.
AUDEN 20:15
side of the German t. with
CHUR 150:7
that with his t.'s heart
GREE 236:12
t.'s heart wrapp'd
SHAK 446:16
t. sniffs the rose
SASS 415:1
t. that hadn't *got* a Christian
PUNCH 402:24
T. well repay the trouble
BELL 38:31

tiger-moth: are the t.'s deep-damask'd
KEATS 289:16

tigers: tamed and shabby t.
HODG 252:2
t. are getting hungry
CHUR 151:3
t. of wrath are wiser than
BLAKE 88:22

tiger-skin: On a t.
ANON 8:23

tight: his shoes were far too t.
LEAR 312:5
ill and terrified and t.
BETJ 44:13
long black hair out t.
ELIOT 205:9
wearing arm-chairs t.
WOD 575:25

tights: she played it in t.
BEER 37:20

tigress: with swiftness of the t.
OWEN 367:11

tike: Or bobtail t., or trundle-tail
SHAK 455:1

tikleth: t. me aboute myn herte
CHAU 143:19

Till: Says Tweed to T.
ANON 7:12

tills: Man comes and t. the field
TENN 543:11

Tillyvally: T., lady
SHAK 488:18

tilt: mammets and to t. with lips
SHAK 438:31

tilth: his full t. and husbandry
SHAK 463:13

timber: beaten by a piece of t.
FRY 219:22
crooked t. of humanity
KANT 288:14
Like season'd t.
HERB 248:17
navy nothing but rotten t.
BURKE 110:5

Timbuctoo: On the plains of T.
WILB 572:3

time: abbreviation of t.
GIBB 224:20
aching t.
KEATS 290:4
All of the olden t.
ANON 6:10
All of the olden t.
AYT 24:11
all t. of our tribulation
PRAY 385:17
annihilate but space and t.
POPE 380:22
antique t. would lie unswept
SHAK 427:17
appeareth for a little t.
BIBLE 80:16
backward and abysm of t.
SHAK 484:24
bank and shoal of t.
SHAK 459:5
been a t. for such a word
SHAK 463:6
been so long t. with you
BIBLE 72:33
be more than biting T.
ELIOT 204:3
besmear'd with sluttish t.
SHAK 493:17
bid t. return
SHAK 479:6
but for all t.
JONS 284:23
choose time is to save t.
BACON 26:7
chronicle of wasted t.
SHAK 494:19
city 'half as old as T.
BURG 108:4
conscious is not to be in t.
ELIOT 202:16
conversing I forget all t.
MILT 348:3
cormorant devouring T.
SHAK 456:14
down the throat of Old T.
DICK 178:4
drew from the womb of t.
HEINE 244:12
entertain conjecture of a t.
SHAK 444:9
envious and calumniating t.
SHAK 487:6
envious T.
MILT 344:17
escaped the shipwreck of t.
BACON 24:18
Even such is T.
RAL 404:15
events in the womb of t.
SHAK 474:11
Fate, T., Occasion
SHEL 503:10
first t. of asking
PRAY 388:23
Fleet the t. carelessly
SHAK 424:20
Footprints on the sands of t.
LONG 317:4
foremost files of t.
TENN 539:7
For T., not Corydon
ARN 15:7
Give peace in our t.
PRAY 385:1
God, who as at this t.
PRAY 386:14
grand Instructor, T.
BURKE 112:1
Grown old before my t.
ROSS 409:7
Have no enemy but t.
YEATS 585:12
have not the t. to meet you
KIPL 298:18
he loved the t. too well
CLARE 152:4
him in the t. of trouble
PRAY 392:4
How goes the t.
TENN 544:9
How soon hath T.
MILT 351:6
How T. is slipping underneath
FITZ 212:22
If the street were t.
ELIOT 202:2
in a t. out-worn
YEATS 585:14
in a t. when thou mayest
PRAY 391:17
inseparable propriety of t.
BACON 25:5
irretrievable t. is flying
VIRG 560:17
it also marks the t.
SHER 505:25
It was the t. of roses
HOOD 254:8
Keeping t.
POE 375:1
let not T. deceive you
AUDEN 18:10

lines to t. thou grow'st
SHAK 492:28
long result of T.
TENN 538:16
long t. ago
FORD 216:19
look into the seeds of t.
SHAK 458:11
Look like the t.
SHAK 459:3
Love's not T.'s fool
SHAK 495:5
me more than t. and space
LAMB 307:26
Men talk of killing t.
BOUC 90:18
my t. has been properly spent
TAYL 531:21
Never the t. and the place
BROW 102:24
night of t. far surpasseth
BROW 97:20
nobility is the act of t.
BACON 26:39
No t. like the present
MANL 328:12
no t. to read play-bills
BURN 112:22
now doth t. waste me
SHAK 480:15
Now is the accepted t.
BIBLE 77:7
Now it is high t. to awake
BIBLE 75:24
Of t.'s eternal motion
FORD 216:20
old common arbitrator, T.
SHAK 487:15
Old T. is still a-flying
HERR 250:5
old T. makes these decay
CAREW 130:12
Old T. the clock-setter
SHAK 452:18
one born out of due t.
BIBLE 76:19
only t. for grief
HOOD 255:9
our bourne of T. and Place
TENN 533:4
O world! O life! O t.
SHEL 501:14
panting T. toil'd after
JOHN 282:25
Perfection is the child of T.
HALL 238:7
precious t. at all to spend
SHAK 493:18
Procrastination is the thief of t.
YOUNG 588:4
ravages of t. not injure
HOR 260:26
Redeeming the t.
BIBLE 78:4
relish of the saltness of t.
SHAK 441:5
remember'd for a very long t.
MCG 325:6
seventy-seven it is t.
JOHN 281:23
shook hands with t.
FORD 216:16
silent touches of t.
BURKE 111:36
spake in t. past
BIBLE 79:28
spare t. and in his working
GILL 229:11
Speech is of T.
CARL 132:23
speech is shallow as T.
CARL 131:13
spirit of the t. shall
SHAK 452:26
stretch'd forefinger of all T.
TENN 541:30
superfluous to demand the t.
SHAK 437:34
superior to t. and place
JOHN 282:7
syllable of recorded t.
SHAK 463:6
temple half as old as T.
ROG 407:9
tether t. or tide
BURNS 115:8
that t. is money
FRAN 218:3
That t. may cease
MARL 329:11
That t. of year thou mayst
SHAK 494:7
thee t.'s furrows I behold
SHAK 493:1
Then do not squander t.
FRAN 218:11
Then while t. serves
HERR 248:26
There's a good t. coming
MACK 325:9
those feet in ancient t.
BLAKE 86:16
three minutes is a T.
HOUS 266:12
through time t. is conquered
ELIOT 202:16
Thus the whirligig of t.
SHAK 490:25
T., a maniac scattering
TENN 536:21
T. and Fate of all their
FITZ 212:17
T. and fevers burn away
AUDEN 19:17
t. and nonsense scorning
BUCK 106:18
T. and the hour runs through
SHAK 458:21
t. and times are done
YEATS 586:21
T. an endless song
YEATS 585:19
T. did beckon to the flow'rs
HERB 247:24
T. doth transfix the flourish
SHAK 493:20
T. for a little something
MILNE 340:15
t. has come
CARR 135:7
'T. has too much credit
COMP 159:12
T. hath, my lord, a wallet
SHAK 487:3
T. held me green and dying
THOM 547:2
T. hovers o'er
JOHN 283:1
T. in hours
VAUG 555:22
t. is all I lacked
DOUG 191:8
t. is come round
SHAK 452:1
T. is fleeting
LONG 317:2
T. is like a fashionable
SHAK 487:5
T. is on our side
GLAD 229:12

T. is our tedious song	MILT 344:15	*timendum:* nobis nil esse in morte t.		Titian: much at heart about T.	RUSK 412:1
t. is out of joint	SHAK 431:26		LUCR 320:9	title: farced t. running 'fore	SHAK 444:25
t. is setting with me	BURNS 114:30	*timeo:* t. Danaos et dona	VIRG 558:1	feel his t. Hang loose	SHAK 462:27
t. is the greatest innovator	BACON 26:28	times: brisk and giddy-paced t.	SHAK 488:26	like my t.	STEV 523:6
T. is the great physician	DISR 186:11	discern the signs of the t.	BIBLE 66:32	t., and possession	PRAY 400:12
T. makes ancient good uncouth	LOW 319:14	It was the best of t.	DICK 183:5	To guard a t. that was	SHAK 452:25
T. may restore us in his	ARN 13:18	my dear t.' waste	SHAK 493:7	Who gain'd no t.	POPE 378:6
t. now with a robber's	SHAK 487:12	My t. be in Thy hand	BROW 104:13	titles: All thy other t. thou hast	SHAK 453:16
t. of the singing of birds	BIBLE 56:22	nature of the t. deceas'd	SHAK 442:3	have t. manifold	WORD 582:3
T. present and time past	ELIOT 202:12	old t.	GOLD 232:19	T. are shadows	DEFOE 173:16
t. remembered is grief	SWIN 528:17	Our t. are in His hand	BROW 104:2	t. of veneration to those	BURKE 111:9
t. requireth	WHIT 571:22	praiser of the t. that	HOR 257:21	titwillow: t., titwillow	GILB 227:15
T.'s eunuch	HOPK 257:3	Praise they that will t. past	HERR 249:17	*Tityre:* T., tu patulae recubans	VIRG 559:11
T.'s fell hand defac'd	SHAK 494:2	revolution of the t.	SHAK 442:1	toad: Give me your arm, old t.	LARK 310:7
t.'s flies	SHAK 486:8	T. are changed with him	STEV 521:32	I had rather be a t.	SHAK 475:21
T.'s glory is to calm	SHAK 492:19	t. begin to wax old	BIBLE 62:7	intelligent Mr T.	GRAH 233:19
T. shall moult away his	SUCK 524:14	T. change	ANON 11:5	pour rose-water over a t.	JERR 273:9
T. shall not lose our passages	DONNE 188:9	*T.* contains more useful	COBD 154:11	should I let the t. *work*	LARK 310:6
T. shall throw a dart	BROW 97:25	T. go by turns	SOUT 514:20	Squat like a t.	MILT 348:10
T.'s noblest offspring	BERK 41:20	t. has made many ministries	BAG 28:24	t. beneath the harrow knows	KIPL 302:1
T.'s printless torrent	SHEL 500:15	t.! Oh, the manners	CIC 151:26	T., that under cold stone	SHAK 462:2
T. stays	DOBS 187:13	t. that try men's souls	PAINE 368:1	t., ugly and venomous	SHAK 424:32
T.'s thievish progress	SHAK 494:10	*timet:* Peiusque leto flagitium t.	HOR 261:19	tree t. is a chef-d'oeuvre	WHIT 570:21
T.'s wheel runs back	BROW 104:10	timing: lucky t. of your death	TAC 531:9	toads: 'imaginary gardens with real t.	
T.'s wingèd chariot hurrying	MARV 332:19	*Timor:* T. mortis conturbat me	DUNB 199:8		MOORE 355:20
T. that is intolerant	AUDEN 19:7	tin: I place a t. wreath upon	POUND 383:9	toast: Let the t. pass	SHER 506:31
t., that takes survey	SHAK 440:23	tine: Lest my jewel it should t.	BURNS 113:1	never had a piece of t.	PAYN 370:9
T., the avenger	BYRON 121:14	tinge: t. with a browner shade	GIBB 224:20	refus'd to pledge my t.	PRIOR 401:10
T. the devourer of everything	OVID 366:18	tingle: that heareth it shall t.	BIBLE 49:37	standing t. that pleased	DIBD 175:20
T. the reaper	THOM 548:28	tingling: whoreson t.	SHAK 441:6	Toasted-cheese: enemies 'T.'	CARR 133:4
T. the refreshing river	AUDEN 20:15	tinkle: grasped it for a t.	BEER 37:14	tobacco: after that tawney weed t.	
t. to audit The accounts	MACN 326:6	tinkling: talk but a t. cymbal	BACON 26:15		JONS 283:17
t. to be born	BIBLE 55:12	t. cymbal	BIBLE 76:14	am going to leave off t.	LAMB 307:28
t. to begin a new	DRYD 197:19	tinklings. t. lull the distant folds	GRAY 234:18	cigarette t.	DOYLE 191:16
t. to every purpose under	BIBLE 55:12	tins: fish gaped among empty t.	PLOM 374:19	damned t.	BURT 116:29
t. to make it shorter	PASC 369:14	tinsel: vainly flapt its t. wing	MARV 331:18	For thy sake, T.	LAMB 308:5
T., to make me grieve	HARDY 240:2	tip: that of a school-boy's t.	THAC 545:11	He who lives without t.	MOL 353:9
t. to murder and create	ELIOT 203:11	t. them to Long Melford	BORR 90:11	superexcellent t.	BURT 116:29
t. to think before I speak	DARW 172:3	t. up bason and a hose	ASHF 17:8	sweeter t. comes from Virginia	THAC 545:30
T. travels in divers paces	SHAK 426:13	Within the nether t.	COL 155:18	taking their roguish t.	JONS 284:5
T. was away and somewhere	MACN 326:11	tipple: that t. in the deep	LOV 318:17	Whether it divine t. were	SPEN 516:15
T. was out of joint	STR 524:4	tippled: Have ye t. drink more fine		tobacker: t., and sleep	DICK 177:9
T. watches from the shadow	AUDEN 18:10		KEATS 290:28	tocsin: t. of the soul	BYRON 123:17
T. we may comprehend	BROW 96:10	tippling: His terrible taste for t.	GILB 225:20	*Tod: auf den T. eines Gefühls*	NIET 363:13
T., which antiquates antiquities	BROW 97:12	tipsy: never gets t. at all	LEAR 311:22	TO-DAY: about them if T. be sweet	
t., which is the author	BACON 24:15	Tip-tilted: T. like the petal	TENN 534:7		FITZ 212:22
t. will come when you will	DISR 184:10	tiptoe: on t. for a flight	KEATS 290:14	Be wise t.	YOUNG 588:3
t. will come	DISR 185:31	t. on the misty mountain	SHAK 483:14	fine day: t.	MALL 327:10
t. will doubt of Rome	BYRON 123:13	Will stand a t. when this	SHAK 445:3	I have lived t.	DRYD 198:15
T. will have his fancy	AUDEN 18:10	Tir'd: T. with all these	SHAK 494:5	live t.	MART 331:8
T. will have meanly run	HOR 259:20	tired: can wait and not be t.	KIPL 299:22	pick t.'s fruits	HOR 259:20
T. will run back	MILT 344:11	He was so t.	ROLFE 407:17	rose the wrong way t.	BEHN 38:20
t. with a gift of tears	SWIN 528:20	hunt down a t. metaphor	BYRON 124:2	such a day to-morrow as t.	SHAK 491:7
t. without injuring eternity	THOR 550:3	I'm t. of Love	BELL 39:18	T. if ye will hear his	PRAY 396:4
T. writes no wrinkle	BYRON 121:25	long process of getting t.	BUTL 118:25	t. I suffer	LESS 313:26
T., you old gypsy man	HODG 252:9	one grows t. of the world	WALP 563:2	t. which the world may	COLL 158:12
t. you were off	HOR 259:6	Thou art t.	ARN 13:14	we are here t.	BEHN 38:13
'tis but the t.	SHAK 450:3	t. her head	BIBLE 51:34	toe: printless t.	BROO 94:21
to sing of T. or Eternity	TENN 533:12	T. of his dark dominion	MER 337:5	t. of the peasant comes	SHAK 436:29
uncertain balance of proud t.	GREE 236:9	t. the sun with talking	CORY 163:4	to t. that line	THOR 550:9
unconscionable t. dying	CHAR 140:30	t. with labour of far travel	CAT 136:28	toes: happier without their t.	LEAR 312:21
unthinking t.	DRYD 197:17	When a man is t. of London	JOHN 277:17	his t. if his nose is warm	LEAR 312:18
use your t.	HERR 250:6	who can ever be t. of Bath	AUST 23:3	Pobble who has no t.	LEAR 312:17
waste of t. and effort	VEBL 556:2	woman who always was t.	ANON 5:13	tread in the bus on my t.	AUDEN 21:2
Wears out his t.	SHAK 473:13	your t., your poor	LAZ 311:13	*togae: Cedant arma t.*	CIC 151:22
weary of t.	BLAKE 87:22	*tirent: pour ceux qui t. le mieux*	VOLT 561:18	together: all that believed were t.	BIBLE 73:24
We have short t. to stay	HERR 249:28	tires: effort nor the failure t.	EMPS 208:17	Are we here t. alone	WHIT 570:13
We take no note of T.	YOUNG 588:2	He t. betimes that spurs	SHAK 478:19	comfortably so long t.	GAY 222:13
What's not destroy'd by T.'s	BRAM 91:23	Tiresias: I T.	ELIOT 205:1	Father and the Son t. is	PRAY 387:11
When t. is broke	SHAK 480:14	T. have foresuffered all	ELIOT 205:2	Let us remain t. still	SHEL 500:17
When T. shall turn those	DRAY 193:12	tiresome: styles are good save the t.		makes them cling t.	WORD 580:11
which are the births of t.	BACON 26:27		VOLT 561:7	never again so much t.	MACN 326:12
which are the rags of t.	DONNE 190:12	tiresomeness: t. of old age	ANON 10:13	Our lives would grow t.	SWIN 530:21
whips and scorns of t.	SHAK 433:8	*Tirez: en disant 'T. le rideau*	RAB 404:1	sufficient to keep them t.	JOHN 276:2
whole length of t. which	BEDE 37:1	Tirra lirra: 'T.	TENN 538:10	Swing, swing t.	CORY 163:2
With leaden foot t. creeps	JAGO 271:1	Titan: like thy glory, T.	SHEL 503:15	they rise or sink T.	TENN 542:18
with the productions of t.	BLAKE 88:17	T.-woman like a lover	SWIN 528:26	t. for the sake of strife	CHUR 149:14
yet t. hath his revolution	CREWE 169:18	Tite: T. tute Tati tibi tanta	ENN 208:20	toil: are the horny hands of t.	LOW 319:9
timebo: quem t.	BIBLE 83:5	tithe: t. of mint and anise	BIBLE 67:24	day in t.	QUAR 403:10
timely: t. utterance gave that	WORD 579:1	t. or toll in our dominions	SHAK 452:17	Death and T.	VIRG 558:21

double t. and trouble — SHAK 462:2
forget his labour an' his t. — BURNS 113:5
Horny-handed sons of t. — KEAR 288:18
In her strong t. of grace — SHAK 424:17
Our love and t. — KIPL 298:10
Remark each anxious t. — JOHN 282:28
slumber is more sweet than t. — TENN 539:17
smeared with t. — HOPK 256:12
some men t. after virtue — LAMB 308:12
they t. not — BIBLE 64:30
T., envy — JOHN 282:29
t. in other men's extremes — KYD 306:4
year with t. of breath — COL 156:17
toil'd: Souls that have t. — TENN 544:3
toiled: we have t. all the night — BIBLE 69:18
toiling: tears and t. breath — ROSS 408:20
Were t. upward in the night — LONG 316:19
toils: alone is worth all these t. — CAT 136:28
token: t. of a covenant between — BIBLE 45:40
tokens: wish there were t. to tell — HOUS 263:7
Words are the t. current — BACON 24:22
Tolbooth-gate: passive resistance of the
T. — SCOTT 418:19
told: grief too much to be t. — VIRG 557:20
I t. my wrath — BLAKE 87:21
'I t. you so — BYRON 124:6
I t. you so — LONG 317:16
Ought to be t. to come — FROST 219:11
our fathers have t. us — PRAY 392:13
They t. me you had been — CARR 134:22
they t. me you were dead — CORY 163:4
t. so as to be understood — BLAKE 88:25
t. you from the beginning — BIBLE 59:9
what we formerly were t. — BLUN 89:3
who bade me fight had t. — EWER 209:12
tolerable: Life would be t. — LEWIS 314:10
t. and not to be endured — SHAK 472:30
tolerate: longer t. the race which has
— BALF 30:3
tolerates: that He t. their existence
— BUTL 118:21
toleration: thus t. produced not only
— GIBB 224:21
toll: tithe or t. in our dominions — SHAK 452:17
To t. me back from thee — KEATS 291:23
Tolle: T. lege — AUG 21:15
tollis: t. peccata mundi — MASS 335:7
tolls: It t. for *thee* — DONNE 190:20
Tom: Poor T.'s a-cold — SHAK 454:25
so no more of T. — BYRON 124:8
T. will make them weep — SHAK 455:1
Tomata: Chops and T. sauce — DICK 182:19
tomb: blossom on the t. — COWP 168:5
buried in the silent t. — WORD 582:15
dozen of Claret on my T. — KEATS 294:22
fair Fidele's grassy t. — COLL 158:16
fourfold t. — BASSE 35:1
gilded t. of a mediocre — SMITH 510:20
heart keeps empty in thy t. — KING 296:11
icy silence of the t. — KEATS 290:30
In her t. by the side — POE 374:23
in the t. of the Capulets — BURKE 108:6
sea was made his t. — BARN 34:5
smell like what it is—a t. — SHEL 501:18
This side the t. — DAV 172:15
T. hideth trouble — POUND 383:19
t. the womb wherein they — SHAK 494:11
totter towards the t. — SAY 415:7
Tombs: ceremonious, like T. — DICK 183:13
from the t. a doleful sound — WATTS 565:28
register'd upon our brazen t. — SHAK 456:14
Some hang above the t. — COL 155:4
through the t. of all regions — CEL 138:6
towers and t. and statues — FLEC 214:6
tombstone: t. white with the name
— KIPL 301:18
tombstones: t. show — HOUS 262:15
Tom Cobbleigh: Old Uncle T. and all
— BALL 32:12
Tommy: it's T. this — KIPL 303:22

Tomnoddy: My Lord T. is thirty-four
— BROU 95:3
tomorrow: about t. there's no knowing
— MED 336:9
Boast not thyself of t. — BIBLE 54:36
gone t. — BEHN 38:13
late t. to be brave — ARMS 12:17
nor t. shall not drive — DONNE 190:26
question what t. may bring — HOR 259:18
such a day t. as to-day — SHAK 491:7
T., and to-morrow — SHAK 463:6
T. do thy worst — DRYD 198:15
T. for the young — AUDEN 20:16
t. I die — LESS 313:26
T. I may be — FITZ 212:16
t. is another day — MITC 352:21
t.'s life's too late — MART 331:8
t.'s uprising to deeds — MORR 358:12
T. we'll be back — HOR 259:17
t. we shall die — BIBLE 58:15
Unborn T. — FITZ 212:22
you can put off till t. — PUNCH 402:13
Tom Pearse: T., lend me your grey
— BALL 32:12
Tom Thumb: attention and thought about
T. — JOHN 282:15
tom-tit: by a river a little t. — GILB 227:15
tonandi: Jovi fulmen viresque t. — MAN 328:11
tone: deep, autumnal t. — SHEL 502:13
in that t. of voice — PUNCH 402:34
Robert Emmet and Wolfe T. — YEATS 586:19
t. of the company that — CHES 145:16
t. of the solid and practical — BURKE 108:16
tones: Sweet t. are remembered — SHEL 501:21
t. as dry and level — AUDEN 20:10
tonge: Englissh sweete upon his t.
— CHAU 141:22
in writyng of oure t. — CHAU 144:17
Kepe wel they t. — CHAU 142:26
mysmetre for defaute of t. — CHAU 144:17
tongs: have the t. and the bones — SHAK 471:3
tongue: administered in the vulgar t.
— PRAY 388:8
bridleth not his t. — BIBLE 80:11
fellows of infinite t. — SHAK 445:13
God's sake hold your t. — DONNE 188:4
Had t. at will and yet — SHAK 474:18
have fallen by the t. — BIBLE 63:11
her t. unbound — CONG 160:2
him whose strenuous t. — KEATS 291:15
his t. as a sweet morsel — HENRY 245:19
his t. Dropt manna — MILT 346:9
his t. is the clapper — SHAK 472:23
his t. to conceive — SHAK 471:10
ignorant of their Mother T. — DRYD 198:14
I held my t. — PRAY 391:30
I mean the t. — WEBS 566:18
I must hold my t. — SHAK 430:1
in a t. not understanded — PRAY 400:8
instead my t. freezes into — SAPP 414:6
is become his mother t. — GOLD 232:15
Keep thy t. from evil — PRAY 391:23
Licked its t. into — ELIOT 203:18
Love's t. is in the eyes — FLET 215:33
men of less truth than t. — SHAK 492:27
my t. from evil-speaking — PRAY 388:17
My t. is the pen — PRAY 392:14
My t. swore — EUR 209:4
nor t. to speak here — LENT 313:23
obnoxious to each carping t. — BRAD 91:13
of a slow t. — BIBLE 47:9
on my t. the taste — HOUS 266:6
our t. with joy — PRAY 398:16
parching t. — KEATS 291:7
senates hang upon thy t. — THOM 549:16
sharp t. is the only edged — IRV 270:21
she had a t. with a tang — SHAK 485:10
Sing, my t. — VEN 556:4
stopp'd his tuneful t. — POPE 377:6
such a t. — SHAK 453:6

their t. a sharp sword — PRAY 393:15
t. can no man tame — BIBLE 80:14
t. cleave to the roof — PRAY 399:3
t. has its desire — AUDEN 20:22
t. In every wound of Caesar — SHAK 451:3
t. like a button-stick — KIPL 298:7
t. of midnight hath told — SHAK 471:20
t. of the dumb sing — BIBLE 58:34
t. our trumpeter — SHAK 427:11
t. proves dainty Bacchus — SHAK 457:8
t. to persuade — CLAR 152:19
T.; well that's a wery — DICK 181:33
t., which is the birth — SHAK 442:15
treasure of our t. — DAN 170:23
'tween my heart and t. — SHAK 449:22
understanding, but no t. — SHAK 430:14
use of my oracular t. — SHER 506:14
vibrates her eternal t. — YOUNG 587:16
while I held my t. — PRAY 391:16
with the valour of my t. — SHAK 459:1
would that my t. could utter — TENN 532:17
Your hand, your t. — SHAK 459:3
your t.'s sweet air — SHAK 469:21
tongueless: t. vigil and all the pain
— SWIN 528:15
tongues: base sale of chapmen's t.
— SHAK 456:20
bestowed that time in the t. — SHAK 487:26
cloven t. like as of fire — BIBLE 73:22
Finds t. in trees — SHAK 424:32
hath a thousand several t. — SHAK 481:14
lack t. to praise — SHAK 494:20
Latin, queen of t., — JONS 285:6
t. of men and of angels — BIBLE 76:14
t., they shall cease — BIBLE 76:14
Walls have t. — SWIFT 528:6
whispering t. can poison truth — COL 156:4
Wild t. that have not Thee — KIPL 302:9
tongue-tied: art made t. by authority
— SHAK 494:5
tonight: t. thou shalt have cramps
— SHAK 484:28
world may end t. — BROW 101:23
Too: T. small to live in — ANON 8:11
took: All which I t. from thee — THOM 548:22
'E went an' t. — KIPL 304:4
person you and I t. me — CARL 131:1
They t. him away in a van — AUDEN 21:7
t. the trouble to be born — BEAU 35:18
ye t. me — BIBLE 68:6
tool: Man is a t.-using animal...Without
— CARL 132:13
t. of honour in my hands — WORD 583:2
Too-late: T., Farewell — ROSS 410:4
tool-making: Man is a t. animal — FRAN 218:15
tools: Give us the t. — CHUR 150:5
secrets are edged t. — DRYD 197:20
t. to work withal — LOW 319:9
tool-shed: rise to a scream on the t.
— AUDEN 20:8
toon: were his legges and his t. — CHAU 142:32
toord: rymyng is nat worth a t. — CHAU 143:15
tooth: danger of her former t. — SHAK 461:12
hadde alwey a coltes t. — CHAU 143:21
Nature, red in t. and claw — TENN 536:29
poison for the age's t. — SHAK 452:10
set my pugging t. on edge — SHAK 491:17
sharper than a serpent's t. — SHAK 453:19
t. for tooth — BIBLE 47:25
toothache: sleeps feels not the t. — SHAK 429:2
That could endure the t. — SHAK 473:7
toothbrush: t. too is airing in this — BETJ 43:12
toothpicks: nothing but a supply of t.
— JERR 273:2
tooth-point: Exactly where each t. goes
— KIPL 302:1
top: beautiful woman on t. — HOR 257:9
is always room at the t. — WEBS 566:9
kick to come to the t. — KEATS 293:31
rise to power at the t. — LUCR 320:6

schoolboy whips his taxed t.	SMITH 511:38	He wants the natural t.	SHAK 462:12	town-crier: lief the t. spoke my lines			
struggle to the t. alone	CAMUS 129:24	if he do but t. the hills	PRAY 397:2		SHAK 433:16		
t. of it reached to heaven	BIBLE 46:18	live to see thee in my t.	SHAK 455:7	Towns: Seven wealthy T. contend for			
t. thing in the world	KEATS 294:23	nothing, Can t. him further	SHAK 461:12	HOMER	ANON 7:14		
toper: poor t. whose untutor'd	COWP 168:8	One t. of nature makes	SHAK 487:6	toy: foolish thing was but a t.	SHAK 490:27		
topics: you have but two t.	JOHN 277:10	puts it not unto the t.	GRAH 233:14	sells eternity to get a t.	SHAK 492:18		
top-mast: strack the t. wi' his hand		To swear to a t. o' sun	KIPL 302:21	toys: All is but t.	SHAK 461:1		
	BALL 30:19	t. his weaknesses with	GOLD 232:8	all my t. beside me lay	STEV 522:20		
topmost: A-top on the t. twig	ROSS 409:13	T. me not	BIBLE 73:9	Deceive boys with t.	LYS 321:18		
tops: think their slender t.	HOOD 254:18	T. not	BIBLE 78:24	make you brooches and t.	STEV 522:29		
torch: bright t.	KEATS 292:4	T. not the cat but a glove	SCOTT 418:9	Not to meddle with my t.	STEV 522:19		
runners relay the t. of life	LUCR 320:7	t. of earthly years	WORD 581:10	of t. and things to eat	STEV 522:21		
t. of her beauty	WOOLF 576:18	t. of Harry in the night	SHAK 444:12	pray'r-books are the t. of age	POPE 379:19		
torches: our little t. at his fire	COK 154:14	touched: he t. the hollow of his	BIBLE 46:23	then cast their t. away	COWP 165:11		
she doth teach the t.	SHAK 482:2	this hath t. thy lips	BIBLE 57:30	Toyshop: They shift the moving T.			
torchlight: t. procession marching		t. a broken girl	FLEC 214:15		POPE 380:30		
	OSUL 365:24	t. none that he did not	JOHN 277:13	trace: can t. my ancestry back	GILB 226:20		
Tories: are T. born wicked	ANON 6:14	T. to the quick	BROW 101:16	tremblers learn'd to t.	GOLD 231:2		
T. own no argument	BROW 97:26	Who t. my clothes	BIBLE 68:32	traces: spring are on winter's t.	SWIN 528:15		
unbending T. who follow	MAC 323:13	touches: silent t. of time	BURKE 111:36	track: Around the ancient t. marched			
torment: measure of our t. is	KIPL 299:11	Such heavenly t. ne'er	SHAK 492:27		MER 337:5		
smoke of their t. ascendeth	BIBLE 82:17	t. a hair of yon gray head	WHIT 571:18	Come flying on our t.	THOM 549:28		
there shall no t. touch them	BIBLE 62:13	t. of sweet harmony	SHAK 468:15	tract: left a little t.	WILDE 572:12		
t. of the night's untruth	DAN 171:1	Who t. this touches a man	WHIT 570:13	trade: adepts in the speaking t.	CHUR 148:27		
t. than a hermit's fast	KEATS 290:24	toucheth: t. pitch shall be defiled	BIBLE 63:2	all is seared with t.	HOPK 256:12		
Tormentarii: Pulveris T., et Acus		Touching: T. all with thine opiate	SHEL 505:3	calling for this idle t.	POPE 376:23		
	BACON 28:9	tough: t. is J.B. Tough	DICK 177:22	craftsman cunning at his t.	KIPL 298:15		
tormented: Am not t. with ten thousand		was interesting, but t.	TWAIN 554:1	dreadful t.	SHAK 455:1		
	MARL 329:7	toujours: est t. dans la majorité	KNOX 305:18	except what t. can give	BROW 105:3		
tormenting: criticism is the most t.		tour: Comme en sa t. d'ivoire	SAIN 413:1	great t. will always be	BURKE 109:3		
	STER 519:30	d'Aquitaine à la t. abolie	NERV 360:26	half a t. and half an art	INGE 270:8		
tormentors: words hereafter thy t.		tourist: loathsome is the British t.	KILV 296:5	It is His t.	HEINE 244:13		
	SHAK 478:21	whisper to the t.	BEER 37:26	I t. both the living	DRYD 197:38		
torments: anybody's t. in this world		tourmente: Malgré moi l'infini me t.		nation was ever ruined by t.	FRAN 218:4		
	CHES 146:3		MUSS 359:4	not accidental, but a t.	SHAK 464:15		
how many t. lie	CIBB 151:9	tournament: We in the t.	BETJ 44:6	not your t. to make tables	JOHN 274:26		
Our t. also may in length	MILT 346:13	tous: à t. points de vue	COUE 163:8	that's my t.	CATH 136:17		
torn: though thy tackle's t.	SHAK 427:26	T. pour un	DUMAS 199:3	This t. of mine	BROW 102:19		
torpedo: than it becomes a t. to him		tout: Habacuc était capable de t.	VOLT 561:23	t. of war I have slain	SHAK 473:20		
	JOHN 274:1	t. for flattery	COLL 158:14	War is the t. of kings	DRYD 196:28		
torpedoes: Damn the t.	FARR 210:24	tout le monde: Quand t. a tort	LA C 306:16	trader: some grave Tyrian t.	ARN 14:21		
torrent: stem the t. of a woman's	ANON 8:20	toves: slithy t.	CARR 134:28	trades: It is the best of all t.	BELL 40:15		
torrents: t. of her myriad universe		toward: I t. thy bed	FLEC 214:12	ugliest of t. have their	JERR 273:6		
	TENN 539:20	tower: Child Roland to the dark t.		tradesmen: bow, ye t.	GILB 225:35		
torrid: t. or the f.ozen zone	CAREW 130:16		SHAK 454:27	Trade Unionism: T. of the married			
tort: Quand tout le monde a t.	LA C 306:16	clock collected in the t.	HOUS 264:28		SHAW 497:31		
Tortis: this 'ere 'T.' is a insect	PUNCH 402:19	intending to build a t.	BIBLE 70:14	Trade-Unionists: There are the T.			
torture: Than on the t. of the mind		Julius Caesar's ill-erected t.	SHAK 480:6		KEYN 296:1		
	SHAK 461:12	length that t. of strength	TENN 541:8	tradition: America is their oldest t.			
t. one poor word ten thousand	DRYD 196:35	name is a t. of strength	SHAK 481:12		WILDE 573:26		
t. them, into believing	NEWM 362:8	nose is as the t. of Lebanon	BIBLE 57:9	from the air a live t.	POUND 382:14		
worms to t. fish	COLM 159:6	Terrace or lofty T.	LEAR 312:3	talk to me about naval t.	CHUR 151:7		
tortured: poisoned air and t. soil	KIPL 300:6	within thy ivory t.	SAIN 413:1	T. means giving votes	CHES 148:5		
torturer: life and the t.'s horse	AUDEN 19:19	Towered: T. cities please us then	MILT 342:24	traducción: original es infiel a la t.			
Tory: hatred for the T. Party	BEVAN 44:16	towers: branchy between t.	HOPK 256:9		BORG 89:24		
I may be a T.	PEEL 371:5	cloud-capp'd t.	SHAK 485:20	traffic: Hushing the latest t.	BRID 92:12		
T. and Whig in turns shall	SMITH 512:6	London's t.	BLAKE 86:12	t. of Jacob's ladder	THOM 548:25		
T. men and Whig measures	DISR 185:38	sleep old palaces and t.	SHEL 502:10	traffick: two hours' t.	SHAK 481:21		
wise T. and a wise Whig	JOHN 278:34	tell the t. thereof	PRAY 392:27	traffickers: Shy t.	ARN 14:21		
toss: chafe and t. in the spray	ARN 13:5	t. and tombs and statues	FLEC 214:6	tragedies: There are two t. in life			
good enough to t.	SHAK 440:12	Ye t. of Julius	GRAY 234:17		SHAW 497:33		
tossed: It t. them down	HOUS 264:28	Towery: T. city and branchy between		t. are finish'd by a death	BYRON 122:28		
t. and gored several persons	BOSW 90:15		HOPK 256:9	tragedy: be out of it simply a t.	WILDE 573:31		
tossing: mind is t. on the ocean	SHAK 465:7	towing-path: after a mile or two of a		first time as t.	MARX 333:9		
t. about in a steamer from	GILB 226:13	t.	TROL 553:9	greatest t. in the world	WELL 567:26		
young men t. on their beds	YEATS 586:14	town: charms the t. with humour		her a most tremendous t.	BEER 37:20		
toss-pots: With t. still had drunken			CHUR 149:12	That is what t. means	STOP 523:18		
	SHAK 490:27	Country in the t.	MART 331:14	t. and therefore not worth	AUST 22:21		
tot: Gott ist t.	NIET 363:6	country retreat near the t.	WYCH 583:24	t., comedy, history	SHAK 432:20		
toujours trop tard ou trop t.	SART 414:9	each and every t. or city	HOLM 253:16	t. is the noblest production	ADD 2:9		
total: What's the demd t.	DICK 180:15	Enormous through the Sacred T.	BELL 39:28	T. is thus a representation	ARIS 12:9		
totter: charming to t. into vogue	WALP 563:3	gives directions to the t.	SWIFT 528:3	t. requires testicles	VOLT 561:22		
t. on in bus'ness	POPE 377:14	go seaward from the t.	HUNT 268:12	t. to those that feel	WALP 563:11		
t. towards the tomb	SAY 415:7	man made the t.	COWP 166:31	tragedye: litel myn t.	CHAU 144:17		
totters: Who t. forth	SHEL 505:7	sounding through the t.	BALL 30:17	tragic: In t. life, God wot	MER 337:14		
totus: et in se ipso t.	HOR 262:10	spreading of the hideous t.	MORR 358:10	tragical: Merry and t.	SHAK 471:13		
touch: child beneath her t.	ROSS 409:22	t. of monks and bones	COL 156:5	trahison: La t. des clercs	BENDA 40:18		
Did but our bodies t.	YEATS 585:20	What little t. by river	KEATS 291:8	Trahit: T. sua quemque voluptas	VIRG 559:17		
Do not t. me	BIBLE 83:24	What's this dull t.	KEPP 295:12	trail: am still on their t.	THOR 550:8		
Fear not to t. the best	RAL 404:10	when he studies it in t.	COWP 166:17	t. that is always new	KIPL 300:23		

trail'd: t. the hunter's javelin	ARN 14:26	**transport:** turned to share the t.	WORD 582:15	t. safely into the unknown'	HASK 243:1
trailing: t. clouds of glory	WORD 579:5	**trappe:** Kaught in a t.	CHAU 141:16	Were it ever so airy a t.	TENN 540:12
T. in the cool stream thy	ARN 14:14	**trappings:** t. and the suits of woe		Where'er we t. 'tis haunted	BYRON 120:15
train: catching a t. is to miss	CHES 148:11		SHAK 429:25	wine-press which ye t.	MAC 322:6

train: catching a t. is to miss — CHES 148:11
descending from the t. — LEL 313:18
her starry t. — MILT 348:5
his t. filled the temple — BIBLE 57:28
next t. has gone ten minutes — PUNCH 402:21
Of heat the express t. — THOM 547:16
take a t. — BROO 94:22
t. and tram alternate go — BETJ 43:17
t. for ill and not — HOUS 264:14
T. up a child in the way — BIBLE 54:22
we rush in the t. — THOM 549:28
world And all her t. — VAUG 555:22
trains: t. all night groan — HOUS 262:16
traitor: Do hate the t. — DAN 170:20
I find myself a t. with — SHAK 480:4
mind by that t. to learning — JOHN 273:17
traitors: flinch and t. sneer — CONN 161:10
Our fears do make us t. — SHAK 462:11
they can see a sort of t. — SHAK 480:4
t. and the treason love — DRYD 196:21
tram: I'm a t. — HARE 242:8
train and t. alternate — BETJ 43:17
trample: light doth t. on my days — VAUG 555:19
t. the vices themselves — AUG 22:3
tramples: Death t. it to fragments — SHEL 499:26
Trams: 'T. and dusty trees — ELIOT 205:5
trance: He fell into a t. — BIBLE 73:37
in mad t. — SHEL 499:20
Tränen: *Wer nie sein Brot mit T.* — GOET 230:12
tranquilles: *t. dans les grands ouvrages* — VOLT 561:16
Tranquillity: divine T. — TENN 539:22
emotion recollected in t. — WORD 583:10
Fame and t. can never be — MONT 354:22
I am restoring t. — BURKE 109:28
moments of t. in great works — VOLT 561:16
t. which religion is powerless — FORB 216:10
transcendental: idle chatter of a t. — GILB 227:21
T. moonshine — CARL 132:7
transform: t. ourselves into beasts — SHAK 475:9
transgression: deceived was in the t. — BIBLE 79:10
there is no t. — BIBLE 74:39
transgressions: was wounded for our t. — BIBLE 59:22
transgressors: was numbered with the t. — BIBLE 59:24
way of t. is hard — BIBLE 53:36
transit: *quam cito t. gloria mundi* THOM 546:7
Sic t. gloria mundi — ANON 11:1
transitory: Action is t. — WORD 577:2
this t. life are in trouble — PRAY 387:16
translate: pudding as well as t. Epictetus — JOHN 273:31
such as cannot write, t. — DENH 174:21
translated: thou art t. — SHAK 470:17
T. Daughter — AUDEN 18:4
t. into another tongue — BIBLE 62:20
translation: be a mistake in the t. VANB 555:4
is only a t. of the Bible — WHAT 569:15
is unfaithful to the t. — BORG 89:24
is what gets lost in t. — FROST 219:16
Not a t. — SHER 505:19
T.'s thief that addeth — MARV 332:17
translations: in a score of bad t. — AUDEN 19:11
Some hold t. not unlike — HOW 266:20
translator: t. of Homer should above — ARN 16:11
translunary: him those brave t. things — DRAY 193:13
transmigrates: it t. — SHAK 422:14

transport: turned to share the t. — WORD 582:15
trappe: Kaught in a t. — CHAU 141:16
trappings: t. and the suits of woe — SHAK 429:25
trash: peasants their vile t. — SHAK 451:21
Traum: *ewige Friede ist ein T.* — MOLT 354:4
traurig: *Dass ich so t. bin* — HEINE 244:9
travail: had my labour for my t. — SHAK 486:20
travaileth: groaneth and t. in pain — BIBLE 75:10
travaille: fyn and guerdoun for t. — CHAU 144:19
travel: Can in a moment t. thither — WORD 579:12
discover we must t. too — FITZ 213:4
English man does not t. — STER 518:31
have discredited your t. — SHAK 421:21
heart turns to t. so that — POUND 383:18
I t. for travel's sake — STEV 521:18
preserve all that t. by land — SWIFT 526:33
ship would *not* t. due West — CARR 133:6
takes me I t. as a visitor — HOR 258:7
tired with labour of far t. — CAT 136:28
t. by land or by water — PRAY 385:20
t. faster than a stagecoach — GOLD 232:18
t. forth without my cloak — SHAK 493:11
t. from Dan to Beersheba — STER 519:2
t. hopefully is a better — STEV 522:9
T., in the younger sort — BACON 27:27
T. light and you can sing — JUV 287:26
travell'd: t. in the realms of gold — KEATS 292:17
travelled: I t. among unknown men — WORD 577:28
Traveller: Farewell, Monsieur T. — SHAK 426:20
Head of a t. — HOUS 266:9
His fellow t. — ANON 8:4
lost t.'s dream — BLAKE 86:1
misled and lonely t. — MILT 341:1
No t. returns — SHAK 433:8
Sentimental T. (meaning — STER 518:30
spurs the lated t. apace — SHAK 461:15
t. betwixt life and death — WORD 581:8
t., by the faithful hound — LONG 316:16
t. came — BLAKE 86:22
t. from an antique land — SHEL 502:15
t. from Lima will visit — WALP 563:9
t.'s journey is done — BLAKE 87:22
World-besotted t. — YEATS 587:3
Travellers: outside at 'The T.' Rest' — HARDY 241:2
t. must be content — SHAK 425:8
traveller's joy: t. beguiles in autumn — HOUS 265:9
travelleth: He that t. into a country — BACON 27:27
poverty come as one that t. — BIBLE 53:22
travelling: Captain is a good t. name — FARQ 210:5
grand object of t. is — JOHN 277:6
That's fairly worth the t. — STEV 523:9
T. is the ruin of all happiness BURN 112:17
travels: t. the fastest who travels KIPL 304:11
T.' will consist of excursions — COL 157:29
trawlers: little fleet of t. under sail BETJ 42:17
Tray: Good T. grew very red — HOFF 252:13
my poor dog T. — CAMP 128:20
T., Blanch, and Sweet-heart — SHAK 454:29
trays: cheap tin t. — MAS 333:19
treachery: fear their subjects' t. — SHAK 446:15
justly kill'd with my own t. — SHAK 437:19
T.! seek it out — SHAK 437:20
which even t. cannot trust — JUN 287:7
treacle: fly that sips t. is lost — GAY 222:30
tread: because you t. on my dreams — YEATS 585:9
face with an undaunted t. — STEV 522:25
t. on classic ground — ADD 2:4
t. on Earth unguess'd — ARN 14:24

t. safely into the unknown' — HASK 243:1
Were it ever so airy a t. — TENN 540:12
Where'er we t. 'tis haunted — BYRON 120:15
wine-press which ye t. — MAC 322:6
treason: condoned high t. — DISR 185:6
greatest t. — ELIOT 204:4
hate traitors and the t. — DRYD 196:21
his office t. was no crime — DRYD 194:16
If *this* be t. — HENRY 245:25
in trust I have found t. — ELIZ 206:3
is a sort of t. — BURKE 110:9
It were t. to our love — THOR 550:28
love grows bitter with t. — SWIN 530:5
none dare call it t. — HAR 242:10
popular humanity is t. — ADD 1:21
reason why gunpowder t. — ANON 7:10
That t. can but peep — SHAK 436:6
They cannot commit t. — COKE 154:24
though they love the t. — DAN 170:20
T. has done his worst — SHAK 461:12
'Twixt t. and convenience — CLEV 153:3
Whilst bloody t. flourish'd — SHAK 450:28
who committed t. enough — SHAK 460:16
treasonous: prompts 'em their t. parles — BROW 99:26
treasons: Is fit for t. — SHAK 468:17
treasure: he that has stoln the t. — CONG 160:8
it as your chiefest t. — BELL 38:23
our delight or as our t. — HERB 248:2
purest t. mortal times — SHAK 478:8
shalt have t. in heaven — BIBLE 67:9
She is your t. — SHAK 484:7
this t. in earthen vessels — BIBLE 77:5
t. of our tongue — DAN 170:23
Where your t. is — BIBLE 64:26
treasures: out t. from an earthen pot — HERB 247:12
yourselves t. upon earth — BIBLE 64:25
yourselves t. in heaven — BIBLE 64:25
treasuries: sunken wrack and sumless t. — SHAK 443:8
Treasury: T. is the spring of business — BAG 28:22
Treasury Bench: plaintive treble of the T. — DISR 184:19
wonder sitting on the T. — CHUR 149:27
treat: All eager for the t. — CARR 135:6
Greek as a t. — CHUR 150:23
something left to t. my friends — MALL 327:12
t. with virtuous scorn — GILB 226:4
who gives a child a t. — MAS 333:25
you're giving a t. — GILB 226:14
treatise: former t. have I made — BIBLE 73:20
T. of Human Nature — HUME 268:1
treaty: signed the t. — THOM 547:5
treble: again towards childish t. — SHAK 425:24
trebled: I would be t. twenty times — SHAK 467:13
tree: be ay sticking in a t. — SCOTT 418:20
billboard lovely as a t. — NASH 360:2
down under a juniper t. — BIBLE 51:13
Eden's dread probationary t. — COWP 166:13
Generations pass while some t. BROW 97:16
Grow to some Southern t. — HARDY 239:9
highly impossible t. — GILB 225:13
his own t. of ancestors — STEV 521:10
I shall be like that t. — SWIFT 527:19
is not growing like a t. — JONS 285:8
it is a t. of life — BIBLE 53:35
leaves of the t. were — BIBLE 83:1
live on this Crumpetty T. — LEAR 312:22
Lord God to grow every t. — BIBLE 45:8
middle t. and highest there — MILT 347:18
more to my taste than a t. — MORR 358:4
'neath a swan-bosomed t. — SITW 508:12
of the t. of the knowledge — BIBLE 45:9
only God can make a t. — KILM 296:4
place where the t. falleth — BIBLE 56:50
pledges of a fruitful t. — HERR 248:20
poem lovely as a t. — KILM 296:3

she gave me of the t.   BIBLE 45:17
some single herb or t.   MARV 331:21
that's why the t.   ANON 4:29
there's a t. of many   WORD 579:5
there vor me the apple t.   BARN 33:28
these things in a green t.   BIBLE 71:10
thocht it was a trustie t.   BALL 32:10
three ravens sat on a t.   BALL 32:7
t. by a river a little   GILB 227:15
t. Continues to be   KNOX 305:22
t. did end their race   MARV 332:2
t. is known by his fruit   BIBLE 66:8
t. of actual life springs   GOET 230:3
t. of diabolical knowledge   SHER 506:10
t. of knowledge of good   BIBLE 45:8
t. of liberty must be refreshed JEFF 272:10
t. of life also   BIBLE 45:8
t. of man was never quiet   HOUS 263:15
t. that a wise man sees   BLAKE 88:16
Under the greenwood t.   SHAK 425:14
was an Old Man in a t.   LEAR 311:16
Was there a t. about which   COWL 164:17
wish I were a t.   HERB 246:23
trees: all the t. are green   KING 297:5
Bosom'd high in tufted t.   MILT 342:20
climbing t. in the Hesperides   SHAK 457:8
did gently kiss the t.   SHAK 468:13
die when the t. were green   CLARE 152:4
fields and leaves to the t.   HOR 261:14
filled the t. and flapped   HODG 252:6
I see men as t.   BIBLE 68:33
might procreate like t.   BROW 96:33
music of its t. at dawn   ARN 14:1
My apple t. will never   FROST 219:9
Of all the t. in England   DE L 174:17
Of all the t. that grow   KIPL 303:25
'O look at the t.   BRID 92:14
Orpheus with his lute made t.   SHAK 447:3
selected the felling of t.   CHUR 149:20
shady t. cover him with   BIBLE 53:10
their tall ancestral t.   HEM 244:21
This lady by the t.   YEATS 584:23
Those t. in whose dim shadow   MAC 323:1
to move and t. to speak   SHAK 461:24
'Trams and dusty t.   ELIOT 205:5
T. did grow and plants   BARN 33:32
t. I see barren of leaves   SHAK 492:26
t. of the Lord also are   PRAY 396:20
T., where you sit   POPE 380:27
unto the root of the t.   BIBLE 63:39
upon the t. that are therein   PRAY 399:3
'whispers through the t.'   POPE 378:21
you lover of t.   BROW 100:12
trek: nations t. from progress   OWEN 367:11
Trelawny: shall T. die   HAWK 243:4
tremble: I t., I expire   SHEL 500:13
Let Sporus t.   POPE 376:30
shall t. at the look of him   PRAY 397:2
start and t. under her feet   TENN 540:12
t. and despoil themselves   SHEL 502:11
t. for my country when   JEFF 272:16
t. like a guilty thing   WORD 579:10
trembled: Laugh at all you t.   COWP 166:14
t. with fear at your frown   ENGL 208:19
tremblers: boding t. learn'd to trace
                                 GOLD 231:2
trembling: brought the t. woman there
                                 BLAKE 85:24
salvation with fear and t.   BIBLE 78:15
T., hoping   POPE 376:3
t. seizes all of me   SAPP 414:6
tremendous: This most t. tale of all BETJ 42:8
white t. daybreak   BROO 94:29
trench: Stand in the t., Achilles SHAW 498:28
trenchant: t. blade   BUTL 117:24
trenched: hoed and t. and weeded
                                 HOUS 264:17
trencher: Dead Caesar's t.   SHAK 422:20
trencher-friends: t., time's flies SHAK 486:8

trencher-man: He is a very valiant t.
                                 SHAK 471:26
trenches: t. in thy beauty's field SHAK 492:23
Trent: silver T. shall run   SHAK 439:24
was Burton built on T.   HOUS 264:12
trépas: vivre le t. de quelqu'un MOL 353:16
tres: omnis divisa in partes t. CAES 126:26
trespass: t. there and go   HOUS 265:10
trespasses: forgive us our t.   PRAY 384:14
tress: corn at midnight by a t. YEATS 586:17
tresses: Knees and t. folded   MER 337:1
t. like the morn   MILT 341:18
trial: is a t. of which you can SHAW 497:3
purity, all t., all obeisance   SHAK 426:29
T. by jury itself   DENM 174:22
which purifies us is t.   MILT 351:24
triangle: eternal t.   ANON 7:23
tribe: All that t.   HOR 261:24
badge of all our t.   SHAK 466:2
purify the dialect of the t.   ELIOT 202:25
Richer than all his t.   SHAK 477:23
tribeless: t., and nationless   SHEL 503:12
tribes: Form'd of two mighty t. BYRON 124:4
thither the t. go up   PRAY 398:11
tribulation: In all time of our t. PRAY 385:17
which came out of great t.   BIBLE 82:2
world ye shall have t.   BIBLE 72:41
Tribunal: its highest T. will accomplish
                                 BURKE 110:28
There's a new t. now   BROW 104:32
tributaries: brooks are Thames's t. ARN 15:8
tribute: majesty shall have t. of me
                                 SHAK 432:16
tribute to whom t. is due   BIBLE 75:22
t. which vice pays to virtue   LA R 310:12
trick: I know a t. worth two   SHAK 438:21
pleasing to t. the trickster   LA F 306:19
win the t.   HOYLE 267:4
trickle: last t. seemed to disappear
                                 PLOM 374:19
tricks: all t. are either knavish JOHN 278:9
of the man of many t.   HOMER 254:4
shap'd for sportive t.   SHAK 480:18
There are no t. in plain   SHAK 451:11
t. and all   BROW 102:19
t. that are vain   HARTE 242:29
Women are like t. by slight   CONG 160:9
tried: to be t. before a jury   JOHN 277:2
t. a little, failed much   STEV 521:5
t. their talents at one   COL 157:26
when he is t.   BIBLE 80:8
trifid: steep and t. God   THOM 547:22
trifle: coffee t. with the spoon POPE 377:7
'twere a careless t.   SHAK 458:22
trifles: man of sense only t.   CHES 145:26
She who t. with all   GAY 223:4
snapper-up of unconsidered t.   SHAK 491:18
T. light as air   SHAK 475:23
t. were worth something   CAT 136:20
write t. with dignity   JOHN 278:23
trifling: mother's deafness is very t.
                                 AUST 22:12
Trigger: Finger do you want on the T.
                                 ANON 8:22
triggers: To dror resolves an' t. LOW 319:3
Trimmer: T.' signifies no more   HAL 237:18
trimmings: mutton with the usual t.
                                 DICK 182:26
Trinities: cold Christ and tangled T.
                                 KIPL 302:2
Trinity: I the T. illustrate   BROW 105:6
T. had never been unkind   NEWM 361:23
we worship one God in T.   PRAY 385:2
trinket: I swung the earth a t. THOM 548:17
joy's a t.   STEP 518:25
trinkets: ye returned to your t. KIPL 300:4
triomphe: on t. sans gloire   CORN 162:16
trip: From fearful t. the victor WHIT 570:8
like a fairy t. upon   SHAK 495:19
t. it as ye go   MILT 342:15

triple: There be t. ways to take KIPL 301:1
t. cord   BURKE 112:5
triplex: robur et aes t.   HOR 259:12
trippingly: t. on the tongue   SHAK 433:16
Triste: Caballero de la T. Figura
                                 CERV 138:12
coitum omne animal t.   ANON 10:17
île t. et noire   BAUD 35:8
jamais t. archy   MARQ 330:21
La chair est t.   MALL 327:9
t. vieillesse vous vous   TALL 531:18
tristement: anglais s'amusent t. SULLY 524:18
tristesse: Bonjour t.   ELUA 206:16
Tristram: christened let call him T.
                                 MAL 327:17
Tristram Shandy: Life and Opinions
of T.   WALP 562:25
T. did not last   JOHN 276:34
Triton: hear old T. blow his wreathed
                                 WORD 582:20
T. blowing loud his wreathed   SPEN 515:21
you this T. of the minnows   SHAK 427:21
triumph: devils'-t. and sorrow   BROW 102:7
forth in t. from the north   MAC 322:6
in ourselves, are t.   LONG 316:27
lives...We shall not see the t. DICK 183:10
meet with T. and Disaster   KIPL 299:22
of the uncircumcised t.   BIBLE 50:16
Poor is the t.   THOM 549:18
ride in t. through Persepolis   MARL 330:7
so be pedestalled in t.   BROW 104:30
there is no glory in the t.   CORN 162:16
t. of hope over experience   JOHN 275:36
t. over death and sin   SPEN 515:17
When learning's t. o'er   JOHN 282:25
triumphant: bound in with the t. sea
                                 SHAK 478:20
mounts exulting on t. wings   POPE 381:14
triumphantes: Laeti t.   ANON 10:4
triumph'd: t. over fate   BYRON 124:28
triumphs: He sicken'd at all t. CHUR 149:4
trivial: away rife t. fond records SHAK 431:15
contests rise from t. things   POPE 380:28
t. and vulgar way of coition   BROW 96:33
t. round   KEBLE 295:4
Trochee: T. trips from long to short
                                 COL 157:3
trod: our forefathers t.   SWIN 530:7
they t. in the wash-tub   CLOU 153:15
t., as on the four winds   MARV 332:13
T. beside me   HOUS 264:1
trodden: little fire is quickly t. SHAK 446:21
t. the winepress alone   BIBLE 60:11
Trois: T. heures, c'est toujours trop tard
                                 SART 414:9
Trojan: T. 'orses will jump out BEVIN 44:19
Trojans: T. and the well-greaved
                                 HOMER 253:28
We T. are at an end   VIRG 558:6
Trolley-bus: T. and windy street BETJ 42:7
trolley buses: kissing of the t. hissing
                                 BETJ 42:16
trompé: amis que d'en être t.   LA R 310:10
tromper: plaisir de t. le trompeur
                                 LA F 306:19
Troop: T. home to churchyards   SHAK 470:25
troops: charged the t. of error BROW 96:5
her Aeneas shall want t.   SHAK 423:10
solemn t. and sweet societies   MILT 343:18
tropes: He rang'd his t.   PRIOR 401:2
trophies: among her cloudy t. hung
                                 KEATS 291:15
Hang their old t. o'er   POPE 380:7
her weedy t. and herself   SHAK 436:19
t. unto the enemies   BROW 96:5
tropic: Under the t. is our language
                                 WALL 562:17
tropics: nuisance of the t. is   BELL 39:31
Trostmittel: Selbstmord ist ein starkes
T.   NIET 363:11

trot: 'Does it t.   LEAR 313:1
troth: thereto I give thee my t.   PRAY 389:4
Trotting: T. through the dark   KIPL 302:22
trouble: charm of powerful t.   SHAK 462:3
  deliver him in the time of t.   PRAY 392:4
  double toil and t.   SHAK 462:2
  full of t.   BIBLE 52:26
  has t. enough of its own   WILC 572:5
  Man is born unto t.   BIBLE 52:17
  No stranger to t. myself   VIRG 557:19
  present help in time of t.   ANON 4:18
  read when they're in t.   HOUS 265:13
  save t. I wed again   CLARE 152:6
  Today the Roman and his t.   HOUS 263:15
  to have your t. doubl'd   DEFOE 173:9
  took the t. to be born   BEAU 35:18
  transcendent capacity of taking t.
     CARL 131:18
  transitory life are in t.   PRAY 387:16
  t. deaf heaven with my   SHAK 493:6
  t. out of King Charles's   DICK 177:7
  t.'s sure   HOUS 264:14
  t. with people is not that   BILL 84:7
  were a t. to my dreams   WORD 580:14
  where all t. seems   SWIN 529:21
  which just make more t.   HOR 260:16
  will t. thine eyes   DONNE 190:23
  women and care and t.   WARD 564:38
  'you ain't see no t. yit   HARR 242:12
troubled: Let not your heart be t. BIBLE 72:30
  no more was by it t.   THAC 546:3
  see that ye be not t.   BIBLE 67:27
  t. midnight and the noon's   ELIOT 202:11
  t. spirit: a broken   PRAY 393:8
  t. with her lonely life   PEPYS 372:8
troubles: all our t. and adversities
     PRAY 385:22
  arms against a sea of t.   SHAK 433:8
  t. of our proud and angry   HOUS 264:22
  t. they reave me of rest   HOUS 266:7
  t. you are yourself spared   LUCR 320:6
  written in t. of the brain   SHAK 463:3
  yet nothing t. me less   LAMB 307:26
troublesome: loud and t. *insects*
     BURKE 111:16
  very t. to everybody else   CONG 160:22
  women are mostly t. cattle   LOVER 318:22
troubling: wicked cease from t. BIBLE 52:13
trousers: bottoms of my t. rolled
     ELIOT 203:25
  like a steam-engine in t.   SMITH 511:10
  never have your best t.   IBSEN 269:19
  shall wear white flannel t.   ELIOT 203:25
  then he hitch'd his t.   BARH 33:23
trout: gray t. lies asleep   HOGG 252:23
  t. for factitious bait   POUND 383:2
  t. that must be caught   SHAK 489:10
  you find a t. in the milk   THOR 550:24
Trouthe: T. and honour   CHAU 141:9
  T. is the hyest thing that   CHAU 142:14
trouts: t. are tickled best   BUTL 118:20
trovato: è molto ben t.   ANON 10:3
trowel: She lays it on with a t. CONG 159:24
  should lay it on with a t.   DISR 185:28
trowth: t. thee shal delivere   CHAU 144:22
Troy: fir'd another T.   DRYD 195:7
  half his T. was burn'd   SHAK 441:1
  heard T. doubted   BYRON 123:11
  ringing plains of windy T.   TENN 543:22
  sacked T.'s sacred city   HOMER 254:4
  T. but a heap of smouldering POUND 382:7
  T. came destined an exile   VIRG 557:8
  Was there another T.   YEATS 586:7
  Where's T.   BRAM 91:23
truant: every t. knew   GOLD 231:2
  have a t. been to chivalry   SHAK 440:16
  t. disposition   SHAK 430:2
truce: t. ought to be allowed   BURKE 111:3
true: any less real and t.   SHAW 496:14
  Arabian Tales were t.   NEWM 361:16

called Faithful and T.   BIBLE 82:25
can the devil speak t.   SHAK 458:16
course of t. love never did run SHAK 469:18
Dare to be t.   HERB 247:2
dark and t. and tender   TENN 542:5
finished yields the t. glory   DRAKE 193:1
having is t. to his wife   VANB 555:6
heart of a t. *Englishman*   ADD 2:19
if I know what t. love is   TENN 534:28
If it is not t.   ANON 10:3
If t., here only   MILT 347:19
I'll prove more t.   SHAK 482:14
is it t.   BETJ 42:8
it is t.   LAWR 311:11
Let God be t.   BIBLE 74:36
let us be t.   ARN 12:23
lived she was a t. lover   MAL 328:2
long enough it will be t.   BENN 40:23
man would like to be t.   BACON 28:7
Minding t. things by what   SHAK 444:13
my shape as t.   SHAK 453:9
My t. love hath my heart   SIDN 507:16
my t. love said   PEELE 371:9
not necessarily t.   WILDE 573:34
ower t. tale   SCOTT 418:8
people as equally t.   GIBB 224:21
ring in the t.   TENN 537:14
speak t.   TENN 534:5
state by proportions t.   MARV 331:20
tell you three times is t.   CARR 133:1
think what is t. and do   HUXL 269:8
thou wast as t. a lover   SHAK 425:9
'Tis easy to be t.   SEDL 419:14
to itself do rest but t.   SHAK 453:1
to thine own self be t.   SHAK 430:19
t. as truth's simplicity   SHAK 487:2
t. beginning of our end   SHAK 471:16
t. king I offer'd free   MAC 322:8
t. paradises are paradises   PROU 402:1
t. pathos and sublime   BURNS 115:15
T. patriots we   BARR 34:23
t. to thyself as thou be   BACON 27:35
unfaithful kept him falsely t. TENN 534:29
we are sure they are t.   SHAK 492:3
whatever for supposing it t. RUSS 412:17
Whatsoever things are t.   BIBLE 78:22
words are t. and faithful   BIBLE 82:31
'You are not t.   WILB 572:4
true-love: do as much for my t. BALL 32:9
  iron pokers into t. knots   COL 157:6
truer: nothing's t. than them   DICK 177:11
truest: paint 'em t. praise   ADD 1:15
  t. and the holiest that   MAL 327:22
trump: at the last t.   BIBLE 76:29
  speaking t. of future fame   BYRON 124:24
  with the sound of the t.   PRAY 392:24
trumpet: Blow up the t. in the new-moon
     PRAY 395:9
  blow your own t.   GILB 228:32
  ever and anon a t. sounds   THOM 548:20
  flute and the t.   AUDEN 20:21
  Glorious the t. and alarm   SMART 509:4
  great voice as of a t.   BIBLE 81:11
  heard the sound of the t.   BIBLE 49:2
  he blew a t.   BIBLE 49:15
  He shifted his t.   GOLD 231:21
  His t. shrill hath thrice   SPEN 515:16
  is the sound of the t.   BIBLE 53:7
  moved more than with a t.   SIDN 508:3
  shrill t. sounds   CIBB 151:13
  t., at whose voice   DONNE 189:33
  t. give an uncertain sound   BIBLE 76:15
  t. in terrible tones went   ENN 208:21
  t. shall sound   BIBLE 76:29
  t. shall be heard on high   DRYD 197:25
  t.'s loud clangour   DRYD 197:23
  t.'s silver sound is still   SCOTT 417:2
  t. will fling out a wonderful CEL 138:6
trumpeter: tongue our t.   SHAK 427:11

trumpets: are the eagles and the t.
     ELIOT 202:5
  He saith among the t.   BIBLE 53:7
  pâtés de foie gras to the sound of t.
     SMITH 511:20
  snarling t. 'gan to chide   KEATS 289:11
  Sound the t.   DRYD 194:26
  Sound the t.   MOR 357:21
  then the t.   CHES 147:3
  thunder of the t. of the night SWIN 530:19
  t. also, and shawms   PRAY 396:8
  t. sounded for him   BUNY 107:38
  t. which sing to battle   SHEL 505:13
  up-lifted Angel t. blow   MILT 340:21
  while the t. blow   TENN 542:7
trumpits: t. en de bangin' er de HARR 242:17
trumps: always having the ace of t.
     LAB 306:10
  if dirt were t.   LAMB 308:9
  Let Spades be t.   POPE 381:5
trundle-tail: Or bobtail tike, or t. SHAK 455:1
trunk: large a t. before   BELL 38:28
trunkless: Though t.   GILB 227:9
  vast and t. legs   SHEL 502:15
trust: absolute t.   SHAK 458:22
  dare t. themselves with men SHAK 486:2
  even treachery cannot t.   JUN 287:7
  frail mortality shall t.   BACON 28:16
  he might t. in the flesh   BIBLE 78:16
  His t. was with th' Eternal   MILT 346:7
  I can but t. that good   TENN 536:26
  I dare not t. it without   BROW 97:5
  If you can t. yourself   KIPL 299:22
  In the People was my t.   WORD 580:22
  in t. Our youth   RAL 404:15
  man assumes a public t.   JEFF 272:17
  my sure t. is in thee   PRAY 394:16
  never should t. experts   SAL 413:18
  no more than power in t.   DRYD 194:10
  not inclined to t. them   VIRG 560:7
  put not your t. in princes   PRAY 399:15
  put their t. in chariots   PRAY 390:14
  put thy t. in God   PRAY 392:12
  So I t.   MAS 333:23
  that put their t. in him   PRAY 389:19
  T. his sworn brother   SHAK 492:7
  t. I have found treason   ELIZ 206:3
  t. in all things high   TENN 542:19
  t. in God   SMITH 510:31
  t. me not at all or all   TENN 535:8
  T. no Future   LONG 317:3
  T. none   SHAK 443:20
  T. one who has gone through VIRG 559:10
  T. the tale   LAWR 311:10
  t. thy honest offer'd courtesy MILT 341:6
  t. to two securities than   CHES 145:30
  was not property but a t.   FOX 217:20
  with pains that conquer t.   TENN 536:21
  woman's t.   SCOTT 418:4
  yet will I t. in him   BIBLE 52:25
trusted: armour wherein he t. BIBLE 69:36
  familiar friend, whom I t.   PRAY 392:5
  few enthusiasts can be t.   BALF 30:4
  He t. in God   PRAY 390:17
  in thee have I t.   PRAY 384:18
  Let no such man be t.   SHAK 468:17
  pays to t. man   THOM 549:23
  to be t. with our selves   CONG 159:17
  unfit to be t.   CHES 146:6
  Who t. God was love indeed TENN 536:29
trustest: t. upon the staff of this BIBLE 51:38
trusteth: blessed is the man that t.
     PRAY 391:21
trustie: thocht it was a t. tree BALL 32:10
trusting: There is no t. appearances
     SHER 506:35
trusts: He's mad that t.   SHAK 454:28
  nor t. them with   CHES 145:26
trustworthiness: With Carthaginian t.
     SALL 413:25

trusty: weapons that t. Achates	VIRG 557:12	let us t., try, try	MOORE 357:3
truth: abode not in the t.	BIBLE 72:13	This t. within thy mind	TENN 543:19	times that t. men's souls	PAINE 368:1
absolute T. belongs	LESS 314:2	thy t. then be thy dower	SHAK 453:3	To t. me with affliction	SHAK 476:18
'Beauty is t.	KEATS 291:11	to handle honesty and t.	SHAW 497:14	t. him afterwards	MOL 353:22
bread of sincerity and t.	BIBLE 75:36	true as t.'s simplicity	SHAK 487:2	T. me	PRAY 399:8
bright countenance of t.	MILT 352:16	trusted to speak the t.	BALF 30:4	'T. not the Pass	LONG 316:15
brightness, purity, and t.	OTWAY 366:4	t. and untruth together	BACON 26:14	t. out my reins and my	PRAY 391:4
bring t. to light	SHAK 492:19	T. away From you is fled	WYATT 583:20	t. the soul's strength	BROW 101:14
casualty when war comes is t.	JOHN 273:18	T. beareth away the victory	BIBLE 62:4	T., try again	HICK 251:1
cause Of t.	MILT 348:26	T. be veiled	SHEL 500:18	**trying:** there is only the t.	ELIOT 202:24
Christianity better than T.	COL 157:18	t. by consecutive reasoning	KEATS 293:16	T. to be glad	HOUS 262:22
closing up truth to t.	MILT 351:26	T. can never be told so	BLAKE 88:25	us is that I am t. to be	BIRK 84:15
Commencing in a t.	SHAK 458:20	T., ever lovely	CAMP 129:9	**trysting:** named a t. day	MAC 322:11
Communist must grasp the t.	MAO 328:19	T., for its own sake	KING 297:17	**tu:** Et t.	CAES 126:28
consecrate to t. and liberty	SHEL 505:6	T. from his lips prevail'd	GOLD 230:24	Et t., Brute	SHAK 450:1
dared to speak the t. to me	TROL 552:20	t. from his face	BUTL 117:34	T. Marcellus eris	VIRG 559:2
dead we owe only t.	VOLT 561:19	t. has such a face	DRYD 196:12	T. regere imperio populos	VIRG 559:1
dearer still is t.	ARIS 12:12	t. in every shepherd's	RAL 404:9	**tua:** Nam t. res agitur	HOR 258:23
divine melodious t.	KEATS 291:1	t. in masquerade	BYRON 123:30	**tub:** mere tale of a t.	WEBS 567:3
does t. sound bitter	BROW 102:9	t. in the groves of Academe	HOR 259:4	**Tuba:** T. mirum sparget sonum	CEL 138:6
enemy of t. and freedom	IBSEN 269:17	t. in the inward parts	PRAY 393:5	t. terribili sonitu taratantara	ENN 208:21
fault and t. discourtesy	HERB 247:6	t. is always strange	BYRON 124:7	**tube:** reeking t. and iron shard	KIPL 302:10
feel certain of any t.	KEATS 294:11	t. is not in us	BIBLE 81:3	**tuberose:** sweet t.	SHEL 503:24
fiction lags after t.	BURKE 109:16	t. is rarely pure	WILDE 572:27	**tubers:** little life with dried t.	ELIOT 204:17
fight for freedom and t.	IBSEN 269:19	T. is the cry of all	BERK 41:22	**tuckets:** Then the t.	CHES 147:3
freeman whom the t. makes free		T. is within ourselves	BROW 103:2	**tucks:** till he t. in his shirt	KIPL 304:28
	COWP 167:22	t. lies within a little	BOL 89:15	**Tucson:** T. and Deadwood and Lost	
full of grace and t.	BIBLE 71:27	T., like a torch	HAM 238:15		BENET 40:19
further to discover t.	BACON 24:15	t. miscall'd simplicity	SHAK 494:5	**tue:** ou je te t.	CHAM 139:18
Great is T.	BIBLE 62:5	t. never hurts the teller	BROW 100:27	**tuer:** t. de temps en temps un	VOLT 561:1
Great is t.	BIBLE 83:26	t. of imagination	KEATS 293:15	**tug of war:** then was the t.	LEE 313:12
great is t.	BROO 95:2	t. serve as a stalking-horse	BOL 89:16	**tulips:** Here t. bloom as they are	BROO 94:18
great ocean of t.	NEWT 362:20	t. shall be thy warrant	RAL 404:10	**tumbled:** Over the t. graves	ELIOT 205:10
have not maintained for t.	SWIFT 526:8	t. shall make you free	BIBLE 72:12	**tumbler:** clean t., and a corkscrew	
here have Pride and T.	YEATS 586:8	T., Sir, is a cow	JOHN 275:3		DICK 180:20
him in possession of t.	LOCKE 315:16	t. sits upon the lips	ARN 14:27	**tumbling:** Fortunes...come t. into some	
him in spirit and in t.	BIBLE 71:40	T. smooth	DONNE 190:6		BACON 25:3
I am the way, the t.	BIBLE 72:32	t. that's told with bad	BLAKE 85:14	**tumult:** of ail the t. and bustle	SMITH 509:8
I mean the t. untold	OWEN 367:1	T. the masculine, of Honour	HARE 242:5	to this t. in the clouds	YEATS 585:15
inquiry of t.	BACON 27:31	T. to her old cavern fled	POPE 375:26	t. and the shouting dies	KIPL 302:7
is the best test of t.	CHES 145:33	t. to o'erpeer	SHAK 427:17	t. Kubla heard from far	COL 156:29
'Leave T. to the police	AUDEN 19:13	t., unity, and concord	PRAY 387:13	t., of the soul	WORD 578:2
lie which is part a t.	TENN 533:25	T., when witty	HARE 242:2	when the t. dwindled	BYRON 126:10
like open t. to cover lies	CONG 159:27	t. which you cannot contradict	PLATO 374:12	**tumultuositas:** t. vulgi semper insaniae	
loins girt about with t.	BIBLE 78:10	T. will come to light	SHAK 466:10		ALC 3:9
lost to love and t.	BURNS 113:7	t. with gold she weighs	POPE 375:13	**tumultuous:** t. joy	SOUT 514:11
love of t.	TENN 534:12	unto the enemies of t.	BROW 96:5	**tun:** t. of man is thy companion	SHAK 439:15
love of t. and right	TENN 537:15	utter what he thinks t.	JOHN 278:15	**tune:** blackbird's t.	BROW 100:13
mainly he told the t.	TWAIN 553:24	was all the test of t.	COWP 168:7	dost thou like this t.	SHAK 488:27
make fiction of the t.	FRY 220:9	We'd see t. dawn together	BROW 99:2	from the t. that they play	KIPL 304:10
men of less t. than tongue	SHAK 492:27	What is t.	BACON 27:28	I am incapable of a t.	LAMB 307:2
Mercy and t. are met	PRAY 395:15	What is t.	BIBLE 72:44	I t. the instrument here	DONNE 189:14
more to disclose t.	BACON 25:5	When I tell any T. it is	BLAKE 87:11	out of t. and harsh	SHAK 433:15
Nobody speaks the t. when	BOWEN 91:4	where deviation from t.	JOHN 277:20	That's sweetly play'd in t.	BURNS 114:27
not t., but things like	CHAP 140:14	Which heavenly t. imparts	KEBLE 295:5	There's many a good t.	BUTL 119:15
out thy light and thy t.	PRAY 392:11	whispering tongues can poison t.	COL 156:4	t. is catching and will	AUDEN 18:13
parsons do not care for t.	STUB 524:5	would keep abreast of T.	LOW 319:14	t. the enchantress plays	HOUS 265:8
possession of t. as of a city	BROW 96:6	yet friend to t.	POPE 378:6	**tuneable:** t. than lark to shepherd's	
rejoiceth in the t.	BIBLE 76:14	you have spoken the t.	BEDE 37:2		SHAK 469:21
Scotland better than t.	JOHN 281:22	**truthful:** have disposition to be t.		**tuneful:** I turn'd the t. art	POPE 380:4
seeming t. which cunning	SHAK 467:11		AUDEN 19:13	untimely stopp'd his t. tongue	POPE 377:16
simple t. his utmost skill	WOTT 583:12	my name is T. James	HARTE 242:32	**tunes:** chanted snatches of old t.	SHAK 436:19
so T. be in the field	MILT 352:5	true Poets must be t.	OWEN 367:1	found out musical t.	BIBLE 63:23
speaketh the t. from his	PRAY 390:4	**truths:** customary fate of new t.	HUXL 269:12	Heft Of Cathedral T.	DICK 184:1
Spirit that strove For t.	SHEL 504:5	Flat and flexible t.	BROW 95:18	like slow old t. of Spain	MAS 333:17
Strict Regard for T.	BELL 39:7	Irrationally held t. may	HUXL 269:11	should have all the good t.	HILL 251:4
strife of T. with Falsehood	LOW 319:14	of darkness tell us t.	SHAK 458:18	well as all the good t.	SHAW 497:22
swear to the t. of a song	PRIOR 400:20	old verities and t.	FAUL 210:30	**tunic:** all-concealing t.	SHEL 502:18
sweet ornament which t.	SHAK 493:16	Some random t. he can impart	WORD 580:5	**tunnel:** Down some profound dull t.	
takes two to speak the t.	THOR 550:23	tell him disagreeable t.	BULW 107:7		OWEN 367:9
tell me the t. about love	AUDEN 21:2	T. as refin'd as ever Athens	ARMS 12:16	t. of green gloom	BROO 94:17
that came of telling t.	DRYD 195:20	t. begin as blasphemies	SHAW 496:2	**tunnies:** blackbird's t.	ARN 14:21
that his simple t. must	SHAK 480:23	t. that wake	WORD 579:11	**turbid:** t. look the most profound	LAND 309:14
that I have look'd on t.	SHAK 495:3	Two t. are told	SHAK 458:19	**turbot:** price of a large t. for it	RUSK 411:18
that she is made of t.	SHAK 495:11	We hold these t. to be	ANON 8:14	'T., Sir,' said the waiter	WELBY 567:17
that stupendous t. believ'd	SMART 509:4	We hold these t. to be	JEFF 272:6	way of t.) an archdeacon	SMITH 512:10
That t. lies somewhere	COWP 165:14	**Truth-teller:** T. was our England's Alfred		**turbulent:** sustained from one t. priest	
there is no other t.	DISR 186:36		TENN 541:13		HENR 246:1
there *is* such a thing as t.	BAG 29:17	**try:** end t. the man	SHAK 441:23	**turf:** Green be the t. above thee	HALL 238:9
they worship T.	BROO 94:24	Guiltier than him they t.	SHAK 463:16		
		'I'll t. the whole cause	CARR 133:19		

Thou t. of the mind | DRYD 196:32
t. custom | SHAK 474:5
t. duke unto a tyrant brother | SHAK 424:28
t. laws restrain | GOLD 231:30
t.'s vein | SHAK 469:27
t. Titus Tatius | ENN 208:20
tyrants: Ask all the t. of thy sex | CONG 160:22
blood of patriots and t. | JEFF 272:10
foe of t. | CAMP 129:9
Kings will be t. from policy | BURKE 111:13
now the t. | KEYN 296:1
Rebellion to t. is obedience | BRAD 91:12
sceptre from t. | TURG 553:22
'Twixt kings and t. there's | HERR 249:8
T. seldom want pretexts | BURKE 111:30
When t.' crests and tombs | SHAK 495:1
with the barbarity of t. | SMITH 511:30
would be t. if they could | DEFOE 173:4
Tyrawley: T. and I have been dead | CHES 146:7
Tyre: one with Nineveh and T. | KIPL 302:8
T., the crowning city | BIBLE 58:16
Tyrian: budded T. | KEATS 292:1
some grave T. trader | ARN 14:21
U: 'U. and 'Non-U' | ROSS 408:19
U. vert, O bleu: voyelles | RIMB 406:9
Ubi: U. Petrus | AMBR 4:1
ubique: Quod semper, quod u. | VINC 557:7
ubiquities: They are blazing u. | EMER 208:14
uffish: in u. thought he stood | CARR 134:29
ugliest: u. of trades have their | JERR 273:6
ugly: There is nothing u. | CONS 162:2
to be good than to be u. | WILDE 573:21
wasn't I born old and u. | DICK 176:1
world u. and bad has made | NIET 363:8
uita: u. breuis, sensus hebes | JOHN 273:17
Ulin: this Lord U.'s daughter | CAMP 129:2
Ulpian: U. at the best | BROW 99:15
Ulster: U. will fight | CHUR 149:18
ulterioris: Tendebantque manus ripae u. | VIRG 558:22
Ultima: U. Cumaei venit iam carminis | VIRG 559:22
U. Thule | VIRG 560:10
ultimate: u. decency of things | STEV 522:15
Ultio: voluptas U. | JUV 288:6
ultor: aliquis nostris ex ossibus u. | VIRG 558:15
ultrices: Luctus et u. posuere cubilia | VIRG 558:21
Ulubris: Est U. | HOR 258:19
Ulysses: Happy he who like U. has | DU B 198:26
U. leaves once more Calypso | SHEL 500:21
umbered: Wenlock Edge was u. | HOUS 265:11
umble: likewise a very 'u. person | DICK 177:6
We are so very 'u. | DICK 177:8
umbra: Pulvis et u. sumus | HOR 261:16
umbrage: Americans have taken u. | PUNCH 402:22
umbrella: u. To keep the scorching | FLET 215:19
unjust steals the just's u. | BOWEN 90:22
umbrellas: who possess u. | FORS 216:26
umbris: u. et imaginibus in veritatem | NEWM 362:6
umpire: Chaos u. sits | MILT 347:4
Umps: 'U.', said Mr Grewgious | DICK 178:5
un: thinking of the old 'u. | DICK 176:30
una: iuvat spinis de pluribus u. | HOR 259:6
U. salus victis nullam | VIRG 558:7
unacceptable: u. face of capitalism | HEATH 244:5
unacknowledged: inspire...Poets are the u. legislators | SHEL 505:13
unacquainted: is u. with your body | BACON 26:17
unadvisedly: u., lightly, or wantonly | PRAY 388:25
unaffected: can be rational and u. | AUST 22:9

unafraid: ruins would strike him u. | HOR 260:19
unalienable: Creator with certain u. rights | ANON 8:14
unalterable: watching Madness with u. | BYRON 121:7
unam: u. sanctam Catholicam et | MASS 334:20
unapt: so u. to perceive how | ARN 15:17
Unarm: U., Eros | SHAK 423:9
unassailable: That u. holds on his rank | SHAK 449:25
unattempted: u. yet in prose or rhyme | MILT 344:21
unattractive: most u. old thing | GILB 227:14
not against the u. | GREE 236:3
unaware: whereof he knew And I was u. | HARDY 239:7
unawares: entertained angels u. | BIBLE 80:3
unbearable: in victory, u. | CHUR 151:5
unbeatable: In defeat, u. | CHUR 151:5
unbecoming: u. a man of quality than | CONG 159:22
u. men that strove with | TENN 544:3
u. the character | ANON 4:20
unbegot: Unborn and u. | HOUS 265:13
unbelief: Blind u. is sure to err | COWP 165:29
did it ignorantly in u. | BIBLE 79:7
help thou mine u. | BIBLE 68:35
help thou mine u. | BUTL 119:11
help thou my u. | FORS 217:10
u. is blind | MILT 341:12
unbelieving: u. husband is sanctified | BIBLE 76:3
unbelov'd: poor u. ones | BETJ 42:7
unbend: u. your noble strength | SHAK 460:10
unbends: There is nothing u. | GAY 222:27
unbent: like an u. bow | DONNE 190:3
She u. her mind afterwards | LAMB 307:9
un-birthday: u. present | CARR 135:20
unborn: To you yet u. these | WHIT 570:2
U. and unbegot | HOUS 265:13
Unborrowed: interest U. from the eye | WORD 578:6
unbought: u. grace of life | BURKE 111:10
unbounded: man Of an u. stomach | SHAK 447:18
unbowed: head is bloody, but u. | HENL 245:4
unbribed: man will do u. | WOLFE 576:6
unbroidered: cramoisi is u. | POUND 382:11
unbroken: ties are u. and whose love | HOR 259:21
unbuild: I arise and u. it again | SHEL 500:7
unburied: friendless bodies of u. | WEBS 567:8
unbusy: sole u. thing | COL 157:14
unbutton: u. here | SHAK 454:20
Uncertain: U., coy | SCOTT 417:21
uncertainty: quit a certainty for an u. | JOHN 281:20
uncharitableness: from all u. | PRAY 385:16
unchaste: No u. action | SHAK 453:6
uncircumcised: daughters of the u. triumph | BIBLE 50:16
uncircumscribed: u., but man | SHEL 503:12
unclassed: u., tribeless | SHEL 503:12
uncle: married with mine u. | SHAK 479:1
nor u. me no uncle | SHAK 429:28
prophetic soul! My u. | SHAK 431:9
unclean: he is u. to you | BIBLE 48:6
midst of a people of u. lips | BIBLE 57:29
u. spirit is gone out | BIBLE 66:13
uncleanness: all u., or covetousness | BIBLE 78:2
unclouded: u. blaze of living light | BYRON 121:37
unclubable: very u. man | JOHN 275:16
uncoffin'd: u., and unknown | BYRON 121:24
uncomfortable: moral when he is only u. | SHAW 497:28
We u. feel | GILB 228:18
uncomfortableness: u. of it all | BROW 104:26

unconcern'd: Thou u. canst hear | POPE 376:21
unconfin'd: Let all her ways be u. | PRIOR 400:23
unconfined: let joy be u. | BYRON 120:21
unconfused: u., unhurried by emotion | JAMES 271:29
unconquerable: man's u. mind | WORD 582:17
nursing the u. hope | ARN 14:20
th' u. will | MILT 345:3
unconquered: eye the u. flame | POUND 382:14
unconscious: irony is generally quite u. | BUTL 118:23
u. hodmen of the men | HEINE 244:12
unconsidered: snapper-up of u. trifles | SHAK 491:18
uncontrollable: less free Than thou, O u. | SHEL 502:12
unconvincing: bald and u. narrative | GILB 227:12
uncorrupt: that leadeth an u. life | PRAY 390:4
Uncorseted: U., her friendly bust | ELIOT 205:14
uncouth: His u. way | MILT 346:16
Time makes ancient good u. | LOW 319:14
U. unkist | SPEN 517:5
uncouther: better the u. | BROW 105:27
Uncover: U., dogs, and lap | SHAK 486:7
uncreated: one u. | PRAY 385:13
womb of u. night | MILT 346:10
uncreating: dies before thy u. word | POPE 376:2
unction: not that flattering u. | SHAK 435:14
Thy blessed U. from above | PRAY 400:5
uncumber'd: u. with a wife | DRYD 196:4
undeceived: only u. Of that | ELIOT 202:20
undefiled: of the Lord is an u. law | PRAY 390:12
Pure religion and u. before | BIBLE 80:11
undemocratic: u. reasons and for motives | KIPL 302:5
under: they shall go u. the earth | PRAY 393:22
u. an English heaven | BROO 94:30
U. bare Ben Bulben's head | YEATS 587:10
U. his own vine what he | SHAK 448:1
under-belly: soft u. of the Axis | CHUR 150:13
Undergraduates: U. owe their happiness | BEER 37:22
underground: thinking Lays lads u. | HOUS 264:6
Till she sunk u. | LEAR 311:17
underlings: that we are u. | SHAK 448:17
under-peep: would u. her lids | SHAK 428:8
undersized: He's a bit u. | GILB 226:14
understand: are said to u. one another | CHAM 139:16
be understood or to u. | GREE 236:7
in the world u. any other | BAG 28:27
invented was easy to u. | AUDEN 18:15
me to u. wisdom secretly | PRAY 393:5
none could u. what she | BUNY 107:37
read and perhaps u. Shakespeare | KEATS 293:26
some who did not u. them | PRAED 384:6
still the less they u. | BUTL 118:6
Then thought I to u. this | PRAY 394:23
things which others u. | WORD 580:5
think I u. people very well | FORS 217:6
to u. them | SPIN 517:7
u. the heath who had not | HARDY 241:20
understanded: tongue not u. of the people | PRAY 400:8
understandeth: Who u. thee not | SHAK 457:2
understanding: all thy getting get u. | BIBLE 53:18
because they appeal to the u. | BAG 28:30
evidence against their own u. | HAL 237:23
good u. have all they that | PRAY 397:13
if thou hast u. | BIBLE 53:2
joke well into a Scotch u. | SMITH 510:28
length of days u. | BIBLE 52:24

likely to propagate u.	JOHN 280:13
obliged to find you an u.	JOHN 279:21
shall light a candle of u.	BIBLE 62:8
spirit of wisdom and u.	BIBLE 58:9
they pass all u.	JAM 271:6
things as pass man's u.	PRAY 386:18
To be totally u. makes	STAEL 517:15
u., but no tongue	SHAK 430:14
where is the place of u.	BIBLE 52:33
which have no u.	PRAY 391:18
which passeth all u.	BIBLE 78:21
yourself ignorant of his u.	COL 157:21

understandings: hearts and muddy u. — BURKE 111:11
understands: she always u. what you — JOHN 278:14

verse and thinks she u.	BROW 100:15

understonde: That thow be u. — CHAU 144:17
understood: all who u. admired — PRAED 384:6

Augurs and u. relations	SHAK 461:24
be told so as to be u.	BLAKE 88:25
something u.	HERB 248:5
those that u. him smiled	SHAK 448:23
u. or to understand I would	GREE 236:7

undertakers: become of the u. vithout
it — DICK 183:1
u.—walk before the hearse — GARR 221:11
Underworld: way down to the U. — VIRG 558:18
undeserving: I'm one of the u. poor — SHAW 498:14
undid: beach u. his corded bales — ARN 14:21

what they u. did	SHAK 422:2

undiscover'd: u. country from whose
bourn — SHAK 433:8
undiscovered: Gold u. (and all the better — HOR 260:20

ocean of truth lay all u.	NEWT 362:20

undisgraced: u. by those extravagancies — CHES 145:24
undo: Now mark me how I will u. — SHAK 480:1

should u. a man	SHAK 446:12
Some to u.	DRYD 198:19
thee does she u. herself	TOUR 551:16
to u. the heavy burdens	BIBLE 60:4
u. this button	SHAK 456:11

undoctored: Against the u. incident — KIPL 298:2
Un-done: Anne Donne, U. — DONNE 190:21

I am u.	BIBLE 57:29
Is not to leave't u.	SHAK 475:18
I was u. by my Auxiliary	STEE 518:14
not thought death had u.	ELIOT 204:20
'save the u. years	OWEN 367:10
some to be u.	DRYD 198:19
Than wishest should be u.	SHAK 459:1
...thou art u.	STER 520:10
u. vast	BROW 101:25
We have left u. those things	PRAY 384:12

undrugged: see u. in evening light — CHES 147:12
Undulate: U. round the world — WHIT 571:13
undulating: expression and an u. throat — BELL 40:2
undurable: delights u. — POUND 383:19
undying: u. Life — BRON 93:19
Unearned: U. increment — MILL 339:4
Uneasy: U. lies the head that wears — SHAK 441:30

You are u.	JACK 270:29

uneatable: full pursuit of the u. — WILDE 573:27
unequal: equal division of u. earnings — ELL 206:11

Men are made by nature u.	FROU 219:18

unexamined: u. life is not worth living — SOCR 512:17
unexpected: Old age is the most u. — TROT 553:16
unexpectedness: which I call u. — PEAC 370:17

unextinguishable: u. laugh in heaven — BROW 95:16
unfabled: blest u. Incense Tree — DARL 171:21
Unfaith: U. in aught is want — TENN 535:6
unfathomable: u. depths of his own
oceanic — COL 158:8

u. deep Forest	THOM 547:19

unfed: houseless heads and u. — SHAK 454:15
unfeeling: Th' u. for his own — GRAY 235:13
unfeignedly: them that u. love thee — PRAY 387:4
unfit: all things u. — GOLD 231:17

often u. a man for society	CHAM 139:14
u. to be trusted	CHES 146:6
U. to hear moral philosophy	SHAK 486:30

unfledg'd: new-hatch'd, u. comrade — SHAK 430:19
unforgetful: teach the u. to forget — ROSS 410:6
unforgiving: fill the u. minute — KIPL 300:2
unforgotten: assuage the u. pain — ROSS 410:6
unfriended: u., melancholy — GOLD 231:23
unfriendly: hostile and the towns u. — ELIOT 203:13

U. to the nose and eyes	STEV 523:13

Unfrowning: U. caryatides — STEV 523:12
unfruitful: he becometh u. — BIBLE 66:17
ungain'd: Men prize the thing u. — SHAK 486:21
Ungeheuern: Wer mit U. kämpft — NIET 363:10
ungentlemanly: knows how u. he can
look — SURT 525:21
unglücklich: u. das Land — BREC 92:1
Unglücklichen: eine andere als die des
U. — WITT 575:16
ungodliness: dwell in the tents of u. — PRAY 395:13
ungodly: hope of the u. away — BIBLE 62:18

in the counsel of the u.	PRAY 389:14
plagues remain for the u.	PRAY 391:18
seen the u. in great power	PRAY 391:29
thyself because of the u.	PRAY 391:20
u. he shall rain snares	PRAY 389:31

ungrateful: I make one u. person — LOUI 318:9
ungratefulness: they call virtue there
u. — SIDN 507:19
unguem: Ad u. Factus — HOR 262:4
unguess'd: tread on Earth u. — ARN 14:24
ungula: putrem sonitu quatit u. — VIRG 559:7
Unhand: 'U. it — TROL 552:17
unhanged: three good men u. in England — SHAK 438:34
unhappiness: Man's u. — CARL 132:19
unhappy: can never be very u. — GAY 223:26

dare to be u.	ROWE 410:25
each u. family is unhappy	TOLS 551:10
instinct for being u. highly	SAKI 413:6
is not cannot be made u.	LUCR 320:9
learning to care for the u.	VIRG 557:19
never as u. as one thinks	LA R 310:18
Not one is respectable or u.	WHIT 570:22
profession an u. ending	JAMES 272:1
that some should be u.	JOHN 277:5
u. alternative is before	AUST 23:15
u. the land that needs	BREC 92:1
which make us so u.	JOYCE 286:22

unhaunted: of a lone u. place possesst — DONNE 190:1
unheard: language of the u. — KING 296:14

those u. Are sweeter	KEATS 291:4

unheavenly: strange u. glare — BRID 92:13
unholy: sights u. — MILT 342:12
unhoming: Men move u. — FRY 220:7
unhonour'd: Mindful of th' u. dead — GRAY 235:3

Unwept, u., and unsung	SCOTT 416:22

unhurried: u. by emotion — JAMES 271:29
Unhurt: U. people are not much — STAR 517:21
unicorn: Sirion, like a young u. — PRAY 391:10
uniform: Should be more u. — HOOD 254:15

that a good u. must work	DICK 182:28

u. 'e wore	KIPL 299:17

uniformity: be preferred before u. — BACON 25:34
unigenitum: Christum Filium Dei u. — MASS 334:20
Unimportant: U., of course — CARR 134:20
uninformed: u. female who ever dared — AUST 24:2
uninitiated: keep far off, you u. — VIRG 558:19
unintelligent: there is anything so u. — ARN 15:17
unintelligible: Of all this u. world — WORD 578:5

u. patter	GILB 228:37

Union: Federal U.: it must be preserved — JACK 270:30

Liberty and U.	WEBS 566:11

Mysterious u. with its native sea — WORD 577:16

Our u. is perfect	DICK 184:4
saved the U. of these States	WHIT 571:21
to an indestructible U.	CHASE 141:3
u. of a deaf man	COL 157:19
u. of hands and hearts	TAYL 532:6
u. of this ever diverse	MER 337:7
U., strong and great	LONG 316:7
u. with Great Britain	SMITH 509:16
yet an u. in partition	SHAK 470:22

unit: Misses an u. — BROW 100:38
unite: Workers of the world, u. — MARX 333:4
United: U. Metropolitan Improved — DICK 179:33
United States: British Empire and the
U. — CHUR 150:3

great Government of the U.	WILS 574:23
rise of the U.	STEV 520:23
These U.	WHIT 571:14

uniting: By u. we stand — DICK 184:5
unity: city: that is at u. — PRAY 398:11

come in the u. of the faith	BIBLE 77:28
'Man can have U. if Man	AUDEN 19:11
preserve the u. of the empire	BURKE 110:4
to dwell together in u.	PRAY 398:26
Trinity in U.	PRAY 385:12
truth, u., and concord	PRAY 387:13

universal: maxim should become a u.
law — KANT 288:9

Nature wears one u. grin	FIEL 211:33
u. dovetailedness with	DICK 180:17
u. frame is without a mind	BACON 25:22
u. good	POPE 379:11

universals: There ain't no u. in this — MACN 326:5
universe: better ordering of the u. — ALF 3:16

hell of a good u.	CUMM 170:12
I accept the u.	CARL 132:30
is the measure of the u.	SHEL 503:8
Prais'd be the fathomless u.	WHIT 571:13
pretend to understand the U.	CARL 132:25
repeat the u. but to fulfil	SANT 414:2
richness and variety of the u.	HOUS 266:15
To mingle with the U.	BYRON 121:22
u. and give me yesterday	JONES 283:10
u. is not hostile	HOLM 253:5
u. is so vast and so ageless	ROS 408:18
We possessed all the u.	SHAW 496:30
will turn the u. to ashes	CEL 138:5

universities: discipline of colleges and
u. — SMITH 509:14
U. incline wits to sophistry — BACON 28:12
University: of the U. as a whole — COL 155:2

servant to be bred at an U.	CONG 160:12
Than his own mother U.	DRYD 197:14
true U. of these days is	CARL 131:35
U. should be a place	DISR 185:10
We are the U.	SPR 517:11

unjust: commended the u. steward — BIBLE 70:25

God all mercy is a God u.	YOUNG 588:9
just and on the u.	BIBLE 64:19

u. steals the just's umbrella BOWEN 90:22
unkind: call'd deform'd but the u.
SHAK 490:18
me not (Sweet) I am u. LOV 318:20
poor when givers prove u. SHAK 433:10
That are sodden and u. BELL 40:9
unkindest: u. cut of all SHAK 450:28
unkindness: his u. may defeat my life
SHAK 476:24
Men loved u. then HOUS 264:4
unkist: Uncouth u. SPEN 517:5
u., and lost CHAU 144:3
unknit: u. that threatening unkind
SHAK 484:15
unknowable: length of time which is
u. BEDE 37:1
world u. THOM 548:24
Unknowe: U., unkist CHAU 144:3
unknowing: Alike u. and unknown
BURNS 114:15
unknown: Alike unknowing and u.
BURNS 114:15
everything u. is held TAC 531:6
keep't u. SHAK 475:18
Of u. modes of being WORD 580:13
some u. regions preserved ELIOT 201:7
TO THE U. GOD BIBLE 74:12
tread safely into the u.' HASK 243:1
unmourned and u. HOR 261:18
unseen, u. POPE 380:24
unlamented: Thus u. let me die POPE 380:24
unleavened: u. bread of sincerity BIBLE 75:36
unleaving: Over Goldengrove u. HOPK 256:25
unlock'd: Lie all u. to your occasions
SHAK 465:16
unlocked: Shakespeare u. his heart'
BROW 101:10
unloose: latchet I am not worthy to u.
BIBLE 71:29
unlovely: Here in the long u. street
TENN 536:5
unlucky: who is so u. MARQ 331:2
unmannerly: them untaught knaves,
u. SHAK 438:14
unmapped: u. country within us which
ELIOT 200:22
unmarried: keep u. as long as he can
SHAW 497:25
unmask: To u. falsehood SHAK 492:19
u. her beauty to the moon SHAK 430:17
unmeaning: u. thing they call a thought
POPE 378:21
unmeritable: This is a slight u. man
SHAK 451:10
unmindfulness: fingers play in skilled
u. HARDY 239:12
Unmiss'd: U. but by his dogs COWP 166:6
unmitigated: ultimate conclusion in u.
KIPL 299:5
unmixed: Nothing is an u. blessing
HOR 260:11
unmourned: u. and unknown HOR 261:18
Unmoved: U., cold SHAK 494:15
unnatural: cruel, not u. SHAK 434:26
Do breed u. troubles SHAK 462:26
Revenge his foul and most u. murder
SHAK 431:6
thoughts u. SHAK 475:20
U. vices ELIOT 203:6
unnecessary: thou u. letter SHAK 453:21
unnoticed: pathway of a life u. HOR 258:24
uno: Crimine ab u. VIRG 558:2
unobtrusive: should be great and u.
KEATS 293:23
unofficial: English u. rose BROO 94:18
unparagon'd: Rubies u. SHAK 428:8
unparallel'd: lass u. SHAK 424:15
unparticular: nice u. man HARDY 241:10
unpitied: u., unreprieved MILT 346:11

unpleasant'st: are a few of the u. words
SHAK 467:15
unpleasing: that are tender and u.
BACON 25:41
U. to a married ear SHAK 457:18
unplumb'd: u., salt ARN 13:13
Unpolicied: Caesar ass U. SHAK 424:14
unpopular: I was not u. there BEER 37:21
u. names ARN 15:25
unpremeditated: strains of u. art SHEL 504:15
u. lay SCOTT 416:10
unpremeditating: Poured forth his u.
strain THOM 549:9
unprepared: Magnificently u. CORN 162:21
unprofitable: flat, and u. SHAK 429:28
months the most idle and u. GIBB 224:7
unpropitious: conditions That seem u.
ELIOT 202:24
unproportion'd: Nor any u. thought
his SHAK 430:19
unprotected: u. race CLARE 152:11
unpunctual: vague u. star BROO 94:19
unquiet: be the earth never so u. PRAY 396:10
sole u. thing COL 156:22
u. heart and brain TENN 536:1
u. slumbers for the sleepers BRON 94:1
unravaged: u. by the fierce intellectual
ARN 15:25
unreasonable: progress depends on the
u. SHAW 498:1
unredressed: there is a wrong left u.
KING 297:18
unrefined: meane and u. stuffe of mine
BRAD 91:15
unreflecting: habit rules the u. herd
WORD 581:17
Unregarded: U. age in corners thrown
SHAK 425:4
unregulated: there the u. sun BROO 94:19
unremembered: nameless, u., acts
WORD 578:4
unremembering: She went her u. way
THOM 547:26
Their u. hearts and heads YEATS 587:8
unrequited: of what u. affection is
DICK 178:2
unrest: frantic-mad with evermore u.
SHAK 495:15
u. which men miscall delight SHEL 499:21
unreturning: Over the u. brave
BYRON 120:26
unreveal'd: rest remaineth u. TENN 536:18
unrighteousness: friends of the mammon
of u. BIBLE 70:26
unruly: it is an u. evil BIBLE 80:14
night has been u. SHAK 460:20
u. wills and affections PRAY 386:12
unsad: u. and evere untrewe CHAU 142:8
unsatisfied: it leaves one u. WILDE 573:20
senses and his heart u. YEATS 585:3
unsavoury: hast the most u. similes
SHAK 438:5
unsealed: my lips are not yet u. BALD 29:29
unseam'd: he u. him from the nave
SHAK 458:3
unsearchable: heart of kings is u.
BIBLE 54:25
What th' u. dispose MILT 351:3
unseemly: how u. is it for my sex
MARL 330:11
unseen: Floats though u. among us
SHEL 501:5
Thou art u. SHEL 504:18
U. before by Gods or wondering
KEATS 290:6
walk the earth U. MILT 348:6
unselfishness: sympathetic u. of an oyster
SAKI 413:7
unsettled: are u. is there any hope
EMER 207:15

unsex: u. me here SHAK 459:2
Unshak'd: U. of motion SHAK 449:25
unshorn: wings presents the god u.
HERR 248:22
Unsifted: U. in such perilous circumstance
SHAK 430:20
unsought: lost, that is u. CHAU 144:3
unsought-for: aye u. slept among his
KEATS 289:24
unsoundness: without a certain u. of
mind MAC 323:23
unspeakable: joy u. and full of glory
BIBLE 80:20
may come to those u. joys PRAY 387:4
u. Turk should be immediately CARL 132:6
u. in full pursuit WILDE 573:27
unspotted: himself u. from the world
BIBLE 80:20
unstable: remember of this u. world
MAL 327:21
U. as water BIBLE 46:39
Unstaid: U. and skittish in all SHAK 488:27
unstitching: Our stitching and u. has
YEATS 584:9
unstoried: still u. FROST 219:6
unstringed: Than an u. viol or a harp
SHAK 478:10
unsubstantial: dwellings and u. realms
of Dis VIRG 558:20
unsuccessful: Like an u. literary man
BELL 40:2
unsung: Unwept, unhonour'd, and u.
SCOTT 416:22
unswept: antique time would lie u.
SHAK 427:17
untainted: breastplate than a heart u.
SHAK 446:6
U. by man's misery SHEL 503:28
untender: So young, and so u. SHAK 453:3
unthinking: u. time DRYD 197:17
untimely: Why came I so u. forth
WALL 562:15
unting: ain't the 'u. as 'urts 'im
PUNCH 402:17
'U. fills my thoughts SURT 525:5
'U. is all that's worth SURT 525:4
untold: I mean the truth u. OWEN 367:11
untouched: If thou appear u. by solemn
WORD 582:1
untravell'd: Gleams that u. world
TENN 543:22
untrewe: unsad and evere u. CHAU 142:8
untried: against the new and u. LINC 314:16
left u. CHES 148:9
untrodden: dwelt among the u. ways
WORD 581:6
untroubled: Untroubling and u. where
CLARE 152:13
Untroubling: U. and untroubled where
CLARE 152:13
untrue: man who's u. to his wife
AUDEN 20:13
untruth: have put more truth and u.
BACON 26:14
should tell one wilful u. NEWM 362:4
torment of the night's u. DAN 171:1
unused: Albeit u. to the melting SHAK 477:23
unutterable: sighed and looked u. things
THOM 549:14
unvanquishable: In u. number SHEL 502:4
unwash'd: Another lean u. artificer
SHAK 452:27
Unwept: U., unhonour'd, and unsung
SCOTT 416:22
unwholesome: boiled very soft is not
u. AUST 22:7
Unwillingly: U. represent GILB 227:5
unwise: In the sight of the u. BIBLE 62:13
wise, and to the u. BIBLE 74:30
unwithered: find u. on its curls HOUS 263:3

victims: little v. play	GRAY 235:12
They are its v.	CONR 161:22
Victor: croyait V. Hugo	COCT 154:13
my shock-headed v.	BETJ 44:6
v. belong the spoils	MARCY 328:21
V. Hugo...A madman	COCT 154:13
V. sat in a corner	AUDEN 21:7
victoree: thy v.	ANON 7:4
victorem: Graecia capta ferum v.	HOR 259:2
Victoria: ticket at V. Station and go	
	BEVIN 44:18
worse at V. and Waterloo	CONN 161:14
victories: Ev'n victors are by v.	DRYD 196:6
Peace hath her v.	MILT 351:17
thousand v. once foil'd	SHAK 493:4
victorious: a' the ills o' life v.	BURNS 115:6
speech in that v. brow	ARN 14:24
victors: Let the v.	ARN 13:15
v. are by victories undone	DRYD 196:6
victory: At every famous v.	SOUT 513:18
glorious thing must be a v.	WELL 567:26
grave, where is thy v.	BIBLE 77:1
he gotten himself the v.	PRAY 396:7
in v., magnanimity	CHUR 150:25
Joy, Empire and V.	SHEL 503:15
One more such v. and we	PYRR 403:7
swallow up death in v.	BIBLE 58:19
Thy v., O Grave	ROSS 408:20
Truth beareth away the v.	BIBLE 62:4
V. at all costs	CHUR 149:30
V. is not a name strong	NELS 360:15
v. is twice itself when	SHAK 471:24
Victrix: V. causa deis placuit	LUCAN 319:22
victuals: About their v.	CALV 127:19
v. and the wine	CALV 127:20
You eat your v. fast enough	HOUS 264:11
vicus: v. of recirculation back	JOYCE 286:2
vida: Que descansada v.	LUIS 320:12
Qué es la v.	CALD 127:5
vidders: careful o' v. all your life	
	DICK 181:36
Video: V. meliora	OVID 366:17
videri: salices et se cupit ante v.	VIRG 559:18
vides: Jupiter est quodcumque v.	
	LUCAN 320:1
vidi: Ut v.	VIRG 560:4
vie: apparié notre v. à un songe	MONT 355:5
et la v. qui est saulve	FRAN 218:1
mis mon génie dans ma v.	WILDE 573:35
que la v. est quotidienne	LAF 306:23
vieille: Quand vous serez bien v.	RONS 407:18
vieillesse: si v. pouvoit	EST 208:25
triste v. vous vous préparez	TALL 531:18
viento: Verde v.	GARC 221:7
vierge: Le v., le vivace et le bel	MALL 327:10
vieux: Eldorado banal de tous les v.	
	BAUD 35:8
view: beam upon my inward v.	ARN 13:4
lends enchantment to the v.	CAMP 129:6
v. of the surplice-question	BROW 100:2
Wheresoe'er I turn my v.	JOHN 280:9
vigil: tongueless v. and all the pain	
	SWIN 528:15
vigilance: liberty to man is eternal v.	
	CURR 170:16
vigilant: Be sober, be v.	BIBLE 80:33
v. as a cat to steal cream	SHAK 440:11
v. eye	SHAK 427:11
v., sober	BIBLE 79:12
vigilat: frustra v. qui custodit	BIBLE 83:12
vigour: v. and a pulse like a cannon	
	EMER 207:10
v. of bone	SHAK 487:6
With all her double v.	SHAK 464:6
Vikings: Stir the V.' blood	KING 296:24
vile: 'beautified' is a v. phrase	SHAK 431:34
change our v. body	PRAY 389:13
goodness to the v. seem	SHAK 455:11
In durance v. here must	BURNS 113:22
make v. things precious	SHAK 454:11

only man is v.	HEBER 244:6
O v., Intolerable	SHAK 484:14
perceive you are a v. Whig	JOHN 276:5
Things base and v.	SHAK 469:22
v. a pun would not scruple	DENN 174:24
vilest: v. things Become themselves	
	SHAK 422:5
villa: v. in summer to dwell	MORR 358:3
village: blaspheming over the v. idiot	
	CHES 148:7
first in a v. than second	CAES 127:3
loveliest v. of the plain	GOLD 230:16
Some v.-Hampden	GRAY 234:23
vegetate in a v.	COLT 159:10
villages: devotees in these peculiar v.	
	IRV 270:26
pleasant v. and farms	MILT 349:13
v. dirty and charging high	ELIOT 203:13
villain: alone the v. of the earth	SHAK 423:2
determined to prove a v.	SHAK 480:19
hungry, lean-fac'd v.	SHAK 427:9
if some eternal v.	SHAK 476:23
Is like a v. with a smiling	SHAK 466:1
lecherous, kindless v.	SHAK 433:4
not fair terms and a v.'s	SHAK 466:5
No v. need be	MER 337:14
One murder made a v.	PORT 381:31
smiling, damned v.	SHAK 431:16
tale condemns me for a v.	SHAK 481:14
V. and he be many miles	SHAK 483:16
Who calls me v.	SHAK 433:3
villains: O v., vipers, damn'd	SHAK 479:9
we were v. by necessity	SHAK 453:11
villainy: species of political v.	PEAC 370:14
villany: clothe my naked v.	SHAK 480:25
v. you teach me I will	SHAK 467:5
Villiers: Great V. lies	POPE 377:33
Villon: V., our sad bad	SWIN 529:2
vina: Ut sint v. proxima	ANON 10:14
vinces: In hoc signo v.	CONS 162:6
Vinci: They spell it V. and pronounce	
	TWAIN 554:9
vincit: Amor v. omnia	CHAU 141:17
Omnia v. Amor	VIRG 560:8
vindicate: v. the ways of God to man	
	POPE 379:2
Vine: Daughter of the V. to Spouse	
	FITZ 213:1
every man under his v.	BIBLE 61:23
foxlike in the v.	TENN 542:16
luscious clusters of the v.	MARV 332:3
maize and v.	TENN 533:5
shall be as the fruitful v.	PRAY 398:20
sweet grape who will the v.	SHAK 492:18
thyme and the gadding v.	MILT 343:6
Under his own v. what he	SHAK 448:1
v. and grapes in gold	FLEC 214:17
With v. leaves in his hair	IBSEN 269:23
vinegar: Marriage from love, like v.	
	BYRON 122:26
Pepper and v. besides	CARR 135:8
thirsty they gave me v.	PRAY 394:12
v., sugar	GOLD 231:16
vines: France With all her v.	COWP 166:34
that spoil the v.	BIBLE 56:23
v. that round the thatch-eaves	KEATS 293:5
vineyard: Give me thy v.	BIBLE 51:17
Jezreelite had a v.	BIBLE 51:17
left as a cottage in a v.	BIBLE 57:16
wellbeloved hath a v. in a very fruitful	
	BIBLE 57:21
who planteth a v.	BIBLE 76:5
vingt-quatre: capitaine de v. soldats	
	ANON 9:8
vintage: draught of v.	KEATS 291:18
Fate of all their V. prest	FITZ 212:17
than the v. of Abi-ezer	BIBLE 49:17
vintager: Since Ariadne was a v.	
	KEATS 289:4

Vintners: often wonder what the V. buy	
	FITZ 213:14
vinum daemonum: indignation call poesy	
v.	BACON 24:27
violations: v. committed by children	
	BOWEN 91:3
viol-de-gamboys: He plays o' the v.	
	SHAK 487:24
violence: essence of war is v.	MAC 323:8
offer it the show of v.	SHAK 429:15
Thus with v. shall that	BIBLE 82:24
V. shall synchronize your	AUDEN 19:11
violent: All v. feelings...produce	
	RUSK 411:11
efforts to do it a v. injury	WOD 575:24
v. hands upon themselves	PRAY 389:10
violently: v. if they must	QUIN 403:24
violet: Fashioned an April v.	WATS 565:12
grave's one v.	BROW 103:24
in the v.-embroidered	MILT 341:3
oxlips and the nodding v.	SHAK 470:10
She is the v.	SKEL 508:18
throw a perfume on the v.	SHAK 452:25
V., amaracus, and asphodel	TENN 541:18
v. by a mossy stone	WORD 581:6
v. of his native land	TENN 536:10
v. smells to him as it	SHAK 444:20
violets: ashen roots the v. blow	TENN 537:18
breathes upon a bank of v.	SHAK 487:20
Fast fading v. cover'd	KEATS 291:21
pied wind-flowers and v.	SHEL 503:18
to mix v. with anything	DISR 186:15
v. dim	SHAK 491:26
When daisies pied and v.	SHAK 457:18
Who are the v. now	SHAK 480:11
would give you some v.	SHAK 436:11
violins: Antonio Stradivari's v.	ELIOT 201:28
v. of autumn	VERL 556:8
violons: v. De l'automne	VERL 556:8
viper: saw a Lawyer killing a v.	COL 156:12
vipers: generation of v.	BIBLE 63:38
O villains, v., damn'd	SHAK 479:9
To extirpate the v.	AYT 24:6
vir: Beatus v. qui timet Dominum	BIBLE 83:9
vires: Ut desint v.	OVID 366:26
Virgil: I just saw V.	OVID 366:24
V. at Mexico	WALP 563:9
V. seems to have composed	ARN 16:12
V. was no good because	BUTL 118:35
Virgile: V., Ovide	CHAU 144:17
virgin: bashful v.'s side-long looks	
	GOLD 230:17
Born of the V. Mary	PRAY 384:26
Every harlot was a v. once	BLAKE 86:1
Gloriously deceitful and a v.	HOR 261:2
Mary ever V.	MASS 334:15
Now too the v. goddess	VIRG 559:22
see the V. blest	MILT 344:15
So though a v.	CAREW 130:15
v. mother born	MILT 344:3
v. shall conceive	BIBLE 58:3
V. shrouded in snow	BLAKE 87:22
v. white integrity	DONNE 187:21
virgin-choir: v. to make delicious moan	
	KEATS 292:2
virgin'd: Hath v. it e'er since	SHAK 428:2
Virginian: I am not a V.	HENRY 245:26
Virginians: Rally behind the V.	BEE 37:3
Virginibus: V. puerisque canto	HOR 260:13
virginité: v. pouvait être une vertu	
	VOLT 561:18
virginity: No, no; for my v.	PRIOR 401:17
That long preserved v.	MARV 332:19
your old v.	SHAK 420:27
virgins: holy v. in their ecstasies	TENN 534:23
v. are soft as the roses	BYRON 120:2
v. that be her fellows	PRAY 392:17
virgo: Iam redit et v.	VIRG 559:22
in omne v. Nobilis	HOR 261:2

waspish: When you are w. SHAK 451:16
wasps: w. and hornets break through
  SWIFT 527:16
wassails: w., wakes HERR 248:18
waste: my dear times' w. SHAK 493:7
  no less than war to w. MILT 349:27
  now doth time w. me SHAK 480:15
  other it is a w. of goods VEBL 556:2
  Over the w. of waters BYRON 122:17
  spirit in a w. of shame SHAK 495:7
  To w. his whole heart TENN 543:9
  And solitary places SHEL 501:10
  w. its sweetness GRAY 234:23
  w. of breath the years YEATS 585:15
  w. remains and kills EMPS 208:17
  w. the remains of life WALP 563:2
  we lay w. our powers WORD 582:19
  were I in the wildest w. BURNS 114:31
  what purpose is this w. BIBLE 68:8
  ye w. places of Jerusalem BIBLE 59:19
wasted: w. his substance with riotous
  BIBLE 70:18
wasteful: w., blundering, low DARW 172:1
waste-paper: Marriage is the w. basket
  WEBB 566:8
Wastes: W. without springs CLARE 152:9
wasting: delightful way of w. time
  MORL 357:23
  w. in despair WITH 575:12
Wat: poor W. SHAK 495:21
  w. their cork-heel'd shoon BALL 31:19
watch: before the morning w. PRAY 398:24
  could ye not w. with me BIBLE 68:15
  done far better by a w. BELL 39:23
  Either he's dead or my w. MARX 333:1
  everlasting w. and moveless BROW 98:8
  Fear gave his w. no look AUDEN 20:19
  if you'd w. a dinner out BROW 99:2
  keeping w. over their flock BIBLE 69:9
  keeping w. above his own LOW 319:13
  like little w. springs SPEN 515:9
  like your w. in a private CHES 145:21
  Lord w. between me BIBLE 46:22
  past as a w. in the night PRAY 395:18
  Set a w., O Lord PRAY 399:9
  She shall w. all night SHAK 484:11
  So here I'll w. the night HOUS 262:18
  some must w. SHAK 434:16
  Thence to a w. SHAK 432:2
  those who w. at that midnight LEAR 312:3
  to w. for her SHAK 456:27
  W. and pray BIBLE 68:16
  'W. and pray ELL 206:9
  w. of the night Jesus went BIBLE 66:25
  w. return'd a silver sound POPE 380:29
  w. the clock for you SHAK 493:18
  W. therefore BIBLE 68:1
  W. the wall KIPL 302:22
  W. ye therefore BIBLE 69:1
  whispers of each other's w. SHAK 444:9
  winding up the w. of his wit SHAK 485:4
watch-chain: too large to hang on a w.
  ANON 8:11
watchdog: w.'s voice that bay'd GOLD 230:21
watched: however w. and tended LONG 317:6
  I w. in vain FLEC 214:19
  w. this famous island descending CHUR 151:4
watcher: like some w. of the skies
  KEATS 292:18
watches: heart That w. and receives
  WORD 582:21
  w. from his mountain walls TENN 533:7
watchful: w. eye and the strong arm
  PALM 368:10
watching: w. and with study faint
  CHUR 149:1
  Weeping and w. for the morrow GOET 230:12
watchman: w. on the lonely tower
  SCOTT 417:1
  w. waketh but in vain PRAY 398:18

W., what of the night BIBLE 58:14
watchmen: w. that went about BIBLE 57:2
watch out: w. for that man HOR 262:3
watchword: Our w. is security PITT 374:1
water: benison of hot w. BROO 94:9
  blackens all the w. about ADD 2:24
  By trinking up ta w. AYT 24:7
  conscious w. saw its God CRAS 169:2
  don't care where the w. CHES 147:28
  Drink no longer w. BIBLE 79:16
  Dripping w. hollows out a stone OVID 366:27
  feet are always in the w. AMES 4:3
  fountain of the w. of life BIBLE 82:32
  good Shall come of w. BROO 94:11
  He asked w. BIBLE 49:10
  I am poured out like w. PRAY 390:19
  I baptize with w. BIBLE 71:29
  'I came like W. FITZ 212:21
  In imperceptible w. HOOD 254:23
  in the w. under the earth BIBLE 47:24
  Is wetter w. BROO 94:12
  King over the W. ANON 7:25
  land where no w. is PRAY 393:21
  Laughing W. LONG 317:11
  Lay a great w. TENN 535:21
  limns the w. BACON 28:16
  more w. glideth by the mill SHAK 486:15
  name was writ in w. KEATS 295:3
  Oft w. fairest meadows COWP 167:29
  plain w. and raw greens AUDEN 21:6
  Plunge in and be deep w. HOR 261:12
  plunge your hands in w. AUDEN 18:10
  ready by w. as by land ELST 206:15
  river of w. of life BIBLE 82:35
  should go across salt w. DICK 183:7
  sound w. escaping from CONS 162:1
  sound of w.'s murmuring SHEL 503:17
  sweet w. and bitter BIBLE 80:15
  that is not filled with w. BIBLE 54:46
  to fare forth on the w. POUND 383:18
  Too much of w. hast thou SHAK 436:20
  travel by land or by w. PRAY 385:20
  Unstable as w. BIBLE 46:39
  virtues We write in w. SHAK 447:20
  wasn't as dull as ditch w. DICK 181:17
  w. clears us of this deed SHAK 460:14
  w. comes down at Lodore SOUT 513:22
  w., every where COL 155:14
  w. flowed in it dazzled BALL 31:3
  w. in the rough rude sea SHAK 479:5
  W. is excellent PIND 373:13
  w. is in water SHAK 423:8
  w., is unsuitable in colour HERB 246:18
  W. like a stone ROSS 409:1
  w. my couch with my tears PRAY 389:26
  w. spilt on the ground BIBLE 50:23
  w. steaming hot PAIN 367:16
  w. suggest her clear DONNE 188:9
  w. the ground where it BACON 26:33
  w. unto wine TENN 539:5
  W. your damned flower-pots BROW 105:5
  We'll o'er the w. to Charlie HOGG 253:1
  What dreadful noise of w. SHAK 480:27
  'What's the w. in French DICK 180:13
  wind and swift-flowing w. CAT 137:7
  with w. and a crust KEATS 290:24
  with w. of affliction BIBLE 51:20
  wood and drawers of w. BIBLE 49:3
  written by drinkers of w. HOR 258:25
water-brooks: hart desireth the w.
  PRAY 392:6
water-colours: amateur painting in w.
  STEV 521:28
water'd: w. heaven with their tears
  BLAKE 87:16
water-drops: women's weapons, w.
  SHAK 454:2
watered: Apollos w. BIBLE 75:31
  is more likely to be w. BUTL 119:4

waterfall: From the w. he named her
  LONG 317:11
water-flags: We saw the w. in flower
  PATM 370:2
water-flies: w. Blow me into abhorring
  SHAK 423:21
water-floods: in the great w. they shall
  PRAY 391:17
water-lilies: floating w. SHEL 503:20
water-lily: inclosed at night in a w.
  LONG 317:23
  She saw the w. bloom TENN 538:11
Waterloo: have not yet met our W.
  DOYLE 192:17
  high at Austerlitz and W. SAND 413:27
  man meets his W. at last PHIL 373:1
  On W.'s ensanguined plain ANON 7:8
  that world-earthquake, W. TENN 541:10
  W. was won on the playing WELL 567:24
  worse at Victoria and W. CONN 161:14
Waterloo House: W. young man GILB 227:28
water-man: great-grandfather was but
  a w. BUNY 107:18
watermen: w., that row one way
  BURT 116:15
water-mill: noise like that of a w.
  SWIFT 526:3
water-pipes: of the noise of the w.
  PRAY 392:8
water-rats: there be land-rats and w.
  SHAK 465:27
Waters: all that move in the W. PRAY 384:25
  beside the w. of comfort PRAY 390:21
  Canst drink the w. DEKK 173:21
  Cast thy bread upon the w. BIBLE 56:5
  chittering w. JOYCE 286:8
  come ye to the w. BIBLE 59:25
  crept by me upon the w. SHAK 484:31
  his chambers in the w. PRAY 396:18
  in perils of w. BIBLE 77:12
  knowledge of man is as the w. BACON 24:20
  lilies by the rivers of w. BIBLE 63:27
  luminous home of w. ARN 15:1
  Many w. cannot quench love BIBLE 57:12
  Midland w. with the gale ARN 14:21
  mighty w. rolling evermore WORD 579:12
  Once more upon the w. BYRON 120:18
  On those cool w. where HOPE 256:4
  Over the rolling w. go TENN 541:31
  quiet w. SCOT 419:5
  shuddering w. saw KIPL 300:6
  sound of many w. BIBLE 81:14
  Stolen w. are sweet BIBLE 53:28
  than all the w. of Israel BIBLE 51:28
  that sitteth upon many w. BIBLE 82:22
  their business in great w. PRAY 397:9
  Though thou the w. warp SHAK 426:1
  upon the face of the w. BIBLE 44:22
  voice of many w. BIBLE 82:15
  w. at their priestlike KEATS 292:11
  w. cover the sea BIBLE 58:11
  w. murmuring MILT 342:8
  w. of affliction BIBLE 58:28
  w. of Babylon we sat PRAY 399:3
  W. on a starry night WORD 578:22
  w. stand in the hills PRAY 396:18
  W. that be above the Firmament PRAY 384:20
  w. to a thirsty soul BIBLE 54:30
  w. to stand on an heap PRAY 395:5
  w. were his winding sheet BARN 34:5
  w. wider HUXL 269:2
  w. wild went o'er his child CAMP 129:5
  wilderness shall w. break BIBLE 58:34
  'with pomp of w. WORD 582:2
water-tower: Under the great grey w.
  CHES 147:8
watery: Robert with his w. smile
  TENN 533:10
  shoreless w. wild ARN 13:12
  weder warmer than after w. LANG 309:28

watter: which makes my teeth w.
    FLEM 214:28
Wattle: ever hear of Captain W. DIBD 175:16
wattles: of clay and w. made YEATS 585:17
  they were all out of w. NASH 360:3
waught: right gude-willie w. BURNS 112:31
waul: We w. and cry SHAK 455:22
wav'd: banner w. without a blast
    SCOTT 416:14
  w. her lily hand GAY 223:30
wave: chin upon an orient w. MILT 344:14
  else save the w.'s slash POUND 383:18
  great w. that echoes round TENN 535:4
  hath seen her w. her hand TENN 538:4
  lift me as a w. SHEL 505:4
  never a w. of all her waves KIPL 303:3
  no w. Of a great flood MER 337:10
  Quivering within the w.'s SHEL 502:10
  translucent w. MILT 341:20
  w. o' the sea SHAK 491:27
  w. to pant beneath thy SHEL 502:12
  weak as is a breaking w. WORD 580:5
  When the blue w. rolls BYRON 122:1
Waverley: W. pen ANON 8:5
waves: came the w. and washed SPEN 515:20
  dolphins of kindlier w. MOORE 355:23
  floods lift up their w. PRAY 396:1
  Him that walked the w. MILT 343:17
  Innumerable twinkling of the w. AESC 3:3
  I see the w. upon the shore SHEL 504:9
  light-hearted Masters of the w. ARN 14:21
  Like as the w. make towards SHAK 493:19
  long'd-for dash of w. is ARN 15:1
  noise of his w. PRAY 394:1
  only on the w. behind us COL 157:20
  save the w. BYRON 123:4
  Though she w. her little hand HARDY 240:16
  w. and storms are gone PRAY 392:8
  w. bound beneath me BYRON 120:18
  w. of thy sweet singing SHEL 500:16
  w. of thy sweet singing SHEL 503:11
  w. roar and whirl ARN 13:7
  w. that beat on Heaven's BLAKE 85:15
  w. thereof are still PRAY 397:10
  w. were more gay YEATS 586:5
  What are the wild w. saying CARP 132:34
  wind sang and the same w. SWIN 529:19
waving: not w. but drowning SMITH 510:26
  w. his wild tail KIPL 304:24
wax: hives with honey and w. SWIFT 525:33
  is even like melting w. PRAY 390:19
  Of wyne and w. WYNT 584:4
  times begin to w. old BIBLE 62:7
  virtue of w. and parchment BURKE 109:24
  w. old as doth a garment PRAY 396:13
  W. to receive BYRON 119:31
  Yet moons swiftly w. again HOR 261:16
wax-works: If you think we're w.
    CARR 135:1
way: all gone out of the w. PRAY 390:3
  broad is the w. BIBLE 65:6
  dangerous w. GOLD 232:25
  each thing give him w. SHAK 421:24
  every one to his own w. BIBLE 59:22
  flowers to strew Thy w. HERB 247:17
  gentleman's w. of thinking ANON 10:14
  have such a winning w. CONG 160:26
  her own w. to perfection BURKE 109:18
  I am the w., the truth BIBLE 72:32
  I have no w. SHAK 455:6
  indirect w. to plant religion BROW 96:16
  must have her w. BURKE 110:15
  mystical w. of Pythagoras BROW 96:11
  of being never in the w. CHAR 140:27
  one w. in to life SEN 420:9
  perish from the right w. PRAY 389:19
  Prepare ye the w. of the Lord BIBLE 59:5
  Prepare ye the w. of the Lord BIBLE 63:36
  ready w. to virtue BROW 96:25
  seeking the w. in life LUCR 320:6

shortest w. is commonly BACON 25:4
Something given that w. FLET 215:14
talked with us by the w. BIBLE 71:18
Teach me thy w. PRAY 391:8
teach thee in the w. wherein PRAY 391:18
That's the w. for Billy HOGG 252:23
that's the w. to the stars VIRG 559:8
that there was a w. to Hell BUNY 107:26
This is the w. BIBLE 58:29
this is the w. of them PRAY 392:28
Thou art my w. QUAR 403:13
w. may be known upon earth PRAY 394:4
w. of all the earth BIBLE 49:5
w. of a man with a maid KIPL 301:1
w. of an eagle in the air BIBLE 55:1
w. of transgressors is BIBLE 53:36
w. plain before my face PRAY 389:24
w. that Providence dictates HITL 251:10
w. to dusty death SHAK 463:6
w. to prevent seditions BACON 27:11
w. to the Better there HARDY 240:1
whole breadth of the w. BUNY 107:15
woman has her w. HOLM 253:15
wayfaring: w. men BIBLE 58:35
ways: all her w. be unconfin'd PRIOR 400:23
  at the parting of the w. BIBLE 60:36
  I knew all her w. HOUS 265:8
  is the chief of the w. BIBLE 53:9
  keep thee in all thy w. PRAY 395:22
  Let me count the w. BROW 98:13
  neither are your ways my w. BIBLE 59:27
  Queer are the w. of a man HARDY 240:15
  That for w. that are dark HARTE 242:29
  There are nine and sixty w. KIPL 300:3
  vindicate the w. of God POPE 379:2
  w. are ways of pleasantness BIBLE 53:17
  w. deep and the weather ELIOT 203:12
  whose heart are thy w. PRAY 395:12
  will maintain mine own w. BIBLE 52:25
  world and its w. have BROW 105:18
wayside: some seeds fell by the w.
    BIBLE 66:16
wayward: w. is this foolish love SHAK 490:31
  What fond and w. thoughts WORD 582:21
we: Even w., Even so MER 336:26
  know that which w. are BYRON 124:9
  people like us are W. KIPL 304:2
  Put it down a w. DICK 182:21
  still it is not w. CHES 147:14
  W. for a certainty are HOUS 264:21
  W. in the tournament BETJ 44:6
weak: concessions of the w. are
    BURKE 109:14
  earth is w. PRAY 394:25
  God hath chosen the w. BIBLE 75:30
  he is w. WORD 580:5
  How very w. the very wise THAC 546:4
  human reason w. BAG 28:30
  in the mind of man so w. BACON 26:2
  Made w. by time and fate TENN 544:3
  Strengthen ye the w. hands BIBLE 58:33
  that are otherwise w. men BACON 25:40
  to be w. is miserable MILT 345:5
  w. alone repent BYRON 121:33
  w. as is a breaking wave WORD 580:5
  w. from your loveliness BETJ 44:6
  w. is their brain-pan BLAKE 87:1
  W. men must fall SHAK 479:5
  w. one is singled SHEL 501:22
  w. piping time of peace SHAK 480:18
  willing but the flesh is w. BIBLE 68:16
  with w. hands though mighty SHEL 499:15
Weakening: W. the will SPEN 515:12
weaker: Is to the w. side inclin'd
    BUTL 118:14
  unto the w. vessel BIBLE 80:29
  w. sex ALEX 3:15
weakest: w. kind of fruit SHAK 467:25
weak-hearted: comfort and help the w.
    PRAY 385:19

weakness: All w. which impairs ARN 14:24
  amiable w. FIEL 211:28
  Girt round with w. SHEL 499:17
  'Is it w. of intellect GILB 227:16
  strength is made perfect in w. BIBLE 77:14
  Stronger by w. WALL 562:9
  thence into a w. SHAK 432:2
  w. of our mortal nature PRAY 386:15
  With too much w. POPE 379:12
weaknesses: his w. are great KIPL 297:23
  We must touch his w. with GOLD 232:8
weal: according to the common w. JAM 271:5
Wealdstone: to the W. turned to waves
    BETJ 42:16
wealth: all that w. e'er gave GRAY 234:21
  all the w. of Indies THAC 546:3
  any means get w. and place POPE 380:9
  gave the little w. he had SWIFT 527:25
  health and w. long to live PRAY 385:5
  His w. a well-spent age CAMP 129:19
  in all time of our w. PRAY 385:17
  insolence of w. will creep JOHN 277:32
  In squandering w. was his DRYD 194:15
  love remember'd such w. SHAK 493:6
  Outshone the w. of Ormus MILT 346:6
  poor man's w. SIDN 507:20
  prevents the rule of w. BAG 29:4
  Say that health and w. HUNT 263:10
  smoke and w. and din HOR 261:7
  Swim'st thou in w. DEKK 173:21
  their w. increaseth MARL 329:20
  There is no w. but life RUSK 412:12
  w. of globèd peonies KEATS 291:15
  w. of thy wit in an instant SHAK 467:19
  w. without producing it SHAW 496:13
  w. ye find, another keeps SHEL 504:3
  What w. to me the show WORD 578:1
  Where w. accumulates GOLD 230:18
wealthy: business of the w. man BELL 39:29
  w. and others have nothing ARIS 12:8
  w. curled darlings SHAK 473:22
wean'd: were we not w. till then
    DONNE 188:29
weaned: w. child shall put his BIBLE 58:11
weapon: folly and his w. wit HOPE 256:2
  other hand held a w. BIBLE 52:1
  So that skill in the w. SHAK 442:15
weaponless: w. himself MILT 350:14
weapons: get your w. ready WHIT 570:10
  let not women's w. SHAK 454:2
  w. of war perished BIBLE 50:17
  wear w., and serve PRAY 400:11
  will hang my w. and my lyre HOR 261:6
wear: have nothing else to w. GILB 225:30
  hue was not the w. HOUS 264:17
  Should so w. out to nought SHAK 455:17
  such qualities as would w. GOLD 232:33
  w. an undeserved dignity SHAK 466:20
  w. him In my heart's core SHAK 434:2
  w. out than to rust out CUMB 170:7
  w. the carpet with their YEATS 586:14
  w. them out in practice BEAU 35:13
  w. your rue with a difference SHAK 436:11
  Will us to w. ourselves MARL 330:8
  you'll w. your eyes out ZOLA 588:19
wearer: by the merit of the w. SHAK 466:20
weareth: it w. the Christian down KIPL 301:18
wearied: Kiss her until she be w. SHEL 505:3
wearies: you say it w. you SHAK 465:7
weariest: w. and most loathed worldly
    SHAK 464:14
wearin: w.' o' the Green ANON 6:6
weariness: In hours of w. WORD 578:4
  much study is a w. BIBLE 56:13
  W. Can snore SHAK 428:18
  w. Of climbing heaven SHEL 505:5
  w., the fever KEATS 291:18
  w. treads on desire PETR 373:5
wearing: not linen you're w. HOOD 255:7
  was w. my powder-blue suit CHAN 139:20

w. arm-chairs tight	WOD 575:25
W. not like destruction	SPEN 515:6
wearisome: miles and make them w.	
	SHAK 478:23
wears: She w. her clothes	SWIFT 526:29
so w. she to him	SHAK 489:1
w. man's smudge and shares	HOPK 256:12
w. the turning globe	HOUS 265:1
weary: Age shall not w. them	BINY 84:10
All with w. task fordone	SHAK 471:21
eyelids are a little w.	PATER 369:18
I am w. of my groaning	PRAY 389:26
I'm w. wi' hunting	BALL 31:5
I sae w. fu' o' care	BURNS 116:6
I was w. and ill at ease	PROC 401:13
Let him be rich and w.	HERB 248:8
not be w. in well doing	BIBLE 77:20
rock in a w. land	BIBLE 58:30
rosy garland and a w. head	SIDN 507:21
So w. with disasters	SHAK 461:10
there the w. be at rest	BIBLE 52:13
weak and w.	POE 375:4
w. haunt for me	KING 296:17
w. reckoning	SHAK 476:6
w., stale, flat	SHAK 429:28
W. with toil	SHAK 493:5
weasel: Methinks it is like a w.	SHAK 434:22
Pop goes the w.	MAND 328:10
w. sucks eggs	SHAK 425:15
weather: again it was gorgeous w.	
	CALV 127:25
first talk is of the w.	JOHN 281:18
her madness and her w.	AUDEN 19:6
If it prove fair w.	SUCK 524:14
In sad or singing w.	SWIN 530:21
in the blue unclouded w.	TENN 538:9
It will be fair w.	BIBLE 66:31
Jolly boating w.	CORY 163:2
like a change in the w.	AUDEN 21:2
no such thing as bad w.	RUSK 412:14
not in fine w.	CLOU 153:16
Plaguy twelvepenny w.	SWIFT 526:11
roof of blue Italian w.	SHEL 501:16
serves for the old June w.	BROW 100:7
'Tis the hard grey w.	KING 296:23
variety about the New England w.	
	TWAIN 554:23
W. and rain have undone	KIPL 303:31
w. on the outward wall	SHAK 466:19
w. the cuckoo likes	HARDY 241:2
w. the shepherd shuns	HARDY 241:3
w. turned around	THOM 547:7
winter and rough w.	SHAK 425:14
you won't hold up the w.	MACN 326:8
weather-beaten: w. sail more willing	
bent	CAMP 129:20
weather-proof: humble roof Is w.	
	HERR 250:14
weather-wise: Some are w.	FRAN 218:7
weave: unwittingly w.	AUDEN 20:6
W. a circle round him thrice	COL 157:1
w. but nets to catch	WEBS 566:17
w. their thread with bones	SHAK 489:3
W. the warp	GRAY 234:15
what a tangled web we w.	SCOTT 417:19
weaver: swifter than a w.'s shuttle	
	BIBLE 52:18
weaving: thread of my own hand's w.	
	KEATS 292:10
web: gives the w. and the pin	SHAK 454:22
She left the w.	TENN 538:11
there's magic in the w.	SHAK 476:4
w. as this will I ensnare	SHAK 474:19
what a tangled w. we weave	SCOTT 417:19
Webb: Captain W. from Dawley	BETJ 44:2
web-foot: Every fork like a white w.	
	HARDY 240:21
webs: Laws are like spider's w.	SOLON 512:23
With swarthy w.	TENN 535:28

Webster: Daniel W. struck me much	
	SMITH 511:10
W. was much possessed	ELIOT 205:13
wed: December when they w.	SHAK 426:23
save trouble I w. again	CLARE 152:6
think to w. it	SHAK 420:25
With this Ring I thee w.	PRAY 389:5
wedde: Cristen man shall w.	CHAU 143:17
wedded: god that I have w. fyve	CHAU 143:17
Hail w. love	MILT 348:8
this Woman to thy w. wife	PRAY 389:3
thou art w. to calamity	SHAK 483:9
w. man so hardy be t'assaille	CHAU 142:9
wedding: get the w. dresses ready	
	BYRON 123:34
has bought her w. clothes	ADD 2:23
Let's have a w.	DICK 178:14
on his w. day	GILB 226:7
she did her w. gown	GOLD 232:33
Wedding-Guest: W. here beat his breast	
	COL 155:8
wedding-ring: small circle of a w.	CIBB 151:9
wedlock: consented together in holy w.	
	PRAY 389:7
W., indeed, hath oft compared	DAV 172:9
yet w.'s the devil	BYRON 124:39
Wednesday: upon W. in Wheeson week	
	SHAK 441:20
Wee: W., sleekit	BURNS 115:20
weed: basest w. outbraves his	SHAK 494:15
gather honey from the w.	SHAK 444:15
It is a w. that grows	BURKE 110:3
Less than the w. that grows	HOPE 256:5
more ought law to w. it	BACON 27:7
No more than Sussex w.	KIPL 303:15
Pernicious w.	COWP 168:26
salt w. sways in the stream	ARN 13:6
thou be than the fat w.	SHAK 431:8
thou w.	SHAK 476:19
w. out the fault without	GOLD 232:8
What is a w.	EMER 207:42
will not w. their own minds	WALP 563:17
weeded: hoed and trenched and w.	
	HOUS 264:17
weeds: all the idle w. that grow	SHAK 455:13
At grubbing w. from gravel	KIPL 299:14
buy yourself w.	GAY 222:34
Long live the w.	HOPK 256:18
pendent boughs her coronet w.	SHAK 436:19
rank fumitor and furrow w.	SHAK 455:13
Rank w.	COWP 168:26
smell far worse than w.	SHAK 494:15
w. and tares of mine own	BROW 96:18
when we're only burning w.	CHES 147:7
Worthless as withered w.	BRON 93:20
week: be accomplished in a w.	STEV 522:8
keep a w. away	SHAK 476:9
mirth to wail a w.	SHAK 492:18
w. is a long time in politics	WILS 574:18
weeks: been fou for w. thegither	BURNS 115:5
weel-stockit: lass wi' the w. farms	
	BURNS 114:6
weep: Babylon we sit down and w.	
	WALP 563:10
Bid me to w.	HERR 249:26
Doth w. full sore	SPEN 516:5
fear of having to w.	BEAU 35:15
If it could w., it could	BROW 98:8
I saw my lady w.	ANON 6:7
I w. for Adonais	SHEL 499:3
I w. like a child	LAWR 311:7
Love made him w. his pints	AUDEN 21:9
make the angels w.	SHAK 464:2
men would w. upon your	HUXL 268:23
milk my ewes and w.	SHAK 492:5
must w. or she will die	TENN 542:10
now you w.	SHAK 450:28
she would w. to see today	DOUG 191:10
should w. for his death	HOR 260:1
Some w. in empty rooms	COL 155:4

'Tis that I may not w.	BYRON 123:10
w. afresh love's long since	SHAK 493:7
W., and you weep alone	WILC 572:5
w. away the life of care	SHEL 504:11
W. for the lives your wishes	AUDEN 18:6
w. over Saul	BIBLE 50:17
'w.!' 'weep	BLAKE 88:5
weep with them that w.	BIBLE 75:16
W. you no more	ANON 8:13
Wherefore w. you	SHAK 485:12
Who would not w.	POPE 376:28
will make them w. and wail	SHAK 455:1
wilt thou w. when I am	BYRON 119:28
women must w.	KING 297:3
You think I'll w.	SHAK 454:2
you *will* w. and know why	HOPK 256:26
weepest: why w. thou	BIBLE 73:8
weeping: all night in a forest, w.	MAL 328:5
are w. in the playtime	BROW 97:36
Doth that bode w.	SHAK 477:1
Ever-w. Paddington	BLAKE 86:3
fierce, w., hungry man	CARL 132:24
hearers w. to their beds	SHAK 480:8
I have full cause of w.	SHAK 454:2
now goeth on his way w.	PRAY 398:17
of my w. something have	OWEN 367:11
Rachel w. for her children	BIBLE 63:34
remembrance of a w. queen	SHAK 479:19
w. and gnashing of teeth	BIBLE 65:17
w. and the laughter	DOWS 191:13
W. and watching	GOET 230:12
W. as fast as they stream	SHAK 450:9
w. late and early	TENN 539:11
w. multitudes	ELIOT 202:5
w. Pleiads wester	HOUS 265:16
wee-things: Th' expectant w.	BURNS 113:5
Wehr: Ein' gute W. und Waffen	LUTH 321:2
Weib: W. und Gesang	LUTH 321:1
Weibliche: Ewig-W. zieht uns hinan	
	GOET 230:6
weigh: more people see than w.	CHES 145:31
Shall w. your Gods	KIPL 304:7
to w. and consider	BACON 27:18
w. this song with the great	YEATS 585:8
w. thy words in a balance	BIBLE 63:12
would w. it down on one side	HAL 237:18
weighed: art w. in the balances	BIBLE 61:7
weighing: counting votes instead of w.	
	INGE 270:7
not w. our merits	PRAY 388:2
weighs: Which w. upon the heart	SHAK 463:3
weight: heavy and the weary w.	WORD 578:5
Knowledge may give w.	CHES 145:31
let us lay aside every w.	BIBLE 79:35
oppression of their prodigal w.	SHAK 479:17
w. of hours has chained	SHEL 502:13
w. of rages will press	SPOO 517:8
whose words are of less w.	BACON 25:41
willing to pull his w.	ROOS 408:2
weights: are deceitful upon the w.	
	PRAY 393:20
w. and measures will be	NAP 359:13
weighty: reserve the more w. voice	
	BACON 25:41
weilest: wo w. du	WAGN 562:1
Wein: Wer nicht liebt W.	LUTH 321:1
weinen: Auf seinem Bette w. sass	
	GOET 230:12
weird: w. sisters	SHAK 458:8
w. women promis'd	SHAK 461:6
weirs: three lone w.	ARN 15:3
welcome: Advice is seldom w.	CHES 145:19
aye be w. back again	BURNS 115:13
bear w. in your eye	SHAK 459:3
ever with a frolic w. took	TENN 544:3
Farewell night, w. day	BUNY 107:37
first to w.	BYRON 124:40
Freely w. to my cup	OLDYS 365:4
hath outstay'd his w. while	COL 157:17
I now bid you a w. adoo	WARD 564:18

you know not w. you came   FITZ 213:9
where: God knows w.   BYRON 123:20
How and W. and Who   KIPL 300:12
'O w. are you going   AUDEN 18:17
when the sun set w. were   BYRON 122:34
W. are the eagles   ELIOT 202:5
W. are you now   HOPE 256:3
w. but here have Pride   YEATS 586:8
W. can we live but days   LARK 310:3
W. is Bohun   CREWE 169:18
'W. is it   COL 156:19
W. is now thy God   PRAY 392:9
w. is your comforting   HOPK 256:19
W. Peter is   AMBR 4:1
w. we are is Hell   MARL 329:8
whereabout: stones prate of my w.

SHAK 460:1
whereabouts: to us to conceal our w.

SAKI 413:12
wherefore: every why he had a w.

BUTL 117:19
occasions and causes why and w.   SHAK 445:8
w. art thou Romeo   SHAK 482:8
w. seeking whom Whence   HOUS 266:9
whereof: he knoweth w. we are made

PRAY 396:17
W. one cannot speak   WITT 575:17
wheresome'er: w. he is   SHAK 443:16
Wherewithal: W. shall a young man
cleanse   PRAY 398:4
whetstone: There is no such w.   ASCH 17:2
which: is which and w. is what   MILNE 340:16
w. of us takes the better   SOCR 512:18
whichever: w. way you move   LUCAN 320:1
whiffling: w. through the tulgey wood

CARR 134:29
Whig: Erastian W.   CHES 146:27
first W. was the Devil   JOHN 278:2
perceive you are a vile W.   JOHN 276:5
Tory and W. in turns shall   SMITH 512:6
Tory men and W. measures   DISR 185:38
wise Tory and a wise W.   JOHN 278:34
Whigs: Gentleman caught the W. bathing

DISR 184:14
W. admit no force but argument   BROW 97:26
W. *not* getting into place   BYRON 123:33
while: w. my pretty one   TENN 541:31
whim: strangest w. has seized   CHES 146:14
tempted by a private w.   BELL 39:24
whimper: Not with a bang but a w.

ELIOT 203:11
whimsies: they have my w.   PRIOR 400:21
whine: w. about their condition   WHIT 570:22
whip: 'Too-slow' will need the w.

TENN 541:26
whip-lash: spindle shank a guid w.

BURNS 115:17
whipp'd: w. the offending Adam out

SHAK 443:5
whipped: child is afraid of being w.

JOHN 273:25
he w. my grandfather   ADD 2:17
whippersnapper: Critic and w.   BROW 99:1
whipping: ought to get a *good* w. VICT 556:14
who should 'scape w.   SHAK 432:26
whips: hath chastised you with w. BIBLE 51:3
w. and scorns of time   SHAK 433:8
whipster: Every puny w. gets my sword

SHAK 477:17
whirled: She w. round and round

LEAR 311:17
whirligig: w. of time brings in his

SHAK 490:25
whirls: flood that w. me to the sea

MER 337:10
whirlwind: comfort serves in a w.

HOPK 256:21
Rides in the w.   ADD 1:14
sweeping w.'s sway   GRAY 234:16
they shall reap the w.   BIBLE 61:11

went up by a w. into heaven   BIBLE 51:22
w. hath blown the dust   DONNE 190:23
whirring: w. pheasant springs   POPE 381:14
whisker: educated w.   TENN 533:10
whiskers: my fur and w.   CARR 133:20
Runcible Cat with crimson w.   LEAR 312:20
whiskey: w. afterwards as he was   ASHF 17:9
Whisky: Freedom and W. gang thegither

BURNS 112:35
tell me w.'s name in Greek   BURNS 112:34
whisper: By all ye cry or w.   KIPL 304:7
fiddled w. music   ELIOT 205:9
Full well the busy w.   GOLD 231:2
His w. came to Me   KIPL 299:3
There's a w. down the field   KIPL 300:23
We wake and w. awhile   DE L 173:25
We w. in her ear   WILB 572:4
w. of a faction should   RUSS 412:18
w. of the south-wind rushing   TENN 538:24
w. softness in chambers   MILT 351:25
W. who dares   MILNE 340:11
whispered: it's w. every where   CONG 160:7
whispering: They've a way of w. to me

HARDY 239:18
...w. from her towers   ARN 15:25
w., with white lips   BYRON 120:25
whisperings: Foul w. are abroad SHAK 462:26
It keeps eternal w. around   KEATS 292:2
whispers: Blood of Jesus w.   BICK 84:4
to be drunk Among w.   ELIOT 203:4
us whom he w. in the ear   BROW 98:21
W. the o'er-fraught heart   SHAK 462:16
whist: my husband from his w.   BROW 100:20
whist upon w. drive   BETJ 42:13
whistle: I'd w. her off and let   SHAK 475:21
was hir joly w. wel ywet   CHAU 143:12
w., and I'll come to you   BURNS 116:4
W. and she'll come to you   FLET 215:24
whistled: w. as he went   DRYD 195:34
whistles: w. blow forlorn   HOUS 262:16
w. in his sound   SHAK 425:24
W. o'er the furrowed land   MILT 342:19
Whistling: W. to keep myself from

DRYD 195:19
W. to the air   SHAK 422:3
white: always goes into w. satin   SHER 565:3
are arrayed in w. robes   BIBLE 82:1
are w. already to harvest   BIBLE 71:41
beloved is w. and ruddy   BIBLE 57:3
black ram Is tupping your w. ewe

SHAK 473:16
called the chess-board w.   BROW 99:5
clear w., inside   KIPL 299:18
curious engine, your w. hand   WEBS 566:21
'elp you a lot with the W.   KIPL 300:15
garment was w. as snow   BIBLE 61:8
hairs were w. like wool   BIBLE 81:14
How ill w. hairs become   SHAK 442:30
Ionian w. and gold   ELIOT 205:4
it here in black and w.   JONS 284:7
Lawn as w. as driven snow   SHAK 492:2
made them w. in the blood   BIBLE 82:2
many a head has turned w.   MULL 359:1
my soul is w.   BLAKE 88:2
nor w. so very white   CANN 129:29
O'er the w. Alps alone   DONNE 188:12
pluck a w. rose with me   SHAK 445:21
read'st black where I read w.   BLAKE 85:22
should be bound in w. vellum   RUSK 412:13
So purely w. they were   SPEN 516:32
so w.! O so soft   JONS 285:4
Take up the W. Man's burden   KIPL 304:6
they shall be as w. as snow   BIBLE 57:18
thunders of w. silence   BROW 98:4
virgin w. integrity   DONNE 187:21
Wearing w. for Eastertide   HOUS 262:14
w. and hairless as an egg   HERR 249:15
w. and small   DUNB 199:11
W. as an angel is the English   BLAKE 88:2
W. as an orchid she rode   AUDEN 18:3

w. dress, her death   SPEN 515:6
w. heat of this revolution   WILS 574:17
W. his shroud as the mountain   SHAK 435:34
W. Horse of the White Horse   CHES 146:15
W. in the moon the long   HOUS 263:20
w. lies to ice a cake   ASQ 17:18
w. races are really pinko-gray   FORS 217:7
W. shall not neutralize   BROW 104:31
w. tremendous daybreak   BROO 94:29
wild w. horses play   ARN 13:5
with w. and bristly beard   SHAK 492:26
world is w. with May   TENN 534:4
whited: like unto w. sepulchres   BIBLE 67:25
white-faced: w. and still in the coffin

WHIT 570:11
Whitefoot: W., come uppe Lightfoot

ING 270:15
white-mossed: from under the w. wonder

BRID 92:14
whiten: w. the green plains under SHEL 500:4
whitens: ptarmigan that w. ere his

TENN 534:37
whiter: Did never w. show   SPEN 516:31
I shall be w. than snow   PRAY 393:5
W. than new snow on a raven's   SHAK 483:7
whites: comparison all w. are ink

SHAK 486:19
w. of their eyes   PUTN 403:6
white-wash'd: w. wall   GOLD 231:3
whitewashed: Guard the decent w. chapel

BETJ 43:7
whither: one knows not w. nor why

MAS 334:8
w. it goeth   BIBLE 71:36
W., O splendid ship   BRID 92:19
W. shall I go then from   PRAY 399:5
whiting: said a w. to a snail   CARR 134:13
w. said with its tail   HOOD 255:17
Whitman: daintily dressed Walt W.

CHES 148:7
pact with you, Walt W.   POUND 383:12
What do you see Walt W.   WHIT 570:12
Whizzing: W. them over the net BETJ 43:20
Who: How and Where and W.   KIPL 300:12
Who is on my side? w.   BIBLE 51:36
W. is this   TENN 538:12
W. killed John Keats   BYRON 125:1
Whoever: W. it is that leaves him

FROST 219:11
whole: faith hath made thee w.   BIBLE 65:26
had I stol'n the w.   STEV 523:6
is greater than the w.   HES 250:19
nothing can be sole or w.   YEATS 584:19
over the measureless w.   LUCR 320:3
parts of one stupendous w.   POPE 379:10
seeing the w. of them   RUSK 411:26
we shall be w.   PRAY 395:8
what a w. Oxford is   COL 155:2
w. breadth of the way   BUNY 107:15
w. man in himself   HOR 262:10
w. need not a physician   BIBLE 65:23
w. wit in a jest   BEAU 35:19
wholesome: labour spread her w. store

GOLD 230:18
nights are w.   SHAK 429:17
steal out of his w. bed   SHAK 449:13
w. salad from the brook   COWP 167:27
wholly: some few to be read w. BACON 27:19
Whom: 'W. the gods love die young'

BYRON 123:11
whoop: we'll w. and we'll holloa WHYT 572:2
whooping: out of all w.   SHAK 426:7
whopping: measures is Latin for a w.

ANST 11:9
whore: dost thou lash that w. SHAK 455:19
Fortune's a right w.   WEBS 567:1
I am the Protestant w.   GWYN 237:8
I' the posture of a w.   SHAK 424:3
judgment of the great w.   BIBLE 82:22
rogue is married to a w.   KIPL 302:18

teach the morals of a w. JOHN 274:10
w. and gambler BLAKE 85:17
w.'s oath SHAK 454:28
woman's a w. JOHN 276:15
you for that cunning w. SHAK 476:21
young man's w. JOHN 275:19
whoremaster: admirable evasion of w.
SHAK 453:11
whoremongers: w., and murderers
BIBLE 83:3
whores: have brought w. for Eleusis
POUND 382:11
Out ye w. PEMB 371:10
whore-shops: Madhouses, prisons, w.
CLARE 152:5
whoring: w. with their own inventions
PRAY 397:6
whose: Never ask me w. HOUS 263:11
Whoso: W. doeth these things PRAY 390:5
Whosoever: W. will be saved PRAY 385:11
why: every w. he had a wherefore
BUTL 117:19
I can't tell you w. MART 331:9
knows not whither nor w. MAS 334:8
What and W. and When KIPL 300:12
w. and wherefore in all SHAK 445:8
w. are we SHEL 499:13
W. are you not here THOR 550:27
W., Edward, tell me why WORD 577:1
W. in the name of Glory KEATS 290:9
wibrated: that had better not be w.
DICK 175:27
wicked: are Tories born w. ANON 6:14
be equally w. and corrupt BURKE 108:20
better than one of the w. SHAK 438:8
desperately w. BIBLE 60:24
fiery darts of the w. BIBLE 78:10
from the deceitful and w. PRAY 392:10
God help the w. SHAK 439:17
It's worse than w. PUNCH 402:26
mercies of the w. are cruel BIBLE 53:34
never wonder to see men w. SWIFT 527:15
pomps and vanity of this w. PRAY 388:13
pretending to be w. WILDE 573:5
seven other spirits more w. BIBLE 66:14
shake their w. sides YEATS 586:8
Something w. this way comes SHAK 462:5
so w. as Lord George Hell BEER 37:16
There is always a w. secret AUDEN 21:1
this mad, w. folly VICT 556:14
unto the w. BIBLE 59:16
war is regarded as w. WILDE 572:22
w. cease from troubling BIBLE 52:13
w. flee when no man pursueth BIBLE 54:41
w. plant KYD 306:7
w. to deserve such pain BROW 99:29
wickedness: I was shapen in w. PRAY 393:5
leaven of malice and w. BIBLE 75:36
leaven of malice and w. PRAY 386:11
little to the w. of a woman BIBLE 63:8
loose the bands of w. BIBLE 60:4
our manifold sins and w. PRAY 384:9
spiritual w. in high places BIBLE 78:10
That is the Path of W. BALL 32:5
w. of the world is print DICK 179:15
w. that he hath committed BIBLE 60:35
w. that hinders loving BROW 102:31
wicket: flannelled fools at the w. KIPL 300:4
Now in Maytime to the w. HOUS 262:22
slow W. of the Night THOM 549:2
wictim: w. o' connubiality DICK 182:1
Widdicombe Fair: I want for to go to
W. BALL 32:12
wide: deep the Poet sees, but w. ARN 14:7
feet long and two feet w. WORD 582:24
nor so w. as a church door SHAK 483:3
w. also the east is from PRAY 396:17
W. is the gate BIBLE 65:6
wider: thee thrice w. SHAK 442:31
W. still and wider shall BENS 40:24

widow: came a certain poor w. BIBLE 68:38
defendeth the fatherless and w. PRAY 399:18
'eard o' the W. at Windsor KIPL 304:9
Here's to the w. of fifty SHER 506:31
to-day or Molly Stark's a w. STARK 517:20
undone w. sits upon my arm MASS 335:21
virgin-w. and a *Mourning Bride* DRYD 197:11
w. bird sate mourning SHEL 500:3
widowhood: comfortable estate of w.
GAY 222:18
Widow-maker: go with the old grey W.
KIPL 299:21
widows: defendeth the cause of w.
PRAY 394:7
devour w.' houses BIBLE 68:37
must ev'n do as other w. GAY 222:34
These w. ADD 2:18
visit the fatherless and w. BIBLE 80:11
When w. exclaim loudly FIEL 211:6
w., and all that are desolate PRAY 385:20
younger w. refuse BIBLE 79:15
wife: accommodated than with a w.
SHAK 442:4
account w. and children BACON 26:32
after his neighbour's w. BIBLE 60:16
all the world and his w. ANST 11:8
animal a husband and w. FIEL 211:30
be 'like Caesar's w. ANON 6:11
Caesar's w. must be above CAES 127:1
casual mistress, but a w. TENN 536:33
centaur, man and w. BYRON 123:19
chaste w. wise SURR 524:21
degrees dwindle into a w. CONG 161:8
every port he finds a w. BICK 84:3
Giant Despair had a w. BUNY 107:21
Giving honour unto the w. BIBLE 80:29
have a w., and so forth CONG 160:33
have quarrelled with my w. PEAC 370:18
having is true to his w. VANB 555:6
Here lies my w. DRYD 196:8
He that hath w. and children BACON 26:31
hope that keeps up a w.'s GAY 222:18
hurling them at his w. DOYLE 191:17
husband is, the w. is TENN 538:19
husband of one w. BIBLE 79:12
I have married a w. BIBLE 70:11
is no fury like an ex-w. CONN 161:13
is sanctified by the w. BIBLE 76:3
Jael Heber's w. BIBLE 49:7
kick his w. out of bed SURT 525:5
kill a w. with kindness SHAK 484:11
lofty character of W. DICK 177:15
Lord Brutus took to w. SHAK 449:16
love your neighbour's w. MAC 324:3
marriage with her brother's w. SHAK 446:28
Match'd with an aged w. TENN 543:21
maxim that man and w. should FARQ 210:9
Mother, W., and Queen TENN 543:15
must be in want of a w. AUST 23:11
Nor winsomeness to w. POUND 383:18
often said to his w. CHES 147:28
One w. is too much GAY 222:36
'oss, my w., and my name SURT 525:17
railing w. SHAK 439:28
Remember Lot's w. BIBLE 70:32
roaring of the wind is my w. KEATS 294:10
sailor's w. had chestnuts SHAK 458:6
shall cleave unto his w. BIBLE 45:13
so as to suit his w. TROL 553:7
Thane of Fife had a w. SHAK 462:21
'thanked God my w. was dead BROW 106:1
Than my sonne's w. ING 270:16
that a man lay down his w. JOYCE 286:28
that they be Man and W. PRAY 389:7
then to have or have no w. BACON 28:17
They took me from my w. CLARE 152:6
to look after a w. SURT 525:24
t'other w. would take ill GAY 222:36
To weans and w. BURNS 115:15
true and honourable w. SHAK 449:15

uncumber'd with a w. DRYD 196:4
upon seeing his w. there TRAV 552:6
Western custom of one w. SAKI 413:13
when his w. talks Greek JOHN 280:18
whose w. shall I take MOORE 356:29
who's untrue to his w. AUDEN 20:13
w. for breed GAY 223:31
w., if you will marry SHAK 485:13
w. looked back BIBLE 46:8
w. shall be as the fruitful PRAY 398:20
w. to be of a studious JOHN 278:21
w. was pretty COWP 168:18
w. who preaches in her HOOD 255:12
Your w. arranges accordingly JUV 287:22
wig: w. with the scorched foretop MAC 324:7
wight: Yonder a maid and her w.
HARDY 240:5
wights: descriptions of the fairest w.
SHAK 494:19
wigwam: Stood the w. of Nokomis
LONG 317:10
wild: bore me in the southern w. BLAKE 88:2
chance to talk a little w. SHAK 446:26
grew more fierce and w. HERB 247:15
I went hunting w. OWEN 367:10
mouth of that w. beast man BOL 89:14
My father is gone w. into SHAK 442:25
nobly w., not mad HERR 249:13
old, w., and incomprehensible VICT 556:15
Revenge is a kind of w. justice BACON 27:7
shoreless watery w. ARN 13:12
this the w. geese spread YEATS 586:19
three w. lads were we SCOTT 418:16
W. he may be DICK 179:19
w., melancholy, and elevating BRON 93:17
w. with all regret TENN 542:4
withered, and so w. SHAK 458:10
wild cats: w. in your kitchens SHAK 474:15
wilder: w. shores of love BLAN 88:30
Wilderness: Beside me singing in the
W. FITZ 212:11
day's journey into the w. BIBLE 51:13
dwellings of the w. PRAY 394:3
given it for a w. of monkeys SHAK 467:7
him that crieth in the w. BIBLE 59:5
in perils in the w. BIBLE 77:12
make a w. and call it peace TAC 531:7
ninety and nine in the w. BIBLE 70:15
of one crying in the w. BIBLE 63:36
of temptation in the w. PRAY 396:4
through the w. of this world BUNY 107:10
To be a little w. MARV 332:14
w. and the solitary place BIBLE 58:32
w. into a glorious empire BURKE 110:7
w. shall waters break out BIBLE 58:34
ye out into the w. to see BIBLE 66:2
wildest: w. beauty in the world OWEN 367:10
wild-fowl: w. than your lion living
SHAK 470:14
wildness: bereft Of wet and w. HOPK 256:18
wile: follow'd with endearing w. GOLD 231:1
wiles: of w. More unexpert MILT 346:8
transient sorrows, simple w. WORD 581:8
wanton w. MILT 342:14
Wilhelmine: His little grandchild W.
SOUT 513:14
Wilkinson: Mr W., a clergyman FITZ 213:21
will: according to the common w. JAM 271:5
can't forge his own w. GILB 228:35
care to stay than w. SHAK 483:15
cause is in my w. SHAK 449:20
consummated in the General W.
AUDEN 19:12
even to have had the w. PROP 401:16
Fix'd fate, free w. MILT 346:19
his w. his law COWP 167:37
if she w. ANON 8:20
Immanent W. and its designs HARDY 239:11
It shows a w. most incorrect SHAK 429:26
I w. not let thee go BRID 92:11

Man has his w. HOLM 253:15
Michael Henchard's W. HARDY 241:18
not because we w. ARN 12:21
not my w., but thine BIBLE 71:8
questions of w. or decision CHOM 148:16
reason and the w. of God ARN 15:15
that the w. is infinite SHAK 486:33
This is the W. of the Yukon SERV 420:13
Thy w. be done in earth BIBLE 64:24
torrent of a woman's w. ANON 8:20
'twur the w. o' the Lord TENN 544:5
war 'twixt will and w. not SHAK 463:18
We *know* our w. is free JOHN 275:24
we will hear Caesar's w. SHAK 450:24
w. be what they will be BUTL 117:10
W. has woven with an absent HARDY 239:12
W. in over-plus SHAK 495:10
w. in us is over-rul'd MARL 329:18
w. most rank SHAK 475:20
w. reigns FRAN 218:10
w. replace reasoned judgement JUV 287:21
w. that my maxim should KANT 288:9
W. you, won't you CARR 134:14
wrote my w. across the sky LAWR 311:12
You w., Oscar WHIS 569:25
willed: All we have w. or hoped BROW 98:15
W. and fulfilled by high KIPL 300:6
w. more mischief than they HOUS 263:13
William: kind W. Maginn LOCK 315:23
Willie: Wee W. Winkie rins through
MILL 340:3
willin: 'When a man says he's w.'
DICK 176:34
willing: spirit indeed is w. but the flesh
BIBLE 68:16
w. to sell for one shilling LEAR 312:13
willingness: w. is to be praised OVID 366:26
willow: green w. is my garland HEYW 250:21
Sang 'W. GILB 227:15
she had a song of 'w. SHAK 476:26
Sing all a green w. SHAK 476:27
Stood Dido with a w. SHAK 468:14
There is a w. grows aslant SHAK 436:19
willows: runs away into the w. VIRG 559:18
w. have overfilled POUND 382:5
w. of the brook compass BIBLE 53:10
w., old rotten planks CONS 162:1
W. whiten TENN 538:3
will-power: *possess the w. to be free*
AUDEN 19:13
Wills: such a lot of people's W. CHES 146:13
talk of w. SHAK 479:10
which our w. are gardeners SHAK 474:8
win: can w. the combat of him BACON 26:2
else had hopes to w. her CONG 160:30
from outward forms to w. COL 156:8
hope to w. by't SHAK 447:12
so who would greatly w. BYRON 125:6
Those who w. heaven BROW 102:27
To w. or lose it all GRAH 233:14
we w. PHEI 373:6
when I saw myself to w. SHAK 495:6
yet wouldst wrongly w. SHAK 459:1
Winchelsea: shall not lie easy at W.
BENET 40:20
wind: Absence is to love what w. BUSS 117:6
all aloud the w. doth blow SHAK 457:19
am a feather for each w. SHAK 491:14
bay'd the whisp'ring w. GOLD 230:21
beat of the off-shore w. KIPL 300:23
blow, thou winter w. SHAK 426:1
both with w. and stream SHAK 475:1
breathing of the common w. WORD 582:17
chiding of the winter's w. SHAK 424:31
clouds and w. without rain BIBLE 54:27
east w. made flesh APPL 11:†2
Fair stood the w. for France DRAY 193:10
fires flare up in a w. FRAN 218:2
fluttering in the w. BROW 101:24
Frisch weht der W. WAGN 562:1

Frosty w. made moan ROSS 409:1
gentle w. does move BLAKE 86:21
God tempers the w. STER 519:11
gone with the w. DOWS 191:12
hear a voice in every w. GRAY 235:11
hears him in the w. POPE 379:5
hiding place from the w. BIBLE 58:30
impatient as the W. WORD 582:15
is best to write in w. CAT 137:7
it were brought forth w. BIBLE 58:20
large a charter as the w. SHAK 425:22
let her down the w. SHAK 475:21
light w. lives or dies KEATS 293:8
like W. I go' FITZ 212:21
Loose as the w. HERB 247:14
Lord was not in the w. BIBLE 51:14
nets to catch the w. WEBS 566:17
Nor ever w. blows loudly TENN 535:27
north w. BIBLE 56:29
Not with this w. blowing KIPL 301:15
observeth the w. shall not sow BIBLE 56:7
of a rushing mighty w. BIBLE 73:22
only the w.'s home ELIOT 205:10
Only w. it into a ball BLAKE 86:8
pass by me as the idle w. SHAK 451:20
piffle before the w. ASHF 17:11
reed shaken with the w. BIBLE 66:2
sand against the w. BLAKE 86:23
Sits the w. in that corner SHAK 472:17
soon as the w. goeth over PRAY 396:17
swoln with w. and the rank MILT 343:13
tears shall drown the w. SHAK 459:6
that which way the w. is SELD 419:22
There's the w. on the heath BORR 90:5
They have sown the w. BIBLE 61:11
thunder-storm *against* the w. BYRON 121:11
trumpet of a prophecy! O, W. SHEL 502:14
upon the wings of the w. PRAY 390:8
upon the wings of the w. PRAY 396:18
warm wind, the west w. MAS 334:9
welter to the parching w. MILT 343:2
Western w. ANON 8:16
western w. was wild KING 296:25
wheel's kick and the w.'s MAS 334:4
When the sweet w. did gently SHAK 468:13
when the w. is southerly SHAK 432:18
whistling mane of every w. THOM 548:13
wild West W. SHEL 502:8
w. and storm PRAY 399:22
w. and the rain SHAK 454:12
w. and the rain SHAK 490:27
w. bloweth where it listeth BIBLE 71:36
w. blow the earth into SHAK 454:3
w. doth blow to-day BALL 32:9
w. extinguishes candles LA R 310:15
w. is my wife and the stars KEATS 294:10
w. of change is blowing MACM 326:1
W. of the western sea TENN 541:31
w. sang and the same waves SWIN 529:19
w.'s feet shine along SWIN 530:18
w.'s in the east DICK 176:5
w. takes me I travel HOR 258:7
w. that blows DIBD 175:20
w. that blows through me LAWR 311:9
w. that follows fast CUNN 170:13
w. was a torrent of darkness NOYES 364:12
with every w. of doctrine BIBLE 77:28
worn window-sill in the w. MACN 326:10
winder: w., a casement DICK 180:4
wind-flowers: pied w. and violets
SHEL 503:18
winding: England's w. sheet BLAKE 85:17
hears its w. murmur ARN 12:22
place is by a w. stair BACON 26:26
waters were his w. sheet BARN 34:5
w. up the watch of his SHAK 485:4
winding-sheet: Her w. is up as high
SCOTT 418:7
w. of Edward's race GRAY 234:15

windmill: cheese and garlic in a w.
SHAK 439:28
window: eating or opening a w. AUDEN 19:18
little w. where the sun HOOD 254:17
Sisera looked out at a w. BIBLE 49:12
stand at the w. AUDEN 18:11
throw it out of the w. BECK 36:17
window-glass: Dash the w. to shivers
SCOTT 418:16
window pane: Good prose is like a w.
ORW 365:13
window-panes: Drift across the w.
ELIOT 204:1
windows: By breaking of w. MORE 357:7
life's five w. of the soul BLAKE 85:23
not by eastern w. only CLOU 154:4
Open the w. AUST 22:15
storied w. richly dight MILT 342:10
then the W. failed DICK 183:19
window-sill: On a worn w. in the wind
MACN 326:10
winds: beteem the w. of heaven SHAK 429:28
imprisoned in the viewless w. SHAK 464:14
Let w. unnoticed whistle BETJ 42:5
seaman tells stories of w. PROP 401:15
Though all the w. of doctrine MILT 352:5
when the w. are churning LUCR 320:6
When the w. are breathing SHEL 501:8
Where the w. are all asleep ARN 13:6
will hear the w. howling ARN 13:7
w., and crack your cheeks SHAK 454:4
w. blew BIBLE 65:11
w. blew BIBLE 65:12
w. come to me from WORD 579:2
w. kiss my parched lips SHAK 452:31
w. of heaven mix for ever SHEL 502:1
w. of March with beauty SHAK 491:26
W. of the World KIPL 298:24
w. shoreward blow ARN 13:5
w. were love-sick with SHAK 422:2
w. will call the darkness SHEL 504:7
ye W. of God PRAY 384:21
Windsmoor: Well-cut W. flapping lightly
BETJ 43:14
Windsor: 'eard o' the Widow at W.
KIPL 304:9
wind up: Excepting to w. the sun
BYRON 126:5
windy: o' the w. side of the law SHAK 490:11
w. night a rainy morrow SHAK 494:14
wine: are fond of Spanish w. MAS 333:20
are lordliest in their w. MILT 350:27
Be not drunk with w. BIBLE 78:5
best fits my little w. HERR 249:20
bin of w. STEV 523:7
blood and w. are red WILDE 572:7
buy w. and milk BIBLE 59:25
Chian w. ARN 14:21
cup of hot w. with not a drop SHAK 427:14
days of w. and roses DOWS 191:13
doesn't get into the w. CHES 147:28
Drinking the blude-red w. BALL 31:16
drink one cup of w. SCOTT 417:12
drink thy w. with a merry BIBLE 55:28
falser than vows made in w. SHAK 426:18
feast of w. on the lees BIBLE 58:18
fetch to me a pint o' w. BURNS 113:31
Flask of W. FITZ 212:11
flown with insolence and w. MILT 345:18
giant refreshed with w. PRAY 395:7
good w. is a good familiar SHAK 475:10
he drinks no w. SHAK 442:14
honest talk and wholesome w. TENN 543:16
'I don't see any w. CARR 133:28
I'll not look for w. JONS 284:12
invisible spirit of w. SHAK 475:8
'I rather like bad w. DISR 186:26
Is not old w. wholesomest WEBS 566:30
'It wasn't the w. DICK 181:28
last Companion: W. BELL 40:8

Let us have w. and women BYRON 122:21
like generous w. BUTL 118:17
Like the best w. BIBLE 57:10
Look not thou upon the w. BIBLE 54:24
love is better than w. BIBLE 56:15
man...having drunk old w. BIBLE 69:19
man that is without w. BIBLE 63:15
mellow, like good w. PHIL 373:10
mouth do crush their w. MARV 332:3
new friend is as new w. BIBLE 62:30
new w. into old bottles BIBLE 65:25
not for kings to drink w. BIBLE 55:2
Not given to w. BIBLE 79:12
not to be rinsed with w. HOPK 256:15
not with w. BIBLE 58:23
of Mr Weston's good w. AUST 22:11
out-did the frolic w. HERR 249:14
pass the rosy w. DICK 180:26
pure cup of rich Canary w. JONS 284:1
Sans W. FITZ 212:18
Sure there was w. HERB 247:14
sweet white w. MAS 333:18
Sweet w. of youth BROO 94:7
take a glass of w. SHER 506:38
temptations both in w. and women
　　　　KITC 305:14
Than mine host's Canary w. KEATS 290:28
thou hast kept the good w. BIBLE 71:34
water unto w. TENN 539:5
when the w. is BECON 36:22
When thirsty grief in w. LOV 318:17
w. and women BURT 116:21
w. for thy stomach's sake BIBLE 79:16
W. has play'd the Infidel FITZ 213:14
w. in rivers SCOTT 418:16
w. inspires us GAY 222:25
W. is a mocker BIBLE 54:15
W. is the strongest BIBLE 62:4
W. loved I deeply SHAK 454:18
W. maketh merry BIBLE 56:4
w. of life is drawn SHAK 461:1
w. that maketh glad PRAY 396:20
w. Was the bright dew SHEL 503:19
with 'W. FITZ 212:7
wine-jar: trusty w. HOR 261:5
wine-lees: thanks to w. and democracy
　　　　BROW 98:28
wine-pots: broken and castaway w.
　　　　CLOU 153:7
wine-press: be the grapes of the w.
　　　　MAC 322:6
trodden the w. alone BIBLE 60:11
wines: old w. GOLD 232:19
wing: flits by on leathern w. COLL 158:13
got to take under my w. GILB 227:14
headlong joy is ever on the w. MILT 350:12
least is longest on the w. COWP 167:29
so long on a broken w. TENN 540:16
vainly flapt its tinsel w. MARV 331:18
winged: Doth the w. life destroy BLAKE 86:18
thoughtless youth was w. DRYD 196:13
W. words HOMER 253:27
wings: all the w. of the Loves SWIN 530:4
Angel of Death spread his w. BYRON 122:2
are no longer w. to fly ELIOT 202:1
bug with gilded w. POPE 377:1
Clap her broad w. FRERE 218:26
covered with silver w. PRAY 394:8
defend thee under his w. PRAY 395:21
exulting on triumphant w. POPE 381:14
great w. beating still YEATS 586:1
hear the beating of his w. BRIG 93:1
her chickens under her w. BIBLE 67:26
His w. were wet with ranging GREE 236:8
is Love without his w. BYRON 124:37
it imped the w. of fame CAREW 130:13
mount up with w. as eagles BIBLE 59:10
O, for a horse with w. SHAK 428:14
of the w. of grasshoppers SHAK 481:28
o' the W. o' the Mornin' KIPL 304:10

resembled the w. of an ostrich MAC 323:5
Sailing on obscene w. COL 156:19
take the w. of the morning PRAY 399:5
that I had w. like a dove PRAY 393:10
them with their woven w. SHAK 465:7
upon the w. of the wind PRAY 390:8
upon the w. of the wind PRAY 396:18
viewless w. of Poesy KEATS 291:20
void his luminous w. ARN 16:10
with ah! bright w. HOPK 256:13
with healing in his w. BIBLE 62:3
wingy: w. mysteries in divinity BROW 96:8
wink: never came a w. too soon HOOD 254:17
w. and hold out mine iron SHAK 443:14
w. a reputation down SWIFT 527:29
winked: An' 'e w. back KIPL 304:5
winners: there are no w. CHAM 139:8
winning: glory of the w. were she MER 337:2
have such a w. way with you CONG 160:26
lips ne'er act the w. part HERR 250:11
w. cause pleased the gods LUCAN 319:22
world be worth thy w. DRYD 195:5
winning-post: boats began to near the
　　w. COKE 154:15
winnings: one heap of all your w. KIPL 300:1
winnowing: hair soft-lifted by the w.
　　　　KEATS 293:6
wins: silly game where nobody w.
　　　　FULL 220:20
winsomeness: Nor w. to wife POUND 383:18
winter: Age makes a w. in the heart
　　　　SPAR 514:22
Bare W. suddenly was changed SHEL 503:17
dark as w. was the flow CAMP 128:21
days of autumn and of w. CLARE 152:16
English w. BYRON 124:3
every w. change to spring TENN 536:26
go south in the w. ELIOT 204:18
Has woven a w. robe HOUS 265:1
If W. comes SHEL 502:14
In w. I get up at night STEV 522:16
In w.'s tedious nights SHAK 480:8
It was not in the w. HOOD 254:8
It was the w. wild MILT 344:5
mountains by the w. sea TENN 535:20
my age is as a lusty w. SHAK 425:6
No enemy But w. SHAK 425:12
No one thinks of w. KIPL 302:15
Our severest w. COWP 168:2
out in the Middle of W. ADD 2:16
sad tale's best for w. SHAK 491:12
Seeming and savour all the w. SHAK 491:22
spring are on w.'s traces SWIN 528:15
summer and w. BIBLE 45:37
Twice a week the w. thorough HOUS 262:22
very dead of W. ANDR 4:7
very dead of w. ELIOT 203:12
W. comes to rule the varied THOM 549:21
w. hath my absence been SHAK 494:16
w. hoar SHEL 501:15
w. I'll not think DONNE 188:9
W. is icummen POUND 382:4
w. is past BIBLE 56:22
W. kept us warm ELIOT 204:17
w. of our discontent SHAK 480:17
w. or summer when they're CHEK 145:3
w., plague and pestilence NASHE 360:8
W. slumbering in the open COL 157:14
w.'s rains and ruins are SWIN 528:17
you will bid the w. come SHAK 452:31
winterfalls: w. of old HOUS 265:1
winters: forty w. shall besiege SHAK 492:23
w. and keeps warm her note CAREW 130:19
wintry: chariotest to their dark w. SHEL 502:8
wipe: God shall w. away all tears BIBLE 82:4
God shall w. away all tears BIBLE 82:31
Let me w. it first SHAK 455:17
w. a bloody nose GAY 223:14
w. the tears for ever from MILT 343:18
wiped: name be w. out likewise SPEN 515:20

them be w. out of the book PRAY 394:14
wipers: let me and you be w. BROW 103:20
wipes: cive, anheling, w. HOLM 253:18
wiping: w. something off a slate KIPL 297:23
wire: By w. and wireless AUDEN 19:11
electric w. the message came ANON 4:17
wireless: By wire and w. AUDEN 19:11
wires: If hairs be w. SHAK 495:8
Wisdom: action W. goes by majorities
　　　　MER 337:35
apply our hearts unto w. PRAY 395:20
celestial W. calms the mind JOHN 283:6
characteristic of w. THOR 550:5
contrivance of human w. to provide
　　　　BURKE 111:8
excess of w. is made a fool EMER 207:18
get w. talk is of bullocks BIBLE 63:20
giveth w. unto the simple PRAY 390:12
increased in w. and stature BIBLE 69:14
infallible criterion of w. BURKE 111:27
in w. hast thou made them PRAY 397:1
is the beginning of w. PRAY 397:13
joy is w. YEATS 585:19
leads to the palace of w. BLAKE 88:13
Love is the w. of the fool JOHN 280:27
man's wit and all men's w. RUSS 412:21
Nature say one thing and W. BURKE 112:8
Of highest w. brings about MILT 351:3
of w. and understanding BIBLE 58:9
politicians chew on w. POPE 377:14
price of w. is above rubies BIBLE 52:34
privilege of w. to listen HOLM 253:20
seen all Solomon's w. BIBLE 50:32
special evidences of our w. TROL 553:1
such w. as many of us have TROL 553:11
teach eternal w. how POPE 379:14
teach his senators w. PRAY 397:4
to the want of human w. LAW 310:22
where shall w. be found BIBLE 52:33
W. and goodness SHAK 455:11
W. and Wit are little seen CHES 145:8
W. be put in a silver rod BLAKE 85:19
w., capacity and virtue SWIFT 526:8
W. denotes the pursuing HUTC 268:3
W. excelleth folly BIBLE 55:10
W. has taught us to be HOLM 253:11
W. hath builded her house BIBLE 53:27
w. (if they have any) BURKE 111:20
W. in minds attentive COWP 167:23
w. in the scorn of consequence TENN 541:19
W. is better than rubies BIBLE 53:26
W. is humble that he knows COWP 167:24
W. is justified of her BIBLE 66:4
W. is the principal thing BIBLE 53:18
w. lingers TENN 539:3
w. of a great minister JUN 287:3
w. of a learned man cometh BIBLE 63:19
w. of human contrivances BURKE 109:18
w. of our ancestors BURKE 108:21
w. of the crocodiles BACON 27:38
w. shall die with you BIBLE 52:23
W.'s self MILT 341:8
w. the world is governed OXEN 367:13
w. we have lost in knowledge ELIOT 202:3
With the ancient is w. BIBLE 52:24
With them the Seed of W. FITZ 212:21
wrath of the lion is the w. BLAKE 88:21
wise: awhile from letters to be w.
　　　　JOHN 282:29
beacons of w. men HUXL 269:10
being darkly w. POPE 379:12
be lowly w. MILT 349:4
be w. BIBLE 53:21
be w. in his own conceit BIBLE 54:31
Be w. to-day YOUNG 588:3
by experience w. POPE 377:5
by the wisest of the w. TENN 539:22
came w. men from the east BIBLE 63:31
confirm the w. COWP 168:9
cunning men pass for w. BACON 25:43

errors of a w. man — BLAKE 87:9
fool than of the w. — BACON 25:29
Great men are not always w. — BIBLE 52:39
Had you been as w. as bold — SHAK 466:17
he is a W. man or a Fool — BLAKE 86:15
How very weak the very w. — THAC 546:4
I heard a w. man say — HOUS 262:20
In a bowl to sea went w. — PEAC 371:3
leave the W. — FITZ 212:19
Let me smile with the w. — JOHN 275:23
man w. in his own conceit — BIBLE 54:33
may then grow w. for spite — SWIFT 527:21
More happy, if less w. — BYRON 124:42
more than woman to be w. — MOORE 356:23
Nature is always w. — THUR 550:33
Nor ever did a w. one — ROCH 406:18
nor talk too w. — KIPL 299:22
not w. in you own conceits — BIBLE 75:17
Obscurely w. — JOHN 278:35
only wretched are the w. — PRIOR 401:8
same tree that a w. man — BLAKE 88:15
so w. as Thurlow looked — FOX 217:21
So w. so young — SHAK 481:3
so witty and so w. — ROCH 406:22
speak to the w. — PIND 373:14
teachings of the w. — LUCR 320:6
that's a w. man and a fool — SHAK 454:8
therefore only are reputed w. — SHAK 465:12
therefore w. as serpents — BIBLE 65:33
things w. and wonderful — ALEX 3:13
'Tis folly to be w. — GRAY 235:13
to be fortunate than w. — WEBS 567:11
To be w., and love — SHAK 487:1
To be w. and eke to love — SPEN 517:2
to think as w. men do — ASCH 17:4
Virtuous and w. he was — ARMS 12:14
What all the w. men promised — MELB 336:11
What leisure to grow w. — ARN 13:10
wherefore thou be w. — TENN 532:15
Who can be w. — SHAK 461:2
w. and masterly inactivity — MACK 325:12
w., and to the unwise — BIBLE 74:30
w. are merry of tongue — YEATS 585:18
w. enough to play the fool — SHAK 489:19
w. father that knows his — SHAK 466:9
w. man will make — BACON 25:38
W. men also die — PRAY 392:28
w. son maketh a glad — BIBLE 53:29
w. want love — SHEL 503:2
Words are w. men's counters — HOBB 251:15
words of the w. are as goads — BIBLE 56:12
world to confound the w. — BIBLE 75:30
wisedoom: what is bettre than w.
— CHAU 142:27
wisely: Be w. worldly — QUAR 403:11
Of one that lov'd not w. — SHAK 477:23
spake w., and could have — BIBLE 63:4
wise-manned: w. to boot — BROW 104:17
wiser: Are w. and nicer — AUDEN 20:12
French are w. than they — BACON 27:14
generation w. than the children — BIBLE 70:25
not the w. grow — POMF 375:8
sadder and a w. man — COL 156:1
sluggard is w. in his own — BIBLE 54:35
that he is w. to-day than — POPE 381:19
Thou speakest w. than thou — SHAK 425:12
to be guided by the w. — CARL 131:16
We are w. than we know — EMER 207:27
young man will be w. — TENN 534:2
wisest: clerkes been noght w. men
— CHAU 143:11
first and w. of them all — MILT 350:9
he was the w. bard — BEHN 38:11
Only the w. of mankind — SMITH 510:11
than the w. man can answer — COLT 159:9
w. and justest and best — PLATO 374:10
w. fool in Christendom — HENR 245:16
w. man the warl' saw — BURNS 114:3
W. men — MILT 350:19
w., virtuousest, discreetest — MILT 349:7

wish: feast at his earnest w. — LEAR 312:21
joy that you can w. — SHAK 467:14
Thy own wish w. I thee — SHAK 456:24
Thy w. was father — SHAK 442:19
To w. myself much better — SHAK 467:13
Who did not w. to die — SHAW 498:27
Whoever hath her w. — SHAK 495:10
who would w. to die — BORR 90:4
willingly believe what they w. — CAES 126:27
w. for what I faintly hope — DRYD 197:16
w. I loved the Human Race — RAL 404:20
w. thine own heart dry — KEATS 290:30
w. 'twere done — ARN 13:23
Wish'd: W. to be with them — SCOTT 416:9
wished: He whom I w. to see — KEPP 295:12
nor w. to change — GOLD 230:22
w. all men as rich as he — GILB 225:28
W. for to hear — KEPP 295:12
w. longer by its readers — JOHN 280:16
wishes: all made of w. — SHAK 426:29
her little w. and ways — HARDY 241:16
there is exact to my w. — ANON 5:13
wishest: Than w. should be undone
— SHAK 459:1
wision: you see my w.'s limited — DICK 182:23
Wissenschaft: *Politik ist keine exakte*
W. — BISM 84:19
wistful: With such a w. eye — WILDE 572:8
wit: accepted w. has — GILB 229:10
are at their w.'s end — PRAY 397:10
attire doth show her w. — ANON 6:20
baiting-place of w. — SIDN 507:20
Beauty, w., High birth — SHAK 487:6
becomes excellent w. — SHAK 442:15
Brevity is the soul of w. — SHAK 431:30
Devise, w. — SHAK 456:19
effusions of w. and humour — AUST 22:31
fancy w. will come — POPE 376:15
folly and his weapon w. — HOPE 256:2
he but have drawn his w. — JONS 284:17
His w. invites you by his — COWP 165:5
His w. was in his own power — JONS 285:1
How the w. brightens — POPE 378:25
I had but a little w. — ANON 8:19
In w., a man — POPE 378:8
is only a w. among Lords — JOHN 274:9
mechanic part of w. — ETH 208:30
mingled with a little w. — DRYD 196:17
Muse gave native w. — HOR 257:23
nature by her mother w. — SPEN 516:20
neither a w. in his own eye — CONG 160:11
no more w. than a Christian — SHAK 487:25
nor all thy Piety nor W. — FITZ 213:7
of that he shoots his w. — SHAK 427:7
of thy w. in an instant — SHAK 467:19
old man's w. may wander — TENN 534:2
pick-purse of another's w. — SIDN 507:26
plays can boast of more w. — ETH 208:27
pleasant smooth w. — AUBR 18:1
plentiful lack of w. — SHAK 432:8
proverb is one man's w. — RUSS 412:21
scintillations of your w. — GOUL 233:5
Some beams of w. on other — DRYD 196:34
spice of w. — STEV 523:7
Staircase w. — DID 184:6
that has a little tiny w. — SHAK 454:12
thirty, the w. — FRAN 218:10
too proud for a w. — GOLD 231:17
to sharpen a good w. — ASCH 17:2
up the watch of his w. — SHAK 485:4
use my w. as a pitchfork — LARK 310:6
ware of mine own w. — SHAK 425:13
wears his w. in his belly — SHAK 486:29
well craves a kind of w. — SHAK 489:19
whole w. in a jest — BEAU 35:19
will be w. in all languages — DRYD 198:1
Wisdom and W. are little — CHES 145:8
w. I e'er was deafen'd — BYRON 124:11
w., if not first — GOLD 231:19
w. is nature to advantage — POPE 378:17

w. is out — BECON 36:22
w. is out — SHAK 472:34
W. is the epitaph — NIET 363:13
w. its soul — COL 156:15
w. Makes such a wound — SHEL 501:20
w., nor words, nor worth — SHAK 451:2
w. of man to say what dream — SHAK 471:9
w.'s a feather — POPE 379:24
W.'s an unruly engine — HERB 247:4
w.'s false mirror held — POPE 380:4
w.'s the noblest frailty — SHAD 420:20
W. to persuade — DAV 172:12
witty fool than a foolish w. — SHAK 488:5
W. will shine — DRYD 197:33
w. with dunces — POPE 375:22
You have a nimble w. — SHAK 426:11
your w. single — SHAK 441:10
Your w.'s too hot — SHAK 456:23
witch: suffer a w. to live — BIBLE 47:26
witchcraft: Nor no w. charm thee
— SHAK 428:22
only is the w. I have us'd — SHAK 474:1
rebellion is as the sin of w. — BIBLE 50:4
w. celebrates — SHAK 460:1
witches: think we're burning w. — CHES 147:7
witching: very w. time of night — SHAK 434:25
with: God knows it I am w. them
— WILDE 572:17
Lord of hosts is w. us — PRAY 392:20
sort of English up w. which — CHUR 151:6
thou art w. me — PRAY 390:22
When you see w. — BLAKE 85:23
w. you in the squeezing — GOLD 232:24
withdraw: (Anthea) must w. from him
— HERR 249:23
to w. one's steps — VIRG 558:18
withdrew: He departed, he w. — CIC 151:27
wither: Age cannot w. her — SHAK 422:5
garlands w. on your brow — SHIR 507:3
I w. slowly in thine arms — TENN 543:11
names that must not w. — BYRON 120:32
wither'd: It could not w. be — JONS 284:12
w. cheek and tresses grey — SCOTT 416:8
w. in my hand — HERB 247:12
w. is the garland — SHAK 423:16
withered: before they be w. — BIBLE 62:11
dried up, and w. — PRAY 395:18
they w. away — BIBLE 66:16
w., and so wild — SHAK 458:10
withereth: Fast w. too — KEATS 290:16
Witherington: W. needs must I wail
— SHEA 498:29
withers: *it w. away* — ENG 208:18
our w. are unwrung — SHAK 434:13
withhold: evening w. not thine hand
— BIBLE 56:8
Sometimes w. in mercy what — MORE 357:10
witholde: man the cours of hire w.
— CHAU 142:29
within: he never went w. — COWL 164:6
I have that w. — SHAK 429:25
kingdom of God is w. you — BIBLE 70:31
they that are w. would — DAV 172:9
thou wert w. me — AUG 21:16
when the fight begins w. — BROW 99:10
without: forasmuch as w. thee we
— PRAY 386:21
much as w. Thee — KNOX 305:21
nor w. you — MART 331:13
that are w. would fain go — DAV 172:9
that is w. sin among you — BIBLE 72:10
those things that are w. — BIBLE 77:12
W. ceasing I make mention — BIBLE 74:29
w. whose never-failing — WOD 575:21
withstand: least we w. Barabbas now
— BROW 101:4
w. in the evil day — BIBLE 78:10
witless: w. nature — HOUS 265:10
witness: shalt not bear false w. — BIBLE 47:24
to bear w. of that Light — BIBLE 71:25

to be a w. for me — BUNY 107:38
w. against you this day — BIBLE 48:18
witnesses: multitude of silent w. — GEOR 224:4
so great a cloud of w. — BIBLE 79:35
w. laid down their clothes — BIBLE 73:28
wits: composed in their w. — ARN 16:9
striving by their w. — LUCR 320:6
they cast on female w. — BRAD 91:13
Universities incline w. to sophistry — BACON 28:12
warming his five w. — TENN 543:10
we have w. to read — JONS 284:19
W. are gamecocks to one — GAY 223:12
youth have ever homely w. — SHAK 490:28
wittiest: is the w. of all things — HARE 242:2
wittles: I live on broken w. — DICK 176:33
They're w. and drink — DICK 177:9
We have no w. — THAC 545:33
witty: am not only w. in myself — SHAK 441:3
fancy my self mighty w. — FARQ 210:20
intelligent, the w., the brave — MILL 339:23
so w. and so wise — ROCH 406:22
w. and it sha'n't be long — CHES 145:7
w., profligate, and thin — YOUNG 588:14
Witz: W. ist das Epigramm auf — NIET 363:13
wive: when I came, alas! to w. — SHAK 490:27
wives: changes when they are w. — SHAK 426:23
divides the w. of aldermen — SMITH 509:8
Fair be their w. — DUNB 199:11
loves into corpses or w. — SWIN 529:10
love your w. — BIBLE 78:27
man so happy in *three* w. — LAMB 308:13
profane and old w.' fables — BIBLE 79:14
sacks to sew up w. — THAC 545:18
we have w. — TENN 543:3
W. are young men's mistresses — BACON 26:34
W., submit yourselves — BIBLE 78:6
wizards: w. haste with odours sweet — MILT 344:4
W. that peep and that mutter — BIBLE 58:5
wo: of w. that is in mariage — CHAU 143:16
woe: balm of w. — SIDN 507:20
Can I see another's w. — BLAKE 88:8
Companions of our w. — WALSH 563:29
Converting all your sounds of w. — SHAK 472:16
Europe made his w. her — ARN 13:9
every secret w. — KIPL 300:6
groan of the martyr's w. — BLAKE 86:6
heavily from w. to woe — SHAK 493:7
Her face was full of w. — ANON 6:7
hideous notes of w. — BYRON 124:6
Joy and w. are woven fine — BLAKE 85:14
me to feel another's w. — POPE 381:13
O Sleep! the friend of W. — SOUT 513:27
pity who has felt the w. — GAY 223:7
prov'd, a very w. — SHAK 495:7
rearward of a conquer'd w. — SHAK 494:14
song of w. — TENN 536:31
to discover sights of w. — MILT 344:25
trappings and the suits of w. — SHAK 429:25
unutterable w. — AYT 24:5
watch and moveless w. — BROW 98:8
with such a draught of w. — SHEL 499:18
W. is me — BIBLE 57:29
W. to her that is filthy — BIBLE 61:27
W. to the bloody city — BIBLE 61:26
W. to thee, O land — BIBLE 56:3
W. to the land that's govern'd — SHAK 481:2
W. unto him that striveth — BIBLE 59:13
W. unto them that join — BIBLE 57:24
W. unto them that rise — BIBLE 57:25
W. weeps out her division — JONS 283:21
woe, w. — POUND 383:15
woe-begone: so dead in look, so w. — SHAK 441:1
woeful: New-hatch'd to the w. time — SHAK 460:20
w. stuff this madrigal — POPE 378:25

woes: Death is the end of w. — SPEN 516:9
Of w. unnumbered — HOMER 253:26
self-consumer of my w. — CLARE 152:12
still her w. at midnight — LYLY 321:12
that sound awakes my w. — BURNS 113:22
To suffer w. which Hope — SHEL 503:15
with old w. new wail — SHAK 493:7
worst of w. that wait on age — BYRON 120:16
Wohlgemutere: Stärkere, Sieghaftere,
W. — NIET 363:2
woke: all w. earlier — BRID 92:13
wolds: Rising in joy over w. — AUDEN 20:6
wolf: grim w. with privy paw — MILT 343:13
his sentinel, the w. — SHAK 460:1
in the tameness of a w. — SHAK 454:28
keep the w. far thence — WEBS 567:9
like the w. on the fold — BYRON 122:1
which man was w. to the man — VANZ 555:8
w. also shall dwell with — BIBLE 58:10
w. behowls the moon — SHAK 471:21
w. that follows — SWIN 528:19
W. that shall keep it may — KIPL 300:20
Wolf's-bane: W., tight-rooted — KEATS 291:13
wolves: eat like w. — SHAK 444:8
herded w. — SHEL 499:16
howling of Irish w. — SHAK 427:1
inwardly they are ravening w. — BIBLE 65:8
w. have prey'd — SHAK 473:11
woman: All your wish is w. to win — THAC 545:31
As w.'s love — SHAK 434:10
beautiful w. on top — HOR 257:9
Believe a w. or an epitaph — BYRON 124:18
between a man and a w. — GIBB 225:4
born of a w. is of few days — BIBLE 52:26
born of a w. hath but a short — PRAY 389:11
-brained w. and large-hearted — BROW 98:15
brawling w. in a wide house — BIBLE 54:20
brought the trembling w. — BLAKE 85:24
by the influence of W. — DICK 177:15
can find a virtuous w. — BIBLE 55:3
civil and obliging young w. — AUST 22:25
Come to my w.'s breasts — SHAK 459:2
day and a contentious w. — BIBLE 54:39
dead w. bites not — GRAY 234:13
dear, deluding W. — BURNS 113:25
deceitful w. — OTWAY 366:1
Die because a w.'s fair — WITH 575:12
dispell'd when a w. appears — GAY 222:26
Each thought on the w. — KING 297:2
e'en a w. and commanded — SHAK 423:17
Eternal W. draws us upward — GOET 230:6
Every w. is infallibly — CHES 146:1
Every w. knows that — BARR 34:22
ev'ry w. is at heart a rake — POPE 377:25
excellent thing in w. — SHAK 456:10
fat white w. whom nobody — CORN 162:22
folly of 'W.'s Rights' — VICT 556:14
Frailty, thy name is w. — SHAK 429:28
gentle w. dare — SOUT 514:6
greatest glory of a w. — PER 372:24
Had we w. ever less — BURNS 114:16
Holmes she is always *the* w. — DOYLE 192:5
if a w. have long hair — BIBLE 76:12
if a w. should continually — JOHN 278:21
I grant I am a w. — SHAK 449:16
ills enow To be a w. — DONNE 190:4
inconstant w. — GAY 223:26
indeed who cheats a w. — GAY 222:29
Is to a w. — DONNE 188:1
Is w.'s happiest knowledge — MILT 348:3
lays his hand upon a w. — TOBIN 551:7
let me not play a w. — SHAK 469:28
Let us look for the w. — DUMAS 199:2
like a w. scorn'd — CONG 160:15
Like to a constant w. — FORD 216:14
Lives a w. true and fair — DONNE 190:9
love a w. for singing — SHAK 453:14
lovely w. stoops to folly — ELIOT 205:3
lovely w. stoops to folly — GOLD 231:31

lovely w. in a rural spot — HUNT 268:13
made he a w. — BIBLE 45:11
made the w. for the man — TENN 533:9
Making a w. of clay — AUDEN 21:7
man and a w. looking — WOOLF 576:21
man to a blind w. — COL 157:19
Many a w. has a past — WILDE 573:9
more in vengeance than a w. — JUV 288:6
more than w. to be wise — MOORE 356:23
most pernicious w. — SHAK 431:16
nakedness of w. is the work — BLAKE 88:21
Nature W.'s cully made — CONG 160:20
never trust a w. — WILDE 573:28
nothing Of w. in me — SHAK 424:4
not thy soul unto a w. — BIBLE 62:29
no w. has ever written — VOLT 561:22
of a weak and feeble w. — ELIZ 206:4
of the enterprise a w. — VIRG 557:15
One hair of a w. can draw — HOW 266:21
opinion is about a w. — JAMES 271:28
other but a w.'s reason — SHAK 490:30
other purgatory but a w. — BEAU 36:12
perfect w. — WORD 581:8
post-chaise with a pretty w. — JOHN 277:15
prison and the w.'s workhouse — SHAW 498:3
Report be an honest w. — SHAK 467:2
She is a w. — SHAK 486:15
she's a w. — RAC 404:3
she shall be called W. — BIBLE 45:12
since a w. must wear chains — FARQ 210:1
So he that tastes w. — GAY 222:30
so long over *such* a w. — HOMER 253:26
sort of bloom on a w. — BARR 34:18
sort of w. who lives for — LEWIS 314:8
So unto the man is w. — LONG 317:12
suffer not a w. to teach — BIBLE 79:9
support of the w. I love — EDW 200:4
sweeter w. ne'er drew breath — ING 270:16
Teaches such beauty as a w.'s — SHAK 457:7
tell a w.'s age — GILB 228:27
than feeling a w.'s pulse — STER 519:6
that he cannot love a w. — ELIOT 201:10
That made a w. cry — MACD 325:4
There is no w.'s sides — SHAK 489:6
There shone one w. — SWIN 530:29
thing but make a man a w. — PEMB 371:11
think my self a very bad w. — ADD 2:2
this Man and this W. — PRAY 388:24
'Tis w.'s whole existence — BYRON 122:14
Titan-w. like a lover — SWIN 528:26
To one of w. born — SHAK 463:8
torrent of a w.'s will — ANON 8:20
unbecoming to a w. — WILDE 573:12
very honest w. — SHAK 424:6
very ordinary little w. — BETJ 43:4
virtuous w. is a crown — BIBLE 53:33
Vitality in a w. is a blind — SHAW 497:20
Was ever w. in this humour — SHAK 480:22
was never yet fair w. — SHAK 454:6
well-born and unhappy w. — ELIOT 201:1
Were w.'s looks — MOORE 356:18
what is w. — COWL 164:23
what's a play without a w. — KYD 306:9
when a w. isn't beautiful — CHEK 145:6
Who takes w. must be — GAY 222:30
wickedness of a w. — BIBLE 63:8
will take some savage w. — TENN 539:6
woman always a w. — WOLL 576:10
w. among all those have — BIBLE 55:23
w. as old as she looks — COLL 158:15
W., behold thy son — BIBLE 73:2
w. being deceived was — FARQ 210:2
w. can be a beauty without — CHEK 145:5
w. can become a man's friend — YEATS 584:19
w. can be proud and stiff — GAY 222:15
w. can forgive another — ELIOT 201:3
w. can hardly ever choose...she — BIBLE 82:10
w. clothed with the sun — SHAK 495:12
w. colour'd ill — ELIOT 201:6
w. dictates before marriage

897

w. drew her long black — ELIOT 205:9
w. drop as an honeycomb — BIBLE 53:20
w. especially — AUST 23:5
w. forget her sucking child — BIBLE 59:17
w. for the hearth — TENN 542:9
w. has haunted me these — KEATS 294:3
w. has her way — HOLM 253:15
W.! in our hours of ease — SCOTT 417:21
w. is a dish for the gods — SHAK 424:9
w. is his game — TENN 542:8
w. is only a woman — KIPL 298:3
w. is so hard — TENN 542:12
W. is the lesser man — TENN 539:5
w. is the worst — GRAN 234:5
w. learn in silence with — BIBLE 79:9
w., let her be as good — ELIOT 201:9
w. liberty to gad abroad — BIBLE 63:9
w. made Society — BRAD 91:8
w. mov'd is like a fountain — SHAK 484:16
w. of real genius — FITZ 213:19
w. of so shining loveliness — YEATS 586:17
w. out-paramoured the Turk — SHAK 454:18
w., rules us still — MOORE 357:1
W.'s at best a contradiction — POPE 377:29
w. sat, in unwomanly rags — HOOD 255:6
w. says to her lusting — CAT 137:7
w.'s business to get married — SHAW 497:25
w.'s cause is man's — TENN 542:18
w.'s desire is rarely — COL 157:33
w. seldom asks advice before — ADD 2:23
W. seldom Writes her Mind — STEE 517:24
W.'s faith — SCOTT 418:4
w.'s friendship ever ends — GAY 223:9
w. should marry a teetotaller — STEV 521:29
w.'s might — SHAK 449:22
W.'s mind — GAY 223:8
w.'s noblest station is — LYTT 321:21
w. sober — PEPYS 372:10
w.'s preaching is like — JOHN 275:10
w.'s whole life is a history — IRV 270:20
w. take An elder — SHAK 489:1
w. taken in adultery — BIBLE 72:9
w. that deliberates is — ADD 1:20
w. that you forsake her — KIPL 299:21
w., therefore to be won — SHAK 446:1
w. wakes to love — TENN 535:9
w. was full of good works — BIBLE 73:36
W. was God's second blunder — NIET 363:4
W., what have I to do — BIBLE 71:33
W.! when I behold thee — KEATS 293:10
w. which is without discretion — BIBLE 53:32
w. who always was tired — ANON 5:13
w. who, between courses — JAMES 271:21
w. who did not care) — KIPL 303:29
w. whom thou gavest — BIBLE 45:17
w. who wrote the book that — LINC 315:6
W., why weepest thou — BIBLE 73:8
W. will be the last thing — MER 337:34
w. with fair opportunities — THAC 545:21
w. yet think him an angel — THAC 545:7
wrapp'd in a w.'s hide — SHAK 446:16
yet a w. too — WORD 581:8
young W. her name was Dull — BUNY 107:30
woman-head: graves have learnt that
w. — DONNE 190:5
womanhood: Heroic w. — LONG 317:7
W. and childhood fleet — LONG 316:20
womankind: faith in w. — TENN 542:19
spoons and packs off its w. — SHAW 497:30
w. than to suppose they — KEATS 294:1
worst he can of w. — HOME 253:23
womanly: blushing w. discovering grace
— DONNE 188:11
So w., Her demeaning — SKEL 508:17
w. feeling and propriety — VICT 556:14
woman's: is semblative a w. part
womb: cloistered in thy dear w. DONNE 189:1
dark w. where I began — MAS 333:22
even so her plenteous w. — SHAK 463:13
events in the w. of time — SHAK 474:11

grave; and the barren w. — BIBLE 54:46
her w. convey sterility — SHAK 453:18
Making their tomb the w. — SHAK 494:11
slayeth the child in the w. — POUND 382:11
this teeming w. of royal — SHAK 478:20
was from his mother's w. — SHAK 463:8
w. of time the body whose — HEINE 244:12
w. of uncreated night — MILT 346:10
wombe: O w.! O bely — CHAU 143:6
women: after the manner of w. — BIBLE 46:6
An' I learned about w. — KIPL 300:16
An' learn about w. from — KIPL 300:17
are not w. truly — JONS 284:11
asham'd that w. are so simple — SHAK 484:19
because w. have cancers — KEATS 293:32
blessed art thou among w. — BIBLE 69:4
by subtleties these w. — MER 337:16
created men and w. different — VICT 556:14
denyin' the w. are foolish — ELIOT 200:19
dry than w.'s tears — WEBS 567:7
England is the paradise of w. — FLOR 216:1
experience of w. which — DOYLE 192:29
fickleness of the w. I love — SHAW 498:9
Fram'd to make w. false — SHAK 474:12
generally like w.'s letters — HAZL 243:8
girls turn into American w. — HAMP 238:17
Half the sorrows of w. — ELIOT 200:24
happiest w. — ELIOT 201:18
hardly any w. at all — AUST 23:4
he hid himself among w. — BROW 97:14
hops, and w. — DICK 181:27
I must have w. — GAY 222:27
is for w. to keep counsel — SHAK 449:22
let not w.'s weapons — SHAK 454:2
Let us have wine and w. — BYRON 122:21
Let your w. keep silence — BIBLE 76:16
love of w. — BYRON 122:24
many w. — JOHN 274:22
Married w. are kept women — SMITH 510:16
men and w. with our race — KIPL 298:10
Men don't know w. — TROL 552:20
men in w. do require — BLAKE 86:1
men that w. marry — LONG 316:21
men, w., and Herveys — MONT 354:6
men, w., and clergymen — SMITH 511:8
Monstrous Regiment of W. — KNOX 305:19
Most w. are not so young — BEER 37:10
Most w. have no characters — POPE 377:17
Music and w. I cannot — PEPYS 372:16
old w. (of both sexes) — STER 520:4
other w. cloy — SHAK 422:5
passing the love of w. — BIBLE 50:17
Phidias Gave w. dreams — YEATS 587:1
poetry w. generally write — BRON 93:17
pretty w. to deserve them — AUST 22:26
proper function of w. — ELIOT 201:20
room the w. come and go — ELIOT 203:18
shame for w. to speak — BIBLE 76:17
Silly w. laden with sins — BIBLE 79:24
Solomon loved many strange w. — BIBLE 51:1
souls of w. are so small — BUTL 118:18
Spare their w. for Thy — BETJ 43:5
spoiled the w.'s chats — BROW 103:15
stir up the zeal of w. — MILL 339:21
temptations both in wine and w. — KITC 305:14
then God help all w. — CAMP 128:7
Though w. all above — SHAK 455:17
thousand business w. — BETJ 42:6
tide in the affairs of w. — BYRON 123:20
to place a w.'s heart — WEBS 566:19
weird w. promis'd — SHAK 461:6
Were w. never so fair — LYLY 321:9
We wage no war with w. — SOUT 514:5
we w. cannot escape it — GIBB 225:3
Where w. walk in public — WHIT 570:15
which w. don't understand — KIPL 301:9
Why need the other w. know — BROW 98:26
wine and w. — BURT 116:21
With many w. I doubt whether — TROL 552:24
w. and care and trouble — WARD 564:38

W. and Champagne) — BELL 39:21
W. and elephants never — SAKI 413:11
W. and Horses and Power — KIPL 297:28
W. and music should never — GOLD 232:29
W. and wine should life — GAY 222:25
'w. are a sex by themselves — BEER 37:24
w. are in furious secret — SHAW 496:27
W. are like tricks by slight — CONG 160:9
w. are mostly troublesome — LOVER 318:22
w. are much more like each — CHES 145:29
W. are strongest — BIBLE 62:4
w. become like their mothers — WILDE 573:2
W. can't forgive failure — CHEK 145:1
w. guide the plot — SHER 506:24
w. in a state of ignorance — KNOX 305:26
w. like that part which — WEBS 566:18
w. Must be half-workers — SHAK 428:11
w. must weep — KING 297:3
W. never look so well — SURT 525:26
w. of good carriage — SHAK 481:28
W.—one half the human — BAG 28:29
w., physical decay, Yourself — AUDEN 19:5
w.'s eyes this doctrine — SHAK 457:6
w.'s eyes this doctrine — SHAK 457:9
w. should be struck regularly — COW 163:14
w.'s rights is the basic — FOUR 217:18
w. the heart argues — ARN 13:20
W., then, are only children — CHES 145:25
W. what they are — BRAD 91:14
w. with perfect courtesy — KITC 305:14
w., worst and best — TENN 535:15
work its way with the w. — DICK 182:28
would have him about w. — SHAK 443:19
you should be w. — SHAK 458:10
womman: is bettre than a good w.
— CHAU 142:27
love a w. that she woot — CHAU 144:3
worthy w. al hir lyve — CHAU 141:31
Wommen: 'W. desiren to have
sovereynetee — CHAU 143:24
won: Duke of Marlbro' w. — SOUT 513:19
gaily you w. — BETJ 44:6
'is never lost till w. — COWP 168:23
not that you w. or lost — RICE 405:23
our Lord the field is w. — MORE 357:1
prize we sought is w. — WHIT 570:7
'She is w. — SCOTT 417:14
therefore may be w. — SHAK 486:10
Things w. are done — SHAK 486:21
to-morrow the ground w. — ARN 14:17
'Where you will never w. — BALL 30:18
woman in this humour w. — SHAK 480:22
woman, therefore to be w. — SHAK 446:1
wonder: all a w. and a wild desire
— BROW 104:19
all knowledge and w. (which — BACON 24:14
all the w. that would be — TENN 538:24
appeared a great w. in heaven — BIBLE 82:10
Have eyes to w. — SHAK 494:20
I w. any man alive will — GAY 222:19
I w. by my troth — DONNE 188:29
may w. at the workmanship — MILT 341:18
still the w. grew — GOLD 231:3
to see the boneless w. — CHUR 149:27
under the white-mossed w. — BRID 92:14
We w. at ourselves like — WORD 577:2
w. how the Devil they got — POPE 376:24
w. of an hour — BYRON 120:9
w. of our age — GREV 236:17
w. of our stage — JONS 284:19
w. what happened to him — COW 163:14
w. what you've missed — AUDEN 18:10
Worship is transcendent w. — CARL 131:29
wonderful: All things wise and w. — ALEX 3:13
knowledge is too w. and excellent
— PRAY 399:5
most w. wonderful — SHAK 426:7
name shall be called W. — BIBLE 58:7
passing strange and w. — SHEL 500:8
speak in our tongues the w. — BIBLE 73:23

There are many w. things   SOPH 513:7
which are too w. for me   BIBLE 55:1
with any thing that is w.   CONG 159:28
w. piece of work which   SHAK 421:21
wonderfully: fearfully and w. made
     PRAY 399:6

wonders: all w. in one sight   CRAS 169:8
carry within us the w.   BROW 96:12
declare the w. that he   PRAY 397:7
Except ye see signs and w.   BIBLE 71:43
his w. in the deep   PRAY 397:9
rich relative work w.   BIRK 84:13
Seven W. of the World   ADD 2:19
signs and my w. in the land of Egypt
     BIBLE 47:11
Signs are taken for w.   ELIOT 203:4
wondrous: tell of all thy w. works
     PRAY 391:5
this is w. strange   SHAK 431:22
What w. life is this   MARV 332:3
won't: if she w.   ANON 8:20
wonynge: w. fer by weste   CHAU 141:29
woo: are April when they w.   SHAK 426:23
Come, w. me   SHAK 426:21
wood: cleave the w. and there   ANON 7:11
God reigned from the w.   VEN 556:6
Heap on more w.   SCOTT 417:15
hewers of w. and drawers   BIBLE 49:3
hollow behind the little w.   TENN 539:25
lath of w. painted   BISM 84:27
must Thou char the w. ere   THOM 548:18
my house in the high w.   BELL 40:11
old w. burn brightest   WEBS 566:30
On Wenlock Edge the w.'s   HOUS 263:14
Out of this w. do not desire   SHAK 470:19
set out to plant a w.   SWIFT 527:28
therefore may be w.   SHAK 486:15
therefore to be w.   SHAK 446:1
whiffling through the tulgey w.   CARR 134:29
You are not w.   SHAK 450:25
you that broke the new w.   POUND 383:12
woodbine: over-canopied with luscious
w.   SHAK 470:10
well-attir'd w.   MILT 343:15
w. spices are wafted abroad   TENN 540:9
woodcock: Now is the w. near the gin
     SHAK 489:12
Spirits of well-shot w.   BETJ 42:11
w. to mine own springe   SHAK 437:19
woodcocks: springes to catch w.   SHAK 430:21
wooden: lies about his w. horse   FLEC 214:18
Sailed off in a w. shoe   FIELD 211:2
this w. O the very casques   SHAK 443:4
wear w. shoes   GOLD 232:6
w. walls are the best walls   COV 163:10
Wooden-shoes: Round-heads and W.
are   ADD 2:1
woodland: a bit of w.   HOR 262:9
stands about the w. ride   HOUS 262:14
woodman: w., spare the beechen
     CAMP 128:17
wood-notes: Warble his native w. wild
     MILT 342:26
woods: Enter these enchanted w.   MER 337:21
green-rob'd senators of mighty w.
     KEATS 290:5
let them be w. of consular   VIRG 559:22
light w. go seaward from   HUNT 268:12
never knew the summer w.   TENN 536:15
pleasure in the pathless w.   BYRON 121:22
road through the w.   KIPL 303:31
sea-blooms and the oozy w.   SHEL 502:11
teachers had been w. and rills   WORD 581:11
there is a spirit in the w.   WORD 578:20
through the Wet Wild W.   KIPL 304:24
too have lived in the w.   VIRG 559:10
when all the w. are still   MILT 351:5
Where are those starry w.   BRID 92:17
w. are lovely   FROST 219:12
w. decay and fall   TENN 543:11

w. with high romances blent   KEATS 292:15
woodshed: Something nasty in the w.
     GIBB 225:2
woodspurge: w. has a cup of three
     ROSS 410:9
wooer: knight to be their w.   BALL 30:14
woof: We know her w.   KEATS 290:27
w. of my tent's thin roof   SHEL 500:6
wooing: w. mind shall be express'd
     SHAK 457:16
w. of it   BACON 27:31
wooings: full length people's w.
     BYRON 122:27
wool: hairs were white like w.   BIBLE 81:14
He giveth snow like w.   PRAY 399:21
his head like the pure w.   BIBLE 61:8
If such as came for w.   BROW 102:17
tease the huswife's w.   MILT 341:18
w. comes not to market   POUND 382:9
woollen: in w.   POPE 377:15
woolly: w., bright   BLAKE 87:26
Woord: W. is but wynd   LYDG 321:4
Woos: W. his own end   TENN 534:37
woot: love a womman that she w.
     CHAU 144:3
Worchyng: W. and wandryng   LANG 309:23
word: been a time for such a w.   SHAK 463:6
before thy uncreating w.   POPE 376:2
beginning was the W.   BIBLE 71:21
beginning was the W.   ELIOT 204:1
be ye doers of the w.   BIBLE 80:10
Bilbo's the w.   CONG 160:21
by every w. that proceedeth   BIBLE 48:22
by every w. that proceedeth   BIBLE 64:1
choke the w.   BIBLE 66:17
comfort of thy holy W.   PRAY 386:5
Every idle w. that men   BIBLE 66:10
father answered never a w.   LONG 317:21
fool can play upon the w.   SHAK 467:18
honour? A w.   SHAK 440:18
in w. mightier than they   MILT 348:26
last kind w. to Christ   BROW 104:25
leave the w. of God   BIBLE 73:27
Lord gave the w.   PRAY 394:8
Man's w. is God in man   TENN 533:31
meanings packed up into one w.   CARR 135:28
meekness the engrafted w.   BIBLE 80:10
nat o w. wol he faille   CHAU 142:31
no w. however sounding   STEV 521:14
once familiar w.   BAYLY 35:10
one Peculiar w.   LAND 309:3
one-while w. for word   ALFR 3:17
plainly repugnant to the W.   PRAY 400:8
Proud w. you never spoke   LAND 308:25
say only the w.   MASS 335:8
sincere milk of the w.   BIBLE 80:22
sincere milk of the w.   BIBLE 83:25
step should sound or a w.   SWIN 529:18
storm, fulfilling his w.   PRAY 399:22
suit the action to the w.   SHAK 433:17
teaching me that w.   SHAK 468:9
Tears wash out a W.   FITZ 213:7
That I kept my w.   DE L 174:8
there is no such w.   BULW 107:5
time lies in one little w.   SHAK 478:13
To-day I pronounced a w.   FLEM 214:27
To honour his own w.   TENN 534:11
torture one poor w. ten   DRYD 196:35
truth of thy holy W.   PRAY 387:13
understanding of thy W.   PRAY 385:18
Was one that kept his w.   HOUS 266:2
We had no w. to say   WILDE 572:11
what the w. did make it   ELIZ 205:19
'When *I* use a w.   CARR 135:21
w., at random spoken   SCOTT 416:23
w. bites like a fish   SPEN 515:15
w. fitly spoken   BIBLE 54:26
w. in its Pickwickian sense…He   DICK 181:22
w. is a lantern unto my   PRAY 398:6
w. is the Verb   HUGO 267:9

w. is too often profaned   SHEL 504:13
w. spoken in due season   BIBLE 54:7
w. takes wing irrevocably   HOR 258:22
w. wad ane o' them speak   BALL 30:21
W. was made flesh   BIBLE 71:27
W. WAS MADE FLESH   MASS 335:12
w. which in wartime has   BETH 42:3
w. within a word   ELIOT 203:4
yesterday the w. of Caesar might
     SHAK 450:23
yet God has not said a w.   BROW 103:30
wordes: glotoun of w.   LANG 309:24
wordless: poem should be w.   MACL 325:13
song was w.   SASS 414:17
words: all sad w. of tongue   WHIT 571:19
All w., And no performance   MASS 335:24
All w. forgotten   DE L 174:15
arched roof in w. deceiving   MILT 344:13
arrangement of your w.   HOR 257:13
barren superfluity of w.   GARTH 221:21
best w. in the best order   COL 157:32
big w. for little   JOHN 275:14
Bright is the ring of w.   STEV 523:1
coiner of sweet w.   ARN 14:25
common, little, easy w.   WESL 568:24
counsel by w. without knowledge
     BIBLE 52:41
deceive you with vain w.   BIBLE 78:3
dressing old w.   SHAK 494:9
empty w. of a dream   BRID 92:10
even from good w.   PRAY 391:30
experience find those w.   CONG 160:27
fear those big w.   JOYCE 286:22
food and not fine w.   MOL 353:10
Fool and his w. are soon   SHEN 505:17
form of sound w.   BIBLE 79:23
for your w.   SHAK 451:31
Garden it abideth not in w.   KIPL 299:13
Give sorrow w.   SHAK 462:16
God spake all these w.   BIBLE 47:24
good w.   SHAK 452:30
heard w. that have been   BEAU 35:19
Hear what comfortable w.   PRAY 387:20
He w. me, girls   SHAK 424:1
his paint-pots and his w.   HOR 257:16
His w. came feebly   WORD 581:1
How often misused w. generate   SPEN 514:31
idiom of w. very little   PRIOR 400:27
I hate false w.   LAND 309:11
In all his w. most wonderful   NEWM 362:12
last w. of Mr Despondency   BUNY 107:37
Let the w. of my mouth   PRAY 390:13
long w. Bother me   MILNE 340:13
matter decocted into few w.   FULL 220:11
Melting melodious w.   HERR 250:9
Men of few w. are the best   SHAK 444:5
multiplieth w. without knowledge
     BIBLE 52:40
my w. among mankind   SHEL 502:14
my w. are my own   CHAR 140:23
My w. echo Thus   ELIOT 202:13
my w. shall not pass away   BIBLE 67:31
of all w. of tongue   HARTE 242:28
Of every four w. I write   BOIL 89:12
of hard w. like a charm   OSB 365:19
of the unpleasant'st w.   SHAK 467:15
on the alms-basket of w.   SHAK 457:12
polite meaningless w.   YEATS 585:1
Proper w. in proper places   SWIFT 526:20
repeats his w.   SHAK 452:20
Th' artillery of w.   SWIFT 527:31
that my w. were now written   BIBLE 52:30
that w. are the daughters   JOHN 281:6
their large confusing w.   AUDEN 18:5
therefore let thy w. be few   BIBLE 55:16
these are very bitter w.   SHAK 441:26
they give good w.   PRAY 393:19
threw w. like stones   SPEN 515:11
times when w. had a meaning   FRAN 217:27
Uncouth w. in disarray   JOHN 280:9

weigh thy w. in a balance — BIBLE 63:12
whose w. are of less weight — BACON 25:41
wild and whirling w. — SHAK 431:18
Winged w. — HOMER 253:27
with these two narrow w. — RAL 404:16
wit, nor w., nor worth — SHAK 451:2
W. are also actions — EMER 207:28
w. are but the signs — JOHN 281:6
w. are images of thought — KEATS 292:20
W. are men's daughters — MADD 326:19
w. are quick and vain — SHEL 502:21
W. are the tokens current — BACON 24:22
w. are true and faithful — BIBLE 82:31
W. are wise men's counters — HOBB 251:15
w. are words — SHAK 474:4
w. but wind — BUTL 118:4
w. clothed in reason's — MILT 346:12
w. divide and rend — SWIN 528:23
w. hereafter thy tormentors — SHAK 478:21
w., like Nature — TENN 535:34
w. no virtue can digest — MARL 330:11
w. of a dead man — AUDEN 19:4
w. of his mouth were softer — PRAY 393:12
w. of learned length — GOLD 231:3
w. of Mercury are harsh — SHAK 457:20
w. oft creep in one dull — POPE 378:20
w. of the wise are as goads — BIBLE 56:12
w. once spoke can never — ROOS 408:9
w. or I shall burst — FARQ 210:12
w. so fair — JONS 285:10
W. strain — ELIOT 202:17
w. That are only fit — FRY 219:30
W. to the heat of deeds — SHAK 460:1
W. without thoughts never — SHAK 434:31
Words, words, mere w. — SHAK 487:17
W., words, words — SHAK 432:7
wrestle With w. and meanings — ELIOT 202:19
Wordsworth: better scholar than W. — HOUS 266:18
Fancy a symphony by W. — BUTL 118:32
W. and out-glittering Keats — BULW 107:3
W., both are thine — STEP 518:22
W. chime his childish verse — BYRON 124:29
W.'s healing power — ARN 13:18
W. sometimes wakes — BYRON 123:7
W.—stupendous genius — BYRON 126:17
W.'s standard of intoxication — SHOR 507:9
W., Tennyson and Browning — BAG 29:20
Wordsworthian: W. or egotistical sublime — KEATS 294:7
work: All hands to w. — ANON 8:24
All out of w. — SHAK 443:7
be as tedious as to w. — SHAK 438:13
Better the rudest w. that — RUSK 411:21
breed one w. that wakes — HOPK 257:3
days when w. was scrappy — CHES 147:22
Did he smile his w. — BLAKE 87:16
do all thy w. — BIBLE 47:24
do the hard and dirty w. — RUSK 411:16
Do the w. that's nearest — KING 296:21
earnestly are you set a-w. — SHAK 487:19
hands wrought in the w. — BIBLE 52:1
he desireth a good w. — BIBLE 79:11
he who has found his w. — CARL 132:10
his six days' w. — MILT 349:2
If any would not w. — BIBLE 79:5
I have finished the w. — OVID 366:19
I have protracted my w. — JOHN 274:14
I like w. — JER 272:26
I'll w. on a new and original — GILB 226:6
'I've got my w. cut out — SQUI 517:13
I want w. — SHAK 438:33
'Know what thou canst w. — CARL 132:18
little w. — DU M 199:6
Look at the end of w. — BROW 101:25
man according to his w. — PRAY 393:20
Man goeth forth to his w. — PRAY 397:1
men must w. — KING 297:3
My medicine, w. — SHAK 476:8
My W. is done — ANON 6:19

noblest w. of man — BUTL 119:7
Old Kaspar's w. was done — SOUT 513:14
one has plenty of w. to do — JER 272:22
patience have her perfect w. — BIBLE 80:7
pleasant and clean w. — RUSK 411:16
should I let the toad w. — LARK 310:6
So the more we w. — KIPL 300:21
stomach sets us to w. — ELIOT 201:4
That do no w. to-day — SHAK 444:27
there is always w. — LOW 319:9
To w., and back to bed — MAS 333:24
To w. my mind — SHAK 493:5
What a piece of w. is a man — SHAK 432:15
When Nature has w. to be — EMER 208:3
when no man can w. — BIBLE 72:14
Who first invented W. — LAMB 307:33
who lives by his own w. — COLL 158:13
woman is the w. of God — BLAKE 88:21
wonderful piece of w. which — SHAK 421:21
W. apace — DEKK 173:20
W. expands so as to fill — PARK 369:1
w. for good to them that — BIBLE 75:11
W. is the curse — WILDE 573:39
w. i' the earth so fast — SHAK 431:21
W. out your own salvation — BIBLE 78:15
w. till we die — LEWIS 314:9
w. upon the vulgar with — POPE 381:18
W. without hope draws nectar — COL 157:15
W. your hands from day — MACN 326:8
Yet the w. itself shall — FRAN 218:20
you don't w., you die — KIPL 299:16
Workers: W. of the world — MARX 333:4
worketh: according to the power that w.** — BIBLE 77:26
w. not the righteousness — BIBLE 80:10
workhouse: prison and the woman's w. — SHAW 498:3
working: according to the mighty w.** — PRAY 389:13
by w. about six weeks — THOR 550:13
each for the joy of the w. — KIPL 304:3
spare time and in his w. — GILL 229:11
w. at something useful — THOM 546:11
working-class: w. which, raw and half-developed — ARN 15:20
working-day: full of briers is this w. — SHAK 424:29
working-house: forge and w. of thought — SHAK 445:6
workmanship: most may wonder at the w.** — MILT 341:18
w. that reconciles Discordant — WORD 580:11
Works: all ye W. of the Lord — PRAY 384:19
believe the w. — BIBLE 72:21
cast away the w. of darkness — PRAY 386:4
cast off the w. of darkness — BIBLE 75:24
devil and all his w. — PRAY 388:13
even the w. of thy fingers — PRAY 389:28
Faith without w. is dead — BIBLE 80:12
forth the fruit of good w. — PRAY 387:2
future, and it w. — STEF 518:15
God now accepteth thy w. — BIBLE 55:28
his w. are the comments — KEATS 294:13
how manifold are thy w. — PRAY 397:1
I know thy w. — BIBLE 81:20
immediately upon your w. — GRANT 234:1
into my w. is my talent — WILDE 573:35
Look on my w. — SHEL 502:16
man according to their w. — BIBLE 82:29
noblest w. and foundations — BACON 27:4
of all thy wondrous w. — PRAY 391:5
proved me, and saw my w. — PRAY 396:4
Rich in good w. — BIBLE 79:20
stained with their own w. — PRAY 397:6
their w. do follow them — BIBLE 82:18
they may see your good w. — BIBLE 64:9
w. and days of hands — ELIOT 203:19
w., begun, continued — PRAY 388:6
W. done least rapidly — BROW 102:26

workshop: suffer England to be the w. — DISR 184:11
workshops: George's w. was burned down — DICK 178:19
worky-day: w. fortune — SHAK 421:14
world: All's right with the w. — BROW 103:21
all the deceits of the w. — PRAY 385:16
all the w. and his wife — ANST 11:8
all the w. should be taxed — BIBLE 69:8
All the w.'s a stage — SHAK 425:24
are the light of the w. — BIBLE 64:8
attracts the envy of the w. — BURKE 109:15
at which the w. grew pale — JOHN 282:31
aught The w. contains — SHEL 504:5
away from the whole w. — VIRG 559:13
aweary of this great w. — SHAK 465:18
'because I am the great w. — FORS 217:4
become fit for this w. — KEATS 293:14
be glad one loves His w. — BROW 103:22
Berkeley destroyed this w. — SMITH 511:33
bestride the narrow w. — SHAK 448:17
blackguard made the w. — HOUS 264:21
bottom of the monstrous w. — MILT 343:16
brave new w. — SHAK 485:26
brought nothing into this w. — BIBLE 79:17
confess that this w.'s spent — DONNE 187:19
contagion of the w.'s — SHEL 499:21
corners of the w. in arms — SHAK 453:1
dark w. of sin — BICK 84:4
Days that Shook the W. — REED 405:8
deed in a naughty w. — SHAK 468:1
despise This wrecched w. — CHAU 144:18
dry a cinder this w. — DONNE 187:20
excellent foppery of the w. — SHAK 453:11
fashion of this w. passeth — BIBLE 76:4
flaming walls of the w. — LUCR 320:3
flood unto the w.'s end — PRAY 394:20
fool in the eye of the w. — CONG 160:11
foutra for the w. — SHAK 442:27
From this vile w. — SHAK 494:6
God so loved the w. — BIBLE 71:38
good be out of the w. — CIBB 151:10
go to bed in another w. — HENS 246:4
greatness of the w. in tears — YEATS 586:22
great while ago the w. begun — SHAK 490:27
had my w. as in my tyme — CHAU 143:19
Had we but w. enough — MARV 332:18
happiness of the next w. — BROW 97:11
heaven commences ere the w. — GOLD 230:20
If there's another w. — BURNS 113:26
If the w. should break — HOR 260:19
I have not loved the w. — BYRON 120:38
I hold the w. — SHAK 465:10
In a w. I never made — HOUS 264:25
into the ends of the w. — PRAY 390:11
is a citizen of the w. — BACON 26:20
kingdoms of the w. — BIBLE 64:3
late to seek a newer w. — TENN 544:3
leave the w. unseen — KEATS 291:10
Let the great w. spin — TENN 539:8
Mad w. — SHAK 452:13
make a hell of this w. — BECK 36:20
Man is one w. — HERB 248:3
mighty frame of the w. — BERK 41:19
milk the cow of the w. — WILB 572:4
monk who shook the w. — MONT 355:10
month in which the w. bigan — CHAU 143:1
much respect upon the w. — SHAK 465:9
My country is the w. — PAINE 368:5
my pains a w. of sighs — SHAK 474:1
naked shingles of the w. — ARN 12:23
Narrows the w. to my neighbour's — MER 337:19
nature makes the whole w. kin — SHAK 487:6
need of a w. of men — BROW 103:9
never have sought the w. — JOHN 279:4
not as the w. giveth — BIBLE 72:35
nourish all the w. — SHAK 457:9
now a w. — POPE 379:4
only interpreted the w. — MARX 333:10

Our country is the w.	GARR 221:18	w. is not thy friend nor	SHAK 483:26	of the star is called W.	BIBLE 82:6
O w.! O life! O time	SHEL 501:14	w. is so full of a number	STEV 522:22	w. and the gall	BIBLE 60:29
passes the glory of the w.	ANON 11:1	w. is still deceived with	SHAK 467:10	worn: comfortless, and w., and old	
perverse creatures in the w.	ADD 2:18	w. is too much with us	WORD 582:19		ROSS 409:2
rack of this tough w.	SHAK 456:12	w. is weary of the past	SHEL 501:3	*short* jacket is always w.	EDW 200:2
remember of this unstable w.	MAL 327:21	w. is white with May	TENN 534:4	when we're w.	SOUT 513:13
roll of the w. eastward	HARDY 241:9	w. knew him not	BIBLE 71:26	worried: w. and scratched by every	
Rose of all the W.	YEATS 586:10	w. made cunningly Of elements	DONNE 189:2		DICK 178:6
Round the w. for ever	ARN 13:6	w. may end to-night	BROW 101:23	worry: In headaches and in w.	AUDEN 18:10
round w. so sure	PRAY 395:24	w. may talk of hereafter	COLL 158:12	worse: bad against the w.	DAY-L 172:23
sea Of the w.'s praise	WORD 582:2	w. must be peopled	SHAK 472:19	better for w.	PRAY 389:4
secure amidst a falling w.	ADD 2:30	w. Of all of us	WORD 580:23	greater feeling to the w.	SHAK 478:17
see how this w. goes	SHAK 455:18	w. of pomp and state	BEAU 36:1	It is w. than a crime	BOUL 90:19
shall gain the whole w.	BIBLE 66:35	w. of the happy is quite	WITT 575:16	kept it from being any w.	HARDY 241:11
shall gain the whole w.	BIBLE 68:34	w.'s a bubble	BACON 28:15	medicine w. than the malady	FLET 215:16
shows how small the w.	GROS 236:22	w.'s a jest	STEP 518:25	More will mean w.	AMIS 4:4
singularly ill-contrived w.	BALF 30:6	w.'s an inn	DRYD 197:10	of finding something w.	BELL 39:3
six days' work, a w.	MILT 349:2	w.'s as ugly	LOCK 315:19	one penny the w.	BARH 33:14
slowest thing in the w.	SHAD 420:21	w.'s at an end	DAV 172:6	other things which were w.	KIPL 304:30
spectacle unto the w.	BIBLE 75:33	w.'s glory passes away	THOM 546:7	remedy is w. than the disease	BACON 27:13
start of the majestic w.	SHAK 448:16	w.'s great age begins	SHEL 500:20	state of that man is w.	BIBLE 66:14
still the w. pursues	ELIOT 204:24	w. shall end when I forget	SWIN 530:16	worst are no w.	SHAK 471:19
that the w.'s grown honest	SHAK 432:11	w. shall glean of me	THOM 548:28	worser: throw away the w. part	SHAK 435:17
Then the w. seemed none	HOUS 264:13	w.'s history is the world's	SCH 415:11	worship: All the earth doth w. thee	
then the w.'s mine oyster	SHAK 469:8	w.'s storm-troubled sphere	BRON 93:18		PRAY 384:16
There is a w. elsewhere	SHAK 427:24	w.'s whole sap is sunk	DONNE 189:28	are come to w. him	BIBLE 63:31
These laid the w. away	BROO 94:7	w., that passeth	CHAU 144:19	him must w. him in spirit	BIBLE 71:40
they only saved the w.	CHES 146:25	w. upside down are come	BIBLE 74:9	is the only object of w.	ANON 7:21
thick rotundity o' the w.	SHAK 454:4	w. will little note	LINC 314:23	let us w. and fall down	PRAY 396:4
This gewgaw w.	DRYD 195:13	w. without end	BIBLE 77:26	Rich in the simple w.	KEATS 291:12
This is the way the w. ends	ELIOT 203:11	w. without end	PRAY 384:15	therefore ye ignorantly w.	BIBLE 74:12
This w.'s no blot for us	BROW 100:31	w. without end	PRAY 395:17	_they w. Truth	BROO 94:24
This w. surely is wide	STER 519:24	w. would go round a deal	CARR 133:25	to w. God in his own way	ROOS 407:26
though the w. perish	FERD 210:33	w. would smell like what	SHEL 501:18	various modes of w.	GIBB 224:21
Though 'twere to buy a w.	SHAK 480:26	W., you have kept faith	HARDY 239:21	with my body I thee w.	PRAY 389:5
Thou seest the w.	SHAK 452:5	You never enjoy the w.	TRAH 551:17	With what deep w. I have	COL 156:20
thrones of all the w.	CHES 147:3	**World-besotted:** W. traveller	YEATS 587:3	w. her by years of noble	TENN 534:12
tied the w. in a tether	SWIN 530:23	**worldes:** thise wrecched w. appetites		W. is transcendent wonder	CARL 131:29
To know the w.	YOUNG 588:11		CHAU 144:19	w. the beast and his image	BIBLE 82:17
to pass through this w.	GREL 236:14	**World-losers:** W. and world-forsakers		w. the Lord in the beauty	PRAY 396:5
to perceive how the w.	ARN 15:17		OSH 365:20	worshipful: w. father and first founder	
triple pillar of the w.	SHAK 421:6	**worldly:** being weary of these w. bars			CAXT 138:2
unshook amidst a bursting w.	POPE 376:21		SHAK 449:3	worshipp'd: w. by the names divine	
warm kind w. is all I know	CORY 163:5	Be wisely w.	QUAR 403:11		BLAKE 86:1
were all the w.'s alarms	YEATS 586:4	breath of w. men cannot	SHAK 479:5	**Worshipped:** W. and served the creature	
were the youth of the w.	BACON 25:10	which flees the w. clamour	LUIS 320:12		BIBLE 74:32
What a w.	SHAW 497:14	w. goods I thee endow	PRAY 389:5	w. stocks and stones	MILT 351:9
What a w. is this	BOL 89:13	**worlds:** best of all possible w.	CAB 126:25	worshipper: Nature mourns her w.	
What is this w.	CHAU 142:22	Between two w. life hovers	BYRON 124:9		SCOTT 416:19
What would the w. be	HOPK 256:18	Exhausted w.	JOHN 282:25	regular w. of the gods	HOR 260:2
When all the w. is young	KING 297:5	Wandering between two w.	ARN 13:8	worshipp'st: w. at the temple's inner	
whereby the w. will be judged	CEL 138:6	what w. away	BROW 99:22		WORD 582:1
where I live unto the w.	SHAK 480:13	w. of wanwood leafmeal	HOPK 256:26	**Worships:** W. language and forgives	
where the w. is quiet	SWIN 529:21	**world-without-end:** w. hour	SHAK 493:18		AUDEN 19:7
which the w. cannot give	PRAY 385:9	**worm:** am but as a crushed w.	PUNCH 402:30	worst: best and the w. of this	SWIN 530:11
whole w. is not sufficient	QUAR 403:9	concealment, like a w.	SHAK 489:7	best and w., and parted	BROO 94:6
who lost the w. for love	DRYD 197:8	I am a w., and no man	PRAY 390:17	best is like the w.	KIPL 301:8
whom the w. was not worthy	BIBLE 79:34	invisible w.	BLAKE 87:12	be the w. of the company	SWIFT 526:15
whoso hath this w.'s good	BIBLE 81:4	is no goodness in the w.	SHAK 424:8	exacts a full look at the w.	HARDY 240:3
Why was this w. created	JOHN 278:5	man may fish with the w.	SHAK 435:27	His w. is better than any	HAZL 243:11
wilderness of this w.	BUNY 107:10	needlessly sets foot upon a w.	COWP 167:28	it was the w. of times	DICK 183:9
wish the estate o' the w.	SHAK 463:7	'Or a rather tough w.	GILB 227:16	me the w. they could do	HOUS 266:7
w. And all her train	VAUG 555:22	wish you all joy of the w.	SHAK 424:7	nor the w. of men	BYRON 120:29
w. and I shall ne'er agree	COWL 164:11	w. at one end and a fool	JOHN 280:28	No w., there is none	HOPK 256:19
w. and its ways have	BROW 105:18	W. nor snail	SHAK 470:12	that democracy is the w.	CHUR 150:19
w. as a vale of tears	BROW 100:6	w. that never dies	BROO 94:14	'This is the w.	SHAK 455:8
w. be worth thy winning	DRYD 195:5	w., the canker	BYRON 125:11	w. friend and enemy	BROO 94:28
w. forgetting	POPE 376:13	**worms:** convocation of politic w.		w. he can of womankind	HOME 253:23
w. has grown grey from	SWIN 530:5		SHAK 435:26	worst inn's w. room	POPE 377:33
w. has lost his youth	BIBLE 62:7	Flies, w., and flowers	WATTS 565:24	w. is death	SHAK 479:8
w. has still Much good	HOUS 264:14	have made w.' meat of me	SHAK 483:4	w. is yet to come	JOHN 273:24
w. he finds himself born	CARL 131:33	He was eaten of w.	BIBLE 74:3	w. of the lot	KIPL 302:12
w. holdeth	POUND 383:19	Impaling w. to torture	COLM 159:6	w. returns to laughter	SHAK 455:5
w., I count it not	BROW 97:3	skin w. destroy this body	BIBLE 52:31	w. speaks something good	HERB 247:12
w. I fill up a place	SHAK 424:24	then w. shall try	MARV 332:19	w. time of the year	ANDR 4:7
W. in a Grain of Sand	BLAKE 85:8	with vilest w. to dwell	SHAK 494:6	**worth:** alone is w. all these toils	CAT 136:28
w. invisible	THOM 548:24	w. that are thy chambermaids	SHAK 483:31	charter of thy w. gives	SHAK 494:13
w. is a comedy to those	WALP 563:11	W., *wäre ich dennoch eingeritten*	LUTH 321:3	flattery is w. his having	JOHN 280:29
W. is crazier and more	MACN 326:14	w. were hallow'd that did	SHAK 476:4	Goodbye is not w. while	HARDY 241:7
w. is everything that is	WITT 575:14	**wormwood:** end is bitter as w.	BIBLE 53:20	his worldly w. for this	TENN 543:9

I am not w. purchasing REED 405:9
I do find that I am w. PEPYS 372:18
If a thing is w. doing CHES 148:10
in the w. and choice JONS 283:23
man's w. something BROW 99:10
not w. going to see JOHN 278:10
rymyng is nat w. a toord CHAU 143:15
therefore not w. reading AUST 22:21
think my trifles were w. CAT 136:20
thy own w. then not knowing SHAK 494:13
turned out w. anything SCOTT 419:3
Were w. a thousand men SCOTT 416:7
what is W. in anything BUTL 117:26
Whose w.'s unknown SHAK 495:5
wit, nor words, nor w. SHAK 451:2
w. a hundred coats-of-arms TENN 537:27
w. an age without a name MORD 357:6
w. by poverty depress'd JOHN 282:24
W. makes the man POPE 379:22
w. of a State MILL 339:14
w. the dust which the rude SHAK 455:10
worthiness: w. of thy Son Jesus Christ
PRAY 388:7
Worthington: Missis W. COW 163:21
worthless: more w. still HOR 260:26
W. as withered weeds BRON 93:20
w. set than Byron and his WELL 568:5
worthy: foemen w. of their steel SCOTT 416:6
found them w. for himself BIBLE 62:13
labourer is w. of his hire BIBLE 69:27
latchet I am not w. to unloose BIBLE 71:29
Lord I am not w. that thou BIBLE 65:14
Lord, I am not w. MASS 335:8
nameless in w. deeds BROW 97:17
philosophical and more w. ARIS 12:10
there be nine w. CAXT 138:3
Who is w. to open the book BIBLE 81:26
whom the world was not w. BIBLE 79:34
w. ends and expectations BACON 26:4
w. of the vocation wherewith BIBLE 77:27
w. to be called thy son BIBLE 70:19
w. womman al hir lyve CHAU 141:31
wot: w. not what they are SHAK 456:15
wotthehell: w. archy wotthehell
MARQ 330:21
would: heaven where they w. be PRAY 397:10
He w., wouldn't he RIC 406:2
I w. that you were all BROW 105:28
I w. they should do PRAY 388:15
what we w. ARN 12:20
w. has heard Sordello's BROW 105:16
W. I were with him SHAK 443:16
wouldest: meat-offering, thou w. not
PRAY 392:2
thee whither thou w. not BIBLE 73:17
wouldst: what thou w. highly SHAK 459:1
wound: Earth felt the w. MILT 349:16
felt a stain like a w. BURKE 111:10
first did help to w. itself SHAK 453:1
heal me of my grievous w. TENN 535:27
Hearts w. up with love SPEN 515:9
keen knife see not the w. SHAK 459:2
long yellow string I w. BROW 103:29
May soothe or w. a heart SCOTT 416:23
now purple with love's w. SHAK 470:8
that never felt a w. SHAK 482:5
thy w. be throughly heal'd SHAK 490:32
to gall a new-healed w. SHAK 441:9
tongue In every w. of Caesar SHAK 451:3
trickling nonsense heal'd my w. CONG 160:2
What w. did ever heal SHAK 475:11
Whose annual w. in Leban MILT 345:17
Willing to w. POPE 376:26
wit Makes such a w. SHEL 501:20
w. for wound BIBLE 47:25
wounded: 'e went to tend the w. KIPL 299:18
heal what is w. LANG 310:1
w. for our transgressions BIBLE 59:22
w. spirit who can bear BIBLE 54:13
'You're w. BROW 101:16

Wounded Knee: Bury my heart at W.
BENET 40:20
wounding: wounded is the w. heart
CRAS 169:3
wounds: bind up the nation's w. LINC 315:3
Faithful are the w. of a friend BIBLE 54:38
many eyes as thou hast w. SHAK 450:9
revenge keeps his own w. green BACON 27:9
soldier details his w. PROP 401:15
'These w. I had on Crispin's SHAK 445:3
to bathe in reeking w. SHAK 458:4
woven: Has w. a winter robe HOUS 265:1
them with their w. wings SHAK 465:7
Wovon: W. man nicht sprechen kann
WITT 575:17
wrack: w. and sumless treasuries SHAK 443:8
Wragg: W. is in custody ARN 15:27
wrang: they may gang a kennin w.
BURNS 112:25
wrangle: shall we begin to w. ANON 7:15
wrapped: w. him in swaddling clothes
BIBLE 69:9
wrapt: All meanly w. in the rude MILT 344:5
wrath: answer turneth away w. BIBLE 54:4
between the dragon and his w. SHAK 453:4
day of w. CEL 138:5
Envy and w. shorten BIBLE 63:13
eternal w. Burnt after MILT 348:27
from the heavy w. of God MARL 329:12
from the w. of the Lamb BIBLE 81:30
great day of his w. is BIBLE 81:30
He who the ox to w. has BLAKE 85:12
if his w. be kindled PRAY 389:19
my w. did end BLAKE 87:21
not your children to w. BIBLE 78:7
Nursing her w. to keep BURNS 115:3
slow to w. BIBLE 80:10
sun go down upon your w. BIBLE 78:1
tigers of w. are wiser BLAKE 88:22
Unto whom I sware in my w. PRAY 396:4
where the grapes of w. HOWE 266:19
w. endureth but the twinkling PRAY 391:13
w. of God upon the children BIBLE 78:3
w. of the lion is the wisdom BLAKE 88:21
you to flee from the w. BIBLE 63:38
wreath: rides homeward with a w.
CHES 147:6
sent thee late a rosy w. JONS 284:12
wreathed: w. the rod of criticism DISR 187:8
wreaths: laurel w. entwine HARTE 242:26
wreck: Beautiful as a w. of Paradise
SHEL 500:12
decay Of that colossal w. SHEL 502:16
king my brother's w. ELIOT 204:26
wrecks: Vomits its w. SHEL 501:17
w. of a dissolving dream SHEL 500:20
Wrekin: forest fleece the W. HOUS 263:14
Wren: considered Sir Christopher W.
BARH 33:7
I bore this w. DRYD 195:12
Mr Christopher W. EVEL 209:8
musician than the w. SHAK 468:19
poor w. SHAK 462:12
robin-red-breast and the w. WEBS 567:8
shall hurt the little w. BLAKE 85:12
Sir Christopher W. BENT 41:9
w. goes to't SHAK 455:16
w. with little quill SHAK 470:18
youngest w. of nine comes SHAK 490:2
Wrest: W. once the law to your SHAK 468:2
wrestle: we w. not against flesh BIBLE 78:10
w. With words and meanings ELIOT 202:19
wrestled: There w. a man with him
BIBLE 46:23
w. with him WALT 564:14
you have w. well SHAK 424:26
wrestles: w. with us strengthens
BURKE 111:23
wrestling: w. with (my God!) HOPK 256:8
wretch: sharp-looking w. SHAK 427:9

shout which hail'd the w. BYRON 121:15
soon the dust of a w. whom DONNE 190:23
w. that dares not die BURNS 114:21
wretched: corruptions made him w.
OTWAY 365:27
is a proud and yet a w. DAV 172:11
ladies most deject and w. SHAK 433:15
Most w. men SHEL 501:13
only w. are the wise PRIOR 401:8
raise the w. than to rise GOLD 230:22
w. child expires BELL 39:2
w. have no friends DRYD 195:14
w. he forsakes YOUNG 587:21
w. in both SHAK 454:1
w. state SHAK 434:28
wretchedness: sum of human w.
BYRON 125:18
w. that glory brings us SHAK 486:10
w. of being rich that you SMITH 510:17
wretches: feel what w. feel SHAK 454:16
gaping w. of the sea HUNT 268:7
How shall w. live like GODL 229:24
Poor naked w. SHAK 454:15
w. hang that jury-men may POPE 381:4
wring: will soon w. their hands WALP 563:24
wrinkle: first w. and the reputation
DRYD 196:36
Time writes no w. on thine BYRON 121:25
What stamps the w. deeper BYRON 120:16
wrinkled: w. deep in time SHAK 421:32
wrist: kiss on the w. STEV 520:20
Plunge them in up to the w. AUDEN 18:10
With gyves upon his w. HOOD 254:12
writ: censure this mysterious w. DRYD 196:17
Hooly w. is the scripture JER 272:21
In all you w. to Rome SHAK 447:8
I never w. SHAK 495:5
name was w. in water KEATS 295:3
Priest w. large MILT 351:15
w. with me in sour misfortune's SHAK 483:28
write: baseness to w. fair SHAK 437:12
can w. the life of a man JOHN 276:3
comfortable I sit down to w. KEATS 294:25
does not w. himself down HAZL 243:10
effect men w. in place lite CHAU 144:16
frustrate of his hope to w. MILT 351:18
he fain would w. a poem BROW 102:32
here to w. me down an ass SHAK 473:5
I always w. of you SHAK 494:9
I will w. for Antiquity LAMB 307:37
I w. so many love-lyrics POUND 382:15
Learn to w. well BUCH 106:15
little more I have to w. HERR 249:5
look in thy heart and w. SIDN 507:17
man may w. at any time JOHN 274:3
many deaths I live and w. HERB 247:22
might w. such stuff for ever JOHN 279:7
much as a man ought to w. TROL 552:13
never to w. for the sake KEATS 294:14
not enough for me to w. LYLY 321:16
Of every four words I w. BOIL 89:1
restraint with which they w. CAMP 128:12
sit down to w. SWIFT 527:34
such as cannot w., translate DENH 174:21
that w. what men do BACON 24:25
this hand wherewith I w. BROW 98:12
Though an angel should w. MOORE 356:1
To make me w. too much DAN 170:24
to w. for him with her ARN 16:8
virtues We w. in water SHAK 447:20
want to read a novel I w. DISR 185:26
we cannot w. like Hazlitt STEV 522:10
When men w. for profit WALP 563:15
will sometimes wish to w. COWP 168:17
w. and read comes by nature SHAK 472:27
W.: for these words are BIBLE 82:31
w. for the general amusement SCOTT 418:10
w. in a book BIBLE 81:18
w. in wind and swift-flowing CAT 137:7
w. it before them BIBLE 58:25

W. me as one that loves   HUNT 268:5
W. sorrow on the bosom   SHAK 479:10
w. such hopeless rubbish   STEP 518:23
w. trifles with dignity   JOHN 278:23
w. upon him my new name   BIBLE 81:19
W. with your spade   CAMP 128:11
writer: alone cannot make a w.   EMER 208:5
every great and original w.   WORD 583:11
Galeotto was the book and w.   DANTE 171:10
original w. is not he who   CHAT 141:5
pen: of a ready w.   PRAY 392:14
plain, rude w.   BURT 116:18
understand a w.'s ignorance   COL 157:21
w. of dictionaries   JOHN 281:5
w. of it be a black man   ADD 2:7
writers: Clear w., like fountains LAND 309:14
Creative w. are always   FORS 217:15
w. become more numerous   GOLD 232:1
W., like teeth   BAG 29:13
writes: He w. as fast as they can HAZL 243:10
w. in dust   BACON 28:16
writing: angel w. in a book of gold
                                       HUNT 268:4
art of w.   DISR 187:9
Charlotte has been w. a book   BRON 94:2
day by day that fine w.   KEATS 294:23
ease in w. comes from art   POPE 378:22
easy w.'s vile hard reading   SHER 506:37
I had in the w.   QUAR 403:8
incurable disease of w.   JUV 287:23
Pardons him for w. well   AUDEN 19:8
recited verses in w.   BIBLE 63:23
rest is mere fine w.   VERL 556:9
sign the w.   BIBLE 61:7
That fairy kind of w. which   DRYD 196:26
this is the w. that was   BIBLE 61:6
w. an exact man   BACON 27:20
w. increaseth rage   GREV 236:17
w., or praying   THOM 546:11
W. their own reproach   SHAK 486:19
your w. and reading   SHAK 472:28
writing-book: You have lost your w.
                                       HOFF 252:17
writing paper: thicker and the w. thinner
                                       MITF 352:25
writings: confess thy w. to be such
                                       JONS 284:18
written: adversary had w. a book   BIBLE 52:38
another until he has w. a book   JOW 285:20
ever w. out of reputation   BENT 41:14
God has w. all the books   BUTL 119:1
has never w. any poetry   CHES 148:4
have written I have w.   BIBLE 73:1
is w. without effort is   JOHN 280:25
large a letter I have w.   BIBLE 77:21
now it is w.   BEDE 37:2
something so w. to after-times   MILT 352:14
that my words were now w.   BIBLE 52:30
those who would make the w.   CONN 161:11
volume of the book it is w.   PRAY 392:2
were all my members w.   PRAY 399:7
w. by mere man that was   JOHN 280:16
w. nothing but his Prefaces   CONG 159:29
w. or created unless Minerva   HOR 258:5
w. three books on the soul   BROW 100:5
You will have w. exceptionally   HOR 257:13
writyng: In Englissh and in w.   CHAU 144:17
wroghte: That first he w.   CHAU 142:1
wrong: absent are always in the w.
                                       DEST 175:14
against injustice and w.   PALM 368:10
Always to advise her w.   SWIFT 527:21
called them by w. names   BROW 99:11
credit in this World much w.   FITZ 213:13
Divine of Kings to govern w.   POPE 375:23
do a little w.   SHAK 468:2
does, not suffers w.   SHEL 502:20
doing no w.   SHAK 467:24
Englishman in the w.   SHAW 498:6

From w. to wrong the exasperated
                                       ELIOT 202:26
His can't be w. whose life   POPE 379:20
if I Called the W. Number   THUR 550:30
is a w. left unredressed   KING 297:18
I would rather be w.   CIC 152:1
keep himself from doing w.   BIBLE 63:10
me when I am in the w.   MELB 336:17
million Frenchmen can't be w.   GUIN 237:6
most divinely in the w.   YOUNG 587:17
multitude is always in the w.   ROOS 408:12
Nature is usually w.   WHIS 569:20
nets of w. and right   YEATS 585:14
noblemen who have gone w.   GILB 228:22
notions are generally w.   MONT 354:9
One w. more to man   BROW 102:7
own he has been in the w.   POPE 381:19
people are never in the w.   BURKE 108:18
persist In doing w.   SHAK 486:31
preserve the stars from w.   WORD 579:16
reason to fear I may be w.   AUST 23:27
right and nothing goes w.   GILB 228:29
right of an excessive w.   BROW 104:23
rose o' the w. side   BROME 93:11
rose the w. way to-day   BEHN 38:20
Should suffer w. no more   MAC 322:11
something must be w.   HOR 261:23
some westward, and all w.   COWP 165:12
surely always in the w.   COWP 164:30
that is a w. one   JOHN 275:34
That the king can do no w.   BLAC 85:5
thou hast seen my w.   BIBLE 60:32
trust not in w. and robbery   PRAY 393:20
We do it w.   SHAK 429:15
When everyone is w.   LA C 306:16
when w., to be put   SCH 415:13
w. because not all was   COWP 168:20
w. could religion induce   LUCR 320:4
w. side of a Turkey tapestry   HOW 266:20
w. stay and her displeasure   SHAK 474:18
w. with our bloody ships   BEAT 35:12
You w. me every way   SHAK 451:18
wronged: w. great soul of an ancient
                                       BROW 102:25
wrongly: yet wouldst w. win   SHAK 459:1
wrongs: abroad redressing human w.
                                       TENN 534:11
are good for righting w.   LOCK 315:21
like w. hushed-up   OWEN 367:7
mass of public w.   KYD 306:3
people's w. his own   DRYD 194:17
wrote: all that he w.   HAZL 243:9
blockhead ever w.   JOHN 277:4
I w. my happy songs   BLAKE 87:25
whatever he w.   JOHN 277:25
Who w. like an angel   GARR 221:13
w. a letter he would put   BACON 25:42
w. her name upon the strand   SPEN 515:20
w. my will across the sky   LAWR 311:12
w. over against the candlestick   BIBLE 61:5
wrought: first miracle that he w. PRAY 388:25
God never w. miracle   BACON 25:23
hands w. in the work   BIBLE 52:1
hand w. to make it grow   FITZ 212:21
last have w. but one hour   BIBLE 67:15
subtly w. me into Shape   FITZ 213:12
though they'd w. it   YEATS 584:16
What hath God w.   BIBLE 48:15
w. about with divers colours   PRAY 392:16
wrung: Not w. from speculations   BROW 96:18
wum: cackle w'en he fine a w.   HARR 242:24
würfelt: *Gott w. nicht*   EINS 200:10
Wye: hushes half the babbling W.
                                       TENN 536:11
is called W. at Monmouth   SHAK 445:5
Wykehamist: rather dirty W.   BETJ 44:14
wyn: to drynken strong w.   CHAU 142:5
wynd: w., the weder gynneth   CHAU 144:4
wyndow: clapte the w.   CHAU 142:28
wyne: Of w. and wax   WYNT 584:4

Wynken: W., Blynken   FIELD 211:2
wys: Ful w. is he that kan hymselven
                                       CHAU 142:30
wyves: w., fieble as in bataille   CHAU 142:10
Xanadu: In X. did Kubla Khan   COL 156:26
Xenophon: X. at New York   WALP 563:9
xiphias: Shoots x. to his aim   SMART 509:3
Yank: boldest thieves, ɔ e Y.   KIPL 302:12
Yankee Doodle: Y. keep it up   BANGS 32:15
yardwand: with his cheating y.   TENN 539:26
yarn: all I ask is a merry y.   MAS 334:6
life is of a mingled y.   SHAK 421:3
yawn: thy everlasting y. confess   POPE 375:25
yawns: Despair y.   HUGO 267:12
yawp: I sound my barbaric y.   WHIT 571:6
ybeten: maker is hymself y.   CHAU 144:2
Yblessed: Y. be god that I have wedded
                                       CHAU 143:17
ydrad: ever was y.   SPEN 515:32
fiend of gods and men y.   SPEN 516:22
ye: then men han seen with y.   CHAU 143:28
yea: Let your y. be yea   BIBLE 80:18
Y., yea; Nay, nay   BIBLE 64:16
year: acceptable y. of the Lord   BIBLE 60:8
Another y.   WORD 581:13
any book that is not a y.   EMER 208:7
beautiful and death-struck y.   HOUS 264:1
bloom of the y.   BROW 98:30
circle of the golden y.   TENN 533:24
days will finish up the y.   SHAK 446:18
does not give you a y.   STEV 522:8
fill the measure of the y.   KEATS 292:14
fit this y.'s fashions   HELL 244:15
Is the y. only lost to me   HERB 247:14
is what the y. teaches   HOR 261:15
measure in a y. of dearth   BLAKE 83:18
pleasure of the fleeting y.   SHAK 494:16
returns with the revolving y.   SHEL 499:10
stood at the gate of the y.   HASK 243:1
that each day is like a y.   WILDE 572:15
That time of y. thou mayst   SHAK 494:7
Thou crownest the y. with   PRAY 394:3
twelve months in all the y.   BALL 31:13
y. is going   TENN 537:14
y.'s at the spring   BROW 103:21
y. wake year to sorrow   SHEL 499:14
yearn: finite hearts that y.   BROW 105:30
Yearn'd: Y. after by the wisest   TENN 539:22
yearning: gray spirit y. in desire TENN 544:1
huddled masses y.   LAZ 311:13
y. like a God in pain   KEATS 289:13
y. thought And aspiration   ROSS 410:7
years: age are threescore y.   PRAY 395:19
Ah, no; the y.   HARDY 239:10
attain y. of discretion   RUSK 412:6
bound him a thousand y.   BIBLE 82:27
cuts off twenty y. of life   SHAK 450:4
down the arches of the y.   THOM 548:8
ever the Knightly y. were   HENL 245:10
gleam on the y. that shall   BULW 107:1
infelicity Seem'd to have y.   WEBS 566:27
Into the vale of y.   SHAK 475:21
It ran a hundred y.   HOLM 253:8
love of finished y.   ROSS 408:26
my y. in the bitterness   BIBLE 59:3
new y. ruin and rend   SWIN 530:6
nor the y. condemn   BINY 84:10
of the y. of my life been   BIBLE 46:38
provoke The y.   WORD 579:8
'save the undone y.   OWEN 367:10
seen sae mony changefu' y.   BURNS 114:15
seventy y. young   HOLM 253:14
seven y. for Rachel   BIBLE 46:21
thousand y. in thy sight   PRAY 395:18
touch of earthly y.   WORD 581:10
y. are slipping by   HOR 260:10
y. as they come bring   HOR 257:21
Y. glide away   BARH 33:8
y. like great black oxen   YEATS 584:17
y. of desolation pass over   JEFF 272:14

y. teach much which — EMER 207:19
y. that the locust hath — BIBLE 61:14
y. to come seemed waste — YEATS 585:15
yet belie thy happy y. — SHAK 488:3
yeas: In russet y. and honest — SHAK 457:16
Yeats: churchyard Y. is laid — YEATS 587:10
William Y. is laid to rest — AUDEN 19:7
yell: such a y. was there — SCOTT 417:20
Yell'ham: That Y. says — HARDY 241:8
yellow: are already y. with August — POUND 383:17
come to her in y. stockings — SHAK 489:17
Come unto these y. sands — SHAK 484:30
islets of y. sand — LEAR 312:16
learn from the Y. an' Brown — KIPL 300:15
sear, the y. leaf — SHAK 463:2
this square old y. Book — BROW 104:14
Was y. like ripe corn — ROSS 409:15
When y. leaves — SHAK 494:7
Y., and black — SHEL 502:8
Y. God forever gazes down — HAYES 243:7
yelping: Faced by the snarled and y. — ELIOT 204:11
yelps: loudest y. for liberty among — JOHN 282:18
yeoman: It did me y.'s service — SHAK 437:12
yeomanly: this the y. — DONNE 190:23
yerde: 'man maketh ofte a y. — CHAU 144:2
Yes: 'Y.', I answered you — BROW 98:5
yes I said yes I will Y. — JOYCE 286:30
y. O at lightning — HOPK 257:6
yesterday: all our pomp of y. — KIPL 302:8
call back y. — SHAK 479:6
dead Y. — FITZ 212:22
Jesus Christ the same y. — BIBLE 80:4
Myself with Y.'s Sev'n — FITZ 212:16
thy sight are but as y. — PRAY 395:18
universe and give me y. — JONES 283:10
We were saying y. — LUIS 320:13
where leaves the Rose of Y. — FITZ 212:10
y. a King — BYRON 125:7
y. doth not usher it — DONNE 190:26
Y. I loved — LESS 313:26
you'd think it was only y. — MILL 339:25
yesterdays: all our y. have lighted — SHAK 463:6
yesteryear: where are the snows of y. — VILL 557:5
Yestreen: Y. the Queen had four Maries — BALL 31:12
yet: as y. there were none — PRAY 399:7
continency—but not y. — AUG 21:14
young man not y. — BACON 26:35
yeux: allez vous user les y. — ZOLA 591:19
Français lève les y. — TOCQ 551:8
yew: never a spray of y. — ARN 14:5
slips of y. — SHAK 462:4
so solemnly to yonder y. — JONS 285:9
stuck all with y. — SHAK 489:4
true wood, of y.-wood — DOYLE 191:14
Y. alone burns lamps — DE L 174:17
yew-tree: that y.'s shade — GRAY 234:20
yield: not make the sickle y. — BLAKE 86:19
Private respects must y. — MILT 350:24
temptation is just to y. — GRAH 233:8
to find, and not to y. — TENN 544:3
year has shot her y. — KIPL 300:23
yielded: by her y. — MILT 347:23
yields: craggy mountains y. — SHAK 495:16
ymage: thilke God that after his y. — CHAU 144:19
Ynde: egre is a tygre yond in Y. — CHAU 142:10
Yo-ho-ho: Y., and a bottle of rum — STEV 521:21
yoke: bear the y. in his youth — BIBLE 60:30
bring the inevitable y. — WORD 579:8
Flanders hath receiv'd our y. — WALL 562:17
his neck unto a savage y. — HERR 250:4
impertinent y. of prelaty — MILT 352:15
savage bull doth bear the y. — SHAK 472:2

Take my y. upon you — BIBLE 66:5
that ye break every y. — BIBLE 60:4
yoked: you are y. with a lamb — SHAK 451:24
yolk: y. runs down the waistcoat — DICK 180:14
yonge: O y., fresshe folkes — CHAU 144:19
Yorick: Alas, poor Y. — SHAK 436:31
you: Here am I, here are y. — AUDEN 19:14
I cannot live with y. — MART 331:13
married My Lord y. — POUND 383:16
y. against me — BETJ 44:6
y. I should love to live — HOR 261:1
Y., that way — SHAK 457:20
young: all of them desirable y. — BIBLE 60:37
America is a country of y. — EMER 208:11
anchored and the y. star-captains — FLEC 214:7
atrocious crime of being a y. — PITT 373:20
been y., and now am old — PRAY 391:28
believe everything a y. — JOW 285:22
both were y. — BYRON 124:12
care for the y. man's whore — JOHN 275:19
crime by corrupting the y. — PLATO 374:8
embarrassing y. — GAV 222:5
fat and look y. till forty — DRYD 196:36
God guide them—y. — TENN 535:5
gods love dies y. — MEN 336:25
hinds to bring forth y. — PRAY 391:11
how y. the policemen look — HICKS 250:23
I was y. — FLEC 214:23
I was y. and foolish — YEATS 584:22
love's y. dream — MOORE 356:12
made y. with young desires — THOM 548:4
Most women are not so y. — BEER 37:10
nor y. enough for a boy — SHAK 488:9
Not so y. — SHAK 453:14
No y. man believes he shall — HAZL 244:3
panting and for ever y. — KEATS 291:7
proper y. men — BURNS 114:17
remember'd that he once was y. — ARMS 12:14
set her six y. on the rail — BROW 101:19
seventy years y. — HOLM 253:14
she died y. — WEBS 566:27
sight to make an old man y. — TENN 533:20
So wise so y. — SHAK 481:3
So y., and so untender — SHAK 453:3
so y., I loved him so — BROW 99:16
those that are with y. — BIBLE 59:7
to be y. was very heaven — WORD 577:21
To find a y. fellow that — CONG 160:11
Tomorrow for the y. — AUDEN 20:16
we knew the worst too y. — KIPL 299:11
When I was y. — MILNE 340:17
When thou wast y. — BIBLE 73:17
While we are y. — ANON 10:13
Wives are y. men's mistresses — BACON 26:34
world and love were y. — RAL 404:9
years to be y. and handsome — SWIFT 526:22
y. a body with so old — SHAK 467:26
y. and easy under the apple — THOM 547:1
y. and lusty as an eagle — PRAY 396:15
y. and sweating devil here — SHAK 476:2
y. are sad and bewildered — SMITH 510:22
y. as beautiful — YOUNG 588:7
y. can do for the old — SHAW 496:25
y. girl miserable may give — FRAN 218:5
Y. in limbs — SHAK 466:17
y. In one another's arms — YEATS 586:11
y. lassie do wi' an auld — BURNS 116:3
y. man cleanse his way — PRAY 398:4
y. man feels his pockets — HOUS 265:2
y. man lands hatless — BETJ 42:12
y. man not yet — BACON 26:35
y. man's dog with them — BIBLE 62:9
y. man's soul — HOUS 262:22
y. man will be wiser — TENN 534:2
Y. men and maidens — PRAY 399:23
Y. men are fitter to invent — BACON 27:39
y. men glittering and sparkling — TRAH 551:19
Y. men have more virtue — JOHN 275:4
Y. men make great mistakes — JOW 285:24
y. men shall see visions — BIBLE 61:15

y. men's vision — DRYD 194:9
y. men think it is — HOUS 266:3
y. to fall asleep for ever — SASS 414:15
you yet call yourself y. — SHAK 441:10
younger: Then let thy love be y. — SHAK 489:2
y. son gathered all together — BIBLE 70:18
Y. than she are happy mothers — SHAK 481:26
y. widows refuse — BIBLE 79:15
youngest: not even the y. of us — THOM 549:5
y. he was little Billee — THAC 545:32
yours: Have these for y. — HOUS 266:5
What I have done is y. — SHAK 492:16
Y. is the Earth and everything — KIPL 300:2
y. till the rending — JOYCE 286:4
yourself: Could love you for y. alone — YEATS 585:5
Keep yourself to y. — DICK 182:9
Live with y. — PERS 372:29
women, physical decay, Y. — AUDEN 19:5
you're not good enough y. — TROL 553:12
yourselves: honey not for y. — VIRG 560:20
youth: After the pleasures of y. — ANON 10:13
banged the y. into dumbness — SHAK 489:27
bear the yoke in his y. — BIBLE 60:30
considered as a debauch of y. — BURKE 108:16
Crabbed age and y. — SHAK 492:13
Creator in the days of thy y. — BIBLE 56:11
days of our y. are — BYRON 125:29
eagle mewing her mighty y. — MILT 352:3
Enjoy'd his y. — DRYD 196:3
every y. cry *Well-a-way* — BALL 30:10
flourish set on y. — SHAK 493:20
flower of their y. — VIRG 560:3
fought against me from my y. — PRAY 398:21
great has been done by y. — DISR 185:39
green unknowing y. engage — DRYD 197:14
heart is evil from his y. — BIBLE 45:36
How beautiful is y. — MED 336:9
If y. knew — EST 208:25
In flow'r of y. and beauty's — DRYD 194:23
informs the Scottish y. — STUB 524:5
In the lexicon of y. — BULW 107:5
in trust Our y. — RAL 404:15
In y. is pleasure — WEVER 569:7
I remember my y. — CONR 161:2
is the measure of our y. — KIPL 299:11
it is y. that must fight — HOOV 255:25
I was a hot-blooded y. — HOR 261:4
Jenny's unsuspecting y. — BURNS 113:7
laugh uproariously in y. — BROO 94:24
Let age approve of y. — BROW 104:13
loves the meat in his y. — SHAK 472:18
might renew our y. — YEATS 587:14
nourishing a y. sublime — TENN 538:16
of my ill adventured y. — DAN 171:1
riband in the cap of y. — SHAK 436:17
sign of an ill-spent y. — SPEN 515:4
sins and offences of my y. — PRAY 391:2
So long as y. and thou — SHAK 493:1
spirit of y. in everything — SHAK 494:17
stretch the folly of our y. — CHES 147:12
submit to be taught by y. — BURKE 110:23
subtle thief of y. — MILT 351:6
Sweet wine of y. — BROO 94:7
That miracle of a y. — EVEL 209:8
that the April of your y. — HERB 246:20
thee in the days of thy y. — BIBLE 56:10
things Y. needed not — WORD 581:12
thou goodly y. — BALL 30:9
Thou hast nor y. nor age — SHAK 464:17
To y. and age in common — ARN 15:13
traitorously corrupted the y. — SHAK 446:14
well-beloved y. — BALL 30:7
were the y. of the world — BACON 25:10
when Y. and Pleasure meet — BYRON 120:21
Where y. grows pale — KEATS 291:17
Whose y. was full of foolish — TENN 536:22
world has lost his y. — BIBLE 62:7
y. And a little beauty — WEBS 566:20
Y. are boarded — DICK 179:34